Features

118th Edition

Statistical Abstract of the United States 1998

The National Data Book

Issued October 1998

U.S. Department of Commerce
William M. Daley, Secretary

Economics and Statistics Administration
Robert J. Shapiro, Under Secretary
for Economic Affairs

BUREAU OF THE CENSUS
James F. Holmes, Acting Director

ECONOMICS
AND STATISTICS
ADMINISTRATION

Economics and Statistics Administration

Robert J. Shapiro, Under Secretary for Economic Affairs

BUREAU OF THE CENSUS

James F. Holmes, Acting Director

Bradford R. Huther, Deputy Director

Nancy A. Potok, Principal Associate Director and Chief Financial Officer

Michael S. McKay, Associate Director for Administration/Controller

ADMINISTRATIVE AND CUSTOMER SERVICES DIVISION
Walter C. Odom, Chief

Acknowledgments

Lars B. Johanson was responsible for the technical supervision and coordination of this volume under the general direction of **Glenn W. King**, Chief, Statistical Compendia Branch. Assisting in the research and analytical phases of assigned sections and in the developmental aspects of new tables were **Rosemary E. Clark**, **Edward C. Jagers,** and **David J. Fleck**. **Geraldine W. Blackburn** provided primary editorial assistance. Other editorial assistance was rendered by **Patricia S. Lancaster**, **Catherine Lavender**, **Joyce Mori**, and **Barbara Shugart**.

The staff of the Administrative and Customer Services Division, under the general supervision of **Walter C. Odom**, Chief, and direct supervision of **Michael G. Garland**, Assistant Chief, performed publication planning, editorial review, design, composition, and printing planning and procurement. **Patricia Heiston**, assisted by **Gloria Davis**, provided publication coordination and editing. **Shirley A. Clark** provided design and graphics services, and **Arlene Duckett** provided printing services.

The cooperation of many contributors to this volume is gratefully acknowledged. The source note below each table credits the various government and private agencies which have collaborated in furnishing information for the **Statistical Abstract**. In a few instances, contributors have requested that their data be designated as subject to copyright restrictions, as indicated in the source notes to the tables affected. Permission to use copyright material should be obtained directly from the copyright owner.

SUGGESTED CITATION

U.S. Bureau of the Census, *Statistical Abstract of the United States: 1998* (118th edition.) Washington, DC, 1998

Reprinted without alteration on acid-free paper ∞
National Technical Information Services
Springfield, Virginia
November 1998
ISBN (cloth) 0-934213-62-3
ISBN (paper) 0-934213-63-1

Preface

The *Statistical Abstract of the United States,* published since 1878, is the standard summary of statistics on the social, political, and economic organization of the United States. It is designed to serve as a convenient volume for statistical reference and as a guide to other statistical publications and sources. The latter function is served by the introductory text to each section, the source note appearing below each table, and Appendix I, which comprises the Guide to Sources of Statistics, the Guide to State Statistical Abstracts, and the Guide to Foreign Statistical Abstracts.

This volume includes a selection of data from many statistical publications, both government and private. Publications cited as sources usually contain additional statistical detail and more comprehensive discussions of definitions and concepts than can be presented here. Data not available in publications issued by the contributing agency but obtained from unpublished records are identified in the source notes as "unpublished data." More information on the subjects covered in the tables so noted may generally be obtained from the source.

Except as indicated, figures are for the United States as presently constituted. Although emphasis in the *Statistical Abstract* is primarily given to national data, many tables present data for regions and individual states and a smaller number for metropolitan areas and cities. Appendix II, Metropolitan Area Concepts and Components, presents explanatory text, a complete current listing and population data for metropolitan statistical areas (MSAs), the primary metropolitan statistical areas (PMSAs), and the consolidated metropolitan statistical areas (CMSAs) defined as of June 1998. Table 43 in Section 1 presents selected population characteristics for MSAs with population of 250,000 or more. Statistics for the Commonwealth of Puerto Rico and for outlying areas of the United States are included in many state tables and are supplemented by information in section

29. Additional information for states, cities, counties, metropolitan areas, and other small units, as well as more historical data, are available in various supplements to the *Abstract* (see inside back cover).

Changes in this edition—This year we have introduced 93 new tables covering a wide range of subject matter. Several based on the *National Survey of Family Growth*, covering issues of fertility, family planning, and women's health, can be found in Sections 2, Vital Statistics, and 3, Health. Other new tables cover such topics as grandchildren living with their grandparents, persons with disabilities, health insurance coverage, ambulatory surgery, educational attainment by state, school violence, household use of public libraries, public library use of the Internet, toxic chemical releases, leisure activity, participation in NCAA sports and high school athletic programs, voter registration, licensed child care centers, foster care, persons with home-based businesses, employee benefits, bank fees and services, home equity debt, use of debit credit cards, alcohol related fatal accidents, computer shipments, and foreign stock market indices. See Appendix V, pp. 964 for a complete list of new tables.

Statistics in this edition are generally for the most recent year or period available by spring 1998. Each year almost 1,500 tables and charts are reviewed and evaluated; new tables and charts of current interest are added, continuing series are updated, and less timely data are condensed or eliminated. Text notes and appendices are revised as appropriate.

USA Statistics in Brief, a pocket-size pamphlet highlighting many statistical series in the *Abstract,* is available separately. Single copies can be obtained free from U.S. Bureau of the Census, Customer Services, Washington, DC 20233 (telephone 301-457-4100).

Statistical Abstract on other media— The *Abstract* is available in its entirety on the Internet and, an enhanced version, on CD-ROM (except for a few copyrighted tables deleted by the request of source organizations). Our Internet site, <http://www.census.gov/statab/www>, contains this 1998 edition and earlier editions of the book, as well as summary items—Statistics in Brief, Frequently Requested Tables, and State Rankings, which will be updated as time allows. State and County Profiles is also on the site.

The CD-ROM version of the *Abstract* has been enriched with links from tables to the Internet sites of appropriate government agencies. In addition, links are provided to the underlying spreadsheets (both .wk1 and .xls) from which the data in the tables are based. Ordering information for the CD-ROM is located in the inside back cover.

Statistics for states and metropolitan areas—Extensive data for the states and metropolitan areas of the United States can be found in the *State and Metropolitan Area Data Book 1997-98*. It features 859 data items covering everything from age and agriculture to wages and welfare for the 50 states and the District of Columbia with the United States totals for comparison. Also included are over 150 data items for metropolitan areas (MAs), 43 items for component counties of MAs, and 3 population items for central cities of MAs.

This publication, as well as selected rankings of the states and metropolitan areas, is available on our Internet site at <http://www.census.gov/statab/www/smadb.html>. Some data items that appear in the book from private sources are not available on the Internet or CD-ROM versions because we did not receive copyright permission to release the data items in these formats. The CD-ROM version also includes links from the data tables to spreadsheets (both .wk1 and .xls) with the data and pertinent geographic information, to contributing government agency Internet sites, and to related source notes and explanations. See the inside back cover for ordering information.

Statistical reliability and responsibility—The contents of this volume were taken from many sources. All data from either censuses and surveys or from administrative records are subject to error arising from a number of factors: Sampling variability (for statistics based on samples), reporting errors in the data for individual units, incomplete coverage, nonresponse, imputations, and processing error. (See also Appendix III, pp. 945-960.) The Bureau of the Census cannot accept the responsibility for the accuracy or limitations of the data presented here, other than those for which it collects. The responsibility for selection of the material and for proper presentation, however, rests with the Bureau.

For additional information on data presented—Please consult the source publications available in local libraries or write to the agency indicated in the source notes. Write to the Bureau of the Census only if it is cited as the source.

Suggestions and comments—Users of the *Statistical Abstract* and its supplements (see inside back cover) are urged to make their data needs known for consideration in planning future editions. Suggestions and comments for improving coverage and presentation of data should be sent to the Director, U.S. Bureau of the Census, Washington, DC 20233.

Contents

[Numbers following subjects are page numbers]

Contents

APPROXIMATE CONVERSION MEASURES

[For assistance on metric usage, call or write the Office of Metric Programs, U.S. Department of Commerce, Washington, DC 20230 (301-975-3690) Internet site <http://www.nist.gov/metric>]

Symbol	When you know conventional	Multiply by	To find metric	Symbol
in	inch	2.54	centimeter	cm
ft	foot	30.48	centimeter	cm
yd	yard	0.91	meter	m
mi	mile	1.61	kilometer	km
in^2	square inch	6.45	square centimeter	cm^2
ft^2	square foot	0.09	square meter	m^2
yd^2	square yard	0.84	square meter	m^2
mi^2	square mile	2.59	square kilometer	km^2
	acre	0.41	hectare	ha
oz	ounce [1]	28.35	gram	g
lb	pound [1]	.45	kilograms	kg
oz (troy)	ounce [2]	31.10	gram	g
	short ton (2,000 lbs)	0.91	metric ton	t
	long ton (2,240 lbs)	1.02	metric ton	t
fl oz	fluid ounce	29.57	milliliter	mL
c	cup	0.24	liter	L
pt	pint	0.47	liter	L
qt	quart	0.95	liter	L
gal	gallon	3.78	liter	L
ft^3	cubic foot	0.03	cubic meter	m^3
yd^3	cubic yard	0.76	cubic meter	m^3
F	degrees Fahrenheit (subtract 32)	0.55	degrees Celsius	C

Symbol	When you know metric	Multiply by	To find conventional	Symbol
cm	centimeter	0.39	inch	in
cm	centimeter	0.33	foot	ft
m	meter	1.09	yard	yd
km	kilometer	0.62	mile	mi
cm^2	square centimeter	0.15	square inch	in^2
m^2	square meter	10.76	square foot	ft^2
m^2	square meter	1.20	square yard	yd^2
km^2	square kilometer	0.39	square mile	mi^2
ha	hectare	2.47	acre	
g	gram	.035	ounce [1]	oz
kg	kilogram	2.21	pounds	lb[1]
g	gram	.032	ounce [2]	oz (troy)
t	metric ton	1.10	short ton (2,000 lbs)	
t	metric ton	0.98	long ton (2,240 lbs)	
mL	milliliter	0.03	fluid ounce	fl oz
L	liter	4.24	cup	c
L	liter	2.13	pint (liquid)	pt
L	liter	1.05	quart (liquid)	qt
L	liter	0.26	gallon	gal
m^3	cubic meter	35.32	cubic foot	ft^3
m^3	cubic meter	1.32	cubic yard	yd^3
C	degrees Celsius	1.80	degrees Fahrenheit (after subtracting 32)	F

[1] For weighing ordinary commodities.   [2] For weighing precious metals, jewels, etc.

Example of table structure:
State and Local Government Retirement Systems—
Beneficiaries and Finances: 1980 to 1991

[**In millions of dollars, except as indicated.** For fiscal years closed during the 12 months ending June 30]

YEAR AND LEVEL OF GOVERNMENT	Number of beneficiaries (1,000)	RECEIPTS					BENEFITS AND WITHDRAWALS			Cash and security holdings
		Total	Employee contributions	Government contributions		Earnings on investments	Total	Benefits	Withdrawals	
				State	Local					
1980: All systems.	(NA)	37,313	6,466	7,581	9,951	13,315	14,008	12,207	1,801	185,226
State-administered . . .	(NA)	28,603	5,285	7,399	5,611	10,308	10,257	8,809	1,448	144,682
Locally administered . .	(NA)	8,710	1,180	181	4,340	3,008	3,752	3,399	353	40,544
1985: All systems.	3,378	71,411	9,468	12,227	15,170	34,546	24,413	21,999	2,414	374,433
State-administered . . .	2,661	55,960	7,901	11,976	8,944	27,139	18,230	16,183	2,047	296,951
Locally administered . .	716	15,451	1,567	251	6,226	7,407	6,183	5,816	367	77,481
1990: All systems.	4,026	111,339	13,853	13,994	18,583	64,907	38,396	35,966	2,430	703,772
State-administered . . .	3,232	89,162	11,648	13,964	11,538	52,012	29,603	27,562	2,041	565,641
Locally administered . .	794	22,177	2,205	32	7,045	12,895	8,793	8,404	389	138,131
1991: All systems.	4,179	108,240	16,268	14,473	18,691	58,808	42,028	39,421	2,607	783,405
State-administered . . .	3,357	85,576	12,563	14,455	11,553	47,006	32,323	30,167	2,156	630,551
Locally administered . .	822	22,664	3,705	18	7,138	11,803	9,706	9,255	451	152,854

NA Not available.
Source: U.S. Bureau of the Census, *Finances of Employee-Retirement Systems of State and Local Governments*, Series GF, No. 2, annual.

Headnotes immediately below table titles provide information important for correct interpretation or evaluation of the table as a whole or for a major segment of it.

Footnotes below the bottom rule of tables give information relating to specific items or figures within the table.

Unit indicators show the *specified quantities* in which data items are presented. They are used for two primary reasons. Sometimes data are not available in absolute form and are estimates (as in the case of many surveys). In other cases we round the numbers in order to save space to show more data, as in the case above.

EXAMPLES OF UNIT INDICATOR INTERPRETATION FROM TABLE

Year	Item	Unit Indicator	Number shown	Multiplier
1991.	Beneficiaries	Thousands.	4,179	1,000
1991.	Receipts.	$ Millions.	108,240	1,000,000

To Determine the Figure it Is Necessary to Multiply the
Number Shown by the Unit Indicator:
Beneficiaries = 4,179 * 1,000 or 4,179,000 (over 4 million).
Receipts = 108,240 * 1,000,000 or 108,240,000,000 (over 108 billion).

When a table presents data with more than one unit indicator, they are found in the headnotes and column headings (shown above), spanner (Table 52), stub (Table 82), or unit column (Table 79). When the data in a table are shown in the same unit indicator, it is shown in boldface as the first part of the headnote (Table 2). If no unit indicator is shown, data presented are in absolute form (Table 1).

Heavy vertical rules are used to separate independent sections of a table, as shown above, or in tables where the stub is continued into one or more additional columns (Table 4).

Averages. An average is a single number or value that is often used to represent the "typical value" of a group of numbers. It is regarded as a measure of "location" or "central tendency" of a group of numbers.

The *arithmetic mean* is the type of average used most frequently. It is derived by summing the individual item values of a particular group and dividing the total by the number of items. The arithmetic mean is often referred to as simply the "mean" or "average."

The *median* of a group of numbers is the middle number or value when each item in the group is arranged according to size (lowest to highest or visa versa); it generally has the same number of items above it as well as below it. If there is an even number if items in the group, the median is taken to be the average of the two middle numbers.

Per capita (or per person) quantities. A per capita figure represents an average computed for every person in a specified group (or population). It is derived by taking the total for an item (such as income, taxes, or retail sales) and dividing it by the number of persons in the specified population.

Index numbers. An index number is the measure of difference or change, usually expressed as a percent, relating one quantity (the variable) of a specified kind to another quantity of the same kind. Index numbers are widely used to express changes in prices over periods of time but may also be used to express differences between related subjects for a single point in time.

To compute a price index, a base year or period is selected. The base year price (of the commodity or service) is then designated as the base or reference price to which the prices for other years or periods are related. Many price indexes use the year 1982 as the base year; in tables this is shown as "1982=100." A method of expressing the price relationship is: The price of a set of one or more items for a related year (e.g. 1990) **divided by** the price of the same set of items for the base year (e.g. 1982). The result multiplied by 100 provides the index number. When 100 is subtracted from the index number, the result equals the percent change in price from the base year.

Average annual percent change. Unless otherwise stated in the *Abstract* (as in Section 1, Population), average annual percent change is computed by use of a *compound interest formula*. This formula assumes that the rate of change is constant throughout a specified compounding period (1 year for average annual rates of change). The formula is similar to that used to compute the balance of a savings account which receives compound interest. According to this formula, at the end of a compounding period the amount of accrued change (e.g. school enrollment or bank interest) is added to the amount which existed at the beginning the period. As a result, over time (e.g., with each year or quarter), the same rate of change is applied to a larger and larger figure.

The *exponential formula,* which is based on continuous compounding, is often used to measure population change. It is preferred by population experts because they view population and population-related subjects as changing without interruption, ever ongoing. Both exponential and compound interest formulas assume a constant rate of change. The former, however, applies the amount of change continuously to the base rather than at the end of each compounding period. When the average annual rates are small (e.g., less than 5 percent) both formulas give virtually the same results. For an explanation

of these two formulas as they relate to population, see U.S. Bureau of the Census, *The Methods and Materials of Demography,* Vol. 2, 3d printing (rev.), 1975, pp. 372-381.

Current and constant dollars. Statistics in some tables in a number of sections are expressed in both current and constant dollars (see, for example, Table 727 in Section 14, Income). Current dollar figures reflect actual prices or costs prevailing during the specified year(s). Constant dollar figures are estimates representing an effort to remove the effects of price changes from statistical series reported in dollar terms. In general, constant dollar series are derived by dividing current dollar estimates by the appropriate price index for the appropriate period (for example, the Consumer Price Index). The result is a series as it would presumably exist if prices were the same throughout, as in the base year—in other words as if the dollar had constant purchasing power. Any changes in this constant dollar series would reflect only changes in real volume of output, income, expenditures, or other measure.

Explanation of Symbols:

The following symbols, used in the tables throughout this book, are explained in condensed form in footnotes to the tables where they appear:

- Represents zero or rounds to less than half the unit of measurement shown.

B Base figure too small to meet statistical standards for reliability of a derived figure.

D Figure withheld to avoid disclosure pertaining to a specific organization or individual.

NA Data not enumerated, tabulated, or otherwise available separately.

NS Percent change irrelevant or insignificant.

S Figure does not meet publication standards for reasons other than that covered by symbol B, above.

X Figure not applicable because column heading and stub line make entry impossible, absurd, or meaningless.

Z Entry would amount to less than half the unit of measurement shown.

In many tables, details will not add to the totals shown because of rounding.

Telephone Contacts List

To help *Abstract* users find more data and information about statistical publications, we are issuing this list of contacts for federal agencies with major statistical programs. The intent is to give a single, first-contact point-of-entry for users of statistics. These agencies will provide general information on their statistical programs and publications, as well as specific information on how to order their publications. We are also including the Internet (World-Wide Web) addresses for many of these agencies. These URLs were current in early September 1998.

Executive Office of the President

Office of Management and Budget

Administrator
Office of Information and Regulatory Affairs
Office of Management and Budget
Washington, DC 20503
Information: 202-395-3080
Publications: 202-395-7332
Internet address:
http://www.whitehouse.gov/WH/EOP/omb

Department of Agriculture

Economic Research Service

Information Center
U.S. Department of Agriculture
Room 3100
1800 M St. N.W.
Washington, DC 20036-5831
Information and Publications: 202-694-5050
Internet address: http://www.econ.ag.gov/

National Agricultural Statistics Service

National Agricultural Statistics Service
U.S. Department of Agriculture
1400 Independence Ave., S.W.
Washington, DC 20250
Information hotline: 1-800-727-9540
Internet address: http://www.usda.gov/nass/

Department of Commerce

Bureau of the Census

Customer Services Branch
Bureau of the Census
U.S. Department of Commerce
Washington, DC 20233
Information and Publications: 301-457-4100
Internet address: http://www.census.gov/

Bureau of Economic Analysis

Current Business Analysis Division, BE-53
Bureau of Economic Analysis
U.S. Department of Commerce
Washington, DC 20230
Information and Publications: 202-606-9900
Internet address: http://www.bea.doc.gov/

Department of Commerce —Con.

International Trade Administration

Trade Statistics Division
Office of Trade and Economic Analysis
International Trade Administration
Room 2814 B
U.S. Department of Commerce
Washington, DC 20230
Information and Publications: 202-482-2185
Internet address:
http://www.ita.doc.gov/tradestats/

National Oceanic and Atmospheric Administration

National Oceanic and Atmospheric
Administration Library
U.S. Department of Commerce
1315 East-West Highway
2nd Floor
Silver Spring, MD 20910
Library: 301-713-2600
Internet address: http://www.lib.noaa.gov/

Department of Defense

Department of Defense
Office of the Assistant to the Secretary of
Defense (Public Affairs)
Room 1E797
Attention: Directorate for Communications
1400 Defense Pentagon
Washington, DC 20301-1400
Information: 703-697-5737
Internet address:
http://web1.whs.osd.mil/mmid/mmidhome.htm

Department of Education

Office of Information Services

Statistical Information Office
U.S. Department of Education
555 New Jersey Ave., N.W.
Washington, DC 20208-5641
Information and Publications:
1-800-424-1616
Internet address: http://www.ed.gov/NCES/

Department of Energy

Energy Information Administration

National Energy Information Center
U.S. Department of Energy
1000 Independence Ave., SW
1F048, EI-30
Washington, DC 20585
Information and Publications: 202-586-8800
Internet address: http://www.eia.doe.gov/

Department of Health and Human Services

Health Resources and Services Administration

HRSA Office of Communications
5600 Fishers Lane, Room 14-45
Rockville, MD 20857
Publications: 301-443-3376
Internet address: http://www.hrsa.dhhs.gov/

Substance Abuse Mental Health Services Administration

U.S. Dept. of Health and Human Services
5600 Fishers Lane, Room 12-105
Rockville, MD 20857
Information: 301-443-4795
Publications: 1-800-729-6686
Internet address: http://www.samhsa.gov/

Centers for Disease Control and Prevention

Office of Information
Centers for Disease Control
1600 Clifton Road, N.E.
Atlanta, GA 30333
Public Inquiries: 1-800-311-3435
Internet address:
http://www.cdc.gov/cdc.html

Health Care Financing Administration

Office of Public Affairs
Health Care Financing Administration
U.S. Dept. of Health and Human Services
Room 403B, Humphrey Building
200 Independence Ave., S.W.
Washington, DC 20201
Media Relations: 202-690-6145
Internet address: http://www.hcfa.gov/

National Center for Health Statistics

Scientific and Technical Information Branch
National Center for Health Statistics
U.S. Department of Health and Human
Services
6525 Belcrest Rd. Rm. 1064
Hyattsville, MD 20782
Information and Publications: 301-436-8500
Internet address:
http://www.cdc.gov/nchswww

Social Security Administration

Office of Research Evaluation and Statistics
4301 Connecticut Ave., N.W. Suite 209
Washington, DC 20008
Information and Publications:
1-800-772-1213
Internet address:
http://www.ssa.gov/statistics/orespubs.htm

Department of Housing and Urban Development

Assistant Secretary for Community Planning and Development

Office of the Assistant Secretary for
Community Planning and Development
U.S. Department of Housing and Urban
Development
451 7th St., S.W.
Washington, DC 20410-0555
Information: 202-708-2690
Publications: 1-800-245-2691
Internet address: http://www.huduser.org/

Department of the Interior

Geological Survey

Earth Science Information Center
Geological Survey
U.S. Department of the Interior
507 National Center
Reston, VA 20192
Information and Publications: 703-648-6045
Internet address for minerals:
http://minerals.er.usgs.gov:80/minerals/
Internet address for other USGS materials:
http://www.usgs.gov/

Department of Justice

Bureau of Justice Statistics

Statistics Division
810 7th St., N.W. 2nd Floor
Washington, DC 20531
Information and Publications: 202-307-0765
Internet address:
http://www.ojp.usdoj.gov/bjs/

National Criminal Justice Reference Service

Box 6000
Rockville, MD 20850
Information and Publications: 301-519-5500
Publications: 1-800-732-3277
Internet address: http://www.ncjrs.org/

Federal Bureau of Investigation

National Crime Information Center
Federal Bureau of Investigation
U.S. Department of Justice
935 Pennsylvania Ave., N.W.
Washington, DC 20535
Information and Publications: 202-324-3691
Publications: 202-324-5611
Internet address: http://www.fbi.gov/

Immigration and Naturalization Service

Statistics Branch
Immigration and Naturalization Service
U.S. Department of Justice
425 I St., NW, Rm. 5309
Washington, DC 20536
Information and Publications: 202-305-1613
Internet address:
http://www.usdoj.gov/ins/index.html

Department of Labor

Bureau of Labor Statistics

Office of Publications and Information
Services
Bureau of Labor Statistics
U.S. Department of Labor
2 Mass. Ave., N.E., Room 2860
Washington, DC 20212
Information and Publications: 202-606-5886
Internet address: http://stats.bls.gov/

Employment and Training Administration

Office of Public Affairs
Employment and Training Administration
U.S. Department of Labor
200 Constitution Ave., N.W., Room S4206
Washington, DC 20210
Information and Publications: 202-219-6871
Internet address: http://www.doleta.gov/

Department of Transportation

Federal Aviation Administration

Public Inquiry Center
APA 200
Federal Aviation Administration
U.S. Department of Transportation
800 Independence Ave., S.W.
Washington, DC 20591
Information and Publications: 202-267-3484
Internet address: http://www.faa.gov/
Bureau of Transportation Statistics
Internet address: http://www.bts.gov/

Federal Highway Administration

Office of Public Affairs
Federal Highway Administration
U.S. Department of Transportation
400 7th St., S.W.
Washington, DC 20590
Information: 202-366-0660
Internet address: http://www.fhwa.dot.gov/

National Highway Traffic Safety Administration

Office of Public & Consumer Affairs
National Highway Traffic Safety
Administration
U.S. Department of Transportation
400 7th St., S.W.
Washington, DC 20590
Information: 202-366-9550
Publications: 202-366-2587
Internet address: http://www.nhtsa.dot.gov/

Department of the Treasury

Internal Revenue Service

Statistics of Income Division
Internal Revenue Service
P.O. Box 2608
Washington, DC 20013-2608
Information and Publications: 202-874-0410
Internet address:
http://www.irs.ustreas.gov/cover.html

Department of Veterans Affairs

Department of Veterans Affairs

Office of Public Affairs
Department of Veterans Affairs
810 Vermont Ave., N.W.
Washington, DC 20420
Information: 202-273-5400
Internet address: http://www.va.gov/

Independent Agencies

Environmental Protection Agency

Information Resource Center, Rm. M2904
Environmental Protection Agency
401 M St., S.W.
Washington, DC 20460
Information: 202-260-5922
Internet address: http://www.epa.gov/

Federal Reserve Board

Division of Research and Statistics
Federal Reserve Board
Washington, DC 20551
Information: 202-452-3301
Publications: 202-452-3245
Internet address: http://www.bog.frb.fed.us/

National Science Foundation

Office of Legislation and Public Affairs
National Science Foundation
4201 Wilson Boulevard
Arlington Virginia 22230
Information: 703-306-1234
Publications: 703-306-1134
Internet address:
http://www.nsf.gov:80/sbe/srs/stats.htm

Securities and Exchange Commission

Office of Public Affairs
Securities and Exchange Commission
450 5th St., N.W.
Washington, DC 20549
Information: 202-942-0020
Publications: 202-942-4040
Internet address: http://www.sec.gov/

Population

This section presents statistics on the growth, distribution, and characteristics of the U.S. population. The principal source of these data is the Bureau of the Census, which conducts a decennial census of population, a monthly population survey, a program of population estimates and projections, and a number of other periodic surveys relating to population characteristics. For a list of relevant publications, see the Guide to Sources of Statistics in Appendix I.

In Brief

Total population, 1997	268 million
Northeast	*19%*
Midwest	*23%*
South	*35%*
West	*22%*
Total households, 1997	101 million
One-person households	*25%*

Decennial censuses—The U.S. Constitution provides for a census of the population every 10 years, primarily to establish a basis for apportionment of members of the House of Representatives among the states. For over a century after the first census in 1790, the census organization was a temporary one, created only for each decennial census. In 1902, the Bureau of the Census was established as a permanent federal agency, responsible for enumerating the population and also for compiling statistics on other subjects.

Historically the census of population has been a complete count. That is, an attempt is made to account for every person, for each person's residence, and for other characteristics (sex, age, family relationships, etc.). Since the 1940 census, in addition to the complete count information, some data have been obtained from representative samples of the population. In the 1990 census, variable sampling rates were employed. For most of the country, 1 in every 6 households (about 17 percent) received the long form or sample questionnaire; in governmental units estimated to have fewer than 2,500 inhabitants, every other household (50 percent) received the sample questionnaire to enhance the reliability of sample data for small areas. Exact agreement is not to be expected between sample data and the complete census count. Sample data may be used with confidence where large numbers are involved and assumed to indicate

trends and relationships where small numbers are involved.

Census data presented here have not been adjusted for underenumeration. Results from the evaluation program for the 1990 census indicate that the overall national undercount was between 1 and 2 percent - the estimate from the Post Enumeration Survey (PES) was 1.6 percent and the estimate from Demographic Analysis (DA) was 1.8 percent. Both the PES and DA estimates show disproportionately high undercounts for some demographic groups. For example, the PES estimates of percent net undercount for Blacks (4.4 percent), Hispanics (5.0 percent), and American Indians (4.5 percent) were higher than the estimated undercount of non-Hispanic Whites (0.7 percent). Historical DA estimates demonstrate that the overall undercount rate in the census has declined significantly over the past 50 years (from an estimated 5.4 percent in 1940 to 1.8 percent in 1990), yet the undercount of Blacks has remained disproportionately high.

Current Population Survey (CPS)—This is a monthly nationwide survey of a scientifically selected sample representing the noninstitutional civilian population. The sample is located in 754 areas comprising 2,121 counties, independent cities, and minor civil divisions with coverage in every state and the District of Columbia and is subject to sampling error. At the present time, about 50,000 occupied households are eligible for interview every month; of these between 4 and 5 percent are, for various reasons, unavailable for interview.

While the primary purpose of the CPS is to obtain monthly statistics on the labor force, it also serves as a vehicle for inquiries on other subjects. Using CPS data, the Bureau issues a series of publications under the general title of *Current Population Reports*, which cover population characteristics (P20), consumer income (P60), special studies (P23), and other topics.

Estimates of population characteristics based on the CPS will not agree with the counts from the census because the CPS and the census use different procedures for collecting and processing the data for racial groups, the Hispanic population, and other topics. Caution should also be used when comparing estimates for various years because of the periodic introduction of changes into the CPS. Beginning in January 1994, a number of changes were introduced into the CPS that effect all data comparisons with prior years. These changes include the results of a major redesign of the survey questionnaire and collection methodology and the introduction of 1990 census population controls, adjusted for the estimated undercount. This change in population controls had relatively little impact on derived measures such as means, medians, and percent distribution, but did have a significant impact on levels.

Population estimates and projections— National population estimates start with decennial census data as benchmarks and add annual population component of change data. Component of change data comes from various agencies, as follows: National Center for Health Statistics (births and deaths), Immigration and Naturalization Service (legal immigrants), Office of Refugee Resettlement (refugees), U.S. Census Bureau's International Programs Center (net movement between Puerto Rico and the U.S. mainland), Armed Forces, Department of Defense, and Office of Personnel Management (movement of military and civilian citizens abroad). Estimated population components of change

included emigration and net undocumented immigration. Estimates for states and smaller areas are based on data series such as births and deaths, school statistics from state departments of education and parochial school systems, and federal income tax returns.

Data for the population by age for April 1, 1990, (shown in Tables 14, 21, and 23) are modified counts. The review of detailed 1990 information indicated that respondents tended to provide their age as of the date of completion of the questionnaire, not their age as of April 1, 1990. In addition, there may have been a tendency for respondents to round up their age if they were close to having a birthday. A detailed explanation of the age modification procedure appears in 1990 Census of Population and Housing Data Paper Listing (CPH-L-74).

Population estimates and projections are published in the P25 series of *Current Population Reports* and *Population Paper Listings (PPLs)*. These estimates and projections are generally consistent with official decennial census figures and do not reflect the amount of estimated census underenumeration. However, these estimates and projections by race have been modified and are not comparable to the census race categories (see section below under "race"). For details on methodology, see the sources cited below the individual tables.

The state population projections, by single year of age, sex, race, and Hispanic origin, prepared for 1995 to 2025 use a cohort–component methodology to generate the projected populations. This method requires separate assumptions for each population component of change: births, deaths, internal migration, and international migration. Data for population components of change derive from various governmental administrative records and census distributions. The 1994 state population estimates serve as the starting point for these projections, which are consistent with the national population projections listed in Current Population Reports, Series P25-1130. The two series of projections (see Table 35) are based on different internal migration assumptions: Series A, the preferred series model, which uses state-to-state migration observed from 1975-76 through 1993-94; and Series B, the economic model, which uses the Bureau of Economic Analysis employment projections.

Immigration—The principal source of immigration data is the *Statistical Yearbook of the Immigration and Naturalization Service*, published annually by the Immigration and Naturalization Service (INS), a unit of the Department of Justice. Immigration statistics are prepared from entry visas and change of immigration status forms. Immigrants are aliens admitted for legal permanent residence in the United States. The procedures for admission depend on whether the alien is residing inside or outside the United States at the time of application for permanent residence. Eligible aliens residing outside the United States are issued immigrant visas by the U.S. Department of State. Eligible aliens residing in the United States are allowed to change their status from temporary to permanent residence at INS district offices. The category, immigrant, includes persons who may have entered the United States as nonimmigrants or refugees, but who subsequently changed their status to that of a permanent resident. Nonresident aliens admitted to the United States for a temporary period are nonimmigrants (Tables 7 and 457). Refugees are considered nonimmigrants when initially admitted into the United States, but are not included in nonimmigrant admission data. A refugee is any person who is outside his or her country of nationality who is unable or unwilling to return to that country because of persecution or a well-founded fear of persecution.

U.S. immigration law gives preferential immigration status to aliens who are related to certain U.S. citizens or legal permanent residents, aliens with needed job skills, or aliens who qualify as refugees. Immigration to the United States can be divided into two general categories: (1) those subject to the annual worldwide limitation, and (2) those exempt from it. The Immigration Act of 1990 established major revisions in the numerical limits

and preference system regulating legal immigration. The numerical limits are imposed on visas issued and not on admissions. The maximum number of visas allowed to be issued under the preference categories in 1996 was 451,819— 311,819 for family-sponsored immigrants and 140,000 for employment-based immigrants. There are nine categories among which the family-sponsored and employment-based immigrant visas are distributed, beginning in fiscal year 1992. The family-sponsored preferences are based on the alien's relationship with a U.S. citizen or legal permanent resident (see Table 6). The employment-based preferences are 1) priority workers (persons of extraordinary ability, outstanding professors and researchers, and certain multinational executives and managers); 2) professionals with advanced degrees or aliens with exceptional ability; 3) skilled workers, professionals without advanced degrees, and needed unskilled workers; 4) special immigrants; and 5) employment creation immigrants (investors). Within the overall limitations the per-country limit for independent countries is set to 7 percent of the total family-sponsored and employment-based limits, while dependent areas are limited to 2 percent of the total. The 1996 limit allowed no more than 31,627 preference visas for any independent country and 9,036 for any dependency. Those exempt from the worldwide limitation include immediate relatives of U.S. citizens, refugees and asylees adjusting to permanent residence, and other various classes of special immigrants (see Table 6).

The Refugee Act of 1980, effective April 1, 1980, provides for a uniform admission procedure for refugees of all countries, based on the United Nations' definition of refugees. Authorized admission ceilings are set annually by the President in consultation with Congress. After 1 year of residence in the United States, refugees are eligible for immigrant status.

The Immigration Reform and Control Act of 1986 (IRCA) allows two groups of illegal aliens to become temporary and then permanent residents of the United States:

aliens who have been in the United States unlawfully since January 1, 1982, (legalization applicants), and aliens who were employed in seasonal agricultural work for a minimum period of time (Special Agricultural Worker (SAW) applicants). The application period for temporary residency for legalization applicants began on May 5, 1987, and ended on May 4, 1988, while the application period for SAW applicants began on June 1, 1987, and ended on November 30, 1988. Legalization applicants became eligible for permanent residence beginning in fiscal year 1989. Beginning 1989 immigrant data include temporary residents who were granted permanent residence under the legalization program of IRCA.

Metropolitan Areas (MAs)—The general concept of a metropolitan area is one of a core area containing a large population nucleus, together with adjacent communities that have a high degree of social and economic integration with that core. Metropolitan statistical areas (MSAs), consolidated metropolitan statistical areas (CMSAs), and primary metropolitan statistical areas (PMSAs) are defined by the Office of Management and Budget (OMB) as a standard for federal agencies in the preparation and publication of statistics relating to metropolitan areas. The entire territory of the United States is classified as metropolitan (inside MSAs or CMSAs—PMSAs are components of CMSAs) or nonmetropolitan (outside MSAs or CMSAs). MSAs, CMSAs, and PMSAs are defined in terms of entire counties except in New England, where the definitions are in terms of cities and towns. The OMB also defines New England County Metropolitan Areas (NECMAs), which are county-based alternatives to the MSAs and CMSAs in the six New England states. Over time, new MAs are created and the boundaries of others change. The analysis of historical trends, therefore, must be made cautiously. For descriptive details and a listing of titles and components of MAs, see Appendix II.

Urban and rural—According to the 1990 census definition, the urban population comprises all persons living in

(a) places of 2,500 or more inhabitants incorporated as cities, villages, boroughs (except in Alaska and New York), and towns (except in the New England states, New York, and Wisconsin), but excluding those persons living in the rural portions of extended cities (places with low population density in one or more large parts of their area); (b) census designated places (previously termed unincorporated) of 2,500 or more inhabitants; and (c) other territory, incorporated or unincorporated, included in urbanized areas. An urbanized area comprises one or more places and the adjacent densely settled surrounding territory that together have a minimum population of 50,000 persons. In all definitions, the population not classified as urban constitutes the rural population

Residence—In determining residence, the Bureau of the Census counts each person as an inhabitant of a usual place of residence (i.e., the place where one usually lives and sleeps). While this place is not necessarily a person's legal residence or voting residence, the use of these different bases of classification would produce the same results in the vast majority of cases.

Race—The Bureau of the Census collects and publishes racial statistics as outlined in Statistical Policy Directive No. 15 issued by the U.S. Office of Management and Budget. This directive provides standards on ethnic and racial categories for statistical reporting to be used by all federal agencies. According to the directive, the basic racial categories are American Indian or Alaska Native, Asian or Pacific Islander, Black, and White. (The directive identifies Hispanic origin as an ethnicity.) The concept of race the Bureau of the Census uses reflects self-identification by respondents; that is the individual's perception of his/her racial identity. The concept is not intended to reflect any biological or anthropological definition. Although the Bureau of the Census adheres to the overall guidelines of Directive No. 15, it recognizes that there are persons who do not identify with a specific racial group. The 1990 census race question includes an "Other race" category with provisions for a write-in entry. Furthermore, the Bureau of the Census recognizes that the categories of the race item include both racial and national origin or socio-cultural groups.

Differences between the 1990 census and earlier censuses affect the comparability of data for certain racial groups and American Indian tribes. The lack of comparability is due to changes in the way some respondents reported their race as well as changes in 1990 census procedures related to the racial classification. (For a fuller explanation, see *1990 Census of Population, Volume I, General Population Characteristics* (1990 CP-1).)

Data for the population by race for April 1, 1990, (shown in Tables 12, 13, 18, 19, 21, and 23) are modified counts and are not comparable to the 1990 census race categories. These numbers were computed using 1990 census data by race which had been modified to be consistent with the guidelines in Federal Statistical Directive No. 15 issued by the Office of Management and Budget. A detailed explanation of the race modification procedure appears in 1990 Census of Population and Housing Data Paper Listing (CPH-L-74).

In the CPS and other household sample surveys in which data are obtained through personal interview, respondents are asked to classify their race as: (1) White, (2) Black, (3) American Indian, Aleut, or Eskimo, or (4) Asian or Pacific Islander. The procedures for classifying persons of mixed races who could not provide a single response to the race question are generally similar to those used in the census.

Hispanic population—In the 1990 census, the Bureau of the Census collected data on the Hispanic-origin population in the United States by using a self-identification question. Persons of Spanish/Hispanic origin are those who classified themselves in one of the specific Hispanic-origin categories listed on the questionnaire—Mexican, Puerto Rican, Cuban, or Other Spanish/Hispanic origin. Both in 1980 and 1990, the

Hispanic-origin question contained prelisted categories for the largest Hispanic origin groups—Mexican, Puerto Rican, and Cuban as well as for the residual category Other Spanish/Hispanic. The 1990 Hispanic-origin question differed from the 1980 question in that in 1990, unlike in 1980, the question contained a write-in line for the subgroups. Another difference between the 1980 and 1990 Hispanic-origin question is that in 1980 the wording of the Hispanic-origin question read: "Is this person of Spanish/Hispanic origin or descent?" while in 1990 the word "descent" was dropped from the question. Persons of Hispanic origin may be of any race.

In the CPS information on Hispanic persons is gathered by using a self-identification question. Persons classify themselves in one of the Hispanic categories in response to the question: "What is the origin or descent of each person in this household?" Hispanic persons in the CPS are persons who report themselves as Mexican-American, Chicano, Mexican, Puerto Rican, Cuban, Central or South American (Spanish countries), or other Hispanic origin.

Nativity—The native population consists of all persons born in the United States, Puerto Rico, or an outlying area of the United States. It also includes persons born in a foreign country who had at least one parent who was a U.S. citizen. All other persons are classified as "foreign born."

Mobility status—The U.S. population is classified according to mobility status on the basis of a comparison between the place of residence of each individual at the time of the survey or census and the place of residence at a specified earlier date. Nonmovers are all persons who were living in the same house or apartment at the end of the period as at the beginning of the period. Movers are all persons who were living in a different house at the end of the period from that in which they were living at the beginning of the period. Movers from abroad include all persons, either U.S. citizens or noncitizens, whose place of residence was outside the United States at the beginning of the period; that is, in Puerto

Rico, an outlying area under the jurisdiction of the United States, or a foreign country.

Living arrangements—Living arrangements refer to residency in households or in group quarters. A "household" comprises all persons who occupy a "housing unit," that is, a house, an apartment or other group of rooms, or a single room that constitutes "separate living quarters." A household includes the related family members and all the unrelated persons, if any, such as lodgers, foster children, wards, or employees who share the housing unit. A person living alone or a group of unrelated persons sharing the same housing unit is also counted as a household. See text, Section 25, Construction and Housing, for definition of housing unit.

All persons not living in households are classified as living in group quarters. These individuals may be institutionalized, e.g., under care or custody in juvenile facilities, jails, correctional facilities, hospitals, or nursing homes; or they may be residents in noninstitutional group quarters such as college dormitories, military barracks, or rooming houses.

Householder—The householder is the first adult household member listed on the questionnaire. The instructions call for listing first the person (or one of the persons) in whose name the home is owned or rented. If a home is owned or rented jointly by a married couple, either the husband or the wife may be listed

first. Prior to 1980, the husband was always considered the household head (householder) in married-couple households.

Family—The term "family" refers to a group of two or more persons related by birth, marriage, or adoption and residing together in a household. A family includes among its members the householder.

Subfamily—A subfamily consists of a married couple and their children, if any, or one parent with one or more never-married children under 18 years old living in a household. Subfamilies are divided into "related" and "unrelated" subfamilies. A related subfamily is related to, but does not include, the householder. Members of a related subfamily are also members of the family with whom they live. The number of related subfamilies, therefore, is not included in the count of families. An unrelated subfamily may include persons such as guests, lodgers, or resident employees and their spouses and/or children; none of whom is related to the householder.

Married couple—A "married couple" is defined as a husband and wife living together in the same household, with or without children and other relatives.

Statistical reliability—For a discussion of statistical collection and estimation, sampling procedures, and measures of statistical reliability applicable to Census Bureau data, see Appendix III.

Figure 1.1
**Ten Fastest-Growing States,
Percent Population Change: 1990 to 1997**

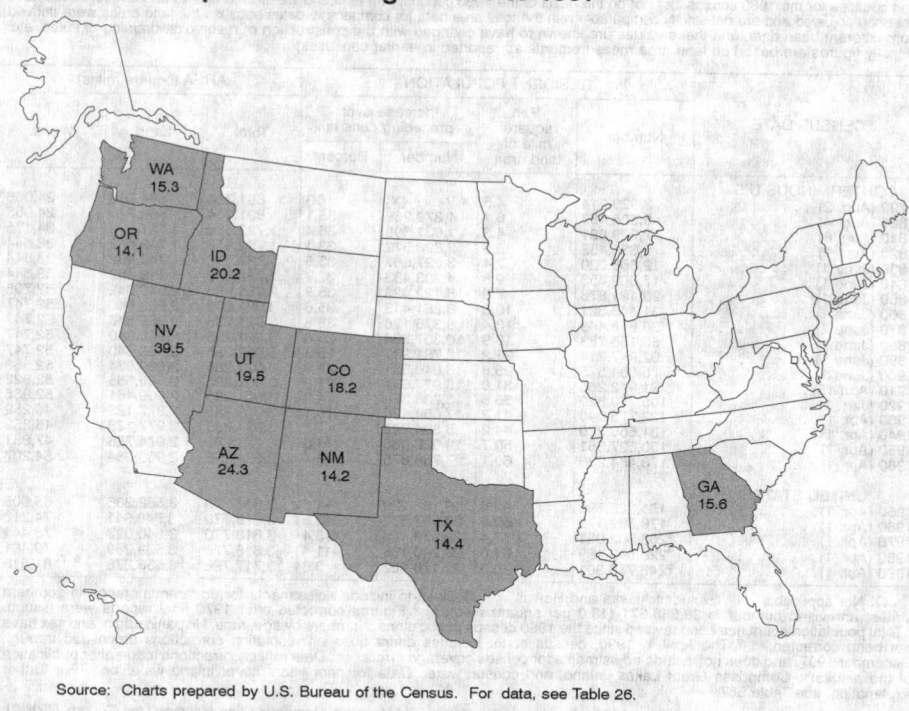

Source: Charts prepared by U.S. Bureau of the Census. For data, see Table 26.

Figure 1.2
**Household Composition—
Percent Change: 1980 to 1997**

1980-90
1990-97

All households

Married-couple households

Male family householder[1]

Female family householder[1]

Nonfamily households

0   10   20   30   40   50   60   70

Percent change

[1] No spouse present.
Source: Charts prepared by U.S. Bureau of the Census. For data, see Table 69.

No. 1. Population and Area: 1790 to 1990

[Area figures represent area on indicated date including in some cases considerable areas not then organized or settled, and not covered by the census. Total area figures for 1790 to 1970 have been recalculated on the basis of the remeasurement of states and counties for the 1980 census, but not on the basis of the 1990 census. The land and water area figures for past censuses have not been adjusted and are not strictly comparable with the total area data for comparable dates because the land areas were derived from different base data, and these values are known to have changed with the construction of reservoirs, draining of lakes, etc. Density figures are based on land area measurements as reported in earlier censuses]

CENSUS DATE	RESIDENT POPULATION				AREA (square miles)		
	Number	Per square mile of land area	Increase over preceding census		Total	Land	Water
			Number	Percent			
CONTERMINOUS U.S. [1]							
1790 (Aug. 2)	3,929,214	4.5	(X)	(X)	891,364	864,746	24,065
1800 (Aug. 4)	5,308,483	6.1	1,379,269	35.1	891,364	864,746	24,065
1810 (Aug. 6)	7,239,881	4.3	1,931,398	36.4	1,722,685	1,681,828	34,175
1820 (Aug. 7)	9,638,453	5.5	2,398,572	33.1	1,792,552	1,749,462	38,544
1830 (June 1)	12,866,020	7.4	3,227,567	33.5	1,792,552	1,749,462	38,544
1840 (June 1)	17,069,453	9.8	4,203,433	32.7	1,792,552	1,749,462	38,544
1850 (June 1)	23,191,876	7.9	6,122,423	35.9	2,991,655	2,940,042	52,705
1860 (June 1)	31,443,321	10.6	8,251,445	35.6	3,021,295	2,969,640	52,747
1870 (June 1)	[2]39,818,449	[2]13.4	8,375,128	26.6	3,021,295	2,969,640	52,747
1880 (June 1)	50,155,783	16.9	10,337,334	26.0	3,021,295	2,969,640	52,747
1890 (June 1)	62,947,714	21.2	12,791,931	25.5	3,021,295	2,969,640	52,747
1900 (June 1)	75,994,575	25.6	13,046,861	20.7	3,021,295	2,969,834	52,553
1910 (Apr. 15)	91,972,266	31.0	15,977,691	21.0	3,021,295	2,969,565	52,822
1920 (Jan. 1)	105,710,620	35.6	13,738,354	14.9	3,021,295	2,969,451	52,936
1930 (Apr. 1)	122,775,046	41.2	17,064,426	16.1	3,021,295	2,977,128	45,259
1940 (Apr. 1)	131,669,275	44.2	8,894,229	7.2	3,021,295	2,977,128	45,259
1950 (Apr. 1)	150,697,361	50.7	19,028,086	14.5	3,021,295	2,974,726	47,661
1960 (Apr. 1)	178,464,236	60.1	27,766,875	18.4	3,021,295	2,968,054	54,207
UNITED STATES							
1950 (Apr. 1)	151,325,798	42.6	19,161,229	14.5	3,618,770	3,552,206	63,005
1960 (Apr. 1)	179,323,175	50.6	27,997,377	18.5	3,618,770	3,540,911	74,212
1970 (Apr. 1)	[3]203,302,031	[3]57.4	23,978,856	13.4	3,618,770	[3]3,540,023	[3]78,444
1980 (Apr. 1)	[4]226,542,199	64.0	23,240,168	11.4	3,618,770	3,539,289	79,481
1990 (Apr. 1)	[5]248,718,301	70.3	22,176,102	9.8	[6]3,717,796	[6]3,536,278	[6][7]181,518

X Not applicable.   [1] Excludes Alaska and Hawaii.   [2] Revised to include adjustments for underenumeration in southern states; unrevised number is 38,558,371 (13.0 per square mile).   [3] Figures corrected after 1970 final reports were issued. [4] Total population count has been revised since the 1980 census publications. Numbers by age, race, Hispanic origin, and sex have not been corrected.   [5] The April 1, 1990, census count includes count question resolution corrections processed through December 1997, and does not include adjustments for census coverage errors.   [6] Data reflect corrections made after publication of the results. [7] Comprises Great Lakes, inland, and coastal water. Data for prior years cover inland water only. For further explanation, see Table 387.

Source: U.S. Bureau of the Census, *1990 Census of Population and Housing, Population and Housing Unit Counts* (CPH-2); 1990 Census of Population and Housing Listing (1990 CPH-L-157); and unpublished data.

No. 2. Population: 1950 to 1997

[In thousands, except percent. Estimates as of July 1. Total population includes Armed Forces abroad; civilian population excludes Armed Forces. For basis of estimates, see text, Section 1]

YEAR	TOTAL		Resident population	Civilian population	YEAR	TOTAL		Resident population	Civilian population
	Population	Percent change				Population	Percent change		
1950	152,271	(X)	151,868	150,790	1974	213,854	0.92	213,342	211,636
1951	154,878	1.71	153,982	151,599	1975	215,973	0.99	215,465	213,789
1952	157,553	1.73	156,393	153,892	1976	218,035	0.95	217,563	215,894
1953	160,184	1.67	158,956	156,595	1977	220,239	1.01	219,760	218,106
1954	163,026	1.77	161,884	159,695	1978	222,585	1.06	222,095	220,467
1955	165,931	1.78	165,069	162,967	1979	225,055	1.11	224,567	222,969
1956	168,903	1.79	168,088	166,055	1980	227,726	1.19	227,225	225,621
1957	171,984	1.82	171,187	169,110	1981	229,966	0.98	229,466	227,818
1958	174,882	1.68	174,149	172,226	1982	232,188	0.97	231,664	229,995
1959	177,830	1.69	177,135	175,277	1983	234,307	0.91	233,792	232,097
1960	180,671	1.60	179,979	178,140	1984	236,348	0.87	235,825	234,110
1961	183,691	1.67	182,992	181,143	1985	238,466	0.90	237,924	236,219
1962	186,538	1.55	185,771	183,677	1986	240,651	0.92	240,133	238,412
1963	189,242	1.45	188,483	186,493	1987	242,804	0.89	242,289	240,550
1964	191,889	1.40	191,141	189,141	1988	245,021	0.91	244,499	242,817
1965	194,303	1.26	193,526	191,605	1989	247,342	0.95	246,819	245,131
1966	196,560	1.16	195,576	193,420	1990	249,949	1.05	249,440	247,799
1967	198,712	1.09	197,457	195,264	1991	252,636	1.08	252,124	250,513
1968	200,706	1.00	199,399	197,113	1992	255,382	1.09	255,002	253,417
1969	202,677	0.98	201,385	199,145	1993	258,089	1.06	257,753	256,280
1970	205,052	1.17	203,984	201,895	1994	260,602	0.97	260,292	258,880
1971	207,661	1.27	206,827	204,866	1995	263,039	0.94	262,761	261,409
1972	209,896	1.08	209,284	207,511	1996	265,453	0.92	265,179	263,893
1973	211,909	0.96	211,357	209,600	1997	267,901	0.92	267,636	266,384

X Not applicable.

Source: U.S. Bureau of the Census, *Current Population Reports*, P25-1045 and P25-1126, and Population Paper Listings PPL-91.

No. 3. Resident Population Projections: 1998 to 2050

[**In thousands**. As of **July 1**. Each series shown assumes middle levels of fertility, life expectancy, and net immigration unless otherwise specified. Middle level components are shown in footnote 1]

YEAR	Middle series [1]	Lowest series [2]	Highest series [3]	FERTILITY		LIFE EXPECTANCY		NET IMMIGRATION	
				Low	High	Low	High	Low	High
1998	270,002	268,396	271,647	269,565	270,392	269,783	270,250	269,050	271,008
1999	272,330	269,861	274,865	271,678	272,915	272,006	272,697	270,835	273,910
2000	274,634	271,237	278,129	273,731	275,448	274,185	275,141	272,581	276,802
2005	285,981	276,990	295,318	283,299	288,471	284,647	287,467	280,949	291,287
2010	297,716	281,468	314,571	292,303	302,893	294,986	300,482	289,423	306,444
2015	310,134	285,472	335,597	301,444	318,595	305,539	314,376	298,356	322,508
2020	322,742	288,807	357,702	310,429	334,889	315,885	328,698	307,290	338,955
2025	335,050	290,789	380,781	318,575	351,554	325,530	343,023	315,709	355,318
2030	346,899	291,070	405,089	325,517	368,732	334,331	357,227	323,414	371,480
2040	369,980	287,685	458,444	336,407	405,660	350,592	385,898	337,416	403,986
2050	393,931	282,524	518,903	345,352	447,502	367,913	415,908	351,354	438,299

[1] Total fertility rate in 2050 = 2,245; life expectancy in 2050 = 82.0 years; and annual net immigration = 820,000. These are middle level assumptions. For explanation of total fertility rate; see headnote, Table 97.   [2] Total fertility rate in 2050 = 1,910; life expectancy in 2050 = 74.8 years; and annual net immigration = 300,000. These are lowest level assumptions.   [3] Total fertility rate in 2050 = 2,580; life expectancy in 2050 = 89.4 years; and annual net immigration = 1,370,000. These are highest level assumptions.

Source: U.S. Bureau of the Census, *Current Population Reports*, P25-1130.

No. 4. Components of Population Change, 1980 to 1997, and Projections, 1998 to 2050

[Resident population. The estimates prior to 1990 are consistent with the original 1990 census count of 248,709,873. Starting with 1990, estimates reflect the revised April 1, 1990, census count of 248,765,170 which includes count resolution corrections processed through August 1997, and does not include adjustments for census coverage errors except for adjustments estimated for the 1995 Census Test in Oakland, California; Patterson, New Jersey; and six Louisiana parishes. These adjustments amounted to a total of 55,297 persons]

YEAR	Popula- tion at start of period (1,000)	TOTAL (Jan. 1-Dec. 31)					RATE PER 1,000 MIDYEAR POPULATION			
		Net increase [1]		Natural increase		Net migra- tion [3] (1,000)	Net growth rate [1]	Natural increase		Net migra- tion rate [3]
		Total (1,000)	Per- cent [2]	Births (1,000)	Deaths (1,000)			Birth rate	Death rate	
1980 [4]	226,546	1,900	0.8	2,743	1,463	724	11.1	16.0	8.6	4.2
1981	228,446	2,200	1.0	3,629	1,978	690	9.6	15.8	8.6	3.0
1982	230,645	2,157	0.9	3,681	1,975	595	9.3	15.9	8.5	2.6
1983	232,803	2,066	0.9	3,639	2,019	592	8.8	15.6	8.6	2.5
1984	234,868	2,070	0.9	3,669	2,039	589	8.8	15.6	8.6	2.5
1985	236,938	2,171	0.9	3,761	2,086	649	9.1	15.8	8.8	2.7
1986	239,109	2,158	0.9	3,757	2,105	661	9.0	15.6	8.8	2.8
1987	241,267	2,195	0.9	3,809	2,123	666	9.1	15.7	8.8	2.7
1988	243,462	2,243	0.9	3,910	2,168	662	9.2	16.0	8.9	2.7
1989 [5]	245,705	2,438	1.0	4,041	2,150	712	9.9	16.4	8.7	2.9
1990 [5]	248,143	2,532	1.0	4,148	2,155	[6]539	10.1	16.6	8.6	[6]2.2
1991	250,689	2,903	1.2	4,111	2,170	[6]962	11.5	16.3	8.6	[6]3.8
1992	253,593	2,893	1.1	4,065	2,176	1,004	11.3	15.9	8.5	3.9
1993	256,486	2,612	1.0	4,000	2,269	880	10.1	15.5	8.8	3.4
1994	259,098	2,477	1.0	3,953	2,279	803	9.5	15.2	8.8	3.1
1995	261,575	2,435	0.9	3,900	2,312	848	9.3	14.8	8.8	3.2
1996	264,010	2,477	0.9	3,915	2,322	884	9.3	14.8	8.8	3.3
1997	266,487	2,435	0.9	3,899	2,333	868	9.1	14.6	8.7	3.2
PROJECTIONS [7]										
1998	268,823	2,342	0.9	3,899	2,377	820	8.7	14.4	8.8	3.0
1999	271,166	2,316	0.9	3,896	2,401	820	8.5	14.3	8.8	3.0
2000	273,482	2,294	0.8	3,899	2,425	820	8.4	14.2	8.8	3.0
2005	284,847	2,278	0.8	4,001	2,543	820	8.0	14.0	8.9	2.9
2010	296,511	2,426	0.8	4,243	2,638	820	8.1	14.3	8.9	2.8
2015	308,875	2,521	0.8	4,450	2,749	820	8.1	14.3	8.9	2.6
2020	321,487	2,504	0.8	4,579	2,895	820	7.8	14.2	9.0	2.5
2025	333,838	2,414	0.7	4,679	3,085	820	7.2	14.0	9.2	2.4
2030	345,730	2,333	0.7	4,822	3,309	820	6.7	13.9	9.5	2.4
2040	368,823	2,319	0.6	5,248	3,749	820	6.3	14.2	10.1	2.2
2050	392,681	2,517	0.6	5,672	3,975	820	6.4	14.4	10.1	2.1

[1] Prior to April 1, 1990, includes "error of closure" (the amount necessary to make the components of change add to the net change between censuses), for which figures are not shown separately.   [2] Percent of population at beginning of period.   [3] Covers net international migration and movement of Armed Forces, federally affiliated civilian citizens, and their dependents.   [4] Data are for period April 1 to December 31.   [5] Net change for 1990 excludes "error of closure" for the 3 months prior to the April 1 census date. Therefore, it may not equal the difference between the populations at the beginning of 1990 and 1991.   [6] Data reflect movement of Armed Forces due to the Gulf War.   [7] Based on middle series of assumptions. See footnote 1, Table 3.

Source: U.S. Bureau of the Census, *Current Population Reports*, P25-1095 and P25-1130; and Population Paper Listings PPL-91.

Population

No. 5. Immigration: 1901 to 1996

[**In thousands, except rate. For fiscal years ending in year shown**; see text, Section 9. For definition of immigrants, see text, Section 1. Data represent immigrants admitted. Rates based on Bureau of the Census estimates as of July 1 for resident population through 1929, and for total population thereafter (excluding Alaska and Hawaii prior to 1959)]

PERIOD	Number	Rate [1]	YEAR	Number	Rate [1]
1901 to 1910	8,795	10.4	1980	531	2.3
1911 to 1920	5,736	5.7	1985	570	2.4
1921 to 1930	4,107	3.5	1989	1,091	4.4
1931 to 1940	528	0.4	1990	1,536	6.1
1941 to 1950	1,035	0.7	1991	1,827	7.2
1951 to 1960	2,515	1.5	1992	974	3.8
1961 to 1970	3,322	1.7	1993	904	3.5
1971 to 1980	4,493	2.1	1994	804	3.1
1981 to 1990	7,338	3.1	1995	720	2.7
1991 to 1996	6,146	4.0	1996	916	3.5

[1] Annual rate per 1,000 U.S. population. Rate computed by dividing sum of annual immigration totals by sum of annual U.S. population totals for same number of years.

Source: U.S. Immigration and Naturalization Service, *Statistical Yearbook*, annual.

No. 6. Immigrants Admitted, by Class of Admission: 1990 to 1996

[**For fiscal year ending September 30**. For definition of immigrants, see text, Section 1]

CLASS OF ADMISSION	1990	1992	1993	1994	1995	1996
Immigrants, total.	**1,536,483**	**973,977**	**904,292**	**804,416**	**720,461**	**915,900**
New arrivals	435,729	511,769	536,294	490,429	380,291	421,405
Adjustments	1,100,754	462,208	367,998	313,987	340,170	494,495
Preference immigrants, total	272,742	329,321	373,788	335,252	323,458	411,673
Family-sponsored immigrants, total.	214,550	213,123	226,776	211,961	238,122	294,174
Unmarried sons/daughters of U.S. citizens and their children.	15,861	12,486	12,819	13,181	15,182	20,909
Spouses, unmarried sons/daughters of alien residents, and their children	107,686	118,247	128,308	115,000	144,535	182,834
Married sons/daughters of U.S. citizens [1]	26,751	22,195	23,385	22,191	20,876	25,452
Brothers or sisters of U.S. citizens [1]	64,252	60,195	62,264	61,589	57,529	64,979
Employment-based immigrants, total.	58,192	116,198	147,012	123,291	85,336	117,499
Priority workers [1]	(X)	5,456	21,114	21,053	17,339	27,501
Professionals with advanced degrees [1]	(X)	58,401	29,468	14,432	10,475	18,462
Skilled workers, professionals, unskilled workers [1]	(X)	47,568	87,689	76,956	50,245	62,756
Special immigrants [1]	4,463	4,063	8,158	10,406	6,737	7,844
Employment creation [1]	(X)	59	583	444	540	936
Professional or highly skilled immigrants [1 2]	26,546	340	(X)	(X)	(X)	(X)
Needed skilled or unskilled workers [1 2]	27,183	311	(X)	(X)	(X)	(X)
Immediate relatives	231,680	235,484	255,059	249,764	220,360	300,430
Spouses of U.S. citizens	125,426	128,396	145,843	145,247	123,238	169,760
Children of U.S. citizens	46,065	42,324	46,788	48,147	48,740	63,971
Orphans.	7,088	6,536	7,348	8,200	9,384	11,366
Parents of U.S. citizens	60,189	64,764	62,428	56,370	48,382	66,699
Refugees and asylees	97,364	117,037	127,343	121,434	114,664	128,565
Cuban Refugee Act, Nov. 1966	5,730	5,365	6,976	8,316	9,579	20,131
Indochinese Refugee Act, Oct. 1977	33	29	24	11	10	5
Refugee-Parolee Act, Oct. 1978.	153	82	53	20	22	9
Asylees, Refugee Act of 1980	4,937	10,658	11,804	5,983	7,837	10,037
Refugees, Refugee Act of 1980	86,511	100,902	108,486	107,104	97,169	98,383
Other refugees	-	1	-	-	47	-
Other immigrants	934,697	292,135	148,102	97,966	61,979	75,232
Children born abroad to resident aliens	2,410	2,116	2,030	1,883	1,894	1,660
Diversity Programs [3]	29,161	36,348	33,480	41,056	47,245	58,790
Amerasians (P.L. 100-202) [4]	13,059	17,253	11,116	2,822	939	956
Immigration Reform and Control Act of 1986 legalization adjustments.	880,372	163,342	24,278	6,022	4,267	4,635
Legalization dependents [5]	(X)	52,272	55,344	34,074	277	184
Other	9,695	20,804	21,854	12,109	7,357	9,007

- Represents zero.   X Not applicable.   [1] Includes spouses and children.   [2] Category was eliminated in 1992 by the Immigration Act of 1990.   [3] Includes categories of immigrants admitted under three laws intended to diversify immigration: P.L. 99-603, P.L. 100-658, and P.L. 101-649.   [4] Under Public Law 100-202, Amerasians are aliens born in Vietnam between January 1, 1962, and January 1, 1976, who were fathered by U.S. citizens.   [5] Spouses and children of persons granted permanent resident status under provisions of the Immigration Reform and Control Act of 1986.

Source: U.S. Immigration and Naturalization Service, *Statistical Yearbook,* annual.

No. 7. Nonimmigrants Admitted, by Class of Admission: 1985 to 1996

[In thousands, except as noted. For fiscal years ending Sept. 30; see text, Section 9. Nonimmigrants are nonresident aliens (non-U.S. citizens) admitted to the United States for a temporary period. Excluded are border crossers, crewmen, and insular travelers]

CLASS OF ADMISSION	1985	1990	1991	1992	1993	1994	1995	1996
Nonimmigrants [1]	9,540	17,574	18,963	20,794	21,566	22,119	22,641	24,843
Temporary visitors, total	8,405	16,080	17,386	19,238	19,879	20,319	20,887	22,880
For pleasure	6,609	13,418	14,734	16,450	16,918	17,155	17,612	19,110
For business [2]	1,797	2,661	2,652	2,788	2,961	3,164	3,275	3,770
Transit aliens [2]	237	306	364	346	331	331	320	326
Foreign government officials [3]	90	97	98	103	102	105	104	118
Treaty traders and investors [3]	97	148	155	152	145	141	132	139
Students [3]	286	355	314	275	403	428	395	459
Representatives to international organizations [3]	57	61	64	70	73	75	72	80
Temporary workers and trainees [4]	75	140	161	163	163	186	197	227
Registered nurses [5]	(X)	(X)	1	7	7	6	7	2
Specialty occupations [6]	(X)	(X)	117	110	93	106	118	144
Workers of distinguished merit or ability [7]	47	100	(X)	(X)	(X)	(X)	(X)	(X)
Performing services unavailable in U.S. [9]	25	36	40	34	29	29	26	24
North America Free-Trade Agreement [8]	(X)	5	8	13	17	25	24	27
Spouses and children of workers and trainees [9]	13	29	35	41	42	49	54	61
Representatives of foreign information media [3]	17	20	21	22	21	28	24	34
Exchange visitors [3]	141	215	224	232	239	259	240	257
NATO officials [3]	8	8	9	9	9	9	9	11
Finances(ees) of U.S. citizens [10]	8	7	8	9	9	9	9	10
Intracompany transferees [3]	107	103	113	121	132	154	174	214
Parolees [11]	64	90	127	137	124	111	114	(NA)
Refugees	68	110	100	123	113	114	96	(NA)

NA Not available.   X Not applicable.   [1] Includes nonimmigrants whose class of admission is unknown.   [2] Includes foreign government officials and their spouses and (unmarried minor or dependent) children, in transit.   [3] Includes spouses and children.   [4] Includes other classes of admission, not shown separately.   [5] Entries began October 1, 1990 (fiscal year 1991). Data for fiscal year 1991 are underreported; an unknown number of H1A entries were counted as H1B entries.   [6] Prior to October 1, 1991, (fiscal year 1992), H1B entries were termed "Distinguished merit or ability." Data for fiscal year 1991 are overreported; an unknown number of H1A entries were counted as H1B entries.   [7] Beginning 1992, as a result of the Immigration Act of 1990, the existing temporary worker and trainee classes of admission have been revised and new worker classes have been created.   [8] Entries under the U.S.-Canada Free Trade Agreement began in January 1989 and under the North American Free Trade Agreement (NAFTA) in January 1994.   [9] Includes spouses and children under NAFTA.   [10] Includes children of fiances(ees) of U.S. citizens.   [11] Aliens allowed to enter the United States for a temporary period of time on emergency conditions or when the entry is determined to be in the public interest (e.g., witness in court).
Source: U.S. Immigration and Naturalization Service, *Statistical Yearbook*, annual.

No. 8. Immigrants, by Country of Birth: 1981 to 1996

[In thousands. For fiscal years ending in year shown; see text, Section 9. For definition of immigrants, see text, Section 1]

COUNTRY OF BIRTH	1981-90, total	1991-94, total	1995	1996
All countries	7,338.1	4,509.9	720.5	915.9
Europe [1]	705.6	599.8	128.2	147.6
France	23.1	11.3	2.5	3.1
Germany	70.1	30.7	6.2	6.7
Greece	29.1	7.3	1.3	1.5
Ireland	32.8	47.8	5.3	1.7
Italy	32.9	10.0	2.2	2.5
Poland	97.4	100.6	13.8	15.8
Portugal	40.0	11.5	2.6	3.0
Romania	38.9	23.6	4.9	5.8
Soviet Union, former [2]	84.0	222.6	54.5	62.8
Armenia	(NA)	(NA)	2.0	2.4
Azerbaijan	(NA)	(NA)	1.9	2.0
Belarus	(NA)	(NA)	3.8	4.3
Moldova	(NA)	(NA)	1.9	1.8
Russia	(NA)	(NA)	14.6	19.7
Ukraine	(NA)	(NA)	17.4	21.1
Uzbekistan	(NA)	(NA)	3.6	4.7
United Kingdom	142.1	69.0	12.4	13.6
Yugoslavia	19.2	11.5	8.3	11.9
Asia [1]	2,817.4	1,366.1	267.9	307.8
Afghanistan	26.6	10.9	1.4	1.3
Bangladesh	15.2	21.1	6.1	8.2
Cambodia	116.6	8.9	1.5	1.6
China	[3]388.8	191.5	35.5	41.7
Hong Kong	63.0	37.8	7.2	7.8
India	261.9	156.9	34.7	44.9
Iran	154.8	59.1	9.2	11.1
Iraq	19.6	15.7	5.6	5.5
Israel	36.3	17.2	2.5	3.1
Japan	43.2	29.1	4.8	6.0
Jordan	32.6	17.0	3.6	4.4
Korea	338.8	79.9	16.0	18.2
Laos	145.6	31.0	3.9	2.8
Lebanon	41.6	21.6	3.9	4.4
Pakistan	61.3	48.2	9.8	12.5
Philippines	495.3	241.6	51.0	55.9
Syria	20.6	11.1	2.4	3.1
Taiwan	(3)	54.0	9.4	13.4
Thailand	64.4	26.6	5.1	4.3
Turkey	20.9	9.1	2.9	3.7
Vietnam	401.4	234.0	41.8	42.1
North America [1]	3,125.0	2,168.6	231.5	340.5
Canada	119.2	61.9	12.9	15.8
Mexico	1,653.3	1,397.9	89.9	163.6
Caribbean [1]	892.7	441.8	96.8	116.8
Cuba	159.2	50.5	17.9	26.5
Dominican Republic	251.8	180.0	38.5	39.6
Haiti	140.2	82.0	14.0	18.4
Jamaica	213.8	74.3	16.4	19.1
Trinidad and Tobago	39.5	28.3	5.4	7.3
Central America [1]	458.7	266.7	31.8	44.3
El Salvador	214.6	118.0	11.7	17.9
Guatemala	87.9	55.3	6.2	8.8
Honduras	49.5	30.6	5.5	5.9
Nicaragua	44.1	39.1	4.4	6.9
Panama	29.0	12.1	2.2	2.6
South America [1]	455.9	236.5	45.7	61.8
Argentina	25.7	12.9	1.8	2.5
Brazil	23.7	22.0	4.6	5.9
Chile	23.4	8.2	1.5	1.7
Colombia	124.4	56.6	10.8	14.3
Ecuador	56.0	30.5	6.4	8.3
Guyana	95.4	36.8	7.4	9.5
Peru	64.4	45.7	8.1	12.9
Venezuela	17.9	10.1	2.6	3.5
Africa [1]	192.3	117.8	42.5	52.9
Egypt	31.4	16.1	5.6	6.2
Ethiopia	27.2	18.9	7.0	6.1
Ghana	14.9	8.3	3.2	6.6
Nigeria	35.3	20.9	6.8	10.2
Other countries [4]	41.9	21.0	4.7	5.3

NA Not available.   [1] Includes countries not shown separately.   [2] Includes other republics and unknown republics, not shown separately.   [3] Data for Taiwan included with China.   [4] Includes Australia, New Zealand, and unknown countries.
Source of Tables 7 and 8: U.S. Immigration and Naturalization Service, *Statistical Yearbook,* annual; and releases.

Population

No. 9. Immigrants Admitted as Permanent Residents Under Refugee Acts, by Country of Birth: 1981 to 1996

[For fiscal years ending in year shown; see text, Section 9. Covers immigrants who were allowed to enter the United States under 1953 Refugee Relief Act and later acts; Hungarian parolees under July 1958 Act; refugee-escapee parolees under July 1960 Act; conditional entries by refugees under Oct. 1965 Act; Cuban parolees under Nov. 1966 Act; Indochina refugees under Act of Oct. 1977; refugee-parolees under the Act of Oct. 1978, and asylees under the Act of March 1980; and refugees under the Act of March 1980]

COUNTRY OF BIRTH	1981-90, total	1991-94, total	1995	1996	COUNTRY OF BIRTH	1981-90, total	1991-94, total	1995	1996
Total	**1,013,620**	**504,893**	**114,664**	**128,565**	China [3]	7,928	3,431	803	845
Europe [1]	**155,512**	**213,840**	**46,998**	**51,977**	Hong Kong	1,916	440	48	47
Albania	353	2,545	314	154	Iran	46,773	17,669	1,245	1,212
Bulgaria	1,197	1,314	105	100	Iraq	7,540	6,814	3,848	3,802
Czechoslovakia	8,204	1,138	38	25	Laos	142,964	28,182	3,364	2,155
Hungary	4,942	1,163	28	40	Philippines	3,403	695	80	80
Poland	33,889	6,782	245	183	Syria	2,145	497	258	208
Romania	29,798	14,100	592	447	Thailand	30,259	14,451	2,932	1,940
Soviet Union, former [2]	72,306	181,711	40,120	42,356	Turkey	1,896	360	58	42
Armenia	(NA)	(NA)	214	182	Vietnam	324,453	111,265	28,595	29,700
Azerbaijan	(NA)	(NA)	1,594	1,446	**North America** [1]	**121,840**	**67,409**	**16,265**	**28,070**
Belarus	(NA)	(NA)	3,421	3,480	Cuba	113,367	41,473	12,355	22,542
Moldova	(NA)	(NA)	1,597	1,415	El Salvador	1,383	3,078	283	262
Russia	(NA)	(NA)	8,176	9,745	Guatemala	(NA)	806	158	234
Ukraine	(NA)	(NA)	14,937	16,636	Nicaragua	5,590	19,759	727	766
Uzbekistan	(NA)	(NA)	3,258	4,144	**South America**	**1,976**	**1,606**	**497**	**922**
Yugoslavia	324	707	4,744	7,820	**Africa** [1]	**22,149**	**21,233**	**7,527**	**5,464**
Asia [1]	**712,092**	**200,735**	**43,314**	**42,076**	Ethiopia	18,542	13,062	1,802	985
Afghanistan	22,946	8,080	616	369	Sudan	(NA)	1,398	935	1,089
Cambodia	114,CS4	5,610	268	210	**Other**	**51**	**70**	**63**	**56**

NA Not available. [1] Includes other countries, not shown separately. [2] Includes other republics and unknown republics, not shown separately. [3] Includes Taiwan.

Source: U.S. Immigration and Naturalization Service, *Statistical Yearbook*, annual; and releases.

No. 10. Estimated Undocumented Immigrants, by Selected States and Countries of Origin: 1996

[As of **October**. Based on estimates of illegal immigrant population who established residence in the United States before 1982 and did not legalize under the Immigration Reform and Control Act (IRCA) and annual estimates of the number of persons who enter surreptitiously across land borders and nonimmigrant overstays who established residence here during the 1982 to 1996 period. The estimates for each country were distributed to States by INS based on U.S. residence pattern of each country's total number of applicants for legalization under IRCA]

STATE	Number (1,000)	COUNTRY	Number (1,000)
United States, total [1]	**5,000**	**Total** [1]	**5,000**
California	2,000	Mexico	2,700
Texas	700	El Salvador	335
New York	540	Guatemala	165
Florida	350	Canada	120
Illinois	290	Haiti	105
New Jersey	135	Philippines	95
Arizona	115	Honduras	90
Massachusetts	85	Bahamas, The	70
Virginia	55	Nicaragua	70
Washington	52	Poland	70
Colorado	45	Colombia	65
Maryland	44	Ecuador	55
New Mexico	37	Jamaica	50
Pennsylvania	37	Dominican Republic	50
Michigan	37	Trinidad & Tobago	50
Oregon	33	Pakistan	41
Georgia	32	India	33
District of Columbia	30	Dominica	32
Connecticut	29	Peru	30
Nevada	24	Korea	30

[1] Includes other states and countries not shown separately.

Source: U.S. Immigration and Naturalization Service, unpublished data.

No. 11. Immigrants Admitted, by Leading Country of Birth and State: 1996

[For year ending September 30. For definition of immigrants, see text, Section 1]

STATE OR OTHER AREA	Total [1]	Mexico	Philippines	India	Vietnam	China	Dominican Republic	Cuba	Ukraine
Total	915,900	163,572	55,876	44,859	42,067	41,728	39,604	26,466	21,079
AL	1,782	162	74	234	74	112	2	3	21
AK	1,280	111	385	28	24	29	24	5	14
AZ	8,900	5,051	316	273	265	251	9	8	48
AR	1,494	446	96	105	138	45	5	-	4
CA	201,529	64,238	23,438	7,757	13,549	10,864	83	346	2,630
CO	8,895	3,138	185	203	753	430	7	6	216
CT	10,874	207	262	681	249	454	278	69	197
DE	1,377	130	60	143	40	66	9	7	14
DC	3,784	40	108	60	350	209	95	3	5
FL	79,461	3,155	1,796	1,393	977	773	2,050	22,217	327
GA	12,608	1,399	252	1,127	1,961	455	46	57	196
HI	8,436	70	5,208	24	328	555	-	1	1
ID	1,825	839	37	42	88	50	-	2	32
IL	42,517	11,715	2,516	3,829	777	1,164	66	109	1,406
IN	4,692	877	219	364	150	282	15	16	106
IA	3,037	620	95	153	447	106	4	-	17
KS	4,303	1,470	131	166	683	160	3	8	88
KY	2,019	98	90	162	150	123	4	16	57
LA	4,092	178	158	336	899	216	28	79	9
ME	1,028	14	39	32	69	74	3	7	13
MD	20,732	319	942	1,421	633	1,095	171	26	391
MA	23,085	141	288	1,075	1,452	1,630	2,051	64	688
MI	17,253	828	391	1,745	455	768	52	24	231
MN	8,977	496	195	376	820	344	10	20	244
MS	1,073	61	117	122	124	72	2	26	4
MO	5,690	451	261	397	710	326	3	56	91
MT	449	15	30	15	-	29	-	-	31
NE	2,150	893	62	69	236	53	2	-	27
NV	5,874	2,263	806	136	83	166	15	255	21
NH	1,512	40	52	90	199	95	38		18
NJ	63,303	1,125	3,544	6,185	630	2,140	5,006	1,593	839
NM	5,780	4,254	91	123	99	69	3	179	10
NY	154,095	1,553	3,719	5,611	971	11,409	20,579	452	9,185
NC	7,011	661	298	682	582	334	40	53	60
ND	606	16	19	42	53	10	1	4	2
OH	10,237	320	343	1,122	294	801	29	19	636
OK	3,511	931	136	216	580	132	5	7	7
OR	7,554	1,942	338	207	888	434	10	27	444
PA	16,938	692	440	1,785	961	1,056	296	62	1,026
RI	3,098	49	65	53	25	102	560	9	68
SC	2,151	148	166	222	121	141	2	-	17
SD	519	15	23	20	20	23	2	9	19
TN	4,343	261	175	384	400	197	3	30	28
TX	83,385	46,403	2,064	3,295	5,793	1,701	108	258	257
UT	4,250	1,036	79	134	280	190	13	7	47
VT	654	19	12	19	81	42	2	-	6
VA	21,375	531	1,446	1,208	1,437	743	50	47	153
WA	18,833	3,482	1,688	577	2,105	774	7	9	1,032
WV	583	18	57	78	2	40	-	2	-
WI	3,607	474	112	287	44	215	16	10	94
WY	280	94	11	10	3	12	-	2	2
GU	2,820	-	2,220	13	14	81	-	-	-
Northern Mariana Islands	176	-	149	-	-	14	-	-	-
PR	8,560	73	7	9	-	66	7,354	257	-
VI	1,384	3	5	15	1	5	442	-	-
Armed Services posts	109	-	60	4	-	1	1	-	-
Other	10	7	-	-	-	-	-	-	-

- Represents zero. [1] Includes other countries, not shown separately.

Source: U.S. Immigration and Naturalization Service, *Statistical Yearbook,* annual.

No. 12. Resident Population—Selected Characteristics, 1790 to 1997, and Projections, 2000 to 2050

[In thousands]

DATE	SEX		RACE					Hispanic origin [1]
					Other			
	Male	Female	White	Black	Total	American Indian, Eskimo, Aleut	Asian and Pacific Islanders	
1790 (Aug. 2) [2]	(NA)	(NA)	3,172	757	(NA)	(NA)	(NA)	(NA)
1800 (Aug. 4) [2]	(NA)	(NA)	4,306	1,002	(NA)	(NA)	(NA)	(NA)
1850 (June 1) [2]	11,838	11,354	19,553	3,639	(NA)	(NA)	(NA)	(NA)
1900 (June 1) [2]	38,816	37,178	66,809	8,834	351	(NA)	(NA)	(NA)
1910 (Apr. 15) [2]	47,332	44,640	81,732	9,828	413	(NA)	(NA)	(NA)
1920 (Jan. 1) [2]	53,900	51,810	94,821	10,463	427	(NA)	(NA)	(NA)
1930 (Apr. 1) [2]	62,137	60,638	110,287	11,891	597	(NA)	(NA)	(NA)
1940 (Apr. 1) [2]	66,062	65,608	118,215	12,866	589	(NA)	(NA)	(NA)
1950 (Apr. 1) [2]	74,833	75,864	134,942	15,042	713	(NA)	(NA)	(NA)
1950 (Apr. 1)	75,187	76,139	135,150	15,045	1,131	(NA)	(NA)	(NA)
1960 (Apr. 1)	88,331	90,992	158,832	18,872	1,620	(NA)	(NA)	(NA)
1970 (Apr. 1) [3]	98,926	104,309	178,098	22,581	2,557	(NA)	(NA)	(NA)
1980 (Apr. 1) [4 5]	110,053	116,493	194,713	26,683	5,150	1,420	3,729	14,609
1990 (Apr. 1) [4 6]	121,271	127,494	208,727	30,511	9,527	2,065	7,462	22,372
1991 (July 1) [7]	122,995	129,130	210,974	31,128	10,024	2,110	7,914	23,432
1992 (July 1) [7]	124,506	130,496	212,885	31,670	10,446	2,147	8,299	24,361
1993 (July 1) [7]	125,913	131,839	214,715	32,180	10,859	2,184	8,675	25,334
1994 (July 1) [7]	127,216	133,076	216,413	32,653	11,227	2,219	9,008	26,302
1995 (July 1) [7]	128,499	134,261	218,066	33,093	11,601	2,252	9,349	27,274
1996 (July 1) [7]	129,746	135,434	219,686	33,514	11,979	2,287	9,692	28,305
1997 (July 1) [7]	131,018	136,618	221,334	33,947	12,355	2,322	10,033	29,348
2000 (July 1) [8]	134,181	140,453	225,532	35,454	13,647	2,402	11,245	31,366
2005 (July 1) [8]	139,785	146,196	232,463	37,734	15,784	2,572	13,212	36,057
2010 (July 1) [8]	145,584	152,132	239,588	40,109	18,019	2,754	15,265	41,139
2015 (July 1) [8]	151,750	158,383	247,193	42,586	20,355	2,941	17,413	46,705
2020 (July 1) [8]	158,021	164,721	254,887	45,075	22,780	3,129	19,651	52,652
2025 (July 1) [8]	164,119	170,931	262,227	47,539	25,284	3,319	21,965	58,930
2050 (July 1) [8]	193,234	200,696	294,615	60,592	38,724	4,371	34,352	96,508

NA Not available.   [1] Persons of Hispanic origin may be of any race.   [2] Excludes Alaska and Hawaii.   [3] The revised 1970 resident population count is 203,302,031; which incorporates changes due to errors found after tabulations were completed. The race and sex data shown here reflect the official 1970 census count.   [4] The race data shown have been modified; see text, Section 1, for explanation.   [5] See footnote 4, Table 1.   [6] The April 1, 1990, census count (248,765,170) includes count resolution corrections processed through August 1997, and does not include adjustments for census coverage errors except for adjustments estimated for the 1995 Census Test in Oakland, California; Patterson, New Jersey; and six Louisiana parishes. These adjustments amounted to a total of 55,297 persons.   [7] Estimated.   [8] Middle series projection; see Table 3.

No. 13. Resident Population Characteristics—Percent Distribution and Median Age, 1850 to 1997, and Projections, 2000 to 2050

[In percent, except as indicated. For definition of median, see Guide to Tabular Presentation]

DATE	SEX		RACE				Hispanic origin [1]	Median age (years)
	Male	Female	White	Black	American Indian, Eskimo, Aleut	Asian and Pacific Islander		
1850 (June 1) [2]	51.0	49.0	84.3	15.7	(NA)	(NA)	(NA)	18.9
1900 (June 1) [2]	51.1	48.9	87.9	11.6	(NA)	(NA)	(NA)	22.9
1910 (Apr. 15) [2]	51.5	48.5	88.9	10.7	(NA)	(NA)	(NA)	24.1
1920 (Jan. 1) [2]	51.0	49.0	89.7	9.9	(NA)	(NA)	(NA)	25.3
1930 (Apr. 1) [2]	50.6	49.4	89.8	9.7	(NA)	(NA)	(NA)	26.4
1940 (Apr. 1) [2]	50.2	49.8	89.8	9.8	(NA)	(NA)	(NA)	29.0
1950 (Apr. 1) [2]	49.7	50.3	89.5	10.0	(NA)	(NA)	(NA)	30.2
1950 (Apr. 1)	49.7	50.3	89.3	9.9	(NA)	(NA)	(NA)	30.2
1960 (Apr. 1)	49.3	50.7	88.6	10.5	(NA)	(NA)	(NA)	29.5
1970 (Apr. 1)	48.7	51.3	87.6	11.1	(NA)	(NA)	(NA)	28.0
1980 (Apr. 1) [3 4]	48.6	51.4	85.9	11.8	0.6	1.6	6.4	30.0
1990 (Apr. 1) [3 5]	48.7	51.3	83.9	12.3	0.8	3.0	9.0	32.8
1995 (July 1) [6]	48.9	51.1	83.0	12.6	0.9	3.6	10.4	34.3
1997 (July 1) [6]	49.0	51.0	82.7	12.7	0.9	3.7	11.0	34.9
2000 (July 1) [7]	48.9	51.1	82.1	12.9	0.9	4.1	11.4	35.7
2025 (July 1) [7]	49.0	51.0	78.3	14.2	1.0	6.6	17.6	38.0
2050 (July 1) [7]	49.1	50.9	74.8	15.4	1.1	8.7	24.5	38.1

NA Not available.   [1] Persons of Hispanic origin may be of any race.   [2] Excludes Alaska and Hawaii.   [3] The race data shown have been modified; see text, Section 1 for explanation.   [4] See footnote 4, Table 1.   [5] See footnote 6, Table 12.   [6] Estimated.   [7] Middle series projection; see Table 3.

Source of tables 12 and 13: U.S. Bureau of the Census, *U.S. Census of Population: 1940*, Vol. II, Part 1, and Vol. IV, Part 1; *1950*, Vol. II, Part 1; *1960*, Vol. I, Part 1; *1970*, Vol. I, Part B; *Current Population Reports*, P25-1095 and P25-1130; and Population Paper Listings PPL-91.

No. 14. Resident Population, by Age and Sex: 1980 to 1997

[In thousands, except as indicated. 1980 and 1990 data are enumerated population as of April 1; data for other years are estimated population as of July 1. Excludes Armed Forces overseas. For definition of median, see Guide to Tabular Presentation]

YEAR AND SEX	Total, all years	Under 5 years	5-9 years	10-14 years	15-19 years	20-24 years	25-29 years	30-34 years	35-39 years	40-44 years	45-49 years	50-54 years	55-59 years	60-64 years	65-74 years	75-84 years	85 years and over	5-13 years	14-17 years	18-24 years	Median age (yr.)
1980, total [1]	226,546	16,348	16,700	18,242	21,168	21,319	19,521	17,561	13,965	11,669	11,090	11,710	11,615	10,088	15,581	7,729	2,240	31,159	16,247	30,022	30.0
Male	110,053	8,362	8,539	9,316	10,755	10,663	9,705	8,677	6,862	5,708	5,388	5,621	5,482	4,670	6,757	2,867	682	15,923	8,298	15,054	28.8
Female	116,493	7,986	8,161	8,926	10,413	10,655	9,816	8,884	7,104	5,961	5,702	6,089	6,133	5,418	8,824	4,862	1,559	15,237	7,950	14,969	31.3
1981, total	229,466	16,893	16,060	18,300	20,541	21,663	20,169	18,731	14,366	12,028	10,985	11,595	11,554	10,359	15,890	7,982	2,349	30,711	15,609	30,245	30.3
1982, total	231,664	17,228	15,958	18,145	19,962	21,682	20,704	18,714	14,566	12,464	11,011	11,414	11,463	10,567	16,147	8,203	2,437	30,528	15,057	30,162	30.5
1983, total	233,792	17,547	16,053	17,869	19,388	21,632	21,141	19,067	16,117	13,150	11,201	11,155	11,457	10,655	16,414	8,429	2,518	30,279	14,740	29,922	30.8
1984, total	235,825	17,695	16,338	17,450	18,931	21,529	21,459	19,503	16,867	13,636	11,429	10,957	11,352	10,803	16,626	8,656	2,595	30,062	14,725	29,461	31.1
1985, total	237,924	17,842	16,665	17,027	18,727	21,265	21,671	20,025	17,604	14,087	11,606	10,854	11,229	10,906	16,858	8,890	2,667	29,893	14,888	28,902	31.4
1986, total	240,133	17,963	17,098	16,474	18,813	21,893	21,893	20,479	18,611	14,398	11,878	10,781	11,135	10,859	17,137	9,129	2,742	30,078	14,824	28,227	31.7
1987, total	242,289	18,052	17,430	16,377	18,698	20,192	21,857	20,984	18,619	15,608	12,294	10,802	10,968	10,783	17,426	9,376	2,823	30,502	14,502	27,694	32.0
1988, total	244,499	18,195	17,759	16,496	18,496	19,655	21,739	21,391	18,993	16,188	12,954	10,995	10,722	10,791	17,626	9,612	2,885	31,028	14,023	27,356	32.3
1989, total	246,819	18,508	17,917	16,797	18,133	19,258	21,560	21,676	19,455	16,960	13,421	11,212	10,534	10,707	17,864	9,850	2,968	31,413	13,536	27,156	32.6
1990, total [2]	248,765	18,763	18,040	17,065	17,890	19,139	21,333	21,837	19,849	17,592	13,746	11,314	10,489	10,626	18,047	10,012	3,022	31,835	13,344	26,955	32.8
Male	121,271	9,602	9,234	8,741	9,177	9,747	10,706	10,865	9,836	8,679	6,741	5,494	5,009	4,947	7,908	3,745	841	16,298	6,860	13,742	31.6
Female	127,494	9,161	8,805	8,324	8,713	9,393	10,627	10,972	10,014	8,914	7,005	5,820	5,479	5,679	10,140	6,267	2,180	15,536	6,484	13,215	34.0
1991, total	252,124	19,187	18,198	17,653	17,232	19,177	20,715	22,152	20,524	18,761	14,101	11,651	10,424	10,582	18,269	10,312	3,185	32,443	13,439	26,378	33.1
1992, total	255,002	19,489	18,285	18,065	17,170	19,085	20,152	22,237	21,092	18,806	15,362	12,059	10,487	10,440	18,440	10,527	3,306	32,907	13,679	26,019	33.4
1993, total	257,753	19,670	18,433	18,464	17,353	18,838	19,593	22,229	21,599	19,207	15,936	12,732	10,682	10,238	18,626	10,723	3,431	33,341	13,952	25,796	33.7
1994, total	260,292	19,694	18,742	18,666	17,707	18,451	19,142	22,141	21,973	19,714	16,685	13,199	10,937	10,079	18,696	10,925	3,542	33,667	14,443	25,456	34.0
1995, total	262,761	19,526	19,083	18,798	18,152	18,046	18,954	21,839	22,293	20,257	17,464	13,647	11,092	10,049	18,748	11,154	3,658	34,142	14,770	25,168	34.3
1996, total	265,179	19,324	19,425	18,949	18,644	17,562	18,993	21,328	22,550	20,809	17,438	13,931	11,362	9,997	18,673	11,432	3,762	34,550	15,149	24,882	34.6
1997, total	267,636	19,150	19,738	19,040	19,068	17,512	18,869	20,741	22,625	21,373	18,470	15,163	11,757	10,056	18,499	11,706	3,871	34,949	15,429	24,979	34.9
Male	131,018	9,801	10,104	9,757	9,827	8,979	9,470	10,340	11,286	10,596	9,074	7,383	5,646	4,745	8,268	4,628	1,112	17,896	7,950	12,821	33.8
Female	136,618	9,349	9,634	9,283	9,241	8,532	9,399	10,401	11,338	10,777	9,396	7,780	6,111	5,311	10,230	7,077	2,759	17,053	7,479	12,158	36.1
Percent:																					
1980 [1]	100.0	7.2	7.4	8.1	9.3	9.4	8.6	7.8	6.2	5.2	4.9	5.2	5.1	4.5	6.9	3.4	1.0	13.8	7.2	13.3	(X)
1990 [2]	100.0	7.5	7.3	6.9	7.2	7.7	8.6	8.8	7.9	7.1	5.5	4.5	4.3	4.2	7.3	4.0	1.2	12.8	5.4	10.8	(X)
1997	100.0	7.2	7.4	7.1	7.1	6.5	7.1	7.7	8.5	8.0	6.9	5.7	4.4	3.8	6.9	4.4	1.4	13.1	5.8	9.3	(X)
Male	100.0	7.5	7.7	7.5	7.5	6.9	7.2	7.9	8.6	8.1	6.9	5.6	4.3	3.6	6.3	3.5	0.8	13.7	6.1	9.8	(X)
Female	100.0	6.8	7.1	6.8	6.8	6.2	6.9	7.6	8.3	7.9	6.9	5.7	4.5	3.9	7.5	5.2	2.0	12.5	5.5	8.9	(X)

X Not applicable.   [1] Total population count has been revised since the 1980 census publications. Numbers by age, race, Hispanic origin, and sex have not been corrected.   [2] The data shown have been modified from the official 1990 census counts. See text, Section 1, for explanation. The April 1, 1990, census count (248,765,170) includes count resolution corrections processed through August 1997, and does not include adjustments for census coverage errors except for adjustments estimated for the 1995 Census Test in Oakland, California; Patterson, New Jersey; and six Louisiana parishes. These adjustments amounted to a total of 55,297 persons.

Source: U.S. Bureau of the Census, Current Population Reports, P25-1095; and Population Paper Listings 91.

No. 15. Ratio of Males to Females, by Age Group, 1980 to 1997, and Projections, 2000 and 2025

[**Number of males per 100 females**. Total resident population]

AGE	1980 (Apr. 1)	1990 [1] (Apr. 1)	1995 (July 1)	1996 (July 1)	1997 (July 1)	PROJECTIONS [2] 2000 (July 1)	PROJECTIONS [2] 2025 (July 1)
All ages.	94.5	95.1	95.7	95.8	95.9	95.5	96.0
Under 14 years	104.6	104.9	104.9	104.9	104.9	104.8	105.1
14 to 24 years	101.9	104.6	105.5	105.7	105.8	104.1	104.2
25 to 44 years	97.4	98.9	99.4	99.4	99.5	98.9	97.7
45 to 64 years	90.7	92.5	93.6	93.7	93.9	93.8	93.5
65 years and over.	67.6	67.2	69.1	69.4	69.8	70.4	82.9

[1] The April 1, 1990, census count (248,765,170) includes count resolution corrections processed through August 1997, and does not include adjustments for census coverage errors except for adjustments estimated for the 1995 Census Test in Oakland, California; Patterson, New Jersey; and six Louisiana parishes. These adjustments amounted to a total of 55,297 persons. [2] Middle series projections; see Table 3.

Source: U.S. Bureau of the Census, *Current Population Reports*, P25-1095 and P25-1130; and Population Paper Listings PPL-91.

No. 16. Resident Population, by Sex and Age: 1997

[**In thousands, except as indicated**. As of **July 1**. For derivation of estimates, see text, Section 1]

AGE	Total	Male	Female	AGE	Total	Male	Female
Total	267,636	131,018	136,618	43 yrs. old	4,098	2,019	2,078
				44 yrs. old	4,128	2,051	2,077
Under 5 yrs. old	19,150	9,801	9,349	45 to 49 yrs. old	18,470	9,074	9,396
Under 1 yr. old	3,797	1,943	1,854	45 yrs. old	3,951	1,951	2,000
1 yr. old	3,773	1,929	1,844	46 yrs. old	3,674	1,806	1,868
2 yrs. old	3,795	1,942	1,852	47 yrs. old	3,681	1,805	1,876
3 yrs. old	3,838	1,965	1,874	48 yrs. old	3,420	1,671	1,749
4 yrs. old	3,947	2,022	1,925	49 yrs. old	3,744	1,840	1,904
5 to 9 yrs. old.	19,738	10,104	9,634				
5 yrs. old	4,022	2,057	1,965	50 to 54 yrs. old	15,163	7,383	7,780
6 yrs. old	4,043	2,069	1,974	50 yrs. old	3,898	1,912	1,986
7 yrs. old	4,029	2,063	1,967	51 yrs. old	2,724	1,326	1,398
8 yrs. old	3,732	1,911	1,821	52 yrs. old	2,770	1,346	1,424
9 yrs. old	3,912	2,004	1,907	53 yrs. old	2,790	1,353	1,437
				54 yrs. old	2,981	1,446	1,534
10 to 14 yrs. old	19,040	9,757	9,283	55 to 59 yrs. old.	11,757	5,646	6,111
10 yrs. old	3,873	1,987	1,887	55 yrs. old	2,532	1,220	1,313
11 yrs. old	3,813	1,954	1,859	56 yrs. old	2,440	1,173	1,268
12 yrs. old	3,799	1,944	1,855	57 yrs. old	2,356	1,131	1,225
13 yrs. old	3,725	1,907	1,818	58 yrs. old	2,168	1,039	1,130
14 yrs. old	3,829	1,965	1,864	59 yrs. old	2,260	1,084	1,176
15 to 19 yrs. old	19,068	9,827	9,241				
15 yrs. old	3,870	1,989	1,881	60 to 64 yrs. old	10,056	4,745	5,311
16 yrs. old	3,815	1,969	1,846	60 yrs. old	2,087	985	1,102
17 yrs. old	3,915	2,027	1,888	61 yrs. old	2,030	963	1,067
18 yrs. old	3,679	1,895	1,784	62 yrs. old	2,048	967	1,081
19 yrs. old	3,789	1,947	1,842	63 yrs. old	1,923	911	1,012
				64 yrs. old	1,968	919	1,049
20 to 24 yrs. old	17,512	8,979	8,532	65 to 69 yrs. old.	9,762	4,461	5,301
20 yrs. old	3,738	1,925	1,813	65 yrs. old	1,947	899	1,048
21 yrs. old	3,510	1,809	1,701	66 yrs. old	1,996	919	1,077
22 yrs. old	3,450	1,773	1,678	67 yrs. old	1,985	915	1,070
23 yrs. old	3,337	1,706	1,632	68 yrs. old	1,889	857	1,032
24 yrs. old	3,476	1,767	1,709	69 yrs. old	1,946	872	1,074
25 to 29 yrs. old	18,869	9,470	9,399				
25 yrs. old	3,637	1,839	1,798	70 to 74 yrs. old.	8,736	3,807	4,929
26 yrs. old	3,876	1,941	1,935	70 yrs. old	1,854	822	1,033
27 yrs. old	3,890	1,951	1,938	71 yrs. old	1,787	784	1,003
28 yrs. old	3,578	1,791	1,787	72 yrs. old	1,788	784	1,004
29 yrs. old	3,888	1,947	1,941	73 yrs. old	1,683	725	958
				74 yrs. old	1,623	692	931
30 to 34 yrs. old	20,741	10,340	10,401	75 to 79 yrs. old.	7,063	2,915	4,148
30 yrs. old	3,882	1,935	1,947	75 yrs. old	1,619	686	933
31 yrs. old	3,901	1,943	1,957	76 yrs. old	1,529	646	884
32 yrs. old	4,146	2,065	2,081	77 yrs. old	1,383	571	812
33 yrs. old	4,288	2,131	2,157	78 yrs. old	1,316	531	785
34 yrs. old	4,524	2,265	2,258	79 yrs. old	1,216	481	734
35 to 39 yrs. old	22,625	11,286	11,338				
35 yrs. old	4,573	2,286	2,287	80 to 84 yrs. old	4,642	1,713	2,929
36 yrs. old	4,492	2,238	2,254	80 yrs. old	1,090	422	667
37 yrs. old	4,572	2,280	2,292	81 yrs. old	1,008	382	626
38 yrs. old	4,249	2,112	2,137	82 yrs. old	930	343	587
39 yrs. old	4,739	2,370	2,368	83 yrs. old	848	302	546
				84 yrs. old	766	264	503
40 to 44 yrs. old	21,373	10,596	10,777	85 to 89 yrs. old	2,456	767	1,689
40 yrs. old	4,583	2,281	2,302	90 to 94 yrs. old	1,058	271	787
41 yrs. old	4,308	2,133	2,175	95 to 99 yrs. old	298	63	234
42 yrs. old	4,257	2,111	2,145	100 yrs. old and over. . .	60	11	50
				Median age (yr.)	34.9	33.8	36.1

Source: U.S. Bureau of the Census, Population Paper Listings PPL-91.

No. 17. Resident Population Projections, by Age and Sex: 1998 to 2050

[In thousands. As of July. See headnote, Table 3]

YEAR	Total	Under 5 years	5 to 13 years	14 to 17 years	18 to 24 years	25 to 34 years	35 to 44 years	45 to 54 years	55 to 64 years	65 to 74 years	75 to 84 years	85 years and over
TOTAL												
Lowest series:												
1998......	268,396	18,626	35,487	15,428	24,972	38,530	44,257	34,432	22,585	18,286	11,851	3,943
1999......	269,861	18,295	35,658	15,547	25,423	37,518	44,450	35,580	23,260	18,068	12,019	4,044
2000......	271,237	17,943	35,790	15,602	25,876	36,740	44,364	36,840	23,798	17,974	12,162	4,148
2005......	276,990	16,896	34,366	16,667	27,491	35,095	41,365	40,992	29,145	17,943	12,465	4,566
2010......	281,468	16,563	31,950	16,319	29,050	36,393	37,049	42,589	34,393	20,245	11,912	5,005
2015......	285,472	16,941	30,832	15,026	28,899	38,644	35,351	39,630	38,217	24,843	11,962	5,128
2020......	288,807	17,168	30,998	14,331	26,671	40,067	36,640	35,487	39,642	29,219	13,598	4,987
2025......	290,789	16,901	31,576	14,234	25,368	38,969	38,834	33,847	36,821	32,395	16,748	5,094
2030......	291,070	16,450	31,454	14,631	25,111	36,312	40,222	35,075	32,948	33,483	19,610	5,776
2040......	287,685	16,200	30,164	14,405	25,849	35,018	36,489	38,475	32,631	27,827	22,376	8,250
2050......	282,524	16,330	30,124	13,925	24,810	35,604	35,185	34,868	35,747	27,700	18,588	9,642
Middle series:												
1998......	270,002	19,117	35,609	15,503	25,160	38,757	44,389	34,520	22,662	18,365	11,925	3,996
1999......	272,330	19,041	35,846	15,661	25,710	37,876	44,661	35,717	23,378	18,186	12,129	4,124
2000......	274,634	18,987	36,043	15,752	26,258	37,233	44,659	37,030	23,962	18,136	12,315	4,259
2005......	285,981	19,127	35,850	16,986	28,268	36,306	42,165	41,507	29,606	18,369	12,898	4,899
2010......	297,716	20,012	35,605	16,894	30,138	38,292	38,521	43,564	35,283	21,057	12,680	5,671
2015......	310,134	21,174	36,698	16,651	30,516	41,084	37,598	41,196	39,650	26,243	13,130	6,193
2020......	322,742	21,979	38,660	16,965	29,919	42,934	39,612	37,740	41,714	31,385	15,375	6,460
2025......	335,050	22,498	40,413	17,872	30,372	43,119	42,391	36,890	39,542	35,425	19,481	7,046
2030......	346,899	23,066	41,589	18,788	31,826	42,744	44,263	38,897	36,348	37,406	23,517	8,455
2040......	369,980	24,980	43,993	19,844	34,570	45,932	44,159	43,530	37,739	33,013	28,668	13,552
2050......	393,931	27,106	47,804	21,207	36,333	49,365	47,393	43,494	42,368	34,731	25,905	18,223
Highest series:												
1998......	271,647	19,563	35,735	15,581	25,352	39,004	44,561	34,615	22,728	18,434	12,011	4,063
1999......	274,865	19,726	36,039	15,780	26,004	38,264	44,932	35,868	23,482	18,290	12,257	4,225
2000......	278,129	19,955	36,300	15,909	26,651	37,766	45,038	37,241	24,105	18,276	12,490	4,399
2005......	295,318	21,350	37,266	17,318	29,064	37,599	43,197	42,119	29,997	18,723	13,367	5,317
2010......	314,571	23,649	39,195	17,467	31,248	40,275	40,302	44,738	36,018	21,696	13,465	6,518
2015......	335,597	25,757	42,763	18,228	32,120	43,587	40,161	43,020	40,839	27,278	14,260	7,583
2020......	357,702	27,273	46,855	19,641	33,084	45,836	42,878	40,263	43,473	32,937	17,007	8,456
2025......	380,781	28,828	50,036	21,737	35,428	47,204	46,208	40,172	41,925	37,593	21,882	9,768
2030......	405,089	30,818	52,876	23,276	38,886	49,091	48,519	42,895	39,398	40,270	26,861	12,198
2040......	458,444	35,901	60,446	26,000	44,069	57,362	51,925	48,560	42,258	37,096	33,907	20,920
2050......	518,903	41,213	70,000	30,005	49,683	64,279	60,324	51,967	47,950	40,319	32,070	31,093
MALE (middle series)												
1998	131,883	9,780	18,232	7,961	12,787	19,325	22,044	16,860	10,805	8,224	4,730	1,134
1999	133,039	9,740	18,355	8,042	13,063	18,869	22,184	17,446	11,150	8,171	4,839	1,179
2000	134,181	9,712	18,454	8,090	13,338	18,535	22,181	18,092	11,433	8,180	4,937	1,228
2005	139,785	9,786	18,353	8,724	14,359	18,014	20,891	20,304	14,166	8,408	5,306	1,473
2010	145,584	10,243	18,232	8,679	15,313	18,990	18,993	21,325	16,922	9,752	5,363	1,771
2015	151,754	10,844	18,801	8,554	15,505	20,393	18,479	20,119	19,077	12,273	5,711	1,995
2020	158,021	11,259	19,813	8,718	15,201	21,319	19,466	18,347	20,120	14,791	6,845	2,141
2025	164,119	11,525	20,712	9,184	15,432	21,405	20,848	17,878	19,048	16,826	8,839	2,422
2030	169,950	11,813	21,311	9,653	16,171	21,214	21,775	18,854	17,441	17,878	10,819	3,021
2040	181,261	12,788	22,534	10,192	17,563	22,808	21,723	21,139	18,093	15,796	13,522	5,103
2050	193,234	13,877	24,488	10,893	18,462	24,533	23,352	21,150	20,403	16,699	12,342	7,036
FEMALE (middle series)												
1998	138,119	9,336	17,377	7,542	12,373	19,432	22,345	17,659	11,857	10,141	7,194	2,862
1999	139,291	9,302	17,492	7,619	12,647	19,007	22,476	18,271	12,228	10,015	7,290	2,945
2000	140,453	9,274	17,589	7,662	12,920	18,699	22,478	18,938	12,529	9,956	7,377	3,031
2005	146,196	9,341	17,498	8,262	13,909	18,291	21,273	21,203	15,440	9,961	7,592	3,426
2010	152,132	9,768	17,373	8,215	14,824	19,301	19,527	22,240	18,362	11,305	7,317	3,899
2015	158,383	10,330	17,897	8,097	15,010	20,691	19,119	21,078	20,572	13,971	7,419	4,199
2020	164,721	10,719	18,847	8,247	14,717	21,615	20,146	19,393	21,594	16,594	8,530	4,319
2025	170,931	10,973	19,701	8,688	14,939	21,715	21,543	19,011	20,495	18,599	10,643	4,624
2030	176,949	11,253	20,278	9,135	15,655	21,529	22,488	20,044	18,907	19,529	12,699	5,433
2040	188,719	12,192	21,459	9,652	17,006	23,125	22,436	22,391	19,646	17,216	15,146	8,449
2050	200,696	13,229	23,316	10,314	17,871	24,832	24,041	22,344	21,965	18,032	13,563	11,188

Source: U.S. Bureau of the Census, *Current Population Reports*, P25-1130.

Population

No. 18. Resident Population, by Race, 1980 to 1997, and Projections, 1998 to 2050

[**In thousands, except as indicated**. As of **July**, except as indicated. These data are consistent with the 1980 and 1990 decennial enumerations and have been modified from the official census counts; see text, Section 1, for explanation. See headnote, Table 3]

YEAR	Total	White	Black	American Indian, Eskimo, Aleut	Asian, Pacific Islander
1980 (April) [1]	226,546	194,713	26,683	1,420	3,729
1981	229,466	196,635	27,133	1,483	4,214
1982	231,664	198,037	27,508	1,537	4,581
1983	233,792	199,420	27,867	1,596	4,909
1984	235,825	200,708	28,212	1,656	5,249
1985	237,924	202,031	28,569	1,718	5,606
1986	240,133	203,430	28,942	1,783	5,978
1987	242,289	204,770	29,325	1,851	6,343
1988	244,499	206,129	29,723	1,923	6,724
1989	246,819	207,540	30,143	2,001	7,134
1990 (April) [2]	248,765	208,727	30,511	2,065	7,462
1991	252,124	210,974	31,128	2,110	7,914
1992	255,002	212,885	31,670	2,147	8,299
1993	257,753	214,715	32,180	2,184	8,675
1994	260,292	216,413	32,653	2,219	9,008
1995	262,761	218,066	33,093	2,252	9,349
1996	265,179	219,686	33,514	2,287	9,692
1997	267,636	221,334	33,947	2,322	10,033
PROJECTIONS					
Lowest series:					
1998	268,396	221,501	34,357	2,328	10,211
1999	269,861	222,346	34,721	2,355	10,440
2000	271,237	223,114	35,074	2,382	10,667
2005	276,990	226,006	36,695	2,514	11,774
2010	281,468	227,841	38,139	2,642	12,845
2015	285,472	229,295	39,491	2,766	13,920
2020	288,807	230,202	40,709	2,881	15,015
2030	291,070	228,310	42,519	3,080	17,161
2040	287,685	221,671	43,674	3,247	19,092
2050	282,524	213,782	44,477	3,383	20,882
Middle series:					
1998	270,002	222,648	34,537	2,337	10,480
1999	272,330	224,103	34,997	2,369	10,861
2000	274,634	225,532	35,454	2,402	11,245
2005	285,981	232,463	37,734	2,572	13,212
2010	297,716	239,588	40,109	2,754	15,265
2015	310,134	247,193	42,586	2,941	17,413
2020	322,742	254,887	45,075	3,129	19,651
2030	346,899	269,046	50,001	3,515	24,337
2040	369,980	281,720	55,094	3,932	29,235
2050	393,931	294,615	60,592	4,371	34,352
Highest series:					
1998	271,647	223,785	34,755	2,346	10,761
1999	274,865	225,848	35,332	2,383	11,302
2000	278,129	227,937	35,919	2,421	11,851
2005	295,318	238,906	39,050	2,627	14,735
2010	314,571	251,262	42,590	2,860	17,859
2015	335,597	264,859	46,435	3,108	21,195
2020	357,702	279,139	50,490	3,365	24,709
2030	405,089	309,404	59,449	3,934	32,302
2040	458,444	343,201	69,844	4,609	40,790
2050	518,903	381,505	81,815	5,384	50,199
PERCENT DISTRIBUTION					
Middle series:					
2000	100.0	82.1	12.9	0.9	4.1
2010	100.0	80.5	13.5	0.9	5.1
2020	100.0	79.0	14.0	1.0	6.1
2030	100.0	77.6	14.4	1.0	7.0
2040	100.0	76.1	14.9	1.1	7.9
2050	100.0	74.8	15.4	1.1	8.7
PERCENT CHANGE (middle series)					
2000-2010	8.4	6.2	13.1	14.6	35.8
2010-2020	8.4	6.4	12.4	13.6	28.7
2020-2030	7.5	5.6	10.9	12.3	23.8
2030-2040	6.7	4.7	10.2	11.8	20.1
2040-2050	6.5	4.6	10.0	11.2	17.5

[1] See footnote 4, Table 1. [2] The April 1, 1990, census count (248,765,170) includes count resolution corrections processed through August 1997, and does not include adjustments for census coverage errors except for adjustments estimated for the 1995 Census Test in Oakland, California; Patterson, New Jersey; and six Louisiana parishes. These adjustments amounted to a total of 55,297 persons.

Source: U.S. Bureau of the Census, *Current Population Reports*, P25-1095 and P25-1130; and Population Paper Listing PPL-91.

No. 19. Resident Population, by Hispanic Origin Status, 1980 to 1997, and Projections, 1998 to 2050

[**In thousands, except as indicated**. As of **July**, except as indicated. These data are consistent with the 1980 and 1990 decennial enumerations and have been modified from the official census counts; see text, Section 1, for explanation. See headnote, Table 3. Minus sign (-) indicates decrease]

YEAR	Total	Hispanic origin [1]	NOT OF HISPANIC ORIGIN			
			White	Black	American Indian, Eskimo, Aleut	Asian, Pacific Islander
1980 (April) [2]	226,546	14,609	180,906	26,142	1,326	3,563
1981	229,466	15,560	181,974	26,532	1,377	4,022
1982	231,664	16,240	182,782	26,856	1,420	4,367
1983	233,792	16,935	183,561	27,159	1,466	4,671
1984	235,825	17,640	184,243	27,444	1,512	4,986
1985	237,924	18,368	184,945	27,738	1,558	5,315
1986	240,133	19,154	185,678	28,040	1,606	5,655
1987	242,289	19,946	186,353	28,351	1,654	5,985
1988	244,499	20,786	187,012	28,669	1,703	6,329
1989	246,819	21,648	187,713	29,005	1,755	6,698
1990 (April) [3]	248,765	22,372	188,307	29,299	1,796	6,992
1991	252,124	23,432	189,590	29,849	1,829	7,425
1992	255,002	24,361	190,657	30,333	1,856	7,794
1993	257,753	25,334	191,606	30,778	1,882	8,153
1994	260,292	26,302	192,426	31,189	1,906	8,469
1995	262,761	27,274	193,198	31,566	1,929	8,794
1996	265,179	28,305	193,875	31,927	1,952	9,120
1997	267,636	29,348	194,571	32,298	1,976	9,443
PROJECTIONS						
Lowest series:						
1998	268,396	29,115	195,037	32,647	1,999	9,598
1999	269,861	29,757	195,307	32,962	2,020	9,815
2000	271,237	30,393	195,505	33,267	2,041	10,030
2005	276,990	33,527	195,589	34,652	2,145	11,077
2010	281,468	36,652	194,628	35,856	2,243	12,088
2015	285,472	39,927	193,150	36,956	2,337	13,102
2020	288,807	43,287	191,047	37,913	2,424	14,136
2030	291,070	49,834	183,295	39,202	2,573	16,166
2040	287,685	56,104	171,054	39,841	2,695	17,991
2050	282,524	62,230	157,701	40,118	2,793	19,683
Middle series:						
1998	270,002	29,566	195,786	32,789	2,005	9,856
1999	272,330	30,461	196,441	33,180	2,029	10,219
2000	274,634	31,366	197,061	33,568	2,054	10,584
2005	285,981	36,057	199,802	35,485	2,183	12,454
2010	297,716	41,139	202,390	37,466	2,320	14,402
2015	310,134	46,705	205,019	39,512	2,461	16,437
2020	322,742	52,652	207,393	41,538	2,601	18,557
2030	346,899	65,570	209,998	45,448	2,891	22,993
2040	369,980	80,164	209,621	49,379	3,203	27,614
2050	393,931	96,508	207,901	53,555	3,534	32,432
Highest series:						
1998	271,647	30,019	196,521	32,971	2,010	10,127
1999	274,865	31,172	197,556	33,457	2,038	10,642
2000	278,129	32,350	198,594	33,952	2,066	11,166
2005	295,318	38,648	203,949	36,589	2,218	13,914
2010	314,571	45,760	209,963	39,572	2,391	16,885
2015	335,597	53,686	216,482	42,800	2,575	20,055
2020	357,702	62,279	223,082	46,183	2,765	23,392
2030	405,089	81,803	235,898	53,604	3,192	30,593
2040	458,444	105,274	248,715	62,132	3,703	38,620
2050	518,903	133,106	262,140	71,863	4,295	47,498
PERCENT DISTRIBUTION						
Middle series:						
2000	100.0	11.4	71.8	12.2	0.7	3.9
2010	100.0	13.8	68.0	12.6	0.8	4.8
2020	100.0	16.3	64.3	12.9	0.8	5.7
2030	100.0	18.9	60.5	13.1	0.8	6.6
2040	100.0	21.7	56.7	13.3	0.9	7.5
2050	100.0	24.5	52.8	13.6	0.9	8.2
PERCENT CHANGE (middle series)						
2000-2010	8.4	31.2	2.7	11.6	12.9	36.1
2010-2020	8.4	28.0	2.5	10.9	12.1	28.9
2020-2030	7.5	24.5	1.3	9.4	11.1	23.9
2030-2040	6.7	22.3	-0.2	8.6	10.8	20.1
2040-2050	6.5	20.4	-0.8	8.5	10.3	17.4

[1] Persons of Hispanic origin may be of any race.   [2] See footnote 4, Table 1.   [3] The April 1, 1990, census count (248,765,170) includes count resolution corrections processed through August 1997, and does not include adjustments for census coverage errors except for adjustments estimated for the 1995 Census Test in Oakland, California; Patterson, New Jersey; and six Louisiana parishes. These adjustments amounted to a total of 55,297 persons.

Source: U.S. Bureau of the Census, *Current Population Reports*, P25-1095 and P25-1130; and Population Paper Listing PPL-91.

No. 20. Components of Population Change, by Race and Hispanic Origin, 1990 to 1997, and Projections, 2000

[The April 1, 1990, census count (248,765,170) includes count resolution corrections processed through August 1997, and does not include adjustments for census coverage errors except for adjustments estimated for the 1995 Census Test in Oakland, California; Patterson, New Jersey; and six Louisiana parishes. These adjustments amounted to a total of 55,297 persons. Minus sign (-) indicates net outmigration]

| YEAR | Population at start of period (1,000) | TOTAL (Jan. 1-Dec. 31) | | | | | RATE PER 1,000 MIDYEAR POPULATION | | | |
| | | Net increase [1] | | Natural increase | | Net migration [3] (1,000) | Net growth rate [1] | Natural increase | | Net migration rate [3] |
		Total (1,000)	Per-cent [2]	Births (1,000)	Deaths (1,000)			Birth rate	Death rate	
WHITE										
1990	208,376	1,673	0.8	3,265	1,860	[4]268	8.0	15.6	8.9	[4]1.3
1993	213,884	1,730	0.8	3,150	1,951	531	8.1	14.7	9.1	2.5
1994	215,614	1,664	0.8	3,121	1,960	503	7.7	14.4	9.1	2.3
1995	217,278	1,634	0.8	3,099	1,987	523	7.5	14.2	9.1	2.4
1996	218,912	1,665	0.8	3,113	2,001	553	7.6	14.2	9.1	2.5
1997	220,577	1,630	0.7	3,091	2,015	554	7.4	14.0	9.1	2.5
2000, proj. [5]	224,818	1,419	0.6	2,986	2,058	491	6.3	13.2	9.1	2.2
BLACK										
1990	30,377	448	1.5	692	266	[4]22	14.6	22.6	8.7	[4]0.7
1993	31,948	484	1.5	659	282	107	15.0	20.5	8.8	3.3
1994	32,432	454	1.4	636	282	100	13.9	19.5	8.6	3.0
1995	32,885	422	1.3	603	286	105	12.8	18.2	8.7	3.2
1996	33,307	432	1.3	596	282	118	12.9	17.8	8.4	3.5
1997	33,739	433	1.3	599	278	112	12.7	17.6	8.2	3.3
2000, proj. [5]	35,225	457	1.3	685	319	90	12.9	19.3	9.0	2.6
AMERICAN INDIAN, ESKIMO, ALEUT										
1990	2,044	36	1.8	42	8	[4]3	17.3	20.1	4.1	[4]1.3
1993	2,166	36	1.7	39	10	7	16.5	17.7	4.4	3.2
1994	2,202	34	1.5	38	10	6	15.3	17.0	4.3	2.6
1995	2,236	33	1.5	37	10	6	14.8	16.6	4.4	2.7
1996	2,269	35	1.5	38	10	7	15.3	16.8	4.5	3.0
1997	2,305	36	1.6	39	10	7	15.4	16.8	4.4	2.9
2000, proj. [5]	2,386	33	1.4	42	13	4	13.7	17.3	5.2	1.6
ASIAN, PACIFIC ISLANDER										
1990	7,345	375	5.1	149	21	[4]246	49.6	19.8	2.7	[4]32.6
1993	8,488	362	4.3	153	25	235	41.8	17.6	2.9	27.1
1994	8,850	326	3.7	158	27	195	36.2	17.5	3.0	21.7
1995	9,176	346	3.8	160	28	214	37.0	17.1	3.0	22.9
1996	9,522	345	3.6	167	30	207	35.5	17.3	3.1	21.3
1997	9,866	337	3.4	171	30	196	33.6	17.0	3.0	19.5
2000, proj. [5]	11,053	386	3.5	186	36	235	34.3	16.6	3.2	20.9
HISPANIC ORIGIN [6]										
1990	22,122	822	3.7	595	84	[4]311	36.4	26.4	3.7	[4]13.8
1993	24,842	969	3.9	661	93	402	38.3	26.1	3.7	15.8
1994	25,812	963	3.7	672	97	387	36.6	25.6	3.7	14.7
1995	26,774	1,018	3.8	680	103	441	37.3	24.9	3.8	16.2
1996	27,792	1,038	3.7	698	106	446	36.7	24.7	3.7	15.8
1997	28,831	1,051	3.6	714	109	446	35.8	24.3	3.7	15.2
2000, proj. [5]	30,913	910	2.9	683	123	350	29.0	21.8	3.9	11.2
WHITE, NON-HISPANIC										
1990	188,160	927	0.5	2,720	1,782	[4]-11	4.9	14.4	9.5	[4]-0.1
1993	191,221	851	0.4	2,546	1,865	170	4.4	13.3	9.7	0.9
1994	192,071	793	0.4	2,508	1,871	156	4.1	13.0	9.7	0.8
1995	192,864	705	0.4	2,478	1,893	120	3.7	12.8	9.8	0.6
1996	193,570	717	0.4	2,476	1,903	145	3.7	12.8	9.8	0.7
1997	194,287	670	0.3	2,437	1,914	147	3.4	12.5	9.8	0.8
2000, proj. [5]	196,751	605	0.3	2,365	1,946	186	3.1	12.0	9.9	0.9
BLACK, NON-HISPANIC										
1990	29,191	397	1.4	659	262	[4]-	13.5	22.4	8.9	[4]-
1993	30,579	421	1.4	620	277	79	13.7	20.1	9.0	2.6
1994	31,000	389	1.3	597	277	69	12.5	19.1	8.9	2.2
1995	31,389	361	1.2	564	281	78	11.4	17.9	8.9	2.5
1996	31,750	371	1.2	556	276	92	11.6	17.4	8.7	2.9
1997	32,121	371	1.2	558	272	85	11.5	17.3	8.4	2.6
2000, proj. [5]	33,374	387	1.2	641	312	57	11.5	19.1	9.3	1.7

- Represents or rounds to zero.   [1] Net change for 1990 excludes "error of closure" for the three months prior to the April 1 census date.   [2] Percent of population at beginning of period.   [3] Covers net international migration and movement of Armed Forces, federally affiliated civilian citizens, and their dependents.   [4] Data reflect movement of Armed Forces due to the Gulf War.   [5] Based on middle series of assumptions. See footnote 1, Table 3.   [6] Persons of Hispanic origin may be of any race.

Source: U.S. Bureau of the Census, *Current Population Reports*, P25-1130; and Population Paper Listing 91.

No. 21. Resident Population, by Age and Race: 1990 to 1997

[In thousands, except percent. As of July, except 1990 as of April. See headnote, Table 18]

YEAR, SEX, AND RACE	Total, all years	Under 5 years	5-9 years	10-14 years	15-19 years	20-24 years	25-29 years	30-34 years	35-39 years	40-44 years	45-49 years	50-54 years	55-59 years	60-64 years	65-74 years	75-84 years	85 years and over	5-13 years	14-17 years	18-24 years
ALL RACES																				
1990 [1]	248,765	18,763	18,040	17,065	17,890	19,139	21,333	21,837	19,849	17,592	13,746	11,314	10,489	10,626	18,047	10,012	3,022	31,835	13,344	26,955
1995	262,761	19,526	19,083	18,798	18,152	18,046	18,954	21,839	22,293	20,257	17,464	13,647	11,092	10,049	18,748	11,154	3,658	34,142	14,770	25,168
1997	267,636	19,150	19,738	19,040	19,068	17,512	18,869	20,741	22,625	21,373	18,470	15,163	11,757	10,056	18,499	11,706	3,871	34,949	15,429	24,979
Male	131,018	9,801	10,104	9,757	9,827	8,979	9,470	10,340	11,286	10,596	9,074	7,383	5,646	4,745	8,268	4,628	1,112	17,896	7,950	12,821
Female	136,618	9,349	9,634	9,283	9,241	8,532	9,399	10,401	11,338	10,777	9,396	7,780	6,111	5,311	10,230	7,077	2,759	17,053	7,479	12,158
WHITE																				
1990 [1]	208,727	14,962	14,504	13,671	14,355	15,642	17,640	18,191	16,653	15,002	11,827	9,745	9,131	9,381	16,175	9,085	2,761	25,560	10,665	21,949
1995	218,066	15,448	15,122	14,956	14,453	14,425	15,348	17,966	18,491	16,954	14,864	11,730	9,539	8,720	16,627	10,105	3,318	27,109	11,731	20,116
1997	221,334	15,184	15,560	15,093	15,151	13,970	15,163	16,903	18,710	17,806	15,564	13,049	10,091	8,683	16,310	10,592	3,504	27,620	12,231	19,922
Male	108,893	7,789	7,978	7,750	7,838	7,219	7,686	8,523	9,431	8,923	7,737	6,421	4,900	4,147	7,349	4,204	998	14,168	6,318	10,298
Female	112,441	7,396	7,582	7,344	7,313	6,750	7,476	8,381	9,278	8,882	7,827	6,629	5,191	4,536	8,961	6,387	2,507	13,453	5,913	9,623
BLACK																				
1990 [1]	30,511	2,942	2,714	2,632	2,717	2,657	2,782	2,720	2,361	1,883	1,415	1,178	1,042	972	1,499	772	223	4,842	2,059	3,819
1995	33,093	3,039	3,018	2,871	2,826	2,647	2,590	2,823	2,791	2,394	1,856	1,383	1,139	990	1,619	830	277	5,316	2,302	3,744
1997	33,947	2,892	3,147	2,937	2,963	2,598	2,615	2,762	2,858	2,582	2,077	1,500	1,208	1,004	1,648	863	292	5,498	2,389	3,757
Male	16,121	1,467	1,597	1,492	1,505	1,285	1,253	1,298	1,343	1,206	949	673	530	430	690	319	86	2,790	1,221	1,869
Female	17,826	1,425	1,550	1,445	1,457	1,313	1,362	1,464	1,515	1,377	1,128	828	679	574	958	544	207	2,707	1,169	1,889
AMERICAN INDIAN, ESKIMO, ALEUT																				
1990 [1]	2,065	220	209	197	191	179	188	181	157	132	99	79	64	53	73	34	9	368	151	256
1995	2,252	204	227	233	203	189	183	187	178	156	126	94	72	58	85	42	15	413	176	264
1997	2,322	202	226	239	219	186	191	184	183	165	134	103	77	61	87	46	18	416	189	266
Male	1,153	102	115	122	111	95	100	93	91	80	65	50	37	28	39	19	6	212	95	135
Female	1,169	100	111	118	109	91	91	90	92	85	69	53	41	32	47	27	12	205	93	131
ASIAN, PACIFIC ISLANDER																				
1990 [1]	7,462	638	612	565	626	661	722	745	678	574	405	312	252	220	300	122	29	1,064	470	931
1995	9,349	835	715	738	670	784	833	862	832	753	619	441	341	281	418	178	47	1,304	559	1,044
1997	10,033	872	805	770	735	758	900	892	874	820	694	510	380	308	453	205	56	1,414	620	1,033
Male	4,851	444	415	393	372	381	431	427	421	387	322	240	180	139	191	87	23	726	316	520
Female	5,182	429	390	377	362	377	469	465	453	433	372	270	200	169	264	118	33	688	305	513
PERCENT																				
Total, 1997	100.0	7.2	7.4	7.1	7.1	6.5	7.1	7.7	8.5	8.0	6.9	5.7	4.4	3.8	6.9	4.4	1.4	13.1	5.8	9.3
White	100.0	6.9	7.0	6.8	6.8	6.3	6.9	7.6	8.5	8.0	7.0	5.9	4.6	3.9	7.4	4.8	1.6	12.5	5.5	9.0
Black	100.0	8.5	9.3	8.7	8.7	7.7	7.7	8.1	8.4	7.6	6.1	4.4	3.6	3.0	4.9	2.5	0.9	16.2	7.0	11.1
American Indian, Eskimo, Aleut	100.0	8.7	9.7	10.3	9.4	8.0	8.2	7.9	7.9	7.1	5.8	4.4	3.3	2.6	3.7	2.0	0.8	17.9	8.1	11.5
Asian, Pacific Islander	100.0	8.7	8.0	7.7	7.3	7.6	9.0	8.9	8.7	7.1	6.9	5.1	3.8	3.1	4.5	2.0	0.6	14.1	6.2	10.3

[1] The April 1, 1990, census count (248,765,170) includes count resolution corrections processed through August 1997, and does not include adjustments for census coverage errors except for adjustments estimated for the 1995 Census Test in Oakland, CA; Patterson, NJ; and six parishes in LA. These adjustments amounted to a total of 55,297 persons.

Source: U.S. Bureau of the Census, Current Population Reports, P25-1095; and Population Paper Listing 91.

Population

No. 22. Resident Population, by Race, Hispanic Origin, and Single Years of Age: 1997

[In thousands, except as indicated. As of July 1. Resident population. For derivation of estimates, see text, Section 1]

AGE	Total	RACE				Hispanic origin [1]	NOT OF HISPANIC ORIGIN			
		White	Black	American Indian, Eskimo, Aleut	Asian, Pacific Islander		White	Black	American Indian, Eskimo, Aleut	Asian, Pacific Islander
Total	**267,636**	**221,334**	**33,947**	**2,322**	**10,033**	**29,348**	**194,571**	**32,298**	**1,976**	**9,443**
Under 5 yrs. old . .	19,150	15,184	2,892	202	872	3,347	12,128	2,703	166	806
Under 1 yr. old .	3,797	3,021	555	41	180	690	2,390	517	33	166
1 yr. old	3,773	3,009	550	39	175	674	2,392	513	32	162
2 yrs. old	3,795	3,016	567	39	172	666	2,408	530	32	159
3 yrs. old	3,838	3,034	591	41	173	658	2,432	554	34	160
4 yrs. old	3,947	3,105	628	42	172	658	2,505	590	35	159
5-9 yrs. old.	19,738	15,560	3,147	226	805	2,928	12,900	2,976	190	745
5 yrs. old	4,022	3,168	634	43	176	657	2,568	597	36	164
6 yrs. old	4,043	3,196	633	42	172	625	2,625	598	36	160
7 yrs. old	4,029	3,185	640	47	157	584	2,656	606	40	145
8 yrs. old	3,732	2,934	607	46	146	521	2,464	575	38	134
9 yrs. old	3,912	3,076	633	48	154	542	2,587	599	40	143
10-14 yrs. old. . . .	19,040	15,093	2,937	239	770	2,515	12,819	2,790	202	714
10 yrs. old	3,873	3,065	612	47	150	521	2,594	580	40	138
11 yrs. old	3,813	3,031	585	47	149	509	2,571	556	39	138
12 yrs. old	3,799	3,011	587	48	154	494	2,564	558	40	143
13 yrs. old	3,725	2,954	566	48	157	488	2,512	539	41	145
14 yrs. old	3,829	3,033	586	49	161	502	2,578	558	42	149
15-19 yrs. old. . . .	19,068	15,151	2,963	219	735	2,580	12,802	2,819	184	683
15 yrs. old	3,870	3,061	604	48	157	503	2,606	575	40	146
16 yrs. old	3,815	3,031	585	46	152	513	2,565	557	39	142
17 yrs. old	3,915	3,106	614	46	150	522	2,630	585	38	139
18 yrs. old	3,679	2,928	576	40	134	503	2,469	548	33	125
19 yrs. old	3,789	3,024	583	40	141	538	2,532	554	34	131
20-24 yrs. old. . . .	17,512	13,970	2,598	186	758	2,571	11,609	2,466	155	711
20 yrs. old	3,738	2,985	572	38	143	537	2,493	543	32	134
21 yrs. old	3,510	2,799	525	37	149	522	2,321	498	31	139
22 yrs. old	3,450	2,764	501	36	149	507	2,297	476	30	139
23 yrs. old	3,337	2,659	490	36	152	492	2,208	465	30	143
24 yrs. old	3,476	2,762	510	38	166	513	2,291	484	32	156
25-29 yrs. old. . . .	18,869	15,163	2,615	191	900	2,567	12,821	2,477	157	847
25 yrs. old	3,637	2,896	526	39	177	504	2,434	500	33	166
26 yrs. old	3,876	3,104	545	40	186	521	2,629	517	33	175
27 yrs. old	3,890	3,139	526	39	186	518	2,666	498	32	174
28 yrs. old	3,578	2,906	471	34	167	489	2,460	445	28	157
29 yrs. old	3,888	3,118	547	38	185	535	2,632	517	31	174
30-34 yrs. old. . . .	20,741	16,903	2,762	184	892	2,664	14,476	2,610	152	839
30 yrs. old	3,882	3,147	527	36	173	531	2,662	497	29	162
31 yrs. old	3,901	3,154	535	36	176	528	2,673	505	29	165
32 yrs. old	4,146	3,378	554	37	178	533	2,892	523	30	168
33 yrs. old	4,288	3,519	557	37	176	528	3,037	527	30	166
34 yrs. old	4,524	3,706	590	39	189	544	3,212	558	32	178
35-39 yrs. old. . . .	22,625	18,710	2,858	183	874	2,415	16,513	2,716	155	825
35 yrs. old	4,573	3,770	586	38	179	513	3,303	557	32	168
36 yrs. old	4,492	3,722	559	36	175	508	3,259	530	31	165
37 yrs. old	4,572	3,772	584	37	178	488	3,329	555	32	168
38 yrs. old	4,249	3,525	529	34	161	435	3,129	504	29	153
39 yrs. old	4,739	3,921	599	38	181	472	3,493	570	32	171
40-44 yrs. old. . . .	21,373	17,806	2,582	165	820	1,976	16,013	2,464	142	778
40 yrs. old	4,583	3,803	571	36	173	437	3,407	544	31	164
41 yrs. old	4,308	3,576	527	34	171	416	3,198	502	29	162
42 yrs. old	4,257	3,546	515	33	163	396	3,187	492	28	154
43 yrs. old	4,098	3,412	490	33	163	363	3,083	468	29	155
44 yrs. old	4,128	3,468	480	30	150	364	3,137	459	26	142

See footnotes at end of table.

No. 22. Resident Population, by Race, Hispanic Origin, and Single Years of Age: 1997—Continued

[See headnote, page 22]

AGE	Total	RACE				Hispanic origin [1]	NOT OF HISPANIC ORIGIN			
		White	Black	American Indian, Eskimo, Aleut	Asian, Pacific Islander		White	Black	American Indian, Eskimo, Aleut	Asian, Pacific Islander
45-49 yrs. old	18,470	15,564	2,077	134	694	1,494	14,205	1,990	118	662
45 yrs. old	3,951	3,325	454	29	143	331	3,024	434	25	136
46 yrs. old	3,674	3,087	419	27	141	316	2,800	401	24	134
47 yrs. old	3,681	3,072	434	28	147	300	2,801	416	24	140
48 yrs. old	3,420	2,906	364	24	126	268	2,661	349	21	120
49 yrs. old	3,744	3,174	406	27	138	280	2,919	389	24	132
50-54 yrs. old	15,163	13,049	1,500	103	510	1,116	12,030	1,438	92	487
50 yrs. old	3,898	3,382	367	25	124	270	3,135	352	22	118
51 yrs. old	2,724	2,319	280	21	105	225	2,113	267	18	100
52 yrs. old	2,770	2,368	285	19	98	214	2,172	273	17	94
53 yrs. old	2,790	2,400	281	19	91	203	2,214	270	17	87
54 yrs. old	2,981	2,582	288	19	92	204	2,395	276	17	88
55-59 yrs. old	11,757	10,091	1,208	77	380	836	9,327	1,161	70	364
55 yrs. old	2,532	2,156	275	17	84	178	1,995	264	16	81
56 yrs. old	2,440	2,100	246	16	78	177	1,937	236	14	75
57 yrs. old	2,356	2,015	249	16	77	170	1,859	239	14	74
58 yrs. old	2,168	1,879	210	14	66	154	1,737	202	12	64
59 yrs. old	2,260	1,942	229	15	74	156	1,799	220	13	70
60-64 yrs. old	10,056	8,683	1,004	61	308	677	8,062	967	55	295
60 yrs. old	2,087	1,797	210	13	67	144	1,665	202	12	64
61 yrs. old	2,030	1,754	201	12	62	141	1,625	193	11	60
62 yrs. old	2,048	1,771	203	12	61	139	1,643	195	11	59
63 yrs. old	1,923	1,668	187	11	57	127	1,551	180	10	55
64 yrs. old	1,968	1,693	204	11	60	126	1,578	197	10	57
65-69 yrs. old	9,762	8,525	935	48	254	579	7,993	903	44	244
65 yrs. old	1,947	1,679	203	11	55	120	1,570	196	10	53
66 yrs. old	1,996	1,736	197	10	53	123	1,623	190	9	51
67 yrs. old	1,985	1,734	191	10	51	119	1,625	184	9	49
68 yrs. old	1,889	1,659	173	9	48	110	1,558	167	8	46
69 yrs. old	1,946	1,717	172	9	48	108	1,618	166	8	46
70-74 yrs. old	8,736	7,785	713	39	199	442	7,376	691	35	192
70 yrs. old	1,854	1,636	165	9	45	98	1,545	160	8	43
71 yrs. old	1,787	1,585	152	8	42	94	1,499	148	7	40
72 yrs. old	1,788	1,600	139	8	41	90	1,516	135	7	40
73 yrs. old	1,683	1,512	128	7	36	82	1,436	124	7	35
74 yrs. old	1,623	1,452	129	7	35	77	1,380	125	6	34
75-79 yrs. old	7,063	6,366	538	28	131	299	6,088	524	26	127
75 yrs. old	1,619	1,456	125	7	32	72	1,389	121	6	31
76 yrs. old	1,529	1,383	112	6	29	67	1,320	109	6	28
77 yrs. old	1,383	1,244	107	5	27	59	1,189	104	5	26
78 yrs. old	1,316	1,188	100	5	23	53	1,139	97	5	22
79 yrs. old	1,216	1,095	95	5	21	47	1,051	93	4	20
80-84 yrs. old	4,642	4,226	325	18	74	182	4,056	317	17	71
80 yrs. old	1,090	991	77	4	18	42	953	75	4	17
81 yrs. old	1,008	920	68	4	16	39	884	66	3	15
82 yrs. old	930	849	63	3	15	37	815	62	3	14
83 yrs. old	848	773	58	3	13	34	742	57	3	13
84 yrs. old	766	692	59	3	12	31	663	57	3	12
85-89 yrs. old	2,456	2,238	172	10	35	100	2,145	168	9	34
90-94 yrs. old	1,058	952	85	5	15	45	910	84	5	14
95-99 yrs. old	298	263	27	2	5	13	251	27	2	5
100 yrs. old and over	60	50	8	1	1	3	48	8	1	1
Median age (yr.) . .	34.9	36.0	29.7	27.2	31.0	26.4	37.4	29.8	27.8	31.3

[1] Persons of Hispanic origin may be of any race.

Source: U.S. Bureau of the Census, Population Paper Listing 91.

No. 23. Resident Population, by Age and Hispanic Origin: 1990 to 1997

[In thousands, except percent. As of July, except 1990 as of April. See headnote, Table 18. Hispanic persons may be of any race]

YEAR AND SEX	Total, all years	Under 5 years	5-9 years	10-14 years	15-19 years	20-24 years	25-29 years	30-34 years	35-39 years	40-44 years	45-49 years	50-54 years	55-59 years	60-64 years	65-74 years	75-84 years	85 years and over	5-13 years	14-17 years	18-24 years
HISPANIC ORIGIN																				
1990 [1]	22,372	2,469	2,180	1,991	2,086	2,322	2,340	2,046	1,643	1,277	937	750	634	550	715	340	91	3,786	1,575	3,217
1995	27,274	3,205	2,593	2,384	2,387	2,466	2,508	2,559	2,202	1,757	1,327	972	766	634	947	428	139	4,499	1,892	3,439
1997	29,348	3,347	2,928	2,515	2,580	2,571	2,567	2,664	2,415	1,976	1,494	1,116	836	677	1,021	481	160	4,941	2,040	3,612
Male	15,074	1,717	1,498	1,289	1,367	1,397	1,400	1,423	1,268	1,013	748	544	398	314	454	192	54	2,529	1,067	1,955
Female	14,274	1,630	1,431	1,226	1,213	1,173	1,167	1,241	1,148	963	746	572	438	363	567	289	106	2,413	975	1,656
NON-HISPANIC																				
WHITE																				
1990 [1]	188,307	12,721	12,516	11,854	12,450	13,524	15,508	16,332	15,162	13,839	10,971	9,058	8,548	8,872	15,511	8,767	2,675	22,106	9,225	19,014
1995	193,198	12,520	12,776	12,795	12,276	12,165	13,064	15,634	16,491	15,359	13,655	10,842	8,838	8,138	15,751	9,706	3,187	23,036	10,011	16,965
1997	194,571	12,128	12,900	12,819	12,803	11,609	12,821	14,476	16,513	16,013	14,205	12,030	9,327	8,062	15,369	10,144	3,354	23,141	10,379	16,610
Male	95,127	6,221	6,618	6,584	6,591	5,931	6,405	7,223	8,277	8,003	7,056	5,923	4,536	3,858	6,930	4,025	947	11,876	5,350	8,499
Female	99,444	5,907	6,282	6,235	6,211	5,678	6,416	7,253	8,236	8,010	7,149	6,107	4,792	4,204	8,439	6,119	2,407	11,264	5,030	8,111
BLACK																				
1990 [1]	29,299	2,801	2,599	2,528	2,608	2,530	2,651	2,602	2,267	1,812	1,364	1,138	1,009	946	1,465	759	219	4,643	1,977	3,644
1995	31,566	2,858	2,864	2,736	2,695	2,520	2,451	2,677	2,661	2,290	1,780	1,328	1,096	955	1,570	811	272	5,053	2,197	3,565
1997	32,298	2,703	2,976	2,790	2,819	2,466	2,477	2,610	2,716	2,464	1,990	1,438	1,161	967	1,594	841	287	5,208	2,275	3,568
Male	15,288	1,370	1,509	1,417	1,430	1,217	1,181	1,219	1,269	1,145	906	643	507	414	667	311	84	2,642	1,161	1,771
Female	17,011	1,334	1,467	1,374	1,389	1,249	1,296	1,391	1,447	1,319	1,084	795	653	553	927	531	203	2,567	1,115	1,797
AMERICAN INDIAN, ESKIMO, ALEUT																				
1990 [1]	1,796	185	179	170	165	151	160	156	138	117	90	72	58	48	68	31	9	316	131	217
1995	1,929	171	191	198	172	158	151	157	152	136	111	84	65	53	76	38	14	349	150	221
1997	1,976	166	190	202	184	155	157	152	155	142	118	92	70	55	79	43	17	350	159	222
Male	972	84	96	102	92	78	81	76	76	69	57	44	33	26	36	18	6	177	80	112
Female	1,003	82	94	99	92	77	76	76	79	74	61	48	37	29	44	25	12	172	79	111
ASIAN, PACIFIC ISLANDER																				
1990 [1]	6,992	586	566	523	582	612	673	701	640	546	385	297	240	210	287	116	27	984	436	863
1995	8,794	772	661	685	623	736	780	811	786	715	591	421	327	269	402	171	45	1,207	519	979
1997	9,443	806	745	714	683	711	847	839	825	778	662	487	364	295	436	198	54	1,310	576	967
Male	4,557	410	384	365	346	356	403	400	397	366	307	229	172	133	183	85	22	673	293	485
Female	4,887	396	361	349	337	355	444	439	428	411	355	258	191	162	253	114	32	637	284	483
1997, PERCENT																				
Hispanic origin	100.0	11.4	10.0	8.6	8.8	8.7	8.8	9.1	8.2	6.7	5.1	3.8	2.8	2.3	3.5	1.6	0.5	16.8	7.0	12.3
Non-Hispanic:																				
White	100.0	6.2	6.6	6.6	6.6	6.0	6.6	7.4	8.5	8.2	7.3	6.2	4.8	4.1	7.9	5.2	1.7	11.9	5.3	8.5
Black	100.0	8.4	9.2	8.6	8.7	7.6	7.7	8.1	8.4	7.6	6.2	4.5	3.6	3.0	4.9	2.6	0.9	16.1	7.0	11.0
American Indian, Eskimo, Aleut	100.0	8.4	9.6	10.2	9.3	7.8	7.9	7.7	7.8	7.2	6.0	4.7	3.5	2.8	4.0	2.2	0.9	17.7	8.0	11.2
Asian, Pacific Is.	100.0	8.5	7.9	7.6	7.2	7.5	9.0	8.9	8.7	8.2	7.0	5.2	3.9	3.1	4.6	2.1	0.6	13.9	6.1	10.2

[1] The April 1, 1990, census count (248,765,170) includes count resolution corrections processed through August 1997, and does not include adjustments for census coverage errors except for adjustments estimated for the 1995 Census Test in Oakland, CA; Patterson, NJ; and six parishes in LA. These adjustments amounted to a total of 55,297 persons.
Source: U.S. Bureau of the Census, Current Population Reports, P25-1095; and Population Paper Listing 91.

No. 24. Projections of Resident Population, by Age, Sex, and Race: 2000 to 2025

[As of **July 1**. Data are for middle series; for assumptions, see Table 3]

AGE, SEX, AND RACE	POPULATION (1,000)				PERCENT DISTRIBUTION			
	2000	2005	2010	2025	2000	2005	2010	2025
Total	**274,634**	**285,981**	**297,716**	**335,050**	**100.0**	**100.0**	**100.0**	**100.0**
Under 5 years old	18,987	19,127	20,012	22,498	6.9	6.7	6.7	6.7
5 to 13 years old	36,043	35,850	35,605	40,413	13.1	12.5	12.0	12.1
14 to 17 years old	15,752	16,986	16,894	17,872	5.7	5.9	5.7	5.3
18 to 24 years old	26,258	28,268	30,138	30,372	9.6	9.9	10.1	9.1
25 to 34 years old	37,233	36,306	38,292	43,119	13.6	12.7	12.9	12.9
35 to 44 years old	44,659	42,165	38,521	42,391	16.3	14.7	12.9	12.7
45 to 54 years old	37,030	41,507	43,564	36,890	13.5	14.5	14.6	11.0
55 to 64 years old	23,962	29,606	35,283	39,542	8.7	10.4	11.9	11.8
65 to 74 years old	18,136	18,369	21,057	35,425	6.6	6.4	7.1	10.6
75 to 84 years old	12,315	12,898	12,680	19,481	4.5	4.5	4.3	5.8
85 years old and over	4,259	4,899	5,671	7,046	1.6	1.7	1.9	2.1
Male	134,181	139,785	145,584	164,119	48.9	48.9	48.9	49.0
Female	140,453	146,196	152,132	170,931	51.1	51.1	51.1	51.0
White, total	**225,532**	**232,463**	**239,588**	**262,227**	**100.0**	**100.0**	**100.0**	**100.0**
Under 5 years old	14,724	14,618	15,142	16,630	6.5	6.3	6.3	6.3
5 to 13 years old	28,254	27,716	27,087	29,949	12.5	11.9	11.3	11.4
14 to 17 years old	12,412	13,177	12,951	13,166	5.5	5.7	5.4	5.0
18 to 24 years old	20,852	22,306	23,489	22,702	9.2	9.6	9.8	8.7
25 to 34 years old	29,837	28,705	30,099	32,831	13.2	12.3	12.6	12.5
35 to 44 years old	36,762	34,201	30,646	32,869	16.3	14.7	12.8	12.5
45 to 54 years old	31,247	34,574	35,911	29,010	13.9	14.9	15.0	11.1
55 to 64 years old	20,600	25,334	29,845	32,246	9.1	10.9	12.5	12.3
65 to 74 years old	15,846	15,844	18,101	29,733	7.0	6.8	7.6	11.3
75 to 84 years old	11,131	11,553	11,208	16,969	4.9	5.0	4.7	6.5
85 years old and over	3,866	4,434	5,108	6,122	1.7	1.9	2.1	2.3
Male	110,799	114,350	118,000	129,596	49.1	49.2	49.3	49.4
Female	114,734	118,113	121,588	132,631	50.9	50.8	50.7	50.6
Black, total	**35,454**	**37,734**	**40,109**	**47,539**	**100.0**	**100.0**	**100.0**	**100.0**
Under 5 years old	3,127	3,244	3,454	3,964	8.8	8.6	8.6	8.3
5 to 13 years old	5,727	5,813	5,962	6,990	16.2	15.4	14.9	14.7
14 to 17 years old	2,414	2,735	2,737	3,104	6.8	7.2	6.8	6.5
18 to 24 years old	3,966	4,233	4,674	5,053	11.2	11.2	11.7	10.6
25 to 34 years old	5,172	5,212	5,489	6,514	14.6	13.8	13.7	13.7
35 to 44 years old	5,649	5,499	5,236	6,017	15.9	14.6	13.1	12.7
45 to 54 years old	4,111	4,909	5,326	5,007	11.6	13.0	13.3	10.5
55 to 64 years old	2,406	2,995	3,801	4,865	6.8	7.9	9.5	10.2
65 to 74 years old	1,675	1,781	2,033	3,901	4.7	4.7	5.1	8.2
75 to 84 years old	890	959	1,002	1,582	2.5	2.5	2.5	3.3
85 years old and over	317	354	396	541	0.9	0.9	1.0	1.1
Male	16,811	17,874	18,981	22,473	47.4	47.4	47.3	47.3
Female	18,643	19,860	21,129	25,066	52.6	52.6	52.7	52.7
American Indian, Eskimo, Aleut, total	**2,402**	**2,572**	**2,754**	**3,319**	**100.0**	**100.0**	**100.0**	**100.0**
Under 5 years old	210	226	245	275	8.7	8.8	8.9	8.3
5 to 13 years old	418	409	429	516	17.4	15.9	15.6	15.5
14 to 17 years old	196	210	197	240	8.2	8.2	7.2	7.2
18 to 24 years old	283	323	342	368	11.8	12.6	12.4	11.1
25 to 34 years old	361	376	421	475	15.0	14.6	15.3	14.3
35 to 44 years old	354	351	349	459	14.7	13.6	12.7	13.8
45 to 54 years old	263	300	321	333	10.9	11.7	11.7	10.0
55 to 64 years old	152	186	225	276	6.3	7.2	8.2	8.3
65 to 74 years old	93	104	122	210	3.9	4.0	4.4	6.3
75 to 84 years old	51	59	65	109	2.1	2.3	2.4	3.3
85 years old and over	22	28	36	59	0.9	1.1	1.3	1.8
Male	1,185	1,266	1,354	1,629	49.3	49.2	49.2	49.1
Female	1,217	1,306	1,400	1,690	50.7	50.8	50.8	50.9
Asian, Pacific Islander, total	**11,245**	**13,212**	**15,265**	**21,965**	**100.0**	**100.0**	**100.0**	**100.0**
Under 5 years old	926	1,040	1,170	1,628	8.2	7.9	7.7	7.4
5 to 13 years old	1,644	1,912	2,126	2,958	14.6	14.5	13.9	13.5
14 to 17 years old	729	864	1,008	1,362	6.5	6.5	6.6	6.2
18 to 24 years old	1,158	1,405	1,633	2,250	10.3	10.6	10.7	10.2
25 to 34 years old	1,863	2,012	2,283	3,300	16.6	15.2	15.0	15.0
35 to 44 years old	1,894	2,114	2,290	3,046	16.8	16.0	15.0	13.9
45 to 54 years old	1,409	1,724	2,006	2,539	12.5	13.0	13.1	11.6
55 to 64 years old	804	1,091	1,412	2,155	7.1	8.3	9.2	9.8
65 to 74 years old	522	640	802	1,581	4.6	4.8	5.3	7.2
75 to 84 years old	242	327	406	821	2.2	2.5	2.7	3.7
85 years old and over	55	83	130	324	0.5	0.6	0.9	1.5
Male	5,386	6,295	7,250	10,421	47.9	47.6	47.5	47.4
Female	5,859	6,918	8,015	11,543	52.1	52.4	52.5	52.6

Source: U.S. Bureau of the Census, *Current Population Reports*, P25-1130.

Population

No. 25. Projections of Hispanic and Non-Hispanic Populations, by Age and Sex: 2000 to 2025

[As of **July 1**. Resident population. Data are for middle series; for assumptions, see Table 3]

AGE AND SEX	POPULATION (1,000)				PERCENT DISTRIBUTION			
	2000	2005	2010	2025	2000	2005	2010	2025
Hispanic origin, total [1]	**31,366**	**36,057**	**41,139**	**58,930**	**100.0**	**100.0**	**100.0**	**100.0**
Under 5 years old	3,203	3,580	4,080	5,662	10.2	9.9	9.9	9.6
5 to 13 years old	5,651	6,215	6,654	9,479	18.0	17.2	16.2	16.1
14 to 17 years old	2,179	2,672	3,007	3,944	6.9	7.4	7.3	6.7
18 to 24 years old	3,679	4,270	5,101	6,560	11.7	11.8	12.4	11.1
25 to 34 years old	5,181	5,414	6,059	8,748	16.5	15.0	14.7	14.8
35 to 44 years old	4,836	5,421	5,562	7,345	15.4	15.0	13.5	12.5
45 to 54 years old	3,049	3,927	4,833	5,791	9.7	10.9	11.7	9.8
55 to 64 years old	1,717	2,260	2,997	5,272	5.5	6.3	7.3	8.9
65 to 74 years old	1,120	1,308	1,606	3,595	3.6	3.6	3.9	6.1
75 to 84 years old	568	748	896	1,771	1.8	2.1	2.2	3.0
85 years old and over	183	242	345	763	0.6	0.7	0.8	1.3
Male	15,799	18,082	20,557	29,276	50.4	50.1	50.0	49.7
Female	15,566	17,975	20,582	29,654	49.6	49.9	50.0	50.3
Non-Hispanic White, total	**197,061**	**199,802**	**202,390**	**209,117**	**100.0**	**100.0**	**100.0**	**100.0**
Under 5 years old	11,807	11,367	11,445	11,510	6.0	5.7	5.7	5.5
5 to 13 years old	23,125	22,072	21,063	21,396	11.7	11.0	10.4	10.2
14 to 17 years old	10,444	10,769	10,230	9,622	5.3	5.4	5.1	4.6
18 to 24 years old	17,510	18,443	18,880	16,785	8.9	9.2	9.3	8.0
25 to 34 years old	25,144	23,806	24,631	24,935	12.8	11.9	12.2	11.9
35 to 44 years old	32,382	29,299	25,628	26,278	16.4	14.7	12.7	12.6
45 to 54 years old	28,485	31,024	31,541	23,797	14.5	15.5	15.6	11.4
55 to 64 years old	19,039	23,285	27,137	27,490	9.7	11.7	13.4	13.1
65 to 74 years old	14,825	14,660	16,653	26,504	7.5	7.3	8.2	12.7
75 to 84 years old	10,607	10,868	10,394	15,373	5.4	5.4	5.1	7.4
85 years old and over	3,694	4,209	4,788	5,428	1.9	2.1	2.4	2.6
Male	96,438	97,946	99,381	103,169	48.9	49.0	49.1	49.3
Female	100,624	101,856	103,009	105,948	51.1	51.0	50.9	50.7
Non-Hispanic Black, total	**33,568**	**35,485**	**37,466**	**43,511**	**100.0**	**100.0**	**100.0**	**100.0**
Under 5 years old	2,929	3,016	3,187	3,571	8.7	8.5	8.5	8.2
5 to 13 years old	5,391	5,430	5,531	6,339	16.1	15.3	14.8	14.6
14 to 17 years old	2,285	2,568	2,547	2,831	6.8	7.2	6.8	6.5
18 to 24 years old	3,751	3,975	4,354	4,609	11.2	11.2	11.6	10.6
25 to 34 years old	4,863	4,883	5,111	5,942	14.5	13.8	13.6	13.7
35 to 44 years old	5,347	5,154	4,877	5,521	15.9	14.5	13.0	12.7
45 to 54 years old	3,922	4,654	5,008	4,613	11.7	13.1	13.4	10.6
55 to 64 years old	2,301	2,850	3,601	4,498	6.9	8.0	9.6	10.3
65 to 74 years old	1,608	1,695	1,921	3,634	4.8	4.8	5.1	8.4
75 to 84 years old	862	919	947	1,457	2.6	2.6	2.5	3.3
85 years old and over	310	344	381	496	0.9	1.0	1.0	1.1
Male	15,871	16,760	17,676	20,494	47.3	47.2	47.2	47.1
Female	17,697	18,725	19,790	23,017	52.7	52.8	52.8	52.9
Non-Hispanic American Indian, Eskimo, Aleut, total	**2,054**	**2,183**	**2,320**	**2,744**	**100.0**	**100.0**	**100.0**	**100.0**
Under 5 years old	180	192	206	229	8.8	8.8	8.9	8.4
5 to 13 years old	352	347	364	429	17.1	15.9	15.7	15.6
14 to 17 years old	165	175	166	198	8.0	8.0	7.1	7.2
18 to 24 years old	239	268	282	304	11.6	12.3	12.1	11.1
25 to 34 years old	303	316	349	390	14.7	14.5	15.0	14.2
35 to 44 years old	301	293	290	372	14.7	13.4	12.5	13.6
45 to 54 years old	231	259	272	275	11.2	11.8	11.7	10.0
55 to 64 years old	136	164	195	227	6.6	7.5	8.4	8.3
65 to 74 years old	82	91	106	176	4.0	4.2	4.6	6.4
75 to 84 years old	46	52	57	92	2.2	2.4	2.4	3.4
85 years old and over	21	27	34	52	1.0	1.2	1.4	1.9
Male	1,008	1,070	1,136	1,342	49.1	49.0	48.9	48.9
Female	1,046	1,113	1,184	1,401	50.9	51.0	51.1	51.1
Non-Hispanic Asian, Pacific Islander, total	**10,584**	**12,454**	**14,402**	**20,748**	**100.0**	**100.0**	**100.0**	**100.0**
Under 5 years old	867	973	1,093	1,526	8.2	7.8	7.6	7.4
5 to 13 years old	1,524	1,787	1,993	2,770	14.4	14.4	13.8	13.4
14 to 17 years old	680	803	944	1,277	6.4	6.4	6.6	6.2
18 to 24 years old	1,080	1,311	1,521	2,114	10.2	10.5	10.6	10.2
25 to 34 years old	1,744	1,887	2,141	3,104	16.5	15.2	14.9	15.0
35 to 44 years old	1,793	1,998	2,165	2,876	16.9	16.0	15.0	13.9
45 to 54 years old	1,344	1,644	1,910	2,415	12.7	13.2	13.3	11.6
55 to 64 years old	770	1,046	1,354	2,055	7.3	8.4	9.4	9.9
65 to 74 years old	500	615	771	1,516	4.7	4.9	5.4	7.3
75 to 84 years old	231	311	387	787	2.2	2.5	2.7	3.8
85 years old and over	51	78	123	308	0.5	0.6	0.9	1.5
Male	5,065	5,928	6,835	9,838	47.9	47.6	47.5	47.4
Female	5,520	6,526	7,567	10,910	52.1	52.4	52.5	52.6

[1] Persons of Hispanic origin may be of any race.

Source: U.S. Bureau of the Census, *Current Population Reports*, P25-1130.

Figure 1.3
Centers of Population: 1790 to 1990

[Prior to 1960, excludes Alaska and Hawaii. The median center is located at the intersection of two median lines, a north-south line constructed so that half of the nation's population lives east and half lives west of it, and an east-west line selected so that half of the Nation's population lives north and half lives south of it. The mean center of population is that point at which an imaginary, flat, weightless, and rigid map of the United States would balance if weights of identical value were placed on it so that each weight represented the location of one person on the date of the census]

YEAR	MEDIAN CENTER		MEAN CENTER		
	Latitude-N	Longitude-W	Latitude-N	Longitude-W	Approximate location
1790 (August 2)	(NA)	(NA)	39 16 30	76 11 12	In Kent County, MD, 23 miles E of Baltimore, MD
1850 (June 1) ..	(NA)	(NA)	38 59 00	81 19 00	In Wirt County, WV, 23 miles SE of Parkersburg, WV[1]
1900 (June 1) ..	40 03 32	84 49 01	39 09 36	85 48 54	In Bartholomew County, IN, 6 miles SE of Columbus, IN
1950 (April 1) ..	40 00 12	84 56 51	38 50 21	88 09 33	In Richland County, IL, 8 miles NNW of Olney, IL
1960 (April 1) ..	39 56 25	85 16 60	38 35 58	89 12 35	In Clinton County, IL, 6.5 miles NW of Centralia, IL
1970 (April 1) ..	39 47 43	85 31 43	38 27 47	89 42 22	In St. Clair County, IL, 5.3 miles ESE of Mascoutah, IL
1980 (April 1) ..	39 18 60	86 08 15	38 08 13	90 34 26	In Jefferson Country, MO, .25 mile W of DeSoto, MO
1990 (April 1) ..	38 57 55	86 31 53	37 52 20	91 12 55	In Crawford Country, MO, 10 miles SE of Steelville, MO

NA Not available. [1] West Virginia was set off from Virginia, Dec. 31, 1862, and admitted as a State, June 19, 1863.

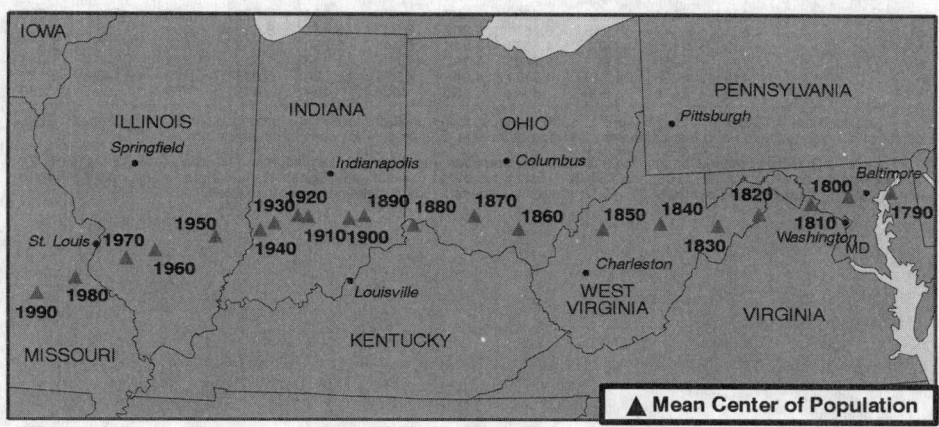

Source: Chart prepared by U.S. Bureau of the Census.

U.S. Census Bureau, the Official Statistics™   Statistical Abstract of the United States: 1998   Sep. 25, 1998

Population

No. 26. Resident Population—States: 1970 to 1997

[In thousands. As of July 1; except 1970, 1980, and 1990, as of April 1. Insofar as possible, population shown for all years is that of present area of state]

STATE	1970	1980 [1]	1985	1990 [2]	1991	1992	1993	1994	1995	1996	1997
U.S.	203,302	226,546	237,924	248,765	252,124	255,002	257,753	260,292	262,761	265,179	267,636
AL	3,444	3,894	3,973	4,040	4,090	4,138	4,193	4,232	4,262	4,287	4,319
AK	303	402	532	550	569	587	597	601	602	605	609
AZ	1,775	2,718	3,184	3,665	3,763	3,868	3,994	4,149	4,308	4,434	4,555
AR	1,923	2,286	2,327	2,351	2,370	2,394	2,424	2,451	2,481	2,506	2,523
CA	19,971	23,668	26,441	29,786	30,413	30,892	31,183	31,369	31,558	31,858	32,268
CO	2,210	2,890	3,209	3,294	3,369	3,462	3,563	3,657	3,742	3,816	3,893
CT	3,032	3,108	3,201	3,287	3,288	3,277	3,273	3,270	3,267	3,267	3,270
DE	548	594	618	666	680	689	698	706	716	723	732
DC	757	638	635	607	594	585	577	566	552	539	529
FL	6,791	9,746	11,351	12,938	13,286	13,501	13,712	13,956	14,181	14,419	14,654
GA	4,588	5,463	5,963	6,478	6,622	6,761	6,896	7,049	7,192	7,334	7,486
HI	770	965	1,040	1,108	1,131	1,150	1,160	1,173	1,179	1,183	1,187
ID	713	944	994	1,007	1,039	1,066	1,101	1,135	1,165	1,188	1,210
IL	11,110	11,427	11,400	11,431	11,518	11,601	11,675	11,737	11,795	11,845	11,896
IN	5,195	5,490	5,459	5,544	5,601	5,648	5,700	5,742	5,788	5,828	5,864
IA	2,825	2,914	2,830	2,777	2,791	2,807	2,820	2,829	2,841	2,848	2,852
KS	2,249	2,364	2,427	2,478	2,493	2,516	2,535	2,554	2,570	2,579	2,595
KY	3,221	3,661	3,695	3,687	3,715	3,752	3,793	3,824	3,856	3,882	3,908
LA	3,645	4,206	4,408	4,222	4,241	4,271	4,285	4,307	4,329	4,341	4,352
ME	994	1,125	1,163	1,228	1,235	1,235	1,237	1,236	1,234	1,239	1,242
MD	3,924	4,217	4,413	4,781	4,857	4,904	4,945	4,989	5,027	5,060	5,094
MA	5,689	5,737	5,881	6,016	5,996	5,991	6,008	6,029	6,061	6,085	6,118
MI	8,882	9,262	9,076	9,295	9,390	9,466	9,524	9,580	9,655	9,731	9,774
MN	3,806	4,076	4,184	4,376	4,428	4,472	4,524	4,567	4,607	4,649	4,686
MS	2,217	2,521	2,588	2,575	2,591	2,610	2,635	2,663	2,691	2,711	2,731
MO	4,678	4,917	5,000	5,117	5,158	5,194	5,238	5,281	5,325	5,364	5,402
MT	694	787	822	799	808	823	840	855	869	877	879
NE	1,485	1,570	1,585	1,578	1,591	1,603	1,613	1,623	1,636	1,649	1,657
NV	489	800	951	1,202	1,285	1,333	1,382	1,459	1,530	1,601	1,677
NH	738	921	997	1,109	1,107	1,113	1,122	1,134	1,146	1,160	1,173
NJ	7,171	7,365	7,566	7,748	7,782	7,824	7,869	7,911	7,956	8,002	8,053
NM	1,017	1,303	1,438	1,515	1,548	1,582	1,617	1,656	1,686	1,711	1,730
NY	18,241	17,558	17,792	17,991	18,028	18,080	18,139	18,154	18,146	18,134	18,137
NC	5,084	5,882	6,254	6,632	6,748	6,833	6,948	7,062	7,187	7,309	7,425
ND	618	653	677	639	634	635	637	640	641	643	641
OH	10,657	10,798	10,735	10,847	10,929	11,000	11,058	11,095	11,133	11,163	11,186
OK	2,559	3,025	3,271	3,146	3,166	3,204	3,229	3,248	3,271	3,295	3,317
OR	2,092	2,633	2,673	2,842	2,920	2,975	3,036	3,089	3,143	3,196	3,243
PA	11,801	11,864	11,771	11,883	11,942	11,981	12,022	12,043	12,046	12,040	12,020
RI	950	947	969	1,003	1,004	1,001	998	994	990	988	987
SC	2,591	3,122	3,303	3,486	3,555	3,593	3,625	3,654	3,683	3,717	3,760
SD	666	691	698	696	708	715	723	730	735	738	738
TN	3,926	4,591	4,715	4,877	4,946	5,013	5,083	5,158	5,235	5,307	5,368
TX	11,199	14,229	16,273	16,986	17,358	17,680	18,035	18,385	18,738	19,091	19,439
UT	1,059	1,461	1,643	1,723	1,771	1,821	1,875	1,929	1,974	2,018	2,059
VT	445	511	530	563	567	570	574	579	583	586	589
VA	4,651	5,347	5,715	6,189	6,282	6,383	6,465	6,538	6,601	6,666	6,734
WA	3,413	4,132	4,400	4,867	5,016	5,144	5,250	5,339	5,436	5,520	5,610
WV	1,744	1,950	1,907	1,793	1,798	1,806	1,816	1,819	1,822	1,820	1,816
WI	4,418	4,706	4,748	4,892	4,946	4,991	5,038	5,075	5,113	5,146	5,170
WY	332	470	500	454	458	464	469	475	479	480	480

[1] See footnote 4, Table 1.   [2] The April 1, 1990, census counts include corrections processed through December 1996, results of special censuses and test censuses, and do not include adjustments for census coverage errors.

Source: U.S. Bureau of the Census, *1990 Census of Population and Housing, Population and Housing Unit Counts* (CPH-2); *Current Population Reports*, P25-1106; and "ST-97-1 Estimates of the Population of States: Annual Time Series, July 1, 1990 to July 1, 1997"; release date: December 31, 1997; <http://www.census.gov/population/estimates/state/ST9097T1.txt>.

No. 27. State Population—Rank, Percent Change, and Population Density: 1980 to 1997

[As of **April 1**, except **1997**, as of **July 1**. For area figures of states, see Table 387. Minus sign (-) indicates decrease]

STATE	RANK			PERCENT CHANGE			POPULATION PER SQ. MILE OF LAND AREA [1]		
	1980	1990	1997	1980-90	1990-95	1995-97	1980	1990	1997
U.S.	(X)	(X)	(X)	9.8	5.6	1.9	64.1	70.3	75.7
AL	22	22	23	3.8	5.5	1.3	76.7	79.6	85.1
AK	50	49	48	36.9	9.4	1.3	0.7	1.0	1.1
AZ	29	24	21	34.9	17.5	5.7	23.9	32.3	40.1
AR	33	33	33	2.8	5.5	1.7	43.9	45.1	48.4
CA	1	1	1	25.8	6.0	2.2	151.7	191.0	206.9
CO	28	26	25	14.0	13.6	4.0	27.9	31.8	37.5
CT	25	27	28	5.8	-0.6	0.1	641.4	678.5	674.9
DE	47	46	46	12.1	7.4	2.2	304.0	340.8	374.2
DC	(X)	(X)	(X)	-4.9	-9.0	-4.2	10,397.9	9,884.4	8,615.0
FL	7	4	4	32.7	9.6	3.3	180.7	239.9	271.7
GA	13	11	10	18.6	11.0	4.1	94.3	111.8	129.3
HI	39	41	41	14.9	6.4	0.7	150.2	172.5	184.7
ID	41	42	40	6.6	15.7	3.9	11.4	12.2	14.6
IL	5	6	6	(Z)	3.2	0.9	205.6	205.6	214.0
IN	12	14	14	1.0	4.4	1.3	153.1	154.6	163.5
IA	27	30	30	-4.7	2.3	0.4	52.1	49.7	51.1
KS	32	32	32	4.8	3.7	1.0	28.9	30.3	31.7
KY	23	23	24	0.7	4.6	1.3	92.1	92.8	98.4
LA	19	21	22	0.4	2.5	0.5	96.5	96.9	99.9
ME	38	38	39	9.1	0.5	0.6	36.5	39.8	40.2
MD	18	19	19	13.4	5.2	1.3	431.4	489.1	521.2
MA	11	13	13	4.9	0.7	0.9	732.0	767.6	780.5
MI	8	8	8	0.4	3.9	1.2	163.0	163.6	172.0
MN	21	20	20	7.4	5.3	1.7	51.2	55.0	58.9
MS	31	31	31	2.2	4.5	1.5	53.7	54.9	58.2
MO	15	15	16	4.1	4.1	1.5	71.4	74.3	78.4
MT	44	44	44	1.6	8.7	1.2	5.4	5.5	6.0
NE	35	36	38	0.5	3.7	1.3	20.4	20.5	21.6
NV	43	39	37	50.1	27.3	9.6	7.3	10.9	15.3
NH	42	40	42	20.5	3.3	2.3	102.6	123.7	130.8
NJ	9	9	9	5.2	2.7	1.2	992.7	1,044.3	1,085.4
NM	37	37	36	16.2	11.3	2.6	10.7	12.5	14.3
NY	2	2	3	2.5	0.9	(-Z)	371.8	381.0	384.1
NC	10	10	11	12.8	8.4	3.3	120.7	136.1	152.4
ND	46	47	47	-2.1	0.4	-0.1	9.5	9.3	9.3
OH	6	7	7	0.5	2.6	0.5	263.7	264.9	273.2
OK	26	28	27	4.0	4.0	1.4	44.1	45.8	48.3
OR	30	29	29	7.9	10.6	3.2	27.4	29.6	33.8
PA	4	5	5	0.2	1.4	-0.2	264.7	265.1	268.2
RI	40	43	43	5.9	-1.4	-0.2	906.4	960.3	944.9
SC	24	25	26	11.7	5.7	2.1	103.6	115.8	124.9
SD	45	45	45	0.8	5.6	0.4	9.1	9.2	9.7
TN	17	17	17	6.2	7.3	2.5	111.4	118.3	130.2
TX	3	3	2	19.4	10.3	3.7	54.3	64.9	74.2
UT	36	35	34	17.9	14.6	4.3	17.8	21.0	25.1
VT	48	48	49	10.0	3.6	1.1	55.3	60.8	63.7
VA	14	12	12	15.8	6.7	2.0	135.0	156.3	170.1
WA	20	18	15	17.8	11.7	3.2	62.1	73.1	84.3
WV	34	34	35	-8.0	1.6	-0.3	81.0	74.5	75.4
WI	16	16	18	4.0	4.5	1.1	86.6	90.1	95.2
WY	49	50	50	-3.4	5.5	0.3	4.8	4.7	4.9

X Not applicable.   Z Less than 0.05 percent.   [1] Persons per square mile were calculated on the basis of land area data from the 1990 census.

Source: U.S. Bureau of the Census, *1990 Census of Population and Housing, Population and Housing Unit Counts* (CPH-2); and "ST-97-1 Estimates of the Population of States: Annual Time Series, July 1, 1990, to July 1, 1997"; release date: December 31, 1997; <http://www.census.gov/population/estimates/state/ST9097T1.txt>.

No. 28. Components of Population Change—States: 1990 to 1997

[In thousands, except percent. Covers period **April 1, 1990**, to **July 1,1997**]

STATE	NET CHANGE [1]		Births	Deaths	NET MOVEMENT FROM ABROAD		Net domestic migration
	Number	Percent			International migration	Net federal movement	
United States	**18,871**	**7.6**	**29,016**	**16,297**	**5,627**	**525**	**-**
Alabama.	279	6.9	446	300	10	7	101
Alaska	59	10.8	79	17	6	8	-17
Arizona.	890	24.3	515	241	87	8	452
Arkansas	172	7.3	257	189	7	2	98
California	2,482	8.3	4,193	1,592	1,789	86	-1,962
Colorado.	598	18.2	396	173	47	14	320
Connecticut.	-17	-0.5	338	210	51	4	-192
Delaware	65	9.8	77	45	7	2	26
District of Columbia	-78	-12.8	72	49	24	3	-128
Florida	1,716	13.3	1,392	1,040	415	33	925
Georgia	1,008	15.6	810	407	74	25	514
Hawaii	78	7.1	140	52	39	19	-65
Idaho.	203	20.2	128	60	14	2	120
Illinois	465	4.1	1,374	768	272	10	-436
Indiana.	320	5.8	610	377	19	1	74
Iowa	76	2.7	275	201	15	(Z)	-10
Kansas.	117	4.7	272	168	21	8	-24
Kentucky	221	6.0	386	265	11	10	79
Louisiana	130	3.1	497	282	20	9	-106
Maine.	14	1.2	110	84	2	2	-15
Maryland	314	6.6	546	293	93	15	-39
Massachusetts.	101	1.7	617	398	112	3	-221
Michigan.	479	5.1	1,021	595	69	2	-162
Minnesota.	310	7.1	473	264	38	1	66
Mississippi	155	6.0	305	191	5	6	35
Missouri	285	5.6	547	383	27	5	86
Montana.	80	10.0	82	54	2	2	49
Nebraska	78	5.0	171	109	11	4	5
Nevada	475	39.5	170	82	34	3	349
New Hampshire.	63	5.7	113	65	4	(Z)	13
New Jersey.	305	3.9	853	526	289	5	-305
New Mexico	215	14.2	200	86	35	6	62
New York	146	0.8	2,045	1,217	841	11	-1,513
North Carolina	793	12.0	746	453	42	37	430
North Dakota.	2	0.3	63	43	3	3	-25
Ohio	339	3.1	1,153	747	39	4	-107
Oklahoma.	172	5.5	339	231	21	10	38
Oregon.	401	14.1	309	197	49	1	244
Pennsylvania.	137	1.2	1,151	912	84	3	-170
Rhode Island.	-16	-1.6	98	60	12	2	-66
South Carolina.	274	7.9	391	233	12	17	91
South Dakota	42	6.0	78	49	3	2	9
Tennessee	491	10.1	535	357	21	6	301
Texas.	2,453	14.4	2,344	969	598	43	461
Utah	336	19.5	280	75	21	2	87
Vermont	26	4.7	54	35	3	(Z)	5
Virginia.	545	8.8	687	371	106	60	70
Washington.	744	15.3	570	289	98	20	352
West Virginia.	22	1.2	158	146	3	(Z)	11
Wisconsin	278	5.7	505	322	19	(Z)	85
Wyoming	26	5.8	47	25	2	1	1

- Represents zero.   Z Less than 500.   [1] Includes residual change, not shown separately. The residual is the effect of national controls on subnational estimates. It is the difference between the implementation of the national estimates model and the county/state estimates model.

Source: U.S. Bureau of the Census, "ST-97-3 Estimates of the Population of States: Annual Time Series, July 1, 1990, to July 1, 1997, and Demographic Components of Population Change, Annual Time Series, July 1, 1990, to July 1, 1997"; release date: January 9, 1998; <http://www.census.gov/population/estimates/state/STCOM97R2.txt>.

No. 29. U.S. Resident Population, by Region and Division: 1970 to 1997

[As of **April 1**; except **1985, 1995**, and **1997**, as of **July 1**. For composition of divisions, see map, inside front cover]

REGION AND DIVISION	POPULATION (millions)						PERCENT DISTRIBUTION					
	1970	1980	1985	1990	1995	1997	1970	1980	1985	1990	1995	1997
United States.....	**203.3**	**226.5**	**237.9**	**248.8**	**262.8**	**267.6**	**100.0**	**100.0**	**100.0**	**100.0**	**100.0**	**100.0**
Northeast............	49.1	49.1	49.9	50.8	51.4	51.6	24.1	21.7	21.0	20.4	19.6	19.3
New England........	11.8	12.3	12.7	13.2	13.3	13.4	5.8	5.5	5.4	5.3	5.1	5.0
Middle Atlantic.......	37.2	36.8	37.1	37.6	38.1	38.2	18.3	16.2	15.6	15.1	14.5	14.3
Midwest.............	56.6	58.9	58.8	59.7	61.8	62.5	27.8	26.0	24.7	24.0	23.5	23.3
East North Central ...	40.3	41.7	41.4	42.0	43.5	43.9	19.8	18.4	17.4	16.9	16.5	16.4
West North Central ...	16.3	17.2	17.4	17.7	18.4	18.6	8.0	7.6	7.3	7.1	7.0	6.9
South..............	62.8	75.4	81.4	85.5	91.8	94.2	30.9	33.3	34.2	34.4	34.9	35.2
South Atlantic........	30.7	37.0	40.2	43.6	47.0	48.2	15.1	16.3	16.9	17.5	17.9	18.0
East South Central ...	12.8	14.7	15.0	15.2	16.0	16.3	6.3	6.5	6.3	6.1	6.1	6.1
West South Central...	19.3	23.7	26.3	26.7	28.8	29.6	9.5	10.5	11.0	10.7	11.0	11.1
West...............	34.8	43.2	47.8	52.8	57.7	59.4	17.1	19.1	20.1	21.2	21.9	22.2
Mountain...........	8.3	11.4	12.7	13.7	15.8	16.5	4.1	5.0	5.4	5.5	6.0	6.2
Pacific	26.5	31.8	35.1	39.2	41.9	42.9	13.1	14.0	14.7	15.7	16.0	16.0

Source: U.S. Bureau of the Census, *1990 Census of Population and Housing, Population and Housing Unit Counts* (CPH-2); and "ST-97-1 Estimates of the Population of States: Annual Time Series, July 1, 1990, to July 1, 1997"; release date: December 31, 1997; <http://www.census.gov/population/estimates/state/ST9097T1.txt>.

No. 30. Resident Population, by Region, Race, and Hispanic Origin: 1990

[As of **April 1**. For composition of regions, see map, inside front cover]

RACE AND HISPANIC ORIGIN	POPULATION (1,000)					PERCENT DISTRIBUTION				
	United States	North-east	Midwest	South	West	United States	North-east	Midwest	South	West
Total............	**248,710**	**50,809**	**59,669**	**85,446**	**52,786**	**100.0**	**20.4**	**24.0**	**34.4**	**21.2**
White..............	199,686	42,069	52,018	65,582	40,017	100.0	21.1	26.0	32.8	20.0
Black..............	29,986	5,613	5,716	15,829	2,828	100.0	18.7	19.1	52.8	9.4
American Indian, Eskimo, Aleut	1,959	125	338	563	933	100.0	6.4	17.2	28.7	47.6
American Indian......	1,878	122	334	557	866	100.0	6.5	17.8	29.7	46.1
Eskimo............	57	2	2	3	51	100.0	2.9	3.5	4.9	88.8
Aleut	24	2	2	3	17	100.0	8.1	8.1	11.5	72.3
Asian or Pacific Islander ..	7,274	1,335	768	1,122	4,048	100.0	18.4	10.6	15.4	55.7
Chinese	1,645	445	133	204	863	100.0	27.0	8.1	12.4	52.4
Filipino	1,407	143	113	159	991	100.0	10.2	8.1	11.3	70.5
Japanese	848	74	63	67	643	100.0	8.8	7.5	7.9	75.9
Asian Indian	815	285	146	196	189	100.0	35.0	17.9	24.0	23.1
Korean............	799	182	109	153	355	100.0	22.8	13.7	19.2	44.4
Vietnamese.........	615	61	52	169	334	100.0	9.8	8.5	27.4	54.3
Laotian............	149	16	28	29	76	100.0	10.7	18.6	19.6	51.0
Cambodian.........	147	30	13	19	85	100.0	20.5	8.8	13.1	57.7
Thai..............	91	12	13	24	43	100.0	12.9	14.2	26.0	46.8
Hmong............	90	2	37	2	50	100.0	1.9	41.3	1.8	55.0
Pakistani...........	81	28	15	22	17	100.0	34.3	18.9	26.5	20.4
Hawaiian...........	211	4	6	12	189	100.0	2.0	2.6	5.8	89.6
Samoan	63	2	2	4	55	100.0	2.4	3.6	6.4	87.6
Guamanian	49	4	3	8	34	100.0	7.3	6.4	16.8	69.5
Other Asian or Pacific Islander	263	49	34	54	126	100.0	18.6	12.9	20.5	48.0
Other races	9,805	1,667	829	2,350	4,960	100.0	17.0	8.5	24.0	50.6
Hispanic origin [1]	22,354	3,754	1,727	6,767	10,106	100.0	16.8	7.7	30.3	45.2
Mexican	13,496	175	1,153	4,344	7,824	100.0	1.3	8.5	32.2	58.0
Puerto Rican	2,728	1,872	258	406	192	100.0	68.6	9.4	14.9	7.0
Cuban	1,044	184	37	735	88	100.0	17.6	3.5	70.5	8.5
Other Hispanic.......	5,086	1,524	279	1,282	2,002	100.0	30.0	5.5	25.2	39.4
Not of Hispanic origin ...	226,356	47,055	57,942	78,679	42,680	100.0	20.8	25.6	34.8	18.9

[1] Persons of Hispanic origin may be of any race.

Source: U.S. Bureau of the Census, *1990 Census of Population, General Population Characteristics, United States* (CP-1-1).

No. 31. Annual Inmigration, Outmigration, and Net Migration for Regions: 1980 to 1997

[In thousands. As of March. For persons 1 year old and over. Excludes members of the Armed Forces except those living off post or with their families on post. Based on Current Population Survey; see text, Section 1, and Appendix III. For composition of regions, see map, inside front cover. Minus sign (-) indicates net outmigration]

PERIOD	North-east	Mid-west	South	West	PERIOD	North-east	Mid-west	South	West
1980-81: Inmigrants	464	650	1,377	871	Net internal migration . .	-328	-31	376	-17
Outmigrants	706	1,056	890	710	Movers from abroad	267	132	451	396
Net internal migration . .	-242	-406	487	161	Net migration	-61	101	827	379
Movers from abroad	207	180	412	514	**1995-96:** Inmigrants	441	842	1,284	792
Net migration	-35	-226	899	675	Outmigrants	675	775	1,134	775
1985-86: Inmigrants	502	1,011	1,355	910	Net internal migration . .	-234	68	150	16
Outmigrants	752	996	1,320	710	Movers from abroad	285	130	470	476
Net internal migration . .	-250	15	35	200	Net migration	51	198	620	492
Movers from abroad	198	158	342	502	**1996-97:**				
Net migration	-52	173	377	702	Total inmigrants	481	661	1,338	688
1990-91: Inmigrants	346	782	1,421	835	From Northeast	(X)	107	392	101
Outmigrants	932	797	987	668	From Midwest	94	(X)	492	228
Net internal migration . .	-585	-15	433	167	From South	256	333	(X)	358
Movers from abroad	209	208	351	617	From West	131	221	454	(X)
Net migration	-376	193	784	784	Total outmigrants	600	814	947	806
1992-93: Inmigrants	313	841	1,145	769	To Northeast	(X)	94	256	131
Outmigrants	647	608	1,044	770	To Midwest	107	(X)	333	221
Net internal migration . .	-334	233	101	-1	To South	392	492	(X)	454
Movers from abroad	230	198	513	364	To West	101	228	358	(X)
Net migration	-104	431	614	363	Net internal migration	-119	-154	391	-118
1993-94: Inmigrants	348	706	1,336	746	Movers from abroad	239	169	445	450
Outmigrants	676	737	960	763	Net migration	120	15	836	332

X Not applicable.

Source: U.S. Bureau of the Census, *Current Population Reports*, P20-510, and earlier reports.

No. 32. Mobility Status of the Population, by Selected Characteristics: 1980 to 1997

[As of March. For persons 1 year old and over. Excludes members of the Armed Forces except those living off post or with their families on post. Based on Current Population Survey; see text, Section 1, and Appendix III. For composition of regions, see map, inside front cover]

MOBILITY PERIOD AND CHARACTERISTIC	Total (1,000)	PERCENT DISTRIBUTION						
		Non-movers	Movers (different house in United States)					Movers from abroad
			Total	Same county	Different county			
					Total	Same state	Different state	
1980-81	221,641	83	17	10	6	3	3	1
1985-86	232,998	82	18	11	7	4	3	1
1990-91	244,884	83	16	10	6	3	3	1
1995-96	260,406	84	16	10	6	3	3	1
1996-97, total persons	**262,976**	**84**	**16**	**11**	**5**	**3**	**2**	**(Z)**
1 to 4 years old	15,965	76	23	16	7	4	3	1
5 to 9 years old	20,271	81	19	13	6	3	3	(Z)
10 to 14 years old	19,505	85	15	10	5	2	2	(Z)
15 to 19 years old	19,164	83	16	11	5	3	2	1
20 to 24 years old	17,489	67	32	21	11	6	5	1
25 to 29 years old	19,260	67	31	21	11	6	5	1
30 to 44 years old	64,956	83	17	11	6	3	3	1
45 to 64 years old	54,488	91	9	6	3	2	1	(Z)
65 to 74 years old	18,015	95	4	3	2	1	1	(Z)
75 to 84 years old	10,954	95	5	3	2	1	1	(Z)
85 years old and over	2,909	94	6	3	3	2	1	(Z)
Northeast	50,876	88	11	8	4	2	2	(Z)
Midwest	61,231	85	15	10	5	3	2	(Z)
South	92,011	82	17	11	6	3	3	(Z)
West	58,858	80	19	13	6	3	3	1
Householders, 15 years and over	101,081	84	15	10	5	3	2	(Z)
Household income:								
Less than $5,000	3,448	74	24	17	7	4	3	2
$5,000 to $9,999	8,460	82	18	12	5	3	2	1
$10,000 to $14,999	8,678	81	19	13	6	3	2	(Z)
$15,000 to $24,999	15,520	81	18	12	6	3	3	(Z)
$25,000 to $34,999	13,810	83	16	11	6	3	2	(Z)
$35,000 to $49,999	16,465	84	15	10	5	3	2	(Z)
$50,000 to $74,999	18,170	87	13	8	5	3	2	(Z)
$75,000 and over	16,529	90	10	6	4	2	2	(Z)
Tenure:								
Owner-occupied units	66,356	93	7	4	2	1	1	(Z)
Renter-occupied units	34,725	67	32	21	11	6	5	1

Z Less than 0.5 percent.

Source: U.S. Bureau of the Census, *Current Population Reports*, P20-510.

No. 33. Resident Population, by Age and State: 1997

[In thousands, except percent. As of July 1. Includes Armed Forces stationed in area. See text, Section 1, for basis of estimates]

STATE	Total	Under 5 years	5 to 17 years	18 to 24 years	25 to 34 years	35 to 44 years	45 to 54 years	55 to 64 years	65 to 74 years	75 to 84 years	85 years and over	Percent 65 years and over
U.S.	267,636	19,150	50,378	24,979	39,610	43,998	33,633	21,813	18,499	11,706	3,871	12.7
AL	4,319	293	779	436	630	684	551	385	312	188	61	13.0
AK	609	49	139	67	80	114	86	42	21	9	2	5.3
AZ	4,555	374	904	425	649	703	536	361	335	208	59	13.2
AR	2,523	177	486	248	336	373	312	230	192	125	42	14.3
CA	32,268	2,661	6,291	3,049	5,285	5,373	3,789	2,249	1,954	1,229	389	11.1
CO	3,893	274	742	363	547	701	553	321	220	130	44	10.1
CT	3,270	217	575	258	489	563	429	269	242	169	59	14.4
DE	732	49	128	65	119	125	91	60	54	31	9	12.9
DC	529	33	74	43	105	88	67	46	40	25	9	13.9
FL	14,654	951	2,520	1,180	1,968	2,261	1,753	1,312	1,458	958	293	18.5
GA	7,486	558	1,430	738	1,220	1,274	955	573	416	245	77	9.9
HI	1,187	88	214	117	161	199	156	95	90	52	15	13.2
ID	1,210	92	260	135	151	187	150	99	72	49	16	11.3
IL	11,896	904	2,271	1,095	1,764	1,950	1,469	963	788	517	177	12.5
IN	5,864	407	1,090	569	859	961	748	496	399	251	84	12.5
IA	2,852	184	542	270	376	445	357	251	214	154	61	15.0
KS	2,595	179	509	252	356	423	317	207	179	124	49	13.5
KY	3,908	257	704	399	563	633	512	351	269	164	55	12.5
LA	4,352	314	877	468	608	686	538	365	280	164	53	11.4
ME	1,242	69	228	110	172	216	169	104	93	59	21	13.9
MD	5,094	347	922	429	819	917	675	402	325	198	61	11.5
MA	6,118	399	1,052	500	1,014	1,028	782	479	446	307	109	14.1
MI	9,774	653	1,852	922	1,434	1,641	1,261	797	664	417	132	12.4
MN	4,686	316	935	427	671	805	587	367	294	205	79	12.3
MS	2,731	202	551	298	385	412	322	228	183	110	39	12.2
MO	5,402	367	1,040	498	756	873	667	462	392	254	95	13.7
MT	879	54	175	87	98	144	123	82	61	41	14	13.2
NE	1,657	114	330	164	218	264	203	135	116	79	33	13.7
NV	1,677	130	313	141	254	279	219	149	119	60	14	11.5
NH	1,173	74	222	94	186	219	152	85	76	49	17	12.1
NJ	8,053	557	1,430	667	1,170	1,385	1,055	683	596	386	124	13.7
NM	1,730	134	365	174	225	281	216	142	110	63	20	11.2
NY	18,137	1,314	3,246	1,579	2,767	2,948	2,312	1,543	1,313	825	290	13.4
NC	7,425	519	1,355	696	1,147	1,201	946	635	524	309	94	12.5
ND	641	41	125	67	85	101	77	54	45	33	14	14.4
OH	11,186	749	2,090	1,045	1,602	1,831	1,423	952	817	513	165	13.4
OK	3,317	226	652	332	437	510	416	300	240	150	55	13.4
OR	3,243	213	598	296	434	542	457	274	224	155	51	13.3
PA	12,020	738	2,126	1,023	1,670	1,963	1,546	1,049	1,015	676	213	15.8
RI	987	62	171	83	157	163	120	75	80	56	20	15.8
SC	3,760	254	702	377	567	603	485	319	262	149	43	12.1
SD	738	49	148	76	93	117	88	61	53	37	15	14.3
TN	5,368	362	963	509	798	875	712	480	371	225	75	12.5
TX	19,439	1,609	3,969	1,993	2,882	3,188	2,353	1,486	1,106	638	216	10.1
UT	2,059	196	492	278	294	282	207	131	98	62	20	8.7
VT	589	35	111	51	86	104	83	47	39	24	9	12.3
VA	6,734	453	1,192	647	1,095	1,159	888	544	425	253	78	11.2
WA	5,610	386	1,068	522	819	983	752	433	343	230	75	11.5
WV	1,816	104	308	184	231	280	253	181	152	93	30	15.1
WI	5,170	335	1,011	484	725	859	650	422	355	240	88	13.2
WY	480	31	101	52	54	80	66	41	31	18	6	11.3

Source: U.S. Bureau of the Census, "Estimates of the Population of the U.S., Regions, and States by Selected Age Groups and Sex: Annual Time Series, July 1, 1990 to July 1, 1997;" published 21 July 1998; <http://www.census.gov/population/estimates/state/97agesex.txt> and "Estimates of the Population of the U.S., Regions, Divisions, and States by 5-Year Age Groups and Sex: Annual Time Series, July 1, 1990 to July 1, 1997;" published 21 July 1998; <http://www.census.gov/population/estimates/state/97ageby5.txt>.

Population

No. 34. Resident Population by Race, Hispanic Origin, and State: 1997

[**In thousands. As of July 1**. These estimates are consistent with data released in PE-64, PE-65, PPL-110, PPL-111 and PPL-112 released July 28, 1998. These estimates are developed using a cohort-component method whereby each component of population change (births, deaths, domestic migration, and international migration) is estimated separately for each birth cohort by sex and race]

STATE	Total	RACE				Black	American Indian, Eskimo, Aleut	Asian, Pacific Islander	Hispanic origin [1]
		White							
		Total	Hispanic	Non-Hispanic					
U.S.	**267,636**	**221,334**	**26,763**	**194,571**	**33,947**	**2,322**	**10,033**	**29,348**
AL.	4,319	3,156	34	3,122	1,120	15	28	39
AK.	609	462	19	443	24	97	27	23
AZ.	4,555	4,046	933	3,113	161	255	93	999
AR.	2,523	2,086	40	2,046	406	13	18	45
CA.	32,268	25,788	9,306	16,482	2,397	307	3,777	9,941
CO	3,893	3,598	522	3,076	168	36	90	556
CT.	3,270	2,886	229	2,657	300	8	76	259
DE.	732	575	21	554	140	2	14	24
DC	529	179	31	148	333	2	16	38
FL.	14,654	12,094	1,952	10,141	2,253	55	253	2,106
GA	7,486	5,206	181	5,024	2,126	17	137	207
HI	1,187	396	49	347	35	7	749	95
ID	1,210	1,174	80	1,094	7	16	13	86
IL	11,896	9,671	1,107	8,564	1,815	27	383	1,183
IN	5,864	5,313	125	5,188	484	14	53	137
IA	2,852	2,753	48	2,704	56	9	36	53
KS.	2,595	2,375	120	2,255	153	23	44	133
KY.	3,908	3,593	26	3,567	283	6	26	30
LA.	4,352	2,882	97	2,785	1,396	19	53	113
ME	1,242	1,222	8	1,214	6	6	9	9
MD	5,094	3,487	150	3,337	1,397	15	195	179
MA	6,118	5,510	284	5,226	384	14	210	359
MI	9,774	8,172	225	7,946	1,392	60	151	254
MN	4,686	4,377	70	4,307	133	57	118	81
MS	2,731	1,709	17	1,691	993	10	18	22
MO	5,402	4,717	73	4,645	607	21	58	82
MT	879	816	13	803	3	55	5	15
NE.	1,657	1,555	62	1,493	66	15	21	68
NV.	1,677	1,448	231	1,218	125	30	74	253
NH	1,173	1,149	15	1,133	8	2	13	17
NJ.	8,053	6,438	826	5,611	1,170	21	424	959
NM	1,730	1,503	663	840	44	158	24	693
NY.	18,137	13,902	1,943	11,958	3,208	74	953	2,570
NC	7,425	5,595	129	5,466	1,643	95	92	149
ND	641	602	6	596	4	30	5	7
OH	11,186	9,763	153	9,610	1,278	22	123	173
OK	3,317	2,757	102	2,655	257	260	43	122
OR	3,243	3,040	174	2,866	58	44	101	190
PA.	12,020	10,648	254	10,394	1,164	17	191	302
RI	987	913	49	864	47	5	22	61
SC.	3,760	2,588	39	2,550	1,130	9	32	46
SD.	738	670	6	664	5	58	5	8
TN.	5,368	4,422	49	4,374	884	12	49	57
TX.	19,439	16,448	5,515	10,933	2,374	93	524	5,723
UT.	2,059	1,962	123	1,838	18	29	51	133
VT.	589	579	5	575	3	2	5	5
VA.	6,734	5,139	209	4,930	1,344	18	233	239
WA	5,610	5,003	302	4,701	196	100	311	340
WV	1,816	1,747	9	1,738	58	2	9	10
WI	5,170	4,761	114	4,646	286	46	77	128
WY	480	461	26	435	4	11	4	28

[1] Persons of Hispanic origin may be of any race.

Source: U.S. Bureau of the Census, "Estimates of the Population of States by Race and Hispanic Origin: July 1, 1997"; published 4 September 1998; <http://www.census.gov/population/estimates/state/srh/srhus97.txt>.

No. 35. State Population Projections: 2000 to 2025

[**In thousands**. As of **July 1**. The two series of projections are based on different internal migration assumptions: 1) Series A, is the preferred series model and uses state-to-state migration observed from 1975-76 through 1993-94; and 2) Series B, the economic model, uses the Bureau of Economic Analysis employment projections. For explanation of methodology, see text, Section 1]

STATE	SERIES A						SERIES B					
	2000	2005	2010	2015	2020	2025	2000	2005	2010	2015	2020	2025
U.S	274,634	285,981	297,716	310,133	322,742	335,050	274,634	285,981	297,716	310,134	322,742	335,050
AL	4,451	4,631	4,798	4,956	5,100	5,224	4,436	4,617	4,802	4,986	5,162	5,319
AK	653	700	745	791	838	885	632	659	690	728	773	825
AZ	4,798	5,230	5,522	5,808	6,111	6,412	4,838	5,432	6,025	6,620	7,193	7,729
AR	2,631	2,750	2,840	2,922	2,997	3,055	2,623	2,757	2,887	3,008	3,109	3,184
CA	32,521	34,441	37,644	41,373	45,278	49,285	32,423	33,511	34,968	36,838	39,034	41,480
CO	4,168	4,468	4,658	4,833	5,012	5,188	4,154	4,510	4,837	5,152	5,454	5,743
CT	3,284	3,317	3,400	3,506	3,621	3,739	3,286	3,291	3,303	3,332	3,376	3,428
DE	768	800	817	832	847	861	758	793	823	851	877	899
DC	523	529	560	594	625	655	530	542	572	611	654	702
FL	15,233	16,279	17,363	18,497	19,634	20,710	15,250	16,273	17,299	18,318	19,262	20,066
GA	7,875	8,413	8,824	9,200	9,552	9,869	7,893	8,540	9,167	9,785	10,386	10,962
HI	1,257	1,342	1,440	1,553	1,677	1,812	1,238	1,297	1,367	1,447	1,537	1,634
ID	1,347	1,480	1,557	1,622	1,683	1,739	1,332	1,489	1,637	1,775	1,900	2,008
IL	12,051	12,266	12,515	12,808	13,121	13,440	12,069	12,314	12,601	12,945	13,323	13,717
IN	6,045	6,215	6,318	6,404	6,481	6,546	6,060	6,301	6,532	6,758	6,969	7,158
IA	2,900	2,941	2,968	2,994	3,019	3,040	2,891	2,939	2,992	3,047	3,095	3,133
KS	2,668	2,761	2,849	2,939	3,026	3,108	2,675	2,788	2,908	3,034	3,158	3,273
KY	3,995	4,098	4,170	4,231	4,281	4,314	3,990	4,109	4,220	4,322	4,411	4,480
LA	4,425	4,535	4,683	4,840	4,991	5,133	4,445	4,558	4,687	4,828	4,972	5,111
ME	1,259	1,285	1,323	1,362	1,396	1,423	1,250	1,259	1,268	1,276	1,282	1,282
MD	5,275	5,467	5,657	5,862	6,071	6,274	5,261	5,426	5,577	5,736	5,904	6,072
MA	6,199	6,310	6,431	6,574	6,734	6,902	6,224	6,361	6,498	6,653	6,824	7,001
MI	9,679	9,763	9,836	9,917	10,002	10,078	9,711	9,835	9,966	10,115	10,272	10,423
MN	4,830	5,005	5,147	5,283	5,406	5,510	4,822	5,014	5,212	5,414	5,606	5,778
MS	2,816	2,908	2,974	3,035	3,093	3,142	2,826	2,949	3,072	3,195	3,310	3,413
MO	5,540	5,718	5,864	6,005	6,137	6,250	5,547	5,750	5,953	6,153	6,336	6,492
MT	950	1,006	1,040	1,069	1,097	1,121	937	998	1,056	1,108	1,152	1,187
NE	1,705	1,761	1,806	1,850	1,892	1,930	1,700	1,766	1,837	1,912	1,984	2,050
NV	1,871	2,070	2,131	2,179	2,241	2,312	1,863	2,130	2,355	2,547	2,712	2,854
NH	1,224	1,281	1,329	1,372	1,410	1,439	1,217	1,267	1,307	1,344	1,377	1,402
NJ	8,178	8,392	8,638	8,924	9,238	9,558	8,185	8,387	8,594	8,832	9,096	9,369
NM	1,860	2,016	2,155	2,300	2,454	2,612	1,858	2,035	2,223	2,425	2,636	2,850
NY	18,146	18,250	18,530	18,916	19,359	19,830	18,174	18,227	18,363	18,616	18,969	19,396
NC	7,777	8,227	8,552	8,840	9,111	9,349	7,789	8,312	8,780	9,206	9,588	9,916
ND	662	677	690	704	717	729	657	677	701	727	754	778
OH	11,319	11,428	11,505	11,588	11,671	11,744	11,352	11,534	11,726	11,937	12,148	12,343
OK	3,373	3,491	3,639	3,789	3,930	4,057	3,370	3,471	3,578	3,684	3,784	3,871
OR	3,397	3,613	3,803	3,992	4,177	4,349	3,397	3,625	3,837	4,036	4,213	4,361
PA	12,202	12,281	12,352	12,449	12,567	12,683	12,220	12,329	12,443	12,580	12,727	12,854
RI	998	1,012	1,038	1,070	1,105	1,141	989	986	986	989	998	1,007
SC	3,858	4,033	4,205	4,369	4,517	4,645	3,852	4,015	4,169	4,318	4,455	4,574
SD	777	810	826	840	853	866	770	811	853	893	930	962
TN	5,657	5,966	6,180	6,365	6,529	6,665	5,668	6,039	6,385	6,707	6,998	7,249
TX	20,119	21,487	22,857	24,280	25,729	27,183	20,178	21,635	23,158	24,775	26,453	28,170
UT	2,207	2,411	2,551	2,670	2,781	2,883	2,216	2,477	2,738	2,995	3,246	3,487
VT	617	638	651	662	671	678	607	623	636	646	655	661
VA	6,997	7,324	7,627	7,921	8,204	8,466	6,965	7,234	7,474	7,708	7,939	8,165
WA	5,858	6,258	6,658	7,058	7,446	7,808	5,829	6,184	6,524	6,857	7,179	7,480
WV	1,841	1,849	1,851	1,851	1,850	1,845	1,833	1,842	1,852	1,861	1,866	1,864
WI	5,326	5,479	5,590	5,693	5,788	5,867	5,324	5,502	5,682	5,864	6,035	6,185
WY	525	568	607	641	670	694	519	559	598	636	671	702

Source: U.S. Bureau of the Census, Population Paper Listings PPL-47.

Population

No. 36. Population Projections, by Age—States: 2000 to 2010

[In thousands. As of July 1. The projections shown here are based on certain internal migration assumptions: Series A, is the preferred series model and uses state-to-state migration observed from 1975-76 through 1993-94]

STATE	UNDER 18 YEARS			18 TO 44 YEARS			45 TO 64 YEARS			65 YEARS AND OVER		
	2000	2005	2010	2000	2005	2010	2000	2005	2010	2000	2005	2010
U.S.	70,782	71,964	72,510	108,151	106,738	106,951	60,991	71,113	78,847	34,710	36,166	39,408
AL	1,105	1,119	1,110	1,731	1,696	1,676	1,033	1,203	1,338	582	613	674
AK	200	213	225	278	286	301	137	155	164	38	46	55
AZ	1,313	1,375	1,387	1,812	1,859	1,863	1,038	1,289	1,465	635	707	807
AR	653	651	636	977	958	929	624	739	824	377	402	451
CA	9,350	9,946	10,689	13,260	13,412	14,407	6,524	7,629	8,759	3,387	3,454	3,789
CO	1,049	1,078	1,080	1,694	1,714	1,707	973	1,153	1,260	452	523	611
CT	791	777	767	1,283	1,234	1,232	749	850	924	461	456	477
DE	191	191	185	311	307	298	169	201	225	97	101	109
DC	125	130	136	215	212	226	114	122	133	69	65	65
FL	3,507	3,563	3,573	5,425	5,443	5,483	3,546	4,362	5,072	2,755	2,911	3,235
GA	2,070	2,155	2,164	3,301	3,326	3,318	1,725	2,080	2,368	779	852	974
HI	328	354	379	495	505	528	277	319	351	157	164	182
ID	378	400	404	516	537	538	296	361	402	157	182	213
IL	3,141	3,151	3,142	4,807	4,665	4,604	2,619	2,956	3,204	1,484	1,494	1,565
IN	1,518	1,524	1,499	2,396	2,330	2,270	1,368	1,567	1,697	763	794	852
IA	706	691	678	1,091	1,052	1,018	661	746	796	442	452	476
KS	698	700	704	1,036	1,026	1,018	575	669	736	359	366	391
KY	963	951	923	1,577	1,516	1,461	946	1,093	1,197	509	538	589
LA	1,214	1,204	1,207	1,722	1,678	1,676	966	1,098	1,190	523	555	610
ME	293	284	281	485	462	449	309	366	407	172	173	186
MD	1,319	1,333	1,330	2,174	2,131	2,106	1,193	1,392	1,557	589	611	664
MA	1,496	1,488	1,452	2,499	2,429	2,393	1,361	1,566	1,723	843	827	863
MI	2,495	2,455	2,400	3,817	3,641	3,540	2,170	2,456	2,620	1,197	1,211	1,276
MN	1,236	1,216	1,212	1,935	1,906	1,858	1,063	1,256	1,391	596	627	686
MS	767	769	751	1,096	1,068	1,048	609	708	782	344	363	393
MO	1,392	1,390	1,378	2,146	2,099	2,053	1,247	1,455	1,603	755	774	830
MT	240	242	242	348	345	337	234	276	297	128	143	164
NE	443	442	443	654	646	636	369	425	462	239	248	265
NV	450	468	456	738	754	718	464	591	662	219	257	295
NH	304	303	300	503	494	486	275	336	380	142	148	163
NJ	2,004	2,024	2,009	3,216	3,136	3,131	1,868	2,139	2,348	1,090	1,093	1,150
NM	534	568	594	717	737	757	403	483	545	206	228	259
NY	4,620	4,610	4,535	7,101	6,817	6,763	4,067	4,502	4,833	2,358	2,321	2,399
NC	1,908	1,934	1,885	3,083	3,065	3,029	1,795	2,147	2,420	991	1,081	1,218
ND	168	163	163	253	249	243	142	162	173	99	103	111
OH	2,817	2,766	2,702	4,411	4,214	4,082	2,566	2,894	3,097	1,525	1,554	1,624
OK	861	852	856	1,265	1,242	1,242	775	893	980	472	504	561
OR	810	821	828	1,277	1,273	1,270	839	997	1,100	471	522	605
PA	2,902	2,845	2,762	4,582	4,363	4,236	2,819	3,206	3,446	1,899	1,867	1,908
RI	245	244	242	390	374	374	215	251	276	148	143	146
SC	970	980	968	1,513	1,479	1,470	897	1,057	1,183	478	517	584
SD	210	211	210	293	292	283	164	193	212	110	114	121
TN	1,376	1,408	1,390	2,238	2,225	2,191	1,336	1,573	1,755	707	760	844
TX	5,708	5,976	6,210	8,122	8,251	8,471	4,188	4,963	5,575	2,101	2,297	2,601
UT	719	759	776	896	941	958	390	477	541	202	234	276
VT	152	150	145	245	238	232	147	173	188	73	77	86
VA	1,697	1,728	1,725	2,912	2,876	2,861	1,600	1,875	2,096	788	845	945
WA	1,459	1,496	1,534	2,346	2,351	2,378	1,368	1,654	1,866	685	757	880
WV	404	394	379	679	636	607	471	523	549	287	296	316
WI	1,344	1,322	1,308	2,090	2,045	1,987	1,187	1,382	1,512	705	730	783
WY	139	146	153	201	205	212	123	146	160	62	71	82

Source: U.S. Bureau of the Census, Population Paper Listings PPL-47.

No. 37. Population Projections, by Race—States: 2000 to 2010

[**In thousands.** As of **July 1**. The projections shown here are based on certain internal migration assumptions: Series A, is the preferred series model and uses state-to-state migration observed from 1975-76 through 1993-94]

STATE	WHITE			BLACK			AMERICAN INDIAN, ESKIMO, ALEUT			ASIAN, PACIFIC ISLANDER		
	2000	2005	2010	2000	2005	2010	2000	2005	2010	2000	2005	2010
U.S.	225,533	232,462	239,588	35,456	37,735	40,110	2,402	2,573	2,754	11,246	13,212	15,265
AL	3,262	3,391	3,509	1,137	1,183	1,227	18	18	20	34	40	44
AK	486	508	524	29	31	33	93	92	91	46	69	96
AZ	4,252	4,623	4,867	177	203	222	262	277	290	107	129	143
AR	2,186	2,286	2,363	409	423	434	15	16	18	19	22	24
CA	25,517	26,583	28,655	2,425	2,511	2,702	292	296	318	4,289	5,051	5,969
CO	3,823	4,068	4,216	196	224	246	41	46	51	108	129	147
CT	2,873	2,862	2,893	324	350	384	8	8	8	80	96	115
DE	603	621	626	147	158	169	2	2	2	15	17	19
DC	184	194	209	321	316	329	-	-	-	15	18	21
FL	12,588	13,332	14,113	2,326	2,573	2,820	51	58	64	267	316	366
GA	5,436	5,713	5,893	2,279	2,515	2,724	17	18	18	142	168	187
HI	423	449	478	31	33	35	6	6	7	796	853	920
ID	1,300	1,425	1,497	8	11	12	21	25	27	17	19	22
IL	9,736	9,839	9,968	1,865	1,914	1,971	26	28	31	423	484	543
IN	5,466	5,599	5,671	502	530	551	16	16	17	60	72	78
IA	2,786	2,810	2,825	62	69	76	9	11	12	43	52	58
KS	2,419	2,487	2,550	173	188	203	27	29	30	50	59	64
KY	3,671	3,760	3,817	287	298	310	6	6	8	29	33	37
LA	2,895	2,923	2,979	1,448	1,521	1,600	20	20	22	62	72	83
ME	1,238	1,261	1,296	5	5	7	6	6	6	9	11	13
MD	3,546	3,580	3,621	1,489	1,609	1,724	16	16	16	223	260	296
MA	5,523	5,534	5,549	417	461	508	14	14	15	246	303	361
MI	8,021	8,024	8,016	1,435	1,486	1,539	61	63	65	163	190	215
MN	4,469	4,580	4,662	158	185	210	64	71	80	139	170	196
MS	1,774	1,826	1,861	1,012	1,049	1,078	8	8	8	19	23	25
MO	4,825	4,957	5,061	628	662	696	24	26	28	63	72	80
MT	879	926	952	3	6	6	61	67	72	7	9	9
NE	1,595	1,636	1,668	72	82	88	16	18	20	23	29	31
NV	1,619	1,777	1,817	138	159	171	31	32	32	85	103	111
NH	1,199	1,251	1,293	9	10	10	2	2	2	14	17	21
NJ	6,442	6,465	6,512	1,239	1,328	1,422	20	23	23	475	578	681
NM	1,615	1,737	1,843	48	56	63	169	186	209	29	35	41
NY	13,747	13,567	13,529	3,299	3,416	3,563	73	76	79	1,028	1,191	1,359
NC	5,851	6,160	6,367	1,738	1,857	1,957	94	98	101	96	113	128
ND	617	628	635	5	5	5	32	37	43	6	6	7
OH	9,835	9,852	9,842	1,320	1,386	1,452	22	24	24	140	166	186
OK	2,759	2,825	2,917	282	311	341	281	295	315	51	58	65
OR	3,167	3,350	3,508	65	74	80	51	55	59	116	135	155
PA	10,741	10,725	10,700	1,224	1,279	1,334	18	22	22	218	258	296
RI	911	911	922	54	60	68	4	6	8	28	35	41
SC	2,660	2,781	2,898	1,156	1,205	1,255	8	8	9	33	38	42
SD	706	730	739	5	5	6	60	66	72	5	6	7
TN	4,658	4,887	5,036	929	999	1,057	12	14	14	57	66	72
TX	16,920	17,916	18,917	2,543	2,797	3,058	95	107	120	562	667	762
UT	2,087	2,267	2,390	22	27	29	37	43	47	62	75	85
VT	606	625	638	2	4	4	2	2	2	6	7	8
VA	5,295	5,457	5,599	1,416	1,526	1,637	19	19	21	267	320	370
WA	5,200	5,506	5,811	192	208	224	107	115	126	358	427	496
WV	1,769	1,774	1,772	58	60	60	2	2	2	11	13	15
WI	4,853	4,937	4,988	326	366	400	49	52	55	100	126	147
WY	501	539	573	6	7	8	13	16	19	4	6	7

- Represents or rounds to zero.

Source: U.S. Bureau of the Census, Population Paper Listings PPL-47.

No. 38. Population Projections, by Hispanic-Origin Status—States: 2000 to 2010

[In thousands. As of July 1. The projections shown here are based on certain internal migration assumptions: Series A, is the preferred series model and uses State-to-State migration observed from 1975-76 through 1993-94. Persons of Hispanic origin may be of any race]

STATE	HISPANIC ORIGIN			NOT OF HISPANIC ORIGIN								
				WHITE			BLACK		AMERICAN INDIAN, ESKIMO, ALEUT		ASIAN, PACIFIC ISLANDER	
	2000	2005	2010	2000	2005	2010	2000	2010	2000	2010	2000	2010
U.S......	31,366	36,057	41,138	197,062	199,802	202,390	33,569	37,466	2,055	2,321	10,585	14,402
AL........	37	42	47	3,231	3,355	3,468	1,133	1,223	18	20	32	42
AK........	31	37	41	461	476	487	27	31	91	91	44	94
AZ........	1,071	1,269	1,450	3,254	3,441	3,518	150	179	232	256	91	119
AR........	33	40	46	2,155	2,249	2,320	407	432	15	18	19	23
CA........	10,647	12,268	14,214	15,562	15,123	15,394	2,138	2,268	170	165	4,006	5,603
CO........	594	682	770	3,268	3,434	3,505	178	216	30	37	98	132
CT........	288	332	386	2,622	2,574	2,561	293	338	6	6	76	109
DE........	25	29	33	582	596	597	143	165	2	2	15	19
DC........	40	46	55	152	156	163	315	322	-	-	13	19
FL........	2,390	2,845	3,319	10,405	10,764	11,145	2,159	2,536	39	44	239	319
GA........	189	226	252	5,270	5,515	5,671	2,262	2,702	15	16	138	181
HI........	107	119	132	363	372	383	27	29	4	5	755	891
ID........	96	121	140	1,211	1,314	1,368	6	8	18	23	15	19
IL........	1,267	1,450	1,637	8,553	8,487	8,445	1,813	1,900	18	19	399	512
IN........	140	162	179	5,338	5,453	5,509	494	540	14	15	58	74
IA........	54	61	71	2,737	2,755	2,762	60	72	8	10	41	56
KS........	138	166	191	2,293	2,337	2,377	167	193	23	26	48	60
KY........	32	38	42	3,643	3,727	3,781	285	306	6	8	27	35
LA........	119	138	156	2,792	2,803	2,841	1,438	1,588	18	20	58	79
ME........	8	10	14	1,230	1,251	1,284	5	5	6	6	9	13
MD........	214	258	300	3,371	3,368	3,372	1,462	1,687	14	14	213	284
MA........	437	524	619	5,182	5,123	5,063	332	391	10	10	239	350
MI........	261	289	319	7,790	7,767	7,732	1,417	1,517	55	59	157	208
MN........	95	114	132	4,387	4,480	4,546	152	202	61	76	135	192
MS........	21	24	27	1,755	1,804	1,836	1,010	1,076	8	8	19	25
MO........	90	105	121	4,745	4,863	4,953	622	689	22	26	61	76
MT........	20	26	28	861	904	926	3	4	59	72	7	9
NE........	61	72	80	1,540	1,572	1,596	70	84	14	18	21	29
NV........	277	350	403	1,366	1,456	1,445	128	156	25	26	77	101
NH........	17	20	22	1,184	1,233	1,273	7	8	2	2	14	21
NJ........	1,044	1,196	1,348	5,558	5,462	5,387	1,104	1,232	14	15	456	656
NM........	736	821	912	912	958	984	34	37	157	195	22	28
NY........	2,805	3,071	3,357	11,640	11,271	11,023	2,668	2,790	53	56	981	1,304
NC........	121	139	154	5,748	6,040	6,233	1,726	1,943	92	99	92	124
ND........	6	8	10	611	620	625	5	5	32	43	6	7
OH........	183	206	230	9,672	9,669	9,638	1,306	1,433	20	22	136	181
OK........	124	143	167	2,653	2,700	2,769	276	332	273	309	47	61
OR........	195	237	278	2,990	3,133	3,253	59	71	45	53	110	147
PA........	334	391	448	10,460	10,398	10,325	1,181	1,276	16	18	210	285
RI........	76	92	112	851	838	834	40	48	4	6	26	39
SC........	42	50	58	2,624	2,738	2,848	1,152	1,249	8	9	31	40
SD........	8	9	10	698	721	729	5	6	60	72	5	7
TN........	57	67	75	4,607	4,828	4,969	925	1,051	12	14	55	70
TX........	5,875	6,624	7,421	11,273	11,587	11,866	2,406	2,833	60	66	506	671
UT........	138	164	185	1,961	2,117	2,219	18	23	33	43	58	81
VT........	6	6	8	600	619	630	2	4	2	2	6	8
VA........	269	322	376	5,061	5,175	5,270	1,394	1,606	16	17	257	358
WA........	360	437	519	4,881	5,115	5,346	179	203	95	112	342	477
WV........	11	15	17	1,758	1,761	1,757	58	58	2	2	11	15
WI........	136	156	173	4,732	4,799	4,833	318	390	45	51	97	143
WY........	35	42	48	469	501	529	4	6	12	17	4	7

Source: U.S. Bureau of the Census, Population Paper Listings PPL-47.

No. 39. Population in Coastal Counties: 1970 to 1997

[Enumerated population as of **April 1**, except as indicated. Areas as defined by U.S. National Oceanic and Atmospheric Agency, 1992. Covers 673 counties and equivalent areas with at least 15 percent of their land area either in a coastal watershed (drainage area) or in a coastal cataloging unit (a coastal area between watersheds)]

YEAR	Total	COUNTIES IN COASTAL REGIONS					Balance of United States
		Total	Atlantic	Gulf of Mexico	Great Lakes	Pacific	
Land area, 1990 (1,000 sq. mi.)	3,536	888	148	114	115	510	2,649
POPULATION							
1970 (mil.).	203.3	110.0	51.1	10.0	26.0	22.8	93.3
1980 (mil.).	226.5	119.8	53.7	13.1	26.0	27.0	106.7
1990 (mil.).	248.7	133.4	59.0	15.2	25.9	33.2	115.3
1995 (July 1) (mil.)	262.8	139.3	61.0	16.5	26.5	35.2	123.5
1997 (July 1) (mil.)	267.6	141.3	61.7	16.9	26.6	36.0	126.3
1970 (percent).	100	54	25	5	13	11	46
1980 (percent).	100	53	24	6	11	12	47
1990 (percent).	100	54	24	6	10	13	46
1995 (July 1) (percent)	100	53	23	6	10	13	47
1997 (July 1) (percent)	100	53	23	6	10	13	47

Source: U.S. Bureau of the Census, *U.S. Census of Population: 1970; 1980 Census of Population*, Vol. 1, Chapter A (PC80-1-A-1), *U.S. Summary; 1990 Census of Population and Housing* (CPH1); and unpublished data.

No. 40. Metropolitan and Nonmetropolitan Area Population: 1970 to 1996

[As of **April 1**, except **1996**, as of **July 1**. Data exclude Puerto Rico. Metropolitan areas are defined by U.S. Office of Management and Budget as of year shown, except as noted]

ITEM	1970	1980 [1] (SMSAs)	MSA'S AND CMSA'S [2]		
			1980	1990	1996
Metropolitan areas: Number of areas	243	318	273	273	273
Population (1,000).	139,480	169,431	177,285	198,170	211,785
Percent change over previous year shown . .	[3]23.6	21.5	(X)	11.8	6.9
Percent of total U.S. population	68.6	74.8	78.3	79.7	79.8
Land area, percent of U.S. land area	10.9	16.0	19.9	19.9	19.9
Nonmetropolitan areas, population (1,000)	63,822	57,115	49,257	50,548	53,498

X Not applicable.   [1] SMSA=standard metropolitan statistical area. Areas are as defined June 30, 1981.   [2] Areas are as defined June 30, 1996.   [3] Percent change from 1960.

Source: U.S. Bureau of the Census, *U.S. Census of Population: 1970; 1990 Census of Population and Housing, Supplementary Reports, Metropolitan Areas as Defined by the Office of Management and Budget, June 30, 1993* (1990 CPH-S-1-1); *1990 Census of Population and Housing, Population and Housing Unit Counts* (CPH-2-1); "Estimates of the Population of Metropolitan Areas: Annual Time Series, July 1, 1991 to July 1, 1996;" published December 1997; <http://www.census.gov/population/estimates/metro-city/ma96-05.txt>; and unpublished data.

No. 41. Number and Population of Metropolitan Areas, by Population Size of Area in 1996: 1990 and 1996

[As of **April 1** for **1990** and as of **July** for **1996**. Data exclude Puerto Rico. CMSA=consolidated metropolitan statistical area. MSA=metropolitan statistical area. PMSA=primary metropolitan statistical area. Areas are as defined by U.S. Office of Management and Budget, June 30, 1996. For area definitions, see Appendix II]

POPULATION SIZE OF METROPOLITAN AREA IN 1996	CMSA'S AND MSA'S				MSA'S AND PMSA'S		
	Number	Population, 1990 (mil.)	Population, 1996		Number	Population, 1996	
			Total (mil.)	Percent in each class		Total (mil.)	Percent in each class
Total, all metropolitan areas . . .	273	198.2	211.8	100	328	211.8	100
1,000,000 or more	47	139.2	148.6	70	59	134.7	63
2,500,000 or more	18	101.3	107.4	51	17	72.0	34
1,000,000 to 2,499,999	29	37.9	41.2	19	42	62.7	29
250,000 to 999,999	93	40.9	43.9	21	116	54.2	26
500,000 to 999,999	29	19.4	20.7	10	37	25.5	12
250,000 to 499,999	64	21.5	23.2	11	79	28.7	14
100,000 to 249,999	114	16.4	17.6	8	134	21.3	10
Less than 100,000	19	1.5	1.6	1	19	1.6	1

Source: U.S. Bureau of the Census, *1990 Census of Population and Housing, Supplementary Reports, Metropolitan Areas as Defined by the Office of Management and Budget, June 30, 1993*, (1990 CPH-S-1-1); and *1990 Census of Population and Housing, Population and Housing Unit Counts* (CPH-2-1); and "Estimates of the Population of Metropolitan Areas"; published December 1997; <http://www.census.gov/population/estimates/metro-city/ma96-07.txt>.

Population

No. 42. Metropolitan and Nonmetropolitan Area Population by State: 1980 to 1996

[As of **April 1**, except **1996**, as of **July**. Metropolitan refers to 255 metropolitan statistical areas and 18 consolidated metropolitan statistical areas as defined by U.S. Office of Management and Budget, June 30, 1996; nonmetropolitan is the area outside metropolitan areas; see Appendix II. Minus sign (-) indicates decrease]

| STATE | METROPOLITAN POPULATION | | | | | | NONMETROPOLITAN POPULATION | | | | | |
| | Total (1,000) | | | Percent change, 1990-96 | Percent of State | | Total (1,000) | | | Percent change, 1990-96 | Percent of State | |
	1980	1990	1996		1990	1996	1980	1990	1996		1990	1996
U.S.	177,285	198,170	211,785	6.9	79.7	79.8	49,257	50,548	53,498	5.8	20.3	20.2
AL.	2,560	2,710	2,894	6.8	67.1	67.7	1,334	1,331	1,379	3.6	32.9	32.3
AK.	174	226	251	11.1	41.1	41.3	227	324	357	10.2	58.9	58.7
AZ.	2,339	3,202	3,878	21.1	87.4	87.6	378	463	550	18.8	12.6	12.4
AR.	1,026	1,109	1,212	9.3	47.2	48.3	1,260	1,242	1,298	4.5	52.8	51.7
CA.	22,907	28,797	30,809	7.0	96.8	96.6	760	961	1,069	11.2	3.2	3.4
CO	2,408	2,779	3,212	15.6	84.4	84.0	482	515	611	18.6	15.6	16.0
CT.	2,982	3,148	3,130	-0.6	95.8	95.6	126	140	144	2.9	4.2	4.4
DE.	496	553	594	7.4	83.0	81.9	98	113	131	15.9	17.0	18.1
DC	638	607	543	-10.5	100.0	100.0	(X)	(X)	(X)	(X)	(X)	(X)
FL.	9,039	12,024	13,381	11.3	92.9	92.9	708	915	1,019	11.4	7.1	7.1
GA	3,507	4,351	5,037	15.8	67.2	68.5	1,956	2,127	2,316	8.9	32.8	31.5
HI	763	836	872	4.3	75.5	73.6	202	272	312	14.7	24.5	26.4
ID	322	362	446	23.2	35.9	37.5	622	645	743	15.2	64.1	62.5
IL	9,461	9,574	9,964	4.1	83.8	84.1	1,967	1,857	1,883	1.4	16.2	15.9
IN	3,885	3,962	4,187	5.7	71.5	71.7	1,605	1,582	1,653	4.5	28.5	28.3
IA	1,198	1,200	1,264	5.3	43.2	44.3	1,716	1,577	1,587	0.6	56.8	55.7
KS.	1,184	1,333	1,425	6.9	53.8	55.4	1,180	1,145	1,147	0.2	46.2	44.6
KY.	1,735	1,780	1,873	5.2	48.3	48.2	1,925	1,907	2,010	5.4	51.7	51.8
LA.	3,125	3,160	3,271	3.5	74.9	75.2	1,082	1,061	1,080	1.8	25.1	24.8
ME	405	443	445	0.5	36.1	35.8	721	785	798	1.7	63.9	64.2
MD	3,920	4,438	4,704	6.0	92.8	92.8	297	343	367	7.0	7.2	7.2
MA	5,530	5,788	5,855	1.2	96.2	96.1	207	229	237	3.5	3.8	3.9
MI	7,719	7,698	7,911	2.8	82.8	82.4	1,543	1,598	1,684	5.4	17.2	17.6
MN	2,674	3,011	3,247	7.8	68.8	69.7	1,402	1,364	1,410	3.4	31.2	30.3
MS	806	874	960	9.8	34.0	35.3	1,715	1,701	1,756	3.2	66.0	64.7
MO	3,314	3,491	3,644	4.4	68.2	68.0	1,603	1,626	1,715	5.5	31.8	32.0
MT	189	191	207	8.4	23.9	23.5	598	608	672	10.5	76.1	76.5
NE.	728	787	847	7.6	49.9	51.3	842	791	805	1.8	50.1	48.7
NV.	666	1,014	1,374	35.5	84.4	85.7	135	188	230	22.3	15.6	14.3
NH	535	659	695	5.5	59.4	59.8	386	450	467	3.8	40.6	40.2
NJ.	7,365	7,730	7,988	3.3	100.0	100.0	(X)	(X)	(X)	(X)	(X)	(X)
NM	675	842	971	15.3	55.6	56.7	628	673	742	10.3	44.4	43.3
NY.	16,144	16,516	16,691	1.1	91.8	91.8	1,414	1,475	1,494	1.3	8.2	8.2
NC	3,749	4,380	4,893	11.7	66.0	66.8	2,131	2,253	2,430	7.9	34.0	33.2
ND	234	257	275	7.0	40.3	42.7	418	381	369	-3.1	59.7	57.3
OH	8,791	8,826	9,056	2.6	81.4	81.1	2,007	2,021	2,117	4.8	18.6	18.9
OK	1,724	1,870	1,988	6.3	59.4	60.2	1,301	1,276	1,313	2.9	40.6	39.8
OR	1,799	1,985	2,249	13.3	69.8	70.2	834	858	955	11.3	30.2	29.8
PA.	10,067	10,084	10,194	1.1	84.9	84.6	1,798	1,799	1,862	3.5	15.1	15.4
RI	886	938	929	-1.0	93.5	93.8	61	65	61	-6.2	6.5	6.2
SC.	2,114	2,422	2,574	6.3	69.5	69.6	1,006	1,064	1,125	5.7	30.5	30.4
SD.	194	221	244	10.4	31.7	33.3	497	475	489	2.9	68.3	66.7
TN.	3,058	3,311	3,617	9.2	67.9	68.0	1,533	1,567	1,702	8.6	32.1	32.0
TX.	11,539	14,166	16,099	13.6	83.4	84.2	2,686	2,821	3,029	7.4	16.6	15.8
UT.	1,132	1,341	1,543	15.1	77.8	77.1	329	382	457	19.6	22.2	22.9
VT.	133	152	163	7.2	26.9	27.7	378	411	426	3.6	73.1	72.3
VA.	3,966	4,775	5,198	8.9	77.2	77.9	1,381	1,414	1,477	4.5	22.8	22.1
WA	3,366	4,036	4,580	13.5	82.9	82.8	766	830	953	14.8	17.1	17.2
WV	796	748	764	2.1	41.7	41.8	1,155	1,045	1,062	1.6	58.3	58.2
WI	3,176	3,331	3,495	4.9	68.1	67.7	1,530	1,561	1,665	6.7	31.9	32.3
WY	141	134	143	6.7	29.6	29.7	329	319	338	6.0	70.4	70.3

X Not applicable.

Source: U.S. Bureau of the Census, *1990 Census of Population and Housing, Supplementary Reports, Metropolitan Areas as Defined by the Office of Management and Budget, June 30, 1993,* (1990 CPH-S-1-1); *1990 Census of Population and Housing, Population and Housing Unit Counts* (CPH-2-1); and unpublished data.

No. 43. Large Metropolitan Areas—Population: 1980 to 1996

[**In thousands, except percent**. As of **April 1**, except as noted. Covers 18 consolidated metropolitan statistical areas (CMSAs), their 73 component primary metropolitan statistical areas (PMSAs), and the remaining 122 MSAs with 250,000 and over population in 1996 as defined by the U.S. Office of Management and Budget as of June 30, 1996. For definitions and components of all metropolitan areas and population of NECMAs (New England County Metropolitan Areas), see Appendix II. Minus sign (-) indicates decrease]

METROPOLITAN AREA	NUMBER (1,000)					Rank, 1996	PERCENT CHANGE	
	1980	1990 [1]	1994 (July)	1995 (July)	1996 (July)		1980-90	1990-96
Albany-Schenectady-Troy, NY MSA	825	862	882	881	879	54	4.5	2.0
Albuquerque, NM MSA	485	589	647	661	670	62	21.4	13.7
Allentown-Bethlehem-Easton, PA MSA	551	595	612	613	614	67	8.0	3.2
Anchorage, AK MSA	174	226	252	251	251	140	29.8	10.7
Appleton-Oshkosh-Neenah, WI MSA	291	315	332	336	341	114	8.2	8.1
Atlanta, GA MSA	2,233	2,960	3,338	3,441	3,541	11	32.5	19.7
Augusta-Aiken, GA-SC MSA	363	415	449	453	454	85	14.2	9.2
Austin-San Marcos, TX MSA	585	846	969	1,007	1,041	43	44.6	23.1
Bakersfield, CA MSA	403	545	611	616	623	65	35.2	14.3
Baton Rouge, LA MSA	494	528	558	563	567	71	6.9	7.4
Beaumont-Port Arthur, TX MSA	373	361	374	376	376	104	-3.2	4.0
Biloxi-Gulfport-Pascagoula, MS MSA	300	312	338	342	343	113	4.1	9.9
Binghamton, NY MSA	263	264	262	258	254	139	0.4	-3.9
Birmingham, AL MSA	815	840	880	888	895	53	3.0	6.5
Boise City, ID MSA	257	296	349	361	373	105	15.2	25.9
Boston-Worcester-Lawrence, MA-NH-ME-CT CMSA	5,122	5,455	5,497	5,534	5,563	7	6.5	2.0
Boston, MA-NH PMSA	3,149	3,228	3,231	3,252	3,263	(X)	2.5	1.1
Brockton, MA PMSA	225	236	242	244	246	(X)	5.1	4.1
Fitchburg-Leominster, MA PMSA	125	138	139	139	139	(X)	10.5	0.9
Lawrence, MA-NH PMSA	298	353	363	368	373	(X)	18.4	5.5
Lowell, MA-NH PMSA	249	281	286	288	291	(X)	12.5	3.6
Manchester, NH PMSA	146	174	178	180	182	(X)	18.9	4.8
Nashua, NH PMSA	134	168	174	176	178	(X)	25.4	6.0
New Bedford, MA PMSA	167	176	175	175	175	(X)	5.4	-0.3
Portsmouth-Rochester, NH-ME PMSA	189	223	226	228	231	(X)	18.0	3.3
Worcester, MA-CT PMSA	439	478	483	483	485	(X)	8.9	1.4
Brownsville-Harlingen-San Benito, TX MSA	210	260	299	308	315	119	24.0	21.1
Buffalo-Niagara Falls, NY MSA	1,243	1,189	1,188	1,182	1,175	36	-4.3	-1.2
Canton-Massillon, OH MSA	404	394	402	402	403	97	-2.6	2.2
Charleston-North Charleston, SC MSA	430	507	516	501	495	78	17.8	-2.3
Charleston, WV MSA	270	250	255	255	255	138	-7.1	1.6
Charlotte-Gastonia-Rock Hill, NC-SC MSA	971	1,162	1,261	1,290	1,321	32	19.6	13.7
Chattanooga, TN-GA MSA	418	424	439	443	446	88	1.6	5.1
Chicago-Gary-Kenosha, IL-IN-WI CMSA	8,115	8,240	8,501	8,547	8,600	3	1.5	4.4
Chicago, IL PMSA	7,246	7,411	7,644	7,686	7,734	(X)	2.3	4.4
Gary, IN PMSA	643	605	618	621	622	(X)	-5.9	2.9
Kankakee, IL PMSA	103	96	101	101	102	(X)	-6.5	5.9
Kenosha, WI PMSA	123	128	138	140	142	(X)	4.1	10.5
Cincinnati-Hamilton, OH-KY-IN CMSA	1,726	1,818	1,895	1,908	1,921	23	5.3	5.7
Cincinnati, OH-KY-IN PMSA	1,468	1,526	1,579	1,588	1,597	(X)	4.0	4.7
Hamilton-Middletown, OH PMSA	259	291	316	320	324	(X)	12.6	11.0
Cleveland-Akron, OH CMSA	2,938	2,860	2,905	2,908	2,913	14	-2.7	1.9
Akron, OH PMSA	660	658	673	676	680	(X)	-0.4	3.4
Cleveland-Lorain-Elyria, OH PMSA	2,278	2,202	2,232	2,232	2,233	(X)	-3.3	1.4
Colorado Springs, CO MSA	309	397	454	465	473	81	28.3	19.1
Columbia, SC MSA	410	454	474	481	488	79	10.7	7.6
Columbus, GA-AL MSA	255	261	273	272	272	134	2.4	4.4
Columbus, OH MSA	1,214	1,345	1,421	1,434	1,448	30	10.8	7.6
Corpus Christi, TX MSA	326	350	376	380	384	101	7.3	9.8
Dallas-Fort Worth, TX CMSA	3,046	4,037	4,378	4,470	4,575	9	32.5	13.3
Dallas, TX PMSA	2,055	2,676	2,911	2,975	3,048	(X)	30.2	13.9
Fort Worth-Arlington, TX PMSA	991	1,361	1,467	1,496	1,527	(X)	37.4	12.2
Davenport-Moline-Rock Island, IA-IL MSA	385	351	357	358	358	108	-8.8	2.0
Dayton-Springfield, OH MSA	942	951	954	952	951	50	1.0	-0.1
Daytona Beach, FL MSA	270	399	443	450	456	83	48.1	14.3
Denver-Boulder-Greeley, CO CMSA	1,742	1,980	2,190	2,233	2,277	20	13.7	15.0
Boulder-Longmont, CO PMSA	190	225	250	254	258	(X)	18.8	14.6
Denver, CO PMSA	1,429	1,623	1,795	1,830	1,867	(X)	13.6	15.0
Greeley, CO PMSA	123	132	145	149	152	(X)	6.8	15.5
Des Moines, IA MSA	368	393	417	423	427	92	6.9	8.8
Detroit-Ann Arbor-Flint, MI CMSA	5,293	5,187	5,239	5,260	5,284	8	-2.0	1.9
Ann Arbor, MI PMSA	455	490	513	521	530	(X)	7.7	8.1
Detroit, MI PMSA	4,388	4,267	4,293	4,305	4,318	(X)	-2.8	1.2
Flint, MI PMSA	450	430	432	434	436	(X)	-4.4	1.3
El Paso, TX MSA	480	592	667	679	684	60	23.3	15.7
Erie, PA MSA	280	276	281	281	281	133	-1.5	1.8
Eugene-Springfield, OR MSA	275	283	299	303	307	123	2.8	8.5
Evansville-Henderson, IN-KY MSA	276	279	287	287	289	128	1.0	3.5
Fayetteville, NC MSA	247	275	284	285	285	131	11.1	3.7
Fayetteville-Springdale-Rogers, AR MSA	179	211	243	253	261	135	18.1	23.7
Fort Myers-Cape Coral, FL MSA	205	335	368	375	380	102	63.3	13.4
Fort Pierce-Port St. Lucie, FL MSA	151	251	278	282	287	129	66.1	14.4
Fort Wayne, IN MSA	445	456	469	472	475	80	2.6	4.2
Fresno, CA MSA	578	756	839	848	862	56	30.8	14.1

See footnotes at end of table.

Population

No. 43. Metropolitan Areas—Population: 1980 to 1996—Continued

[See headnote, page 41]

METROPOLITAN AREA	NUMBER (1,000)					Rank, 1996	PERCENT CHANGE	
	1980	1990 [1]	1994 (July)	1995 (July)	1996 (July)		1980-90	1990-96
Grand Rapids-Muskegon-Holland, MI MSA	841	938	990	1,003	1,015	46	11.5	8.2
Greensboro—Winston-Salem—High Point, NC MSA	951	1,050	1,109	1,125	1,141	38	10.5	8.7
Greenville-Spartanburg-Anderson, SC MSA	744	831	873	884	897	52	11.6	8.0
Harrisburg-Lebanon-Carlisle, PA MSA	556	588	610	612	615	66	5.7	4.6
Hartford, CT MSA	1,081	1,158	1,149	1,145	1,145	37	7.1	-1.1
Hickory-Morganton, NC MSA	270	292	306	311	315	120	8.1	7.7
Honolulu, HI MSA	763	836	869	871	872	55	9.7	4.2
Houston-Galveston-Brazoria, TX CMSA	3,118	3,731	4,108	4,178	4,253	10	19.6	14.0
Brazoria, TX PMSA	170	192	213	216	221	(X)	13.0	15.2
Galveston-Texas City, TX PMSA	196	217	235	238	241	(X)	11.1	10.7
Houston, TX PMSA	2,753	3,322	3,660	3,724	3,792	(X)	20.7	14.1
Huntington-Ashland, WV-KY-OH MSA	336	313	317	317	317	118	-7.1	1.3
Huntsville, AL MSA	243	293	328	328	330	116	20.6	12.7
Indianapolis, IN MSA	1,306	1,380	1,460	1,476	1,492	28	5.7	8.1
Jackson, MS MSA	362	395	412	416	421	93	9.2	6.5
Jacksonville, FL MSA	722	907	972	982	1,009	47	25.5	11.2
Johnson City-Kingsport-Bristol, TN-VA MSA	434	436	450	454	458	82	0.6	5.1
Kalamazoo-Battle Creek, MI MSA	421	429	440	442	444	89	2.1	3.5
Kansas City, MO-KS MSA	1,449	1,583	1,658	1,673	1,690	24	9.2	6.8
Killeen-Temple, TX MSA	215	255	289	292	297	126	19.0	16.3
Knoxville, TN MSA	546	586	630	641	649	63	7.2	10.8
Lafayette, LA MSA	331	345	361	365	369	106	4.3	6.8
Lakeland-Winter Haven, FL MSA	322	405	430	436	441	91	26.0	8.8
Lancaster, PA MSA	362	423	443	448	451	86	16.7	6.6
Lansing-East Lansing, MI MSA	420	433	445	446	448	87	3.1	3.4
Las Vegas, NV-AZ MSA	528	853	1,082	1,143	1,201	35	61.5	40.9
Lexington, KY MSA	371	406	431	435	441	90	9.4	8.7
Little Rock-North Little Rock, AR MSA	474	513	538	543	548	72	8.1	6.9
Los Angeles-Riverside-Orange County, CA CMSA	11,498	14,532	15,266	15,353	15,495	2	26.4	6.6
Los Angeles-Long Beach, CA PMSA	7,477	8,863	9,081	9,078	9,128	(X)	18.5	3.0
Orange County, CA PMSA	1,933	2,411	2,564	2,599	2,637	(X)	24.7	9.4
Riverside-San Bernardino, CA PMSA	1,558	2,589	2,920	2,969	3,016	(X)	66.1	16.5
Ventura, CA PMSA	529	669	701	707	715	(X)	26.4	6.8
Louisville, KY-IN MSA	954	949	981	986	992	49	-0.5	4.5
Macon, GA MSA	273	291	307	309	313	122	6.6	7.4
Madison, WI MSA	324	367	390	393	395	98	13.5	7.7
McAllen-Edinburg-Mission, TX MSA	283	384	465	482	496	77	35.4	29.2
Melbourne-Titusville-Palm Bay, FL MSA	273	399	443	450	454	84	46.2	13.8
Memphis, TN-AR-MS MSA	939	1,007	1,055	1,067	1,078	42	7.3	7.0
Miami-Fort Lauderdale, FL CMSA	2,644	3,193	3,397	3,459	3,514	12	20.8	10.1
Fort Lauderdale, FL PMSA	1,018	1,256	1,386	1,413	1,438	(X)	23.3	14.6
Miami, FL PMSA	1,626	1,937	2,012	2,046	2,076	(X)	19.2	7.2
Milwaukee-Racine, WI CMSA	1,570	1,607	1,637	1,639	1,643	25	2.4	2.2
Milwaukee-Waukesha, WI PMSA	1,397	1,432	1,454	1,455	1,458	(X)	2.5	1.8
Racine, WI PMSA	173	175	183	184	185	(X)	1.1	5.7
Minneapolis-St. Paul, MN-WI MSA	2,198	2,539	2,693	2,730	2,765	15	15.5	8.9
Mobile, AL MSA	444	477	509	514	519	75	7.5	8.8
Modesto, CA MSA	266	371	407	411	416	94	39.3	12.2
Montgomery, AL MSA	273	293	309	312	315	121	7.3	7.7
Nashville, TN MSA	851	985	1,071	1,095	1,117	40	15.8	13.4
New London-Norwich, CT-RI MSA	273	291	285	286	287	130	6.5	-1.4
New Orleans, LA MSA	1,304	1,285	1,310	1,314	1,313	33	-1.5	2.1
New York-Northern New Jersey-Long Island, NY-NJ-CT-PA CMSA	18,906	19,550	19,820	19,881	19,938	1	3.4	2.0
Bergen-Passaic, NJ PMSA	1,293	1,279	1,301	1,307	1,311	(X)	-1.1	2.6
Bridgeport, CT PMSA	439	444	442	443	444	(X)	1.2	0.0
Danbury, CT PMSA	175	194	196	198	199	(X)	10.3	3.0
Dutchess County, NY PMSA	245	259	261	262	263	(X)	5.9	1.2
Jersey City, NJ PMSA	557	553	551	551	551	(X)	-0.7	-0.4
Middlesex-Somerset-Hunterdon, NJ PMSA	886	1,020	1,068	1,079	1,091	(X)	15.1	7.0
Monmouth-Ocean, NJ PMSA	849	986	1,036	1,051	1,065	(X)	16.1	8.0
Nassau-Suffolk, NY PMSA	2,606	2,609	2,649	2,655	2,660	(X)	0.1	2.0
New Haven-Meriden, CT PMSA	500	530	527	524	524	(X)	5.9	-1.2
New York, NY PMSA	8,275	8,547	8,616	8,631	8,643	(X)	3.3	1.1
Newark, NJ PMSA	1,964	1,916	1,935	1,938	1,940	(X)	-2.4	1.3
Newburgh, NY-PA PMSA	278	336	355	359	363	(X)	20.8	8.0
Stamford-Norwalk, CT PMSA	326	330	330	331	332	(X)	1.3	0.6
Trenton, NJ PMSA	308	326	329	330	330	(X)	5.8	1.4
Waterbury, CT PMSA	205	222	222	222	222	(X)	8.1	0.1
Norfolk-Virginia Beach-Newport News, VA-NC MSA	1,201	1,445	1,528	1,535	1,540	27	20.3	6.6
Oklahoma City, OK MSA	861	959	1,009	1,017	1,027	44	11.4	7.1
Omaha, NE-IA MSA	605	640	664	671	682	61	5.6	6.6
Orlando, FL MSA	805	1,225	1,363	1,386	1,417	31	52.2	15.7
Pensacola, FL MSA	290	344	373	378	386	99	18.9	12.0
Peoria-Pekin, IL MSA	366	339	344	346	347	112	-7.3	2.2

See footnotes at end of table.

No. 43. Metropolitan Areas—Population: 1980 to 1996—Continued

[See headnote, page 41]

METROPOLITAN AREA	NUMBER (1,000)					Rank, 1996	PERCENT CHANGE	
	1980	1990 [1]	1994 (July)	1995 (July)	1996 (July)		1980-90	1990-96
Philadelphia-Wilmington-Atlantic City, PA-NJ-DE-MD CMSA	5,649	5,893	5,960	5,969	5,973	6	4.3	1.4
Atlantic-Cape May, NJ PMSA	276	319	330	332	334	(X)	15.6	4.5
Philadelphia, PA-NJ PMSA	4,781	4,922	4,951	4,953	4,953	(X)	2.9	0.6
Vineland-Millville-Bridgeton, NJ PMSA	133	138	139	138	136	(X)	3.9	-1.5
Wilmington-Newark, DE-MD PMSA	459	513	540	546	551	(X)	11.9	7.3
Phoenix-Mesa, AZ MSA	1,600	2,238	2,485	2,657	2,747	16	39.9	22.7
Pittsburgh, PA MSA	2,571	2,395	2,400	2,389	2,379	19	-6.9	-0.6
Portland-Salem, OR-WA CMSA	1,584	1,793	1,990	2,031	2,078	22	13.3	15.9
Portland-Vancouver, OR-WA PMSA	1,334	1,515	1,682	1,717	1,759	(X)	13.6	16.1
Salem, OR PMSA	250	278	308	314	319	(X)	11.3	14.9
Providence-Fall River-Warwick, RI-MA MSA	1,077	1,134	1,130	1,126	1,124	39	5.4	-0.9
Provo-Orem, UT MSA	218	264	302	311	320	117	20.9	21.3
Raleigh-Durham-Chapel Hill, NC MSA	665	858	968	997	1,025	45	29.1	19.4
Reading, PA MSA	313	337	349	350	352	110	7.7	4.7
Reno, NV MSA	194	255	284	291	299	125	31.5	17.3
Richmond-Petersburg, VA MSA	761	866	917	926	935	51	13.7	8.0
Rochester, NY MSA	1,031	1,062	1,088	1,087	1,088	41	3.1	2.4
Rockford, IL MSA	326	330	346	349	352	109	1.2	6.9
Sacramento-Yolo, CA CMSA	1,100	1,481	1,588	1,609	1,632	26	34.7	10.2
Sacramento, CA PMSA	986	1,340	1,441	1,460	1,482	(X)	35.8	10.6
Yolo, CA PMSA	113	141	146	148	150	(X)	24.6	6.2
Saginaw-Bay City-Midland, MI MSA	422	399	403	403	403	96	-5.3	1.0
St. Louis, MO-IL MSA	2,414	2,492	2,531	2,540	2,548	18	3.2	2.2
Salinas, CA MSA	290	356	333	334	339	115	22.5	-4.7
Salt Lake City-Ogden, UT MSA	910	1,072	1,178	1,197	1,218	34	17.8	13.6
San Antonio, TX MSA	1,089	1,325	1,433	1,463	1,490	29	21.7	12.5
San Diego, CA MSA	1,862	2,498	2,615	2,627	2,655	17	34.2	6.3
San Francisco-Oakland-San Jose, CA CMSA	5,368	6,250	6,502	6,543	6,605	5	16.4	5.7
Oakland, CA PMSA	1,762	2,080	2,180	2,193	2,210	(X)	18.1	6.2
San Francisco, CA PMSA	1,489	1,604	1,639	1,645	1,655	(X)	7.7	3.2
San Jose, CA PMSA	1,295	1,498	1,555	1,574	1,600	(X)	15.6	6.8
Santa Cruz-Watsonville, CA PMSA	188	230	235	236	238	(X)	22.1	3.5
Santa Rosa, CA PMSA	300	388	412	416	421	(X)	29.5	8.4
Vallejo-Fairfield-Napa, CA PMSA	334	450	480	479	482	(X)	34.6	7.1
Santa Barbara-Santa Maria-Lompoc, CA MSA	299	370	384	384	386	100	23.7	4.3
Sarasota-Bradenton, FL MSA	351	489	519	525	529	74	39.6	8.0
Savannah, GA MSA	231	258	276	280	283	132	11.8	9.6
Scranton—Wilkes-Barre—Hazleton, PA MSA	659	639	636	632	628	64	-3.2	-1.6
Seattle-Tacoma-Bremerton, WA CMSA	2,409	2,970	3,222	3,272	3,321	13	23.3	11.8
Bremerton, WA PMSA	147	190	217	226	232	(X)	28.9	22.1
Olympia, WA PMSA	124	161	188	193	197	(X)	29.8	22.2
Seattle-Bellevue-Everett, WA PMSA	1,652	2,033	2,179	2,204	2,235	(X)	23.1	9.9
Tacoma, WA PMSA	486	586	639	649	657	(X)	20.7	12.1
Shreveport-Bossier City, LA MSA	377	376	378	379	380	103	-0.1	0.9
South Bend, IN MSA	242	247	255	257	258	137	2.2	4.3
Spokane, WA MSA	342	361	397	402	405	95	5.7	12.1
Springfield, MO MSA	228	264	288	294	296	127	15.9	12.1
Springfield, MA MSA	570	588	581	578	577	70	3.2	-1.9
Stockton-Lodi, CA MSA	347	481	519	526	533	73	38.4	11.0
Syracuse, NY MSA	723	742	752	749	746	59	2.7	0.5
Tallahassee, FL MSA	190	234	255	257	259	136	22.7	11.0
Tampa-St. Petersburg-Clearwater, FL MSA	1,614	2,068	2,159	2,181	2,199	21	28.2	6.3
Toledo, OH MSA	617	614	612	611	611	68	-0.4	-0.4
Tucson, AZ MSA	531	667	735	755	768	57	25.5	15.1
Tulsa, OK MSA	657	709	743	747	756	58	7.9	6.7
Utica-Rome, NY MSA	320	317	315	308	302	124	-1.1	-4.5
Visalia-Tulare-Porterville, CA MSA	246	312	346	348	350	111	26.9	12.2
Washington-Baltimore, DC-MD-VA-WV CMSA	5,791	6,726	7,050	7,107	7,165	4	16.2	6.5
Baltimore, MD PMSA	2,199	2,382	2,458	2,468	2,474	(X)	8.3	3.9
Hagerstown, MD PMSA	113	121	126	127	127	(X)	7.3	4.8
Washington, DC-MD-VA-WV PMSA	3,478	4,223	4,465	4,512	4,563	(X)	21.4	8.1
West Palm Beach-Boca Raton, FL MSA	577	864	958	976	993	48	49.7	15.0
Wichita, KS MSA	442	485	507	509	513	76	9.7	5.7
York, PA MSA	313	340	360	365	368	107	8.5	8.5
Youngstown-Warren, OH MSA	645	601	603	600	599	69	-6.8	-0.4

X Not applicable.   [1] The April 1, 1990, census count includes resolution corrections processed through March 1996, and does not include adjustments for census coverage errors.

Source: U.S. Bureau of the Census, *1990 Census of Population and Housing, Supplementary Reports, Metropolitan Areas as Defined by the Office of Management and Budget, June 30, 1993* (CPH-S-1-1); *1990 Census of Population and Housing, Population and Housing Unit Counts* (CPH-2-1); "Estimates of the Population of Metropolitan Areas: Annual Time Series, July 1, 1991 to July 1, 1996"; published: December 1997; <http://www.census.gov/population/estimates/metro-city/ma96-05.txt>; and unpublished data.

No. 44. 75 Largest Metropolitan Areas—Racial and Hispanic Origin Populations: 1996

[As of **July 1**. Areas as defined by U.S. Office of Management and Budget, June 30, 1996. Covers 273 metropolitan areas: 17 consolidated metropolitan statistical area (CMSAs) and 245 metropolitan statistical areas (MSAs) located outside of New England as well as 11 New England county metropolitan areas (NECMAs) in New England. For area definitions, see Appendix II]

METROPOLITAN AREA [1]	Total population (1,000)	PERCENT OF TOTAL METROPOLITAN POPULATION			
		Black	American Indian, Eskimo, Aleut	Asian and Pacific Islander	Hispanic origin [2]
New York-Northern New Jersey-Long Island, NY-NJ-CT-PA CMSA/NECMA [3]	19,847	19.3	0.3	6.2	16.8
Los Angeles-Riverside-Orange County, CA CMSA	15,495	8.4	0.7	11.1	37.8
Chicago-Gary-Kenosha, IL-IN-WI CMSA	8,600	19.3	0.2	3.9	13.1
Washington-Baltimore, DC-MD-VA-WV CMSA	7,165	25.7	0.3	4.8	4.9
San Francisco-Oakland-San Jose, CA CMSA	6,605	8.7	0.7	18.1	18.6
Philadelphia-Wilmington-Atlantic City, PA-NJ-DE-MD CMSA	5,973	19.4	0.2	2.7	4.7
Boston-Worcester-Lawrence-Lowell-Brockton, MA-NH NECMA	5,796	5.7	0.2	3.4	5.1
Detroit-Ann Arbor-Flint, MI CMSA	5,284	21.0	0.4	1.9	2.3
Dallas-Fort Worth, TX CMSA	4,575	14.2	0.6	3.4	15.1
Houston-Galveston-Brazoria, TX CMSA	4,253	18.3	0.4	4.8	23.6
Atlanta, GA MSA	3,541	25.8	0.2	2.6	3.0
Miami-Fort Lauderdale, FL CMSA	3,514	19.6	0.2	1.8	36.6
Seattle-Tacoma-Bremerton, WA CMSA	3,321	5.0	1.3	7.7	4.0
Cleveland-Akron, OH CMSA	2,913	16.5	0.2	1.3	2.2
Minneapolis-St. Paul, MN-WI MSA	2,765	4.4	1.0	3.4	2.0
Phoenix-Mesa, AZ MSA	2,747	4.0	2.4	2.2	19.5
San Diego, CA MSA	2,655	6.4	0.9	10.2	25.1
St. Louis, MO-IL MSA	2,548	17.6	0.2	1.2	1.3
Pittsburgh, PA MSA	2,379	8.3	0.1	0.9	0.7
Denver-Boulder-Greeley, CO CMSA	2,277	5.2	0.8	2.8	14.0
Tampa-St. Petersburg-Clearwater, FL MSA	2,199	10.2	0.3	1.6	8.6
Portland-Salem, OR-WA CMSA	2,078	2.7	1.0	3.9	5.6
Cincinnati-Hamilton, OH-KY-IN CMSA	1,921	11.5	0.1	1.0	0.6
Kansas City, MO-KS MSA	1,690	13.3	0.5	1.4	3.5
Milwaukee-Racine, WI CMSA	1,643	14.8	0.6	1.6	4.6
Sacramento-Yolo, CA CMSA	1,632	7.0	1.3	9.7	14.4
Norfolk-Virginia Beach-Newport News, VA-NC MSA	1,540	29.7	0.3	3.2	2.9
Indianapolis, IN MSA	1,492	13.6	0.2	1.0	1.1
San Antonio, TX MSA	1,490	6.6	0.4	1.6	52.1
Columbus, OH MSA	1,448	13.1	0.2	1.9	1.0
Orlando, FL MSA	1,417	13.8	0.4	2.5	10.5
Charlotte-Gastonia-Rock Hill, NC-SC MSA	1,321	20.4	0.4	1.4	1.5
New Orleans, LA MSA	1,313	35.0	0.3	2.1	4.8
Salt Lake City-Ogden, UT MSA	1,218	1.2	0.8	3.0	7.3
Las Vegas, NV-AZ MSA	1,201	9.1	1.2	4.2	14.1
Buffalo-Niagara Falls, NY MSA	1,175	11.4	0.7	1.3	2.5
Greensboro—Winston-Salem—High Point, NC MSA	1,141	19.6	0.4	1.0	1.2
Nashville, TN MSA	1,117	15.7	0.2	1.4	1.1
Hartford, CT NECMA	1,110	9.4	0.2	2.2	8.1
Rochester, NY MSA	1,088	9.9	0.4	1.8	3.7
Memphis, TN-AR-MS MSA	1,078	41.9	0.2	1.1	1.1
Austin-San Marcos, TX MSA	1,041	10.0	0.5	3.0	24.3
Oklahoma City, OK MSA	1,027	10.8	4.7	2.2	4.6
Raleigh-Durham-Chapel Hill, NC MSA	1,025	24.2	0.3	2.4	2.1
Grand Rapids-Muskegon-Holland, MI MSA	1,015	7.5	0.6	1.2	3.7
Jacksonville, FL MSA	1,009	22.1	0.3	2.5	3.3
West Palm Beach-Boca Raton, FL MSA	993	14.4	0.2	1.5	9.8
Louisville, KY-IN MSA	992	13.0	0.2	0.8	0.8
Dayton-Springfield, OH MSA	951	14.3	0.2	1.2	0.9
Richmond-Petersburg, VA MSA	935	29.9	0.3	1.8	1.4
Providence-Warwick-Pawtucket, RI NECMA	907	4.8	0.5	2.2	6.3
Greenville-Spartanburg-Anderson, SC MSA	897	17.9	0.2	0.8	1.0
Birmingham, AL MSA	895	28.9	0.2	0.6	0.6
Albany-Schenectady-Troy, NY MSA	879	5.1	0.2	1.7	2.1
Honolulu, HI MSA	872	3.8	0.5	64.3	7.3
Fresno, CA MSA	862	5.0	1.4	9.3	41.2
Tucson, AZ MSA	768	3.7	3.4	2.3	27.9
Tulsa, OK MSA	756	8.5	6.6	1.1	2.7
Syracuse, NY MSA	746	6.2	0.6	1.5	1.7
El Paso, TX MSA	684	3.6	0.5	1.4	73.5
Omaha, NE-IA MSA	682	8.5	0.6	1.5	4.3
Albuquerque, NM MSA	670	3.3	5.7	1.9	38.4
Knoxville, TN MSA	649	6.4	0.3	1.1	0.8
Scranton—Wilkes-Barre—Hazleton, PA MSA	628	1.0	0.1	0.7	0.7
Bakersfield, CA MSA	623	6.4	1.8	4.4	33.8
Harrisburg-Lebanon-Carlisle, PA MSA	615	7.6	0.1	1.5	2.2
Allentown-Bethlehem-Easton, PA MSA	614	2.5	0.1	1.5	5.8
Toledo, OH MSA	611	12.2	0.3	1.2	3.9
Youngstown-Warren, OH MSA	599	10.2	0.2	0.5	1.5
Springfield, MA NECMA	592	7.7	0.2	1.9	9.8
Baton Rouge, LA MSA	567	31.1	0.2	1.3	1.6
Little Rock-North Little Rock, AR MSA	548	20.8	0.3	0.8	1.5
Stockton-Lodi, CA MSA	533	5.8	1.1	15.2	27.7
Sarasota-Bradenton, FL MSA	529	6.8	0.3	0.8	4.1
Mobile, AL MSA	519	28.0	0.5	0.9	1.2

[1] Metropolitan areas are shown in rank order of total population.   [2] Persons of Hispanic origin may be of any race.
[3] Includes data for New Haven-Bridgeport-Stamford-Waterbury-Danbury, CT NECMA.
Source: U.S. Bureau of the Census, *State and Metropolitan Area Data Book, 1997-98*, 1998.

No. 45. Metropolitan Areas With Large Numbers of Selected Racial Groups and of Hispanic Origin Population: 1996

[As of July 1. For Black, Hispanic origin, and Asian and Pacific Islander populations, areas selected had 100,000 or more of specified group; for American Indian, Eskimo, and Aleut population, areas selected are ten areas with largest number of that group. See headnote, Table 44]

BLACK

METROPOLITAN AREA	Number of specified group (1,000)	Percent of total metro. area
New York-Northern New Jersey-Long Island, NY-NJ-CT-PA CMSA/NECMA [2]	3,839	19.3
Washington-Baltimore, DC-MD-VA-WV CMSA	1,840	25.7
Chicago-Gary-Kenosha, IL-IN-WI CMSA	1,656	19.3
Los Angeles-Riverside-Orange County, CA CMSA	1,306	8.4
Philadelphia-Wilmington-Atlantic City, PA-NJ-DE-MD CMSA	1,160	19.4
Detroit-Ann Arbor-Flint, MI CMSA	1,108	21.0
Atlanta, GA MSA	914	25.8
Houston-Galveston-Brazoria, TX CMSA	778	18.3
Miami-Fort Lauderdale, FL CMSA	688	19.6
Dallas-Fort Worth, TX CMSA	651	14.2
San Francisco-Oakland-San Jose, CA CMSA	573	8.7
Cleveland-Akron, OH CMSA	481	16.5
New Orleans, LA MSA	459	35.0
Norfolk-Virginia Beach-Newport News, VA-NC MSA	458	29.7
Memphis, TN-AR-MS MSA	452	41.9
St. Louis, MO-IL MSA	449	17.6
Boston-Worcester-Lawrence-Lowell-Brockton, MA-NH NECMA	331	5.7
Richmond-Petersburg, VA MSA	280	29.9
Charlotte-Gastonia-Rock Hill, NC-SC MSA	270	20.4
Birmingham, AL MSA	259	28.9
Raleigh-Durham-Chapel Hill, NC MSA	248	24.2
Milwaukee-Racine, WI CMSA	243	14.8
Kansas City, MO-KS MSA	225	13.3
Tampa-St. Petersburg-Clearwater, FL MSA	224	10.2
Greensboro—Winston-Salem—High Point, NC MSA	224	19.6
Jacksonville, FL MSA	223	22.1
Cincinnati-Hamilton, OH-KY-IN CMSA	222	11.5
Indianapolis, IN MSA	203	13.6
Pittsburgh, PA MSA	197	8.3
Orlando, FL MSA	195	13.8
Columbus, OH MSA	189	13.1
Jackson, MS MSA	182	43.3
Baton Rouge, LA MSA	176	31.1
Nashville, TN MSA	176	15.7
San Diego, CA MSA	169	6.4
Seattle-Tacoma-Bremerton, WA CMSA	165	5.0
Greenville-Spartanburg-Anderson, SC MSA	161	17.9
Charleston-North Charleston, SC MSA	154	31.1
Augusta-Aiken, GA-SC MSA	149	32.9
Columbia, SC MSA	147	30.2
Mobile, AL MSA	145	28.0
West Palm Beach-Boca Raton, FL MSA	143	14.4
Shreveport-Bossier City, LA MSA	138	36.3
Dayton-Springfield, OH MSA	136	14.3
Buffalo-Niagara Falls, NY MSA	134	11.4
Louisville, KY-IN MSA	129	13.0
Minneapolis-St. Paul, MN-WI MSA	122	4.4
Denver-Boulder-Greeley, CO CMSA	119	5.2
Macon, GA MSA	119	38.0
Montgomery, AL MSA	116	36.7
Sacramento-Yolo, CA CMSA	115	7.0
Little Rock-North Little Rock, AR MSA	114	20.8
Oklahoma City, OK MSA	111	10.8
Phoenix-Mesa, AZ MSA	110	4.0
Las Vegas, NV-AZ MSA	109	9.1
Rochester, NY MSA	108	9.9
Columbus, GA-AL MSA	108	39.6
Lafayette, LA MSA	107	29.1
Austin-San Marcos, TX MSA	104	10.0
Hartford, CT NECMA	104	9.4
Savannah, GA MSA	104	36.6

HISPANIC ORIGIN [1]

METROPOLITAN AREA	Number of specified group (1,000)	Percent of total metro. area
Los Angeles-Riverside-Orange County, CA CMSA	5,850	37.8
New York-Northern New Jersey-Long Island, NY-NJ-CT-PA CMSA/NECMA [2]	3,325	16.8
Miami-Fort Lauderdale, FL CMSA	1,286	36.6
San Francisco-Oakland-San Jose, CA CMSA	1,228	18.6
Chicago-Gary-Kenosha, IL-IN-WI CMSA	1,125	13.1
Houston-Galveston-Brazoria, TX CMSA	1,005	23.6
San Antonio, TX MSA	777	52.1
Dallas-Fort Worth, TX CMSA	690	15.1
San Diego, CA MSA	666	25.1
Phoenix-Mesa, AZ MSA	536	19.5
El Paso, TX MSA	503	73.5
McAllen-Edinburg-Mission, TX MSA	433	87.3
Fresno, CA MSA	355	41.2
Washington-Baltimore, DC-MD-VA-WV CMSA	351	4.9
Denver-Boulder-Greeley, CO CMSA	320	14.0
Boston-Worcester-Lawrence-Lowell-Brockton, MA-NH NECMA	297	5.1
Philadelphia-Wilmington-Atlantic City, PA-NJ-DE-MD CMSA	278	4.7
Brownsville-Harlingen-San Benito, TX MSA	266	84.4
Albuquerque, NM MSA	257	38.4
Austin-San Marcos, TX MSA	253	24.3
Sacramento-Yolo, CA CMSA	235	14.4
Corpus Christi, TX MSA	217	56.5
Tucson, AZ MSA	214	27.9
Bakersfield, CA MSA	211	33.8
Tampa-St. Petersburg-Clearwater, FL MSA	189	8.6
Las Vegas, NV-AZ MSA	169	14.1
Laredo, TX MSA	168	94.9
Visalia-Tulare-Porterville, CA MSA	157	44.9
Orlando, FL MSA	149	10.5
Stockton-Lodi, CA MSA	148	27.7
Salinas, CA MSA	135	39.9
Seattle-Tacoma-Bremerton, WA CMSA	133	4.0
Detroit-Ann Arbor-Flint, MI MSA	124	2.3
Santa Barbara-Santa Maria-Lompoc, CA MSA	124	32.1
Portland-Salem, OR-WA CMSA	115	5.6
Modesto, CA MSA	111	26.7
Atlanta, GA MSA	105	3.0

ASIAN AND PACIFIC ISLANDER

METROPOLITAN AREA	Number of specified group (1,000)	Percent of total metro. area
Los Angeles-Riverside-Orange County, CA CMSA	1,713	11.1
New York-Northern New Jersey-Long Island, NY-NJ-CT-PA CMSA/NECMA [2]	1,222	6.2
San Francisco-Oakland-San Jose, CA CMSA	1,198	18.1
Honolulu, HI MSA	561	64.3
Washington-Baltimore, DC-MD-VA-WV CMSA	342	4.8
Chicago-Gary-Kenosha, IL-IN-WI CMSA	340	3.9
San Diego, CA MSA	272	10.2
Seattle-Tacoma-Bremerton, WA CMSA	254	7.7
Houston-Galveston-Brazoria, TX CMSA	206	4.8
Boston-Worcester-Lawrence-Lowell-Brockton, MA-NH NECMA	195	3.4
Philadelphia-Wilmington-Atlantic City, PA-NJ-DE-MD CMSA	164	2.7
Sacramento-Yolo, CA CMSA	159	9.7
Dallas-Fort Worth, TX CMSA	154	3.4

AMERICAN INDIAN, ESKIMO, ALEUT

METROPOLITAN AREA	Number of specified group (1,000)	Percent of total metro. area
Los Angeles-Riverside-Orange County, CA CMSA	113	0.7
Phoenix-Mesa, AZ MSA	65	2.4
New York-Northern New Jersey-Long Island, NY-NJ-CT-PA CMSA/NECMA [2]	61	0.3
Tulsa, OK MSA	50	6.6
San Francisco-Oakland-San Jose, CA CMSA	49	0.7
Oklahoma City, OK MSA	48	4.7
Seattle-Tacoma-Bremerton, WA CMSA	45	1.3
Albuquerque, NM MSA	38	5.7
Flagstaff, AZ-UT MSA	34	28.4
Minneapolis-St. Paul, MN-WI MSA	28	1.0

[1] Persons of Hispanic origin may be of any race. [2] Includes data for New Haven-Bridgeport-Stamford-Waterbury-Danbury, CT NECMA.

Source: U.S. Bureau of the Census, State and Metropolitan Area Data Book, 1997-98, 1998.

No. 46. Urban and Rural Population, 1960 to 1990, and by State, 1990

[In thousands, except percent. As of April 1. Resident population]

STATE	Total	URBAN		Rural	STATE	Total	URBAN		Rural
		Number	Percent				Number	Percent	
1960	179,323	125,269	69.9	54,054	MN	4,375	3,056	69.9	1,319
1970	[1]203,212	149,647	73.6	53,565	MS	2,573	1,211	47.1	1,362
1980	[2]226,546	167,051	73.7	59,495	MO	5,117	3,516	68.7	1,601
1990, total . .	**[2]248,710**	**187,053**	**75.2**	**61,656**	MT	799	420	52.5	379
					NE.	1,578	1,044	66.1	534
AL.	4,041	2,440	60.4	1,601	NV.	1,202	1,061	88.3	140
AK.	550	371	67.5	179	NH	1,109	566	51.0	544
AZ.	3,665	3,207	87.5	458					
AR.	2,351	1,258	53.5	1,093	NJ.	7,730	6,910	89.4	820
CA.	29,760	27,571	92.6	2,189	NM	1,515	1,106	73.0	409
					NY.	17,990	15,164	84.3	2,826
CO	3,294	2,716	82.4	579	NC	6,629	3,338	50.4	3,291
CT.	3,287	2,602	79.1	686	ND	639	340	53.3	298
DE.	666	487	73.0	180					
DC	607	607	100.0	-	OH	10,847	8,039	74.1	2,808
FL.	12,938	10,967	84.8	1,971	OK	3,146	2,130	67.7	1,015
					OR	2,842	2,003	70.5	839
GA	6,478	4,097	63.2	2,381	PA.	11,882	8,188	68.9	3,693
HI	1,108	986	89.0	122	RI	1,003	863	86.0	140
ID	1,007	578	57.4	429					
IL	11,431	9,669	84.6	1,762	SC	3,487	1,905	54.6	1,581
IN	5,544	3,598	64.9	1,946	SD.	696	348	50.0	348
					TN.	4,877	2,970	60.9	1,907
IA	2,777	1,683	60.6	1,094	TX.	16,987	13,635	80.3	3,352
KS.	2,478	1,713	69.1	765	UT.	1,723	1,499	87.0	224
KY.	3,685	1,910	51.8	1,775					
LA.	4,220	2,872	68.1	1,348	VT.	563	181	32.2	382
ME	1,228	548	44.6	680	VA.	6,187	4,293	69.4	1,894
					WA	4,867	3,718	76.4	1,149
MD	4,781	3,888	81.3	893	WV	1,793	648	36.1	1,145
MA	6,016	5,070	84.3	947	WI	4,892	3,212	65.7	1,680
MI	9,295	6,556	70.5	2,739	WY	454	295	65.0	159

- Represents zero.   [1] The revised 1970 resident population count is 203,302,031; which incorporates changes due to errors found after tabulations were completed.   [2] Total population count has been revised since the 1980 and 1990 census publications to 226,542,199 and 248,718,301, respectively.

Source: U.S. Bureau of the Census, *1990 Census of Population and Housing, Population and Housing Unit Counts* (1990 CPH-2).

No. 47. Incorporated Places, by Population Size: 1970 to 1996

POPULATION SIZE	NUMBER OF INCORPORATED PLACES				POPULATION (mil.)				PERCENT OF TOTAL			
	1970	1980	1990	1996	1970	1980	1990	1996	1970	1980	1990	1996
Total	18,666	19,097	19,262	19,335	131.9	140.3	152.9	162.6	100.0	100.0	100.0	100.0
1,000,000 or more. . .	6	6	8	10	18.8	17.5	20.0	22.3	14.2	12.5	13.0	13.7
500,000 to 999,999 . . .	20	16	15	14	13.0	10.9	10.1	8.8	9.8	7.8	6.6	5.4
250,000 to 499,999 . . .	30	33	41	42	10.5	11.8	14.2	15.3	7.9	8.4	9.3	9.4
100,000 to 249,999 . . .	97	114	131	153	13.9	16.6	19.1	22.2	10.5	11.8	12.5	13.7
50,000 to 99,999.	232	250	309	347	16.2	17.6	21.2	23.4	12.2	12.3	13.9	14.4
25,000 to 49,999.	455	526	567	597	15.7	18.4	20.0	20.7	11.9	13.1	13.0	12.7
10,000 to 24,999.	1,127	1,260	1,290	1,366	17.6	19.8	20.3	21.4	13.3	14.1	13.3	13.2
Under 10,000	16,699	16,892	16,901	16,806	26.4	28.0	28.2	28.5	20.0	20.0	18.4	17.5

Source: U.S. Bureau of the Census, *Census of Population: 1970* and *1980*, Vol. I; *1990 Census of Population and Housing, Population and Housing Unit Counts* (CPH-2-1); computer diskette PE-59; and unpublished data.

No. 48. Cities With 100,000 or More Inhabitants in 1996—Population, 1980 to 1996, and Land Area, 1990

[**Population**: As of **April 1**; except **1996**, as of **July 1**. Data refer to boundaries in effect December 1994. Minus sign (-) indicates decrease]

CITY	1980, total (1,000)	POPULATION 1990 Total (1,000)	1990 Percent— Black	1990 Percent— American Indian, Eskimo, Aleut	1990 Percent— Asian, Pacific Islander	1990 Percent— Hispanic[1]	1996 Total (1,000)	1996 Rank	1996 Percent change, 1990-96	Land area, 1990 (square miles)
Abilene, TX	98	107	7.0	0.4	1.3	15.5	108	192	1.7	103.1
Akron, OH	237	223	24.5	0.3	1.2	0.7	217	74	-2.8	62.2
Albany, NY	102	100	20.6	0.3	2.3	3.1	104	204	3.5	21.4
Albuquerque, NM	332	385	3.0	3.0	1.7	34.5	420	37	9.0	132.2
Alexandria, VA	103	111	21.9	0.3	4.2	9.7	118	167	5.8	15.3
Allentown, PA	104	105	5.0	0.2	1.3	11.7	102	207	-2.9	17.7
Amarillo, TX	149	158	6.0	0.8	1.9	14.7	170	112	7.6	87.9
Anaheim, CA	219	266	2.5	0.5	9.4	31.4	289	57	8.5	44.3
Anchorage, AK	174	226	6.4	6.4	4.8	4.1	251	66	10.7	1,697.6
Ann Arbor, MI	108	110	9.0	0.4	7.7	2.6	109	191	-0.8	25.9
Arlington, TX	160	262	8.4	0.5	3.9	8.9	295	56	12.6	93.0
Arlington, VA[2]	153	171	10.5	0.3	6.8	13.5	175	107	2.6	25.9
Atlanta, GA	425	394	67.1	0.1	0.9	1.9	402	38	2.0	131.8
Aurora, CO	159	222	11.4	0.6	3.8	6.6	252	65	13.6	132.5
Aurora, IL	81	100	11.9	0.2	1.3	23.0	116	169	16.8	33.5
Austin, TX	346	472	12.4	0.4	3.0	23.0	541	22	14.7	217.8
Bakersfield, CA	106	176	9.4	1.1	3.6	20.5	206	77	16.6	91.8
Baltimore, MD	787	736	59.2	0.3	1.1	1.0	675	15	-8.2	80.8
Baton Rouge, LA	220	220	43.9	0.1	1.7	1.6	216	75	-1.7	73.9
Beaumont, TX	118	114	41.3	0.2	1.7	4.3	111	182	-2.7	80.1
Berkeley, CA	103	103	18.8	0.6	14.8	8.4	103	206	0.5	10.5
Birmingham, AL	284	265	63.3	0.1	0.6	(Z)	259	63	-2.6	148.5
Boise City, ID	102	127	0.6	0.6	1.6	2.7	153	120	20.6	46.1
Boston, MA	563	574	25.6	0.3	5.3	10.8	558	20	-2.8	48.4
Bridgeport, CT	143	142	26.6	0.3	2.3	26.5	138	139	-2.6	16.0
Brownsville, TX	85	107	0.2	0.1	0.3	90.1	132	148	23.4	27.9
Buffalo, NY	358	328	30.7	0.8	1.0	4.9	311	54	-5.4	40.6
Cedar Rapids, IA	110	109	2.9	0.2	1.0	1.1	113	173	4.3	53.5
Chandler, AZ	30	90	2.6	1.2	2.4	17.3	143	134	59.0	47.6
Charlotte, NC	315	420	31.8	0.4	1.8	1.4	441	32	5.2	174.3
Chattanooga, TN	170	152	33.7	0.2	1.0	0.6	150	125	-1.3	118.4
Chesapeake, VA	114	152	27.4	0.3	1.2	1.3	192	87	26.6	340.7
Chicago, IL	3,005	2,784	39.1	0.3	3.7	19.6	2,722	3	-2.2	227.2
Chula Vista, CA	84	135	4.6	0.6	8.9	37.3	152	122	12.4	29.0
Cincinnati, OH	385	364	37.9	0.2	1.1	0.7	346	49	-5.0	77.2
Clearwater, FL	85	99	9.0	0.2	1.0	2.9	100	219	1.5	24.9
Cleveland, OH	574	506	46.6	0.3	1.0	4.6	498	25	-1.5	77.0
Colorado Springs, CO	215	280	7.0	0.8	2.4	9.1	345	50	23.1	183.2
Columbia, SC	101	111	43.7	0.3	1.4	2.0	113	178	1.8	117.1
Columbus, GA[3]	169	179	38.1	0.3	1.4	3.0	183	99	2.3	216.1
Columbus, OH	565	633	22.6	0.2	2.4	1.1	657	16	3.8	190.9
Concord, CA	104	111	2.4	0.7	8.7	11.5	115	172	3.2	29.5
Coral Springs, FL	37	79	3.5	0.2	2.1	7.1	105	198	33.5	23.5
Corona, CA	38	76	2.8	0.8	7.1	30.4	100	217	32.0	28.5
Corpus Christi, TX	232	257	4.8	0.4	0.9	50.4	280	59	8.9	135.0
Costa Mesa, CA	83	96	1.3	0.5	6.6	20.0	101	214	4.8	15.6
Dallas, TX	905	1,008	29.5	0.5	2.2	20.9	1,053	9	4.5	342.4
Dayton, OH	194	182	40.4	0.2	0.6	0.7	173	109	-5.0	55.0
Denver, CO	493	468	12.8	1.2	2.4	23.0	498	26	6.5	153.3
Des Moines, IA	191	193	7.1	0.4	2.4	2.4	193	85	0.1	75.3
Detroit, MI	1,203	1,028	75.7	0.4	0.8	2.8	1,000	10	-2.7	138.7
Durham, NC	101	139	45.7	0.2	2.0	1.2	150	128	7.9	69.3
Elizabeth, NJ	106	110	19.8	0.3	2.7	39.1	110	186	0.1	12.3
El Monte, CA	79	106	1.0	0.6	11.8	72.5	110	188	3.6	9.5
El Paso, TX	425	515	3.4	0.4	1.2	69.0	600	17	16.4	245.4
Erie, PA	119	109	12.0	0.2	0.5	2.4	105	199	-3.2	22.0
Escondido, CA	64	109	1.5	0.8	3.7	23.4	116	170	6.9	35.6
Eugene, OR	106	113	1.3	0.9	3.5	2.7	124	157	9.7	38.0
Evansville, IN	130	126	9.5	0.2	0.6	0.6	123	158	-2.2	40.7
Flint, MI	160	141	47.9	0.7	0.5	2.9	135	144	-4.3	33.8
Fontana, CA	37	88	8.7	0.9	4.5	36.1	104	203	19.0	35.6
Fort Collins, CO	65	87	1.0	0.5	2.4	7.1	104	202	19.1	41.2
Fort Lauderdale, FL	153	149	28.1	0.2	0.9	7.2	152	123	1.7	31.4
Fort Wayne, IN	172	192	16.7	0.3	1.0	2.7	185	96	-3.7	62.7
Fort Worth, TX	385	448	22.0	0.4	2.0	19.5	480	28	7.2	281.1
Fremont, CA	132	173	3.8	0.7	19.4	13.3	188	94	8.3	77.0
Fresno, CA	217	354	8.3	1.1	12.5	29.9	396	39	11.8	99.1
Fullerton, CA	102	114	2.2	0.5	12.2	21.3	120	163	5.3	22.1
Garden Grove, CA	123	143	1.5	0.6	20.5	23.5	149	129	4.4	17.9
Garland, TX	139	181	8.9	0.5	4.5	11.6	190	92	5.2	57.3
Gary, IN	152	117	80.6	0.2	0.2	5.7	111	184	-4.9	50.2
Glendale, AZ	97	148	3.0	0.9	2.1	15.5	182	100	23.2	52.2
Glendale, CA	139	180	1.3	0.3	14.1	21.0	184	97	2.4	30.6
Grand Prairie, TX	71	100	9.7	0.8	3.0	20.5	109	190	9.7	68.5
Grand Rapids, MI	182	189	18.5	0.8	1.1	5.0	188	93	-0.5	44.3

See footnotes at end of table.

No. 48. Cities With 100,000 or More Inhabitants in 1996—Population, 1980 to 1996, and Land Area, 1990—Continued

[See headnote, p. 47]

CITY	1980, total (1,000)	POPULATION 1990 Total (1,000)	1990 Percent— Black	1990 Percent— American Indian, Eskimo, Aleut	1990 Percent— Asian, Pacific Islander	1990 Percent— Hispanic[1]	1996 Total (1,000)	1996 Rank	1996 Percent change, 1990-96	Land area, 1990 (square miles)
Greensboro, NC	156	184	33.9	0.5	1.4	1.0	195	83	6.3	79.8
Green Bay, WI	88	96	0.5	2.5	2.3	1.1	102	209	5.8	43.8
Hampton, VA	123	134	38.9	0.3	1.7	2.0	139	137	3.7	51.8
Hartford, CT	136	140	38.9	0.3	1.4	31.6	133	147	-4.8	17.3
Hayward, CA	94	115	9.8	1.0	15.5	23.9	122	162	6.0	43.5
Henderson, NV	24	65	2.7	1.0	2.0	8.1	122	160	88.4	71.5
Hialeah, FL	145	188	1.9	0.1	0.5	87.6	205	78	8.9	19.2
Hollywood, FL	121	122	8.5	0.2	1.3	11.9	128	151	5.1	27.3
Honolulu, HI[4]	365	377	1.3	0.3	70.5	4.6	423	35	12.3	85.7
Houston, TX	1,595	1,638	28.1	0.3	4.1	27.6	1,744	4	6.5	539.9
Huntington Beach, CA	171	182	0.9	0.6	8.3	11.2	191	90	5.1	26.4
Huntsville, AL	143	160	24.4	0.5	2.1	1.2	170	111	6.6	164.4
Independence, MO	112	112	1.4	0.6	1.0	2.0	110	185	-1.8	78.2
Indianapolis, IN[3]	701	731	22.6	0.2	0.9	1.1	747	12	2.1	361.7
Inglewood, CA	94	110	51.9	0.4	2.5	38.5	111	183	1.3	9.2
Irvine, CA	62	110	1.8	0.2	18.1	6.3	128	152	15.9	42.3
Irving, TX	110	155	7.5	0.6	4.6	16.3	177	104	14.2	67.6
Jackson, MS	203	202	55.7	0.1	0.5	0.4	193	86	-4.5	109.0
Jacksonville, FL[3]	541	635	25.2	0.3	1.9	2.6	680	14	7.0	758.7
Jersey City, NJ	224	229	29.7	0.3	11.4	24.2	229	72	0.2	14.9
Kansas City, KS	161	152	29.3	0.7	1.2	7.1	143	135	-5.9	107.8
Kansas City, MO	448	435	29.6	0.5	1.2	3.9	441	33	1.5	311.5
Knoxville, TN	175	170	15.8	0.2	1.0	0.7	168	113	-1.3	77.2
Lafayette, LA	81	102	27.2	0.2	1.3	1.7	105	201	3.0	40.9
Lakewood, CO	114	126	1.0	0.7	1.9	9.1	135	143	6.7	40.8
Lancaster, CA	48	97	7.4	0.9	3.7	15.2	116	171	18.9	88.8
Lansing, MI	130	127	18.6	1.0	1.8	7.9	126	153	-1.2	33.9
Laredo, TX	91	123	0.1	0.2	0.4	93.9	165	115	34.2	32.9
Las Vegas, NV	165	258	11.4	0.9	3.6	12.5	377	41	46.0	83.3
Lexington-Fayette, KY	204	225	13.4	0.2	1.6	1.1	240	68	6.5	284.5
Lincoln, NE	172	192	2.4	0.6	1.7	2.0	209	76	9.0	63.3
Little Rock, AR	159	176	34.0	0.3	0.9	0.8	176	106	(Z)	102.9
Livonia, MI	105	101	0.3	0.2	1.3	1.3	105	200	4.2	35.7
Long Beach, CA	361	429	13.7	0.6	13.6	23.6	422	36	-1.7	50.0
Los Angeles, CA	2,969	3,486	14.0	0.5	9.8	39.9	3,554	2	2.0	469.3
Louisville, KY	299	270	29.7	0.2	0.7	0.7	261	61	-3.3	62.1
Lowell, MA	92	103	2.4	0.2	11.1	10.1	101	212	-2.4	13.8
Lubbock, TX	174	186	8.6	0.3	1.4	22.5	194	84	4.0	104.1
Macon, GA	117	107	52.2	0.1	0.4	0.6	113	175	5.6	47.9
Madison, WI	171	191	4.2	0.4	3.9	2.0	198	81	3.6	57.8
Manchester, NH	91	99	1.0	0.2	1.1	2.1	101	213	1.6	33.0
McAllen, TX	66	84	0.3	0.2	0.7	77.0	103	205	23.0	32.4
Memphis, TN	646	619	54.8	0.2	0.8	0.7	597	18	-3.5	256.0
Mesa, AZ	152	289	1.9	1.0	1.5	10.9	345	51	19.2	108.6
Mesquite, TX	67	101	5.8	0.5	2.6	8.8	112	180	10.3	42.8
Miami, FL	347	359	27.4	0.2	0.6	62.5	365	44	1.8	35.6
Milwaukee, WI	636	628	30.5	0.9	1.9	6.3	591	19	-6.0	96.1
Minneapolis, MN	371	368	13.0	3.3	4.3	2.1	359	46	-2.6	54.9
Mobile, AL	200	196	38.9	0.2	1.0	1.0	203	79	3.2	118.0
Modesto, CA	107	165	2.7	1.0	7.9	16.3	179	103	8.4	30.2
Montgomery, AL	178	190	42.3	0.2	0.7	0.8	196	82	3.2	135.0
Moreno Valley, CA	(5)	119	13.8	0.7	6.6	22.9	141	136	18.7	49.1
Naperville, IL	43	86	2.1	0.1	4.8	1.8	107	194	24.7	27.9
Nashville-Davidson, TN[3]	456	488	24.3	0.2	1.4	0.9	511	24	4.7	473.3
Newark, NJ	329	275	58.5	0.2	1.2	26.1	269	60	-2.4	23.8
New Haven, CT	126	130	36.1	0.3	2.4	13.2	125	156	-4.5	18.9
New Orleans, LA	558	497	61.9	0.2	1.9	3.5	477	29	-4.1	180.6
Newport News, VA	145	171	33.6	0.3	2.3	2.8	176	105	2.7	68.3
New York, NY	7,072	7,323	28.7	0.4	7.0	24.4	7,381	1	0.8	308.9
Norfolk, VA	267	261	39.1	0.4	2.6	2.9	233	70	-10.6	53.8
Norwalk, CA	85	94	3.2	0.9	12.4	47.9	100	216	6.3	9.8
Oakland, CA	339	372	43.9	0.6	14.8	13.9	367	43	-1.3	56.1
Oceanside, CA	77	128	7.9	0.7	6.1	22.6	146	130	13.9	40.7
Oklahoma City, OK	404	445	16.0	4.2	2.4	5.0	470	30	5.7	608.2
Omaha, NE	314	343	13.1	0.7	1.0	3.1	364	45	6.2	100.6
Ontario, CA	89	133	7.3	0.7	3.9	41.7	145	131	8.8	36.7
Orange, CA	91	111	1.4	0.5	7.9	22.8	120	164	8.3	23.3
Orlando, FL	128	165	26.9	0.3	1.6	8.7	174	108	5.6	67.3
Overland Park, KS	82	112	1.8	0.3	1.9	2.0	131	150	17.2	55.7
Oxnard, CA	108	143	5.2	0.8	8.6	54.4	151	124	5.9	24.4
Palmdale, CA	12	70	6.4	0.9	4.4	22.0	107	196	51.6	77.6
Pasadena, CA	118	132	19.0	0.4	8.1	27.3	134	146	1.9	23.0
Pasadena, TX	113	120	1.0	0.5	1.6	28.8	132	149	10.0	43.8
Paterson, NJ	138	141	36.0	0.3	1.4	41.0	150	126	6.7	8.4
Pembroke Pines, FL	36	66	5.3	0.2	2.0	11.5	101	215	53.5	31.9
Peoria, IL	124	114	20.9	0.2	1.7	1.6	112	179	-1.1	40.9
Philadelphia, PA	1,688	1,586	39.9	0.2	2.7	5.6	1,478	5	-6.8	135.1

See footnotes at end of table.

No. 48. Cities With 100,000 or More Inhabitants in 1996—Population, 1980 to 1996, and Land Area, 1990—Continued

[See headnote, p. 47]

CITY	1980, total (1,000)	POPULATION 1990 Total (1,000)	Percent— Black	American Indian, Eskimo, Aleut	Asian, Pacific Islander	His-panic [1]	1996 Total (1,000)	Rank	Per-cent change, 1990-96	Land area, 1990 (square miles)
Phoenix, AZ	790	984	5.2	1.9	1.7	20.0	1,159	7	17.7	419.9
Pittsburgh, PA	424	370	25.8	0.2	1.6	0.9	350	48	-5.3	55.6
Plano, TX	72	128	4.1	0.3	4.0	6.2	192	88	50.4	66.2
Pomona, CA	93	132	14.4	0.6	6.7	51.3	135	145	2.3	22.8
Portland, OR	368	464	7.7	1.2	5.3	3.2	481	27	3.7	124.7
Portsmouth, VA	105	104	47.3	0.3	0.8	1.3	101	211	-2.5	33.1
Providence, RI	157	161	14.8	0.9	5.9	15.5	153	121	-5.1	18.5
Raleigh, NC	150	212	27.6	0.3	2.5	1.4	244	67	15.0	88.1
Rancho Cucamonga, CA	55	101	5.9	0.6	5.4	20.0	117	168	15.0	37.8
Reno, NV	101	134	2.9	1.4	4.9	11.1	155	118	16.2	57.5
Richmond, VA	219	203	55.2	0.2	0.9	0.9	198	80	-2.2	60.1
Riverside, CA	171	227	7.4	0.8	5.2	26.0	255	64	12.6	77.7
Rochester, NY	242	230	31.5	0.5	1.8	8.7	222	73	-3.8	35.8
Rockford, IL	140	142	15.0	0.3	1.5	4.2	144	132	1.2	45.0
Sacramento, CA	276	369	15.3	1.2	15.0	16.2	376	42	1.9	96.3
St. Louis, MO	453	397	47.5	0.2	0.9	1.3	352	47	-11.4	61.9
St. Paul, MN	270	272	7.4	1.4	7.1	4.2	260	62	-4.6	52.8
St. Petersburg, FL	239	240	19.6	0.2	1.7	2.6	236	69	-1.8	59.2
Salem, OR	89	108	1.5	1.6	2.4	6.1	123	159	13.7	41.5
Salinas, CA	80	109	3.0	0.9	8.1	50.6	112	181	2.7	18.6
Salt Lake City, UT	163	160	1.7	1.6	4.7	9.7	173	110	7.9	109.0
San Antonio, TX	786	959	7.0	0.4	1.1	55.6	1,068	8	11.3	333.0
San Bernardino, CA	119	170	16.0	1.0	4.0	34.6	183	98	7.9	55.1
San Diego, CA	876	1,111	9.4	0.6	11.8	20.7	1,171	6	5.4	324.0
San Francisco, CA	679	724	10.9	0.5	29.1	13.9	735	13	1.6	46.7
San Jose, CA	629	782	4.7	0.7	19.5	26.6	839	11	7.2	171.3
Santa Ana, CA	204	294	2.6	0.5	9.7	65.2	302	55	2.9	27.1
Santa Clarita, CA	(5)	120	1.5	0.6	4.2	13.4	125	155	4.3	40.5
Santa Rosa, CA	83	113	1.8	1.2	3.4	9.5	122	161	7.6	33.7
Savannah, GA	142	138	51.3	0.2	1.1	1.4	136	141	-1.1	62.6
Scottsdale, AZ	89	130	0.8	0.6	1.2	4.8	179	102	37.6	184.4
Seattle, WA	494	516	10.1	1.4	11.8	3.6	525	23	1.6	83.9
Shreveport, LA	206	199	44.8	0.2	0.5	1.1	192	89	-3.5	98.6
Simi Valley, CA	78	100	1.5	0.6	5.5	12.7	107	195	6.7	33.0
Sioux Falls, SD	81	101	0.7	1.6	0.7	0.6	113	176	12.3	45.1
South Bend, IN	110	106	20.9	0.4	0.9	3.4	102	208	-3.2	36.4
Spokane, WA	171	177	1.9	2.0	2.1	2.1	187	95	5.3	55.9
Springfield, IL	100	105	13.0	0.2	1.0	0.8	113	177	7.1	42.5
Springfield, MA	152	157	19.2	0.2	1.0	16.9	150	127	-4.5	32.1
Springfield, MO	133	140	2.5	0.7	0.9	1.0	143	133	2.1	68.0
Stamford, CT	102	108	17.8	0.1	2.6	9.8	110	187	1.9	37.7
Sterling Heights, MI	109	118	0.4	0.2	2.9	1.1	119	166	0.8	36.6
Stockton, CA	150	211	9.6	1.0	22.8	25.0	233	71	10.3	52.6
Sunnyvale, CA	107	117	3.4	0.5	19.3	13.2	125	154	6.7	21.9
Syracuse, NY	170	164	20.3	1.3	2.2	2.9	156	117	-4.9	25.1
Tacoma, WA	159	177	11.4	2.0	6.9	3.8	179	101	1.4	48.0
Tallahassee, FL	82	125	29.1	0.2	1.8	3.0	137	140	9.6	63.3
Tampa, FL	272	280	25.0	0.3	1.4	15.0	285	58	1.9	108.7
Tempe, AZ	107	142	3.2	1.3	4.1	10.9	163	116	14.6	39.5
Thousand Oaks, CA	77	104	1.2	0.4	4.8	9.6	113	174	8.6	49.6
Toledo, OH	355	333	19.7	0.3	1.0	4.0	318	53	-4.6	80.6
Topeka, KS	119	120	10.6	1.3	0.8	5.8	120	165	-0.2	55.2
Torrance, CA	130	133	1.5	0.4	21.9	10.1	136	142	2.3	20.5
Tucson, AZ	331	411	4.3	1.6	2.2	29.3	449	31	9.1	156.3
Tulsa, OK	361	367	13.6	4.7	1.4	2.6	378	40	3.0	183.5
Vallejo, CA	80	109	21.2	0.7	23.0	10.8	110	189	0.4	30.2
Virginia Beach, VA	262	393	13.9	0.4	4.3	3.1	430	34	9.5	248.3
Waco, TX	101	104	23.1	0.3	0.9	16.3	108	193	4.7	75.8
Warren, MI	161	145	0.7	0.5	1.3	1.1	138	138	-4.7	34.3
Washington, DC	638	607	65.8	0.2	1.8	5.4	543	21	-10.5	61.4
Waterbury, CT	103	109	13.0	0.3	0.7	13.4	106	197	-2.3	28.6
West Covina, CA	80	96	8.5	0.5	17.2	34.6	102	210	5.5	16.2
Wichita, KS	280	304	11.3	1.2	2.6	5.0	320	52	5.4	115.1
Wichita Falls, TX	94	96	11.2	0.7	1.8	10.0	100	218	4.0	54.1
Winston-Salem, NC	132	151	39.3	0.2	0.8	0.9	154	119	1.7	71.1
Worcester, MA	162	170	4.5	0.3	2.8	9.6	166	114	-2.0	37.6
Yonkers, NY	195	188	14.1	0.2	3.0	16.7	190	91	1.2	18.1

Z Less than .05 percent.   [1] Hispanic persons may be of any race.   [2] Data are for Arlington CDP (census designated place) which is not incorporated as a city but is recognized for census purposes as a large urban place. Arlington CDP is coextensive with Arlington County.   [3] Represents the portion of a consolidated city that is not within one or more separately incorporated places. [4] The population shown in this table is for the CDP; the 1990 census population for the City and County of Honolulu is 836,231. [5] Not incorporated.

Source: U.S. Bureau of the Census, *1980 Census of Population*, Vol. 1, Chapters A and B; *1990 Census of Population and Housing, Population and Housing Unit Counts*, (CPH-2) and *General Population Characteristics*, (CP-1); and "Estimates of the Population of Cities with Populations of 100,000 and Greater"; <http://www.census.gov/population/estimates/metro-city/SC100K96.txt>; published November 1997.

Population

No. 49. Population 65 Years Old and Over, by Age Group and Sex, 1980 to 1997, and Projections, 2000

[As of **April**, except **1997** and **2000**, as of **July**. Projection based on middle series, see Table 3]

AGE GROUP AND SEX	NUMBER (1,000)				PERCENT DISTRIBUTION			
	1980	1990 [1]	1997	2000, proj.	1980	1990 [1]	1997	2000, proj.
Persons 65 yrs. and over	25,549	31,082	34,076	34,709	100	100	100	100
65 to 69 years old	8,782	10,067	9,762	9,410	34	32	29	27
70 to 74 years old	6,798	7,980	8,736	8,726	27	26	26	25
75 to 79 years old	4,794	6,103	7,063	7,415	19	20	21	21
80 to 84 years old	2,935	3,909	4,642	4,900	12	13	14	14
85 years old and over	2,240	3,022	3,871	4,259	9	10	11	12
Males, 65 yrs. and over..........	10,305	12,494	14,010	14,346	100	100	100	100
65 to 69 years old.............	3,903	4,508	4,461	4,321	38	36	32	30
70 to 74 years old.............	2,854	3,400	3,807	3,859	28	27	27	27
75 to 79 years old.............	1,848	2,389	2,915	3,092	18	19	21	22
80 to 84 years old.............	1,019	1,356	1,713	1,846	10	11	12	13
85 years old and over	682	841	1,112	1,228	7	7	8	9
Females, 65 yrs. and over........	15,245	18,587	20,066	20,364	100	100	100	100
65 to 69 years old.............	4,880	5,559	5,301	5,089	32	30	26	25
70 to 74 years old.............	3,945	4,581	4,929	4,867	26	25	25	24
75 to 79 years old.............	2,946	3,714	4,148	4,323	19	20	21	21
80 to 84 years old.............	1,916	2,553	2,929	3,055	13	14	15	15
85 years old and over	1,559	2,180	2,759	3,031	10	12	14	15

[1] The April 1, 1990, census count (248,765,170) includes count resolution corrections processed through August 1997 and does not include adjustments for census coverage errors except for adjustments estimated for the 1995 Census Test in Oakland, CA, Patterson, NJ, and six parishes in LA. These adjustments amounted to a total of 55,297 persons.

Source: U.S. Bureau of the Census, *Current Population Reports*, P25-1095 and P25-1130; and Population Paper Listing 91.

No. 50. Persons 65 Years Old and Over—Characteristics, by Sex: 1980 to 1997

[As of **March, except as noted.** Covers civilian noninstitutional population. See headnote, Table 51]

CHARACTERISTIC	TOTAL				MALE				FEMALE			
	1980	1990	1995	1997	1980	1990	1995	1997	1980	1990	1995	1997
Total [1] (million)	24.2	29.6	31.7	31.9	9.9	12.3	13.2	13.4	14.2	17.2	18.5	18.5
White (million)	21.9	26.5	28.4	28.5	9.0	11.0	11.9	12.0	12.9	15.4	16.6	16.4
Black (million)	2.0	2.5	2.6	2.6	0.8	1.0	1.0	1.0	1.2	1.5	1.6	1.6
Percent below poverty level [2]	15.2	11.4	11.7	10.8	11.1	7.8	7.2	6.8	17.9	13.9	14.9	13.6
PERCENT DISTRIBUTION												
Marital status:												
Single...............	5.5	4.6	4.2	4.2	4.9	4.2	4.2	4.1	5.9	4.9	4.2	4.3
Married................	55.4	56.1	56.9	55.6	78.0	76.5	77.0	74.2	37.9	41.4	42.5	42.1
Spouse present	53.6	54.1	54.7	53.3	76.1	74.2	74.5	71.8	37.9	39.7	40.6	39.9
Spouse absent	1.8	2.0	2.2	2.3	1.9	2.3	2.5	2.4	1.7	1.7	1.9	2.2
Widowed................	35.7	34.2	33.2	33.4	13.5	14.2	13.5	15.7	51.2	48.6	47.3	46.3
Divorced	3.5	5.0	5.7	6.8	3.6	5.0	5.2	6.0	3.4	5.1	6.0	7.4
Family status:												
In families [3]	67.6	66.7	66.6	67.2	83.0	81.9	80.6	79.6	56.8	55.8	56.7	56.8
Nonfamily householders	31.2	31.9	32.4	32.2	15.7	16.6	18.4	18.4	42.0	42.8	42.4	42.2
Secondary individuals	1.2	1.4	1.0	1.1	1.3	1.5	1.0	2.0	1.1	1.4	0.9	0.9
Living arrangements:												
Living in household	99.8	99.7	99.9	100.0	99.9	99.9	100.0	100.0	99.7	99.5	99.9	100.0
Living alone	30.3	31.0	31.5	31.2	14.9	15.7	17.3	17.3	41.0	42.0	41.7	41.2
Spouse present.	53.6	54.1	54.7	53.5	76.1	74.3	74.5	71.8	37.9	39.7	40.6	39.9
Living with someone else . . .	15.9	14.6	13.7	15.3	8.9	9.9	8.1	10.9	20.8	17.8	17.6	18.9
Not in household [4]	0.2	0.3	0.1	-	0.1	0.1	-	-	0.3	0.5	0.1	-
Years of school completed:												
8 years or less	43.1	28.5	21.0	18.8	45.3	30.0	22.0	19.5	41.6	27.5	20.3	18.3
1 to 3 years of high school . . .	16.2	16.1	[5]15.2	[5]15.7	15.5	15.7	[5]14.5	[5]14.6	16.7	16.4	[5]15.6	[5]16.4
4 years of high school	24.0	32.9	[6]33.8	[6]34.3	21.4	29.0	[6]29.2	[6]29.6	25.8	35.6	[6]37.1	[6]37.7
1 to 3 years of college	8.2	10.9	[7]17.1	[7]16.5	7.5	10.8	[7]17.1	[7]16.3	8.6	11.0	[7]17.0	[7]16.6
4 years or more of college	8.6	11.6	[8]13.0	[8]14.8	10.3	14.5	[8]17.2	[8]19.9	7.4	9.5	[8]9.9	[8]11.1
Labor force participation: [9]												
Employed	12.2	11.5	11.7	11.8	18.4	15.9	16.1	16.5	7.8	8.4	8.5	8.3
Unemployed	0.4	0.4	0.5	0.4	0.6	0.5	0.7	0.5	0.3	0.3	0.3	0.3
Not in labor force	87.5	88.1	87.9	87.8	81.0	83.6	83.2	82.9	91.9	91.3	91.2	91.4

- Represents zero. [1] Includes other races, not shown separately. [2] Poverty status based on income in preceding year. [3] Excludes those living in unrelated subfamilies. [4] In group quarters other than institutions. [5] Represents those who completed 9th to 12th grade, but have no high school diploma. [6] High school graduate. [7] Some college or associate degree. [8] Bachelor's or advanced degree. [9] Annual averages of monthly figures. Source: U.S. Bureau of Labor Statistics, *Employment and Earnings*, January issues. Data for each year are not directly comparable with other years. See text, Section 13, and February 1994, March 1996, and February 1997 issues of *Employment and Earnings*.

Source: Except as noted, U.S. Bureau of the Census, *Current Population Reports*, P20-491, and earlier reports; P60-198; and unpublished data.

No. 51. Social and Economic Characteristics of the White and Black Populations: 1990 to 1997

[As of **March, except labor force status, annual average**. Excludes members of Armed Forces except those living off post or with their families on post. Data for 1990 are based on 1980 census population controls; 1995 and 1997 data based on 1990 census population controls. Based on Current Population Survey; see text, Section 1, and Appendix III]

CHARACTERISTIC	NUMBER (1,000)						PERCENT DISTRIBUTION			
	White			Black			White		Black	
	1990	1995	1997	1990	1995	1997	1990	1997	1990	1997
Total persons	206,983	216,751	220,070	30,392	33,531	34,218	100.0	100.0	100.0	100.0
Under 5 years old	15,161	15,915	15,546	2,932	3,342	3,127	7.3	7.1	9.6	9.1
5 to 14 years old	28,405	30,786	31,228	5,546	6,268	6,464	13.7	14.2	18.2	18.9
15 to 44 years old	96,656	97,876	98,314	14,660	16,101	16,320	46.6	44.7	48.2	47.7
45 to 64 years old	40,282	44,189	46,517	4,766	5,264	5,691	19.5	21.1	15.7	16.6
65 years old and over.	26,479	27,985	28,464	2,487	2,557	2,616	12.8	12.9	8.2	7.6
EDUCATIONAL ATTAINMENT										
Persons 25 years old and over	134,687	141,113	144,058	16,751	18,457	19,072	100.0	100.0	100.0	100.0
Elementary: 0 to 8 years.	14,131	11,101	10,837	2,701	1,800	1,685	10.5	7.5	16.1	8.8
High school: 1 to 3 years	14,080	[1]12,882	[1]13,590	2,969	[1]3,041	[1]3,106	10.5	[1]9.4	17.7	[1]16.3
4 years	52,449	[2]47,986	[2]48,860	6,239	[2]6,686	[2]6,835	38.9	[2]33.9	37.2	[2]35.8
College: 1 to 3 years	24,350	[3]35,321	[3]35,339	2,952	[3]4,486	[3]4,912	18.1	[3]24.5	17.6	[3]25.8
4 years or more.	29,677	[4]33,824	[4]35,431	1,890	[4]2,444	[4]2,534	22.0	[4]24.6	11.3	[4]13.3
LABOR FORCE STATUS [5]										
Civilians 16 years old and over	160,625	166,914	169,993	21,477	23,246	24,003	100.0	100.0	100.0	100.0
Civilian labor force	107,447	111,950	114,693	13,740	14,817	15,529	66.9	67.5	64.0	64.7
Employed	102,261	106,490	109,856	12,175	13,279	13,969	63.7	64.6	56.7	58.2
Unemployed	5,186	5,459	4,836	1,565	1,538	1,560	3.2	2.8	7.3	6.5
Unemployment rate [6]	4.8	4.9	4.2	11.4	10.4	10.0	(X)	(X)	(X)	(X)
Not in labor force.	53,178	54,965	55,301	7,737	8,429	8,474	33.1	32.5	36.0	35.3
FAMILY TYPE										
Total families . . . . [7] . . .	56,590	58,437	58,934	7,470	8,093	8,455	100.0	100.0	100.0	100.0
With own children . . .	26,718	27,951	28,236	4,378	4,682	4,886	47.2	47.9	58.6	57.8
Married couple . . . . [7] . . .	46,981	47,899	47,650	3,750	3,842	3,851	83.0	80.9	50.2	45.5
With own children [7].	21,579	22,005	21,914	1,972	1,926	1,974	38.1	37.2	26.4	23.3
Female householder, no spouse present . .	7,306	8,031	8,339	3,275	3,716	3,947	12.9	14.2	43.8	46.7
With own children [7].	4,199	4,841	4,997	2,232	2,489	2,594	7.4	8.5	29.9	30.7
Male householder, no spouse present . . . . [7]. . . .	2,303	2,507	2,944	446	536	657	4.1	5.0	6.0	7.8
With own children [7].	939	1,105	1,325	173	267	319	1.7	2.2	2.3	3.8
FAMILY INCOME IN PREVIOUS YEAR IN CONSTANT (1996) DOLLARS										
Total families	56,590	58,437	58,934	7,470	8,093	8,455	100.0	100.0	100.0	100.0
Less than $5,000.	1,019	1,227	1,164	583	631	662	1.8	2.0	7.8	7.8
$5,000 to $9,999	1,924	2,455	2,276	934	987	939	3.4	3.9	12.5	11.1
$10,000 to $14,999	2,830	3,331	3,191	747	882	907	5.0	5.4	10.0	10.7
$15,000 to $24,999	7,187	7,948	7,651	1,419	1,432	1,487	12.7	13.0	19.0	17.6
$25,000 to $34,999	7,640	8,241	7,927	964	1,133	1,210	13.5	13.5	12.9	14.3
$35,000 to $49,999	10,809	10,754	10,761	1,173	1,165	1,279	19.1	18.3	15.7	15.1
$50,000 or more	25,069	24,605	25,965	1,658	1,869	1,972	44.3	44.1	22.2	23.3
Median income (dol.) [8]	45,520	43,284	44,756	25,571	26,148	26,522	(X)	(X)	(X)	(X)
Families below poverty level [9] .	4,409	5,312	5,059	2,077	2,212	2,206	7.8	8.6	27.8	26.1
Persons below poverty level [9] .	20,785	25,379	24,650	9,302	10,196	9,694	10.0	11.2	30.7	28.3
HOUSING TENURE										
Total occupied units	80,163	83,737	85,059	10,486	11,655	12,109	100.0	100.0	100.0	100.0
Owner-occupied	54,094	57,449	58,826	4,445	4,888	5,510	67.5	69.2	42.4	45.5
Renter-occupied	24,685	24,793	24,802	5,862	6,547	6,400	30.8	29.2	55.9	52.9
No cash rent.	1,384	1,494	1,432	178	220	200	1.7	1.7	1.7	1.6

X Not applicable.   [1] Represents those who completed 9th to 12th grade, but have no high school diploma.   [2] High school graduate.   [3] Some college or associate degree.   [4] Bachelor's or advanced degree.   [5] Source: U.S. Bureau of Labor Statistics, *Employment and Earnings*, January issues. Data for each year are not directly comparable with other years.   [6] Total unemployment as percent of civilian labor force.   [7] Children under 18 years old.   [8] For definition of median, see Guide to Tabular Presentation.   [9] For explanation of poverty level, see text, Section 14.

Source: Except as noted, U.S. Bureau of the Census, *Current Population Reports*, P20-509, and earlier reports; P60-197; P60-198; and unpublished data.

No. 52. Social and Economic Characteristics of the Asian and Pacific Islander Population: 1990 and 1997

[As of **March**. Excludes members of Armed Forces except those living off post or with their families on post. Data for 1990 are based on 1980 census population controls; 1997 data are based on 1990 census population controls. Based on Current Population Survey; see text, Section 1, and Appendix III]

CHARACTERISTIC	NUMBER (1,000)		PERCENT DISTRIBUTION	
	1990	1997	1990	1997
Total persons	**6,679**	**10,071**	**100.0**	**100.0**
Under 5 years old	602	885	9.0	8.8
5 to 14 years old	1,112	1,607	16.6	16.0
15 to 44 years old	3,345	5,091	50.1	50.6
45 to 64 years old	1,155	1,841	17.3	18.3
65 years old and over	465	647	7.0	6.4
EDUCATIONAL ATTAINMENT				
Persons 25 years old and over	**3,961**	**6,107**	**100.0**	**100.0**
Elementary: 0 to 8 years	543	599	13.7	9.8
High school: 1 to 3 years	234	[1]321	5.9	[1]5.3
4 years	1,038	[2]1,417	26.2	[2]23.2
College: 1 to 3 years	568	[3]1,194	14.3	[3]19.6
4 years or more	1,578	[4]2,576	39.9	[4]42.2
LABOR FORCE STATUS [5]				
Civilians 16 years old and over	**4,849**	**7,378**	**100.0**	**100.0**
Civilian labor force	3,216	5,036	66.3	68.3
Employed	3,079	4,797	63.5	65.0
Unemployed	136	239	2.8	3.2
Unemployment rate [6]	4.2	4.7	(X)	(X)
Not in labor force	1,634	2,342	33.7	31.7
FAMILY TYPE				
Total families	**1,531**	**2,246**	**100.0**	**100.0**
Married couple	1,256	1,763	82.1	78.5
Female householder, no spouse present	188	297	12.3	13.2
Male householder, no spouse present	86	186	5.6	8.3
FAMILY INCOME IN PREVIOUS YEAR IN CONSTANT (1996) DOLLARS				
Total families	**1,531**	**2,246**	**100.0**	**100.0**
Less than $5,000	(NA)	88	(NA)	3.9
$5,000 to $9,999	(NA)	85	(NA)	3.8
$10,000 to $14,999	(NA)	119	(NA)	5.3
$15,000 to $24,999	(NA)	256	(NA)	11.4
$25,000 to $34,999	(NA)	245	(NA)	10.9
$35,000 to $49,999	(NA)	355	(NA)	15.8
$50,000 or more	(NA)	1,094	(NA)	48.7
Median income [7]	51,057	49,105	(X)	(X)
Families below poverty level [8]	182	284	11.9	12.6
Persons below poverty level [8]	938	1,454	14.1	14.4
HOUSING TENURE				
Total occupied units	**1,988**	**2,998**	**100.0**	**100.0**
Owner-occupied	977	1,568	49.1	52.3
Renter-occupied	982	1,394	49.4	46.5
No cash rent	30	36	1.5	1.2

NA Not available.   X Not applicable.   [1] Represents those who completed 9th to 12th grade, but have no high school diploma.   [2] High school graduate.   [3] Some college or associate degree.   [4] Bachelor's or advanced degree.   [5] Data beginning 1994 not directly comparable with earlier years. See text, Section 13.   [6] Total unemployment as percent of civilian labor force.   [7] For definition of median, see Guide to Tabular Presentation.   [8] For explanation of poverty level, see text, Section 14.

Source: U.S. Bureau of the Census, *Current Population Reports*, P20-459; and unpublished data.

No. 53. Population Living on Selected Reservations and Trust Lands and American Indian Tribes With 10,000 or More American Indians: 1990

[As of **April**]

RESERVATION AND TRUST LANDS WITH 5,000 OR MORE AMERICAN INDIANS, ESKIMOS, AND ALEUTS	Total population	AMERICAN INDIANS, ESKIMOS, ALEUTS		AMERICAN INDIAN TRIBE	Number	Percent distribution
		Number	Percent of total			
All reservation and trust lands	**808,163**	**437,431**	**54.1**	**American Indian population, total** [2]	**1,878,285**	**100.0**
Navajo and Trust Lands, AZ-NM-UT. .	148,451	143,405	96.6	Cherokee	308,132	16.4
Pine Ridge and Trust Lands, NE-SD	12,215	11,182	91.5	Navajo	219,198	11.7
				Chippewa	103,826	5.5
Fort Apache, AZ.	10,394	9,825	94.5	Sioux [3]	103,255	5.5
Gila River, AZ	9,540	9,116	95.6	Choctaw	82,299	4.4
Papago, AZ.	8,730	8,480	97.1	Pueblo	52,939	2.8
Rosebud and Trust Lands, SD.	9,696	8,043	83.0	Apache	50,051	2.7
				Iroquois [4]	49,038	2.6
San Carlos, AZ	7,294	7,110	97.5	Lumbee	48,444	2.6
				Creek.	43,550	2.3
Zuni Pueblo, AZ-NM	7,412	7,073	95.4	Blackfoot	32,234	1.7
Hopi and Trust Lands, AZ . . .	7,360	7,061	95.9	Canadian and Latin American. .	22,379	1.2
Blackfeet, MT	8,549	7,025	82.2	Chickasaw	20,631	1.1
Turtle Mountain and Trust Lands, ND-SD	7,106	6,772	95.3	Potawatomi [4]	16,763	0.9
				Tohono O'Odham.	16,041	0.9
Yakima and Trust Lands, WA . .	27,668	6,307	22.8	Pima	14,431	0.8
				Tlingit.	13,925	0.7
Osage, OK [1]	41,645	6,161	14.8	Seminole	13,797	0.7
Fort Peck, MT	10,595	5,782	54.6	Alaskan Athabaskans	13,738	0.7
Wind River, WY	21,851	5,676	26.0	Cheyenne	11,456	0.6
Eastern Cherokee, NC	6,527	5,388	82.5	Comanche	11,322	0.6
Flathead, MT.	21,259	5,130	24.1	Paiute	11,142	0.6
Cheyenne River, SD	7,743	5,100	65.9	Puget Sound Salish	10,246	0.5

[1] The Osage Reservation is coextensive with Osage County. Data shown for the reservation are for the entire reservation. [2] Includes other American Indian tribes, not shown separately. [3] Any entry with the spelling "Siouan" was miscoded to Sioux in North Carolina. [4] Reporting and/or processing problems have affected the data for this tribe.

Source: U.S. Bureau of the Census, *1990 Census of Population, General Population Characteristics, American Indian and Alaska Native Areas* (CP-1-1A); and press releases CB91-232 and CB92-244.

No. 54. Social and Economic Characteristics of the American Indian Population: 1990

[**As of April**. Based on a sample and subject to sampling variability]

CHARACTERISTIC	American Indian, total [1]	Cherokee	Navajo	Sioux [2]	Chippewa	Choctaw	Pueblo	Apache	Iroquois [3]	Lumbee
Total persons	**1,937,391**	**369,035**	**225,298**	**107,321**	**105,988**	**86,231**	**55,330**	**53,330**	**52,557**	**50,888**
Percent under 5 years old	9.7	6.3	13.6	12.3	10.3	8.2	10.3	10.2	8.1	8.3
Percent 18 years old and over .	65.8	73.3	57.7	60.0	64.0	68.8	64.2	64.7	71.1	66.2
Percent 65 years old and over .	5.9	7.2	4.6	4.4	4.7	8.0	5.8	3.4	6.7	5.6
EDUCATIONAL ATTAINMENT										
Persons 25 years old and over	1,040,955	229,231	100,594	51,014	54,804	49,128	28,597	27,717	30,882	27,343
Percent high school graduates or higher	65.6	68.2	51.0	69.7	69.7	70.3	71.5	63.8	71.9	51.6
Percent bachelor's degree or higher	9.4	11.1	4.5	8.9	8.2	13.3	7.3	6.9	11.3	9.4
FAMILY TYPE										
Total families	449,281	98,610	44,845	22,669	25,077	21,856	11,825	12,314	12,988	12,650
Percent distribution:										
Married couple.	65.8	73.1	61.1	54.2	58.4	75.2	61.2	66.9	67.5	68.5
Female householder, no spouse present	26.2	20.8	28.6	36.0	33.1	20.0	29.2	24.7	25.5	23.9
Male householder, no spouse present	8.0	6.1	10.3	9.8	8.5	4.8	9.6	8.4	7.0	7.6
INCOME IN 1989										
Median family (dol.) [4]	21,619	24,907	13,940	16,525	20,249	24,467	19,845	19,690	27,025	23,934
Median household (dol.) [4]	19,900	21,922	12,817	15,611	18,801	21,640	19,097	18,484	23,460	21,708
Per capita (dol.).	8,284	10,469	4,788	6,508	7,777	9,463	6,679	7,271	10,568	8,625
Families below poverty level [5] .	122,237	19,100	21,204	8,939	7,814	4,347	3,691	3,913	2,249	2,554
Percent below poverty level . .	27.2	19.4	47.3	39.4	31.2	19.9	31.2	31.8	17.3	20.2
Persons below poverty level [5] .	585,273	79,271	107,526	45,658	35,231	19,453	17,981	19,246	10,253	10,966
Percent below poverty level .	31.2	22.0	48.8	44.4	34.3	23.0	33.2	37.5	20.1	22.1

[1] Includes other American Indian tribes not shown separately. [2] Any entry with the spelling "Siouan" was miscoded to Sioux in North Carolina. [3] Reporting and/or processing problems have affected the data for this tribe. [4] For definition of median, see Guide to Tabular Presentation. [5] For explanation of poverty level, see text, Section 14.

Source: U.S. Bureau of the Census, *1990 Census of Population, Characteristics of American Indians by Tribe and Language*, 1990 CP-3-7.

Population

No. 55. Social and Economic Characteristics of the Hispanic Population: 1997

[As of March, except labor force status, annual average. Excludes members of the Armed Forces except those living off post or with their families on post. Based on Current Population Survey; see text, Section 1, and Appendix III]

CHARACTERISTIC	NUMBER (1,000)						PERCENT DISTRIBUTION					
	His-panic, total	Mexi-can	Puer-to Rican	Cuban	Cen-tral and South Amer-ican	Other His-panic	His-panic, total	Mexi-can	Puer-to Rican	Cuban	Cen-tral and South Amer-ican	Other His-panic
Total persons	29,703	18,795	3,152	1,258	4,292	2,206	100.0	100.0	100.0	100.0	100.0	100.0
Under 5 years old	3,443	2,415	313	77	410	228	11.6	12.8	9.9	6.1	9.6	10.3
5 to 14 years old	5,560	3,783	639	126	632	380	18.7	20.1	20.3	10.0	14.7	17.2
15 to 44 years old	15,106	9,554	1,532	509	2,394	1,104	50.9	51.0	48.7	40.4	55.8	50.0
45 to 64 years old	4,079	2,274	499	286	677	341	13.8	12.1	15.8	22.8	15.8	15.5
65 years old and over	1,516	757	167	260	179	154	5.1	4.1	5.3	20.7	4.2	7.0
EDUCATIONAL ATTAINMENT												
Persons 25 years old and over.	15,476	9,157	1,669	946	2,473	1,231	100.0	100.0	100.0	100.0	100.0	100.0
High school graduate or higher	8,471	4,449	1,019	617	1,564	820	54.7	48.6	61.1	65.2	63.3	66.6
Bachelor's degree or higher	1,601	682	180	186	367	184	10.3	7.4	10.8	19.7	14.8	14.9
LABOR FORCE STATUS [1]												
Civilians 16 years old and over	20,321	12,443	2,139	1,025	3,164	1,550	100.0	100.0	100.0	100.0	100.0	100.0
Civilian labor force	13,796	8,546	1,293	646	2,293	1,018	67.9	68.7	60.4	63.0	72.5	65.7
Employed.	12,726	7,884	1,166	603	2,133	940	62.6	63.4	54.5	58.9	67.4	60.6
Unemployed	1,069	662	127	43	160	77	5.3	5.3	5.9	4.2	5.1	5.0
Unemployment rate [2] .	7.7	7.7	9.8	6.6	7.0	7.6	(X)	(X)	(X)	(X)	(X)	(X)
Male	7.0	7.0	9.6	6.0	(NA)	(NA)	(X)	(X)	(X)	(X)	(X)	(X)
Female	8.9	8.9	10.1	7.6	(NA)	(NA)	(X)	(X)	(X)	(X)	(X)	(X)
Not in labor force	6,526	3,897	846	379	871	533	32.1	31.3	39.6	37.0	27.5	34.4
FAMILY TYPE												
Total families	6,631	4,007	780	367	962	515	100.0	100.0	100.0	100.0	100.0	100.0
Married couple	4,520	2,892	424	282	627	295	68.2	72.2	54.3	76.9	65.2	57.3
Female householder, no spouse present	1,617	807	307	62	258	183	24.4	20.2	39.4	16.9	26.8	35.5
Male householder, no spouse present	494	307	49	23	77	37	7.4	7.7	6.3	6.2	8.0	7.1
FAMILY INCOME IN 1996												
Total families	6,631	4,007	780	367	962	515	100.0	100.0	100.0	100.0	100.0	100.0
Less than $5,000	326	166	70	6	44	41	4.9	4.1	9.0	1.5	4.4	8.0
$5,000 to $9,999	646	378	118	32	57	62	9.8	9.4	15.1	8.6	5.9	12.0
$10,000 to $14,999	768	493	77	33	99	67	11.6	12.3	9.9	8.7	10.2	13.0
$15,000 to $24,999	1,425	941	143	61	203	78	21.5	23.4	18.3	16.7	21.1	15.3
$25,000 to $34,999	1,037	651	98	49	172	66	15.5	16.3	12.6	13.6	17.8	13.0
$35,000 to $49,999	1,005	605	131	57	139	75	15.1	15.0	16.5	15.6	14.4	14.8
$50,000 or more	1,425	775	146	129	251	123	21.5	19.4	18.7	35.3	26.1	23.9
Median income (dol.) [3]	26,179	25,347	23,646	35,616	29,960	26,171	(X)	(X)	(X)	(X)	(X)	(X)
Families below poverty level [4]	1,748	1,111	258	46	183	151	26.4	27.7	33.1	12.5	19.0	29.3
Persons below poverty level [4]	8,697	5,815	1,116	217	892	657	29.4	31.0	35.7	17.3	20.8	29.9
HOUSING TENURE												
Total occupied units .	8,225	4,830	1,043	496	1,164	691	100.0	100.0	100.0	100.0	100.0	100.0
Owner-occupied	3,543	2,237	322	274	400	311	43.1	46.3	30.8	55.2	34.3	45.0
Renter-occupied [5]	4,681	2,592	722	222	765	381	56.9	53.7	69.1	44.8	65.7	55.0

NA Not available. X Not applicable. [1] Source: U.S. Bureau of Labor Statistics, *Employment and Earnings*, January 1998. [2] Total unemployment as percent of civilian labor force. [3] For definition of median, see Guide to Tabular Presentation. [4] For explanation of poverty level, see text, Section 14. [5] Includes no cash rent.

Source: Except as noted, U.S. Bureau of the Census, unpublished data.

No. 56. Native and Foreign-Born Population, by Place of Birth: 1950 to 1990

[In thousands, except percent. Data are based on a sample from the census; for details, see text, Section 1. See source for sampling variability]

YEAR	Total population	NATIVE POPULATION						FOREIGN BORN	
		Total	Born in state of residence	Born in other states	State of birth not reported	Born in outlying areas [1]	Born abroad or at sea of American parents	Number	Percent of total population
1950	150,216	139,869	102,788	35,284	1,370	330	96	10,347	6.9
1960	178,467	168,806	118,802	44,264	4,526	817	397	9,661	5.4
1970	203,194	193,454	131,296	51,659	8,882	873	744	9,740	4.8
1980	226,546	212,466	144,871	65,452	(NA)	1,088	1,055	14,080	6.2
1990	248,710	228,943	153,685	72,011	(NA)	1,382	1,864	19,767	7.9

NA Not available. [1] 1950, includes Alaska and Hawaii. Includes Puerto Rico.

Source: U.S. Bureau of the Census, *1970 Census of Population*, Vol. II, PC(2)-2A; and *1990 Census of Population Listing* (1990CPH-L-121).

No. 57. Native and Foreign-Born Population, by Selected Characteristics: 1997

[In thousands. The foreign-born population includes some undocumented immigrants, refugees, and temporary residents such as students and temporary workers as well as legally-admitted immigrants. Based on Current Population Survey; see text, Section 1 and Appendix III]

CHARACTERISTIC	Native population	FOREIGN-BORN POPULATION				
		Total	Year of entry			
			Before 1970	1970 to 1979	1980 to 1989	1990 to 1997
Total.	241,014	25,779	4,749	4,936	8,555	7,539
Under 5 years old.	19,482	299	(X)	(X)	(X)	299
5 to 17 years old.	49,124	2,319	(X)	13	810	1,498
18 to 24 years old.	22,047	2,940	(X)	395	990	1,555
25 to 29 years old.	16,489	2,770	25	408	1,149	1,190
30 to 34 years old.	17,843	3,154	146	514	1,499	995
35 to 44 years old.	38,664	5,296	526	1,477	2,209	1,084
45 to 64 years old.	48,276	6,211	2,226	1,778	1,490	716
65 years old and over	29,088	2,789	1,827	350	408	203
Male.	117,690	12,946	2,081	2,453	4,476	3,937
Female.	123,324	12,832	2,669	2,482	4,080	3,601
White.	202,566	17,504	4,060	3,195	5,362	4,887
Black	32,190	2,028	233	413	833	550
American Indian/Eskimo/Aleut.	2,291	142	13	17	43	69
Asian or Pacific Islander	3,967	6,105	444	1,310	2,318	2,032
Hispanic origin [1]	18,311	11,393	1,550	2,276	4,236	3,331
EDUCATIONAL ATTAINMENT						
Persons 25 years old and over	150,361	20,220	4,749	4,528	6,755	4,188
Not high school graduate	23,515	7,009	1,499	1,548	2,526	1,436
High school grad/some college	91,098	8,261	2,299	1,823	2,612	1,526
Bachelor's degree.	24,185	3,172	571	747	1,079	776
Graduate or professional degree	11,563	1,778	380	410	538	450
LABOR FORCE STATUS						
Persons 16 years old and over [2]	179,733	23,649	4,749	4,935	7,991	5,971
In the civilian labor force	119,635	15,593	2,299	3,717	5,769	3,806
Employed	113,156	14,524	2,197	3,496	5,383	3,447
Unemployed	6,479	1,069	102	221	386	359
Not in the labor force.	59,275	8,013	2,447	1,195	2,209	2,162
INCOME IN 1996						
Persons 16 years old and over	179,733	23,649	4,749	4,935	7,991	5,971
Without income	11,310	3,376	313	434	1,171	1,455
With income	168,423	20,273	4,436	4,501	6,820	4,516
$1 to $9,999 or loss.	50,469	7,036	1,494	1,257	2,317	1,970
$10,000 to $19,999	39,068	5,565	1,072	1,135	2,009	1,349
$20,000 to $34,999	39,380	4,023	857	1,051	1,456	658
$35,000 to $49,999	19,773	1,728	474	495	500	259
$50,000 or more	19,733	1,921	539	563	538	280
POVERTY STATUS [3]						
In poverty	31,117	5,412	497	651	1,943	2,320
Not in poverty	209,342	20,347	4,252	4,284	6,611	5,201
HOMEOWNERSHIP						
In owner-occupied unit.	169,581	12,442	3,602	3,109	3,756	1,975
In renter-occupied unit.	71,433	13,336	1,147	1,826	4,799	5,564

X Not applicable. [1] Persons of Hispanic origin may be of any race. [2] Includes persons in Armed Forces, not shown separately. [3] Persons for whom poverty status is determined.

Source: U.S. Bureau of the Census, *Current Population Reports*, P20-507 and Population Paper Listing PPL-92.

No. 58. Population, by Selected Ancestry Group and Region: 1990

[As of **April 1**. Covers persons who reported single and multiple ancestry groups. Persons who reported a multiple ancestry group may be included in more than one category. Major classifications of ancestry groups do not represent strict geographic or cultural definitions. Based on a sample and subject to sampling variability; see text, Section 1]

ANCESTRY GROUP	Total (1,000)	PERCENT DISTRIBUTION, BY REGION				ANCESTRY GROUP	Total (1,000)	PERCENT DISTRIBUTION, BY REGION			
		North-east	Mid-west	South	West			North-east	Mid-west	South	West
European:[1]						Central & South America[3] and Spain:					
Austrian	865	38	21	19	22	Cuban	860	18	3	69	9
British	1,119	17	18	39	26	Dominican	506	86	1	10	2
Croatian	544	21	43	20	16	Hispanic[4]	1,113	13	6	31	50
Czech	1,296	10	52	22	16	Mexican	11,587	1	9	33	57
Danish	1,635	9	34	12	45	Puerto Rican	1,955	66	11	15	8
Dutch	6,227	16	34	29	21	Salvadoran	499	13	2	23	62
English	32,652	18	22	35	25	Spanish	2,024	16	8	30	45
European	467	14	17	31	39	West Indian:[1]					
Finnish	659	14	47	11	27	Jamaican	435	59	5	31	6
French[2]	10,321	26	26	29	20	Asia:					
German	57,947	17	39	25	19	Asian Indian	570	32	19	26	24
Greek	1,110	37	23	21	19	Chinese	1,505	25	8	12	55
Hungarian	1,582	36	32	17	16	Filipino	1,451	10	9	13	68
Irish	38,736	24	25	33	17	Japanese	1,005	9	8	11	72
Italian	14,665	51	17	17	15	Korean	837	22	14	20	44
Lithuanian	812	43	28	16	13	Vietnamese	536	9	8	28	54
Norwegian	3,869	6	52	10	33	North America:					
Polish	9,366	37	37	15	11	Acadian/Cajun	668	1	2	91	5
Portuguese	1,153	49	3	8	41	Afro-American	23,777	15	21	54	10
Russian	2,953	44	16	18	22	American Indian	8,708	9	22	47	23
Scandinavian	679	8	33	15	45	American	12,396	10	18	61	11
Scotch-Irish	5,618	14	19	47	20	Canadian	550	34	18	21	28
Scottish	5,394	20	21	33	26	French Canadian	2,167	45	20	20	15
Slovak	1,883	40	34	14	11	United States	644	16	18	53	13
Swedish	4,681	14	40	14	32	White	1,800	7	13	53	28
Swiss	1,045	16	36	17	30						
Ukrainian	741	51	22	14	13						
Welsh	2,034	22	24	27	27						
Yugoslavian	258	23	28	12	37						

[1] Non-Hispanic groups.   [2] Excludes French Basque.   [3] Hispanic groups.   [4] A general type of response which may encompass several ancestry groups.

Source: U.S. Bureau of the Census, *1990 Census of Population, Supplementary Reports, Detailed Ancestry Groups for States* (1990 CP-S-1-2).

No. 59. Persons Speaking a Language Other Than English at Home, by Age and Language: 1990

[As of **April**. Based on a sample and subject to sampling variability]

AGE GROUP AND LANGUAGE SPOKEN AT HOME	Persons who speak language (1,000)	Percent who speak English less than "very well"	LANGUAGE	Persons, 5 years old and over who speak language (1,000)
Persons 5 years old and over	230,446	(X)	Speak only English	198,601
Speak only English	198,601	(X)	Spanish	17,339
Speak other language	31,845	43.9	French	1,702
Speak Spanish or Spanish Creole	17,345	47.9	German	1,547
Speak Asian or Pacific Island language	4,472	54.1	Italian	1,309
Speak other language	10,028	32.4	Chinese	1,249
			Tagalog	843
Persons 5 to 17 years old	45,342	(X)	Polish	723
Speak only English	39,020	(X)	Korean	626
Speak other language	6,323	37.8	Vietnamese	507
Speak Spanish or Spanish Creole	4,168	39.3	Portuguese	430
Speak Asian or Pacific Island language	816	44.2	Japanese	428
Speak other language	1,340	29.2	Greek	388
			Arabic	355
Persons 18 to 64 years old	153,908	(X)	Hindi (Urdu)	331
Speak only English	132,200	(X)	Russian	242
Speak other language	21,708	45.1	Yiddish	213
Speak Spanish or Spanish Creole	12,121	49.6	Thai (Laotian)	206
Speak Asian or Pacific Island language	3,301	54.7	Persian	202
Speak other language	6,286	31.4	French Creole	188
			Armenian	150
Persons 65 years old and over	31,195	(X)	Navaho	149
Speak only English	27,381	(X)	Hungarian	148
Speak other language	3,814	47.2	Hebrew	144
Speak Spanish or Spanish Creole	1,057	62.3	Dutch	143
Speak Asian or Pacific Island language	355	72.0	Mon-Khmer (Cambodian)	127
Speak other language	2,402	36.9	Gujarathi	102

X Not applicable.

Source: U.S. Bureau of the Census, *1990 Census of Population and Housing Data Paper Listing* (CPH-L-133); and Summary Tape File 3C.

No. 60. Living Arrangements of Persons 15 Years Old and Over, by Selected Characteristics: 1997

[In thousands. As of March. Based on Current Population Survey which includes members of Armed Forces living off post or with families on post, but excludes other Armed Forces; see text, Section 1, and Appendix III]

LIVING ARRANGEMENT	Total	15 to 19 years old	20 to 24 years old	25 to 34 years old	35 to 44 years old	45 to 54 years old	55 to 64 years old	65 to 74 years old	75 years old and over
Total [1]	207,235	19,164	17,489	40,256	43,960	33,013	21,475	18,015	13,863
Alone	25,402	95	988	3,630	3,878	3,760	3,117	4,361	5,573
With spouse.	109,331	355	3,266	21,627	29,164	22,933	14,999	11,288	5,699
With other persons	72,502	18,714	13,235	14,999	10,918	6,320	3,359	2,366	2,591
White	173,296	15,195	14,043	32,639	36,438	28,071	18,447	15,983	12,482
Alone	21,513	78	804	2,857	3,171	3,117	2,579	3,819	5,088
With spouse.	96,790	298	2,916	18,923	25,437	20,167	13,371	10,415	5,263
With other persons	54,993	14,819	10,323	10,859	7,830	4,787	2,497	1,749	2,131
Black	24,627	3,047	2,508	5,350	5,415	3,524	2,167	1,570	1,046
Alone	3,126	13	114	545	553	541	484	468	409
With spouse.	7,764	36	234	1,598	2,241	1,745	994	633	283
With other persons	13,737	2,998	2,160	3,207	2,621	1,238	689	469	354
Hispanic origin [2]	20,700	2,631	2,592	5,495	4,388	2,461	1,618	992	524
Alone	1,195	7	53	204	233	178	161	218	141
With spouse.	9,729	90	617	2,993	2,781	1,545	990	545	168
With other persons	9,776	2,534	1,922	2,298	1,374	738	467	229	215

[1] Includes persons of other races and persons not of Hispanic origin, not shown separately. [2] Persons of Hispanic origin may be of any race.

No. 61. Marital Status of the Population, by Sex, Race, and Hispanic Origin: 1980 to 1997

[In millions, except percent. As of March. Persons 18 years old and over. Excludes members of Armed Forces except those living off post or with their families on post. Based on Current Population Survey, see text, Section 1, and Appendix III]

MARITAL STATUS, RACE, AND HISPANIC ORIGIN	TOTAL				MALE				FEMALE			
	1980	1990	1995	1997	1980	1990	1995	1997	1980	1990	1995	1997
Total [1]	159.5	181.8	191.6	195.6	75.7	86.9	92.0	94.2	83.8	95.0	99.6	101.4
Never married	32.3	40.4	43.9	45.9	18.0	22.4	24.6	25.4	14.3	17.9	19.3	20.5
Married.	104.6	112.6	116.7	116.6	51.8	55.8	57.7	57.9	52.8	56.7	58.9	58.7
Widowed.	12.7	13.8	13.4	13.7	2.0	2.3	2.3	2.7	10.8	11.5	11.1	11.1
Divorced	9.9	15.1	17.6	19.3	3.9	6.3	7.4	8.2	6.0	8.8	10.3	11.1
Percent of total	100.0	100.0	100.0	100.0	100.0	100.0	100.0	100.0	100.0	100.0	100.0	100.0
Never married	20.3	22.2	22.9	23.5	23.8	25.8	26.8	27.0	17.1	18.9	19.4	20.2
Married.	65.5	61.9	60.9	59.7	68.4	64.3	62.7	61.5	63.0	59.7	59.2	57.9
Widowed.	8.0	7.6	7.0	7.0	2.6	2.7	2.5	2.9	12.8	12.1	11.1	10.9
Divorced	6.2	8.3	9.2	9.9	5.2	7.2	8.0	8.7	7.1	9.3	10.3	11.0
White, total	139.5	155.5	161.3	164.1	66.7	74.8	78.1	79.8	72.8	80.6	83.2	84.3
Never married	26.4	31.6	33.2	34.5	15.0	18.0	19.2	19.7	11.4	13.6	14.0	14.7
Married.	93.8	99.5	102.0	101.8	46.7	49.5	50.6	50.8	47.1	49.9	51.3	50.9
Widowed.	10.9	11.7	11.3	11.7	1.6	1.9	1.9	2.3	9.3	9.8	9.4	9.4
Divorced	8.3	12.6	14.8	16.1	3.4	5.4	6.3	6.9	5.0	7.3	8.4	9.2
Percent of total	100.0	100.0	100.0	100.0	100.0	100.0	100.0	100.0	100.0	100.0	100.0	100.0
Never married	18.9	20.3	20.6	21.0	22.5	24.1	24.6	24.7	15.7	16.9	16.9	17.5
Married.	67.2	64.0	63.2	62.1	70.0	66.2	64.9	63.8	64.7	61.9	61.7	60.4
Widowed.	7.8	7.5	7.0	7.1	2.5	2.6	2.5	2.8	12.8	12.2	11.3	11.2
Divorced	6.0	8.1	9.1	9.8	5.0	7.2	8.1	8.7	6.8	9.0	10.1	10.9
Black, total	16.6	20.3	22.1	22.8	7.4	9.1	9.9	10.2	9.2	11.2	12.2	12.6
Never married	5.1	7.1	8.5	8.9	2.5	3.5	4.1	4.2	2.5	3.6	4.4	4.7
Married.	8.5	9.3	9.6	9.7	4.1	4.5	4.6	4.6	4.5	4.8	4.9	5.0
Widowed.	1.6	1.7	1.7	1.6	0.3	0.3	0.3	0.3	1.3	1.4	1.4	1.3
Divorced	1.4	2.1	2.4	2.6	0.5	0.8	0.8	1.0	0.9	1.3	1.5	1.6
Percent of total	100.0	100.0	100.0	100.0	100.0	100.0	100.0	100.0	100.0	100.0	100.0	100.0
Never married	30.5	35.1	38.4	39.1	34.3	38.4	41.7	41.5	27.4	32.5	35.8	37.2
Married.	51.4	45.8	43.2	42.4	54.6	49.2	46.7	45.3	48.7	43.0	40.4	40.0
Widowed.	9.8	8.5	7.6	7.2	4.2	3.7	3.1	3.3	14.3	12.4	11.3	10.4
Divorced	8.4	10.6	10.7	11.3	7.0	8.8	8.5	9.9	9.5	12.0	12.5	12.4
Hispanic, [2] total	7.9	13.6	17.6	19.1	3.8	6.7	8.8	9.7	4.1	6.8	8.8	9.4
Never married	1.9	3.7	5.0	5.8	1.0	2.2	3.0	3.5	0.9	1.5	2.1	2.3
Married.	5.2	8.4	10.4	11.1	2.5	4.1	5.1	5.5	2.6	4.3	5.3	5.6
Widowed.	0.4	0.5	0.7	0.7	0.1	0.1	0.2	0.1	0.3	0.4	0.6	0.6
Divorced	0.5	1.0	1.4	1.4	0.2	0.4	0.6	0.6	0.3	0.6	0.8	0.9
Percent of total	100.0	100.0	100.0	100.0	100.0	100.0	100.0	100.0	100.0	100.0	100.0	100.0
Never married	24.1	27.2	28.6	30.6	27.3	32.1	33.8	35.7	21.1	22.5	23.5	25.2
Married.	65.6	61.7	59.3	58.1	67.1	60.9	57.9	56.9	64.3	62.4	60.7	59.3
Widowed.	4.4	4.0	4.2	3.8	1.6	1.5	1.8	1.5	7.1	6.5	6.6	6.1
Divorced	5.8	7.0	7.9	7.6	4.0	5.5	6.6	5.8	7.6	8.5	9.2	9.3

[1] Includes persons of other races and not of Hispanic origin, not shown separately. [2] Hispanic persons may be of any race.

Source of tables 60 and 61: U.S. Bureau of the Census, Current Population Reports, P20-506, and earlier reports; and unpublished data.

No. 62. Marital Status of the Population, by Sex and Age: 1997

[As of **March. Persons 18 years old and over.** Excludes members of Armed Forces except those living off post or with their families on post. Based on Current Population Survey; see text, Section 1, and Appendix III]

SEX AND AGE	NUMBER OF PERSONS (1,000)					PERCENT DISTRIBUTION				
	Total	Never married	Mar- ried	Wid- owed	Di- vorced	Total	Never married	Mar- ried	Wid- owed	Di- vorced
Male	**94,154**	**25,375**	**57,886**	**2,686**	**8,208**	**100.0**	**27.0**	**61.5**	**2.9**	**8.7**
18 to 19 years old............	3,783	3,687	89	-	7	100.0	97.5	2.4	-	0.2
20 to 24 years old............	8,751	7,266	1,363	2	121	100.0	83.0	15.6	0.1	1.4
25 to 29 years old............	9,613	4,947	4,249	11	406	100.0	51.5	44.2	0.1	4.2
30 to 34 years old............	10,426	3,155	6,367	20	884	100.0	30.3	61.1	0.2	8.5
35 to 39 years old............	11,323	2,177	7,908	25	1,212	100.0	19.2	69.8	0.2	10.7
40 to 44 years old............	10,470	1,607	7,481	33	1,349	100.0	15.3	71.5	0.3	12.9
45 to 54 years old............	16,119	1,393	12,286	156	2,285	100.0	8.6	76.2	1.0	14.2
55 to 64 years old............	10,265	595	8,205	331	1,134	100.0	5.8	79.9	3.2	11.0
65 to 74 years old............	8,085	348	6,392	758	588	100.0	4.3	79.1	9.4	7.3
75 years old and over	5,318	199	3,547	1,351	221	100.0	3.7	66.7	25.4	4.2
Female..............	**101,414**	**20,503**	**58,748**	**11,056**	**11,107**	**100.0**	**20.2**	**57.9**	**10.9**	**11.0**
18 to 19 years old............	3,715	3,426	277	4	8	100.0	92.2	7.5	0.1	0.2
20 to 24 years old............	8,737	6,145	2,362	17	214	100.0	70.3	27.0	0.2	2.4
25 to 29 years old............	9,647	3,708	5,337	25	576	100.0	38.4	55.3	0.3	6.0
30 to 34 years old............	10,570	2,070	7,407	52	1,041	100.0	19.6	70.1	0.5	9.8
35 to 39 years old............	11,432	1,549	8,259	100	1,523	100.0	13.5	72.2	0.9	13.3
40 to 44 years old............	10,735	1,093	7,725	178	1,738	100.0	10.2	72.0	1.7	16.2
45 to 54 years old............	16,894	1,192	12,092	650	2,960	100.0	7.1	71.6	3.8	17.5
55 to 64 years old............	11,210	523	7,517	1,485	1,685	100.0	4.7	67.1	13.2	15.0
65 to 74 years old............	9,930	413	5,310	3,294	913	100.0	4.2	53.5	33.2	9.2
75 years old and over	8,544	385	2,460	5,251	449	100.0	4.5	28.8	61.5	5.3

- Represents or rounds to zero.

Source: U.S. Bureau of the Census, *Current Population Reports*, P20-506.

No. 63. Marital Status of the Population—Projections, by Age and Sex: 2000 and 2010

[These numbers are based on the 1990 census, as enumerated, with modifications for age and race, and household estimates from 1991 to 1994, and are projected forward using alternative marital status and household-type proportions. Series 1, shown here, is based on a time series model and is the preferred projection. For Series 1, assumptions about future changes in family and household situation extend trends of the past 30 years]

CHARACTERISTIC	NUMBER (1,000)		PERCENT DISTRIBU- TION		CHARACTERISTIC	NUMBER (1,000)		PERCENT DISTRIBU- TION	
	2000	2010	2000	2010		2000	2010	2000	2010
Population 18 years and over	203,852	225,206	100.0	100.0	55 to 64 years old	23,962	35,283	100.0	100.0
Never married (single) ...	44,459	50,747	21.8	22.5	Never married (single)..	1,254	1,905	5.2	5.4
Ever married...........	159,393	174,459	78.2	77.5	Ever married	22,707	33,379	94.8	94.6
Married, spouse present.	111,408	119,016	54.7	52.8	Married, spouse present	16,424	23,360	68.5	66.2
Other	47,985	55,443	23.5	24.6	Other	6,283	10,019	26.2	28.4
18 to 24 years old	26,258	30,138	100.0	100.0	65 to 74 years old	18,136	21,057	100.0	100.0
Never married (single)..	20,917	24,429	79.7	81.1	Never married (single)..	825	899	4.5	4.3
Ever married	5,341	5,708	20.3	18.9	Ever married	17,311	20,159	95.5	95.7
Married, spouse present	3,750	4,003	14.3	13.3	Married, spouse present	11,309	13,305	62.4	63.2
Other	1,591	1,705	6.1	5.7	Other	6,002	6,854	33.1	32.5
25 to 34 years old	37,233	38,292	100.0	100.0	75 years and over	16,574	18,351	100.0	100.0
Never married (single)..	12,288	14,006	33.0	36.6	Never married (single)..	943	1,012	5.7	5.5
Ever married	24,946	24,286	67.0	63.4	Ever married	15,631	17,339	94.3	94.5
Married, spouse present	18,967	18,115	50.9	47.3	Married, spouse present	6,293	7,394	38.0	40.3
Other	5,979	6,171	16.1	16.1	Other	9,338	9,944	56.3	54.2
35 to 44 years old	44,659	38,521	100.0	100.0	Females, 18 years and over	105,927	116,776	100.0	100.0
Never married (single)..	5,886	5,660	13.2	14.7	Never married (single)..	19,955	22,904	18.8	19.6
Ever married	38,774	32,860	86.8	85.3	Ever married	85,972	93,872	81.2	80.4
Married, spouse present	28,930	23,628	64.8	61.3	Married, spouse present	55,682	59,485	52.6	50.9
Other	9,844	9,233	22.0	24.0	Other	30,290	34,387	28.6	29.4
45 to 54 years old	37,030	43,564	100.0	100.0	Males, 18 years and over .	97,925	108,430	100.0	100.0
Never married (single)..	2,346	2,836	6.3	6.5	Never married (single)..	24,504	27,843	25.0	25.7
Ever married	34,684	40,729	93.7	93.5	Ever married	73,421	80,587	75.0	74.3
Married, spouse present	25,736	29,212	69.5	67.1	Married, spouse present	55,726	59,531	56.9	54.9
Other	8,948	11,517	24.2	26.4	Other	17,695	21,056	18.1	19.4

Source: U.S. Bureau of the Census, *Current Population Reports*, P25-1129.

No. 64. Cohabitation Experience of Women 15 to 44 Years of Age, by Selected Characteristics: 1995

[In percent, except as indicated. Based on the National Survey of Family Growth, a sample survey of women 15 to 44 years of age in the civilian noninstitutionalized population; for details, see source]

| CHARACTERISTIC | Number (1,000) | Ever married or cohabited | Ever married | EVER COHABITED | | | | Never cohabited | Currently cohabiting |
				Total	Never married	Before first marriage	After first marriage		
Total women	**60,201**	**72.5**	**62.3**	**41.1**	**10.2**	**23.6**	**7.3**	**58.9**	**7.0**
15 to 19 years old.	8,961	11.4	4.5	8.9	7.0	1.8	0.1	91.1	4.1
20 to 24 years old.	9,041	54.5	34.3	38.4	20.2	17.2	0.9	61.6	11.2
25 to 29 years old.	9,693	79.7	64.3	49.3	15.4	30.1	3.8	50.7	9.8
30 to 34 years old.	11,065	89.2	79.9	51.4	9.3	33.8	8.3	48.6	7.5
35 to 39 years old.	11,211	92.9	86.5	50.0	6.4	31.0	12.6	50.0	5.2
40 to 44 years old.	10,230	94.5	90.4	43.0	4.1	23.0	15.9	57.0	4.4
Hispanic	6,702	71.8	61.4	36.7	10.4	19.2	7.1	63.3	8.2
Non-Hispanic White.	42,522	75.3	66.4	42.6	8.9	25.6	8.1	57.4	7.0
Non-Hispanic Black.	8,210	60.3	43.1	40.1	17.3	17.9	5.0	59.9	6.9
Non-Hispanic other	2,767	66.8	58.5	31.7	8.3	19.8	3.6	68.3	4.6
Never married	22,679	27.0	(X)	27.0	27.0	(X)	(X)	73.0	11.4
Currently married	29,673	100.0	100.0	45.4	(X)	36.8	8.6	54.6	(X)
Formerly married	7,849	100.0	100.0	65.4	(X)	41.8	23.7	34.6	20.7
Education: [1]									
No high school diploma or GED [2] . .	5,424	91.4	76.8	60.1	14.6	31.1	14.5	39.9	11.6
High school diploma or GED [2]	18,169	91.3	81.9	52.0	9.4	30.1	12.5	48.0	8.0
Some college, no bachelor's degree.	12,399	82.9	72.8	46.3	10.1	28.7	7.5	53.7	6.8
Bachelor's degree or higher.	11,748	79.8	70.5	37.8	9.2	25.1	3.5	62.2	5.1

X Not applicable. [1] Covers only women 22 to 44 years old at time of interview. [2] GED is general equivalency diploma.

Source: U.S. National Center for Health Statistics, *"Fertility, Family Planning, and Women's Health: New data from the 1995 National Survey of Family Growth"*, Vital and Health Statistics, Series 23, No. 19, 1997.

No. 65. Women 15 to 44 Years of Age by Number of Husbands or Cohabiting Partners: 1995

[In percent, except as indicated. Based on the National Survey of Family Growth, a sample survey of women 15 to 44 years of age in the civilian noninstitutionalized population; for details, see source]

| CHARACTERISTIC | Number (1,000) | Never married and never cohabited | NUMBER OF HUSBANDS OR COHABITING PARTNERS [1] | | | |
			One	Two	Three	Four or more
Total women	**60,201**	**27.5**	**49.8**	**16.0**	**4.8**	**1.9**
15 to 19 years old.	8,961	88.6	10.8	0.4	0.2	0.1
20 to 24 years old.	9,041	45.5	46.1	6.9	1.3	0.2
25 to 29 years old.	9,693	20.3	60.2	16.0	2.8	0.7
30 to 34 years old.	11,065	10.8	59.0	21.6	6.0	2.6
35 to 39 years old.	11,211	7.1	59.1	21.6	8.6	3.6
40 to 44 years old.	10,230	5.5	57.5	25.2	8.3	3.5
Hispanic	6,702	28.2	51.8	16.0	3.1	0.9
Non-Hispanic White	42,522	24.7	50.9	16.7	5.4	2.2
Non-Hispanic Black	8,210	39.7	42.3	13.1	3.6	1.3
Non-Hispanic other	2,767	33.2	51.7	12.1	2.3	0.7
Never married	22,679	73.0	19.4	5.5	1.5	0.5
Currently married	29,673	(X)	74.2	19.4	5.0	1.5
Formerly married	7,849	(X)	45.7	33.5	13.5	7.3
Education: [2]						
No high school diploma or GED [3]	5,424	8.6	52.8	25.9	8.9	3.8
High school diploma or GED [3]	18,169	8.7	58.4	22.7	7.1	3.0
Some college, no bachelor's degree	12,399	17.1	56.8	18.2	5.9	2.0
Bachelor's degree or higher	11,748	20.2	61.9	14.0	2.9	1.0

X Not applicable. [1] Husbands with whom a woman also cohabited (outside of marriage) are counted only once. [2] Covers only women 22 to 44 years old at time of interview. [3] GED is general equivalency diploma.

Source: U.S. National Center for Health Statistics, *"Fertility, Family Planning, and Women's Health: New data from the 1995 National Survey of Family Growth"*, Vital and Health Statistics, Series 23, No. 19, 1997.

No. 66. Unmarried Couples, by Selected Characteristics: 1980 to 1997

[In thousands. As of March. An "unmarried couple" is two unrelated adults of the opposite sex sharing the same household. See headnote, Table 69]

PRESENCE OF CHILDREN AND AGE OF HOUSEHOLDER	1980	1985	1990	1995	1997
Unmarried couples, total.	1,589	1,983	2,856	3,668	4,130
No children under 15 years old	1,159	1,380	1,966	2,349	2,660
Some children under 15 years old	431	603	891	1,319	1,470
Under 25 years old	411	425	596	742	782
25 to 44 years old	837	1,203	1,775	2,188	2,429
45 to 64 years old	221	239	358	558	723
65 years old and over	119	116	127	180	195

Source: U.S. Bureau of the Census, *Current Population Reports*, P20-506, and earlier reports; and unpublished data.

No. 67. Married Couples of Same or Mixed Races and Origins: 1980 to 1997

[In thousands. As of March. Persons 15 years old and over. Persons of Hispanic origin may be of any race. Except as noted, based on Current Population Survey; see headnote, Table 69]

RACE AND ORIGIN OF SPOUSES	1980	1990	1995	1997
Married couples, total	49,714	53,256	54,937	54,666
RACE				
Same race couples	48,264	50,889	51,733	51,489
White/White.	44,910	47,202	48,030	47,791
Black/Black	3,354	3,687	3,703	3,698
Interracial couples	651	964	1,392	1,264
Black/White	167	211	328	311
Black husband/White wife	122	150	206	201
White husband/Black wife	45	61	122	110
White/other race [1]	450	720	988	896
Black/other race [1]	34	33	76	57
All other couples [1]	799	1,401	1,811	1,912
HISPANIC ORIGIN				
Hispanic/Hispanic	1,906	3,085	3,857	4,034
Hispanic/other origin (not Hispanic)	891	1,193	1,434	1,662
All other couples (not of Hispanic origin)	46,917	48,979	49,646	48,970

[1] Excluding White and Black.

Source: U.S. Bureau of the Census, *Current Population Reports*, P20-509, and earlier reports; and unpublished data.

No. 68. Householder and Marital Status of Population, 15 Years Old and Over: 1997

[In thousands. As of March. See headnote, Table 69]

HOUSEHOLDER AND MARITAL STATUS	Total, 15 yrs. and over	MALE					FEMALE				
		Total [1]	20 to 24 years	25 to 44 years	45 to 64 years	65 yr. and over	Total [1]	20 to 24 years	25 to 44 years	45 to 64 years	65 yr. and over
Total persons	207,235	100,159	8,751	41,832	26,384	13,403	107,076	8,737	42,384	28,104	18,474
Householder	101,018	60,073	2,157	26,885	20,047	10,734	40,945	2,341	16,253	11,265	10,674
Never married.	16,927	8,339	1,295	5,258	1,171	411	8,589	1,636	4,787	1,197	609
Married, spouse present .	53,604	42,519	788	18,312	15,503	7,872	11,085	466	5,845	3,516	1,223
Married, spouse absent . .	4,880	1,832	36	911	644	241	3,047	115	1,686	924	311
Widowed	11,473	1,998	-	65	365	1,569	9,475	12	301	1,814	7,345
Divorced	14,134	5,384	38	2,339	2,365	642	8,749	111	3,634	3,814	1,186
Not householder.	106,217	40,086	6,595	14,949	6,336	2,670	66,131	6,397	26,131	16,840	7,798
Never married.	40,461	22,976	5,970	6,630	817	137	17,484	4,508	3,634	518	188
Married, spouse present .	55,728	12,147	384	5,990	3,982	1,745	43,581	1,629	20,646	14,931	6,146
Married, spouse absent . .	2,540	1,425	156	791	361	82	1,115	152	554	239	90
Widowed	2,276	692	2	24	123	539	1,584	5	54	321	1,200
Divorced	5,213	2,846	83	1,512	1,055	165	2,367	102	1,244	831	175

- Represents or rounds to zero.   [1] Includes 15 to 19 year olds.

Source: U.S. Bureau of the Census, unpublished data.

No. 69. Households, Families, Subfamilies, and Married Couples: 1970 to 1997

[In thousands, except as indicated. As of **March**. Based on Current Population Survey; includes members of Armed Forces living off post or with their families on post, but excludes all other members of Armed Forces; see text, Section 1, and Appendix III. For definition of terms, see text, Section 1. Minus sign (-) indicates decrease]

TYPE OF UNIT	1970	1975	1980	1985	1990	1995	1996	1997	PERCENT CHANGE		
									1970-80	1980-90	1990-97
Households	63,401	71,120	80,776	86,789	93,347	98,990	99,627	101,018	27	16	8
Average size	3.14	2.94	2.76	2.69	2.63	2.65	2.65	2.64	(X)	(X)	(X)
Family households	51,456	55,563	59,550	62,706	66,090	69,305	69,594	70,241	16	11	6
Married couple	44,728	46,951	49,112	50,350	52,317	53,858	53,567	53,604	10	7	2
Male householder[1]	1,228	1,485	1,733	2,228	2,884	3,226	3,513	3,847	41	66	33
Female householder[1]	5,500	7,127	8,705	10,129	10,890	12,220	12,514	12,790	58	25	17
Nonfamily households	11,945	15,557	21,226	24,082	27,257	29,686	30,033	30,777	78	28	13
Male householder	4,063	5,912	8,807	10,114	11,606	13,190	13,348	13,707	117	32	18
Female householder	7,882	9,645	12,419	13,968	15,651	16,496	16,685	17,070	58	26	9
One person	10,851	13,939	18,296	20,602	22,999	24,732	24,900	25,402	69	26	10
Families	51,586	55,712	59,550	62,706	66,090	69,305	69,594	70,241	15	11	6
Average size	3.58	3.42	3.29	3.23	3.17	3.19	3.20	3.19	(X)	(X)	(X)
Married couple	44,755	46,971	49,112	50,350	52,317	53,858	53,567	53,604	10	7	2
Male householder[1]	1,239	1,499	1,733	2,228	2,884	3,226	3,513	3,847	40	66	33
Female householder[1]	5,591	7,242	8,705	10,129	10,890	12,220	12,514	12,790	56	25	17
Unrelated subfamilies	130	149	360	526	534	674	588	615	177	48	15
Married couple	27	20	20	46	68	64	51	50	(B)	(B)	(B)
Male reference persons[1]	11	14	36	85	45	59	45	77	(B)	(B)	(B)
Female reference persons[1]	91	115	304	395	421	550	493	487	234	39	16
Related subfamilies	1,150	1,349	1,150	2,228	2,403	2,878	2,942	2,907	-	109	21
Married couple	617	576	582	719	871	1,015	1,046	1,012	-6	50	16
Father-child[1]	48	69	54	116	153	195	189	244	(B)	(B)	59
Mother-child[1]	484	705	512	1,392	1,378	1,668	1,706	1,651	6	169	20
Married couples	45,373	47,547	49,714	51,114	53,256	54,937	54,664	54,666	10	7	3
With own household	44,728	46,951	49,112	50,350	52,317	53,858	53,567	53,604	10	7	2
Without own household	645	596	602	764	939	1,079	1,097	1,062	-7	56	13
Percent without	1.4	1.3	1.2	1.5	1.8	2.0	2.0	1.9	(X)	(X)	(X)

- Represents or rounds to zero.   B Not shown; base less than 75,000.   X Not applicable.   [1] No spouse present.

Source: U.S. Bureau of the Census, *Current Population Reports*, P20-509 and unpublished data.

No. 70. Households—Projections, by Type of Household: 1998 to 2010

[In thousands. These numbers are based on the **1990** census, as enumerated, with modifications for age and race, and household estimates from **1991 to 1994**, and are projected forward using alternative marital status and household-type proportions. Series 2 reflects the consequences of projected changes in the age/sex structure of the population only assuming no change from the composition in 1990 of the proportion maintaining households for specific types by age and sex. For details of assumptions for Series 1 and 3, see Tables 74 and 75]

TYPE OF HOUSEHOLD	1998	1999	2000	2005	2010
TOTAL HOUSEHOLDS					
Series 1	101,043	102,119	103,246	108,819	114,825
Series 2	100,924	101,966	103,058	108,426	114,200
Series 3	100,684	101,683	102,734	107,892	113,426
TYPE OF HOUSEHOLD (Series 1)					
Total	101,043	102,119	103,246	108,819	114,825
Family households	70,387	71,015	71,669	74,733	77,895
Married couple	54,707	55,092	55,496	57,371	59,308
Female householder, no spouse present	11,935	12,101	12,272	13,084	13,927
Male householder, no spouse present	3,745	3,822	3,901	4,278	4,660
With children under 18	33,001	33,058	33,117	32,699	32,203
Married couple	24,740	24,713	24,686	23,958	23,126
Female householder, no spouse present	6,624	6,679	6,737	6,944	7,189
Male householder, no spouse present	1,638	1,666	1,694	1,797	1,888
Without children under 18	37,386	37,957	38,552	42,034	45,692
Married couple	29,968	30,378	30,810	33,413	36,182
Female householder, no spouse present	5,311	5,422	5,535	6,140	6,738
Male householder, no spouse present	2,107	2,157	2,208	2,481	2,772
Nonfamily households	30,656	31,104	31,577	34,086	36,931
Female householder, total	16,671	16,875	17,095	18,301	19,702
Living alone[1]	14,664	14,844	15,035	16,093	17,327
Male householder, total	13,985	14,228	14,482	15,784	17,229
Living alone[1]	10,789	10,989	11,195	12,244	13,400

[1] These counts cover individuals 15 years of age or older.

Source: U.S. Bureau of the Census, *Current Population Reports*, P25-1129.

No. 71. Households, 1980 to 1997, and Persons in Households, 1997, by Type of Household and Presence of Children

[As of **March**. Based on Current Population Survey; see headnote, Table 69]

TYPE OF HOUSEHOLD AND PRESENCE OF CHILDREN	HOUSEHOLDS					PERSONS IN HOUSEHOLDS, 1997		Persons per house-hold, 1997
	Number (1,000)			Percent distribution				
	1980	1990	1997	1990	1997	Num-ber (1,000)	Percent distribu-tion	
Total households	80,776	93,347	101,018	100	100	266,682	100	2.64
Family households	59,550	66,090	70,241	71	70	228,305	86	3.25
With own children under age 18.	31,022	32,289	34,665	35	34	(NA)	(NA)	(NA)
Without own children under age 18. . .	28,528	33,801	35,575	36	35	(NA)	(NA)	(NA)
Married couple family.	49,112	52,317	53,604	56	53	175,501	66	3.27
With own children under age 18.	24,961	24,537	25,083	26	25	(NA)	(NA)	(NA)
Without own children under age 18. . .	24,151	27,780	28,521	30	28	(NA)	(NA)	(NA)
Male householder, no spouse present. .	1,733	2,884	3,847	3	4	12,382	5	3.22
With own children under age 18.	616	1,153	1,709	1	2	(NA)	(NA)	(NA)
Without own children under age 18. . .	1,117	1,731	2,138	2	2	(NA)	(NA)	(NA)
Female householder, no spouse present .	8,705	10,890	12,790	12	13	40,422	15	3.16
With own children under age 18.	5,445	6,599	7,874	7	8	(NA)	(NA)	(NA)
Without own children under age 18. . .	3,261	4,290	4,916	5	5	(NA)	(NA)	(NA)
Nonfamily households.	21,226	27,257	30,777	29	30	38,377	14	1.25
Living alone	18,296	22,999	25,402	25	25	25,402	10	1.00
Male householder.	8,807	11,606	13,707	12	14	18,534	7	1.35
Living alone	6,966	9,049	10,442	10	10	10,442	4	1.00
Female householder	12,419	15,651	17,070	17	17	19,843	7	1.16
Living alone	11,330	13,950	14,961	15	15	14,961	6	1.00

NA Not available.

Source: U.S. Bureau of the Census, *Current Population Reports*, P20-509, and earlier reports; and unpublished data.

No. 72. Household Characteristics, by Type of Household: 1997

[As of **March**. Based on Current Population Survey; see headnote, Table 69]

CHARACTERISTIC	NUMBER OF HOUSEHOLDS (1,000)					PERCENT DISTRIBUTION				
		Family households			Non-family house-holds		Family households			Non-family house-holds
	Total	Total [1]	Married couple	Female house-holder [2]		Total	Total [1]	Married couple	Female house-holder [2]	
Total.	101,018	70,241	53,604	12,790	30,777	100	100	100	100	100
Age of householder:										
15 to 24 years old.	5,160	2,964	1,333	1,245	2,197	5	4	2	10	7
25 to 29 years old.	8,647	5,686	3,960	1,218	2,961	9	8	7	10	10
30 to 34 years old.	10,667	8,051	5,942	1,585	2,616	11	11	11	12	8
35 to 44 years old.	23,823	19,026	14,254	3,769	4,797	24	27	27	29	16
45 to 54 years old.	18,843	14,383	11,484	2,198	4,459	19	20	21	17	14
55 to 64 years old.	12,469	8,997	7,536	1,126	3,472	12	13	14	9	11
65 to 74 years old.	11,679	7,120	5,949	933	4,559	12	10	11	7	15
75 years old and over	9,729	4,014	3,146	716	5,715	10	6	6	6	19
Size of household:										
One person	25,402	(X)	(X)	(X)	25,402	25	(X)	(X)	(X)	83
Two persons	32,736	28,367	21,268	5,462	4,369	32	40	40	43	14
Three persons	17,065	16,380	11,416	3,866	685	17	23	21	30	2
Four persons	15,396	15,206	12,524	2,025	190	15	22	23	16	1
Five persons	6,774	6,680	5,544	880	94	7	10	10	7	(Z)
Six persons	2,311	2,289	1,874	297	22	2	3	3	2	(Z)
Seven persons or more . . .	1,334	1,318	978	262	15	1	2	2	2	(Z)
Marital status of householder:										
Never married (single)	16,927	5,238	(X)	3,720	11,689	17	7	(X)	29	38
Married, spouse present. . .	53,604	53,604	53,604	(X)	(X)	53	76	100	(X)	(X)
Married, spouse absent . . .	4,880	2,690	(X)	2,159	2,189	5	4	(X)	17	7
Widowed	11,473	2,677	(X)	2,264	8,796	11	4	(X)	18	29
Divorced	14,134	6,032	(X)	4,648	8,102	14	9	(X)	36	26

X Not applicable.   Z Less than 0.5 percent.   [1] Includes male householder, no spouse present.   [2] No spouse present.

Source: U.S. Bureau of the Census, *Current Population Reports*, P20-509.

No. 73. Households, by Age of Householder and Size of Household: 1980 to 1997

[**In millions**. As of **March**. Based on Current Population Survey; see headnote, Table 69]

AGE OF HOUSEHOLDER AND SIZE OF HOUSEHOLD	1980	1985	1990	1995	1996	1997			
						Total [1]	White	Black	Hispanic [2]
Total	80.8	86.8	93.3	99.0	99.6	101.0	85.1	12.1	8.2
Age of householder:									
15 to 24 years old	6.6	5.4	5.1	5.4	5.3	5.2	4.0	0.9	0.7
25 to 29 years old	9.3	9.6	9.4	8.4	8.4	8.6	6.9	1.3	1.0
30 to 34 years old	9.3	10.4	11.0	11.1	10.9	10.7	8.7	1.4	1.2
35 to 44 years old	14.0	17.5	20.6	22.9	23.2	23.8	19.6	3.1	2.2
45 to 54 years old	12.7	12.6	14.5	17.6	18.0	18.8	15.9	2.2	1.3
55 to 64 years old	12.5	13.1	12.5	12.2	12.4	12.5	10.6	1.4	0.9
65 to 74 years old	10.1	10.9	11.7	11.8	11.9	11.7	10.4	1.1	0.6
75 years old and over	6.4	7.3	8.4	9.6	9.6	9.7	8.8	0.7	0.3
One person	18.3	20.6	23.0	24.7	24.9	25.4	21.5	3.1	1.2
Male	7.0	7.9	9.0	10.1	10.3	10.4	8.7	1.3	0.6
Female	11.3	12.7	14.0	14.6	14.6	15.0	12.8	1.8	0.6
Two persons	25.3	27.4	30.1	31.8	32.5	32.7	28.5	3.2	1.8
Three persons	14.1	15.5	16.1	16.8	16.7	17.1	14.0	2.3	1.7
Four persons	12.7	13.6	14.5	15.3	15.1	15.4	12.7	1.9	1.6
Five persons	6.1	6.1	6.2	6.6	6.6	6.8	5.5	1.0	1.0
Six persons	2.5	2.3	2.1	2.3	2.4	2.3	1.8	0.3	0.5
Seven persons or more	1.8	1.3	1.3	1.4	1.4	1.3	0.9	0.3	0.4

[1] Includes other races, not shown separately.   [2] Hispanic persons may be of any race.

Source: U.S. Bureau of the Census, *Current Population Reports*, P20-509, and earlier reports; and unpublished data.

No. 74. Households—Projections, by Age of Householder: 1998 to 2010

[**In thousands**. These numbers are based on the **1990** census, as enumerated, with modifications for age and race, and household estimates from **1991** to **1994**, and are projected forward using alternative marital status and household-type proportions. Series 1, shown here, is based on a time series model and is the preferred projection. For Series 1, assumptions about future changes in family and household situation extend trends of the past 30 years]

AGE OF HOUSEHOLDER	1998	1999	2000	2005	2010
Households, total	**101,043**	**102,119**	**103,246**	**108,819**	**114,825**
Under 25 years old	4,758	4,854	4,966	5,399	5,724
25 to 34 years old	17,746	17,336	17,045	16,547	17,426
35 to 44 years old	23,767	23,916	23,914	22,560	20,581
45 to 54 years old	19,727	20,434	21,210	23,924	25,283
55 to 64 years old	13,237	13,658	14,002	17,331	20,693
65 to 74 years old	11,588	11,475	11,446	11,597	13,298
75 years and over	10,221	10,447	10,663	11,462	11,821

Source: U.S. Bureau of the Census, *Current Population Reports*, P25-1129.

No. 75. Households—Projections, by Race and Hispanic Origin of Householder: 1998 to 2010

[**In thousands**. These numbers are based on the **1990** census, as enumerated, with modifications for age and race, and household estimates from **1991** to **1994**, and are projected forward using alternative marital status and household-type proportions. Race and Hispanic origin of householders were not tabulated for either series 1 or series 2. Series 3, shown here, reflects the consequences of projected change in both the age/sex structure and race/origin composition of the population. Current patterns of family and householdership are assumed to remain at their **1990** proportions]

CHARACTERISTIC OF HOUSEHOLDER	1998	1999	2000	2005	2010
Households, total	**100,684**	**101,683**	**102,734**	**107,892**	**113,426**
White	85,271	85,952	86,676	90,204	94,010
Black	11,753	11,948	12,149	13,137	14,185
American Indian, Eskimo, Aleut.	727	740	754	827	906
Asian, Pacific Islander.	2,933	3,043	3,155	3,724	4,324
Hispanic origin [1]	8,195	8,474	8,761	10,236	11,866

[1] Persons of Hispanic origin may be of any race.

Source: U.S. Bureau of the Census, *Current Population Reports*, P25-1129.

No. 76. Households—States: 1980 to 1996

[As of **April 1**, except **beginning 1993**, as of **July 1**. Minus sign (-) indicates decrease]

STATE	NUMBER (1,000)					1996		PERCENT CHANGE		PERSONS PER HOUSEHOLD		
	1980	1990	1993	1994	1995	Total	House-holder 65 yrs. and over	1980-90	1990-96	1980	1990	1996
U.S.	80,390	91,946	95,358	95,988	97,386	98,751	21,381	14.4	7.4	2.75	2.63	2.62
AL	1,342	1,507	1,574	1,582	1,603	1,624	367	12.3	7.8	2.84	2.62	2.56
AK	131	189	206	207	210	214	20	43.7	13.4	2.93	2.80	2.76
AZ	957	1,369	1,466	1,518	1,624	1,687	366	43.0	23.3	2.79	2.62	2.59
AR	816	891	919	925	938	951	236	9.2	6.7	2.74	2.57	2.51
CA	8,630	10,381	10,812	10,829	10,941	11,101	2,153	20.3	6.9	2.68	2.79	2.79
CO	1,061	1,282	1,388	1,424	1,466	1,502	246	20.8	17.1	2.65	2.51	2.47
CT	1,094	1,230	1,227	1,222	1,225	1,231	287	12.5	-	2.76	2.59	2.65
DE	207	247	262	264	270	276	58	19.5	11.4	2.79	2.61	2.62
DC	253	250	243	238	233	231	50	-1.4	-7.3	2.40	2.26	2.24
FL	3,744	5,135	5,379	5,451	5,551	5,648	1,640	37.1	10.0	2.55	2.46	2.45
GA	1,872	2,366	2,533	2,587	2,654	2,723	465	26.4	15.1	2.84	2.66	2.65
HI	294	356	376	380	384	389	87	21.2	9.0	3.15	3.01	2.97
ID	324	361	395	405	419	430	86	11.3	19.1	2.85	2.73	2.68
IL	4,045	4,202	4,294	4,295	4,322	4,352	942	3.9	3.6	2.76	2.65	2.65
IN	1,927	2,065	2,149	2,156	2,182	2,209	472	7.2	6.9	2.77	2.61	2.57
IA	1,053	1,064	1,084	1,084	1,093	1,103	275	1.1	3.6	2.68	2.52	2.51
KS	872	945	962	965	975	982	224	8.3	3.9	2.62	2.53	2.54
KY	1,263	1,380	1,430	1,437	1,457	1,478	322	9.2	7.1	2.82	2.60	2.55
LA	1,412	1,499	1,539	1,543	1,559	1,572	324	6.2	4.8	2.91	2.74	2.67
ME	395	465	474	473	477	483	109	17.7	3.8	2.75	2.56	2.54
MD	1,461	1,749	1,816	1,830	1,853	1,871	356	19.7	7.0	2.82	2.67	2.70
MA	2,033	2,247	2,264	2,269	2,297	2,322	536	10.5	3.3	2.72	2.58	2.61
MI	3,195	3,419	3,494	3,500	3,534	3,576	765	7.0	4.6	2.84	2.66	2.66
MN	1,445	1,648	1,702	1,716	1,740	1,763	366	14.0	7.0	2.74	2.58	2.58
MS	827	911	941	948	964	979	222	10.2	7.4	2.97	2.75	2.66
MO	1,793	1,961	2,001	2,009	2,031	2,052	478	9.4	4.6	2.67	2.53	2.51
MT	284	306	321	326	335	341	75	7.9	11.3	2.70	2.53	2.50
NE	571	602	615	616	624	631	147	5.4	4.8	2.66	2.54	2.54
NV	304	466	535	562	591	619	115	53.2	32.8	2.59	2.53	2.53
NH	323	411	419	423	431	439	85	27.1	6.7	2.75	2.62	2.62
NJ	2,549	2,795	2,839	2,841	2,866	2,889	674	9.7	3.4	2.84	2.70	2.75
NM	441	543	578	592	607	619	122	22.9	14.1	2.90	2.74	2.64
NY	6,340	6,639	6,702	6,684	6,709	6,737	1,524	4.7	1.5	2.70	2.63	2.65
NC	2,043	2,517	2,646	2,680	2,738	2,796	589	23.2	11.1	2.78	2.54	2.53
ND	228	241	242	242	244	247	60	5.8	2.4	2.75	2.55	2.51
OH	3,834	4,088	4,187	4,187	4,223	4,260	956	6.6	4.2	2.76	2.59	2.54
OK	1,119	1,206	1,235	1,238	1,250	1,265	291	7.8	4.9	2.62	2.53	2.50
OR	992	1,103	1,180	1,197	1,223	1,249	273	11.3	13.2	2.60	2.52	2.51
PA	4,220	4,496	4,559	4,552	4,575	4,594	1,211	6.6	2.2	2.74	2.57	2.58
RI	339	378	378	376	376	378	96	11.6	-0.1	2.70	2.55	2.56
SC	1,030	1,258	1,328	1,331	1,352	1,376	289	22.1	9.4	2.93	2.68	2.64
SD	243	259	265	267	270	273	68	6.8	5.4	2.74	2.59	2.56
TN	1,619	1,854	1,941	1,965	2,002	2,041	431	14.5	10.1	2.77	2.56	2.52
TX	4,929	6,071	6,458	6,570	6,741	6,894	1,240	23.2	13.6	2.82	2.73	2.69
UT	449	537	586	600	621	639	112	19.8	19.0	3.20	3.15	3.06
VT	178	211	218	220	223	227	45	18.1	7.5	2.75	2.57	2.57
VA	1,863	2,292	2,414	2,439	2,476	2,511	469	23.0	9.6	2.77	2.61	2.61
WA	1,541	1,872	2,019	2,049	2,097	2,139	406	21.5	14.2	2.61	2.53	2.53
WV	686	689	705	705	709	714	187	0.3	3.7	2.79	2.55	2.50
WI	1,652	1,822	1,883	1,891	1,917	1,943	432	10.3	6.6	2.77	2.61	2.61
WY	166	169	176	178	181	184	35	1.9	8.8	2.78	2.63	2.55

- Represents or rounds to zero.

Source: U.S. Bureau of the Census, *1980 Census of Population*, Vol. 1, Chapter B; *1990 Census of Population, General Population Characteristics, United States* (1990 CP-1-1); and unpublished data.

No. 77. Family and Nonfamily Households, by Race, Hispanic Origin, and Type: 1980 to 1997

[As of **March**, except as noted. Based on Current Population Survey, except as noted; see headnote, Table 69]

RACE, HISPANIC ORIGIN, AND TYPE	NUMBER (1,000)					PERCENT DISTRIBUTION				
	1980	1985	1990	1995	1997	1980	1985	1990	1995	1997
TOTAL HOUSEHOLDS										
Total [1]	**80,776**	**86,789**	**93,347**	**98,990**	**101,018**	**100**	**100**	**100**	**100**	**100**
White	70,766	75,328	80,163	83,737	85,059	88	87	86	85	84
Black	8,586	9,480	10,486	11,655	12,109	11	11	11	12	12
Hispanic [2]	3,684	4,883	5,933	7,735	8,225	5	6	6	8	8
FAMILY HOUSEHOLDS										
White, total	**52,243**	**54,400**	**56,590**	**58,437**	**58,934**	**100**	**100**	**100**	**100**	**100**
Married couple	44,751	45,643	46,981	47,899	47,650	86	84	83	82	81
Male householder [3]	1,441	1,816	2,303	2,507	2,944	3	3	4	4	5
Female householder [3]	6,052	6,941	7,306	8,031	8,339	12	13	13	14	14
Black, total	**6,184**	**6,778**	**7,470**	**8,093**	**8,455**	**100**	**100**	**100**	**100**	**100**
Married couple	3,433	3,469	3,750	3,842	3,851	56	51	50	47	46
Male householder [3]	256	344	446	536	657	4	5	6	7	8
Female householder [3]	2,495	2,964	3,275	3,716	3,947	40	44	44	46	47
Asian or Pacific Islander, total [4]	**818**	**(NA)**	**1,531**	**1,588**	**2,246**	**100**	**(NA)**	**100**	**100**	**100**
Married couple	691	(NA)	1,256	1,290	1,763	84	(NA)	82	81	78
Male householder [3]	39	(NA)	86	98	186	5	(NA)	6	6	8
Female householder [3]	88	(NA)	188	200	297	11	(NA)	12	13	13
Hispanic, total [2]	**3,029**	**3,939**	**4,840**	**6,200**	**6,631**	**100**	**100**	**100**	**100**	**100**
Married couple	2,282	2,824	3,395	4,235	4,520	75	72	70	68	68
Male householder [3]	138	210	329	479	494	5	5	7	8	7
Female householder [3]	610	905	1,116	1,485	1,617	20	23	23	24	24
NONFAMILY HOUSEHOLDS										
White, total	**18,522**	**20,928**	**23,573**	**25,300**	**26,125**	**100**	**100**	**100**	**100**	**100**
Male householder	7,499	8,608	9,951	11,093	11,481	40	41	42	44	44
Female householder	11,023	12,320	13,622	14,207	14,644	60	59	58	56	56
Black, total	**2,402**	**2,703**	**3,015**	**3,562**	**3,654**	**100**	**100**	**100**	**100**	**100**
Male householder	1,146	1,244	1,313	1,653	1,669	48	46	44	46	46
Female householder	1,256	1,459	1,702	1,909	1,985	52	54	56	54	54
Hispanic, total [2]	**654**	**944**	**1,093**	**1,535**	**1,593**	**100**	**100**	**100**	**100**	**100**
Male householder	365	509	587	790	854	56	54	54	51	54
Female householder	289	435	506	745	740	44	46	46	49	46

NA Not available.   [1] Includes other races not shown separately.   [2] Hispanic persons may be of any race.   [3] No spouse present.   [4] 1980 data as of April and are from 1980 Census of Population. When comparing 1995 estimates of number of households with other years, caution should be used.
Source: U.S. Bureau of the Census, *Current Population Reports*, P20-509, and earlier reports; and unpublished data.

No. 78. Family Groups with Children Under 18 Years Old, by Race and Hispanic Origin: 1980 to 1997

[As of **March**. Family groups comprise family households, related subfamilies, and unrelated subfamilies. Excludes members of Armed Forces except those living off post or with their families on post. Based on Current Population Survey; see text, Section 1, and Appendix III]

RACE AND HISPANIC ORIGIN OF HOUSEHOLDER OR REFERENCE PERSON	NUMBER (1,000)				PERCENT DISTRIBUTION			
	1980	1990	1995	1997	1980	1990	1995	1997
All races, total [1]	**32,150**	**34,670**	**37,168**	**37,619**	**100**	**100**	**100**	**100**
Two-parent family groups	25,231	24,921	25,640	25,577	79	72	69	68
One-parent family groups	6,920	9,749	11,528	12,042	22	28	31	32
Maintained by mother	6,230	8,398	9,834	10,012	19	24	26	27
Maintained by father	690	1,351	1,694	2,030	2	4	5	5
White, total	**27,294**	**28,294**	**29,846**	**30,242**	**100**	**100**	**100**	**100**
Two-parent family groups	22,628	21,905	22,320	22,294	83	77	75	74
One-parent family groups	4,664	6,389	7,525	7,948	17	23	25	26
Maintained by mother	4,122	5,310	6,239	6,396	15	19	21	21
Maintained by father	542	1,079	1,286	1,552	2	4	4	5
Black, total	**4,074**	**5,087**	**5,491**	**5,679**	**100**	**100**	**100**	**100**
Two-parent family groups	1,961	2,006	1,962	2,020	48	39	36	36
One-parent family groups	2,114	3,081	3,529	3,659	52	61	64	64
Maintained by mother	1,984	2,860	3,197	3,268	49	56	58	58
Maintained by father	129	221	332	391	3	4	6	7
Hispanic, total [2]	**2,194**	**3,429**	**4,527**	**4,870**	**100**	**100**	**100**	**100**
Two-parent family groups	1,626	2,289	2,879	3,115	74	67	64	64
One-parent family groups	568	1,140	1,647	1,756	26	33	36	36
Maintained by mother	526	1,003	1,404	1,500	24	29	31	31
Maintained by father	42	138	243	256	2	4	5	5

[1] Includes other races, not shown separately.   [2] Hispanic persons may be of any race.
Source: U.S. Bureau of the Census, *Current Population Reports*, P20-509, and earlier reports; and unpublished data.

No. 79. Family Groups With Children Under 18 Years Old, by Type, Race, and Hispanic Origin: 1997

[As of **March**. Excludes members of Armed Forces except those living off post or with their families on post. Based on Current Population Survey; see text, Section 1, and Appendix III]

RACE AND HISPANIC ORIGIN OF HOUSEHOLDER OR REFERENCE PERSON	NUMBER (1,000)					PERCENT DISTRIBUTION				
	Total	Family house-holds	Subfamilies			Total	Family house-holds	Subfamilies		
			Total	Related	Unre-lated			Total	Related	Unre-lated
All races, total [1]	**37,619**	**34,665**	**2,954**	**2,360**	**594**	**100**	**100**	**100**	**100**	**100**
Two-parent family groups	25,577	25,083	494	465	29	68	72	17	20	5
One-parent family groups	12,042	9,583	2,459	1,895	564	32	28	83	80	95
Maintained by mother.	10,012	7,874	2,138	1,651	487	27	23	72	70	82
Maintained by father.	2,030	1,709	321	244	77	5	5	11	10	13
White, total.	**30,242**	**28,236**	**2,006**	**1,509**	**497**	**100**	**100**	**100**	**100**	**100**
Two-parent family groups	22,294	21,914	379	353	26	74	78	19	23	5
One-parent family groups	7,948	6,322	1,627	1,156	471	26	22	81	77	95
Maintained by mother	6,396	4,997	1,399	988	411	21	18	70	65	83
Maintained by father.	1,552	1,325	228	168	60	5	5	11	11	12
Black, total.	**5,679**	**4,886**	**793**	**713**	**80**	**100**	**100**	**100**	**100**	**100**
Two-parent family groups	2,020	1,974	46	46	-	36	40	6	6	-
One-parent family groups	3,659	2,913	747	667	80	64	60	94	94	100
Maintained by mother	3,268	2,594	674	607	67	58	53	85	85	84
Maintained by father.	391	319	73	60	13	7	7	9	8	16
Hispanic, total [2]	**4,870**	**4,305**	**565**	**477**	**88**	**100**	**100**	**100**	**100**	**100**
Two-parent family groups	3,115	2,962	152	137	15	64	69	27	29	17
One-parent family groups	1,756	1,342	412	340	72	36	31	73	71	82
Maintained by mother	1,500	1,138	361	297	64	31	26	64	62	73
Maintained by father.	256	204	51	43	8	5	5	9	9	9

- Represents or rounds to zero.　[1] Includes other races, not shown separately.　[2] Hispanic persons may be of any race.

Source: U.S. Bureau of the Census, *Current Population Reports*, P20-509.

No. 80. Families, by Size and Presence of Children: 1980 to 1997

[In thousands, except as indicated. As of **March**. Excludes members of Armed Forces except those living off post or with their families on post. Based on Current Population Survey; see text, Section 1, and Appendix III. For definition of families, see text, Section 1]

CHARACTERISTIC	NUMBER					PERCENT DISTRIBUTION				
	1980	1985	1990	1995	1997	1980	1985	1990	1995	1997
Total.	**59,550**	**62,706**	**66,090**	**69,305**	**70,241**	**100**	**100**	**100**	**100**	**100**
Size of family:										
Two persons	23,461	25,349	27,606	29,176	29,780	39	40	42	42	42
Three persons	13,603	14,804	15,353	15,903	16,239	23	24	23	23	23
Four persons	12,372	13,259	14,026	14,624	14,602	21	21	21	21	21
Five persons	5,930	5,894	5,938	6,283	6,326	10	9	9	9	9
Six persons	2,461	2,175	1,997	2,106	2,108	4	4	3	3	3
Seven or more persons . . .	1,723	1,225	1,170	1,213	1,186	3	2	2	2	2
Average per family	3.29	3.23	3.17	3.19	3.19	(X)	(X)	(X)	(X)	(X)
Own children under age 18:										
None	28,528	31,594	33,801	35,009	35,575	48	50	51	51	51
One	12,443	13,108	13,530	14,088	14,334	21	21	20	20	20
Two	11,470	11,645	12,263	13,213	13,295	19	19	19	19	19
Three	4,674	4,486	4,650	5,044	5,100	8	7	7	7	7
Four or more	2,435	1,873	1,846	1,951	1,937	4	3	3	3	3
Own children under age 6:										
None	46,063	48,505	50,905	53,695	54,847	77	77	77	77	78
One	9,441	9,677	10,304	10,733	10,685	16	15	16	15	15
Two or more	4,047	4,525	4,882	4,876	4,709	7	7	7	7	7

X Not applicable.

Source: U.S. Bureau of the Census, *Current Population Reports*, P20-509, and earlier reports; and unpublished data.

No. 81. Families, by Number of Own Children Under 18 Years Old: 1980 to 1997

[As of **March** and based on Current Population Survey; see headnote, Table 80]

RACE, HISPANIC ORIGIN, AND YEAR	NUMBER OF FAMILIES (1,000)					PERCENT DISTRIBUTION				
	Total	No children	One child	Two children	Three or more children	Total	No children	One child	Two children	Three or more children
ALL FAMILIES [1]										
1980....................	59,550	28,528	12,443	11,470	7,109	100	48	21	19	12
1985....................	62,706	31,594	13,108	11,645	6,359	100	50	21	19	10
1990....................	66,090	33,801	13,530	12,263	6,496	100	51	20	19	10
1995....................	69,305	35,009	14,088	13,213	6,995	100	51	20	19	10
1996....................	69,594	35,391	14,041	13,206	6,957	100	51	20	19	10
1997....................	70,241	35,575	14,334	13,295	7,037	100	51	20	19	10
Married couple	53,604	28,521	9,510	10,152	5,420	100	53	18	19	10
Male householder [2] ...	3,847	2,138	1,003	513	192	100	56	26	13	5
Female householder [2] ..	12,790	4,916	3,821	2,629	1,423	100	38	30	21	11
WHITE FAMILIES										
1980....................	52,243	25,769	10,727	9,977	5,769	100	49	21	19	11
1985....................	54,400	28,169	11,174	9,937	5,120	100	52	21	18	9
1990....................	56,590	29,872	11,186	10,342	5,191	100	53	20	18	9
1995....................	58,437	30,486	11,491	10,983	5,478	100	52	20	19	9
1996....................	58,869	30,783	11,455	11,110	5,521	100	52	19	19	9
1997....................	58,934	30,698	11,594	11,046	5,595	100	52	20	19	10
BLACK FAMILIES										
1980....................	6,184	2,364	1,449	1,235	1,136	100	38	23	20	18
1985....................	6,778	2,887	1,579	1,330	982	100	43	23	20	15
1990....................	7,470	3,093	1,894	1,433	1,049	100	41	25	19	14
1995....................	8,093	3,411	1,971	1,593	1,117	100	42	24	20	14
1996....................	8,055	3,472	1,958	1,485	1,140	100	43	24	18	14
1997....................	8,455	3,569	2,071	1,654	1,162	100	42	25	20	14
HISPANIC FAMILIES [3]										
1980....................	3,029	946	680	698	706	100	31	22	23	23
1985....................	3,939	1,337	904	865	833	100	34	23	22	21
1990....................	4,840	1,790	1,095	1,036	919	100	37	23	21	19
1995....................	6,200	2,216	1,408	1,406	1,171	100	36	23	23	19
1996....................	6,287	2,238	1,450	1,437	1,160	100	36	23	23	18
1997....................	6,631	2,326	1,589	1,516	1,200	100	35	24	23	18

[1] Includes other races, not shown separately.   [2] No spouse present.   [3] Hispanic persons may be of any race.

Source: U.S. Bureau of the Census, *Current Population Reports*, P20-509, and earlier reports; and unpublished data.

No. 82. Female Family Householders With No Spouse Present—Characteristics, by Race and Hispanic Origin: 1980 to 1997

[As of **March**. Covers persons 15 years old and over. Based on Current Population Survey; see headnote, Table 80]

CHARACTERISTIC	Unit	WHITE			BLACK			HISPANIC ORIGIN [1]		
		1980	1990	1997	1980	1990	1997	1980	1990	1997
Female family householder.	1,000	6,052	7,306	8,339	2,495	3,275	3,947	610	1,116	1,617
Marital status:										
Never married (single)........	Percent...	11	15	20	27	39	46	23	27	39
Married, spouse absent	Percent...	17	16	16	29	21	19	32	29	23
Widowed................	Percent...	33	26	20	22	17	13	15	16	11
Divorced	Percent...	40	43	44	22	23	22	30	29	27
Presence of children under age 18:										
No own children	Percent...	41	43	40	28	32	34	25	33	30
With own children	Percent...	59	58	60	72	68	66	75	67	70
One child	Percent...	28	30	30	26	30	30	28	25	31
Two children............	Percent...	20	19	21	23	22	21	23	22	24
Three children...........	Percent...	7	7	7	11	9	10	15	13	10
Four or more children.......	Percent...	3	2	2	11	7	6	9	6	5
Children per family	Number...	1.03	0.95	1.01	1.51	1.26	1.22	1.56	1.37	1.40

[1] Persons of Hispanic origin may be of any race.

Source: U.S. Bureau of the Census, *Current Population Reports*, P20-506, and earlier reports; and unpublished data.

No. 83. Family Households With Own Children Under Age 18, by Type of Family, 1980 to 1997, and by Age of Householder, 1997

[As of **March.** Excludes members of Armed Forces except those living off post or with their families on post. Based on Current Population Survey; see text, Section 1, and Appendix III]

FAMILY TYPE	1980	1990	1997						
			Total	15 to 24 years old	25 to 34 years old	35 to 44 years old	45 to 54 years old	55 to 64 years old	65 years old and over
NUMBER (1,000)									
Family households with children .	**31,022**	**32,289**	**34,665**	**1,862**	**10,429**	**15,496**	**5,991**	**743**	**144**
Married couple. . . .	24,961	24,537	25,083	738	7,241	11,668	4,739	599	97
Male householder [1]	616	1,153	1,709	121	541	649	327	48	23
Female householder [1]	5,445	6,599	7,874	1,003	2,647	3,180	925	96	24
PERCENT DISTRIBUTION									
Family households with children .	**100**	**100**	**100**	**100**	**100**	**100**	**100**	**100**	**100**
Married couple. . . .	81	76	72	40	69	75	79	80	67
Male householder [1]	2	4	5	6	5	4	5	6	16
Female householder [1]	18	20	23	54	25	20	15	13	17
HOUSEHOLDS WITH CHILDREN, AS A PERCENT OF ALL FAMILY HOUSEHOLDS, BY TYPE									
Family households with children, total	**52**	**49**	**49**	**63**	**78**	**81**	**42**	**8**	**1**
Married couple. . . .	51	47	47	55	73	82	41	8	1
Male householder [1]	36	40	44	31	52	65	47	14	6
Female householder [1]	63	61	62	81	94	84	42	9	1

[1] No spouse present.

Source: U.S. Bureau of the Census, *Current Population Reports*, P20-509, and earlier reports; and unpublished data.

No. 84. Children Under 18 Years Old, by Presence of Parents: 1980 to 1997

[As of **March.** Excludes persons under 18 years old who maintained households or family groups. Based on Current Population Survey; see headnote, Table 80]

RACE, HISPANIC ORIGIN, AND YEAR	Number (1,000)	Both parents	PERCENT LIVING WITH—					Father only	Neither parent
			Mother only						
			Total	Divorced	Married, spouse absent	Never married	Wid-owed		
ALL RACES [1]									
1980	63,427	77	18	8	6	3	2	2	4
1985	62,475	74	21	9	5	6	2	3	3
1990	64,137	73	22	8	5	7	2	3	3
1995	70,254	69	23	9	6	8	1	4	4
1997	70,983	68	24	8	5	9	1	4	4
WHITE									
1980	52,242	83	14	7	4	1	2	2	2
1985	50,836	80	16	8	4	2	1	2	2
1990	51,390	79	16	8	4	3	1	3	2
1995	55,327	76	18	8	5	4	1	3	3
1997	55,869	75	18	8	4	5	1	4	3
BLACK									
1980	9,375	42	44	11	16	13	4	2	12
1985	9,479	40	51	11	12	25	3	3	7
1990	10,018	38	51	10	12	27	2	4	8
1995	11,301	33	52	11	11	29	2	4	11
1997	11,369	35	52	9	11	31	1	5	8
HISPANIC [2]									
1980	5,459	75	20	6	8	4	2	2	4
1985	6,057	68	27	7	11	7	2	2	3
1990	7,174	67	27	7	10	8	2	3	3
1995	9,843	63	28	8	9	10	1	4	4
1997	10,526	64	27	7	7	12	1	4	5

[1] Includes other races not shown separately.   [2] Hispanic persons may be of any race.

Source: U.S. Bureau of the Census, *Current Population Reports*, P20-506, and earlier reports; and unpublished data.

No. 85. Living Arrangements of Children Under 18 Years Old Living With One or Both Parents: 1997

[In thousands. As of March. Covers only those persons under 18 years old who are living with one or both parents. Characteristics are shown for the householder or reference person in married-couple situations. See also headnote, Table 80]

CHARACTERISTIC OF PARENT	ALL RACES [1] Total	Living with— Both parents	Mother only	Father only	WHITE Total	Living with— Both parents	Mother only	Father only	BLACK Total	Living with— Both parents	Mother only	Father only	HISPANIC [2] Total	Living with— Both parents	Mother only	Father only
Children under 18 years old	**68,185**	**48,386**	**16,740**	**3,059**	**54,198**	**41,654**	**10,204**	**2,339**	**10,409**	**3,940**	**5,888**	**581**	**10,008**	**6,748**	**2,819**	**441**
Age:																
15 to 24 years old	4,014	1,262	2,527	226	2,664	1,079	1,408	177	1,193	128	1,035	30	936	359	510	68
25 to 29 years old	7,786	4,657	2,717	412	5,765	4,005	1,457	302	1,769	487	1,184	98	1,566	1,023	489	54
30 to 34 years old	13,881	9,564	3,690	626	10,869	8,174	2,221	474	2,241	798	1,339	103	2,417	1,681	624	111
35 to 39 years old	17,641	13,181	3,728	732	14,267	11,379	2,302	586	2,523	1,102	1,302	119	2,225	1,554	586	85
40 to 44 years old	13,849	10,873	2,513	463	11,649	9,571	1,720	358	1,492	733	668	91	1,635	1,233	335	67
45 to 54 years old	9,783	7,881	1,409	493	8,114	6,709	1,006	399	981	595	311	75	1,048	769	232	47
55 to 64 years old	1,023	832	119	73	740	631	73	36	163	89	38	36	159	112	38	8
65 years old and over	208	138	36	34	130	106	18	6	47	7	12	28	22	18	4	-
Educational attainment:																
Less than 9th grade	4,004	2,748	1,047	209	3,272	2,399	710	163	358	110	207	41	2,733	1,947	657	129
9th to 12th grade, no diploma	8,004	4,231	3,232	541	5,747	3,587	1,725	435	1,940	439	1,417	84	2,278	1,336	837	104
High school graduate [3]	22,133	14,653	6,228	1,252	17,176	12,453	3,830	893	4,085	1,553	2,215	316	2,569	1,687	758	125
Some college, no degree or associate degree	18,578	13,054	4,821	703	14,757	11,328	2,885	544	3,057	1,171	1,777	109	1,683	1,163	454	66
Bachelor's degree	10,172	8,852	1,065	255	8,711	7,708	783	220	765	514	228	23	553	442	100	11
Graduate or professional degree	5,293	4,847	347	99	4,535	4,179	272	84	205	153	43	9	191	173	13	5
Employment status: [4]																
In the civilian labor force	57,236	42,510	12,056	2,670	46,429	36,732	7,611	2,085	7,926	3,414	4,035	478	7,632	5,591	1,636	404
Employed	53,989	41,027	10,505	2,456	44,322	35,553	6,840	1,929	6,953	3,194	3,323	436	6,962	5,240	1,360	361
Both parents employed	28,936	28,936	(X)	(X)	25,004	25,004	(X)	(X)	2,415	2,415	(X)	(X)	2,965	2,965	(X)	(X)
Unemployed	3,247	1,483	1,550	214	2,106	1,179	771	157	973	219	712	42	671	351	276	44
Not in the labor force	10,116	5,088	4,663	365	7,060	4,224	2,590	246	2,398	466	1,835	97	2,316	1,101	1,179	37
Family income:																
Under $5,000	2,837	532	2,158	147	1,584	417	1,080	87	1,118	31	1,031	57	587	112	453	21
$5,000 to $9,999	4,648	904	3,451	293	2,936	769	1,977	191	1,498	74	1,329	95	1,184	354	789	42
$10,000 to $14,999	4,561	1,773	2,458	330	3,061	1,415	1,378	268	1,191	203	940	49	1,351	750	481	120
$15,000 to $24,999	8,687	4,723	3,302	663	6,412	3,939	1,979	494	1,866	517	1,200	150	2,221	1,595	533	94
$25,000 to $29,999	4,669	3,137	1,246	286	3,715	2,616	888	211	732	358	319	55	889	677	175	37
$30,000 to $39,999	8,676	6,526	1,693	457	6,978	5,472	1,146	360	1,280	716	485	79	1,258	1,045	164	49
$40,000 to $49,999	7,597	6,282	1,030	285	6,504	5,535	732	237	756	450	277	29	849	734	92	23
$50,000 and over	26,511	24,510	1,403	598	23,006	21,492	1,024	490	1,967	1,591	308	68	1,668	1,481	132	55
Tenure: [5]																
Owned	43,801	36,247	5,982	1,571	37,568	32,088	4,222	1,257	4,104	2,337	1,525	242	4,208	3,469	564	175
Rented	24,384	12,139	10,757	1,488	16,630	9,566	5,982	1,082	6,306	1,602	4,363	340	5,800	3,279	2,255	267

- Represents or rounds to zero. X Not applicable. [1] Includes other races, not shown separately. [2] Persons of Hispanic origin may be of any race. [3] Includes equivalency. [4] Excludes children whose parent is in the Armed Forces. [5] Refers to the tenure of the householder (who may or may not be the child's parent).

Source: U.S. Bureau of the Census, *Current Population Reports*, P20-506; and unpublished data.

No. 86. Grandchildren Living in the Home of Their Grandparents: 1980 to 1997

[In thousands. Except as noted, based on Current Population Survey; see headnote, Table 80]

LIVING ARRANGEMENTS	1980 [1]	1990	1992	1993	1994	1995	1996	1997
Total children under 18 years old. . .	63,369	64,137	65,965	66,893	69,508	70,254	70,908	70,983
Children living in home of grandparents	**2,306**	**3,155**	**3,253**	**3,368**	**3,735**	**3,965**	**4,060**	**3,894**
With parent(s) present	1,318	2,221	2,386	2,351	2,375	2,498	2,629	2,585
Both parents present	310	467	502	475	436	427	467	554
Mother only present	922	1,563	1,740	1,647	1,764	1,876	1,943	1,785
Father only present	86	191	144	229	175	195	220	247
Without parent(s) present	988	935	867	1,017	1,359	1,466	1,431	1,309

[1] Based on census of population.

Source: U.S. Bureau of the Census, *1980 Census of Population*, PC80-2-4B, *Living Arrangements of Children and Adults*, and *Current Population Reports*, P20-506, and earlier reports.

No. 87. Nonfamily Households, by Sex and Age of Householder: 1990 and 1997

[In thousands. As of March. See headnote, Table 80]

ITEM	MALE HOUSEHOLDER					FEMALE HOUSEHOLDER				
	Total	15 to 24 yr. old	25 to 44 yr. old	45 to 64 yr. old	65 yr. old and over	Total	15 to 24 yr. old	25 to 44 yr. old	45 to 64 yr. old	65 yr. old and over
1990, total	**11,606**	**1,236**	**5,780**	**2,536**	**2,053**	**15,651**	**1,032**	**3,697**	**3,545**	**7,377**
One person (living alone).	9,049	674	4,231	2,203	1,943	13,950	536	2,881	3,300	7,233
Nonrelatives present. . . .	2,557	560	1,551	334	112	1,701	497	817	245	143
Never married	5,844	1,175	3,689	696	285	4,382	976	2,406	510	491
Married [1]	1,117	28	513	391	187	794	15	261	320	198
Widowed	1,417	-	29	221	1,166	7,428	4	52	1,333	6,038
Divorced.	3,228	33	1,550	1,229	416	3,046	37	977	1,382	649
1997, total	**13,707**	**1,189**	**6,538**	**3,508**	**2,471**	**17,070**	**1,007**	**3,836**	**4,423**	**7,803**
One person (living alone).	10,442	566	4,615	2,947	2,314	14,961	519	2,893	3,931	7,619
Nonrelatives present. . . .	3,265	625	1,922	562	157	2,110	488	944	493	184
Single (never married). . .	6,820	1,130	4,311	1,012	368	4,869	960	2,563	826	520
Married [1]	1,301	32	609	455	205	889	21	242	404	221
Widowed	1,585	-	26	233	1,326	7,211	7	83	995	6,126
Divorced.	4,000	28	1,590	1,808	573	4,102	19	949	2,198	937

- Represents or rounds to zero. [1] No spouse present.

Source: U.S. Bureau of the Census, *Current Population Reports*, P20-509, and earlier reports.

No. 88. Persons Living Alone, by Sex and Age: 1980 to 1997

[As of March. Based on Current Population Survey; see headnote, Table 80]

SEX AND AGE	NUMBER OF PERSONS (1,000)					PERCENT DISTRIBUTION				
	1980	1985	1990	1995	1997	1980	1985	1990	1995	1997
Both sexes	**18,296**	**20,602**	**22,999**	**24,732**	**25,402**	**100**	**100**	**100**	**100**	**100**
15 to 24 years old	1,726	1,324	1,210	1,196	1,083	9	6	5	5	4
25 to 34 years old	[1]4,729	3,905	3,972	3,653	3,630	[1]26	19	17	15	14
35 to 44 years old	([1])	2,322	3,138	3,663	3,878	([1])	11	14	15	15
45 to 64 years old	4,514	4,939	5,502	6,377	6,877	25	24	24	26	27
65 to 74 years old	3,851	4,130	4,350	4,374	4,361	21	20	19	18	17
75 years old and over	3,477	3,982	4,825	5,470	5,573	19	19	21	22	22
Male	**6,966**	**7,922**	**9,049**	**10,140**	**10,442**	**38**	**39**	**39**	**41**	**41**
15 to 24 years old	947	750	674	623	566	5	4	3	3	2
25 to 34 years old	[1]2,920	2,307	2,395	2,213	2,235	[1]16	11	10	9	9
35 to 44 years old	([1])	1,406	1,836	2,263	2,380	([1])	7	8	9	9
45 to 64 years old	1,613	1,845	2,203	2,787	2,947	9	9	10	11	12
65 to 74 years old	775	868	1,042	1,134	1,178	4	4	5	5	5
75 years old and over	711	746	901	1,120	1,136	4	4	4	5	4
Female	**11,330**	**12,680**	**13,950**	**14,592**	**14,961**	**62**	**62**	**61**	**59**	**59**
15 to 24 years old	779	573	536	572	519	4	3	2	2	2
25 to 34 years old	[1]1,809	1,598	1,578	1,440	1,395	[1]10	8	7	6	5
35 to 44 years old	([1])	916	1,303	1,399	1,498	([1])	4	6	6	6
45 to 64 years old	2,901	3,095	3,300	3,589	3,931	16	15	14	15	15
65 to 74 years old	3,076	3,262	3,309	3,240	3,183	17	16	14	13	13
75 years old and over	2,766	3,236	3,924	4,351	4,436	15	16	17	18	17

[1] Data for persons 35 to 44 years old included with persons 25 to 34 years old.

Source: U.S. Bureau of the Census, *Current Population Reports*, P20-506, and earlier reports; and unpublished data.

No. 89. Religious Bodies—Selected Data

[Includes the self-reported membership of religious bodies with 60,000 or more as reported to the *Yearbook of American and Canadian Churches*. Groups may be excluded if they do not supply information. The data are not standardized so comparisons between groups are difficult. The definition of "church member" is determined by the religious body]

RELIGIOUS BODY	Year reported	Churches reported	Member-ship (1,000)	Pastors serving parishes [1]
African Methodist Episcopal Church [2]	1991	8,000	3,500	(NA)
African Methodist Episcopal Zion Church	1997	3,098	1,252	2,571
American Baptist Churches in the U.S.A.	1996	5,807	1,503	4,323
Armenian Apostolic Church of America	1995	28	180	23
Assemblies of God	1996	11,884	2,468	18,100
Baptist Bible Fellowship International, The	1995	3,600	1,500	(NA)
Baptist General Conference	1996	875	136	(NA)
Baptist Missionary Association of America	1996	1,349	232	1,250
Buddhist [3]	1990	(NA)	401	(NA)
Christian and Missionary Alliance, The	1996	1,850	312	1,578
Christian Brethren (a.k.a. Plymouth Brethren)	1997	1,150	100	(NA)
Christian Church (Disciples of Christ)	1996	3,840	910	3,359
Christian Churches and Churches of Christ	1988	5,579	1,072	5,525
Christian Congregation, Inc., The	1996	1,437	115	1,433
Christian Methodist Episcopal Church	1983	2,340	719	(NA)
Christian Reformed Church in North America	1996	737	202	635
Church of God (Anderson, IN)	1996	2,327	229	2,921
Church of God (Cleveland, TN)	1995	6,060	753	3,121
Church of God in Christ, The	1991	15,300	5,500	28,988
Church of God of Prophecy, The	1996	1,910	70	5,155
Church of Jesus Christ of Latter-day Saints, The	1996	11,000	4,800	(NA)
Church of the Brethren	1996	1,106	142	838
Church of the Nazarene	1996	5,135	608	5,111
Churches of Christ	1996	14,000	2,250	11,000
Community Churches, International Council of	1995	517	250	491
Conservative Baptist Association of America	1992	1,084	200	(NA)
Coptic Orthodox Church	1992	85	180	65
Cumberland Presbyterian Church	1996	774	88	(NA)
Diocese of the Armenian Church of America	1991	72	414	49
Episcopal Church, The	1996	7,415	2,537	8,037
Evangelical Covenant Church, The	1997	615	93	565
Evangelical Free Church of America	1995	1,224	243	1,936
Evangelical Lutheran Church in America	1996	10,936	5,181	9,778
Free Methodist Church of North America	1996	1,050	75	(NA)
Free Will Baptists, National Association of	1996	2,491	210	2,800
Full Gospel Fellowship of Churches & Ministers International	1995	650	195	725
General Association of Regular Baptist Churches	1996	1,440	116	(NA)
General Baptists (General Association of)	1996	830	68	798
General Conference Mennonite Brethren Churches	1996	368	82	590
Grace Gospel Fellowship	1992	128	60	160
Greek Orthodox Archdiocese of North and South America	1997	532	1,950	(NA)
Hindu [3]	1990	(NA)	227	(NA)
Independent Fundamental Churches of America	1995	670	70	(NA)
International Church of the Foursquare Gospel	1996	1,773	230	2,322
International Pentecostal Holiness Church	1996	1,658	164	1,452
Jehovah's Witnesses	1996	10,671	976	(NA)
Jewish [3]	1990	(NA)	3,137	(NA)
Lutheran Church - Missouri Synod, The	1996	6,099	2,601	5,315
Mennonite Church	1996	1,004	91	1,525
Muslim / Islamic [3]	1990	(NA)	527	(NA)
National Association of Congregational Christian Churches	1997	429	69	558
National Baptist Convention of America, Inc.	1987	2,500	3,500	8,000
National Baptist Convention, U.S.A., Inc.	1992	33,000	8,200	32,832
National Missionary Baptist Convention of America	1992	(NA)	2,500	(NA)
Old Order Amish Church	1993	898	81	3,592
Orthodox Church in America	1995	600	2,000	650
Pentecostal Assemblies of the World	1994	1,760	1,000	4,262
Pentecostal Church of God, Inc.	1996	1,230	112	(NA)
Presbyterian Church in America	1995	1,299	268	1,522
Presbyterian Church (U.S.A.)	1996	11,328	3,637	9,532
Progressive National Baptist Convention, Inc.	1995	2,000	2,500	(NA)
Reformed Church in America	1996	909	304	915
Religious Society of Friends (Conservative)	1994	1,200	104	(NA)
Reorganized Church of Jesus Christ of Latter-day Saints	1995	1,160	178	16,671
Roman Catholic Church, The	1996	22,728	61,208	(NA)
Romanian Orthodox Episcopate of America	1996	37	65	37
Salvation Army, The	1995	1,264	453	3,645
Serbian Orthodox Church in the U.S.A. and Canada	1986	68	67	60
Seventh-day Adventist Church	1996	4,363	809	2,337
Southern Baptist Convention	1996	40,565	15,692	37,955
Unitarian Universalist [3]	1990	(NA)	502	(NA)
United Church of Christ	1996	6,110	1,453	4,627
United Methodist Church, The	1996	36,361	8,495	36,666
Wesleyan Church (USA), The	1996	1,580	118	1,800
Wisconsin Evangelical Lutheran Synod	1996	1,235	413	1,217

NA Not available. [1] Does not include retired clergy or clergy not working with congregations. [2] Figures obtained from the *Directory of African American Religious Bodies, 1991.* [3] Figures obtained from the National Survey of Religious Identification, a survey conducted by the City University of New York in 1990 and published in *One Nation Under God: Religion in Contemporary American Society,* by Barry Kosmin and Seymour Lachman (1993).

Source: National Council of the Churches of Christ in the USA, New York, NY, *1998 Yearbook of American and Canadian Churches,* annual (copyright).

Population

No. 90. Religious Preference, Church Membership, and Attendance: 1980 to 1997

[In percent. Covers civilian noninstitutional population, 18 years old and over. Data represent averages of the combined results of several surveys during year or period indicated. Data are subject to sampling variability, see source]

YEAR	RELIGIOUS PREFERENCE					Church/syna-gogue members	Persons attend-ing church/syna-gogue [1]	AGE AND REGION	Church/syna-gogue members, 1997
	Protes-tant	Catho-lic	Jewish	Other	None				
1980	61	28	2	2	7	69	40	18-29 years old. . . .	63
1985	57	28	2	4	9	71	42	30-49 years old. . . .	66
1990	56	25	2	6	11	65	40	50-64 years old. . . .	71
1993	57	26	1	8	[2]8	68	40	65 years and over . .	75
1994	60	24	2	6	[2]8	68	42	East [3]	70
1995	58	25	2	(NA)	(NA)	69	43	Midwest [4]	73
1996	58	25	3	5	[2]9	65	38	South [5]	73
1997	58	26	2	6	[2]8	67	40	West [6]	51

NA Not available. [1] Persons who attended a church or synagogue in the last 7 days. [2] Includes those respondents who did not designate. [3] ME, NH, RI, NY, CT, VT, MA, NJ, PA, WV, DE, MD, and DC. [4] OH, IN, IL, MI, MN, WI, IA, ND, SD, KS, NE, and MO. [5] KY, TN, VA, NC, SC, GA, FL, AL, MS, TX, AR, OK, and LA. [6] AZ, NM, CO, NV, MT, ID, WY, UT, CA, WA, OR, AK, and HI.

Source: Princeton Religion Research Center, Princeton, NJ, *Religion in America*, annual. Based on surveys conducted by the Gallup Organization, Inc.

No. 91. Christian Church Adherents, 1990, and Jewish Population, 1996—States

[Christian church adherents were defined as "all members, including full members, their children and the estimated number of other regular participants who are not considered as communicant, confirmed or full members." Data on Christian church adherents are based on reports of 133 church groupings and exclude 34 church bodies that reported more than 100,000 members to the *Yearbook of American and Canadian Churches*. The Jewish population includes Jews who define themselves as Jewish by religion as well as those who define themselves as Jewish in cultural terms. Data on Jewish population are based primarily on a compilation of individual estimates made by local Jewish federations. Additionally, most large communities have completed Jewish demographic surveys from which the Jewish population can be determined]

REGION, DIVISION, AND STATE	CHRISTIAN ADHERENTS, 1990		JEWISH POPULATION, 1996		REGION, DIVISION, AND STATE	CHRISTIAN ADHERENTS, 1990		JEWISH POPULATION, 1996	
	Number (1,000)	Percent of population [1]	Number (1,000)	Percent of population [1]		Number (1,000)	Percent of population [1]	Number (1,000)	Percent of population [1]
U.S.	**131,084**	**52.7**	**5,900**	**2.2**	MO	2,892	56.6	62	1.2
AL	2,858	70.7	9	0.2	MT	341	42.7	1	0.1
AK	175	31.8	3	0.5	NE	1,000	63.4	7	0.4
AZ	1,505	41.1	72	1.8	NV	366	29.6	21	1.4
AR	1,423	60.5	2	0.1	NH	431	38.9	10	0.8
CA	11,665	39.2	921	2.9	NJ	4,305	55.7	435	5.5
CO	1,244	37.8	52	1.4	NM	883	58.3	9	0.5
CT	1,933	58.9	97	3.0	NY	9,970	55.5	1,652	9.1
DE	297	44.6	14	1.9	NC	3,949	59.6	22	0.3
DC	349	57.5	26	4.6	ND	485	75.9	1	0.1
FL	5,106	39.5	644	4.5	OH	5,313	48.9	129	1.2
GA	3,659	56.5	84	1.2	OK	2,097	66.5	6	0.2
HI	391	35.3	7	0.6	OR	904	31.8	20	0.6
ID	507	50.4	(Z)	0.1	PA	6,960	58.6	325	2.7
IL	6,579	57.5	268	2.3	RI	754	75.1	16	1.6
IN	2,615	47.1	18	0.3	SC	2,149	61.7	9	0.2
IA	1,674	60.3	6	0.2	SD	474	68.1	(Z)	0.1
KS	1,346	54.3	15	0.6	TN	2,968	60.8	18	0.3
KY	2,213	60.1	11	0.3	TX	10,788	63.5	113	0.6
LA	2,959	70.1	17	0.4	UT	1,371	79.6	4	0.2
ME	439	36.1	8	0.6	VT	233	40.4	6	1.0
MD	2,101	43.9	212	4.2	VA	2,898	46.8	75	1.1
MA	3,666	60.9	268	4.4	WA	1,579	32.4	34	0.6
MI	4,580	49.2	107	1.1	WV	740	41.3	2	0.1
MN	2,807	64.2	42	0.9	WI	3,125	63.9	29	0.6
MS	1,804	70.1	1	0.1	WY	216	47.6	(Z)	0.1

Z Fewer than 500. [1] Based on U.S. Bureau of the Census data for resident population enumerated as of April 1, 1990, and estimated as of July 1, 1996.

Source: Christian church adherents—M. Bradley; N. Green, Jr.; D. Jones; M. Lynn; and L. McNeil; *Churches and Church Membership in the United States 1990*, Glenmary Research Center, Atlanta, GA, 1992 (copyright); Jewish population—American Jewish Committee, New York, NY, *American Jewish Year Book, 1996* (copyright).

Vital Statistics

This section presents vital statistics data on births, deaths, abortions, fetal deaths, fertility, life expectancy, marriages, and divorces. Vital statistics are compiled for the country as a whole by the National Center for Health Statistics (NCHS) and published in its annual report, *Vital Statistics of the United States,* in certain reports of the *Vital and Health Statistics* series, and in the *Monthly Vital Statistics Report.* Reports in this field are also issued by the various state bureaus of vital statistics. Data on fertility, on age of persons at first marriage, and on marital status and marital history are compiled by the Bureau of the Census from its Current Population Survey (CPS; see text, Section 1) and published in *Current Population Reports,* P20 series. Data on abortions are published by the Alan Guttmacher Institute, New York, NY, in selected issues of *Family Planning Perspectives.*

Registration of vital events—The registration of births, deaths, fetal deaths, and other vital events in the United States is primarily a state and local function. The civil laws of every state provide for a continuous and permanent birth- and death-registration system. Many states also provide for marriage- and divorce-registration systems. Vital events occurring to U.S. residents outside the United States are not included in the data.

Births and deaths—The live-birth, death, and fetal-death statistics prepared by NCHS are based on vital records filed in the registration offices of all states, of New York City, and of the District of Columbia. The annual collection of death statistics on a national basis began in 1900 with a national death-registration area of 10 states and the District of Columbia; a similar annual collection of birth statistics for a national birth-registration area began in 1915, also with 10 reporting states and the District of Columbia. Since 1933, the birth- and death-registration areas have comprised the entire United States, including Alaska (beginning 1959) and Hawaii (beginning 1960). National statistics on fetal

In Brief		
	1996	
	Number	Rate
Births	*3,915,000*	*14.8*
Deaths	*2,322,000*	*8.8*
Marriages	*1,840,000*	*8.1*
Divorces	*920,000*	*4.2*

deaths were first compiled for 1918 and annually since 1922.

Prior to 1951, birth statistics came from a complete count of records received in the Public Health Service (now received in NCHS). From 1951 through 1971, they were based on a 50-percent sample of all registered births (except for a complete count in 1955 and a 20- to 50-percent sample in 1967). Beginning in 1972, they have been based on a complete count for states participating in the Vital Statistics Cooperative Program (VSCP) (for details, see the technical appendix in *Vital Statistics of the United States*) and on a 50-percent sample of all other areas. Beginning 1986, all reporting areas participated in the VSCP. Mortality data have been based on a complete count of records for each area (except for a 50-percent sample in 1972). Beginning in 1970, births to and deaths of nonresident aliens of the United States and U.S. citizens outside the United States have been excluded from the data. Fetal deaths and deaths among Armed Forces abroad are excluded. Data based on samples are subject to sampling error; for details, see annual issues of *Vital Statistics of the United States.*

Mortality statistics by cause of death are compiled in accordance with World Health Organization regulations according to the *International Classification of Diseases* (ICD). The ICD is revised approximately every 10 years. The ninth revision of the ICD was employed beginning in 1979. Deaths for prior years were classified according to the revision of the ICD in use at the time. Each revision of the ICD introduces a number of discontinuities in mortality statistics; for a discussion of those between the eighth and ninth revisions of the ICD, see *Monthly Vital Statistics Report,* Vol. 28, No. 11, supplement.

Some of the tables present age-adjusted death rates in addition to crude death rates. Age-adjusted death rates shown in this section were prepared using the direct method, in which age-specific death rates for a population of interest are applied to a standard population distributed by age. Age adjustment eliminates the differences in observed rates between points in time or among compared population groups that result from age differences in population composition.

Fertility and life expectancy—The total fertility rate, defined as the number of births that 1,000 women would have in their lifetime if, at each year of age, they experienced the birth rates occurring in the specified year, is compiled and published by NCHS. Other data relating to social and medical factors which affect fertility rates, such as contraceptive use and birth expectations, are collected and made available by both NCHS and the Bureau of the Census. NCHS figures are based on information in birth and fetal death certificates and on the periodic National Surveys of Family Growth; Bureau of the Census data are based on decennial censuses and the CPS.

Data on life expectancy, the average remaining lifetime in years for persons who attain a given age, are computed and published by NCHS. For details, see the technical appendix in *Vital Statistics of the United States.*

Marriage and divorce—The compilation of nationwide statistics on marriages and divorces in the United States began in 1887-88 when the National Office of Vital Statistics prepared estimates for the years 1867-86. Although periodic updates took place after 1888, marriage and divorce statistics were not collected and published annually until 1944 by that office. In 1957 and 1958, respectively, the same office established marriage- and divorce-registration areas. Beginning in 1957, the marriage-registration area comprised 30 states, plus Alaska, Hawaii, Puerto Rico, and the Virgin Islands; it currently includes 42 states

and the District of Columbia. The divorce-registration area, starting in 1958 with 14 states, Alaska, Hawaii, and the Virgin Islands, currently includes a total of 31 states and the Virgin Islands. Procedures for estimating the number of marriages and divorces in the registration states are discussed in *Vital Statistics of the United States,* Vol. III— *Marriage and Divorce.* Total counts of events for registration and nonregistration states are gathered by collecting already summarized data on marriages and divorces reported by state offices of vital statistics and by county offices of registration.

Another important source of data on marriage and divorce trends in the United States is the March supplement to the Current Population Survey conducted by the Bureau of the Census. For information on marital status, see Section 1.

Vital statistics rates—Except as noted, vital statistics rates computed by NCHS are based on decennial census population figures as of April 1 for 1940, 1950, 1960, 1970, 1980, and 1990; and on midyear population figures for other years, as estimated by the Bureau of the Census (see text, Section 1).

Race—Data by race for births, deaths, marriages, and divorces from NCHS are based on information contained in the certificates of registration. The Census Bureau's Current Population Survey obtains information on race by asking respondents to classify their race as: (1) White, (2) Black, (3) American Indian, Eskimo, or Aleut, or (4) Asian or Pacific Islander.

Beginning with the 1989 data year, NCHS is tabulating its birth data primarily by race of the mother. In 1988 and prior years, births were tabulated by the race of the child, which was determined from the race of the parents as entered on the birth certificate.

Trend data by race shown in this section are by race of mother beginning with the 1980 data. Hispanic origin of the mother is reported and tabulated, independently of race. Thus persons of Hispanic origin may be or any race. In 1994, 91 percent of women of Hispanic origin were reported as White.

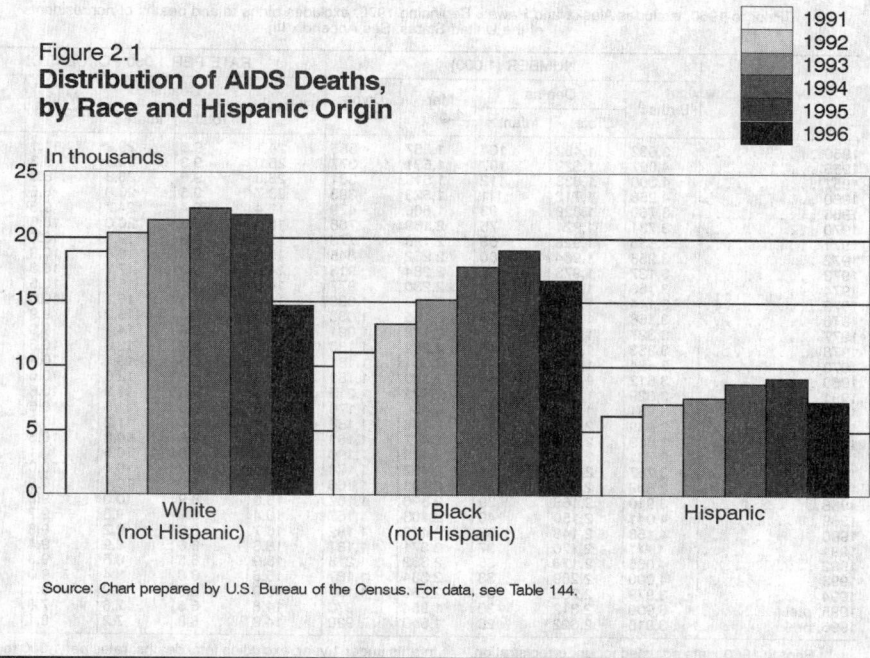

Figure 2.1
**Distribution of AIDS Deaths,
by Race and Hispanic Origin**

In thousands

Legend: 1991, 1992, 1993, 1994, 1995, 1996

White (not Hispanic)   Black (not Hispanic)   Hispanic

Source: Chart prepared by U.S. Bureau of the Census. For data, see Table 144.

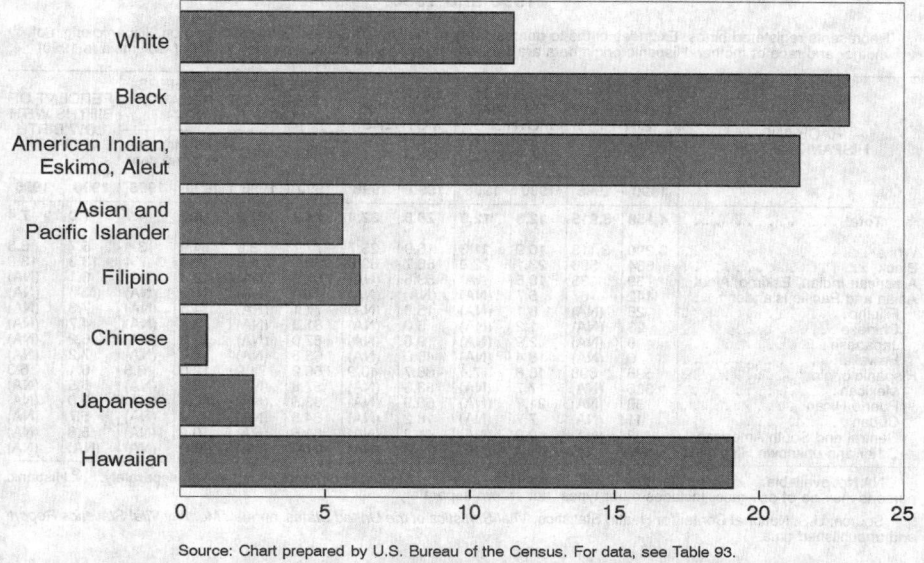

Figure 2.2
**Births to Teenage Mothers as a Percent
of Total Births, by Race: 1995**

White
Black
American Indian, Eskimo, Aleut
Asian and Pacific Islander
Filipino
Chinese
Japanese
Hawaiian

Source: Chart prepared by U.S. Bureau of the Census. For data, see Table 93.

No. 92. Live Births, Deaths, Marriages, and Divorces: 1950 to 1996

[Prior to 1960, excludes Alaska and Hawaii. Beginning 1970, excludes births to and deaths of nonresidents of the United States. See Appendix III]

YEAR	NUMBER (1,000)					RATE PER 1,000 POPULATION				
	Births [1]	Deaths		Mar-riages [3]	Divor-ces [4]	Births [1]	Deaths		Mar-riages [3]	Divor-ces [4]
		Total	Infant [2]				Total	Infant [2]		
1950	3,632	1,452	104	1,667	385	24.1	9.6	29.2	11.1	2.6
1955	4,097	1,529	107	1,531	377	25.0	9.3	26.4	9.3	2.3
1957	4,300	1,633	112	1,518	381	25.3	9.6	26.3	8.9	2.2
1960	4,258	1,712	111	1,523	393	23.7	9.5	26.0	8.5	2.2
1965	3,760	1,828	93	1,800	479	19.4	9.4	24.7	9.3	2.5
1970	3,731	1,921	75	2,159	708	18.4	9.5	20.0	10.6	3.5
1971	3,556	1,928	68	2,190	773	17.2	9.3	19.1	10.6	3.7
1972	3,258	1,964	60	2,282	845	15.6	9.4	18.5	10.9	4.0
1973	3,137	1,973	56	2,284	915	14.8	9.3	17.7	10.8	4.3
1974	3,160	1,934	53	2,230	977	14.8	9.1	16.7	10.5	4.6
1975	3,144	1,893	51	2,153	1,036	14.6	8.8	16.1	10.0	4.8
1976	3,168	1,909	48	2,155	1,083	14.6	8.8	15.2	9.9	5.0
1977	3,327	1,900	47	2,178	1,091	15.1	8.6	14.1	9.9	5.0
1978	3,333	1,928	46	2,282	1,130	15.0	8.7	13.8	10.3	5.1
1979	3,494	1,914	46	2,331	1,181	15.6	8.5	13.1	10.4	5.3
1980	3,612	1,990	46	2,390	1,189	15.9	8.8	12.6	10.6	5.2
1981	3,629	1,978	43	2,422	1,213	15.8	8.6	11.9	10.6	5.3
1982	3,681	1,975	42	2,456	1,170	15.9	8.5	11.5	10.6	5.1
1983	3,639	2,019	41	2,446	1,158	15.6	8.6	11.2	10.5	5.0
1984	3,669	2,039	40	2,477	1,169	15.6	8.6	10.8	10.5	5.0
1985	3,761	2,086	40	2,413	1,190	15.8	8.8	10.6	10.1	5.0
1986	3,757	2,105	39	2,407	1,178	15.6	8.8	10.4	10.0	4.9
1987	3,809	2,123	38	2,403	1,166	15.7	8.8	10.1	9.9	4.8
1988	3,910	2,168	39	2,396	1,167	16.0	8.9	10.0	9.8	4.8
1989	4,041	2,150	40	2,403	1,157	16.4	8.7	9.8	9.7	4.7
1990	4,158	2,148	38	2,443	1,182	16.7	8.6	9.2	9.8	4.7
1991	4,111	2,170	37	2,371	1,187	16.3	8.6	8.9	9.4	4.7
1992	4,065	2,176	35	2,362	1,215	15.9	8.5	8.5	9.3	4.8
1993	4,000	2,269	33	2,334	1,187	15.5	8.8	8.4	9.0	4.6
1994	3,979	2,286	31	2,362	1,191	15.0	8.8	8.0	9.1	4.6
1995, prel.	3,900	2,312	30	1,954	973	14.8	8.8	7.9	7.6	4.1
1996, prel.	3,915	2,322	28	1,840	920	14.8	8.8	7.2	8.1	4.2

[1] Prior to 1960, data adjusted for underregistration. [2] Infants under 1 year, excluding fetal deaths; rates per 1,000 registered live births. [3] Includes estimates for some states through 1965 and also for 1976 and 1977 and marriage licenses for some states for all years except 1973 and 1975. Beginning 1978, includes nonlicensed marriages in California. [4] Includes reported annulments and some estimated state figures for all years.

Source: U.S. National Center for Health Statistics, *Vital Statistics of the United States*, annual, *Monthly Vital Statistics Report*; and unpublished data.

No. 93. Live Births, by Race and Type of Hispanic Origin—Selected Characteristics: 1990 and 1996

[Represents registered births. Excludes births to nonresidents of the United States. Data are based on Hispanic origin of mother and race of mother. Hispanic origin data are available from only 48 states and the District of Columbia in 1990]

RACE AND HISPANIC ORIGIN	NUMBER OF BIRTHS (1,000)		BIRTHS TO TEENAGE MOTHERS, PERCENT OF TOTAL		BIRTHS TO UNMARRIED MOTHERS, PERCENT OF TOTAL		PERCENT OF MOTHERS BEGINNING PRENATAL CARE DURING—				PERCENT OF BIRTHS WITH LOW BIRTH WEIGHT [1]	
							First trimester		Third trimes-ter or no care			
	1990	1996	1990	1996	1990	1996	1990	1996	1990	1996	1990	1996
Total	4,158	3,915	12.8	12.9	26.6	32.4	74.2	81.8	6.0	4.1	7.0	7.4
White	3,290	3,113	10.9	11.3	16.9	25.7	77.7	83.9	4.9	3.4	5.7	6.3
Black	684	596	23.1	22.9	66.7	69.8	60.7	71.3	10.9	7.4	13.3	13.0
American Indian, Eskimo, Aleut	39	38	19.5	(NA)	53.6	(NA)	57.9	(NA)	12.9	(NA)	6.1	(NA)
Asian and Pacific Islander [2]	142	167	5.7	(NA)	(NA)	(NA)	(NA)	(NA)	(NA)	(NA)	(NA)	(NA)
Filipino	26	(NA)	6.1	(NA)	15.9	(NA)	77.1	(NA)	4.5	(NA)	7.3	(NA)
Chinese	23	(NA)	1.2	(NA)	5.0	(NA)	81.3	(NA)	3.4	(NA)	4.7	(NA)
Japanese	9	(NA)	2.9	(NA)	9.6	(NA)	87.0	(NA)	2.9	(NA)	6.2	(NA)
Hawaiian	6	(NA)	18.4	(NA)	45.0	(NA)	65.8	(NA)	8.7	(NA)	7.2	(NA)
Hispanic origin [3]	595	698	16.8	17.4	36.7	40.9	60.2	71.9	12.0	6.8	6.1	6.3
Mexican	386	(NA)	17.7	(NA)	33.3	(NA)	57.8	(NA)	13.2	(NA)	5.5	(NA)
Puerto Rican	59	(NA)	21.7	(NA)	55.9	(NA)	63.5	(NA)	10.6	(NA)	9.0	(NA)
Cuban	11	(NA)	7.7	(NA)	18.2	(NA)	84.8	(NA)	2.8	(NA)	5.7	(NA)
Central and South American	83	(NA)	9.0	(NA)	41.2	(NA)	61.5	(NA)	10.9	(NA)	5.8	(NA)
Other and unknown Hispanic	(NA)	(NA)	(NA)	(NA)	(NA)	(NA)	(NA)	(NA)	(NA)	(NA)	(NA)	(NA)

NA Not available. [1] Births less than 2,500 grams (5 lb.-8 oz.). [2] Includes other races not shown separately. [3] Hispanic persons may be of any race. Includes other types, not shown separately.

Source: U.S. National Center for Health Statistics, *Vital Statistics of the United States*, annual, *Monthly Vital Statistics Report*; and unpublished data.

No. 94. Births and Birth Rates: 1980 to 1996

[Births in thousands. Births by race of child. Excludes births to nonresidents of the United States. For population bases used to derive these data, see text, Section 2, and Appendix III]

ITEM	1980	1985	1988	1989	1990	1991	1992	1993	1994	1995	1996
Live births [1]	3,612	3,761	3,910	4,041	4,158	4,111	4,065	4,000	3,953	3,900	3,915
White	2,936	3,038	3,102	3,192	3,290	3,241	3,202	3,126	3,121	2,753	3,113
Black	568	582	639	673	684	683	674	695	636	394	596
American Indian	29	34	37	39	39	39	39	39	38	26	38
Asian or Pacific Islander	74	105	129	133	142	145	150	153	158	135	167
Male	1,853	1,928	2,002	2,069	2,129	2,102	2,082	2,049	2,023	1,996	(NA)
Female	1,760	1,833	1,907	1,971	2,029	2,009	1,983	1,951	1,930	1,903	(NA)
Males per 100 females	105	105	105	105	105	105	105	105	105	105	(NA)
Age of mother:											
Under 20 years old	562	478	489	518	533	532	518	514	518	512	506
20 to 24 years old	1,226	1,141	1,067	1,078	1,094	1,090	1,070	1,038	1,001	966	951
25 to 29 years old	1,108	1,201	1,239	1,263	1,277	1,220	1,179	1,129	1,089	1,064	1,078
30 to 34 years old	550	696	804	842	886	885	895	901	906	905	904
35 to 39 years old	141	214	270	294	318	331	345	357	372	384	401
40 years old or more	24	29	41	46	50	54	58	61	66	70	75
Birth rate per 1,000 population	15.9	15.8	16.0	16.4	16.7	16.3	15.9	15.5	15.2	14.8	14.8
White	15.1	15.0	15.0	15.4	15.8	15.4	15.0	14.7	14.4	14.2	(NA)
Black	21.3	20.4	21.5	22.3	22.4	21.9	21.3	20.5	19.5	18.2	(NA)
American Indian	20.7	19.8	19.3	19.7	18.9	18.3	18.4	17.8	17.1	16.6	(NA)
Asian or Pacific Islander	19.9	18.7	19.2	18.7	19.0	18.2	18.0	17.7	17.5	17.3	(NA)
Male	16.8	16.7	16.8	17.2	17.6	17.1	16.7	(NA)	(NA)	(NA)	(NA)
Female	15.1	15.0	15.2	15.6	15.9	15.6	15.2	(NA)	(NA)	(NA)	(NA)
Plural birth ratio [2]	19.3	21.0	22.4	23.0	23.3	23.9	24.4	25.2	25.7	26.1	(NA)
White	18.5	20.4	22.0	22.5	22.9	23.4	24.0	24.9	25.5	26.0	(NA)
Black	24.1	25.3	25.8	26.9	27.0	27.8	28.2	28.7	29.4	28.8	(NA)
Fertility rate per 1,000 women [3]	68.4	66.2	67.2	69.2	70.9	69.6	68.9	67.6	66.7	65.6	65.7
White [3]	64.8	64.1	64.5	66.4	68.3	67.0	66.5	65.4	64.9	64.4	64.7
Black [3]	84.7	78.8	82.6	86.2	86.8	85.2	83.2	80.5	76.9	72.3	70.8
American Indian [3]	82.7	78.6	76.8	79.0	76.2	75.1	75.4	73.4	70.9	69.1	69.8
Asian or Pacific Islander [3]	73.2	68.4	70.2	68.2	69.6	67.6	67.2	66.7	66.8	66.4	66.6
Age of mother:											
10 to 14 years old	1.1	1.2	1.3	1.4	1.4	1.4	1.4	1.4	1.4	1.3	1.2
15 to 19 years old	53.0	51.0	53.0	57.3	59.9	62.1	60.7	59.6	58.9	56.8	54.7
20 to 24 years old	115.1	108.3	110.2	113.8	116.5	115.7	114.6	112.6	111.1	109.8	111.1
25 to 29 years old	112.9	111.0	114.4	117.6	120.2	118.2	117.4	115.5	113.9	112.2	113.9
30 to 34 years old	61.9	69.1	74.8	77.4	80.8	79.5	80.2	80.8	81.5	82.5	84.5
35 to 39 years old	19.8	24.0	28.1	29.9	31.7	32.0	32.5	32.9	33.7	34.3	35.4
40 to 44 years old	3.9	4.0	4.8	5.2	5.5	5.5	5.9	6.1	6.4	6.6	6.8
45 to 49 years old	0.2	0.2	0.2	0.2	0.2	0.2	0.3	0.3	0.3	0.3	0.3

NA Not available. [1] Includes other races not shown separately. [2] Number of multiple births per 1,000 live births. [3] Per 1,000 women, 15 to 44 years old in specified group. The rate for *age of mother 45 to 49 years old* computed by relating births to mothers 45 years old and over to women 45 to 49 years old.

Source: U.S. National Center for Health Statistics, *Vital Statistics of the United States,* annual; *Monthly Vital Statistics Report;* and unpublished data.

No. 95. Teenagers—Births and Birth Rates, by Race and Sex: 1980 to 1996

[Birth rates per 1,000 women in specified group, see text, Section 2]

ITEM	1980	1985	1988	1989	1990	1991	1992	1993	1994	1995	1996
NUMBER OF BIRTHS											
All races, total [1]	552,161	467,485	478,353	506,503	521,826	519,577	505,415	501,093	505,488	(NA)	(NA)
15-17 years	198,222	167,789	176,624	181,044	183,327	188,226	187,549	190,535	195,169	(NA)	(NA)
18-19 years	353,939	299,696	301,729	325,459	338,499	331,351	317,866	310,558	310,319	(NA)	(NA)
White	393,564	324,590	323,830	340,472	354,482	352,359	342,739	341,817	348,081	(NA)	(NA)
15-17 years	129,341	107,993	109,739	111,736	114,934	118,809	118,786	121,309	126,388	(NA)	(NA)
18-19 years	264,223	216,597	214,091	228,736	239,548	233,550	223,953	220,508	221,693	(NA)	(NA)
Black	147,378	130,857	140,608	150,699	151,613	150,956	146,800	143,153	140,968	(NA)	(NA)
15-17 years	65,069	55,656	61,856	63,832	62,881	63,571	63,002	63,156	62,563	(NA)	(NA)
18-19 years	82,309	75,201	78,752	86,867	88,732	87,385	83,798	79,997	78,405	(NA)	(NA)
BIRTH RATE											
All races, total [1]	53.0	51.0	53.0	57.3	59.9	62.1	60.7	59.6	58.9	56.8	54.7
15-17 years	32.5	31.0	33.6	36.4	37.5	38.7	37.8	37.8	37.6	36.0	34.0
18-19 years	82.1	79.6	79.9	84.2	88.6	94.4	94.5	92.1	91.5	89.1	86.5
White	45.4	43.3	44.4	47.9	50.8	52.8	51.8	51.1	51.1	50.1	48.4
15-17 years	25.5	24.4	26.0	28.1	29.5	30.7	30.1	30.3	30.7	30.0	28.6
18-19 years	73.2	70.4	69.6	72.9	78.0	83.5	83.8	82.1	82.1	81.2	78.8
Black	97.8	95.4	102.7	111.5	112.8	115.5	112.4	108.6	104.5	96.1	91.7
15-17 years	72.5	69.3	75.7	81.9	82.3	84.1	81.3	79.8	76.3	69.7	64.9
18-19 years	135.1	132.4	142.7	151.9	152.9	158.6	157.9	151.9	148.3	137.1	133.0

[1] Includes races other than White and Black.

Source: U.S. National Center for Health Statistics, *Monthly Vital Statistics Report,* Vol. 45, No. 5, Supplement.

Vital Statistics

No. 96. Live Births, by State: 1995

[Number of births, except rate. Registered births. Excludes births to nonresidents of the United States. By race of mother. See Appendix III]

STATE	All races [1]	WHITE		BLACK		Hispanic [2]	Birth rate [3]	Fertility rate [4]
		Total	Non-Hispanic	Total	Non-Hispanic			
United States	**3,899,589**	**3,098,885**	**2,382,638**	**603,139**	**587,781**	**679,768**	**14.8**	**65.6**
Alabama	60,329	39,759	39,073	19,868	19,830	758	14.2	61.9
Alaska	10,244	7,014	6,581	445	421	574	17.0	73.2
Arizona	72,463	63,777	38,474	2,238	2,166	25,504	17.2	79.5
Arkansas	35,175	26,984	25,962	7,676	7,648	1,004	14.2	65.0
California	552,045	449,889	196,695	40,260	39,284	254,001	17.5	76.6
Colorado	54,332	49,634	38,142	2,619	2,518	11,523	14.5	62.5
Connecticut	44,334	37,643	30,867	5,396	4,974	5,505	13.5	61.0
Delaware	10,266	7,689	7,134	2,362	2,326	585	14.3	61.2
Dist. of Columbia	9,014	2,023	1,354	6,780	6,736	685	16.3	65.3
Florida	188,723	142,326	108,831	42,142	41,191	34,509	13.3	64.9
Georgia	112,282	71,811	66,497	38,462	38,217	5,067	15.6	64.5
Hawaii	18,595	4,968	4,311	564	540	2,029	15.7	72.2
Idaho	18,035	17,477	15,375	74	71	2,040	15.5	70.5
Illinois	185,812	142,225	110,180	37,507	37,308	32,166	15.7	69.3
Indiana	82,835	73,145	70,525	8,737	8,674	2,546	14.3	62.2
Iowa	36,810	34,931	33,463	992	963	1,279	13.0	59.9
Kansas	37,201	33,125	30,010	2,890	2,857	2,828	14.5	66.1
Kentucky	52,377	47,127	46,634	4,784	4,759	493	13.6	59.0
Louisiana	65,641	37,519	36,448	26,844	26,784	1,158	15.1	65.2
Maine	13,896	13,554	13,248	79	66	112	11.2	49.7
Maryland	72,396	46,970	43,477	22,674	22,348	3,155	14.4	60.6
Massachusetts	81,648	70,242	63,067	7,778	6,272	8,109	13.4	57.9
Michigan	134,642	106,509	95,715	25,015	24,679	4,781	14.1	61.3
Minnesota	63,263	56,702	49,834	2,905	2,705	1,915	13.7	60.5
Mississippi	41,344	21,578	21,321	19,244	19,241	220	15.3	66.5
Missouri	73,028	60,720	59,423	11,017	10,990	1,288	13.7	61.5
Montana	11,142	9,858	9,226	40	33	282	12.8	60.2
Nebraska	23,243	21,294	19,289	1,220	1,209	1,615	14.2	64.5
Nevada	25,056	21,567	15,459	1,895	1,863	6,124	16.4	75.2
New Hampshire	14,665	14,386	13,659	89	75	214	12.8	54.2
New Jersey	114,828	87,435	69,375	20,973	19,518	18,835	14.5	64.8
New Mexico	26,920	22,694	9,914	508	473	12,900	16.0	71.6
New York	271,369	199,079	121,349	56,213	49,730	54,193	15.0	66.1
North Carolina	101,592	71,413	67,262	26,909	26,833	4,244	14.1	61.7
North Dakota	8,476	7,634	7,375	70	68	147	13.2	61.3
Ohio	154,064	129,185	126,215	22,802	22,702	2,801	13.8	61.0
Oklahoma	45,672	36,038	33,727	4,497	4,469	2,356	13.9	64.3
Oregon	42,811	39,736	34,781	873	860	5,002	13.6	62.2
Pennsylvania	151,850	126,987	120,544	21,445	21,062	6,572	12.6	57.8
Rhode Island	12,776	11,289	8,256	915	683	1,554	12.9	57.3
South Carolina	50,926	31,875	31,127	18,410	18,393	763	13.9	59.3
South Dakota	10,475	8,693	8,590	100	97	116	14.4	66.9
Tennessee	73,173	55,964	54,875	16,156	16,130	1,111	13.9	60.6
Texas	322,753	275,090	137,816	38,727	38,434	137,131	17.2	74.5
Utah	39,577	37,610	34,496	243	231	3,110	20.3	86.2
Vermont	6,783	6,659	6,268	39	33	27	11.6	50.2
Virginia	92,578	67,450	62,660	21,307	21,209	4,841	14.0	58.6
Washington	77,228	67,306	56,839	2,962	2,757	8,502	14.2	62.1
West Virginia	21,162	20,237	20,162	807	806	90	11.6	52.7
Wisconsin	67,479	58,155	55,365	6,518	6,476	2,856	13.2	58.8
Wyoming	6,261	5,910	5,368	69	69	548	13.0	59.3

[1] Includes other races not shown separately.   [2] Persons of Hispanic origin may be of any race. Births by Hispanic origin of mother.   [3] Per 1,000 estimated population.   [4] Per 1,000 women aged 15-44 years estimated.

Source: U.S. National Center for Health Statistics, *Vital Statistics of the United States*, annual, and *Monthly Vital Statistics Report*.

No. 97. Total Fertility Rate and Intrinsic Rate of Natural Increase: 1960 to 1996

[Based on race of child and registered births only, thru 1979. Beginning 1980, based on race of mother. Beginning 1970, excludes births to nonresidents of United States. The *total fertility rate* is the number of births that 1,000 women would have in their lifetime if, at each year of age, they experienced the birth rates occurring in the specified year. A total fertility rate of 2,110 represents "replacement level" fertility for the total population under current mortality conditions (assuming no net immigration). The *intrinsic rate of natural increase* is the rate that would eventually prevail if a population were to experience, at each year of age, the birth rates and death rates occurring in the specified year and if those rates remained unchanged over a long period of time. Minus sign (-) indicates decrease. See also Appendix III]

ANNUAL AVERAGE AND YEAR	TOTAL FERTILITY RATE			INTRINSIC RATE OF NATURAL INCREASE		
	Total	White	Black and other	Total	White	Black and other
1960-64 ...	3,449	3,326	4,326	18.6	17.1	27.7
1965-69 ...	2,622	2,512	3,362	8.2	6.4	18.6
1970-74 ...	2,094	1,997	2,680	-0.7	-2.5	9.1
1975-79 ...	1,774	1,685	2,270	-6.6	-8.5	3.0
1980-84 ...	1,819	1,731	2,262	-5.4	-7.3	3.0
1985-88 ...	1,870	1,769	2,339	-4.2	-6.3	4.3
1970	2,480	2,385	3,067	6.0	4.5	14.4
1971	2,267	2,161	2,920	2.6	0.8	12.6
1972	2,010	1,907	2,628	-2.0	-3.9	8.6
1973	1,879	1,783	2,443	-4.5	-6.5	5.7
1974	1,835	1,749	2,339	-5.4	-7.2	4.0
1975	1,774	1,686	2,276	-6.7	-8.6	3.0
1976	1,738	1,652	2,223	-7.4	-9.3	2.1
1977	1,790	1,703	2,279	-6.2	-8.1	3.2
1978	1,760	1,668	2,265	-6.8	-8.8	2.9
1979	1,808	1,716	2,310	-5.7	-7.7	3.8
1980	1,840	1,773	2,177	-5.1	-7.0	4.0
1981	1,812	1,748	2,118	-5.6	-7.4	3.0
1982	1,828	1,767	2,107	-5.2	-7.0	3.0
1983	1,799	1,741	2,066	-5.8	-7.5	2.2
1984	1,807	1,749	2,071	-5.6	-7.3	2.1
1985	1,844	1,787	2,109	-4.8	-6.5	2.7
1986	1,838	1,776	2,136	-4.9	-6.7	2.8
1987	1,872	1,805	2,198	-4.1	-6.1	4.0
1988	1,934	1,857	2,298	-2.9	-5.1	5.7
1989	2,014	1,931	2,433	-1.4	-3.6	7.4
1990	2,081	2,003	2,480	-0.1	-2.3	8.3
1991	2,073	1,996	2,480	-0.2	-2.4	8.2
1992	2,065	1,994	2,442	-0.4	-2.5	7.5
1993	2,046	1,982	2,385	-0.7	-1.9	3.7
1994	2,036	1,985	2,300	(NA)	(NA)	(NA)
1995	2,019	1,989	2,175	(NA)	(NA)	(NA)
1996	2,040	2,019	2,149	(NA)	(NA)	(NA)

NA Not available.

Source: U.S. National Center for Health Statistics, *Vital Statistics of the United States*, annual; and unpublished data.

No. 98. Projected Fertility Rates, by Race and Age Group: 1997 and 2010

[For definition of total fertility rate, see headnote, Table 97. Birth rates represent live births per 1,000 women in age group indicated. Projections are based on middle fertility assumptions. For explanations of methodology, see text, Section 1]

AGE GROUP	ALL RACES [1]		WHITE		BLACK		AMERICAN INDIAN, ESKIMO, ALEUT		ASIAN AND PACIFIC ISLANDER		HISPANIC [2]	
	1997	2010	1997	2010	1997	2010	1997	2010	1997	2010	1997	2010
Total fertility rate ..	2,063	2,108	1,992	2,046	2,428	2,438	2,153	2,159	1,952	1,954	2,977	2,977
Birth rates:												
10 to 14 years old. ...	1.4	1.6	0.8	0.9	4.8	4.8	1.7	1.7	0.9	0.8	2.6	2.6
15 to 19 years old. ...	59.6	63.6	50.9	56.0	110.1	111.5	78.4	81.8	28.1	28.7	103.7	103.7
20 to 24 years old. ...	115.9	118.2	109.5	112.6	157.7	158.7	143.4	143.7	80.0	79.5	184.7	184.1
25 to 29 years old. ...	118.1	119.5	119.0	120.7	112.6	113.1	108.8	109.0	121.6	121.7	152.4	152.4
30 to 34 years old. ...	78.8	81.0	79.8	82.0	66.5	67.8	61.7	62.9	100.7	101.1	96.7	96.7
35 to 39 years old. ...	31.6	32.1	31.5	31.7	27.7	27.7	27.4	27.4	47.9	47.3	45.3	45.3
40 to 44 years old. ...	5.6	5.9	5.4	5.6	5.4	5.3	6.0	6.0	10.4	10.3	10.8	10.8
45 to 49 years old. ...	0.3	0.3	0.2	0.2	0.5	0.5	0.3	0.3	1.0	1.0	0.6	0.6

[1] Includes other races not shown separately. [2] Persons of Hispanic origin may be of any race.

Source: U.S. Bureau of the Census, *Current Population Reports*, P25-1130.

No. 99. Birth Rates, by Live-Birth Order and Race: 1980 to 1996

[**Births per 1,000 women 15 to 44 years old in specified racial group.** Live-birth order refers to number of children born alive. Figures for births of order not stated are distributed. See also headnote, Table 94]

LIVE-BIRTH ORDER	ALL RACES [1]					WHITE					BLACK				
	1980	1990	1994	1995	1996	1980	1990	1994	1995	1996	1980	1990	1994	1995	1996
Total	68.4	70.9	66.7	65.6	65.7	65.6	68.3	64.9	64.4	64.7	84.9	86.8	76.9	72.3	70.8
First birth	29.5	29.0	27.5	27.3	27.0	28.8	28.4	27.0	26.9	26.7	33.7	32.4	29.8	28.7	27.6
Second birth	21.8	22.8	21.5	21.1	21.3	21.3	22.4	21.4	21.1	21.4	24.7	25.6	22.2	20.7	20.6
Third birth	10.3	11.7	10.7	10.5	10.6	9.6	11.1	10.4	10.3	10.4	14.0	15.6	13.1	12.0	12.0
Fourth birth [2]	3.9	4.5	4.2	4.0	6.8	3.4	4.0	3.8	3.8	6.1	6.5	7.4	6.3	5.7	10.6
Fifth birth	1.5	1.7	1.6	1.5	(NA)	1.3	1.4	1.3	1.3	(NA)	2.9	3.2	2.9	2.6	(NA)
Sixth and seventh	1.0	1.0	1.0	0.9	(NA)	0.8	0.8	0.8	0.7	(NA)	2.1	2.0	2.0	1.8	(NA)
Eighth and over	0.4	0.3	0.3	0.3	(NA)	0.3	0.2	0.2	0.2	(NA)	0.9	0.5	0.6	0.6	(NA)

NA Not available. [1] Includes other races not shown separately. [2] 1996 data represents 'fourth child and over'.

Source: U.S. National Center for Health Statistics, *Vital Statistics of the United States*, annual; and *Monthly Vital Statistics Reports*.

No. 100. Births to Teens, Unmarried Mothers, and Prenatal Care: 1985 to 1995

[In percent. Represents registered births. See headnote, Table 93]

CHARACTERISTIC	1985	1990	1991	1992	1993	1994	1995
Percent of births to teenage mothers . .	12.7	12.8	12.9	12.7	12.8	13.1	13.1
White	10.8	10.9	11.0	10.9	11.0	11.3	11.5
Black	23.0	23.1	23.1	22.7	22.7	23.2	23.1
American Indian, Eskimo, Aleut.	19.1	19.5	20.3	20.0	20.3	21.0	21.4
Asian and Pacific Islander [1]	5.5	5.7	5.8	5.6	5.7	5.7	5.6
Filipino	5.8	6.1	6.1	5.6	5.8	6.0	6.2
Chinese.	1.1	1.2	1.1	1.0	1.0	1.0	0.9
Japanese.	2.9	2.9	2.7	2.6	2.7	2.8	2.5
Hawaiian.	15.9	18.4	18.1	18.4	18.5	19.6	19.1
Other . . . . . [2]	(NA)	(NA)	(NA)	(NA)	6.5	6.4	6.3
Hispanic origin [2]	16.5	16.8	17.2	17.1	17.4	17.8	17.9
Mexican	17.5	17.7	18.1	18.0	18.2	18.6	18.8
Puerto Rican	20.9	21.7	21.7	21.4	22.3	23.2	23.5
Cuban.	7.1	7.7	7.1	7.1	6.8	7.3	7.7
Central and South American	8.2	9.0	9.4	9.6	9.9	10.4	10.6
Other and unknown Hispanic.	(NA)	(NA)	(NA)	(NA)	21.0	20.8	20.1
Percent births to unmarried mothers . . .	22.0	26.6	28.0	30.1	31.0	32.6	32.2
White	14.5	16.9	18.0	22.6	23.6	25.4	25.3
Black	60.1	66.7	68.2	68.1	68.7	70.4	69.9
American Indian, Eskimo, Aleut.	40.7	53.6	55.3	55.3	55.8	57.0	57.2
Asian and Pacific Islander [1]	10.1	(NA)	(NA)	14.7	15.7	16.2	16.3
Filipino	12.1	15.9	16.8	16.8	17.7	18.5	19.5
Chinese.	3.7	5.0	5.5	6.1	6.7	7.2	7.9
Japanese.	7.9	9.6	9.8	9.8	10.0	11.2	10.8
Hawaiian.	(NA)	45.0	45.0	45.7	47.8	48.6	49.0
Hispanic origin [2].	29.5	36.7	38.5	39.1	40.0	43.1	40.8
Mexican	25.7	33.3	35.3	36.3	37.0	40.8	38.1
Puerto Rican	51.1	55.9	57.5	57.5	59.4	60.2	60.0
Cuban.	16.1	18.2	19.5	20.2	21.0	22.9	23.8
Central and South American	34.9	41.2	43.1	43.9	45.2	45.9	44.1
Percent of mothers beginning prenatal care 1st trimester	76.2	74.2	76.2	77.7	78.9	80.2	81.3
White	79.4	77.7	79.5	80.8	81.8	82.8	83.6
Black	61.8	60.7	61.9	63.9	66.0	68.3	70.4
American Indian, Eskimo, Aleut.	60.3	57.9	59.9	62.1	63.4	65.2	66.7
Asian and Pacific Islander [1]	75.0	(NA)	(NA)	76.6	77.6	79.7	79.9
Filipino	77.2	77.1	77.1	78.7	79.3	81.3	80.9
Chinese.	82.4	81.3	82.3	83.8	84.6	86.2	85.7
Japanese.	85.8	87.0	87.7	88.2	87.2	89.2	89.7
Hawaiian.	(NA)	65.8	68.1	69.9	70.6	77.0	75.9
Hispanic origin [2].	61.2	60.2	61.0	64.2	66.6	68.9	70.8
Mexican	59.9	57.8	58.7	62.1	64.8	67.3	69.1
Puerto Rican	58.3	63.5	65.0	67.8	70.0	71.7	74.0
Cuban.	82.5	84.8	85.4	86.8	88.9	90.1	89.2
Central and South American	60.6	61.5	63.4	66.8	68.7	71.2	73.2
Percent of mothers beginning prenatal care 3d trimester or no care.	5.7	6.0	5.8	5.2	4.8	4.4	4.2
White	4.7	4.9	4.7	4.2	3.9	3.6	3.5
Black	10.0	10.9	10.7	9.9	9.0	8.2	7.6
American Indian, Eskimo, Aleut.	11.5	12.9	12.2	11.0	10.3	9.8	9.5
Asian and Pacific Islander [1]	6.1	(NA)	(NA)	4.9	4.6	4.1	4.3
Filipino	4.6	4.5	5.0	4.3	4.0	3.6	4.1
Chinese.	4.2	3.4	3.4	2.9	2.9	2.7	3.0
Japanese.	2.6	2.9	2.5	2.4	2.8	1.9	2.3
Hawaiian.	(NA)	8.7	7.5	7.0	6.7	4.7	5.1
Hispanic origin [2].	12.5	12.0	11.0	9.5	8.8	7.6	7.4
Mexican	12.9	13.2	12.2	10.5	9.7	8.3	8.1
Puerto Rican	15.5	10.6	9.1	8.0	7.1	6.5	5.5
Cuban.	3.7	2.8	2.4	2.1	1.8	1.6	2.1
Central and South American	12.5	10.9	9.5	7.9	7.3	6.5	6.1
Percent of births with low birth weight [3] .	6.8	7.0	7.1	7.1	7.2	7.3	7.3
White	5.6	5.7	5.8	5.8	6.0	6.1	6.2
Black	12.4	13.3	13.6	13.3	13.3	13.2	13.1
American Indian, Eskimo, Aleut.	5.9	6.1	6.2	6.2	6.4	6.4	6.6
Asian and Pacific Islander [1]	6.1	(NA)	(NA)	6.6	6.6	6.8	6.9
Filipino	6.9	7.3	7.3	7.4	7.0	7.8	7.8
Chinese.	5.0	4.7	5.1	5.0	4.9	4.8	5.3
Japanese.	5.9	6.2	5.9	7.0	6.5	6.9	7.3
Hawaiian.	6.4	7.2	6.7	6.9	6.8	7.2	6.8
Hispanic origin [2].	6.2	6.1	6.1	6.1	6.2	6.2	6.3
Mexican	5.8	5.5	5.6	5.6	5.8	5.8	5.8
Puerto Rican	8.7	9.0	9.4	9.2	9.2	9.1	9.4
Cuban.	6.0	5.7	5.6	6.1	6.2	6.3	6.5
Central and South American	5.7	5.8	5.9	5.8	5.9	6.0	6.2

NA Not available.   [1] Includes other races not shown separately.   [2] Hispanic persons may be of any race. Includes other types, not shown separately.   [3] Births less than 2,500 grams (5 lb.-8 oz.).

Source: U.S. National Center for Health Statistics, *Vital Statistics of the United States*, annual; and *Monthly Vital Statistics Reports*.

No. 101. Births to Unmarried Women, by Race of Child and Age of Mother: 1980 to 1995

[Excludes births to nonresidents of United States. Marital status is inferred from a comparison of the child's and parents' surnames on the birth certificate for those states that do not report on marital status. No estimates included for misstatements on birth records or failures to register births. See also Appendix III]

RACE OF CHILD AND AGE OF MOTHER	1980	1990	1993	1994	1995	RACE OF CHILD AND AGE OF MOTHER	1980	1990	1993	1994	1995
NUMBER (1,000)						20 to 24 years	35.6	34.7	35.4	34.8	34.5
Total live births [1]	**666**	**1,165**	**1,240**	**1,290**	**1,254**	25 to 29 years	15.0	19.7	18.9	18.4	18.2
White	320	647	742	794	785	30 to 34 years	6.2	10.1	10.7	10.6	10.6
Black	326	473	452	448	421	35 years and over	2.4	4.5	5.4	5.6	5.8
Under 15 years	9	11	11	12	11	AS PERCENT OF ALL BIRTHS IN RACIAL GROUPS					
15 to 19 years	263	350	357	381	376						
20 to 24 years	237	404	439	449	432	**Total** [1]	**18.4**	**28.0**	**31.0**	**32.6**	**32.2**
25 to 29 years	100	230	234	238	229	White	11.0	20.1	23.6	25.4	25.3
30 to 34 years	41	118	132	137	133	Black	55.2	65.2	68.7	70.4	69.9
35 years and over	16	53	67	72	73	BIRTH RATE [2]					
PERCENT DISTRIBUTION						**Total** [1][3]	**29.4**	**43.8**	**45.3**	**46.9**	**45.1**
						White [3]	17.6	31.8	35.9	38.3	37.5
Total [1]	**100.0**	**100.0**	**100.0**	**100.0**	**100.0**	Black [3]	82.9	93.9	84.0	82.1	75.9
White	48.1	55.6	59.8	61.6	62.6	15 to 19 years	27.6	42.5	44.5	46.4	44.4
Black	48.9	40.6	36.5	34.8	33.6	20 to 24 years	40.9	65.1	69.2	72.2	70.3
Under 15 years	1.4	0.9	0.9	0.9	0.9	25 to 29 years	34.0	56.0	57.1	59.0	56.1
15 to 19 years	39.5	30.0	28.8	29.6	30.0	30 to 34 years	21.1	37.6	38.5	40.1	39.6

[1] Includes other races not shown separately.   [2] Rate per 1,000 unmarried women (never-married, widowed, and divorced) estimated as of July 1.   [3] Covers women aged 15 to 44 years.

Source: U.S. National Center for Health Statistics, *Vital Statistics of the United States*, annual; *Monthly Vital Statistics Report*; and unpublished data.

No. 102. Live Births by Plurality of Birth and Ratios, and Race of Mother: 1994 and 1995

PLURALITY AND RACE OF MOTHER	1994	1995—AGE OF MOTHER								
		All ages	Under 15 yrs.	15 to 19 yrs.	20 to 24 yrs.	25 to 29 yrs.	30 to 34 yrs.	35 to 39 yrs.	40 to 44 yrs.	45 to 49 yrs.
NUMBER										
Live births, total [1]	3,952,767	3,899,589	12,242	499,873	965,547	1,063,539	904,666	383,745	67,250	2,727
White	3,121,004	3,098,885	5,854	349,635	743,123	873,022	754,662	316,166	54,232	2,191
Black	636,391	603,139	5,927	133,694	183,435	133,535	96,084	42,507	7,702	255
Live births in single deliveries [1]	3,851,109	3,797,880	12,097	492,655	945,971	1,035,896	875,002	368,957	64,893	2,409
White	3,041,559	3,018,184	5,784	345,108	729,224	850,825	729,562	303,608	52,182	1,891
Black	617,689	585,787	5,858	131,231	178,299	129,068	92,577	40,985	7,518	251
Live births in twin deliveries [1]	97,064	96,736	142	7,131	19,235	26,385	27,699	13,693	2,173	278
White	75,318	76,196	70	4,472	13,631	21,062	23,259	11,548	1,894	260
Black	18,344	17,000	66	2,431	5,072	4,367	3,423	1,472	165	4
Live births in higher-order multiple deliveries [1][2] . . .	4,594	4,973	3	87	341	1,258	1,965	1,095	184	40
White	4,127	4,505	-	55	268	1,135	1,841	1,010	156	40
Black	358	352	3	32	64	100	84	50	19	-
RATIO PER 1,000 LIVE BIRTHS										
All multiple births [1]	25.7	26.1	11.8	14.4	20.3	26.0	32.8	38.5	35.0	116.6
White	25.5	26.0	12.0	12.9	18.7	25.4	33.3	39.7	37.8	136.9
Black	29.4	28.8	11.6	18.4	28.0	33.5	36.5	35.8	23.9	(B)
Twin births [1]	24.6	24.8	11.6	14.3	19.9	24.8	30.6	35.7	32.3	101.9
White	24.1	24.6	12.0	12.8	18.3	24.1	30.8	36.5	34.9	118.7
Black	28.8	28.2	11.1	18.2	27.7	32.7	35.6	34.6	21.4	(B)
RATIO PER 100,000 LIVE BIRTHS										
Higher-order multiple births [1][2]	116.2	127.5	(B)	17.4	35.3	118.3	217.2	285.3	273.6	1,466.8
White	132.2	145.4	(B)	15.7	36.1	130.0	244.0	319.5	287.7	1,825.7
Black	56.3	58.4	(B)	23.9	34.9	74.9	87.4	117.6	(B)	(B)

- Represents or rounds to zero.   B Does not meet standard of reliability or precision.   [1] Includes races other than White and Black.   [2] Births is greater than twin deliveries.

Source: U.S. National Center for Health Statistics, Advance Report of Final Natality Statistics, *Monthly Vital Statistics Report*.

Vital Statistics

No. 103. Low Birth Weight and Births to Teenage Mothers and to Unmarried Women—States: 1990 to 1996

[Represents registered births. Excludes births to nonresidents of the United States. Based on 100 percent of births in all states and the District of Columbia. See Appendix III]

STATE	PERCENT OF BIRTHS WITH LOW BIRTH WEIGHT[1]			BIRTHS TO TEENAGE MOTHERS, PERCENT OF TOTAL			BIRTHS TO UNMARRIED WOMEN, PERCENT OF TOTAL		
	1990	1995	1996	1990	1995	1996	1990	1995	1996
U.S.	7.0	7.3	7.4	12.8	13.1	12.9	28.0	32.2	32.4
AL................	8.4	9.0	9.3	18.2	18.5	18.3	30.1	34.5	33.5
AK................	4.8	5.3	5.5	9.7	11.2	11.2	26.2	29.9	31.3
AZ................	6.4	6.8	6.6	14.2	15.1	15.0	32.7	38.2	39.0
AR................	8.2	8.2	8.5	19.7	19.6	19.8	[2]29.4	32.9	33.9
CA................	5.8	6.1	6.0	11.6	12.4	12.0	[2]31.6	32.1	31.6
CO................	8.0	8.4	8.8	11.3	12.1	11.9	21.2	24.9	24.8
CT................	6.6	7.1	7.2	8.2	8.6	8.2	[2]26.6	30.6	31.3
DE................	7.6	8.4	8.5	11.9	13.2	13.7	29.0	34.9	35.5
DC................	15.1	13.4	14.2	17.8	16.3	16.8	64.9	65.8	66.0
FL................	7.4	7.7	7.9	13.9	13.7	13.4	31.7	35.8	36.0
GA................	8.7	8.8	8.5	16.7	16.3	15.9	32.8	35.2	35.0
HI................	7.1	7.0	7.3	10.5	10.1	10.3	24.8	29.2	30.2
ID................	5.7	5.9	5.7	12.3	14.0	13.5	16.7	19.9	21.3
IL................	7.6	7.9	8.0	13.1	12.9	12.7	31.7	33.8	33.7
IN................	6.6	7.5	7.7	14.5	14.7	14.5	26.2	31.9	32.6
IA................	5.4	6.0	6.4	10.2	11.0	11.0	21.0	25.2	26.3
KS................	6.2	6.4	6.9	12.3	13.1	13.1	21.5	25.9	26.9
KY................	7.1	7.6	7.8	17.5	17.2	17.0	23.6	28.5	29.8
LA................	9.2	9.7	9.8	17.6	19.1	18.9	36.8	42.4	43.4
ME................	5.1	6.1	5.9	10.8	10.3	9.7	22.6	27.8	28.7
MD................	7.8	8.5	8.5	10.5	10.3	10.3	[2]29.6	33.3	33.4
MA................	5.9	6.3	6.3	8.0	7.5	7.3	24.7	25.6	25.6
MI................	7.6	7.7	7.6	13.5	12.5	12.2	[2]26.2	34.3	33.8
MN................	5.1	5.9	5.8	8.0	8.4	8.5	20.9	23.9	24.4
MS................	9.6	9.8	9.9	21.3	22.2	21.3	40.5	45.3	45.1
MO................	7.1	7.6	7.5	14.4	14.4	14.4	28.6	32.1	33.1
MT................	6.2	5.8	6.4	11.5	12.6	12.5	[2]23.7	26.5	27.8
NE................	5.3	6.3	6.3	9.8	10.0	10.6	20.7	24.3	24.7
NV................	7.2	7.4	7.5	12.6	13.7	13.3	[2]25.4	42.0	42.7
NH................	4.9	5.5	4.8	7.2	7.6	7.4	16.9	22.2	23.4
NJ................	7.0	7.6	7.6	8.4	8.2	7.7	24.3	27.6	27.9
NM................	7.4	7.5	7.5	16.3	18.4	17.9	35.4	42.6	42.1
NY................	7.6	7.6	7.6	9.1	9.3	9.2	[2]33.0	37.9	38.8
NC................	8.0	8.7	8.7	16.2	15.2	15.0	29.4	31.4	32.0
ND................	5.5	5.3	5.7	8.6	9.6	9.6	18.4	23.5	25.2
OH................	7.1	7.6	7.3	13.8	13.7	13.3	[2]28.9	33.0	32.9
OK................	6.6	7.0	7.4	16.2	17.1	17.2	25.2	30.5	30.9
OR................	5.0	5.5	5.3	12.0	13.0	13.2	25.7	28.9	29.7
PA................	7.1	7.4	7.5	10.9	10.8	10.6	28.6	32.4	32.3
RI................	6.2	6.8	6.9	10.5	10.1	10.3	26.3	31.1	32.9
SC................	8.7	9.3	9.2	17.1	17.3	16.8	32.7	37.4	37.2
SD................	5.1	5.6	5.8	10.8	11.4	11.5	22.9	28.0	29.5
TN................	8.2	8.7	8.8	17.6	16.9	16.8	30.2	33.1	33.4
TX................	6.9	7.1	7.2	15.6	16.6	16.2	[2]17.5	30.0	30.5
UT................	5.7	6.3	6.5	10.3	10.8	10.6	13.5	15.7	16.0
VT................	5.3	5.4	6.2	8.5	8.2	8.9	20.1	24.9	26.4
VA................	7.2	7.7	7.7	11.7	11.4	11.0	26.0	29.3	28.8
WA................	5.3	5.5	5.6	10.8	11.5	11.3	23.7	26.7	27.3
WV................	7.1	7.9	7.9	17.8	17.2	16.8	25.4	30.5	31.4
WI................	5.9	6.0	6.2	10.2	10.5	10.6	24.2	27.4	27.4
WY................	7.4	7.4	8.4	13.6	15.2	14.4	19.8	26.4	27.0

[1] Less than 2,500 grams (5 pounds-8 ounces).   [2] Marital status of mother is inferred.

Source: U.S. National Center for Health Statistics, *Vital Statistics of the United States,* annual; and *Monthly Vital Statistics Report.*

No. 104. Live Births, by Place of Delivery, Median and Low Birth Weight, and Prenatal Care: 1980 to 1995

[Represents registered births. Excludes births to nonresidents of the United States. For total number of births, see Table 94. See Appendix III]

ITEM	1980	1985	1990	1992	1993	1994	1995
Births attended (1,000):							
In hospital [1]	3,576	3,722	4,110	4,022	3,959	3,912	3,861
By physician, not in hospital	12	10	14	10	8	7	6
By midwife and other, not in hospital [2]	24	29	21	21	20	21	21
Median birth weight [3]	7 lb.-7 oz.	7 lb.-7 oz.	7 lb.-7 oz.	7 lb.-7 oz.	7 lb.-7 oz.	(NA)	(NA)
Percent of births with low birth weight	6.8	6.8	7.0	7.1	7.2	7.3	7.3
White	5.7	5.6	5.7	5.8	6.0	6.1	6.2
Black	12.5	12.4	13.3	13.3	13.3	13.2	13.1
Percent of births by period in which prenatal care began:							
1st trimester	76.3	76.2	74.2	77.7	78.9	80.2	81.3
3d trimester or no prenatal care	5.1	5.7	6.0	5.2	4.8	4.4	4.2

NA Not available. [1] Includes all births in hospitals or institutions and in clinics. [2] Includes births with attendant not specified. [3] Beginning 1990, median birth weight based on race of mother; prior to 1990, based on race of child.

No. 105. Cesarean Section Deliveries, by Age of Mother: 1990 to 1995

[In thousands, except rate. 1990 excludes data for Oklahoma, which did not report method of delivery on the birth certificate]

AGE OF MOTHER	1990	1994	1995	AGE OF MOTHER	1990	1994	1995
Births by method of delivery	4,111	3,953	3,900	Black births by method of delivery	679	636	603
Vaginal	3,111	3,088	3,064	Vaginal	517	494	469
After previous cesarean	84	110	112	Cesarean deliveries	146	138	130
Cesarean deliveries	914	831	807	RATE			
Primary	575	521	510				
Repeat	339	310	297	Cesarean delivery rate [1]	23	21	21
White births by method of delivery	3,252	3,121	3,099	Primary [2]	16	15	15
Vaginal	2,215	2,436	2,435	Rate of vaginal cesarean birth after previous cesarean [3]	19	26	28
Cesarean deliveries	733	656	640				

[1] Percent of all live births by cesarean delivery. [2] Number of primary cesareans per 100 live births to women who have not had a previous cesarean. [3] Number of vaginal births after previous cesarean delivery per 100 live births to women with a previous cesarean delivery.

No. 106. Live Births and Births to Teen Mothers—20 Largest Metro Areas: 1993

[Excludes births to nonresidents of the United States. Data are by place of residence. Metropolitan statistical areas (MSAs), consolidated metropolitan statistical areas (CMSAs), and New England County Metropolitan Areas (NECMAs) are defined by the U.S. Office of Management and Budget as of June 30, 1990. See Appendix II for definitions and components]

METROPOLITAN AREA	ALL BIRTHS		BIRTHS TO TEENS	
	Number	Rate per 1,000 population	Number of teen births	Percent of total births
New York-Northern New Jersey-Long Island, NY-NJ-CT-PA CMSA/NECMA	290,532	16	22,950	8
Los Angeles-Anaheim-Riverside, CA CMSA	310,792	20	36,390	12
Chicago-Gary-Lake County, IL-IN-WI CMSA	146,678	18	17,688	12
Washington, DC-MD-VA MSA	66,625	16	5,262	8
San Francisco-Oakland-San Jose, CA CMSA	101,011	16	8,753	9
Philadelphia-Wilmington-Trenton, PA-NJ-DE-MD CMSA	89,732	15	9,609	11
Boston-Lawrence-Salem-Lowell-Brockton, MA NECMA	54,291	14	3,402	6
Detroit-Ann Arbor, MI CMSA	72,354	15	8,347	12
Dallas-Fort Worth, TX CMSA	73,645	18	9,788	13
Houston-Galveston-Brazoria, TX CMSA	74,277	19	10,226	14
Miami-Fort Lauderdale, FL CMSA	52,393	16	5,476	10
Seattle-Tacoma, WA CMSA	40,565	15	3,458	9
Atlanta, GA MSA	51,280	17	5,955	12
Cleveland-Akron-Lorain, OH CMSA	40,822	15	4,891	12
Minneapolis-St.Paul, MN-WI MSA	40,314	16	2,972	7
San Diego, CA MSA	48,935	19	5,207	11
St. Louis, MO-IL MSA	38,042	15	4,953	13
Pittsburgh-Beaver Valley, PA CMSA	27,177	12	2,548	9
Phoenix, AZ MSA	40,406	18	5,643	14
Tampa-St. Petersburg-Clearwater, FL MSA	27,658	13	3,653	13
Baltimore, MD MSA	36,237	15	4,028	11
Denver-Boulder, CO CMSA	31,139	16	3,330	11
Cinncinati-Hamilton, OH-KY-IN CMSA	27,104	15	3,611	13
Milwaukee-Racine, WI CMSA	25,099	15	3,235	13
Kansas City, MO-KS MSA	24,787	15	3,011	12

Source of Tables 104-106: U.S. National Center for Health Statistics, *Vital Statistics of the United States*, annual; and unpublished data.

No. 107. Women Who Have Had a Child in the Last Year, by Age: 1980 to 1995

[See headnote, Table 108]

AGE OF MOTHER	WOMEN WHO HAD A CHILD IN LAST YEAR (1,000)			TOTAL BIRTHS PER 1,000 WOMEN			FIRST BIRTHS PER 1,000 WOMEN		
	1980	1990	1995	1980	1990	1995	1980	1990	1995
Total	3,247	3,913	3,696	71.1	67.0	61.4	28.5	26.4	23.2
15 to 29 years old [1] . . .	2,476	2,568	2,252	103.7	90.8	81.2	48.6	43.2	38.1
15 to 19 years old .	(NA)	338	340	(NA)	39.8	37.7	(NA)	30.1	26.9
20 to 24 years old [2] .	1,396	1,038	957	96.6	113.4	105.7	(NA)	51.8	52.5
25 to 29 years old . .	1,081	1,192	955	114.8	112.1	98.8	(NA)	46.2	35.1
30 to 44 years old	770	1,346	1,444	35.4	44.7	44.4	6.3	10.6	10.4
30 to 34 years old . .	519	892	926	60.0	80.4	83.8	(NA)	21.9	21.2
35 to 39 years old . .	192	377	410	26.9	37.3	36.7	(NA)	6.5	7.8
40 to 44 years old . .	59	77	107	9.9	8.6	10.5	(NA)	1.2	1.5

NA Not available.   [1] For 1980, 18 to 29 years old.   [2] For 1980, 18 to 24 years old.

Source: U.S. Bureau of the Census, *Current Population Reports*, P20-375, P20-454, P20-470 and P20-499.

No. 108. Characteristics of Women Who Have Had a Child in the Last Year: 1995

[As of **June.** Covers civilian noninstitutional population. Since the number of women who had a birth during the 12-month period was tabulated and not the actual numbers of births, some small underestimation of fertility for this period may exist due to the omission of: (1) Multiple births, (2) Two or more live births spaced within the 12-month period (the woman is counted only once), (3) Women who had births in the period and who did not survive to the survey date, and (4) Women who were in institutions and therefore not in the survey universe. These losses may be somewhat offset by the inclusion in the CPS of births to immigrants who did not have their children born in the United States and births to nonresident women. These births would not have been recorded in the vital registration system. Based on Current Population Survey (CPS); see text, Section 1, and Appendix III]

CHARACTERISTIC	TOTAL, 15 TO 44 YEARS OLD			15 TO 29 YEARS OLD			30 TO 44 YEARS OLD		
	Num- ber of women (1,000)	Women who have had a child in the last year		Num- ber of women (1,000)	Women who have had a child in the last year		Num- ber of women (1,000)	Women who have had a child in the last year	
		Total births per 1,000 women	First births per 1,000 women		Total births per 1,000 women	First births per 1,000 women		Total births per 1,000 women	First births per 1,000 women
Total [1]	60,225	61.4	23.2	27,742	81.2	38.1	32,483	44.4	10.4
White	48,603	59.2	22.6	22,001	76.6	36.5	26,602	44.8	11.1
Black	8,617	70.6	26.4	4,276	109.0	49.6	4,342	32.7	3.7
Hispanic [2]	6,632	79.6	25.0	3,511	99.9	40.6	3,120	56.8	7.5
Currently married	31,616	85.5	30.3	8,445	168.2	76.1	23,171	55.3	13.6
Married, spouse present	29,202	87.2	31.4	7,720	172.4	78.9	21,482	56.6	14.3
Married, spouse absent [3]	2,414	64.5	17.4	725	123.4	46.6	1,689	39.3	4.9
Widowed or divorced	5,762	28.4	4.1	1,015	65.2	11.8	4,748	20.6	2.5
Never married	22,846	36.3	18.0	18,282	41.9	22.0	4,564	14.0	2.1
Educational attainment:									
Less than high school	12,629	57.3	19.6	9,005	65.6	26.2	3,624	36.9	3.1
High school, 4 years	18,404	67.4	25.5	7,050	119.6	56.6	11,354	35.0	6.2
College:									
1 or more years.	29,192	59.3	23.2	11,687	70.0	36.2	17,505	52.2	14.6
No degree	12,724	56.1	21.2	6,578	71.1	34.3	6,147	40.0	7.2
Associate degree.	4,663	56.9	19.2	1,451	102.6	47.1	3,213	36.2	6.7
Bachelor's degree	8,884	65.3	27.0	3,149	56.2	34.2	5,735	70.2	23.1
Grad. or prof. degree	2,921	59.2	26.8	510	48.8	41.7	2,411	61.4	23.7
Labor force status:									
Employed	39,989	46.5	20.9	16,596	61.8	35.4	23,393	35.6	10.6
Unemployed	3,287	53.5	22.8	2,086	59.8	30.4	1,202	42.6	9.6
Not in labor force	16,949	98.1	28.5	9,060	121.7	44.8	7,889	71.0	9.8
Occupation of employed women:									
Managerial-professional	11,059	46.2	22.3	3,148	65.3	40.2	7,911	38.6	15.2
Tech., sales, admin. support . . .	16,997	48.6	21.5	7,754	63.8	36.6	9,243	35.9	8.8
Service workers	7,612	44.0	16.6	4,001	53.0	25.6	3,611	34.0	6.6
Farming, forestry, and fishing . .	501	41.0	27.9	235	40.7	40.7	266	41.3	16.5
Precision prod., craft, repair . . .	813	56.6	37.5	272	87.4	70.4	541	41.1	21.0
Operators, fabricators, laborers .	3,007	39.5	17.8	1,186	67.3	39.1	1,821	21.5	3.8
Family income: Under $10,000 . . .	6,957	91.0	32.8	4,081	124.1	49.7	2,875	44.1	8.8
$10,000 to $19,999	8,159	64.3	25.8	4,358	93.1	44.5	3,801	31.4	4.3
$20,000 to $24,999	4,542	60.6	20.3	2,355	83.5	37.6	2,188	36.0	1.7
$25,000 to $29,999	4,364	57.0	18.9	2,104	77.8	34.1	2,259	37.7	4.7
$30,000 to $34,999	4,076	60.6	24.3	1,840	75.6	43.4	2,236	48.2	8.6
$35,000 to $49,999	9,949	59.1	20.8	4,160	80.8	32.9	5,789	43.5	12.2
$50,000 to $74,999	9,720	52.5	23.3	3,735	62.8	41.0	5,985	46.0	12.3
$75,000 and over	7,088	53.1	19.2	2,765	34.8	13.6	4,323	64.8	22.8

[1] Includes women of other races and women with family income not reported, not shown separately.   [2] Persons of Hispanic origin may be of any race.   [3] Includes separated women.

Source: U.S. Bureau of the Census, *Current Population Reports*, P20-375, P20-454, and P20-482.

No. 109. Women Who Have Had a Child in the Last Year, by Age and Labor Force Status: 1980 to 1995

[See headnote, Table 108]

YEAR	TOTAL, 18 TO 44 YEARS OLD			18 TO 29 YEARS OLD			30 TO 44 YEARS OLD		
	Number (1,000)	In the labor force		Number (1,000)	In the labor force		Number (1,000)	In the labor force	
		Number (1,000)	Percent		Number (1,000)	Percent		Number (1,000)	Percent
1980	3,247	1,233	38	2,476	947	38	770	287	37
1981	3,381	1,411	42	2,499	1,004	40	881	407	46
1982	3,433	1,508	44	2,445	1,040	43	988	469	48
1983	3,625	1,563	43	2,682	1,138	42	942	425	45
1984	3,311	1,547	47	2,375	1,058	45	936	489	52
1985	3,497	1,691	48	2,512	1,204	48	984	488	50
1986	3,625	1,805	50	2,452	1,185	48	1,174	620	53
1987	3,701	1,881	51	2,521	1,258	50	1,180	623	53
1988	3,667	1,866	51	2,384	1,177	49	1,283	688	54
1990 [1]	3,913	2,068	53	2,568	1,275	50	1,346	793	59
1992 [1]	3,688	1,985	54	2,346	1,182	50	1,342	802	60
1994 [1]	3,890	2,066	53	2,389	1,209	51	1,501	857	57
1995 [1]	3,696	2,034	55	2,252	1,150	51	1,444	884	61

[1] Lower age limit is 15 years old.
Source: U.S. Bureau of the Census, *Current Population Reports*, P20-482; and unpublished data from the June 1995 Current Population Survey.

No. 110. Childless Women and Children Ever Born, by Race, Age, and Marital Status: 1995

[See headnote, Table 103]

CHARACTERISTIC	Total number of women (1,000)	WOMEN BY NUMBER OF CHILDREN EVER BORN (percent)				CHILDREN EVER BORN	
		Total	None	One	Two or more	Total number (1,000)	Per 1,000 women
ALL RACES [1]							
Women ever married	37,378	100	19.0	22.3	58.7	65,948	1,764
15 to 19 years old	319	100	43.9	45.5	10.6	218	684
20 to 24 years old	3,036	100	36.7	34.4	28.9	3,096	1,020
25 to 29 years old	6,105	100	28.8	29.2	42.0	8,112	1,329
30 to 34 years old	9,006	100	18.7	23.0	58.4	15,634	1,736
35 to 39 years old	9,660	100	13.2	16.9	69.8	19,578	2,027
40 to 44 years old	9,252	100	12.3	17.9	69.8	19,310	2,087
Women never married	22,846	100	79.1	10.8	10.2	8,886	389
15 to 19 years old	8,701	100	92.4	6.3	1.3	826	95
20 to 24 years old	6,018	100	78.3	12.6	9.1	2,106	350
25 to 29 years old	3,564	100	69.6	13.4	17.0	2,181	612
30 to 34 years old	2,050	100	61.7	14.9	23.4	1,684	821
35 to 39 years old	1,523	100	60.5	15.4	24.1	1,315	863
40 to 44 years old	992	100	65.9	14.6	19.5	775	782
WHITE							
Women ever married	31,819	100	19.6	22.3	58.1	55,113	1,732
15 to 19 years old	269	100	40.1	48.6	11.3	197	732
20 to 24 years old	2,651	100	37.5	34.3	28.3	2,636	994
25 to 29 years old	5,243	100	29.7	29.6	40.7	6,758	1,289
30 to 34 years old	7,652	100	19.3	22.8	58.1	12,958	1,693
35 to 39 years old	8,233	100	13.6	16.6	69.9	16,519	2,006
40 to 44 years old	7,771	100	12.5	17.9	69.6	16,045	2,065
Women never married	16,784	100	87.0	8.0	5.0	3,597	214
15 to 19 years old	6,806	100	94.6	4.5	0.9	456	67
20 to 24 years old	4,516	100	84.1	10.2	6.7	1,075	238
25 to 29 years old	2,517	100	80.5	10.6	8.8	872	346
30 to 34 years old	1,306	100	77.0	9.9	13.0	605	463
35 to 39 years old	946	100	81.3	10.9	7.8	312	329
40 to 44 years old	693	100	80.4	11.8	7.9	277	400
BLACK							
Women ever married	3,746	100	14.1	22.8	63.1	7,417	1,980
15 to 19 years old	23	(B)	(B)	(B)	(B)	13	(B)
20 to 24 years old	235	100	29.4	36.7	33.9	297	1,263
25 to 29 years old	568	100	16.4	29.1	54.9	951	1,676
30 to 34 years old	888	100	13.9	24.3	61.7	1,841	2,073
35 to 39 years old	986	100	10.7	18.0	71.4	2,079	2,109
40 to 44 years old	1,046	100	11.7	19.4	69.0	2,236	2,137
Women never married	4,872	100	52.1	20.6	27.4	4,773	980
15 to 19 years old	1,439	100	82.9	14.6	2.5	302	210
20 to 24 years old	1,160	100	54.7	22.3	23.0	933	804
25 to 29 years old	851	100	37.4	22.2	40.4	1,166	1,370
30 to 34 years old	641	100	30.9	26.0	43.1	974	1,519
35 to 39 years old	521	100	22.9	23.1	54.0	953	1,831
40 to 44 years old	260	100	28.8	22.5	48.8	444	1,711

B Base figure too small to meet statistical standards for reliability.   [1] Includes other races, not shown separately.
Source: U.S. Bureau of the Census, *Current Population Reports*, P20-482.

No. 111. Number of Male Sexual Partners in Lifetime, by Selected Characteristics: 1995

[Based on responses from the National Survey of Family Growth (NSFG) sponsored by the National Center for Health Statistics. Based on interview conducted in person in homes of 10,847 women between January and October 1995, using computer-assisted personal intervewing. A small part of the NSFG was conducted with self-administered technique called Audio-Assisted Self Interviewing. See source for details]

WOMEN 15-44 YEARS OF AGE	Number (1,000)	NUMBER OF PARTNERS IN LIFETIME BY PERCENT DISTRIBUTION							
		0 [1]	1	2	3	4	5	6-9	10 or more
All women................	60,201	10.5	23.5	12.3	9.6	8.4	8.1	12.1	15.5
Age:									
15-19 years old..............	8,961	45.8	19.4	11.0	7.9	3.6	2.9	5.7	3.7
20-24 years old..............	9,041	11.0	21.6	13.4	11.5	9.0	7.7	11.9	13.9
25-29 years old..............	9,693	4.3	22.0	13.5	10.1	9.2	10.1	13.8	16.9
30-34 years old..............	11,065	2.8	23.4	11.8	9.1	11.5	9.7	13.7	18.0
35-39 years old..............	11,211	1.8	24.3	11.7	9.4	8.5	9.3	14.5	20.5
40-44 years old..............	10,230	2.4	29.4	12.6	9.7	8.0	8.4	11.7	17.7
Married........................	29,673	0.5	34.5	13.8	9.9	8.9	8.0	11.2	13.2
Unmarried.....................	30,528	20.2	12.8	10.9	9.4	7.9	8.2	12.8	17.7
First intercourse:									
Under 16 years old	13,944	(X)	11.3	11.2	10.2	8.6	10.6	18.5	29.0
16 years old................	8,750	(X)	18.6	12.6	12.9	10.9	9.4	16.5	18.8
17 years old................	8,754	(X)	17.3	14.4	11.4	12.3	12.5	13.1	18.8
18 years old................	6,941	(X)	26.0	14.3	11.0	11.0	9.0	13.1	14.9
19 years old................	4,759	(X)	37.6	14.7	11.6	8.0	7.2	11.0	9.2
20 years old and over	10,653	(X)	52.2	16.5	8.6	6.3	4.7	5.9	4.6
Education: [2]									
No high school diploma or GED [3]..	5,424	1.3	27.7	15.8	10.1	7.6	10.1	11.7	15.8
High school diploma or GED	18,169	2.5	23.5	13.0	10.8	9.8	9.6	13.7	17.1
Some college, no bachelor's degree.................	12,399	4.6	22.3	10.3	9.6	9.1	10.2	14.1	19.9
Bachelor's degree or higher.	11,748	4.7	26.1	11.7	8.6	9.5	7.1	13.5	18.9
Poverty level income: [2]									
0-149 percent	10,072	3.8	21.8	13.7	9.9	9.4	10.1	13.6	17.7
Race and Hispanic origin:									
Hispanic	6,702	12.1	37.1	15.8	8.9	5.1	5.7	6.9	8.5

X Not applicable.   [1] Never had intercourse, or never had voluntary intercourse if first intercourse was not voluntary.
[2] Limited to women 22-44 years of age at time of interview.   [3] GED = general equivalency diploma.

No. 112. Unmarried Women Who Have Had Intercourse in the 12 Months Prior to Interview: 1995

[Represents women 15-44 years of age. See headnote, Table 111]

WOMEN 15-44 YEARS OF AGE	Number (1,000)	PARTNERS USED CONDOMS FOR DISEASE PREVENTION—PERCENT DISTRIBUTION				
		Every time	More than half the time	Half the time	Less than half the time	Not at all
Total [1]	12,708	31.3	13.9	8.4	13.9	32.5
Age and number of partners: [2]						
One partner	8,197	31.6	9.0	6.1	10.9	42.3
Two or more partners..................	4,504	30.9	22.7	12.6	19.4	14.5
15-29 years old.................	8,570	32.2	15.1	9.6	13.8	29.3
One partner	5,315	32.7	10.1	7.3	10.4	39.5
Two or more partners	3,252	31.4	23.2	13.4	19.4	12.5
30-44 years old.................	4,139	29.5	11.4	5.9	14.1	39.2
One partner	2,882	29.6	7.0	3.9	11.8	47.6
Two or more partners	1,251	29.5	21.4	10.4	19.4	19.4
Race and Hispanic origin of partners: [2]						
Hispanic	1,077	30.9	15.4	11.3	13.7	28.7
One partner	707	29.8	12.5	9.4	11.5	36.8
Two or more partners	370	33.1	21.0	14.9	17.8	13.2
Non-Hispanic White.................	8,202	27.7	13.0	8.1	14.7	36.5
One partner	5,341	28.6	7.7	5.9	10.5	47.4
Two or more partners	2,861	26.2	23.0	12.1	22.5	16.3
Non-Hispanic Black	3,042	39.2	15.4	9.2	12.8	23.4
One partner	1,890	38.4	12.0	6.4	12.3	30.8
Two or more partners	1,153	40.5	21.0	13.8	13.6	11.2
Education: [3]						
No high school diploma or GED [4]...........	2,128	26.6	13.9	7.6	10.8	41.1
High school diploma or GED...........	5,247	26.2	12.5	7.6	14.5	39.1
Some college, no bachelor's degree........	3,779	29.7	10.6	6.1	13.9	39.7
Bachelor's degree or higher	3,111	32.4	13.6	7.0	12.0	35.1

[1] Includes women with missing information on number of partners in the 12 months prior to interview.   [2] Number of male partners in the 12 months prior to interview.   [3] Limited to women 22-44 years of age at time of interview.   [4] GED is general equivalency diploma.

Source of Tables 111 and 112: U.S. National Center for Health Statistics, *Fertility, Family Planning, and Women's Health: New data from the 1995 National Survey of Family Growth, Vital and Health Statistics,* Series 23, No. 19, 1997.

No. 113. Ever Received Any Infertility Services, by Women 15-44 Years of Age, by Selected Characteristics: 1995

[In percents, except as indicated]

CHARACTERISTICS	Number (1,000)	Any services [1]	Advice	Tests on woman or man	Ovulation drugs	Surgery or treatment for blocked tubes	Assisted reproductive technology [2]
Total	60,201	15.4	6.4	4.2	3.0	1.5	1.0
AGE							
15-24 years old	18,002	4.4	1.1	0.2	0.3	0.1	(Z)
25-34 years old	20,758	17.1	6.3	3.7	3.1	1.2	0.8
35-44 years old	21,440	22.9	10.9	8.1	5.2	2.9	2.1
PARITY, AGE, AND MARITAL STATUS							
One or more births	34,958	21.8	7.7	4.6	3.6	1.8	0.9
15-24 years old.	3,889	16.1	3.3	0.3	0.6	0.5	-
25-34 years old.	13,620	21.5	6.2	3.1	3.1	1.3	0.6
35-44 years old.	17,449	23.4	9.8	6.7	4.6	2.4	1.4
Married	23,988	24.1	9.2	6.0	4.6	2.1	1.1
Unmarried	10,970	16.8	4.3	1.6	1.3	0.9	0.5
EDUCATION [3]							
No high school diploma or GED [4]	5,424	14.9	3.3	2.0	1.2	0.7	0.2
High school diploma or GED	18,169	20.0	7.8	4.9	3.9	2.0	1.1
Some college, no bachelor's degree	12,399	19.4	7.8	5.6	3.3	2.0	1.2
Bachelor's degree or higher	11,748	18.0	10.3	7.1	5.3	1.9	2.2
POVERTY LEVEL INCOME [3]							
0-149 percent	10,072	16.6	4.8	2.1	1.5	0.9	0.2

- Rounds to zero.   Z Less than 0.5 percent.   [1] Includes services to help get pregnant as well as to help prevent miscarriage.   [2] Includes artificial insemination, in vitro fertilization (IVF, gamete intrafallopian transfer (GIFT), and other techniques not shown separately.   [3] Limited to women 22-44 years of age at time of interiew. The poverty index ratio was calculated by dividing the total family income by the weighted average threshold income of families whose head of household was under 65 years of age, based on the 1994 poverty levels defined by the U.S. Census Bureau.   [4] GED = General equivalency diploma.

Source: U.S. National Center for Health Statistics, *Fertility, Family Planning, and Women's Health: New data from the 1995 National Survey of Family Growth, Vital and Health Statistics,* Series 23, No. 19, 1997.

No. 114. Pregnancies Ending in Live Birth to Women 15-44 Years Old, and Months Pregnant When Prenatal Care Began: 1991-95

CHARACTERISTIC	Number (1,000)	PERCENT DISTRIBUTION			
		Total	Months pregnant when prenatal care began		
			Less than 3 months	3-4 months	5 months or more or no prenatal care
All pregnancies [1]	17,052	100.0	88.1	5.4	6.6
AGE AT TIME OF BIRTH					
Under 20 years old.	2,023	100.0	75.3	10.7	14.0
20-24 years old	4,388	100.0	84.5	7.3	8.2
25-29 years old	5,088	100.0	91.3	4.0	4.7
30-44 years old	5,553	100.0	92.5	3.1	4.3
MARITAL STATUS AT TIME OF BIRTH					
Never married	3,940	100.0	77.3	9.6	13.1
Married	12,171	100.0	91.5	4.0	4.5
Formerly married	942	100.0	88.6	5.3	6.1
WANTEDNESS STATUS AT CONCEPTION [2]					
Intended.	11,833	100.0	91.2	3.9	4.9
Mistimed.	3,715	100.0	82.2	9.1	8.7
Unwanted.	1,485	100.0	78.0	8.2	13.8
EDUCATION [3]					
No high school diploma or GED [4]	2,368	100.0	78.9	6.9	14.3
High school diploma or GED	6,076	100.0	88.5	6.3	5.2
Some college, no bachelor's degree	3,582	100.0	94.5	3.0	2.5
Bachelor's degree or higher	3,144	100.0	93.8	2.3	3.9

[1] Includes pregnancies with missisng information on prenatal care or wantedness status.   [2] Based on new questions in Cycle 5. See source "Definitions of Terms."   [3] Limited to women 22-44 yeaers of age at time of interview.   [4] GED is general equivalency diploma.

Source: U.S. National Center for Health Statistics, *Fertility, Family Planning, and Women's Health: New data from the 1995 National Survey of Family Growth, Vital and Health Statistics,* Series 23, No. 19, 1997.

No. 115. Pregnancies, Number and Outcome: 1976 to 1992

[**Live births:** source of data is statistics of registered births published annually by National Center for Health Statistics (NCHS). **Induced abortions:** derived from published reports by the Alan Guttmacher Institute. **Fetal losses:** based on the National Survey of Family Growth conducted by NCHS]

YEAR	NUMBER (1,000)				RATE PER 1,000 WOMEN, 15 TO 44 YEARS OLD			
	Total	Live births	Induced abortions	Fetal losses	Total	Live births	Induced abortions	Fetal losses
1976	5,002	3,168	1,179	655	102.7	65.0	24.2	13.4
1977	5,331	3,327	1,317	687	107.0	66.8	26.4	13.8
1978	5,433	3,333	1,410	690	106.7	65.5	27.7	13.5
1979	5,714	3,494	1,498	722	109.9	67.2	28.8	13.9
1980	5,912	3,612	1,554	746	111.9	68.4	29.4	14.1
1981	5,958	3,629	1,577	751	110.5	67.3	29.3	13.9
1982	6,024	3,681	1,574	769	110.1	67.3	28.8	14.1
1983	5,977	3,639	1,575	763	108.0	65.7	28.5	13.8
1984	6,019	3,669	1,577	773	107.4	65.5	28.1	13.8
1985	6,144	3,761	1,589	795	108.3	66.3	28.0	14.0
1986	6,129	3,757	1,574	798	106.7	65.4	27.4	13.9
1987	6,183	3,809	1,559	815	106.8	65.8	26.9	14.1
1988	6,341	3,910	1,591	840	109.1	67.3	27.4	14.5
1989	6,480	4,041	1,567	873	111.0	69.2	26.8	15.0
1990	6,668	4,158	1,609	902	113.8	70.9	27.4	15.4
1991	6,563	4,111	1,557	896	111.1	69.6	26.3	15.2
1992	6,484	4,065	1,529	890	109.9	68.9	25.9	15.1

Source: U.S. National Center for Health Statistics, *Monthly Vital Statistics Report,* Vol. 41, No. 6, Supplement.

No. 116. Pregnancies, by Outcome, Age of Woman, and Race: 1991

[See headnote, Table 115]

ITEM	Total	Under 15 years old	15 to 19 years old	20 to 24 years old	25 to 29 years old	30 to 34 years old	35 to 39 years old	40 years old and over
PREGNANCIES								
Non-Hispanic:								
White, pregnancies	3,964	8	489	1,007	1,145	884	368	63
Live births	2,635	3	250	637	834	640	235	36
Induced abortions	774	4	164	264	163	106	58	16
Fetal losses	556	1	75	107	148	138	76	11
Black, pregnancies	1,344	14	272	439	320	202	81	15
Live births	673	6	149	216	160	98	37	6
Induced abortions	507	7	101	178	119	67	29	7
Fetal losses	164	1	22	45	41	37	15	3
Hispanic:								
Pregnancies	965	5	177	306	250	149	64	14
Live births	623	2	105	199	170	100	39	8
Induced abortions	208	1	40	73	50	28	13	4
Fetal losses	134	1	32	33	30	22	12	2
RATE PER 1,000 WOMEN								
Non-Hispanic:								
White, pregnancies	91.8	1.3	84.7	151.4	154.7	107.6	47.3	8.6
Live births	61.0	0.5	43.4	95.7	112.7	77.9	30.2	4.8
Induced abortions	17.9	0.7	28.4	39.6	22.0	12.9	7.4	2.2
Fetal losses	12.9	0.2	13.0	16.0	20.0	16.8	9.7	1.6
Black, pregnancies	174.8	11.0	216.7	337.2	232.3	142.7	63.9	14.4
Live births	87.6	4.9	118.9	166.1	116.3	69.3	28.9	5.7
Induced abortions	65.9	5.1	80.5	136.4	86.3	47.1	23.0	6.2
Fetal losses	21.3	0.9	17.2	34.7	29.7	26.3	12.1	2.4
Hispanic:								
Pregnancies	167.4	4.8	180.2	285.6	224.3	143.9	74.8	19.8
Live births	108.1	2.4	106.7	186.3	152.8	96.1	44.9	11.1
Induced abortions	36.2	1.4	40.4	68.1	44.4	27.1	15.5	5.2
Fetal losses	23.2	1.0	33.1	31.2	27.1	20.7	14.4	3.6

Source: U.S. National Center for Health Statistics, *Monthly Vital Statistics Report,* Vol. 43, No. 12.

No. 117. Unintended Birth Whether Mistimed or Unwanted, by Women 15-44 Years of Age: 1995

[See headnote, Table 111]

CHARACTERISTICS	Number of women, total 15-44 years of age	WOMEN WHO HAD AN UNINTENDED BIRTH [1]		
		Number (1,000)	First birth unintended	
			Percent mistimed	Percent unwanted
Total	**60,201**	**17,077**	**80.4**	**19.6**
AGE AT BIRTH				
Under 20 years	8,961	7,666	83.4	16.6
20-24 years	9,041	5,674	84.7	15.3
25-29 years	9,693	2,440	73.6	26.4
30-44 years	11,065	1,292	56.8	43.2
BIRTH ORDER				
First birth	(NA)	12,540	84.9	15.1
Second birth	(NA)	2,926	77.5	22.5
Third or higher birth	(NA)	1,611	51.1	48.9
POVERTY LEVEL [2]				
0-149 percent	10,072	5,386	75.5	24.5
0-99 percent	5,992	3,417	73.2	26.8
RACE AND HISPANIC ORIGIN				
Hispanic	6,702	2,293	74.8	25.2
Non-Hispanic White	45,522	10,641	84.4	15.6
Non-Hispanic Black	8,210	3,469	72.9	27.1
Non-Hispanic other	2,767	674	74.8	25.2

NA Not available. [1] Based on "traditional" version (comparable to Cycle 4 and previous cycles) of wantedness status. See source "Definition of Terms." [2] Limited to women 22-44 years of age at time of interview.
Source: U.S. National Center for Health Statistics, *Fertility, Family Planning, and Women's Health: New data from the 1995 National Survey of Family Growth, Vital and Health Statistics,* Series 23, No. 19, 1997.

No. 118. Single Babies Born in 1990-93 Who Were Ever Breastfed, Duration, and Mean Duration of Breastfeeding in Weeks, by Selected Characteristics: 1995

CHARACTERISTICS	Percent breastfed at all	PERCENT DISTRIBUTION				Mean duration in weeks
		Total	Duration of breastfeeding			
			0-2 months	3-4 months	5 or more months	
All babies [1]	**55.2**	**100.0**	**40.3**	**8.6**	**51.1**	**28.7**
Under 20 years	36.0	100.0	69.7	4.5	25.8	17.5
20-24 years	46.4	100.0	46.6	12.4	41.0	24.1
25 years and over	63.0	100.0	35.0	7.8	57.3	31.5
25-29 years	56.4	100.0	39.8	8.7	51.5	28.2
30-44 years	69.1	100.0	31.3	7.1	61.6	34.0
MARITAL STATUS AT TIME OF BIRTH						
Never married	31.4	100.0	54.8	8.3	36.8	20.8
Married	63.4	100.0	37.7	8.5	53.8	30.1
Formerly married	50.2	100.0	45.3	11.3	43.4	26.4
WANTEDNESS STATUS AT CONCEPTION						
Intended	60.4	100.0	38.1	9.4	52.6	29.7
Mistimed	46.3	100.0	50.7	6.7	42.6	23.3
Unwanted	36.9	100.0	38.1	4.7	57.3	31.6
EDUCATION						
No high school diploma or GED [2]	38.9	100.0	44.9	8.8	46.4	26.8
High school diploma or GED	49.0	100.0	44.0	9.8	46.2	27.2
Some college, no bachelor's degree	63.0	100.0	43.9	7.1	49.1	26.5
Bachelor's degree or higher	81.1	100.0	28.7	8.5	62.8	35.2
POVERTY LEVEL INCOME [3]						
0-149 percent	42.6	100.0	42.4	8.3	49.2	30.2
150-299 percent	58.1	100.0	39.5	9.6	50.8	29.4
300 percent or higher	68.2	100.0	38.8	8.1	53.1	28.3
RACE AND HISPANIC ORIGIN						
Hispanic	62.2	100.0	42.7	7.1	50.2	26.7
Non-Hispanic White	59.1	100.0	38.5	8.1	53.3	29.8
Non-Hispanic Black	25.1	100.0	45.0	14.0	40.9	22.9

[1] Includes babies born to women of other race and origin groups not shown separately. [2] GED = general equivalence diploma. [3] The poverty index ratio was calculated by dividing the total family income by the weighted average threshold income of families whose head of household was under 65 years of age, based on the U.S. Census Bureau. Limited to women 22-44 years of age at time of interview.
Source: U.S. National Center for Health Statistics, *Fertility, Family Planning, and Women's Health: New data from the 1995 National Survey of Family Growth, Vital and Health Statistics,* Series 23, No. 19, 1997.

No. 119. Contraceptive Use by Women, 15 to 44 Years of Age: 1995

[Based on samples of the female population of of the United States; see source for details. See Appendix III]

CONTRACEPTIVE STATUS AND METHOD	All women [1]	AGE			RACE			MARITAL STATUS		
		15-24 years	25-34 years	35-44 years	Non-Hispanic White	Non-Hispanic Black	His-panic	Never mar-ried	Cur-rently mar-ried	For-merly married
All women (1,000)	60,201	18,002	20,758	21,440	42,522	8,210	6,702	22,679	29,673	7,849
PERCENT DISTRIBUTION										
Sterile [2] . . .	29.7	2.6	25.0	57.0	30.2	31.5	28.4	6.9	43.2	45.1
Surgically sterile	27.9	1.8	23.6	54.0	28.5	29.7	26.3	5.7	41.1	42.5
Noncontraceptively sterile [3] . . .	3.1	0.1	1.2	7.4	3.2	3.7	2.3	0.9	4.1	5.8
Contraceptively sterile [4]	24.8	1.7	22.4	46.6	25.3	26.0	24.0	4.8	37.0	36.7
Nonsurgically sterile [5] . . .	1.7	0.7	1.3	2.8	1.6	1.8	2.0	1.1	2.0	2.2
Pregnant, postpartum	4.6	5.9	6.9	1.3	4.3	4.5	6.3	3.1	6.4	1.9
Seeking pregnancy	4.0	2.1	6.2	3.5	3.7	4.6	4.0	1.5	6.4	2.1
Other nonusers	22.3	44.4	13.3	12.6	21.1	23.1	26.3	46.8	4.7	18.4
Never had intercourse	10.9	30.8	3.4	1.4	10.4	8.9	12.1	28.9	-	-
No intercourse in last month [6] .	6.2	7.0	5.3	6.5	5.7	7.2	8.6	11.5	0.5	12.7
Had intercourse in last month [6]	5.2	6.6	4.6	4.7	5.0	7.0	5.6	6.4	4.2	5.7
Nonsurgical contraceptors	39.7	45.0	49.1	26.1	41.2	36.1	35.1	41.8	39.7	32.4
Pill	17.3	23.1	23.7	6.3	18.8	14.8	13.6	20.4	15.6	14.6
IUD	0.5	0.1	0.6	0.8	0.5	0.5	0.9	0.3	0.7	0.4
Diaphragm	1.2	0.2	1.2	2.0	1.5	0.5	0.4	0.5	1.8	0.9
Condom	13.1	13.9	15.0	10.7	13.0	12.5	12.1	13.9	13.3	10.1
Periodic abstinence	1.5	0.5	1.8	2.0	1.6	0.7	1.3	0.6	2.3	0.7
Natural family planning	0.2	-	0.3	0.3	0.3	-	0.1	-	0.4	-
Withdrawal	2.0	1.6	2.3	1.9	2.1	0.9	2.0	1.5	2.3	1.8
Other methods [7]	3.9	5.6	4.2	2.1	3.4	6.2	4.7	4.6	3.3	3.9

- Represents or rounds to zero. [1] Includes other races, not shown separately. [2] Total sterile includes male sterile for unknown reasons. [3] Persons who had sterilizing operation and who gave as one reason that they had medical problems with their female organs. [4] Includes all other sterilization operations, and sterilization of the husband or current partner. [5] Persons sterile from illness, accident, or congenital conditions. [6] Data refer to no intercourse in the 3 months prior to interview. [7] Includes implants, injectables, morning-after-pill, suppository, Today(TM) sponge and less frequently used methods.
Source: U.S. National Center for Health Statistics, *Advance Data from Vital and Health Statistics*, No. 182.

No. 120. Women Who Have Ever Had a Live Birth, and Use of Maternity Leave for the Most Recent Birth: 1995

[Women 15-44 years of age]

CHARACTERISTICS OF THE MOTHER	Number (1,000)	PERCENT DISTRIBUTION						
		Total	Not employed	Employed	Took mater-nity leave	Did not take leave [1]		
						Not needed	Not offered	Other reasons
All women	34,958	100.0	48.0	52.0	37.3	2.3	0.9	11.6
AGE AT TIME OF BIRTH								
15-19 years old	3,436	100.0	71.9	28.1	14.8	0.7	0.1	12.5
20-24 years old	10,094	100.0	52.8	47.2	29.8	1.3	1.3	14.9
25-29 years old	11,629	100.0	44.8	55.2	41.1	2.7	0.8	10.5
30-44 years old	9,799	100.0	38.3	61.7	48.3	3.5	0.8	9.1
YEAR OF CHILD's BIRTH								
1991-95	13,999	100.0	43.2	56.8	43.5	2.2	0.9	10.3
1981-90	15,344	100.0	47.4	52.6	37.2	2.7	0.8	11.8
1980 and before	5,616	100.0	61.5	38.5	22.0	1.6	0.9	14.0
MARITAL STATUS AT TIME OF BIRTH								
Never married	6,379	100.0	58.4	41.6	26.8	0.8	1.0	13.0
Married	26,439	100.0	44.9	55.1	40.3	2.8	0.8	11.1
Formerly married	2,140	100.0	54.3	45.7	31.1	0.8	1.3	12.5
BIRTH ORDER								
First	10,901	100.0	35.8	64.2	46.9	1.8	1.1	14.4
Second	13,965	100.0	47.7	52.3	38.1	2.6	1.0	10.7
Third or higher	10,092	100.0	61.5	38.5	25.8	2.5	0.4	9.7
EDUCATION AT INTERVIEW [2]								
No high school diploma or GED [3]	4,961	100.0	69.6	30.4	16.5	0.7	0.4	12.8
High school diploma or GED	14,295	100.0	48.8	51.2	36.2	1.6	1.0	12.4
Some college, no bachelor's degree . . .	7,967	100.0	40.1	59.9	44.4	2.6	1.1	11.8
Bachelor's degree or higher	5,929	100.0	32.8	67.2	52.8	5.6	0.7	7.9
RACE AND HISPANIC ORIGIN								
Hispanic	4,372	100.0	57.8	42.2	28.9	1.1	0.8	11.4

[1] The group labeled "not needed" includes women who did not need to take maternity leave: (1) Due to the timing of their birth relative to their job schedule (for example, teachers who delivered during summer break. (2) Due to the nature of their jobs (for example, worked out of their homes, self-employed). (3) Because they decided to quit their jobs after delivery. The group labeled "not offered" includes: (1) Woman whose employers did not offer (or denied) maternity leave at all (for example, woman would be fired if she took leave. (2) woman whose job benefits did not include maternity leave. The final group labeled "other reasons" includes women who decided to quit their jobs before delivery, who could not afford to take maternity leave for personal or financial reasons, and who continued to work right after delivery. [2] Women 22-44 years of age at time of interview. [3] GED is general equivalency diploma.
Source: U.S. National Center for Health Statistics, *Fertility, Family Planning, and Women's Health: New data from the 1995 National Survey of Family Growth, Vital and Health Statistics*, Series 23, No. 19, 1997.

No. 121. Live Births—Mothers Who Smoked During Pregnancy: 1995

[In thousands, except percents. Excludes California, Indiana, New York, and South Dakota, which did not require reporting of tobacco use during pregnancy]

SMOKING MEASURE AND RACE OF MOTHER	Total	YEARS OF SCHOOL COMPLETED BY MOTHER					
		0-8 years	9-11 years	12 years	13-15 years	16 years or more	Not stated
All races [1]	3,108,918	149,716	494,124	1,065,576	681,065	668,533	49,904
White	2,441,118	123,398	341,516	815,105	542,248	583,779	35,072
Black	539,173	19,034	135,809	209,567	114,430	49,581	10,752
Percent:							
Smoker [1]	13.9	12.6	26.2	17.7	10.5	2.7	12.6
White	15.0	13.4	30.6	20.0	11.4	2.8	12.8
Black	10.6	9.5	16.1	10.5	7.3	3.0	14.2
PERCENT DISTRIBUTION							
All races smoker	100.0	100.0	100.0	100.0	100.0	100.0	100.0
10 cigarettes or less	65.4	59.7	64.5	64.9	67.7	72.9	67.7
11-20 cigarettes	30.1	32.9	30.4	30.8	28.6	24.5	27.5
21 cigarettes or more	4.6	7.4	5.1	4.4	3.7	2.7	4.8
White smoker	100.0	100.0	100.0	100.0	100.0	100.0	100.0
10 cigarettes or less	62.8	57.4	61.1	62.5	65.6	72.0	63.7
11-20 cigarettes	32.3	34.6	33.3	32.8	30.4	25.2	30.8
21 cigarettes or more	4.9	8.0	5.6	4.7	4.0	2.9	5.5
Black smoker	100.0	100.0	100.0	100.0	100.0	100.0	100.0
10 cigarettes or less	80.0	76.6	79.3	80.3	82.0	81.4	77.3
11-20 cigarettes	17.6	20.2	17.8	17.5	16.4	17.7	19.5
21 cigarettes or more	2.4	3.1	2.9	2.2	1.6	(B)	3.2

B Base data too small to meet statistical standards for reliability of a derived figure. [1] Includes races other than White and Black.

No. 122. Percent Low Birthweight, by Smoking Status, Age, and Race of Mother: 1995

[Low birth weight is defined as weight of less than 2,500 grams (5 lb. 8 oz.). Excludes California, Indiana, New York, and South Dakota, which did not require reporting of tobacco use during pregnancy]

SMOKING STATUS AND RACE OF MOTHER	All ages	AGE OF MOTHER								
		Under 15 years	15-19 years			20-24 years	25-29 years	30-34 years	35-39 years	40-49 years
			Total	15-17 years	18-19 years					
All races [1]	7.6	14.2	9.7	10.6	9.1	7.6	6.6	6.9	8.3	9.8
Smoker	12.2	15.2	11.3	12.0	10.9	10.6	11.6	13.7	16.8	19.6
Nonsmoker	6.8	14.1	9.3	10.3	8.7	7.0	5.9	5.9	7.1	8.7
White	6.4	11.6	8.2	8.9	7.8	6.4	5.6	5.9	7.1	8.5
Smoker	10.6	14.8	10.8	11.3	10.5	9.7	9.9	11.2	13.9	16.5
Nonsmoker	5.6	11.1	7.4	8.2	6.9	5.5	4.9	5.2	6.2	7.6
Black	13.2	16.7	13.2	13.8	12.7	12.1	12.8	14.3	16.4	17.4
Smoker	22.9	18.3	16.9	19.0	15.7	18.2	22.8	26.9	29.5	32.2
Nonsmoker	12.0	16.6	12.9	13.5	12.5	11.5	11.2	11.7	13.4	15.0

[1] Includes races other than White and Black.

No. 123. Live Births—Drinking Status of Mother: 1995

[In absolutes, except percents. Excludes California, New York, and South Dakota, which did not require reporting of alcohol use during pregnancy]

DRINKING STATUS, DRINKING MEASURE, AND RACE OF MOTHER	All ages	AGE OF MOTHER								
		Under 15 years	15-19 years			20-24 years	25-29 years	30-34 years	35-39 years	40-49 years
			Total	15-17 years	18-19 years					
All races [1]	3,337,069	10,586	431,930	166,266	265,664	829,905	911,556	774,300	322,225	56,567
Drinker	50,820	61	3,844	1,373	2,471	9,612	12,573	15,303	8,045	1,382
Nondrinker	3,231,681	10,374	421,579	162,431	259,148	807,392	884,616	745,621	308,119	53,980
White	2,640,303	4,610	293,384	105,572	187,812	629,126	748,670	650,689	267,770	46,054
Drinker	36,464	37	2,833	987	1,846	6,644	8,574	11,216	6,108	1,052
Nondrinker	2,561,196	4,502	285,993	102,910	183,083	612,729	728,701	628,546	256,699	44,026
Black	562,779	5,658	126,281	56,113	70,168	172,492	123,656	88,488	38,897	7,307
Drinker	12,578	18	773	297	476	2,493	3,569	3,673	1,754	298
Nondrinker	541,238	5,567	123,907	55,153	68,754	167,543	117,972	83,052	36,350	6,847
Percent:										
Drinker [1]	1.5	0.6	0.9	0.8	0.9	1.2	1.4	2.0	2.5	2.5
White	1.4	0.8	1.0	0.9	1.0	1.1	1.2	1.8	2.3	2.3
Black	2.3	(B)	0.6	0.5	0.7	1.5	2.9	4.2	4.6	4.2

B Less than 50. [1] Includes races other than White or Black.

Source of Tables 121-123: U.S. National Center for Health Statistics, *Monthly Vital Statistics Reports*.

No. 124. Abortions—Number, Rate, and Ratio, by Race: 1975 to 1995

YEAR	ALL RACES				WHITE				BLACK AND OTHER			
	Women 15-44 years old (1,000)	Abortions			Women 15-44 years old (1,000)	Abortions			Women 15-44 years old (1,000)	Abortions		
		Number (1,000)	Rate per 1,000 women	Ratio per 1,000 live births [1]		Number (1,000)	Rate per 1,000 women	Ratio per 1,000 live births [1]		Number (1,000)	Rate per 1,000 women	Ratio per 1,000 live births [1]
1975 ..	47,606	1,034	21.7	331	40,857	701	17.2	276	6,749	333	49.3	565
1979 ..	52,016	1,498	28.8	420	44,266	1,062	24.0	373	7,750	435	56.2	625
1980 ..	53,048	1,554	29.3	428	44,942	1,094	24.3	376	8,106	460	56.5	642
1981 ..	53,901	1,577	29.3	430	45,494	1,108	24.3	377	8,407	470	55.9	645
1982 [2]	54,679	1,574	28.8	428	46,049	1,095	23.8	373	8,630	479	55.5	646
1983 [2]	55,340	1,575	28.5	436	46,506	1,084	23.3	376	8,834	491	55.5	670
1984 ..	56,061	1,577	28.1	423	47,023	1,087	23.1	366	9,038	491	54.3	646
1985 ..	56,754	1,589	28.0	422	47,512	1,076	22.6	360	9,242	513	55.5	659
1986 [2]	57,483	1,574	27.4	416	48,010	1,045	21.8	350	9,473	529	55.9	661
1987 ..	57,964	1,559	27.1	405	48,288	1,017	21.1	338	9,676	542	56.0	648
1988 [2]	58,192	1,591	27.3	401	48,325	1,026	21.2	333	9,867	565	57.3	638
1989 [2]	58,365	1,567	26.8	380	48,104	1,006	20.9	309	10,261	561	54.7	650
1990 [2]	58,700	1,609	27.4	389	48,224	1,039	21.5	318	10,476	570	54.4	655
1991 ..	59,080	1,557	26.3	379	48,406	982	20.3	303	10,674	574	53.8	661
1992 ..	59,020	1,529	25.9	380	48,161	943	19.6	298	10,859	585	53.9	681
1993 [2]	59,143	1,500	25.4	378	48,137	911	18.9	291	11,007	589	53.5	700
1994 [2]	59,284	1,431	24.1	364	48,121	861	17.9	277	11,163	570	51.1	699
1995 ..	59,442	1,364	22.9	351	48,140	820	17.0	265	11,302	544	48.1	686

[1] Live births are those which occurred from July 1 of year shown through June 30 of the following year (to match time of conception with abortions). Births are classified by race of child 1972-1988, and by race of mother after 1988. [2] Total numbers of abortions in 1983 and 1986 have been estimated by interpolation; 1989, 1990, 1993, and 1994 have been estimated using trends in CDC data.

No. 125. Abortions, by Selected Characteristics: 1990 to 1995

[Number of abortions from surveys conducted by source; characteristics from the U.S. Centers for Disease Control's (CDC) annual abortion surveillance summaries, with adjustments for changes in states reporting data to the CDC each year]

CHARACTERISTIC	NUMBER (1,000)			PERCENT DISTRIBUTION			ABORTION RATIO [2]		
	1990 [1]	1992	1995	1990 [1]	1992	1995	1990 [1]	1992	1995
Total abortions	1,609	1,529	1,364	100	100	100	280	275	260
Age of woman:									
Less than 15 years old	13	13	11	1	1	1	515	511	480
15 to 19 years old	351	295	264	22	19	19	403	370	348
20 to 24 years old	532	526	442	33	34	32	328	333	317
25 to 29 years old	360	341	308	22	22	23	224	228	225
30 to 34 years old	216	213	196	13	14	14	196	192	179
35 to 39 years old	108	110	110	7	7	8	249	239	179
40 years old and over.	29	31	32	2	2	2	354	338	310
Race of woman:									
White.	1,039	944	820	65	62	60	241	229	210
Black and other	570	585	544	35	38	40	396	405	409
Marital status of woman: [3]									
Married	284	257	221	18	17	16	88	84	77
Unmarried	1,325	1272	1,143	82	83	84	527	508	477
Number of prior live births:									
None	780	691	614	49	45	45	316	298	277
One.	396	396	359	25	26	26	230	233	223
Two.	280	281	248	17	18	18	292	299	285
Three	102	105	95	6	7	7	279	290	284
Four or more	50	57	48	3	4	4	223	244	228
Number of prior induced abortions:									
None.	891	810	721	55	53	53	(NA)	(NA)	(NA)
One.	443	431	383	28	28	28	(NA)	(NA)	(NA)
Two or more	275	288	260	17	19	19	(NA)	(NA)	(NA)
Weeks of gestation: [4]									
Less than 9 weeks.	817	799	728	51	52	53	(NA)	(NA)	(NA)
9 to 10 weeks	418	378	317	26	25	23	(NA)	(NA)	(NA)
11 to 12 weeks	199	182	153	12	12	11	(NA)	(NA)	(NA)
13 weeks or more	175	171	166	11	11	12	(NA)	(NA)	(NA)

NA Not available. [1] Total numbers of abortions in 1990, 1993 and 1994 have been estimated using trends in CDC data.
[2] Number of abortions per 1,000 abortions and live births. Live births are those which occurred from July 1 of year shown through June 30 of the following year (to match time of conception with abortions). [3] Separated women included with unmarried women. [4] Data not exactly comparable with prior years because of a change in the method of calculation.

Source of Tables 124 and 125: S.K. Henshaw and J. Van Vort, eds., *Abortion Factbook, 1992. Edition: Readings, Trends, and State and Local Data to 1988*, The Alan Guttmacher Institute, New York, NY, 1992 (copyright); S.K. Henshaw and J. Van Vort, *Abortion Services in the United States, 1991 and 1992; Family Perspectives, 26:100, 1994;* and unpublished data.

No. 126. Abortions—Number and Rate, by State: 1992 and 1995

[Number of abortions from surveys of hospitals, clinics, and physicians identified as providers of abortion services conducted by The Alan Guttmacher Institute. Abortion rates are computed per 1,000 women 15 to 44 years of age on **July 1** of specified year]

STATE	ABORTIONS (1,000)		RATE [1]		STATE	ABORTIONS (1,000)		RATE [1]	
	1992	1995	1992	1995		1992	1995	1992	1995
U.S..	1,529	1,364	25.9	22.9	MO	14	11	11.6	8.9
AL	17	15	18.2	15.0	MT	3	3	18.2	16.2
AK	2	2	16.5	14.2	NE	6	4	15.7	12.1
AZ	21	18	24.1	19.1	NV	13	16	44.2	46.7
AR	7	6	13.5	11.1	NH	4	3	14.6	12.0
CA	304	240	42.1	33.4	NJ	55	61	31.0	34.5
CO	20	16	23.6	18.0	NM	6	5	17.7	14.4
CT	20	17	26.2	23.0	NY	195	176	46.2	42.8
DE	6	6	35.2	34.4	NC	36	35	22.4	21.0
DC	21	21	138.4	151.7	ND	1	1	10.7	9.6
FL	85	88	30.0	30.0	OH	50	41	19.5	16.2
GA	40	37	24.0	21.2	OK	9	9	12.5	12.9
HI	12	8	46.0	29.3	OR	16	16	23.9	22.6
ID	2	2	7.2	5.8	PA	50	41	18.6	15.5
IL	68	68	25.4	25.6	RI	7	6	30.0	25.5
IN	16	14	12.0	10.6	SC	12	11	14.2	12.9
IA	7	6	11.4	9.8	SD	1	1	6.8	6.6
KS	13	10	22.4	18.3	TN	19	18	16.2	15.2
KY	10	8	11.4	8.8	TX	97	89	23.1	20.5
LA	14	15	13.4	14.7	UT	4	4	9.3	8.1
ME	4	3	14.7	9.6	VT	3	2	21.2	17.9
MD	31	31	26.4	25.6	VA	35	31	22.7	20.0
MA	41	41	28.4	29.2	WA	33	25	27.7	20.2
MI	56	49	25.2	22.6	WV	3	3	7.7	7.6
MN	16	15	15.6	14.2	WI	15	13	13.6	11.6
MS	8	3	12.4	5.5	WY	-	-	4.3	2.7

- Represents or rounds to zero.   [1] Rate per 1,000 women, 15 to 44 years old.

Source: S.K. Henshaw and J. Van Vort, eds., *Abortion Factbook, 1992 Edition: Readings, Trends, and State and Local Data to 1988,* The Alan Guttmacher Institute, New York, NY, 1992 (copyright); and S.K. Henshaw and J. Van Vort, *Abortion Services in the United States, 1991 and 1992, Family Planning Perspectives,* 26:100, 1994; and unpublished data.

No. 127. Average Lifetime in Years by Race, by State: 1989-91

STATE	Total	White	Black	STATE	Total	White	Black
U.S.	75.37	76.13	69.16	MO	75.25	76.02	68.81
				MT	76.23	76.72	(S)
AL	73.64	75.01	69.23	NE	76.92	77.21	(S)
AZ	76.10	76.42	70.84	NV	74.18	74.44	(S)
AR	74.33	75.20	68.93	NH	76.72	76.68	(S)
CA	75.86	75.92	69.65				
CO	76.96	77.06	72.41	NJ	75.42	76.46	68.47
				NM	75.74	76.08	(S)
CT	76.91	77.44	70.84	NY	74.68	75.61	69.33
DE	74.76	75.76	69.26	NC	74.48	75.89	69.38
DC	67.99	76.09	64.44	ND	77.62	77.99	(S)
FL	75.84	76.82	68.77				
GA	73.61	75.24	68.79	OH	75.32	75.93	70.15
				OK	75.10	75.21	70.85
HI	78.21	77.92	(S)	OR	76.44	76.51	(S)
ID	76.88	76.89	(S)	PA	75.38	76.15	68.27
IL	74.90	76.16	67.46	RI	76.54	76.80	(S)
IN	75.39	75.82	69.80				
IA	77.29	77.38	(S)	SC	73.51	75.33	68.82
				SD	76.91	77.91	(S)
KS	76.76	77.06	71.22	TN	74.32	75.27	68.97
KY	74.37	74.65	70.16	TX	75.14	75.75	69.79
LA	73.05	74.87	68.62	UT	77.70	77.77	(S)
ME	76.35	76.35	(S)				
MD	74.79	76.30	69.69	VT	76.54	76.50	(S)
				VA	75.22	76.34	70.05
MA	76.72	76.90	72.45	WA	76.82	76.92	71.34
MI	75.04	76.18	68.49	WV	74.26	74.37	69.75
MN	77.76	77.97	(S)	WI	76.87	77.18	70.96
MS	73.03	74.78	69.41	WY	76.21	76.34	(S)

S Does not meet standards of reliability and precision.

Source: U.S. National Center for Health Statistics, U.S. Decennial Life Tables for 1989-91 Volume II.

No. 128. Expectation of Life at Birth, 1970 to 1996, and Projections, 1995 to 2010

[In years. Excludes deaths of nonresidents of the United States]

YEAR	TOTAL			WHITE			BLACK AND OTHER			BLACK		
	Total	Male	Female	Total	Male	Female	Total	Male	Female	Total	Male	Female
1970	70.8	67.1	74.7	71.7	68.0	75.6	65.3	61.3	69.4	64.1	60.0	68.3
1975	72.6	68.8	76.6	73.4	69.5	77.3	68.0	63.7	72.4	66.8	62.4	71.3
1980	73.7	70.0	77.4	74.4	70.7	78.1	69.5	65.3	73.6	68.1	63.8	72.5
1982	74.5	70.8	78.1	75.1	71.5	78.7	70.9	66.8	74.9	69.4	65.1	73.6
1983	74.6	71.0	78.1	75.2	71.6	78.7	70.9	67.0	74.7	69.4	65.2	73.5
1984	74.7	71.1	78.2	75.3	71.8	78.7	71.1	67.2	74.9	69.5	65.3	73.6
1985	74.7	71.1	78.2	75.3	71.8	78.7	71.0	67.0	74.8	69.3	65.0	73.4
1986	74.7	71.2	78.2	75.4	71.9	78.8	70.9	66.8	74.9	69.1	64.8	73.4
1987	74.9	71.4	78.3	75.6	72.1	78.9	71.0	66.9	75.0	69.1	64.7	73.4
1988	74.9	71.4	78.3	75.6	72.2	78.9	70.8	66.7	74.8	68.9	64.4	73.2
1989	75.1	71.7	78.5	75.9	72.5	79.2	70.9	66.7	74.9	68.8	64.3	73.3
1990	75.4	71.8	78.8	76.1	72.7	79.4	71.2	67.0	75.2	69.1	64.5	73.6
1991	75.5	72.0	78.9	76.3	72.9	79.6	71.5	67.3	75.5	69.3	64.6	73.8
1992	75.8	72.3	79.1	76.5	73.2	79.8	71.8	67.7	75.7	69.6	65.0	73.9
1993	75.5	72.2	78.8	76.3	73.1	79.5	71.5	67.3	75.5	69.2	64.6	73.7
1994	75.7	72.3	79.0	76.4	73.2	79.6	71.7	67.5	75.8	69.6	64.9	74.1
1995	75.8	72.5	78.9	76.5	73.4	79.6	71.9	67.9	75.7	69.6	65.2	73.9
1996	76.1	73.0	79.0	76.8	73.8	79.6	(NA)	(NA)	(NA)	70.3	66.1	74.2
Projections: [1] 1995	75.9	72.5	79.3	76.9	73.6	80.1	(NA)	(NA)	(NA)	69.7	64.8	74.5
2000	76.4	73.0	79.7	77.4	74.2	80.5	(NA)	(NA)	(NA)	69.7	64.6	74.7
2005	76.9	73.5	80.2	77.9	74.7	81.0	(NA)	(NA)	(NA)	69.9	64.5	75.0
2010	77.4	74.1	80.6	78.6	75.5	81.6	(NA)	(NA)	(NA)	70.4	65.1	75.5

NA Not available. [1] Based on middle mortality assumptions; for details, see source. Source: U.S. Bureau of the Census, *Current Population Reports*, P25-1130.

Source: Except as noted, U.S. National Center for Health Statistics, *Vital Statistics of the United States*, annual, and *Monthly Vital Statistics Reports*.

No. 129. Selected Life Table Values: 1979 to 1996

AGE AND SEX	TOTAL [1]			WHITE			BLACK		
	1979-1981	1990	1996	1979-1981	1990	1996	1979-1981	1990	1996
AVERAGE EXPECTATION OF LIFE IN YEARS									
At birth: Male	70.1	71.8	73.0	70.8	72.7	73.8	64.1	64.5	66.1
Female	77.6	78.8	79.0	78.2	79.4	79.6	72.9	73.6	74.2
Age 20: Male	51.9	53.3	54.2	52.5	54.0	54.8	46.4	46.7	48.0
Female	59.0	59.8	59.9	59.4	60.3	60.4	54.9	55.3	55.7
Age 40: Male	33.6	35.1	35.9	34.0	35.6	36.3	29.5	30.1	31.0
Female	39.8	40.6	40.7	40.2	41.0	41.0	36.3	36.8	37.0
Age 50: Male	25.0	26.4	27.1	25.3	26.7	27.5	22.0	22.5	23.4
Female	30.7	31.3	31.5	31.0	31.6	31.7	27.8	28.2	28.6
Age 65: Male	14.2	15.1	15.7	14.3	15.2	15.8	13.3	13.2	13.9
Female	18.4	18.9	18.9	18.6	19.1	19.0	17.1	17.2	17.2
EXPECTED DEATHS PER 1,000 ALIVE AT SPECIFIED AGE [2]									
At birth: Male	13.9	10.3	(NA)	12.3	8.6	(NA)	23.0	19.7	(NA)
Female	11.2	8.2	(NA)	9.7	6.6	(NA)	19.3	16.3	(NA)
Age 20: Male	1.8	1.6	(NA)	1.8	1.4	(NA)	2.2	2.7	(NA)
Female	0.6	0.5	(NA)	0.6	0.5	(NA)	0.7	0.7	(NA)
Age 40: Male	3.0	3.1	(NA)	2.6	2.7	(NA)	6.9	7.1	(NA)
Female	1.6	1.4	(NA)	1.4	1.2	(NA)	3.2	3.1	(NA)
Age 50: Male	7.8	6.2	(NA)	7.1	5.6	(NA)	14.9	12.8	(NA)
Female	4.2	3.5	(NA)	3.8	3.2	(NA)	7.7	6.6	(NA)
Age 65: Male	28.2	12.9	(NA)	27.4	23.0	(NA)	38.5	36.8	(NA)
Female	14.3	13.5	(NA)	13.6	12.8	(NA)	21.6	21.4	(NA)
NUMBER SURVIVING TO SPECIFIED AGE PER 1,000 BORN ALIVE									
Age 20: Male	973	979	(NA)	975	981	(NA)	961	963	(NA)
Female	982	986	(NA)	984	988	(NA)	972	976	(NA)
Age 40: Male	933	938	(NA)	940	946	(NA)	885	880	(NA)
Female	965	971	(NA)	969	975	(NA)	941	944	(NA)
Age 50: Male	890	899	(NA)	901	912	(NA)	801	801	(NA)
Female	941	950	(NA)	947	957	(NA)	896	904	(NA)
Age 65: Male	706	741	(NA)	724	760	(NA)	551	571	(NA)
Female	835	851	(NA)	848	864	(NA)	733	751	(NA)

NA Not available. [1] Includes other races not shown separately. [2] See footnote 1, Table 130.

Source: U.S. National Center for Health Statistics, *U.S. Life Tables and Actuarial Tables, 1959-61, 1969-71, and 1979-81; Vital Statistics of the United States*, annual; and unpublished data.

No. 130. Expectation of Life and Expected Deaths, by Race, Sex, and Age: 1995

AGE IN 1990 (years)	EXPECTATION OF LIFE IN YEARS					EXPECTED DEATHS PER 1,000 ALIVE AT SPECIFIED AGE [1]				
	Total	White		Black		Total	White		Black	
		Male	Female	Male	Female		Male	Female	Male	Female
At birth	75.8	73.4	79.6	65.2	73.9	7.57	6.98	5.55	16.22	13.74
1	75.4	72.9	79.0	65.3	73.9	0.58	0.57	0.44	1.10	0.82
2	74.4	72.0	78.1	64.3	73.0	0.43	0.41	0.33	0.79	0.66
3	73.4	71.0	77.1	63.4	72.0	0.33	0.31	0.26	0.60	0.53
4	72.5	70.0	76.1	62.4	71.0	0.27	0.26	0.21	0.49	0.42
5	71.5	69.1	75.1	61.5	70.1	0.23	0.23	0.18	0.43	0.34
6	70.5	68.1	74.1	60.5	69.1	0.21	0.22	0.16	0.40	0.28
7	69.5	67.1	73.1	59.5	68.1	0.20	0.21	0.15	0.36	0.24
8	68.5	66.1	72.2	58.5	67.1	0.18	0.19	0.14	0.31	0.21
9	67.5	65.1	71.2	57.5	66.1	0.16	0.17	0.13	0.25	0.21
10	66.6	64.1	70.2	56.6	65.2	0.15	0.15	0.12	0.20	0.21
11	65.6	63.1	69.2	55.6	64.2	0.16	0.16	0.13	0.20	0.23
12	64.6	62.1	68.2	54.6	63.2	0.21	0.22	0.16	0.32	0.26
13	63.6	61.2	67.2	53.6	62.2	0.31	0.35	0.21	0.59	0.31
14	62.6	60.2	66.2	52.6	61.2	0.45	0.54	0.28	0.95	0.36
15	61.6	59.2	65.2	51.7	60.2	0.61	0.74	0.35	1.37	0.43
16	60.7	58.3	64.3	50.8	59.3	0.75	0.94	0.42	1.77	0.50
17	59.7	57.3	63.3	49.8	58.3	0.87	1.09	0.47	2.11	0.57
18	58.8	56.4	62.3	48.9	57.3	0.94	1.20	0.48	2.36	0.62
19	57.8	55.4	61.3	48.1	56.4	0.98	1.26	0.47	2.54	0.67
20	56.9	54.5	60.4	47.2	55.4	1.01	1.32	0.45	2.72	0.72
21	55.9	53.6	59.4	46.3	54.4	1.05	1.38	0.44	2.91	0.77
22	55.0	52.7	58.4	45.4	53.5	1.08	1.42	0.43	3.07	0.84
23	54.1	51.7	57.4	44.6	52.5	1.10	1.43	0.44	3.17	0.92
24	53.1	50.8	56.5	43.7	51.6	1.11	1.43	0.46	3.25	1.02
25	52.2	49.9	55.5	42.9	50.6	1.12	1.42	0.48	3.30	1.12
26	51.2	48.9	54.5	42.0	49.7	1.13	1.41	0.50	3.37	1.23
27	50.3	48.0	53.6	41.1	48.7	1.17	1.44	0.53	3.49	1.34
28	49.3	47.1	52.6	40.3	47.8	1.23	1.53	0.56	3.69	1.45
29	48.4	46.2	51.6	39.4	46.9	1.32	1.65	0.60	3.94	1.57
30	47.5	45.2	50.6	38.6	46.0	1.42	1.79	0.64	4.21	1.70
31	46.5	44.3	49.7	37.7	45.0	1.51	1.92	0.68	4.49	1.83
32	45.6	43.4	48.7	36.9	44.1	1.61	2.04	0.73	4.76	1.97
33	44.7	42.5	47.7	36.1	43.2	1.70	2.14	0.79	5.02	2.12
34	43.8	41.6	46.8	35.3	42.3	1.79	2.23	0.85	5.28	2.27
35	42.8	40.7	45.8	34.5	41.4	1.89	2.32	0.92	5.55	2.43
36	41.9	39.8	44.9	33.6	40.5	1.99	2.42	0.99	5.84	2.60
37	41.0	38.8	43.9	32.8	39.6	2.10	2.53	1.06	6.18	2.78
38	40.1	37.9	42.9	32.0	38.7	2.22	2.66	1.13	6.56	2.97
39	39.2	37.0	42.0	31.2	37.8	2.34	2.79	1.20	6.99	3.18
40	38.3	36.1	41.0	30.5	36.9	2.47	2.94	1.28	7.45	3.40
41	37.3	35.3	40.1	29.7	36.1	2.62	3.10	1.37	7.92	3.63
42	36.4	34.4	39.2	28.9	35.2	2.76	3.27	1.47	8.40	3.86
43	35.5	33.5	38.2	28.2	34.3	2.92	3.43	1.59	8.88	4.10
44	34.6	32.6	37.3	27.4	33.5	3.07	3.60	1.72	9.37	4.34
45	33.8	31.7	36.3	26.7	32.6	3.25	3.80	1.87	9.88	4.60
46	32.9	30.8	35.4	25.9	31.7	3.46	4.02	2.04	10.43	4.89
47	32.0	29.9	34.5	25.2	30.9	3.70	4.30	2.24	11.02	5.21
48	31.1	29.1	33.5	24.5	30.1	4.00	4.64	2.47	11.67	5.56
49	30.2	28.2	32.6	23.7	29.2	4.35	5.04	2.75	12.38	5.95
50	29.3	27.3	31.7	23.0	28.4	4.74	5.49	3.05	13.15	6.37
51	28.5	26.5	30.8	22.3	27.6	5.16	5.99	3.39	13.97	6.84
52	27.6	25.6	29.9	21.6	26.8	5.62	6.52	3.75	14.82	7.35
53	26.8	24.8	29.0	21.0	26.0	6.11	7.10	4.12	15.68	7.93
54	25.9	24.0	28.1	20.3	25.2	6.64	7.73	4.52	16.58	8.58
55	25.1	23.2	27.3	19.6	24.4	7.21	8.41	4.96	17.48	9.26
56	24.3	22.4	26.4	19.0	23.6	7.84	9.17	5.44	18.48	9.99
57	23.5	21.6	25.5	18.3	22.8	8.58	10.07	5.99	19.73	10.82
58	22.7	20.8	24.7	17.7	22.1	9.45	11.14	6.62	21.32	11.78
59	21.9	20.0	23.9	17.0	21.3	10.42	12.36	7.33	23.17	12.83
60	21.1	19.3	23.0	16.4	20.6	11.50	13.70	8.11	25.29	14.01
61	20.4	18.5	22.2	15.9	19.9	12.62	15.11	8.93	27.45	15.24
62	19.6	17.8	21.4	15.3	19.2	13.77	16.59	9.79	29.36	16.40
63	18.9	17.1	20.6	14.7	18.5	14.92	18.12	10.67	30.84	17.44
64	18.2	16.4	19.8	14.2	17.8	16.11	19.73	11.59	32.02	18.42
65	17.4	15.7	19.1	13.6	17.1	17.35	21.43	12.57	32.99	19.34
70	14.1	12.5	15.4	11.0	13.9	26.18	32.69	19.52	48.22	29.73
75	11.0	9.7	12.0	8.8	11.1	39.26	49.26	30.73	65.70	41.08
80	8.3	7.2	8.9	6.8	8.4	60.15	75.57	49.53	89.94	59.43
85 and over . .	6.0	5.2	6.3	5.1	6.2	1,000.0	1,000.0	1,000.0	1,000.0	1,000.0

[1] Based on the proportion of the cohort who are alive at the beginning of an indicated age interval who will die before reaching the end of that interval. For example, out of every 1,000 people alive and exactly 50 years old at the beginning of the period, between 4 and 5 (4.74) will die before reaching their 51st birthdays.

Source: U.S. National Center for Health Statistics, *Vital Statistics of the United States*, annual; and unpublished data.

No. 131. Deaths and Death Rates, by Sex and Race: 1980 to 1996

[Rates are per 1,000 population for specified groups. Excludes deaths of nonresidents of the United States and fetal deaths. For explanation of age-adjustment, see text, Section 2. The standard population for this table is the total population of the United States enumerated in 1940. See Appendix III]

SEX AND RACE	1980	1985	1987	1988	1989	1990	1991	1992	1993	1994	1995	1996
Deaths [1] (1,000)	1,990	2,086	2,123	2,168	2,150	2,148	2,170	2,176	2,269	2,279	2,312	2,322
Male [1] (1,000)	1,075	1,098	1,108	1,126	1,114	1,113	1,122	1,122	1,162	1,163	1,173	1,169
Female [1] (1,000)	915	989	1,015	1,042	1,036	1,035	1,048	1,053	1,107	1,116	1,139	1,154
White (1,000)	1,739	1,819	1,843	1,877	1,854	1,853	1,869	1,874	1,951	1,960	1,987	2,001
Male (1,000)	934	950	953	965	951	951	956	957	988	989	997	997
Female (1,000)	805	869	890	911	903	902	912	917	963	971	990	1,004
Black (1,000)	233	244	255	264	268	266	270	269	282	282	286	282
Male (1,000)	130	134	140	144	146	145	147	147	154	153	154	149
Female (1,000)	103	111	115	120	121	120	122	123	129	129	132	132
Death rates [1]	8.8	8.8	8.8	8.8	8.7	8.6	8.6	8.5	8.8	8.8	8.8	8.8
Male [1]	9.8	9.5	9.4	9.5	9.3	9.2	9.1	9.0	9.2	9.2	9.1	9.0
Female [1]	7.9	8.1	8.2	8.3	8.2	8.1	8.1	8.1	8.4	8.4	8.5	8.5
White	8.9	9.0	9.0	9.1	8.9	8.9	8.9	8.8	9.1	9.1	9.1	9.1
Male	9.8	9.6	9.5	9.6	9.4	9.3	9.3	9.2	9.4	9.3	9.3	9.2
Female	8.1	8.4	8.5	8.7	8.5	8.5	8.5	8.4	8.8	8.8	8.9	9.0
Black	8.8	8.5	8.7	8.9	8.9	8.8	8.6	8.5	8.8	8.6	8.6	8.4
Male	10.3	9.9	10.1	10.3	10.3	10.1	10.0	9.8	10.1	9.9	9.8	9.4
Female	7.3	7.3	7.5	7.6	7.6	7.5	7.4	7.4	7.6	7.5	7.6	7.5
Age-adjusted death [1]	5.9	5.5	5.4	5.4	5.3	5.2	5.1	5.0	5.1	5.1	5.0	4.9
Male [1]	7.8	7.2	7.1	7.1	6.9	6.8	6.7	6.6	6.6	6.5	6.5	6.3
Female [1]	4.3	4.1	4.0	4.1	4.0	3.9	3.9	3.8	3.9	3.9	3.9	3.8
White	5.6	5.2	5.1	5.1	5.0	4.9	4.9	4.8	4.9	4.8	4.8	4.7
Male	7.5	6.9	6.7	6.7	6.5	6.4	6.3	6.2	6.3	6.2	6.1	5.9
Female	4.1	3.9	3.8	3.9	3.8	3.7	3.7	3.6	3.7	3.6	3.6	3.6
Black	8.4	7.9	8.0	8.1	8.1	7.9	7.8	7.7	7.9	7.7	7.7	7.4
Male	11.1	10.5	10.6	10.8	10.8	10.6	10.5	10.3	10.5	10.3	10.2	9.7
Female	6.3	5.9	5.9	6.0	5.9	5.8	5.8	5.7	5.8	5.7	5.7	5.6

[1] Includes other races not shown separately.

No. 132. Death Rates, by Age, Sex, and Race: 1970 to 1996

[Number of deaths per 100,000 population in specified group. See headnote, Table 131]

SEX, YEAR, AND RACE	All ages [1]	Under 1 yr. old	1-4 yr. old	5-14 yr. old	15-24 yr. old	25-34 yr. old	35-44 yr. old	45-54 yr. old	55-64 yr. old	65-74 yr. old	75-84 yr. old	85 yr. old and over
MALE [2]												
1970	1,090	2,410	93	51	189	215	403	959	2,283	4,874	10,010	17,822
1980	977	1,429	73	37	172	196	299	767	1,815	4,105	8,817	18,801
1990	918	1,083	52	29	147	204	310	610	1,553	3,492	7,889	18,057
1994	915	899	47	27	146	209	333	599	1,444	3,332	7,441	17,972
1995	914	844	45	27	141	205	333	599	1,417	3,285	7,377	17,979
1996	900	821	43	26	132	180	301	577	1,397	3,248	7,271	17,580
White: 1970	1,087	2,113	84	48	171	177	344	883	2,203	4,810	10,099	18,552
1980	983	1,230	66	35	167	171	257	699	1,729	4,036	8,830	19,097
1990	931	896	46	26	131	176	268	549	1,467	3,398	7,845	18,268
1994	932	740	41	24	124	180	287	536	1,365	3,247	7,386	18,196
1995	932	718	39	25	122	178	288	535	1,331	3,199	7,321	18,153
1996	923	683	37	24	115	156	263	519	1,314	3,176	7,230	17,903
Black: 1970	1,187	4,299	151	67	321	560	957	1,778	3,257	5,803	9,455	12,222
1980	1,034	2,587	111	47	209	407	690	1,480	2,873	5,131	9,232	16,099
1990	1,008	2,112	86	41	252	431	700	1,261	2,618	4,946	9,130	16,955
1994	988	1,797	84	42	278	434	732	1,268	2,423	4,654	8,830	16,267
1995	981	1,591	78	40	249	417	721	1,273	2,438	4,611	8,779	16,729
1996	940	1,698	73	39	235	363	632	1,190	2,397	4,423	8,588	16,017
FEMALE [2]												
1970	808	1,864	75	32	68	102	231	517	1,099	2,580	6,678	15,518
1980	785	1,142	55	24	58	76	159	413	934	2,145	5,440	14,747
1990	812	856	41	19	49	74	138	343	879	1,991	4,883	14,274
1994	838	736	38	18	48	78	146	330	842	1,990	4,871	14,265
1995	847	690	36	18	48	78	150	328	841	1,986	4,883	14,492
1996	852	673	34	18	46	75	146	325	831	1,989	4,879	14,441
White: 1970	813	1,615	66	30	62	84	193	463	1,015	2,471	6,699	15,980
1980	806	963	49	23	56	65	138	373	876	2,067	5,402	14,980
1990	847	690	36	18	46	62	117	309	823	1,924	4,839	14,401
1994	880	605	32	16	44	64	122	297	792	1,930	4,822	14,416
1995	891	572	31	17	44	64	126	294	788	1,925	4,831	14,639
1996	899	557	28	16	43	63	123	292	784	1,930	4,840	14,647
Black: 1970	829	3,369	129	44	112	231	533	1,044	1,986	3,861	6,692	10,707
1980	733	2,124	84	31	71	150	324	768	1,561	3,057	6,212	12,367
1990	748	1,736	68	28	69	160	299	639	1,453	2,866	5,688	13,310
1994	753	1,453	70	27	72	168	327	629	1,342	2,816	5,779	13,166
1995	759	1,342	63	27	70	167	328	619	1,350	2,824	5,840	13,472
1996	752	1,407	63	26	67	155	317	611	1,311	2,790	5,766	13,315

[1] Includes unknown age.   [2] Includes other races not shown separately.

Source of Tables 131 and 132: U.S. National Center for Health Statistics, *Vital Statistics of the United States,* annual; *Monthly Vital Statistics Report;* and unpublished data.

No. 133. Deaths and Death Rates, by State: 1990 to 1996

[By state of residence. Excludes deaths of nonresidents of the United States, except as noted. Caution should be used in comparing death rates by state, rates are affected by the population composition of the area. See also Appendix III]

STATE	NUMBER OF DEATHS (1,000)							RATE PER 1,000 POPULATION [1]						
	1990	1991	1992	1993	1994	1995	1996	1990	1991	1992	1993	1994	1995	1996
United States..	2,148	2,165	2,176	2,269	2,279	2,312	2,322	8.6	8.6	8.5	8.8	8.8	8.8	8.8
Alabama.........	39	38	39	41	42	42	43	9.7	9.3	9.5	9.9	9.9	10.0	10.0
Alaska..........	2	2	2	2	2	3	3	4.0	3.8	3.9	3.8	4.0	4.2	4.3
Arizona.........	29	29	31	33	34	35	39	7.9	7.8	8.1	8.2	8.4	8.4	8.8
Arkansas	25	24	25	27	26	27	27	10.5	10.2	10.4	10.9	10.7	10.8	10.6
California	214	219	216	222	224	224	231	7.2	7.2	7.0	7.0	7.1	7.1	7.2
Colorado........	22	22	22	24	24	25	26	6.6	6.6	6.5	6.7	6.6	6.7	6.8
Connecticut......	28	28	28	29	29	29	30	8.4	8.4	8.6	8.9	8.9	9.0	9.0
Delaware	6	6	6	6	6	6	7	8.7	8.6	8.6	8.7	9.0	8.8	9.0
Dist. of Columbia . . .	7	7	7	7	7	7	7	12.0	11.7	12.1	11.6	12.6	12.4	12.1
Florida	134	135	140	147	149	153	154	10.4	10.2	10.4	10.7	10.7	10.8	10.7
Georgia	52	53	53	56	57	58	59	8.0	8.0	7.8	8.1	8.0	8.1	8.0
Hawaii	7	7	7	7	7	8	8	6.1	5.9	6.0	6.2	6.2	6.4	6.7
Idaho	7	8	8	8	8	9	9	7.4	7.5	7.4	7.6	7.5	7.3	7.3
Illinois	103	105	102	107	107	108	106	9.0	9.1	8.8	9.2	9.1	9.2	9.0
Indiana.........	50	52	50	52	52	53	55	8.9	9.2	8.8	9.1	9.1	9.2	9.3
Iowa	27	26	27	28	28	28	28	9.7	9.3	9.5	9.9	9.8	9.9	9.7
Kansas.........	22	23	22	24	23	24	24	9.0	9.0	8.8	9.2	9.1	9.3	9.3
Kentucky	35	35	35	37	37	37	37	9.5	9.5	9.3	9.7	9.7	9.6	9.6
Louisiana.......	38	38	38	40	39	40	40	8.9	9.0	8.8	9.3	9.0	9.1	9.3
Maine..........	11	11	11	12	12	12	11	9.0	8.9	9.0	9.3	9.4	9.5	8.9
Maryland	38	38	39	40	41	42	42	8.0	7.8	7.9	8.7	8.2	8.3	8.2
Massachusetts.....	53	51	54	56	55	55	55	8.8	8.6	9.0	9.4	9.1	9.1	9.1
Michigan........	79	80	79	83	83	84	84	8.5	8.5	8.4	8.7	8.7	8.8	8.7
Minnesota........	35	35	35	36	37	38	37	7.9	8.0	7.8	8.0	8.0	8.1	8.0
Mississippi	25	26	25	26	27	27	27	9.8	9.9	9.7	10.1	10.0	10.0	9.8
Missouri	50	53	51	54	54	54	54	9.8	10.4	9.8	10.8	10.2	10.2	10.1
Montana........	7	7	7	7	7	8	8	8.6	8.7	8.6	8.9	8.6	8.8	8.7
Nebraska	15	15	15	15	15	15	16	9.4	9.2	9.2	9.6	9.3	9.3	9.4
Nevada	9	9	10	11	12	13	13	7.8	7.2	7.7	7.8	8.2	8.2	8.2
New Hampshire	8	9	9	9	9	9	9	7.7	7.7	7.7	7.9	7.8	8.0	8.1
New Jersey......	70	70	71	73	72	74	72	9.1	9.0	9.1	9.2	9.1	9.3	9.0
New Mexico	11	11	11	12	12	13	13	7.0	7.2	7.1	7.3	7.3	7.4	7.3
New York	169	167	166	171	169	168	163	9.4	9.2	9.2	9.4	9.3	9.3	8.9
North Carolina.....	57	59	60	62	63	65	66	8.6	8.7	8.7	9.0	8.9	9.0	9.1
North Dakota......	6	6	6	6	6	6	6	8.9	8.9	9.0	9.3	9.2	9.3	9.3
Ohio	99	99	99	103	103	106	105	9.1	9.1	9.0	9.1	9.3	9.5	9.4
Oklahoma........	30	30	31	32	32	33	33	9.7	9.6	9.5	10.1	9.9	10.0	10.0
Oregon.........	25	25	26	28	27	28	29	8.8	8.6	8.7	9.0	8.9	9.0	9.0
Pennsylvania.....	122	124	124	126	128	128	130	10.3	10.3	10.3	10.5	10.6	10.6	10.7
Rhode Island......	10	9	9	10	9	10	10	9.5	9.2	9.5	9.7	9.4	9.8	9.6
South Carolina.....	30	30	31	32	32	34	34	8.5	8.4	8.5	8.6	8.8	9.1	9.3
South Dakota	6	7	7	7	7	7	7	9.1	9.4	9.5	9.6	9.4	9.5	9.3
Tennessee	46	45	47	49	51	51	51	9.5	9.2	9.3	9.7	9.8	9.8	9.7
Texas..........	125	129	129	135	136	138	138	7.4	7.4	7.3	7.5	7.4	7.4	7.2
Utah	9	9	10	10	10	11	11	5.3	5.2	5.4	5.5	5.5	5.6	5.5
Vermont........	5	5	5	5	5	5	5	8.2	8.0	8.4	8.5	8.2	8.5	8.3
Virginia.........	48	49	49	52	52	53	53	7.8	7.8	7.7	8.0	8.0	8.0	7.9
Washington......	37	38	38	40	40	41	42	7.6	7.5	7.4	8.0	7.5	7.5	7.6
West Virginia.....	19	20	20	20	20	20	20	10.8	11.0	10.9	11.0	11.1	11.1	11.2
Wisconsin.......	43	44	42	45	44	45	45	8.7	8.8	8.5	8.7	8.7	8.8	8.7
Wyoming	3	3	3	3	3	4	4	7.1	6.9	7.1	7.5	7.3	7.7	7.5

[1] Rates based on enumerated resident population as of April 1 for 1990; estimated resident population as of July 1 for all other years.

Source: U.S. National Center for Health Statistics, *Vital Statistics of the United States,* annual; and *Monthly Vital Statistics Report.*

No. 134. Infant, Maternal, and Neonatal Mortality Rates and Fetal Mortality Ratios, by Race: 1980 to 1996

[Deaths per 1,000 live births, except as noted. Excludes deaths of nonresidents of U.S. Race for live births tabulated according to race of mother, for infant and neonatal mortality rates. Beginning 1989, race for live births tabulated according to race of mother, for maternal mortality rates and mortality rates. See also Appendix III]

ITEM	1980	1990	1991	1992	1993	1994	1995	1996
Infant deaths [1]	**12.6**	**9.2**	**8.9**	**8.5**	**8.4**	**8.0**	**7.6**	**7.2**
White	10.9	7.6	7.3	6.9	6.8	6.6	6.3	6.0
Black and other	20.2	15.5	15.1	14.4	14.1	13.5	(NA)	(NA)
Black	22.2	18.0	17.6	16.8	16.5	15.8	15.1	14.2
Maternal deaths [2]	**9.2**	**8.2**	**7.9**	**7.8**	**7.5**	**8.3**	**7.1**	**(NA)**
White	6.7	5.4	5.8	5.0	4.8	6.2	4.2	(NA)
Black and other	19.8	19.1	15.6	18.2	17.6	16.2	18.5	(NA)
Black	21.5	22.4	18.3	20.8	20.5	18.5	22.1	(NA)
Fetal deaths [3]	**9.2**	**7.5**	**7.3**	**7.4**	**(NA)**	**(NA)**	**(NA)**	**(NA)**
White	8.2	6.4	6.2	6.3	(NA)	(NA)	(NA)	(NA)
Black and other	13.4	11.9	11.4	11.7	(NA)	(NA)	(NA)	(NA)
Neonatal deaths [4]	**8.5**	**5.8**	**5.6**	**5.4**	**5.3**	**5.1**	**4.9**	**4.7**
White	7.4	4.8	4.5	4.3	4.3	4.2	4.1	3.9
Black and other	13.2	9.9	9.5	9.2	9.0	8.6	(NA)	(NA)
Black	14.6	11.6	11.2	10.8	10.7	10.2	9.8	9.2

NA Not available.   [1] Represents deaths of infants under 1 year old, exclusive of fetal deaths.   [2] Per 100,000 live births from deliveries and complications of pregnancy, childbirth, and the puerperium. Deaths are classified according to the ninth revision of the *International Classification of Diseases;* earlier years classified according to the revision in use at the time; see text, Section 2.   [3] Includes only those deaths with stated or presumed period of gestation of 20 weeks or more.   [4] Represents deaths of infants under 28 days old, exclusive of fetal deaths.

No. 135. Fetal and Infant Deaths—Number and Percent Distribution: 1970 to 1993

[State requirements for reporting of fetal deaths vary. Most states require reporting of fetal deaths of gestations of 20 weeks or more. There is substantial evidence that not all fetal deaths for which reporting is required are reported. For details of methodology, see Appendix III and source]

YEAR	NUMBER						PERCENT DISTRIBUTION					
	Total	Fetal deaths		Infant deaths			Total	Fetal deaths		Infant deaths		
		Early [1]	Late [2]	Neonatal		Post-neo-natal [5]		Early [1]	Late [2]	Neonatal		Post-neo-natal [5]
				Early [3]	Late [4]					Early [3]	Late [4]	
1970	127,628	17,170	35,791	50,821	5,458	18,388	100.0	13.5	28.0	39.8	4.3	14.4
1980	78,879	10,754	22,599	25,492	5,126	14,908	100.0	13.6	28.7	32.3	6.5	18.9
1982	75,095	11,028	21,666	23,706	4,629	14,066	100.0	14.7	28.9	31.6	6.2	18.7
1983	71,379	10,933	19,819	22,315	4,192	14,120	100.0	15.3	27.8	31.3	5.9	19.8
1984	69,679	10,963	19,136	21,566	4,125	13,889	100.0	15.7	27.5	31.0	5.9	19.9
1985	69,691	10,958	18,703	21,865	4,314	13,851	100.0	15.7	26.8	31.4	6.2	19.9
1986	67,863	11,100	17,872	21,053	4,159	13,679	100.0	16.4	26.3	31.0	6.1	20.2
1987	67,757	11,656	17,693	20,471	4,156	13,781	100.0	17.2	26.1	30.2	6.1	20.3
1988	68,352	11,833	17,609	20,471	4,219	14,220	100.0	17.3	25.8	29.9	6.2	20.8
1989	70,124	12,397	18,072	20,796	4,372	14,487	100.0	17.7	25.8	29.7	6.2	20.7
1990	67,696	12,554	16,791	20,020	4,289	14,042	100.0	18.5	24.8	29.6	6.3	20.7
1991	65,000	12,310	15,924	18,916	4,062	13,788	100.0	18.9	24.5	29.1	6.2	21.2
1992	63,153	12,704	15,821	17,798	4,051	12,779	100.0	20.1	25.1	28.2	6.4	21.8
1993	55,387	12,588	14,243	(NA)	(NA)	(NA)	100.7	22.7	25.7	(NA)	(NA)	(NA)

NA Not available.   [1] 20-27 weeks gestation.   [2] 28 weeks or more gestation.   [3] Less than 7 days.   [4] 7-27 days.   [5] 28 days-11 months.

No. 136. Infant Deaths and Infant Mortality Rates, by Cause of Death: 1980 to 1995

[Excludes deaths of nonresidents of the United States. Deaths classified according to ninth revision of *International Classification of Diseases.* See also Appendix III]

CAUSE OF DEATH	NUMBER			PERCENT DISTRIBUTION			INFANT MORTALITY RATE [1]		
	1980	1990	1995	1980	1990	1995	1980	1990	1995
Total	**45,526**	**38,351**	**29,583**	**100**	**100**	**100**	**12.6**	**9.2**	**7.6**
Congenital anomalies	9,220	8,239	6,554	20	21	22	2.6	2.0	1.7
Disorders relating to short gestation and unspecified low birth weight	3,648	4,013	3,933	8	10	13	1.0	1.0	1.0
Sudden infant death syndrome	5,510	5,417	3,397	12	14	11	1.5	1.3	0.9
Respiratory distress syndrome	4,989	2,850	1,454	11	7	5	1.4	0.7	0.4
Newborn affected by maternal complications of pregnancy	1,572	1,655	1,309	4	4	4	0.4	0.4	0.3
Newborn affected by complications of placenta, cord, and membranes	985	975	962	2	3	3	0.3	0.2	(NA)
Accidents and adverse effects	1,166	930	787	3	2	3	0.3	0.2	(NA)
Infections specific to the perinatal period	971	875	788	2	2	3	0.3	0.2	(NA)
Pneumonia and influenza	1,012	634	492	2	2	2	0.3	0.2	(NA)
Intrauterine hypoxia and birth asphyxia	1,497	762	475	3	2	2	0.4	0.2	(NA)
All other causes	14,956	12,001	9,432	33	31	32	4.1	2.9	(NA)

NA Not available   [1] Deaths of infants under 1 year old per 1,000 live births.
Sources of Tables 134-136: U.S. National Center for Health Statistics, *Vital Statistics of the United States,* annual, and *Monthly Vital Statistics Report;* and unpublished data.

No. 137. Infant Mortality Rates, by Race—States: 1980 to 1995

[**Deaths per 1,000 live births, by place of residence.** Represents deaths of infants under 1 year old, exclusive of fetal deaths. Excludes deaths of nonresidents of the United States. See Appendix III]

STATE	TOTAL [1]				WHITE				BLACK			
	1980	1985	1990	1995	1980	1985	1990	1995	1980	1985	1990	1995
U.S	12.6	10.6	9.2	7.6	11.0	9.3	7.3	6.3	21.4	18.2	18.0	15.1
Alabama	15.1	12.6	10.8	9.8	11.6	10.4	8.1	7.1	21.6	17.0	16.0	15.2
Alaska	12.3	10.8	10.5	7.7	9.4	9.6	7.6	6.1	19.5	20.5	(S)	(B)
Arizona	12.4	9.7	8.8	7.5	11.8	9.4	7.8	7.2	18.4	12.4	20.6	17.0
Arkansas	12.7	11.6	9.2	8.8	10.3	10.9	8.4	7.2	20.0	14.2	13.9	14.3
California	11.1	9.5	7.9	6.3	10.6	9.2	7.0	5.8	18.0	16.3	16.8	14.4
Colorado	10.1	9.4	8.8	6.5	9.8	9.1	7.8	6.0	19.1	15.9	19.4	16.8
Connecticut	11.2	10.0	7.9	7.2	10.2	8.5	6.3	6.5	19.1	20.9	17.6	12.6
Delaware	13.9	14.8	10.1	7.5	9.8	11.6	9.7	6.0	27.9	25.8	20.1	13.1
District of Columbia	25.0	20.8	20.7	16.2	17.8	10.8	0.0	(B)	26.7	23.7	24.6	19.6
Florida	14.6	11.3	9.6	7.5	11.8	9.2	6.7	6.0	22.8	17.8	16.8	13.0
Georgia	14.5	12.7	12.4	9.4	10.8	9.5	7.4	6.5	21.0	19.0	18.3	15.1
Hawaii	10.3	8.8	6.7	5.8	11.6	7.5	6.1	(B)	11.8	20.0	(S)	(B)
Idaho	10.7	10.4	8.7	6.1	10.7	10.5	8.6	5.8	(NA)	(NA)	(S)	(B)
Illinois	14.8	11.7	10.7	9.4	11.7	9.3	7.9	7.2	26.3	21.4	22.4	18.7
Indiana	11.9	10.9	9.6	8.4	10.5	10.0	7.9	7.3	23.4	19.5	17.4	17.5
Iowa	11.8	9.5	8.1	8.2	11.5	9.4	7.9	7.8	27.2	12.3	21.9	21.2
Kansas	10.4	9.3	8.4	7.0	9.5	9.0	8.0	6.2	20.6	14.4	17.7	17.6
Kentucky	12.9	11.2	8.5	7.6	12.0	10.3	8.2	7.4	22.0	20.5	14.3	10.7
Louisiana	14.3	11.9	11.1	9.8	10.5	8.6	8.1	6.2	20.6	17.2	16.7	15.3
Maine	9.2	9.1	6.2	6.5	9.4	9.2	6.7	6.3	(S)	12.0	(S)	(B)
Maryland	14.0	11.9	9.5	8.9	11.6	9.1	6.8	6.0	20.4	18.9	17.1	15.3
Massachusetts	10.5	9.1	7.0	5.2	10.1	8.2	6.1	4.7	16.8	20.8	11.9	9.0
Michigan	12.8	11.4	10.7	8.3	10.6	9.3	7.4	6.2	24.2	22.4	21.6	17.3
Minnesota	10.0	8.8	7.3	6.7	9.6	8.8	6.7	6.0	20.0	15.5	23.7	17.6
Mississippi	17.0	13.7	12.1	10.5	11.1	9.3	7.4	7.0	23.7	18.9	16.2	14.7
Missouri	12.4	10.2	9.4	7.4	11.1	9.0	7.9	6.4	20.7	17.0	18.2	13.8
Montana	12.4	10.3	9.0	7.0	11.8	9.8	6.0	7.0	(NA)	13.2	(S)	(B)
Nebraska	11.5	9.6	8.3	7.4	10.7	9.0	6.9	7.3	25.2	17.7	18.9	(B)
Nevada	10.7	8.5	8.4	5.7	10.0	8.7	8.2	5.5	20.6	11.7	14.2	(B)
New Hampshire	9.9	9.3	7.1	5.5	9.9	9.2	6.0	5.5	22.5	29.9	(S)	(B)
New Jersey	12.5	10.6	9.0	6.6	10.3	8.8	6.4	5.3	21.9	18.8	18.4	13.3
New Mexico	11.5	10.6	9.0	6.2	11.3	10.6	7.6	6.1	23.1	14.4	(S)	(B)
New York	12.5	10.8	9.6	7.7	10.8	9.4	7.4	6.2	20.0	16.1	18.1	13.9
North Carolina	14.5	11.8	10.6	9.2	11.4	9.4	8.0	6.7	20.0	17.8	16.5	15.9
North Dakota	12.1	8.5	8.0	7.2	11.7	8.4	7.2	6.7	27.5	6.9	(S)	(B)
Ohio	12.8	10.3	9.8	8.7	11.2	9.3	7.8	7.3	23.0	16.9	19.5	17.5
Oklahoma	12.7	10.9	9.2	8.3	12.1	10.8	9.1	8.0	21.8	18.5	14.3	15.1
Oregon	12.2	9.9	8.3	6.1	12.2	9.7	7.0	5.9	15.9	17.3	(S)	(B)
Pennsylvania	13.2	11.0	9.6	7.8	11.9	9.5	7.4	6.2	23.1	20.4	20.5	17.6
Rhode Island	11.0	8.2	8.1	7.2	10.9	8.1	7.0	7.0	(S)	(S)	(S)	(B)
South Carolina	15.6	14.2	11.7	9.6	10.8	9.6	8.1	6.7	22.9	21.8	17.3	14.6
South Dakota	10.9	9.9	10.1	9.5	9.0	8.9	8.0	7.9	(NA)	(NA)	(S)	(B)
Tennessee	13.5	11.4	10.3	9.3	11.9	8.9	7.3	6.8	19.3	20.2	17.9	17.9
Texas	12.2	9.8	8.1	6.5	11.2	9.0	6.7	5.9	18.8	15.5	14.7	11.7
Utah	10.4	9.6	7.5	5.4	10.5	9.7	6.0	5.3	27.3	3.3	(S)	(B)
Vermont	10.7	8.5	6.4	6.0	10.7	8.5	5.9	6.2	(S)	(NA)	(S)	(B)
Virginia	13.6	11.5	10.2	7.8	11.9	9.3	7.4	5.7	19.8	19.2	19.5	15.3
Washington	11.8	10.7	7.8	5.9	11.5	10.9	7.3	5.6	16.4	12.6	20.6	16.2
West Virginia	11.8	10.7	9.9	7.9	11.4	10.4	8.1	7.6	21.5	20.6	(S)	(B)
Wisconsin	10.3	9.1	8.2	7.3	9.7	8.5	7.7	6.3	18.5	17.4	19.0	18.6
Wyoming	9.8	12.2	8.6	7.7	9.3	12.2	7.5	6.8	25.9	9.9	(S)	(B)

B Base figure too small to meet statistical standards for reliability. NA Not available. S Figure does not meet publication standards. [1] Includes other races, not shown separately.

Source: U.S. National Center for Health Statistics, *Vital Statistics of the United States,* annual; and unpublished data.

No. 138. Deaths and Death Rates, by Selected Causes: 1990 to 1996

[Excludes deaths of nonresidents of the United States, except as noted. Beginning 1980, deaths classified according to ninth revision of *International Classification of Diseases;* for earlier years, classified according to revision in use at that time. See also Appendix III]

CAUSE OF DEATH	DEATHS (1,000)				CRUDE DEATH RATE PER 100,000 POPULATION [2]			
	1990	1994 [1]	1995	1996	1990	1994 [1]	1995	1996
All causes	2,148.5	2,286.0	2,312.1	2,322.4	863.8	876.9	880.0	875.4
Major cardiovascular diseases	916.0	945.2	951.4	951.3	368.3	362.6	362.1	358.6
Diseases of heart	720.1	734.1	737.6	733.8	289.5	281.6	280.7	276.6
Percent of total	33.5	32.1	31.9	31.6	33.5	32.1	31.9	31.6
Rheumatic fever and rheumatic heart disease	6.0	5.5	5.1	5.0	2.4	2.1	2.0	1.9
Hypertensive heart disease [3]	23.4	23.8	25.0	25.9	9.5	9.1	9.5	9.8
Ischemic heart disease	489.2	487.5	481.3	476.8	196.7	187.0	183.2	179.7
Other diseases of endocardium	13.0	14.5	16.2	17.3	5.2	5.6	6.2	6.5
All other forms of heart disease	188.4	200.1	207.4	206.3	75.8	76.8	78.9	77.8
Hypertension [3]	9.2	11.7	12.5	12.9	3.7	4.5	4.8	4.9
Cerebrovascular diseases	144.1	154.4	158.0	160.4	57.9	59.2	60.1	60.5
Atherosclerosis	18.0	18.0	16.7	16.8	7.3	6.9	6.4	6.3
Other	24.6	27.1	26.6	27.3	9.9	10.4	10.1	10.3
Malignancies [4]	505.3	534.3	538.5	544.3	203.2	205.2	204.9	205.2
Percent of total	23.5	23.4	23.3	23.4	23.5	23.4	23.3	23.4
Of respiratory and intrathoracic organs	146.4	154.3	156.4	158.6	58.9	59.2	59.5	59.8
Of digestive organs and peritoneum	120.8	127.2	126.6	127.7	48.6	48.8	48.2	48.1
Of genital organs	57.5	62.1	60.5	60.4	23.1	23.8	23.0	22.8
Of breast	43.7	43.3	44.2	44.1	17.6	16.6	16.8	16.6
Of urinary organs	20.7	22.0	22.6	23.2	8.3	8.4	8.6	8.7
Leukemia	18.6	20.1	20.1	20.5	7.5	7.7	7.7	7.7
Accidents and adverse effects	92.0	90.1	93.3	93.9	37.0	34.6	35.5	35.4
Motor vehicle	46.8	42.2	43.4	43.4	18.8	16.2	16.5	16.4
All other	45.2	48.0	50.0	50.4	18.2	18.4	19.0	19.0
Chronic obstructive pulmonary diseases and allied conditions	86.7	101.9	102.9	106.1	34.9	39.1	39.2	40.0
Bronchitis, chronic and unspecified	3.6	3.6	3.3	3.2	1.4	1.4	1.3	1.2
Emphysema	15.7	17.3	16.9	17.4	6.3	6.6	6.4	6.5
Asthma	4.8	5.7	5.6	5.6	1.9	2.2	2.1	2.1
Other	62.6	75.3	77.0	80.0	25.2	28.9	29.3	30.1
Pneumonia and influenza	79.5	82.1	82.9	82.6	32.0	31.5	31.6	31.1
Pneumonia	77.4	80.8	82.3	82.0	31.1	31.0	31.3	30.9
Influenza	2.1	1.3	0.6	0.6	0.8	0.5	0.2	0.2
Diabetes mellitus	47.7	55.4	59.3	61.6	19.2	21.2	22.6	23.2
Suicide	30.9	32.4	31.3	30.9	12.4	12.4	11.9	11.6
Chronic liver disease and cirrhosis	25.8	25.7	25.2	25.1	10.4	9.9	9.6	9.5
Other infectious and parasitic diseases	32.2	48.5	50.3	39.7	13.0	18.6	19.1	15.0
Homicide and legal intervention	24.9	23.7	22.9	20.7	10.0	9.1	8.7	7.8
Nephritis, nephrotic syndrome, and nephrosis	20.8	23.6	23.7	24.4	8.3	9.1	9.0	9.2
Septicemia	19.2	19.9	21.0	21.4	7.7	7.6	8.0	8.1
Certain conditions originating in the perinatal period	17.7	14.1	13.5	12.8	7.1	5.4	5.1	4.8
Congenital anomalies	13.1	11.9	11.9	11.9	5.3	4.6	4.5	4.5
Benign neoplasms [5]	6.8	7.0	7.8	7.8	2.7	2.7	3.0	2.9
Ulcer of stomach and duodenum	6.2	6.0	5.5	5.1	2.5	2.3	2.1	1.9
Hernia of abdominal cavity and intestinal obstruction [6]	5.8	6.0	6.2	6.5	2.3	2.3	2.4	2.5
Anemias	4.1	4.2	4.6	4.4	1.6	1.6	1.7	1.6
Cholelithiasis and other disorders of gall bladder	3.0	2.6	2.8	2.8	1.2	1.0	1.0	1.1
Nutritional deficiencies	3.0	3.2	3.6	3.7	1.2	1.2	1.4	1.4
Tuberculosis	1.8	1.6	1.3	1.2	0.7	0.6	0.5	0.5
Infections of kidney	1.3	1.0	0.9	0.9	0.5	0.4	0.3	0.3
Viral hepatitis	1.6	2.8	3.4	3.8	0.6	1.1	1.3	1.4
Meningitis	1.0	0.9	0.8	0.8	0.4	0.4	0.3	0.3
Acute bronchitis and bronchiolitis	0.6	0.5	0.5	0.5	0.3	0.2	0.2	0.2
Hyperplasia of prostate	0.5	0.5	0.4	0.5	0.2	0.2	0.2	0.2
Symptoms, signs, and ill-defined conditions	24.1	26.6	27.3	30.4	9.7	10.2	10.4	11.4
All other causes	172.9	206.1	214.1	222.4	69.5	79.1	81.5	83.8

[1] Based on a 10-percent sample of deaths. Includes deaths of nonresidents. [2] 1990 based on resident population enumerated as of April 1. Other years based on resident population estimated as of July 1. [3] With or without renal disease. [4] Includes other types of malignancies not shown separately. [5] Includes neoplasms of unspecified nature; beginning 1990 also includes carcinoma in situ. [6] Without mention of hernia.

Source: U.S. National Center for Health Statistics, *Vital Statistics of the United States,* annual; *Monthly Vital Statistics Report;* and unpublished data.

No. 139. Age-Adjusted Death Rates, by Selected Causes: 1990 to 1996

[Rates per 100,000 population. For explanation of age-adjustment, see text, Section 2. The standard population for this table is the total population of the United States enumerated in 1940. See also headnote, Table 138]

CAUSE OF DEATH	1990	1991	1992	1993	1994	1995	1996
All causes	**520.2**	**513.7**	**504.5**	**513.3**	**507.4**	**503.9**	**494.1**
Major cardiovascular diseases	189.8	185.0	180.4	181.8	176.8	174.9	171.0
Diseases of heart	152.0	148.2	144.3	145.3	140.4	138.3	134.6
Rheumatic fever and rheumatic heart disease	1.5	1.4	1.3	1.3	1.2	1.1	1.1
Hypertensive heart disease [1]	4.8	4.7	4.8	4.9	5.0	5.1	5.1
Hypertensive heart and renal disease	0.5	0.5	0.5	0.5	0.5	0.4	0.4
Ischemic heart disease	102.6	99.1	95.7	94.9	91.4	89.5	87.0
Other diseases of endocardium	2.5	2.5	2.6	2.6	2.6	2.6	2.7
Acute myocardial infraction	53.7	51.5	49.1	47.5	45.6	43.8	42.2
Old myocardial infraction and other	47.8	46.6	45.7	46.5	45.0	44.9	44.0
Hypertension [1]	1.9	1.9	2.0	2.2	2.2	2.3	2.3
Cerebrovascular diseases	27.7	26.8	26.2	26.5	26.5	26.7	26.5
Atherosclerosis	2.7	2.6	2.4	2.4	2.3	2.3	2.2
Intracerebral/intracranial hemorrage	5.2	5.1	5.1	5.1	5.0	5.1	5.2
Cerebral thrombosis	3.3	2.9	2.7	2.5	2.4	2.2	2.1
Cerebral embolism	0.1	0.1	0.1	0.1	0.1	0.1	0.1
Malignancies [2]	135.0	134.5	133.1	132.6	131.5	129.9	129.1
Of respiratory and intrathoracic organs	41.4	41.1	40.8	40.8	40.1	39.7	39.6
Of digestive organs and peritoneum	30.2	29.9	29.6	29.5	29.3	29.1	28.8
Of genital organs	13.6	13.6	13.5	13.2	13.2	12.8	12.5
Of breast	12.7	12.4	12.0	11.8	11.6	11.5	11.2
Of urinary organs	5.1	5.1	5.1	5.0	5.1	5.1	5.1
Leukemia	5.0	5.0	4.9	4.9	4.9	4.8	4.9
Of lip, oral cavity, and pharynx	2.4	2.4	2.3	2.3	2.1	2.1	2.0
Accidents and adverse effects	32.5	31.0	29.4	30.3	30.3	30.5	30.1
Motor vehicle	18.5	17.0	15.8	16.0	16.1	16.3	16.2
All other	14.0	13.9	13.7	14.4	14.2	14.2	13.9
Chronic obstructive pulmonary diseases and allied conditions [3]	19.7	20.1	19.9	21.4	21.0	20.8	21.0
Bronchitis, chronic and unspecified	0.8	0.8	0.8	0.8	0.7	0.6	0.6
Emphysema	3.7	3.8	3.7	3.9	3.7	3.6	3.6
Asthma	1.4	1.5	1.4	1.4	1.5	1.5	1.5
Other	13.7	14.1	14.0	15.2	15.1	15.0	15.2
Pneumonia and influenza	14.0	13.4	12.7	13.5	13.0	12.9	12.6
Pneumonia	13.7	13.2	12.5	13.3	12.8	12.8	12.5
Influenza	0.3	0.2	0.2	0.2	0.2	0.1	0.1
Diabetes mellitus	11.7	11.8	11.9	12.4	12.9	13.3	13.6
Suicide	11.5	11.4	11.1	11.3	11.2	11.2	10.8
Chronic liver disease and cirrhosis	8.6	8.3	8.0	7.9	7.9	7.6	7.5
Homicide and legal intervention	10.2	10.9	10.5	10.7	10.3	9.4	8.4
Nephritis, nephrotic syndrome, and renal failure	3.9	3.9	4.0	4.1	3.9	4.0	4.0
Acute glomerulonephritis/nephrotic syndrome	0.1	0.1	0.1	(NA)	0.1	-	0.1
Septicemia	4.1	4.1	4.0	4.1	4.0	4.1	4.1
Other infectious and parasitic diseases	12.0	13.3	14.7	15.9	17.5	17.6	13.6
Benign neoplasms [4]	1.7	1.7	1.7	1.7	1.7	1.7	1.7
Ulcer of stomach and duodenum	1.3	1.2	1.2	1.2	1.2	1.0	0.9
Hernia of abdominal cavity and intestinal obstruction [5]	1.1	1.1	1.1	1.0	1.1	1.0	1.0
Anemias	0.9	0.9	0.9	0.9	0.9	0.9	0.9
Cholelithiasis and other disorders of gallbladder	0.6	0.5	0.5	0.5	0.5	0.5	0.5
Nutritional deficiencies	0.5	0.5	0.5	0.5	0.5	0.5	0.5
Tuberculosis	0.5	0.5	0.4	0.4	0.4	0.3	0.3
Tuberculosis of respiratory system	0.4	0.4	0.3	0.3	0.3	0.2	0.2
Other tuberculosis	0.1	0.1	0.1	0.1	0.1	0.1	0.1
Infections of kidney	0.2	0.2	0.2	0.2	0.2	0.2	0.2
Viral hepatitis	0.5	0.6	0.6	0.8	0.9	1.0	1.1
Meningitis	0.3	0.3	0.2	0.3	0.3	0.2	0.3
Acute bronchitis and bronchiolitis	0.1	0.1	0.1	0.1	0.1	0.1	0.1
Hyperplasia of prostate	0.1	0.1	0.1	0.1	0.1	0.1	0.1
Symptoms, signs, and ill-defined conditions	7.3	7.2	6.7	7.4	6.8	7.2	8.1
Meningococcal infection	0.1	0.1	0.1	0.1	0.1	0.1	0.1
Angina pectoris	0.2	0.2	0.2	0.2	0.1	0.1	0.1
Appendicitis	0.1	0.1	0.1	0.1	0.1	0.1	0.1
Complications of pregnancy, childbirth	0.1	0.1	0.1	0.1	0.1	0.1	0.1
Congenital anomalies	5.0	4.7	4.6	4.6	4.5	4.4	4.3
Perinatal period conditions	6.9	6.4	6.0	5.9	4.8	5.4	5.2
Birth trauma, intrauterine hypoxia, etc.	1.5	1.3	1.1	1.0	0.9	0.9	0.8

- Represents or rounds to zero.   NA Not available.   [1] With or without renal disease.   [2] Includes other types of malignancies not shown separately.   [3] Prior to 1980, data are shown for bronchitis, emphysema, and asthma.   [4] Includes neoplasms of unspecified nature; also includes carcinoma in situ.   [5] Without mention of hernia.

Source: U.S. National Center for Health Statistics, *Vital Statistics of the United States*, annual; *Monthly Vital Statistics Reports*; and unpublished data.

No. 140. Deaths, by Selected Causes and Selected Characteristics: 1995

[In thousands. Excludes deaths of nonresidents of the U.S. Deaths classified according to ninth revision of *International Classification of Diseases.* See also Appendix III]

AGE, SEX, AND RACE	Total [1]	Heart disease	Cancer	Accidents and adverse effects	Cerebrovascular diseases	Chronic obstructive pulmonary diseases [2]	Pneumonia, flu	Suicide	Chronic liver disease, cirrhosis	Diabetes mellitus	Homicide and legal intervention
ALL RACES [3]											
Both sexes, total [4]	**2,312.1**	**737.6**	**538.5**	**93.3**	**158.0**	**102.9**	**82.9**	**31.3**	**25.2**	**59.3**	**22.9**
Under 1 years old	29.6	0.7	0.1	0.8	0.2	(Z)	0.5	(X)	(Z)	-	0.3
1 to 4 years old	6.4	0.3	0.5	2.3	0.1	(Z)	0.2	(X)	(Z)	(Z)	0.5
5 to 9 years old	3.8	0.1	0.5	1.6	(Z)	(Z)	0.1	(Z)	(Z)	(Z)	0.2
10 to 14 years old	4.8	0.2	0.5	1.9	(Z)	0.1	0.1	0.3	(Z)	(Z)	0.4
15 to 19 years old	15.1	0.4	0.7	6.6	0.1	0.1	0.1	1.9	(Z)	(Z)	3.3
20 to 24 years old	19.2	0.6	1.0	7.2	0.1	0.1	0.1	2.9	(Z)	0.1	4.0
25 to 29 years old	22.7	1.1	1.6	6.4	0.2	0.1	0.2	2.9	0.1	0.2	3.2
30 to 34 years old	35.1	2.4	3.3	7.1	0.5	0.2	0.4	3.4	0.5	0.4	2.9
35 to 39 years old	46.5	4.9	6.3	7.5	1.1	0.3	0.7	3.3	1.3	0.8	2.3
40 to 44 years old	55.8	8.7	10.8	6.7	1.7	0.5	0.8	3.1	2.4	1.1	1.8
45 to 49 years old	65.6	14.2	18.0	5.3	2.4	0.9	1.0	2.6	2.7	1.6	1.2
50 to 54 years old	77.4	20.3	26.2	4.0	3.0	1.8	1.1	2.0	2.6	2.4	0.8
55 to 59 years old	96.6	27.0	36.1	3.3	3.9	3.4	1.3	1.4	2.5	3.4	0.6
60 to 64 years old	138.9	41.2	51.8	3.4	5.8	6.5	2.1	1.4	2.9	4.8	0.4
65 to 69 years old	204.3	62.2	73.6	3.8	9.6	12.2	3.8	1.4	3.0	7.1	0.3
70 to 74 years old	276.5	87.8	89.2	4.6	16.1	18.0	6.9	1.5	2.9	9.1	0.3
75 to 79 years old	315.5	106.8	83.7	5.3	23.1	20.5	10.7	1.3	2.1	9.4	0.2
80 to 84 years old	336.7	123.3	68.4	5.7	30.6	18.7	15.3	1.0	1.3	8.7	0.1
85 years old and over	561.3	235.3	66.2	9.7	59.4	19.1	37.6	0.8	0.8	10.1	0.1
WHITE											
Both sexes, total [4]	**1,987.4**	**649.1**	**468.9**	**77.7**	**136.5**	**95.1**	**73.6**	**28.2**	**21.4**	**47.5**	**11.4**
Under 1 years old	19.5	0.5	0.1	0.5	0.2	(Z)	0.3	(X)	(Z)	-	0.2
1 to 4 years old	4.4	0.2	0.4	1.6	(Z)	(Z)	0.1	(X)	(Z)	(Z)	0.2
5 to 9 years old	2.7	0.1	0.4	1.2	(Z)	(Z)	(Z)	(Z)	(Z)	(Z)	0.1
10 to 14 years old	3.5	0.1	0.4	1.5	(Z)	0.1	(Z)	0.3	(Z)	(Z)	0.2
15 to 19 years old	10.9	0.3	0.5	5.6	(Z)	0.1	0.1	1.6	(Z)	(Z)	1.4
20 to 24 years old	13.3	0.4	0.7	6.0	0.1	0.1	0.1	2.4	(Z)	0.1	1.6
25 to 29 years old	15.7	0.7	1.3	5.2	0.1	0.1	0.1	2.4	0.1	0.1	1.5
30 to 34 years old	24.9	1.6	2.5	5.8	0.4	0.1	0.3	3.0	0.4	0.3	1.4
35 to 39 years old	33.1	3.5	5.0	6.0	0.7	0.2	0.4	3.0	1.0	0.5	1.2
40 to 44 years old	40.1	6.4	8.5	5.3	1.0	0.4	0.5	2.9	1.9	0.8	1.0
45 to 49 years old	49.3	10.7	14.5	4.2	1.6	0.7	0.7	2.4	2.1	1.2	0.7
50 to 54 years old	60.5	15.9	21.4	3.3	2.1	1.5	0.8	1.8	2.1	1.7	0.5
55 to 59 years old	77.3	21.5	30.1	2.7	2.7	3.0	1.0	1.3	2.0	2.4	0.3
60 to 64 years old	114.3	33.8	43.7	2.8	4.4	5.9	1.7	1.3	2.5	3.5	0.3
65 to 69 years old	174.0	52.7	64.0	3.2	7.6	11.2	3.1	1.3	2.7	5.5	0.2
70 to 74 years old	241.3	76.3	78.8	4.0	13.5	16.7	6.0	1.4	2.7	7.3	0.2
75 to 79 years old	281.8	95.3	75.1	4.7	20.1	19.3	9.6	1.3	2.0	7.9	0.1
80 to 84 years old	304.6	112.0	61.7	5.1	27.5	17.7	13.9	1.0	1.2	7.4	0.1
85 years old and over	515.9	217.3	59.8	9.0	54.5	18.1	34.9	0.8	0.8	8.7	0.1
BLACK											
Both sexes, total [4]	**286.4**	**78.6**	**60.6**	**12.7**	**18.5**	**6.7**	**7.8**	**2.2**	**3.1**	**10.4**	**10.8**
Under 1 years old	9.1	0.2	(Z)	0.2	0.1	(Z)	0.2	(X)	(Z)	-	0.1
1 to 4 years old	1.7	0.1	0.1	0.5	(Z)	(Z)	0.1	(X)	(Z)	(Z)	0.2
5 to 9 years old	0.9	(Z)	0.1	0.4	(Z)	(Z)	(Z)	(Z)	-	(Z)	0.1
10 to 14 years old	1.1	0.1	0.1	0.4	(Z)	0.1	(Z)	(Z)	(Z)	(Z)	0.2
15 to 19 years old	3.7	0.1	0.1	0.8	(Z)	0.1	(Z)	0.2	(Z)	(Z)	1.8
20 to 24 years old	5.0	0.2	0.2	0.9	(Z)	0.1	(Z)	0.3	(Z)	(Z)	2.3
25 to 29 years old	6.2	0.3	0.3	0.9	0.1	0.1	0.1	0.3	(Z)	0.1	1.7
30 to 34 years old	9.2	0.7	0.6	1.0	0.1	0.1	0.1	0.3	0.1	0.1	1.4
35 to 39 years old	12.2	1.3	1.1	1.2	0.4	0.1	0.2	0.3	0.2	0.2	1.1
40 to 44 years old	14.3	2.2	2.0	1.2	0.6	0.2	0.2	0.2	0.4	0.3	0.7
45 to 49 years old	14.7	3.2	3.0	0.9	0.7	0.2	0.3	0.1	0.5	0.4	0.4
50 to 54 years old	14.9	4.0	4.1	0.6	0.8	0.3	0.3	0.1	0.4	0.6	0.2
55 to 59 years old	17.1	4.9	5.2	0.5	1.0	0.4	0.3	0.1	0.4	0.8	0.2
60 to 64 years old	21.7	6.7	7.1	0.5	1.2	0.6	0.4	0.1	0.3	1.1	0.1
65 to 69 years old	26.8	8.6	8.5	0.5	1.8	0.9	0.6	0.1	0.3	1.4	0.1
70 to 74 years old	30.9	10.2	9.2	0.5	2.3	1.1	0.8	0.1	0.2	1.6	0.1
75 to 79 years old	29.4	10.1	7.5	0.5	2.5	1.0	0.9	(Z)	0.1	1.3	0.1
80 to 84 years old	27.8	9.9	5.9	0.4	2.7	0.8	1.1	(Z)	0.1	1.2	(Z)
85 years old and over	39.5	15.7	5.5	0.6	4.2	0.9	2.2	(Z)	(Z)	1.2	(Z)

- Represents zero.　X Not applicable.　Z Fewer than 50.　[1] Includes other causes, not shown separately.　[2] Includes allied conditions.　[3] Includes other races, not shown separately.　[4] Includes those deaths with age not stated.

Source: U.S. National Center for Health Statistics, *Vital Statistics of the United States,* annual.

No. 141. Deaths, by Age and Leading Cause: 1995

[Excludes deaths of nonresidents of the United States. Deaths classified according to ninth revision of *International Classification of Diseases.* See also Appendix III]

AGE AND LEADING CAUSE OF DEATH	NUMBER OF DEATHS			DEATH RATE PER 100,000 POPULATION		
	Total	Male	Female	Total	Male	Female
All ages [1]	**2,312,132**	**1,172,959**	**1,139,173**	**880.0**	**914.1**	**847.3**
1 to 4 yrs. old, total	**6,393**	**3,609**	**2,784**	**40.6**	**44.8**	**36.2**
Leading causes of death:						
Accidents	2,280	1,354	926	14.5	16.8	12.0
Congenital anomalies	695	374	321	4.4	4.6	4.2
Malignant neoplasms (cancer)	488	290	198	3.1	3.6	2.6
Homicide and legal intervention	452	253	199	2.9	3.1	2.6
Heart disease	251	136	115	1.6	1.7	1.5
HIV infection [2]	210	96	114	1.3	1.2	1.5
Pneumonia and influenza	156	69	87	1.0	0.9	1.1
Certain conditions originating in the perinatal period	87	45	42	0.6	0.6	0.5
Septicemia	80	38	42	0.5	0.5	0.5
Cerebrovascular diseases	57	36	(X)	0.4	0.4	(X)
5 to 14 yrs. old, total	**8,596**	**5,219**	**3,377**	**22.5**	**26.7**	**18.2**
Leading causes of death:						
Accidents	3,544	2,288	1,256	9.3	11.7	6.8
Malignant neoplasms (cancer)	1,026	587	439	2.7	3.0	2.4
Homicide and legal intervention	562	374	188	1.5	1.9	1.0
Congenital anomalies	449	230	219	1.2	1.2	1.2
Suicide	337	260	77	0.9	1.3	0.4
Heart disease	294	163	131	0.8	0.8	0.7
HIV infections [2]	189	103	86	0.5	0.5	0.5
Chronic obstructive pulmonary diseases	143	98	45	0.4	0.5	0.2
Pneumonia and influenza	128	58	70	0.3	0.3	0.4
Benign neoplasms & carcinoma in situ	105	52	53	0.3	0.3	0.3
15 to 24 yrs. old, total	**34,244**	**25,777**	**8,467**	**95.3**	**140.5**	**48.1**
Leading causes of death:						
Accidents	13,842	10,313	3,529	38.5	56.2	20.1
Homicide and legal intervention	7,284	6,224	1,060	20.3	33.9	6.0
Suicide	4,784	4,132	652	13.3	22.5	3.7
Malignant neoplasms (cancer)	1,642	1,009	633	4.6	5.5	3.6
Heart disease	1,039	659	380	2.9	3.6	2.2
HIV infection [2]	629	377	252	1.7	2.1	1.4
Congenital anomalies	452	258	194	1.3	1.4	1.1
Chronic obstructive pulmonary disease	246	133	113	0.7	0.7	0.6
Pneumonia and influenza	207	119	88	0.6	0.6	0.5
Cerebrovascular diseases	172	97	75	0.5	0.5	0.4
25 to 44 yrs. old, total	**160,015**	**111,957**	**48,058**	**192.0**	**269.8**	**114.8**
Leading causes of death:						
HIV infection [2]	30,754	25,615	5,139	36.9	61.7	12.3
Accidents	27,660	21,096	6,564	33.2	50.8	15.7
Malignant neoplasms (cancer)	21,985	10,069	11,916	26.4	24.3	28.5
Heart disease	17,064	12,268	4,796	20.5	29.6	11.5
Suicide	12,759	10,314	2,445	15.3	24.9	5.8
Homicide and legal intervention	10,280	7,910	2,370	12.3	19.1	5.7
Chronic liver disease and cirrhosis	4,309	3,119	1,190	5.2	7.5	2.8
Cerebrovascular diseases	3,492	1,863	1,629	4.2	4.5	3.9
Diabetes mellitus	2,458	1,421	1,037	2.9	3.4	2.5
Pneumonia and influenza	2,102	1,302	800	2.5	3.1	1.9
45 to 64 yrs. old, total	**378,512**	**233,212**	**145,300**	**725.0**	**924.5**	**538.5**
Leading causes of death:						
Malignant neoplasms (cancer)	132,084	70,077	62,007	253.0	277.8	229.8
Heart disease	102,738	72,337	30,401	196.8	286.8	112.7
Accidents	16,004	11,429	4,575	30.7	45.3	17.0
Cerebrovascular diseases	15,208	8,365	6,843	29.1	33.2	25.4
Chronic obstructive pulmonary diseases	12,744	6,673	6,071	24.4	26.5	22.5
Diabetes mellitus	12,184	6,462	5,722	23.3	25.6	21.2
Chronic liver disease and cirrhosis	10,603	7,557	3,046	20.3	30.0	11.3
HIV infection [2]	10,499	9,119	1,380	20.1	36.1	5.1
Suicide	7,336	5,679	1,657	14.1	22.5	6.1
Pneumonia and influenza	5,537	3,400	2,137	10.6	13.5	7.9
65 yrs. old and over, total	**1,694,326**	**776,232**	**918,094**	**5,052.8**	**5,670.6**	**4,626.6**
Leading causes of death:						
Heart disease	615,426	276,756	338,670	1,835.3	2,021.8	1,706.7
Malignant neoplasms (cancer)	381,142	199,536	181,606	1,136.6	1,457.7	915.2
Cerebrovascular diseases	138,762	51,030	87,732	413.8	372.8	442.1
Chronic obstructive pulmonary diseases	88,478	46,425	42,053	263.9	339.1	211.9
Pneumonia and influenza	74,297	32,557	41,740	221.6	237.8	210.3
Diabetes millitus	44,452	18,144	26,308	132.6	132.5	132.6
Accidents	29,099	14,399	14,700	86.8	105.2	74.1
Alzheimer's disease	20,230	6,837	13,393	60.3	49.9	67.5
Nephritis, nephrotic syndrome, and nephrosis	20,182	9,421	10,761	60.2	68.8	54.2
Septicemia	16,899	6,764	10,135	50.4	49.4	51.1

X Not applicable.   [1] Includes those deaths with age not stated.   [2] Human immunodeficiency virus.

Source: U.S. National Center for Health Statistics, *Vital Statistics of the United States,* annual; and unpublished data.

No. 142. Death Rates, by Leading Causes and Age: 1980 to 1995

[**Deaths per 100,000 population in specified group.** Except as noted, excludes deaths of nonresidents of the United States. See text, Section 2]

YEAR, RACE, AND AGE	Heart disease	Malignant neo- plasms	Acci- dents and adverse effects	Cere- bro- vas- cular dis- eases	Chronic obstruc- tive pulmo- nary dis- eases [1]	Pneu- monia, flu	Suicide	Chronic liver dis- ease, cirrho- sis	Dia- betes mellitus	Homi- cide and legal inter- vention
All races, both sexes: [2]										
1980	336.0	183.9	46.7	75.1	24.7	24.1	11.9	13.5	15.4	10.7
1990	289.5	203.2	37.0	57.9	34.9	32.0	12.4	10.4	19.2	10.0
1994	281.3	205.2	35.1	58.9	39.0	31.3	12.0	9.8	21.8	(NA)
1995	280.7	204.9	35.5	60.1	39.2	31.6	11.9	9.6	21.8	(NA)
1 to 4 years old	1.8	3.3	15.9	(NA)	(NA)	1.1	(NA)	(NA)	22.6	(NA)
5 to 14 years old	0.9	2.8	9.3	(NA)	0.3	0.3	0.9	(NA)	(NA)	3.0
15 to 24 years old . . .	2.8	4.8	38.7	0.5	0.6	0.6	13.8	(NA)	(NA)	1.5
25 to 44 years old . . .	20.2	26.4	32.5	4.2	(NA)	2.6	15.3	5.3	3.0	22.6
45 to 64 years old . . .	202.3	261.0	29.9	29.3	25.6	10.8	14.0	20.8	22.5	13.8
65 years old and over	1,840.7	1,134.5	85.4	405.2	262.5	219.4	(NA)	(NA)	128.5	(NA)
All races, males: 1995	282.7	219.5	47.9	48.0	42.0	29.4	19.8	(NA)	20.4	13.8
1 to 4 years old	1.8	3.5	18.7	(NA)	(NA)	1.2	(NA)	(NA)	(NA)	3.3
5 to 14 years old	0.9	3.1	12.0	(NA)	0.4	0.3	1.2	(NA)	(NA)	1.9
15 to 24 years old . . .	3.4	5.8	56.8	0.5	0.8	0.6	23.4	(NA)	(NA)	38.3
25 to 44 years old . . .	28.8	24.4	50.2	4.5	(NA)	3.2	24.8	7.7	3.6	21.7
45 to 64 years old . . .	295.5	289.6	43.9	33.3	28.2	13.7	22.1	30.5	24.4	(NA)
65 years old and over . .	2,043.6	1,463.6	105.0	370.4	341.0	237.6	(NA)	(NA)	127.6	(NA)
All races, females: 1995	278.8	191.0	23.7	71.7	36.4	33.6	(NA)	(NA)	(NA)	(NA)
1 to 4 years old	1.8	3.0	12.9	(NA)	(NA)	1.0	(NA)	(NA)	24.6	(NA)
5 to 14 years old	0.8	2.4	6.6	(NA)	0.2	0.2	0.5	(NA)	(NA)	2.7
15 to 24 years old . . .	2.1	3.9	19.8	(NA)	0.5	0.6	3.7	(NA)	(NA)	1.2
25 to 44 years old . . .	11.7	28.3	15.1	4.0	(NA)	2.0	5.9	3.0	2.4	6.2
45 to 64 years old . . .	115.3	234.4	16.7	25.7	23.1	8.1	6.4	11.7	20.8	5.8
65 years old and over . .	1,701.7	909.2	72.0	429.0	208.8	207.0	(NA)	(NA)	129.1	(NA)
White, both sexes: 1995	297.6	215.0	35.7	62.6	43.6	33.8	12.9	9.8	21.8	(NA)
1 to 4 years old	1.4	3.3	13.9	(NA)	(NA)	0.9	(NA)	(NA)	(NA)	2.1
5 to 14 years old	0.8	2.8	8.5	(NA)	0.2	0.2	0.9	(NA)	(NA)	1.0
15 to 24 years old . . .	2.2	4.9	40.1	0.5	0.5	0.6	14.2	(NA)	(NA)	10.9
25 to 44 years old . . .	17.2	25.1	31.7	3.2	(NA)	2.0	16.3	5.0	2.6	8.1
45 to 64 years old . . .	188.7	252.8	27.9	24.1	26.0	9.6	15.2	19.7	19.2	(NA)
65 years old and over . .	1,848.9	6,126.3	85.4	401.3	274.7	223.0	(NA)	(NA)	118.8	(NA)
White males: 1995	297.9	228.1	47.4	48.6	46.1	30.8	21.4	13.2	20.0	(NA)
1 to 4 years old	1.4	3.7	16.5	0.4	(NA)	1.0	(NA)	(NA)	(NA)	2.3
5 to 14 years old	0.8	3.1	10.9	(NA)	0.3	0.2	1.3	(NA)	(NA)	1.1
15 to 24 years old . . .	2.8	5.9	58.3	0.5	0.5	0.6	24.1	(NA)	(NA)	17.4
25 to 44 years old . . .	25.4	23.2	48.8	3.4	(NA)	2.5	26.1	7.4	3.2	12.3
45 to 64 years old	280.8	275.7	40.4	27.1	28.3	11.9	23.8	28.8	21.4	(NA)
65 years old and over . .	2,051.4	1,437.8	103.4	361.4	351.8	237.9	(NA)	(NA)	120.9	(NA)
White females: 1995	297.4	202.4	24.4	76.0	41.2	36.6	(NA)	(NA)	23.5	(NA)
1 to 4 years old	1.4	2.9	11.2	(NA)	(NA)	0.9	(NA)	(NA)	(NA)	1.9
5 to 14 years old	0.8	2.5	6.0	0.2	(NA)	0.2	0.5	(NA)	(NA)	0.8
15 to 24 years old . . .	1.6	3.9	21.0	0.4	(NA)	0.5	3.8	(NA)	(NA)	3.9
25 to 44 years old	8.9	27.0	14.3	2.9	(NA)	1.5	6.5	2.6	2.0	3.7
45 to 64 years old . . .	100.9	231.0	15.9	21.4	23.9	7.4	7.0	10.9	17.1	(NA)
65 years old and over . .	1,709.5	911.9	73.1	428.7	221.6	212.7	(NA)	(NA)	117.4	(NA)
Black, both sexes: 1995 . . .	237.3	182.9	38.5	55.9	20.1	23.5	(NA)	(NA)	31.4	32.5
1 to 4 years old	4.2	3.3	26.3	(NA)	(NA)	1.9	(NA)	(NA)	(NA)	7.4
5 to 14 years old	1.3	2.9	13.8	(NA)	1.1	0.4	0.7	(NA)	(NA)	4.3
15 to 24 years old . . .	5.7	4.8	23.4	(NA)	1.7	(NA)	11.6	(NA)	(NA)	88.1
25 to 44 years old . . .	43.5	37.6	41.3	11.6	(NA)	6.8	10.5	7.8	6.0	53.0
45 to 64 years old	353.4	373.2	47.9	74.5	27.8	22.7	(NA)	31.8	52.8	18.5
65 years old and over .	1,988.3	1,349.2	89.0	478.4	167.3	196.7	(NA)	(NA)	240.1	(NA)
Black males: 1995	244.2	209.1	56.2	51.0	24.9	25.6	(NA)	(NA)	26.1	56.3
1 to 4 years old	3.9	3.2	30.8	(NA)	(NA)	2.1	(NA)	(NA)	(NA)	8.4
5 to 14 years old	1.5	3.3	18.0	(NA)	1.3	(S)	1.1	(NA)	(NA)	5.6
15 to 24 years old . . .	6.8	5.4	52.6	(NA)	2.1	(NA)	20.6	(NA)	1.0	157.6
25 to 44 years old . . .	57.6	35.4	65.3	12.3	(NA)	8.5	18.9	10.7	7.1	90.9
45 to 64 years old	484.7	468.2	78.4	92.1	34.1	32.9	(NA)	49.0	54.9	33.4
65 years old and over . .	2,203.6	1,933.5	126.4	485.2	264.5	244.6	(NA)	(NA)	211.1	(NA)
Black females: 1995	231.3	159.1	22.5	60.4	15.8	21.7	(NA)	(NA)	36.1	(NA)
1 to 4 years old	4.4	3.4	21.7	(NA)	(NA)	1.8	(NA)	(NA)	(NA)	6.4
5 to 14 years old	1.2	2.5	9.5	(NA)	0.8	(NA)	(S)	(NA)	(NA)	3.0
15 to 24 years old . . .	4.7	4.2	15.0	(NA)	1.2	(NA)	2.7	(NA)	(NA)	18.7
25 to 44 years old . . .	31.0	39.6	9.7	11.0	3.5	5.3	(NA)	5.3	5.0	19.5
45 to 64 years old	247.8	296.8	23.3	60.3	22.7	14.0	(NA)	18.0	51.2	(NA)
65 years old and over . .	1,852.6	981.0	65.5	474.1	106.0	166.5	(NA)	(NA)	258.4	(NA)

NA Not available. S Figure does not meet publication standards. [1] Includes allied conditions. [2] Includes other races not shown separately.

Source: U.S. National Center for Health Statistics, *Vital Statistics of the United States*, annual; and *Monthly Vital Statistics Report*.

No. 143. Death Rates, by Leading Cause—States: 1995

[Deaths per 100,000 resident population enumerated as of April 1. By place of residence. Excludes nonresidents of the United States. Causes of death classified according to ninth revisions of International Classification of Diseases]

STATE	Total [1]	Heart disease	Cancer	Cerebrovascular diseases [2]	Accidents and adverse effects	Motor vehicle accidents	Chronic obstructive pulmonary diseases [2]	Diabetes mellitus	HIV [3]	Suicide	Homicide
U.S.	880.0	280.7	204.9	60.1	35.5	16.5	39.2	22.6	(NA)	11.9	8.7
AL	996.1	314.2	221.4	65.2	52.5	26.8	39.5	27.3	9.2	13.2	12.5
AK	423.0	90.6	95.1	24.0	56.2	16.1	17.7	9.3	5.0	17.1	8.9
AZ	837.9	242.6	190.1	51.8	47.0	23.5	48.3	19.5	11.5	19.1	12.7
AR	1,075.1	339.8	244.7	91.5	48.8	26.3	45.0	22.4	6.8	14.5	11.6
CA	709.8	216.3	162.8	51.4	29.3	14.1	34.2	16.2	20.4	11.7	11.6
CO	667.6	172.1	145.9	42.7	39.8	18.6	42.3	14.3	10.9	17.5	5.7
CT	899.5	298.9	215.6	57.2	32.9	10.7	35.5	18.1	18.4	9.9	-
DE	875.9	276.1	227.3	47.8	37.1	17.6	36.0	26.9	22.7	11.2	5.9
DC	1,244.2	302.4	267.2	66.8	34.8	12.3	24.2	39.5	117.8	7.0	56.8
FL	1,081.3	351.6	263.5	69.9	38.1	19.8	52.9	26.0	30.8	15.3	8.8
GA	810.8	242.4	177.3	56.2	41.1	21.4	34.2	16.7	22.0	11.5	10.3
HI	643.1	196.0	156.4	51.5	27.6	12.0	20.4	14.2	10.4	12.0	4.9
ID	732.1	212.3	172.4	54.8	45.2	22.7	38.2	17.7	3.7	16.0	4.0
IL	916.9	304.4	212.2	63.3	33.9	14.7	38.0	22.5	12.1	9.5	11.0
IN	918.2	294.3	216.3	68.9	38.0	17.1	41.3	24.8	6.7	12.0	7.8
IA	986.0	332.0	219.1	77.5	41.1	19.2	48.3	22.4	-	11.8	
KS	933.0	297.7	205.9	70.6	38.7	17.6	44.9	22.5	5.6	11.3	6.3
KY	963.7	315.8	229.2	63.9	44.2	22.0	48.1	25.1	5.6	12.4	6.5
LA	914.4	279.4	214.3	58.6	42.4	21.0	32.7	34.4	16.8	12.5	17.6
ME	946.8	293.9	242.9	59.9	32.1	14.7	54.3	25.4	6.1	13.0	
MD	829.8	236.4	201.9	52.5	27.6	13.5	31.6	27.0	25.6	10.1	12.7
MA	913.4	275.8	231.9	57.0	20.1	8.0	38.8	21.8	15.5	8.1	3.7
MI	876.1	294.8	203.5	61.4	33.2	17.0	37.5	23.4	8.4	10.3	9.9
MN	813.7	225.2	188.6	67.8	36.1	14.4	36.3	18.7	5.6	11.3	
MS	1,002.0	356.0	213.1	69.3	59.6	33.5	37.9	18.1	9.5	11.8	15.9
MO	1,021.9	345.3	230.7	72.9	43.5	20.6	46.1	23.4	8.8	13.5	8.9
MT	876.6	230.3	203.4	68.3	43.7	22.4	55.2	24.1	-	23.1	5.4
NE	932.6	312.0	206.2	71.2	35.2	15.5	44.6	17.5	-	11.4	
NV	818.6	246.9	194.5	46.4	36.0	19.9	52.0	15.4	13.2	25.8	11.2
NH	803.6	256.9	205.2	55.2	25.0	11.8	41.5	22.6	4.1	11.9	
NJ	932.5	303.3	231.9	53.4	29.1	10.6	34.5	30.1	30.7	7.3	5.4
NM	744.3	196.1	159.5	42.7	54.6	26.7	41.5	26.1	9.1	17.6	10.1
NY	928.4	350.2	213.3	44.8	27.5	9.9	33.8	19.4	44.1	7.6	8.7
NC	902.2	269.5	206.8	72.3	41.0	20.7	39.7	24.3	14.1	12.6	9.6
ND	931.6	304.3	214.4	77.3	32.7	13.1	37.9	24.3	-	14.7	
OH	950.1	317.4	226.1	60.0	29.1	12.4	44.2	30.0	7.9	9.7	
OK	1,002.3	340.4	217.9	72.5	44.9	22.1	48.1	19.5	7.1	15.3	13.5
OR	898.4	240.1	214.7	77.7	43.5	18.9	45.4	21.7	9.2	15.8	4.7
PA	1,059.2	359.7	250.7	68.6	35.3	13.1	43.9	28.2	11.5	12.1	6.5
RI	975.7	334.1	250.4	64.8	21.9	8.1	42.0	24.7	10.0	9.0	
SC	912.7	277.6	201.9	75.2	44.5	23.1	38.4	27.4	15.2	11.9	8.9
SD	948.5	312.3	214.5	73.2	44.4	22.1	44.4	23.0	-	11.8	
TN	976.1	308.2	220.9	79.8	47.3	24.5	41.9	23.4	9.7	13.0	11.1
TX	736.1	222.9	168.9	52.3	34.3	17.8	33.3	24.4	14.8	11.9	9.6
UT	560.6	148.1	108.6	39.9	32.4	17.2	24.1	21.3	4.8	14.8	3.9
VT	846.7	278.2	198.9	57.1	32.8	16.1	41.2	24.5	4.6	13.0	
VA	799.9	240.2	190.4	57.5	33.4	13.9	34.1	17.6	12.6	12.5	7.8
WA	751.0	208.6	183.0	60.7	34.9	13.7	39.7	19.4	10.9	14.4	5.5
WV	1,107.0	378.9	259.4	67.9	40.4	21.2	60.0	32.8	-	15.1	5.5
WI	880.1	281.4	206.3	69.8	35.6	15.1	36.7	21.6	-	12.1	4.7
WY	774.7	203.3	186.6	55.8	50.0	27.1	55.4	22.1	-	17.1	

- Represents or rounds to zero.   NA Not available.   [1] Includes other causes not shown separately.   [2] Includes allied conditions.   [3] Human immunodeficiency virus.

Source: U.S. National Center for Health Statistics, *Monthly Vital Statistics Report;* and unpublished data.

No. 144. Estimated Deaths of Persons With Acquired Immunodeficiency Syndrome (AIDS) Deaths, by Selected Characteristics: 1991 to 1996

[Estimates adjusted for delays in reporting of deaths. Total estimates of less than 1,000, 1,000 to 2,499, 2,500 to 4,999, and 5,000 or more are rounded to the nearest 10, 25, 50, and 100 respectively. Annual estimates are through the most recent year for which reliable estimates are available. Because there is uncertainty in the estimates of deaths of persons with AIDS, changes over time in estimates of deaths of persons with AIDS should not be computed from these rounded estimates. See souce, "Technical notes"]

CHARACTERISTICS	1991	1992	1993	1994	1995	1996
Total	36,600	41,100	44,600	49,400	50,700	39,200
RACE/ETHNICITY						
White, not Hispanic.	18,900	20,400	21,400	22,300	21,800	14,700
Black, not Hispanic.	11,100	13,300	15,200	17,800	19,100	16,700
Hispanic	6,200	7,100	7,600	8,700	9,100	7,300
Asian/Pacific Islander	250	270	300	400	360	290
American Indian/Alaska Native	90	80	130	140	180	100
MALE ADULT/ADOLESCENT EXPOSURE CATEGORY						
Male total.	31,900	35,600	38,100	41,400	42,000	31,400
Men who have sex with men	21,000	22,800	23,700	25,100	24,900	17,300
Injecting drug use.	6,800	8,000	9,100	10,200	10,800	9,000
Men who have sex with men and inject drugs . . .	2,425	2,700	3,000	3,300	3,300	2,500
Hemophilia/coagulation disorder	270	320	340	330	310	220
Heterosexual contact.	820	1,175	1,525	1,925	2,300	2,125
Receipt of blood transfusion, blood components, or tissue	380	330	320	310	280	240
Risk not reported or identified	210	240	200	170	130	80
FEMALE ADULT/ADOLESCENT EXPOSURE CATEGORY						
Female total.	4,250	5,100	6,000	7,400	8,100	7,300
Injecting drug use.	2,250	2,700	3,050	3,650	3,850	3,450
Hemophilia/coagulation disorder	10	20	20	20	20	20
Heterosexual contact.	1,625	1,950	2,600	3,450	4,000	3,650
Receipt of blood transfusion, blood components, or tissue	250	260	240	240	250	200
Risk not reported or identified	80	120	90	70	60	40
Pediatric [1] exposure category	390	420	530	560	530	440

[1] Less than 13 years old.

Source: U.S. Centers for Disease Control and Prevention, HIV/AIDS Surveillance Report, 1996; 8 (No.1).

No. 145. Death Rates From Heart Disease, by Sex and Age: 1980 to 1995

[**Deaths per 100,000 population in specified age groups.** Excludes deaths of nonresidents of the United States. Deaths classified according to the ninth revision of the *International Classification of Diseases,* classified according to the revision in use at the time; see text, Section 2. See Appendix III]

AGE AT DEATH AND SELECTED TYPE OF HEART DISEASE	MALE					FEMALE				
	1980	1990	1993	1994	1995	1980	1990	1993	1994	1995
Total U.S. rate [1]	369	298	292	284	283	305	282	285	279	279
25 to 34 years old	11	10	11	11	11	5	5	6	6	6
35 to 44 years old	69	48	47	47	47	21	15	17	17	17
45 to 54 years old	283	183	173	171	169	85	61	58	57	56
55 to 64 years old	747	537	499	478	465	272	216	205	196	194
65 to 74 years old	1,728	1,250	1,175	1,133	1,102	829	617	589	566	558
75 to 84 years old	3,834	2,968	2,754	2,655	2,615	2,497	1,894	1,808	1,741	1,715
85 years old and over	8,753	7,418	7,332	7,123	7,040	7,351	6,478	6,415	6,253	6,268
Persons 45 to 54 years old:										
Ischemic heart	217.3	123.8	112.0	109.2	107.5	52.2	33.6	30.8	30.6	29.4
Rheumatic heart	3.1	1.1	0.9	1.0	0.7	4.3	1.9	1.7	1.4	1.3
Hypertensive heart [2]	8.3	7.6	(NA)	8.7	8.8	5.5	4.3	(NA)	4.1	3.9
Persons 55 to 64 years old:										
Ischemic heart	581.1	375.4	337.9	323.4	312.6	189.0	135.4	124.5	120.4	116.8
Rheumatic heart	6.2	3.4	2.7	2.4	2.2	9.2	4.7	3.9	3.7	3.4
Hypertensive heart [2]	21.8	18.1	(NA)	17.3	18.2	13.3	10.9	(NA)	9.5	9.3
Persons 65 to 74 years old:										
Ischemic heart	1,355.5	898.5	823.7	794.0	770.5	605.3	415.2	383.6	368.1	362.8
Rheumatic heart	11.8	7.1	6.0	5.9	4.5	18.6	10.5	9.7	9.1	8.3
Hypertensive heart [2]	44.3	33.2	(NA)	29.4	30.9	36.2	25.9	(NA)	21.4	22.1
Persons 75 to 84 years old:										
Ischemic heart	2,953.7	2,129.6	1,962.7	1,863.9	1,824.0	1,842.7	1,287.6	1,188.3	1,142.9	1,116.3
Rheumatic heart	16.7	12.3	12.4	11.1	10.7	25.4	22.5	19.6	18.5	17.9
Hypertensive heart [2]	90.7	67.9	(NA)	59.3	59.7	101.1	69.7	(NA)	61.7	62.4
Persons 85 years old and over:										
Ischemic heart	6,501.6	5,120.7	4,920.7	4,771.9	4,674.4	5,280.6	4,257.8	4,097.6	3,980.8	3,948.8
Rheumatic heart	19.5	18.7	24.6	19.2	21.5	25.8	33.3	31.3	28.1	28.8
Hypertensive heart [2]	180.3	154.3	(NA)	143.0	154.9	250.8	212.1	(NA)	216.3	223.2

NA Not available. [1] Includes persons under 25 years old not shown separately. [2] With or without renal disease.

Source: U.S. National Center for Health Statistics, *Vital Statistics of the United States,* annual; and unpublished data.

No. 146. Death Rates From Cancer, by Sex and Age: 1980 to 1995

[Deaths per 100,000 population in the specified age groups. See headnote, Table 145]

AGE AT DEATH AND SELECTED TYPE OF CANCER	MALE					FEMALE				
	1980	1990	1993	1994	1995	1980	1990	1993	1994	1995
Total [1]	205.3	221.3	222.1	220.7	219.5	163.6	186.0	189.8	190.5	191.0
25 to 34 years	13.4	12.6	11.9	(NA)	11.7	14.0	12.6	12.3	(NA)	12.2
35 to 44 years	44.0	38.5	38.0	(NA)	36.5	53.1	48.1	44.1	(NA)	44.0
45 to 54 years	188.7	162.5	150.7	(NA)	143.7	171.8	155.5	145.2	(NA)	140.7
55 to 64 years	520.8	532.9	507.4	(NA)	480.5	361.7	375.2	366.7	(NA)	357.5
65 to 74 years	1,093.2	1,122.2	1,113.3	(NA)	1,089.9	607.1	677.4	688.4	(NA)	690.7
75 to 84 years	1,790.5	1,914.4	1,885.4	(NA)	1,842.3	903.1	1,010.3	1,046.1	(NA)	1,061.5
85 years old and over	2,369.5	2,739.9	2,830.7	(NA)	2,837.3	1,255.7	1,372.1	1,415.3	(NA)	1,429.1
Persons, 35 to 44 years old:										
Respiratory, intrathoracic	12.6	9.1	8.3	8.0	7.6	6.8	5.4	5.0	4.9	5.1
Digestive organs, peritoneum	9.5	8.9	9.1	8.9	8.9	6.5	5.5	5.5	5.4	5.5
Breast	-	(B)	(B)	(B)	(B)	17.9	17.8	15.2	15.2	15.0
Genital organs	0.7	0.6	0.6	0.6	0.7	8.3	7.3	6.8	6.6	6.7
Lymphatic and hematopoietic tissues, excl. leukemia	4.3	4.5	4.7	(NA)	(NA)	2.4	2.1	2.0	(NA)	(NA)
Urinary organs	1.4	1.5	1.5	1.3	1.5	0.6	0.6	0.7	0.7	0.7
Lip, oral cavity, and pharynx	1.8	1.3	1.3	1.1	1.1	0.5	0.3	0.4	0.4	0.4
Leukemia	3.2	2.5	2.5	2.2	2.4	2.6	2.2	2.0	1.8	1.7
Persons, 45 to 54 years old:										
Respiratory, intrathoracic	79.8	63.0	54.6	51.9	49.9	34.8	35.3	31.6	30.4	30.1
Digestive organs, peritoneum	44.3	40.4	37.6	38.7	37.3	27.8	23.3	21.5	21.3	21.0
Breast	0.2	0.3	0.3	0.2	0.3	48.1	45.4	42.0	41.6	41.4
Genital organs	3.4	2.9	2.7	2.9	2.6	24.1	19.4	17.9	18.1	17.6
Lymphatic and hematopoietic tissues, excl. leukemia	10.2	10.9	10.3	(NA)	(NA)	6.6	6.0	6.0	(NA)	(NA)
Urinary organs	7.4	7.2	7.4	7.1	7.1	3.3	2.9	3.0	2.8	2.8
Lip, oral cavity, and pharynx	8.2	5.9	6.0	5.6	5.3	2.6	1.6	1.7	1.3	1.3
Leukemia	6.2	5.6	5.2	5.2	4.8	4.4	4.1	3.9	3.8	3.5
Persons, 55 to 64 years old:										
Respiratory, intrathoracic	223.8	232.6	216.0	206.8	196.1	74.5	107.6	107.3	105.3	104.8
Digestive organs, peritoneum	129.3	124.0	122.0	120.0	120.9	79.1	69.3	67.9	66.4	66.0
Breast	0.7	0.6	0.7	0.7	0.7	80.5	78.6	72.2	69.8	69.8
Genital organs	23.5	27.9	24.9	24.0	23.6	46.8	40.1	38.1	39.0	37.2
Lymphatic and hematopoietic tissues, excl. leukemia	24.4	27.2	26.1	(NA)	(NA)	16.8	16.7	18.4	(NA)	(NA)
Urinary organs	22.9	23.5	22.3	22.5	21.9	8.9	8.8	8.4	8.8	9.1
Lip, oral cavity, and pharynx	17.9	16.2	14.2	13.5	12.7	6.0	4.7	4.3	4.0	4.3
Leukemia	14.7	14.7	14.7	14.8	14.5	9.3	8.8	8.7	8.5	8.7
Persons, 65 to 74 years old:										
Respiratory, intrathoracic	422.0	447.3	441.2	434.5	432.4	106.1	181.7	199.2	203.6	205.0
Digestive organs, peritoneum	284.1	267.4	259.6	260.8	256.9	173.6	153.0	151.8	149.7	149.9
Breast	1.1	1.1	1.2	1.4	1.1	101.1	111.7	105.7	105.6	103.3
Genital organs	107.6	123.5	117.9	115.1	110.0	73.6	71.0	67.0	69.2	66.7
Lymphatic and hematopoietic tissues, excl. leukemia	48.1	56.8	59.0	(NA)	(NA)	34.4	39.5	42.5	(NA)	(NA)
Urinary organs	56.9	50.7	53.3	52.1	50.9	19.7	19.8	19.5	20.9	19.8
Lip, oral cavity, and pharynx	25.4	21.5	20.1	18.0	19.3	8.8	8.3	7.5	7.9	7.5
Leukemia	35.3	36.0	36.7	35.6	37.2	18.7	18.8	19.1	19.1	18.9
Persons, 75 to 84 years old:										
Respiratory, intrathoracic	511.5	594.4	384.8	576.7	573.4	98.0	194.5	226.3	236.4	245.1
Digestive organs, peritoneum	496.6	468.0	441.7	437.2	430.6	326.3	293.3	287.7	284.0	283.4
Breast	2.1	1.6	2.3	2.0	2.4	126.4	146.3	146.4	145.9	142.0
Genital organs	315.4	358.5	356.6	350.7	333.9	95.7	95.3	97.4	96.7	96.3
Lymphatic and hematopoietic tissues, excl. leukemia	80.0	104.5	107.8	(NA)	(NA)	57.8	71.2	78.4	(NA)	(NA)
Urinary organs	112.4	107.5	103.4	105.3	105.4	37.4	38.5	38.0	39.9	39.3
Lip, oral cavity, and pharynx	31.4	26.1	24.6	23.5	23.2	10.9	11.6	10.4	10.6	10.3
Leukemia	71.5	71.9	71.4	71.5	75.1	38.5	38.8	37.8	38.3	39.9
Persons, 85 years old and over:										
Respiratory, intrathoracic	386.3	538.0	559.7	556.1	567.6	96.3	142.8	173.9	171.8	187.5
Digestive organs, peritoneum	705.8	699.5	668.5	661.4	667.2	504.3	497.6	487.0	477.2	478.8
Breast	2.6	2.4	5.1	3.9	4.2	169.3	196.8	206.0	197.5	203.7
Genital organs	612.3	750.0	842.2	822.5	821.5	115.9	115.6	114.4	115.3	120.5
Lymphatic and hematopoietic tissues, excl. leukemia	93.2	140.5	145.6	(NA)	(NA)	63.0	90.0	95.5	(NA)	(NA)
Urinary organs	177.0	186.3	190.3	189.6	192.2	63.8	68.5	64.5	67.3	68.4
Lip, oral cavity, and pharynx	40.2	37.4	31.1	30.0	34.1	16.0	17.5	16.8	16.0	17.7
Leukemia	117.1	116.0	115.6	118.5	123.0	61.1	65.0	68.2	68.1	65.5

- Represents zero.   B Base figure too small to meet statistical standards for reliability.   NA Not available.   [1] Includes persons under 25 years of age and malignant neoplasms of other and unspecified sites, not shown separately.

Source: U.S. National Center for Health Statistics, *Vital Statistics of the United States,* annual; and unpublished data.

No. 147. Death Rates From Accidents and Violence, by Race and Sex: 1980 to 1995

[Rates are per 100,000 population. Excludes deaths of nonresidents of the United States. Deaths classified according to the ninth revision of the *International Classification of Diseases*. See text, Section 2. See Appendix III]

CAUSE OF DEATH	WHITE						BLACK					
	Male			Female			Male			Female		
	1980	1990	1995	1980	1990	1995	1980	1990	1995	1980	1990	1995
Total [1]	97.1	81.2	(NA)	36.3	32.1	(NA)	154.0	142.0	(NA)	42.6	38.6	(NA)
Motor vehicle accidents	35.9	26.1	22.6	12.8	11.4	10.8	31.1	28.1	24.6	8.3	9.4	9.0
All other accidents. . . .	30.4	23.6	24.7	14.4	12.4	13.5	46.0	32.7	31.6	18.6	13.4	13.5
Suicide	19.9	22.0	21.4	5.9	5.3	(NA)	10.3	12.0	(NA)	2.2	2.3	(NA)
Homicide	10.9	9.0	(NA)	3.2	2.8	(NA)	66.6	69.2	56.3	13.5	13.5	(NA)

NA Not available.   [1] Includes persons under 15 years old, not shown separately.

No. 148. Deaths and Death Rates From Accidents, by Type: 1980 to 1995

[See headnote, Table 147 and Appendix III]

TYPE OF ACCIDENT	DEATHS (number)					RATE PER 100,000 POPULATION				
	1980	1990	1993	1994	1995	1980	1990	1993	1994	1995
Total	105,718	91,983	90,523	(NA)	(NA)	46.7	37.0	35.1	(NA)	(NA)
Motor vehicle accidents	53,172	46,814	41,893	42,524	43,363	23.5	18.8	16.3	16.3	16.5
Traffic	51,930	45,827	40,899	41,507	42,331	22.9	18.4	15.9	15.9	16.1
Nontraffic	1,242	987	994	1,017	1,032	0.5	0.4	0.4	0.4	0.4
Water-transport accidents	1,429	923	763	723	762	0.6	0.4	0.3	0.3	0.3
Air and space transport accidents . .	1,494	941	859	1,075	851	0.7	0.4	0.3	0.4	0.3
Railway accidents	632	663	670	635	569	0.3	0.3	0.3	0.2	0.2
Accidental falls	13,294	12,313	13,141	13,450	13,986	5.9	5.0	5.1	5.2	5.3
Accidental drowning.	6,043	3,979	3,807	3,404	3,790	2.7	1.6	1.5	1.3	1.4
Accidents caused by—										
Fires and flames	5,822	4,175	3,900	3,986	3,761	2.6	1.7	1.5	1.5	1.4
Firearms, unspecified and other . .	1,667	1,175	1,261	1,123	992	0.7	0.5	0.5	0.4	0.4
Handguns.	288	241	260	233	233	0.1	0.1	0.1	0.1	0.1
Electric current	1,095	670	548	561	559	0.5	0.3	0.2	0.2	0.2
Accidental poisoning by—										
Drugs and medicines	2,492	4,506	7,382	7,828	8,000	1.1	1.8	2.9	3.0	3.0
Other solid and liquid substances .	597	549	495	481	461	0.3	0.2	0.2	0.2	0.2
Gases and vapors	1,242	748	660	685	611	0.5	0.3	0.3	0.3	0.2
Complications due to medical procedures	2,282	2,669	2,724	2,616	2,712	1.0	1.1	1.1	1.0	1.0
Inhalation and ingestion of objects . .	3,249	3,303	3,160	3,065	3,185	1.4	1.3	1.2	1.2	1.2

NA Not available.

Source of Tables 147-148: U.S. National Center for Health Statistics, *Vital Statistics of the United States*, annual; and unpublished data.

No. 149. Death Rates for Injury by Firearms, Sex, Race, and Age: 1995

[**Death rate per 100,000 population.** Deaths classified according to the ninth revision of the *International Classification of Diseases*]

ITEM	5-14 yrs. old	15-24 yrs. old	25-34 yrs. old	35-44 yrs. old	45-54 yrs. old	55-64 yrs. old	65-74 yrs. old	75-84 yrs. old	85 yrs. and over
MALE									
Firearms: White	2.5	31.4	26.1	21.2	19.6	19.9	26.1	39.8	50.8
Black	5.5	140.2	94.4	46.6	32.1	24.3	22.0	20.9	(B)
Accidents: White	0.7	1.8	0.8	0.6	0.5	0.4	0.6	0.7	(B)
Black.	0.8	4.3	1.5	(B)	(B)	(B)	(B)	(B)	(B)
Suicide: White	0.8	15.4	15.1	14.2	14.9	16.6	23.9	38.2	49.5
Black.	(B)	13.2	11.9	7.6	6.9	7.5	10.2	13.9	(B)
Homicide: White	0.9	13.6	9.8	6.3	4.0	2.8	1.5	0.8	(B)
Black.	4.1	121.0	80.7	38.3	24.6	15.9	10.8	(B)	(B)
FEMALE									
Firearms: White	0.8	4.6	5.0	4.9	4.4	3.6	3.1	3.0	1.8
Black	1.4	13.5	11.9	7.9	4.4	3.7	3.1	(B)	(B)
Accidents: White.	0.1	0.2	0.2	0.2	(B)	(B)	(B)	(B)	(B)
Black.	(B)	(B)	(B)	(B)	(B)	(B)	(B)	(B)	(B)
Suicide: White	0.3	2.0	2.4	2.8	3.0	2.6	2.3	2.0	1.2
Black.	(B)	1.5	1.4	0.8	(B)	(B)	(B)	(B)	(B)
Homicide: White	0.4	2.2	2.3	1.8	1.2	0.8	0.7	0.8	(B)
Black.	1.2	11.8	10.2	6.7	3.4	2.3	(B)	(B)	(B)

B Does not meet standard of reliability or precision.

Source: U.S. National Center for Health Statistics, *Advance Data from Vital and Health Statistics*, No. 231.

No. 150. Suicides, by Race, Age, and Method: 1980 to 1995

[Death rates per 100,000 population. In specified group]

SEX, AGE, AND METHOD	1980	1985	1987	1988	1989	1990	1991	1992	1993	1994	1995
All races, both sexes	26,869	29,453	30,796	30,407	30,232	30,906	30,810	30,484	31,102	31,142	31,284
5 to 9 years old	3	3	1	6	4	6	1	10	6	4	7
10 to 14 years old	139	275	250	237	236	258	265	304	315	318	330
15 to 19 years old	1,797	1,849	1,902	2,059	2,009	1,979	1,899	1,847	1,884	1,948	1,890
20 to 24 years old	3,442	3,272	3,022	2,870	2,861	2,890	2,852	2,846	2,965	3,008	2,894
25 to 29 years old	3,228	3,364	3,372	3,355	3,299	3,192	3,086	2,864	2,979	3,026	2,880
30 to 34 years old	2,692	3,012	3,283	3,355	3,266	3,358	3,428	3,308	3,328	3,328	3,412
35 to 39 years old	2,150	2,528	2,799	2,909	2,937	3,098	3,089	3,177	3,248	3,328	3,332
40 to 44 years old	1,785	2,098	2,333	2,296	2,394	2,619	2,678	2,832	2,922	2,978	3,135
White, both sexes	24,829	27,087	28,217	27,790	27,424	28,086	27,996	27,611	28,035	27,976	28,187
5 to 9 years old	2	3	-	1	6	2	4	-	6	4	2	5
10 to 14 years old	130	243	218	195	196	219	228	265	258	269	284
15 to 19 years old	1,635	1,643	1,679	1,819	1,743	1,701	1,628	1,531	1,594	1,588	1,587
20 to 24 years old	3,057	2,866	2,649	2,489	2,399	2,481	2,450	2,404	2,443	2,490	2,416
25 to 29 years old	2,876	2,985	2,940	2,940	2,847	2,731	2,629	2,464	2,504	2,557	2,443
30 to 34 years old	2,391	2,674	2,910	2,904	2,850	2,952	3,045	2,895	2,940	2,933	2,977
35 to 39 years old	1,979	2,316	2,517	2,626	2,628	2,779	2,799	2,845	2,902	3,003	2,985
40 to 44 years old	1,639	1,948	2,157	2,124	2,189	2,404	2,470	2,582	2,665	2,719	2,857
Black, both sexes	1,607	1,795	1,963	2,022	2,153	2,111	2,097	2,143	2,259	2,271	2,231
5 to 9 years old	1	-	-	-	2	2	1	1	2	2	1
10 to 14 years old	9	22	25	29	32	29	31	33	39	39	30
15 to 19 years old	108	135	162	167	175	183	183	223	213	263	229
20 to 24 years old	307	289	263	298	350	282	296	313	395	366	323
25 to 29 years old	278	294	341	325	340	357	344	303	353	325	321
30 to 34 years old	245	262	311	360	349	318	301	331	296	282	312
35 to 39 years old	133	175	225	226	244	252	237	257	265	296	266
40 to 44 years old	128	115	129	131	168	171	153	194	183	201	218
Method total, both sexes:											
Drugs, medicaments, & biologicals	2,761	2,668	2,891	2,910	2,988	2,920	3,095	3,215	2,975	3,022	2,874
Other solid or liquid substances	274	269	215	223	227	223	219	223	204	207	178
Gases and vapors	2,418	2,767	3,215	2,692	2,228	2,281	2,230	2,057	2,092	2,044	2,095
Suicide by hanging [1]	3,691	4,264	4,235	4,375	4,484	4,444	4,561	4,678	4,627	4,745	5,217
Handgun	169	179	228	235	216	246	271	261	282	302	3,700
Other and unspecified firearms	13,287	14,382	14,841	14,972	15,058	15,421	14,907	14,714	15,354	15,059	14,803
All other	2,329	2,122	2,104	2,038	2,127	2,153	2,179	2,142	2,264	2,359	2,417
Method, white:											
Drugs, medicaments, & biologicals	2,620	2,503	2,676	2,694	2,774	2,703	2,894	2,979	2,742	2,756	2,643
Other solid or liquid substances	246	234	187	200	195	190	195	194	180	171	153
Gases and vapors	2,375	2,713	3,122	2,623	2,154	2,227	2,172	1,994	2,017	1,987	2,018
Suicide by hanging [1]	3,288	3,712	3,667	3,807	3,853	3,812	3,945	4,050	3,943	4,063	4,493
Handgun	1,940	2,802	3,067	2,962	2,904	3,218	3,348	3,194	3,304	3,404	3,392
Other and unspecified firearms	12,346	13,318	13,686	13,763	13,767	14,126	13,626	13,412	13,967	13,603	13,468
All other	2,014	1,805	1,812	1,741	1,777	1,810	1,816	1,788	1,882	1,992	2,020
Method, black:											
Drugs, medicaments, & biologicals	106	120	158	167	164	159	144	160	164	188	157
Other solid or liquid substances	17	26	20	15	23	22	14	12	14	24	13
Gases and vapors	29	39	67	52	53	30	44	46	49	33	57
Hanging [1]	263	334	350	376	408	374	375	379	418	394	406
Handgun	151	146	184	176	171	178	191	185	205	201	213
Other and unspecified firearms	795	886	959	1,006	1,070	1,085	1,062	1,096	1,160	1,192	1,091
All other	246	244	225	230	264	263	267	265	249	239	294

- Represents or rounds to zero.   [1] Includes strangulation and suffocation.
Source: U.S. National Center for Health Statistics, *Vital Statistics of the United States*, annual, and unpublished data.

No. 151. Homicide Rates by Race, Sex, and Age: 1990 to 1995

AGE	WHITE				BLACK			
	Male		Female		Male		Female	
	1990	1995	1990	1995	1990	1995	1990	1995
Total [1]	9.0	7.8	2.8	2.7	69.2	56.3	13.5	11.1
Under 1 year	6.4	7.1	5.1	5.0	21.4	19.4	22.8	19.2
1-4 yrs.	1.8	2.1	1.4	1.8	7.6	8.7	7.2	6.8
5-9 yrs.	0.5	0.7	0.7	0.6	2.1	2.1	2.5	1.5
10-14 yrs.	1.7	2.0	0.9	1.0	8.1	8.2	4.8	3.0
15-19 yrs.	12.5	14.7	3.6	3.9	115.7	110.5	15.6	16.4
20-24 yrs.	18.1	18.2	4.5	4.2	162.2	155.5	22.1	17.2
25-29 yrs.	16.6	14.3	4.4	4.4	140.0	113.9	26.5	19.6
30-34 yrs.	13.6	11.7	4.3	4.1	110.2	83.8	24.0	20.6
35-39 yrs.	12.3	9.4	3.4	3.5	92.8	61.1	18.7	17.0
40-44 yrs.	10.5	9.0	3.0	3.3	69.0	50.3	11.7	11.8
45-49 yrs.	8.9	6.7	2.9	2.6	52.9	44.5	8.2	6.9
50-54 yrs.	7.6	5.9	2.3	2.4	41.3	32.1	6.2	6.0
55-59 yrs.	5.7	5.4	1.9	2.0	32.8	29.4	6.7	5.5
60-64 yrs.	5.3	4.6	1.8	1.4	35.4	24.5	4.5	4.3
65-69 yrs.	4.3	3.8	1.5	1.5	24.4	21.4	7.4	5.7
70-74 yrs.	3.9	2.4	2.1	2.2	24.1	21.7	6.0	(B)
75-79 yrs.	3.8	2.5	2.6	2.0	29.7	19.5	8.9	9.2
80-84 yrs.	4.1	2.6	3.1	2.6	28.5	(B)	15.3	(B)
85 yrs. and over	4.9	3.5	2.5	2.1	(B)	(B)	19.2	14.4

B Base figure to small to meet statistical standards for reliability of a derived figure.   [1] Includes persons under 15 years old, not shown separately.
Source: U.S. National Center for Health Statistics, *Vital Statistics of the United States*, annual.

No. 152. Deaths and Death Rates for Injury by Firearms, by Race and Sex: 1980 to 1995

[Age-adjusted rates per 100,000]

YEAR	ALL RACES Both sexes	Male	Female	WHITE Both sexes	Male	Female	ALL OTHER Total Both sexes	Male	Female	Black Both sexes	Male	Female
NUMBER												
1980	33,780	28,322	5,458	24,849	20,714	4,135	8,931	7,608	1,323	8,505	7,265	1,240
1985	31,566	26,382	5,184	24,507	20,389	4,118	7,059	5,993	1,066	6,565	5,584	981
1990	37,155	31,736	5,419	26,299	22,249	4,050	10,856	9,487	1,369	10,175	8,922	1,253
1993	39,595	33,711	5,884	26,948	22,608	4,268	12,647	11,031	1,616	11,763	10,310	1,453
1994	38,505	33,021	5,484	26,403	22,408	3,995	12,102	10,613	1,489	11,223	9,880	1,343
1995	35,957	30,724	5,233	25,438	21,510	3,928	10,519	9,214	1,305	9,643	8,494	1,149
RATE [1]												
1980	14.8	25.3	4.8	12.4	21.1	4.2	29.1	53.0	8.1	33.5	61.8	9.1
1985	12.7	21.8	4.2	11.4	19.4	3.9	19.7	35.4	5.7	23.2	42.2	6.5
1990	14.6	25.4	4.2	11.9	20.5	3.7	26.9	48.9	6.5	33.4	61.5	7.8
1993	15.6	26.9	4.6	12.2	20.7	3.9	30.1	54.4	7.3	37.6	68.8	8.8
1994	15.1	26.2	4.2	11.9	20.4	3.6	28.4	51.6	6.6	35.5	65.1	8.0
1995	13.9	24.1	4.0	11.3	19.3	3.5	24.4	44.4	5.7	30.3	55.6	6.8

[1] Age-adjusted death rate. For method of computation see source.

No. 153. Deaths and Death Rates for Drug-Induced Causes, by Race and Sex: 1980 to 1995

[Age-adjusted rates per 100,000]

YEAR	ALL RACES Both sexes	Male	Female	WHITE Both sexes	Male	Female	ALL OTHER Total Both sexes	Male	Female	Black Both sexes	Male	Female
NUMBER												
1980	6,900	3,771	3,129	5,814	3,088	2,726	1,086	683	403	1,006	648	358
1985	8,663	5,342	3,321	6,946	4,172	2,774	1,717	1,170	547	1,600	1,107	493
1990	9,463	5,897	3,566	7,603	4,646	2,957	1,860	1,251	609	1,703	1,155	548
1993	13,275	9,052	4,223	10,394	7,005	3,389	2,881	2,047	834	2,688	1,924	764
1994	13,923	9,491	4,432	10,895	7,339	3,556	3,028	2,152	876	2,780	1,995	785
1995	14,218	9,909	4,309	11,173	7,730	3,443	3,045	2,179	866	2,800	2,011	789
RATE [1]												
1980	3.0	3.4	2.6	2.9	3.2	2.6	3.7	4.9	2.5	4.1	5.8	2.7
1985	3.5	4.5	2.6	3.3	4.0	2.5	4.9	7.2	2.9	5.9	8.9	3.3
1990	3.6	4.6	2.6	3.3	4.2	2.5	4.6	6.7	2.8	5.7	8.4	3.4
1993	4.8	6.8	3.0	4.5	6.2	2.8	6.6	10.0	3.6	8.3	13.0	4.4
1994	5.0	7.0	3.0	4.7	6.5	2.9	6.8	10.5	3.7	8.6	13.4	4.4
1995	5.1	7.3	3.0	4.8	6.8	2.8	6.7	10.4	3.5	8.5	13.3	4.4

[1] Age-adjusted death rate. For method of computation see source.

No. 154. Deaths and Death Rates for Alcohol-Induced Causes, by Race and Sex: 1980 to 1995

[Age-adjusted rates per 100,000]

YEAR	ALL RACES Both sexes	Male	Female	WHITE Both sexes	Male	Female	ALL OTHER Total Both sexes	Male	Female	Black Both sexes	Male	Female
NUMBER												
1980	19,765	14,447	5,318	14,815	10,936	3,879	4,950	3,511	1,439	4,451	3,170	1,281
1985	17,741	13,216	4,525	13,216	9,922	3,294	4,525	3,294	1,231	4,114	3,030	1,084
1990	19,757	14,842	4,915	14,904	11,334	3,570	4,853	3,508	1,345	4,337	3,172	1,165
1993	19,557	14,873	4,684	15,293	11,716	3,577	4,264	3,157	1,107	3,663	2,759	904
1994	20,163	15,293	4,870	15,853	12,154	3,699	4,310	3,139	1,171	3,648	2,700	948
1995	20,231	15,443	4,788	15,991	12,338	3,653	4,240	3,105	1,135	3,538	2,614	924
RATE [1]												
1980	8.4	13.0	4.3	6.9	10.8	3.5	18.8	29.5	10.0	20.4	32.4	10.6
1985	7.0	11.0	3.4	5.8	9.2	2.8	14.6	23.5	7.2	16.8	27.7	8.0
1990	7.2	11.4	3.4	6.2	9.9	2.8	13.6	22.0	6.8	16.1	26.6	7.7
1993	6.7	10.8	3.0	6.1	9.7	2.7	10.8	17.8	5.0	12.5	21.3	5.5
1994	6.8	10.9	3.1	6.2	9.9	2.7	10.6	17.3	5.2	12.2	20.4	5.6
1995	6.7	10.8	3.0	6.2	9.9	2.7	10.1	16.7	4.8	11.5	19.4	5.3

[1] Age-adjusted death rate. For method of computation see source.

Source of Tables 152-154: U.S. National Center for Health Statistics, *Monthly Vital Statistics Reports*.

No. 155. Deaths—Life Years Lost and Mortality Costs, by Age, Sex, and Cause: 1994

[**Life years lost:** Number of years person would have lived in absence of death. **Mortality cost:** value of lifetime earnings lost by persons who die prematurely, discounted at 6 percent]

CHARACTERIS-TIC	Number of deaths (1,000)	LIFE YEARS LOST [1]		MORTALITY COST [2]		CHARACTERIS-TIC	Number of deaths (1,000)	LIFE YEARS LOST [1]		MORTALITY COST [2]	
		Total (1,000)	Per death	Total (mil.)	Per death			Total (1,000)	Per death	Total (mil.)	Per death
Total	2,279	38,450	17	356,632	156,487	Heart disease . . .	361	4,829	13	44,032	121,880
Under 5 yrs. . . .	39	2,897	75	20,868	541,885	Cancer.	280	4,220	15	40,875	145,741
5-14 yrs.	8	575	68	6,127	723,930	Cerebrovascular					
15-24 yrs.	35	2,018	57	33,116	939,713	diseases.	60	721	12	5,844	97,034
25-44 yrs.	159	6,749	43	136,819	861,709	Injuries.	61	2,167	36	38,567	637,384
45-64 yrs.	375	9,461	25	120,314	320,823	Other.	400	8,870	22	123,705	309,053
65 yrs. and over .	1,663	16,751	10	39,388	23,691						
Heart disease . . .	732	9,216	13	60,786	82,994	**Female. . . . .**	1,116	17,643	16	103,608	92,818
Cancer.	534	8,811	16	71,070	133,013	Under 5 yrs.	17	1,332	79	8,129	482,267
Cerebrovascular						5-14 yrs.	3	237	72	2,082	634,449
diseases.	153	1,800	12	10,091	65,824	15-24 yrs.	8	529	62	6,653	784,321
Injuries.	91	3,164	35	48,774	533,418	25-44 yrs.	47	2,164	46	31,311	668,305
Other.	768	15,459	20	165,911	216,162	45-64 yrs.	143	3,996	28	36,957	257,772
Male	1,163	20,807	18	253,024	217,609	65 yrs. and over .	897	9,386	10	18,476	20,591
Under 5 yrs. . . .	22	1,565	72	12,739	588,288	Heart disease . . .	371	4,387	12	16,753	45,141
5-14 yrs.	5	338	65	4,045	780,602	Cancer.	254	4,591	18	30,195	118,949
15-24 yrs.	27	1,490	56	26,463	988,976	Cerebrovascular					
25-44 yrs.	112	4,585	41	105,507	942,669	diseases.	93	1,079	12	4,247	45,631
45-64 yrs.	232	5,465	24	83,357	359,846	Injuries.	31	997	32	10,207	330,013
65 yrs. and over .	765	7,365	10	20,912	27,326	Other.	367	6,589	18	42,206	114,922

[1] Based on life expectancy at year of death.   [2] Cost estimates based on the person's age, sex, life expectancy at the time of death, labor force participation rates, annual earnings, value of homemaking services, and a 4 percent discount rate by which to convert to present worth the potential aggregate earnings lost over the years.

Source: Institute for Health and Aging, University of California, San Francisco, CA, unpublished data.

No. 156. Marriages and Divorces: 1970 to 1996

YEAR	MARRIAGES [1]						DIVORCES AND ANNULMENTS		
	Number (1,000)	Rate per 1,000 population					Number (1,000)	Rate per 1,000 population	
		Total	Men, 15 yrs. old and over [2]	Women, 15 yrs. old and over [2]	Unmarried women			Total [2]	Married women, 15 yrs. old and over
					15 yrs. old and over	15 to 44 yrs. old			
1970.	2,159	10.6	31.1	28.4	76.5	140.2	708	3.5	14.9
1975.	2,153	10.0	27.9	25.6	66.9	118.5	1,036	4.8	20.3
1980.	2,390	10.6	28.5	26.1	61.4	102.6	1,189	5.2	22.6
1983.	2,446	10.5	28.0	25.7	59.9	99.3	1,158	5.0	21.3
1984.	2,477	10.5	28.0	25.8	59.5	99.0	1,169	5.0	21.5
1985.	2,413	10.1	27.0	24.9	57.0	94.9	1,190	5.0	21.7
1986.	2,407	10.0	26.6	24.5	56.2	93.9	1,178	4.9	21.2
1987.	2,403	9.9	26.3	24.3	55.7	92.4	1,166	4.8	20.8
1988.	2,396	9.8	26.0	24.0	54.6	91.0	1,167	4.8	20.7
1989.	2,403	9.7	25.8	23.9	54.2	91.2	1,157	4.7	20.4
1990.	2,443	9.8	26.0	24.1	54.5	91.3	1,182	4.7	20.9
1991.	2,371	9.4	(NA)	(NA)	54.2	86.8	1,189	4.7	20.9
1992.	2,362	9.3	(NA)	(NA)	53.3	88.2	1,215	4.8	21.2
1993.	2,334	9.0	(NA)	(NA)	52.3	86.8	1,187	4.6	20.5
1994.	2,362	9.1	(NA)	(NA)	51.5	84.0	1,191	4.6	20.5
1995.	2,336	8.9	(NA)	(NA)	50.8	83.0	1,169	4.4	19.8
1996 provisional . .	2,344	8.8	(NA)	(NA)	49.7	81.5	1,150	4.3	19.5

NA Not available.   [1] Beginning 1980, includes nonlicensed marriages registered in California.   [2] Rates for 1981-88 are revised and may differ from rates published previously.

No. 157. Percent Distribution of Marriages, by Marriage Order: 1970 to 1988

[Excludes marriages with marriage order not stated. See headnote, Table 159]

MARRIAGE ORDER	1970	1980	1981	1982	1983	1984	1985	1986	1987	1988
Total.	100.0	100.0	100.0	100.0	100.0	100.0	100.0	100.0	100.0	100.0
First marriage of bride and groom . . .	68.6	56.2	54.7	54.8	54.4	54.4	54.3	53.9	53.9	54.1
First marriage of bride, remarriage of groom . . .	7.6	11.3	11.8	11.6	11.6	11.5	11.5	11.3	11.3	11.1
Remarriage of bride, first marriage of groom . . .	7.3	9.8	10.1	10.3	10.5	10.7	10.9	11.2	11.3	11.4
Remarriage of bride and groom	16.5	22.7	23.4	23.3	23.3	23.5	23.4	23.6	23.5	23.4

Source of Tables 156 and 157: U.S. National Center for Health Statistics, *Vital Statistics of the United States*, annual; *Monthly Vital Statistics Report*; and unpublished data.

No. 158. Percent Distribution of Marriages, by Age, Sex, and Previous Marital Status: 1980 and 1990

[Data cover marriage registration area; see text, Section 2. Based on a sample and subject to sampling variability; for details, see source]

SEX AND PREVIOUS MARITAL STATUS	Total	Under 20 years old	20-24 years old	25-29 years old	30-34 years old	35-44 years old	45-64 years old	65 years old and over
WOMEN								
All marriages: [1]								
1980.	100.0	21.1	37.1	18.7	9.3	7.8	5.0	1.0
1990.	100.0	10.6	29.3	24.6	14.2	13.9	6.1	1.0
First marriages: [2]								
1980.	100.0	30.4	47.3	16.0	4.0	1.6	0.6	0.1
1990.	100.0	16.6	40.8	27.2	10.1	4.5	0.7	0.1
Remarriages: [2][3]								
1980.	100.0	1.7	15.3	24.4	20.6	20.8	14.3	2.9
1990.	100.0	0.6	8.0	19.9	21.7	31.3	16.0	2.7
Previously divorced: [4]								
1980.	100.0	1.7	16.7	26.7	22.5	21.6	10.0	0.6
1990.	100.0	0.6	8.6	20.9	23.0	32.5	13.6	0.6
MEN								
All marriages: [1]								
1980.	100.0	8.5	35.7	23.8	12.3	10.5	7.4	1.8
1990.	100.0	4.3	24.7	27.1	16.6	16.4	9.1	1.9
First marriages: [2]								
1980.	100.0	12.7	50.0	25.7	7.5	2.9	1.1	0.1
1990.	100.0	6.6	36.0	34.3	14.8	7.1	1.1	0.1
Remarriages: [2][3]								
1980.	100.0	0.2	7.2	20.1	21.9	25.6	20.0	5.1
1990.	100.0	0.1	3.6	13.8	19.9	33.8	23.8	5.1
Previously divorced: [4]								
1980.	100.0	0.2	7.7	21.7	24.1	27.7	17.3	1.4
1990.	100.0	0.1	3.8	14.8	21.2	35.8	22.6	1.7

[1] Includes marriage order not stated. [2] Excludes data for Iowa. [3] Includes remarriages of previously widowed. [4] Excludes remarriages in Michigan, Ohio, and South Carolina.

No. 159. Marriage Rates and Median Age of Bride and Groom, by Previous Marital Status: 1970 to 1990

[Data cover marriage registration area; see text, Section 2. Figures for previously divorced and previously widowed exclude data for Michigan and Ohio for all years, for South Carolina beginning 1975, and for the District of Columbia for 1970. Based on a sample and subject to sampling variability; for details, see source. For definition of median, see Guide to Tabular Presentation]

	MARRIAGE RATES [1]						MEDIAN AGE AT MARRIAGE (years)					
	Women			Men			Women			Men		
YEAR	Single	Divorced	Wid-owed	Single	Divorced	Wid-owed	First mar-riage	Remarriage		First mar-riage	Remarriage	
								Divorced	Widowed		Divorced	Widowed
1970	93.4	123.3	10.2	80.4	204.5	40.6	20.6	30.1	51.2	22.5	34.5	58.7
1975	75.9	117.2	8.3	61.5	189.8	40.4	20.8	30.2	52.4	22.7	33.6	59.4
1980	66.0	91.3	6.7	54.7	142.1	32.2	21.8	31.0	53.6	23.6	34.0	61.2
1985	61.5	81.8	5.7	50.1	121.6	27.7	23.0	32.8	54.6	24.8	36.1	62.7
1986	59.7	79.5	5.5	49.1	117.8	26.8	23.3	33.1	54.3	25.1	36.6	62.9
1987	58.9	80.7	5.4	48.8	115.7	26.1	23.6	33.3	53.9	25.3	36.7	62.8
1988	58.4	78.6	5.3	48.3	109.7	25.1	23.7	33.6	53.9	25.5	37.0	63.0
1989	58.7	75.6	5.1	48.2	105.6	24.5	23.9	34.0	53.8	25.9	37.3	62.9
1990	57.7	76.2	5.2	47.0	105.9	23.8	24.0	34.2	54.0	25.9	37.4	63.1

[1] Rate per 1,000 population 15 years old and over in specified group.

No. 160. Divorces and Annulments—Duration of Marriage, Age at Divorce and Children Involved: 1970 to 1990

[Data cover divorce-registration area; see text, Section 2. Based on a sample and subject to sampling variability; for details, see source. Median age computed on data by single years of age]

DURATION OF MARRIAGE, AGE AT DIVORCE, AND CHILDREN INVOLVED	1970	1975	1980	1983	1984	1985	1986	1987	1988	1989	1990
Median duration of marriage (years)	6.7	6.5	6.8	7.0	6.9	6.8	6.9	7.0	7.1	7.2	7.2
Men (years)	32.9	32.2	32.7	34.0	34.3	34.4	34.6	34.9	35.1	35.4	35.6
Women (years)	29.8	29.5	30.3	31.5	31.7	31.9	32.1	32.5	32.6	32.9	33.2
Estimated number of children involved in divorce (1,000).	870	1,123	1,174	1,091	1,081	1,091	1,064	1,038	1,044	1,063	1,075
Avg. number of children per decree.	1.22	1.08	0.98	0.94	0.92	0.92	0.90	0.89	0.89	0.91	0.90
Rate per 1,000 children under 18 years of age .	12.5	16.7	17.3	17.4	17.2	17.3	16.8	16.3	16.4	16.8	16.8

Source of Tables 158-160: U.S. National Center for Health Statistics of the United States, *Vital Statistics of the United States,* annual, *Monthly Vital Statistics Report;* and unpublished data.

No. 161. First Marriage Dissolution and Years Until Remarriage for Women, by Race and Hispanic Origin: 1988

[For women 15 to 44 years old. Based on 1988 National Survey of Family Growth; see Appendix III. Marriage dissolution includes death of spouse, separation because of marital discord, and divorce]

ITEM	Number (1,000)	YEARS UNTIL REMARRIAGE (cumulative percent)					
		All	1	2	3	4	5
ALL RACES [1]							
Year of dissolution of first marriage:							
All years	11,577	56.8	20.6	32.8	40.7	46.2	49.7
1980-84	3,504	47.5	16.3	28.1	36.4	[2]41.1	[2]45.4
1975-79	3,235	65.3	21.9	36.0	44.7	52.7	55.4
1970-74	1,887	83.2	24.9	38.6	47.9	56.4	61.2
1965-69	1,013	89.9	32.6	48.7	60.2	65.0	72.8
WHITE							
Year of dissolution of first marriage:							
All years	10,103	59.9	21.9	35.2	43.5	49.4	53.0
1980-84	3,030	51.4	18.2	31.1	40.3	[2]45.2	[2]49.8
1975-79	2,839	69.5	23.2	38.5	46.9	55.6	58.4
1970-74	1,622	87.5	24.9	39.8	49.8	59.3	64.3
1965-69	893	91.0	34.7	52.3	64.9	69.3	76.9
BLACK							
Year of dissolution of first marriage:							
All years	1,166	34.0	10.9	16.5	19.6	22.7	25.0
1980-84	380	19.7	[3]4.7	[3]10.6	[3]12.9	[2]14.8	[2]14.8
1975-79	301	32.3	[3]11.4	[3]15.6	18.5	22.2	24.9
1970-74	227	59.0	22.3	29.4	35.3	38.7	42.3
1965-69	98	81.2	[3]20.9	[3]27.3	[3]31.3	40.8	52.1
Hispanic, [4] all years	942	44.7	12.5	16.6	22.7	27.8	29.9

[1] Includes other races. [2] The percent having remarried is biased downward because the women had not completed the indicated number of years since dissolution of first marriage at the time of the survey. [3] Figure does not meet standard of reliability or precision. [4] Hispanic persons may be of any race.

Source: National Center for Health Statistics, *Advance Data from Vital and Health Statistics*, No. 194.

No. 162. Marriage Experience for Women, by Age and Race: 1980 and 1990

[**In percent.** As of **June.** Based on Current Population Survey; see text, Section 1]

MARITAL STATUS AND AGE	ALL RACES		WHITE		BLACK		HISPANIC [1]	
	1980	1990	1980	1990	1980	1990	1980	1990
EVER MARRIED								
20 to 24 years old	49.5	38.5	52.2	41.3	33.3	23.5	55.4	45.8
25 to 29 years old	78.6	69.0	81.0	73.2	62.3	45.0	80.2	69.6
30 to 34 years old	89.9	82.2	91.6	85.6	77.9	61.1	88.3	83.0
35 to 39 years old	94.3	89.4	95.3	91.4	87.4	74.9	91.2	88.9
40 to 44 years old	95.1	92.0	95.8	93.4	89.7	82.1	94.2	92.8
45 to 49 years old	95.9	94.4	96.4	95.1	92.5	89.7	94.4	91.7
50 to 54 years old	95.3	95.5	95.8	96.1	92.1	91.9	95.0	91.8
DIVORCED AFTER FIRST MARRIAGE								
20 to 24 years old	14.2	12.5	14.7	12.8	10.5	9.6	9.4	6.8
25 to 29 years old	20.7	19.2	21.0	19.8	20.2	17.8	13.9	13.5
30 to 34 years old	26.2	28.1	25.8	28.6	31.4	26.6	21.1	19.9
35 to 39 years old	27.2	34.1	26.7	34.6	32.9	35.8	21.9	29.7
40 to 44 years old	26.1	35.8	25.5	35.2	33.7	45.1	19.7	26.6
45 to 49 years old	23.1	35.2	22.7	35.5	29.0	39.8	23.9	24.6
50 to 54 years old	21.8	29.5	21.0	28.5	29.0	39.2	22.5	22.9
REMARRIED AFTER DIVORCE								
20 to 24 years old	45.5	38.1	47.0	39.3	(B)	(B)	(B)	(B)
25 to 29 years old	53.4	51.8	56.4	52.8	27.9	44.4	(B)	49.5
30 to 34 years old	60.9	59.6	63.3	61.4	42.0	42.0	58.3	45.9
35 to 39 years old	64.9	65.0	66.9	66.5	50.6	54.0	45.2	51.2
40 to 44 years old	67.4	67.1	68.6	69.5	58.4	50.3	(B)	53.9
45 to 49 years old	69.2	65.9	70.4	67.2	62.7	55.0	(B)	51.0
50 to 54 years old	72.0	63.0	72.6	65.4	72.7	50.2	(B)	62.2
REDIVORCED AFTER REMARRIAGE								
20 to 24 years old	8.5	13.1	(NA)	(NA)	(NA)	(NA)	(NA)	(NA)
25 to 29 years old	15.6	17.8	(NA)	(NA)	(NA)	(NA)	(NA)	(NA)
30 to 34 years old	19.1	22.7	(NA)	(NA)	(NA)	(NA)	(NA)	(NA)
35 to 39 years old	24.7	28.5	(NA)	(NA)	(NA)	(NA)	(NA)	(NA)
40 to 44 years old	28.4	30.6	(NA)	(NA)	(NA)	(NA)	(NA)	(NA)
45 to 49 years old	25.1	36.4	(NA)	(NA)	(NA)	(NA)	(NA)	(NA)
50 to 54 years old	29.0	34.5	(NA)	(NA)	(NA)	(NA)	(NA)	(NA)

B Base is less than 75,000. NA Not available. [1] Persons of Hispanic origin may be of any race.

Source: U.S. Bureau of the Census, *Current Population Reports*, P23-180.

No. 163. Marriages and Divorces—Number and Rate, by State: 1980 to 1996

[By place of occurrence]

STATE	MARRIAGES [1]						DIVORCES [3]					
	Number (1,000)			Rate per 1,000 population [2]			Number (1,000)			Rate per 1,000 population [2]		
	1980	1990	1996, prov.	1980	1990	1995	1980	1990	1996, prov.	1980	1990	1995
U.S.	2,390.3	2,443.0	2,344.0	10.6	9.8	8.9	1,189.0	1,182.0	1,150.0	5.2	4.7	4.4
Alabama	49.0	43.3	47.4	12.6	10.6	9.9	26.7	25.3	25.8	6.9	6.1	6.1
Alaska	5.4	5.7	5.4	13.3	10.2	9.0	3.5	2.9	2.8	8.8	5.5	5.0
Arizona	30.2	37.0	39.2	11.1	10.0	9.2	19.9	25.1	25.8	7.3	6.9	6.6
Arkansas	26.5	35.7	36.2	11.6	15.3	14.7	15.9	16.8	15.2	6.9	6.9	6.5
California [4]	210.9	236.7	202.8	8.9	7.9	6.3	133.5	128.0	(NA)	5.6	4.3	(NA)
Colorado	34.9	31.5	34.5	12.1	9.8	9.2	18.6	18.4	(NA)	6.4	5.5	(NA)
Connecticut	26.0	27.8	21.4	8.4	7.9	6.7	13.5	10.3	10.5	4.3	3.2	2.9
Delaware	4.4	5.6	5.2	7.5	8.4	7.5	2.3	3.0	3.3	3.9	4.4	5.1
Dist. of Columbia	5.2	4.7	3.4	8.1	8.2	6.4	4.7	2.7	(NA)	7.3	4.5	3.4
Florida	108.3	142.3	149.9	11.1	10.9	10.2	71.6	81.7	80.2	7.3	6.3	5.6
Georgia	70.6	64.4	60.1	12.9	10.3	8.5	34.7	35.7	35.9	6.4	5.5	5.2
Hawaii	11.9	18.1	19.5	12.3	16.4	15.8	4.4	5.2	4.8	4.6	4.6	4.6
Idaho	13.4	15.0	15.0	14.2	13.9	13.3	6.6	6.6	7.0	7.0	6.5	5.8
Illinois	109.8	97.1	90.2	9.6	8.8	7.0	51.0	44.3	40.4	4.5	3.8	3.3
Indiana	57.9	54.3	49.2	10.5	9.6	8.7	40.0	(NA)	(NA)	7.3	(NA)	(NA)
Iowa	27.5	24.8	23.8	9.4	9.0	7.8	11.9	11.1	9.9	4.1	3.9	3.7
Kansas	24.8	23.4	20.6	10.5	9.2	8.6	13.4	12.6	11.7	5.7	5.0	4.2
Kentucky	32.7	51.3	43.3	8.9	13.5	12.3	16.7	21.8	21.2	4.6	5.8	5.9
Louisiana	43.5	41.2	38.9	10.3	9.6	9.4	18.1	(NA)	(NA)	4.3	(NA)	(NA)
Maine	12.0	11.8	(NA)	10.7	9.7	8.7	6.2	5.3	(NA)	5.5	4.3	4.4
Maryland	46.3	46.1	41.8	11.0	9.7	8.5	17.5	16.1	16.3	4.1	3.4	3.0
Massachusetts	46.3	47.8	40.6	8.1	7.9	7.2	17.9	16.8	12.4	4.9	4.3	4.2
Michigan	86.9	76.1	69.1	9.4	8.2	7.4	45.0	40.2	38.7	4.9	4.3	4.2
Minnesota	37.6	33.7	33.2	9.2	7.7	7.1	15.4	15.4	15.2	3.8	3.5	3.4
Mississippi	27.9	24.3	21.3	11.1	9.4	8.0	13.8	14.4	15.7	5.5	5.5	4.8
Missouri	54.6	49.3	46.1	11.1	9.6	8.4	27.6	26.4	26.3	5.6	5.1	5.0
Montana	8.3	7.0	6.6	10.6	8.6	7.6	4.9	4.1	4.3	6.3	5.1	4.8
Nebraska	14.2	12.5	12.8	9.1	8.0	7.4	6.4	6.5	6.1	4.1	4.0	3.8
Nevada	114.3	123.4	141.2	142.8	99.0	88.1	13.8	13.3	15.9	17.3	11.4	8.1
New Hampshire	9.3	10.6	9.7	10.0	9.5	8.4	5.3	5.3	5.0	5.7	4.7	4.2
New Jersey	55.8	58.0	51.7	7.6	7.6	6.7	27.8	23.6	25.0	3.8	3.0	3.1
New Mexico	16.6	13.2	16.0	12.8	8.8	9.0	10.4	7.7	10.9	8.0	4.9	6.7
New York	144.5	169.3	152.3	8.2	8.6	8.1	62.0	57.9	60.8	3.5	3.2	3.1
North Carolina	46.7	52.1	61.9	7.9	7.8	8.6	28.1	34.0	35.9	4.8	5.1	5.1
North Dakota	6.1	4.8	5.0	9.3	7.5	7.2	2.1	2.3	2.2	3.3	3.6	3.4
Ohio	99.8	95.8	82.8	9.2	9.0	8.1	58.8	51.0	44.6	5.4	4.7	4.4
Oklahoma	46.5	33.2	26.7	15.4	10.6	8.7	24.2	24.9	19.3	8.0	7.7	6.7
Oregon	23.0	25.2	25.6	8.7	8.9	8.2	17.8	15.9	15.0	6.7	5.5	4.8
Pennsylvania	93.7	86.8	70.2	7.9	7.1	6.3	34.9	40.1	38.3	2.9	3.3	3.3
Rhode Island	7.5	8.1	7.8	7.9	8.1	7.5	3.6	3.8	3.2	3.8	3.7	3.7
South Carolina	53.9	55.8	43.1	17.3	15.9	12.1	13.6	16.1	15.2	4.4	4.5	4.0
South Dakota	8.8	7.7	6.7	12.7	11.1	10.0	2.8	2.6	2.7	4.1	3.7	4.0
Tennessee	59.2	66.6	82.1	12.9	13.9	15.7	30.2	32.3	34.4	6.6	6.5	6.3
Texas	181.8	182.8	179.7	12.8	10.5	10.1	96.8	94.0	(NA)	6.8	5.5	5.3
Utah	17.0	19.0	22.0	11.6	11.2	11.1	7.8	8.8	9.3	5.3	5.1	4.6
Vermont	5.2	6.1	5.9	10.2	10.9	10.3	2.6	2.6	2.5	5.1	4.5	4.8
Virginia	60.2	71.3	65.4	11.3	11.4	10.3	23.6	27.3	28.6	4.4	4.4	4.4
Washington	47.7	48.6	39.2	11.6	9.5	7.7	28.6	28.8	26.5	6.9	5.9	5.5
West Virginia	17.4	13.2	11.1	8.9	7.2	6.1	10.3	9.7	8.0	5.3	5.3	5.1
Wisconsin	41.1	41.2	36.2	8.7	7.9	7.1	17.5	17.8	17.3	3.7	3.6	3.4
Wyoming	6.9	4.8	4.9	14.6	10.7	10.7	4.0	3.1	3.1	8.5	6.6	6.7

NA Not available.   [1] Data are counts of marriages performed, except as noted.   [2] Based on total population residing in area; population enumerated as of April 1 for 1980; estimated as of July 1 for all other years.   [3] Includes annulments.   [4] Marriage data include nonlicensed marriages registered.

Source: U.S. National Center for Health Statistics, *Vital Statistics of the United States,* annual; and *Monthly Vital Statistics Reports.*

Health and Nutrition

This section presents statistics on health expenditures and insurance coverage, including medicare and medicaid, medical personnel, hospitals, nursing homes and other care facilities, incidence of acute and prevalence of chronic conditions, nutritional intake of the population, and food consumption. Summary statistics showing recent trends on health care and discussions of selected health issues are published annually by the U.S. National Center for Health Statistics (NCHS) in *Health, United States.* Data on national health expenditures, medical costs, and insurance coverage are compiled by the U.S. Health Care Financing Administration (HCFA) and appear in the quarterly *Health Care Financing Review* and in the annual *Medicare and Medicaid Statistical Supplement* to the *Health Care Financing Review.* Statistics on health insurance are also collected by NCHS and are published in Series 10 of *Vital and Health Statistics.* The Census Bureau also publishes data on insurance coverage. Statistics on health facilities are collected by NCHS and are published in Series 14 of *Vital and Health Statistics.* Statistics on hospitals are published annually by the American Hospital Association, Chicago, IL, in *Hospital Statistics.* Primary sources for data on nutrition are the quarterly *National Food Review* and the annual *Food Consumption, Prices, and Expenditures,* both issued by the U.S. Department of Agriculture. NCHS also conducts periodic surveys of nutrient levels in the population, including estimates of food and nutrient intake, overweight and obesity, hypercholesterolemia, hypertension, and clinical signs of malnutrition.

National health expenditures—HCFA compiles estimates of national health expenditures (NHE) to measure spending for health care in the United States. The NHE accounts are structured to show spending by type of expenditure (i.e., hospital care, physician care, dental care, and other professional care; home health; drugs and other medical nondurables; vision products and other medical durables; nursing home care and other personal health expenditures; plus nonpersonal health expenditures for such items as public health,

In Brief

In 1996:
42 million with no health insurance.

1995: Persons with—
Arthritis	33 million
Deformities, orthopedic impairments	32 million
Hypertension	30 million

Per capita consumption of fresh fruit:
1980	105 pounds
1996	129 pounds

research, construction of medical facilities, administration and the net cost of private health insurance) and by source of funding (e.g., private health insurance, out-of-pocket payments, and a range of public programs including medicare, medicaid, and those operated by the Department of Veterans Affairs (VA)).

Data used to estimate health expenditures come from existing sources which are tabulated for other purposes. The type of expenditure estimates rely upon statistics produced by such groups as the American Hospital Association, the Internal Revenue Service, the Department of Commerce, and the Department of Health and Human Services (HHS). Source of funding estimates are constructed using administrative and statistical records from the medicare and medicaid programs, the Department of Defense and VA medical programs, the Social Security Administration, Census Bureau's *Governmental Finances,* state and local governments, other HHS agencies, and other nongovernment sources. Detailed descriptions of sources and methods are published in an article titled "National health accounts: Lessons from the U.S. experience" in the summer 1992 edition of the *Health Care Financing Review,* Volume 13, Number 4. Revisions to the sources and methods, along with the most recent analysis of health care expenditure estimates, are published in the *Health Care Financing Review's* annual article on national health expenditures.

Medicare and medicaid—Since July 1966, the federal medicare program has provided two coordinated plans for nearly all people age 65 and over: (1) A hospital insurance plan which covers hospital and related services and (2) a voluntary supplementary medical insurance plan, financed partially by monthly premiums paid by participants, which partly covers physicians' and related medical services. Such insurance also applies, since July 1973, to disabled beneficiaries of any age after 24 months of entitlement to cash benefits under the social security or railroad retirement programs and to persons with end stage renal disease.

Under medicaid, all states offer basic health services to certain very poor people: Individuals who are pregnant, aged, disabled or blind, and families with dependent children. Medicaid eligibility is automatic for almost all cash welfare recipients in these states. Thirty-nine states also extend medicaid to certain other persons who qualify, except for incomes above regular eligibility levels; those persons include those who have medical expenses which, when subtracted from their income, spend down to a state "medically needy" level or those who meet the higher "medically needy" income restrictions. Within federal guidelines, each state determines its own medicaid eligibility criteria and the health services to be provided under medicaid. The cost of providing medicaid services is jointly shared by the federal government and the states.

Health resources—Hospital statistics based on data from the American Hospital Association's yearly survey are published annually in *Hospital Statistics,* and cover all hospitals accepted for registration by the Association. To be accepted for registration, a hospital must meet certain requirements relating to number of beds, construction, equipment, medical and nursing staff, patient care, clinical records, surgical and obstetrical facilities, diagnostic and treatment facilities, laboratory services, etc. Data obtained from NCHS cover all U.S. hospitals which meet certain criteria for inclusion. The criteria are published in *Vital and Health Statistics* reports, Series 13. NCHS defines a hospital as a nonfederal short-term general or special facility with six or more inpatient beds with an average stay of less than 60 days.

Statistics on the demographic characteristics of persons employed in the health occupations are compiled by the U.S. Bureau of Labor Statistics and reported in *Employment and Earnings* (monthly) (see Table 672, Section 13). Data based on surveys of health personnel and utilization of health facilities providing long-term care, ambulatory care, and hospital care are presented in NCHS Series 13 and Series 14, *Data on Health Resources Utilization* and *Data on Health Resources: Manpower and Facilities.* Statistics on patient visits to health care providers, as reported in health interviews, appear in NCHS Series 10, *National Health Interview Survey Data.*

The HCFA's *Health Care Financing Review* and its annual *Medicare and Medicaid Statistical Supplement* present data for hospitals and nursing homes as well as extended care facilities and home health agencies. These data are based on records of the medicare program and differ from those of other sources because they are limited to facilities meeting federal eligibility standards for participation in medicare.

Data on patients in hospitals for the mentally ill and on mental health facilities are collected by the National Institute of Mental Health (NIMH) and appear in *Mental Health, U.S.;* the *Mental Health Statistics* reports; (series CN); and the Mental Health Statistical Note series.

Disability and illness—General health statistics, including morbidity, disability, injuries, preventive care, and findings from physiological testing are collected by NCHS in its National Health Interview Survey and its National Health and Nutrition Examination Surveys and appear in *Vital and Health Statistics,* Series 10 and 11, respectively. The Department of Labor compiles statistics on occupational injuries (see Section 13). Annual incidence data on notifiable diseases are compiled by the Public Health Service (PHS) at its Centers for Disease Control and Prevention in Atlanta, Georgia, and are published as a supplement to its *Morbidity and Mortality Weekly Report.*

The list of diseases is revised annually and includes those which, by mutual agreement of the states and PHS, are communicable diseases of national importance.

Nutrition—Statistics on annual per capita consumption of food and its nutrient value are estimated by the U.S. Department of Agriculture and published quarterly in *National Food Review.* Historical data can be found in *Food Consumption, Prices, and Expenditures,* issued annually.

Statistics on food insufficiency and food and nutrient intake are collected by NCHS to estimate the diet of the Nation's population. NCHS also collects physical examination data to assess the population's nutritional status, including growth, overweight/obesity, nutritional deficiencies, and prevalence of nutrition-related conditions, such as hypertension, hypercholesterolemia, and diabetes.

Statistical reliability—For discussion of statistical collection, estimation, and sampling procedures and measures of reliability applicable to data from NCHS and HCFA, see Appendix III.

Figure 3.1
Per Capita Food Consumption, by Selected Products: 1970 to 1996

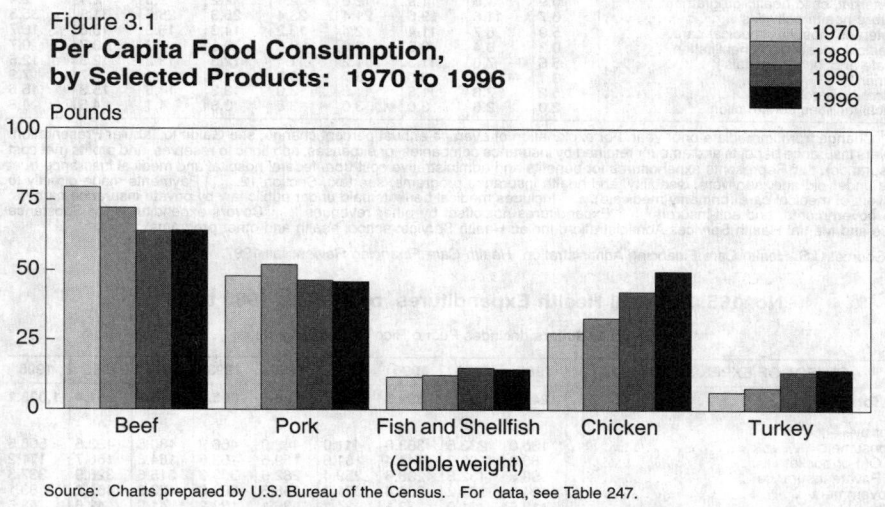

Source: Charts prepared by U.S. Bureau of the Census. For data, see Table 247.

Figure 3.2
Consumer Price Indexes: Medical Services

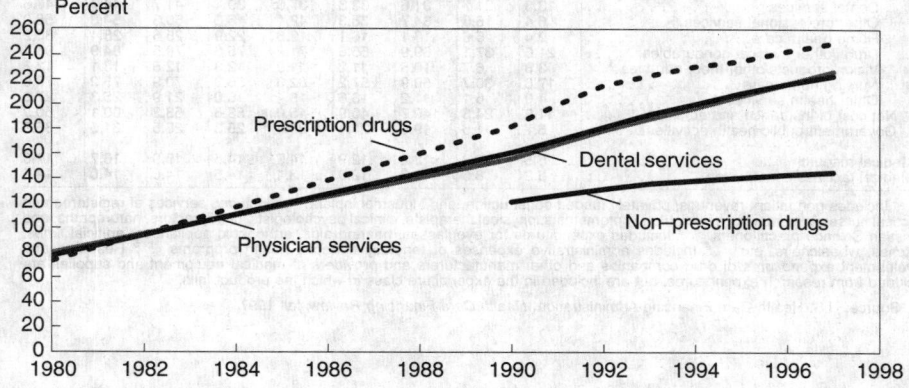

Source: Chart prepared by U.S. Bureau of the Census. For data, see Tables 179 and 773.

No. 164. National Health Expenditures, by Type: 1980 to 1996

[In billions of dollars, except percent. Includes Puerto Rico and outlying areas]

TYPE OF EXPENDITURE	1980	1985	1990	1991	1992	1993	1994	1995	1996
Total	**247.3**	**428.7**	**699.5**	**766.8**	**836.6**	**895.1**	**945.7**	**991.4**	**1,035.1**
Annual percent change [1]	14.9	9.9	12.2	9.6	9.1	7.0	5.6	4.8	4.4
Private expenditures	**142.5**	**254.5**	**415.1**	**445.2**	**478.1**	**506.2**	**521.8**	**536.2**	**552.0**
Health services and supplies	138.0	248.0	404.9	435.0	467.1	494.3	510.0	525.3	540.9
Out-of-pocket payments	60.3	100.7	144.4	151.6	159.5	163.6	164.8	166.7	171.2
Insurance premiums [2]	69.8	132.8	238.6	259.4	282.5	303.3	315.6	326.9	337.3
Other	8.0	14.5	21.9	24.0	25.1	27.3	29.6	31.7	32.4
Medical research	0.3	0.5	1.0	1.1	1.2	1.2	1.3	1.3	1.4
Medical facilities construction	4.2	6.0	9.3	9.0	9.8	10.7	10.5	9.6	9.7
Public expenditures	**104.8**	**174.2**	**284.4**	**321.7**	**358.5**	**389.0**	**423.9**	**455.2**	**483.1**
Percent federal of public	68.7	70.7	68.9	70.2	71.7	71.9	71.7	72.2	72.6
Health services and supplies	97.6	164.3	270.1	306.9	342.0	371.9	405.2	435.4	462.7
Medicare [3]	37.5	72.1	112.1	124.4	141.4	153.0	169.8	187.9	203.1
Public assistance medical payments [4] . . .	28.0	44.4	80.4	99.1	111.9	125.6	136.4	145.6	153.1
Temporary disability insurance [5]	0.1	0.1	0.1	0.1	0.1	0.1	0.1	0.1	0.1
Workers' compensation (medical) [5]	5.1	8.0	16.1	17.2	19.0	18.5	18.6	18.2	17.3
Defense Dept. hospital, medical	4.4	7.5	11.6	12.8	13.0	13.3	13.2	13.4	13.4
Maternal, child health programs	0.9	1.3	1.9	2.0	2.1	2.2	2.3	2.4	2.4
Public health activities	6.7	11.6	19.6	21.4	23.4	25.3	28.5	31.5	35.5
Veterans' hospital, medical care	5.9	8.7	11.4	12.4	13.2	14.3	15.3	15.6	16.7
Medical vocational rehabilitation	0.3	0.4	0.6	0.6	0.6	0.6	0.7	0.7	0.7
State and local hospitals [6]	5.6	7.0	11.3	11.2	11.1	12.3	13.2	12.3	12.5
Other [7]	3.1	3.3	5.0	5.7	6.2	6.6	7.1	7.7	7.9
Medical research	5.2	7.3	11.3	11.8	13.0	13.3	14.6	15.3	15.6
Medical facilities construction	2.0	2.6	3.0	3.0	3.5	3.8	4.1	4.5	4.8

[1] Change from immediate prior year. For explanation of average annual percent change, see Guide to Tabular Presentation. [2] Covers insurance benefits and amount retained by insurance companies for expenses, additions to reserves, and profits (net cost of insurance). [3] Represents expenditures for benefits and administrative cost from federal hospital and medical insurance trust funds under old-age, survivors, disability, and health insurance programs; see text, Section 12. [4] Payments made directly to suppliers of medical care (primarily medicaid). [5] Includes medical benefits paid under public law by private insurance carriers, state governments, and self-insurers. [6] Expenditures not offset by other revenues. [7] Covers expenditures for Substance Abuse and Mental Health Services Administration, Indian Health Service; school health and other programs.

Source: U.S. Health Care Financing Administration, *Health Care Financing Review*, fall 1997.

No. 165. National Health Expenditures, by Object: 1980 to 1996

[In billions of dollars. Includes Puerto Rico and outlying areas]

OBJECT OF EXPENDITURE	1980	1985	1990	1991	1992	1993	1994	1995	1996
Total	**247.3**	**428.7**	**699.5**	**766.8**	**836.6**	**895.1**	**945.7**	**991.4**	**1,035.1**
Spent by—									
Consumers	130.0	233.5	383.0	411.0	442.0	466.9	480.5	493.6	508.5
Out-of-pocket	60.3	100.7	144.4	151.6	159.5	163.6	164.8	166.7	171.2
Private insurance	69.8	132.8	238.6	259.4	282.5	303.3	315.6	326.9	337.3
Government	104.8	174.2	284.4	321.7	358.5	389.0	423.9	455.2	483.1
Other [1]	12.5	21.0	32.1	34.1	36.1	39.2	41.3	42.6	43.5
Spent for—									
Health services and supplies	235.6	412.3	675.0	741.9	809.1	866.1	915.2	960.7	1,003.6
Personal health care expenses	217.0	376.4	614.7	679.6	740.7	787.0	828.5	869.0	907.2
Hospital care	102.7	168.3	256.4	282.3	305.3	323.0	335.7	346.7	358.5
Physician services	45.2	83.6	146.3	162.2	175.9	183.6	190.4	196.4	202.1
Dental services	13.3	21.7	31.6	33.3	37.0	39.1	41.7	44.7	47.6
Other professional services [2]	6.4	16.6	34.7	38.3	42.1	46.3	50.3	54.3	58.0
Home health care	2.4	5.6	13.1	16.1	19.6	22.9	25.6	28.4	30.2
Drugs/other medical nondurables	21.6	37.1	59.9	65.6	71.2	75.6	79.5	84.9	91.4
Vision products/other med. durables [3] . .	3.8	6.7	10.5	11.2	11.9	12.3	12.5	13.1	13.3
Nursing home care	17.6	30.7	50.9	57.2	62.3	66.3	70.9	75.2	78.5
Other health services	4.0	6.1	11.2	13.6	15.4	18.0	21.9	25.3	27.6
Net cost of insurance and admin. [4]	11.9	24.3	40.7	40.9	45.0	53.8	58.2	60.1	60.9
Government public health activities	6.7	11.6	19.6	21.4	23.4	25.3	28.5	31.5	35.5
Medical research [5]	5.5	7.8	12.2	12.9	14.2	14.5	15.9	16.7	17.0
Medical facilities construction	6.2	8.5	12.3	12.0	13.4	14.5	14.6	14.0	14.5

[1] Includes nonpatient revenues, privately funded construction, and industrial inplant. [2] Includes services of registered and practical nurses in private duty, podiatrists, optometrists, physical therapists, clinical psychologists, chiropractors, naturopaths, and Christian Science practitioners. [3] Includes expenditures for eyeglasses, hearing aids, orthopedic appliances, artificial limbs, crutches, wheelchairs, etc. [4] Includes administrative expenses of federally financed health programs. [5] Research and development expenditures of drug companies and other manufacturers and providers of medical equipment and supplies are excluded from research expenditures, but are included in the expenditure class in which the product falls.

Source: U.S. Health Care Financing Administration, *Health Care Financing Review*, fall 1997.

No. 166. Health Services and Supplies—Per Capita Consumer Expenditures, by Object: 1980 to 1996

[In dollars, except percent. Based on Social Security Administration estimates of total U.S. population as of July 1, including Armed Forces and federal employees abroad and civilian population of outlying areas. Excludes research and construction]

OBJECT OF EXPENDITURE	1980	1985	1990	1991	1992	1993	1994	1995	1996
Total, national	**1,002**	**1,668**	**2,596**	**2,825**	**3,050**	**3,233**	**3,384**	**3,521**	**3,645**
Annual percent change [1]	13.9	9.3	11.1	8.8	8.0	6.0	4.7	4.0	3.5
Hospital care	437	681	986	1,075	1,151	1,206	1,241	1,270	1,302
Physicians' services	192	338	563	618	663	685	704	720	734
Dentists' services	57	88	121	127	140	146	154	164	173
Other professional services [2]	27	67	133	146	159	173	186	199	211
Home health care	10	23	50	61	74	86	97	105	110
Drugs and other medical nondurables	92	150	230	250	268	282	294	311	332
Vision products and other medical durables [2]	16	27	40	43	45	46	46	48	48
Nursing home care	75	124	196	218	235	248	262	276	285
Other health services	17	25	43	52	58	67	81	93	100
Net cost of insurance and administration [2]	50	98	157	156	170	201	215	220	221
Government public health activities	29	47	75	82	88	95	105	116	129
Total, private consumer [3]	**553**	**945**	**1,473**	**1,565**	**1,666**	**1,743**	**1,777**	**1,809**	**1,847**
Hospital care	178	274	404	422	436	451	446	444	445
Physicians' services	135	234	381	421	454	466	473	472	477
Dentists' services	54	85	117	122	134	138	146	156	164
Other professional services [2]	19	50	99	106	115	124	132	140	148
Home health care	4	8	23	26	30	33	35	34	33
Drugs and other medical nondurables	85	137	205	220	237	247	256	268	284
Vision products and other medical durables [2]	13	21	29	29	30	30	29	28	27
Nursing home care	32	58	92	97	99	98	101	105	104
Net cost of insurance	33	76	123	122	132	156	162	162	163

[1] Change from immediate prior year.   [2] See footnotes for corresponding objects in Table 165.   [3] Represents out-of-pocket payments and private health insurance.

Source: U.S. Health Care Financing Administration, *Health Care Financing Review*, fall 1997.

No. 167. Government Expenditures for Health Services and Supplies: 1996

[In millions of dollars. Includes Puerto Rico and outlying areas. Excludes medical research and construction]

TYPE OF SERVICE	Total [1]	Federal	State and local	Medi-care [2] (OASDHI)	Public assis-tance [3]	OTHER HEALTH SERVICES		
						Veterans	Defense Dept. [4]	Workers' compensa-tion [5]
Total [1]	**462,689**	**336,577**	**126,112**	**203,127**	**153,100**	**16,732**	**13,364**	**17,262**
Hospital care	220,643	181,569	39,074	118,316	55,871	13,736	10,339	7,699
Physician services	66,508	54,179	12,329	42,570	15,411	163	1,646	5,867
Home health care	17,851	15,865	1,986	13,595	4,256	-	-	-
Nursing home care	48,303	32,182	16,121	8,940	37,653	1,711	-	-
Administration	15,216	10,067	5,148	5,300	7,964	72	195	1,417
Public health activities	35,487	3,919	31,568	-	-	-	-	-

- Represents zero.   [1] Includes other items not shown separately.   [2] Covers hospital and medical insurance payments and administrative costs under old-age, survivors, disability, and health insurance program.   [3] Covers medicaid and other medical public assistance. Excludes funds paid into medicare trust fund by states to cover premiums for public assistance recipients and medically indigent persons.   [4] Includes care for retirees and military dependents.   [5] Medical benefits.

Source: U.S. Health Care Financing Administration, *Health Care Financing Review*, fall 1997.

No. 168. Expenditures for Health Services and Supplies, by Type of Payer: 1980 to 1995

[In billions of dollars. Beginning 1985 data are not consistent with later revisions shown in Table 165]

TYPE OF PAYER	1980	1985	1988	1989	1990	1991	1992	1993	1994	1995
Total expenditures	**235.6**	**411.8**	**538.3**	**599.8**	**672.9**	**736.8**	**806.7**	**863.1**	**906.7**	**957.8**
Private	158.4	282.2	371.5	411.0	450.8	483.4	522.4	547.0	569.5	597.4
Business	61.7	108.6	144.0	165.4	185.8	200.1	217.9	229.5	239.0	249.4
Share of private health insurance premiums	45.3	79.1	104.1	121.4	138.4	148.2	162.4	172.3	177.1	183.8
Households [1]	89.5	160.5	209.2	226.8	245.3	261.8	282.2	293.7	306.7	323.3
Share of private health insurance premiums	14.6	30.7	40.1	45.8	51.3	56.8	62.6	66.4	66.0	68.5
Out-of-pocket spending	60.3	100.6	129.2	136.2	148.4	155.0	165.8	171.6	176.0	182.6
Nonpatient revenues [2]	7.2	13.1	18.3	18.8	19.8	21.6	22.4	23.8	23.7	24.7
Public	77.3	129.6	166.8	188.9	222.1	253.3	284.2	316.1	337.3	360.4
Federal government	42.4	68.4	84.1	96.3	115.1	135.7	159.1	179.5	189.1	203.4
State/local government	34.8	61.2	82.7	92.5	107.0	117.6	125.2	136.6	148.1	157.0

[1] Includes other items not shown separately.   [2] Includes philanthropy.

Source: U.S. Health Care Financing Administration, *Health Care Financing Review*, spring 1997.

No. 169. Personal Health Care—Third Party Payments and Private Consumer Expenditures: 1980 to 1996

[In billions of dollars, except percent. See headnote, Table 170]

ITEM	1980	1985	1990	1991	1992	1993	1994	1995	1996
Personal health care expenditures......	217.0	376.4	614.7	679.6	740.7	787.0	828.5	869.0	907.2
Third party payments, total	**156.8**	**275.8**	**470.3**	**528.0**	**581.1**	**623.4**	**663.6**	**702.3**	**736.0**
Percent of personal health care	72.2	73.3	76.5	77.7	78.5	79.2	80.1	80.8	81.1
Private insurance payments..........	62.0	114.1	206.7	227.4	247.5	261.6	271.9	282.6	292.3
Government expenditures...........	87.0	147.7	242.3	277.1	309.1	335.0	362.7	388.5	412.0
Other [1]	7.8	14.0	21.3	23.4	24.5	26.7	29.0	31.1	31.7
Private consumer expenditures [2]	**122.3**	**214.7**	**351.1**	**379.0**	**407.1**	**425.2**	**436.8**	**449.4**	**463.5**
Percent met by private insurance	50.7	53.1	58.9	60.0	60.8	61.5	62.3	62.9	63.1
Hospital care	41.8	67.8	104.9	110.9	115.7	120.9	120.7	121.2	122.6
Percent met by private insurance	87.2	87.0	90.2	89.9	89.9	90.2	91.1	92.1	92.5
Physicians' services	31.8	57.9	99.0	110.5	120.5	124.8	127.8	128.9	131.3
Percent met by private insurance	53.9	57.8	67.4	69.7	71.9	73.9	76.1	77.5	77.5

[1] Includes nonpatient revenues and industrial inplant health services. [2] Includes expenditures not shown separately. Represents out-of-pocket payments and private health insurance benefits. Excludes net cost of insurance.

No. 170. Personal Health Care Expenditures, by Object and Source of Payment: 1996

[In millions of dollars, except as indicated. Includes Puerto Rico and outlying areas. Covers all expenditures for health services and supplies, except net cost of insurance and administration, government public health activities, and expenditures of philanthropic agencies for fund raising activities]

OBJECT OF PAYMENT	Total	PRIVATE PAYMENTS					Govern-ment	Third party pay-ments [2]
		Total	Consumer			Other [1]		
			Total	Out of pocket pay-ments	Private health insur-ance			
Total	**907,211**	**495,224**	**463,516**	**171,176**	**292,340**	**31,708**	**411,986**	**736,035**
Hospital care..............	358,546	137,903	122,624	9,201	113,424	15,278	220,643	349,345
Physicians' services	202,057	135,548	131,331	29,552	101,779	4,217	66,508	172,505
Dentists' services.............	47,551	45,465	45,283	22,116	23,166	183	2,086	25,435
Other professional services [3]	58,012	44,676	40,870	22,530	18,340	3,805	13,336	35,482
Home health care.............	30,192	12,340	9,022	5,852	3,170	3,319	17,851	24,340
Drugs/other medical nondurables ...	91,442	78,134	78,134	50,329	27,806	-	13,308	41,114
Vision products/other med. durables [3] .	13,271	7,523	7,523	6,914	609	-	5,748	6,357
Nursing home care.............	78,511	30,207	28,728	24,682	4,046	1,479	48,303	53,828
Other health services............	27,629	3,427	-	-	-	3,427	24,202	27,629

- Represents zero. [1] Includes nonpatient revenues and industrial plant. [2] Covers private health insurance, other private payments, and government. [3] See footnotes for corresponding items on Table 165.

Source of tables 169 and 170: U.S. Health Care Financing Administration, *Health Care Financing Review*, fall 1997.

No. 171. Medicare Enrollees and Expenditures: 1980 to 1996

[Enrollment as of July 1. Includes Puerto Rico and outlying areas and enrollees in foreign countries and unknown place of residence]

ITEM	1980	1985	1990	1992	1993	1994	1995	1996
ENROLLEES (mil.)								
Total..................	**28.5**	**31.1**	**34.2**	**35.6**	**36.3**	**36.9**	**37.5**	**38.1**
Hospital insurance	28.1	30.6	33.7	35.2	35.9	36.5	37.1	37.7
Supplementary medical insurance	27.4	30.0	32.6	33.9	34.6	35.2	35.7	36.1
EXPENDITURES (mil. dol.)								
Total..................	**36,802**	**72,294**	**110,984**	**135,845**	**150,370**	**164,862**	**184,204**	**200,338**
Hospital insurance [1]	25,557	48,414	66,997	85,015	94,391	104,545	117,604	129,929
Inpatient hospital	24,116	44,940	59,451	71,660	76,773	81,697	89,127	97,802
Skilled nursing facility	395	548	2,575	3,960	5,671	7,407	9,595	11,129
Home health agency	540	1,913	3,666	7,225	9,787	12,503	15,571	17,527
Hospice	-	43	358	846	1,059	1,486	1,883	1,999
Supplementary medical insurance [1] ...	11,245	23,880	43,987	50,830	55,979	60,317	66,600	70,409
Physician	8,187	17,312	29,609	32,480	34,589	36,935	40,457	41,232
Outpatient hospital	1,897	4,319	8,482	10,702	12,632	14,042	15,625	16,447
Home health agency	234	38	74	78	120	154	200	227
Group practice prepayment.......	203	720	2,827	4,124	4,632	6,439	6,808	8,847
Independent laboratory	114	558	1,476	1,876	2,006	2,048	2,065	1,846

- Represents zero. [1] Includes administrative expenses and, for hospital insurance, peer review activity, not shown separately.

Source: U.S. Health Care Financing Administration, Office of the Actuary, unpublished data.

No. 172. Medicare—Persons Served and Reimbursements: 1990 to 1996

[Persons served are enrollees who use covered services, incurred expenses greater than the applicable deductible amounts and for whom medicare paid benefits. Reimbursements are amounts paid to providers for covered services. Excluded are retroactive adjustments resulting from end of fiscal year cost settlements and certain lump-sum interim payments. Also excluded are beneficiary (or third party payor) liabilities for applicable deductibles, coinsurance amounts, and charges for noncovered services. Includes data for enrollees living in outlying territories and foreign countries]

TYPE OF COVERAGE AND SERVICE	Unit	PERSONS 65 YEARS OLD AND OVER			DISABLED PERSONS [1]		
		1990	1995	1996	1990	1995	1996
Persons served, total [2]	1,000	24,809	27,379	27,263	2,390	3,333	3,476
Hospital insurance [2]	1,000	6,367	7,147	7,139	680	933	964
Inpatient hospital	1,000	5,906	6,148	6,091	644	844	868
Skilled-nursing services	1,000	615	1,186	1,321	23	54	63
Home health services	1,000	1,818	3,185	3,290	122	272	293
Supplementary medical insurance [2]	1,000	24,687	27,234	27,113	2,365	3,299	3,442
Physicians' and other medical services	1,000	24,193	26,621	26,432	2,249	3,184	3,315
Outpatient services	1,000	14,055	17,597	17,875	1,496	2,281	2,407
Home health services	1,000	38	42	45	-	-	-
Persons served per 1,000 enrollees, total [2]	Rate	802	826	816	734	759	749
Hospital insurance [2]	Rate	209	218	216	209	212	208
Inpatient hospital	Rate	194	188	185	198	192	187
Skilled-nursing services	Rate	20	36	40	7	12	14
Home health services	Rate	60	97	100	38	62	63
Supplementary medical insurance [2]	Rate	832	858	848	804	837	828
Physicians' and other medical services	Rate	815	839	826	764	808	798
Outpatient services	Rate	474	554	559	508	579	579
Home health services	Rate	1	1	1	-	-	-
Reimbursements, total	Mil. dol	88,778	138,948	145,322	11,239	21,024	22,647
Per person served	Dollars	3,578	5,075	5,330	4,703	6,308	6,515
Hospital insurance	Mil. dol	54,244	89,631	95,404	6,694	12,752	13,790
Inpatient hospital	Mil. dol	48,952	68,213	71,191	6,346	11,079	11,848
Skilled-nursing services	Mil. dol	1,886	7,504	9,157	85	374	464
Home health services	Mil. dol	3,406	13,914	15,056	264	1,300	1,478
Supplementary medical insurance	Mil. dol	34,533	49,317	49,918	4,545	8,272	8,858
Physicians' and other medical services	Mil. dol	27,379	37,069	36,865	2,831	4,888	5,125
Outpatient services	Mil. dol	7,077	12,045	12,838	1,714	3,384	3,733
Home health services	Mil. dol	78	203	215	-	-	-

- Represents or rounds to zero.   [1] Age under 65; includes persons enrolled because of end-stage renal disease (ESRD) only.
[2] Persons are counted once for each type of covered service used, but are not double counted in totals.

Source: U.S. Health Care Financing Administration, *Medicare Program Statistics*, annual; and unpublished data.

No. 173. Medicare—Utilization and Charges: 1980 to 1996

[**Fiscal year data, except as indicated.** Data reflect date expense was incurred based on bills submitted for payment and recorded in Health Care Financing Administration central records through September 1997. Includes Puerto Rico, Virgin Islands, Guam, other outlying areas, and enrollees in foreign countries]

ITEM	Unit	PERSONS 65 YEARS OLD AND OVER				DISABLED PERSONS [1]			
		1980	1990	1995	1996	1980	1990	1995	1996
Hospital inpatient care:									
Admissions [2]	1,000	9,258	9,216	10,574	10,521	1,271	1,257	1,442	1,572
Per 1,000 enrollees [3]	Rate	369	309	323	319	429	396	328	339
Covered days of care	Millions	98	82	76	72	13	11	10	10
Per 1,000 enrollees [3]	Rate	3,885	2,702	2,313	2,153	4,549	3,464	2,351	2,289
Per admission	Days	10.5	8.9	7.2	6.8	10.6	8.8	7.2	6.8
Hospital covered charges	Mil. dol	28,615	90,846	138,489	140,606	4,087	11,910	18,885	21,011
Per covered day	Dollars	293	1,104	1,828	1,978	303	1,083	1,828	1,978
Percent of covered charges reimbursed [4]	Percent	70.0	47.5	47.5	48.8	68.6	46.5	47.5	48.8
Physician allowed charges [5]	Mil. dol	9,011	30,447	41,409	36,212	1,112	2,907	5,647	5,411
Percent reimbursed	Percent	78.0	77.0	76.2	76.0	78.7	75.7	76.2	76.0

[1] Disabled persons under age 65 and persons enrolled solely because of end-stage renal disease.   [2] Beginning 1990, represents number of discharges and includes pass-through amounts, except for kidney acquisition.   [3] Based on Hospital Insurance (HI) enrollment as of July 1.   [4] Prior to 1990, billing reimbursements exclude: (1) PPS pass-through amounts for capital, direct medical education, kidney acquisitions, and bad debts by medicare patients; (2) certain lump-sum interim payments. All years exclude retroactive adjustments resulting from end-of-fiscal year cost reports.   [5] Calendar year data.

Source: U.S. Health Care Financing Administration, unpublished data.

No. 174. Medicare—Summary, by State and Other Areas: 1995 and 1997

STATE AND OTHER AREA	ENROLLMENT [1] (1,000)		PAYMENTS [2] (mil. dol.)		STATE AND OTHER AREA	ENROLLMENT [1] (1,000)		PAYMENTS [2] (mil. dol.)	
	1995	1997	1995	1997		1995	1997	1995	1997
All areas ..	37,496	38,342	176,884	207,123	MO	832	843	3,821	4,579
U.S.....	36,703	37,514	175,976	206,064	MT	130	133	489	496
					NE.........	249	251	840	1,030
AL........	641	660	3,042	3,583	NV.........	192	212	894	1,123
AK........	34	37	133	163	NH.........	156	162	597	714
AZ........	597	632	2,717	3,211	NJ.........	1,169	1,181	5,603	6,573
AR........	422	429	1,638	1,906	NM.........	211	221	710	873
CA........	3,633	3,727	20,406	22,088	NY.........	2,639	2,657	13,904	16,451
CO........	421	442	1,835	2,216	NC.........	1,025	1,071	4,276	5,079
CT........	502	508	2,584	3,082	ND.........	103	103	412	468
DE........	100	105	445	471	OH.........	1,666	1,679	7,262	8,556
DC........	78	76	1,164	1,264	OK.........	487	495	2,178	2,677
FL	2,610	2,703	14,828	17,525	OR.........	467	475	1,685	1,887
GA........	832	866	4,090	4,725	PA.........	2,069	2,079	10,796	12,445
HI	149	156	580	655	RI	168	169	772	989
ID	150	155	463	565	SC.........	508	533	1,926	2,366
IL.........	1,617	1,620	7,276	8,314	SD.........	117	118	563	476
IN	823	833	3,491	4,080	TN.........	770	794	4,083	4,722
IA	474	475	1,527	1,738	TX.........	2,076	2,153	11,504	14,275
KS........	383	386	1,545	1,691	UT.........	187	195	708	887
KY........	586	601	2,401	2,889	VT	83	86	284	328
LA........	580	591	3,448	4,286	VA	817	847	2,979	3,636
ME........	202	208	707	879	WA	687	707	2,603	3,033
MD........	601	618	2,868	3,438	WV	329	332	1,208	1,504
MA........	933	945	5,496	6,455	WI	761	770	2,673	3,109
MI	1,348	1,368	6,237	7,401	WY	60	63	180	216
MN........	631	639	2,378	2,733	PR	477	502	875	1,025
MS........	397	406	1,723	2,214	Other areas .	317	325	33	35

[1] Hospital and/or medical insurance enrollment as of September.   [2] Benefit payments for all areas represent 100 percent fee for service experience and actual HMO expenditures through the fiscal year and relate to the state of the provider.

Source: U.S. Health Care Financing Administration, unpublished data.

No. 175. Medicaid—Summary, by State and Other Areas: 1995 and 1996

[Data are for fiscal years]

STATE AND OTHER AREA	RECIPIENTS [1] (1,000)		PAYMENTS [2] (mil. dol.)		STATE AND OTHER AREA	RECIPIENTS [1] (1,000)		PAYMENTS [2] (mil. dol.)	
	1995	1996	1995	1996		1995	1996	1995	1996
All areas ..	36,282	36,118	120,141	121,685	MO	695	636	2,039	2,018
U.S.....	35,210	35,028	119,885	121,419	MT	99	101	326	352
					NE.........	168	191	608	678
AL........	539	546	1,455	1,461	NV.........	105	109	350	365
AK........	68	69	252	278	NH.........	97	100	473	547
AZ........	494	528	218	211	NJ.........	790	714	3,813	3,726
AR........	353	363	1,376	1,224	NM.........	287	318	714	878
CA........	5,017	5,107	10,521	11,124	NY.........	3,035	3,281	22,086	22,347
CO........	294	271	1,063	1,032	NC.........	1,084	1,130	3,175	3,678
CT........	380	329	2,125	2,030	ND.........	61	61	297	298
DE........	79	82	324	308	OH.........	1,533	1,478	5,585	5,512
DC........	138	143	532	710	OK.........	394	358	1,055	1,021
FL	1,735	1,638	4,802	4,670	OR.........	452	450	1,327	1,313
GA........	1,147	1,185	3,076	3,085	PA.........	1,230	1,168	4,633	4,663
HI	52	41	258	266	RI	135	130	673	684
ID	115	119	360	405	SC.........	496	503	1,438	1,523
IL.........	1,552	1,454	5,600	5,365	SD.........	74	77	305	316
IN	559	594	1,878	2,452	TN.........	1,466	1,409	2,772	2,886
IA	304	308	1,036	1,088	TX.........	2,562	2,572	6,565	6,871
KS........	256	251	831	860	UT.........	160	152	464	422
KY........	641	641	1,945	1,931	VT	100	102	320	302
LA........	785	778	2,708	2,453	VA	681	623	1,833	1,776
ME........	153	167	760	723	WA	639	621	1,461	1,393
MD........	414	399	2,019	2,047	WV	389	395	1,169	1,128
MA........	728	715	3,972	3,777	WI	460	434	1,894	1,904
MI	1,168	1,172	3,409	3,359	WY	51	51	171	183
MN........	473	455	2,550	2,430	PR	1,055	1,074	244	256
MS........	520	510	1,266	1,342	Virgin Islands	17	17	12	9

[1] Persons who had payments made on their behalf at any time during the fiscal year.   [2] Payments are for fiscal year and reflect federal and state contribution payments. Data exclude disproportionate hospital share payments.

Source: U.S. Health Care Financing Administration, unpublished data.

No. 176. Medicaid—Selected Utilization Measures: 1980 to 1996

[**In thousands.** For fiscal years ending in year shown. Includes Virgin Islands. See text, Section 3]

MEASURE	1980	1985	1990	1992	1993	1994	1995	1996
General hospitals:								
Recipients discharged	2,255	2,390	3,261	3,866	4,050	3,890	3,743	3,300
Total days of care	24,089	29,562	27,471	29,921	31,095	28,941	25,711	23,072
Nursing facilities: [1]								
Total recipients	1,395	1,375	1,461	1,573	1,610	1,639	1,667	1,594
Total days of care	273,497	277,996	360,044	408,191	422,965	400,785	400,123	409,663
Intermediate care facilities: [2]								
Total recipients	121	147	146	151	149	159	151	140
Total days of care	250,124	47,324	49,730	53,538	44,952	54,105	56,878	56,625

[1] Includes skilled nursing facilities and intermediate care facilities for all other than the mentally retarded. [2] Mentally retarded.

Source: U.S. Health Care Financing Administration, Office of Information Systems, *Statistical Report on Medical Care: Eligibles, Recipients, Payments, and Services.*

No. 177. Medicaid—Selected Characteristics of Persons Covered: 1990 to 1996

[**In thousands, except percent.** Represents number of persons as of March of following year who were enrolled at any time in year shown. Person did not have to receive medical care paid for by medicaid in order to be counted. See headnote, Table 606]

POVERTY STATUS	1990	1995	1996							
			Total [1]	White	Black	His-panic [2]	Under 18 years old	18-44 years old	45-64 years old	65 years and over
Persons covered, total	24,160	31,621	31,236	20,710	8,521	6,230	15,287	9,282	3,452	3,215
Below poverty level	15,175	16,900	16,631	10,050	5,526	4,100	9,051	4,959	1,587	1,035
Above poverty level	8,985	14,721	14,605	10,660	2,995	2,130	6,236	4,323	1,865	2,180
Percent of population										
covered	9.7	12.0	11.7	9.4	25.0	21.0	21.6	8.5	6.3	10.1
Below poverty level	45.2	46.4	45.5	40.8	57.0	47.1	62.6	35.7	33.5	30.2
Above poverty level	4.2	6.5	6.4	5.5	12.3	10.2	11.1	4.5	3.7	7.7

[1] Includes other races not shown separately. [2] Persons of Hispanic origin may be of any race.

Source: U.S. Bureau of the Census, *Current Population Reports,* P60-198, earlier reports; and unpublished data.

No. 178. Medicaid—Recipients and Payments: 1980 to 1996

[**For fiscal year ending in year shown;** see text, Section 10. Includes Puerto Rico and outlying areas. Medical vendor payments are those made directly to suppliers of medical care]

BASIS OF ELIGIBILITY AND TYPE OF SERVICE	RECIPIENTS (1,000)					PAYMENTS (mil. dol.)				
	1980	1985	1990	1995	1996	1980	1985	1990	1995	1996
Total [1] **. . . . .**	**21,605**	**21,814**	**25,255**	**36,282**	**36,118**	**23,311**	**37,508**	**64,859**	**120,141**	**121,685**
Age 65 and over	3,440	3,061	3,202	4,119	4,285	8,739	14,096	21,508	36,527	36,947
Blindness	92	80	83	92	95	124	249	434	848	869
Disabled [2]	2,819	2,937	3,635	5,767	6,126	7,497	13,203	23,969	48,570	51,196
AFDC [3] program	14,210	15,275	17,230	24,767	23,866	6,354	9,160	17,690	31,487	29,819
Other and unknown	1,499	1,214	1,105	1,537	1,746	596	798	1,257	2,708	2,853
Inpatient services in—										
General hospital	3,680	3,434	4,593	5,561	5,362	6,412	9,453	16,674	26,331	25,176
Mental hospital	66	60	92	84	93	775	1,192	1,714	2,511	2,040
Intermediate care facilities:										
Mentally retarded	121	147	147	151	140	1,989	4,731	7,354	10,383	9,555
Nursing facility services [4]	1,398	1,375	1,461	1,667	1,594	7,887	11,587	17,693	29,052	29,630
Physicians	13,765	14,387	17,078	23,789	22,861	1,875	2,346	4,018	7,360	7,238
Dental	4,652	4,672	4,552	6,383	6,208	462	458	593	1,019	1,028
Other practitioner	3,234	3,357	3,873	5,528	5,342	198	251	372	986	1,094
Outpatient hospital	9,705	10,072	12,370	16,712	15,905	1,101	1,789	3,324	6,627	6,504
Clinic	1,531	2,121	2,804	5,322	5,070	320	714	1,688	4,280	4,222
Laboratory [5]	3,212	6,354	8,959	13,064	12,607	121	337	721	1,180	1,208
Home health	392	535	719	1,639	1,727	332	1,120	3,404	9,406	10,868
Prescribed drugs	13,707	13,921	17,294	23,723	22,585	1,318	2,315	4,420	9,791	10,697
Family planning	1,129	1,636	1,752	2,501	2,366	81	195	265	514	474

[1] Recipient data do not add due to small number of recipients that are reported in more than one category. Includes recipients of, and payments for, other care not shown separately. [2] Permanently and totally. [3] Aid to Families with Dependent Children. [4] Nursing facility services includes skilled nursing facility services and intermediate care facility services for all other than the mentally retarded. [5] Includes radiological services.

Source: U.S. Health Care Financing Administration, Office of Information Systems, *Statistical Report on Medical Care: Eligibles, Recipients, Payments, and Services.*

No. 179. Consumer Price Indexes of Medical Care Prices: 1980 to 1997

[1982-1984=100. Indexes are annual averages of monthly data based on components of consumer price index for all urban consumers; for explanation, see text, Section 15]

YEAR	Medical care	MEDICAL CARE SERVICES				Medical care commodities	ANNUAL PERCENT CHANGE [2]				Medical care commodities
		Total [1]	Professional services				Medical care	Medical care services			
			Total [1]	Physicians	Dental			Total [1]	Physicians	Dental	
1980	74.9	74.8	77.9	76.5	78.9	75.4	11.0	11.3	10.5	11.9	9.3
1985	113.5	113.2	113.5	113.3	114.2	115.2	6.3	6.1	5.9	6.2	7.2
1989	149.3	148.9	146.4	150.1	146.1	150.8	7.7	7.7	7.4	6.3	7.8
1990	162.8	162.7	156.1	160.8	155.8	163.4	9.0	9.3	7.1	6.6	8.4
1991	177.0	177.1	165.7	170.5	167.4	176.8	8.7	8.9	6.0	7.4	8.2
1992	190.1	190.5	175.8	181.2	178.7	188.1	7.4	7.6	6.3	6.8	6.4
1993	201.4	202.9	184.7	191.3	188.1	195.0	5.9	6.5	5.6	5.3	3.7
1994	211.0	213.4	192.5	199.8	197.1	200.7	4.8	5.2	4.4	4.8	2.9
1995	220.5	224.2	201.0	208.8	206.8	204.5	4.5	5.1	4.5	4.9	1.9
1996	228.2	232.4	208.3	216.4	216.5	210.4	3.5	3.7	3.6	4.7	2.9
1997	234.6	239.1	215.4	222.9	226.6	215.3	2.8	2.9	3.0	4.7	2.3

[1] Includes other services not shown separately.   [2] Percent change from the immediate prior year.

Source: U.S. Bureau of Labor Statistics, *CPI Detailed Report,* January 1998.

No. 180. Average Annual Expenditures per Consumer Unit for Health Care: 1985 to 1995

[In dollars, except percent. See text, Section 14, and headnote, Table 733. For composition of regions, see map, inside front cover]

ITEM	HEALTH CARE, TOTAL		Health insurance	Medical services	Drugs and medical supplies [1]	PERCENT DISTRIBUTION		
	Amount	Percent of total expenditures				Health insurance	Medical services	Drugs and medical supplies [1]
1985	1,108	4.7	375	496	238	33.8	44.8	21.5
1988	1,298	5.0	474	529	294	36.5	40.8	22.7
1989	1,407	5.1	537	542	327	38.2	38.5	23.2
1990	1,480	5.2	581	562	337	39.3	38.0	22.8
1991	1,554	5.2	656	555	344	42.2	35.7	22.1
1992	1,634	5.5	725	533	375	44.4	32.6	22.9
1993	1,776	5.8	800	574	402	45.0	32.3	22.6
1994	1,755	5.5	815	571	369	46.4	32.5	21.0
1995	1,732	5.4	860	511	360	49.7	29.5	20.8
Age of reference person:								
Under 25 years old	465	2.5	209	157	99	44.9	33.8	21.3
25 to 34 years old	1,096	3.5	517	380	199	47.2	34.7	18.2
35 to 44 years old	1,609	4.2	726	596	286	45.1	37.0	17.8
45 to 54 years old	1,850	4.4	817	664	369	44.2	35.9	19.9
55 to 64 years old	1,909	5.9	896	587	427	46.9	30.7	22.4
65 to 74 years old	2,617	10.3	1,528	471	618	58.4	18.0	23.6
75 years old and over	2,683	14.4	1,557	487	639	58.0	18.2	23.8
Origin of reference person:								
Hispanic	1,055	3.9	477	394	184	45.2	37.3	17.4
Non-Hispanic	1,790	5.5	893	521	375	49.9	29.1	20.9
Black	1,057	4.5	572	223	262	54.1	21.1	24.8
Other	1,878	5.5	932	557	389	49.6	29.7	20.7
Region of residence:								
Northeast	1,757	5.3	890	541	325	50.7	30.8	18.5
Midwest	1,759	5.5	890	479	390	50.6	27.2	22.2
South	1,790	5.9	907	483	399	50.7	27.0	22.3
West	1,584	4.5	720	567	296	45.5	35.8	18.7
Size of consumer unit:								
One person	1,109	5.7	560	308	241	50.5	27.8	21.7
Two or more persons	1,977	5.3	979	591	407	49.5	29.9	20.6
Two persons	2,126	6.4	1,132	511	482	53.2	24.0	22.7
Three persons	1,775	4.7	826	588	361	46.5	33.1	20.3
Four persons	1,969	4.6	924	701	345	46.9	35.6	17.5
Five persons or more	1,856	4.5	828	686	342	44.6	37.0	18.4
Income before taxes:								
Complete income reporters [2] . . .	1,747	5.2	864	502	380	49.5	28.7	21.8
Quintiles of income:								
Lowest 20 percent	1,111	7.6	565	259	288	50.9	23.3	25.9
Second 20 percent	1,603	7.2	851	358	395	53.1	22.3	24.6
Third 20 percent	1,687	5.8	871	441	374	51.6	26.1	22.2
Fourth 20 percent	1,912	4.9	971	568	373	50.8	29.7	19.5
Highest 20 percent	2,417	3.9	1,063	881	473	44.0	36.5	19.6
Incomplete reporters of income .	1,683	6.2	844	552	286	50.1	32.8	17.0

[1] Includes prescription and nonprescription drugs.   [2] A complete reporter is a consumer unit providing values for at least one of the major sources of income.

Source: Bureau of Labor Statistics, *Consumer Expenditure Survey,* annual.

No. 181. Health Insurance Coverage Status, by Selected Characteristics: 1990 to 1996

[Persons as of following year for coverage in the year shown. Government health insurance includes medicare, medicaid, and military plans. Based on Current Population Survey; see text, Section 1, and Appendix III]

CHARACTERISTIC	NUMBER (mil.)							PERCENT			
	Total persons	Covered by private or government health insurance					Not covered by health insur- ance	Covered by private or government health insurance			Not covered by health insur- ance
		Total [1]	Private		Government			Total [1]	Private	Medi- caid	
			Total	Group health [2]	Medi- care	Medi- caid					
1990	248.9	214.2	182.1	150.2	32.3	24.3	34.7	86.1	73.2	9.7	13.9
1991	251.4	216.0	181.4	150.1	32.9	26.9	35.4	85.9	72.1	10.7	14.1
1992 [3]	256.8	218.2	181.5	148.8	33.2	29.4	38.6	85.0	70.7	11.5	15.0
1993 [3]	259.8	220.0	182.4	148.3	33.1	31.7	39.7	84.7	70.2	12.2	15.3
1994 [3]	262.1	222.4	184.3	159.6	33.9	31.6	39.7	84.8	70.3	12.1	15.2
1995 [3]	264.3	223.7	185.9	161.5	34.7	31.9	40.6	84.6	70.3	12.1	15.4
1996, total [3][4] . .	**266.8**	**225.1**	**187.4**	**163.2**	**35.2**	**31.5**	**41.7**	**84.4**	**70.2**	**11.8**	**15.6**
Age: Under 6 years .	23.9	20.6	14.9	14.1	0.2	6.6	3.3	86.2	62.1	27.8	13.8
6 to 11 years	24.0	20.5	16.1	15.2	0.1	5.2	3.5	85.4	66.9	21.6	14.6
12 to 17 years . . .	23.3	19.5	16.3	14.8	0.2	3.7	3.8	83.9	70.0	15.8	16.1
18 to 24 years . . .	25.0	17.8	15.1	12.4	0.2	2.9	7.2	71.1	60.3	11.6	28.9
25 to 34 years . . .	40.3	31.3	27.9	26.2	0.4	3.3	9.0	77.7	69.3	8.1	22.3
35 to 44 years . . .	44.0	36.8	33.4	31.2	0.8	3.1	7.2	83.7	76.1	7.1	16.3
45 to 54 years . . .	33.0	28.5	26.3	24.3	0.9	1.9	4.5	86.3	79.6	5.7	13.7
55 to 64 years . . .	21.5	18.5	16.3	14.0	1.8	1.6	3.0	86.2	75.7	7.3	13.8
65 years and over.	31.9	31.5	21.2	10.9	30.6	3.2	0.3	98.9	66.6	10.1	1.1
Sex: Male	130.6	108.3	92.2	81.6	15.1	13.4	22.3	82.9	70.6	10.3	17.1
Female	136.2	116.8	95.2	81.6	20.1	18.0	19.4	85.8	69.9	13.2	14.2
Race: White	220.1	188.3	161.8	139.9	30.9	20.9	31.7	85.6	73.5	9.5	14.4
Black	34.2	26.8	17.7	16.4	3.4	8.6	7.4	78.3	51.8	25.1	21.7
Hispanic origin [5]	29.7	19.7	13.2	12.1	1.8	6.3	10.0	66.4	44.3	21.1	33.6

[1] Includes other government insurance, not shown separately. Persons with coverage counted only once in total, even though they may have been covered by more that one type of policy. [2] Related to employment of self or other family members. [3] Beginning 1992, data based on 1990 census adjusted population controls. [4] Includes other races not shown separately. [5] Persons of Hispanic origin may be of any race.

Source: U.S. Bureau of the Census, *Current Population Reports*, P60-199; and unpublished data.

No. 182. Medical Care Benefit Coverage and Costs of Private Employees: 1980 to 1995

[Covers full-time employees in private establishments with 100 or more employees. Based on a sample survey of establishments; for details, see source]

YEAR	Percent of employees covered	EMPLOYEES WITH SINGLE COVERAGE		EMPLOYEES WITH FAMILY COVERAGE		YEAR AND TYPE OF PLAN	Percent distribution of covered employees
		Percent required to contribute toward cost	Average monthly employee contribution (dol.)	Percent required to contribute toward cost	Average monthly employee contribution (dol.)		
1980	97	26	(NA)	46	(NA)	**1988, total . . . . .**	100
1981	97	27	(NA)	49	(NA)	Fee-for-service	74
1982	97	27	(NA)	51	(NA)	HMO [1]	19
1983	96	33	10.13	54	32.51	PPO [2]	7
1984	97	36	11.93	58	35.93	**1991, total . . . . .**	100
1985	96	36	12.05	56	38.33	Fee-for-service	67
1986	95	43	12.80	63	41.40	HMO [1]	17
1988	90	44	19.29	64	60.07	PPO [2]	16
1989	92	47	25.31	66	72.10	**1995, total . . . . .**	100
1991	83	51	26.60	69	96.97	Fee-for-service	37
1993	82	61	(NA)	76	107.42	HMO [1]	27
1995	77	(NA)	(NA)	(NA)	(NA)	PPO [2]	34

NA Not available. [1] Health maintenance organization. [2] Preferred provider organization.

Source: U.S. Bureau of Labor Statistics, *Employee Benefits in Medium and Large Private Establishments*, periodic.

No. 183. Private Establishments Offering Health Insurance, by Selected Characteristics: 1993

[As of December 31. Based on the National Employer Health Insurance Survey; for details on sample survey, see source]

FIRM SIZE [1] AND INDUSTRY GROUP	ESTABLISHMENTS OFFERING—							Private employees, percent working in establishments offering health insurance
	One or more major health plans [2]		Two or more major plans [2] (percent)	Fee-for-service plan [3] (percent)	Any managed care plan [4] (percent)	Health maintenance organization [5] (HMO) (percent)	Preferred provider organization [6] (PPO) (percent)	
	Number (1,000)	Percent of all establishments						
Total [7]	3,245	51.6	18.6	52.0	55.5	25.9	35.0	83.1
Less than 10 employees	1,311	33.2	10.1	56.0	47.5	20.5	28.7	39.2
10 to 24 employees	583	67.1	11.7	47.9	56.9	25.3	34.7	68.8
25 to 99 employees	493	83.0	17.3	43.4	63.6	29.6	39.6	84.2
100 to 499 employees	295	93.9	24.1	44.1	64.8	31.5	43.3	94.9
500 to 999 employees	90	96.8	29.3	53.0	59.1	27.0	42.6	98.6
1,000 or more employees	473	96.7	46.4	59.9	61.1	33.9	41.7	99.3
Agriculture, forestry, and fishing	66	30.2	8.7	55.4	47.1	16.3	32.8	54.7
Mining	22	67.3	21.4	64.7	41.4	11.6	34.9	91.9
Construction	214	40.4	20.6	57.1	51.6	23.5	30.8	63.1
Manufacturing	311	60.8	19.1	50.2	58.8	29.6	34.3	93.3
Transportation, communication, and utilities	168	65.8	23.2	49.9	60.7	27.0	40.1	91.2
Wholesale trade	330	64.9	17.1	52.0	56.1	23.3	37.0	86.9
Retail trade	637	43.6	19.3	54.6	52.7	25.2	33.2	72.1
Finance, insurance, and real estate	352	64.8	26.6	50.6	59.2	30.8	38.2	91.3
Services	1,147	51.3	15.6	50.5	55.6	25.5	34.8	82.8

[1] Number of employees nationwide as reported by respondent.   [2] Major health plans typically cover hospital care and doctor visits.   [3] A plan in which the covered person seeks care from his or her own choice of providers on a fee-for-service basis. Either the patient or the provider submits the claims. Plans reported as fee-for-service with PPO riders were counted as PPO plans. [4] Covers both health maintenance organizations and preferred provider organizations.   [5] Offers comprehensive health care from a specified set of providers for fixed periodic payments. HMO providers may be employees or under contract to the HMO. Care from providers outside the HMO is only covered in emergencies or when the patient is referred by an HMO provider. For this report, open-ended HMOs and Point of Service (POS) plans that include some HMO-like features but allow patients to use providers outside the HMO with higher patient costs, have been combined with HMOs. Exclusive Provider Organizations (EPO) are also combined with HMOs.   [6] A plan in which the covered person may seek care from a provider associated with the plan (preferred provider) or a provider outside the plan (nonpreferred provider). Typically the patient pays more when he or she sees a nonpreferred provider.   [7] Includes establishments with unknown characteristics.

No. 184. Percent of Private Employees Eligible and Enrolled in Employer's Health Plan: 1993

[As of December 31. Based on the National Employer Health Insurance Survey; for details on sample survey, see source]

FIRM SIZE [1] AND INDUSTRY GROUP	ALL EMPLOYEES				FULL-TIME EMPLOYEES		PART-TIME EMPLOYEES	
	Number (1,000)	Percent eligible for health benefits	Percent enrolled in employer's plan	Percent of eligible employees enrolled	Number (1,000)	Percent enrolled in employer's plan	Number (1,000)	Percent enrolled in employer's plan
Total [2]	98,323	67.9	57.6	84.8	76,861	70.8	21,462	10.2
Less than 25 employees	26,453	41.7	33.3	79.9	19,494	43.9	6,959	3.5
25 to 99 employees	16,250	66.6	53.8	80.8	12,634	68.2	3,616	3.5
100 to 999 employees	20,911	77.2	65.0	84.1	16,892	78.7	4,019	7.1
1,000 or more employees	34,710	82.9	73.4	88.5	27,842	86.0	6,868	22.3
Agriculture, forestry, and fishing	1,590	38.1	30.8	81.0	1,140	42.2	450	2.0
Mining	771	87.3	82.1	94.0	723	86.8	48	[3]9.8
Construction	4,545	51.9	42.4	81.7	4,053	46.6	492	7.8
Manufacturing	19,211	86.5	78.3	90.5	18,080	82.4	1,131	13.1
Transportation, communication, and utilities	6,231	80.2	72.5	90.3	5,251	81.5	979	24.0
Wholesale trade	6,590	77.2	67.2	87.0	5,788	75.2	802	9.3
Retail trade	17,843	45.2	34.3	75.9	10,481	54.2	7,362	5.9
Finance, insurance, and real estate	8,035	80.2	67.9	84.7	6,850	77.3	1,184	13.6
Services	33,509	65.5	53.7	82.0	24,495	69.0	9,014	12.0

[1] Number of employees nationwide as reported by respondent.   [2] Includes establishments with unknown characteristics. [3] Figure does not meet standards of reliability or precision.

Source of Tables 183 and 184: U.S. National Center for Health Statistics, *Employer-Sponsored Health Insurance, State and National Estimates, 1997.*

No. 185. Private Establishments Offering Health Insurance and Employees Enrolled, by State: 1993

[As of December 31. Based on the National Employer Health Insurance Survey; for details on sample survey, see source]

STATE	ESTABLISHMENTS OFFERING—			Percent of employees enrolled in employer's plan	STATE	ESTABLISHMENTS OFFERING—			Percent of employees enrolled in employer's plan
	One or more major health plans[1]		Any managed care plan[2] (percent)			One or more major health plans[1]		Any managed care plan[2] (percent)	
	Number (1,000)	Percent of all establishments				Number (1,000)	Percent of all establishments		
U.S.	3,244.7	51.6	55.5	57.6	MO	71.2	52.2	64.8	56.7
AL	48.5	52.0	57.5	57.2	MT	11.7	40.0	40.7	41.2
AK	7.0	46.2	36.1	51.7	NE	22.2	46.2	36.6	47.8
AZ	46.8	49.7	75.5	53.7	NV	17.4	52.1	71.0	53.4
AR	25.9	40.3	37.2	51.8	NH	19.5	57.5	36.9	55.0
CA	379.8	47.0	84.2	54.4					
CO	54.6	53.1	67.2	54.2	NJ	94.0	52.0	41.5	62.5
CT	50.9	60.4	40.1	62.9	NM	21.3	49.4	54.9	46.7
DE	10.1	64.2	45.5	62.2	NY	227.1	54.6	50.9	61.3
DC	12.7	66.0	74.7	68.7	NC	86.6	51.9	37.5	62.6
FL	169.9	47.5	61.5	52.8	ND	10.1	49.1	29.0	46.1
GA	91.1	54.8	47.9	60.6	OH	135.6	54.7	48.1	60.8
HI	24.8	85.8	81.2	74.9	OK	36.7	43.9	57.1	47.4
ID	17.0	49.9	36.6	46.2	OR	47.0	51.6	69.3	57.2
IL	139.4	53.2	54.7	62.5	PA	158.7	61.0	37.1	64.1
IN	69.0	50.3	42.9	59.9	RI	16.2	64.5	65.9	63.9
IA	41.7	44.0	48.6	53.2	SC	40.1	48.8	34.9	59.7
KS	34.9	48.3	48.3	53.6	SD	10.5	44.7	24.6	44.7
KY	43.0	49.5	46.3	54.9	TN	53.5	48.2	57.1	61.5
LA	39.7	43.9	48.0	51.1	TX	186.5	44.7	48.6	53.3
ME	19.8	56.7	31.1	59.0	UT	21.3	47.3	61.6	48.4
MD	65.0	56.8	63.5	57.6	VT	11.1	55.0	47.3	50.6
MA	89.7	60.4	65.3	60.5	VA	85.1	55.7	51.6	57.6
MI	114.0	60.1	48.2	61.9	WA	81.9	56.4	75.0	58.4
MN	65.8	51.1	57.3	56.1	WV	19.3	51.9	26.9	54.0
MS	24.6	43.3	38.6	55.0	WI	66.2	52.6	50.3	54.8
					WY	8.0	47.3	20.6	44.4

[1] Major health plans typically cover hospital care and doctor visits. [2] Covers both health maintenance organizations and preferred provider organizations.
Source: U.S. National Center for Health Statistics, *Employer-Sponsored Health Insurance, State and National Estimates, 1997.*

No. 186. Persons With and Without Health Insurance Coverage, by State: 1996

[Based on the Current Population Survey and subject to sampling error; see text, Section 1, and Appendix III]

STATE	Total persons covered (1,000)	TOTAL PERSONS NOT COVERED		CHILDREN NOT COVERED		STATE	Total persons covered (1,000)	TOTAL PERSONS NOT COVERED		CHILDREN NOT COVERED	
		Number (1,000)	Percent of total	Number (1,000)	Percent of total			Number (1,000)	Percent of total	Number (1,000)	Percent of total
U.S.	225,077	41,716	15.6	10,554	14.8	MO	4,591	700	13.2	168	11.7
AL	3,726	550	12.9	144	12.8	MT	788	124	13.6	29	11.1
AK	569	89	13.5	27	11.6	NE	1,483	190	11.4	46	9.8
AZ	3,642	1,159	24.1	357	25.0	NV	1,381	255	15.6	78	19.0
AR	2,041	566	21.7	155	20.7	NH	1,033	109	9.5	27	9.6
CA	25,853	6,514	20.1	1,631	17.8						
CO	3,240	644	16.6	191	18.4	NJ	6,546	1,317	16.7	349	18.6
CT	2,985	368	11.0	108	11.6	NM	1,435	412	22.3	108	17.5
DE	636	98	13.4	24	12.9	NY	15,265	3,132	17.0	735	15.1
DC	459	80	14.8	18	14.6	NC	6,103	1,160	16.0	310	17.2
FL	11,654	2,722	18.9	615	18.4	ND	568	62	9.8	16	9.7
GA	6,080	1,319	17.8	297	15.2	OH	9,974	1,292	11.5	305	10.1
HI	1,073	101	8.6	16	5.3	OK	2,784	570	17.0	195	20.6
ID	990	196	16.5	44	13.2	OR	2,743	496	15.3	138	17.0
IL	10,511	1,337	11.3	322	9.8	PA	10,763	1,133	9.5	214	7.3
IN	5,081	600	10.6	132	9.6	RI	847	93	9.9	13	6.3
IA	2,565	335	11.6	78	9.4	SC	3,077	634	17.1	199	20.7
KS	2,280	292	11.4	82	11.0	SD	639	67	9.5	16	8.7
KY	3,295	601	15.4	177	17.4	TN	4,702	841	15.2	281	18.7
LA	3,378	890	20.9	260	22.4	TX	14,557	4,680	24.3	1,367	24.5
ME	1,058	146	12.1	33	12.9	UT	1,758	240	12.0	73	11.1
MD	4,507	581	11.4	107	8.1	VT	522	65	11.1	9	6.0
MA	5,392	766	12.4	143	9.2	VA	5,680	811	12.5	160	10.9
MI	8,739	857	8.9	189	7.3	WA	4,881	761	13.5	171	11.2
MN	4,229	480	10.2	114	8.4	WV	1,487	261	14.9	27	7.9
MS	2,279	518	18.5	154	18.4	WI	4,781	438	8.4	90	6.2
						WY	422	66	13.5	14	10.5

Source: U.S. Bureau of the Census; "Health Insurance Coverage: 1996 - Table F"; published 3 April 1998; <http://www.census.gov/hhes/hlthins/cover96/c96tabf.html>; and unpublished data.

No. 187. Health Maintenance Organizations (HMOs): 1980 to 1997

[As of **January 1,** except as noted. An HMO is a prepaid health plan delivering comprehensive care to members through designated providers, having a fixed periodic payment for health care services, and requiring members to be in a plan for a specified period of time (usually 1 year). A group HMO delivers health services through a physician group that is controlled by the HMO unit or contracts with one or more independent group practices to provide health services. An individual practice association (IPA) HMO contracts directly with physicians in independent practice, and/or contracts with one or more associations of physicians in independent practice, and/or contracts with one or more multispecialty group practices. Data are based on a census of HMOs. For composition of regions, see map, inside front cover]

TYPE OF PRACTICE AND SIZE	1980 (June 30)	1985 (Dec. 31)	1990	1992	1993	1994	1995	1996	1997
NUMBER OF PLANS									
Total..........	235	478	572	555	551	540	550	628	651
Model type:									
I.P.A............	97	244	360	340	332	319	323	366	284
Network.......	138	234	212	166	150	117	107	122	109
Mixed..........	(NA)	(NA)	(NA)	49	69	104	120	140	258
Region:									
Northeast........	55	81	115	111	102	101	99	111	110
Midwest........	72	157	160	165	169	159	154	181	184
South..........	45	141	176	161	167	173	190	217	236
West..........	63	99	121	118	113	107	107	119	121
ENROLLMENT [1] (mil.)									
Total..........	9.1	21.0	33.0	36.1	38.4	42.2	46.2	52.5	66.8
Model type:									
I.P.A............	1.7	6.4	13.7	14.7	15.3	16.1	17.4	21.7	26.7
Group..........	7.4	14.6	19.3	16.5	15.4	13.6	12.9	13.5	11.1
Mixed..........	(NA)	(NA)	(NA)	4.9	7.7	12.5	15.9	17.2	29.0
Federal program: [2]									
Medicaid [3]......	0.3	0.6	1.2	1.7	1.7	2.6	3.5	4.7	5.5
Medicare.......	0.4	1.1	1.8	2.2	2.2	2.5	2.9	3.7	4.8

NA Not available. [1] Excludes enrollees participating in open-ended plans. [2] Refers to enrollment by medicaid or medicare beneficiaries, where the program contracts directly with the HMO to pay the appropriate annual premium. [3] Enrollment for 1990 as of June 30.

Source: Interstudy, Minneapolis, MN, *The InterStudy Competitive Edge,* annual (copyright).

No. 188. Annual Receipts/Revenue for the Health Service Industries: 1990 to 1996

[**In millions of dollars.** Unless otherwise noted, receipts estimates are obtained from a sample of employer and nonemployer firms. Revenue estimates are obtained from a sample of employer firms only]

INDUSTRY	1987 SIC code [1]	1990	1992	1993	1994	1995	1996
TAXABLE FIRMS—RECEIPTS							
Health services [2]......	80	271,212	321,653	335,108	351,419	376,279	399,185
Offices and clinics of MD's...........	801	128,871	151,824	154,242	159,616	167,969	173,483
Offices and clinics of dentists.......	802	31,502	36,939	38,946	41,663	44,909	47,417
Offices and clinics of doctors of osteopathy..	803	3,254	4,008	4,159	4,354	4,698	4,760
Offices and clinics of other practitioners [2]...	804	20,139	23,893	25,367	25,891	27,357	28,594
Offices and clinics of chiropractors......	8041	5,467	6,555	6,936	6,757	6,742	6,958
Offices and clinics of optometrists.......	8042	4,799	5,333	5,715	6,021	6,113	6,313
Offices and clinics of podiatrists.......	8043	1,811	2,102	2,156	2,190	2,388	2,440
Nursing and personal care facilities........	805	30,162	34,743	36,172	37,320	41,135	44,254
Hospitals [3]......	806	26,487	31,083	33,331	35,143	38,417	44,669
General medical and surgical hospitals [3]..	8062	20,442	24,162	26,683	27,993	30,704	36,496
Psychiatric hospitals [3]......	8063	4,129	4,396	3,730	3,764	3,847	3,508
Specialty hospitals, except psychiatric [3]....	8069	1,916	2,525	2,918	3,386	3,866	4,665
Medical and dental laboratories.........	807	12,033	15,172	15,066	15,427	15,524	16,042
Medical laboratories.............	8071	9,996	12,882	12,735	13,007	12,909	13,266
Dental laboratories.............	8072	2,037	2,290	2,331	2,420	2,615	2,776
Home health care services.........	808	7,556	11,208	13,178	15,394	17,987	19,542
Miscellaneous allied services, n.e.c. [2][4].....	809	11,208	12,783	14,647	16,611	18,283	20,423
Kidney dialysis centers............	8092	1,451	2,140	2,468	2,898	3,259	3,385
Specialty outpatient facilities, n.e.c. [4].....	8093	5,326	6,476	6,999	7,965	8,616	9,586
TAX EXEMPT FIRMS—REVENUE [3]							
Selected health services [2]...........	80 pt.	267,858	324,416	345,081	363,112	385,210	401,047
Offices and clinics of doctors of medicine...	801	12,888	16,548	19,647	21,882	24,873	26,153
Nursing and personal care facilities.......	805	12,132	15,221	15,972	16,564	17,570	18,510
Hospitals.............	806	233,615	279,736	294,757	308,105	325,033	337,822
General medical and surgical hospitals...	8062	210,503	254,391	268,885	281,430	297,407	309,681
Psychiatric hospitals......	8063	11,008	10,933	10,243	9,848	9,211	9,291
Specialty hospitals, exc. psychiatric.....	8069	12,104	14,412	15,629	16,827	18,415	18,850
Home health care services.........	808	3,874	5,714	6,608	7,428	7,943	8,043
Miscellaneous allied services, n.e.c. [2][4]....	809	5,285	7,123	8,007	9,025	9,666	10,388
Kidney dialysis centers........	8092	305	400	462	526	620	676
Specialty outpatient facilities, n.e.c. [4].....	8093	3,519	4,437	4,737	5,320	5,661	5,957

[1] Based on the 1987 Standard Industrial Classification code; see text, Section 13. [2] Includes other industries not shown separately. [3] Estimates are obtained from a sample of employer firms only. [4] N.e.c. means not elsewhere classified.

Source: U.S. Bureau of the Census, *Current Business Reports, Service Annual Survey: 1996,* BS/96.

No. 189. Employment in the Health Service Industries: 1980 to 1997

[In thousands. See headnote Table 687]

INDUSTRY	1987 SIC code [1]	1980	1985	1990	1995	1996	1997
Health services [2]	80	5,278	6,293	7,814	9,230	9,469	9,687
Offices and clinics of MDs	801	802	1,028	1,338	1,609	1,679	1,743
Offices and clinics of dentists	802	(NA)	439	513	592	609	622
Offices and clinics of other practitioners	804	96	165	277	397	414	429
Nursing and personal care facilities	805	997	1,198	1,415	1,691	1,732	1,761
Skilled nursing care facilities	8051	(NA)	791	989	1,253	1,289	1,312
Intermediate care facilities	8052	(NA)	(NA)	200	211	212	213
Other, n.e.c. [3]	8059	(NA)	(NA)	227	227	231	235
Hospitals	806	2,750	2,997	3,549	3,772	3,814	3,876
General medical and surgical hospitals	8062	(NA)	2,811	3,268	3,474	3,517	3,576
Psychiatric hospitals	8063	(NA)	59	104	91	87	86
Specialty hospitals, exc. psychiatric	8069	(NA)	126	176	208	209	214
Medical and dental laboratories	807	(NA)	119	166	190	196	206
Home health care services	808	(NA)	(NA)	291	629	665	682

NA Not available. [1] Based on the 1987 Standard Industrial Classification code; see text, Section 13. [2] Includes other industries not shown separately. [3] N.e.c. means not elsewhere classified.

Source: U.S. Bureau of Labor Statistics, Bulletins 2445 and 2481, and *Employment and Earnings*, monthly, March and June issues.

No. 190. Physicians, by Selected Activity: 1980 to 1996

[In thousands. 1980, 1985, 1995, and 1996, as of Dec. 31; other years as of Jan. 1, except as noted. Includes Puerto Rico and outlying areas]

ACTIVITY	1980	1985	1990	1993	1994	1995	1996
Doctors of medicine, total	**467.7**	**552.7**	**615.4**	**670.3**	**684.4**	**720.3**	**737.8**
Professionally active	435.5	511.1	560.0	605.7	619.8	646.0	663.9
Place of medical education:							
U.S. medical graduates	343.6	398.4	437.2	466.6	475.0	492.2	505.7
Foreign medical graduates [1]	91.8	112.7	122.8	139.1	144.8	153.8	158.3
Sex: Male	386.7	436.3	463.9	488.5	494.9	505.9	515.6
Female	48.7	74.8	96.1	117.2	124.9	140.1	148.3
Active nonfederal	417.7	489.5	539.5	584.0	597.3	624.9	643.5
Patient care	361.9	431.5	487.8	531.7	543.2	564.1	580.7
Office-based practice	271.3	329.0	359.9	398.8	407.0	427.3	445.8
General and family practice	47.8	53.9	57.6	58.1	58.2	59.9	61.8
Cardiovascular diseases	6.7	9.1	10.7	12.1	12.9	13.7	14.3
Dermatology	4.4	5.3	6.0	6.5	6.7	7.0	7.2
Gastroenterology	2.7	4.1	5.2	6.3	6.7	7.3	7.6
Internal medicine	40.5	52.7	57.8	67.3	67.9	72.6	77.9
Pediatrics	17.4	22.4	26.5	30.8	31.5	33.9	35.5
Pulmonary diseases	2.0	3.0	3.7	4.4	4.6	5.0	4.9
General surgery	22.4	24.7	24.5	24.3	24.2	24.1	25.4
Obstetrics and gynecology	19.5	23.5	25.5	27.6	28.2	29.1	29.9
Ophthalmology	10.6	12.2	13.1	13.9	14.3	14.6	14.9
Orthopedic surgery	10.7	13.0	14.2	16.3	16.6	17.1	17.6
Otolaryngology	5.3	5.8	6.4	6.7	6.9	7.1	7.2
Plastic surgery	2.4	3.3	3.8	4.1	4.3	4.6	5.0
Urological surgery	6.2	7.1	7.4	7.8	7.8	8.0	8.2
Anesthesiology	11.3	15.3	17.8	20.6	22.0	23.8	24.9
Diagnostic radiology	4.2	7.7	9.8	11.9	12.1	12.8	13.3
Emergency medicine	(NA)	(NA)	8.4	9.8	10.6	11.7	12.3
Neurology	3.2	4.7	5.6	6.8	7.1	7.6	7.9
Pathology, anatomical/clinical	6.0	6.9	7.3	8.5	8.7	9.0	9.7
Psychiatry	15.9	18.5	20.0	22.3	22.6	23.3	24.4
Other specialty	31.9	35.8	28.8	32.4	33.2	35.0	35.8
Hospital-based practice	90.6	102.5	127.9	132.9	136.1	136.8	134.9
Residents and interns [2]	59.6	72.2	89.9	89.0	91.5	93.7	90.6
Full-time hospital staff	31.0	30.3	38.0	43.9	44.6	43.1	44.3
Other professional activity [3]	35.2	44.0	39.0	37.7	39.9	40.3	42.8
Not classified	20.6	14.0	12.7	14.7	14.3	20.6	20.0
Federal	17.8	21.6	20.5	21.7	22.5	21.1	20.4
Patient care	14.6	17.3	16.1	18.8	19.3	18.1	18.2
Office-based practice	0.7	1.2	1.1	0.1	-	-	-
Hospital-based practice	13.9	16.1	15.0	18.7	19.3	18.1	18.2
Other professional activity [3]	3.2	4.3	4.4	2.9	3.2	3.0	2.2
Inactive/unknown address	32.1	41.6	55.4	64.7	64.7	74.3	73.8
Doctors of osteopathy [4]	**18.8**	**24.0**	**30.9**	**33.4**	**35.0**	**35.7**	**37.3**

- Represents zero. NA Not available. [1] Foreign medical graduates received their medical education in schools outside the United States and Canada. [2] Includes clinical fellows. [3] Includes medical teaching, administration, research, and other. [4] As of July. Total DOs. Source: American Osteopathic Association, Chicago, IL.

Source: Except as noted, American Medical Association, Chicago, IL, *Physician Characteristics and Distribution in the U.S.*, annual (copyright).

No. 191. Dentists and Nurses: 1980 to 1996

[As of **end of year**. Excludes Puerto Rico and outlying areas]

ITEM	Unit	1980	1985	1990	1991	1992	1993	1994	1995	1996
Dentists, number [1]	1,000...	141	156	[2]173	179	183	187	191	194	196
Active (exc. in federal service) [3]	1,000...	121	136	147	150	152	154	157	159	162
Rate per 100,000 population [4]	Rate ...	53	57	59	59	60	60	60	61	61
Nurses, number (active registered)	1,000...	1,273	1,538	1,790	1,853	1,907	1,976	2,044	2,116	2,162
Rate per 100,000 population [4]	Rate ...	560	644	713	730	748	767	785	805	815

[1] Includes current year's graduates. [2] Revised since originally published. [3] Source: American Dental Association, Bureau of Economic and Behavioral Research, Master Membership file and periodic censuses. [4] Based on Bureau of Census estimated resident population as of July 1. Estimates reflect revisions based on the 1990 Census of Population.

Source: Except as noted, U.S. Dept. of Health and Human Services, Health Resources and Services Administration, unpublished data.

No. 192. Health Professions Schools—Number, Enrollment, and Graduates: 1980 to 1997

[Data on the number of schools are reported as of the beginning of the academic year; all other data are reported as of the end of the academic year. Data are based on reporting by health professions schools]

YEAR	Medi-cine	Osteo-pathy	REGISTERED NURSING				Licensed practical nursing	Den-tistry	Optom-etry	Phar-macy
			Total	Bacca-laureate	Associ-ate degree	Diploma				
NUMBER OF SCHOOLS [1]										
1980	126	14	1,385	377	697	311	1,299	60	16	72
1985	127	15	1,477	427	777	273	1,254	60	17	72
1988	127	15	1,465	467	789	209	1,068	58	17	74
1989	127	15	1,442	479	792	171	1,095	58	17	74
1990	127	15	1,457	488	812	157	1,171	58	17	74
1991	126	15	1,470	489	829	152	1,154	56	17	74
1992	126	15	1,484	501	838	145	1,125	55	17	74
1993	126	15	1,484	501	848	135	1,154	55	17	74
1994	126	16	1,493	507	857	129	1,159	54	17	74
1995	125	16	1,501	509	868	124	1,185	54	17	74
1996	125	16	1,516	521	876	119	1,210	54	17	74
1997	125	17	1,508	523	876	109	(NA)	54	17	78
FIRST-YEAR ENROLLMENT										
1980	16,930	1,426	105,952	35,414	53,633	16,905	56,316	6,132	1,202	8,035
1985	16,997	1,750	118,224	39,573	63,776	14,875	47,034	5,047	1,187	6,986
1988	16,713	1,692	94,269	28,505	57,375	8,389	43,774	4,370	1,268	7,751
1989	16,868	1,780	103,025	29,042	63,973	10,010	47,602	4,196	1,271	7,990
1990	16,756	1,844	108,580	29,858	68,634	10,088	52,969	3,979	1,258	8,033
1991	16,876	1,950	113,526	33,437	69,869	10,220	56,176	4,001	1,239	8,267
1992	17,071	1,974	122,656	37,886	74,079	10,691	58,245	4,047	1,355	8,343
1993	17,079	2,035	126,837	41,290	75,382	10,165	60,749	4,072	1,395	8,664
1994	17,121	2,162	129,897	42,953	77,343	9,601	60,632	4,100	1,351	8,970
1995	17,085	2,217	127,184	43,451	76,016	7,717	57,906	4,121	1,390	9,157
1996	17,058	2,274	119,205	40,048	72,930	6,227	(NA)	4,237	1,438	8,740
1997	16,935	2,535	(NA)	(NA)	(NA)	(NA)	(NA)	4,255	1,362	8,790
TOTAL ENROLLMENT										
1980	63,800	4,571	234,659	98,939	92,069	43,651	52,202	22,482	4,517	23,074
1985	67,016	6,547	237,232	95,008	104,968	37,256	48,840	20,588	4,569	18,646
1988	65,735	6,586	182,947	73,621	90,399	18,927	40,035	17,885	4,646	21,424
1989	65,300	6,614	184,924	70,078	95,986	18,860	42,808	17,094	4,708	22,447
1990	65,016	6,615	201,458	74,865	106,175	20,418	46,720	16,412	4,723	23,013
1991	65,163	6,792	221,170	81,788	117,413	21,969	52,749	15,951	4,760	23,238
1992	65,602	7,012	237,598	90,877	123,816	22,905	56,762	15,882	4,864	23,482
1993	66,142	7,375	257,983	102,128	132,603	23,252	59,095	15,980	5,078	26,287
1994	66,629	7,822	270,228	110,693	137,300	22,235	61,007	16,250	(NA)	27,143
1995	67,072	8,146	268,350	112,659	135,895	19,796	59,428	16,353	5,201	27,667
1996	66,907	8,475	261,219	109,505	135,235	16,479	56,028	16,552	5,312	28,060
1997	67,276	8,961	238,244	103,213	122,242	12,789	(NA)	16,570	5,210	28,027
GRADUATES										
1980	15,113	1,059	75,523	24,994	36,034	14,495	41,892	5,256	1,073	7,432
1985	16,318	1,474	82,075	24,975	45,208	11,892	36,955	5,353	1,114	5,735
1988	15,919	1,572	64,839	21,504	37,397	5,938	26,912	4,581	1,106	6,184
1989	15,630	1,609	61,660	18,997	37,837	4,826	30,368	4,312	1,143	6,560
1990	15,398	1,529	66,088	18,571	42,318	5,199	35,417	4,233	1,115	6,956
1991	15,427	1,534	72,230	19,264	46,794	6,172	38,100	3,995	1,224	7,122
1992	15,365	1,532	80,839	21,415	52,896	6,528	41,951	3,918	1,150	7,113
1993	15,466	1,606	88,149	24,442	56,770	6,937	44,822	3,778	1,167	7,380
1994	15,555	1,752	94,870	28,912	58,839	7,119	45,083	3,875	1,125	7,504
1995	15,888	1,843	97,052	31,254	58,749	7,049	44,234	3,908	1,219	7,837
1996	15,907	1,932	94,757	32,413	56,641	5,703	(NA)	3,810	1,210	8,003
1997	15,923	2,020	(NA)	(NA)	(NA)	(NA)	(NA)	(NA)	(NA)	(NA)
2000, proj.	16,112	1,934	79,660	26,490	47,790	5,380	(NA)	3,242	1,200	7,120

NA Not available. [1] Some nursing schools offer more than one type of program. Numbers shown for nursing are number of nursing programs.

Source: U.S. National Center for Health Statistics, *Health United States*, annual.

No. 193. Active Nonfederal Physicians and Nurses, by State: 1996

[As of December. Excludes doctors of osteopathy, federally-employed persons, and physicians with addresses unknown. Includes all physicians not classified according to activity status]

STATE	PHYSICIANS		NURSES		STATE	PHYSICIANS		NURSES	
	Total	Rate [1]	Total	Rate [1]		Total	Rate [1]	Total	Rate [1]
United States..	634,785	239	2,161,700	815	Missouri	11,970	223	51,200	955
Alabama.	8,134	190	32,800	765	Montana	1,626	185	7,100	810
Alaska	929	154	6,300	1,041	Nebraska	3,295	200	15,200	922
Arizona.	8,724	197	33,200	749	Nevada	2,602	163	9,900	618
Arkansas	4,516	180	17,900	714	New Hampshire	2,577	222	11,200	965
California	76,689	241	179,700	564	New Jersey.	22,340	279	67,100	839
Colorado.	8,523	223	30,900	810	New Mexico	3,491	204	11,700	684
Connecticut.	11,015	337	33,400	1,022	New York	66,410	366	167,600	924
Delaware	1,617	224	7,700	1,064	North Carolina	16,073	220	62,000	848
District of Columbia .	3,699	686	8,900	1,650	North Dakota	1,304	203	7,000	1,089
Florida	32,718	227	119,300	827	Ohio	24,917	223	101,200	907
Georgia	14,621	199	53,600	731	Oklahoma	5,360	163	19,600	595
Hawaii	2,892	244	8,900	752	Oregon.	6,966	218	26,500	829
Idaho	1,719	145	7,100	598	Pennsylvania.	33,130	275	126,300	1,049
Illinois	29,512	249	104,700	884	Rhode Island.	3,048	308	11,400	1,154
Indiana.	10,797	185	46,900	805	South Carolina.	7,259	195	27,400	737
Iowa	4,806	169	29,100	1,022	South Dakota	1,298	176	7,700	1,044
Kansas	5,094	198	21,600	837	Tennessee	12,386	233	46,400	874
Kentucky	7,571	195	30,400	783	Texas.	36,307	190	124,200	651
Louisiana	10,030	231	32,400	746	Utah	3,860	191	13,000	644
Maine.	2,594	209	13,300	1,074	Vermont	1,624	277	5,300	904
Maryland	17,696	350	43,000	850	Virginia.	15,155	227	54,400	816
Massachusetts.	23,932	393	73,300	1,205	Washington.	12,412	225	43,500	788
Michigan.	20,704	213	79,600	818	West Virginia.	3,713	204	15,000	824
Minnesota.	11,182	241	46,200	994	Wisconsin	11,189	217	45,600	886
Mississippi	3,984	147	19,900	734	Wyoming	775	161	4,200	875

[1] Per 100,000 resident population. Based on U.S. Bureau of the Census estimates as of July 1, 1996.

Source: Physicians: American Medical Association, Chicago, IL, *Physician Characteristics and Distribution in the U.S.,* annual (copyright); Nurses: U.S. Dept. of Health and Human Services, Health Resources and Services Administration, unpublished data.

No. 194. Physician Contacts, by Patient Characteristics: 1980 to 1995

[See headnote, Table 220. Based on National Health Interview Survey; see Appendix III]

| YEAR | TOTAL VISITS (mil.) | | | | VISITS PER PERSON PER YEAR | | | | | | | | | |
| | Sex | | Race | | Sex | | Race | | Age (years) | | | | | |
	Male	Fe-male	White	Black	Male	Fe-male	White	Black	Under 5	5 to 17	18 to 24	25 to 44	45 to 64	65 and over
1980	426	610	903	115	4.0	5.4	4.8	4.5	[1]6.7	[2]3.2	[3]4.0	4.6	5.1	6.4
1985	498	733	1,074	132	4.4	6.1	5.4	4.7	[1]6.3	[2]3.1	[3]4.2	4.9	6.1	8.3
1987	523	765	1,118	140	4.5	6.2	5.5	4.9	6.7	3.3	4.4	4.8	6.4	8.9
1988	530	774	1,139	136	4.5	6.2	5.6	4.6	7.0	3.4	3.8	5.1	6.1	8.7
1989	552	771	1,148	140	4.7	6.1	5.6	4.7	6.7	3.5	3.9	5.1	6.1	8.9
1990	558	806	1,178	148	4.7	6.4	5.7	4.9	6.9	3.2	4.3	5.1	6.4	9.2
1991	589	842	1,243	152	4.9	6.6	6.0	4.9	7.1	3.4	3.9	5.1	6.6	10.4
1992	624	889	1,286	181	5.1	6.9	6.1	5.8	6.9	3.5	4.1	5.4	7.2	10.6
1993	634	917	1,314	183	5.1	7.0	6.2	5.7	7.2	3.6	4.0	5.4	7.1	10.9
1994	652	930	1,350	179	5.2	7.0	6.3	5.4	6.8	3.5	3.9	5.5	7.3	11.3
1995	626	922	1,325	170	4.9	6.9	6.1	5.2	6.5	3.4	3.9	5.2	7.1	11.1

[1] Under 6 years.   [2] 6 to 16 years.   [3] 17 to 24 years.

Source: U.S. National Center for Health Statistics, *Vital and Health Statistics,* Series 10, No. 193, and earlier reports; and unpublished data.

No. 195. Visits to Office Based Physicians: 1996

[Based on the 1996 National Ambulatory Medical Care Survey and subject to sampling error; see source for details]

CHARACTERISTIC	Number of visits (1,000)	Per-cent distri-bution	Visits per person per year	CHARACTERISTIC	Number of visits (1,000)	Per-cent distri-bution	Visits per person per year
All visits	734,493	100.0	2.8	New patient	102,512	14.0	(X)
Age:				Expected source of payment: [1]			
Under 15 years old	140,851	19.2	2.4	Insurance [2]	639,065	87.0	(X)
15 to 24 years old	59,086	8.0	1.6	Blue Cross/Blue Shield	114,640	15.6	(X)
25 to 44 years old	184,449	25.1	2.2	Other private insurance	230,839	31.4	(X)
45 to 64 years old	170,229	23.2	3.2	Medicare	160,329	21.8	(X)
65 to 74 years old	93,879	12.8	5.1	Medicaid	89,583	12.2	(X)
75 years old and over	85,999	11.7	6.3	Worker's compensation	13,992	1.9	(X)
Sex:				Other source of insurance . .	71,084	9.7	(X)
Male	299,984	40.8	2.3	Unknown source of			
Female	434,510	59.2	3.2	insurance [3]	40,660	5.5	(X)
Race:				Self pay	64,016	8.7	(X)
White	625,472	85.2	2.9	No charge	8,142	1.1	(X)
Black	81,813	11.1	2.4	Other and no answer	23,271	3.1	(X)
Asian/Pacific Islander	24,033	3.3	2.4	Disposition: [1]			
American Indian/Eskimo/Aleut .	3,174	0.4	1.4	Return at specified time	459,061	62.5	(X)
Visit status:				Return if needed	210,242	28.6	(X)
Old patient	631,982	86.0	(X)	No follow-up planned	54,520	7.4	(X)
Old problem	487,127	66.3	(X)	Admit to hospital	5,683	0.8	(X)
New problem	144,855	19.7	(X)	Other	28,390	3.9	(X)

X Not applicable.   [1] More than one source of payment or disposition may be reported.   [2] Equal to all visits minus self pay, no charge, other source, and no answer.   [3] Type of payment indicated, expected source was left blank.

Source: U.S. National Center for Health Statistics, *Advance Data*, No. 295, December 17, 1997.

No. 196. Medical Practice Characteristics, by Selected Specialty: 1985 to 1995

[**Dollar figures in thousands.** Based on a sample telephone survey of 4,000 nonfederal office and hospital based patient care physicians, excluding residents. For details see source. For definition of mean, see Guide to Tabular Presentation]

SPECIALTY	1985	1990	1991	1992	1993	1994	1995
MEAN PATIENT VISITS PER WEEK							
All physicians [1]	117.1	120.9	118.4	114.8	112.4	109.6	107.6
General/Family practice	138.1	146.0	144.4	138.4	137.0	133.5	133.7
Internal medicine	105.2	112.0	110.7	109.4	105.3	105.4	99.7
Surgery	108.2	107.6	106.9	101.6	98.3	98.8	97.1
Pediatrics	130.8	134.0	133.5	126.9	130.9	125.5	125.9
Obstetrics/Gynecology	112.0	120.0	112.2	110.5	111.0	102.9	94.0
MEAN HOURS IN PATIENT CARE PER WEEK							
All physicians [1]	51.3	53.3	53.3	52.9	52.9	52.1	51.3
General/Family practice	53.6	55.0	54.7	53.1	54.0	51.9	52.9
Internal medicine	52.4	55.7	56.3	55.5	56.0	56.6	53.9
Surgery	51.2	53.1	53.4	53.0	54.3	53.4	53.2
Pediatrics	50.6	52.4	52.4	52.6	53.8	51.6	50.4
Obstetrics/Gynecology	56.9	60.4	59.5	58.8	58.9	58.1	54.6
MEAN NET INCOME							
All physicians [1]	112.2	164.3	170.6	181.7	189.3	182.4	195.5
General/Family practice	77.9	102.7	111.5	114.4	116.8	121.2	131.2
Internal medicine	102.0	152.5	149.6	162.1	180.8	174.9	185.7
Surgery	155.0	236.4	233.8	250.5	262.7	255.2	269.4
Pediatrics	76.2	106.5	119.3	123.9	135.4	126.2	140.5
Obstetrics/Gynecology	124.3	207.3	221.8	220.7	221.9	200.4	244.3
MEAN PROFESSIONAL EXPENSES							
All physicians [1]	102.7	150.0	168.4	183.4	182.2	183.1	201.6
General/Family practice	96.5	134.5	146.4	162.9	162.4	190.5	179.4
Internal medicine	90.0	139.2	159.0	174.1	185.2	186.4	200.4
Surgery	135.7	201.0	215.6	245.1	245.9	249.9	265.1
Pediatrics	87.3	138.0	145.4	173.7	167.4	157.8	208.5
Obstetrics/Gynecology	131.9	212.6	236.2	239.7	238.1	196.8	266.9
MEAN LIABILITY PREMIUM							
All physicians [1]	10.5	14.5	14.9	13.8	14.4	15.1	15.0
General/Family practice	6.8	7.8	8.1	8.2	7.9	10.2	9.0
Internal medicine	5.8	9.2	8.0	8.6	9.0	8.6	9.4
Surgery	16.6	22.8	22.5	20.9	22.7	22.3	23.3
Pediatrics	4.7	7.8	8.4	7.7	8.6	7.6	7.9
Obstetrics/Gynecology	23.5	34.3	34.9	34.4	33.7	37.4	38.6

[1] Includes other specialties not shown separately.

Source: American Medical Association, Chicago IL, *Socioeconomic Characteristics of Medical Practice,* annual (copyright).

No. 197. Percent of Adult Persons with a Dental Visit Within Past Year, by Patient Characteristics: 1990 to 1993

[Covers civilian noninstitutional population, 25 years old and over. Data are age-adjusted. Estimates are based on one adult member per sample household. Excludes persons with unknown dental data. Based on National Health Interview Survey; see Appendix III]

CHARACTERISTIC	1990	1991	1993	CHARACTERISTIC	1990	1991	1993
Total [1]	62.3	58.2	60.8	White, non-Hispanic	64.9	61.5	64.0
				Black, non-Hispanic	49.1	44.3	47.3
25 to 34 years old	65.1	59.1	60.3	Hispanic origin [2]	53.8	43.1	46.2
35 to 44 years old	69.1	64.8	66.9				
45 to 64 years old	62.8	59.2	62.0	Years of school completed:			
65 years old and over	49.6	47.2	51.7	Less than 12 years	41.2	35.2	38.0
65 to 74 years old	53.5	51.1	56.3	12 years	61.3	56.7	58.7
75 years old and over	43.4	41.3	44.9	13 years or more	75.7	72.2	73.8
				Poverty status: [3]			
Male	58.8	55.5	58.2	Below poverty	38.2	33.0	35.9
Female	65.6	60.8	63.4	At or above poverty	65.4	61.9	64.3

[1] Includes all other races not shown separately and unknown education level and poverty status.   [2] Persons of Hispanic origin may be of any race.   [3] For explanation of poverty level, see text, Section 14.

Source: U.S. National Center for Health Statistics, *Health, United States, 1995.*

No. 198. Percent of Women, 15 to 44 Years Old, Who Received Selected Medical Services From a Medical Care Provider: 1995

[In percent, except as indicated. See headnote, Table 64]

CHARACTERISTIC	Number (1,000)	Pregnancy test	Pap smear	Pelvic exam	HIV test [1]	Other STD [2] test or treatment	Test or treatment for infection [3]
Total	60,201	16.0	61.9	61.3	17.3	7.6	21.0
AGE AT INTERVIEW							
15-19 years old	8,961	16.1	33.5	32.4	14.6	9.4	16.9
15-17 years old	5,452	11.4	23.0	23.4	12.1	7.1	12.2
18-19 years old	3,508	23.3	49.9	46.4	18.5	13.0	24.2
20-24 years old	9,041	27.4	68.7	66.5	23.7	14.0	28.1
25-29 years old	9,693	25.3	70.9	69.3	23.6	10.3	25.7
30-34 years old	11,065	17.4	69.5	70.3	18.5	6.5	21.8
35-39 years old	11,211	8.1	62.9	62.6	14.2	4.7	19.2
40-44 years old	10,230	4.3	62.7	63.2	10.0	2.2	15.1
RACE AND HISPANIC ORIGIN							
Hispanic	6,702	19.8	52.2	52.6	21.9	7.2	20.4
Non-Hispanic White	42,522	14.8	63.2	63.2	14.5	7.1	20.9
Non-Hispanic Black	8,210	19.8	67.6	63.0	28.7	11.4	24.8
Non-Hispanic other	2,767	14.3	47.7	47.7	14.7	(B)	13.6
MARITAL STATUS							
Never married	22,679	15.5	52.1	49.8	18.9	10.7	20.1
Currently married	29,673	17.3	68.5	69.0	14.5	4.7	20.9
Formerly married	7,849	12.4	64.8	65.3	23.1	9.7	24.2

B Figure does not meet standard of reliability.   [1] Excludes HIV (human immunodeficiency virus) tests done as part of blood donation.   [2] STD is sexually transmitted disease.   [3] Refers to vaginal, urinary tract, and pelvic infections.

Source: U.S. National Center for Health Statistics, *Fertility, Family Planning, and Women's Health: New data from the 1995 National Survey of Family Growth, Vital and Health Statistics,* Series 23, No. 19, 1997.

No. 199. Use of Mammography for Women 40 Years Old and Over by Patient Characteristics: 1990 to 1994

[Percent of women having a mammogram within the past 2 years. Covers civilian noninstitutional population. Based on National Health Interview Survey; see Appendix III]

CHARACTERISTIC	1990	1993	1994	CHARACTERISTIC	1990	1993	1994
Total [1]	51.4	59.7	60.9	Years of school completed:			
40 to 49 years old	55.1	59.9	61.3	Less than 12 years	36.4	46.4	48.2
50 years old and over	49.7	59.7	60.6	12 years	52.7	59.0	61.0
50 to 64 years old	56.0	65.1	66.5	13 years or more	62.8	69.5	69.7
65 years old and over	43.4	54.2	55.0				
White, non-Hispanic	52.7	60.6	61.3	Poverty status: [3]			
Black, non-Hispanic	46.0	59.2	64.4	Below poverty	28.7	41.6	43.3
Hispanic origin [2]	45.2	50.9	51.9	At or above poverty	54.8	62.8	64.2

[1] Includes all other races not shown separately and unknown education level and poverty status.   [2] Persons of Hispanic origin may be of any race.   [3] For explanation of poverty level, see text, Section 14.

Source: U.S. National Center for Health Statistics, *Health United States, 1996-97 and Injury Chartbook,* 1997.

Health and Nutrition

No. 200. Hospitals—Summary Characteristics: 1980 to 1996

[Covers hospitals accepted for registration by the American Hospital Association; see text, Section 3. Short-term hospitals have an average patient stay of less than 30 days; long-term, an average stay of longer duration. Special hospitals include obstetrics and gynecology; eye, ear, nose, and throat; rehabilitation; orthopedic; and chronic and other special hospitals except psychiatric, tuberculosis, alcoholism, and chemical dependency hospitals]

ITEM	1980	1985	1990	1991	1992	1993	1994	1995	1996
NUMBER									
All hospitals	6,965	6,872	6,649	6,634	6,539	6,467	6,374	6,291	6,201
With 100 beds or more	3,755	3,805	3,620	3,611	3,572	3,558	3,492	3,376	3,347
Nonfederal [1]	6,606	6,529	6,312	6,300	6,214	6,151	6,067	5,992	5,911
Community hospitals [2]	5,830	5,732	5,384	5,342	5,292	5,261	5,229	5,194	5,134
Nongovernmental nonprofit	3,322	3,349	3,191	3,175	3,173	3,154	3,139	3,092	3,045
For profit	730	805	749	738	723	717	719	752	759
State and local government	1,778	1,578	1,444	1,429	1,396	1,390	1,371	1,350	1,330
Long-term general and special	157	128	131	126	115	117	110	112	112
Psychiatric	534	610	757	800	774	741	696	657	653
Tuberculosis	11	7	4	4	4	4	5	3	3
Federal	359	343	337	334	325	316	307	299	290
BEDS (1,000)									
All hospitals [3]	1,365	1,318	1,213	1,202	1,178	1,163	1,128	1,081	1,062
Rate per 1,000 population [4]	6.0	5.5	4.9	4.8	4.6	4.5	4.3	4.1	4.0
Beds per hospital	196	190	182	180	180	179	177	172	171
Nonfederal [1]	1,248	1,197	1,113	1,101	1,085	1,071	1,044	1,004	989
Community hospitals [2]	988	1,001	927	924	921	919	902	873	862
Rate per 1,000 population [4]	4.3	4.2	3.7	3.7	3.6	3.6	3.5	3.3	3.3
Nongovernmental nonprofit	692	707	657	656	656	649	637	610	598
For profit	87	104	102	100	99	99	101	106	109
State and local government	209	189	169	168	167	169	164	157	155
Long-term general and special	39	31	25	25	23	21	19	19	19
Psychiatric	215	169	158	150	139	131	121	110	106
Tuberculosis	2	1	(Z)	(Z)	(Z)	(Z)	1	(Z)	(Z)
Federal	117	112	98	95	89	87	84	78	73
AVERAGE DAILY CENSUS (1,000)									
All hospitals	1,060	910	844	827	807	783	745	710	685
Community hospitals [2]	747	649	619	611	604	592	568	548	531
Nongovernmental nonprofit	542	476	455	451	445	432	413	393	379
For profit	57	54	54	52	51	51	50	55	56
State and local government	149	119	111	108	108	109	104	100	96
EXPENSES (bil. dol.) [5]									
All hospitals	91.9	153.3	234.9	258.5	282.5	301.5	310.8	320.3	330.5
Nonfederal [1]	84.0	141.0	219.6	241.7	264.3	281.9	290.8	300.0	308.3
Community hospitals [2]	76.9	130.5	203.7	225.0	248.1	266.1	275.8	285.6	293.8
Nongovernmental nonprofit	55.8	96.1	150.7	166.8	183.8	197.2	204.2	209.6	216.0
For profit	5.8	11.5	18.8	20.5	22.5	23.1	23.4	26.7	28.4
State and local government	15.2	22.9	34.2	37.7	41.8	45.8	48.1	49.3	49.4
Long-term general and special	1.2	1.9	2.7	2.9	2.7	2.7	2.3	2.2	2.3
Psychiatric	5.8	8.3	12.9	13.5	13.2	12.7	12.3	11.7	12.0
Tuberculosis	0.1	0.1	0.1	(Z)	(Z)	0.1	0.7	0.4	(Z)
Federal	7.9	12.3	15.2	16.8	18.2	19.6	20.0	20.2	22.3
PERSONNEL (1,000) [6]									
All hospitals	3,492	3,625	4,063	4,165	4,236	4,289	4,270	4,273	4,276
Nonfederal [1]	3,213	3,326	3,760	3,864	3,929	3,970	3,969	3,971	3,981
Community hospitals [2]	2,873	2,997	3,420	3,535	3,620	3,677	3,692	3,714	3,725
Nongovernmental nonprofit	2,086	2,216	2,533	2,624	2,692	2,711	2,719	2,702	2,711
For profit	189	221	273	281	285	289	301	343	359
State and local government	598	561	614	630	643	676	672	670	654
Long-term general and special	56	58	55	55	49	45	38	38	40
Psychiatric	275	263	280	269	256	242	233	215	212
Tuberculosis	3	2	1	1	1	1	1	1	1
Federal	279	299	303	301	306	320	301	301	295
PERSONNEL PER 100 PATIENTS [6]									
All hospitals	329	398	482	504	525	548	573	602	624
Nonfederal [1]	333	403	487	510	533	554	582	607	629
Community hospitals [2]	380	462	552	579	599	621	650	677	701
Nongovernmental nonprofit	385	466	557	582	605	627	658	687	715
For profit	334	408	510	537	556	572	599	626	642
State and local government	401	471	555	584	596	622	644	669	682
Long-term general and special	170	212	257	259	257	259	233	240	248
Psychiatric	150	180	215	217	226	230	241	243	249
Tuberculosis	290	378	405	277	281	272	278	408	526
Federal	297	351	424	434	444	479	480	538	565
Outpatient visits (mil.)	263.0	282.1	368.2	387.7	417.9	435.7	453.6	483.2	505.5
Emergency	82.0	80.1	92.8	93.5	95.8	97.4	96.0	99.9	97.6

Z Less than 500 beds or $50 million.   [1] Short term (average length of stay less than 30 days) general and special (e.g., obstetrics and gynecology; eye, ear, nose, and throat; rehabilitation etc. except psychiatric, tuberculosis, alcoholism and chemical dependency). Includes hospital units of institutions.   [2] Excludes hospital units of institutions.   [3] Beginning 1990, number of beds at end of reporting period; prior years, average number in 12 month period.   [4] Based on Bureau of the Census estimated resident population as of July 1. Estimates reflect revisions based on the 1990 Census of Population.   [5] Excludes new construction.   [6] Includes full-time equivalents of part-time personnel.

Source: American Hospital Association, Chicago, IL, *Hospital Statistics*, annual (copyright).

No. 201. Community Hospitals—States: 1990 to 1996

[For definition of community hospitals see footnotes 1 and 2, Table 200]

STATE	NUMBER OF HOSPITALS			BEDS (1,000)			PATIENTS ADMITTED (1,000)		AVERAGE DAILY CENSUS [1] (1,000)		OUTPATIENT VISITS (mil.)	
	1990	1995	1996	1990	1995	1996	1995	1996	1995	1996	1995	1996
United States	5,384	5,194	5,134	928.1	872.7	862.4	30,945	31,099	547.6	530.8	414.3	439.9
Alabama.	120	115	113	18.6	18.3	18.7	642	673	10.7	10.8	6.4	7.6
Alaska	16	17	17	1.2	1.3	1.1	40	38	0.7	0.6	0.8	0.8
Arizona.	61	61	61	9.9	9.9	10.3	427	452	5.6	6.2	4.0	4.2
Arkansas	86	85	84	10.9	10.1	10.3	342	344	6.0	5.8	3.6	4.1
California	445	424	420	80.5	75.0	75.7	3,029	3,072	45.0	44.6	39.5	41.7
Colorado.	69	69	68	10.4	9.3	9.1	340	351	5.4	5.2	5.5	6.1
Connecticut.	35	34	33	9.6	7.5	7.3	338	338	5.5	5.2	5.7	6.1
Delaware	8	8	6	2.0	1.9	1.6	81	74	1.5	1.3	1.4	1.2
District of Columbia	11	12	12	4.5	3.8	3.7	154	146	2.7	2.8	1.2	1.4
Florida	224	212	210	50.7	49.7	50.0	1,772	1,816	29.4	28.8	16.9	18.9
Georgia	163	160	159	25.7	26.1	25.9	859	838	15.8	15.5	9.6	10.1
Hawaii	18	21	21	2.9	3.0	3.0	97	100	2.4	2.3	2.1	2.3
Idaho.	43	41	42	3.2	3.4	3.4	104	116	1.8	1.9	1.7	2.0
Illinois	210	207	205	45.8	42.0	40.7	1,452	1,444	25.0	23.9	20.6	21.6
Indiana.	113	115	115	21.8	19.4	19.5	699	693	11.3	11.1	11.8	12.3
Iowa	124	116	115	14.3	12.6	12.4	361	365	7.1	7.1	6.2	7.0
Kansas.	138	132	131	11.8	10.8	10.9	291	292	5.8	5.6	4.0	4.4
Kentucky	107	104	104	15.9	15.1	15.0	534	529	9.0	8.6	6.1	6.6
Louisiana	140	130	129	19.1	19.1	19.3	622	635	10.6	10.2	8.0	8.4
Maine.	39	39	39	4.5	4.0	3.9	142	146	2.6	2.5	2.5	2.7
Maryland	52	50	51	13.6	12.6	12.5	574	570	8.8	8.5	4.9	5.0
Massachusetts.	101	96	88	21.7	18.9	18.0	751	730	13.0	12.1	13.5	13.7
Michigan.	176	167	164	33.9	29.6	28.8	1,120	1,116	19.3	18.4	19.2	21.0
Minnesota.	152	142	142	19.4	17.4	17.6	496	497	11.3	11.5	5.7	5.4
Mississippi	103	97	97	12.9	12.6	13.3	388	416	7.6	8.2	3.2	4.3
Missouri	135	126	125	24.3	21.9	21.5	714	728	12.6	12.1	9.9	10.2
Montana.	55	55	53	4.6	4.2	4.2	96	93	2.7	2.8	1.3	1.5
Nebraska	90	91	90	8.5	7.9	8.2	183	187	4.5	4.5	2.5	2.7
Nevada	21	20	20	3.4	3.6	3.6	149	152	2.2	2.2	1.4	1.4
New Hampshire	27	29	28	3.5	3.4	3.2	110	108	2.1	1.9	1.8	2.1
New Jersey.	95	92	89	28.9	29.9	28.1	1,068	1,059	21.4	19.8	12.8	13.5
New Mexico	37	36	36	4.2	3.7	3.7	156	159	2.1	2.1	2.5	2.8
New York	235	230	227	74.7	73.9	72.1	2,398	2,385	59.1	55.2	38.9	40.8
North Carolina	120	119	119	22.0	22.7	22.7	833	844	15.5	15.3	8.8	9.6
North Dakota.	50	43	43	4.4	4.2	4.2	89	88	2.7	2.6	1.3	1.5
Ohio	190	180	178	43.1	37.8	36.9	1,375	1,373	22.2	21.2	22.0	23.0
Oklahoma.	111	110	108	12.4	11.5	10.8	368	368	6.1	5.7	3.8	4.3
Oregon.	70	64	63	8.1	7.2	7.1	296	302	3.8	3.7	5.8	5.8
Pennsylvania.	238	225	223	52.6	48.5	47.0	1,810	1,756	33.8	31.6	26.9	27.1
Rhode Island.	12	11	11	3.2	2.7	2.6	119	118	1.8	1.8	1.7	1.8
South Carolina.	69	66	66	11.3	11.3	11.0	410	412	7.2	7.0	4.7	4.9
South Dakota	53	50	49	4.2	4.6	4.5	94	94	3.0	2.9	1.0	1.2
Tennessee	134	126	124	23.6	20.9	20.6	740	754	12.5	12.4	7.4	7.9
Texas.	428	416	408	59.2	57.2	56.3	2,029	2,074	31.1	30.7	22.7	24.4
Utah	42	42	41	4.4	4.2	4.3	171	174	2.2	2.2	3.2	3.6
Vermont	15	14	14	1.7	1.8	1.6	55	55	1.3	1.2	1.0	0.9
Virginia.	97	96	95	20.0	18.6	18.5	699	700	11.5	11.6	7.2	7.9
Washington	91	88	90	12.0	10.8	11.1	467	470	6.0	6.1	8.4	8.4
West Virginia	59	59	59	8.4	8.1	8.0	271	271	4.9	4.7	4.0	4.4
Wisconsin	129	127	124	18.6	17.0	16.5	550	541	10.2	9.6	8.2	9.0
Wyoming	27	25	25	2.2	2.0	2.0	43	43	1.1	1.0	0.7	0.8

[1] Inpatients receiving treatment each day; excludes newborn.

Source: American Hospital Association, Chicago, IL, *Hospital Statistics*, annual (copyright).

No. 202. Hospital Use Rates, by Type of Hospital: 1980 to 1996

TYPE OF HOSPITAL	1980	1985	1990	1992	1993	1994	1995	1996
Community hospitals: [1]								
Admissions per 1,000 population [2]	159	141	125	122	119	118	118	117
Admissions per bed	37	33	34	34	33	34	35	28
Average length of stay [3] (days)	7.6	7.1	7.2	7.1	7.0	6.7	6.5	6.2
Outpatient visits per admission	5.6	6.5	9.7	11.2	11.9	12.5	13.4	14.1
Outpatient visits per 1,000 population [2]	890	919	1,208	1,367	1,423	1,471	1,577	1,659
Surgical operations (million)	18.8	20.1	21.9	22.9	22.8	23.0	23.2	23.6
Number per admission	0.5	0.6	0.7	0.7	0.7	0.7	0.7	0.8
Nonfederal psychiatric:								
Admissions per 1,000 population [2]	2.5	2.5	2.9	2.9	2.9	2.9	2.7	2.7
Days in hospital per 1,000 population [2]	295	224	190	162	149	136	124	117

[1] For definition of community hospitals, see footnotes 1 and 2, Table 200.   [2] Based on Bureau of the Census estimated resident population as of July 1. Estimates reflect revisions based on the 1990 Census of Population.   [3] Number of inpatient days divided by number of admissions.

Source: American Hospital Association, Chicago, IL, *Hospital Statistics*, annual (copyright).

No. 203. Average Cost to Community Hospitals per Patient: 1980 to 1996

[In dollars, except percent. Covers nonfederal short-term general or special hospitals (excluding psychiatric or tuberculosis hospitals and hospital units of institutions). Total cost per patient based on total hospital expenses (payroll, employee benefits, professional fees, supplies, etc.). Data have been adjusted for outpatient visits]

TYPE OF EXPENSE AND HOSPITAL	1980	1985	1989	1990	1991	1992	1993	1994	1995	1996
Average cost per day, total	**245**	**460**	**637**	**687**	**752**	**820**	**881**	**931**	**968**	**1,006**
Annual percent change [1]	12.9	11.9	8.7	7.8	9.5	9.0	7.4	5.7	4.0	3.9
Nongovernmental nonprofit	246	463	642	692	758	828	898	950	994	1,042
For profit	257	500	708	752	820	889	914	924	947	945
State and local government	239	433	582	634	696	754	800	859	878	903
Average cost per stay, total	**1,851**	**3,245**	**4,588**	**4,947**	**5,360**	**5,794**	**6,132**	**6,230**	**6,216**	**6,225**
Nongovernmental nonprofit	1,902	3,307	4,649	5,001	5,393	5,809	6,178	6,257	6,279	6,344
For profit	1,676	3,033	4,406	4,727	5,134	5,548	5,643	5,529	5,425	5,207
State and local government	1,750	3,106	4,430	4,838	5,340	5,871	6,206	6,513	6,445	6,419

[1] Change from immediate prior year.

Source: American Hospital Association, Chicago, IL, *Hospital Statistics*, annual (copyright).

No. 204. Average Cost to Community Hospitals per Patient, by State: 1990 to 1995

[In dollars. See headnote, Table 203]

STATE	AVERAGE COST PER DAY			AVERAGE COST PER STAY			STATE	AVERAGE COST PER DAY			AVERAGE COST PER STAY		
	1990	1994	1995	1990	1994	1995		1990	1994	1995	1990	1994	1995
U.S.	687	931	968	4,947	6,230	6,216	MO	679	915	967	5,022	6,249	6,228
AL	588	781	819	4,175	4,895	5,028	MT	405	470	493	3,973	4,965	5,184
AK	1,070	1,263	1,341	6,249	8,168	8,282	NE	490	606	661	4,675	6,006	5,880
AZ	867	1,091	1,191	4,877	5,375	5,613	NV	854	1,016	1,072	5,511	6,526	6,014
AR	534	724	704	3,730	4,514	4,459	NH	671	825	915	4,544	5,978	6,188
CA	939	1,301	1,315	5,709	7,252	7,111	NJ	613	934	962	4,573	6,933	7,007
CO	725	993	1,069	5,209	6,241	6,289	NM	734	1,047	1,073	4,172	5,564	5,358
CT	825	1,121	1,264	6,238	7,835	7,358	NY	641	854	909	6,397	8,127	8,077
DE	771	1,042	1,058	5,112	7,303	7,298	NC	595	806	832	4,408	5,701	5,631
DC	995	1,304	1,346	7,876	9,021	8,632	ND	427	515	521	4,468	5,547	5,589
FL	769	975	1,004	5,312	6,106	6,040	OH	720	1,008	1,061	4,801	6,103	6,141
GA	630	797	836	4,303	5,621	5,618	OK	632	848	861	4,302	5,291	5,188
HI	638	958	956	6,048	8,428	8,445	OR	800	1,077	1,141	4,432	5,492	5,325
ID	547	679	719	3,701	4,448	4,686	PA	662	892	963	5,120	6,332	6,482
IL	717	988	1,050	5,253	6,372	6,584	RI	663	970	1,092	4,839	5,984	6,202
IN	667	955	963	4,390	5,715	5,610	SC	590	876	923	4,168	6,056	5,935
IA	495	672	702	4,135	5,077	5,049	SD	391	470	476	3,905	4,797	5,494
KS	532	715	732	4,161	5,240	5,308	TN	633	870	871	4,340	5,621	5,355
KY	563	748	795	3,762	4,873	4,838	TX	752	1,055	1,063	4,663	6,051	5,879
LA	701	929	902	4,575	5,916	5,612	UT	832	1,115	1,213	4,409	5,378	5,676
ME	574	802	916	4,604	5,685	6,083	VT	598	651	714	4,343	5,400	5,883
MD	678	981	1,064	4,640	5,833	5,899	VA	635	885	901	4,408	5,518	5,423
MA	788	1,131	1,157	5,709	7,018	7,099	WA	817	1,206	1,318	4,519	5,909	6,180
MI	716	929	994	5,358	6,169	6,218	WV	565	727	763	3,918	4,839	4,974
MN	536	695	736	4,782	6,029	6,241	WI	554	802	794	4,083	5,536	5,679
MS	439	584	584	3,116	4,235	4,265	WY	462	504	545	3,990	4,639	4,817

Source: American Hospital Association, Chicago, IL, *Hospital Statistics*, annual (copyright).

No. 205. Hospital Utilization Rates: 1980 to 1996

[Represents estimates of inpatients discharged from noninstitutional, short-stay hospitals, exclusive of federal hospitals. Excludes newborn infants. Based on sample data collected from the National Hospital Discharge Survey, a sample survey of hospital records of patients discharged in year shown; subject to sampling variability. For composition of regions, see map, inside front cover]

SELECTED CHARACTERISTIC	Patients dis-charged (1,000)	PATIENTS DISCHARGED PER 1,000 PERSONS [1]			DAYS OF CARE PER 1,000 PERSONS [1]			AVERAGE STAY (days)		
		Total	Male	Female	Total	Male	Female	Total	Male	Female
1980.	37,832	168	139	194	1,217	1,068	1,356	7.3	7.7	7.0
1985	35,056	148	124	171	954	849	1,053	6.5	6.9	6.2
1990 [2]	30,788	124	102	144	792	704	875	6.4	6.9	6.1
1991 [2]	31,098	124	103	144	795	715	869	6.4	7.0	6.0
1992 [2]	30,951	122	101	142	751	680	818	6.2	6.7	5.8
1993 [2]	30,825	120	98	141	720	644	792	6.0	6.5	5.6
1994 [2]	30,843	119	98	139	684	610	755	5.7	6.2	5.4
1995 [2]	30,722	118	96	138	630	561	695	5.4	5.8	5.0
1996, [2] total	30,545	116	94	136	606	543	665	5.2	5.8	4.9
Age:										
Under 1 year old	736	195	215	175	1,154	1,292	1,009	5.9	6.0	5.8
1 to 4 years old	649	42	47	36	140	151	128	3.3	3.2	3.5
5 to 14 years old	822	21	23	20	92	103	81	4.3	4.5	4.1
15 to 24 years old	2,849	80	33	128	258	164	356	3.2	5.0	2.8
25 to 34 years old	4,077	102	44	160	360	241	477	3.5	5.5	3.0
35 to 44 years old	3,399	79	64	93	373	368	377	4.7	5.7	4.1
45 to 64 years old	6,294	117	121	114	624	659	592	5.3	5.5	5.2
65 to 74 years old	4,804	257	271	247	1,604	1,675	1,546	6.2	6.2	6.3
75 years old and over. . .	6,914	455	477	443	3,075	3,160	3,025	6.8	6.6	6.8
Region:										
Northeast	6,665	129	113	145	803	746	855	6.2	6.6	5.9
Midwest	7,107	115	95	133	574	519	626	5.0	5.4	4.7
South	11,085	120	96	143	621	554	684	5.2	5.8	4.8
West	5,688	98	74	122	440	378	502	4.5	5.1	4.1

[1] Based on Bureau of the Census estimated civilian population as of July 1. Estimates for 1980-90 do not reflect revisions based on the 1990 Census of Population.   [2] Comparisons beginning 1990 with data for earlier years should be made with caution as estimates of change may reflect improvements in the design rather than true changes in hospital use.
Source: U.S. National Center for Health Statistics, *Vital and Health Statistics*, series 13; and unpublished data.

No. 206. Hospital Discharges and Days of Care: 1996

[See headnote, Table 205]

AGE AND FIRST-LISTED DIAGNOSIS	DISCHARGES		Days of care per 1,000 per-sons [1]	Aver-age stay (days)	AGE AND FIRST-LISTED DIAGNOSIS	DISCHARGES		Days of care per 1,000 per-sons [1]	Aver-age stay (days)
	Num-ber (1,000)	Per 1,000 per-sons [1]				Num-ber (1,000)	Per 1,000 per-sons [1]		
MALE					**FEMALE**				
All ages [2]	**12,110**	**89.7**	**511.8**	**5.7**	**All ages [2]**	**18,435**	**115.3**	**531.6**	**4.6**
Under 15 years [3]	1,240	42.0	193.2	4.6	Under 15 years [3]	967	34.3	154.6	4.5
Pneumonia	178	6.0	21.8	3.6	Pneumonia	142	5.0	18.5	3.7
Injuries and poisoning	142	4.8	17.1	3.6	Injuries and poisoning	81	2.9	12.4	4.3
Asthma	123	4.2	11.6	2.8	Asthma	72	2.5	6.4	2.5
15 to 44 years [3]	2,831	47.7	263.2	5.5	15 to 44 years [3]	7,495	126.1	404.4	3.2
Injuries and poisoning	550	9.3	43.9	4.7	Delivery	3,817	64.2	140.2	2.2
Psychoses	277	4.7	44.6	9.5	Injuries and poisoning	315	5.3	20.1	3.8
Diseases of heart	166	2.8	10.5	3.7	Psychoses	299	5.0	48.2	9.6
Intervertebral disk disorders.	90	1.5	4.3	2.8					
					45 to 64 years [3]	3,156	113.8	592.0	5.2
45 to 64 years [3]	3,138	120.8	658.7	5.5	Diseases of heart	455	16.4	75.8	4.6
Diseases of heart	793	30.5	139.3	4.6	Malignant neoplasms	249	9.0	53.3	5.9
Injuries and poisoning	269	10.4	56.1	5.4	Injuries and poisoning	215	7.8	39.8	5.1
Malignant neoplasms	200	7.7	55.8	7.3	Pneumonia	93	3.4	20.9	6.2
Cerebrovascular diseases. .	105	4.1	25.1	6.2	Diabetes	78	2.8	17.8	6.3
65 to 74 years [3]	2,253	270.6	1,675.3	6.2	65 to 74 years [3]	2,551	246.6	1,546.3	6.3
Diseases of heart	612	73.5	396.2	5.4	Diseases of heart	553	53.4	298.5	5.6
Malignant neoplasms	196	23.5	171.0	7.3	Injuries and poisoning	209	20.2	135.3	6.7
Injuries and poisoning	132	15.8	103.3	6.5	Malignant neoplasms	205	19.8	133.9	6.8
Cerebrovascular diseases. .	127	15.3	92.0	6.0	Cerebrovascular diseases. .	125	12.0	76.9	6.4
Pneumonia	108	13.0	89.2	6.9	Pneumonia	111	10.8	79.5	7.4
75 years old and older [3] .	2,648	476.6	3,160.4	6.6	75 years old and older [3] .	4,266	442.8	3,025.3	6.8
Diseases of heart	635	114.3	616.5	5.4	Diseases of heart	922	95.7	576.8	6.0
Pneumonia	213	38.3	291.7	7.6	Injuries and poisoning	453	47.0	315.0	6.7
Malignant neoplasms	155	28.0	199.5	7.1	Cerebrovascular diseases. .	289	30.0	207.6	6.9
Injuries and poisoning	184	33.2	239.2	7.2	Pneumonia	270	28.1	199.5	7.1
Cerebrovascular diseases. .	186	33.4	228.3	6.8	Malignant neoplasms	181	18.8	148.7	7.9

[1] Based on Bureau of the Census estimated civilian population as of July 1.   [2] Average length of stay and rates per 1,000 population are age-adjusted.   [3] Includes other first-listed diagnoses not shown separately.
Source: U.S. National Center for Health Statistics, and unpublished data.

No. 207. Hospital Discharges—Principal Source of Expected Payment: 1996

[See headnote, Table 205]

CHARACTERISTIC	Total dis-charges [1] (1,000)	PRINCIPAL SOURCE OF EXPECTED PAYMENT—PERCENT DISTRIBUTION							
		Private insur-ance	Government				Self-pay	No charge	Other [2]
			Medicare	Medicaid	Workers' compen-sation	Other			
All ages	30,545	35.1	38.1	14.4	0.7	1.5	4.7	0.3	3.3
Under 15 years old. . . .	2,207	43.9	0.8	37.5	(X)	2.3	5.2	0.2	7.9
15 to 44 years old	10,325	49.6	5.3	25.6	1.2	2.2	8.3	0.6	4.6
45 to 64 years old	6,294	55.8	16.5	11.9	1.2	2.2	5.8	0.5	4.1
65 years old and over. . .	11,718	9.6	85.7	1.7	0.2	0.3	0.7	([3])	1.0
SEX									
Male, all ages	12,110	33.8	41.2	10.8	1.3	1.7	5.5	0.4	3.4
Under 15 years old. . . .	1,240	44.1	0.8	37.4	(X)	2.5	5.2	0.2	7.9
15 to 44 years old	2,831	44.8	10.7	16.2	3.2	3.0	13.4	1.0	4.5
45 to 64 years old	3,138	54.9	18.2	10.2	1.6	2.4	5.9	0.4	4.2
65 years old and over. . .	4,901	11.3	83.8	1.4	0.2	0.5	0.8	([3])	1.1
Female, all ages	18,435	36.0	36.1	16.8	0.4	1.3	4.1	0.3	3.3
Under 15 years old. . . .	967	43.6	0.8	37.6	(X)	2.2	5.2	0.2	8.0
15 to 44 years old	7,495	51.4	3.3	29.1	0.4	2.0	6.3	0.4	4.6
45 to 64 years old	3,156	56.7	14.8	13.5	0.8	2.1	5.8	0.5	3.9
65 years old and over. . .	6,817	8.3	87.0	1.8	0.2	0.2	0.6	([3])	0.9
RACE									
White.	19,738	36.1	42.4	10.5	0.8	1.2	4.1	0.3	2.8
All other.	5,131	28.5	27.4	28.1	0.6	2.6	6.9	0.7	3.8
Not stated.	5,676	37.7	32.9	15.6	0.5	1.5	4.6	([3])	4.9
REGION									
Northeast	6,665	36.2	38.7	14.8	0.9	0.7	4.4	0.5	2.9
Midwest	7,107	38.0	40.0	10.7	0.6	1.3	4.6	([3])	3.8
South.	11,085	32.3	39.8	14.8	0.8	1.9	5.7	0.5	2.7
West	5,688	35.7	31.2	18.0	0.7	1.9	3.1	0.5	4.7

X Not applicable.   [1] Includes discharges for whom expected source of payment was unknown.   [2] Includes all other nonprofit source of payment such as church, welfare, or United Way.   [3] Figure does not meet standards of reliability or precision.

Source: U.S. National Center for Health Statistics, unpublished data.

No. 208. Procedures for Inpatients Discharged From Short-Stay Hospitals: 1980 to 1996

[**Rates per 1,000 population** based on Bureau of the Census estimated civilian population as of July 1. Excludes newborn infants and discharges from federal hospitals. Comparisons between data for 1980 and 1985 with data for 1990 and subsequent years should be made with caution as estimates of change may reflect improvements in the design rather than true changes in hospital use. See headnote, Table 205]

SEX AND TYPE OF PROCEDURE	1980	1985	1990	1992	1993	1994	1995	1996
Surgical procedures, total [1][2]	108.6	104.6	92.4	91.7	88.8	87.4	86.2	87.0
Cardiac catheterization	1.5	2.9	4.0	4.1	3.9	4.0	4.1	4.4
Removal of coronary artery obstruction [3]	(S)	0.3	1.2	1.6	1.6	1.7	1.7	2.5
Reduction of fracture [4]	2.7	2.9	2.4	2.5	2.6	2.2	2.2	2.3
Coronary artery bypass graft	0.6	1.0	1.6	1.8	1.9	1.9	2.2	2.3
Male, total [1][2]	78.1	76.8	70.6	70.2	67.1	66.5	65.9	67.2
Prostatectomy	3.1	3.2	3.0	2.9	2.5	2.1	1.9	1.6
Female, total [1][2]	137.1	130.6	113.0	112.0	109.3	107.1	105.3	105.9
Procedures to assist delivery [2]	20.5	20.4	19.4	18.7	18.4	18.1	17.0	16.0
Repair of current obstetric laceration	3.0	4.5	6.2	6.1	6.5	6.8	7.2	7.8
Cesarean section	5.3	7.2	7.4	7.1	7.0	6.5	5.8	6.2
Hysterectomy	5.6	5.5	4.6	4.4	4.3	4.2	4.3	4.4
Diagnostic and other nonsurgical procedures [2][5]	30.7	50.5	70.0	76.5	73.5	69.8	66.1	66.0
Angiocardiography and arteriography [6].	2.5	4.7	7.0	7.0	6.7	7.0	7.0	7.4
Respiratory therapy	(S)	0.3	4.7	4.7	3.4	4.5	4.3	4.1
CAT scan [7]	1.4	5.8	6.0	5.0	4.5	4.0	3.7	3.8
Male, total [2][4]	31.1	51.4	61.0	66.2	62.5	59.6	57.1	57.1
Angiocardiography and arteriography [6].	3.3	6.0	8.7	8.6	8.2	8.4	8.5	9.1
Respiratory therapy	(S)	0.3	4.9	4.7	3.4	4.6	4.5	4.3
CAT scan [7]	1.4	5.9	6.1	4.9	4.5	4.0	3.7	3.8
Female, total [2][5]	30.3	49.6	78.5	86.1	83.8	79.5	74.6	74.4
Manual assisted delivery	0.6	1.6	5.9	6.2	7.2	7.3	6.5	7.6
Fetal EKG and fetal monitoring.	1.1	2.2	10.8	9.5	8.7	8.3	7.0	6.6
Diagnostic ultrasound	1.7	6.2	7.3	6.7	6.4	5.8	5.1	5.0

S Figure does not meet standard of reliability or precision.   [1] Includes other types of surgical procedures not shown separately.   [2] Beginning in 1990, the definition of some surgical and diagnostic and other nonsurgical procedures was revised, causing a discontinuity in the trends for some totals.   [3] Beginning 1996 includes separately coded "insertion of stent".   [4] Excluding skull, face, and jaw.   [5] Includes other nonsurgical procedures not shown separately.   [6] Using contrast material.   [7] Computerized axial tomography.

Source: U.S. National Center for Health Statistics, Vital and Health Statistics, Series 13; and unpublished data.

No. 209. Organ Transplants and Grafts: 1985 to 1996

[As of end of year. Based on reports of procurement programs and transplant centers in the United States, except as noted]

PROCEDURE	NUMBER OF PROCEDURES							NUMBER OF CENTERS		Number of people waiting, 1996	1-year patient survival rates, 1996 (percent)
	1985	1990	1992	1993	1994	1995	1996	1990	1996		
Transplant: [1]											
Heart.	719	2,108	2,171	2,297	2,341	2,361	2,344	148	166	3,698	86.9
Liver	602	2,690	3,064	3,439	3,652	3,925	4,064	85	120	7,467	85.8
Kidney	7,695	9,877	10,231	11,020	11,392	11,891	12,080	232	253	34,550	98.0
Heart-lung	30	52	48	60	70	70	39	79	99	237	(NA)
Lung	2	203	535	667	723	871	811	70	93	2,309	74.1
Pancreas/Islet cell	130	528	557	774	842	1,027	1,022	84	121	323	95.0
Cornea grafts [2] . . .	26,300	40,631	42,337	40,215	43,743	44,652	46,300	[3]107	[3]110	2,013	(NA)
Bone grafts	(NA)	350,000	350,000	(NA)	(NA)	450,000	475,000	30	(NA)	(NA)	(NA)
Skin grafts [4]	(NA)	5,500	5,500	(NA)	(NA)	5,500	9,000	25	(NA)	(NA)	(NA)

NA Not available.   [1] Simultaneous kidney-pancreas transplants are counted twice, both in kidney transplants and in pancreas transplants. Double kidney, double lung, and heart-lung transplants are counted as one transplant.   [2] 1985 through 1992, number of procedures and eye banks include Canada.   [3] Eye banks.   [4] Procedure data are shown in terms of square feet.

Source: Transplants: through 1992, U.S. Department of Health and Human Services, Public Health Service, Division of Organ Transplantation; beginning 1993, United Network for Organ Sharing, Richmond, VA; American Association of Tissue Banks, McLean, VA; and Eye Bank Association of America, Washington, DC; and unpublished data.

No. 210. Visits to Hospital Outpatient and Emergency Departments: 1995 and 1996

[In thousands. An outpatient department is a hospital facility where nonurgent ambulatory care is provided under the supervision of a physician. Data for outpatient departments exclude clinics where only ancillary services, such as radiology, are provided. An emergency department is a hospital facility staffed by physicians for the provision of outpatient services to patients whose conditions require immediate attention and is staffed 24 hours a day. Data are for nonfederal short stay and general hospitals. Based on the National Hospital Ambulatory Care Surveys and subject to sampling error; see source for details]

CHARACTERISTIC	OUTPATIENT DEPARTMENT		EMERGENCY DEPARTMENT		CHARACTERISTIC	OUTPATIENT DEPARTMENT		EMERGENCY DEPARTMENT	
	1995	1996	1995	1996		1995	1996	1995	1996
All visits	67,232	67,186	96,545	90,347	New problem	10,436	10,473	(NA)	(NA)
Age:					New patient	12,491	11,833	(NA)	(NA)
Under 15 years old.	15,039	15,196	22,709	20,872	Expected source of payment: [2]				
15 to 24 years old	8,307	8,310	15,681	14,366	Insurance [3]	53,921	53,273	75,890	70,514
25 to 44 years old	18,588	18,547	30,086	28,036	Blue Cross/Blue Shield.	8,269	8,471	10,987	10,084
45 to 64 years old	14,811	14,911	13,978	13,745	Other private insurance	14,489	13,565	25,056	24,314
65 to 74 years old	6,004	5,799	6,057	5,945	Medicare.	10,876	10,890	14,949	14,462
75 years old and over. . .	4,482	4,422	8,033	7,382	Medicaid.	19,333	20,640	22,041	19,884
Sex:					Worker's compensation	834	729	3,776	3,058
Male	26,221	25,888	46,501	42,473	Other source of insurance	4,594	3,497	4,544	4,254
Female	41,011	41,298	50,044	47,873	Unknown source of insurance	2,002	2,851	3,474	2,978
Race:					Self pay	7,113	6,622	16,113	15,188
White.	50,110	46,644	74,593	68,702	No charge	990	1,898	519	1,097
Black	15,022	18,377	19,284	19,604	Other.	2,930	3,085	2,471	1,874
Asian/Pacific Islander . . .	1,926	1,993	1,963	1,639	Unknown source of payment	2,278	2,307	1,552	1,674
American Indian/Eskimo/Aleut	[1]174	171	705	401					
Visit status:									
Old patient	54,741	55,353	(NA)	(NA)					
Old problem	44,305	44,879	(NA)	(NA)					

NA Not available.   [1] Figure does not meet standard of reliability or precision.   [2] More than one reported source of payment may be reported.   [3] Equal to all visits minus self pay, no charge, other source, and no answer.

Source: U.S. National Center for Health Statistics, Advance Data Nos. 293 and 294, December 17, 1997 and prior issues.

No. 211. Skilled Nursing Facilities: 1980 to 1996

[Covers facilities and beds certified for participation under medicare as of midyear. Includes facilities which have transfer agreements with one or more participating hospitals, and are engaged primarily in providing skilled nursing care and related services for the rehabilitation of injured, disabled, or sick persons]

ITEM	Unit	1980	1990	1992	1993	1994	1995	1996
Skilled nursing facilities	Number .	5,155	9,008	10,910	11,472	12,584	13,281	14,177
Beds	1,000. . .	448	512	606	623	649	657	672
Per 1,000 medicare enrollees [1] .	Rate . . .	16.0	15.2	17.2	17.3	17.8	17.7	17.8

[1] Based on total number of beneficiaries enrolled in the medicare hospital insurance program as of July 1 of year stated.

Source: U.S. Health Care Financing Administration, Medicare Participating Providers and Suppliers of Health Services, 1980; and unpublished data.

No. 212. Ambulatory Surgery Visits and Procedures, by Type of Facility: 1994 and 1995

[Excludes ambulatory surgery patients admitted to hospitals as inpatients. Hospital data cover only nonfederal short-stay and general hospitals. Freestanding facilities specializing in dentistry, podiatry, pain block, abortion, family planning, or birthing are excluded. Based on data collected from the National Survey of Ambulatory Surgery; for details, see source]

UTILIZATION MEASURE	ALL FACILITIES		HOSPITALS		FREESTANDING CENTERS	
	1994	1995	1994	1995	1994	1995
Number of visits (1,000).	18,850	19,638	15,973	16,413	2,877	3,225
Rate per 1,000 population [1]	72.8	75.1	61.7	62.8	11.1	12.3
Number of procedures (1,000)	28,278	29,433	23,969	24,562	4,309	4,871
Rate per 1,000 population [1]	109.2	112.6	92.6	94.0	16.6	18.6

[1] Based on Bureau of the Census estimated civilian population, including institutionalized persons, as of July 1.

Source: U.S. National Center for Health Statistics, *Advance Data*, Nos. 283 and 296, March 14, 1997, and December 24, 1997.

No. 213. Ambulatory Surgery Procedures, by Sex and Age: 1996

[In thousands. Covers procedures done on an ambulatory (outpatient) basis in hospitals and freestanding ambulatory surgery centers. Excluded specialties include dentistry, podiatry, abortion, family planning, birthing, pain block, and small procedures. Based on sample data collected from the National Survey of Ambulatory Surgery, a sample survey of medical records in hospitals and free- standing ambulatory surgery centers; subject to sampling variability]

TYPE OF PROCEDURE	Total	SEX		AGE			
		Male	Female	Under 15 years	15-44 years	45-64 years	65 years and over
Total [1]	**31,507**	**13,882**	**17,625**	**2,381**	**9,561**	**8,825**	**10,740**
Injection of agent into spinal canal.	534	224	310	(B)	166	199	169
Release of carpal tunnel	358	120	238	(B)	132	142	84
Extraction of lens	2,367	881	1,486	(B)	46	331	1,977
Insertion of prosthetic lens (pseudophakos). .	1,816	696	1,120	(B)	36	270	1,501
Myringotomy with insertion of tube.	524	313	211	490	16	(B)	(B)
Operations on nasal sinuses.	463	229	234	33	223	163	43
Tonsillectomy with or without adenoidectomy .	383	164	219	263	109	(B)	(B)
Cardiac catheterization	472	298	175	(B)	47	206	213
Endoscopy of small intestine [2]	1,563	668	895	28	419	502	614
Endoscopy of large intestine [2]	1,913	855	1,058	15	380	696	822
Endoscopic polypectomy of large intestine . .	555	317	238	(B)	59	201	291
Repair of inguinal hernia	531	477	54	75	165	146	146
Laparoscopy	422	55	367	(B)	334	63	18
Cystoscopy with or without biopsy	703	422	281	26	137	205	336
Bilateral destruction or occlusion of fallopian tubes	320	(X)	320	-	314	(B)	(B)
Dilation and curettage of uterus.	530	(X)	530	(B)	318	160	51
Arthroscopy of knee	629	357	272	9	325	212	83
Excision of semilunar cartilage of knee.	455	275	180	(B)	198	178	76
Operations on muscle, tendon, fascia, and bursa	664	320	345	28	260	254	123
Local excision of lesion of breast (lumpectomy)	341	12	329	(B)	127	130	81
Excision or destruction of lesion or tissue of skin and subcutaneous tissue	877	412	465	71	330	258	217
Arteriography and angiocardiography using contrast material.	791	476	316	(B)	66	319	404
Injection or infusion of therapeutic or prophylactic substance.	464	203	260	(B)	135	165	155

- Represents zero.   B Figure too small to meet statistical standard for reliability.   X Not applicable.   [1] Includes other procedures not shown separately.   [2] With or without biopsy.

Source: U.S. National Center for Health Statistics, *Advance Data*, No. 300, August 12, 1998.

No. 214. Home Health and Hospice Care Agencies, by Selected Characteristics: 1996

[In percent, except as indicated. Based on the National Home and Hospice Care Survey. Home health care is provided to individuals and families in their place of residence. Hospice care is available in both the home and inpatient settings. Agencies which provide both types of care are classified according to how the majority of their patients are cared for. See source for details. For composition of regions, see map, inside front cover]

AGENCY CHARACTERISTIC	Agencies, total	CURRENT PATIENTS [1]			DISCHARGES [2]		
		Total	Home health care	Hospice care	Total	Home health care	Hospice care
Total (1,000)................	13.5	2,486.8	2,427.5	59.4	8,168.9	7,775.7	393.2
PERCENT DISTRIBUTION							
Ownership:							
Proprietary...............	54.3	40.9	41.6	11.0	31.1	32.0	13.3
Voluntary nonprofit	34.3	49.9	49.0	84.0	61.5	60.3	85.2
Government and other...........	11.4	9.2	9.3	4.4	7.4	7.7	1.5
Certification:							
Medicare................	88.2	92.5	92.4	96.8	95.3	95.3	95.3
Medicaid	86.0	93.6	93.6	93.8	95.7	95.8	94.3
Region:							
Northeast................	15.0	26.2	26.5	15.0	29.7	30.2	18.2
Midwest.................	27.0	26.9	26.6	35.9	21.1	20.9	25.2
South	40.1	32.6	32.6	32.0	24.9	24.2	38.5
West	18.0	14.3	14.2	17.1	24.4	24.7	18.1

[1] Patients on the rolls of the agency as of midnight the day prior to the survey. [2] Patients removed from the rolls of the agency during the 12 months prior to the day of the survey. A patient could be included more than once if the individual had more than one episode of care during the year.

Source: U.S. National Center for Health Statistics, *Advance Data*, No. 297, April 16, 1998.

No. 215. Home Health and Hospice Care Patients, by Selected Characteristics: 1996

[See headnote, Table 214]

ITEM	CURRENT PATIENTS [1]			DISCHARGES [2]		
	Total	Home health care	Hospice care	Total	Home health care	Hospice care
Total (1,000)...................	2,486.8	2,427.5	59.4	8,168.9	7,775.7	393.2
PERCENT DISTRIBUTION						
Age: [3]						
Under 45 years old	14.1	14.3	7.3	19.0	19.5	8.1
45-54 years old....................	5.3	5.4	4.5	6.0	5.9	7.9
55-64 years old...................	7.8	7.7	10.3	8.7	8.4	14.8
65 years old and over	72.4	72.2	77.7	66.1	66.1	67.5
65-69 years old	8.8	8.8	8.4	10.7	10.8	8.7
70-74 years old	13.0	12.9	16.2	13.3	13.2	15.6
75-79 years old	17.1	17.1	16.6	12.5	12.4	14.5
80-84 years old	16.6	16.7	15.2	14.1	14.2	12.3
85 years old and over..............	16.8	16.7	21.3	15.5	15.4	16.4
Sex:						
Male	33.2	32.9	44.9	37.2	36.5	50.3
Female	66.8	67.1	55.1	62.8	63.5	49.7
Race:						
White	65.5	65.1	83.7	63.5	62.8	78.9
Black	12.0	12.0	8.3	7.6	7.4	11.2
Other or unknown	22.5	22.9	8.0	28.9	29.8	9.9
Marital status: [4]						
Married	29.3	29.0	43.7	37.5	37.0	48.4
Widowed	35.3	35.3	32.2	24.8	24.6	29.4
Divorced or separated	4.2	4.1	9.3	5.0	5.0	6.5
Never married.	18.5	18.7	8.5	18.0	18.4	9.3
Unknown	12.7	12.8	[5]6.3	14.6	15.0	6.4
Primary admission diagnosis:						
Neoplasms.	6.5	5.2	59.6	11.6	8.6	70.6
Endocrine, nutritional and metabolic and immunity disorders.	9.9	10.2	[5]	5.6	5.8	[5]
Diseases of the nervous system and sense organs	5.8	5.7	8.1	3.3	3.2	3.2
Diseases of the circulatory system	25.1	25.4	12.3	21.8	22.4	9.6
Diseases of the musculoskeletal system and connective tissue	8.5	8.7	[5]	7.7	8.1	[5]
Injuries and poisoning	6.7	6.9	[5]	11.9	12.5	[5]

[1] Patients on the rolls of the agency as of midnight the day prior to the survey. [2] Patients removed from the rolls of the agency during the 12 months prior to the day of the survey. A patient could be included more than once if the individual had more than one episode of care during the year. [3] Excludes unknown. [4] For current patients, marital status at admission; for discharged patients, status at time of discharge. [5] Figure does not meet standard of reliability or precision.

Source: U.S. National Center for Health Statistics, *Advance Data*, No. 297, April 16, 1998.

No. 216. Elderly Home Health Patients: 1996

[Covers the civilian population 65 years old and over who are home health care patients. Home health care is provided to individuals and families in their place of residence. Based on the 1996 National Home and Hospice Care Survey]

ITEM	CURRENT PATIENTS [1]		DIS-CHARGES [2]		ITEM	CURRENT PATIENTS [1]		DIS-CHARGES [2]	
	Number (1,000)	Per-cent	Number (1,000)	Per-cent		Number (1,000)	Per-cent	Number (1,000)	Per-cent
Total 65 yrs. old & over	**1,753**	**100.0**	**5,138**	**100.0**	Own income	36	2.0	18	0.3
Received help with—					Medicare	1,396	79.6	3,612	66.7
Bathing or showering	933	53.2	1,896	36.9	Medicaid	123	7.0	693	12.8
Dressing	804	45.8	1,707	33.2					
Eating	162	9.2	347	6.7	Services rendered last billing period:				
Transferring in/out of a bed or chair	519	29.6	1,296	25.2	Nursing services	1,476	84.2	4,505	87.7
Using the toilet	396	22.6	963	18.7	Social services	186	10.6	633	12.3
Doing light housework	682	38.9	1,216	23.7	Counseling	40	2.3	830	1.6
Managing money	49	2.8	29	0.6	Medications	171	9.8	368	7.2
Shopping for groceries or clothes	247	14.1	475	9.2	Physical therapy	348	19.8	1,524	29.7
Using the telephone	47	2.7	76	1.5	Homemaker-household services	493	28.1	967	18.8
Preparing meals	404	23.0	639	12.4	Nutrition services	58	3.3	99	1.9
Taking medications	410	23.4	855	16.6	Physician services	64	3.7	110	2.1
Primary source of payment of last billing:					Occupational therapy	86	4.9	286	5.6
Private insurance	64	3.7	724	13.4	Speech therapy/audiology	27	1.6	86	1.7

[1] Patients on the rolls of the agency as of midnight the day prior to the survey.   [2] Patients removed from the rolls of the agency during the 12 months prior to the day of the survey. A patient could be included more than once if the individual had more than one episode of care during the year.

Source: U.S. National Center for Health Statistics, unpublished data.

No. 217. Nursing Homes—Selected Characteristics: 1985 and 1995

[Covers nursing and related care homes in the conterminous United States that had three or more beds, were staffed for use by residents, and routinely provided nursing and personal care services. Excludes places providing only room and board and places serving specific health problems. Based on the 1995 National Nursing Home Survey, a two-stage survey sample of nursing homes and their residents. Subject to sampling variability. For composition of regions, see map, inside front cover]

CHARACTERISTIC	Nursing homes	BEDS		CURRENT RESIDENTS		FULL-TIME EQUIVALENT EMPLOYMENT			
						Administrative, medical, and therapeutic		Nursing	
		Number (1,000)	Per nursing home	Number (1,000)	Occu-pancy rate [1]	Number (1,000)	Rate per 100 beds	Number (1,000)	Rate per 100 beds
1985	19,100	1,624	85	1,491	91.8	(NA)	(NA)	(NA)	(NA)
1995, total	**16,700**	**1,771**	**106**	**1,549**	**87.4**	**20.1**	**1.1**	**914**	**51.6**
OWNERSHIP									
Proprietary	11,000	1,152	105	990	85.9	13.6	1.2	574	49.8
Voluntary nonprofit	4,300	468	109	421	89.9	4.9	1.0	254	54.3
Government and other	1,400	151	108	138	91.5	1.6	1.1	85	56.3
CERTIFICATION									
Medicare and medicaid certified	11,600	1,378	118	1,214	88.0	15.0	1.1	728	52.8
Medicare only	[2]1,000	60	60	50	83.9	1.9	3.2	36	60.0
Medicaid only	3,400	280	82	241	85.8	2.8	1.0	128	45.5
Not certified	[2]700	53	75	44	84.2	0.4	0.8	22	42.4
BED SIZE									
Less than 50 beds	2,800	87	31	71	81.4	4.7	5.4	50	56.8
50-99 beds	5,900	430	73	378	87.9	5.2	1.2	221	51.4
100-199 beds	6,700	903	135	794	88.0	8.4	0.9	469	51.9
200 beds or more	1,300	351	270	305	86.9	1.8	0.5	174	49.6
REGION									
Northeast	2,900	379	131	347	91.5	4.2	1.1	215	56.6
Midwest	5,600	564	101	495	87.7	4.8	0.9	264	46.8
South	5,500	573	104	495	86.4	6.3	1.1	300	52.3
West	2,800	255	91	212	83.2	4.8	1.9	135	52.9
AFFILIATION [3]									
Chain	9,100	978	108	857	87.7	(NA)	(NA)	(NA)	(NA)
Independent	7,600	788	91	689	87.4	(NA)	(NA)	(NA)	(NA)

NA Not available.   [1] Number of residents divided by number of available beds multiplied by 100.   [2] Figure does not meet standards of reliability or precision.   [3] Excludes a small number of homes, beds, and residents with unknown affiliation.

Source: U.S. National Center for Health Statistics, *Advance Data*, No. 280, January 23, 1997.

No. 218. Nursing Home Residents 65 Years Old and Over, by Selected Characteristics: 1995

[Covers nursing and related care homes in the conterminous United States that had three or more beds, were staffed for use by residents, and routinely provided nursing and personal care services. Excludes places providing only room and board and places serving specific health problems. Based on the 1995 National Nursing Home Survey, a two-stage survey sample of nursing homes and their residents. Subject to sampling variability]

CHARACTERISTIC [1]	Number (1,000)	Percent distri- bution	ITEM	Percent of elderly resi- dents	FUNCTIONAL STATUS	Percent of elderly residents receiving assis- tance
Total [2]	1,385	100.0	Type of aids used:		ADLs: [9]	
			Wheelchair	64.5	Bathing, showering. . .	96.3
Male.	343	24.7	Walker.	24.9	Dressing.	86.6
Female	1,043	75.3	Hospital bed	78.4	Eating	45.1
					Transferring in or	
65 to 74 years	242	17.5	Vision impaired.	26.4	out of beds or chair .	23.8
75 to 84 years	586	42.3	Hearing impaired.	22.4	Using toilet room	57.8
85 years and over.	557	40.2				
			Type of nursing care:		IADLs: [10]	
White	1,240	89.5	Skilled care [3]	46.1	Care of personal	
Black	118	8.5	Intermediate care [4]. . .	50.4	possessions	77.6
			Residential care [5] . . .	3.5	Managing money	69.2
Hispanic	32	2.3			Securing personal . . .	
Non-Hispanic.	1,276	92.1	Primary source of		items	76.8
			payment: [6]		Using telephone	69.2
Living quarters:			Private sources [7]	28.9		
Private residence	510	36.8	Medicare	12.7		
Retirement home.	31	2.2	Medicaid	55.7		
Board and care and/or			Other [8]	2.7		
residential facility	69	4.9				
Nursing home.	160	11.6				
Hospital.	562	40.6				
Mental health facility	15	1.1				

[1] At time of admission.   [2] Includes other and/or unknown, not shown separately.   [3] Skilled care indicates the greatest degree of medical care. Every patient is under the supervision of a physician and the facility has a transfer agreement with a nearby hospital. Twenty-four hour nursing care is provided with a physician on call to furnish medical care in case of emergency. [4] Intermediate care is provided to individuals who do not require the degree of care or treatment normally given by a hospital or skilled nursing facility, but who do require health-related institutionalized care above the level of room and board.   [5] Residential care usually means providing residents with room, board, laundry services, some forms of personal care, and recreational activities and social services.   [6] In month before interview.   [7] Includes private insurance, own income, family support, social security benefits, and retirement funds.   [8] Includes supplemental security income, welfare, religious organizations, foundations, agencies, Veterans Administration contract, pensions, or other compensation, payment source not yet determined, and other and unknown sources.   [9] Activities of daily living.   [10] Instrumental activities of daily living.

Source: U.S. National Center for Health Statistics, *Advance Data*, No. 289, July 2, 1997.

No. 219. Mental Health Facilities—Summary, by Type of Facility: 1994

[Facilities, beds and inpatients as of year-end; other data are for calendar year or fiscal year ending in a month other than December since facilities are permitted to report on either a calendar or fiscal year basis. Excludes private psychiatric office practice and psychiatric service modes of all types in hospitals or outpatient clinics of federal agencies other than U.S. Dept. of Veterans Affairs. Excludes data from Puerto Rico, Virgin Islands, Guam, and other territories]

TYPE OF FACILITY	Num- ber of facili- ties	INPATIENT BEDS		INPATIENTS		Average daily inpatients (1,000)	Inpatient care epi- sodes [2] (1,000)	EXPENDI- TURES		Patient care staff [4] (1,000)
		Total (1,000)	Rate [1]	Total (1,000)	Rate [1]			Total (mil. dol.)	Per capita [3] (dol.)	
Total	5,392	248.4	97.0	190.8	73.5	190.5	2,388	33,135	128.0	370.9
Mental hospitals:										
State and county	256	79.3	30.6	70.0	26.9	69.5	308	7,824	30.2	100.2
Private [5]	889	69.0	27.8	50.1	19.4	48.8	568	8,829	34.1	72.4
General hospitals [6]	1,612	53.0	20.5	35.8	13.8	37.1	1,102	5,344	20.6	74.3
Veterans Administration [7] . .	161	21.1	8.2	15.4	5.9	15.2	186	1,386	5.4	21.6
Other [8][9]	2,474	26.0	9.9	19.5	7.5	19.9	224	9,752	37.7	102.4

[1] Rate per 100,000 population. Based on Bureau of the Census estimated civilian population as of July 1.   [2] "Inpatient care episodes" is defined as the number of residents in inpatient facilities at the beginning of the year plus the total additions to inpatient facilities during the year.   [3] Based on Bureau of the Census estimated civilian population as of July 1.   [4] Full-time equivalent. [5] Includes residential treatment centers for emotionally disturbed children.   [6] Nonfederal hospitals with separate psychiatric services.   [7] Includes U.S. Department of Veterans Affairs (VA) neuropsychiatric hospitals, VA general hospitals with separate psychiatric settings and VA freestanding psychiatric outpatient clinics.   [8] Includes free-standing psychiatric outpatient facilities that provide only psychiatric outpatient services.   [9] Includes other multiservice mental health facilities with two or more settings, which are not elsewhere classified, as well as freestanding partial care facilities which only provide psychiatric partial care services. Number of facilities, expenditures, and staff data also include freestanding psychiatric partial care facilities.

Source: U.S. Substance Abuse and Mental Health Services Administration, Center for Mental Health Services, unpublished data.

No. 220. Days of Disability, by Type and Selected Characteristics: 1980 to 1995

[Covers civilian noninstitutional population. Beginning 1985, the levels of estimates may not be comparable to estimates for 1980 because the later data are based on a revised questionnaire and field procedures; for further information, see source. Based on National Health Interview Survey; see Appendix III. For composition of regions, see map, inside front cover]

ITEM	TOTAL DAYS OF DISABILITY (millions)						DAYS PER PERSON					
	1980	1985	1990	1993	1994	1995	1980	1985	1990	1993	1994	1995
Restricted-activity days [1] . . .	4,165	3,453	3,669	4,346	4,143	4,097	19.1	14.8	14.9	17.1	16.0	15.6
Male	1,802	1,442	1,558	1,844	1,723	1,748	17.1	12.8	13.1	14.9	13.6	13.7
Female	2,363	2,011	2,111	2,502	2,420	2,349	21.0	16.6	16.7	19.2	18.2	17.5
White	3,518	2,899	3,057	3,598	3,375	3,392	18.7	14.5	14.8	17.0	15.7	15.6
Black	580	489	536	616	608	558	22.7	17.4	17.7	19.2	18.4	17.0
Under 65 years	3,228	2,557	2,734	3,289	3,070	3,091	16.6	12.4	12.6	14.7	13.4	13.4
65 years and over	937	895	936	1,057	1,073	1,006	39.2	33.1	31.4	33.8	34.6	32.0
Northeast	862	689	656	798	803	754	17.9	13.8	13.2	15.9	15.9	14.7
Midwest	989	744	836	978	879	865	17.2	12.7	14.0	15.8	13.9	13.9
South	1,415	1,308	1,404	1,564	1,443	1,561	19.8	16.3	16.7	18.3	16.4	16.9
West	899	712	773	1,006	1,017	917	22.0	15.7	14.8	17.7	17.6	16.4
Family income:												
Under $10,000	(NA)	893	662	741	681	649	(NA)	25.8	27.3	30.2	29.1	30.0
$10,000 to $19,999	(NA)	781	758	857	801	794	(NA)	16.7	19.1	22.3	21.5	21.0
$20,000 to $34,999	(NA)	791	715	849	825	824	(NA)	12.1	13.5	15.7	15.2	15.1
$35,000 or more	(NA)	568	912	1,086	1,051	1,133	(NA)	9.9	10.3	11.2	10.5	10.6
Bed-disability days [2]	1,520	1,436	1,521	1,708	1,603	1,593	7.0	6.1	6.2	6.7	6.2	6.1
Male	616	583	625	688	623	678	5.9	5.2	5.2	5.6	4.9	5.3
Female	904	852	896	1,020	980	915	8.0	7.1	7.1	7.8	7.4	6.8
Under 65 years	1,190	1,064	1,115	1,286	1,155	1,181	6.1	5.1	5.2	5.8	5.1	5.1
65 years and over	330	371	406	422	448	412	13.8	13.7	13.6	13.5	14.4	13.1
Work-loss days [3]	485	575	621	666	642	657	5.0	5.3	5.3	5.6	5.2	5.3
Male	271	287	303	315	311	307	4.9	4.8	4.7	4.8	4.6	4.5
Female	215	288	319	351	332	349	5.1	6.0	5.9	6.4	5.9	6.1
School-loss days [4]	204	217	212	250	225	229	5.3	4.8	4.6	5.3	4.5	4.5
Male	95	100	100	121	104	107	4.8	4.4	4.3	5.0	4.1	4.2
Female	109	117	112	129	121	122	5.7	5.3	5.0	5.5	5.0	4.9

NA Not available.   [1] A day when a person cuts down on his activities for more than half a day because of illness or injury. Includes bed-disability, work-loss, and school-loss days. Total includes other races and unknown income, not shown separately. [2] A day when a person stayed in bed more than half a day because of illness or injury. Includes those work-loss and school-loss days actually spent in bed.   [3] A day when a person lost more than half a workday because of illness or injury. Computed for persons 17 years of age and over (beginning 1985, 18 years of age and over) in the currently employed population, defined as those who were working or had a job or business from which they were not on layoff during the 2-week period preceding the week of interview.   [4] Child's loss of more than half a school day because of illness or injury. Computed for children 6-16 years of age. Beginning 1985, children 5-17 years old.

Source: U.S. National Center for Health Statistics, *Vital and Health Statistics,* Series 10, No. 193, and earlier reports; and unpublished data.

No. 221. Injuries, by Sex, Age and Type: 1980 to 1995

[Covers civilian noninstitutional population and comprises incidents leading to restricted activity and/or medical attention. Beginning 1985, data not strictly comparable with other years. See headnote, Table 220. Based on National Health Interview Survey; see Appendix III]

YEAR	INJURIES (mil.)			RATE PER 100 POPULATION		
	Total	Male	Female	Total	Male	Female
1980	68.1	39.0	29.1	31.2	37.1	25.8
1985	62.6	34.6	28.0	26.8	30.6	23.1
1990	60.1	33.6	26.6	24.4	28.1	21.0
1993	62.1	33.4	28.7	24.4	27.0	22.0
1994	61.9	32.6	29.2	23.8	25.8	22.0
1995, total	**64.6**	**34.7**	**29.9**	**24.7**	**27.2**	**22.3**
Under 5 years	5.5	3.3	2.2	27.0	31.7	22.0
5 to 17 years	15.2	9.4	5.8	30.2	36.4	23.7
18 to 44 years	25.7	14.3	11.4	23.8	26.9	20.8
45 years and over	18.2	7.7	10.5	21.9	20.2	23.3
Fractures [1]	8.2	4.9	3.3	3.1	3.8	2.5
Sprains and strains	13.0	6.5	6.5	4.9	5.1	4.8
Open wounds and lacerations	12.4	7.3	5.1	4.7	5.7	3.8
Contusions [2]	12.3	6.7	5.6	4.7	5.2	4.2
Other	18.7	9.3	9.4	7.2	7.3	7.0

[1] Includes dislocations.   [2] Includes superficial injuries.

Source: U.S. National Center for Health Statistics, *Vital and Health Statistics,* Series 10, No. 190, and earlier reports; and unpublished data.

No. 222. Injuries Associated With Consumer Products: 1995

[For products associated with more than 20,000 injuries in 1995. Estimates calculated from a representative sample of hospitals with emergency treatment departments in the United States. Data are estimates of the number of emergency room treated cases nationwide associated with various products. Product involvement does not necessarily mean the product caused the accident. Products were selected from the U.S. Consumer Product Safety Commission's National Electronic Injury Surveillance System]

PRODUCT	1995	PRODUCT	1995
Home workshop equipment:		Fences or fence posts	112,886
Saws (hand or power)	87,397	House repair and construction materials	75,301
Hammers	43,157	Glass doors	44,916
Household packaging and containers:		Door sills or frames	41,287
Household containers and packaging	185,725	Handrails, railings, or banisters	38,852
Bottles and jars	87,760	General household appliances:	
Bags	20,473	Ranges	32,017
Housewares:		Refrigerators	26,731
Knives	455,657	Heating, cooling equipment: [3]	
Drinking glasses	126,030	Pipes (excl. smoking pipes)	29,683
Tableware and flatware	105,995	Home entertainment equipment:	
Scissors	32,026	Televisions	36,959
Cookware, bowls, and canisters	31,514	Sound recording equipment [4]	20,209
Waste containers, trash baskets, etc.	28,437	Personal use items:	
Home furnishing: [1]		Jewelry	50,937
Beds	395,623	Razors and shavers	36,327
Tables	321,828	Hair grooming equipment and	
Chairs	276,745	accessories	26,207
Mirrors, mirror glass	224,551	Coins	24,787
Bathtubs and showers	156,749	Yard and garden equipment:	
Ladders	138,894	Lawn mowers	74,582
Carpets, rugs	125,267	Pruning, trimming, and edging equipment	36,091
Sofas, couches, davenports, etc.	115,037	Chain saws	31,356
Other furniture	59,112	Other unpowered garden tools	22,645
Toilets	43,687	Sports and recreation equipment:	
Misc. decorating items	26,382	Bicycles	586,808
Benches	24,726	Swings or swing sets	83,748
Electric lighting equipment	22,905	Swimming pools	78,336
Home structures, construction: [2]		Playground climbing equipment	76,744
Floors or flooring materials	1,012,282	Trampolines	66,174
Stairs or steps	978,911	All-terrain vehicles	62,400
Other doors (excl. garage)	323,671	Sleds	51,557
Ceilings and walls	239,654	Slides or sliding boards	47,832
Household cabinets, racks, and shelves	217,183	Skateboards	30,353
Nails, screws, tacks, or bolts	198,849	Minibikes or trail bikes	28,994
Windows	148,906	BBs or pellets	20,422
Porches, balconies, open-side floors	124,539		

[1] Includes accessories.　[2] Includes materials.　[3] Includes ventilating equipment.　[4] Includes reproducing equipment.

Source: National Safety Council, Itasca, IL, *Accident Facts*, 1997 Edition (copyright).

No. 223. Costs of Unintentional Injuries: 1996

[Covers costs of deaths or disabling injuries together with vehicle accidents and fires]

COST	AMOUNT (bil. dol.)					PERCENT DISTRIBUTION				
	Total [1]	Motor vehicle	Work	Home	Other	Total [1]	Motor vehicle	Work	Home	Other
Total	**444.1**	**176.1**	**121.0**	**95.7**	**65.3**	**100.0**	**100.0**	**100.0**	**100.0**	**100.0**
Wage and productivity losses [2]	224.7	63.8	60.2	60.1	43.9	50.6	36.2	49.8	62.8	67.2
Medical expense	74.6	21.2	19.0	22.4	13.1	16.8	12.0	15.7	23.4	20.1
Administrative expenses [3]	76.3	50.0	25.6	4.6	3.8	17.2	28.4	21.2	4.8	5.8
Motor vehicle damage	39.5	39.5	1.6	(NA)	(NA)	8.9	22.4	1.3	(NA)	(NA)
Employer cost [4]	19.8	1.6	11.3	4.0	3.2	4.5	0.9	9.3	4.2	4.9
Fire loss	9.2	(NA)	3.3	4.6	1.3	2.1	(NA)	2.7	4.8	2.0

NA Not available.　[1] Excludes duplication between work and motor vehicle ($13.9 billion in 1996).　[2] Actual loss of wages and household production, and the present value of future earnings lost.　[3] Includes the administrative cost of public and private insurance, and police and legal costs.　[4] Estimate of the uninsured costs incurred by employers, representing the money value of time lost by noninjured workers.

Source: National Safety Council, Itasca, IL, *Accident Facts*, 1997 Edition (copyright).

No. 224. Specified Reportable Diseases—Cases Reported: 1980 to 1996

[Figures should be interpreted with caution. Although reporting of some of these diseases is incomplete, the figures are of value in indicating trends of disease incidence. Includes cases imported from outside the United States]

DISEASE	1980	1985	1990	1991	1992	1993	1994	1995	1996
AIDS [1]	(NA)	8,249	41,595	43,672	45,472	103,533	78,279	71,547	66,885
Amebiasis	5,271	4,433	3,328	2,989	2,942	2,970	2,983	(2)	(2)
Aseptic meningitis	8,028	10,619	11,852	14,526	12,223	12,848	8,932	(2)	(2)
Botulism [3]	89	122	92	114	91	97	143	97	119
Brucellosis (undulant fever)	183	153	85	104	105	120	119	98	112
Chickenpox [4] (1,000)	190.9	178.2	173.1	147.1	158.4	134.7	151.2	120.6	83.5
Diphtheria	3	3	4	5	4	-	-	2	2
Encephalitis:									
Primary infectious	1,362	1,376	1,341	1,021	774	919	717	(2)	(2)
Post infectious	40	161	105	82	129	170	143	(2)	(2)
Escherichia coli 0157:H7	(2)	(2)	(2)	(2)	(2)	(2)	1,420	2,139	2,741
Haemophilius influenza	(2)	(2)	(2)	2,764	1,412	1,419	1,174	1,180	1,170
Hepatitis: B (serum) (1,000)	19.0	26.6	21.1	18.0	16.1	13.4	12.5	10.8	10.6
A (infectious) (1,000)	29.1	23.2	31.4	24.4	23.1	24.2	29.8	31.6	31.0
Unspecified (1,000)	11.9	5.5	1.7	1.3	0.9	0.6	0.4	(2)	(2)
C/Non-A, non-B (1,000) [5]	(2)	4.2	2.6	3.6	6.0	4.8	4.4	4.6	3.7
Legionellosis	(2)	830	1,370	1,317	1,339	1,280	1,615	1,241	1,198
Leprosy (Hansen disease)	223	361	198	154	172	187	136	144	112
Leptospirosis	85	57	77	58	54	51	38	(2)	(2)
Lyme disease	(2)	(2)	(2)	9,465	9,895	8,257	13,043	11,700	16,455
Malaria	2,062	1,049	1,292	1,278	1,087	1,411	1,229	1,419	1,800
Measles (1,000)	13.5	2.8	27.8	9.6	2.2	0.3	1.0	0.3	0.5
Meningococcal infections	2,840	2,479	2,451	2,130	2,134	2,637	2,886	3,243	3,437
Mumps (1,000)	8.6	3.0	5.3	4.3	2.6	1.7	1.5	0.9	0.8
Pertussis [6] (1,000)	1.7	3.6	4.6	2.7	4.1	6.6	4.6	5.1	7.8
Plague	18	17	2	11	13	10	17	9	5
Poliomyelitis, acute [7]	9	7	6	10	6	4	8	6	5
Psittacosis	124	119	113	94	92	60	38	64	42
Rabies, animal	6,421	5,565	4,826	6,910	8,589	9,377	8,147	7,811	6,982
Rabies, human	-	1	1	3	1	3	6	5	3
Rheumatic fever, acute [8]	432	90	108	127	75	112	112	(2)	(2)
Rubella [9] (1,000)	3.9	0.6	1.1	1.4	0.2	0.2	0.2	0.1	0.2
Salmonellosis [10] (1,000)	33.7	65.3	48.6	48.2	40.9	41.6	43.3	46.0	45.5
Shigellosis [11] (1,000)	19.0	17.1	27.1	23.5	23.9	32.2	29.8	32.1	26.0
Tetanus	95	83	64	57	45	48	51	41	36
Toxic-shock syndrome	(2)	384	322	280	244	212	192	191	145
Trichinosis	131	61	129	62	41	16	32	29	11
Tuberculosis [12] (1,000)	27.7	22.2	25.7	26.3	26.7	25.3	24.4	22.9	21.3
Tularemia	234	177	152	193	159	132	96	(2)	(2)
Typhoid fever	510	402	552	501	414	440	441	369	396
Typhus fever:									
Flea-borne (endemic-murine)	81	37	50	43	28	25	(2)	(2)	(2)
Tick-borne (Rocky Mt. spotted fever)	1,163	714	651	628	502	456	465	590	831
Sexually transmitted diseases:									
Gonorrhea (1,000)	1,004	911	690	620	501	440	418	393	326
Syphilis (1,000)	69	68	134	129	113	101	82	69	53
Chlamydia (1,000)	(2)	(2)	(2)	(2)	(2)	(2)	(2)	478	499
Chancroid (1,000)	0.8	2.1	4.2	3.5	1.9	1.4	0.8	0.6	0.4

- Represents zero.   NA Not available.   [1] Acquired immunodeficiency syndrome was not a notifiable disease until 1984. Figures are shown for years in which cases were reported to the CDC. Beginning 1993, based on revised classification system and expanded surveillance case definition.   [2] Disease was not notifiable.   [3] Includes foodborne, infant, wound, and unspecified cases.   [4] Chickenpox was taken off the nationally notifiable list in 1991 but many states continue to report.   [5] Includes some persons positive for antibody to hepatitis C virus who do not have hepatitis.   [6] Whooping cough.   [7] Revised. Data subject to annual revisions.   [8] Based on reports from states: 37 in 1980, 31 in 1985, 30 in 1990, 23 in 1991, 26 in 1992 and 1993, and 27 in 1994.   [9] German measles.   [10] Excludes typhoid fever.   [11] Bacillary dysentery.   [12] Newly reported active cases.

Source: U.S. Centers for Disease Control and Prevention, Atlanta, GA, *Summary of Notifiable Diseases, United States, 1996, Morbidity and Mortality Weekly Report,* Vol. 45, No. 53, October 31, 1997.

No. 225. Selected Measures of Hospital Utilization for Patients Discharged With the Diagnosis of Human Immunodeficiency Virus (HIV): 1985 to 1996

[See headnote, Table 205]

MEASURE OF UTILIZATION	Unit	1985	1990	1993	1994	1995	1996
Number of patients discharged [1]	1,000	23	146	225	234	249	227
Rate of patient discharges [2]	Rate	1.0	5.9	8.8	9.0	9.5	8.6
Number of days of care	1,000	387	2,188	2,561	2,317	2,326	2,123
Rate of days of care [2]	Rate	16.3	87.7	99.9	89.5	89.0	80.4
Average length of stay [3]	Days	17.1	14.9	11.4	9.9	9.3	9.4

[1] Comparisons beginning 1990 with data for earlier years should be made with caution as estimates of change may reflect improvements in the 1988 sample design rather than true changes in hospital use.   [2] Per 10,000 population. Based on Bureau of the Census estimated civilian population as of July 1. Population estimates for the 1980s do not reflect revised estimates based on the 1990 Census of Population.   [3] For similar data on all patients, see Table 205.

Source: National Center for Health Statistics, *Vital and Health Statistics,* Series 13, and unpublished data.

No. 226. AIDS Cases Reported, by Patient Characteristic: 1981 to 1997

[Provisional. For cases reported in the year shown. For data on AIDS deaths, see Table 144. Data are subject to retrospective changes and may differ from those data in Table 224]

CHARACTERISTIC	1981-1997, total	1990	1993	1994	1995	1996	1997
Total.	620,077	41,549	102,166	77,170	70,935	66,545	58,493
Age:							
Under 5 years old	6,041	583	674	751	554	483	306
5 to 12 years old	1,661	139	198	221	192	170	145
13 to 19 years old	2,992	173	560	401	385	378	363
20 to 29 years old	107,302	8,061	18,370	12,636	11,117	9,770	8,234
30 to 39 years old	280,672	18,801	46,458	34,980	31,848	29,834	25,795
40 to 49 years old	157,328	9,640	26,108	20,309	19,375	18,774	16,954
50 to 59 years old	46,602	2,921	7,270	5,834	5,552	5,278	4,957
60 years old and over	17,479	1,231	2,528	2,038	1,912	1,858	1,739
Sex:							
Male.	522,430	36,684	85,781	63,357	57,512	53,009	45,738
Female	97,647	4,865	16,385	13,813	13,423	13,536	12,755
Race/ethnic group:							
Non-Hispanic White.	288,422	22,267	47,507	32,750	29,412	26,189	20,188
Non-Hispanic Black.	229,804	13,206	38,014	30,954	29,097	28,661	27,018
Hispanic	94,719	5,661	15,438	12,568	11,552	10,804	10,394
Other/unknown.	7,132	415	1,207	898	874	891	893
Transmission category:							
Males, 13 years and over.	518,443	36,294	85,352	62,882	57,150	52,677	45,495
Men who have sex with men	305,750	23,809	49,595	35,278	30,983	27,475	20,912
Injecting drug use.	109,858	6,960	20,104	15,141	13,343	11,806	9,744
Men who have sex with men and injecting drug use	38,993	2,809	7,265	4,533	3,807	3,154	2,265
Hemophilia/coagulation disorder . .	4,427	333	1,053	482	427	304	180
Heterosexual contact [1]	11,729	260	1,837	1,891	1,930	2,349	2,090
Heterosexual contact with injecting drug user	6,847	457	1,177	933	877	827	703
Transfusion [2]	4,604	449	603	369	341	272	217
Undetermined [3]	36,235	1,217	3,718	4,255	5,442	6,490	9,384
Females, 13 years and over . . .	93,932	4,533	15,942	13,316	13,039	13,215	12,547
Injecting drug use.	41,483	2,327	8,047	5,911	5,294	4,730	4,046
Hemophilia/coagulation disorder . .	198	16	32	28	26	22	16
Heterosexual contact [1]	20,374	506	3,288	3,433	3,522	3,783	3,295
Heterosexual contact with injecting drug user	15,405	1,036	2,770	2,031	1,874	1,871	1,349
Transfusion [2].	3,391	335	485	310	271	267	182
Undetermined [3]	13,081	313	1,320	1,603	2,052	2,542	3,659

[1] Includes persons who have had heterosexual contact with a person with human immunodeficiency virus (HIV) infection or at risk of HIV infection.   [2] Receipt of blood transfusion, blood components, or tissue.   [3] Includes persons for whom risk information is incomplete (because of death, refusal to be interviewed, or loss to followup), persons still under investigation, men reported only to have had heterosexual contact with prostitutes, and interviewed persons for whom no specific risk is identified.
Source: U.S. Centers for Disease Control and Prevention, Atlanta, GA, *HIV/AIDS Surveillance Reports*, semiannual.

No. 227. AIDS, Syphilis, Tuberculosis, and Measles Cases Reported, by State: 1997

[Diseases selected are those included in the Healthy People 2000 Indicators series]

STATE	AIDS	Syphilis [1]	Tuber-culosis	Measles	STATE	AIDS	Syphilis [1]	Tuber-culosis	Measles
U.S. [2] . .	58,443	8,550	18,534	148	MO	577	114	248	1
AL.	570	410	416	-	MT.	41	-	17	-
AK.	52	1	78	-	NE.	91	5	22	-
AZ.	448	132	272	5	NV.	592	10	46	2
AR.	242	173	179	-	NH.	55	-	17	1
CA.	7,029	386	3,527	30	NJ	3,226	151	728	3
CO.	380	15	93	1	NM.	169	9	60	-
CT.	1,222	62	126	1	NY.	13,189	138	2,271	16
DE.	231	22	18	-	NC.	850	721	462	2
DC.	998	117	106	2	ND.	13	-	12	-
FL.	6,098	296	1,401	9	OH.	848	218	286	-
GA.	1,722	515	595	1	OK.	283	117	194	1
HI	94	1	167	6	OR.	305	10	157	-
ID	52	1	17	-	PA.	1,912	123	459	8
IL.	1,842	435	974	8	RI	152	2	39	-
IN	523	151	160	-	SC.	779	378	293	1
IA	101	7	73	-	SD.	11	1	19	8
KS.	159	29	78	-	TN.	784	747	358	-
KY.	361	135	199	-	TX.	4,718	676	1,817	7
LA.	1,094	364	345	-	UT.	152	5	36	1
ME.	51	2	21	1	VT.	29	-	6	-
MD.	1,875	891	340	2	VA.	1,175	236	349	1
MA.	863	78	254	16	WA.	641	17	298	1
MI	882	153	161	8	WV.	130	1	54	1
MN.	214	16	318	2	WI	255	89	130	1
MS.	347	390	236	-	WY	16	-	2	-

- Represents zero.   [1] Primary and secondary only.   [2] Excludes cases with state not reported.
Source: U.S. Centers for Disease Control and Prevention, Atlanta, GA, *Morbidity and Mortality Weekly Report*, Vol. 46, Nos. 52 and 53, January 9, 1998, and unpublished data.

Health and Nutrition

No. 228. Children Immunized Against Specified Diseases: 1994 to 1996

[In percent. Covers civilian noninstitutionalized population ages 19 months to 35 months. Based on estimates from the National Immunization Survey. The health care providers of the children are contacted to verify and/or complete vaccination information. Results are based on race/ethnic status of the child]

VACCINATION	1994, total	1995, total	1996					
			Total	White non-Hispanic	Hispanic	Black non-Hispanic	American Indian/ Alaskan Native	Asian/ Pacific Islander
Diphtheria-tetanus-pertussis (DPT)/ diphtheria-tetanus:								
3+ doses	94	95	95	96	93	93	93	96
4+ doses	76	79	81	83	77	79	83	84
Polio: 3+ doses	83	88	91	92	89	90	89	90
Hib [1]: 3+ doses	86	92	92	93	89	90	90	92
Measles containing (MCV)	89	90	91	92	88	89	87	94
Hepatitis B: 3+ doses	37	68	82	82	80	82	78	84
4 DPT/3 polio/1 MCV	74	76	78	80	73	76	81	81
4 DPT/3 polio/1 MCV/3 hiB	69	74	77	79	71	74	80	78

[1] Haemophilus B.

Source: U.S. Centers for Disease Control and Prevention, *Morbidity and Mortality Weekly Report*, Vol. 46, No. 41, October 17, 1997, and unpublished data.

No. 229. Acute Conditions, by Type: 1980 to 1995

[Covers civilian noninstitutional population. Estimates include only acute conditions which were medically attended or caused at least 1 day of restricted activity. Based on National Health Interview Survey; see Appendix III. See headnote, Table 220. For composition of regions, see map, inside front cover]

YEAR AND CHARACTERISTIC	NUMBER OF CONDITIONS (mil.)					RATE PER 100 POPULATION				
	Infective and parasitic	Respiratory		Digestive system	Injuries	Infective and parasitic	Respiratory		Digestive system	Injuries
		Common cold	Influenza				Common cold	Influenza		
1980	53.6	(NA)	(NA)	24.9	72.7	24.6	(NA)	(NA)	11.4	33.4
1985	47.8	(NA)	(NA)	16.3	64.0	20.5	(NA)	(NA)	7.0	27.4
1990	51.7	61.5	106.8	13.0	60.1	21.0	25.0	43.4	5.3	24.4
1993	54.3	68.2	132.6	16.1	62.1	21.3	26.8	52.2	6.3	24.4
1994	54.2	66.0	90.4	15.9	61.9	20.9	25.4	34.8	6.1	23.8
1995, total [1]	52.6	60.6	108.0	15.8	64.6	20.1	23.1	41.2	6.0	24.7
Under 5 years old	10.5	10.9	10.9	2.4	5.5	52.0	53.7	53.6	11.7	27.0
5 to 17 years old	19.9	16.6	30.0	3.7	15.2	39.6	33.0	59.4	7.3	30.2
18 to 24 years old	4.6	5.4	10.7	1.6	6.3	18.3	21.8	43.1	6.3	25.1
25 to 44 years old	11.2	15.4	37.6	4.2	19.4	13.5	18.6	45.2	5.0	23.4
45 to 64 years old	4.5	8.3	14.5	2.3	12.0	8.7	16.1	28.0	4.5	23.3
65 years old and over	1.9	3.8	4.4	1.7	6.2	5.9	12.2	14.0	5.4	19.7
Male	23.8	28.4	49.8	7.2	34.7	18.6	22.3	39.0	5.7	27.2
Female	28.8	32.1	58.3	8.6	29.9	21.5	23.9	43.4	6.4	22.3
White	46.0	47.8	95.5	12.3	56.7	21.2	22.0	44.0	5.7	26.1
Black	5.8	8.8	8.7	3.1	5.9	17.6	26.9	26.5	9.6	18.1
Northeast	12.2	10.9	16.1	2.8	12.5	23.7	21.2	31.4	5.5	24.2
Midwest	10.3	14.8	34.4	3.7	18.5	16.5	23.8	55.3	6.0	29.7
South	23.1	18.8	27.0	5.5	20.1	25.0	20.4	29.3	5.9	21.8
West	7.0	16.0	30.4	3.8	13.6	12.6	28.7	54.5	6.8	24.3
Family income:										
Under $10,000	4.7	6.5	10.3	2.4	6.3	21.6	30.1	47.7	11.2	29.1
$10,000 to $19,999	8.2	8.3	15.0	2.4	9.2	21.6	21.8	39.7	6.4	24.3
$20,000 to $34,999	9.9	14.2	22.7	2.8	20.1	18.2	26.0	41.6	5.1	26.0
$35,000 or more	23.7	22.0	47.9	5.8	25.9	22.2	20.6	44.8	5.4	24.3

NA Not available. [1] Includes other races and unknown income not shown separately.

Source: U.S. National Center for Health Statistics, *Vital and Health Statistics*, Series 10, No. 193, and earlier reports; and unpublished data.

No. 230. Osteoporosis—Prevalence Among Women 50 Years Old and Over: 1988-91

[In percent. Osteopenia is defined as a bone mineral density 1-2.5 standard deviations below the mean of White, non-Hispanic women 20-29 years of age as measured in the National Health and Nutrition Examination Survey III (NHANES) (Phase I). Osteoporosis is defined as a bone mineral density value of more than 2.5 standard deviations below the mean of young White, non-Hispanic women. Osteoporosis is an important cause of hip fractures among older women, with decreased bone mass density predicting future hip fracture risk. Based on sample data collected from NHANES III (Phase I)]

DEGREE OF BONE LOSS	50 to 59 years old	60 to 69 years old	70 to 79 years old	80 years old and over
Total	55	69	88	95
Osteopenia	51	50	57	45
Osteoporosis	4	19	31	50

Source: U.S. National Center for Health Statistics, *Health, United States, 1995*.

No. 231. Prevalence of Selected Chronic Conditions, by Age and Sex: 1995

[Covers civilian noninstitutional population. Conditions classified according to ninth revision of International Classification of Diseases. Based on National Health Interview Survey; see Appendix III. See headnote, Table 220]

CHRONIC CONDITION	Condi- tions (1,000)	Male				Female			
		Under 45 years old	45 to 64 years old	65 to 74 years old	75 years old and over	Under 45 years old	45 to 64 years old	65 to 74 years old	75 years old and over
Arthritis.	32,663	22.4	176.7	385.5	437.0	36.0	285.4	498.2	616.1
Dermatitis, including eczema	9,333	33.3	25.1	[2]23.6	[2]31.8	40.5	45.8	34.2	[2]23.8
Trouble with—									
Dry (itching) skin.	6,440	16.0	26.8	38.0	50.1	21.9	33.4	49.1	53.6
Ingrown nails	5,371	15.6	20.4	[2]20.8	44.0	15.0	36.9	39.9	43.2
Corns and calluses	4,347	5.7	15.5	[2]21.4	[2]33.4	11.0	41.0	42.8	74.1
Visual impairments	8,511	27.7	60.3	68.7	135.6	12.8	37.1	43.1	88.7
Cataracts	6,256	[2]1.8	16.8	72.1	214.0	[2]1.1	21.6	132.1	247.0
Hearing impairments	22,465	41.4	203.6	332.8	423.5	26.3	89.7	159.0	307.3
Tinnitus	6,805	13.2	66.3	94.2	68.8	7.3	44.1	55.3	56.7
Deformities or orthopedic									
impairments.	31,784	90.0	186.6	167.1	163.9	101.3	165.2	168.0	210.5
Ulcer	4,297	10.4	29.9	[2]19.9	[2]17.9	12.0	27.7	38.7	[2]19.6
Hernia of abdominal cavity	4,664	9.2	29.1	67.0	53.6	5.0	35.4	44.6	56.1
Frequent constipation	3,644	2.7	[2]7.2	[2]9.4	[2]43.0	14.5	26.4	33.0	72.6
Diabetes.	8,693	6.2	62.1	131.4	110.6	9.7	65.4	134.3	121.1
Migraine	11,897	21.8	31.7	[2]15.2	[2]13.8	70.7	82.6	35.2	[2]10.1
Heart conditions.	21,114	24.0	143.1	316.3	439.4	34.0	100.0	229.3	318.0
High blood pressure									
(Hypertension)	29,954	34.0	233.2	352.0	344.5	30.3	212.9	423.8	465.3
Varicose veins of lower									
extremities.	7,398	4.1	17.1	46.9	[2]41.1	23.3	73.4	101.6	115.0
Hemorrhoids	9,077	20.9	63.8	49.0	58.2	24.2	63.4	58.4	57.7
Chronic bronchitis.	14,533	44.2	37.4	58.1	45.6	58.9	88.7	72.4	70.9
Asthma	14,878	60.7	31.4	47.8	[2]16.9	61.0	73.6	44.3	40.0
Hay fever, allergic rhinitis without asthma	25,730	96.0	96.4	76.1	61.7	99.5	133.0	84.8	61.2

[1] Conditions per 1,000 persons. [2] Figure does not meet standards of reliability or precision.

Source: U.S. National Center for Health Statistics, *Vital and Health Statistics*, Series 10, No. 193, and earlier reports; and unpublished data.

No. 232. Persons Using Assistive Technology Devices, by Age: 1994

[In thousands, except as indicated. For the civilian noninstitutionalized population. Based on the National Health Interview Survey; see Appendix III]

ASSISTIVE DEVICE	Total	Under 45 years old	45 to 64 years old	65 years old and over
Any anatomical device [1]	**4,565**	**2,491**	**1,325**	**748**
Rate per 1,000 persons	17.6	14.0	26.3	24.1
Back brace.	1,688	795	614	279
Neck brace.	168	76	78	[2]13
Hand brace	332	171	119	42
Arm brace	320	209	86	[2]25
Leg brace.	596	266	138	192
Foot brace	282	191	59	31
Knee brace.	989	694	199	96
Other brace	399	239	104	56
Any artificial limb	199	69	59	70
Artificial leg or foot	173	58	50	65
Any mobility device [1]	**7,394**	**1,151**	**1,699**	**4,544**
Crutch	575	227	188	160
Cane	4,762	434	1,116	3,212
Walker.	1,799	109	295	1,395
Medical shoes.	677	248	226	203
Wheelchair	1,564	335	365	863
Scooter	140	12	53	75
Any hearing device [1]	**4,484**	**439**	**969**	**3,076**
Hearing aid.	4,156	370	849	2,938
Amplified telephone	675	73	175	427
TDD/TTY [3]	104	58	[2]25	[2]21
Closed caption television.	141	66	[2]32	43
Listening device	106	[2]26	[2]22	58
Signaling device	95	[2]37	[2]23	35
Interpreter	57	[2]27	[2]21	[2]9
Any vision device [1]	**527**	**123**	**135**	**268**
Telescopic lenses.	158	40	[2]49	70
Braille	59	[2]28	[2]23	[2]8
Readers.	68	[2]15	[2]14	39
White cane.	130	[2]35	48	47

[1] Numbers do not add to totals because a person could have used more than one device. [2] Figure does not meet standards of reliability or precision. [3] TDD/TTY is a typewriter-like device for the deaf that communicates over telephone lines using text.

Source: U.S. National Center for Health Statistics, *Advance Data*, No. 292, November 13, 1997.

No. 233. Disability Status of Children Under 15 Years Old: 1994-95

[For period October 1994 through January 1995. Covers civilian noninstitutional population and members of the Armed Forces living off post or with their families on post. The criteria for presence of disability varied by age. In general, a disability is considered a reduced ability to perform tasks one would normally do at a given stage in life. Based on the Survey of Income and Program Participation; for details, see source]

AGE AND DISABILITY STATUS	Number (1,000)	Percent distribution	AGE AND DISABILITY STATUS	Number (1,000)	Percent distribution
Children under 3 years old	11,942	100.0	Children 6 to 14 years old	35,011	100.0
With a developmental condition [1] . . .	313	2.6	With any disability [3]	4,462	12.7
			With a severe disability	659	1.9
Children 3 to 5 years old	12,427	100.0	Difficulty doing regular schoolwork . . .	2,170	6.2
With any disability [2]	652	5.2	With a learning disability	1,559	4.5
With a developmental condition [1] . . .	510	4.1	With a developmental disability [4] . . .	451	1.3
Difficulty walking, running,			Difficulty with one or more ADLs [5] . . .	381	1.1
or using stairs	235	1.9	Needs personal assistance	272	0.8

[1] A developmental condition for which the child has received therapy or diagnostic services. [2] Covers children with a developmental condition and/or difficulty walking, running, or using stairs. [3] Includes in addition to the disabilities listed below those children who have difficulty seeing, hearing, walking, running, or using stairs and those who use wheelchairs, canes, crutches, or walkers. [4] Includes the conditions of mental retardation, autism, and cerebral palsy. [5] See headnote, Table 235.

No. 234. Disability Status of Persons 15 Years Old and Over: 1994-95

[In thousands, except as noted. See headnote, Table 233]

DISABILITY STATUS	Total	15 to 21 years	22 to 44 years	45 to 54 years	55 to 64 years	65 to 79 years	80 years and over
Total	**202,368**	**25,146**	**95,002**	**30,316**	**20,647**	**24,471**	**6,785**
With any disability.	48,481	3,047	14,105	7,412	7,497	11,568	4,853
Percent of total	24.0	12.1	14.9	24.5	36.3	47.3	71.5
With a severe disability	25,309	813	6,071	3,472	4,528	6,798	3,627
Difficulty with one or more ADLs [1]	8,194	154	1,425	952	1,235	2,565	1,864
Needs personal assistance	3,806	91	663	324	509	1,181	1,039
Difficulty with one or more IADLs [1]	12,260	385	2,364	1,360	1,662	3,747	2,743
Needs personal assistance with one or more ADLs or IADLs [1]	9,473	318	1,777	984	1,268	2,814	2,312

[1] See headnote, Table 235.

No. 235. Receipt of Personal Assistance by Persons with Disabilities: 1994-95

[See headnote, Table 233. ADLs are activities of daily living and include getting around inside the home, getting in or out of a bed or chair, taking a bath or shower, dressing, eating, and using the toilet. IADLs are instrumental activities of daily living and include going outside the home, keeping track of money and bills, preparing meals, doing light housework, and using the telephone]

	PERSONS 15 YEARS OLD AND OVER				PERSONS 65 YEARS OLD AND OVER			
RELATIONSHIP OF FIRST HELPER TO PERSON RECEIVING ASSISTANCE	Receiving assistance with an ADL or an IADL		Receiving assistance with an ADL		Receiving assistance with an ADL or an IADL		Receiving assistance with an ADL	
	Number (1,000)	Percent distribution	Number (1,000)	Percent distribution	Number (1,000)	Percent distribution	Number (1,000)	Percent distribution
Persons receiving assistance	**9,342**	**100.0**	**3,777**	**100.0**	**5,046**	**100.0**	**2,202**	**100.0**
Household member	4,478	47.9	2,154	57.0	2,360	46.8	1,208	54.9
Not a household member	4,864	52.1	1,623	43.0	2,686	53.2	994	45.1
Spouse	2,607	27.9	1,298	34.4	1,366	27.1	724	32.9
Daughter	1,710	18.3	688	18.2	1,120	22.2	465	21.1
Son	1,183	12.7	392	10.4	711	14.1	245	11.1
Parent	800	8.6	280	7.4	(X)	(X)	(X)	(X)
Other relative	1,231	13.2	447	11.8	755	15.0	312	14.2
Nonrelative.	1,018	10.9	300	7.9	468	9.3	151	6.9
Paid help.	794	8.5	372	9.9	626	12.4	305	13.8

X Not applicable.

Source of Tables 233-235: U.S. Bureau of the Census, *Current Population Reports*, P70-61.

No. 236. Substance Abuse Treatment Facilities and Clients: 1995 and 1996

[As of October 1. Based on the Uniform Facility Data Set Survey (UFDS), a census of all facilities that treat only substance abuse and specialized substance abuse units within multi-purpose health care institutions in the United States and associated jurisdictions. Data were collected in cooperation with state agencies which defined what constitutes a provider for reporting purposes. Selected missing data for responding facilities were imputed]

FACILITY SERVICE ORIENTATION	Number	TYPE OF CARE AND TYPE OF PROBLEM	Number of clients, 1996	CLIENT CHARACTERISTIC	Number of clients, 1996
FACILITIES		Total	940,141	Total	940,141
1995	10,746	Outpatient rehab	825,176	Under 18 years old	76,687
1996, total.	10,641	24-hour rehab.	100,469	18 to 24 years old	122,739
Freestanding substance abuse					
treatment	6,167	24-hour detoxification. . .	14,496	25 to 34 years old	283,673
Mental health services	1,984			35 to 44 years old	295,780
Physical health services	1,340			45 to 64 years old	145,819
Other community settings & services.	572	Drug only.	273,232	65 years old and over . .	15,443
Correctional settings & services	578	Alcohol only	261,977		
		Both alcohol & drug	404,932	Male	640,369
CLIENTS				Female	299,772
1995	1,009,127				
1996, total.	940,141	Total with a drug		White, non-Hispanic. . . .	550,496
Freestanding substance abuse					
treatment	514,265	problem [1]	678,164	Black, non-Hispanic. . . .	219,409
Mental health services	189,853	Total with an alcohol		Hispanic	130,140
Physical health services	120,015	problem [2]	666,909	Asian, Pacfic Islander. . .	8,987
Other community settings & services.	38,382			American Indian [3]	25,011
Correctional settings & services	77,626			Other	6,098

[1] The sum of clients with a drug problem and clients with both diagnoses.   [2] The sum of clients with an alcohol problem and clients with both diagnoses.   [3] Includes Alaskan native.

Source: U.S. Substance Abuse and Mental Health Services Administration, *Uniform Facility Data Set (UFDS): Data for 1996 and 1980-1996*, 1997.

No. 237. Drug Use, by Type of Drug and Age Group: 1979 to 1996

[In percent. Current users are those who used drugs at least once within month prior to this study. Based on national samples of respondents residing in households. Subject to sampling variability; see source]

AGE AND TYPE OF DRUG	EVER USED					CURRENT USER				
	1979	1985	1990	1995	1996	1979	1985	1990	1995	1996
12 YEARS OLD AND OVER										
Marijuana and hashish	27.9	29.4	30.5	31.0	32.0	13.2	9.7	5.4	4.7	4.7
Cocaine	8.6	11.2	11.2	10.3	10.3	2.6	3.0	0.9	0.7	0.8
Inhalants	(NA)	7.9	5.7	5.7	5.6	(NA)	0.6	0.4	0.4	0.4
Hallucinogens	8.9	6.9	7.9	9.5	9.7	1.9	1.2	0.4	0.7	0.6
Heroin	1.3	0.9	0.8	1.2	1.1	0.1	0.1	-	0.1	0.1
Stimulants [1]	(NA)	7.3	5.5	4.9	4.7	(NA)	1.8	0.6	0.4	0.4
Sedatives [1]	(NA)	4.8	2.8	2.7	2.3	(NA)	0.5	0.2	0.2	0.1
Tranquilizers [1]	(NA)	7.6	4.0	3.9	3.6	(NA)	2.2	0.6	0.4	0.4
Analgesics [1]	(NA)	7.6	6.3	6.1	5.5	(NA)	1.4	0.9	0.6	0.9
Alcohol.	88.5	84.9	82.2	82.3	82.6	63.2	60.2	52.6	52.2	51.0
Cigarettes	(NA)	78.0	75.4	71.8	71.6	(NA)	38.7	32.6	28.8	28.9
12 to 17 YEARS OLD										
Marijuana and hashish	26.7	20.1	12.7	16.2	16.8	14.2	10.2	4.4	8.2	7.1
Alcohol.	70.8	56.1	48.8	40.6	38.8	49.6	41.2	32.5	21.1	18.8
Cigarettes.	(NA)	50.7	45.1	38.1	36.3	(NA)	29.4	22.4	20.2	18.3
18 TO 25 YEARS OLD										
Marijuana and hashish	66.1	57.6	50.4	41.4	44.0	35.6	21.7	12.7	12.0	13.2
Alcohol.	(NA)	(NA)	87.6	84.4	83.8	75.1	70.1	62.8	61.3	60.0
Cigarettes.	(NA)	75.3	70.7	67.7	68.5	(NA)	47.4	40.9	35.3	38.3
26 TO 34 YEARS OLD										
Marijuana and hashish	45.0	54.1	56.5	51.8	50.5	19.7	19.0	9.5	6.7	6.3
Alcohol.	(NA)	(NA)	(NA)	90.1	90.3	71.6	70.6	64.4	63.0	61.6
Cigarettes.	(NA)	84.7	84.1	75.8	73.8	(NA)	45.7	42.4	34.7	35.0
35 YEARS OLD AND OVER										
Marijuana and hashish	9.0	13.9	19.6	25.3	27.0	2.9	2.6	2.4	1.8	2.0
Alcohol.	(NA)	(NA)	83.5	87.1	87.8	59.7	57.5	49.5	52.6	51.7
Cigarettes.	(NA)	82.2	79.0	77.5	77.8	(NA)	35.5	28.9	27.2	27.0

- Represents or rounds to zero.   NA Not available.   [1] Nonmedical use; does not include over-the-counter drugs.

Source: U.S. Substance Abuse and Mental Health Services Administration, *National Household Survey on Drug Abuse*, annual.

Health and Nutrition

No. 238. Current Cigarette Smoking: 1979 to 1995

[In percent. Prior to 1992, a current smoker is a person who has smoked at least 100 cigarettes and who now smokes. Beginning 1992, definition includes persons who smoke only "some days". Excludes unknown smoking status. Based on the National Health Interview Survey; for details, see Appendix III]

SEX, AGE, AND RACE	1979	1985	1990	1991	1992	1993	1994	1995
Total smokers, 18 years old and over.................	33.5	30.1	25.5	25.6	26.5	25.0	25.5	24.7
Male, total........................	37.5	32.6	28.4	28.1	28.6	27.7	28.2	27.0
18 to 24 years.............	35.0	28.0	26.6	23.5	28.0	28.8	29.8	27.8
25 to 34 years.............	43.9	38.2	31.6	32.8	32.8	30.2	31.4	(NA)
35 to 44 years.............	41.8	37.6	34.5	33.1	32.9	32.0	33.2	(NA)
45 to 64 years.............	39.3	33.4	29.3	29.3	28.6	29.2	28.3	27.1
65 years and over.........	20.9	19.6	14.6	15.1	16.1	13.5	13.2	14.3
White, total....................	36.8	31.7	28.0	27.4	28.2	27.0	27.7	(NA)
18 to 24 years.............	34.3	28.4	27.4	25.1	30.0	30.4	31.8	(NA)
25 to 34 years.............	43.6	37.3	31.6	32.1	33.5	29.9	32.5	(NA)
35 to 44 years.............	41.3	36.6	33.5	32.1	30.9	31.2	32.0	(NA)
45 to 64 years.............	38.3	32.1	28.7	28.0	28.1	27.8	26.9	(NA)
65 years and over.........	20.5	18.9	13.7	13.7	14.9	12.5	11.9	(NA)
Black, total....................	44.1	39.9	32.5	35.0	32.2	32.7	33.7	(NA)
18 to 24 years.............	40.2	27.2	21.3	15.0	16.2	19.9	18.7	(NA)
25 to 34 years.............	47.5	45.6	33.8	39.4	29.5	30.7	29.8	(NA)
35 to 44 years.............	48.6	45.0	42.0	44.4	47.5	36.9	44.5	(NA)
45 to 64 years.............	50.0	46.1	36.7	42.0	35.4	42.4	41.2	(NA)
65 years and over.........	26.2	27.7	21.5	24.3	28.3	27.9	25.6	(NA)
Female, total.................	29.9	27.9	22.8	23.5	24.6	22.5	23.1	22.6
18 to 24 years.............	33.8	30.4	22.5	22.4	24.9	22.9	25.2	21.8
25 to 34 years.............	33.7	32.0	28.2	28.4	30.1	27.3	28.8	(NA)
35 to 44 years.............	37.0	31.5	24.8	27.6	27.3	27.4	26.8	(NA)
45 to 64 years.............	30.7	29.9	24.8	24.6	26.1	23.0	22.8	24.0
65 years and over.........	13.2	13.5	11.5	12.0	12.4	10.5	11.1	11.5
White, total....................	30.1	27.7	23.4	23.7	25.1	23.1	23.7	(NA)
18 to 24 years.............	34.5	31.8	25.4	25.1	28.5	26.8	28.5	(NA)
25 to 34 years.............	34.1	32.0	28.5	28.4	31.5	28.4	30.2	(NA)
35 to 44 years.............	37.2	31.0	25.0	27.0	27.6	27.3	27.1	(NA)
45 to 64 years.............	30.6	29.7	25.4	25.3	25.8	23.4	23.2	(NA)
65 years and over.........	13.8	13.3	11.5	12.1	12.6	10.5	11.1	(NA)
Black, total....................	31.1	31.0	21.2	24.4	24.2	20.8	21.7	(NA)
18 to 24 years.............	31.8	23.7	10.0	11.8	10.3	8.2	11.8	(NA)
25 to 34 years.............	35.2	36.2	29.1	32.4	26.9	24.7	24.8	(NA)
35 to 44 years.............	37.7	40.2	25.5	35.3	32.4	31.5	28.2	(NA)
45 to 64 years.............	34.2	33.4	22.6	23.4	30.9	21.3	23.5	(NA)
65 years and over.........	8.5	14.5	11.1	9.6	11.1	10.2	13.6	(NA)

NA Not available.
Source: U.S. National Center for Health Statistics, *Health United States, 1996-97 and Injury Chartbook*, 1997, and U.S. Centers for Disease Control and Prevention, *Morbidity and Mortality Weekly Report*, Vol. 46, No. 51, December 26, 1997.

No. 239. Cancer—Estimated New Cases, 1998, and Survival Rates, 1977-79 to 1986-93

[The 5-year relative survival rate, which is derived by adjusting the observed survival rate for expected mortality, represents the likelihood that a person will not die from causes directly related to their cancer within 5 years. Survival data shown are based on those patients diagnosed while residents of an area listed below during the time periods shown. Data are based on information collected as part of the National Cancer Institute's Surveillance, Epidemiology, and End Results (SEER) program; a collection of population-based registries in Connecticut, New Mexico, Utah, Iowa, Hawaii, Atlanta, Detroit, Seattle-Puget Sound, and San Francisco-Oakland]

SITE	ESTIMATED NEW CASES, [1] 1998 (1,000)			5-YEAR RELATIVE SURVIVAL RATES (percent)							
				White				Black			
	Total	Male	Female	1977-79	1980-82	1983-85	1986-93	1977-79	1980-82	1983-85	1986-93
All sites [2].........	1,229	628	601	51.0	52.0	54.2	59.5	39.1	39.6	39.7	44.4
Lung................	172	91	80	13.6	13.5	14.0	14.1	10.9	12.2	11.5	11.1
Breast [3]...........	180	2	179	75.4	77.1	79.6	85.5	63.1	65.9	63.5	69.9
Colon and rectum......	132	64	67	52.2	54.8	58.3	62.3	45.5	46.3	47.7	52.4
Colon.............	96	44	51	52.9	55.6	59.1	63.1	47.9	49.0	48.9	52.6
Rectum............	36	20	16	50.6	53.0	56.5	60.6	38.6	37.8	43.9	52.1
Prostate.............	185	185	(X)	72.1	74.5	77.5	90.2	62.4	64.6	63.9	75.3
Bladder.............	54	40	15	75.8	79.0	79.2	82.5	55.3	58.4	58.6	60.9
Corpus uteri..........	36	(X)	36	86.8	83.5	85.6	86.5	57.7	55.4	55.3	57.2
Non-Hodgkin's lymphoma [4].	55	31	24	48.5	51.8	54.7	52.2	51.1	50.5	45.1	43.7
Oral cavity and pharynx...	30	21	10	54.4	55.3	55.6	54.9	36.6	30.6	34.9	33.5
Leukemia [4].........	29	16	13	37.9	39.2	41.5	42.8	30.2	32.8	33.4	33.4
Melanoma of skin.......	42	24	17	82.1	82.9	84.9	88.1	50.8	62.0	75.6	66.8
Pancreas............	29	14	15	2.3	2.9	2.9	3.7	3.8	5.0	5.5	5.1
Kidney..............	30	18	13	50.6	51.2	56.4	59.9	51.6	55.5	54.5	55.3
Stomach............	23	14	8	16.1	16.4	16.3	19.4	15.1	19.4	18.4	20.1
Ovary..............	25	(X)	25	37.7	38.8	40.3	46.5	40.0	38.3	41.7	41.9
Cervix uteri [5].......	14	(X)	14	69.4	67.9	70.4	71.4	62.1	61.0	59.9	57.1

X Not applicable. [1] Estimates provided by American Cancer Society are based on rates from the National Cancer Institute's SEER program. [2] Includes other sites not shown separately. [3] Survival rates for female only. [4] All types combined. [5] Invasive cancer only.
Source: U.S. National Institutes of Health, National Cancer Institute, *Cancer Statistics Review*, annual

No. 240. Cumulative Percent Distribution of Population, by Height and Sex: 1988-94

[For persons 20 to 79 years old. Height was measured without shoes. Based on sample and subject to sampling variability; see source]

HEIGHT	MALES						FEMALES					
	20-29 years	30-39 years	40-49 years	50-59 years	60-69 years	70-79 years	20-29 years	30-39 years	40-49 years	50-59 years	60-69 years	70-79 years
Percent under—												
4'8"	-	-	-	-	-	-	0.6	0.1	-	-	0.2	1.7
4'9"	-	-	-	-	-	-	0.7	0.2	0.3	0.1	0.7	3.3
4'10"	-	-	-	-	0.1	-	1.2	0.7	0.7	1.9	1.7	4.9
4'11"	-	-	-	-	0.1	0.1	3.1	2.6	1.7	3.1	4.4	9.8
5'	0.1	-	0.2	-	0.4	0.1	6.0	5.5	5.3	6.6	9.9	15.4
5'1"	0.1	-	0.4	0.1	0.5	0.6	11.5	10.4	9.9	11.9	19.0	28.9
5'2"	0.5	0.8	0.7	0.2	0.7	1.9	21.8	18.5	18.8	24.4	34.3	45.6
5'3"	1.3	1.4	0.9	1.0	2.2	2.7	34.3	30.7	31.9	38.6	48.3	61.2
5'4"	3.4	2.2	1.7	2.5	5.8	7.8	48.9	42.9	49.2	52.6	65.5	74.5
5'5"	6.9	5.1	5.6	6.0	9.4	16.5	62.7	59.1	64.3	69.9	76.5	85.9
5'6"	11.7	10.1	12.1	11.7	15.8	27.3	74.0	71.8	77.0	81.6	87.8	93.9
5'7"	20.8	18.9	19.6	20.5	27.4	39.5	84.7	84.1	87.0	89.3	92.5	97.3
5'8"	32.0	28.3	28.0	32.6	38.6	53.4	92.4	91.6	94.5	95.6	96.7	99.2
5'9"	46.3	44.3	42.1	43.9	55.1	68.7	96.2	95.6	97.3	99.0	99.3	99.9
5'10"	58.7	58.0	58.1	60.6	68.8	79.5	98.6	98.1	98.9	99.6	99.8	100.0
5'11"	70.1	70.4	71.1	75.2	81.4	89.2	99.5	99.5	99.4	100.0	100.0	100.0
6'	81.2	79.7	81.5	85.4	90.0	94.1	100.0	100.0	100.0	100.0	100.0	100.0
6'1"	87.4	86.2	89.0	92.4	95.2	97.2	100.0	100.0	100.0	100.0	100.0	100.0
6'2"	94.7	92.4	94.4	96.4	98.2	99.3	100.0	100.0	100.0	100.0	100.0	100.0
6'3"	97.9	98.1	97.2	98.2	99.5	99.9	100.0	100.0	100.0	100.0	100.0	100.0

- Represents or rounds to zero.

Source: U.S. National Center for Health Statistics, unpublished data.

No. 241. Cumulative Percent Distribution of Population, by Weight and Sex: 1988-94

[For persons 20 to 79 years old. Weight measured includes clothes weight, estimated as ranging from .20 pounds to .62 pounds. Based on sample and subject to sampling variability; see source]

WEIGHT	MALES						FEMALES					
	20-29 years	30-39 years	40-49 years	50-59 years	60-69 years	70-79 years	20-29 years	30-39 years	40-49 years	50-59 years	60-69 years	70-79 years
Percent under—												
90 pounds ...	-	-	-	-	-	-	0.5	0.5	-	0.3	0.2	1.8
100 pounds ..	-	-	-	-	-	0.2	3.8	2.0	1.6	1.3	1.7	4.7
110 pounds ..	0.5	0.1	0.2	0.1	0.8	0.4	13.3	7.7	5.5	3.7	5.6	9.2
120 pounds ..	1.8	1.0	0.7	0.6	1.5	1.7	27.0	17.8	12.6	9.5	13.8	19.0
130 pounds ..	6.7	3.4	3.3	2.2	3.1	5.8	46.1	31.4	25.1	19.7	24.3	31.6
140 pounds ..	15.8	7.8	6.7	5.4	7.5	13.2	58.7	44.3	37.4	30.0	36.2	46.6
150 pounds ..	29.0	17.0	14.1	9.9	15.5	23.3	70.4	55.5	49.4	42.0	48.8	57.3
160 pounds ..	42.1	27.6	23.0	16.2	24.5	35.2	76.5	65.3	59.3	52.7	61.3	67.9
170 pounds ..	54.9	42.0	32.4	28.9	36.1	48.4	82.6	72.6	70.0	61.5	71.3	77.6
180 pounds ..	66.7	54.9	48.6	41.5	48.2	59.5	87.6	78.3	78.6	70.9	79.0	84.6
190 pounds ..	76.2	66.4	61.0	55.2	60.5	73.1	90.1	82.2	82.6	77.0	84.3	90.2
200 pounds ..	82.1	74.8	70.1	68.5	72.5	82.6	92.5	86.2	87.4	83.8	89.1	92.8
210 pounds ..	86.8	81.2	78.0	77.4	81.0	87.8	94.5	89.3	90.5	89.0	92.6	94.6
220 pounds ..	90.4	86.3	83.8	84.4	87.1	93.2	96.0	92.1	93.2	92.1	94.7	95.7
230 pounds ..	92.9	91.6	88.8	89.3	92.6	95.7	97.7	94.2	94.9	93.7	96.4	96.3
240 pounds ..	95.4	94.3	92.6	92.6	95.7	96.7	98.7	96.0	97.3	95.1	97.3	97.5
250 pounds ..	96.2	95.5	94.1	94.5	97.2	97.4	99.0	96.7	97.6	96.7	97.6	98.8
260 pounds ..	97.2	96.6	95.7	96.3	98.0	98.5	99.4	97.5	98.1	97.9	98.8	99.3
270 pounds ..	97.9	97.4	96.5	97.3	98.6	99.4	99.7	98.7	98.4	98.1	99.2	99.5
280 pounds ..	98.7	97.6	97.5	98.1	98.9	99.8	99.8	98.7	98.7	98.7	99.4	99.8
290 pounds ..	99.0	98.0	97.8	98.6	99.5	100.0	99.9	99.1	99.0	98.8	99.6	99.9
300 pounds ..	99.3	98.2	98.7	99.0	99.5	100.0	100.0	99.4	99.2	99.5	99.8	99.9
310 pounds ..	99.3	98.5	98.9	99.2	100.0	100.0	100.0	99.7	99.4	99.9	99.8	100.0
320 pounds ..	99.5	98.6	99.2	99.5	100.0	100.0	100.0	99.9	99.5	99.5	99.8	100.0
330 pounds ..	99.5	98.8	99.3	99.5	100.0	100.0	100.0	99.9	99.6	100.0	99.8	100.0
340 pounds ..	99.5	99.3	99.3	99.9	100.0	100.0	100.0	99.9	99.6	100.0	99.9	100.0
350 pounds ..	99.6	99.7	99.3	100.0	100.0	100.0	100.0	99.9	100.0	100.0	99.9	100.0
360 pounds ..	99.6	99.8	99.3	100.0	100.0	100.0	100.0	99.9	100.0	100.0	100.0	100.0
370 pounds ..	99.6	98.8	99.3	100.0	100.0	100.0	100.0	99.9	100.0	100.0	100.0	100.0
380 pounds ..	99.6	99.8	99.4	100.0	100.0	100.0	100.0	99.9	100.0	100.0	100.0	100.0

- Represents or rounds to zero.

Source: U.S. National Center for Health Statistics, unpublished data.

No. 242. Percent of Population Overweight, by Age, Sex, and Race: 1976 to 1994

[In percent. Overweight is defined for men as body mass index greater than or equal to 27.8 kilograms/meter squared, and for women as body mass index greater than or equal to 27.3 kilograms/meter squared. These points were used because they represent the sex-specific 85th percentiles for persons 20-29 years of age in the 1976-80 National Health and Nutrition Examination Survey (NHANES). Data are based on physical examinations of a sample of the civilian noninstitutional population in the NHANES]

SEX, AGE, AND RACE	1976-80	1988-94	SEX, AGE, AND RACE	1976-80	1988-94	SEX, AGE, AND RACE	1976-80	1988-94
Persons 20 to 74 years old, [1]	**25.4**	**34.8**	MALE			FEMALE [2]		
Male..	24.0	33.7	20 to 34 years old..	17.3	25.4	20 to 34 years old..	16.8	25.6
Female [2]	26.5	35.9	35 to 44 years old..	28.9	34.9	35 to 44 years old..	27.0	36.8
			45 to 54 years old..	31.0	37.7	45 to 54 years old..	32.5	45.4
White male .	24.2	34.3	55 to 64 years old..	28.1	43.7	55 to 64 years old..	37.0	48.2
White female [2]	24.4	33.9	65 to 74 years old..	25.2	42.9	65 to 74 years old..	38.4	42.3
Black male .	25.7	34.0	75 years old and over	(NA)	27.7	75 years old and over	(NA)	35.1
Black female [2]	44.3	53.0						

NA Not available. [1] Age-adjusted. Includes other races not shown separately. [2] Excludes pregnant women.

Source: U.S. National Center for Health Statistics, *Health, United States, 1996-97* and *Injury Chartbook*, 1997.

No. 243. Self-Perception of Being Overweight: 1988-94

[In percent. See headnote, Table 242]

AGE	PERCENT OF OVERWEIGHT PEOPLE WHO THINK THEY ARE OVERWEIGHT						PERCENT OF POPULATION NOT OVERWEIGHT WHO THINK THEY ARE OVERWEIGHT					
	Total [1]		Non-Hispanic White		Non-Hispanic Black		Total [1]		Non-Hispanic White		Non-Hispanic Black	
	Male	Female	Male	Female	Male	Female	Male	Female	Male	Female	Male	Female
Total..........	81.7	91.6	84.4	93.8	71.2	86.4	25.4	44.1	28.0	45.9	14.8	34.9
20 to 39 years old....	82.4	93.7	86.6	95.7	73.4	90.0	24.4	45.0	27.3	46.1	12.7	37.6
40 to 59 years old....	85.8	96.3	88.9	99.2	71.1	90.6	30.9	51.5	33.5	54.2	21.5	41.6
60 years old and over .	73.9	82.8	75.0	85.7	64.4	71.0	19.7	33.3	21.3	35.9	10.5	15.1

[1] Includes other races and persons of Hispanic origin not shown separately.

Source: U.S. National Center for Health Statistics, unpublished data.

No. 244. Healthy Eating Indexes, by Selected Food Groups and Dietary Guidelines: 1996

[Healthy Eating Index is comprised of the sum of 10 dietary component indices for a maximum possible score of 100. A score of 80 or above was judged to reflect a "good" diet. Each of the dietary components has a scoring range of zero to 10. Individuals with an intake at the recommended level received a maximum score of 10 points. A score of zero was assigned when no foods in a particular group were eaten. Intermediate scores were calculated proportionately. The indexes for grains, vegetables, fruits, milk, and meat groups measure the degree to which a person's diet conforms to the U.S. Department of Agriculture's (USDA) "Food Guide Pyramid" serving recommendations. The index was applied to USDA one-day food and nutrient intake data from the Continuing Survey of Food Intakes by Individuals. The data are based on a representative sample of individuals 2 years old and over excluding women who were pregnant or lactating at the time of the survey]

FOOD GROUP AND DIETARY GUIDELINE	Average score on one day	Percent receiving score of 10	Perfect score of 10 [1]	Score of zero
Healthy Eating Index..........	63.8	[2]12.2	(X)	(X)
Grains [3]............	6.7	22.2	6-11 servings	0 servings
Vegetables [4]............	6.3	31.8	3-5 servings	0 servings
Fruits [5]............	3.8	17.1	2-4 servings	0 servings
Milk [5]............	5.4	25.5	2-3 servings	0 servings
Meat [6]............	6.4	26.4	2-3 servings	0 servings
Total fat [7]............	6.9	37.5	30% or less energy from fat	45% or more energy from fat
Saturated fat [7]............	6.4	40.1	Less than 10% energy from saturated fat	15% or more energy from saturated fat
Cholesterol............	7.9	71.9	300 mg. or less	450 mg. or more
Sodium............	6.3	34.7	2,400 mg. or less	4,800 mg or more
Variety [8]............	7.6	53.0	8 different food items over 1 day	Fewer than 4 items over 1 day

X Not applicable. [1] Depends on recommended energy intake. All amounts listed are based on a per day basis. [2] Percent receiving a score of 80 or higher. [3] One serving: a slice of bread, one-half cup of cooked pasta, or one-half cup of cooked cereal grains. [4] One serving: one-half cup of cooked vegetables, 1 cup of raw leafy vegetables, or one-half cup of raw nonleafy chopped vegetables. Fruits are similar. [5] One serving: one cup of milk or equivalent. [6] Includes eggs, nuts, and some legumes. One serving: 2.5 ounces of lean meat or equivalent. [7] Consumption of specified fat as a percentage of total food energy intake. [8] Amount of variety in a person's diet over a 1-day period.

Source: U.S. Department of Agriculture, Center for Nutrition Policy and Promotion, unpublished data.

No. 245. Percentage of Adults Engaging in Leisure-Time Physical Activity: 1992

[Covers persons 18 years old and over. Based on response to question about physical activity in prior month. Based on a sample survey of approximately 96,000 persons in 48 states and the District of Columbia; for details, see source]

CHARACTERISTIC	No participation in physical activity	Participates in regular, sustained activity[1]	Participates in regular, vigorous activity[2]
Total	28.7	20.1	14.4
Male	26.5	21.5	12.9
Female	30.7	18.9	15.8
White, non-Hispanic.....	26.8	20.8	15.3
Black, non-Hispanic.....	38.5	15.2	9.4
Hispanic............	34.8	20.1	11.9
Other..............	31.4	17.3	11.8
Males:			
18 to 29 years old	18.9	26.8	8.0
30 to 44 years old	25.0	17.4	11.1
45 to 64 years old	32.0	18.9	16.3
65 to 74 years old	33.2	26.8	20.6
75 years old and over ..	38.2	23.2	20.6
Females:			
18 to 29 years old	25.4	19.9	11.4

CHARACTERISTIC	No participation in physical activity	Participates in regular, sustained activity[1]	Participates in regular, vigorous activity[2]
30 to 44 years old	26.9	18.5	18.0
45 to 64 years old	32.1	19.4	17.7
65 to 74 years old	36.6	19.0	16.5
75 years old and over ..	50.5	15.0	12.8
School years completed:			
Less than 12 years....	46.5	15.6	8.2
12 years...........	32.8	17.8	11.5
Some college (13-15 years).............	22.6	22.7	14.9
College (16 or more years).............	17.8	23.5	21.9
Household income:			
Less than $10,000	41.5	17.6	9.0
$10,000 to $19,999....	34.6	18.7	10.8
$20,000 to $34,999....	26.9	20.3	14.2
$35,000 to $49,999....	23.0	20.9	16.3
$50,000 and over	17.7	23.5	20.5

[1] Any type or intensity of activity that occurs 5 times or more per week and 30 minutes or more per occasion. [2] Rhythmic contraction of large muscle groups performed at 50 percent or more of estimated age- and sex-specific maximum cardiorespiratory capacity, 3 times per week or more for at least 20 minutes per occasion.

Source: U.S. National Center for Chronic Disease Prevention and Health Promotion, *Physical Activity and Health: A Report of the Surgeon General, 1996.*

No. 246. Nutrition—Nutrients in Foods Available for Civilian Consumption per Capita per Day: 1970 to 1994

[Computed by the Center for Nutrition Policy and Promotion (CNPP). Based on Economic Research Service (ERS) estimates of per capita quantities of food available for consumption from "Food Consumption, Prices, and, Expenditures," on imputed consumption data for foods no longer reported by ERS, and on CNPP estimates of quantities of produce from home gardens. Food supply estimates do not reflect loss of food or nutrients from further marketing or home processing. Enrichment and fortification levels of iron, thiamin, riboflavin, niacin, vitamin A, vitamin B_6, vitamin B_{12}, and ascorbic acid are included]

NUTRIENT	Unit	1970-79	1980-89	1990	1993	1994
Food energy	Calories.........	3,300	3,400	3,600	3,700	3,800
Carbohydrate.............	Grams...........	391	417	458	482	491
Protein.................	Grams...........	95	100	105	108	110
Total fat [1]	Grams...........	151	157	156	161	159
Saturated..............	Grams...........	52	53	51	52	52
Monounsaturated	Grams...........	61	63	63	66	65
Polyunsaturated	Grams...........	28	31	32	32	31
Cholesterol	Milligrams........	440	420	400	410	410
Vitamin A...............	Micrograms RE [2]....	1,530	1,510	1,530	1,530	1,520
Carotenes...............	Micrograms RE [2]....	580	620	670	670	660
Vitamin E...............	Milligrams α-TE [3]....	14.2	15.7	16.6	17.6	16.9
Vitamin C...............	Milligrams........	109	114	111	122	124
Thiamin................	Milligrams........	2.1	2.4	2.6	2.7	2.7
Riboflavin..............	Milligrams........	2.4	2.5	2.6	2.6	2.6
Niacin.................	Milligrams........	23.6	26.4	28.0	29.0	29.0
Vitamin B_6..............	Milligrams........	2.0	2.1	2.2	2.3	2.3
Folacin................	Micrograms........	289	303	311	329	331
Vitamin B_{12}.............	Micrograms........	9.1	8.4	8.2	8.0	8.1
Calcium................	Milligrams........	880	900	940	950	960
Phosphorus	Milligrams........	1,460	1,530	1,620	1,650	1,680
Magnesium..............	Milligrams........	320	340	370	380	380
Iron	Milligrams........	18.7	18.2	20.2	20.9	21.2
Zinc	Milligrams........	12.1	12.3	12.7	13.0	13.2
Copper	Milligrams........	1.6	1.7	1.8	1.9	1.9
Potassium..............	Milligrams........	3,470	3,530	3,650	3,750	3,780

[1] Includes other types of fat not shown separately. [2] Retinol equivalents. [3] Alpha-Tocopherol equivalents.

Source: U.S. Dept. of Agriculture, Center for Nutrition Policy and Promotion. Data published by Economic Research Service in *Food Consumption, Prices, and Expenditures,* annual.

No. 247. Per Capita Consumption of Major Food Commodities: 1980 to 1996

[In pounds, retail weight except as indicated. Consumption represents the residual after exports, nonfood use and ending stocks are subtracted from the sum of beginning stocks, domestic production, and imports. Based on Bureau of the Census estimated population. Estimates reflect revisions based on the 1990 Census of Population]

COMMODITY	1980	1985	1990	1992	1993	1994	1995	1996
Red meat, total (boneless, trimmed weight) [1][2]	126.4	124.9	112.3	114.1	112.1	114.7	114.7	112.0
Beef	72.1	74.6	64.0	62.8	61.5	63.6	64.0	64.2
Veal	1.3	1.5	0.9	0.8	0.8	0.8	0.8	1.0
Lamb and mutton	1.0	1.1	1.0	1.0	1.0	0.9	0.9	0.8
Pork (excluding lard)	52.1	47.7	46.4	49.5	48.9	49.5	49.0	46.0
Fish and shellfish (edible weight) [3]	12.4	15.0	15.0	14.7	14.9	15.1	14.9	14.7
Fresh and frozen	7.8	9.7	9.6	9.8	10.1	10.3	9.9	9.9
Canned	4.3	5.0	5.1	4.6	4.5	4.5	4.7	4.5
Tuna	3.0	3.3	3.7	3.5	3.5	3.3	3.4	3.2
Cured	0.3	0.3	0.3	0.3	0.3	0.3	0.3	0.3
Poultry products: (boneless weight) [2][4]	40.8	45.5	56.3	60.8	62.5	63.3	62.9	64.3
Chicken	32.7	36.4	42.5	46.7	48.5	49.3	48.8	49.8
Turkey	8.1	9.1	13.8	14.1	14.0	14.1	14.1	14.6
Eggs (number)	271.1	254.7	234.3	235.0	235.6	237.6	234.6	236.2
Shell	236.2	216.5	186.3	180.7	179.1	176.9	173.8	174.1
Processed	34.9	38.2	48.0	54.3	56.5	60.6	60.8	62.1
Dairy products:								
Total (milk equivalent, milkfat basis) [5]	543.2	593.7	568.5	565.9	574.0	585.8	584.1	575.6
Fluid milk and cream [6]	245.5	240.8	233.4	230.5	225.7	226.3	223.2	223.5
Beverage milks	237.4	229.7	221.8	218.3	213.4	213.5	209.7	210.0
Plain whole milk	141.7	119.7	87.7	81.2	77.4	76.0	72.6	72.1
Plain reduced-fat milk (2%)	54.7	68.5	78.4	78.1	76.0	74.9	70.4	69.1
Plain light and skim milks	26.9	27.4	42.8	46.2	47.3	49.7	53.9	55.7
Flavored whole milk	4.7	3.7	2.8	2.7	2.7	2.7	2.7	2.7
Flavored reduced-fat, light, and skim milks	5.3	6.0	6.6	6.9	6.9	7.1	7.3	7.7
Buttermilk	4.1	4.4	3.5	3.2	3.0	2.9	2.8	2.7
Yogurt (excl. frozen)	2.5	4.0	4.0	4.2	4.3	4.7	5.1	4.8
Cream [7]	3.4	4.4	4.6	4.8	4.9	4.9	5.1	5.4
Sour cream and dips	1.8	2.3	2.5	2.7	2.7	2.8	2.9	2.9
Condensed and evaporated milks:								
Whole milk	3.8	3.6	3.2	3.2	3.0	2.6	2.3	2.3
Skim milk	3.3	3.8	4.8	5.2	5.2	5.5	4.5	4.1
Cheese [8]	17.5	22.5	24.6	26.0	26.2	26.8	27.3	27.7
American	9.6	12.2	11.1	11.3	11.4	11.5	11.8	12.0
Cheddar	6.9	9.8	9.0	9.2	9.1	9.1	9.1	9.2
Italian	4.4	6.5	9.0	10.0	9.8	10.3	10.4	10.8
Mozzarella	3.0	4.6	6.9	7.7	7.6	7.9	8.0	8.5
Other [9]	3.4	3.9	4.5	4.7	5.0	5.0	5.0	5.0
Swiss	1.3	1.3	1.4	1.2	1.2	1.2	1.1	1.1
Cream and Neufchatel	1.0	1.2	1.7	2.0	2.1	2.2	2.1	2.2
Cottage cheese	4.5	4.1	3.4	3.1	2.9	2.8	2.7	2.6
Ice cream	17.5	18.1	15.8	16.3	16.1	16.1	15.7	15.9
Ice milk	7.1	6.9	7.7	7.1	6.9	7.6	7.5	7.6
Frozen yogurt	(NA)	(NA)	2.8	3.1	3.5	3.5	3.5	2.7
Fats and oils:								
Total, fat content only	57.2	64.3	62.8	67.4	70.2	68.5	66.8	65.6
Butter (product weight)	4.5	4.9	4.4	4.4	4.7	4.8	4.5	4.3
Margarine (product weight)	11.3	10.8	10.9	11.0	11.1	9.9	9.2	9.1
Lard (direct use)	2.6	1.8	1.9	1.7	1.7	2.3	2.2	2.3
Edible tallow (direct use)	1.1	1.9	0.5	2.4	2.2	2.4	2.7	3.0
Shortening	18.2	22.9	22.2	22.4	25.1	24.1	22.5	22.2
Salad and cooking oils	21.2	23.6	24.8	27.2	26.8	26.2	26.8	26.0
Other edible fats and oils	1.5	1.6	1.2	1.4	1.7	1.6	1.6	1.4
Flour and cereal products	144.7	156.6	182.0	186.2	191.0	194.1	192.5	198.5
Wheat flour	116.9	124.6	136.0	138.8	143.3	144.5	141.8	148.8
Rye flour	0.7	0.7	0.6	0.6	0.6	0.6	0.6	0.6
Rice, milled	9.4	9.1	16.2	17.5	17.6	19.3	20.1	18.9
Corn products	12.9	17.2	21.9	22.1	22.3	22.5	22.7	22.9
Oat products	3.9	4.0	6.5	6.5	6.5	6.5	6.5	6.6
Barley products	1.0	1.0	0.8	0.7	0.7	0.7	0.7	0.7
Breakfast cereals	12.0	12.8	15.4	16.6	17.3	17.4	17.1	16.8
Ready-to-eat	9.7	10.5	12.6	13.9	14.6	14.8	14.6	14.3
Ready-to-cook	2.3	2.3	2.9	2.6	2.7	2.6	2.5	2.5
Caloric sweeteners, total [10]	123.0	128.8	137.0	141.2	144.4	147.3	149.8	152.0
Sugar, refined cane and beet	83.6	62.7	64.4	64.6	64.3	65.0	65.5	66.2
Corn sweeteners (dry weight)	38.2	64.8	71.1	75.2	78.7	81.0	83.0	84.5
Other:								
Cocoa beans	3.4	4.6	5.4	5.7	5.4	4.8	4.6	4.6
Coffee (green beans)	10.3	10.5	10.3	10.0	9.1	8.2	8.0	9.0
Peanuts (shelled)	4.8	6.3	6.0	6.2	6.0	5.8	5.7	5.7
Tree nuts (shelled)	1.8	2.5	2.4	2.2	2.2	2.3	1.9	2.1

NA Not available.   [1] Excludes edible offals.   [2] Excludes shipments to Puerto Rico and the other U.S. possessions. [3] Excludes game fish consumption.   [4] Includes skin, neck meat, and giblets.   [5] Includes other products, not shown separately.   [6] Fluid milk figures are aggregates of commercial sales and milk produced and consumed on farms.   [7] Heavy cream, light cream, and half and half.   [8] Excludes cottage, pot, and baker's cheese.   [9] Includes other cheeses not shown separately.   [10] Dry weight. Includes edible syrups (maple, molasses, etc.) and honey not shown separately.

Source: U.S. Department of Agriculture, Economic Research Service, *Food Consumption, Prices, and Expenditures, 1997: Annual Data, 1970-1995;* and *Agricultural Outlook,* monthly.

No. 248. Per Capita Utilization of Selected Commercially Produced Fruits and Vegetables: 1980 to 1996

[In pounds, farm weight. Domestic food use of fresh fruits and vegetables reflects the fresh-market share of commodity production plus imports and minus exports. All data are on a calendar year basis except for citrus fruits, October or November; apples, August; grapes and pears, July. See headnote, Table 247]

COMMODITY	1980	1985	1990	1991	1992	1993	1994	1995	1996
Fresh fruits.	104.8	110.6	116.3	113.0	123.5	124.9	126.4	124.5	129.2
Noncitrus	78.8	89.2	95.0	93.9	99.1	98.9	101.4	100.4	104.3
Bananas	20.8	23.5	24.4	25.1	27.3	26.8	28.1	27.4	28.0
Apples	19.2	17.3	19.6	18.2	19.2	19.2	19.6	18.9	19.3
Grapes	4.0	6.8	7.9	7.3	7.2	7.0	7.3	7.5	6.9
Nectarines and peaches	7.1	5.5	5.5	6.4	6.0	6.0	5.5	5.4	4.3
Pears	2.6	2.8	3.2	3.2	3.1	3.4	3.5	3.4	3.1
Strawberries	2.0	3.0	3.2	3.6	3.6	3.6	4.1	4.2	4.4
Pineapples	1.5	1.5	2.1	1.9	2.0	2.1	2.0	1.9	1.9
Plums and prunes	1.5	1.4	1.5	1.4	1.8	1.3	1.6	0.9	1.4
Watermelons	10.7	13.5	13.3	12.8	14.8	14.6	15.4	15.7	17.4
Cantaloups	5.8	8.5	9.2	8.7	8.5	8.7	8.6	9.2	10.6
Honeydews	1.4	2.1	2.1	1.9	2.1	1.7	1.8	1.9	2.3
Other [1]	2.2	3.3	3.0	3.4	3.5	4.6	3.9	4.0	4.7
Citrus	26.1	21.5	21.4	19.1	24.4	26.0	25.0	24.1	24.8
Oranges	14.3	11.6	12.4	8.5	12.9	14.2	13.1	12.0	12.8
Grapefruit	7.3	5.5	4.4	5.9	5.9	6.2	6.1	6.1	5.8
Other [2]	4.5	4.4	4.6	4.7	5.6	5.6	5.8	6.0	6.2
Processed fruits	153.1	153.3	150.5	147.4	137.5	154.4	151.4	155.1	154.0
Noncitrus	55.5	58.3	63.3	61.4	63.1	64.6	63.6	60.8	60.1
Apples	20.6	26.0	28.5	25.7	27.5	29.5	30.1	26.8	27.6
Grapes	11.7	12.3	11.8	12.7	11.5	12.7	11.8	14.2	11.6
Pineapples	10.6	10.7	12.7	12.8	13.3	11.8	10.7	10.6	10.6
Other [3]	12.7	9.4	10.4	10.1	10.9	10.4	11.0	9.2	10.3
Citrus	97.6	95.0	87.1	86.0	74.4	89.9	87.8	94.3	93.9
Oranges	81.0	78.4	72.0	73.7	63.5	74.6	72.5	78.9	76.7
Other [4]	16.6	16.6	15.2	12.3	10.9	15.3	15.2	15.5	17.2
Selected fresh vegetables	149.3	156.1	166.2	163.3	171.3	172.3	175.6	176.3	178.7
Asparagus	0.3	0.5	0.6	0.6	0.6	0.6	0.6	0.6	0.6
Broccoli	1.4	2.6	3.4	3.1	3.4	2.9	3.9	4.0	4.1
Cabbage	8.1	8.8	8.8	8.5	8.9	9.7	9.7	8.7	9.1
Carrots	6.2	6.5	8.3	7.7	8.3	8.2	8.7	9.0	10.2
Cauliflower	1.1	1.8	2.2	2.0	1.8	1.7	1.6	1.4	1.4
Celery	7.4	6.9	7.2	6.8	7.4	7.1	6.8	6.4	6.3
Corn	6.5	6.4	6.7	5.9	6.9	7.0	8.2	7.8	8.3
Cucumbers	3.9	4.4	4.7	4.6	5.0	5.3	5.5	5.7	6.0
Head lettuce	25.6	23.7	27.8	26.1	25.9	24.6	24.3	22.5	23.3
Mushrooms	1.2	1.8	2.0	1.9	2.0	2.0	2.0	2.1	2.1
Onions	11.4	13.6	15.1	15.7	16.2	16.5	16.5	17.6	17.9
Snap beans	1.3	1.3	1.1	1.1	1.5	1.5	1.6	1.7	1.4
Bell peppers	2.9	3.8	4.5	5.1	5.7	6.2	6.5	6.3	7.1
Potatoes	51.1	46.3	45.8	46.4	48.9	49.7	48.6	50.7	48.8
Sweet potatoes [5]	4.4	5.4	4.6	4.0	4.3	3.9	4.7	4.5	4.6
Tomatoes	12.8	14.9	15.5	15.4	15.5	16.0	16.5	17.2	16.6
Other fresh vegetables [6]	3.7	7.4	7.9	8.4	9.0	9.4	9.9	10.1	10.9
Selected vegetables for freezing	51.6	64.5	70.5	72.8	71.6	76.7	81.4	78.2	83.3
Selected vegetables for canning . . .	102.7	99.4	110.9	113.3	111.6	112.1	107.6	110.4	109.4
Potatoes for chips	16.5	17.6	17.0	17.3	17.5	17.6	17.1	16.9	16.9
Pulses [7]	5.8	7.6	7.1	7.8	8.2	7.8	8.4	8.5	8.0

[1] Includes apricots, avocados, cherries, cranberries, kiwi fruit, mangos, and papayas.   [2] Includes tangerines, tangelos, lemons, and limes.   [3] Includes peaches, pears, and strawberries.   [4] Includes grapefruit, lemons, limes, tangelos, and tangerines.   [5] Fresh and processed.   [6] Includes artichokes, Brussels sprouts, eggplant, escarole/endive, garlic, romaine and leaf lettuce (after 1984), radishes, and spinach.   [7] Dry edible beans, dry field peas, and lentils.

No. 249. Per Capita Consumption of Selected Beverages, by Type: 1980 to 1996

[In gallons. See headnote, Table 247]

COMMODITY	1980	1985	1990	1991	1992	1993	1994	1995	1996
Nonalcoholic	(NA)	(NA)	128.6	130.8	130.6	131.0	133.0	133.0	136.9
Milk (plain and flavored)	27.6	26.7	25.7	25.7	25.3	24.7	24.8	24.3	24.3
Whole	17.0	14.3	10.5	10.2	9.8	9.3	9.2	8.8	8.7
Reduced-fat, light, and skim	10.5	12.3	15.2	15.5	15.6	15.4	15.6	15.6	15.7
Tea	7.3	7.1	6.9	7.4	8.1	8.4	8.2	8.0	8.0
Coffee	26.7	27.4	26.9	26.8	25.9	23.4	21.1	20.5	23.1
Bottled water	2.4	4.5	8.0	8.0	8.2	9.4	10.7	11.6	12.4
Soft drinks	35.1	35.7	46.3	47.9	48.5	50.1	51.3	51.6	51.9
Diet	5.1	7.1	10.7	11.7	11.6	11.7	11.8	11.8	11.7
Regular	29.9	28.7	35.6	36.3	36.9	38.4	39.5	39.8	40.2
Selected fruit juices	6.8	7.4	8.1	7.6	7.6	7.3	8.6	8.2	8.7
Fruit drinks, cocktails, and ades	(NA)	(NA)	6.3	6.9	6.5	7.0	7.4	7.8	7.4
Canned iced tea	(NA)	(NA)	0.1	0.2	0.2	0.4	0.6	0.7	0.8
Vegetable juices	(NA)	(NA)	0.3	0.3	0.3	0.3	0.3	0.3	0.3
Alcoholic (adult population)	42.8	40.7	39.5	37.8	37.3	36.7	36.6	35.9	36.1
Beer	36.6	34.6	34.4	33.2	32.7	32.4	32.2	31.6	31.6
Wine [1]	3.2	3.5	2.9	2.7	2.7	2.5	2.5	2.6	2.7
Distilled spirits	3.0	2.6	2.2	2.0	2.0	1.9	1.8	1.8	1.8

NA Not available.   [1] Beginning 1985, includes wine coolers.

Source of Tables 248 and 249: U.S. Dept. of Agriculture, Economic Research Service, *Food Consumption, Prices, and Expenditures*, annual; and *Agricultural Outlook*, monthly.

Figure 4.1
Educational Attainment, by Race, and Hispanic Origin
(For persons 25 years old and over)

Completed 4 Years of High School or More

White
Black
Hispanic

[1] High school graduates or more.

Completed 4 Years of College or More

[1] B.A. degree or more.

Source: Chart prepared by U.S. Bureau of the Census. For data, see Table 260.

This section presents data primarily concerning formal education as a whole, at various levels, and for public and private schools. Data shown relate to the school-age population and school enrollment, educational attainment, education personnel, and financial aspects of education. In addition, data are shown for libraries, computer usage in schools, and adult education. The chief sources are the decennial census of population and the Current Population Survey (CPS), both conducted by the Bureau of the Census (see text, Section 1); annual, biennial, and other periodic surveys conducted by the National Center for Education Statistics, a part of the U.S. Department of Education; and surveys conducted by the National Education Association.

The censuses of population have included data on school enrollment since 1840 and on educational attainment since 1940. The CPS has reported on school enrollment annually since 1945 and on educational attainment periodically since 1947.

The National Center for Education Statistics is continuing the pattern of statistical studies and surveys conducted by the U.S. Office of Education since 1870. The annual *Digest of Education Statistics* provides summary data on pupils, staff, finances, including government expenditures, and organization at the elementary, secondary, and higher education levels. It is also a primary source for detailed information on federal funds for education, projections of enrollment, graduates, and teachers. *The Condition of Education,* issued annually, presents a summary of information on education of particular interest to policymakers.

Other sources of data include special studies by the National Center for Education Statistics and annual or biennial reports of education agencies in individual states. The census of governments, conducted by the Bureau of the Census

In Brief

The enrollment rate of 3 to 5 year olds in preprimary school:

1970	*37 percent*
1996	*61 percent*

Persons 25 years old and over completing college:

1970	*11 percent*
1997	*24 percent*

Public elementary and secondary schools with internet access:

1994	*35 percent*
1997	*78 percent*

every 5 years (for the years ending in "2" and "7"), provides data on school district finances and state and local government expenditures for education. Reports published by the Bureau of Labor Statistics contain data relating civilian labor force experience to educational attainment (see also Tables 648, 674, and 681 in Section 13).

Types and sources of data—The statistics in this section are of two general types. One type, exemplified by data from the Bureau of the Census, is based on direct interviews with individuals to obtain information about their own and their family members' education. Data of this type relate to school enrollment and level of education attained, classified by age, sex, and other characteristics of the population. The school enrollment statistics reflect attendance or enrollment in any regular school within a given period; educational attainment statistics reflect the highest grade completed by an individual or, beginning in 1992, the highest diploma or degree received.

For enrollment data starting in October 1994, the CPS used 1990 census population controls plus adjustments for undercount. Also the survey changed from paper to computer assisted technology; for years 1981 through 1993, 1980 population controls were used; 1971 through 1980, 1970 census population controls had been used. These changes had little impact on summary measures (e.g., medians) and proportional measures (e.g., enrollment rates); however, use of the controls may have significant impact on absolute numbers.

Beginning with data for 1986, a new edit and tabulation package for school enrollment has been introduced. In 1988, a new edit and tabulation package was introduced for educational attainment data.

The second type, generally exemplified by data from the National Center for Education Statistics and the National Education Association, is based on reports from administrators of educational institutions and of state and local agencies having jurisdiction over education. Data of this type relate to enrollment, attendance, staff, and finances for the Nation, individual states, and local areas.

Unlike the National Center for Education Statistics, the Census Bureau does not regularly include specialized vocational, trade, business, or correspondence schools in its surveys. The National Center for Education Statistics includes nursery schools and kindergartens that are part of regular grade schools in their enrollment figures. The Census Bureau includes all nursery schools and kindergartens. At the higher education level, the statistics of both agencies are concerned with institutions granting degrees or offering work acceptable for degree-credit, such as junior colleges.

School attendance—All states require that children attend school. While state laws vary as to the ages and circumstances of compulsory attendance, generally they require that formal schooling begin by age 6 and continue to age 16.

Schools—The National Center for Education Statistics defines a *school* as "a division of the school system consisting of students composing one or more grade groups or other identifiable groups, organized as one unit with one or more teachers to give instruction of a defined type, and housed in a school plant of one

or more buildings. More than one school may be housed in one school plant, as is the case when the elementary and secondary programs are housed in the same school plant."

Regular schools are those which advance a person toward a diploma or degree. They include public and private nursery schools, kindergartens, graded schools, colleges, universities, and professional schools.

Public schools are schools controlled and supported by local, state, or federal governmental agencies; *private* schools are those controlled and supported mainly by religious organizations or by private persons or organizations.

The Bureau of the Census defines *elementary* schools as including grades 1 through 8; *high* schools as including grades 9 through 12; and *colleges* as including junior or community colleges, regular 4-year colleges, and universities and graduate or professional schools. Statistics reported by the National Center for Education Statistics and the National Education Association by type of organization, such as elementary level and secondary level, may not be strictly comparable with those from the Bureau of the Census because the grades included at the two levels vary, depending on the level assigned to the middle or junior high school by the local school systems.

School year—Except as otherwise indicated in the tables, data refer to the school year which, for elementary and secondary schools, generally begins in September of the preceding year and ends in June of the year stated. For the most part, statistics concerning school finances are for a 12-month period, usually July 1 to June 30. Enrollment data generally refer to a specific point in time, such as fall, as indicated in the tables.

Statistical reliability—For a discussion of statistical collection, estimation, and sampling procedures and measures of statistical reliability applicable to Census Bureau and the National Center for Education Statistics data, see Appendix III.

No. 250. School Enrollment: 1965 to 2008

[In thousands. As of fall]

YEAR	TOTAL	ALL LEVELS		K THROUGH GRADE 8		GRADES 9 THROUGH 12		COLLEGE	
		Public	Private	Public	Private	Public	Private	Public	Private
1965	54,394	46,143	8,251	30,563	4,900	11,610	1,400	3,970	1,951
1970	59,838	52,322	7,516	32,558	4,052	13,336	1,311	6,428	2,153
1975	61,004	53,654	7,350	30,515	3,700	14,304	1,300	8,835	2,350
1980	58,305	50,335	7,971	27,647	3,992	13,231	1,339	9,457	2,640
1981	57,916	49,691	8,225	27,280	4,100	12,764	1,400	9,647	2,725
1982	57,591	49,262	8,330	27,161	4,200	12,405	1,400	9,696	2,730
1983	57,432	48,935	8,497	26,981	4,315	12,271	1,400	9,683	2,782
1984	57,150	48,686	8,465	26,905	4,300	12,304	1,400	9,477	2,765
1985	57,226	48,901	8,325	27,034	4,195	12,388	1,362	9,479	2,768
1986	57,709	49,467	8,242	27,420	4,116	12,333	1,336	9,714	2,790
1987	58,254	49,982	8,272	27,933	4,232	12,076	1,247	9,973	2,793
1988	58,485	50,349	8,136	28,501	4,036	11,687	1,206	10,161	2,894
1989	59,436	51,120	8,316	29,152	4,162	11,390	1,193	10,578	2,961
1990	60,267	52,061	8,206	29,878	4,095	11,338	1,137	10,845	2,974
1991	61,605	53,357	8,248	30,506	4,074	11,541	1,125	11,310	3,049
1992	62,686	54,208	8,478	31,088	4,212	11,735	1,163	11,385	3,103
1993	63,241	54,654	8,587	31,504	4,280	11,961	1,191	11,189	3,116
1994	63,986	55,245	8,741	31,898	4,360	12,213	1,236	11,134	3,145
1995, prel.	64,788	55,932	8,856	32,341	4,427	12,500	1,260	11,092	3,169
1996, prel.	65,713	56,720	8,993	32,778	4,486	12,852	1,297	11,090	3,210
1997, proj.	66,526	57,516	9,010	33,206	4,545	13,103	1,322	11,208	3,143
1998, proj.	67,307	58,187	9,121	33,522	4,588	13,270	1,339	11,395	3,194
1999, proj.	67,870	58,668	9,203	33,722	4,616	13,420	1,354	11,525	3,233
2000, proj.	68,334	59,065	9,269	33,903	4,640	13,537	1,366	11,626	3,263
2001, proj.	68,728	59,403	9,325	34,055	4,661	13,643	1,376	11,705	3,287
2002, proj.	69,041	59,675	9,366	34,124	4,671	13,800	1,392	11,751	3,303
2003, proj.	69,337	59,924	9,413	34,124	4,671	13,951	1,407	11,849	3,335
2004, proj.	69,657	60,196	9,461	33,958	4,648	14,263	1,439	11,975	3,374
2005, proj.	69,942	60,436	9,506	33,756	4,620	14,579	1,471	12,101	3,415
2006, proj.	70,160	60,610	9,549	33,584	4,597	14,785	1,491	12,242	3,461
2007, proj.	70,305	60,720	9,584	33,489	4,584	14,854	1,498	12,378	3,502
2008, proj.	70,351	60,735	9,616	33,455	4,579	14,746	1,488	12,534	3,549

Source: U.S. National Center for Education Statistics, *Digest of Education Statistics*, annual, and *Projections of Education Statistics*, annual.

No. 251. School Expenditures, by Type of Control and Level of Instruction in Constant (1996-97) Dollars: 1960 to 1997

[In millions of dollars. For school years ending in year shown. Total expenditures for public elementary and secondary schools include current expenditures, interest on school debt, and capital outlay. Data deflated by the Consumer Price Index, wage earners, and clerical workers through 1975; thereafter, all urban consumers, on a school year basis (supplied by the National Center for Education Statistics). See also Appendix III]

YEAR	Total	ELEMENTARY AND SECONDARY SCHOOLS			COLLEGES AND UNIVERSITIES		
		Total	Public	Private [1]	Total	Public	Private [1]
1960	129,041	90,388	84,439	5,949	38,653	21,112	17,541
1970	287,987	181,660	171,143	10,517	106,327	68,292	38,035
1975	333,402	211,233	198,960	12,273	122,170	82,738	39,431
1980	339,023	211,163	196,425	14,738	127,861	84,812	43,049
1983	343,366	208,410	191,734	16,676	134,956	87,975	46,982
1984	356,896	217,013	199,058	17,954	139,883	90,746	49,137
1985	372,090	224,464	205,834	18,630	147,626	95,713	51,913
1986	393,535	236,280	217,004	19,276	157,255	102,323	54,932
1987	417,115	250,292	229,863	20,429	166,824	106,505	60,319
1988	429,875	257,890	236,902	20,988	171,985	109,548	62,437
1989	454,835	274,538	253,034	21,504	180,298	114,215	66,082
1990	477,475	289,056	266,279	22,777	188,418	120,627	67,792
1991	489,658	295,384	272,245	23,139	194,274	123,922	70,352
1992	497,837	300,384	277,159	23,225	197,453	124,943	72,511
1993	508,394	305,869	282,009	23,860	202,525	128,407	74,218
1994	518,659	312,461	288,334	24,127	206,198	129,951	76,246
1995, prel.	532,366	319,453	294,731	24,722	212,913	134,805	78,108
1996, est.	548,618	330,158	304,651	25,508	218,460	138,440	80,020
1997, est.	564,200	339,700	313,500	26,200	224,500	142,600	81,900

[1] Estimated.

Source: U.S. National Center for Education Statistics, *Digest Education Statistics*, annual.

No. 252. School Enrollment, Faculty, Graduates, and Finances, With Projections: 1985 to 2008

[As of **fall, except as indicated**]

ITEM	Unit	1985	1990	1995, prel.	1996, est.	2000, proj.	2005, proj.	2008, proj.
ELEMENTARY AND SECONDARY SCHOOLS								
School enrollment, total	1,000	44,979	46,448	50,527	51,413	53,445	54,426	54,268
Kindergarten through grade 8	1,000	31,229	33,973	36,768	37,264	38,543	38,376	38,034
Grades 9 through 12	1,000	13,750	12,475	13,760	14,149	14,902	16,050	16,234
Public	1,000	39,422	41,217	44,840	45,630	47,439	48,335	48,201
Kindergarten through grade 8	1,000	27,034	29,878	32,341	32,778	33,903	33,756	33,455
Grades 9 through 12	1,000	12,388	11,338	12,500	12,852	13,537	14,579	14,746
Private	1,000	5,557	5,232	5,687	5,783	6,006	6,091	6,067
Kindergarten through grade 8	1,000	4,195	4,095	4,427	4,486	4,640	4,620	4,579
Grades 9 through 12	1,000	1,362	1,137	1,260	1,297	1,366	1,471	1,488
Enrollment rate:								
5 and 6 year olds	Percent	96.1	96.5	96.0	94.0	(NA)	(NA)	(NA)
7 to 13 year olds	Percent	99.2	99.6	98.9	97.7	(NA)	(NA)	(NA)
14 to 17 year olds	Percent	94.9	95.8	96.3	95.4	(NA)	(NA)	(NA)
Classroom teachers, total [1]	1,000	2,549	2,753	2,978	3,032	3,211	3,394	3,460
Public	1,000	2,206	2,398	2,598	2,645	2,802	2,963	3,022
Private	1,000	343	355	380	387	409	430	438
High school graduates, total [2]	1,000	2,643	2,503	2,557	2,623	2,856	2,984	(NA)
Public	1,000	2,383	2,235	2,293	2,358	2,560	2,675	(NA)
Public schools: [2]								
Constant (**1996-97**) dollars:								
Teachers' average salary	Dol.	36,799	39,165	38,632	38,509	(NA)	(NA)	(NA)
Current school expenditures per pupil	Dol.	5,081	5,817	5,939	6,060	(NA)	(NA)	(NA)
HIGHER EDUCATION								
Enrollment, total	1,000	12,247	13,819	14,262	14,300	14,889	15,516	16,083
Male	1,000	5,818	6,284	6,343	6,344	6,442	6,684	6,906
Full time	1,000	3,608	3,808	3,807	3,816	3,816	4,010	4,182
Part time	1,000	2,211	2,476	2,535	2,528	2,626	2,674	2,724
Female	1,000	6,429	7,535	7,919	7,956	8,447	8,833	9,177
Full time	1,000	3,468	4,013	4,321	4,398	4,727	5,075	5,380
Part time	1,000	2,961	3,521	3,598	3,558	3,720	3,758	3,797
Public	1,000	9,479	10,845	11,092	11,090	11,626	12,101	12,534
Four-year institutions	1,000	5,210	5,848	5,815	5,807	6,114	6,413	6,670
Two-year institutions	1,000	4,270	4,996	5,278	5,283	5,512	5,688	5,864
Private	1,000	2,768	2,974	3,169	3,210	3,263	3,415	3,549
Four-year institutions	1,000	2,506	2,730	2,955	2,996	3,024	3,165	3,288
Two-year institutions	1,000	261	244	215	214	239	250	260
Undergraduate	1,000	10,597	11,959	12,232	12,259	12,915	13,511	14,045
Graduate	1,000	1,376	1,586	1,732	1,743	1,706	1,728	1,752
First-time professional	1,000	274	273	298	298	269	278	286
Full-time equivalent	1,000	8,943	9,983	10,335	10,402	10,829	11,401	11,910
Public	1,000	6,668	7,558	7,752	7,775	8,168	8,593	8,974
Private	1,000	2,276	2,425	2,583	2,627	2,661	2,809	2,937
Faculty, total	1,000	715	817	932	890	947	(NA)	(NA)
Public	1,000	503	574	657	633	673	(NA)	(NA)
Private	1,000	212	244	275	257	274	(NA)	(NA)
Degrees conferred, total [2]	1,000	1,830	2,025	2,247	2,243	2,231	2,404	(NA)
Associate's	1,000	446	482	532	529	535	579	(NA)
Bachelor's	1,000	988	1,095	1,186	1,183	1,151	1,253	(NA)
Master's	1,000	289	337	406	410	426	446	(NA)
Doctorate's	1,000	34	39	44	44	46	48	(NA)
First-professional	1,000	74	72	79	77	73	78	(NA)

NA Not available.   [1] Full-time equivalents.   [2] For school year ending June the following year.

Source: U.S. National Center for Education Statistics, *Digest of Education Statistics*, annual, and *Projections of Educational Statistics*, annual.

No. 253. Federal Funds for Education and Related Programs: 1995 to 1997

[In millions of dollars, except percent. For fiscal years ending in September. Figures represent on-budget funds]

LEVEL, AGENCY, AND PROGRAM	1995	1996	1997 [1]
Total, all programs	71,636.3	70,743.4	73,070.4
Percent of federal budget outlays	4.7	4.5	4.5
Elementary/secondary education programs	33,623.8	34,391.5	36,634.8
Department of Education [2]	14,029.0	14,323.8	15,663.1
Grants for the disadvantaged	6,808.0	7,020.5	7,234.8
School improvement programs	1,397.0	1,247.4	1,520.6
Indian education	71.0	77.4	67.5
Education for the handicapped	3,177.0	3,222.2	3,425.9
Vocational and adult education	1,482.0	1,348.1	1,597.4
Education reform—Goals 2000	61.0	271.5	690.5
Department of Agriculture [2]	8,201.3	8,408.1	8,795.2
Child nutrition programs [3]	7,644.8	7,875.0	8,264.0
Agricultural Marketing Service—commodities [4]	400.0	400.0	400.0
Department of Defense [2]	1,295.5	1,313.1	1,373.1
Overseas dependents schools	855.8	813.3	856.3
Section VI schools [5]	284.2	336.1	349.1
Department of Energy	12.6		
Department of Health and Human Services	5,116.6	5,185.9	4,946.6
Head Start	3,534.0	3,570.0	3,981.0
Social security student benefits	953.0	931.0	324.0
Department of the Interior [2]	493.1	486.5	603.8
Mineral Leasing Act and other funds	56.2	56.9	134.3
Indian Education	435.9	428.5	468.5
Department of Justice	128.9	175.9	196.9
Department of Labor	3,957.8	4,084.0	4,593.0
Job Corps	1,029.0	1,114.0	1,146.0
Department of Veterans Affairs	311.8	344.3	371.4
Vocational rehab for disabled veterans	298.1	349.6	377.4
Other agencies and programs	77.2	70.0	91.7
Higher education programs [2]	17,614.9	15,772.3	15,417.7
Department of Education [2]	14,234.0	12,257.6	11,735.3
Student financial assistance	7,047.0	6,861.6	7,599.0
Federal Family Education Loans	6,030.0	4,258.7	2,974.3
Department of Agriculture	33.4	3.4	32.6
Department of Commerce	3.5	3.4	3.5
Department of Defense	729.5	864.9	872.1
Tuition assistance for military personnel	127.0	260.3	258.7
Service academies [6]	163.3	171.7	176.2
Senior ROTC	219.4	218.2	231.1
Professional development education [2]	219.8	214.7	206.1
Department of Energy [2]	28.0		
Department of Health and Human Services [2]	796.0	798.6	862.3
Health professions training programs	298.3	2,733.5	313.9
National Health Service Corps scholarships	78.2	28.8	31.2
National Institutes of Health training grants [7]	380.5	457.0	476.0
Department of the Interior [2]	159.1	132.5	146.5
Shared revenues, Mineral Leasing Act and other receipts—estimated education share	82.8	59.0	71.0
Indian programs	76.2	73.5	75.5
Department of State	3.0	2.0	-
Department of Transportation	56.1	50.3	50.6
Department of Veterans Affairs [2]	1,010.1	1,074.7	1,183.8
Post-Vietnam veterans	33.6	44.4	59.9
All-volunteer-force educational assistance	868.4	922.8	1,017.8
Other agencies and programs [2]	562.3	555.5	530.9
National Endowment for the Humanities	56.5	30.9	30.9
National Science Foundation	211.8	262.0	273.0
United States Information Agency	260.8	239.4	198.6
Other education programs [2]	4,719.7	4,828.0	5,125.2
Department of Education [2]	2,861.0	3,085.6	3,293.0
Administration	404.0	502.9	414.3
Libraries	117.0	167.6	167.7
Rehabilitative services and handicapped research	2,333.0	2,410.2	2,702.2
Department of Agriculture	422.9	412.9	408.8
Department of Health and Human Services	138.0	117.0	145.0
Department of Justice	36.3	35.1	33.7
Department of State	51.6	53.3	54.1
Department of the Treasury [2]	48.0	59.0	61.0
Other agencies and programs [2]	1,161.8	1,065.2	1,129.5
Agency for International Development	260.4	307.0	290.0
Library of Congress	241.0	252.0	269.0
National Endowment for the Arts	2.3	0.5	6.2
National Endowment for the Humanities	94.2	62.4	62.4
Research programs at universities and related institutions	15,677.9	15,751.6	15,892.7
Department of Agriculture	434.5	423.1	420.6
Department of Defense	1,854.0	1,602.8	1,490.7
Department of Energy	2,651.6	2,558.8	2,609.3
Department of Health and Human Services	6,419.0	7,013.7	7,109.1
National Aeronautics and Space Administration [2]	1,752.0	1,611.4	1,512.0
National Science Foundation	1,874.4	1,861.2	1,969.0

- Represents zero. [1] Estimated. [2] Includes other programs and agencies, not shown separately. [3] The Special Milk Program is included in the Child Nutrition Program. [4] Purchased under Section 32 of the Act of August 1935 for use in child nutrition programs. [5] Program provides for the education of dependents of federal employees residing on federal property where free public education is unavailable in the nearby community. [6] Instructional costs only including academics, audiovisual, academic computer center, faculty training, military training, physical education, and libraries. [7] Includes alcohol, drug abuse, and mental health training programs.

Source: U.S. National Center for Education Statistics, *Digest of Education Statistics*, 1997.

No. 254. School Expenditures, by Source of Funds in Constant (1996-97) Dollars: 1980 to 1995

[For school years ending in year shown. Includes nursery, kindergarten, and special programs when provided by school system. Data are deflated by the Consumer Price Index for all urban consumers, on a school year basis (supplied by the U.S. National Center for Education Statistics). Distribution by source of funds is estimated]

SOURCE OF FUNDS AND CONTROL OF SCHOOL	EXPENDITURES (bil. dol.)					PERCENT DISTRIBUTION				
	1980	1985	1990	1994	1995	1980	1985	1990	1994	1995
Total.	339.0	372.2	477.5	518.7	532.4	100.0	100.0	100.0	100.0	100.0
Federal.	38.7	32.0	39.5	45.7	46.2	11.4	8.6	8.3	8.8	8.7
State	131.6	144.4	177.9	178.4	187.9	38.8	38.8	37.3	34.4	35.3
Local	88.6	95.1	122.6	135.9	134.8	26.1	25.6	25.7	26.2	25.3
All other	80.0	100.5	137.5	158.6	163.4	23.6	27.0	28.8	30.6	30.7
Public.	281.2	301.5	386.9	418.3	429.5	100.0	100.0	100.0	100.0	100.0
Federal	30.3	23.7	28.7	34.7	35.0	10.8	7.9	7.4	8.3	8.1
State	130.8	143.5	176.2	176.8	186.2	46.5	47.6	45.5	42.3	43.4
Local	88.2	94.8	122.1	135.3	134.4	31.4	31.4	31.6	32.4	31.3
All other	31.9	39.5	59.9	71.5	74.0	11.4	13.1	15.5	17.1	17.2
Private	57.7	70.6	90.6	100.5	102.8	100.0	100.0	100.0	100.0	100.0
Federal	8.4	8.3	10.8	11.1	11.2	14.5	11.7	11.9	11.0	10.9
State and local	1.2	1.4	2.3	2.2	2.1	2.1	1.9	2.5	2.2	2.1
All other	48.1	61.0	77.5	87.2	89.5	83.3	86.4	85.6	86.8	87.0
Elementary and secondary .	211.2	224.5	289.1	312.5	319.5	100.0	100.0	100.0	100.0	100.0
Federal	19.2	13.7	16.3	20.3	20.1	9.1	6.1	5.6	6.5	6.3
State	91.5	100.4	125.9	130.2	137.8	43.3	44.7	43.6	41.7	43.1
Local	85.2	91.3	117.6	130.1	129.0	40.3	40.7	40.7	41.7	40.4
All other	15.4	19.2	29.2	31.8	32.6	7.3	8.6	10.1	10.2	10.2
Public	196.5	205.8	266.3	288.3	294.7	100.0	100.0	100.0	100.0	100.0
Federal	19.2	13.7	16.3	20.3	20.1	9.8	6.6	6.1	7.1	6.8
State	91.5	100.4	125.9	130.2	137.8	46.6	48.8	47.3	45.2	46.8
Local	85.2	91.3	117.6	130.1	129.0	43.3	44.4	44.2	45.1	43.8
All other [1]	0.6	0.6	6.4	7.7	7.9	0.3	0.3	2.4	2.7	2.7
Private	14.7	18.6	22.8	24.1	24.7	100.0	100.0	100.0	100.0	100.0
Higher education	127.9	147.7	188.4	206.2	212.9	100.0	100.0	100.0	100.0	100.0
Federal	19.4	18.3	23.2	25.4	26.2	15.2	12.4	12.3	12.3	12.3
State	40.1	44.2	52.0	48.2	50.1	31.4	29.9	27.6	23.4	23.5
Local	3.5	3.8	4.9	5.7	5.8	2.7	2.5	2.6	2.8	2.7
All other	64.7	81.3	108.2	126.8	130.8	50.6	55.0	57.4	61.5	61.5
Public	84.7	95.7	120.6	130.0	134.8	100.0	100.0	100.0	100.0	100.0
Federal	11.1	10.1	12.4	14.3	14.9	13.0	10.5	10.3	11.0	11.1
State	39.3	43.1	50.3	46.6	48.4	46.4	45.1	41.7	35.9	35.9
Local	3.1	3.5	4.4	5.2	5.4	3.6	3.6	3.7	4.0	4.0
All other	31.3	38.9	53.5	63.8	66.1	37.0	40.7	44.3	49.1	49.0
Private	43.0	52.0	67.8	76.2	78.1	100.0	100.0	100.0	100.0	100.0
Federal	8.4	8.3	10.8	11.1	11.2	19.5	15.9	15.9	14.5	14.4
State and local	1.2	1.4	2.2	2.1	2.1	2.9	2.6	3.3	2.8	2.7
All other	33.4	42.4	54.8	63.0	64.7	77.6	81.5	80.8	82.7	82.9

[1] Beginning in 1989-90, includes all fees for transportation, books, and food services.

Source: U.S. National Center for Education Statistics, Digest of Education Statistics, annual.

No. 255. Enrollment in Public and Private Schools, by Control and Level, With Projections: 1980 to 2008

[In thousands. As of fall. Data are for regular day schools and exclude independent nursery schools and kindergartens, residential schools for exceptional children, subcollegiate departments of colleges, federal schools for Indians, and federally operated schools on federal installations. College data include degree-credit and nondegree-credit enrollment]

CONTROL OF SCHOOL AND LEVEL	1980	1985	1990	1995, prel.	2000, proj.	2003, proj.	2004, proj.	2005, proj.	2006, proj.	2007, proj.	2008, proj.
Total.	58,305	57,226	60,267	64,789	68,335	69,337	69,657	69,942	70,160	70,305	70,351
Public.	50,335	48,901	52,061	55,932	59,066	59,924	60,196	60,436	60,611	60,721	60,735
Private	7,971	8,325	8,206	8,857	9,269	9,413	9,461	9,506	9,549	9,584	9,616
Kindergarten through 8 . .	31,639	31,229	33,973	36,768	38,543	38,795	38,606	38,376	38,181	38,073	38,034
Public.	27,647	27,034	29,878	32,341	33,903	34,124	33,958	33,756	33,584	33,489	33,455
Private	3,992	4,195	4,095	4,427	4,640	4,671	4,648	4,620	4,597	4,584	4,579
Grades 9 through 12. . . .	14,570	13,750	12,475	13,760	14,902	15,358	15,702	16,050	16,276	16,352	16,234
Public	13,231	12,388	11,338	12,500	13,537	13,951	14,263	14,579	14,785	14,854	14,746
Private	1,339	1,362	1,137	1,260	1,366	1,407	1,439	1,471	1,491	1,498	1,488
College.	12,097	12,247	13,819	14,262	14,889	15,185	15,349	15,516	15,703	15,880	16,083
Public.	9,457	9,479	10,845	11,092	11,626	11,849	11,975	12,101	12,242	12,378	12,534
Private	2,640	2,768	2,974	3,169	3,263	3,335	3,374	3,415	3,461	3,502	3,549

Source: U.S. National Center for Education Statistics, Digest of Education Statistics, annual; Projections of Education Statistics, annual; and unpublished data.

No. 256. School Enrollment, by Age: 1970 to 1996

[As of **October.** Covers civilian noninstitutional population enrolled in nursery school and above. Based on Current Population Survey, see text, Section 1, Population]

AGE	1970	1980	1985	1990	1991	1992	1993	1994	1995	1996
ENROLLMENT										
Total 3 to 34 years old . . .	**60,357**	**57,348**	**58,013**	**60,588**	**61,276**	**62,084**	**62,730**	**66,427**	**66,939**	**67,317**
3 and 4 years old.	1,461	2,280	2,801	3,292	3,068	3,063	3,275	3,917	4,042	3,959
5 and 6 years old.	7,000	5,853	6,697	7,207	7,178	7,252	7,298	7,752	7,901	7,893
7 to 13 years old	28,943	23,751	22,849	25,016	25,445	25,768	26,110	26,768	27,003	26,936
14 and 15 years old	7,869	7,282	7,362	6,555	6,634	6,861	7,011	7,519	7,651	7,598
16 and 17 years old	6,927	7,129	6,654	6,098	6,155	6,272	6,339	6,895	6,997	7,220
18 and 19 years old	3,322	3,788	3,716	4,044	3,969	4,012	4,063	4,180	4,274	4,539
20 and 21 years old	1,949	2,515	2,708	2,852	3,041	3,027	2,810	3,133	3,025	3,017
22 to 24 years old	1,410	1,931	2,068	2,231	2,365	2,577	2,579	2,724	2,545	2,605
25 to 29 years old	1,011	1,714	1,942	2,013	2,045	1,907	1,942	2,070	2,216	2,265
30 to 34 years old	466	1,105	1,218	1,281	1,377	1,344	1,303	1,468	1,284	1,286
35 years old and over	(NA)	1,290	1,766	2,439	2,620	2,473	2,634	2,845	2,830	2,979
ENROLLMENT RATE										
Total 3 to 34 years old . . .	**56.4**	**49.7**	**48.3**	**50.2**	**50.7**	**51.4**	**51.8**	**53.3**	**53.7**	**54.1**
3 and 4 years old.	20.5	36.7	38.9	44.4	40.5	39.7	40.4	47.3	48.7	48.3
5 and 6 years old.	89.5	95.7	96.1	96.5	95.4	95.5	95.4	96.7	96.0	94.0
7 to 13 years old	99.2	99.3	99.2	99.6	99.7	99.4	99.5	99.3	98.9	97.7
14 and 15 years old	98.1	98.2	98.1	99.0	98.8	99.1	98.9	98.8	98.9	98.0
16 and 17 years old	90.0	89.0	91.7	92.5	93.3	94.1	94.0	94.4	93.6	92.8
18 and 19 years old	47.7	46.4	51.6	57.3	59.6	61.4	61.6	60.2	59.4	61.5
20 and 21 years old	31.9	31.0	35.3	39.7	42.0	44.0	42.7	44.9	44.9	44.4
22 to 24 years old	14.9	16.3	16.9	21.0	22.2	23.7	23.6	24.1	23.2	24.8
25 to 29 years old	7.5	9.3	9.2	9.7	10.2	9.8	10.2	10.8	11.6	11.9
30 to 34 years old	4.2	6.4	6.1	5.8	6.2	6.1	5.9	6.7	6.0	6.1
35 years old and over	(NA)	1.4	1.6	2.1	2.2	2.1	2.2	2.3	2.2	2.3

NA Not available.

Source: U.S. Bureau of the Census, *Current Population Reports*, P20-500; and earlier reports.

No. 257. School Enrollment, by Race, Hispanic Origin, and Age: 1980 to 1996

[See headnote, Table 256]

AGE	WHITE			BLACK			HISPANIC ORIGIN [1]		
	1980	1990	1996	1980	1990	1996	1980	1990	1996
ENROLLMENT									
Total 3 to 34 years	**47,673**	**48,899**	**52,987**	**8,251**	**8,854**	**10,443**	**4,263**	**6,073**	**8,570**
3 and 4 years old	1,844	2,700	3,052	371	452	687	172	249	502
5 and 6 years old	4,781	5,750	6,215	904	1,129	1,233	491	835	1,188
7 to 13 years old	19,585	20,076	21,175	3,598	3,832	4,326	2,009	2,794	3,710
14 and 15 years old	6,038	5,265	5,997	1,088	1,023	1,197	568	739	978
16 and 17 years old	5,937	4,858	5,680	1,047	962	1,151	454	592	862
18 and 19 years old	3,199	3,271	3,645	494	596	613	226	329	470
20 and 21 years old	2,206	2,402	2,428	242	305	389	111	213	244
22 to 24 years old.	1,669	1,781	2,070	196	274	300	93	121	272
25 to 29 years old.	1,473	1,706	1,741	187	162	349	84	130	217
30 to 34 years old.	942	1,090	984	124	119	197	54	72	127
35 years old and over	1,104	2,096	2,392	186	238	408	(NA)	145	248
ENROLLMENT RATE									
Total 3 to 34 years	**48.9**	**49.5**	**53.4**	**53.9**	**51.9**	**56.2**	**49.8**	**47.4**	**50.3**
3 and 4 years old	36.3	44.9	47.9	38.2	41.6	49.9	28.5	29.8	38.1
5 and 6 years old	95.8	96.5	94.8	95.4	96.3	90.5	94.5	94.8	89.5
7 to 13 years old	99.2	99.6	97.7	99.4	99.8	97.4	99.2	99.4	97.2
14 and 15 years old	98.3	99.1	98.0	97.9	99.2	98.9	94.3	99.0	96.6
16 and 17 years old	88.6	92.5	92.8	90.6	91.7	92.1	81.8	85.4	88.7
18 and 19 years old	46.3	57.1	62.5	45.7	55.2	52.8	37.8	44.1	47.0
20 and 21 years old	31.9	41.0	44.9	23.4	28.4	37.0	19.5	27.2	25.3
22 to 24 years old.	16.4	20.2	24.6	13.6	20.0	21.0	11.7	9.9	17.6
25 to 29 years old.	9.2	9.9	11.3	8.8	6.1	13.7	6.9	6.3	8.6
30 to 34 years old.	6.3	5.9	5.7	6.8	4.4	7.1	5.1	3.6	5.0
35 years old and over	1.3	2.1	2.2	1.8	2.1	3.0	(NA)	2.1	2.5

NA Not available.   [1] Persons of Hispanic origin may be of any race.

Source: U.S. Census Bureau, *Current Population Reports*, P20-500; and earlier reports.

No. 258. Enrollment in Public and Private Schools: 1960 to 1996

[In millions, except percent. As of October. For civilian noninstitutional population. For 1960, 5 to 34 years old; for 1970 to 1985, 3 to 34 years old; beginning 1986, for 3 years old and over]

YEAR	PUBLIC						PRIVATE					
	Total	Nur-sery	Kinder-garten	Ele-mentary	High School	College	Total	Nur-sery	Kinder-garten	Ele-mentary	High School	College
1960	39.0	(NA)	(1)	27.5	9.2	2.3	7.2	(NA)	(1)	4.9	1.0	1.3
1970	52.2	0.3	2.6	30.0	13.5	5.7	8.1	0.8	0.5	3.9	1.2	1.7
1975	52.8	0.6	2.9	27.2	14.5	7.7	8.2	1.2	0.5	3.3	1.2	2.0
1978	50.0	0.6	2.5	25.3	14.2	7.4	8.6	1.2	0.5	3.2	1.2	2.4
1979	50.0	0.6	2.6	24.8	14.0	7.7	8.2	1.2	0.4	3.1	1.1	2.3
1980	(NA)	0.6	2.7	24.4	(NA)	(NA)	(NA)	1.4	0.5	3.1	(NA)	(NA)
1981	49.7	0.7	2.6	24.8	13.5	8.2	8.7	1.4	0.5	3.0	1.1	2.6
1982	49.2	0.7	2.7	24.4	13.0	8.4	8.2	1.4	0.6	3.0	1.1	2.6
1983	48.7	0.8	2.7	24.2	12.8	8.2	9.0	1.5	0.7	3.0	1.2	2.6
1984	49.0	0.8	3.0	24.1	12.7	8.5	8.3	1.6	0.5	2.7	1.1	2.4
1985 2	49.0	0.9	3.2	23.8	12.8	8.4	9.0	1.6	0.6	3.1	1.2	2.5
1986 2	51.2	0.8	3.4	24.2	13.0	9.8	9.4	1.7	0.6	3.0	1.2	2.9
1987 2	51.7	0.8	3.4	24.8	12.7	10.0	8.9	1.7	0.6	2.8	1.1	2.8
1988 2	52.2	0.9	3.4	25.5	12.2	10.3	8.9	1.8	0.5	2.8	1.0	2.8
1989 2	52.5	0.9	3.3	25.9	12.1	10.3	8.9	1.9	0.6	2.7	0.8	2.9
1990 2	53.8	1.2	3.3	26.6	11.9	10.7	9.2	2.2	0.6	2.7	0.9	2.9
1991 2	54.5	1.1	3.5	26.6	12.2	11.1	9.4	1.8	0.6	3.0	1.0	3.0
1992 2	55.0	1.1	3.5	27.1	12.3	11.1	9.4	1.8	0.6	3.1	1.0	3.0
1993 2	56.0	1.2	3.5	27.7	12.6	10.9	9.4	1.8	0.7	2.9	1.0	3.0
1994 2	58.6	1.9	3.3	28.1	13.5	11.7	10.7	2.3	0.6	3.4	1.1	3.3
1995 2	58.7	2.0	3.2	28.4	13.7	11.4	11.1	2.4	0.7	3.4	1.2	3.3
1996 2	59.5	1.9	3.4	28.1	14.1	12.0	10.8	2.3	0.7	3.4	1.2	3.2
Percent White:												
1960.	85.7	(NA)	(1)	84.3	88.2	92.2	95.7	(NA)	(1)	95.3	96.7	96.3
1970.	84.5	59.5	84.4	83.1	85.6	90.7	93.4	91.1	88.2	94.1	96.1	92.8
1980.	(NA)	68.2	80.7	80.9	(NA)	(NA)	(NA)	89.0	87.0	90.7	(NA)	(NA)
1990.	79.8	71.7	78.3	78.9	79.2	84.1	87.4	89.6	83.2	88.2	89.4	85.0
1995.	78.0	71.3	76.9	77.5	76.9	81.9	85.0	88.7	84.1	86.1	86.0	81.1
1996.	77.7	70.3	77.4	77.4	77.9	79.6	84.5	84.0	83.4	86.5	88.0	81.7

NA Not available.   1 Included in elementary school.   2 See Table 305 for college enrollment 35 years old and over. Also data beginning 1986 based on a revised edit and tabulation package.

Source: U.S. Bureau of the Census, Current Population Reports, P20-500; and earlier reports.

No. 259. School Enrollment, by Sex and Level: 1960 to 1996

[In millions. As of Oct. For the civilian noninstitutional population. For 1960, persons 5 to 34 years old; 1970-1979, 3 to 34 years old; beginning 1980, 3 years old and over. Elementary includes kindergarten and grades 1-8; high school, grades 9-12; and college, 2-year and 4-year colleges, universities, and graduate and professional schools. Data for college represent degree-credit enrollment]

YEAR	ALL LEVELS 1			ELEMENTARY			HIGH SCHOOL			COLLEGE		
	Total	Male	Female	Total	Male	Female	Total	Male	Female	Total	Male	Female
1960	46.3	24.2	22.0	32.4	16.7	15.7	10.2	5.2	5.1	3.6	2.3	1.2
1970	60.4	31.4	28.9	37.1	19.0	18.1	14.7	7.4	7.3	7.4	4.4	3.0
1975	61.0	31.6	29.4	33.8	17.3	16.5	15.7	8.0	7.7	9.7	5.3	4.4
1978	58.6	30.1	28.6	31.5	16.1	15.3	15.5	7.8	7.6	9.8	5.1	4.7
1979	57.9	29.5	28.3	30.9	15.9	15.0	15.1	7.7	7.4	10.0	5.0	5.0
1980 2	58.6	29.6	29.1	30.6	15.8	14.9	14.6	7.3	7.3	11.4	5.4	6.0
1981 2	58.4	29.5	28.9	30.1	15.5	14.7	14.4	7.3	7.1	11.8	5.6	6.2
1981 3	59.9	30.3	29.6	31.0	15.9	15.0	14.7	7.5	7.3	12.1	5.8	6.3
1982	59.4	30.0	29.4	30.7	15.8	14.9	14.2	7.2	7.0	12.3	5.9	6.4
1983	59.3	30.1	29.2	30.6	15.7	14.8	14.1	7.1	7.0	12.4	6.0	6.3
1984	58.9	29.9	29.0	30.3	15.6	14.7	13.9	7.1	6.8	12.3	6.0	6.3
1985	59.8	30.0	29.7	30.7	15.7	15.0	14.1	7.2	6.9	12.5	5.9	6.6
1986 4	60.1	30.4	29.7	31.1	16.1	15.0	14.0	7.1	6.9	12.4	5.8	6.6
1986 4	60.5	30.6	30.0	31.1	16.1	15.0	14.2	7.2	7.0	12.7	6.0	6.7
1987	60.6	30.7	29.9	31.6	16.3	15.3	13.8	7.0	6.8	12.7	6.0	6.7
1988	61.1	30.7	30.5	32.2	16.6	15.6	13.2	6.7	6.4	13.1	5.9	7.2
1989	61.5	30.8	30.7	32.5	16.7	15.8	12.9	6.6	6.3	13.2	6.0	7.2
1990	63.0	31.5	31.5	33.2	17.1	16.0	12.8	6.5	6.4	13.6	6.2	7.4
1991	63.9	32.1	31.8	33.8	17.3	16.4	13.1	6.8	6.4	14.1	6.4	7.6
1992	64.6	32.2	32.3	34.3	17.7	16.6	13.3	6.8	6.5	14.0	6.2	7.8
1993	65.4	32.9	32.5	34.8	17.9	16.9	13.6	7.0	6.6	13.9	6.3	7.6
1994	69.3	34.6	34.6	35.4	18.2	17.2	14.6	7.4	7.2	15.0	6.8	8.2
1995	69.8	35.0	34.8	35.7	18.3	17.4	15.0	7.7	7.3	14.7	6.7	8.0
1996	70.3	35.1	35.2	35.5	18.3	17.3	15.3	7.9	7.4	15.2	6.8	8.4

1 Beginning 1970, includes nursery schools, not shown separately.   2 Based on 1970 population controls.   3 Based on 1980 population controls.   4 Revised. Data beginning 1986, based on a revised edit and tabulation package.

Source: U.S. Bureau of the Census, Current Population Reports, P20-500; and earlier reports.

No. 260. Educational Attainment, by Race and Hispanic Origin: 1960 to 1997

[In percent. **For persons 25 years old and over. 1960, 1970, and 1980 as of April 1** and based on sample data from the censuses of population. **Other years as of March** and based on the Current Population Survey; see text, Section 1, Population, and Appendix III. See Table 261 for data by sex]

YEAR	Total [1]	White	Black	Asian and Pacific Islander	HISPANIC [2] Total [3]	Mexican	Puerto Rican	Cuban
COMPLETED 4 YEARS OF HIGH SCHOOL OR MORE								
1960	41.1	43.2	20.1	(NA)	(NA)	(NA)	(NA)	(NA)
1965	49.0	51.3	27.2	(NA)	(NA)	(NA)	(NA)	(NA)
1970	52.3	54.5	31.4	(NA)	32.1	24.2	23.4	43.9
1975	62.5	64.5	42.5	(NA)	37.9	31.0	28.7	51.7
1980	66.5	68.8	51.2	(NA)	44.0	37.6	40.1	55.3
1985	73.9	75.5	59.8	(NA)	47.9	41.9	46.3	51.1
1990	77.6	79.1	66.2	80.4	50.8	44.1	55.5	63.5
1994 [4]	80.9	82.0	72.9	84.8	53.3	46.7	59.4	64.1
1995 [4]	81.7	83.0	73.8	(NA)	53.4	46.5	61.3	64.7
1996 [4]	81.7	82.8	74.3	83.2	53.1	46.9	60.4	63.8
1997 [4]	82.1	83.0	74.9	84.9	54.7	48.6	61.1	65.2
COMPLETED 4 YEARS OF COLLEGE OR MORE								
1960	7.7	8.1	3.1	(NA)	(NA)	(NA)	(NA)	(NA)
1965	9.4	9.9	4.7	(NA)	(NA)	(NA)	(NA)	(NA)
1970	10.7	11.3	4.4	(NA)	4.5	2.5	2.2	11.1
1975	13.9	14.5	6.4	(NA)	(NA)	(NA)	(NA)	(NA)
1980	16.2	17.1	8.4	(NA)	7.6	4.9	5.6	16.2
1985	19.4	20.0	11.1	(NA)	8.5	5.5	7.0	13.7
1990	21.3	22.0	11.3	39.9	9.2	5.4	9.7	20.2
1994 [4]	22.2	22.9	12.9	41.2	9.1	6.3	9.7	16.2
1995 [4]	23.0	24.0	13.2	(NA)	9.3	6.5	10.7	19.4
1996 [4]	23.6	24.3	13.6	41.7	9.3	6.5	11.0	18.8
1997 [4]	23.9	24.6	13.3	42.2	10.3	7.5	10.7	19.7

NA Not available.   [1] Includes other races, not shown separately.   [2] Persons of Hispanic origin may be of any race. [3] Includes persons of other Hispanic origin, not shown separately.   [4] Beginning 1994, persons high school graduates and those with a BA degree or higher.

Source: U.S. Bureau of the Census, *U.S. Census of Population, U.S. Summary,* PC80-1-C1 and *Current Population Reports* P20-455, P20-459, P20-462, P20-465RV, P20-489, P20-493, P20-505; and unpublished data.

No. 261. Educational Attainment, by Race, Hispanic Origin, and Sex: 1960 to 1997

[See Table 260 for headnote and totals for both sexes]

YEAR	ALL RACES [1] Male	Female	WHITE Male	Female	BLACK Male	Female	ASIAN AND PACIFIC ISLANDER Male	Female	HISPANIC [2] Male	Female
COMPLETED 4 YEARS OF HIGH SCHOOL OR MORE										
1960	39.5	42.5	41.6	44.7	18.2	21.8	(NA)	(NA)	(NA)	(NA)
1965	48.0	49.9	50.2	52.2	25.8	28.4	(NA)	(NA)	(NA)	(NA)
1970	51.9	52.8	54.0	55.0	30.1	32.5	(NA)	(NA)	37.9	34.2
1975	63.1	62.1	65.0	64.1	41.6	43.3	(NA)	(NA)	39.5	36.7
1980	67.3	65.8	69.6	68.1	50.8	51.5	(NA)	(NA)	67.3	65.8
1985	74.4	73.5	76.0	75.1	58.4	60.8	(NA)	(NA)	48.5	47.4
1990	77.7	77.5	79.1	79.0	65.8	66.5	84.0	77.2	50.3	51.3
1994 [3]	81.0	80.7	82.1	81.9	71.7	73.8	88.6	81.5	53.4	53.2
1995 [3]	81.7	81.6	83.0	83.0	73.4	74.1	(NA)	(NA)	52.9	53.8
1996 [3]	81.9	81.6	82.7	82.8	74.3	74.2	86.0	80.7	53.0	53.3
1997 [3]	82.0	82.2	82.9	83.2	73.5	76.0	(NA)	(NA)	54.9	54.6
COMPLETED 4 YEARS OF COLLEGE OR MORE										
1960	9.7	5.8	10.3	6.0	2.8	3.3	(NA)	(NA)	(NA)	(NA)
1965	12.0	7.1	12.7	7.3	4.9	4.5	(NA)	(NA)	(NA)	(NA)
1970	13.5	8.1	14.4	8.4	4.2	4.6	(NA)	(NA)	7.8	4.3
1975	17.6	10.6	18.4	11.0	6.7	6.2	(NA)	(NA)	8.3	4.6
1980	20.1	12.8	21.3	13.3	8.4	8.3	(NA)	(NA)	9.4	6.0
1985	23.1	16.0	24.0	16.3	11.2	11.0	(NA)	(NA)	9.7	7.3
1990	24.4	18.4	25.3	19.0	11.9	10.8	44.9	35.4	9.8	8.7
1994 [3]	25.1	19.6	26.1	20.0	12.8	13.0	45.8	37.2	9.6	8.6
1995 [3]	26.0	20.2	27.2	21.0	13.6	12.9	(NA)	(NA)	10.1	8.4
1996 [3]	26.0	21.4	26.9	21.8	12.4	14.6	46.4	37.3	10.3	8.3
1997 [3]	26.2	21.7	27.0	22.3	12.5	13.9	(NA)	(NA)	10.6	10.1

NA Not available.   [1] Includes other races, not shown separately.   [2] Persons of Hispanic origin may be of any race. [3] Beginning 1994, persons high school graduates and those with a BA degree or higher.

Source: U.S. Bureau of the Census, *U.S. Census of Population, 1960, 1970, and 1980, Vol.1;* and *Current Population Reports* P20-459, P20-489, P20-493, P20-505; and unpublished data.

No. 262. Educational Attainment, by Selected Characteristic: 1997

[**For persons 25 years old and over.** As of **March.** Based on Current Population Survey; see text, Section 1, Population, and Appendix III. For composition of regions, see map, inside front cover]

CHARACTERISTIC	Population (1,000)	PERCENT OF POPULATION—HIGHEST LEVEL					
		Not a high school graduate	High school graduate	Some college, but no degree	Associate's degree [1]	Bachelor's degree	Advanced degree
Total persons	170,581	17.9	33.8	17.2	7.3	16.0	7.8
Age:							
25 to 34 years old	40,256	12.7	31.6	20.0	8.6	21.1	6.0
35 to 44 years old	43,960	11.9	34.6	18.9	8.9	17.7	7.9
45 to 54 years old	33,013	13.2	32.8	17.5	8.1	16.8	11.6
55 to 64 years old	21,475	22.4	36.7	14.7	5.4	12.0	8.7
65 to 74 years old	18,015	30.5	35.7	13.4	4.1	10.1	6.2
75 years old or over	13,862	39.6	32.5	12.2	3.0	8.3	4.5
Sex:							
Male	81,620	18.0	32.1	17.2	6.5	16.8	9.4
Female	88,961	17.8	35.5	17.2	8.0	15.4	6.3
Race: White	144,058	17.0	33.9	17.2	7.4	16.5	8.1
Black	19,072	25.1	35.8	19.1	6.7	9.5	3.8
Other	7,451	17.5	25.4	13.5	7.0	23.7	12.9
Hispanic origin: Hispanic	15,476	45.3	25.9	13.3	5.2	7.5	2.9
Non-Hispanic	155,105	15.2	34.5	17.6	7.5	16.9	8.3
Region: Northeast	34,031	17.5	35.8	13.3	6.8	17.3	9.3
Midwest	39,505	14.8	38.2	16.8	7.6	15.4	7.1
South	59,924	20.7	33.5	17.2	6.7	14.5	7.4
West	37,121	16.9	27.5	21.3	8.3	18.0	7.9
Marital status:							
Never married	25,354	16.4	29.9	18.8	6.9	20.1	7.8
Married spouse present	105,710	15.0	34.2	16.9	7.7	17.3	8.9
Married spouse absent	6,833	29.7	32.9	17.4	6.2	9.4	4.4
Separated	4,642	28.0	35.7	18.1	6.5	8.0	3.7
Widowed	13,720	39.7	34.2	12.1	3.9	6.8	3.2
Divorced	18,965	16.2	36.5	20.4	8.3	12.4	6.2
Civilian labor force status:							
Employed	109,399	10.7	32.8	18.6	8.7	19.4	9.8
Unemployed	5,035	25.6	37.5	17.8	5.8	9.3	3.9
Not in the labor force	55,437	31.7	35.4	14.3	4.5	9.9	4.2

[1] Includes vocational degrees.

Source: U.S. Bureau of the Census, *Current Population Reports,* P20-505; and unpublished data.

No. 263. Earnings, by Highest Degree Earned: 1997

[**For persons 18 years old and over with earnings. Persons as of March.** Earnings for prior year. Based on Current Population Survey; see text, section 1, Population, and Appendix III. For definition of mean, see Guide to Tabular Presentation]

CHARACTERISTIC	Total persons	LEVEL OF HIGHEST DEGREE							
		Not a high school graduate	High school graduate only	Some college, no degree	Asso- ciate's	Bache- lor's	Master's	Profes- sional	Doctorate
MEAN EARNINGS (dol.)									
All persons [1]	28,106	15,011	22,154	23,937	28,514	38,112	50,162	94,038	72,464
Age:									
18 to 24 years old	10,394	6,950	11,221	9,125	14,277	18,026	26,621	5,000	(B)
25 to 34 years old	25,010	14,692	20,373	23,608	26,770	32,431	35,626	52,476	44,282
35 to 44 years old	33,451	17,975	25,613	29,640	30,438	43,830	58,624	109,588	81,400
45 to 54 years old	36,720	19,865	27,133	34,141	33,086	44,523	56,022	115,498	75,426
55 to 64 years old	32,152	19,098	24,829	34,178	32,570	41,874	45,391	95,146	79,498
65 years old and over .	20,256	12,051	14,536	15,771	15,694	32,272	29,689	68,056	75,976
Sex:									
Male	34,705	17,826	27,642	30,057	35,484	46,702	62,145	102,913	81,492
Female	20,570	10,421	16,161	17,475	22,480	28,701	36,483	72,015	51,865
White	28,844	15,358	22,782	24,229	28,867	38,936	50,813	92,612	73,647
Male	35,821	18,246	28,591	30,847	36,222	48,014	63,113	103,490	82,615
Female	20,590	10,290	16,270	16,959	22,122	28,667	36,687	64,618	53,862
Black	21,978	13,110	18,722	23,148	25,220	31,955	37,592	(B)	(B)
Male	25,067	15,461	22,267	25,594	29,561	35,558	40,313	(B)	(B)
Female	19,271	10,337	15,379	21,155	22,793	29,311	35,909	(B)	(B)
Hispanic [2]	19,439	13,287	18,528	21,303	25,014	32,955	36,827	(B)	(B)
Male	21,870	14,986	21,593	25,795	29,693	38,130	36,370	(B)	(B)
Female	15,841	9,867	14,635	15,659	20,192	27,407	37,660	(B)	(B)

B Base figure too small to meet statistical standards for reliability of a derived figure.   [1] Includes other races, not shown separately.   [2] Persons of Hispanic origin may be of any race.

Source: U.S. Bureau of the Census, *Current Population Reports,* P20-505.

No. 264. Educatonal Attainment—25 Largest States: 1997

[In percent. As of March. For persons 25 years old and over. Twenty five largest states based on total resident population. For data on smaller states, see Table 265. Based on the Current Population Survey; see text, Section 1, Population, and Appendix III]

ITEM	Total	AGE			SEX		RACE		His-panic origin [1]
		25 to 44 yrs. old	45 to 64 yrs. old	65 yrs. old and over	Male	Female	White	Black	
U.S. total: High school graduate or more .	**82.1**	**87.7**	**83.2**	**65.5**	**82.0**	**82.2**	**83.0**	**74.9**	**54.7**
Bachelor's degree or more	**23.9**	**26.3**	**25.4**	**14.8**	**26.2**	**21.7**	**24.6**	**13.3**	**10.3**
Alabama: High school graduate or more	77.6	87.9	78.5	54.4	78.4	76.9	81.1	66.6	(B)
Bachelor's degree or more	19.3	24.4	20.0	7.7	19.0	19.6	21.5	12.4	(B)
Arizona: High school graduate or more.	82.6	82.4	82.9	82.5	82.9	82.3	83.3	74.7	54.8
Bachelor's degree or more	19.5	18.3	24.2	15.9	21.4	17.7	19.8	15.5	7.4
California: High school graduate or more	80.7	81.1	83.4	74.4	81.2	80.2	79.7	85.1	49.5
Bachelor's degree or more	27.5	27.0	31.7	21.3	30.2	24.8	26.2	20.5	8.8
Florida: High school graduate or more	81.4	85.8	81.8	73.4	80.8	82.0	83.3	64.7	65.7
Bachelor's degree or more	21.7	21.9	24.9	17.3	25.1	18.6	22.8	9.6	17.1
Georgia: High school graduate or more	78.8	85.3	78.9	58.0	77.6	79.9	82.6	70.5	85.6
Bachelor's degree or more	22.3	26.6	20.6	12.0	22.3	22.4	26.0	12.7	27.6
Illinois: High school graduate or more.	84.4	89.3	86.2	67.4	83.5	85.3	84.8	81.9	54.0
Bachelor's degree or more	25.0	28.5	26.4	12.6	28.1	22.3	26.2	12.0	8.2
Indiana: High school graduate or more	81.9	90.5	82.4	61.5	84.4	79.6	82.2	74.3	(B)
Bachelor's degree or more	16.2	19.1	17.4	7.8	17.0	15.4	16.1	7.5	(B)
Kentucky: High school graduate or more.	75.4	86.0	74.0	50.3	75.0	75.7	75.0	80.4	(B)
Bachelor's degree or more	17.6	21.1	14.9	12.7	19.7	15.8	17.9	9.6	(B)
Louisiana: High school graduate or more	75.7	83.0	75.4	56.3	75.3	76.0	79.5	65.3	(B)
Bachelor's degree or more	18.1	19.7	20.1	10.6	20.1	16.4	21.7	8.9	(B)
Maryland: High school graduate or more	84.7	90.0	88.1	63.4	84.3	85.1	85.6	79.9	63.8
Bachelor's degree or more	32.2	33.2	35.2	24.0	34.5	30.1	35.1	15.5	32.0
Massachusetts: High school graduate or more .	85.9	90.7	86.7	70.7	85.5	86.2	86.7	74.2	63.9
Bachelor's degree or more	33.5	39.7	35.5	12.5	35.0	32.0	34.0	13.3	10.3
Michigan: High school graduate or more	86.0	92.3	88.9	66.1	85.4	86.5	86.9	79.3	65.2
Bachelor's degree or more	21.0	23.2	22.1	14.0	23.0	19.2	21.9	11.4	10.0
Minnesota: High school graduate or more. . . .	87.9	93.6	89.6	64.4	86.6	89.2	87.8	93.9	(B)
Bachelor's degree or more	28.3	32.0	31.3	8.5	31.8	24.9	28.1	27.2	(B)
Missouri: High school graduate or more.	80.1	86.7	83.3	61.5	80.5	79.8	82.1	67.1	(B)
Bachelor's degree or more	22.9	27.7	21.6	14.4	24.2	21.8	23.7	14.1	(B)
New Jersey: High school graduate or more . . .	84.8	92.6	86.2	62.6	85.1	84.5	85.2	79.7	64.3
Bachelor's degree or more	28.5	33.7	29.0	14.5	32.5	24.9	28.4	15.6	13.7
New York: High school graduate or more	80.0	86.1	81.0	62.5	81.2	79.0	82.3	68.6	52.0
Bachelor's degree or more	25.8	29.5	26.8	14.3	27.9	23.9	27.7	11.6	8.7
North Carolina: High school graduate or more . .	78.4	86.3	77.8	58.0	76.6	80.1	79.8	74.1	54.7
Bachelor's degree or more	22.6	26.1	20.9	16.1	24.2	21.0	24.8	13.7	17.8
Ohio: High school graduate or more.	86.2	92.0	89.2	67.3	86.5	85.9	87.2	76.2	60.1
Bachelor's degree or more	21.5	25.3	24.2	8.3	25.5	17.9	22.0	12.4	13.4
Pennsylvania: High school graduate or more . .	82.4	92.0	83.8	60.1	83.0	81.9	83.3	76.2	55.0
Bachelor's degree or more	22.9	29.1	21.6	11.8	25.7	20.5	23.8	12.2	7.0
South Carolina: High school graduate or more .	77.3	87.0	73.8	54.8	76.2	78.4	81.3	66.1	(B)
Bachelor's degree or more	19.2	20.7	20.0	12.9	21.0	17.7	22.6	10.0	(B)
Tennessee: High school graduate or more . . .	76.1	87.7	73.1	51.0	75.0	77.0	75.0	80.9	(B)
Bachelor's degree or more	17.1	20.4	15.3	11.5	19.0	15.5	18.0	11.1	(B)
Texas: High school graduate or more	78.5	83.6	77.7	62.1	78.1	78.9	77.4	83.9	52.4
Bachelor's degree or more	22.4	23.9	23.9	14.0	24.6	20.4	22.5	16.9	9.0
Virginia: High school graduate or more.	81.3	89.8	77.0	65.5	78.5	83.8	83.2	71.7	73.6
Bachelor's degree or more	28.0	31.9	25.8	21.4	30.9	25.4	30.3	15.0	27.8
Washington: High school graduate or more . . .	88.8	90.1	90.9	79.1	88.0	89.6	89.0	(B)	37.9
Bachelor's degree or more	26.1	25.0	30.3	19.5	27.6	24.6	26.2	(B)	4.6
Wisconsin: High school graduate or more	87.1	94.3	90.2	60.9	88.0	86.4	87.8	77.1	(B)
Bachelor's degree or more	22.4	25.9	22.2	12.4	24.9	20.1	22.9	9.8	(B)

B Base too small to meet statistical standards for reliability of a derived figure.   [1] Persons of Hispanic origin may be of any race.

Source: U.S. Bureau of the Census, *Current Population Reports*, P20-505.

No. 265. Educational Attainment for Smaller States: 1997

[See headnote, Table 264]

STATE	High school graduate or more	Bachelor's degree or more	STATE	High school graduate or more	Bachelor's degree or more
U.S. total	**82.1**	**23.9**	Montana	88.6	25.2
			Nebraska	86.0	21.3
Alaska	92.1	27.5	Nevada	85.4	19.9
Arkansas	76.9	14.6	New Hampshire.	85.1	27.0
Colorado	87.6	28.9	New Mexico	78.0	23.6
Connecticut	84.0	30.0	North Dakota	82.6	20.5
Delaware	84.4	26.8	Oklahoma	85.2	20.5
District of Columbia	80.3	33.7	Oregon	84.7	24.3
Hawaii	83.7	22.5	Rhode Island	77.5	25.7
Idaho	85.7	19.4	South Dakota	85.6	20.1
Iowa	86.7	21.7	Utah	89.5	26.7
Kansas	88.1	27.5	Vermont	84.4	23.7
Maine	85.8	20.0	West Virginia	77.3	14.7
Mississippi	77.5	20.9	Wyoming	91.3	22.2

Source: U.S. Bureau of the Census, *Current Population Reports*, P20-505.

No. 266. Preprimary School Enrollment—Summary: 1970 to 1996

[As of **October**. Civilian noninstitutional population. Includes public and nonpublic nursery school and kindergarten programs. Excludes 5 year olds enrolled in elementary school. Based on Current Population Survey; see text, Section 1, Population, and Appendix III]

ITEM	1970	1975	1980	1985	1990	1993	1994	1995	1996
NUMBER OF CHILDREN (1,000)									
Population, 3 to 5 years old	10,949	10,183	9,284	10,733	11,207	11,954	12,328	12,518	12,378
Total enrolled [1]	4,104	4,954	4,878	5,865	6,659	6,581	7,514	7,739	7,580
Nursery	1,094	1,745	1,981	2,477	3,378	2,984	4,162	4,331	4,147
Public	332	570	628	846	1,202	1,204	1,848	1,950	1,830
Private	762	1,174	1,353	1,631	2,177	1,779	2,314	2,381	2,317
Kindergarten	3,010	3,211	2,897	3,388	3,281	3,597	3,352	3,408	3,433
Public	2,498	2,682	2,438	2,847	2,767	3,020	2,819	2,799	2,853
Private	511	528	459	541	513	577	534	608	580
White	3,443	4,105	3,994	4,757	5,389	5,224	5,889	6,144	5,902
Black	586	731	725	919	964	1,011	1,289	1,236	1,245
Hispanic [2]	(NA)	(NA)	370	496	642	657	851	1,040	1,068
3 years old.	454	683	857	1,035	1,205	1,097	1,385	1,489	1,506
4 years old.	1,007	1,418	1,423	1,765	2,086	2,179	2,532	2,553	2,454
5 years old.	2,643	2,852	2,598	3,065	3,367	3,306	3,597	3,697	3,621
ENROLLMENT RATE									
Total enrolled [1]	37.5	48.6	52.5	54.6	59.4	55.1	61.0	61.8	61.2
White	37.8	48.6	52.7	54.7	59.7	55.7	60.9	63.0	61.2
Black	34.9	48.1	51.8	55.8	57.8	52.7	64.2	58.9	60.8
Hispanic [2]	(NA)	(NA)	43.3	43.3	49.0	43.9	47.7	51.1	52.7
3 years old.	12.9	21.5	27.3	28.8	32.6	27.1	33.9	35.9	37.2
4 years old.	27.8	40.5	46.3	49.1	56.0	53.9	60.3	61.6	59.2
5 years old.	69.3	81.3	84.7	86.5	88.8	85.7	88.9	87.5	86.5

NA Not available.   [1] Includes races not shown separately.   [2] Persons of Hispanic origin may be of any race. The method of identifying Hispanic children was changed in 1980 from allocation based on status of mother to status reported for each child. The number of Hispanic children using the new method is larger.

Source: U.S. Bureau of the Census, *Current Population Reports*, P20-500.

No. 267. School Enrollment of 3 to 5 Year Olds, by Education and Labor Force Status of Mother and Family Income: 1996

[**In thousands.** As of **October**. Civilian noninstitutional population. Based on Current Population Survey; see text, Section 1, Population, and Appendix III]

CHARACTERISTIC	Total popula- tion [1]	ENROLLED IN NURSERY SCHOOL			ENROLLED IN KINDERGARTEN			Enrolled in elemen- tary school
		Total	Public	Private	Total	Public	Private	
Total children 3 to 5 years	12,378	4,147	1,830	2,317	3,433	2,853	580	214
3- and 4- year olds	8,193	3,655	1,540	2,115	305	202	103	-
5-year olds	4,185	492	290	202	3,129	2,652	477	214
Education of mother:								
Children living with mother	11,531	3,899	1,673	2,225	3,177	2,621	555	207
Elementary: 0 to 8 years.	667	132	120	12	166	158	8	4
High school: 1-3 years	1,312	313	254	59	332	328	4	22
High school graduate	3,696	1,106	639	466	964	859	105	81
College: Less than a BA degree . .	3,428	1,226	436	790	1,065	831	234	49
BA degree or higher	2,430	1,122	224	898	651	446	205	50
Labor force status of mother:								
Children living with mother	11,531	3,899	1,673	2,225	3,177	2,621	555	207
Mother in the labor force.	7,341	2,688	1,113	1,575	2,134	1,728	406	138
Employed	6,792	2,511	992	1,519	1,986	1,595	390	125
Full time	4,639	1,665	658	1,007	1,352	1,082	271	98
Part time	2,153	846	334	512	633	514	120	27
Unemployed	549	177	120	57	149	133	16	13
Mother not in the labor force	4,190	1,211	561	650	1,042	893	149	69
Children not living with mother.	847	249	157	92	256	232	25	8
Family income:								
Less than $10,000	1,645	434	371	63	401	366	34	28
$10,000 to 14,999.	999	275	194	81	283	265	18	13
$15,000 to 19,999.	797	233	185	49	237	219	18	14
$20,000 to 24,999.	1,130	337	197	140	299	265	34	29
$25,000 to 29,999.	796	244	129	115	220	198	22	13
$30,000 to 34,999.	740	206	93	114	225	187	38	3
$35,000 to 39,999.	801	272	121	151	235	188	47	15
$40,000 to 49,999.	1,186	433	140	293	293	244	49	22
$50,000 to 74,999.	1,979	785	166	619	571	408	164	26
$75,000 and over	1,336	651	105	546	393	277	116	28
Not reported	968	277	130	147	276	235	41	24

- Represents zero.   [1] Includes those not enrolled, not shown separately.

Source: U.S. Bureau of the Census, *Current Population Reports*, P20-500.

No. 268. Public Elementary and Secondary Schools—Summary: 1980 to 1997

[For school year ending in year shown, except as indicated. Data are estimates]

ITEM	Unit	1980	1985	1990	1994	1995	1996	1997
School districts, total.............	Number .	16,044	15,812	15,552	15,056	14,947	14,910	14,891
ENROLLMENT								
Population 5-17 years old [1]........	1,000...	48,041	44,787	44,949	47,293	48,110	48,912	49,699
Percent of resident population.....	Percent .	21.4	19.0	18.2	18.3	18.5	18.6	18.7
Fall enrollment [2]................	1,000...	41,778	39,354	40,527	43,274	43,898	44,649	45,346
Percent of population 5-17 years old [3]	Percent .	87.0	87.9	90.2	91.5	91.2	91.3	91.2
Elementary [3]................	1,000...	24,397	23,830	26,253	28,147	28,148	28,581	28,926
Secondary [4]................	1,000...	17,381	15,524	14,274	15,127	15,750	16,068	16,419
Average daily:								
Attendance (ADA).............	1,000...	38,411	36,530	37,573	40,144	40,794	41,477	42,143
High school graduates	1,000...	2,762	2,424	2,327	2,227	2,282	2,283	2,336
INSTRUCTIONAL STAFF								
Total [5]	1,000...	2,521	2,473	2,685	2,865	2,929	2,970	3,042
Classroom teachers............	1,000...	2,211	2,175	2,362	2,512	2,567	2,606	2,668
Average salaries:								
Instructional staff..............	Dollar ..	16,715	24,666	32,638	37,446	38,331	39,465	40,562
Classroom teachers............	Dollar ..	15,970	23,600	31,367	35,737	36,685	37,716	38,562
REVENUES								
Revenue receipts...............	Mil. dol. .	97,635	141,013	208,656	259,587	273,364	286,927	301,404
Federal......................	Mil. dol. .	9,020	9,553	13,184	18,434	18,766	19,323	20,387
State	Mil. dol. .	47,929	69,107	100,787	119,443	130,139	138,045	147,396
Local	Mil. dol. .	40,686	62,373	94,685	121,710	124,459	129,560	133,621
Percent of total:								
Federal......................	Percent .	9.2	6.8	6.3	7.1	6.9	6.7	6.8
State	Percent .	49.1	49.0	48.3	46.0	47.6	48.1	48.9
Local	Percent .	41.7	44.2	45.4	46.9	45.5	45.2	44.3
EXPENDITURES								
Total	Mil. dol. .	96,105	139,382	209,698	262,485	276,502	292,323	308,077
Current expenditures (day schools) ....[6].....	Mil. dol. .	85,661	127,230	186,583	230,773	242,729	254,254	268,026
Other current expenditures [6]......	Mil. dol. .	1,859	2,109	3,341	5,199	5,464	5,902	6,397
Capital outlay................	Mil. dol. .	6,504	7,529	16,012	20,578	21,904	25,189	25,849
Interest on school debt	Mil. dol. .	2,081	2,514	3,762	5,934	6,406	6,978	7,806
Percent of total:								
Current expenditures (day schools)	Percent .	89.1	91.3	89.0	87.9	87.8	87.0	87.0
Other current expenditures [6]......	Percent .	1.9	1.5	1.6	2.0	2.0	2.0	2.1
Capital outlay................	Percent .	6.8	5.4	7.6	7.8	7.9	8.6	8.4
Interest on school debt	Percent .	2.2	1.8	1.8	2.3	2.3	2.4	2.5
In current dollars:								
Revenue receipts per pupil enrolled.................	Dollar ..	2,337	3,583	5,149	5,999	6,227	6,426	6,647
Current expenditures per pupil enrolled.................	Dollar ..	2,050	3,233	4,604	5,333	5,529	5,695	5,911
In constant (1997) dollars: [7]								
Revenue receipts per pupil enrolled.................	Dollar ..	4,785	5,382	6,442	6,520	6,579	6,609	6,647
Current expenditures per pupil enrolled.................	Dollar ..	4,199	4,856	5,760	5,796	5,842	5,857	5,911

[1] Estimated resident population as of July 1 of the previous year. Estimates reflect revisions based on the 1990 Census of Population.   [2] Fall enrollment of the previous year.   [3] Kindergarten through grade 6.   [4] Grades 7 through 12.   [5] Full-time equivalent.   [6] Current expenses for summer schools, adult education, post-high school vocational education, personnel retraining, etc., when operated by local school districts and not part of regular public elementary and secondary day-school program.   [7] Compiled by U.S. Bureau of the Census. Deflated by the Consumer Price Index, all urban consumers (for school year) supplied by U.S. National Center for Education Statistics.

Source: Except as noted, National Education Association, Washington, DC, Estimates of School Statistics Database (copyright).

No. 269. Elementary and Secondary Schools—Teachers and Pupil-Teacher Ratios With Projections: 1960 to 1997

[In thousands, except ratios. As of fall. Data are for full-time equivalents. Schools are classified by type of organization, rather than by grade group; elementary includes kindergarten and secondary includes junior high]

ITEM	TOTAL			PUBLIC			PRIVATE		
	Total	Elemen-tary	Second-ary	Total	Elemen-tary	Second-ary	Total	Elemen-tary	Second-ary
Number of teachers:									
1960	1,600	991	609	1,408	858	550	192	133	59
1970	2,292	1,283	1,009	2,059	1,130	929	233	153	80
1975	2,453	1,353	1,100	2,198	1,181	1,017	255	172	83
1980	2,485	1,401	1,084	2,184	1,189	995	301	212	89
1985	2,549	1,483	1,066	2,206	1,237	969	343	246	97
1987	2,632	1,564	1,068	2,279	1,307	973	353	257	95
1988	2,668	1,604	1,064	2,323	1,353	970	345	251	94
1989	2,734	1,662	1,072	2,357	1,387	970	377	275	102
1990	2,753	1,680	1,073	2,398	1,426	972	355	254	101
1991	2,787	1,713	1,074	2,432	1,459	973	355	254	101
1992	2,822	1,752	1,070	2,459	1,492	967	363	260	103
1993	2,870	1,775	1,095	2,504	1,513	991	366	262	104
1994	2,926	1,794	1,132	2,552	1,528	1,024	373	266	108
1995	2,978	1,814	1,164	2,598	1,546	1,053	380	269	111
1996, prel.	3,023	1,836	1,186	2,638	1,564	1,073	385	272	113
1997, proj.	3,071	1,861	1,211	2,682	1,586	1,096	390	275	115
Pupil-teacher ratio:									
1960	26.4	29.4	21.4	25.8	28.4	21.7	30.7	36.1	18.6
1970	22.4	24.6	19.5	22.3	24.3	19.8	23.0	26.5	16.4
1975	20.3	21.7	18.6	20.4	21.7	18.8	19.6	21.5	15.7
1980	18.6	20.1	16.6	18.7	20.4	16.8	17.7	18.8	15.0
1985	17.6	19.1	15.6	17.9	19.5	15.8	16.2	17.1	14.0
1987	17.3	18.8	15.0	17.6	19.3	15.2	15.5	16.4	13.1
1988	17.0	18.6	14.7	17.3	19.0	14.9	15.2	16.1	12.8
1989	16.8	18.4	14.3	17.2	19.0	14.6	14.2	15.1	11.7
1990	16.9	18.5	14.3	17.2	19.0	14.6	14.7	16.1	11.3
1991	17.0	18.5	14.5	17.3	18.9	14.9	14.6	16.0	11.1
1992	17.1	18.4	14.8	17.4	18.8	15.2	14.8	16.2	11.3
1993	17.1	18.5	14.7	17.4	18.9	15.1	14.9	16.3	11.5
1994	17.1	18.6	14.7	17.3	18.9	15.1	15.0	16.4	11.4
1995	17.0	18.6	14.5	17.3	18.9	14.8	15.0	16.5	11.4
1996, prel.	16.9	18.5	14.4	17.1	18.8	14.7	15.0	16.5	11.4
1997, proj.	17.0	18.6	14.5	17.3	19.0	14.9	15.0	16.5	11.5

Source: U.S. National Center for Education Statistics, *Digest of Education Statistics*, annual.

No. 270. Public Elementary and Secondary Schools, by Type and Size of School: 1995-96

[Data reported by schools, rather than school districts]

ENROLLMENT SIZE OF SCHOOL	NUMBER OF SCHOOLS					ENROLLMENT (1,000) [1]				
	Total	Ele-men-tary [2]	Second-ary [3]	Com-bined [4]	Other [5]	Total	Ele-men-tary [2]	Second-ary [3]	Com-bined [4]	Other [5]
Total	87,125	61,165	20,997	2,796	2,167	44,682	29,120	14,343	1,122	98
PERCENT DISTRIBUTION										
Total	100.0	100.0	100.0	100.0	100.0	100.0	100.0	100.0	100.0	100.0
Under 100 students.	8.9	5.8	13.5	30.4	59.9	0.8	0.6	0.9	3.3	18.9
100 to 199 students	9.5	8.9	10.5	14.7	18.5	2.7	2.8	2.2	5.3	18.9
200 to 299 students	11.2	12.2	8.6	10.2	10.8	5.4	6.5	3.0	6.2	19.6
300 to 399 students	13.5	15.8	7.8	7.9	5.1	9.0	11.6	3.8	6.9	13.2
400 to 499 students	13.4	16.0	7.1	6.7	2.5	11.5	15.1	4.5	7.5	8.1
500 to 599 students	11.8	13.8	6.8	7.1	1.1	12.3	15.9	5.3	9.7	4.3
600 to 699 students	8.8	9.8	6.4	5.1	0.3	10.8	13.4	5.9	8.2	1.4
700 to 799 students	6.2	6.7	5.4	4.3	0.3	8.9	10.5	5.7	7.9	1.5
800 to 999 students . . .	7.2	6.8	9.0	5.3	0.7	12.2	12.6	11.4	11.9	4.7
1,000 to 1,499 students . . .	6.3	3.9	13.7	5.1	0.7	14.3	9.5	23.9	15.4	6.4
1,500 to 1,999 students . . .	2.0	0.4	6.8	2.1	-	6.5	1.3	16.7	8.9	-
2,000 to 2,999 students . . .	1.0	0.1	4.0	0.8	-	4.6	0.3	13.3	4.5	-
3,000 or more students . . .	0.2	-	0.6	0.4	0.1	1.2	-	3.2	4.4	3.2
Average enrollment	(X)	(X)	(X)	(X)	(X)	525	476	703	401	136

- Represents zero.   X Not applicable.   [1] Data for those schools reporting enrollment.   [2] Includes schools beginning with grade 6 or below and with no grade higher than 8.   [3] Includes schools with no grade lower than 7.   [4] Includes schools with both elementary and secondary grades.   [5] Includes special education, alternative, and other schools not classified by grade span.

Source: U.S. National Center for Education Statistics, *Digest of Education Statistics*, annual.

No. 271. Public Elementary and Secondary School Enrollment, by State: 1980 to 1995

[In thousands, except rate. As of fall. Includes unclassified students]

STATE	ENROLLMENT								ENROLLMENT RATE [2]			
	K through grade 8 [1]				Grades 9 through 12							
	1980	1985	1990	1995, prel.	1980	1985	1990	1995, prel.	1980	1985	1990	1995, prel.
United States . . .	27,647	27,034	29,878	32,341	13,231	12,388	11,338	12,500	86.2	87.7	91.3	91.6
Alabama.	528	517	527	539	231	213	195	207	87.6	89.6	93.3	95.8
Alaska.	60	77	85	93	26	30	29	34	94.0	99.4	97.4	94.8
Arizona.	357	386	479	549	157	162	161	195	88.9	90.8	93.3	93.5
Arkansas	310	304	314	322	138	130	123	131	90.3	91.8	95.9	94.9
California	2,730	2,927	3,615	4,041	1,347	1,329	1,336	1,495	87.1	89.5	92.8	92.8
Colorado.	374	379	420	479	172	172	154	177	92.2	92.7	94.6	92.5
Connecticut.	364	321	347	384	168	141	122	134	83.3	83.4	90.2	91.7
Delaware	62	63	73	77	37	30	27	31	79.5	80.1	87.4	86.6
District of Columbia .	71	62	61	62	29	25	19	18	91.8	96.8	100.9	105.7
Florida	1,042	1,086	1,370	1,614	468	476	492	563	84.4	86.7	92.6	91.0
Georgia	742	757	849	966	327	323	303	345	86.8	88.2	93.6	95.7
Hawaii	110	113	123	136	55	51	49	52	83.4	84.2	87.6	88.3
Idaho	144	149	160	170	59	59	61	74	95.4	93.6	96.9	95.2
Illinois	1,335	1,246	1,310	1,390	649	580	512	553	82.6	83.3	86.9	88.1
Indiana.	708	654	676	684	347	312	279	293	88.0	88.4	90.4	90.6
Iowa	351	324	345	344	183	161	139	158	88.4	89.1	92.1	93.2
Kansas.	283	286	320	329	133	125	117	134	88.7	91.0	92.6	91.7
Kentucky	464	449	459	468	206	195	177	192	83.7	85.8	90.5	93.0
Louisiana	544	573	586	580	234	215	199	217	80.2	83.9	88.2	88.5
Maine.	153	142	155	156	70	64	60	58	91.6	93.3	96.5	93.5
Maryland	493	446	527	590	258	225	188	215	83.9	84.9	89.1	89.0
Massachusetts.	676	559	604	675	346	285	230	240	88.6	86.3	88.8	90.2
Michigan.	1,227	1,086	1,145	1,192	570	517	440	450	86.9	87.8	90.3	88.9
Minnesota.	482	468	546	586	272	237	211	249	87.2	89.4	91.2	90.8
Mississippi	330	330	372	366	147	141	131	140	79.6	81.0	91.3	91.8
Missouri	567	544	588	636	277	251	228	254	83.8	84.9	86.5	87.9
Montana.	106	108	111	116	50	46	42	49	92.9	93.8	93.8	93.6
Nebraska	189	184	198	203	91	82	76	87	86.6	87.7	88.7	88.6
Nevada	101	107	150	196	49	48	51	69	93.4	93.3	98.7	95.7
New Hampshire	112	107	126	142	55	54	46	52	85.3	87.5	89.1	89.6
New Jersey.	820	740	784	880	426	376	306	317	81.5	82.9	86.1	86.5
New Mexico	186	187	208	229	85	90	94	100	89.5	91.6	94.3	91.7
New York	1,838	1,703	1,828	1,980	1,033	918	770	833	80.8	82.3	86.6	88.6
North Carolina	786	749	783	871	343	337	304	312	90.1	91.2	94.8	92.0
North Dakota.	77	84	85	82	40	35	33	37	85.9	89.2	92.8	93.2
Ohio	1,312	1,206	1,258	1,297	645	588	514	539	84.8	85.6	88.0	88.4
Oklahoma.	399	414	425	446	179	178	154	171	92.9	94.3	95.1	95.5
Oregon.	319	305	340	376	145	142	132	152	88.5	89.7	90.7	90.1
Pennsylvania.	1,231	1,093	1,172	1,257	678	591	496	531	80.4	80.3	83.6	84.6
Rhode Island.	98	90	102	110	51	44	37	40	80.1	81.2	87.3	88.1
South Carolina.	426	424	452	463	193	183	170	182	88.1	89.6	94.0	94.9
South Dakota	86	88	95	101	42	37	34	43	87.4	90.7	89.7	94.5
Tennessee	602	575	598	651	252	239	226	243	87.8	88.3	93.5	94.7
Texas.	2,049	2,261	2,511	2,757	851	871	872	991	92.4	93.2	98.4	98.9
Utah	250	299	325	328	93	105	122	149	98.2	96.3	97.7	97.4
Vermont	66	63	71	75	29	27	25	30	87.9	89.3	93.9	95.9
Virginia.	703	665	728	788	307	303	270	292	90.7	94.0	94.2	93.4
Washington.	515	507	613	680	242	243	227	277	91.7	92.2	94.0	92.9
West Virginia	270	249	224	211	113	109	98	96	92.6	92.2	95.7	96.6
Wisconsin.	528	501	566	603	303	267	232	267	82.1	83.8	86.0	87.0
Wyoming	70	74	71	69	28	29	27	31	97.3	97.0	97.3	97.0

[1] Data include a small number of pre-kindergarten students.   [2] Percent of persons 5-17 years old. Based on enumerated resident population as of April 1, 1980, and 1990, and estimated resident population as of July 1 for other years. Data not adjusted for revisions based on the 1990 Census of Population.

Source: U.S. National Center for Education Statistics, *Digest of Education Statistics*, annual.

No. 272. Public Elementary and Secondary School Enrollment, by Grade: 1980 to 1995

[In thousands. As of fall of year. Kindergarten includes nursery schools]

GRADE	1980	1985	1987	1988	1989	1990	1991	1992	1993	1994	1995, prel.
Pupils enrolled	40,877	39,422	40,008	40,189	40,543	41,217	42,047	42,823	43,465	44,111	44,840
Kindergarten and grades 1 to 8 .	27,647	27,034	27,933	28,501	29,152	29,878	30,506	31,088	31,504	31,898	32,341
Kindergarten	2,689	3,192	3,388	3,433	3,486	3,610	3,686	3,817	3,922	4,047	4,173
First.	2,894	3,239	3,407	3,460	3,485	3,499	3,556	3,542	3,529	3,593	3,671
Second.	2,800	2,941	3,173	3,223	3,289	3,327	3,360	3,431	3,429	3,440	3,507
Third	2,893	2,895	3,046	3,167	3,235	3,297	3,334	3,361	3,437	3,439	3,445
Fourth	3,107	2,771	2,938	3,051	3,182	3,248	3,315	3,342	3,361	3,426	3,431
Fifth	3,130	2,776	2,901	2,945	3,067	3,197	3,268	3,325	3,350	3,372	3,438
Sixth	3,038	2,789	2,811	2,937	2,987	3,110	3,239	3,303	3,356	3,381	3,395
Seventh	3,085	2,938	2,910	2,905	3,027	3,067	3,181	3,299	3,355	3,404	3,422
Eighth	3,086	2,982	2,839	2,853	2,853	2,979	3,020	3,129	3,249	3,302	3,356
Unclassified [1]	924	511	520	527	540	543	545	539	515	494	502
Grades 9 to 12	13,231	12,388	12,076	11,687	11,390	11,338	11,541	11,735	11,961	12,213	12,500
Ninth	3,377	3,439	3,143	3,106	3,141	3,169	3,313	3,352	3,487	3,604	3,704
Tenth	3,368	3,230	3,020	2,895	2,868	2,896	2,915	3,027	3,050	3,131	3,237
Eleventh	3,195	2,866	2,936	2,749	2,629	2,612	2,645	2,656	2,751	2,748	2,826
Twelfth	2,925	2,550	2,681	2,650	2,473	2,381	2,392	2,431	2,424	2,488	2,487
Unclassified [1]	366	303	296	288	279	282	275	269	248	242	245

[1] Includes ungraded and special education.

Source: U.S. National Center for Education Statistics, *Digest of Education Statistics,* annual.

No. 273. Public Elementary and Secondary School Teachers—Selected Characteristics: 1993-94

[**For school year.** Based on survey and subject to sampling error; for details, see source. Excludes prekindergarten teachers. See Table 289 for similar data on private school teachers]

CHARACTERISTIC	Unit	AGE				SEX		RACE/ETHNICITY		
		Under 30 years old	30 to 39 years old	40 to 49 years old	Over 50 years old	Male	Female	White [1]	Black [1]	His-panic
Total teachers [2]	1,000 . .	280	573	1,070	637	694	1,867	2,217	188	109
Highest degree held:										
Bachelor's	Percent .	83.9	59.4	46.3	40.9	46.2	54.1	51.8	48.4	62.8
Master's	Percent .	14.5	36.6	47.0	50.4	45.7	40.6	42.5	44.6	29.8
Education specialist.	Percent .	1.0	3.0	5.4	6.1	5.1	4.4	4.4	5.4	4.6
Doctorate	Percent .	0.1	0.3	0.7	1.4	1.3	0.5	0.7	0.9	1.4
Full-time teaching experience:										
Less than 3 years	Percent .	47.8	10.5	4.3	1.3	8.9	10.0	9.4	8.5	16.7
3 to 9 years	Percent .	52.2	48.7	16.9	7.3	21.6	26.9	25.5	20.8	32.1
10 to 20 years	Percent .	(X)	40.8	47.5	24.2	29.9	37.0	35.1	35.5	34.1
20 years or more	Percent .	(X)	(X)	31.3	67.1	39.6	26.1	30.0	35.2	17.1
Full-time teachers	1,000 . .	259	517	974	590	643	1,697	2,012	182	103
Earned income	Dol. . . .	27,151	31,596	38,106	42,243	41,031	34,781	36,576	36,200	35,197
Salary	Dol. . . .	24,737	29,270	35,751	39,931	36,182	33,384	34,221	33,889	32,996
Supplemental contract during school year:										
Teachers receiving	1,000 . .	114	205	329	168	349	467	723	49	32
Salary.	Dol. . . .	1,777	2,163	2,107	2,109	2,923	1,442	2,067	2,325	1,930
Supplemental contract during summer:										
Teachers receiving	1,000 . .	52	102	161	86	147	254	328	41	24
Salary	Dol. . . .	1,819	1,942	2,053	2,404	2,530	1,803	2,015	2,221	2,477
Teachers with nonschool employment:										
Teaching/tutoring	1,000 . .	12	25	50	32	37	81	100	11	6
Education related	1,000 . .	8	20	34	18	39	41	69	5	4
Not education related	1,000 . .	28	50	101	59	124	113	208	16	7

X Not applicable.   [1] Non-Hispanic.   [2] Includes teachers with no degrees and associates degrees, not shown separately.

Source: U.S. National Center for Education Statistics, *Digest of Education Statistics,* 1997; and unpublished data.

No. 274. Newly Hired Teachers, by Selected Characteristics: 1988 to 1994

[In percent. Based on sample and subject to sampling error; see source for details]

CHARACTERISTIC	PUBLIC SCHOOLS			PRIVATE SCHOOLS		
	1988	1991	1994	1988	1991	1994
Total newly hired teachers	100.0	100.0	100.0	100.0	100.0	100.0
First-time teachers	30.6	41.7	45.8	25.2	34.0	42.4
Transfers.	36.6	34.3	31.4	38.1	36.1	34.3
Within state and sector.	20.8	21.6	20.2	19.0	18.1	14.6
Across state	8.3	7.1	7.1	8.3	7.0	11.5
Across sector	7.5	5.6	4.1	10.9	11.0	8.1
Reentrants	32.8	24.0	22.9	36.7	30.0	23.3
Main previous year activity:						
First-time teachers.	100.0	100.0	100.0	100.0	100.0	100.0
Work in education (nonteaching).	5.7	5.2	10.7	4.8	7.5	13.6
Work outside education.	11.0	10.0	11.6	24.5	20.6	19.9
College	66.5	58.4	56.7	51.8	48.7	43.1
Homemaking and childrearing	3.6	4.4	2.1	7.7	5.8	5.8
Other.	13.3	22.0	18.9	11.3	17.4	17.6
Substitute teaching	(NA)	18.0	17.2	(NA)	12.0	15.2
Reentrants.	100.0	100.0	100.0	100.0	100.0	100.0
Work in education (nonteaching).	10.3	19.1	15.0	8.9	11.7	19.9
Work outside education.	17.4	17.9	19.2	21.2	26.1	26.0
College	18.0	10.4	18.1	20.0	5.6	11.9
Homemaking and childrearing	27.8	19.3	14.6	28.6	23.1	21.4
Other.	26.5	33.3	33.1	21.3	33.6	20.9
Substitute teaching	(NA)	23.8	29.6	(NA)	18.7	18.1

NA Not available.

Source: U.S. Department of Education, National Center for Education Statistics, *Condition of Education, 1996.*

No. 275. Public Elementary and Secondary Schools—Number and Average Salary of Classroom Teachers, 1970 to 1997, and by State, 1997

[Estimates for school year ending in June of year shown. Schools classified by type of organization rather than by grade-group; elementary includes kindergarten]

YEAR AND STATE	TEACHERS [1] (1,000)			AVG. SALARY ($1,000)			YEAR AND STATE	TEACHERS [1] (1,000)			AVG. SALARY ($1,000)		
	Total	Ele-men-tary	Sec-ondary	All teach-ers	Ele-men-tary	Sec-ond-ary		Total	Ele-men-tary	Sec-ondary	All teach-ers	Ele-men-tary	Sec-ond-ary
1970	2,008	1,109	899	8.6	8.4	8.9	LA	48.2	33.8	14.4	29.0	29.0	29.0
1975	2,171	1,169	1,001	11.7	11.3	12.0	ME.	14.7	10.2	4.5	33.8	33.3	34.5
1980	2,211	1,206	1,005	16.0	15.6	16.5	MD.	47.1	26.6	20.5	41.1	40.3	42.3
1985	2,175	1,212	963	23.6	23.2	24.2	MA.	61.6	26.5	35.1	42.7	42.7	42.7
1987	2,249	1,274	975	26.6	26.1	27.2	MI	84.7	61.3	23.5	48.2	48.2	48.2
1988	2,282	1,308	974	28.0	27.5	28.8	MN.	48.6	27.7	20.8	38.3	38.5	38.0
1989	2,324	1,354	970	29.6	29.0	30.2	MS.	29.2	16.0	13.2	27.7	28.1	27.3
1990	2,362	1,390	972	31.4	30.8	32.0	MO	59.3	30.6	28.7	33.2	32.5	33.9
1991	2,409	1,435	974	33.1	32.5	33.9	MT	10.2	7.0	3.2	30.0	29.6	30.7
1992	2,429	1,466	963	34.1	33.5	34.8	NE	20.0	11.5	8.5	31.8	31.8	31.8
1993	2,466	1,496	970	35.0	34.4	35.9	NV	14.7	8.5	6.3	37.3	37.0	37.8
1994	2,512	1,517	995	35.7	35.2	36.6	NH	12.7	8.9	3.8	36.0	36.0	36.0
1995	2,567	1,535	1,033	36.7	36.2	37.5	NJ	89.2	56.2	33.0	49.8	48.7	51.6
1996	2,606	1,559	1,047	37.7	37.3	38.4	NM	19.4	13.9	5.5	30.1	29.4	30.4
1997, U.S.	2,668	1,607	1,061	38.6	38.2	39.1	NY	195.8	97.7	98.0	48.0	47.0	49.3
AL	44.9	26.9	18.0	32.5	32.5	32.5	NC	74.3	46.4	27.9	31.2	31.0	31.4
AK	8.0	5.3	2.7	50.6	50.6	50.6	ND	7.9	5.1	2.8	27.7	27.9	27.4
AZ	40.4	31.1	9.3	33.3	33.3	33.3	OH	106.0	70.5	35.5	38.7	38.3	39.4
AR	27.5	13.5	14.0	30.3	29.5	31.1	OK	39.6	20.6	19.0	30.4	30.1	30.6
CA	244.6	180.5	64.1	43.0	42.5	44.5	OR	27.4	17.7	9.7	41.0	40.6	41.5
CO	36.4	18.4	18.0	36.3	36.1	36.5	PA	106.4	55.1	51.3	47.1	46.6	47.7
CT	37.2	26.6	10.6	50.4	50.0	51.6	RI	11.4	6.4	4.9	43.1	43.0	43.1
DE	6.6	3.3	3.4	41.4	41.3	41.6	SC	39.7	27.2	12.5	32.8	32.6	33.4
DC	5.8	3.6	2.3	45.0	45.5	46.3	SD	9.6	6.7	2.9	26.8	26.9	26.6
FL	122.4	63.4	59.0	33.9	33.9	33.9	TN	50.9	36.8	14.1	34.2	33.9	35.2
GA	82.2	48.2	34.0	35.6	35.1	36.3	TX	247.7	129.7	117.9	33.0	32.3	33.8
HI	10.9	6.0	4.8	35.8	35.8	35.8	UT	20.7	10.9	9.8	31.9	32.0	32.0
ID	13.1	6.7	6.4	31.8	31.8	31.9	VT	7.6	4.0	3.6	37.2	37.9	36.5
IL	118.2	82.9	35.4	42.1	40.4	46.2	VA	76.1	46.7	29.5	35.7	34.7	37.3
IN	56.7	30.4	26.3	38.8	39.0	38.7	WA	48.2	27.9	20.3	37.8	37.8	37.9
IA	32.8	15.4	17.4	33.3	32.3	34.1	WV	20.9	12.4	8.5	33.3	32.9	33.7
KS	30.8	16.3	14.5	35.7	35.7	35.7	WI	54.5	37.3	17.2	39.1	38.7	39.9
KY	38.4	27.1	11.3	33.8	33.5	35.1	WY	6.7	3.3	3.4	31.7	31.8	31.6

[1] Full-time equivalent.

Source: National Education Association, Washington, DC, Estimates of School Statistics Database (copyright).

No. 276. Average Salary and Wages Paid in Public School Systems: 1980 to 1998

[**In dollars.** For school year ending in year shown. Data reported by a stratified sample of school systems enrolling 300 or more pupils. Data represent unweighted means of average salaries paid school personnel reported by each school system]

POSITION	1980	1985	1990	1993	1994	1995	1996	1997	1998
ANNUAL SALARY									
Central office administrators:									
Superintendent (contract salary) . . .	39,344	56,954	75,425	85,120	87,717	90,198	94,229	98,106	101,519
Deputy/assoc. superintendent	37,440	52,877	69,623	77,057	78,672	81,266	84,077	88,564	90,226
Assistant superintendent	33,452	48,003	62,698	70,525	72,701	75,236	77,007	80,176	82,339
Administrators for—									
Finance and business	27,147	40,344	52,354	57,864	59,997	61,323	63,840	65,797	67,724
Instructional services	29,790	43,452	56,359	62,508	64,676	66,767	68,463	70,788	73,058
Public relations/information	24,021	35,287	44,926	50,622	52,366	53,263	53,860	55,928	57,224
Staff personnel services	29,623	44,182	56,344	62,162	63,690	65,819	67,760	70,088	71,073
Subject area supervisors	23,974	34,422	45,929	51,407	52,837	54,534	56,145	58,776	60,359
School building administrators:									
Principals:									
Elementary.	25,165	36,452	48,431	54,905	56,906	58,589	60,922	62,903	64,653
Junior high/middle	27,625	39,650	52,163	58,620	60,651	62,311	64,452	66,859	68,740
Senior high.	29,207	42,094	55,722	63,054	64,993	66,596	69,277	72,410	74,380
Assistant principals:									
Elementary.	20,708	30,496	40,916	45,377	47,057	48,491	50,537	52,284	53,206
Junior high/middle	23,507	33,793	44,570	49,925	51,518	52,942	54,355	56,451	57,768
Senior high.	24,816	35,491	46,486	52,348	54,170	55,556	57,555	59,739	60,999
Classroom teachers.	15,913	23,587	31,278	35,291	36,531	37,264	38,706	39,580	40,133
Auxiliary professional personnel:									
Counselors	18,847	27,593	35,979	40,413	41,355	42,486	44,073	45,365	46,162
Librarians	16,764	24,981	33,469	37,945	39,319	40,418	41,761	43,315	44,310
School nurses	13,788	19,944	26,090	29,555	30,630	31,066	32,786	33,720	34,619
Secretarial/clerical personnel:									
Central office:									
Secretaries.	10,331	15,343	20,238	22,770	23,495	23,935	24,809	25,709	26,316
Accounting/payroll clerks.	10,479	15,421	20,088	22,605	23,275	24,042	25,009	25,881	26,249
Typists/data entry clerks	8,359	12,481	16,125	17,772	18,296	18,674	19,447	20,726	21,633
School building level:									
Secretaries.	8,348	12,504	16,184	18,104	18,692	19,170	20,076	20,709	21,215
Library clerks	6,778	9,911	12,152	13,311	13,809	14,381	14,791	15,349	15,742
HOURLY WAGE RATE									
Other support personnel:									
Teacher aides:									
Instructional	4.06	5.89	7.43	8.31	8.50	8.77	9.04	9.25	9.46
Noninstructional	3.89	5.60	7.08	7.82	8.14	8.29	8.52	8.88	8.82
Custodians	4.88	6.90	8.54	9.51	9.76	10.05	10.35	10.65	10.79
Cafeteria workers	3.78	5.42	6.77	7.56	7.72	7.89	8.15	8.30	8.56
Bus drivers	5.21	7.27	9.21	10.15	10.35	10.69	11.04	11.50	11.55

Source: Educational Research Service, Arlington, VA, *National Survey of Salaries and Wages in Public Schools,* annual, Vols. 2 and 3. (All rights reserved. Copyright.)

No. 277. Public School Employment: 1982 and 1996

[**In thousands.** Covers full-time employment. Excludes Hawaii. 1982 also excludes District of Columbia and New Jersey. 1982 based on sample survey of school districts with 250 or more students. 1996 based on sample survey of school districts with 100 or more employees; see source for sampling variability]

OCCUPATION	1982					1996				
	Total	Male	Female	White [1]	Black [1]	Total	Male	Female	White [1]	Black [1]
All occupations	**3,082**	**1,063**	**2,019**	**2,498**	**432**	**3,718**	**1,013**	**2,705**	**2,915**	**506**
Officials, administrators	41	31	10	36	3	47	27	19	39	5
Principals and assistant										
principals.	90	72	19	76	11	101	55	45	79	15
Classroom teachers [2]	1,680	534	1,146	1,435	186	2,051	522	1,529	1,735	198
Elementary schools	798	129	669	667	98	1,024	137	887	854	101
Secondary schools	706	363	343	619	67	755	324	431	651	69
Other professional staff	235	91	144	193	35	263	60	203	219	30
Teachers aides [3]	215	14	200	146	45	365	38	327	238	78
Clerical, secretarial staff.	210	4	206	177	19	258	6	252	200	29
Service workers [4]	611	316	295	434	132	633	304	330	407	151

[1] Excludes individuals of Hispanic origin. [2] Includes other classroom teachers, not shown separately. [3] Includes technicians. [4] Includes craftworkers and laborers.

Source: U.S. Equal Employment Opportunity Commission, *Elementary-Secondary Staff Information (EEO-5),* biennial.

No. 278. Public Elementary and Secondary School Price Indexes: 1975 to 1996

[1983=100. For years ending **June 30**. Reflects prices paid by public elementary-secondary schools. For explanation of average annual percent change, see Guide to Tabular Presentation]

YEAR	Index, total	PERSONNEL COMPENSATION				CONTRACTED SERVICES, SUPPLIES AND EQUIPMENT						
		Total	Professional salaries	Nonprofessional salaries	Fringe benefits	Total	Services	Supplies and materials	Equipment replacement	Library materials and textbooks	Utilities	Fixed costs
1975 ..	52.7	53.4	56.0	55.6	40.9	50.4	55.7	58.0	53.7	53.8	34.5	45.2
1980 ..	76.6	75.9	76.7	77.8	71.0	79.2	77.4	85.9	79.6	82.1	71.1	77.9
1983 ..	100.0	100.0	100.0	100.0	100.0	100.0	100.0	100.0	100.0	100.0	100.0	100.0
1984 ..	105.0	106.0	105.7	104.5	108.3	101.7	105.6	99.6	103.4	107.8	94.3	105.4
1985 ..	112.0	113.7	113.4	111.3	117.1	105.5	112.4	103.2	107.2	111.0	96.1	110.8
1986 ..	118.5	121.1	121.4	117.6	123.3	108.3	117.4	103.0	109.3	120.8	93.7	116.2
1987 ..	123.3	127.4	128.4	121.9	128.8	107.5	123.7	101.5	112.9	126.5	75.3	122.7
1988 ..	129.8	134.5	135.5	127.5	137.0	111.8	126.1	105.9	113.4	140.0	78.1	128.4
1989 ..	136.3	141.6	142.2	133.3	147.0	116.2	131.8	112.0	116.0	149.4	75.1	134.6
1990 ..	144.3	150.0	150.1	139.4	159.3	122.6	137.7	119.2	121.2	171.7	82.1	140.3
1991 ..	152.3	158.3	158.1	146.5	169.8	129.7	142.5	122.7	125.7	189.4	92.6	144.9
1992 ..	158.5	165.4	165.8	152.4	175.8	132.0	148.0	122.5	128.5	199.0	90.8	148.9
1993 ..	162.2	169.6	169.2	155.1	184.5	133.9	151.5	121.9	131.8	205.6	90.4	153.8
1994 ..	167.1	175.1	175.1	159.3	190.2	136.5	154.0	122.7	135.4	218.4	90.6	158.7
1995 ..	170.9	179.2	178.9	163.7	194.9	139.3	157.2	124.4	138.7	230.7	89.7	163.9
1996 ..	177.3	185.6	185.7	169.2	200.3	145.9	161.8	138.7	143.2	227.9	91.0	169.1

Source: Research Associates of Washington, Arlington, VA, *Inflation Measures for Schools, Colleges, and Libraries*, annual (copyright).

No. 279. Finances of Public Elementary and Secondary School Systems, by Enrollment-Size Group: 1994-95

[**In millions of dollars, except as indicated.** Data are estimates subject to sampling variability. For details, see source. See also Appendix III]

ITEM	All school systems	SCHOOL SYSTEMS WITH ENROLLMENT OF—							
		50,000 or more	25,000 to 49,999	15,000 to 24,999	7,500 to 14,999	5,000 to 7,499	3,000 to 4,999	Under 3,000
Fall enrollment (1,000)	44,111	8,302	4,799	4,141	6,773	4,066	5,273	10,758
General revenue	275,186	52,551	27,980	23,497	40,687	25,663	33,479	71,328
From federal sources	18,136	4,528	2,018	1,478	2,374	1,348	1,746	4,644
Through state	16,473	4,240	1,838	1,374	2,165	1,250	1,581	4,026
Compensatory programs	6,388	1,814	704	509	815	470	613	1,463
Handicapped programs	2,082	353	209	179	286	178	215	661
Child nutrition programs	5,025	1,299	613	451	688	391	502	1,081
Direct	1,664	288	180	105	210	98	165	618
From state sources [1]	130,602	24,076	14,073	12,346	19,913	11,572	14,793	33,828
General formula assistance	89,912	15,328	9,273	8,739	14,156	8,128	10,659	23,629
Handicapped programs	8,333	1,537	1,100	872	1,196	696	816	2,116
From local sources	126,448	23,947	11,890	9,673	18,399	12,743	16,940	32,856
Taxes	85,687	12,422	8,216	6,432	12,961	9,090	12,320	24,246
Contributions from parent government	21,450	8,543	1,776	1,577	2,700	1,899	2,250	2,705
From other local governments	2,920	391	269	231	299	245	425	1,059
Current charges	7,440	1,053	754	678	1,097	723	920	2,215
School lunch	4,154	557	414	387	672	430	564	1,130
Other	8,952	1,540	873	755	1,342	787	1,024	2,631
General expenditure	276,874	53,432	28,585	23,817	41,170	25,710	33,111	71,048
Current spending	246,611	47,682	25,065	20,895	36,392	23,002	29,676	63,899
By function:								
Instruction	148,488	29,195	14,771	12,605	22,146	14,042	18,205	37,523
Support services	82,958	15,352	8,598	6,891	12,005	7,630	9,809	22,672
Other current spending	15,165	3,134	1,696	1,399	2,241	1,330	1,661	3,704
By object:								
Total salaries and wages	159,902	31,056	16,640	13,847	23,945	15,133	19,449	39,832
Total employee benefits	38,932	8,417	3,847	3,186	5,835	3,488	4,492	9,666
Other	47,777	8,209	4,577	3,861	6,612	4,381	5,735	14,401
Capital outlay	24,304	4,759	2,972	2,330	3,817	2,142	2,658	5,628
Interest on debt	5,187	961	522	523	820	474	686	1,201
Payments to other governments	772	30	27	69	141	92	92	320
Debt outstanding	97,672	17,837	9,621	9,280	15,415	9,220	13,312	22,987
Long-term	94,641	17,801	9,313	9,137	14,897	8,923	12,830	21,739
Short-term	3,032	36	308	143	517	298	482	1,248
Long-term debt issued	16,307	2,912	1,349	1,307	2,386	1,721	2,490	4,143
Long-term debt retired	7,062	1,250	692	611	1,076	725	897	1,811

[1] Includes other sources, not shown separately.

Source: U.S. Bureau of the Census, Internet site <http://www.census.gov/govs/www/school.html> (expected release July 1998).

No. 280. Public Elementary and Secondary Estimated Finances, 1980 to 1997, and by State, 1997

[**In millions of dollars, except as noted.** For school years ending in June of year shown]

YEAR AND STATE	RECEIPTS						EXPENDITURES				
	Total	Revenue receipts				Non-revenue re-ceipts [1]	Total [2]	Per capita [3] (dol.)	Current expenditures		
		Total	Source						Ele-mentary and second-ary day schools	Average per pupil in ADA [4]	
			Federal	State	Local					Amount (dol.)	Rank
1980	101,724	97,635	9,020	47,929	40,686	4,089	96,105	428	85,661	2,230	(X)
1985	146,976	141,013	9,533	69,107	62,373	5,963	139,382	591	127,230	3,483	(X)
1990	218,126	208,656	13,184	100,787	94,685	9,469	209,698	850	186,583	4,966	(X)
1991	243,817	223,896	14,178	108,021	101,697	19,921	227,459	915	200,911	5,262	(X)
1992	248,958	235,122	15,707	111,530	107,885	13,836	236,786	939	208,512	5,357	(X)
1993	263,460	247,912	17,381	115,924	114,606	15,548	248,898	976	219,297	5,538	(X)
1994	275,121	259,587	18,434	119,443	121,710	15,534	262,485	1,018	230,773	5,749	(X)
1995	288,658	273,364	18,766	130,139	124,459	15,294	276,502	1,062	242,729	5,950	(X)
1996	306,148	286,927	19,323	138,045	129,560	19,221	292,323	1,113	254,254	6,134	(X)
1997, total . . .	319,920	301,404	20,387	147,396	133,621	18,516	308,077	1,162	268,026	6,360	(X)
Alabama	4,147	3,883	397	2,517	969	264	4,558	1,063	3,895	5,478	36
Alaska	1,279	1,143	144	726	273	136	1,257	2,078	1,156	10,393	1
Arizona	4,574	4,057	292	1,976	1,789	517	4,493	1,013	3,556	4,777	47
Arkansas	2,429	2,267	189	1,495	583	162	2,206	880	1,904	4,498	48
California	35,528	34,780	2,909	20,832	11,038	748	34,137	1,072	29,657	5,327	41
Colorado	4,490	4,022	226	1,774	2,022	468	4,225	1,107	3,466	5,550	34
Connecticut	4,798	4,794	202	1,886	2,706	4	4,798	1,468	4,417	8,845	4
Delaware	917	900	69	594	238	17	902	1,246	818	8,098	6
District of Columbia	533	496	70	-	425	38	608	1,127	573	8,167	5
Florida	15,138	13,864	1,022	6,768	6,074	1,274	14,873	1,031	12,023	5,988	30
Georgia	9,456	8,260	545	4,343	3,372	1,196	9,328	1,272	7,904	6,459	20
Hawaii	1,325	1,325	98	1,198	30	-	1,273	1,076	1,054	6,066	26
Idaho	1,346	1,240	85	792	363	106	1,265	1,065	1,104	4,794	46
Illinois	14,150	12,997	973	3,513	8,512	1,153	12,754	1,077	10,699	6,048	27
Indiana	7,095	6,851	341	3,603	2,906	245	6,885	1,181	5,784	6,411	21
Iowa	3,289	3,090	117	1,657	1,316	199	2,988	1,049	2,632	5,546	35
Kansas	3,257	3,001	164	1,730	1,107	256	2,874	1,114	2,572	6,157	23
Kentucky	3,740	3,697	295	2,460	943	43	3,669	945	3,399	5,959	31
Louisiana	4,547	4,109	485	2,088	1,535	439	4,027	928	3,661	5,092	43
Maine	1,494	1,454	95	669	690	40	1,494	1,206	1,395	6,775	14
Maryland	6,044	5,783	324	2,315	3,144	261	5,988	1,183	5,360	7,052	12
Massachusetts . . .	7,145	7,145	383	2,571	4,192	-	6,948	1,142	6,573	7,628	8
Michigan	13,454	12,806	848	8,685	3,273	648	12,722	1,307	11,207	7,318	11
Minnesota	6,690	5,937	237	3,260	2,440	753	6,739	1,450	5,110	6,529	19
Mississippi	2,423	2,311	325	1,272	714	112	2,347	866	2,059	4,351	50
Missouri	5,926	5,500	327	2,178	2,995	426	5,183	966	4,401	5,375	39
Montana	980	965	95	469	401	15	986	1,125	891	6,006	29
Nebraska	1,621	1,606	66	604	936	14	1,737	1,053	1,527	5,636	32
Nevada	1,805	1,639	72	550	1,017	166	1,955	1,221	1,413	5,384	38
New Hampshire . .	1,387	1,304	39	87	1,178	84	1,295	1,117	1,183	6,557	17
New Jersey	12,392	12,296	422	4,815	7,059	96	12,240	1,530	11,657	10,284	2
New Mexico	2,338	2,022	197	1,326	499	316	2,152	1,257	1,628	5,457	37
New York	28,871	26,754	1,624	10,471	14,659	2,116	27,621	1,523	24,346	9,628	3
North Carolina . . .	7,121	6,740	500	4,424	1,817	381	7,094	971	6,311	5,623	33
North Dakota	659	645	76	272	298	14	615	958	567	5,016	44
Ohio	13,099	12,159	771	5,141	6,247	940	12,432	1,114	10,384	6,132	24
Oklahoma	3,257	3,007	269	1,880	858	250	3,033	920	2,600	4,486	49
Oregon	3,773	3,376	241	1,871	1,264	398	3,769	1,179	3,216	6,602	16
Pennsylvania	14,795	14,775	824	6,114	7,837	20	13,265	1,102	12,570	7,568	9
Rhode Island	1,202	1,202	71	477	654	-	1,150	1,164	1,113	8,030	7
South Carolina . . .	4,261	3,918	310	2,063	1,545	344	3,876	1,043	3,288	5,357	40
South Dakota	767	747	74	239	435	19	730	989	632	4,990	45
Tennessee	4,441	4,240	357	2,153	1,731	201	4,541	856	4,367	5,286	42
Texas	25,188	22,958	1,789	9,839	11,330	2,229	24,481	1,282	21,255	6,041	28
Utah	2,185	2,183	137	1,368	678	1	2,133	1,057	1,719	3,822	51
Vermont	814	788	40	228	521	26	775	1,321	702	7,561	10
Virginia	6,477	6,410	346	2,358	3,706	67	7,196	1,079	6,489	6,370	22
Washington	7,253	6,523	389	4,473	1,661	730	6,936	1,257	5,543	6,084	25
West Virginia	2,140	2,093	180	1,315	598	47	2,135	1,173	1,914	6,769	15
Wisconsin	7,155	6,682	293	3,643	2,747	473	6,696	1,301	5,733	6,999	13
Wyoming	725	659	43	319	298	65	695	1,448	600	6,541	18

- Represents or rounds to zero.   X Not applicable.   [1] Amount received by local education agencies from the sales of bonds and real property and equipment, loans, and proceeds from insurance adjustments.   [2] Includes interest on school debt and other current expenditures not shown separately.   [3] Based on Bureau of the Census estimated resident population, as of July 1, the previous year. Estimates reflect revisions based on the 1990 Census of Population.   [4] Average daily attendance.

Source: National Education Association, Washington, DC, Estimates of School Statistics Database (copyright).

No. 281. Computers for Student Instruction in Elementary and Secondary Schools: 1985 and 1998

[Market Data Retrieval collects student use computer information in elementary and secondary schools nationwide through a comprehensive annual technology survey that utilizes both mail and telephone methods]

LEVEL	1984-85				1997-98			
	Total schools	Total enrollment (1,000)	Number of computers [1]	Students per computer [2]	Total schools	Total enrollment (1,000)	Number of computers [1]	Students per computer
U.S. total	**105,509**	**44,091**	**631,983**	**62.7**	**108,526**	**51,866**	**8,049,875**	**6.4**
Public schools, total	81,100	39,186	569,825	63.5	86,641	46,769	7,415,007	6.3
Elementary	50,967	19,373	215,393	79.3	51,143	23,499	3,401,082	6.9
Middle/junior high	9,791	6,662	100,331	61.2	13,063	8,549	1,348,058	6.3
Senior high	15,152	11,191	228,726	51.5	15,489	12,287	2,180,520	5.6
K-12/other	5,190	1,959	25,375	45.8	6,946	2,434	485,345	5.0
Catholic schools, total . . .	9,463	2,813	28,427	73.5	8,232	2,653	311,822	8.5
Elementary	7,831	2,065	15,863	85.1	6,830	1,970	222,942	8.8
Secondary	1,481	700	12,147	57.8	1,244	631	81,178	7.8
K-12/other	151	48	417	(NA)	158	52	7,701	6.7
Other private schools, total	14,946	2,093	33,731	40.5	13,653	2,444	323,045	7.6
Elementary	8,226	1,049	13,400	42.7	6,765	1,058	129,249	8.2
Secondary	950	79	6,266	40.1	1,048	218	41,335	5.3
K-12/other	5,770	965	14,065	(NA)	5,840	1,168	152,461	7.7

NA Not available.   [1] Includes estimates for schools not reporting number of computers.   [2] Excludes schools with no computers.

Source: Market Data Retrieval, Shelton, CT, unpublished data (copyright).

No. 282. Public Schools with Access or Planned Access to the Internet: 1994 to 1997

[**In percent.** As of **fall.** Excludes special education, vocational education, and alternative based on sample and subject to sampling error; see source for details]

SCHOOL CHARACTERISTIC	PERCENT OF SCHOOLS WITH INTERNET ACCESS				PERCENT OF INSTRUCTIONAL ROOMS WITH INTERNET ACCESS				Percent of schools in 1996 having or expecting to have access to the Internet by the year 2000
	1994	1995	1996	1997	1994	1995	1996	1997	
Total [1]	**35**	**50**	**65**	**78**	**3**	**8**	**14**	**27**	**95**
Instructional level:									
Elementary	30	46	61	75	3	8	13	24	94
Secondary	49	65	77	89	4	8	16	32	98
Size of enrollment:									
Less than 300	30	39	57	75	3	9	15	27	93
300 to 999	35	52	66	78	3	8	13	28	96
1,000 or more	58	69	80	89	3	4	16	25	97
Percent minority enrollment:									
Less than 6 percent	(NA)	52	65	84	(NA)	9	18	37	95
6 to 20 percent	(NA)	58	72	87	(NA)	10	18	35	97
21 to 49 percent	(NA)	54	65	73	(NA)	9	12	22	98
50 percent or more	(NA)	40	56	63	(NA)	3	5	13	91
Percent of students eligible for free or reduced-price lunch:									
Less than 11 percent	(NA)	62	78	88	(NA)	9	18	36	97
11 to 30 percent	(NA)	59	72	83	(NA)	10	16	32	98
31 to 70 percent	(NA)	47	58	78	(NA)	7	14	27	93
71 percent or more	(NA)	31	53	63	(NA)	3	7	14	93

NA Not available.   [1] Includes combined schools.

Source: U.S. National Center for Education Statistics, "Internet Access in Public Schools," Issue Brief, February 1998.

No. 283. Student Use of Computers at School: 1984 and 1993

[In percent. As of **October.** Based on the Current Population Survey and subject to sampling error; see Appendix III and source]

CHARACTERISTIC	1984, total	1993					
		Total	Prekinder-garten and kinder-garden	Grades 1-8	Grades 9-12	1st to 4th year of college	5th or later year of college
Total	27.3	59.0	26.2	68.9	58.2	55.2	52.1
Sex:							
Male.	29.0	59.4	25.9	69.5	56.5	57.5	56.7
Female	25.5	58.7	26.5	68.4	60.0	53.3	47.8
Race/ethnicity:							
White [1]	30.0	61.6	29.4	73.7	59.9	54.9	49.8
Black [1]	16.8	51.5	16.5	56.5	54.5	56.9	57.9
Hispanic	18.6	52.3	19.2	58.4	54.1	51.9	53.7
Other	28.6	59.0	23.5	65.7	57.3	60.9	69.4
Household income:							
Less than $5,000	18.7	51.2	19.6	55.0	50.6	61.7	66.7
$5,000 to $9,999	21.0	53.3	24.4	60.3	51.9	53.9	56.2
$10,000 to $14,999	22.4	56.4	20.1	64.7	56.7	50.7	76.1
$15,000 to $19,999	25.9	58.1	23.8	67.5	57.4	51.2	58.5
$20,000 to $24,999	26.7	56.4	23.7	64.3	53.0	57.4	52.4
$25,000 to $29,999	30.5	60.0	28.0	70.1	60.3	51.5	58.0
$30,000 to $34,999	30.5	59.1	23.7	69.6	59.7	51.7	45.3
$35,000 to $39,999	32.3	60.7	27.1	72.1	61.7	49.2	47.9
$40,000 to $49,999	32.8	59.3	28.5	70.3	57.2	53.9	48.6
$50,000 to $74,999	35.5	62.6	28.6	75.6	61.5	57.4	44.2
$75,000 or more	36.0	64.6	33.5	78.7	62.5	60.9	47.7
Control of school:							
Public	27.4	60.2	30.1	68.6	58.1	53.9	54.1
Private	26.5	52.1	18.7	72.5	60.7	60.7	48.0

[1] Non-Hispanic.

Source: U.S. National Center for Education Statistics, *Digest of Education Statistics,* 1994.

No. 284. Availability and Use of Selected Teaching Resources: 1996

[In percent. For resources available at the worksite or used for instructional purposes. Based in a sample survey conducted in the spring of 1996. For details, see source]

RESOURCE	All teach-ers	SEX		LEVEL [1]		SCHOOL SYSTEM SIZE			RACE	
		Male	Female	Ele-men-tary	Sec-ondary	Less than 3,000	3,000 to 24,999	25,000 or more	White	Minority
RESOURCE AVAILABLE										
Personal computers.	83.7	81.6	84.4	86.9	80.9	85.5	86.8	76.7	84.7	77.1
Computers with CD-ROM drive . . .	58.2	62.8	56.6	58.9	57.6	60.5	60.9	51.1	59.7	44.4
Networked computers	45.0	50.5	43.1	41.2	48.4	48.6	46.0	39.1	45.5	41.6
Computers with modems	37.5	43.7	35.4	35.8	39.0	39.4	37.0	36.4	38.4	30.8
VCR	92.9	93.4	92.7	93.3	92.9	94.7	92.2	92.1	93.6	85.3
Television monitor	85.4	87.4	84.6	82.0	88.9	84.9	85.1	86.2	86.0	78.0
Hypermedia or multimedia soft-ware	39.9	43.6	38.6	41.3	38.8	40.0	40.4	38.9	40.7	33.7
Standard software	71.3	76.8	69.4	68.3	74.3	73.7	72.5	66.6	73.1	55.9
Specialized instructional software. .	56.3	52.4	57.6	62.7	50.6	60.6	53.7	56.3	57.2	50.5
Online services/networks	35.3	42.8	32.6	29.3	40.7	40.4	35.0	30.1	36.7	24.5
Instructional laser/video disks	37.3	41.2	36.0	34.9	39.8	32.6	40.0	37.7	38.0	32.7
Instructional videotapes	79.7	77.6	80.4	78.5	80.7	81.3	81.2	75.4	80.8	70.8
Distance learning/video conferencing.	11.2	13.9	10.2	7.9	14.2	14.2	9.7	10.4	10.9	14.2
RESOURCE USED										
Personal computers.	60.8	58.8	61.5	68.8	53.7	63.3	63.8	53.1	61.7	52.7
Computers with CD-ROM drive . . .	29.4	34.0	27.8	32.0	26.8	33.2	30.8	22.9	30.5	17.0
Networked computers	23.9	28.4	22.3	23.6	24.1	27.1	24.1	20.1	24.5	19.6
Computers with modems	12.8	18.2	10.9	13.3	12.6	12.8	13.2	12.2	13.2	8.7
VCR	72.3	72.7	72.2	72.2	72.7	74.6	73.8	67.3	73.3	61.1
Television monitor	63.6	66.0	62.8	58.3	68.9	64.3	64.9	60.5	64.5	52.0
Hypermedia or multimedia soft-ware	20.0	20.3	19.9	23.5	16.8	18.8	21.9	17.8	20.5	15.0
Standard software	44.3	51.7	41.6	40.6	47.9	43.8	46.0	41.8	45.6	34.3
Specialized instructional software. .	38.3	32.4	40.4	47.2	30.4	42.2	36.8	37.0	39.5	31.4
Online services/networks	8.9	13.4	7.3	7.9	9.8	9.4	9.3	7.7	9.6	3.8
Instructional laser/video disks	16.1	17.5	15.7	16.4	16.0	13.5	17.7	16.1	16.4	12.7
Instructional videotapes	62.7	59.7	63.7	63.7	62.2	65.9	64.0	56.6	63.6	54.3
Distance learning/video conferencing.	2.7	3.7	2.4	1.9	3.6	3.2	2.5	2.8	2.4	4.7

[1] Level as determined by respondent.

Source: National Education Association, Washington, DC, *Status of the American Public School Teacher, 1995-1996* (copyright).

No. 285. Technology in Public Schools: 1992 to 1997

[For school year ending in year shown. Based on surveys of school districts conducted in the spring and summer of the school year. For details, see source]

TECHNOLOGY	NUMBER					PERCENT OF TOTAL	
	1992	1994	1995	1996	1997	1992	1997
Schools with interactive videodisk players [1]	6,502	19,189	27,059	29,759	30,417	8	36
Elementary [2]	2,921	10,043	14,594	16,200	16,614	6	32
Junior high [3]	1,258	3,844	5,460	6,009	6,124	10	43
Senior high [4]	2,106	5,026	6,661	7,195	7,322	14	42
Students represented (1,000)	5,781	13,434	18,552	20,258	20,706	14	45
Schools with modems [1]	13,597	24,277	35,696	40,147	40,876	16	48
Elementary [2]	5,831	11,679	18,858	21,733	22,234	11	43
Junior high [3]	2,608	4,531	6,546	7,286	7,417	20	53
Senior high [4]	5,001	7,853	9,930	10,682	10,781	30	63
Students represented (1,000)	10,717	16,476	22,372	24,688	25,136	25	54
Schools with networks [1]	4,184	19,272	27,805	31,986	32,299	5	38
Elementary [2]	1,583	8,477	13,582	16,189	16,441	3	32
Junior high [3]	776	3,611	5,194	5,971	6,035	6	43
Senior high [4]	1,736	7,104	8,839	9,562	9,565	10	55
Students represented (1,000)	3,754	12,713	17,540	19,997	20,193	9	44
Schools with CD-ROM's [1]	5,706	24,526	40,509	45,918	46,388	7	54
Elementary [2]	1,897	11,794	22,305	25,965	26,377	4	51
Junior high [3]	1,231	4,874	7,501	8,341	8,410	9	60
Senior high [4]	2,543	7,724	10,354	11,150	11,140	15	65
Students represented (1,000)	5,298	15,576	24,121	27,070	27,347	12	59
Schools with satellite dishes [1]	1,129	12,580	15,400	16,298	16,232	1	19
Elementary [2]	351	4,269	5,565	6,014	6,001	1	11
Junior high [3]	166	2,497	3,214	3,409	3,377	1	24
Senior high [4]	606	5,770	6,550	6,782	6,769	4	39
Students represented (1,000)	1,906	6,740	8,963	9,270	9,232	4	20
Schools with cable [1]	(NA)	58,652	63,639	64,310	64,171	(NA)	75
Elementary [2]	(NA)	35,325	38,336	38,714	38,678	(NA)	74
Junior high [3]	(NA)	10,696	11,518	11,575	11,554	(NA)	82
Senior high [4]	(NA)	12,198	13,114	13,282	13,208	(NA)	77
Students represented (1,000)	(NA)	33,510	36,284	36,950	36,870	(NA)	80

NA Not available.   [1] Includes schools for special education and adult education, not shown separately.   [2] Includes K-12, preschool, preschool through 3, K-6, and K-8.   [3] Includes schools with grade spans of 4-8, 7-8, and 7-9.   [4] Includes 7-12, 9-12, 10-12, vocational technical, and alternative high schools.

Source: Quality Education Data, Denver, CO, National Education Database.

No. 286. Student Participation in School Programs: 1993-94

[As of fall. Based on survey and subject to sampling error; for details see source]

CONTROL AND LEVEL	TOTAL STUDENTS		PERCENT OF STUDENTS PARTICIPATING IN PROGRAM OR SERVICE							
	Number	Percent distribution	Bilingual education	English as a second language	Remedial reading	Remedial mathematics	Programs for the disabled	Programs for the gifted and talented	Diagnostic and prescriptive [1]	Extended day
Public total	41,622	100.0	3.07	3.97	10.88	6.90	6.88	6.43	0.27	2.50
School level [2]:										
Elementary	26,886	64.6	3.98	4.75	13.46	7.77	6.76	6.25	0.31	3.58
Secondary	13,758	33.1	1.39	2.58	5.63	5.03	6.54	6.90	0.20	0.48
Combined	978	2.3	1.80	1.88	13.70	9.39	14.84	4.72	0.44	1.31
Private total	4,971	100.0	0.81	0.58	6.35	4.16	2.98	4.93	0.89	9.20
School level [2]:										
Elementary	2,803	56.4	0.77	0.45	7.22	4.33	0.93	3.34	0.94	12.48
Secondary	811	16.3	0.19	0.62	4.24	3.06	3.43	8.56	0.47	0.23
Combined	1,356	27.3	1.25	0.83	5.82	4.46	6.95	6.05	1.03	7.76

[1] Includes testing for reading and cognitive disabilities, for example.   [2] Elementary schools have grade 6 or lower and no grade higher than 8. Secondary schools have no grade lower than 7. Combined schools have grades lower than 7 and higher than 8.

Source: U.S. National Center for Education Statistics, *Digest of Education Statistics*, 1997.

No. 287. Children and Youth With Disabilities Served by Selected Programs: 1990 to 1996

[**For school year ending in year shown.** Excludes outlying areas. For persons age 6 to 21 years old served under IDEA (Individuals with Disabilities Act), Part B and Chapter 1 of ESEA (Elementary and Secondary Education Act), SOP (State Operated Program)]

ITEM	1990	1991	1992	1993	1994	1995	1996
All conditions (1,000)...............	4,210.8	4,320.3	4,459.2	4,586.2	4,730.4	4,859.1	5,028.7
PERCENT DISTRIBUTION							
Specific learning disabilities	48.6	49.3	50.1	51.3	50.9	51.2	51.3
Speech or language impairments	23.1	22.8	22.3	21.7	21.4	20.9	20.3
Mental retardation..................	13.0	12.4	12.0	11.3	11.3	11.4	11.3
Serious emotional disturbance	9.0	9.0	8.9	8.7	8.7	8.8	8.7
Hearing impairments.................	1.3	1.3	1.3	1.3	1.3	1.3	1.3
Orthopedic impairments..............	1.1	1.1	1.1	1.1	1.2	1.2	1.2
Other health impairments.............	1.2	1.3	1.3	1.4	1.7	2.2	2.6
Visually impaired	0.5	0.5	0.5	0.5	0.5	0.5	0.5
Multiple disabilities	2.0	2.2	2.2	2.2	2.3	1.8	1.8
Deaf-blind........................	(Z)	(Z)	(Z)	(Z)	(Z)	(Z)	(Z)
Autism	(NA)	(NA)	0.1	0.3	0.4	0.5	0.6
Traumatic brain injury	(NA)	(NA)	-	0.1	0.1	0.1	0.2

- Represents zero.   Z less than .05 percent.   NA Not available.

Source: U.S. Department of Education, Office of Special Education Programs, Data Analysis System (DANS).

No. 288. Catholic Elementary and Secondary Schools: 1960 to 1996

[As of **October 1**. Regular sessions only]

ITEM	Unit	1960	1970	1980	1985	1990	1992	1993	1994	1995	1996
Elementary schools .	Number	10,501	9,362	8,043	7,806	7,291	7,174	7,114	7,055	7,022	7,005
Pupils enrolled . . .	1,000..	4,373	3,359	2,269	2,057	1,884	1,984	1,992	2,004	2,011	2,033
Teachers, total [1] .	1,000..	108	112	97	97	91	110	112	118	119	108
Religious	1,000..	79	52	25	18	11	11	12	11	10	8
Lay.........	1,000..	29	60	72	79	80	98	100	107	109	99
Secondary schools .	Number	2,392	1,981	1,516	1,430	1,296	1,249	1,231	1,238	1,228	1,226
Pupils enrolled . .	1,000..	880	1,008	837	762	592	584	585	615	624	631
Teachers, total [1] .	1,000..	44	54	49	50	40	45	45	47	48	46
Religious	1,000..	33	28	14	11	6	6	7	6	6	5
Lay.........	1,000..	11	26	35	39	34	38	38	40	42	41

[1] Beginning 1992, includes part-time teachers.

Source: National Catholic Educational Association, (NCEA) Washington, DC; from the NCEA Data Bank—*U.S. Catholic Schools 1967-1968*, (copyright) and *U.S. Catholic Elementary and Secondary Schools 1996-1997 Annual Statistical Report on Schools, Enrollment & Staffing*, NCEA, annual (copyright); and NCEA/Ganley's *Catholic Schools in America*, 1997 edition, annual (copyright).

No. 289. Private Elementary and Secondary School Teachers—Selected Characteristics: 1993-94

[For school year. Based on survey and subject to sampling error; for details, see source. See Table 273 for similar data on public school teachers]

CHARACTERISTIC	Unit	AGE				SEX		RACE/ETHNICITY		
		Under 30 years old	30 to 39 years old	40 to 49 years old	Over 50 years old	Male	Fe-male	White [1]	Black [1]	His-panic
Total teachers [2] . . .	1,000 . . .	**65**	**94**	**131**	**88**	**93**	**285**	**348**	**12**	**12**
Highest degree held:										
Bachelor's	Percent .	78.8	63.1	54.0	47.2	47.3	62.8	59.4	55.8	57.4
Master's..........	Percent .	10.8	25.7	35.1	40.5	40.6	26.3	30.2	26.4	19.9
Education specialist .	Percent .	1.0	2.6	3.4	3.8	2.6	3.0	2.6	4.8	4.4
Doctorate	Percent .	0.2	1.4	2.0	2.6	4.3	0.8	1.6	1.0	2.3
Full-time teaching experience:										
Less than 3 years . .	Percent .	54.9	21.7	12.6	7.2	21.7	20.6	20.4	26.9	25.5
3 to 9 years	Percent .	44.9	51.2	29.8	13.4	28.2	35.8	33.6	34.9	41.8
10 to 20 years.....	Percent .	0.1	27.1	45.5	30.2	28.7	29.9	30.0	27.9	21.6
20 years or more . . .	Percent .	(Z)	(Z)	12.1	49.2	21.4	13.7	16.0	10.3	11.1
Full-time teachers . . .	1,000 . . .	53	82	103	62	70	231	277	9	9
Earned income	Dol....	18,384	21,344	22,190	24,113	27,196	20,007	21,578	23,094	22,912
Salary	Dol....	16,062	19,108	20,631	22,500	23,003	18,815	19,717	20,333	20,740

Z Less than .05 percent.   [1] Non-Hispanic.   [2] Includes teachers with no degrees and associates degrees, not shown separately.

Source: U.S. National Center for Education Statistics, *Digest of Education Statistics*, 1997.

No. 290. Scholastic Assessment Test (SAT) Scores and Characteristics of College-Bound Seniors: 1967 to 1997

[For school year ending in year shown. Data are for the SAT I: Reasoning Tests. Scores between the two tests have been equated to the same 200-800 scale and are thus comparable. Scores for 1995 and prior years have been recentered and revised. SAT I: Reasoning Test replaced the SAT in March 1994]

TYPE OF TEST AND CHARACTERISTIC	Unit	1967	1970	1975	1980	1985	1990	1994	1995	1996	1997
AVERAGE TEST SCORES [1]											
Verbal, total [2]	Point . . .	543	537	512	502	509	500	499	504	505	505
Male	Point . . .	540	536	515	506	514	505	501	505	507	507
Female	Point . . .	545	538	509	498	503	496	497	502	503	503
Math, total [2]	Point . . .	516	512	498	492	500	501	504	506	508	511
Male	Point . . .	535	531	518	515	522	521	523	525	527	530
Female	Point . . .	495	493	479	473	480	483	487	490	492	494
PARTICIPANTS											
Total	1,000 . . .	(NA)	(NA)	996	922	977	1,026	1,050	1,068	1,085	1,127
Male	Percent .	(NA)	(NA)	49.9	48.2	48.3	47.8	46.9	46.4	46.5	46.1
White	Percent .	(NA)	(NA)	86.0	82.1	81.0	73.0	69.4	69.2	68.7	68.0
Black	Percent .	(NA)	(NA)	7.9	9.1	7.5	10.0	10.8	10.7	10.8	10.8
Obtaining scores [1] of—											
600 or above:											
Verbal	Percent .	(NA)	(NA)	(NA)	(NA)	(NA)	20.3	21.1	21.9	21.1	20.9
Math	Percent .	(NA)	(NA)	(NA)	(NA)	(NA)	20.4	22.0	23.4	22.7	23.4
Below 400:											
Verbal	Percent .	(NA)	(NA)	(NA)	(NA)	(NA)	17.3	21.0	16.4	15.9	16.1
Math	Percent .	(NA)	(NA)	(NA)	(NA)	(NA)	15.8	15.5	16.0	16.0	15.2
Selected intended area of study:											
Business and commerce	Percent .	(NA)	(NA)	11.5	18.6	21.0	20.9	13.8	13.3	12.8	12.8
Engineering	Percent .	(NA)	(NA)	6.7	11.1	11.7	10.2	9.4	8.8	8.5	8.4
Social science	Percent .	(NA)	(NA)	7.7	7.8	7.5	12.6	12.1	11.6	11.3	11.0
Education	Percent .	(NA)	(NA)	9.1	6.1	4.7	7.5	8.0	8.1	8.2	8.6

NA Not available.   [1] Minimum score 200; maximum score, 800.   [2] 1967 and 1970 are estimates based on total number of persons taking SAT.

Source: College Entrance Examination Board, New York, NY, *National College-Bound Senior,* annual (copyright).

No. 291. American College Testing (ACT) Program Scores and Characteristics of College-Bound Students: 1970 to 1997

[For academic year ending in year shown. Except as indicated, test scores and characteristics of college-bound students. Through 1980, data based on 10 percent sample; thereafter, based on all ACT tested seniors]

TYPE OF TEST AND CHARACTERISTIC	Unit	1970	1975	1980	1985	1990 [1]	1993 [1]	1994 [1]	1995 [1]	1996 [1]	1997 [1]
TEST SCORES [2]											
Composite	Point . . .	19.9	18.6	18.5	18.6	20.6	20.7	20.8	20.8	20.9	21.0
Male	Point . . .	20.3	19.5	19.3	19.4	21.0	21.0	20.9	21.0	21.0	21.1
Female	Point . . .	19.4	17.8	17.9	17.9	20.3	20.5	20.7	20.7	20.8	20.8
English	Point . . .	18.5	17.7	17.9	18.1	20.5	20.3	20.3	20.2	20.3	20.3
Male	Point . . .	17.6	17.1	17.3	17.6	20.1	19.8	19.8	19.8	19.8	19.9
Female	Point . . .	19.4	18.3	18.3	18.6	20.9	20.6	20.7	20.6	20.7	20.7
Math	Point . . .	20.0	17.6	17.4	17.2	19.9	20.1	20.2	20.2	20.2	20.6
Male	Point . . .	21.1	19.3	18.9	18.6	20.7	20.8	20.8	20.9	20.9	21.3
Female	Point . . .	18.8	16.2	16.2	16.0	19.3	19.6	19.6	19.7	19.7	20.1
Reading [3]	Point . . .	19.7	17.4	17.2	17.4	(NA)	21.2	21.2	21.3	21.3	21.3
Male	Point . . .	20.3	18.7	18.2	18.3	(NA)	21.2	21.1	21.1	21.0	21.2
Female	Point . . .	19.0	16.4	16.4	16.6	(NA)	21.2	21.4	21.4	21.6	21.5
Science reasoning [4]	Point . . .	20.8	21.1	21.1	21.2	(NA)	20.8	20.9	21.0	21.1	21.1
Male	Point . . .	21.6	22.4	22.4	22.6	(NA)	21.5	21.6	21.6	21.7	21.7
Female	Point . . .	20.0	20.0	20.0	20.0	(NA)	20.3	20.4	20.5	20.5	20.6
PARTICIPANTS [5]											
Total	1,000 . . .	788	714	822	739	817	876	892	945	925	959
Male	Percent .	52	46	45	46	46	45	45	44	44	44
White	Percent .	(NA)	77	83	82	79	77	76	75	77	74
Black	Percent .	4	7	8	8	9	10	10	10	10	10
Obtaining composite scores [6]											
of— 27 or above	Percent .	14	14	13	14	12	12	13	13	13	14
18 or below	Percent .	21	33	33	32	35	35	34	34	34	33
Planned educational major:											
Business [7]	Percent .	18	21	20	21	20	15	14	14	13	11
Engineering	Percent .	8	6	8	9	9	10	9	9	9	8
Social science [8]	Percent .	10	9	6	7	10	10	9	9	9	8
Education	Percent .	16	12	9	6	8	9	10	9	9	9

NA Not available.   [1] Beginning 1990, not comparable with previous years because a new version of the ACT was introduced. Estimated average composite scores for prior years: 1989, 20.6; 1988, 1987, and 1986, 20.8.   [2] Minimum score, 1; maximum score, 36.   [3] Prior to 1990, social studies; data not comparable with previous years.   [4] Prior to 1990, natural sciences; data not comparable with previous years.   [5] Beginning 1985, data are for seniors who graduated in year shown and had taken the ACT in their junior or senior years. Data by race are for those responding to the race question.   [6] Prior to 1990, 26 or above and 15 or below.   [7] Includes political and persuasive (e.g. sales) fields through 1975; thereafter, business and commerce.   [8] Includes religion through 1975.

Source: The ACT, Inc., Iowa City, IA, *High School Profile Report,* annual.

No. 292. Proficiency Test Scores for Selected Subjects, by Characteristic: 1977 to 1996

[Based on The National Assessment of Educational Progress Tests which are administered to a representative sample of students in public and private schools. Test scores can range from 0 to 500. For details, see source]

TEST AND YEAR	Total	SEX		RACE		His-panic origin	PARENTAL EDUCATION				
		Male	Female	White[1]	Black[1]		Less than high school	High school	More than high school		
									Total	Some college	College graduate
READING											
9 year olds:											
1979-80	215	210	220	221	189	190	194	213	226	(NA)	(NA)
1987-88	212	208	216	218	189	194	193	211	220	(NA)	(NA)
1993-94	211	207	215	218	185	186	189	207	221	(NA)	(NA)
1995-96	212	207	218	220	190	194	197	207	220	(NA)	(NA)
13 year olds:											
1979-80	259	254	263	264	233	237	239	254	271	(NA)	(NA)
1987-88	258	252	263	261	243	240	247	253	265	(NA)	(NA)
1993-94	258	251	266	265	234	235	237	251	269	(NA)	(NA)
1995-96	259	253	265	267	236	240	241	252	270	(NA)	(NA)
17 year olds:											
1979-80	286	282	289	293	243	261	262	278	299	(NA)	(NA)
1987-88	290	286	294	295	274	271	267	282	300	(NA)	(NA)
1993-94	288	282	295	296	266	263	268	276	299	(NA)	(NA)
1995-96	287	280	294	294	265	265	267	273	297	(NA)	(NA)
WRITING [2]											
4th graders:											
1983-84	204	201	208	211	182	189	179	192	217	208	218
1987-88	206	199	213	215	173	190	194	199	212	211	212
1993-94	205	196	214	214	173	189	188	202	(NA)	212	212
1995-96	207	200	214	216	182	191	190	203	(NA)	205	214
8th graders:											
1983-84	267	258	276	272	247	247	258	261	276	271	278
1987-88	264	254	274	269	246	250	254	258	271	275	271
1993-94	265	254	278	272	245	252	250	259	(NA)	270	275
1995-96	264	251	276	271	242	246	245	258	(NA)	270	274
11th graders:											
1983-84	290	281	299	297	270	259	274	284	299	298	300
1987-88	291	282	299	296	275	274	276	285	298	296	299
1993-94	285	276	293	291	267	271	269	279	(NA)	286	293
1995-96	283	275	292	289	267	269	260	275	(NA)	287	291
MATHEMATICS											
9 year olds:											
1977-78	219	217	220	224	192	203	200	219	231	230	231
1985-86	222	222	222	227	202	205	201	218	231	229	231
1993-94	231	232	230	237	212	210	210	225	(NA)	239	238
1995-96	231	233	229	237	212	215	220	221	(NA)	238	240
13 year olds:											
1977-78	264	264	265	272	230	238	245	263	280	273	284
1985-86	269	270	268	274	249	254	252	263	278	274	280
1993-94	274	276	273	281	252	256	255	266	(NA)	277	285
1995-96	274	276	272	281	252	256	254	267	(NA)	278	283
17 year olds:											
1977-78	300	304	297	306	268	276	280	294	313	305	317
1985-86	302	305	299	308	279	283	279	293	310	305	314
1993-94	306	309	304	312	286	291	284	295	(NA)	305	318
1995-96	307	310	305	313	286	292	281	297	(NA)	307	317
SCIENCE											
9 year olds:											
1976-77	220	222	218	230	175	192	199	223	233	237	232
1985-86	224	227	221	232	196	199	204	220	235	236	235
1993-94	231	232	230	240	201	201	211	225	(NA)	239	239
1995-96	230	232	228	239	201	207	215	222	(NA)	242	240
13 year olds:											
1976-77	247	251	244	256	208	213	224	245	264	260	266
1985-86	251	256	247	259	222	226	229	245	262	258	264
1993-94	257	259	254	267	224	232	234	247	(NA)	260	269
1995-96	256	261	252	266	226	232	232	248	(NA)	260	266
17 year olds:											
1976-77	290	297	282	298	240	262	265	284	304	296	309
1985-86	289	295	282	298	253	259	258	277	300	295	304
1993-94	294	300	289	306	257	261	256	279	(NA)	295	311
1995-96	296	300	292	307	260	269	261	282	(NA)	297	308
HISTORY, 1993-94											
4th graders	205	203	206	215	177	180	177	197	(NA)	214	216
8th graders:	259	259	259	267	239	243	241	251	(NA)	264	270
12th graders	286	288	285	292	265	267	263	276	(NA)	287	296
GEOGRAPHY, 1993-94											
4th graders	206	208	203	218	168	183	186	197	(NA)	216	216
8th graders	260	262	258	270	229	239	238	250	(NA)	265	272
12th graders	285	288	281	291	258	268	263	274	(NA)	286	294

NA Not available. [1] Non-Hispanic. [2] Writing scores revised from previous years; previous writing scores were recorded on a 0 to 400 rather than 0 to 500 scale.

Source: U.S. National Center for Education Statistics, *Digest of Education Statistics*, annual.

No. 293. Students Taking Advanced Placement Examinations, 1984 to 1995 and Exams Taken, 1996

ITEM	Total [1]	SEX		RACE/ETHNICITY		
		Male	Female	White [2]	Black [2]	Hispanic
STUDENTS TAKING EXAMS [3]						
1984	24	24	25	23	4	10
1985	29	29	29	29	5	14
1986	33	33	33	32	6	14
1987	36	35	37	34	8	17
1988	39	38	40	40	9	22
1989	44	42	47	45	11	31
1990	48	46	51	48	13	32
1991	53	51	56	54	15	32
1992	57	53	62	58	14	37
1993	62	56	68	61	16	40
1994	60	53	68	60	14	34
1995	66	58	74	65	18	42
EXAMINATIONS TAKEN						
Total, 1996 [4]	824,329	386,061	438,268	535,055	31,554	59,752
Social studies	262,388	126,235	136,153	176,126	9,993	14,200
Foreign language	67,019	24,048	42,971	29,970	1,811	21,419
Calculus	122,852	67,208	55,644	80,805	4,042	3,320
Computer science	11,065	9,246	1,819	6,910	363	467
Science	137,511	75,299	62,212	86,810	4,769	5,622
With scores of 3 or higher, 1996 [4][5]	523,321	256,095	267,226	344,026	11,078	36,454
Social studies	159,173	82,688	76,485	109,750	3,530	6,189
Foreign language	47,846	16,855	30,991	18,132	890	19,374
Calculus	78,185	45,915	32,270	52,370	1,316	2,437
Computer science	6,231	5,406	825	4,042	85	187
Science	85,126	50,319	34,807	54,375	2,396	2,396

[1] Includes other races, not shown separately.   [2] Non-Hispanic.   [3] Rates per 1,000 11th- and 12th-grade student. Includes a small number of college students who took exams, about 2 percent of all candidates in 1995.   [4] Includes other exams, not shown separately.   [5] A score of 3 or higher usually receives college credit.

Source: 1984-1995, U.S. National Center for Education Statistics, *The Condition of Education,* 1997; 1996, The College Entrance Examination Board, New York, NY, *The National School Grade Distribution Report,* annual, (copyright).

No. 294. Foreign Language Enrollment in Public High Schools: 1970 to 1994

[**In thousands, except percent**. As of **fall**, for grades 9 through 12]

LANGUAGE	1970	1974	1976	1978	1982	1985	1990	1994
Total enrollment	13,301.9	13,648.9	13,952.1	13,941.4	12,879.3	12,466.5	11,099.6	11,847.5
Enrolled in all foreign languages	3,779.3	3,294.5	3,174.0	3,200.1	2,909.8	4,028.9	4,256.9	5,001.9
Percent of all students	28.4	24.1	22.7	23.0	22.6	32.3	38.4	42.2
Enrolled in modern foreign languages [1]	3,514.1	3,127.3	3,023.5	3,048.3	2,740.2	3,852.0	4,093.0	4,813.0
Spanish	1,810.8	1,678.1	1,717.0	1,631.4	1,562.8	2,334.4	2,611.4	3,219.8
French	1,230.7	977.9	888.4	856.0	858.0	1,133.7	1,089.4	1,105.9
German	410.5	393.0	352.7	330.6	266.9	312.2	295.4	326.0
Italian	27.3	40.2	45.6	45.5	44.1	47.3	40.4	43.8
Japanese	(NA)	(NA)	(NA)	(NA)	6.2	8.6	25.1	42.3
Russian	20.2	15.1	11.3	8.8	5.7	6.4	16.5	16.4
Percent of all students [1]	26.4	22.9	21.7	21.9	21.3	30.9	36.9	40.6
Spanish	13.6	12.3	12.3	11.7	12.1	18.7	23.5	27.2
French	9.3	7.2	6.4	6.1	6.7	9.1	9.8	9.3
German	3.1	2.9	2.5	2.4	2.1	2.5	2.7	2.8
Italian	0.2	0.3	0.3	0.3	0.3	0.4	0.4	0.4
Japanese	(NA)	(NA)	(NA)	(NA)	0.1	0.1	0.2	0.4
Russian	0.2	0.1	0.1	0.1	(Z)	0.1	0.2	0.1

NA Not available.   Z Less than .05 percent.   [1] Includes other foreign languages, not shown separately.

Source: The American Council on the Teaching of Foreign Languages, Yonkers, NY, *Foreign Language Enrollments in Public Secondary Schools, Fall 1994.*

No. 295. Public High School Graduates, by State: 1980 to 1997

[In thousands. For school year ending in year shown]

STATE	1980	1990	1995	1997, est.	STATE	1980	1990	1995	1997, est.
U.S.	2,747.7	2,320.3	2,273.5	2,357.6	Missouri	62.3	49.0	48.9	50.0
Alabama	45.2	40.5	36.3	35.3	Montana	12.1	9.4	10.1	10.6
Alaska	5.2	5.4	5.8	6.4	Nebraska	22.4	17.7	18.0	20.7
Arizona	28.6	32.1	31.0	31.8	Nevada	8.5	9.5	10.0	11.3
Arkansas	29.1	26.5	24.6	24.9	New Hampshire	11.7	10.8	10.1	9.4
California	249.2	236.3	255.2	265.4	New Jersey	94.6	69.8	67.4	70.8
Colorado	36.8	33.0	32.4	34.7	New Mexico	18.4	14.9	14.9	15.9
Connecticut	37.7	27.9	26.4	26.6	New York	204.1	143.3	132.4	137.4
Delaware	7.6	5.6	5.2	5.8	North Carolina	70.9	64.8	59.5	58.0
District of Columbia	5.0	3.6	3.0	3.0	North Dakota	9.9	7.7	7.8	8.1
Florida	87.3	88.9	89.8	96.1	Ohio	144.2	114.5	109.4	103.8
Georgia	61.6	56.6	56.7	59.4	Oklahoma	39.3	35.6	33.3	30.6
Hawaii	11.5	10.3	9.4	10.1	Oregon	29.9	25.5	26.7	27.2
Idaho	13.2	12.0	14.2	15.6	Pennsylvania	146.5	110.5	104.1	112.9
Illinois	135.6	108.1	105.2	107.8	Rhode Island	10.9	7.8	7.8	7.7
Indiana	73.1	60.0	56.1	57.7	South Carolina	38.7	32.5	30.7	35.8
Iowa	43.4	31.8	31.3	32.5	South Dakota	10.7	7.7	8.4	9.4
Kansas	30.9	25.4	26.1	26.5	Tennessee	49.8	46.1	43.6	43.9
Kentucky	41.2	38.0	37.6	37.5	Texas	171.4	172.5	170.3	176.0
Louisiana	46.3	36.1	36.5	36.1	Utah	20.0	21.2	27.7	30.2
Maine	15.4	13.8	11.5	13.3	Vermont	6.7	6.1	5.9	6.0
Maryland	54.3	41.6	41.4	42.5	Virginia	66.6	60.6	58.3	61.4
Massachusetts	73.8	55.9	47.7	50.5	Washington	50.4	45.9	49.3	53.8
Michigan	124.3	93.8	84.6	90.6	West Virginia	23.4	21.9	20.1	19.9
Minnesota	64.9	49.1	49.4	52.5	Wisconsin	69.3	52.0	51.7	55.5
Mississippi	27.6	25.2	23.8	23.2	Wyoming	6.1	5.8	5.9	5.9

Source: U.S. National Center for Education Statistics, *Digest of Education Statistics*, annual.

No. 296. High School Dropouts, by Race and Hispanic Origin: 1975 to 1996

[In percent. As of October]

ITEM	1975	1980	1985	1988 [1]	1989	1990	1991	1992	1993	1994	1995	1996
EVENT DROPOUTS [2]												
Total [3]	**5.8**	**6.0**	**5.2**	**4.8**	**4.5**	**4.0**	**4.0**	**4.3**	**4.2**	**5.0**	**5.4**	**4.7**
White	5.4	5.6	4.8	4.7	3.9	3.8	3.7	4.1	4.1	4.7	5.1	4.5
Male	5.0	6.4	4.9	5.1	4.1	4.1	3.6	3.8	4.1	4.6	5.4	4.8
Female	5.8	4.9	4.7	4.3	3.8	3.5	3.8	4.4	4.1	4.9	4.8	4.1
Black	8.7	8.3	7.7	6.3	7.7	5.1	6.2	4.9	5.4	6.2	6.1	6.3
Male	8.3	8.0	8.3	6.7	6.9	4.1	5.5	3.3	5.7	6.5	7.9	4.6
Female	9.0	8.5	7.2	6.0	8.6	6.0	7.0	6.7	5.0	5.7	4.4	7.8
Hispanic [4]	10.9	11.5	9.7	10.5	7.7	8.0	7.3	7.9	5.4	9.2	11.6	8.4
Male	10.1	16.9	9.3	12.3	7.6	8.7	10.4	5.8	5.7	8.4	10.9	9.2
Female	11.6	6.9	9.8	8.4	7.7	7.2	4.8	8.6	5.0	10.1	12.5	7.6
STATUS DROPOUTS [5]												
Total [3]	**15.6**	**15.6**	**13.9**	**14.6**	**14.4**	**13.6**	**14.2**	**12.7**	**12.7**	**13.3**	**13.9**	**12.8**
White	13.9	14.4	13.5	14.2	14.1	13.5	14.2	12.2	12.2	12.7	13.6	12.5
Male	13.5	15.7	14.7	15.4	15.4	14.2	15.4	13.3	13.0	13.6	14.3	12.9
Female	14.2	13.2	12.3	13.0	12.8	12.8	13.1	11.1	11.5	11.7	13.0	12.1
Black	27.3	23.5	17.6	17.7	16.4	15.1	15.6	16.3	16.4	15.5	14.4	16.0
Male	27.8	26.0	18.8	18.9	18.6	13.6	15.4	15.5	15.6	17.5	14.2	17.4
Female	26.9	21.5	16.6	16.6	14.5	16.2	15.8	17.1	17.2	13.7	14.6	14.7
Hispanic [4]	34.9	40.3	31.5	39.6	37.7	37.3	39.6	33.9	32.7	34.7	34.7	34.5
Male	32.6	42.6	35.8	40.2	40.3	39.8	44.4	38.4	34.7	36.1	34.2	36.2
Female	36.8	38.1	27.0	38.8	35.0	34.5	34.5	29.6	31.0	33.1	35.4	32.7

[1] Beginning 1988 reflects new editing procedures for cases with missing data on school enrollment. [2] Percent of students who drop out in a single year without completing high school. For grades 10 to 12. [3] Includes other races, not shown separately. [4] Persons of Hispanic origin may be of any race. [5] Percent of the population who have not completed high school and are not enrolled, regardless of when they dropped out. For persons 18 to 24 years old.

Source: U.S. Bureau of the Census, *Current Population Reports*, P20-500.

No. 297. High School Dropouts by Age, Race, and Hispanic Origin: 1970 to 1996

[As of **October. For persons 14 to 24 years old.** See Table 299 for definition of dropouts]

AGE AND RACE	NUMBER OF DROPOUTS (1,000)					PERCENT OF POPULATION				
	1970	1980	1990	1995	1996	1970	1980	1990	1995	1996
Total dropouts [1]	**4,670**	**5,212**	**3,854**	**3,963**	**3,763**	**12.2**	**12.0**	**10.1**	**9.9**	**9.4**
16 to 17 years	617	709	418	406	464	8.0	8.8	6.3	5.4	6.0
18 to 21 years	2,138	2,578	1,921	1,980	1,841	16.4	15.8	13.4	14.2	13.0
22 to 24 years	1,770	1,798	1,458	1,491	1,306	18.7	15.2	13.8	13.6	12.4
White [2]	3,577	4,169	3,127	3,098	2,951	10.8	11.3	10.1	9.7	9.2
16 to 17 years	485	619	334	314	369	7.3	9.2	6.4	5.4	6.0
18 to 21 years	1,618	2,032	1,516	1,530	1,411	14.3	14.7	13.1	13.8	12.6
22 to 24 years	1,356	1,416	1,235	1,181	1,047	16.3	14.0	14.0	13.4	12.4
Black [2]	1,047	934	611	605	672	22.2	16.0	10.9	10.0	11.0
16 to 17 years	125	80	73	70	77	12.8	6.9	6.9	5.8	6.1
18 to 21 years	500	486	345	328	368	30.5	23.0	16.0	15.8	16.6
22 to 24 years	397	346	185	194	213	37.8	24.0	13.5	12.5	14.9
Hispanic [2][3]	(NA)	919	1,122	1,355	1,350	(NA)	29.5	26.8	24.7	24.6
16 to 17 years	(NA)	92	89	94	105	(NA)	16.6	12.9	10.7	10.8
18 to 21 years	(NA)	470	502	652	665	(NA)	40.3	32.9	29.9	33.8
22 to 24 years	(NA)	323	523	598	545	(NA)	40.6	42.8	37.4	35.3

NA Not available.   [1] Includes other groups not shown separately.   [2] Includes persons 14 to 15 years, not shown separately.
[3] Persons of Hispanic origin may be of any race.

Source: U.S. Bureau of the Census, *Current Population Reports*, P20-500; and earlier reports.

No. 298. Enrollment Status, by Race, Hispanic Origin, and Sex: 1975 and 1996

[As of **October. For persons 18 to 21 years old.** For the civilian noninstitutional population. Based on the Current Population Survey; see text, Section 1, Population, and Appendix III]

CHARACTERISTIC	TOTAL PERSONS 18 TO 21 YEARS OLD (1,000)		PERCENT DISTRIBUTION							
			Enrolled in high school		High school graduates				Not high school graduates	
					Total		In college			
	1975	1996	1975	1996	1975	1996	1975	1996	1975	1996
Total [1]	**15,693**	**14,176**	**5.7**	**9.4**	**78.0**	**77.5**	**33.5**	**43.8**	**16.3**	**13.0**
White	13,448	11,243	4.7	8.7	80.6	78.7	34.6	45.3	14.7	12.6
Black	1,997	2,211	12.5	14.0	60.4	69.3	24.9	31.3	27.0	16.6
Hispanic [2]	899	1,965	12.0	13.2	57.2	52.9	24.4	23.1	30.8	33.8
Male [1]	7,584	6,979	7.4	11.8	76.6	74.6	35.4	41.1	15.9	13.6
White	6,545	5,591	6.2	10.9	79.7	76.1	36.9	41.9	14.1	13.1
Black	911	1,022	15.9	18.6	55.0	63.5	23.9	29.4	29.0	17.8
Hispanic [2]	416	992	17.3	15.7	54.6	48.1	25.2	17.7	27.9	36.3
Female [1]	8,109	7,197	4.2	7.1	79.2	80.4	31.8	46.5	16.6	12.4
White	6,903	5,651	3.2	6.6	81.4	81.4	32.4	48.7	15.3	12.0
Black	1,085	1,190	9.7	10.1	65.0	74.3	25.8	32.9	25.4	15.5
Hispanic [2]	484	973	7.6	10.6	59.3	58.0	23.6	28.6	33.1	31.3

[1] Includes other races not shown separately.   [2] Persons of Hispanic origin may be of any race.

Source: U.S. Bureau of the Census, *Current Population Reports*, P20-500; and earlier reports.

No. 299. Employment Status of High School Graduates and School Dropouts: 1980 to 1997

[**In thousands, except percent**. As of **October.** For civilian noninstitutional population 16 to 24 years old. Based on the Current Population Survey; see text, Section 1, Population, and Appendix III]

EMPLOYMENT STATUS, SEX, AND RACE	GRADUATES [1]				DROPOUTS [2]			
	1980	1990	1995 [3]	1997 [3]	1980	1990	1995 [3]	1997 [3]
Civilian population	**11,622**	**8,370**	**6,627**	**6,662**	**5,254**	**3,800**	**3,876**	**3,624**
In labor force	9,795	7,107	5,530	5,633	3,549	2,506	2,443	2,411
Percent of population	84.3	84.9	83.4	84.6	67.5	66.0	63.0	66.5
Employed	8,567	6,279	4,863	5,010	2,651	1,993	1,894	1,933
Percent of labor force	87.5	88.3	87.9	88.9	74.7	79.5	77.5	80.2
Unemployed	1,228	828	667	623	898	513	549	478
Unemployment rate, total [4]	12.5	11.7	12.1	11.1	25.3	20.5	22.5	19.8
Male	13.5	11.1	11.7	10.8	23.5	18.8	19.2	17.8
Female	11.5	12.3	12.5	11.4	28.7	23.5	28.8	23.5
White	10.8	9.0	10.5	9.1	21.6	17.0	19.1	17.4
Black	26.1	26.0	20.3	22.2	43.9	43.3	48.0	35.2
Not in labor force	1,827	1,262	1,097	1,029	1,705	1,294	1,433	1,214
Percent of population	15.7	15.1	16.6	15.4	32.5	34.1	37.0	33.5

[1] For persons not enrolled in college who have completed 4 years of high school only.   [2] For persons not in regular school and who have not completed the 12th grade nor received a general equivalency degree.   [3] See footnote 2, Table 644.
[4] Includes other races not shown separately.

Source: U.S. Bureau of Labor Statistics, Bulletin 2307; *News*, USDL 98-171, May 1, 1998; and unpublished data.

No. 300. General Educational Development (GED) Credentials Issued: 1974 to 1995

[Includes outlying areas]

YEAR	GEDs issued (1,000)	PERCENT DISTRIBUTION BY AGE OF TEST TAKER				
		Under 19 years old	20 to 24 years old	25 to 29 years old	30 to 34 years old	35 years old and over
1974	295	35	27	13	9	17
1975	342	33	26	14	9	18
1980	488	37	27	13	8	15
1985	427	33	26	15	10	16
1990	419	35	25	14	10	17
1991	471	33	27	14	10	17
1992	465	32	28	13	11	16
1993	476	33	27	14	11	16
1994	499	34	26	13	10	16
1995	513	37	25	13	10	15

Source: U.S. National Center for Education Statistics, *Digest of Education Statistics*, 1997.

No. 301. College Enrollment of Recent High School Graduates: 1965 to 1996

[For persons 16 to 24 who graduated from high school in the preceeding 12 months. Includes persons receiving GEDs. Based on surveys and subject to sampling error]

YEAR	NUMBER OF HIGH SCHOOL GRADUATES (1,000)					PERCENT ENROLLED IN COLLEGE [2]				
	Total [1]	Male	Female	White	Black	Total [1]	Male	Female	White	Black
1965	2,659	1,254	1,405	2,417	(NA)	50.9	57.3	45.3	51.7	(NA)
1970	2,757	1,343	1,414	2,461	(NA)	51.8	55.2	48.5	52.0	(NA)
1975	3,186	1,513	1,673	2,825	(NA)	50.7	52.6	49.0	51.2	(NA)
1980	3,089	1,500	1,589	2,682	361	49.3	46.7	51.8	49.9	41.8
1981	3,053	1,490	1,563	2,626	359	53.9	54.8	53.1	54.6	42.9
1982	3,100	1,508	1,592	2,644	384	50.6	49.0	52.1	52.0	36.5
1983	2,964	1,390	1,574	2,496	392	52.7	51.9	53.4	55.0	38.5
1984	3,012	1,429	1,583	2,514	438	55.2	56.0	54.5	57.9	40.2
1985	2,666	1,286	1,380	2,241	333	57.7	58.6	56.9	59.4	42.3
1986	2,786	1,331	1,455	2,307	386	53.8	55.9	51.9	56.0	36.5
1987	2,647	1,278	1,369	2,207	337	56.8	58.4	55.3	56.6	51.9
1988	2,673	1,334	1,339	2,187	382	58.9	57.0	60.8	60.7	45.0
1989	2,454	1,208	1,245	2,051	337	59.6	57.6	61.6	60.4	52.8
1990	2,355	1,169	1,185	1,921	341	59.9	57.8	62.0	61.5	46.3
1991	2,276	1,139	1,137	1,867	320	62.4	57.6	67.1	64.6	45.6
1992	2,398	1,216	1,182	1,900	353	61.7	59.6	63.8	63.4	47.9
1993	2,338	1,118	1,219	1,910	302	62.6	59.7	65.4	62.8	55.6
1994	2,517	1,244	1,273	2,065	318	61.9	60.6	63.2	63.6	50.9
1995	2,599	1,238	1,361	2,088	356	61.9	62.6	61.4	62.6	51.4
1996	2,660	1,297	1,363	2,092	416	65.0	60.1	69.7	65.8	55.3

NA Not available. [1] Includes other races, not shown separately. [2] As of October.

Source: U.S. National Center for Education Statistics, *Digest of Education Statistics*, annual.

No. 302. College Enrollment, by Sex and Attendance Status: 1983 to 1995

[As of **fall. In thousands**]

SEX AND AGE	1983		1989		1991		1993		1995, prel.	
	Total	Part time	Total	Part time	Total	Part time	Total	Part time	Total	Part time
Total	12,465	5,204	13,539	5,878	14,359	6,244	14,305	6,177	14,262	6,133
Male	6,024	2,264	6,190	2,450	6,502	2,572	6,427	2,537	6,343	2,535
14 to 17 years old	102	16	71	12	46	6	83	10	61	7
18 to 19 years old	1,256	158	1,342	113	1,217	121	1,224	138	1,338	246
20 to 21 years old	1,241	205	1,189	198	1,306	230	1,294	209	1,282	283
22 to 24 years old	1,158	382	1,090	367	1,214	378	1,260	392	1,153	365
25 to 29 years old	1,115	624	1,038	639	1,082	587	950	564	962	508
30 to 34 years old	570	384	603	439	664	475	661	484	561	378
35 years old and over	583	494	857	682	972	775	955	739	986	748
Female	6,441	2,940	7,349	3,428	7,857	3,671	7,877	3,640	7,919	3,598
14 to 17 years old	142	16	101	12	76	-	93	6	87	18
18 to 19 years old	1,496	179	1,515	184	1,496	186	1,416	172	1,557	261
20 to 21 years old	1,125	204	1,253	213	1,462	240	1,414	279	1,424	313
22 to 24 years old	884	378	1,104	470	1,072	411	1,263	493	1,258	529
25 to 29 years old	947	658	1,052	732	1,053	679	1,058	689	1,159	704
30 to 34 years old	721	553	750	563	804	591	811	575	675	427
35 years old and over	1,126	953	1,574	1,253	1,895	1,563	1,824	1,427	1,760	1,345

- Represents or rounds to zero.

Source: U.S. National Center for Education Statistics, *Digest of Education Statistics*, annual.

No. 303. College Enrollment, by Selected Characteristics: 1980 to 1996

[In thousands. As of fall. Totals may differ from other tables because of adjustments to underreported and nonreported racial/ethnic data. Nonresident alien students are not distributed among racial/ethnic groups]

CHARACTERISTIC	1980	1988	1990	1992	1993	1994	1995, prel.	1996, est.
Total	12,086.8	13,819.5	14,359.0	14,487.4	14,304.8	14,278.8	14,261.8	14,300.3
Male	5,868.1	6,284.4	6,501.8	6,524.0	6,427.5	6,371.9	6,342.5	6,344.0
Female	6,218.7	7,535.1	7,857.1	7,963.4	7,877.4	7,906.9	7,919.2	7,956.3
Public	9,456.4	10,844.7	11,309.6	11,384.6	11,189.1	11,133.7	11,092.4	11,090.2
Private	2,630.4	2,974.8	3,049.4	3,101.7	3,115.7	3,145.1	3,169.4	3,210.1
2-year	4,521.4	5,240.1	5,651.9	5,722.4	5,565.9	5,529.7	5,492.5	5,497.4
4-year	7,565.4	8,579.4	8,707.1	8,765.0	8,738.9	8,749.1	8,769.3	8,802.8
Undergraduate.	10,469.1	11,959.2	12,439.3	12,537.7	12,324.0	12,262.6	12,232.0	12,259.4
Graduate	1,340.9	1,586.2	1,639.1	1,668.7	1,688.4	1,721.5	1,732.0	1,743.1
First professional . . .	276.8	274.1	280.5	280.9	292.4	294.7	297.6	297.7
White [1]	9,833.0	10,723.0	10,989.8	10,875.4	10,600.0	10,427.0	10,311.2	10,226.0
Male	4,772.9	4,861.3	4,962.2	4,884.6	4,755.0	4,650.7	4,594.1	4,553.0
Female	5,060.1	5,861.7	6,027.6	5,990.8	5,845.1	5,776.3	5,717.2	5,673.1
Public	7,656.1	8,385.4	8,622.2	8,492.8	8,226.6	8,056.3	7,945.4	7,848.3
Private	2,176.9	2,337.6	2,367.5	2,382.6	2,373.4	2,370.6	2,365.9	2,377.7
2-year	3,558.5	3,954.3	4,198.8	4,131.2	3,960.6	3,861.7	3,794.0	3,742.8
4-year	6,274.5	6,768.7	6,791.0	6,744.3	6,639.5	6,565.3	6,517.2	6,483.2
Undergraduate.	8,480.7	9,272.6	9,507.7	9,387.6	9,100.4	8,916.0	8,805.6	8,730.9
Graduate	1,104.7	1,228.4	1,258.0	1,267.2	1,273.8	1,286.8	1,282.3	1,273.9
First professional . . .	247.7	222.0	224.0	220.6	225.9	224.2	223.3	221.2
Black [1]	1,106.8	1,247.1	1,335.4	1,392.9	1,412.8	1,448.6	1,473.7	1,499.4
Male	463.7	484.7	517.0	536.9	543.7	549.7	555.9	563.6
Female	643.0	762.4	818.4	856.0	869.1	898.9	917.8	935.8
Public	876.1	976.5	1,053.4	1,100.5	1,114.3	1,144.6	1,160.7	1,177.3
Private	230.7	270.6	281.9	292.3	298.5	304.1	313.0	322.2
2-year	472.5	524.3	577.6	601.6	599.0	615.0	621.5	629.3
4-year	634.3	722.8	757.7	791.2	813.7	833.6	852.2	870.2
Undergraduate.	1,018.8	1,147.2	1,229.3	1,280.6	1,290.4	1,317.3	1,333.6	1,352.6
Graduate	75.1	83.9	88.9	94.1	102.2	110.6	118.6	125.5
First professional . . .	12.8	16.0	17.2	18.2	20.2	20.7	21.4	21.4
Hispanic	471.7	782.6	866.6	955.0	988.8	1,045.6	1,093.8	1,152.2
Male	231.6	354.0	390.5	427.7	441.2	464.0	480.2	501.3
Female	240.1	428.6	476.0	527.3	547.6	581.6	613.7	650.9
Public	406.2	671.4	742.1	822.3	851.3	898.7	937.1	987.6
Private	65.5	111.1	124.5	132.7	137.5	146.8	156.8	164.7
2-year	255.1	424.2	483.7	545.0	556.8	582.9	608.4	644.2
4-year	216.6	358.3	382.9	409.9	432.0	462.7	485.5	508.1
Undergraduate.	433.1	724.6	804.2	887.8	918.1	968.3	1,012.0	1,065.6
Graduate	32.1	47.2	50.9	55.3	57.9	63.9	68.0	72.7
First professional . . .	6.5	10.9	11.4	12.0	12.8	13.4	13.8	14.0
American Indian [1] .	83.9	102.8	113.7	119.3	121.7	127.4	131.3	134.0
Male	37.8	43.1	47.6	50.2	51.2	53.0	54.8	55.7
Female	46.1	59.7	66.1	69.1	70.5	74.4	76.5	78.2
Public	74.2	90.4	100.2	103.3	106.4	110.7	113.8	116.3
Private	9.7	12.4	13.6	15.9	15.3	16.6	17.5	17.7
2-year	47.0	54.9	62.6	64.4	63.2	66.2	65.6	66.7
4-year	36.9	47.9	51.2	54.9	58.5	61.2	65.7	67.2
Undergraduate.	77.9	95.5	105.8	110.9	112.7	117.4	120.7	122.9
Graduate	5.2	6.2	6.6	7.0	7.3	8.1	8.5	8.9
First professional . . .	0.8	1.1	1.3	1.5	1.7	1.8	2.1	2.2
Asian [1]	286.4	572.5	637.2	697.0	724.4	774.3	797.4	823.6
Male	151.3	294.9	325.1	351.5	363.1	385.0	393.3	403.6
Female	135.2	277.6	312.0	345.6	361.3	389.3	404.1	420.0
Public	239.7	461.0	516.3	565.9	586.3	622.1	638.0	657.1
Private	46.7	111.6	120.9	131.1	138.2	152.2	159.4	166.5
2-year	124.3	215.2	255.7	289.5	295.0	312.5	314.9	322.9
4-year	162.1	357.3	381.5	407.5	429.4	461.8	482.4	500.7
Undergraduate.	248.7	500.5	558.7	613.0	634.2	674.1	692.2	713.2
Graduate	31.6	53.2	57.6	61.5	65.2	72.6	75.6	79.0
First professional . . .	6.1	18.8	20.8	22.5	25.0	27.6	29.6	31.4
Nonresident alien .	305.0	391.5	416.4	447.7	457.1	455.9	454.4	464.9
Male	210.8	246.3	259.4	273.1	273.4	269.5	264.3	266.7
Female	94.2	145.2	157.0	174.6	183.7	186.4	190.1	198.2
Public	204.1	260.0	275.3	299.5	304.3	301.2	297.5	303.7
Private	100.8	131.5	141.0	148.1	152.7	154.7	156.9	161.3
2-year	64.1	67.1	73.5	90.6	91.2	91.4	88.1	91.5
4-year	240.9	324.4	342.8	357.0	365.9	364.5	366.2	373.5
Undergraduate.	209.9	218.7	233.6	257.9	268.2	269.4	267.6	274.1
Graduate	92.2	167.3	177.0	183.6	182.0	179.5	179.5	183.2
First professional . . .	2.9	5.4	5.8	6.2	6.9	7.0	7.3	7.7

[1] Non-Hispanic.
Source: U.S. National Center for Education Statistics, *Digest of Education Statistics,* annual.

No. 304. Foreign (Nonimmigrant) Student Enrollment in College: 1976 to 1997

[For **fall** of the previous year]

| REGION OF ORIGIN | ENROLLMENT (1,000) | | | | | | | | | PERCENT ENROLLED IN— | | | | | |
| | | | | | | | | | | Engineering | | Science[1] | | Business | |
	1976	1980	1985	1990	1993	1994	1995	1996	1997	1980	1996	1980	1996	1980	1996
All regions . . .	179	286	342	387	439	449	453	454	458	25	16	8	8	16	21
Africa	25	36	40	25	21	21	21	21	22	20	14	9	8	19	20
Nigeria	11	16	18	4	2	2	2	2	2	19	11	9	10	22	18
Asia[2]	97	165	200	245	291	294	292	290	291	32	19	8	9	16	22
China: Taiwan . . .	11	18	23	31	37	37	36	33	30	17	18	15	6	17	25
Hong Kong	12	10	10	11	14	14	13	12	11	22	15	9	4	26	37
India	10	9	15	26	36	35	34	32	31	31	36	16	9	21	15
Indonesia	1	2	7	9	11	11	12	13	12	27	21	7	2	21	45
Iran	20	51	17	7	4	4	3	3	2	45	31	7	17	11	7
Japan	7	12	13	30	43	44	45	46	46	7	3	5	4	19	18
Malaysia	2	4	22	14	13	14	14	14	15	13	31	14	3	22	36
Saudi Arabia	3	10	8	4	4	4	4	4	4	30	29	4	4	14	14
South Korea	3	5	16	22	29	31	34	36	37	17	12	11	8	15	16
Thailand	7	7	7	7	9	9	11	12	13	17	17	6	3	26	40
Europe	14	23	33	46	58	62	65	67	68	15	9	9	9	14	22
Latin America[3]	30	42	49	48	43	45	47	47	50	20	13	8	7	14	23
Mexico	5	6	6	7	8	8	9	9	9	16	16	7	6	11	22
Venezuela	5	10	10	3	3	4	4	4	5	30	16	8	5	11	25
North America	10	16	16	19	22	23	23	24	24	8	5	6	7	13	11
Canada	10	15	15	18	21	22	23	23	23	8	5	6	7	12	11
Oceania	3	4	4	4	4	4	4	4	4	5	5	7	7	16	16

[1] Physical and life sciences.   [2] Includes countries not shown separately.   [3] Includes Central America, Caribbean, and South America.

Source: Institute of International Education, New York, NY, *Open Doors*, annual (copyright).

No. 305. College Enrollment, by Sex, Age, Race, and Hispanic Origin: 1980 to 1996

[**In thousands.** As of **October** for the civilian noninstitutional population, 14 years old and over. Based on the Current Population Survey; see text, Section 1, Population, and Appendix III]

CHARACTERISTIC	1980	1985	1988[1]	1989	1990	1991	1992	1993	1994	1995	1996
Total[2]	11,387	12,524	13,116	13,180	13,621	14,057	14,035	13,898	15,022	14,715	15,226
Male[3]	5,430	5,906	5,950	5,950	6,192	6,439	6,192	6,324	6,764	6,703	6,820
18 to 24 years	3,604	3,749	3,770	3,717	3,922	3,954	3,912	3,994	4,152	4,089	4,187
25 to 34 years	1,325	1,464	1,395	1,443	1,412	1,605	1,392	1,406	1,589	1,561	1,523
35 years old and over . .	405	561	727	716	772	832	789	873	958	985	1,013
Female[3]	5,957	6,618	7,166	7,231	7,429	7,618	7,844	7,574	8,258	8,013	8,406
18 to 24 years	3,625	3,788	4,021	4,085	4,042	4,218	4,429	4,199	4,576	4,452	4,582
25 to 34 years	1,378	1,599	1,568	1,639	1,749	1,680	1,732	1,688	1,830	1,788	1,920
35 years old and over . .	802	1,100	1,452	1,396	1,546	1,636	1,575	1,616	1,766	1,684	1,765
White[3]	9,925	10,781	11,140	11,243	11,488	11,686	11,710	11,434	12,222	12,021	12,189
18 to 24 years	6,334	6,500	6,659	6,631	6,635	6,813	6,916	6,763	7,118	7,011	7,123
25 to 34 years	2,328	2,604	2,448	2,597	2,698	2,661	2,582	2,505	2,735	2,686	2,644
35 years old and over . .	1,051	1,448	1,896	1,868	2,023	2,107	2,053	2,068	2,267	2,208	2,254
Male	4,804	5,103	5,078	5,136	5,235	5,304	5,210	5,222	5,524	5,535	5,453
Female	5,121	5,679	6,063	6,107	6,253	6,382	6,499	6,212	6,698	6,486	6,735
Black[3]	1,163	1,263	1,321	1,287	1,393	1,477	1,424	1,545	1,800	1,772	1,901
18 to 24 years	688	734	752	835	894	828	886	861	1,001	988	983
25 to 34 years	289	295	330	275	258	373	302	386	440	426	519
35 years old and over . .	156	213	206	146	207	257	208	284	323	334	354
Male	476	552	494	480	587	629	527	636	745	710	764
Female	686	712	827	807	807	848	897	909	1,054	1,062	1,136
Hispanic origin[3][4]	443	580	747	754	748	830	918	995	1,187	1,207	1,223
18 to 24 years	315	375	450	453	435	516	586	602	662	745	706
25 to 34 years	118	189	191	170	168	196	214	249	312	250	310
35 years old and over . .	(NA)	(NA)	93	114	130	109	102	129	205	193	184
Male	222	279	355	353	364	347	388	442	529	568	529
Female	221	299	391	401	384	483	530	553	659	639	693

NA Not available.   [1] Beginning 1988, based on a revised edit and tabulation package.   [2] Includes other races not shown separately.   [3] Includes persons 14 to 17 years old, not shown separately.   [4] Persons of Hispanic origin may be of any race.

Source: U.S. Bureau of the Census, *Current Population Reports*, P20-500; and earlier reports.

No. 306. Higher Education—Summary: 1970 to 1996

[Institutions, staff, and enrollment as of fall. Finances for fiscal year ending in the following year. Covers universities, colleges, professional schools, junior and teachers colleges, both publicly and privately controlled, regular session. Includes estimates for institutions not reporting. See also Appendix III]

ITEM	Unit	1970	1980	1985	1990	1992	1993	1994	1995	1996, est.
ALL INSTITUTIONS										
Number of institutions [1]	Number .	2,556	3,231	3,340	3,559	3,638	3,632	3,688	3,706	(NA)
4-year	Number .	1,665	1,957	2,029	2,141	2,169	2,190	2,215	2,244	(NA)
2-year	Number .	891	1,274	1,311	1,418	1,469	1,442	1,473	1,462	(NA)
Instructional staff—										
(Lecturer or above) [2]	1,000. . .	474	686	715	817	877	915	915	932	890
Percent full-time	Percent .	78	66	64	61	(NA)	60	(NA)	59	(NA)
Total enrollment [3]	1,000. .	8,581	12,097	12,247	13,819	14,486	14,305	14,279	14,262	14,300
Male	1,000. .	5,044	5,874	5,818	6,284	6,524	6,427	6,372	6,343	6,344
Female	1,000. .	3,537	6,223	6,429	7,535	7,963	7,877	7,907	7,919	7,956
4-year institutions	1,000. .	6,262	7,571	7,716	8,579	8,765	8,739	8,749	8,769	8,803
2-year institutions	1,000. .	2,319	4,526	4,531	5,240	5,722	5,566	5,530	5,493	5,497
Full-time	1,000. .	5,816	7,098	7,075	7,821	8,162	8,128	8,138	8,129	8,213
Part-time	1,000. .	2,765	4,999	5,172	5,998	6,325	6,177	6,141	6,133	6,087
Public	1,000. .	6,428	9,457	9,479	10,845	11,385	11,189	11,134	11,092	11,090
Private	1,000. .	2,153	2,640	2,768	2,974	3,102	3,116	3,145	3,169	3,210
Undergraduate [4]	1,000. .	7,376	10,475	10,597	11,959	12,538	12,324	12,263	12,232	12,259
Men	1,000. .	4,254	5,000	4,962	5,380	5,583	5,484	5,422	5,401	5,411
Women	1,000. .	3,122	5,475	5,635	6,579	6,955	6,840	6,840	6,831	6,848
First-time freshmen	1,000. .	2,063	2,588	2,292	2,257	2,184	2,161	2,133	2,169	2,193
First professional	1,000. .	173	278	274	273	281	292	295	298	298
Men	1,000. .	159	199	180	167	169	173	174	174	172
Women	1,000. .	15	78	94	107	112	120	121	124	125
Graduate [4]	1,000. .	1,031	1,343	1,376	1,586	1,669	1,688	1,721	1,732	1,743
Men	1,000. .	630	675	677	737	772	771	776	768	760
Women	1,000. .	400	670	700	849	896	917	946	965	983
Current funds revenues [5]	Mil. dol. .	23,879	65,585	100,438	149,766	170,881	179,227	189,121	(NA)	(NA)
Tuition and fees	Mil. dol. .	5,021	13,773	23,117	37,434	45,346	48,647	51,507	(NA)	(NA)
Federal government	Mil. dol. .	4,190	9,748	12,705	18,236	21,015	22,076	23,243	(NA)	(NA)
State government	Mil. dol. .	6,503	20,106	29,912	39,481	41,248	41,910	44,343	(NA)	(NA)
Auxiliary enterprises	Mil. dol. .	3,125	7,287	10,674	14,903	16,663	17,538	18,336	(NA)	(NA)
Plant funds [6]	Mil. dol. .	(NA)	4,774	7,713	(NA)	(NA)	(NA)	(NA)	(NA)	(NA)
Increase in fund balance [7]	Mil. dol. .	498	2,793	7,239	(NA)	(NA)	(NA)	(NA)	(NA)	(NA)
Current funds expenditures [5]	Mil. dol. .	23,375	64,053	97,536	146,088	165,241	173,351	182,969	(NA)	(NA)
Educational and general [8]	Mil. dol. .	17,616	50,074	76,128	114,140	128,978	136,024	144,158	(NA)	(NA)
Auxiliary enterprises [9]	Mil. dol. .	2,988	7,288	10,528	14,272	15,562	16,429	17,205	(NA)	(NA)
Gross addition to plant value. . .	Mil. dol. .	4,165	6,471	10,149	19,672	(NA)	(NA)	(NA)	(NA)	(NA)
Value of plant	Mil. dol. .	46,054	88,761	122,261	190,355	(NA)	(NA)	(NA)	(NA)	(NA)
Endowment (market value)	Mil. dol. .	13,714	23,465	50,281	72,049	(NA)	(NA)	(NA)	(NA)	(NA)
2-YEAR INSTITUTIONS										
Number of institutions [1][10]	Number .	891	1,274	1,311	1,418	1,469	1,442	1,473	1,462	(NA)
Public	Number .	654	945	932	972	1,024	1,021	1,036	1,047	(NA)
Private	Number .	237	329	379	446	445	421	437	415	(NA)
Instructional staff—										
(Lecturer or above) [2]	1,000. . .	92	192	211	(NA)	(NA)	290	(NA)	285	(NA)
Enrollment [3][4]	1,000. . .	2,319	4,526	4,531	5,240	5,722	5,566	5,530	5,493	5,497
Public	1,000. . .	2,195	4,329	4,270	4,996	5,485	5,337	5,308	5,278	5,283
Private	1,000. . .	124	198	261	244	238	229	221	215	214
Male	1,000. . .	1,375	2,047	2,002	2,233	2,413	2,345	2,323	2,329	2,348
Female	1,000. . .	945	2,479	2,529	3,007	3,309	3,220	3,207	3,164	3,149
Current funds revenue [5]	Mil. dol. .	2,504	8,505	12,293	18,021	20,805	21,961	22,977	(NA)	(NA)
Tuition and fees	Mil. dol. .	413	1,618	2,618	4,029	5,218	5,594	5,643	(NA)	(NA)
State government	Mil. dol. .	926	3,961	5,659	8,001	8,647	8,730	9,252	(NA)	(NA)
Local government	Mil. dol. .	701	1,623	2,027	3,044	3,524	3,524	3,936	(NA)	(NA)
Current funds expenditures	Mil. dol. .	2,327	8,212	11,976	17,494	19,941	21,187	22,078	(NA)	(NA)
Education and general [8]	Mil. dol. .	2,073	7,608	11,118	16,270	18,578	19,763	20,616	(NA)	(NA)
Instruction	Mil. dol. .	1,205	3,764	5,398	7,903	9,018	9,182	9,476	9,829	(NA)

NA Not available. [1] Beginning 1980, number of institutions includes count of branch campuses. Due to revised survey procedures, data beginning 1990 are not comparable with previous years. [2] Due to revised survey methods, data beginning 1990 not comparable with previous years. [3] Beginning 1980, branch campuses counted according to actual status, e.g., 2-year branch in 2-year category; previously a 2-year branch included in university category. [4] Includes unclassified students. (Students taking courses for credit, but are not candidates for degrees.) [5] Includes items not shown separately. [6] Annual net increase in plant funds. [7] Includes endowment, and, beginning 1980, annuity and student loans. [8] Data for 1970 are not strictly comparable with later years. [9] Includes activities. [10] Beginning 1980, includes schools accredited by the National Association of Trade and Technical Schools.

Source: U.S. National Center for Education Statistics, Digest of Education Statistics, annual; Projections of Education Statistics, annual; and unpublished data.

No. 307. Colleges—Number, 1995 and Enrollment, 1996, by State

[Number of institutions beginning in academic year. Opening fall enrollment of resident and extension students attending full time or part time. Excludes students taking courses for credit by mail, radio, or TV, and students in branches of U.S. institutions operated in foreign countries. See Appendix III]

STATE	Number of institutions, 1995 [1]	1996 ENROLLMENT, prel. (1,000)										
		Total	Male	Female	Public	Private	Full time	White [2]	Minority enrollment			Non-resident alien
									Total [3]	Black [2]	His-panic	
United States. .	**3,706**	**14,300**	**6,344**	**7,956**	**11,090**	**3,210**	**8,213**	**10,226**	**3,609**	**1,499**	**1,152**	**465**
Alabama.	82	219	96	124	197	23	150	157	58	52	2	4
Alaska	9	29	12	17	28	1	12	22	5	1	1	1
Arizona.	45	277	125	152	253	23	131	200	69	9	40	8
Arkansas	38	101	43	58	89	11	68	80	18	15	1	2
California	348	1,883	841	1,041	1,625	258	887	923	878	144	383	82
Colorado.	59	243	111	132	209	34	131	194	43	8	23	6
Connecticut.	42	155	68	88	98	58	83	123	26	12	8	6
Delaware	9	45	19	26	37	8	26	35	8	6	1	1
District of Columbia .	19	74	33	41	7	67	49	36	30	22	3	8
Florida	114	641	277	364	531	110	309	418	203	88	92	20
Georgia	120	318	135	183	249	69	214	215	95	81	5	8
Hawaii	17	61	27	34	47	14	35	16	39	1	1	6
Idaho	12	60	27	33	49	11	41	55	4	(Z)	2	1
Illinois	169	721	316	405	532	189	371	504	199	92	64	18
Indiana.	78	286	131	155	221	65	191	246	31	18	7	9
Iowa	59	177	81	96	126	51	122	157	13	5	3	7
Kansas.	54	172	77	95	155	17	96	146	21	8	6	6
Kentucky	61	178	74	104	147	30	118	158	17	12	1	3
Louisiana	36	204	86	118	175	29	145	133	64	54	5	6
Maine.	33	56	22	33	38	18	32	53	2	(Z)	(Z)	1
Maryland	57	261	108	152	217	43	128	170	81	59	6	10
Massachusetts.	118	410	179	231	173	237	261	317	68	23	18	25
Michigan.	109	547	239	308	459	88	278	437	93	60	12	18
Minnesota.	107	275	122	154	209	67	164	244	24	8	4	7
Mississippi	46	126	54	72	115	11	93	84	41	38	1	2
Missouri	101	291	127	164	189	101	170	244	39	26	5	8
Montana.	26	43	20	23	38	5	33	37	5	(Z)	1	1
Nebraska	35	119	54	66	100	20	68	107	9	3	2	3
Nevada	10	73	33	41	72	2	24	55	16	4	6	2
New Hampshire	30	64	27	37	36	28	39	60	3	1	1	1
New Jersey	61	328	143	186	265	64	177	223	94	39	32	11
New Mexico	35	104	43	60	98	6	51	57	45	3	33	2
New York	311	1,028	437	591	572	455	665	672	312	137	103	44
North Carolina	121	373	160	213	303	70	241	276	91	75	5	6
North Dakota.	20	41	20	20	37	4	32	36	3	(Z)	(Z)	1
Ohio	156	538	240	297	405	132	337	448	73	51	8	16
Oklahoma.	45	177	81	96	154	23	107	134	35	13	4	8
Oregon.	45	165	76	89	141	24	92	138	21	3	6	6
Pennsylvania.	217	622	293	329	335	287	391	519	86	52	12	17
Rhode Island.	12	72	32	40	37	35	46	61	9	3	3	3
South Carolina.	59	174	72	102	148	26	111	127	45	40	2	3
South Dakota	21	35	16	20	29	7	26	31	3	(Z)	(Z)	1
Tennessee	76	247	108	139	194	53	162	198	44	37	3	5
Texas.	179	955	437	519	838	117	521	582	347	95	202	27
Utah	17	152	76	76	114	37	96	137	10	1	4	5
Vermont	22	35	15	20	20	15	24	33	2	(Z)	(Z)	1
Virginia.	89	354	154	200	292	61	202	260	86	58	8	8
Washington.	64	292	129	164	252	40	180	232	51	11	11	9
West Virginia.	28	86	38	48	75	11	60	79	5	4	1	2
Wisconsin.	66	299	132	167	245	54	182	264	28	13	6	7
Wyoming	9	31	13	18	30	1	18	28	2	(Z)	1	(Z)
U.S. military [4] . .	10	82	69	13	82	-	20	65	16	11	3	1

- Represents zero.   Z Fewer than 500.   [1] Branch campuses counted as separate institutions.   [2] Non-Hispanic.
[3] Includes other races not shown separately.   [4] Service schools.

Source: U.S. National Center for Education Statistics, *Digest of Education Statistics,* annual.

No. 308. Higher Education Price Indexes: 1970 to 1996

[1983=100. For years ending June 30. Reflects prices paid by colleges and universities]

YEAR	Index, total	PERSONNEL COMPENSATION				CONTRACTED SERVICES, SUPPLIES, AND EQUIPMENT					
		Total	Professional salaries	Nonprofessional salaries	Fringe benefits	Total	Services	Supplies and materials	Equipment	Library acquisitions	Utilities
1970 ..	39.5	42.1	47.7	38.8	24.7	31.9	42.8	37.6	41.9	25.7	16.3
1971 ..	42.1	44.8	50.1	41.8	28.0	34.1	45.1	39.0	43.5	30.8	18.0
1972 ..	44.3	47.1	52.0	44.9	31.1	36.0	47.8	39.8	45.1	34.9	19.2
1973 ..	46.7	49.8	54.3	47.6	34.7	37.6	49.9	41.1	46.5	37.7	20.2
1974 ..	49.9	52.8	57.2	50.6	38.6	41.4	52.2	46.5	49.4	41.6	24.8
1975 ..	54.3	56.3	60.3	54.6	42.9	48.5	56.8	58.0	58.3	46.7	31.8
1976 ..	57.8	60.0	63.5	59.0	47.8	51.3	59.1	60.7	61.7	52.1	34.4
1977 ..	61.5	63.5	66.4	63.1	52.8	55.7	62.6	63.8	64.8	56.8	40.5
1978 ..	65.7	67.6	69.9	68.1	58.4	60.2	66.6	66.6	69.3	63.2	45.9
1979 ..	70.5	72.4	74.1	73.4	64.5	65.1	71.2	71.7	74.7	70.0	50.3
1980 ..	77.5	78.4	79.4	80.2	72.6	75.0	77.0	84.6	81.6	77.8	64.1
1981 ..	85.8	85.8	86.3	87.7	81.8	85.9	85.2	95.6	89.6	85.9	79.7
1982 ..	93.9	93.5	93.7	94.6	91.5	94.9	94.2	100.4	96.4	93.5	92.4
1983 ..	100.0	100.0	100.0	100.0	100.0	100.0	100.0	100.0	100.0	100.0	100.0
1984 ..	104.8	105.4	104.7	105.1	108.3	103.0	104.9	99.7	102.3	105.3	102.5
1985 ..	110.8	112.0	111.4	109.2	117.7	107.1	110.8	103.0	104.8	111.3	105.3
1986 ..	116.3	118.8	118.2	112.8	127.7	109.0	115.1	102.6	107.2	121.2	103.1
1987 ..	120.9	125.4	125.0	116.3	137.4	107.4	119.7	99.0	108.9	132.9	91.0
1988 ..	126.1	131.7	130.9	120.6	147.1	109.8	123.0	101.1	120.5	140.5	87.7
1989 ..	132.8	139.5	138.8	125.3	158.7	112.8	128.8	108.3	115.1	153.5	85.3
1990 ..	140.8	148.3	147.6	130.3	171.3	118.7	134.0	114.3	119.6	167.0	90.1
1991 ..	148.2	156.5	155.6	135.4	184.4	123.2	139.8	116.4	123.3	179.8	92.2
1992 ..	153.4	162.4	160.8	140.2	193.8	126.9	145.7	115.2	126.3	193.9	93.3
1993 ..	157.9	167.6	165.0	144.2	204.2	129.4	149.5	113.2	128.6	203.4	94.7
1994 ..	163.3	173.4	170.3	148.2	214.1	133.8	154.8	114.3	130.8	214.9	98.7
1995 ..	168.3	179.1	176.1	152.5	221.4	136.0	158.0	115.7	133.5	227.1	96.8
1996 ..	173.3	184.1	181.7	157.3	224.5	141.1	163.8	130.1	137.0	242.9	93.3

Source: Research Associates of Washington, Arlington, VA, *Inflation Measures for Schools, Colleges, and Libraries,* annual (copyright).

No. 309. Institutions of Higher Education—Finances: 1980 to 1995

[In millions of dollars. For fiscal years ending in year shown. For coverage, see headnote, Table 306. See also Appendix III]

ITEM	1980	1985	1990	1992	1993	1994	1995		
							Total	Public	Private
Current funds revenues.	58,520	92,473	139,635	161,396	170,881	179,227	189,121	119,312	69,808
Tuition and fees	11,930	21,283	33,926	41,559	45,346	48,647	51,507	21,908	29,599
Federal government	8,902	11,509	17,255	19,833	21,015	22,076	23,243	13,192	10,051
State government	18,378	27,583	38,349	40,587	41,248	41,910	44,343	42,855	1,488
Local government	1,588	2,387	3,640	4,160	4,445	4,998	5,166	4,757	409
Private gifts, grants, and contracts [1]	2,808	4,896	7,781	8,977	9,660	10,203	10,867	4,738	6,129
Endowment earnings	1,177	2,096	3,144	3,442	3,628	3,670	3,988	693	3,295
Educational activities [2]	1,239	2,127	3,632	4,521	5,038	5,294	5,603	3,616	1,987
Auxiliary enterprises	6,481	10,100	13,938	15,759	16,663	17,538	18,336	11,374	6,962
Hospitals	([3])	7,475	13,217	17,240	18,124	18,960	19,100	12,528	6,572
Other funds revenues [4]	6,015	3,015	4,753	5,318	5,715	5,931	6,967	3,652	3,315
Current funds expenditures [5] . . .	56,914	89,951	134,656	156,189	165,241	173,351	182,969	115,465	67,504
Educational and general	44,543	70,061	105,585	121,567	128,978	136,023	144,158	92,174	51,984
Instruction	18,497	28,777	42,146	47,997	50,341	52,776	55,720	37,599	18,121
Institutional support	5,054	8,587	12,674	14,475	15,250	15,926	16,845	9,929	6,916
Research	5,099	7,552	12,506	14,262	15,291	16,118	17,110	11,830	5,280
Plant operation [6]	4,700	7,345	9,458	10,347	10,784	11,368	11,746	7,669	4,077
Academic support	3,876	6,074	9,438	10,577	11,073	11,678	12,279	8,463	3,815
Libraries	1,624	2,362	3,254	3,596	3,685	3,908	4,166	2,615	1,551
Student services	2,567	4,178	6,388	7,509	8,165	8,563	9,060	5,614	3,446
Scholarships and fellowships .	2,200	3,670	6,656	9,060	10,148	11,238	12,285	4,662	7,623
Unrestricted funds	905	1,962	3,854	5,206	5,949	6,645	7,329	2,149	5,180
Restricted funds	1,296	1,709	2,802	3,854	4,199	4,593	4,956	2,513	2,443
Public service	1,817	2,861	4,690	5,489	5,935	6,242	6,691	5,034	1,657
Mandatory transfers	732	1,016	1,630	1,851	1,991	2,115	2,423	1,373	1,049
Auxiliary enterprises [5]	6,486	10,012	13,204	14,966	15,562	16,429	17,205	11,235	5,970
Hospitals [5]	4,757	8,010	12,679	16,104	17,050	17,510	18,071	11,802	6,270
Independent operations [5]	1,128	1,868	3,187	3,552	3,652	3,387	3,534	254	3,280

[1] Private grants represent nongovernmental revenue for sponsored research and other sponsored programs; includes private contracts. [2] Sales and service of educational departments only. [3] Included in other. [4] Includes sales and services of federally funded research and development centers, and others sources. [5] Includes mandatory transfers which are primarily current expenditures for plant. [6] Includes maintenance.

Source: U.S. National Center for Education Statistics, *Digest of Education Statistics,* annual.

No. 310. Major Federal Student Financial Assistance Programs: 1970 to 1997

[For award years July 1 of year shown to the following June 30, except as indicated. Funds utilized exclude operating costs, etc., and represent funds given to students]

PROGRAM	Unit	1970	1980	1985	1990	1993	1994	1995	1996, est.	1997, est.
Pell Grants:										
Number of recipients	1,000..	(X)	2,708	2,813	3,405	3,756	3,675	3,612	3,660	3,683
Funds utilized	Mil. dol.	(X)	2,387	3,597	4,935	5,654	5,519	5,472	5,762	6,256
Average grant	Dollars.	(X)	882	1,279	1,449	1,506	1,502	1,515	1,574	1,699
Supplemental Educational Opportunity Grants: [1]										
Number of recipients	1,000..	253.4	716.5	686.0	761.2	1,068	1,056	1,082	1,191	991
Funds utilized	Mil. dol.	134	368	410	503	752	755	764	762	738
Average grant	Dollars.	527	513	598	661	705	715	706	640	745
College Work-Study:										
Number of recipients	1,000..	425.0	819.1	728.4	687.4	711	700	702	691	945
Funds utilized [2]	Mil. dol.	200	660	656	727	771	757	764	776	1,007
Average annual earnings	Dollars.	470	806	901	1,059	1,084	1,081	1,087	1,123	1,065
Perkins Loans: [3]										
Number of recipients	1,000..	452.0	813.4	700.9	660.2	684	663	687	674	788
Loan funds utilized [2]	Mil. dol.	241	694	703	870	918	970	1,029	1,021	1,058
Average loan	Dollars.	532	853	1,003	1,318	1,342	1,464	1,497	1,516	1,342
Loans in default [4]	Mil. dol.	(NA)	612.0	690.0	727.5	733	760	818	(NA)	(NA)
Default rate	Percent.	(NA)	11.6	8.3	6.2	11.42	10.75	12.57	(NA)	(NA)
Federal Family Education Loans [5]										
Number of loans	1,000..	1,017	2,905	3,833	4,493	5,647	6,512	5,243	5,531	5,737
Loan funds utilized [6]	Mil. dol.	1,015	6,200	8,913	12,291	17,863	22,891	19,152	20,729	21,453
Average loan	Dollars.	998	2,135	2,374	2,734	3,163	3,515	3,653	3,748	3,792
Default rate [7]	Percent.	(NA)	10.1	9.0	10.4	13.4	12.9	12.5	11.9	11.9

NA Not available. X Not applicable. [1] For 1970, data represents Educational Opportunity Grants Program. [2] Includes institutional matching funds. [3] Formerly National Direct Student Loans. [4] Loans in default represents all loans in institutions' portfolio. [5] Formerly Guaranteed Student Loans. Beginning with 1985, data include activity under the Stafford program, the PLUS (Parent Loans for Undergraduate Students), FISL (Federally Insured Student Loans), and SLS (Supplemental Loans Students) programs. [6] Represents dollar amount of commitments. [7] Cumulative dollar amount of default claims to lenders, minus cumulative collections as a percent of all loans that have ever gone into repayment.

Source: U.S. Dept. of Education, Office of Postsecondary Education, unpublished data.

No. 311. Finances of Public Colleges, 1990 to 1995, and by State, 1996

[For academic years ending in year shown. Data provided by the state higher education finance officers, except as noted]

STATE	FTE [1] enrollment (1,000)	Appropriations for current operations [2] (mil. dol.)	Net tuition revenues (mil. dol.) [3]	STATE	FTE [1] enrollment (1,000)	Appropriations for current operations [2] (mil. dol.)	Net tuition revenues (mil. dol.) [3]
Total, 1990	7,960.3	33,784.0	11,277.0	Michigan	316.4	1,633.5	1,232.0
Total, 1991	8,140.7	35,040.0	12,449.0	Minnesota	161.0	862.4	361.3
Total, 1992	8,326.0	35,013.0	14,194.0	Mississippi	101.6	458.7	208.5
Total, 1993	8,398.3	35,179.0	15,765.0	Missouri	129.4	689.5	457.4
Total, 1994	8,334.6	36,465.0	16,638.0	Montana	32.4	113.7	76.9
Total, 1995	8,263.2	38,582.0	17,425.0	Nebraska	67.5	308.0	120.5
Total, 1996	**8,268.8**	**39,699.0**	**18,346.1**	Nevada	36.8	199.9	41.7
Alabama	177.4	681.2	406.7	New Hampshire	27.9	78.8	160.0
Alaska	17.4	155.8	38.8	New Jersey [4]	185.6	1,119.7	495.3
Arizona	161.9	761.0	346.8	New Mexico	70.9	441.9	98.9
Arkansas	74.3	334.8	162.3	New York	439.3	2,226.7	1,080.9
California	1,263.1	6,059.9	1,362.0	North Carolina	238.9	1,403.5	355.2
Colorado	136.1	482.3	432.5	North Dakota	30.7	122.7	65.0
Connecticut	57.0	428.7	192.8	Ohio	338.4	1,414.5	1,069.1
Delaware	26.8	134.0	168.6	Oklahoma	111.4	493.3	213.3
District of Columbia	7.9	49.9	9.3	Oregon	93.5	388.7	267.7
Florida	403.0	1,660.5	509.8	Pennsylvania	279.9	1,410.8	1,237.6
Georgia	212.8	1,186.6	369.2	Rhode Island	25.2	128.1	108.9
Hawaii	32.7	242.7	33.4	South Carolina	123.9	490.8	352.7
Idaho	39.0	226.1	49.0	South Dakota	21.9	87.9	61.6
Illinois	353.2	1,844.9	459.6	Tennessee	153.4	724.6	302.5
Indiana	174.0	802.2	551.2	Texas	617.9	2,955.0	1,085.9
Iowa	100.4	555.5	284.7	Utah	81.6	383.1	148.4
Kansas	105.8	496.9	214.7	Vermont	15.3	36.7	132.6
Kentucky	115.8	440.7	254.7	Virginia	219.0	818.1	664.8
Louisiana	136.2	433.4	325.0	Washington	192.4	879.5	314.3
Maine	26.9	161.7	92.9	West Virginia	60.8	198.3	160.8
Maryland	155.1	716.8	432.2	Wisconsin	180.9	1,034.2	425.1
Massachusetts	116.7	593.5	311.3	Wyoming	21.3	147.5	39.7

[1] Full-time equivalent (FTE). Credit and noncredit program enrollment including summer session. Excludes medical enrollments. [2] State and local appropriations. Includes aid to students attending in-state public institutions. Excludes sums for research, agriculture stations and cooperative extension, and hospitals and medical schools. [3] Excludes appropriated aid to students attending in-state public institutions. [4] Estimated by source.

Source: Research Associates of Washington, Arlington, VA, State Profiles: Financing Public Higher Education, annual (copyright).

No. 312. Institutions of Higher Education—Charges: 1985 to 1997

[In dollars. Estimated. **For the entire academic year ending in year shown.** Figures are average charges per full-time equivalent student. Room and board are based on full-time students]

ACADEMIC CONTROL AND YEAR	TUITION AND REQUIRED FEES [1]				BOARD RATES [2]				DORMITORY CHARGES			
	All institu-tions	2-yr. col-leges	4-yr. col-leges	Other 4-yr. schools	All institu-tions	2-yr. col-leges	4-yr. col-leges	Other 4-yr. schools	All institu-tions	2-yr. col-leges	4-yr. col-leges	Other 4-yr. schools
Public:												
1985	971	584	1,386	1,117	1,241	1,302	1,276	1,201	1,196	921	1,237	1,200
1989	1,285	730	1,846	1,515	1,533	1,488	1,576	1,504	1,457	965	1,483	1,506
1990	1,356	756	2,035	1,608	1,635	1,581	1,728	1,561	1,513	962	1,561	1,554
1991	1,454	824	2,159	1,707	1,691	1,594	1,767	1,641	1,612	1,050	1,658	1,655
1992	1,624	937	2,410	1,933	1,780	1,612	1,852	1,745	1,731	1,074	1,789	1,782
1993	1,782	1,025	2,604	2,192	1,841	1,668	1,982	1,761	1,756	1,106	1,856	1,787
1994	1,942	1,125	2,820	2,360	1,880	1,681	1,993	1,828	1,873	1,190	1,897	1,958
1995	2,057	1,192	2,977	2,499	1,949	1,712	2,108	1,866	1,959	1,232	1,992	2,044
1996 [3] . . .	2,179	1,239	3,151	2,660	2,020	1,681	2,192	1,937	2,057	1,297	2,104	2,133
1997 [3] . . .	2,277	1,283	3,321	2,778	2,110	1,782	2,283	2,023	2,148	1,346	2,189	2,228
Private:												
1985	5,315	3,485	6,843	5,135	1,462	1,294	1,647	1,405	1,426	1,424	1,753	1,309
1989	7,461	4,817	9,451	7,172	1,880	1,609	2,269	1,762	1,849	1,540	2,353	1,686
1990	8,174	5,196	10,348	7,778	1,948	1,811	2,339	1,823	1,923	1,663	2,411	1,774
1991	8,772	5,570	11,379	8,389	2,074	1,989	2,470	1,943	2,063	1,744	2,654	1,889
1992	9,434	5,752	12,192	9,053	2,252	2,090	2,727	2,098	2,221	1,789	2,860	2,038
1993	9,942	6,059	13,055	9,533	2,344	1,875	2,825	2,197	2,348	1,970	3,018	2,151
1994	10,572	6,370	13,874	10,100	2,434	1,970	2,946	2,278	2,490	2,067	3,277	2,261
1995	11,111	6,914	14,537	10,653	2,509	2,023	3,035	2,362	2,587	2,233	3,469	2,347
1996 [3] . . .	11,864	7,094	15,605	11,297	2,606	2,098	3,218	2,429	2,738	2,371	3,680	2,473
1997 [3] . . .	12,537	7,190	16,531	11,911	2,661	2,186	3,140	2,518	2,873	2,513	3,820	2,597

[1] For in-State students.   [2] Beginning 1988, rates reflect 20 meals per week, rather than meals served 7 days a week. [3] Preliminary.

Source: U.S. National Center for Education Statistics, *Digest of Education Statistics,* annual.

No. 313. Voluntary Financial Support of Higher Education: 1970 to 1996

[For school years ending in years shown; enrollment as of fall of preceding year. Voluntary support, as defined in Gift Reporting Standards, excludes income from endowment and other invested funds as well as all support received from federal, state, and local governments and their agencies and contract research]

ITEM	Unit	1970	1980	1985	1990	1993	1994	1995	1996
Estimated support, total [1]	Mil. dol.	1,780	3,800	6,320	9,800	11,200	12,350	12,750	14,250
Individuals	Mil. dol .	822	1,757	2,876	4,770	5,510	6,210	6,540	7,440
Alumni	Mil. dol .	381	910	1,460	2,540	2,980	3,410	3,600	4,040
Business corporations	Mil. dol .	269	696	1,574	2,170	2,400	2,510	2,560	2,800
Foundations	Mil. dol .	434	903	1,175	1,920	2,200	2,540	2,460	2,815
Religious organizations	Mil. dol .	102	155	208	240	250	240	250	255
Current operations	Mil. dol .	960	2,250	3,800	5,440	6,300	6,710	7,230	7,850
Capital purposes	Mil. dol .	820	1,550	2,520	4,360	4,900	5,640	5,520	6,400
Enrollment, higher education . . .	1,000 . .	8,094	11,570	12,242	13,539	14,486	14,306	14,279	14,210
Support per student	Dollars .	220	328	516	724	773	863	893	1,003
In 1995-96 dollars	Dollars .	899	652	754	811	838	913	917	1,003
Expenditures, higher education .	Bil. dol .	24.7	62.47	98.26	150.56	182.69	191.58	201.60	211.20
Expenditures per student	Dollars .	3,052	5,399	8,026	11,120	12,611	13,392	14,119	14,863
In 1995-96 dollars	Dollars .	12,476	10,733	11,730	13,526	13,671	14,166	14,506	14,863
Institutions reporting support	Number.	1,045	1,019	1,114	1,056	1,106	992	1,086	1,104
Total support reported	Mil. dol .	1,472	3,055	5,295	8,214	9,491	10,326	10,992	12,251
Private 4-year institutions	Mil. dol .	1,154	2,178	3,522	5,072	5,767	6,103	6,500	7,163
Public 4-year institutions.	Mil. dol .	292	856	1,728	3,056	3,610	4,138	4,382	4,943
2-year colleges	Mil. dol .	26	20	45	85	115	84	110	145

[1] Includes other contributions, not shown separately.

Source: Council for Aid to Education, New York, NY, *Voluntary Support of Education,* annual.

No. 314. Average Salaries for College Faculty Members: 1995 to 1997

[In thousands of dollars. For academic year ending in year shown. Figures are for 9 months teaching for full-time faculty members in 4-year institutions. Fringe benefits averaged in 1995, $12,400 in public institutions and $14,300 in private institutions, in 1996, $12,600 in public institutions and $14,600 in private institutions and in 1997, $12,600 in public institutions and $14,700 in private institutions]

TYPE OF CONTROL AND ACADEMIC RANK	1995	1996	1997	TYPE OF CONTROL AND ACADEMIC RANK	1995	1996	1997
Public: All ranks.	49.1	50.4	52.0	Private: [1] All ranks	55.4	57.5	59.3
Professor	62.0	63.9	65.8	Professor	73.2	75.6	78.2
Associate professor	47.0	48.2	49.7	Associate professor	50.0	51.5	52.7
Assistant professor	39.2	40.2	41.3	Assistant professor	41.2	42.4	43.4
Instructor	29.6	30.8	31.8	Instructor	31.7	32.9	33.1

[1] Excludes church-related colleges and universities.

Source: American Association of University Professors, Washington, DC, *AAUP Annual Report on the Economic Status of the Profession.*

No. 315. Employees in Higher Education Institutions, by Sex and Occupation: 1976 to 1995

[In thousands. As of fall. Based on survey and subject to sampling error; see source]

YEAR AND STATUS	Total	PROFESSIONAL STAFF									Nonprofessional staff, total
		Total	Executive, administrative, and managerial		Faculty [1]		Research/ instruction assistants		Other		
			Male	Female	Male	Female	Male	Female	Male	Female	
1976, total	**1,863.8**	**1,073.1**	**74.6**	**26.6**	**460.6**	**172.7**	**106.5**	**53.6**	**87.5**	**91.0**	**790.7**
Full time.	1,339.9	709.4	72.0	25.0	326.8	107.2	18.6	9.4	76.2	74.1	630.5
Part time.	523.9	363.7	2.6	1.7	133.7	65.4	87.9	44.2	11.3	16.9	160.2
1991, total	**2,545.2**	**1,595.5**	**85.4**	**59.3**	**525.6**	**300.7**	**119.1**	**78.6**	**165.4**	**261.3**	**949.8**
Full time.	1,812.9	1,031.8	82.9	56.2	366.2	169.4	(NA)	(NA)	142.2	214.8	781.1
Part time.	732.3	563.7	2.5	3.1	159.4	131.2	119.1	78.6	23.2	46.4	168.7
1993, total	**2,602.6**	**1,687.3**	**82.7**	**60.9**	**561.1**	**354.4**	**120.4**	**82.4**	**166.7**	**258.6**	**915.3**
Full time.	1,783.5	1,039.1	80.1	57.7	363.4	182.3	(NA)	(NA)	142.7	212.9	744.4
Part time.	819.1	648.2	2.7	3.2	197.7	172.1	120.4	82.4	24.0	45.8	170.9
1995, total	**2,662.1**	**1,744.9**	**82.1**	**65.3**	**562.9**	**368.8**	**124.0**	**91.9**	**177.2**	**272.7**	**917.2**
Full time.	1,801.4	1,066.5	79.2	61.8	360.2	190.7	(NA)	(NA)	151.5	223.2	734.9
Part time.	860.7	678.4	2.9	3.6	202.7	178.1	124.0	91.9	25.6	49.5	182.3

NA Not available.   [1] Instruction and research.

Source: U.S. Center for Education Statistics, *Fall Staff in Postsecondary Institutions, 1995,* March 1998.

No. 316. Faculty in Institutions of Higher Education: 1970 to 1995

[In thousands, except percent. As of fall. Based on survey and subject to sampling error; see source]

YEAR	Total	EMPLOYMENT STATUS		CONTROL		LEVEL		PERCENT		
		Full time	Part time	Public	Private	4-Year	2-Year	Part time	Public	2-Year
1970	474	369	104	314	160	382	92	22	66	19
1975	628	440	188	443	185	467	161	30	71	26
1976	633	434	199	449	184	467	166	31	71	26
1977	678	448	230	492	186	485	193	34	73	28
1979	675	445	230	488	187	494	182	34	72	27
1980	686	450	236	495	191	494	192	34	72	28
1981	705	461	244	509	196	493	212	35	72	30
1982	710	462	248	506	204	493	217	35	71	30
1983	724	471	254	512	212	504	220	35	71	31
1984	717	462	255	505	212	504	213	36	70	30
1985	715	459	256	503	212	504	211	36	70	30
1986	722	459	263	510	212	506	216	36	71	30
1987	793	523	270	553	240	548	246	34	70	31
1989	824	524	300	577	247	584	241	36	70	29
1991	826	536	291	581	245	591	235	35	70	28
1993	915	546	370	650	265	626	289	40	71	32
1995	932	551	381	657	275	647	285	41	70	31

Source: U.S. Center for Education Statistics, *Fall Staff in Postsecondary Institutions, 1995,* March 1998.

No. 317. Higher Education Registrations in Foreign Languages: 1970 to 1995

[As of **fall**]

ITEM	1970	1972	1974	1977	1980	1983	1986	1990	1995
Registrations [1] (1,000)	**1,111.5**	**1,008.9**	**946.6**	**933.5**	**924.8**	**966.0**	**1,003.2**	**1,184.1**	**1,138.8**
Index (1960=100)	171.8	155.9	146.3	144.3	142.9	149.3	155.0	183.0	176.0
By selected language (1,000):									
Spanish	389.2	364.5	362.2	376.7	379.4	386.2	411.3	533.9	606.3
French	359.3	293.1	253.1	246.1	248.4	270.1	275.3	272.5	205.4
German	202.6	177.1	152.1	135.4	126.9	128.2	121.0	133.3	96.3
Italian	34.2	33.3	33.0	33.3	34.8	38.7	40.9	49.7	43.8
Japanese	6.6	8.3	9.6	10.7	11.5	16.1	23.5	45.7	44.7
Russian	36.1	36.4	32.5	27.8	24.0	30.4	34.0	44.6	24.7
Latin	27.6	24.4	25.2	24.4	25.0	24.2	25.0	28.2	25.9
Chinese	6.2	10.0	10.6	9.8	11.4	13.2	16.9	19.5	26.5
Ancient Greek	16.7	20.6	24.4	25.8	22.1	19.4	16.9	16.4	16.3
Hebrew	16.6	21.1	22.4	19.4	19.4	18.2	17.6	16.4	16.3
Portuguese	5.1	4.8	5.1	5.0	4.9	4.4	15.6	13.0	13.1
Arabic.	1.3	1.7	2.0	3.1	3.5	3.4	5.1	6.2	6.5
12 languages as percent of total .	99.1	98.7	98.5	98.3	98.5	98.6	98.6	98.5	97.8

[1] Includes other foreign languages, not shown separately.

Source: Association of Departments of Foreign Languages, New York, NY, *ADFL Bulletin,* Vol. 28, No. 2, and earlier issues (copyright).

No. 318. College Freshmen—Summary Characteristics: 1970 to 1997

[**In percent**. As of **fall** for first-time, full-time freshmen. Based on sample survey and subject to sampling error; see source]

CHARACTERISTIC	1970	1980	1985	1990	1993	1994	1995	1996	1997
Sex: Male	55	49	48	46	45	46	46	46	46
Female	45	51	52	54	55	54	54	54	54
Applied to three or more colleges	[1]15	26	29	36	37	36	36	37	36
Average grade in high school:									
A- to A+	16	21	21	23	27	28	28	32	32
B- to B+	58	60	59	58	57	56	56	54	54
C to C+	27	19	20	19	16	15	15	14	14
D	1	1	1	-	-	-	-	-	-
Political orientation:									
Liberal	34	20	21	23	25	23	21	22	22
Middle of the road	45	60	57	55	50	53	54	53	55
Conservative	17	17	19	20	21	21	20	21	19
Probable field of study:									
Arts and humanities	16	9	8	9	8	8	10	10	9
Biological sciences	4	4	4	4	6	7	7	7	6
Business	16	24	27	21	16	16	16	16	16
Education	11	7	7	10	10	10	10	11	10
Engineering	9	12	11	8	9	8	7	8	9
Physical science	2	3	2	2	3	2	2	2	2
Social science	14	7	8	10	9	10	9	9	8
Professional	(NA)	15	13	15	20	19	18	16	15
Technical	4	6	5	4	3	3	4	2	4
Data processing/computer programming	(NA)	2	2	1	1	1	1	1	2
Other [2]	(NA)	(NA)	16	16	17	17	17	19	19
Communications	(NA)	2	2	2	2	2	2	2	2
Computer science	(NA)	1	2	2	2	2	2	3	3
Recipient of financial aid:									
Pell grant	(NA)	33	19	23	24	23	23	20	22
Supplemental educational opportunity grant	(NA)	8	5	7	6	6	6	6	6
State scholarship or grant	(NA)	16	14	16	14	16	16	17	17
College grant	(NA)	13	19	22	24	26	26	29	27
Federal guaranteed student loan	(NA)	21	23	23	28	29	29	26	25
Perkins loan [3]	(NA)	9	6	8	8	9	9	9	9
College loan	(NA)	4	4	6	6	8	10	9	11
College work-study grant	(NA)	15	10	10	12	13	13	12	12
Attitudes—agree or strongly agree:									
Activities of married women are best confined to home and family	48	27	22	25	24	25	24	24	25
Capital punishment should be abolished	56	34	27	22	22	20	21	22	24
Legalize marijuana	38	39	22	19	28	32	34	33	35
There is too much concern for the rights of criminals	52	66	(NA)	(NA)	68	73	73	72	70
Abortion should be legalized	(NA)	54	55	65	62	60	58	56	54
Aspires to an advanced degree	49	49	51	61	65	64	64	67	67
Male	57	50	52	60	64	62	61	65	63
Female	41	47	50	62	67	66	66	68	69
Median family income ($1,000)	12	23	34	43	46	48	49	53	53

- Represents or rounds to zero.   NA Not available.   [1] 1969 data.   [2] Includes other fields, not shown separately.
[3] National Direct Student Loan prior to 1990.

Source: The Higher Education Research Institute, University of California, Los Angeles, CA, *The American Freshman: National Norms*, annual.

No. 319. Freshman Enrollment in Remedial Courses, by Institutional Characteristic: 1995

[**In percent, except number of freshmen**. As of **fall**. Remedial courses are those developed for students lacking skills necessary to perform college-level work as required by the institution. Based on survey and subject to sampling error; for details, see source]

INSTITUTIONAL CHARACTERISTIC	Number of freshmen (1,000)	INSTITUTIONS OFFERING COURSES				FRESHMEN TAKING COURSES			
		Total	Reading	Writing	Math	Total	Reading	Writing	Math
All institutions	2,128	78	57	71	72	29	13	17	24
Control: Public, 2 year	943	100	99	99	99	41	20	25	34
Private, 2 year	56	63	29	61	62	26	11	18	23
Public, 4 year	726	81	52	71	78	22	8	12	18
Private, 4 year	403	63	34	52	51	13	7	8	9
Minority enrollment:									
High [1]	338	94	87	85	93	43	25	29	35
Low [2]	1,790	76	53	70	70	26	11	15	21

[1] Total enrollment, excluding nonresident aliens, is less than 50 percent White, non-Hispanic.   [2] Total enrollment, excluding nonresident aliens, is more than 50% White, Non-Hispanic.

Source: U.S. National Center for Education Statistics, "Remedial Education at Higher Education Institutions in Fall of 1995," NCES 97-584.

No. 320. College Population, by Selected Characteristics: 1987 and 1996

[In thousands, except percent. As of October. Based on the Current Population Survey. See text, Section 1, Population, and Appendix III]

CHARACTERISTIC	Total popu-lation	ENROLLED IN COLLEGE							
		Total	Type of school			Percent enrolled full time	Percent employed		
			2-year	4-year	Graduate school		Total	Full time	Part time
Total, 1987 [1]	**190,058**	**12,719**	**3,648**	**6,656**	**2,415**	**62.6**	**60.4**	**31.7**	**28.7**
Male	90,610	6,030	1,522	3,356	1,152	67.2	60.6	31.7	28.9
Female.	99,449	6,689	2,127	3,299	1,264	58.4	60.1	31.6	28.5
White.	162,757	10,731	3,039	5,617	2,075	61.6	62.2	32.6	29.6
Black.	21,520	1,351	422	748	181	66.3	50.5	28.6	21.9
Hispanic origin [2].	13,687	739	307	342	90	57.3	65.5	37.0	28.6
14 to 19 years old	21,410	3,284	1,111	2,172	1	88.1	44.0	7.6	36.4
20 and 21 years old	7,078	2,642	624	1,961	58	84.4	53.3	14.5	38.8
22 to 24 years old	11,712	2,006	457	1,055	494	67.2	62.5	29.8	32.7
25 to 34 years old	42,374	2,985	851	996	1,137	36.4	74.0	55.8	18.2
35 years and older	107,484	1,802	605	471	725	22.3	83.1	62.8	20.3
Total, 1996 [1]	**205,108**	**15,226**	**4,174**	**8,130**	**2,922**	**64.6**	**63.1**	**33.5**	**29.6**
Male	98,529	6,820	1,752	3,781	1,288	68.6	62.5	35.2	27.3
Female.	106,579	8,406	2,423	4,349	1,634	61.4	63.6	32.1	31.5
White.	171,804	12,189	3,295	6,565	2,328	64.4	65.9	34.2	31.7
Black.	24,335	1,901	580	1,013	308	62.0	54.6	35.3	19.3
Hispanic origin [2].	19,903	1,223	444	605	174	57.9	61.7	33.7	28.0
15 to 19 years old	18,993	3,546	1,223	2,303	18	88.8	46.2	9.6	36.6
20 and 21 years old	6,800	2,907	669	2,187	52	86.1	56.8	14.6	42.2
22 to 24 years old	10,495	2,551	515	1,502	534	75.9	64.1	27.9	36.3
25 to 34 years old	40,093	3,443	922	1,304	1,217	45.3	74.3	53.9	20.4
35 years and older	128,729	2,778	845	835	1,098	24.9	76.5	63.8	12.7

[1] Includes other races, not shown separately.   [2] Persons of Hispanic origin may be of any race.

Source: U.S. Bureau of the Census, *Current Population Reports*, P20-443 and P20-500.

No. 321. Salary Offers to Candidates for Degrees: 1995 to 1997

[In dollars. Data are average beginning salaries based on offers made by business, industrial, government, and nonprofit and educational employers to graduating students. Data from representative colleges throughout the United States]

FIELD OF STUDY	BACHELOR'S			MASTER'S [1]			DOCTOR'S		
	1995	1996	1997	1995	1996	1997	1995	1996	1997
Accounting	27,926	29,375	30,154	31,474	32,965	33,636	(NA)	(NA)	(NA)
Business, general [2]	25,711	27,274	29,346	39,293	42,193	42,618	(NA)	(NA)	(NA)
Marketing	25,400	26,777	28,031	40,899	[3]42,046	[3]47,422	(NA)	(NA)	(NA)
Engineering:									
Civil	30,618	31,308	33,031	34,600	35,702	37,947	42,323	[3]51,198	[3]49,746
Chemical.	39,880	41,443	42,802	41,757	43,733	45,469	57,299	60,179	[3]59,536
Computer	34,941	37,529	40,093	40,889	43,488	50,485	59,280	[3]55,332	[3]63,367
Electrical	36,049	38,025	39,546	43,137	45,655	50,166	56,065	62,447	[3]64,158
Mechanical	35,744	37,036	[3]38,287	42,067	43,181	45,974	51,989	[3]54,676	[3]61,037
Nuclear [4].	38,531	37,453	[3]37,050	45,167	[3]40,840	[3]43,001	(NA)	(NA)	(NA)
Petroleum	37,476	39,770	43,444	43,517	[3]42,630	[3]48,350	(NA)	(NA)	(NA)
Engineering technology . . .	31,663	33,826	35,498	(NA)	(NA)	(NA)	(NA)	(NA)	(NA)
Chemistry.	29,340	29,743	34,135	38,000	[3]37,360	[3]37,050	52,907	[3]55,160	[3]54,671
Mathematics	30,271	29,745	32,151	35,570	[3]36,996	[3]38,360	52,057	[3]52,000	[3]53,969
Physics	31,996	30,484	[3]35,554	37,835	[3]40,305	[3]42,500	53,660	[3]56,787	[3]62,403
Humanities . . . . . [5] . . .	22,811	24,285	25,078	(NA)	(NA)	(NA)	(NA)	(NA)	(NA)
Social sciences [5]	24,010	24,635	25,103	(NA)	(NA)	(NA)	(NA)	(NA)	(NA)
Computer science	33,712	35,222	37,215	42,885	44,204	44,331	48,000	[3]61,352	[3]63,058

NA Not available.   [1] Candidates with 1 year or less of full-time nonmilitary employment.   [2] For master's degree, offers are after nontechnical undergraduate degree.   [3] Fewer than 50 offers reported.   [4] Includes engineering physics.   [5] Excludes economics.

Source: National Association of Colleges and Employers, Bethlehem, PA, Salary Survey, *A Study of Beginning Offers*, annual (copyright).

No. 322. Time Spent Earning Bachelor's Degree, by Selected Characteristic: 1993

[As of **spring**. Based on Survey of Income and Program Participation; for details, see source]

CHARACTERISTIC	Total with bache- lor's degrees (1,000)	YEARS TO BA DEGREE FROM END OF HIGH SCHOOL						Mean duration [1]
		Number (1,000)			Percent			
		4 years or less	5 years or less	6 years or less	4 years or less	5 years or less	6 years or less	
All persons	36,787	15,624	23,810	27,334	42.5	64.7	74.3	6.29
Male.	19,351	7,321	11,695	13,827	37.8	60.4	71.5	6.28
Female	17,436	8,302	12,115	13,508	47.6	69.5	77.5	6.30
White	32,279	14,161	21,201	24,235	43.9	65.7	75.1	6.24
Male.	17,258	6,717	10,537	12,411	38.9	61.1	71.9	6.22
Female	15,021	7,444	10,664	11,824	49.6	71.0	78.7	6.26
Black	2,314	713	1,258	1,473	30.8	54.4	63.7	7.19
Male.	926	264	493	570	28.5	53.2	61.6	6.98
Female	1,388	448	764	904	32.3	55.0	65.1	7.33
Hispanic origin [2]	1,367	363	689	852	26.6	50.4	62.3	6.79
Male.	693	187	308	407	27.0	44.4	58.7	7.06
Female	674	176	381	445	26.1	56.5	66.0	6.50
Field of bachelor's degree: [3]								
Agriculture/Forestry	395	103	209	293	26.1	52.9	74.2	5.78
Biology	624	241	416	471	38.6	66.7	75.5	6.34
Business/Management.	5,282	1,952	3,117	3,628	37.0	59.0	68.7	6.72
Economics.	660	321	433	479	48.6	65.6	72.6	6.35
Education	3,613	1,522	2,338	2,658	42.1	64.7	73.6	7.03
Engineering	2,577	729	1,392	1,733	28.3	54.0	67.2	6.66
English/Journalism	1,137	553	743	854	48.6	65.3	75.1	6.28
Home Economics	337	177	262	284	52.5	77.7	84.3	4.71
Law	145	73	98	104	(B)	(B)	(B)	6.33
Liberal Arts/Humanities	2,188	894	1,413	1,592	40.9	64.6	72.8	6.44
Mathematics/Statistics	567	283	412	457	49.9	72.7	80.6	5.28
Medicine/Dentistry.	142	39	74	104	(B)	(B)	(B)	6.32
Nursing/Pharmacy/Technical Health .	1,626	498	914	1,092	30.6	56.2	67.2	7.10
Physical/Earth Sciences.	614	194	362	470	31.6	59.0	76.5	6.25
Police Science/Law Enforcement . . .	326	95	182	240	29.1	55.8	73.6	6.11
Psychology	815	328	555	619	40.2	68.1	76.0	6.02
Religion/Theology	138	52	66	71	(B)	(B)	(B)	7.64
Social Sciences	1,760	683	1,113	1,333	38.8	63.2	75.7	6.44
Vo-tech Studies	181	64	121	135	(B)	(B)	(B)	7.39
Other	1,816	735	1,082	1,302	40.5	59.6	71.7	6.63
Advanced degree.	11,843	6,089	8,507	9,417	51.4	71.8	79.5	5.67

B Base is less than 200,000 persons.   [1] For definition of mean, see Guide to Tabular Presentation.   [2] Persons of Hispanic origin may be of any race.   [3] For persons whose highest degree is the BA.

Source: U.S. Bureau of the Census, unpublished data.

No. 323. Earned Degrees Conferred, by Level and Sex: 1960 to 1995

[**In thousands, except percent**. Includes Alaska and Hawaii]

YEAR ENDING	ALL DEGREES		ASSOCIATE'S		BACHELOR'S		MASTER'S		FIRST PROFESSIONAL		DOCTOR'S	
	Total	Percent male	Male	Female	Male	Female	Male	Female	Male	Female	Male	Female
1960 [1]	477	65.8	(NA)	(NA)	254	138	51	24	(NA)	(NA)	9	1
1965	660	61.5	(NA)	(NA)	282	212	81	40	27	1	15	2
1970	1,271	59.2	117	89	451	341	126	83	33	2	26	4
1975	1,666	56.0	191	169	505	418	162	131	49	7	27	7
1980	1,731	51.1	184	217	474	456	151	147	53	17	23	10
1981	1,752	50.3	189	228	470	465	147	149	53	19	23	10
1982	1,788	49.8	197	238	473	480	146	150	52	20	22	10
1983	1,815	49.6	204	246	479	490	145	145	51	22	22	11
1984	1,819	49.6	203	250	482	492	144	141	51	23	22	11
1985	1,828	49.3	203	252	483	497	143	143	50	25	22	11
1986	1,830	49.0	196	250	486	502	144	145	49	25	22	12
1987	1,823	48.4	191	245	481	510	141	148	47	25	22	12
1988	1,835	48.0	190	245	477	518	145	154	45	25	23	12
1989	1,873	47.3	186	250	483	535	149	161	45	26	23	13
1990	1,940	46.6	191	264	492	560	154	171	44	27	24	14
1991	2,025	45.8	199	283	504	590	156	181	44	28	25	15
1992	2,108	45.6	207	297	521	616	162	191	45	29	26	15
1993	2,167	45.5	212	303	533	632	169	200	45	30	26	16
1994	2,206	45.1	215	315	532	637	176	211	45	31	27	17
1995	2,218	44.9	218	321	526	634	179	219	45	31	27	18

NA Not available.   [1] First-professional degrees are included with bachelor's degrees.

Source: U.S. National Center for Education Statistics, *Digest of Education Statistics*, annual.

No. 324. Degrees and Awards Earned Below Bachelor's, by Field: 1995

[Covers associate degrees and other awards based on postsecondary curriculums of less than 4 years in institutions of higher education]

FIELD OF STUDY	LESS THAN 1-YEAR AWARDS		1- TO LESS THAN 4-YEAR AWARDS		ASSOCIATE DEGREES	
	Total	Women	Total	Women	Total	Women
Total	**85,195**	**42,559**	**152,037**	**89,391**	**539,691**	**321,339**
Agriculture and natural resources	1,705	385	4,067	1,825	5,730	1,729
Architecture and related programs	15	11	10	8	277	207
Area, ethnic, and cultural studies	118	90	136	126	68	51
Biological/life sciences	297	145	62	30	1,879	1,127
Business management and administrative services	14,598	10,437	29,449	24,035	96,300	68,145
Communications and communications technologies	1,802	557	675	343	5,144	2,222
Computer and information sciences	2,154	1,034	5,295	2,822	9,152	4,409
Construction trades	2,310	177	4,582	254	1,728	130
Consumer and personal services	1,518	1,093	6,120	4,749	5,626	1,879
Education	355	318	1,461	1,309	9,658	6,600
Engineering and engineering technologies	2,259	460	7,800	869	36,964	4,213
English language and literature/letters	98	70	50	36	1,548	1,043
Foreign languages and literatures	248	162	196	78	616	439
Health professions and related sciences	25,428	18,643	42,467	35,877	98,474	81,944
Home economics and vocational home economics	5,218	3,089	8,582	6,944	7,821	7,006
Law and legal studies	902	772	1,686	1,405	9,140	7,977
Liberal/general studies and humanities	334	85	1,273	850	170,817	102,983
Library science	73	68	53	45	101	92
Mathematics	5	1	1	1	782	344
Mechanics and repairers	4,850	495	20,835	1,708	11,497	743
Multi/interdisciplinary studies	181	164	130	74	8,692	4,464
Parks, recreation, leisure, and fitness	86	43	145	72	864	363
Physical sciences	32	16	79	32	2,456	1,032
Precision production trades	2,956	532	7,179	1,334	9,344	1,891
Protective services	8678	1882	3536	908	19709	5507
Psychology	33	24	69	50	1,600	1,154
Public administration and services	608	373	732	502	3,882	3,099
R.O.T.C. and military technologies	1	-	-	-	364	33
Social sciences and history	136	22	96	55	3,634	2,173
Theological studies, religion and philosophy	111	59	1,100	576	688	327
Transportation and material moving	7,759	1,158	668	202	1,446	220
Visual and performing arts	324	193	3,401	2,210	12,544	7,269
Undistributed and unclassified	3	1	102	62	1,146	524

- Represents zero.

Source: U.S. National Center for Education Statistics, *Digest of Education Statistics, 1997.*

No. 325. Bachelor's Degrees Earned, by Field: 1971 to 1995

FIELD OF STUDY	1971	1980	1985	1990	1995	PERCENT FEMALE	
						1971	1995
Total	**839,730**	**929,417**	**979,477**	**1,051,344**	**1,160,134**	**43.4**	**54.6**
Agriculture and natural resources	12,672	22,802	18,107	12,900	19,841	4.2	36.0
Architecture and environmental design	5,570	9,132	9,325	9,364	8,756	11.9	34.4
Area, ethnic and cultural studies	2,582	2,840	2,985	4,613	5,706	52.4	63.3
Biological sciences/life sciences	35,743	46,370	38,445	37,204	55,984	29.1	52.3
Business and management	114,729	184,867	232,636	248,698	234,323	9.1	48.0
Communications [1]	10,802	28,616	42,002	51,308	48,803	35.3	58.2
Computer and information sciences	2,388	11,154	38,878	27,257	24,404	13.6	28.4
Education	176,307	118,038	88,072	105,112	106,079	74.5	75.8
Engineering [1]	50,046	68,893	95,828	81,322	78,154	0.8	15.6
English language and literature/letters	64,342	32,541	33,218	47,519	51,901	65.6	65.7
Foreign languages	20,536	12,089	10,827	12,386	13,775	74.0	69.2
Health sciences	25,226	63,920	64,422	58,302	79,855	77.1	81.9
Home economics	11,167	18,411	15,157	14,491	15,345	97.3	88.2
Law	545	683	1,157	1,592	2,032	5.0	70.7
Liberal/general studies	7,481	23,196	21,818	27,985	33,356	33.6	60.6
Library and archival sciences	1,013	398	197	77	50	92.0	96.0
Mathematics	24,937	11,872	15,861	15,176	13,723	37.9	46.8
Military technologies	357	38	299	196	27	0.3	11.1
Multi/interdisciplinary studies	6,286	11,277	12,978	16,267	26,033	22.8	64.8
Parks and recreation	1,621	5,753	4,725	4,582	12,889	34.7	47.8
Philosophy, religion, and theology	11,890	13,276	12,447	12,068	12,854	25.5	31.0
Physical sciences [1]	21,412	23,410	23,704	16,066	19,177	13.8	34.8
Protective services	2,045	15,015	12,510	15,354	24,157	9.2	37.7
Psychology	38,187	42,093	39,900	53,952	72,083	44.4	72.9
Public affairs	5,466	16,644	11,754	13,908	18,586	68.4	78.8
Social sciences [2]	155,324	103,662	91,570	118,083	128,154	36.8	46.8
Visual and performing arts	30,394	40,892	38,140	39,934	48,690	59.7	59.4
Unclassified	662	1,535	2,515	5,628	5,397	0.9	16.6

[1] Includes technologies.   [2] Includes history.

Source: U.S. National Center for Education Statistics, *Digest of Education Statistics,* annual.

No. 326. Master's and Doctorate's Degrees Earned, by Field: 1971 to 1995

LEVEL AND FIELD OF STUDY	1971	1980	1985	1990	1995	PERCENT FEMALE	
						1971	1995
MASTER'S DEGREES							
Total	230,509	298,081	286,251	324,301	397,629	40.1	55.1
Agriculture and natural resources	2,457	3,976	3,928	3,382	4,252	5.9	40.0
Architecture and related programs	1,705	3,139	3,275	3,499	3,923	13.8	41.1
Area, ethnic and cultural studies	1,032	852	904	1,212	1,639	38.3	53.3
Biological sciences/life sciences	5,728	6,510	5,059	4,869	5,393	33.6	51.8
Business management and administrative services	25,977	54,484	66,996	76,676	93,809	3.9	37.0
Communications and technologies	1,856	3,082	3,669	4,362	5,609	34.6	62.4
Computer and information sciences	1,588	3,647	7,101	9,677	10,326	10.3	26.1
Education	87,666	101,819	74,654	84,881	101,242	56.2	76.5
Engineering and engineering technologies	16,443	16,243	21,555	24,772	29,670	1.1	16.3
English language and literature/letters	10,686	6,189	5,187	6,567	7,845	60.6	64.8
Foreign languages	5,217	2,854	2,471	2,760	3,136	64.2	68.3
Health sciences	5,749	15,704	17,385	20,321	31,243	55.3	78.4
Home economics	1,452	2,690	2,375	2,100	2,864	93.9	82.8
Law and legal studies	955	1,817	1,796	1,888	2,511	4.8	33.1
Liberal arts and sciences, general studies and humanities	885	2,646	1,696	1,999	2,565	44.6	64.0
Library science	7,001	5,374	3,870	4,341	5,057	81.3	79.2
Mathematics	5,695	3,382	3,413	4,146	4,181	27.1	39.2
Military technologies	2	46	119	-	124	-	5.6
Multi/interdisciplinary studies	821	2,306	2,583	2,834	2,457	25.0	55.5
Parks and recreation	218	647	596	529	1,755	29.8	49.2
Philosophy, religion, and theology	4,036	5,126	5,602	6,265	6,620	27.1	38.8
Physical sciences and science technologies	6,367	5,219	5,796	5,449	5,753	13.3	30.2
Protective services	194	1,805	1,235	1,151	1,706	10.3	46.5
Psychology	5,717	9,938	9,891	10,730	13,921	40.6	72.0
Public administration and services	7,785	17,560	15,575	17,399	23,501	50.0	70.8
Social sciences [1]	16,539	12,176	10,503	11,634	14,845	28.5	44.7
Visual and performing arts	6,675	8,708	8,718	8,481	10,277	47.4	57.4
Unclassified	63	142	299	2,377	1,405		10.7
DOCTORATE'S DEGREES							
Total	32,107	32,615	32,943	38,371	44,446	14.3	39.4
Agriculture and natural resources	1,086	991	1,213	1,295	1,264	2.9	23.9
Architecture and related programs	36	79	89	103	141	8.3	32.6
Area, ethnic and cultural studies	144	151	140	131	186	16.7	57.0
Biological sciences/life sciences	3,645	3,636	3,432	3,844	4,645	16.3	40.3
Business management and administrative services	757	753	831	1,093	1,394	2.8	27.3
Communications and technologies	145	193	234	273	321	13.1	49.5
Computer and information sciences	128	240	248	627	884	2.3	18.2
Education	6,041	7,314	6,612	6,502	6,905	21.0	62.0
Engineering and engineering technology	3,638	2,507	3,230	4,981	6,128	0.6	11.9
English language and literature/letters	1,650	1,294	1,041	1,078	1,561	28.8	57.4
Foreign languages	988	755	635	724	905	34.6	56.4
Health sciences	466	786	1,199	1,536	2,069	16.5	58.1
Home economics	123	192	273	301	388	61.0	74.5
Law and legal studies	20	40	105	111	88	-	29.5
Liberal arts and sciences, general studies and humanities	32	192	112	63	90	31.3	54.4
Library science	39	73	87	42	55	28.2	63.6
Mathematics	1,249	763	734	966	1,226	7.6	22.1
Multi/interdisciplinary studies	59	209	219	272	238	6.8	45.8
Parks and recreation	2	21	36	35	149	50.0	41.6
Philosophy, religion, and theology	866	1,693	1,612	1,756	2,098	5.8	17.1
Physical sciences and science technologies	4,390	3,089	3,403	4,164	4,483	5.6	23.5
Protective services	1	18	33	38	26	-	46.2
Psychology	2,144	3,395	3,447	3,811	3,822	24.0	62.6
Public administration and services	174	342	431	508	556	24.1	50.7
Social sciences [1]	3,660	3,230	2,851	3,010	3,725	13.9	37.7
Visual and performing arts	621	655	696	849	1,080	22.2	49.5
Unclassified	3	4	-	258	19	-	5.3

- Represents zero.   [1] Includes history.

Source: U.S. National Center for Education Statistics, *Digest of Education Statistics*, annual.

No. 327. First Professional Degrees Earned in Selected Professions: 1970 to 1995

[First professional degrees include degrees which require at least 6 years of college work for completion (including at least 2 years of preprofessional training). See Appendix III]

TYPE OF DEGREE AND SEX OF RECIPIENT	1970	1975	1980	1985	1990	1991	1992	1993	1994	1995
Medicine (M.D.):										
Institutions conferring degrees.....	86	104	112	120	124	121	120	122	121	119
Degrees conferred, total.........	8,314	12,447	14,902	16,041	15,075	15,043	15,243	15,531	15,368	15,537
Percent to women	8.4	13.1	23.4	30.4	34.2	36.0	35.7	37.7	37.9	38.8
Dentistry (D.D.S. or D.M.D.):										
Institutions conferring degrees.....	48	52	58	59	57	55	52	55	53	53
Degrees conferred, total.........	3,718	4,773	5,258	5,339	4,100	3,699	3,593	3,605	3,787	3,897
Percent to women	0.9	3.1	13.3	20.7	30.9	32.1	32.3	33.9	38.5	36.4
Law (LL.B. or J.D.):										
Institutions conferring degrees.....	145	154	179	181	182	179	177	184	185	183
Degrees conferred, total.........	14,916	29,296	35,647	37,491	36,485	37,945	38,848	40,302	40,044	39,349
Percent to women	5.4	15.1	30.2	38.5	42.2	43.0	42.7	42.5	43.0	42.6
Theological (B.D., M.Div., M.H.L.):										
Institutions conferring degrees.....	(NA)	(NA)	(NA)	(NA)	(NA)	(NA)	(NA)	(NA)	186	192
Degrees conferred, total.........	5,298	5,095	7,115	7,221	5,851	5,695	5,251	5,447	5,967	5,978
Percent to women	2.3	6.8	13.8	18.5	24.8	23.4	23.3	24.8	24.8	25.7

NA Not available.

Source: U.S. National Center for Education Statistics, *Digest of Education Statistics*, annual.

No. 328. Degrees Earned, by Level and Race/Ethnicity: 1981 to 1995

[For **school year ending in year shown.** Data exclude some institutions not reporting field of study and are slight undercounts of degrees awarded]

LEVEL OF DEGREE AND RACE/ETHNICITY	TOTAL						PERCENT DISTRIBUTION	
	1981	1985	1990	1993	1994	1995, prel.	1981	1995, prel.
Associate's degrees, total	410,174	429,815	450,263	508,154	529,106	538,545	100.0	100.0
White, non-Hispanic	339,167	355,343	369,580	405,883	418,301	419,323	82.7	77.9
Black, non-Hispanic.........	35,330	35,791	35,327	42,340	45,461	47,142	8.6	8.8
Hispanic	17,800	19,407	22,195	29,991	32,074	36,013	4.3	6.7
Asian or Pacific Islander......	8,650	9,914	13,482	16,632	18,433	20,717	2.1	3.8
American Indian/Alaskan Native...............	2,584	2,953	3,530	4,379	4,871	5,492	0.6	1.0
Nonresident alien	6,643	6,407	6,149	8,929	9,966	9,858	1.6	1.8
Bachelor's degrees, total	934,800	968,311	1,048,631	1,159,931	1,165,973	1,158,788	100.0	100.0
White, non-Hispanic	807,319	826,106	884,376	947,309	936,227	913,377	86.4	78.8
Black, non-Hispanic.........	60,673	57,473	61,063	77,872	83,576	87,203	6.5	7.5
Hispanic	21,832	25,874	32,844	45,376	50,241	54,201	2.3	4.7
Asian or Pacific Islander......	18,794	25,395	39,248	51,463	55,660	60,478	2.0	5.2
American Indian/Alaskan Native...............	3,593	4,246	4,392	5,671	6,189	6,606	0.4	0.6
Nonresident alien	22,589	29,217	26,708	32,240	34,080	36,923	2.4	3.2
Master's degrees, total	294,183	280,421	322,465	368,701	385,419	397,052	100.0	100.0
White, non-Hispanic	241,216	223,628	251,690	278,829	288,288	292,784	82.0	73.7
Black, non-Hispanic.........	17,133	13,939	15,446	19,780	21,937	24,171	5.8	6.1
Hispanic	6,461	6,864	7,950	10,665	11,913	12,907	2.2	3.3
Asian or Pacific Islander......	6,282	7,782	10,577	13,866	15,267	16,842	2.1	4.2
American Indian/Alaskan Native...............	1,034	1,256	1,101	1,407	1,697	1,621	0.4	0.4
Nonresident alien	22,057	26,952	35,701	44,154	46,317	48,727	7.5	12.3
Doctor's degrees, total	32,839	32,307	38,113	42,021	43,149	44,427	100.0	100.0
White, non-Hispanic	25,908	23,934	25,880	26,700	27,156	27,826	78.9	62.6
Black, non-Hispanic.........	1,265	1,154	1,153	1,352	1,393	1,667	3.9	3.8
Hispanic	456	677	788	827	903	984	1.4	2.2
Asian or Pacific Islander......	877	1,106	1,235	1,582	2,025	2,690	2.7	6.1
American Indian/Alaskan Native...............	130	119	99	106	134	130	0.4	0.3
Nonresident alien	4,203	5,317	8,958	11,454	11,538	11,130	12.8	25.1
First professional degrees, total	71,340	71,057	70,744	74,960	75,418	75,800	100.0	100.0
White, non-Hispanic	64,551	63,219	60,240	60,830	60,140	59,402	90.5	78.4
Black, non-Hispanic.........	2,931	3,029	3,410	4,100	4,444	4,747	4.1	6.3
Hispanic	1,541	1,884	2,427	2,984	3,134	3,231	2.2	4.3
Asian or Pacific Islander......	1,456	1,816	3,362	5,160	5,892	6,397	2.0	8.4
American Indian/Alaskan Native................	192	248	257	368	371	412	0.3	0.5
Nonresident alien	669	861	1,048	1,518	1,437	1,611	0.9	2.1

Source: U.S. National Center for Education Statistics, *Digest of Education Statistics*, annual.

No. 329. College and University Libraries—Summary: 1975 to 1995

[For school year ending in year shown, except enrollment as of fall of the prior year. Prior to 1982, includes outlying areas]

ITEM	1975	1982	1985	1988	1990	1992	1995
Number of libraries	2,972	3,104	3,322	3,438	3,274	3,274	3,639
Total enrollment (1,000)	10,322	12,372	12,242	12,767	13,539	14,359	14,279
COLLECTIONS (1,000)							
Number of volumes	447,059	567,826	631,727	706,504	717,042	749,429	792,707
Volumes added during year.	23,242	19,507	20,658	21,907	19,003	20,982	22,460
Number of serial subscriptions.	4,434	4,890	6,317	6,416	5,748	6,966	6,780
STAFF							
Total	56,836	58,476	58,476	67,251	69,359	67,166	68,920
Librarians and professional	23,530	23,816	21,822	25,115	26,101	26,341	27,376
OPERATING EXPENDITURES ($1,000)							
Total [1]	1,091,784	1,943,769	2,404,524	2,770,075	3,257,813	3,648,654	4,317,847
Salaries.	592,568	1,081,894	1,156,138	1,451,551	1,693,813	1,889,368	2,058,375
Collection.	327,904	561,199	750,282	891,281	1,040,928	1,197,293	1,374,407

[1] Includes other expenditures, not shown separately.

Source: U.S. National Center for Education Statistics, *Digest of Education Statistics,* 1997; and Academic Library Survey.

No. 330. Libraries—Number, by Type: 1980 to 1996

TYPE	1980	1985	1990	1996	TYPE	1980	1985	1990	1996
Total [1]	31,564	32,323	34,613	37,258	Junior college . . .	1,191	1,188	1,233	1,262
					Colleges,				
United States . . .	28,638	29,843	30,761	32,666	universities	3,400	3,846	3,360	3,468
Public.	8,717	8,849	9,060	9,165	Departmental .	1,489	1,824	1,454	1,491
Public branches . . .	5,936	6,330	5,833	6,205	Law,				
Special [2]	7,649	7,530	9,051	10,282	medicine,				
Medicine	1,674	1,667	1,861	1,982	religious . .	269	531	501	491
Religious	913	839	946	1,042	Government.	1,260	1,574	1,735	1,875
Law [3]	417	435	647	1,155	Armed Forces	485	526	489	409
Academic	4,591	5,034	4,593	4,730	Outlying areas . .	113	114	110	110

[1] Includes Canadian libraries, and libraries in regions administered by the United States, not shown separately. Data are exclusive of elementary and secondary school libraries. Law libraries with fewer than 10,000 volumes are included only if they specialize in a particular field.   [2] Includes other types of special libraries, not shown separately. Increase between 1980 and 1990 is due mainly to revised criteria for identifying special libraries and improved methods of counting.   [3] Increase beginning 1996 due to increased effort in identifying special libraries.

Source: R.R. Bowker Co., New York, NY, *The Bowker Annual: Library and Book Trade Almanac* and *American Library Directory,* annual. (Copyright by Reed Publishing (USA) Inc.)

No. 331. Public Libraries, Selected Characteristics: 1995

[Based on survey of public libraries. Data are for public libraries in the 50 states and the District of Columbia. The response rates for these items are between 97 and 100 percent]

POPULATION OF SERVICE AREA	NUMBER OF—		OPERATING INCOME			PAID STAFF [3]		Books and serial volumes (per capita)
	Public libraries	Stationary outlets [1]	Total (mil. dol.) [2]	Source (percent)		Total	Librarians with ALA-MLS [4]	
				State government	Local government			
Total	8,981	15,994	5,594	12.0	78.3	115,968	26,636	2.8
1,000,000 or more	20	858	759	11.0	74.7	14,011	4,078	2.5
500,000 to 999,000	50	1,091	927	17.4	74.6	16,942	4,430	2.6
250,000 to 499,999	92	1,063	659	10.4	82.4	12,637	3,248	2.4
100,000 to 249,999	306	1,906	885	9.8	82.8	18,290	4,296	2.2
50,000 to 99,999	509	1,587	706	13.8	78.3	15,083	3,448	2.4
25,000 to 49,999	863	1,636	680	11.8	79.4	14,746	3,335	2.9
10,000 to 24,999	1,657	2,133	601	9.9	79.0	13,524	2,732	3.4
5,000 to 9,999	1,508	1,685	227	11.5	74.1	5,778	781	4.2
2,500 to 4,999	1,339	1,376	87	7.2	74.3	2,587	204	5.3
1,000 to 2,499	1,644	1,664	50	5.8	68.2	1,722	71	7.7
Fewer than 1,000	993	995	14	7.1	67.2	646	13	13.7

[1] The sum of central and branches libraries. The total number of central libraries was 8,937; the total of branch libraries was 7,057.   [2] Includes income from the federal government (1.0%) and other sources (8.7%), not shown separately.   [3] Full-time equivalents.   [4] Librarians with master's degrees from a graduate library education program accredited by the American Library Association (ALA). Total librarians, including those without ALA-MLS, were 38,694.

Source: U.S. National Center for Education Statistics, *Public Libraries in the United States: 1995.*

No. 332. Household Use of Public Library Services: 1996

[For the 50 states and DC. Based on a survey conducted between January and April 1996; see source for details]

ITEM	All households	Households with children under 18 years old	Households with no children under 18 years old
Number of households (1,000)	99,088	36,225	62,863
PERCENT USING PUBLIC LIBRARIES			
Used in the past year	65	82	54
Used on the past month	44	61	35
Way of using—			
Borrow or drop off books or tapes	36	53	26
Go for other purpose [1]	18	26	14
Called library to renew book or to get information [2]	14	18	12
Linked to library from home computer	4	5	3
Had material mailed or delivered to home	2	3	2
Visited a bookmobile	2	4	1
Purpose for using—			
Enjoyment or hobbies [3]	32	45	24
To get information for personal use	20	22	18
School or class assignment	19	38	7
Work assignment or to keep up to date at work	8	10	7
To get information to help find a job	5	5	5
For program or activity for children 6 to 12 years old	4	7	2
For activity for children under 6	4	8	1
To work with a tutor or take a class to learn to read	1	2	1

[1] Including a lecture, story hour, or using equipment.　[2] Information other than library hours or directions.　[3] Including borrowing books or tapes or to attend activities.

Source: U.S. Center for Education Statistics, *Use of Public Library Services by Households in the United States: 1996*, February 1997.

No. 333. Public Library Use of the Internet: 1997

[**As of spring.** Based on sample survey; see source for details]

ITEM	Total	POPULATION OF LEGAL SERVICE AREA					
		Less than 5,000	5,000 to 24,999	25,000 to 99,999	100,000 to 499,999	500,000 to 99,999	One million or more
All libraries systems	8,921	3,950	3,143	1,367	392	49	20
Percent connected to the Internet: [1]							
1996	44.6	31.3	46.9	74.1	92.2	93.1	82.0
1997	72.3	56.3	79.2	92.5	93.1	95.5	100.0
Percent not connected in 1997 planing to connect for staff and public use in 1998	41.8	32.1	61.6	57.1	89.9	100.0	(X)
Percent of connected libraries offering various services to patrons: [1]							
E-mail accounts	18.0	25.5	15.0	13.7	9.5	18.3	20.4
Access to newsgroup services	28.1	29.4	29.3	26.8	18.5	26.9	20.4
Access to FTP or telnet services	40.6	28.1	48.1	45.6	43.2	47.9	41.9
Text-based World-Wide Web browsing	40.8	28.8	51.2	38.4	44.3	61.1	46.9
Graphical based World-Wide Web browsing	72.1	68.5	76.2	70.4	68.8	79.5	84.2
Online database services	26.3	14.4	28.6	33.7	45.7	68.3	57.7
Online CD services	30.7	23.9	31.7	35.4	39.8	59.0	73.9
Online reference services	29.7	38.3	25.8	25.2	22.7	27.0	20.8
Special software/hardware for individuals with disabilities	10.6	7.2	7.4	15.4	27.3	50.0	58.5
Average operating expenditures ($000) [2]	632.9	37.3	251.3	1,056.0	3,953.8	1,8075.7	3,7404.8
For information technology ($000)	69.0	12.5	24.6	85.7	289.7	1,448.1	2,471.6
Percent distribution: [3]							
System/server hardware costs	24.7	14.7	31.4	26.6	18.4	14.7	27.6
Software costs	10.6	8.6	11.7	11.5	8.4	9.8	6.7
Communications hardware (e.g. modems)	11.1	8.6	11.7	9.4	9.7	7.4	12.3
Telecommunication fees (e.g leased lines)	17.8	24.6	17.0	13.7	9.7	7.7	8.6
Facilities upgrading (e.g. wiring)	10.1	14.5	7.8	9.8	7.0	2.8	10.0
Training and education	8.8	14.9	5.7	7.3	6.2	4.9	2.7
Content/resource development (e.g. web page development)	6.0	3.8	5.4	8.8	6.3	4.0	2.0
Program planning/management	4.7	5.3	2.9	6.3	6.3	2.6	6.0
Staffing costs	15.9	21.5	12.3	16.0	16.7	12.9	13.5
Maintenance for information technology	10.3	12.7	10.2	8.7	9.6	6.4	13.2
Percent of IT expenditures spent on Internet	46.5	42.0	45.0	55.9	54.1	41.2	52.9

X Not applicable.　[1] At least one outlet in the system connected or offering services. Out of the 8,921 library systems in the United States, 1,455 have a total of 7,024 branches.　[2] For the last completed fiscal year.　[3] Includes duplication.

Source: The American Library Association, Washington, DC, *The 1997 Survey of U.S. Public Libraries and the Internet: Final Report, 1998*.

No. 334. Participation in Adult Education: 1994-95

[For the civilian noninstitutional population 17 years old and over not enrolled full time in elementary or secondary school at the time of the survey. Adult education is considered any enrollment in any educational activity at any time in the prior 12 months. Based on survey and subject to sampling error; source for details]

CHARACTERISTIC	Adult population (1,000)	Number taking adult ed. courses (1,000)	PARTICIPANTS IN ADULT EDUCATION				
			Percent of total	Reason for taking course (percent) [1]			
				Personal/ social	Advance on the job	Train for a new job	Complete degree or diploma
Total	**189,543**	**76,261**	**40**	**44**	**54**	**11**	**10**
Age: 17 to 24 years old	22,407	10,539	47	39	33	21	19
25 to 34 years old	40,326	19,508	48	41	56	14	8
35 to 44 years old	42,304	20,814	49	40	64	10	9
45 to 54 years old	31,807	14,592	46	39	65	7	10
55 to 64 years old	21,824	6,117	28	52	54	4	6
65 years old and over	30,876	4,691	15	86	14	1	3
Sex: Male	90,256	34,450	38	34	60	10	10
Female	99,287	41,811	42	51	49	12	9
Race/ethnicity:							
White [2]	144,587	59,982	41	44	57	10	9
Black [2]	20,806	7,704	37	45	48	13	12
Hispanic	15,689	5,281	34	40	37	13	11
Other races [2]	8,461	3,294	39	40	45	16	13
Marital status:							
Never married	38,627	17,094	44	37	44	20	15
Currently married	114,678	48,200	42	45	58	8	8
Other	36,238	10,967	30	48	52	9	8
Children under 18 in household:							
Yes	77,787	36,103	46	43	56	11	9
No	111,756	40,158	36	44	52	11	10
Educational attainment:							
Up to 8th grade	12,808	1,283	10	52	20	8	9
9th to 12th grade	16,511	3,332	20	45	27	10	18
High school diploma or GED	62,956	19,341	31	44	49	10	6
Vocational school after high school	6,327	2,648	42	44	57	8	8
Some college	34,433	16,978	49	45	47	16	13
Associate's degree	9,975	5,601	56	39	64	9	9
Bachelor's or higher	46,535	27,078	58	43	65	9	9
Labor force status:							
Employed	117,826	59,734	51	37	64	10	10
Unemployed	8,155	2,983	37	39	27	25	13
Not in the labor force	63,562	13,544	21	72	15	11	8
Occupation: [3]							
Professional	16,814	12,219	73	37	74	8	10
Executive, administrative and managerial	12,500	7,070	57	37	76	8	10
Technical and related support	4,812	3,300	69	32	73	9	11
Sales workers	15,666	7,131	46	41	53	12	11
Administrative support [4]	20,460	10,727	52	43	62	11	6
Service	17,355	8,238	47	37	51	14	12
Agriculture, forestry, and fishing	1,908	500	26	40	49	6	12
Precision production, craft and repair	11,441	4,977	43	30	62	8	11
Machine operators, assemblers [5]	8,309	2,515	30	28	58	10	9
Transportation and materials moving	4,488	1,295	29	35	60	13	12
Handlers, equipment cleaners, helpers and laborers	1,989	519	26	33	43	24	5
Nonclassifiable, undetermined	2,022	1,194	59	35	71	6	4
Household income:							
Under $10,000	30,198	6,883	23	48	25	20	12
$10,001 to $15,000	13,523	3,610	27	51	32	17	10
$15,001 to $20,000	13,116	4,176	32	45	38	15	12
$20,001 to $25,000	13,812	4,339	31	47	44	13	11
$25,001 to $30,000	16,386	6,208	38	45	46	13	11
$30,001 to $40,000	28,628	12,220	43	45	55	11	9
$40,001 to $50,000	20,446	9,567	47	41	61	10	8
$50,001 to $75,000	29,161	15,169	52	39	67	7	8
More than $75,000	24,274	14,089	58	43	64	7	9

[1] Reason for taking at least one course. Includes duplication. Excludes "to improve basic skills," cited by no more than 6 percent of participants. [2] Non-Hispanic. [3] For those employed in the 12 months prior to the interview. Excludes those participating exclusively in full-time credential programs. [4] Includes clerical. [5] Includes inspectors.

Source: U.S. Department of Education, National Center for Education Statistics, *1995 National Household Education Survey*.

Figure 5.1
Criminal Victimization: 1993 to 1996

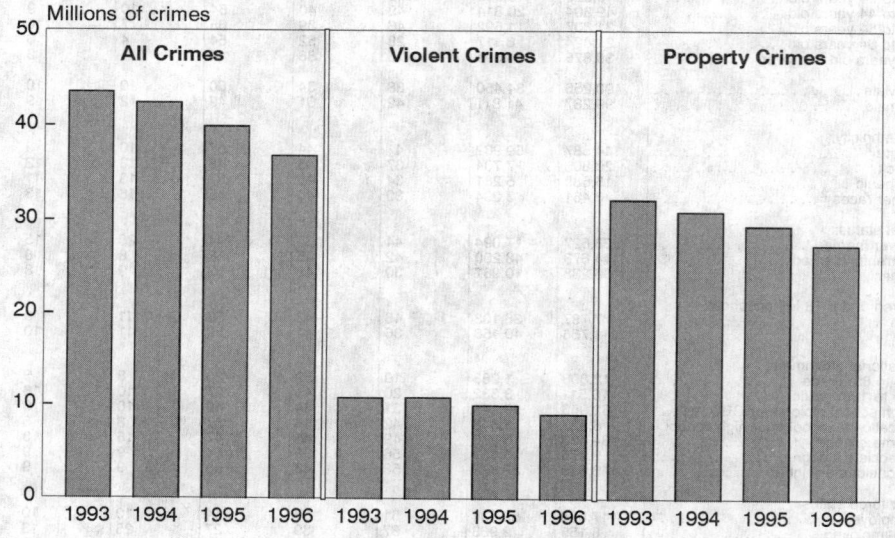

Source: Chart prepared by U.S. Bureau of the Census. For data, see Table 346.

Figure 5.2
Federal and State Prisoners: 1970 to 1996

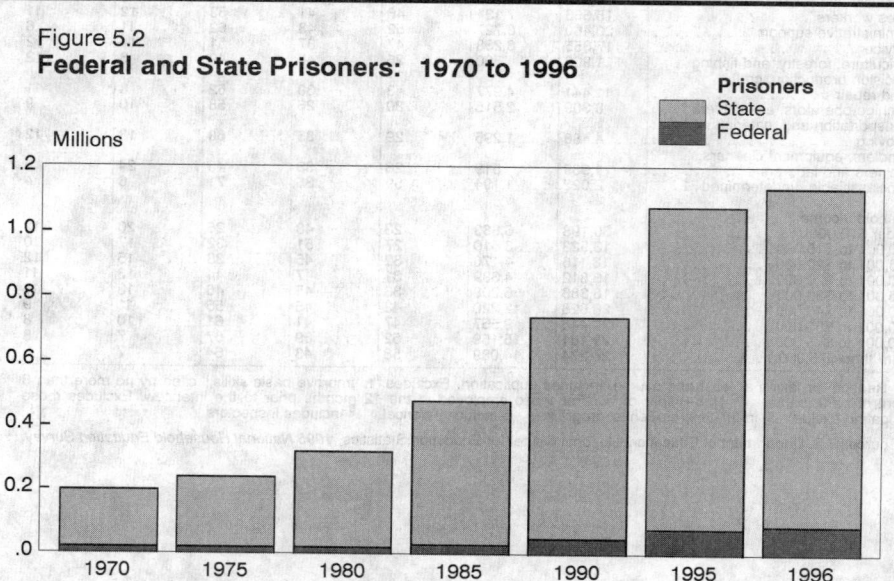

Source: Chart prepared by U.S. Bureau of the Census. For data, see Table 377.

Law Enforcement, Courts, and Prisons

This section presents data on crimes committed, victims of crimes, arrests, and data related to criminal violations and the criminal justice system. The major sources of these data are the Bureau of Justice Statistics (BJS), the Federal Bureau of Investigation (FBI), and the Administrative Office of the U.S. Courts. BJS issues several reports, including *Sourcebook of Criminal Justice Statistics, Criminal Victimization in the United States, Prisoners in State and Federal Institutions, Children in Custody, National Survey of Courts, Census of State Correctional Facilities* and *Survey of Prison Inmates, Census of Jails* and *Survey of Jail Inmates, Parole in the United States, Capital Punishment,* and the annual *Expenditure and Employment Data for the Criminal Justice System.* The Federal Bureau of Investigation's major annual report is *Crime in the United States,* which presents data on reported crimes as gathered from state and local law enforcement agencies.

Legal jurisdiction and law enforcement—Law enforcement is, for the most part, a function of state and local officers and agencies. The U.S. Constitution reserves general police powers to the states. By act of Congress, federal offenses include only offenses against the U.S. Government and against or by its employees while engaged in their official duties, and offenses which involve the crossing of state lines or an interference with interstate commerce. Excluding the military, there are 52 separate criminal law jurisdictions in the United States: 1 in each of the 50 states, 1 in the District of Columbia, and the federal jurisdiction. Each of these has its own criminal law and procedure and its own law enforcement agencies. While the systems of law enforcement are quite similar among the states, there are often substantial differences in the penalties for like offenses.

Law enforcement can be divided into three parts: Investigation of crimes and arrests of persons suspected of committing them; prosecution of those charged with crime;

In Brief

The number of reported crimes declined for the fifth straight year in 1996 to 13.5 million offenses from 14.9 million in 1991, a 9.4 percent drop according to the FBI. The number of murders over the same period declined from 24,700 to 19,700.

Almost 8,800 incidents of hate crimes were recorded in 1996. Sixty–two percent of the incidents were motivated by race, 11 percent by ethnic or national origin, 16 percent by religion, and 12 percent by sexual orientation.

The Nation's prisons and jails both reached new record highs in 1996 with 1,137,000 and 518,000 inmates, respectively, incarcerated.

and the punishment or treatment of persons convicted of crime.

Crime—There are two major approaches taken in determining the extent of crime. One perspective is provided by the FBI through its Uniform Crime Reporting Program (UCR). The FBI receives monthly and annual reports from law enforcement agencies throughout the country, currently representing 95 percent of the national population. Each month, city police, sheriffs, and state police file reports on the number of index offenses that become known to them.

The FBI Crime Index offenses are as follows: *Murder and nonnegligent manslaughter,* is based on police investigations, as opposed to the determination of a medical examiner or judicial body, includes willful felonious homicides, and excludes attempts and assaults to kill, suicides, accidental deaths, justifiable homicides, and deaths caused by negligence; *forcible rape* includes forcible rapes and attempts; *robbery* includes stealing or taking anything of value by force or violence or threat of force or violence and includes attempted robbery; *aggravated assault* includes assault with intent to kill; *burglary* includes any unlawful entry to commit a felony or a theft and includes attempted burglary and burglary followed by larceny; *larceny* includes theft of property or articles of value without use of force and violence or fraud and excludes embezzlement, "con games," forgery, etc.; *motor vehicle theft* includes all cases where vehicles are driven away and abandoned, but excludes vehicles taken for temporary use and returned by the taker. Arson was added as the eighth Index offense in April 1979 following a Congressional mandate. *Arson* includes any willful or malicious burning or attempt to burn with or without intent to defraud, a dwelling house, public building, motor vehicle or aircraft, personal property of another, etc.

The monthly Uniform Crime Reports also contain data on crimes cleared by arrest and on characteristics of persons arrested for all criminal offenses. In summarizing and publishing crime data, the FBI depends primarily on the adherence to the established standards of reporting for statistical accuracy, presenting the data as information useful to persons concerned with the problem of crime and criminal-law enforcement.

National Crime Victimization Survey (NCVS)—A second perspective on crime is provided by this survey (formerly the National Crime Survey until August 1991) of the Bureau of Justice Statistics. Details about the crimes come directly from the victims. No attempt is made to validate the information against police records or any other source.

The NCVS measures rape, robbery, assault, household and personal larceny, burglary, and motor vehicle theft. The NCVS includes offenses reported to the police, as well as those not reported. Police reporting rates (percent of victimizations) varied by type of crime. In 1994, for instance, 32 percent of the rapes/sexual assaults were reported; 55 percent of the robberies; 40 percent of assaults; 33 percent of personal thefts; 51 percent of the household burglaries; and 78 percent of motor vehicle thefts.

Murder and kidnaping are not covered. Commercial burglary and robbery were dropped from the program during 1977. The so-called victimless crimes, such as drunkenness, drug abuse, and prostitution, also are excluded, as are crimes for which it is difficult to identify knowledgeable respondents or to locate data records.

Crimes of which the victim may not be aware also cannot be measured effectively. Buying stolen property may fall into this category, as may some instances of embezzlement. Attempted crimes of many types probably are under recorded for this reason. Events in which the victim has shown a willingness to participate in illegal activity also are excluded.

In any encounter involving a personal crime, more than one criminal act can be committed against an individual. For example; a rape may be associated with a robbery; or a household offense, such as a burglary, can escalate into something more serious in the event of a personal confrontation. In classifying the survey-measured crimes, each criminal incident has been counted only once—by the most serious act that took place during the incident and ranked in accordance with the seriousness classification system used by the Federal Bureau of Investigation. The order of seriousness for crimes against persons is as follows: Rape, robbery, assault, and larceny. Consequently, if a person were both robbed and assaulted, the event would be classified as robbery; if the victim suffered physical harm, the crime would be categorized as robbery with injury. Personal crimes take precedence over household offenses.

A *victimization,* basic measure of the occurrence of a crime, is a specific criminal act as it affects a single victim. The number of victimizations is determined by the number of victims of such acts. Victimization counts serve as key elements in computing rates of victimization. For crimes against persons, the rates are based on the total number of individuals age 12 and over or on a portion of that population sharing a particular characteristic or set of traits. As general indicators of the danger of having been victimized during the reference period, the rates are not sufficiently refined to represent true measures of risk for specific individuals or households.

An *incident* is a specific criminal act involving one or more victims; therefore, the number of incidents of personal crimes lower than that of victimizations.

A major redesign of the survey was recently implemented involving such changes as a new screening questionnaire, improved measurement of rape and sexual assault categories, improvements to measurement of domestic violence, changes in crime definitions, and increased automation through the use of computer-assisted telephone interviewing (CATI). The effects of the redesign show that the new methods elicit more reports of victimizations.

Courts—Statistics on criminal offenses and the outcome of prosecutions are incomplete for the country as a whole, although data are available for many states individually. The only national compilations of such statistics were made by the Bureau of the Census for 1932 to 1945 covering a maximum of 32 states and by the Bureau of Justice Statistics for 1986, 1988, 1990, and 1992 based on a nationally representative sample survey.

The bulk of civil and criminal litigation in the country is commenced and determined in the various state courts. Only when the U.S. Constitution and acts of Congress specifically confer jurisdiction upon the federal courts may civil litigation be heard and decided by them. Generally, the federal courts have jurisdiction over the following types of cases: Suits or proceedings by or against the United States; civil actions between private parties arising under the Constitution, laws, or treaties of the United States; civil actions between private litigants who are citizens of different states; civil cases involving admiralty, maritime, or prize jurisdiction; and all matters in bankruptcy.

There are several types of courts with varying degrees of legal jurisdiction. These jurisdictions include original, appellate, general, and limited or special. A *court of original jurisdiction* is one having the authority initially to try a case and pass judgment on the law and the facts; a *court of appellate jurisdiction* is one with the legal authority to review cases and hear appeals; a *court of general jurisdiction* is a trial court of unlimited original jurisdiction in civil and/or criminal cases, also called a "major trial court"; a *court of limited or spe-*

cial jurisdiction is a trial court with legal authority over only a particular class of cases, such as probate, juvenile, or traffic cases.

The 94 federal courts of original jurisdiction are known as the U.S. district courts. One or more of these courts is established in every state and one each in the District of Columbia, Puerto Rico, the Virgin Islands, the Northern Mariana Islands, and Guam. Appeals from the district courts are taken to intermediate appellate courts of which there are 13, known as U.S. courts of appeals and the United States Court of Appeals for the Federal Circuit. The Supreme Court of the United States is the final and highest appellate court in the federal system of courts.

Juvenile offenders—For statistical purposes, the FBI and most states classify as juvenile offenders persons under the age of 18 years who have committed a crime or crimes.

Delinquency cases are all cases of youths referred to a juvenile court for violation of a law or ordinance or for seriously "antisocial" conduct. Several types of facilities are available for those adjudicated delinquent, ranging from the short-term physically unrestricted environment to the long-term very restrictive atmosphere.

Prisoners—Data on prisoners in federal and state prisons and reformatories were collected annually by the Bureau of the Census until 1950, by the Federal Bureau of Prisons until 1971, transferred then to the Law Enforcement Assistance Administration and, in 1979, to the Bureau of Justice Statistics. Adults convicted of criminal activity may be given a prison or jail sentence. A *prison* is a confinement facility having custodial authority over adults sentenced to confinement of more than one year. A *jail* is a facility, usually operated by a local law enforcement agency, holding persons detained pending adjudication and/or persons committed after adjudication to 1 year or less. Nearly every state publishes annual data either for its whole prison system or for each separate state institution.

Statistical reliability—For discussion of statistical collection, estimation, and sampling procedures and measures of statistical reliability pertaining to the National Crime Victimization Survey and Uniform Crime Reporting Program, see Appendix III.

No. 335. Crimes and Crime Rates, by Type of Offense: 1986 to 1996

[Data refer to offenses known to the police. Rates are based on Bureau of the Census estimated resident population as of July 1, 1990, enumerated as of April 1. See source for details. Minus sign (-) indicates decrease. For definitions of crimes, see text, Section 5]

ITEM AND YEAR	Total	VIOLENT CRIME					PROPERTY CRIME			
		Total	Mur-der [1]	Forci-ble rape	Rob-bery	Aggra-vated assault	Total	Bur-glary	Larce-ny—theft	Motor vehi-cle theft
Number of offenses (1,000):										
1986	13,212	1,489	20.6	91.5	543	834	11,723	3,241	7,257	1,224
1987	13,509	1,484	20.1	91.1	518	855	12,025	3,236	7,500	1,289
1988	13,923	1,566	20.7	92.5	543	910	12,357	3,218	7,706	1,433
1989	14,251	1,646	21.5	94.5	578	952	12,605	3,168	7,872	1,565
1990	14,476	1,820	23.4	102.6	639	1,055	12,656	3,074	7,946	1,636
1991	14,873	1,912	24.7	106.6	688	1,093	12,961	3,157	8,142	1,662
1992	14,438	1,932	23.8	109.1	672	1,127	12,506	2,980	7,915	1,611
1993	14,142	1,926	24.5	106.0	660	1,136	12,219	2,835	7,821	1,563
1994	13,990	1,858	23.3	102.2	619	1,113	12,132	2,713	7,880	1,539
1995	13,863	1,799	21.6	97.5	581	1,099	12,064	2,594	7,998	1,472
1996	13,474	1,682	19.7	95.8	537	1,030	11,791	2,502	7,895	1,395
Percent change, number of offenses:										
1986 to 1996	2.0	12.9	-4.4	4.7	-1.1	23.5	0.6	-22.8	8.8	14.0
1993 to 1994	-1.1	-3.5	-5.0	-3.6	-6.2	-2.0	-0.7	-4.3	0.8	-1.5
1994 to 1995	-0.9	-3.2	-7.3	-4.6	-6.1	-1.3	-0.6	-4.4	1.5	-4.4
1995 to 1996	-2.8	-6.5	-8.8	-1.7	-7.6	-6.3	-2.3	-3.5	-1.3	-5.2
Rate per 100,000 population:										
1986	5,480.4	617.7	8.6	37.9	225.1	346.1	4,862.6	1,344.6	3,010.3	507.8
1987	5,550.0	609.7	8.3	37.4	212.7	351.3	4,940.3	1,329.6	3,081.3	529.4
1988	5,664.2	637.2	8.4	37.6	220.9	370.2	5,027.1	1,309.2	3,134.9	582.9
1989	5,741.0	663.7	8.7	38.1	233.0	383.4	5,077.9	1,276.3	3,171.3	630.4
1990	5,820.3	731.8	9.4	41.2	257.0	424.1	5,088.5	1,235.9	3,194.8	657.8
1991	5,897.8	758.1	9.8	42.3	272.7	433.3	5,139.7	1,252.0	3,228.8	659.0
1992	5,660.2	757.5	9.3	42.8	263.6	441.8	4,902.7	1,168.2	3,103.0	631.5
1993	5,484.4	746.8	9.5	41.1	255.9	440.3	4,737.6	1,099.2	3,032.4	606.1
1994	5,374.4	714.0	9.0	39.3	237.7	428.0	4,660.0	1,041.8	3,027.0	591.2
1995	5,275.9	684.6	8.2	37.1	220.9	418.3	4,591.3	987.1	3,043.8	560.4
1996	5,078.9	634.1	7.4	36.1	202.4	388.2	4,444.8	943.0	2,975.9	525.9
Percent change, rate per 100,000 population:										
1986 to 1996	-7.3	2.7	-14.0	-4.7	-10.1	12.2	-8.6	-29.9	-1.1	3.6
1993 to 1994	-2.0	-4.4	-5.3	-4.4	-7.1	-2.8	-1.6	-5.2	-0.2	-2.5
1994 to 1995	-1.8	-4.1	-8.9	-5.6	-7.1	-2.3	-1.5	-5.3	0.6	-5.2
1995 to 1996	-3.7	-7.4	-9.8	-2.7	-8.4	-7.2	-3.2	-4.5	-2.2	-6.2

[1] Includes nonnegligent manslaughter.

Source: U.S. Federal Bureau of Investigation, *Crime in the United States,* annual.

No. 336. Crimes and Crime Rates, by Type and Area: 1996

[In thousands, except rate. Rate per 100,000 population; see headnote, Table 335. Estimated totals based on reports from city and rural law enforcement agencies representing 96 percent of the national population. For definitions of crimes, see text, Section 5]

TYPE OF CRIME	UNITED STATES		METROPOLITAN AREAS [1]		OTHER CITIES		RURAL AREAS	
	Total	Rate	Total	Rate	Total	Rate	Total	Rate
Total	13,474	5,079	11,650	5,512	1,166	5,328	657	2,050
Violent crime	1,683	634	1,510	715	101	461	71	222
Murder and nonnegligent manslaughter	20	7	17	8	1	5	1	5
Forcible rape	96	36	81	38	8	35	8	24
Robbery	537	202	516	244	16	72	5	16
Aggravated assault	1,030	388	897	424	77	350	58	177
Property crime	11,791	4,445	10,141	4,798	1,065	4,867	586	1,828
Burglary	2,502	943	2,098	993	205	935	199	620
Larceny-theft	7,895	2,976	6,739	3,188	809	3,695	347	1,083
Motor vehicle theft	1,395	526	1,303	616	52	238	40	126

[1] For definition, see Appendix II.

Source: U.S. Federal Bureau of Investigation, *Crime in the United States,* annual.

No. 337. Crime Rates, by State, 1994 to 1996, and by Type, 1996

[Offenses known to the police per 100,000 population. Based on Bureau of the Census estimated resident population as of **July 1.** For definitions of crimes, see text, Section 5]

STATE	1994, total	1995, total	1996									
				Violent crime					Property crime			
			Total	Total	Mur-der [1]	Forci-ble rape	Rob-bery	Aggra-vated assault	Total	Bur-glary	Larce-ny—theft	Motor vehicle theft
United States . . .	5,374	5,276	5,079	634	7.4	36.1	202	388	4,445	943	2,976	526
Alabama	4,903	4,848	4,820	565	10.4	32.7	167	356	4,255	1,002	2,887	366
Alaska.	5,708	5,754	5,450	728	7.4	65.6	117	538	4,723	843	3,387	493
Arizona	7,925	8,214	7,067	632	8.5	31.2	168	424	6,436	1,256	4,253	927
Arkansas	4,799	4,691	4,699	524	8.7	41.7	114	360	4,175	953	2,909	313
California	6,174	5,831	5,208	863	9.1	32.1	296	526	4,345	979	2,605	761
Colorado	5,318	5,396	5,119	405	4.7	46.2	98	255	4,714	901	3,416	398
Connecticut	4,548	4,503	4,228	412	4.8	23.1	170	215	3,816	842	2,484	489
Delaware	4,148	5,159	4,895	668	4.3	62.6	180	422	4,227	804	2,988	434
District of Columbia [2] . .	11,085	12,174	11,897	2,470	73.1	47.9	1,187	1,162	9,427	1,810	5,780	1,837
Florida.	8,250	7,702	7,497	1,051	7.5	52.1	289	702	6,446	1,521	4,205	721
Georgia	6,010	6,004	6,310	639	8.6	32.1	205	393	5,671	1,115	3,928	629
Hawaii.	6,681	7,199	6,585	281	3.4	27.5	136	114	6,304	1,080	4,620	605
Idaho [3]	4,077	4,402	4,013	267	3.6	26.3	20	217	3,745	709	2,849	188
Illinois [3]	5,626	5,456	5,316	886	10.0	34.2	279	563	4,430	913	3,026	490
Indiana	4,593	4,632	4,498	537	7.2	34.1	124	372	3,961	784	2,753	425
Iowa	3,655	4,102	3,649	273	1.9	19.7	45	206	3,376	665	2,521	191
Kansas [3]	4,894	4,887	4,682	414	6.6	42.6	96	268	4,268	981	3,038	248
Kentucky [3]	3,499	3,352	3,166	321	5.9	31.7	94	189	2,846	688	1,896	261
Louisiana.	6,671	6,676	6,839	929	17.5	41.5	277	594	5,910	1,296	3,982	632
Maine	3,273	3,285	3,394	125	2.0	20.9	24	79	3,269	748	2,378	143
Maryland	6,123	6,295	6,062	931	11.6	37.6	393	489	5,131	992	3,427	711
Massachusetts	4,441	4,342	3,837	642	2.6	29.0	128	483	3,195	704	1,963	528
Michigan	5,445	5,183	5,118	635	7.5	57.0	176	395	4,482	895	2,886	701
Minnesota	4,341	4,497	4,463	339	3.6	50.0	116	170	4,124	763	2,977	385
Mississippi	4,837	4,515	4,523	488	11.1	36.1	134	307	4,035	1,132	2,552	351
Missouri.	5,308	5,121	5,084	591	8.1	29.2	171	383	4,493	894	3,151	448
Montana [3]	5,019	4,797	4,494	161	3.9	27.1	30	100	4,333	558	3,519	256
Nebraska.	4,440	4,545	4,437	435	2.9	27.1	64	341	4,002	615	3,046	342
Nevada	6,677	6,579	5,992	811	13.7	53.4	308	437	5,181	1,220	3,262	698
New Hampshire	2,741	2,655	2,824	118	1.7	34.8	27	54	2,705	436	2,118	152
New Jersey	4,661	4,704	4,333	532	4.2	24.7	236	267	3,801	792	2,428	581
New Mexico	6,188	6,428	6,602	841	11.5	63.5	162	603	5,762	1,377	3,803	582
New York.	5,071	4,560	4,132	727	7.4	23.0	340	357	3,405	714	2,197	494
North Carolina	5,625	5,640	5,526	588	8.5	31.3	164	385	4,938	1,346	3,257	336
North Dakota	2,736	2,866	2,669	84	2.2	24.1	11	47	2,585	309	2,086	190
Ohio	4,461	4,405	4,456	429	4.8	41.3	164	218	4,027	835	2,784	408
Oklahoma	5,570	5,597	5,653	597	6.8	46.8	107	437	5,056	1,256	3,317	483
Oregon	6,296	6,564	5,997	463	4.0	39.7	122	297	5,534	988	4,014	531
Pennsylvania	3,272	3,365	3,393	433	5.7	25.3	201	200	2,960	551	1,997	412
Rhode Island	4,119	4,245	3,994	347	2.5	29.0	83	232	3,646	822	2,360	464
South Carolina	6,001	6,064	6,214	997	9.0	49.2	172	767	5,217	1,284	3,505	429
South Dakota	3,102	3,061	2,970	177	1.2	41.0	19	116	2,793	557	2,122	114
Tennessee	5,120	5,363	5,449	774	9.5	46.5	224	494	4,675	1,164	2,865	647
Texas	5,872	5,684	5,709	644	7.7	43.8	172	421	5,065	1,069	3,447	549
Utah	5,301	6,091	5,986	332	3.2	41.8	69	218	5,654	848	4,377	429
Vermont	3,250	3,434	3,003	121	1.9	27.0	15	77	2,882	673	2,058	150
Virginia	4,048	3,989	3,968	341	7.5	26.7	123	185	3,627	588	2,760	279
Washington	6,028	6,270	5,909	431	4.6	51.1	119	256	5,478	1,058	3,899	522
West Virginia	2,528	2,458	2,483	210	3.8	19.6	40	146	2,273	547	1,550	177
Wisconsin	3,944	3,886	3,821	253	4.0	21.0	97	131	3,569	588	2,635	346
Wyoming	4,290	4,320	4,254	250	3.3	29.1	20	197	4,004	662	3,203	139

[1] Includes nonnegligent manslaughter.   [2] Includes offenses reported by the police at the National Zoo.   [3] Complete data were not available; therefore, it was necessary for the crime counts to be estimated for 1995 and 1996.

Source: U.S. Federal Bureau of Investigation, *Crime in the United States,* annual.

No. 338. Crime Rates, by Type—Selected Large Cities: 1996

[**Offenses known to the police per 100,000 population.** Based on Bureau of the Census estimated resident population as of **July 1.** For definitions of crimes, see text, Section 5]

CITY RANKED BY POPULATION SIZE, 1995 [1]	Crime index, total	VIOLENT CRIME					PROPERTY CRIME			
		Total	Murder	Forcible rape	Robbery	Aggravated assault	Total	Burglary	Larceny—theft	Motor vehicle theft
New York, NY	5,212.2	1,344.2	13.4	31.8	676.7	622.3	3,868.0	834.8	2,210.6	822.7
Los Angeles, CA	6,725.2	1,796.3	20.3	41.8	720.1	1,014.2	4,928.9	1,025.3	2,717.7	1,185.9
Chicago, IL [2]	(NA)	(NA)	28.6	(NA)	975.3	1,347.0	7,046.1	1,469.6	4,338.7	1,237.8
Houston, TX	7,636.5	1,267.2	14.7	56.5	467.0	728.9	6,369.3	1,433.4	3,672.4	1,263.5
Philadelphia, PA	6,920.0	1,528.9	27.1	46.1	1,013.1	442.6	5,391.2	1,060.2	2,817.6	1,513.4
San Diego, CA	5,270.0	868.6	6.8	31.5	256.6	573.7	4,401.5	736.8	2,712.2	952.5
Phoenix, AZ	9,541.1	923.8	16.3	40.4	329.6	537.5	8,617.4	1,716.0	5,313.7	1,587.7
Dallas, TX	9,466.6	1,535.0	20.5	69.8	577.2	867.5	7,931.6	1,693.4	4,621.8	1,616.4
San Antonio, TX	8,586.6	464.1	11.5	62.4	230.1	160.3	8,122.5	1,339.7	5,921.6	861.1
Detroit, MI	11,991.2	2,318.6	42.7	111.6	948.2	1,216.0	9,672.7	2,144.2	4,109.9	3,418.6
Honolulu, HI	6,840.1	313.0	3.1	25.3	161.8	122.8	6,527.1	1,028.0	4,773.7	725.5
San Jose, CA	6,849.8	1,011.5	19.4	57.1	439.1	496.0	5,838.3	1,402.1	3,482.7	953.4
Las Vegas, NV	4,129.1	731.6	4.8	41.1	132.2	553.5	3,397.5	566.0	2,383.6	447.9
San Francisco, CA	7,594.9	1,326.8	11.0	40.0	743.4	532.4	6,268.2	950.0	4,168.7	1,149.5
Baltimore, MD	12,001.2	2,722.7	45.8	89.5	1,450.6	1,136.9	9,278.4	2,066.0	5,656.0	1,556.4
Jacksonville, FL	8,623.5	1,414.5	12.3	98.6	404.4	899.1	7,209.1	1,907.8	4,613.8	687.5
Columbus, OH	9,539.8	970.8	13.9	89.2	518.2	349.5	8,569.0	2,032.3	5,348.1	1,188.5
Memphis, TN	11,127.0	1,984.6	25.5	124.9	945.2	889.0	9,142.4	2,633.5	4,247.5	2,261.5
Milwaukee, WI	7,912.6	952.6	20.7	44.8	534.7	352.4	6,960.0	1,215.4	4,137.5	1,607.1
El Paso, TX	7,485.5	852.1	5.0	40.6	198.2	608.3	6,633.4	653.8	5,256.5	723.1
Washington, DC	11,889.0	2,469.8	73.1	47.9	1,186.7	1,162.1	9,419.2	1,809.9	5,772.2	1,837.0
Boston, MA	8,092.2	1,656.8	10.7	74.9	628.0	943.1	6,435.4	914.4	3,843.1	1,678.0
Charlotte, NC	9,659.1	1,609.0	12.8	55.2	468.2	1,072.8	8,050.1	1,845.8	5,450.4	753.9
Seattle, WA	10,310.8	841.9	6.9	48.4	363.8	422.9	9,468.8	1,455.7	6,835.4	1,177.7
Austin, TX	7,865.9	710.9	7.4	50.2	256.0	397.2	7,155.0	1,409.3	5,058.2	687.5
Nashville-Davidson, TN	11,218.9	1,890.5	16.8	91.9	549.0	1,232.9	9,328.4	1,514.0	6,262.5	1,551.9
Denver, CO	6,647.1	742.3	12.4	69.3	257.1	403.5	5,904.8	1,508.6	3,345.3	1,050.9
Cleveland, OH	7,541.4	1,538.4	20.8	129.6	818.9	569.1	6,003.0	1,553.9	2,709.6	1,739.5
New Orleans, LA	11,042.2	2,257.0	71.9	79.9	1,167.3	937.9	8,785.2	2,038.5	4,663.9	2,082.7
Oklahoma City, OK	12,158.5	1,130.2	14.3	101.6	314.7	699.7	11,028.2	2,276.3	7,656.4	1,095.5
Fort Worth, TX	8,272.6	1,059.9	14.5	67.8	359.8	617.8	7,212.7	1,683.6	4,568.0	961.2
Portland, OR	10,751.3	1,674.5	10.9	85.9	439.6	1,138.0	9,076.8	1,526.4	6,160.0	1,390.5
Tucson, AZ	9,819.3	1,100.6	9.7	59.7	272.7	758.5	8,718.7	1,420.5	6,024.7	1,273.5
Kansas City, MO	11,661.8	1,981.2	23.2	91.9	642.4	1,223.7	9,680.6	1,995.0	6,271.0	1,414.6
Long Beach, CA	5,978.8	1,152.0	21.6	35.9	552.5	542.0	4,826.8	1,137.0	2,652.4	1,037.4
Virginia Beach, VA	4,733.2	244.4	4.5	28.9	103.4	107.5	4,488.8	696.4	3,566.7	225.8
Albuquerque, NM	11,307.5	1,468.6	16.4	87.9	468.2	896.1	9,838.9	2,117.7	6,083.6	1,637.5
Atlanta, GA	17,070.2	3,316.0	47.4	94.9	1,163.1	2,010.5	13,754.3	2,534.6	8,981.3	2,238.3
Fresno, CA	10,633.1	1,392.9	17.6	55.1	532.3	787.9	9,240.2	1,751.8	5,147.3	2,341.0
Miami, FL	13,745.8	3,114.5	32.2	52.2	1,334.9	1,695.2	10,631.3	2,546.7	6,086.4	1,998.3
Tulsa, OK	7,207.3	1,165.9	8.2	80.0	228.5	849.1	6,041.4	1,614.3	3,303.1	1,124.0
Sacramento, CA	8,906.3	977.4	11.3	40.6	494.1	431.3	7,928.9	1,884.6	4,440.5	1,603.8
St. Louis, MO	15,128.8	2,727.8	44.4	71.9	1,092.4	1,519.1	12,401.0	2,643.3	7,814.1	1,943.6
Oakland, CA	10,526.5	2,194.8	25.0	86.5	973.3	1,110.1	8,331.7	1,627.9	5,341.5	1,362.4
Cincinnati, OH	7,616.7	1,087.8	8.9	87.4	492.2	499.4	6,528.9	1,577.7	4,445.7	505.5
Minneapolis, MN	11,290.5	1,882.8	23.0	142.7	896.6	820.5	9,407.8	2,123.4	5,721.9	1,562.5
Pittsburgh, PA	5,296.0	803.8	13.3	58.1	441.7	290.7	4,492.1	860.6	2,838.5	793.1
Omaha, NE	7,683.5	1,352.5	7.7	59.0	223.0	1,062.7	6,331.0	1,013.1	4,278.0	1,039.9
Mesa, AZ	7,551.0	721.5	5.3	32.3	148.5	535.5	6,829.5	1,139.3	4,571.9	1,118.2
Colorado Springs, CO	6,199.9	481.8	3.6	71.9	136.8	269.5	5,718.1	998.1	4,304.3	415.7
Toledo, OH	8,468.0	811.7	9.2	85.3	399.6	317.6	7,656.3	1,724.2	4,996.1	935.9
Buffalo, NY	8,506.0	1,446.8	19.2	86.8	837.7	503.1	7,059.2	2,010.6	3,612.0	1,436.6
Wichita, KS	7,956.7	758.5	7.7	72.6	263.2	415.1	7,198.1	1,660.7	4,776.4	761.1
Arlington, TX	7,136.5	829.8	5.7	52.2	206.9	564.9	6,306.8	1,136.9	4,408.4	761.5
Santa Ana, CA	4,479.5	756.4	15.6	21.0	399.4	320.4	3,723.2	617.7	2,204.0	901.5
Tampa, FL	14,549.5	2,948.7	14.6	89.6	906.4	1,938.1	11,600.8	2,502.1	7,054.3	2,044.3
Anaheim, CA	5,126.8	723.8	4.9	28.3	341.8	348.8	4,403.0	942.9	2,638.5	821.6
Corpus Christi, TX	10,628.3	1,053.5	6.3	96.3	169.2	781.8	9,574.8	1,316.2	7,676.7	581.9
Louisville, KY	7,661.0	1,233.1	23.0	47.7	660.1	502.4	6,427.9	1,759.5	3,454.9	1,213.5
Birmingham, AL	10,759.1	1,622.5	41.5	84.1	675.3	821.5	9,136.6	2,194.6	5,614.2	1,327.9
St. Paul, MN	7,745.8	911.7	9.7	87.5	327.4	487.1	6,834.1	1,544.0	4,303.9	986.2
Newark, NJ	13,148.5	3,345.1	35.1	68.3	1,610.9	1,630.7	9,803.4	2,287.4	4,464.5	3,051.4
Aurora, CO	6,096.1	621.4	4.2	73.6	213.2	330.3	5,474.7	987.5	3,954.0	533.2
Anchorage, AK	6,349.9	815.6	9.8	77.7	219.0	509.1	5,534.3	923.6	3,989.0	621.7
Norfolk, VA	7,665.6	948.1	24.8	57.7	438.7	426.9	6,717.5	1,124.6	4,900.5	692.4
Riverside, CA	6,321.6	1,293.0	7.3	46.9	356.6	882.2	5,028.5	1,180.8	2,905.6	942.1
St. Petersburg, FL	9,683.3	1,920.2	10.6	67.4	560.5	1,281.7	7,763.1	1,841.8	5,025.0	896.3
Raleigh, NC	6,966.4	860.2	10.2	36.7	298.6	514.7	6,106.2	1,280.3	4,264.7	561.2
Lexington-Fayette, KY	6,356.2	828.5	5.8	50.6	240.1	532.0	5,527.7	1,199.7	3,948.6	379.4
Rochester, NY	9,045.2	981.1	22.9	51.4	587.8	319.0	8,064.1	1,933.7	4,966.5	1,163.9
Baton Rouge, LA	11,922.0	1,480.6	30.9	51.4	527.2	871.0	10,441.3	2,430.1	6,613.9	1,397.4
Jersey City, NJ	7,312.7	1,659.6	11.4	39.8	813.8	794.6	5,653.1	1,499.4	2,624.1	1,529.6
Stockton, CA	8,592.2	1,379.5	20.4	54.5	581.5	723.2	7,212.6	1,513.7	4,346.8	1,352.1

NA Not available.   [1] Crime data were not available for Indianapolis, IN.   [2] The rates for forcible rape, violent crime, and crime index are not shown because the forcible rape figures were not in accordance with national Uniform Crime Reporting guidelines.

Source: U.S. Federal Bureau of Investigation, *Crime in the United States,* annual.

No. 339. Murder Victims—Circumstances and Weapons Used or Cause of Death: 1990 to 1996

[Based solely on police investigation. For definition of murder, see text, Section 5]

CHARACTERISTIC	1990	1994	1995	1996	CHARACTERISTIC	1990	1994	1995	1996
Murders, total . . .	**20,273**	**22,084**	**20,232**	**15,848**	Other motives	19.4	20.7	21.6	17.9
Percent distribution . . .	100.0	100.0	100.0	100.0	Unknown	24.8	28.0	28.9	28.9
CIRCUMSTANCES					TYPE OF WEAPON OR CAUSE OF DEATH				
Felonies, total	20.8	18.4	17.7	19.0					
Robbery	9.2	9.4	9.3	9.4	Guns	64.3	70.0	68.2	67.8
Narcotics	6.7	5.6	5.1	5.2	Handguns	49.8	57.8	55.8	54.2
Sex offenses	1.1	0.2	0.2	0.2	Cutting or stabbing . . .	17.4	12.7	12.6	13.5
Other felonies	3.7	3.2	3.2	4.2	Blunt objects [1]	5.4	4.1	4.5	4.6
Suspected felonies . . .	0.7	0.6	0.6	0.5	Personal weapons [2] . . .	5.5	5.3	5.9	5.9
Argument, total	34.4	32.3	31.2	33.7	Strangulations,				
Property or money . .	2.5	1.8	1.7	2.1	asphyxiations	2.0	1.8	1.8	2.1
Romantic triangle . . .	2.0	1.7	1.4	1.2	Fire	1.4	0.9	0.8	1.0
Other arguments . . .	29.8	28.8	28.2	30.4	All other [3]	4.0	5.2	6.1	5.1

[1] Refers to club, hammer, etc.   [2] Hands, fists, feet, etc.   [3] Includes poison, drowning, explosives, narcotics, and unknown.
Source: U.S. Federal Bureau of Investigation, *Crime in the United States,* annual.

No. 340. Murder Victims, by Age, Sex, and Race: 1996

AGE	Total	SEX			RACE			
		Male	Female	Unknown	White	Black	Other	Unknown
Total	**15,848**	**12,195**	**3,631**	**22**	**7,647**	**7,638**	**425**	**138**
Percent distribution	100.0	76.9	22.9	0.1	48.3	48.2	2.7	0.9
Under 18 yrs. old	1,960	1,385	572	3	973	907	57	23
18 yrs. old and over.	13,669	10,661	3,003	5	6,564	6,659	364	82
Infant (under 1 yr. old)	247	124	120	3	153	80	7	7
1 to 4 yrs. old.	375	204	171	-	198	159	15	3
5 to 8 yrs. old.	101	57	44	-	63	36	2	-
9 to 12 yrs. old	81	42	39	-	46	34	1	-
13 to 16 yrs. old	692	557	135	-	320	344	21	7
17 to 19 yrs. old	1,669	1,447	222	-	667	954	36	12
20 to 24 yrs. old	2,739	2,379	360	-	1,050	1,601	72	16
25 to 29 yrs. old	2,219	1,807	411	1	908	1,234	63	14
30 to 34 yrs. old	1,838	1,389	447	2	867	904	53	14
35 to 39 yrs. old	1,685	1,235	450	-	878	756	39	12
40 to 44 yrs. old	1,212	897	315	-	660	511	32	9
45 to 49 yrs. old	877	628	248	1	493	358	24	2
50 to 54 yrs. old	539	398	141	-	320	190	25	4
55 to 59 yrs. old	362	277	85	-	232	116	12	2
60 to 64 yrs. old	276	205	71	-	179	91	5	1
65 to 69 yrs. old	223	152	71	-	156	62	5	-
70 to 74 yrs. old	174	106	68	-	125	44	5	-
75 yrs. old and over.	320	142	177	1	222	92	4	2
Age unknown	219	149	56	14	110	72	4	33

- Represents zero.
Source: U.S. Federal Bureau of Investigation, *Crime in the United States,* annual.

No. 341. Homicide Victims, by Race and Sex: 1970 to 1995

[**Rates per 100,000 resident population in specified group.** Excludes deaths to nonresidents of United States. Beginning 1980, deaths classified according to the ninth revision of the *International Classification of Diseases;* for earlier years, classified according to revision in use at the time; see text, Section 2]

YEAR	HOMICIDE VICTIMS					HOMICIDE RATE [2]				
	Total [1]	White		Black		Total [1]	White		Black	
		Male	Female	Male	Female		Male	Female	Male	Female
1970	16,848	5,865	1,938	7,265	1,569	8.3	6.8	2.1	67.6	13.3
1980	24,278	10,381	3,177	8,385	1,898	10.7	10.9	3.2	66.6	13.5
1981	23,646	9,941	3,125	8,312	1,825	10.3	10.4	3.1	64.8	12.7
1982	22,358	9,260	3,179	7,730	1,743	9.6	9.6	3.1	59.1	12.0
1983	20,191	8,355	2,880	6,822	1,672	8.6	8.6	2.8	51.4	11.3
1984	19,796	8,171	2,956	6,563	1,677	8.4	8.3	2.9	48.7	11.2
1985	19,893	8,122	3,041	6,616	1,666	8.3	8.2	2.9	48.4	11.0
1986	21,731	8,567	3,123	7,634	1,861	9.0	8.6	3.0	55.0	12.1
1987	21,103	7,979	3,149	7,518	1,969	8.7	7.9	3.0	53.3	12.6
1988	22,032	7,994	3,072	8,314	2,089	9.0	7.9	2.9	58.0	13.2
1989	22,909	8,337	2,971	8,888	2,074	9.2	8.2	2.8	61.1	12.9
1990	24,932	9,147	3,006	9,981	2,163	10.0	9.0	2.8	69.2	13.5
1991	26,513	9,581	3,201	10,628	2,330	10.5	9.3	3.0	72.0	14.2
1992	25,488	9,456	3,012	10,131	2,187	10.0	9.1	2.8	67.5	13.1
1993	26,009	9,054	3,232	10,640	2,297	10.1	8.6	3.0	69.7	13.6
1994	24,926	9,055	2,921	10,083	2,124	9.6	8.5	2.6	65.1	12.4
1995	22,895	8,336	3,028	8,847	1,936	8.7	7.8	2.7	56.3	11.1

[1] Includes races not shown separately.   [2] Rate based on enumerated population figures as of April 1 for 1970, 1980, and 1990; July 1 estimates for other years.
Source: U.S. National Center for Health Statistics, *Vital Statistics of the United States,* annual, and unpublished data.

No. 342. Forcible Rape—Number and Rate: 1980 to 1996

[For definition of rape, see text, Section 5]

ITEM	1980	1985	1989	1990	1991	1992	1993	1994	1995	1996
NUMBER										
Total.	82,990	88,670	94,500	102,560	106,590	109,060	106,010	102,220	97,460	95,770
By force	63,599	71,060	78,411	86,541	91,522	93,825	92,360	89,297	85,249	83,633
Attempt	19,391	17,610	16,089	16,019	15,068	15,235	13,650	12,923	12,211	12,137
RATE										
Per 100,000 population	36.8	37.1	38.1	41.2	42.3	42.8	41.1	39.3	37.1	36.1
Per 100,000 females	71.6	72.3	74.3	80.5	82.5	83.5	80.3	76.7	72.5	70.7
Per 100,000 females 12 years old and over	86.3	86.6	89.3	96.6	100.9	100.5	96.4	92.0	87.1	84.9
AVERAGE ANNUAL PERCENT CHANGE IN RATE [1]										
Per 100,000 population	6.1	3.9	1.3	8.1	2.7	1.2	-4.0	-4.4	-5.6	-2.7
Per 100,000 females 12 years old and over	6.0	4.3	1.4	8.2	4.5	-0.4	-4.1	-4.6	-5.3	-2.6

[1] Represents annual average from prior year shown except for 1980, from 1979; for 1985, from 1984; and for 1989, from 1988.

Source: U.S. Federal Bureau of Investigation, *Population-at-Risk Rates and Selected Crime Indicators,* annual.

No. 343. Robbery and Property Crimes, by Type and Selected Characteristic: 1980 to 1996

[For definition of crime, see text, Section 5]

ITEM	NUMBER OF OFFENSES (1,000)				RATE PER 100,000 INHABITANTS				AVERAGE VALUE LOST (dol.)	
	1980	1990	1995	1996	1980	1990	1995	1996	1995	1996
Robbery, total [1]	**566**	**639**	**581**	**537**	**251.1**	**257.0**	**220.9**	**202.4**	**873**	**929**
Type of crime:										
Street or highway	293	359	315	275	130.1	144.2	120.0	103.7	645	667
Commercial house	78	73	71	72	34.6	29.5	27.2	27.2	1,351	1,477
Gas station	23	18	13	13	10.4	7.1	5.1	4.9	959	487
Convenience store	38	39	30	32	17.0	15.6	11.4	11.9	400	567
Residence	60	62	63	57	26.8	25.1	24.0	21.5	1,082	1,133
Bank	8	9	9	11	3.8	3.8	3.5	4.0	4,015	4,207
Weapon used:										
Firearm	228	234	238	219	101.3	94.1	90.6	82.4	(NA)	(NA)
Knife or cutting instrument	73	76	53	48	32.3	30.7	20.1	18.1	(NA)	(NA)
Other dangerous weapon	51	61	53	62	22.8	24.5	20.2	23.5	(NA)	(NA)
Strongarm	214	268	236	208	94.8	107.7	90.0	78.4	(NA)	(NA)
Burglary, total	**3,795**	**3,074**	**2,595**	**2,502**	**1,684.1**	**1,235.9**	**987.6**	**943.0**	**1,259**	**1,332**
Forcible entry	2,789	2,150	1,737	1,647	1,237.5	864.5	661.2	621.0	(NA)	(NA)
Unlawful entry	711	678	657	649	315.6	272.8	250.1	244.5	(NA)	(NA)
Attempted forcible entry	295	245	201	206	131.0	98.7	76.4	77.5	(NA)	(NA)
Residence	2,525	2,033	1,736	1,663	1,120.6	817.4	660.6	627.0	1,211	1,350
Nonresidence	1,270	1,041	859	838	563.5	418.5	327.0	316.0	1,257	1,296
Occurred during the night	1,508	1,135	905	866	669.0	456.4	344.4	326.5	(NA)	(NA)
Occurred during the day	1,263	1,151	1,000	900	560.3	462.8	380.5	339.3	(NA)	(NA)
Larceny-theft, total	**7,137**	**7,946**	**8,001**	**7,895**	**3,167.0**	**3,194.8**	**3,044.9**	**2,975.9**	**535**	**532**
Pocket picking	85	81	51	35	37.9	32.4	19.4	13.3	350	320
Purse snatching	107	82	51	47	47.5	32.8	19.5	17.5	279	296
Shoplifting	773	1,291	1,205	1,213	343.0	519.1	458.4	457.2	108	120
From motor vehicles	1,231	1,744	1,940	1,997	546.4	701.3	738.5	752.7	531	518
Motor vehicle accessories	1,366	1,185	964	843	606.2	476.3	367.0	317.9	329	387
Bicycles	715	443	501	438	317.5	178.2	190.5	165.3	286	263
From buildings	1,187	1,118	1,004	1,006	526.9	449.4	382.1	379.1	891	894
From coin-operated machines	58	63	50	47	25.8	25.4	18.9	17.9	283	296
Other	1,613	1,940	2,235	2,268	715.7	780.0	850.5	855.1	770	723
Motor vehicles, total [2]	**1,132**	**1,636**	**1,473**	**1,395**	**502.2**	**657.8**	**560.5**	**525.9**	**5,129**	**5,372**
Automobiles	845	1,304	1,154	1,093	374.8	524.3	439.2	412.1	(NA)	(NA)
Trucks and buses	149	238	240	230	66.1	95.5	91.2	86.7	(NA)	(NA)

NA Not available. [1] Includes other crimes not shown separately. [2] Includes other types of motor vehicles not shown separately.

Source: U.S. Federal Bureau of Investigation, *Population-at-Risk Rates and Selected Crime Indicators,* annual.

No. 344. Hate Crimes—Number of Incidents, Offenses, Victims, and Offenders, by Bias Motivation: 1996

[The FBI collects statistics on hate crimes from 11,354 law enforcement agencies representing over 223 million inhabitants. Hate crime offenses cover incidents motivated by race, religion, sexual orientation, and ethnicity/national origin]

BIAS MOTIVATION	Incidents	Offenses	Victims	Known offenders
Total bias motivations	**8,759**	**10,706**	**11,039**	**8,935**
Race, total	5,396	6,767	6,994	6,122
Anti-White	1,106	1,384	1,445	1,783
Anti-Black	3,674	4,469	4,600	3,701
Anti-American Indian/Alaskan native	51	69	71	56
Anti-Asian/Pacific Islander	355	527	544	374
Anti-multi-racial group	210	318	334	208
Ethnicity/national origin, total	940	1,163	1,207	1,095
Anti-Hispanic	564	710	728	734
Anti-other ethnicity/national origin	376	453	479	361
Religion, total	1,401	1,500	1,535	523
Anti-Jewish	1,109	1,182	1,209	371
Anti-Catholic	35	37	38	17
Anti-Protestant	75	80	81	44
Anti-Islamic	27	33	33	16
Anti-other religious group	129	139	145	64
Anti-multi-religious group	24	27	27	11
Anti-atheism/agnosticism/etc	2	2	2	-
Sexual orientation, total	1,016	1,256	1,281	1,180
Anti-male homosexual	757	927	940	925
Anti-female homosexual	150	185	192	150
Anti-homosexual	84	94	99	93
Anti-heterosexual	15	38	38	4
Anti-bisexual	10	12	12	8
Multiple bias	6	20	22	15

- Represents zero.

Source: U.S. Federal Bureau of Investigation, <http://WWW.fbi.GOV/ucr/hateinfo.htm>.

No. 345. Hate Crimes Reported, by State: 1996

[See headnote, Table 344]

STATE	Number of participating agencies	Population	Agencies submitting incidents	Incidents reported	STATE	Number of participating agencies	Population	Agencies submitting incidents	Incidents reported
United States	**11,354**	**223,346,702**	**1,834**	**8,759**	Mississippi	129	1,716,566	3	3
					Missouri	230	4,270,323	25	150
					Montana	95	858,174	4	10
Alabama	289	4,167,898	-	-	Nebraska	10	207,564	2	3
Alaska	1	254,774	1	9	Nevada	4	1,169,351	3	44
Arizona	81	4,253,428	19	250	New Hampshire	2	81,381	1	1
Arkansas	191	2,510,000	1	1	New Jersey	568	7,995,838	273	839
California	718	31,502,681	256	2,052	New Mexico	70	1,298,291	8	44
Colorado	230	3,820,118	27	133					
Connecticut	98	2,772,165	44	114	New York	499	17,645,588	40	903
Delaware	50	724,747	9	67	North Carolina	83	2,888,221	19	34
District of Columbia	1	543,000	1	16	North Dakota	101	640,486	2	2
					Ohio	405	8,873,634	55	234
Florida	394	14,658,195	51	187	Oklahoma	293	3,294,345	27	83
Georgia	2	413,123	2	28	Oregon	174	3,155,762	27	172
Hawaii	(1)	(1)	(1)	(1)	Pennsylvania	1,137	11,833,651	43	205
Idaho	112	1,202,496	32	72	Rhode Island	46	990,000	11	40
Illinois	113	5,412,562	113	348	South Carolina	340	3,677,033	24	42
Indiana	179	3,634,883	12	36					
Iowa	231	2,841,077	25	43	South Dakota	32	255,844	2	3
Kansas	1	312,706	1	28	Tennessee	191	2,904,931	13	33
Kentucky	527	3,848,633	49	109	Texas	915	19,026,891	88	350
Louisiana	140	2,697,770	5	6	Utah	124	1,988,036	25	59
Maine	131	1,235,309	10	58	Vermont	3	35,462	3	4
Maryland	148	5,071,690	37	387	Virginia	409	6,678,025	32	100
					Washington	230	5,466,381	62	198
Massachusetts	405	6,091,117	102	454	West Virginia	22	179,467	3	4
Michigan	485	7,958,039	159	486	Wisconsin	338	5,160,000	21	43
Minnesota	307	4,648,824	58	268	Wyoming	70	480,222	4	4

- Represents zero.   [1] Did not report.

Source: U.S. Federal Bureau of Investigation, <http://WWW.fbi.GOV/ucr/hateinfo.htm>.

No. 346. Criminal Victimizations and Victimization Rates: 1993 to 1996

[Based on National Crime Victimization Survey; see text, Section 5, and Appendix III]

TYPE OF CRIME	NUMBER OF VICTIMIZATIONS (1,000)				VICTIMIZATION RATES [1]			
	1993	1994	1995	1996	1993	1994	1995	1996
All crimes, total	43,547	42,359	39,926	36,796	(X)	(X)	(X)	(X)
Personal crimes [2]	11,365	11,349	10,436	9,443	53.7	53.1	46.2	43.5
Crimes of violence	10,848	10,860	10,022	9,125	51.3	50.8	44.5	42.0
Completed violence	3,213	3,205	2,960	2,700	15.2	15.0	12.9	12.4
Attempted/threatened violence	7,635	7,654	7,061	6,425	36.1	35.8	31.6	29.6
Rape/sexual assault	485	433	363	307	2.3	2.0	1.6	1.4
Rape/attempted rape	313	316	252	197	1.5	1.5	1.1	0.9
Rape	160	168	153	98	0.8	0.8	0.7	0.4
Attempted rape	152	149	99	99	0.7	0.7	0.4	0.5
Sexual assault	173	117	112	110	0.8	0.5	0.5	0.5
Robbery	1,291	1,299	1,171	1,134	6.1	6.1	5.3	5.2
Completed/property taken	815	795	753	757	3.9	3.7	3.5	3.5
With injury	274	288	224	250	1.3	1.3	1.0	1.1
Without injury	541	507	529	508	2.6	2.4	2.4	2.3
Attempted to take property	476	504	418	377	2.3	2.4	1.8	1.7
With injury	96	122	84	79	0.5	0.6	0.4	0.4
Without injury	381	382	335	298	1.8	1.8	1.4	1.4
Assault	9,072	9,128	8,487	7,683	42.9	42.7	37.6	35.4
Aggravated	2,563	2,478	2,050	1,910	12.1	11.6	8.8	8.8
With injury	713	679	533	513	3.4	3.2	2.4	2.4
Threatened with weapon	1,850	1,799	1,517	1,397	8.7	8.4	6.4	6.4
Simple	6,509	6,650	6,437	5,773	30.8	31.1	28.9	26.6
With minor injury	1,356	1,466	1,426	1,240	6.4	6.9	6.0	5.7
Without injury	5,153	5,184	5,012	4,533	24.4	24.3	22.9	20.9
Personal theft [3]	517	489	414	318	2.4	2.3	1.7	1.5
Property crimes	32,182	31,011	29,490	27,353	322.1	307.6	279.5	266.3
Household burglary	5,984	5,482	5,004	4,845	59.9	54.4	47.4	47.2
Completed	4,824	4,573	4,232	4,056	48.3	45.4	40.0	39.5
Attempted forcible entry	1,160	910	773	789	11.6	9.0	7.4	7.7
Motor vehicle theft	1,961	1,764	1,717	1,387	19.6	17.5	16.2	13.5
Completed	1,291	1,172	1,163	938	12.9	11.6	10.8	9.1
Attempted	670	591	554	449	6.7	5.9	5.5	4.4
Theft . . . . [4]	24,238	23,765	22,769	21,120	242.6	235.7	215.9	205.7
Completed [4]	23,020	22,743	21,857	20,303	230.4	225.6	207.6	197.7
Attempted	1,218	1,022	911	818	14.3	10.1	8.4	8.0

X Not applicable. [1] Per 1,000 persons age 12 older or per 1,000 households. [2] The victimization survey cannot measure murder because of the inability to question the victim. [3] Includes pocket picking, purse snatching, and attempted purse snatching. [4] Includes thefts in which the amount taken was not ascertained. In 1993, this category accounted for 1,433,000 victimizations and in 1994, 1,241,000.

Source: U.S. Bureau of Justice Statistics, *Criminal Victimization 1996*, November 1997, and previous bulletins.

No. 347. Victimization Rates, by Type of Violent Crime and Characteristic of the Victim: 1996

[Rate per 1,000 persons age 12 years or older. Based on National Crime Victimization Survey; see text, Section 5, and Appendix III]

CHARACTERISTIC	CRIMES OF VIOLENCE						Personal theft
	All crimes of violence	Rape/ sexual assault	Robbery	Assault			
				Total	Aggravated	Simple	
Total	42.0	1.4	5.2	35.4	8.8	26.6	1.5
Male	49.9	0.4	7.2	42.3	11.6	30.8	1.3
Female	34.6	2.3	3.4	28.9	6.2	22.7	1.6
12 to 15 yrs. old	95.0	2.6	10.0	82.3	15.6	66.8	3.3
16 to 19 yrs. old	102.7	4.9	12.0	85.7	25.3	60.4	2.5
20 to 24 yrs. old	74.3	2.1	10.0	62.2	15.9	46.4	2.9
25 to 34 yrs. old	51.1	1.8	7.1	42.2	9.8	32.4	1.2
35 to 49 yrs. old	32.8	1.3	3.8	27.7	7.4	20.3	1.0
50 to 64 yrs. old	15.7	0.1	1.8	13.8	3.8	10.0	1.2
65 yrs. old and over	4.9	-	1.1	3.8	0.8	3.0	0.7
White	40.9	1.3	4.2	35.3	8.2	27.2	1.4
Black	52.3	1.8	11.4	39.1	13.4	25.6	1.9
Other	33.2	2.1	7.4	23.8	7.2	16.6	1.3
Hispanic	44.0	1.2	8.4	34.5	10.6	23.9	2.7
Non-Hispanic	41.6	1.4	4.9	35.3	8.5	26.8	1.3
Household income:							
Less than $7,500	65.3	2.9	9.9	52.5	17.3	35.2	2.6
$7,500-$14,999	52.1	1.8	8.5	41.9	11.9	30.0	1.1
$15,000-$24,999	44.1	1.4	5.4	37.3	10.3	26.9	1.5
$25,000-$34,999	43.0	1.9	5.5	35.6	6.8	28.8	0.9
$35,000-$49,999	43.0	1.4	4.5	37.1	8.6	28.5	1.5
$50,000-$74,999	37.5	0.8	3.3	33.3	7.9	25.4	1.8
$75,000 or more	30.5	1.0	2.0	27.5	5.5	22.0	1.5

- Represents zero.
Source: U.S. Bureau of Justice Statistics, *Criminal Victimization 1996*, November 1997.

No. 348. Victim-Offender Relationship in Crimes of Violence, by Characteristics of the Criminal Incident: 1996

[In percent. Covers only crimes of violence. Based on National Crime Victimization Survey; see text, Section 5, and Appendix III]

CHARACTERISTICS OF INCIDENT	Total	Rape/ sexual assault	Robbery	ASSAULT		
				Total	Aggravated[1]	Simple
Total	**100**	**100**	**100**	**100**	**100**	**100**
Victim/offender relationship: [2]						
Relatives	10	17	7	10	10	10
Well-known	24	32	12	26	25	27
Casual acquaintance	16	30	6	17	13	19
Stranger	50	36	75	47	52	45
Time of day:						
6 a.m. to 6 p.m.	55	35	44	57	48	60
6 p.m. to midnight	33	38	39	32	36	30
Midnight to 6 a.m.	11	22	14	10	14	8
Location of crime:						
At or near victim's home or lodging	27	40	25	27	24	27
Friend's/relative's/neighbor's home	8	20	6	8	10	7
Commercial places	13	11	5	14	11	15
Parking lots/garages	8	7	11	7	9	7
School	13	7	7	15	6	17
Streets other than near victim's home	19	6	35	17	27	14
Other [3]	13	10	12	13	14	13
Victim's activity:						
At work or traveling to or from work	21	17	10	23	20	24
School	12	6	9	13	7	15
Activities at home	22	36	18	22	21	23
Shopping/errands	5	3	12	4	5	3
Leisure activities away from home	23	24	26	23	26	21
Traveling	9	2	16	8	12	6
Other	8	12	7	8	9	8
Distance from victim's home:						
Inside home or lodging	14	35	12	14	12	14
Near victim's home	15	7	14	15	17	14
1 mile or less	21	13	29	21	23	20
5 miles or less	23	17	23	24	20	25
50 miles or less	22	23	17	23	23	23
More than 50 miles	4	6	4	4	5	3
Weapons:						
No weapons present	72	91	45	75	4	100
Weapons present	28	9	55	25	96	-
Firearm	11	4	32	8	32	-
Other type of weapon [4]	17	5	23	17	64	-

- Represents zero. [1] An aggravated assault is any assault in which an offender possesses or uses a weapon or inflicts serious injury. [2] Excludes "don't know" relationships. [3] Includes areas on public transportation or inside station, in apartment yard, park, field, playground, or other areas. [4] Includes knives, other sharp objects, blunt objects, and other types of weapons.
Source: U.S. Bureau of Justice Statistics, *Criminal Victimization 1996*, November 1997.

No. 349. Property Victimization Rates, by Selected Household Characteristic: 1996

[Victimizations per 1,000 households. Based on National Crime Victimization Survey; see text, Section 5, and Appendix III]

CHARACTERISTIC	Total	Burglary	Motor vehicle theft	Theft
Total	**266.3**	**47.2**	**13.5**	**205.7**
Race:				
White	259.9	44.3	12.1	203.5
Black	310.0	69.3	22.2	218.5
Other	268.4	39.4	16.5	212.5
Ethnicity:				
Hispanic	328.1	56.2	24.6	247.3
Non-Hispanic	261.2	46.4	12.5	202.3
Household income:				
Less than $7,500	282.7	74.5	11.8	196.5
$7,500-$14,999	247.5	59.5	11.5	176.5
$15,000-$24,999	273.1	45.9	14.1	213.1
$25,000-$34,999	285.1	47.8	14.5	222.8
$35,000-$49,999	287.6	39.3	16.1	232.1
$50,000-$74,999	284.0	38.1	14.4	231.6
$75,000 or more	304.6	41.8	14.4	248.3
Residence:				
Urban	334.5	64.2	20.3	250.0
Suburban	250.5	37.8	12.9	199.8
Rural	206.0	43.7	5.4	156.9
Form of tenure:				
Home owned	233.7	38.9	10.7	184.1
Home rented	327.1	62.6	18.8	245.8

Source: U.S. Bureau of Justice Statistics, *Criminal Victimization 1996*, November 1997.

No. 350. Reported Criminal Victimization at School, by Selected Characteristics and Perceptions of Conditions at School: 1989 and 1995

[Percent of students ages 12 through 19 reporting. Based on the National Crime Victimization Survey, special School Crime Supplement; see text, Section 5, and Appendix III]

STUDENT CHARACTERISTICS	1989 Number of students (1,000)	1989 Percent reporting any victimization [1]	1995 Number of students (1,000)	1995 Percent reporting any victimization [1]	STUDENT CHARACTERISTICS	1989 Number of students (1,000)	1989 Percent reporting any victimization [1]	1995 Number of students (1,000)	1995 Percent reporting any victimization [1]
Total	21,554	14.5	23,933	14.6	PERCEPTIONS OF CONDITIONS AT SCHOOL				
CHARACTERISTICS					Student reports of street gangs at school:				
White, non-Hispanic . .	15,349	14.3	16,351	14.5	Yes	3,301	21.8	6,796	21.4
Black, non-Hispanic . .	3,391	14.9	3,752	16.8	No	17,042	13.1	13,687	11.8
Hispanic	2,027	14.7	2,898	12.4	Student reports of				
Other, non-Hispanic . .	787	14.7	932	13.7	knowing a student who				
					brought a gun to school:				
Student age:					Yes	(NA)	(NA)	3,042	24.6
12 years old	3,221	17.8	3,735	19.8	No	(NA)	(NA)	20,608	13.2
13 years old	3,319	18.0	3,781	17.9	Student reports of				
14 years old	3,264	16.8	3,732	17.0	seeing a student with				
15 years old	3,214	15.3	3,688	14.4	a gun at school:				
16 years old	3,275	12.0	3,674	11.9	Yes	(NA)	(NA)	1,270	31.2
17 years old	3,274	10.6	3,172	9.9	No	(NA)	(NA)	22,359	13.7
18 years old	1,756	8.6	1,820	6.8	Student reports of drug				
19 years old	231	5.3	331	8.8	availability:[2]				
					Any available	13,630	16.8	15,630	16.0
Student school type:					None available	2,560	10.3	3,922	12.9
Public	19,265	14.7	21,719	14.8					
Private	1,873	12.8	2,163	12.4					

NA Not available. [1] Includes reported violent and property victimization. If the student reported an incident either, he or she is counted as having experienced any victimization. [2] Includes marijuana, cocaine, crack, and upper/downers.

Source: U.S. Bureau of Justice Statistics, *Students' Reports of School Crime: 1989 and 1995.*

No. 351. Aliens Expelled and Immigration Violations: 1980 to 1995

[For fiscal years ending in year shown. See text, Section 9]

ITEM	Unit	1980	1985	1989	1990	1991	1992	1993	1994	1995
Aliens expelled	1,000	737	1,062	860	1,045	1,091	1,144	1,280	1,074	1,363
Deported	1,000	17	21	30	26	28	38	37	40	42
Other [1]	1,000	719	1,041	830	1,019	1,063	1,106	1,243	1,035	1,321
Prosecution	Number . .	14,863	17,688	18,580	20,079	18,882	14,655	19,650	15,348	17,273
Immigration violations	Number . .	14,498	16,976	17,992	19,351	18,297	14,138	18,958	14,842	16,947
Nationality violations	Number . .	365	712	588	728	585	517	692	506	326
Convictions	Number . .	12,935	9,833	12,561	12,719	11,509	9,865	12,538	10,646	12,294
Immigration violations	Number . .	12,678	9,635	12,379	12,515	11,392	9,766	12,252	10,486	12,182
Nationality violations	Number . .	257	198	182	204	117	99	286	160	112

[1] Through 1993, covers required departures; beginning 1994, covers required departures, exclusions, and voluntary departures.

No. 352. Immigration Border Patrol and Investigation Activities: 1980 to 1995

[In thousands, except where indicated. For fiscal years ending in year shown. See text, Section 9]

ITEM	Unit	1980	1985	1989	1990	1991	1992	1993	1994	1995
BORDER PATROL										
Border patrol agents:										
Authorized number	Number . . .	2,484	3,228	4,804	4,852	4,968	4,948	4,143	4,559	5,259
On duty	Number . . .	2,329	3,023	3,857	4,360	4,312	4,759	3,991	4,226	4,881
Border patrol obligations . . .	Mil. dol. . .	82.5	141.9	246.4	261.1	295.5	325.8	354.5	376.8	457.2
Persons apprehended [1] . . .	1,000	766.6	1,272.4	906.5	1,123.2	1,152.7	1,221.9	1,281.7	1,046.6	1,336.5
Deportable aliens located [2] . .	1,000	759.4	1,262.4	893.0	1,103.4	1,132.9	1,199.6	1,263.5	1,031.7	1,324.2
Mexican	1,000	734.2	1,218.7	832.2	1,054.8	1,095.1	1,168.9	1,230.1	999.9	1,293.5
Canadian	1,000	5.3	5.9	5.3	5.7	6.7	6.2	5.2	3.4	3.5
Other	1,000	19.9	37.8	55.5	42.8	31.1	24.4	28.1	28.4	27.2
Number of seizures	Number . . .	1,920	7,827	10,789	17,275	14,261	11,391	10,995	9,134	9,327
Value of seizures	Mil. dol. . .	116.1	122.0	1,212.7	843.6	950.2	1,247.9	1,383	1,598	733.0
Narcotics	Mil. dol. . .	110.3	119.8	1,191.5	797.8	910.1	1,216.8	1,338	1,556	686.6
INVESTIGATIONS										
Deportable aliens located	1,000	150.9	83.9	61.1	64.1	63.6	57.4	60.4	61.6	68.9
Mexican	1,000	83.3	48.3	33.1	35.8	35.5	36.2	38.8	40.1	46.3
Canadian	1,000	1.5	1.1	0.5	0.4	0.5	0.4	0.4	0.5	0.5
Other	1,000	66.1	34.5	28.5	30.0	29.7	20.8	21.1	21.1	22.0

[1] Covers deportable aliens located and U.S. citizens engaged in smuggling or other immigration violations. [2] Beginning 1988, includes apprehension by the antismuggling unit.

Source of tables 351 and 352: U.S. Immigration and Naturalization Service, *Statistical Yearbook,* annual; and unpublished data.

No. 353. Juvenile Arrests for Selected Offenses: 1980 to 1996

[Juveniles are persons between the ages 10-17]

OFFENSE	1980	1985	1990	1991	1992	1993	1994	1995	1996
Number of contributing agencies	8,178	11,263	10,765	10,148	11,058	10,277	10,693	10,037	10,033
Population covered (1,000)	169,439	206,269	204,543	189,962	217,754	213,705	208,035	206,762	196,048
NUMBER									
Violent crime, total	77,220	75,077	97,103	95,677	118,358	122,434	125,141	123,131	104,598
Murder	1,475	1,384	2,661	2,626	3,025	3,473	3,114	2,812	2,188
Forcible rape	3,668	5,073	4,971	4,766	5,451	5,490	4,873	4,556	4,234
Robbery.	38,529	31,833	34,944	35,632	42,639	44,598	47,046	47,240	39,817
Aggravated assault	33,548	36,787	54,527	52,653	67,243	68,873	70,108	68,523	58,359
Weapon law violations	21,203	27,035	33,123	37,575	49,903	54,414	52,278	46,506	40,178
Drug abuse, total	86,685	78,660	66,300	58,603	73,232	90,618	124,931	149,236	149,065
Sale and manufacturing	13,004	14,846	24,575	22,929	25,331	27,635	32,746	34,077	32,590
Heroin/cocaine.	1,318	2,851	17,511	16,915	17,881	18,716	20,327	19,187	17,478
Marijuana	8,876	8,646	4,372	3,579	4,853	6,144	8,812	10,682	11,504
Synthetic narcotics	465	414	346	570	663	455	465	701	618
Dangerous nonnarcotic drugs . . .	2,345	2,935	2,346	1,865	1,934	2,320	3,142	3,507	2,990
Possession.	73,681	63,814	41,725	35,674	47,901	62,983	92,185	115,159	116,475
Heroin/cocaine.	2,614	7,809	15,194	13,747	16,855	17,726	21,004	21,253	17,574
Marijuana	64,465	50,582	20,940	16,490	25,004	37,915	61,003	82,015	87,938
Synthetic narcotics	1,524	1,085	1,155	885	897	1,008	1,227	2,047	1,717
Dangerous nonnarcotic drugs . . .	5,078	4,338	4,436	4,552	5,145	6,334	8,951	9,844	9,246

Source: U.S. Federal Bureau of Investigation, *Crime in the United States*, annual.

No. 354. Persons Arrested, by Charge and Race: 1996

[Represents arrests (not charges) reported by 10,027 agencies with a total 1996 population 196 million as estimated by FBI]

OFFENSE CHARGED	TOTAL ARRESTS (1,000)					PERCENT DISTRIBUTION				
	Total	White	Black	American Indian or Alaskan Native	Asian or Pacific Islander	Total	White	Black	American Indian or Alaskan Native	Asian or Pacific Islander
Total.	11,392.5	7,637.0	3,479.2	144.2	132.2	100.0	67.0	30.5	1.3	1.2
Serious crimes [1]	2,109.9	1,311.4	740.7	24.2	33.6	100.0	62.2	35.1	1.1	1.6
Murder and nonnegligent manslaughter.	14.7	6.3	8.0	0.2	0.2	100.0	43.0	54.4	1.1	1.5
Forcible rape	24.9	14.0	10.4	0.3	0.3	100.0	56.2	41.5	1.1	1.2
Robbery	124.3	49.4	72.4	0.7	1.8	100.0	39.7	58.3	0.5	1.5
Aggravated assault.	395.1	235.9	150.2	4.0	5.0	100.0	59.7	38.0	1.0	1.3
Burglary	271.9	185.3	80.3	2.9	3.5	100.0	68.1	29.5	1.1	1.3
Larceny/theft	1,130.0	734.0	361.7	14.4	19.9	100.0	65.0	32.0	1.3	1.8
Motor vehicle theft	134.7	76.0	54.4	1.6	2.7	100.0	56.4	40.4	1.2	2.0
Arson	14.1	10.5	3.4	0.1	0.1	100.0	74.0	24.0	0.9	1.0
All other nonserious crimes . . .	9,282.6	6,325.6	2,738.5	120.0	98.6	100.0	68.1	29.5	1.3	1.1
Other assaults	1,001.7	626.0	350.8	13.4	11.5	100.0	62.5	35.0	1.3	1.1
Forgery and counterfeiting . .	91.5	58.9	30.4	0.7	1.6	100.0	64.3	33.2	0.8	1.7
Fraud	330.7	211.8	114.8	1.6	2.6	100.0	64.0	34.7	0.5	0.8
Embezzlement	11.7	7.5	4.0	0.1	0.2	100.0	63.7	34.3	0.5	1.5
Stolen property—buying, receiving, possessing	116.8	67.8	46.6	0.9	1.5	100.0	58.1	39.9	0.8	1.3
Vandalism	244.0	179.0	58.7	3.3	2.9	100.0	73.4	24.1	1.4	1.2
Weapons; carrying, possessing, etc.	164.4	95.5	65.7	1.2	1.9	100.0	58.1	40.0	0.7	1.2
Prostitution and commercialized vice.	83.4	49.1	32.0	0.5	1.8	100.0	58.9	38.3	0.6	2.1
Sex offenses (except forcible rape and prostitution)	73.6	54.7	17.2	0.8	0.9	100.0	74.3	23.3	1.1	1.3
Drug abuse violations	1,160.7	701.9	445.8	5.7	7.3	100.0	60.5	38.4	0.5	0.6
Gambling	17.2	7.9	8.7	0.1	0.6	100.0	45.6	50.4	0.4	3.6
Offenses against family and children.	106.8	70.8	33.0	1.3	1.7	100.0	66.2	30.9	1.2	1.6
Driving under the influence. .	1,050.2	911.5	107.1	17.9	13.7	100.0	86.8	10.2	1.7	1.3
Liquor laws	499.0	403.8	79.2	12.6	3.4	100.0	80.9	15.9	2.5	0.7
Drunkenness	525.4	426.3	84.6	12.5	2.0	100.0	81.1	16.1	2.4	0.4
Disorderly conduct	641.2	401.6	227.1	8.2	4.2	100.0	62.6	35.4	1.3	0.7
Vagrancy	22.7	12.3	9.9	0.4	0.1	100.0	54.2	43.5	1.9	0.4
All other offenses (except traffic).	2,848.6	1,818.6	962.0	35.5	32.5	100.0	63.8	33.8	1.2	1.1
Suspicion	4.9	3.3	1.5	0.1	-	100.0	67.8	30.6	1.1	0.5
Curfew and loitering law violations	142.7	103.6	34.9	1.7	2.5	100.0	72.6	24.5	1.2	1.7
Runaways.	145.6	113.9	24.4	1.7	5.7	100.0	78.2	16.7	1.2	3.9

- Represents zero. [1] Includes arson.

Source: U.S. Federal Bureau of Investigation, *Crime in the United States*, annual.

No. 355. Persons Arrested, by Charge, Sex, and Age: 1996

[Represents arrests (not charges) reported by 10,033 agencies (reporting 12 months) with a total 1996 population of 196 million as estimated by FBI]

CHARGE	Total (1,000)	PERCENT DISTRIBUTION							
		Male	Under 15 years	Under 18 years	18-24 years	25-44 years	45-54 years	55-64 years	65 yr. and over
Total arrests	**11,428**	**79.4**	**6.1**	**19.0**	**27.0**	**47.4**	**6.4**	**1.7**	**0.7**
Serious crimes [1]	**2,114**	**75.5**	**11.8**	**30.8**	**25.2**	**37.7**	**4.5**	**1.2**	**0.6**
Murder and nonnegligent manslaughter	15	89.7	1.8	15.0	41.1	36.7	4.8	1.6	1.0
Forcible rape	25	98.8	5.8	17.0	26.6	48.1	5.7	1.8	0.7
Robbery	124	90.3	8.6	32.1	32.7	33.0	2.0	0.3	0.1
Aggravated assault	396	82.1	4.7	14.7	25.4	50.6	6.6	1.8	0.8
Burglary [2]	272	88.7	14.0	37.0	27.3	32.5	2.6	0.4	0.1
Larceny—theft	1,133	66.2	14.2	33.8	23.2	36.2	4.8	1.3	0.8
Motor vehicle theft	135	86.4	11.0	41.5	28.6	27.5	2.0	0.3	0.1
Arson	14	85.1	35.5	53.1	16.6	24.6	4.0	1.3	0.5
All other nonserious crimes	**9,314**	**80.2**	**4.8**	**16.3**	**27.4**	**49.7**	**6.8**	**1.8**	**0.7**
Other assaults	1,004	79.7	7.2	17.6	22.8	51.3	6.1	1.6	0.6
Forgery and counterfeiting	92	64.6	0.9	7.1	31.4	55.3	5.0	0.9	0.3
Fraud	331	58.3	1.7	5.8	26.7	58.2	7.3	1.6	0.6
Embezzlement	12	55.1	0.6	8.4	35.8	48.3	5.8	1.4	0.4
Stolen property [3]	117	85.4	7.3	27.2	33.0	35.7	3.2	0.7	0.2
Vandalism	244	86.2	19.8	44.1	24.7	27.8	2.8	0.6	0.3
Weapons (carrying, etc.)	165	92.1	7.3	24.4	32.9	35.5	4.9	1.6	0.7
Prostitution and commercialized vice	83	40.0	0.2	1.4	19.5	70.6	6.4	1.5	0.6
Sex offenses [4]	74	92.0	9.0	17.9	19.1	47.4	9.4	3.9	2.1
Drug abuse violations	1,162	83.3	2.4	14.0	31.6	48.7	4.8	0.8	0.2
Gambling	17	86.2	1.7	13.3	26.1	39.1	11.8	6.6	3.1
Offenses against family and children	108	77.6	1.8	5.6	19.4	64.7	7.7	1.7	0.6
Driving under the influence	1,066	85.2	(Z)	1.3	21.2	61.3	11.3	3.6	1.3
Liquor laws	501	80.5	2.5	22.9	46.6	23.9	4.6	1.5	0.5
Drunkenness	526	87.9	0.5	3.3	20.3	58.9	12.4	3.9	1.3
Disorderly conduct	642	78.9	8.6	25.5	28.6	39.2	5.0	1.3	0.5
Vagrancy	23	79.9	2.9	13.2	26.9	48.0	8.3	2.6	0.9
Suspicion	5	80.0	9.0	33.0	26.3	35.2	4.1	1.0	0.4
Curfew, loitering (juveniles)	143	70.6	27.6	100.0	(X)	(X)	(X)	(X)	(X)
Runaways (juveniles)	146	42.7	41.0	100.0	(X)	(X)	(X)	(X)	(X)
All other offenses, except traffic	2,854	81.3	3.3	11.9	27.7	51.4	6.6	1.7	0.7

X Not applicable.   Z Less than 0.05 percent.   [1] Includes arson arrests, a newly established index offense in 1979.   [2] Breaking or entering.   [3] Buying, receiving, possessing.   [4] Excludes forcible rape and prostitution, shown separately.

Source: U.S. Federal Bureau of Investigation, *Crime in the United States,* annual.

No. 356. Drug Use by Arrestees in Major U.S. Cities, by Type of Drug and Sex: 1997

[**Percent testing positive.** Based on data from the Arrestee Drug Abuse Monitoring Program]

CITY	MALE				FEMALE			
	Any drug [1]	Mari-juana	Cocaine	Heroin	Any drug [1]	Mari-juana	Cocaine	Heroin
Atlanta, GA	72	36	51	2	74	28	61	3
Birmingham, AL	67	43	39	5	67	25	49	5
Chicago, IL	80	48	49	22	(NA)	(NA)	(NA)	(NA)
Cleveland, OH	64	46	27	4	57	39	22	4
Dallas, TX	63	44	32	4	53	28	34	4
Denver, CO	71	42	40	4	69	32	50	6
Detroit, MI	62	44	23	5	69	28	48	9
Fort Lauderdale, FL	73	38	51	3	68	24	57	4
Houston, TX	63	24	40	10	45	17	29	5
Indianapolis, IN	63	44	31	3	67	30	45	3
Los Angeles, CA	59	27	38	6	70	18	49	11
Manhattan, NY	79	32	58	19	81	25	62	20
Miami, FL	61	32	46	2	(NA)	(NA)	(NA)	(NA)
New Orleans, LA.	67	38	46	11	40	12	32	3
Omaha, NE	62	50	21	2	54	33	17	4
Philadelphia, PA	67	41	34	11	75	21	58	16
Phoenix, AZ	64	30	32	9	66	21	33	8
Portland, OR	71	38	37	14	78	19	45	27
St. Louis, MO	74	48	41	10	70	31	53	9
San Antonio, TX	52	34	26	10	38	17	18	9
San Diego, CA	73	38	21	7	73	24	23	12
San Jose, CA.	51	29	14	6	53	17	16	12
Washington, DC	69	39	33	10	57	19	39	11

NA Not available.   [1] Includes other drugs not shown separately.

Source: U.S. National Institute of Justice, *Drug Use Forecasting,* annual.

No. 357. Drug Arrest Rates for Drug Abuse Violations, 1980 to 1996, and by Region, 1996

[Rate per 100,000 inhabitants. Based on Bureau of the Census estimated resident population as of July 1, except 1980 and 1990, enumerated as of April 1. For composition of regions, see inside front cover]

OFFENSE	1980	1990	1995	1996				
				Total	Region			
					North-east	Mid-west	South	West
Drug arrest rate, total	256.0	435.3	564.7	558.6	645.7	390.3	490.7	681.2
Sale and/or manufacture	57.9	139.0	140.7	137.0	213.3	100.7	99.1	140.5
Heroin or cocaine [1]	10.8	93.7	83.7	78.1	159.8	29.2	58.6	64.7
Marijuana....................	28.4	26.4	32.7	35.0	41.5	31.6	29.1	38.5
Synthetic or manufactured drugs	2.8	2.7	3.9	3.4	3.1	1.7	3.7	4.4
Other dangerous nonnarcotic drugs ..	15.9	16.2	20.3	20.5	8.9	38.3	7.7	32.8
Possession.........................	198.1	296.3	423.9	421.6	432.4	289.6	391.6	540.8
Heroin or cocaine [1]	22.2	144.4	157.4	142.7	187.5	60.8	112.1	197.3
Marijuana....................	146.2	104.9	192.7	205.4	220.0	175.8	242.5	170.9
Synthetic or manufactured drugs	6.7	6.6	8.5	7.9	5.0	5.0	9.8	10.4
Other dangerous nonnarcotic drugs ..	23.0	40.4	65.4	65.6	19.9	48.0	27.2	162.2

[1] Includes other derivatives such as morphine, heroin, and codeine.

Source: U.S. Federal Bureau of Investigation, *Crime in the United States*, annual.

No. 358. Federal Drug Seizures, by Type of Drug: 1990 to 1996

[For fiscal years ending in year shown. Reflects the combined drug seizure effort of the Drug Enforcement Administration, the Federal Bureau of Investigation, the U.S. Customs Services, and beginning October 1993 the U.S. Border Patrol within the jurisdiction of the United States as well as maritime seizures by the U.S. Coast Guard. Based on reports to the federal-wide Drug Seizure System, which eliminates duplicate reporting of a seizure involving more than one federal agency]

DRUG	1990	1991	1992	1993	1994	1995	1996
AMOUNTS (lbs.)							
Total......................	**737,318**	**926,635**	**1,093,334**	**1,046,203**	**1,355,646**	**1,575,579**	**1,720,509**
Heroin	1,794	3,030	2,551	3,514	2,887	2,567	3,378
Cocaine	235,214	246,324	303,260	244,302	309,709	234,097	254,191
Marijuana....................	483,248	499,070	783,475	772,307	1,041,425	1,306,895	1,429,922
Hashish	17,062	178,211	4,048	26,080	1,625	32,020	33,018
PERCENT CHANGE FROM PRIOR YEAR SHOWN [1]							
Heroin	-25.7	68.9	-15.8	37.7	-17.8	-11.1	31.6
Cocaine	7.6	4.7	23.1	-19.4	26.8	-24.4	8.6
Marijuana....................	-54.9	3.3	57.0	-1.4	34.8	25.5	9.4
Hashish	-66.9	944.5	-97.7	544.3	-93.8	1870.4	3.1

[1] For 1990, change from 1989.

Source: U.S. Bureau of Justice Statistics, *Fact Sheet: Drug Data Summary*, July 1994, series NCJ-148213; and unpublished data.

No. 359. Authorized Intercepts of Communication—Summary: 1980 to 1996

[Data for jurisdictions with statutes authorizing or approving interception of wire or oral communication]

ITEM	1980	1985	1987	1988	1989	1990	1991	1992	1993	1994	1995	1996
Jurisdictions: [1]												
With wiretap statutes	28	32	33	34	37	40	41	41	41	41	41	46
Reporting interceptions	22	22	22	23	25	25	23	23	23	18	19	24
Intercept applications autho-rized	564	784	673	738	763	872	856	919	976	1,154	1,058	1,149
Intercept installations........	524	722	634	678	720	812	802	846	938	1,100	1,024	1,035
Federal	79	235	233	286	305	321	349	332	444	549	527	574
State...................	445	487	401	392	415	491	453	514	494	551	497	461
Intercepted communications, average [2]	1,058	1,320	1,299	1,251	1,656	1,487	1,584	1,861	1,801	2,139	2,028	1,969
Incriminating	315	275	230	316	337	321	290	347	364	373	459	422
Persons arrested [3]	1,871	2,469	2,226	2,486	2,804	2,057	2,364	2,685	2,428	2,852	2,577	2,464
Convictions [3]	259	660	506	543	706	420	605	607	413	772	494	502
Major offense specified:												
Gambling	199	206	135	126	111	116	98	66	96	86	95	114
Drugs..................	282	434	379	435	471	520	536	634	679	876	732	821
Homicide and assault	13	25	18	14	20	21	21	35	28	19	30	41
Other	70	119	141	163	161	204	201	184	173	173	201	173

[1] Jurisdictions include federal government, states, and District of Columbia. [2] Average per authorized installation. [3] Based on information received from intercepts installed in year shown; additional arrests/convictions will occur in subsequent years but are not shown here.

Source: Administrative Office of the U.S. Courts, *Report on Applications for Orders Authorizing or Approving the Interception of Wire, Oral or Electronic Communications* (Wiretap Report), annual.

No. 360. U.S. Population Who Had Face-to-Face Contact With Police, by Race and Ethnicity, and Reason for Contact: 1996

[Persons having multiple contacts or more than one reason for any single contact appear in table more than once; therefore, may not add to total. Covers persons 12 years old and over. Based on the Police-Public Contact Survey of 6,421 persons; data subject to sampling variability]

REASON FOR CONTACT	NUMBER HAVING CONTACT (1,000)				PERCENT HAVING CONTACT			
	Total	White	Black	Hispanic [1]	Total	White	Black	Hispanic [1]
Population total	**215,529**	**163,883**	**25,394**	**17,159**	(X)	(X)	(X)	(X)
For any reason	44,556	36,262	3,964	2,593	20.7	22.1	15.6	15.1
I reported a crime.	12,722	10,640	1,049	634	5.9	6.5	4.1	3.7
I asked police for help.	10,087	8,393	744	500	4.7	5.1	2.9	2.9
I reported a problem.	7,892	6,449	508	557	3.7	3.9	2.0	3.2
Police ticketed me	10,947	8,988	815	865	5.1	5.5	3.2	5.0
I was in a traffic accident.	5,454	4,501	501	241	2.5	2.7	2.0	1.4
I witnessed an accident.	2,326	2,007	151	102	1.1	1.2	0.6	0.6
I was the victim of a crime	6,755	5,753	343	360	3.1	3.5	1.4	2.1
I witnessed a crime.	3,467	2,776	419	179	1.6	1.7	1.6	1.0
Police suspected me of a crime	2,611	1,945	197	326	1.2	1.2	0.8	1.9
Police asked why I was there	2,690	2,070	361	84	1.2	1.3	1.4	0.5
Police had a warrant for my arrest. . . .	492	378	84	30	0.2	0.2	0.3	0.2
I had a casual encounter	8,042	6,901	640	327	3.7	4.2	2.5	1.9
I attended a community meeting	2,437	1,986	285	32	1.1	1.2	1.1	0.2
Some other reason.	14,066	11,760	1,075	724	6.5	3.9	2.0	3.2

X Not applicable.   [1] Persons of Hispanic origin may be of any race.

Source: U.S. Bureau of Justice Statistics, *Police Use of Force, National Collection of Data*, November 1997.

No. 361. Full-Time Sworn Police Officers in State and Local Government— Number and Rate: 1996

[**In thousands, except rate per 10,000 population.** As of **June.** Rate based on Bureau of the Census estimated resident population as of July 1]

STATE	Number [1]	Rate per 10,000 [2]	TYPE OF AGENCY			STATE	Number [1]	Rate per 10,000 [2]	TYPE OF AGENCY		
			Local	State	Sheriff				Local	State	Sheriff
U.S.	**663,535**	**25**	**410,956**	**54,587**	**152,922**	MO	12,998	24	8,836	996	2,421
AL	9,767	23	6,484	581	1,963	MT	1,682	19	690	212	616
AK	1,254	21	740	290	-	NE	3,297	20	1,929	464	794
AZ	10,088	23	6,967	952	1,563	NV	4,363	27	2,565	375	935
AR	5,819	23	3,244	522	1,410	NH	2,305	20	1,862	245	129
CA	69,134	22	35,939	6,219	22,869	NJ	28,058	35	19,891	2,702	3,145
CO	9,896	26	5,451	581	3,324	NM	4,134	24	2,462	435	889
CT	8,525	26	6,411	1,022	886	NY	71,221	39	54,657	3,972	5,852
DE	1,660	23	923	540	24	NC	16,953	23	9,505	1,380	5,264
DC	3,909	72	3,587	-	-	ND	1,141	18	561	120	364
FL.	37,395	26	19,652	1,740	14,124	OH	23,811	21	15,932	1,391	5,179
GA	19,115	26	10,241	878	6,752	OK	7,232	22	4,951	756	1,014
HI	2,989	25	2,746	-	-	OR	6,064	19	3,245	824	1,921
ID	2,524	21	1,142	192	1,053	PA	24,873	21	17,655	4,114	1,239
IL	38,192	32	26,151	1,988	8,426	RI	2,422	24	1,958	193	153
IN	10,931	19	6,426	1,207	2,618	SC	8,675	23	4,004	892	3,037
IA	5,043	18	3,037	433	1,343	SD	1,464	20	847	155	344
KS	6,183	24	3,616	552	1,683	TN	12,152	23	7,076	768	3,520
KY	6,466	17	4,089	984	1,113	TX	47,767	25	28,269	2,873	11,326
LA	16,125	37	5,733	873	8,720	UT	3,699	18	1,882	355	1,198
ME	2,318	19	1,426	337	321	VT	981	17	548	290	87
MD	13,828	27	8,923	1,625	1,438	VA	18,448	28	8,911	1,662	6,605
MA	17,935	29	13,068	2,565	1,540	WA	9,292	17	5,430	906	2,553
MI	20,568	21	13,288	2,164	4,435	WV	2,977	16	1,416	595	726
MN	7,994	17	5,006	484	2,139	WI	12,678	25	7,640	497	3,886
MS	5,813	21	3,326	535	1,474	WY	1,377	29	618	151	507

- Represents zero.   [1] Includes special police not shown separately.   [2] Based on resident population as of July 1.

Source: U.S. Bureau of Justice Statistics, *Census of State and Local Law Enforcement Agencies, 1996*, series NCJ 164618, June 1998.

No. 362. General Purpose Law Enforcement Agencies—Number, Employment, and Expenditures: 1993

[Includes both full-time and part-time employees. State police data are based on the 49 main state police agencies; Hawaii does not have a state police agency. Expenditure data cover fiscal years ending in year stated]

TYPE OF AGENCY	Number of agencies [1]	NUMBER OF EMPLOYEES						Operating expenditures (bil. dol.)
		Full-time			Part-time			
		Total	Sworn	Civilian	Total	Sworn	Civilian	
Total	17,120	828,435	622,913	205,522	87,875	42,890	44,985	41.9
Local police	12,361	474,072	373,554	100,518	58,146	28,186	29,960	24.3
Sheriff	3,084	224,236	155,815	68,421	19,660	11,048	8,612	10.7
State police	49	76,972	51,874	25,098	845	228	617	4.2
Special police	1,626	53,156	41,670	11,485	9,224	3,428	5,796	2.8

[1] The number of agencies reported here is the result of a weighted sample and not an exact enumeration.

Source: U.S. Bureau of Justice Statistics, *Local Police Departments, 1993*, April 1996.

No. 363. Federal Agencies Employing 500 or More Full-Time Officers With Authority to Carry Firearms and Make Arrests—Number of Officers: 1993 and 1996

[As of December]

AGENCY	1993	1996
All agencies [1]	68,825	74,493
U.S. Customs Service	10,120	9,749
Federal Bureau of Investigation	10,075	10,389
Federal Bureau of Prisons	9,984	11,329
Immigration and Naturalization Service.	9,466	12,403
Administrative Office of the U.S. Courts	3,763	2,777
Internal Revenue Service	3,621	3,784
U.S. Postal Inspection Service	3,587	3,576
Drug Enforcement Administration	2,813	2,946
U.S. Secret Service	2,186	3,185
National Park Service	2,160	2,148
U.S. Marshals Service.	2,153	2,650
Bureau of Alcohol, Tobacco and Firearms	1,959	1,869
U.S. Capitol Police	1,080	1,031
U.S. Forest Service	732	619
GSA - Federal Protective Services.	732	643
U.S. Fish and Wildlife Service.	620	869

[1] Includes agencies not shown separately.

Source: U.S. Bureau of Justice Statistics, *Federal Law Enforcement Officers, 1993* and *1996*.

No. 364. Law Enforcement Officers Killed and Assaulted: 1988 to 1996

[Covers officers killed feloniously and accidentally in line of duty; includes federal officers. For composition of regions, see inside front cover]

ITEM	1988	1989	1990	1991	1992	1993	1994	1995	1996
OFFICERS KILLED									
Total killed	155	145	133	124	129	129	141	131	100
Northeast	17	23	13	16	16	12	17	16	16
Midwest	18	22	20	26	15	27	30	19	21
South.	77	67	69	55	68	57	50	61	46
West	39	23	23	18	23	22	30	32	16
Puerto Rico	-	8	8	8	7	11	9	2	1
Outlying areas, foreign countries	4	2	-	1	-	-	5	1	-
ASSAULTS									
Population (1,000) [1]	186,418	189,641	199,065	191,397	217,997	210,658	221,572	194,781	166,038
Number of—									
Agencies represented	8,866	9,213	9,483	9,263	10,862	9,809	10,626	8,938	7,808
Police officers.	369,743	380,232	412,314	405,069	460,430	454,105	480,343	421,414	373,575
Total assaulted	58,752	62,172	71,794	62,852	81,252	66,975	64,912	56,686	46,695
Firearm	2,759	3,154	3,662	3,532	4,455	4,002	3,168	2,238	1,887
Knife or cutting instrument . . .	1,367	1,379	1,641	1,493	2,095	1,574	1,513	1,301	871
Other dangerous weapon . . .	5,573	5,778	7,390	7,014	8,604	7,551	7,210	6,299	5,084
Hands, fists, feet, etc	49,053	51,861	59,101	50,813	66,098	53,848	53,021	46,848	38,853

- Represents zero. [1] Represents the number of persons covered by agencies shown.

Source: U.S. Federal Bureau of Investigation, *Law Enforcement Officers Killed and Assaulted*, annual.

No. 365. U.S. Supreme Court—Cases Filed and Disposition: 1980 to 1996

[Statutory term of court begins first Monday in **October**]

ACTION	1980	1985	1990	1991	1992	1993	1994	1995	1996
Total cases on docket	**5,144**	**5,158**	**6,316**	**6,770**	**7,245**	**7,786**	**8,100**	**7,565**	**7,602**
Appellate cases on docket	2,749	2,571	2,351	2,451	2,441	2,442	2,515	2,456	2,430
From prior term	527	400	365	365	379	342	377	361	375
Docketed during present term	2,222	2,171	1,986	2,086	2,062	2,100	2,138	2,095	2,055
Cases acted upon [1]	2,324	2,185	2,042	2,125	2,140	2,099	2,185	2,130	2,124
Granted review	167	166	114	103	83	78	83	92	74
Denied, dismissed, or withdrawn	1,999	1,863	1,802	1,914	1,920	1,947	2,016	1,945	1,955
Summarily decided	90	78	81	52	84	34	52	62	66
Cases not acted upon	425	386	309	326	301	343	330	326	306
Pauper cases on docket	2,371	2,577	3,951	4,307	4,792	5,332	5,574	5,098	5,165
Cases acted upon	2,027	2,189	3,436	3,768	4,261	4,621	4,983	4,514	4,613
Granted review	17	20	27	17	14	21	10	13	13
Denied, dismissed, or withdrawn	1,968	2,136	3,369	3,716	4,209	4,566	4,955	4,439	4,582
Summarily decided	32	24	28	22	25	30	14	55	15
Cases not acted upon	344	388	515	539	531	711	591	584	552
Original cases on docket	24	10	14	12	12	12	11	11	7
Cases disposed of during term	7	2	3	1	1	1	2	5	2
Total cases available for argument .	**264**	**276**	**201**	**196**	**166**	**145**	**136**	**145**	**140**
Cases disposed of	162	175	131	130	120	105	97	93	92
Cases argued	154	171	125	127	116	99	94	90	90
Cases dismissed or remanded without argument	8	4	6	3	4	6	3	3	2
Cases remaining	102	101	70	66	46	40	39	52	48
Cases decided by signed opinion	144	161	121	120	111	93	91	87	87
Cases decided by per curiam opinion	8	10	4	3	4	6	3	3	3
Number of signed opinions	123	146	112	107	107	84	82	75	80

[1] Includes cases granted review and carried over to next term, not shown separately.

Source: Office of the Clerk, Supreme Court of the United States, unpublished data.

No. 366. U.S. Courts of Appeals—Cases Commenced and Disposition: 1980 to 1996

[For years ending **June 30**]

ITEM	1980	1985	1990	1991	1992	1993	1994	1995	1996
Cases commenced [1]	23,200	33,360	40,898	42,033	46,032	49,770	48,815	49,671	51,524
Criminal	4,405	4,989	9,493	9,949	10,956	11,885	11,052	10,171	10,653
U.S. civil	4,654	6,744	6,626	6,663	7,113	7,758	7,518	7,761	8,681
Private civil	10,200	16,827	20,490	20,798	22,862	24,030	24,781	25,992	27,188
Administrative appeals . . .	2,950	3,179	2,578	2,764	3,052	3,824	3,560	3,345	2,858
Cases terminated [1]	20,887	31,387	38,520	41,414	42,933	47,466	48,546	50,085	49,359
Criminal	3,993	4,892	7,509	9,198	9,830	11,043	11,519	11,320	9,995
U.S. civil	4,346	6,363	6,379	6,579	6,797	7,462	7,637	7,710	7,831
Private civil	8,942	15,743	20,369	20,698	21,628	23,437	23,943	25,574	25,999
Administrative appeals . .	2,643	2,760	2,582	3,148	2,801	3,464	3,480	3,254	3,131
Cases disposed of [2]	10,607	16,369	21,006	22,707	23,162	25,567	26,475	28,187	26,988
Affirmed or granted	8,017	12,286	16,629	17,988	18,463	20,604	21,371	22,825	21,696
Reversed or denied	1,845	2,770	2,565	2,503	2,681	2,514	2,636	2,679	2,533
Other	745	1,313	1,812	2,216	2,018	2,449	2,468	2,683	2,759
Median months [3]	8.9	10.3	10.1	10.2	10.5	10.4	10.5	10.5	10.3

[1] Includes original proceedings and bankruptcy appeals not shown separately.   [2] Terminated on the merits after hearing or submission.   [3] Prior to 1985, the figure is from filing of complete record to final disposition; beginning 1985, figure is from filing notice of appeal to final disposition. For definition of median, see Guide to Tabular Presentation.

No. 367. U.S. District Courts—Civil and Criminal Cases: 1980 to 1996

[In thousands, except percent. For years ending **June 30**]

ITEM	1980	1985	1990	1991	1992	1993	1994	1995	1996
Civil cases: Commenced	168.8	273.7	217.9	207.7	226.9	228.6	236.0	239.0	272.7
Cases terminated [1]	155.0	268.6	213.4	211.7	239.6	225.2	228.9	226.1	246.4
No court action	68.7	129.4	51.6	44.6	51.4	44.0	40.5	37.0	36.8
Court action, total	86.2	139.2	161.8	166.5	187.6	181.2	188.4	189.1	209.6
Before pretrial	53.8	95.5	127.0	136.9	153.4	152.3	159.6	161.6	183.3
Pretrial	22.4	31.1	25.5	21.1	26.2	21.1	21.0	19.7	18.8
Trials	10.1	12.6	9.2	8.4	8.0	7.9	7.8	7.7	7.5
Percent reaching trial . . .	6.5	4.7	4.3	4.0	3.4	3.5	3.4	3.4	3.1
Criminal cases: Commenced [2]	28.0	38.5	46.5	45.1	47.5	45.7	44.9	44.2	47.1
Defendants disposed of [3]	36.6	47.4	56.5	56.7	58.4	59.5	61.2	55.3	59.5
Not convicted	8.0	8.8	9.8	10.0	10.0	9.2	10.0	9.0	8.5
Convicted	28.6	38.5	46.7	46.8	48.4	50.4	51.1	46.3	51.0
Imprisonment	13.2	18.7	27.8	29.2	31.1	34.2	34.5	31.7	36.5
Probation	11.1	14.4	14.2	13.8	13.1	12.6	12.8	11.5	11.6
Fine and other	4.4	5.4	4.7	3.8	4.3	3.7	3.9	3.2	2.9

[1] Excludes land condemnation cases.   [2] Excludes transfers.   [3] Includes Guam, Virgin Islands, and Northern Mariana Islands; 1980 includes Canal Zone.

Source of Tables 366 and 367: Administrative Office of the U.S. Courts, *Statistical Tables for the Federal Judiciary,* annual.

No. 368. U.S. District Courts—Civil Cases Commenced and Pending: 1993 to 1996

[For years ending June 30]

TYPE OF CASE	CASES COMMENCED				CASES PENDING			
	1993	1994	1995	1996	1993	1994	1995	1996
Cases total [1]	**228,562**	**235,996**	**239,013**	**272,661**	**215,574**	**217,963**	**224,378**	**250,233**
Contract actions [1]	38,240	31,988	31,619	33,413	40,525	29,697	27,337	29,934
Recovery of overpayments [2]	7,255	2,591	2,099	3,583	5,995	1,227	1,041	2,379
Real property actions	8,436	7,468	7,282	6,276	7,743	5,855	5,073	4,554
Tort actions	40,939	48,067	44,511	67,029	45,148	47,186	52,334	69,309
Personal injury	37,409	44,734	41,102	63,222	41,324	43,638	48,789	65,527
Personal injury product liability [1]	16,545	23,977	17,631	38,170	15,208	20,694	24,166	37,261
Asbestos	4,900	7,111	6,821	6,760	7,154	3,704	3,524	4,503
Other personal injury	20,864	20,757	23,471	25,052	26,116	22,944	24,623	28,266
Personal property damage	3,530	3,333	3,409	3,807	3,824	3,548	3,545	3,782
Actions under statutes [1]	140,811	148,344	155,495	165,922	121,964	135,020	139,487	146,303
Civil rights [1]	26,483	31,521	35,566	40,476	26,477	33,271	37,512	42,961
Employment	12,221	15,256	18,225	22,150	12,530	17,359	20,375	24,428
Bankruptcy suits	6,192	5,675	5,138	4,737	4,203	4,705	4,541	4,087
Commerce (ICC rates, etc.)	1,475	1,228	613	1,622	1,238	693	446	795
Environmental matters	1,077	1,059	1,136	1,158	1,943	1,864	1,823	1,866
Prisoner petitions	52,454	56,283	62,597	69,352	39,512	45,417	47,382	51,428
Forfeiture and penalty	4,832	3,548	2,670	2,255	4,850	3,359	2,399	2,058
Labor laws	16,174	15,800	15,030	15,068	13,026	12,346	11,829	11,942
Protected property rights [3]	6,202	7,051	6,990	6,800	5,281	5,963	5,998	6,387
Securities commodities and exchanges	1,875	1,742	1,870	1,741	3,983	3,130	2,969	2,881
Social Security laws	11,602	11,142	10,168	8,517	8,304	12,302	11,310	9,226
Tax suits	2,267	2,275	2,144	2,078	2,255	1,884	1,692	1,669
Freedom of information	425	566	481	465	498	502	500	497

[1] Includes other types not shown separately.   [2] Includes enforcement of judgments in student loan cases, and overpayments of veterans benefits.   [3] Includes copyright, patent, and trademark rights.

Source: Administrative Office of the U.S. Courts, *Statistical Tables for the Federal Judiciary,* annual.

No. 369. U.S. District Courts—Offenders Convicted and Sentenced to Prison, and Length of Sentence: 1996

MOST SERIOUS OFFENSE OF CONVICTION	Offenders convicted	Convicted offenders sentenced to prison	Length of sentence (mo.)	MOST SERIOUS OFFENSE OF CONVICTION	Offenders convicted	Convicted offenders sentenced to prison	Length of sentence (mo.)
Total [1]	**53,076**	**36,373**	**61.2**	Drug offenses [2]	19,020	16,492	82.4
				Possession	1,791	1,209	51.9
Violent offenses	2,870	2,475	90.7	Trafficking and manufacturing	17,229	15,283	84.8
Property offenses	14,179	7,192	22.5	Public-order offenses	16,978	10,206	47.5
Fraudulent offenses [2]	10,512	5,751	19.7	Regulatory offenses	1,677	737	25.8
Embezzlement	1,207	521	15.8	Other offenses	15,301	9,469	49.1
Fraud [3]	8,096	4,597	20.5	Weapons	3,435	2,785	99.4
Forgery	299	136	13.4	Immigration	5,308	4,492	22.1
Other offenses [2]	3,667	1,441	33.6	Tax law violations [4]	800	339	30.3
Larceny	2,618	805	22.2				

[1] Total may include offenders for whom offense category could not be determined.   [2] Includes offenses not shown separately.   [3] Excludes tax fraud.   [4] Includes tax fraud.

Source: U.S. Bureau of Justice Statistics, *Compendium of Federal Justice Statistics,* annual.

No. 370. Federal Prosecutions of Public Corruption: 1980 to 1996

[As of Dec. 31. Prosecution of persons who have corrupted public office in violation of Federal Criminal Statutes]

PROSECUTION STATUS	1980	1985	1987	1988	1989	1990	1991	1992	1993	1994	1995	1996
Total: [1] Indicted	727	1,157	1,276	1,274	1,348	1,176	1,452	1,189	1,371	1,165	1,051	952
Convicted	602	997	1,081	1,067	1,149	1,084	1,194	1,081	1,362	969	878	878
Awaiting trial	213	256	368	288	375	300	346	380	403	332	323	240
Federal officials: Indicted	123	563	651	629	695	615	803	624	627	571	527	440
Convicted	131	470	545	529	610	583	665	532	595	488	438	450
Awaiting trial	16	90	118	86	126	103	149	139	133	124	120	64
State officials: Indicted	72	79	102	66	71	96	115	84	113	99	61	66
Convicted	51	66	76	69	54	79	77	92	133	97	61	55
Awaiting trial	28	20	26	14	18	28	42	24	39	17	23	21
Local officials: Indicted	247	248	246	276	269	257	242	232	309	248	236	232
Convicted	168	221	204	229	201	225	180	211	272	202	191	190
Awaiting trial	82	49	89	79	122	98	88	91	132	96	89	74

[1] Includes individuals who are neither public officials nor employees but who were involved with public officials or employees in violating the law, not shown separately.

Source: U.S. Department of Justice, *Federal Prosecutions of Corrupt Public Officials, 1970-1980* and *Report to Congress on the Activities and Operations of the Public Integrity Section,* annual.

No. 371. Delinquency Cases Disposed by Juvenile Courts, by Reason for Referral: 1985 to 1995

[In thousands. A delinquency offense is an act committed by a juvenile for which an adult could be prosecuted in a criminal court. Disposition of a case involves taking a definite action such as waiving the case to criminal court, dismissing the case, placing the youth on probation, placing the youth in a facility for delinquents, or such actions as fines, restitution, and community service]

REASON FOR REFERRAL	1985	1986	1987	1988	1989	1990	1991	1992	1993	1994	1995
All delinquency offenses .	**1,112**	**1,180**	**1,181**	**1,190**	**1,236**	**1,320**	**1,413**	**1,485**	**1,515**	**1,607**	**1,714**
Case rate [1]	42.2	45.5	46.0	46.8	48.9	51.5	54.2	55.6	55.6	57.9	60.7
Violent offenses.	67	71	66	70	80	97	109	121	124	135	142
Criminal homicide.	1	2	1	2	2	2	2	2	3	3	3
Forcible rape	4	5	4	4	5	5	6	6	7	6	7
Robbery	26	26	22	22	23	28	31	33	35	37	40
Aggravated assault	36	39	38	43	51	62	70	79	80	88	93
Property offenses.	489	518	519	518	545	565	614	618	593	594	623
Burglary	139	142	134	132	136	146	154	158	149	142	140
Larceny	307	327	331	325	334	342	381	381	374	382	419
Motor vehicle theft	36	43	48	55	68	71	72	71	63	61	53
Arson	7	6	6	7	7	7	7	8	8	9	10
Delinquency offenses	555	590	595	601	611	658	691	747	798	878	949
Simple assault	92	101	105	109	114	128	139	155	171	184	205
Vandalism	84	87	86	84	85	100	112	119	119	124	122
Drug law violations	76	72	72	81	78	71	65	73	91	125	159
Obstruction of justice.	68	72	74	75	77	80	76	80	90	102	110
Other [2]	235	258	258	253	256	278	298	320	328	343	353

[1] Number of cases disposed per 1,000 youth (ages 10 to 17) at risk.   [2] Includes such offenses as stolen property offenses, trespassing, weapons offenses, other sex offenses, liquor law violations, disorderly conduct, and miscellaneous offenses.

Source: National Center for Juvenile Justice, Pittsburgh, PA, *Juvenile Court Statistics*, annual.

No. 372. Delinquency Cases and Case Rates, by Sex and Race: 1986 to 1995

[A delinquency offense is an act committed by a juvenile for which an adult could be prosecuted in a criminal court. Disposition of a case involves taking a definite action such as waiving the case to criminal court, dismissing the case, placing the youth on probation, placing the youth in a facility for delinquents, or such actions as fines, restitution, and community service. Offenses may not add to toal sex and race categories due to rounding]

SEX, RACE, AND OFFENSE	NUMBER OF CASES			CASE RATE [1]		
	1986	1991	1995	1986	1991	1995
Male, total	**955,900**	**1,146,900**	**1,338,600**	**71.9**	**85.8**	**92.4**
Person	152,900	221,700	285,400	11.5	16.6	19.7
Property	580,100	686,900	676,300	43.6	51.4	46.7
Drugs	60,000	57,200	137,000	4.5	4.3	9.5
Public order	163,000	181,100	239,900	12.3	13.5	16.6
Female, total	**224,100**	**266,300**	**375,800**	**17.7**	**21.0**	**27.3**
Person	37,400	55,900	91,900	3.0	4.4	6.7
Property	129,900	159,800	195,400	10.3	12.6	14.2
Drugs	12,400	7,900	22,200	1.0	0.6	1.6
Public order	44,400	42,700	66,300	3.5	3.4	4.8
White, total	**844,300**	**927,900**	**1,127,800**	**40.0**	**44.4**	**50.0**
Person	109,900	156,700	219,600	5.2	7.5	9.7
Property	524,400	594,600	609,500	24.9	28.4	27.0
Drugs	53,700	32,100	102,100	2.5	1.5	4.5
Public order	156,300	144,600	196,600	7.4	6.9	8.7
Black, total	**304,700**	**439,300**	**522,900**	**79.3**	**112.0**	**123.7**
Person	76,000	112,400	145,000	19.8	28.7	34.3
Property	165,700	223,100	224,900	43.2	56.9	53.2
Drugs	17,100	31,600	53,500	4.4	8.1	12.7
Public order	46,000	72,300	99,600	12.0	18.4	23.6
Other races, total	**31,000**	**46,000**	**63,600**	**30.7**	**37.2**	**44.0**
Person	4,400	8,500	12,700	4.4	6.9	8.8
Property	19,900	29,100	37,300	19.7	23.6	25.8
Drugs	1,600	1,400	3,500	1.6	1.1	2.4
Public order	5,100	7,000	10,100	5.0	5.7	7.0

[1] Cases per 1,000 youth at risk.

Source: National Center for Juvenile Justice, Pittsburgh, PA, *Juvenile Court Statistics*, annual.

No. 373. Child Abuse and Neglect Cases Substantiated and Indicated— Victim Characteristics: 1990 to 1996

[Based on reports alleging child abuse and neglect that were referred for investigation by the respective child protective services agency in each state. The reporting period may be either calendar or fiscal year. The majority of states provided duplicated counts. Also, varying number of states reported the various characteristics presented below. A substantiated case represents a type of investigation disposition that determines that there is sufficient evidence under state law to conclude that maltreatment occurred or that the child is at risk of maltreatment. An indicated case represents a type of disposition that concludes that there was a reason to suspect maltreatment had occurred]

ITEM	1990		1994		1995		1996	
	Number	Percent	Number	Percent	Number	Percent	Number	Percent
TYPES OF SUBSTANTIATED MALTREATMENT								
Victims, total [1][2]	690,658	(X)	1,011,595	(X)	970,285	100.0	969,018	100.0
Neglect	338,770	49.1	520,550	51.5	507,015	52.3	500,032	51.6
Physical abuse	186,801	27.0	241,338	23.9	237,840	24.5	229,332	23.7
Sexual abuse	119,506	17.3	136,362	13.5	122,964	12.7	119,397	12.3
Emotional maltreatment	45,621	6.6	47,337	4.7	42,051	4.3	55,473	5.7
Medical Neglect	(NA)	(NA)	24,593	2.4	28,541	2.9	25,758	2.7
SEX OF VICTIM								
Victims, total [2]	794,101	100.0	903,195	100.0	809,634	100.0	808,370	100.0
Male	357,367	45.0	420,817	46.6	381,075	47.1	384,280	47.5
Female	405,409	51.1	472,535	52.3	425,193	52.5	419,656	51.9
AGE OF VICTIM								
Victims, total [2]	807,965	100.0	901,573	100.0	808,575	100.0	807,854	100.0
1 year and younger	106,507	13.2	119,203	13.2	103,335	12.8	101,055	12.5
2 to 5 years old	192,018	23.8	240,925	26.7	215,303	26.6	208,754	25.8
6 to 9 years old	175,609	21.7	210,334	23.3	195,400	24.2	200,888	24.9
10 to 13 years old	150,507	18.6	172,800	19.2	154,682	19.1	158,247	19.6
14 to 17 years old	116,015	14.4	132,566	14.7	121,548	15.0	123,872	15.3
18 and over	5,464	0.7	6,821	0.8	7,506	0.9	6,466	0.8

NA Not available.   X Not applicable.   [1] More than one type of maltreatment may be substantiated per child. Therefore, totals for this category will add up to more than 100 percent. Victim totals and maltreatment types are based on subset of states which reported both the number of child victims and maltreatment incidences by type for that year. [2] Includes other and unknown not shown separately.

No. 374. Child Abuse and Neglect Cases Reported and Investigated, by State: 1996

[Based on reports alleging child abuse and neglect that were referred for investigation by the respective child protective services agency in each state. The reporting period may be either calendar or fiscal year. The majority of states were unable to provide unduplicated counts. Only nine jurisdictions (Alaska, Hawaii, Michigan, Montana, Ohio, Oregon, South Carolina, Vermont, and Washington) provided unduplicated counts of children subject of report. Excludes the Armed Forces]

STATE	Population under 18 years old	REPORTS Number of reports[1]	REPORTS Number of children subject of a report	Investigation disposition, number of children substantiated[2]	STATE	Population under 18 years old	REPORTS Number of reports[1]	REPORTS Number of children subject of a report	Investigation disposition, number of children substantiated[2]
U.S.	69,048,323	2,050,801	3,031,597	969,018	MO	1,394,199	52,548	83,875	23,522
AL	1,076,436	26,384	39,361	18,640	MT	232,751	8,943	17,732	3,664
AK	184,387	[3]10,100	10,100	7,544	NE	442,186	8,346	16,749	3,612
AZ	1,150,186	28,418	46,716	20,603	NV	416,750	13,558	21,838	8,135
AR	659,448	20,121	38,211	8,571	NH	295,866	6,160	8,337	1,063
CA	8,866,413	370,521	463,072	182,160	NJ	1,986,972	[3]67,817	67,817	10,537
CO	997,938	30,960	49,867	6,906	NM	501,233	[3]28,661	28,661	8,845
CT	797,950	33,152	49,344	19,906	NY	4,540,534	141,376	236,241	70,602
DE	176,015	5,335	9,751	2,337	NC	1,833,617	60,687	102,168	33,133
DC	109,559	5,022	12,018	5,867	ND	168,643	4,341	7,292	270
FL	3,423,067	124,354	184,442	74,587	OH	2,847,841	95,514	154,202	56,336
GA	1,952,456	51,981	87,006	48,572	OK	880,796	[3]40,916	40,916	11,646
HI	306,523	[3]5,384	5,384	2,555	OR	808,406	24,515	39,486	9,238
ID [2]	348,509	11,987	32,496	8,816	PA	2,894,676	[3]23,666	23,666	6,183
IL [2]	3,155,905	70,222	124,129	43,973	RI	235,283	8,699	14,160	4,181
IN	1,498,524	43,744	66,097	22,861	SC	937,765	20,389	39,063	8,917
IA	719,339	22,131	32,801	9,967	SD	204,156	[3]9,051	9,051	2,617
KS	687,314	[3]30,552	30,552	3,264	TN	1,322,161	[3]34,293	34,293	11,439
KY	968,660	39,241	60,896	27,293	TX	5,452,277	99,780	151,261	44,704
LA	1,233,455	27,950	45,981	14,911	UT	678,803	18,858	24,857	8,538
ME	299,519	4,470	9,616	4,656	VT	146,648	2,259	2,561	1,221
MD	1,286,190	29,900	48,160	(NA)	VA	1,631,836	34,630	53,271	10,280
MA	1,421,929	35,505	60,199	27,219	WA	1,436,804	33,913	47,631	20,033
MI	2,537,014	58,655	142,700	21,073	WV	421,933	16,439	26,478	(NA)
MN	1,247,008	16,685	25,435	10,200	WI	1,343,034	[3]45,479	45,479	16,667
MS	756,134	18,116	29,179	(NA)	WY	133,275	3,821	6,154	895

NA Not available.   [1] Except as noted, reports are on incident/family based basis or based on number of reported incidents regardless of the number of children involved in the incidents.   [2] Type of investigation disposition that determines that there is sufficient evidence under state law to conclude that maltreatment occurred or that the child is at risk of maltreatment. [3] Child-based report that enumerates each child who is a subject of a report.

Source of Tables 373 and 374: U.S. Department of Health and Human Services, National Center on Child Abuse and Neglect, National Child Abuse and Neglect Data System, *Child Maltreatment 1996: Reports From the States to the National Child Abuse and Neglect System,* April 1998.

No. 375. Jail Inmates, by Race and Detention Status: 1986 to 1996

[Data are for midyear. Excludes federal and state prisons or other correctional institutions; institutions exclusively for juveniles; state-operated jails in Alaska, Connecticut, Delaware, Hawaii, Rhode Island, and Vermont; and other facilities which retain persons for less than 48 hours. As of **June 30.** Data for 1993 based on National Jail Census; for other years, based on sample survey and subject to sampling variability]

CHARACTERISTIC	1986	1990	1991	1992	1993	1994	1995	1996
Total inmates [1]	274,444	405,320	426,479	444,584	459,804	486,474	507,044	518,492
Percent of rated capacity. .	96	104	101	99	97	96	93	92
Male	251,235	368,002	386,865	403,768	415,576	437,600	455,400	462,400
Female	21,501	37,318	39,614	40,816	44,228	48,800	51,600	56,100
White [2]	159,178	186,989	190,333	191,362	180,914	253,500	266,200	288,900
Black [2]	112,522	174,335	187,618	195,156	203,463	224,900	232,000	221,000
Other races [2]	2,744	5,321	5,391	5,831	6,178	8,100	8,800	8,600
Hispanic [3]	38,422	57,449	60,129	62,961	69,200	74,900	74,400	81,000
Non-Hispanic.	236,022	347,871	366,350	381,623	390,600	411,600	432,600	437,500
Adult [4]	272,736	403,019	424,129	441,781	455,500	479,800	499,300	510,400
Juvenile [5]	1,708	2,301	2,350	2,804	4,300	6,700	7,800	8,100

[1] 1990 to 1993, includes 31,356, 38,675, 43,138, and 52,235 persons, respectively, of unknown race not shown separately. [2] Beginning 1993, data represent White, non-Hispanic and Black, non-Hispanic and rounded to nearest 100. [3] Hispanic persons may be of any race. Data for 1993 to 1996 are estimated and rounded to nearest 100. [4] Includes inmates not classified by conviction status. [5] Juveniles are persons defined by state statute as being under a certain age, usually 18, and subject initially to juvenile court authority even if tried as adults in criminal court. In 1994 the definition was changed to include all persons under age 18.

Source: U.S. Bureau of Justice Statistics, through 1994, *Jail Inmates*, annual; beginning 1995, *Prison and Jail Inmates at Midyear*, annual.

No. 376. State and Federal Correctional Facilities—Inmates and Staff: 1990 and 1995

[Covers all state and federal correctional institutions or places of confinement such as prisons, prison farms, boot camps, and community based halfway houses and work release centers. Excludes jails and other regional detention centers, private facilities, facilities for the military, Immigration and Naturalization Service, Bureau of Indian Affairs, U.S. Marshall Service, and correctional hospital wards not operated by correctional authorities]

CHARACTERISTIC	1990	1995	Percent change, 1990-95	CHARACTERISTIC	1990	1995	Percent change, 1990-95
FACILITIES				Male.	675,624	961,210	42.3
Total	**1,287**	**1,500**	**16.6**	Female	40,025	62,362	55.8
Type of facility:				Type of facility:			
Confinement [1]	1,037	1,196	15.3	Confinement.	698,570	992,333	42.1
Community.	250	304	21.6	Community.	17,079	31,239	82.9
Federal	80	125	56.3	Federal	56,821	81,930	44.2
State.	1,207	1,375	13.9	State.	658,828	941,642	42.9
Size of facility:				Custody level:			
Fewer than 500.	816	854	4.7	Maximum/close/high.	150,205	202,174	34.6
500-999.	260	286	10.0	Medium	292,372	415,688	42.2
1,000-2,499	185	306	65.4	Minimum/low	219,907	366,227	66.5
2,500 or more.	26	54	107.7	Not classified	53,165	39,483	-25.7
Age of facility:				**STAFF**			
Less than 10 years	314	497	58.3	**Total**	**264,201**	**347,320**	**31.5**
10-19 years old.	163	273	67.5	Federal.	18,451	25,379	37.5
20-49 years old.	373	366	-1.9	State	245,750	321,941	31.0
50-99 years old.	379	310	-18.2	Custody/security staff	169,587	220,892	30.3
100 years old or more . . .	58	45	-22.4	**INMATES PER EMPLOYEE**			
Not reported	-	9	(NA)				
INMATES				All staff.	2.7	2.9	7.4
Total	**715,649**	**1,023,572**	**43.0**	Custody/security staff	4.2	4.6	9.5

- Represents or round to zero.   NA Not available.

Source: U.S. Bureau of Justice Statistics, *Census of State and Federal Correctional Facilities, 1995.*

No. 377. Federal and State Prisoners: 1970 to 1996

[Based on Bureau of the Census estimated resident population, as of **July 1.** Beginning 1980, includes all persons under jurisdiction of federal and state authorities rather than those in the custody of such authorities. Represents inmates sentenced to maximum term of more than a year]

YEAR	PRESENT AT END OF YEAR						RECEIVED FROM COURTS					
	All institutions		Federal		State		All institutions		Federal		State	
	Number	Rate [1]	Number	Rate [1]	Number	Rate [1]	Number	Rate [1]	Number	Rate [1]	Number	Rate [1]
1970 ...	196,429	96.7	20,038	9.8	176,391	86.8	79,351	39.1	12,047	5.9	67,304	33.1
1975 ...	240,593	113.3	24,131	11.4	216,462	102.0	129,573	61.0	16,770	7.9	112,803	53.1
1980 ...	315,974	139.2	20,611	9.1	295,363	130.1	142,122	62.7	10,907	4.8	131,215	57.9
1985 ...	480,568	216.5	32,695	13.6	447,873	187.6	198,499	82.7	15,368	6.4	183,131	76.3
1986 ...	522,084	230.4	36,531	15.0	485,553	201.4	219,382	91.0	16,067	7.0	203,315	84.0
1987 ...	560,812	229.0	39,523	16.0	521,289	214.2	241,887	99.0	16,260	7.0	225,627	92.0
1988 ...	603,732	244.0	42,738	17.0	560,994	227.0	261,242	106.0	15,932	6.4	245,310	99.3
1989 ...	680,907	274.3	47,168	19.0	633,739	255.3	316,215	127.4	18,388	7.4	297,827	120.0
1990 ...	739,980	295.0	50,403	20.1	689,577	274.9	(NA)	(NA)	(NA)	(NA)	323,069	128.8
1991 ...	789,610	309.6	56,696	22.2	732,914	287.3	(NA)	(NA)	(NA)	(NA)	317,237	124.4
1992 ...	846,277	331.8	65,706	25.8	780,571	306.0	(NA)	(NA)	(NA)	(NA)	334,301	130.3
1993 ...	932,074	359.4	74,399	28.8	857,675	330.7	(NA)	(NA)	(NA)	(NA)	(NA)	(NA)
1994 ...	1,016,691	388.6	79,795	30.5	936,896	358.1	345,035	131.9	23,956	9.2	321,079	122.7
1995 ...	1,085,022	411.0	83,663	31.7	1,001,359	379.3	361,464	136.9	23,972	9.1	337,492	127.8
1996 ...	1,136,819	426.6	88,815	33.3	1,048,004	393.3	353,893	132.8	27,346	10.3	326,547	122.5

NA Not available. [1] Rate per 100,000 estimated population.

Source: U.S. Bureau of Justice Statistics, *Prisoners in State and Federal Institutions on December 31,* annual.

No. 378. Prisoners Under Jurisdiction of State and Federal Correctional Authorities—Summary, by State: 1980 to 1996

[For years ending **December 31**]

SEX, JURISDIC-TION, AND STATE	1980	1990	1995	1996 Total	1996 Per-cent change, 1995-1996	SEX, JURISDIC-TION, AND STATE	1980	1990	1995	1996 Total	1996 Per-cent change, 1995-1996
U.S. [1] .	**329,821**	**773,919**	**1,125,874**	**1,180,524**	**4.9**	MI [3][4]	15,124	34,267	41,112	42,349	3.0
						MN.	2,001	3,176	4,846	5,158	6.4
Male.....	316,401	729,840	1,057,406	1,105,945	4.6	MS.	3,902	8,375	12,684	13,859	9.3
Female ...	13,420	44,079	68,468	74,579	8.9	MO	5,726	14,943	19,134	22,003	15.0
						MT.	739	1,425	1,999	2,293	14.7
Federal...	24,363	65,526	100,250	105,544	5.3	NE.	1,446	2,403	3,074	3,287	6.9
State	305,458	708,393	1,025,624	1,074,980	4.8	NV.	1,839	5,322	7,713	8,439	9.4
AL [2]	6,543	15,665	20,718	21,760	5.0	NH.	326	1,342	2,015	2,062	2.3
AK [2]	822	2,622	3,522	3,716	5.5	NJ	5,884	21,128	27,066	27,490	1.6
AZ [3]	4,372	14,261	21,341	22,493	5.4	NM......	1,279	3,187	4,078	4,724	15.8
AR......	2,911	7,322	8,910	9,407	5.6	NY......	21,815	54,895	68,486	69,709	1.8
CA......	24,569	97,309	135,646	146,049	7.7	NC......	15,513	18,411	29,253	30,647	4.8
CO [2]	2,629	7,671	11,063	12,438	12.4	ND......	253	483	608	722	18.8
CT [2]	4,308	10,500	14,802	15,007	1.4	OH......	13,489	31,822	44,663	46,174	3.4
DE [2]	1,474	3,471	4,836	5,110	5.7	OK [4]	4,796	12,285	18,151	19,593	7.9
DC [2]	3,145	9,947	9,800	9,376	-4.3	OR......	3,177	6,492	7,886	8,661	9.8
FL [3]	20,735	44,387	63,879	63,763	-0.2	PA [2]	8,171	22,290	32,416	34,537	6.5
GA [3]	12,178	22,411	34,266	35,139	2.5	RI [2]	813	2,392	2,902	3,271	12.7
HI [2]	985	2,533	3,560	4,011	12.7	SC......	7,862	17,319	19,611	20,446	4.3
ID	817	1,961	3,328	3,832	15.1	SD......	635	1,341	1,871	2,063	10.3
IL [3]	11,899	27,516	37,658	38,852	3.2	TN......	7,022	10,388	15,206	15,626	2.8
IN	6,683	12,736	16,125	16,960	5.2	TX......	29,892	50,042	127,766	132,383	3.6
IA [3]	2,481	3,967	5,906	6,342	7.4	UT......	932	2,496	3,471	3,972	14.4
KS......	2,494	5,775	7,054	7,756	10.0	VT [2]	480	1,049	1,279	1,119	-12.5
KY......	3,588	9,023	12,060	12,910	7.0	VA......	8,920	17,593	27,415	27,655	0.9
LA......	8,889	18,599	25,195	26,779	6.3	WA......	4,399	7,995	11,608	12,527	7.9
ME......	814	1,523	1,396	1,426	2.1	WV	1,257	1,565	2,512	2,749	9.4
MD [2]	7,731	17,848	21,453	22,050	2.8	WI	3,980	7,465	11,199	12,991	16.0
MA [3][4] ...	3,185	8,345	11,687	11,796	0.9	WY	534	1,110	1,395	1,499	7.5

[1] State-level data excludes federal inmates. [2] Includes both jail and prison inmates (state has combined jail and prison system). [3] Numbers are for custody rather than jurisdiction counts. [4] Data are for custody counts until 1995 when jurisdiction counts are reported.

Source: U.S. Bureau of Justice Statistics, *Prisoners in 1996,* and earlier reports.

No. 379. Adults on Probation, in Jail or Prison, or on Parole: 1980 to 1996

[As of December 31, except jail counts as June 30]

ITEM	Total [1]	Probation	Jail	Prison	Parole
1980	1,840,400	1,118,097	[2]182,288	319,598	220,438
1981	2,006,600	1,225,934	[2]195,085	360,029	225,539
1982	2,192,600	1,357,264	207,853	402,914	224,604
1983	2,475,100	1,582,947	221,815	423,898	246,440
1984	2,689,200	1,740,948	233,018	448,264	266,992
1985	3,011,400	1,968,712	254,986	487,593	300,203
1986	3,239,400	2,114,621	272,735	526,436	325,638
1987	3,459,600	2,247,158	294,092	562,814	355,505
1988	3,714,100	2,356,483	341,893	607,766	407,977
1989	4,055,600	2,522,125	393,303	683,367	456,803
1990	4,348,100	2,670,234	403,019	743,382	531,407
1991	4,536,200	2,729,322	424,129	792,535	590,198
1992	4,762,600	2,811,611	441,781	850,566	658,601
1993	4,879,600	2,843,400	455,500	909,200	671,500
1994	5,129,700	2,964,171	483,717	991,612	690,159
1995	5,374,500	3,096,500	499,300	1,078,500	700,200
1996	5,531,100	3,180,400	518,500	1,127,500	704,700

[1] Totals may not add due to individuals having multiple correctional statuses.　[2] Estimated.

Source: U.S. Bureau of Justice Statistics, *Correctional Populations in the United States*, annual.

No. 380. Prisoners Under Sentence of Death: 1980 to 1996

[As of **December 31.** Excludes prisoners under sentence of death who remained within local correctional systems pending exhaustion of appellate process or who had not been committed to prison]

CHARACTERISTIC	1980	1985	1987	1988	1989	1990	1991	1992	1993	1994	1995	1996
Total [1]	688	1,575	1,967	2,117	2,243	2,346	2,466	2,575	2,727	2,905	3,064	3,219
White	418	896	1,128	1,235	1,308	1,368	1,450	1,508	1,575	1,653	1,732	1,820
Black and other	270	679	839	882	935	978	1,016	1,067	1,152	1,252	1,332	1,399
Under 20 years	11	13	10	11	6	8	14	12	13	19	20	16
20 to 24 years	173	212	222	195	191	168	179	188	211	231	264	281
25 to 34 years	334	804	969	1,048	1,080	1,110	1,087	1,078	1,066	1,088	1,068	1,076
35 to 54 years	186	531	744	823	917	1,006	1,129	1,212	1,330	1,449	1,583	1,707
55 years and over	10	31	39	47	56	64	73	85	96	103	119	139
Years of school completed:												
7 years or less	68	147	181	180	183	178	173	181	185	186	191	196
8 years	74	159	183	184	178	186	181	180	183	198	195	199
9 to 11 years	204	483	650	692	739	775	810	836	885	930	979	1,026
12 years	162	440	591	657	695	729	783	831	887	939	995	1,034
More than 12 years	43	127	168	180	192	209	222	232	244	255	272	280
Unknown	163	235	211	231	263	279	313	315	332	382	422	484
Marital status:												
Never married	268	655	856	898	956	998	1,071	1,132	1,222	1,320	1,412	1,498
Married	229	487	571	594	610	632	663	663	671	707	718	731
Divorced [2]	217	449	557	632	684	726	746	780	823	863	924	990
Time elapsed since sentencing:												
Less than 12 months	185	273	295	293	231	231	252	265	262	280	287	285
12 to 47 months	389	739	804	812	809	753	718	720	716	755	784	815
48 to 71 months	102	303	412	409	408	438	441	444	422	379	423	447
72 months and over	38	276	473	610	802	934	1,071	1,146	1,316	1,476	1,560	1,672
Legal status at arrest:												
Not under sentence	384	861	1,123	1,207	1,301	1,345	1,415	1,476	1,562	1,662	1,764	1,863
Parole or probation [3]	115	350	480	545	585	578	615	702	754	800	866	892
Prison or escaped	45	81	91	93	94	128	102	101	102	103	110	111
Unknown	170	299	290	279	270	305	321	296	298	325	314	353

[1] Revisions to the total number of prisoners were not carried to the characteristics except for race.　[2] Includes persons married but separated, widows, widowers, and unknown.　[3] Includes prisoners on mandatory conditional release, work release, leave, AWOL, or bail. Covers 24 prisoners in 1989, 28 in 1990, 29 in 1991 and 1992, 33 in 1993 and 1995, and 31 in 1994 and 1996.

Source: U.S. Bureau of Justice Statistics, *Capital Punishment,* annual.

No. 381. Movement of Prisoners Under Sentence of Death: 1980 to 1996

[Prisoners reported under sentence of death by civil authorities. The term "under sentence of death" begins when the court pronounces the first sentence of death for a capital offense]

STATUS	1980	1985	1987	1988	1989	1990	1991	1992	1993	1994	1995	1996
Under sentence of death, Jan. 1	595	1,420	1,800	1,967	2,117	2,243	2,346	2,465	2,580	2,727	2,905	3,064
Received death sentence [1] [2]	203	281	299	296	251	244	266	265	282	306	310	299
White	125	165	190	196	133	147	163	147	146	162	168	174
Black	77	114	106	91	114	94	101	114	130	136	138	119
Dispositions other than executions . . .	101	108	90	128	102	108	116	124	108	112	105	99
Executions	-	18	25	11	16	23	14	31	38	31	56	45
Under sentence of death, Dec. 31 [1] [2] .	688	1,575	1,967	2,117	2,243	2,346	2,466	2,575	2,727	2,890	3,054	3,219
White	425	896	1,128	1,238	1,308	1,368	1,450	1,508	1,575	1,645	1,730	1,820
Black	268	664	813	853	898	940	1,016	1,029	1,111	1,197	1,275	1,349

- Represents zero.   [1] Includes races other than White or Black.   [2] Revisions to total number of prisoners under death sentence not carried to this category.

Source: U.S. Bureau of Justice Statistics, Capital Punishment, annual.

No. 382. Prisoners Executed Under Civil Authority: 1930 to 1996

[Excludes executions by military authorities. The Army (including the Air Force) carried out 160 (148 between 1942 and 1950; 3 each in 1954, 1955, and 1957; and 1 each in 1958, 1959, and 1961). Of the total, 106 were executed for murder (including 21 involving rape), 53 for rape, and 1 for desertion. The Navy carried out no executions during the period]

YEAR OR PERIOD	Total [1]	White	Black	EXECUTED FOR MURDER			EXECUTED FOR RAPE			EXECUTED, OTHER OFFENSES [2]		
				Total [1]	White	Black	Total [1]	White	Black	Total [1]	White	Black
All years	4,217	1,971	2,201	3,692	1,884	1,770	455	48	405	70	39	31
1930 to 1939.	1,667	827	816	1,514	803	687	125	10	115	28	14	14
1940 to 1949.	1,284	490	781	1,064	458	595	200	19	179	20	13	7
1950 to 1959.	717	336	376	601	316	280	102	13	89	14	7	7
1960 to 1967.	191	98	93	155	87	68	28	6	22	8	5	3
1968 to 1976.	-	-	-	-	-	-	-	-	-	-	-	-
1977 to 1984.	32	22	10	32	22	15	-	-	-	-	-	-
1985	18	11	7	18	11	7	-	-	-	-	-	-
1986	18	11	7	18	11	7	-	-	-	-	-	-
1987	25	13	12	25	13	12	-	-	-	-	-	-
1988	11	6	5	11	6	5	-	-	-	-	-	-
1989	16	8	8	16	8	8	-	-	-	-	-	-
1990	23	16	7	23	16	7	-	-	-	-	-	-
1991	14	7	7	14	7	7	-	-	-	-	-	-
1992	31	19	11	31	19	11	-	-	-	-	-	-
1993	38	23	14	38	23	14	-	-	-	-	-	-
1994	31	20	11	31	20	11	-	-	-	-	-	-
1995	56	33	22	56	33	22	-	-	-	-	-	-
1996	45	31	14	45	31	14	-	-	-	-	-	-

- Represents zero.   [1] Includes races other than White or Black.   [2] Includes 25 armed robbery, 20 kidnapping, 11 burglary, 8 espionage (6 in 1942 and 2 in 1953), and 6 aggravated assault.

Source: Through 1978, U.S. Law Enforcement Assistance Administration; thereafter, U.S. Bureau of Justice Statistics, Correctional Populations in the United States, annual.

No. 383. Prisoners Under Sentence of Death and Executed Under Civil Authority, by States: 1977 to 1996

[Alaska, District of Columbia, Hawaii, Iowa, Maine, Massachusetts, Michigan, Minnesota, New York, North Dakota, Rhode Island, Vermont, West Virginia, and Wisconsin are jurisdictions without a death penalty]

STATE	1977 to 1996	1993	1994	1995	1996	STATE	1977 to 1996	1993	1994	1995	1996	STATE	1977 to 1996	1993	1994	1995	1996
U.S..	358	38	31	56	45	ID	1	-	1	-	-	NC . . .	8	-	1	2	-
						IL	8	-	1	5	1	OK . . .	8	-	-	3	2
AL . . .	13	-	-	2	1	IN	4	-	1	-	1	SC . . .	11	-	-	1	6
AZ . . .	6	2	-	1	2	LA	23	1	-	1	1	TX . . .	107	17	14	19	3
AR . . .	12	-	5	2	1	MD	1	-	1	-	-	UT . . .	5	-	-	-	1
CA . . .	4	1	-	-	2	MS	4	-	-	-	-	VA . . .	37	5	2	5	8
DE . . .	8	2	1	1	3	MO . . .	23	4	-	6	6	WA . . .	2	1	-	-	-
FL . . .	38	3	1	3	2	NE . . .	2	-	1	-	1	WY . . .	1	-	-	-	-
GA . . .	22	2	1	2	2	NV . . .	6	-	-	-	1						

- Represents zero.

Source: Through 1978, U.S. Law Enforcement Assistance Administration; thereafter, U.S. Bureau of Justice Statistics, Capital Punishment, annual.

No. 384. Fire Losses—Total and Per Capita: 1980 to 1996

[Includes allowance for uninsured and unreported losses but excludes losses to government property and forests. Represents incurred losses]

YEAR	Total (mil. dol.)	Per capita [1]	YEAR	Total (mil. dol.)	Per capita [1]	YEAR	Total (mil. dol.)	Per capita [1]
1980	5,579	24.56	1986	8,488	35.21	1992	13,588	48.24
1981	5,625	24.53	1987	8,504	34.96	1993	11,331	43.96
1982	5,894	25.61	1988	9,626	39.11	1994	12,778	49.08
1983	6,320	27.20	1989	9,514	38.33	1995	11,887	45.14
1984	7,602	32.35	1990	9,495	38.26	1996	13,837	52.16
1985	7,753	32.70	1991	11,302	44.83			

[1] Based on Bureau of the Census estimated resident population as of July 1.

Source: Insurance Information Institute, New York, NY, *Insurance Facts,* annual.

No. 385. Fires—Number and Loss, by Type and Property Use: 1993 to 1996

[Based on annual sample survey of fire departments. No adjustments were made for unreported fires and losses. Property loss includes direct property loss only]

TYPE AND PROPERTY USE	NUMBER (1,000)				PROPERTY LOSS (mil. dol.)			
	1993	1994	1995	1996	1993	1994	1995	1996
Fires, total.	**1,953**	**2,054**	**1,966**	**1,975**	**8,546**	**8,151**	**8,918**	**9,406**
Structure	621	614	574	578	7,406	6,867	7,620	7,933
Outside of structure [1]	52	66	61	63	63	120	77	91
Brush and rubbish	732	795	778	766	-	-	-	-
Vehicle.	421	422	406	414	1,030	1,111	1,152	1,333
Other.	127	157	147	154	47	53	69	49
Structure by property use:								
Public assembly	16	17	15	16	298	334	336	330
Educational	9	9	9	9	64	91	84	65
Institutional	10	11	9	8	30	20	31	24
Stores and offices	29	30	29	27	741	598	[2]681	665
Residential.	470	451	426	428	4,843	4,317	4,363	4,962
1-2 family units [3]	358	341	320	324	[4]4,111	3,537	3,615	4,121
Apartments.	100	97	94	93	653	678	649	748
Other residential [5]	12	13	12	11	79	102	99	93
Storage [6].	39	43	39	41	651	568	710	949
Industry, utility, defense [6] . .	19	19	18	18	623	758	[7]1,248	[8]733
Special structures	29	34	29	31	156	181	167	205

- Represents zero. [1] Includes outside storage, crops, timber, etc. [2] Includes an estimated $135 million in property loss that occurred in the explosion and fire in the federal office building in Oklahoma City on April 19, 1995. [3] Includes mobile homes. [4] Reflects wildfires that occurred in southern California in 1993 that resulted in $809 million in property damage. [5] Includes hotels and motels, college dormitories, boarding houses, etc. [6] Data underreported as some incidents were handled by private fire brigades or fixed suppression systems which do not report. [7] Includes estimated losses of $500 million in an industrial complex fire in Massachusetts and $200 million in a manufacturing plant in Georgia in 1995. [8] Includes $280 million in property in a storage property fire in New Orleans, Louisiana in 1996.

Source: National Fire Protection Association, Quincy, MA, "1996 U.S. Fire Loss", *NFPA Journal,* September 1997, and prior issues (copyright 1997).

No. 386. Fires and Property Loss for Incendiary and Suspicious Fires and Civilian Fire Deaths and Injuries, by Selected Property Type: 1993 to 1996

[Based on sample survey of fire departments]

ITEM	1993	1994	1995	1996	ITEM	1993	1994	1995	1996
NUMBER (1,000)					CIVILIAN FIRE DEATHS				
Structure fires, total. . .	621	614	574	578	Deaths, total [4]	4,635	4,275	4,585	4,990
Structure fires of incendiary or suspicious origin	85	86	91	85	Residential property.	3,825	3,465	3,695	4,080
					One- and two-family dwellings	3,035	2,785	3,035	3,470
Fires of incendiary origin .	54	53	58	52	Apartments	685	640	605	565
Fires of suspicious origin .	31	33	33	33	Vehicles	595	630	535	710
PROPERTY LOSS [1] (mil. dol.)					CIVILIAN FIRE INJURIES				
Structure fires, total. . .	7,406	6,867	7,620	7,933	Injuries, total [4]	30,475	27,250	25,775	25,550
Structure fires of incendiary or suspicious origin	2,351	1,447	1,647	1,405	Residential property.	22,600	20,025	19,125	19,300
					One- and two-family dwellings.	15,700	14,000	13,450	13,700
Fires of incendiary origin .	[2]1,901	964	[3]1,116	897	Apartments	6,300	5,475	5,200	5,175
Fires of suspicious origin .	450	483	531	508	Vehicles	2,675	2,625	2,525	2,225

[1] Direct property loss only. [2] Includes fire losses that occurred during the wildfires in California and the World Trade Center bombing in New York city, which resulted in combined estimated losses of $1.039 billion. [3] Includes $135 million in property loss that occurred in the explosion and fire in the federal office building in Oklahoma City on April 19, 1995. [4] Includes other not shown separately.

Source: National Fire Protection Association, Quincy, MA, "1996 U.S. Fire Loss", *NFPA Journal,* September 1997, and prior issues (copyright 1997).

Geography and Environment

This section presents a variety of information on the physical environment of the United States, starting with basic area measurement data and ending with climatic data for selected weather stations around the country. The subjects covered between those points are mostly concerned with environmental trends, but include such related subjects as land use, water consumption, air pollutant emissions, toxic releases, oil spills, hazardous waste sites, threatened and endangered wildlife, and weather-related events.

The information in this section is selected from a wide range of federal agencies that compile the data for various administrative or regulatory purposes, such as the Environmental Protection Agency, U.S. Geological Survey, National Oceanic and Atmospheric Administration, Soil Conservation Service, and General Services Administration. Other agencies include the Bureau of the Census, which presents nationwide area measurement information and the Bureau of Economic Analysis, which compiles data on pollution abatement and control expenditures.

Area—For the 1990 census, area measurements were calculated by computer based on the information contained in a single, consistent geographic database, the TIGER[TM] File (described below), rather than relying on historical, local, and manually calculated information. This especially affects water area figures reported in 1990; these had only included those bodies of water of least 40 acres and those streams with a width of at least one-eighth of a statute mile from 1940 to 1980. Water area figures for 1990 increased because the data reflected all water recorded in the Census Bureau's geographic database including coastal, Great Lakes, and territorial waters.

Geography—The U.S. Geological Survey conducts investigations, surveys, and research in the fields of geography,

In Brief

Wastewater treatment facilities served almost 190 million people in 1996 or 72 percent of the population.

Emissions of CFC (choroflurocarbon) gases in the United States declined 67 percent between 1990 and 1996 from 223,000 metric tons annually to 73,000 tons.

Forty-one percent of the municipal paper waste was recovered in 1996 compared to 28 percent in 1990. The recovery rate also increased for ferrous metals from 20 percent to 38 percent of the waste generated.

New Jersey leads the Nation in the number of hazardous waste sites on the Superfund list with 110 of the country's 1,231 sites as of the end of 1997.

geology, topography, geographic information systems, mineralogy, hydrology, and geothermal energy resources as well as natural hazards. In cooperation with state and local agencies, the U.S. Geological Survey prepares and publishes topographic, land use/land cover, geologic, and hydrologic maps and digital data compilations. The U.S. Geological Survey provides United States cartographic data through the Earth Sciences Information Center, water resources data through the National Water Data Exchange (NAWDEX), and a variety of research and Open-File reports which are announced monthly in New Publications of the U.S. Geological Survey. In a joint project with the Census Bureau, the U.S. Geological Survey provided the basic information on geographic features for input into a national geographic and cartographic database prepared by the Census Bureau, called the TIGER[TM] (Topologically Integrated Geographic Encoding and Referencing) System.

Maps prepared by the Bureau of the Census show the names and boundaries of various types of legal and statistical entities, such as places, county subdivisions, and larger areas and are available as of the specific decennial census. An inventory is available for the 1990 census, both on computer tape and CD-ROM as the 1990 TIGER/GICS (Geographic Identification Code Scheme) and for the 1992 economic censuses in the *Geographic Reference Manual* (EC92-R-1). The Census Bureau maintains a current inventory of governmental units and their legal boundaries through its Boundary and Annexation Survey. The TIGER™ System contains information on the legal and statistical entities used by the Census Bureau, as well as on both manmade and natural features, such as streets, roads, railroads, rivers, and lakes; information is available to the public in the form of machine-readable TIGER™ extract files.

An inventory of the Nation's land resources by type of use/cover was conducted by the Soil Conservation Service in 1982, 1987, and 1992. The results, published in the *1992 National Inventory of Land Resources*, cover all nonfederal land in Puerto Rico, the Virgin Islands, and the United States except Alaska.

Environment—The principal federal agency responsible for pollution abatement and control activities is the Environmental Protection Agency (EPA). It is responsible for establishing and monitoring national air quality standards, water quality activities, solid and hazardous waste disposal, and control of toxic substances.

National Ambient Air Quality Standards (NAAQS) for suspended particulate matter, sulfur dioxide, photochemical oxidants, carbon monoxide, and nitrogen dioxide were originally set by the EPA in April 1971. Every 5 years, each of the NAAQS is reviewed and revised if new health or welfare data indicates that a change is necessary. The standard for photochemical oxidants, now called ozone, was revised in February 1979. Also, a new NAAQS for lead was promulgated in October 1978 and for suspended particulate matter in 1987. Table 398 gives some of the health-related standards for the six air pollutants having NAAQS. Responsibility for demonstrating compliance with or progress toward achieving these standards lies with the state agencies. In 1996, there were 1,734 nonfederal sampling stations for particulates, 690 for sulfur dioxide, 554 for carbon monoxide, 1,037 for ozone, 415 for nitrogen dioxide, and 428 for lead. Data from these state networks are periodically submitted to EPA's National Aerometric Information Retrieval System (AIRS) for summarization in annual reports on the nationwide status and trends in air quality; for details, see *National Air Quality and Emissions Trends Report, 1996.*

Climate—NOAA, through the National Weather Service and the National Environmental Satellite, Data and Information Service, is responsible for data on climate. NOAA maintains about 11,600 weather stations, of which over 3,000 produce autographic precipitation records, about 600 take hourly readings of a series of weather elements, and the remainder record data once a day. These data are reported monthly in the *Climatological Data* (published by state), and monthly and annually in the *Local Climatological Data* (published by location for major cities).

The normal climatological temperatures, precipitation, and degree days listed in this publication are derived for comparative purposes and are averages for the 30-year period, 1961-90. For stations that did not have continuous records for the entire 30 years from the same instrument site, the normals have been adjusted to provide representative values for the current location. The information in all other tables is based on data from the beginning of the record at that location through 1995, except as noted.

No. 387. Land and Water Area of States and Other Entities: 1990

[One square mile=2.59 square kilometers. Excludes territorial water, which was included in the 1993 edition of the *Statistical Abstract*]

STATE AND OTHER AREA	TOTAL AREA		LAND AREA		WATER AREA				
					Total		Inland sq. mi.	Coastal sq. mi.	Great Lakes sq. mi.
	Sq. mi.	Sq. km.	Sq. mi.	Sq. km.	Sq. mi.	Sq. km.			
United States.....	3,717,796	9,629,091	3,536,278	9,158,960	181,518	470,131	78,937	42,528	60,052
Alabama.	52,237	135,293	50,750	131,443	1,486	3,850	968	519	-
Alaska	615,230	1,593,444	570,374	1,477,268	44,856	116,177	17,501	27,355	-
Arizona.	114,006	295,276	113,642	294,333	364	943	364	-	-
Arkansas	53,182	137,742	52,075	134,875	1,107	2,867	1,107	-	-
California	158,869	411,470	155,973	403,971	2,895	7,499	2,674	222	-
Colorado.	104,100	269,618	103,729	268,658	371	960	371	-	-
Connecticut.	5,544	14,358	4,845	12,550	698	1,808	161	538	-
Delaware	2,396	6,206	1,955	5,062	442	1,144	71	371	-
District of Columbia	68	177	61	159	7	18	7	-	-
Florida	59,928	155,214	53,937	139,697	5,991	15,517	4,683	1,308	-
Georgia	58,977	152,750	57,919	150,010	1,058	2,740	1,011	47	-
Hawaii	6,459	16,729	6,423	16,636	36	93	36	-	-
Idaho	83,574	216,456	82,751	214,325	823	2,131	823	-	-
Illinois	57,918	150,007	55,593	143,987	2,325	6,021	750	-	1,575
Indiana.	36,420	94,328	35,870	92,904	550	1,424	315	-	235
Iowa	56,276	145,754	55,875	144,716	401	1,038	401	-	-
Kansas.	82,282	213,110	81,823	211,922	459	1,189	459	-	-
Kentucky	40,411	104,665	39,732	102,907	679	1,759	679	-	-
Louisiana	49,651	128,595	43,566	112,836	6,085	15,759	4,153	1,931	-
Maine.	33,741	87,388	30,865	79,939	2,876	7,449	2,263	613	-
Maryland	12,297	31,849	9,775	25,316	2,522	6,533	680	1,842	-
Massachusetts.	9,241	23,934	7,838	20,300	1,403	3,634	424	979	-
Michigan.	96,705	250,465	56,809	147,136	39,895	103,329	1,704	-	38,192
Minnesota.	86,943	225,182	79,617	206,207	7,326	18,975	4,780	-	2,546
Mississippi	48,286	125,060	46,914	121,506	1,372	3,553	781	591	-
Missouri	69,709	180,546	68,898	178,446	811	2,100	811	-	-
Montana.	147,046	380,849	145,556	376,991	1,490	3,859	1,490	-	-
Nebraska	77,358	200,358	76,878	199,113	481	1,245	481	-	-
Nevada	110,567	286,367	109,806	284,396	761	1,971	761	-	-
New Hampshire	9,283	24,044	8,969	23,231	314	813	314	-	-
New Jersey	8,215	21,277	7,419	19,215	796	2,062	371	425	-
New Mexico	121,598	314,939	121,364	314,334	234	605	234	-	-
New York	53,989	139,833	47,224	122,310	6,766	17,523	1,888	976	3,901
North Carolina	52,672	136,421	48,718	126,180	3,954	10,241	3,954	-	-
North Dakota	70,704	183,123	68,994	178,695	1,710	4,428	1,710	-	-
Ohio	44,828	116,103	40,953	106,067	3,875	10,036	376	-	3,499
Oklahoma.	69,903	181,048	68,679	177,877	1,224	3,171	1,224	-	-
Oregon.	97,132	251,571	96,002	248,646	1,129	2,925	1,050	80	-
Pennsylvania.	46,058	119,291	44,820	116,083	1,239	3,208	490	-	749
Rhode Island.	1,231	3,189	1,045	2,707	186	482	168	18	-
South Carolina	31,189	80,779	30,111	77,988	1,078	2,791	1,006	72	-
South Dakota	77,121	199,744	75,896	196,571	1,225	3,174	1,225	-	-
Tennessee	42,146	109,158	41,219	106,758	926	2,400	926	-	-
Texas.	267,277	692,248	261,914	678,358	5,363	13,890	4,959	404	-
Utah	84,904	219,902	82,168	212,815	2,736	7,086	2,736	-	-
Vermont	9,615	24,903	9,249	23,956	366	947	366	-	-
Virginia	42,326	109,625	39,598	102,558	2,729	7,067	1,000	1,728	-
Washington.	70,637	182,949	66,581	172,445	4,055	10,503	1,545	2,511	-
West Virginia	24,231	62,759	24,087	62,384	145	375	145	-	-
Wisconsin	65,499	169,643	54,314	140,672	11,186	28,971	1,831	-	9,355
Wyoming	97,818	253,349	97,105	251,501	714	1,848	714	-	-
Other areas:									
Puerto Rico	3,508	9,085	3,427	8,875	81	210	65	16	-
American Samoa	90	233	77	200	13	33	7	6	-
Guam	217	561	210	543	7	18	7	-	-
No. Mariana Islands . .	189	490	179	464	10	26	2	8	-
Palau	241	624	177	458	64	165	40	24	-
Virgin Islands of the U.S.	171	443	134	346	37	96	17	20	-

- Represents or rounds to zero.

Source: U.S. Bureau of the Census, *1990 Census of Population and Housing*, series CPH-2; and unpublished data from the TIGER/Geographic Information Control System (TIGER/GICS)computer file. Corrections have been made subsequent to the 1990 census reports.

No. 388. Area and Acquisition of the Federal Public Domain: 1781 to 1994

[In millions of acres. Areas of acquisitions are as computed in 1912, and do not agree with figures in square miles shown in Table 387 which include later adjustments and reflect subsequent remeasurement. Excludes outlying areas of the United States amounting to 645,949 acres in 1978]

YEAR	Land area, total [1]	YEAR	LAND AREA [1]			YEAR AND ACQUISITION	ACREAGE		
			Total	Public domain	Acquired		Total	Land	Inland water
1802 ...	200.0	1980 ...	719.5	648.0	71.5	**Aggregate**	**1,840.7**	**1,807.5**	**33.2**
1850 ...	1,200.0	1981 ...	730.8	668.7	62.2				
1880 ...	900.0	1982 ...	729.8	670.0	59.8	1781-1802 (State Cessions)	236.8	233.4	3.4
1912 ...	600.0	1983 ...	732.0	672.4	59.6	1803, Louisiana Purchase [2]......	529.9	523.4	6.5
1946 ...	413.0	1984 ...	726.6	658.9	67.7	1819, Cession from Spain	46.1	43.3	2.8
1950 ...	412.0	1985 ...	726.7	656.2	70.5	Red River Basin [3]	29.6	29.1	0.5
1955 ...	407.9	1986 ...	727.1	662.7	64.4				
1959 ...	768.6	1987 ...	724.3	661.0	63.3	1846, Oregon Compromise	183.4	180.6	2.7
1960 ...	771.5	1988 ...	688.2	623.2	65.0	1848, Mexican Cession [2]	338.7	334.5	4.2
1965 ...	765.8	1989 ...	662.2	597.9	64.3	1850, Purchase from Texas......	78.9	78.8	0.1
1970 ...	761.3	1990 ...	649.8	587.4	62.4	1853, Gadsden Purchase	19.0	19.0	(Z)
1975 ...	760.4	1991 ...	649.3	587.6	61.8	1867, Alaska Purchase	378.3	365.3	12.9
1976 ...	762.2	1992 ...	651.1	590.9	60.2				
1977 ...	741.5	1993 ...	650.3	590.5	59.9				
1978 ...	775.2	1994 ...	657.3	573.2	84.1				
1979 ...	744.1								

Z Less than 50,000.   [1] Owned by federal government. Comprises original public domain plus acquired lands. Estimated from imperfect data available for indicated years. Prior to 1959, excludes Alaska, and 1960, Hawaii. Source: Beginning 1955, U.S. General Services Administration, *Inventory Report on Real Property Owned by the United States Throughout the World,* annual. [2] Data for Louisiana Purchase exclude areas eliminated by Treaty of 1819 with Spain. Such areas are included in figures for Mexican Cession.   [3] Represents drainage basin of Red River of the North, south of 49th parallel. Authorities differ as to method and date of its acquisition. Some hold it as part of the Louisiana Purchase; others, as acquired from Great Britain.

Source: Except as noted, U.S. Dept. of the Interior. Estimated area, Bureau of Land Management; all other data, Office of the Secretary, *Areas of Acquisitions to the Territory of the U.S.,* 1922.

No. 389. Total and Federally Owned Land, by State: 1996

[As of **end of fiscal year;** see text, Section 9. Total land area figures are not comparable with those in Table 387]

STATE	Total (1,000 acres)	Not owned by federal government (1,000 acres)	OWNED BY FEDERAL GOVERNMENT [1]		STATE	Total (1,000 acres)	Not owned by federal government (1,000 acres)	OWNED BY FEDERAL GOVERNMENT [1]	
			Acres (1,000)	Percent				Acres (1,000)	Percent
United States..	**2,271,343**	**1,708,214**	**563,129**	**24.8**	Missouri	44,248	42,590	1,658	3.7
Alabama	32,678	31,598	1,080	3.3	Montana	93,271	67,786	25,485	27.3
Alaska	365,482	193,694	171,788	47.0	Nebraska	49,032	48,517	515	1.1
Arizona	72,688	41,351	31,337	43.1	Nevada	70,264	14,183	56,082	79.8
Arkansas	33,599	30,860	2,740	8.2	New Hampshire ...	5,769	5,035	734	12.7
California	100,207	55,449	44,757	44.7	New Jersey.......	4,813	4,712	102	2.1
Colorado	66,486	42,356	24,129	36.3	New Mexico	77,766	51,550	26,217	33.7
Connecticut	3,135	3,128	7	0.2	New York	30,681	30,484	197	0.6
Delaware	1,266	1,264	2	0.2	North Carolina ...	31,403	29,374	2,028	6.5
District of Columbia ..	39	30	9	23.4	North Dakota	44,452	43,040	1,413	3.2
Florida	34,721	32,077	2,645	7.6	Ohio	26,222	25,942	280	1.1
Georgia	37,295	35,835	1,460	3.9	Oklahoma	44,088	43,410	678	1.5
Hawaii	4,106	3,755	350	8.5	Oregon	61,599	29,789	31,809	51.6
Idaho	52,933	19,941	32,992	62.3	Pennsylvania.....	28,804	28,182	623	2.2
Illinois	35,795	35,390	405	1.1	Rhode Island	677	674	3	0.5
Indiana	23,158	22,764	394	1.7	South Carolina ...	19,374	18,440	935	4.8
Iowa	35,860	35,831	30	0.1	South Dakota	48,882	46,304	2,577	5.3
Kansas	52,511	52,161	350	0.7	Tennessee	26,728	25,152	1,576	5.9
Kentucky	25,512	24,430	1,083	4.2	Texas	168,218	166,210	2,008	1.2
Louisiana	28,868	28,123	745	2.6	Utah	52,697	18,799	33,898	64.3
Maine	19,848	19,654	193	1.0	Vermont	5,937	5,560	377	6.3
Maryland	6,319	6,162	157	2.5	Virginia	25,496	23,217	2,279	8.9
Massachusetts	5,035	4,983	52	1.0	Washington	42,694	30,755	11,939	28.0
Michigan	36,492	32,513	3,980	10.9	West Virginia	15,411	14,333	1,077	7.0
Minnesota	51,206	47,137	4,069	7.9	Wisconsin	35,011	33,278	1,733	5.0
Mississippi	30,223	28,946	1,276	4.2	Wyoming	62,343	31,465	30,878	49.5

[1] Excludes trust properties.

Source: U.S. General Services Administration, *Inventory Report on Real Property Owned by the United States Throughout the World,* annual.

No. 390. Land Cover/Use, by State: 1992

[In thousands of acres. Excludes Alaska and District of Columbia]

STATE	Total surface area [1]	Federal land	NONFEDERAL LAND							
			Total	Devel-oped [2]	Rural					
					Total	Crop-land	Pasture land	Range-land	Forest land	Minor cover/ use
Total	**1,940,011**	**407,989**	**1,483,126**	**92,352**	**1,390,774**	**382,317**	**125,927**	**398,949**	**394,958**	**88,624**
United States	1,937,678	407,899	1,480,916	91,946	1,388,970	381,950	125,215	398,803	394,437	88,565
Alabama	33,091	921	31,192	2,046	29,147	3,147	3,760	67	20,968	1,205
Arizona	72,960	30,280	42,408	1,404	41,004	1,198	76	32,227	4,718	2,785
Arkansas	34,040	3,207	29,803	1,322	28,480	7,730	5,727	159	14,267	598
California	101,572	46,792	52,892	5,001	47,892	10,052	1,161	17,140	14,794	4,746
Colorado	66,618	23,923	42,240	1,694	40,547	8,940	1,256	23,537	3,755	3,059
Connecticut	3,212	15	3,054	816	2,238	229	110	-	1,760	140
Delaware	1,309	33	1,213	205	1,008	499	26	-	353	130
Florida	37,545	3,791	30,406	4,645	25,761	2,997	4,373	3,467	12,378	2,545
Georgia	37,702	2,087	34,599	3,077	31,523	5,173	3,075	-	21,714	1,560
Hawaii	4,093	432	3,621	170	3,451	274	88	925	1,483	680
Idaho	53,481	33,298	19,521	587	18,934	5,600	1,243	6,668	4,024	1,399
Illinois	36,061	521	34,766	3,094	31,672	24,100	2,764	-	3,419	1,390
Indiana	23,159	487	22,287	2,095	20,193	13,513	1,866	-	3,626	1,188
Iowa	36,016	184	35,363	1,779	33,584	24,988	3,712	-	1,931	2,953
Kansas	52,658	606	51,488	1,997	49,491	26,565	2,306	15,723	1,331	3,565
Kentucky	25,862	1,201	23,985	1,653	22,332	5,092	5,859	-	10,312	1,069
Louisiana	30,561	1,264	26,373	1,764	24,609	5,972	2,269	227	12,961	3,181
Maine	21,290	164	19,517	697	18,820	448	111	-	17,557	705
Maryland	6,695	167	6,034	1,095	4,939	1,673	545	-	2,364	356
Massachusetts	5,302	89	4,839	1,309	3,530	272	170	-	2,778	310
Michigan	37,457	3,166	33,040	3,686	29,354	8,985	2,353	-	15,608	2,408
Minnesota	54,017	3,383	47,092	2,418	44,674	21,356	3,282	-	13,815	6,222
Mississippi	30,521	1,726	27,992	1,337	26,655	5,726	4,047	-	15,765	1,117
Missouri	44,606	2,017	41,710	2,336	39,374	13,347	11,911	126	11,656	2,332
Montana	94,109	27,122	65,656	1,096	64,561	15,035	3,370	36,835	5,156	4,165
Nebraska	49,507	739	48,137	1,252	46,885	19,239	2,066	22,669	777	2,135
Nevada	70,759	60,290	10,025	394	9,631	762	297	7,854	353	364
New Hampshire	5,938	747	4,952	563	4,389	142	98	-	3,932	217
New Jersey	4,984	159	4,549	1,588	2,961	650	159	-	1,766	386
New Mexico	77,819	27,394	50,196	866	49,330	1,892	212	39,792	4,600	2,835
New York	31,429	231	29,788	3,005	26,783	5,616	3,001	-	17,178	987
North Carolina	33,708	2,448	28,476	3,542	24,933	5,960	2,019	-	15,979	975
North Dakota	45,250	1,951	42,187	1,344	40,843	24,743	1,168	10,325	426	4,181
Ohio	26,451	375	25,654	3,558	22,096	11,929	2,269	-	6,624	1,275
Oklahoma	44,772	1,202	42,395	1,875	40,520	10,081	7,720	14,061	6,988	1,672
Oregon	62,127	32,291	29,155	1,125	28,030	3,776	1,900	9,375	11,839	1,142
Pennsylvania	28,997	682	27,813	3,432	24,381	5,596	2,326	-	15,316	1,143
Rhode Island	776	4	661	190	472	25	24	-	393	30
South Carolina	19,912	1,156	17,961	1,856	16,105	2,983	1,190	-	10,922	1,010
South Dakota	49,354	2,907	45,459	1,135	44,324	16,436	2,158	21,933	540	3,257
Tennessee	26,972	1,379	24,740	2,161	22,579	4,857	5,165	-	11,580	977
Texas	170,756	3,203	163,687	8,231	155,456	28,261	16,710	94,155	9,960	6,369
Utah	54,336	35,582	16,866	561	16,305	1,815	665	10,050	1,626	2,148
Vermont	6,153	368	5,521	324	5,197	635	349	-	4,138	75
Virginia	26,091	2,389	22,774	2,183	20,591	2,901	3,444	-	13,539	707
Washington	43,608	12,479	29,931	1,851	28,081	6,745	1,352	5,476	12,547	1,960
West Virginia	15,508	1,201	14,138	689	13,449	915	1,609	-	10,534	391
Wisconsin	35,938	1,829	32,747	2,357	30,390	10,813	2,954	-	13,410	3,212
Wyoming	62,598	30,020	32,012	541	31,471	2,272	901	26,015	975	1,309
Caribbean	2,334	90	2,211	407	1,804	367	712	145	521	59

- Represents zero.   [1] Includes water area not shown separately.   [2] Includes urban and built-up areas in units of 10 acres or greater, and rural transportation.

Source: U.S. Dept. of Agriculture, Soil Conservation Service, and Iowa State University, Statistical Laboratory; *Summary Report, 1992 National Resources Inventory.*

No. 391. Extreme and Mean Elevations States and Other Areas

[One foot=.305 meter]

STATE OR OTHER AREA	HIGHEST POINT Name	Elevation Feet	Elevation Meters	LOWEST POINT Name	Elevation Feet	Elevation Meters	APPROXIMATE MEAN ELEVATION Feet	APPROXIMATE MEAN ELEVATION Meters
U.S.....	**Mt. McKinley (AK)........**	**20,320**	**6,198**	**Death Valley (CA).....**	**-282**	**-86**	**2,500**	**763**
AL........	Cheaha Mountain.........	2,405	733	Gulf of Mexico......	(¹)	(¹)	500	153
AK........	Mount McKinley......	20,320	6,198	Pacific Ocean......	(¹)	(¹)	1,900	580
AZ........	Humphreys Peak......	12,633	3,853	Colorado River......	70	21	4,100	1,251
AR........	Magazine Mountain......	2,753	840	Ouachita River......	55	17	650	198
CA........	Mount Whitney......	14,494	4,419	Death Valley......	-282	-86	2,900	885
CO........	Mt. Elbert........	14,433	4,402	Arkansas River........	3,350	1,022	6,800	2,074
CT........	Mt. Frissell on South slope...	2,380	726	Long Island Sound....	(¹)	(¹)	500	153
DE........	Ebright Road,[2] New Castle County	448	137	Atlantic Ocean......	(¹)	(¹)	60	18
DC........	Tenleytown at Reno Reservoir.	410	125	Potomac River......	1	(Z)	150	46
FL........	Sec. 30, T6N, R20W, Walton County	345	105	Atlantic Ocean......	(¹)	(¹)	100	31
GA........	Brasstown Bald......	4,784	1,459	Atlantic Ocean......	(¹)	(¹)	600	183
HI........	Puu Wekiu......	13,796	4,208	Pacific Ocean......	(¹)	(¹)	3,030	924
ID........	Borah Peak.....	12,662	3,862	Snake River......	710	217	5,000	1,525
IL........	Charles Mound......	1,235	377	Mississippi River......	279	85	600	183
IN........	Franklin Twp., Wayne Co....	1,257	383	Ohio River......	320	98	700	214
IA........	Sec. 29, T100N, R41W, Osceola County[3]	1,670	509	Mississippi River......	480	146	1,100	336
KS........	Mount Sunflower......	4,039	1,232	Verdigris River......	679	207	2,000	610
KY........	Black Mountain......	4,139	2,162	Mississippi River......	257	78	750	229
LA........	Driskill Mountain.....	535	163	New Orleans......	-8	-2	100	31
ME........	Mount Katahdin......	5,267	1,606	Atlantic Ocean......	(¹)	(¹)	600	183
MD........	Backbone Mountain......	3,360	1,025	Atlantic Ocean......	(¹)	(¹)	350	107
MA........	Mount Greylock......	3,487	1,064	Atlantic Ocean......	(¹)	(¹)	500	153
MI........	Mount Arvon......	1,979	604	Lake Erie......	571	174	900	275
MN........	Eagle Mountain, Cook Co....	2,301	702	Lake Superior......	600	183	1,200	366
MS........	Woodall Mountain......	806	246	Gulf of Mexico......	(¹)	(¹)	300	92
MO........	Taum Sauk Mountain.....	1,772	540	St. Francis River......	230	70	800	244
MT........	Granite Peak......	12,799	3,904	Kootenai River......	1,800	549	3,400	1,037
NE........	Johnson Twp., Kimball Co....	5,424	1,654	Missouri River......	840	256	2,600	793
NV........	Boundary Peak......	13,140	4,007	Colorado River......	479	146	5,500	1,678
NH........	Mount Washington......	6,288	1,918	Atlantic Ocean......	(¹)	(¹)	1,000	305
NJ........	High Point......	1,803	550	Atlantic Ocean......	(¹)	(¹)	250	76
NM........	Wheeler Peak......	13,161	4,014	Red Bluff Reservoir....	2,842	867	5,700	1,739
NY........	Mount Marcy......	5,344	1,630	Atlantic Ocean......	(¹)	(¹)	1,000	305
NC........	Mount Mitchell......	6,684	2,039	Atlantic Ocean......	(¹)	(¹)	700	214
ND........	White Butte, Slope Co....	3,506	1,069	Red River......	750	229	1,900	580
OH........	Campbell Hill......	1,549	472	Ohio River......	455	139	850	259
OK........	Black Mesa......	4,973	1,517	Little River......	289	88	1,300	397
OR........	Mount Hood......	11,239	3,428	Pacific Ocean......	(¹)	(¹)	3,300	1,007
PA........	Mount Davis......	3,213	980	Delaware River......	(¹)	(¹)	1,100	336
RI........	Jerimoth Hill......	812	248	Atlantic Ocean......	(¹)	(¹)	200	61
SC........	Sassafras Mountain......	3,560	1,086	Atlantic Ocean......	(¹)	(¹)	350	107
SD........	Harney Peak....	7,242	2,209	Big Stone Lake......	966	295	2,200	671
TN........	Clingmans Dome......	6,643	2,026	Mississippi River......	178	54	900	275
TX........	Guadalupe Peak......	8,749	2,668	Gulf of Mexico......	(¹)	(¹)	1,700	519
UT........	Kings Peak......	13,528	4,126	Beaverdam Wash....	2,000	610	6,100	1,861
VT........	Mount Mansfield......	4,393	1,340	Lake Champlain......	95	29	1,000	305
VA........	Mount Rogers......	5,729	1,747	Atlantic Ocean......	(¹)	(¹)	950	290
WA........	Mount Rainier......	14,410	4,395	Pacific Ocean......	(¹)	(¹)	1,700	519
WV........	Spruce Knob......	4,861	1,483	Potomac River......	240	73	1,500	458
WI........	Timms Hill......	1,951	595	Lake Michigan......	579	177	1,050	320
WY........	Gannett Peak......	13,804	4,210	Belle Fourche River....	3,099	945	6,700	2,044
Other areas:								
Puerto Rico....	Cerro de Punta..........	4,390	1,339	Atlantic Ocean......	(¹)	(¹)	1,800	549
American Samoa...	Lata Mountain......	3,160	964	Pacific Ocean......	(¹)	(¹)	1,300	397
Guam....	Mount Lamlam......	1,332	406	Pacific Ocean......	(¹)	(¹)	330	101
Virgin Is...	Crown Mountain......	1,556	475	Atlantic Ocean......	(¹)	(¹)	750	229

Z Less than 0.5 meter. [1] Sea level. [2] At DE-PA state line. [3] "Sec." denotes section; "T," township; "R," range; "N," north; and "W," west.

Source: U.S. Geological Survey, for highest and lowest points, *Elevations and Distances in the United States, 1990*; for mean elevations, 1983 edition.

No. 392. Water Areas for Selected Major Bodies of Water: 1990

[Includes only that portion of body of water under the jurisdiction of the United States, excluding Hawaii. One square mile=2.59 square kilometers]

BODY OF WATER AND STATE	AREA Sq. mi.	AREA Sq. km.	BODY OF WATER AND STATE	AREA Sq. mi.	AREA Sq. km.
Atlantic Coast water bodies:			Leech Lake (MN)	162	419
Chesapeake Bay (MD-VA)	2,747	7,115	Lake St. Clair (MI) [1]	161	416
Pamlico Sound (NC)	1,622	4,200	Eufaula Lake (OK)	157	407
Long Island Sound (CT-NY)	914	2,368			
Delaware Bay (DE-NJ)	614	1,591	Sam Rayburn Reservoir (TX)	150	389
Cape Cod Bay (MA)	598	1,548	Goose Lake (CA-OR)	147	381
Albemarle Sound (NC)	492	1,274	Utah Lake (UT)	139	361
Biscayne Bay (FL)	218	565	Lake Marion (SC)	139	360
Buzzards Bay (MA)	215	558	Lake Francis Case (SD)	134	346
Tangier Sound (MD-VA)	172	445	Lake Pend Oreille (ID)	133	343
Currituck Sound (NC)	116	301	Lake Texoma (OK-TX)	132	342
Pocomoke Sound (MD-VA)	111	286	Yellowstone Lake (WY)	131	339
Chincoteague Bay (MD-VA)	105	272	Livingston Reservoir (TX)	127	330
Great South Bay (NY)	94	243	Franklin D. Roosevelt Lake (WA)	124	322
Core Sound (NC)	88	229	Moosehead Lake (ME)	116	301
			Clark Hill Lake (GA-SC)	105	272
Gulf Coast water bodies:			Lake Maurepas (LA)	91	235
Mississippi Sound (AL-LA-MS)	813	2,105	Lake Moultrie (SC)	89	230
Laguna Madre (TX)	733	1,897	Lake Winnibigoshish (MN)	87	225
Lake Pontchartrain (LA)	631	1,635	Hartwell Lake (GA-SC)	86	224
Florida Bay (FL)	616	1,596	Upper Klamath Lake (OR)	85	221
Breton Sound (LA)	511	1,323	Harry S. Truman Reservoir (MO)	84	217
Mobile Bay (AL)	310	802	Oneida Lake (NY)	80	207
Lake Borgne (LA-MS)	271	702	Malheur Lake (OR)	75	195
Matagorda Bay (TX)	253	656			
Atchafalaya Bay (LA)	245	635	**Alaska water bodies:**		
Galveston Bay (TX)	236	611	Chatham Strait	1,559	4,039
			Prince William Sound	1,382	3,579
Tampa Bay (FL)	212	549	Clarence Strait	1,199	3,107
Vermilion Bay (LA)	189	489	Iliamna Lake	1,022	2,646
Corpus Christi Bay (TX)	151	392	Frederick Sound	792	2,051
West Cote Blanche Bay (LA)	146	378	Sumner Strait	791	2,048
Trinity Bay (TX)	129	335	Stephens Passage	702	1,819
Choctawhatchee Bay (FL)	122	315	Kvichak Bay	640	1,659
San Antonio Bay (TX)	118	306	Montague Strait	463	1,198
Timbalier Bay (LA)	112	291	Becharof Lake	447	1,158
Charlotte Harbor (FL)	112	291	Icy Strait	436	1,130
Aransas Bay (TX)	104	268	Hotham Inlet	433	1,120
Apalachicola Bay (FL)	101	262	Selawik Lake	403	1,044
Terrebonne Bay (LA)	99	256	Nushagak Bay	393	1,018
East Cote Blanche Bay (LA)	94	243	Baird Inlet	348	902
St. George Sound (FL)	93	240			
Sabine Lake (LA-TX)	89	229	Yakutat Bay	345	894
White Lake (LA)	85	221	Teshekpuk Lake	324	839
Old Tampa Bay (FL)	83	214	Behm Canal	324	839
Bon Secour Bay (AL)	79	204	Turnagain Arm	322	834
Pine Island Sound (FL)	75	194	Kachemak Bay	310	803
			Glacier Bay	310	803
Pacific Coast water bodies:			Stefansson Sound	301	780
Puget Sound (WA)	808	2,092	Revillagigedo Channel	295	764
San Francisco Bay (CA)	264	684	Kasegaluk Lagoon	293	759
Willapa Bay (WA)	125	325	Cordova Bay	241	623
Hood Canal (WA)	117	303	Sitka Sound	229	593
			Naknek Lake	225	582
Interior water bodies:			Eschscholtz Bay	210	543
Lake Michigan (IL-IN-MI-WI)	22,342	57,866	Stepovak Bay	206	534
Lake Superior (MI-MN-WI) [1]	20,557	53,243	Keku Strait	206	534
Lake Huron (MI) [1]	8,800	22,792			
Lake Erie (MI-NY-OH-PA) [1]	5,033	13,036	Port Clarence	187	486
Lake Ontario (NY) [1]	3,446	8,926	Orca Bay	184	476
Great Salt Lake (UT)	1,836	4,756	Knik Arm	169	437
Green Bay (MI-WI)	1,396	3,617	Dall Lake	167	433
Lake Okeechobee (FL)	663	1,717	Knight Island Passage	167	432
Lake Sakakawea (ND)	563	1,459	Scammon Bay	163	423
Lake Oahe (ND-SD)	538	1,394	Port Moller	159	412
Lake of the Woods (MN) [1]	462	1,196	Ernest Sound	158	410
Lake Champlain (NY-VT) [1]	414	1,072	Spafarief Bay	157	405
Fort Peck Lake (MT)	379	981	Pavlov Bay	153	396
Salton Sea (CA)	364	944	Shishmaref Inlet	153	395
			Smith Bay	140	363
Toledo Bend Reservoir (LA-TX)	268	694	Seymour Canal	140	361
Lower Red Lake (MN)	257	666	Sitkalidak Strait	135	349
Lake Powell (AZ-UT)	250	649	Tlevak Strait	135	349
Kentucky Lake (KY-TN)	234	605			
Lake Mead (AZ-NV)	233	603			
Lake Winnebago (WI)	206	535	Lake Clark	130	336
Mille Lacs Lake (MN)	200	518	Lynn Canal	130	336
Flathead Lake (MT)	191	495	Chignik Bay	119	309
Lake Tahoe (CA-NV)	187	486	Elson Lagoon	119	309
Upper Red Lake (MN)	186	483	Bucareli Bay	119	307
Pyramid Lake (NV)	170	440	Hinchinbrook Entrance	118	306

[1] Area measurements for Lake Champlain, Lake Erie, Lake Huron, Lake Ontario, Lake St. Clair, Lake Superior, and Lake of the Woods include only those portions under the jurisdiction of the United States.

Source: U.S. Bureau of the Census, unpublished data from the Census TIGER [TM] database.

No. 393. Flows of Largest U.S. Rivers—Length, Discharge, and Drainage Area

RIVER	Location of mouth	Source stream (name and location)	Length (miles) [1]	Average discharge at mouth (1,000 cubic ft. per second)	Drainage area (1,000 sq. mi.)
Missouri	Missouri	Red Rock Creek, MT	2,540	76.2	[5]529
Mississippi	Louisiana	Mississippi River, MN	[2]2,340	[3]593	[4][5]1,150
Yukon	Alaska	McNeil River, Canada	1,980	225	[5]328
St. Lawrence	Canada	North River, MN	1,900	348	[5]396
Rio Grande	Mexico-Texas	Rio Grande, CO	1,900	-	336
Arkansas	Arkansas	East Fork Arkansas River, CO	1,460	41	161
Colorado	Mexico	Colorado River, CO	1,450	-	246
Atchafalaya [6]	Louisiana	Tierra Blanca Creek, NM	1,420	58	95.1
Ohio	Illinois-Kentucky	Allegheny River, PA	1,310	281	203
Red	Louisiana	Tierra Blanca Creek, NM	1,290	56	93.2
Brazos	Texas	Blackwater Draw, NM	1,280	-	45.6
Columbia	Oregon-Washington	Columbia River, Canada	1,240	265	[5]258
Snake	Washington	Snake River, WY	1,040	56.9	108
Platte	Nebraska	Grizzly Creek, CO	990	-	84.9
Pecos	Texas	Pecos River, NM	926	-	44.3
Canadian	Oklahoma	Canadian River, CO	906	-	46.9
Tennessee	Kentucky	Courthouse Creek, NC	886	68	40.9
Colorado (of Texas)	Texas	Colorado River, TX	862	-	42.3
North Canadian	Oklahoma	Corrumpa Creek, NM	800	-	17.6
Mobile	Alabama	Tickanetley Creek, GA	774	67.2	44.6
Kansas	Kansas	Arikaree River, CO	743	-	59.5
Kuskokwim	Alaska	South Fork Kuskokwim River, AK	724	67	48
Yellowstone	North Dakota	North Folk Yellowstone River, WY	692	-	70
Tanana	Alaska	Nabesna River, AK	659	41	44.5
Gila	Arizona	Middle Fork Gila River, NM	649	-	58.2

- Represents zero.   [1] From source to mouth.   [2] The length from the source of the Missouri River to the Mississippi River and thence to the Gulf of Mexico is about 3,710 miles.   [3] Includes about 167,000 cubic ft. per second diverted from the Mississippi into the Atchafalaya River but excludes the flow of the Red River.   [4] Excludes the drainage areas of the Red and Atchafalaya Rivers.   [5] Drainage area includes both the United States and Canada.   [6] In east-central Louisiana, the Red River flows into the Atchafalaya River, a distributary of the Mississippi River. Data on average discharge, length, and drainage area include the Red River, but exclude all water diverted into the Atchafalaya from the Mississippi River.

Source: U.S. Geological Survey, *Largest Rivers in the United States*, Open File Report 87-242, May 1990.

No. 394. U.S. Water Withdrawals and Consumptive Use Per Day, by End Use: 1940 to 1995

[Includes Puerto Rico. Withdrawal signifies water physically withdrawn from a source. Includes fresh and saline water; excludes water used for hydroelectric power]

YEAR	Total (bil. gal.)	Per capita [1] (gal.)	Irrigation (bil. gal.)	PUBLIC SUPPLY [2] Total (bil. gal.)	PUBLIC SUPPLY [2] Per capita [3] (gal.)	Rural [4] (bil. gal.)	Industrial and misc. [5] (bil. gal.)	Steam electric utilities (bil. gal.)
WITHDRAWALS								
1940	140	1,027	71	10	75	3.1	29	23
1950	180	1,185	89	14	145	3.6	37	40
1955	240	1,454	110	17	148	3.6	39	72
1960	270	1,500	110	21	151	3.6	38	100
1965	310	1,602	120	24	155	4.0	46	130
1970	370	1,815	130	27	166	4.5	47	170
1975	420	1,972	140	29	168	4.9	45	200
1980	440	1,953	150	34	183	5.6	45	210
1985	399	1,650	137	38	189	7.8	31	187
1990	408	1,620	137	41	195	7.9	30	195
1995	402	1,500	134	43	192	8.9	26	190
CONSUMPTIVE USE								
1960	61	339	52	3.5	25	2.8	3.0	0.2
1965	77	403	66	5.2	34	3.2	3.4	0.4
1970	87	427	73	5.9	36	3.4	4.1	0.8
1975	96	451	80	6.7	38	3.4	4.2	1.9
1980	100	440	83	7.1	38	3.9	5.0	3.2
1985	92	380	74	[6]	[6]	9.2	6.1	6.2
1990	94	370	76	[6]	[6]	8.9	6.7	4.0
1995	100	374	81	[6]	[6]	9.9	4.8	3.7

[1] Based on Bureau of the Census resident population as of July 1.   [2] Includes commercial water withdrawals.   [3] Based on population served.   [4] Rural farm and nonfarm household and garden use, and water for farm stock and dairies.   [5] For 1940 to 1960, includes manufacturing and mineral industries, rural commercial industries, air-conditioning, resorts, hotels, motels, military and other state and federal agencies, and miscellaneous; thereafter, includes manufacturing, mining and mineral processing, ordnance, construction, and miscellaneous.   [6] Public supply consumptive use included in end-use categories.

Source: 1940-1960, U.S. Bureau of Domestic Business Development, based principally on committee prints, *Water Resources Activities in the United States*, for the Senate Committee on National Water Resources, U.S. Senate, thereafter, U.S. Geological Survey, *Estimated Use of Water in the United States in 1995*, circular 1200, and previous quinquennial issues.

No. 395. National Ambient Water Quality in Rivers and Streams—Violation Rate: 1980 to 1995

[In percent. Violation level based on U.S. Environmental Protection Agency water quality criteria. Violation rate represents the proportion of all measurements of a specific water quality pollutant which exceeds the "violation level" for that pollutant. "Violation" does not necessarily imply a legal violation. Data based on U.S. Geological Survey's National Stream Quality Accounting Network (NASQAN) data system; for details, see source. Years refer to water years. A water year begins in Oct. and ends in Sept. μg=micrograms; mg=milligrams. For metric conversion, see page ix]

POLLUTANT	VIOLATION LEVEL	1980	1985	1989	1990	1991	1992	1993	1994	1995
Fecal coliform bacteria....	Above 200 cells per 100 ml..	31	28	30	26	15	28	31	28	35
Dissolved oxygen.......	Below 5 mg per liter.......	5	3	3	2	2	2	(Z)	2	1
Phosphorus, total, as phosporous........	Above 1.0 mg per liter.....	4	3	2	3	2	2	2	2	4
Lead, dissolved........	Above 50 μg per liter......	(Z)	(Z)	(Z)	(Z)	(Z)	(Z)	(NA)	(NA)	(NA)
Cadmium, dissolved.....	Above 10 μg per liter......	1	(Z)	(Z)	(Z)	(Z)	(Z)	(NA)	(NA)	(NA)

NA Not available. Z Less than 1.

Source: U.S. Geological Survey, national-level data, unpublished; state-level data, *Water-Data Report*, annual series prepared in cooperation with the state governments.

No. 396. Oil Polluting Incidents Reported in and Around U.S. Waters: 1973 to 1993

YEAR	Incidents	Gallons	YEAR	Incidents	Gallons
1973.	11,054	15,289,188	1986.	5,818	4,427,544
1974.	12,083	15,739,792	1987.	5,693	3,759,983
1975.	10,998	21,528,444	1988.	6,733	10,650,138
1976.	11,066	18,517,384	1989.	8,562	25,531,292
1977.	10,979	8,188,398	1990.	10,186	13,907,783
1978.	12,174	11,035,890	1991.	10,405	2,156,063
1979.	11,556	10,051,271	1992.	9,131	1,572,341
1980.	9,886	12,638,848			
1981.	9,589	8,919,789	1993.	9,672	1,543,578
1982.	9,416	10,404,646	Tankships.	185	14,138
1983.	10,530	8,378,719	Tank barges	338	295,243
1984.	10,089	19,007,332	Other vessels	5,220	412,430
1985.	7,740	8,465,055	Nonvessels.	3,929	821,767

Source: U.S. Coast Guard. Based on unpublished data from the *Marine Safety Information System*.

No. 397. Wastewater Treatment Facilities: 1988 to 1996

[Covers treatment facilities, which are structures designed to treat wastewater, storm water, or combined sewer overflows prior to discharging to the environment. Treatment is accomplished by subjecting the wastewater to a combination of physical, chemical, and/or biological processes that reduce the concentration of contaminants]

LEVEL OF TREATMENT	NUMBER OF FACILITIES			1996		
	1988	1992	1996	Present design capacity	Number of persons served	
					Number	Percent of U.S.
Total.....................	15,591	15,613	16,024	42,225	189,710,899	71.8
Non-discharge [1]...............	1,854	1,981	2,032	1,421	7,660,876	2.9
Less than secondary.............	1,789	868	176	3,054	17,177,492	6.5
Secondary....................	8,536	9,086	9,388	17,734	81,944,349	31.0
Greater than secondary...........	3,412	3,678	4,428	20,016	82,928,182	31.4

[1] Facilities that do not discharge effluent to surface waters.

Source: U.S. Environmental Protection Agency, Office of Wastewater Management, *1996 Clean Water Needs Survey Report to Congress*.

No. 398. National Ambient Air Pollutant Concentrations: 1990 to 1996

[Data represent annual composite averages of pollutant based on daily 24-hour averages of monitoring stations, except carbon monoxide is based on the second-highest, non-overlapping, 8-hour average; ozone, average of the second-highest daily maximum 1-hour value; and lead, quarterly average of ambient lead levels. Based on data from the Aerometric Information Retrieval System. µg/m³=micrograms of pollutant per cubic meter of air; ppm=parts per million]

POLLUTANT	Unit	Monitoring stations, number	Air quality standard [1]	1990	1991	1992	1993	1994	1995	1996
Carbon monoxide	ppm....	334	[2]9	5.90	5.60	5.20	4.90	5.10	4.5	4.2
Ozone	ppm....	573	[3].12	0.113	0.114	0.106	0.108	0.108	0.113	0.106
Sulfur dioxide	ppm....	473	.03	0.008	0.0078	0.0073	0.0071	0.0068	0.0056	0.0056
Particulates (PM-10) [4]	µg/m³....	955	50	29.4	29.1	26.8	26.0	26.2	25.1	24.2
Nitrogen dioxide	ppm....	212	.053	0.020	0.020	0.019	0.019	0.020	0.019	0.019
Lead	µg/m³....	189	[5]1.5	0.07	0.09	0.07	0.06	0.05	0.04	0.04

[1] Refers to the primary National Ambient Air Quality Standard that protects the public health.   [2] Based on 8-hour standard of 9 ppm.   [3] Based on 1-hour standard of .12 ppm.   [4] The particulates (PM-10) standard replaced the previous standard for total suspended particulates in 1987.   [5] Based on 3-month standard of 1.5 µg/m³.
Source: U.S. Environmental Protection Agency, *National Air Quality and Emissions Trends Report*, annual.

No. 399. National Air Pollutant Emissions: 1970 to 1996

[In thousands of tons, except as indicated. PM-10=Particulate matter of less than ten microns. Methodologies to estimate data for 1970 to 1984 period and 1985 to present emissions differ. Beginning with 1985, the estimates are based on a modified National Acid Precipitation Assessment Program inventory]

YEAR	PM-10	PM-10, fugitive dust[1]	Sulfur dioxide	Nitrogen dioxides	Volatile organic compounds	Carbon monoxide	Lead
1970	13,190	(NA)	31,161	21,639	30,817	128,761	220,869
1975	7,803	(NA)	28,011	23,151	25,895	115,968	159,659
1980	7,287	(NA)	25,905	24,875	26,167	116,702	74,153
1984	6,220	(NA)	23,470	23,172	25,572	114,262	42,217
1985	4,695	40,889	23,230	23,488	24,227	115,644	22,890
1986	4,553	46,582	22,544	23,329	23,480	110,437	14,763
1987	4,492	38,041	22,308	22,806	23,193	108,879	7,681
1988	5,424	55,851	22,767	24,526	24,167	117,169	7,053
1989	4,590	48,650	22,907	24,057	22,383	104,447	5,468
1990	4,639	25,308	23,136	23,792	20,985	96,535	4,975
1991	4,299	25,258	22,496	23,772	21,100	98,461	4,168
1992	4,198	25,308	22,240	24,137	20,695	95,123	3,808
1993	4,086	23,937	21,879	24,482	20,895	95,291	3,911
1994	4,353	26,572	21,262	24,892	21,546	99,677	4,043
1995	4,068	22,820	18,552	23,935	20,586	89,721	3,943
1996	4,068	27,233	19,113	23,393	19,086	88,822	3,869

NA Not available.   [1] Sources such as agricultural tilling, construction, mining and quarrying, paved roads, unpaved roads, and wind erosion.

No. 400. Air Pollutant Emissions, by Pollutant and Source: 1996

[In thousands of tons, except as indicated. See headnote, Table 399]

SOURCE	Particulates[1]	Sulfur dioxide	Nitrogen oxides	Volatile organic compounds	Carbon monoxide	Lead
Total	31,301	19,113	23,393	19,086	88,822	3,869
Fuel combustion, stationary sources	1,186	16,785	10,493	1,075	5,962	493
Electric utilities	282	12,604	6,034	45	377	62
Industrial	306	3,399	3,170	208	1,072	17
Other fuel combustion	598	782	1,289	822	4,513	414
Residential	472	173	838	758	3,993	(NA)
Industrial processes	828	1,594	770	1,462	4,584	2,174
Chemical and allied product manufacturing	67	287	159	436	1,223	117
Metals processing	211	530	98	70	2,378	2,000
Petroleum and related industries	40	368	110	517	348	(NA)
Other	510	409	403	439	635	638
Solvent utilization	6	1	3	6,273	6	(NA)
Storage and transport	109	2	6	1,312	25	(NA)
Waste disposal and recycling	290	48	100	433	1,203	57
Highway vehicles	274	307	7,171	5,502	52,944	19
Light-duty gas vehicles and motorcycles	(NA)	144	3,403	3,323	33,144	14
Light-duty trucks	(NA)	(NA)	1,510	1,582	14,746	5
Heavy-duty gas vehicles	(NA)	(NA)	326	286	3,601	-
Diesels	172	80	1,933	312	1,453	(NA)
Off highway [2]	591	368	4,610	2,426	17,002	545
Miscellaneous [3]	28,018	9	239	601	7,099	(NA)

- Represents zero.   NA Not available.   [1] Represents both PM-10 and PM-10 fugitive dust; see Table 399.   [2] Includes emissions from farm tractors and other farm machinery, construction equipment, industrial machinery, recreational marine vessels, and small general utility engines such as lawn mowers.   [3] Includes emissions such as from forest fires and other kinds of burning, various agricultural activities, fugitive dust from paved and unpaved roads, and other construction and mining activities, and natural sources.
Source of Tables 399 and 400: U.S. Environmental Protection Agency, *National Air Pollutant Emission Trends, 1900-1996*.

No. 401. Emissions of Greenhouse Gases, by Type and Source: 1990 to 1996

[Emission estimates were mandated by Congress through Section 1605(a) of the Energy Policy Act of 1992 (Title XVI). Gases that contain carbon can be measured either in terms of the full molecular weight of the gas or just in terms of their carbon content]

TYPE AND SOURCE	Unit	1990	1991	1992	1993	1994	1995	1996, prel.
Carbon dioxide:								
Carbon content, total [1]	Mil. metric tons	1,373.7	1,360.2	1,379.9	1,411.6	1,433.5	1,444.6	1,495.9
Energy sources	Mil. metric tons	1,345.8	1,330.6	1,351.5	1,380.9	1,401.3	1,411.4	1,463.0
Methane:								
Gas, total [1]	Mil. metric tons	31.6	31.6	31.7	30.8	31.4	30.9	30.9
Energy sources	Mil. metric tons	12.1	12.0	12.0	11.1	11.4	11.2	11.6
Landfills	Mil. metric tons	11.1	11.0	10.9	10.8	10.7	10.6	10.4
Agricultural sources	Mil. metric tons	8.3	8.6	8.8	8.8	9.1	9.1	8.8
Nitrous oxide, total	1,000 metric tons	449	452	452	463	472	454	446
Agriculture	1,000 metric tons	164	167	168	176	179	159	146
Mobile sources	1,000 metric tons	150	148	150	147	147	148	148
Stationary combustion	1,000 metric tons	38	37	37	38	39	39	41
Industrial sources	1,000 metric tons	97	100	96	101	107	108	111
Nitrogen oxide, total [1]	Mil. metric tons	20.9	20.6	20.7	21.1	21.5	19.7	(NA)
Energy related	Mil. metric tons	19.8	19.5	19.7	20.1	20.3	18.8	(NA)
Stationary source fuel combustion	Mil. metric tons	10.4	10.3	10.4	10.6	10.5	9.1	(NA)
Transportation	Mil. metric tons	9.4	9.2	9.4	9.5	9.8	9.6	(NA)
Nonmethane volatile organic compounds (VOCs), total [1]	Mil. metric tons	21.4	20.8	20.3	20.5	21.1	20.7	(NA)
Energy related	Mil. metric tons	9.0	8.7	8.4	8.4	8.7	8.2	(NA)
Transportation	Mil. metric tons	8.1	7.8	7.5	7.5	7.9	7.6	(NA)
Industrial processes	Mil. metric tons	9.4	9.3	9.5	9.6	9.8	9.9	(NA)
Solid waste disposal	Mil. metric tons	2.1	2.1	2.1	2.1	2.1	2.2	(NA)
Carbon monoxide, total	Mil. metric tons	91.3	88.3	85.3	85.4	89.6	83.5	(NA)
Energy related	Mil. metric tons	74.9	74.4	72.9	72.9	74.7	70.9	(NA)
Transportation	Mil. metric tons	70.3	69.6	67.8	68.5	70.3	67.4	(NA)
Stationary source fuel combustion	Mil. metric tons	4.6	4.8	5.0	4.5	4.4	3.5	(NA)
Industrial processes	Mil. metric tons	4.7	4.6	4.7	4.8	4.9	5.2	(NA)
Chlorofluorocarbons (CFCs) gases [2]	1,000 metric tons	223	201	173	149	113	105	73
Hydrofluorocarbons	1,000 metric tons	5	5	8	11	18	22	34
Hydrochlorofluorocarbons (HCFCs) gases [3]	1,000 metric tons	74	89	101	118	135	129	146
Other chemicals:								
Carbon tetrachloride	1,000 metric tons	30	-	26	22	16	5	5
Methyl Cloroform	1,000 metric tons	316	224	215	122	78	46	26
Sulfur hexafluoride	1,000 metric tons	1	1	1	1	1	1	1

- Represents zero.   NA Not available.   [1] Includes minor sources not shown separately.   [2] Covers principally CFC-11, CFC-12, and CFC-113.   [3] Covers principally HCFC-22.

Source: U.S. Energy Information Administration, *Emissions of Greenhouse Gases in the United States*, annual.

No. 402. Municipal Solid Waste Generation, Recovery, and Disposal: 1980 to 1996

[In millions of tons, except as indicated. Covers post-consumer residential and commercial solid wastes which comprise the major portion of typical municipal collections. Excludes mining, agricultural and industrial processing, demolition and construction wastes, sewage sludge, and junked autos and obsolete equipment wastes. Based on material-flows estimating procedure and wet weight as generated]

ITEM AND MATERIAL	1980	1985	1990	1991	1992	1993	1994	1995	1996
Waste generated	151.5	164.4	205.2	204.6	208.9	211.8	214.2	211.5	209.7
Per person per day (lb.)	3.7	3.8	4.5	4.4	4.5	4.5	4.5	4.4	4.3
Materials recovered	14.5	16.4	33.6	37.0	40.6	43.8	50.9	55.1	57.3
Per person per day (lb.)	0.35	0.38	0.7	0.8	0.9	0.9	1.1	1.1	1.2
Combustion for energy recovery	2.7	7.6	29.7	30.1	30.5	30.9	31.2	34.5	36.1
Per person per day (lb.)	0.06	0.17	0.7	0.7	0.7	0.7	0.7	0.7	0.7
Combustion without energy recovery	11.0	4.1	2.2	2.2	2.2	1.6	1.3	1.0	(NA)
Per person per day (lb.)	0.27	0.10	0.05	0.05	0.05	0.03	0.03	0.02	(NA)
Landfill, other disposal	123.3	136.4	139.7	135.3	135.7	135.5	130.8	120.8	116.2
Per person per day (lb.)	2.97	3.13	3.1	2.9	2.9	2.9	2.8	2.5	2.4
Percent distribution of generation:									
Paper and paperboard	36.1	37.4	35.4	34.7	35.5	36.6	37.7	38.6	38.1
Glass	9.9	8.0	6.4	6.2	6.3	6.4	6.2	6.1	5.9
Metals	9.6	8.6	8.1	8.1	7.7	7.5	7.6	7.5	7.7
Plastics	5.2	7.1	8.3	8.7	8.8	9.0	9.0	8.9	9.4
Rubber and leather	2.8	2.3	2.8	2.9	2.8	2.7	2.9	2.9	3.0
Textiles	1.7	1.7	2.8	3.0	3.2	3.2	3.4	3.5	3.7
Wood	4.4	5.0	6.0	6.2	5.9	5.8	5.3	4.9	5.2
Food wastes	8.7	8.0	10.1	10.2	10.1	10.0	10.0	10.3	10.4
Yard wastes	18.2	18.2	17.1	17.1	16.8	15.7	14.7	14.1	13.4
Other wastes	3.4	3.6	3.0	3.1	2.9	3.0	3.2	3.2	3.2

NA Not available.

Source: Franklin Associates, Ltd., Prairie Village, KS, *Characterization of Municipal Solid Waste in the United States: 1996.* Prepared for the U.S. Environmental Protection Agency.

No. 403. Generation and Recovery of Selected Materials in Municipal Solid Waste: 1980 to 1996

[In millions of tons, except as indicated. Covers post-consumer residential and commercial solid wastes which comprise the major portion of typical municipal collections. Excludes mining, agricultural and industrial processing, demolition and construction wastes, sewage sludge, and junked autos and obsolete equipment wastes. Based on material-flows estimating procedure and wet weight as generated]

ITEM AND MATERIAL	1980	1985	1990	1991	1992	1993	1994	1995	1996
Waste generated, total	**151.5**	**164.4**	**205.2**	**204.6**	**208.9**	**211.8**	**214.2**	**211.5**	**209.7**
Paper and paperboard	54.7	61.5	72.7	71.0	74.3	77.4	80.8	81.7	79.9
Ferrous metals	11.6	10.9	12.6	12.7	12.1	11.9	11.8	11.6	11.8
Aluminum	1.8	2.3	2.8	2.8	2.9	2.9	3.0	3.0	3.0
Other nonferrous metals	1.1	1.0	1.1	1.1	1.1	1.1	1.4	1.3	1.3
Glass	15.0	13.2	13.1	12.6	13.1	13.6	13.4	12.8	12.4
Plastics	7.9	11.6	17.1	17.7	18.4	19.0	19.3	18.9	19.8
Yard wastes	27.5	30.0	35.0	35.0	35.0	33.3	31.5	29.8	28.0
Other wastes	31.9	33.9	50.7	51.7	52.1	52.5	53.0	52.5	53.5
Materials recovered, total	**14.5**	**16.4**	**33.6**	**37.0**	**40.6**	**43.8**	**50.9**	**55.1**	**57.3**
Paper and paperboard	11.9	13.1	20.2	22.5	24.5	25.5	29.5	32.7	32.6
Ferrous metals	0.4	0.4	2.6	3.1	3.4	3.9	4.1	4.2	4.5
Aluminum	0.3	0.6	1.0	1.0	1.1	1.0	1.2	1.0	1.0
Other nonferrous metals	0.5	0.5	0.7	0.7	0.7	0.7	1.0	0.8	0.8
Glass	0.8	1.0	2.6	2.6	2.9	3.0	3.1	3.1	3.2
Plastics	-	0.1	0.4	0.5	0.6	0.7	0.9	1.0	1.1
Yard wastes	-	-	4.2	4.8	5.4	6.9	8.0	9.0	10.8
Other wastes	0.6	0.7	1.8	1.9	2.0	2.1	3.1	3.2	3.3
Percent of generation recovered, total	**9.6**	**10.0**	**16.4**	**18.1**	**19.4**	**20.7**	**23.8**	**26.1**	**27.3**
Paper and paperboard	21.8	21.3	27.8	31.7	33.0	32.9	36.5	40.0	40.8
Ferrous metals	3.4	3.7	20.4	24.1	27.7	32.8	35.0	36.4	38.0
Aluminum	16.7	26.1	35.9	35.5	38.7	35.7	37.8	34.6	34.2
Other nonferrous metals	45.5	50.0	66.4	65.5	63.4	63.1	73.3	64.3	66.7
Glass	5.3	7.6	20.0	20.3	22.0	22.1	23.3	24.5	25.7
Plastics	-	0.9	2.2	2.5	3.3	3.5	4.9	5.2	5.4
Yard wastes	-	-	12.0	13.7	15.4	20.8	25.4	30.3	38.6
Other wastes	1.9	2.1	3.6	3.7	3.9	4.0	5.9	6.1	6.2

- Represents zero.

Source: Franklin Associates, Ltd., Prairie Village, KS, *Characterization of Municipal Solid Waste in the United States: 1996.* Prepared for the U.S. Environmental Protection Agency.

No. 404. Toxic Chemical Releases and Transfers, by Media: 1988 to 1995

[In thousands of pounds. Based on reports filed as required by section 313 of the Emergency Planning and Community Right-to-Know Act (EPCRA, or Title III of the Superfund Amendments and Reauthorization Act of 1986), Public Law 99-499. Owners and operators of facilities that are classified within Standard Classification Code groups 20 through 39, have 10 or more full-time employees, and that manufacture, process, or otherwise uses any listed toxic chemical in quantities greater than the established threshold in the course of a calendar year are covered and required to report]

MEDIA	CORE CHEMICALS [1]						Expanded chemical list [2], 1995
	1988	1993	1994	1995			
				Total	Change, 1988-95	Percent change, 1988-95	
Total facilities reporting	20,412	21,260	20,697	19,968	-444	-2.2	19,968
Total releases and transfers	**4,015,275**	**4,899,836**	**4,963,568**	**4,884,330**	**869,056**	**21.6**	**5,743,577**
Total releases	2,962,349	1,893,560	1,700,851	1,610,448	-1,351,901	-45.6	2,208,749
Total air emissions	2,176,712	1,317,366	1,263,917	1,172,651	-1,004,061	-46.1	1,262,322
Fugitive air	679,934	375,914	349,635	302,210	-377,724	-55.6	85,095
Point source air	1,496,778	941,452	914,283	870,441	-626,337	-41.8	1,177,228
Surface water	164,467	194,864	39,975	35,794	-128,672	-78.2	136,316
Underground injection	161,939	113,290	114,170	136,752	-25,188	-15.6	234,980
Releases to land	459,232	268,040	282,798	265,252	-193,980	-42.2	275,132
Total transfers	1,052,925	3,006,276	3,262,707	3,273,882	(NA)	(NA)	3,534,828
Tranfers to recycling	(NA)	1,937,016	2,168,767	2,141,325	(NA)	(NA)	2,213,731
Transfers to energy recovery	(NA)	444,763	455,461	485,656	(NA)	(NA)	512,030
Transfers to treatment	369,160	208,232	217,217	235,231	-133,929	-36.3	287,577
Transfers to POTWs[3]	254,723	163,233	158,465	154,662	-100,061	-39.3	239,837
Transfers to disposal	386,183	250,671	259,377	254,785	-131,398	-34.0	279,222
Other off-site transfers	42,859	2,360	3,421	2,222	-40,637	-94.8	2,431

NA Not available. [1] Excludes chemicals removed from the list, those added in 1990, 1991, 1994, and 1995, and aluminum oxide, ammonia, hydrochloric acid, and sulfuric acid. Chemicals covered for all reporting years. [2] The Environmental Protection Agency added 286 chemicals and chemical categories to the EPCRA section list of 313 list of toxic chemicals. [3] Publicly Owned Treatment Works is a waste water treatment facility that is owned by a state or municipality.

Source: U.S. Environmental Protection Agency, *1995 Toxics Release Inventory.*

No. 405. Toxic Chemical Releases, by Industry: 1988 to 1995

[**In thousands of pounds.** Based on reports filed as required by section 313 of the Emergency Planning and Community Right-to-Know Act (EPCRA, or Title III of the Superfund Amendments and Reauthorization Act of 1986), Public Law 99-499. Owners and operators of facilities that are classified within Standard Classification Code groups 20 through 39, have 10 or more full-time employees, and that manufacture, process, or otherwise uses any listed toxic chemical in quantities greater than the established threshold in the course of a calendar year are covered and required to report]

INDUSTRY	1987 SIC [1] code	CORE CHEMICALS [2]						1995, expanded chemical list [3]
		1988	1993	1994	1995			
					Total	Change, 1988-95	Percent change, 1988-95	
Total	(X)	2,962,349	1,893,560	1,700,861	1,610,448	-1,351,901	-45.6	2,208,749
Food and kindred products	20	7,288	7,528	6,160	5,281	-2,007	-27.5	86,013
Tobacco products	21	342	137	135	95	-247	-72.2	1,748
Textile mill products	22	34,154	17,450	15,773	14,990	-19,163	-56.1	17,766
Apparel and other textile products	23	922	1,003	1,311	1,232	310	33.6	1,259
Lumber and wood products	24	31,050	29,264	32,345	29,497	-1,552	-5.0	31,289
Furniture and fixtures	25	61,363	54,276	51,525	40,712	-20,651	-33.7	40,961
Paper and allied products	26	201,459	146,849	180,646	176,176	-25,283	-12.6	233,225
Printing and publishing	27	60,694	36,148	34,313	31,375	-29,319	-48.3	31,625
Chemical and allied products	28	979,850	679,468	495,871	492,005	-487,846	-49.8	787,752
Petroleum and coal products	29	67,649	49,334	42,535	40,190	-27,460	-40.6	59,943
Rubber and misc. plastic products	30	146,535	119,295	112,865	100,928	-45,607	-31.1	112,219
Leather and leather products	31	11,928	4,473	3,620	2,649	-9,279	-77.8	3,069
Stone, clay, glass products	32	23,923	12,161	10,836	12,648	-11,276	-47.1	36,042
Primary metal industries	33	471,664	281,310	273,635	291,697	-179,967	-38.2	331,200
Fabricated metals products	34	130,537	88,873	86,511	78,245	-52,292	-40.1	82,585
Industrial machinery and equip.	35	59,463	26,566	23,576	19,293	-40,170	-67.6	23,159
Electronic, electric equipment	36	115,408	32,723	28,850	23,445	-91,963	-79.7	30,489
Transportation equipment	37	188,630	121,900	118,900	104,852	-83,777	-44.4	110,018
Instruments and related products	38	47,210	20,255	13,540	12,202	-35,008	-74.2	16,866
Miscellaneous	39	28,471	15,279	13,828	11,188	-17,283	-60.7	11,450
Multiple codes	20-39	283,311	131,240	137,651	114,132	-169,179	-59.7	149,652
No codes	20-39	10,499	18,029	16,394	7,617	-2,882	-27.5	10,418

X Not applicable.   [1] Standard Industrial Classification, see text, Section 13.   [2] Chemicals covered for all reporting years.
[3] The Environmental Protection Agency added 286 chemicals and chemical categories to the EPCRA section list of 313 list of toxic chemicals.

Source: U.S. Environmental Protection Agency, *1995 Toxics Release Inventory.*

No. 406. Toxic Releases, by State: 1988 to 1995

[**In thousands of pounds**. Excludes delisted chemicals, chemicals added in 1990, 1991, 1994, and 1995, and aluminum oxide, ammonia, hydorchloric acid, and sulfuric acid. See headnote, Table 405]

STATE AND OUTLYING AREAS	1988	1993	1994	1995	STATE AND OUTLYING AREAS	1988	1993	1994	1995
Total	2,962,349	1,893,560	1,700,861	1,610,448	MT	35,587	44,485	46,348	42,615
U.S. total	2,947,832	1,881,528	1,690,827	1,600,889	NE	13,510	9,498	7,989	7,303
AL	103,600	90,151	84,093	88,803	NV	2,288	2,946	3,002	3,175
AK	3,713	2,104	1,095	2,158	NH	12,279	3,185	2,235	1,840
AZ	65,969	11,813	30,504	33,525	NJ	36,331	14,070	12,541	10,882
AR	35,988	23,853	27,568	22,863	NM	30,246	22,938	17,132	17,869
CA	90,474	41,417	33,852	26,460	NY	87,704	33,468	29,394	25,618
CO	13,222	3,958	3,726	3,190	NC	121,477	76,501	77,888	69,164
CT	32,536	12,393	10,062	7,201	ND	1,130	918	977	1,183
DE	6,925	3,914	3,642	2,822	OH	157,020	95,508	90,806	94,078
DC	1	-	29	30	OK	28,263	14,964	12,719	12,862
FL	59,370	45,794	70,223	50,666	OR	17,836	13,985	15,833	17,746
GA	67,892	36,394	41,140	36,503	PA	97,147	43,982	44,628	40,237
HI	834	499	514	398	RI	6,321	3,382	3,026	2,556
ID	7,283	1,870	2,393	2,625	SC	60,584	44,670	42,442	44,180
IL	107,659	69,935	71,707	67,396	SD	2,312	1,891	1,998	1,757
IN	160,767	78,980	65,019	62,657	TN	115,218	95,015	87,016	88,368
IA	38,598	22,572	21,081	19,184	TX	302,813	197,101	187,319	188,296
KS	28,564	16,636	15,843	14,582	UT	123,311	84,202	65,671	68,622
KY	49,698	30,870	29,578	28,013	VT	1,594	616	607	511
LA	241,889	263,611	113,098	119,733	VA	109,750	43,669	42,088	39,248
ME	14,673	8,076	6,055	5,821	WA	25,877	16,707	19,863	20,959
MD	17,996	10,333	10,611	10,106	WV	31,331	18,493	17,898	15,861
MA	26,065	10,045	8,581	6,937	WI	48,633	29,233	29,095	24,266
MI	94,915	71,910	75,924	54,148	WY	16,739	794	875	1,110
MN	54,343	22,078	19,589	16,771	Am. Samoa	-	(Z)	-	-
MS	54,595	42,546	41,332	38,178	Puerto Rico	12,669	10,453	9,073	8,370
MO	85,229	47,557	44,176	39,813	Virgin Island	1,848	1,579	961	1,186

- Represents zero.   Z Less than 500 pounds.

Source: U.S. Environmental Protection Agency, Office of Pollution Prevention and Toxics, *1995 Toxics Release Inventory*, annual.

No. 407. Hazardous Waste Sites on the National Priority List, by State: 1997

[Includes both proposed and final sites listed on the National Priorities List for the Superfund program as authorized by the Comprehensive Environmental Response, Compensation, and Liability Act of 1980 and the Superfund Amendments and Reauthorization Act of 1986]

STATE AND OUTLYING AREAS	Total sites	Rank	Percent distribution	Federal	Non-federal	STATE AND OUTLYING AREAS	Total sites	Rank	Percent distribution	Federal	Non-federal
Total	1,245	(X)	(X)	157	1,088	Montana	9	40	0.73	-	9
						Nebraska	10	37	0.81	1	9
United States. .	**1,231**	**(X)**	**100.00**	**155**	**1,076**	Nevada	1	49	0.08	-	1
Alabama	13	30	1.06	3	10	New Hampshire	18	19	1.46	1	17
Alaska	7	43	0.57	6	1	New Jersey	110	1	8.94	6	104
Arizona	10	37	0.81	3	7	New Mexico	10	37	0.81	1	9
Arkansas	11	33	0.89	-	11	New York	80	4	6.50	4	76
California	94	3	7.64	23	71	North Carolina	23	17	1.87	2	21
Colorado.	17	20	1.38	3	14	North Dakota	-	50	0.00	-	-
Connecticut	14	29	1.14	1	13	Ohio	37	10	3.01	5	32
Delaware	17	20	1.38	1	16	Oklahoma	11	33	0.89	1	10
District of Columbia .	-	(X)	0.00	-	-	Oregon.	11	33	0.89	2	9
Florida	54	6	4.39	6	48	Pennsylvania	99	2	8.04	6	93
Georgia	16	24	1.30	2	14	Rhode Island.	12	31	0.97	2	10
Hawaii	4	45	0.32	3	1	South Carolina.	26	15	2.11	2	24
Idaho	9	40	0.73	2	7	South Dakota	2	48	0.16	1	1
Illinois	41	8	3.33	4	37	Tennessee	16	24	1.30	4	12
Indiana	30	12	2.44	-	30	Texas	27	14	2.19	4	23
Iowa	17	20	1.38	1	16	Utah	16	24	1.30	4	12
Kansas	11	33	0.89	2	9	Vermont	8	42	0.65	-	8
Kentucky	16	24	1.30	1	15	Virginia	25	16	2.03	7	18
Louisiana	17	20	1.38	1	16	Washington	47	7	3.82	14	33
Maine	12	31	0.97	3	9	West Virginia	7	43	0.57	2	5
Maryland	16	24	1.30	6	10	Wisconsin	39	9	3.17	-	39
Massachusetts	31	11	2.52	8	23	Wyoming	3	46	0.24	1	2
Michigan	74	5	6.01	1	73						
Minnesota	28	13	2.27	2	26	Guam	2	(X)	(X)	1	1
Mississippi	3	46	0.24	-	3	Puerto Rico	10	(X)	(X)	1	9
Missouri	22	18	1.79	3	19	Virgin Islands.	2	(X)	(X)	-	2

- Represents zero. X Not applicable.

Source: U.S. Environmental Protection Agency, *Supplementary Materials: National Priorities List, Proposed Rule*, December 1997.

No. 408. Environmental Industry—Revenues and Employment, by Industry Segment: 1980 to 1997

[Covers approximately 59,000 private and public companies engaged in environmental activities]

INDUSTRY SEGMENT	REVENUE (bil. dol.)					EMPLOYMENT (1,000)				
	1980	1990	1995	1996	1997	1980	1990	1995	1996	1997
Industry total	**55.0**	**149.0**	**179.0**	**181.1**	**185.1**	**462.5**	**1,174.3**	**1,327.0**	**1,338.0**	**1,348.0**
Analytical services [1]	0.4	1.5	1.2	1.2	1.1	6.0	20.2	14.1	14.0	12.7
Wastewater treatment works [2]	10.9	20.4	23.4	24.0	24.7	53.9	95.0	101.5	103.1	104.8
Solid waste management [3]	8.5	26.1	32.5	33.9	34.9	83.2	209.5	243.4	245.7	249.9
Hazardous waste management [4] . .	0.6	6.3	6.2	6.0	5.8	6.8	56.9	52.5	51.6	49.4
Remediation/industrial services . . .	0.4	8.0	8.6	8.6	8.7	6.9	107.2	98.1	95.7	96.0
Consulting & engineering	1.5	12.5	15.5	15.2	15.0	20.5	144.2	180.2	178.9	174.4
Water equipment & chemicals	6.9	13.5	16.5	17.5	18.0	62.4	97.9	110.2	115.3	117.0
Instrument manufacturing	0.2	2.0	3.0	3.1	3.2	2.5	18.8	26.2	28.5	28.7
Air pollution control equipment [5] . .	3.3	13.1	15.0	15.7	16.2	28.3	82.7	107.2	108.7	111.2
Waste management equipment [6] . .	4.0	10.4	11.7	12.0	12.2	41.9	88.8	93.8	93.5	94.2
Process & prevention technology . .	0.1	0.4	0.8	0.8	0.9	2.1	8.9	19.5	20.0	21.2
Water utilities [7]	11.9	19.8	25.3	26.4	27.0	76.9	104.7	118.2	119.8	121.3
Resource recovery [8]	4.4	13.1	16.9	14.3	15.0	48.7	118.4	136.0	136.6	141.2
Environmental energy sources [9] . .	1.5	1.8	2.3	2.4	2.4	22.4	21.1	26.1	26.4	26.4

[1] Covers environmental laboratory testing and services. [2] Mostly revenues collected by municipal entities. [3] Covers such activities as collection, transportation, transfer stations, disposal, landfill ownership, and management for solid waste. [4] Transportation and disposal of hazardous, medical, and nuclear waste. [5] Includes stationery and mobile sources. [6] Includes vehicles, containers, liners, processing, and remediation equipment. [7] Revenues generated from the sale of water. [8] Revenues generated from the sale of recovered metals, paper, plastic, etc. [9] Includes solar, wind, geothermal, and conservation devices.

Source: Environmental Business International, Inc., San Diego, CA, *Environmental Business Journal*, monthly (copyright).

No. 409. Value of Selected Product Shipments for Environmental or Potential Environmental Use: 1995

[In millions of dollars. Based on a sample survey of private businesses involved in the commercial activities of the environmental industry. The environmental industry is defined as the manufacture of products, performance of services and the construction of projects used, or that potentially could be used, for measuring, preventing, limiting, or correcting environmental damage to air, water, and soil]

PRODUCTS	Total [1]	For environmental use	Not for environmental use	PRODUCTS	Total [1]	For environmental use	Not for environmental use
Total products	**36,864**	**14,378**	**15,199**	Solid waste [2]	1,741	713	609
Air treatment [2]	4,740	4,629	82	Storage containers (including			
Particulate emissions				metal and concrete)	879	260	266
collectors	793	793	-	Energy conservation [2]	7,633	2,448	4,880
Catalytic converters	2,702	2,702	-	Wind energy conversion			
Water and wastewater				(including turbines, turbine			
treatment [2]	10,503	5,230	4,321	sets, windmills, and parts)	4,054	12	4,042
Storage tanks and process				Industrial heat exchangers	1,279	678	384
vessels (including pressure)	1,338	488	731	Ethanol	1,714	1,464	229
Fluid filters (including				Noise pollution control	100	63	23
housings)	729	232	366	Monitoring and analysis [2]	12,148	1,296	5,284
Sewage treatment equipment	792	792	-	Industrial process monitoring			
Deionization equipment	811	811	-	devices	3,438	530	2,471
Pumps	2,101	362	1,380	Flow measurement devices	5,347	108	573

- Represents or rounds to zero. [1] Includes unknown use not shown separately. [2] Includes products not shown separately.

No. 410. Receipts for Selected Services for Environmental or Potential Environmental Purposes: 1995

[In millions of dollars. See headnote, Table 409]

SERVICES	Total [1]	For environmental purposes	Not for environmental purposes	SERVICES	Total [1]	For environmental purposes	Not for environmental purposes
Total services	**111,106**	**55,720**	**54,313**	Operation of sorting &			
Air treatment [2]	1,249	1,249	-	separation systems	1,093	1,093	-
Emissions monitoring	704	704	-	Site remediation	2,743	2,743	-
Water and wastewater				Incinerator operations	837	837	-
treatment [2]	9,439	9,398	2	Hazardous clean-up and			
Hydrogeological services	1,036	1,036	-	containment	1,235	1,235	-
Water treatment planning and				Monitoring, assessment and			
analysis	1,487	1,487	-	analysis [2]	4,895	4,071	809
Sewerage systems (including				Facility assessment &			
design and operation)	2,569	2,569	-	monitoring	2,263	2,263	-
Private water supply (including				Analytical laboratory services	1,694	870	809
operation & mgt.)	3,168	3,168	-	Administrative, management			
Solid waste [2]	35,839	34,728	929	and engineering [2]	59,684	6,275	52,573
Dump trucking	1,599	488	929	Management consulting	41,292	1,993	38,859
Waste collection and				Information management	1,522	331	1,175
hauling	17,018	17,018	-	Regulatory and compliance report			
Hazardous material hauling	2,666	2,666	-	(incl. Phase 1 & Phase 2 audits)	680	680	-
Waste disposal	6,331	6,331	-	Engineering design [2]	14,384	2,234	11,818

- Represents or rounds to zero. [1] Includes unknown use not shown separately. [2] Includes products not shown separately.

Source of Tables 409 and 410: U.S. Environmental Protection Agency and U.S. International Trade Administration, *Survey of Environmental Products and Services,* February 1998.

No. 411. Threatened and Endangered Wildlife and Plant Species—Number: 1998

[As of **April**. Endangered species: One in danger of becoming extinct throughout all or a significant part of its natural range. Threatened species: One likely to become endangered in the foreseeable future]

ITEM	Mammals	Birds	Reptiles	Amphibians	Fishes	Snails	Clams	Crustaceans	Insects	Arachnids	Plants
Total listings	333	274	114	25	119	23	71	19	41	5	672
Endangered species, total	**310**	**253**	**80**	**17**	**78**	**16**	**63**	**16**	**32**	**5**	**554**
United States	59	75	14	9	67	15	61	16	28	5	553
Foreign	251	178	66	8	11	1	2	-	4	-	1
Threatened species, total	**23**	**21**	**34**	**8**	**41**	**7**	**8**	**3**	**9**	**-**	**118**
United States	7	15	20	7	41	7	8	3	9	-	116
Foreign	16	6	14	1	-	-	-	-	-	-	2

- Represents zero.

Source: U.S. Fish and Wildlife Service, *Endangered Species Technical Bulletin,* quarterly.

No. 412. Major U.S. Weather Disasters: 1980 to 1998

[Covers only weather related disasters costing $1 billion or more]

EVENT	Description	Time period	Esti mated cost (bil. dol.)	Deaths
Southeast severe weather	Tornadoes and flooding related to strong El Nino in the southeast	Winter/Spring 1998	$1	Over 130
Northern plains flooding	Severe flooding in Dakotas and Minnesota due to heavy spring snowmelt	April-May 1977	$2	11
MS and OH valleys flooding and tornadoes	Tornadoes and severe flooding hit the states of AR, MO, MS, TN, IL, IN, KY, OH, and WV	March 1997	$1	67
West Coast flooding	Flooding from rains and snowmelt in CA, WA, OR, ID, NV, & MT	Dec. 1996- Jan. 1997	$2-$3	36
Hurricane Fran	Category 3 hurricane in NC and VA.	Sept. 1996	$5	37
Southern Plains severe drought	Drought in agricultural areas of TX & OK	Fall 1995- summer 1996	Over $4	(NA)
Pacific Northwest severe flooding	Flooding from heavy rain & snowmelt in OR, WA, ID, and MT .	Feb. 1996	$1	9
Blizzard of '96 followed by flooding	Heavy snowstorm followed by severe flooding in Appalachians, Mid-Atlantic, and Northeast.	Jan. 1996	$3	187
Hurricane Opal	Category 3 hurricane in FL, AL, parts of GA, TN, & Carolinas. .	Oct. 1995	Over $3	27
Hurricane Marilyn	Category 2 hurricane in Virgin Islands	Sept. 1995	$2	13
TX/OK/LA/MS severe weather and flooding	Flooding, hail, & tornadoes across TX, OK, parts of LA, MS, Dallas & New Orleans hardest hit	May 1995	$5-$6	32
California flooding	Flooding from frequent winter storms across much of CA	Jan.-Mar. 1995	$3	27
Texas flooding	Flooding from torrential rain & thunderstorms across southeast TX	Oct. 1994	$1	19
Tropical storm Alberto	Flooding due to 10 to 25 inch rain across GA, AL, part of FL . .	July 1994	$1	32
Southeast ice storm	Intense ice storm in pts of TX, OK, AR, LA, MS, AL, TN, GA, SC, NC, & VA	Feb. 1994	$3	9
California wildfires	Out-of-control wildfires over southern CA	Fall 1993	$1	4
Midwest flooding	Extreme flooding across central U.S.	Summer 1993	$15-$20	48
Drought/heat wave	Extreme drought/heatwave across southeastern U.S.	Summer 1993	$1	(NA)
Storm/blizzard	Storm/blizzard over eastern U.S.	Mar. 1993	$3-$6	270
Nor'easter of 1992	Slow-moving storm batters northeast U.S. coast, New England hardest hit	Dec. 1992	$1-$2	19
Hurricane Iniki	Category 4 hurricane hit Hawaiian island of Kauai	Sept. 1992	1.8	7
Hurricane Andrew	Category 4 hurricane hit FL & LA	Aug. 1992	$27	58
Oakland firestorm	Oakland, CA firestorm due to low humidity & high winds	Oct. 1991	$1.5	25
Hurricane Bob	Category 2 hurricane—mainly coastal NC, Long Island, & New England	Aug. 1991	$1.5	18
Hurricane Hugo	Category 4 hurricane hit Puerto Rico & Virgin Islands, devastated NC & SC.	Sept. 1989	Over $9	86
Drought/heat wave	Drought/heatwave over central & eastern U.S.	Summer 1988	$40	5,000-10,000
Hurricane Juan	Category 1 hurricane, flooding most severe problem, hit LA and southeast U.S.	Oct.-Nov. 1985	$1.5	63
Hurricane Elena	Category 3 hurricane across FL to LA	Aug.-Sept. 1985	$1.3	4
Florida freeze	Severe freeze central/northern FL, damage to citrus industry . .	Dec. 1983	$2	-
Hurricane Alicia	Category 3 hurricane across TX	Aug. 1983	$3	21
Drought/heat wave	Drought/heatwave over central & eastern U.S.	June-Sept. 1980	$20	10,000

- Represents zero.   NA Not available or not reported.

Source: U.S. National Oceanic and Atmospheric Administration, National Climatic Data Center. *"Billion Dollar U.S. Weather Disaster, 1980-1998,"* June 1, 1998. <http://www.ncdc.noaa.gov/publications/billionz.html>.

No. 413. Tornadoes, Floods, and Tropical Storms: 1986 to 1996

ITEM	1986	1987	1988	1989	1990	1991	1992	1993	1994	1995	1996
Tornadoes, number [1]	764	656	702	856	1,133	1,132	1,298	1,176	1,082	1,235	1,170
Tornado days	168	151	156	160	181	179	195	186	199	178	196
Lives lost, total	15	59	32	50	53	39	39	33	69	30	25
Most in a single tornado	3	30	5	21	29	17	12	7	22	6	5
Floods and flash floods:											
Lives lost.	80	71	31	85	142	61	39	103	89	79	164
North Atlantic tropical storms and hurricanes [2]	6	7	12	11	14	8	7	8	7	19	13
Number of hurricanes reaching U.S. mainland.	2	1	1	3	-	1	1	1	-	2	2
Total direct deaths from tropical storms and hurricanes	9	3	550	84	123	17	28	273	1,175	121	138
Direct deaths on U.S. mainland .	9	-	6	56	10	17	26	9	38	29	33
Property loss in U.S.	17	8	59	7,670	57	1,500	26,500	57	973	3,729	3,600

- Represents zero.   [1] A violent, rotating column of air descending from a cumulonimbus cloud in the form of a tubular- or funnel-shaped cloud, usually characterized by movements along a narrow path and wind speeds from 100 to over 300 miles per hour. Also known as a "twister" or "waterspout."   [2] Source: National Hurricane Center, Coral Gables, FL, unpublished data. Tropical storms have maximum winds of 39 to 73 miles per hour; hurricanes have maximum winds of 74 miles per hour or higher.

Source: Except as noted, U.S. National Oceanic and Atmospheric Administration, *Storm Data,* monthly.

No. 414. Highest and Lowest Temperatures, by State Through 1996

STATE	HIGHEST TEMPERATURES			LOWEST TEMPERATURES		
	STATION	Temperature (F)	Date	STATION	Temperature (F)	Date
U.S. . . .	Greenland Ranch, CA. .	134	Jul. 10, 1913	Prospect Creek, AK . . .	-80	Jan. 23, 1971
AL	Centerville	112	Sep. 5, 1925	New Market	-27	Jan. 30, 1966
AK	Fort Yukon	100	Jun. 27, 1915	Prospect Creek.	-80	Jan. 23, 1971
AZ	Lake Havasu City	128	Jun. 29, 1994	Hawley Lake	-40	Jan. 7, 1971
AR	Ozark	120	Aug. 10, 1936	Pond.	-29	Feb. 13, 1905
CA	Greenland Ranch	134	Jul. 10, 1913	Boca.	-45	Jan. 20, 1937
CO	Bennett	118	Jul. 11, 1888	Maybell	-61	Feb. 1, 1985
CT	Danbury	105	Jul. 21, 1991 [1]	Falls Village	-32	Feb. 16, 1943
DE	Millsboro	110	Jul. 21, 1930	Millsboro	-17	Jan. 17, 1893
FL	Monticello	109	Jun. 29, 1931	Tallahassee	-2	Feb. 13, 1899
GA	Louisville	112	Jul. 24, 1952	CCC Camp F-16.	-17	Jan. 27, 1940
HI.	Pahala	100	Apr. 27, 1931	Mauna Kea Obs. 111.2. .	12	May 17, 1979
ID.	Orofino	118	Jul. 28, 1934	Island Park Dam	-60	Jan. 18, 1943
IL.	East St. Louis.	117	Jul. 14, 1954	Elizabeth	-35	Feb. 3, 1996 [1]
IN.	Collegeville	116	Jul. 14, 1936	New Whiteland	-36	Jan. 19, 1994
IA.	Keokuk	118	Jul. 20, 1934	Elkader	-47	Feb. 3, 1996 [1]
KS	Alton (near)	121	Jul. 24, 1936 [1]	Lebanon	-40	Feb. 13, 1905
KY	Greensburg	114	Jul. 28, 1930	Cynthiana	-34	Jan. 28, 1963
LA	Plain Dealing	114	Aug. 10, 1936	Minden	-16	Feb. 13, 1899
ME	North Bridgton	105	Jul. 10, 1911 [1]	Van Buren	-48	Jan. 19, 1925
MD	Cumberland	109	Jul. 10, 1936 [1]	Oakland	-40	Jan. 13, 1912
MA	New Bedford	107	Aug. 2, 1975	Chester	-35	Jan. 12, 1981
MI	Mio.	112	Jul. 13, 1936	Vanderbilt	-51	Feb. 9, 1934
MN	Moorhead	114	Jul. 6, 1936 [1]	Tower	-60	Feb. 2, 1996
MS	Holly Springs	115	Jul. 29, 1930	Corinth	-19	Jan. 30, 1966
MO	Warsaw.	118	Jul. 14, 1954 [1]	Warsaw.	-40	Feb. 13, 1905
MT	Medicine Lake	117	Jul. 5, 1937	Rogers Pass	-70	Jan. 20, 1954
NE	Minden	118	Jul. 24, 1936 [1]	Camp Clarke	-47	Feb. 12, 1899
NV	Laughlin	125	Jun. 29, 1994	San Jacinto	-50	Jan. 8, 1937
NH	Nashua	106	Jul. 4, 1911	Pittsburg	-46	Jan. 28, 1925
NJ	Runyon	110	Jul. 10, 1936	River Vale	-34	Jan. 5, 1904
NM	Waste Isolat Pilot Plt . . .	122	Jun. 27, 1994	Gavilan	-50	Feb. 1, 1951
NY	Troy	108	Jul. 22, 1926	Old Forge	-52	Feb. 18, 1979 [1]
NC	Fayetteville.	110	Aug. 21, 1983	Mt. Mitchell	-34	Jan. 21, 1985
ND	Steele.	121	Jul. 6, 1936	Parshall.	-60	Feb. 15, 1936
OH	Gallipolis (near).	113	Jul. 21, 1934 [1]	Milligan	-39	Feb. 10, 1899
OK	Tipton	120	Jun. 27, 1994 [1]	Watts	-27	Jan. 18, 1930
OR	Pendleton	119	Aug. 10, 1898	Seneca	-54	Feb. 10, 1933 [1]
PA	Phoenixville	111	Jul. 10, 1936 [1]	Smethport	-42	Jan. 5, 1904
RI.	Providence.	104	Aug. 2, 1975	Greene	-25	Feb. 5, 1996
SC	Camden	111	Jun. 28, 1954 [1]	Caesars Head	-19	Jan. 21, 1985
SD	Gannvalley.	120	Jul. 5, 1936	McIntosh	-58	Feb. 17, 1936
TN	Perryville	113	Aug. 9, 1930 [1]	Mountain City.	-32	Dec. 30, 1917
TX	Seymour	120	Aug. 12, 1936	Seminole	-23	Feb. 8, 1933 [1]
UT	Saint George	117	Jul. 5, 1985	Peter's Sink	-69	Feb. 1, 1985
VT	Vernon	105	Jul. 4, 1911	Bloomfield	-50	Dec. 30, 1933
VA	Balcony Falls	110	Jul. 15, 1954	Mtn. Lake Bio. Stn.	-30	Jan. 22, 1985
WA	Ice Harbor Dam	118	Aug. 5, 1961 [1]	Mazama	-48	Dec. 30, 1968
WV	Martinsburg	112	Jul. 10, 1936 [1]	Lewisburg	-37	Dec. 30, 1917
WI	Wisconsin Dells	114	Jul. 13, 1936	Danbury	-54	Jan. 24, 1922
WY	Basin	114	Jul. 12, 1900	Riverside R.S.	-66	Feb. 9, 1933

[1] Also on earlier dates at the same or other places.

Source: U.S. National Oceanic and Atmospheric Administration, (accessed December 11, 1997).

No. 415. Normal Daily Mean, Maximum, and Minimum Temperatures—Selected Cities

[In **Fahrenheit degrees.** Airport data except as noted. Based on standard 30-year period, 1961 through 1990]

STATE	STATION	DAILY MEAN TEMPERATURE			DAILY MAXIMUM TEMPERATURE			DAILY MINIMUM TEMPERATURE		
		Jan.	July	Annual average	Jan.	July	Annual average	Jan.	July	Annual average
AL	Mobile.	49.9	82.3	67.5	59.7	91.3	77.4	40.0	73.2	57.4
AK	Juneau	24.2	56.0	40.6	29.4	63.9	46.9	19.0	48.1	34.1
AZ	Phoenix.	53.6	93.5	72.6	65.9	105.9	85.9	41.2	81.0	59.3
AR	Little Rock	39.1	81.9	61.8	49.0	92.4	72.5	29.1	71.5	51.0
CA	Los Angeles	56.8	69.1	63.0	65.7	75.3	70.4	47.8	62.8	55.5
	Sacramento	45.2	75.7	60.8	52.7	93.2	73.5	37.7	58.1	48.1
	San Diego	57.4	71.0	64.2	65.9	76.2	70.8	48.9	65.7	57.6
	San Francisco	48.7	62.7	57.1	55.6	71.6	65.2	41.8	53.9	49.0
CO	Denver	29.7	73.5	50.3	43.2	88.2	64.2	16.1	58.6	36.2
CT	Hartford.	24.6	73.7	49.9	33.2	85.0	60.2	15.8	62.2	39.5
DE	Wilmington.	30.6	76.4	54.2	38.7	85.6	63.6	22.4	67.1	44.8
DC	Washington	34.6	80.0	58.0	42.3	88.5	66.9	26.8	71.4	49.2
FL	Jacksonville	52.4	81.6	68.0	64.2	91.4	78.9	40.5	71.9	57.1
	Miami	67.2	82.6	75.9	75.2	89.0	82.8	59.2	76.2	69.0
GA	Atlanta	41.0	78.8	61.3	50.4	88.0	71.2	31.5	69.5	51.3
HI	Honolulu	72.9	80.5	77.2	80.1	87.5	84.4	65.6	73.5	70.0
ID	Boise	29.0	74.0	50.9	36.4	90.2	62.8	21.6	57.7	39.1
IL	Chicago.	21.0	73.2	49.0	29.0	83.7	58.6	12.9	62.6	39.5
	Peoria.	21.6	75.5	50.7	29.9	85.7	60.4	13.2	65.4	41.0
IN	Indianapolis	25.5	75.4	52.3	33.7	85.5	62.1	17.2	65.2	42.4
IA	Des Moines	19.4	76.6	49.9	28.1	86.7	59.8	10.7	66.5	40.0
KS	Wichita	29.5	81.4	56.2	39.8	92.8	67.4	19.2	69.9	45.0
KY	Louisville	31.7	77.2	56.1	40.3	87.0	66.0	23.2	67.3	46.0
LA	New Orleans	51.3	81.9	68.1	60.8	90.6	77.6	41.8	73.1	58.5
ME	Portland	20.8	68.6	45.4	30.3	78.8	54.9	11.4	58.3	35.8
MD	Baltimore	31.8	77.0	55.1	40.2	87.2	65.0	23.4	66.8	45.2
MA	Boston	28.6	73.5	51.3	35.7	81.8	59.0	21.6	65.1	43.6
MI	Detroit.	22.9	72.3	48.6	30.3	83.3	58.1	15.6	61.3	39.0
	Sault Ste. Marie . . .	12.9	63.8	39.7	21.1	76.3	49.6	4.6	51.3	29.8
MN	Duluth.	7.0	66.1	38.5	16.2	77.1	47.9	-2.2	55.1	29.0
	Minneapolis-St. Paul	11.8	73.6	44.9	20.7	84.0	54.3	2.8	63.1	35.3
MS	Jackson.	44.1	81.5	64.2	55.6	92.4	76.4	32.7	70.5	52.0
MO	Kansas City	25.7	78.5	53.6	34.7	88.7	63.6	16.7	68.2	43.7
	St. Louis	29.3	79.8	56.1	37.7	89.3	65.4	20.8	70.4	46.7
MT	Great Falls.	21.2	68.2	44.8	30.6	83.3	56.4	11.6	53.2	33.1
NE	Omaha	21.1	76.9	50.6	31.3	87.9	61.5	10.9	65.9	39.5
NV	Reno	32.9	71.6	50.8	45.1	91.9	66.8	20.7	51.3	34.7
NH	Concord	18.6	69.5	45.1	29.8	82.4	57.0	7.4	56.5	33.1
NJ	Atlantic City	30.9	74.7	53.0	40.4	84.5	63.2	21.4	64.8	42.8
NM	Albuquerque.	34.2	78.5	56.2	46.8	92.5	70.1	21.7	64.4	42.2
NY	Albany	20.6	71.8	47.4	30.2	84.0	58.1	11.0	59.6	36.6
	Buffalo	23.6	71.1	47.7	30.2	80.2	55.8	17.0	61.9	39.5
	New York [1]	31.5	76.8	54.7	37.6	85.2	62.3	25.3	68.4	47.1
NC	Charlotte	39.3	79.3	60.1	49.0	88.9	70.4	29.6	69.6	49.7
	Raleigh	38.9	78.1	59.3	48.9	88.0	70.1	28.8	68.1	48.4
ND	Bismarck	9.2	70.4	41.6	20.2	84.4	53.8	-1.7	56.4	29.4
OH	Cincinnati.	28.1	75.1	53.2	36.6	85.5	63.2	19.5	64.8	43.2
	Cleveland	24.8	71.9	49.6	31.9	82.4	58.7	17.6	61.4	40.5
	Columbus	26.4	73.2	51.4	34.1	83.7	61.2	18.5	62.7	41.6
OK	Oklahoma City	35.9	82.0	60.0	46.7	93.4	71.1	25.2	70.6	48.8
OR	Portland	39.6	68.2	53.6	45.4	79.9	62.6	33.7	56.5	44.5
PA	Philadelphia	30.4	76.7	54.3	37.9	86.1	63.4	22.8	67.2	45.1
	Pittsburgh	26.1	72.1	50.3	33.7	82.6	59.9	18.5	61.6	40.7
RI	Providence.	27.9	72.7	50.4	36.6	82.1	59.8	19.1	63.2	41.0
SC	Columbia.	43.8	80.8	63.1	55.3	91.6	75.1	32.1	70.0	50.9
SD	Sioux Falls.	13.8	74.3	45.5	24.3	86.3	56.8	3.3	62.3	34.2
TN	Memphis	39.7	82.6	62.3	48.5	92.3	72.1	30.9	72.9	52.4
	Nashville	36.2	79.3	59.1	45.9	89.5	69.8	26.5	68.9	48.4
TX	Dallas-Fort Worth . .	43.4	85.3	65.4	54.1	96.5	76.3	32.7	74.1	54.6
	El Paso	42.8	82.3	63.2	56.1	96.1	77.5	29.4	68.4	49.0
	Houston	50.4	82.6	67.9	61.0	92.7	78.6	39.7	72.4	57.3
UT	Salt Lake City	27.9	77.9	52.0	36.4	92.2	63.6	19.3	63.7	40.3
VT	Burlington	16.3	70.5	44.6	25.1	81.2	54.0	7.5	59.7	35.2
VA	Norfolk	39.1	78.2	59.2	47.3	86.4	67.8	30.9	70.0	50.6
	Richmond	35.7	78.0	57.7	45.7	88.4	68.8	25.7	67.5	46.6
WA	Seattle-Tacoma. . . .	40.1	65.2	52.0	45.0	75.2	59.4	35.2	55.2	44.6
	Spokane	27.1	68.8	47.3	33.2	83.1	57.5	20.8	54.4	36.9
WV	Charleston	32.1	75.1	55.0	41.2	85.7	65.8	23.0	64.4	44.2
WI	Milwaukee	18.9	70.9	46.1	26.1	79.9	54.3	11.6	62.0	37.9
WY	Cheyenne	26.5	68.4	45.6	37.7	82.2	58.0	15.2	54.6	33.2
PR	San Juan.	77.0	82.6	80.2	83.2	88.5	86.4	70.8	76.8	74.0

[1] City office data.

Source: U.S. National Oceanic and Atmospheric Administration, *Climatography of the United States*, No. 81.

No. 416. Highest Temperature of Record—Selected Cities

[In Fahrenheit degrees. Airport data, except as noted. For period of record through 1995]

STATE	STATION	Length of record (yr.)	Jan.	Feb.	Mar.	Apr.	May	June	July	Aug.	Sept.	Oct.	Nov.	Dec.	Annual
AL	Mobile	54	84	82	90	94	100	102	104	102	99	93	87	81	104
AK	Juneau	51	57	57	59	72	82	86	90	83	72	61	56	54	90
AZ	Phoenix	58	88	92	100	105	113	122	121	116	118	107	93	88	122
AR	Little Rock	54	83	85	91	95	98	105	112	108	106	97	86	80	112
CA	Los Angeles	60	88	92	95	102	97	104	97	98	110	106	101	94	110
	Sacramento	45	70	76	88	93	105	115	114	109	108	101	87	72	115
	San Diego	55	88	90	93	98	96	101	95	98	111	107	97	88	111
	San Francisco	68	72	78	85	92	97	106	105	100	103	99	85	75	106
CO	Denver	61	73	76	84	90	96	104	104	101	97	89	79	75	104
CT	Hartford	41	65	73	87	96	97	100	102	101	99	91	81	74	102
DE	Wilmington	48	75	78	86	94	95	100	102	101	100	91	85	74	102
DC	Washington	54	79	82	89	95	99	101	104	103	101	94	86	75	104
FL	Jacksonville	54	85	88	91	95	100	103	105	102	100	96	88	84	105
	Miami	53	88	89	92	96	96	98	98	98	97	95	89	87	98
GA	Atlanta	47	79	80	89	93	95	101	105	102	98	95	84	79	105
HI	Honolulu	26	87	88	88	89	93	92	94	93	95	94	93	89	95
ID	Boise	56	63	71	81	92	98	109	111	110	102	94	74	65	111
IL	Chicago	37	65	71	88	91	93	104	104	101	99	91	78	71	104
	Peoria	56	70	72	86	92	93	105	103	103	100	90	81	71	105
IN	Indianapolis	56	71	74	85	89	93	102	104	102	100	90	81	74	104
IA	Des Moines	56	65	73	91	93	98	103	105	108	101	95	76	69	108
KS	Wichita	43	75	84	89	96	100	110	113	110	107	95	85	83	113
KY	Louisville	48	77	77	86	91	95	102	105	101	104	92	84	76	105
LA	New Orleans	49	83	85	89	92	96	100	101	102	101	92	87	84	102
ME	Portland	55	64	64	86	85	94	98	99	103	95	88	74	69	103
MD	Baltimore	45	75	79	87	94	98	101	104	105	100	92	83	77	105
MA	Boston	44	66	70	81	94	95	100	102	102	100	90	79	73	102
MI	Detroit	37	62	65	81	89	93	104	102	100	98	91	77	68	104
	Sault Ste. Marie	55	45	47	75	85	89	93	97	98	95	80	67	60	98
MN	Duluth	54	52	55	78	88	90	94	97	97	95	86	70	55	97
	Minneapolis-St. Paul	57	58	60	83	95	96	102	105	102	98	89	75	63	105
MS	Jackson	32	82	85	89	94	99	105	106	102	104	95	88	84	106
MO	Kansas City	23	69	77	86	93	92	105	107	109	102	92	82	70	109
	St. Louis	50	76	81	87	93	93	101	113	106	104	93	80	77	113
MT	Great Falls	58	67	70	78	89	93	101	105	106	98	91	76	69	106
NE	Omaha	59	69	78	89	97	99	105	114	110	104	96	80	72	114
NV	Reno	54	70	75	83	89	96	103	104	105	101	91	77	70	105
NH	Concord	54	68	66	85	95	97	98	102	101	98	90	80	68	102
NJ	Atlantic City	52	78	75	87	94	99	106	104	102	99	90	84	75	106
NM	Albuquerque	56	69	76	85	89	98	107	105	101	100	91	77	72	107
NY	Albany	49	65	67	86	92	94	99	100	99	100	89	82	71	100
	Buffalo	52	72	65	81	94	90	96	97	99	98	87	80	74	99
	New York [1]	127	72	75	86	96	99	101	106	104	102	94	84	72	106
NC	Charlotte	56	78	81	90	93	100	103	103	103	104	98	85	77	104
	Raleigh	51	79	84	92	95	97	104	105	104	104	98	88	79	105
ND	Bismarck	56	62	69	81	93	98	107	109	109	105	95	75	65	109
OH	Cincinnati	34	69	73	84	89	93	102	103	102	98	88	81	75	103
	Cleveland	54	73	69	83	88	92	104	103	102	101	90	82	77	104
	Columbus	56	74	73	85	89	94	102	100	101	100	90	80	76	102
OK	Oklahoma City	42	80	84	93	100	104	105	109	110	102	96	87	86	110
OR	Portland	55	63	71	80	87	100	100	107	107	105	92	73	65	107
PA	Philadelphia	54	74	74	87	94	97	100	104	101	100	96	81	72	104
	Pittsburgh	43	69	69	82	89	91	98	103	100	97	87	82	74	103
RI	Providence	42	69	72	80	98	94	97	102	104	100	86	78	70	104
SC	Columbia	48	84	84	91	94	101	107	107	107	101	101	90	83	107
SD	Sioux Falls	50	66	70	87	94	100	110	108	108	104	94	76	61	110
TN	Memphis	54	78	81	85	94	99	104	108	105	103	95	85	81	108
	Nashville	56	78	84	86	91	97	106	107	104	105	94	84	79	107
TX	Dallas-Fort Worth	42	88	88	96	95	103	113	110	108	106	102	89	68	113
	El Paso	56	80	83	89	98	104	114	112	108	104	96	87	80	114
	Houston	26	84	91	91	95	97	103	104	107	102	96	89	85	107
UT	Salt Lake City	67	62	69	78	86	93	104	107	106	100	89	75	69	107
VT	Burlington	52	66	62	84	91	93	100	100	101	94	85	75	65	101
VA	Norfolk	47	78	81	88	97	100	101	103	104	99	95	86	80	104
	Richmond	66	80	83	93	96	100	104	105	102	103	99	86	80	105
WA	Seattle-Tacoma	51	64	70	75	85	93	96	100	99	98	89	74	64	100
	Spokane	48	59	63	71	90	96	101	103	108	98	86	67	56	108
WV	Charleston	48	79	78	89	94	93	98	104	101	102	92	85	80	104
WI	Milwaukee	55	62	65	82	91	93	101	103	103	98	89	77	63	103
WY	Cheyenne	60	66	71	74	83	90	100	100	96	95	83	73	69	100
PR	San Juan	41	92	96	96	97	96	97	95	97	97	98	96	94	98

[1] City office data.

Source: U.S. National Oceanic and Atmospheric Administration, *Comparative Climatic Data,* annual.

No. 417. Lowest Temperature of Record—Selected Cities

[In Fahrenheit degrees. Airport data, except as noted. For period of record through 1995]

STATE	STATION	Length of record (yr.)	Jan.	Feb.	Mar.	Apr.	May	June	July	Aug.	Sept.	Oct.	Nov.	Dec.	Annual
AL	Mobile	54	3	11	21	32	43	49	60	59	42	30	22	8	3
AK	Juneau	51	-22	-22	-15	6	25	31	36	27	23	11	-5	-21	-22
AZ	Phoenix	58	17	22	25	32	40	50	61	60	47	34	25	22	17
AR	Little Rock	54	-4	-5	11	28	40	46	54	52	37	29	17	-1	-5
CA	Los Angeles	60	23	32	34	39	43	48	49	51	47	41	34	32	23
	Sacramento	45	23	23	26	32	36	41	48	49	43	36	26	18	18
	San Diego	55	29	36	39	41	48	51	55	57	51	43	38	34	29
	San Francisco	68	24	25	30	31	36	41	43	42	38	34	25	20	20
CO	Denver	61	-25	-30	-11	-2	22	30	43	41	17	3	-8	-25	-30
CT	Hartford	41	-26	-21	-6	9	28	37	44	36	30	17	1	-14	-26
DE	Wilmington	48	-14	-6	2	18	30	41	48	43	36	24	14	-7	-14
DC	Washington	54	-5	4	11	24	34	47	54	49	39	29	16	1	-5
FL	Jacksonville	54	7	19	23	34	45	47	61	63	48	36	21	11	7
	Miami	53	30	32	32	46	53	60	69	68	68	51	39	30	30
GA	Atlanta	47	-8	5	10	26	37	46	53	55	36	28	3	-	-8
HI	Honolulu	26	53	53	55	57	60	65	66	67	66	61	57	54	53
ID	Boise	56	-17	-15	6	19	22	31	35	34	23	11	-3	-25	-25
IL	Chicago	37	-27	-17	-8	7	24	36	40	41	28	17	1	-25	-27
	Peoria	56	-25	-18	-10	14	25	39	47	41	26	19	-2	-25	-27
IN	Indianapolis	56	-27	-21	-7	16	28	37	44	41	28	17	-2	-23	-27
IA	Des Moines	56	-24	-20	-22	9	30	38	47	40	26	14	-4	-22	-24
KS	Wichita	43	-12	-21	-2	15	31	43	51	48	31	18	1	-16	-21
KY	Louisville	48	-22	-19	-1	22	31	42	50	46	33	23	-1	-15	-22
LA	New Orleans	49	14	19	25	32	41	50	60	60	42	35	24	11	11
ME	Portland	55	-26	-39	-21	8	23	33	40	33	23	15	3	-21	-39
MD	Baltimore	45	-7	-3	6	20	32	40	50	45	35	25	13	-	-7
MA	Boston	44	-12	-4	6	16	34	45	50	47	38	28	15	-7	-12
MI	Detroit	37	-21	-15	-4	10	25	36	41	38	29	17	9	-10	-21
	Sault Ste. Marie	55	-36	-35	-24	-2	18	26	36	29	25	16	-10	-31	-36
MN	Duluth	54	-39	-33	-29	-5	17	27	35	32	22	8	-23	-34	-39
	Minneapolis-St. Paul	57	-34	-28	-32	2	18	34	43	39	26	15	-17	-29	-34
MS	Jackson	32	2	11	15	27	38	47	51	55	35	26	17	4	2
MO	Kansas City	23	-17	-19	-10	12	30	42	52	43	31	17	1	-23	-23
	St. Louis	38	-18	-10	-5	22	31	43	51	47	36	23	1	-16	-18
MT	Great Falls	58	-37	-35	-29	-6	15	31	40	30	20	-11	-25	-43	-43
NE	Omaha	59	-23	-21	-16	5	27	38	44	43	25	13	-9	-23	-23
NV	Reno	54	-16	-16	-2	13	18	25	33	24	20	8	1	-16	-16
NH	Concord	54	-33	-37	-16	8	21	30	35	29	21	10	-5	-22	-37
NJ	Atlantic City	52	-10	-11	5	12	25	37	42	40	32	20	10	-7	-11
NM	Albuquerque	56	-17	-5	8	19	28	40	52	50	37	21	-7	-7	-17
NY	Albany	49	-28	-21	-21	10	26	36	40	34	24	16	5	-22	-28
	Buffalo	52	-16	-20	-7	12	26	35	43	38	32	20	9	-10	-20
	New York[1]	127	-6	-15	3	12	32	44	52	50	39	28	5	-13	-15
NC	Charlotte	56	-5	5	4	24	32	45	53	53	39	24	11	2	-5
	Raleigh	51	-9	5	11	23	31	38	48	46	37	19	11	4	-9
ND	Bismarck	56	-44	-43	-31	-12	15	30	35	33	11	-10	-30	-43	-44
OH	Cincinnati	34	-25	-11	-11	17	27	39	47	43	31	16	1	-20	-25
	Cleveland	54	-20	-15	-5	10	25	31	41	38	32	19	3	-15	-20
	Columbus	56	-22	-13	-6	14	25	35	43	39	31	20	5	-17	-22
OK	Oklahoma City	42	-4	-3	3	20	37	47	53	51	36	16	11	-8	-8
OR	Portland	55	-2	-3	19	29	29	39	43	44	34	26	13	6	-3
PA	Philadelphia	54	-7	-4	7	19	28	44	51	44	35	25	15	1	-7
	Pittsburgh	43	-22	-12	-1	14	26	34	42	39	31	16	-1	-12	-22
RI	Providence	42	-13	-7	1	14	29	41	48	40	33	20	6	-10	-13
SC	Columbia	48	-1	5	4	26	34	44	54	53	40	23	12	4	-1
SD	Sioux Falls	50	-36	-31	-23	5	17	33	38	34	22	9	-17	-28	-36
TN	Memphis	54	-4	-11	12	29	38	48	52	48	36	25	9	-13	-13
	Nashville	56	-17	-13	2	23	34	42	51	47	36	26	-1	-10	-17
TX	Dallas-Fort Worth	42	4	7	15	29	41	51	59	56	43	29	20	-1	-1
	El Paso	56	-8	8	14	23	31	46	57	56	41	25	20	1	-8
	Houston	26	12	20	22	31	44	52	62	60	48	29	25	19	7
UT	Salt Lake City	67	-22	-30	2	14	25	35	40	37	27	16	-14	-21	-30
VT	Burlington	52	-30	-30	-20	2	24	33	39	35	25	15	-2	-26	-30
VA	Norfolk	47	-3	8	18	28	36	45	54	49	45	27	20	7	-3
	Richmond	66	-12	6	11	23	31	40	51	46	35	21	10	-1	-12
WA	Seattle-Tacoma	51	-	1	11	29	28	38	43	44	35	28	6	6	-
	Spokane	48	-22	-17	-7	17	24	33	37	35	24	10	-21	-25	-25
WV	Charleston	48	-16	-6	-	19	26	33	37	35	24	10	-21	-25	-25
WI	Milwaukee	55	-26	-19	-10	12	21	33	40	44	28	18	-5	-20	-26
WY	Cheyenne	60	-29	-34	-21	-8	16	25	38	36	8	-1	-16	-28	-34
PR	San Juan	41	61	62	60	64	66	69	69	70	69	67	66	63	60

- Represents zero.   [1] City office data.

Source: U.S. National Oceanic and Atmospheric Administration, *Comparative Climatic Data*, annual.

No. 418. Normal Monthly and Annual Precipitation—Selected Cities

[**In inches.** Airport data, except as noted. Based on standard 30-year period, 1961 through 1990]

STATE	STATION	Jan.	Feb.	Mar.	Apr.	May	June	July	Aug.	Sept.	Oct.	Nov.	Dec.	Annual
AL	Mobile	4.76	5.46	6.41	4.48	5.74	5.04	6.85	6.96	5.91	2.94	4.10	5.31	63.96
AK	Juneau	4.54	3.75	3.28	2.77	3.42	3.15	4.16	5.32	6.73	7.84	4.91	4.44	54.31
AZ	Phoenix	0.67	0.68	0.88	0.22	0.12	0.13	0.83	0.96	0.86	0.65	0.66	1.00	7.66
AR	Little Rock	3.42	3.61	4.91	5.49	5.17	3.57	3.60	3.26	4.05	3.75	5.20	4.83	50.86
CA	Los Angeles	2.40	2.51	1.98	0.72	0.14	0.03	0.01	0.15	0.31	0.34	1.76	1.66	12.01
	Sacramento	3.73	2.87	2.57	1.16	0.27	0.12	0.05	0.07	0.37	1.08	2.72	2.51	17.52
	San Diego	1.80	1.53	1.77	0.79	0.19	0.07	0.02	0.10	0.24	0.37	1.45	1.57	9.90
	San Francisco	4.35	3.17	3.06	1.37	0.19	0.11	0.03	0.05	0.20	1.22	2.86	3.09	19.70
CO	Denver	0.50	0.57	1.28	1.71	2.40	1.79	1.91	1.51	1.24	0.98	0.87	0.64	15.40
CT	Hartford	3.41	3.23	3.63	3.85	4.12	3.75	3.19	3.65	3.79	3.57	4.04	3.91	44.14
DE	Wilmington	3.03	2.91	3.43	3.39	3.84	3.55	4.23	3.40	3.43	2.88	3.27	3.48	40.84
DC	Washington	2.72	2.71	3.17	2.71	3.66	3.38	3.80	3.91	3.31	3.02	3.12	3.12	38.63
FL	Jacksonville	3.31	3.93	3.68	2.77	3.55	5.69	5.60	7.93	7.05	2.90	2.19	2.72	51.32
	Miami	2.01	2.08	2.39	2.85	6.21	9.33	5.70	7.58	7.63	5.64	2.66	1.83	55.91
GA	Atlanta	4.75	4.81	5.77	4.26	4.29	3.56	5.01	3.66	3.42	3.05	3.86	4.33	50.77
HI	Honolulu	3.55	2.21	2.20	1.54	1.13	0.50	0.59	0.44	0.78	2.28	3.00	3.80	22.02
ID	Boise	1.45	1.07	1.29	1.24	1.08	0.81	0.35	0.43	0.80	0.75	1.48	1.36	12.11
IL	Chicago	1.53	1.36	2.69	3.64	3.32	3.78	3.66	4.22	3.82	2.41	2.92	2.47	35.82
	Peoria	1.51	1.42	2.91	3.77	3.70	3.99	4.20	3.10	3.87	2.65	2.69	2.44	36.25
IN	Indianapolis	2.32	2.46	3.79	3.70	4.00	3.49	4.47	3.64	2.87	2.63	3.23	3.34	39.94
IA	Des Moines	0.96	1.11	2.33	3.36	3.66	4.46	3.78	4.20	3.53	2.62	1.79	1.32	33.12
KS	Wichita	0.79	0.96	2.43	2.38	3.81	4.31	3.13	3.02	3.24	2.22	1.59	1.20	29.33
KY	Louisville	2.86	3.30	4.66	4.23	4.62	3.46	4.51	3.54	3.16	2.71	3.70	3.64	44.39
LA	New Orleans	5.05	6.01	4.90	4.50	4.56	5.84	6.12	6.17	5.51	3.05	4.42	5.75	61.88
ME	Portland	3.53	3.33	3.67	4.08	3.62	3.44	3.09	2.87	3.09	3.90	5.17	4.55	44.34
MD	Baltimore	3.05	3.12	3.38	3.09	3.72	3.67	3.69	3.92	3.41	2.98	3.32	3.41	40.76
MA	Boston	3.59	3.62	3.69	3.60	3.25	3.09	2.84	3.24	3.06	3.30	4.22	4.01	41.51
MI	Detroit	1.76	1.74	2.55	2.95	2.92	3.61	3.18	3.43	2.89	2.10	2.67	2.82	32.62
	Sault Ste. Marie	2.42	1.74	2.30	2.35	2.71	3.14	2.71	3.61	3.69	3.23	3.45	2.88	34.23
MN	Duluth	1.22	0.80	1.91	2.25	3.03	3.82	3.61	3.99	3.84	2.49	1.80	1.24	30.00
	Minneapolis-St. Paul	0.95	0.88	1.94	2.42	3.39	4.05	3.53	3.62	2.72	2.19	1.55	1.08	28.32
MS	Jackson	5.24	4.70	5.82	5.57	5.05	3.18	4.51	3.77	3.55	3.26	4.81	5.91	55.37
MO	Kansas City	1.09	1.10	2.51	3.12	5.04	4.72	4.38	4.01	4.86	3.29	1.92	1.58	37.62
	St. Louis	1.81	2.12	3.58	3.50	3.97	3.72	3.85	2.85	3.12	2.68	3.28	3.03	37.51
MT	Great Falls	0.91	0.57	1.10	1.41	2.52	2.39	1.24	1.54	1.24	0.78	0.66	0.85	15.21
NE	Omaha	0.74	0.77	2.04	2.66	4.52	3.87	3.51	3.24	3.72	2.28	1.49	1.02	29.86
NV	Reno	1.07	0.99	0.71	0.38	0.69	0.46	0.28	0.32	0.39	0.38	0.87	0.99	7.53
NH	Concord	2.51	2.53	2.72	2.91	3.14	3.15	3.23	3.32	2.81	3.23	3.66	3.16	36.37
NJ	Atlantic City	3.46	3.06	3.62	3.56	3.33	2.64	3.83	4.14	2.93	2.82	3.58	3.32	40.29
NM	Albuquerque	0.44	0.46	0.54	0.52	0.50	0.59	1.37	1.64	1.00	0.89	0.43	0.50	8.88
NY	Albany	2.36	2.27	2.93	2.99	3.41	3.62	3.18	3.47	2.95	2.83	3.23	2.93	36.17
	Buffalo	2.70	2.31	2.68	2.87	3.14	3.55	3.08	4.17	3.49	3.09	3.83	3.67	38.58
	New York [1]	3.42	3.27	4.08	4.20	4.42	3.67	4.35	4.01	3.89	3.56	4.47	3.91	47.25
NC	Charlotte	3.71	3.84	4.43	2.68	3.82	3.39	3.92	3.73	3.50	3.36	3.23	3.48	43.09
	Raleigh	3.48	3.69	3.77	2.59	3.92	3.68	4.01	4.02	3.19	2.86	2.98	3.24	41.43
ND	Bismarck	0.45	0.43	0.77	1.67	2.18	2.72	2.14	1.72	1.49	0.90	0.49	0.51	15.47
OH	Cincinnati	2.59	2.69	4.24	3.75	4.28	3.84	4.24	3.35	2.88	2.86	3.46	3.15	41.33
	Cleveland	2.04	2.19	2.91	3.14	3.49	3.70	3.52	3.40	3.44	2.54	3.17	3.09	36.63
	Columbus	2.18	2.24	3.27	3.21	3.93	4.04	4.31	3.72	2.96	2.15	3.22	2.86	38.09
OK	Oklahoma City	1.13	1.56	2.71	2.77	5.22	4.31	2.61	2.60	3.84	3.23	1.98	1.40	33.36
OR	Portland	5.35	3.85	3.56	2.39	2.06	1.48	0.63	1.09	1.75	2.67	5.34	6.13	36.30
PA	Philadelphia	3.21	2.79	3.46	3.62	3.75	3.74	4.28	3.80	3.42	2.62	3.34	3.38	41.41
	Pittsburgh	2.54	2.39	3.41	3.15	3.59	3.71	3.75	3.21	2.97	2.36	2.85	2.92	36.85
RI	Providence	3.88	3.61	4.05	4.11	3.76	3.33	3.18	3.63	3.48	3.69	4.43	4.38	45.53
SC	Columbia	4.42	4.12	4.82	3.28	3.68	4.80	5.50	6.09	3.67	3.04	2.90	3.59	49.91
SD	Sioux Falls	0.51	0.64	1.64	2.52	3.03	3.40	2.68	2.85	3.02	1.78	1.09	0.70	23.86
TN	Memphis	3.73	4.35	5.41	5.46	4.98	3.57	3.79	3.43	3.53	3.01	5.10	5.74	52.10
	Nashville	3.58	3.81	4.85	4.37	4.88	3.57	3.97	3.46	3.46	2.62	4.12	4.61	47.30
TX	Dallas-Fort Worth	1.83	2.18	2.77	3.50	4.88	2.98	2.31	2.21	3.39	3.52	2.29	1.84	33.70
	El Paso	0.40	0.41	0.29	0.20	0.25	0.67	1.54	1.58	1.70	0.76	0.44	0.57	8.81
	Houston	3.29	2.96	2.92	3.21	5.24	4.96	3.60	3.49	4.89	4.27	3.79	3.45	46.07
UT	Salt Lake City	1.11	1.23	1.91	2.12	1.80	0.93	0.81	0.86	1.28	1.44	1.29	1.40	16.18
VT	Burlington	1.82	1.63	2.23	2.76	3.12	3.47	3.65	4.06	3.30	2.88	3.13	2.42	34.47
VA	Norfolk	3.78	3.47	3.70	3.06	3.81	3.82	5.06	4.81	3.90	3.15	2.85	3.23	44.64
	Richmond	3.24	3.16	3.61	2.96	3.84	3.62	5.03	4.40	3.34	3.53	3.17	3.26	43.16
WA	Seattle-Tacoma	5.38	3.99	3.54	2.33	1.70	1.50	0.76	1.14	1.88	3.23	5.83	5.91	37.19
	Spokane	1.98	1.49	1.49	1.18	1.41	1.26	0.67	0.72	0.73	0.99	2.15	2.42	16.49
WV	Charleston	2.91	3.04	3.63	3.31	3.94	3.59	4.99	4.01	3.24	2.89	3.59	3.39	42.53
WI	Milwaukee	1.60	1.45	2.67	3.50	2.84	3.24	3.47	3.53	3.38	2.41	2.51	2.33	32.93
WY	Cheyenne	0.40	0.39	1.03	1.37	2.39	2.08	2.09	1.69	1.27	0.74	0.53	0.42	14.40
PR	San Juan	2.81	2.15	2.35	3.76	5.93	4.00	4.37	5.32	5.28	5.71	5.94	4.72	52.34

[1] City office data.

Source: U.S. National Oceanic and Atmospheric Administration, *Climatography of the United States*, No. 81.

No. 419. Average Number of Days With Precipitation of .01 Inch or More— Selected Cities

[Airport data, except as noted. For period of record through 1995, except as noted]

STATE	STATION	Length of record (yr.)	Jan.	Feb.	Mar.	Apr.	May	June	July	Aug.	Sept.	Oct.	Nov.	Dec.	Annual
AL	Mobile	54	11	10	10	7	9	11	16	14	10	6	8	10	122
AK	Juneau	51	18	17	18	17	17	15	17	17	20	24	20	21	222
AZ	Phoenix	56	4	4	4	2	1	1	4	5	3	3	3	4	36
AR	Little Rock	53	10	9	10	10	10	8	8	7	7	7	8	9	105
CA	Los Angeles	60	6	6	6	3	1	1	1	1	1	2	3	5	35
	Sacramento	56	10	9	9	5	3	1	(Z)	(Z)	1	4	7	9	58
	San Diego	55	7	6	7	4	2	1	(Z)	(Z)	1	3	4	6	42
	San Francisco	68	11	10	10	6	3	1	1	(Z)	1	4	7	10	62
CO	Denver	61	6	6	9	9	11	9	9	9	6	5	6	5	89
CT	Hartford	41	11	10	12	11	12	11	10	10	9	9	11	12	127
DE	Wilmington	48	11	9	11	11	11	10	9	9	9	8	11	10	116
DC	Washington	54	10	9	11	10	11	9	10	9	8	7	9	9	112
FL	Jacksonville	54	8	8	8	6	8	12	15	14	13	9	7	8	116
	Miami	53	7	6	6	6	8	10	15	16	17	17	9	8	130
GA	Atlanta	61	11	10	11	9	9	10	12	10	8	7	9	10	115
HI	Honolulu	46	9	9	9	9	7	6	7	6	7	9	9	10	98
ID	Boise	56	12	10	10	8	8	6	2	3	4	6	10	11	90
IL	Chicago	37	11	9	12	13	11	10	10	9	9	9	11	11	126
	Peoria	56	9	8	11	12	11	10	9	9	9	8	11	11	114
IN	Indianapolis	56	12	10	13	12	12	10	9	8	8	8	11	12	126
IA	Des Moines	56	8	7	10	11	11	11	9	9	9	8	8	8	108
KS	Wichita	42	6	5	8	8	8	9	8	8	7	7	6	6	86
KY	Louisville	48	11	11	13	12	12	10	10	8	8	8	10	11	124
LA	New Orleans	47	10	9	9	7	8	11	14	13	10	6	7	10	114
ME	Portland	55	11	10	11	12	12	11	10	9	9	9	12	12	129
MD	Baltimore	45	11	9	11	11	11	9	9	9	8	8	9	9	114
MA	Boston	44	12	11	12	11	11	11	9	10	9	9	11	12	127
MI	Detroit	37	13	11	13	13	11	10	10	10	10	10	12	14	136
	Sault Ste. Marie	54	19	15	13	11	11	11	10	11	13	14	17	19	166
MN	Duluth	54	12	10	11	11	12	13	11	11	12	10	11	12	135
	Minneapolis-St. Paul	57	9	7	10	10	11	12	10	10	10	8	8	9	115
MS	Jackson	32	11	9	10	8	8	8	10	8	7	7	8	9	109
MO	Kansas City	23	7	7	10	11	12	11	9	9	8	7	8	10	106
	St. Louis	38	9	8	11	11	11	9	8	8	7	7	8	8	111
MT	Great Falls	58	9	8	9	9	12	12	8	8	7	6	7	8	101
NE	Omaha	59	6	7	9	10	12	11	9	9	8	6	6	7	99
NV	Reno	53	6	6	6	4	4	3	2	2	2	3	5	6	51
NH	Concord	54	11	10	11	12	12	11	10	10	9	9	11	11	126
NJ	Atlantic City	52	11	10	11	11	11	9	9	9	8	7	9	11	112
NM	Albuquerque	56	4	4	5	3	5	4	9	9	6	5	3	4	61
NY	Albany	49	12	11	12	12	13	11	10	10	10	9	12	12	134
	Buffalo	52	20	17	16	14	12	10	10	10	11	11	16	19	169
	New York[1]	126	11	10	11	11	11	10	11	10	8	8	9	10	121
NC	Charlotte	56	10	10	11	9	10	10	10	10	7	7	8	10	111
	Raleigh	51	10	10	10	9	9	10	11	10	8	7	8	9	112
ND	Bismarck	56	8	7	8	8	10	11	9	8	7	6	6	8	96
OH	Cincinnati	48	12	11	13	13	12	11	10	9	8	8	11	12	130
	Cleveland	54	16	14	15	14	13	11	10	10	10	10	13	16	155
	Columbus	56	13	11	14	13	13	11	10	10	9	8	11	12	137
OK	Oklahoma City	56	6	6	7	8	10	9	6	6	7	6	5	6	83
OR	Portland	55	18	16	17	14	12	9	4	5	7	12	18	19	151
PA	Philadelphia	55	11	9	11	11	11	10	9	9	8	8	9	10	116
	Pittsburgh	43	16	14	16	14	13	12	11	10	10	10	13	16	153
RI	Providence	42	11	10	12	11	11	11	9	9	8	9	11	12	124
SC	Columbia	48	10	10	10	8	9	10	12	11	8	6	7	9	110
SD	Sioux Falls	50	6	7	9	10	11	11	10	9	8	6	7	6	98
TN	Memphis	45	10	9	11	10	10	9	9	7	7	6	9	10	107
	Nashville	54	11	11	12	11	11	9	9	10	9	8	10	11	119
TX	Dallas-Fort Worth	42	7	7	7	8	9	6	5	5	7	6	6	7	79
	El Paso	56	4	3	2	2	2	3	8	8	5	4	3	4	49
	Houston	26	11	9	9	7	9	9	9	9	9	7	8	9	106
UT	Salt Lake City	67	10	9	10	10	8	5	5	5	6	8	8	9	91
VT	Burlington	52	14	12	13	12	14	12	12	13	12	12	14	14	154
VA	Norfolk	47	11	10	11	10	10	9	11	10	8	8	8	9	115
	Richmond	58	10	9	11	9	11	10	11	10	8	8	8	8	113
WA	Seattle-Tacoma	51	18	16	17	14	10	9	5	6	9	13	18	19	154
	Spokane	48	14	11	11	9	8	8	5	5	6	9	13	15	112
WV	Charleston	48	15	14	15	14	13	11	13	11	10	10	12	14	151
WI	Milwaukee	55	11	10	12	12	11	11	10	9	9	9	11	11	125
WY	Cheyenne	60	6	6	9	10	12	11	11	10	8	6	6	6	101
PR	San Juan	40	17	13	12	13	16	15	19	18	17	17	18	19	196

Z Less than 1/2 day.   [1] City office data.

Source: U.S. National Oceanic and Atmospheric Administration, *Comparative Climatic Data*, annual.

No. 420. Snow and Ice Pellets—Selected Cities

[In inches. Airport data, except as noted. For period of record through 1995. T denotes trace]

STATE	STATION	Length of record (yr)	Jan.	Feb.	Mar.	Apr.	May	June	July	Aug.	Sept.	Oct.	Nov.	Dec.	Annual
AL	Mobile	54	0.1	0.1	0.1	T	T	-	T	-	-	-	T	0.1	0.4
AK	Juneau	51	26.3	19.1	15.3	3.4	-	T	-	-	T	1	12.9	22.7	100.7
AZ	Phoenix	58	T	-	T	T	T	-	-	-	-	T	-	-	T
AR	Little Rock	53	2.4	1.4	0.5	T	-	-	-	-	-	T	0.2	0.6	5.1
CA	Los Angeles	60	T	T	T	-	-	-	-	-	-	-	T	T	T
	Sacramento	47	T	-	T	-	T	-	-	-	-	-	-	T	T
	San Diego	55	T	-	T	-	-	-	-	-	-	-	T	T	T
	San Francisco	68	-	T	T	-	-	-	-	-	-	-	-	-	T
CO	Denver	61	8.1	7.5	12.5	8.9	1.6	-	T	T	1.6	3.7	9.1	7.3	60.3
CT	Hartford	41	12.3	11.8	9.8	1.5	-	T	-	-	-	0.1	2.1	10.3	47.9
DE	Wilmington	48	6.4	6.1	3.3	0.2	T	T	T	-	-	0.1	0.9	3.3	20.3
DC	Washington	52	5.3	5.2	2.1	-	T	-	T	T	-	-	0.8	3	16.4
FL	Jacksonville	54	T	-	-	-	-	-	T	-	-	-	-	-	T
	Miami	53	-	-	-	-	-	-	-	-	-	-	-	-	-
GA	Atlanta	61	0.9	0.5	0.4	T	-	-	-	-	-	T	-	0.2	2.0
HI	Honolulu	49	-	-	-	-	-	-	-	-	-	-	-	-	-
ID	Boise	56	6.6	3.6	1.6	0.6	0.1	T	-	T	-	0.1	2.3	5.8	20.7
IL	Chicago	37	10.8	8.4	6.7	1.6	0.1	T	T	T	T	0.4	1.9	8.3	38.2
	Peoria	52	6.6	5.5	4.0	0.8	-	T	-	T	T	0.1	2.0	5.8	24.8
IN	Indianapolis	64	6.3	5.8	3.3	0.5	-	T	-	T	-	0.2	1.8	5.0	22.9
IA	Des Moines	56	8.1	7.2	6.1	1.8	-	T	T	-	T	0.3	3.1	6.7	33.3
KS	Wichita	42	4.4	4.2	2.5	0.2	T	T	T	T	T	-	1.2	3.2	15.7
KY	Louisville	48	5.2	4.4	3.2	0.1	T	T	T	-	-	0.1	1	2.1	16.1
LA	New Orleans	49	-	0.1	T	T	T	-	-	-	-	-	T	0.1	0.2
ME	Portland	55	19.3	17.3	12.8	3.0	0.2	-	-	-	T	0.2	3.0	15.0	70.8
MD	Baltimore	45	5.7	6.5	3.7	0.1	T	-	T	-	-	-	1.0	3.4	20.4
MA	Boston	60	12.3	11.7	7.9	0.9	-	-	-	T	-	-	1.3	7.6	41.7
MI	Detroit	37	10.5	9.2	6.8	1.7	T	-	-	-	T	0.2	2.9	10.0	41.3
	Sault Ste. Marie	54	28.7	18.4	14.8	5.7	0.5	T	-	T	0.1	2.4	15.7	30.8	117.1
MN	Duluth	52	17.1	13.3	13.4	6.7	0.7	-	T	T	0.1	1.5	12.7	15.4	78.9
	Minneapolis-St. Paul	57	9.9	8.4	10.5	2.8	0.1	T	T	T	-	0.5	7.9	9.4	49.5
MS	Jackson	32	0.5	0.2	0.2	-	-	-	-	-	-	-	-	-	0.9
MO	Kansas City	61	5.6	4.5	3.5	0.8	T	T	T	-	T	-	1.1	4.4	19.9
	St. Louis	59	5.2	4.6	4.1	0.4	-	T	T	-	-	T	1.4	3.8	19.5
MT	Great Falls	58	9.6	8.3	10.3	7.3	1.7	0.3	T	0.1	1.5	3.4	7.5	8.4	58.4
NE	Omaha	60	7.3	6.6	6.3	1	0.1	T	T	-	T	0.3	2.6	5.6	29.8
NV	Reno	53	5.9	5.2	4.3	1.2	0.8	-	-	-	-	0.3	2.4	4.3	24.4
NH	Concord	54	17.9	14.6	11.0	2.3	0.1	T	-	-	-	0.1	3.9	13.6	63.5
NJ	Atlantic City	51	5.0	5.3	2.5	0.3	T	T	T	-	-	T	0.4	2.2	15.7
NM	Albuquerque	56	2.5	2.1	1.8	0.6	-	T	T	T	T	0.1	1.2	2.5	10.8
NY	Albany	49	16.3	14.4	11.1	2.6	0.1	T	T	-	T	0.2	4.2	14.9	63.8
	Buffalo	52	23.5	18.6	11.5	3.2	0.2	T	T	T	T	0.3	11.3	23.2	91.8
	New York [1]	127	7.5	8.6	5.0	0.9	T	T	-	T	-	-	0.9	5.4	28.3
NC	Charlotte	56	2.0	1.6	1.2	-	T	-	T	-	-	T	0.1	0.5	5.4
	Raleigh	51	2.2	2.5	1.3	-	T	-	T	-	-	-	0.1	0.8	6.9
ND	Bismarck	56	7.4	6.8	8.4	3.8	0.9	T	T	T	0.2	1.7	6.5	7.0	42.7
OH	Cincinnati	48	7.0	5.5	4.3	0.5	-	T	T	T	-	0.3	2.0	3.8	23.4
	Cleveland	54	13.0	12.3	10.4	2.3	0.1	T	T	-	T	0.6	5.0	12.0	55.7
	Columbus	48	8.5	6.2	4.5	0.9	-	T	T	-	T	0.1	2.2	5.5	27.9
OK	Oklahoma City	56	3.0	2.4	1.5	-	T	T	T	-	T	-	0.5	1.8	9.2
OR	Portland	55	3.2	1.1	0.4	T	-	T	-	T	T	-	0.4	1.4	6.5
PA	Philadelphia	53	6.2	6.6	3.7	0.3	T	T	T	-	-	-	0.7	3.3	20.8
	Pittsburgh	43	11.6	9.3	8.7	1.7	0.1	T	T	T	T	0.4	3.5	8.2	43.5
RI	Providence	42	9.5	10.0	7.5	0.7	0.2	-	-	-	-	0.1	1.1	6.8	35.9
SC	Columbia	48	0.4	0.8	0.2	T	-	-	-	T	-	-	T	0.3	1.7
SD	Sioux Falls	50	6.5	8.1	9.4	2.7	-	T	T	-	-	0.8	5.5	7.1	40.1
TN	Memphis	45	2.2	1.4	0.8	T	T	T	-	T	-	T	0.1	0.6	5.1
	Nashville	54	3.7	3.0	1.4	-	-	-	T	-	T	-	0.4	1.4	9.9
TX	Dallas-Fort Worth	42	1.1	0.9	0.2	T	T	-	-	-	-	T	0.1	0.2	2.5
	El Paso	56	1.3	0.8	0.4	0.3	T	T	-	T	-	T	0.9	1.6	5.3
	Houston	61	0.2	0.2	-	-	T	T	T	-	-	-	T	-	0.4
UT	Salt Lake City	67	13.4	9.5	9.3	4.9	0.6	T	T	T	0.1	1.2	6.9	11.8	57.7
VT	Burlington	52	19.0	17.0	12.7	3.9	0.2	T	-	T	-	0.2	6.6	18.4	78.0
VA	Norfolk	47	2.7	2.8	1.0	-	T	T	-	T	-	-	-	0.9	7.4
	Richmond	58	4.8	4.0	2.4	0.1	T	-	-	T	-	T	0.4	2.0	13.7
WA	Seattle-Tacoma	51	4.8	1.6	1.3	0.1	T	-	T	-	T	-	1.1	2.4	11.3
	Spokane	48	15.6	7.6	3.9	0.6	0.1	T	T	-	T	0.4	6.4	14.9	49.5
WV	Charleston	48	10.6	8.6	5.1	0.9	-	T	T	T	T	0.2	2.4	5.3	33.1
WI	Milwaukee	55	13.1	10.0	8.6	1.7	0.1	T	T	T	T	0.2	3.2	10.3	47.2
WY	Cheyenne	60	6.5	6.4	11.9	9.0	3.3	0.2	-	-	0.9	3.7	7.3	6.2	55.4
PR	San Juan	40	-	-	-	-	-	-	-	-	-	-	-	-	-

- Represents zero or rounds to zero.   [1] City office data.

Source: U.S. National Oceanic and Atmospheric Administration, Comparative Climatic Data, annual.

No. 421. Sunshine, Average Wind Speed, Heating and Cooling Degree Days, and Average Relative Humidity—Selected Cities

[Airport data, except as noted. For period of record through 1995, except as noted. M=morning. A=afternoon]

STATE	STATION	Average percentage of possible sunshine [1] — Length of record (yr.)	Average percentage of possible sunshine [1] — Annual	Average Wind Speed (m.p.h.) — Length of record (yr.)	Average Wind Speed — Annual	Average Wind Speed — Jan.	Average Wind Speed — July	Heating degree days	Cooling degree days	Avg. Rel. Humidity — Length of record (yr.)	Annual — Length of record (yr.)	Annual — Mean number (days)	Jan. M	Jan. A	July M	July A
AL	Mobile	46	60	47	8.9	10.2	6.9	1,702	2,627	33	87	57	82	61	90	61
AK	Juneau	44	23	50	8.3	8.1	7.5	8,897	-	29	84	73	82	78	83	70
AZ	Phoenix	57	81	50	6.2	5.3	7.1	1,350	4,162	35	51	23	67	33	44	20
AR	Little Rock	35	60	53	7.8	8.4	6.7	3,155	2,005	35	84	57	80	62	88	56
CA	Los Angeles	59	72	47	7.5	6.7	7.9	1,458	727	36	79	65	70	60	86	68
	Sacramento	46	72	45	7.9	7.2	8.9	2,749	1,237	34	83	46	90	70	77	29
	San Diego	54	72	55	7.0	6.0	7.5	1,256	984	35	77	62	71	57	82	66
	San Francisco	67	71	68	10.6	7.2	13.6	3,016	145	36	84	62	86	67	86	59
CO	Denver	60	67	47	8.6	8.6	8.3	6,020	679	35	68	40	64	49	69	34
CT	Hartford	40	52	41	8.4	9.0	7.3	6,151	677	36	77	52	71	56	79	51
DE	Wilmington	47	55	47	9.0	9.8	7.8	4,937	1,046	48	78	55	75	60	80	54
DC	Washington	46	55	47	9.4	10.0	8.3	4,047	1,549	35	75	53	70	55	77	53
FL	Jacksonville	46	61	47	7.9	8.1	7.0	1,434	2,551	59	88	56	87	58	88	58
	Miami	45	68	46	9.2	9.5	7.9	200	4,198	31	84	61	84	59	84	63
GA	Atlanta	60	59	57	9.1	10.4	7.7	2,991	1,667	35	82	56	79	59	88	59
HI	Honolulu	45	74	46	11.3	9.5	13.1	-	4,474	26	72	55	81	61	67	51
ID	Boise	55	58	56	8.7	8.0	8.4	5,861	754	56	69	43	81	71	54	22
IL	Chicago	36	52	52	10.4	11.7	8.4	6,536	752	37	80	60	77	68	82	57
	Peoria	51	53	52	10.0	11.1	7.8	6,148	982	36	83	62	79	69	87	59
IN	Indianapolis	63	51	47	9.6	10.9	7.5	5,615	1,014	36	84	62	81	70	87	60
IA	Des Moines	45	55	46	10.7	11.5	8.9	6,497	1,036	34	80	60	76	68	83	58
KS	Wichita	39	62	42	12.2	12.0	11.3	4,791	1,628	42	80	56	79	63	79	49
KY	Louisville	47	53	48	8.3	9.5	6.8	4,514	1,288	35	81	59	77	64	85	58
LA	New Orleans	46	60	47	8.1	9.3	6.1	1,513	2,655	47	88	63	85	66	91	66
ME	Portland	54	55	55	8.7	9.1	7.6	7,378	268	55	79	59	76	61	80	59
MD	Baltimore	44	58	45	9.1	9.7	7.9	4,707	1,137	42	77	54	72	57	80	53
MA	Boston	59	55	38	12.5	13.8	11.0	5,641	678	31	72	58	68	57	74	56
MI	Detroit	36	49	37	10.4	12.0	8.5	6,569	626	37	81	60	80	69	82	54
	Sault Ste. Marie	53	43	54	9.2	9.7	7.8	9,316	131	54	85	67	81	74	89	62
MN	Duluth	46	49	46	11.0	11.6	9.4	9,818	180	34	81	63	77	70	85	59
	Minneapolis-St. Paul	56	54	57	10.5	10.5	9.4	7,981	682	36	79	60	75	67	81	55
MS	Jackson	30	59	32	7.3	8.4	5.8	2,467	2,215	32	91	58	87	65	94	59
MO	Kansas City	22	59	23	10.7	11.3	9.4	5,393	1,288	23	81	60	77	64	85	58
	St. Louis	46	55	46	9.7	10.6	8.0	4,758	1,534	35	83	59	81	66	84	56
MT	Great Falls	57	51	54	12.6	15.1	10.0	7,741	388	34	67	45	67	61	67	31
NE	Omaha	49	59	59	10.5	10.9	8.8	6,300	1,072	31	82	59	78	66	85	58
NV	Reno	52	69	53	6.6	5.6	7.2	5,674	508	32	70	31	79	50	62	18
NH	Concord	53	55	53	6.7	7.3	5.7	7,554	328	30	81	54	76	59	84	51
NJ	Atlantic City	36	56	37	9.9	10.9	8.3	5,169	826	31	82	57	78	58	84	58
NM	Albuquerque	55	76	56	8.9	8.0	8.9	4,425	1,244	35	60	29	70	40	59	27
NY	Albany	56	49	47	8.9	9.8	7.5	6,894	507	30	80	57	77	63	81	55
	Buffalo	51	43	56	11.9	14.1	10.3	6,747	477	35	80	62	79	72	78	55
	New York [2]	42	58	58	9.4	10.7	7.6	4,805	1,096	61	72	56	68	60	75	55
NC	Charlotte	46	58	46	7.4	7.8	6.6	3,341	1,582	35	82	53	78	56	86	56
	Raleigh	46	59	46	7.7	8.5	6.7	3,457	1,417	31	85	54	79	55	89	58
ND	Bismarck	55	55	56	10.2	10.0	9.2	8,968	488	36	81	57	75	69	84	48
OH	Cincinnati	43	49	48	9.0	10.6	7.2	5,248	996	33	82	60	79	68	85	57
	Cleveland	53	45	54	10.5	12.2	8.6	6,201	621	35	79	62	78	70	81	57
	Columbus	45	48	46	8.3	9.8	6.5	5,708	797	36	80	59	77	68	84	56
OK	Oklahoma City	44	64	47	12.3	12.6	10.9	3,659	1,859	30	80	55	78	59	80	50
OR	Portland	46	39	47	7.9	10.0	7.6	4,522	371	55	86	59	85	75	82	45
PA	Philadelphia	54	56	55	9.5	10.3	8.2	4,954	1,101	36	76	54	73	59	79	54
	Pittsburgh	42	44	45	9.1	10.6	7.3	5,968	654	35	79	57	76	66	82	54
RI	Providence	41	55	42	10.5	11.1	9.4	5,884	606	32	75	55	71	56	77	56
SC	Columbia	47	60	47	6.8	7.2	6.3	2,649	1,966	29	87	51	82	54	89	54
SD	Sioux Falls	49	57	47	11.1	11.0	9.8	7,809	744	32	82	60	77	69	83	54
TN	Memphis	42	59	47	8.8	10.0	7.5	3,082	2,118	56	81	57	79	63	85	57
	Nashville	53	57	54	8.0	9.1	6.5	3,729	1,616	30	84	57	80	63	89	57
TX	Dallas-Fort Worth	41	64	42	10.7	10.9	9.8	2,407	2,603	32	82	56	80	61	81	49
	El Paso	52	80	53	8.8	8.3	8.3	2,708	2,094	35	57	28	66	35	62	29
	Houston	25	56	26	7.9	8.3	7.1	1,599	2,700	26	90	60	86	64	93	57
UT	Salt Lake City	66	62	66	8.8	7.5	9.5	5,765	1,047	36	68	43	79	69	52	22
VT	Burlington	51	44	52	9.0	9.8	8.0	7,771	388	30	77	59	72	64	79	53
VA	Norfolk	46	58	47	10.6	11.5	8.9	3,495	1,422	47	78	57	74	59	81	59
	Richmond	49	56	47	7.7	8.1	6.9	3,963	1,348	61	83	53	80	57	85	56
WA	Seattle-Tacoma [3]	50	38	47	9.0	9.6	8.3	4,908	190	36	83	62	81	74	82	49
	Spokane	47	48	48	8.9	8.8	8.6	6,842	398	36	78	52	86	79	65	28
WV	Charleston	47	48	48	6.1	7.3	4.9	4,646	1,031	48	83	56	78	63	90	59
WI	Milwaukee	54	52	55	11.5	12.6	9.7	7,324	479	35	80	64	76	68	82	61
WY	Cheyenne	59	64	38	12.9	15.3	10.4	7,326	285	36	65	44	58	50	70	38
PR	San Juan	39	76	40	8.4	8.5	9.7	-	5,558	40	79	65	82	64	79	67

- Represents zero.   [1] Percent of days that are either clear or partly cloudy.   [2] Airport data for sunshine.   [3] Does not represent airport data.

Source: U.S. National Oceanic and Atmospheric Administration, *Comparative Climatic Data*, annual.

Parks, Recreation, and Travel

This section presents data on national parks and forests, state parks, recreational activities, the arts and humanities, and domestic and foreign travel.

Parks and recreation—The Department of the Interior has responsibility for administering the national parks. As part of this function, it issues reports relating to the usage of public parks for recreation purposes. The National Park Service publishes information on visits to national park areas in its annual report, *National Park Statistical Abstract. The National Parks: Index (year)* is a biannual report which has appeared under a variety of *Index* titles prior to 1985. Beginning with the 1985 edition, the report has appeared under the current title. The *Index* contains brief descriptions, with acreages, of each area administered by the Service, plus certain "related" areas. A statistical summary of service-administered areas is also presented. The annual *Federal Recreation Fee Report* summarizes the prior year's recreation fee receipts and recreation visitation statistics for seven federal land managing agencies.

Statistics for state parks are compiled by the National Association of State Park Directors which issues its annual *Information Exchange.* The Department of Agriculture's Forest Service, in its *Report of the Forest Service,* issues data on recreational uses of the national forests.

Visitation—Data on visitation to reporting areas are collected by several different agencies and groups. The methodology used to collect these results may vary accordingly, from visual counts and estimates to the use of electromagnetic traffic counters. In using and comparing these data, one should also be aware of several different definitions that follow: Recreation visit, which is the entry of any person into an area for recreation purposes; nonrecreation visits, which include visits going to and from inholdings, through traffic, tradespeople and personnel with business in the area; and visitor hour, which constitutes the presence of a person in a recreation area or site for recreational purposes for periods of time aggregating 60 minutes.

In Brief

In 1997
Percent of adults attending:

Movies	66%
Sports events	41%
Amusement park	57%

In 1996
Expenditures for:

Fishing	$37.8 billion
Hunting	$20.6 billion
Wildlife watching	$29.2 billion

Recreation and leisure activities—Statistics on the participation in various recreation and leisure time activities are based on several sample surveys. Data on participation in fishing, hunting, and other forms of wildlife-associated recreation are published periodically by the U.S. Department of Interior, Fish and Wildlife Service. The most recent data are from the 1991 survey. Data on participation in various sports recreation activities are published by the National Sporting Goods Association.

Travel—Information on foreign travel and personal expenditures abroad, as well as expenditures by foreign citizens traveling in the United States, is compiled annually by the U.S. Bureau of Economic Analysis and published in selected issues of the monthly *Survey of Current Business.* Statistics on arrivals to the United States are reported by the U.S. International Trade Administration (ITA). Sources of statistics on departures from the United States include the Department of Transportation's *International Air Travel Statistics*, and other sources. Data on domestic travel, business receipts and employment of the travel industry, and travel expenditures are published by the U.S. Travel Data Center, which is the research department of the Travel Industry Association and is the national nonprofit center for travel and tourism research which is located in Washington, DC. Other data on household transportation characteristics may be found in Section 21.

No. 422. National Park System—Summary: 1985 to 1996

[For fiscal years ending in year shown, except as noted; see text, Section 10, Federal Government . Includes data for five areas in Puerto Rico and Virgin Islands, one area in American Samoa, and one area in Guam]

ITEM	1985	1990	1991	1992	1993	1994	1995	1996
Finances (mil. dol.): [1]								
Expenditures reported	848.1	986.1	1,104.4	1,268.7	1,429.4	1,404.0	1,445.0	1,391.0
Salaries and wages	369.4	459.1	495.3	518.1	596.1	627.2	633.0	650.0
Improvements, maintenance	127.4	160.0	179.6	212.1	224.8	222.9	234.0	234.0
Construction	84.7	108.5	134.1	193.3	226.8	205.6	192.0	168.0
Other	266.6	258.5	295.4	345.2	379.7	348.3	386.0	339.0
Funds available	1,248.2	1,505.5	1,988.4	2,274.8	2,346.5	2,307.7	2,225.0	2,116.0
Appropriations	821.6	1,052.5	1,284.7	1,392.8	1,334.0	1,388.8	1,325.0	1,346.0
Other [2]	426.6	453.0	703.7	882.0	1,012.5	918.9	900.0	770.0
Revenue from operations	50.6	78.6	78.1	88.3	89.5	97.0	106.3	133.2
Recreation visits (millions): [3]								
All areas	263.4	258.7	267.8	274.7	273.1	268.6	269.6	265.8
National parks [4]	50.0	57.7	57.4	58.7	59.8	63.0	64.8	63.1
National monuments	15.9	23.9	25.8	26.6	26.5	23.6	23.5	23.6
National historical, commemorative, archaeological [5]	61.9	57.5	61.0	63.3	61.9	59.5	56.9	59.0
National parkways	40.0	29.1	28.8	30.7	30.4	29.3	31.3	30.9
National recreation areas [4]	49.4	47.2	49.8	50.3	50.8	52.3	53.7	52.6
National seashores and lakeshores	25.3	23.3	24.4	23.9	24.1	24.0	22.5	20.3
National Capital Parks	8.3	7.5	7.5	8.1	9.1	5.4	5.5	6.1
Miscellaneous other areas	12.6	12.5	13.1	13.1	10.5	11.8	11.4	11.3
Recreation overnight stays (millions) [3]	15.8	17.6	17.7	18.3	17.7	18.3	16.8	16.6
In commercial lodgings	3.5	3.9	4.0	4.1	4.0	3.9	3.8	3.7
In Park Service campgrounds	7.3	7.9	7.8	8.1	7.5	7.6	7.1	6.5
In tents	3.6	4.1	4.2	4.4	4.1	4.2	3.9	3.7
In recreation vehicles	3.8	3.8	3.6	3.7	3.4	3.4	3.2	2.8
In backcountry	1.7	1.7	2.0	2.2	2.4	2.4	2.2	2.1
Other	3.2	4.2	3.9	3.9	3.8	4.4	3.7	3.7
Land (1,000 acres): [6]								
Total	75,749	76,362	76,607	76,492	75,515	74,905	77,355	77,458
Parks	45,739	46,089	46,135	46,208	45,521	48,111	49,307	49,315
Recreation areas	3,335	3,344	3,346	3,347	3,349	3,351	3,353	3,353
Other	26,675	26,929	27,126	26,937	26,645	23,443	24,695	24,790
Acquisition, gross	34	21	66	23	39	32	27	103
By purchase	29	18	15	21	29	29	25	16
By gift	2	2	43	1	10	1	1	3
By transfer or exchange	3	3	8	1	1	(Z)	1	84
Exclusion	(Z)	1	(Z)	(Z)	(Z)	(Z)	(Z)	(Z)
Acquisition, net	34	21	66	23	39	32	27	103

Z Less than 500 acres. [1] Financial data are those associated with the National Park System. Certain other functions of the National Park Service (principally the activities absorbed from the former Heritage Conservation and Recreation Service in 1981) are excluded. [2] Includes funds carried over from prior years. [3] For calendar year. [4] Through 1990, combined data for North Cascades National Park and two adjacent National Recreation Areas are included in National Parks total. [5] Includes military areas. [6] Federal land only, as of Dec. 31. Federal land acreages, in addition to National Park Service administered lands, also include lands within national park system area boundaries but under the administration of other agencies. Year-to-year changes in the federal lands figures include changes in the acreages of these other lands and hence often differ from "net acquisition."

Source: U.S. National Park Service, Visits, National Park Statistical Abstract, annual; and unpublished data. Other data are unpublished.

No. 423. National Forest Recreation Use, Summary: 1980 to 1996

[For year ending September 30. Estimated. Represents recreational use of National Forest land and water in states which have a Forest Service recreation program]

YEAR AND ACTIVITY	Recreation visitor-days [1] (1,000)	Per-cent	STATE	Recreation visitor-days [1], 1996 (1,000)	STATE OR OTHER AREA	Recreation visitor-days [1], 1996 (1,000)
1980	233,549	100.0	U.S.	341,200	NV	3,857
1984	227,554	100.0			NH	3,354
1985	225,407	100.0	AL	689	NM	9,326
1986	226,533	100.0	AK	6,962	NY	39
1987	238,458	100.0	AZ	35,000	NC	6,979
1988	242,316	100.0	AR	2,210	ND	133
1989	252,495	100.0	CA	71,165	OH	524
1990	263,051	100.0	CO	30,971	OK	393
1991	278,849	100.0	FL	2,960	OR	37,030
1992	287,691	100.0	GA	2,925	PA	3,268
1993	295,473	100.0	ID	15,365	SC	1,011
1994	330,348	100.0	IL	1,188	SD	3,571
1995	345,083	100.0	IN	684	TN	3,309
1996, total	341,200	100.0	KS	86	TX	2,302
Mechanized travel and viewing scenery	122,141	35.8	KY	2,326	UT	19,378
Camping, picnicking, and swimming	87,082	25.5	LA	599	VT	1,395
Hiking, horseback riding, and water travel	33,099	9.7	MA	158	VA	4,927
Winter sports	19,708	5.8	MI	4,866	WA	24,797
Hunting	19,384	5.7	MN	5,982	WV	1,499
Resorts, cabins, and organization	17,702	5.2	MS	1,828	WI	2,527
Fishing	18,160	5.3	MO	2,518	WY	9,114
Nature studies	3,299	1.0	MT	13,495		
Other [2]	20,627	6.0	NE	320	PR	171

[1] One recreation visitor-day is the recreation use of National Forest land or water that aggregates 12 visitor-hours. This may entail 1 person for 12 hours, 12 persons for 1 hour, or any equivalent combination of individual or group use, either continuous or intermittent. [2] Includes team sports, gathering forest products, attending talks and programs, and other uses.

Source: U.S. Forest Service, Annual Report.

No. 424. State Parks and Recreation Areas—States: 1996

[For year ending June 30. Data are shown as reported by state park directors. In some states, park agency has under its control forests, fish and wildlife areas, and/or other areas. In other states, agency is responsible for state parks only]

STATE	Acreage (1,000)	Visitors (1,000) [1]	REVENUE Total ($1,000)	REVENUE Percent of operating expenditures	STATE	Acreage (1,000)	Visitors (1,000) [1]	REVENUE Total ($1,000)	REVENUE Percent of operating expenditures
United States ...	12,318	747,812	559,754	43.6	Missouri	137	16,112	6,100	23.5
					Montana	49	1,646	1,126	21.9
Alabama.........	50	5,915	25,724	91.0	Nebraska	133	9,188	11,003	92.3
Alaska	3,250	4,270	1,957	37.0	Nevada.........	149	3,447	1,362	21.7
Arizona.........	46	2,301	2,301	36.1	New Hampshire ...	154	910	5,492	106.4
Arkansas........	51	7,614	12,805	54.8	New Jersey	327	13,915	6,914	26.4
California........	1,345	70,952	63,689	36.4	New Mexico......	91	5,002	3,345	25.2
Colorado........	347	12,700	10,708	67.9	New York	261	65,358	42,299	34.1
Connecticut......	176	8,029	3,571	40.2	North Carolina	143	10,968	2,481	17.6
Delaware........	17	3,002	5,013	56.8	North Dakota.....	20	1,129	803	40.9
Florida	454	12,491	21,606	48.3	Ohio...........	204	58,598	20,997	36.8
Georgia	67	13,945	16,917	31.0	Oklahoma.......	71	16,990	16,679	53.2
Hawaii	25	15,000	(NA)	(NA)	Oregon.........	92	40,786	12,185	45.6
Idaho	42	2,380	2,801	41.5	Pennsylvania	283	37,001	9,350	15.5
Illinois..........	408	40,038	4,282	11.8	Rhode Island	9	3,046	3,039	50.6
Indiana	175	17,029	23,120	100.9	South Carolina....	82	9,999	14,431	66.9
Iowa...........	63	12,983	2,700	31.0	South Dakota.....	93	6,638	5,923	77.1
Kansas.........	29	7,360	3,057	54.0	Tennessee.......	134	30,101	24,538	56.6
Kentucky........	43	8,663	42,260	69.7	Texas..........	669	23,340	18,822	60.8
Louisiana	39	1,343	3,598	42.4	Utah...........	114	7,333	5,494	32.7
Maine..........	567	1,987	1,789	29.9	Vermont	65	788	4,963	95.3
Maryland........	249	10,061	11,163	41.9	Virginia	66	4,891	3,978	33.1
Massachusetts....	276	12,505	3,310	11.0	Washington	260	48,456	9,337	30.6
Michigan........	266	24,325	24,143	74.3	West Virginia	196	8,891	15,250	60.8
Minnesota	247	8,391	9,201	44.0	Wisconsin	140	12,993	10,230	92.5
Mississippi......	24	4,831	5,442	41.2	Wyoming.......	120	2,171	643	15.2

NA Not available.   [1] Includes overnight visitors.

Source: National Association of State Park Directors, Tuscon, AZ, *1997 Annual Information Exchange.*

No. 425. Personal Consumption Expenditures for Recreation: 1990 to 1996

[In billions of dollars, except percent. Represents market value of purchases of goods and services by individuals and nonprofit institutions]

TYPE OF PRODUCT OR SERVICE	1990	1991	1992	1993	1994	1995	1996
Total recreation expenditures	281.6	292.0	310.8	340.2	370.2	402.5	431.1
Percent of total personal consumption [1]	7.3	7.3	7.4	7.6	7.8	8.1	8.3
Books and maps	16.5	16.9	17.7	19.0	20.6	22.1	23.2
Magazines, newspapers, and sheet music	21.5	21.9	21.6	22.7	24.5	25.5	26.5
Nondurable toys and sport supplies..................	31.6	32.8	34.2	36.6	39.7	42.2	45.4
Wheel goods, sports and photographic equipment [2]	29.8	29.5	29.9	32.6	35.6	39.1	42.0
Video and audio products, computer equipment, and musical instruments	53.8	57.3	61.2	68.1	78.5	85.2	89.7
Radio and television repair.......................	4.2	4.0	4.2	4.5	4.5	4.9	5.1
Flowers, seeds, and potted plants..................	11.1	11.3	12.3	12.7	13.4	13.9	14.9
Admissions to specified spectator amusements	15.1	15.7	16.6	18.1	19.0	20.2	22.1
Motion picture theaters	5.2	5.3	5.0	5.2	5.6	6.0	6.3
Legitimate theaters and opera, and entertainments of nonprofit institutions [3]..................	5.6	6.0	6.8	7.8	8.2	8.7	9.3
Spectator sports [4]	4.4	4.5	4.8	5.1	5.2	5.5	6.4
Clubs and fraternal organizations except insurance [5]	8.9	9.6	10.3	11.2	11.8	12.7	13.0
Commercial participant amusements [6]...............	23.0	23.8	27.2	31.5	36.2	41.5	46.2
Pari-mutuel net receipts.........................	3.4	3.3	3.3	3.3	3.3	3.3	3.5
Other [7]	62.7	65.9	72.4	80.0	83.1	91.9	99.6

[1] See Table 723.   [2] Includes boats and pleasure aircraft.   [3] Except athletic.   [4] Consists of admissions to professional and amateur athletic events and to racetracks, including horse, dog, and auto.   [5] Consists of dues and fees excluding insurance premiums.   [6] Consists of billiard parlors; bowling alleys; dancing, riding, shooting, skating, and swimming places; amusement devices and parks; golf courses; sightseeing buses and guides; private flying operations; casino gambling; and other commercial participant amusements.   [7] Consists of net receipts of lotteries and expenditures for purchases of pets and pet care services, cable TV, film processing, photographic studios, sporting and recreation camps, video cassette rentals, and recreational services, not elsewhere classified.

Source: U.S. Bureau of Economic Analysis, *The National Income and Product Accounts of the United States, 1929-94,* Vol.1, and *Survey of Current Business,* August, 1997.

No. 426. Expenditures per Consumer Unit for Entertainment and Reading: 1985 to 1995

[Data are **annual averages. In dollars, except as indicated.** Based on Consumer Expenditure Survey; see text, Section 14, Income, Expendures, and Wealth, for description of survey. See also headnote, Table 733. For composition of regions, see inside front cover]

YEAR AND CHARACTERISTIC	ENTERTAINMENT AND READING		ENTERTAINMENT				Reading
	Total	Percent of total expenditures	Total	Fees and admissions	Television, radios, and sound equipment	Other equipment and services [1]	
1985.	1,311	5.6	1,170	320	371	479	141
1986.	1,289	5.4	1,149	308	371	470	140
1987.	1,335	5.5	1,193	323	379	491	142
1988.	1,479	5.7	1,329	353	416	560	150
1989.	1,581	5.7	1,424	377	429	618	157
1990.	1,575	5.6	1,422	371	454	597	153
1991.	1,635	5.5	1,472	378	468	627	163
1992.	1,662	5.6	1,500	379	492	629	162
1993.	1,792	5.8	1,626	414	590	621	166
1994.	1,732	5.5	1,567	439	533	595	165
1995, total	**1,775**	**5.5**	**1,612**	**433**	**542**	**637**	**163**
Age of reference person:							
Under 25 years old.	1,152	6.3	1,081	225	456	400	71
25 to 34 years old.	1,816	5.8	1,682	394	580	708	134
35 to 44 years old.	2,124	5.5	1,951	531	657	763	173
45 to 54 years old.	2,337	5.5	2,138	585	664	889	199
55 to 64 years old.	1,765	5.4	1,577	418	492	666	188
65 to 74 years old.	1,336	5.3	1,156	377	397	382	180
75 years old and over.	790	4.3	652	223	260	170	138
Origin of reference person:							
Hispanic.	1,134	4.2	1,060	231	459	369	74
Non-Hispanic.	1,829	5.6	1,659	450	549	660	170
Black.	1,008	4.3	935	147	516	273	73
Other.	1,929	5.7	1,747	487	553	708	182
Region of residence:							
Northeast.	1,730	5.2	1,544	429	520	595	186
Midwest.	1,772	5.5	1,602	419	572	612	170
South.	1,594	5.3	1,459	373	514	572	135
West.	2,116	6.0	1,939	552	570	816	177
Size of consumer unit:							
One person.	1,112	5.7	992	265	367	360	120
Two or more persons.	2,035	5.5	1,856	499	611	747	179
Two persons.	1,854	5.6	1,667	459	516	693	187
Three persons.	2,010	5.3	1,834	452	618	764	176
Four persons.	2,376	5.6	2,187	650	739	797	189
Five persons or more.	2,132	5.1	1,986	476	701	809	146

[1] Other equipment and services includes pets, toys, and playground equipment; sports, exercise, and photographic equipment; and recreational vehicles.

Source: U.S. Bureau of Labor Statistics, *Consumer Expenditure Survey*, annual.

No. 427. Motion Pictures and Amusement and Recreation Services—Annual Receipts: 1990 to 1996

[**In millions of dollars.** For taxable employer and nonemployer firms]

KIND OF BUSINESS	1987 SIC code [1]	1990	1992	1993	1994	1995	1996
Motion pictures.	78	39,982	45,662	49,799	53,504	57,184	60,205
Production, distribution, and allied services	781, 782	28,888	34,288	37,653	40,256	43,264	46,223
Theaters	783	6,088	5,879	5,977	6,233	6,530	7,036
Video tape rental.	784	5,006	5,495	6,169	7,015	7,390	6,946
Amusement and recreation services.	79	50,126	57,699	63,651	68,453	77,452	85,769
Dance studios, schools, and halls.	791	626	784	880	906	947	1,036
Theatrical producers (except motion picture), bands, orchestras, and entertainers	792	10,735	13,054	15,408	16,050	17,479	19,679
Bowling centers.	793	2,800	2,915	2,724	2,709	2,681	2,719
Commercial sports.	794	8,636	9,010	9,870	11,090	13,056	14,632
Professional sports clubs and promoters	7941	3,702	3,978	5,056	6,138	7,695	8,877
Racing, including track operation	7948	4,934	5,032	4,814	4,952	5,360	5,755
Miscellaneous amusement and recreation services [2].	799	27,329	31,936	34,769	37,698	43,290	47,702
Physical fitness facilities	7991	3,623	4,135	3,961	4,033	4,412	4,970
Public golf courses.	7992	2,254	2,609	2,828	3,059	3,584	3,976
Coin-operated amusement devices	7993	2,146	2,566	2,763	2,965	3,254	3,486
Amusement parks.	7996	4,922	5,366	5,641	5,858	6,298	6,775
Membership sports and recreation clubs	7997	4,825	5,397	5,965	6,379	6,765	7,439

[1] 1987 Standard Industrial Classification code; see text, Section 13.   [2] Includes kinds of businesses, not shown separately.

Source: U.S. Bureau of the Census, *Current Business Reports, Service Annual Survey: 1996*, BS/96.

No. 428. Quantity of Books Sold and Value of U.S. Domestic Consumer Expenditures: 1982 to 1996

[Includes all titles released by publishers in the United States and imports which appear under the imprints of American publishers. Multi-volume sets, such as encyclopedias, are counted as one unit]

TYPE OF PUBLICATION AND MARKET AREA	UNITS SOLD (mil.)					CONSUMER EXPENDITURES (mil. dol.)				
	1982	1985	1990	1995	1996	1982	1985	1990	1995	1996
Total [1]	**1,723**	**1,788**	**2,005**	**2,186**	**2,212**	**9,889**	**12,611**	**19,043**	**25,154**	**26,109**
Hardbound, total	646	694	824	827	837	6,190	7,969	11,789	15,011	15,468
Softbound, total	1,077	1,094	1,181	1,359	1,375	3,699	4,642	7,254	10,143	10,641
Trade	459	553	705	813	819	2,484	3,660	6,498	9,340	9,474
Adult	315	360	403	465	440	2,028	2,871	4,777	7,060	6,925
Juvenile	144	193	301	348	379	456	789	1,721	2,280	2,549
Religious	144	134	130	148	155	706	926	1,362	1,792	1,909
Professional	106	110	131	146	144	1,630	2,043	2,957	4,153	4,288
Bookclubs	133	130	108	123	132	510	582	705	949	1,061
Elhi text	233	234	209	237	245	1,067	1,415	1,948	2,384	2,522
College text	115	110	137	142	150	1,388	1,575	2,319	2,708	2,920
Mail order publications	134	121	138	92	93	581	650	752	578	599
Mass market paperbacks-rack sized	382	382	433	470	458	1,102	1,244	1,775	2,322	2,374
General retailers	756	829	1,010	1,145	1,153	3,743	5,103	8,465	11,888	12,211
College stores	224	225	255	274	275	1,910	2,309	3,403	4,311	4,528
Libraries and institutions [2]	80	80	88	97	96	888	1,090	1,592	2,111	2,169
Schools [2]	262	260	244	273	281	1,313	1,685	2,365	2,896	3,060
Direct to consumers	319	300	304	289	299	1,889	2,214	2,901	3,544	3,745
Other	82	94	104	108	108	146	210	316	404	396

[1] Types of publications include university press publications and subscription reference works, not shown separately.   [2] Elhi libraries included in schools.

Source: Book Industry Study Group, Inc., New York, NY, *Book Industry Trends, 1997,* annual (copyright).

No. 429. Book Purchasing by Adults: 1991 and 1996

[**In percent.** Excludes books purchased for or by children under age 13. Based on a survey of 16,000 households conducted over 12 months ending in December of year shown. For details, see source]

CHARACTERISTIC	TOTAL		MASS MARKET [1]		TRADE [2]		HARDCOVER	
	1991	1996	1991	1996	1991	1996	1991	1996
Total	**100.0**	**100.0**	**100.0**	**100.0**	**100.0**	**100.0**	**100.0**	**100.0**
Age of purchaser:								
Under 25 years old	4.3	3.9	3.7	3.6	5.2	4.4	4.4	3.6
25 to 34 years old	18.8	15.7	13.9	13.7	25.4	17.9	19.6	14.8
35 to 44 years old	23.7	25.9	22.8	22.1	25.2	29.7	23.7	26.5
45 to 54 years old	22.4	22.3	26.0	21.5	18.5	21.9	20.5	23.7
55 to 64 years old	15.6	15.6	15.8	16.5	13.9	14.1	17.2	16.0
65 years old and over	15.2	16.6	17.8	22.6	11.8	12.0	14.6	15.4
Household income:								
Under $30,000	37.1	32.7	41.7	40.9	32.6	28.3	34.1	27.6
$30,000 to 49,999	27.2	23.8	27.3	22.4	27.7	24.6	26.5	24.6
$50,000 to 59,999	11.0	7.9	9.8	6.9	12.3	8.4	11.5	8.3
$60,000 to 69,999	6.9	9.1	7.0	7.9	7.2	9.9	6.3	9.6
$70,000 and over	17.8	26.5	14.2	21.9	20.2	28.8	21.6	29.9
Household size:								
Singles	20.8	18.7	17.7	20.1	24.1	17.8	22.8	18.1
Families with no children	40.4	43.4	42.3	42.1	38.0	43.2	39.7	45.1
Families with children	38.8	37.9	40.0	37.8	37.9	39.0	37.5	36.8
Age of reader:								
Under 25 years old	7.3	6.9	5.2	5.1	10.1	9.2	7.7	6.3
25 to 34 years old	18.7	16.6	14.1	14.2	24.7	19.2	20.2	16.2
35 to 44 years old	22.9	24.8	22.3	21.6	24.0	28.0	22.7	25.2
45 to 54 years old	20.8	20.2	24.9	20.0	16.5	19.6	18.4	21.6
55 to 64 years old	14.9	14.4	15.9	16.9	12.7	11.8	15.6	14.3
65 years old and over	15.4	17.1	17.6	22.2	12.0	12.2	15.6	16.4
Category of book:								
Popular fiction	54.9	50.9	93.0	93.6	14.9	14.5	31.8	40.4
General nonfiction	10.3	9.4	3.6	2.7	15.6	12.2	16.5	14.4
Cooking/crafts	10.2	10.2	0.4	0.4	20.6	16.9	18.2	14.3
Other	24.6	29.5	3.0	3.3	48.9	56.4	33.5	30.9
Sales outlet:								
Independent	32.5	18.6	26.5	11.3	44.9	27.6	29.0	17.2
Chain book store	22.0	25.6	17.2	22.0	27.4	27.6	25.2	27.7
Book clubs	16.6	18.0	17.8	18.7	9.5	13.6	22.6	22.0
Other [3]	28.9	37.8	38.5	48.0	18.2	31.2	23.2	33.1

[1] "Pocket size" books sold primarily through magazine and news outlets, supermarkets, variety stores, etc.   [2] All paperbound books, except mass market.   [3] Includes mail order, price clubs, discount stores, food/drug stores, used book stores, and other outlets.

Source: Book Industry Study Group, Inc., New York, NY, *Consumer Research Study on Book Purchasing,* annual (copyright).

No. 430. Profile of Consumer Expenditures for Sound Recordings: 1990 to 1997

[In percent, except total value. Based on monthly telephone surveys of the population 10 years old and over]

ITEM	1990	1995	1997	ITEM	1990	1995	1997
Total value (mil. dol.)	7,541.1	12,320.3	12,236.8	Mail order.	2.5	4.0	2.7
PERCENT DISTRIBUTION [1]				Internet	(NA)	(NA)	0.3
Age: 10 to 14 years.	7.6	8.0	8.9	Music type: [2]			
15 to 19 years.	18.3	17.1	16.8	Rock	36.1	33.5	32.5
20 to 24 years.	16.5	15.3	13.8	Country	9.6	16.7	14.4
25 to 29 years.	14.6	12.3	11.7	R&B	11.6	11.3	11.2
30 to 34 years.	13.2	12.1	11.0	Pop.	13.7	10.1	9.4
35 to 39 years.	10.2	10.8	11.6	Rap.	8.5	6.7	10.1
40 to 44 years.	7.8	7.5	8.8	Classical	3.1	2.9	2.8
45 years and over	11.1	16.1	16.5	Jazz	4.8	3.0	2.8
Sex: Male	54.4	53.0	48.6	Oldies	0.8	1.0	0.8
Female	45.6	47.0	51.4	Gospel.	2.5	3.1	4.5
Sales outlet:				Soundtracks	0.8	0.9	1.2
Record store.	69.8	52.0	51.8	New age	1.1	0.7	0.8
Other store.	18.5	28.2	31.9	Children's.	0.5	0.5	0.9
Music club	8.9	14.3	11.6	Other.	5.6	7.0	5.7

NA Not available.   [1] Percent distributions exclude nonresponses and responses of don't know.   [2] As classified by respondent.

Source: Recording Industry Association of America, Inc., Washington, DC, *1997 Consumer Profile.*

No. 431. Household Pet Ownership: 1996

[Based on a sample survey of 80,000 households in 1996; for details, see source]

ITEM	Unit	Dog	Cat	Pet bird	Horse
Households owning companion pets [1]	Million	31.2	27.0	4.6	1.5
Percent of all households.	Percent . . .	31.6	27.3	4.6	1.5
Average number owned.	Number. . .	1.7	2.2	2.7	2.7
Total companion pet population [1].	Million	52.9	59.1	12.6	4.0
Households obtaining veterinary care [2]	Percent . . .	88.7	72.9	15.8	66.3
Average visits per household per year	Number. . .	2.6	1.9	0.2	2.3
Average annual costs per household	Dollars	186.80	112.24	10.95	226.26
Total expenditures.	Mil. dol.	5,828	3,030	50	339
PERCENT DISTRIBUTION OF HOUSEHOLDS OWNING PETS					
Annual household income: Under $12,500	Percent . . .	12.7	13.9	17.3	9.5
$12,500 to $24,999	Percent . . .	19.1	19.7	20.9	20.3
$25,000 to $39,999	Percent . . .	21.6	21.5	22.0	21.8
$40,000 to $59,999	Percent . . .	21.5	21.2	17.5	23.1
$60,000 and over	Percent . . .	25.2	23.7	22.3	25.4
Family size: [1] One person	Percent . . .	13.2	16.8	12.7	12.1
Two persons	Percent . . .	31.0	32.6	27.9	29.1
Three persons	Percent . . .	21.4	20.6	20.4	22.0
Four or more persons	Percent . . .	34.5	29.9	38.9	36.7

[1] As of December.   [2] During 1996.

Source: American Veterinary Medical Association, Schaumburg, IL, *U.S. Pet Ownership and Demographics Sourcebook, 1997,* (copyright).

No. 432. Household Participation in Lawn and Garden Activities: 1992 to 1996

[For calendar year. Based on national household sample survey conducted by the Gallup Organization. Subject to sampling variability; see source]

ACTIVITY	PERCENT HOUSEHOLDS ENGAGED IN—					RETAIL SALES (mil. dol.)				
	1992	1993	1994	1995	1996	1992	1993	1994	1995	1996
Total.	75	71	74	72	64	22,824	22,410	25,897	22,242	22,519
Lawn care.	54	54	56	53	47	7,460	6,446	8,417	7,621	6,925
Indoor houseplants.	34	31	37	30	31	926	689	999	864	791
Flower gardening	39	39	44	38	37	2,167	2,396	3,147	2,107	2,987
Insect control.	27	24	28	24	24	1,593	1,080	1,127	1,049	1,734
Shrub care	27	28	30	25	25	1,437	1,274	1,133	774	1,059
Vegetable gardening.	31	26	31	28	26	1,440	1,063	1,476	1,359	1,341
Tree care	20	21	22	17	20	1,664	2,011	1,408	1,002	1,362
Landscaping	22	24	26	20	22	4,444	5,006	5,797	5,524	3,964
Flower bulbs	23	22	28	21	21	503	453	635	377	521
Fruit trees.	13	13	14	11	12	350	759	389	241	349
Container gardening.	9	11	12	12	10	239	441	359	377	387
Raising transplants [1]	8	10	11	8	8	169	201	182	187	238
Herb gardening	7	8	10	8	9	135	175	112	140	144
Growing berries	6	6	6	5	5	62	126	85	55	90
Ornamental gardening.	6	6	5	5	5	235	290	264	144	158
Water gardening	(NA)	(NA)	5	5	4	(NA)	(NA)	367	421	469

NA Not available.   [1] Starting plants in advance of planting in ground.

Source: The National Gardening Association, Burlington, VT, *National Gardening Survey,* annual (copyright).

No. 433. Participants in Wildlife Related Recreation Activities: 1996

[In thousands. For persons 16 years old and over engaging in activity at least once in 1996. Based on survey and subject to sampling error; see source for details]

PARTICIPANT	Number	Days of participation	Trips	PARTICIPANT	Number	Days of participation
Total sportsmen [1]	**39,694**	**882,569**	**729,495**	**Wildlife watchers** [1]	**62,868**	**(X)**
Total anglers	35,246	625,893	506,557	Nonresidential [2]	23,652	313,790
Freshwater	29,734	515,115	420,010	Observe wildlife	22,878	278,683
Excluding Great Lakes	28,921	485,474	402,814	Photograph wildlife	12,038	79,342
Great Lakes	2,039	20,095	17,195	Feed wildlife	9,976	89,606
Saltwater	9,438	103,034	86,547			
				Residential [3]	60,751	(X)
Total hunters	13,975	256,676	222,938	Observe wildlife	44,063	(X)
Big game	11,288	153,784	113,971	Photograph wildlife	16,021	(X)
Small game	6,945	75,117	63,744	Feed wild birds [4]	54,122	(X)
Migratory birds	3,073	26,501	22,509	Visit public parks	11,011	(X)
Other animals	1,521	24,522	22,714	Maintain plantings or natural areas	13,401	(X)

X Not applicable. [1] Detail does not add to total due to multiple responses and nonresponse. [2] Persons taking a trip of at least one mile for activity. [3] Activity within one mile of home. [4] Or other wildlife.

No. 434. Expenditures For Wildlife Related Recreation Activities: 1996

[See headnote, Table 433]

TYPE OF EXPENDITURE	FISHING			HUNTING			WILDLIFE WATCHING		
	Expenditures (mil. dol.)	Spenders		Expenditures (mil. dol.)	Spenders		Expenditures (mil. dol.)	Spenders	
		Number (1,000)	Percent of anglers		Number (1,000)	Percent of hunters		Number (1,000)	Percent of watchers
Total [1]	**37,797**	**34,002**	**96**	**20,613**	**13,769**	**99**	**29,228**	**52,729**	**84**
Food and lodging	5,990	28,452	81	2,512	11,073	79	5,352	17,922	76
Food	4,256	28,267	80	2,078	11,060	79	3,447	17,761	75
Lodging	1,734	8,020	23	434	1,909	14	1,905	6,783	29
Transportation	3,730	28,741	82	1,780	12,022	86	2,943	20,260	86
Public	559	1,780	5	145	479	3	811	2,229	9
Private	3,171	28,382	81	1,634	11,926	85	2,132	19,863	84
Other trip-related costs	5,661	28,398	81	864	4,378	31	1,150	9,340	39
Sport specific equipment [2]	5,309	24,726	70	5,519	11,278	81	8,230	47,355	75
Auxiliary equipment [3]	1,037	6,006	17	1,233	5,730	41	858	4,763	8
Special equipment [4]	12,828	3,599	10	4,521	805	6	7,564	1,094	2
Other expenditures [5]	3,242	24,944	71	4,185	12,471	89	3,132	23,827	40

[1] Total not adjusted for multiple responses or nonresponse. [2] Items owned primarily for each specific activity, such as rods and reels for fishing and guns and rifles for hunting. [3] Equipment such as camping gear owned for wildlife-associated recreation. [4] "Big ticket" equipment such as campers and boats owned for wildlife-associated recreation. [5] Books, magazines, membership dues and contributions, land leasing and ownership, licenses and plantings.

Source of Tables 433 and 434: U.S. Fish and Wildlife Service, *1996 National Survey of Fishing, Hunting, and Wildlife Associated Recreation.*

No. 435. Participation in NCAA Sports: 1996-97

[Excludes sports sponsored by fewer than 10 institutions]

SPORT	MALES			FEMALES		
	Teams	Athletes	Average squad	Teams	Athletes	Average squad
Total	**7,705**	**200,627**	**(X)**	**7,684**	**128,209**	**(X)**
Baseball	829	24,442	29.5	(X)	(X)	(X)
Basketball	950	15,141	15.9	966	13,392	13.9
Crew [1]	49	1,820	37.2	(X)	(X)	(X)
Cross Country	792	10,271	13.0	838	10,141	12.1
Fencing	36	657	18.3	42	558	13.3
Field Hockey	(X)	(X)	(X)	228	4,857	21.3
Football	601	53,984	89.8	(X)	(X)	(X)
Golf	678	7,197	10.6	282	2,323	8.2
Gymnastics	28	413	14.8	91	1,311	14.4
Ice Hockey [2]	125	3,608	28.9	22	436	19.8
Lacrosse	182	5,705	31.4	182	4,068	22.4
Rifle	42	408	9.7	(X)	(X)	(X)
Rowing	(X)	(X)	(X)	97	3,951	40.7
Skiing	40	575	14.4	40	455	11.4
Soccer	681	17,053	25.0	691	14,829	21.5
Softball	(X)	(X)	(X)	770	13,167	17.1
Squash [1]	25	418	16.7	26	381	14.6
Swimming	368	7,508	20.4	432	8,745	20.2
Tennis	776	7,999	10.3	859	8,223	9.6
Track, Indoor	512	15,957	31.2	528	13,061	24.7
Track, Outdoor	625	19,305	30.9	644	15,578	24.2
Volleyball	74	1,052	14.2	923	12,284	13.3
Water Polo [2]	42	893	21.3	23	452	19.6
Wrestling	250	6,219	24.9	(X)	(X)	(X)

X Not applicable. [1] Sport recognized by the NCAA but does not have an NCAA championship. [2] Sport recognized by the NCAA but does not have an NCAA championship for women.

Source: The National Collegiate Athletic Association (NCAA), Overland Park, KS, 1996-97 Participation Study.

No. 436. Selected Spectator Sports: 1985 to 1996

SPORT	Unit	1985	1987	1990	1992	1993	1994	1995	1996
Baseball, major leagues: [1]									
Attendance	1,000	47,742	53,182	55,512	56,852	71,237	50,010	51,288	61,665
Regular season	1,000	46,824	52,011	54,824	55,873	70,257	50,010	50,469	60,097
National League	1,000	22,292	24,734	24,492	24,113	36,924	25,808	25,110	30,379
American League	1,000	24,532	27,277	30,332	31,760	33,333	24,202	25,359	29,718
Playoffs [2]	1,000	591	784	479	668	636	(X)	533	1,300
World Series	1,000	327	387	209	311	344	(X)	286	268
Players' salaries: [3]									
Average	$1,000	371	412	598	1,029	1,076	1,168	1,111	1,120
Basketball: [4] [5]									
NCAA—Men's college:									
Teams	Number	753	760	767	813	831	858	868	866
Attendance	1,000	26,584	26,798	28,741	29,378	28,527	28,390	28,548	28,225
NCAA—Women's college:									
Teams	Number	746	756	782	815	826	859	864	874
Attendance	1,000	2,072	2,156	2,777	3,397	4,193	4,557	4,962	5,234
Pro: [6]									
Teams	Number	23	23	27	27	27	27	27	29
Attendance, total [7]	1,000	11,534	13,190	18,586	18,609	19,120	19,350	19,883	21,797
Regular season	1,000	10,506	12,065	17,369	17,367	17,778	17,984	18,516	20,513
Average per game	Number	11,141	12,795	15,690	15,689	16,060	16,246	16,727	17,253
Players' salaries:									
Average	$1,000	325	440	817	1,202	1,348	1,700	1,900	2,100
Football:									
NCAA College: [5]									
Teams	Number	509	507	533	552	560	568	565	566
Attendance	1,000	34,952	35,008	35,330	35,225	34,871	36,460	35,638	36,083
National Football League: [8]									
Teams	Number	28	28	28	28	28	(NA)	(NA)	(NA)
Attendance, total [9]	1,000	14,058	[10]15,180	17,666	17,784	14,772	(NA)	(NA)	(NA)
Regular season	1,000	13,345	[10]11,406	13,960	13,829	13,967	(NA)	(NA)	(NA)
Average per game	Number	59,567	[10]54,315	62,321	61,736	62,352	(NA)	(NA)	(NA)
Postseason games [11]	1,000	711	656	848	815	805	(NA)	(NA)	(NA)
Players' salaries: [12]									
Average	$1,000	194	203	352	645	683	637	714	(NA)
Median base salary	$1,000	140	175	236	325	330	325	335	(NA)
National Hockey league: [13]									
Regular season attendance	1,000	11,621	12,118	12,344	13,917	15,714	(NA)	15,658	16,237
Playoffs attendance	1,000	1,153	1,337	1,442	1,346	1,440	(NA)	1,447	1,423
Horseracing: [14] [15]									
Racing days	Number	13,745	14,208	13,841	13,644	13,237	13,082	13,243	12,457
Attendance	1,000	73,346	70,105	63,803	49,275	45,688	42,065	38,934	43,367
Pari-mutuel turnover	Mil. dol	12,222	13,122	7,162	14,078	13,718	14,143	14,592	14,902
Revenue to government	Mil. dol	625	608	624	491	472	452	456	444
Greyhound: [14]									
Total performances	Number	9,590	11,156	14,915	17,528	17,976	17,035	16,110	15,151
Attendance	1,000	23,853	26,215	28,660	28,003	(NA)	(NA)	(NA)	(NA)
Pari-mutuel turnover	Mil. dol	2,702	3,193	3,422	3,306	3,255	2,948	2,730	2,433
Revenue to government	Mil. dol	201	221	235	204	195	183	157	139
Jai alai: [14]									
Total performances	Number	2,736	2,906	3,620	3,288	3,200	3,146	2,748	2,542
Games played	Number	32,260	38,476	(NA)	45,067	43,056	42,607	37,052	34,346
Attendance	1,000	4,722	6,816	5,329	4,634	4,194	3,684	3,208	(NA)
Total handle	Mil. dol	664.0	707.5	545.5	425.9	384.2	330.7	296.4	273.4
Revenue to government	Mil. dol	50	51	39	30	27	22	13	12
Professional rodeo: [16]									
Rodeos	Number	617	637	754	770	791	782	739	742
Performances	Number	1,887	1,832	2,159	2,203	2,269	2,245	2,217	2,229
Members	Number	5,239	5,342	5,693	5,714	5,760	6,415	6,894	7,084
Permit-holders (rookies)	Number	2,534	2,746	3,290	3,290	2,857	2,888	3,346	4,141

NA Not available.   X Not applicable.   [1] Source: The National League of Professional Baseball Clubs, New York, NY, *National League Green Book;* and The American League of Professional Baseball Clubs, New York, NY, *American League Red Book.* [2] Beginning 1996, two rounds of playoffs were played. Prior years had one round.   [3] Source: Major League Baseball Players Association, New York, NY.   [4] Season ending in year shown.   [5] Source: National Collegiate Athletic Assn., Overland Park, KS. For women's attendance total, excludes double-headers with men's teams.   [6] Source: National Basketball Assn., New York, NY. For season ending in year shown.   [7] Includes All-Star game, not shown separately.   [8] Source: National Football League, New York, NY.   [9] 1987 through 1992 includes preseason attendance, not shown separately.   [10] Season was interrupted by a strike.   [11] Includes Pro Bowl, a nonchampionship game and Super Bowl.   [12] Source: National Football League Players Association, Washington, DC.   [13] For season beginning in year shown. Source: National Hockey League, Montreal, Quebec. [14] Source: Association of Racing Commissioners International, Inc., Lexington, KY.   [15] Includes thoroughbred, harness, quarter horse, and fairs.   [16] Source: Professional Rodeo Cowboys Association, Colorado Springs, CO., *Official Professional Rodeo Media Guide,* annual, (copyright).

Source: Compiled from sources listed in footnotes.

No. 437. Selected Recreational Activities: 1975 to 1996

ACTIVITY	Unit	1975	1980	1985	1990	1993	1994	1995	1996
Softball, amateur: [1]									
Total participants [2]	Million ..	26	30	41	41	42	42	42	42
Youth participants	1,000...	450	650	712	1,100	1,208	1,209	1,350	1,416
Adult teams [3]	1,000...	66	110	152	188	200	196	187	184
Youth teams [3]	1,000...	9	18	31	46	62	68	74	79
Golfers (one round or more) [4][5]	1,000...	13,036	15,112	17,520	27,800	24,600	24,300	25,000	24,737
Golf rounds played [5]	1,000...	308,562	357,701	414,777	502,000	498,600	464,800	490,200	477,400
Golf facilities	Number .	11,370	12,005	12,346	12,846	13,439	13,683	14,074	14,341
Classification:									
Private	Number .	4,770	4,839	4,861	4,810	4,492	4,367	4,324	4,306
Daily fee	Number .	5,014	5,372	5,573	6,024	6,803	7,126	7,491	7,729
Municipal	Number .	1,586	1,794	1,912	2,012	2,144	2,190	2,259	2,306
Tennis: [6]									
Players	1,000...	[7]34,000	(NA)	13,000	21,000	21,500	16,500	17,820	19,499
Courts	1,000...	130	(NA)	220	220	230	240	240	245
Indoor	1,000...	8	(NA)	14	14	14	15	15	15
Tenpin bowling: [8]									
Participants, total	Million ..	62.5	72.0	67.0	71.0	79.0	79.0	79.0	91.0
Male	Million ..	29.9	34.0	32.0	35.4	36.3	36.3	36.3	41.8
Female	Million ..	32.6	38.0	35.0	35.6	42.6	42.6	42.6	49.2
Establishments	Number .	8,577	8,591	8,275	7,611	7,250	7,183	7,049	6,880
Lanes	1,000...	141	154	155	148	143	142	139	136
Membership, total [9]	1,000...	8,751	9,664	8,064	6,588	5,599	5,201	4,925	4,662
American Bowling Congress	1,000...	4,300	4,688	3,657	3,036	2,576	2,455	2,370	2,261
Women's Bowling Congress	1,000...	3,692	4,187	3,714	2,859	2,403	2,191	2,036	1,917
Young American Bowling Alliance [10]	1,000...	759	789	693	693	620	555	519	484
Motion picture theaters [11]	1,000...	15	18	21	24	26	26	28	30
Four-wall	1,000...	11	14	18	23	25	26	27	29
Drive-in	1,000...	4	4	3	1	1	(Z)	1	1
Receipts, box office	Mil. dol.	2,115	2,749	3,749	5,022	5,154	5,396	5,494	5,912
Admission, average price	Dollars .	2.05	2.69	3.55	4.23	4.14	4.18	4.35	4.42
Attendance	Million ..	1,033	1,022	1,056	1,187	1,244	1,292	1,263	1,339
Boating: [12]									
Recreational boats owned	1,000...	(NA)	11,832	13,778	15,987	16,212	16,239	15,375	15,830
Retail expenditures on boating [13]	Mil. dol.	4,800	7,370	13,284	13,731	11,254	14,071	17,226	17,753
Retail units purchased:									
Total all boats [14]	1,000...	(NA)	570	637	504	487	563	649	619
Outboard boats	1,000...	(NA)	290	305	227	205	220	231	215
Inboard boats	1,000...	(NA)	8	17	15	10	11	12	11
Sterndrive boats	1,000...	(NA)	56	115	97	75	90	94	95
Jet boats [15]	1,000...	(NA)	69	34	19	(NA)	(NA)	15	14
Canoes	1,000...	(NA)	105	79	75	90	100	98	93
Personal watercraft [16]	1,000...	(NA)	21	50	42	107	142	200	191
Boat trailers	1,000...	(NA)	176	192	165	163	176	207	194
Outboard motors	1,000...	(NA)	315	392	352	283	308	317	308
Sterndrive and inboard engines	1,000...	(NA)	88	155	134	95	114	120	120

NA Not available.   Z Fewer than 500.   [1] Source: Amateur Softball Association, Oklahoma City, OK.   [2] Amateur Softball Association teams and other amateur softball teams.   [3] Amateur Softball Association teams only.   [4] Source: National Golf Foundation, Jupiter, FL.   [5] Prior to 1990, for persons 5 years of age and over; thereafter for persons 12 years of age and over.   [6] Source: Tennis Industry Association, North Palm Beach, FL. Players for persons 12 years old and over who played at least once.   [7] 1974 data.   [8] For season ending in year shown. Persons 5 years old and over. Source: Bowling Headquarters, Greendale, WI.   [9] Membership totals are for U.S., Canada and for U.S. military personnel worldwide.   [10] Prior to 1985, represents American Jr. Bowling Congress and ABC/WIBC Collegiate Division.   [11] Source: Motion Picture Association of America, Inc., Encino, CA. Prior to 1975, figures represent theaters; thereafter, screens.   [12] Source: National Marine Manufacturers Association, Chicago, IL.   [13] Represents estimated expenditures for new and used boats, motors and engines, accessories, safety equipment, fuel, insurance, docking, maintenance, launching, storage, repairs, and other expenses.   [14] 1980 through 1990 includes auxiliary sailboats; 1980 through 1992 includes inflatable boats, not shown separately.   [15] 1980 through 1990, count of nonpowered sailboats.   [16] 1980 through 1990, count of sailboats.

Source: Compiled from sources listed in footnotes.

No. 438. Participation in Selected Sports Activities: 1996

[In thousands, except rank. For persons 7 years of age or older. Except as indicated, a participant plays a sport more than once in the year. Based on a sampling of 15,000 households]

ACTIVITY	ALL PERSONS Number	ALL PERSONS Rank	SEX Male	SEX Female	AGE 7-11 years	AGE 12-17 years	AGE 18-24 years	AGE 25-34 years	AGE 35-44 years	AGE 45-54 years	AGE 55-64 years	AGE 65 years and over	HOUSEHOLD INCOME (dol.) Under 15,000	15,000-24,999	25,000-34,999	35,000-49,999	50,000-74,999	75,000 and over
Total	237,745	(X)	115,443	122,301	19,177	22,701	24,615	40,373	43,312	32,333	21,360	33,873	43,372	36,377	35,382	42,878	50,791	28,944
Number participated in—																		
Aerobic exercising [1]	24,119	11	5,314	18,805	757	1,981	4,067	6,168	5,206	2,982	1,371	1,587	3,117	3,024	3,462	4,619	5,739	4,159
Backpacking [2]	11,469	22	7,240	4,229	1,229	2,008	2,002	2,725	2,065	986	332	122	1,825	1,990	1,539	2,107	2,309	1,698
Badminton	6,084	28	2,909	3,175	987	1,398	820	1,018	1,230	411	149	72	866	710	1,054	1,259	1,415	780
Baseball	14,823	18	11,610	3,213	4,529	4,144	1,465	1,874	1,764	520	200	327	1,851	1,736	2,318	2,948	3,875	2,095
Basketball	33,281	9	22,375	10,906	6,424	9,157	4,665	6,112	4,717	1,281	418	506	4,296	4,660	4,825	6,886	7,908	4,706
Bicycle riding [1]	53,342	3	28,595	24,747	11,774	10,397	4,973	8,495	8,409	4,317	2,469	2,508	7,802	6,775	7,883	10,287	12,575	8,020
Billiards	34,477	8	21,841	12,636	2,044	3,924	7,611	9,912	6,774	2,737	910	567	5,432	5,290	5,054	7,118	7,160	4,422
Bowling	42,895	6	22,579	20,316	5,239	6,744	7,006	9,185	7,760	3,571	1,537	1,853	5,542	6,150	6,515	8,636	10,648	5,404
Calisthenics [1]	10,064	25	5,023	5,041	1,307	2,132	1,056	2,007	1,777	1,016	320	449	1,116	1,045	1,438	2,047	2,523	1,894
Camping [3]	44,695	5	24,102	20,593	5,594	6,200	5,306	9,186	9,374	4,610	2,493	1,932	6,214	6,907	7,039	9,323	10,691	4,521
Exercise walking [1]	73,307	1	26,666	46,641	2,701	3,522	7,104	13,151	14,827	12,499	8,433	11,070	12,821	10,945	10,464	13,534	15,846	9,698
Exercising with equipment [1]	47,823	4	22,200	25,622	664	4,066	6,625	11,482	10,521	6,970	3,918	3,576	5,525	5,788	6,711	8,904	12,372	8,522
Fishing—fresh water	40,208	7	27,160	13,048	4,302	4,393	5,087	7,869	8,210	5,146	2,844	2,356	6,653	6,229	6,346	7,746	9,031	4,203
Fishing—salt water	11,045	23	7,926	3,119	787	979	1,212	2,089	2,575	1,626	909	867	1,501	1,341	1,219	2,049	3,115	1,820
Football—tackle	8,953	27	7,969	983	1,639	3,472	1,786	1,170	568	98	46	174	1,569	1,624	1,286	1,723	1,825	925
Football—touch	11,645	20	9,603	2,042	2,252	3,772	1,768	2,166	1,251	253	50	133	1,893	1,676	1,757	2,137	2,981	1,202
Golf	23,082	12	18,219	4,863	834	1,952	2,410	5,376	5,036	3,457	1,860	2,157	1,575	2,069	2,641	4,233	7,119	5,444
Hiking	26,457	10	14,465	11,992	3,009	3,261	3,166	5,885	5,812	3,230	1,169	926	3,960	3,429	3,729	4,753	6,164	4,423
Hunting with firearms	19,251	15	16,317	2,933	642	1,861	2,704	4,862	4,269	2,503	1,238	1,171	2,662	2,960	3,160	4,329	4,151	1,989
Martial arts	4,673	30	3,286	1,387	1,239	929	635	768	630	340	56	76	755	625	736	794	1,084	679
Racquetball	5,582	29	3,768	1,814	351	522	1,169	1,804	1,014	529	79	114	517	809	695	1,015	1,569	976
Running/jogging [1]	22,239	13	12,320	9,919	2,005	4,739	4,113	4,714	3,864	1,727	613	464	2,847	3,121	2,940	4,139	5,455	3,737
Skiing—alpine/downhill	10,466	24	6,277	4,188	777	1,618	1,849	2,370	2,237	1,049	469	97	726	992	801	1,597	2,979	3,370
Skiing—cross country	3,385	31	1,820	1,566	209	341	392	665	825	597	183	174	249	310	327	752	976	772
Soccer	13,876	19	8,626	5,251	4,420	4,063	1,599	1,729	1,325	358	98	284	1,658	1,430	2,244	2,760	3,521	2,264
Softball	19,873	14	10,837	9,035	3,605	4,274	2,301	4,513	3,221	1,196	350	413	2,750	2,659	2,886	4,175	5,024	2,379
Swimming [1]	60,223	2	29,145	31,078	10,465	10,517	7,141	10,286	10,300	5,460	2,881	3,172	7,944	7,482	8,181	11,115	15,859	9,643
Table tennis	9,542	26	5,907	3,635	1,261	2,354	1,174	1,725	1,854	677	292	205	1,136	1,165	1,178	1,680	2,600	1,783
Target shooting	15,695	17	11,097	4,598	869	1,645	2,037	3,788	3,370	1,969	1,032	985	2,416	2,528	2,507	3,141	3,244	1,859
Tennis	11,485	21	6,381	5,105	1,196	2,081	2,156	2,631	1,893	850	325	354	1,057	1,214	1,484	2,420	2,719	2,591
Volleyball	18,535	16	8,970	9,565	1,460	4,721	3,471	4,534	2,945	934	256	215	2,694	2,282	2,760	3,771	4,458	2,571

X Not applicable.   [1] Participant engaged in activity at least six times in the year.   [2] Includes wilderness camping.   [3] Vacation/overnight.

Source: National Sporting Goods Association, Mt. Prospect, IL, *Sports Participation in 1996: Series I* (copyright).

No. 439. Participation in Selected Sports Activities: 1996

[In thousands, except rank. For persons 7 years of age or older. Based on a sampling of 20,000 households]

ACTIVITY	ALL PERSONS		SEX		AGE								HOUSEHOLD INCOME (dol.)					
	Number	Rank	Male	Female	7-11 years	12-17 years	18-24 years	25-34 years	35-44 years	45-54 years	55-64 years	65 years and over	Under 15,000	15,000-24,999	25,000-34,999	35,000-49,999	50,000-74,999	75,000 and over
Total	237,745	(X)	115,443	122,303	19,177	22,703	24,615	40,374	43,311	32,333	21,360	33,873	43,885	35,864	35,367	42,638	54,226	25,766
Number participating in—																		
Archery (target)	5,297	14	4,097	1,200	959	1,090	552	1,030	976	488	132	69	666	633	877	1,063	1,471	586
Boating, motor/power	28,835	1	16,560	12,275	2,238	3,080	3,444	6,882	6,175	3,685	1,938	1,392	3,172	3,421	4,035	5,659	7,732	4,815
Canoeing	9,666	8	5,648	4,018	929	1,477	1,159	2,061	2,243	1,073	429	295	1,037	1,105	1,260	1,884	2,623	1,757
Dart throwing	21,320	4	12,804	8,516	1,660	2,174	4,000	6,659	4,377	1,610	463	379	3,549	2,997	3,726	4,228	4,605	2,215
Hunting with bow arrow	5,495	13	5,108	387	179	527	1,025	1,372	1,212	750	343	88	791	791	1,014	1,240	1,247	412
Ice hockey	2,064	20	1,749	315	358	495	514	385	242	37	33	-	163	214	339	602	482	264
Ice/figure skating	8,356	9	3,185	5,170	1,901	2,208	1,012	1,423	1,226	391	108	87	809	736	855	1,778	2,801	1,376
Mountain biking-off road	7,276	11	4,928	2,348	735	1,162	1,278	1,953	1,229	624	170	125	1,008	1,134	1,081	1,267	1,681	1,106
Mountain biking-on road	11,261	7	6,671	4,590	1,341	1,703	1,665	3,568	1,806	794	287	97	1,415	1,616	1,607	2,166	2,859	1,598
Roller hockey	3,412	18	2,654	758	1,000	1,267	484	385	162	46	34	34	312	250	410	720	1,156	564
Roller skating/in-line	25,507	2	12,877	12,630	7,877	7,020	3,361	3,837	2,389	641	132	251	2,504	3,031	3,907	4,976	7,438	3,651
Roller skating/traditional																		
2x2 wheel	15,134	5	5,450	9,684	4,558	3,627	1,569	2,205	2,027	648	268	233	2,756	1,868	2,215	3,339	3,564	1,391
Sailing	4,014	16	2,345	1,669	231	391	475	850	848	613	293	314	322	306	428	801	987	1,169
Scuba (open water)	2,424	19	1,740	684	25	161	331	788	707	317	82	13	166	245	327	354	698	633
Skate boarding	4,664	15	3,704	961	1,710	1,983	473	239	148	41	16	54	585	497	474	975	1,436	697
Snorkeling	7,088	12	3,939	3,149	323	736	794	1,722	1,685	1,206	418	204	370	541	743	1,219	2,265	1,949
Snowboarding	3,711	17	2,726	985	365	1,393	901	673	281	85	-	14	328	394	366	905	1,039	679
Step aerobics	11,270	6	1,519	9,750	140	665	2,342	3,444	2,557	1,221	488	413	1,441	1,521	1,580	1,958	3,084	1,685
Water skiing	7,370	10	4,419	2,951	436	1,046	1,544	2,189	1,416	517	140	81	735	650	1,066	1,469	2,131	1,318
Wind surfing	691	21	428	264	-	113	179	102	165	65	34	32	33	68	25	63	299	203
Work out at club	22,455	3	10,492	11,964	350	1,207	4,611	6,627	4,685	2,555	1,353	1,067	2,422	2,389	2,697	3,975	6,428	4,544

- Represents or rounds to zero. X Not applicable.

Source: National Sporting Goods Association, Mt. Prospect, IL, *Sports Participation in 1996: Series II* (copyright).

No. 440. High School Students Engaged in Organized Physical Activity: 1995

[In percent. For students in grades 9 to 12. Based on school-based survey and subject to sampling error; for details see source]

CHARACTERISTIC	PARTICIPATION ON SPORTS TEAM		ENROLLMENT IN PHYSICAL EDUCATION CLASS		
	Run by school	Run by other organization	Total	Exercised 20 minutes or more per class [1]	Attended daily
All students	50.3	36.9	59.6	69.7	25.4
Male	57.8	46.4	62.2	74.8	27.0
Grade 9	61.7	52.8	80.5	76.5	42.1
Grade 10.	55.6	46.9	72.6	73.1	34.8
Grade 11.	56.0	43.1	51.5	75.8	17.4
Grade 12.	58.3	42.8	45.4	73.7	14.8
Female.	42.4	26.8	56.8	63.7	23.5
Grade 9	43.7	32.0	80.8	65.6	39.7
Grade 10.	47.9	32.4	71.4	63.9	33.8
Grade 11.	39.4	23.8	41.2	57.2	12.3
Grade 12.	38.8	19.8	39.1	66.0	11.1
White, non-Hispanic	53.9	39.1	62.9	71.3	21.7
Male.	59.9	47.2	64.2	74.8	23.3
Female	47.1	29.9	61.7	67.1	19.9
Black, non-Hispanic	45.0	32.4	50.2	59.0	33.8
Male.	57.9	46.8	56.8	71.8	37.7
Female	34.9	21.1	44.4	46.6	30.1
Hispanic.	37.8	32.0	51.0	68.5	33.1
Male.	48.6	43.2	57.6	76.0	36.2
Female	27.3	21.2	44.6	59.0	30.1

[1] Exercised or played sports.

Source: U.S. National Center for Chronic Disease Prevention and Health Promotion, *Physical Activity and Health: A Report of the Surgeon General*, 1996.

No. 441. Participation in High School Athletic Programs: 1971 to 1997

[Data based on number of state associations reporting and may underrepresent the number of schools with and participants in athletic programs]

YEAR	PARTICIPANTS [1]		SEX AND SPORT	MOST POPULAR SPORTS, 1996-97 [2]	
	Males	Females		Schools	Participants
1971	3,666,917	294,105	MALE		
1972-73	3,770,621	817,073			
1973-74	4,070,125	1,300,169	Basketball	16,704	544,025
1975-76	4,109,021	1,645,039	Track & field (outdoor)	14,580	468,061
1977-78	4,367,442	2,083,040	Baseball	14,212	444,248
1978-79	3,709,512	1,854,400	Football	13,119	957,507
1979-80	3,517,829	1,750,264	Golf	11,573	150,578
1980-81	3,503,124	1,853,789	Cross country	11,485	174,599
1981-82	3,409,081	1,810,671	Tennis	9,322	136,451
1982-83	3,355,558	1,779,972	Wrestling	8,738	227,596
1983-84	3,303,599	1,747,346	Soccer	8,432	296,587
1984-85	3,354,284	1,757,884	Swimming & diving	5,028	93,523
1985-86	3,344,275	1,807,121			
1986-87	3,364,082	1,836,356	FEMALE		
1987-88	3,425,777	1,849,684	Basketball	16,325	447,687
1988-89	3,416,844	1,839,352	Track & field (outdoor)	14,525	393,946
1989-90	3,398,192	1,858,659	Volleyball	12,986	370,957
1990-91	3,406,355	1,892,316	Softball (fast pitch).	11,895	313,607
1991-92	3,429,853	1,940,801	Soccer	6,971	226,636
1992-93	3,416,389	1,997,489	Tennis	9,228	150,346
1993-94	3,472,967	2,130,315	Cross country	10,934	145,624
1994-95	3,536,359	2,240,461	Swimming & diving	5,270	123,886
1995-96	3,634,052	2,367,936	Field hockey.	1,462	56,502
1996-97	3,706,225	2,472,043	Track & field (indoor)	1,874	41,024

[1] A participant is counted in the number of sports participated in. [2] Ten most popular sports for each sex in terms of number of participants.

Source: National Federation of State High School Associations, Kansas City, MO, *The 1997 High School Athletics Participation Survey* (copyright).

No. 442. Sporting Goods Sales, by Product Category: 1988 to 1997

[In millions of dollars, except percent. Based on a sample survey of consumer purchases of 80,000 households, (100,000 beginning 1995), except recreational transport, which was provided by industry associations. Excludes Alaska and Hawaii]

SELECTED PRODUCT CATEGORY	1988	1989	1990	1991	1992	1993	1994	1995	1996	1997, proj.
Sales, all products	**43,937**	**48,585**	**48,250**	**47,104**	**47,110**	**49,129**	**53,453**	**58,428**	**61,254**	**62,932**
Annual percent change [1] . . .	19.4	10.6	-0.7	-2.4	(Z)	4.3	8.8	9.3	4.8	2.7
Percent of retail sales	2.7	2.8	2.6	2.5	2.4	2.4	2.4	2.5	2.5	2.5
Athletic and sport clothing [2] . . .	9,555	10,286	10,130	10,731	8,990	9,096	9,521	10,311	11,127	11,399
Athletic and sport footwear [2] . . .	6,797	10,435	11,654	11,787	11,733	11,084	11,120	11,415	12,815	13,345
Walking shoes	1,471	2,419	2,950	2,689	2,688	2,673	2,543	2,841	3,079	3,202
Gym shoes, sneakers	1,602	2,303	2,536	2,545	2,397	2,016	1,869	1,741	1,996	2,076
Jogging and running shoes. . . .	987	1,106	1,110	1,192	1,232	1,231	1,069	1,043	1,132	1,223
Tennis shoes	448	645	740	759	748	599	556	480	541	541
Aerobic shoes	514	667	611	600	590	500	356	372	401	413
Basketball shoes	493	631	918	974	984	874	867	999	1,192	1,252
Golf shoes.	183	186	226	249	260	275	238	225	231	254
Athletic and sport equipment [2] . . .	10,705	11,504	11,964	12,062	12,846	13,880	15,257	17,442	17,618	18,064
Firearms and hunting.	1,894	2,139	2,202	2,091	2,533	2,722	3,490	3,003	2,427	2,184
Exercise equipment.	1,452	1,748	1,824	2,106	2,050	2,602	2,449	2,960	3,225	3,387
Golf	1,111	1,167	1,219	1,149	1,338	1,248	1,342	3,194	3,560	3,916
Camping	945	996	1,072	1,006	903	906	1,017	1,205	1,122	1,156
Bicycles (10-12-15-18+ speed) .	819	906	1,092	(NA)	(NA)	(NA)	(NA)	(NA)	(NA)	(NA)
Fishing tackle.	766	769	776	711	678	716	717	737	725	696
Snow skiing	710	606	606	577	627	611	652	646	767	825
Tennis.	264	315	287	295	296	267	257	241	240	240
Archery	235	261	265	270	334	285	306	287	272	273
Baseball and softball	174	206	217	214	245	323	295	251	287	293
Water skis	160	96	88	63	55	51	51	54	54	54
Bowling accessories	129	143	155	155	164	159	157	156	154	154
Recreational transport.	16,880	16,360	14,502	12,524	13,541	15,069	17,555	19,259	19,693	20,124
Pleasure boats	9,637	9,319	7,644	5,862	5,765	6,246	7,679	9,064	9,243	9,474
Recreational vehicles.	4,839	4,481	4,113	3,615	4,412	4,775	5,690	5,895	6,327	6,454
Bicycles and supplies	2,131	2,259	2,423	2,686	2,973	3,534	3,470	3,390	3,187	3,251
Snowmobiles	273	301	322	362	391	515	715	910	936	946

NA Not available.   Z Less than .05 percent.   [1] Represents change from immediate prior year.   [2] Includes other products not shown separately.

Source: National Sporting Goods Association, Mt. Prospect, IL, *The Sporting Goods Market in 1997*; and prior issues (copyright).

No. 443. Consumer Purchases of Sporting Goods, by Consumer Characteristics: 1996

[In percent. Based on sample survey of consumer purchases of 100,000 households. Excludes Alaska and Hawaii]

CHARACTERISTIC	Total house-holds	FOOTWEAR				EQUIPMENT					
		Aero-bic shoes	Gym shoes/sneak-ers	Jog-ging/run-ning shoes	Walk-ing shoes	Fish-ing tackle	Camp-ing equip-ment	Exer-cise equip-ment	Hunt-ing equip-ment guns	Team sports equip-ment	Golf equip-ment
Total.	**100**	**100**	**100**	**100**	**100**	**100**	**100**	**100**	**100**	**100**	**100**
Age of user:											
Under 14 years old	20	7	46	13	6	4	17	-	3	48	2
14 to 17 years old	6	5	14	13	3	5	9	3	3	24	4
18 to 24 years old	9	11	5	10	4	6	9	4	5	6	5
25 to 34 years old	15	31	10	19	11	21	22	22	26	10	22
35 to 44 years old	16	25	10	20	18	22	18	26	26	7	22
45 to 64 years old	21	19	10	22	36	27	14	34	31	4	29
65 years old and over	13	3	4	4	22	9	3	8	5	-	16
Multiple ages	-	-	-	-	-	6	8	3	1	1	-
Sex of user:											
Male	49	12	54	56	38	84	64	41	92	77	91
Female	51	89	47	44	62	11	29	56	7	22	9
Both sexes	-	-	-	-	-	5	7	3	1	1	
Education of household head:											
Less than high school	10	5	7	4	7	8	6	5	8	5	2
High school	26	21	28	14	26	30	19	22	26	20	15
Some college	36	38	37	36	35	38	37	36	39	38	30
College graduate.	29	36	28	47	32	24	38	37	27	37	53
Annual household income:											
Under $15,000	22	10	13	8	15	13	12	7	9	7	3
$15,000 to $24,999	17	13	16	11	15	14	13	12	21	11	6
$25,000 to $34,999	14	10	14	12	14	11	15	11	15	13	9
$35,000 to $49,999	17	23	21	18	19	23	20	22	16	22	21
$50,000 to $74,999	22	33	28	33	27	28	28	30	23	34	37
$75,000 and over	8	13	9	19	11	11	12	18	16	13	24

- Represents or rounds to zero.

Source: National Sporting Goods Association, Mt. Prospect, IL, *The Sporting Goods Market in 1997* (copyright).

No. 444. Participation in Various Leisure Activities: 1997

[In percent, except as indicated. Covers activities engaged in at least once in the prior 12 months. See headnote, Table 446. See also Table 447]

ITEM	Adult population (mil.)	ATTENDANCE AT—			PARTICIPATION IN—				
		Movies	Sports events	Amusement park	Exercise program	Playing sports	Charity work	Home improvement/ repair	Computer hobbies
Total	195.6	66	41	57	76	45	43	66	40
Sex: Male	94.2	66	49	58	75	56	40	71	44
Female	101.4	65	34	57	77	35	46	61	37
Race: Hispanic	19.1	59	35	66	69	35	31	61	25
White	146.1	68	44	56	78	48	45	70	43
African American	22.1	60	35	55	74	34	44	51	37
American Indian	3.0	65	34	59	83	49	34	58	37
Asian	5.3	76	29	58	70	48	41	58	62
Age: 18 to 24 years old	23.7	88	51	76	85	67	35	57	68
25 to 34 years old	40.1	79	51	70	82	63	41	63	51
35 to 44 years old	45.3	73	46	68	79	52	50	76	47
45 to 54 years old	33.7	65	42	53	77	40	46	75	40
55 to 64 years old	20.9	46	33	40	69	19	44	71	23
65 to 74 years old	19.6	38	21	29	65	23	40	55	11
75 years old and over	12.3	28	16	18	56	13	40	44	7
Education: Grade school	13.7	14	13	34	46	13	20	40	1
Some high school	26.9	52	25	54	66	30	31	59	19
High school graduate	62.0	62	38	58	74	41	36	65	35
Some college	50.3	78	48	64	81	54	50	71	52
College graduate	25.2	82	59	61	87	61	55	76	63
Graduate school	17.4	81	55	53	88	57	67	73	59
Income: $10,000 or less	15.0	37	15	39	55	19	32	42	19
$10,001 to $20,000	26.5	46	26	51	69	27	34	53	22
$20,001 to $30,000	29.4	56	28	55	72	40	37	61	30
$30,001 to $40,000	32.1	71	42	64	77	46	47	68	40
$40,001 to $50,000	25.9	73	51	67	80	51	42	75	47
$50,001 to $75,000	35.0	82	54	65	86	60	50	80	54
$75,001 to $100,000	16.2	81	66	64	86	61	51	79	64
Over $100,000	15.5	87	65	56	90	66	59	81	69

Source: U.S. National Endowment for the Arts, *1997 Survey of Public Participation in the Arts* Research Division Note #70, July 1998.

No. 445. Arts and Humanities—Selected Federal Aid Programs: 1980 to 1996

[In millions of dollars, except as indicated. For fiscal years ending in year shown, see text, Section 9, State and Local Government]

TYPE OF FUND AND PROGRAM	1980	1985	1990	1991	1992	1993	1994	1995	1996
National Endowment for the Arts:									
Funds available [1]	188.1	171.7	170.8	166.5	163.0	159.7	158.1	152.1	86.9
Program appropriation	97.0	118.7	124.3	124.6	123.0	120.0	116.3	109.0	63.5
Matching funds [2]	42.9	29.5	32.4	32.4	30.3	27.4	29.4	28.5	17.2
Grants awarded (number)	5,505	4,801	4,475	4,239	4,229	4,096	3,843	3,685	1,751.0
Funds obligated [3]	166.4	149.4	157.6	158.0	154.6	148.4	145.2	147.9	72.2
Music	13.6	15.3	16.5	14.1	14.9	12.4	10.9	10.9	5.1
State programs	22.1	24.4	26.1	37.7	37.0	42.0	40.7	39.2	25.9
Museums	11.2	11.9	12.1	11.3	11.1	9.9	9.4	9.0	3.8
Theater	8.4	10.6	10.6	9.4	9.4	8.3	8.8	7.3	5.2
Dance	8.0	9.0	9.6	8.5	8.2	7.9	7.6	7.1	4.2
Media arts	8.4	9.9	13.9	11.8	12.0	10.2	10.9	8.9	3.0
Challenge [4]	50.8	20.7	19.7	19.7	13.8	11.7	9.6	21.1	4.0
Visual arts	7.3	6.2	5.9	5.3	5.6	5.1	4.8	4.4	1.2
Other	36.6	41.3	43.1	40.2	42.7	40.9	42.5	40.0	19.8
National Endowment for the Humanities:									
Funds available [1]	186.2	125.6	140.6	152.1	156.5	158.5	157.9	151.4	93.1
Program appropriation	100.3	95.2	114.2	125.1	131.2	131.9	131.4	125.7	77.2
Matching funds [2]	38.4	30.4	26.3	27.0	25.2	26.5	26.5	25.7	15.9
Grants awarded (number)	2,917	2,241	2,195	2,171	2,199	2,197	1,881	1,871	815.0
Funds obligated [3]	185.5	125.7	141.0	149.8	159.1	160.3	159.0	151.8	93.4
Education programs	18.3	17.9	16.3	18.5	20.0	20.8	19.6	19.2	13.5
State programs	26.0	24.4	29.6	30.8	31.8	32.4	32.2	32.0	29.0
Research grants	32.0	24.4	22.5	24.0	25.3	23.7	23.4	22.2	5.1
Fellowship program	18.0	15.3	15.3	16.2	17.4	18.9	17.7	16.5	5.1
Challenge [4]	53.5	19.6	14.6	15.1	12.4	14.2	14.4	13.8	9.9
Public programs	25.1	24.1	25.4	25.3	27.0	26.7	27.5	25.8	12.5
Preservation and access	(X)	(X)	17.5	19.9	25.1	23.5	24.1	22.2	18.3
National Capital Arts and Cultural Affairs Program	(X)	(X)	(X)	(X)	(X)	(X)	(X)	(X)	(X)
Other	12.6	(X)	(X)	(X)	(X)	(X)	(X)	(X)	(X)

X Not applicable. [1] Includes other funds, shown separately. Excludes administrative funds. Gifts are included through 1980; excluded thereafter. [2] Represents federal funds obligated only upon receipt or certification by Endowment of matching non-federal gifts. [3] Includes obligations for new grants, supplemental awards on previous years' grants, and program contracts. [4] Program designed to stimulate new sources and higher levels of giving to institutions for the purpose of guaranteeing long-term stability and financial independence. Program requires a match of at least 3 private dollars to each federal dollar. Funds for challenge grants are not allocated by program area because they are awarded on a grant-by-grant basis.

Source: U.S. National Endowment for the Arts, *Annual Report;* and U.S. National Endowment for the Humanities, *Annual Report.*

No. 446. Attendance Rates for Various Arts Activities: 1997

[In percent. For persons 18 years old and over. Excludes elementary and high school performances. Based on the 1997 household survey Public Participation in the Arts. Data are subject to sampling error; see source. See also Tables 444 and 447]

ITEM	ATTENDANCE AT LEAST ONCE IN THE PRIOR 12 MONTHS AT—								
	Jazz perfor- mance	Classical music perfor- mance	Opera	Musical play	Non- musical play	Ballet	Art museum	Historic park	Reading literature[1]
Total.	**12**	**16**	**5**	**25**	**16**	**6**	**35**	**47**	**63**
Sex: Male.	13	14	4	22	15	4	34	48	55
Female.	11	17	5	27	17	8	36	46	71
Race: Hispanic	7	8	3	16	10	5	29	33	50
White	12	18	5	27	17	7	36	51	65
African American	16	10	2	22	16	4	31	37	60
American Indian	11	9	5	15	5	1	22	42	56
Asian	10	16	7	20	18	4	42	44	69
Age: 18 to 24 years old . .	15	16	5	26	20	7	38	46	70
25 to 34 years old	13	11	4	23	13	5	37	49	61
35 to 44 years old	14	14	4	26	15	7	37	52	64
45 to 54 years old	13	20	6	29	20	7	40	54	66
55 to 64 years old	9	16	5	23	14	5	30	45	58
65 to 74 years old	8	18	4	24	15	5	28	37	59
75 years old and over . .	4	14	3	15	13	4	20	25	61
Education: Grade school . .	2	2	-	6	3	2	6	13	29
Some high school.	3	4	2	13	7	2	14	27	46
High school graduate . .	7	8	2	16	9	4	25	41	58
Some college	15	18	5	28	19	7	43	56	72
College graduate	21	28	10	44	28	11	58	67	80
Graduate school.	28	45	14	50	37	14	70	73	86
Income: $10,000 or less . .	5	4	2	12	10	2	16	23	45
$10,001 to $20,000. . . .	6	8	2	12	7	3	20	29	53
$20,001 to $30,000. . . .	8	10	2	17	10	4	26	39	62
$30,001 to $40,000. . . .	11	13	3	21	16	5	32	50	62
$40,001 to $50,000. . . .	11	15	5	23	15	6	37	52	64
$50,001 to $75,000. . . .	16	22	8	32	20	8	46	62	72
$75,001 to $100,000. . .	23	26	6	41	27	10	55	65	75
Over $100,000	27	35	13	51	32	13	60	69	76

[1] Includes novels, short stories, poetry, or and plays.

Source: U.S. National Endowment for the Arts, *1997 Survey of Public Participation in the Arts* Research Division Note #70, July 1998.

No. 447. Participation in Various Arts Activities: 1997

[In percent. Covers activities engaged in at least once in the prior 12 months. See Table 444 and headnote, Table 446]

ITEM	Playing classical music	Modern danc- ing[1]	Drawing	Pottery work[2]	Weaving	Photo- graphy[3]	Creative writing	Buying art work	Singing in groups
Total	1	13	16	15	28	17	12	35	10
Sex: Male	9	13	15	16	5	16	10	36	9
Female	13	12	17	14	49	18	14	34	12
Race: Hispanic.	7	14	17	11	17	12	8	33	7
White	12	12	15	16	30	17	12	36	8
African American	8	11	16	11	25	18	14	43	26
American Indian	9	21	18	25	28	28	10	35	7
Asian	12	17	27	13	28	22	21	19	9
Age: 18 to 24 years old . . .	13	20	39	21	22	28	32	42	14
25 to 34 years old	10	13	18	17	25	18	13	43	9
35 to 44 years old	11	13	15	18	29	18	12	40	9
45 to 54 years old	15	11	13	18	29	18	10	37	13
55 to 64 years old	9	8	9	10	29	10	5	31	11
65 to 74 years old	6	14	7	10	32	10	5	23	10
75 years old and over . .	6	9	4	3	28	5	6	8	7
Education: Grade school . .	2	4	4	7	14	8	2	24	11
Some high school	4	11	13	15	22	12	8	35	9
High school graduate . . .	8	12	15	16	28	13	9	31	9
Some college	14	16	20	18	32	22	17	35	13
College graduate	18	10	18	13	32	23	14	41	9
Graduate school	20	15	18	13	26	22	19	41	12
Income: $10,000 or less. . .	5	9	15	8	28	11	8	29	13
$10,001 to $20,000	7	10	13	12	27	14	8	27	9
$20,001 to $30,000	8	12	17	16	26	14	12	26	11
$30,001 to $40,000	10	14	15	20	29	18	11	44	13
$40,001 to $50,000	11	12	16	17	29	18	13	35	8
$50,001 to $75,000	15	13	17	18	28	18	17	32	10
$70,001 to $100,000 . . .	15	18	18	17	24	23	13	41	11
Over $100,000	18	12	18	14	23	23	11	46	9

[1] Dancing other than ballet (e.g. folk and tap).   [2] Includes ceramics, jewelry, leatherwork, and metalwork.   [3] Includes making movies or video as an artistic activity.

Source: U.S. National Endowment for the Arts, *1997 Survey of Public Participation in the Arts* Research Division Note #70, July 1998.

No. 448. Performing Arts—Selected Data: 1980 to 1996

[Receipts and expenditures in millions of dollars. For season ending in year shown, except as indicated]

ITEM	1980	1985	1989	1990	1991	1992	1993	1994	1995	1996
Legitimate theater: [1]										
Broadway shows:										
New productions [3]	61	33	30	35	28	37	33	37	29	38
Playing weeks [2][3]	1,540	1,075	1,097	1,061	970	903	1,019	1,061	1,118	1,146
Attendance (mil.)	9.6	7.3	8.0	8.0	7.3	7.4	7.9	8.1	9.0	9.5
Receipts	146	208	265	282	267	293	328	356	406	436
Nonprofit professional theatres: [4]										
Companies reporting	147	217	192	185	184	182	177	231	215	228
Gross income	113.6	234.7	349.0	307.6	333.9	359.1	342.5	455.1	444.4	450.7
Earned income	67.3	146.1	224.6	188.4	202.6	222.5	209.7	277.4	281.2	274.0
Contributed income	46.3	88.6	124.4	119.2	131.3	136.6	132.8	177.7	163.1	176.7
Gross expenses	113.6	239.3	349.2	306.3	336.7	365.6	349.3	460.2	444.9	439.5
Productions	1,852	2,710	2,469	2,265	2,277	2,310	2,319	2,929	2,646	3,074
Performances	42,109	52,341	53,263	46,131	48,695	46,184	44,933	59,542	56,608	56,954
Total attendance (mil.)	14.2	14.2	18.7	15.2	16.9	16.0	16.5	20.7	18.6	17.1
OPERA America professional member companies: [5]										
Number of companies reporting [6]	79	97	101	98	98	100	85	86	88	83
Expenses [6]	122.4	216.4	311.7	321.2	346.7	371.8	389.5	404.9	435.0	466.7
Performances [7]	1,372	1,909	2,429	2,336	2,283	2,424	1,945	1,982	2,251	2,296
Total attendance (mil.) [7][8]	5.5	6.7	7.4	7.5	7.6	7.3	5.5	6.0	6.5	6.5
Main season attendance (mil.) [7][9]	(NA)	3.3	4.0	4.1	4.3	4.3	3.6	3.7	3.9	3.9
Symphony orchestras: [10]										
Concerts	(NA)	19,573	20,630	18,931	18,074	19,778	18,389	17,795	29,328	28,887
Attendance (mil.)	(NA)	24.0	25.8	24.7	26.7	26.3	24.0	24.4	30.9	31.1
Gross revenue	(NA)	252.4	353.2	377.5	394.5	414.0	430.5	442.5	536.2	558.9
Concert income	(NA)	168.6	231.0	253.3	273.8	284.1	294.1	303.6	368.6	383.7
Endowment income	(NA)	(NA)	46.8	52.1	52.5	55.3	59.7	60.4	76.2	79.9
Other earned income	(NA)	83.8	75.4	72.1	68.2	74.6	76.8	78.5	91.4	95.3
Operating expenses	(NA)	426.1	583.5	621.7	662.2	683.0	689.9	710.0	858.8	892.4
Artistic personnel	(NA)	231.9	310.2	327.3	355.8	398.9	378.8	389.9	464.7	473.9
Concert production	(NA)	69.2	89.0	104.3	110.3	117.2	114.3	129.3	160.6	166.0
Advertising and promotion	(NA)	32.5	47.5	51.3	57.3	58.3	63.1	67.3	75.2	82.9
General and administrative	(NA)	51.3	68.4	73.3	75.6	76.2	73.6	74.4	87.2	88.2
Other	(NA)	41.3	68.4	65.6	63.2	32.4	60.1	49.1	71.1	81.5
Support	(NA)	188.1	249.0	257.8	281.2	279.6	293.0	293.1	351.0	382.8
Tax supported grants	(NA)	42.2	54.5	55.6	58.3	49.1	48.0	46.4	55.5	57.6
Private sector support	(NA)	145.9	194.5	202.1	222.9	230.5	245.0	246.7	295.5	325.3
Development expenses	(NA)	20.8	30.9	31.4	36.7	36.0	38.0	37.9	38.8	42.8
Net support	(NA)	167.3	218.2	226.4	244.6	243.6	255.0	255.2	312.2	340.0

NA Not available. [1] Source: The League of American Theaters and Producers, Inc, New York, NY. [2] All shows (new productions and holdovers from previous seasons). [3] Eight performances constitute one playing week. [4] Source: Theatre Communications Group, New York, NY. For years ending on or prior to Aug. 31. [5] Source: OPERA America, Washington, DC. For years ending on or prior to Aug 31. [6] United States companies. [7] Prior to 1993, United States and Canadian companies; beginning 1993, U.S. companies only. [8] Includes educational performances, outreach, etc. [9] For paid performances. [10] Source: American Symphony Orchestra League, Inc., Washington, DC. For years ending Aug. 31. Prior to 1995 represents 254 U.S. orchestras; beginning 1995, represesnts all United States. Orchestras, excluding college/university and youth orchestras. Also, beginning 1995, data based on 1,200 orchestras; prior data based on 254.

Source: Compiled from sources listed in footnotes.

No. 449. Boy Scouts and Girl Scouts—Membership and Units: 1970 to 1997

[In thousands. Boy Scouts as of Dec. 31; Girl Scouts as of Sept. 30. Includes Puerto Rico and outlying areas]

ITEM	1970	1975	1980	1985	1990	1992	1993	1994	1995	1996	1997
BOY SCOUTS OF AMERICA											
Membership	6,287	5,318	4,318	4,845	5,448	5,334	5,354	5,378	5,457	5,629	5,835
Boys	4,683	3,933	3,207	3,755	4,293	4,146	4,165	4,188	4,256	4,399	4,574
Adults	1,604	1,385	1,110	1,090	1,155	1,188	1,189	1,190	1,201	1,230	1,262
Total units (packs, troops, posts, groups)	157	150	129	134	130	128	128	129	132	135	139
GIRL SCOUTS OF THE U.S.A.											
Membership	3,922	3,234	2,784	2,802	3,269	3,510	3,438	3,363	3,318	3,390	3,525
Girls	3,248	2,723	2,250	2,172	2,480	2,647	2,612	2,561	2,534	2,584	2,671
Adults	674	511	534	630	788	863	826	802	784	807	855
Total units (troops, groups)	164	159	154	166	202	219	221	218	215	219	223

Source: Boy Scouts of America, National Council, Irving, TX, Annual Report; and Girl Scouts of the United States of America, New York, NY, Annual Report.

No. 450. Travel by U.S. Residents—Summary: 1985 to 1997

[In millions, except party size. See headnote, Table 451]

TYPE OF TRIP	1985	1990	1991	1992	1993	1994	1995	1996	1997
All travel: Total trips [1]	497.8	589.4	592.4	650.7	648.2	665.3	669.7	682.8	715.9
Person trips	808.3	956.0	980.1	1,063.0	1,057.5	1,139.1	1,172.6	1,161.2	1,256.1
Party size	1.6	1.6	1.7	1.6	1.6	1.7	1.8	1.7	1.8
Business travel: Total trips	156.6	182.8	176.9	210.8	210.4	193.2	207.8	192.8	207.4
Person trips	196.1	221.8	224.0	278.0	275.4	246.7	275.2	251.2	275.5
Party size	1.3	1.2	1.3	1.3	1.3	1.3	1.3	1.3	1.3
Pleasure travel: Total trips	301.2	361.1	364.3	411.7	413.4	434.3	413.0	432.5	443.2
Person trips	539.5	649.4	666.6	736.4	740.0	781.2	809.5	807.8	862.4
Party size	1.8	1.8	1.8	1.8	1.8	1.8	1.9	1.9	1.9
Vacation travel: Total trips	264.5	328.7	327.7	352.8	352.2	343.4	349.7	375.5	388.6
Person trips	487.8	591.6	605.3	637.1	633.2	664.6	680.4	706.1	751.8
Party size	1.8	1.8	1.9	1.8	1.8	1.9	1.9	1.9	1.9

[1] Includes other trips, not shown separately.

Source: Travel Industry Association of America, Washington, DC, *National Travel Survey,* annual, (copyright).

No. 451. Characteristics of Business Trips and Pleasure Trips: 1985 to 1997

[Represents trips to places 100 miles or more from home by one or more household members traveling together. Based on a monthly telephone survey of 1,500 U.S. adults. For details, see source]

CHARACTERISTIC	Unit	BUSINESS TRIPS				PLEASURE TRIPS			
		1985	1990	1995	1997	1985	1990	1995	1997
Total trips	Millions.	156.6	182.8	207.8	207.4	301.2	361.1	413.0	443.2
Average household members on trip	Number .	1.3	1.2	1.3	1.3	1.8	1.8	1.9	1.9
Average nights per trip [1]	Nights . .	3.6	3.7	3.1	3.2	5.6	4.4	3.8	3.8
Average miles per trip [2]	Miles . . .	1,180	1,020	1,022	1,128	1,010	867	781	901
Traveled primarily by auto/truck/RV [3] rental car	Percent .	51	58	63	60	73	77	84	80
Traveled primarily by air	Percent .	44	37	35	38	21	18	13	16
Used a rental car while on trip	Percent .	20	14	22	25	6	7	8	9
Stayed in a hotel while on trip	Percent .	62	71	66	65	39	37	39	39
Used a travel agent	Percent .	28	21	24	27	13	12	9	11
Also a vacation trip	Percent .	13	17	14	18	80	82	74	74
Male travelers	Percent .	67	71	74	70	48	49	53	53
Female travelers	Percent .	33	29	26	30	52	51	47	47
Household income:									
Less than $40,000	Percent .	58	42	25	25	73	63	47	42
$40,000 or more	Percent .	42	56	75	75	27	38	53	58

[1] Includes no overnight stays.   [2] United States only.   [3] Recreational vehicle.

Source: Travel Industry Association of America, Washington, DC, *National Travel Survey,* annual, (copyright).

No. 452. Arrangement of Passenger Transportation—Receipts and and Expenses, by Source: 1990 to 1996

[In millions of dollars. For taxable employer firms. Data are for SIC 472. Based on the 1987 Standard Industrial Classification code; see text, Section 13, Labor Force]

ITEM	1990	1991	1992	1993	1994	1995	1996
RECEIPTS							
Total	**10,921**	**10,152**	**10,573**	**11,032**	**11,710**	**12,754**	**13,725**
Air carriers	5,837	5,527	5,881	6,211	6,544	7,174	7,689
Water carriers	474	520	523	529	584	679	653
Hotels and motels	771	676	744	773	846	951	1,045
Motor coaches	403	385	379	363	348	342	421
Railroads	127	130	110	122	116	122	147
Rental cars	175	171	187	216	264	335	363
Packaged tours	2,250	1,931	1,989	2,143	2,397	2,539	2,706
Other	884	812	760	671	609	612	701
EXPENSES							
Total	**9,912**	**9,469**	**9,705**	**10,051**	**10,706**	**11,258**	**12,238**
Annual payroll	3,891	3,740	3,924	4,013	4,489	4,745	5,114
Employer contributions to Social Security and other supplemental benefits	519	516	526	573	664	718	791
Lease and rental payments	919	874	873	838	767	786	850
Advertising and promotion	722	636	653	670	652	607	697
Taxes and licenses	158	134	135	140	153	160	152
Utilities	352	341	371	417	448	505	544
Depreciation	409	379	326	339	365	393	412
Purchased office supplies	321	295	300	288	313	324	337
Purchased repair services	156	139	124	129	142	151	161
Other	2,465	2,415	2,473	2,644	2,713	2,869	3,180

Source: U.S. Bureau of the Census, *Current Business Reports, Service Annual Survey: 1996,* BS/96.

No. 453. Domestic Travel Expenditures, by State: 1995

[Represents U.S. spending on domestic overnight trips and day trips of 100 miles or more away from home. Excludes spending by foreign visitors and by U.S. residents in U.S. territories and abroad]

STATE	Total (mil. dol.)	Share of total (percent)	Rank	STATE	Total (mil. dol.)	Share of total (percent)	Rank	STATE	Total (mil. dol.)	Share of total (percent)	Rank
U.S., total .	360,314	100.0	(X)	KY	4,034	1.0	29	OH	9,641	2.4	11
AL	4,092	1.0	28	LA	6,059	1.6	21	OK	3,015	0.7	36
AK	1,157	0.3	46	ME	1,600	0.4	42	OR	4,263	1.1	27
AZ	6,333	1.8	19	MD	5,667	1.4	22	PA	11,186	2.9	8
AR	3,078	0.7	34	MA	8,031	2.3	14	RI	744	0.2	51
CA	46,672	13.8	1	MI	8,396	2.1	13	SC	5,366	1.4	23
CO	6,707	1.7	17	MN	4,931	1.2	24	SD	909	0.2	48
CT	3,810	1.0	30	MS	3,185	0.8	32	TN	7,679	1.9	15
DE	886	0.2	50	MO	6,989	1.7	16	TX	22,562	6.1	3
DC	3,245	1.2	31	MT	1,546	0.4	43	UT	3,046	0.8	35
FL	30,879	10.2	2	NE	2,058	0.5	39	VT	1,136	0.3	47
GA	10,457	2.7	9	NV	15,006	4.0	6	VA	9,996	2.5	10
HI	6,434	3.1	18	NH	1,676	0.4	40	WA	6,060	1.7	20
ID	1,650	0.4	41	NJ	11,708	2.9	7	WV	1,467	0.4	44
IL	15,852	4.1	5	NM	2,931	0.7	37	WI	4,809	1.2	25
IN	4,634	1.2	26	NY	21,647	7.0	4	WY	1,232	0.3	45
IA	3,172	0.8	33	NC	9,056	2.2	12				
KS	2,729	0.7	38	ND	897	0.2	49				

X Not applicable.

Source: Travel Industry Association of America, Washington, DC, *Impact of Travel on State Economies, 1995* (copyright).

No. 454. International Travelers and Expenditures, With Projections: 1988 to 1997

[For coverage, see Table 455. Minus sign (-) indicates deficit]

YEAR	TRAVEL AND PASSENGER FARE (mil. dol.)				U.S. net travel and passenger payments (mil. dol.)	U.S. travelers to foreign countries (1,000)	Foreign visitors to the U.S. (1,000)
	Payments by U.S. travelers		Receipts from foreign visitors				
	Total [1]	Expenditures abroad	Total [1]	Travel receipts			
1988	39,843	32,114	38,409	29,434	-1,434	40,669	33,942
1989	41,665	33,416	46,863	36,205	5,198	41,138	36,365
1990	47,880	37,349	58,305	43,007	10,425	44,623	39,363
1991	45,334	35,322	64,237	48,384	18,903	41,566	42,674
1992	49,108	38,552	71,359	54,742	22,251	43,898	47,261
1993	52,026	40,713	73,986	57,875	21,960	44,411	45,779
1994	56,667	43,782	75,500	58,417	18,833	46,450	44,753
1995	60,486	46,053	82,520	63,395	22,034	50,763	43,318
1996, est. . .	64,515	48,739	90,465	69,908	25,950	52,311	46,489
1997, proj. .	75,032	57,183	88,928	68,043	13,896	53,991	46,216

[1] Includes passenger fares not shown separately.

Source: U.S. Dept. of Commerce, International Trade Administration, Internet site <http://www.tinet.ita.doc.gov/free> (Accessed 14 April 1998).

No. 455. Foreign Travel: 1989 to 1996

[**In thousands.** U.S. travelers cover residents of the United States, its territories and possessions. Foreign travelers to the United States include travelers for business and pleasure, international travelers in transit through the United States, and students; excludes travel by international personnel and international businessmen employed in the United States]

ITEM AND AREA	1989	1990	1991	1992	1993	1994	1995	1996, est.
U.S. travelers to foreign countries. . . .	41,138	44,623	41,566	43,898	44,411	46,450	50,763	52,311
Canada	12,184	12,252	12,003	11,819	12,024	12,542	12,933	12,909
Mexico	14,163	16,381	15,042	16,114	15,285	15,759	18,771	19,616
Total overseas	14,791	15,990	14,521	15,965	17,102	18,149	19,059	19,786
Europe	7,233	8,043	6,316	7,136	7,491	8,167	8,596	8,706
Foreign travelers to the U.S.	36,365	39,363	42,674	47,262	45,779	44,753	43,318	46,489
Canada	15,325	17,263	19,113	18,598	17,293	14,974	14,663	15,301
Mexico	7,041	7,041	7,406	10,872	9,824	11,321	8,016	8,530
Total overseas	13,999	15,059	16,155	17,791	18,662	18,458	20,639	22,658
Europe	6,251	6,659	7,360	8,262	8,630	8,119	8,793	9,727
South America	1,134	1,328	1,575	1,770	2,026	2,112	2,449	2,461
Central America	384	412	444	481	545	513	509	524
Caribbean	1,109	1,137	1,061	1,004	1,098	1,031	1,044	1,133
Far East	4,023	4,360	4,579	5,097	5,165	5,551	6,616	7,500
Middle East	356	365	357	373	419	403	454	480
Oceania	605	662	641	654	609	556	588	629
Africa	137	137	139	150	169	173	186	205

Source: U.S. Dept. of Commerce, International Trade Administration, Internet site <http://www.tinet.ita.doc.gov/abstract> (Accessed 10 April 1998).

No. 456. Top States and Cities Visited by Overseas Travelers: 1995 and 1996

[Includes travelers for business and pleasure, international travelers in transit through the United States, and students; excludes travel by international personnel and international businessmen employed in the United States]

STATE	OVERSEAS VISITORS (1,000)		MARKET SHARE (percent)		CITY	OVERSEAS VISITORS (1,000)		MARKET SHARE (percent)	
	1995	1996	1995	1996		1995	1996	1995	1996
Total overseas travelers .	20,639	22,658	100.0	100.0					
California.	5,304	6,004	25.7	26.5	New York City	4,252	4,532	20.6	20.0
Florida	5,345	5,710	25.9	25.2	Los Angeles	3,323	3,603	16.1	15.9
New York	4,479	4,804	21.7	21.2	Miami.	2,951	3,127	14.3	13.8
Hawaii	2,910	3,059	14.1	13.5	San Francisco	2,539	2,923	12.3	12.9
Nevada.	1,858	2,062	9.0	9.1	Orlando	2,621	2,583	12.7	11.4
Guam	1,238	1,292	6.0	5.7	Oahu/Honolulu.	2,373	2,402	11.5	10.6
Illinois.	1,115	1,178	5.4	5.2	Las Vegas	1,754	1,971	8.5	8.7
Massachusetts	1,053	1,156	5.1	5.1	Washington, DC.	1,589	1,382	7.7	6.1
Arizona.	887	997	4.3	4.4	Chicago	1,053	1,110	5.1	4.9
Texas	867	974	4.2	4.3	Boston	970	1,065	4.7	4.7
Pennsylvania	599	702	2.9	3.1	San Diego.	722	702	3.5	3.1
Georgia	599	657	2.9	2.9	Tampa/St. Petersburg	516	589	2.5	2.6
New Jersey	599	634	2.9	2.8	Anaheim.	495	589	2.4	2.6
Washington	599	612	2.9	2.7	Atlanta	495	566	2.4	2.5
Colorado.	433	566	2.1	2.5	Seattle	537	544	2.6	2.4
Utah.	433	498	2.1	2.2	Philadelphia	330	431	1.6	1.9
Louisiana	413	408	2.0	1.8	Phoenix	351	408	1.7	1.8
Ohio.	351	385	1.7	1.7	Houston	433	408	2.1	1.8
North Carolina	310	363	1.5	1.6	San Jose	289	408	1.4	1.8
Michigan	372	363	1.8	1.6	Dallas/Ft. Worth	310	385	1.5	1.7
Virginia	351	340	1.7	1.5	New Orleans	372	363	1.8	1.6
Minnesota	206	272	1.0	1.2	Denver	248	363	1.2	1.6
Maryland.	248	272	1.2	1.2	Ft. Lauderdale	413	317	2.0	1.4
Oregon	248	249	1.2	1.1	Florida Keys	413	317	2.0	1.4
Tennessee.	268	227	1.3	1.0	Detroit	268	249	1.3	1.1
Connecticut	227	227	1.1	1.0	Minneapolis/St. Paul	165	227	0.8	1.0
South Carolina	227	181	1.1	0.8	Monterey	227	227	1.1	1.0
Wisconsin	144	159	0.7	0.7	Riverside/San Bernandino .	186	227	0.9	1.0
Wyoming	165	159	0.8	0.7	Sarasota.	144	227	0.7	1.0
Missouri	144	159	0.7	0.7	Ft. Myers	206	227	1.0	1.0

Source: U.S. Dept. of Commerce, International Trade Administration, Internet site <http://www.tinet.ita.doc.gov/free> (Accessed 08 April 1998).

No. 457. Foreign Visitors for Pleasure Admitted, by Country of Last Residence: 1985 to 1996

[In thousands. For years ending September 30. See headnote, Table 7, Section 1, Population]

COUNTRY	1985	1990	1995	1996	COUNTRY	1985	1990	1995	1996
Total [1]	6,609	13,418	17,612	19,110	Africa [2]	101	105	137	157
					Egypt.	16	16	16	19
Europe [2]	2,048	5,383	7,012	7,478	Nigeria.	25	11	10	12
Austria	34	87	146	158					
Belgium	39	95	153	170	Oceania [2]	282	562	478	512
Denmark	36	75	78	89	Australia.	195	380	327	342
Finland	24	83	47	53	New Zealand.	74	153	115	127
France	226	566	738	767	North America.	1,664	2,463	2,240	2,314
Greece	34	43	44	43	Canada	79	119	127	121
Ireland	55	81	126	151	Mexico.	773	1,061	893	908
Italy.	155	308	427	437	Caribbean [2]	584	963	831	907
Netherlands	82	214	308	325	Bahamas, The	211	332	234	292
Norway	41	80	71	80	Barbados	17	34	36	37
Poland	40	55	36	45	Cayman Islands	18	31	31	34
Soviet Union	2	53	54	71	Dominican Republic . . .	57	137	138	140
Spain.	64	183	248	262	Haiti	56	57	43	39
Sweden	71	230	142	165	Jamaica	74	132	130	144
Switzerland.	110	236	321	337	Netherlands Antilles . . .	27	31	32	27
United Kingdom.	598	1,899	2,342	2,495	Trinidad and Tobago . .	71	81	64	70
Germany [3]	373	969	1,550	1,624	Central America [2].	228	320	387	376
					Costa Rica	41	62	91	87
Asia [2]	1,866	3,830	5,666	5,445	El Salvador	38	46	63	62
China (Mainland China					Guatemala	53	91	99	97
and Taiwan)	83	187	378	363	Panama	38	43	54	54
Hong Kong.	64	111	162	174	South America [2]	606	1,016	1,978	2,000
India	52	75	75	84	Argentina	66	136	320	339
Israel.	80	128	160	186	Brazil.	148	300	710	723
Japan	1,277	2,846	3,986	3,621	Chile	28	54	117	121
Korea	26	120	427	513	Colombia	123	122	174	187
Philippines	59	76	85	86	Ecuador	42	57	77	78
Saudi Arabia	31	33	45	42	Peru	44	97	98	101
Singapore	23	32	61	72	Venezuela	122	199	400	362

[1] Includes countries unknown or not reported. [2] Includes countries not shown separately. [3] Data prior to 1995 for former West Germany.

Source: U.S. Immigration and Naturalization Service, Statistical Yearbook, annual.

Figure 8.1
Participation in Elections for President and Representatives—
Percent of Voting-Age Population

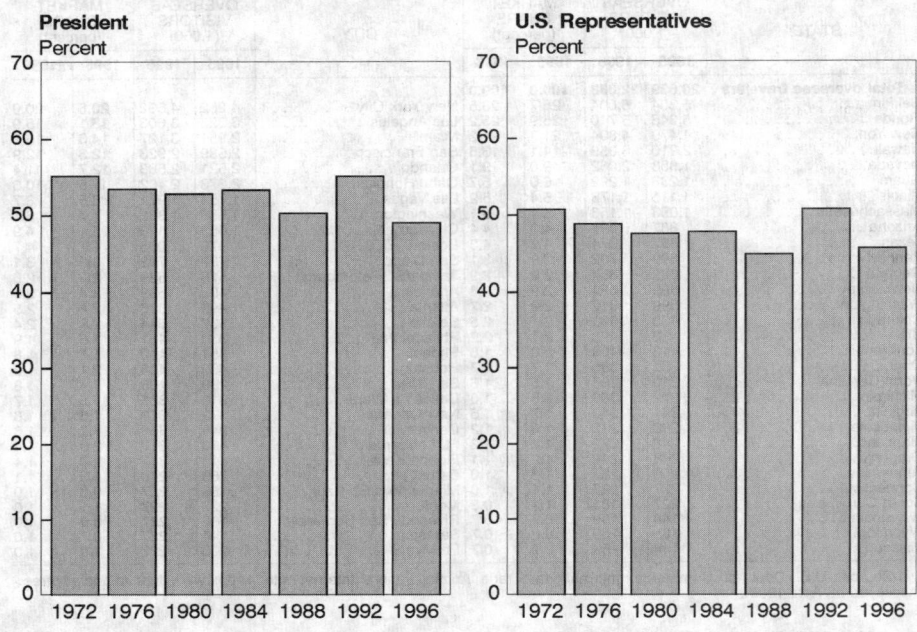

President
Percent

U.S. Representatives
Percent

Source: Chart prepared by U.S. Bureau of the Census. For data, see Table 485.

Figure 8.2
Political Campaign Receipts

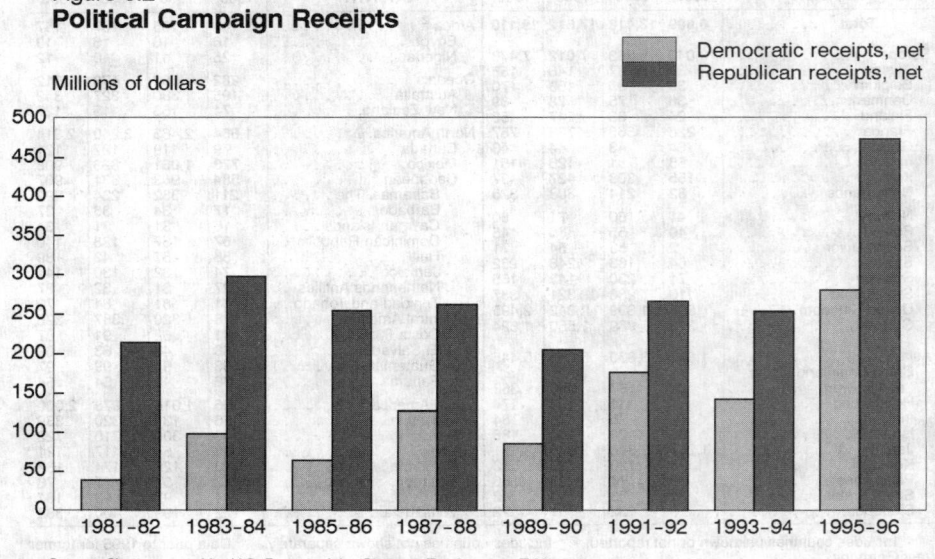

Millions of dollars

Democratic receipts, net
Republican receipts, net

Source: Chart prepared by U.S. Bureau of the Census. For data, see Table 488.

Elections

This section relates primarily to presidential, congressional, and gubernatorial elections. Also presented are summary tables on congressional legislation; state legislatures; Black, Hispanic, and female officeholders; population of voting age; voter participation; and campaign finances.

Official statistics on federal elections, collected by the Clerk of the House, are published biennially in *Statistics of the Presidential and Congressional Election* and *Statistics of the Congressional Election*. Federal and state elections data appear also in *America Votes*, a biennial volume published by Congressional Quarterly, Inc., Washington, DC. Federal elections data also appear in the U.S. Congress, *Congressional Directory*, and in official state documents. Data on reported registration and voting for social and economic groups are obtained by the U.S. Bureau of the Census as part of the Current Population Survey (CPS) and are published in *Current Population Reports*, P20 (see text, Section 1).

Almost all federal, state, and local governmental units in the United States conduct elections for political offices and other purposes. The conduct of elections is regulated by state laws or, in some cities and counties, by local charter. An exception is that the U.S. Constitution prescribes the basis of representation in Congress and the manner of electing the President, and grants to Congress the right to regulate the times, places, and manner of electing federal officers. Amendments to the Constitution have prescribed national criteria for voting eligibility. The 15th Amendment, adopted in 1870, gave all citizens the right to vote regardless of race, color, or previous condition of servitude. The 19th Amendment, adopted in 1919, further extended the right to vote to all citizens regardless of sex. The payment of poll taxes as a prerequisite to voting in federal elections was banned by the 24th Amendment in 1964. In 1971, as a result of the 26th Amendment, eligibility to vote in national

In Brief	
Percent of voting-age population voting for Representatives:	
1992	*50.8%*
1994	*36.0%*
Voter registration sources 1995–96:	
Motor vehicle offices	*33.1%*
By mail	*29.7%*
Public assistance offices	*6.3%*
State designated sites	*4.2%*
Disability services	*0.4%*
Armed Forces offices	*0.2%*
Other	*26.1%*

elections was extended to all citizens, 18 years old and over.

Presidential election—The Constitution specifies how the President and Vice President are selected. Each state elects, by popular vote, a group of electors equal in number to its total of members of Congress. The 23d Amendment, adopted in 1961, grants the District of Columbia three presidential electors, a number equal to that of the least populous state. Subsequent to the election, the electors meet in their respective states to vote for President and Vice President. Usually, each elector votes for the candidate receiving the most popular votes in his or her state. A majority vote of all electors is necessary to elect the President and Vice President. If no candidate receives a majority, the House of Representatives, with each state having one vote, is empowered to elect the President and Vice President, again, with a majority of votes required.

The 22d Amendment to the Constitution, adopted in 1951, limits presidential tenure to two elective terms of 4 years each, or to one elective term for any person who, upon succession to the Presidency, has held the office or acted as President for more than 2 years.

Congressional election—The Constitution provides that Representatives be apportioned among the states according to their population; that a census of population be taken every 10 years as a basis for apportionment; and that each state have at least one Representative. At the time of each apportionment, Congress decides what the total number of Representatives will be. Since 1912, the total has been 435, except during 1960 to 1962 when it increased to 437, adding one Representative each for Alaska and Hawaii. The total reverted to 435 after reapportionment following the 1960 census. Members are elected for 2-year terms, all terms covering the same period. The District of Columbia, American Samoa, Guam, and the Virgin Islands each elect one nonvoting Delegate and Puerto Rico elects a nonvoting Resident Commissioner.

The Senate is composed of 100 members, 2 from each state, who are elected to serve for a term of 6 years. One-third of the Senate is elected every 2 years. Senators were originally chosen by the state legislatures. The 17th Amendment to the Constitution, adopted in 1913, prescribed that Senators be elected by popular vote.

Voter eligibility and participation—The Census Bureau publishes estimates of the population of voting age and the percent casting votes in each state for Presidential and congressional election years. These voting-age estimates include a number of persons who meet the age requirement but are not eligible to vote, (e.g. aliens and some institutionalized persons). In addition, since 1964, voter participation and voter characteristics data have been collected during November of election years as part of the CPS. These survey data include noncitizens in the voting age population estimates, but exclude members of the Armed Forces and the institutional population.

Statistical reliability—For a discussion of statistical collection and estimation, sampling procedures, and measures of statistical reliability applicable to Census Bureau data, see Appendix III.

Figure 8.3
Popular Vote Cast for President, by Major Political Party

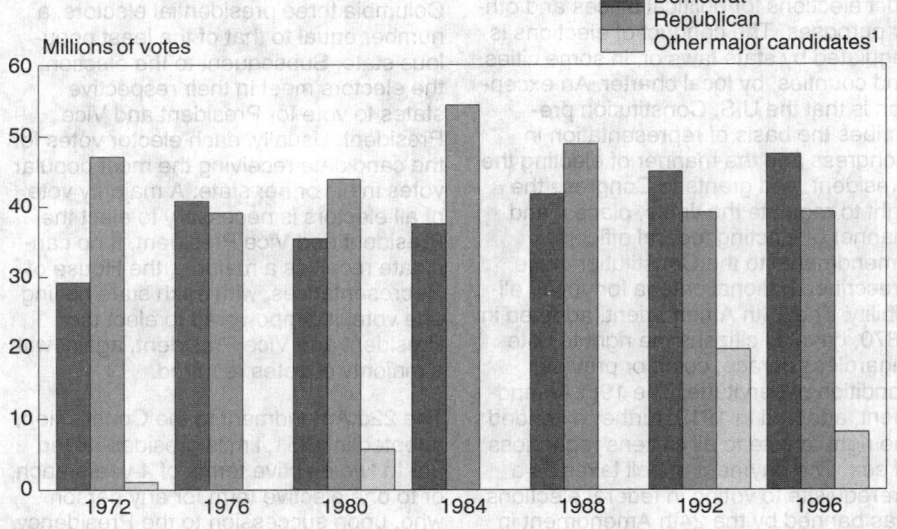

Millions of votes

Legend: Democrat, Republican, Other major candidates[1]

[1] 1972—American, John Schmitz; 1980—Independent, John Anderson; 1992—Independent, Ross Perot; 1996 Reform, Ross Perot.

Source: Chart prepared by U.S. Bureau of the Census. For data, see Tables 458 and 459.

No. 458. Vote Cast for President, by Major Political Party: 1936 to 1996

[Prior to 1960, excludes Alaska and Hawaii; prior to 1964, excludes DC. Vote cast for major party candidates include the votes of minor parties cast for those candidates]

	CANDIDATES FOR PRESIDENT			VOTE CAST FOR PRESIDENT					
				Democratic			Republican		
YEAR	Democratic	Republican	Total popular vote [1] (1,000)	Popular vote		Electoral vote	Popular vote		Electoral vote
				Number (1,000)	Per-cent		Number (1,000)	Per-cent	
1936	F. D. Roosevelt . .	Landon	45,655	27,757	60.8	523	16,684	36.5	8
1940	F. D. Roosevelt . .	Willkie	49,900	27,313	54.7	449	22,348	44.8	82
1944	F. D. Roosevelt . .	Dewey	47,977	25,613	53.4	432	22,018	45.9	99
1948	Truman	Dewey	48,794	24,179	49.6	303	21,991	45.1	189
1952	Stevenson	Eisenhower.	61,551	27,315	44.4	89	33,936	55.1	442
1956	Stevenson	Eisenhower.	62,027	26,023	42.0	73	35,590	57.4	457
1960	Kennedy	Nixon.	68,838	34,227	49.7	303	34,108	49.5	219
1964	Johnson.	Goldwater.	70,645	43,130	61.1	486	27,178	38.5	52
1968	Humphrey	Nixon.	73,212	31,275	42.7	191	31,785	43.4	301
1972	McGovern	Nixon.	77,719	29,170	37.5	17	47,170	60.7	520
1976	Carter	Ford	81,556	40,831	50.1	297	39,148	48.0	240
1980	Carter	Reagan	86,515	35,484	41.0	49	43,904	50.7	489
1984	Mondale.	Reagan	92,653	37,577	40.6	13	54,455	58.8	525
1988	Dukakis	Bush	91,595	41,809	45.6	111	48,886	53.4	426
1992	Clinton.	Bush	104,425	44,909	43.0	370	39,104	37.4	168
1996	Clinton.	Dole	96,278	47,402	49.2	379	39,199	40.7	159

[1] Include votes for minor party candidates, independents, unpledged electors, and scattered write-in votes.

Source: Congressional Quarterly, Inc., Washington, DC, *America at the Polls 2,* 1965, and *America Votes,* biennial (copyright).

No. 459. Vote Cast for Leading Minority Party Candidates for President: 1936 to 1996

[See headnote, Table 458]

YEAR	Candidate	Party	Popular vote (1,000)	Candidate	Party	Popular vote (1,000)
1936 . .	William Lemke.	Union	892	Norman Thomas . . .	Socialist	188
1940 . .	Norman Thomas . . .	Socialist	116	Roger Babson	Prohibition.	59
1944 . .	Norman Thomas . . .	Socialist	79	Claude Watson	Prohibition.	75
1948 . .	Strom Thurmond . . .	States' Rights.	1,176	Henry Wallace.	Progressive	1,157
1952 . .	Vincent Hallinan. . . .	Progressive	140	Stuart Hamblen	Prohibition.	73
1956 . .	T. Coleman Andrews.	States' Rights.	111	Eric Hass	Socialist Labor	44
1960 . .	Eric Hass	Socialist Labor	48	Rutherford Decker . .	Prohibition.	46
1964 . .	Eric Hass	Socialist Labor	45	Clifton DeBerry	Socialist Workers	33
1968 . .	George Wallace	American Independent.	9,906	Henning Blomen . . .	Socialist Labor	53
1972 . .	John Schmitz.	American.	1,099	Benjamin Spock. . . .	People's	79
1976 . .	Eugene McCarthy . .	Independent	757	Roger McBride.	Libertarian	173
1980 . .	John Anderson	Independent	5,720	Ed Clark.	Libertarian	921
1984 . .	David Bergland	Libertarian.	228	Lyndon H. LaRouche.	Independent	79
1988 . .	Ron Paul	Libertarian.	432	Lenora B. Fulani . . .	New Alliance	217
1992 . .	H. Ross Perot	Independent	19,742	Andre Marrou	Libertarian	292
1996 . .	H. Ross Perot	Reform Party	8,085	Ralph Nader	Green.	685

Source: Congressional Quarterly, Inc. Washington, DC, *America at the Polls 1920-1996,* 1997; and *America Votes,* biennial (copyright).

No. 460. Democratic and Republican Percentages of Two-Party Presidential Vote, by Selected Characteristics of Voters: 1988 and 1992

[In percent. Covers citizens of voting age living in private housing units in the contiguous United States. Percentages for Democratic Presidential vote are computed by subtracting the percentage Republican vote from 100 percent; third-party or independent votes are not included as valid data. Data are from the National Election Studies and are based on a sample and subject to sampling variability; for details, see source]

	1988		1992			1988		1992	
CHARACTERISTIC	Demo-cratic	Repub-lican	Demo-cratic	Repub-lican	CHARACTERISTIC	Demo-cratic	Repub-lican	Demo-cratic	Repub-lican
Total [1]	47	53	58	42	Race:				
Year of birth:					White.	41	59	53	47
1959 or later	48	52	58	42	Black.	92	8	94	6
1943 to 1958	47	53	58	42					
1927 to 1942	49	51	57	43	Education:				
1911 to 1926.	44	56	62	38	Grade school	61	39	70	30
1895 to 1910	47	53	58	42	High school.	51	49	63	37
					College	42	58	55	45
Sex:									
Male	44	56	55	45	Union household. . . .	59	41	68	32
Female	50	50	61	39	Nonunion household . .	44	56	56	44

[1] Includes other characteristics, not shown separately.

Source: Center for Political Studies, University of Michigan, Ann Arbor, MI, unpublished data (copyright).

No. 461. Electoral Vote Cast for President, by Major Political Party—States: 1956 to 1996

[D=Democratic, R=Republican. For composition of regions, see inside front cover]

STATE	1956 [1]	1960 [2]	1964	1968 [3]	1972 [4]	1976 [5]	1980	1984	1988 [6]	1992	1996
Democratic	73	303	486	191	17	297	49	13	111	370	379
Republican	457	219	52	301	520	240	489	525	426	168	159
AL	[1]D-10	[2]D-5	R-10	([3])	R-9	D-9	R-9	R-9	R-9	R-9	R-9
AK	(X)	R-3	D-3	R-3	R-3	R-3	R-3	R-3	R-3	R-3	R-3
AZ	R-4	R-4	R-5	R-5	R-6	R-6	R-6	R-7	R-7	R-8	D-8
AR	D-8	D-8	D-6	D-6	R-6	R-6	R-6	R-6	R-6	D-6	D-6
CA	R-32	R-32	D-40	R-40	R-45	R-45	R-45	R-47	R-47	D-54	D-54
CO	R-6	R-6	D-6	R-6	R-7	R-7	R-7	R-8	R-8	R-8	R-8
CT	R-8	D-8	D-8	D-8	R-8	R-8	R-8	R-8	R-8	D-8	D-8
DE	R-3	D-3	D-3	D-3	R-3	R-3	D-3	R-3	R-3	D-3	D-3
DC	(X)	(X)	D-3	D-3	D-3	D-3	D-3	D-3	D-3	D-3	D-3
FL	R-10	R-10	D-14	R-14	R-17	D-17	R-17	R-21	R-21	R-25	D-25
GA	D-12	D-12	R-12	([3])	R-12	D-12	D-12	R-12	R-12	D-13	R-13
HI	(X)	D-3	D-4	D-4	R-4	D-4	D-4	R-4	D-4	D-4	D-4
ID	R-4	R-4	R-4	R-4	R-4	R-4	R-4	R-4	R-4	R-4	R-4
IL	R-27	D-27	D-26	R-26	R-26	R-26	R-26	R-24	R-24	D-22	D-22
IN	R-13	R-13	D-13	R-13	R-13	R-13	R-13	R-12	R-12	R-12	R-12
IA	R-10	R-10	D-9	R-9	R-8	R-8	R-8	R-8	D-8	D-7	D-7
KS	R-8	R-8	D-7	R-7	R-7	R-7	R-7	R-7	R-7	R-6	R-6
KY	R-10	R-10	D-9	R-9	R-9	D-9	R-9	R-9	R-9	D-8	D-8
LA	R-10	D-10	R-10	([3])	R-10	D-10	R-10	R-10	R-10	D-9	D-9
ME	R-5	R-5	D-4	D-4	R-4	R-4	R-4	R-4	R-4	D-4	D-4
MD	R-9	D-9	D-10	D-10	R-10	D-10	D-10	R-10	R-10	D-10	D-10
MA	R-16	D-16	D-14	D-14	D-14	D-14	D-14	R-13	D-13	D-12	D-12
MI	R-20	D-20	D-21	D-21	R-21	R-21	R-21	R-20	R-20	D-18	D-18
MN	R-11	D-11	D-10	D-10	R-10	D-10	D-10	D-10	D-10	D-10	D-10
MS	D-8	([2])	R-7	([3])	R-7	D-7	R-7	R-7	R-7	R-7	R-7
MO	D-13	D-13	D-12	R-12	R-12	D-12	R-12	R-11	R-11	D-11	D-11
MT	R-4	R-4	D-4	R-4	R-4	R-4	R-4	R-4	R-4	D-3	R-3
NE	R-6	R-6	D-5	R-5	R-5	R-5	R-5	R-5	R-5	R-5	R-5
NV	R-3	D-3	D-3	R-3	R-3	R-3	R-3	R-4	R-4	D-4	R-5
NH	R-4	R-4	D-4	R-4	R-4	R-4	R-4	R-4	R-4	D-4	D-4
NJ	R-16	R-16	D-17	R-17	R-17	R-17	R-17	R-16	R-16	D-15	D-15
NM	R-4	D-4	D-4	R-4	R-4	R-4	R-4	R-5	R-5	D-5	D-5
NY	R-45	D-45	D-43	D-43	R-41	D-41	R-41	R-36	R-36	D-33	D-33
NC	D-14	D-14	D-13	[3]R-12	R-13	D-13	R-13	R-13	R-13	R-14	R-14
ND	R-4	R-4	D-4	R-4	R-3	R-3	R-3	R-3	R-3	R-3	R-3
OH	R-25	R-25	D-26	R-26	R-25	D-25	R-25	R-23	R-23	D-21	D-21
OK	R-8	[2]R-7	D-8	R-8	R-8	R-8	R-8	R-8	R-8	R-8	R-8
OR	R-6	R-6	D-6	R-6	R-6	R-6	R-6	R-7	D-7	D-7	D-7
PA	R-32	D-32	D-29	D-29	R-27	D-27	R-27	R-25	R-25	D-23	D-23
RI	R-4	D-4	D-4	D-4	D-4	D-4	D-4	D-4	D-4	D-4	D-4
SC	D-8	D-8	R-8	R-8	R-8	D-8	R-8	R-8	R-8	R-8	R-8
SD	R-4	R-4	D-4	R-4	R-4	R-4	R-4	R-3	R-3	R-3	R-3
TN	R-11	R-11	D-11	R-11	R-10	D-10	R-10	R-11	R-11	D-11	D-11
TX	R-24	D-24	D-25	D-25	R-26	D-26	R-26	R-29	R-29	R-32	R-32
UT	R-4	R-4	D-4	R-4	R-4	R-4	R-4	R-5	R-5	R-5	R-5
VT	R-3	R-3	D-3	R-3	R-3	R-3	R-3	R-3	R-3	R-3	D-3
VA	R-12	R-12	D-12	R-12	[4]R-11	R-12	R-12	R-12	R-12	R-13	R-13
WA	R-9	R-9	D-9	D-9	R-9	[5]R-8	R-9	R-10	D-10	D-11	D-11
WV	R-8	D-8	D-7	D-7	R-6	D-6	D-6	R-6	[6]D-5	D-5	D-5
WI	R-12	R-12	D-12	R-12	R-11	D-11	R-11	R-11	D-11	D-11	D-11
WY	R-3	R-3	D-3	R-3	R-3	R-3	R-3	R-3	R-3	R-3	R-3

- Represents zero.   X Not applicable.   [1] Excludes one electoral vote cast for Walter B. Jones in Alabama.   [2] Excludes 15 electoral votes cast for Harry F. Byrd as follows: AL 6, MS 8, and OK 1.   [3] Excludes 46 electoral votes cast for American Independent George C. Wallace as follows: AL 10, AR 6, GA 12, LA 10, MS 7, and NC 1.   [4] Excludes one electoral vote cast for Libertarian John Hospers in Virginia.   [5] Excludes one electoral vote cast for Ronald Reagan in Washington.   [6] Excludes one electoral vote cast for Lloyd Bentsen for President in West Virginia.

Source: 1956-72, U.S. Congress, Clerk of the House, *Statistics of the Presidential and Congressional Election*, quadrennial; 1976-96, Congressional Quarterly, Inc., Washington DC, *America Votes*, biennial (copyright).

No. 462. Popular Vote Cast for President, by Political Party—States: 1992 and 1996

[In thousands, except percent]

STATE	1992				1996				Percent of total vote		
	Total [1]	Demo-cratic Party	Repub-lican Party	Perot (Reform Party)	Total [1]	Demo-cratic Party	Repub-lican Party	Perot (Reform Party)	Demo-cratic Party	Repub-lican Party	Perot (Reform Party)
United States..	104,425	44,909	39,104	19,742	96,278	47,402	39,199	8,085	49.2	40.7	8.4
Alabama.	1,688	690	804	183	1,534	662	769	92	43.2	50.1	6.0
Alaska	259	78	102	73	242	80	123	26	33.3	50.8	10.9
Arizona.	1,487	543	572	354	1,404	653	622	112	46.5	44.3	8.0
Arkansas	951	506	337	99	884	475	325	70	53.7	36.8	7.9
California	11,132	5,121	3,631	2,296	10,019	5,120	3,828	698	51.1	38.2	7.0
Colorado.	1,569	630	563	366	1,511	671	692	100	44.4	45.8	6.6
Connecticut.	1,616	682	578	349	1,393	736	483	140	52.8	34.7	10.0
Delaware	290	126	102	59	271	140	99	29	51.8	36.6	10.6
District of Columbia . .	228	193	21	10	186	158	17	4	85.2	9.3	1.9
Florida	5,314	2,073	2,173	1,053	5,304	2,547	2,245	484	48.0	42.3	9.1
Georgia	2,321	1,009	995	310	2,299	1,054	1,081	146	45.8	47.0	6.4
Hawaii	373	179	137	53	360	205	114	27	56.9	31.6	7.6
Idaho	482	137	203	130	492	165	257	63	33.6	52.2	12.7
Illinois	5,050	2,453	1,734	841	4,311	2,342	1,587	346	54.3	36.8	8.0
Indiana.	2,306	848	989	456	2,136	887	1,007	224	41.5	47.1	10.5
Iowa	1,355	586	505	253	1,234	620	493	105	50.3	39.9	8.5
Kansas.	1,157	390	450	312	1,074	388	583	93	36.1	54.3	8.6
Kentucky	1,493	665	617	204	1,389	637	623	120	45.8	44.9	8.7
Louisiana	1,790	816	733	211	1,784	928	713	123	52.0	39.9	6.9
Maine.	679	263	207	207	606	313	186	86	51.6	30.8	14.2
Maryland	1,985	989	707	281	1,781	966	682	116	54.3	38.3	6.5
Massachusetts.	2,774	1,319	805	631	2,557	1,572	718	227	61.5	28.1	8.9
Michigan.	4,275	1,871	1,555	825	3,849	1,990	1,481	337	51.7	38.5	8.7
Minnesota.	2,348	1,021	748	563	2,193	1,120	766	258	51.1	35.0	11.8
Mississippi	982	400	488	86	894	394	440	52	44.1	49.2	5.8
Missouri	2,392	1,054	811	519	2,158	1,026	890	217	47.5	41.2	10.1
Montana.	411	155	144	107	407	168	180	55	41.3	44.1	13.6
Nebraska	738	217	344	174	677	237	363	71	35.0	53.7	10.5
Nevada	506	189	176	133	464	204	199	44	43.9	42.9	9.5
New Hampshire. . . .	538	209	202	121	499	246	196	48	49.3	39.4	9.7
New Jersey.	3,344	1,436	1,357	522	3,076	1,652	1,103	262	53.7	35.9	8.5
New Mexico	570	262	213	92	556	273	233	32	49.2	41.9	5.8
New York	6,927	3,444	2,347	1,091	6,316	3,756	1,933	503	59.5	30.6	8.0
North Carolina	2,612	1,114	1,135	358	2,516	1,108	1,226	168	44.0	48.7	6.7
North Dakota.	308	99	136	71	266	107	125	33	40.1	46.9	12.2
Ohio	4,940	1,985	1,894	1,036	4,534	2,148	1,860	483	47.4	41.0	10.7
Oklahoma.	1,390	473	593	320	1,207	488	582	131	40.4	48.3	10.8
Oregon.	1,463	621	476	354	1,378	650	538	121	47.2	39.1	8.8
Pennsylvania	4,960	2,239	1,792	903	4,506	2,216	1,801	431	49.2	40.0	9.6
Rhode Island.	453	213	132	105	390	233	105	44	59.7	26.8	11.2
South Carolina.	1,203	480	578	139	1,152	506	573	64	44.0	49.8	5.6
South Dakota	336	125	137	73	324	139	151	31	43.0	46.5	9.7
Tennessee	1,983	934	841	200	1,894	909	864	106	48.0	45.6	5.6
Texas.	6,154	2,282	2,496	1,355	5,612	2,460	2,736	379	43.8	48.8	6.7
Utah	744	183	323	203	666	222	362	66	33.3	54.4	10.0
Vermont	290	134	88	66	258	138	80	31	53.4	31.1	12.0
Virginia.	2,559	1,039	1,151	349	2,417	1,091	1,138	160	45.1	47.1	6.6
Washington.	2,288	993	731	542	2,254	1,123	841	201	49.8	37.3	8.9
West Virginia.	684	331	242	109	636	328	234	72	51.5	36.8	11.3
Wisconsin.	2,531	1,041	931	544	2,196	1,072	845	227	48.8	38.5	10.4
Wyoming	201	68	79	51	212	78	105	26	36.8	49.8	12.3

[1] Includes other parties not shown.

Source: Congressional Quarterly, Inc., Washington, DC, *America Votes*, biennial (copyright).

No. 463. Vote Cast for United States Senators, 1994 and 1996, and Incumbent Senators, 1996—States

[D=Democrat; R=Republican]

STATE	1994 Total (1,000)[1]	1994 Percent for leading party	1996 Total (1,000)[1]	1996 Percent for leading party	INCUMBENT SENATORS AND YEAR TERM EXPIRES — Name, party, and year	INCUMBENT SENATORS AND YEAR TERM EXPIRES — Name, party, and year
Alabama	(X)	(X)	1,499	R-52.5	Jeff Sessions (R) 2003	Richard C. Shelby (R) 1999
Alaska	(X)	(X)	232	R-76.7	Frank H. Murkowski (R) 1999	Ted Stevens (R) 2003
Arizona	1,119	R-53.7	(X)	(X)	John McCain (R) 1999	Jon Kyl (R) 2001
Arkansas	(X)	(X)	846	R-52.7	Dale Bumpers (D) 1999	Tim Hutchinson (R) 2003
California	8,503	D-46.8	(X)	(X)	Barbara Boxer (D) 1999	Dianne Feinstein (D) 2001
Colorado	(X)	(X)	1,470	R-51.1	Ben N. Campbell (R) 1999	Wayne Allard (R) 2003
Connecticut	1,080	D-67.0	(X)	(X)	Christopher J. Dodd (D) 1999	Joseph I. Lieberman (D) 2000
Delaware	199	R-55.8	276	D-60.0	Joseph R. Biden Jr. (D) 2003	William V. Roth, Jr. (R) 2001
Florida	4,105	R-70.5	(X)	(X)	Bob Graham (D) 1999	Connie Mack (R) 2001
Georgia	(X)	(X)	2,259	D-48.9	Paul Coverdell (R) 1999	Max Cleland (D) 2003
Hawaii	357	D-71.8	(X)	(X)	Daniel K. Akaka (D) 2001	Daniel K. Inouye (D) 1999
Idaho	(X)	(X)	497	R-57.0	Larry E. Craig (R) 2003	Dirk Kempthorne (R) 1999
Illinois	(X)	(X)	4,251	D-56.1	Carol Moseley-Braun (D) 1999	Richard J. Durbin (D) 2003
Indiana	1,544	R-67.4	(X)	(X)	Dan Coats (R) 1999	Richard G. Lugar (R) 2001
Iowa	(X)	(X)	1,224	D-51.8	Tom Harkin (D) 2003	Charles E. Grassley (R) 1998
Kansas	(X)	(X)	[2]1,065	R-53.9	Sam Brownback (R) 1999	Pat Roberts (R) 2003
Kentucky	(X)	(X)	1,307	R-55.5	Wendell H. Ford (D) 1999	Mitch McConnell (R) 2003
Louisiana	(X)	(X)	1,700	D-50.2	John B. Breaux (D) 1999	Mary Landrieu (D) 2003
Maine	511	R-60.3	607	R-49.2	Susan Collins (R) 2003	Olympia Snowe (R) 2001
Maryland	1,369	D-59.1	(X)	(X)	Barbara A. Mikulski (D) 1999	Paul S. Sarbanes (D) 2001
Massachusetts	2,179	D-58.1	2,556	D-52.2	Edward M. Kennedy (D) 2001	John F. Kerry (D) 2003
Michigan	3,043	R-51.9	3,763	D-58.4	Carl Levin (D) 2003	Spencer Abraham (R) 2001
Minnesota	1,773	R-49.1	2,183	D-50.3	Paul David Wellstone (D) 2003	Rod Grams (R) 2001
Mississippi	608	R-68.8	879	R-71.0	Thad Cochran (R) 2003	Trent Lott (R) 2001
Missouri	1,775	R-59.7	(X)	(X)	Christopher S. Bond (R) 1999	John Ashcroft (R) 2001
Montana	350	R-62.4	407	D-49.6	Max Baucus (D) 2003	Conrad Burns (R) 2001
Nebraska	579	D-54.8	677	R-56.1	Chuck Hagel (R) 2003	J. Robert Kerrey (D) 2001
Nevada	368	D-52.7	(X)	(X)	Harry Reid (D) 1999	Richard H. Bryan (D) 2001
New Hampshire	(X)	(X)	493	R-49.2	Judd Gregg (R) 1999	Robert C. Smith (R) 2003
New Jersey	2,055	D-50.3	2,884	D-52.7	Robert G. Torricelli (D) 2003	Frank R. Lautenberg (D) 2000
New Mexico	463	D-54.0	552	R-64.7	Jeff Bingaman (D) 2001	Pete V. Domenici (R) 2003
New York	4,790	D-55.2	(X)	(X)	Daniel P. Moynihan (D) 2001	Alfonse M. D'Amato (R) 1999
North Carolina	(X)	(X)	2,556	R-52.6	Lauch Faircloth (R) 1999	Jesse Helms (R) 2003
North Dakota	237	D-58.0	(X)	(X)	Byron L. Dorgan (D) 1999	Kent Conrad (D) 2001
Ohio	3,437	R-53.4	(X)	(X)	John Glenn (D) 1999	Mike DeWine (R) 2001
Oklahoma	982	R-55.2	1,183	R-56.7	James Inhofe (R) 2003	Don Nickles (R) 1999
Oregon	[3]1,197	[3]D-47.8	1,360	R-49.8	Gordon Smith (R) 2003	Ron Wyden (D) 1999
Pennsylvania	3,513	R-49.4	(X)	(X)	Rick Santorum (R) 2001	Arlen Specter (R) 1999
Rhode Island	345	R-64.5	363	D-63.5	Jack Reed (D) 2003	John H. Chafee (R) 2001
South Carolina	(X)	(X)	1,161	R-53.4	Ernest F. Hollings (D) 1999	Strom Thurmond (R) 2003
South Dakota	(X)	(X)	324	D-51.3	Thomas A. Daschle (D) 1999	Tim Johnson (D) 2003
Tennessee	[4]1,480	[4]R-56.4	1,779	R-61.4	Fred Thompson (R) 2003	Bill Frist (R) 2001
Texas	4,280	R-60.8	5,527	R-54.8	Kay Bailey Hutchison (R) 2001	Phil Gramm (R) 2003
Utah	519	R-68.8	(X)	(X)	Robert F. Bennett (R) 1999	Orrin G. Hatch (R) 2001
Vermont	212	R-50.3	(X)	(X)	Patrick J. Leahy (D) 1999	James M. Jeffords (R) 2001
Virginia	2,057	D-45.6	2,355	R-52.5	Charles S. Robb (D) 2001	John W. Warner (R) 2003
Washington	1,700	R-55.7	(X)	(X)	Patty Murray (D) 1999	Slade Gorton (R) 2001
West Virginia	421	D-69.0	596	D-76.6	Robert C. Byrd (D) 2001	John D. Rockefeller IV (D) 20
Wisconsin	1,565	D-58.3	(X)	(X)	Herb Kohl (D) 2001	Russell Feingold (D) 2003
Wyoming	202	R-58.9	211	R-54.1	Mike Enzi (R) 2003	Craig Thomas (R) 2001

X Not applicable.   [1] Includes vote cast for minor parties.   [2] Kansas had elections to fill two Senate seats in 1996. Pat Roberts was elected to fill the full-term seat vacated by the retiring Nancy Kassenbaum. Sam Brownback was elected to fill the short-term seat vacated by Robert Dole, who resigned in 1996 to run for President.   [3] Special election in January 1996 to fill the unexpired term of Senator Packwood.   [4] In a special election in 1994 to fill an unexpired term, the Republican candidate received 60.4 percent of 1,465,835 total votes cast. Tennessee had elections to fill two Senate seats in 1994. Bill Frist was elected to fill the full term. Fred Thompson was elected to fill the short-term seat vacated by Harlan Mathews. Vote is for the full-term seat.

Source: Congressional Quarterly, Inc., Washington, D.C. *America Votes*, biennial (copyright).

No. 464. Vote Cast for United States Representatives, by Major Political Party—States: 1990 to 1996

[In thousands, except percent. In each state, totals represent the sum of votes cast in each Congressional District or votes cast for Representative at Large in states where only one member is elected. In all years there are numerous districts within the state where either the Republican or Democratic party had no candidate. In some states the Republican and Democratic vote includes votes cast for the party candidate by endorsing parties]

STATE	1990				1994				1996			
	Total[1]	Demo-cratic	Repub-lican	Percent for leading party	Total[1]	Demo-cratic	Repub-lican	Percent for leading party	Total[1]	Demo-cratic	Repub-lican	Percent for leading party
U.S.[2]...	61,513	32,565	27,648	D-52.9	69,770	31,698	36,590	R-52.4	89,863	43,626	43,902	R-48.9
AL........	1,017	690	315	D-67.9	1,115	554	558	R-50.1	1,469	656	786	R-53.5
AK........	192	92	99	R-51.7	208	68	119	R-56.9	234	85	139	R-59.4
AZ........	966	345	621	R-64.3	1,099	410	653	R-59.4	1,356	521	801	R-59.0
AR[3]......	665	369	296	D-55.5	709	336	373	R-52.6	863	396	456	R-52.8
CA........	7,287	3,568	3,347	D-49.0	8,328	3,958	4,066	R-48.8	9,482	4,707	4,292	D-49.6
CO........	1,001	504	487	D-50.3	1,056	364	687	R-65.1	1,461	597	833	R-57.0
CT........	1,037	489	546	R-52.6	1,069	506	516	R-48.3	1,294	724	547	D-55.9
DE........	177	116	58	D-65.5	195	52	138	R-70.7	267	73	186	R-69.5
DC[3,4]....	160	98	42	D-61.7	(NA)	(NA)	(NA)	(NA)	(NA)	(NA)	(NA)	(NA)
FL[3,4]....	2,378	1,213	1,163	D-51.0	2,852	1,156	1,694	R-59.4	4,692	2,037	2,640	R-56.3
GA........	1,394	855	539	D-61.3	1,498	681	816	R-54.5	2,163	1,011	1,152	R-53.3
HI........	341	216	118	D-63.3	354	219	120	D-61.9	353	196	136	D-55.5
ID........	315	183	131	D-58.2	393	138	255	R-65.0	494	194	290	R-58.7
IL........	3,077	1,646	1,349	D-53.5	3,044	1,460	1,577	R-51.8	4,128	2,267	1,813	D-54.9
IN........	1,514	831	683	D-54.9	1,546	667	875	R-56.6	2,105	944	1,119	R-53.1
IA........	792	401	385	D-50.4	977	407	560	R-57.3	1,201	533	650	R-54.1
KS........	781	394	387	D-50.4	817	298	519	R-63.5	1,049	425	591	R-56.4
KY........	764	353	397	R-52.0	784	316	451	R-57.5	1,238	507	731	R-59.0
LA........	106	106	-	D-100.0	(X)	(X)	(X)	(X)	660	262	398	R-60.3
ME........	517	284	233	D-55.0	503	236	234	D-47.0	600	379	211	D-63.2
MD........	1,091	566	517	D-51.9	1,345	662	683	R-50.7	1,639	877	762	D-53.5
MA........	2,051	1,420	567	D-69.2	1,976	1,363	593	D-69.0	2,409	1,585	781	D-65.8
MI........	2,434	1,321	1,089	D-54.3	3,001	1,418	1,532	R-51.0	3,700	1,945	1,679	D-52.6
MN........	1,781	1,042	736	D-58.5	1,748	884	847	D-50.6	2,141	1,180	895	D-55.1
MS........	369	299	69	D-81.2	620	354	256	D-57.1	904	397	488	R-54.0
MO........	1,353	728	625	D-53.8	1,766	894	834	D-50.6	[5]2,116	1,116	833	D-52.8
MT........	317	157	160	R-50.5	352	171	149	D-48.7	404	175	212	R-52.4
NE........	587	277	309	R-52.7	571	203	365	R-64.0	662	204	450	R-68.0
NV........	313	144	151	R-48.2	376	138	216	R-57.4	450	173	249	R-55.3
NH........	291	141	149	R-51.2	309	117	180	R-58.2	491	221	247	R-50.3
NJ........	1,827	837	911	R-49.9	2,005	880	1,091	R-54.4	2,823	1,352	1,399	R-49.6
NM........	359	146	214	R-59.5	462	188	263	R-57.1	548	271	261	D-49.4
NY[6].....	3,662	1,830	1,662	D-50.0	4,611	2,213	2,251	R-48.8	5,551	3,041	2,358	D-54.8
NC........	2,011	1,076	935	D-53.5	1,588	681	907	R-57.1	2,514	1,136	1,340	R-53.3
ND........	234	153	81	D-65.2	235	123	106	D-52.3	263	145	114	D-55.1
OH........	3,418	1,807	1,590	D-52.9	3,298	1,328	1,925	R-58.4	4,388	2,031	2,192	R-49.9
OK........	857	519	338	D-60.6	969	368	555	R-57.3	1,180	430	723	R-61.3
OR........	1,053	667	342	D-63.4	1,193	647	499	D-54.2	1,335	724	558	D-54.3
PA........	2,851	1,293	1,552	R-54.5	3,371	1,492	1,831	R-54.3	4,316	2,223	2,038	D-51.5
RI........	347	182	165	D-52.5	342	209	132	D-61.3	360	241	108	D-66.9
SC........	670	383	275	D-57.2	867	313	552	R-63.6	1,057	345	683	R-64.6
SD........	257	174	83	D-67.6	306	183	112	D-59.8	323	120	186	R-57.7
TN........	717	369	289	D-51.5	1,416	615	776	R-54.8	1,784	856	889	R-49.8
TX[7].....	3,278	1,763	1,498	D-53.8	4,120	1,734	2,294	R-55.7	[8]5,219	2,323	2,785	R-53.4
UT........	442	234	191	D-52.9	504	216	252	R-50.0	664	264	386	R-58.2
VT........	210	6	83	[9]I-56.0	211	-	99	[9]I-49.9	255	24	83	I-58.1
VA........	1,153	663	411	D-57.5	1,908	753	1,089	R-57.1	2,199	1,027	1,117	R-50.8
WA........	1,313	696	596	D-53.0	1,687	827	854	R-50.6	2,174	1,130	1,021	D-52.0
WV........	375	251	123	D-67.1	407	269	138	D-66.1	522	458	64	D-87.8
WI........	1,256	597	652	R-51.9	1,459	548	893	R-61.2	2,150	1,012	1,121	R-52.1
WY........	158	71	87	R-55.1	196	81	104	R-53.2	210	86	116	R-55.2

- Represents zero. NA Not available. X Not applicable. [1] Includes vote cast for minor parties. Total for 1996 includes results from 431 districts, including 14 where members were elected without major party opposition (7 won by the Republicans and 7 by the Democrats). In four districts (three in Louisiana and 1 in Florida) candidates ran unopposed and no vote was recorded. [2] Includes vote cast for nonvoting Delegate at Large in District of Columbia, except for 1994 and 1996. [3] State law does not require tabulation of votes for unopposed candidates. [4] In 1990 Districts 8, 10, 12, 13, and 16 were unopposed; in 1994 Districts 4, 10, 13, 14, 18, and 23 were unopposed; in 1996 District 4 was unopposed. [5] Total vote includes 112,472 votes cast for an Independent candidate who was precluded from running as a Republican due to a filing technicality. This candidate won the election and joined Congress as a Republican. [6] Includes votes cast by other endorsing parties for Democratic and Republican candidates. [7] 1990 data are for a general election runoff in one district. 1990 open primary totals—total, 1,186,253; Democratic, 706,004; Republican, 450,867. In 1994 all Representatives won their seats in the open primary. In 1996, Districts 1, 2, and 3 were unopposed. Districts 4 and 6 were contested in the September primary election but the Republican candidate in both won a majority and did not have to run again in the November general election. In Districts 5 and 7 no candidate in the primary won a majority; as a result the top two finishers in the primary ran in the general election. 1996 data are for the open primary. [8] Total includes votes from races held on November 5. Court-ordered redistricting in the Houston area, however, required runoff elections in three districts where no candidate received a majority. These runoffs were held December 5; they are not included in the total vote count reported here. [9] Leading party candidate was Independent.

Source: Congressional Quarterly, Inc., Washington, DC, *America Votes*, biennial (copyright).

No. 465. Vote Cast for United States Representatives, by Major Political Party—Congressional Districts: 1996

[In some states the Democratic and Republican vote includes votes cast for the party candidate by endorsing parties]

STATE AND DISTRICT	DEMOCRATIC CANDIDATE Name	Percent of total	REPUBLICAN CANDIDATE Name	Percent of total	STATE AND DISTRICT	DEMOCRATIC CANDIDATE Name	Percent of total	REPUBLICAN CANDIDATE Name	Percent of total
AL....	(X)	(X)	(X)	(X)	44th..	Rufus	38.5	Bono	57.7
1st..	Womack	33.8	Callahan	64.4	45th..	Alexander	33.2	Rohrabacher	61.0
2d...	Gaines	35.4	Everett	63.2	46th..	Sanchez	46.8	Dornan	45.8
3d...	Little	47.3	Riley	50.4	47th..	Laine	28.9	Cox	65.7
4th..	Wilson	48.2	Aderholt	49.9	48th..	Farrell	26.9	Packard	65.9
5th..	Cramer	55.7	Parker	42.2	49th..	Navarro	41.9	Bilbray	52.6
6th..	Bates	27.3	Bachus	70.9	50th..	Filner	61.9	Baize	32.4
7th..	Hilliard	71.1	Powell	27.1	51st..	Tamerius	28.9	Cunningham	65.1
AK....	Lincoln	36.4	Young	59.4	52d..	Wesley	29.8	Hunter	65.5
AZ....	(X)	(X)	(X)	(X)	CO....	(X)	(X)	(X)	(X)
1st..	Cox	39.8	Salmon	60.2	1st..	DeGette	56.9	Rogers	40.2
2d...	Pastor	65.0	Buster	30.8	2d...	Skaggs	57.0	Miller	38.3
3d...	Schneider	33.5	Stump	66.5	3d...	Gurule	31.1	McInnis	68.9
4th..	Milton	33.2	Shadegg	66.8	4th..	Kelley	38.0	Schaffer	56.1
5th..	Nelson	25.9	Kolbe	68.7	5th..	Robinson	28.1	Hefley	71.9
6th..	Owens	46.6	Hayworth	47.6	6th..	Fitz-Gerald	37.8	Schaefer	62.2
AR....	(X)	(X)	(X)	(X)	CT....	(X)	(X)	(X)	(X)
1st..	Berry	52.8	Dupwe	44.3	1st..	Kennelly	73.5	Sleath	24.9
2d...	Snyder	52.3	Cummins	47.7	2d...	Gejdenson	51.6	Munster	44.9
3d...	Henry	41.8	Hutchinson	55.7	3d...	DeLauro	71.3	Coppola	28.1
4th..	Tolliver	36.5	Dickey	63.5	4th..	Finch	37.6	Shays	60.5
CA....	(X)	(X)	(X)	(X)	5th..	Maloney	52.0	Franks	45.9
1st..	Alioto	43.5	Riggs	49.6	6th..	Koskoff	48.9	Johnson	49.6
2d...	Braden	33.7	Herger	60.8	DE....	Williams	27.5	Castle	69.5
3d...	Fazio	53.5	LeFever	41.1	FL....	(X)	(X)	(X)	(X)
4th..	Hirning	36.1	Doolittle	60.5	1st..	Beck	27.4	Scarborough	72.5
5th..	Matsui	70.4	Dinsmore	26.1	2d...	Boyd	59.4	Sutton	40.5
6th..	Woolsey	61.8	Hughes	34.0	3d...	Brown	61.2	Fields	38.8
7th..	Miller	71.8	Reece	22.3	4th..	(1)	(1)	Fowler	(NA)
8th..	Pelosi	84.3	Raimondo	12.4	5th..	Thurman	61.7	Gentry	38.3
9th..	Dellums	77.0	Wright	18.5	6th..	O'Brien	32.8	Stearns	67.2
10th..	Tauscher	48.6	Baker	47.2	7th..	Stuart	37.9	Mica	62.0
11th..	Silva	36.2	Pombo	59.3	8th..	Krulick	32.5	McCollum	67.5
12th..	Lantos	71.7	Jenkins	23.7	9th..	Provenzano	31.3	Bilirakis	68.7
13th..	Stark	65.2	Fay	30.4	10th..	Green	33.4	Young	66.6
14th..	Eshoo	64.9	Brink	31.1	11th..	Davis	57.9	Sharpe	42.1
15th..	Lane	34.8	Campbell	58.5	12th..	Canady	38.4	Canady	61.6
16th..	Lofgren	65.7	Wojslaw	30.2	13th..	Gordon	35.6	Miller	64.3
17th..	Farr	58.9	Brown	37.8	14th..	Nolan	26.5	Goss	73.5
18th..	Condit	65.7	Conrad	31.8	15th..	Byron	42.9	Weldon	51.4
19th..	Barile	28.3	Radanovich	66.6	16th..	Stuber	36.0	Foley	64.0
20th..	Dooley	56.5	Harvey	39.1	17th..	Meek	88.8	Rolle	11.2
21st..	Vollmer	26.5	Thomas	65.8	18th..	(1)	(1)	Ros-Lehtinen	100.0
22d..	Capps	48.4	Seastrand	44.2	19th..	Wexler	65.6	Kennedy	34.4
23d..	Unruhe	35.1	Gallegly	59.6	20th..	Deutsch	65.0	Jacobs	35.0
24th..	Sherman	49.4	Sybert	43.6	21st..	(1)	(1)	Diaz-Balart	100.0
25th..	Trautman	33.2	McKeon	62.4	22d..	Cooper	38.1	Shaw	61.9
26th..	Berman	65.9	Glass	28.6	23d..	Hastings	73.5	Brown	26.5
27th..	Kahn	43.2	Rogan	50.2	GA....	(X)	(X)	(X)	(X)
28th..	Levering	36.9	Dreier	60.7	1st..	Kaszans	31.8	Kingston	68.2
29th..	Waxman	67.6	Stepanek	24.6	2d...	Bishop	54.0	Ealum	46.0
30th..	Becerra	72.3	Parker	18.7	3d...	Chafin	38.9	Collins	61.1
31st..	Martinez	67.5	Flores	28.0	4th..	McKinney	57.8	Mitnick	42.2
32d..	Dixon	82.4	Ardito	12.4	5th..	Lewis	100.0	(1)	(1)
33d..	Roybal-Allard	82.1	Leonard	14.1	6th..	Coles	42.2	Gingrich	57.8
34th..	Torres	68.4	Nunez	26.6	7th..	Watts	42.2	Barr	57.8
35th..	Waters	85.5	Carlson	12.1	8th..	Wiggins	47.4	Chambliss	52.6
36th..	Harman	52.5	Brooks	43.9	9th..	Poston	34.5	Deal	65.5
37th..	Millender-McDonald	85.0	Voetee	15.0	10th..	Bell	47.7	Norwood	52.3
38th..	Zbur	42.7	Horn	52.6	11th..	Stephenson	35.7	Linder	64.3
39th..	Davis	31.9	Royce	62.8	HI....	(X)	(X)	(X)	(X)
40th..	Conaway	29.0	Lewis	64.9	1st..	Abercrombie	50.4	Swindle	46.5
41st..	Waldron	33.0	Kim	58.5	2d...	Mink	60.3	Pico	30.8
42d..	Brown	50.5	Wilde	49.5	ID....	(X)	(X)	(X)	(X)
43d..	Kimbrough	37.9	Calvert	54.7	1st..	Williams	47.5	Chenoweth	50.0
					2d...	Seidi	29.5	Crapo	68.8

See footnotes at end of table.

No. 465. Vote Cast for United States Representatives, by Major Political Party—Congressional Districts: 1996—Continued

[See headnote, p. 284]

STATE AND DIS-TRICT	DEMOCRATIC CANDIDATE Name	Percent of total	REPUBLICAN CANDIDATE Name	Per-cent of total	STATE AND DIS-TRICT	DEMOCRATIC CANDIDATE Name	Percent of total	REPUBLICAN CANDIDATE Name	Per-cent of total
IL.....	(X)......	(X)	(X)......	(X)	4th...	Frank.....	71.6	Raymond.....	28.3
1st...	Rush	85.7	Naughton.	12.6	5th...	Meehan	99.1	(X)......	(X)
2d...	Jackson	94.1	(1)	(1)	6th...	Tierney.	48.2	Torkildsen	48.0
3d...	Lipinski.	65.3	Nalepa	32.0	7th...	Markey.	69.8	Long	30.1
4th...	Gutierrez	93.6	(1)	(1)	8th...	Kennedy	84.3	Hyde.	15.6
5th...	Blagojevich	64.1	Flanagan	35.9	9th...	Moakley	72.2	Gryska	27.7
6th...	de la Rosa	33.4	Hyde.	64.3	10th...	Delahunt.	54.3	Teague	41.7
7th...	Davis	82.6	Borow.	15.0	MI.....	(X)	(X)	(X)	(X)
8th...	Hull	36.1	Crane	62.2	1st...	Stupak	70.7	Carr	27.2
9th...	Yates	63.4	Walsh	36.6	2d...	Kruszynski	33.0	Hoekstra	65.3
10th...	Torf	30.9	Porter	69.1	3d...	Flory	29.5	Ehlers.	68.6
11th...	Balanoff	48.2	Weller	51.8	4th...	Donaldson	32.7	Camp	65.5
12th...	Costello	71.6	Hunter.	26.6	5th...	Barcia	70.0	Sims	28.2
13th...	Hynes	40.1	Fawell	59.9	6th...	Annen	30.7	Upton	67.7
14th...	Mains.	35.6	Hastert	64.4	7th...	Tunnicliff.	42.9	Smith	55.0
15th...	Prussing	42.7	Ewing	57.3	8th...	Stabenow	53.8	Chrysler.	44.1
16th...	Lee	39.7	Manzullo	60.3	9th...	Kildee	59.2	Nowak.	38.8
17th...	Evans	51.9	Baker	47.3	10th...	Bonior	54.4	Heintz	43.6
18th...	Curran	40.7	LaHood	59.3	11th...	Frumin	35.9	Knollenberg	61.2
19th...	Poshard	66.7	Winters	31.8	12th...	Levin	57.4	Pappageorge	40.5
20th...	Hoffman	49.7	Shimkus	50.3	13th...	Rivers	56.6	Fitzsimmons.	41.3
IN.....	(X)	(X)	(X)	(X)	14th...	Conyers	85.9	Ashe	12.1
1st...	Visclosky	69.2	Petyo	29.2	15th...	Kilpatrick.	88.4	Hume	9.8
2d...	Carmichael	40.0	McIntosh	57.8	16th...	Dingell	62.0	DeSana.	35.7
3d...	Roemer	57.9	Zakas	40.9	MN.....	(X)	(X)	(X)	(X)
4th...	Houseman	39.3	Souder	58.4	1st...	Rieder	47.2	Gutknecht	52.7
5th...	Clark	35.7	Buyer	61.9	2d...	Minge.	54.9	Revier.	41.1
6th...	Dillard-Trammell	23.0	Burton.	75.0	3d...	Leino	29.8	Ramstad	70.1
7th...	Hellmann	34.6	Pease.	62.0	4th...	Vento	57.0	Newinski	36.8
8th...	Weinzapfel	48.3	Hostettler	50.0	5th...	Sabo	64.3	Uldrich	28.5
9th...	Hamilton	56.5	Leising	42.5	6th...	Luther	55.8	Jude	44.0
10th...	Carson.	52.9	Blankenbaker	44.8	7th...	Peterson.	67.9	McKigney.	31.8
IA.....	(X)	(X)	(X)	(X)	8th...	Oberstar.	67.3	Larson	25.2
1st...	Rush	45.6	Leach	52.8	MS.....	(X)	(X)	(X)	(X)
2d...	Smith	45.9	Nussle.	53.4	1st...	Boyd	30.6	Wicker.	67.6
3d...	Boswell	49.4	Mahaffey	47.6	2d...	Thompson	59.6	Covington	38.0
4th...	McBurney	46.7	Ganske	52.0	3d...	Eaves	36.5	Pickering	61.4
5th...	Smith	33.6	Latham	65.4	4th...	Antoine	36.4	Parker.	61.2
KS.....	(X)	(X)	(X)	(X)	5th...	Taylor.	58.3	Dollar	40.1
1st...	Divine	24.5	Moran	73.5	MO.....	(X)	(X)	(X)	(X)
2d...	Frieden.	45.5	Ryun.	52.2	1st...	Clay.	70.2	O'Sullivan	27.6
3d...	Hancock	45.4	Snowbarger	49.8	2d...	Horn	37.1	Talent	61.3
4th...	Rathbun	46.6	Tiahrt	50.1	3d...	Gephardt	59.0	Wheelehan	38.8
KY.....	(X)	(X)	(X)	(X)	4th...	Skelton.	63.8	Phelps	33.9
1st...	Null	46.4	Whitfield	53.6	5th...	McCarthy	67.4	Bennett	28.9
2d...	Wright	41.9	Lewis	58.1	6th...	Danner.	68.6	Bailey	29.3
3d...	Ward	49.7	Northrup	50.3	7th...	Bamberger	31.6	Blunt.	64.9
4th...	Bowman	31.6	Bunning.	68.4	8th...	Firebaugh	37.3	Emerson [5]	50.5
5th...	(1)	(1)	Rogers	100.0	9th...	Volkmer	47.0	Hulshof	49.4
6th...	Baesler.	55.7	Fletcher.	44.3	MT....	Yellowtail	43.2	Hill	52.4
LA [2]...	(X)	(X)	(X)	(X)	NE.....	(X)	(X)	(X)	(X)
1st...	(X)	(X)	Livingston [3]	(X)	1st...	Combs	29.9	Bereuter	70.0
2d...	Jefferson [3]	(X)	(X)	(X)	2d...	Davis	40.1	Christensen	56.8
3d...	(X)	(X)	Tauzin [3]	(X)	3d...	Webster	22.5	Barrett.	77.4
4th...	(X)	(X)	McCrery [3]	(X)	NV.....	(X)	(X)	(X)	(X)
5th...	Thompson	41.7	Cooksey	58.3	1st...	Coffin	43.5	Ensign	50.1
6th...	(X)	(X)	Baker [3]	(X)	2d...	Wilson	35.3	Gibbons	58.6
7th...	John [4]	53.1	(1)	(1)	NH.....	(X)	(X)	(X)	(X)
ME.....	(X)	(X)	(X)	(X)	1st...	Keefe.	46.6	Sununu	50.0
1st...	Allen	55.3	Longley	44.7	2d...	Arnesen	43.5	Bass.	50.5
2d...	Baldacci	71.9	Young	24.8	NJ.....	(X)	(X)	(X)	(X)
MD.....	(X)	(X)	(X)	(X)	1st...	Andrews	76.1	Suplee	21.0
1st...	Eastaugh	38.4	Gilchrest	61.6	2d...	Katz.	38.0	LoBiondo	60.3
2d...	DeJuliis	38.2	Ehrlich.	61.8	3d...	Leonardi	33.3	Saxton	64.2
3d...	Cardin	67.3	McDonough	32.7	4th...	Meara	33.7	Smith	63.6
4th...	Wynn	85.2	Kimble.	14.8	5th...	Auer	24.8	Roukema	71.3
5th...	Hoyer.	56.9	Morgan	43.1	6th...	Pallone	61.3	Corodemus	36.1
6th...	Crawford.	43.2	Bartlett	56.8	7th...	Lerner	41.8	Franks.	55.4
7th...	Cummings	83.5	Kondner	16.5	8th...	Pascrell	51.2	Martini.	48.0
8th...	Mooers.	38.6	Morella	61.2	9th...	Rothman	55.8	Donovan	42.2
MA.....	(X)	(X)	(X)	(X)	10th...	Payne	84.2	Williams.	14.6
1st...	Olver	52.7	Swift	47.2	11th...	Evangel	30.9	Frelinghuy-sen.	66.3
2d...	Neal.	71.7	Steele	21.9	12th...	Del Vecchio.	46.7	Pappas	50.4
3d...	McGovern	52.9	Blute.	45.4	13th...	Menendez.	78.8	Munoz.	17.4

See footnotes at end of table.

No. 465. Vote Cast for United States Representatives, by Major Political Party—Congressional Districts: 1996—Continued

[See headnote, p. 284]

STATE AND DISTRICT	DEMOCRATIC CANDIDATE Name	Percent of total	REPUBLICAN CANDIDATE Name	Percent of total	STATE AND DISTRICT	DEMOCRATIC CANDIDATE Name	Percent of total	REPUBLICAN CANDIDATE Name	Percent of total
NM....	(X)	(X)	(X)	(X)	13th..	Brown	60.5	Blair	35.9
1st...	Wertheim	37.1	Schiff	56.6	14th..	Sawyer	54.3	George	41.7
2d...	Baca	44.1	Skeen	55.9	15th..	Arnebeck	29.2	Pryce	70.8
3d...	Richardson	67.2	Redmond	30.5	16th..	Burkhart	28.0	Regula	68.7
NY....	(X)	(X)	(X)	(X)	17th..	Traficant	91.0	(1)	(1)
1st...	Bredes	45.3	Forbes	54.7	18th..	Burch	46.3	Ney	50.2
2d...	Herman	33.2	Lazio	64.2	19th..	Coyne	41.0	LaTourette	54.7
3d...	LaMagna	42.1	King	55.3	OK....	(X)	(X)	(X)	(X)
4th...	McCarthy	57.5	Frisa	40.5	1st...	Amen	27.6	Largent	68.2
5th...	Ackerman	63.7	Lally	35.0	2d...	Johnson	44.5	Coburn	55.5
6th...	Flake	84.9	Misir	15.1	3d...	Roberts	45.2	Watkins	51.4
7th...	Manton	71.1	Birtley	28.9	4th...	Crocker	39.9	Watts	57.7
8th...	Nadler	82.3	Benjamin	16.2	5th...	Forsythe	27.1	Istook	69.7
9th...	Schumer	74.8	Verga	21.3	6th...	Barby	36.1	Lucas	63.9
10th..	Towns	91.3	Parker	7.9	OR....	(X)	(X)	(X)	(X)
11th..	Owens	92.0	Hayle	8.0	1st...	Furse	51.9	Witt	45.3
12th..	Velazquez	84.6	Prado	13.6	2d...	Dugan	36.5	Smith	61.7
13th..	Butler	34.7	Molinari	61.6	3d...	Blumenauer	66.9	Bruun	26.3
14th..	Maloney	72.4	Livingston	23.7	4th...	DeFazio	65.7	Newkirk	28.4
15th..	Rangel	91.3	Adams	4.8	5th...	Hooley	51.2	Bunn	46.0
16th..	Serrano	96.3	Torres	2.9	PA....	(X)	(X)	(X)	(X)
17th..	Engel	85.0	McCarthy	13.3	1st...	Foglietta	87.5	Cella	12.5
18th..	Lowey	63.6	Katsorhis	32.0	2d...	Fattah	88.0	Murphy	12.0
19th..	Klein	39.4	Kelly	46.3	3d...	Borski	68.9	McColgan	31.1
20th..	Aggarwal	37.6	Gilman	57.1	4th...	Klink	64.2	Adametz	35.8
21st..	McNulty	66.1	Norman	26.9	5th...	Rudy	39.7	Peterson	60.3
22d...	James	39.5	Solomon	60.5	6th...	Holden	58.6	Leinbach	40.7
23d...	Hapanowicz	26.0	Boehlert	64.3	7th...	Innelli	32.4	Weldon	66.9
24th..	Ravenscroft	25.0	McHugh	71.1	8th...	Murray	35.3	Greenwood	59.1
25th..	Mack	44.9	Walsh	55.1	9th...	Kemmler	26.3	Shuster	73.7
26th..	Hinchey	55.2	Wittig	42.3	10th..	Cullen	36.2	McDade	59.8
27th..	Fricano	40.1	Paxon	59.9	11th..	Kanjorski	68.0	Urban	32.0
28th..	Slaughter	57.3	Rosenberger	42.7	12th..	Murtha	70.0	Choby	30.0
29th..	LaFalce	62.0	Callard	38.0	13th..	Hoeffel	48.9	Fox	48.9
30th..	Pordum	45.2	Quinn	54.8	14th..	Coyne	60.7	Ravotti	39.0
31st..	MacBain	25.4	Houghton	71.6	15th..	McHale	54.8	Kilbanks	41.3
NC....	(X)	(X)	(X)	(X)	16th..	Blaine	37.5	Pitts	59.4
1st...	Clayton	65.9	Tyler	33.1	17th..	Kettl	27.8	Gekas	72.2
2d...	Etheridge	52.5	Funderburk	45.7	18th..	Doyle	56.0	Fawcett	40.4
3d...	Parrott	36.5	Jones	62.7	19th..	Chronister	35.9	Goodling	62.6
4th...	Price	54.4	Heineman	43.8	20th..	Mascara	53.9	McCormick	46.1
5th...	Cashion	35.4	Burr	62.1	21st..	DiNicola	49.3	English	50.7
6th...	Costley	25.4	Coble	73.4	RI....	(X)	(X)	(X)	(X)
7th...	McIntyre	52.9	Caster	45.8	1st...	Kennedy	69.4	Cicione	28.0
8th...	Hefner	55.2	Blackwood	43.7	2d...	Weygand	64.5	Wild	31.7
9th...	Daisley	35.4	Myrick	63.0	SC....	(X)	(X)	(X)	(X)
10th..	Neill	28.7	Ballenger	70.0	1st...	(1)	(1)	Sanford	96.4
11th..	Ferguson	40.0	Taylor	58.3	2d...	(1)	(1)	Spence	89.8
12th..	Watt	71.5	Martino	26.7	3d...	Dorn	38.7	Graham	60.3
ND....	Pomeroy	55.1	Cramer	43.2	4th...	Curry	27.8	Inglis	70.9
OH....	(X)	(X)	(X)	(X)	5th...	Spratt	54.1	Bigham	45.3
1st...	Longabaugh	43.4	Chabot	54.2	6th...	Clyburn	69.4	McLeod	30.0
2d...	Chandler	22.6	Portman	72.0	SD....	Weiland	37.0	Thune	57.7
3d...	Hall	63.6	Westbrock	33.3	TN....	(X)	(X)	(X)	(X)
4th...	McClain	30.3	Oxley	64.8	1st...	Smith	32.3	Jenkins	64.8
5th...	Saunders	34.1	Gillmor	61.1	2d...	Smith	28.6	Duncan	70.7
6th...	Strickland	51.3	Cremeans	48.7	3d...	Jolly	42.5	Wamp	56.3
7th...	Blain	26.4	Hobson	67.8	4th...	Stewart	41.2	Hilleary	57.9
8th...	Kitchen	26.1	Boehner	70.3	5th...	Clement	72.4	Edmondson	23.8
9th...	Kaptur	77.1	Whitman	20.8	6th...	Gordon	54.4	Gill	41.6
10th..	Kucinich	49.1	Hoke	46.3	7th...	Trotter	34.6	Bryant	64.1
11th..	Stokes	81.2	Sykora	15.2	8th...	Tanner	67.3	Watson	29.9
12th..	Ruccia	33.2	Kasich	63.9	9th...	Ford	61.1	DeBerry	37.3

See footnotes at end of table.

No. 465. Vote Cast for United States Representatives, by Major Political Party— Congressional Districts: 1996

[See headnote, p. 284]

STATE AND DIS-TRICT	DEMOCRATIC CANDIDATE Name	Percent of total	REPUBLICAN CANDIDATE Name	Per-cent of total	STATE AND DIS-TRICT	DEMOCRATIC CANDIDATE Name	Percent of total	REPUBLICAN CANDIDATE Name	Per-cent of total
TX	(X)........	(X)	(X)........	(X)	**VA**	(X)........	(X)	(X)........	(X)
1st...	Sandlin.....	51.6	Merritt......	46.7	1st...	(1)........	(1)	Bateman.....	99.0
2d...	Turner.....	52.2	Babin.......	45.6	2d...	Pickett.....	64.8	Tate......	35.1
3d...	Cole......	24.4	Johnson.....	73.0	3d...	Scott......	82.1	Holland.....	17.9
4th...	Hall......	63.8	Hall.......	34.3	4th...	Sisisky.....	78.6	Zevgolis.....	21.4
5th...	Pouland....	46.9	Sessions.....	53.1	5th...	Goode Jr....	60.8	Landrith.....	35.8
6th...	(1)........	(1)	Barton......	77.1	6th...	Grey......	30.8	Goodlatte....	67.0
7th...	Siegmund....	15.1	Archer......	81.4	7th...	Slayton.....	20.3	Bliley......	75.1
8th...	Newman [6]	13.6	Brady [7]	41.5	8th...	Moran.....	66.4	Otey......	28.1
9th...	Lampson [8]	44.1	Stockman....	46.4	9th...	Boucher....	65.0	Muldoon.....	30.7
10th...	Doggett.....	56.2	Doggett.....	41.4	10th...	Weinberg....	25.2	Wolf......	72.0
11th...	Edwards....	56.8	Mathis......	42.4	11th...	Horton.....	34.5	Davis III....	64.1
12th...	Parmer.....	41.0	Granger.....	57.8	**WA**	(X)........	(X)	(X)........	(X)
13th...	Silverman....	32.3	Thornberry...	66.9	1st...	Coopersmith..	46.3	White......	53.7
14th...	Morris.....	47.6	Paul.......	51.1	2d...	Quigley.....	47.8	Metcalf.....	48.5
15th...	Hinojosa....	62.3	Haughey....	36.7	3d...	Baird......	49.8	Smith......	50.2
16th...	Reyes......	70.6	Ledesma....	27.6	4th...	Locke......	47.0	Hastings....	53.0
17th...	Stenholm...	51.6	Izzard......	47.4	5th...	Olson......	44.4	Nethercutt...	55.6
18th...	Jackson-Lee..	77.1	White......	10.1	6th...	Dicks......	65.9	Tinsley.....	30.2
19th...	Sawyer.....	19.6	Combest.....	80.4	7th...	McDermott...	81.0	Kleschen....	19.0
20th...	Gonzalez....	63.7	Walker.....	34.4	8th...	Little......	34.6	Dunn......	65.4
21st...	Wharton....	22.4	Smith......	76.4	9th...	Smith......	50.1	Tate......	47.3
22d...	Cunningham..	31.9	DeLay......	68.1	**WV**	(X)........	(X)	(X)........	(X)
23d...	Jones......	36.4	Bonilla......	61.8	1st...	Mollohan....	100.0	(1)........	(1)
24th...	Frost......	55.7	Harrison [10]	39.1	2d...	Wise......	68.9	Morris.....	31.1
25th...	Bentsen [9]	34.0	McKenna [10]	17.1	3d...	Rahall.....	100.0	(1)........	(1)
26th...	Frankel.....	26.4	Armey......	73.6	**WI**	(X)........	(X)	(X)........	(X)
27th...	Ortiz......	64.6	Gardner.....	33.8	1st...	Spottswood..	49.0	Neumann....	50.9
28th...	Tejeda.....	75.4	Cude......	23.4	2d...	Soglin......	41.0	Klug......	57.4
29th...	Green [11]	67.5	Rodriguez....	31.0	3d...	Kind......	52.0	Harsdorf....	47.8
30th...	Johnson [11]	54.6	Hendry [12]	18.3	4th...	Kleczka.....	57.6	Reynolds....	42.2
UT	(X)........	(X)	(X)........	(X)	5th...	Barrett.....	73.3	Melotik.....	24.6
1st...	Sanders.....	30.0	Hansen.....	68.3	6th...	Lindskoog....	23.9	Petri......	73.0
2d...	Anderson....	42.4	Cook......	55.0	7th...	Obey......	57.0	West......	42.9
3d...	Orton......	47.3	Cannon.....	51.1	8th...	Johnson.....	52.0	Prosser.....	47.9
					9th...	Brenholt....	25.5	Sensenbrenner.	74.4
VT[13]	(X)........	9.4	Sweetser.....	32.6	**WY**	Maxfield....	40.8	Cubin.......	55.2

NA Not available.   X Not applicable.   [1] No candidate.   [2] Louisiana holds an open-primary election with candidates from all parties running on the same ballot. Any candidate who receives a majority is elected; if no candidate receives 50 percent, there is a run-off election in November between the top two finishers.   [3] Candidate listed won seat in open-primary.   [4] There were two Democratic candidates; Hunter Lundy received 46.9 percent of Democratic votes.   [5] Jo Ann Emerson ran as an independent but caucused in the 105th Congress with the Democrats.   [6] There were two Democratic candidates; Robert Musemeche received 6.0 percent of Democratic votes.   [7] There were two Republican candidates; Gene Fontenot received 38.9 percent of Republican votes.   [8] There were two Democratic candidates; Geraldine Sam received 9.4 percent of Democratic votes.   [9] There were two Democratic candidates; Beverly Clark received 16.9 percent of Democratic votes.   [10] There were seven additional Republican candidates who received a total of 31.7 percent of Republican votes.   [11] There were two additional Democratic candidates who received a total of 15.7 percent of Democratic candidates.   [12] There were two Republican candidates; Lisa Kitterman received 6.9 percent of Republican votes.   [13] The winning candidate was Bernard Sanders, an Independent, who received 49.9 percent of the vote.

Source: Congressional Quarterly Inc., *Congressional Quarterly Weekly Report* (copyright).

No. 466. Composition of Congress, by Political Party: 1971 to 1996

[D=Democratic, R=Republican. Data for beginning of first session of each Congress (as of January 3), except as noted. Excludes vacancies at beginning of session]

YEAR	Party and President	Congress	HOUSE Majority party	HOUSE Minority party	HOUSE Other	SENATE Majority party	SENATE Minority party	SENATE Other
1971 [1]	R (Nixon)...........	92d...	D-254	R-180	-	D-54	R-44	2
1973 [1][2]	R (Nixon)...........	93d...	D-239	R-192	1	D-56	R-42	2
1975 [3]	R (Ford)...........	94th..	D-291	R-144	-	D-60	R-37	2
1977 [4]	D (Carter)..........	95th..	D-292	R-143	-	D-61	R-38	1
1979 [4]	D (Carter)..........	96th..	D-276	R-157	-	D-58	R-41	1
1981 [4]	R (Reagan).........	97th..	D-243	R-192	-	R-53	D-46	1
1983	R (Reagan).........	98th..	D-269	R-165	-	R-54	D-46	-
1985	R (Reagan).........	99th..	D-252	R-182	-	R-53	D-47	-
1987	R (Reagan).........	100th.	D-258	R-177	-	D-55	R-45	-
1989	R (Bush)..........	101st.	D-259	R-174	-	D-55	R-45	-
1991 [5]	R (Bush)..........	102d..	D-267	R-167	1	D-56	R-44	-
1993 [5]	D (Clinton).........	103d..	D-258	R-176	1	D-57	R-43	-
1995 [5]	D (Clinton).........	104th.	R-230	D-204	1	R-52	D-48	-
1996 [5][6]	D (Clinton).........	104th.	R-236	D-197	1	R-53	D-46	-

- Represents zero.   [1] Senate had one Independent and one Conservative-Republican.   [2] House had one Independent-Democrat.   [3] Senate had one Independent, one Conservative-Republican, and one undecided (New Hampshire).   [4] Senate had one Independent.   [5] House had one Independent-Socialist.   [6] As of beginning of second session.
Source: U.S. Congress, Joint Committee on Printing, *Congressional Directory*, annual; beginning 1977, biennial.

No. 467. Composition of Congress, by Political Party Affiliation—States: 1989 to 1997

[Figures are for the beginning of the first session (as of January 3), except as noted. Dem.=Democratic; Rep.=Republican]

STATE	REPRESENTATIVES								SENATORS							
	101st Cong.,[1] 1989		102d Cong.,[2] 1991		103rd Cong.,[2] 1993		104th Cong.,[2 3 4] 1997		101st Cong., 1989		102d Cong., 1991		103rd Cong., 1993		104th Cong.,[3 5] 1997	
	Dem.	Rep.	Dem.	Rep.	Dem.	Rep.	Dem.	Rep.	Dem.	Rep.	Dem.	Rep.	Dem.	Rep.	Dem.	Rep.
U.S.	259	174	267	167	258	176	197	236	55	45	56	44	57	43	46	53
AL.	4	2	5	2	4	3	2	5	2	-	2	-	2	-	-	2
AK.	-	1	-	1	-	1	-	1	-	2	-	2	-	2	-	2
AZ.	1	4	1	4	3	3	1	5	1	1	1	1	1	1	-	2
AR.	3	1	3	1	2	2	2	2	2	-	2	-	2	-	1	1
CA.	27	18	26	19	30	22	29	23	1	1	1	1	2	-	2	-
CO	3	3	3	3	2	4	2	4	1	1	1	1	1	1	-	2
CT.	3	3	3	3	3	3	4	2	2	-	2	-	2	-	2	-
DE.	1	-	1	-	-	1	-	1	1	1	1	1	1	1	1	1
FL.	10	9	9	10	10	13	8	15	1	1	1	1	1	1	1	1
GA.	9	1	9	1	7	4	3	8	2	-	2	-	1	1	1	1
HI	1	1	2	-	2	-	2	-	2	-	2	-	2	-	2	-
ID	1	1	2	-	1	1	-	2	-	2	-	2	-	2	-	2
IL	14	8	15	7	12	8	10	10	2	-	2	-	2	-	2	-
IN	6	3	8	2	7	3	4	6	-	2	-	2	-	2	-	2
IA	2	4	2	4	1	4	1	4	1	1	1	1	1	1	1	1
KS.	2	3	2	3	2	2	-	4	-	2	-	2	-	2	-	2
KY.	4	3	4	3	4	2	1	5	1	1	1	1	1	1	1	1
LA.	4	4	4	4	4	3	2	5	2	-	2	-	2	-	2	-
ME.	1	1	1	1	1	1	2	-	1	1	1	1	1	1	-	2
MD.	6	2	5	3	4	4	4	4	2	-	2	-	2	-	2	-
MA.	10	1	10	1	8	2	10	-	2	-	2	-	2	-	2	-
MI	11	7	11	7	10	6	10	6	2	-	2	-	2	-	1	1
MN.	5	3	6	2	6	2	6	2	-	2	1	1	1	1	1	1
MS.	4	1	5	-	5	-	2	3	-	2	-	2	-	2	-	2
MO.	5	4	6	3	6	3	5	4	-	2	-	2	-	2	-	2
MT.	1	1	1	1	1	-	-	1	1	1	1	1	1	1	1	1
NE.	1	2	1	2	1	2	-	3	2	-	2	-	2	-	1	1
NV.	1	1	1	1	1	1	-	2	2	-	2	-	2	-	1	1
NH	-	2	1	1	1	1	-	2	-	2	-	2	-	2	-	2
NJ.	8	6	8	6	7	6	6	7	2	-	2	-	2	-	2	-
NM	1	2	1	2	1	2	-	3	1	1	1	1	1	1	1	1
NY.	21	13	21	13	18	13	18	13	1	1	1	1	1	1	1	1
NC.	8	3	7	4	8	4	6	6	1	1	1	1	-	2	-	2
ND	1	-	1	-	1	-	1	-	2	-	2	-	2	-	2	-
OH	11	10	11	10	10	9	8	11	2	-	2	-	2	-	1	1
OK	4	2	4	2	4	2	-	6	1	1	1	1	1	1	-	2
OR	3	2	4	1	4	1	4	1	-	2	-	2	-	2	1	1
PA.	12	11	11	12	11	10	11	10	-	2	-	2	1	1	1	1
RI	-	2	1	1	1	1	2	-	1	1	1	1	1	1	1	1
SC.	4	2	4	2	3	3	2	4	1	1	1	1	1	1	1	1
SD.	1	-	1	-	1	-	-	1	1	1	1	1	1	1	2	-
TN.	6	3	6	3	6	3	4	5	2	-	2	-	2	-	-	2
TX.	19	8	19	8	21	9	17	13	1	1	1	1	1	1	-	2
UT.	1	2	2	1	2	1	-	3	-	2	-	2	-	2	-	2
VT.	-	1	-	-	-	-	-	-	1	1	1	1	1	1	1	1
VA.	5	5	6	4	7	4	6	5	1	1	1	1	1	1	1	1
WA.	5	3	5	3	8	1	3	6	1	1	1	1	1	1	1	1
WV.	4	-	4	-	3	-	3	-	2	-	2	-	2	-	2	-
WI	5	4	4	5	4	5	5	4	1	1	1	1	2	-	2	-
WY	-	1	-	1	-	1	-	1	-	2	-	2	-	2	-	2

- Represents zero.   [1] Alabama and Indiana had one vacancy each.   [2] Vermont had one Independent-Socialist Representative.   [3] As of beginning of second session.   [4] California had one vacancy.   [5] Oregon had one vacancy.

Source: U.S. Congress, Joint Committee on Printing, *Congressional Directory,* biennial; and unpublished data.

No. 468. Members of Congress—Incumbents Re-elected: 1964 to 1996

YEAR	REPRESENTATIVES						SENATORS					
	Retire-ments[1]	Incumbent candidates					Retire-ments[1]	Incumbent candidates				
		Total	Re-elected		Defeated in—			Total	Re-elected		Defeated in—	
			Num-ber	Per-cent of candi-dates	Pri-mary	General election			Num-ber	Per-cent of candi-dates	Pri-mary	General election
PRESIDENTIAL-YEAR ELECTIONS												
1964	33	397	344	86.6	8	45	2	33	28	84.8	1	4
1968	23	409	396	96.8	4	9	6	28	20	71.4	4	4
1972	40	390	365	93.6	12	13	6	27	20	74.1	2	5
1976	47	384	368	95.8	3	13	8	25	16	64.0	-	9
1980	34	398	361	90.7	6	31	5	29	16	55.2	4	9
1984	22	411	392	95.4	3	16	4	29	26	89.7	-	3
1988	23	409	402	98.3	1	6	6	27	23	85.2	-	4
1992	65	368	325	88.3	[2]19	[3]24	7	28	23	82.1	1	4
1996	50	384	361	94.0	2	21	13	21	19	90.5	1	1
MIDTERM ELECTIONS												
1966	22	411	362	88.1	8	41	3	32	28	87.5	3	1
1970	29	401	379	94.5	10	12	4	31	24	77.4	1	6
1974	43	391	343	87.7	8	40	7	27	23	85.2	2	2
1978	49	382	358	93.7	5	19	10	25	15	60.0	3	7
1982	40	393	354	90.1	[2]10	29	3	30	28	93.3	-	2
1986	40	394	385	97.7	3	6	6	28	21	75.0	-	7
1990	27	406	390	96.1	1	15	3	32	31	96.9	-	1
1994	48	387	349	90.2	4	34	9	26	24	92.3	-	2

- Represents zero. [1] Does not include persons who died or resigned before the election. [2] Number of incumbents defeated in primaries by other incumbents due to redistricting: six in 1982 and four in 1992. [3] Five incumbents defeated in general election by other incumbents due to redistricting.

Source: Ornstein, Norman J., Thomas E. Mann, and Michael J. Malbin, *Vital Statistics on Congress, 1993-1994*, Congressional Quarterly, Inc., Washington, DC, 1995; Congressional Quarterly, Inc., Washington, DC, *America Votes*, biennial (copyright).

No. 469. Members of Congress—Selected Characteristics: 1981 to 1995

[As of beginning of first session of each Congress, (January 3). Figures for Representatives exclude vacancies]

MEMBERS OF CONGRESS AND YEAR	Male	Fe-male	Black[1]	Asian, Pacific Islan-der[2]	His-panic[3]	AGE[4] (in years)					SENIORITY[5]				
						Under 40	40 to 49	50 to 59	60 to 69	70 and over	Less than 2 yrs.	2 to 9 yrs.	10 to 19 yrs.	20 to 29 yrs.	30 yrs. or more
REPRESENTATIVES															
97th Cong., 1981 . . .	416	19	17	3	6	94	142	132	54	13	77	231	96	23	8
98th Cong., 1983 . . .	413	21	21	3	8	86	145	132	57	14	83	224	88	28	11
99th Cong., 1985 . . .	412	22	20	3	10	71	154	131	59	19	49	237	104	34	10
100th Cong., 1987 . .	412	23	23	4	11	63	153	137	56	26	51	221	114	37	12
101st Cong., 1989 . .	408	25	24	5	10	41	163	133	74	22	39	207	139	35	13
102d Cong., 1991 . .	407	28	25	3	11	39	152	134	86	24	55	178	147	44	11
103d Cong., 1993[6] .	388	47	38	4	17	47	151	128	89	15	118	141	132	32	12
104th Cong., 1995 . .	388	47	40	4	17	53	155	135	79	13	92	188	110	36	9
SENATORS															
97th Cong., 1981 . . .	98	2	-	3	-	9	35	36	14	6	19	51	17	11	2
98th Cong., 1983 . . .	98	2	-	2	-	7	28	39	20	6	5	61	21	10	3
99th Cong., 1985 . . .	98	2	-	2	-	4	27	38	25	6	8	56	27	7	2
100th Cong., 1987 . .	98	2	-	2	-	5	30	36	22	7	14	41	36	7	2
101st Cong., 1989 . .	98	2	-	2	-	-	30	40	22	8	23	22	43	10	2
102d Cong., 1991 . .	98	2	-	2	-	2	23	46	24	7	5	34	47	10	4
103d Cong., 1993[6] .	93	7	1	2	-	1	16	48	22	12	15	30	39	11	5
104th Cong., 1995 . .	92	8	1	2	-	1	14	41	27	17	12	38	30	15	5

- Represents zero. [1] Source: Joint Center for Political and Economic Studies, Washington, DC, Black Elected Officials: A National Roster, annual, (copyright). [2] Source: Library of Congress, Congressional Research Service, "Asian Pacific Americans in the United States Congress", Report 94-767 GOV. [3] Source: National Association of Latino Elected and Appointed Officials, Washington, DC, *National Roster of Hispanic Elected Officials*, annual. [4] Some members do not provide date of birth. [5] Represents consecutive years of service. [6] Includes members elected to fill vacant seats through June 14, 1993.

Source: Except as noted, compiled by U.S. Bureau of the Census from data published in *Congressional Directory*, biennial.

No. 470. U.S. Congress—Measures Introduced and Enacted and Time in Session: 1979 to 1996

[Excludes simple and concurrent resolutions]

ITEM	96th Cong., 1979-80	97th Cong., 1981-82	98th Cong., 1983-84	99th Cong., 1985-86	100th Cong., 1987-88	101st Cong., 1989-90	102d Cong., 1991-92	103d Cong., 1993-94	104th Cong., 1995-96
Measures introduced............	12,583	11,490	11,156	9,885	9,588	6,664	6,775	8,544	6,808
Bills	11,722	10,582	10,134	8,697	8,515	5,977	6,212	7,883	6,545
Joint resolutions	861	908	1,022	1,188	1,073	687	563	661	263
Measures enacted	736	529	677	483	761	666	609	473	337
Public	613	473	623	466	713	650	589	465	333
Private.................	123	56	54	17	48	16	20	8	4
HOUSE OF REPRESENTATIVES									
Number of days	326	303	266	281	298	281	280	265	290
Number of hours...............	1,876	1,420	1,705	1,794	1,659	1,688	1,796	1,887	2,445
Number of hours per day	5.8	4.7	6.4	6.4	5.6	6.0	6.4	7.1	8.4
SENATE									
Number of days	333	312	281	313	307	274	287	291	343
Number of hours...............	2,324	2,158	1,951	2,531	2,341	2,254	2,292	2,514	2,876
Number of hours per day	7.0	6.9	6.9	8.1	7.6	8.2	8.0	8.6	8.4

Source: U.S. Congress, *Congressional Record* and *Daily Calendar*, selected issues.

No. 471. Congressional Bills Vetoed: 1961 to 1997

PERIOD	President	Total vetoes	Regular vetoes	Pocket vetoes	Vetoes sustained	Bills passed over veto
1961-63	Kennedy	21	12	9	21	-
1963-69	Johnson	30	16	14	30	-
1969-74	Nixon	43	26	17	36	7
1974-77	Ford	66	48	18	54	12
1977-81	Carter................	31	13	18	29	2
1981-89	Reagan	78	39	39	69	9
1989-93	Bush.................	44	29	15	43	1
1993-97	Clinton	20	20	-	19	1

- Represents zero.

Source: U.S. Congress, Senate Library, *Presidential Vetoes ... 1789-1968*; U.S. Congress, *Calendars of the U.S. House of Representatives and History of Legislation*, annual.

No. 472. Congressional Staff, by Location of Employment: 1972 to 1995

[Excludes those persons employed in Congressional support agencies such as the U.S. General Accounting Office, the Library of Congress, and the Congressional Budget Office]

YEAR	PERSONAL STAFF House	PERSONAL STAFF Senate	YEAR	STANDING COMMITTEE STAFF House	STANDING COMMITTEE STAFF Senate	LOCATION OF EMPLOYMENT	1985	1990	1991	1993	1995
1972 ..	5,280	2,426	1970..	702	635	Total..................	18,136	17,625	17,851	(NA)	16,184
1980 ..	7,371	3,746	1980..	1,917	1,191						
1981 ..	7,487	3,945	1981..	1,843	1,022	House of Representatives....	11,636	11,064	11,041	10,791	9,913
1982 ..	7,511	4,041	1982..	1,839	1,047	Committee staff [2]	2,146	2,173	2,321	2,070	1,266
1983 ..	7,606	4,059	1983..	1,970	1,075	Personal staff............	7,528	7,496	7,278	7,390	7,186
1984 ..	7,385	3,949	1984..	1,944	1,095	Leadership staff	144	156	149	137	134
1985 ..	7,528	4,097	1985..	2,009	1,080	Officers of House, staff.....	1,818	1,239	1,293	1,194	1,327
1986 ..	[1]7,920	[1]3,774	1986..	1,954	1,075						
1987 ..	7,584	4,075	1987..	2,024	1,074	Senate	6,369	6,425	6,665	6,529	6,163
			1988..	1,976	970	Committee staff [2]	1,178	1,207	1,154	1,032	796
1989 ..	7,569	3,837	1989..	1,986	1,013	Personal staff	4,097	4,162	4,294	4,200	4,247
1990 ..	7,496	4,162	1990..	1,993	1,090	Leadership staff	118	94	125	132	126
1991 ..	7,278	4,294	1991..	2,201	1,030	Officers of Senate, staff	976	962	1,092	1,165	994
1992 ..	7,597	4,249	1992..	2,178	1,008						
1993 ..	7,400	4,138	1993..	2,118	897						
1994 ..	7,390	4,200	1994..	2,046	958						
1995 ..	7,186	4,247	1995..	1,246	732	Joint committee staff	131	136	145	(NA)	108

NA Not available.   [1] House figure is average for year, and Senate figure only covers period following implementation of Gramm-Rudman budget reductions.   [2] Covers standing, select, and special committees.

Source: Ornstein, Norman J., Thomas E. Mann, and Michael J. Malbin, *Vital Statistics on Congress, 1993-1994*, Congressional Quarterly, Inc., Washington, DC, 1994, and unpublished data (copyright).

No. 473. Number of Governors, by Political Party Affiliation: 1970 to 1998

[Reflects figures after inaugurations for each year]

YEAR	Demo-cratic	Re-pub-lican	Inde-pen-dent	YEAR	Demo-cratic	Re-pub-lican	Inde-pen-dent	YEAR	Demo-cratic	Re-pub-lican	Inde-pen-dent
1970......	18	32	-	1989......	28	22	-	1995......	19	30	1
1975......	36	13	1	1990......	29	21	-	1996......	18	31	1
1980......	31	19	-	1991[1]......	29	19	2	1997......	17	32	1
1985......	34	16	-	1992......	28	20	2	1998......	17	32	1
1987......	26	24	-	1993......	30	18	2				
1988......	27	23	-	1994......	29	19	2				

- Represents zero.   [1] Reflects result of runoff election in Arizona in February 1991.

Source: National Governors' Association, Washington, DC, 1970-87 and 1991-97, *Directory of Governors of the American States, Commonwealths & Territories*, annual; and 1988-90, *Directory of Governors*, annual (copyright).

No. 474. Vote Cast for and Governor Elected, by State: 1990 to 1996

[**In thousands, except percent**. D=Democratic, R=Republican, I=Independent]

STATE	1990		1992		1994		1996		Candidate elected at most recent election
	Total vote [1]	Percent leading party	Total vote [1]	Percent leading party	Total vote [1]	Percent leading party	Total vote [1]	Percent leading party	
AL.........	1,216	R-52.1	(X)	(X)	1,202	R-50.3	(X)	(X)	Fob James, Jr.
AK.........	195	I-38.9	(X)	(X)	213	D-41.1	(X)	(X)	James Campbell
AZ.........	[2]941	[2]R-52.4	(X)	(X)	1,129	R-52.5	(X)	(X)	Fife Symington
AR.........	696	D-57.5	(X)	(X)	717	D-59.8	(X)	(X)	Jim Guy Tucker
CA.........	7,699	R-49.2	(X)	(X)	8,659	R-55.2	(X)	(X)	Pete Wilson
CO.........	1,011	D-61.9	(X)	(X)	1,116	D-55.5	(X)	(X)	Roy Romer
CT.........	1,141	I-40.4	(X)	(X)	1,147	R-36.2	(X)	(X)	John Rowland
DE.........	(X)	(X)	277	D-64.7	(X)	(X)	271	D-69.5	Thomas R. Carper
FL.........	3,531	D-56.5	(X)	(X)	4,206	D-50.8	(X)	(X)	Lawton Chiles
GA.........	1,450	D-52.9	(X)	(X)	1,545	D-51.1	(X)	(X)	Zell Miller
HI.........	340	D-59.8	(X)	(X)	369	D-36.6	(X)	(X)	Ben Cayetano
ID.........	321	D-68.2	(X)	(X)	413	R-52.3	(X)	(X)	Phil Batt
IL.........	3,257	R-50.7	(X)	(X)	3,107	R-63.9	(X)	(X)	Jim Edgar
IN.........	(X)	(X)	2,229	D-62.0	(X)	(X)	2,110	D-51.5	Frank L. O'Bannon
IA.........	976	R-60.6	(X)	(X)	997	R-56.8	(X)	(X)	Terry Branstad
KS.........	783	D-48.6	(X)	(X)	821	R-64.1	(X)	(X)	Bill Graves
KY [3]......	(X)	(X)	835	D-64.7	(X)	(X)	984	D-50.9	Paul Patton
LA.........	(X)	(X)	[4]1,728	[4]D-61.2	(X)	(X)	1,550	[5]R-63.5	Mike Foster
ME.........	522	R-46.7	(X)	(X)	511	I-35.4	(X)	(X)	Angus King
MD.........	1,111	D-59.8	(X)	(X)	1,410	D-50.2	(X)	(X)	Parris Glendening
MA.........	2,343	R-50.2	(X)	(X)	2,164	R-70.9	(X)	(X)	William Weld
MI.........	2,565	R-49.8	(X)	(X)	3,088	R-61.5	(X)	(X)	John Engler
MN [3]......	1,807	R-49.6	(X)	(X)	1,766	R-62.0	(X)	(X)	Arne Carlson
MS [3]......	(X)	(X)	711	R-50.8	(X)	(X)	819	R-55.6	Kirk Fordice
MO.........	(X)	(X)	2,344	D-58.7	(X)	(X)	2,143	D-57.2	Mel Carnahan
MT.........	(X)	(X)	408	R-51.3	(X)	(X)	405	R-79.2	Marc Racicot
NE.........	587	D-49.9	(X)	(X)	580	D-73.0	(X)	(X)	Ben Nelson
NV.........	321	D-64.8	(X)	(X)	371	D-53.9	(X)	(X)	Bob Miller
NH.........	295	D-60.3	516	R-56.0	312	R-69.9	497	D-57.2	Jeanne Shaheen
NJ [6]......	2,254	D-61.2	(X)	(X)	2,506	R-49.3	(X)	(X)	Christine T. Whitman
NM.........	411	D-54.6	(X)	(X)	468	R-49.8	(X)	(X)	Gary Johnson
NY.........	4,057	D-53.2	(X)	(X)	5,204	R-48.8	(X)	(X)	George Pataki
NC.........	(X)	(X)	2,595	D-52.7	(X)	(X)	2,566	D-56.0	James B. Hunt
ND.........	(X)	(X)	305	R-57.9	(X)	(X)	264	R-66.2	Edward T. Schafer
OH.........	3,478	R-55.7	(X)	(X)	3,346	R-71.8	(X)	(X)	George Voinovich
OK.........	911	D-57.4	(X)	(X)	995	R-46.9	(X)	(X)	Frank Keating
OR.........	1,113	D-45.7	(X)	(X)	1,221	D-50.9	(X)	(X)	John Kitzhaber
PA.........	3,053	D-67.7	(X)	(X)	3,585	R-45.4	(X)	(X)	Thomas Ridge
RI.........	357	D-74.1	425	D-61.5	361	R-47.4	(X)	(X)	Lincoln Almond
SC.........	761	R-69.5	(X)	(X)	934	R-50.4	(X)	(X)	David Beasley
SD.........	257	R-58.9	(X)	(X)	312	R-55.4	(X)	(X)	William Janklow
TN.........	790	D-60.8	(X)	(X)	1,487	R-54.3	(X)	(X)	Don Sundquist
TX.........	3,893	D-49.5	(X)	(X)	4,396	R-53.5	(X)	(X)	George W. Bush
UT.........	(X)	(X)	763	R-42.2	(X)	(X)	672	R-75.0	Mike Leavitt
VT.........	211	R-51.8	286	D-74.7	212	D-68.7	255	D-70.5	Howard Dean
VA [6]......	1,789	D-50.1	(X)	(X)	1,794	R-58.3	(X)	(X)	George F. Allen
WA.........	(X)	(X)	2,271	D-52.2	(X)	(X)	2,237	D-58.0	Gary Locke
WV.........	(X)	(X)	657	D-56.0	(X)	(X)	629	R-51.6	Cecil H. Underwood
WI.........	1,380	R-58.2	(X)	(X)	1,563	R-67.3	(X)	(X)	Tommy Thompson
WY.........	160	D-65.4	(X)	(X)	201	R-58.7	(X)	(X)	Jim Geringer

X Not applicable.   [1] Includes minor party and scattered votes.   [2] Result of runoff election in February 1991. [3] Voting years 1987, 1991, and 1995.   [4] Result of runoff election in 1991.   [5] Result of runoff election in November 1995.   [6] Voting years 1989 and 1993.

Source: Congressional Quarterly Inc., Washington, DC, *America Votes*, biennial; and unpublished data (copyright).

No. 475. Composition of State Legislatures, by Political Party Affiliation: 1990 to 1996

[Data reflect election results in year shown for most states; and except as noted, results in previous year for other states. Figures reflect immediate results of elections, including holdover members in state houses which do not have all of their members running for re-election. Dem.=Democrat, Rep.=Republican. In general, Lower House refers to body consisting of State Representatives; Upper House, of State Senators]

STATE	LOWER HOUSE								UPPER HOUSE							
	1990 [1,2]		1992 [3,4]		1994 [5,6]		1996 [5,6]		1990 [1,8]		1992 [3,9]		1994 [5,10]		1996 [5,10]	
	Dem.	Rep.	Dem.	Rep.	Dem.	Rep.	Dem.	Rep.	Dem.	Rep.	Dem.	Rep.	Dem.	Rep.	Dem.	Rep.
U.S.	3,242	2,202	3,186	2,223	2,817	2,603	2,886	2,539	1,186	757	1,132	799	1,021	905	998	931
AL [10]	82	23	82	23	74	31	72	33	28	7	27	8	23	12	22	12
AK [11]	23	17	20	18	17	22	16	24	10	10	10	10	8	12	7	13
AZ [12]	27	33	25	35	22	38	22	38	17	13	12	18	11	19	12	18
AR [11]	90	9	88	11	88	12	86	13	31	4	30	5	28	7	28	6
CA [11]	47	33	47	33	39	40	43	37	25	13	21	16	21	17	25	15
CO [11]	27	38	31	34	24	41	24	41	12	23	16	19	16	19	15	20
CT [12]	87	64	85	64	90	61	97	54	20	16	19	17	17	19	19	17
DE [11]	17	24	18	23	14	27	14	27	15	6	15	6	12	9	13	8
FL [11]	74	46	71	49	63	57	59	61	22	18	20	20	19	21	17	23
GA [12]	145	35	128	51	114	65	106	74	45	11	41	15	35	20	34	22
HI [11]	45	6	47	4	44	7	39	12	22	3	22	3	23	2	23	2
ID [12]	28	56	20	50	13	57	11	59	21	21	12	23	8	27	5	30
IL [11]	72	46	67	51	54	64	60	58	31	28	27	32	26	33	28	31
IN [11]	52	48	55	45	44	56	50	50	24	26	22	28	20	30	19	31
IA [11]	55	45	49	51	36	64	46	54	29	21	27	23	27	23	21	29
KS [11]	63	62	59	66	45	80	48	77	18	22	13	27	13	27	13	27
KY [11]	68	32	71	29	64	36	64	36	27	11	25	13	21	17	20	18
LA [10]	89	16	88	16	86	17	76	28	34	5	33	6	33	6	25	14
ME [12]	97	54	93	58	77	74	81	69	21	14	20	15	16	18	19	15
MD [10]	116	25	116	25	100	41	100	41	38	9	38	9	32	15	32	15
MA [12]	118	37	123	34	125	34	134	25	25	15	31	9	30	10	34	6
MI [11]	61	49	55	55	53	56	58	52	18	20	16	22	16	22	16	22
MN [11]	78	56	85	49	71	63	70	64	46	21	45	22	43	21	42	24
MS [10]	98	23	91	29	89	31	86	33	43	9	37	15	36	14	34	18
MO [11]	99	64	98	65	87	76	88	75	23	11	20	14	19	15	19	15
MT [11]	61	39	47	53	33	67	35	65	29	21	30	20	19	31	16	34
NE.	(13)	(13)	(13)	(13)	(13)	(13)	(13)	(13)	(13)	(13)	(13)	(13)	(13)	(13)	(13)	(13)
NV [11]	22	19	27	12	21	21	25	17	10	10	10	11	8	13	9	12
NH [12]	125	268	136	258	112	286	143	255	11	13	11	13	6	18	9	15
NJ [11]	22	58	27	53	28	52	30	50	13	27	16	24	16	24	16	24
NM [11]	49	21	53	17	46	24	42	28	26	16	27	15	27	15	25	17
NY [12]	95	55	100	50	94	56	96	54	26	35	26	35	25	36	26	35
NC [12]	81	39	78	42	52	68	59	61	36	14	39	11	26	24	30	20
ND [11]	48	58	33	65	23	75	26	72	27	26	25	24	20	29	19	30
OH [11]	61	38	53	46	43	56	39	60	12	21	13	20	13	20	12	21
OK [11]	68	33	70	31	65	36	65	36	37	11	37	11	35	13	33	15
OR [11]	28	32	28	32	26	34	29	31	20	10	16	14	11	19	10	20
PA [12]	107	94	105	98	101	102	99	104	24	26	24	25	21	29	20	30
RI [12]	89	11	85	15	84	16	84	16	45	5	39	11	40	10	41	9
SC [11]	79	43	71	52	58	62	53	70	33	13	30	16	29	17	26	20
SD [12]	25	45	28	42	24	46	23	47	17	18	20	15	16	19	13	22
TN [11]	57	42	63	36	59	40	61	38	20	13	19	14	18	15	18	15
TX [11]	93	57	91	58	89	61	82	68	22	9	18	13	17	14	14	16
UT [11]	31	44	26	49	20	55	20	55	10	19	11	18	10	19	9	20
VT [12]	73	75	87	57	86	61	89	57	15	15	14	16	12	18	17	13
VA [11]	58	41	52	47	52	47	53	46	22	18	22	18	22	18	20	20
WA [11]	58	40	65	33	38	60	45	53	24	25	28	21	25	24	23	26
WV [11]	74	26	79	21	69	30	74	25	33	1	32	2	26	8	25	9
WI [11]	58	41	51	47	48	51	47	52	19	14	16	17	16	17	17	16
WY [11]	22	42	19	41	13	47	17	43	10	20	10	20	10	20	9	21

[1] Status as of May 1992; reflects results of elections held in LA, KY, MS, and NJ in 1991.   [2] Excludes one Independent each for MA, MS, NH, SC, and VA; one Independent Democrat for NH; two Independents for VT; one vacancy each for AR, NV, and SC; two vacancies for PA; four vacancies for MA; and five vacancies for NH.   [3] Status as of November 11, 1993.   [4] Excludes one Independent each for AR, LA, NH, SC, and VA; two Independents each for AK and MS; four Independents for VT; members of political parties other than Democratic, Republican, or Independent (one in MA, two in VT, and four in NH); one vacancy each for GA, NH, TX, and WI; two vacancies each for CT and MA; and three vacancies for NV.   [5] Status as of December 7, 1994.   [6] Excludes one Independent each for AK, CA, LA, and VA; two Independents each for MS and VT; four Independents for SC; members of political parties other than Democratic, Republican, or Independent (one each in MA and VT and two in NH); one undecided in GA; and one vacancy each in LA, MI, and WV.   [7] Excludes two Independents for CA; and one vacancy for NV.   [8] Excludes two Independents for CA; and one vacancy each for CA and PA.   [9] Excludes one Independent in ME, two independents in CA, one vacancy in GA, two vacancies in MS, and three vacancies in MN.   [10] Members of both houses serve 4-year terms.   [11] Upper House members serve 4-year terms and Lower House members serve 2-year terms.   [12] Members of both houses serve 2-year terms.   [13] Single chamber (unicameral body) of 49 members, elected without party designation.

Source: 1990, The Council of State Governments, Lexington, KY, *State Elective Officials and the Legislatures*, biennial (copyright); 1992 and 1994, National Conference of State Legislatures, Denver, CO, unpublished data (copyright).

No. 476. Political Party Control of State Legislatures, by Party: 1975 to 1997

[As of beginning of year. Until 1972 there were two nonpartisan legislatures in Minnesota and Nebraska. Since then only Nebraska has had a nonpartisan legislature]

YEAR	LEGISLATURES UNDER— Democratic control	Split control or tie	Republican control	YEAR	LEGISLATURES UNDER— Democratic control	Split control or tie	Republican control	YEAR	LEGISLATURES UNDER— Democratic control	Split control or tie	Republican control
1975...	37	7	5	1985...	27	11	11	1993...	25	16	8
1977...	36	8	5	1987...	28	12	9	1994...	24	17	8
1979...	30	7	12	1989 [2]...	28	13	8	1995...	18	12	19
1981 [1]...	28	6	15	1990...	29	11	9	1996...	16	15	18
1983...	34	4	11trol	1992...	29	14	6	1997...	20	11	18

[1] Two 1984 midterm recall elections resulted in a change in control of the Michigan State Senate. At the time of the 1984 election, therefore, Democrats controlled 33 legislatures. [2] A party change during the year by a Democratic representative broke the tie in the Indiana House of Representatives, giving the Republicans control of both chambers.

Source: National Conference of State Legislatures, Denver, CO, *State Legislatures*, periodic.

No. 477. Local Elected Officials, by Sex, Race, Hispanic Origin, and Type of Government: 1992

SEX, RACE, AND HISPANIC ORIGIN	Total	GENERAL PURPOSE County	GENERAL PURPOSE Municipal	GENERAL PURPOSE Town, township	SPECIAL PURPOSE School district	SPECIAL PURPOSE Special district
Total	493,830	58,818	135,531	126,958	88,434	84,089
Male	324,255	43,563	94,808	76,213	54,443	55,228
Female	100,531	12,525	26,825	27,702	24,730	8,749
Sex not reported	69,044	2,730	13,898	23,043	9,261	20,112
White	405,905	52,705	114,880	102,676	73,894	61,750
Black	11,542	1,715	4,566	369	4,222	670
American Indian, Eskimo, Aleut	1,800	147	776	86	564	227
Asian, Pacific Islander	514	80	97	16	184	137
Hispanic	5,859	906	1,701	216	2,466	570
Non-Hispanic	413,902	53,741	118,618	102,931	76,398	62,214
Race, Hispanic origin not reported	74,069	4,171	15,212	23,811	9,570	21,305

Source: U.S. Bureau of the Census, *1992 Census of Governments, Popularly Elected Officials* (GC92(1)-2).

No. 478. Women Holding State Public Offices, by Office and State: 1997

[As of **January**. For data on women in U.S. Congress, see Table 469]

STATE	State-wide elective executive office [1]	State legislature	STATE	State-wide elective executive office [1]	State legislature	STATE	State-wide elective executive office [1]	State legislature
United States	82	1,605	Kentucky	-	13	North Dakota	4	24
Alabama	3	6	Louisiana	1	17	Ohio	2	29
Alaska	1	8	Maine	-	48	Oklahoma	4	15
Arizona	4	34	Maryland	1	56	Oregon	1	23
Arkansas	2	23	Massachusetts	-	46	Pennsylvania	1	31
California	2	27	Michigan	2	34	Rhode Island	1	39
Colorado	3	35	Minnesota	3	62	South Carolina	1	22
Connecticut	2	54	Mississippi	-	22	South Dakota	4	18
Delaware	4	16	Missouri	[2]2	42	Tennessee	1	18
Florida	1	38	Montana	2	35	Texas	1	33
Georgia	1	39	Nebraska	2	13	Utah	2	17
Hawaii	1	13	Nevada	1	21	Vermont	-	60
Idaho	2	25	New Hampshire	1	130	Virginia	-	21
Illinois	2	46	New Jersey	1	20	Washington	4	58
Indiana	3	28	New Mexico	1	30	West Virginia	-	20
Iowa	1	32	New York	1	39	Wisconsin	-	31
Kansas	3	49	North Carolina	1	29	Wyoming	2	16

- Represents zero. [1] Excludes women elected to the judiciary, women appointed to state cabinet-level positions, women elected to executive posts by the legislature, and elected members of university Board of Trustees or board of education. [2] Includes one official who was appointed to an elective position.

Source: Center for the American Woman and Politics, Eagleton Institute of Politics, Rutgers University, New Brunswick, NJ, information releases (copyright).

No. 479. Black Elected Officials, by Office, 1970 to 1993, and by Region and State, 1993

[As of **January 1993**, no Black elected officials had been identified in Hawaii, Idaho, Montana, North Dakota, or Utah]

STATE	Total	U.S. and State legisla-tures[1]	City and county offices[2]	Law enforce-ment[3]	Educa-tion[4]	STATE	Total	U.S. and State legisla-tures[1]	City and county offices[2]	Law enforce-ment[3]	Educa-tion[4]
1970 (Feb.)	1,469	179	715	213	362	MA	30	8	18	2	2
1980 (July)	4,890	326	2,832	526	1,206	MI	333	17	133	68	115
1985 (Jan.)	6,016	407	3,517	661	1,431	MN	16	1	2	10	3
1990 (Jan.)	7,335	436	4,485	769	1,645	MS	751	42	495	88	126
1991 (Jan.)	7,445	473	4,496	847	1,629	MO	185	18	134	14	19
1992 (Jan.)	7,517	499	4,557	847	1,614	NE	6	1	2	-	3
1993 (Jan.)	**7,984**	**561**	**4,819**	**922**	**1,682**	NV	10	3	4	1	2
						NH	2	2	-	-	-
AL	699	23	529	58	89	NJ	211	13	113	-	85
AK	3	1	2	-	-	NM	3	-	-	2	1
AZ	15	4	3	3	5	NY	299	30	63	70	136
AR	380	13	214	51	102	NC	468	28	328	31	81
CA	273	13	72	82	106	OH	219	16	124	30	49
CO	20	4	4	10	2	OK	123	6	95	1	21
CT	62	14	38	2	8	OR	10	4	2	4	-
DE	23	3	14	-	6	PA	158	18	55	52	33
DC	198	[5]4	185	-	9	RI	12	9	3	-	-
FL	200	22	133	28	17	SC	450	26	269	15	140
GA	545	43	371	32	99	SD	3	1	2	-	-
IL	465	25	282	37	121	TN	168	16	104	24	24
IN	72	12	50	4	6	TX	472	18	323	40	91
IA	11	1	6	1	3	VT	2	2	-	-	-
KS	21	6	7	3	5	VA	155	14	126	-	15
KY	63	4	47	5	7	WA	19	2	9	5	3
LA	636	33	346	104	153	WV	21	1	17	3	-
ME	1	-	1	-	-	WI	30	8	15	4	3
MD	140	32	79	23	6	WY	1	-	-	-	1

- Represents zero. [1] Includes elected State administrators. [2] County commissioners and councilmen, mayors, vice mayors, aldermen, regional officials, and other. [3] Judges, magistrates, constables, marshals, sheriffs, justices of the peace, and other. [4] Members of state education agencies, college boards, school boards, and other. [5] Includes two shadow senators and one shadow representative.

Source: Joint Center for Political and Economic Studies, Washington, DC, *Black Elected Officials: A National Roster*, annual, (copyright).

No. 480. Hispanic Public Officials, by Office, 1985 to 1994, and by State, 1994

[As of **September**. For states not shown, no Hispanic public officials had been identified]

STATE	Total	State execu-tives and legisla-tors[1]	County and munici-pal officials	Judicial and law enforce-ment	Educa-tion and school boards	STATE	Total	State execu-tives and legisla-tors[1]	County and munici-pal officials	Judicial and law enforce-ment	Educa-tion and school boards
1985 (Sept.)	3,147	129	1,316	517	1,185	KS	7	5	1	-	1
1986 (Sept.)	3,202	132	1,352	530	1,188	LA	12	3	1	8	-
1987 (Sept.)	3,317	138	1,412	568	1,199	MD	2	-	1	-	1
1988 (Sept.)	3,360	135	1,425	574	1,226	MA	1	-	-	-	1
1989 (Sept.)	3,783	143	1,724	575	1,341	MI	8	-	5	1	2
1990 (Sept.)	4,004	144	1,819	583	1,458	MN	3	2	-	1	-
1991 (Sept.)	4,202	151	1,867	596	1,588	MO	1	-	1	-	-
1992 (Sept.)	4,994	150	1,908	628	2,308	MT	2	-	-	1	1
1993 (Sept.)	5,170	182	2,023	633	2,332	NE	3	-	2	-	1
1994	**5,459**	**199**	**2,197**	**651**	**2,412**	NV	4	1	-	1	2
AK	1	1	-	-	-	NJ	37	2	17	1	17
AZ	341	11	144	50	136	NM	716	50	410	105	151
AR	2	1	-	-	1	NY	83	12	13	11	47
CA	796	16	349	50	381	OH	4	-	1	2	1
CO	201	9	140	10	42	OK	1	-	1	-	-
CT	26	12	9	-	5	OR	5	-	3	1	1
DE	1	-	1	-	-	PA	8	1	3	1	3
DC	1	-	-	1	-	RI	1	1	-	-	-
FL	64	16	33	12	3	TX	2,215	41	1,022	389	763
HI	2	2	-	-	-	UT	1	1	-	-	-
ID	2	1	1	-	-	WA	14	2	4	2	6
IL	881	7	26	3	[2]845	WI	2	-	2	-	-
IN	8	1	5	1	1	WY	3	1	2	-	-

- Represents zero. [1] Includes U.S. Representatives. [2] Includes local school council members in the Chicago area.

Source: National Association of Latino Elected and Appointed Officials, Washington, DC, *National Roster of Hispanic Elected Officials*, annual.

No. 481. Public Confidence Levels in Selected Public and Private Institutions: 1996

[Based on a sample survey of 2,719 persons 18 years old and over conducted during the spring and subject to sampling variability; see source]

INSTITUTION	LEVEL OF CONFIDENCE				
	A great deal	Quite a lot	Some	Very little	Can't say/ no answer
Religious organizations	23.6	31.1	31.3	12.3	1.7
Higher education (colleges or univ.)	18.3	38.7	28.3	7.5	7.1
Private elementary or secondary education	15.1	35.3	33.4	9.7	6.5
Youth development and recreation organizations	14.8	35.2	32.7	11.6	5.7
Federated charitable appeals	12.6	26.3	34.9	21.6	4.5
Health organizations	10.8	28.2	42.0	15.9	3.1
Environmental organizations	9.4	23.1	41.0	20.3	6.2
Human service organizations	9.1	28.1	42.6	15.1	5.0
Recreational organizations (adult)	7.8	27.5	41.9	13.4	9.4
Arts, culture, & humanities organizations	9.3	26.7	39.8	14.3	9.9
Private and community foundations	7.6	24.0	42.3	13.5	12.6
Public /society benefit organizations [1]	7.5	22.7	43.4	20.8	5.6
International/foreign organizations [2]	6.3	19.1	37.5	24.2	12.8
Small businesses	15.3	40.8	32.6	7.6	3.6
Military	16.9	37.0	31.0	12.1	3.1
Public higher educ. (colleges or univ.)	15.0	36.4	34.2	11.6	2.8
Public elementary or secondary education	13.3	31.7	37.2	15.3	2.4
Organized labor	6.6	17.7	40.9	29.3	5.6
Media (e.g. newspapers, TV, radio)	6.3	22.7	39.5	29.7	1.8
Work-related organizations	6.1	21.5	47.2	17.4	7.9
Major corporations	4.9	18.7	44.2	27.4	4.8
State government	4.1	22.2	44.9	26.4	2.5
Organizations that lobby for a particular cause	4.0	15.7	42.7	29.5	8.1
Political organizations, parties	3.8	10.8	39.2	42.6	3.7
Local government	5.4	25.9	43.3	23.1	2.3
Federal government	5.2	17.5	43.9	31.1	2.2
Congress	3.4	12.4	41.7	39.0	3.5

[1] Civil rights, social justice, or community improvement organizations.   [2] Culture exchange or relief organizations.

Source: Hodgkinson, Virginia, Murray Weitzman, and the Gallup Organization, Inc., *Giving & Volunteering in the United States: 1996 Edition.* (Copyright and published by INDEPENDENT SECTOR, Washington, DC, 1996.)

No. 482. Political Party Identification of the Adult Population, by Degree of Attachment, 1972 to 1994, and by Selected Characteristics, 1994

[In percent. Covers citizens of voting-age living in private housing units in the contiguous United States. Data are from the National Election Studies and are based on a sample and subject to sampling variability; for details, see source]

YEAR AND SELECTED CHARACTERISTIC	Total	Strong Demo- crat	Weak Demo- crat	Inde- pendent Demo- crat	Inde- pendent	Inde- pendent Repub- lican	Weak Repub- lican	Strong Repub- lican	Apolitical
1972	100	15	26	11	13	11	13	10	1
1980	100	18	23	11	13	10	14	9	2
1984	100	17	20	11	11	12	15	12	2
1986	100	18	22	10	12	11	15	11	2
1988	100	18	18	12	11	13	14	14	2
1990	100	20	19	12	11	12	15	10	2
1992	100	18	18	14	12	12	14	11	1
1994, total [1]	100	15	19	13	10	12	15	16	1
Age:									
17 to 24 years old	100	9	20	22	10	8	19	10	1
25 to 34 years old	100	11	19	14	12	11	16	16	1
35 to 44 years old	100	13	18	14	12	11	14	18	-
45 to 54 years old	100	15	16	15	7	16	12	17	1
55 to 64 years old	100	18	22	8	8	16	12	15	-
65 to 74 years old	100	28	17	6	8	13	14	15	-
75 to 99 years old	100	19	26	9	9	5	17	13	2
Sex:									
Male	100	13	17	12	11	14	14	18	1
Female	100	18	21	13	10	9	15	13	1
Race:									
White	100	12	19	12	10	13	16	17	1
Black	100	38	23	20	8	4	2	3	1
Education:									
Grade school	100	26	26	7	13	7	11	6	4
High school	100	15	22	14	13	10	13	11	1
College	100	14	16	13	7	13	16	21	-

- Represents zero.   [1] Includes other characteristics, not shown separately.

Source: Center for Political Studies, University of Michigan, Ann Arbor, MI, unpublished data. Data prior to 1988 published in Warren E. Miller and Santa A. Traugott, *American National Election Studies Data Sourcebook, 1952-1986,* Harvard University Press, Cambridge, MA, 1989 (copyright).

No. 483. Voting-Age Population, Percent Reporting Registered, and Voted: 1980 to 1996

[As of **November**. Covers civilian noninstitutional population 18 years old and over. Includes aliens. Figures are based on Current Population Survey (see text, Section 1, and Appendix III) and differ from those in Table 485 based on population estimates and official vote counts]

Column groups: **VAP** = Voting-Age Population (mil.); **Reg Pres / Reg Cong** = Percent Reporting They Registered (Presidential / Congressional election years); **Voted Pres / Voted Cong** = Percent Reporting They Voted (Presidential / Congressional election years).

CHARACTERISTIC	VAP 1980	VAP 1984	VAP 1986	VAP 1988	VAP 1990	VAP 1992	VAP 1994	VAP 1996	Reg Pres 1980	Reg Pres 1988	Reg Pres 1992	Reg Pres 1996	Reg Cong 1982	Reg Cong 1986	Reg Cong 1990	Reg Cong 1994	Voted Pres 1980	Voted Pres 1988	Voted Pres 1992	Voted Pres 1996	Voted Cong 1982	Voted Cong 1986	Voted Cong 1990	Voted Cong 1994
Total[1]	157.1	170.0	173.9	178.1	182.1	185.7	190.3	193.7	66.9	66.6	68.2	65.9	64.1	64.3	62.2	62.0	59.2	57.4	61.3	54.2	48.5	46.0	45.0	44.6
18 to 20 years old	12.3	11.2	10.7	10.7	10.8	9.7	10.3	10.8	44.7	44.9	48.3	45.6	35.0	35.4	35.4	37.2	35.7	33.2	38.5	31.2	19.8	18.6	18.4	16.5
21 to 24 years old	15.9	16.7	15.7	14.8	14.0	14.6	14.9	13.9	52.7	50.6	55.3	51.2	47.8	46.6	43.3	45.5	43.1	38.3	45.7	33.4	28.4	24.2	22.3	22.3
25 to 34 years old	35.7	40.3	41.9	42.7	42.4	41.6	41.1	40.1	62.0	57.8	60.6	56.9	57.1	55.8	52.0	51.5	54.6	48.0	53.2	43.1	40.4	35.1	33.8	32.2
35 to 44 years old	25.6	30.7	33.0	35.2	37.9	39.7	41.9	43.3	70.6	69.3	69.2	66.5	67.5	67.9	65.5	63.3	64.4	61.3	63.6	54.9	52.2	49.3	48.4	46.0
45 to 64 years old	43.6	44.3	44.8	45.9	46.9	49.1	50.9	53.7	75.8	75.5	75.3	73.5	75.6	74.8	71.4	71.0	69.3	67.9	70.0	64.4	62.2	58.7	55.8	56.0
65 years old and over	24.1	26.7	27.7	28.8	29.9	30.8	31.1	31.9	74.6	78.4	78.0	77.0	75.2	76.9	76.5	75.6	65.1	68.8	70.1	67.0	59.9	60.9	60.3	60.7
Male	74.1	80.3	82.4	84.5	86.6	88.6	91.0	92.6	66.6	65.2	66.9	64.4	63.7	63.4	61.2	60.8	59.1	56.4	60.2	52.8	48.7	45.8	44.6	44.4
Female	83.0	89.6	91.5	93.6	95.5	97.1	99.3	101.0	67.1	67.8	69.3	67.3	64.4	65.0	63.1	63.2	59.4	58.3	62.3	55.5	48.4	46.1	45.4	44.9
White	137.7	146.8	149.9	152.9	155.6	157.8	160.3	162.8	68.4	67.9	70.1	67.7	65.6	65.3	63.8	64.2	60.9	59.1	63.6	56.0	49.9	47.0	46.7	46.9
Black	16.4	18.4	19.0	19.7	20.4	21.0	21.8	22.5	60.0	64.5	63.9	63.5	59.1	64.0	58.8	58.3	50.5	51.5	54.0	50.6	43.0	43.2	39.2	37.0
Hispanic[2]	8.2	9.5	11.8	12.9	13.8	14.7	17.5	18.4	36.3	35.5	35.0	35.7	35.3	35.9	32.3	30.0	29.9	28.8	28.9	26.7	25.3	24.2	21.0	19.1
Region:[3] Northeast	35.5	36.9	37.3	37.9	38.1	38.3	38.4	38.3	64.8	64.8	67.0	64.7	62.5	62.0	61.0	60.9	58.5	57.4	61.2	54.5	49.8	44.4	45.2	45.2
Midwest	41.5	42.1	42.8	43.3	43.9	44.4	44.5	45.2	73.8	72.5	74.6	71.6	71.1	70.7	68.2	68.7	65.8	62.9	67.2	59.3	54.7	49.5	48.6	48.8
South	50.6	57.6	59.2	60.7	62.4	63.7	64.4	68.1	62.2	65.6	67.2	65.9	61.7	63.0	61.3	60.7	55.6	54.5	59.0	52.2	41.8	41.8	42.4	40.5
West	29.5	33.4	34.6	36.2	37.7	39.3	41.0	42.1	63.3	63.0	63.6	60.8	60.6	60.8	57.7	58.1	57.2	55.6	58.5	51.8	50.7	48.4	45.0	46.4
School years completed: 8 years or less	22.7	20.6	19.6	19.1	17.7	15.4	14.7	14.1	53.0	47.5	43.9	40.7	52.3	50.5	44.0	40.1	42.6	36.7	35.1	28.1	35.7	32.7	27.7	23.2
High school: 1 to 3 years	22.5	22.1	21.4	21.1	21.0	[4]21.0	[4]20.7	21.0	54.6	52.8	[4]50.4	47.9	53.3	52.4	47.9	[4]44.7	45.6	41.3	[4]41.2	33.8	37.7	33.8	30.9	[4]27.0
4 years	61.2	67.8	68.6	70.0	71.5	[5]65.3	[5]64.9	65.2	66.4	64.6	[5]64.9	62.2	62.9	62.9	60.0	[5]58.9	58.9	54.7	[5]57.5	49.1	47.1	44.4	42.2	[5]40.5
College: 1 to 3 years	26.7	30.9	33.0	34.3	36.3	[6]46.7	[6]50.4	50.9	74.4	73.5	[6]75.4	72.9	70.0	70.0	68.7	[6]68.4	67.2	64.5	[6]68.7	60.5	53.3	49.9	50.0	[6]49.1
4 years or more	24.0	28.6	31.3	33.6	35.6	[7]37.4	[7]39.4	42.5	84.3	83.1	[7]84.8	80.4	79.4	77.8	77.3	[7]76.3	79.9	77.6	[7]81.0	73.0	66.5	62.5	62.5	[7]63.1
Employed	95.0	104.2	108.5	113.8	115.5	116.3	122.6	125.6	68.7	67.1	69.9	67.0	65.5	64.4	62.6	62.9	61.8	58.4	63.8	55.2	50.0	45.7	45.1	45.2
Unemployed	6.9	7.4	6.6	5.8	6.7	8.3	6.5	6.4	50.3	50.4	53.7	52.5	49.8	50.6	44.6	46.4	41.2	38.6	46.2	37.2	34.1	31.2	27.9	28.3
Not in labor force	55.2	58.4	58.8	58.5	59.9	61.1	61.2	61.6	65.8	67.2	66.8	65.1	64.3	65.4	63.4	61.9	57.0	57.3	58.7	54.1	48.7	48.2	46.7	45.3

NA Not available.

[1] Includes other races not shown separately.   [2] Hispanic persons may be of any race.   [3] For composition of regions, see map, inside front cover.   [4] Represents those who completed 9th to 12th grade, but have no high school diploma.   [5] High school graduate.   [6] Some college or associate degree.   [7] Bachelor's or advanced degree.

Source: U.S. Bureau of the Census, *Current Population Reports*, P20-453 and P20-466; and unpublished data.

No. 484. Persons Reported Registered and Voted, by State: 1994

[See headnote, Table 483]

STATE	Voting-age population (1,000)	PERCENT OF VOTING-AGE POPULATION		STATE	Voting-age population (1,000)	PERCENT OF VOTING-AGE POPULATION	
		Registered	Voted			Registered	Voted
U.S.	**190,267**	**62.0**	**44.6**	MO	3,797	72.3	54.5
AL	3,136	70.6	45.8	MT	619	73.2	60.7
AK	393	71.7	59.1	NE	1,156	72.6	54.3
AZ	2,971	56.0	41.6	NV	1,081	49.5	40.1
AR	1,801	60.0	41.6	NH	832	64.3	41.2
CA	22,639	54.2	45.0	NJ	5,918	61.6	40.3
CO	2,703	64.3	46.4	NM	1,175	58.8	46.8
CT	2,431	68.4	51.3	NY	13,599	56.8	44.6
DE	528	58.7	41.2	NC	5,211	60.8	35.7
DC	440	66.9	55.6	ND	441	93.3	61.1
FL	10,582	55.5	42.3	OH	8,152	64.6	46.6
GA	5,105	54.9	35.4	OK	2,325	65.8	46.8
HI	833	51.5	46.0	OR	2,309	72.7	60.9
ID	798	63.0	50.7	PA	9,004	58.9	42.7
IL	8,561	63.0	42.8	RI	729	64.2	50.6
IN	4,191	55.6	38.7	SC	2,681	60.8	45.2
IA	2,059	71.7	52.5	SD	495	75.4	63.9
KS	1,798	65.3	50.5	TN	3,856	63.7	43.0
KY	2,807	62.5	34.5	TX	13,134	58.2	37.6
LA	3,013	70.6	34.2	UT	1,231	59.4	44.1
ME	909	81.6	58.2	VT	432	70.7	48.8
MD	3,726	62.6	46.2	VA	4,760	60.0	45.7
MA	4,532	65.6	51.6	WA	3,924	66.8	46.3
MI	6,921	73.7	52.2	WV	1,396	60.8	33.9
MN	3,296	80.9	58.4	WI	3,638	77.2	49.6
MS	1,863	72.6	44.3	WY	333	69.0	63.5

Source: U.S. Bureau of the Census, unpublished data.

No. 485. Participation in Elections for President and U.S. Representatives: 1932 to 1996

[As of **November**. Estimated resident population 21 years old and over, 1932-70, except as noted, and 18 years old and over thereafter; includes Armed Forces. Prior to 1960, excludes Alaska and Hawaii. District of Columbia is included in votes cast for President beginning 1964 and in votes cast for Representative from 1972 to 1992]

YEAR	Resident population (incl. aliens) of voting age[1] (1,000)	For President[2] (1,000)	Percent of voting-age population	For U.S. Representatives (1,000)	Percent of voting-age population	YEAR	Resident population (incl. aliens) of voting age[1] (1,000)	For President[2] (1,000)	Percent of voting-age population	For U.S. Representatives (1,000)	Percent of voting-age population
1932	75,768	39,758	52.5	37,657	49.7	1966	116,638	(X)	(X)	52,908	45.4
1934	77,997	(X)	(X)	32,256	41.4	1968	120,285	73,212	60.9	66,288	55.1
1936	80,174	45,654	56.9	42,886	53.5	1970	124,498	(X)	(X)	54,173	43.5
1938	82,354	(X)	(X)	36,236	44.0	1972	140,777	77,719	55.2	71,430	50.7
1940	84,728	49,900	58.9	46,951	55.4	1974	146,338	(X)	(X)	52,495	35.9
1942	86,465	(X)	(X)	28,074	32.5	1976	152,308	81,556	53.5	74,422	48.9
1944	85,654	47,977	56.0	45,103	52.7	1978	158,369	(X)	(X)	55,332	34.9
1946	92,659	(X)	(X)	34,398	37.1	1980	163,945	86,515	52.8	77,995	47.6
1948	95,573	48,794	51.1	45,933	48.1	1982	169,643	(X)	(X)	64,514	38.0
1950	98,134	(X)	(X)	40,342	41.1	1984	173,995	92,653	53.3	83,231	47.8
1952	99,929	61,551	61.6	57,571	57.6	1986	177,922	(X)	(X)	59,619	33.5
1954	102,075	(X)	(X)	42,580	41.7	1988	181,956	91,595	50.3	81,786	44.9
1956	104,515	62,027	59.3	58,426	55.9	1990	185,812	(X)	(X)	61,513	33.1
1958	106,447	(X)	(X)	45,818	43.0	1992	189,524	104,425	55.1	96,239	50.8
1960	109,672	68,838	62.8	64,133	58.5	1994	193,650	(X)	(X)	70,780	37.4
1962	112,952	(X)	(X)	51,267	45.4	1996	196,507	96,278	49.0	89,863	45.8
1964	114,090	70,645	61.9	65,895	57.8						

X Not applicable.   [1] Population 18 and over in Georgia, 1944-70, and in Kentucky, 1956-70; 19 and over in Alaska and 20 and over in Hawaii, 1960-70.   [2] Source: 1932-58, U.S. Congress, Clerk of the House, *Statistics of the Presidential and Congressional Election*, biennial.

Source: Except as noted, U.S. Bureau of the Census, *Current Population Reports*, P25-1085; Congressional Quarterly Inc., Washington, DC, *America Votes*, biennial (copyright).

No. 486. Resident Population of Voting Age and Percent Casting Votes—States: 1988 to 1996

[As of **November. Estimated population, 18 years old and over**. Includes Armed Forces stationed in each state, aliens, and institutional population]

STATE	VOTING-AGE POPULATION							PERCENT CASTING VOTES FOR—				
	1988 (1,000)	1990 (1,000)	1992 (1,000)	1994 (1,000)	1996, proj. (1,000)			Presidential electors		U.S. Representatives		
					Total	Black	His-panic [1]	1992	1996	1992	1994	1996
U.S.	181,956	185,812	189,524	193,650	196,509	22,857	18,609	55.1	49.0	50.8	36.0	45.6
AL	2,950	2,995	3,080	3,138	3,218	744	20	54.8	50.4	49.9	37.1	46.6
AK	369	382	405	429	425	17	14	63.8	56.6	58.6	44.0	53.6
AZ	2,610	2,696	2,812	2,923	3,094	85	602	52.9	64.5	71.8	54.0	63.9
AR	1,717	1,737	1,774	1,817	1,860	253	18	53.6	58.0	61.0	36.7	57.1
CA	21,250	22,124	22,521	23,225	23,133	1,716	6,323	49.4	58.6	65.6	49.3	57.8
CO	2,397	2,447	2,579	2,713	2,843	113	351	60.8	55.3	56.6	43.3	52.1
CT	2,525	2,534	2,508	2,486	2,468	199	173	64.4	52.0	51.9	44.8	48.0
DE	490	507	521	534	547	92	15	55.6	56.4	57.2	43.0	52.4
DC	503	481	467	452	435	269	20	48.7	48.3	46.9	34.6	44.1
FL	9,651	10,180	10,422	10,856	11,043	1,375	1,409	51.0	46.5	43.2	33.8	40.9
GA	4,631	4,791	5,006	5,159	5,396	1,368	101	46.4	51.2	50.2	33.6	47.0
HI	804	841	866	900	882	24	69	43.1	49.0	50.1	36.6	46.9
ID	683	707	750	803	845	4	49	64.3	54.2	58.5	41.2	52.6
IL	8,411	8,495	8,598	8,712	8,764	1,245	728	58.7	52.6	56.6	38.5	50.8
IN	4,046	4,105	4,209	4,298	4,369	331	81	54.8	54.3	55.8	39.7	52.5
IA	2,053	2,061	2,073	2,112	2,138	38	30	65.3	48.9	52.7	36.0	47.7
KS	1,809	1,819	1,840	1,889	1,898	107	75	62.9	49.2	56.2	34.9	47.1
KY	2,710	2,740	2,798	2,857	2,924	201	15	53.4	54.5	55.9	43.0	52.3
LA	3,006	2,988	3,045	3,100	3,137	902	75	58.8	57.4	65.0	38.6	56.2
ME	902	924	932	931	939	4	6	72.9	58.1	63.3	47.7	56.9
MD	3,536	3,640	3,705	3,750	3,811	982	110	53.6	64.3	69.5	52.0	62.8
MA	4,642	4,646	4,616	4,564	4,623	234	229	60.1	57.7	59.9	46.3	56.1
MI	6,774	6,851	6,947	6,983	7,067	972	159	61.5	54.2	61.0	45.2	53.2
MN	3,167	3,222	3,272	3,362	3,412	65	44	71.8	56.3	64.5	50.4	55.6
MS	1,816	1,832	1,873	1,905	1,961	632	12	52.4	61.1	65.9	58.6	60.9
MO	3,770	3,813	3,851	3,902	3,980	397	47	62.1	56.1	61.1	47.9	54.8
MT	574	579	600	623	647	2	9	68.4	56.6	61.1	43.3	55.3
NE	1,145	1,152	1,164	1,192	1,208	41	35	63.4	45.9	45.9	30.2	40.7
NV	824	929	1,011	1,088	1,180	72	145	50.1	46.0	46.7	30.3	41.8
NH	817	835	838	843	860	5	9	64.2	49.5	53.0	36.5	48.8
NJ	5,905	5,927	5,964	5,974	6,005	819	632	56.1	46.7	48.8	35.9	43.0
NM	1,047	1,075	1,121	1,167	1,210	22	505	50.8	42.7	42.1	(NA)	(NA)
NY	13,659	13,683	13,705	13,646	13,579	2,292	1,616	50.5	47.5	48.8	38.4	43.2
NC	4,903	5,061	5,190	5,364	5,499	1,126	69	50.3	45.0	40.9	29.3	36.9
ND	470	462	462	467	473	3	3	66.7	45.8	48.7	29.6	45.7
OH	7,986	8,066	8,207	8,313	8,358	866	112	60.2	41.5	41.8	31.7	38.1
OK	2,300	2,310	2,352	2,394	2,419	164	69	59.1	42.6	44.2	29.0	40.1
OR	2,055	2,140	2,220	2,311	2,396	37	101	65.9	48.0	[2]47.2	[2]26.3	42.5
PA	9,037	9,091	9,161	9,212	9,196	814	196	54.1	47.1	49.0	33.3	44.5
RI	772	776	768	764	750	29	39	59.0	47.5	48.6	27.5	42.3
SC	2,505	2,587	2,669	2,740	2,777	771	27	45.1	47.1	45.5	36.2	44.3
SD	498	498	505	522	530	3	4	66.6	47.7	52.0	35.5	45.6
TN	3,609	3,685	3,796	3,913	4,021	589	29	52.2	45.6	51.5	32.6	46.1
TX	11,878	12,222	12,681	13,166	13,622	1,564	3,730	48.5	45.1	42.7	28.3	36.8
UT	1,070	1,104	1,169	1,246	1,323	10	69	63.6	47.5	50.1	39.0	46.4
VT	411	422	429	429	441	2	3	67.5	56.9	[3]22.4	[3](X)	15.1
VA	4,572	4,716	4,855	4,967	5,089	924	133	52.7	49.9	54.2	40.5	48.8
WA	3,465	3,650	3,812	4,000	4,122	111	193	60.0	41.2	44.3	31.3	38.3
WV	1,358	1,349	1,376	1,389	1,414	40	7	49.7	47.0	51.0	38.8	45.1
WI	3,559	3,616	3,675	3,777	3,824	180	76	68.9	49.7	55.3	40.7	48.6
WY	321	319	329	343	352	3	20	61.0	62.9	67.3	56.5	62.4

NA Not available.　　X Not applicable.　　[1] Persons of Hispanic origin may be of any race.　　[2] State law does not require tabulation of votes for unopposed candidates.　　[3] See footnote 3, Table 464.

Source: Compiled by U.S. Bureau of the Census. Population data from U.S. Bureau of the Census, *Current Population Reports*, P25-1117 and *Statistical Brief* (SB/96-2); votes cast from Elections Research Center, Chevy Chase, MD, *America Votes*, biennial (copyright); and 1994, Congressional Quarterly Inc., *Congressional Quarterly Weekly Report*, Vol. 53, No. 15, April 15, 1995 (copyright).

No. 487. Sources of Voter Registration Applications: 1995-96

[Based on a report to the United States Congress on the impact of the National Voter Registration Act of 1993 on the administration of elections for federal office during the preceding 2-year period, 1995 through 1996. Based on survey results from 43 states and the District of Columbia. Six states are exempt from the provisions of the Act. Vermont is excluded because of state constitutional impediments]

STATE	Total	MOTOR VEHICLE OFFICES		By mail	Public assistance offices	Disability services	Armed Forces offices	State designated sites	All other services
		Total	Percent of total						
United States..	41,452,428	13,722,233	33.1	12,330,015	2,602,748	178,015	76,008	1,732,475	10,810,934
Alabama.........	560,500	90,356	16.1	106,199	80,096	3,202	4,730	17,512	258,405
Alaska.........	170,669	55,215	32.4	21,264	3,673	133	8	40,668	49,708
Arizona.........	524,042	81,317	15.5	272,550	17,845	2,662	7,278	57,108	85,282
Arkansas	282,023	114,325	40.5	52,305	28,324	1,570	956	6,670	77,873
California	5,761,575	818,927	14.2	2,372,689	129,273	4,132	2,094	25,219	2,409,241
Colorado....	554,343	303,422	54.7	52,644	12,255	1,460	2,292	3,264	179,006
Connecticut.......	338,203	35,323	10.4	97,829	21,061	221	919	9,843	173,007
Delaware	159,302	128,626	80.7	5,956	7,889	2,135	917	632	13,147
District of Columbia .	320,968	276,653	86.2	13,743	14,268	129	387	15,788	-
Florida	2,723,303	1,202,599	44.2	706,163	158,836	9,396	4,787	56,231	585,291
Georgia	1,469,269	772,419	52.6	295,283	103,942	2,046	231	140,762	154,586
Hawaii	139,399	27,370	19.6	103,709	1,040	-	-	2,606	4,674
Idaho [1]	(X)	(X)	(X)	(X)	(X)	(X)	(X)	(X)	(X)
Illinois	887,874	295,255	33.3	94,681	33,837	26,676	1,706	5,068	430,651
Indiana.........	1,059,666	287,198	27.1	478,351	83,853	8,388	2,697	55,208	143,971
Iowa	731,514	240,316	32.9	142,058	26,345	950	507	-	321,338
Kansas.........	377,279	186,604	49.5	56,228	8,419	1,028	630	11,122	113,248
Kentucky	1,495,553	731,840	48.9	50,505	63,477	4,624	1,061	23,402	620,644
Louisiana	1,345,799	291,805	21.7	226,014	74,636	5,709	4,826	35,605	707,204
Maine..........	269,673	106,434	39.5	46,254	16,849	118	54	7,538	92,426
Maryland	473,449	165,267	34.9	222,233	982	671	188	25,802	58,306
Massachusetts.....	619,966	96,097	15.5	301,088	10,895	2,258	1,043	92,910	115,675
Michigan........	1,493,541	1,211,238	81.1	64,717	79,538	8,371	4,237	-	125,440
Minnesota [1]......	(X)	(X)	(X)	(X)	(X)	(X)	(X)	(X)	(X)
Mississippi	268,459	-	-	77,938	33,203	4,255	1,097	-	151,966
Missouri	937,209	409,323	43.7	135,076	143,135	4,507	1,361	15,851	227,956
Montana	90,017	51,690	57.4	21,553	473	211	232	-	15,858
Nebraska	294,282	125,477	42.6	25,784	9,564	1,929	780	204	130,544
Nevada	289,345	150,695	52.1	94,025	13,200	340	512	-	30,573
New Hampshire [1] ...	(X)	(X)	(X)	(X)	(X)	(X)	(X)	(X)	(X)
New Jersey.......	1,425,826	172,607	12.1	39,358	54,579	6,790	-	374,686	777,806
New Mexico	203,052	35,650	17.6	78,109	16,668	543	170	6,671	65,241
New York	3,275,102	699,644	21.4	2,020,088	358,105	32,216	892	90,292	73,865
North Carolina.....	1,449,659	539,287	37.2	229,122	74,882	8,097	3,496	139,477	455,298
North Dakota [1]....	(X)	(X)	(X)	(X)	(X)	(X)	(X)	(X)	(X)
Ohio	1,866,048	528,762	28.3	360,675	100,129	4,041	2,155	240,236	630,050
Oklahoma........	554,679	228,138	41.1	124,795	58,811	1,213	178	1,760	139,784
Oregon.........	802,724	199,065	24.8	401,234	38,446	5,174	-	3,432	155,373
Pennsylvania......	1,846,786	597,625	32.4	959,041	59,462	950	4,953	6,342	218,413
Rhode Island......	41,131	-	75.9	5,569	3,822	523	-	-	-
South Carolina.....	117,197	93,881	80.1	-	20,615	2,051	650	-	-
South Dakota	94,117	5,030	5.3	14,993	13,906	648	2,022	3,582	53,936
Tennessee	776,156	186,563	24.0	222,871	147,830	-	4,568	28,126	186,198
Texas..........	3,340,587	1,494,846	44.8	1,050,413	353,550	7,690	5,991	129,066	299,031
Utah	330,169	84,743	25.7	93,404	24,913	754	2,165	47,229	76,961
Vermont[2]	(X)	(X)	(X)	(X)	(X)	(X)	(X)	(X)	(X)
Virginia.........	664,754	181,128	27.3	228,418	54,051	2,428	906	775	197,048
Washington.......	883,722	350,304	39.6	330,403	22,859	5,360	2,292	7,313	165,191
West Virginia......	143,497	37,952	26.5	34,683	23,212	2,416	40	4,475	40,719
Wisconsin [1]......	(X)	(X)	(X)	(X)	(X)	(X)	(X)	(X)	(X)
Wyoming [1]	(X)	(X)	(X)	(X)	(X)	(X)	(X)	(X)	(X)

- Represents zero.   X Not applicable   [1] Exempt from the National Voter Registration Act of 1993.   [2] Has not yet implemented to National Voter Registration Act of 1993.

Source: Federal Election Commission, Executive Summary—*Report to the Congress, June 1997.*

No. 488. Political Party Financial Activity, by Major Political Party: 1981 to 1996

[In millions of dollars. Covers financial activity during 2-year calendar period indicated. Some political party financial activities, such as building funds and state and local election spending, are not reported to the source. Also excludes contributions earmarked to federal candidates through the party organizations, since some of those funds never passed through the committees' accounts]

YEAR AND TYPE OF COMMITTEE	DEMOCRATIC				REPUBLICAN			
	Receipts, net[1]	Disburse-ments, net[1]	Contribu-tions to candi-dates	Monies spent on behalf of party's nomi-nees[2]	Receipts, net[1]	Disburse-ments, net[1]	Contribu-tions to candi-dates	Monies spent on behalf of party's nomi-nees[2]
1981-82	39.3	40.1	1.7	3.3	215.0	214.0	5.6	14.3
1983-84	98.5	97.4	2.6	9.0	297.9	300.8	4.9	20.1
1985-86	64.8	65.9	1.7	9.0	255.2	258.9	3.4	14.3
1987-88	127.9	121.9	1.8	17.9	263.3	257.0	3.4	22.7
1989-90	85.8	90.9	1.5	8.7	206.3	213.5	2.9	10.7
1991-92	177.7	171.9	1.9	28.1	267.3	256.1	3.0	33.9
1993-94, total	**143.3**	**141.8**	**2.2**	**21.2**	**254.4**	**243.7**	**3.0**	**20.6**
National committee	41.8	44.0	0.1	-0.3	87.4	85.3	0.5	4.7
Senatorial committee	26.4	26.4	0.5	12.3	65.3	65.4	0.6	10.9
Congressional committee	19.4	19.4	1.0	7.7	26.7	26.3	0.8	3.9
Other national	7.8	8.1	-	-	-	-	-	-
State and local	47.8	44.0	0.6	1.5	75.0	66.7	1.0	1.1
1995-96, total	**281.5**	**274.8**	**2.1**	**22.6**	**474.0**	**465.3**	**3.8**	**31.0**
National committee	108.4	105.6	-	6.7	193.0	192.4	0.5	22.8
Senatorial committee	30.8	30.8	0.5	8.4	64.5	66.1	0.7	0.3
Congressional committee	26.6	26.4	1.0	5.7	74.2	73.6	1.3	7.3
Other national	22.5	23.1	-	-	13.9	13.0	-	-
State and local	93.2	88.9	0.6	1.8	128.4	120.2	1.3	0.6

- Represents zero.   [1] Excludes monies transferred between affiliated committees.   [2] Monies spent in the general election. Minus sign (-) indicates refunds for expenditures.

Source: U.S. Federal Election Commission, *FEC Reports on Financial Activity, Final Report, Party and Non-Party Political Committees*, biennial.

No. 489. Independent Expenditures for Presidential and Congressional Campaigns: 1985 to 1996

[In thousands of dollars. Covers campaign finance activity during 2-year calendar period indicated. An "independent expenditure" is money spent to support or defeat a clearly identified candidate. According to federal election law, such an expenditure must be made without cooperation or consultation with the candidate or his/her campaign. Independent expenditures are not limited, as are contributions]

TYPE OF OFFICE AND YEAR	ALL PARTIES			DEMOCRATS		REPUBLICANS		OTHERS	
	Total	For	Against	For	Against	For	Against	For	Against
TOTAL									
1985-86	10,205	8,832	1,373	3,450	888	5,376	485	6	-
1987-88	21,341	16,654	4,687	2,865	4,248	13,784	439	6	-
1989-90	5,774	4,177	1,597	1,530	735	2,645	862	2	-
1991-92	11,052	8,710	2,342	3,044	1,483	5,548	847	118	12
1993-94	4,980	3,256	1,724	672	1,119	2,571	590	13	15
1995-96	21,744	11,016	10,728	1,186	6,491	9,714	4,228	116	9
PRESIDENTIAL									
1985-86	841	795	45	76	28	719	17	-	-
1987-88	14,127	10,628	3,499	568	3,352	10,054	146	6	-
1989-90	497	322	174	5	169	318	5	-	-
1991-92	4,431	3,695	736	583	561	3,052	163	60	12
1993-94	112	27	85	12	84	15	(Z)	-	1
1995-96	1,436	601	835	111	761	459	74	31	-
SENATE									
1985-86	5,312	4,331	980	988	632	3,343	348	-	-
1987-88	4,401	3,641	761	831	617	2,810	143	(Z)	-
1989-90	3,506	2,362	1,144	756	428	1,604	716	2	-
1991-92	2,604	1,912	692	1,025	462	886	230	1	-
1993-94	2,627	1,612	1,015	261	476	1,351	539	(Z)	-
1995-96	14,821	7,041	7,780	347	5,499	6,668	2,280	26	1
HOUSE OF REPRESENTATIVES									
1985-86	4,053	3,706	347	2,386	227	1,314	120	6	-
1987-88	2,813	2,385	427	1,466	279	920	149	(Z)	-
1989-90	1,772	1,493	279	770	138	723	141	-	-
1991-92	4,017	3,103	914	1,436	460	1,610	454	57	-
1993-94	2,241	1,617	624	399	559	1,205	51	13	14
1995-96	5,487	3,374	2,113	728	231	2,587	1,874	59	8

- Represents zero.   Z Less than $500.

Source: U.S. Federal Election Commission, *FEC Index of Independent Expenditures, 1987-88*, May 1989; press release of May 19, 1989; and unpublished data.

No. 490. Political Action Committees—Number, by Committee Type: 1980 to 1996

[As of **December 31**]

COMMITTEE TYPE	1980	1985	1990	1991	1992	1993	1994	1995	1996
Total	**2,551**	**3,992**	**4,172**	**4,094**	**4,195**	**4,210**	**3,954**	**4,016**	**4,079**
Corporate	1,206	1,710	1,795	1,738	1,735	1,789	1,660	1,674	1,642
Labor	297	388	346	338	347	337	333	334	332
Trade/membership/health	576	695	774	742	770	761	792	815	838
Nonconnected	374	1,003	1,062	1,083	1,145	1,121	980	1,020	1,103
Cooperative	42	54	59	57	56	56	53	44	41
Corporation without stock	56	142	136	136	142	146	136	129	123

Source: U.S. Federal Election Commission, press release of January 23, 1996.

No. 491. Political Action Committees—Financial Activity Summary, by Committee Type: 1991 to 1996

[**In millions of dollars.** Covers financial activity during 2-year calendar period indicated. Data have not been adjusted for transfers between affiliated committees]

COMMITTEE TYPE	RECEIPTS			DISBURSEMENTS [1]			CONTRIBUTIONS TO CANDIDATES		
	1991-92	1993-94	1995-96	1991-92	1993-94	1995-96	1991-92	1993-94	1995-96
Total	**385.5**	**391.8**	**437.5**	**394.8**	**388.1**	**430.0**	**188.9**	**189.6**	**217.9**
Corporate	112.5	115.0	133.8	112.4	116.8	130.6	68.4	69.6	78.2
Labor	89.9	90.3	104.1	94.6	88.4	99.8	41.4	41.9	48.0
Trade/membership/health	95.7	96.4	106.0	97.5	94.1	105.4	53.9	52.9	60.2
Nonconnected	73.8	76.9	81.2	76.2	75.1	81.3	18.3	18.2	24.0
Cooperative	4.8	4.4	3.9	4.9	4.5	4.2	3.0	3.0	3.0
Corporation without stock	8.7	8.9	8.5	9.2	9.2	8.7	4.0	4.1	4.5

[1] Comprises contributions to candidates, independent expenditures, and other disbursements.

Source: U.S. Federal Election Commission, *FEC Reports on Financial Activity, Final Report, Party and Non-Party Political Committees,* biennial.

No. 492. Presidential Campaign Finances—Federal Funds for General Election: 1980 to 1996

[**In millions of dollars.** Based on FEC certifications, audit reports, and Dept. of Treasury reports]

1980		1988		1992		1996	
Candidate	Amount	Candidate	Amount	Candidate	Amount	Candidate	Amount
Total	**62.7**	**Total**	**92.2**	**Total**	**110.4**	**Total**	**152.6**
Anderson [1]	4.2	Bush	46.1	Bush	55.2	Clinton	61.8
Carter	29.4	Dukakis	46.1	Clinton	55.2	Dole	61.8
Reagan	29.2			Perot	-	Perot	29.0

- Represents zero.   [1] John Anderson, as the candidate of a new party, was permitted to raise funds privately. Total receipts for the Anderson campaign, including federal funds, were $17.6 million, and total expenditures were $15.6 million.

Source: U.S. Federal Election Commission, periodic press releases.

No. 493. Presidential Campaign Finances—Primary Campaign Receipts and Disbursements: 1987 to 1996

[**In millions of dollars**. Covers campaign finance activity during 2-year calendar period indicated. Covers candidates who received federal matching funds or who had significant financial activity]

ITEM	TOTAL			DEMOCRATIC			REPUBLICAN		
	1987-88 [1]	1991-92 [2]	1995-96	1987-88	1991-92	1995-96	1987-88	1991-92	1995-96
Receipts, total [3]	**213.8**	**125.2**	**243.9**	**91.9**	**70.0**	**46.2**	**116.0**	**49.7**	**187.0**
Individual contributions	141.1	82.4	126.4	59.4	44.7	31.3	76.8	34.4	93.1
Federal matching funds	65.7	41.5	56.0	30.1	24.4	14.0	34.7	15.0	41.6
Disbursements	**210.7**	**118.7**	**(NA)**	**90.2**	**64.4**	**(NA)**	**114.6**	**48.8**	**(NA)**

NA Not available.   [1] Includes a minor party candidate who sought several party nominations and a Democratic candidate who did not receive federal matching funds, but who had significant financial activity.   [2] Includes other parties, not shown separately.   [3] Includes other types of receipts, not shown separately.

Source: U.S. Federal Election Commission, *FEC Reports on Financial Activity, Final Report, Presidential Pre-Nomination Campaigns,* quadrennial.

No. 494. Congressional Campaign Finances—Receipts and Disbursements: 1991 to 1996

[Covers all campaign finance activity during 2-year calendar period indicated for primary, general, run-off, and special elections. For 1991-92 relates to 2,585 House of Representatives candidates and 365 Senate candidates. For 1993-94 relates to 2,045 House of Representatives candidates and 331 Senate candidates; Data have been adjusted to eliminate transfers between all committees within a campaign. For further information on legal limits of contributions, see Federal Election Campaign Act of 1971, as amended]

ITEM	HOUSE OF REPRESENTATIVES						SENATE					
	Amount (mil. dol.)			Percent distribution			Amount (mil. dol.)			Percent distribution		
	1991-92	1993-94	1995-96	1991-92	1993-94	1995-96	1991-92	1993-94	1995-96	1991-92	1993-94	1995-96
Total receipts [1]	395.9	421.3	505.4	100	100	100	263.4	319.1	285.1	100	100	100
Individual contributions.	192.4	216.1	276.5	49	51	55	162.8	186.4	167.5	62	58	59
Other committees	127.4	132.4	155.8	32	31	31	51.2	47.2	45.6	19	15	16
Candidate loans	43.0	43.9	42.6	11	10	8	28.7	43.5	40.3	11	14	14
Candidate contributions	11.4	10.3	7.3	3	2	1	6.5	24.9	16.4	2	8	6
Democrats.	217.7	216.7	233.1	55	51	46	143.8	133.6	126.5	55	42	44
Republicans.	174.3	201.8	266.9	44	48	53	118.3	183.6	157.7	45	58	55
Others	3.9	2.8	5.4	1	1	1	1.3	2.0	0.9	(Z)	1	(Z)
Incumbents	203.5	224.1	281.7	51	53	56	99.7	113.3	81.8	38	36	29
Challengers [2]	91.3	100.6	121.6	23	24	24	95.6	119.2	79.2	36	37	28
Open seats [2]	101.1	96.6	72.2	26	23	14	68.2	86.6	124.1	26	27	44
Total disbursements . . .	407.6	407.2	477.8	100	100	95	272.1	318.8	287.5	100	100	100
Democrats.	228.3	213.4	221.1	56	46	44	147.6	136.3	127.4	54	43	44
Republicans.	176.0	191.0	251.4	43	50	50	123.2	180.6	159.1	45	57	55
Others	3.3	2.8	5.3	1	1	1	1.2	2.0	0.9	(Z)	1	(Z)
Incumbents	217.9	213.5	258.1	53	54	51	107.2	115.1	85.4	39	36	30
Challengers [2]	90.0	99.1	119.6	22	25	24	95.3	118.3	78.9	35	37	27
Open seats [2]	99.7	94.6	100.2	24	21	20	69.6	85.5	123.1	26	27	43

Z Less than $50,000 or 0.5 percent. [1] Includes other types of receipts, not shown separately. [2] Elections in which an incumbent did not seek re-election.

Source: U.S. Federal Election Commission, *FEC Reports on Financial Activity, Final Report, U.S. Senate and House Campaigns*, biennial.

No. 495. Contributions to Congressional Campaigns by Political Action Committees (PAC), by Type of Committee: 1981 to 1996

[In millions of dollars. Covers amounts given to candidates in primary, general, run-off, and special elections during the 2-year calendar period indicated. For number of political action committees, see Table 490]

TYPE OF COMMITTEE	Total [1]	Democrats	Republicans	Incumbents	Challengers	Open seats [2]
HOUSE OF REPRESENTATIVES						
1981-82	61.1	34.2	26.8	40.8	10.9	9.4
1983-84	75.7	46.3	29.3	57.2	11.3	7.2
1985-86	87.4	54.7	32.6	65.9	9.1	12.4
1987-88	102.2	67.4	34.7	82.2	10.0	10.0
1989-90	108.5	72.2	36.2	87.5	7.3	13.6
1991-92	127.4	85.4	41.7	94.4	12.2	20.8
1993-94	132.4	88.2	43.9	101.4	12.7	18.3
1995-96, total [3]	**159.8**	**79.4**	**79.7**	**117.2**	**21.4**	**20.1**
Corporate	53.2	16.2	36.8	45.8	1.9	5.2
Trade association [4]	45.4	16.8	28.4	35.5	3.8	5.9
Labor.	40.2	37.3	2.7	22.0	11.8	6.0
Nonconnected [5]	15.6	6.8	8.7	9.5	3.5	2.5
SENATE						
1981-82	22.6	11.2	11.4	14.3	5.2	3.0
1983-84	29.7	14.0	15.6	17.9	6.3	5.4
1985-86	45.3	20.2	25.1	23.7	10.2	11.4
1987-88	45.7	24.2	21.5	28.7	8.0	9.0
1989-90	41.2	20.2	21.0	29.5	8.2	3.5
1991-92	51.2	29.0	22.2	31.9	9.4	10.0
1995-96, total [3]	**55.4**	**19.3**	**36.0**	**28.6**	**7.6**	**19.3**
Corporate	23.4	4.9	18.5	13.7	2.7	7.1
Trade association [4]	14.5	4.1	10.3	7.7	1.7	5.1
Labor.	7.7	7.0	0.7	2.4	1.5	3.8
Nonconnected [5]	7.9	2.7	5.2	3.8	1.3	2.7

[1] Includes other parties, not shown separately. [2] Elections in which an incumbent did not seek re-election. [3] Includes other types of political action committees not shown separately. [4] Includes membership organizations and health organizations. [5] Represents "ideological" groups as well as other issue groups not necessarily ideological in nature.

Source: U.S. Federal Election Commission, *FEC Reports on Financial Activity, Party and Non-Party Political Committees, Final Report*, biennial.

State and Local Government Finances and Employment

This section presents data on revenues, expenditures, debt, and employment of state and local governments. Nationwide statistics relating to state and local governments, their numbers, finances, and employment, are compiled primarily by the Bureau of the Census through a program of censuses and surveys. Every fifth year (for years ending in "2" and "7") the Bureau conducts a census of governments involving collection of data for all governmental units in the United States. In addition, the Bureau conducts annual surveys which cover all the state governments and a sample of local governments.

Annually, the Bureau of the Census releases information on the Internet which present financial data for the federal government, nationwide totals for state and local governments, and state-local data by states. Also released annually is a series on state, city, county, and school finances, and on state and local public employment. There is also a series of quarterly data releases covering tax revenue and finances of major public employee retirement systems.

Basic information for Census Bureau statistics on governments is obtained by mail canvass from state and local officials; however, financial data for each of the state governments and for many of the large local governments are compiled from their official records and reports by Census Bureau personnel. In over two thirds of the states, all or part of local government financial data are obtained through central collection arrangements with state governments. Financial data on the federal government is primarily based on the *Budget* published by the Office of Management and Budget (see text, Section 10).

Governmental units—The governmental structure of the United States includes, in addition to the federal government and the states, thousands of local

In Brief	
State government revenue (from own sources) in 1995: $691 billion	
Taxes	58%
Insurance trust funds	23%
Charges and misc.	9%
Interest earnings	4%
Utility and liquor stores	1%
State government direct expenditures in 1995: $596 billion	
Public welfare	27%
Education	17%
Insurance trust funds	16%
Health and hospitals	8%
Highways	8%

governments—counties, municipalities, townships, school districts, and numerous kinds of "special districts." In 1997, 87,453 local governments were identified by the census of governments. As defined by the census, governmental units include all agencies or bodies having an organized existence, governmental character, and substantial autonomy. While most of these governments can impose taxes, many of the special districts—such as independent public housing authorities, and numerous local irrigation, power, and other types of districts—are financed from rentals, charges for services, benefit assessments, grants from other governments, and other non-tax sources. The count of governments excludes semi-autonomous agencies through which states, cities, and counties sometimes provide for certain functions—for example, "dependent" school systems, state institutions of higher education, and certain other "authorities" and special agencies which are under the administrative or fiscal control of an established governmental unit.

Finances—The financial statistics relate to government fiscal years ending June 30, or at some date within the 12 previous months. The following governments are exceptions and are included as though they were part of the June 30 group; ending September 30, the state governments of Alabama and Michigan, the District of Columbia, and Alabama school districts; and ending August 31, the state government of Texas and Texas school districts. New York State ends its fiscal year on March 31. The federal government ended the fiscal year June 30 until 1976 when its fiscal year, by an act of Congress, was revised to extend from Oct. 1 to Sept. 30. A 3-month quarter (July 1 to Sept. 30, 1976) bridged the transition.

Nationwide government finance statistics have been classified and presented in terms of uniform concepts and categories, rather than according to the highly diverse terminology, organization, and fund structure utilized by individual governments. Accordingly, financial statistics which appear here for the federal government and for individual states or local governments have been standardized and may not agree directly with figures appearing in the original sources.

Statistics on governmental finances distinguish among general government, utilities, liquor stores, and insurance trusts. *General government* comprises all activities except utilities, liquor stores, and insurance trusts. Utilities include government water supply, electric light and power, gas supply, and transit systems. Liquor stores are operated by 17 states and by local governments in 6 states. Insurance trusts relate to employee retirement, unemployment compensation, and other social insurance systems administered by the federal, state, and local governments.

Data for cities or counties relate only to municipal or county governments and their dependent agencies and do not include amounts for other local governments in the same geographic location. Therefore, expenditure figures for "education" do not include spending by the separate school districts which administer public schools within most municipal or county areas. Variations in the assignment of governmental responsibility for public assistance, health, hospitals, public housing, and other functions to a lesser degree also have an important effect upon reported amounts of city or county expenditure, revenue, and debt. Therefore, any comparisons based upon these figures should be made with caution and with due recognition of variations that exist among areas.

Employment and payrolls—These data are based mainly on mail canvassing of state and local governments. Payroll includes all salaries, wages, and individual fee payments for the month specified, and employment relates to all persons on governmental payrolls during a pay period of the month covered—including paid officials, temporary help, and (unless otherwise specified) part-time as well as full-time personnel. Beginning 1986, statistics for full-time equivalent employment have been computed with a formula using hours worked by part-time employees. A payroll based formula was used prior to 1985. Full-time equivalent employment statistics were not computed for 1985. Figures shown for individual governments cover major dependent agencies such as institutions of higher education, as well as the basic central departments and agencies of the government.

Statistical reliability—For a discussion of statistical collection and estimation, sampling procedures, and measures of statistical reliability applicable to Census Bureau data, see Appendix III.

No. 496. Number of Governmental Units, by Type: 1942 to 1997

TYPE OF GOVERNMENT	1942	1952 [1]	1962	1967	1972	1977	1982	1987	1992	1997
Total	155,116	116,807	91,237	81,299	78,269	79,913	81,831	83,237	85,006	87,504
U.S. government	1	1	1	1	1	1	1	1	1	1
State government	48	50	50	50	50	50	50	50	50	50
Local governments	155,067	116,756	91,186	81,248	78,218	79,862	81,780	83,186	84,955	87,453
County.	3,050	3,052	3,043	3,049	3,044	3,042	3,041	3,042	3,043	3,043
Municipal	16,220	16,807	18,000	18,048	18,517	18,862	19,076	19,200	19,279	19,372
Township and town	18,919	17,202	17,142	17,105	16,991	16,822	16,734	16,691	16,656	16,629
School district	108,579	67,355	34,678	21,782	15,781	15,174	14,851	14,721	14,422	13,726
Special district.	8,299	12,340	18,323	21,264	23,885	25,962	28,078	29,532	31,555	34,683

[1] Adjusted to include units in Alaska and Hawaii which adopted statehood in 1959.

No. 497. Number of Local Governments, by Type—States: 1997

[Governments in existence in January. Limited to governments actually in existence. Excludes, therefore, a few counties and numerous townships and "incorporated places" existing as areas for which statistics can be presented as to population and other subjects, but lacking any separate organized county, township, or municipal government]

STATE	All local governmental units	County	Municipal	Township [1]	School district	Special district
United States	**87,453**	**3,043**	**19,372**	**16,629**	**13,726**	**34,683**
Alabama.	1,131	67	446	-	127	491
Alaska	175	12	149	-	-	14
Arizona.	637	15	87	-	231	304
Arkansas	1,516	75	491	-	311	639
California	4,607	57	471	-	1,069	3,010
Colorado.	1,869	62	269	-	180	1,358
Connecticut.	583	-	30	149	17	387
Delaware	336	3	57	-	19	257
District of Columbia	2	-	1	-	-	1
Florida	1,081	66	394	-	95	526
Georgia	1,344	156	535	-	180	473
Hawaii	19	3	1	-	-	15
Idaho.	1,147	44	200	-	114	789
Illinois	6,835	102	1,288	1,433	944	3,068
Indiana.	3,198	91	569	1,008	294	1,236
Iowa	1,876	99	950	-	394	433
Kansas.	3,950	105	627	1,370	324	1,524
Kentucky	1,366	119	434	-	176	637
Louisiana	467	60	302	-	66	39
Maine.	832	16	22	467	98	229
Maryland	420	23	156	-	-	241
Massachusetts.	861	12	44	307	85	413
Michigan.	2,775	83	534	1,242	584	332
Minnesota.	3,501	87	854	1,794	360	406
Mississippi	936	82	295	-	164	395
Missouri	3,416	114	944	324	537	1,497
Montana.	1,144	54	128	-	362	600
Nebraska	2,894	93	535	455	681	1,130
Nevada	205	16	19	-	17	153
New Hampshire	575	10	13	221	166	165
New Jersey	1,421	21	324	243	552	281
New Mexico	881	33	99	-	96	653
New York	3,413	57	615	929	686	1,126
North Carolina	952	100	527	-	-	325
North Dakota.	2,758	53	363	1,341	237	764
Ohio	3,597	88	941	1,310	666	592
Oklahoma.	1,799	77	592	-	578	552
Oregon.	1,493	36	240	-	258	959
Pennsylvania.	5,070	66	1,023	1,546	516	1,919
Rhode Island.	119	-	8	31	4	76
South Carolina	716	46	269	-	91	310
South Dakota	1,810	66	309	956	177	302
Tennessee	940	93	343	-	14	490
Texas.	4,700	254	1,177	-	1,087	2,182
Utah	683	29	230	-	40	384
Vermont	691	14	49	237	279	112
Virginia.	483	95	231	-	1	156
Washington	1,812	39	275	-	296	1,202
West Virginia.	704	55	232	-	55	362
Wisconsin	3,059	72	583	1,266	442	696
Wyoming	654	23	97	-	56	478

- Represents zero. [1] Includes "town" governments in the six New England States and in Minnesota, New York, and Wisconsin.

Source of Tables 496 and 497: U.S. Bureau of the Census, *1997 Census of Governments, Government Organization*, Series GC97(1); <http://www.census.gov/govs/www/govstruc.html> (accessed 26 June 1998).

No. 498. County, Municipal, and Township Governments: 1992

[Number of governments as of **January 1997**. Population enumerated as of **July 1, 1994**. Consolidated city-county governments are classified as municipal rather than county governments. Township governments include "towns" in the six New England States, Minnesota, New York, and Wisconsin]

POPULATION-SIZE GROUP	COUNTY GOVERNMENTS			MUNICIPAL GOVERNMENTS			TOWNSHIP GOVERNMENTS		
	Number, 1997	Population, 1994		Number, 1997	Population, 1994		Number, 1997	Population, 1994	
		Number (1,000)	Percent		Number (1,000)	Percent		Number (1,000)	Percent
Total	3,043	236,107	100	19,372	161,605	100	16,629	54,662	100
250,000 or more	183	128,741	55	66	46,417	29	4	1,758	3
100,000 to 299,999	264	40,234	17	142	20,687	13	31	4,259	8
50,000 to 99,999	378	26,583	11	346	23,595	15	84	5,626	10
25,000 to 49,999	604	21,543	9	590	20,623	13	257	8,750	16
10,000 to 24,999	908	15,047	6	1,378	21,606	13	744	11,509	21
5,000 to 9,999	413	3,105	1	1,618	11,504	7	1,064	7,403	14
2,500 to 4,999	178	668	–	2,096	7,426	5	1,836	6,422	12
1,000 to 2,499	86	165	–	3,723	5,965	4	3,606	5,766	11
Less than 1,000	29	21	–	9,413	3,782	2	9,003	3,169	6

– Represents or rounds to zero.

Source: U.S. Bureau of the Census, *1997 Census of Governments, Government Organization*, Series GC97(1); <http://www.census.gov/govs/www/govstruc.html> (accessed July 17, 1998).

Figure 9.1
Lottery Ticket Sales—Type of Game and Use of Proceeds: 1997

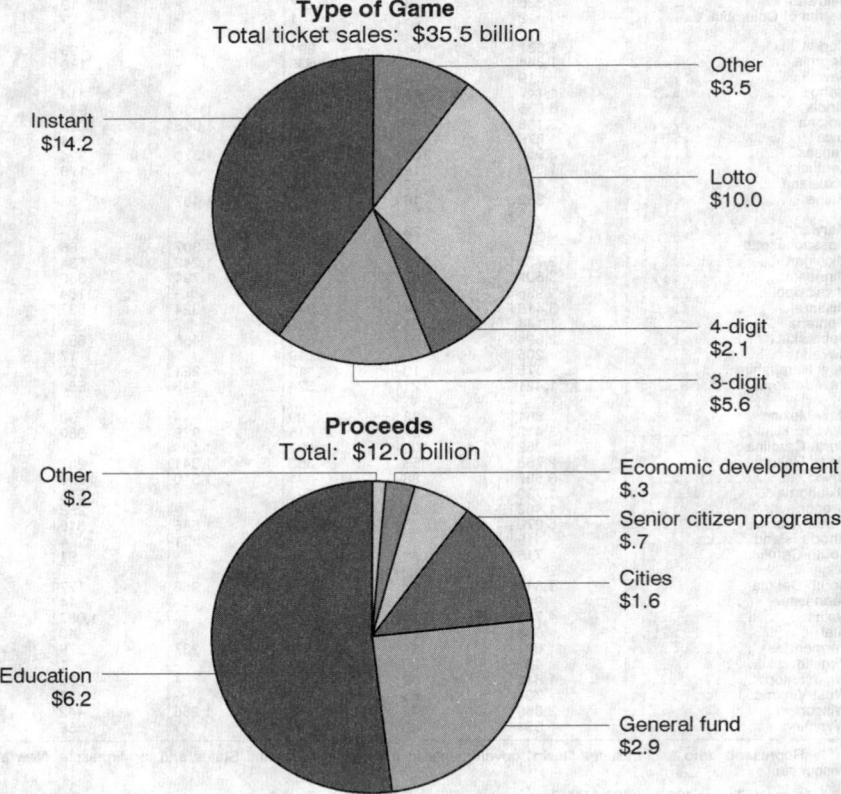

Type of Game
Total ticket sales: $35.5 billion

Instant $14.2
Other $3.5
Lotto $10.0
4-digit $2.1
3-digit $5.6

Proceeds
Total: $12.0 billion

Other $.2
Education $6.2
Economic development $.3
Senior citizen programs $.7
Cities $1.6
General fund $2.9

Source: Chart prepared by U.S. Bureau of the Census. For data, see Table 523.

No. 499. All Governments—Revenue, Expenditure, and Debt: 1980 to 1995

[For fiscal year ending in year shown; see text, Section 9. Local government amounts are estimates subject to sampling variation; see Appendix III and source]

ITEM	All governments (bil. dol.)	FEDERAL [1]		STATE AND LOCAL (bil. dol.)			PER CAPITA [2] (dollars)		
		Total (bil. dol.)	Percent of total	Total	State	Local	Total	Federal	State and local
Revenue: [3] 1980	[4]932	565	60.7	[4]452	277	258	[4]4,115	2,496	1,993
1990	[4]2,047	1,155	56.4	[4]1,032	632	580	[4]8,229	4,641	4,150
1994	[4]2,513	1,401	55.7	[4]1,331	842	721	[4]9,656	5,381	5,115
1995	[4]2,759	1,573	57.0	[4]1,418	906	757	[4]10,500	5,985	5,396
Intergovernmental: 1980. . . .	(X)	2	(X)	[4]83	64	102	(X)	8	367
1990	(X)	3	(X)	[4]137	126	191	(X)	12	550
1994	(X)	3	(X)	[4]215	205	242	(X)	12	828
1995	(X)	3	(X)	[4]229	216	259	(X)	12	871
General, own sources:									
1980	717	417	58.2	299	169	130	3,163	1,842	1,321
1990	1,493	780	52.2	713	391	322	6,002	3,137	2,865
1994	1,831	946	51.7	885	488	397	7,033	3,633	3,400
1995	1,956	1,015	51.9	941	523	417	7,444	3,863	3,580
Taxes: [3] 1980	574	351	61.1	223	137	86	2,535	1,548	986
1990	1,134	632	55.7	502	301	201	4,558	2,542	2,016
1994	1,406	780	55.5	626	373	252	5,401	2,998	2,403
1995	1,505	844	56.1	661	399	261	5,728	3,214	2,514
Property: 1980.	68	(X)	(X)	68	3	66	302	(X)	302
1990.	156	(X)	(X)	156	6	150	626	(X)	626
1994.	197	(X)	(X)	197	8	189	757	(X)	757
1995.	203	(X)	(X)	203	10	194	773	(X)	774
Individual income:									
1980.	286	244	85.3	42	37	5	1,263	1,077	186
1990.	573	467	81.6	106	96	10	2,301	1,877	425
1994.	672	543	80.8	129	117	12	2,581	2,086	495
1995.	728	590	81.0	138	126	12	2,771	2,245	525
Corporate income:									
1980.	78	65	82.9	13	13	-	344	285	59
1990.	117	94	80.3	24	22	2	471	376	95
1994.	169	140	83.2	28	26	3	648	539	109
1995.	188	157	83.5	31	29	2	715	598	120
Sales or gross receipts:									
1980.	112	[5]32	28.6	80	68	12	494	[5]141	353
1990.	232	[5]54	23.3	178	147	31	932	[5]217	715
1994.	298	[5]75	25.0	224	186	38	1,146	[5]287	859
1995.	312	[5]75	24.0	237	197	40	1,189	[5]286	903
Current charges and miscellaneous: 1980. . .	142	67	46.7	76	32	44	629	294	335
1990	359	148	41.3	211	91	120	1,444	596	849
1994	425	165	38.9	259	114	145	1,632	635	997
1995	451	171	37.9	280	124	156	1,716	649	1,066
Expenditures: [3] 1980 . . .	[4]959	617	64.4	[4]434	258	261	[4]4,232	2,724	1,916
1990.	[4]2,219	1,393	62.8	[4]976	572	581	[4]8,921	5,601	3,924
1994.	[4]2,673	1,630	60.8	[4]1,264	775	719	[4]10,267	6,262	4,856
1995.	[4]2,820	1,705	60.5	[4]1,351	837	759	[4]11,630	6,491	5,143
Intergovernmental: 1980. . .	(X)	91	(X)	[4]2	85	2	(X)	401	8
1990	(X)	147	(X)	[4]3	175	6	(X)	591	13
1994	(X)	218	(X)	[4]4	225	9	(X)	837	14
1995	(X)	233	(X)	[4]4	241	8	(X)	888	14
Direct: [3] 1980.	959	526	54.9	432	173	259	4,232	2,323	1,908
1990.	2,219	1,246	56.2	973	397	575	8,919	5,009	3,911
1994.	2,673	1,412	52.8	1,261	550	710	10,269	5,425	4,843
1995.	2,820	1,472	52.2	1,348	596	751	10,732	5,602	5,129
Current operation: 1980 .	517	209	40.5	308	108	200	2,282	923	1,359
1990	1,190	490	41.2	700	258	442	4,785	1,970	2,814
1994	1,422	494	34.8	928	368	560	5,462	1,899	3,565
1995	1,471	486	33.0	986	396	590	5,598	1,850	3,751
Capital outlay: 1980	99	36	36.7	63	23	40	439	161	278
1990	221	98	44.3	123	46	78	888	394	495
1994	217	80	36.7	138	53	85	835	307	528
1995	226	75	33.2	151	58	94	860	284	576
Debt outstanding: [6] 1980. . .	1,250	914	73.2	336	122	214	5,522	4,036	1,486
1990.	4,127	3,266	79.2	861	318	542	16,589	13,129	3,459
1994.	5,796	4,721	81.5	1,075	411	664	22,267	18,138	4,129
1995.	6,116	5,001	81.8	1,115	427	688	23,276	19,033	4,243

- Represents or rounds to zero.   X Not applicable.   [1] Data adjusted to system for reporting state and local data; therefore, differ from figures in Section 10 tables.   [2] 1980 and 1990 based on enumerated resident population as of April 1, all other years based on estimated resident population as of July 1.   [3] Includes amounts not shown separately.   [4] Excludes duplicate transactions between levels of government; see source.   [5] Includes customs.   [6] End of fiscal year.

Source: U.S. Bureau of the Census; *Government Finances*, GF, No. 5, annual, 1980-90; <http://www.census.gov/govs/www/index.html> (accessed 29 June 1998).

No. 500. All Governments—Detailed Finances: 1995

[For fiscal year ending in year shown, see text, Section 9. Local government amounts are estimates subject to sampling variation; see Appendix III and source]

ITEM	All govern- ments (mil. dol.)	Federal (mil. dol.)	STATE AND LOCAL (mil. dol.) Total	State	Local	PER CAPITA[1] (dol.) Federal	State and local
Revenue	**2,758,681**	**1,572,588**	**1,417,925**	**906,404**	**757,400**	**5,985**	**5,396**
Intergovernmental revenue	(²)	3,060	228,771	215,558	259,093	12	871
Revenue from own sources	2,758,681	1,569,528	1,189,153	690,846	498,307	5,973	4,526
General revenue from own sources	1,955,775	1,015,042	940,733	523,466	417,268	3,863	3,580
Taxes ³	1,504,992	844,415	660,577	399,147	261,430	3,214	2,514
Property	203,451	(X)	203,451	9,518	193,933	-	774
Individual income	728,174	590,243	137,931	125,610	12,320	2,246	525
Corporation income	188,410	157,004	31,406	29,075	2,331	598	120
Sales and gross receipts	312,453	75,185	237,268	196,850	40,418	286	903
Customs duties	19,438	19,438	(X)	(X)	(X)	74	(X)
General	160,166	(X)	160,166	132,236	27,930	(X)	610
Selective ³	132,849	55,747	77,102	64,614	12,488	212	293
Motor fuel	54,875	28,669	26,206	25,440	766	109	100
Alcoholic beverages	11,429	7,523	3,906	3,597	309	29	15
Tobacco products	13,414	5,878	7,536	7,348	188	22	29
Public utilities	24,355	9,365	14,990	8,062	6,928	36	57
Motor vehicle and operators' licenses	14,644	(X)	14,644	13,559	1,085	(X)	56
Death and gift	19,684	14,763	4,921	4,904	17	56	19
Charges and miscellaneous ³	450,783	170,627	280,156	124,319	155,838	649	1,066
Current charges ³	267,922	95,860	172,062	64,783	107,280	365	655
National defense and international relations	9,612	9,612	(X)	(X)	(X)	37	(X)
Postal service	53,311	53,311	(X)	(X)	(X)	203	(X)
Education ³	47,548	(X)	47,548	35,812	11,736	(X)	181
School lunch sales	4,129	(X)	4,129	24	4,105	(X)	16
Higher education	39,751	(X)	39,751	35,317	4,434	(X)	151
Natural resources	15,204	13,042	2,162	1,656	507	50	8
Hospitals	47,193	223	46,970	15,344	31,626	1	179
Sewerage	19,723	(X)	19,723	30	19,693	(X)	75
Solid waste management	8,638	2	8,636	373	8,263	-	33
Parks and recreation	4,741	113	4,628	970	3,658	-	18
Housing and community development	5,979	2,459	3,520	298	3,222	9	13
Airports	7,690	27	7,663	695	6,968	-	29
Sea and inland port facilities	3,414	1,491	1,923	479	1,444	6	7
Highways	5,425	(X)	5,425	3,416	2,009	(X)	21
Interest earnings	66,430	12,973	53,457	27,351	26,106	49	203
Special assessments	3,106	(X)	3,106	180	2,926	(X)	12
Sale of property	5,618	4,666	952	221	732	18	4
Utility and liquor store revenue	72,271	(X)	72,271	6,919	65,352	(X)	275
Insurance trust revenue	730,635	554,486	176,149	160,462	15,687	2,110	670
Expenditure	**2,819,860**	**1,705,486**	**1,351,438**	**837,082**	**759,368**	**6,491**	**5,143**
Intergovernmental expenditure	(²)	233,389	3,675	240,757	7,930	888	14
Direct expenditure	2,819,860	1,472,097	1,347,763	596,325	751,438	5,602	5,129
General expenditure ³	2,059,994	913,806	1,146,188	492,525	653,663	3,478	4,362
Education ³	404,933	26,660	378,273	101,510	276,763	101	1,440
Elementary and secondary education	264,240	(X)	264,240	2,187	262,053	(X)	1,006
Higher education	97,048	(X)	97,048	82,339	14,710	(X)	369
Public welfare	250,356	57,246	193,110	160,421	32,689	218	735
Hospitals	79,916	11,990	67,926	28,883	39,044	46	259
Health	52,551	14,531	38,020	20,604	17,416	55	145
Highways	77,840	731	77,109	46,893	30,216	3	293
Police protection	47,917	6,862	41,055	5,735	35,320	26	156
Fire protection	17,009	(X)	17,009	-	17,009	(X)	65
Corrections	38,922	3,065	35,857	24,091	11,766	12	136
Natural resources	54,993	39,742	15,251	11,980	3,271	151	58
Sewerage	23,583	(X)	23,583	1,462	22,121	(X)	90
Solid waste management	17,701	2,711	14,990	1,658	13,331	10	57
Housing and community development	37,787	16,278	21,509	2,085	19,424	62	82
Governmental administration	52,881	(X)	52,881	22,977	29,904	(X)	201
Parks and recreation	20,138	2,250	17,888	2,965	14,924	9	68
Interest on general debt	290,195	233,225	56,970	24,485	32,485	888	217
Utility and liquor store expenditure	94,235	(X)	94,235	10,108	84,127	(X)	359
Insurance trust expenditure	665,631	558,291	107,340	93,692	13,648	2,125	409
By character and object:							
Current operation	1,471,734	486,041	985,693	396,035	589,658	1,850	3,751
Capital outlay	226,088	74,648	151,440	57,829	93,611	284	576
Construction	119,941	9,929	110,012	46,113	63,899	38	419
Equip., land, and existing structures	106,148	64,719	41,429	11,716	29,713	246	158
Assistance and subsidies	156,759	119,892	36,867	23,511	13,356	456	140
Interest on debt (general and utility)	299,648	233,225	66,423	25,259	41,165	888	253
Insurance benefits and repayments	665,631	558,291	107,340	93,692	13,648	2,125	409
Expenditure for salaries	593,342	162,392	430,950	125,432	305,518	618	1,640

- Represents or rounds to zero.   X Not applicable.   [1] Based on estimated resident population as of July 1. See Table 2.
[2] Aggregates exclude duplicative transactions between levels of government; see source.   [3] Includes amounts not shown separately.   [4] Included in items shown above.

Source: U.S. Bureau of the Census; <http://www.census.gov/pub/govs/www/index.html> (accessed 5 June 1998); and unpublished data.

No. 501. All Governments—Capital Outlays: 1980 to 1995

[In millions of dollars, except percent. **For fiscal year ending in year shown;** see text, Section 9. Local government amounts are subject to sampling variation; see Appendix III and source]

LEVEL AND FUNCTION	1980	1985	1990	1991	1992	1993	1994	1995
Total	**99,386**	**156,912**	**220,960**	**227,225**	**227,798**	**221,227**	**217,305**	**226,088**
Federal government:								
Total	36,492	77,014	97,891	95,575	93,095	85,328	79,804	74,648
Annual percent change [1]	10.9	6.3	-1.9	-2.4	-2.6	-8.3	-6.5	-6.5
Direct expenditure	526,330	924,889	1,246,131	900,262	889,494	1,364,873	1,412,364	1,472,097
Percent of direct expenditure .	6.9	8.3	7.9	10.6	10.5	6.3	5.7	5.1
By function:								
National defense [2]	28,161	64,154	75,624	72,775	69,061	61,754	59,160	53,826
Education	97	39	41	97	90	86	145	221
Highways	132	121	181	143	310	210	203	185
Health and hospitals	673	916	1,096	1,387	1,594	1,703	1,508	1,740
Natural resources	4,046	4,092	4,698	4,721	5,466	6,122	2,990	3,261
Housing [3]	317	1,935	4,343	4,147	4,017	3,942	3,557	3,918
Air transportation	151	785	664	778	879	916	909	791
Water transportation [4]	1,003	583	385	459	506	739	495	369
Other	1,912	4,389	10,859	11,068	11,172	9,856	10,837	10,337
State and local governments:								
Total	62,894	79,898	123,069	131,650	134,703	135,899	137,501	151,440
Annual percent change [1]	7.0	13.1	9.9	7.0	2.3	0.9	1.2	10.1
Direct expenditure	432,328	656,188	972,662	1,059,806	1,146,853	1,213,723	1,115,997	1,347,763
Percent of direct expenditure .	14.5	12.2	12.7	12.4	11.7	11.2	12.3	11.2
By function:								
Education [5]	10,737	13,477	25,997	27,251	30,845	31,359	29,012	35,708
Higher education	2,972	4,629	7,441	7,064	9,180	8,949	8,959	10,461
Elementary and secondary .	7,362	8,358	18,057	19,852	21,319	22,102	19,693	24,808
Highways	19,133	23,900	33,867	36,409	37,031	36,980	39,503	42,561
Health and hospitals	2,443	2,709	3,848	4,142	4,331	5,291	4,464	4,883
Natural resources	1,052	1,736	2,545	2,474	2,266	2,137	2,349	2,891
Housing [3]	2,248	3,217	3,997	4,389	4,182	4,890	4,066	4,527
Air transportation	1,391	1,875	3,434	3,941	4,605	5,413	5,170	3,802
Water transportation [4]	623	717	924	984	778	996	1,483	1,101
Sewerage	6,272	5,926	8,356	9,104	8,926	10,261	7,989	8,894
Parks and recreation	2,023	2,196	3,877	4,702	3,934	3,849	3,919	4,085
Utilities	9,933	13,435	16,601	17,028	17,785	15931	18,180	19,028
Water	3,335	4,160	6,873	7,499	7,567	6,490	6,893	7,466
Electric	4,572	5,247	3,976	3,579	3,950	3,760	4,030	3,715
Transit	1,921	3,830	5,443	5,636	5,836	5,253	6,966	7,507
Gas	105	198	310	314	432	428	290	340
Other	7,039	10,711	19,623	21,226	20,020	18,793	21,366	23,961

[1] Change from prior year shown. [2] Includes international relations and U.S. service schools. [3] Includes community development. [4] Includes terminals. [5] Includes other education.

Source: U.S. Bureau of the Census, *Historical Statistics on Governmental Finances and Employment*; and *Government Finances*, Series GF, No. 5, annual, 1980-92; <http://www.census.gov/govs/www/index.html> (accessed 22 July 1998).

No. 502. All Governments—Expenditure for Public Works: 1980 to 1995

[In millions of dollars. Public works include expenditures on highways, airports, water transport and terminals, sewerage, solid waste management, water supply, and mass transit systems. Represents direct expenditures excluding intergovernmental grants]

ITEM	Total	High-ways	Airport transpor-tation	Water transport and ter-minals	Sewer-age	Solid waste manage-ment	Water supply	Mass transit
1980: Total	72,177	33,745	5,071	3,278	9,892	3,322	9,228	7,641
Federal	5,114	434	2,570	2,110	-	-	-	-
State	22,832	20,661	360	360	334	-	91	1,026
Local	44,231	12,650	2,141	808	9,558	3,322	9,137	6,615
Capital expenditures (percent) . . .	48	57	30	50	63	11	36	25
1990: Total	146,762	61,913	10,983	4,524	18,309	10,144	22,101	18,788
Federal	7,911	856	4,499	2,556	-	-	-	-
State	43,787	36,464	635	504	636	891	136	4,521
Local	95,064	24,593	5,848	1,464	17,673	9,253	21,966	14,267
Capital expenditures (percent) . . .	42	55	37	29	46	18	31	29
1994: Total	180,634	72,758	15,896	5,476	21,624	14,041	26,617	24,221
Federal	10,021	691	6,482	2,848	-	-	-	-
State	52,534	43,812	788	635	1,318	1,370	176	4,434
Local	118,079	28,255	8,626	1,993	20,305	12,671	26,441	19,788
Capital expenditures (percent) . . .	40	55	38	36	37	13	26	29
1995: Total	192,985	77,840	15,085	5,016	23,583	17,701	28,041	25,719
Federal	12,837	731	6,688	2,707	-	2,711	-	-
State	56,392	46,893	783	604	1,462	1,658	178	4,814
Local	123,756	30,216	7,614	1,706	22,121	13,331	27,863	20,904
Capital expenditures (percent) . . .	39	55	30	29	38	11	27	29

- Represents or rounds to zero.

Source: U.S. Bureau of the Census, *Government Finances*, Series GF, No. 5, annual 1980-90; <http://www.census.gov/govs/index.html> *State and Local Government Finance Estimates by State,* annual (accessed 5 June 1998); and unpublished data.

No. 503. Federal Grants-in-Aid Summary: 1970 to 1998

[For fiscal year ending in year shown; see text, Section 9. Minus sign (-) indicates decrease]

| | CURRENT DOLLARS | | | | | | | CONSTANT (1992) DOLLARS | |
| | | | Grants to individuals | | Grants as percent of— | | | | |
YEAR	Total grants (mil. dol.)	Annual percent change [1]	Total (mil. dol.)	Percent of total grants	State-local govt. outlays [2]	Federal outlays	Gross domestic product	Total grants (mil. dol.)	Annual percent change [1]
1970	24,065	19.3	8,727	36.3	19.0	12.3	2.4	86.9	11.8
1975	49,791	14.8	16,762	33.7	23.5	15.0	3.2	126.6	3.3
1980	91,385	9.6	32,652	35.7	26.3	15.5	3.4	155.7	-1.1
1985	105,852	8.5	49,352	46.6	21.3	11.2	2.6	135.6	4.7
1990	135,325	11.0	77,132	57.0	18.7	10.8	2.4	144.7	6.2
1991	154,519	14.2	92,497	59.9	19.5	11.7	2.6	158.6	9.6
1992	178,065	15.2	112,185	63.0	20.8	12.9	2.9	178.1	12.3
1993	193,612	8.7	124,289	64.2	21.2	13.7	3.0	188.7	6.0
1994	210,596	8.8	135,232	64.2	21.8	14.4	3.1	200.5	6.3
1995	224,991	6.8	145,793	64.8	22.2	14.8	3.1	208.2	3.8
1996	227,811	1.3	147,598	64.8	(NA)	14.6	3.0	205.5	-1.3
1997	234,160	2.8	148,847	63.6	(NA)	14.6	2.9	205.8	0.1
1998 est.	250,922	7.2	161,063	64.2	(NA)	15.0	3.0	215.9	4.9

NA Not available.   [1] Average annual percent change from prior year shown. For explanation, see Guide to Tabular Presentation. 1970, change from 1969.   [2] Outlays as defined in the national income and product accounts.

Source: Office of Management and Budget, based on *Historical Tables, Budget of the United States Government*, FY 99.

No. 504. Federal Aid to State and Local Governments: 1970 to 1998

[In millions of dollars. For fiscal year ending in year shown; see text, Section 9. Includes trust funds]

PROGRAM	1970	1980	1990	1994	1995	1996	1997	1998, est.
Grant-in-aid shared revenue [1]	[2]24,065	91,385	135,325	210,596	224,991	227,811	234,160	250,922
National defense	37	93	241	169	68	38	(NA)	(NA)
Energy	25	499	461	466	492	481	440	424
Natural resources and environment	411	5,363	3,745	3,765	4,148	3,900	4,121	4,220
Environmental Protection Agency	194	4,603	2,874	2,700	2,912	2,779	2,907	2,748
Agriculture	604	569	1,285	937	780	641	634	702
Transportation [1]	4,599	13,022	19,174	23,633	25,787	25,957	26,846	27,744
Airports	83	590	1,220	1,620	1,826	1,665	1,489	1,554
Highways	4,395	9,208	14,171	18,667	19,475	19,366	20,304	21,423
Urban mass transit	104	3,129	3,730	3,267	4,353	4,291	4,499	4,068
Community and regional development [1]	1,780	6,486	4,965	7,789	7,230	7,850	8,161	9,188
Appalachian development	184	335	124	181	182	230	236	159
Community development block grants	(X)	3,902	2,818	3,651	4,333	4,545	4,517	4,989
Education, employment, training, social services [1]	6,417	21,862	23,359	32,744	34,125	34,034	34,735	36,202
Education for the disadvantaged	1,470	3,370	4,437	6,819	6,785	7,006	7,187	6,231
School improvement programs	86	523	1,080	1,358	1,288	1,140	1,187	1,282
Bilingual and immigrant education [3]	-	166	152	176	189	160	171	268
Federally affected areas impact aid	622	622	799	797	803	945	651	1,001
Vocational and adult education	285	854	1,287	1,292	1,449	1,323	1,382	1,312
Payments to States for Family Support Activities	81	383	265	839	953	931	445	152
Social services-block grants to States	574	2,763	2,749	2,728	2,797	2,484	2,571	2,443
Human development services	390	1,548	2,618	3,998	4,463	4,494	4,876	5,233
Training and employment assistance	954	6,191	3,042	3,310	3,620	3,231	3,324	3,643
Office of libraries	105	158	127	125	109	156	132	171
Health [1]	3,849	15,758	43,890	86,265	93,587	97,650	98,974	105,404
Alcohol, drug abuse, and mental health [3] . .	146	679	1,241	2,132	2,444	2,083	1,622	2,164
Medicaid [3]	2,727	13,957	41,103	82,034	89,070	91,990	95,552	100,960
Income security [1]	5,795	18,495	35,189	51,532	55,122	53,375	54,965	61,160
Family support payments to States [3]	4,142	6,888	12,246	16,508	17,133	16,670	5,345	4,376
Food stamps-administration [4]	559	412	2,130	2,688	2,740	3,030	3,122	3,673
Child nutrition and special milk programs [3] . .	380	3,388	4,871	6,938	7,387	7,757	8,141	8,664
Housing assistance [3]	436	3,435	9,516	15,791	18,416	16,762	17,717	19,159
Veterans benefits and services	18	90	134	199	253	266	277	290
Administration of justice	42	529	574	992	1,222	1,547	2,845	3,293
General government [5]	479	8,616	2,309	2,098	2,172	2,064	2,153	2,284

- Represents or rounds to zero.   X Not applicable.   NA Not available.   [1] Includes items not shown separately.   [2] Includes $5 million for international affairs subsequently provided to a private institution.   [3] Includes grants for payments to individuals.   [4] Includes Puerto Rico.   [5] Includes general purpose fiscal assistance.

Source: U.S. Office of Management and Budget, *Historical Tables, Budget of the United States Government*, FY 99.

No. 505. Federal Aid to State and Local Governments—Selected Programs, by State: 1997

[In millions of dollars, except per capita. For fiscal year ending September 30]

STATE AND OUTLYING AREA	FEDERAL AID [1]		OE [3] compensatory education [4]	EPA [5] waste treatment facilities construction	HHS [6]		HUD [8]		ETA [10] employment/ training	DOT [11] highway trust fund
	Total	Per capita [2] (dol.)			Administration for Children and Families [7]	Medicaid	Lower income housing assistance [9]	Community development		
United States [12]	229,778	859	10,414	2,679	20,650	95,552	12,032	4,585	5,308	20,467
Alabama	3,483	806	207	31	160	1,565	166	86	76	299
Alaska	1,303	2,139	99	19	110	232	102	17	26	240
Arizona	3,355	737	237	23	221	1,248	171	27	88	334
Arkansas	2,283	905	111	22	189	1,014	84	33	47	285
California	27,014	837	1,136	245	3,319	9,424	1,325	413	949	2,097
Colorado	2,444	628	108	17	307	840	129	46	61	207
Connecticut	2,905	888	86	30	231	1,340	215	75	77	368
Delaware	629	860	30	19	64	226	35	10	12	86
District of Columbia	2,740	5,179	198	8	185	481	121	52	36	94
Florida	8,504	580	398	71	816	3,536	398	156	215	736
Georgia	5,469	730	250	43	398	2,302	247	106	95	473
Hawaii	1,184	998	66	17	151	352	78	17	30	207
Idaho	936	773	40	16	82	295	25	6	28	161
Illinois	9,296	781	448	124	1,238	3,510	674	250	217	704
Indiana	3,539	604	155	45	231	1,566	152	60	67	429
Iowa	1,977	693	75	39	180	839	63	20	42	229
Kansas	1,620	624	102	27	155	643	56	22	33	186
Kentucky	3,702	947	179	43	202	1,816	155	59	68	293
Louisiana	4,457	1,024	262	33	208	2,464	150	51	82	256
Maine	1,378	1,109	48	20	107	709	65	19	33	118
Maryland	3,950	775	108	48	666	1,456	244	126	71	419
Massachusetts	6,365	1,041	218	236	397	2,485	531	160	122	1,025
Michigan	7,237	740	407	145	558	3,380	300	73	177	605
Minnesota	3,952	843	129	42	440	1,639	185	48	72	302
Mississippi	2,626	962	167	24	162	1,264	94	33	49	195
Missouri	4,231	783	204	50	322	1,916	214	66	81	444
Montana	991	1,127	68	14	64	286	43	13	20	171
Nebraska	1,227	741	57	20	144	465	62	19	17	167
Nevada	983	586	32	11	74	260	73	10	34	148
New Hampshire	842	718	25	12	63	378	46	10	22	105
New Jersey	6,602	820	220	68	534	2,845	517	157	173	644
New Mexico	2,152	1,244	138	25	209	757	81	17	37	201
New York	24,384	1,344	799	318	2,667	12,548	1,675	806	361	1,201
North Carolina	6,284	846	225	54	500	3,128	210	97	100	448
North Dakota	1,074	1,676	49	12	64	227	34	11	17	141
Ohio	8,327	744	379	69	711	3,909	477	199	178	763
Oklahoma	2,510	757	151	26	249	900	176	41	62	270
Oregon	2,853	880	108	20	191	991	122	36	75	340
Pennsylvania	10,268	854	392	89	1,158	4,585	587	253	265	934
Rhode Island	1,144	1,158	33	15	134	503	108	18	33	106
South Carolina	2,987	794	132	27	146	1,555	114	32	70	252
South Dakota	982	1,330	56	22	44	224	58	15	12	146
Tennessee	4,555	849	170	43	226	2,333	183	74	73	378
Texas	13,184	678	816	100	788	6,199	479	201	314	1,179
Utah	1,355	658	55	12	91	485	34	8	36	153
Vermont	601	1,020	27	9	47	240	26	6	16	89
Virginia	3,518	522	164	49	303	1,223	206	93	91	442
Washington	4,496	801	193	50	437	1,757	176	73	142	467
West Virginia	2,100	1,157	92	32	125	945	71	20	47	219
Wisconsin	3,617	700	185	59	348	1,617	158	63	79	329
Wyoming	762	1,588	32	20	29	135	12	6	12	134
Outlying areas	4,370	346	52	203	141	327	102	157		124

- Represents or rounds to zero. [1] Includes programs not shown separately. [2] Based on estimated resident population as of July 1, 1997. [3] Department of Education, Office of Elementary and Secondary Education. [4] For the disadvantaged. [5] Environmental Protection Agency. [6] Department of Health and Human Services. [7] Includes family support payments (Aid to Families with Dependent Children), social services block grants, children and family services, foster care and adoption assistance, low-income home energy assistance, community services block grants, refugee assistance, and assistance for legalized aliens. [8] Department of Housing and Urban Development. [9] Includes public housing, housing payments (section 8) to public agencies, and college housing. [10] Department of Labor, Employment and Training Administration, Insurance and Employment Service Operations, and Community Service. [11] Department of Transportation, Highway Trust Fund. [12] Includes undistributed amounts not shown separately.

Source: U.S. Bureau of the Census, *Federal Expenditures by State for Fiscal Year 1997.*

No. 506. State and Local Governments—Summary of Finances: 1980 to 1995

[For fiscal year ending in year shown; see text, Section 9. Local government amounts are estimates subject to sampling variation; see Appendix III and source]

ITEM	TOTAL (mil. dol.)				PER CAPITA [1] (dol.)			
	1980	1990	1994	1995	1980	1990	1994	1995
Revenue [2]	451,537	1,032,115	1,331,442	1,417,925	1,993	4,150	5,115	5,396
From Federal Government	83,029	136,802	215,445	228,771	367	550	828	871
Public welfare	24,921	59,961	111,315	115,799	110	241	428	441
Highways	8,980	14,368	18,259	19,879	40	58	70	76
Education	14,435	23,233	30,413	34,045	-	93	117	130
Health and hospitals	2,513	5,904	9,364	11,113	11	24	36	42
Housing and community development	3,905	9,655	13,108	15,255	17	39	50	58
Other and unallocable	28,275	23,683	32,987	32,681	125	95	127	124
From State and local sources	368,509	895,313	1,100,441	1,189,153	1,627	3,600	4,228	4,526
General, net intergovernmental	299,293	712,700	884,996	940,733	1,321	2,865	3,400	3,580
Taxes	223,463	501,619	625,527	660,577	986	2,017	2,403	2,514
Property	68,499	155,613	197,140	203,451	302	626	757	774
Sales and gross receipts	79,927	177,885	223,628	237,268	353	715	859	903
Individual income	42,080	105,640	128,810	137,931	186	425	495	525
Corporation income	13,321	23,566	28,320	31,406	59	95	109	120
Other	19,636	38,915	47,630	50,521	87	156	183	192
Charges and miscellaneous	75,830	211,081	259,469	280,156	335	849	997	1,066
Utility and liquor stores	25,560	58,642	70,075	72,271	113	236	269	275
Water supply system	6,766	17,674	22,692	23,879	30	71	87	91
Electric power system	11,387	29,268	33,808	34,627	50	118	130	132
Transit system	2,397	5,216	3,713	6,540	11	21	14	25
Gas supply system	1,809	3,043	6,256	3,588	8	12	24	14
Liquor stores	3,201	3,441	3,607	3,637	14	14	14	14
Insurance trust revenue [3]	43,656	123,970	160,927	176,149	193	498	618	670
Employee retirement	25,441	94,268	114,304	122,595	112	379	439	467
Unemployment compensation	13,529	18,441	29,901	37,225	60	74	115	142
Direct expenditure	432,328	972,662	1,260,642	1,347,763	1,908	3,911	4,843	5,129
By function:								
Direct general expenditure [3]	367,340	834,786	1,074,017	1,146,188	1,622	3,356	4,126	4,362
Education [3]	133,211	288,148	353,287	378,273	588	1,159	1,357	1,440
Elementary and secondary	92,930	202,009	246,981	264,240	410	812	949	1,006
Higher education	33,919	73,418	90,871	97,048	150	295	349	369
Highways	33,311	61,057	72,067	77,109	147	245	277	293
Public welfare	45,552	110,518	179,829	193,110	201	444	691	735
Health	8,387	24,223	35,329	38,020	37	97	136	145
Hospitals	23,787	50,412	65,101	67,926	105	203	250	259
Police protection	13,494	30,577	38,645	41,055	60	123	148	156
Fire protection	5,718	13,186	16,123	17,009	25	53	62	65
Natural resources	5,509	12,330	13,987	15,251	24	50	54	58
Sanitation and sewerage	13,214	28,453	35,665	38,573	58	114	137	147
Housing and community development	6,062	15,479	19,899	21,509	27	62	76	82
Parks and recreation	6,520	14,326	16,676	17,888	29	58	64	68
Financial administration	6,719	16,217	20,577	22,380	30	65	79	85
Interest on general debt [4]	14,747	49,739	54,960	56,970	65	200	211	217
Utility and liquor stores [4]	36,191	77,801	91,163	94,235	160	313	350	359
Water supply system	9,228	22,101	26,617	28,041	41	89	102	107
Electric power system	15,016	30,997	33,829	34,021	66	125	130	129
Gas supply system	1,715	2,989	3,510	25,719	8	12	13	98
Transit system	7,641	18,788	24,221	3,434	34	76	93	13
Liquor stores	2,591	2,926	2,985	3,020	11	12	11	11
Insurance trust expenditure [3]	28,797	63,321	95,462	107,340	127	255	367	409
Employee retirement	14,008	38,355	51,662	61,427	56	154	198	234
Unemployment compensation	12,070	16,499	28,624	35,204	53	66	110	134
By character and object:								
Current operation	307,811	700,131	927,899	985,693	1,359	2,815	3,565	3,751
Capital outlay	62,894	123,069	137,501	151,440	278	495	528	576
Construction	51,492	89,114	101,992	110,012	227	358	392	419
Equipment, land, and existing structures	11,402	33,955	35,509	41,429	50	137	136	158
Assistance and subsidies	15,222	27,227	35,295	36,867	67	109	136	140
Interest on debt (general and utility)	17,604	58,914	64,624	66,423	78	237	248	253
Insurance benefits and repayments	28,797	63,321	95,462	107,340	127	255	367	409
Expenditure for salaries and wages	*163,896*	*341,158*	*410,610*	*430,950*	*723*	*1,372*	*1,577*	*1,640*
Debt outstanding, year end	335,603	860,584	1,074,660	1,115,370	1,481	3,460	4,129	4,245
Long-term	322,456	841,278	1,047,994	1,088,331	1,423	3,382	4,026	4,142
Short-term	13,147	19,306	26,666	27,039	58	78	102	103
Long-term debt:								
Issued	42,364	108,468	207,807	129,337	187	436	798	492
Retired	17,404	64,831	166,552	95,070	77	261	640	362

NA Not available   [1] 1980 and 1990 based on enumerated resident population as of April 1. Other years based on estimated resident population as of July 1; see Table 2.   [2] Aggregates exclude duplicative transactions between state and local governments; see source.   [3] Includes amounts not shown separately.   [4] Interest on utility debt included in "utility expenditure." For total interest on debt, see "Interest on debt (general and utility)."

Source: U.S. Bureau of the Census, *Government Finances*, Series GF, No. 5, annual 1980-90; <http://www.census.gov/govs/estimate.html> (accessed 9 June 1998).

No. 507. State and Local Government Receipts and Current Expenditures in the National Income and Product Accounts: 1980 to 1997

[In billions of dollars. For explanation of national income, see text, Section 14]

ITEM	1980	1985	1990	1991	1992	1993	1994	1995	1996	1997
Receipts.	361.4	528.7	728.9	784.2	844.3	894.4	949.2	999.0	1,043.4	1,090.4
Personal tax and nontax receipts . .	56.2	94.0	139.1	147.8	159.7	167.4	176.8	189.4	200.2	214.3
Income taxes	42.6	72.1	106.3	110.4	118.1	124.2	131.2	140.3	149.1	159.8
Nontaxes	5.0	9.9	15.6	19.2	22.5	23.4	24.8	26.7	28.8	31.0
Other	8.6	11.9	17.3	18.2	19.1	19.8	20.8	22.4	22.3	23.5
Corporate profits tax accruals	14.5	20.2	22.5	23.6	24.4	26.9	29.9	31.1	34.5	37.6
Indirect business tax and nontax accruals [1]	172.3	271.4	377.6	398.4	423.7	445.6	469.8	489.3	508.9	528.1
Sales taxes.	82.9	131.1	183.2	190.0	202.2	214.8	228.2	239.4	249.8	257.4
Property taxes.	68.8	107.0	155.5	167.6	177.5	185.0	191.4	197.4	202.3	208.8
Contributions for social insurance. .	29.7	42.8	57.4	60.9	64.3	68.7	73.4	77.3	81.4	86.2
Federal grants-in-aid	88.7	100.3	132.4	153.4	172.2	185.8	199.2	211.9	218.3	224.2
Current expenditures.	307.0	437.8	648.8	708.4	758.0	807.0	852.3	895.9	938.0	982.6
Consumption expenditures	261.3	382.6	550.1	579.4	603.6	631.6	663.8	698.6	730.9	762.9
Transfer payments to persons	65.7	101.9	166.5	199.0	227.2	247.2	264.3	280.6	294.8	311.8
Net interest paid	-19.3	-38.9	-51.7	-53.3	-54.7	-52.4	-55.1	-59.6	-61.7	-65.2
Interest received by government.	38.7	81.0	112.1	116.8	119.4	116.9	118.8	123.7	126.3	129.8
Less: Dividends received	1.9	4.5	9.0	9.5	10.1	10.5	11.4	12.5	13.6	14.6
Subsidies.	0.4	0.3	0.4	0.4	0.4	0.4	0.4	0.3	0.3	0.3
Less: Current surplus of government enterprises	-0.9	3.7	7.5	7.6	8.4	9.3	9.7	11.5	12.7	12.6
Current surplus or deficit. .	54.4	91.0	80.1	75.8	86.3	87.4	96.8	103.1	105.3	107.8
Social insurance funds	26.9	47.0	59.9	64.3	68.0	67.8	68.9	70.5	71.3	71.4
Other	27.5	44.0	20.2	11.5	18.3	19.7	27.9	32.5	34.1	36.3

[1] Includes other items not shown separately.

Source: U.S. Bureau of Economic Analysis, *National Income and Product Accounts of the United States, 1929-94*, Vol.1 and *Survey of Current Business*, August 1997.

No. 508. State and Local Government Consumption Expenditures and Transfers in the National Income and Product Accounts: 1980 to 1997

[In billions of dollars. For explanation of national income, see text, Section 14]

EXPENDITURE	1980	1985	1990	1991	1992	1993	1994	1995	1996	1997
Consumption expenditures and gross investment [1]	324.4	464.9	672.6	703.4	735.8	765.0	802.8	846.0	886.7	928.9
Consumption expenditures.	261.3	382.6	550.1	579.4	603.6	631.6	663.8	698.6	730.9	762.9
Durable goods [2]	4.7	7.4	10.9	11.7	12.4	13.2	13.9	14.7	15.3	15.8
Nondurable goods.	28.8	38.7	56.5	58.4	60.9	64.3	67.8	73.0	78.2	80.6
Services	227.8	336.5	482.8	509.4	530.3	554.2	582.1	610.9	637.5	666.5
Gross investment	63.1	82.3	122.5	123.9	132.2	133.4	138.9	147.4	155.7	166.0
Structures	55.1	67.6	98.5	100.5	108.1	108.7	113.4	121.0	128.5	138.4
Equipment	8.1	14.8	23.9	23.4	24.0	24.7	25.6	26.4	27.3	27.6
Transfers	65.7	101.9	166.5	199.0	227.2	247.2	264.3	280.6	294.8	(NA)
Benefits from social insurance funds	17.8	30.4	49.6	55.1	61.0	66.0	71.1	76.8	83.5	(NA)
State and local employee retirement.	15.1	25.5	40.6	44.7	49.6	54.8	60.3	66.3	72.9	(NA)
Temporary disability insurance . . .	0.8	1.4	2.2	2.8	3.0	2.3	2.2	2.1	2.1	(NA)
Workers' compensation.	2.0	3.5	6.9	7.6	8.4	8.9	8.6	8.4	8.6	(NA)
Public assistance	42.8	65.7	108.1	134.4	156.0	170.0	180.9	190.3	197.0	(NA)
Medical care.	24.6	41.8	76.7	100.2	119.7	132.5	141.7	151.3	159.9	(NA)
Family Assistance [3]	12.4	15.4	19.8	22.0	23.3	24.0	24.3	23.3	21.7	(NA)
Supplemental Security Income [4]. .	2.0	2.3	3.8	3.8	4.1	3.9	3.8	3.8	3.6	(NA)
General assistance	1.4	2.4	3.0	2.9	3.3	3.3	3.4	3.4	3.5	(NA)
Energy assistance	1.3	2.1	1.6	1.6	1.6	1.5	2.0	1.5	1.4	(NA)
Other [5]	1.0	1.6	3.2	3.8	4.0	4.8	5.7	7.0	6.8	(NA)
Education	2.4	3.5	5.3	5.7	6.0	6.6	7.6	8.5	9.1	(NA)
Employment and training	1.7	0.9	0.9	0.9	1.1	1.1	1.1	1.2	1.1	(NA)
Other [6]	0.8	1.3	2.5	2.9	3.1	3.4	3.7	3.9	4.1	(NA)

NA Not available. [1] Gross government investment consists of general government and government enterprise expenditures for fixed assets; inventory investment is included in government consumption expenditures. [2] Consumption expenditures for durable goods excludes expenditures classified as investment, except for goods transferred to foreign countries by the federal government. [3] Consists of aid to families with dependent children. Beginning with 1996, assistance programs operating under the personal responsibility and work opportunity act of 1996. [4] Prior to 1974, consists of old-age assistance, aid to the blind, and aid to the permanently and totally disabled, which were partly federally funded. [5] Consists of emergency assistance and medical insurance premium payments paid on behalf of indigents. [6] Consists largely of foster care, veterans benefits, Alaska dividends, and crime victim payments.

Source: U.S. Bureau of Economic Analysis, *National Income and Product Accounts of the United States 1929-94*, Vol. 1 and *Survey of Current Business*, August 1997.

No. 509. Long Term Municipal New Bond Issues for State and Local Governments: 1980 to 1997

[In billions of dollars]

ITEM	1980	1985	1990	1991	1992	1993	1994	1995	1996	1997
Long-term municipal new issues [1]	**45.6**	**202.4**	**125.9**	**169.5**	**231.7**	**289.9**	**162.3**	**156.2**	**181.7**	**215.1**
General obligation	13.7	39.6	40.2	57.0	80.3	91.4	55.6	60.2	64.2	72.1
Revenue	31.9	162.8	85.7	112.5	151.3	198.5	106.7	96.0	117.5	142.9
Competitive	19.3	27.8	30.2	40.2	44.3	55.6	49.5	41.0	47.0	47.8
Negotiated	26.4	174.6	95.9	129.3	187.3	234.3	112.8	115.4	134.7	167.2
States with largest issuance: [2]										
California	3.6	25.3	15.7	23.6	25.9	38.3	25.4	20.2	24.9	27.8
New York	2.9	12.7	16.9	20.9	22.0	30.7	18.8	18.8	21.1	27.9
Texas	3.8	21.2	6.5	11.3	17.1	16.3	10.3	10.4	11.6	15.5
Florida	2.2	13.2	5.9	8.7	13.3	17.7	7.7	9.1	10.0	10.5
Illinois	2.3	9.2	6.3	6.5	10.9	11.7	7.9	6.6	8.8	10.0
All others	30.8	120.8	74.6	98.5	142.5	175.2	92.2	91.1	105.3	123.4
Type of issuer: [3]										
City, town, or village	8.5	36.5	22.7	31.2	44.5	51.3	26.6	27.9	30.3	35.3
College or university	0.2	2.9	1.5	3.6	3.7	4.7	2.4	2.5	4.5	3.3
County/parish	4.6	15.8	10.0	14.8	20.1	24.4	17.2	13.3	16.8	15.5
Direct issuer	-	0.4	0.2	0.2	0.7	0.8	0.6	0.4	1.0	0.8
District	3.9	15.6	15.2	23.3	31.8	38.2	21.7	22.4	27.5	33.7
Local authority	9.2	51.1	20.7	27.8	41.0	56.5	26.3	27.9	33.7	41.9
State authority	14.1	68.1	40.6	49.1	64.6	85.7	47.6	47.2	53.5	66.0
State	5.1	12.1	15.0	19.5	25.2	28.2	19.8	14.6	14.3	18.6
Refunding	1.6	70.5	25.3	53.6	122.2	194.6	49.8	47.5	60.8	81.4
New Capital	45.6	202.4	125.9	169.5	231.6	289.9	162.3	156.2	181.7	215.1
General use of proceeds:										
Airports	0.4	3.0	5.2	4.3	7.2	5.7	4.3	4.7	5.2	6.0
Combined utilities	0.3	2.4	1.0	1.4	2.8	1.9	1.2	0.7	1.2	1.5
Economic development	0.2	2.5	2.1	3.4	4.6	6.0	4.2	2.5	1.8	2.9
Education	4.0	20.4	20.5	25.5	35.0	43.4	26.9	28.5	35.0	42.6
Health care	3.1	30.0	12.6	16.5	20.8	29.2	13.8	11.5	16.6	22.2
Industrial development	1.0	2.9	1.9	2.3	2.4	2.4	2.1	3.2	2.8	3.5
Multi family housing	2.5	20.2	3.1	3.5	5.7	6.2	4.9	6.1	6.7	5.4
Nursing homes/life care retirement	0.3	1.2	1.6	1.5	2.4	2.5	2.4	1.9	3.0	3.6
Other miscellaneous	11.1	37.3	36.2	52.9	67.1	82.7	48.8	44.2	55.3	57.5
Polution control	2.3	10.0	2.5	5.2	6.2	8.1	7.0	5.0	5.4	5.5
Electric & public power	4.4	23.2	5.2	8.9	15.7	27.8	6.3	4.8	5.9	6.5
Single family housing	10.6	16.4	12.5	10.4	8.9	8.2	10.5	10.0	10.4	13.6
Solid waste/resource recovery	0.4	3.8	3.0	2.6	3.4	5.1	3.8	3.3	2.2	3.6
Student loans	0.2	4.0	0.4	2.0	5.1	4.8	3.3	4.4	4.2	3.9
Transportation	1.3	11.0	7.6	11.9	17.9	21.0	9.4	11.3	10.2	17.2
Water, sewer, and gas facilities	3.1	13.4	9.3	16.7	25.0	33.2	12.5	13.2	14.5	18.2
Waterfront/seaports	0.5	1.5	0.5	0.4	1.5	1.6	0.8	0.8	1.3	1.3

- Represents or rounds to zero.   [1] Excludes notes and new issues with a final maturity of less than 13 months. Also private placements and not-for-profit cooperative utilities.   [2] Ranked by 1997 long-term municipal new issue volume.   [3] Includes outlying areas.

Source: Securities Data Company, Newark, NJ, Municipal New Issues Database (copyright).

No. 510. State and Local Governments—Indebtedness: 1980 to 1995

[In billions of dollars, except per capita. For fiscal year ending in year shown; see text, Section 9. Local government amounts are estimates subject to sampling variation; see Appendix III and source]

ITEM	DEBT OUTSTANDING						LONG TERM		
	Total	Per capita [1] (dol.)	Long-term			Short-term	Net long term	Debt issued	Debt retired
			Local schools [2]	Utilities	All other				
1980: Total	335.6	1,481	32.3	55.2	235.0	13.1	262.9	42.4	17.4
State	122.0	540	3.8	4.6	111.5	2.1	79.8	16.4	5.7
Local	213.6	943	28.5	50.6	123.5	11.0	183.1	25.9	11.7
1985: Total	568.6	2,390	43.8	90.8	414.5	19.6	430.5	101.2	43.5
State	211.9	893	6.7	8.6	193.8	2.8	110.4	41.7	16.4
Local	356.7	1,499	37.1	82.2	220.6	16.8	320.1	59.5	27.2
1990: Total	860.6	3,459	60.4	134.8	646.1	19.3	477.0	108.5	64.8
State	318.3	1,282	4.4	12.3	298.8	2.8	125.5	43.5	22.9
Local	542.3	2,180	56.0	122.4	347.4	16.5	351.5	65.0	42.0
1992: Total	970.5	3,806	78.4	150.4	720.4	21.3	561.6	155.1	99.2
State	372.3	1,463	7.6	13.7	348.1	2.9	125.4	70.2	45.0
Local	598.1	2,345	70.9	136.7	373.1	18.4	409.1	85.0	54.3
1993: Total	1,016.2	3,943	89.2	157.6	746.8	22.6	617.1	195.0	146.3
State	389.7	1,515	9.4	14.8	361.7	3.9	176.9	77.1	60.7
Local	628.0	2,436	79.8	142.7	385.2	18.9	440.2	118.4	86.3
1994: Total	1,074.7	4,129	143.5	164.9	438.0	26.7	672.8	207.8	166.6
State	411.0	1,582	10.4	16.7	162.0	4.9	200.8	78.5	61.3
Local	663.7	2,550	86.2	148.2	276.0	21.8	472.0	129.3	105.3
1995: Total	1,115.4	4,243	118.2	163.9	756.0	27.0	835.3	129.3	95.1
State	427.2	1,629	11.3	17.0	345.0	6.1	205.3	52.6	37.5
Local	688.1	2,619	107.0	146.9	411.0	20.9	629.9	76.8	57.6

[1] 1980 and 1990 based on enumerated resident population as of April 1; other years based on estimated resident population as of July 1; see Table 2.   [2] Includes debt for education activities other than higher education.

Source: U.S. Bureau of the Census, State and Local Government Finance Estimates, annual thru 1992; <http://www.census.gov/govs/www/estimate.html> (accessed 10 June 1998).

No. 511. Bond Ratings for State Governments, by State: 1997

[**As of fourth quarter.** Key to investment grade ratings are in declining order of quality. The ratings from AA to CCC may be modified by the addition of a plus or minus sign to show relative standing within the major rating categories. **S&P:** AAA, AA, A, BBB, BB, B, CCC, CC, C; **Moody's:** Aaa, Aa, A, Baa, Ba, B, Caa, Ca, C; Numerical modifiers 1, 2, and 3 are added to letter-rating. **Fitch:** AAA, AA, A, BBB, BB, B, CCC, CC, C]

STATE	Standard & Poor's	Moody's	Fitch	STATE	Standard & Poor's	Moody's	Fitch
Alabama	AA	Aa	AA	Montana	AA-	Aa3	(1)
Alaska	AA	Aa	AA	Nebraska	(1)	(1)	(1)
Arizona	(1)	(1)	(1)	Nevada	AA	Aa2	(1)
Arkansas	AA	Aa3	(1)	New Hampshire	AA+	Aa2	AA+
California	A+	A1	AA-	New Jersey	AA+	Aa1	AA+
Colorado	(1)	(1)	(1)	New Mexico	AA+	Aa1	(1)
Connecticut	AA-	Aa	AA	New York	A-	A2	A+
Delaware	AA+	Aa1	(1)	North Carolina	AAA	Aaa	AAA
Florida	AA	Aa2	AA	North Dakota	AA-	Aa3	(1)
Georgia	AA+	Aaa	AAA	Ohio	AA+	Aa1	(1)
Hawaii	AA	A1	AA	Oklahoma	AA	Aa3	AA
Idaho	(1)	(1)	(1)	Oregon	AA	Aa2	AA
Illinois	AA-	Aa3	AA	Pennsylvania	AA-	Aa3	AA-
Indiana	AA+	(1)	(1)	Rhode Island	AA-	A1	AA-
Iowa	(1)	(1)	(1)	South Carolina	AAA	Aaa	AAA
Kansas	(1)	(1)	(1)	South Dakota	(1)	(1)	(1)
Kentucky	(1)	(1)	(1)	Tennessee	AA+	Aaa	AAA
Louisiana	A-	A2	A	Texas	AA	Aa2	AA+
Maine	AA+	Aa3	AA	Utah	AAA	Aaa	AAA
Maryland	AAA	Aaa	AAA	Vermont	AA-	Aa2	AA
Massachusetts	A+	Aa3	A+	Virginia	AAA	Aaa	AAA
Michigan	AA	Aa1	AA	Washington	AA+	Aa1	AA
Minnesota	AA+	Aaa	AAA	West Virginia	AA-	A1	A+
Mississippi	AA	Aa3	AA	Wisconsin	AA	Aa2	(2)
Missouri	AAA	Aaa	AAA	Wyoming	(1)	(1)	(1)

[1] Not reviewed. [2] Under general review.

Sources: Standard & Poors, New York, NY; Moody's Investors Service, New York, NY (copyright); and Fitch IBCA, New York, NY.

No. 512. Bond Ratings for City Governments, by Largest Cities: 1997

[**As of fourth quarter.** For key to ratings, see headnote in table above]

CITIES RANKED BY 1994 POPULATION	Standard & Poors	Moody's	Fitch	CITIES RANKED BY 1994 POPULATION	Standard & Poors	Moody's	Fitch
New York, NY	BBB+	A3	A-	Honolulu, HI	AA	Aa2	(1)
Los Angeles, CA	AA	Aa2	(1)	Tulsa, OK	AA	Aa2	(1)
Chicago, IL	A	A1	A+	Sacramento, CA	AA	Aa2	(1)
Houston, TX	AA-	Aa3	AA	Miami, FL	BB	Ba1	(1)
Philadelphia, PA	BBB	Baa	BBB	St. Louis, MO	A-	Baa1	BBB
San Diego, CA	AA	Aa1	(1)	Oakland, CA	AA-	A1	(1)
Phoenix, AZ	AA+	Aa1	(1)	Pittsburgh, PA	BBB	Baa1	BBB+
Dallas, TX	AAA	Aaa	(1)	Cincinnati, OH	AA+	Aa2	(1)
San Antonio, TX	AA	Aa2	AA	Minneapolis, MN	AAA	Aaa	(1)
Detroit, MI	BBB+	Baa2	BBB+	Omaha, NE	AAA	Aaa	(1)
San Jose, CA	(1)	NR	(1)	Toledo, OH	A	Baa1	(1)
Indianapolis, IN	AAA	Aaa	AAA	Colorado Springs, CO	AA-	Aa3	(1)
San Francisco, CA	AA-	Aa3	AA	Mesa, AZ	AA-	A1	(1)
Baltimore, MD	A	A1	AAA	Buffalo, NY	BBB	Baa3	(1)
Jacksonville, FL	AA	Aa2	AA	Wichita, KS	AA	Aa2	(1)
Columbus, OH	AAA	Aaa	(1)	Santa Ana, CA	(1)	(1)	(1)
Milwaukee, WI	AA+	Aa1	AA+	Arlington, TX	AA	Aa3	(1)
Memphis, TN	AA	Aa3	AA	Tampa, FL	(1)	(1)	(1)
El Paso, TX	AA	Aa3	(1)	Anaheim, CA	AA	Aa2	(1)
Washington, DC	B	Ba1	BB	Corpus Christi, TX	A+	A3	(1)
Boston, MA	A+	A1	A+	Louisville, KY	AA-	A1	(1)
Seattle, WA	AA+	Aa1	(1)	Birmingham, AL	AA	Aa3	(1)
Austin, TX	AA	Aa2	AA	St. Paul, MN	AA+	Aa2	(1)
Nashville-Davidson, TN	AA	Aa2	(1)	Newark, NJ	A	Baa1	(1)
Denver, CO	AA	Aa2	AA	Anchorage, AK	A	A1	(1)
Cleveland, OH	A	A2	A	Aurora, CO	AA-	A1	(1)
New Orleans, LA	BBB+	Baa2	(1)	Riverside, CA	(1)	(1)	(1)
Oklahoma City, OK	AA	Aa2	(1)	Norfolk, VA	AA	A1	(1)
Fort Worth, TX	AA	Aa2	AA	St Petersburg, FL	A+	A1	(1)
Portland, OR	AA+	Aaa	(1)	Lexington-Fayette, KY	NR	(1)	(1)
Kansas City, MO	AA	Aa3	(1)	Raleigh, NC	AAA	Aaa	(1)
Charlotte, NC	AAA	Aaa	(1)	Rochester, NY	AA	A1	(1)
Tucson, AZ	AA	Aa3	(1)	Baton Rouge, LA	(1)	(1)	(1)
Long Beach, CA	AA-	(1)	(1)	Jersey City, NJ	BBB	Baa3	(1)
Virginia Beach, VA	AA	Aa2	(1)	Stockton, CA	(1)	(1)	(1)
Albuquerque, NM	AA	Aa3	AA	Akron, OH	AA-	A2	(1)
Atlanta, GA	AA	Aa3	(1)	Mobile, AL	A+	A	(1)
Fresno, CA	(1)	(1)	(1)	Richmond, VA	AA	A1	(1)

[1] Not rated.

Sources: Standard & Poors, New York, NY; Moody's Investors Service, New York, NY (copyright); and Fitch IBCA, New York, NY.

No. 513. State Resources, Expenditures, and Balances: 1996 and 1997

[In millions of dollars. For fiscal year ending in year shown; see text; Section 9. **General funds** exclude special funds earmarked for particular purposes, such as highway trust funds and federal funds; they support most on-going broad-based State services and are available for appropriation to support any governmental activity. Minus sign (-) indicates deficit]

STATE	EXPENDITURES BY FUND SOURCE Total, 1996	1997[1] Total[2]	Gen-eral fund	Federal funds	Other state funds	STATE GENERAL FUND Resources[3][4] 1996	1997[1]	Expenditures[4] 1996	1997[1]	Balance[5] 1996	1997[1]
United States . . .	750,733	782,815	374,601	201,731	191,572	389,031	408,065	371,421	386,702	16,259	18,800
Alabama	11,652	11,852	4,481	3,470	3,888	4,298	4,498	4,240	4,475	58	23
Alaska	4,168	4,242	2,320	983	939	2,347	(NA)	2,347	(NA)	(NA)	(NA)
Arizona	12,766	13,808	4,884	3,537	5,319	4,933	5,413	4,533	4,897	400	516
Arkansas	7,609	8,271	2,624	2,053	3,529	2,632	2,772	2,632	2,772	-	-
California	90,211	96,251	48,443	32,011	13,593	46,078	49,994	45,393	49,088	[6]685	[6]906
Colorado	8,968	9,266	4,508	1,905	2,853	4,758	5,049	4,408	4,534	[6]369	[6]375
Connecticut	13,715	13,737	9,200	1,977	1,527	9,111	9,582	8,861	9,320	250	263
Delaware	3,743	4,049	1,766	601	1,532	2,030	2,159	1,651	1,766	[6]379	[6]393
Florida	38,131	40,101	15,405	8,553	14,628	14,997	16,136	14,710	15,447	287	689
Georgia	19,906	19,824	9,884	4,830	4,543	10,928	11,776	10,439	11,043	489	733
Hawaii	6,310	6,317	3,186	1,014	1,669	3,284	3,322	3,124	3,186	161	136
Idaho	2,870	2,963	1,392	871	696	1,349	1,405	1,337	1,392	12	13
Illinois	27,131	28,163	13,539	6,312	7,844	18,267	19,280	18,041	18,474	426	806
Indiana	14,304	15,212	7,931	3,699	3,554	8,249	9,069	7,344	7,538	805	1,138
Iowa	8,867	9,407	4,139	2,055	3,213	4,095	4,471	3,781	4,014	253	349
Kansas	7,629	7,884	3,559	1,875	2,386	3,818	4,066	3,439	3,538	379	528
Kentucky	12,589	11,983	5,649	3,323	3,011	5,789	6,187	5,286	5,649	223	284
Louisiana	13,749	14,733	5,263	4,593	4,651	5,311	5,993	5,090	5,838	318	135
Maine	3,906	3,950	1,748	1,201	947	1,723	1,816	1,682	1,769	13	16
Maryland	14,559	15,054	7,380	3,386	3,838	7,396	7,581	7,383	7,374	13	207
Massachusetts	19,736	20,942	14,779	4,233	875	18,054	18,263	16,881	18,064	[6]1,172	199
Michigan	30,778	30,619	8,273	8,392	13,950	8,673	8,366	8,673	8,313	[6]0	53
Minnesota	14,647	15,545	9,730	3,139	2,430	10,421	11,546	9,078	9,551	[6]1,343	1,995
Mississippi	7,066	7,699	2,732	2,652	2,204	2,816	2,942	2,731	2,755	[6]86	94
Missouri	12,428	12,974	6,483	2,814	3,528	6,285	6,716	5,822	6,482	464	234
Montana	2,333	2,370	993	790	587	1,017	1,028	985	993	30	30
Nebraska	4,247	4,546	1,860	1,124	1,558	2,005	2,226	1,758	1,870	248	355
Nevada	(NA)	(NA)	(NA)	(NA)	(NA)	1,393	1,660	1,257	1,552	159	108
New Hampshire	2,247	2,306	855	797	604	808	893	852	848	-44	-1
New Jersey	23,301	23,422	15,889	4,920	2,427	16,234	16,939	15,532	15,858	[6]867	[6]1,108
New Mexico	6,209	6,616	2,916	2,037	1,663	2,937	3,054	2,773	2,975	144	[6]81
New York	68,688	66,929	30,636	20,318	14,396	33,331	33,330	32,679	32,897	287	[6]433
North Carolina	18,194	20,693	10,465	5,551	4,032	10,411	11,226	9,685	10,467	[6]291	[6]319
North Dakota	1,789	1,997	668	695	634	699	767	651	685	48	[6]82
Ohio	30,516	32,834	16,404	4,649	10,813	16,645	17,504	15,858	16,404	251	149
Oklahoma	8,175	8,567	3,836	2,180	2,435	3,838	4,105	3,549	3,880	289	225
Oregon	11,900	12,895	3,866	2,669	6,360	4,060	4,628	3,531	3,900	529	794
Pennsylvania	31,619	33,209	16,466	9,655	6,749	16,347	17,058	16,279	16,548	156	403
Rhode Island	3,585	3,609	1,714	1,015	826	1,714	1,817	1,714	1,772	-	46
South Carolina	10,918	12,499	4,769	3,719	3,872	4,935	5,187	4,336	4,613	[6]599	[6]574
South Dakota	1,656	1,718	635	603	477	631	649	616	639	-	-
Tennessee	13,603	14,750	6,056	5,144	3,078	5,471	5,796	5,326	5,500	[6]125	276
Texas	39,987	39,855	24,736	11,485	3,585	26,682	27,115	24,636	24,736	2,046	2,379
Utah	4,967	5,504	3,014	1,231	1,228	2,793	3,046	2,595	2,981	197	65
Vermont	1,610	1,658	690	575	339	707	771	702	771	-	-
Virginia	17,181	18,081	7,988	3,097	6,644	7,759	8,438	7,655	8,183	104	255
Washington	17,297	18,651	9,051	3,732	5,139	9,175	9,626	8,619	9,113	556	513
West Virginia	4,915	5,309	1,986	2,008	1,103	2,539	2,640	2,338	2,457	158	149
Wisconsin	16,678	17,939	9,305	3,786	4,848	8,747	9,608	8,132	9,284	[6]582	321
Wyoming	1,680	2,012	505	472	1,028	512	551	459	499	53	[6]52

- Represents zero.   NA Not available.   [1] Estimated.   [2] Includes bonds not shown separately.   [3] Includes funds budgeted, adjustments, and balances from previous year.   [4] May or may not include budget stabilization fund transfers, depending on state accounting practices.   [5] Resources less expenditures.   [6] Ending balance is held in a budget stabilization fund.

Source: National Association of State Budget Officers, Washington, DC, *1997 State Expenditure Report,* and National Governors' Association and NASBO, *Fiscal Survey of the States,* semi-annual (copyright).

No. 514. State Governments—Summary of Finances: 1980 to 1996

[For fiscal year ending in year shown; see text; Section 9]

ITEM	TOTAL (mil. dol.)				PER CAPITA [1] (dollars)			
	1980	1990	1995	1996	1980	1990	1995	1996
Borrowing and revenue	293,356	672,994	957,452	1,026,450	1,299	2,712	3,651	3,879
Borrowing	16,394	40,532	53,697	60,152	73	163	205	227
Revenue	276,962	632,462	903,756	966,298	1,226	2,549	3,447	3,651
General revenue	233,592	517,720	739,016	770,006	1,034	2,087	2,818	2,910
Taxes	137,075	300,779	399,148	418,264	607	1,212	1,522	1,581
Sales and gross receipts	67,855	147,404	196,851	205,687	300	594	751	777
General	43,168	99,929	132,236	139,279	191	403	504	526
Motor fuels	9,722	19,379	25,440	25,981	43	78	97	98
Alcoholic beverages	2,478	3,191	3,597	3,667	11	13	14	14
Tobacco products	3,738	5,541	7,348	7,338	17	22	28	28
Other	8,750	19,365	28,230	29,423	39	78	108	111
Licenses	8,690	18,849	26,083	27,036	38	76	99	102
Motor vehicles	4,936	9,850	12,433	12,740	22	40	47	48
Corporations in general	1,388	3,096	5,018	5,158	6	12	19	19
Other	2,366	5,903	8,632	9,138	10	24	33	35
Individual income	37,089	96,076	125,610	133,976	164	387	479	506
Corporation net income	13,321	21,751	29,075	29,316	59	88	111	111
Property	2,892	5,775	9,518	9,974	13	23	36	38
Other	7,227	10,922	12,014	12,275	32	44	46	46
Charges and miscellaneous	32,190	90,612	124,310	130,273	142	365	474	492
Intergovernmental revenue	64,326	126,329	215,558	221,469	285	509	822	837
From Federal Government	61,892	118,353	202,485	208,100	274	477	772	786
Public welfare	24,680	59,397	114,945	118,154	109	239	438	446
Education	12,765	21,271	31,944	34,055	57	86	122	129
Highways	8,860	13,931	19,419	18,809	39	56	74	71
Other	15,587	23,754	25,834	26,015	69	96	99	98
From local governments	2,434	7,976	13,073	13,370	11	32	50	51
Utility revenue	1,304	3,305	3,845	3,919	6	13	15	15
Liquor store revenue	2,765	2,907	3,073	3,160	12	12	12	12
Insurance trust revenue [2]	39,301	108,530	157,821	189,213	174	437	602	715
Employee retirement	21,146	78,898	104,451	139,316	94	318	398	526
Unemployment compensation	13,468	18,370	37,041	33,685	60	74	141	127
Expenditure and debt redemption	263,494	592,213	874,365	902,353	1,166	2,387	3,335	3,410
Expenditure	257,812	572,318	836,894	859,959	1,141	2,307	3,192	3,250
General expenditure	228,223	508,284	733,504	755,277	1,010	2,049	2,797	2,854
Education	87,939	184,935	249,670	263,519	389	745	952	996
Public welfare	44,219	104,971	194,854	195,731	196	423	743	740
Health and hospitals	17,855	42,666	60,003	62,033	79	172	229	234
Highways	25,044	44,249	57,374	58,255	111	178	219	220
Police protection	2,263	5,166	6,451	7,173	10	21	25	27
Correction	4,449	17,266	26,069	27,324	20	70	99	103
Natural resources	4,346	9,909	12,534	12,862	19	40	48	49
Housing and community development	601	2,856	3,466	3,836	3	12	13	14
Other and unallocable	41,507	96,266	97,003	99,877	184	388	370	377
Utility expenditure	2,401	7,131	7,586	8,043	11	29	29	30
Liquor store expenditure	2,206	2,452	2,522	2,593	10	10	10	10
Insurance trust expenditure [2]	24,981	54,452	93,282	94,045	111	219	356	355
Employee retirement	10,256	29,562	47,541	53,083	45	119	181	201
Unemployment compensation	12,006	16,423	35,032	29,337	53	66	134	111
By character and object:								
Intergovernmental expenditure	84,504	175,028	240,978	252,102	374	705	919	953
Direct expenditure	173,307	397,291	595,916	607,856	767	1,601	2,273	2,297
Current operation	108,131	258,046	396,035	405,416	479	1,040	1,510	1,532
Capital outlay	23,325	45,524	57,829	58,915	103	183	221	223
Construction	19,736	34,803	46,113	46,924	87	140	176	177
Land and existing structure	1,345	3,471	2,676	2,968	6	14	10	11
Equipment	2,243	7,250	9,039	9,022	10	29	34	34
Assistance and subsidies	9,818	16,902	23,511	23,313	43	68	90	88
Interest on debt	7,052	22,367	25,259	26,167	31	90	96	99
Insurance benefits [3]	24,981	54,452	93,282	94,045	111	219	356	355
Debt redemption	5,682	19,895	37,471	42,395	25	80	143	160
Debt outstanding, year end	121,958	318,254	427,239	447,339	540	1,283	1,629	1,690
Long-term	119,821	315,490	421,139	441,489	530	1,272	1,606	1,668
Full-faith and credit	49,364	74,972	116,195	118,549	219	302	443	448
Nonguaranteed	70,457	240,518	304,944	322,940	312	969	1,163	1,220
Short-term	2,137	2,764	6,100	5,849	9	11	23	22
Net long-term [4]	79,810	125,524	205,348	219,392	353	506	783	829
Full-faith and credit only	39,357	63,481	106,571	108,955	174	256	406	412

[1] 1980 and 1990 based on enumerated resident population as of April 1; other years based on estimated resident population as of July 1.   [2] Includes other items not shown separately.   [3] Includes repayments.   [4] Less cash and investment assets specifically held for redemption of long-term debt.

Source: U.S. Bureau of the Census, *State Government Finances,* Series GF, No. 3, annual, 1980-92; <http://www.census.gov/ftp/pub/govs/www/state.html> (accessed 10 June 1998).

No. 515. State Governments—Revenue, by State: 1996

[**In millions of dollars, except as noted.** For fiscal year ending in year shown; see text, Section 9]

STATE	Total revenue [1]	GENERAL REVENUE							
		Total	Per capita [2]		Intergovernmental revenue			Charges and miscellaneous		
			Total (dol.)	Rank	Total	From federal government	From local governments	Total	Current charges	Miscellaneous general revenue
United States..	966,298	770,006	2,910	X	221,469	208,100	13,370	130,273	67,145	63,128
Alabama	12,741	10,894	2,541	40	3,347	3,301	46	2,290	1,641	649
Alaska.	8,254	6,819	11,272	1	1,017	1,012	5	4,283	294	3,988
Arizona	12,594	10,867	2,451	45	3,105	2,767	338	1,352	666	686
Arkansas	8,653	7,023	2,802	25	2,163	2,156	7	1,152	736	415
California.	123,342	98,185	3,082	21	29,087	26,731	2,356	11,351	6,743	4,609
Colorado	11,866	9,461	2,479	43	2,746	2,726	20	1,895	1,071	824
Connecticut	14,349	12,357	3,782	6	2,734	2,729	5	1,793	845	948
Delaware.	3,619	3,303	4,565	2	662	633	29	952	466	487
Florida.	41,680	32,994	2,288	49	8,493	8,171	322	4,801	1,818	2,983
Georgia	22,409	18,345	2,501	41	5,420	5,319	101	2,633	1,425	1,207
Hawaii.	6,383	5,379	4,547	3	1,228	1,220	8	1,072	756	316
Idaho	4,384	3,305	2,783	27	850	844	7	597	280	318
Illinois	36,991	30,306	2,559	38	8,394	7,873	521	4,635	1,891	2,744
Indiana	16,550	15,065	2,585	37	3,750	3,625	125	2,878	1,678	1,200
Iowa	9,245	8,133	2,856	24	2,139	2,057	82	1,554	979	574
Kansas	7,864	6,892	2,672	34	1,694	1,658	37	1,219	729	490
Kentucky	13,788	11,571	2,981	22	3,152	3,141	11	1,929	1,085	844
Louisiana	14,296	11,833	2,726	33	4,111	4,084	26	2,816	1,621	1,195
Maine	4,267	3,836	3,097	20	1,245	1,242	3	694	287	407
Maryland	16,041	14,011	2,769	28	3,240	3,126	114	2,605	1,318	1,286
Massachusetts . . .	25,197	22,845	3,754	7	5,827	5,354	474	4,562	1,814	2,748
Michigan	38,047	32,129	3,302	14	7,760	7,313	447	5,240	3,200	2,040
Minnesota	20,525	16,192	3,483	9	3,620	3,461	159	2,330	1,325	1,005
Mississippi	8,865	7,461	2,752	30	2,696	2,608	88	904	675	229
Missouri.	17,051	13,022	2,428	46	3,711	3,690	20	2,101	1,103	998
Montana	3,476	2,831	3,229	15	991	977	15	583	250	334
Nebraska.	4,999	4,536	2,751	31	1,190	1,164	26	977	640	337
Nevada	5,997	4,146	2,590	36	804	764	40	452	254	199
New Hampshire . .	3,561	2,706	2,333	48	1,011	862	149	858	372	486
New Jersey	35,857	26,615	3,326	12	6,663	6,424	240	5,567	2,529	3,038
New Mexico	8,129	6,318	3,692	8	1,794	1,749	45	1,464	599	865
New York.	94,277	71,219	3,927	5	27,668	22,373	5,296	9,401	3,941	5,460
North Carolina . . .	23,387	20,047	2,743	32	5,758	5,300	458	2,407	1,525	882
North Dakota	2,569	2,144	3,337	11	660	631	29	499	361	138
Ohio	43,823	29,467	2,640	35	8,726	8,485	241	5,091	2,882	2,209
Oklahoma	10,609	8,156	2,475	44	2,197	2,119	78	1,341	934	407
Oregon	15,432	9,958	3,115	19	3,334	3,267	67	2,208	1,141	1,067
Pennsylvania	42,796	33,512	2,783	26	9,151	9,063	88	6,066	3,512	2,554
Rhode Island	4,271	3,346	3,385	10	1,110	1,053	57	686	253	433
South Carolina . . .	12,602	10,261	2,761	29	3,187	3,062	125	1,961	1,414	547
South Dakota	2,284	1,886	2,557	39	695	687	8	461	181	280
Tennessee	14,749	12,510	2,357	47	4,726	4,689	38	1,599	1,133	466
Texas	51,118	42,616	2,232	50	13,077	12,612	465	8,268	3,344	4,924
Utah	6,773	5,831	2,890	23	1,757	1,712	45	1,160	826	335
Vermont	2,146	1,950	3,325	13	650	647	4	459	286	173
Virginia	20,072	16,617	2,493	42	3,515	3,377	138	4,201	2,483	1,719
Washington	24,790	17,195	3,115	18	3,891	3,834	56	2,718	1,685	1,034
West Virginia	6,866	5,836	3,206	16	2,094	2,079	15	971	555	416
Wisconsin	24,365	16,071	3,123	17	3,860	3,578	282	2,626	1,505	1,121
Wyoming	2,348	2,004	4,175	4	768	753	15	610	95	515

See footnote at end of table.

No. 515. State Governments—Revenue, by State: 1996—Continued

[See headnote, page 318]

STATE	GENERAL REVENUE							Utility revenue	Liquor store revenue	Insurance trust revenue
		Taxes								
	Total	General sales	Selective sales [3]	License taxes	Indi- vidual income	Corpo- ration net income	Other taxes			
United States	**418,264**	**139,279**	**66,409**	**27,036**	**133,976**	**29,316**	**22,248**	**3,919**	**3,160**	**189,213**
Alabama	5,258	1,439	1,335	423	1,578	218	265	(X)	136	1,710
Alaska	1,519	(X)	99	79	(X)	326	1,015	17	(X)	1,418
Arizona	6,409	2,720	938	391	1,494	448	418	21	(X)	1,706
Arkansas	3,709	1,376	564	216	1,162	229	162	(X)	(X)	1,630
California	57,747	18,980	5,113	3,035	20,760	5,831	4,028	143	(X)	25,014
Colorado	4,820	1,322	716	256	2,274	206	47	(X)	(X)	2,405
Connecticut	7,830	2,445	1,487	331	2,614	641	311	21	(X)	1,972
Delaware	1,688	(X)	253	533	632	166	105	7	(X)	309
Florida	19,699	11,429	3,812	1,315	(X)	1,008	2,136	5	(X)	8,681
Georgia	10,292	3,824	962	420	4,244	719	123	(X)	(X)	4,064
Hawaii	3,079	1,432	473	85	1,000	66	24	(X)	(X)	1,004
Idaho	1,857	600	252	156	655	153	41	(X)	47	1,032
Illinois	17,277	5,057	3,428	952	5,781	1,621	437	(X)	(X)	6,684
Indiana	8,437	2,868	894	202	3,478	894	102	(X)	(X)	1,485
Iowa	4,441	1,456	691	414	1,588	203	88	(X)	87	1,024
Kansas	3,979	1,401	530	203	1,377	255	213	(X)	(X)	973
Kentucky	6,489	1,784	1,282	381	2,075	285	683	(X)	(X)	2,218
Louisiana	4,906	1,622	937	418	1,160	328	441	(X)	(X)	2,463
Maine	1,897	658	278	114	709	71	66	(X)	70	361
Maryland	8,167	2,000	1,555	358	3,485	331	439	89	(X)	1,941
Massachusetts	12,455	2,610	1,278	398	6,707	1,228	235	69	(X)	2,283
Michigan	19,129	6,587	1,738	982	5,868	2,190	1,764	(X)	475	5,443
Minnesota	10,243	2,900	1,592	769	4,136	703	142	(X)	(X)	4,333
Mississippi	3,861	1,832	770	247	742	202	67	(X)	134	1,269
Missouri	7,210	2,465	986	516	2,741	426	76	(X)	(X)	4,029
Montana	1,256	(X)	269	148	383	76	380	(X)	39	606
Nebraska	2,369	815	410	158	840	127	20	(X)	(X)	463
Nevada	2,889	1,572	863	313	(X)	(X)	141	46	(X)	1,806
New Hampshire	837	(X)	429	108	52	180	69	-	223	632
New Jersey	14,385	4,318	3,045	753	4,734	1,155	379	447	(X)	8,796
New Mexico	3,061	1,284	452	165	643	163	354	(X)	(X)	1,811
New York	34,150	6,963	4,950	974	17,399	2,730	1,134	2,156	(X)	20,902
North Carolina	11,882	2,971	2,173	733	4,929	939	137	(X)	(X)	3,340
North Dakota	985	282	278	78	152	74	122	(X)	(X)	424
Ohio	15,649	4,991	2,613	1,219	5,903	807	116	(X)	373	13,983
Oklahoma	4,618	1,210	660	658	1,512	164	413	246	(X)	2,207
Oregon	4,416	(X)	591	581	2,823	300	120	(X)	184	5,290
Pennsylvania	18,295	5,701	3,056	1,809	5,214	1,504	1,010	(X)	693	8,592
Rhode Island	1,549	465	313	80	581	87	23	8	(X)	917
South Carolina	5,113	1,919	684	389	1,813	251	56	644	(X)	1,697
South Dakota	730	383	189	90	(X)	38	29	(X)	(X)	397
Tennessee	6,185	3,537	1,207	610	114	534	182	(X)	(X)	2,239
Texas	21,271	10,811	6,424	3,048	(X)	(X)	988	(X)	(X)	8,502
Utah	2,914	1,170	300	99	1,139	177	29	(X)	88	854
Vermont	841	183	221	72	281	45	40	(X)	28	168
Virginia	8,900	1,996	1,593	419	4,301	363	229	(X)	249	3,206
Washington	10,586	6,182	1,685	493	(X)	(X)	2,226	(X)	254	7,341
West Virginia	2,771	797	655	156	751	235	177	-	45	985
Wisconsin	9,586	2,708	1,322	614	4,151	621	170	(X)	(X)	8,294
Wyoming	626	211	63	74	(X)	(X)	278	(X)	34	310

- Represents or rounds to zero.   X Not applicable.   [1] Includes items not shown separately.   [2] Based on estimated resident population as of July 1.   [3] Special tax rate on specific items.

Source: U.S. Bureau of the Census; <http://www.census.gov/govs/www/state.html> (accessed 10 June 1998).

No. 516. State Governments—Expenditures and Debt, by State: 1996

[In millions of dollars, except as indicated. For fiscal year ending in year shown; see text, Section 9]

STATE	Total expenditure [1]	GENERAL EXPENDITURE								
		Total		Inter-govern-mental	Direct expen-ditures	Selected functions				
		Amount	Per capita [2] (dol.)			Educa-tion	Public welfare	Health and hospitals	High-ways	Police protection
United States .	859,959	755,277	2,854	252,102	503,174	263,519	195,731	62,033	58,255	7,173
Alabama	12,127	10,992	2,564	3,077	7,915	4,872	2,325	1,330	881	87
Alaska	5,630	5,105	8,438	1,058	4,047	1,236	713	191	623	53
Arizona	11,898	10,818	2,440	4,255	6,563	3,788	2,605	600	1,143	120
Arkansas	7,050	6,481	2,586	1,636	4,845	2,509	1,583	589	698	52
California	113,361	98,783	3,101	48,759	50,024	34,780	28,805	8,344	4,522	1,012
Colorado	10,312	8,902	2,333	2,850	6,052	3,945	2,081	381	796	52
Connecticut	13,530	11,736	3,592	2,424	9,311	2,888	2,815	1,340	712	105
Delaware	3,248	2,926	4,044	511	2,414	962	463	211	257	48
Florida	36,454	33,619	2,332	11,140	22,479	10,872	7,318	2,606	3,241	295
Georgia	20,013	18,589	2,535	5,285	13,304	7,933	4,623	1,289	1,228	150
Hawaii	5,947	5,229	4,420	144	5,085	1,548	915	487	270	9
Idaho	3,501	3,083	2,596	999	2,083	1,361	528	106	346	30
Illinois	34,111	30,092	2,540	8,549	21,543	8,773	9,377	2,310	2,435	295
Indiana	15,368	14,422	2,475	5,091	9,331	6,142	3,155	608	1,532	146
Iowa	8,853	8,183	2,873	2,672	5,511	3,263	1,710	698	1,046	61
Kansas	7,276	6,680	2,590	2,263	4,417	2,961	1,102	565	996	40
Kentucky	11,842	10,603	2,731	2,825	7,778	4,263	2,770	638	1,059	115
Louisiana	14,030	12,591	2,901	3,026	9,565	4,348	2,976	1,494	858	166
Maine	4,240	3,735	3,016	743	2,992	1,080	1,256	235	362	34
Maryland	15,554	13,355	2,639	3,238	10,117	4,050	2,923	1,072	1,220	274
Massachusetts . .	24,950	22,790	3,745	5,160	17,630	4,492	5,999	2,182	1,803	287
Michigan	35,080	31,644	3,252	13,299	18,345	13,812	6,440	3,406	1,936	229
Minnesota	17,325	15,749	3,388	6,068	9,681	5,783	4,129	1,117	1,214	89
Mississippi	8,217	7,437	2,744	2,506	4,931	2,724	1,658	623	718	52
Missouri	12,841	11,751	2,191	3,434	8,317	4,387	2,898	1,032	1,152	130
Montana	3,136	2,729	3,113	699	2,030	1,014	510	168	340	30
Nebraska	4,490	4,320	2,620	1,176	3,144	1,514	976	503	574	43
Nevada	4,831	4,024	2,514	1,624	2,400	1,539	653	140	400	39
New Hampshire . .	3,240	2,841	2,449	392	2,449	579	988	146	224	27
New Jersey	32,315	26,035	3,254	7,771	18,264	7,750	6,744	1,588	1,812	259
New Mexico	6,740	6,222	3,636	2,055	4,166	2,457	1,118	577	651	56
New York	82,420	68,866	3,798	25,417	43,449	17,326	26,146	6,433	2,841	353
North Carolina . . .	21,221	19,410	2,656	6,653	12,757	8,051	4,419	1,577	1,733	195
North Dakota . . .	2,064	1,860	2,895	411	1,449	705	361	84	209	6
Ohio	35,517	28,492	2,552	10,054	18,439	10,315	7,392	2,268	2,203	192
Oklahoma	9,265	7,912	2,401	2,537	5,375	3,476	1,658	593	832	51
Oregon	11,858	9,633	3,014	3,110	6,523	3,473	2,116	809	933	120
Pennsylvania . . .	38,699	33,136	2,752	9,676	23,460	10,526	9,835	3,005	2,427	625
Rhode Island . . .	4,061	3,400	3,441	505	2,895	886	882	332	210	30
South Carolina . .	12,400	10,683	2,874	2,720	7,963	3,832	2,554	1,308	616	140
South Dakota . . .	1,975	1,861	2,523	369	1,492	529	393	107	265	20
Tennessee	13,829	12,885	2,428	3,517	9,367	4,383	3,958	1,058	1,233	87
Texas	46,082	41,519	2,175	12,364	29,154	17,049	10,636	3,079	3,563	292
Utah	6,172	5,663	2,807	1,527	4,136	2,751	952	440	357	44
Vermont	2,061	1,918	3,270	313	1,605	623	516	60	189	34
Virginia	17,717	16,307	2,446	4,463	11,844	6,430	2,916	1,613	2,011	313
Washington	21,086	17,587	3,186	5,430	12,157	7,475	3,804	1,405	1,435	172
West Virginia . . .	6,970	5,623	3,089	1,325	4,297	2,079	1,588	203	705	39
Wisconsin	16,990	15,251	2,964	6,290	8,961	5,324	3,193	969	1,172	61
Wyoming	2,062	1,807	3,764	687	1,120	659	253	118	270	12

See footnotes at end of table.

No. 516. State Governments—Expenditures and Debt, by State: 1996—Continued

[In millions of dollars, except as indicated. For fiscal year ending in year shown; see text, Section 9]

STATE	GENERAL EXPENDITURE					Utility expen-ditures	Liquor stores expen-ditures	Insur-ance trust expen-ditures	Cash and security holdings	DEBT OUTSTANDING	
	Selected functions									Total	Per capita [2] (dol.)
	Correc-tions	Natural resources	Parks and recre-ation	Govern-mental adminis-tration	Inter-est on general debt						
United States .	27,324	12,862	3,479	24,666	25,402	8,043	2,593	94,045	1,558,249	447,339	1,690
Alabama	220	174	8	283	217	(X)	147	988	18,014	3,645	850
Alaska	150	267	15	294	240	21	(X)	504	31,310	3,177	5,251
Arizona	499	169	29	335	181	25	(X)	1,056	21,216	2,936	662
Arkansas	171	136	39	206	121	(X)	(X)	569	10,668	2,142	855
California	3,843	1,876	210	3,095	2,448	100	(X)	14,479	194,354	45,859	1,439
Colorado	353	158	43	294	335	5	(X)	1,405	26,043	3,577	937
Connecticut	465	72	48	536	912	186	(X)	1,608	20,152	16,415	5,024
Delaware	113	44	43	171	270	54	(X)	269	7,889	4,279	5,914
Florida	1,647	1,241	125	1,253	1,112	63	(X)	2,772	59,587	15,515	1,076
Georgia	817	355	184	399	345	(X)	(X)	1,424	32,554	6,200	845
Hawaii	106	75	109	224	333	-	(X)	717	9,676	5,117	4,326
Idaho.	98	115	20	99	93	(X)	37	382	7,014	1,454	1,224
Illinois	873	266	203	836	1,493	(X)	(X)	4,019	50,536	22,676	1,914
Indiana	378	160	43	293	271	(X)	(X)	946	21,813	6,117	1,050
Iowa	184	204	17	300	125	(X)	60	610	12,990	2,065	725
Kansas	195	159	5	235	72	(X)	(X)	596	7,557	1,161	450
Kentucky	226	255	91	429	376	8	(X)	1,232	19,462	7,030	1,811
Louisiana	384	319	132	319	745	(X)	(X)	1,439	23,556	7,452	1,717
Maine	64	106	8	120	170	(X)	47	458	6,372	3,160	2,551
Maryland	743	303	68	621	594	393	(X)	1,805	30,394	9,691	1,915
Massachusetts . .	729	228	97	901	1,708	88	(X)	2,072	33,203	29,295	4,814
Michigan	1,241	401	59	684	696	(X)	370	3,066	46,643	13,668	1,405
Minnesota	302	329	88	461	288	(X)	(X)	1,576	30,369	4,858	1,045
Mississippi	230	168	108	133	136	(X)	108	672	13,089	2,232	823
Missouri.	312	231	28	375	307	(X)	(X)	1,090	29,305	7,128	1,329
Montana	66	110	6	122	136	(X)	30	377	6,492	2,244	2,560
Nebraska	94	130	21	119	85	(X)	(X)	170	6,260	1,402	850
Nevada	151	57	14	163	129	83	(X)	725	10,136	2,259	1,411
New Hampshire. .	62	35	13	130	376	-	182	217	8,373	5,833	5,027
New Jersey	875	163	382	907	1,329	1,422	(X)	4,857	56,754	25,602	3,199
New Mexico	175	89	31	211	110	(X)	(X)	519	16,901	2,147	1,254
New York	2,377	326	291	2,750	3,354	4,657	(X)	8,897	142,507	73,122	4,032
North Carolina. . .	873	403	87	582	251	(X)	(X)	1,810	38,110	4,513	618
North Dakota . . .	17	77	7	59	55	(X)	(X)	203	4,173	819	1,274
Ohio	1,144	284	80	898	822	(X)	260	6,765	105,128	12,628	1,131
Oklahoma	296	133	50	326	159	231	(X)	1,123	14,607	3,889	1,180
Oregon	291	239	32	613	343	1	111	2,113	22,294	6,086	1,904
Pennsylvania . . .	1,077	432	113	1,028	1,088	(X)	648	4,915	67,402	15,046	1,250
Rhode Island . . .	116	28	30	181	295	37	(X)	624	7,600	5,506	5,571
South Carolina . .	391	171	51	221	185	654	(X)	1,062	18,468	5,324	1,433
South Dakota . . .	44	86	18	79	108	(X)	(X)	113	5,110	1,704	2,310
Tennessee	445	166	82	284	192	4	(X)	941	18,538	3,069	578
Texas	2,351	643	67	932	741	(X)	(X)	4,563	103,090	14,576	763
Utah	158	133	35	235	128	(X)	66	443	11,470	2,464	1,221
Vermont.	43	53	9	85	105	1	26	116	2,734	1,718	2,929
Virginia	809	138	69	678	550	4	214	1,192	31,094	8,793	1,319
Washington	497	438	57	406	509	(X)	219	3,280	40,086	8,991	1,629
West Virginia . . .	82	140	40	266	163	5	39	1,303	5,860	2,830	1,555
Wisconsin.	513	496	57	427	548	(X)	(X)	1,739	44,764	9,127	1,773
Wyoming	32	83	16	71	54	(X)	30	225	6,530	799	1,665

- Represents or rounds to zero.   X Not applicable.   [1] Includes items not shown separately.   [2] Based on estimated resident population as of July 1.

Source: U.S. Bureau of the Census, <http://www.census.gov/govs/www/state.html> (accessed 10 June 1998).

No. 517. State Government Tax Collections, by State: 1997

[In millions of dollars, except as indicated. For fiscal year ending in year shown; see text; Section 9. Includes local shares of state-imposed taxes. N.e.c.= Not elsewhere classified]

STATE	ALL TAXES Total[1]	Per capita Total (dol.)	Per capita Rank	Total property taxes	SALES AND GROSS RECEIPTS TAXES Total[1]	Total general sales taxes	Selective sales taxes Total[1]	Alcoholic beverages and tobacco sales	Insurance premiums	Motor fuels sales	Public utilities
United States ...	443,493	1,660	(X)	10,275	215,802	147,147	68,655	11,129	9,017	27,081	8,606
Alabama	5,484	1,270	46	131	2,866	1,506	1,361	187	156	473	414
Alaska	1,619	2,657	1	54	96	(X)	96	27	28	36	3
Arizona	6,834	1,500	32	257	3,803	2,855	948	214	138	505	88
Arkansas	3,777	1,497	33	8	2,018	1,429	588	121	66	352	(X)
California	61,667	1,911	11	3,612	25,222	19,974	5,248	942	1,284	2,822	43
Colorado	5,290	1,359	44	(X)	2,179	1,413	766	92	114	491	7
Connecticut	8,146	2,491	3	-	4,165	2,598	1,567	165	186	544	179
Delaware	1,743	2,383	5	(X)	253	(X)	253	33	43	102	23
Florida	21,080	1,439	39	788	16,081	12,068	4,013	996	487	1,481	576
Georgia	10,898	1,456	37	38	4,905	3,916	990	215	222	553	(X)
Hawaii	3,088	2,602	2	(X)	1,926	1,457	469	75	77	75	114
Idaho	1,961	1,620	23	(X)	924	622	302	36	47	212	3
Illinois	18,545	1,559	26	204	8,796	5,296	3,500	485	127	1,221	889
Indiana	9,101	1,552	27	4	4,132	3,043	1,089	123	138	617	5
Iowa	4,686	1,643	20	(X)	2,228	1,500	728	112	106	386	(X)
Kansas	4,230	1,630	21	44	2,007	1,476	531	119	90	303	1
Kentucky	6,819	1,745	15	415	3,194	1,883	1,311	81	276	407	(X)
Louisiana	5,646	1,297	45	25	2,759	1,828	931	138	250	495	13
Maine	2,019	1,626	22	42	965	683	282	78	43	156	-
Maryland	8,604	1,689	17	236	3,695	2,095	1,600	127	166	614	156
Massachusetts	13,305	2,175	6	-	4,217	2,876	1,341	343	298	603	(X)
Michigan	20,326	2,080	7	1,688	8,872	7,132	1,740	674	186	841	(X)
Minnesota	11,223	2,395	4	10	4,776	3,115	1,661	245	181	539	-
Mississippi	4,017	1,471	34	23	2,665	1,916	749	96	103	356	(X)
Missouri	7,816	1,447	38	16	3,702	2,592	1,110	138	186	649	(X)
Montana	1,259	1,433	40	213	260	(X)	260	31	32	171	11
Nebraska	2,548	1,538	28	5	1,281	866	416	64	40	277	3
Nevada	3,034	1,809	12	61	2,601	1,699	903	72	97	217	6
New Hampshire	915	780	50	1	459	(X)	459	62	53	111	57
New Jersey	14,415	1,790	14	3	7,192	4,415	2,777	326	294	465	1,162
New Mexico	3,102	1,793	13	34	1,807	1,346	461	60	61	237	7
New York	34,865	1,922	10	(X)	12,140	7,353	4,787	851	681	474	1,683
North Carolina	12,633	1,701	16	(X)	5,396	3,135	2,261	198	259	998	321
North Dakota	1,064	1,660	19	2	606	311	295	29	21	104	27
Ohio	16,421	1,468	35	18	8,055	5,234	2,821	378	346	1,368	713
Oklahoma	5,061	1,526	30	(X)	1,941	1,273	668	134	143	347	15
Oregon	4,946	1,525	31	-	674	(X)	674	166	76	421	9
Pennsylvania	19,377	1,612	24	203	9,221	6,055	3,166	491	377	790	718
Rhode Island	1,644	1,665	18	4	813	490	324	63	33	124	69
South Carolina	5,381	1,431	41	14	2,735	2,032	703	148	78	328	38
South Dakot	768	1,041	49	(X)	609	411	198	31	34	95	2
Tennessee	6,616	1,233	47	(X)	5,087	3,840	1,247	153	244	723	7
Texas	23,025	1,184	48	(X)	18,404	11,362	7,042	1,086	673	2,383	368
Utah	3,011	1,462	36	(X)	1,580	1,265	315	52	45	217	(X)
Vermont	899	1,527	29	10	409	184	225	27	19	58	8
Virginia	9,628	1,430	42	22	3,767	2,119	1,648	125	219	735	124
Washington	11,202	1,997	8	1,927	8,289	6,572	1,717	417	212	685	241
West Virginia	2,906	1,600	25	-	1,515	831	683	42	77	228	193
Wisconsin	10,187	1,970	9	76	4,231	2,865	1,366	254	102	694	312
Wyoming	662	1,381	43	86	282	215	67	6	13	47	(X)

See footnotes at end of table.

No. 517. State Government Tax Collections, by State: 1997—Continued

[See headnote, page 322]

STATE	LICENSE TAXES					OTHER TAXES				
	Total[1]	Corporation license	Hunting and fishing license	Motor vehicle and operators license	Occupancy and business license, n.e.c.	Total[1]	Individual income	Corporation net income	Death and gift	Severance
United States . . .	28,204	5,871	1,075	14,065	5,768	189,212	145,162	30,557	5,913	4,606
Alabama.	424	110	17	187	100	2,062	1,688	227	45	80
Alaska	78	1	16	29	31	1,392	(X)	331	2	1,059
Arizona.	437	6	15	334	50	2,336	1,668	601	67	(X)
Arkansas	222	8	20	113	66	1,529	1,247	230	19	13
California	2,963	41	74	1,622	1,122	29,871	23,273	5,804	757	37
Colorado.	261	4	54	154	41	2,850	2,560	224	35	30
Connecticut.	341	11	3	238	78	3,640	2,807	530	227	(X)
Delaware	579	391	1	28	149	911	663	173	32	(X)
Florida	1,370	122	15	908	251	2,841	(X)	1,233	537	76
Georgia	405	31	21	238	70	5,549	4,741	726	60	(X)
Hawaii	90	2	-	62	17	1,072	977	68	22	(X)
Idaho	148	1	23	52	39	889	712	138	4	3
Illinois	1,215	124	24	820	237	8,329	6,287	1,804	199	(X)
Indiana.	194	5	15	116	45	4,771	3,751	904	115	1
Iowa	422	35	18	274	70	2,036	1,720	221	88	(X)
Kansas.	212	21	12	138	32	1,967	1,513	291	76	87
Kentucky	427	148	17	161	90	2,783	2,205	293	95	187
Louisiana	436	248	22	105	55	2,426	1,560	380	78	408
Maine.	117	3	12	65	33	895	772	97	15	(X)
Maryland	350	13	11	206	117	4,324	3,769	343	106	(X)
Massachusetts.	431	20	6	307	56	8,657	7,182	1,213	203	(X)
Michigan.	1,016	11	45	691	216	8,750	6,400	2,229	79	41
Minnesota.	821	3	37	537	228	5,616	4,779	699	48	3
Mississippi.	266	75	11	131	40	1,062	791	226	12	33
Missouri	562	89	27	256	155	3,536	3,038	411	81	-
Montana.	144	1	25	37	45	643	434	89	15	56
Nebraska	165	6	10	81	51	1,097	937	137	15	2
Nevada	303	15	-	109	95	69	(X)	(X)	28	39
New Hampshire	121	4	6	65	36	335	53	208	41	(X)
New Jersey.	742	130	12	429	111	6,478	4,825	1,264	313	(X)
New Mexico	134	2	11	91	25	1,128	748	173	18	189
New York	945	67	31	708	72	21,780	17,554	3,042	889	(X)
North Carolina.	767	214	15	419	101	6,471	5,455	870	145	2
North Dakota.	77	(X)	7	42	27	379	163	75	5	136
Ohio	1,358	481	30	595	220	6,990	6,141	737	102	9
Oklahoma.	701	40	12	551	88	2,419	1,698	221	81	404
Oregon.	512	5	26	352	115	3,760	3,273	384	34	53
Pennsylvania.	1,920	971	45	558	280	8,033	5,575	1,576	615	(X)
Rhode Island.	80	10	1	48	20	747	640	89	13	(X)
South Carolina.	411	40	14	113	97	2,221	1,933	239	28	(X)
South Dakota	94	1	12	32	41	65	(X)	37	21	7
Tennessee	738	401	19	238	72	791	128	480	61	1
Texas.	3,265	1,831	65	869	429	1,355	(X)	(X)	207	1,148
Utah	90	4	14	57	13	1,341	1,128	177	10	25
Vermont	68	1	5	42	17	412	323	45	18	(X)
Virginia.	431	26	19	288	87	5,409	4,728	425	92	2
Washington.	510	11	29	269	150	477	(X)	(X)	88	82
West Virginia.	151	6	15	79	25	1,237	786	251	17	177
Wisconsin.	614	71	49	249	236	5,265	4,538	639	51	2
Wyoming.	78	5	19	47	3	217	(X)	-	4	213

- Represents or rounds to zero.   X Not applicable.   [1] Includes amounts not shown separately.

Source: U.S. Bureau of the Census, <http://www.census.gov/govs/www/sttax97.html> (accessed 11 June 1998).

No. 518. Local Governments—Revenue, by State: 1995

[In millions of dollars, except as noted. For fiscal year ending in year shown; see text, Section 9]

STATE	Total revenue[1]	GENERAL REVENUE								Utility revenue
		Total	Per capita[2] (dol.)	Intergovernmental revenue		Total charges and miscellaneous	Taxes			
				From federal government	From state governments		Total	General sales	Other taxes	
United States..	757,400	676,361	2,574	26,286	232,807	155,838	261,430	27,930	205,233	64,788
Alabama	9,010	7,538	1,769	300	2,647	2,384	2,208	889	1,078	1,389
Alaska.	2,560	2,328	3,869	110	821	625	771	107	632	204
Arizona.	11,962	9,847	2,286	392	3,896	2,117	3,442	683	2,614	2,042
Arkansas.	3,894	3,489	1,406	103	1,468	926	992	253	663	387
California	115,059	99,863	3,164	4,158	41,946	25,842	27,917	4,072	21,525	11,601
Colorado	11,214	9,899	2,646	353	2,833	2,503	4,210	1,210	2,854	1,151
Connecticut	8,452	7,901	2,419	279	2,246	773	4,602	-	4,602	367
Delaware	1,423	1,279	1,787	47	583	305	344	-	311	120
District of Columbia . . .	5,663	4,910	8,890	1,924	(X)	548	2,438	486	792	365
Florida.	41,616	37,116	2,617	1,106	10,418	12,251	13,341	342	11,136	4,057
Georgia.	19,370	17,093	2,377	416	4,969	5,248	6,460	1,308	4,680	2,105
Hawaii.	1,600	1,439	1,221	116	179	388	755	-	631	161
Idaho	2,440	2,333	2,003	55	971	641	665	-	652	106
Illinois	34,333	30,349	2,573	1,355	8,534	6,070	14,391	1,088	11,971	2,117
Indiana	13,699	12,546	2,168	304	4,546	2,970	4,727	-	4,283	1,100
Iowa	7,198	6,739	2,372	224	2,188	1,723	2,604	61	2,482	445
Kansas	6,873	6,056	2,357	97	2,065	1,582	2,312	266	1,941	787
Kentucky	6,975	6,283	1,629	235	2,557	1,667	1,824	-	1,212	666
Louisiana.	9,747	9,007	2,081	340	2,992	2,369	3,306	1,745	1,410	654
Maine	2,446	2,363	1,914	77	692	345	1,248	-	1,240	84
Maryland	12,301	11,537	2,295	537	3,131	2,025	5,844	-	3,880	297
Massachusetts . . .	16,127	13,902	2,294	852	4,426	2,124	6,500	-	6,438	1,586
Michigan	26,007	23,964	2,482	840	12,049	5,368	5,707	-	5,238	1,144
Minnesota	16,078	14,630	3,176	351	5,831	3,964	4,484	15	4,371	1,038
Mississippi	5,707	5,282	1,963	181	2,228	1,682	1,192	1	1,138	423
Missouri.	10,994	9,877	1,855	316	2,628	2,250	4,683	941	3,119	933
Montana	1,698	1,648	1,897	105	618	366	559	-	551	50
Nebraska.	5,557	3,713	2,269	156	939	912	1,705	136	1,525	1,754
Nevada	4,271	4,053	2,650	135	1,468	1,221	1,229	75	946	217
New Hampshire . .	2,337	2,278	1,987	59	274	260	1,685	-	1,684	58
New Jersey	24,382	23,691	2,978	308	7,221	3,672	12,490	-	12,433	684
New Mexico	3,777	3,538	2,098	175	1,815	774	773	295	434	240
New York	87,381	80,065	4,412	2,913	26,258	13,868	37,026	5,971	23,814	3,180
North Carolina . . .	18,321	15,712	2,186	493	6,274	4,472	4,473	861	3,510	2,320
North Dakota	1,289	1,217	1,898	73	430	274	441	30	404	63
Ohio	27,896	26,175	2,351	1,033	8,379	5,127	11,636	854	7,989	1,667
Oklahoma	6,628	6,107	1,867	215	2,244	1,722	1,927	765	1,084	498
Oregon	8,998	8,360	2,660	640	2,842	1,911	2,967	-	2,818	630
Pennsylvania	29,540	27,368	2,272	1,440	9,011	5,281	11,636	93	9,344	1,639
Rhode Island	2,023	1,918	1,937	104	524	146	1,144	-	1,143	77
South Carolina . . .	7,881	6,988	1,897	194	2,130	2,367	2,296	52	2,191	891
South Dakota	1,418	1,275	1,736	63	276	236	701	109	578	112
Tennessee	14,447	9,943	1,899	303	3,071	3,067	3,502	973	2,261	4,298
Texas	48,330	42,923	2,291	1,052	13,405	10,065	18,401	2,227	15,160	4,948
Utah	4,873	3,802	1,926	172	1,315	974	1,341	227	1,052	1,071
Vermont	1,237	1,123	1,926	112	250	118	643	-	641	112
Virginia	14,931	13,693	2,074	429	4,235	2,544	6,486	577	5,157	992
Washington	17,837	14,686	2,702	517	5,594	3,955	4,620	1,008	3,122	3,088
West Virginia	3,148	3,032	1,664	87	1,288	815	842	-	810	101
Wisconsin	14,850	13,955	2,729	410	5,549	2,521	5,476	142	5,305	698
Wyoming	1,601	1,529	3,194	31	554	479	465	66	384	69

- Represents or rounds to zero.   X Not applicable.   [1] Includes items not shown separately.   [2] Based on estimated resident population as of July 1.

Source: U.S. Bureau of the Census, <http://www.census.gov/govs/www/esti95.html> (accessed 25 June 1998); and unpublished data.

No. 519. Local Governments—Expenditures and Debt, by State: 1995

[In millions of dollars, except as indicated. For fiscal year ending in year shown; see text, Section 9]

STATE	Total expendi-ture [1]	GENERAL EXPENDITURE								Utility expendi-tures	Debt out-standing
		Total		Direct expendi-tures	Selected functions (direct expenditures)						
		Amount	Per capita [2] (dol.)		Educa-tion	Public welfare	Health and hospi-tals	High-ways	Police protec-tion		
United States . . .	759,368	661,593	2,518	653,663	276,763	32,689	56,460	30,216	35,320	83,629	688,131
Alabama.	9,447	7,876	1,848	7,866	3,008	35	1,605	429	405	1,516	7,462
Alaska	2,595	2,301	3,825	2,301	907	19	107	112	100	286	3,836
Arizona.	11,973	10,036	2,330	9,774	4,223	395	415	457	607	1,877	15,412
Arkansas	3,910	3,535	1,425	3,535	1,879	4	282	233	181	364	3,133
California	116,580	97,675	3,095	96,311	30,952	11,011	9,839	3,396	5,600	15,956	93,784
Colorado.	11,498	9,991	2,670	9,947	3,739	524	695	569	520	1,373	15,631
Connecticut.	8,330	7,805	2,389	7,803	3,946	216	78	295	416	384	3,971
Delaware	1,411	1,296	1,810	1,293	756	1	9	73	71	101	1,165
District of Columbia .	5,925	4,303	7,792	4,303	706	1,137	425	111	238	1,125	4,371
Florida	41,647	36,719	2,589	36,606	14,424	258	3,403	1,564	2,593	4,635	49,082
Georgia	19,111	16,211	2,254	16,176	7,057	75	3,099	614	767	2,731	17,152
Hawaii	1,780	1,486	1,261	1,486	-	15	18	72	177	294	1,988
Idaho	2,448	2,348	2,015	2,339	1,146	32	292	173	117	100	841
Illinois	32,790	27,894	2,365	27,866	12,231	339	1,372	1,577	1,873	3,631	26,853
Indiana.	13,277	12,037	2,080	11,933	5,633	414	1,445	508	437	1,155	7,916
Iowa	7,305	6,708	2,361	6,631	3,028	126	642	689	295	589	5,259
Kansas	6,763	5,968	2,323	5,967	2,871	36	458	493	303	768	6,794
Kentucky	7,034	6,260	1,623	6,258	3,015	36	436	235	253	761	12,265
Louisiana	9,326	8,480	1,959	8,471	3,638	51	1,150	411	520	762	8,794
Maine.	2,373	2,283	1,850	2,283	1,212	29	53	142	91	90	1,571
Maryland	12,141	11,439	2,275	11,361	5,603	42	254	460	655	363	11,977
Massachusetts.	16,597	13,260	2,188	12,727	6,102	78	605	504	791	2,504	10,487
Michigan.	26,251	24,321	2,519	24,218	11,919	441	2,120	1,404	1,198	1,320	17,553
Minnesota.	16,361	14,709	3,193	14,617	5,913	1,015	1,341	1,326	540	1,314	17,195
Mississippi	5,621	5,207	1,935	5,206	2,494	22	932	375	216	413	3,695
Missouri	11,109	9,829	1,846	9,827	5,137	73	630	585	566	1,100	6,512
Montana.	1,707	1,660	1,911	1,655	956	23	70	90	67	46	722
Nebraska	5,530	3,700	2,261	3,693	1,976	52	238	280	139	1,773	4,697
Nevada	4,377	4,144	2,709	4,142	1,297	50	393	269	272	231	5,422
New Hampshire	2,288	2,221	1,937	2,166	1,132	118	17	121	114	67	1,168
New Jersey.	24,698	24,048	3,023	23,682	11,284	1,239	533	830	1,515	637	15,423
New Mexico	3,752	3,491	2,071	3,469	1,613	42	201	205	205	260	3,104
New York	90,122	79,528	4,383	75,584	27,576	9,213	6,353	2,931	3,933	6,616	73,695
North Carolina	18,557	15,636	2,176	15,369	6,747	670	2,674	274	725	2,672	17,444
North Dakota.	1,256	1,166	1,817	1,154	564	34	9	124	44	86	971
Ohio	27,665	25,570	2,297	25,437	11,220	1,325	2,076	1,294	1,416	2,030	16,050
Oklahoma.	6,634	6,114	1,869	6,112	3,068	17	684	315	326	500	5,107
Oregon.	8,988	7,903	2,515	7,899	3,724	32	552	507	378	1,045	5,936
Pennsylvania.	29,101	25,783	2,140	25,773	11,774	1,362	1,212	907	1,051	2,752	38,539
Rhode Island.	1,918	1,808	1,827	1,808	1,015	13	3	53	128	71	793
South Carolina.	7,723	6,786	1,842	6,763	3,140	10	1,333	120	289	935	7,116
South Dakota	1,508	1,382	1,881	1,379	678	14	39	143	58	103	713
Tennessee	14,189	9,788	1,870	9,747	3,968	101	1,312	494	509	4,215	18,257
Texas.	46,112	39,335	2,099	39,288	19,656	232	3,930	1,538	2,118	6,449	55,816
Utah	4,951	3,825	1,937	3,820	1,994	15	156	185	201	1,126	8,751
Vermont	1,079	956	1,641	956	619	-	4	107	34	121	523
Virginia.	15,189	13,790	2,089	13,739	6,322	663	544	386	703	1,190	13,364
Washington.	18,428	14,228	2,617	14,195	5,960	29	1,072	956	647	4,116	24,601
West Virginia	3,166	2,980	1,636	2,977	1,779	1	241	39	86	171	3,909
Wisconsin.	15,256	14,279	2,793	14,256	6,436	1,007	860	1,180	769	830	10,232
Wyoming	1,573	1,496	3,127	1,495	722	7	249	60	61	75	1,081

- Represents or rounds to zero.   [1] Includes items not shown separately.   [2] Based on estimated resident population as of July 1.

Source: U.S. Bureau of the Census, <http://www.census.gov/govs/www/esti95.html> (accessed 25 June 1998); and unpublished data.

No. 520. Estimated State and Local Taxes Paid by a Family of Four in Selected Cities: 1996

[Data based on average family of four (two wage earners and two school age children) owning their own home and living in a city where taxes apply. Comprises state and local sales, income, auto, and real estate taxes. For definition of median, see Guide to Tabular Presentation]

CITY	TOTAL TAXES PAID, BY GROSS FAMILY INCOME LEVEL (dollars)					TOTAL TAXES PAID AS PERCENT OF INCOME				
	$25,000	$50,000	$75,000	$100,000	$150,000	$25,000	$50,000	$75,000	$100,000	$150,000
Albuquerque, NM . . .	1,607	3,698	6,380	8,958	15,009	6.4	7.4	8.5	9.0	10.0
Atlanta, GA	1,756	4,204	7,241	9,960	15,625	7.0	8.4	9.7	10.0	10.4
Baltimore, MD	2,688	5,450	8,529	11,296	17,108	10.8	10.9	11.4	11.3	11.4
Boston, MA	2,418	5,216	8,368	11,191	16,734	9.7	10.4	11.2	11.2	11.2
Charlotte, NC	1,947	4,271	7,098	9,929	15,116	7.8	8.5	9.5	9.9	10.1
Chicago, IL	2,048	4,034	6,351	8,352	12,334	8.2	8.1	8.5	8.4	8.2
Columbus, OH	2,181	4,564	7,442	10,267	15,989	8.7	9.1	9.9	10.3	10.7
Denver, CO	1,938	3,933	6,245	8,377	12,815	7.8	7.9	8.3	8.4	8.5
Detroit, MI	2,505	5,305	8,223	10,911	16,280	10.0	10.6	11.0	10.9	10.9
Honolulu, HI	1,934	4,453	7,457	10,229	16,907	7.7	8.9	9.9	10.2	11.3
Houston, TX	1,681	2,969	4,636	5,890	8,392	6.7	5.9	6.2	5.9	5.6
Indianapolis, IN	1,887	3,687	5,726	7,518	10,810	7.6	7.4	7.6	7.5	7.2
Jacksonville, FL	964	1,766	2,916	3,779	5,478	3.9	3.5	3.9	3.8	3.7
Kansas City, MO . . .	2,032	4,084	6,517	8,961	13,807	8.1	8.2	8.7	9.0	9.2
Las Vegas, NV . . .	1,447	2,273	3,513	4,459	6,249	5.8	4.5	4.7	4.5	4.2
Los Angeles, CA . . .	1,838	4,069	7,469	10,951	17,648	7.4	8.1	10.0	11.0	11.8
Memphis, TN.	1,524	2,483	4,022	5,230	7,718	6.1	5.0	5.4	5.2	5.1
Milwaukee, WI	2,650	5,811	9,100	12,095	18,218	10.6	11.6	12.1	12.1	12.1
Minneapolis, MN . . .	1,889	4,492	7,694	10,531	16,234	7.6	9.0	10.3	10.5	10.8
New Orleans, LA . . .	1,446	3,325	5,711	7,774	11,849	5.8	6.7	7.6	7.8	7.9
New York City, NY . .	2,420	6,370	10,905	15,031	23,288	9.7	12.7	14.5	15.0	15.5
Oklahoma City, OK. .	2,039	4,092	6,778	9,309	14,654	8.2	8.2	9.0	9.3	9.8
Omaha, NE.	2,391	4,717	7,941	10,915	17,118	9.6	9.4	10.6	10.9	11.4
Philadelphia, PA. . . .	3,119	5,930	8,815	11,463	16,749	12.5	11.9	11.8	11.5	11.2
Phoenix, AZ	2,145	4,082	6,539	8,885	13,551	8.6	8.2	8.7	8.9	9.0
Portland, ME.	2,723	6,115	10,160	13,785	20,981	10.9	12.2	13.5	13.8	14.0
Seattle, WA.	2,085	3,424	5,278	6,785	9,598	8.3	6.8	7.0	6.8	6.4
Virginia Beach, VA . .	2,385	4,515	7,331	9,880	14,662	9.5	9.0	9.8	9.9	9.8
Washington, DC. . . .	2,144	4,653	7,922	10,937	17,055	8.6	9.3	10.6	11.0	11.4
Wichita, KS.	2,041	3,866	6,625	9,180	14,126	8.2	7.7	8.8	9.2	9.4
Average [1]	2,071	4,312	7,025	9,486	14,476	8.3	8.6	9.4	9.5	9.7
Median [1]	1,989	4,092	6,989	9,555	14,659	8.0	8.2	9.3	9.6	9.8

[1] Based on selected cities and District of Columbia. For complete list of cities, see Table 521.

Source: Government of the District of Columbia, Department of Finance and Revenue, *Tax Rates and Tax Burdens in the District of Columbia: A Nationwide Comparison*, annual.

No. 521. Residential Property Tax Rates in Selected Cities: 1996

[Effective tax rate is amount each jurisdiction considers based upon assessment level used. Assessment level is ratio of assessed value to assumed market value. Nominal rate is announced rates it levied at taxable value of house]

CITY	EFFECTIVE TAX RATE PER $100		Assessment level (percent)	Nominal rate per $100	CITY	EFFECTIVE TAX RATE PER $100		Assessment level (percent)	Nominal rate per $100
	Rank	Rate				Rank	Rate		
Newark, NJ.	1	4.02	17.6	22.85	Billings, MT.	28	1.48	3.9	37.95
Bridgeport, CT.	2	3.96	58.6	6.75	Columbia, SC	29	1.42	4.0	35.47
Manchester, NH.	3	3.48	113.0	3.08	Louisville, KY	30	1.38	100.0	1.38
Milwaukee, WI.	4	3.32	94.9	3.50	Wichita, KS.	31	1.38	12.0	11.47
Providence, RI	5	3.04	100.0	3.04	Albuquerque, NM. . . .	32	1.38	33.3	4.13
Des Moines, IA	6	2.95	68.0	4.34	Boston, MA	33	1.37	100.0	1.37
Detroit, MI	7	2.76	46.9	5.88	Minneapolis, MN	34	1.34	91.6	1.46
Philadelphia, PA	8	2.64	32.0	8.26	Little Rock, AR	35	1.25	18.6	6.71
Houston, TX	9	2.61	100.0	2.61	Kansas City, MO	36	1.20	19.0	6.33
Portland, ME.	10	2.46	100.0	2.46	Seattle, WA	37	1.14	88.1	1.30
Omaha, NE	11	2.43	90.0	2.70	Wilmington, DE	38	1.13	51.9	2.19
Baltimore, MD	12	2.42	40.0	6.06	Virginia Beach, VA . . .	39	1.12	92.2	1.22
Sioux Falls, SD	13	2.23	87.6	2.55	Charlotte, NC	40	1.12	88.9	1.26
Atlanta, GA.	14	2.04	40.0	5.09	Jacksonville, FL.	41	1.11	100.0	1.11
Burlington, VT.	15	1.98	98.0	2.02	Oklahoma City, OK . .	42	1.10	11.0	10.00
Fargo, ND	16	1.97	4.2	46.85	Las Vegas, NV	43	1.00	35.0	2.85
Indianapolis, IN	17	1.93	15.0	12.86	Jackson, MS.	44	0.95	10.0	9.53
Charleston, WV.	18	1.84	60.0	3.07	Washington, DC	45	0.95	98.9	0.96
Boise City, ID	19	1.83	99.2	1.84	New York City, NY . . .	46	0.86	8.0	10.73
Phoenix, AZ	20	1.83	10.0	18.25	Denver, CO	47	0.84	10.4	8.07
Columbus, OH	21	1.82	35.0	5.20	Cheyenne, WY	48	0.77	9.5	8.10
Chicago, IL.	22	1.79	19.0	9.44	Los Angeles, CA	49	0.74	70.0	1.05
New Orleans, LA	23	1.61	10.0	16.13	Birmingham, AL.	50	0.70	10.0	6.95
Portland, OR.	24	1.55	100.0	1.55	Honolulu, HI	51	0.33	95.0	0.35
Salt Lake City, UT . . .	25	1.55	80.3	1.93					
Anchorage, AK	26	1.54	95.0	1.62	Unweighted average .	(X)	1.75	54.9	7.42
Memphis, TN	27	1.53	24.1	6.34	Median	(X)	1.54	(X)	(X)

X Not applicable.

Source: Government of the District of Columbia, Department of Finance and Revenue, *Tax Rates and Tax Burdens in the District of Columbia: A Nationwide Comparison*, annual.

No. 522. Gross Revenue From Parimutuel and Amusement Taxes and Lotteries, by State: 1996

[Millions of dollars. For fiscal years; see text, Section 9]

STATE	Gross revenue	Amusement taxes [1]	Parimutuel taxes	LOTTERY REVENUE			
				Total [2] (mil. dol.)	Apportionment of funds		
					Prizes	Administra-tion	Proceeds available from ticket sales
United States..	34,035	1,862	459	31,713	18,693	1,767	11,253
Alabama.........	5	-	5	-	-	-	-
Alaska..........	2	2	-	-	-	-	-
Arizona.........	253	1	8	243	135	24	84
Arkansas........	8	1	8	-	-	-	-
California.......	2,250	-	105	2,145	1,132	204	808
Colorado........	319	1	8	310	192	27	92
Connecticut......	841	160	11	670	402	28	241
Delaware........	127	-	-	127	58	4	64
Florida.........	2,044	1	82	1,962	1,024	117	821
Georgia.........	1,435	-	-	1,435	789	107	539
Hawaii..........	(X)	(X)	(X)	(X)	(X)	(X)	(X)
Idaho..........	91	-	-	91	55	16	20
Illinois.........	1,825	309	42	1,474	839	57	578
Indiana.........	576	-	3	573	350	32	191
Iowa...........	278	103	4	170	103	25	42
Kansas.........	174	1	5	168	96	20	51
Kentucky........	531	-	21	509	322	31	157
Louisiana.......	272	2	4	266	145	18	103
Maine..........	152	-	3	149	84	16	49
Maryland........	1,061	5	3	1,053	609	49	394
Massachusetts.....	2,869	8	11	2,850	2,140	70	641
Michigan........	1,338	-	9	1,329	736	52	542
Minnesota.......	423	66	2	356	231	60	64
Mississippi......	216	216	-	-	-	-	-
Missouri........	497	100	-	396	230	38	129
Montana........	30	-	-	30	16	6	8
Nebraska.......	92	9	1	82	43	17	23
Nevada........	488	488	-	-	-	-	-
New Hampshire....	160	2	5	153	98	7	48
New Jersey......	1,810	306	2	1,502	796	43	663
New Mexico......	2	1	1	-	-	-	-
New York.......	3,341	-	45	3,295	1,827	83	1,386
North Carolina.....	(X)	(X)	(X)	(X)	(X)	(X)	(X)
North Dakota.....	12	12	-	-	-	-	-
Ohio..........	2,247	-	12	2,235	1,363	83	788
Oklahoma.......	17	14	3	-	-	-	-
Oregon.........	947	-	2	945	599	201	145
Pennsylvania.....	1,607	1	21	1,585	891	61	634
Rhode Island.....	402	-	6	396	303	5	88
South Carolina.....	28	28	-	-	-	-	-
South Dakota.....	119	-	-	119	16	8	95
Tennessee.......	-	-	-	-	-	-	-
Texas..........	3,139	25	12	3,102	1,951	63	1,087
Utah..........	(X)	(X)	(X)	(X)	(X)	(X)	(X)
Vermont........	75	-	-	75	44	6	25
Virginia........	901	-	-	901	480	86	335
Washington......	393	-	3	390	224	56	110
West Virginia.....	177	-	5	172	94	19	59
Wisconsin.......	463	1	5	457	277	32	148
Wyoming........	-	-	-	-	-	-	-

- Represents or rounds to zero.   X Not applicable.   [1] Represents nonlicense taxes.   [2] Excludes commissions.
Source: U.S. Bureau of the Census, unpublished data.

No. 523. Lottery Sales—Type of Game, 1980 to 1997 and Use of Profits, 1965-95

[In millions of dollars. For fiscal years]

GAME	1980	1985	1990	1995	1997	USE OF PROFITS	Cumu-lative [1] 1965-95	Govern-ment profits 1997
Total ticket sales.........	2,393	9,035	20,017	31,931	35,486	Total [2]...........	92,922	11,959
Passive [3]...............	206	88	(NA)	(NA)	(NA)	Education............	52,061	6,204
Instant [4]..............	527	1,296	5,204	11,511	14,217	General fund.........	21,133	2,946
Three-digit [5]...........	1,554	3,376	4,572	5,737	5,639	Cities..............	9,013	1,580
Four-digit [5]...........	55	693	1,302	1,941	2,111	Senior citizen programs ..	8,708	701
Lotto [6]..............	52	3,583	8,563	10,594	9,996	Taxes..............	(NA)	32
Other [7]..............	(NA)	(NA)	409	2,148	3,523	Economic development...	1,385	349
						Infrastructure.........	(NA)	81
State proceeds (net income) [8]..	978	3,735	7,703	11,100	11,959	Environment..........	485	31

NA Not available.   [1] Cumulative profits tracks lottery revenue to government from March 12, 1964 - June 30, 1995.
[2] Includes other not shown separately.   [3] Also known as draw game or ticket. Player must match his ticket to winning numbers drawn by lottery. Players cannot choose their numbers.   [4] Player scratches a latex section on ticket which reveals instantly whether ticket is a winner.   [5] Players choose and bet on three or four digits, depending on game, with various payoffs for different straight order or mixed combination bets.   [6] Players typically select six digits out of a large field of numbers. Varying prizes are offered for matching three through six numbers drawn by lottery.   [7] Includes breakopen tickets, spiel, keno, video lottery, etc.
[8] Sales minus prizes and expenses equal net government income.
Source: TLF Publications, Inc., Boyds, MD, 1998 World Lottery Almanac annual; LaFleur's Fiscal 1997 Lottery Special Report; and LaFleur's Lottery World Government Profits Report (copyright).

No. 524. City Governments—Total and Per Capita Finances for Largest Cities: 1995

[For fiscal year ending in year shown; see text, Section 9. Cities ranked by size of population estimated as of July 1, 1994, except Honolulu ranked by county population. Data reflect inclusion of fiscal activity of dependent school systems where applicable. Inter-city comparisons should be made with caution due to variations in responsibilities among urban areas; for details see text, Section 9, and source]

CITIES RANKED BY 1994 POPULATION	REVENUE		GENERAL REVENUE		TAXES		GENERAL EXPENDITURE		DEBT OUTSTANDING	
	Total (mil. dol.)	Per capita [1] (dol.)	Total (mil. dol.)	Per capita [1] (dol.)	Total (mil. dol.)	Per capita [1] (dol.)	Total (mil. dol.)	Per capita [1] (dol.)	Total (mil. dol.)	Per capita [1] (dol.)
New York City, NY [2]	47,303	6,416	40,877	5,544	17,792	2,413	38,644	5,241	43,017	5,834
Los Angeles, CA	7,631	2,155	4,523	1,277	1,850	522	4,436	1,252	8,830	2,493
Chicago, IL	4,732	1,730	3,867	1,414	1,662	608	3,833	1,401	7,173	2,623
Houston, TX	1,971	1,139	1,583	915	830	479	1,694	979	3,793	2,191
Philadelphia, PA [2]	4,169	2,780	3,395	2,264	1,626	1,084	3,032	2,022	3,590	2,394
San Diego, CA	1,578	1,361	1,285	1,109	420	362	1,231	1,062	1,815	1,565
Phoenix, AZ	1,373	1,211	1,198	1,056	406	358	1,191	1,051	2,881	2,541
Dallas, TX	1,487	1,420	1,217	1,162	532	508	1,204	1,150	3,943	3,765
San Antonio, TX	1,680	1,596	710	675	275	261	678	644	4,167	3,959
Detroit, MI	2,193	2,189	1,707	1,704	610	609	1,474	1,471	1,956	1,953
Honolulu, HI [2]	1,114	1,281	993	1,142	526	605	1,023	1,177	1,581	1,819
San Jose, CA	921	1,118	810	983	365	442	746	905	1,482	1,798
Indianapolis, IN [2]	1,121	1,502	1,086	1,454	513	688	1,136	1,521	1,722	2,306
San Francisco, CA [2]	3,765	5,154	3,106	4,251	952	1,303	2,799	3,831	3,777	5,170
Baltimore, MD [2]	2,186	3,171	1,940	2,815	677	983	1,711	2,482	1,248	1,811
Jacksonville, FL [2]	1,649	2,482	826	1,244	339	510	977	1,470	4,861	7,316
Columbus, OH	798	1,218	693	1,058	341	521	637	972	1,378	2,104
Memphis, TN	2,094	3,467	1,050	1,739	222	367	1,023	1,694	803	1,330
Milwaukee, WI	811	1,360	658	1,103	165	278	696	1,168	532	892
El Paso, TX	409	687	328	551	162	273	322	541	595	1,000
Washington, DC [2]	5,086	9,171	4,647	8,380	2,438	4,397	4,484	8,086	4,047	7,297
Boston, MA [2]	2,126	3,793	1,902	3,393	726	1,294	1,762	3,144	1,168	2,084
Seattle, WA	1,276	2,439	847	1,619	404	772	912	1,744	1,472	2,813
Austin, TX	1,367	2,562	712	1,335	227	425	758	1,421	3,293	6,174
Nashville-Davidson, TN [2]	1,816	3,569	1,111	2,183	597	1,174	1,068	2,099	1,818	3,572
Cleveland, OH	814	1,625	597	1,191	297	593	675	1,348	1,371	2,738
Denver, CO [2]	1,464	2,959	1,325	2,680	474	959	1,815	3,670	4,960	10,029
New Orleans, LA	769	1,594	681	1,412	311	645	658	1,365	1,037	2,149

[1] Based on estimated population as of July 1, 1995.   [2] Represents, in effect, city-county consolidated government.
Source: U.S. Bureau of the Census, unpublished data.

No. 525. City Governments—Revenue for Largest Cities: 1995

[In millions of dollars. For fiscal year ending in year shown; see text, Section 9. See headnote, Table 524]

CITIES RANKED BY 1994 POPULATION	Total revenue	GENERAL REVENUE									Utility revenue
		Total	Intergovernmental		General revenue from own sources						
			Total	From federal government	Total	Taxes			Current charges	Miscellaneous general revenue	
						Total	Property	Sales and gross receipts			
New York City, NY [1]	47,303	40,877	17,006	2,279	23,871	17,792	7,530	3,755	4,594	1,486	2,290
Los Angeles, CA	7,631	4,523	1,018	522	3,505	1,850	665	790	1,216	438	2,350
Chicago, IL	4,732	3,867	1,054	312	2,813	1,662	637	838	708	442	280
Houston, TX	1,971	1,583	122	81	1,461	830	428	374	465	167	254
Philadelphia, PA [1]	4,169	3,395	1,230	374	2,165	1,626	339	130	416	123	603
San Diego, CA	1,578	1,285	292	132	994	420	135	230	260	313	162
Phoenix, AZ	1,373	1,198	407	104	790	406	119	260	268	116	132
Dallas, TX	1,487	1,217	85	68	1,132	532	281	240	452	147	141
San Antonio, TX	1,680	710	146	27	565	275	134	130	208	82	939
Detroit, MI	2,193	1,707	745	175	961	610	236	49	243	108	179
Honolulu, HI [1]	1,114	993	142	80	851	526	419	62	215	110	121
San Jose, CA	921	810	110	20	700	365	117	164	239	96	11
Indianapolis, IN [1]	1,121	1,086	321	65	765	513	423	24	212	39	7
San Francisco, CA [1]	3,765	3,106	1,214	194	1,892	952	458	258	618	322	253
Baltimore, MD [1]	1,649	826	130	69	696	339	211	115	173	184	749
Jacksonville, FL [1]	2,186	1,940	1,056	90	885	677	471	45	100	107	65
Columbus, OH	798	693	103	31	590	341	26	7	173	76	105
Memphis, TN	2,094	1,050	673	27	377	222	178	32	109	47	959
Milwaukee, WI	811	658	348	64	310	165	153	6	92	52	49
El Paso, TX	409	328	40	26	287	162	86	72	82	43	51
Washington, DC [1]	5,086	4,647	1,692	1,628	2,955	2,438	730	795	260	257	51
Boston, MA [1]	2,126	1,902	849	43	1,052	726	680	28	230	97	90
Seattle, WA	1,276	847	138	26	710	404	133	177	235	71	399
Austin, TX	1,367	712	62	11	651	227	114	101	357	67	584
Nashville-Davidson, TN [1]	1,816	1,111	260	1	851	597	342	213	187	67	648
Cleveland, OH	814	597	145	68	452	297	52	6	107	48	217
Denver, CO [1]	1,464	1,325	335	30	991	474	130	294	405	111	105
New Orleans, LA	769	681	146	90	535	311	135	155	149	76	56

- Represents or rounds to zero.   [1] Represents, in effect, city-county consolidated government.
Source: U.S. Bureau of the Census, unpublished data.

No. 526. City Governments—Expenditures for Largest Cities: 1995

[In millions of dollars. For fiscal year ending in year shown; see text, Section 9. See headnote, Table 524]

CITIES RANKED BY 1994 POPULATION	Total expenditure	GENERAL EXPENDITURE								Utility expenditure
		Total	Education	Housing and community development	Public welfare	Health and hospitals	Police protection	Fire protection	Highways	
New York City, NY [1]	47,881	38,644	9,394	2,681	7,783	4,339	2,291	806	479	5,260
Los Angeles, CA	7,494	4,436	15	234	-	32	729	274	64	2,273
Chicago, IL	4,641	3,833	1	154	125	116	771	239	268	249
Houston, TX	2,148	1,694	-	40	-	69	352	169	54	363
Philadelphia, PA [1]	4,018	3,032	16	148	283	409	330	123	48	643
San Diego, CA	1,524	1,231	-	112	-	2	174	72	31	234
Phoenix, AZ	1,401	1,191	11	73	-	1	181	103	34	179
Dallas, TX	1,456	1,204	-	24	-	18	165	79	29	141
San Antonio, TX	1,528	678	23	3	30	27	118	77	26	827
Detroit, MI	2,017	1,474	5	77	-	94	282	87	-	294
Honolulu, HI [1]	1,278	1,023	-	110	-	11	120	50	10	256
San Jose, CA	822	746	-	101	-	3	121	62	18	17
Indianapolis, IN [1]	1,204	1,136	1	109	126	214	93	43	34	26
San Francisco, CA [1]	3,744	2,799	62	91	365	668	215	137	33	661
Baltimore, MD [1]	1,704	977	-	75	10	41	99	66	14	673
Jacksonville, FL [1]	1,892	1,711	615	82	1	78	189	92	25	63
Columbus, OH	774	637	-	13	-	27	131	83	20	137
Memphis, TN	1,963	1,023	516	25	-	7	84	69	19	853
Milwaukee, WI	822	696	-	67	-	17	138	68	19	34
El Paso, TX	449	322	-	7	1	24	60	29	8	102
Washington, DC [1]	5,077	4,484	706	192	1,137	425	238	101	103	97
Boston, MA [1]	2,022	1,762	503	72	102	234	164	100	19	56
Seattle, WA	1,470	912	-	61	-	17	110	74	75	502
Austin, TX	1,384	758	-	8	7	232	72	46	16	603
Nashville-Davidson, TN [1]	1,797	1,068	388	-	13	113	81	59	-	673
Cleveland, OH	990	675	-	56	-	24	142	70	29	315
Denver, CO [1]	1,964	1,815	-	29	168	182	104	56	41	119
New Orleans, LA	770	658	-	94	2	22	62	34	9	75
Salt Lake City, UT	340	314	-	13	-	-	30	19	10	26

- Represents or rounds to zero. [1] Represents, in effect, city-county consolidated government.

Source: U.S. Bureau of the Census, unpublished data.

No. 527. County Governments—Total and Per Capita Finances for Largest Counties: 1995

[For fiscal year ending in year shown; see text, Section 9. Counties ranked by size of population estimated as of July 1, 1994, Data relate only to county governments and their dependent agencies and do not include amounts for other local governments in the same geographic location such as separate school districts; excluded are areas having certain type of county characteristics but included as part of another government. See Tables 524-526, for details see text, Section 9, and source]

COUNTIES RANKED BY 1994 POPULATION	REVENUE		GENERAL REVENUE		TAXES		TOTAL EXPENDITURE		DEBT OUTSTANDING	
	Total (mil. dol.)	Per capita [1] (dol.)	Total (mil. dol.)	Per capita [1] (dol.)	Total (mil. dol.)	Per capita [1] (dol.)	Total (mil. dol.)	Per capita [1] (dol.)	Total (mil. dol.)	Per capita [1] (dol.)
Los Angeles, CA	12,583	1,375	11,576	1,265	1,650	180	12,276	1,342	5,904	645
Cook, IL	2,131	414	1,902	370	1,145	223	1,997	388	1,581	307
Harris, TX	1,592	523	1,592	523	719	236	1,607	528	5,045	1,657
San Diego, CA	2,433	925	2,204	838	308	117	2,291	870	401	152
Orange, CA	2,325	914	2,205	867	311	122	2,191	861	4,239	1,667
Maricopa, AZ	1,349	575	1,349	575	304	129	1,310	558	1,255	535
Wayne, MI	1,321	640	1,244	602	235	114	1,310	635	1,005	487
Dade, FL	3,885	1,918	3,686	1,820	1,153	570	4,052	2,001	5,678	2,804
Dallas, TX	849	437	840	432	344	177	849	437	793	408
King, WA	1,375	866	1,317	830	678	427	1,462	921	1,988	1,253
Santa Clara, CA	1,606	1,031	1,606	1,031	307	197	1,732	1,112	758	487
San Bernadino, CA	1,799	1,158	1,720	1,107	180	116	1,948	1,254	1,548	996
Middlesex, MA	93	67	62	44	10	7	-	-	-	-
Cuyahoga, OH	1,124	801	1,124	801	358	255	1,134	808	1,251	891
Broward, FL	1,117	808	1,085	785	470	340	1,083	783	2,449	1,771
Riverside, CA	1,468	1,085	1,467	1,085	251	186	1,484	1,097	1,396	1,032
Suffolk, NY	1,705	1,264	1,620	1,201	972	720	1,650	1,223	1,474	1,093
Allegheny, PA	1,087	823	1,051	796	337	256	1,041	788	1,564	1,184
Alameda, CA	1,594	1,208	1,507	1,142	282	214	1,583	1,200	534	404
Nassau, NY	2,090	1,605	2,090	1,605	1,248	958	2,295	1,762	2,441	1,874
Bexar, TX	572	447	571	446	213	167	603	471	1,220	953
Tarrant, TX	542	431	542	431	236	188	494	393	953	758
Oakland, CA	677	593	620	543	169	148	572	500	342	300
Sacramento, CA	1,626	1,481	1,555	1,416	310	283	1,656	1,508	1,577	1,436
Hennepin, MN	1,183	1,126	1,183	1,126	349	333	1,085	1,033	412	392
Franklin, OH	572	570	571	568	240	239	578	575	706	703
St Louis, MO	434	431	422	420	296	295	456	454	350	348

- Represents or rounds to zero. [1] Based on estimated population as of July 1, 1995.

Source: U.S. Bureau of the Census, unpublished data.

No. 528. County Governments—Revenue for Largest Counties: 1995

[In millions of dollars. For fiscal year ending in year shown; see text, Section 9. See headnote, Table 527]

COUNTIES RANKED BY 1994 POPULATION	Total revenue [1]	GENERAL REVENUE									Utility revenue
		Total [1]	Intergovernmental		General revenue from own sources						
			Total	From federal government	Total	Taxes			Current charges	Miscellaneous general revenue	
						Total [1]	Property	Sales and gross receipts			
Los Angeles, CA	12,583	11,576	8,497	190	3,079	1,650	1,504	90	707	722	28
Cook, IL	2,131	1,902	353	17	1,549	1,145	756	377	332	72	-
Harris, TX	1,592	1,592	398	18	1,194	719	661	21	225	251	-
San Diego, CA	2,433	2,204	1,636	57	569	308	262	15	161	100	1
Orange, CA	2,325	2,205	1,186	28	1,019	311	285	9	221	487	-
Maricopa, AZ	1,349	1,349	700	36	649	304	269	19	227	118	-
Wayne, MI	1,321	1,244	708	140	536	235	230	-	240	61	-
Dade, FL	3,885	3,686	727	313	2,958	1,153	840	253	1,437	368	199
Dallas, TX	849	840	162	2	677	344	310	2	273	61	-
King, WA	1,375	1,317	252	35	1,066	678	333	250	297	90	58
Santa Clara, CA	1,606	1,606	1,073	32	533	307	283	4	119	108	-
San Bernadino, CA	1,799	1,720	1,224	52	496	180	157	16	161	155	3
Middlesex, MA	93	62	26	-	35	10	-	-	24	2	-
Cuyahoga, OH	1,124	1,124	426	8	698	358	202	125	227	112	-
Broward, FL	1,117	1,085	138	21	948	470	393	52	322	156	32
Riverside, CA	1,468	1,467	937	17	530	251	208	27	131	148	-
Suffolk, NY	1,705	1,620	480	14	1,140	972	391	568	99	69	85
Allegheny, PA	1,087	1,051	490	27	560	337	326	9	174	49	-
Alameda, CA	1,594	1,507	1,015	10	492	282	182	89	113	97	-
Nassau, NY	2,090	2,090	479	30	1,612	1,248	624	620	279	84	-
Bexar, TX	572	571	123	2	448	213	195	5	121	113	-
Tarrant, TX	542	542	177	9	366	236	215	6	68	61	-
Oakland, CA	677	620	364	5	256	169	164	-	49	37	17
Sacramento, CA	1,626	1,555	832	19	722	310	167	111	259	153	4
Hennepin, MN	1,183	1,183	485	32	699	349	347	-	282	67	-

- Represents or rounds to zero.   [1] Includes items not shown separately.

Source: U.S. Bureau of the Census, and unpublished data.

No. 529. County Governments—Expenditures for Largest Counties: 1995

[In millions of dollars. For fiscal year ending in year shown; see text, Section 9. See headnote, Table 527]

COUNTIES RANKED BY 1994 POPULATION	Total expenditure [1]	GENERAL EXPENDITURE								Utility expenditure
		Total [1]	Education	Housing and community development	Public welfare	Health and hospitals	Police protection	Fire protection	Highways	
Los Angeles, CA	12,276	11,464	366	194	4,330	2,555	663	363	70	33
Cook, IL	1,997	1,870	2	15	3	688	50	-	64	-
Harris, TX	1,607	1,607	-	10	16	514	99	1	35	-
San Diego, CA	2,291	2,188	84	48	901	263	94	-	16	8
Orange, CA	2,191	2,104	62	23	568	164	117	79	78	-
Maricopa, AZ	1,310	1,310	16	16	416	297	46	-	20	-
Wayne, MI	1,310	1,239	-	8	94	301	21	-	-	-
Dade, FL	4,052	3,648	-	196	51	688	294	119	30	404
Dallas, TX	849	847	-	1	15	440	21	-	6	-
King, WA	1,462	1,189	1	10	6	187	62	5	42	274
Santa Clara, CA	1,732	1,732	103	4	529	357	37	30	19	-
San Bernadino, CA	1,948	1,876	68	9	722	360	116	39	-	7
Middlesex, MA	-	-	-	-	-	-	-	-	-	-
Cuyahoga, OH	1,134	1,134	-	7	210	536	15	-	16	-
Broward, FL	1,083	976	-	11	19	77	125	15	24	107
Riverside, CA	1,484	1,484	76	23	466	203	95	22	28	-
Suffolk, NY	1,650	1,547	213	7	355	104	283	3	17	104
Allegheny, PA	1,041	1,005	25	32	114	257	22	1	31	-
Alameda, CA	1,583	1,508	18	8	534	409	25	15	28	-
Nassau, NY	2,295	2,293	220	23	391	377	386	11	26	2
Bexar, TX	603	602	-	2	8	38	267	16	7	-
Tarrant, TX	494	494	-	8	9	224	12	-	-	-
Oakland, CA	572	546	3	7	2	136	26	-	21	14
Sacramento, CA	1,656	1,585	51	99	588	97	62	1	36	7
Hennepin, MN	1,085	1,085	-	5	174	477	37	-	42	-

- Represents or rounds to zero.   [1] Includes items not shown separately.

Source: U.S. Bureau of the Census, and unpublished data.

No. 530. Governmental Employment and Payrolls: 1980 to 1995

[For **October.** Covers both full-time and part-time employees. Local government data are estimates subject to sampling variation; see Appendix III and source]

TYPE OF GOVERNMENT	1980	1985	1988	1989	1990	1991	1992	1993	1994	1995
EMPLOYEES (1,000)										
Total	**16,213**	**16,690**	**17,588**	**17,879**	**18,369**	**18,554**	**18,745**	**18,823**	**19,420**	**19,521**
Federal (civilian) [1]	2,898	3,021	3,112	3,114	3,105	3,103	3,047	2,999	2,952	2,895
State and local	13,315	13,669	14,476	14,765	15,263	15,452	15,698	15,824	16,468	16,626
Percent of total	82	82	82	83	83	83	84	84	85	85
State	3,753	3,984	4,236	4,365	4,503	4,521	4,595	4,673	4,694	4,719
Local	9,562	9,685	10,240	10,400	10,760	10,930	11,103	11,151	11,775	11,906
Counties	1,853	1,891	2,024	2,085	2,167	2,196	2,253	2,270	(NA)	(NA)
Municipalities	2,561	2,467	2,570	2,569	2,642	2,662	2,665	2,644	(NA)	(NA)
School districts	4,270	4,416	4,679	4,774	4,950	5,045	5,134	(NA)	(NA)	(NA)
Townships	394	392	415	405	418	415	424	(NA)	(NA)	(NA)
Special districts	484	519	552	568	585	612	627	(NA)	(NA)	(NA)
OCTOBER PAYROLLS (mil. dol.)										
Total	**19,935**	**28,945**	**34,203**	**36,763**	**39,228**	**41,237**	**43,120**	**(NA)**	**(NA)**	**(NA)**
Federal (civilian) [1]	5,205	7,580	7,976	8,636	8,999	9,687	9,937	(NA)	(NA)	(NA)
State and local	14,730	21,365	26,227	28,127	30,229	31,551	33,183	34,540	36,545	37,714
Percent of total	74	74	77	77	77	77	77	(NA)	(NA)	(NA)
State	4,285	6,329	7,842	8,443	9,083	9,437	9,828	10,288	10,666	10,927
Local	10,445	15,036	18,385	19,684	21,146	22,113	23,355	24,252	25,878	26,787
Counties	1,936	2,819	3,532	3,855	4,192	4,404	4,698	4,839	(NA)	(NA)
Municipalities	2,951	4,191	4,979	5,274	5,564	5,784	6,207	6,328	(NA)	(NA)
School districts	4,683	6,746	8,298	8,852	9,551	9,975	10,394	(NA)	(NA)	(NA)
Townships	330	446	556	599	642	664	685	(NA)	(NA)	(NA)
Special districts	546	834	1,020	1,104	1,197	1,287	1,370	(NA)	(NA)	(NA)

NA Not available.   [1] Includes employees outside the United States.

Source: U.S. Bureau of the Census, *Historical Statistics on Governmental Finances and Employment,* and *Public Employment,* Series GE, No. 1, annual, 1980-92; <http://www.census.gov/govs/www/apes.html> (accessed 8 July 1998).

No. 531. All Governments—Employment and Payroll, by Function: 1995

[For **October.** Covers both full-time and part-time employees. Local government amounts are estimates subject to sampling variation; see Appendix III and source]

FUNCTION	EMPLOYEES (1,000)					OCTOBER PAYROLLS (mil. dol.)				
	Total	Federal (civilian) [1]	State and local			Total	Federal (civilian) [1]	State and local		
			Total	State	Local			Total	State	Local
Total	**19,521**	**2,895**	**16,626**	**4,719**	**11,906**	**(NA)**	**(NA)**	**37,714**	**10,927**	**26,787**
National defense [2]	831	831	(X)	(X)	(X)	(NA)	(NA)	(X)	(X)	(X)
Postal Service	849	849	(X)	(X)	(X)	(NA)	(NA)	(X)	(X)	(X)
Space research and technology	22	22	(X)	(X)	(X)	(NA)	(NA)	(X)	(X)	(X)
Elem and secondary educ	6,252	(X)	6,252	50	6,202	13,939	(NA)	13,939	119	13,820
Higher education	2,414	(X)	2,414	1,954	461	4,591	(NA)	4,591	3,794	797
Other education	129	12	117	117	(X)	260	(NA)	260	260	(X)
Health	544	141	403	166	238	(NA)	(NA)	977	431	546
Hospitals	1,303	174	1,129	522	608	(NA)	(NA)	37	14	23
Public welfare	526	10	516	230	286	(NA)	(NA)	1,145	549	597
Social insurance administration .	167	68	98	98	-	(NA)	(NA)	254	254	(X)
Police protection	926	86	840	91	749	(NA)	(NA)	3,427	287	3,140
Fire protection	360	(X)	360	(X)	360	950	(NA)	950	(X)	950
Correction	655	28	627	413	213	(NA)	(NA)	1,620	1,062	559
Streets & highways	564	4	560	257	303	(NA)	(NA)	1,357	667	690
Air transportation	86	49	37	3	35	(NA)	(NA)	104	8	96
Water transport/Terminals	27	15	12	5	7	(NA)	(NA)	37	14	23
Solid waste management	115	(X)	115	2	114	263	(NA)	263	6	258
Sewerage	130	(X)	130	1	128	345	(NA)	345	4	341
Parks & recreation	387	26	361	47	314	(NA)	(NA)	502	81	421
Natural resources	421	210	211	168	43	(NA)	(NA)	475	395	80
Housing & community dev.	151	20	131	(X)	131	(NA)	(NA)	315	(X)	315
Water supply	165	-	165	1	164	410	(NA)	410	3	407
Electric power	82	-	82	6	76	296	(NA)	296	26	270
Gas supply	11	-	11	(X)	11	28	(NA)	28	(X)	28
Transit	210	(X)	210	20	190	676	(NA)	676	80	595
Libraries	152	5	147	1	147	(NA)	(NA)	207	1	206
State liquor stores	10	(X)	10	10	(X)	18	(NA)	18	18	(X)
Financial administration	520	131	388	168	220	(NA)	(NA)	916	444	472
Other government administration	436	24	413	53	359	(NA)	(NA)	644	137	507
Judicial and legal	401	53	349	130	219	(NA)	(NA)	994	428	565
Other & unallocable	673	138	535	206	329	(NA)	(NA)	1,256	603	653

- Represents zero.   NA Not available.   X Not applicable.   [1] Includes employees outside the United States.   [2] Includes international relations.

Source: U.S. Bureau of the Census; <http://www.census.gov/pub/govs/www/apes.html>; (accessed 8 July 1998).

No. 532. State and Local Government—Employer Costs per Hour Worked: 1997

[In dollars. As of March. Based on a sample; see source for details. For additional data, see Table 701]

ITEM	Total compensation	Wages and salaries	BENEFITS						
			Total	Paid leave	Supplemental pay	Insurance	Retirement and savings	Legally required benefits	Other [1]
All state & local government workers	**26.58**	**18.61**	**7.97**	**2.06**	**0.23**	**2.09**	**1.95**	**1.61**	**0.04**
Occupational group:									
White-collar occupations	29.54	21.21	8.33	2.14	0.14	2.20	2.08	1.73	0.04
Professional specialty and technical	34.92	25.78	9.14	2.12	0.15	2.33	2.49	1.99	0.06
Teachers	38.86	29.20	9.66	1.97	0.06	2.54	2.89	2.13	0.07
Executive, admin., & managerial	33.78	23.43	10.35	3.40	0.18	2.24	2.48	2.03	(Z)
Admin. support including clerical	17.04	11.28	5.76	1.55	0.09	1.93	1.09	1.08	0.02
Blue-collar occupations	21.50	13.93	7.57	2.03	0.38	2.03	1.58	1.53	0.03
Service occupations	19.50	12.51	6.99	1.78	0.44	1.74	1.76	1.24	0.03
Industry group:									
Services	27.88	20.15	7.73	1.87	0.15	2.11	1.93	1.63	0.04
Health services	21.99	14.67	7.32	2.28	0.58	1.71	1.14	1.59	0.03
Hospitals	22.53	15.10	7.43	2.35	0.56	1.68	1.19	1.62	0.03
Educational services	29.21	21.37	7.84	1.79	0.09	2.19	2.09	1.66	0.05
Elementary and secondary education	28.94	21.29	7.66	1.63	0.06	2.28	2.02	1.61	0.06
Higher education	30.53	22.10	8.43	2.23	0.17	1.90	2.31	1.81	(Z)
Public administration	24.07	15.73	8.33	2.40	0.33	1.99	2.10	1.49	0.03

Z Cost per hour worked is less than one cent.   [1] Includes severance pay and supplemental unemployment benefits.

Source: U.S. Bureau of Labor Statistics, News, Employer Costs for Employee Compensation-March 1997, USDL 97-371.

No. 533. State and Local Government—Employee Benefits: 1994

[In percent. For January through July. Covers full-time employees in state and local governments. Covers only benefits for which the employer pays part or all of the premium or expenses involved, except unpaid maternity and paternity leave, and long-term care insurance. Based on sample. For data on employee benefits in businesses, see Table 703]

BENEFIT	All employees	White collar employees [1]	Teachers [2]	Blue collar employees [3]	BENEFIT	All employees	White collar employees [1]	Teachers [2]	Blue collar employees [3]
Paid:					Life	87	87	85	87
Vacations	66	84	9	91	Noncontributory	86	85	85	88
Holidays	73	86	33	91	Accident/sickness	21	24	11	26
Jury duty leave	94	94	94	93	Noncontributory	76	72	86	79
Funeral leave	62	59	58	70	Long-term disability	30	31	37	23
Family leave	4	4	3	6	Noncontributory	77	77	77	79
Military leave	75	80	61	82	Retirement and savings plans:				
Sick leave	94	93	96	94	Defined benefit pension	91	90	93	91
Personal leave	38	30	58	31	Noncontributory	28	30	20	31
Unpaid:					Defined contribution	9	10	7	9
Family leave	93	93	96	90	Money purchase pension [4]	7	7	5	7
Insurance plans:					Additional benefits:				
Medical	87	89	84	86	Child care	9	11	5	9
Dental	62	62	59	66	Educational assistance:				
Extended care facility	81	83	81	78	Job related	64	69	51	66
Home health care	84	84	86	84	Not job related	20	22	15	20
Hospital/room & board	100	100	100	100	Sabbatical leave	27	19	59	9
In HMO's	30	34	24	28	Employee assistance program	68	73	55	74
Inpatient surgery	100	100	100	100	Flexible benefits plans	5	5	7	3
Mental health care:					Financial counciling	6	7	6	4
Inpatient	99	99	100	99	Long-term care insurance	4	5	2	3
Outpatient	97	98	97	97	Nonproduction bonuses, cash	34	40	17	41
Vision	35	36	30	37	Subsidized commuting	7	8	4	9
Alcohol abuse treatment:					Recreation facilities	14	13	19	13
Inpatient detox	99	99	99	99	Reimbursement accounts [5]	64	68	59	61
Inpatient rehab	77	76	78	76	Severance pay	29	26	32	32
Outpatient	83	83	83	82	Travel accident insurance	13	13	14	12
Drug abuse treatment:					Wellness programs	34	38	29	32
Inpatient detox	98	98	99	94					
Inpatient rehab	74	73	76	74					
Outpatient	80	79	82	80					

[1] Includes all professional, administrative, technical, and clerical employees except teachers.   [2] Includes all personnel in primary and secondary schools, junior colleges, and universities whose primary duty is teaching or closely related activities.
[3] Includes police, firefighters, and all production and service employees.   [4] Fixed contributions are periodically placed in an employee's account and benefits are based on how much money has accumulated at retirement.   [5] Account which is used throughout the year to pay for plan premiums or to reimburse the employee for benefit related expenses. Account may be financed by employer, employee, or both.

Source: U.S. Bureau of Labor Statistics, Employee Benefits in State and Local Governments, 1994.

No. 534. State and Local Government Employment and Average Earnings, by State: 1990 and 1995

[For **October**]

STATE	FULL-TIME EQUIVALENT EMPLOYMENT (1,000)				FULL-TIME EQUIVALENT EMPLOYMENT PER 10,000 POPULATION [2]				AVERAGE OCTOBER EARNINGS [3] (dol.)			
	State		Local [1]		State		Local [1]		State		Local [1]	
	1990	1995	1990	1995	1990	1995	1990	1995	1990	1995	1990	1995
United States....	3,840	3,971	9,239	10,119	154	151	371	385	2,472	2,854	2,364	2,763
Alabama........	79	81	148	165	196	191	367	389	2,196	2,421	1,749	2,017
Alaska.........	22	22	21	24	401	366	385	391	3,543	3,727	3,491	4,051
Arizona........	50	58	136	161	137	135	370	373	2,334	2,570	2,540	2,689
Arkansas.......	43	48	78	90	182	192	330	364	1,922	2,353	1,545	1,823
California......	325	338	1,091	1,141	109	107	367	362	3,209	3,664	3,073	3,523
Colorado.......	54	57	130	148	165	153	395	394	2,765	3,234	2,292	2,612
Connecticut.....	58	63	98	102	178	193	299	311	3,018	3,321	2,854	3,491
Delaware.......	21	22	17	19	314	307	250	269	2,245	2,743	2,458	2,755
District of Columbia	(X)	(X)	57	47	(X)	(X)	939	927	(X)	(X)	3,024	3,425
Florida........	160	175	497	534	123	123	384	377	2,095	2,488	2,247	2,485
Georgia........	112	115	270	333	173	159	418	462	2,037	2,456	1,872	2,164
Hawaii.........	49	51	13	14	445	436	120	119	2,317	2,624	2,536	3,013
Idaho.........	19	21	37	46	186	179	372	396	2,100	2,476	1,772	2,165
Illinois........	145	141	416	444	127	119	364	377	2,520	3,027	2,463	2,985
Indiana........	89	89	196	217	161	153	354	375	2,496	2,583	2,036	2,375
Iowa..........	57	53	107	116	207	187	387	408	2,936	3,126	2,024	2,367
Kansas.........	50	48	104	118	200	187	421	461	2,077	2,325	1,979	2,315
Kentucky.......	75	73	114	133	204	190	310	344	2,141	2,488	1,823	2,523
Louisiana.......	85	93	155	171	200	214	368	394	2,047	2,359	1,713	1,860
Maine.........	22	21	42	45	179	172	345	364	2,352	2,618	1,978	2,349
Maryland.......	89	81	159	172	186	161	333	341	2,609	2,835	2,776	3,159
Massachusetts....	93	82	196	220	155	135	325	362	2,541	3,068	2,554	2,961
Michigan.......	144	141	316	324	155	148	340	339	2,858	3,342	2,646	3,255
Minnesota.......	70	73	163	196	160	157	374	425	2,936	3,266	2,552	2,830
Mississippi......	47	50	105	122	183	186	407	453	1,824	2,394	1,543	1,798
Missouri.......	74	79	171	192	145	149	334	361	1,965	2,232	2,052	2,297
Montana........	17	18	35	38	211	208	434	439	2,072	2,534	1,959	2,347
Nebraska.......	29	30	68	76	186	181	430	465	2,075	2,290	2,089	2,413
Nevada	19	21	42	53	160	134	348	345	2,502	2,864	2,574	3,085
New Hampshire....	16	17	33	38	145	147	301	335	2,352	2,669	2,215	2,641
New Jersey......	112	125	304	312	145	157	393	393	2,859	3,563	2,698	3,553
New Mexico......	40	42	57	68	262	251	379	404	2,100	2,390	1,783	2,119
New York.......	285	257	866	856	158	142	482	471	2,997	3,423	2,795	3,479
North Carolina....	107	115	244	281	161	159	368	389	2,372	2,570	2,065	2,287
North Dakota.....	15	16	20	22	234	257	314	340	2,057	2,440	2,138	2,450
Ohio	139	143	385	425	128	128	355	381	2,510	3,083	2,236	2,696
Oklahoma.......	65	68	116	129	208	206	369	393	1,975	2,018	1,761	2,113
Oregon.........	52	52	100	114	184	166	353	362	2,302	2,848	2,322	2,896
Pennsylvania.....	127	152	361	369	107	126	304	306	2,437	3,025	2,403	2,911
Rhode Island.....	21	20	27	29	205	203	266	288	2,586	3,240	2,656	3,169
South Carolina....	79	78	116	136	227	213	333	370	1,956	2,318	1,848	2,141
South Dakota	13	14	24	27	192	194	349	364	1,979	2,355	1,733	2,004
Tennessee......	79	84	175	188	163	161	358	359	2,055	2,389	1,883	2,196
Texas.........	223	268	706	858	131	143	415	456	2,192	2,492	1,952	2,229
Utah	37	42	51	63	216	214	294	321	2,000	2,524	2,092	2,460
Vermont........	13	13	18	21	233	216	312	363	2,302	2,471	2,090	2,455
Virginia........	117	116	221	247	188	175	356	373	2,267	2,553	2,248	2,505
Washington......	91	96	164	188	187	175	336	344	2,459	3,094	2,515	3,338
West Virginia.....	34	35	59	60	188	189	326	327	1,919	2,212	1,862	2,203
Wisconsin.......	67	64	183	201	136	126	375	393	2,503	3,153	2,372	2,900
Wyoming........	11	11	24	27	239	227	539	565	2,045	2,203	2,110	2,309

X Not applicable.   [1] Estimates subject to sampling variation; see Appendix III and source.   [2] 1990 based on enumerated resident population as of April 1, 1990. 1995 based on estimated resident population as of July 1.   [3] For full-time employees.

Source: U.S. Bureau of the Census, *Public Employment,* Series GE, No. 90-1, annual; <http://www.census.gov/pub/govs/www/apes/95SL.html> (accessed 8 July 1998).

No. 535. State and Local Government Full-Time Equivalent Employment, by Selected Function and State: 1995

[In thousands, for October. Local government amounts are estimates subject to sampling variation; see Appendix III and source]

STATE	EDUCATION						PUBLIC WELFARE		HEALTH		HOSPITALS	
	Total		Elem. & secondary		Higher education							
	State [1]	Local	State	Local	State	Local	State	Local	State	Local	State	Local
United States..	1,468.7	5,619.2	41.4	5,341.2	1,330.8	278.0	226.8	265.1	160.1	208.6	496.2	551.4
Alabama.........	34.2	86.7	-	86.7	30.3	-	4.3	1.1	6.8	3.9	12.2	20.1
Alaska..........	7.3	11.4	2.9	11.4	3.9	-	1.8	0.1	0.5	0.6	0.3	0.2
Arizona..........	24.8	90.8	-	83.6	22.4	7.2	5.3	4.0	2.1	2.7	0.7	4.6
Arkansas........	18.6	58.2	-	58.2	15.3	-	3.7	0.2	4.0	0.3	4.9	3.8
California	117.2	553.1	-	490.9	112.6	62.1	3.7	52.0	10.1	33.3	34.5	75.4
Colorado........	32.7	77.4	-	76.0	31.5	1.4	1.0	4.4	1.2	2.4	4.6	7.9
Connecticut......	18.0	67.0	-	67.0	15.2	-	4.8	1.8	2.6	1.4	12.3	-
Delaware	6.8	13.7	-	13.7	6.5	-	2.0	-	1.8	0.2	2.3	-
District of Columbia .	(X)	10.0	(X)	8.8	(X)	1.1	(X)	1.8	(X)	2.1	(X)	3.8
Florida	42.2	274.4	-	253.0	39.6	21.4	11.2	5.8	14.7	5.8	16.4	36.8
Georgia	40.7	181.4	-	180.7	35.0	0.7	7.7	1.4	4.4	8.2	14.4	42.0
Hawaii	30.4	-	23.2	-	7.1	-	1.1	0.1	2.8	0.2	3.2	-
Idaho	7.6	27.1	-	26.2	7.1	0.9	1.8	0.2	1.2	0.9	1.0	4.3
Illinois	55.3	232.1	-	212.6	52.4	19.5	13.4	7.1	3.2	6.7	15.2	15.2
Indiana.........	46.6	123.0	-	123.0	41.8	-	5.2	1.6	1.7	2.7	11.1	23.0
Iowa	25.9	72.8	-	66.6	24.7	6.2	2.7	1.5	0.3	2.0	8.1	8.9
Kansas.........	21.0	70.6	-	64.9	20.3	5.7	1.7	0.8	0.9	3.2	6.6	7.3
Kentucky	30.3	90.7	-	90.7	26.2	-	4.6	0.5	2.0	4.5	5.5	3.2
Louisiana	34.1	102.0	-	102.0	30.2	-	6.0	0.7	5.3	0.9	18.7	13.3
Maine..........	6.8	31.1	-	31.1	5.6	-	1.9	0.2	1.1	0.2	1.5	1.1
Maryland	19.7	104.9	-	96.0	17.7	8.9	7.9	2.3	6.0	3.6	6.9	-
Massachusetts.....	23.7	129.5	-	129.5	23.0	-	6.6	2.7	3.9	2.1	11.8	6.1
Michigan........	63.4	196.2	-	184.2	62.8	12.0	14.6	2.6	2.1	9.7	15.6	13.2
Minnesota.......	38.7	109.8	-	106.1	37.2	3.7	2.2	11.0	2.1	3.7	7.2	13.3
Mississippi	16.8	69.5	-	63.9	15.3	5.7	3.4	0.3	3.3	0.3	9.0	18.0
Missouri	26.3	118.1	-	113.0	24.4	5.1	7.5	2.1	3.3	3.5	12.4	7.8
Montana........	7.1	26.7	-	26.5	6.4	0.1	1.3	0.9	0.4	0.6	1.3	0.8
Nebraska	10.8	43.7	-	41.2	10.1	2.5	2.9	1.1	0.7	0.4	4.4	4.3
Nevada	6.1	27.3	-	27.3	6.0	-	1.0	0.4	0.7	0.8	1.7	3.6
New Hampshire....	5.7	24.7	-	24.7	5.3	-	1.3	2.5	0.8	0.1	1.0	-
New Jersey......	45.8	178.9	14.8	169.2	27.6	9.8	5.4	11.5	2.5	4.0	17.1	6.4
New Mexico	16.9	43.3	-	40.9	15.9	2.4	1.4	0.5	2.9	0.4	5.4	2.6
New York	49.0	400.8	-	375.3	43.9	25.5	7.5	51.8	8.9	17.2	55.6	61.4
North Carolina.....	45.6	162.5	-	149.0	42.6	13.5	1.3	13.4	2.0	13.9	15.6	17.8
North Dakota......	7.8	13.6	-	13.6	7.3	-	0.3	0.9	1.3	0.3	1.4	-
Ohio...........	68.0	212.7	-	207.5	65.6	5.2	2.2	22.3	3.8	17.5	17.7	15.1
Oklahoma........	25.5	80.0	-	79.6	23.5	0.4	5.8	0.4	3.8	1.0	6.1	9.5
Oregon.........	16.2	68.2	-	61.0	15.2	7.2	4.6	0.8	1.5	3.5	7.3	2.3
Pennsylvania......	50.6	208.4	-	200.1	47.6	8.3	11.6	21.7	1.7	5.2	21.0	2.8
Rhode Island.....	7.0	18.1	0.4	18.1	5.8	-	1.8	0.1	1.3	0.1	1.5	-
South Carolina.....	27.2	80.4	-	80.4	24.3	-	4.9	0.2	8.1	2.0	9.8	14.3
South Dakota	5.6	16.8	-	16.8	5.1	-	1.0	0.2	0.6	0.2	1.4	0.4
Tennessee	38.6	100.7	-	100.7	36.5	-	4.6	3.7	3.6	3.3	10.6	12.3
Texas..........	91.5	547.9	-	517.3	86.8	30.7	24.0	3.7	10.4	16.1	40.3	43.7
Utah	22.0	39.0	-	39.0	21.1	-	3.0	0.4	1.4	1.1	3.9	1.0
Vermont	4.6	16.6	-	16.6	4.2	-	1.1	-	0.5	-	0.3	-
Virginia.........	44.9	149.2	-	149.2	42.2	-	2.3	7.5	5.8	5.3	18.0	3.5
Washington......	36.8	87.0	-	87.0	36.1	-	7.3	1.2	7.0	4.1	8.1	8.9
West Virginia.....	13.6	41.0	-	41.0	12.1	-	2.6	-	0.7	1.5	1.5	3.3
Wisconsin.......	29.8	114.1	-	105.2	28.5	8.9	1.2	13.3	1.7	4.7	7.6	3.9
Wyoming	3.3	16.1	-	14.4	3.2	1.7	0.3	-	0.5	0.2	1.4	4.1

See footnotes at end of table.

No. 535. State and Local Government Full-Time Equivalent Employment, by Selected Function and State: 1995—Continued

[In thousands, for October. Local government amounts are estimates subject to sampling variation; see Appendix III and source]

STATE	HIGHWAYS		POLICE PROTECTION		FIRE PROTECTION		CORRECTIONS		PARKS AND RECREATION		GOVERNMENT ADMINISTRATION	
	State	Local	State	Local	State	Local	State	Local	State	Local	State	Local
United States..	**253.3**	**289.9**	**89.6**	**689.2**	**(X)**	**274.3**	**409.2**	**205.8**	**38.6**	**207.3**	**339.6**	**586.1**
Alabama.........	4.3	6.6	1.0	9.9	(X)	4.5	4.3	2.4	0.8	2.9	5.4	6.8
Alaska..........	2.8	0.9	0.4	1.4	(X)	0.7	1.3	-	0.1	0.6	2.5	1.9
Arizona.........	2.9	4.0	1.7	11.1	(X)	3.9	7.6	4.8	0.7	3.5	5.5	13.0
Arkansas........	3.6	3.6	0.9	5.4	(X)	2.3	3.4	1.2	0.8	0.8	2.6	5.8
California	17.3	21.6	11.0	79.5	(X)	30.0	43.1	27.8	3.7	32.2	23.6	78.4
Colorado........	3.1	5.3	1.1	9.5	(X)	3.7	4.2	2.9	0.3	5.8	5.3	9.4
Connecticut......	4.0	3.8	1.6	8.0	(X)	4.1	7.4	-	0.4	2.2	7.0	4.4
Delaware........	1.5	0.7	0.8	1.2	(X)	0.3	1.8	-	0.3	0.3	2.3	0.9
District of Columbia .	(X)	0.8	(X)	4.5	(X)	1.6	(X)	4.2	(X)	0.4	(X)	3.3
Florida	10.6	13.6	3.8	44.9	(X)	18.2	31.1	13.3	1.1	15.6	21.2	35.6
Georgia	6.1	7.8	2.3	18.8	(X)	12.2	19.1	6.2	2.9	4.3	5.0	16.4
Hawaii	0.8	1.0	-	3.3	(X)	1.6	2.1	-	0.3	1.9	3.6	2.2
Idaho..........	1.8	1.6	0.4	2.9	(X)	0.9	1.5	0.8	0.2	0.7	1.8	3.4
Illinois	8.4	11.5	3.7	39.4	(X)	14.6	13.6	8.1	0.8	17.5	11.8	29.0
Indiana.........	4.6	6.4	2.0	12.5	(X)	5.8	6.3	3.8	0.1	3.9	4.1	14.3
Iowa	2.7	5.5	0.9	5.7	(X)	1.7	2.3	0.9	0.2	2.2	4.0	5.4
Kansas.........	3.8	5.6	1.0	6.6	(X)	2.5	3.6	1.9	0.5	2.4	4.6	6.7
Kentucky	5.4	3.0	1.7	6.0	(X)	2.8	5.3	2.2	2.2	1.5	8.1	4.8
Louisiana	5.7	4.9	1.1	12.4	(X)	4.1	6.8	2.6	0.9	2.8	5.3	10.6
Maine..........	2.8	1.5	0.5	2.4	(X)	1.6	1.2	0.6	0.2	0.6	2.0	2.3
Maryland	5.0	4.6	2.3	13.4	(X)	6.1	10.6	2.5	0.7	6.4	8.2	7.5
Massachusetts.....	4.6	5.9	1.9	16.4	(X)	12.8	6.1	5.0	1.1	2.1	12.6	9.1
Michigan........	3.8	10.1	3.0	20.3	(X)	7.7	16.5	4.8	0.8	5.8	7.1	21.1
Minnesota.......	4.9	7.5	0.9	9.0	(X)	2.3	3.4	3.8	0.6	4.3	5.3	12.5
Mississippi	3.4	5.3	1.0	6.6	(X)	2.6	3.7	1.0	0.4	0.8	2.0	6.5
Missouri	6.7	5.3	2.2	14.1	(X)	5.0	6.7	2.3	0.7	3.5	5.9	9.5
Montana........	1.8	1.3	0.4	1.7	(X)	0.5	0.8	0.3	0.1	0.4	1.4	2.1
Nebraska.......	2.4	3.1	0.7	3.5	(X)	1.1	2.0	0.8	0.4	1.1	1.6	4.0
Nevada........	1.5	1.3	0.6	4.1	(X)	1.6	2.9	1.3	0.2	2.2	1.9	4.8
New Hampshire....	2.0	1.3	0.4	2.6	(X)	1.4	1.0	0.5	0.2	0.3	1.5	1.7
New Jersey......	8.0	10.7	3.7	28.5	(X)	7.7	9.0	7.1	2.4	5.6	18.0	20.9
New Mexico......	2.7	1.6	0.6	4.4	(X)	1.6	3.9	1.3	0.7	1.6	4.2	4.0
New York	14.1	30.1	5.4	71.1	(X)	19.7	33.9	24.2	2.6	10.7	40.5	39.6
North Carolina.....	12.6	3.3	3.3	16.5	(X)	5.4	12.4	3.6	0.7	4.0	10.0	10.4
North Dakota.....	1.0	1.1	0.2	1.1	(X)	0.3	0.5	0.2	0.1	0.7	1.1	1.5
Ohio	8.6	13.3	2.5	27.2	(X)	18.5	14.7	7.5	0.9	7.8	11.7	30.6
Oklahoma.......	4.1	5.6	1.7	7.9	(X)	3.9	7.8	1.1	1.8	2.2	5.1	6.1
Oregon.........	3.4	4.0	1.2	6.2	(X)	3.2	2.9	2.8	0.5	2.2	6.5	6.1
Pennsylvania.....	13.7	10.6	6.4	25.1	(X)	5.7	12.8	10.7	1.0	4.2	13.6	26.6
Rhode Island.....	0.9	1.0	0.3	2.6	(X)	2.0	1.7	-	0.1	0.8	2.5	1.6
South Carolina.....	5.1	2.4	2.3	8.5	(X)	3.2	8.1	2.0	0.6	2.3	4.3	7.6
South Dakota	1.2	1.6	0.3	1.3	(X)	0.4	0.7	0.3	0.1	0.7	1.4	1.7
Tennessee	4.7	6.7	1.6	12.0	(X)	5.9	7.0	4.3	1.1	3.7	4.9	9.8
Texas..........	14.0	18.9	3.4	53.4	(X)	18.5	43.0	20.9	1.2	13.4	16.3	39.4
Utah	1.8	1.5	0.7	4.0	(X)	1.6	2.5	0.7	0.3	2.3	2.9	3.4
Vermont	1.1	1.0	0.5	0.8	(X)	0.3	0.9	-	0.2	0.2	1.3	1.0
Virginia.........	12.0	3.9	2.5	14.2	(X)	7.0	12.7	6.2	0.9	6.0	7.4	13.2
Washington.......	6.2	6.7	1.8	10.6	(X)	5.4	7.4	3.5	0.5	4.9	5.2	13.9
West Virginia.....	6.1	0.8	0.9	2.4	(X)	0.9	0.8	0.4	1.0	0.9	3.0	3.2
Wisconsin........	2.0	9.1	0.9	13.3	(X)	4.8	6.5	2.4	0.3	3.8	5.5	10.7
Wyoming	1.7	0.7	0.2	1.4	(X)	0.3	0.5	0.3	0.1	0.6	0.9	1.5

- Represents or rounds to zero.   X Not applicable.   [1]Includes items not shown separately.

Source: U.S. Bureau of the Census, <http://www.census.gov/ftp/pub/govs/www/apes/95SL.html> (accessed 8 July 1998).

No. 536. City Government Employment and Payroll—Largest Cities: 1990 and 1995

[For October. See footnote 2, Table 524, for those areas representing city-county consolidated governments]

CITIES RANKED BY 1994 POPULATION	TOTAL EMPLOYMENT (1,000)		FULL-TIME EQUIVALENT EMPLOYMENT[1]				OCTOBER PAYROLL (mil. dol.)		AVERAGE EARNINGS IN OCTOBER, FULL-TIME EMPLOYEES (dol.)	
			Total (1,000)		Per 10,000 population[1]					
	1990	1995	1990	1995	1990	1995	1990	1995	1990	1995
New York, NY [2][3]	456	425	395	388	539	545	1,092	1,306	2,783	3,454
Los Angeles, CA	51	48	51	47	146	140	177	191	3,488	4,133
Chicago, IL	42	41	42	41	149	147	125	156	3,002	3,757
Houston, TX	20	23	20	23	120	117	40	57	2,061	2,459
Philadelphia, PA	32	30	32	29	201	187	89	92	2,843	3,220
San Diego, CA	10	12	10	10	88	92	29	34	2,876	3,472
Phoenix, AZ	12	12	11	12	116	113	32	38	2,876	3,281
Dallas, TX	15	15	15	14	144	135	28	41	1,945	2,876
San Antonio, TX	13	16	13	15	134	133	28	37	2,227	2,539
Detroit, MI	22	18	21	17	206	166	50	50	2,390	2,908
Honolulu, HI	10	10	9	9	110	112	24	28	2,600	3,083
San Jose, CA	6	7	5	6	62	72	16	27	3,453	4,700
Indianapolis, IN	13	12	12	12	171	159	23	33	1,910	2,490
San Francisco, CA	26	26	26	26	356	341	94	98	3,648	3,710
Baltimore, MD [2]	30	28	29	27	395	381	73	81	2,540	3,010
Jacksonville, FL	11	10	10	9	154	145	24	28	2,582	3,064
Columbus, OH	8	8	7	8	118	109	18	26	2,416	3,324
Memphis, TN [2]	22	22	21	21	341	332	48	54	2,287	2,679
Milwaukee, WI	9	9	9	9	137	136	21	23	2,431	2,793
El Paso, TX [2][3]	5	6	5	6	94	104	9	13	1,973	2,302
Washington, DC [2][3]	50	40	48	39	789	720	139	124	2,930	3,269
Boston, MA [2]	21	22	21	22	363	381	50	49	2,391	2,279
Seattle, WA	11	11	10	11	198	201	32	40	3,274	3,985
Austin, TX [2]	10	13	10	12	203	244	21	28	2,186	2,512
Nashville-Davidson, TN [2]	18	21	17	19	347	383	42	41	2,510	2,135
Cleveland, OH	9	10	8	9	163	173	21	24	2,521	2,805
Denver, CO	13	16	12	14	254	279	31	45	2,649	3,126
New Orleans, LA	10	9	10	9	194	215	16	19	1,623	2,226
Portland, OR	5	6	5	5	97	106	15	19	3,305	3,950
Fort Worth, TX	5	6	5	5	117	112	11	12	2,171	2,403
Oklahoma City, OK	5	5	4	5	101	110	11	14	2,430	3,084
Kansas City, MO	6	7	6	7	145	150	15	17	2,390	2,685
Tucson, AZ	5	6	5	5	114	119	12	14	2,528	2,882
Charlotte, NC [2]	5	5	5	5	115	112	11	13	2,399	2,847
Virginia Beach, VA [2]	14	17	13	15	334	358	28	35	2,232	2,385
Long Beach, CA	6	6	5	5	126	126	18	21	3,413	3,947
Albuquerque, NM	7	8	6	8	161	151	12	15	2,040	2,432
Atlanta, GA	8	8	8	8	205	199	18	20	2,286	2,541
Baton Rouge, LA	6	6	5	6	132	153	11	14	2,255	2,550
Fresno, CA	3	3	3	3	77	72	8	10	2,944	3,652
Tulsa, OK	4	4	4	4	115	113	11	11	2,555	2,734
Oakland, CA	5	5	4	5	111	123	15	19	3,948	4,482
Sacramento, CA	4	4	4	4	105	104	11	14	3,021	3,713
St. Louis, MO	8	8	7	8	186	188	17	20	2,363	2,606
Minneapolis, MN	6	7	6	6	154	170	15	23	2,815	3,921
Pittsburgh, PA	6	6	6	5	152	147	12	16	2,240	3,221
Miami, FL	4	4	4	3	113	105	15	12	3,771	3,503
Omaha, NE	3	3	3	3	79	82	8	10	3,051	3,533
Cincinnati, OH	7	8	6	7	173	200	16	23	2,634	3,480
Las Vegas, NV	2	2	2	2	77	67	5	7	2,563	3,570
Colorado Springs, CO	6	6	5	6	188	195	13	19	2,618	3,242
Toledo, OH	3	3	3	3	91	91	9	10	2,847	3,191
Buffalo, NY [2]	13	12	12	12	379	414	31	40	2,596	3,733
Mesa, AZ	2	3	2	3	81	86	7	9	2,898	3,307
Wichita, KS	3	4	3	3	87	97	5	8	2,083	2,617
Santa Ana, CA	2	2	2	2	58	65	7	8	4,144	4,813
Arlington, TX	2	2	2	2	68	75	5	6	2,538	2,991
Anaheim, CA	4	4	3	3	99	92	9	10	3,728	4,635
Tampa, FL	4	4	4	4	151	143	10	13	2,505	3,176
Corpus Christi, TX	3	3	3	3	116	117	6	8	2,009	2,384
Newark, NJ	5	6	5	5	177	194	8	18	1,698	3,544
Louisville, KY	5	5	4	4	159	155	9	9	2,180	2,224
Birmingham, AL	4	4	4	4	142	155	8	9	2,243	2,354
St. Paul, MN	4	4	3	3	124	124	10	11	3,265	3,601
Anchorage, AK	9	11	8	8	351	346	28	39	3,706	4,683
Riverside, CA	2	2	2	2	88	80	7	9	3,459	4,122
Aurora, CO [2]	2	2	2	2	84	85	5	6	2,586	2,972
Norfolk, VA [2]	10	12	10	11	376	454	22	27	2,268	2,583
St Petersburg, FL	3	4	3	3	125	126	7	9	2,412	2,836
Lexington-Fayette, KY	3	4	3	4	133	168	6	8	1,929	2,159
Raleigh, NC	3	3	3	3	141	129	5	7	2,297	2,705
Jersey City, NJ	4	4	3	4	131	175	10	13	3,172	3,755
Rochester, NY	9	10	8	9	347	398	27	33	3,315	3,630
Stockton, CA	2	2	1	2	47	88	5	6	3,554	3,330
Akron, OH	6	6	5	6	224	275	11	14	2,255	2,550
Lincoln, NE	4	4	3	3	156	147	7	9	2,367	2,724

[1] 1990 based on enumerated resident population as of April 1, 1990. 1995 based on estimated resident population as of July 1, 1995.   [2] Includes city-operated elementary and secondary schools.   [3] Includes city-operated university or college.

Source: U.S. Bureau of the Census, *City Employment*, GE-90-2; and unpublished data.

Federal Government Finances and Employment

This section presents statistics relating to the financial structure and the civilian employment of the federal government. The fiscal data cover taxes, other receipts, outlays, and debt. The principal sources of fiscal data are *The Budget of the United States Government* and related documents, published annually by the Office of Management and Budget (OMB), and the Department of the Treasury's *United States Government Annual Report* and its *Appendix*. Detailed data on tax returns and collections are published annually by the Internal Revenue Service. Personnel data relating to staffing and payrolls for the various public functions and agencies, to employee characteristics, and to civil service status; are published by the Office of Personnel Management and the Bureau of Labor Statistics. The primary source for data on public lands is *Public Land Statistics*, published annually by the Bureau of Land Management, Department of the Interior. Data on federally-owned land and real property are collected by the General Services Administration and presented in its annual *Inventory Report on Real Property Owned by the United States Throughout the World*.

Budget concept—Under the unified budget concept, all federal monies are included in one comprehensive budget. These monies comprise both federal funds and trust funds. Federal funds are derived mainly from taxes and borrowing and are not restricted by law to any specific government purpose. Trust funds, such as the Unemployment Trust Fund, collect certain taxes and other receipts for use in carrying out specific purposes or programs in accordance with the terms of the trust agreement or statute. Fund balances include both cash balances with Treasury and investments in U.S. securities. Part of the balance is obligated, part unobligated. Prior to 1985, the budget totals, under provisions of law, excluded some federal activities—including the Federal Financing Bank,

In Brief	
	1998
Gross Federal debt	*$5,544 bil.*
Interest on	
the public debt	*$362 bil.*
Net interest	*$243 bil.*

the Postal Service, the Synthetic Fuels Corporation, and the lending activities of the Rural Electrification Administration. The Balanced Budget and Emergency Deficit Control Act of 1985 (P.L.99-177) repealed the off-budget status of these entities and placed social security (federal old-age and survivors insurance and the federal disability insurance trust funds) off-budget. Though social security is now off-budget and, by law, excluded from coverage of the congressional budget resolutions, it continues to be a federal program.

Receipts arising from the government's sovereign powers are reported as governmental receipts; all other receipts, i.e., from business-type or market-oriented activities, are offset against outlays. Outlays are reported on a checks-issued (net) basis (i.e., outlays are recorded at the time the checks to pay bills are issued).

Debt concept—For most of U.S. history, the total debt consisted of debt borrowed by the Treasury (i.e., public debt). The present debt series includes both public debt and agency debt. The *gross federal debt* includes money borrowed by the Treasury and by various federal agencies; it is the broadest generally used measure of the federal debt. *Total public debt* is covered by a statutory debt limitation and includes only borrowing by the Treasury.

Treasury receipts and outlays—All receipts of the government, with a few exceptions, are deposited to the credit of the U.S. Treasury regardless of ultimate disposition. Under the Constitution, no money may be withdrawn from the

Treasury unless appropriated by the Congress.

The day-to-day cash operations of the federal government clearing through the accounts of the U.S. Treasury are reported in the *Daily Treasury Statement*. Extensive detail on the public debt is published in the *Monthly Statement of the Public Debt of the United States*.

Budget receipts such as taxes, customs duties, and outlays represented by checks issued and cash payments made by disbursing officers as well as government agencies are reported in the *Daily Treasury Statement of Receipts and Outlays of the United States Government* and in the Treasury's *United States Government Annual Report* and its *Appendix*. These deposits in and payments from accounts maintained by government agencies are on the same basis as the unified budget.

The quarterly *Treasury Bulletin* contains data on fiscal operations and related Treasury activities, including financial statements of government corporations and other business-type activities.

Income tax returns and tax collections—Tax data are compiled by the Internal Revenue Service of the Treasury Department. The *Annual Report of the Commissioner and Chief Counsel of the Internal Revenue Service Data Book* gives a detailed account of tax collections by kind of tax and by regions, districts, and states. The agency's annual *Statistics of Income* reports present detailed data from individual income tax returns and corporation income tax returns. The quarterly *Statistics of Income Bulletin* has, in general, replaced the supplemental *Statistics of Income* publications which presented data on such diverse subjects as tax-exempt organizations, unincorporated businesses, fiduciary income tax and estate tax returns, sales of capital assets by individuals, international income and taxes reported by corporations and individuals, and estate tax wealth.

Employment and payrolls—The Office of Personnel Management collects employment and payroll data from all departments and agencies of the federal government, except the Central

Intelligence Agency, the National Security Agency, and the Defense Intelligence Agency. Employment figures represent the number of persons who occupied civilian positions at the end of the report month shown and who are paid for personal services rendered for the federal government, regardless of the nature of appointment or method of payment.

Federal payrolls include all payments for personal services rendered during the report month and payments for accumulated annual leave of employees who separate from the service. Since most federal employees are paid on a biweekly basis, the calendar month earnings are partially estimated on the basis of the number of work days in each month where payroll periods overlap.

Federal employment and payroll figures are published by the Office of Personnel Management in its *Federal Civilian Workforce Statistics—Employment and Trends*. It also publishes biennial employment data for minority groups, data on occupations of white- and blue-collar workers, and data on employment by geographic area; reports on salary and wage distribution of federal employees are published annually. General schedule is primarily white-collar; wage system primarily blue-collar. Data on federal employment are also issued by the Bureau of Labor Statistics in its *Monthly Labor Review* and in *Employment and Earnings* and by the Bureau of the Census in its annual *Public Employment*.

Public lands—These data refer to transactions which involve the disposal, under public land laws, of federal public lands to nonfederal owners. In general, original entries and selections are applications to secure title to public lands which have been accepted as properly filed (i.e., allowed). Some types of applications, however, are not reported until issuance of the final certificate, which passes equitable title to the land to the applicant. Applications are approved when full compliance with the requirements of the laws is shown and become final entries (perfected entries) upon issuance of a final certificate. Patents are government deeds which pass legal title to the land to the applicant. Certifications are issued in lieu of patents in connection with certain state selections.

No. 537. Federal Budget—Summary: 1945 to 1998

[In millions of dollars, except percent. For fiscal years ending in year shown; see text, Section 9. The Balanced Budget and Emergency Deficit Control Act of 1985 put all the previously off-budget federal entities into the budget and moved Social Security off-budget. Minus sign (-) indicates deficit or decrease]

YEAR	Receipts	Outlays	Surplus or deficit(-)	Outlays as percent of GDP [1]	GROSS FEDERAL DEBT [2]				
					Total	Federal gov't account	Held by the public		
							Total	Federal Reserve System	As percent of GDP [1]
1945	45,159	92,712	-47,553	41.9	260,123	24,941	235,182	21,792	117.5
1950	39,443	42,562	-3,119	15.6	256,853	37,830	219,023	18,331	93.9
1955	65,451	68,444	-2,993	17.3	274,366	47,751	226,616	23,607	69.4
1960	92,492	92,191	301	17.8	290,525	53,686	236,840	26,523	56.1
1965	116,817	118,228	-1,411	17.2	322,318	61,540	260,778	39,100	46.9
1970	192,807	195,649	-2,842	19.4	380,921	97,723	283,198	57,714	37.8
1975	279,090	332,332	-53,242	21.4	541,925	147,225	394,700	84,993	34.9
1980	517,112	590,947	-73,835	21.7	909,050	199,212	709,838	120,846	33.4
1981	599,272	678,249	-78,976	22.2	994,845	209,507	785,338	124,466	32.6
1982	617,766	745,755	-127,989	23.2	1,137,345	217,560	919,785	134,497	35.4
1983	600,562	808,380	-207,818	23.6	1,371,710	240,114	1,131,596	155,527	40.1
1984	666,486	851,874	-185,388	22.3	1,564,657	264,159	1,300,498	155,122	41.0
1985	734,088	946,423	-212,334	23.1	1,817,521	317,612	1,499,908	169,806	44.3
1986	769,215	990,460	-221,245	22.6	2,120,629	383,919	1,736,709	190,855	48.5
1987	854,353	1,004,122	-149,769	21.8	2,346,125	457,444	1,888,680	212,040	50.9
1988	909,303	1,064,489	-155,187	21.5	2,601,307	550,507	2,050,799	229,218	52.5
1989	991,190	1,143,671	-152,481	21.4	2,868,039	678,157	2,189,882	220,088	53.6
1990	1,031,969	1,253,163	-221,194	22.0	3,206,564	795,841	2,410,722	234,410	56.4
1991	1,055,041	1,324,400	-269,359	22.6	3,598,498	910,362	2,688,137	258,591	61.4
1992	1,091,279	1,381,681	-290,402	22.5	4,002,136	1,003,302	2,998,834	296,397	65.1
1993	1,154,401	1,409,414	-255,013	21.8	4,351,416	1,103,945	3,247,471	325,653	67.2
1994	1,258,627	1,461,731	-203,104	21.4	4,643,705	1,211,588	3,432,117	355,150	67.8
1995	1,351,830	1,515,729	-163,899	21.1	4,921,018	1,317,645	3,603,373	374,114	68.4
1996	1,453,062	1,560,512	-107,450	20.7	5,181,934	1,448,967	3,732,968	390,924	68.8
1997	1,579,292	1,601,235	-21,943	20.1	5,369,707	1,598,559	3,771,148	424,507	67.4
1998, est.	1,657,858	1,667,815	-9,957	20.0	5,543,589	1,746,773	3,796,816	(NA)	66.4

NA Not available.   [1] Gross domestic product as of fiscal year; for calendar year GDP, see Section 14.   [2] See text, Section 10 for discussion of debt concept.

Source: U.S. Office of Management and Budget, *Historical Tables*, annual.

No. 538. Federal Budget Outlays—Defense, Human and Physical Resources, and Net Interest Payments: 1980 to 1998

[In millions of dollars. For fiscal year ending in year shown. Minus sign (-) indicates offsets]

OUTLAYS	1980	1985	1990	1993	1994	1995	1996	1997	1998, est.
Federal outlays, total	590,947	946,423	1,253,163	1,409,414	1,461,731	1,515,729	1,560,512	1,601,235	1,667,815
National defense	133,995	252,748	299,331	291,086	281,642	272,066	265,748	270,473	264,112
Human resources	313,374	471,822	619,329	827,535	869,414	923,765	958,254	1,002,323	1,048,983
Education, training, employment, and social services	31,843	29,342	38,755	50,012	46,307	54,263	52,001	53,008	55,114
Health	23,169	33,542	57,716	99,415	107,122	115,418	119,378	123,843	131,772
Medicare	32,090	65,822	98,102	130,552	144,747	159,855	174,225	190,016	198,135
Income security	86,557	128,230	147,076	207,299	214,089	220,493	225,989	230,886	239,349
Social security	118,547	188,623	248,623	304,585	319,565	335,846	349,676	365,257	381,499
Veterans benefits and services	21,169	26,262	29,058	35,671	37,584	37,890	36,985	39,313	43,114
Physical resources	65,985	56,821	126,004	46,762	70,575	59,197	64,236	60,000	81,087
Energy	10,156	5,609	3,341	4,319	5,219	4,936	2,844	1,483	403
Natural resources and environment	13,858	13,357	17,080	20,239	21,064	22,078	21,614	21,369	23,822
Commerce and housing credit	9,390	4,337	67,600	-21,853	-4,228	-17,808	-10,472	-14,624	3,525
Transportation	21,329	25,838	29,485	35,004	38,066	39,350	39,565	40,767	41,535
Community and regional development	11,252	7,680	8,498	9,052	10,454	10,641	10,685	11,005	11,802
Net interest	52,538	129,504	184,221	198,811	202,957	232,169	241,090	244,013	242,694
International affairs	12,714	16,176	13,764	17,248	17,083	16,434	13,496	15,228	14,480
General science, space/ technology	5,832	8,627	14,444	17,030	16,227	16,724	16,709	17,174	17,093
Agriculture	8,839	25,565	11,958	20,363	15,046	9,778	9,159	9,032	10,580
Administration of justice	4,584	6,270	9,993	14,955	15,256	16,216	17,548	20,197	22,274
General government	13,028	11,588	10,734	13,009	11,303	13,835	11,892	12,768	12,878
Undistributed offsetting receipts	-19,942	-32,698	-36,615	-37,386	-37,772	-44,455	-37,620	-49,973	-46,366

Source: U. S. Office of Management and Budget, *Historical Tables* annual.

No. 539. Federal Receipts, by Source: 1980 to 1998

[In millions of dollars. For fiscal years ending in year shown; see text, Section 9. Receipts reflect collections. Covers both federal funds and trust funds; see text, Section 10. Excludes government-sponsored but privately-owned corporations, Federal Reserve System, District of Columbia government, and money held in suspense as deposit funds]

SOURCE	1980	1985	1990	1995	1996	1997	1998, est.
Total receipts [1]	517,112	734,088	1,031,969	1,351,830	1,453,062	1,579,292	1,657,858
Individual income taxes	244,069	334,531	466,884	590,244	656,417	737,466	767,768
Corporation income taxes	64,600	61,331	93,507	157,004	171,824	182,293	190,842
Social insurance and retirement receipts	157,803	265,163	380,047	484,473	509,414	539,371	571,374
Excise taxes	24,329	35,992	35,345	57,484	54,014	56,924	55,540
Social insurance and retirement receipts [1]	157,803	265,163	380,047	484,473	509,414	539,371	571,374
Employment and general retirement	138,748	234,646	353,891	451,045	476,361	506,751	538,124
Old-age and survivors insurance:							
Trust funds (off-budget)	96,581	169,822	255,031	284,091	311,869	336,729	358,949
Disability insurance (off-budget)	16,628	16,348	26,625	66,988	55,623	55,261	57,042
Hospital insurance	23,217	44,871	68,556	96,024	104,997	110,710	118,029
Railroad retirement/pension fund:							
Trust funds	2,323	2,213	2,292	2,424	2,362	2,440	2,493
Railroad social security equivalent account	(NA)	1,391	1,387	1,518	1,510	1,611	1,611
Unemployment insurance	15,336	25,758	21,635	28,878	28,584	28,202	28,922
Trust funds	15,336	25,758	21,635	28,878	28,584	28,202	28,922
Total excise taxes [1]	24,329	35,992	35,345	57,484	54,014	56,924	55,540
Federal funds:							
Alcohol	5,601	5,562	5,695	7,216	7,220	7,257	7,251
Tobacco	2,443	4,779	4,081	5,878	5,795	5,873	5,926
Telephone	(NA)	2,147	2,995	3,794	4,234	4,543	4,864
Ozone depleting chemicals/products	(NA)	(NA)	360	616	320	130	55
Transportation fuels	(NA)	(NA)	(NA)	8,491	7,468	7,107	442
Trust funds:							
Highway	6,620	13,015	13,867	22,611	24,651	23,867	26,063
Airport and airway	1,874	2,851	3,700	5,534	2,369	4,007	7,975
Black lung disability	272	581	665	608	614	614	640
Inland waterway	(NA)	40	63	103	108	96	116
Hazardous substance superfund	(NA)	273	818	867	313	71	101
Post-closure liability (hazardous waste)	(NA)	7	-1	(NA)	(NA)	(NA)	(NA)
Oil spill liability	(NA)	(NA)	143	211	34	1	46
Aquatic resources	(NA)	126	218	306	315	316	281
Leaking underground storage tank	(NA)	(NA)	122	165	48	-2	140
Vaccine injury compensation	(NA)	(NA)	159	138	115	123	111

NA Not available. [1] Totals reflect interfund and intragovernmental transactions and/or other functions, not shown separately.

Source: U.S. Office of Management and Budget, *Historical Tables,* annual.

No. 540. Federal Trust Fund Receipts, Outlays, and Balances: 1995 to 1997

[In billions of dollars. For fiscal years ending in year shown. Receipts deposited. Outlays on a checks-issued basis less refunds collected. Balances: That which have not been spent. See text, Section 10, for discussion of the budget concept and trust funds]

DESCRIPTION	INCOME			OUTLAYS			BALANCES [1]		
	1995	1996	1997	1995	1996	1997	1995	1996	1997
Total [2]	786	835	878	687	720	752	1,282	1,391	1,515
Airport and airway trust fund	6	3	5	7	7	6	12	8	6
Federal employees health benefits fund	16	16	16	16	16	17	8	7	7
Federal civilian employees retirement funds	67	68	71	39	40	42	374	402	431
Federal old-age, survivors and disability insurance trust funds	399	418	449	338	352	367	483	550	631
Foreign military sales trust fund	13	15	15	13	14	15	6	6	-
Highway trust fund	(NA)	(NA)	25	(NA)	(NA)	25	(NA)	(NA)	22
Health insurance trust funds:									
Medicare: Federal hospital insurance (HI) trust fund	115	124	129	115	128	138	130	125	116
Federal supplemental medical insurance	58	82	81	65	69	73	14	27	35
Military retirement fund	35	33	38	28	29	30	127	131	139
Railroad retirement trust funds	12	9	9	11	8	8	14	14	15
Unemployment trust funds	33	32	33	25	26	24	48	54	62
Veterans life insurance trust funds	2	2	2	2	2	2	14	14	14
Other trust funds [3]	11	10	10	9	9	9	35	31	31

- Represents or rounds to zero. NA Not available. [1] Balances available on a cash basis (rather than an authorization basis) at the end of the year. Balances are primarily invested in federal debt securities. [2] Includes funds not shown separately. [3] Effective August 9, 1989, the permanent insurance fund of the FDIC was classified under law as a federal fund.

Source: U.S. Office of Management and Budget, *Analytical Perspectives,* annual.

No. 541. Federal Budget Outlays in Constant (1992) Dollars: 1980 to 1998

[Dollar amounts in billions of dollars. For fiscal years ending in year shown; see text, Section 9. Given the inherent imprecision in deflating outlays, the data shown in constant dollars present a reasonable perspective—not precision. The deflators and the categories that are deflated are as comparable over time as feasible. Minus sign (-) indicates offset]

OUTLAYS	1980	1985	1990	1991	1992	1993	1994	1995	1996	1997	1998, est.
Constant (1992) dollar outlays, total	**1,015.9**	**1,209.0**	**1,353.7**	**1,366.1**	**1,381.7**	**1,374.8**	**1,392.8**	**1,407.8**	**1,412.0**	**1,414.0**	**1,441.0**
National defense [1]	229.4	306.1	324.6	283.3	298.4	286.6	271.9	256.4	240.3	239.3	229.3
Nondefense, total	786.5	903.0	1,029.1	1,082.8	1,083.3	1,088.1	1,120.9	1,151.4	1,171.6	1,174.7	1,211.8
Payments for individuals	484.5	564.4	632.3	671.8	727.6	761.1	780.9	808.8	822.5	836.7	855.3
Direct payments [2]	427.7	499.1	548.9	576.2	615.5	640.3	652.5	674.0	689.0	705.6	716.3
Grants to state and local governments	56.8	65.2	83.4	95.5	112.2	120.9	128.5	134.8	133.5	131.1	138.9
All other grants	98.8	70.2	61.1	62.9	65.6	67.5	71.8	73.3	72.1	74.7	77.0
Net Interest [2]	88.6	165.2	197.8	200.2	199.4	193.7	193.1	215.3	218.6	216.4	211.3
All other [2]	149.7	145.7	178.0	188.2	130.0	101.3	109.6	93.3	90.2	88.0	105.6
Undistributed offsetting receipts[2]	-35.1	-42.6	-40.0	-40.4	-39.3	-35.6	-34.5	-39.3	-31.6	-41.1	-37.4
Total outlays as percent of GDP	21.7	23.1	22.0	22.6	22.5	21.8	21.4	21.1	20.7	20.1	20.0
National defense [1]	4.9	6.2	5.3	4.7	4.9	4.5	4.1	3.8	3.5	3.4	3.2
Nondefense, total	16.8	16.9	16.8	17.9	17.6	17.3	17.2	17.3	17.2	16.7	16.8
Payments for individuals	10.2	10.4	10.3	11.1	11.8	12.1	12.0	12.2	12.1	11.9	11.9
Direct payments [2]	9.0	9.2	8.9	9.5	10.0	10.2	10.0	10.1	10.1	10.0	9.9
Grants to state and local governments	1.2	1.2	1.4	1.6	1.8	1.9	2.0	2.0	2.0	1.9	1.9
All other grants	2.2	1.4	1.0	1.1	1.1	1.1	1.1	1.1	1.1	1.1	1.1
Net Interest [2]	1.9	3.2	3.2	3.3	3.2	3.1	3.0	3.2	3.2	3.1	2.9
All other [2]	3.2	2.8	2.9	3.1	2.1	1.6	1.7	1.4	1.4	1.3	1.5
Undistributed offsetting receipts[2]	-0.7	-0.8	-0.6	-0.7	-0.6	-0.6	-0.6	-0.6	-0.5	-0.6	-0.6
Percent of outlays, total	**100.0**	**100.0**	**100.0**	**100.0**	**100.0**	**100.0**	**100.0**	**100.0**	**100.0**	**100.0**	**100.0**
National defense [1]	22.7	26.7	23.9	20.6	21.6	20.7	19.3	17.9	17.0	16.9	15.8
Nondefense, total	77.3	73.3	76.1	79.4	78.4	79.3	80.7	82.1	83.0	83.1	84.2
Payments for individuals	47.1	45.1	46.6	49.1	52.7	55.5	56.2	57.7	58.3	59.3	59.4
Direct payments [2]	41.6	39.9	40.5	42.1	44.5	46.7	47.0	48.1	48.8	50.0	49.8
Grants to state and local governments	5.5	5.2	6.2	7.0	8.1	8.8	9.3	9.6	9.5	9.3	9.7
All other grants	9.9	6.0	4.6	4.7	4.7	4.9	5.1	5.2	5.1	5.3	5.4
Net Interest [2]	8.9	13.7	14.7	14.7	14.4	14.1	13.9	15.3	15.4	15.2	14.6
All other [2]	14.8	12.0	13.1	13.9	9.4	7.5	8.0	6.7	6.5	6.3	7.6
Undistributed offsetting receipts[2]	-3.4	-3.5	-2.9	-3.0	-2.8	-2.7	-2.6	-2.9	-2.4	-3.1	-2.8

[1] Includes a small amount of grants to state and local governments and direct payments for individuals. [2] Includes some off-budget amounts; most of the off-budget amounts are direct payments for individuals (social security benefits).

No. 542. Federal Outlays, by Agency: 1990 to 1998

[In millions of dollars]

DEPARTMENT OR OTHER UNIT	1990	1993	1994	1995	1996	1997	1998, est.
Total outlays	**1,253,163**	**1,409,414**	**1,461,731**	**1,515,729**	**1,560,512**	**1,601,235**	**1,667,815**
Legislative Branch	2,241	2,406	2,552	2,625	2,273	2,363	2,855
The Judiciary	1,646	2,628	2,677	2,903	3,059	3,259	3,719
Agriculture	46,012	63,144	60,753	56,665	54,352	52,547	55,015
Commerce	3,734	2,798	2,915	3,401	3,702	3,783	4,065
Defense-Military	289,755	278,574	268,646	259,556	253,253	258,322	251,385
Education	22,972	30,109	24,557	31,205	29,727	30,009	30,747
Energy	12,084	16,942	17,839	17,617	16,203	14,467	14,366
Health and Human Services	175,531	253,835	278,901	303,081	319,803	339,535	359,106
Housing and Urban Development	20,167	25,181	25,845	29,044	25,236	27,527	30,950
Interior	5,790	6,784	6,900	7,378	6,725	6,720	7,937
Justice	6,507	10,170	10,005	10,788	11,954	14,310	15,474
Labor	25,215	44,651	37,047	32,092	32,492	30,458	32,125
State	3,979	5,384	5,718	5,344	4,951	5,237	5,261
Transportation	28,650	34,457	37,228	38,777	38,780	39,832	40,465
Treasury	255,172	298,804	307,577	348,579	364,629	379,345	387,222
Veterans Affairs	28,998	35,487	37,401	37,771	36,920	39,280	43,074
Corps of Engineers	3,324	3,354	3,483	3,745	3,627	3,598	4,064
Other Defense-Civil Programs	21,692	25,961	26,971	27,977	28,952	30,282	31,494
Environmental Protection Agency	5,108	5,930	5,855	6,351	6,046	6,164	6,440
Executive Office of the President	158	194	231	215	202	221	240
Federal Emergency Management Admin.	2,183	3,253	4,154	3,136	3,102	3,326	3,698
General Services Administration	-93	825	448	831	732	1,084	944
International Assistance Programs	10,086	11,526	10,498	11,129	9,665	10,126	9,609
National Aeronautics and Space Admin.	12,429	14,305	13,695	13,378	13,881	14,360	13,729
National Science Foundation	1,838	2,452	2,642	2,845	3,012	3,130	3,165
Office of Personnel Management	31,949	36,794	38,596	41,276	42,870	45,404	46,418
Small Business Administration	692	785	779	677	873	333	-62
Social Security Administration (On-budget)	18,147	28,944	31,936	31,753	31,365	34,939	38,641
Social Security Administration (Off-budget)	244,998	298,349	313,881	330,370	343,869	358,372	371,839
Other Independent Agencies (On-budget)	69,501	-16,342	4,367	-5,179	3,434	-2,080	12,276
Other Independent Agencies (Off-budget)	1,626	1,441	1,103	-1,969	-180	-49	1,721
Undistributed offsetting receipts	-98,930	-119,711	-123,469	-137,632	-134,997	-154,969	-160,167

Source of Tables 541 and 542: U.S. Office of Management and Budget, *Historical Tables*, annual.

No. 543. Federal Outlays, by Detailed Function: 1990 to 1998

[In millions of dollars]

FUNCTION AND SUBFUNCTION	1990	1993	1994	1995	1996	1997	1998, est.
Total outlays	**1,253,163**	**1,409,414**	**1,461,731**	**1,515,729**	**1,560,512**	**1,601,235**	**1,667,815**
National defense, total [1]	299,331	291,086	281,642	272,066	265,748	270,473	264,112
Department of Defense-Military [1]	289,755	278,561	268,622	259,442	253,187	258,311	251,385
Military personnel	75,622	75,904	73,137	70,809	66,669	69,724	69,649
Operation and maintenance	88,340	94,094	87,929	91,078	88,759	92,461	92,393
Procurement	80,972	69,936	61,769	54,982	48,913	47,690	43,733
Research, development, test, & evaluation	37,458	36,968	34,762	34,594	36,494	37,015	35,770
Military construction	5,080	4,831	4,979	6,823	6,683	6,187	5,545
Family housing	3,501	3,255	3,316	3,571	3,828	4,003	3,960
Atomic energy defense activities	8,988	11,017	11,892	11,777	11,639	11,267	11,640
Defense-related activities	587	1,508	1,128	847	922	895	1,087
International affairs, total	13,764	17,248	17,083	16,434	13,496	15,228	14,480
International development and humanitarian assistance	5,498	5,827	7,049	7,599	6,160	6,054	5,750
International security assistance	8,652	7,639	6,642	5,252	4,565	4,632	5,214
Conduct of foreign affairs	3,050	4,325	4,557	4,192	3,761	3,919	3,908
Foreign information and exchange activities	1,103	1,352	1,398	1,417	1,187	1,173	1,149
International financial programs	-4,539	-1,896	-2,564	-2,026	-2,177	-550	-1,541
General science, space and technology, total	14,444	17,030	16,227	16,724	16,709	17,174	17,093
General science and basic research	2,835	3,938	3,863	4,131	4,016	4,118	4,906
Space flight, research, & supporting activities	11,609	13,092	12,363	12,593	12,693	13,056	12,187
Energy, total	3,341	4,319	5,219	4,936	2,844	1,483	403
Energy supply	1,976	3,286	3,899	3,584	1,654	634	-342
Energy conservation	365	521	582	671	624	572	551
Emergency energy preparedness	442	336	275	223	141	23	13
Energy information, policy, and regulation	559	176	462	458	425	254	181
Natural resources and environment, total [1]	17,080	20,239	21,064	22,078	21,614	21,369	23,822
Water resources	4,401	4,258	4,528	4,791	4,617	4,536	5,302
Conservation and land management	3,553	4,777	5,161	5,318	5,396	5,067	5,606
Recreational resources	1,876	2,620	2,619	2,801	2,673	2,785	3,518
Pollution control and abatement	5,170	6,061	6,050	6,512	6,180	6,290	6,606
Agriculture, total	11,958	20,363	15,046	9,778	9,159	9,032	10,580
Farm income stabilization	9,761	17,720	12,350	7,020	6,477	6,272	7,740
Agricultural research and services	2,197	2,643	2,695	2,758	2,682	2,760	2,840
Commerce and housing credit, total [1]	67,600	-21,853	-4,228	-17,808	-10,472	-14,624	3,525
Mortgage credit	3,845	1,554	-501	-1,038	-5,025	-4,006	-2,631
Postal Service	2,116	1,602	1,233	-1,839	-58	77	1,807
Deposit insurance	57,891	-27,957	-7,570	-17,827	-8,394	-14,384	-4,546
Transportation, total [1]	29,485	35,004	38,066	39,350	39,565	40,767	41,535
Ground transportation	18,954	21,251	23,940	25,297	25,650	26,795	27,358
Air transportation	7,234	10,049	10,146	10,020	10,135	10,138	10,553
Water transportation	3,151	3,423	3,648	3,732	3,460	3,554	3,390
Community and regional development, total	8,498	9,052	10,454	10,641	10,685	11,005	11,802
Community development	3,530	3,681	4,133	4,744	4,860	4,962	5,646
Area and regional development	2,868	2,443	2,166	2,615	2,667	2,691	2,763
Disaster relief and insurance	2,100	2,928	4,156	3,282	3,158	3,352	3,393
Education, training, employment, & social services, [1]	38,755	50,012	46,307	54,263	52,001	53,008	55,114
Elementary, secondary, and vocational education	9,918	13,481	14,258	14,694	14,871	15,073	15,357
Higher education	11,107	14,483	7,876	14,172	12,191	12,298	12,418
Research and general education aids	1,577	2,040	2,086	2,120	2,215	2,136	2,434
Training and employment	5,619	6,700	7,097	7,430	7,030	6,681	7,542
Social services	9,723	12,360	14,031	14,882	14,769	15,811	16,324
Health, total	57,716	99,415	107,122	115,418	119,378	123,843	131,772
Health care services	47,642	86,860	94,259	101,931	106,622	109,973	116,100
Health research and training	8,611	10,794	11,000	11,569	10,827	11,847	13,513
Consumer and occupational health & safety	1,462	1,762	1,863	1,918	1,929	2,023	2,159
Medicare	98,102	130,552	144,747	159,855	174,225	190,016	198,135
Income security, total [1]	147,076	207,299	214,089	220,493	225,989	230,886	239,349
General retirement and disability insurance [2]	5,148	4,347	5,720	5,106	5,234	4,721	4,658
Federal employee retirement and disability	52,037	60,095	62,545	65,882	68,093	71,526	74,165
Unemployment compensation	18,889	37,802	28,729	23,638	24,898	22,888	23,438
Housing assistance	15,891	21,542	23,884	27,520	26,754	27,798	28,752
Food and nutrition assistance	23,964	35,148	36,773	37,594	37,933	36,061	36,137
Social security	248,623	304,585	319,565	335,846	349,676	365,257	381,499
Veterans benefits and services, total [1]	29,058	35,671	37,584	37,890	36,985	39,313	43,114
Income security for veterans	15,241	17,758	19,613	18,966	18,201	20,407	21,833
Veterans education, training & rehabilitation	278	826	1,115	1,124	1,114	1,156	1,116
Hospital and medical care for veterans	12,134	14,812	15,678	16,428	16,586	17,093	18,415
Veterans housing	517	1,299	197	329	66	-342	713
Administration of justice, total	9,993	14,955	15,256	16,216	17,548	20,197	22,274
General government, total	10,734	13,009	11,303	13,835	11,892	12,768	12,878
Net interest, total	184,221	198,811	202,957	232,169	241,090	244,013	242,694
Interest on the public debt	264,724	292,502	296,278	332,414	343,955	355,796	362,120
Interest received by on-budget trust funds	-46,321	-55,537	-56,494	-59,871	-60,869	-63,776	-65,951
Interest received by off-budget trust funds	-15,991	-26,788	-29,203	-33,305	-36,507	-41,214	-46,730
Undistributed offsetting receipts, total	-36,615	-37,386	-37,772	-44,455	-37,620	-49,973	-46,366

[1] Includes functions not shown separately. [2] Includes social security.
Source: U.S. Office of Management and Budget, *Historical Tables,* annual.

No. 544. Tax Expenditures Estimates, by Function: 1997 to 2000

[In millions of dollars. For years ending, **Sept. 30, except as noted.** Tax expenditures are defined as *revenue losses* attributable to provisions of the federal tax laws which allow a special exclusion, exemption, or deduction from gross income or which provide a special credit, a preferential rate of tax, or a deferral of liability. Represents tax expenditures of **$1.5 billion or more in 2000**]

PROVISION	1997	1998	1999	2000
National defense:				
Exclusion of benefits and allowances to Armed Forces personnel	2,080	2,095	2,120	2,140
International affairs:				
Exclusion of income earned abroad by United States citizens	1,790	1,985	2,205	2,450
Exclusion of income of foreign sales corporations	1,600	1,700	1,800	1,900
Inventory property sales source rules exception	1,500	1,600	1,700	1,800
Deferral of income from controlled foreign corps [1]	2,200	2,400	2,600	2,800
Exclusion of interest on life insurance savings.	12,765	13,465	14,200	14,990
Housing:				
Exclusion of interest on owner-occupied mortgage subsidy bonds . . .	1,750	1,670	1,595	1,520
Deductibility of mortgage interest on owner-occupied homes	49,060	51,245	53,695	56,515
Deductibility of state and local property tax on owner-occupied homes	16,915	17,700	18,440	19,220
Exclusion of capital gains on home sales for persons age 55 and over	3,740	1,110	-	-
Capital gains exclusion on home sales	8,750	9,100	9,465	9,845
Exception from passive loss rules for $25,000 of rental loss	4,175	3,910	3,680	3,465
Credit for low-income housing investment	2,300	2,420	2,365	2,340
Accelerated depreciation on rental housing [1]	1,365	1,585	1,845	2,100
Commerce:				
Capital gains (other than agriculture, timber, iron ore and coal) [1]	24,620	25,360	26,120	26,900
Step-up basis of capital gains at death	8,750	9,100	9,465	9,845
Accelerated depreciation of buildings other than rental housing [1]	5,830	4,690	3,470	2,530
Accelerated depreciation of machinery and equipment [1]	24,970	26,655	28,535	29,410
Graduated corporation income tax rate [1]	4,695	4,950	5,085	5,280
Education, training, employment, and social services:				
Education:				
HOPE tax credit	-	205	4,160	4,870
Lifetime Learning tax credit	-	115	2,550	2,590
Child credit	-	3,590	19,175	19,240
Deductibility of charitable contributions (education)	2,670	2,890	3,010	3,145
Training, employment, and social services:				
Credit for child and dependent care expenses	2,515	2,510	2,510	2,505
Deductibility of charitable contributions, other than education and health	17,080	18,700	19,565	20,530
Health:				
Exclusion of employer contributions for medical insurance premiums and medical care	67,050	71,465	76,230	81,295
Deductibility of medical expenses.	4,175	4,550	4,815	5,110
Exclusion of interest on hospital construction bonds	1,675	1,740	1,795	1,845
Deductibility of charitable contributions (health).	2,365	2,570	2,685	2,805
Income security:				
Exclusion of workmen's compensation benefits.	4,410	4,950	5,210	5,480
Net exclusion of pension contributions and earnings:				
Employer plans	71,145	72,135	72,375	73,500
Individual Retirement Accounts	9,770	10,275	10,780	11,085
Keogh plans	3,520	3,655	3,755	3,895
Exclusion of other employee benefits:				
Premiums on group term life insurance	2,065	2,110	2,150	2,200
Additional deduction for the elderly	1,545	1,710	1,785	1,800
Earned income credit.	6,065	6,210	4,635	4,515
Social Security:				
Exclusion of social security benefits:				
Social security benefits for retired workers	17,470	18,330	19,115	20,025
Social security benefits for disabled	2,270	2,495	2,685	2,875
Social security benefits for dependents and survivors.	3,825	4,000	4,160	4,310
Veterans benefits and services:				
Exclusion of veterans disability compensation	2,770	2,930	3,100	3,280
General purpose fiscal assistance:				
Exclusion of interest on public purpose bonds	13,800	14,315	14,760	15,125
Deductibility of nonbusiness state and local taxes other than on owner-occupied homes	30,720	32,145	33,490	34,910
Tax credit for corporations receiving income from doing business in U.S. possessions	2,700	2,770	2,800	2,885
Addendum—Aid to state and local governments:				
Deductibility of—				
Property taxes on owner-occupied homes	16,915	17,700	18,440	19,220
Nonbusiness state and local taxes other than on owner-occupied homes	30,720	32,145	33,490	34,910
Exclusion of interest on—				
Public purpose bonds.	13,800	14,315	14,760	15,125
Owner-occupied mortgage revenue bonds	1,750	1,670	1,595	1,520
Hospital construction bonds.	1,675	1,740	1,795	1,845

- Representa zero. [1] Normal tax method.

Source: U.S. Office of Management and Budget, *Analytical Perspectives*, annual.

No. 545. United States Government—Balance Sheet: 1985 to 1997

[In millions of dollars. For fiscal year ending in year shown]

ITEM	1985	1990	1995	1996	1997
Assets, total	**55,204**	**70,415**	**89,349**	**103,432**	**119,395**
Cash and monetary assets, total	39,839	60,839	84,080	86,056	81,372
U.S. Treasury operating cash:					
Federal Reserve account	4,174	7,638	8,620	7,700	7,692
Tax and loan note accounts	12,886	32,517	29,329	36,525	35,930
Special drawing rights (SDR):					
Total holdings	6,847	10,666	11,035	10,177	9,997
SDRs certificates issued to Federal Reserve banks	-4,618	-8,518	-10,168	-9,718	-9,200
Monetary assets with IMF [1]	11,678	8,883	14,682	15,428	14,045
Other cash and monetary assets:					
U.S. Treasury monetary assets	1,310	1,572	356	87	87
Cash and other assets held outside the Treasury Account	7,558	8,079	29,697	21,133	18,609
U.S. Treasury time deposits	(NA)	(NA)	528	4,724	4,214
Loan financing accounts:					
Guaranteed loans	(NA)	(NA)	-12,714	-13,750	-13,892
Direct loans	(NA)	(NA)	19,732	32,780	53,803
Miscellaneous asset accounts	(NA)	9,576	-1,748	-1,654	-1,888
Total assets and excess of liabilities over assets	1,567,780	2,479,165	3,674,266	3,795,179	3,832,638
Excess of liabilities over assets at beginning of fiscal year	1,301,228	2,188,926	3,421,723	3,584,917	3,691,747
Add: Total deficit for fiscal year	211,931	220,388	163,916	107,445	21,968
Subtotal	(NA)	(NA)	3,585,639	3,692,362	3,713,715
Deduct: Other transactions not applied to surplus or deficit	582	564	722	615	472
Excess of liabilities over assets at close of fiscal year	1,512,576	2,408,750	3,584,917	3,691,747	3,713,243
Liabilities, total	1,567,780	2,479,165	3,674,266	3,795,179	3,832,638
Borrowing from the public, total	1,509,857	2,470,166	3,603,299	3,732,957	3,771,141
Public debt securities outstanding	1,823,103	3,233,313	4,973,985	5,224,812	5,413,147
Premium and discount on public debt securities	(NA)	59,811	-79,996	-77,932	-76,633
Total public debt securities	(NA)	(NA)	4,893,989	5,146,880	5,336,514
Agency securities outstanding	4,366	32,758	26,955	35,043	33,187
Federal securities, total	(NA)	3,266,073	4,920,944	5,181,923	5,369,700
Deduct: Net federal securities held as investments by government accounts	(NA)	795,907	1,317,645	1,448,967	1,598,559
Accrued interest payable	26,709	43,799	50,611	45,605	46,083
Special drawing rights allocated by IMF [1]	5,191	6,823	7,380	7,052	6,689
Deposit fund liabilities	14,385	8,306	8,186	7,213	6,800
Miscellaneous liability accounts (checks outstanding, etc.)	11,639	9,882	4,790	2,352	1,925

NA Not available.   [1] IMF = International Monetary Funds.

Source: U.S. Dept of Treasury, *United States Government Annual Report*.

No. 546. Direct Loan Transactions and Primary Guaranteed Loans: 1994 to 1998

ITEM	1994	1995	1996	1997	1998	PERCENT CHANGE			
						1994-95	1995-96	1996-97	1997-98
DIRECT LOAN TRANSACTIONS									
Obligations	22,702	30,901	23,387	33,580	28,079	36.1	-24.3	43.6	-16.4
Loan disbursements	19,281	21,982	23,566	32,181	31,985	14.0	7.2	36.6	-0.6
Change in outstandings	-800	1,628	3,978	12,715	5,535	-303.5	144.3	219.6	-56.5
Outstandings	**159,211**	**163,323**	**166,534**	**181,375**	**186,910**	**2.6**	**2.0**	**8.9**	**3.1**
PRIMARY GUARANTEED LOANS [1]									
Commitments	204,142	138,272	174,430	172,258	194,033	-32.3	26.1	-1.2	12.6
New guaranteed loans	194,221	117,875	143,885	144,699	155,476	-39.3	22.1	0.6	7.4
Change in outstandings	38,678	26,170	89,887	57,763	88,108	-32.3	243.5	-35.7	52.5
Outstandings	**698,813**	**726,770**	**806,104**	**821,891**	**909,999**	**4.0**	**10.9**	**2.0**	**10.7**

[1] When guaranteed loans result in loans receivable, they are shown in direct loans.

Source: U.S. Office of Management and Budget, *Budget of the United States Government*, annual.

No. 547. Summary of Federal Debt: 1985 to 1996

[In millions of dollars. Based on end of fiscal year]

ITEM	1985	1990	1994	1995	1996
Debt outstanding, total	**1,827,470**	**3,266,073**	**4,721,293**	**5,000,945**	**5,259,854**
Public debt securities	1,823,103	3,233,313	4,692,750	4,973,983	5,224,811
Agency securities	4,366	32,758	28,543	26,962	35,043
Government accounts, total	317,612	795,907	1,213,115	1,320,800	1,454,608
Public debt securities	316,545	795,762	1,213,098	1,320,784	1,447,001
Agency securities	1,067	145	17	16	7,606
The public, total	1,509,857	2,470,166	3,508,178	3,680,145	3,805,246
Public debt securities	1,506,558	2,437,551	3,479,652	3,653,199	3,777,810
Agency securities	3,299	32,613	28,526	26,946	27,437
Interest-bearing public debt, total	**1,821,010**	**3,210,943**	**4,689,524**	**4,950,644**	**5,220,790**
Marketable, total	1,360,179	2,092,759	3,091,602	3,260,447	3,418,371
Treasury bills	384,220	482,454	697,295	742,462	761,232
Treasury notes	776,449	1,218,081	1,867,507	1,980,343	2,098,670
Treasury bonds	199,510	377,224	511,800	522,643	543,469
Nonmarketable, total	460,831	1,118,184	1,597,922	1,690,197	1,802,419
U.S. savings bonds	77,011	122,152	176,413	181,181	184,147
Foreign series: Government	6,638	36,041	41,996	40,950	37,488
Government account series, total	313,928	779,412	1,211,689	1,324,270	1,454,690
Airport and airway trust fund	7,410	14,312	12,206	11,145	7,682
Bank insurance fund	16,130	8,438	13,972	20,117	22,186
Employees life insurance fund	6,312	9,561	14,929	15,839	16,962
Exchange stabilization fund	2,073	1,863	7,326	2,399	11,853
Federal disability insurance trust fund	5,443	11,254	6,025	35,150	50,051
Federal employees retirement funds	127,253	223,229	329,602	357,539	377,677
Federal hospital insurance trust fund	20,721	96,249	128,716	129,864	125,805
Federal Housing Administration	3,485	6,678	5,933	6,277	7,894
Fed. old-age & survivors insurance trust	30,968	203,717	413,425	447,947	499,403
Fed. S&L Corp., resolution fund	4,953	929	1,649	528	694
Fed. supplementary medical insur. trust	10,736	14,286	21,489	13,513	27,175
Government life insurance fund	269	184	114	106	99
Highway trust fund	9,422	9,530	7,751	8,954	11,660
National service life insurance fund	9,296	10,917	11,852	11,954	12,007
Postal Service fund	2,362	3,063	1,270	1,249	860
Railroad retirement account	4,232	8,356	10,596	12,129	14,763
Treasury deposit funds	681	304	130	130	77
Unemployment trust fund	16,454	50,186	39,745	47,098	53,849
Other	35,728	106,376	184,959	202,332	213,993
State and local government series	62,778	161,248	137,386	113,368	95,674
Domestic series	(X)	18,886	29,995	29,995	29,995
Other	477	447	445	432	424
MATURITY DISTRIBUTION					
Amount outstanding, total	**1,185,675**	**1,841,903**	**2,719,861**	**2,870,781**	**3,011,185**
Maturity class:					
Within 1 year	472,661	626,297	877,932	1,002,875	1,058,558
1-5 years	402,766	630,144	1,128,322	1,157,492	1,212,258
5-10 years	159,383	267,573	289,998	290,111	306,643
10-20 years	62,853	82,713	88,208	87,297	111,360
20 years and over	88,012	235,176	335,401	333,006	322,366

X Not applicable.

Source: U.S. Department of the Treasury, *Treasury Bulletin*, quarterly.

No. 548. U.S. Savings Bonds: 1980 to 1996

[In billions of dollars, except percent. As of end of fiscal year, see text, Section 9]

ITEM	1980	1985	1988	1989	1990	1991	1992	1993	1994	1995	1996
Amounts outstanding, total [1]	73	77	107	114	123	134	149	167	177	182	184
Funds from sales	5	5	7	8	8	9	14	17	9	7	6
Accrued discounts	4	5	8	8	8	10	9	9	9	9	10
Redemptions [2]	17	6	6	7	8	8	7	8	9	12	2
Percent of total outstanding	23.0	7.4	5.6	6.3	6.1	5.6	5.0	4.7	5.3	6.5	1.4

[1] Interest-bearing debt only for amounts end of year. [2] Matured and unmatured bonds.

Source: U.S. Dept. of the Treasury, *Treasury Bulletin*, quarterly.

No. 549. Federal Funds—Summary Distribution, by State: 1997

[In millions of dollars. For year ending Sept. 30. Data for grants, salaries and wages, and direct payments to individuals are on an expenditures basis; procurement is on obligation basis]

STATE	FEDERAL FUNDS		Defense	Non-defense	Direct payments to individuals	Procurement	Grants to state and local governments	Salaries and wages
	Total [1]	Per capita [2] (dol.)						
United States [3]	1,428,815	5,339	218,136	1,210,679	781,880	193,071	229,778	166,145
Alabama.	24,563	5,687	4,311	20,252	14,177	3,231	3,483	2,902
Alaska.	4,701	7,715	1,491	3,210	1,056	856	1,303	1,284
Arizona.	22,108	4,854	3,906	18,202	12,872	2,636	3,355	2,574
Arkansas	12,668	5,021	954	11,715	8,339	455	2,283	1,067
California	160,874	4,985	31,183	129,690	84,090	26,247	27,014	17,587
Colorado.	19,702	5,061	4,095	15,607	9,332	3,494	2,444	3,386
Connecticut.	17,864	5,463	3,139	14,725	10,045	2,918	2,905	1,353
Delaware	3,452	4,718	417	3,034	2,186	157	629	383
District of Columbia	23,112	43,692	2,417	20,695	2,845	4,184	2,740	11,598
Florida	82,060	5,600	13,266	68,794	56,224	8,083	8,504	7,666
Georgia	35,778	4,779	7,964	27,814	18,839	4,774	5,469	5,707
Hawaii	8,266	6,966	3,179	5,087	3,430	1,077	1,184	2,330
Idaho.	5,683	4,695	503	5,180	2,981	888	936	627
Illinois	52,818	4,440	3,311	49,506	32,892	3,190	9,296	5,404
Indiana.	25,115	4,283	2,520	22,595	15,741	2,329	3,539	1,781
Iowa	13,557	4,753	712	12,845	8,003	806	1,977	943
Kansas.	12,507	4,820	1,626	10,881	7,287	989	1,620	1,589
Kentucky	21,261	5,440	2,593	18,668	11,773	2,755	3,702	2,273
Louisiana	23,156	5,321	3,047	20,109	13,171	2,777	4,457	2,066
Maine.	7,184	5,784	1,481	5,703	3,840	1,018	1,378	755
Maryland	39,137	7,683	7,253	31,884	15,749	8,477	3,950	7,556
Massachusetts.	37,378	6,110	5,840	31,538	19,716	6,121	6,365	2,824
Michigan.	40,652	4,159	1,883	38,769	27,371	2,010	7,237	2,741
Minnesota.	20,088	4,287	1,540	18,548	11,243	1,684	3,952	1,638
Mississippi	15,026	5,503	2,655	12,371	8,590	1,727	2,626	1,542
Missouri	31,697	5,868	6,146	25,551	16,365	6,324	4,231	3,033
Montana	5,132	5,840	348	4,784	2,525	260	991	595
Nebraska	7,809	4,713	942	6,867	4,384	521	1,227	974
Nevada	7,085	4,226	989	6,096	4,512	550	983	824
New Hampshire	5,041	4,299	679	4,362	3,022	487	842	480
New Jersey	39,537	4,910	4,556	34,982	24,525	4,097	6,602	3,476
New Mexico	12,441	7,192	1,616	10,825	4,679	3,534	2,152	1,595
New York	95,622	5,272	4,826	90,795	55,163	5,778	24,384	7,039
North Carolina	34,731	4,677	5,152	29,579	20,298	1,960	6,284	4,887
North Dakota	4,331	6,758	490	3,842	1,828	229	1,074	575
Ohio	50,707	4,533	4,823	45,884	32,186	4,605	8,327	4,298
Oklahoma	17,317	5,221	2,790	14,527	10,206	1,188	2,510	2,629
Oregon.	14,633	4,511	718	13,915	9,107	580	2,853	1,422
Pennsylvania.	65,314	5,434	5,166	60,148	42,286	5,126	10,268	5,267
Rhode Island.	5,879	5,954	775	5,104	3,443	356	1,144	709
South Carolina.	18,815	5,004	3,064	15,751	10,887	2,404	2,987	2,077
South Dakota	4,149	5,622	322	3,827	2,034	253	982	511
Tennessee	28,558	5,320	2,145	26,413	16,209	4,386	4,555	2,624
Texas.	88,332	4,544	15,251	73,081	47,835	13,293	13,184	10,897
Utah	8,436	4,097	1,285	7,151	4,125	1,206	1,355	1,388
Vermont	2,728	4,632	192	2,536	1,581	150	601	267
Virginia.	52,908	7,857	21,431	31,477	20,026	16,254	3,518	11,312
Washington.	30,321	5,404	6,366	23,955	15,295	4,601	4,496	4,574
West Virginia.	10,409	5,733	445	9,964	6,649	502	2,100	863
Wisconsin	20,805	4,024	984	19,821	13,481	1,307	3,617	1,363
Wyoming	2,643	5,510	268	2,375	1,250	149	762	375

[1] Includes other programs not shown separately. [2] Based on Bureau of the Census resident population as of July 1. [3] Includes outlying areas, not shown separately.

Source: U.S. Bureau of the Census, *Federal Expenditures by State for Fiscal Year*, annual.

No. 550. Tax Returns Filed—Examination Coverage: 1988 to 1996

[In thousands, except as indicated. Return classification as Schedule C or C-EZ (nonfarm sole proprietorships) or Schedule F (farm proprietorships) for audit examination purposes was based on the largest source of income on the return and certain other characteristics. Therefore, some returns with business activity are reflected in the nonbusiness individual income tax return statistics in the table below (and vise versa), so that the statistics for the number of returns with Schedule C is not comparable to the number of nonfarm sole proprietorship returns in Table 858. Series completely revised starting with fiscal year 1988; data not comparable to earlier years]

YEAR AND ITEM	Returns filed [1]	RETURNS EXAMINED					AVERAGE TAX AND PENALTY PER RETURN (dollars)		
		Total	Per-cent cover-age	By—			Revenue agents [3]	Tax audi-tors	Service centers
				Rev-enue agents	Tax audi-tors	Serv-ice cent-ers [2]			
INDIVIDUAL RETURNS									
1988	103,251	1,621	1.57	353	532	736	997,696	2,188	1,950
1989	107,029	1,385	1.29	243	543	599	246,371	1,827	1,649
1990	109,868	1,145	1.04	202	517	426	309,566	1,962	2,432
1991	112,305	1,313	1.17	200	500	613	664,440	2,398	2,738
1992	113,829	1,206	1.06	210	537	459	1,365,896	2,280	2,539
1993	114,719	1,059	0.92	251	506	303	103,250	2,625	2,974
1994	113,754	1,226	1.08	364	456	406	246,785	3,113	1,963
1995	114,683	1,919	1.67	339	459	1,122	204,616	3,497	1,404
1996 [4]									
Individual, total	116,060	1,942	1.67	252	509	1,180	818,753	3,051	1,714
1040A, TPI under $25,000 [5]	45,985	922	2	43	145	733	14,742	3,017	1,837
Non 1040, TPI under $25,000 [5]	13,227	155	1.17	18	61	76	8,551	1,912	1,634
TPI $25,000 under $50,000 [5]	27,263	260	0.95	27	111	122	32,438	2,016	769
TPI $50,000 under $100,000 [5]	17,019	197	1.16	23	77	96	16,504	2,344	563
TPI $100,000 and over [5]	4,541	129	2.85	40	37	53	561,834	5,124	3,826
Sch C—TGR under $25,000 [6]	2,436	103	4.21	24	32	46	7,579	3,845	2,242
Sch C—TGR $25,000 under $100,000 [6]	3,082	88	2.85	29	31	28	9,787	5,061	1,324
Sch C—TGR $100,000 and over [6]	1,738	71	4.09	43	11	16	1,867,030	10,509	3,180
Sch F—TGR under $100,000 [6]	501	8	1.59	2	3	4	6,051	1,688	675
Sch F—TGR $100,000 and over [6]	268	10	3.61	3	2	5	556,717	2,750	1,352
Corporation (except S Corporation)	2,553	60	2.34	58	(NA)	2	5,232,788	(NA)	14,332
Fiduciary	3,191	5	0.15	2	(NA)	3	21,786	(NA)	464
Estate	82	12	14.4	12	(NA)	0.3	82,472	(NA)	33,582
Gift	216	2	0.89	2	(NA)	0.004	(NA)	(NA)	(NA)
Employment	28,679	56	0.17	47	9	0.2	134,781	10,508	265
Excise	789	33	4.17	31	1	0.001	63,771	746	43,416
Windfall profit	(NA)	(NA)	(NA)	(NA)	(NA)	(NA)	(NA)	(NA)	(NA)
Misc. taxable	(NA)	0.4	(NA)	0.04	(NA)	0.02	446,690	(NA)	15,879
Partnerships	1,549	8	0.49	5	(NA)	2	(NA)	(NA)	(NA)
S Corporations (nontaxable)	2,161	20	0.49	18	(NA)	1	(NA)	(NA)	(NA)
Miscellaneous nontaxable [7]	(NA)	0.6	(NA)	0.06	(NA)	(NA)	(NA)	(NA)	(NA)

NA Not available. [1] Returns filed in previous calender year. [2] Includes taxpayer contacts by correspondence. [3] Mostly reflects coordinated examination of large corporations and related returns. [4] Includes activities to protect release of funds in Treasury in response to taxpayer efforts to recoup tax previously assessed and paid with penalty. [5] Total positive income, i.e., excludes losses. [6] Total gross receipts. [7] Includes Domestic International Sales Corporations, InterestCharge Domestic International Sales Corporations, Real Estate Investment Morgage Conduits, and other.

Source: U.S. Internal Revenue Service, *IRS Data Book, 1995* Publication 55B.

No. 551. Internal Revenue Gross Collections, by Source: 1980 to 1996

[For fiscal year ending in year shown; see text, Section 9]

SOURCE OF REVENUE	COLLECTIONS (bil. dol.)					PERCENT OF TOTAL				
	1980	1985	1990	1995	1996	1980	1985	1990	1995	1996
All taxes	519	743	1,078	1,389	1,500	100.0	100.0	100.0	100.0	100.0
Individual income taxes	288	397	540	676	745	54.9	53.4	50.1	48.7	50.0
Withheld by employers	224	299	388	534	533	43.1	40.2	36.0	38.4	35.5
Employment taxes [1]	128	225	367	465	492	24.7	30.2	34.0	33.5	32.8
Old-age and disability insurance	123	216	358	455	482	23.6	29.0	33.2	32.8	32.1
Unemployment insurance	3	6	6	6	6	0.6	0.8	0.6	0.4	0.4
Corporation income taxes	72	77	110	174	189	13.9	10.4	10.2	12.5	12.6
Estate and gift taxes	7	7	12	15	18	1.3	0.9	1.1	1.1	1.2
Excise taxes	25	37	49	59	56	4.7	5.0	4.5	4.2	3.7

[1] Includes railroad retirement, not shown separately.

Source: U.S. Internal Revenue Service, *Annual Report,* and Bureau of Alcohol, Tobacco, and Firearms, Tobacco Tax Collections.

No. 552. Federal Individual Income Tax Returns With Adjusted Gross Income (AGI)—Summary: 1980 to 1995

[Includes Puerto Rico and Virgin Islands. Includes returns of resident aliens, based on a sample of unaudited returns as filed. Data are not comparable for all years because of tax changes and other changes, as indicated. See *Statistics of Income, Individual Income Tax Returns* publications for a detailed explanation. See Appendix III]

ITEM	NUMBER OF RETURNS (1,000)				AMOUNT (mil. dol.)				AVERAGE AMOUNT (dollars)			
	1980	1990	1994	1995	1980	1990	1994	1995	1980	1990	1994	1995
Total returns	93,902	113,717	115,943	118,218	1,613,731	3,405,427	3,907,518	4,189,354	17,185	29,947	33,702	35,473
Form 1040	57,123	69,270	66,381	64,775	1,310,088	2,772,625	3,056,958	3,199,476	22,935	40,026	46,045	49,394
Salaries and wages	83,802	96,730	99,356	101,139	1,349,843	2,599,401	3,026,778	3,201,457	16,108	26,873	30,464	31,654
Interest received	49,020	70,370	65,340	67,029	102,009	227,084	126,169	154,781	2,081	3,227	1,931	2,309
Dividends in AGI	10,739	22,904	25,235	26,214	38,761	80,169	82,410	94,592	3,609	3,500	3,266	3,608
Business or profession profit less loss	8,881	11,222	15,944	16,173	55,129	141,430	166,204	169,343	6,207	12,603	10,424	10,471
Sales of capital assets, net gain less loss, in AGI	9,971	14,288	18,823	19,963	30,029	114,231	142,288	170,415	3,012	7,995	7,559	8,537
Pensions and annuities in AGI	7,374	17,041	17,894	18,415	43,340	159,294	205,423	221,053	5,878	9,348	11,480	12,004
Rents and royalties, net income less loss	8,208	10,317	10,126	10,224	4,105	-3156	15,967	17,193	500	-306	1,577	1,682
Partnerships and S Corporations [1], profit less loss	3,910	5,977	5,590	5,622	10,099	67,022	114,386	125,752	2,583	11,213	20,464	22,369
Farm profit less loss	2,608	2,321	2,242	2,219	-1,792	-434	-7,378	-7,850	-687	-187	-3,290	-3,537
Statutory adjustments, total	13,149	16,648	17,859	18,209	28,614	33,974	39,103	41,140	2,176	2,041	2,190	2,259
Individual Retirement Arrangements	2,564	5,224	4,319	4,301	3,431	9,858	8,389	8,338	1,338	1,887	1,942	1,939
Self-employed retirement (Keogh) plan	569	824	996	1,032	2,008	6,778	8,195	8,734	3,529	8,226	8,229	8,462
Married couples who both work	(NA)	(NA)	(NA)	(NA)	(NA)	(NA)	(NA)	(NA)	(NA)	(NA)	(NA)	(NA)
Exemptions, total [2]	227,925	227,549	232,716	237,164	227,569	485,985	562,559	584,509	998	2,135	2,417	2,465
Age 65 or older	11,847	(NA)	(NA)	(NA)	(NA)	(NA)	(NA)	(NA)	(NA)	(NA)	(NA)	(NA)
Blind	185	(NA)	(NA)	(NA)	(NA)	(NA)	(NA)	(NA)	(NA)	(NA)	(NA)	(NA)
Standard and itemized deductions, total [3]	88,105	112,796	114,965	117,230	362,776	789,942	890,760	940,359	4,118	7,003	7,748	8,027
Itemized deductions, total [3]	28,950	32,175	33,018	34,008	218,028	458,485	493,654	527,374	7,531	14,250	14,951	15,507
Medical and dental expenses	19,458	5,091	5,229	5,351	14,972	21,457	26,378	26,964	769	4,215	5,044	5,039
Taxes paid	28,749	31,594	32,569	33,530	69,404	140,011	175,848	188,644	2,414	4,432	5,399	5,626
Interest paid	26,677	29,395	27,873	28,705	91,187	208,354	197,240	215,078	3,418	7,088	7,076	7,493
Contributions	26,601	29,230	29,849	30,541	25,810	57,243	70,545	74,992	970	1,958	2,363	2,455
Taxable income [4]	88,105	93,148	92,793	94,612	1,279,985	2,263,661	2,597,980	2,813,826	14,528	24,302	27,998	29,741
Income tax before credits	76,136	93,089	92,702	94,498	256,294	453,128	541,571	596,169	3,366	4,868	5,842	6,309
Tax credits, total [2]	19,674	12,484	15,042	15,240	7,216	6,831	8,927	10,040	367	547	594	659
Child care	4,231	6,144	6,012	5,964	956	2,549	2,526	2,518	226	415	420	422
Elderly and disabled	562	339	222	252	135	61	47	48	240	180	210	191
Residential energy	4,670	(NA)	(NA)	(NA)	562	(NA)	(NA)	(NA)	120	(NA)	(NA)	(NA)
Foreign tax [5]	393	772	1,546	1,731	1,342	1,682	2,309	2,965	3,415	2,179	1,494	1,713
General business credit [6]	(NA)	263	301	268	616	690	690	703	(NA)	2,342	2,291	2,627
Income tax, total [6]	73,906	89,862	87,619	89,253	250,341	447,127	534,856	588,419	3,387	4,976	6,104	6,593

NA Not available. [1]S Corporations are certain small corporations with up to 35 shareholders, mostly individuals, electing to be taxed at the shareholder level. [2]Includes items not shown separately. Beginning 1994, total exemptions amount is after limitation. [3]Starting 1990, includes additional standard deductions for age 65 or older or for blindness. Beginning 1994, total itemized deductions are after limitation. [4]For 1980, includes amounts "taxed" at zero percent. [5]Investment credit was included in the more-inclusive general business tax credit starting with 1984. With exceptions, investment credit was repealed effective 1986. [6]Includes minimum tax or alternative minimum tax.

Source: U.S. Internal Revenue Service, *Statistics of Income Bulletin*, and *Statistics of Income, Individual Income Tax Returns*, annual.

No. 553. Individual Income Tax Returns—Number, Income Tax, and Average Tax, by Size of Adjusted Gross Income: 1994 and 1995

[Number in thousands; money amounts in billions of dollars, except as indicated]

SIZE OF ADJUSTED GROSS INCOME	NUMBER OF RETURNS		ADJUSTED GROSS INCOME (AGI)		TAXABLE INCOME		INCOME TAX TOTAL [1]		TAX AS PERCENT OF AGI [2]		AVERAGE TAX ($1,000) [2]	
	1994	1995, prel.	1994	1995, prel.	1994	1995, prel.	1994	1995, prel.	1994	1995, prel.	1994	1995, prel.
Total..........	115,943	118,218	3,907.5	4,189.4	2,598.0	2,813.8	534.9	588.4	14.3	14.1	6.1	6.8
Less than $1,000 [3] .	3,342	3,204	-52.2	-53.9	0.1	0.1	0.1	0.1	-2.9	-0.2	0.2	0.2
$1,000-$2,999	6,389	6,526	12.8	13.0	0.7	0.9	0.1	0.2	4.7	1.2	0.1	0.1
$3,000-$4,999	5,854	5,860	23.5	23.2	1.3	1.3	0.2	0.2	2.9	1.0	0.1	0.1
$5,000-$6,999	5,577	5,680	33.5	34.0	2.9	2.9	0.4	0.4	4.3	1.3	0.3	0.2
$7,000-$8,999	5,840	5,593	46.8	44.9	7.1	6.7	1.0	1.0	3.7	2.2	0.3	0.3
$9,000-$10,999 ...	5,496	5,372	54.9	53.7	11.3	10.7	1.7	1.6	5.4	3.0	0.5	0.5
$11,000-$12,999...	5,401	5,555	64.8	66.6	17.3	17.2	2.4	2.6	6.2	3.9	0.7	0.8
$13,000-$14,999 ..	5,385	5,344	75.2	74.8	24.2	23.9	3.2	3.2	6.5	4.3	0.9	0.9
$15,000-$16,999 ..	4,955	4,837	79.1	77.3	30.4	29.2	4.0	3.8	7.5	4.9	1.2	1.1
$17,000-$18,999 ..	4,318	4,402	77.7	79.3	33.7	34.0	4.3	4.3	7.4	5.5	1.3	1.3
$19,000-$21,999 ..	6,281	6,507	128.7	133.4	63.9	64.9	8.7	8.6	7.6	6.5	1.6	1.5
$22,000-$24,999 ..	5,521	5,610	129.5	131.8	70.0	71.1	10.1	10.1	8.1	7.6	1.9	1.9
$25,000-$29,999 ..	8,121	7,848	222.5	215.2	130.4	125.1	19.4	18.5	8.8	8.6	2.4	2.4
$30,000-$39,999 ..	12,014	12,380	418.1	430.5	265.1	270.6	41.9	42.4	10.1	9.9	3.5	3.5
$40,000-$49,999 ..	9,024	9,099	403.8	406.6	269.1	269.4	43.6	43.6	10.8	10.7	4.9	4.8
$50,000-$74,999 ..	13,127	13,679	794.7	828.3	555.5	579.8	96.8	100.3	12.2	12.1	7.4	8.2
$75,000-$99,999 ..	4,784	5,374	409.0	458.5	300.3	335.0	61.5	67.7	15.1	14.8	12.9	16.0
$100,000-$199,999..	3,405	4,075	446.5	532.0	346.3	411.6	82.7	97.2	18.5	18.3	24.3	31.3
$200,000-$499,999..	890	1,007	256.2	292.1	218.0	249.4	65.6	74.6	25.6	25.6	73.7	95.0
$500,000-$999,999..	149	178	100.7	120.3	88.9	106.6	30.4	36.3	30.2	30.2	203.7	258.2
$1,000,000 or more.	70	87	181.8	227.6	161.5	203.5	56.6	71.5	31.2	31.4	810.7	1,077.0

[1] Consists of income after credits, and alternative minimum tax. [2] Computed using taxable returns only. [3] In addition to low income taxpayers, this size class (and others) includes taxpayers with "tax preferences," not reflected in adjusted gross income or taxable income which are subject to the "alternative minimum tax" (included in total income tax).

Source: U.S. Internal Revenue Service, *Statistics of Income Bulletin,* quarterly and *Statistics of Income, Individual Income Tax Returns,* annual.

No. 554. Individual Income Tax Returns—Itemized Deductions and Statutory Adjustments, by Size of Adjusted Gross Income: 1995

[Preliminary]

ITEM	Unit	ADJUSTED GROSS INCOME CLASS						
		Total	Under $10,000	$10,000 to $19,999	$20,000 to $29,999	$30,000 to $39,999	$40,000 to $49,999	$50,000 to $99,999	$100,000 and over
Returns with itemized deductions:									
Number [1]	1,000 ..	34,008	739	2,146	3,326	4,197	4,457	14,169	4,972
Amount.................	Mil. dol .	527,374	7,248	21,423	32,514	43,544	51,310	203,725	167,608
Medical and dental expenses:									
Returns..............	1,000 ..	5,351	471	1,140	1,035	888	679	1,011	128
Amount..............	Mil. dol .	26,964	2,740	6,541	3,931	3,566	2,773	5,521	1,892
Taxes paid: Returns, total.....	1,000 ..	33,530	671	1,991	3,252	4,140	4,420	14,105	4,952
State, local income taxes..	1,000 ..	28,641	352	1,347	2,652	3,577	3,862	12,502	4,349
Real estate taxes......	1,000 ..	30,111	540	1,668	2,753	3,593	3,894	13,019	4,643
Amount, total	Mil. dol .	188,644	1,361	3,892	7,431	11,661	14,601	70,734	78,964
State, local income taxes.	Mil. dol .	113,996	178	891	2,711	5,410	7,392	40,303	57,111
Real estate taxes.......	Mil. dol .	67,000	1,040	2,775	4,222	5,560	6,391	27,157	19,854
Interest paid: Returns	1,000 ..	28,705	460	1,422	2,676	3,524	3,830	12,566	4,228
Amount	Mil. dol .	215,078	2,853	7,965	12,864	19,304	22,990	88,591	60,512
Home mortgages interest:									
Returns	1,000 ..	28,350	446	1,401	2,646	3,494	3,803	12,483	4,078
Amount	Mil. dol .	203,074	2,770	7,827	12,609	19,017	22,623	86,750	51,479
Contributions: Returns	1,000 ..	30,541	505	1,633	2,835	3,623	3,940	13,251	4,753
Amount	Mil. dol .	74,992	577	2,247	3,332	4,596	6,553	25,990	31,697
Employee business expense:									
Returns................	1,000 ..	10,435	69	360	880	1,402	1,531	4,937	1,257
Amount................	Mil. dol .	32,568	158	1,102	2,513	3,936	4,172	13,781	6,906
Returns with statutory adjus'mts: [2]									
Returns................	1,000 ..	18,209	2,970	3,117	2,647	2,191	1,812	3,569	1,903
Amount of adjustments	Mil. dol .	41,140	2,317	3,699	3,779	3,877	3,025	9,860	14,582
Payments to IRAs: [3] Returns ..	1,000 ..	4,301	302	632	977	811	586	671	322
Amount	Mil. dol .	8,338	554	1,223	1,498	1,476	895	1,720	971
Payments to Keogh plans:									
Returns	1,000 ..	1,032	14	39	55	49	74	341	461
Amount	Mil. dol .	8,734	46	83	158	178	217	1,890	6,161
Alimony paid: Returns........	1,000 ..	568	37	51	71	75	53	169	112
Amount..............	Mil. dol .	5,226	283	202	336	469	248	1,221	2,467

[1] After limitations. [2] Includes disability income exclusion, employee business expenses, moving expenses, forfeited interest penalty, alimony paid, deduction for expense of living abroad, and other data not shown separately. [3] Individual Retirement Account.

Source: U.S. Internal Revenue Service, *Statistics of Income, Individual Income Tax Returns,* annual.

No. 555. Federal Individual Income Tax Returns—Adjusted Gross Income (AGI), by Source of Income and Income Class for Taxable Returns: 1995

[In millions of dollars, except as indicated. Minus sign (-) indicates net loss was greater than net income. See headnote, Table 552]

ITEM	Total [1]	Under $10,000	$10,000 to $19,999	$20,000 to $29,999	$30,000 to $39,999	$40,000 to $49,999	$50,000 to $99,999	$100,000 and over
Number of returns(1,000)	89,253	10,273	16,497	16,762	12,295	9,065	19,018	5,343
Source of income:								
Adjusted gross income (AGI)	4,007,580	55,988	248,323	415,112	427,540	405,133	1,284,470	1,171,014
Salaries and wages	3,009,987	47,772	179,841	337,470	362,139	337,926	1,055,136	689,704
Percent of AGI for taxable returns	75.1	85.3	72.4	81.3	84.7	83.4	82.1	58.9
Interest received	141,385	4,733	16,164	13,283	11,425	10,257	31,853	53,671
Dividends in AGI	89,030	2,131	5,262	5,699	4,617	4,959	20,520	45,842
Business; profession, net profit less loss	154,113	1,724	7,358	11,888	11,481	11,189	42,027	68,446
Pensions and annuities in AGI	207,062	3,683	30,913	34,134	24,103	22,409	65,579	26,241
Sales of property, [2] net gain less loss	164,637	2,506	2,056	3,011	3,366	4,237	20,953	128,509
Rents and royalties, net income less loss	17,193	-1,238	1,060	937	-193	442	831	15,353
Other sources, [3] net	271,473	-3,202	9,356	13,219	14,729	16,974	58,215	162,179
Percent of all returns: [4]								
Number of returns	75.5	8.7	14.0	14.2	10.4	7.7	16.1	4.5
Adjusted gross income	95.7	1.3	5.9	9.9	10.2	9.7	30.7	28.0
Salaries and wages	94.0	1.5	5.6	10.5	11.3	10.6	33.0	21.4
Interest received	91.4	3.1	10.4	8.6	7.4	6.6	20.6	34.7
Dividends in AGI	94.1	2.3	5.6	6.0	4.9	5.2	21.7	48.5
Business; profession net profit less loss	91.0	1.0	4.4	7.0	6.8	6.6	24.8	40.4
Pensions and annuities in AGI	93.7	1.7	14.0	15.4	10.9	10.1	29.7	11.9
Sales of property [2] net gain less loss	98.4	1.5	1.2	1.8	2.0	2.5	12.5	76.8

[1] Includes a small number of taxable returns with no adjusted gross income.   [2] Includes sales of capital assets and other property; net gain less loss.   [3] Excludes rental passive losses disallowed in the computation of adjusted gross income; net income less loss.   [4] Without regard to taxability.

Source: U.S. Internal Revenue Service, *Statistics of Income,* annual.

No. 556. Federal Individual Income Tax Returns, by State, 1995

STATE AND OTHER AREA	Number of returns [1] (1,000)	Adjusted gross income (AGI) [2]	INCOME TAX Total [3] (mil. dol.)	INCOME TAX Per capita [4] (dol.)	STATE AND OTHER AREA	Number of returns [1] (1,000)	Adjusted gross income (AGI) [2]	INCOME TAX Total [3] (mil. dol.)	INCOME TAX Per capita [4] (dol.)
U.S.	118,782	4,182,770	620,972	2,363	MT	393	10,577	1,382	1,589
AL	1,817	55,941	7,631	1,794	NE	776	23,765	3,364	2,055
AK	363	10,737	1,676	2,775	NV	754	28,184	4,581	2,994
AZ	1,838	60,878	8,546	2,026	NH	562	20,789	3,120	2,718
AR	1,052	29,618	3,869	1,558	NJ	3,801	167,510	26,965	3,394
CA	13,393	497,133	74,372	2,354	NM	736	20,792	2,690	1,596
CO	1,783	65,016	9,758	2,604	NY	7,921	318,702	50,650	2,793
CT	1,564	74,987	13,168	4,021	NC	3,319	107,004	14,461	2,010
DE	344	12,761	1,813	2,529	ND	293	8,251	1,121	1,749
DC	272	10,486	1,738	3,137	OH	5,292	172,218	24,270	2,176
FL	6,553	221,515	34,968	2,468	OK	1,366	39,278	5,164	1,575
GA	3,205	109,626	15,692	2,179	OR	1,427	47,971	6,640	2,114
HI	550	19,057	2,511	2,115	PA	5,461	189,238	27,790	2,302
ID	495	15,249	2,034	1,749	RI	452	15,643	2,183	2,205
IL	5,437	210,915	33,575	2,838	SC	1,648	49,579	6,426	1,750
IN	2,657	89,205	12,612	2,173	SD	332	9,340	1,344	1,844
IA	1,289	39,953	5,323	1,873	TN	2,376	75,925	11,226	2,136
KS	1,135	38,272	5,480	2,136	TX	8,058	264,968	40,823	2,180
KY	1,612	48,441	6,444	1,669	UT	813	27,071	3,510	1,799
LA	1,764	52,275	7,338	1,690	VT	274	8,436	1,128	1,928
ME	561	16,668	2,139	1,724	VA	3,019	113,394	16,228	2,452
MD	2,367	95,237	13,587	2,695	WA	2,485	92,305	14,048	2,587
MA	2,853	116,899	18,688	3,077	WV	715	20,425	2,631	1,439
MI	4,314	158,420	23,775	2,490	WI	2,389	82,049	11,277	2,201
MN	2,149	78,927	11,308	2,453	WY	220	7,093	1,065	2,219
MS	1,106	29,525	3,734	1,385	Other [5]	1,061	27,011	4,096	(NA)
MO	2,376	77,411	11,010	2,068					

NA Not available.   [1] Includes returns constructed by Internal Revenue Service for certain self-employment tax returns.   [2] Less deficit.   [3] Includes additional tax for tax preferences, self-employment tax, tax from investment credit recapture and other income-related taxes. Total is before earned income credit.   [4] Based on resident population as of July 1.   [5] Includes returns filed from Army Post Office and Fleet Post Office addresses by members of the Armed Forces stationed overseas; returns by other U.S. citizens abroad; and returns filed by residents of Puerto Rico with income from sources outside of Puerto Rico or with income earned as U.S. Government employees.

Source: U.S. Internal Revenue Service, *Statistics of Income Bulletin.* Quarterly.

No. 557. Federal Individual Income Tax—Tax Liability, Effective and Marginal Tax Rates, for Selected Income Groups: 1990 to 1997

[Refers to income after exclusions. Effective rate represents tax liability divided by stated income. The marginal tax rate is the percentage of the first additional dollar of income which would be paid in income tax. Computations assume the low income allowance, standard deduction, zero bracket amount, or itemized deductions equal to 10 percent of adjusted gross income, whichever is greatest. Excludes self employment tax]

ADJUSTED GROSS INCOME	1990	1992	1993	1994	1995	1996	1997
TAX LIABILITY							
Single person, no dependents:							
$5,000	-	-	-	-306	-314	-323	-332
$10,000	705	615	593	563	540	518	480
$20,000	2,205	2,115	2,093	2,063	2,040	2,018	1,980
$25,000	2,988	2,865	2,843	2,813	2,790	2,768	2,730
$35,000	5,718	5,360	5,233	5,093	4,973	4,846	4,692
$50,000	9,498	9,168	9,069	8,957	8,865	8,766	8,654
$75,000	16,718	15,867	15,719	15,555	15,418	15,270	15,107
Married couple, two dependents: [1]							
$5,000	-700	-920	-975	-1,500	-1,800	-2,000	-2,000
$10,000	-953	-1,384	-1,511	-2,528	-3,110	-3,556	-3,556
$20,000	926	409	235	-359	-832	-1,324	-1,414
$25,000	1,703	1,470	1,410	1,275	929	479	389
$35,000	3,203	2,970	2,910	2,828	2,768	2,715	2,625
$50,000	5,960	5,220	5,160	5,078	5,018	4,965	4,875
$75,000	12,386	11,670	11,471	11,216	11,030	10,831	10,576
EFFECTIVE RATE							
Single person, no dependents:							
$5,000 [2]	-	-	-	-6.1	-6.3	-6.5	-6.6
$10,000	7.1	6.2	5.9	5.6	5.4	5.2	4.8
$20,000	11.0	10.6	10.5	10.3	10.2	10.1	9.9
$25,000	12.0	11.5	11.4	11.3	11.2	11.1	10.9
$35,000	16.3	15.3	15.0	14.6	14.2	13.8	13.4
$50,000	19.0	18.3	18.1	17.9	17.7	17.5	17.3
$75,000	22.3	21.2	21.0	20.7	20.6	20.4	20.1
Married couple, two dependents: [1]							
$5,000 [3]	-14.0	-18.4	-19.5	-30.0	-36.0	-40.0	-40.0
$10,000 [4]	-9.5	-13.8	-15.1	-25.3	-31.1	-35.6	-35.6
$20,000 [4]	4.6	2.0	1.2	-1.8	-4.2	-6.6	-7.1
$25,000	6.8	5.9	5.6	5.1	3.7	1.9	1.6
$35,000	9.2	8.5	8.3	8.1	7.9	7.8	7.5
$50,000	11.9	10.4	10.3	10.2	10.0	9.9	9.8
$75,000	16.5	15.6	15.3	15.0	14.7	14.4	14.1
MARGINAL TAX RATE							
Single person, no dependents:							
$5,000	-	-	-	8	-	-	-
$10,000	15	15	15	15	15	15	15
$20,000	15	15	15	15	15	15	15
$25,000	28	15	15	15	15	15	15
$35,000	28	28	28	28	28	28	28
$50,000	28	28	28	28	28	28	28
$75,000	33	31	31	31	31	31	31
Married couple, two dependents: [1]							
$5,000 [3]	-14	-18	-20	-30	-36	-40	-40
$10,000 [4]	-	-	-	-	-	-	-
$20,000 [4]	25	28	29	33	35	36	36
$25,000	15	15	15	33	35	36	36
$35,000	15	15	15	15	15	15	15
$50,000	28	15	15	15	15	15	15
$75,000	28	28	28	28	28	28	28

- Represents zero.   [1] Only one spouse is assumed to work.   [2] Beginning 1994, refundable earned income credit.
[3] Refundable earned income credit.

Source: U.S. Dept. of the Treasury, Office of Tax Analysis, unpublished data.

No. 558. Federal Individual Income Tax—Current Income Equivalent to 1995 Constant Income for Selected Income Groups: 1990 to 1997

[Constant 1995 dollar incomes calculated by using the NIPA Personal Consumption Expenditure (PCE) Implicit Price Deflator (1992=100): 1990, 92.9; 1992, 100.0; 1993 ,102.7; 1994, 105.2; 1995, 107.9; 1996, 110.5; and 1997, 112.7]

ADJUSTED GROSS INCOME	1990	1992	1993	1994	1995	1996	1997
REAL INCOME EQUIVALENT							
Single person, no dependents:							
$5,000	4,310	4,630	4,760	4,870	5,000	5,120	5,220
$10,000	8,610	9,270	9,520	9,750	10,000	10,240	10,450
$20,000	17,220	18,540	19,030	19,490	20,000	20,480	20,890
$25,000	21,530	23,170	23,790	24,370	25,000	25,600	26,120
$35,000	30,140	32,440	33,300	34,110	35,000	35,840	36,560
$50,000	43,060	46,340	47,580	48,730	50,000	51,200	52,230
$75,000	64,590	69,520	71,360	73,100	75,000	76,790	78,350
Married couple, two dependents: [1]							
$5,000	4,310	4,630	4,760	4,870	5,000	5,120	5,220
$10,000	8,610	9,270	9,520	9,750	10,000	10,240	10,450
$20,000	17,220	18,540	19,030	19,490	20,000	20,480	20,890
$25,000	21,530	23,170	23,790	24,370	25,000	25,600	26,120
$35,000	30,140	32,440	33,300	34,110	35,000	35,840	36,560
$50,000	43,060	46,340	47,580	48,730	50,000	51,200	52,230
$75,000	64,590	69,520	71,360	73,100	75,000	76,790	78,350
EFFECTIVE RATE (percent)							
Single person, no dependents:							
$5,000 [2]	-	-	-	-6.3	-6.3	-6.3	-6.4
$10,000	5.8	5.5	5.5	5.4	5.4	5.4	5.2
$20,000	10.4	10.2	10.2	10.2	10.2	10.2	10.1
$25,000	11.3	11.2	11.2	11.2	11.2	11.2	11.1
$35,000	14.7	14.3	14.3	14.2	14.2	14.2	14.0
$50,000	18.0	17.8	17.8	17.7	17.7	17.7	17.8
$75,000	21.1	20.6	20.6	20.6	20.6	20.5	20.5
Married couple, two dependents: [1]							
$5,000 [3]	-14.0	-18.4	-19.5	-30.0	-36.0	-40.0	-40.0
$10,000 [4]	-11.0	-14.9	-15.9	-25.9	-31.1	-34.7	-34.0
$20,000 [4]	1.3	-	-0.2	-2.7	-4.2	-5.6	-5.2
$25,000	5.5	5.2	5.2	4.4	3.7	2.7	3.0
$35,000	8.2	8.0	8.0	7.9	7.9	7.9	7.8
$50,000	10.2	10.1	10.1	10.0	10.0	10.0	10.0
$75,000	15.1	14.8	14.8	14.7	14.7	14.7	14.6
MARGINAL TAX RATE (percent)							
Single person, no dependents:							
$5,000	-	-	-	-	-	-	-
$10,000	15	15	15	15	15	15	15
$20,000	15	15	15	15	15	15	15
$25,000	15	15	15	15	15	15	15
$35,000	28	28	28	28	28	28	28
$50,000	28	28	28	28	28	28	28
$75,000	33	31	31	31	31	31	31
Married couple, two dependents: [1]							
$5,000 [3]	-14	-18.4	-19.5	-30	-36	-40	-40
$10,000 [4]	-	-	-	-	-	-	-
$20,000 [4]	25	28.1	28.9	32.7	35.2	36.1	36.1
$25,000	15	15	15	32.7	35.2	36.1	36.1
$35,000	15	15	15	15	15	15	15
$50,000	15	15	15	15	15	15	15
$75,000	28	28	28	28	28	28	28

- Represents zero.   [1] Only one spouse is assumed to work.   [2] Beginning 1994, refundable earned income credit.   [3] Refundable earned income credit.   [4] Refundable earned income credit.

Source: U.S. Dept. of the Treasury, Office of Tax Analysis, unpublished data.

No. 559. Federal Civilian Employment, by Branch and Agency: 1990 to 1997

[For fiscal year ending in year shown; excludes Central Intelligence Agency, National Security Agency; and, as of November 1984, the Defense Intelligence Agency; and, as of October 1996, the National Imagery and Mapping Agency]

AGENCY	1990	1995	1996	1997	PERCENT CHANGE	
					1990-95	1996-97
Total, all agencies	**3,128,267**	**2,920,277**	**2,847,392**	**2,783,704**	**-6.6**	**-2.2**
Legislative Branch, total.	37,495	33,367	31,547	31,355	-11.0	-0.6
Judicial Branch	23,605	28,993	29,581	30,641	22.8	3.6
Executive Branch, total	3,067,167	2,857,917	2,786,264	2,721,708	-6.8	-2.3
Executive Departments	2,065,542	[1]1,782,834	1,714,460	1,655,788	-13.7	-3.4
State	25,288	24,859	24,489	24,108	-1.7	-1.6
Treasury	158,655	155,951	146,137	140,369	-1.7	-3.9
Defense.	1,034,152	832,352	795,921	749,461	-19.5	-5.8
Justice.	83,932	103,262	109,794	117,261	23.0	6.8
Interior.	77,679	76,439	71,028	67,865	-1.6	-4.5
Agriculture	122,594	113,321	109,586	106,539	-7.6	-2.8
Commerce	69,920	36,803	35,156	34,792	-47.4	-1.0
Labor	17,727	16,204	15,230	15,787	-8.6	3.7
Health & Human Services	123,959	[1]59,788	58,491	59,490	-51.8	1.7
Housing & Urban Development	13,596	11,822	11,462	10,908	-13.0	-4.8
Transportation.	67,364	63,552	63,309	64,179	-5.7	1.4
Energy.	17,731	19,589	18,237	17,078	10.5	-6.4
Education.	4,771	4,988	4,721	4,640	4.5	-1.7
Veterans Affairs [2]	248,174	263,904	250,899	243,311	6.3	-3.0
Independent agencies:						
American Battle Monuments Comm	396	375	371	359	-5.3	-3.2
Armed Forces Retirement Home	966	960	908	910	(X)	0.2
Arms Control & Disarmament Agency . .	216	266	244	240	23.1	-1.6
Board of Gov Fed Reserve System	1,525	1,704	1,740	1,716	11.7	-1.4
Commodity Futures Trading Comm	542	544	553	571	0.4	3.3
Consumer Product Safety Comm.	520	486	468	475	-6.5	1.5
Corp Natl & Community Service	(X)	574	516	539	(X)	4.5
Defense Nuclear Facilities Safety Bd	25	106	106	102	324.0	-3.8
Environmental Protection Agency.	17,123	17,910	17,160	18,045	4.6	5.2
Equal Employment Opportunity Comm . .	2,880	2,796	2,655	2,631	-2.9	-0.9
Export-Import Bank of US.	343	443	426	419	29.2	-1.6
Farm Credit Administration	515	380	332	303	-26.2	-8.7
Federal Communications Commission . .	1,778	2,116	2,069	2,080	19.0	0.5
Federal Deposit Insurance Corporation. .	17,641	14,765	10,008	8,265	-16.3	-17.4
Federal Election Commission	250	327	294	300	30.8	2.0
Fed. Emergency Managmt Agency.	3,137	5,256	6,569	4,888	67.5	-25.6
Federal Housing Finance Board [3]	65	113	119	113	73.8	-5.0
Federal Labor Relations Auth	251	221	232	216	-12.0	-6.9
Federal Maritime Commission	230	169	150	138	-26.5	-8.0
Federal Med & Concil Svc	316	297	293	279	-6.0	-4.8
Fed Ret Thrift Invest Board.	93	110	110	112	18.3	1.8
Federal Trade Commission.	988	996	941	965	0.8	2.6
General Services Administration	20,277	16,500	15,654	14,309	-18.6	-8.6
Holocaust Memorial Council	26	207	217	210	696.2	-3.2
Int Boun & Wat Comm (US & Mex)	260	236	246	248	-9.2	0.8
International Trade Commission.	491	442	391	387	-10.0	-1.0
National Archives & Recds Admin	3,120	2,833	3,061	2,832	-9.2	-7.5
National Aeronautics & Space Admin . . .	24,872	21,635	21,006	19,844	-13.0	-5.5
Natl Credit Union Admin.	900	912	935	931	1.3	-0.4
Natl Fnd Arts & Humanities.	547	493	337	336	-9.9	-0.3
Natl Labor Relations Board.	2,263	2,050	1,970	1,992	-9.4	1.1
Natl Science Foundation	1,318	1,292	1,249	1,210	-2.0	-3.1
Natl Trans Safety Board.	366	368	370	388	0.5	4.9
Nuclear Regulatory Commission	3,353	3,212	3,148	3,081	-4.2	-2.1
Office of Personnel Management.	6,636	4,354	3,524	3,603	-34.4	2.2
Panama Canal Commission	8,240	9,060	9,335	9,777	10.0	4.7
Peace Corps	1,178	1,179	1,122	1,094	0.1	-2.5
Pension Benefit Guar Corp	574	716	763	743	24.7	-2.6
Railroad Retirement Board	1,772	1,544	1,440	1,327	-12.9	-7.8
Securities & Exchange Comm	2,302	2,852	2,838	2,861	23.9	0.8
Selective Service System	288	218	221	203	-24.3	-8.1
Small Business Administration.	5,128	5,085	4,839	4,380	-0.8	-9.5
Smithsonian Institution, Summary	5,092	5,444	5,188	5,188	6.9	-
Social Security Admin	(X)	[1]66,850	66,314	67,033	(X)	1.1
Tennessee Valley Authority	28,392	16,545	16,022	14,510	-41.7	-9.4
U.S. Information Agency.	8,555	7,480	6,850	6,534	-12.6	-4.6
U.S. International Development						
Cooperation Agency	4,698	3,755	3,267	2,968	-20.1	-9.2
U.S. Postal Service	816,886	845,393	852,285	853,298	3.5	0.1

- Represents zero.   X Not applicable.   [1] Sizable changes due to the Social Security Administration which was separated from the Department of Health and Human Services to become an independent agency effective April 1995.   [2] Formerly Veterans Administration.   [3] Formerly Federal Home Loan Bank Board.

Source: U.S. Office of Personnel Management, *Federal Civilian Workforce Statistics— Employment and Trends,* bimonthly.

No. 560. Federal Civilian Employment and Annual Payroll, by Branch: 1970 to 1997

[Average annual employment. For fiscal year ending in year shown; see text, Section 9. Includes employees in U.S. territories and foreign countries. Data represent employees in active-duty status, including intermittent employees. Annual employment figures are averages of monthly figures. Excludes Central Intelligence Agency, National Security Agency, and, as of November 1984, the Defense Intelligence Agency, and as of October 1996, the National Imagery and Mapping Agency]

| YEAR | EMPLOYMENT | | | | | | PAYROLL (mil. dol.) | | | | |
| | Total (1,000) | Percent of U.S. employed [1] | Executive | | Legis-lative (1,000) | Judicial (1,000) | Total | Executive | | Legis-lative | Judicial |
			Total (1,000)	Defense				Total	Defense		
1970	[2]2,997	3.8	2,961	1,263	29	7	27,322	26,894	11,264	338	89
1971	2,899	3.7	2,861	1,162	31	7	29,475	29,007	11,579	369	98
1972	2,882	3.5	2,842	1,128	32	8	31,626	31,102	12,181	411	112
1973	2,822	3.3	2,780	1,076	33	9	33,240	32,671	12,414	447	121
1974	2,825	3.3	2,781	1,041	35	9	35,661	35,035	12,789	494	132
1975	2,877	3.4	2,830	1,044	37	10	39,126	38,423	13,418	549	154
1976	2,879	3.2	2,831	1,025	38	11	42,259	41,450	14,699	631	179
1977	2,855	3.1	2,803	997	39	12	45,895	44,975	15,696	700	219
1978	2,875	3.0	2,822	987	40	13	49,921	48,899	16,995	771	251
1979	2,897	2.9	2,844	974	40	13	53,590	52,513	18,065	817	260
1980	[3]2,987	3.0	2,933	971	40	14	58,012	56,841	18,795	883	288
1981	2,909	2.9	2,855	986	40	15	63,793	62,510	21,227	922	360
1982	2,871	2.9	2,816	1,019	39	16	65,503	64,125	22,226	980	398
1983	2,878	2.9	2,823	1,033	39	16	69,878	68,420	23,406	1,013	445
1984	2,935	2.8	2,879	1,052	40	17	74,616	73,084	25,253	1,081	451
1985	3,001	2.8	2,944	1,080	39	18	80,599	78,992	28,330	1,098	509
1986	3,047	2.8	2,991	1,089	38	19	82,598	80,941	29,272	1,112	545
1987	3,075	2.7	3,018	1,084	38	19	85,543	83,797	29,786	1,153	593
1988	3,113	2.7	3,054	1,073	38	21	88,841	86,960	29,609	1,226	656
1989	3,133	2.7	3,074	1,067	38	22	92,847	90,870	30,301	1,266	711
1990	[4]3,233	2.7	3,173	1,060	38	23	99,138	97,022	31,990	1,329	787
1991	3,101	2.7	3,038	1,015	38	25	104,273	101,965	32,956	1,434	874
1992	3,106	2.6	3,040	1,004	39	27	108,054	105,402	31,486	1,569	1,083
1993	3,043	2.5	2,976	952	39	28	114,323	111,523	32,755	1,609	1,191
1994	2,993	2.4	2,928	900	37	28	116,138	113,264	32,144	1,613	1,260
1995	2,943	2.4	2,880	852	34	28	118,304	115,328	31,753	1,598	1,379
1996	2,881	2.3	2,819	811	32	29	119,321	116,385	31,569	1,519	1,417
1997	2,816	2.2	2,755	768	31	30	119,549	116,639	31,446	1,515	1,396

[1] Civilian only. See Table 646.   [2] Includes 33,000 temporary census workers.   [3] Includes 81,116 temporary census workers. [4] Includes 111,020 temporary census workers.

Source: U.S. Office of Personnel Management, *Federal Civilian Workforce Statistics—Employment and Trends*, bimonthly; and unpublished data.

No. 561. Federal Executive Branch (Non-Postal) Employment, by Race and National Origin: 1990 to 1997

[As of **Sept. 30.** Covers total employment for only Executive branch agencies participating in OPMs Central Personnel Data File (CPDF)]

PAY SYSTEM	1990	1994	1995	1996	1997
All personnel	2,150,359	2,043,449	1,960,577	1,890,406	1,830,300
White, non-Hispanic	1,562,846	1,462,185	1,394,690	1,341,157	1,293,244
General schedule and related	1,218,188	1,146,990	1,101,108	1,060,863	1,027,440
Grades 1-4 ($12,669 - $22,685)	132,028	90,029	79,195	67,988	63,775
Grades 5-8 ($19,520 - $34,814)	337,453	303,999	288,755	275,093	264,288
Grades 9-12 ($29,577 - $55,760)	510,261	484,681	465,908	451,651	434,228
Grades 13-15 ($51,003 - $92,161)	238,446	268,281	267,250	266,131	265,149
Total executives/senior pay levels [1]	9,337	13,114	13,307	13,319	13,465
Wage pay system	244,220	202,440	186,184	174,364	164,755
Other pay systems	91,101	99,641	94,091	92,611	87,584
Black	356,867	340,512	327,302	313,810	303,415
General schedule and related	272,657	265,926	258,586	249,959	243,932
Grades 1-4 ($12,669 - $22,685)	65,077	46,189	41,381	34,993	32,439
Grades 5-8 ($19,520 - $34,814)	114,993	115,966	112,962	109,571	106,037
Grades 9-12 ($29,577 - $55,760)	74,985	80,284	79,795	80,065	79,124
Grades 13-15 ($51,003 - $92,161)	17,602	23,487	24,448	25,330	26,332
Total executives/senior pay levels [1]	479	865	942	967	1,002
Wage pay system	72,755	60,335	55,637	51,189	47,261
Other pay systems	10,976	13,386	12,137	11,695	11,220
Hispanic	115,170	116,863	115,964	115,644	114,740
General schedule and related	83,218	86,816	86,762	86,598	87,427
Grades 1-4 ($12,669 - $22,685)	15,738	12,033	11,081	9,798	9,320
Grades 5-8 ($19,520 - $34,814)	28,727	30,749	31,152	31,437	31,843
Grades 9-12 ($29,577 - $55,760)	31,615	34,104	34,056	34,431	34,742
Grades 13-15 ($51,003 - $92,161)	7,138	9,930	10,473	10,932	11,522
Total executives/senior pay levels [1]	154	323	382	376	409
Wage pay system	26,947	23,122	22,128	21,416	20,565
Other pay systems	4,851	6,602	6,692	7,254	6,339
American Indian, Alaska Natives, and Asian and Pacific Islander	115,476	123,889	122,621	119,795	118,901

[1] General schedule pay rates and Senior Pay Levels effective as of January 1997.

Source: Office of Personnel Management, Central Personnel Data File.

No. 562. Paid Civilian Employment in the Federal Government: 1996

[As of **December 31**. Excludes Central Intelligence Agency, Defense Intelligence Agency, seasonal and on-call employees, and National Security Agency]

STATE	Total (1,000)	Percent Defense	Percent change, 1994-96	STATE	Total (1,000)	Percent Defense	Percent change, 1994-96
United States.	**2,735**	**26.2**	**-5.8**	Missouri	58	21.9	-9.9
Alabama	52	42.0	-5.3	Montana	11	10.5	-13.4
Alaska	14	32.4	-6.9	Nebraska	15	23.9	-6.4
Arizona	40	21.6	-1.0	Nevada	12	18.1	-2.7
Arkansas	20	19.3	-0.8	New Hampshire	8	15.1	-7.7
California	269	31.1	-8.7	New Jersey	68	28.1	-5.8
Colorado	52	23.6	-8.5	New Mexico	26	31.2	-4.4
Connecticut	22	13.4	-10.2	New York	139	9.3	-4.3
Delaware	5	28.9	-13.2	North Carolina	55	31.6	1.5
District of Columbia	185	7.3	-9.4	North Dakota	8	23.3	-0.4
Florida	112	25.6	-1.8	Ohio	86	32.1	-6.8
Georgia	87	37.5	-5.2	Oklahoma	42	46.7	-0.3
Hawaii	24	72.9	-2.4	Oregon	28	10.1	-6.7
Idaho	11	13.1	-0.4	Pennsylvania	112	26.7	-11.6
Illinois	97	15.6	-8.4	Rhode Island	11	41.6	1.1
Indiana	40	30.2	-4.1	South Carolina	26	38.8	-14.5
Iowa	20	7.2	-4.5	South Dakota	10	13.3	-0.6
Kansas	25	22.2	-5.5	Tennessee	52	10.1	-1.5
Kentucky	34	28.9	-5.8	Texas	172	29.9	-2.0
Louisiana	34	24.5	-2.3	Utah	29	44.3	-7.0
Maine	13	42.5	-4.5	Vermont	6	9.9	5.2
Maryland	126	26.2	-4.9	Virginia	151	58.4	-5.8
Massachusetts	54	15.2	-9.4	Washington	62	38.8	-6.5
Michigan	55	14.9	-8.9	West Virginia	18	10.0	1.7
Minnesota	33	7.5	-3.8	Wisconsin	29	11.1	-4.0
Mississippi	24	39.9	-4.4	Wyoming	6	16.2	-10.7

Source: U.S. Office of Personnel Management, *Biennial Report of Employment by Geographic Area.*

No. 563. Paid Full-Time Federal Civilian Employment, All Areas: 1990 to 1997

[As of **March 31**. Excludes employees of Congress and federal courts, maritime seamen of Dept. of Commerce, and small number for whom rates were not reported. See text, Section 10, for explanation of general schedule and wage system]

COMPENSATION AUTHORITY	EMPLOYEES (1,000)				AVERAGE PAY			
	1990	1995	1996	1997	1990	1995	1996	1997
Total	**2,697**	**2,620**	**2,564**	**2,506**	**31,174**	**(NA)**	**42,195**	**43,873**
General Schedule	1,506	1,417	1,381	1,290	31,239	40,568	42,139	43,239
Wage System	369	269	252	237	26,565	32,084	32,976	33,834
Postal pay system [1]	661	753	761	765	29,264	33,665	33,952	35,069
Other	161	181	170	214	41,149	53,839	56,298	58,782

NA Not available. [1] Source: Employees—U.S. Postal Service, *Annual Report of the Postmaster General.* Average pay—U.S. Postal Service, *Comprehensive Statement of Postal Operations*, annual.

Source: Except as noted, U.S. Office of Personnel Management, *Pay Structure of the Federal Civil Service*, annual.

No. 564. Federal General Schedule Employee Pay Increases: 1965 to 1997

[Percent change from prior year shown, except 1965, change from 1964. Represents legislated pay increases. For some years data based on range for details see source]

DATE	Pay increase	DATE	Pay increase	DATE	Pay increase
1965	3.6	1975	5.0	1987	3.0
1966	2.9	1976	5.2	1988	2.0
1967	4.5	1977	7.0	1989	4.1
1968	4.9	1978	5.5	1990	3.6
1969	9.1	1979	7.0	1991	4.1
1970	6.0	1980	9.1	1992	4.2
1971	6.0	1981	4.8	1993	3.7
1972	5.5	1982	4.0	1994	-
1972	5.1	1984	4.0	1995	2.0
1973	4.8	1985	3.5	1996	2.0
1974	5.5	1986	-	1997	2.3

- Represents zero.

Source: U.S. Office of Personnel Management, *Pay Structure of the Federal Civil Service*, annual.

No. 565. Accessions to and Separations From Employment in the Federal Government: 1995 and 1997

[As of September 30]

AGENCY	ACCESSIONS				SEPARATIONS			
	Number		Rate		Number		Rate	
	1995	1997	1995	1997	1995	1997	1995	1997
Total, all agencies	556,695	509,669	19.2	18.4	638,733	539,116	22.1	19.5
Legislative Branch, total [1]	1,074	963	6.6	6.8	1,985	1,733	12.2	12.3
General Accounting Office	39	70	0.9	2.1	392	355	8.9	10.5
Government Printing Office.	77	140	1.8	3.8	318	328	7.6	9.0
Library of Congress.	540	396	11.6	8.9	642	553	13.8	12.4
Judicial Branch	-	-	-	-	-	-	-	-
Executive Branch, total	555,621	508,706	19.3	18.5	636,748	537,383	22.1	19.5
Executive Office of the President	384	500	24.3	31.7	373	425	23.6	27.0
Executive Departments	257,125	261,491	14.0	15.6	422,606	306,913	23.0	18.3
State.	3,338	3,591	13.3	14.9	3,919	3,539	15.6	14.6
Treasury	24,532	47,313	15.0	31.2	52,634	52,979	32.2	35.0
Defense.	104,088	95,515	12.2	12.4	155,722	136,468	18.3	17.8
Justice.	14,958	1,336	14.9	13.1	7,496	6,049	7.5	5.3
Interior.	12,936	15,111	17.1	22.0	16,147	13,086	21.4	19.0
Agriculture	25,365	26,753	23.3	26.0	41,384	28,568	37.9	27.8
Commerce	5,900	5,377	15.8	15.5	6,460	5,686	17.3	16.4
Labor	1,438	2,044	8.7	13.2	2,003	1,457	12.2	9.4
Health & Human Services [2].	8,774	9,612	9.3	16.2	78,780	8,156	83.7	13.8
Housing & Urban Development	489	573	4.0	5.1	1,952	1,553	15.8	13.9
Transportation.	2,673	4,512	4.2	7.1	4,740	4,192	7.4	6.6
Energy	2,087	837	10.5	4.8	2,671	1,924	13.4	11.0
Education.	683	488	13.8	10.6	354	435	7.2	9.4
Veterans Affairs [3].	49,864	34,866	19.0	14.2	48,344	42,821	18.5	17.4
Independent agencies [1]	298,112	246,715	28.6	23.0	213,769	230,045	20.5	21.4
Board of Governors, Fed RSRV System . . .	231	151	13.7	8.7	199	260	11.8	15.0
Environmental Protection Agency	2,232	2,407	12.3	13.7	2,078	1,435	11.5	8.2
Equal Employment Opportunity Comm	129	103	4.5	3.9	156	71	5.4	2.7
Federal Deposit Insurance Corporation . . .	360	457	2.2	5.1	4,404	2,266	26.8	25.1
Fed Emergency Management Agency	3,165	2,058	60.2	36.5	3,059	3,791	58.2	67.2
General Services Administration	292	512	1.7	3.5	2,552	647	14.8	4.4
National Aeronautics & Space Admin	2,004	1,274	8.9	6.3	3,673	2,482	16.2	12.2
National Archives & Records Admin	583	457	20.0	15.6	307	229	10.5	7.8
Nuclear Regulatory Commission.	98	132	3.0	4.2	263	201	8.0	6.4
Office of Personnel Management	506	514	10.3	14.5	1,407	538	28.6	15.2
Panama Canal Comm	1,744	1,485	19.6	15.5	1,246	1,043	14.0	10.9
Railroad Retirement Board	46	37	2.9	2.7	185	150	11.6	10.9
Securities and Exchange Commission. . . .	584	505	21.1	17.9	356	410	12.8	14.5
Small Business Administration	1,065	1,259	18.1	27.3	2,799	1,686	47.6	36.5
Smithsonian Institution	707	628	13.1	14.4	980	800	18.2	15.6
Tennessee Valley Authority	674	217	4.1	1.4	2,873	1,310	17.3	8.5
U.S. Information Agency	356	254	4.7	3.8	836	689	11.0	10.4
U.S. International Dev. Coop. Agency	333	181	8.6	5.9	665	422	17.2	13.7
U.S. Postal Service	210,447	225,188	25.0	26.2	179,494	203,945	21.3	23.7

- Represents zero.   [1] Includes other branches, or other agencies, not shown separately.   [2] Sizable changes due to the Social Security Administration which was separated from the Department of Health and Human Services to become an independent agency effective April 1995.   [3] Formerly Veterans Administration.

Source: U.S. Office of Personnel Management, Federal Civilian Workforce Statistics—*Employment and Trends*, bimonthly.

No. 566. Federal Land and Buildings Owned and Leased, and Predominant Land Usage: 1990 to 1996

[For fiscal years ending in years shown; see text, Section 9. Covers federal real property throughout the world, except as noted. Cost of land figures represent total cost of property owned in year shown. For further details see source. For data on federal land by state, see Table 389]

ITEM AND AGENCY	Unit	1990	1992	1993	1994	1995	1996
Federally owned:							
Land, worldwide	1,000 acres. .	650,014	651,286	650,513	677,802	549,670	563,278
United States	1,000 acres. .	649,802	651,094	650,322	676,615	549,474	563,129
Buildings	1,000	(NA)	(NA)	(NA)	(NA)	(NA)	(NA)
United States	1,000	446	449	440	448	424	430
Buildings floor area (sq. ft.). . . .	Mil. sq/ft. . . .	(NA)	(NA)	(NA)	(NA)	(NA)	(NA)
United States	Mil. sq/ft. . . .	2,859	2,898	2,783	2,944	2,793	2,930
Costs	Mil. dol. . . .	187,865	193,047	194,181	209,318	199,387	217,857
Land	Mil. dol. . . .	(NA)	19,673	20,134	20,947	18,972	22,952
Buildings	Mil. dol. . . .	(NA)	95,254	96,223	115,633	113,018	123,897
Structures and facilities.	Mil. dol. . . .	(NA)	78,120	77,824	72,738	67,398	71,008
Federally leased:							
Land, worldwide	1,000 acres. .	994	974	941	1,119	1,385	1,373
United States	1,000 acres. .	938	932	898	1,055	1,351	1,339
Buildings	1,000	(NA)	(NA)	(NA)	(NA)	(NA)	(NA)
United States	Number	47,291	46,568	43,130	53,128	77,896	77,232
Buildings floor area (sq. ft.). . . .	Mil. sq/ft. . . .	(NA)	(NA)	(NA)	(NA)	(NA)	(NA)
United States	Mil. sq/ft. . . .	234	248	252	276	275	277
Annual rental	Mil. dol. . . .	2,590	3,074	3,706	3,766	3,633	3,739
United States	Mil. dol. . . .	2,125	2,524	2,727	3,105	3,174	3,214

NA Not available.

Source: U.S. General Services Administration, *Inventory Report on Real Property Owned by the United States Throughout the World*, annual.

National Defense and Veterans Affairs

This section presents data on national defense and its human and financial costs; active and reserve military personnel; ships, equipment and aircraft; and federally sponsored programs and benefits for veterans. The principal sources of these data are the annual *Selected Manpower Statistics* and the *Atlas/Data Abstract for the United States and Selected Areas* issued by the Office of the Secretary of Defense; *Annual Report of Secretary of Veterans Affairs, Department of Veterans Affairs,* and *The Budget of the United States Government,* Office of Management and Budget. For more data on expenditures, personnel, and ships, see Section 31.

Department of Defense (DOD)—DOD is responsible for providing military forces of the United States. The President serves as Commander in Chief of the Armed Forces; from him, the authority flows to the Secretary of Defense and through the Joint Chiefs of Staff to the commanders of unified and specified commands (e.g., United States European Command).

Reserve components—Reserve personnel of the Armed Forces consist of the Army National Guard, Army Reserve, Naval Reserve, Marine Corps Reserve, Air National Guard, Air Force Reserve, and Coast Guard Reserve. They provide trained personnel available for active duty in the Armed Forces in time of war or national emergency and at such other times as authorized by law. The National Guard has dual federal-state responsibilities and uses jointly provided equipment, facilities, and budget support. The President is empowered to mobilize the National Guard and to use such of the Armed Forces as he considers necessary to enforce federal authority in any state.

The ready reserve includes selected reservists who are intended to assist active forces in a war and the individual ready reserve who, in a major war, would be used to fill out active and reserve units

In Brief	
	1997
U.S. defense outlays	$264.1 bil.
Defense outlays as percent of gross domestic product	3.2%

and later would be a source of combat replacements; a portion of the ready reserve serves in an active status. The standby reserve cannot be called to active duty unless the Congress gives explicit approval. The retired reserve represents a low potential for mobilization.

Department of Veterans Affairs— The Department of Veterans Affairs administers laws authorizing benefits for eligible former and present members of the Armed Forces and for the beneficiaries of deceased members. Veterans benefits available under various acts of Congress include compensation for service-connected disability or death; pensions for nonservice-connected disability or death; vocational rehabilitation, education, and training; home loan insurance; life insurance; health care; special housing and automobiles or other conveyances for certain disabled veterans; burial and plot allowances; and educational assistance to families of deceased or totally disabled veterans, servicemen missing in action, or prisoners of war. Since these benefits are legislated by Congress, the dates they were enacted and the dates they apply to veterans may be different from the actual dates the conflicts occurred.

VA estimates of veterans cover all persons with active duty service during periods of war or armed conflict and until 1982 include those living outside the United States. Veteran population estimates for September 1982 are for the 50 states, the District of Columbia and Puerto Rico. Veterans whose active duty service was entirely during periods of peacetime are eligible for some veterans benefits and, where appropriate, are included in VA estimates.

No. 567. National Defense Outlays and Veterans Benefits: 1960 to 1998

[For fiscal year ending in year shown; see text, Section 9. Includes outlays of Department of Defense, Department of Veterans Affairs, and other agencies for activities primarily related to national defense and veterans programs. For explanation of average annual percent change, see Guide to Tabular Presentation. Minus sign (-) indicates decline]

YEAR	NATIONAL DEFENSE AND VETERANS OUTLAYS				ANNUAL PERCENT CHANGE [1]			DEFENSE OUTLAYS, PERCENT OF—	
	Total outlays (bil. dol.)	Defense outlays		Veterans outlays (bil. dol.)	Total outlays	Defense outlays	Veterans outlays	Federal outlays	Gross domestic product [2]
		Current dollars (bil. dol.)	Constant (1992) dollars (bil. dol.)						
1960	53.5	48.1	260.3	5.4	2.5	2.4	3.1	52.2	9.3
1965	56.3	50.6	248.9	5.7	-6.8	-7.6	0.7	42.8	7.4
1966	64.0	58.1	274.0	5.9	13.7	14.8	3.5	43.2	7.7
1967	78.1	71.4	323.4	6.7	22.1	22.9	13.8	45.4	8.8
1968	88.9	81.9	352.2	7.0	13.8	14.7	4.4	46.0	9.4
1969	90.1	82.5	337.4	7.6	1.3	0.7	8.5	44.9	8.7
1970	90.4	81.7	315.4	8.7	0.3	-1.0	13.6	41.8	8.1
1971	88.7	78.9	287.1	9.8	-1.9	-3.5	12.7	37.5	7.3
1972	89.9	79.2	263.7	10.7	1.4	0.4	9.8	34.3	6.7
1973	88.7	76.7	239.6	12.0	1.3	-3.1	12.0	31.2	5.9
1974	92.7	79.3	228.3	13.4	4.6	3.5	11.4	29.5	5.5
1975	103.1	86.5	224.1	16.6	11.2	9.0	24.0	26.0	5.6
1976	108.0	89.6	216.8	18.4	4.8	3.6	11.0	24.1	5.2
1976, TQ [3] . . .	26.2	22.3	52.1	4.0	(X)	(X)	(X)	23.2	4.9
1977	115.2	97.2	216.4	18.0	6.7	8.5	-2.1	23.8	4.9
1978	123.5	104.5	217.4	19.0	7.1	7.5	5.2	22.8	4.7
1979	136.2	116.3	221.9	19.9	10.4	11.3	5.0	23.1	4.7
1980	155.2	134.0	229.4	21.2	13.9	15.2	6.3	22.7	4.9
1981	180.5	157.5	241.8	23.0	16.3	17.6	8.5	23.2	5.2
1982	209.3	185.3	263.6	24.0	15.9	17.6	4.2	24.8	5.8
1983	234.7	209.9	284.0	24.8	12.1	13.3	3.3	26.0	6.1
1984	253.0	227.4	287.4	25.6	7.8	8.3	3.2	26.7	6.0
1985	279.0	252.7	306.1	26.3	10.3	11.1	2.7	26.7	6.2
1986	299.8	273.4	324.7	26.4	7.4	8.2	0.4	27.6	6.2
1987	308.8	282.0	330.0	26.8	3.0	3.1	1.5	28.1	6.1
1988	319.8	290.4	333.9	29.4	3.6	3.0	9.7	27.3	5.9
1989	333.7	303.6	338.3	30.1	4.3	4.5	2.4	26.5	5.7
1990	328.4	299.3	324.6	29.1	-1.6	-1.4	-3.3	23.9	5.3
1991	304.6	273.3	283.3	31.3	-7.2	-8.7	7.6	20.6	4.7
1992	332.5	298.4	298.4	34.1	12.0	12.4	8.0	21.6	4.9
1993	326.8	291.1	286.6	35.7	-1.9	-2.4	4.6	20.7	4.5
1994	319.2	281.6	271.9	37.6	-2.3	-3.3	5.3	19.3	4.1
1995	310.0	272.1	256.4	37.9	-2.9	-3.4	0.8	17.9	3.8
1996	302.7	265.7	240.3	37.0	-2.4	-2.3	-2.4	17.0	3.5
1997	309.8	270.5	239.3	39.3	2.3	1.8	6.3	16.9	3.4
1998, est.	307.2	264.1	229.3	43.1	-0.8	-2.4	9.7	15.8	3.2

X Not applicable.   [1] Change from prior year shown; for 1960, change from 1955.   [2] Represents fiscal year GDP; for definition, see text, Section 14.   [3] Transition quarter, July-Sept.

Source: U.S. Office of Management and Budget, *Historical Tables,* annual.

No. 568. Federal Budget Outlays for National Defense Functions: 1980 to 1998

[In billions of dollars, except percent. For fiscal year ending in year shown; see text, Section 9. Minus sign (-) indicates decline]

DEFENSE FUNCTION	1980	1985	1989	1990	1991	1992	1993	1994	1995	1996	1997	1998, est.
Total.	134.0	252.7	303.6	299.3	273.3	298.4	291.1	281.6	272.1	265.7	270.5	264.1
Percent change [1]	15.2	11.1	4.5	-1.4	-8.7	9.2	-2.4	0.6	-3.4	-2.3	1.8	-2.4
Defense Dept., military	130.9	245.2	294.9	289.8	262.4	286.9	278.6	268.6	259.4	253.2	258.3	251.4
Military personnel	40.9	67.8	80.7	75.6	83.4	81.2	75.9	73.1	70.8	66.7	69.7	69.6
Percent of military	31.2	27.7	27.0	26.1	31.8	28.3	27.2	27.2	27.3	26.3	27.0	27.7
Operation, maintenance	44.8	72.4	87.0	88.3	101.8	92.0	94.1	87.9	91.1	88.8	92.5	92.4
Procurement	29.0	70.4	81.6	81.0	82.0	74.9	69.9	61.8	55.0	48.9	47.7	43.7
Research and development . .	13.1	27.1	37.0	37.5	34.6	34.6	37.0	34.8	34.6	36.5	37.0	35.8
Military construction	2.5	4.3	5.3	5.1	3.5	4.3	4.8	5.0	6.8	6.7	6.2	5.5
Family housing.	1.7	2.6	3.3	3.5	3.3	3.3	3.3	3.3	3.6	3.8	4.0	4.0
Other [2]	-1.1	0.6	0.1	-1.2	-46.2	-3.3	-6.4	2.7	-2.4	1.8	1.2	0.3
Atomic energy activities [3] . . .	2.9	7.1	8.1	9.0	10.0	10.6	11.0	11.9	11.8	11.6	11.3	11.6
Defense-related activities [4] . . .	0.2	0.5	0.6	0.6	0.9	0.9	0.8	1.5	1.1	0.8	0.9	1.1

[1] Change from immediate prior year.   [2] Revolving and management funds, trust funds, special foreign currency program, allowances, and offsetting receipts.   [3] Defense activities only.   [4] Includes civil defense activities.

Source: U.S. Office of Management and Budget, *Historical Tables,* annual.

No. 569. National Defense—Budget Authority and Outlays: 1980 to 1998

[In billions of dollars, except percent. For fiscal year ending in year shown, except as noted; see text, Section 9]

ITEM	1980	1985	1990	1991	1992	1993	1994	1995	1996	1997	1998, est.
Budget authority [1]	143.9	294.7	303.3	288.9	295.1	281.1	263.3	266.3	266.0	270.3	267.6
Department of Defense-Military [2]	140.6	286.8	293.0	276.2	282.1	267.2	251.4	255.7	254.4	258.0	254.9
Atomic energy [1][3]	3.2	7.3	9.7	11.6	12.0	12.1	10.9	10.1	10.7	11.3	11.7
Outlays (Defense) [1]	134.0	252.7	299.3	273.3	298.4	291.1	281.6	272.1	265.7	270.5	264.1
Department of Defense-Military	130.9	245.2	289.8	262.4	286.9	278.6	268.6	259.4	253.2	258.3	251.4
Atomic energy [1][3]	3.1	7.6	9.6	10.0	10.6	11.0	11.9	11.8	11.6	11.3	11.6

[1] Includes defense budget authority, balances, and outlays by other departments. [2] Excluding accruals. [3] Includes other defense related activities.

Source: U.S. Office of Management and Budget, *Historical Tables*, annual.

No. 570. Defense-Related Agencies: 1980 to 1995

[In thousands, except percent. Annual averages]

EMPLOYMENT	1980	1985	1989	1990	1991	1992	1993	1994	1995
Total U.S. employment [1]	100,907	108,856	119,030	120,430	119,282	120,058	121,744	123,060	124,900
Federal	4,386	4,608	4,662	4,577	4,541	4,549	4,403	(NA)	(NA)
Resident Armed Forces	1,604	1,706	1,688	1,637	1,564	1,566	1,485	(NA)	(NA)
Civilian personnel [2]	2,987	3,001	3,133	3,233	3,101	2,983	2,918	2,993	2,943
DOD—Civilian employment	948	1,073	1,067	1,024	1,083	1,044	973	926	874
Percent of federal civilian personnel	31.7	35.8	34.1	31.7	34.9	35.0	33.3	30.9	(NA)
DOD—Military and civilian employment	2,552	2,779	2,755	2,661	2,647	2,610	2,458	(NA)	(NA)
Percent of total federal	58.2	60.3	59.1	58.1	58.3	57.4	55.8	(NA)	(NA)
Percent of total U.S.	2.5	2.6	2.3	2.2	2.2	2.2	2.0	(NA)	(NA)

NA Not available. [1] Includes resident Armed Forces. [2] See Table 560.

Source: U.S. Dept. of Defense, *Civilian Manpower Statistics*, annual (Sept. issues).

No. 571. Military and Civilian Personnel and Expenditures: 1990 to 1996

ITEM	1990	1992	1993	1994	1995	1996
Personnel, total [1] (1,000)	3,693	3,889	3,762	3,623	3,391	3,252
Active duty military	1,185	1,214	1,171	1,131	1,085	1,056
Civilian	931	899	847	810	768	732
Reserve and National Guard	1,577	1,777	1,744	1,682	1,538	1,464
Expenditures, total (mil. dol.)	209,904	211,534	214,655	210,138	209,695	211,740
Payroll outlays	88,650	99,250	100,510	99,822	98,396	99,794
Active duty military pay	33,705	39,447	38,782	37,694	35,188	38,389
Civilian pay	28,230	31,205	31,619	30,587	29,932	29,230
Retired military pay	21,159	23,936	25,658	26,386	27,595	27,817
Reserve and National Guard pay	5,556	4,661	4,451	5,154	5,681	4,357
Prime contract awards [2] (mil. dol.)	121,254	112,285	114,145	110,316	109,005	109,408
Supply contracts	66,895	54,880	54,856	48,642	46,471	47,725
Service contracts	28,540	30,503	32,163	33,040	34,981	35,366
R and D contracts	21,955	21,508	22,076	21,513	21,266	20,033
Construction contracts	2,088	2,894	2,829	4,786	3,846	3,974
Civil function contracts	1,775	2,500	2,222	2,335	2,440	2,309
Major area of work (mil. dol.):						
Aircraft, fixed wing	6,329	8,197	6,926	6,277	7,543	6,521
Research, devel'mt, testing and evaluation (RDTE	(NA)	1,266	1,422	3,256	(NA)	(NA)
RDTE/Aircraft-Engineering development	(NA)	1,266	1,422	1,769	(NA)	(NA)
RDTE/Missile and space systems-op systems	(NA)	(NA)	(NA)	1,487	(NA)	(NA)
Gas turbines and jet engines	1,856	974	(NA)	(NA)	(NA)	(NA)
Guided missiles	928	(NA)	793	494	495	625
Guided missile handling and servicing equip.	446	(NA)	757	(NA)	(NA)	(NA)
Major location of expenditures (mil. dol.):						
San Diego, CA	4,820	5,289	6,405	4,748	5,280	5,245
Pico Rivera, CA	(NA)	4,284	2,428	3,272	(NA)	(NA)
St. Louis, MO	5,616	3,462	5,442	6,087	5,770	7,049
Norfolk, VA	2,741	3,257	3,265	3,228	3,399	3,170
Arlington, VA	2,527	2,974	3,246	3,284	3,483	3,573
Fort Worth, TX	3,594	2,948	3,136	2,492	3,343	3,239
Washington, DC	2,771	2,828	3,045	2,347	2,347	2,759
Marietta, GA	(NA)	2,573	2,734	2,828	2,349	2,612
Long Beach, CA	(NA)	(NA)	2,236	3,550	2,563	3,030
Sunnyvale, CA	(NA)	(NA)	2,625	3,088	2,222	2,061

NA Not available. [1] Includes those based ashore and excludes those temporarily shore-based, in a transient status, or afloat. [2] Represents contract awards over $25,000.

Source: U.S. Dept. of Defense, *Atlas/Data Abstract for the United States and Selected Areas*, annual.

No. 572. Military Prime Contract Awards to All Businesses, by Program: 1980 to 1997

[In billions of dollars. Net values for **fiscal year ending in year shown;** see text, Section 9. Includes all new prime contracts; debit or credit changes in contracts are also included. Actions cover official awards, amendments, or other changes in prime contracts to obtain military supplies, services, or construction. Excludes term contracts and contracts which do not obligate a firm total dollar amount or fixed quantity, but includes job orders, task orders, and delivery orders against such contracts]

DOD PROCUREMENT PROGRAM	1980	1990	1991	1992	1993	1994	1995	1996	1997
Total	83.7	144.7	150.9	136.3	138.3	132.2	131.4	132.2	128.4
Intragovernmental [1]	10.2	10.0	11.9	9.6	12.9	11.1	12.3	13.0	11.5
For work outside the U.S.	5.4	7.1	9.2	5.9	5.8	5.6	5.6	6.4	6.4
Educ. and nonprofit institutions	1.5	3.5	3.6	3.4	3.4	3.3	3.3	3.3	3.6
With business firms for work in the U.S. [2] .	66.7	123.8	125.9	117.2	116.0	112.0	110.0	109.5	106.9
Major hard goods	41.0	79.1	74.1	67.1	64.5	59.2	56.0	55.1	52.5
Aircraft	12.5	24.0	23.6	24.1	23.0	23.5	18.8	20.3	18.4
Electronics and communication equip..	9.6	18.5	15.2	14.2	14.2	12.4	12.3	11.5	12.1
Missiles and space systems	7.9	17.1	16.4	13.1	12.1	11.6	10.6	10.2	9.5
Ships	6.0	10.3	9.3	8.3	9.0	6.8	9.1	7.1	6.8
Tanks, ammo. and weapons	5.1	9.2	9.6	7.4	6.2	4.9	5.3	5.9	5.7
Services	5.9	14.6	16.9	17.3	17.5	17.7	18.6	19.2	20.2

[1] Covers only purchases from other federal agencies and reimbursable purchases on behalf of foreign governments. [2] Includes Department of Defense. Includes other business not shown separately. Contracts awarded for work in U.S. possessions, and other areas subject to complete sovereignty of United States; contracts in a classified location; and any intragovernmental contracts entered into overseas.

Source: U.S. Dept. of Defense, *Prime Contract Awards*, semiannual.

No. 573. Department of Defense Contract Awards, Payroll, and Civilian and Military Personnel—States: 1996

[For years ending **Sept. 30. Contracts** refer to awards made in year specified; expenditures relating to awards may extend over several years. **Civilian employees** include United States citizen and foreign national direct hire civilians subject to Office of Management and Budget (OMB) ceiling controls and civilian personnel involved in civil functions in the United States. Excludes indirect hire civilians and those direct hire civilian not subject to OMB ceiling controls. **Military personnel** include active duty personnel based ashore. Excludes personnel temporarily shore-based in a transient status, or afloat. **Payroll outlays** include the gross earnings of civilian and active duty military personnel for services rendered to the government and for cash allowances for benefits. Excludes employer's share of employee benefits, accrued military retirement benefits and most permanent change of station costs]

STATE	Contract awards [1] (mil. dol.)	Payroll (mil. dol.)	PERSONNEL (1,000)		STATE	Contract awards [1] (mil. dol.)	Payroll (mil. dol.)	PERSONNEL (1,000)	
			Civilian	Military				Civilian	Military
U.S. . . .	**109,408**	**99,794**	**732.0**	**1,056.1**	MO	7,093	1,630	15.8	14.6
AL	1,838	2,183	22.0	14.6	MT	91	298	1.1	3.7
AK	565	879	4.4	16.6	NE	322	711	3.7	9.4
AZ	2,911	1,865	8.8	21.8	NV	285	777	2.2	7.8
AR	249	730	3.9	5.0	NH	568	240	1.3	0.4
CA	18,230	12,332	84.7	118.8	NJ	2,564	1,419	19.4	7.6
CO	2,045	2,157	12.5	29.4	NM	676	1,168	8.5	14.4
CT	2,638	613	3.4	5.8	NY	3,501	1,688	12.8	20.4
DE	102	332	1.6	4.0	NC	1,421	4,259	17.5	96.3
DC	1,483	1,237	14.0	14.5	ND	106	439	1.7	9.5
FL.	5,863	6,670	29.0	56.1	OH	2,733	2,337	28.4	8.4
GA	3,966	4,332	32.9	63.0	OK	771	2,172	19.7	28.1
HI	928	2,331	16.8	34.4	OR	203	481	2.9	0.9
ID	133	346	1.4	4.0	PA	3,687	2,218	30.9	3.3
IL	1,256	1,988	15.3	29.0	RI	334	437	4.3	3.0
IN	1,552	1,022	12.3	1.2	SC	1,012	2,263	10.4	33.8
IA	371	244	1.4	0.4	SD	110	258	1.2	3.3
KS	763	1,079	5.6	17.2	TN	1,137	1,072	5.1	5.8
KY	874	1,723	10.1	33.4	TX	8,819	8,383	51.7	115.2
LA	1,078	1,333	8.4	16.3	UT	395	916	12.7	5.0
ME	797	525	5.5	1.8	VT	225	90	0.5	0.1
MD	4,137	3,265	35.6	29.9	VA	9,563	11,356	89.4	89.0
MA	4,675	843	8.6	3.0	WA	2,382	3,813	25.2	36.4
MI	1,241	764	8.4	1.2	WV	199	242	1.7	0.5
MN	960	393	2.5	0.9	WI	551	413	3.3	0.4
MS	1,912	1,301	10.3	12.5	WY	92	233	1.0	3.6

[1] Military awards for supplies, services, and construction. Net value of contracts of over $25,000 for work in each state and DC. Figures reflect impact of prime contracting on state distribution of defense work. Often the state in which a prime contractor is located in is not the state where the subcontracted work is done. See also headnote, Table 572. Undistributed civilians and military personnel, their payrolls, and prime contract awards for performance in classified locations are excluded.

Source: U.S. Dept. of Defense, *Atlas/Data Abstract for the United States and Selected Areas*, annual.

No. 574. Worldwide Military Expenditures: 1987 to 1995

[In billions of dollars. For military expenditures and Armed Forces by country, see Section 30. GNP=Gross national product]

COUNTRY GROUP	1987	1988	1989	1990	1991	1992	1993	1994	1995
Current dollars, total [1]	**1,051**	**1,080**	**1,089**	**1,106**	**1,049**	**974**	**912**	**879**	**865**
United States	288	293	304	306	280	305	298	288	278
Percent of total	27.4	27.1	27.9	27.7	26.7	31.3	32.6	32.8	32.1
Developed countries [2]	881	911	922	912	848	771	732	695	668
Developing countries [2]	170	169	167	193	200	203	180	184	197
NATO countries [3]	464	472	492	504	483	504	496	485	471
Constant (1995) dollars, total [1]	**1,360**	**1,349**	**1,305**	**1,271**	**1,159**	**1,048**	**957**	**901**	**865**
United States	373	366	364	352	310	328	312	295	278
Percent of total	27.4	27.1	27.9	27.7	26.7	31.3	32.6	32.8	32.1
Developed countries [2]	1,140	1,138	1,105	1,048	937	829	768	712	668
Developing countries [2]	220	211	200	222	221	219	189	189	197
NATO countries [3]	601	590	590	579	533	542	519	497	471
Percent of GNP	**5.0**	**4.8**	**4.5**	**4.3**	**3.9**	**3.6**	**3.3**	**3.0**	**2.8**
United States	6.1	5.8	5.6	5.3	4.7	4.9	4.5	4.2	3.8
Developed countries [2]	5.1	4.8	4.6	4.3	3.8	3.6	3.3	3.0	2.8
Developing countries [2]	4.9	4.4	4.1	4.4	4.3	3.6	3.0	2.8	2.8
NATO countries [3]	4.6	4.3	4.2	4.0	3.7	3.7	3.5	3.3	3.0

[1] Includes countries not shown separately. [2] Twenty-eight developed countries; see Table 575 for selected countries; for complete list, see source. [3] North Atlantic Treaty Organization.

No. 575. Arms Trade in Constant (1995) Dollars—Selected Countries: 1993 to 1995

[In millions of dollars, except percent. Because some countries exclude arms imports or exports from their trade statistics and their "total" imports and exports are therefore understated, and because arms transfers may be estimated independently of trade data, the ratio of arms to total imports or exports may be overstated and may even exceed 100 percent]

COUNTRY	1993	1994	1995 Total	Arms imports as percent of total imports	COUNTRY	1993	1994	1995 Total	Arms imports as percent of total imports
World total [1]	**32,220**	**26,720**	**31,940**	**0.7**	Iran	1,153	400	270	2.2
					Iraq	-	-	-	-
Exporters: [1]					Israel	1,153	615	340	1.1
Canada	786	277	280	0.1	Italy	115	123	110	0.1
China: Mainland	1,153	743	625	0.6	Japan	603	718	625	0.2
Czech Republic	220	308	120	-					
France	1,153	1,538	2,200	0.1	Jordan	31	41	70	1.9
Poland	10	51	40	0.3	Kuwait	970	226	900	11.6
United Kingdom	4,823	5,228	5,200	0.1	Libya	-	10	-	-
United States	15,940	12,200	15,600	0.1	Morocco	73	113	50	0.6
Germany	1,782	1,435	1,200	0.1	Nicaragua	5	-	-	-
Importers: [1]					North Korea	5	92	100	5.8
Afghanistan	5	21	20	(NA)	Oman	147	297	460	10.8
Algeria	21	144	230	2.2	Pakistan	577	297	480	4.2
Angola	294	718	90	(NA)	Peru	42	62	280	3.0
Argentina	21	10	40	0.2	Poland	5	5	90	0.3
Australia	708	410	900	1.5					
					Romania	-	-	-	-
Canada	231	277	210	0.1	Saudi Arabia	7,968	6,560	8,600	31.3
Cuba	105	-	-	-	South Korea	1,153	1,435	1,100	0.8
Czech Republic	5	92	-	-	Spain	335	564	675	0.6
Egypt	1,468	1,230	1,900	16.2	Syria	283	41	70	1.5
El Salvador	42	31	20	0.7					
					Turkey	1,258	1,128	700	2.0
Ethiopia	5	-	-	(NA)	United Kingdom	335	215	190	0.1
Germany	681	308	310	0.1	*United States*	*1,468*	*1,128*	*1,000*	*0.1*
Greece	891	482	825	(NA)	Venezuela	73	82	90	0.8
Hungary	970	10	30	0.2	Vietnam	10	82	200	2.7
India	283	236	410	1.2	Yemen (Sanaa)	21	256	140	(NA)

- Represents or rounds to zero. NA Not available. [1] Includes countries not shown separately.

Source of Tables 574 and 575: U.S. Arms Control and Disarmament Agency, *World Military Expenditures and Arms Transfers*, annual.

No. 576. Arms Transfers—Cumulative Value for Period 1993-95, by Major Supplier and Recipient Country

[In millions of dollars]

RECIPIENT	Total [1]	SUPPLIER					
		United States	United Kingdom	Russia	West Germany	France	China: Mainland
World, total	**88,915**	**42,775**	**14,955**	**7,925**	**4,335**	**4,760**	**2,470**
Africa [1]	3,350	370	10	795	10	360	105
North Africa	740	230	10	260	-	70	-
Algeria	395	10	-	260	-	-	-
Libya	10	-	-	-	-	-	-
Morocco	235	140	-	-	-	-	-
Subsahara Africa	1,810	140	-	535	10	160	95
Angola	1,060	-	-	525	-	-	-
Nigeria	50	-	-	-	-	-	-
Rwanda	100	80	-	-	-	-	-
Zimbabwe	10	-	-	-	-	-	-
Americas:							
Central America & Carribean . .	305	180	-	105	-	10	-
Cuba	100	-	-	100	-	-	-
El Salvador	100	100	-	-	-	-	-
North America (NAFTA)	4,440	490	1,200	70	310	430	100
Canada	710	400	-	-	-	290	-
Mexico	155	90	-	-	-	-	-
United States	3,575	(X)	1,200	-	310	130	100
South America	2,230	370	150	120	200	250	25
Brazil	430	80	80	-	160	60	-
Chile	525	20	-	-	-	-	-
Colombia	155	80	-	-	-	-	-
Venezuela	250	80	-	-	-	60	-
Asia:							
Central Asia & Caucasus	535	-	-	445	-	-	-
Middle East	36,940	18,415	11,450	1,715	380	2,020	8,470
Egypt	4,495	4,100	-	-	-	130	-
Iran	1,780	-	-	1,000	-	-	490
Israel	2,060	1,700	-	-	300	-	60
Kuwait	2,055	1,600	160	240	-	-	-
Saudi Arabia	22,555	10,100	10,300	-	60	1,400	90
Syria	380	-	-	120	-	-	-
United Arab Emirates	1,735	500	260	280	-	270	-
Yemen	410	-	-	-	-	-	160
East Asia	15,895	8,130	1,670	2,235	1,650	170	535
Burma	370	-	-	-	-	-	310
China:							
Mainland	1,610	40	-	1,200	-	-	(X)
Taiwan	3,215	3,200	-	-	-	-	-
Indonesia	300	70	100	-	110	-	-
Japan	1,960	1,900	-	-	-	-	-
Korea, South	3,505	1,400	290	-	1,500	100	-
Malaysia	1,920	40	1,200	550	-	-	-
Singapore	560	220	-	-	-	-	-
Thailand	1,575	1,100	-	-	-	-	110
South Asia	2,660	115	120	740	-	430	865
India	890	100	-	675	-	-	-
Pakistan	1,300	10	90	-	-	430	625
Europe	15,740	8,915	325	1,700	1,280	1,090	-
Eastern Europe	2,470	30	-	1,315	125	-	-
Hungary	950	10	-	-	110	-	-
Western Europe	13,270	8,885	325	385	1,155	1,090	-
Belgium	775	300	-	-	-	280	-
Denmark	220	190	-	-	-	-	-
Finland	375	40	100	-	-	160	-
France	370	260	-	-	-	(X)	-
Germany	1,270	1,000	-	-	(X)	-	-
Greece	2,195	1,200	-	-	-	525	60
Italy	330	250	60	-	-	-	-
Netherlands	560	525	-	-	-	-	-
Norway	390	210	-	-	-	120	-
Portugal	515	410	60	-	-	-	-
Spain	1,580	1,300	-	-	-	-	-
Sweden	395	100	-	5	280	-	-
Switzerland	290	60	-	-	160	-	-
Turkey	3,020	2,300	-	350	90	170	-
United Kingdom	735	725	(X)	-	-	-	-
Oceania	2,170	1,140	30	-	500	-	-
Australia	2,030	1,100	-	-	500	-	-
New Zealand	120	40	-	-	-	-	-

- Represents $2.5 million or less.   X Not applicable.   [1] Includes countries not shown separately.

Source: U.S. Arms Control and Disarmament Agency, *World Military Expenditures and Arms Transfers*, annual.

No. 577. U.S. Military Sales and Assistance to Foreign Governments: 1988 to 1996

[In millions of dollars, except as indicated. For fiscal year ending in year shown; see text, Section 9. Department of Defense (DOD) sales deliveries cover deliveries against DOD sales orders sales orders authorized under Arms Export Control Act, as well as earlier and applicable legislation. For details regarding individual programs, see source]

ITEM	1988	1989	1990	1991	1992	1993	1994	1995	1996
Military sales agreements	10,959	9,738	13,861	17,673	14,290	31,777	13,413	8,868	10,386
Military constr. sales agrmts	219	75	644	770	148	589	59	25	83
Military sales deliveries [1]	9,137	7,589	8,074	9,058	10,409	11,453	9,566	11,923	12,732
Military sales financing . . . . [2] . .	4,049	4,273	4,758	4,693	4,274	4,124	3,917	3,712	3,836
Military assistance programs [2] . [3] .	697	535	137	177	116	540	321	112	337
Military assist. program delivery [3] .	56	53	27	150	87	55	1	8	44
IMET program/deliveries [3]	45	46	43	46	42	43	22	26	39

[1] Includes military construction sales deliveries. [2] Also includes Military Assistance Service Funded (MASF) program data, section 506(a) drawdown authority, and MAP Merger Funds. [3] Includes Military Assistance Service Funded (MASF) program data and section 506(a) drawdown authority.

No. 578. U.S. Military Sales Deliveries, by Country: 1988 to 1996

[In millions of dollars. For fiscal years ending in year shown; see text, Section 9. Represents Department of Defense military sales]

COUNTRY	1988	1989	1990	1991	1992	1993	1994	1995	1996
Total [1]	9,137	7,589	8,074	9,158	10,410	11,453	9,566	11,923	12,732
Australia	850	583	381	205	156	259	362	303	232
Canada	214	144	118	164	123	230	159	128	146
China: Taiwan	503	394	455	549	711	738	739	1,200	1,192
Egypt.	497	322	441	572	1,091	1,276	1,029	1,740	1,262
Germany	382	632	366	476	511	356	148	240	411
Greece	129	137	114	124	163	226	234	224	212
Israel	754	230	146	238	721	782	446	329	388
Italy	62	64	61	61	52	48	105	54	180
Japan	218	206	267	490	579	380	784	727	811
Kuwait	41	46	52	111	858	873	221	487	651
Netherlands	321	387	398	392	244	114	140	159	397
Portugal	15	32	72	40	89	83	228	91	21
Saudi Arabia	1,297	965	1,139	3,018	2,611	3,595	2,118	3,697	2,937
South Korea	326	316	328	230	309	306	374	431	393
Spain	637	656	407	155	138	203	402	171	435
Thailand	290	210	176	178	100	106	151	357	350
Turkey	688	619	723	617	703	756	892	345	618
United Kingdom	211	131	205	243	154	227	202	108	153

[1] Includes countries not shown.

Source of Tables 577 and 578: U.S. Defense Security Assistance Agency, *Foreign Military Sales, Foreign Military Construction Sales,* and *Military Assistance Facts,* annual.

No. 579. Summary of Active and Reserve Military Personnel and Forces

ITEM	Cold War (1990)	1998	Force target	ITEM	Cold War (1990)	1998	Force target
Military personnel (1,000):				Battle force ships [2]	546	346	330-346
Active	2,069	1,431	1,422	Marine Corps:			
Guard and Reserve	1,128	892	889	Divisions:			
Military Forces:				Active	3	3	3
Army divisions:				Reserve	1	1	1
Active	18	10	10	Air wings:			
National Guard	10	[1]8	[1]8	Active	3	3	3
Air Force:				Reserve	1	1	1
Fighter wing:				Strategic nuclear forces:			
Active	24	13	13	Intercontinental ballistic			
Reserve	12	7	7	missiles	1,000	550	500
Navy aircraft carriers:				Warheads	2,450	2,000	[3]500
Active	15	11	11	Ballistic missile submarines . . .	31	18	[3]14
Training	1	1	1	Sea-launched ballistic missiles.	568	432	336
Navy air wings:				Warheads	4,864	3,456	[3][4]1,750
Active	13	10	10	Heavy bombers	324	[5]87	[5]92
Reserve	2	1	1				

[1] Plus 15 enhanced readiness brigades. [2] Includes active and reserve ships. [3] Upon entry-into-force of START II. [4] Not over 1,750. [5] Does not include 95 B-1 bombers dedicated to conventional missions.

Source: U.S. Office of Management and Budget, *Budget of the United States Government,* annual.

No. 580. Department of Defense Manpower: 1950 to 1995

[In thousands. As of end of fiscal year; see text, Section 9. Includes National Guard, Reserve, and retired regular personnel on extended or continuous active duty. Excludes Coast Guard. Other officer candidates are included under enlisted personnel]

YEAR	Total [1,2]	ARMY Total [2]	ARMY White	ARMY Black	ARMY Officers	ARMY Enlisted	NAVY [3] Total [2]	NAVY White	NAVY Black	NAVY Officers	NAVY Enlisted	MARINE CORPS Total [2]	MARINE CORPS White	MARINE CORPS Black	MARINE CORPS Officers	MARINE CORPS Enlisted	AIR FORCE Total [2]	AIR FORCE White	AIR FORCE Black	AIR FORCE Officers	AIR FORCE Enlisted
1950	1,459	593	(NA)	(NA)	73	519	381	(NA)	(NA)	45	333	74	(NA)	(NA)	7	67	411	(NA)	(NA)	57	354
1955	2,935	1,109	(NA)	(NA)	122	986	661	(NA)	(NA)	75	583	205	(NA)	(NA)	18	187	960	(NA)	(NA)	137	823
1960	2,475	873	(NA)	(NA)	101	770	617	(NA)	(NA)	70	545	171	(NA)	(NA)	16	154	815	(NA)	(NA)	130	683
1965	2,654	969	(NA)	(NA)	112	855	670	(NA)	(NA)	78	588	190	(NA)	(NA)	17	173	825	(NA)	(NA)	132	690
1966	3,092	1,200	(NA)	(NA)	118	1,080	743	(NA)	(NA)	80	659	262	(NA)	(NA)	21	241	887	(NA)	(NA)	131	753
1967	3,375	1,442	(NA)	(NA)	144	1,297	750	(NA)	(NA)	82	664	285	(NA)	(NA)	24	262	897	(NA)	(NA)	135	759
1968	3,546	1,570	(NA)	(NA)	166	1,402	764	(NA)	(NA)	85	674	307	(NA)	(NA)	25	283	905	(NA)	(NA)	140	762
1969	3,458	1,512	(NA)	(NA)	173	1,337	774	(NA)	(NA)	85	684	310	(NA)	(NA)	26	284	862	(NA)	(NA)	135	723
1970	3,065	1,323	(NA)	(NA)	167	1,153	691	(NA)	(NA)	81	606	260	(NA)	(NA)	25	235	791	(NA)	(NA)	130	657
1971	2,713	1,124	(NA)	(NA)	149	972	622	(NA)	(NA)	75	542	212	(NA)	(NA)	22	191	755	(NA)	(NA)	126	625
1972	2,322	811	(NA)	(NA)	121	687	587	(NA)	(NA)	73	511	198	(NA)	(NA)	20	178	726	(NA)	(NA)	122	600
1973	2,252	801	(NA)	(NA)	116	682	564	(NA)	(NA)	71	490	196	(NA)	(NA)	19	177	691	(NA)	(NA)	115	572
1974	2,162	783	(NA)	(NA)	106	674	546	(NA)	(NA)	67	475	189	(NA)	(NA)	19	170	644	(NA)	(NA)	110	529
1975	2,128	784	(NA)	(NA)	103	678	535	(NA)	(NA)	66	466	196	(NA)	(NA)	19	177	613	(NA)	(NA)	105	503
1976	2,082	779	(NA)	(NA)	99	678	525	(NA)	(NA)	64	458	192	(NA)	(NA)	19	174	585	(NA)	(NA)	100	481
1977	2,075	782	(NA)	(NA)	98	680	530	(NA)	(NA)	63	462	192	(NA)	(NA)	19	173	571	(NA)	(NA)	96	470
1978	2,062	772	(NA)	(NA)	98	670	530	(NA)	(NA)	63	463	191	(NA)	(NA)	18	172	570	(NA)	(NA)	96	470
1979	2,027	759	(NA)	(NA)	97	657	523	(NA)	(NA)	62	457	185	(NA)	(NA)	18	167	559	(NA)	(NA)	95	459
1980	2,051	777	503	229	99	674	527	436	55	63	460	188	142	39	18	170	558	460	80	98	456
1981	2,083	781	502	232	102	675	540	443	58	65	470	191	145	39	18	172	570	468	83	99	467
1982	2,109	780	504	230	103	673	553	450	62	67	481	192	149	38	19	173	583	476	87	102	476
1983	2,123	780	512	220	106	669	558	462	66	68	485	194	152	37	20	174	592	483	88	105	483
1984	2,138	780	520	215	108	668	565	455	67	69	491	196	153	36	20	176	597	486	89	106	486
1985	2,151	781	523	211	110	667	571	459	70	71	495	198	152	37	20	178	602	488	90	108	489
1986	2,169	781	524	210	110	667	581	464	75	72	504	199	151	38	20	179	608	491	92	109	495
1987	2,174	781	519	212	108	668	587	467	81	72	510	200	150	38	20	179	607	489	92	107	495
1988	2,138	772	507	213	107	660	593	466	85	72	516	197	147	38	20	177	576	462	88	105	467
1989	2,130	770	497	218	107	658	593	461	91	72	516	197	146	38	20	177	571	458	87	104	463
1990	2,044	732	466	213	104	624	579	446	93	72	503	197	145	38	20	177	535	428	82	100	431
1991	1,986	711	452	204	104	603	570	439	92	71	495	194	144	36	20	174	510	409	77	97	409
1992	1,807	610	388	173	95	511	542	415	88	69	468	185	138	32	19	165	470	377	70	90	376
1993	1,705	572	365	158	88	480	510	390	84	66	439	178	134	30	18	160	444	357	65	84	356
1994	1,610	541	344	147	85	452	469	355	78	62	403	174	131	28	18	156	426	341	62	81	341
1995	1,518	509	322	137	83	422	435	326	75	59	372	175	130	28	18	157	400	318	58	78	318

NA Not available.   [1] Beginning 1980, excludes Navy Reserve personnel on active duty for Training and Administration of Reserves (TARS). From 1969, the full-time Guard and Reserve.   [2] Includes Cadets and other not shown separately.   [3] Prior to 1980, includes Navy Reserve personnel on active duty for Training and Administration of Reserves (TARS).

Source: U.S. Dept. of Defense, Selected Manpower Statistics, annual.

No. 581. Military Installations in the United States: 1997

[Represents bases with active-duty populations of 300 or more. Excludes the Coast Guard]

STATE AND BRANCH	Active duty personnel	Family members	Civilians	STATE AND BRANCH	Active duty personnel	Family members	Civilians
United States	**1,275,596**	**1,568,828**	**624,294**	Michigan	1,026	-	1,335
Alabama	20,219	14,969	28,633	Air Force	1,026	-	1,335
Army	11,297	11,895	20,633	Minnesota	(X)	(X)	(X)
Navy	4,461	1,537	4,000	Mississippi	19,394	18,301	7,841
Air Force	4,461	1,537	4,000	Navy	7,088	1,655	2,435
Alaska	16,688	24,453	4,409	Air Force	12,306	16,646	5,406
Army	6,700	9,600	2,580	Missouri	7,828	12,200	4,635
Navy	475	(NA)	46	Army	4,800	6,000	4,000
Air Force	9,513	14,853	1,783	Air Force	3,028	6,200	635
Arizona	23,061	45,897	7,463	Montana	3,871	5,159	441
Army	5,750	11,700	4,000	Air Force	3,871	5,159	441
Marine Corps	5,311	7,197	1,064	Nebraska	9,780	15,500	2,920
Air Force	12,000	27,000	2,399	Air Force	9,780	15,500	2,920
Arkansas	13,678	14,910	2,714	Nevada	7,863	12,133	2,900
Army	6839	7455	1357	Navy	1,100	2,000	1,400
Air Force	6,839	7,455	1,357	Air Force	6,763	10,133	1,500
California	188,871	159,238	73,398	New Hampshire	401	967	3,630
Army	7,698	9,384	5,351	Navy	401	967	3,630
Navy	100,884	41,044	29,333	New Jersey	9,748	11,725	15,725
Marine Corps	56,589	68,847	9,755	Army	2,048	2,220	9,968
Air Force	23,700	39,963	28,959	Navy	2,199	1,100	2,795
Colorado	34,815	49,671	8,982	Air Force	5,501	8,405	2,962
Army	15,000	32,000	3,300	New Mexico	15,194	25,356	21,876
Air Force	19,815	17,671	5,682	Army	786	1,637	6,927
Connecticut	9,000	22,000	1,800	Air Force	14,408	23,719	14,949
Navy	9,000	22,000	1,800	New York	14,395	22,187	6,069
Delaware	4,040	6,000	1,128	Army	11,895	19,187	6,069
Air Force	4,040	6,000	1,128	Navy	2,500	3,000	-
District of Columbia	9,115	4,190	9,200	North Carolina	112,424	173,762	17,380
Army	3,555	4,150	3,540	Army	49,000	78,000	4,783
Navy	2,920	-	4,620	Marine Corps	54,003	88,535	11,083
Marine Corps	1,168	40	-	Air Force	9,421	7,227	1,514
Air Force	1,472	-	1,040	North Dakota	9,940	13,546	1,712
Florida	65,936	108,699	27,378	Air Force	9,940	13,546	1,712
Navy	39,151	54,312	14,346	Ohio	8,900	12,750	16,650
Air Force	26,785	54,387	13,032	Air Force	8,900	12,750	16,650
Georgia	68,839	100,181	40,309	Oklahoma	26,966	44,682	21,762
Army	53,696	70,376	20,005	Army	14,585	38,982	5,668
Navy	5,907	19,950	4,308	Air Force	12,381	5,700	16,094
Marine Corps	900	1,700	3,175	Oregon	(X)	(X)	(X)
Air Force	8,336	8,155	12,821	Pennsylvania	2,284	4,616	1,729
Hawaii	50,984	42,140	19,744	Army	713	1,866	951
Army	15,787	12,895	3,223	Navy	1,571	2,750	778
Navy	23,128	22,962	12,554	Rhode Island	3,652	3,000	3,976
Marine Corps	8,671	6,283	2,674	Navy	3,677	3,000	3,897
Air Force	3,398	-	1,293	South Carolina	25,661	33,326	5,852
Idaho	4,274	3,400	430	Army	8,679	7,762	931
Navy	(1)	(1)	(1)	Navy	1,072	-	669
Air Force	4,274	3,400	430	Marine Corps	5,750	9,164	1,477
Illinois	25,635	22,877	13,347	Air Force	10,160	16,400	2,775
Army	2,120	3,560	8,390	South Dakota	3,500	5,050	500
Navy	16,719	10,000	2,418	Air Force	3,500	5,050	500
Air Force	6,796	9,317	2,539	Tennessee	2,272	2,192	1,707
Indiana	(1)	(1)	(1)	Navy	2,272	2,192	1,707
Army	(1)	(1)	(1)	Texas	120,456	150,118	59,368
Iowa	(X)	(X)	(X)	Army	67,934	109,854	18,854
Kansas	18,621	27,350	5,755	Navy	7,996	8,378	8,016
Army	15,641	20,600	5,330	Air Force	44,526	31,886	32,498
Air Force	2,980	6,750	425	Utah	4,700	-	9,800
Kentucky	29,906	46,373	11,491	Air Force	4,700	-	9,800
Army	29,906	46,373	11,491	Vermont	(X)	(X)	(X)
Louisiana	18,506	15,362	7,559	Virginia	161,678	167,722	77,403
Army	8,851	13,782	2,363	Army	23,526	19,472	24,314
Navy	3,638	1,580	3,352	Navy	130,152	144,750	50,289
Air Force	6,017	-	1,844	Marine Corps	8,000	3,500	2,800
Maine	3,474	3,550	891	Air Force	8,985	13,000	2,256
Navy	3,474	3,550	891	Washington	60,884	91,517	23,892
Maryland	30,691	24,988	45,829	Army	20,000	22,100	5,400
Army	14,255	14,304	35,755	Navy	31,837	56,704	15,325
Navy	10,446	2,684	7,981	Marine Corps	5,339	14,679	541
Air Force	5,990	8,000	2,093	Air Force	9,047	12,713	3,167
Massachusetts	2,622	1,755	1,872	West Virginia	(X)	(X)	(X)
Army	(1)	(1)	(1)	Wisconsin	304	816	2,259
Navy	(1)	(1)	(1)	Army	304	816	2,259
Air Force	2,622	1,755	1,872	Wyoming	3,500	4,200	600
				Air Force	3,500	4,200	600

- Represents or rounds to zero.   NA Not available.   X Not applicable.   [1]Closed or scheduled to close.

Source: Army Times Publishing Co. Springfield, VA 22159, *Guide to Military Installations in the U.S.*, annual.

No. 582. Military Personnel on Active Duty, by Location: 1980 to 1996

[In thousands. As of end of fiscal year; see text, Section 9]

ITEM	1980	1985	1988	1989	1990	1991	1992	1993	1994	1995	1996
Total.	2,051	2,151	2,138	2,130	2,044	1,986	1,807	1,705	1,611	1,518	1,472
Shore-based [1]	1,840	1,920	1,891	1,884	1,794	1,743	1,589	1,505	1,431	1,351	1,317
Afloat [2]	211	231	248	246	252	243	218	200	180	167	155
United States [3]	1,562	1,636	1,598	1,620	1,437	1,539	1,463	1,397	1,324	1,280	1,231
Foreign countries	488	516	541	510	609	448	344	308	287	238	240

[1] Includes Navy personnel temporarily on shore.   [2] Includes Marine Corps.   [3] Includes outlying areas.

Source: U.S. Dept. of Defense, *Selected Manpower Statistics*, annual.

No. 583. U.S. Military Personnel on Active Duty in Foreign Countries: 1996

[As of end of fiscal year]

COUNTRY	1996	COUNTRY	1996	COUNTRY	1996
In foreign countries [1] .	**240,421**	Estonia.	2	Nicaragua	15
Ashore	213,467	Ethopia.	10	Niger	6
Afloat	26,954	Fiji.	2	Nigeria	16
Albania.	3	Finland	17	Norway.	104
Algeria.	8	France	73	Oman.	30
Angola	3	Georgia	2	Pakistan	26
Antarctica	19	Germany.	48,878	Panama	6,435
Antigua.	2	Ghana	7	Paraguay	10
Argentina	25	Gibraltar	4	Peru.	26
Armenia	1	Greece	507	Philippines.	138
Australia	328	Greenland	141	Poland	20
Austria	37	Guatemala	17	Portugal	1,075
Azerbaijan	1	Guinea	6	Qatar	43
Bahamas, The	53	Haiti	277	Rep. of Korea	36,539
Bahrain.	598	Honduras	865	Romania	12
Bangladesh	10	Hong Kong	29	Russia	74
Barbados	11	Hungary	6,523	Saudi Arabia	1,587
Belarus	2	Iceland	1,893	Senegal	11
Belgium	1,646	India.	24	Serbia.	8
Belize	2	Indonesia	43	Sierra Leone	6
Bolivia	24	Ireland	8	Singapore	158
Bosnia and Herzegovina . . .	15,003	Israel	44	Slovakia	4
Botswana	7	Italy	12,401	South Africa.	23
Brazil	47	Jamaica	10	Spain	2,746
Bulgaria	14	Japan	42,962	Sri Lanka	7
Burma	11	Jordan	24	St. Helena	3
Burundi	5	Kazakhstan	7	Suriname	2
Cambodia	5	Kenya.	29	Sweden	13
Cameroon	9	Korea, Republic of	36,539	Switzerland	24
Canada.	208	Kuwait	5,531	Syria	11
Chad	9	Kyrgyzstan	1	Tanzania, U. Rep. of . . .	5
Chile	24	Laos.	3	Thailand	242
China	32	Latvia	1	Togo.	6
Colombia.	34	Lebanon	2	Trinidad and Tabago . . .	32
Congo	5	Liberia	9	Tunisia	19
Costa Rica	9	Lithuania	2	Turkey	2,922
Cote D'Ivoire	19	Luxembourg	9	Turkmenistan	1
Croatia	4,007	Macedonia	501	Uganda	9
Cuba (Guantanamo)	1,886	Madagascar.	6	Ukraine.	8
Cyprus	50	Malaysia	19	United Arab Emirates. . . .	23
Czech Republic	10	Mali	6	United Kingdom	11,662
Denmark.	38	Malta	8	Uruguay	9
Diego Garcia	878	Mexico	35	Uzbekistan	1
Djibouti	7	Moldova	1	Venezuela	30
Dominican Republic	10	Morocco	17	Vietnam	6
Ecuador	70	Mozambique	5	Yemen	11
Egypt	1,066	Nepal	6	Zaire	9
El Salvador	26	Netherlands.	747	Zambabwe	8
Eritrea	1	New Zealand	32	Zambia.	6

[1] Includes areas not shown separately.

Source: U.S. Department of Defense, *Selected Manpower Statistics*, annual.

No. 584. Coast Guard Personnel on Active Duty: 1970 to 1997

[As of end of fiscal year; see text, Section 9]

YEAR	Total	Officers	Cadets	Enlisted	YEAR	Total	Officers	Cadets	Enlisted
1970.	37,689	5,512	653	31,524	1992.	39,388	7,507	919	30,962
1975.	36,788	5,630	1,177	29,981	1993.	39,234	7,628	907	30,699
1980.	39,381	6,463	877	32,041	1994.	37,802	7,656	881	29,265
1985.	38,595	6,775	733	31,087	1995.	36,731	7,462	841	28,401
1990.	36,939	6,876	927	29,136	1996.	35,229	7,270	830	27,129
1991.	38,377	7,192	900	30,285	1997.	34,890	7,100	845	26,945

Source: U.S. Dept. of Transportation, *Annual Report of the Secretary of Transportation*.

No. 585. Armed Forces Personnel—Summary of Major Conflicts

[For Revolutionary War, number of personnel serving not known, but estimates range from 184,000 to 250,000; for War of 1812, 286,730 served; for Mexican War, 78,718 served. Dates of the major conflicts may differ from those specified in various laws providing benefits for veterans]

ITEM	Unit	Civil War [1]	Spanish-American War	World War I	World War II	Korean conflict	Vietnam conflict
Personnel serving [2]	1,000	2,213	307	4,735	[3]16,113	[4]5,720	[5]8,744
Average duration of service	Months	20	8	12	33	19	23
Service abroad:							
Personnel serving [8]	Percent	(NA)	[6]29	53	73	[7]56	(NA)
Average duration [8]	Months	(NA)	1.5	6	16	13	(NA)
Casualties:[9]							
Battle deaths [2]	1,000	140	(Z)	53	292	34	[10]47
Wounds not mortal [2]	1,000	282	2	204	671	103	[10]153
Draftees:							
Classified	1,000	777	(X)	24,234	36,677	9,123	[5]75,717
Examined	1,000	522	(X)	3,764	17,955	3,685	[5]8,611
Rejected	1,000	160	(X)	803	6,420	1,189	[5]3,880
Inducted	1,000	46	(X)	2,820	10,022	1,560	[5]1,759

NA Not available. X Not applicable. Z Fewer than 500. [1] Union forces only. Estimates of the number serving in Confederate forces range from 600,000 to 1.5 million. [2] Source: U.S. Department of Defense, *Selected Manpower Statistics*, annual. [3] Covers Dec. 1, 1941, to Dec. 31, 1946. [4] Covers June 25, 1950, to July 27, 1953. [5] Covers Aug. 4, 1964, to Jan. 27, 1973. [6] Army and Marines only. [7] Excludes Navy. Covers July 1950 through Jan. 1955. Far East area only. [8] During hostilities only. [9] For periods covered, see footnotes 3, 4, and 5. [10] Covers Jan. 1, 1961, to Jan. 27, 1973. Includes known military service personnel who have died from combat related wounds.

Source: Except as noted, the President's Commission on Veterans' Pensions, Veterans' *Benefits in the United States*, Vol. I, 1956; and U.S. Dept. of Defense, unpublished data.

No. 586. Enlisted Military Personnel Accessions: 1990 to 1996

[In thousands. For years ending Sept. 30]

BRANCH OF SERVICE	1990	1994	1995	1996	BRANCH OF SERVICE	1990	1994	1995	1996
Total	**461.1**	**373.1**	**357.3**	**367.6**	First enlistments	62.1	37.6	36.4	39.2
First enlistments	216.4	160.5	160.0	174.6	Reenlistments	58.6	45.0	41.4	40.6
Reenlistments	237.0	188.5	180.8	181.6	Marine Corps	47.7	44.6	46.7	48.7
Reserves to active duty	15.6	24.0	16.6	12.0	First enlistments	32.9	32.2	34.4	34.5
Army	181.7	138.0	135.9	146.0	Reenlistments	14.4	11.7	11.9	0.4
First enlistments	84.8	60.3	57.7	69.7	Air Force	104.4	84.5	81.3	81.6
Reenlistments	96.5	77.6	77.7	76.2	First enlistments	36.6	30.5	31.4	31.2
Navy	135.3	105.9	93.4	91.3	Reenlistments	67.5	54.0	49.7	50.3

Source: U.S. Dept. of Defense, *Selected Manpower Statistics*, annual.

No. 587. Military Personnel on Active Duty: 1990 to 1996

[In thousands. As of Sept. 30]

RANK/GRADE	1990	1991	1992	1993	1994	1995	1996
Total [1]	**2,043.7**	**1,985.6**	**1,807.2**	**1,705.1**	**1,610.5**	**1,518.2**	**1,471.7**
Recruit—E-1	97.6	74.6	83.2	75.4	73.3	63.4	69.3
Private—E-2	140.3	125.8	110.9	114.1	108.2	99.7	99.0
Pvt. 1st class—E-3	280.1	275.6	233.5	214.6	208.4	197.1	200.4
Corporal—E-4	427.8	426.1	383.5	352.2	322.2	317.2	283.8
Sergeant—E-5	361.5	355.5	305.1	295.6	281.0	261.4	254.8
Staff Sgt.—E-6	239.1	238.9	227.4	214.6	198.1	180.5	172.6
Sgt. 1st class—E-7	134.1	134.2	130.5	124.7	119.7	109.3	107.7
Master Sgt.—E-8	38.0	36.1	33.2	31.6	29.9	28.8	28.8
Sgt. Major—E-9	15.3	14.8	13.5	12.8	12.1	11.1	10.7
Warrant Officer—W-1	3.2	2.8	2.2	2.4	2.4	2.0	2.1
Chief Warrant—W-4	3.0	3.0	2.7	2.4	2.4	2.2	2.0
2d Lt.—0-1	31.9	27.3	25.8	25.0	24.8	25.6	25.2
1st Lt.—0-2	37.9	37.6	33.5	29.7	27.3	26.1	25.8
Captain—0-3	106.6	106.1	100.2	93.0	89.2	84.3	81.0
Major—0-4	53.2	53.1	50.4	48.0	44.8	43.9	43.9
Lt. Colonel—0-5	32.3	32.2	30.9	29.5	29.0	28.7	28.2
Colonel—0-6	14.0	13.7	13.2	12.5	12.2	11.7	11.6
Brig. General—0-7	0.5	0.5	0.5	0.4	0.5	0.4	0.4
Major General—0-8	0.4	0.3	0.3	0.3	0.3	0.3	0.3
Lt. General—0-9	0.1	0.1	0.1	0.1	0.1	0.1	0.1
General—0-10	(Z)	(Z)	(Z)	(Z)	(Z)	(Z)	(Z)

Z Fewer than 50. [1] Includes cadets and midshipmen and warrant officers, W-2 and W-3.

Source: U.S. Dept. of Defense, *Selected Manpower Statistics*, annual, and Office of the Comptroller, unpublished data.

No. 588. Military Reserve Personnel: 1980 to 1997

[In thousands. As of end of fiscal year; see text, Section 9. Excludes U.S. Coast Guard Reserve. The ready reserve includes selected reservists who are intended to assist active forces in a war and the individual ready reserve who, in a major war, would be used to fill out active and reserve units and later would be a source of combat replacements; a portion of the ready reserve serves in an active status. The standby reserve cannot be called to active duty unless the Congress gives its explicit approval. The retired reserve represents a low potential for mobilization]

RESERVE STATUS AND BRANCH OF SERVICE	1980	1985	1987	1988	1989	1990	1991	1992	1993	1994	1995	1996	1997
Total reserves	**1,349**	**1,610**	**1,657**	**1,677**	**1,661**	**1,671**	**1,786**	**1,883**	**1,867**	**1,805**	**1,659**	**1,550**	**1,461**
Ready reserve	1,263	1,566	1,620	1,642	1,631	1,641	1,758	1,858	1,841	1,779	1,633	1,523	1,438
Standby reserve	86	44	38	34	29	29	28	25	26	26	26	28	23
Retired reserve	338	372	412	469	477	462	474	442	461	482	506	530	550
Army	804	1,045	1,064	1,070	1,062	1,050	1,124	1,156	1,132	1,077	1,001	921	862
Navy	207	214	238	244	248	252	271	297	302	317	280	262	238
Marine Corp	94	92	88	87	82	83	96	107	112	109	104	102	100
Air Force	243	259	268	275	270	286	295	323	321	302	274	265	261

Source: U.S. Dept. of Defense, *Official Guard and Reserve Manpower Strengths and Statistics*, quarterly.

No. 589. Ready Reserve Personnel Profile—Race, and Sex: 1990 to 1997

ITEM	RACE					PERCENT DISTRIBUTION			
	Total	White	Black	Asian	American Indian	White	Black	Asian	American Indian
1990	1,641,475	1,289,367	271,470	14,616	7,695	78.5	16.5	0.9	0.5
1993	1,840,650	1,425,255	309,699	21,089	9,068	77.4	16.8	1.1	0.5
1994	1,779,436	1,366,387	297,519	22,190	8,870	76.8	16.7	1.2	0.5
1995	1,633,497	1,254,592	273,847	21,792	8,591	76.8	16.8	1.3	0.5
1996	1,522,451	1,166,628	249,114	21,240	8,226	76.6	16.4	1.4	0.5
1997, total [1]	**1,437,722**	**1,102,234**	**229,950**	**21,412**	**8,115**	**76.7**	**16.0**	**1.5**	**0.6**
Male	1,214,511	956,215	170,425	18,224	6,580	78.7	14.0	1.5	0.5
Officers	187,339	160,468	12,729	2,370	469	85.7	6.8	1.3	0.3
Enlisted	1,027,172	795,747	157,696	15,854	6,111	77.5	15.4	1.5	0.6
Female	223,080	145,992	59,519	3,185	1,535	65.4	26.7	1.4	0.7
Officers	42,988	32,516	6,715	549	112	75.6	15.6	1.3	0.3
Enlisted	180,092	113,476	52,804	2,636	1,423	63.0	29.3	1.5	0.8

[1] Includes unknown sex.

Source: U.S. Dept. of Defense, *Official Guard and Reserve Manpower Strengths and Statistics*, annual.

No. 590. Military Reserve Costs: 1980 to 1995

[In millions of dollars. As of end of fiscal year; see text, Section 9. Army and Air Force data include National Guard]

TYPE OF COST	1980	1985	1989	1990	1991	1992	1993	1994	1995
Total	**7,969**	**19,414**	**19,797**	**21,526**	**21,811**	**21,867**	**22,825**	**20,269**	**20,424**
Operations and maintenance	3,526	5,734	6,694	6,687	7,398	7,714	8,095	8,173	8,832
Personnel	2,456	7,703	8,637	8,621	8,543	9,272	9,062	9,564	9,258
Procurement	1,459	5,009	3,520	4,914	4,480	3,533	4,398	1,168	1,102
Active-duty support	408	566	611	638	700	731	682	632	658
Construction	120	402	605	666	690	617	588	732	574

Source: U.S. Dept. of Defense, unpublished data.

No. 591. National Guard—Summary: 1980 to 1996

[As of end of fiscal year; see text, Section 9. Includes Puerto Rico]

ITEM	Unit	1980	1985	1990	1991	1992	1993	1994	1995	1996
Army National Guard:										
Units	Number	3,379	4,353	4,055	6,470	6,727	6,339	6,000	5,872	5,643
Personnel [1]	1,000	368	438	444	446	427	410	397	375	373
Funds obligated [2]	Bil. dol.	1.8	4.4	5.2	5.4	6.3	6.3	6.0	6.0	5.9
Value of equipment	Bil. dol.	7.6	18.8	29.0	29.0	29.0	31.0	31.0	33.0	33.0
Air National Guard:										
Units	Number	1,054	1,184	1,339	1,450	1,425	1,330	1,665	1,604	1,588
Personnel [1]	1,000	96	109	118	115	119	117	114	110	110
Funds obligated [2]	Bil. dol.	1.7	2.8	3.2	1.2	1.9	2.6	3.1	4.2	4.6
Value of equipment (est.) [3]	Bil. dol.	5.2	21.4	26.4	27.1	38.3	41.7	40.2	38.3	40.1

[1] Officers and enlisted personnel.　[2] Federal funds; includes personnel, operations, maintenance, and military construction.　[3] Beginning 1985, increase due to repricing of aircraft to current year dollars to reflect true replacement value. Beginning 1993 includes value of aircraft and support equipment.

Source: National Guard Bureau, *Annual Review of the Chief, National Guard Bureau;* and unpublished data.

No. 592. Veterans—States: 1997

[In thousands. As of end of fiscal year; see text, Section 9. Data were estimated starting with veteran's place of residence as of April 1, 1990, based on 1990 census, extended to later years on the basis of estimates of veteran interstate migration, separations from the Armed Forces, and mortality; not directly comparable with earlier estimates previously published by the VA. Excludes 541,000 whose only active-duty military service of less than 2 years occurred since Sept. 30, 1980, and who failed to satisfy the minimum service requirement. Also excludes a small indeterminate number of National Guard personnel or reservists who incurred service-connected disabilities while on an initial tour of active duty for training only]

STATE	Total veterans [1]	War veterans [1]	World War I	World War II	Korean conflict	Vietnam era [2]	Persian Gulf War
United States.	25,422	19,519	7	6,674	4,257	8,177	1,853
Alabama.	418	325	-	106	76	135	42
Alaska	64	44	-	7	7	30	3
Arizona.	452	346	-	127	81	146	27
Arkansas	252	198	-	70	44	79	24
California	2,747	2,060	1	684	470	936	156
Colorado.	374	286	-	81	63	144	26
Connecticut.	327	250	-	93	54	97	18
Delaware	77	58	-	20	12	24	6
District of Columbia	48	38	-	14	10	14	5
Florida	1,686	1,315	1	560	311	488	105
Georgia	673	497	-	136	104	246	57
Hawaii	114	84	-	24	19	42	8
Idaho	109	84	-	28	17	36	10
Illinois	1,038	811	-	282	170	316	75
Indiana.	580	443	-	144	92	180	46
Iowa	283	227	-	77	50	86	24
Kansas.	255	200	-	68	43	85	17
Kentucky	360	282	-	93	59	117	31
Louisiana	362	286	-	97	60	116	37
Maine.	151	115	-	36	24	51	13
Maryland	519	380	-	120	82	172	36
Massachusetts.	573	441	-	171	98	164	30
Michigan.	927	713	-	232	140	290	76
Minnesota.	451	345	-	107	73	149	30
Mississippi	227	178	-	62	41	67	26
Missouri	572	445	-	150	99	182	44
Montana.	92	73	-	24	15	30	8
Nebraska	163	128	-	42	30	51	13
Nevada	186	138	-	44	36	65	8
New Hampshire	133	99	-	30	21	46	9
New Jersey.	714	554	-	216	125	199	39
New Mexico	168	129	-	41	28	60	13
New York	1,485	1,146	-	423	244	411	112
North Carolina.	698	528	-	169	115	231	56
North Dakota.	57	45	-	14	10	18	5
Ohio	1,160	901	-	310	183	353	95
Oklahoma.	336	267	-	92	61	116	23
Oregon.	364	283	-	96	57	124	25
Pennsylvania.	1,329	1,041	-	401	219	376	95
Rhode Island.	106	83	-	33	18	31	7
South Carolina.	373	282	-	88	61	129	35
South Dakota	72	57	-	18	14	21	7
Tennessee	507	390	-	124	83	170	42
Texas.	1,599	1,223	-	383	265	576	124
Utah	134	106	-	37	23	44	10
Vermont	61	46	-	14	10	20	5
Virginia.	691	511	-	151	116	258	51
Washington.	620	466	-	140	100	231	41
West Virginia.	194	157	-	56	35	59	17
Wisconsin.	496	380	-	127	79	151	38
Wyoming	45	36	-	11	8	16	4

- Represents zero.   [1] Veterans who served in more than one wartime period are counted only once. "All Veterans" includes Vietnam era (no prior wartime service), Korean conflict (no prior wartime service), World War II, post Vietnam era, Persian Gulf War era, and other.   [2] Excludes reservists.

Source: U.S. Dept. of Veterans Affairs, Management Sciences Service (008B2), Annual Report of the Secretary of Veterans Affairs.

No. 593. Veterans Living in the United States and Puerto Rico, by Age and by Service: 1997

[In thousands, except as indicated. As of July, 1. Estimated. Excludes whose active military service of less than 2 years occurred since Sept. 30, 1980. See headnote, Table 592]

AGE	Total veterans	WARTIME VETERANS						Peace-time veterans
		Total [1]	Persian Gulf	Vietnam era	Korean conflict	World War II	World War I	
All ages	25,551	19,614	1,864	8,212	4,290	6,694	7	5,937
Under 30 years old. . . .	1,000	842	842	-	-	-	-	158
30-34 years old	1,192	403	403	-	-	-	-	788
35-39 years old	1,470	247	191	58	-	-	-	1,223
40-44 years old	1,798	1,149	189	1,060	-	-	-	650
45-49 years old	2,922	2,781	153	2,755	-	-	-	141
50-54 years old	3,152	2,793	61	2,778	-	-	-	358
55-59 years old	2,312	942	18	878	65	-	-	1,370
60-64 years old	2,555	1,543	5	297	1,380	-	-	1,012
65 years old and over . . .	9,149	8,913	1	385	2,844	6,694	7	236

- Represents zero.   [1] Veterans who served in more than one wartime period are counted only once.

Source: U.S. Dept. of Veterans Affairs, Office of Policy and Planning, *Veteran Population*, annual.

No. 594. Disabled Veterans Receiving Compensation: 1980 to 1997

[In thousands, except as indicated. As of end of fiscal year; see text, Section 9. Represents veterans receiving compensation for service-connected disabilities. Totally disabled refers to veterans with any disability, mental or physical, deemed to be total and permanent which prevents the individual from maintaining a livelihood and are rated for disability at 100 percent]

MILITARY SERVICE	1980	1985	1990	1991	1992	1993	1994	1995	1996	1997
Disabled, all periods [1]	2,274	2,240	2,184	2,179	2,181	2,198	2,218	2,236	2,253	2,263
Peace-time.	262	352	444	468	500	471	492	514	529	539
World War I [1]	30	12	3	3	2	1	1	1	(Z)	(Z)
World War II.	1,193	1,049	876	841	805	769	731	692	655	616
Korea.	236	223	209	205	202	198	195	191	187	182
Vietnam.	553	604	652	662	671	682	694	705	714	724
Persian Gulf.	(X)	(X)	(X)	(X)	(X)	76	106	134	168	202
Totally disabled, all periods [1] .	121	136	131	131	132	135	138	143	150	156
Peace-time.	20	26	27	27	28	28	29	30	32	33
World War I [1]	3	1	(Z)	(Z)	(Z)	(Z)	(Z)	(Z)	(Z)	(Z)
World War II.	51	54	43	41	39	37	36	34	33	31
Korea.	16	17	16	16	15	15	15	15	15	15
Vietnam.	31	38	44	46	49	52	56	61	67	73
Persian Gulf.	(X)	(X)	(X)	(X)	(X)	2	2	3	3	4
Compensation (mil. dol.)	6,104	8,270	9,284	9,612	10,031	10,545	11,056	11,644	11,072	13,004

X Not applicable.   Z Less than 500.   [1] Includes Spanish-American War and Mexican Border service, not shown separately.

Source: U.S. Dept. of Veterans Affairs, *Annual Report of the Secretary of Veterans Affairs;* and unpublished data.

No. 595. Veterans Benefits—Expenditures, by Program: 1980 to 1997

[In millions of dollars. For fiscal years ending in year shown; see text, Section 9. Beginning with fiscal year 1989, data are for outlays]

PROGRAM	1980	1985	1990	1992	1993	1994	1995	1996	1997
Total.	23,187	29,359	28,998	33,900	35,460	37,401	37,775	36,915	39,277
Medical programs.	6,042	9,227	11,582	13,815	14,603	15,430	16,255	16,337	16,900
Construction	300	557	661	639	622	695	641	698	597
General operating expenses.	605	765	811	920	904	906	954	961	1,063
Compensation and pension	11,044	14,037	14,674	16,282	16,882	17,188	17,765	17,056	19,284
Vocational rehabilitation and education.	2,350	1,164	452	695	863	1,119	1,127	1,212	1,287
All other [1]	2,846	3,609	818	1,549	1,586	2,062	1,034	652	145

[1] Includes insurance and indemnities, and miscellaneous funds and expenditures. (Excludes expenditures from personal funds of patients.)

Source: U.S. Dept. of Veterans Affairs, *Trend Data*, annual.

No. 596. Veterans Compensation and Pension Benefits—Number on Rolls and Average Payment, by Period of Service and Status: 1980 to 1996

[As of **Sept. 30.** Living refers to veterans receiving compensation for disability incurred or aggravated while on active duty and war veterans receiving pension and benefits for nonservice connected disabilities. Deceased refers to deceased veterans whose dependents were receiving pensions and compensation benefits]

PERIOD OF SERVICE AND VETERAN STATUS	VETERANS ON ROLLS (1,000)							AVERAGE PAYMENT (annual basis) [1] (dol.)			
	1980	1990	1992	1993	1994	1995	1996	1980	1990	1991	1992
Total.	4,646	3,584	3,428	3,374	3,342	3,330	3,308	2,370	4,335	4,552	4,712
Living veterans	3,195	2,746	2,674	2,660	2,659	2,669	2,671	2,600	4,320	4,491	4,611
Service connected	2,273	2,184	2,181	2,198	2,218	2,236	2,253	2,669	4,250	4,406	4,593
Nonservice connected.	922	562	493	462	441	433	418	2,428	4,591	4,837	4,689
Deceased veterans	1,451	838	754	714	683	662	637	1,863	4,382	4,761	5,071
Service connected	358	320	314	310	308	307	306	3,801	7,349	7,815	8,244
Nonservice connected.	1,093	518	440	404	376	355	332	1,228	2,548	2,748	2,810
Prior to World War I	14	4	3	3	2	2	2	1,432	2,616	2,921	3,073
Living.	(Z)	(Z)	(Z)	(Z)	(Z)	(Z)	(Z)	2,634	10,502	10,441	8,176
World War I	692	198	146	124	105	89	74	1,683	3,435	3,674	3,754
Living.	198	18	9	6	4	3	2	2,669	6,922	7,239	6,476
World War II	2,520	1,723	1,543	1,453	1,375	1,307	1,237	2,307	4,052	4,238	4,334
Living.	1,849	1,294	1,153	1,083	1,018	961	902	2,462	4,123	4,278	4,333
Korean conflict [2]	446	390	387	377	371	368	360	2,691	5,105	5,330	5,462
Living.	317	305	300	296	292	290	285	2,977	5,103	5,288	5,390
Peacetime	312	495	550	518	539	559	574	3,080	4,132	4,216	4,292
Living.	262	444	500	471	492	514	529	2,828	3,709	3,789	3,866
Vietnam era [3]	662	774	804	821	842	868	889	2,795	4,945	5,242	5,551
Living.	569	685	711	727	746	766	784	2,709	4,671	4,936	5,234
Persian Gulf War [4]	(X)	(X)	(Z)	78	108	138	173	(X)	(X)	(X)	1,673
Living.	(X)	(X)	(Z)	76	106	134	169	(X)	(X)	(X)	1,386

X Not applicable. Z Fewer than 500. [1] Annual basis. Averages calculated by multiplying average monthly payment by 12. [2] Service during period June 27, 1950, to Jan. 31, 1955. [3] Service from Aug. 5, 1964, to May 7, 1975. [4] Service from August 2, 1990, to the present.

Source: U.S. Dept. of Veterans Affairs, *Annual Report of the Secretary of Veterans Affairs;* and unpublished data.

No. 597. Veterans Administration Health Care Summary: 1990 to 1996

[For years ending **Sept. 30**]

ITEM	Unit	1990	1995	1996	ITEM	Unit	1990	1995	1996
Facilities operating:					Obligations [2]	Mil. dol. .	11,827	16,548	16,791
Hospitals	Number .	172	173	173	Prescriptions dispensed .	Millions. .	58.6	66.1	66.5
Domiciliaries.	Number .	32	39	40	Laboratory.	Millions. .	188	(NA)	(NA)
Outpatient clinics. . . .	Number .	339	391	398	Inpatients treated [3]	1,000 . . .	1,113	1,035	961
Nursing home units . .	Number .	126	131	133	Average daily	1,000 . . .	88	81	75
Employment [1]	1,000 . . .	199	205	199	Outpatient visits	Millions. .	22.6	27.6	29.3

NA Not available. [1] Net full-time equivalent. [2] 1980, cost basis; thereafter, obligation basis. [3] Based on the number of discharges and deaths during the fiscal year, plus the number on the rolls (bed occupants and patients on authorized leave of absence) at the end of the fiscal year. Excludes interhospital transfers.

Source: U.S. Dept. of Veterans Affairs, *Annual Report of the Secretary of Veterans Affairs; Directory of VA Facilities,* biennial; and unpublished data.

No. 598. Veterans Assistance—Education and Training: 1980 to 1996

[In thousands, except where indicated. For fiscal years ending in year shown; see text, Section 9. Represents persons in training during year]

PROGRAM	1980	1990	1991	1992	1993	1994	1995	1996
Veteran Education Assistance [1]	1,107	102	143	195	246	284	292	296
Institutions of higher education	842	94	132	177	223	258	264	270
Resident schools other than college	149	6	9	14	18	19	19	18
Correspondence schools	42	1	1	3	3	4	(NA)	3
On-the-job training	74	1	1	2	2	2	4	5
Children's Educational Assistance	82.6	37.5	37.3	37.2	36.4	35.7	34.8	36
Institutions of higher education	75.5	35.3	35.2	35.1	34.3	33.7	33.1	34
Schools other than college	6.5	2.1	2.1	2.1	2.0	1.9	1.7	1.6
Special restorative training	0.1	(Z)	(Z)	(Z)	(Z)	(Z)	(Z)	(Z)
On-the-job training	0.5	0.1	(Z)	(Z)	(Z)	(Z)	(Z)	(Z)
Spouses, Widows/Widowers Educational Assistance Program	13.0	4.5	4.4	4.5	4.4	4.6	4.6	5.0
Institutions of higher education	10.8	4.1	4.0	4.0	4.0	4.1	4.2	4.5
Schools other than college	2.2	0.4	0.4	0.4	0.4	0.4	0.4	0.4
Disabled Veterans Vocational Rehab.	25.5	27.8	35.9	36.8	40.7	44.2	47.9	51.8
Guaranteed and insured loans, (1,000)	297.4	196.6	181.2	266.0	383.3	602.2	263.1	320.8
Guaranteed and insured loans, (mil. dol.) . .	14,815	15,779	15,454	22,960	34,635	55,141	25,341	32,609
Guaranty and insurance (mil. dol.)	6,370	5,561	5,299	7,819	11,601	18,332	8,383	10,525

NA Not available. Z Fewer than 50. [1] Data for 1980-85 are for Post-Korean Conflict GI Bill (Title 38 USC Chapter 34). Data for 1990-94 are for the Active Duty Montgomery GI Bill (Title 38 USC Chapter 30).

Source: U.S. Dept. of Veterans Affairs, *Annual Report of the Secretary of Veterans Affairs;* and unpublished data.

Figure 12.1
Social Security Trust Funds: 1980 to 1996

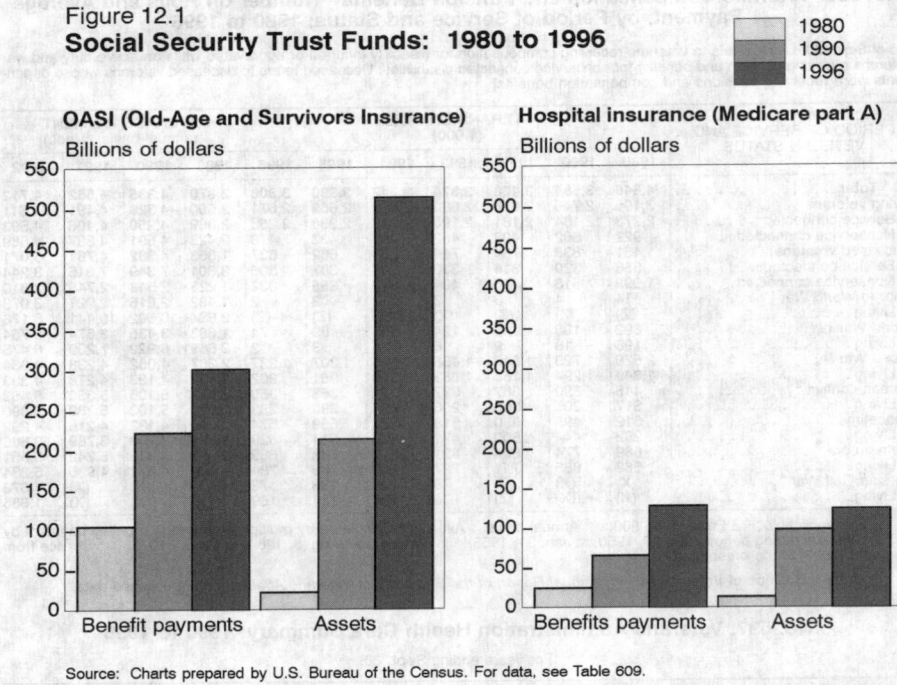

Source: Charts prepared by U.S. Bureau of the Census. For data, see Table 609.

Figure12.2.
Percent Distribution of Households Contributing to Charity by Annual Dollar Amount: 1995

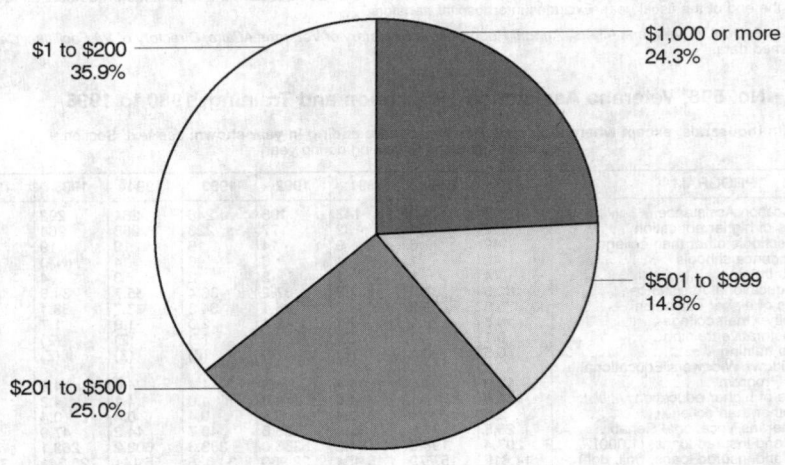

Source: Chart prepared by U.S. Bureau of the Census. For data, see Table 640.

Social Insurance and Human Services

This section presents data related to governmental expenditures for social welfare; governmental programs for old-age, survivors, disability, and health insurance (OASDHI); governmental employee retirement; private pension plans; government unemployment and temporary disability insurance; federal supplemental security income payments and aid to the needy; child and other welfare services; and federal food programs. Also included here are selected data on workers' compensation and vocational rehabilitation, child support, child care, charity contributions, and philanthropic trusts and foundations.

The principal sources for these data are the Social Security Administration's quarterly *Social Security Bulletin* and the *Annual Statistical Supplement to the Social Security Bulletin* which present current data on many of the programs. Current data on employment security are published annually in the Department of Labor's *Unemployment Insurance, Financial Data.*

Social insurance under the Social Security Act—Programs established by the Social Security Act provide protection against wage loss resulting from retirement, prolonged disability, death, or unemployment, and protection against the cost of medical care during old age and disability. The federal OASDI program provides monthly benefits to retired or disabled insured workers and their dependents and to survivors of insured workers. To be eligible, a worker must have had a specified period of employment in which OASDI taxes were paid. A worker becomes eligible for full benefits at age 65, although reduced benefits may be obtained up to 3 years earlier; the worker's spouse is under the same limitations. Survivor benefits are payable to dependents of deceased insured workers. Disability benefits are payable to an insured worker under age 65 with a

In Brief

In 1996 percent of families receiving:

Social Security	23%
Private pensions	9%
Educational assistance	7%

Social Security beneficiaries, 1996:

Total	44 million
Retired workers	27 million

prolonged disability and to the disabled worker's dependents on the same basis as dependents of retired workers. Disability benefits are provided at age 50 to the disabled widow or widower of a deceased worker who was fully insured at the time of death. Disabled children, aged 18 or older, of retired, disabled, or deceased workers are also eligible for benefits. A lump-sum benefit is generally payable on the death of an insured worker to a spouse or minor children. For information on the medicare (HI) program, see Section 3.

Retirement, survivors, disability, and hospital insurance benefits are funded by a payroll tax on annual earnings (up to a maximum of earnings set by law) of workers, employers, and the self-employed. The maximum taxable earnings are adjusted annually to reflect increasing wage levels (see Table 608). Effective January 1994, there is no dollar limit on wages and self-employment income subject to hospital insurance tax. Tax receipts and benefit payments are administered through federal trust funds. Special benefits for uninsured persons; hospital benefits for persons 65 and over with specified amounts of social security coverage less than that required for cash benefit eligibility; and that part of the cost of supplementary medical insurance not financed by contributions from participants are financed from federal general revenues.

Unemployment insurance is presently administered by the U.S. Employment and Training Administration and each state's employment security agency. By agreement with the U.S. Secretary of Labor, state agencies also administer unemployment compensation for eligible ex-service members and federal employees, unemployment assistance under the Disaster Relief Act of 1970, and workers assistance and relocation allowances under the Trade Act. Under state unemployment insurance laws, benefits related to the individual's past earnings are paid to unemployed eligible workers. State laws vary concerning the length of time benefits are paid and their amount. In most states, benefits are payable for 26 weeks and, during periods of high unemployment, extended benefits are payable under a federal-state program to those who have exhausted their regular state benefits. The basic benefit can vary among states by over 100 percent. Some states also supplement the basic benefit with allowances for dependents.

Unemployment insurance is funded by a federal unemployment tax levied on the taxable payrolls of most employers. Taxable payroll under the federal act and 12 state laws is the first $7,000 in wages paid each worker during a year. Forty-one states have taxable payrolls above $7,000. Employers are allowed a percentage credit of taxable payroll for contributions paid to states under state unemployment insurance laws. The remaining percent of the federal tax finances administrative costs, the federal share of extended benefits, and advances to states. About 93 percent of wage and salary workers are covered by unemployment insurance.

Retirement programs for government employees—The Civil Service Retirement System (CSRS) and the Federal Employees' Retirement System (FERS) are the two major programs providing age and service, disability, and survivor annuities for federal civilian employees. In general, employees hired after December 31, 1983, are covered under FERS and the social security program

(OASDHI), and employees on staff prior to that date are members of CSRS and are covered under medicare. CSRS employees were offered the option of transferring to FERS during 1987. There are separate retirement systems for the uniformed services (supplementing OASDHI) and for certain special groups of federal employees. State and local government employees are covered for the most part by state and local retirement systems similar to the federal civil service retirement system. In many jurisdictions these benefits supplement OASDHI coverage.

Workers' compensation—All states provide protection against work-connected injuries and deaths, although some states exclude certain workers (e.g., domestic help). Federal laws cover federal employees, private employees in the District of Columbia, and longshoremen and harbor workers. In addition, the Social Security Administration and the Department of Labor administer "Black Lung" benefits programs for coal miners disabled by pneumoconiosis and for specified dependents and survivors. Specified occupational diseases are compensable to some extent. In most states, benefits are related to the worker's salary. The benefits may or may not be augmented by dependents' allowances or automatically adjusted to prevailing wage levels.

Income support—Income support programs are designed to provide benefits for persons with limited income and resources. The Supplemental Security Income (SSI) program and the Temporary Assistance for Needy Families (TANF) program are the major programs providing monthly payments. In addition, a number of programs provide money payments or in-kind benefits for special needs or purposes. Several programs offer food and nutritional services. Also, various federal–state programs provide energy assistance, public housing, and subsidized housing to individuals and families with low incomes. General assistance may also be available at the state or local level.

The SSI program, administered by the Social Security Administration, provides income support of persons aged 65 or older and blind or disabled adults and children. Eligibility requirements and federal payment standards are nationally uniform. Most states supplement the basic SSI payment for all or selected categories of persons.

The Personal Responsibility and Work Opportunity Reconciliation Act of 1996 contained provisions that replaced the Aid to Families with Dependent Children (AFDC), Job Opportunities and Basic Skills (JOBS), and Emergency Assistance programs with the Temporary Assistance for Needy Families block grant program. This law contains strong work requirements, comprehensive child support enforcement, support for families moving from welfare to work, and other features. The TANF became effective as soon as each state submitted a complete plan implementing TANF, but no later than July 1, 1997. Statistical data in this issue of the *Abstract* reflect the AFDC program in effect through 1996 (before the passage of this legislation). The AFDC program provided cash assistance based on need, income, resources, and family size.

Federal food stamp program—Under the food stamp program, single persons and those living in households meeting nationwide standards for income and assets may receive coupons redeemable for food at most retail food stores. The monthly amount of coupons a unit receives is determined by household size and income. Households without income receive the determined monthly cost of a nutritionally adequate diet for their household size. This amount is updated to account for food price increases. Households with income receive the difference between the amount of a nutritionally adequate diet and 30 percent of their income, after certain allowable deductions.

To qualify for the program, a household must have less than $2,000 in disposable assets ($3,000 if one member is aged 60 or older), gross income below 130 percent of the official poverty guidelines, and net income below 100 percent of the poverty guidelines. Households with a person aged 60 or older or a disabled person receiving SSI, social security, or veterans' disability benefits may have gross income exceeding 130 percent of the poverty guidelines. All households must meet these requirements, even those receiving other federal assistance payments. Households are certified for varying lengths of time, depending on their income sources and individual circumstances.

Health and welfare services—Programs providing health and welfare services are aided through federal grants to states for child welfare services, vocational rehabilitation, activities for the aged, maternal and child health services, maternity and infant care projects, comprehensive health services, and a variety of public health activities. For information about the medicaid program, see Section 3.

Noncash benefits—The Bureau of the Census annually collects data on the characteristics of recipients of noncash (in-kind) benefits to supplement the collection of annual money income data in the Current Population Survey (see text, Section 1, and Section 15). Noncash benefits are those benefits received in a form other than money which serve to enhance or improve the economic well-being of the recipient. As for money income, the data for noncash benefits are for the calendar year prior to the date of the interview. The major categories of noncash benefits covered are public transfers (e.g. food stamps, school lunch, public housing, and medicaid) and employer or union-provided benefits to employees.

Statistical reliability—For discussion of statistical collection, estimation, and sampling procedures and measures of statistical reliability applicable to HHS and Census Bureau data, see Appendix III.

No. 599. Social Welfare Expenditures Under Public Programs: 1980 to 1994

[In billions of dollars, except percent. See headnote, Table 601]

YEAR	Total	Social insurance	Public aid	Health and medical programs [1]	Veterans programs	Education	Housing	Other social welfare	All health and medical care [2]
Total:									
1980	493	230	73	27	21	121	7	14	100
1985	732	370	98	39	27	172	13	14	171
1990	1,049	514	147	61	31	258	19	18	274
1991	1,160	561	181	66	33	277	22	20	314
1992	1,267	619	208	70	36	292	21	22	353
1993	1,366	659	221	75	36	332	20	23	382
1994	1,435	684	238	79	38	344	28	25	408
Federal:									
1980	303	191	49	13	21	13	6	9	69
1985	451	310	63	18	27	14	11	8	122
1990	617	422	93	27	30	18	17	9	190
1991	676	454	113	30	32	19	19	10	214
1992	750	496	139	32	35	20	18	11	250
1993	804	534	152	33	36	20	18	11	275
1994	853	557	163	35	37	24	25	12	295
State and local:									
1980	190	39	23	14	(Z)	108	1	5	31
1985	281	59	35	21	(Z)	158	2	6	49
1990	432	92	54	34	(Z)	240	3	9	84
1991	483	108	68	36	1	258	3	10	100
1992	517	123	69	38	1	272	3	11	103
1993	561	125	69	42	1	311	2	12	107
1994	582	126	75	45	1	320	2	13	113
Percent federal:									
1980	62	83	68	47	99	11	91	65	69
1985	62	84	64	46	99	8	88	56	71
1990	59	82	63	44	98	7	85	50	69
1991	59	80	67	45	98	7	87	50	71
1992	59	81	69	44	98	6	91	48	72
1994	59	82	68	44	98	7	92	48	72
Per capita (current dollars): [3]									
1980	2,126	990	314	118	92	523	30	59	434
1985	3,009	1,516	405	161	111	708	52	56	705
1990	4,123	2,017	579	243	120	1,018	77	71	1,081
1992	4,870	2,377	801	270	133	1,126	79	83	1,359
1993	5,234	2,523	849	287	137	1,274	76	87	1,466
1994	5,442	2,591	905	301	141	1,308	102	94	1,551
Per capita (constant (1994) dollars): [3] [4]									
1980	3,700	1,723	547	205	160	911	52	102	746
1985	4,035	2,032	543	217	148	950	70	75	942
1990	4,631	2,265	650	273	135	1,143	86	79	1,214
1992	5,119	2,498	842	284	140	1,183	85	87	1,428
1993	5,361	2,585	869	294	141	1,305	78	89	1,501
1994	5,442	2,591	905	301	141	1,308	102	94	1,551

Z Less than $500 million. [1] Excludes program parts of social insurance, public aid, veterans, and other social welfare. [2] Combines "Health and medical programs" with medical services included in social insurance, public aid, veterans, vocational rehabilitation, and antipoverty programs. [3] Excludes payments within foreign countries for education, veterans, OASDHI, and civil service retirement. [4] Constant dollar figures are based on implicit price deflators for personal consumption expenditures published by U.S. Bureau of Economic Analysis in Survey of Current Business.

No. 600. Social Welfare Expenditures Under Public Programs as Percent of GDP and Total Government Outlays: 1980 to 1994

[See headnote, Table 601]

YEAR	TOTAL EXPENDITURES				FEDERAL				STATE AND LOCAL GOVERNMENT			
			Percent of—				Percent of—				Percent of—	
	Total (bil. dol.)	Percent change [1]	Total GDP [2]	Total govt. outlays	Total (bil. dol.)	Percent change [1]	Total GDP [2]	Total Federal outlays	Total (bil. dol.)	Percent change [1]	Total GDP [2]	Total State and local outlays
1980	493	14.7	18.6	57.2	303	15.2	11.4	54.4	190	13.8	7.2	62.9
1985	732	8.0	18.4	54.4	451	7.1	11.3	48.7	281	9.3	7.1	68.8
1990	1,049	9.6	18.5	58.2	617	9.1	10.9	51.4	432	10.3	7.6	74.0
1991	1,160	10.6	19.8	60.3	676	9.7	11.5	52.8	483	11.8	8.2	77.4
1992	1,267	9.2	20.6	63.7	750	10.8	12.2	57.4	517	7.0	8.4	77.6
1993	1,366	7.8	21.1	66.7	804	7.2	12.4	60.0	561	8.5	8.7	81.3
1994	1,435	21.8	21.8	63.3	853	6.1	13.0	56.6	582	3.7	8.8	78.6

[1] Percent change from immediate prior year. [2] Gross domestic product.
Source of Tables 599 and 600: U.S. Social Security Administration, Social Security Bulletin, Vol. 60, No. 3, 1997; and unpublished data.

No. 601. Social Welfare Expenditures, by Source of Funds and Public Program: 1980 to 1994

[In millions of dollars. For fiscal years ending in year shown; see text, Section 9. Represents outlays from trust funds (mostly social insurance funds built up by earmarked contributions from insured persons, their employers, or both) and budgetary outlays from general revenues. Includes administrative expenditures, capital outlay, and some expenditures and payments outside the United States]

PROGRAM	FEDERAL				STATE AND LOCAL			
	1980	1990	1993	1994	1980	1990	1993	1994
Total	303,167	616,639	804,424	852,622	189,060	432,167	561,357	582,023
Social insurance	191,162	422,257	534,229	557,389	38,592	91,565	124,998	126,458
Old-age, survivors, disability, health	152,110	355,264	449,277	477,340	(X)	(X)	(X)	(X)
Health insurance (medicare)	34,992	109,709	148,094	161,393	(X)	(X)	(X)	(X)
Public employee retirement [1]	26,983	53,541	61,699	63,801	12,507	36,851	50,928	55,520
Railroad employee retirement	4,769	7,230	7,921	8,025	(X)	(X)	(X)	(X)
Unemployment insurance and employment services [2]	4,408	3,096	12,124	4,972	13,919	16,878	28,597	26,279
Other railroad employee insurance [3]	224	105	86	83	(X)	(X)	(X)	(X)
State temporary disability insurance [4]	(X)	(X)	(X)	(X)	1,377	3,224	3,316	3,201
Workers' compensation [5]	2,668	3,021	3,173	3,168	10,789	34,613	42,157	41,458
Hospital and medical benefits	130	457	597	688	3,596	13,849	17,116	15,512
Public aid [6]	49,394	92,858	151,850	162,675	23,309	53,953	69,149	75,351
Public assistance [7]	23,542	54,747	95,340	100,209	21,522	50,347	65,285	71,546
Medical assistance payments [7]	14,550	40,690	77,367	81,192	13,020	35,485	47,771	53,012
Social services	1,757	2,065	2,785	2,734	586	688	928	911
Supplemental security income	6,440	13,625	22,642	26,281	1,787	3,605	3,864	3,805
Food stamps	9,083	16,254	24,497	25,274	(X)	(X)	(X)	(X)
Other [8]	10,329	8,232	9,372	10,911	(X)	(X)	(X)	(X)
Health and medical programs	12,840	27,204	33,189	34,770	13,935	34,282	41,554	44,526
Hospital and medical care	6,636	14,816	18,575	18,601	5,667	11,155	12,108	12,357
Civilian programs	2,438	3,654	5,166	5,466	5,667	11,155	12,108	12,357
Defense Department [9]	4,198	11,162	13,409	13,134	(X)	(X)	(X)	(X)
Maternal and child health programs	351	492	595	615	519	1,374	1,590	1,657
Medical research	4,428	9,172	10,690	11,739	496	1,676	2,090	2,228
Medical facilities construction	210	413	166	102	1,409	1,922	2,878	3,137
Other	1,215	2,311	3,164	3,714	5,844	18,155	22,888	25,147
Veterans programs	21,255	30,428	35,806	37,262	212	488	572	633
Pensions and compensation	11,306	15,793	17,205	17,481	(X)	(X)	(X)	(X)
Health and medical programs	6,204	12,004	15,410	16,231	(X)	(X)	(X)	(X)
Hospital and medical care	5,750	11,321	14,382	15,160	(X)	(X)	(X)	(X)
Hospital construction	323	445	750	779	(X)	(X)	(X)	(X)
Medical and prosthetic research	131	238	279	292	(X)	(X)	(X)	(X)
Education [10]	2,401	523	938	1,098	(X)	(X)	(X)	(X)
Life insurance [10]	665	1,038	905	972	(X)	(X)	(X)	(X)
Welfare and other	679	1,070	1,348	1,479	212	488	572	633
Education [11]	13,452	18,374	20,455	24,084	107,597	240,011	311,455	320,112
Elementary and secondary [12]	7,430	9,944	13,238	15,514	79,720	189,333	239,182	245,597
Construction [13]	41	23	5	9	6,483	10,613	22,283	19,684
Higher	4,468	6,747	5,285	6,577	21,708	50,678	72,273	74,514
Construction [13]	42	-	35	23	1,486	3,953	8,955	8,959
Vocational and adult [13]	1,207	1,293	1,495	1,504	6,169	([12])	([12])	([12])
Housing	6,278	16,612	18,006	24,724	601	2,856	1,798	2,045
Other social welfare	8,786	8,905	10,838	11,718	4,813	9,012	11,832	12,899
Vocational rehabilitation	1,006	1,661	1,830	1,904	245	466	549	511
Medical services and research	237	415	458	476	56	116	137	128
Institutional care [14]	74	143	143	150	408	486	579	633
Child nutrition [15]	4,209	5,470	7,139	7,626	643	1,696	2,253	2,473
Child welfare [16]	57	253	295	295	743	(NA)	(NA)	(NA)
Special CSA and ACTION programs [17]	2,303	169	208	204	(X)	(X)	(X)	(X)
Welfare, not elsewhere classified [18]	1,137	1,209	1,223	1,540	2,774	6,365	8,451	9,282

- Represents zero. NA Not available. X Not applicable. [1] Excludes refunds to those leaving service. Federal data include military retirement. [2] Includes compensation for federal employees and ex-servicemen, trade adjustment and cash training allowance, and payments under extended, emergency, disaster, and special unemployment insurance programs. [3] Unemployment and temporary disability insurance. [4] Cash and medical benefits in five areas. Includes private plans where applicable. [5] Benefits paid by private insurance carriers, state funds, and self-insurers. Federal includes black lung benefit programs. [6] Includes payments under state general assistance programs and work incentive activities, not shown separately. [7] Medicaid payments and state and local general assistance medical payments. [8] Refugee assistance, surplus food for the needy, and work-experience training programs under the Comprehensive Employment and Training Act. Beginning 1990, includes low-income energy assistance program. [9] Includes medical care for military dependent families. [10] Excludes servicemen's group life insurance. [11] Federal expenditures include administrative costs (Department of Education) and research, not shown separately. [12] Beginning 1990, all State and local vocational education costs included with elementary-secondary. [13] Construction costs of vocational and adult education programs included under elementary-secondary expenditures. [14] Federal expenditures represent primarily surplus foods for nonprofit institutions. [15] Surplus food for schools and programs under National School Lunch and Child Nutrition Acts. [16] Represents primarily child welfare services under Title V of the Social Security Act. [17] Includes domestic volunteer programs under ACTION and community action and migrant workers programs under Community Services Administration. Beginning 1990, represents ACTION funds only. [18] Federal expenditures include administrative expenses of the Secretary of Health and Human Services; Indian welfare and guidance; and aging and juvenile delinquency activities. State and local include antipoverty and manpower programs, child care and adoption services, legal assistance, and other unspecified welfare services.

Source: U.S. Social Security Administration, *Social Security Bulletin*, Vol. 60, No. 3, 1997; and unpublished data.

No. 602. Private Expenditures for Social Welfare, by Type: 1980 to 1994

[In millions of dollars, except percent]

TYPE	1980	1985	1989	1990	1991	1992	1993	1994
Total expenditures	251,507	464,643	671,722	723,154	766,892	833,552	877,604	924,994
Percent of gross domestic product	9.0	11.1	12.4	12.6	13.0	13.3	13.4	13.3
Health.	142,500	253,900	369,800	413,100	441,000	477,000	505,100	528,600
Income maintenance . . . . [1] [2]	53,564	118,871	167,260	164,772	170,754	187,461	192,340	204,736
Private pension plan payments [1] [2] . .	37,605	98,570	141,286	138,114	143,314	158,857	163,158	174,452
Short-term sickness and disability [2] . .	8,630	10,570	13,616	13,680	13,844	14,684	15,132	15,901
Long-term disability [2]	1,282	1,937	2,892	2,926	3,172	3,143	2,900	2,895
Life insurance and death	5,075	7,489	9,063	9,278	9,472	10,184	10,693	11,229
Supplemental unemployment.	972	305	403	774	952	593	457	259
Education	32,667	52,873	75,350	80,699	86,140	93,069	99,265	105,361
Welfare and other services	22,776	38,999	59,312	64,583	68,998	76,022	80,899	86,297

[1] Covers benefits paid for solely by employers and all benefits of employment-related pension plans to which employee contributions are made. Excludes individual savings plans such as IRAs and Keogh plans. Pension plan benefits include monthly benefits and lump-sum distributions to retired and disabled employees and their dependents and to survivors of deceased employees. Also includes preretirement lump-sum distributions. [2] Covers wage and salary workers in private industry.

Source: U.S. Social Security Administration, *Annual Statistical Supplement* to the *Social Security Bulletin*, annual.

No. 603. Public Income-Maintenance Programs—Cash Benefit Payments: 1980 to 1996

[In billions of dollars. Includes payments outside the United States and benefits to dependents, where applicable]

PROGRAM	1980	1985	1988	1989	1990	1991	1992	1993	1994	1995	1996
Total [1] . . . . [2]	228.1	335.2	393.8	421.9	455.8	503.3	543.5	549.1	576.4	(NA)	(NA)
Percent of personal income [2] . .	10.1	9.9	9.7	9.6	9.8	10.4	10.5	10.2	10.0	(NA)	(NA)
OASDI [3]	120.3	186.1	216.4	229.6	245.6	265.6	284.3	296.3	311.6	327.9	369.2
Public employee retirement [4]	40.6	63.0	78.0	83.8	90.4	97.3	103.7	112.6	119.3	(NA)	(NA)
Railroad retirement.	4.9	6.3	6.7	6.9	7.2	7.5	7.3	7.9	8.0	8.1	8.8
Veterans' pensions, compensation. . . .	11.4	14.1	14.7	15.3	15.8	16.3	16.5	16.9	18.7	18.0	20.3
Unemployment benefits [5]	18.9	14.4	13.2	16.4	20.0	31.3	37.3	21.5	21.6	22.0	23.9
Temporary disability benefits.	1.4	1.8	2.8	2.9	3.2	3.9	4.0	3.3	3.2	(NA)	(NA)
Workers' compensation [6]	9.7	22.3	30.3	33.8	37.6	41.7	45.7	45.3	44.6	(NA)	(NA)
Public assistance	12.1	15.3	17.0	17.4	19.3	20.1	22.4	21.0	23.3	22.8	(NA)
Supplemental security income	7.9	11.1	14.7	14.9	15.2	18.5	22.3	24.7	26.1	27.9	31.8

NA Not available. [1] Includes lump sum death benefits, not shown separately. Lump sum death benefits for state and local government employee retirement systems are not available beginning 1988. [2] For base data, see Table 724. [3] Old-age, survivors, and disability insurance under federal Social Security Act; see text, Section 12. [4] Excludes refunds of contributions to employees who leave service. [5] Beginning 1985, covers state unemployment insurance, Ex-Servicemen's Compensation Act and railroad unemployment insurance only. [6] Includes black lung benefits.

Source: U.S. Social Security Administration, *Social Security Bulletin*, quarterly; and unpublished data.

No. 604. Number of Families Receiving Specified Sources of Income, by Characteristic of Householder and Family Income: 1996

[In thousands. Families as of March 1997. Based on Current Population Survey; see text, Sections 1 and 14, and Appendix III]

SOURCE OF INCOME	Total families [1]	Under 65 years old	65 years old and over	White	Black	His-panic origin [2]	Under $15,000	$15,000 to $24,999	$25,000 to $34,999
Total	70,241	59,107	11,133	58,934	8,455	6,631	9,606	9,499	9,469
Earnings	59,919	55,359	4,560	50,504	6,934	5,763	5,464	6,955	7,917
Wages and salary	58,452	54,247	4,205	49,184	6,852	5,658	5,156	6,694	7,675
Social security, railroad retirement . . .	16,147	5,890	10,257	14,053	1,691	924	2,555	3,643	3,017
Supplemental security income (SSI) . .	2,587	2,010	577	1,684	754	403	1,186	570	300
Public assistance	3,397	3,334	63	1,992	1,217	695	2,424	540	190
Veterans payments	1,559	914	646	1,346	179	71	167	214	171
Unemployment compensation	4,564	4,350	215	3,822	552	483	483	584	747
Workers compensation.	1,517	1,390	127	1,322	146	166	122	182	225
Retirement income	9,791	4,109	5,682	8,807	754	311	407	1,565	1,993
Private pensions	6,386	2,345	4,041	5,788	439	191	285	1,184	1,437
Military retirement	828	582	246	678	122	28	21	44	127
Federal employee pensions.	1,096	421	676	976	97	44	38	127	192
State or local employee pensions . .	1,767	734	1,032	1,624	116	55	58	189	347
Other income	10,377	9,995	382	8,433	1,493	756	1,699	1,372	1,479
Alimony	256	252	4	231	22	10	31	30	39
Child support	4,445	4,415	30	3,550	785	288	994	753	845
Education assistance	4,932	4,786	146	4,010	682	371	542	550	551

[1] Includes other items not shown separately. [2] Persons of Hispanic origin may be of any race.

Source: U.S. Bureau of the Census, "Current Population Survey, Annual Demographic Survey, March Supplement"; published 29 September 1997; <http://ferret.bls.census.gov/macro/031997/faminc/09000.htm>.

No. 605. Cash and Noncash Benefits for Persons With Limited Income: 1995 and 1996

[For years ending September 30, except as noted. Programs covered provide cash, goods, or services to persons who make no payment and render no service in return. In case of job and training programs and some educational benefits, recipients must work or study for wages, training allowances, stipends, grants, or loans. Most of the programs base eligibility on individual, household, or family income, but some use group or area income tests; and a few offer help on the basis of presumed need]

PROGRAM	AVERAGE MONTHLY RECIPIENTS (1,000)		EXPENDITURES (mil. dol.)					
			Total		Federal		State and local	
	1995	1996	1995	1996	1995	1996	1995	1996
Total	(X)	(X)	366,594	367,712	258,382	261,311	108,212	106,401
Medical care [1]	(X)	(X)	174,556	177,575	101,338	103,568	73,218	74,007
Medicaid [2][3]	41,388	41,284	156,395	159,357	89,070	91,205	67,325	68,152
Veterans [4][5][6]	1,561	1,587	8,642	8,697	8,642	8,697	-	-
General assistance [6]	(NA)	(NA)	5,464	5,429	-	-	5,464	5,429
Indian health services [2][3]	1,257	1,285	1,960	1,984	1,960	1,984	-	-
Maternal and child health services	12,200	13,000	1,113	1,105	684	679	429	426
Cash aid [1]	(X)	(X)	91,598	91,673	67,923	69,637	23,675	22,036
Supplemental security income (SSI) [3][7]	6,715	6,894	30,567	30,367	26,839	26,934	3,728	3,433
A.F.D.C. [3][8]	13,619	12,649	25,553	23,677	13,788	12,698	11,765	10,979
Earned income tax credit (refunded portion) [9]	52,128	53,706	19,040	21,566	19,040	21,566	-	-
Foster care	261	267	5,747	5,853	3,066	3,114	2,681	2,739
General assistance [9]	989	767	3,559	2,880	-	-	3,559	2,880
Pensions for needy veterans [10][11]	798	705	3,018	3,086	3,018	3,086	-	-
Food benefits [1]	(X)	(X)	38,627	39,036	36,797	37,116	1,830	1,921
Food stamps [3][12]	28,000	26,800	27,438	27,344	25,678	25,494	1,760	1,850
School lunch program [13][14]	14,400	14,600	4,581	4,784	4,581	4,784	(NA)	(NA)
Women, infants and children [3][15]	6,900	7,200	3,451	3,688	3,451	3,688	-	-
School breakfast [13]	5,500	6,200	1,021	1,088	1,021	1,088	-	-
Child and adult care food program [16]	1,300	1,300	905	945	905	945	-	-
Nutrition program for elderly [17]	3,401	(NA)	690	691	620	620	70	71
Housing benefits [1]	(X)	(X)	27,272	27,208	24,948	25,096	2,325	2,113
Low-income housing asst. (Sec. 8) [18]	3,012	3,095	15,824	15,015	15,824	15,015	-	-
Low-rent public housing [18][19]	1,411	1,414	4,449	4,710	4,449	4,710	(NA)	(NA)
Rural housing loans [20][21]	32	41	1,983	2,716	1,983	2,716	-	-
Interest reduction payments [18]	501	493	661	651	661	651	-	-
Home investment partnerships [3][21][22]	67	71	3,269	3,136	963	1,039	2,306	2,097
Education aid [1]	(X)	(X)	16,092	16,275	15,137	15,320	955	955
Pell grants [23][24]	3,952	3,600	6,634	6,144	6,634	6,144	-	-
Head Start	751	752	4,417	4,461	3,534	3,569	883	892
Stafford loans [23]	3,516	3,716	2,702	3,339	2,702	3,339	-	-
Services [1]	(X)	(X)	11,329	10,136	6,012	5,452	5,317	4,684
Social services (Title 20) [25]	(NA)	(NA)	7,168	6,095	2,800	2,381	4,368	3,714
Child care for AFDC recipients and ex-recipients [26]	583	(NA)	1,675	1,737	950	980	725	757
Child care and development block grant	663	(NA)	935	935	935	935	-	-
Jobs and training [1]	(X)	(X)	5,437	4,567	4,626	3,955	811	612
Training for disadvantaged adults and youth [27]	507	426	1,124	977	1,124	977	-	-
JOBS (for AFDC recipients) [28]	632	650	1,767	1,280	1,051	765	716	516
Job Corps	100	100	1,089	1,094	1,089	1,094	-	-
Summer youth employment program [29]	489	409	867	625	867	625	-	-
Energy assistance [1]	(X)	(X)	1,682	1,239	1,601	1,167	81	73
Low-income energy assistance [3][30][31]	5,500	4,300	1,402	1,064	1,386	1,055	16	9

- Represents zero.   NA Not available.   X Not applicable.   [1] Includes other programs not shown separately.   [2] Recipient data represent unduplicated annual number.   [3] Expenditures include administrative expenses.   [4] Medical care for veterans with a nonservice-connected disability.   [5] Recipients are estimated number of inpatients.   [6] Estimated expenditures.   [7] Includes state-administered SSI supplements.   [8] Aid to families with dependent children program. Excludes data for foster care program and child support operations (cost and collections).   [9] Estimated recipients.   [10] Estimated recipients as of September.   [11] Includes dependents and survivors.   [12] Includes Puerto Rico's nutritional assistance program.   [13] Free and reduced-price segments.   [14] Includes estimate of commodity assistance.   [15] Special supplemental food program for women, infants and children.   [16] Recipient data are numbers of children receiving free or reduced price meals and snacks in child care centers and estimates of children in family day care homes with incomes below 185 percent of poverty.   [17] No income test required but preference given to those with greatest need.   [18] Recipient data represent units eligible for payment at end of year.   [19] Includes operating subsidies and HUD-administered Indian housing.   [20] Recipient data represent total families or dwelling units during year.   [21] Expenditure data represent amounts obligated.   [22] Recipient data are housing units provided or rehabilitated.   [23] Recipient data are total numbers for the school year ending in year shown.   [24] Expenditure data are appropriations available for school year ending the fiscal year named.   [25] Nonfederal expenditure data are rough estimates.   [26] Recipient data are estimated number of children served.   [27] Recipient data are total number of participants.   [28] Job opportunities and basic skills training program (JOBS).   [29] Total participants (June-August).   [30] Households served during the year with heating and winter crisis aid.   [31] Federal funds include amounts transferred to other programs serving the needy.

Source: Library of Congress, Congressional Research Service, "Cash and Noncash Benefits for Persons With Limited Income: Eligibility Rules, Recipient and Expenditure Data, FYs 1994-96," CRS Report, forthcoming.

No. 606. Households Receiving Means-Tested Noncash Benefits: 1980 to 1996

[In thousands, except percent. Households as of **March** of following year. Covers civilian noninstitutional population, including persons in the Armed Forces living off post or with their families on post. A means-tested benefit program requires that the household's income and/or assets fall below specified guidelines in order to qualify for benefits. The means-tested noncash benefits covered are food stamps, free or reduced-price school lunches, public or subsidized housing, and medicaid. There are general trends toward underestimation of noncash beneficiaries. Households are classified according to poverty status of family or nonfamily householder; for explanation of poverty level, see text, Section 14. Data for 1980-90 based on 1980 census population controls; beginning 1995, based on 1990 census population controls. Based on Current Population Survey; see text, Section 1, and Appendix III]

TYPE OF BENEFIT RECEIVED	1980	1985	1990	1995	1996			
						Below poverty level		Above poverty level
					Total	Number	Percent distribution	
Total households	82,368	88,458	94,312	99,627	101,018	13,102	100	87,916
Receiving at least one noncash benefit . .	14,266	14,466	16,098	21,148	21,666	8,383	64	13,283
Not receiving cash public assistance . .	7,860	7,860	8,819	13,335	13,895	4,020	31	9,875
Receiving cash public assistance [1] . . .	6,407	6,607	7,279	7,813	7,770	4,363	33	3,407
Total households receiving—								
Food stamps.	6,769	6,779	7,163	8,388	8,263	5,399	41	2,864
School lunch.	5,532	5,752	6,252	8,607	8,922	3,881	30	5,041
Public housing.	2,777	3,799	4,339	4,846	4,981	2,622	20	2,359
Medicaid	8,287	8,178	10,321	14,111	14,486	6,373	49	8,113

[1] Households receiving money from aid to families with dependent children program, supplemental security income program or other public assistance programs.

Source: U.S. Bureau of the Census, *Current Population Reports*, P60-155, and earlier reports; and unpublished data.

No. 607. Persons Participating in Selected Means-Tested Government Assistance Programs, by Selected Characteristics: 1993

[In percent, except as indicated. **Average monthly participation**. Covers noninstitutionalized population. Persons are considered participants in aid to families with dependent children (AFDC), general assistance, and food stamp programs if they are the primary recipient or if they are covered under another person's allotment. Persons receiving supplemental security income (SSI) payments are considered to be participants in an assistance program as are persons covered by medicaid or living in public or subsidized rental housing. Based on the Survey of Income and Program Participation; for details on sample survey, see source]

SELECTED CHARACTERISTIC	Major means-tested assistance programs [1]	AFDC or general assistance	SSI	Food stamps	Medicaid	Housing assistance
Number of recipients (1,000)	35,968	12,790	4,987	22,553	26,453	10,759
PERCENT OF POPULATION PARTICIPATING						
Total	14.0	5.0	1.9	8.7	10.3	4.2
Under 18 years old	23.7	11.4	-	16.9	19.5	6.6
18 to 64 years old	10.0	3.0	2.0	6.1	6.6	3.0
65 years old and over	12.0	0.2	5.9	3.9	8.1	4.8
White	10.6	3.1	1.5	6.2	7.7	2.7
White, non-Hispanic	8.7	2.4	1.4	4.9	6.2	2.3
Black	35.5	16.4	4.7	25.4	27.0	13.7
Hispanic origin [2]	28.9	10.9	2.9	18.9	21.6	7.9
Poverty status: [3]						
Below the poverty level	57.3	26.8	6.6	45.7	44.9	18.0
At or above the poverty level	6.5	1.2	1.1	2.4	4.3	1.8
Family status:						
In married-couple families.	7.7	1.7	0.9	4.3	5.2	1.6
In families with female householder, no spouse present	42.9	23.9	3.6	32.6	34.8	14.4
Unrelated individuals	12.8	0.8	5.2	4.9	8.1	5.7

- Represents or rounds to zero. [1] Covers AFDC, general assistance, SSI, food stamps, medicaid, and housing assistance. [2] Persons of Hispanic origin may be of any race. [3] For explanation of poverty level, see text, Section 14.

Source: U.S. Bureau of the Census, *Current Population Reports*, P70-58.

No. 608. Social Security—Covered Employment, Earnings, and Contribution Rates: 1980 to 1996

[Includes Puerto Rico, Virgin Islands, American Samoa, and Guam. Represents all reported employment. Data are estimated. OASDHI=Old-age, survivors, disability, and health insurance; SMI=Supplementary medical insurance]

ITEM	Unit	1980	1985	1989	1990	1991	1992	1993	1994	1995	1996
Workers with insured status [1]	Million. .	137.4	148.3	158.3	161.3	164.0	165.9	167.4	168.8	170.4	172.4
Male	Million. .	75.4	79.6	83.8	85.2	86.4	87.2	87.8	88.3	88.9	89.8
Female	Million. .	62.0	68.6	74.5	76.1	77.5	78.7	79.6	80.5	81.5	82.6
Under 25 years old	Million. .	25.5	22.4	21.3	21.4	21.3	20.8	20.1	19.3	18.9	18.4
25 to 34 years old	Million. .	34.9	39.4	41.3	41.5	41.6	41.3	40.8	40.2	39.8	39.3
35 to 44 years old	Million. .	22.4	28.6	33.5	34.9	36.4	37.2	38.0	38.9	39.7	40.5
45 to 54 years old	Million. .	18.6	19.0	21.4	22.1	22.8	24.1	25.5	26.8	28.1	29.4
55 to 59 years old	Million. .	9.2	9.1	8.7	8.7	8.7	8.8	9.0	9.2	9.5	9.7
60 to 64 years old	Million. .	7.9	8.7	8.7	8.7	8.8	8.7	8.5	8.4	8.3	8.4
65 to 69 years old	Million. .	6.7	7.3	7.9	8.1	8.2	8.1	8.2	8.2	8.1	8.1
70 years old and over	Million. .	12.1	13.9	15.4	15.8	16.3	16.8	17.3	17.7	18.1	18.5
Workers reported with—											
Taxable earnings [2]	Million. .	113	120	132	134	133	134	136	139	143	144
Maximum earnings [2]	Million. .	10	8	8	8	8	8	8	8	8	8
Earnings in covered employment [2]	Bil. dol	1,329	1,942	2,573	2,704	2,761	2,916	3,033	3,171	3,369	3,577
Reported taxable [2]	Bil. dol	1,178	1,725	2,238	2,358	2,422	2,533	2,644	2,784	2,924	3,080
Percent of total	Percent.	88.6	88.8	87.0	87.2	87.7	86.9	87.2	87.8	86.8	86.1
Annual maximum taxable earnings [3]	Dollars .	25,900	39,600	48,000	51,300	53,400	55,500	57,600	60,600	61,200	62,700
Contribution rates for OASDHI: [4]											
Each employer and employee	Percent.	6.13	7.05	7.51	7.65	7.65	7.65	7.65	7.65	7.65	7.65
Self-employed [5]	Percent.	8.10	14.10	15.02	15.30	15.30	15.30	15.30	15.30	15.30	15.30
SMI, monthly premium [6]	Dollars .	9.60	15.50	31.90	28.60	29.90	31.80	36.60	41.10	46.10	42.50

[1] Estimated number fully insured for retirement and/or survivor benefits as of beginning of year. [2] Includes self-employment. [3] The maximum taxable earnings for HI was $125,000 in 1991; $130,200 in 1992, and 135,000 in 1993. Beginning 1994 upper limit on earnings subject to HI taxes was repealed. [4] As of January 1, 1997, and 1998, each employee and employer pays 7.65 percent and the self-employed pay 15.3 percent. [5] Self-employed pays 11.8 percent in 1985 and 13.02 percent in 1989. The additional amount is supplied from general revenues. Beginning 1990, self-employed pays 15.3 percent, and half of the tax is deductible for income tax purposes and for computing self-employment income subject to social security tax. [6] 1980, as of July 1; beginning 1985, as of January 1. As of January 1, 1997, the monthly premium is $43.80; as of January 1, 1998, $43.80.

Source: U.S. Social Security Administration, *Annual Statistical Supplement* to the *Social Security Bulletin;* and unpublished data.

No. 609. Social Security Trust Funds: 1980 to 1996

[In billions of dollars]

TYPE OF TRUST FUND	1980	1985	1990	1991	1992	1993	1994	1995	1996
Old-age and survivors insurance (OASI):									
Net contribution income [1]	103.5	180.2	272.4	278.4	286.8	296.2	298.3	310.1	328.0
Interest received [2]	1.8	1.9	16.4	20.8	24.3	27.0	29.9	32.8	35.7
Benefit payments [3]	105.1	167.2	223.0	240.5	[4]254.9	[4]267.8	279.1	291.6	302.9
Assets, end of year	22.8	[5]35.8	214.2	267.8	319.2	369.3	413.5	458.5	514.0
Disability insurance (DI):									
Net contribution income [1]	13.3	17.4	28.7	29.3	30.4	31.5	51.7	54.7	57.7
Interest received [2]	0.5	0.9	0.9	1.1	1.1	0.8	1.2	2.2	3.0
Benefit payments [3]	15.5	18.8	24.8	27.7	[4]31.1	[4]34.6	37.7	40.9	44.2
Assets, end of year	3.6	[6]6.3	11.1	12.9	12.3	9.0	22.9	37.6	52.9
Hospital insurance (HI):									
Net contribution income [1][7]	23.9	47.7	72.2	78.4	82.4	84.9	97.9	103.3	115.9
Interest received [2]	1.1	3.4	8.5	9.5	10.5	12.5	10.7	10.8	10.2
Benefit payments	25.1	47.5	66.2	71.5	83.9	93.5	103.3	116.4	128.6
Assets, end of year	13.7	[8]20.5	98.9	115.2	124.0	127.8	132.8	130.3	124.9
Supplementary medical insurance (SMI):									
Net premium income	3.0	5.6	11.3	11.9	14.1	14.2	17.4	19.7	18.8
Transfers from general revenue	7.5	18.3	33.0	37.6	41.4	41.5	36.2	39.0	65.0
Interest received	0.4	1.2	1.6	1.7	1.8	2.0	2.0	1.6	1.8
Benefit payments	10.6	22.9	42.5	47.3	49.3	55.8	58.6	65.0	68.6
Assets, end of year	4.5	10.9	15.5	17.8	24.2	24.1	19.4	13.1	28.3

[1] Includes deposits by states and deductions for refund of estimated employee-tax overpayment. Beginning in 1985, includes government contributions on deemed wage credits for military service in 1957 and later. Includes tax credits on net earnings from self-employment in 1985-89. Includes taxation of benefits beginning in 1985 for OASI and DI and in 1994 for HI. [2] In 1985-90, includes interest on advance tax transfers. Beginning 1985, includes interest on reimbursement for unnegotiated checks. Data for 1985 reflect interest on interfund borrowing. [3] Includes payments for vocational rehabilitation services furnished to disabled persons receiving benefits because of their disabilities. Beginning in 1985, amounts reflect deductions for unnegotiated benefit checks. [4] Data adjusted to reflect 12 months of benefit payments. [5] Includes $13.2 billion borrowed from the DI and HI Trust Funds. [6] Excludes $2.5 billion lent to the OASI Trust Fund. [7] Includes premiums from aged ineligibles enrolled in HI. [8] Excludes $10.6 billion lent to the OASI Trust Fund.

Source: U.S. Social Security Administration, *Annual Report of Board of Trustees, OASI, DI, HI, and SMI Trust Funds.* Also published in *Social Security Bulletin,* quarterly.

No. 610. Social Security (OASDI)—Benefits, by Type of Beneficiary: 1980 to 1996

[A person eligible to receive more than one type of benefit is generally classified or counted only once as a retired-worker beneficiary. OASDI=Old-age, survivors, and disability insurance. See also headnote, Table 608 and Appendix III]

TYPE OF BENEFICIARY	1980	1985	1989	1990	1991	1992	1993	1994	1995	1996
BENEFITS IN CURRENT-PAYMENT STATUS [1] (end of year)										
Number of benefits (1,000)	35,585	37,058	39,151	39,832	40,592	41,507	42,246	42,883	43,387	43,737
Retired workers [2] (1,000)	19,562	22,432	24,327	24,838	25,289	25,758	26,104	26,408	26,673	26,898
Disabled workers [3] (1,000)	2,859	2,657	2,895	3,011	3,195	3,468	3,726	3,963	4,185	4,386
Wives and husbands [2][4] (1,000)	3,477	3,375	3,365	3,367	3,370	3,382	3,367	3,337	3,290	3,194
Children (1,000)	4,607	3,319	3,165	3,187	3,268	3,391	3,527	3,654	3,734	3,803
Under age 18	3,423	2,699	2,488	2,497	2,558	2,664	2,777	2,887	2,956	3,010
Disabled children [5]	450	526	586	600	616	637	656	673	686	697
Students [6]	733	94	91	89	95	90	94	94	92	96
Of retired workers	639	457	423	422	426	432	436	440	442	443
Of deceased workers	2,610	1,917	1,780	1,776	1,791	1,808	1,836	1,864	1,884	1,898
Of disabled workers	1,358	945	962	989	1,052	1,151	1,255	1,350	1,409	1,463
Widowed mothers [7] (1,000)	562	372	312	304	301	294	289	283	275	242
Widows and widowers [2][8] (1,000)	4,411	4,863	5,071	5,111	5,158	5,205	5,224	5,232	5,226	5,210
Parents [2] (1,000)	15	10	6	6	5	5	5	4	4	4
Special benefits [9] (1,000)	93	32	10	7	5	4	2	2	1	1
Average monthly benefit, current dollars										
Retired workers [2]	341	479	567	603	629	653	674	697	720	745
Retired worker and wife [2]	567	814	966	1,027	1,072	1,111	1,145	1,184	1,221	1,262
Disabled workers [3]	371	484	556	587	609	626	642	661	682	704
Wives and husbands [2][4]	164	236	281	298	311	322	332	343	354	369
Children of retired workers	140	198	242	259	273	285	297	309	322	337
Children of deceased workers	240	330	385	406	420	432	443	456	469	487
Children of disabled workers	110	142	157	164	168	170	173	178	183	194
Widowed mothers [7]	246	332	388	409	424	438	448	464	478	515
Widows and widowers, nondisabled [2]	311	433	522	557	584	608	630	655	680	699
Parents [2]	276	378	454	482	506	526	547	570	591	614
Special benefits [9]	105	138	158	167	173	178	183	187	192	197
Average monthly benefit, constant (1996) dollars [10]										
Retired workers [2]	627	695	713	715	723	730	733	738	744	745
Retired worker and wife [2]	1,042	1,181	1,215	1,217	1,233	1,242	1,246	1,254	1,262	1,262
Disabled workers [3]	682	702	699	696	700	700	698	700	705	704
Wives and husbands [2][4]	301	342	353	353	358	360	361	363	366	369
Children of deceased workers	441	480	484	481	483	483	482	483	485	487
Widowed mothers [7]	452	482	488	485	488	490	487	492	494	515
Widows and widowers, nondisabled [2]	572	628	657	659	671	680	685	694	703	699
BENEFITS AWARDED DURING YEAR (1,000)										
Number of benefits	4,215	3,796	3,646	3,717	3,865	4,051	4,001	3,940	3,882	3,793
Retired workers [2]	1,620	1,690	1,657	1,665	1,695	1,708	1,661	1,625	1,609	1,581
Disabled workers [3]	389	377	426	468	536	637	635	632	646	624
Wives and husbands [2][4]	469	440	380	379	380	383	365	345	322	302
Children	1,174	714	675	695	727	795	816	824	809	798
Widowed mothers [7]	108	72	60	58	58	56	56	55	52	49
Widows and widowers [2][8]	452	502	449	452	469	472	466	459	445	438
Parents [2]	1	(Z)	(Z)	(Z)	(Z)	(Z)	(Z)	(Z)	(Z)	(Z)
Special benefits [9]	1	1	(Z)	(Z)	(Z)	(Z)	(Z)	(Z)	(Z)	(Z)
BENEFIT PAYMENTS DURING YEAR (bil. dol.)										
Total amount [11]	120.5	186.2	230.9	247.8	268.1	286.0	302.4	316.6	332.6	347.1
Monthly benefits [12]	120.1	186.0	230.6	247.6	267.9	285.8	302.2	316.6	332.4	346.9
Retired workers [2]	70.4	116.8	146.0	156.8	169.1	179.4	188.4	196.4	205.3	213.4
Disabled workers [3]	12.8	16.5	20.3	22.1	24.7	27.9	30.9	33.7	36.6	39.6
Wives and husbands [2][4]	7.0	11.1	13.6	14.5	15.5	16.4	16.9	17.4	17.9	18.2
Children	10.5	10.7	11.5	12.0	12.8	13.6	14.6	15.4	16.1	17.1
Under age 18	7.4	8.5	8.7	9.0	9.5	10.1	10.8	11.4	11.9	12.6
Disabled children [5]	1.0	1.8	2.3	2.5	2.8	3.0	3.3	3.4	3.6	3.8
Students [6]	2.1	0.4	0.5	0.5	0.5	0.5	0.5	0.6	0.6	0.6
Of retired workers	1.1	1.1	1.2	1.3	1.4	1.5	1.6	1.6	1.7	1.8
Of deceased workers	7.4	7.8	8.3	8.6	9.0	9.4	9.9	10.3	10.7	11.2
Of disabled workers	2.0	1.8	2.0	2.2	2.4	2.7	3.1	3.4	3.7	4.0
Widowed mothers [7]	1.6	1.5	1.4	1.4	1.5	1.5	1.5	1.6	1.6	1.5
Widows and widowers [2][8]	17.6	29.3	37.7	40.7	44.1	47.1	49.7	52.1	54.8	57.0
Parents [2]	0.1	0.1	(Z)	(Z)	(Z)	(Z)	(Z)	(Z)	(Z)	(Z)
Special benefits [9]	0.1	0.1	(Z)	(Z)	(Z)	(Z)	(Z)	(Z)	(Z)	(Z)
Lump sum	0.4	0.2	0.2	0.2	0.2	0.2	0.2	0.2	0.2	0.2

Z Fewer than 500 or less than $50 million.   [1] Benefit payment actually being made at a specified time with no deductions or with deductions amounting to less than a month's benefits; i.e., the benefits actually being received.   [2] 62 years and over.   [3] Disabled workers under age 65.   [4] Includes wife beneficiaries with entitled children in their care and entitled divorced wives.   [5] 18 years old and over. Disability began before age 18 and, beginning 1973, before age 22.   [6] Full-time students aged 18-21 through 1984 and aged 18 and 19 beginning 1985.   [7] Includes surviving divorced mothers with entitled children in their care and widowed fathers with entitled children in their care.   [8] Includes widows aged 60-61, surviving divorced wives aged 60 and over, disabled widows and widowers aged 50 and over; and widowers aged 60-61.   [9] Benefits for persons aged 72 and over not insured under regular or transitional provisions of Social Security Act.   [10] Constant dollar figures are based on the consumer price index for December as published by the U.S. Bureau of Labor Statistics.   [11] Represents total disbursements of benefit checks by the U.S. Dept. of the Treasury during the years specified.   [12] Distribution by type estimated.

Source: U.S. Social Security Administration, *Annual Statistical Supplement* to the *Social Security Bulletin;* and unpublished data.

No. 611. Social Security—Beneficiaries, Annual Payments, and Average Monthly Benefit, 1980 to 1996, and by State and Other Area, 1996

[Number of beneficiaries in current-payment status and average monthly benefit as of **December**. Data for number of beneficiaries and average monthly benefit based on 10-percent sample of administrative records. See also headnote, Table 610, and Appendix III]

YEAR, STATE, AND OTHER AREA	NUMBER OF BENEFICIARIES (1,000)				ANNUAL PAYMENTS (mil. dol.)				AVERAGE MONTHLY BENEFIT (dol.)		
	Total	Retired workers and dependents [1]	Survivors	Disabled workers and dependents	Total	Retired workers and dependents [1]	Survivors [2]	Disabled workers and dependents	Retired workers [3]	Disabled workers	Widows and widowers [4]
1980.	35,585	23,309	7,598	4,678	120,472	78,025	27,010	15,437	341	371	311
1985.	37,058	25,989	7,162	3,907	186,195	128,536	38,824	18,836	479	484	433
1990.	39,832	28,369	7,197	4,266	247,796	172,042	50,951	24,803	603	587	557
1993.	42,238	29,633	7,341	5,264	302,402	206,365	61,440	34,598	674	642	630
1994.	42,878	29,913	7,371	5,592	316,835	214,895	64,223	37,717	697	661	655
1995.	43,380	30,139	7,379	5,862	332,581	224,381	67,302	40,898	720	682	680
1996, total [5]	**43,737**	**30,314**	**7,347**	**6,077**	**347,088**	**232,938**	**69,976**	**44,174**	**745**	**705**	**707**
United States.	**42,712**	**29,691**	**7,126**	**5,893**	**341,753**	**230,042**	**68,570**	**43,139**	**(NA)**	**(NA)**	**(NA)**
Alabama	787	486	157	143	5,777	3,462	1,344	971	696	678	632
Alaska	46	29	9	8	348	218	73	57	735	693	651
Arizona	720	522	103	95	5,758	4,041	995	722	754	729	732
Arkansas	507	319	92	96	3,650	2,223	773	655	679	672	618
California	4,023	2,885	622	515	32,467	22,475	6,087	3,905	757	714	738
Colorado	505	347	79	79	3,898	2,568	756	574	725	699	709
Connecticut	569	427	79	62	5,003	3,687	838	478	818	721	785
Delaware	124	89	19	16	1,034	717	195	123	775	730	752
District of Columbia	77	53	15	9	539	355	114	70	629	648	587
Florida	3,034	2,269	428	337	24,195	17,498	4,190	2,507	743	713	729
Georgia	1,027	646	190	191	7,677	4,716	1,626	1,335	705	681	642
Hawaii	169	132	22	15	1,317	1,002	205	110	733	717	676
Idaho	181	130	28	24	1,395	963	265	166	723	694	723
Illinois	1,827	1,291	315	221	15,447	10,536	3,221	1,690	786	731	762
Indiana	967	673	162	132	8,055	5,432	1,651	971	777	716	750
Iowa	539	392	89	58	4,313	2,996	896	421	744	694	723
Kansas	436	313	72	51	3,545	2,464	725	356	764	681	744
Kentucky	720	422	137	161	5,274	2,963	1,203	1,109	693	704	633
Louisiana	701	413	159	129	5,117	2,866	1,383	868	692	713	644
Maine	242	165	36	42	1,777	1,175	332	270	687	642	667
Maryland	685	485	122	78	5,545	3,766	1,171	608	746	729	717
Massachusetts	1,052	746	153	154	8,548	5,874	1,542	1,132	748	697	741
Michigan	1,598	1,098	278	221	13,677	9,065	2,880	1,732	798	761	759
Minnesota	715	523	115	77	5,641	3,945	1,133	563	733	686	706
Mississippi	498	292	98	109	3,430	1,969	764	697	659	653	585
Missouri	977	668	162	146	7,622	5,048	1,540	1,034	731	688	701
Montana	153	105	25	23	1,179	780	235	163	726	703	705
Nebraska	282	205	46	31	2,212	1,541	461	210	733	672	731
Nevada	241	177	32	33	1,939	1,373	306	260	751	741	733
New Hampshire	188	136	26	26	1,529	1,078	262	188	750	707	740
New Jersey	1,314	967	202	144	11,614	8,339	2,115	1,160	820	744	780
New Mexico	262	173	47	43	1,890	1,215	392	283	697	689	667
New York.	2,968	2,103	458	408	25,268	17,455	4,619	3,194	794	746	755
North Carolina	1,255	833	204	218	9,467	6,153	1,766	1,548	708	675	633
North Dakota	116	82	22	12	864	576	206	82	699	671	675
Ohio.	1,910	1,306	352	252	15,644	10,193	3,571	1,881	762	720	738
Oklahoma	580	395	106	79	4,416	2,886	969	560	711	688	680
Oregon	548	404	78	65	4,451	3,175	793	484	758	700	743
Pennsylvania	2,332	1,690	399	242	19,419	13,455	4,119	1,845	767	724	744
Rhode Island	189	138	25	26	1,532	1,096	251	185	743	676	735
South Carolina	638	411	109	118	4,776	3,026	909	842	708	686	623
South Dakota	135	95	25	15	992	669	224	99	687	635	662
Tennessee	940	595	172	172	7,029	4,329	1,507	1,193	706	671	647
Texas	2,498	1,672	493	333	19,064	12,252	4,501	2,311	722	697	687
Utah	228	162	36	31	1,782	1,242	339	201	750	688	746
Vermont	100	69	15	16	773	522	142	108	732	676	707
Virginia	965	650	167	148	7,372	4,790	1,518	1,063	715	698	662
Washington	802	583	117	101	6,641	4,670	1,205	765	774	708	755
West Virginia	386	231	81	74	3,019	1,710	756	553	736	749	674
Wisconsin	884	643	137	104	7,263	5,101	1,397	764	763	705	742
Wyoming.	72	51	11	10	569	392	105	73	750	712	712
Puerto Rico	625	338	123	165	3,207	1,577	719	911	483	591	438
Guam	8	5	2	1	41	23	13	5	522	642	494
American Samoa. . . .	5	2	2	2	21	7	9	6	440	504	371
Virgin Islands	12	8	2	1	75	49	16	10	616	673	549
Abroad	371	265	89	17	1,994	1,239	643	106	482	613	509

NA Not available. [1] Includes special benefits; see footnote 9, Table 610. [2] Includes lump-sum payments to survivors of deceased workers. [3] Excludes persons with special benefits. [4] Nondisabled only. [5] Number of beneficiaries includes those with state or area unknown.

Source: U.S. Social Security Administration, *Social Security Bulletin*, quarterly.

No. 612. Public Employee Retirement Systems—Participants and Finances: 1980 to 1996

[For fiscal year of retirement system, except data for the Thrift Savings Plan are for calendar year]

RETIREMENT PLAN	Unit	1980	1985	1990	1991	1992	1993	1994	1995	1996
TOTAL PARTICIPANTS [1]										
Federal retirement systems:										
Defined benefit:										
Civil Service Retirement System	1,000 .	4,629	4,919	4,167	4,086	4,014	3,808	3,808	3,731	3,663
Federal Employees Retirement System [2].	1,000 .	(X)	(X)	1,180	1,325	1,367	1,764	1,764	1,512	1,615
Military Service Retirement System [3] . . .	1,000 .	3,380	3,672	3,763	3,732	3,579	3,511	3,451	3,387	3,372
Thrift Savings Plan [4]	1,000 .	(X)	(X)	1,625	1,776	1,900	2,036	2,119	2,195	2,300
State and local retirement systems [5][6]	1,000 .	(NA)	15,234	16,858	17,502	18,310	13,466	13,290	14,734	15,153
ACTIVE PARTICIPANTS										
Federal retirement systems:										
Defined benefit:										
Civil Service Retirement System	1,000 .	2,700	2,800	1,826	1,726	1,654	1,525	1,443	1,525	1,343
Federal Employees Retirement System [2].	1,000 .	(X)	(X)	1,136	1,260	1,276	1,318	1,375	1,318	1,447
Military Service Retirement System [3] . . .	1,000 .	2,050	2,192	2,130	2,064	1,868	1,763	1,666	1,572	1,525
Thrift Savings Plan [4]	1,000 .	(X)	(X)	1,419	1,593	1,300	1,812	1,876	1,930	1,800
State and local retirement systems [5][6]	1,000 .	(NA)	10,364	11,345	11,696	11,998	11,940	11,849	12,524	13,051
ASSETS										
Total	Bil. dol.	258	529	1,047	1,150	1,276	1,384	1,519	1,655	1,854
Federal retirement systems	Bil. dol.	73	154	326	367	411	455	494	537	581
Defined benefit	Bil. dol.	73	154	318	355	394	434	468	502	534
Civil Service Retirement System	Bil. dol.	73	142	220	237	256	277	294	311	328
Federal Employees Retirement System [2].	Bil. dol.	(X)	(X)	18	24	32	41	50	60	71
Military Service Retirement System [3] . . .	Bil. dol.	([7])	12	80	94	106	116	124	131	135
Thrift Savings Plan [4]	Bil. dol.	(X)	(X)	8	12	16	21	26	35	47
State and local retirement systems [5]	Bil. dol.	185	374	721	783	866	929	1,025	1,118	1,273
CONTRIBUTIONS										
Total	Bil. dol.	83	106	103	111	107	120	121	127	129
Federal retirement systems	Bil. dol.	19	54	61	65	68	68	67	67	66
Defined benefit	Bil. dol.	19	54	59	62	64	63	62	61	60
Civil Service Retirement System	Bil. dol.	19	27	28	29	30	31	31	31	32
Federal Employees Retirement System [2].	Bil. dol.	(X)	(X)	4	5	6	6	6	6	6
Military Service Retirement System [3] . . .	Bil. dol.	([7])	27	27	28	28	26	25	24	22
Thrift Savings Plan [4]	Bil. dol.	(X)	(X)	2	3	4	5	5	6	6
State and local retirement systems [5]	Bil. dol.	64	52	42	46	39	52	54	60	63
BENEFITS										
Total	Bil. dol.	39	62	89	96	101	117	124	125	131
Federal retirement systems	Bil. dol.	27	40	53	56	58	63	65	66	66
Defined benefit	Bil. dol.	27	40	53	56	58	62	64	65	69
Civil Service Retirement System	Bil. dol.	15	23	31	33	33	35	36	37	39
Federal Employees Retirement System [2].	Bil. dol.	(X)	(X)	(Z)	(Z)	(Z)	(Z)	(Z)	1	1
Military Service Retirement System [3] . . .	Bil. dol.	12	17	22	23	25	27	28	28	29
Thrift Savings Plan [4]	Bil. dol.	(X)	(X)	(Z)	(Z)	(Z)	1	1	1	1
State and local retirement systems [5]	Bil. dol.	12	22	36	39	44	54	59	59	65

NA Not available.　 X Not applicable.　 Z Less than $500 million.　 [1] Includes active, separated vested, retired employees, and survivors.　 [2] The Federal Employees Retirement System was established June 6, 1986.　 [3] Includes nondisability and disability retirees, surviving families, and all active personnel with the exception of active reserves.　 [4] The Thrift Savings Plan (a defined contribution plan) was established April 1, 1987.　 [5] Excludes state and local plans that are fully supported by employee contributions.　 [6] Not adjusted for double counting of individuals participating in more than one plan.　 [7] The Military Retirement System was unfunded until October 1, 1984.

Source: Employee Benefit Research Institute, Washington, DC, *EBRI Databook on Employee Benefits, Sixth Edition* (copyright).

No. 613. Federal Civil Service Retirement: 1980 to 1997

[As of **Sept. 30** or for **year ending Sept. 30**. Covers both Civil Service Retirement System and Federal Employees Retirement System]

ITEM	Unit	1980	1985	1990	1992	1993	1994	1995	1996	1997
Employees covered [1]	1,000 . .	2,720	2,750	2,945	2,933	2,843	2,778	2,668	2,629	2,681
Annuitants, total	**1,000** . .	**1,675**	**1,955**	**2,143**	**2,185**	**2,242**	**2,263**	**2,311**	**2,333**	**2,352**
Age and service	1,000 . .	905	1,122	1,288	1,322	1,378	1,398	1,441	1,459	1,474
Disability	1,000 . .	343	332	297	282	274	268	263	260	257
Survivors	1,000 . .	427	501	558	581	589	597	607	614	621
Receipts, total [2]	**Mil. dol.**	**24,389**	**40,790**	**52,689**	**59,737**	**62,878**	**63,390**	**65,684**	**67,339**	**70,227**
Employee contributions	Mil. dol .	3,686	4,679	4,501	4,713	4,703	4,610	4,498	4,398	4,358
Federal government contributions	Mil. dol .	15,562	22,301	27,368	30,785	32,668	32,434	33,130	33,991	35,386
Disbursements, total [3]	**Mil. dol.**	**14,977**	**23,203**	**31,416**	**33,187**	**35,123**	**36,532**	**38,435**	**39,711**	**41,722**
Age and service annuitants [4]	Mil. dol .	12,639	19,414	26,495	27,684	29,288	30,440	32,070	32,970	34,697
Survivors	Mil. dol .	1,912	3,158	4,366	5,093	5,377	5,607	5,864	6,221	6,518
Average monthly benefit:										
Age and service	Dollars .	992	1,189	1,369	1,493	1,537	1,587	1,643	1,698	1,749
Disability	Dollars .	723	881	1,008	1,094	1,120	1,141	1,164	1,184	1,204
Survivors	Dollars .	392	528	653	731	760	789	819	849	881
Cash and security holdings.	Bil. dol . .	73.7	142.3	238.0	289.6	317.4	344.3	366.2	394.1	422.2

[1] Excludes employees in leave without pay status.　 [2] Includes interest on investments.　 [3] Includes refunds, death claims, and administration.　 [4] Includes disability annuitants.

Source: U.S. Office of Personnel Management, *Civil Service Retirement and Disability Trust Fund Annual Report.*

No. 614. State and Local Government Retirement Systems—Beneficiaries and Finances: 1980 to 1996

[In billions of dollars, except as indicated. For fiscal years closed during the 12 months ending June 30]

YEAR AND LEVEL OF GOVERNMENT	Number of beneficiaries (1,000)	RECEIPTS					BENEFITS AND WITHDRAWALS			Cash and security holdings
		Total	Employee contributions	Government contributions		Earnings on investments	Total	Benefits	Withdrawals	
				State	Local					
1980: All systems.........	(NA)	37.3	6.5	7.6	10.0	13.3	14.0	12.2	1.8	185
State-administered....	(NA)	28.6	5.3	7.4	5.6	10.3	10.3	8.8	1.4	145
Locally administered...	(NA)	8.7	1.2	0.2	4.3	3.0	3.8	3.4	0.4	41
1990: All systems.........	4,026	111.3	13.9	14.0	18.6	64.9	38.4	36.0	2.4	721
State-administered....	3,232	89.2	11.6	14.0	11.5	52.0	29.6	27.6	2.0	575
Locally administered...	794	22.2	2.2	(Z)	7.0	12.9	8.8	8.4	0.4	145
1995: All systems.........	4,979	148.8	18.6	16.6	24.4	89.2	61.4	58.8	2.7	1,118
State-administered....	4,025	123.3	15.7	16.2	15.4	76.0	48.0	45.8	2.2	914
Locally administered...	954	25.5	2.9	0.4	9.0	13.3	13.5	13.0	0.5	204
1996: All systems.........	5,128	192.6	19.4	19.5	24.2	129.4	68.1	64.7	3.3	1,273
State-administered....	4,166	156.3	16.4	19.1	16.1	106.9	53.2	50.5	2.6	1,045
Locally administered...	962	34.0	3.0	0.4	8.1	22.5	14.9	14.2	0.7	228

NA Not available.   Z Less than $50 million.

Source: U.S. Bureau of the Census, *Finances of Employee-Retirement Systems of State and Local Governments*, Series GF, No. 2, annual.

No. 615. Private Pension Plans—Summary, by Type of Plan: 1980 to 1994

["Pension plan" is defined by the Employee Retirement Income Security Act (ERISA) as "any plan, fund, or program which was heretofore or is hereafter established or maintained by an employer or an employee organization, or by both, to the extent that such plan (a) provides retirement income to employees, or (b) results in a deferral of income by employees for periods extending to the termination of covered employment or beyond, regardless of the method of calculating the contributions made to the plan, the method of calculating the benefits under the plan, or the method of distributing benefits from the plan." A defined benefit plan provides a definite benefit formula for calculating benefit amounts - such as a flat amount per year of service or a percentage of salary times years of service. A defined contribution plan is a pension plan in which the contributions are made to an individual account for each employee. The retirement benefit is dependent upon the account balance at retirement. The balance depends upon amounts contributed, investment experience, and, in the case of profit sharing plans, amounts which may be allocated to the account due to forfeitures by terminating employees. Employee Stock Ownership Plans (ESOP) and 401(k) plans (see Table 617) are included among defined contribution plans. Data are based on Form 5500 series reports filed with the Internal Revenue Service]

ITEM	Unit	TOTAL				DEFINED CONTRIBUTION PLAN				DEFINED BENEFIT PLAN			
		1980	1985	1990	1994	1980	1985	1990	1994	1980	1985	1990	1994
Number of plans [1]	1,000...	488.9	632.1	712.3	690.3	340.8	462.0	599.2	615.9	148.1	170.2	113.1	74.4
Total participants [2][3]	Million ..	57.9	74.7	76.9	85.1	19.9	35.0	38.1	44.8	38.0	39.7	38.8	40.3
Active participants [2][4]	Million ..	49.0	62.3	61.8	65.0	18.9	33.2	35.5	40.4	30.1	29.0	26.3	24.6
Contributions [5]	Bil. dol..	66.2	95.1	98.8	144.4	23.5	53.1	75.8	105.3	42.6	42.0	23.0	39.0
Benefits [6]	Bil. dol..	35.3	101.9	129.4	163.9	13.1	47.4	63.0	81.3	22.1	54.5	66.4	82.6

[1] Excludes all plans covering only one participant.   [2] Includes double counting of workers in more than one plan.   [3] Total participants include active participants, vested separated workers, and retirees.   [4] Any workers currently in employment covered by a plan and who are earning or retaining credited service under a plan. Includes any nonvested former employees who have not yet incurred breaks in service.   [5] Includes both employer and employee contributions.   [6] Benefits paid directly from trust and premium payments made from plan to insurance carriers. Excludes benefits paid directly by insurance carriers.

Source: U.S. Dept. of Labor, Pension and Welfare Benefits Administration, *Private Pension Plan Bulletin*, winter 1996.

No. 616. Pension Plan Coverage of Workers, by Selected Characteristics: 1996

[Covers workers as of **March 1997** who had earnings in 1996. Based on Current Population Survey; see text, Section 1, and Appendix III]

SEX AND AGE	NUMBER WITH COVERAGE (1,000)				PERCENT OF TOTAL WORKERS			
	Total [1]	White	Black	Hispanic [2]	Total [1]	White	Black	Hispanic [2]
Total	59,923	51,168	6,351	3,835	41.9	42.3	40.5	28.0
Male................	33,363	29,023	3,004	2,236	43.8	44.3	40.9	27.4
Under 65 years old	32,724	28,458	2,953	2,209	44.6	45.3	41.1	27.4
15 to 24 years old	1,501	1,277	166	170	12.0	12.0	12.6	9.8
25 to 44 years old	18,768	16,147	1,773	1,427	48.4	49.2	43.7	30.4
45 to 64 years old	12,456	11,034	1,013	612	56.5	56.9	55.9	37.9
65 years old and over	639	564	51	27	22.5	22.0	31.6	23.2
Female...............	26,560	22,145	3,347	1,599	39.8	40.0	40.1	28.9
Under 65 years old	26,082	21,725	3,312	1,574	40.4	40.6	40.5	28.9
15 to 24 years old	1,176	969	164	98	10.3	10.3	10.6	8.7
25 to 44 years old	15,091	12,436	1,976	1,002	45.0	45.4	43.5	32.1
45 to 64 years old	9,815	8,320	1,172	474	50.0	49.8	56.1	39.6
65 years old and over	478	420	35	25	22.4	22.0	21.5	29.8

[1] Includes other races, not shown separately.   [2] Hispanic persons may be of any race.

Source: U.S. Bureau of the Census, unpublished data.

No. 617. 401(k) Plans—Summary: 1985 to 1993

[A 401(k) plan is a qualified retirement plan that allows participants to have a portion of their compensation (otherwise payable in cash) contributed pretax to a retirement account on their behalf]

ITEM	1985	1988	1989	1990	1991	1992	1993
Number of plans [1]	29,869	68,121	83,301	97,614	111,314	139,704	154,527
Active participants [2] (1,000)	10,339	15,203	17,337	19,548	19,126	22,404	23,138
Assets (mil. dol.)	143,939	276,995	357,015	384,854	440,259	552,959	616,316
Contributions (mil. dol.)	24,322	39,412	46,081	48,998	51,533	64,345	69,322
Benefits (mil. dol.)	16,399	25,235	30,875	32,028	32,734	43,166	44,206
Percentage of all private defined contribution plans:							
Assets	34	47	52	54	53	58	58
Contributions	46	61	63	65	64	69	68
Benefits	35	43	47	51	51	58	57

[1] Excludes single-participant plans. [2] May include some employees who are eligible to participate in the plan but have not elected to join. 401(k) participants may participate in one or more additional plans.

Source: Employee Benefit Research Institute, Washington, DC, *EBRI Databook on Employee Benefits, Fifth Edition* (copyright).

No. 618. State Unemployment Insurance—Summary: 1980 to 1996

[Includes unemployment compensation for state and local government employees where covered by state law]

ITEM	Unit	1980	1985	1989	1990	1991	1992	1993	1994	1995	1996
Insured unemployment, avg. weekly	1,000	3,356	2,617	2,158	2,522	3,342	3,245	2,751	2,670	2,572	2,595
Percent of covered employment [1]	Percent	3.9	2.9	2.1	2.4	3.1	3.1	2.6	2.5	2.3	2.3
Percent of civilian unemployed	Percent	43.9	31.5	33.1	36.7	39.7	34.6	31.5	33.4	34.7	35.9
Unemployment benefits, avg. weekly	Dollars	100	128	152	162	170	174	180	182	187	190
Percent of weekly wage	Percent	36.6	35.3	35.4	36.0	36.4	35.4	36.0	35.7	35.5	34.5
Weeks compensated	Million	149.0	119.3	97.6	116.0	155.1	150.2	125.6	123.4	118.3	119.0
Beneficiaries, first payments [2]	1,000	9,992	8,372	7,369	8,629	10,075	9,243	7,884	7,959	8,035	7,995
Average duration of benefits [2]	Weeks	14.9	14.2	13.2	13.4	15.4	16.2	15.9	15.5	14.7	14.9
Claimants exhausting benefits	1,000	3,072	2,575	1,940	2,323	3,472	3,838	3,204	2,977	2,662	2,739
Percent of first payment [3]	Percent	33.2	31.2	28.0	29.4	34.8	39.9	39.2	36.3	34.3	33.4
Contributions collected [4]	Bil. dol.	11.4	19.3	16.5	15.2	14.5	17.0	19.8	21.8	22.0	21.6
Benefits paid	Bil. dol.	13.8	14.1	13.6	17.3	24.6	24.0	20.7	20.4	20.1	20.6
Funds available for benefits [5]	Bil. dol.	11.6	16.2	37.5	38.4	31.5	27.1	28.2	31.3	35.4	38.6
Average employer contribution rate [6]	Percent	2.4	3.1	2.2	2.0	2.0	2.2	2.5	2.6	2.4	2.3

[1] Insured unemployment as percent of average covered employment in preceding year. [2] Weeks compensated divided by first payment. [3] Based on first payments for 12-month period ending June 30. [4] Contributions from employers; also employees in states which tax workers. [5] End of year. Sum of balances in state clearing accounts, benefit-payment accounts, and state accounts in federal unemployment trust funds. [6] As percent of taxable wages.

No. 619. State Unemployment Insurance, by State and Other Area: 1996

[See headnote, Table 618. For state data on insured unemployment, see Table 683]

STATE AND OTHER AREA	Benefi- ciaries, first pay- ments (1,000)	Benefits paid (mil. dol.)	Avg. weekly unem- ploy- ment benefits (dol.)	STATE AND OTHER AREA	Benefi- ciaries, first pay- ments (1,000)	Benefits paid (mil. dol.)	Avg. weekly unem- ploy- ment benefits (dol.)	STATE AND OTHER AREA	Benefi- ciaries, first pay- ments (1,000)	Benefits paid (mil. dol.)	Avg. weekly unem- ploy- ment benefits (dol.)
Total	7,995	20,634	190	KY	120	221	171	OH	269	700	202
AL	146	206	142	LA	77	143	128	OK	49	98	175
AK	45	113	172	ME	47	103	171	OR	146	367	191
AZ	76	159	151	MD	118	339	195	PA	467	1,502	219
AR	96	174	170	MA	193	720	254	RI	54	183	228
CA	1,178	2,806	152	MI	404	947	205	SC	114	192	165
CO	75	189	208	MN	117	339	234	SD	9	16	150
CT	133	418	222	MS	70	128	141	TN	176	312	155
DE	27	96	224	MO	147	287	154	TX	350	920	189
DC	22	85	236	MT	30	59	165	UT	34	68	198
FL	264	639	178	NE	29	51	161	VT	23	48	168
GA	192	284	166	NV	56	144	194	VA	114	195	173
HI	41	173	270	NH	24	39	153	WA	229	795	212
ID	49	96	182	NJ	312	1,357	255	WV	59	141	176
IL	354	1,221	213	NM	30	74	157	WI	234	470	202
IN	128	233	187	NY	542	1,824	206	WY	13	30	181
IA	79	178	200	NC	235	382	193	PR	127	215	94
KS	55	114	202	ND	15	32	175	VI	2	7	155

Source of Tables 618 and 619: U.S. Employment and Training Administration, *Unemployment Insurance Financial Handbook*, annual.

No. 620. Workers' Compensation Payments: 1980 to 1995

[In billions of dollars, except as indicated. See headnote, Table 621]

ITEM	1980	1985	1987	1988	1989	1990	1991	1992	1993	1994	1995
Workers covered [1] (mil.)	79	84	88	91	104	106	104	104	106	109	113
Premium amounts paid [2] . .	**22.3**	**29.2**	**38.1**	**43.3**	**48.0**	**53.1**	**55.2**	**57.4**	**60.8**	**60.5**	**57.1**
Private carriers [2]	15.7	19.5	25.4	28.5	31.9	35.1	35.7	34.5	35.6	34.0	31.6
State funds	3.0	3.5	5.5	6.7	7.2	8.0	8.7	9.6	10.9	11.2	10.5
Federal programs [3]	1.1	1.7	1.7	1.9	2.0	2.2	2.1	2.5	2.5	2.5	2.6
Self-insurers	2.4	4.5	5.4	6.2	6.9	7.9	8.7	10.8	11.8	12.8	12.4
Annual benefits paid [2]	**13.6**	**22.2**	**27.3**	**30.7**	**34.3**	**38.2**	**42.2**	**45.7**	**45.3**	**44.7**	**43.5**
By private carriers [2]	7.0	12.3	15.5	17.5	19.9	22.2	24.5	25.3	24.1	22.6	21.4
From state funds [4]	4.3	5.7	6.8	7.4	8.0	8.7	9.7	10.7	10.6	10.6	10.9
Employers' self-insurance [5]	2.3	4.1	5.1	5.7	6.4	7.2	7.9	9.7	10.6	11.5	11.2
Type of benefit:											
Medical/hospitalization	3.9	7.5	9.9	11.5	13.4	15.2	16.8	17.6	17.5	17.2	16.7
Compensation payments	9.7	14.7	17.4	19.2	20.9	23.1	25.3	28.1	27.8	27.5	26.7
Disability.	8.4	13.1	15.8	17.6	19.2	21.2	23.3	26.0	25.4	25.5	24.8
Survivor	1.3	1.7	1.6	1.6	1.7	1.8	2.0	2.1	2.4	2.0	2.0
Percent of covered payroll: [1]											
Workers' compensation costs [6] [7] .	1.96	1.82	2.07	2.16	2.04	2.13	2.16	2.13	2.17	2.05	1.83
Benefits [7]	1.07	1.30	1.43	1.49	1.42	1.53	1.62	1.66	1.59	1.49	1.37

[1] Data for period 1980 to 1988 not comparable with later years. [2] Premium and benefit amounts include estimated benefit payments under insurance policy deductible provisions. Deductible benefits are allocated to private carriers and state funds. [3] Includes federal employer compensation program and that portion of federal black lung benefits program financed from employer contributions. [4] Net cash and medical benefits paid by competitive and exclusive state funds and by federal workers' compensation programs, including black lung benefit program. [5] Cash and medical benefits paid by self-insurers, plus value of medical benefits paid by employers carrying workers' compensation policies that exclude standard medical coverage. [6] Premiums written by private carriers and state funds, and benefits paid by self-insurers increased by 5-10 percent prior to 1992 and by 11 percent for 1992-95 for administrative costs. Also includes benefits paid and administrative costs of federal system for government employees. [7] Excludes programs financed from general revenue—black lung benefits and supplemental pensions in some states.

Source: 1980-1993, U.S. Social Security Administration, *Annual Statistical Supplement* to the *Social Security Bulletin*. Beginning 1994, Jack Schmulowitz, *Workers' Compensation: Benefits, Coverage, and Costs, 1994-95*, National Academy of Social Insurance, Washington, DC, 1997.

No. 621. Workers' Compensation Payments, by State: 1990 to 1995

[In millions of dollars. Calendar-year data, except fiscal-year data for federal civilian and other programs and for some states with state funds. Payments represent compensation and medical benefits and include insurance losses paid by private insurance carriers (compiled from state workers' compensation agencies and A.M. Best Co); disbursements of state funds (compiled from the A.M. Best Co., state workers' compensation agencies and U.S. Bureau of the Census); and self-insurance payments, estimated from available state data. Includes benefit payments under Longshore and Harbor Workers' Compensation Act for states in which such payments are made]

STATE	1990	1992	1993	1994	1995	STATE	1990	1992	1993	1994	1995
Total [1]	**38,238**	**45,668**	**45,330**	**44,697**	**43,512**	Nevada	339	529	553	432	365
						New Hampshire	169	206	194	178	169
Alabama.	444	481	[2]479	[2]480	516	New Jersey.	844	956	968	[2]957	[2]972
Alaska.	113	127	122	112	106	New Mexico	228	216	182	162	145
Arizona.	371	399	402	406	386	New York	1,752	2,317	2,370	[2]2,725	[2]2,780
Arkansas	229	244	224	209	159	North Carolina.	480	705	671	565	495
California	6,065	7,907	7,625	7,390	[2]7,177	North Dakota.	60	71	60	75	71
Colorado.	595	722	683	612	584	Ohio	1,960	2,364	2,353	2,149	2,303
Connecticut	694	783	[2]848	[2]773	[2]733	Oklahoma	369	476	493	550	580
Delaware	75	89	[2]88	[2]103	[2]103						
						Oregon.	573	476	468	468	463
District of Columbia .	86	126	122	115	113	Pennsylvania	2,019	2,531	[2]2,774	[2]2,582	[2]2,663
Florida	1,976	1,861	2,296	2,720	2,518	Rhode Island.	219	266	185	160	138
Georgia	735	1,004	911	812	699	South Carolina.	277	350	[2]344	[2]339	[2]353
Hawaii	216	288	324	343	326	South Dakota	56	69	72	78	63
Idaho.	105	123	125	147	148	Tennessee	463	522	487	449	400
Illinois	1,607	1,750	1,668	1,582	1,438	Texas	2,896	[2]3,082	[2]2,694	[2]2,232	[2]2,006
Indiana.	350	375	364	378	361						
Iowa	231	259	240	233	233	Utah	187	160	165	152	140
Kansas.	266	297	307	[2]302	[2]280	Vermont	61	73	73	67	65
Kentucky	383	475	595	585	498	Virginia.	507	542	539	591	557
						Washington.	883	1,018	1,068	1,087	1,129
Louisiana	575	586	531	531	516	West Virginia.	389	456	476	510	529
Maine.	380	429	341	282	286	Wisconsin	561	598	608	609	608
Maryland	505	565	548	558	522	Wyoming	49	66	76	77	75
Massachusetts.	1,235	1,205	[2]1,017	[2]917	[2]773						
Michigan.	1,205	1,428	[2]1,594	[2]1,589	[2]1,585	Federal programs:					
Minnesota.	582	822	809	[2]783	[2]733	Civilian employ-					
Mississippi	198	247	214	[2]213	[2]218	ees.	1,448	1,751	1,822	1,859	1,880
Missouri	496	698	656	785	733	Black lung					
Montana.	150	165	167	154	151	benefits [3]	1,435	1,396	1,356	1,306	1,222
Nebraska	137	157	160	156	141	Other [4]	11	11	11	(NA)	(NA)

NA Not available. [1] Beginning 1992 total includes an amount for benefits under deductible provisions not distributed by state. [2] Includes benefits under deductible provisions. [3] Includes payments by Social Security Administration and by Department of Labor. [4] Primarily payments made to dependents of reservists who died while on active duty in the Armed Forces.

Source: U.S. Social Security Administration, *Social Security Bulletin*, summer 1995, and selected prior issues. Beginning 1994, Jack Schmulowitz, *Workers' Compensation: Benefits, Coverage, and Costs, 1994-95*, National Academy of Social Insurance, Washington, DC, 1997.

No. 622. Persons With Work Disability, by Selected Characteristics: 1997

[In thousands, except percent. As of March. Covers civilian noninstitutional population and members of Armed Forces living off post or with their families on post. Persons are classified as having a work disability if they (1) have a health problem or disability which prevents them from working or which limits the kind or amount of work they can do; (2) have a service-connected disability or ever retired or left a job for health reasons; (3) did not work in survey reference week or previous year because of long-term illness or disability; or (4) are under age 65, and are covered by medicare or receive supplemental security income. Based on Current Population Survey; see text, Section 1, and Appendix III]

AGE AND PARTICIPATION STATUS IN ASSISTANCE PROGRAMS	Total [1]	Male	Female	White	Black	Hispanic [2]
Persons with work disability	**17,439**	**8,454**	**8,985**	**13,293**	**3,456**	**1,701**
16 to 24 years old.	1,390	686	703	955	341	180
25 to 34 years old.	2,622	1,237	1,386	1,916	612	278
35 to 44 years old.	4,075	2,034	2,041	3,024	907	416
45 to 54 years old.	4,368	2,128	2,241	3,419	785	369
55 to 64 years old.	4,983	2,370	2,614	3,980	811	457
Percent work disabled of total population . . .	10.2	10.0	10.4	9.4	16.2	9.1
16 to 24 years old.	4.2	4.1	4.3	3.6	6.9	3.8
25 to 34 years old.	6.5	6.2	6.9	5.9	11.4	5.1
35 to 44 years old.	9.3	9.3	9.2	8.3	16.8	9.5
45 to 54 years old.	13.2	13.2	13.3	12.2	22.3	15.0
55 to 64 years old.	23.1	23.1	23.3	21.6	37.4	28.3
Percent of work disabled—						
Receiving social security income.	30.3	31.9	28.9	31.6	26.5	25.4
Receiving food stamps	23.6	19.5	27.3	19.9	36.9	35.5
Covered by medicaid.	34.7	30.5	38.7	30.4	49.0	48.4
Residing in public housing	7.0	5.3	8.7	4.9	14.4	12.2
Residing in subsidized housing	3.4	2.7	4.1	2.5	6.6	5.8

[1] Includes other races not shown separately.   [2] Hispanic persons may be of any race.
Source: U.S. Bureau of the Census, unpublished data.

No. 623. Vocational Rehabilitation—Summary: 1980 to 1997

[For fiscal years ending in year shown; see text, Section 9. Includes Puerto Rico, Guam, Virgin Islands, American Samoa, Northern Mariana Islands, and the Republic of Palau. State agencies, using matching state and federal funds, provide vocational rehabilitation services to eligible individuals with disabilities to enable them to prepare for and engage in gainful employment. Services may include counseling, guidance and work related placement services, physical and mental restoration, training and rehabilitation technology]

ITEM	Unit	1980	1985	1990	1992	1993	1994	1995	1996	1997
Federal and State expenditures [1]	Mil. dol. .	1,076	1,452	1,910	2,240	2,241	2,517	2,714	2,844	3,046
Federal expenditures.	Mil. dol. .	817	1,100	1,525	1,731	1,691	1,891	2,054	2,104	2,164
Applicants processed for program eligibility .	1,000 . . .	717	594	625	713	713	675	625	578	617
Percent accepted into program	Percent . .	58	60	57	57	61	72	76	76	79
Total persons rehabilitated [2]	1,000 . . .	277	228	216	192	194	203	210	213	212
Rehabilitation rate [3]	Percent . .	64	64	62	58	56	49	46	61	61
Severely disabled persons rehabilitated [2][4] . . .	1,000 . . .	143	135	146	134	139	149	159	166	168
Rehabilitation rate [3]	Percent . .	61	62	62	57	55	49	46	60	60
Percent of total persons rehabilitated . . .	Percent . .	51	59	68	70	72	74	76	78	79
Persons served, total [5]	1,000 . . .	1,095	932	938	949	1,049	1,194	1,250	1,226	1,267
Persons served, severely disabled [4][5]	1,000 . . .	606	581	640	668	762	882	940	951	1,005
Percent of total persons served	Percent . .	55	62	68	70	73	74	75	78	79

[1] Includes expenditures only under the basic support provisions of the Rehabilitation Act.   [2] Persons successfully placed into gainful employment.   [3] Persons rehabilitated as a percent of all active case closures (whether rehabilitated or not); beginning 1996, as a percent of persons who required services.   [4] An individual with a severe disability is an individual whose severe physical or mental impairment seriously limits one or more functional capacities in terms of an employment outcome, and whose vocational rehabilitation can be expected to require multiple vocational rehabilitation services over an extended period of time.
[5] Includes active cases accepted for rehabilitation services during year plus active cases on hand at beginning of year.
Source: U.S. Dept. of Education, Rehabilitation Services Administration, Caseload Statistics of State Vocational Rehabilitation Agencies in Fiscal Years, and State Vocational Rehabilitation Agency Program Data in Fiscal Years, both annual.

No. 624. Protection Against Short-Term Sickness Income Loss: 1980 to 1994

[In millions of dollars, except percent. "Short-term sickness" refers to short-term or temporary nonwork-connected disability (lasting not more than 6 months) and the first 6 months of long-term disability]

ITEM	1980	1985	1988	1989	1990	1991	1992	1993	1994
Short-term sickness: Income loss	33,746	48,484	60,185	63,862	68,296	69,542	73,783	76,816	81,101
Total protection provided [1]	**17,480**	**22,918**	**27,922**	**30,006**	**31,683**	**32,991**	**35,464**	**35,889**	**36,874**
Protection as percent of loss	51.8	47.3	46.4	47.0	46.4	47.4	48.1	46.7	45.5
Benefits provided by protection:									
Individual insurance.	1,280	1,796	2,057	2,451	2,701	2,588	3,497	3,560	3,263
Group benefits to workers in private									
employment	9,984	12,440	15,392	16,364	16,835	17,555	18,456	18,310	19,039
Private cash insurance [2]	3,271	2,601	2,903	2,732	2,711	2,605	2,703	2,608	2,558
Publicly operated cash sickness funds [3] . .	770	1,179	1,779	1,907	2,269	2,817	2,975	2,349	2,370
Sick leave	5,943	8,660	10,710	11,725	11,855	12,133	12,778	13,353	14,111
Sick leave for government employees.	6,041	8,487	10,266	10,967	11,873	12,537	13,115	13,616	14,160

[1] Provided by individual insurance, group benefits to workers in private employment, and sick leave for government employees. Includes benefits for the sixth month of disability payable under old-age, survivors, disability, and health insurance program, not shown separately.   [2] Group accident and sickness insurance and self-insurance privately written either on a voluntary basis or in compliance with state temporary disability insurance laws in CA, HI, NJ, and NY. Includes a small but undetermined amount of group disability insurance benefits paid to government workers and to self-employed persons through farm, trade, or professional associations.   [3] Includes state-operated plans in RI, CA, and NJ; State Insurance Fund and special fund for disabled unemployed in New York; and provisions of Railroad Unemployment Insurance Act.
Source: U.S. Social Security Administration, Social Security Bulletin, fall 1994, and unpublished data.

No. 625. Supplemental Security Income—Recipients and Payments: 1980 to 1996

[Recipients and average monthly payments, as of **December**. See also Appendix III]

PROGRAM	Unit	1980	1985	1990	1991	1992	1993	1994	1995	1996
Recipients, total [1]	1,000 . .	4,142	4,138	4,817	5,118	5,566	5,984	6,296	6,514	6,614
Aged.	1,000 . .	1,808	1,504	1,454	1,465	1,471	1,475	1,466	1,446	1,413
Blind.	1,000 . .	78	82	84	85	85	85	85	84	82
Disabled	1,000 . .	2,256	2,551	3,279	3,569	4,010	4,424	4,745	4,984	5,119
Payments, total [2]	Mil. dol .	7,941	11,060	16,599	18,524	22,233	24,557	25,877	27,628	28,792
Aged.	Mil. dol .	2,734	3,035	3,736	3,890	4,140	4,248	4,367	4,467	4,507
Blind.	Mil. dol .	190	264	334	347	371	375	372	375	372
Disabled	Mil. dol .	5,014	7,755	12,521	14,268	17,711	19,928	21,131	22,782	23,906
Average monthly payment, total [1] .	Dollars .	168	226	299	321	358	345	351	358	363
Aged.	Dollars .	128	164	213	221	227	237	243	251	261
Blind.	Dollars .	213	274	342	351	362	359	364	370	379
Disabled	Dollars .	198	261	337	361	407	381	384	389	391

[1] Federally administered payments only.   [2] Includes data not available by reason for eligibility.

No. 626. Supplemental Security Income (SSI)—Recipients and Payments, by State and Other Area: 1995 and 1996

[Recipients as of **December**. Data cover federal SSI payments and/or federally-administered state supplementation. For explanation of methodology, see Appendix III]

STATE AND OTHER AREA	RECIPIENTS (1,000)		PAYMENTS FOR YEAR (mil. dol.)		STATE AND OTHER AREA	RECIPIENTS (1,000)		PAYMENTS FOR YEAR (mil. dol.)	
	1995	1996	1995	1996		1995	1996	1995	1996
Total	6,514	6,614	27,037	28,252	MO	114	116	431	455
U.S	6,513	6,613	27,035	28,250	MT	14	14	53	55
AL	165	167	600	631	NE	21	22	76	81
AK	7	7	27	29	NV	21	22	79	86
AZ	73	76	288	308	NH	11	11	39	42
AR	94	94	326	335	NJ	144	146	594	616
CA	1,032	1,045	5,391	5,594	NM	45	46	166	174
CO	57	58	217	229	NY	589	606	2,724	2,895
CT	45	46	181	194	NC	191	195	639	687
DE	11	11	40	43	ND	9	9	29	30
DC	20	20	83	85	OH	248	254	1,044	1,106
FL	338	353	1,300	1,408	OK	74	75	266	279
GA	199	201	692	728	OR	47	48	183	196
HI	19	20	82	88	PA	265	270	1,159	1,214
ID	17	17	63	67	RI	24	25	100	107
IL	267	268	1,160	1,199	SC	111	112	384	402
IN	89	91	348	367	SD	14	14	47	50
IA	42	42	148	153	TN	180	179	648	667
KS	38	38	141	150	TX	404	412	1,391	1,460
KY	165	170	635	672	UT	20	21	80	85
LA	182	182	717	731	VT	13	13	50	50
ME	31	28	96	99	VA	130	133	471	497
MD	82	85	332	353	WA	92	95	398	424
MA	164	166	700	728	WV	68	70	276	294
MI	210	214	896	943	WI	112	95	487	377
MN	62	64	235	250	WY	6	6	21	23
MS	141	141	504	517	N. Mariana	1	1	2	2

Source of Tables 625 and 626: U.S. Social Security Administration, *Social Security Bulletin*, quarterly, and *Annual Statistical Supplement* to the *Social Security Bulletin*.

No. 627. Public Assistance—Recipients and Payments Under Aid to Families With Dependent Children (AFDC): 1980 to 1996

[See text, Section 12 for changes in AFDC program. Includes Puerto Rico, Guam, and Virgin Islands]

PROGRAM	1980	1985	1990	1991	1992	1993	1994	1995	1996
RECIPIENTS (1,000)									
Families [1]	3,843	3,721	4,218	4,708	4,936	5,050	4,979	4,641	4,166
Recipients [1]	11,101	10,924	12,159	13,489	14,035	14,257	13,961	12,923	11,533
Children	7,599	7,247	8,208	9,104	9,471	9,598	9,463	8,840	7,965
Families [2]	3,642	3,692	3,974	4,374	4,768	4,981	5,046	4,876	4,553
Recipients [2]	10,597	10,813	11,460	12,592	13,625	14,143	14,226	13,652	12,649
Children	7,419	7,198	7,917	8,715	9,303	9,539	9,590	9,283	8,673
Adults	3,178	3,615	3,543	3,877	4,322	4,604	4,636	4,382	3,976
Total payments (mil. dol.)	12,475	15,196	19,078	20,931	22,106	22,688	22,867	22,032	20,411
AVG. MONTHLY PAYMENTS[1] (dol.)									
Families	288	341	392	388	381	377	376	383	383
Recipients	100	118	136	135	134	133	134	137	138

[1] As of December.   [2] Average monthly recipients.

Source: U.S. Administration for Children and Families, *Quarterly Public Assistance Statistics*, annual; "Welfare Caseloads: Families and Recipients 1936-1997;" <http://www.acf.dhhs.gov/news/3697.htm>; (accessed 25 March 1998) and "Welfare Caseloads: Adults and Children 1960-1997;" <http://www.acf.dhhs.gov/news/6097ac.htm>; (accessed 22 September 1997).

No. 628. Aid to Families With Dependent Children (AFDC)— Recipients and Payments, by State and Other Area: 1995 and 1996

[Recipients as of **December**. See text, Section 12 for changes in AFDC program]

STATE AND OTHER AREA	RECIPIENTS (1,000)		PAYMENTS FOR YEAR (mil. dol.)		Average monthly payment per family, 1996	STATE AND OTHER AREA	RECIPIENTS (1,000)		PAYMENTS FOR YEAR (mil. dol.)		Average monthly payment per family, 1996
	1995	1996	1995	1996			1995	1996	1995	1996	
Total	12,923	11,533	22,032	20,411	$374	MT	32	28	48	45	350
U.S.	12,757	11,373	21,945	20,329	377	NE	39	37	57	54	315
AL	109	92	83	75	148	NV	40	31	52	48	272
AK	34	35	107	107	731	NH	25	21	57	50	435
AZ	176	157	251	228	300	NJ	297	261	510	463	345
AR	59	55	49	52	189	NM	102	92	154	153	376
CA	2,645	2,490	6,125	5,908	549	NY	1,206	1,090	3,042	2,929	565
CO	101	89	143	129	304	NC	286	256	334	300	221
CT	164	157	383	323	463	ND	14	12	23	21	358
DE	23	23	36	35	279	OH	556	527	849	763	308
DC	71	68	124	121	391	OK	112	89	152	122	262
FL	583	491	764	680	267	OR	92	67	181	155	385
GA	368	310	414	385	246	PA	553	488	905	821	360
HI	67	65	173	173	657	RI	59	55	134	125	492
ID	23	20	32	30	278	SC	125	100	107	101	184
IL	665	611	882	833	310	SD	17	14	23	22	300
IN	152	121	197	153	242	TN	260	206	199	190	160
IA	93	81	149	131	333	TX	715	624	520	496	162
KS	71	58	114	98	324	UT	41	36	70	64	363
KY	176	164	183	191	222	VT	26	23	62	56	512
LA	242	214	151	130	154	VA	168	139	222	199	256
ME	56	51	101	99	401	WA	274	261	606	585	493
MD	212	174	308	285	321	WV	98	67	109	101	231
MA	245	217	646	560	528	WI	186	137	389	291	404
MI	542	472	1,000	779	365	WY	14	11	21	17	295
MN	171	162	356	333	476	PR	158	147	68	63	104
MS	131	112	75	68	118	GU	8	9	14	14	550
MO	239	211	276	254	256	VI	5	5	4	4	249

Source: U.S. Administration for Children and Families, *Quarterly Public Assistance Statistics*, annual.

No. 629. Mothers Who Receive AFDC and/or Food Stamp Benefits—Socioeconomic Characteristics: 1993

[As of **summer**. Covers mothers 15 to 44 years old. AFDC=Aid to Families with Dependent Children program. Based on Survey of Income and Program Participation; see text, Section 14]

CHARACTERISTIC	AFDC MOTHERS		FOOD STAMP MOTHERS		CHARACTERISTIC	AFDC MOTHERS		FOOD STAMP MOTHERS	
	Number (1,000)	Percent distribution	Number (1,000)	Percent distribution		Number (1,000)	Percent distribution	Number (1,000)	Percent distribution
Total	3,754	100	5,303	100	Married, husband absent [2]	648	17	906	17
Age:					Widowed or divorced . .	851	23	1,244	23
15 to 19 years old. . . .	191	5	204	4	Never married	1,783	48	2,065	39
20 to 24 years old. . . .	866	23	1,162	22	Educational attainment:				
25 to 29 years old. . . .	865	23	1,150	22	Not a high school				
30 to 34 years old. . . .	921	25	1,335	25	graduate	1,633	44	2,169	41
35 to 39 years old. . . .	604	16	922	17	High school, 4 years . .	1,422	38	2,141	40
40 to 44 years old. . . .	307	8	530	10	College: 1 or more years	698	19	992	19
Race:					Labor force status:				
White	2,074	55	3,176	60	Worked all or some				
Black	1,471	39	1,903	36	weeks	474	13	1,159	22
Hispanic origin:					No job last month	3,280	87	4,144	78
Hispanic [1]	784	21	1,060	20	Monthly family income: [3]				
Not Hispanic	2,970	79	4,242	80	Less than $500	1,351	36	1,635	31
Marital status:					$500 to $999	1,360	36	1,797	34
Married, husband					$1,000 to $1,499	479	13	924	17
present	472	13	1,087	20	$1,500 and over	552	15	861	16

[1] Persons of Hispanic origin may be of any race.   [2] Includes separated women.   [3] Excludes those who did not report income.

Source: U.S. Bureau of the Census, *Statistical Brief*, Nos. SB/95-2 and SB/95-22.

No. 630. Federal Food Programs: 1980 to 1997

[**For fiscal years ending in year shown**; see text, Section 9. Program data include Puerto Rico, Virgin Islands, Guam, American Samoa, Northern Marianas, and the former Trust Territory when a federal food program was operated in these areas. Participation data are average monthly figures except as noted. Participants are not reported for the nutrition program for the elderly and the commodity distribution programs. Cost data are direct federal benefits to recipients; they exclude federal administrative payments and applicable state and local contributions. Federal costs for commodities and cash-in-lieu of commodities are shown separately from direct cash benefits for those programs receiving both]

PROGRAM	Unit	1980	1985	1990	1993	1994	1995	1996	1997
Food stamp:									
Participants	Million . .	21.1	19.9	20.1	27.0	27.5	26.6	25.5	22.8
Federal cost.	Mil. dol . .	8,721	10,744	14,187	22,006	22,749	22,765	22,441	19,555
Monthly average coupon value per recipient	Dollars . .	34.47	44.99	58.92	67.96	69.01	71.27	73.22	71.35
Nutrition assistance program for Puerto Rico: [1]									
Federal cost.	Mil. dol . .	(X)	825	937	1,040	1,079	1,131	1,143	1,174
National school lunch program (NSLP):									
Free lunches served	Million . .	1,671	1,657	1,662	1,981	2,049	2,090	2,128	2,189
Reduced-price lunches served	Million . .	308	255	273	287	298	309	326	351
Children participating [2]	Million . .	26.6	23.6	24.1	24.9	25.3	25.7	25.9	26.4
Federal cost.	Mil. dol . .	2,279	2,578	3,214	4,081	4,291	4,467	4,662	4,930
School breakfast (SB):									
Children participating [2]	Million . .	3.6	3.4	4.1	5.4	5.8	6.3	6.6	6.9
Federal cost.	Mil. dol . .	288	379	596	869	959	1,048	1,119	1,212
Special supplemental food program (WIC): [3]									
Participants	Million . .	1.9	3.1	4.5	5.9	6.5	6.9	7.2	7.4
Federal cost.	Mil. dol . .	584	1,193	1,637	2,115	2,325	2,516	2,690	2,814
Commodity supplemental food program (CS): [4]									
Participants	Million . .	0.1	0.2	0.3	0.4	0.4	0.4	0.4	0.4
Federal cost.	Mil. dol . .	19	42	71	94	87	79	80	81
Child and adult care (CC): [5]									
Participants	Million . .	0.7	1.0	1.5	2.0	2.2	2.4	2.4	2.5
Federal cost.	Mil. dol . .	207	390	720	1,082	1,196	1,296	1,360	1,386
Summer feeding (SF): [7]									
Children participating [8]	Million . .	1.9	1.5	1.7	2.1	2.2	2.1	2.2	2.3
Federal cost.	Mil. dol . .	104	103	145	195	205	212	225	213
Nutrition program for the elderly:									
Meals served	Million . .	166	225	246	244	247	251	246	248
Federal cost.	Mil. dol . .	75	134	142	153	152	148	145	145
Federal cost of commodities donated to— [9]									
Child nutrition (NSLP, CC, SF, and SB)	Mil. dol . .	930	840	646	704	764	733	734	659

X Not applicable.   [1] Puerto Rico was included in the food stamp program until June 30, 1982.   [2] Average monthly participation (excluding summer months of June through August). Includes children in public and private elementary and secondary schools and in residential child care institutes.   [3] WIC serves pregnant and postpartum women, infants, and children up to age five.   [4] CS is a food distribution alternative to WIC which also serves needy elderly persons.   [5] Program provides year-round subsidies to feed preschool children in child care centers and family day care homes. Certain care centers serving disabled or elderly adults also receive meal subsidies.   [6] Average quarterly daily attendance at participating institutions.   [7] Program provides free meals to children in poor areas during summer months.   [8] Peak month (July) average daily attendance at participating institutions.   [9] Includes the federal cost of commodity entitlements, cash-in-lieu of commodities, and bonus foods.

Source: U.S. Dept. of Agriculture, Food and Nutrition Service. In "Annual Historical Review of FNS Programs" and unpublished data.

No. 631. Federal Food Stamp and National School Lunch Programs, by State: 1990 to 1997

[For years ending Sept. 30. Participation data are average monthly number participating in year ending Sept. 30. National school lunch outlets include public and private elementary and secondary schools and residential child care institutions. Food stamp costs are for benefits only and exclude administrative expenditures. National school lunch program costs are for federal cash reimbursements at rates set by law for each meal served but do not include the value of USDA donated commodities utilized in this program]

STATE	FOOD STAMP PROGRAM								NATIONAL SCHOOL LUNCH PROGRAM					
	Households participating (1,000)		Persons (1,000)			Cost (mil. dol.)			Persons (1,000)			Cost (mil. dol.)		
	1995	1997	1990	1995	1997	1990	1995	1997	1990	1995	1997	1990	1995	1997
Total [1] . .	10,879	9,450	20,067	26,619	22,837	14,187	22,765	19,555	24,133	25,685	26,358	3,214	4,467	4,930
U.S.	10,867	9,438	20,036	26,579	22,799	14,153	22,714	19,504	23,583	25,171	25,903	3,098	4,343	4,814
AL	209	186	454	525	469	328	441	393	554	551	548	77	93	100
AK	15	15	25	45	45	25	50	52	38	44	49	8	13	15
AZ	178	133	317	480	364	239	414	316	324	400	420	47	77	88
AR	107	105	235	272	266	155	212	214	296	313	311	41	53	57
CA	1,176	1,045	1,955	3,175	2,815	968	2,473	2,379	2,135	2,344	2,491	396	587	663
CO	103	91	221	252	217	156	217	182	277	303	311	31	43	48
CT	100	94	133	226	210	72	169	169	223	230	242	23	34	38
DE	21	20	33	57	54	25	47	41	57	66	67	6	9	10
DC	43	40	62	94	90	43	93	91	47	50	51	10	14	14
FL	588	514	781	1,395	1,192	609	1,307	1,061	1,107	1,195	1,268	158	249	279
GA	329	284	536	816	698	382	700	597	892	979	1,025	106	159	181
HI	55	57	77	125	127	81	177	189	141	138	145	14	20	24
ID	30	27	59	80	70	40	59	53	129	139	139	14	19	21
IL	488	434	1,013	1,151	1,020	835	1,056	933	908	965	1,004	131	175	197
IN	183	140	311	470	348	226	382	293	608	596	598	54	70	76
IA	75	67	170	184	161	109	141	125	375	383	387	31	40	44
KS	75	64	142	184	149	96	144	112	311	310	310	29	40	43
KY	187	174	458	520	444	334	413	372	490	507	521	61	79	84
LA	267	220	727	711	575	549	629	512	676	668	667	104	126	132
ME	60	58	94	132	124	63	112	103	106	104	104	11	16	17
MD	169	152	255	399	354	203	365	320	343	367	376	40	60	67
MA	178	149	347	410	340	207	315	262	439	467	492	44	67	75
MI	418	366	917	971	839	663	806	678	714	763	759	82	113	124
MN	131	110	263	308	260	165	240	192	482	530	546	42	58	63
MS	185	155	499	480	399	352	383	313	418	407	403	76	87	92
MO	237	199	431	576	478	312	488	401	538	570	578	58	79	87
MT	28	27	57	71	67	41	57	55	83	86	84	10	13	13
NE	43	41	95	105	97	59	77	72	187	206	212	18	24	26
NV	46	38	50	99	82	41	91	74	73	96	102	8	16	20
NH	25	21	31	58	46	20	44	35	87	89	94	6	10	11
NJ	233	212	382	551	490	289	506	449	484	523	543	60	91	102
NM	87	75	157	239	205	117	196	168	174	187	191	30	40	44
NY	1,027	899	1,548	2,183	1,914	1,086	2,065	1,775	1,510	1,660	1,704	232	332	367
NC	258	250	419	614	586	282	495	478	737	763	791	91	123	141
ND	17	16	39	41	38	25	32	29	92	87	84	8	9	10
OH	506	389	1,089	1,155	874	861	1,017	744	888	987	973	109	138	145
OK	153	129	267	375	308	186	315	256	354	370	367	46	64	68
OR	132	121	216	289	259	168	254	216	230	250	258	26	39	43
PA	516	440	952	1,173	1,009	661	1,006	865	969	987	1,008	102	143	157
RI	40	37	64	93	85	42	82	70	55	57	57	7	12	14
SC	140	140	299	364	349	240	297	281	446	453	458	60	82	89
SD	19	18	50	50	47	35	40	39	101	106	105	12	14	15
TN	281	253	527	662	586	372	554	475	576	599	606	68	90	100
TX	946	751	1,880	2,558	2,034	1,429	2,246	1,765	1,982	2,176	2,287	304	429	486
UT	44	38	99	119	98	71	90	78	230	248	258	24	33	35
VT	27	25	38	59	53	22	46	41	46	49	51	4	7	7
VA	235	206	346	546	476	247	450	379	573	614	634	60	87	96
WA	204	198	340	476	442	229	417	387	360	429	440	43	69	77
WV	123	117	262	309	287	192	253	239	200	208	210	29	33	36
WI	119	87	286	320	232	180	220	158	462	495	518	45	60	65
WY	13	11	28	34	29	21	28	23	56	57	56	5	7	8

[1] Food stamp totals include Guam and the Virgin Islands; national school lunch totals include Puerto Rico, Guam, the Virgin Islands, Dept. of Defense overseas schools, and (in FY 1990 only) American Samoa and the Northern Marianas. Several outlying areas receive nutrition assistance grants in lieu of food stamp assistance (e.g., Puerto Rico, American Samoa and the Northern Marianas).

Source: U.S. Dept. of Agriculture, Food and Consumer Service. In "Annual Historical Review of FNS Programs" and unpublished data.

No. 632. Child Support—Award and Recipiency Status of Custodial Parent: 1991

[In thousands except as noted. Custodial parents 15 years and older with own children under 21 years of age present from absent parents as of spring 1992. Covers civilian noninstitutional population. Based on Current Population Survey; see text, section 1, and Appendix III. For definition of mean, see Guide to Tabular Presentation]

AWARD AND RECIPIENCY STATUS	ALL CUSTODIAL PARENTS				CUSTODIAL PARENTS BELOW THE POVERTY LEVEL			
	Total		Mothers	Fathers	Total		Mothers	Fathers
	Number	Percent distribu- tion			Number	Percent distribu- tion		
Total	**11,502**	(X)	**9,918**	**1,584**	**3,720**	(X)	**3,513**	**207**
With child support agreement or award . . .	6,190	(X)	5,542	648	1,438	(X)	1,368	71
Supposed to receive payments in 1991. .	5,326	100.0	4,883	443	1,257	100.0	1,200	57
Actually received payments in 1991 . .	4,006	75.2	3,728	278	859	68.3	845	14
Received full amount	2,742	51.5	2,552	189	499	39.7	497	2
Received partial payments.	1,265	23.8	1,176	89	360	28.6	348	12
Did not receive payments in 1991. . . .	1,320	24.8	1,156	164	398	31.7	355	43
Child support not awarded	5,312	(X)	4,376	936	2,282	(X)	2,145	136
MEAN INCOME AND CHILD SUPPORT								
Received child support payments in 1991:								
Mean total money income (dol.).	19,217	(X)	18,144	33,579	5,734	(X)	5,687	(B)
Mean child support received (dol.)	2,961	(X)	3,011	2,292	1,910	(X)	1,922	(B)
Received the full amount due:								
Mean total money income (dol.) . . .	20,050	(X)	19,310	30,012	5,980	(X)	6,004	(B)
Mean child support received (dol.). .	3,543	(X)	3,618	2,536	2,670	(X)	2,660	(B)
Received partial payments:								
Mean total money income (dol.) . . .	17,411	(X)	15,611	41,163	5,392	(X)	5,235	(B)
Mean child support received (dol.). .	1,699	(X)	1,694	1,773	857	(X)	871	(B)
Received no payments in 1991:								
Mean total money income (dol.).	15,919	(X)	14,602	25,184	5,399	(X)	5,525	(B)
Without child support agreement or award:								
Mean total money income (dol.).	13,283	(X)	10,226	27,578	4,979	(X)	4,942	5,560

B Base too small to meet statistical standards for reliability.   X Not applicable.
Source: U.S. Bureau of the Census, *Current Population Reports*, P60-187.

No. 633. Child Support Enforcement Program—Caseload and Collections: 1980 to 1996

[For years ending Sept. 30. Includes Puerto Rico, Guam, and the Virgin Islands. The child support enforcement program locates absent parents, establishes paternity of children born out-of-wedlock, and establishes and enforces support orders. By law, these services are available to all families that need them. The program is operated at the state and local government level but 68 percent of administrative costs are paid by the federal government. Child support collected for families not receiving Aid to Families with Dependent Children (AFDC) goes to the family to help it remain self-sufficient. Most of the child support collected on behalf of AFDC families goes to federal and state governments to offset AFDC payments. Based on data reported by state agencies. Minus sign (-) indicates net outlay]

ITEM	Unit	1980	1985	1990	1992	1993	1994	1995	1996
Total cases	**1,000** . . .	**5,432**	**8,401**	**12,796**	**15,158**	**17,125**	**18,610**	**19,162**	**19,319**
AFDC and AFDC arrears only caseload . .	1,000 . . .	(NA)	(NA)	7,953	8,717	9,638	10,420	10,379	9,971
AFDC cases	1,000 . . .	4,583	6,242	5,872	6,752	7,472	7,986	7,880	7,380
AFDC arrears only cases [1]	1,000 . . .	(NA)	(NA)	2,082	1,965	2,166	2,434	2,499	2,591
Non-AFDC cases	1,000 . . .	849	2,159	4,843	6,441	7,487	8,190	8,783	9,348
Cases for which a collection was made:									
AFDC cases	1,000 . . .	503	684	701	837	879	926	976	940
AFDC arrears only cases [1]	1,000 . . .	(NA)	(NA)	224	255	289	308	343	402
Non-AFDC cases	1,000 . . .	243	654	1,363	1,749	1,958	2,169	2,408	2,612
Percentage of cases with collections:									
AFDC cases	Percent .	11.0	11.0	11.9	12.4	11.8	11.6	12.4	12.7
AFDC arrears only cases [1]	Percent .	(NA)	(NA)	10.8	13.0	13.4	12.7	13.7	15.5
Non-AFDC cases	Percent .	28.7	30.3	28.1	27.2	26.1	26.5	27.4	27.9
Absent parents located, total	1,000 . . .	643	878	2,062	3,152	3,777	4,204	4,950	5,779
Paternities established, total	1,000 . . .	144	232	393	512	554	592	659	718
Support orders established, total [2]	1,000 . . .	374	669	1,022	879	1,026	1,025	1,051	1,082
FINANCES									
Collections, total . [3]	**Mil. dol** .	**1,478**	**2,694**	**6,010**	**7,964**	**8,907**	**9,850**	**10,828**	**12,020**
AFDC collections [3]	Mil. dol. .	603	1,090	1,750	2,259	2,416	2,550	2,690	2,855
State share	Mil. dol. .	274	415	620	787	847	891	939	1,014
Incentive payments to states	Mil. dol. .	72	145	264	299	339	407	400	409
Federal share	Mil. dol. .	246	341	533	738	777	762	822	888
Payments to AFDC families [4]	Mil. dol. .	10	189	334	435	446	457	474	480
Non-AFDC collections	Mil. dol. .	874	1,604	4,260	5,705	6,491	7,300	8,138	9,165
Administrative expenditures, total	Mil. dol. .	466	814	1,606	1,995	2,241	2,556	3,012	3,055
State share	Mil. dol. .	117	243	545	652	724	816	917	1,015
Federal share.	Mil. dol. .	349	571	1,061	1,343	1,517	1,741	2,095	2,040
Program savings, total.	Mil. dol. .	127	86	-190	-170	-278	-496	-852	-744
State share	Mil. dol. .	230	317	338	434	462	482	422	408
Federal share.	Mil. dol. .	-103	-231	-528	-605	-740	-978	-1,273	-1,151
Total fees and costs recovered for non-AFDC cases	Mil. dol. .	5	3	22	29	31	33	33	37
Percentage of AFDC payments recovered	Percent .	5.2	7.3	10.3	11.4	12.0	12.5	13.6	15.5

NA Not available.   [1] Reflects cases that are no longer receiving AFDC but still have outstanding child support due.
[2] Through 1990 includes modifications to orders.   [3] Beginning 1993 includes medical support payments not shown separately.
[4] Beginning 1985, states were required to pass along to the family the first $50 of any current child support collected each month.
Source: U.S. Department of Health and Human Services, Office of Child Support Enforcement, *Annual Report to Congress*.

No. 634. Regular Child Care Arrangements for Children Under 6 Years Old, by Type of Arrangement: 1995

[In percent, except as indicated. Estimates are based on children under 6 years old who have yet to enter kindergarten. Based on 14,064 interviews from a sample survey of the civilian, noninstitutional population in households with telephones; see source for details]

CHARACTERISTIC	CHILDREN		TYPE OF NONPARENTAL ARRANGEMENT				No nonparental arrange-ment
	Number (1,000)	Percent distri-bution	Total [1]	In relative care	In nonrelative care	In center-based program [2]	
Total.................	21,421	100	60	21	18	31	40
Race-ethnicity:							
White, non-Hispanic	13,996	65	62	18	21	33	38
Black, non-Hispanic............	3,344	16	66	31	12	33	34
Hispanic	2,838	13	46	23	12	17	54
Other	1,243	6	58	25	13	28	42
Mother's employment status: [3]							
35 or more hours per week.......	7,101	34	88	33	32	39	12
Less than 35 hours per week	4,034	19	75	30	26	35	25
Looking for work.............	1,635	8	42	16	4	25	58
Not in labor force	8,354	40	32	7	6	22	68
Household income:							
Less than $10,001	4,502	21	50	22	10	25	50
$10,001 to $20,000...........	2,909	14	54	27	12	24	46
$20,001 to $30,000...........	3,385	16	53	22	14	25	47
$30,001 to $40,000...........	3,047	14	60	23	20	27	40
$40,001 to $50,000...........	2,304	11	63	19	22	32	37
$50,001 to $75,000...........	3,063	14	74	20	26	40	26
$75,001 or more.............	2,211	10	77	14	30	49	23

[1] Columns do not add to total because some children participated in more than one type of nonparental arrangement. [2] Center-based programs include day care centers, head start programs, preschool, prekindergartens, and other early childhood programs. [3] Children without mothers are not included.

Source: U.S. National Center for Education Statistics, *Statistics in Brief*, October 1995 (NCES 95-824).

No. 635. Licensed Child Care Centers, 1998, and Family Child Care Providers, 1997, by State

[Centers as of February; family child care providers as of August]

STATE	Licensed child care centers, 1998	Licensed family child care providers, 1997	STATE	Licensed child care centers, 1998	Licensed family child care providers, 1997
U.S.	98,374	282,883			
			MO	1,515	2,651
AL................	1,335	3,366	MT.................	251	1,726
AK................	226	515	NE.................	743	3,844
AZ................	1,483	1,503	NV.................	405	636
AR................	1,935	1,345	NH.................	790	453
CA................	12,885	36,390			
			NJ.................	3,200	4,100
CO................	2,396	6,287	NM.................	600	233
CT................	1,555	5,082	NY.................	3,374	16,882
DE................	262	1,976	NC.................	3,670	4,824
DC................	360	236	ND.................	98	2,887
FL................	5,971	7,604			
			OH.................	3,760	4,181
GA................	1,148	6,309	OK.................	1,818	4,022
HI................	494	489	OR.................	930	11,167
ID................	511	1,326	PA.................	3,416	4,486
IL................	2,725	9,359	RI.................	340	716
IN................	659	2,821			
			SC.................	1,689	2,534
IA................	1,555	5,087	SD.................	153	1,237
KS................	1,377	8,667	TN.................	2,693	2,518
KY................	1,861	798	TX.................	7,575	13,860
LA................	1,907	10,000	UT.................	320	2,690
ME................	904	2,365			
			VT.................	500	1,620
MD................	2,125	12,292	VA.................	2,340	4,840
MA................	2,221	10,993	WA.................	1,837	8,725
MI................	4,619	17,022	WV.................	307	4,450
MN................	1,514	15,559	WI.................	2,269	7,516
MS................	1,543	1,863	WY.................	210	831

Source: Children's Foundation, Washington, DC, *1998 Child Care Licensing Study* and *1997 Family Child Care Licensing Study,* (copyright).

No. 636. Foster Care—Homes and Children in Out-of-Home Care, by State: 1995

[Number of foster homes covers only licensed, certified and approved foster homes. Out-of-home care includes children placed into family foster care, kinship (relative) foster care, group homes, and residential group care]

STATE	Number of foster homes	CHILDREN IN OUT-OF-HOME CARE		STATE	Number of foster homes	CHILDREN IN OUT-OF-HOME CARE	
		Number	Rate per 1,000 children			Number	Rate per 1,000 children
U.S.	142,374	483,629	6.3	MO	4,135	9,423	7.7
				MT............	(NA)	1,606	7.2
AL.............	1,528	3,593	2.9	NE............	629	3,326	7.0
AK.............	931	1,881	8.7	NV............	711	2,486	6.2
AZ.............	1,669	5,979	4.9	NH............	880	1,527	5.3
AR.............	612	2,507	3.6				
CA.............	(NA)	74,364	8.1	NJ............	3,598	8,014	4.1
				NM............	633	2,064	3.4
CO.............	3,347	7,186	7.1	NY............	20,410	53,562	11.2
CT.............	1,427	7,839	9.0	NC............	4,098	12,692	8.2
DE.............	300	851	4.8	ND............	560	1,102	6.3
FL.............	4,929	10,789	3.1				
				OH............	9,145	17,134	5.7
GA.............	3,614	14,582	7.5	OK............	1,516	5,063	6.0
HI.............	1,086	1,652	5.2	OR............	3,134	5,937	7.1
ID.............	759	913	2.9	PA............	(NA)	23,653	7.8
IL.............	13,667	53,342	17.1	RI............	611	3,284	14.0
IN.............	4,991	9,649	6.9				
				SC............	1,620	5,181	4.9
IA.............	2,365	4,195	5.0	SD............	481	922	4.6
KS.............	(NA)	6,345	9.1	TN............	2,724	9,511	6.5
KY.............	1,636	3,800	3.7	TX............	3,452	15,734	2.9
LA.............	2,628	6,034	5.1	UT............	1,029	2,118	3.0
ME.............	1,169	2,312	7.9				
				VT............	990	1,483	9.2
MD.............	3,341	11,818	8.8	VA............	4,500	6,973	4.7
MA.............	7,033	13,241	9.1	WA............	6,867	9,715	6.9
MI.............	6,850	14,987	5.6	WV............	791	2,954	7.8
MN.............	5,000	8,452	6.4	WI............	(NA)	7,875	5.0
MS.............	978	2,945	3.8	WY............	(NA)	1,034	7.7

NA Not available.

Source: Petit, M.R. & Curtis, P.A., *Child Abuse and Neglect: A Look at the States, 1997 CWLA Stat Book*, Child Welfare League of America, Washington, DC, 1997, (copyright).

No. 637. Head Start—Enrollment and Congressional Appropriations: 1970 to 1997

[For fiscal years ending in year shown; see text, Section 9]

YEAR	Enrollment (1,000)	Appro-priation (mil. dol.)	YEAR	Enrollment (1,000)	Appro-priation (mil. dol.)	AGE AND RACE	Enrollment, 1997 (percent)
1970 ...	477	326	1984 ...	442	996	Under 3 years old	4
1971 ...	398	360	1985 ...	452	1,075	3 years old...........	30
1972 ...	379	376	1986 ...	452	1,040	4 years old...........	60
1973 ...	379	401	1987 ...	447	1,131	5 years old and over ...	6
1974 ...	353	404	1988 ...	448	1,206		
1975 ...	349	404	1989 ...	451	1,235	White	31
1976 ...	349	441	1990 ...	541	1,552	Black	36
1977 ...	333	475	1991 ...	583	1,952	Hispanic	26
1978 ...	391	625	1992 ...	621	2,202	American Indian	4
1979 ...	388	680	1993 ...	714	2,776	Asian	3
1980 ...	376	735	1994 ...	740	3,326		
1981 ...	387	819	1995 ...	751	3,534		
1982 ...	396	912	1996 ...	752	3,569		
1983 ...	415	912	1997 ...	794	3,981		

Source: U.S. Administration for Children and Families, "Head Start 1998 Fact Sheet;" <http://www.acf.dhhs.gov/programs/hsb/facts98.htm>; (accessed 22 July 1998).

No. 638. Percent of Adult Population Doing Volunteer Work: 1995

[Volunteers are persons who worked in some way to help others for no monetary pay during the previous year. Based on a sample survey of 2,719 persons 18 years old and over conducted during the spring of the following year and subject to sampling variability; see source]

AGE, SEX, RACE, AND HISPANIC ORIGIN	Percent of population volunteering	Average hours volunteered per week	EDUCATIONAL ATTAINMENT AND HOUSEHOLD INCOME	Percent of population volunteering	Average hours volunteered per week	TYPE OF ACTIVITY	Percent of population involved in activity
Total.	48.8	4.2	Elementary school	18.7	(B)	Arts, culture, humanities. .	6.2
			Some high school.	26.1	3.3	Education	17.5
18-24 years old	38.4	2.8	High school graduate	43.1	4.0	Environment	7.1
25-34 years old	50.8	4.3	Technical, trade, or			Health.	13.2
35-44 years old	55.0	4.3	business school	51.2	4.4	Human services	12.7
45-54 years old	55.3	4.5	Some college	56.3	3.9		
55-64 years old	47.9	4.8	College graduate	70.7	4.8	Informal	20.3
65-74 years old	44.7	4.1				International, foreign	1.6
75 years old and over.	33.7	4.4	Under $10,000.	34.7	3.6	Political organizations . . .	3.8
			$10,000-$19,999	34.3	3.2	Private, community	
Male	45.1	4.2	$20,000-$29,999	45.2	3.7	foundations	2.7
Female	52.2	4.2	$30,000-$39,999	46.0	3.7		
			$40,000-$49,999	52.7	5.8	Public and societal benefit .	6.7
White.	51.9	4.2	$50,000-$59,999	64.1	5.1	Recreation - adults	7.3
Black.	35.3	4.5	$60,000-$74,999	56.4	4.4	Religion	25.8
			$75,000-$99,999	64.8	4.0	Work-related organizations	7.9
Hispanic [1]	40.4	4.3	$100,000 or more.	69.4	4.4	Youth development	15.4

B Base figure too small to meet statistical standards for reliability.　　[1] Hispanic persons may be of any race.

No. 639. Charity Contributions—Average Dollar Amount and Percent of Household Income, 1991 to 1995, and by Age of Respondent and Household Income, 1995

[Estimates cover households' contribution activity for the year and are based on respondents' replies as to contribution and volunteer activity of household. See headnote, Table 638]

YEAR AND AGE	ALL CONTRIBUTING HOUSEHOLDS Average amount (dol.)	ALL CONTRIBUTING HOUSEHOLDS Percent of household income	CONTRIBUTORS AND VOLUNTEERS Average amount (dol.)	CONTRIBUTORS AND VOLUNTEERS Percent of household income	HOUSEHOLD INCOME	ALL CONTRIBUTING HOUSEHOLDS Average amount (dol.)	ALL CONTRIBUTING HOUSEHOLDS Percent of household income	CONTRIBUTORS AND VOLUNTEERS Average amount (dol.)	CONTRIBUTORS AND VOLUNTEERS Percent of household income
1991	899	2.2	1,155	2.6	**1995—**				
1993	880	2.1	1,193	2.6	Under $10,000 . . .	295	4.3	(B)	(B)
1995, total.	1,017	2.2	1,279	2.6	$10,000-$19,999 . .	425	2.8	444	2.9
18-24 years	287	0.7	344	0.7	$20,000-$29,999 . .	578	2.3	658	2.6
25-34 years	743	1.6	922	2.0	$30,000-$39,999 . .	722	2.1	928	2.7
35-44 years	1,342	2.6	1,653	3.0	$40,000-$49,999 . .	576	1.3	677	1.5
45-54 years	955	1.8	1,142	2.1	$50,000-$59,999 . .	1,001	1.8	1,142	2.1
55-64 years	1,791	3.6	2,473	4.5	$60,000-$74,999 . .	1,301	1.9	1,443	2.1
65-74 years	980	2.8	1,125	3.0	$75,000-$99,999 . .	1,582	1.8	1,682	2.0
75 years and over. .	839	3.7	1,078	5.0	$100,000 and over. .	3,379	3.4	4,195	4.2

B Base too small to meet statistical standards for reliability.

No. 640. Charity Contributions—Percent of Households Contributing, by Dollar Amount, 1991 to 1995, and Type of Charity, 1995

[In percent, except as noted. See headnote, Tables 638 and 639]

ANNUAL AMOUNT OF HOUSEHOLD CONTRIBUTIONS	ALL HOUSEHOLDS 1991	ALL HOUSEHOLDS 1993	ALL HOUSEHOLDS 1995	GIVERS 1991	GIVERS 1993	GIVERS 1995	TYPE OF CHARITY	1995 Percentage of households	1995 Average contribution [1] (dol.)
None	27.8	26.6	31.5	(X)	(X)	(X)	Arts, culture, humanities .	9.4	216
Givers	72.2	73.4	68.5	100.0	100.0	100.0	Education	20.3	318
$1 to $100. . . .	14.9	20.9	15.2	24.9	32.3	24.3	Environment.	11.5	106
$101 to $200 . .	8.1	9.8	7.2	13.5	15.2	11.6	Health.	27.3	214
$201 to $300 . .	7.3	5.6	5.7	12.2	8.6	9.2	Human services	25.1	271
$301 to $400 . .	3.3	3.7	4.7	5.6	5.8	7.5	International	6.1	283
$401 to $500 . .	3.2	4.0	5.2	5.4	6.2	8.3	Private, community		
$501 to $600 . .	2.6	3.0	3.0	4.4	4.6	4.7	foundations	6.1	181
$601 to $700 . .	2.5	2.0	2.6	4.2	3.1	4.1	Public, societal benefit . .	10.3	122
$701 to $999 . .	3.4	2.9	3.7	5.7	4.6	6.0	Recreation - adults	7.0	161
$1,000 or more. .	14.5	12.8	15.2	24.2	19.7	24.3	Religion.	48.0	868
Not reported . .	12.4	8.6	5.9	(X)	(X)	(X)	Youth development	20.9	137

X Not applicable.　　[1] Average contribution per contributing household.

Source of Tables 638-640: Hodgkinson, Virginia, Murray Weitzman, and the Gallup Organization, Inc., *Giving and Volunteering in the United States: 1996 Edition*. (Copyright and published by INDEPENDENT SECTOR, Washington, DC, fall 1996.)

No. 641. Private Philanthropy Funds, by Source and Allocation: 1980 to 1996

[In billions of dollars. Estimates for sources of funds based on U.S. Internal Revenue Service reports of individual charitable deductions, household surveys of giving by Independent Sector, and, for 1980 and 1985, an econometric model. For corporate giving, data are those prepared by the Council for Aid to Education. Data about foundation donations are based upon surveys of foundations and data provided by the Foundation Center. Estimates of the allocation of funds were derived from surveys of nonprofits conducted by source and other groups]

SOURCE AND ALLOCATION	1980	1985	1987	1988	1989	1990	1991	1992	1993	1994	1995	1996
Total funds	48.6	73.0	90.0	98.1	106.7	111.5	117.2	121.1	126.5	129.3	140.5	150.7
Individuals	40.7	58.7	72.3	80.1	87.8	91.2	96.1	98.4	102.1	103.8	112.2	119.9
Foundations	2.8	4.9	5.9	6.2	6.6	7.2	7.7	8.6	9.5	9.7	10.6	11.8
Corporations	2.3	4.6	5.2	5.3	5.5	5.5	5.6	5.9	6.3	7.0	7.9	8.5
Charitable bequests	2.9	4.8	6.6	6.6	7.0	7.6	7.8	8.2	8.5	8.8	9.8	10.5
Allocation:												
Religion	22.2	38.2	43.5	45.2	47.8	49.8	53.9	54.9	56.3	60.2	66.3	69.4
Health	5.3	7.7	9.2	9.6	9.9	9.9	9.7	10.2	10.8	11.5	12.6	13.9
Education	5.0	8.2	9.8	10.2	11.0	12.4	13.5	14.3	15.4	16.6	17.6	18.8
Human service	4.9	8.5	9.8	10.5	11.4	11.8	11.1	11.6	12.5	11.7	11.7	12.2
Arts, culture and humanities . .	3.2	5.1	6.3	6.8	7.5	7.9	8.8	9.3	9.6	9.7	10.0	10.9
Public/societal benefit	1.5	2.2	2.9	3.2	3.8	4.9	4.9	5.1	5.4	6.1	7.1	7.6
Environment/wildlife	(¹)	(¹)	2.1	2.4	2.0	2.6	2.9	3.1	3.2	3.5	4.0	4.0
International	(¹)	(¹)	0.9	1.0	1.2	1.5	1.8	1.7	1.9	2.2	2.1	2.0
Unclassified	6.6	3.1	5.4	5.4	7.8	6.8	6.2	5.9	5.1	1.4	1.7	3.6
Gifts to foundations	(¹)	(¹)	(¹)	3.9	4.4	3.8	4.5	5.0	6.3	6.3	7.5	8.3

¹ Included in "Unclassified."

Source: AAFRC Trust for Philanthropy, New York, NY, *Giving USA*, annual, (copyright).

No. 642. Foundations—Number and Finances, by Asset Size: 1995

[Figures are for latest year reported by foundations. Covers nongovernmental nonprofit organizations with funds and programs managed by their own trustees or directors, whose goals were to maintain or aid social, educational, religious, or other activities deemed to serve the common good. Excludes organizations that make general appeals to the public for funds, act as trade associations for industrial or other special groups, or do not currently award grants]

ASSET SIZE	Number	Assets (mil. dol.)	Gifts received (mil. dol.)	Expenditures (mil. dol.)	Grants (mil. dol.)	PERCENT DISTRIBUTION				
						Number	Assets	Gifts received	Expenditures	Grants
Total	40,140	226,736	10,261	15,115	12,262	100.0	100.0	100.0	100.0	100.0
Under $50,000	8,298	148	251	331	303	20.7	0.1	2.4	2.2	2.5
$50,000–$99,999	3,554	260	90	119	103	8.9	0.1	0.9	0.8	0.8
$100,000–$249,999.	6,539	1,072	201	235	203	16.3	0.5	2.0	1.6	1.7
$250,000–$499,999.	5,258	1,895	262	290	243	13.1	0.8	2.6	1.9	2.0
$500,000–$999,999.	4,898	3,484	362	405	342	12.2	1.5	3.5	2.7	2.8
$1,000,000–$4,999,999	7,560	16,878	1,561	1,711	1,434	18.8	7.4	15.2	11.3	11.7
$5,000,000–$9,999,999	1,686	11,873	918	1,028	851	4.2	5.2	8.9	6.8	6.9
$10,000,000–$49,999,999 . . .	1,791	37,562	2,539	3,018	2,443	4.5	16.6	24.7	20.0	19.9
$50,000,000–$99,999,999 . . .	269	18,776	886	1,363	1,102	0.7	8.3	8.6	9.0	9.0
$100,000,000–$249,999,999 . .	169	25,889	1,339	1,628	1,302	0.4	11.4	13.1	10.8	10.6
$250,000,000 or more	118	108,898	1,852	4,988	3,936	0.3	48.0	18.1	33.0	32.1

Source: The Foundation Center, New York, NY, *Guide to U.S. Foundations, Their Trustees, Officers, and Donors*, Vol. 1, 1996.

No. 643. Foundations—Grants Reported, by Subject Field and Recipient Organization: 1996

[Covers grants of $10,000 or more in size. Based on reports of 1,010 foundations. Grant sample totaling $7.3 billion represented over half of all grant dollars awarded by private, corporate, and community foundations. For definition of foundations, see headnote, Table 642]

SUBJECT FIELD	NUMBER OF GRANTS		DOLLAR VALUE		RECIPIENT ORGANIZATION ¹	NUMBER OF GRANTS		DOLLAR VALUE	
	Number	Percent distribution	Amount (mil. dol.)	Percent distribution		Number	Percent distribution	Amount (mil. dol.)	Percent distribution
Total	78,296	100.0	7,279	100.0	Arts/humanities org.	2,813	3.6	227	3.1
Arts and culture	11,137	14.2	900	12.4	Community improvement				
Education	16,358	20.9	1,852	25.4	organizations	3,735	4.8	301	4.1
Environment & animals. . . .	4,404	5.6	394	5.4	Educational institutions.	21,712	27.7	2,723	37.4
Health	10,420	13.3	1,180	16.2	Colleges & universities . . .	11,013	14.1	1,559	21.4
Human services	18,036	23.0	1,262	17.3	Educational support				
International affairs,					agencies.	4,588	5.9	641	8.8
development & peace. . . .	2,468	3.2	235	3.2	Schools	4,208	5.4	294	4.0
Public/societal benefit.	9,509	12.1	847	11.6	Hospitals/medical care				
Science and technology . . .	2,259	2.9	251	3.5	facilities	3,605	4.6	394	5.4
Social sciences	1,296	1.7	189	2.6	Human service agencies. . . .	14,435	18.4	781	10.7
Religion.	2,317	3.0	160	2.2	Museums/historical societies .	3,291	4.2	327	4.5
Other	92	0.1	8	0.1	Recreation organizations . . .	856	1.1	265	3.6

¹ Grants may be awarded to multiple types of recipient organizations and would thereby be double-counted.

Source: The Foundation Center, New York, NY, *The Foundation Grants Index*, 1997.

Figure 13.1
**Employment Growth, by Occupation:
1996 to 2006**

In percent

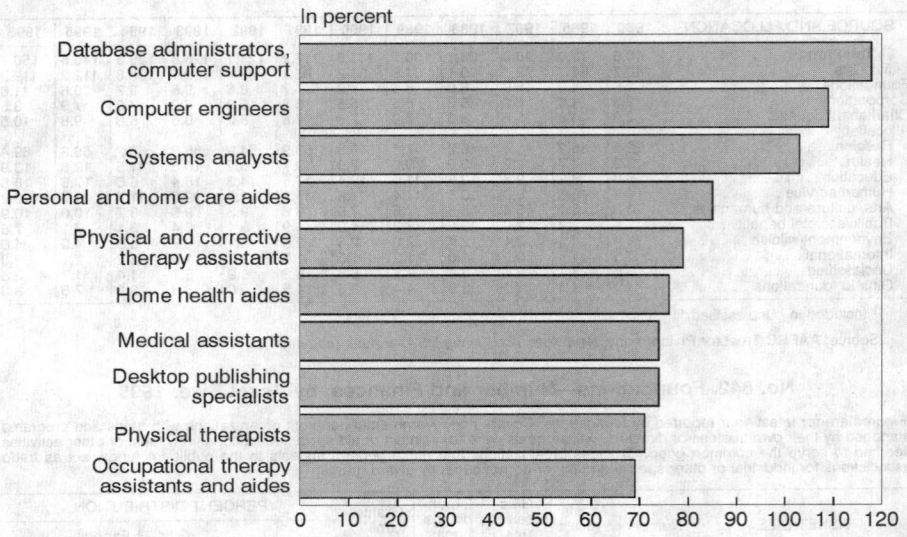

Source: Chart prepared by U.S. Bureau of the Census. For data, see Table 673.

Figure 13.2
**Unemployed Persons 20 Years Old and Over,
by Reason of Unemployment: 1997**

In millions

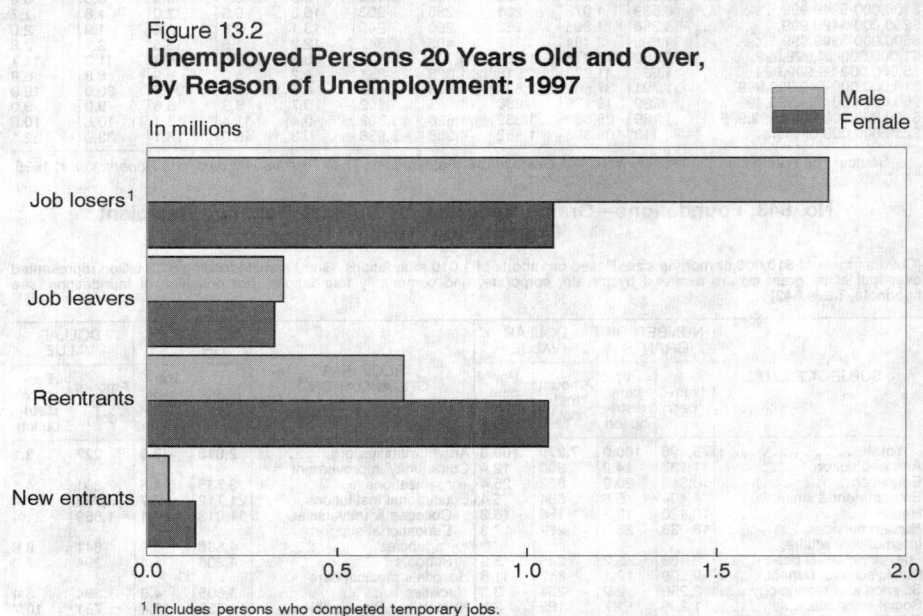

1 Includes persons who completed temporary jobs.
Source: Chart prepared by U.S. Bureau of the Census. For data, see Table 682.

Labor Force, Employment, and Earnings

This section presents statistics on the labor force; its distribution by occupation and industry affiliation; and the supply of, demand for, and conditions of labor. The chief source of these data is the Current Population Survey (CPS) conducted by the Bureau of the Census for the Bureau of Labor Statistics (BLS). Comprehensive historical and current data are available from the BLS Internet site (http://stats.bls.gov/cpshome.htm). These data are published on a current basis in the BLS monthly publication, *Employment and Earnings*. Detailed data on the labor force also are available from the decennial census of population.

Types of data—Most statistics in this section are obtained by two methods: household interviews or questionnaires and reports of establishment payroll records. Each method provides data which the other cannot suitably supply. Population characteristics, for example, are readily obtainable only from the household survey, while detailed industrial classifications can be readily derived only from establishment records.

Household data are obtained from a monthly sample survey of the population. The CPS is used to gather data for the calendar week including the 12th of the month and provides current comprehensive data on the labor force (see text, Section 1). The CPS provides information on the work status of the population without duplication since each person is classified as employed, unemployed, or not in the labor force. Employed persons holding more than one job are counted only once, according to the job at which they worked the most hours during the survey week.

Monthly, quarterly, and annual data from the CPS are published by the Bureau of Labor Statistics in *Employment and Earnings*. Data presented include national totals of the number of persons in the civilian labor force by sex, race, Hispanic origin, and age; the number employed; hours of work;

In Brief	
Labor force participation rate of married women with children under 6 years old:	
1960	18.6%
1970	30.3%
1980	45.1%
1997	63.6%
Fastest growing occupations, 1996-2006:	
Data base administrators and computer specialists	+118%
Computer engineers	+109%
Systems analysts	+103%

industry and occupational groups; and the number unemployed, reasons for, and duration of unemployment. Annual data shown in this section are averages of monthly figures for each calendar year, unless otherwise specified.

The CPS also produces annual estimates of employment and unemployment for each state, 50 large metropolitan statistical areas, and selected cities. These estimates are published by BLS in its annual *Geographic Profile of Employment and Unemployment.* More detailed geographic data (e.g., for counties and cities) are provided by the decennial population censuses.

Data based on establishment records are compiled by BLS and cooperating state agencies as part of an ongoing Current Employment Statistics program. Survey data, gathered monthly from a sample of employers through mail questionnaires or electronic interviewing, are supplemented by data from other government agencies and adjusted at intervals to data from government social insurance program reports. The estimates exclude self-employed persons, private household workers, unpaid family workers, agricultural workers, and the Armed Forces. In March 1997, reporting establishments employed 9 million manufacturing workers (47 percent of the total manufacturing employment at the time), 20 million workers in nonmanufacturing industries (24 percent of the total in nonmanufacturing), and 15 million federal, state, and local government employees (77 percent of total government).

The establishment survey counts workers each time they appear on a payroll during the reference period (as with the CPS, the week including the 12th of the month). Thus, unlike the CPS, a person with two jobs is counted twice. The establishment survey is designed to provide detailed industry information for the Nation, states, and metropolitan areas on nonfarm wage and salary employment, average weekly hours, and average hourly and weekly earnings. Establishment survey data also are published in *Employment and Earnings*. Historical national data are available on the Internet site: <http://stats.bls.gov/ceshome.htm>.

Labor force—According to the CPS definitions, the civilian labor force comprises all civilians in the noninstitutional population 16 years and over classified as "employed" or "unemployed" according to the following criteria: Employed civilians comprise (a) all civilians, who, during the reference week, did any work for pay or profit (minimum of an hour's work) or worked 15 hours or more as unpaid workers in a family enterprise, and (b) all civilians who were not working but who had jobs or businesses from which they were temporarily absent for noneconomic reasons (illness, weather conditions, vacation, labor-management dispute, etc.) whether they were paid for the time off or were seeking other jobs. Unemployed persons comprise all civilians who had no employment during the reference week, who made specific efforts to find a job within the previous 4 weeks (such as applying directly to an employer, or to a public employment service, or checking with friends), and who were available for work during that week, except for temporary illness. Persons on layoff from a job and expecting recall also are classified as unemployed. All other civilian persons, 16 years old and over, are "not in the labor force."

Beginning in 1982, changes in the estimation procedures and the introduction of 1980 census data caused substantial increases in the population and estimates of persons in all labor force categories. Rates on labor force characteristics, however, were essentially unchanged. In order to avoid major breaks in series, some 30,000 labor force series were adjusted back to 1970. The effect of the 1982 revisions on various data series and an explanation of the adjustment procedure used are described in "Revisions in the Current Population Survey in January 1982," in the February 1982 issue of *Employment and Earnings.* The revisions did not, however, smooth out the breaks in series occurring between 1972 and 1979, and data users should make allowances for them in making certain data comparisons.

Beginning in January 1985, and again in January 1986, the CPS estimation procedures were revised due to the implementation of a new sample design (for the 1985 revision) and to reflect an explicit estimate of the number of undocumented immigrants (for the 1986 revision). The greatest impact of these revisions was on estimates of persons of Hispanic origin. Where possible, these estimates were revised back to January 1980. A description of the changes and an indication of their effect on the national estimates of labor force characteristics appear in the February 1985 and February 1986 issues of *Employment and Earnings,* respectively.

Beginning in January 1994, several changes were introduced into the CPS that effect all data comparisons with prior years. These changes include the results of a major redesign of the survey questionnaire and collection methodology, revisions to some of the labor force concepts and definitions, and the introduction of 1990 census population controls, adjusted for the estimated undercount. An explanation of the changes and their effects on the labor force data appears in "Revisions in the Current Population Survey Effective January 1994" in the February 1994 issue of *Employment and Earnings.*

Beginning in 1996, 1990 census population controls, adjusted for the estimated undercount were extended back to

January 1990. A discussion of the changes and their effects on the labor force data appears in "Revisions in Household Survey Data Effective February 1996" in the March 1996 issue of *Employment and Earnings.*

Beginning in January 1997, the CPS reflects updated 1990 census–based population controls. The greatest impact of the new population controls was on estimates for persons of Hispanic origin. An explanation of the changes and their effect on labor force estimates appear in "Revisions in the Current Population Survey Effective January 1997" in the February 1997 issue of *Employment and Earnings.*

Hours and earnings—Average hourly earnings, based on establishment data, are gross earnings (i.e., earnings before payroll deductions) and include overtime premiums; they exclude irregular bonuses and value of payments-in-kind. Hours are those for which pay was received. Wages and salaries from the CPS consist of total monies received for work performed by an employee during the income year. It includes wages, salaries, commissions, tips, piece-rate payments, and cash bonuses earned before deductions were made for taxes, bonds, union dues, etc. Persons who worked 35 hours or more are classified as working full time.

Industrial and occupational groups—Establishments responding to the establishment survey are classified into industries on the basis of their principal product or activity (determined by annual sales volume) in accordance with the *1987 Standard Industrial Classification (SIC) Manual,* Office of Management and Budget. The SIC is a classification structure for the entire national economy. The structure provides data on a division and industry code basis, according to the level of industrial detail. For example, manufacturing is a major industrial division; food and kindred products (code 20) is one of its major groups. One of the ways this group is further divided is into meat products (code 201) and meat packing plants (code 2011).

Industry data derived from the CPS for 1983-91 utilize the 1980 census industrial classification developed from the 1972 SIC. CPS data from 1971 to 1982 were based on the 1970 census classification system which was developed from the 1967 SIC. Most of the industry categories were not affected by the change in classification.

The occupational classification system used in the 1980 census and in the CPS for 1983-91 evolved from the 1980 Standard Occupational Classification (SOC) system, first introduced in 1977. Occupational categories used in the 1980 census classification system are so radically different from the 1970 census system used in the CPS through 1982, that their implementation represented a break in historical data series. In cases where data have not yet been converted to the 1980 classifications and still reflect the 1970 classifications (e.g., Table 698), comparisons between the two systems should not be made. To help users bridge the data gap, a limited set of estimates was developed for the 1972-82 period based on the new classifications. The estimates were developed by means of applying conversion factors created by double coding a 20-percent sample of CPS occupational records for 6 months during 1981-82. For further details, contact BLS.

Beginning in January 1992, the occupational and industrial classification systems used in the 1990 census were introduced into the CPS. (These systems were largely based on the 1980 Standard Occupational Classification and the 1987 Standard Industrial Classification.) There were a few breaks in comparability between the 1980 and 1990 census-based systems, particularly within the "technical, sales, and administrative support" categories. The most notable changes in industry classification were the shift of several industries from "business services" to "professional services" and the splitting of some industries into smaller, more detailed categories. A number of industry titles were changed as well, with no change in content.

Productivity—BLS publishes data on productivity as measured by output per hour (labor productivity), output per combined unit of labor and capital input (multifactor productivity), and, for manufacturing industries, output per combined unit of capital, labor, energy, materials, and purchased service inputs. Labor productivity and related indexes are published for the business sector as a whole and its major subsectors: nonfarm business, manufacturing, nonfinancial corporations, 178 specific industries, and various functional areas of the federal government. Multifactor productivity and related measures are published for the private business sector and its major subsectors. Productivity indexes which take into account capital, labor, energy, materials, and service inputs are published for the 21 major industry groups which comprise the manufacturing sector and for the following industries: cotton and synthetic broadwoven fabrics, household furniture, tire and inner tubes, footwear, steel, metal stampings, farm and garden machinery, refrigeration and heating equipment, motor vehicles, and railroad transportation industries. The major sector data are published in the BLS quarterly news release, *Productivity and Costs* and in the annual *Multifactor Productivity Measures* release. The specific industry productivity measures are published annually in the BLS Bulletin, *Productivity Measures for Selected Industries and Government Services.* Detailed information on methods, limitations, and data sources appears in the *BLS Handbook of Methods,* BLS Bulletin 2490 (1997), Chapters 10 and 11.

Unions—As defined here, unions include traditional labor unions and employee associations similar to labor unions. Data on union membership status provided by BLS are for employed wage and salary workers and relate to their principal job. Earnings by union membership status are usual weekly earnings of full-time wage and salary workers. The information is collected through the Current Population Survey. Collective bargaining settlements data had been collected for bargaining situations involving 1,000 or more workers in private industry and state and local government. These data series were discontinued with 1995 data.

Work stoppages—Work stoppages include all strikes and lockouts known to BLS which last for at least 1 full day or shift and involve 1,000 or more workers. All stoppages, whether or not authorized by a union, legal or illegal, are counted. Excluded are work slowdowns and instances where employees report to work late, or leave early, to attend mass meetings or mass rallies.

Seasonal adjustment—Many economic statistics reflect a regularly recurring seasonal movement which can be estimated on the basis of past experience. By eliminating that part of the change which can be ascribed to usual seasonal variation (e.g., climate or school openings and closings), it is possible to observe the cyclical and other nonseasonal movements in the series. However, in evaluating deviations from the seasonal pattern—that is, changes in a seasonally adjusted series—it is important to note that seasonal adjustment is merely an approximation based on past experience. Seasonally adjusted estimates have a broader margin of possible error than the original data on which they are based, since they are subject not only to sampling and other errors, but also are affected by the uncertainties of the adjustment process itself.

Statistical reliability—For discussion of statistical collection, estimation, sampling procedures, and measures of statistical reliability applicable to Census Bureau and BLS data, see Appendix III.

No. 644. Employment Status of the Civilian Population: 1950 to 1997

[In thousands, except as indicated. Annual averages of monthly figures. For the civilian noninstitutional population 16 years old and over. Based on Current Population Survey; see text, Section 1, Population, and Appendix III]

YEAR	Civilian noninsti-tutional population	CIVILIAN LABOR FORCE						NOT IN LABOR FORCE	
		Total	Percent of population	Employed	Employ-ment/population ratio [1]	Unemployed Number	Unemployed Percent of labor force	Number	Percent of population
1950	104,995	62,208	59.2	58,918	56.1	3,288	5.3	42,787	40.8
1960	117,245	69,628	59.4	65,778	56.1	3,852	5.5	47,617	40.6
1970	137,085	82,771	60.4	78,678	57.4	4,093	4.9	54,315	39.6
1980	167,745	106,940	63.8	99,303	59.2	7,637	7.1	60,806	36.2
1981	170,130	108,670	63.9	100,397	59.0	8,273	7.6	61,460	36.1
1982	172,271	110,204	64.0	99,526	57.8	10,678	9.7	62,067	36.0
1983	174,215	111,550	64.0	100,834	57.9	10,717	9.6	62,665	36.0
1984	176,383	113,544	64.4	105,005	59.5	8,539	7.5	62,839	35.6
1985	178,206	115,461	64.8	107,150	60.1	8,312	7.2	62,744	35.2
1986	180,587	117,834	65.3	109,597	60.7	8,237	7.0	62,752	34.7
1987	182,753	119,865	65.6	112,440	61.5	7,425	6.2	62,888	34.4
1988	184,613	121,669	65.9	114,968	62.3	6,701	5.5	62,944	34.1
1989 [2]	186,393	123,869	66.5	117,342	63.0	6,528	5.3	62,523	33.5
1990 [2]	189,164	125,840	66.5	118,793	62.8	7,047	5.6	63,324	33.5
1991	190,925	126,346	66.2	117,718	61.7	8,628	6.8	64,578	33.8
1992	192,805	128,105	66.4	118,492	61.5	9,613	7.5	64,700	33.6
1993 [2]	194,838	129,200	66.3	120,259	61.7	8,940	6.9	65,638	33.7
1994 [2]	196,814	131,056	66.6	123,060	62.5	7,996	6.1	65,758	33.4
1995	198,584	132,304	66.6	124,900	62.9	7,404	5.6	66,280	33.4
1996 [2]	200,591	133,943	66.8	126,708	63.2	7,236	5.4	66,647	33.2
1997 [2]	203,133	136,297	67.1	129,558	63.8	6,739	4.9	66,837	32.9

[1] Civilian employed as a percent of the civilian noninstitutional population. [2] Data not strictly comparable with data for earlier years. See text, Section 13, and February 1994, March 1996, and February 1997 issues of *Employment and Earnings*.

Source: U.S. Bureau of Labor Statistics, Bulletin 2307; and *Employment and Earnings*, monthly.

No. 645. Civilian Labor Force and Participation Rates, With Projections: 1980 to 2006

[For civilian noninstitutional population 16 years old and over. Annual averages of monthly figures. Rates are based on annual average civilian noninstitutional population of each specified group and represent proportion of each specified group in the civilian labor force. Based on Current Population Survey; see text, Section 1, Population, and Appendix III]

RACE, SEX, AND AGE	CIVILIAN LABOR FORCE (millions)						PARTICIPATION RATE (percent)					
	1980	1990 [1]	1995	1996	1997 [1]	2006, proj.	1980	1990 [1]	1995	1996	1997 [1]	2006, proj.
Total [2]	106.9	125.8	132.3	133.9	136.3	148.8	63.8	66.5	66.6	66.8	67.1	67.6
White	93.6	107.4	112.0	113.1	114.7	123.6	64.1	66.9	67.1	67.2	67.5	68.1
Male	54.5	59.6	61.1	61.8	62.6	66.0	78.2	77.1	75.7	75.8	75.9	74.3
Female	39.1	47.8	50.8	51.3	52.1	57.6	51.2	57.4	59.0	59.1	59.5	62.0
Black	10.9	13.7	14.8	15.1	15.5	17.2	61.0	64.0	63.7	64.1	64.7	64.9
Male	5.6	6.8	7.2	7.3	7.4	8.0	70.3	71.0	69.0	68.7	68.3	69.6
Female	5.3	6.9	7.6	7.9	8.2	9.2	53.1	58.3	59.5	60.4	61.7	61.3
Hispanic [3]	6.1	10.7	12.3	12.8	13.8	17.4	64.0	67.4	65.8	66.5	67.9	67.4
Male	3.8	6.5	7.4	7.6	8.3	10.2	81.4	81.4	79.1	79.6	80.1	77.1
Female	2.3	4.2	4.9	5.1	5.5	7.2	47.4	53.1	52.6	53.4	55.1	57.2
Male	61.5	69.0	71.4	72.1	73.3	78.2	77.4	76.4	75.0	74.9	75.0	73.6
16 to 19 years.	5.0	4.1	4.0	4.0	4.1	4.6	60.5	55.7	54.8	53.2	52.3	52.5
20 to 24 years.	8.6	7.9	7.3	7.1	7.2	8.3	85.9	84.4	83.1	82.5	82.5	76.5
25 to 34 years.	17.0	19.9	18.7	18.4	18.1	16.5	95.2	94.1	93.0	93.2	93.0	92.3
35 to 44 years.	11.8	17.5	19.2	19.6	20.1	18.5	95.5	94.3	92.3	92.4	92.6	90.6
45 to 54 years.	9.9	11.1	13.4	14.0	14.6	18.0	91.2	90.7	88.8	89.1	89.5	87.5
55 to 64 years.	7.2	6.6	6.5	6.7	7.0	9.9	72.1	67.8	66.0	67.0	67.6	70.2
65 years and over . . .	1.9	2.0	2.2	2.2	2.3	2.6	19.0	16.3	16.8	16.9	17.1	17.8
Female	45.5	56.8	60.9	61.9	63.0	70.6	51.5	57.5	58.9	59.3	59.8	61.4
16 to 19 years.	4.4	3.7	3.7	3.8	3.8	4.4	52.9	51.6	52.2	51.3	51.0	51.1
20 to 24 years.	7.3	6.8	6.3	6.3	6.3	7.2	68.9	71.3	70.3	71.3	72.7	71.8
25 to 34 years.	12.3	16.1	15.5	15.4	15.3	14.4	65.5	73.5	74.9	75.2	76.0	77.6
35 to 44 years.	8.6	14.7	16.6	17.0	17.3	17.0	65.5	76.4	77.2	77.5	77.7	80.2
45 to 54 years.	7.0	9.1	11.8	12.4	13.0	17.2	59.9	71.2	74.4	75.4	76.0	79.9
55 to 64 years.	4.7	4.9	5.4	5.5	5.7	8.8	41.3	45.2	49.2	49.6	50.9	55.8
65 years and over . .	1.2	1.5	1.6	1.6	1.6	1.7	8.1	8.6	8.8	8.6	8.6	8.7

[1] See footnote 2, Table 644. [2] Includes other races, not shown separately. [3] Persons of Hispanic origin may be of any race.

Source: U.S. Bureau of Labor Statistics, *Employment and Earnings*, monthly, January issues; *Monthly Labor Review*, November 1997; and unpublished data.

No. 646. Employment Status of the Civilian Population: 1970 to 1997

[In thousands, except as indicated. Annual averages of monthly figures. For the civilian noninstitutional population 16 years old and over. Based on Current Population Survey; see text, Section 1, Population, and Appendix III]

| YEAR, SEX, RACE, AND HISPANIC ORIGIN | Civilian noninsti-tutional popula-tion | CIVILIAN LABOR FORCE | | | | | | | NOT IN LABOR FORCE | |
| | | Total | Percent of popula-tion | Employed | Employ-ment/ popula-tion ratio [1] | Unemployed | | | | |
						Number	Percent of labor force	Number	Percent of population
Total: [2]									
1970	137,085	82,771	60.4	78,678	57.4	4,093	4.9	54,315	39.6
1980	167,745	106,940	63.8	99,303	59.2	7,637	7.1	60,806	36.2
1985	178,206	115,461	64.8	107,150	60.1	8,312	7.2	62,744	35.2
1990 [3]	189,164	125,840	66.5	118,793	62.8	7,047	5.6	63,324	33.5
1994 [3]	196,814	131,056	66.6	123,060	62.5	7,996	6.1	65,758	33.4
1995	198,584	132,304	66.6	124,900	62.9	7,404	5.6	66,280	33.4
1996	200,591	133,943	66.8	126,708	63.2	7,236	5.4	66,647	33.2
1997 [3]	203,133	136,297	67.1	129,558	63.8	6,739	4.9	66,837	32.9
Male:									
1970.	64,304	51,228	79.7	48,990	76.2	2,238	4.4	13,076	20.3
1980.	79,398	61,453	77.4	57,186	72.0	4,267	6.9	17,945	22.6
1985.	84,469	64,411	76.3	59,891	70.9	4,521	7.0	20,058	23.7
1990 [3]	90,377	69,011	76.4	65,104	72.0	3,906	5.7	21,367	23.6
1994 [3]	94,355	70,817	75.1	66,450	70.4	4,367	6.2	23,538	24.9
1995.	95,178	71,360	75.0	67,377	70.8	3,983	5.6	23,818	25.0
1996.	96,206	72,087	74.9	68,207	70.9	3,880	5.4	24,119	25.1
1997 [3]	97,715	73,261	75.0	69,685	71.3	3,577	4.9	24,454	25.0
Female:									
1970.	72,782	31,543	43.3	29,688	40.8	1,855	5.9	41,239	56.7
1980.	88,348	45,487	51.5	42,117	47.7	3,370	7.4	42,861	48.5
1985.	93,736	51,050	54.5	47,259	50.4	3,791	7.4	42,686	45.5
1990 [3]	98,787	56,829	57.5	53,689	54.3	3,140	5.5	41,957	42.5
1994 [3]	102,460	60,239	58.8	56,610	55.3	3,629	6.0	42,221	41.2
1995.	103,406	60,944	58.9	57,523	55.6	3,421	5.6	42,462	41.1
1996.	104,385	61,857	59.3	58,501	56.0	3,356	5.4	42,528	40.7
1997 [3]	105,418	63,036	59.8	59,873	56.8	3,162	5.0	42,382	40.2
White:									
1970.	122,174	73,556	60.2	70,217	57.5	3,339	4.5	48,618	39.8
1980.	146,122	93,600	64.1	87,715	60.0	5,884	6.3	52,523	35.9
1985.	153,679	99,926	65.0	93,736	61.0	6,191	6.2	53,753	35.0
1990 [3]	160,625	107,447	66.9	102,261	63.7	5,186	4.8	53,178	33.1
1994 [3]	165,555	111,082	67.1	105,190	63.5	5,892	5.3	54,473	32.9
1995.	166,914	111,950	67.1	106,490	63.8	5,459	4.9	54,965	32.9
1996.	168,317	113,108	67.2	107,808	64.1	5,300	4.7	55,209	32.8
1997 [3]	169,993	114,693	67.5	109,856	64.6	4,836	4.2	55,301	32.5
Black:									
1973.	14,917	8,976	60.2	8,128	54.5	846	9.4	5,941	39.8
1980.	17,824	10,865	61.0	9,313	52.2	1,553	14.3	6,959	39.0
1985.	19,664	12,364	62.9	10,501	53.4	1,864	15.1	7,299	37.1
1990 [3]	21,477	13,740	64.0	12,175	56.7	1,565	11.4	7,737	36.0
1994 [3]	22,879	14,502	63.4	12,835	56.1	1,666	11.5	8,377	36.6
1995.	23,246	14,817	63.7	13,279	57.1	1,538	10.4	8,429	36.3
1996.	23,604	15,134	64.1	13,542	57.4	1,592	10.5	8,470	35.9
1997 [3]	24,003	15,529	64.7	13,969	58.2	1,560	10.0	8,474	35.3
Hispanic: [4]									
1980.	9,598	6,146	64.0	5,527	57.6	620	10.1	3,451	36.0
1985.	11,915	7,698	64.6	6,888	57.8	811	10.5	4,217	35.4
1990 [3]	15,904	10,720	67.4	9,845	61.9	876	8.2	5,184	32.6
1994 [3]	18,117	11,975	66.1	10,788	59.5	1,187	9.9	6,142	33.9
1995.	18,629	12,267	65.8	11,127	59.7	1,140	9.3	6,362	34.2
1996.	19,213	12,774	66.5	11,642	60.6	1,132	8.9	6,439	33.5
1997 [3]	20,321	13,796	67.9	12,726	62.6	1,069	7.7	6,526	32.1
Mexican:									
1986.	7,377	4,941	67.0	4,387	59.5	555	11.2	2,436	33.0
1990 [3]	9,752	6,707	68.8	6,146	63.0	561	8.4	3,045	31.2
1994 [3]	11,174	7,567	67.7	6,800	60.9	766	10.1	3,608	32.3
1995.	11,609	7,765	66.9	7,016	60.4	750	9.7	3,844	33.1
1996.	11,762	7,943	67.5	7,209	61.3	734	9.2	3,819	32.5
1997 [3]	12,443	8,546	68.7	7,884	63.4	662	7.7	3,897	31.3
Puerto Rican:									
1986.	1,494	804	53.8	691	46.3	113	14.0	690	46.2
1990 [3]	1,718	960	55.9	870	50.6	91	9.5	758	44.1
1994 [2]	1,854	1,026	55.4	907	48.9	119	11.6	828	44.6
1995.	1,896	1,098	57.9	974	51.4	123	11.2	798	42.1
1996.	2,017	1,170	58.0	1,057	52.4	112	9.6	848	42.0
1997 [3]	2,139	1,293	60.4	1,166	54.5	127	9.8	846	39.6
Cuban:									
1986.	842	570	67.7	533	63.3	36	6.4	272	32.3
1990 [3]	918	603	65.7	559	60.9	44	7.2	315	34.3
1994 [3]	1,002	604	60.3	555	55.4	49	8.1	398	39.7
1995.	1,019	613	60.2	568	55.7	45	7.4	406	39.8
1996.	991	637	64.3	591	59.7	46	7.2	354	35.7
1997 [3]	1,025	646	63.0	603	58.8	43	6.6	379	37.0

[1] Civilian employed as a percent of the civilian noninstitutional population.   [2] Includes other races, not shown separately.   [3] See footnote 2, Table 644.   [4] Persons of Hispanic origin may be of any race. Includes persons of other Hispanic origin, not shown separately.

Source: U.S. Bureau of Labor Statistics, Bulletin 2307; and *Employment and Earnings*, monthly, January issues.

No. 647. Civilian Labor Force—Percent Distribution, by Sex and Age: 1960 to 1997

[For civilian noninstitutional population 16 years old and over. Annual averages of monthly figures. Based on Current Population Survey; see text, Section 1, Population, and Appendix III]

YEAR AND SEX	Civilian labor force (1,000)	PERCENT DISTRIBUTION						
		16 to 19 years	20 to 24 years	25 to 34 years	35 to 44 years	45 to 54 years	55 to 64 years	65 yrs. and over
Total: 1960	69,628	7.0	9.6	20.7	23.4	21.3	13.5	4.6
1970	82,771	8.8	12.8	20.6	19.9	20.5	13.6	3.9
1980	106,940	8.8	14.9	27.3	19.1	15.8	11.2	2.9
1990 [1]	125,840	6.2	11.7	28.6	25.5	16.1	9.2	2.7
1995	132,304	5.9	10.3	25.8	27.0	19.1	9.0	2.9
1997 [1]	136,297	5.8	9.9	24.5	27.4	20.2	9.3	2.9
Male: 1960	46,388	6.0	8.9	22.1	23.6	20.6	13.8	4.9
1970	51,228	7.8	11.2	22.1	20.4	20.3	13.9	4.2
1980	61,453	8.1	14.0	27.6	19.3	16.1	11.8	3.1
1990 [1]	69,011	5.9	11.4	28.8	25.3	16.1	9.6	2.9
1995	71,360	5.7	10.3	26.2	26.9	18.8	9.1	3.1
1997 [1]	73,261	5.6	9.8	24.7	27.4	19.9	9.5	3.1
Female: 1960	23,240	8.8	11.1	17.8	22.8	22.7	12.8	3.9
1970	31,543	10.3	15.5	18.1	18.9	20.7	13.2	3.3
1980	45,487	9.6	16.1	26.9	19.0	15.4	10.4	2.6
1990 [1]	56,829	6.5	12.0	28.3	25.8	16.1	8.7	2.6
1995	60,944	6.1	10.4	25.5	27.2	19.4	8.8	2.7
1997 [1]	63,036	6.1	10.1	24.2	27.4	20.6	9.1	2.5

[1] See footnote 2, Table 644.

Source: U.S. Bureau of Labor Statistics, Bulletin 2307, and *Employment Earnings,* monthly, January issues.

No. 648. Civilian Labor Force and Participation Rates, by Educational Attainment, Sex, Race, and Hispanic Origin: 1992 to 1997

[As of March. For the civilian noninstitutional population 25 to 64 years of age. See Table 681 for unemployment data. Based on Current Population Survey; see text, Section 1, Population, and Appendix III]

YEAR, SEX, AND RACE	CIVILIAN LABOR FORCE					PARTICIPATION RATE [1]				
	Total (1,000)	Percent distribution				Total	Less than high school diploma	High school gradu-ates, no degree	Less than a bach-elor's degree	College graduate
		Less than high school diploma	High school graduate, no degree	Less than a bach-elor's degree	College graduate					
Total: [2]										
1992 . . .	102,387	12.2	36.2	25.2	26.4	79.0	60.3	78.3	83.5	88.4
1993 . . .	103,504	11.5	35.2	26.3	27.0	78.9	59.6	77.7	82.9	88.3
1994 [3] . .	104,868	11.0	34.0	27.6	27.3	78.9	58.3	77.8	83.2	88.2
1995 . . .	106,519	10.8	33.1	27.8	28.3	79.3	59.8	77.3	83.2	88.7
1996 . . .	108,037	10.9	32.9	27.7	28.5	79.4	60.2	77.9	83.7	87.8
1997 [3] . .	110,514	10.9	33.0	27.4	28.6	80.1	61.7	82.5	83.7	88.5
Male:										
1992	55,917	13.9	34.7	23.8	27.5	88.6	75.1	89.0	91.8	93.7
1993	56,544	13.2	33.9	24.7	28.1	88.1	74.9	88.1	90.6	93.7
1994 [3]	56,633	12.7	32.9	25.8	28.6	87.0	71.5	86.8	90.3	93.2
1995	57,454	12.2	32.3	25.7	29.7	87.4	72.0	86.9	90.1	93.8
1996	58,121	12.7	32.2	26.0	29.1	87.5	74.3	86.9	90.0	92.9
1997 [3]	59,268	12.8	32.2	25.8	29.2	87.7	75.2	86.4	90.6	93.5
Female:										
1992	46,469	10.2	37.9	26.9	25.0	70.0	45.6	69.1	76.2	82.2
1993	46,961	9.3	36.7	28.2	25.8	70.0	44.2	68.8	76.1	82.2
1994 [3]	48,235	9.1	35.3	29.8	25.8	71.1	44.7	70.0	77.0	82.5
1995	49,065	9.1	34.1	30.2	26.6	71.5	47.2	68.9	77.3	82.8
1996	49,916	8.8	33.7	29.7	27.8	71.8	45.7	69.8	78.1	82.3
1997 [3]	51,246	8.7	34.0	29.3	28.0	72.8	47.1	71.4	77.6	83.2
White:										
1992	87,656	11.3	36.1	25.5	27.1	79.8	61.5	78.7	83.8	88.7
1993	88,457	10.7	35.0	26.4	27.9	79.7	61.1	78.2	83.1	88.8
1994 [3]	89,009	10.5	33.7	27.7	28.1	79.8	60.3	78.3	83.5	88.5
1995	90,192	10.0	32.8	27.8	29.3	80.1	61.6	77.9	83.4	88.8
1996	91,506	10.4	32.8	27.5	29.3	80.4	62.5	78.6	83.9	88.2
1997 [3]	93,179	10.4	32.8	27.3	29.5	81.0	63.8	79.2	83.9	89.0
Black:										
1992	10,936	19.2	40.3	24.9	15.6	74.4	55.4	76.9	83.4	89.1
1993	11,051	16.8	39.5	27.6	16.1	73.8	53.4	74.7	83.0	89.6
1994 [3]	11,368	14.5	39.3	29.2	17.0	73.5	49.4	75.2	82.5	89.5
1995	11,695	14.1	38.6	29.6	17.7	74.2	51.0	74.5	82.8	90.9
1996	11,891	14.2	37.2	31.2	17.4	73.7	50.1	74.3	83.0	87.9
1997 [3]	12,253	14.3	37.8	31.3	16.6	74.9	52.9	75.0	83.8	89.0
Hispanic: [4]										
1992	7,702	39.1	30.2	19.3	11.4	73.8	64.6	77.5	84.2	87.1
1993	8,010	38.7	29.4	21.0	10.9	73.9	64.9	76.8	84.0	87.3
1994 [3]	8,984	38.6	28.7	21.5	11.1	73.2	63.9	77.5	81.9	86.3
1995	9,298	38.9	28.2	21.3	11.6	73.2	64.7	75.9	81.9	87.9
1996	9,683	38.9	28.5	21.2	11.3	74.2	65.0	78.2	83.7	87.2
1997 [3]	10,556	37.4	28.1	22.1	12.4	75.9	66.4	79.4	85.3	87.7

[1] See headnote, Table 645.   [2] Includes other races, not shown separately.   [3] See footnote 2, Table 644.   [4] Persons of Hispanic origin may be of any race.

Source: U.S. Bureau of Labor Statistics, unpublished data.

No. 649. Characteristics of the Civilian Labor Force, by State: 1996

[In thousands, except ratio and rate. Preliminary. For civilian noninstitutional population, 16 years old and over. Annual averages of monthly figures. Because of separate processing and weighting procedures, the totals for the United States may differ from results obtained by aggregrating totals for states]

STATE	TOTAL		EMPLOYED		Employed/population ratio [1]	UNEMPLOYED					PARTICIPATION RATE [3]	
						Total		Rate [2]				
	Number	Female	Total	Female		Number	Female	Total	Male	Female	Male	Female
United States...	**133,943**	**61,857**	**126,708**	**58,501**	**63.2**	**7,236**	**3,356**	**5.4**	**5.4**	**5.4**	**74.9**	**59.3**
Alabama	2,088	989	1,981	936	60.3	107	53	5.1	4.9	5.4	71.9	56.3
Alaska	316	147	291	137	68.4	25	9	7.8	9.1	6.3	80.3	68.2
Arizona	2,249	1,017	2,125	958	62.8	124	59	5.5	5.3	5.8	75.3	58.2
Arkansas	1,234	582	1,168	550	61.2	67	31	5.4	5.4	5.4	71.7	58.4
California	15,596	6,846	14,470	6,351	60.8	1,126	495	7.2	7.2	7.2	75.0	56.4
Colorado	2,102	956	2,013	917	69.3	89	39	4.2	4.4	4.0	79.0	65.7
Connecticut	1,720	826	1,621	779	64.3	99	47	5.7	5.7	5.7	74.5	62.5
Delaware	382	188	363	180	65.0	20	9	5.2	5.8	4.5	73.9	63.7
District of Columbia	272	141	249	129	58.2	23	12	8.5	8.7	8.4	67.8	60.1
Florida	6,938	3,227	6,586	3,053	58.8	352	175	5.1	4.8	5.4	69.9	54.8
Georgia	3,753	1,767	3,580	1,673	64.7	173	94	4.6	4.0	5.3	76.4	60.2
Hawaii	591	286	553	270	64.0	38	17	6.4	6.9	5.8	75.7	61.9
Idaho	619	275	587	260	66.7	32	15	5.2	5.1	5.4	77.7	62.9
Illinois	6,100	2,809	5,778	2,663	64.9	322	146	5.3	5.3	5.2	77.1	60.7
Indiana	3,072	1,412	2,945	1,351	66.3	127	62	4.1	3.9	4.4	76.9	61.9
Iowa	1,599	769	1,539	738	70.8	60	31	3.8	3.5	4.1	79.4	68.1
Kansas	1,340	622	1,279	591	66.9	60	31	4.5	4.1	5.0	77.4	63.2
Kentucky	1,867	878	1,762	827	59.0	105	52	5.6	5.4	5.9	69.6	56.1
Louisiana	1,997	947	1,863	872	57.9	135	75	6.7	5.6	8.0	70.0	55.2
Maine	669	317	635	302	65.5	34	15	5.1	5.4	4.8	74.8	63.5
Maryland	2,786	1,341	2,650	1,275	68.5	136	66	4.9	4.9	4.9	77.6	66.8
Massachusetts	3,189	1,512	3,052	1,456	64.6	137	56	4.3	4.9	3.7	74.0	61.5
Michigan	4,807	2,220	4,572	2,118	63.1	234	102	4.9	5.1	4.6	74.8	58.6
Minnesota	2,609	1,216	2,505	1,179	71.7	104	37	4.0	4.8	3.1	80.9	68.7
Mississippi	1,262	588	1,185	545	58.5	77	42	6.1	5.2	7.2	70.9	54.7
Missouri	2,898	1,407	2,765	1,347	68.5	132	60	4.6	4.9	4.3	77.9	66.3
Montana	447	208	423	199	63.0	24	10	5.3	5.9	4.6	72.9	60.6
Nebraska	913	431	886	417	72.0	27	14	2.9	2.7	3.2	81.1	67.7
Nevada	844	373	798	350	65.4	46	23	5.4	4.8	6.2	77.5	60.8
New Hampshire	624	291	598	278	67.3	26	13	4.2	3.9	4.5	78.2	62.9
New Jersey	4,124	1,908	3,869	1,786	63.1	255	122	6.2	6.0	6.4	75.6	59.5
New Mexico	800	363	735	335	57.9	64	28	8.1	8.4	7.6	71.3	55.2
New York	8,639	4,018	8,100	3,780	57.8	540	238	6.2	6.5	5.9	70.5	53.9
North Carolina	3,796	1,771	3,631	1,692	65.5	165	79	4.3	4.3	4.5	76.1	61.5
North Dakota	343	163	333	158	69.8	11	5	3.1	3.1	3.0	78.0	66.4
Ohio	5,643	2,605	5,365	2,479	63.0	278	126	4.9	5.0	4.8	74.6	58.6
Oklahoma	1,577	730	1,513	696	61.3	64	34	4.1	3.6	4.6	72.9	55.8
Oregon	1,721	786	1,619	741	65.2	102	46	5.9	6.0	5.8	76.6	62.2
Pennsylvania	5,903	2,727	5,590	2,602	60.2	313	125	5.3	5.9	4.6	72.4	55.6
Rhode Island	496	237	470	224	62.3	25	13	5.1	4.9	5.4	73.3	58.9
South Carolina	1,848	861	1,737	807	61.5	111	54	6.0	5.8	6.2	73.3	58.2
South Dakota	390	183	377	177	70.0	13	6	3.2	3.2	3.2	78.0	66.7
Tennessee	2,751	1,301	2,609	1,230	63.5	142	71	5.2	4.9	5.4	73.8	60.8
Texas	9,748	4,345	9,200	4,080	65.2	549	265	5.6	5.3	6.1	79.0	59.7
Utah	998	441	964	425	68.8	35	16	3.5	3.3	3.7	81.4	61.6
Vermont	324	158	310	150	68.3	15	7	4.6	4.5	4.6	77.5	66.3
Virginia	3,389	1,621	3,240	1,546	64.3	149	74	4.4	4.2	4.6	74.5	60.8
Washington	2,887	1,319	2,699	1,224	64.4	188	94	6.5	5.9	7.2	77.1	61.1
West Virginia	808	370	747	346	51.4	61	24	7.5	8.3	6.6	64.6	47.7
Wisconsin	2,918	1,378	2,815	1,333	72.1	103	44	3.5	3.8	3.2	79.9	69.6
Wyoming	258	119	245	113	67.4	13	6	5.0	5.1	5.0	78.9	63.5

[1] Civilian employment as a percent of civilian noninstitutional population.　[2] Percent unemployed of the civilian labor force.
[3] Percent of civilian noninstitutional population of each specified group in the civilian labor force.

Source: U.S. Bureau of Labor Statistics, *Employment and Earnings*, monthly, May 1997; and unpublished data.

No. 650. Civilian Labor Force, by Selected Metropolitan Area: 1997

[For the civilian noninstitutional population 16 years old and over. Annual averages of monthly figures. Data are derived from the Local Area Unemployment Statistics Program. For composition of metropolitan areas, see Appendix II]

METROPOLITAN AREAS RANKED BY LABOR FORCE SIZE, 1997	Civilian labor force (1,000)	Unemployment rate [1]	METROPOLITAN AREAS RANKED BY LABOR FORCE SIZE, 1997	Civilian labor force (1,000)	Unemployment rate [1]
U.S. total	136,297	4.9	Indianapolis, IN MSA	829	2.8
Los Angeles-Long Beach, CA PMSA . . .	4,497	6.8	Orlando, FL MSA.	813	3.4
Chicago, IL PMSA	4,084	4.5	Milwaukee-Waukesha, WI PMSA . . .	806	3.6
New York, NY PMSA	3,373	9.4	Columbus, OH MSA.	806	2.9
Washington, DC-MD-VA-WV PMSA. . . .	2,519	3.7	Charlotte-Gastonia-Rock Hill, NC-SC		
Philadelphia, PA-NJ PMSA	2,497	4.9	MSA	751	3.0
Detroit, MI PMSA.	2,233	3.9	Fort Lauderdale, FL PMSA	749	4.9
Atlanta, GA MSA	2,061	3.7	San Antonio, TX MSA.	744	4.1
Houston, TX PMSA	2,054	5.0	Sacramento, CA PMSA.	740	5.4
Dallas, TX PMSA.	1,814	3.7	Norfolk-Virginia Beach-Newport News,		
Boston, MA-NH PMSA	1,808	3.4	VA-NC MSA	722	4.8
Minneapolis-St. Paul, MN-WI MSA	1,637	2.5	Bergen-Passaic, NJ PMSA	679	5.2
Phoenix-Mesa, AZ MSA	1,422	3.0	Salt Lake City-Ogden, UT MSA . . .	670	2.9
Nassau-Suffolk, NY PMSA	1,393	3.9	Las Vegas, NV-AZ MSA	666	4.1
Orange County, CA PMSA.	1,379	3.3	Austin-San Marcos, TX MSA	650	3.1
Riverside-San Bernardino, CA PMSA . .	1,354	6.9	Greensboro-Winston-Salem-High Point,		
St. Louis, MO-IL MSA.	1,347	4.1	NC MSA.	641	2.8
Seattle-Bellevue-Everett, WA PMSA . . .	1,346	3.3	Middlesex-Somerset-Hunterdon,		
Baltimore, MD PMSA	1,320	5.6	NJ PMSA	637	3.6
San Diego, CA MSA.	1,282	4.2	New Orleans, LA MSA	619	5.5
Oakland, CA PMSA	1,176	4.3	Nashville, TN MSA.	618	3.5
Pittsburgh, PA MSA	1,158	5.0	Raleigh-Durham-Chapel Hill, NC MSA. .	609	1.9
Tampa-St. Petersburg-Clearwater,			Hartford, CT MSA	588	5.4
FL MSA	1,133	3.5	Grand Rapids-Muskegon-Holland, MI		
Cleveland-Lorain-Elyria, OH PMSA . . .	1,115	4.8	MSA	584	3.4
Denver, CO PMSA.	1,088	2.8	Buffalo-Niagara Falls, NY MSA. . . .	583	5.4
Miami, FL PMSA	1,041	7.1	Providence-Fall River-Warwick, RI-MA		
Portland-Vancouver, OR-WA PMSA. . .	1,026	4.3	MSA	577	5.6
Newark, NJ PMSA.	1,022	5.1	Rochester, NY MSA	576	4.1
Kansas City, MO-KS MSA.	961	3.7	Louisville, KY-IN MSA.	549	4.1
San Jose, CA PMSA	938	3.0	Memphis, TN-AR-MS MSA	530	4.6
San Francisco, CA PMSA	932	3.3	Jacksonville, FL MSA	530	3.6
Fort Worth-Arlington, TX PMSA	847	3.7	Oklahoma City, OK MSA	527	3.3
Cincinnatti, OH-KY-IN PMSA	839	3.8	Monmouth-Ocean, NJ PMSA	521	4.8

[1] Percent unemployed of the civilian labor force.

Source: U.S. Bureau of Labor Statistics, Local Area Unemployment Statistics program.

No. 651. School Enrollment and Labor Force Status: 1980 and 1997

[In thousands, except percent. As of October. For the civilian noninstitutional population 16 to 24 years old. Based on Current Population Survey; see text, Section 1, Population, and Appendix III]

CHARACTERISTIC	POPULATION		CIVILIAN LABOR FORCE		EMPLOYED		UNEMPLOYED		
	1980	1997 [1]	1980	1997 [1]	1980	1997 [1]	1980, total	1997 [1] Total	Rate [2]
Total, 16 to 24 years [3]	37,103	32,965	24,918	20,993	21,454	18,810	3,464	2,183	10.4
Enrolled in school [3]	15,713	18,140	7,454	8,841	6,433	7,957	1,021	884	10.0
16 to 19 years	11,126	12,156	4,836	5,087	4,029	4,406	807	681	13.4
20 to 24 years	4,587	5,985	2,618	3,754	2,404	3,550	214	204	5.4
Sex:									
Male	7,997	9,059	3,825	4,286	3,259	3,775	566	511	11.9
Female	7,716	9,081	3,629	4,555	3,174	4,182	455	373	8.2
College level	7,664	9,373	3,996	5,372	3,632	5,016	364	356	6.6
Full-time.	6,396	7,906	2,854	4,083	2,554	3,778	300	304	7.5
Race:									
White	13,242	14,376	6,687	7,519	5,889	6,862	798	657	8.7
Below college	6,566	6,756	3,095	2,951	2,579	2,575	516	376	12.7
College level	6,678	7,620	3,592	4,568	3,310	4,287	282	281	6.1
Black.	2,028	2,619	595	924	406	732	189	192	20.8
Below college	1,282	1,511	294	406	174	278	120	128	31.6
College level	747	1,109	300	519	230	455	70	64	12.4
Not enrolled [3]	21,390	14,825	17,464	12,152	15,021	10,853	2,443	1,299	10.7
White	18,103	11,881	15,121	9,980	13,318	9,095	1,803	885	8.9
Black	2,864	2,337	2,055	1,710	1,451	1,333	604	377	22.1

[1] See footnote 2, Table 644.   [2] Percent of civilian labor force in each category.   [3] Includes other races, not shown separately.

Source: U.S. Bureau of Labor Statistics, Bulletin 2307; News, USDL 98-171, May 1, 1998; and unpublished data.

No. 652. Labor Force Participation Rates, by Marital Status, Sex, and Age: 1960 to 1997

[Annual averages of monthly figures. See Table 649 for definition of participation rate. Based on Current Population Survey; see text, Section 1, Population, and Appendix III]

MARITAL STATUS AND YEAR	MALE PARTICIPATION RATE							FEMALE PARTICIPATION RATE						
	Total	16-19 years	20-24 years	25-34 years	35-44 years	45-64 years	65 and over	Total	16-19 years	20-24 years	25-34 years	35-44 years	45-64 years	65 and over
Single:														
1960 ..	69.8	42.6	80.3	91.5	88.6	80.1	31.2	58.6	30.2	77.2	83.4	82.9	79.8	24.3
1970 ..	65.5	54.6	73.8	87.9	86.2	75.7	25.2	56.8	44.7	73.0	81.4	78.6	73.0	19.7
1975 ..	68.7	57.9	77.9	86.7	83.2	69.9	21.0	59.8	49.6	72.5	80.8	78.6	68.3	15.8
1980 ..	72.6	59.9	81.3	89.2	82.2	66.9	16.8	64.4	53.6	75.2	83.3	76.9	65.6	13.9
1985 ..	73.8	56.3	81.5	89.4	84.6	65.5	15.6	66.6	52.3	76.3	82.4	80.8	67.9	9.8
1990 [1]	74.8	55.1	81.6	89.9	84.5	67.3	15.7	66.7	51.7	74.5	80.9	80.8	66.2	12.1
1993 ..	74.2	52.6	80.5	89.2	84.3	68.4	15.0	66.2	49.6	73.8	78.9	78.9	68.8	12.4
1994 [1]	73.9	53.6	80.5	88.4	83.1	67.8	17.8	66.7	51.4	73.6	78.9	78.7	68.8	12.7
1995 ..	73.7	54.4	80.3	88.7	81.4	67.0	17.9	66.8	52.2	72.9	80.2	79.5	67.3	11.6
1996 ..	73.3	52.8	79.8	89.1	82.1	67.4	18.2	67.1	51.5	73.3	80.9	79.4	68.5	12.2
1997 [1]	73.1	51.9	80.1	89.0	82.1	68.5	14.8	67.9	51.0	75.1	82.3	80.1	70.8	11.5
Married: [2]														
1960 ..	89.2	91.5	97.1	98.8	98.6	93.7	36.6	31.9	27.2	31.7	28.8	37.2	36.0	6.7
1970 ..	86.1	92.3	94.7	98.0	98.1	91.2	29.9	40.5	37.8	47.9	38.8	46.8	44.0	7.3
1975 ..	83.0	92.9	95.3	97.4	97.1	86.8	23.3	44.3	46.2	57.0	48.4	52.0	43.8	7.0
1980 ..	80.9	91.3	96.9	97.5	97.2	84.3	20.5	49.8	49.3	61.4	58.8	61.8	46.9	7.3
1985 ..	78.7	91.0	95.6	97.4	96.8	81.7	16.8	53.8	49.6	65.7	65.8	68.1	49.4	6.6
1990 [1]	78.6	92.1	95.6	96.9	96.7	82.6	17.5	58.4	49.5	66.1	69.6	74.0	56.5	8.5
1993 ..	77.6	91.3	95.0	96.5	96.0	82.5	16.5	59.4	49.8	65.1	70.6	74.7	59.9	7.6
1994 [1]	77.4	88.7	94.2	95.9	95.6	81.9	18.1	60.7	48.9	65.8	71.6	75.8	61.9	9.4
1995 ..	77.5	89.2	94.9	96.3	95.4	82.4	18.0	61.0	51.6	64.7	72.0	75.7	62.7	9.1
1996 ..	77.6	84.4	94.5	96.4	95.4	83.2	18.3	61.2	48.6	66.0	71.7	75.8	63.7	9.0
1997 [1]	77.7	84.6	94.9	96.1	95.7	83.6	18.3	61.6	50.1	66.1	71.9	76.0	64.6	8.9
Other: [3]														
1960 ..	63.1	(B)	96.9	95.2	94.4	83.2	22.7	41.6	43.5	58.0	63.1	70.0	60.0	11.4
1970 ..	60.7	(B)	90.4	93.7	91.1	78.5	19.3	40.3	48.6	60.3	64.6	68.8	61.9	10.0
1975 ..	63.4	(B)	88.8	92.4	89.4	73.4	15.4	40.1	47.6	65.3	68.6	69.2	59.0	8.3
1980 ..	67.5	(B)	92.6	94.1	91.9	73.3	13.7	43.6	50.0	68.4	76.5	77.1	60.2	8.2
1985 ..	68.7	(B)	95.1	93.7	91.8	72.8	11.4	45.1	51.9	66.2	76.9	81.6	61.0	7.5
1990 [1]	68.9	(B)	93.1	93.0	90.7	74.9	12.0	47.2	53.9	65.4	77.0	82.1	65.0	8.4
1993 ..	67.9	(B)	91.9	91.9	89.5	74.5	12.0	47.2	53.0	64.8	75.0	81.4	66.9	8.2
1994 [1]	66.8	(B)	91.0	90.3	88.6	72.6	11.9	47.5	46.2	66.6	74.3	80.4	67.6	8.7
1995 ..	66.2	(B)	92.7	90.9	88.2	72.4	12.1	47.4	55.8	67.2	77.1	80.7	67.2	8.4
1996 ..	66.4	(B)	90.6	92.0	88.8	73.1	11.5	48.1	42.6	70.7	78.5	82.1	67.7	8.0
1997 [1]	67.4	60.8	89.9	92.1	89.6	74.7	13.2	48.6	49.7	70.4	80.2	81.9	68.6	8.1

B For 1960, percentage not shown where base is less than 50,000; beginning 1970, 35,000.   [1] See footnote 2, Table 644.   [2] Spouse present.   [3] Widowed, divorced, and married (spouse absent).

Source: U.S. Bureau of Labor Statistics, Bulletins 2217 and 2340; and unpublished data.

No. 653. Marital Status of Women in the Civilian Labor Force: 1960 to 1997

[Annual averages of monthly figures. For civilian noninstitutional population 16 years old and over. Based on Current Population Survey; see text, Section 1, Population, and Appendix III]

YEAR	FEMALE LABOR FORCE (1,000)				FEMALE PARTICIPATION RATE [3]			
	Total	Single	Married [1]	Other [2]	Total	Single	Married [1]	Other [2]
1960	23,240	5,410	12,893	4,937	37.7	58.6	31.9	41.6
1965	26,200	5,976	14,829	5,396	39.3	54.5	34.9	40.7
1970	31,543	7,265	18,475	5,804	43.3	56.8	40.5	40.3
1975	37,475	9,125	21,484	6,866	46.3	59.8	44.3	40.1
1980	45,487	11,865	24,980	8,643	51.5	64.4	49.9	43.6
1981	46,696	12,124	25,428	9,144	52.1	64.5	50.5	44.6
1982	47,755	12,460	25,971	9,324	52.6	65.1	51.1	44.8
1983	48,503	12,659	26,468	9,376	52.9	65.0	51.8	44.4
1984	49,709	12,867	27,199	9,644	53.6	65.6	52.8	44.7
1985	51,050	13,163	27,894	9,993	54.5	66.6	53.8	45.1
1986	52,413	13,512	28,623	10,277	55.3	67.2	54.9	45.6
1987	53,658	13,885	29,381	10,393	56.0	67.4	55.9	45.7
1988	54,742	14,194	29,921	10,627	56.6	67.7	56.7	46.2
1989	56,030	14,377	30,548	11,104	57.4	68.0	57.8	47.0
1990 [4]	56,829	14,612	30,901	11,315	57.5	66.7	58.4	47.2
1991	57,178	14,681	31,112	11,385	57.4	66.2	58.5	46.8
1992	58,141	14,872	31,700	11,570	57.8	66.2	59.3	47.1
1993	58,795	15,031	31,980	11,784	57.9	66.2	59.4	47.2
1994 [4]	60,239	15,333	32,888	12,018	58.8	66.7	60.7	47.5
1995	60,944	15,467	33,359	12,118	58.9	66.8	61.0	47.4
1996	61,857	15,842	33,618	12,397	59.3	67.1	61.2	48.1
1997 [4]	63,036	16,492	33,802	12,742	59.8	67.9	61.6	48.6

[1] Husband present.   [2] Widowed, divorced, or separated.   [3] See Table 649 for definition of participation rate.   [4] See footnote 2, Table 644.

Source: U.S. Bureau of Labor Statistics, Bulletin 2307; and unpublished data.

No. 654. Employment Status of Women, by Marital Status and Presence and Age of Children: 1960 to 1997

[As of **March.** For 1960, civilian noninstitutional persons 14 years and over, thereafter 16 years old and over. Based on Current Population Survey; see text, Section 1, Population, and Appendix III]

ITEM	TOTAL			WITH ANY CHILDREN								
				Total			Children 6 to 17 only			Children under 6		
	Single	Mar- ried [1]	Other [2]	Single	Mar- ried [1]	Other [2]	Single	Mar- ried [1]	Other [2]	Single	Mar- ried [1]	Other [2]
IN LABOR FORCE (mil.)												
1960	5.4	12.3	4.9	(NA)	6.6	1.5	(NA)	4.1	1.0	(NA)	2.5	0.4
1970	7.0	18.4	5.9	(NA)	10.2	1.9	(NA)	6.3	1.3	(NA)	3.9	0.6
1980	11.2	24.9	8.8	0.6	13.7	3.6	0.2	8.4	2.6	0.3	5.2	1.0
1985	12.9	27.7	10.3	1.1	14.9	4.0	0.4	8.5	2.9	0.7	6.4	1.1
1990 [3]	14.0	31.0	11.2	1.5	16.5	4.2	0.6	9.3	3.0	0.9	7.2	1.2
1994 [3]	14.9	32.9	11.9	2.2	17.6	4.4	0.8	9.9	3.2	1.4	7.7	1.2
1995	15.0	33.6	12.0	2.1	18.0	4.6	0.8	10.2	3.3	1.3	7.8	1.3
1996 [3]	15.4	33.4	12.4	2.2	17.8	4.7	0.9	10.2	3.4	1.4	7.6	1.3
1997 [3]	16.2	33.9	12.8	2.8	18.2	4.7	1.0	10.6	3.4	1.8	7.6	1.3
PARTICIPATION RATE [4]												
1960	44.1	30.5	40.0	(NA)	27.6	56.0	(NA)	39.0	65.9	(NA)	18.6	40.5
1970	53.0	40.8	39.1	(NA)	39.7	60.7	(NA)	49.2	66.9	(NA)	30.3	52.2
1980	61.5	50.1	44.0	52.0	54.1	69.4	67.6	61.7	74.6	44.1	45.1	60.3
1985	65.2	54.2	45.6	51.6	60.8	71.9	64.1	67.8	77.8	46.5	53.4	59.7
1990 [3]	66.4	58.2	46.8	55.2	66.3	74.2	69.7	73.6	79.7	48.7	58.9	63.6
1994 [3]	65.1	60.6	47.3	56.9	69.0	73.1	67.5	76.0	78.4	52.2	61.7	62.2
1995	65.5	61.1	47.3	57.5	70.2	75.3	67.0	76.2	79.5	53.0	63.5	66.3
1996 [3]	65.2	61.1	48.2	60.5	70.0	77.0	71.8	76.7	80.6	55.1	62.7	69.2
1997 [3]	66.8	62.1	48.7	68.1	71.1	79.1	74.0	77.6	81.1	65.1	63.6	74.2
EMPLOYMENT (mil.)												
1960	5.1	11.6	4.6	(NA)	6.2	1.3	(NA)	3.9	0.9	(NA)	2.3	0.4
1970	6.5	17.5	5.6	(NA)	9.6	1.8	(NA)	6.0	1.2	(NA)	3.6	0.6
1980	10.1	23.6	8.2	0.4	12.8	3.3	0.2	8.1	2.4	0.2	4.8	0.9
1985	11.6	26.1	9.4	0.9	13.9	3.5	0.3	8.1	2.6	0.5	5.9	0.9
1990 [3]	12.9	29.9	10.5	1.2	15.8	3.8	0.5	8.9	2.7	0.7	6.9	1.1
1994 [3]	13.4	31.4	11.0	1.7	16.8	4.0	0.7	9.5	2.9	1.1	7.3	1.0
1995	13.7	32.3	11.3	1.8	17.2	4.2	0.7	9.8	3.1	1.1	7.3	1.2
1996 [3]	14.1	32.3	11.7	1.8	17.1	4.4	0.7	9.8	3.2	1.1	7.3	1.2
1997 [3]	14.7	32.8	12.1	2.3	17.5	4.3	0.9	10.3	3.1	1.4	7.3	1.1
UNEMPLOY- MENT RATE [5]												
1960	6.0	5.4	6.2	(NA)	6.0	8.4	(NA)	4.9	6.8	(NA)	7.8	12.5
1970	7.1	4.8	4.8	(NA)	6.0	7.2	(NA)	4.8	5.9	(NA)	7.9	9.8
1980	10.3	5.3	6.4	23.2	5.9	9.2	15.6	4.4	7.9	29.2	8.3	12.8
1985	10.2	5.7	8.5	23.8	6.6	6.6	15.4	5.5	10.6	28.5	8.0	16.1
1990 [3]	8.2	3.5	5.7	18.4	4.2	8.5	14.5	3.8	7.7	20.8	4.8	10.2
1994 [3]	10.0	4.5	7.4	19.5	5.0	9.8	13.2	4.5	7.7	23.0	5.6	15.1
1995	8.7	3.9	5.8	16.6	4.3	8.1	11.8	3.6	7.1	19.5	5.3	10.8
1996 [3]	8.6	3.4	5.5	18.5	3.5	6.4	15.7	3.2	5.1	20.3	3.9	9.7
1997 [3]	8.8	3.2	5.8	16.9	3.5	9.0	13.5	2.9	7.9	18.8	4.4	11.7

NA Not available.   [1] Husband present.   [2] Widowed, divorced, or separated.   [3] See footnote 2, Table 644.   [4] Percent of women in each specific category in the labor force.   [5] Unemployed as a percent of civilian labor force in specified group.
Source: U.S. Bureau of Labor Statistics, Bulletin 2307; and unpublished data.

No. 655. Labor Force Participation Rates for Wives, Husband Present, by Age of Own Youngest Child: 1975 to 1997

[As of **March.** For civilian noninstitutional population, 16 years old and over. For definition of participation rate, see Table 654. Based on Current Population Survey; see text, Section 1, Population, and Appendix III]

PRESENCE AND AGE OF CHILD	TOTAL			WHITE			BLACK		
	1975	1985	1997 [1]	1975	1985	1997 [1]	1975	1985	1997 [1]
Wives, total	**44.4**	**54.2**	**62.1**	**43.6**	**53.3**	**61.5**	**54.1**	**63.8**	**69.2**
No children under 18	43.8	48.2	54.2	43.6	47.5	53.8	47.6	55.2	57.4
With children under 18	44.9	60.8	71.1	43.6	59.9	70.6	58.4	71.7	80.1
Under 6, total..........	36.7	53.4	63.6	34.7	52.1	62.9	54.9	69.6	78.1
Under 3.............	32.7	50.5	61.3	30.7	49.4	61.1	50.1	66.2	73.7
1 year or under	30.8	49.4	59.5	29.2	48.6	58.9	50.0	63.7	69.5
2 years............	37.1	54.0	66.6	35.1	52.7	66.5	56.4	69.9	81.5
3 to 5 years........	42.2	58.4	67.0	40.1	56.6	66.5	61.2	73.8	82.8
3 years............	41.2	55.1	65.1	39.0	52.7	64.6	62.7	72.3	79.4
4 years............	41.2	59.7	64.6	38.7	58.4	63.2	64.9	70.6	79.5
5 years............	44.4	62.1	71.2	43.8	59.9	70.0	56.3	79.1	78.7
6 to 13 years	51.8	68.2	76.5	50.7	67.7	76.2	65.7	73.3	81.3
14 to 17 years	53.5	67.0	80.1	53.4	66.6	80.0	52.3	74.4	82.9

[1] See footnote 2, Table 644.
Source: U.S. Bureau of Labor Statistics, Bulletin 2340; and unpublished data.

No. 656. Families With Own Children—Employment Status of Parents: 1995 and 1996

[Annual average of monthly figures. For families with own children. Based on the Current Population Survey, see text, Section 1, Population, and Appendix III]

CHARACTERISTIC	NUMBER (1,000) 1995	1996	PERCENT DISTRIBUTION 1995	1996
WITH OWN CHILDREN UNDER 18				
Total families	33,544	33,980	100.0	100.0
Parent(s) employed	29,659	30,296	88.4	89.2
No parent employed	3,886	3,683	11.6	10.8
Married-couple families	24,604	24,818	100.0	100.0
Parent(s) employed	23,643	23,960	96.1	96.5
Mother employed	16,629	16,950	67.6	68.3
Both parents employed	15,491	15,851	63.0	63.9
Mother employed, not father	1,137	1,098	4.6	4.4
Father employed, not mother	7,014	7,010	28.5	28.2
Neither parent employed . .	962	859	3.9	3.5
Families maintained by women [1]	7,433	7,469	100.0	100.0
Mother employed	4,755	4,919	64.0	65.9
Mother not employed	2,678	2,550	36.0	34.1
Families maintained by men [1] .	1,507	1,692	100.0	100.0
Father employed	1,261	1,417	83.7	83.7
Father not employed	245	275	16.3	16.3
WITH OWN CHILDREN 6 to 17				
Total families	18,270	18,694	100.0	100.0
Parent(s) employed	16,391	16,892	89.7	90.4
No parent employed	1,878	1,802	10.3	9.6
Married-couple families	13,001	13,257	100.0	100.0
Parent(s) employed	12,484	12,786	96.0	96.4
Mother employed	9,562	9,896	73.6	74.7
Both parents employed	8,846	9,210	68.0	69.5

CHARACTERISTIC	NUMBER (1,000) 1995	1996	PERCENT DISTRIBUTION 1995	1996
Mother employed, not father	717	687	5.5	5.2
Father employed, not mother	2,921	2,890	22.5	21.8
Neither parent employed . .	517	470	4.0	3.6
Families maintained by women [1]	4,360	4,393	100.0	100.0
Mother employed	3,142	3,221	72.1	73.3
Mother not employed	1,219	1,172	27.9	26.7
Families maintained by men [1] .	908	1,044	100.0	100.0
Father employed	766	885	84.3	84.7
Father not employed	143	160	15.7	15.3
WITH OWN CHILDREN UNDER 6				
Total families	15,275	15,286	100.0	100.0
Parent(s) employed	13,267	13,405	86.9	87.7
No parent employed	2,007	1,881	13.1	12.3
Married-couple families	11,604	11,562	100.0	100.0
Parent(s) employed	11,159	11,174	96.2	96.6
Mother employed	7,066	7,053	60.9	61.0
Both parents employed	6,646	6,641	57.3	57.4
Mother employed, not father	421	412	3.6	3.6
Father employed, not mother	4,092	4,121	35.3	35.6
Neither parent employed . .	445	388	3.8	3.4
Families maintained by women [1]	3,073	3,076	100.0	100.0
Mother employed	1,613	1,699	52.5	55.2
Mother not employed	1,460	1,378	47.5	44.8
Families maintained by men [1] .	598	648	100.0	100.0
Father employed	496	532	82.8	82.2
Father not employed	102	115	17.1	17.8

[1] No spouse present.
Source: U.S. Bureau of Labor Statistics, News, USDL97-195, June 16, 1997.

No. 657. Employed Civilians and Weekly Hours: 1970 to 1997

[In thousands, except as indicated. For civilian noninstitutional population 16 years old and over. Annual averages of monthly figures. Based on Current Population Survey; see text, Section 1, Population, and Appendix III]

ITEM	1970	1980	1990 [1]	1992	1994 [1]	1995	1996	1997 [1]
Total employed	78,678	99,303	118,793	120,259	123,060	124,900	126,708	129,558
Age:								
16 to 19 years old	6,144	7,710	6,581	5,805	6,161	6,419	6,500	6,661
20 to 24 years old	9,731	14,087	13,401	12,840	12,758	12,443	12,138	12,380
25 to 34 years old	16,318	27,204	33,935	32,385	32,286	32,356	32,077	31,809
35 to 44 years old	15,922	19,523	30,817	32,666	33,599	34,202	35,051	35,908
45 to 54 years old	16,473	16,234	19,525	22,175	23,348	24,378	25,514	26,744
55 to 64 years old	10,974	11,586	11,189	11,058	11,228	11,435	11,739	12,296
65 years old and over	3,118	2,960	3,346	3,331	3,681	3,666	3,690	3,761
Class of worker:								
Nonagriculture	75,215	95,938	115,570	117,144	119,651	121,460	123,264	126,159
Wage and salary worker	69,491	88,525	106,598	107,966	110,517	112,448	114,171	116,983
Self-employed	5,221	7,000	8,719	8,959	9,003	8,902	8,971	9,056
Unpaid family workers	502	413	253	218	131	110	122	120
Agriculture	3,463	3,364	3,223	3,115	3,409	3,440	3,443	3,399
Wage and salary worker	1,154	1,425	1,740	1,689	1,715	1,814	1,869	1,890
Self-employed	1,810	1,642	1,378	1,320	1,645	1,580	1,518	1,457
Unpaid family workers	499	297	105	106	49	45	56	51
Weekly hours:								
Nonagriculture:								
Wage and salary workers	38.3	38.1	39.2	39.2	39.1	39.2	39.2	39.4
Self-employed	45.0	41.2	40.8	40.6	39.5	39.4	39.6	39.7
Unpaid family workers	37.9	34.7	34.0	34.2	33.7	33.5	34.1	32.6
Agriculture:								
Wage and salary workers	40.0	41.6	41.2	40.7	41.0	41.1	41.5	41.6
Self-employed	51.0	49.3	46.8	46.4	43.0	43.5	43.1	42.7
Unpaid family workers	40.0	38.6	38.5	36.9	39.0	42.0	38.0	44.3

[1] See footnote 2, Table 644.
Source: U.S. Bureau of Labor Statistics, Employment and Earnings, monthly, January issues; and unpublished data.

No. 658. Employed Workers Actively Seeking a New Job: 1997

[As of February. In thousands, except percent. For employed wage and salary workers 16 years old and over responding to the question on actively seeking work in the prior 3 months. Based on the Current Population Survey; see text, Section 1, and Appendix III]

CHARACTERISTIC	Total employed	PERSONS RESPONDING TO SEARCH QUESTION			CHARACTERISTIC	Total employed	PERSONS RESPONDING TO SEARCH QUESTION		
		Total	Actively seeking work	Percent			Total	Actively seeking work	Percent
Total	**112,819**	**110,546**	**5,528**	**5.0**	Professional specialty . .	17,477	17,186	921	5.4
Age:					Technical and related				
16 to 19 years old	5,951	5,828	400	6.9	support	4,042	3,998	206	5.2
20 to 24 years old	11,645	11,326	949	8.4	Sales	12,493	12,247	774	6.3
25 to 34 years old	29,278	28,590	1,825	6.4	Administrative support,				
35 to 44 years old	31,126	30,579	1,396	4.6	including clerical	17,843	17,585	816	4.6
45 to 54 years old	22,474	22,078	732	3.3	Private household.	731	644	20	3.1
55 to 64 years old	9,843	9,698	203	2.1	Protective service	2,138	2,097	80	3.8
65 years old and over . .	2,502	2,447	23	0.9	Service, except private				
Sex:					households and protec				
Male	58,797	57,655	3,071	5.3	tive	12,808	12,425	658	5.3
Female.	54,022	52,891	2,457	4.6	Precision production, craft,				
Educational attainment:					and repair	11,803	11,586	458	4.0
Less than high school					Machine operators,				
diploma.	14,371	13,976	609	4.4	assemblers, and inspec				
High school diploma,					tors	7,691	7,534	330	4.4
no college	36,613	35,821	1,347	3.8	Transportation and mate				
Some college or associ					rial moving occupations	4,787	4,653	178	3.8
ate degree.	32,827	32,269	1,742	5.4	Handlers, equipment				
Bachelor's degree or more	29,009	28,480	1,829	6.4	cleaners, helpers and				
Occupation:					laborers	4,517	4,396	314	7.1
Executive, administrative,					Farming, forestry and				
and managerial	14,887	14,639	694	4.7	fishing	1,604	1,558	78	5.0

Source: U.S. Bureau of Labor Statistics, Current Population Survey, February 1997, unpublished data.

No. 659. Persons At Work, by Hours Worked: 1997

[For civilian noninstitutional population 16 years old and over. Annual averages of monthly figures. Based on Current Population Survey; see text, Section 1, Population, and Appendix III]

HOURS OF WORK	PERSONS AT WORK (1,000)			PERCENT DISTRIBUTION		
	Total	Agriculture industries	Non-agriculture industries	Total	Agriculture industries	Non-agriculture industries
Total	**124,003**	**3,233**	**120,770**	**100.0**	**100.0**	**100.0**
1 to 34 hours	30,733	984	29,749	24.8	30.4	24.6
1 to 4 hours	1,297	81	1,216	1.0	2.5	1.0
5 to 14 hours	4,811	225	4,586	3.9	7.0	3.8
15 to 29 hours	15,290	462	14,828	12.3	14.3	12.3
30 to 34 hours	9,335	216	9,120	7.5	6.7	7.6
35 hours and over	93,270	2,248	91,021	75.2	69.6	75.4
35 to 39 hours	8,635	164	8,470	7.0	5.1	7.0
40 hours	45,121	725	44,396	36.4	22.4	36.8
41 hours and over.	39,515	1,359	38,155	31.9	42.0	31.6
41 to 48 hours.	14,428	246	14,182	11.6	7.6	11.7
49 to 58 hours.	14,530	400	14,130	11.7	12.4	11.7
60 hours and over	10,556	713	9,844	8.5	22.1	8.2
Average weekly hours:						
Total at work.	39.5	42.1	39.4	(X)	(X)	(X)
Persons usually working full time	43.4	48.8	43.3	(X)	(X)	(X)

X Not applicable.
Source: U.S. Bureau of Labor Statistics, *Employment and Earnings*, monthly, January, 1997 issue.

No. 660. Persons With a Job But Not at Work: 1970 to 1997

[In thousands, except percent. For civilian noninstitutional population 16 years old and over. Annual averages of monthly figures. Based on Current Population Survey; see text, Section 1, Population, and Appendix III]

REASON FOR NOT WORKING	1970	1975	1980	1985	1990 [1]	1992	1993	1994 [1]	1995	1996	1997 [1]
All industries, number	**4,645**	**5,221**	**5,881**	**5,789**	**6,160**	**6,088**	**6,041**	**5,619**	**5,582**	**5,768**	**5,555**
Percent of employed	**5.9**	**6.1**	**5.9**	**5.4**	**5.2**	**5.1**	**5.0**	**4.6**	**4.5**	**4.6**	**4.3**
Reason for not working:											
Vacation	2,341	2,815	3,320	3,338	3,529	3,409	3,328	2,877	2,982	3,085	2,942
Illness	1,324	1,343	1,426	1,308	1,341	1,259	1,295	1,184	1,084	1,090	1,114
Bad weather	128	139	155	141	90	128	153	165	122	256	146
Industrial dispute	156	95	105	42	24	19	24	15	21	11	20
All other	696	829	876	960	1,177	1,272	1,241	1,378	1,373	1,325	1,334

[1] See footnote 2, Table 644.
Source: U.S. Bureau of Labor Statistics, *Employment and Earnings*, monthly, January issues; and unpublished data.

No. 661. Self-Employed Workers, by Industry and Occupation: 1970 to 1997

[In thousands. For civilian noninstitutional population 16 years old and over. Annual averages of monthly figures. Data from 1992 forward are not fully comparable with data for prior years because of the introduction of the occupational and industrial classification used in the 1990 census. Based on the Current Population Survey; see text, Section 1, Population, and Appendix III]

ITEM	1970	1980	1990 [1]	1993	1994 [1]	1995	1996	1997 [1]
Total self-employed.	7,031	8,642	10,097	10,280	10,648	10,482	10,490	10,513
Industry:								
Agriculture	1,810	1,642	1,378	1,320	1,645	1,580	1,518	1,457
Nonagriculture	5,221	7,000	8,719	8,960	9,003	8,902	8,971	9,056
Mining	14	28	24	17	13	16	15	14
Construction	687	1,173	1,457	1,549	1,506	1,460	1,496	1,492
Manufacturing	264	358	427	439	426	433	406	422
Transportation and public utilities	196	282	301	372	385	396	432	438
Trade	1,667	1,899	1,851	1,886	1,906	1,772	1,760	1,761
Finance, insurance, and real estate	254	458	630	655	625	660	674	629
Services	2,140	2,804	4,030	4,041	4,142	4,166	4,189	4,300
Occupation:								
Managerial and professional specialty	(NA)	(NA)	3,050	3,078	3,106	3,147	3,288	3,432
Technical, sales, and administrative support. .	(NA)	(NA)	2,240	2,319	2,380	2,341	2,304	2,219
Service occupations	(NA)	(NA)	1,207	1,044	1,178	1,190	1,198	1,179
Precision production, craft, and repair.	(NA)	(NA)	1,675	1,888	1,740	1,618	1,595	1,651
Operators, fabricators, and laborers	(NA)	(NA)	567	631	639	631	634	629
Farming, forestry, and fishing	(NA)	(NA)	1,358	1,320	1,605	1,556	1,471	1,403

NA Not available.   [1] See footnote 2, Table 644.

Source: U.S. Bureau of Labor Statistics, Bulletin 2307; *Employment and Earnings*, monthly, January issues; and unpublished data.

No. 662. Self-Employed Persons With Home-Based Businesses: 1997

[As of May. For persons at work 16 years and over in nonagriculture industries in home-based businesses as part of their primary job. Based on the Current Population Survey; see text Section 1, Population and Appendix III]

CHARACTERISTIC	Total [1] (1,000)	PERCENT DISTRIBUTION BY HOURS WORKED AT HOME			MEAN HOURS	
		Less than 8 hours	8 hours or more		Worked at home	Total at work on primary job
			Total	35 hours or more		
Total	4,125	30.4	69.6	29.3	23.0	37.3
SEX						
Male.	2,157	36.2	63.8	25.5	20.4	42.1
Female	1,968	24.2	75.8	33.5	25.9	31.9
RACE AND HISPANIC ORIGIN						
White	3,868	30.5	69.5	29.0	22.9	36.9
Black	135	29.2	70.8	47.0	29.1	42.7
Hispanic origin [2]	156	27.8	72.2	31.3	23.8	35.9
OCCUPATION						
Managerial and professional	1,714	28.3	71.7	28.2	23.1	37.0
Exec., admin., and managerial.	1,014	28.3	71.7	29.0	23.8	39.6
Professional	700	28.3	71.7	27.1	22.1	33.2
Technical, sales, and administrative [3]	1,016	33.4	66.6	22.5	19.5	32.0
Sales	722	34.4	65.6	24.1	20.2	35.8
Administrative support	259	33.1	66.9	15.5	16.7	20.1
Service	616	12.0	88.0	58.3	36.9	42.1
Precision production, craft, and repair.	564	50.1	49.9	15.1	14.8	41.9
Operators, fabricators, and laborers	215	36.1	63.9	22.4	20.0	38.0
INDUSTRY						
Construction	726	49.5	50.5	14.3	14.3	44.3
Manufacturing	193	13.6	86.4	38.5	29.1	36.5
Transportation and public utilities.	132	52.8	47.2	18.0	14.9	35.7
Wholesale trade	185	28.9	71.1	30.2	22.3	39.4
Retail trade	532	38.9	61.1	19.2	19.1	30.5
Finance, insurance, and real estate	291	22.5	77.5	23.6	20.9	34.5
Services	2,054	23.0	77.0	37.8	27.4	36.8

[1] Includes persons who worked at home but did not report the number of hours worked. These persons are excluded from the distribution.   [2] Persons of Hispanic origin may be of any race.   [3] Includes other occupations, not shown separately.

Source: U.S. Bureau of Labor Statistics, *News*, USDL 98-93, March 11, 1998.

No. 663. Persons Doing Job-Related Work at Home: 1991 and 1997

[As of May. For persons at work 16 years and over in nonagriculture industries doing job-related work at home as part of their primary job. Based on the Current Population Survey; see text, Section 1, Population, and Appendix III]

| CHARACTERISTIC | Total (1,000) [1] | Rate [2] | PERCENT DISTRIBUTION | | | | MEAN HOURS WORKED | | | |
| | | | Wage and salary workers | | Self-employed [3] | | Persons paid to work at home | | Persons not paid to work at home | |
			Paid	Unpaid	Total	Home based business	Total house worked [4]	Worked at home	Total house worked [4]	Worked at home
Total, 1991	**19,967**	**18.3**	**9.4**	**60.9**	**27.8**	(NA)	(NA)	**8.0**	(NA)	**6.0**
Total, 1997	**21,478**	**17.8**	**17.0**	**51.5**	**30.1**	**19.2**	**40.8**	**14.9**	**46.5**	**8.9**
SEX										
Male	11,202	17.3	15.0	50.1	33.8	19.3	46.6	17.0	49.1	8.7
Female	10,275	18.3	19.1	53.1	26.2	19.2	35.9	13.1	43.9	9.1
RACE AND HISPANIC ORIGIN										
White	19,646	19.2	17.0	50.7	30.9	19.7	40.7	14.7	46.8	8.8
Black . . . . [5]	1,117	8.5	16.6	64.8	16.2	12.1	43.9	17.0	43.8	10.5
Hispanic origin [5]	830	7.2	17.5	53.9	27.8	18.8	38.8	18.2	47.0	9.2
OCCUPATION										
Exec., admin., and managerial	5,940	34.0	14.6	54.8	29.8	17.1	43.8	14.6	49.5	8.7
Professional	7,180	39.2	13.5	67.5	18.2	9.7	40.7	14.3	45.1	9.6
Technical and related support	417	10.6	26.9	60.3	11.3	8.6	44.4	16.2	43.5	6.8
Sales	3,356	22.4	19.1	39.1	40.4	21.5	42.8	16.6	48.2	9.5
Administrative support	1,684	9.7	36.3	39.0	20.5	15.4	34.5	11.2	40.4	6.3
Service	1,250	7.2	20.4	23.0	54.0	49.3	38.5	24.4	43.9	5.8
Precision production, craft, and repair	1,145	8.2	10.1	26.5	62.0	49.2	42.0	11.3	46.7	6.3
Operators, fabricators, and laborers	506	2.9	14.4	31.2	51.1	42.5	(B)	(B)	49.9	10.6

B Base figure too small to meet statistical standards for reliability of a derived figure.   NA Not available.   [1] Includes persons who worked 15 hours or more in an unpaid capacity in a family business.   [2] Persons working at home as a percent of the total at work. 1997 excludes persons not responding to the questions on working at home.   [3] Includes incorporated and unincorporated self-employed.   [4] On primary job.   [5] Persons of Hispanic origin may be of any race.
Source: U.S. Bureau of Labor Statistics, News, USDL 98-93, March 11, 1998.

No. 664. Persons on Flexible Schedules: 1997

[As of May. For full-time wage and salary workers 16 years old and over. Data relate to the primary job. Based on the Current Population Survey; see text, Section 1, Population, and Appendix III]

| ITEM | TOTAL | | | MALE | | | FEMALE | | |
| | Total [1] | With flexible schedules | | Total [1] | With flexible schedules | | Total [1] | With flexible schedules | |
		Number	Percent		Number	Percent		Number	Percent
Total, 1997	**90,549**	**25,031**	**27.6**	**52,073**	**14,952**	**28.7**	**38,476**	**10,079**	**26.2**
AGE									
16 to 19 years old	1,640	339	20.7	1,050	177	16.9	590	161	27.4
20 to 24 years old	8,462	1,923	22.7	4,968	1,111	22.4	3,494	812	23.2
25 to 34 years old	25,208	7,161	28.4	14,721	4,231	28.7	10,486	2,931	27.9
35 to 44 years old	26,755	7,781	29.1	15,434	4,730	30.6	11,321	3,051	26.9
45 to 54 years old	19,596	5,355	27.3	10,806	3,118	28.9	8,790	2,237	25.4
55 to 64 years old	7,778	2,129	27.4	4,431	1,334	30.1	3,347	796	23.8
65 years old and over	1,110	344	31.0	662	251	38.0	448	93	20.7
RACE AND HISPANIC ORIGIN									
White	75,683	21,698	28.7	44,495	13,186	29.6	31,188	8,512	27.3
Black	10,884	2,191	20.1	5,323	1,068	20.1	5,561	1,123	20.2
Hispanic origin [2]	9,635	1,769	18.4	6,283	1,147	18.3	3,352	622	18.5
OCCUPATION									
Executive, administrative, and managerial	13,469	5,705	42.4	7,213	3,251	45.1	6,255	2,454	39.2
Professional specialty	13,915	4,947	35.5	6,668	3,156	47.3	7,247	1,791	24.7
Technical and related support	3,376	1,040	30.8	1,724	611	35.4	1,651	429	26.0
Sales	9,001	3,687	41.0	5,106	2,315	45.3	3,895	1,372	35.2
Administrative support, including clerical	13,402	3,101	23.1	3,162	687	21.7	10,240	2,414	23.6
Private household	308	125	40.5	21	16	(B)	287	109	37.8
Protective service	1,891	314	16.6	1,619	254	15.7	272	60	22.2
Service, exc. private household and protective	8,855	1,934	21.8	4,665	986	21.1	4,190	947	22.6
Precision production, craft and repair . .	11,519	2,023	17.6	10,506	1,861	17.7	1,013	162	16.0
Operators, fabricators, and laborers . .	14,812	2,156	14.6	11,388	1,815	15.9	3,424	342	10.0

B Percent not shown where base is less than 75,000.   [1] Includes persons who did not provide information on flexible schedules.   [2] Persons of Hispanic origin may be of any race.
Source: U.S. Bureau of Labor Statistics, News, USDL98-119, March 26, 1998.

No. 665. Employed Persons in Alternative and Traditional Work Arrangements, by Selected Characteristic: 1997

[As of February. For all employed persons, except unpaid family members, 16 years old and over. See source for definitions of working arrangements. Based on the Current Population Survey and subject to sampling error; see source and Appendix III]

CHARACTERISTIC	WORKERS IN ALTERNATIVE ARRANGEMENTS				Workers in traditional arrangements
	Independent contractors	On-call workers	Temporary help agency workers	Workers provided by contract firms	
Total (1,000)............................	8,456	1,996	1,300	809	114,199
AGE AND SEX					
Total (percent)........................	100.0	100.0	100.0	100.0	100.0
16 to 19 years old....................	0.8	9.6	6.1	1.9	5.0
20 to 24 years old....................	2.4	11.9	16.5	8.1	9.8
25 to 34 years old....................	18.3	22.5	30.3	34.2	25.4
35 to 44 years old....................	31.1	25.4	21.5	31.1	27.7
45 to 54 years old....................	26.5	14.4	16.2	14.2	20.4
55 to 64 years old....................	13.9	9.7	6.7	7.7	9.2
65 years and over....................	7.0	6.5	2.8	2.8	2.5
Male...............................	66.6	49.0	44.7	69.8	52.7
16 to 19 years old....................	0.3	5.3	2.9	1.1	2.5
20 to 24 years old....................	1.5	6.4	9.6	7.7	5.1
25 to 34 years old....................	11.4	11.8	15.1	24.0	13.7
35 to 44 years old....................	20.7	12.1	6.9	21.9	14.6
45 to 54 years old....................	17.7	6.9	6.2	9.1	10.5
55 to 64 years old....................	9.9	3.9	2.2	5.1	4.9
65 years and over....................	5.1	2.6	1.7	0.9	1.4
Female..............................	33.4	51.0	55.3	30.2	47.3
16 to 19 years old....................	0.5	4.3	3.2	0.8	2.4
20 to 24 years old....................	0.9	5.4	6.9	0.4	4.7
25 to 34 years old....................	7.0	10.6	15.1	10.3	11.7
35 to 44 years old....................	10.4	13.4	14.6	9.2	13.1
45 to 54 years old....................	8.8	7.5	10.0	5.1	9.9
55 to 64 years old....................	4.0	5.8	4.4	2.6	4.3
65 years and over....................	1.9	3.9	1.1	1.9	1.1

Source: U.S. Bureau of Labor Statistics, *News,* USDL97-422, December 2, 1997.

No. 666. Multiple Jobholders: 1997

[Annual average of monthly figures. For the civilian noninstitutional population 16 years old and over. Multiple jobholders are employed persons who, either 1) had jobs as wage or salary workers with two employers or more; 2) were self-employed and also held a wage and salary job; or 3) were unpaid family workers on their primary jobs but also held wage and salary job. Based on the Current Population Survey; see text, Section 1, Population, and Appendix III]

CHARACTERISTIC	TOTAL		MALE		FEMALE	
	Number (1,000)	Percent of employed	Number (1,000)	Percent of employed	Number (1,000)	Percent of employed
Total [1]............................	7,955	6.1	4,237	6.1	3,718	6.2
Age:						
16 to 19 years old....................	331	5.0	144	4.2	187	5.7
20 to 24 years old....................	809	6.5	385	5.9	424	7.3
25 to 54 years old....................	6,076	6.4	3,278	6.5	2,798	6.4
55 to 64 years old....................	625	5.1	356	5.3	268	4.8
65 years old and over................	115	3.1	74	3.3	40	2.6
Race and Hispanic origin:						
White..............................	6,909	6.3	3,693	6.2	3,216	6.4
Black..............................	758	5.4	388	5.9	370	5.0
Hispanic origin [2]...................	494	3.9	305	3.9	190	3.8
Marital status:						
Married, spouse present..............	4,434	5.9	2,675	6.3	1,758	5.4
Widowed, divorced, or separated......	1,388	6.8	495	6.0	893	7.4
Single, never married................	2,133	6.3	1,067	5.7	1,067	7.1
Full- or part-time status:						
Primary job full time, secondary job part time..	4,888	(X)	2,661	(X)	1,827	(X)
Both jobs part time..................	1,689	(X)	521	(X)	1,168	(X)
Both jobs full time..................	237	(X)	169	(X)	68	(X)
Hours vary on primary or secondary job.....	1,509	(X)	869	(X)	640	(X)

X Not applicable.   [1] Includes a small number of persons who work part time on their primary job and full time on their secondary job(s), not shown separately. Includes other races, not shown separately.   [2] Persons of Hispanic origin may be of any race.

Source: U.S. Bureau of Labor Statistics, *Employment and Earnings,* monthly, January 1998 issue.

No. 667. Distribution of Workers, by Tenure with Current Employer, by Selected Characteristic: 1996

[As of **February**. For employed wage and salary workers 16 years old and over. Based on the Current Population Survey and subject to sampling error; see source and Appendix III]

CHARACTERISTIC	Number employed (1,000)	12 months or less	13 to 23 months	2 years	3 to 4 years	5 to 9 years	10 to 14 years	15 to 19 years	20 years or more	Median years [1]
		PERCENT DISTRIBUTION BY TENURE WITH CURRENT EMPLOYER								
Total	110,281	26.0	8.5	4.8	15.2	19.8	10.0	6.8	9.0	3.8
AGE AND SEX										
16 to 19 years old.	5,749	77.6	11.8	5.5	5.0	0.2	-	-	-	0.7
20 years old and over	104,531	23.1	8.3	4.8	15.8	20.8	10.5	7.1	9.5	4.2
20 to 24 years old	11,468	52.2	14.1	8.9	18.3	6.3	0.1	-	-	1.2
25 to 34 years old	29,474	29.5	10.8	5.7	20.3	24.7	7.8	1.2	(Z)	2.8
35 to 44 years old	30,316	17.9	7.4	4.3	14.9	24.2	14.3	11.3	5.8	5.3
45 to 54 years old	21,330	13.0	5.1	3.0	12.1	20.0	13.5	11.1	22.3	8.3
55 to 64 years old	9,398	10.6	4.6	2.7	11.0	18.0	12.2	12.0	28.9	10.2
65 years old and over.	2,545	13.0	5.1	3.4	11.8	19.3	13.1	7.4	26.9	8.4
Male.	57,291	25.1	8.0	4.7	15.1	19.1	10.0	6.9	11.0	4.0
16 to 19 years old	2,932	77.3	9.9	6.8	5.8	0.2	-	-	-	0.7
20 years old and over.	54,359	22.3	7.9	4.6	15.6	20.2	10.6	7.3	11.6	4.4
20 to 24 years old	5,979	52.7	13.2	8.2	19.1	6.6	0.2	-	-	1.2
25 to 34 years old	15,779	28.2	10.0	5.8	20.8	25.3	8.3	1.5	(Z)	3.0
35 to 44 years old	15,756	16.3	7.0	3.8	14.0	23.1	15.7	13.0	7.1	6.1
45 to 54 years old	10,712	11.9	4.6	2.6	10.7	17.7	12.3	11.0	29.3	10.1
55 to 64 years old	4,846	10.3	5.3	3.0	10.6	17.0	10.0	9.4	34.4	10.5
65 years old and over	1,287	12.2	5.8	3.1	14.6	16.7	12.4	5.7	29.5	8.3
Female.	52,989	27.0	9.0	4.9	15.4	20.5	9.9	6.6	6.8	3.5
16 to 19 years old	2,817	77.9	13.7	4.0	4.2	0.2	-	-	-	0.7
20 years old and over.	50,172	24.1	8.7	5.0	16.0	21.6	10.4	7.0	7.2	3.9
20 to 24 years old	5,489	51.7	15.0	9.8	17.4	6.0	0.1	-	-	1.2
25 to 34 years old	13,695	30.9	11.6	5.7	19.7	24.0	7.2	0.9	-	2.7
35 to 44 years old	14,561	19.6	7.8	4.7	15.9	25.5	12.7	9.5	4.4	4.8
45 to 54 years old	10,617	14.1	5.5	3.3	13.5	22.3	14.8	11.3	15.2	7.0
55 to 64 years old	4,551	11.0	3.9	2.4	11.4	19.1	14.5	14.8	23.1	10.0
65 years old and over	1,258	13.9	4.3	3.8	8.9	22.0	13.8	9.2	24.2	8.4

- Represents zero.   Z Less than 0.05 percent.   [1] For definition of median, see Guide to Tabular Presentation.

Source: U. S. Bureau of Labor Statistics, News, USDL 97-25, January 30, 1997, and unpublished data.

No. 668. Part-Time Workers, by Reason: 1997

[In thousands, except hours. For persons working 1 to 34 hours per week. For civilian noninstitutional population 16 years old and over. Annual average of monthly figures. Based on the Current Population Survey and subject to sampling error; see text, Section 1, Population, and Appendix III]

REASON	ALL INDUSTRIES			NONAGRICULTURAL INDUSTRIES		
	Total	Usually work—		Total	Usually work—	
		Full time	Part time		Full time	Part time
Total working fewer than 35 hours	**30,733**	**9,922**	**20,811**	**29,749**	**9,618**	**20,131**
Economic reasons	4,068	1,407	2,662	3,879	1,313	2,567
Slack work or business conditions	2,286	1,141	1,144	2,167	1,074	1,093
Could find only part-time work	1,468	-	1,468	1,433	-	1,433
Seasonal work	129	79	50	99	58	41
Job started or ended during the week	186	186	-	180	180	-
Noneconomic reasons.	26,665	8,516	18,149	25,870	8,306	17,564
Child-care problems	823	82	742	812	81	731
Other family or personal obligations	5,496	683	4,813	5,327	668	4,658
Health or medical limitations	705	-	705	673	-	673
In school or training	6,160	88	6,072	6,028	87	5,942
Retired or Social Security limit on earnings . . .	1,861	-	1,861	1,732	-	1,732
Vacation or personal day	3,303	3,303	-	3,248	3,248	-
Holiday, legal, or religious	876	876	-	867	867	-
Weather related curtailment.	635	635	-	570	570	-
Other	6,804	2,849	3,955	6,613	2,785	3,827
Average hours per week:						
Economic reasons.	23.0	24.0	22.4	23.1	24.1	22.5
Noneconomic reasons.	21.4	25.6	19.5	21.5	25.7	19.6

- Represents or rounds to zero.

Source: U.S. Bureau of Labor Statistics, Employment and Earnings, monthly, January 1998 issue.

No. 669 Displaced Workers, by Selected Characteristics: 1996

[In percent, except total. As of February. For persons 20 years old and over with tenure of 3 years or more who lost or left a job between January 1993 and December 1995 because of plant closings or moves, slack work, or the abolishment of their positions. Data revised since originally published. Based on Current Population Survey and subject to sampling error; see source and and Appendix III]

CHARACTERISTIC	Total (1,000)	EMPLOYMENT STATUS			REASON FOR JOB LOSS		
		Employed	Unem-ployed	Not in the labor force	Plant or company closed down or moved	Slack work	Position or shift abolished
Total [1]	4,171	73.6	12.5	13.9	44.0	24.2	31.8
20 to 24 years old	149	71.3	17.9	10.7	52.9	30.0	17.1
25 to 54 years old	3,397	78.5	12.0	9.5	43.1	25.3	31.6
55 to 64 years old	487	52.1	16.6	31.3	45.3	15.1	39.7
65 years old and over	139	31.6	4.1	64.3	50.4	22.5	27.1
Males	2,358	77.8	13.1	9.1	42.8	27.3	29.9
20 to 24 years old	82	77.4	17.1	5.4	53.5	34.9	11.6
25 to 54 years old	1,929	82.0	13.2	4.8	42.4	28.6	28.9
55 to 64 years old	276	60.7	12.6	26.7	41.5	14.8	43.7
65 years old and over	71	(2)	(2)	(2)	(2)	(2)	(2)
Females	1,813	68.2	11.8	20.0	45.5	20.2	34.4
20 to 24 years old	67	(2)	18.9	17.2	52.3	23.9	23.8
25 to 54 years old	1,468	73.9	10.6	15.6	44.0	21.0	35.1
55 to 64 years old	211	40.8	21.9	37.3	50.1	15.5	34.4
65 years old and over	67	(2)	(2)	(2)	(2)	(2)	(2)
White	3,632	74.1	12.0	13.9	43.0	24.7	32.4
Black	420	67.4	17.1	15.5	51.8	20.0	28.2
Hispanic origin [3]	383	66.5	22.8	10.7	49.5	37.0	13.4

[1] Includes other races, not shown separately.   [2] Data not shown where base is less than 75,000.   [3] Persons of Hispanic origin may be of any race.
Source: U.S. Bureau of Labor Statistics, *News*, USDL 96-446.

No. 670. Percent Distribution of Employed Persons by Disability Status: 1991 to 1994

[Data from the Survey of Income and Program Participation]

DISABILITY STATUS	1991	1993	1994	DISABILITY STATUS	1991	1993	1994
All employed persons (1,000)	119,432	122,614	125,591	Lifting and carrying	2.3	2.6	2.5
Total of employed persons	100.0	100.0	100.0	Climbing stairs	2.3	2.6	2.6
				Walking 3 city blocks	2.4	2.6	2.7
With no disability	86.6	86.2	86.2	With an ADL [1] limitation	0.8	1.0	0.9
With a disability	13.4	13.8	13.8	With an IADL [2] limitation	1.1	1.3	1.4
Severe	2.8	3.2	3.4	Needs personal assistance and			
Not severe	10.6	10.6	10.4	an ADL or IADL	0.7	0.9	0.9
With a functional limitation	8.4	8.9	7.9	Uses a wheelchair	0.1	0.1	0.1
Severe	1.7	2.0	2.1	Does not use a wheelchair, but			
With difficulty:				uses a cane, crutches, or a			
Seeing words and letters	2.0	2.2	1.6	walker	0.4	0.5	0.4
Hearing normal conversation	3.2	3.5	2.7				

[1] ADLs are activities of daily living and include getting around inside the home, getting in or out of a bed or chair, taking a bath or shower, dressing, eating, and using the toilet.   [2] IADLs are instrumental activities of daily living and include going outside the home, keeping track of money and bills, preparing meals, doing light housework, and using the telephone.
Source: U.S. Census Bureau, Internet site <http://www.census.gov/hhes/www/disable/dissipp.html> (Accessed 18 June 1997)

No. 671. Persons Not in the Labor Force: 1997

[In thousands. Annual average of monthly figures. For the civilian noninstitutional population 16 years old and over. Based on the Current Population Survey; see text, Section 1, Population, and Appendix III]

STATUS AND REASON	Total	AGE			SEX	
		16 to 24 years old	25 to 54 years old	55 years old and over	Male	Female
Total not in the labor force	66,837	11,343	18,552	36,942	24,454	42,382
Do not want a job now [1]	61,895	9,434	16,311	36,151	22,420	39,475
Want a job now	4,941	1,909	2,241	791	2,034	2,907
In the previous year—						
Did not search for a job	2,857	1,034	1,245	579	1,118	1,739
Did search for a job [2]	2,084	875	997	212	917	1,168
Not available for work now	669	346	289	34	257	412
Available for work now, not looking for work	1,416	529	708	178	659	756
Reason for not currently looking:						
Discouraged over job prospects [3]	343	107	184	52	200	143
Family responsibilities	139	26	97	16	21	117
In school or training	235	188	45	2	113	121
Ill health or disability	116	17	71	28	52	64
Other [4]	583	191	311	81	273	311

[1] Includes some persons who are not asked if they want a job.   [2] Persons who had a job in the prior 12 months must have searched since the end of that job.   [3] Includes such things as believes no work available, could not find work, lacks necessary schooling or training, employer thinks too young or old, and other types of discrimination.   [4] Includes such things as child care and transportation problems.
Source: U.S. Bureau of Labor Statistics, *Employment and Earnings*, monthly, January 1998 issue.

No. 672. Employed Civilians, by Occupation, Sex, Race, and Hispanic Origin: 1983 and 1997

[For civilian noninstitutional population 16 years old and over. Annual average of monthly figures. Based on Current Population Survey; see text, Section 1, Population, and Appendix III. Persons of Hispanic origin may be of any race. See headnote, Table 661]

OCCUPATION	1983				1997 [1]			
	Total employed (1,000)	Percent of total			Total employed (1,000)	Percent of total		
		Female	Black	Hispanic		Female	Black	Hispanic
Total	100,834	43.7	9.3	5.3	129,558	46.2	10.8	9.8
Managerial and professional specialty	23,592	40.9	5.6	2.6	37,686	48.9	7.3	5.0
Executive, administrative, and managerial [2]	10,772	32.4	4.7	2.8	18,440	44.3	6.9	5.4
Officials and administrators, public	417	38.5	8.3	3.8	606	49.5	11.9	5.6
Financial managers	357	38.6	3.5	3.1	688	49.3	5.6	5.1
Personnel and labor relations managers	106	43.9	4.9	2.6	108	63.4	7.5	2.9
Purchasing managers	82	23.6	5.1	1.4	114	40.9	6.4	4.6
Managers, marketing, advertising and public relations	396	21.8	2.7	1.7	711	34.6	3.7	4.8
Administrators, education and related fields	415	41.4	11.3	2.4	733	61.3	10.7	5.8
Managers, medicine and health	91	57.0	5.0	2.0	701	76.8	7.4	4.3
Managers, properties and real estate	305	42.8	5.5	5.2	535	49.4	7.1	10.3
Management-related occupations [2]	2,966	40.3	5.8	3.5	4,604	57.7	8.4	5.1
Accountants and auditors	1,105	38.7	5.5	3.3	1,625	56.6	7.9	5.0
Professional specialty [2]	12,820	48.1	6.4	2.5	19,245	53.3	7.8	4.5
Architects	103	12.7	1.6	1.5	169	17.9	1.7	5.1
Engineers [2]	1,572	5.8	2.7	2.2	2,036	9.6	3.9	3.8
Aerospace engineers	80	6.9	1.5	2.1	87	4.7	1.3	2.2
Chemical engineers	67	6.1	3.0	1.4	92	17.3	7.4	1.1
Civil engineers	211	4.0	1.9	3.2	248	7.7	2.2	4.2
Electrical and electronic	450	6.1	3.4	3.1	652	9.2	5.5	3.8
Industrial engineers	210	11.0	3.3	2.4	258	16.4	4.1	5.6
Mechanical	259	2.8	3.2	1.1	352	5.9	2.5	3.2
Mathematical and computer scientists [2]	463	29.6	5.4	2.6	1,494	30.4	7.5	3.1
Computer systems analysts, scientists	276	27.8	6.2	2.7	1,236	28.6	7.7	3.1
Operations and systems researchers and analysts	142	31.3	4.9	2.2	201	40.5	7.0	3.3
Natural scientists [2]	357	20.5	2.6	2.1	529	31.0	5.1	2.2
Chemists, except biochemists	98	23.3	4.3	1.2	144	25.5	5.5	4.2
Biological and life scientists	55	40.8	2.4	1.8	106	44.7	5.7	0.9
Medical scientists	(3)	(3)	(3)	(3)	77	46.9	9.6	1.1
Health diagnosing occupations [2]	735	13.3	2.7	3.3	1,027	25.2	3.6	4.0
Physicians	519	15.8	3.2	4.5	724	26.2	4.2	4.8
Dentists	126	6.7	2.4	1.0	138	17.3	2.6	1.1
Health assessment and treating occupations	1,900	85.8	7.1	2.2	2,886	86.5	8.4	3.3
Registered nurses	1,372	95.8	6.7	1.8	2,065	93.5	8.3	2.9
Pharmacists	158	26.7	3.8	2.6	200	45.9	4.1	2.6
Dietitians	71	90.8	21.0	3.7	101	88.7	28.5	6.0
Therapists [2]	247	76.3	7.6	2.7	455	75.4	6.6	4.0
Respiratory therapists	69	69.4	6.5	3.7	85	59.4	7.7	2.0
Physical therapists	55	77.0	9.7	1.5	110	64.0	5.0	4.1
Speech therapists	51	90.5	1.5	-	102	95.0	3.6	3.7
Physicians' assistants	51	36.3	7.7	4.4	65	63.2	5.5	8.7
Teachers, college and university	606	36.3	4.4	1.8	869	42.7	6.5	3.4
Teachers, except college and university [2]	3,365	70.9	9.1	2.7	4,798	75.7	10.2	5.4
Prekindergarten and kindergarten	299	98.2	11.8	3.4	574	97.8	13.2	9.7
Elementary school	1,350	83.3	11.1	3.1	1,872	83.9	10.9	5.4
Secondary school	1,209	51.8	7.2	2.3	1,173	58.4	8.3	4.0
Special education	81	82.2	10.2	2.3	384	82.9	10.8	3.2
Counselors, educational and vocational	184	53.1	13.9	3.2	248	66.2	12.4	4.1
Librarians, archivists, and curators	213	84.4	7.8	1.6	217	77.1	6.3	4.7
Librarians	193	87.3	7.9	1.8	188	80.5	6.5	5.4
Social scientists and urban planners [2]	261	46.8	7.1	2.1	441	54.9	8.1	4.5
Economists	98	37.9	6.3	2.7	135	52.2	6.6	3.7
Psychologists	135	57.1	8.6	1.1	256	59.3	9.2	4.5
Social, recreation, and religious workers [2]	831	43.1	12.1	3.8	1,357	54.8	17.2	6.9
Social workers	407	64.3	18.2	6.3	781	69.3	21.7	8.7
Recreation workers	65	71.9	15.7	2.0	126	70.8	13.4	4.9
Clergy	293	5.6	4.9	1.4	350	13.6	12.4	5.0
Lawyers and judges	651	15.8	2.7	1.0	925	26.7	2.8	3.8
Lawyers	612	15.3	2.6	0.9	885	26.6	2.7	3.8
Writers, artists, entertainers, and athletes [2]	1,544	42.7	4.8	2.9	2,234	49.3	5.0	5.8
Authors	62	46.7	2.1	0.9	137	53.6	1.7	2.1
Technical writers	(3)	(3)	(3)	(3)	61	51.1	3.9	3.7
Designers	393	52.7	3.1	2.7	658	58.5	2.9	6.6
Musicians and composers	155	28.0	7.9	4.4	155	36.6	10.5	9.3
Actors and directors	60	30.8	6.6	3.4	136	38.2	7.3	5.1
Painters, sculptors, craft-artists, and artist printmakers	186	47.4	2.1	2.3	251	45.8	3.0	5.6
Photographers	113	20.7	4.0	3.4	132	29.2	6.6	5.3
Editors and reporters	204	48.4	2.9	2.1	257	51.2	4.8	1.7
Public relations specialists	157	50.1	6.2	1.9	148	65.7	7.4	6.7
Announcers	(3)	(3)	(3)	(3)	61	14.2	9.2	9.9
Athletes	58	17.6	9.4	1.7	92	27.0	7.1	5.5

See footnotes at end of table.

No. 672. Employed Civilians, by Occupation, Sex, Race, and Hispanic Origin: 1983 and 1997—Continued

[See headnote, page 417]

OCCUPATION	1983 Total employed (1,000)	1983 Female	1983 Black	1983 Hispanic	1997 [1] Total employed (1,000)	1997 Female	1997 Black	1997 Hispanic
Technical, sales, and administrative support	**31,265**	**64.6**	**7.6**	**4.3**	**38,309**	**64.1**	**10.5**	**7.9**
Technicians and related support	3,053	48.2	8.2	3.1	4,214	51.9	9.7	6.1
Health technologists and technicians [2]	1,111	84.3	12.7	3.1	1,693	80.2	13.0	6.3
Clinical laboratory technologists and technicians	255	76.2	10.5	2.9	388	75.9	16.1	7.4
Dental hygienists	66	98.6	1.6	-	107	98.2	1.5	2.3
Radiologic technicians	101	71.7	8.6	4.5	148	69.5	7.5	1.6
Licensed practical nurses	443	97.0	17.7	3.1	408	94.1	15.4	5.6
Engineering and related technologists and technicians [2]	822	18.4	6.1	3.5	960	18.6	7.4	6.7
Electrical and electronic technicians	260	12.5	8.2	4.6	391	14.2	7.4	6.8
Drafting occupations	273	17.5	5.5	2.3	222	16.7	3.9	4.6
Surveying and mapping technicians	(3)	(3)	(3)	(3)	76	10.2	5.1	5.3
Science technicians [2]	202	29.1	6.6	2.8	287	39.5	9.4	8.3
Biological technicians	52	37.7	2.9	2.0	106	57.2	11.2	6.0
Chemical technicians	82	26.9	9.5	3.5	85	22.8	10.4	3.7
Technicians, except health, engineering, and science [2]	917	35.3	5.0	2.7	1,275	42.2	7.1	4.8
Airplane pilots and navigators	69	2.1	-	1.6	120	1.2	1.8	2.4
Computer programmers	443	32.5	4.4	2.1	626	30.0	5.9	4.5
Legal assistants	128	74.0	4.3	3.6	346	83.9	9.8	5.8
Sales occupations	11,818	47.5	4.7	3.7	15,734	50.2	8.1	7.6
Supervisors and proprietors	2,958	28.4	3.6	3.4	4,635	38.4	4.8	6.8
Sales representatives, finance and business services [2]	1,853	37.2	2.7	2.2	2,613	44.0	6.9	4.5
Insurance sales	551	25.1	3.8	2.5	594	42.8	7.7	4.7
Real estate sales	570	48.9	1.3	1.5	781	50.0	4.6	5.1
Securities and financial services sales	212	23.6	3.1	1.1	429	31.2	5.5	2.6
Advertising and related sales	124	47.9	4.5	3.3	173	56.6	10.0	4.2
Sales representatives, commodities, except retail	1,442	15.1	2.1	2.2	1,507	24.9	3.0	5.0
Sales workers, retail and personal services	5,511	69.7	6.7	4.8	6,887	65.7	11.9	10.0
Cashiers	2,009	84.4	10.1	5.4	3,007	78.4	15.6	12.1
Sales-related occupations	54	58.7	2.8	1.3	91	73.5	5.0	4.6
Administrative support, including clerical	16,395	79.9	9.6	5.0	18,361	78.8	12.8	8.6
Supervisors	676	53.4	9.3	5.0	685	59.8	14.4	6.1
Computer equipment operators	605	63.9	12.5	6.0	392	58.5	15.4	7.0
Computer operators	597	63.7	12.1	6.0	385	58.4	15.0	7.1
Secretaries, stenographers, and typists [2]	4,861	98.2	7.3	4.5	3,692	97.9	9.8	6.9
Secretaries	3,891	99.0	5.8	4.0	3,033	98.6	8.7	6.4
Typists	906	95.6	13.8	6.4	555	94.4	17.0	9.7
Information clerks	1,174	88.9	8.5	5.5	1,993	88.4	11.3	9.5
Receptionists	602	96.8	7.5	6.6	1,005	96.5	8.8	9.7
Records processing occupations, except financial [2]	866	82.4	13.9	4.8	935	80.5	15.3	9.5
Order clerks	188	78.1	10.6	4.4	231	74.1	15.9	11.0
Personnel clerks, except payroll and time keeping	64	91.1	14.9	4.6	69	85.0	18.5	13.2
Library clerks	147	81.9	15.4	2.5	155	76.3	13.2	6.6
File clerks	287	83.5	16.7	6.1	295	84.7	15.5	11.7
Records clerks	157	82.8	11.6	5.6	175	82.6	15.0	5.1
Financial records processing [2]	2,457	89.4	4.6	3.7	2,196	92.2	7.1	6.4
Bookkeepers, accounting, and auditing clerks	1,970	91.0	4.3	3.3	1,735	92.3	6.3	5.9
Payroll and time keeping clerks	192	82.2	5.9	5.0	155	92.7	10.2	10.4
Billing clerks	146	88.4	6.2	3.9	161	93.8	12.2	6.0
Cost and rate clerks	96	75.6	5.9	5.3	(3)	(3)	(3)	(3)
Billing, posting, and calculating machine operators	(3)	(3)	(3)	(3)	98	91.6	8.2	10.1
Duplicating, mail and other office machine operators	68	62.6	16.0	6.1	77	59.4	18.4	12.3
Communications equipment operators	256	89.1	17.0	4.4	185	81.5	21.6	9.7
Telephone operators	244	90.4	17.0	4.3	173	83.5	21.5	8.4
Mail and message distributing occupations	799	31.6	18.1	4.5	977	38.0	20.8	9.5
Postal clerks, except mail carriers	248	36.7	26.2	5.2	320	45.1	27.9	7.0
Mail carrier, postal service	259	17.1	12.5	2.7	314	30.7	15.8	9.3
Mail clerks, except postal service	170	50.0	15.8	5.9	181	51.7	24.2	12.7
Messengers	122	26.2	16.7	5.2	161	22.7	12.4	11.3
Material recording, scheduling, and distributing [2][4]	1,562	37.5	10.9	6.6	1,953	44.2	14.8	11.4
Dispatchers	157	45.7	11.4	4.3	233	51.3	14.7	9.0
Production coordinators	182	44.0	6.1	2.2	263	54.1	5.3	4.3
Traffic, shipping, and receiving clerks	421	22.6	9.1	11.1	638	30.5	17.2	15.2
Stock and inventory clerks	532	38.7	13.3	5.5	454	41.1	16.9	12.8
Weighers, measurers, and checkers	79	47.2	16.9	5.8	53	56.2	11.9	10.9
Expediters	112	57.5	8.4	4.3	245	69.4	14.0	10.1
Adjusters and investigators	675	69.9	11.1	5.1	1,701	74.4	14.0	8.9
Insurance adjusters, examiners, and investigators	199	65.0	11.5	3.3	434	72.5	11.1	8.5
Investigators and adjusters, except insurance	301	70.1	11.3	4.8	983	74.8	14.4	8.6
Eligibility clerks, social welfare	69	88.7	12.9	9.4	112	86.9	15.1	13.6
Bill and account collectors	106	66.4	8.5	6.5	172	68.6	18.3	8.4
Miscellaneous administrative support [2]	2,397	85.2	12.5	5.9	3,576	83.4	14.6	9.4
General office clerks	648	80.6	12.7	5.2	818	80.6	12.7	9.8
Bank tellers	480	91.0	7.5	4.3	446	90.1	9.8	9.0
Data entry keyers	311	93.6	18.6	5.6	664	81.9	18.3	9.8
Statistical clerks	96	75.7	7.5	3.4	89	89.0	22.9	3.2
Teachers' aides	348	93.7	17.8	12.6	623	93.1	15.2	12.6

See footnotes at end of table.

No. 672. Employed Civilians, by Occupation, Sex, Race, and Hispanic Origin: 1983 and 1997—Continued

[See headnote, page 417]

OCCUPATION	1983 Total employed (1,000)	1983 Percent of total Female	1983 Percent of total Black	1983 Percent of total Hispanic	1997[1] Total employed (1,000)	1997[1] Percent of total Female	1997[1] Percent of total Black	1997[1] Percent of total Hispanic
Service occupations	**13,857**	**60.1**	**16.6**	**6.8**	**17,537**	**59.4**	**17.6**	**14.6**
Private household [2]	980	96.1	27.8	8.5	795	95.4	16.2	26.6
Child care workers	408	96.9	7.9	3.6	260	96.8	11.8	17.4
Cleaners and servants	512	95.8	42.4	11.8	512	94.9	17.8	31.3
Protective service	1,672	12.8	13.6	4.6	2,300	17.9	18.7	8.8
Supervisors, protective service	127	4.7	7.7	3.1	181	12.5	16.5	8.5
Supervisors, police and detectives	58	4.2	9.3	1.2	108	17.4	14.8	6.0
Firefighting and fire prevention	189	1.0	6.7	4.1	233	3.4	11.9	5.7
Firefighting occupations	170	1.0	7.3	3.8	218	3.1	12.4	4.6
Police and detectives	645	9.4	13.1	4.0	1,005	16.4	18.1	7.6
Police and detectives, public service	412	5.7	9.5	4.4	579	11.8	13.4	9.1
Sheriffs, bailiffs, and other law enforcement officers	87	13.2	11.5	4.0	142	22.2	18.6	7.2
Correctional institution officers	146	17.8	24.0	2.8	284	22.9	27.4	4.9
Guards	711	20.6	17.0	5.6	881	24.4	21.6	11.0
Guards and guards, except public service	602	13.0	18.9	6.2	738	18.2	23.7	11.6
Service except private household and protective	11,205	64.0	16.0	6.9	14,442	64.0	17.5	14.9
Food preparation and service occupations [2]	4,860	63.3	10.5	6.8	5,999	56.8	11.6	16.4
Bartenders	338	48.4	2.7	4.4	310	57.2	2.0	6.3
Waiters and waitresses	1,357	87.8	4.1	3.6	1,375	77.8	4.7	10.2
Cooks	1,452	50.0	15.8	6.5	2,126	41.8	16.7	20.4
Food counter, fountain, and related occupations	326	76.0	9.1	6.7	322	69.4	12.4	8.5
Kitchen workers, food preparation	138	77.0	13.7	8.1	278	72.6	9.8	14.2
Waiters' and waitresses' assistants	364	38.8	12.6	14.2	536	48.5	9.9	18.4
Health service occupations	1,739	89.2	23.5	4.8	2,447	88.2	30.8	9.2
Dental assistants	154	98.1	6.1	5.7	231	96.7	6.1	11.5
Health aides, except nursing	316	86.8	16.5	4.8	341	76.0	27.6	6.2
Nursing aides, orderlies, and attendants	1,269	88.7	27.3	4.7	1,875	89.4	34.5	9.5
Cleaning and building service occupations [2]	2,736	38.8	24.4	9.2	3,108	43.2	21.5	21.3
Maids and housemen	531	81.2	32.3	10.1	643	80.1	27.1	24.8
Janitors and cleaners	2,031	28.6	22.6	8.9	2,226	34.0	19.9	21.0
Personal service occupations [2]	1,870	79.2	11.1	6.0	2,888	80.9	14.3	9.6
Barbers	92	12.9	8.4	12.1	79	22.8	36.6	7.8
Hairdressers and cosmetologists	622	88.7	7.0	5.7	748	90.3	10.2	8.7
Attendants, amusement and recreation facilities	131	40.2	7.1	4.3	206	34.8	13.8	7.8
Public transportation attendants	63	74.3	11.3	5.9	115	82.7	10.5	6.2
Welfare service aides	77	92.5	24.2	10.5	95	86.2	25.8	11.3
Family child care providers	(NA)	(NA)	(NA)	(NA)	513	98.2	11.0	11.2
Early childhood teachers' assistants	(NA)	(NA)	(NA)	(NA)	432	95.6	17.2	10.8
Precision production, craft, and repair	**12,328**	**8.1**	**6.8**	**6.2**	**14,124**	**8.9**	**8.1**	**12.1**
Mechanics and repairers	4,158	3.0	6.8	5.3	4,675	3.9	7.9	10.2
Mechanics and repairers, except supervisors [2]	3,906	2.8	7.0	5.5	4,428	3.7	8.0	10.6
Vehicle and mobile equipment mechanics/repairers [2]	1,683	0.8	6.9	6.0	1,898	1.3	7.0	12.0
Automobile mechanics	800	0.5	7.8	6.0	905	1.5	7.8	13.2
Aircraft engine mechanics	95	2.5	4.0	7.6	135	2.9	8.4	10.2
Electrical and electronic equipment repairers [2]	674	7.4	7.3	4.5	726	9.5	10.7	9.8
Data processing equipment repairers	98	9.3	6.1	4.5	190	13.3	7.1	8.5
Telephone installers and repairers	247	9.9	7.8	3.7	197	13.1	12.2	6.4
Construction trades	4,289	1.8	6.6	6.0	5,378	2.4	7.1	13.7
Construction trades, except supervisors	3,784	1.9	7.1	6.1	4,685	2.4	7.4	14.6
Carpenters	1,160	1.4	5.0	5.0	1,335	1.6	6.6	12.9
Extractive occupations	196	2.3	3.3	6.0	145	1.3	8.6	14.2
Precision production occupations	3,685	21.5	7.3	7.4	3,926	24.1	9.7	12.2
Operators, fabricators, and laborers	**16,091**	**26.6**	**14.0**	**8.3**	**18,399**	**24.7**	**15.1**	**15.4**
Machine operators, assemblers, and inspectors [2]	7,744	42.1	14.0	9.4	7,962	37.7	14.8	17.9
Textile, apparel, and furnishings machine operators [2]	1,414	82.1	18.7	12.5	1,083	72.1	18.8	28.0
Textile sewing machine operators	806	94.0	15.5	14.5	607	82.0	16.0	33.8
Pressing machine operators	141	66.4	27.1	14.2	102	70.6	22.4	44.1
Fabricators, assemblers, and hand working occupations	1,715	33.7	11.3	8.7	2,113	34.3	14.1	14.1
Production inspectors, testers, samplers, and weighers	794	53.8	13.0	7.7	787	47.6	12.9	16.9
Transportation and material moving occupations	4,201	7.8	13.0	5.9	5,389	9.6	15.2	11.0
Motor vehicle operators	2,978	9.2	13.5	6.0	4,089	11.3	15.3	10.9
Trucks drivers	2,195	3.1	12.3	5.7	3,075	5.7	13.4	11.1
Transportation occupations, except motor vehicles	212	2.4	6.7	3.0	174	3.3	11.3	2.6
Material moving equipment operators	1,011	4.8	12.9	6.3	1,125	4.5	15.4	12.7
Industrial truck and tractor operators	369	5.6	19.6	8.2	526	7.2	19.4	17.9
Handlers, equipment cleaners, helpers, and laborers [2]	4,147	16.8	15.1	8.6	5,048	20.3	15.5	16.3
Freight, stock, and material handlers	1,488	15.4	15.3	7.1	1,930	24.5	16.0	12.9
Laborers, except construction	1,024	19.4	16.0	8.6	1,323	21.3	16.1	15.6
Farm operators and managers	1,450	12.1	1.3	0.7	1,317	23.1	1.2	2.4
Other agricultural and related occupations	2,072	19.9	11.7	14.0	2,030	17.9	6.6	33.6
Farm workers	1,149	24.8	11.6	15.9	796	19.0	4.8	41.3
Forestry and logging occupations	126	1.4	12.8	2.1	108	5.1	6.7	6.8

- Represents or rounds to zero.   NA Not available.   [1] See footnote 2, Table 644.   [2] Includes other occupations, not shown separately.   [3] Level of total employment below 50,000.   [4] Includes clerks.

Source: U.S. Bureau of Labor Statistics, *Employment and Earnings,* monthly, January issues; and unpublished data.

No. 673. Employment Projections, by Occupation: 1996 and 2006

[**In thousands, except percent**. Estimates based on the Current Employment Statistics estimates and the Occupational Employment Statistics estimates. See source for methodological assumptions]

OCCUPATION	EMPLOYMENT		CHANGE		Education and training category
	1996	2006	Number	Percent	
LARGEST JOB GROWTH					
Cashiers	3,146	3,677	530	17	Short-term on-the-job training
Systems analysts	506	1,025	520	103	Bachelor's degree
General managers and top executives	3,210	3,677	467	15	Work experience plus bachelor's or higher degree
Registered nurses	1,971	2,382	411	21	Associate's degree
Salespersons, retail	4,072	4,481	408	10	Short-term on-the-job training
Truck drivers light and heavy	2,719	3,123	404	15	Short-term on-the-job training
Home health aides	495	873	378	76	Short-term on-the-job training
Teacher aides and educational assistants	981	1,352	370	38	Short-term on-the-job training
Nursing aides, orderlies, and attendants	1,312	1,645	333	25	Short-term on-the-job training
Receptionists and information clerks	1,074	1,392	318	30	Short-term on-the-job training
Teachers, secondary school	1,406	1,718	312	22	Bachelor's degree
Child care workers	830	1,129	299	36	Short-term on-the-job training
Clerical supervisors and managers	1,369	1,630	262	19	Work experience in a related occupation
Database administrators, computer support specialists [1]	212	461	249	118	Bachelor's degree
Marketing and sales worker supervisors	2,316	2,562	246	11	Work experience in a related occupation
Maintenance repairers, general utility	1,362	1,608	246	18	Long-term on-the-job training
Food counter, fountain, and related workers	1,720	1,963	243	14	Short-term on-the-job training
Teachers, special education	407	648	241	59	Bachelor's degree
Computer engineers	216	451	235	109	Bachelor's degree
Food preparation workers	1,253	1,487	234	19	Short-term on-the-job training
Hand packers and packagers	986	1,208	222	23	Short-term on-the-job training
Guards	955	1,175	221	23	Short-term on-the-job training
General office clerks	3,111	3,326	215	7	Short-term on-the-job training
Waiters and waitresses	1,957	2,163	206	11	Short-term on-the-job training
Social workers	585	772	188	32	Bachelor's degree
Adjustment clerks	401	584	183	46	Short-term on-the-job training
Cooks, short order and fast food	804	978	174	22	Short-term on-the-job training
Personal and home care aides	202	374	171	85	Short-term on-the-job training
Food service and lodging managers	589	757	168	28	Work experience in a related occupation
Medical assistants	225	391	166	74	Moderate-term on-the-job training
FASTEST GROWING					
Database administrators, computer support specialists [1]	212	461	249	118	Bachelor's degree
Computer engineers	216	451	235	109	Bachelor's degree
Systems analysts	506	1,025	520	103	Bachelor's degree
Personal and home care aides	202	374	171	85	Short-term on-the-job training
Physical and corrective therapy assistants and aides	84	151	66	79	Moderate-term on-the-job training
Home health aides	495	873	378	76	Short-term on-the-job training
Medical assistants	225	391	166	74	Moderate-term on-the-job training
Desktop publishing specialists	30	53	22	74	Long-term on-the-job training
Physical therapists	115	196	81	71	Bachelor's degree
Occupational therapy assistants and aides	16	26	11	69	Moderate-term on-the-job training
Paralegals	113	189	76	68	Associate's degree
Occupational therapists	57	95	38	66	Bachelor's degree
Teachers, special education	407	648	241	59	Bachelor's degree
Human services workers	178	276	98	55	Moderate-term on-the-job training
Data processing equipment repairers	80	121	42	52	Postsecondary vocational training
Medical records technicians	87	132	44	51	Associate's degree
Speech-language pathologists and audiologists	87	131	44	51	Master's degree
Dental hygienists	133	197	64	48	Associate's degree
Amusement and recreation attendants	288	426	138	48	Short-term on-the-job training
Physician assistants	64	93	30	47	Bachelor's degree
Respiratory therapists	82	119	37	46	Associate's degree
Adjustment clerks	401	584	183	46	Short-term on-the-job training
Engineering, science, and computer systems managers	343	498	155	45	Work experience plus bachelor's or higher degree
Emergency medical technicians	150	217	67	45	Postsecondary vocational training
Manicurists	43	62	19	45	Postsecondary vocational training
Bill and account collectors	269	381	112	42	Short-term on-the-job training
Residential counselors	180	254	74	41	Bachelor's degree
Instructors and coaches, sports and physical training	303	427	123	41	Moderate-term on-the-job training
Dental assistants	202	278	77	38	Moderate-term on-the-job training
Securities and financial services sales workers	263	363	100	38	Bachelor's degree

[1] Includes all other computer specialists.

Source: U.S. Bureau of Labor Statistics, *Monthly Labor Review*, November 1997.

No. 674. Occupations of the Employed, by Selected Characteristics: 1997

[In thousands. Annual averages of monthly figures. For civilian noninstitutional population 25 to 64 years old. Based on Current Population Survey; see text, Section 1, Population, and Appendix III]

SEX, RACE, AND EDUCATIONAL ATTAINMENT	Total employed	Managerial/ professional	Tech./ sales/ administrative	Service [1]	Precision production [2]	Operators/ fabricators [3]	Farming, forestry, fishing
Male, total [4]	57,507	17,574	11,029	4,816	11,273	10,816	2,000
Less than a high school diploma	6,724	364	461	902	1,841	2,495	661
High school graduates, no college	18,492	2,131	3,034	1,832	5,334	5,422	739
Less than a bachelor's degree	14,977	3,547	3,857	1,500	3,346	2,346	379
College graduates	17,314	11,533	3,676	581	751	551	222
White	49,360	15,601	9,519	3,639	10,018	8,756	1,828
Less than a high school diploma	5,628	318	396	671	1,615	2,046	582
High school graduates, no college	15,756	1,923	2,602	1,328	4,779	4,450	674
Less than a bachelor's degree	12,797	3,167	3,289	1,161	2,980	1,838	363
College graduates	15,178	10,193	3,232	478	645	420	210
Black	5,531	1,017	952	883	895	1,666	116
Less than a high school diploma	818	31	40	157	165	366	58
High school graduates, no college	2,141	148	301	404	434	807	47
Less than a bachelor's degree	1,608	267	418	260	245	411	7
College graduates	963	571	192	62	52	81	4
Female, total [4]	49,250	16,872	19,431	7,538	1,107	3,778	524
Less than a high school diploma	4,022	231	843	1,585	202	1,047	115
High school graduates, no college	16,444	2,396	7,816	3,558	540	1,932	202
Less than a bachelor's degree	14,556	4,225	7,384	1,888	267	652	139
College graduates	14,229	10,020	3,388	507	98	148	69
White	40,917	14,612	16,462	5,649	878	2,818	497
Less than a high school diploma	3,108	189	699	1,153	168	794	106
High school graduates, no college	13,675	2,134	6,841	2,642	428	1,439	190
Less than a bachelor's degree	12,047	3,662	6,111	1,451	208	481	133
College graduates	12,087	8,628	2,810	403	75	104	67
Black	6,102	1,518	2,207	1,534	141	687	16
Less than a high school diploma	661	32	108	351	16	147	6
High school graduates, no college	2,192	201	751	771	76	387	7
Less than a bachelor's degree	2,017	448	1,034	362	39	133	2
College graduates	1,233	837	314	51	10	20	1

[1] Includes private household workers.   [2] Includes craft and repair.   [3] Includes laborers.   [4] Includes other races, not shown separately.

Source: U.S. Bureau of Labor Statistics, unpublished data.

No. 675. Employment, by Industry: 1970 to 1997

[In thousands, except percent. See headnote, Table 647. Data from 1985 to 1990, and also beginning 1995, not strictly comparable with other years due to changes in industrial classification]

INDUSTRY	1970	1980	1990 [1]	1995	1997 [1] Total	Percent Female	Percent Black	Percent Hispanic[2]
Total employed	78,678	99,303	118,793	124,900	129,558	46.2	10.8	9.8
Agriculture	3,463	3,364	3,223	3,440	3,399	24.9	3.4	19.4
Mining	516	979	724	627	634	14.4	4.2	9.4
Construction	4,818	6,215	7,764	7,668	8,302	9.4	6.8	11.8
Manufacturing	20,746	21,942	21,346	20,493	20,835	32.1	10.4	11.2
Transportation, communication, and other public utilities	5,320	6,525	8,168	8,709	9,182	28.8	14.9	8.6
Wholesale and retail trade	15,008	20,191	24,622	26,071	26,777	47.3	8.9	11.1
Wholesale trade	2,672	3,920	4,669	4,986	4,907	29.6	6.3	10.7
Retail trade	12,336	16,270	19,953	21,086	21,869	51.2	9.4	11.2
Finance, insurance, real estate	3,945	5,993	8,051	7,983	8,297	58.4	9.7	7.2
Services [3]	20,385	28,752	39,267	43,953	46,393	62.0	12.1	8.5
Business and repair services [3]	1,403	3,848	7,485	7,526	8,450	37.2	11.6	11.0
Advertising	147	191	277	267	298	53.5	5.8	5.4
Services to dwellings and buildings	(NA)	370	827	829	829	48.5	15.3	23.4
Personnel supply services	(NA)	235	710	853	1,018	62.6	21.1	10.5
Computer and data processing	(NA)	221	805	1,136	1,535	31.0	6.5	4.4
Detective/protective services	(NA)	213	378	506	555	20.3	23.6	11.8
Automobile services	600	952	1,457	1,459	1,635	14.5	9.6	15.4
Personal services [3]	4,276	3,839	4,733	4,375	4,404	68.9	13.6	16.8
Private households	1,782	1,257	1,036	971	921	90.9	17.6	25.6
Hotels and lodging places	979	1,149	1,818	1,495	1,549	53.4	14.5	19.0
Entertainment and recreation	717	1,047	1,526	2,238	2,465	44.5	9.0	9.1
Professional and related services [3]	12,904	19,853	25,351	29,661	30,935	69.4	12.3	6.6
Hospitals	2,843	4,036	4,700	4,961	5,130	76.3	16.2	6.3
Health services, except hospitals	1,628	3,345	4,673	5,967	6,395	79.1	14.4	7.3
Elementary, secondary schools	6,126	5,550	5,994	6,653	6,866	75.4	12.2	7.2
Colleges and universities	([4])	2,108	2,637	2,768	2,759	52.0	10.0	5.7
Social services	828	1,590	2,239	2,979	3,182	81.6	17.1	9.0
Legal services	429	776	1,215	1,335	1,398	56.1	5.6	5.8
Public administration [5]	4,476	5,342	5,627	5,957	5,738	44.5	16.5	6.5

NA Not available.   [1] See footnote 2, Table 644.   [2] Persons of Hispanic origin may be of any race.   [3] Includes industries not shown separately.   [4] Included with elementary/secondary schools.   [5] Includes workers involved in uniquely governmental activities, e.g., judicial and legislative.

Source: U.S. Bureau of Labor Statistics, Employment and Earnings, monthly, January issues; and unpublished data.

No. 676. Employment by Selected Industry, With Projections: 1986 to 2006

[Figures may differ from those in other tables since these data exclude establishments not elsewhere classified (SIC 99); in addition, agriculture services (SIC 074, 5, 8) are included in agriculture, not services. See source for details. Minus sign (-) indicates decrease]

INDUSTRY	1987 SIC [1] code	EMPLOYMENT (1,000)			ANNUAL GROWTH RATE	
		1986	1996	2006, proj.	1986-1996	1996-2006, proj.
Total	(X)	111,374	132,352	150,927	1.7	1.3
Nonfarm wage and salary	(X)	98,727	118,732	136,318	1.9	1.4
Goods-producing (excluding agriculture)	(X)	24,538	24,431	24,451	-0.0	0.0
Mining	10-14	778	574	443	-3.0	-2.5
Construction	15,16,17	4,810	5,400	5,900	1.2	0.9
Manufacturing	20-39	18,951	18,457	18,108	-0.3	-0.2
Durable manufacturing	24,25,32-39	11,200	10,766	10,514	-0.4	-0.2
Lumber and wood products	24	724	780	797	0.7	0.2
Furniture and fixtures	25	498	504	509	0.1	0.1
Stone, clay and glass products	32	558	541	497	-0.3	-0.8
Primary metal industries	33	752	711	633	-0.6	-1.2
Blast furnaces/basic steel products	331	273	240	197	-1.3	-2.0
Fabricated metal products	34	1,422	1,448	1,378	0.2	-0.5
Industrial machinery and equipment	35	2,074	2,112	2,087	0.2	-0.1
Computer and equipment	357	469	363	314	-2.5	-1.4
Electronic and other electric equipment [2]	36	1,774	1,651	1,627	-0.7	-0.1
Communications equipment	366	296	269	255	-0.9	-0.5
Electronic components	367	610	610	700	-0.0	1.4
Transportation equipment	37	2,003	1,781	1,792	-1.2	0.1
Motor vehicles and equipment	371	872	963	929	1.0	-0.4
Instruments and related products [2]	38	1,036	854	787	-1.9	-0.8
Measuring/controlling devices	382	312	297	265	-0.5	-1.1
Medical instruments and supplies	384	213	268	310	2.3	1.5
Miscellaneous manufacturing industries	39	361	387	408	0.7	0.5
Nondurable manufacturing	20-23,26-31	7,751	7,691	7,593	-0.1	-0.1
Food and kindred products	20	1,605	1,693	1,713	0.5	0.1
Tobacco manufactures	21	59	41	30	-3.4	-3.1
Textile mill products	22	703	624	588	-1.2	-0.6
Apparel and other textile products	23	1,100	864	714	-2.4	-1.9
Paper and allied products	26	667	681	702	0.2	0.3
Printing and publishing	27	1,456	1,538	1,501	0.5	-0.2
Chemicals and allied products	28	1,021	1,032	1,070	0.1	0.4
Petroleum and coal products	29	169	142	118	-1.7	-1.8
Rubber/misc. plastics products	30	822	981	1,091	1.8	1.1
Leather and leather products	31	149	96	65	-4.3	-3.8
Service producing	(X)	74,189	94,300	111,867	2.4	1.7
Transportation, communications, utilities	40-42,44-49	5,247	6,260	7,111	1.8	1.3
Transportation	40-42,44-47	3,051	4,038	4,774	2.8	1.7
Communications	48	1,275	1,337	1,360	0.5	0.2
Electric, gas, and sanitary services	49	921	885	976	-0.4	1.0
Wholesale trade	50,51	5,751	6,483	7,228	1.2	1.1
Retail trade	52-59	17,878	21,625	23,875	1.9	1.0
Eating and drinking places	58	5,902	7,499	8,884	2.4	1.7
Finance, insurance, and real estate	60-67	6,275	6,899	7,651	1.0	1.0
Services	70-87,89	22,346	33,586	44,852	4.2	2.9
Hotels and other lodging places	70	1,378	1,716	1,978	2.2	1.4
Personal services [2]	72	1,008	1,184	1,294	1.6	0.9
Business services [2]	73	3,931	7,254	10,835	6.3	4.1
Advertising	731	204	242	270	1.7	1.1
Services to buildings	734	685	897	1,097	2.7	2.0
Personnel supply services	736	990	2,646	4,039	10.3	4.3
Computer and data processing services	737	588	1,208	2,509	7.5	7.6
Auto repair, services, and garages	75	762	1,084	1,482	3.6	3.2
Miscellaneous repair shops	76	322	375	425	1.5	1.3
Motion pictures	78	320	522	628	5.0	1.9
Video tape rental	784	94	155	173	5.1	1.1
Amusement and recreation services	79	895	1,466	1,998	5.1	3.1
Health services	80	6,528	9,469	12,620	3.8	2.9
Offices of health practitioners	801,2,3,4	1,752	2,751	4,046	4.6	3.9
Nursing and personal care facilities	805	1,245	1,732	2,377	3.4	3.2
Hospitals, private	806	3,037	3,814	4,229	2.3	1.0
Health services, n.e.c. [3]	807,8,9	494	1,172	1,968	9.0	5.3
Legal services	81	747	930	1,187	2.2	2.5
Educational services	82	1,421	2,020	2,478	3.6	2.1
Social services	83	1,406	2,403	3,461	5.5	3.7
Museums, botanical, zoological gardens	84	52	85	109	5.0	2.5
Membership organizations	86	1,536	2,185	2,428	3.6	1.1
Engineering, management, and services	87,89	2,042	2,893	3,930	3.5	3.1
Government	(X)	16,693	19,447	21,150	1.5	0.8
Federal government	(X)	2,899	2,757	2,670	-0.5	-0.3
State and local government	(X)	13,794	16,690	18,480	1.9	1.0
Agriculture	01,02,07,08,0	3,327	3,642	3,618	0.9	-0.1
Private households	88	1,235	928	775	-2.8	-1.8
Nonagriculture self-employed and unpaid family	(X)	8,085	9,051	10,216	1.1	1.2

X Not applicable. [1] 1987 Standard Industrial Classification; see text, Section 13, Labor Force. [2] Includes other industries, not shown separately. [3] N.e.c. means not elsewhere classified.

Source: U.S. Bureau of Labor Statistics, *Monthly Labor Review*, November 1997.

No. 677. Unemployed Workers—Summary: 1980 to 1997

[In thousands, except as indicated. For civilian noninstitutional population 16 years old and over. Annual averages of monthly figures. For data on unemployment insurance, see Table 618]

AGE, SEX, RACE, HISPANIC ORIGIN	1980	1985	1990 [1]	1993	1994 [1]	1995	1996	1997 [1]
UNEMPLOYED								
Total [2]	7,637	8,312	7,047	8,940	7,996	7,404	7,236	6,739
16 to 19 years old	1,669	1,468	1,212	1,365	1,320	1,346	1,306	1,271
20 to 24 years old	1,835	1,738	1,299	1,514	1,373	1,244	1,239	1,152
25 to 44 years old	2,964	3,681	3,323	4,291	3,694	3,390	3,262	2,989
45 to 64 years old	1,075	1,331	1,109	1,662	1,456	1,269	1,289	1,199
65 years and over	94	93	105	108	153	153	139	127
Male	4,267	4,521	3,906	5,055	4,367	3,983	3,880	3,577
16 to 19 years old	913	806	667	768	740	744	733	694
20 to 24 years old	1,076	944	715	865	768	673	675	636
25 to 44 years old	1,619	1,950	1,803	2,387	1,968	1,776	1,689	1,504
45 to 64 years old	600	766	662	972	803	697	707	674
65 years and over	58	55	59	64	88	94	76	69
Female	3,370	3,791	3,140	3,885	3,629	3,421	3,356	3,162
16 to 19 years old	755	661	544	597	580	602	573	577
20 to 24 years old	760	794	584	648	605	571	564	516
25 to 44 years old	1,345	1,732	1,519	1,905	1,726	1,615	1,574	1,486
45 to 64 years old	473	566	447	690	653	574	582	525
65 years and over	36	39	46	45	66	60	63	58
White [3]	5,884	6,191	5,186	6,655	5,892	5,459	5,300	4,836
16 to 19 years old	1,291	1,074	903	992	960	952	939	912
20 to 24 years old	1,364	1,235	899	1,057	952	866	854	765
Black [3]	1,553	1,864	1,565	1,844	1,666	1,538	1,592	1,560
16 to 19 years old	343	357	268	313	300	325	310	302
20 to 24 years old	426	455	349	387	351	311	327	327
Hispanic [3][4]	620	811	876	1,248	1,187	1,140	1,132	1,069
16 to 19 years old	145	141	161	201	198	205	199	197
20 to 24 years old	138	171	167	237	220	209	217	206
Full-time workers	6,269	6,793	5,677	7,305	6,513	5,909	5,803	5,395
Part-time workers	1,369	1,519	1,369	1,635	1,483	1,495	1,433	1,344
UNEMPLOYMENT RATE (percent) [5]								
Total [2]	7.1	7.2	5.6	6.9	6.1	5.6	5.4	4.9
16 to 19 years old	17.8	18.6	15.5	19.0	17.6	17.3	16.7	16.0
20 to 24 years old	11.5	11.1	8.8	10.5	9.7	9.1	9.3	8.5
25 to 44 years old	6.0	6.2	4.9	6.2	5.3	4.8	4.6	4.2
45 to 64 years old	3.7	4.5	3.5	4.8	4.0	3.4	3.3	3.0
65 years and over	3.1	3.2	3.0	3.2	4.0	4.0	3.6	3.3
Male	6.9	7.0	5.7	7.2	6.2	5.6	5.4	4.9
16 to 19 years old	18.3	19.5	16.3	20.4	19.0	18.4	18.1	16.9
20 to 24 years old	12.5	11.4	9.1	11.3	10.2	9.2	9.5	8.9
25 to 44 years old	5.6	5.9	4.8	6.3	5.2	4.7	4.4	3.9
45 to 64 years old	3.5	4.5	3.7	5.1	4.1	3.5	3.4	3.1
65 years and over	3.1	3.1	3.0	3.2	4.0	4.3	3.4	3.0
Female	7.4	7.4	5.5	6.6	6.0	5.6	5.4	5.0
16 to 19 years old	17.2	17.6	14.7	17.5	16.2	16.1	15.2	15.0
20 to 24 years old	10.4	10.7	8.5	9.7	9.2	9.0	9.0	8.1
25 to 44 years old	6.4	6.6	4.9	6.1	5.4	5.0	4.9	4.6
45 to 64 years old	4.0	4.6	3.2	4.4	3.9	3.3	3.3	2.8
65 years and over	3.1	3.3	3.1	3.1	4.0	3.7	4.0	3.6
White [3]	6.3	6.2	4.8	6.1	5.3	4.9	4.7	4.2
16 to 19 years old	15.5	15.7	13.5	16.2	15.1	14.5	14.2	13.6
20 to 24 years old	9.9	9.2	7.3	8.8	8.1	7.7	7.8	6.9
Black [3]	14.3	15.1	11.4	13.0	11.5	10.4	10.5	10.0
16 to 19 years old	38.5	40.2	30.9	38.8	35.2	35.7	33.6	32.4
20 to 24 years old	23.6	24.5	19.9	21.9	19.5	17.7	18.8	18.3
Hispanic [3][4]	10.1	10.5	8.2	10.8	9.9	9.3	8.9	7.7
16 to 19 years old	22.5	24.3	19.5	26.1	24.5	24.1	23.6	21.6
20 to 24 years old	12.1	12.6	9.1	13.1	11.8	11.5	11.8	10.3
Experienced workers [6]	6.9	6.8	5.3	6.6	5.9	5.4	5.2	4.7
Women maintaining families	9.2	10.4	8.3	9.7	8.9	8.0	8.2	8.1
Married men, wife present [2]	4.2	4.3	3.4	4.4	3.7	3.3	3.0	2.7
White	3.9	4.0	3.1	4.1	3.4	3.0	2.8	2.5
Black	7.4	8.0	6.2	7.2	6.0	5.0	4.9	4.3
Percent without work for—								
Fewer than 5 weeks	43.2	42.1	46.3	36.5	34.1	36.5	36.4	37.7
5 to 10 weeks	23.4	22.2	23.5	20.6	20.6	22.0	21.8	21.9
11 to 14 weeks	9.0	8.0	8.5	8.3	9.5	9.6	9.8	9.9
15 to 26 weeks	13.8	12.3	11.7	14.5	15.5	14.6	14.6	14.8
27 weeks and over	10.7	15.4	10.0	20.1	20.3	17.3	17.4	15.8
Unemployment duration, average (weeks)	11.9	15.6	12.0	18.0	18.8	16.6	16.7	15.8

[1] See footnote 2, Table 644.   [2] Includes other races, not shown separately.   [3] Includes other ages, not shown separately.
[4] Persons of Hispanic origin may be of any race.   [5] Unemployed as percent of civilian labor force in specified group.   [6] Wage and salary workers.

Source: U.S. Bureau of Labor Statistics, Employment and Earnings, monthly, January issues; and unpublished data.

No. 678. Unemployed Persons, by Sex and Reason: 1970 to 1997

[**In thousands.** For civilian noninstitutional population 16 years old and over. Annual averages of monthly figures. Based on Current Population Survey; see text, Section 1, Population, and Appendix III]

SEX AND REASON	1970	1980	1985	1989	1990 [1]	1991	1992	1993	1994 [1]	1995	1996	1997 [1]
Male, total	2,238	4,442	4,267	4,521	3,906	4,946	5,523	5,055	4,367	3,983	3,880	3,577
Job losers [2]	1,199	2,909	2,649	2,749	2,257	3,172	3,593	3,150	2,416	2,190	2,158	1,902
Job leavers	282	375	438	409	528	507	495	507	408	407	372	414
Reentrants	533	782	776	876	806	891	978	939	1,265	1,113	1,076	1,004
New entrants	224	377	405	487	315	375	457	459	278	273	273	257
Female, total	1,855	3,486	3,370	3,791	3,140	3,683	4,090	3,885	3,629	3,421	3,356	3,162
Job losers [2]	614	1,478	1,297	1,390	1,130	1,522	1,796	1,699	1,399	1,286	1,212	1,135
Job leavers	267	452	453	468	513	497	507	469	383	417	402	381
Reentrants	696	1,110	1,152	1,380	1,124	1,247	1,307	1,259	1,521	1,412	1,435	1,334
New entrants	279	447	468	552	373	416	480	459	326	306	307	312

[1] See footnote 2, Table 644. [2] Beginning 1994, persons who completed temporary jobs are identified separately and are included as job losers.

Source: U.S. Bureau of Labor Statistics, *Employment and Earnings*, monthly, January issues; and Bulletin 2307.

No. 679. Unemployment Rates, by Industry, 1975 to 1997, and by Sex, 1980 and 1997

[**In percent.** For civilian noninstitutional population 16 years old and over. Annual averages of monthly figures. Rate represents unemployment as a percent of labor force in each specified group. Data for 1985-90 not strictly comparable with other years due to changes in industrial classification]

INDUSTRY	1975	1980	1985	1990 [1]	1995 [1]	1997 [1]	MALE 1980	MALE 1997 [1]	FEMALE 1980	FEMALE 1997 [1]
All unemployed [2]	8.5	7.1	7.2	5.6	5.6	4.9	6.9	4.9	7.4	5.0
Industry: [3]										
Agriculture	10.4	11.0	13.2	9.8	11.1	9.1	9.7	9.1	15.1	9.1
Mining	4.1	6.4	9.5	4.8	5.2	3.8	6.7	3.7	4.5	4.1
Construction	18.0	14.1	13.1	11.1	11.5	9.0	14.6	9.2	8.9	6.9
Manufacturing	10.9	8.5	7.7	5.8	4.9	4.2	7.4	3.5	10.8	5.5
Transportation and public utilities	5.6	4.9	5.1	3.9	4.5	3.5	5.1	3.4	4.4	3.8
Wholesale and retail trade	8.7	7.4	7.6	6.4	6.5	6.2	6.6	5.6	8.3	6.9
Finance, insurance, and real estate	4.9	3.4	3.5	3.0	3.3	3.0	3.2	3.0	3.5	3.0
Services	7.1	5.9	6.2	5.0	5.4	4.6	6.3	4.8	5.8	4.5
Government	4.1	4.1	3.9	2.7	2.9	2.6	3.9	2.8	4.3	2.5

[1] See footnote 2, Table 644. [2] Includes the self-employed, unpaid family workers, and persons with no previous work experience, not shown separately. [3] Covers unemployed wage and salary workers.

Source: U.S. Bureau of Labor Statistics, *Employment and Earnings*, monthly, January issues.

No. 680. Unemployment by Occupation, 1990 to 1997, and by Sex, 1997

[**For civilian noninstitutional population 16 years old and over.** Annual averages of monthly data. Rate represents unemployment as a percent of the labor force for each specified group. Based on Current Population Survey; see text, Section 1, Population, and Appendix III. See also headnote, Table 661]

OCCUPATION	NUMBER (1,000) 1990 [1]	NUMBER (1,000) 1995 [1]	NUMBER (1,000) 1997 [1]	UNEMPLOYMENT RATE 1990 [1]	UNEMPLOYMENT RATE 1995 [1]	1997 [1] Total	1997 [1] Male	1997 [1] Female
Total [2]	7,047	7,404	6,739	5.6	5.6	4.9	4.9	5.0
Managerial and professional specialty	666	880	761	2.1	2.4	2.0	1.9	2.1
Executive, administrative, and managerial	350	420	359	2.3	2.4	1.9	1.8	2.0
Professional specialty	316	460	403	2.0	2.5	2.0	2.0	2.1
Technical sales, and administrative support	1,641	1,744	1,646	4.3	4.5	4.1	3.6	4.4
Technicians and related support	116	113	104	2.9	2.8	2.4	2.2	2.6
Sales occupations	720	795	814	4.8	5.0	4.9	3.6	6.2
Administrative support, including clerical	804	836	728	4.1	4.3	3.8	4.2	3.7
Service occupations	1,139	1,378	1,255	6.6	7.5	6.7	6.5	6.8
Private household	47	99	73	5.6	10.7	8.4	12.6	8.2
Protective service	74	86	89	3.6	3.7	3.7	3.4	5.2
Service except private household and protective	1,018	1,193	1,093	7.1	7.9	7.0	7.6	6.7
Precision production, craft, and repair	861	860	719	5.9	6.0	4.8	4.8	5.1
Mechanics and repairers	175	182	167	3.8	4.0	3.5	3.4	4.5
Construction trades	483	501	406	8.5	9.0	7.0	7.0	7.2
Other precision production, craft, and repair	202	177	145	4.7	4.2	3.4	3.0	5.0
Operators, fabricators, and laborers	1,714	1,618	1,490	8.7	8.2	7.5	7.1	8.8
Machine operators, assemblers, inspectors	727	629	551	8.1	7.4	6.5	5.1	8.6
Transportation and material moving occupations	329	329	306	6.3	6.0	5.4	5.3	6.0
Handlers, equipment cleaners, helpers, laborers	657	660	633	11.6	11.7	11.1	11.3	10.5
Construction laborers	177	179	167	18.1	18.7	17.1	16.9	20.8
Farming, forestry, and fishing	237	311	267	6.4	7.9	7.1	6.9	7.8

[1] See footnote 2, Table 644. [2] Includes persons with no previous work experience and those whose last job was in the Armed Forces.

Source: U.S. Bureau of Labor Statistics, *Employment and Earnings*, monthly, January issues.

No. 681. Unemployed and Unemployment Rates, by Educational Attainment, Sex, Race, and Hispanic Origin: 1992 to 1997

[As of **March.** For the civilian noninstitutional population 25 to 64 years old. See Table 648 for civilian labor force and participation rate data. Based on Current Population Survey; see text, Section 1, Population, and Appendix III]

YEAR, SEX, AND RACE	UNEMPLOYED (1,000)					UNEMPLOYMENT RATE [1]				
	Total	Less than high school diploma	High school gradu- ates, no degree	Less than a bach- elor's degree	College graduate	Total	Less than high school diploma	High school gradu- ate, no degree	Less than a bach- elor's degree	College graduate
Total: [2]										
1992	6,846	1,693	2,851	1,521	782	6.7	13.5	7.7	5.9	2.9
1995	5,065	1,150	1,833	1,329	753	4.8	10.0	5.2	4.5	2.5
1996	5,147	1,285	1,947	1,239	675	4.8	10.9	5.5	4.1	2.2
1997 [3]	4,902	1,253	1,853	1,157	640	4.4	10.4	5.1	3.8	2.0
Male:										
1992	4,207	1,151	1,709	854	493	7.5	14.8	8.8	6.4	3.2
1995	2,925	765	1,064	656	440	5.1	10.9	5.7	4.4	2.6
1996	3,088	815	1,205	682	385	5.3	11.0	6.4	4.5	2.3
1997 [3]	2,797	752	1,069	616	359	4.7	9.9	5.6	4.0	2.1
Female:										
1992	2,639	542	1,142	666	289	5.7	11.4	6.5	5.3	2.5
1995	2,140	385	770	673	313	4.4	8.6	4.6	4.5	2.4
1996	2,059	471	742	556	289	4.1	10.7	4.4	3.8	2.1
1997 [3]	2,105	500	783	541	281	4.1	11.3	4.5	3.6	2.0
White:										
1992	5,247	1,285	2,146	1,176	641	6.0	12.9	6.8	5.3	2.7
1993	5,129	1,175	2,025	1,166	763	5.8	12.4	6.5	5.0	3.1
1995	3,858	831	1,362	1,054	612	4.3	9.2	4.6	4.2	2.3
1996	3,865	969	1,386	934	575	4.2	10.2	4.6	3.7	2.1
1997 [3]	3,674	910	1,395	867	502	3.9	9.4	4.6	3.4	1.8
Black:										
1992	1,353	361	619	291	81	12.4	17.2	14.1	10.7	4.8
1995	905	225	377	218	86	7.7	13.7	8.4	6.3	4.1
1996	1,061	258	479	255	69	8.9	15.3	10.8	6.9	3.3
1997 [3]	997	291	381	235	89	8.1	16.6	8.2	6.1	4.4
Hispanic: [4]										
1992	757	408	224	88	36	9.8	13.6	9.6	5.9	4.2
1995	746	393	211	102	40	8.0	10.9	8.1	5.2	3.7
1996	826	462	202	118	44	8.5	12.3	7.3	5.7	4.0
1997 [3]	768	379	221	128	39	7.3	9.6	7.5	5.5	3.0

[1] Percent unemployed of the civilian labor force. [2] Includes other races, not shown separately. [3] See footnote 2, Table 644. [4] Persons of Hispanic origin may be of any race.

Source: U.S. Bureau of Labor Statistics, unpublished data.

No. 682. Unemployed Persons, by Reason of Unemployment: 1997

[Annual averages of monthly data. Based on Current Population Survey; see text, Section 1, Population, and Appendix III]

AGE, SEX, AND REASON	Total unem- ployed (1,000)	PERCENT DISTRIBUTION BY DURATION				
		Less than 5 weeks	5 to 14 weeks	15 weeks and over		
				Total	15 to 26 weeks	27 weeks or longer
Total 16 years old and over	6,739	37.7	31.7	30.6	14.8	15.8
16 to 19 years old	1,271	47.1	34.0	18.9	10.9	8.0
Total 20 years old and over	**5,467**	**35.5**	**31.2**	**33.3**	**15.7**	**17.7**
Males	2,882	34.5	30.6	35.0	16.2	18.8
Job losers and persons who completed temporary . .	1,795	36.1	31.2	32.7	16.0	16.7
On temporary layoff.	567	54.1	31.2	14.7	10.1	4.7
Not on temporary layoff	1,228	27.8	31.2	41.0	18.7	22.3
Permanent job losers	833	25.1	30.2	44.7	20.0	24.8
Persons who completed temporary jobs.	395	33.7	33.4	33.0	15.9	17.0
Job leavers	358	40.1	30.8	29.1	15.3	13.7
Reentrants	675	27.8	28.8	43.4	17.4	26.0
New entrants.	55	24.7	30.4	44.9	14.1	30.8
Females	2,585	36.6	31.9	31.5	15.1	16.4
Job losers and persons who completed temporary . .	1,069	38.9	32.0	29.1	15.6	13.5
On temporary layoff.	304	57.6	28.3	14.2	8.3	5.9
Not on temporary layoff	764	31.5	33.5	35.0	18.5	16.5
Permanent job losers	541	29.1	33.7	37.1	19.6	17.6
Persons who completed temporary jobs.	224	37.2	32.9	29.9	16.1	13.8
Job leavers	333	41.8	32.4	25.8	13.0	12.8
Reentrants	1,057	33.7	31.9	34.3	15.3	19.1
New entrants.	126	27.8	29.4	42.8	14.9	27.9

Source: U.S. Bureau of Labor Statistics, *Employment and Earnings*, monthly, January 1998 issue.

No. 683. Total Unemployed and Insured Unemployed—States: 1980 to 1997

[For civilian noninstitutional population 16 years old and over. Annual averages of monthly figures. Total unemployment estimates based on the Current Population Survey; see text, Section 1, Population, and Appendix III. U.S. totals derived by independent population controls; therefore state data may not add to U.S. totals]

STATE	TOTAL UNEMPLOYED								INSURED UNEMPLOYED [3]			
	Number (1,000)				Percent [1]				Number (1,000)		Percent [4]	
	1980	1985	1990 [2]	1997 [2]	1980	1985	1990 [2]	1997 [2]	1995	1996	1995	1996
United States . . .	7,637	8,312	7,047	6,739	7.1	7.2	5.6	4.9	[5]2,572.0	[5]2,595.5	[5]2.3	[5]2.3
Alabama	147	160	130	110	8.8	8.9	6.9	5.1	30.7	33.7	1.9	2.0
Alaska	18	24	19	25	9.7	9.7	7.0	7.9	12.9	13.1	5.5	5.5
Arizona	83	96	99	101	6.7	6.5	5.5	4.6	25.2	25.4	1.5	1.4
Arkansas	76	91	78	64	7.6	8.7	7.0	5.3	26.5	29.6	2.7	2.9
California	790	934	874	1,006	6.8	7.2	5.8	6.3	450.2	443.1	3.7	3.6
Colorado	88	101	89	70	5.9	5.9	5.0	3.3	21.9	22.5	1.3	1.3
Connecticut	94	83	95	88	5.9	4.9	5.2	5.1	44.4	41.2	3.0	2.7
Delaware	22	17	19	15	7.7	5.3	5.2	4.0	6.4	8.0	1.9	2.3
District of Columbia .	24	27	22	20	7.3	8.4	6.6	7.9	8.8	8.0	2.1	1.9
Florida	251	320	390	338	5.9	6.0	6.0	4.8	90.7	87.3	1.6	1.5
Georgia	163	188	182	177	6.4	6.5	5.5	4.5	39.1	39.2	1.3	1.2
Hawaii	21	27	16	38	4.9	5.6	2.9	6.4	15.3	15.1	3.0	3.0
Idaho	34	37	29	34	7.9	7.9	5.9	5.3	14.5	14.1	3.2	3.0
Illinois	459	513	369	288	8.3	9.0	6.2	4.7	119.8	129.7	2.3	2.4
Indiana	252	215	149	109	9.6	7.9	5.3	3.5	30.9	34.1	1.2	1.3
Iowa	82	112	62	51	5.8	8.0	4.3	3.3	18.8	21.3	1.5	1.6
Kansas	53	62	57	52	4.5	5.0	4.5	3.8	16.5	15.9	1.5	1.4
Kentucky	133	161	104	104	8.0	9.5	5.9	5.4	29.0	30.1	1.9	1.9
Louisiana	121	229	117	124	6.7	11.5	6.3	6.1	27.3	26.7	1.7	1.6
Maine	39	30	33	36	7.8	5.4	5.2	5.4	15.1	14.8	3.0	2.9
Maryland	140	104	122	142	6.5	4.6	4.7	5.1	44.1	43.7	2.2	2.2
Massachusetts	162	120	195	131	5.6	3.9	6.0	4.0	73.4	70.2	2.6	2.5
Michigan	534	433	350	210	12.4	9.9	7.6	4.2	88.3	99.1	2.2	2.4
Minnesota	125	133	117	86	5.9	6.0	4.9	3.3	35.6	36.1	1.6	1.6
Mississippi	79	116	90	73	7.5	10.3	7.6	5.7	21.5	23.6	2.1	2.3
Missouri	167	158	151	122	7.2	6.4	5.8	4.2	42.9	44.7	1.8	1.9
Montana	23	31	24	24	6.1	7.7	6.0	5.4	9.5	9.8	3.0	3.0
Nebraska	31	44	18	24	4.1	5.5	2.2	2.6	7.1	7.7	0.9	1.0
Nevada	27	41	33	36	6.2	8.0	4.9	4.1	16.5	16.4	2.3	2.1
New Hampshire	22	21	36	20	4.7	3.9	5.7	3.1	5.7	5.8	1.1	1.1
New Jersey	260	217	206	215	7.2	5.7	5.1	5.1	106.8	110.6	3.2	3.2
New Mexico	42	57	46	51	7.5	8.8	6.5	6.2	11.1	11.8	1.8	1.9
New York	597	544	467	564	7.5	6.5	5.3	6.4	227.7	210.1	3.0	2.8
North Carolina	187	168	144	139	6.6	5.4	4.2	3.6	47.6	54.0	1.5	1.6
North Dakota	15	20	13	9	5.0	5.9	4.0	2.5	4.0	3.9	1.5	1.4
Ohio	426	455	310	262	8.4	8.9	5.7	4.6	80.8	84.4	1.7	1.7
Oklahoma	66	112	86	66	4.8	7.1	5.7	4.1	15.5	14.4	1.3	1.2
Oregon	107	116	83	101	8.3	8.8	5.6	5.8	44.4	45.9	3.3	3.3
Pennsylvania	425	443	315	311	7.8	8.0	5.4	5.2	165.9	167.5	3.4	3.4
Rhode Island	34	25	35	27	7.2	4.9	6.8	5.3	19.1	18.4	4.6	4.4
South Carolina	96	107	83	86	6.9	6.8	4.8	4.5	27.6	29.6	1.8	1.9
South Dakota	16	18	13	12	4.9	5.1	3.9	3.1	2.3	2.6	0.7	0.8
Tennessee	152	180	126	146	7.3	8.0	5.3	5.4	41.1	47.3	1.8	2.0
Texas	352	565	544	531	5.2	7.0	6.3	5.4	123.7	121.7	1.7	1.6
Utah	40	43	35	32	6.3	5.9	4.3	3.1	7.9	8.4	1.0	1.0
Vermont	16	13	15	13	6.4	4.8	5.0	4.0	7.3	7.2	2.9	2.8
Virginia	128	160	141	135	5.0	5.6	4.3	4.0	29.5	28.0	1.1	1.0
Washington	156	170	125	142	7.9	8.1	4.9	4.8	90.2	84.5	4.0	3.7
West Virginia	74	100	64	55	9.4	13.0	8.4	6.9	18.6	19.2	3.0	3.0
Wisconsin	167	171	114	108	7.2	7.2	4.4	3.7	51.7	56.9	2.2	2.3
Wyoming	9	18	13	13	4.0	7.1	5.5	5.1	3.9	4.2	2.0	2.0

[1] Total unemployment as percent of civilian labor force. [2] See footnote 2, Table 644. [3] Source: U.S. Employment and Training Administration, *Unemployment Insurance, Financial Handbook*, annual updates. [4] Insured unemployment as percent of average covered employment in the previous year. [5] Includes 56,500 in Puerto Rico and the Virgin Islands in 1995 and 55,000 in 1996.

Source: Except as noted, U.S. Bureau of Labor Statistics, *Geographic Profile of Employment and Unemployment*, annual.

No. 684. Job Openings and Placements and Help-Wanted Advertising: 1970 to 1996

[Openings 1970 and 1980, for years ending Sept. 30; beginning 1985, for years ending June 30]

ITEM	1970	1980	1985	1990	1992	1993	1994	1995	1996
Job openings: [1] Received (1,000) . . .	6,130	8,122	7,529	5,651	5,752	6,343	6,619	5,917	6,039
Average per month	511	677	627	471	479	529	552	493	503
Nonagricultural placements [1] (1,000) .	4,604	5,610	3,270	3,714	3,396	3,375	3,360	3,216	3,255
Index of help-wanted advertising in newspapers [2] (1987=100)	60	84	91	84	62	69	83	85	83

[1] As reported by state employment agencies. Beginning 1985, all placements. Placements include duplication for individuals placed more than once. [2] Source: The Conference Board, New York, NY (copyright). Index based on the number of advertisements in classified sections of 51 newspapers, each in a major employment area.

Source: Except as noted, U.S. Employment and Training Administration, unpublished data.

No. 685. Nonfarm Establishments—Employees, Hours, and Earnings, by Industry: 1970 to 1997

[Based on data from establishment reports. Includes all full- and part-time employees who worked during, or received pay for, any part of the pay period reported. Excludes proprietors, the self-employed, farm workers, unpaid family workers, private household workers, and Armed Forces. Establishment data shown here conform to industry definitions in the 1987 Standard Industrial Classification and are adjusted to March 1997 employment benchmarks, and reflect historical corrections to previously published data. Based on the Current Employment Statistics Program; see Appendix III]

| ITEM AND YEAR | Total | GOODS-PRODUCING | | | | SERVICE-PRODUCING | | | | | | |
		Total	Mining	Con-struc-tion	Manu-factur-ing	Total	Trans-portation and public utilities	Whole-sale trade	Retail trade	Finance, insur-ance, and real estate	Serv-ices	Govern-ment
EMPLOYEES (1,000)												
1970	70,880	23,578	623	3,588	19,367	47,302	4,515	4,006	11,034	3,645	11,548	12,554
1980	90,406	25,658	1,027	4,346	20,285	64,748	5,146	5,292	15,018	5,160	17,890	16,241
1985	97,387	24,842	927	4,668	19,248	72,544	5,233	5,727	17,315	5,948	21,927	16,394
1990	109,403	24,905	709	5,120	19,076	84,497	5,777	6,173	19,601	6,709	27,934	18,304
1991	108,249	23,745	689	4,650	18,406	84,504	5,755	6,081	19,284	6,646	28,336	18,402
1992	108,601	23,231	635	4,492	18,104	85,370	5,718	5,997	19,356	6,602	29,052	18,645
1993	110,713	23,352	610	4,668	18,075	87,361	5,811	5,981	19,773	6,757	30,197	18,841
1994	114,163	23,908	601	4,986	18,321	90,256	5,984	6,162	20,507	6,896	31,579	19,128
1995	117,191	24,265	581	5,160	18,524	92,925	6,132	6,378	21,187	6,806	33,117	19,305
1996	119,608	24,493	580	5,418	18,495	95,115	6,253	6,482	21,597	6,911	34,454	19,419
1997	122,690	24,934	592	5,686	18,657	97,756	6,395	6,648	22,011	7,091	36,040	19,570
PERCENT DISTRIBUTION												
1970	100.0	33.3	0.9	5.1	27.3	66.7	6.4	5.7	15.6	5.1	16.3	17.7
1980	100.0	28.4	1.1	4.8	22.4	71.6	5.7	5.9	16.6	5.7	19.8	18.0
1985	100.0	25.5	1.0	4.8	19.8	74.5	5.4	5.9	17.8	6.1	22.5	16.8
1990	100.0	22.8	0.6	4.7	17.4	77.2	5.3	5.6	17.9	6.1	25.5	16.7
1991	100.0	21.9	0.6	4.3	17.0	78.1	5.3	5.6	17.8	6.1	26.2	17.0
1992	100.0	21.4	0.6	4.1	16.7	78.6	5.3	5.5	17.8	6.1	26.8	17.2
1993	100.0	21.1	0.6	4.2	16.3	78.9	5.2	5.4	17.9	6.1	27.3	17.0
1994	100.0	20.9	0.5	4.4	16.0	79.1	5.2	5.4	18.0	6.0	27.7	16.8
1995	100.0	20.7	0.5	4.4	15.8	79.3	5.3	5.5	18.1	5.8	28.2	16.5
1996	100.0	20.5	0.5	4.5	15.5	79.5	5.2	5.4	18.1	5.8	28.8	16.2
1997	100.0	20.3	0.5	4.6	15.2	79.7	5.2	5.4	17.9	5.8	29.4	16.0
WEEKLY HOURS [1]												
1970	37.1	(NA)	42.7	37.3	39.8	(NA)	40.5	39.9	33.8	36.7	34.4	(NA)
1980	35.3	(NA)	43.3	37.0	39.7	(NA)	39.6	38.4	30.2	36.2	32.6	(NA)
1985	34.9	(NA)	43.4	37.7	40.5	(NA)	39.5	38.4	29.4	36.4	32.5	(NA)
1990	34.5	(NA)	44.1	38.2	40.8	(NA)	38.4	38.1	28.8	35.8	32.5	(NA)
1991	34.3	(NA)	44.4	38.1	40.7	(NA)	38.1	38.1	28.6	35.7	32.4	(NA)
1992	34.4	(NA)	43.9	38.0	41.0	(NA)	38.3	38.2	28.8	35.8	32.5	(NA)
1993	34.5	(NA)	44.3	38.5	41.4	(NA)	39.3	38.2	28.8	35.8	32.5	(NA)
1994	34.7	(NA)	44.8	38.9	42.0	(NA)	39.7	38.4	28.9	35.8	32.5	(NA)
1995	34.5	(NA)	44.7	38.9	41.6	(NA)	39.4	38.3	28.8	35.9	32.4	(NA)
1996	34.4	(NA)	45.3	39.0	41.6	(NA)	39.6	38.3	28.8	35.9	32.4	(NA)
1997	34.6	(NA)	45.4	38.9	42.0	(NA)	39.7	38.4	28.9	36.1	32.6	(NA)
HOURLY EARNINGS [1]												
1970	3.23	(NA)	3.85	5.24	3.35	(NA)	3.85	3.43	2.44	3.07	2.81	(NA)
1980	6.66	(NA)	9.17	9.94	7.27	(NA)	8.87	6.95	4.88	5.79	5.85	(NA)
1985	8.57	(NA)	11.98	12.32	9.54	(NA)	11.40	9.15	5.94	7.94	7.90	(NA)
1990	10.01	(NA)	13.68	13.77	10.83	(NA)	12.92	10.79	6.75	9.97	9.83	(NA)
1991	10.32	(NA)	14.19	14.00	11.18	(NA)	13.20	11.15	6.94	10.39	10.23	(NA)
1992	10.57	(NA)	14.54	14.15	11.46	(NA)	13.43	11.39	7.12	10.82	10.54	(NA)
1993	10.83	(NA)	14.60	14.38	11.74	(NA)	13.55	11.74	7.29	11.35	10.78	(NA)
1994	11.12	(NA)	14.88	14.73	12.07	(NA)	13.78	12.06	7.49	11.83	11.04	(NA)
1995	11.43	(NA)	15.30	15.09	12.37	(NA)	14.13	12.43	7.69	12.32	11.39	(NA)
1996	11.82	(NA)	15.62	15.47	12.77	(NA)	14.45	12.87	7.99	12.80	11.79	(NA)
1997	12.28	(NA)	16.17	16.03	13.17	(NA)	14.93	13.44	8.34	13.33	12.28	(NA)
WEEKLY EARNINGS [1]												
1970	120	(NA)	164	195	133	(NA)	156	137	82	113	97	(NA)
1980	235	(NA)	397	368	289	(NA)	351	267	147	210	191	(NA)
1985	299	(NA)	520	464	386	(NA)	450	351	175	289	257	(NA)
1990	345	(NA)	603	526	442	(NA)	496	411	194	357	319	(NA)
1991	354	(NA)	630	533	455	(NA)	503	425	198	371	331	(NA)
1992	364	(NA)	638	538	470	(NA)	514	435	205	387	343	(NA)
1993	374	(NA)	647	554	486	(NA)	533	448	210	406	350	(NA)
1994	386	(NA)	667	573	507	(NA)	547	463	216	424	359	(NA)
1995	394	(NA)	684	587	515	(NA)	557	476	221	442	369	(NA)
1996	407	(NA)	708	603	531	(NA)	572	493	230	460	382	(NA)
1997	425	(NA)	734	624	553	(NA)	593	516	241	481	400	(NA)

NA Not available. [1] Average hours and earnings. Private production and related workers in mining, manufacturing, and construction; nonsupervisory employees in other industries.

Source: U.S. Bureau of Labor Statistics, *Employment and Earnings*, monthly, June issues and Internet site <http://stats.bls.gov/ceshome.htm>

No. 686. Employees in Nonfarm Establishments—States: 1980 to 1997

[In thousands. For coverage, see headnote, Table 685. National totals differ from the sum of the State figures because of differing benchmarks among States and differing industrial and geographic stratification. Based on 1987 *Standard Industrial Classification Manual*, see text, Section 13, Labor Force, Employment and Earnings]

STATE	1980	1995	1997							
			Total [1]	Construction	Manufacturing	Transportation and public utilities	Wholesale and retail trade	Finance, insurance, and real estate	Services	Government
United States	90,406	117,191	122,690	5,686	18,657	6,395	28,659	7,091	36,040	19,570
Alabama............	1,356	1,804	1,863	97	380	91	427	84	428	346
Alaska.............	169	262	268	13	15	24	56	12	65	73
Arizona............	1,014	1,796	1,977	131	207	96	481	127	599	324
Arkansas	742	1,069	1,103	48	253	66	252	44	254	184
California	9,849	12,422	13,167	554	1,914	663	3,057	756	4,051	2,144
Colorado...........	1,251	1,834	1,977	118	204	122	481	127	597	315
Connecticut........	1,427	1,562	1,616	57	276	75	354	131	497	226
Delaware	259	366	388	22	57	16	86	47	107	53
District of Columbia	616	643	615	9	13	18	49	28	266	233
Florida	3,576	5,996	6,427	333	491	327	1,652	410	2,265	943
Georgia	2,159	3,402	3,620	169	589	230	916	187	944	578
Hawaii	404	533	532	[2]22	17	41	135	36	169	112
Idaho.............	330	477	509	32	74	24	129	25	122	99
Illinois	4,850	5,593	5,773	235	974	337	1,324	399	1,686	806
Indiana............	2,130	2,787	2,860	141	677	140	682	139	683	391
Iowa	1,110	1,358	1,405	60	254	65	345	79	365	234
Kansas............	945	1,198	1,268	59	206	72	310	61	317	236
Kentucky	1,210	1,643	1,714	82	316	97	410	69	425	291
Louisiana	1,579	1,772	1,847	116	190	110	430	86	498	364
Maine.............	418	538	554	24	88	23	140	28	158	93
Maryland	1,712	2,183	2,257	138	176	106	536	131	752	417
Massachusetts.......	2,654	2,977	3,119	100	448	134	711	213	1,107	405
Michigan...........	3,443	4,274	4,446	180	967	173	1,044	206	1,219	649
Minnesota..........	1,770	2,379	2,485	94	434	124	600	146	700	380
Mississippi	829	1,075	1,106	51	241	53	237	41	258	219
Missouri	1,970	2,521	2,636	122	419	164	623	154	736	413
Montana...........	280	351	366	18	24	21	99	16	105	77
Nebraska..........	628	816	856	39	116	53	210	55	229	153
Nevada	400	786	890	82	41	45	179	40	382	106
New Hampshire......	385	540	568	21	107	19	148	29	165	78
New Jersey.........	3,060	3,601	3,725	131	482	257	872	239	1,172	569
New Mexico........	465	682	707	43	46	32	168	31	195	177
New York	7,207	7,872	8,027	264	921	408	1,640	720	2,696	1,374
North Carolina.......	2,380	3,460	3,667	204	835	170	838	166	871	579
North Dakota........	245	302	313	15	23	18	81	15	87	71
Ohio	4,367	5,221	5,386	224	1,090	233	1,311	287	1,469	760
Oklahoma..........	1,138	1,316	1,387	51	180	79	324	69	378	275
Oregon............	1,045	1,418	1,525	82	244	74	378	95	401	250
Pennsylvania........	4,753	5,253	5,398	214	936	278	1,217	313	1,707	713
Rhode Island........	398	440	449	15	80	15	98	27	151	64
South Carolina.......	1,189	1,646	1,722	100	362	75	414	75	395	299
South Dakota.......	238	344	354	15	49	16	88	21	92	70
Tennessee	1,747	2,499	2,582	116	517	150	609	120	683	383
Texas.............	5,851	8,023	8,602	458	1,081	514	2,046	464	2,392	1,482
Utah	551	908	995	65	133	56	239	53	270	172
Vermont	200	270	279	13	47	12	65	12	84	45
Virginia	2,157	3,070	3,231	186	404	168	724	168	974	596
Washington.........	1,608	2,347	2,512	136	369	133	607	128	677	458
West Virginia........	646	688	709	35	82	39	162	28	199	139
Wisconsin..........	1,938	2,559	2,653	109	609	123	605	140	678	386
Wyoming	210	219	224	15	11	14	53	8	49	58

[1] Includes mining, not shown separately.   [2] Includes mining.

Source: U.S. Bureau of Labor Statistics, *Employment and Earnings*, monthly, May issues. Compiled from data supplied by cooperating state agencies.

No. 687. Nonfarm Industries—Employees and Earnings: 1980 to 1997

[Annual averages of monthly figures. Covers all full- and part-time employees who worked during, or received pay for, any part of the pay period including the 12th of the month. For mining and manufacturing, data refer to production and related workers; for construction, to employees engaged in actual construction work; and for other industries, to nonsupervisory employees and working supervisors. See also headnote, Table 685]

INDUSTRY	1987 SIC [1] code	ALL EMPLOYEES TOTAL (1,000)			PRODUCTION WORKERS Total (1,000)			PRODUCTION WORKERS Average hourly earnings (dollars)		
		1980	1990	1997	1980	1990	1997	1980	1990	1997
Total	(X)	90,406	109,403	122,690	(NA)	(NA)	(NA)	(NA)	(NA)	(NA)
Private sector [2]	(X)	74,166	91,098	103,120	60,331	73,774	84,529	6.66	10.01	12.28
Mining	(B)	1,027	709	592	762	509	446	9.17	13.68	16.17
Metal mining	10	98	58	54	74	46	41	10.26	14.05	17.82
Coal mining	12	246	147	96	204	119	79	10.86	16.71	19.01
Oil and gas extraction	13	560	395	335	389	261	245	8.59	12.94	15.66
Nonmetallic minerals, except fuels	14	123	110	108	96	83	81	7.52	11.58	14.19
Construction	(C)	4,346	5,120	5,686	3,421	3,974	4,409	9.94	13.77	16.03
General building contractors	15	1,173	1,298	1,316	900	938	928	9.22	13.01	15.21
Heavy construction, except building	16	895	770	795	720	643	664	9.20	13.34	15.60
Special trade contractors	17	2,278	3,051	3,575	1,802	2,393	2,817	10.63	14.20	16.41
Manufacturing	(D)	20,285	19,076	18,657	14,214	12,947	12,896	7.27	10.83	13.17
Durable goods	(X)	12,159	11,109	10,987	8,416	7,363	7,539	7.75	11.35	13.73
Lumber and wood products [3]	24	704	733	793	587	603	653	6.57	9.08	10.77
Logging	241	88	85	82	71	70	66	8.64	11.22	12.18
Sawmills and planing mills	242	215	198	182	190	172	159	6.70	9.22	10.86
Millwork, plywood, and structural members	243	206	262	294	170	210	236	6.44	9.04	10.88
Wood containers	244	43	45	54	37	38	46	4.95	6.64	8.37
Mobile homes	2451	46	41	70	36	33	59	6.08	8.67	11.05
Furniture and fixtures [3]	25	466	506	510	376	400	405	5.49	8.52	10.55
Household furniture	251	301	289	277	253	241	234	5.12	7.87	9.96
Office furniture	252	51	68	63	40	51	47	5.91	9.64	11.63
Partitions and fixtures	254	63	78	87	47	57	65	6.68	9.77	11.30
Stone, clay, and glass products [3]	32	629	556	552	486	432	431	7.50	11.12	13.18
Flat glass	321	18	17	17	14	13	14	9.65	15.15	18.65
Glass and glassware, pressed and blown	322	124	83	72	105	72	60	7.97	12.40	14.98
Products of purchased glass	323	45	60	63	32	46	49	6.50	9.75	11.92
Cement, hydraulic	324	31	18	17	25	14	13	10.55	13.90	17.48
Structural clay products	325	46	36	34	34	28	27	6.14	9.55	11.49
Pottery and related products	326	47	39	39	39	31	31	6.25	9.62	11.47
Concrete, gypsum, and plaster	327	204	206	217	157	157	166	7.45	10.76	12.60
Primary metal industries [3]	33	1,142	756	711	878	574	556	9.77	12.92	15.22
Blast furnaces and basic steel products	331	512	276	235	396	212	181	11.39	14.82	18.03
Iron and steel foundries	332	209	132	130	167	105	107	8.20	11.55	13.81
Primary nonferrous metals	333	71	46	39	53	34	30	10.63	14.36	16.66
Nonferrous rolling and drawing	335	211	172	168	151	124	129	8.81	12.29	14.48
Nonferrous foundries (castings)	336	90	84	91	72	66	74	7.30	10.21	12.05
Fabricated metal products [3]	34	1,609	1,419	1,475	1,194	1,045	1,112	7.45	10.83	12.79
Metal cans and shipping containers	341	75	50	38	63	43	32	9.84	14.27	16.29
Cutlery, handtools, and hardware	342	164	131	125	125	96	96	7.02	10.78	12.46
Plumbing and heating, exc. electric	343	71	60	59	52	43	42	6.59	9.75	11.71
Fabricated structural metal products	344	506	427	451	351	303	331	7.27	10.16	12.11
Screw machine products	345	109	96	104	84	73	82	6.96	10.70	12.89
Metal forgings and stampings	346	260	225	255	205	178	203	8.56	12.70	14.95
Industrial machinery and equipment [3]	35	2,517	2,095	2,163	1,614	1,260	1,362	8.00	11.77	14.07
Engines and turbines	351	135	89	83	87	58	53	9.73	14.55	16.83
Farm and garden machinery	352	169	106	104	116	78	76	8.78	10.99	13.78
Construction and related machinery	353	389	229	243	255	141	159	8.60	11.92	13.53
Metalworking machinery	354	398	330	349	290	236	249	8.13	12.27	14.90
Special industry machinery	355	194	159	180	125	94	100	7.53	11.90	14.68
General industrial machinery	356	300	247	263	196	158	168	7.95	11.32	13.78
Computer and office equipment	357	420	438	375	181	137	139	6.75	11.51	14.31
Refrigeration and service machinery	358	175	177	202	120	125	146	7.23	10.93	12.81
Electronic and other elec. equip. [3]	36	1,771	1,673	1,688	([4])	1,055	1,068	([4])	10.30	12.70
Electric distribution equipment	361	117	97	82	82	67	56	6.96	10.15	12.66
Electrical industrial apparatus	362	232	169	154	163	119	108	([4])	10.00	12.16
Household appliances	363	162	124	115	128	99	90	6.95	10.26	12.19
Electric lighting and wiring equip	364	211	189	181	157	136	129	6.43	10.12	12.70
Household audio and video equip	365	109	85	79	79	59	51	6.42	9.68	11.11
Communications equipment	366	([4])	264	276	([4])	133	131	([4])	11.03	13.88
Electronic components and accessories	367	539	582	652	325	329	395	6.05	10.00	12.53
Transportation equipment [3]	37	1,881	1,989	1,842	1,220	1,224	1,254	9.35	14.08	17.56
Motor vehicles and equipment	371	789	812	985	575	617	779	9.85	14.56	18.06
Aircraft and parts	372	633	712	500	344	345	251	9.28	14.79	18.86
Ship and boat building and repairing	373	221	188	157	176	141	119	8.22	10.94	13.20
Railroad equipment	374	71	33	33	53	25	25	9.93	13.41	16.81
Guided missiles, space vehicles, and parts	376	111	185	91	35	57	24	9.22	14.39	19.54

See footnotes at end of table.

No. 687. Nonfarm Industries—Employees and Earnings: 1980 to 1997—Continued

[See headnote, p. 429]

INDUSTRY	1987 SIC [1] code	ALL EMPLOYEES TOTAL (1,000)			PRODUCTION WORKERS					
					Total (1,000)			Average hourly earnings (dollars)		
		1980	1990	1997	1980	1990	1997	1980	1990	1997
Durable goods—Continued . . .	(X)									
Instruments and related products	38	1,022	1,006	863	[4]	499	426	[4]	11.29	13.51
Search and navigation equipment . . .	381	[4]	284	161	[4]	94	44	[4]	14.62	16.82
Measuring and controlling devices . . .	382	[4]	323	299	[4]	180	153	[4]	10.68	13.53
Medical instruments and supplies . . .	384	[4]	246	276	[4]	144	161	[4]	9.85	12.51
Ophthalmic goods	385	44	43	35	31	30	22	5.30	8.18	10.16
Photographic equipment and supplies	386	135	100	84	67	43	40	8.83	14.08	15.93
Watches, clocks, watchcases, and parts	387	22	11	8	17	8	6	5.24	7.70	9.90
Misc. manufacturing industries [3]	39	418	375	389	313	272	273	5.46	8.61	10.59
Jewelry, silverware, and plated ware .	391	56	52	49	40	37	34	5.76	9.23	10.98
Toys and sporting goods	394	117	104	110	88	76	76	5.01	7.94	10.02
Pens, pencils, office and art supplies .	395	37	34	31	27	24	21	5.58	8.89	11.09
Costume jewelry and notions	396	[4]	33	24	[4]	25	17	[4]	7.40	9.38
Nondurable goods [3]	(X)	**8,127**	**7,968**	**7,670**	**5,798**	**5,584**	**5,357**	**6.56**	**10.12**	**12.33**
Food and kindred products [3]	20	1,708	1,661	1,691	1,175	1,194	1,256	6.85	9.62	11.49
Meat products	201	358	422	489	298	359	415	6.99	7.94	9.35
Dairy products	202	175	155	142	96	95	94	6.86	10.56	13.21
Preserved fruits and vegetables	203	246	247	232	202	206	195	5.94	8.95	11.02
Grain mill products	204	144	128	125	99	89	90	7.67	11.52	14.38
Bakery products	205	230	213	207	139	133	139	7.14	10.85	12.46
Sugar and confectionery products . . .	206	108	99	98	81	78	78	6.56	10.26	12.73
Fats and oils	207	44	31	33	32	22	23	7.03	10.10	12.65
Beverages	208	234	184	181	105	78	88	8.12	13.51	16.00
Tobacco products	21	69	49	41	54	36	32	7.74	16.23	19.27
Cigarettes	211	46	35	28	35	26	21	9.23	19.57	24.76
Textile mill products [3]	22	848	691	616	737	593	522	5.07	8.02	10.03
Broadwoven fabric mills, cotton . . .	221	150	91	72	135	82	65	5.25	8.31	10.44
Broadwoven fabric mills, synthetics . .	222	116	77	64	104	68	54	5.30	8.63	10.98
Broadwoven fabric mills, wool	223	19	17	14	16	14	12	5.21	8.61	10.50
Narrow fabric mills	224	23	24	21	20	20	18	4.63	7.39	9.19
Knitting mills	225	224	205	173	194	179	148	4.77	7.37	9.14
Textile finishing, except wool	226	74	62	67	62	50	54	5.39	8.45	10.27
Carpets and rugs	227	54	61	64	44	50	55	5.20	8.25	10.02
Yarn and thread mills	228	125	103	86	113	92	76	4.76	7.68	9.73
Apparel and other textile products [3] . . .	23	1,264	1,036	826	1,079	869	674	4.56	6.57	8.25
Men's and boys' suits and coats	231	77	50	29	67	42	24	5.34	7.34	8.40
Men's and boys' furnishings	232	362	274	207	310	235	175	4.23	6.06	7.73
Women's and misses outerwear	233	417	328	252	360	274	205	4.61	6.26	7.85
Women's and children's undergarments	234	90	62	35	76	51	28	4.15	6.18	7.84
Girls' and children's outerwear	236	64	56	31	55	47	25	4.20	5.95	7.54
Paper and allied products [3]	26	685	697	685	519	522	522	7.84	12.31	15.04
Papermills	262	178	180	159	133	136	124	9.05	15.10	19.08
Paperboard mills	263	65	52	50	51	40	39	9.28	15.26	18.79
Paperboard containers and boxes . . .	265	205	209	220	157	162	171	6.94	10.39	12.80
Misc. converted paper products	267	220	241	244	163	174	180	6.89	10.79	13.14
Printing and publishing [3]	27	1,252	1,569	1,553	699	871	847	7.53	11.24	13.05
Newspapers	271	420	474	441	164	166	148	7.72	11.17	12.90
Periodicals	272	90	129	136	16	47	46	7.16	11.95	14.40
Books	273	101	121	128	52	66	67	6.76	10.10	12.31
Commercial printing	275	410	552	573	304	401	409	7.85	11.52	13.28
Blankbooks and bookbinding	278	62	72	66	51	56	51	5.78	8.83	10.19
Chemicals and allied products [3]	28	1,107	1,086	1,034	626	600	572	8.30	13.54	16.58
Industrial inorganic chemicals	281	161	138	117	88	70	57	9.07	14.66	18.56
Plastics materials and synthetics	282	205	180	158	137	116	105	8.21	13.97	17.42
Drugs	283	196	237	267	97	105	120	7.69	12.90	16.39
Soap, cleaners, and toilet goods	284	141	159	156	86	98	96	7.67	11.71	13.28
Paints and allied products	285	65	61	52	33	31	28	7.39	11.99	14.06
Industrial organic chemicals	286	174	155	138	88	86	79	9.67	15.97	19.86
Agricultural chemicals	287	72	56	52	45	34	31	8.12	13.73	16.60
Petroleum and coal products [3]	29	198	157	140	125	103	92	10.10	16.24	20.18
Petroleum refining	291	155	118	97	93	75	63	10.94	17.58	22.52
Asphalt paving and roofing materials .	295	31	27	29	24	21	21	7.69	12.87	15.02
Rubber and misc. plastics products [3] . . .	30	764	888	995	588	687	772	6.58	9.76	11.57
Tires and inner tubes	301	115	84	78	81	62	57	9.74	15.42	18.59
Rubber and plastics footwear	302	22	11	7	20	9	6	4.43	6.66	9.71
Leather and leather products [3]	31	233	133	90	197	109	69	4.58	6.91	8.98
Leather tanning and finishing	311	19	15	13	16	12	11	6.10	9.04	11.88
Footwear, except rubber	314	144	74	41	123	63	33	4.42	6.61	8.49
Luggage	316	16	11	10	12	8	8	4.90	6.91	8.82
Handbags and personal leather goods	317	30	15	10	25	12	6	4.33	6.08	7.92

See footnotes at end of table.

No. 687. Nonfarm Industries—Employees and Earnings: 1980 to 1997—Continued

[See headnote, p. 429]

INDUSTRY	1987 SIC [1] code	ALL EMPLOYEES TOTAL (1,000)			PRODUCTION WORKERS					
					Total (1,000)			Average hourly earnings (dollars)		
		1980	1990	1997	1980	1990	1997	1980	1990	1997
Transp. and public utilities [3]	(E)	**5,146**	**5,777**	**6,395**	**4,293**	**4,781**	**5,355**	**8.87**	**12.92**	**14.93**
Railroad transportation	40	532	279	227	[4]	[4]	[4]	[4]	[4]	[4]
Class I railroads, plus Amtrak [5]	4011	482	241	202	(4)			[6]9.92	[6]16.08	[6]18.10
Local and interurban passenger transit	41	265	338	451	244	308	412	6.34	9.23	10.90
Trucking and warehousing	42	[4]	1,395	1,667	(NA)	1,215	1,459	[4]	11.68	13.23
Water transportation	44	211	177	180	[4]	[4]	[4]	[4]	[4]	[4]
Transportation by air	45	[4]	968	1,128	[4]	[4]	[4]	[4]	[4]	[4]
Pipelines, except natural gas	46	21	19	14	15	14	12	10.50	17.04	20.54
Transportation services	47	[4]	336	439	159	270	357	6.94	10.38	13.14
Communication [3]	48	1,357	1,309	1,424	1,014	978	1,093	8.50	13.51	16.92
Telephone communication	481	1,072	913	975	779	658	730	8.72	14.13	17.51
Radio and television broadcasting	483	192	234	243	154	193	202	7.44	12.71	17.03
Cable and other pay television services	484	[4]	126	175	[4]	105	147	[4]	10.50	13.51
Electric, gas, and sanitary services [3]	49	829	957	866	678	759	689	8.90	15.23	19.09
Electric services	491	391	454	368	316	351	294	9.12	15.80	20.08
Gas production and distribution	492	168	165	143	138	129	110	8.27	14.25	17.99
Combination utility services	493	197	193	160	162	156	124	9.64	17.58	23.16
Sanitary services	495	50	115	162	44	99	134	7.16	11.55	14.70
Wholesale trade	(F)	**5,292**	**6,173**	**6,648**	**4,328**	**4,959**	**5,355**	**6.95**	**10.79**	**13.44**
Retail trade [3]	(G)	**15,018**	**19,601**	**22,011**	**13,484**	**17,358**	**19,375**	**4.88**	**6.75**	**8.34**
General merchandise stores	53	2,245	2,540	2,718	2,090	2,380	2,528	4.77	6.83	8.16
Food stores	54	2,384	3,215	3,496	2,202	2,953	3,173	6.24	7.31	8.69
Automotive dealers and service stations	55	1,689	2,063	2,314	1,430	1,718	1,936	5.66	8.92	11.42
Apparel and accessory stores	56	957	1,183	1,098	820	991	913	4.30	6.25	8.06
Furniture and home furnishings stores	57	606	820	1,009	502	670	828	5.53	8.53	11.26
Eating and drinking places	58	4,626	6,509	7,636	4,256	5,905	6,876	3.69	4.97	6.05
Finance, insurance, real estate	(H)	**5,160**	**6,709**	**7,091**	**3,907**	**4,860**	**5,180**	**5.79**	**9.97**	**13.33**
Depository institutions	60	[4]	2,251	2,027	[4]	1,632	1,457	[4]	8.43	10.29
Nondepository institutions	61	[4]	373	567	[4]	270	402	[4]	10.40	13.68
Security and commodity brokers	62	227	424	597	[4]	[4]	[4]	[4]	[4]	[4]
Insurance carriers	63	1,224	1,462	1,535	854	982	1,117	6.29	11.18	15.83
Insurance agents, brokers, service	64	464	663	724	[4]	[4]	[4]	[4]	[4]	[4]
Real estate	65	989	1,315	1,419	[4]	[4]	[4]	[4]	[4]	[4]
Holding and other investment offices	67	115	221	222	[4]	[4]	[4]	[4]	[4]	[4]
Services [3]	(I)	**17,890**	**27,934**	**36,040**	**15,921**	**24,387**	**31,513**	**5.85**	**9.83**	**12.28**
Hotels and other lodging places	70	1,076	1,631	1,744	[4]	[4]	[4]	[4]	[4]	[4]
Hotels and motels	701	1,038	1,578	1,693	954	1,398	1,490	4.45	6.98	8.55
Personal services [3]	72	818	1,104	1,182	[4]	[4]	[4]	[4]	[4]	[4]
Laundry, cleaning, garment services	721	356	426	439	318	379	386	4.47	6.82	8.07
Beauty shops	723	284	372	397	264	333	353	4.26	7.10	9.12
Business services [3]	73	2,564	5,139	7,983	[4]	4,522	7,091	[4]	9.48	11.83
Advertising	731	153	235	255	116	169	185	8.07	13.51	16.85
Personnel supply services	736	543	1,535	2,968	[4]	[4]	[4]	[4]	[4]	[4]
Employment agencies	7361	[4]	246	323	[4]	[4]	[4]	[4]	[4]	[4]
Help supply services	7363	[4]	1,288	2,646	[4]	1,245	2,573	[4]	8.09	9.64
Computer and data processing services	737	304	772	1,411	254	603	1,125	7.16	15.11	20.09
Prepackaged software	7372	[4]	113	230	[4]	[4]	[4]	[4]	[4]	[4]
Data processing and preparation	7374	[4]	197	249	[4]	[4]	[4]	[4]	[4]	[4]
Auto repair, services, and parking	75	571	914	1,124	488	756	925	6.10	8.77	10.59
Automotive repair shops	753	350	524	622	297	429	500	6.52	9.67	11.91
Motion pictures	78	[4]	408	548	[4]	344	460	[4]	10.95	14.17
Motion picture theaters	783	124	112	132	[4]	[4]	[4]	[4]	[4]	[4]
Amusement and recreation services	79	[4]	1,076	1,573	[4]	944	1,379	[4]	8.11	9.20
Health services [3]	80	5,278	7,814	9,420	4,712	6,948	8,614	5.68	10.41	13.26
Offices and clinics of medical doctors	801	802	1,338	1,743	[4]	1,105	1,431	[4]	10.58	13.78
Nursing and personal care facilities	805	997	1,415	1,755	898	1,279	1,578	4.17	7.24	9.34
Hospitals	806	2,750	3,549	3,869	2,522	3,248	3,545	6.06	11.79	15.03
Home health care services	808	[4]	291	713	[4]	269	657	[4]	8.72	11.35
Legal services	81	498	908	947	427	748	756	7.35	14.16	17.30
Educational services	82	1,138	1,661	2,114	[4]	[4]	[4]	[4]	[4]	[4]
Social services	83	1,134	1,734	2,514	990	1,494	2,183	4.26	7.11	8.82
Membership organizations	86	1,539	1,946	2,248	[4]	[4]	[4]	[4]	[4]	[4]
Engineering and management services	87	[4]	2,478	3,005	[4]	1,886	2,295	[4]	13.56	17.14
Government	(J)	**16,241**	**18,304**	**19,570**	**(NA)**	**(NA)**	**(NA)**	**(NA)**	**(NA)**	**(NA)**
Federal government	(X)	2,866	3,085	2,699	(NA)	(NA)	(NA)	(NA)	(NA)	(NA)
State government	(X)	3,610	4,305	4,594	(NA)	(NA)	(NA)	(NA)	(NA)	(NA)
Local government	(X)	9,765	10,914	12,276	(NA)	(NA)	(NA)	(NA)	(NA)	(NA)

NA Not available.   X Not applicable.   [1] 1987 Standard Industrial Classification, see text, Section 13, Labor Force.   [2] Excludes government.   [3] Includes industries not shown separately.   [4] Included in totals; not available separately.   [5] For changes in "Class I" classification, see text, Section 21, Water Transportation.   [6] Includes all employees except executives, officials, and staff assistants who received pay during the month.

Source: U.S. Bureau of Labor Statistics, *Employment and Earnings*, monthly, June issues and Internet site <http://stats.bls.gov/ceshome.htm>

No. 688. Indexes of Output per Hour—Selected Industries: 1975 to 1996

[See text, Section 13, Labor Force. Minus sign (-) indicates decrease]

INDUSTRY	1987 SIC code [1]	INDEXES (1987=100)						Average annual percent change [2], 1975-96
		1975	1980	1985	1990	1995	1996	
Mining:	(B)							
Coal mining	12	57.7	61.7	85.1	118.3	155.5	169.4	5.3
Crude petroleum and natural gas	131	142.8	97.2	83.0	97.0	119.4	126.5	-0.6
Nonmetallic minerals, except fuels	14	81.0	86.9	95.1	101.4	104.5	104.3	1.2
Manufacturing:	(D)							
Red meat products	2011,13	71.3	89.7	102.2	96.3	101.8	95.4	1.4
Poultry dressing and processing	2015	67.6	81.6	100.5	108.6	121.9	120.0	2.8
Dairy products	202	65.0	75.2	92.4	106.2	114.9	114.1	2.7
Preserved fruits and vegetables	203	77.2	82.9	94.3	95.5	109.1	109.4	1.7
Grain mill products	204	57.2	70.8	92.4	105.2	114.9	107.0	3.0
Bakery products	2051,52	81.8	82.4	96.0	92.7	97.3	95.4	0.7
Bottled and canned soft drinks	2086	55.7	66.5	85.2	126.7	160.2	163.0	5.2
Cotton and synthetic broadwoven fabrics	221,2	66.2	78.5	95.1	108.3	141.3	146.3	3.8
Yarn spinning mills	2281	67.4	65.5	89.6	106.0	135.5	151.6	3.9
Sawmills and planing mills, general	2421	68.2	71.5	93.5	99.9	110.2	116.0	2.6
Millwork	2431	98.8	97.6	97.4	97.8	85.5	86.8	-0.6
Wood kitchen cabinets	2434	82.3	94.1	87.1	93.6	102.6	100.1	0.9
Household furniture	251	82.1	93.2	93.4	104.5	116.9	122.2	1.9
Pulp, paper, and paperboard mills	261,2,3	63.5	77.1	87.6	103.2	122.0	117.1	3.0
Corrugated and solid fiber boxes	2653	78.6	90.5	99.6	98.8	100.2	101.9	1.2
Industrial inorganic chemicals	281	66.9	75.4	84.0	104.5	105.1	106.3	2.2
Synthetic fibers	2823,24	46.9	71.2	79.3	103.6	123.8	121.0	4.6
Cosmetics and other toiletries	2844	92.2	83.8	90.3	101.1	115.4	123.8	1.4
Industrial organic chemicals, n.e.c. [3]	2869	69.8	81.3	87.8	99.0	94.1	93.3	1.4
Petroleum refining	291	80.0	81.7	84.7	109.2	132.3	142.0	2.8
Tires and inner tubes	301	54.1	60.7	89.3	103.0	131.1	138.8	4.6
Miscellaneous plastics products, n.e.c. [3]	308	66.7	75.1	88.2	105.1	120.0	124.1	3.0
Concrete products	3271,72	91.1	88.8	99.4	104.1	113.8	124.5	1.5
Ready-mixed concrete	3273	93.3	90.0	93.6	100.2	95.6	94.0	0.0
Steel	331	59.3	65.4	85.8	109.6	142.7	153.6	4.6
Gray and ductile iron foundries	3321	90.3	86.3	96.9	107.9	111.7	116.6	1.2
Fabricated structural metal	3441	82.0	86.0	99.0	101.2	111.9	113.0	1.5
Metal doors, sash, and trim	3442	88.3	90.5	104.8	103.1	96.5	99.4	0.6
Fabricated plate work	3443	(NA)	(NA)	87.5	94.1	106.9	109.3	[4]1.1
Metal stampings	3465,66,6	80.6	84.0	91.8	95.0	109.4	114.0	1.7
Valves and pipe fittings	3491,92,9	84.0	93.5	94.4	105.4	115.0	117.6	1.6
Farm and garden machinery	352	94.2	91.3	92.8	116.5	134.7	136.6	1.8
Construction machinery	3531	87.7	88.5	92.2	109.6	128.8	126.3	1.8
Pumps and compressors	3561,63,9	79.9	87.2	92.1	98.3	108.6	114.0	1.7
Refrigeration and heating equipment	3585	85.3	90.7	98.1	106.3	115.1	115.1	1.4
Motors and generators	3621	82.7	87.9	94.9	100.9	143.8	151.0	2.9
Major household appliances	3631,32,3	71.2	79.3	93.8	104.2	125.0	123.2	2.6
Lighting fixtures and equipment	3645,46,4	80.5	84.4	96.7	96.2	110.6	113.3	1.6
Motor vehicles and equipment	371	70.2	71.6	95.3	102.2	105.9	106.1	2.0
Aircraft	3721	80.9	97.9	94.2	112.9	131.4	142.0	2.7
Instruments to measure electricity	3825	67.2	76.2	95.4	110.7	178.7	182.7	4.9
Photographic equipment and supplies	386	60.9	72.9	86.1	107.8	129.5	129.0	3.6
Service producing:	(E,G,H,I)							
United States postal service [5]	43	86.1	94.8	98.4	104.0	106.5	104.7	0.9
Air transportation [6]	4512,13,2	55.6	70.8	92.0	92.9	108.6	111.0	3.3
Telephone communications	481	49.3	67.6	88.9	113.3	147.0	160.7	5.8
Gas and electric utilities	491,2,3	107.0	107.2	98.0	106.2	128.1	138.0	1.2
Scrap and waste materials	5093	(NA)	79.2	93.4	98.6	109.6	115.4	[7]1.8
Hardware stores	525	82.4	94.9	95.6	110.5	111.0	119.2	1.8
Department stores	531	63.7	73.6	92.6	94.2	108.5	112.7	2.8
Variety stores	533	151.6	128.6	129.2	151.2	157.3	175.0	0.7
Food stores	54	106.1	107.6	104.1	95.9	91.1	88.7	-0.8
New and used car dealers	551	83.9	87.9	99.8	106.1	106.5	107.3	1.2
Auto and home supply stores	553	70.3	82.8	94.5	102.7	106.0	105.6	2.0
Gasoline service stations	554	58.5	72.1	93.5	102.6	117.1	114.5	3.2
Apparel and accessory stores	56	74.0	82.4	101.3	101.8	122.4	128.8	2.7
Home furniture, furnishings, and equipment stores	57	64.7	75.1	92.9	107.7	138.3	142.2	3.8
Eating and drinking places	58	107.9	106.8	96.2	104.0	101.5	98.2	-0.4
Drug stores and proprietary stores	591	90.0	104.5	102.5	103.6	104.4	105.6	0.8
Liquor stores	592	90.4	95.7	101.9	105.2	102.6	110.1	0.9
Miscellaneous shopping goods stores	594	(NA)	88.4	94.1	104.2	112.7	117.0	[7]1.3
Commercial banks	602	76.3	78.5	94.3	107.7	127.6	131.5	2.6
Hotels and motels	701	99.9	103.9	101.2	96.1	110.1	109.5	0.4
Laundry, cleaning, and garment services	721	109.8	103.2	103.3	101.8	105.2	108.2	-0.1
Beauty and barber shops	723,4	80.2	85.7	94.6	97.4	104.4	106.9	1.4
Automotive repair shops	753	106.7	100.4	99.4	106.9	118.5	112.9	0.3

NA Not available.   [1] 1987 Standard Industrial Classification; see text, Section 13.   [2] Average annual percent change based on compound rate formula.   [3] N.e.c. means not elsewhere classified.   [4] Change from 1985-96.   [5] Refers to output per full-time equivalent employee years on fiscal basis.   [6] Refers to output per employee.   [7] Change from 1980-96.

Source: U.S. Bureau of Labor Statistics, Internet site <http://stats.bls.gov/iprhome.htm>

No. 689. Productivity and Related Measures: 1970 to 1997

[See text, Section 13, Labor Force. Minus sign (-) indicates decrease]

ITEM	1970	1980	1985	1990	1993	1994	1995	1996	1997
INDEXES (1992=100)									
Output per hour, business sector	70.5	84.2	91.7	96.1	100.2	100.6	100.5	102.6	104.5
Nonfarm business	72.6	86.0	92.3	96.2	100.1	100.5	100.7	102.6	104.3
Manufacturing	55.1	71.0	83.8	94.3	102.2	104.7	108.1	112.1	117.1
Output, [1] business sector	52.0	73.0	85.7	98.6	102.7	107.0	109.5	113.3	118.4
Nonfarm business	52.1	73.4	85.8	98.8	103.0	107.0	109.8	113.6	118.7
Manufacturing	57.6	76.4	87.8	98.8	103.6	108.7	112.5	116.1	122.6
Hours, [2] business sector	73.7	86.6	93.5	102.6	102.6	106.3	108.9	110.4	113.3
Nonfarm business	71.8	85.4	92.9	102.7	102.8	106.4	109.0	110.7	113.7
Manufacturing	104.5	107.6	104.7	104.9	101.4	103.8	104.1	103.6	104.7
Compensation per hour, [3] business sector	23.6	54.5	73.0	90.7	102.6	104.3	106.9	111.1	115.4
Nonfarm business	23.8	54.8	73.4	90.6	102.3	104.1	106.7	110.8	115.0
Manufacturing	23.8	55.8	75.3	91.0	102.9	105.6	108.7	112.1	116.1
Real hourly compensation, [3] business sector	85.4	92.7	95.2	97.4	99.6	98.7	98.4	99.3	100.9
Nonfarm business	86.1	93.3	95.7	97.3	99.3	98.5	98.3	99.1	100.6
Manufacturing	86.1	94.9	98.1	97.6	99.9	100.0	100.1	100.3	101.5
Unit labor costs, [4] business sector	33.5	64.7	79.7	94.4	102.4	103.7	106.3	108.3	110.5
Nonfarm business	32.8	63.8	79.5	94.1	102.2	103.6	106.0	108.0	110.2
Manufacturing	43.2	78.5	89.8	96.5	100.7	100.8	100.6	100.0	99.1
ANNUAL PERCENT CHANGE [5]									
Output per hour, business sector	2.0	-0.3	1.6	0.7	0.2	0.4	0.1	2.0	1.9
Nonfarm business	1.4	-0.4	1.0	0.5	0.1	0.4	0.2	1.9	1.7
Manufacturing	3.2	0.5	3.8	1.8	2.2	2.5	3.2	3.7	4.4
Output, [1] business sector	-0.1	-1.2	3.9	0.8	2.7	4.1	2.3	3.5	4.5
Nonfarm business	-0.2	-1.2	3.6	0.7	3.0	3.9	2.6	3.5	4.5
Manufacturing	-2.9	-4.1	3.0	-0.4	3.6	4.9	3.5	3.2	5.6
Hours, [2] business sector	-2.0	-0.9	2.2	0.1	2.6	3.7	2.4	1.4	2.6
Nonfarm business	-1.6	-0.8	2.5	0.2	2.8	3.5	2.4	1.6	2.7
Manufacturing	-5.9	-4.6	-0.7	-2.2	1.4	2.4	0.3	-0.5	1.1
Compensation per hour, [3] business sector	7.8	10.8	4.9	5.7	2.6	1.6	2.5	3.9	3.9
Nonfarm business	7.2	10.8	4.6	5.5	2.3	1.7	2.5	3.8	3.8
Manufacturing	7.1	11.9	5.4	4.8	2.9	2.6	2.9	3.2	3.5
Real hourly compensation, [3] business sector	1.9	-2.4	1.3	0.3	-0.4	-0.9	-0.3	0.9	1.6
Nonfarm business	1.4	-2.4	1.0	0.1	-0.7	-0.8	-0.3	0.8	1.5
Manufacturing	1.3	-1.4	1.8	-0.5	-0.1	-	0.1	0.2	1.2
Unit labor costs, [4] business sector	5.7	11.1	3.2	5.0	2.4	1.2	2.6	1.8	2.0
Nonfarm business	5.7	11.2	3.6	5.0	2.2	1.4	2.4	1.9	2.1
Manufacturing	3.8	11.4	1.6	2.9	0.7	0.1	-0.3	-0.5	-0.9

- Represents zero.   [1] Refers to gross sectoral product, annual weighted.   [2] Hours at work of all persons engaged in the business and nonfarm business sectors (employees, proprietors, and unpaid family workers); employees' and proprietors' hours in manufacturing.   [3] Wages and salaries of employees plus employers' contributions for social insurance and private benefit plans. Also includes an estimate of same for self-employed. Real compensation deflated by the consumer price index for all urban consumers, see text, Section 15, Prices.   [4] Hourly compensation divided by output per hour.   [5] All changes are from the immediate prior year.

Source: U.S. Bureau of Labor Statistics, News USDL 98-92, *Productivity and Costs*.

No. 690. Drug Testing in the Workplace: 1992-93 and 1995

[For private industry establishments with 50 or more workers. Based on sample survey; see source for details]

CHARACTERISTIC	1992-93			1995		
	Total work-sites (1,000)	Percent of worksites that test—		Total work-sites (1,000)	Percent of worksites that test—	
		For drug use	For alcohol use		For drug use	For alcohol use
All worksites	162.8	48.4	23.0	188.5	55.8	36.0
EMPLOYEE SIZE						
50 to 99 employees	61.6	40.2	16.5	73.2	49.7	31.4
100 to 249 employees	66.0	48.2	22.9	66.2	54.2	33.6
250 to 999 employees	29.0	61.4	32.7	36.9	62.3	42.9
1,000 employees or more	6.2	70.9	42.1	12.3	73.2	55.2
INDUSTRY						
Wholesale and retail trade	32.2	53.7	22.1	40.3	52.0	33.1
Communications, utilities, and transportation	13.5	72.4	34.9	14.6	74.2	52.7
Finance, insurance, and real estate	14.2	22.6	7.8	13.9	28.9	11.0
Mining and construction	5.6	69.6	28.6	5.9	77.5	45.5
Services	43.3	27.9	17.4	59.5	40.9	26.5
Manufacturing	54.0	60.2	28.3	54.3	71.9	49.5

Source: U.S. Bureau of Labor Statistics, *Monthly Labor Review*, November 1996; and unpublished data.

No. 691. Annual Total Compensation and Wages and Salary Accruals Per Full-Time Equivalent Employee, by Industry: 1990 to 1996

[In dollars. Wage and salary accruals include executives' compensation, bonuses, tips, and payments-in-kind; total compensation includes in addition to wages and salaries, employer contributions for social insurance, employer contributions to private and welfare funds, director's fees, jury and witness fees, etc. Based on the 1987 Standard Industrial Classification Code (SIC); See text, Section 13, Labor Force]

INDUSTRY	ANNUAL TOTAL COMPENSATION				ANNUAL WAGES AND SALARIES			
	1990	1994	1995	1996	1990	1994	1995	1996
Domestic industries	32,093	37,007	37,855	38,988	26,396	30,020	30,919	32,006
Agriculture, forestry, and fisheries	18,638	20,777	21,258	21,685	16,014	17,833	18,331	18,870
Mining	46,053	55,069	57,203	58,878	38,081	44,482	46,683	48,329
Construction	33,701	37,275	37,417	38,456	27,832	30,191	30,453	31,649
Manufacturing	37,048	43,970	44,934	46,232	30,148	34,725	35,852	37,165
Transportation	36,636	40,586	40,830	41,481	29,019	31,882	32,279	32,994
Communication	46,481	56,743	59,508	61,200	38,930	46,802	49,316	50,716
Electric, gas, and sanitary services	48,057	58,667	61,163	63,011	39,538	46,725	48,857	50,433
Wholesale trade	37,394	43,515	44,549	46,104	31,810	36,504	37,817	39,256
Retail trade	18,678	21,131	21,250	21,757	16,065	18,130	18,300	18,821
Finance, insurance, and real estate	37,905	46,860	49,602	52,778	32,071	39,282	41,698	44,629
Services	29,141	32,959	34,065	34,922	24,996	27,886	28,987	29,935
Government	37,142	43,771	45,034	46,983	28,195	32,921	33,992	35,300

Source: U.S. Bureau of Economic Analysis, *National Income and Product Accounts of the United States, 1929-94*, vol.2; and *Survey of Current Business*, August 1997.

No. 692. Average Hourly and Weekly Earnings, by Private Industry Group: 1980 to 1997

[Average earnings include overtime. Data are for production and related workers in mining, manufacturing, and construction, and nonsupervisory employees in other industries. Excludes agriculture. See headnote, Table 685]

PRIVATE INDUSTRY GROUP	CURRENT DOLLARS					CONSTANT (1982) DOLLARS [1]				
	1980	1985	1990	1995	1997	1980	1985	1990	1995	1997
TOTAL AVERAGE HOURLY EARNINGS										
Total	6.66	8.57	10.01	11.43	12.28	7.78	7.77	7.52	7.39	7.55
Mining	9.17	11.98	13.68	15.30	16.17	10.71	10.86	10.28	9.90	9.94
Construction	9.94	12.32	13.77	15.09	16.03	11.61	11.17	10.35	9.76	9.86
Manufacturing	7.27	9.54	10.83	12.37	13.17	8.49	8.65	8.14	8.00	8.10
Transportation, public utilities	8.87	11.40	12.92	14.13	14.93	10.36	10.34	9.71	9.14	9.18
Wholesale trade	6.95	9.15	10.79	12.43	13.44	8.12	8.30	8.11	8.04	8.27
Retail trade	4.88	5.94	6.75	7.69	8.34	5.70	5.39	5.07	4.97	5.13
Finance, insurance, real estate	5.79	7.94	9.97	12.32	13.33	6.76	7.20	7.49	7.97	8.20
Services	5.85	7.90	9.83	11.39	12.28	6.83	7.16	7.39	7.37	7.55
TOTAL AVERAGE WEEKLY EARNINGS										
Total	235	299	345	394	425	275	271	259	255	261
Mining	397	520	603	684	734	464	471	453	442	451
Construction	368	464	526	587	624	430	421	395	380	384
Manufacturing	289	386	442	515	553	337	350	332	333	340
Transportation, public utilities	351	450	496	557	593	410	408	373	360	365
Wholesale trade	267	351	411	476	516	312	319	309	308	317
Retail trade	147	175	194	221	241	172	158	146	143	148
Finance, insurance, real estate	210	289	357	442	481	245	262	268	286	296
Services	191	257	319	369	400	223	233	240	239	246

[1] Earnings in current dollars divided by the Consumer Price Index (CPI-W) on a 1982 base; see text, Section 15, Prices.

Source: U.S. Bureau of Labor Statistics, *Employment and Earnings*, monthly, June issues; and Internet site <http://stats.bls.gov/ceshome.htm>

No. 693. Annual Percent Changes in Earnings and Compensation: 1980 to 1997

[Annual percent change from immediate prior year. Minus sign (-) indicates decrease]

ITEM	1980	1985	1990	1992	1993	1994	1995	1996	1997
Current dollars:									
Hourly earnings, total [1]	8.1	3.0	3.6	2.4	2.5	2.7	2.8	3.3	3.8
Hourly earnings, manufacturing [2]	8.5	3.8	3.3	2.5	2.4	2.8	2.5	3.3	3.1
Compensation per employee-hour [3]	10.7	4.5	5.5	5.2	2.3	1.7	2.5	3.8	3.8
Constant (1982) dollars:									
Hourly earnings, total [1]	-4.8	-0.4	-1.6	-0.5	-0.3	0.1	0.1	0.5	1.5
Hourly earnings, manufacturing [2]	-4.5	0.3	-1.7	-0.4	-0.4	0.2	-0.4	0.5	0.7
Compensation per employee-hour [3]	-2.5	0.9	0.1	2.1	-0.7	-0.8	-0.3	0.8	1.5
Consumer Price Index (CFI-U) [4]	13.5	3.6	5.4	3.0	3.0	2.6	2.8	3.0	2.3

[1] Production or nonsupervisory workers on private nonfarm payrolls.　[2] Production and related workers.　[3] Nonfarm business sector.　[4] See text, Section 15, Prices.

Source: U.S. Bureau of Labor Statistics, News USDL 98-92, *Productivity and Costs*.

No. 694. Average Annual Pay, by State: 1995 and 1996

[In dollars, except percent change. For workers covered by state unemployment insurance laws and for federal civilian workers covered by unemployment compensation for federal employees, approximately 97 percent of wage and salary civilian employment in 1996. Excludes most agricultural workers on small farms, all Armed Forces, elected officials in most states, railroad employees, most domestic workers, most student workers at school, employees of certain nonprofit organizations, and most self-employed individuals. Pay includes bonuses, cash value of meals and lodging, and tips and other gratuities]

STATE	AVERAGE ANNUAL PAY		Percent change, 1995-96 [1]	STATE	AVERAGE ANNUAL PAY		Percent change, 1995-96 [1]
	1995	1996 [1]			1995	1996 [1]	
United States	27,846	28,946	4.0	Missouri	25,669	26,601	3.6
Alabama	24,396	25,180	3.2	Montana	20,516	21,146	3.1
Alaska	32,685	32,461	-0.7	Nebraska	22,389	23,294	4.0
Arizona	25,324	26,387	4.2	Nevada	26,647	27,788	4.3
Arkansas	21,590	22,294	3.3	New Hampshire	26,637	27,691	4.0
California	30,717	31,776	3.4	New Jersey	34,533	35,928	4.0
Colorado	27,122	28,520	5.2	New Mexico	23,040	23,716	2.9
Connecticut	35,127	36,592	4.2	New York	34,938	36,816	5.4
Delaware	29,123	30,711	5.5	North Carolina	24,403	25,410	4.1
District of Columbia	42,453	44,458	4.7	North Dakota	20,492	21,242	3.7
Florida	24,709	25,641	3.8	Ohio	26,868	27,776	3.4
Georgia	26,308	27,492	4.5	Oklahoma	22,671	23,329	2.9
Hawaii	26,977	27,363	1.4	Oregon	25,833	27,028	4.6
Idaho	22,839	23,353	2.3	Pennsylvania	27,904	28,973	3.8
Illinois	30,101	31,296	4.0	Rhode Island	26,375	27,194	3.1
Indiana	25,571	26,477	3.5	South Carolina	23,292	24,049	3.3
Iowa	22,875	23,679	3.5	South Dakota	19,931	20,724	4.0
Kansas	23,709	24,609	3.8	Tennessee	25,046	25,963	3.7
Kentucky	23,502	24,463	4.1	Texas	26,899	28,129	4.6
Louisiana	23,895	24,541	2.7	Utah	23,626	24,572	4.0
Maine	23,125	23,850	3.1	Vermont	23,583	24,480	3.8
Maryland	29,143	30,295	4.0	Virginia	26,899	28,003	4.1
Massachusetts	32,352	33,937	4.9	Washington	27,453	28,881	5.2
Michigan	30,545	31,522	3.2	West Virginia	23,488	24,075	2.5
Minnesota	27,363	28,866	5.5	Wisconsin	25,099	26,021	3.7
Mississippi	21,120	21,822	3.3	Wyoming	22,351	22,870	2.3

[1] Revised since originally published.

Source: U.S. Bureau of Labor Statistics, *News* USDL 97-315, September 11, 1997, *Average Annual Pay by State and Industry.*

No. 695. Average Annual Pay, by Selected Metropolitan Areas: 1995 and 1996

[In dollars. Metropolitan areas ranked by average pay 1996. Includes data for Metropolitan Statistical Areas and Primary Metropolitan Statistical Areas defined as of June 30, 1995. In the New England areas, the New England County Metropolitan Area (NECMA) definitions were used. See source for details. See also headnote, Table 694]

METROPOLITAN AREA	1995	1996 [1]	METROPOLITAN AREA	1995	1996 [1]
Metropolitan areas	29,099	30,250	Brazoria, TX	29,892	30,781
New York, NY	42,272	45,028	Rochester, MN	29,107	30,662
San Jose, CA	42,409	44,824	Dutchess County, NY	29,707	30,546
San Francisco, CA	37,975	40,015	Rochester, NY	29,301	30,241
Middlesex-Somerset-Hunterdon, NJ . .	37,925	39,631	Bloomington-Normal, IL	29,023	29,969
New Haven-Bridgeport-Stamford-			Baltimore, MD	28,733	29,953
Waterbury-Danbury, CT	37,546	39,496	Portland-Vancouver, OR-WA	28,358	29,940
Newark, NJ	37,224	38,886	Monmouth-Ocean, NJ	29,033	29,920
Trenton, NJ	36,614	37,598	Cleveland-Lorain-Elyria, OH	28,742	29,706
Bergen-Passaic, NJ.	35,746	36,840	Springfield, IL.	28,615	29,703
Jersey City, NJ	34,621	36,833	Sacramento, CA	29,289	29,565
Washington, DC-MD-VA-WV.	34,910	36,385	St. Louis, MO-IL	28,599	29,471
Detroit, MI	34,710	35,748	Charlotte-Gastonia-Rock Hill, NC-SC .	27,859	29,290
Hartford, CT.	33,948	34,842	Lansing-East Lansing, MI	28,149	29,245
Kokomo, IN	33,967	34,779	Indianapolis, IN	28,081	29,137
Oakland, CA	33,180	34,428	Raleigh-Durham-Chapel Hill, NC . . .	27,925	29,098
Boston-Worcester-Lawrence-Lowell-			Milwaukee-Waukesha, WI	27,926	29,079
Brockton, MA-NH	32,798	34,382	Pittsburgh, PA	28,051	29,069
Chicago, IL	32,523	33,921	Yolo, CA	28,616	29,067
Seattle-Bellevue-Everett, WA	31,550	33,589	West Palm Beach-Boca Raton, FL. . .	27,912	29,057
Anchorage, AK.	33,650	33,501	Cincinnati, OH-KY-IN	28,057	29,043
Los Angeles-Long Beach, CA	32,445	33,476	San Diego, CA	27,842	28,845
Flint, MI	33,389	33,294	Kansas City, MO-KS	27,597	28,773
Wilmington-Newark, DE-MD	31,439	33,221	Allentown-Bethlehem-Easton, PA. . . .	27,804	28,771
Philadelphia, PA-NJ.	31,695	33,080	Albany-Schenectady-Troy, NY	27,694	28,719
Dallas, TX	31,500	32,996	Richmond-Petersburg, VA	27,598	28,714
Houston, TX	31,390	32,895	Austin-San Marcos, TX	26,922	28,707
Nassau-Suffolk, NY.	31,635	32,883	Dayton-Springfield, OH	27,676	28,665
Orange County, CA	30,904	32,179	Kalamazoo-Battle Creek, MI	27,259	28,611
New London-Norwich, CT.	30,892	32,003	Birmingham, AL	27,337	28,520
Minneapolis-St. Paul, MN-WI	30,170	31,935	Fort Worth-Arlington, TX	27,454	28,511
Denver, CO	30,059	31,627	Gary, IN	27,498	28,504
Huntsville, AL.	31,233	31,473	Grand Rapids-Muskegon-Holland, MI .	27,298	28,485
Atlanta, GA	29,959	31,358	Decatur, IL	27,339	28,424
Saginaw-Bay City-Midland, MI.	29,863	31,135	Miami, FL	27,453	28,382
Ann Arbor, MI.	30,013	31,027	Honolulu, HI.	27,936	28,336
Boulder-Longmont, CO	28,441	30,968	Ventura, CA.	27,262	28,289

[1] Revised since originally published.

Source: U.S. Bureau of Labor Statistics, *News* USDL 97-379, October 30, 1997 *Average Annual Pay Levels in Metropolitan Areas.*

No. 696. Full-Time Wage and Salary Workers—Number and Earnings: 1985 to 1997

[In current dollars of usual weekly earnings. Data represent annual averages of quarterly data. See text, Section 13, Labor Force, and headnote Table 661, for a discussion of occupational data. Based on Current Population Survey; see text, Section 1, Population, and Appendix III. For definition of median, see Guide to Tabular Presentation]

CHARACTERISTIC	NUMBER OF WORKERS (1,000)				MEDIAN WEEKLY EARNINGS (dol.)			
	1985	1990 [1]	1995 [1]	1997 [1]	1985	1990 [1]	1995 [1]	1997 [1]
All workers [2]	77,002	85,804	89,282	93,578	343	412	479	503
Male	45,589	49,564	51,222	53,220	406	481	538	579
16 to 24 years old	6,956	6,824	6,118	6,174	240	282	303	317
25 years old and over	38,632	42,740	45,104	47,046	442	512	588	615
Female	31,414	36,239	38,060	40,358	277	346	406	431
16 to 24 years old	5,621	5,227	4,366	4,522	210	254	275	292
25 years old and over	25,793	31,012	33,695	35,836	296	369	428	462
White	66,481	72,811	74,874	77,973	355	424	494	519
Male	40,030	42,797	43,747	45,349	417	494	566	595
Female	26,452	30,014	31,127	32,624	281	353	415	444
Black	8,393	9,820	10,596	11,356	277	329	383	400
Male	4,367	4,983	5,279	5,517	304	361	411	432
Female	4,026	4,837	5,317	5,839	252	308	355	375
Hispanic origin [3]	(NA)	7,812	8,719	9,996	(NA)	304	329	351
Male	(NA)	5,000	5,597	6,456	(NA)	318	350	371
Female	(NA)	2,812	3,122	3,540	(NA)	278	305	318
Occupation, male:								
Managerial and professional	11,078	12,255	13,684	14,359	583	729	829	875
Exec., admin., managerial	5,835	6,389	7,172	7,466	593	740	833	868
Professional specialty	5,243	5,866	6,512	6,894	571	719	827	883
Technical, sales, and administrative support	8,803	9,677	9,894	10,239	420	493	556	588
Tech. and related support	1,563	1,762	1,688	1,803	472	567	641	667
Sales	4,227	4,692	5,000	5,174	431	502	579	603
Admin. support, incl. clerical	3,013	3,224	3,206	3,262	391	436	489	514
Service	3,947	4,602	4,779	5,071	272	317	357	372
Private household	13	12	15	24	(B)	(B)	(B)	(B)
Protective	1,327	1,531	1,691	1,654	391	477	552	575
Other service	2,607	3,059	3,073	3,393	230	271	300	317
Precision production [4]	10,026	10,259	10,046	10,511	408	486	534	569
Mechanics and repairers	3,752	3,687	3,658	3,860	400	475	538	581
Construction trades	3,308	3,650	3,541	3,813	394	478	507	538
Other	2,966	2,922	2,847	2,838	433	508	574	588
Operators, fabricators and laborers	10,585	11,464	11,529	11,709	325	375	413	436
Machine operators, assemblers, and inspectors	4,403	4,594	4,576	4,610	341	387	421	449
Transportation and material moving	3,459	3,752	3,870	4,033	369	416	482	505
Handlers, equipment cleaners, helpers, and laborers	2,724	3,118	3,083	3,065	261	306	328	343
Farming, forestry, and fishing	1,150	1,306	1,290	1,331	216	261	294	302
Occupation, female:								
Managerial and professional	8,302	10,575	12,609	13,893	399	510	605	632
Exec., admin., managerial	3,492	4,758	5,803	6,500	383	484	570	605
Professional specialty	4,810	5,816	6,806	7,393	408	534	632	662
Technical, sales, and administrative support	14,622	16,290	16,004	16,552	269	331	383	403
Tech. and related support	1,200	1,476	1,506	1,691	331	417	480	498
Sales	2,929	3,554	3,862	4,231	226	290	330	352
Admin. support, incl. clerical	10,494	11,260	10,636	10,630	270	332	384	403
Service	3,963	4,577	4,838	5,101	185	230	264	282
Private household	330	305	324	324	130	171	193	213
Protective	156	217	266	308	278	405	438	451
Other service	3,477	4,055	4,249	4,469	188	230	264	280
Precision production [4]	906	900	957	984	268	316	371	382
Mechanics and repairers	144	139	150	160	392	458	550	489
Construction trades	53	50	66	65	265	393	400	445
Other	709	711	741	760	253	299	346	362
Operators, fabricators and laborers	3,482	3,722	3,462	3,630	216	261	297	313
Machine operators, assemblers, and inspectors	2,778	2,878	2,559	2,625	216	259	296	313
Transportation and material moving	189	227	261	292	252	314	354	373
Handlers, equipment cleaners, helpers and laborers	514	616	642	713	209	249	284	299
Farming, forestry, and fishing	138	175	190	198	185	216	249	257

B Data not shown where base is less than 50,000.　NA Not available.　[1] See footnote 2, Table 644.　[2] Includes other races, not shown separately.　[3] Persons of Hispanic origin may be of any race.　[4] Includes craft and repair.

Source: U.S. Bureau of Labor Statistics, Bulletin 2307, and Employment and Earnings, monthly, January issues; and unpublished data.

No. 697. Workers With Earnings, by Occupation of Longest Held Job and Sex: 1996

[Covers persons 15 years old and over as of **March 1997**. Based on Current Population Survey; see text, Section 1, Population, and Appendix III. For definition of median, see Guide to Tabular Presentation]

MAJOR OCCUPATION OF LONGEST JOB HELD	ALL WORKERS				YEAR ROUND, FULL TIME			
	Women		Men		Women		Men	
	Number (1,000)	Median earnings	Number (1,000)	Median earnings	Number (1,000)	Median earnings	Number (1,000)	Median earnings
Total [1]	**66,661**	**16,028**	**76,121**	**25,785**	**36,430**	**23,710**	**53,787**	**32,144**
Executive, administrators, and managerial	8,493	27,369	10,396	42,681	6,480	31,208	9,066	46,654
Professional specialty	10,821	27,721	9,118	42,309	6,230	34,537	7,085	50,012
Technical and related support	2,404	24,011	2,056	32,608	1,569	27,239	1,638	36,775
Sales	9,326	10,112	8,324	27,493	3,988	21,350	5,997	35,104
Admin. support, incl. clerical	15,663	17,029	4,294	22,450	9,435	21,758	2,875	30,381
Precision production, craft and repair	1,345	16,640	13,993	26,296	851	21,165	10,278	30,421
Machine operators, assemblers, and inspectors	3,499	13,243	5,327	22,096	2,139	17,456	4,032	25,625
Transportation and material moving	577	12,740	5,234	23,692	235	17,681	3,634	27,723
Handlers, equipment cleaners, helpers, and laborers	1,205	9,050	5,055	10,908	448	16,856	2,231	20,793
Service workers	12,545	7,756	8,340	12,569	4,754	14,976	4,654	21,028
Private household	900	4,428	34	(B)	257	11,365	9	(B)
Service, except private household	11,645	8,122	8,305	12,612	4,497	15,225	4,645	21,036
Farming, forestry, and fishing	707	5,332	3,284	11,355	233	17,251	1,672	18,127

B Base less than 75,000.   [1] Includes persons whose longest job was in the Armed Forces.

Source: U.S. Bureau of the Census, *Current Population Reports* P60-197.

No. 698. Employment Cost Index (ECI), by Industry and Occupation: 1982 to 1997

[As of **December.** The ECI is a measure of the rate of change in employee compensation (wages, salaries, and employer costs for employee benefits). Data are not seasonally adjusted: 1982-85 based on fixed employment counts from 1970 Census of Population; 1986-94 based on fixed employment counts from the 1980 Census of Population; Beginning 1995 based primarily on 1990 Occupational Employment Survey]

ITEM	INDEXES (June 1989=100)						PERCENT CHANGE FOR 12 MONTHS ENDING DEC.—				
	1982	1985	1990	1995	1996	1997	1985	1990	1995	1996	1997
Civilian workers [1]	**74.8**	**86.8**	**107.6**	**127.2**	**130.9**	**135.2**	**4.3**	**4.9**	**2.7**	**2.9**	**3.3**
Workers, by occupational group:											
White-collar occupations	72.9	85.8	108.3	128.0	131.9	136.5	4.9	5.2	2.9	3.0	3.5
Blue-collar occupations	78.2	88.4	106.5	125.8	129.1	132.4	3.3	4.4	2.5	2.6	2.6
Service occupations	74.3	87.2	108.0	127.4	131.0	135.6	3.9	5.1	2.5	2.8	3.5
Workers, by industry division:											
Manufacturing	76.9	87.8	107.2	128.3	132.1	135.3	3.3	5.1	2.6	3.0	2.4
Nonmanufacturing	73.9	86.4	107.8	126.8	130.5	135.1	4.7	4.9	2.8	2.9	3.5
Service industries	70.5	84.1	110.2	129.4	133.2	137.6	4.7	6.3	2.4	2.9	3.3
Public administration [2]	71.9	85.4	108.7	128.3	131.8	135.1	4.9	5.3	3.3	2.7	2.5
Private industry workers [3]	**75.8**	**87.3**	**107.0**	**126.7**	**130.6**	**135.1**	**3.9**	**4.6**	**2.6**	**3.1**	**3.4**
Workers, by occupational group:											
White-collar occupations	73.7	86.4	107.4	127.6	131.7	136.7	4.9	4.9	2.8	3.2	3.8
Blue-collar occupations	78.4	88.5	106.4	125.6	129.0	132.3	3.1	4.4	2.4	2.7	2.6
Service occupations	76.3	88.4	107.3	125.2	128.9	134.1	3.0	4.7	1.9	3.0	4.0
Workers, by industry division:											
Manufacturing	76.9	87.8	107.2	128.3	132.1	135.3	3.3	5.1	2.6	3.0	2.4
Nonmanufacturing	75.1	87.0	106.9	125.9	129.8	134.7	4.3	4.5	2.7	3.1	3.8
Service industries	(NA)	84.1	109.3	129.4	133.4	138.5	(NA)	6.2	2.2	3.1	3.8
Business services	(NA)	(NA)	107.4	126.3	131.8	138.6	(NA)	6.0	2.7	4.4	5.2
Health services	(NA)	83.7	110.8	132.2	134.5	138.1	(NA)	6.8	2.7	1.7	2.7
Hospitals	(NA)	(NA)	110.7	131.3	133.7	136.5	(NA)	7.0	2.1	1.8	2.1
Workers by bargaining status:											
Union	79.6	90.1	106.2	127.7	130.8	133.5	2.6	4.3	2.8	2.4	2.1
Nonunion	74.3	86.3	107.3	126.5	130.4	135.3	4.6	4.8	2.7	3.1	3.8
State and local government	**70.8**	**84.6**	**110.4**	**129.3**	**132.7**	**135.7**	**5.6**	**5.8**	**2.9**	**2.6**	**2.3**
Workers, by occupational group:											
White-collar occupations	70.4	84.2	110.9	129.1	132.5	135.5	5.8	6.0	2.9	2.6	2.3
Blue-collar workers	73.9	86.7	108.7	128.0	131.2	134.2	5.3	4.8	2.6	2.5	2.3
Workers, by industry division:											
Service industries	70.0	84.0	111.3	129.6	133.1	136.0	5.9	6.3	2.8	2.7	2.2
Schools	69.0	83.6	111.6	129.8	133.4	136.2	6.2	6.0	2.8	2.8	2.1
Elementary and secondary	68.6	83.6	112.1	130.1	133.1	135.8	6.4	6.3	2.8	2.3	2.0
Colleges and universities	(NA)	(NA)	110.2	128.7	134.0	137.2	(NA)	5.3	2.5	4.1	2.4
Services, excluding schools [4]	73.1	85.2	110.2	129.4	132.0	135.3	4.7	6.8	3.0	2.0	2.5
Public administration [2]	71.9	85.4	108.7	128.3	131.8	135.1	4.9	5.3	3.3	2.7	2.5

NA Not available.   [1] Includes private industry and state and local government workers and excludes farm, household, and federal government workers.   [2] Consists of legislative, judicial, administrative, and regulatory activities.   [3] Excludes farm and household workers.   [4] Includes library, social, and health services. Formerly called hospitals and other services.

Source: U.S. Bureau of Labor Statistics, *News, Employment Cost Index,* quarterly; and Internet site <http://stats.bls.gov/ecthome.htm>

No. 699. Federal Minimum Wage Rates: 1955 to 1996

YEAR	VALUE OF THE MINIMUM WAGE [1]		YEAR	VALUE OF THE MINIMUM WAGE [1]	
	Current dollars	Constant (1996) dollars [2]		Current dollars	Constant (1996) dollars [2]
1955	0.75	4.39	1976	2.30	6.34
1956	1.00	5.77	1977	2.30	5.95
1957	1.00	5.58	1978	2.65	6.38
1958	1.00	5.43	1979	2.90	6.27
1959	1.00	5.39	1980	3.10	5.90
1960	1.00	5.30	1981	3.35	5.78
1961	1.15	6.03	1982	3.35	5.45
1962	1.15	5.97	1983	3.35	5.28
1963	1.25	6.41	1984	3.35	5.06
1964	1.25	6.33	1985	3.35	4.88
1965	1.25	6.23	1986	3.35	4.80
1966	1.25	6.05	1987	3.35	4.63
1967	1.40	6.58	1988	3.35	4.44
1968	1.60	7.21	1989	3.35	4.24
1969	1.60	6.84	1990	3.80	4.56
1970	1.60	6.47	1991	4.25	4.90
1971	1.60	6.20	1992	4.25	4.75
1972	1.60	6.01	1993	4.25	4.61
1973	1.60	5.65	1994	4.25	4.50
1974	2.00	6.37	1995	4.25	4.38
1975	2.10	6.12	1996	4.75	4.75

[1] Effective September 1, 1997 the federal minimum wage rose to $5.15; $5.03 in constant 1996 dollars. [2] Adjusted for inflation using the CPI-U; see text, Section 15, Prices.

Source: U.S. Employment Standards Administration, Internet site: <http://www.dol.gov/esa/public/minwage> (accessed 24 June 1998).

No. 700. Workers Paid Hourly Rates, by Selected Characteristics: 1997

[Data are for the fourth quarter of 1997, not seasonally adjusted. For employed wage and salary workers. Based on Current Population Survey; see text, Section 1, and Appendix III]

CHARACTERISTIC	NUMBER OF WORKERS [1] (1,000)				PERCENT OF ALL WORKERS PAID HOURLY RATES			Median hourly earnings of workers paid hourly rates [2]
	Total paid hourly rates	At or below $5.15			At or below $5.15			
		Total	At $5.15	Below $5.15	Total	At $5.15	Below $5.15	
Total, 16 years and over [3]	71,081	6,237	2,115	4,122	8.8	3.0	5.8	$8.84
16 to 24 years	15,793	3,225	1,145	2,080	20.4	7.3	13.2	6.22
16 to 19 years	5,973	1,838	654	1,184	30.8	10.9	19.8	5.64
25 years and over	55,287	3,013	970	2,043	5.4	1.8	3.7	9.91
Male, 16 years and over	35,326	2,390	755	1,635	6.8	2.1	4.6	9.89
16 to 24 years	8,107	1,450	520	930	17.9	6.4	11.5	6.61
16 to 19 years	3,021	895	334	561	29.6	11.1	18.6	5.70
25 years and over	27,219	940	235	705	3.5	0.9	2.6	11.16
Women, 16 years and over	35,755	3,846	1,359	2,487	10.8	3.8	7.0	8.02
16 to 24 years	7,687	1,774	624	1,150	23.1	8.1	15.0	6.03
16 to 19 years	2,952	943	320	623	31.9	10.8	21.1	5.59
25 years and over	28,068	2,073	735	1,338	7.4	2.6	4.8	8.83
White	58,395	4,863	1,632	3,231	8.3	2.8	5.5	8.97
Black	9,562	1,116	423	693	11.7	4.4	7.2	8.06
Hispanic origin [4]	8,765	984	388	596	11.2	4.4	6.8	7.61
Full-time workers	53,422	2,510	841	1,669	4.7	1.6	3.1	9.82
Part-time workers [5]	17,529	3,714	1,272	2,442	21.2	7.3	13.9	6.24
Private sector industries	62,889	5,812	1,991	3,821	9.2	3.2	6.1	8.60
Goods-producing [6]	19,243	741	257	484	3.9	1.3	2.5	10.15
Service-producing [7]	43,646	5,071	1,734	3,337	10.9	3.7	7.2	7.92
Public sector	8,192	425	124	301	5.2	1.5	3.7	10.88

[1] Excludes the incorporated self-employed. [2] For definition of median, see Guide to Tabular Presentation. [3] Includes races not shown separately. Also includes a small number of multiple jobholders whose full- part- time status can not be determined for their principal job. [4] Persons of Hispanic origin may be of any race. [5] Working fewer than 35 hours per week. [6] Includes agriculture, mining, construction, and manufacturing. [7] Includes transportation and public utilities; wholesale trade; finance, insurance, and real estate; private households; and other service industries.

Source: U.S. Bureau of Labor Statistics, unpublished data.

No. 701. Employer Costs for Employee Compensation per Hour Worked: 1997

[In dollars. As of March, for private industry workers. Based on a sample of establishments; see source for details]

COMPENSATION COMPONENT	Total	Goods produc- ing [1]	Service produc- ing [2]	Manufac- turing	Non- manufac- turing	Union mem- bers	Non- union mem- bers	Full- time workers	Part- time workers
Total compensation . . .	**17.97**	**21.86**	**16.73**	**21.84**	**17.10**	**23.48**	**17.21**	**20.37**	**9.60**
Wages and salaries	13.04	14.92	12.44	14.79	12.64	15.13	12.75	14.55	7.75
Total benefits.	4.94	6.94	4.29	7.05	4.46	8.34	4.46	5.82	1.85
Paid leave	1.14	1.45	1.04	1.66	1.02	1.56	1.08	1.38	0.27
Vacation.	0.57	0.76	0.50	0.85	0.50	0.86	0.53	(NA)	(NA)
Holiday	0.39	0.53	0.35	0.61	0.34	0.49	0.38	(NA)	(NA)
Sick	0.13	0.11	0.14	0.12	0.13	0.14	0.13	(NA)	(NA)
Other	0.05	0.05	0.05	0.09	0.04	0.06	0.05	(NA)	(NA)
Supplemental pay	0.51	0.82	0.42	0.88	0.43	0.91	0.46	0.62	0.14
Premium pay	0.21	0.45	0.13	0.45	0.15	0.59	0.15	(NA)	(NA)
Nonproduction bonuses .	0.26	0.30	0.25	0.33	0.24	0.19	0.27	(NA)	(NA)
Shift pay	0.05	0.07	0.04	0.09	0.04	0.13	0.04	(NA)	(NA)
Insurance	1.09	1.64	0.92	1.70	0.95	2.19	0.94	1.33	0.25
Health insurance	0.99	1.49	0.83	1.55	0.86	2.01	0.85	(NA)	(NA)
Retirement and savings . . .	0.55	0.85	0.45	0.79	0.49	1.33	0.44	0.66	0.13
Defined benefit	0.26	0.49	0.19	0.44	0.22	1.06	0.15	(NA)	(NA)
Defined contributions . . .	0.29	0.36	0.26	0.35	0.27	0.26	0.29	(NA)	(NA)
Legally required [3]	1.62	2.11	1.46	1.94	1.55	2.27	1.53	1.79	1.04
Social Security	1.08	1.27	1.03	1.27	1.04	1.30	1.05	(NA)	(NA)
Federal unemployment . .	0.03	0.03	0.03	0.03	0.03	0.03	0.03	(NA)	(NA)
State unemployment . . .	0.12	0.14	0.11	0.13	0.11	0.15	0.11	(NA)	(NA)
Workers compensation . .	0.39	0.68	0.30	0.51	0.36	0.79	0.34	(NA)	(NA)
Other benefits [4]	0.03	0.07	-	0.08	-	0.08	0.02	0.03	-

- Represents or rounds to zero. NA Not available. [1] Mining, construction, and manufacturing. [2] Transportation, communications, and public utilities, wholesale and retail trade, finance, insurance, and real estate, and services. [3] Includes railroad retirement, railroad unemployment, railroad supplemental unemployment, and other legally required benefits, not shown separately. [4] Includes severance pay, and supplemental unemployment benefits.

Source: U.S. Bureau of Labor Statistics, *News, Employer Costs for Employee Compensation*, USDL, 97-371.

No. 702. Employees With Employer- or Union-Provided Pension Plans or Group Health Plans: 1996

[For wage and salary workers 15 years old and over as of March 1997. Based on Current Population Survey; see text, Section 1, and Appendix III. Data based on 1990 population controls]

OCCUPATION	Total (1,000)	PERCENT— Included in pen- sion plan	PERCENT— With group health plan	CHARACTERISTIC	Total (1,000)	PERCENT— Included in pen- sion plan	PERCENT— With group health plan
Total	142,909	41.9	53.0	AGE			
Executive, admin., managerial . . .	18,898	55.0	67.9	Total.	142,909	41.9	53.0
Professional specialty	19,942	60.1	66.5	15 to 24 years	23,914	11.2	21.6
				25 to 44 years old	72,348	46.8	58.2
Technical/related support	4,460	57.7	67.0	45 to 64 years	41,677	53.4	63.3
Sales workers	17,665	29.9	43.0	65 years and over	4,970	22.5	41.2
Admin. support, inc. clerical	19,995	47.6	57.6	WORK EXPERIENCE			
				Worked.	142,909	41.9	53.0
Precision prod., craft/repair	15,351	42.8	57.0	Full time	112,387	50.0	62.4
				50 weeks or more	90,257	55.6	68.2
Mach. operators, assemblers [1] . . .	8,826	43.4	60.3	27 to 49 weeks	12,998	35.2	48.7
Transportation/material moving. . .	5,812	41.1	57.1	26 weeks or fewer	9,132	16.2	24.6
Handlers, equipment cleaners [2] . .	6,270	26.6	36.9	Part time	30,521	12.2	18.3
				50 weeks or more	13,465	17.4	23.7
Service workers	20,901	22.7	32.0	27 to 49 weeks	6,694	12.7	18.1
Private households	935	1.4	7.4	26 weeks or fewer	10,362	5.1	11.3
Other	19,967	23.7	33.2	EMPLOYER SIZE			
				Under 25 persons	42,985	13.7	28.1
Farming, forestry and fishing	4,014	9.5	22.3	25 to 99 persons.	18,139	35.4	53.7
				100 to 499 persons	19,504	50.4	62.9
Armed Forces	775	74.6	30.7	500 to 999 persons	8,059	56.6	65.8
				Over 1,000 persons	54,222	61.3	67.0

[1] Includes inspectors. [2] Includes helpers and laborers.

Source: U.S. Bureau of the Census, unpublished data.

No. 703. Employee Benefits in Medium and Large Firms: 1995

[In percent. Covers full-time employees in private industry. Medium and large establishments exclude establishments with fewer than 100 workers. Covers only benefits for which the employer pays part or all of the premium or expenses involved, except unpaid family leave. Based on a sample survey of establishments; for details, see sources. For data on employee benefits in state and local governments and in small establishments, see Tables 533 and 704]

EMPLOYEE BENEFIT PROGRAM	All employees	Professional, technical and related	Clerical and sales	Blue collar and service	EMPLOYEE BENEFIT PROGRAM	All employees	Professional, technical and related	Clerical and sales	Blue collar and service
Paid time off:					With no employer contribution	9	13	8	7
Holidays	89	88	93	88	Income contribution plans:				
Vacations	96	97	99	94	Severance pay	35	47	43	24
Personal leave	22	24	34	15	Supplemental unemployment benefits	4	1	1	6
Funeral leave	80	83	85	75					
Jury duty leave	85	91	89	79	Family benefits:				
Military leave	44	59	45	35	Employer assistance for child care	8	15	7	3
Sick leave	58	74	78	39	Employer provided funds	4	7	4	2
Family leave	2	3	2	1	On-site child care	3	8	2	1
					Off-site child care	1	2	1	(Z)
Unpaid family leave	84	89	86	80					
Insurance:					Health promotion programs:				
Short-term disability	53	48	52	57	Wellness programs	34	47	32	27
Long-term disability	42	60	53	26	Employee assistance programs	58	72	60	49
Medical care	77	80	76	75	Fitness center	19	31	16	13
Fee-for-service [1]	37	29	30	45					
HMO [1]	27	33	32	21	Miscellaneous benefits:				
PPO [1]	34	36	36	33	Job-related travel accident insurance	41	58	47	28
Exclusive provider [1]	1	1	2	1	Nonproduction bonuses	39	40	37	38
Dental care	57	66	57	51	Subsidized commuting	5	8	5	3
Life insurance	87	93	89	83	Educational assistance:				
Retirement	80	87	85	73	Job-related	65	79	65	56
Defined benefit	52	53	55	50	Non-job related	18	25	17	15
Defined contribution	55	67	64	45					
401(k) plans:									
With employer contribution	45	55	50	37					

Z Less than 0.5 percent.   [1] Percent of participants receiving medical care insurance.
Source: U.S. Bureau of Labor Statistics, News, USDL 97-246, July 25, 1997.

No. 704. Employee Benefits in Small Firms: 1996

[In percent. Covers full-time employees in private industry. Small establishments are establishments with fewer than 100 workers. Covers only benefits for which the employer pays part or all of the premium or expenses involved, except certain tax deferred earnings arrangements. Based on a sample survey of establishments; for details, see sources. For data on employee benefits in state and local governments and in large establishments, see Tables 533 and 703]

EMPLOYEE BENEFIT PROGRAM	All employees	Professional, technical and related	Clerical and sales	Blue collar and service	EMPLOYEE BENEFIT PROGRAM	All employees	Professional, technical and related	Clerical and sales	Blue collar and service
Paid time off:					Income contribution plans:				
Holidays	80	86	91	71	Severance pay	15	23	19	9
Vacations	86	90	95	79	Supplemental unemployment benefits	(Z)	(Z)	(Z)	(Z)
Personal leave	14	21	18	8					
Funeral leave	51	60	60	42	Family benefits:				
Jury duty leave	59	74	68	47	Employer assistance for child care	2	4	2	(Z)
Military leave	18	25	23	12	Employer provided funds	1	2	2	(Z)
Sick leave	50	66	64	35	On-site child care	1	2	(Z)	(Z)
Family leave	2	3	3	1	Off-site child care	1	2	(Z)	(Z)
Insurance:									
Short-term disability	29	32	33	25	Health promotion programs:				
Long-term disability	22	39	30	10	Wellness programs	8	11	9	5
Medical care	64	76	69	56	Employee assistance programs	14	18	19	10
Fee-for-service [1]	36	31	34	41	Fitness center	4	6	5	3
HMO [1]	27	27	28	25					
PPO [1]	35	41	36	32	Miscellaneous benefits:				
Dental care	31	40	35	24	Job-related travel accident insurance	12	17	16	7
Life insurance	62	72	68	54	Nonproduction bonuses	44	44	46	43
Retirement	46	56	53	37	Subsidized commuting	1	3	2	1
Defined benefit	15	12	16	15	Educational assistance:				
Defined contribution	38	51	46	28	Job-related	38	56	45	27
Tax deferred earnings arrangements:					Non-job related	5	6	6	4
With employer contribution	24	30	31	17					
With no employer contribution	4	8	4	3					

Z Less than 0.5 percent.   [1] Percent of participants receiving medical care insurance.
Source: U.S. Bureau of Labor Statistics, News, USDL 98-240, June 15, 1998.

No. 705. Workers Killed or Disabled on the Job: 1960 to 1996

[Data for 1996 are preliminary estimates. Excludes homicides and suicides. Estimates based on data from the U.S. National Center for Health Statistics, state vital statistics departments, state industrial commissions and beginning 1992, Bureau of Labor Statisitcs, Census of Occupational Fatalities. Numbers of workers based on data from the U.S. Bureau of Labor Statistics]

YEAR	DEATHS						Dis-abling injur-ies [2] (mil.)	YEAR AND INDUSTRY GROUP	DEATHS		Dis-abling injur-ies [2] (1,000)
	Total		Manufacturing		Nonmanu-facturing						
	Num-ber (1,000)	Rate [1]	Num-ber (1,000)	Rate [1]	Num-ber (1,000)	Rate [1]			Num-ber	Rate [1]	
1960 ...	13.8	21	1.7	10	12.1	25	2.0	Total, 1996 [3]	4,800	4	3,900
1965 ...	14.1	20	1.8	10	12.3	24	2.1	Agriculture [4].........	710	21	150
1970 ...	13.8	18	1.7	9	12.1	21	2.2	Mining and quarrying [5]..	150	25	20
1975 ...	13.0	15	1.6	9	11.4	17	2.2	Construction.........	1,000	15	350
1980 ...	13.2	13	1.7	8	11.5	15	2.2	Manufacturing.........	610	3	610
1985 ...	11.5	11	1.2	6	10.3	12	2.0	Transportation and			
1986 ...	11.1	10	1.0	5	10.1	11	1.8	utilities.............	750	12	310
1987 ...	11.3	10	1.0	5	10.3	11	1.8	Trade [6]..........	460	2	880
1988 ...	11.0	10	1.1	6	9.9	10	1.8	Services [7].........	610	1	1,000
1989 ...	10.9	9	1.1	6	9.8	10	1.7	Government.........	510	3	580
1990 ...	10.1	9	1.0	5	9.1	9	3.9				
1991 ...	9.8	8	0.8	4	9.0	9	3.5				
1992 ...	5.0	4	0.7	4	4.3	4	3.3				
1993 ...	5.0	4	0.7	4	4.3	4	3.2				
1994 ...	5.3	4	0.7	4	4.3	4	3.5				
1995 ...	5.0	4	0.6	4	4.3	4	3.6				
1996 ...	4.8	4	0.6	3	4.2	4	3.9				

[1] Per 100,000 workers.   [2] Disabling injury defined as one which results in death, some degree of physical impairment, or renders the person unable to perform regular activities for a full day beyond the day of the injury. Due to change in methodology, data beginning 1990 not comparable with prior years.   [3] Includes deaths where industry is not known.   [4] Includes forestry and fishing.   [5] Includes oil and gas extraction.   [6] Includes wholesale and retail trade.   [7] Includes finance, insurance, and real estate.

Source: National Safety Council, Itasca, IL, *Accident Facts,* annual (copyright).

No. 706. Worker Deaths and Injuries and Production Time Lost: 1994 to 1996

ITEM	DEATHS (1,000)			DISABLING INJURIES [1] (mil.)			PRODUCTION TIME LOST (mil. days)					
							In the current year			In future years [2]		
	1994	1995	1996	1994	1995	1996	1994	1995	1996	1994	1995	1996
All accidents	41.1	45.7	43.9	9.1	9.9	10.2	215	225	230	410	455	430
On the job	5.0	5.3	4.8	3.5	3.6	3.9	75	75	80	60	65	60
Off the job.............	36.1	40.4	39.1	5.6	6.3	6.3	140	150	150	350	390	370
Motor vehicle	19.6	22.9	22.2	0.9	1.2	1.3	(NA)	(NA)	(NA)	(NA)	(NA)	(NA)
Public nonmotor vehicle ...	7.6	7.5	7.4	2.4	2.3	2.4	(NA)	(NA)	(NA)	(NA)	(NA)	(NA)
Home	8.9	10.0	9.5	2.3	2.8	2.6	(NA)	(NA)	(NA)	(NA)	(NA)	(NA)

NA Not available.   [1] See footnote 2, Table 705 for a definition of disabling injuries.   [2] Based on an average of 5,850 days lost in future years per fatality and 565 days lost in future years per permanent injury.

Source: National Safety Council, Itasca, IL, *Accident Facts,* annual (copyright).

No. 707. Industries with the Highest Total Case Incidence Rates for Nonfatal Injuries and Illnesses: 1995 and 1996

[Rates per 100 full-time employees. Industries shown are those with highest rates in 1996. See headnote, Table 708]

INDUSTRY	1987 SIC [1] code	1995	1996	INDUSTRY	1987 SIC [1] code	1995	1996
Private industry	(X)	8.1	7.4	Aluminum die-castings...........	3363	23.1	19.9
Meat packing plants	2011	36.6	30.3	Motor homes	3716	14.3	19.8
Metal sanitary ware.............	3431	21.0	29.4	Travel trailers and campers	3792	22.7	19.7
Ship building and repairing........	3731	32.7	27.4	Truck trailers	3715	31.2	19.4
Steel foundries, n.e.c.	3325	26.4	26.4	Iron and steel forgings..........	3462	19.7	19.4
Mobile homes	2451	24.3	26.2	Air transportation, scheduled [3]	451	14.5	19.3
Motor vechicles and car bodies.....	3711	31.5	26.1	Knit underwear mills	2254	17.2	19.2
Gray and ductile iron foundries	3321	29.2	25.8	Leather tanning and finishing	311	18.5	19.1
Automotive stampings	3465	23.8	23.2	Prepared flour mixes and doughs ...	2045	18.2	18.6
Steel springs, except wire.........	3493	(NA)	22.7	Raw cane sugar................	2061	18.2	18.4
Secondary nonferrous metals	334	26.1	21.0	Poultry slaughtering and processing...	2015	18.3	17.8
Truck and bus bodies	3713	22.5	21.0	Distilled and blended liquors.......	2085	13.7	17.5
Public building and related furniture ..	253	19.4	20.6	Commercial laundry equipment.....	3582	(NA)	17.4
Structural wood members, n.e.c. [2]..	2439	21.0	20.5	Fabricated pipe and fittings.......	3498	12.9	17.2

NA Not available.   X Not applicable.   [1] 1987 Standard Industrial Classification; see text, Section 13.   [2] N.e.c. means not elsewhere classified.   [3] Due to reclassification of air courier operations into SIC 451, data for 1996 are not comparable with earlier years.

Source: U.S. Bureau of Labor Statistics, *Occupational Injuries and Illnesses in the United States by Industry,* annual.

No. 708. Nonfatal Occupational Injury and Illness Incidence Rates: 1995 and 1996

[Rates per 100 full-time employees. For nonfarm employment data, see table 687. Rates refer to any occupational injury or illness resulting in (1) lost workday cases, or (2) nonfatal cases without lost workdays. Incidence rates were calculated as: Number of injuries and illnesses divided by total hours worked by all employees during year multiplied by 200,000 as base for 100 full-time equivalent workers (working 40 hours per week, 50 weeks a year)]

INDUSTRY	1987 SIC [1] code	1995	1996	INDUSTRY	1987 SIC [1] code	1995	1996
Private sector [2]	(X)	8.1	7.4	Local passenger transit	41	10.3	10.3
Agriculture, forestry, fishing [2]	A	9.7	8.7	Trucking and warehousing [4]	42	13.8	10.4
Mining [3]	B	6.2	5.4	Water transportation	44	9.0	9.8
Metal mining [3]	10	5.2	5.0	Transportation by air [4]	45	13.7	17.9
Coal mining [3]	12	9.1	8.0	Pipelines, except natural gas	46	1.6	2.0
Oil and gas extraction	13	5.9	5.0	Transportation services [4]	47	4.5	3.5
Nonmetallic minerals, exc. fuels	14	5.4	4.8	Communications	48	3.3	3.5
Construction	C	10.6	9.9	Electric, gas, sanitary services	49	7.5	6.9
General building contractors	15	9.8	9.0	**Wholesale and retail trade**	F, G	7.5	6.8
Heavy construction, except building	16	9.9	9.0	Wholesale trade	F	7.5	6.6
Special trade contractors	17	11.1	10.4	Retail trade	G	7.5	6.9
Manufacturing	D	11.6	10.6	**Finance, insurance, real estate**	H	2.6	2.4
Durable goods	(X)	12.8	11.6	Depository institutions	60	2.2	1.8
Lumber and wood products	24	14.9	14.2	Nondepository institutions	61	1.3	1.1
Furniture and fixtures	25	13.9	12.2	Security and commodity brokers	62	0.8	0.6
Stone, clay, and glass products	32	12.3	12.4	Insurance carriers	63	2.3	2.1
Primary metal industries	33	16.5	15.0	Insurance agents, brokers, and service	64	1.2	1.4
Fabricated metal products	34	15.8	14.4	Real estate	65	5.7	5.4
Industrial machinery and equip.	35	11.2	9.9	Holding and other investment offices	67	2.6	2.8
Electronic/other electric equip.	36	7.6	6.8	**Services** [5]	I	6.4	6.0
Transportation equipment	37	18.6	16.3	Hotels and other lodging places	70	9.7	9.0
Instruments/related products	38	5.3	5.1	Personal services	72	4.1	3.8
Miscellaneous manufacturing industries	39	9.1	9.5	Business services	73	4.6	3.9
Nondurable goods	(X)	9.9	9.2	Auto repair, services, and parking	75	6.7	5.9
Food and kindred products	20	16.3	15.0	Miscellaneous repair services	76	8.1	6.3
Tobacco products	21	5.6	6.7	Motion pictures	78	3.3	(NA)
Textile mill products	22	8.2	7.8	Amusement and recreation services	79	9.5	9.5
Apparel and other textile products	23	8.2	7.4	Health services	80	9.2	9.1
Paper and allied products	26	8.5	7.9	Legal services	81	1.0	1.1
Printing and publishing	27	6.4	6.0	Educational services	82	3.9	3.4
Chemicals and allied products	28	5.5	4.8	Social services	83	7.6	7.2
Petroleum and coal products	29	4.8	4.6	Museums, botanical, zoological gardens	84	7.2	(NA)
Rubber and misc. plastics products	30	12.9	12.3	Engineering and management services	87	2.3	2.0
Leather and leather products	31	11.4	10.7	Services, n.e.c. [6]	89	2.4	(NA)
Transportation/public utilities [3][4]	E	9.1	8.7				
Railroad transportation [3]	40	4.2	3.5				

NA Not available.   X Not applicable.   [1] 1987 Standard Industrial Classification; see text, Section 13.   [2] Excludes farms with fewer than 11 employees.   [3] Data conforming to OSHA definitions for employers in the railroad industry and for mining operators in coal, metal, and nonmetal mining. Independent mining contractors are excluded from the coal, metal, and nonmetal mining industries.   [4] Due to reclassification of air courier operations into SIC 451, data for 1996 are not comparable with earlier years.   [5] Includes categories not shown separately.   [6] N.e.c means not elsewhere classified.

Source: U.S. Bureau of Labor Statistics, *Occupational Injuries and Illnesses in the United States by Industry*, annual.

No. 709. Fatal Work Injuries, by Cause: 1996

[For the 50 States and DC. Based on the 1996 Census of Fatal Occupational Injuries. Due to methodological differences, data differ from those in table 705. For details, see source]

CAUSE	Number of fatalities	Percent distribution	CAUSE	Number of fatalities	Percent distribution
Total	**6,112**	**100**	Contacts with objects and equipment [1]	1,005	16
			Struck by object [1]	579	9
Transportation accidents [1]	2,556	42	Struck by falling objects	402	7
Highway accidents [1]	1,324	22	Struck by flying object	58	1
Collision between vehicles, mobile equipment	656	11	Caught in or compressed by—		
Noncollision accidents	348	6	Equipment or objects	283	5
Nonhighway accident (farm, industrial premises)	369	6	Collapsing materials	130	2
Aircraft accidents	320	5	Falls	684	11
Workers struck by a vehicle	349	6	Exposure to harmful substances or		
Water vehicle accidents	107	2	environments [1]	523	9
Railway accidents	75	1	Contact with electric current	279	5
			Exposure to caustic, noxious or allergenic substances	119	2
Assaults and violent acts [1]	1,144	19	Oxygen deficiency	92	2
Homicides [1]	912	15	Drowning, submersion	67	1
Shooting	751	12			
Stabbing	79	1	Fires and explosions	184	3
Self-inflicted injury	199	3	Other events and exposures	16	(Z)

Z Less than 0.5 percent.   [1] Includes other causes, not shown separately.

Source: U.S. Bureau of Labor Statistics, *USDL News*, Bulletin 97-226, August 7, 1997.

No. 710. Fatal Occupational Injuries, by Industry and Event: 1996

[See headnote, Table 709]

INDUSTRY	1987 SIC [1] code	Fatal-ities [2]	EVENT OR EXPOSURE—PERCENT DISTRIBUTION					Rate [5]
			Trans-portation incidents	Assaults/ violent acts	Contact with objects [3]	Falls	Expo-sure [4]	
Total.	(X)	6,112	42	19	16	11	9	5
Private industry	(X)	5,521	40	19	17	12	9	5
Agriculture, forestry, fishing	A	798	47	9	24	9	10	22
Mining [6]	B	152	34	-	41	6	7	27
Coal mining.	12	39	23	-	69	-	-	40
Oil and gas extraction	13	82	37	-	27	7	12	27
Construction	C	1,039	25	2	21	32	16	14
General building contractors	15	183	17	3	21	45	12	-
Heavy construction, except building.	16	247	48	2	24	9	16	-
Special trade contractors	17	599	18	2	20	38	18	-
Manufacturing [6]	D	715	30	9	39	7	8	4
Food and kindred products.	20	70	31	10	26	11	14	4
Lumber and wood products	24	203	25	3	65	3	2	26
Transportation and public utilities [6] . . .	E	947	71	9	8	4	7	13
Local passenger transit	41	78	24	71	-	-	-	16
Trucking and warehousing	42	511	78	5	9	4	3	21
Transportation by air	45	113	97	-	-	-	-	15
Electric, gas, sanitary services	49	88	43	-	11	-	33	8
Wholesale trade	F	267	51	13	16	10	5	5
Retail trade [6].	G	672	21	68	4	3	2	3
Food stores.	54	173	9	86	2	2	-	5
Automotive dealer and service stations	55	98	39	44	8	-	-	5
Eating and drinking places	58	166	8	86	-	-	-	3
Finance, insurance, real estate.	H	114	33	45	4	11	7	2
Services [6].	I	767	41	29	8	10	8	2
Business services.	73	168	40	29	10	12	8	3
Auto repair, services, and parking	75	103	35	34	17	-	6	6
Government.	J	591	57	21	7	5	6	3

- No data reported or data do not meet publication standards.   X Not applicable.   [1] 1987 Standard Industrial Classification code, see text Section 13, Labor Force.   [2] Includes 50 fatalities for which there was insufficient information to determine industry classification. Includes fatalities caused by fires and explosions, not shown separately.   [3] Includes equipment.   [4] Exposure to harmful substances or environments.   [5] Rate per 100,000 employed civilians 16 years old and over.   [6] Includes other industries, not shown separately.

Source: U.S. Bureau of Labor Statistics, *USDL News*, 97-226, August 7, 1997; and unpublished data.

No. 711. Work Stoppages: 1960 to 1997

[Excludes work stoppages involving fewer than 1,000 workers and lasting less than 1 day. Information is based on reports of labor disputes appearing in daily newspapers, trade journals, and other public sources. The parties to the disputes are contacted by telephone, when necessary, to clarify details of the stoppages]

YEAR	Number of work stop-pages [1]	Workers involved [2] (1,000)	DAYS IDLE		YEAR	Number of work stop-pages [1]	Workers involved [2] (1,000)	DAYS IDLE	
			Number [3] (1,000)	Percent esti-mated working time [4]				Number [3] (1,000)	Percent esti-mated working time [4]
1960.	222	896	13,260	0.09	1982.	96	656	9,061	0.04
1965.	268	999	15,140	0.10	1983.	81	909	17,461	0.08
1969.	412	1,576	29,397	0.16	1984.	62	376	8,499	0.04
1970.	381	2,468	52,761	0.29	1985.	54	324	7,079	0.03
1971.	298	2,516	35,538	0.19	1986.	69	533	11,861	0.05
1972.	250	975	16,764	0.09	1987.	46	174	[5]4,481	0.02
1973.	317	1,400	16,260	0.08	1988.	40	118	[5]4,381	0.02
1974.	424	1,796	31,809	0.16	1989.	51	452	16,996	0.07
1975.	235	965	17,563	0.09	1990.	44	185	5,926	0.02
1976.	231	1,519	23,962	0.12	1991.	40	392	4,584	0.02
1977.	298	1,212	21,258	0.10	1992.	35	364	3,989	0.01
1978.	219	1,006	23,774	0.11	1993.	35	182	3,981	0.01
1979.	235	1,021	20,409	0.09	1994.	45	322	5,020	0.02
1980.	187	795	20,844	0.09	1995.	31	192	5,771	0.02
1981.	145	729	16,908	0.07	1996.	37	273	4,887	0.02
					1997.	29	339	4,497	0.01

[1] Beginning in year indicated.   [2] Workers counted more than once if involved in more than one stoppage during the year.   [3] Resulting from all stoppages in effect in a year, including those that began in an earlier year.   [4] Agricultural and government employees are included in the total working time; private household and forestry and fishery employees are excluded.   [5] Revised since originally published.

Source: U.S. Bureau of Labor Statistics, *Compensation and Working Conditions*, monthly through 1995, thereafter quarterly.

No. 712. Labor Union Membership, by Sector: 1983 to 1997

[See headnote, Table 714]

SECTOR	1983	1985	1990	1992	1993	1994	1995	1996	1997
TOTAL (1,000)									
Wage and salary workers:									
Union members	17,717.4	16,996.1	16,739.8	16,390.3	16,598.1	16,740.3	16,359.6	16,269.4	16,109.9
Covered by unions	20,532.1	19,358.1	19,057.8	18,540.1	18,646.4	18,842.5	18,346.3	18,158.1	17,923.0
Public sector workers:									
Union members	5,737.2	5,743.1	6,485.0	6,653.1	7,017.8	7,091.0	6,927.4	6,854.4	6,746.7
Covered by unions	7,112.2	6,920.6	7,691.4	7,840.6	8,162.4	8,191.8	7,986.6	7,829.7	7,668.0
Private sector workers:									
Union members	11,980.2	11,253.0	10,254.8	9,737.2	9,580.3	9,649.4	9,432.1	9,415.0	9,363.3
Covered by unions	13,419.9	12,437.5	11,366.4	10,699.5	10,484.0	10,650.6	10,359.8	10,328.4	10,255.0
PERCENT									
Wage and salary workers:									
Union members	20.1	18.0	16.1	15.8	15.8	15.5	14.9	14.5	14.1
Covered by unions	23.3	20.5	18.3	17.9	17.7	17.4	16.7	16.2	15.6
Public sector workers:									
Union members	36.7	35.7	36.5	36.6	37.7	38.7	37.7	37.6	37.2
Covered by unions	45.5	43.1	43.3	43.2	43.8	44.7	43.5	43.0	42.3
Private sector workers:									
Union members	16.5	14.3	11.9	11.4	11.1	10.8	10.3	10.0	9.7
Covered by unions	18.5	15.9	13.2	12.5	12.1	11.9	11.3	11.0	10.6

Source: The Bureau of National Affairs, Inc., Washington, DC, *Union Membership and Earnings Data Book: Compilations from the Current Population Survey (1998 edition),* (copyright by BNA PLUS); authored by Barry Hirsch and David Macpherson of Florida State University. Internet site <http://www.bna.com/bnaplus>

No. 713. Union Members, by Selected Characteristics: 1997

[**Annual averages of monthly data.** Covers employed wage and salary workers 16 years old and over. Excludes self-employed workers whose businesses are incorporated although they technically qualify as wage and salary workers. Based on Current Population Survey, see text, Section 1, Population, and Appendix III]

CHARACTERISTIC	EMPLOYED WAGE AND SALARY WORKERS			MEDIAN USUAL WEEKLY EARNINGS [3] (dol.)			
	Total (1,000)	Percent		Total	Union members [1]	Represented by unions [2]	Not represented by unions
		Union members [1]	Represented by unions [2]				
Total [4]	**114,533**	**14.1**	**15.6**	**503**	**640**	**632**	**478**
16 to 24 years old	18,571	5.2	6.1	306	385	384	302
25 to 34 years old	29,408	11.7	13.2	481	579	572	466
35 to 44 years old	31,461	15.9	17.7	579	675	666	548
45 to 54 years old	22,714	20.5	22.4	607	704	697	578
55 to 64 years old	9,871	19.2	20.7	558	661	657	512
65 years and over	2,509	7.3	8.2	393	614	609	374
Men	59,825	16.3	17.7	579	683	679	539
Women	54,708	11.6	13.4	431	577	568	411
White	**96,104**	**13.6**	**15.1**	**519**	**663**	**654**	**494**
Men	50,941	16.0	17.4	595	699	695	569
Women	45,163	10.9	12.6	444	595	587	421
Black	**13,346**	**17.9**	**20.1**	**400**	**533**	**523**	**371**
Men	6,201	20.2	22.2	432	577	573	396
Women	7,145	16.0	18.3	375	504	496	349
Hispanic [5]	**11,881**	**11.8**	**13.5**	**351**	**506**	**501**	**331**
Men	7,153	12.6	14.3	371	538	526	348
Women	4,728	10.6	12.2	318	440	430	309
Full-time workers	93,578	15.6	17.3	503	640	632	478
Part-time workers	20,710	7.0	8.0	(X)	(X)	(X)	(X)
Managerial and professional specialty	31,946	13.2	15.5	738	776	766	731
Technical sales, and admin. support	34,796	9.1	10.5	456	550	541	441
Service occupations	16,204	13.2	14.5	313	516	505	293
Precision, production, craft, and repair	12,069	22.6	23.7	548	724	718	501
Operators, fabricators, and laborers	17,629	21.5	22.7	401	572	561	365
Farming, forestry, and fishing	1,890	4.6	5.1	295	505	475	290
Agricultural wage and salary workers	1,681	2.2	2.4	306	(B)	(B)	305
Private nonagri. wage and salary workers	94,705	9.8	10.8	490	610	603	476
Mining	607	13.9	14.3	680	717	717	668
Construction	5,739	18.6	19.5	518	771	760	484
Manufacturing	19,961	16.3	17.2	517	595	592	503
Transportation and public utilities	6,949	26.0	27.5	617	718	714	580
Wholesale and retail trade, total	23,676	5.6	6.2	391	457	451	387
Finance, insurance, and real estate	7,070	2.2	2.8	546	487	501	548
Services	30,704	5.4	6.5	475	517	512	470
Government	18,147	37.2	42.3	605	681	671	530

B Data not shown where base is less than 50,000. X Not applicable. [1] Members of a labor union or an employee association similar to a labor union. [2] Members of a labor union or an employee association similar to a union as well as workers who report no union affiliation but whose jobs are covered by a union or an employee association contract. [3] For full-time employed wage and salary workers. [4] Includes races not shown separately. Also includes a small number of multiple jobholders whose full- part-time status can not be determined for their principal job. [5] Persons of Hispanic origin may be of any race.
Source: U.S. Bureau of Labor Statistics, *Employment and Earnings,* monthly, January 1998 issue.

No. 714. Labor Union Membership, by State: 1983 and 1997

[Annual averages of monthly figures. For wage and salary workers in agriculture and non-agriculture. Data represent union members by place of residence. Based on the Current Population Survey and subject to sampling error. For methodological details, see source]

| STATE | UNION MEMBERS (1,000) | | WORKERS COVERED BY UNIONS (1,000) | | PERCENT OF WORKERS— | | | | | |
| | | | | | Union members | | Covered by unions | | Private manufacturing sector union members | |
	1983	1997	1983	1997	1983	1997	1983	1997	1983	1997
United States..	17,717.4	16,109.9	20,532.1	17,923.0	20.1	14.1	23.3	15.6	27.8	16.3
Alabama [1]........	228.2	184.5	268.2	212.2	16.9	10.2	19.8	11.7	25.9	17.0
Alaska..........	41.7	50.1	49.2	55.9	24.9	20.0	29.3	22.3	23.3	5.3
Arizona [1].......	125.0	131.7	156.4	155.3	11.4	7.0	14.3	8.2	7.8	4.9
Arkansas [1]......	82.2	59.4	103.2	68.3	11.0	5.9	13.8	6.8	18.7	9.2
California........	2,118.9	2,066.7	2,505.2	2,320.6	21.9	16.0	25.9	18.0	21.0	9.7
Colorado.........	177.9	174.2	209.6	200.7	13.6	9.6	16.0	11.1	13.1	12.0
Connecticut.......	314.0	247.8	345.1	262.3	22.7	16.9	25.0	17.9	28.1	14.2
Delaware........	49.2	39.2	54.1	44.7	20.1	11.7	22.1	13.3	27.3	17.6
District of Columbia ..	52.4	30.1	69.4	37.2	19.5	13.6	25.9	16.8	17.6	20.3
Florida [1]........	393.7	403.0	532.9	533.1	10.2	6.8	13.8	9.0	11.3	4.5
Georgia [1].......	267.0	238.1	345.1	267.5	11.9	7.1	15.3	8.0	16.9	8.8
Hawaii..........	112.6	126.7	124.9	135.9	29.2	26.3	32.4	28.2	35.6	14.8
Idaho [1].........	41.3	43.4	53.7	52.0	12.5	8.5	16.2	10.1	19.0	10.4
Illinois..........	1,063.8	970.8	1,205.1	1,041.0	24.2	18.5	27.4	19.9	32.4	21.4
Indiana..........	503.3	398.6	544.5	438.0	24.9	14.6	27.0	16.0	48.7	24.8
Iowa [1].,.......	185.9	172.4	231.3	204.5	17.2	13.2	21.5	15.7	40.3	19.2
Kansas [1]........	125.2	86.9	170.4	113.6	13.7	7.8	18.7	10.2	25.5	13.6
Kentucky........	223.7	193.1	259.8	220.7	17.9	12.2	20.8	13.9	37.4	24.2
Louisiana [1]......	204.2	118.7	267.8	149.7	13.8	7.0	18.1	8.9	24.9	16.3
Maine...........	88.0	72.0	100.4	79.8	21.0	13.5	24.0	15.0	24.8	24.5
Maryland	346.5	348.7	423.1	403.1	18.5	14.9	22.6	17.3	29.2	20.0
Massachusetts.....	603.2	423.1	661.4	462.9	23.7	15.1	26.0	16.6	26.7	10.8
Michigan........	1,005.4	969.0	1,084.6	1,024.1	30.4	23.1	32.8	24.4	46.2	32.8
Minnesota........	393.9	436.1	439.4	459.6	23.2	19.9	25.9	20.9	22.3	16.1
Mississippi [1].....	79.4	57.5	99.7	85.8	9.9	5.4	12.5	8.0	18.9	8.2
Missouri.........	374.4	359.3	416.7	388.5	20.8	14.6	23.2	15.8	36.6	24.7
Montana.........	49.5	47.3	55.5	53.0	18.3	13.8	20.5	15.5	33.0	13.6
Nebraska [1]......	80.6	68.8	94.8	91.1	13.6	9.3	16.0	12.3	19.1	13.0
Nevada [1].......	90.0	147.1	106.7	185.7	22.4	19.1	26.6	24.1	10.8	8.9
New Hampshire	48.5	55.6	60.8	62.7	11.5	10.2	14.4	11.5	10.6	6.6
New Jersey.......	822.1	802.1	918.2	866.5	26.9	22.0	30.0	23.7	31.4	22.0
New Mexico......	52.6	55.6	70.6	74.8	11.8	8.4	15.8	11.3	11.9	6.7
New York ...,....	2,155.6	1,949.4	2,385.9	2,050.2	32.5	26.3	36.0	27.7	31.0	22.3
North Carolina [1]....	178.7	126.2	238.1	152.7	7.6	3.8	10.2	4.6	6.9	2.5
North Dakota [1].....	28.4	23.9	35.1	28.2	13.2	8.6	16.3	10.1	27.4	17.4
Ohio	1,011.0	931.3	1,125.0	1,002.7	25.1	18.9	27.9	20.3	40.9	28.5
Oklahoma........	131.5	109.5	168.2	133.6	11.5	8.4	14.7	10.2	25.2	15.8
Oregon..........	222.9	242.2	261.9	272.1	22.3	17.6	26.2	19.8	28.7	15.2
Pennsylvania.....	1,195.7	866.0	1,350.0	923.8	27.5	17.1	31.1	18.2	42.3	21.6
Rhode Island......	85.8	80.9	93.7	84.8	21.5	18.7	23.5	19.5	16.9	9.6
South Carolina [1] ...	69.6	61.3	100.6	82.9	5.9	3.7	8.6	5.0	5.5	5.6
South Dakota [1]	26.8	21.0	34.8	26.2	11.5	6.9	14.9	8.6	19.0	8.7
Tennessee [1]......	252.4	192.9	300.9	234.2	15.1	8.6	18.0	10.5	21.4	10.9
Texas [1].........	583.7	538.6	712.8	650.9	9.7	6.4	11.9	7.8	16.1	9.5
Utah [1].........	81.6	74.0	100.9	86.5	15.2	8.3	18.9	9.7	14.9	5.9
Vermont.........	25.9	21.8	31.5	25.8	12.6	8.5	15.3	10.0	13.5	6.2
Virginia [1].......	268.3	192.6	346.1	220.2	11.7	6.5	15.1	7.4	21.2	8.7
Washington......	419.9	508.2	499.7	563.4	27.1	20.5	32.3	22.7	35.5	26.1
West Virginia.....	142.7	105.6	160.6	112.4	25.3	15.6	28.5	16.6	41.3	24.6
Wisconsin........	465.5	468.0	526.7	499.2	23.8	18.8	26.9	20.0	36.0	21.4
Wyoming [1].......	27.1	18.7	31.8	22.0	13.9	9.3	16.2	10.9	14.6	13.1

[1] Right to work state.

Source: The Bureau of National Affairs, Inc., Washington, DC, *Union Membership and Earnings Data Book: Compilations from the Current Population Survey, (1998 edition)* (copyright by BNA PLUS); authored by Barry Hirsch and David Macpherson of Florida State University. Internet site <http://www.bna.com/bnaplus/databook.html>

Figure 14.1
Gross Private Saving and Gross Investment: 1960 to 1997

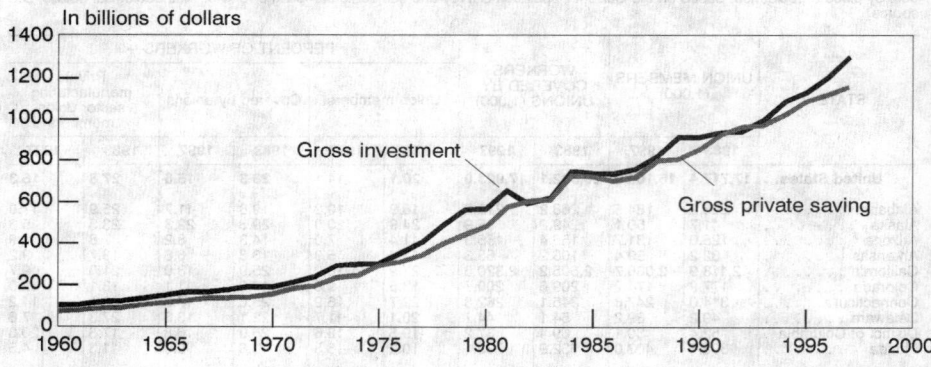

Source: Chart prepared by U.S. Bureau of the Census. For data, see Table 725.

Figure 14.2
Personal Income Per Capita, by State: 1997

(In constant 1992 dollars)

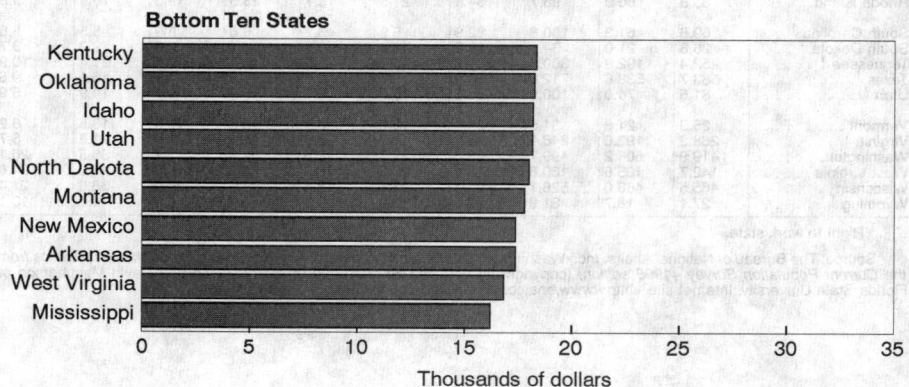

Source: Chart prepared by U.S. Bureau of the Census. For data, see Table 727.

Income, Expenditures, and Wealth

This section presents data on gross domestic product (GDP), gross national product (GNP), national and personal income, saving and investment, money income, poverty, and national and personal wealth. The data on income and expenditures measure two aspects of the U.S. economy. One aspect relates to the national income and product accounts (NIPAs), a summation reflecting the entire complex of the Nation's economic income and output and the interaction of its major components; the other relates to the distribution of money income to families and individuals, or consumer income.

The primary source for data on GDP, GNP, national and personal income, gross saving and investment, and fixed reproducible tangible wealth is the *Survey of Current Business,* published monthly by the Bureau of Economic Analysis (BEA). A comprehensive revision to the NIPAs was completed in January 1996. Discussions of the revision appeared in the July, September, and October 1995 the January/February 1996, and the May 1997 issues of the *Survey of Current Business*. Summary historical estimates appeared in the August 1997 issue of the *Survey of Current Business*. Detailed historical data appear in the *National Income and Product Accounts of the United States, 1929-94.*

Sources of income distribution data are the decennial censuses of population and the Current Population Survey (CPS), both products of the Bureau of the Census (see text, Section 1). Annual data on income of families, individuals, and households are presented in *Current Population Reports-Consumer Income,* P60 series.

Data on individuals' saving and assets are published by the Board of Governors of the Federal Reserve System in the quarterly *Flow of Funds Accounts;* and detailed information on personal wealth is published periodically by the Internal Revenue Service (IRS) in *SOI Bulletin.*

In Brief

Real Gross Domestic Product (GDP) rose in 1997 at an annual rate of 3.8% marking the sixth consecutive annual increase. Real GDP per capita also increased in 1997 to $26,835.

The number of persons in poverty fell 2.7 million between 1993 and 1996 to 36.5 million.

The median net worth of families was $56,400 in 1995, up slightly from 1992 in real terms, but unchanged from 1989.

National income and product—

Gross domestic product is the total output of goods and services produced by labor and property located in the United States, valued at market prices. GDP can be viewed in terms of the expenditure categories that comprise its major components—purchases of goods and services by consumers and government, gross private domestic investment, and net exports of goods and services. The goods and services included are largely those bought for final use (excluding illegal transactions) in the market economy. A number of inclusions, however, represent imputed values, the most important of which is rental value of owner-occupied housing. GDP, in this broad context, measures the output attributable to the factors of production located in the United States. *Gross State product* (GSP) is the gross market value of the goods and services attributable to labor and property located in a state. It is the state counterpart of the Nation's gross domestic product.

As part of the comprehensive revision released in January 1996, BEA replaced its fixed-weighted (1987 dollars) index as the featured measure of real GDP with an index based on chain-type annual weights. Changes in the new featured measures of real output and prices are calculated as the average of changes based on weights for the current and preceding years. (Components of real output are weighted by price and components of prices are weighted by output.) These annual changes are "chained" (multiplied) together to form a time series that allows for the effects of changes in relative prices and changes in the composition of output over time. Quarterly and monthly changes are also based on annual weights. The new output indexes are expressed as 1992 = 100, and for recent years, in 1992 dollars; the new price indexes are based to 1992 = 100.

Chained (1992) dollar estimates of most components of GDP are not published for periods prior to 1982, because during periods far from the base period, the levels of the components may provide misleading information about their contributions to an aggregate. Values are published in index form (1992 = 100) for 1929 to the present to allow users to calculate the percent changes for all components, changes which are accurate for all periods. In addition, the Bureau of Economic Analysis publishes estimates of the contribution of major components to the percent change in GDP for all periods.

Gross national product measures the output attributable to all labor and property supplied by United States residents. GNP differs from "national income" mainly in that GNP includes allowances for depreciation and for indirect business taxes (sales and property taxes); see Table 721.

In December 1991, the Bureau of Economic Analysis began featuring gross domestic product rather than gross national product as the primary measure of U.S. production. GDP is now the standard measure of growth because it is the appropriate measure for much of the short-term monitoring and analysis of the economy. In addition, the use of GDP facilitates comparisons of economic activity in the United States with that in other countries.

National income is the aggregate of labor and property earnings which arises in the current production of goods and services. It is the sum of employee compensation, proprietors' income, rental income of persons, corporate profits, and net interest. It measures the total factor costs of the goods and services produced by the economy. Income is measured before deduction of taxes.

Capital consumption adjustment for corporations and for nonfarm sole proprietorships and partnerships is the difference between capital consumption based on income tax returns and capital consumption measured using empirical evidence on prices of used equipment and structures in resale markets, which have shown that depreciation for most types of assets approximates a geometric pattern. The tax return data are valued at historical costs and reflect changes over time in service lives and depreciation patterns as permitted by tax regulations. *Inventory valuation adjustment* represents the difference between the book value of inventories used up in production and the cost of replacing them.

Personal income is the current income received by persons from all sources minus their personal contributions for social insurance. Classified as "persons" are individuals (including owners of unincorporated firms), nonprofit institutions that primarily serve individuals, private trust funds, and private noninsured welfare funds. Personal income includes transfers (payments not resulting from current production) from government and business such as Social Security benefits, public assistance, etc., but excludes transfers among persons. Also included are certain nonmonetary types of income—chiefly estimated net rental value to owner-occupants of their homes and the value of services furnished without payment by financial intermediaries. Capital gains (net losses) are excluded.

Disposable personal income is personal income less personal tax and nontax payments. It is the income available to persons for spending or saving. Personal tax and nontax payments are tax payments (net of refunds) by persons (except personal contributions for social insurance) that are not chargeable to business expense, and certain personal payments to general government that are treated like taxes. Personal taxes include income, estate and gift, and personal property taxes and motor vehicle licenses. Nontax payments include passport fees, fines and forfeitures, and donations.

Consumer Expenditure Survey—The Consumer Expenditure Survey program was begun in late 1979. The principal objective of the survey is to collect current consumer expenditure data which provide a continuous flow of data on the buying habits of American consumers. The data are necessary for future revisions of the Consumer Price Index.

The survey conducted by the Bureau of the Census for the Bureau of Labor Statistics, consists of two components: (1) An interview panel survey in which the expenditures of consumer units are obtained in five interviews conducted every 3 months; and (2) a diary or recordkeeping survey completed by participating households for two consecutive 1-week periods.

Each component of the survey queries an independent sample of consumer units representative of the U.S. total population. Over 52 weeks of the year, 5,000 consumer units are sampled for the diary survey. Each consumer unit keeps a diary for two 1-week periods yielding approximately 10,000 diaries a year. The interview sample is selected on a rotating panel basis, targeted at 5,000 consumer units per quarter. Data are collected in 88 urban and 16 rural areas of the country that are representative of the U.S. total population. The survey includes students in student housing. Data from the two surveys are combined; integration is necessary to permit analysis of total family expenditures because neither the diary nor quarterly interview survey was designed to collect a complete account of consumer spending.

The Diary survey is designed to obtain expenditures on small, frequently purchased items which are normally difficult for respondents to recall. Detailed records of expenses are kept for food and beverages, both at home and in eating places, tobacco, housekeeping supplies, nonprescription drugs, and personal care products and services.

The Interview survey is designed to obtain data on the types of expenditures which respondents can be expected to recall for a period of 3 months or longer. In general, these include relatively large expenditures, such as those for property, automobiles, and major appliances, or expenditures which occur on a fairly regular basis, such as rent, utilities, or insurance premiums. Including "global estimates" for food, it is estimated that about 95 percent of expenditures are covered in the interview. Excluded are nonprescription drugs, household supplies, and personal care items. The interview survey also provides data on expenditures incurred while on trips. Both surveys exclude all business related expenditures for which the family is reimbursed.

Distribution of money income to families and individuals—Money income statistics are based on data collected in various field surveys of income conducted since 1936. Since 1947, the Bureau of the Census has collected the data on an annual basis and published them in *Current Population Reports,* P60 series. In each of the surveys, field representatives interview samples of the population with respect to income received during the previous year. Money income as defined by the Bureau of the Census differs from the BEA concept of "personal income."

Data on consumer income collected in the CPS by the Bureau of the Census cover money income received (exclusive of certain money receipts such as capital gains) before payments for personal income taxes, social security, union dues, medicare deductions, etc. Therefore, money income does not reflect the fact that some families receive part of their income in the form of noncash benefits (see Section 12) such as food stamps, health benefits, and subsidized housing; that some farm families receive noncash benefits in the form of rent-free housing and goods produced and consumed on the farm; or that noncash benefits are also received by some nonfarm residents which often take the form of the use of business transportation and facilities, full or partial payments by business for retirement programs, medical and educational expenses, etc. These elements should be considered when comparing income levels. For data on noncash benefits, see Section 12. None of the aggregate income concepts (GDP, national income, or personal income) is exactly comparable with money income, although personal income is the closest.

Several changes were made in the collection and processing of the March 1994 CPS data. These changes included (1) a change in the data collection method from paper and pencil to computer-assisted interviewing, (2) revisions allowing for the coding of different income amounts on selected questionnaire items (limits either increased or decreased in the following categories: earnings increased to $999,999, social security increased to $49,999, supplemental security income and Public Assistance increased to $24,999, veterans' benefits increased to $99,999, child support and alimony decreased to $49,999), and (3) the introduction of 1990 census population controls. A detailed description of these changes and their effects on estimates can be found in *Current Population Reports*, Series P60–189.

In October 1983, the Census Bureau began to collect data under the new Survey of Income and Program Participation (SIPP). The information supplied by this survey is expected to provide better measures of the status and changes in income distribution and poverty of households and persons in the United States. The data collected in SIPP will be used to study Federal and state aid programs (such as food stamps, welfare, medicaid, and subsidized housing), to estimate program costs and coverage, and to assess the effects of proposed changes in program eligibility rules or benefit levels. The core questions are repeated at each interview and cover labor force activity, the types and amounts of income received, and participation status in various programs. The core also contains questions covering attendance in postsecondary schools and private health insurance coverage. Various supplements or topical modules covering areas such as educational attainment, assets and liabilities, and pension plan coverage are periodically included.

Poverty—Families and unrelated individuals are classified as being above or below the poverty level using the poverty index originated at the Social Security Administration in 1964 and revised by Federal Interagency Committees in 1969 and 1980. The poverty index is based solely on money income and does not reflect the fact that many low-income persons receive noncash benefits such as food stamps, Medicaid, and public housing. The index is based on the Department of Agriculture's 1961 Economy Food Plan and reflects the different consumption requirements of families based on their size and composition. The poverty thresholds are updated every year to reflect changes in the Consumer Price Index. The following technical changes to the thresholds were made in 1981: (1) distinctions based on sex of householder have been eliminated; (2) separate thresholds for farm families have been dropped; and (3) the matrix has been expanded to families of nine or more persons from the old cutoff of seven or more persons. These changes have been incorporated in the calculation of poverty data beginning with 1981.

In the recent past, the Bureau of the Census has published a number of technical papers that presented experimental poverty estimates based on income definitions that counted the value of selected government noncash benefits. The Census Bureau has also published annual reports on after-tax income. The *Current Population Reports,* series P60-186RD brings together the benefit and tax data that previously appeared in the separate reports. This report shows the distribution of income among households and the prevalence of poverty under the official definition of money income and under definitions that add or subtract income components.

The poverty statistics presented by the Bureau of the Census and Congressional Budget Office reflect alternative adjustments for inflation. The study used a variation of the Consumer Price Index to adjust poverty thresholds for the effects of changing prices since 1967. The alternative measure of inflation uses estimates of the cost of renting equivalent housing to assess homeownership costs; this methodology has been used in the official Consumer Price Index since 1983. See text, Section 15, and source for more details.

Statistical reliability—For a discussion of statistical collection and estimation, sampling procedures, and measures of statistical reliability pertaining to Census Bureau data, see Appendix III.

No. 715. GDP in Current and Real (1992) Dollars: 1960 to 1997

[In billions of dollars. For explanation of gross domestic product and chained dollars, see text, Section 14]

ITEM	1960	1970	1980	1983	1984	1985	1986	1987	1988
CURRENT DOLLARS									
Gross domestic product (GDP)..	**526.6**	**1,035.6**	**2,784.2**	**3,514.5**	**3,902.4**	**4,180.7**	**4,422.2**	**4,692.3**	**5,049.6**
Personal consumption expenditures	332.2	648.1	1,760.4	2,283.4	2,492.3	2,704.8	2,892.7	3,094.5	3,349.7
Durable goods................	43.3	85.0	213.5	279.8	325.1	361.1	398.7	416.7	451.0
Nondurable goods	152.9	272.0	695.5	830.3	883.6	927.6	957.2	1,014.0	1,081.1
Services....................	136.0	291.1	851.4	1,173.3	1,283.6	1,416.1	1,536.8	1,663.8	1,817.6
Gross private domestic investment.....	78.8	150.2	465.9	547.1	715.6	715.1	722.5	747.2	773.9
Fixed investment	75.5	148.1	473.5	552.0	648.1	688.9	712.9	722.9	763.1
Change in business inventories	3.2	2.2	-7.6	-4.9	67.5	26.2	9.6	24.2	10.9
Net exports of goods and services	2.4	1.2	-14.9	-51.7	-102.0	-114.2	-131.5	-142.1	-106.1
Exports	25.3	57.0	278.9	277.0	303.1	303.0	320.7	365.7	447.2
Imports	22.8	55.8	293.8	328.6	405.1	417.2	452.2	507.9	553.2
Government consumption expenditures and gross investment..........	113.2	236.1	572.8	735.7	796.6	875.0	938.5	992.8	1,032.0
Federal	65.6	115.9	248.4	344.5	372.6	410.1	435.2	455.7	457.3
National defense	54.9	90.6	174.2	255.0	282.7	312.4	332.4	350.4	354.0
State and local	47.6	120.2	324.4	391.2	424.0	464.9	503.3	537.2	574.7
CHAINED (1992) DOLLARS									
Gross domestic product (GDP)..	**2,262.9**	**3,397.6**	**4,615.0**	**4,803.7**	**5,140.1**	**5,323.5**	**5,487.7**	**5,649.5**	**5,865.2**
Personal consumption expenditures	1,432.6	2,197.8	3,009.7	3,240.6	3,407.6	3,566.5	3,708.7	3,822.3	3,972.7
Durable goods................	105.2	187.0	282.6	327.4	374.9	411.4	448.4	454.9	483.5
Nondurable goods	615.4	859.1	1,065.1	1,112.4	1,151.8	1,178.3	1,215.9	1,239.3	1,274.4
Services....................	717.4	1,155.4	1,670.7	1,809.0	1,883.0	1,977.3	2,041.4	2,126.9	2,212.4
Gross private domestic investment.....	270.5	426.1	628.3	642.1	833.4	823.8	811.8	821.5	828.2
Fixed investment	269.2	432.1	648.4	654.2	762.4	799.3	805.0	799.4	818.3
Change in business inventories	10.5	5.4	-10.2	-5.7	75.3	30.2	11.1	26.4	11.7
Net exports of goods and services	-21.3	-65.0	10.1	-63.3	-127.3	-147.9	-163.9	-156.2	-114.4
Exports	86.8	158.1	331.4	303.3	328.4	337.3	362.2	402.0	465.8
Imports	108.1	223.1	321.3	366.6	455.7	485.2	526.1	558.2	580.2
Government consumption expenditures and gross investment..........	617.2	866.8	941.4	987.3	1,018.4	1,080.1	1,135.0	1,165.9	1,180.9
Federal	349.4	427.2	399.3	452.7	463.7	495.6	518.4	534.4	524.6
National defense	301.3	349.0	280.7	334.6	348.1	374.1	393.4	409.2	405.5
State and local	267.2	440.0	543.6	534.9	555.0	584.7	616.9	631.8	656.6

	1989	1990	1991	1992	1993	1994	1995	1996	1997
CURRENT DOLLARS									
Gross domestic product (GDP)..	**5,438.7**	**5,743.8**	**5,916.7**	**6,244.4**	**6,558.1**	**6,947.0**	**7,265.4**	**7,636.0**	**8,079.9**
Personal consumption expenditures	3,594.8	3,839.3	3,975.1	4,219.8	4,459.2	4,717.0	4,957.7	5,207.6	5,485.8
Durable goods................	472.8	476.5	455.2	488.5	530.2	579.5	608.5	634.5	659.3
Nondurable goods	1,163.8	1,245.3	1,277.6	1,321.8	1,370.7	1,428.4	1,475.8	1,534.7	1,592.0
Services....................	1,958.1	2,117.5	2,242.3	2,409.4	2,558.4	2,709.1	2,873.4	3,038.4	3,234.5
Gross private domestic investment.....	829.2	799.7	736.2	790.4	876.2	1,007.9	1,038.2	1,116.5	1,242.5
Fixed investment	797.5	791.6	738.5	783.4	855.7	946.6	1,008.1	1,090.7	1,174.1
Change in business inventories	31.7	8.0	-2.3	7.0	20.5	61.2	30.1	25.9	68.4
Net exports of goods and services	-80.4	-71.3	-20.5	-29.5	-60.7	-90.9	-86.0	-94.8	-101.1
Exports	509.3	557.3	601.8	639.4	658.6	721.2	818.4	870.9	957.1
Imports	589.7	628.6	622.3	669.0	719.3	812.1	904.5	965.7	1,058.1
Government consumption expenditures and gross investment..........	1,095.1	1,176.1	1,225.9	1,263.8	1,283.4	1,313.0	1,355.5	1,406.7	1,452.7
Federal	477.2	503.6	522.6	528.0	518.3	510.2	509.6	520.0	523.8
National defense	360.6	373.1	383.5	375.8	360.7	349.2	344.6	352.8	350.3
State and local	617.9	672.6	703.4	735.8	765.0	802.8	846.0	886.7	928.9
CHAINED (1992) DOLLARS									
Gross domestic product (GDP)..	**6,062.0**	**6,136.3**	**6,079.4**	**6,244.4**	**6,389.6**	**6,610.7**	**6,742.1**	**6,928.4**	**7,188.8**
Personal consumption expenditures	4,064.6	4,132.2	4,105.8	4,219.8	4,343.6	4,486.0	4,595.3	4,714.1	4,867.5
Durable goods................	496.2	493.3	462.0	488.5	523.8	561.2	583.6	611.1	645.5
Nondurable goods	1,303.5	1,316.1	1,302.9	1,321.8	1,351.0	1,389.9	1,412.6	1,432.3	1,458.5
Services....................	2,262.3	2,321.3	2,341.0	2,409.4	2,468.9	2,535.5	2,599.6	2,671.0	2,764.1
Gross private domestic investment.....	863.5	815.0	738.1	790.4	863.6	975.7	991.5	1,069.1	1,197.0
Fixed investment	832.0	805.8	741.3	783.4	842.8	915.5	962.1	1,041.7	1,123.6
Change in business inventories	33.3	10.4	-3.0	7.0	22.1	60.6	27.3	25.0	65.7
Net exports of goods and services	-82.7	-61.9	-22.3	-29.5	-70.2	-104.6	-98.8	-114.4	-146.5
Exports	520.2	564.4	599.9	639.4	658.2	712.4	791.2	857.0	962.7
Imports	603.0	626.3	622.2	669.0	728.4	817.0	890.1	971.5	1,109.2
Government consumption expenditures and gross investment..........	1,213.9	1,250.4	1,258.0	1,263.8	1,252.1	1,252.3	1,251.9	1,257.9	1,269.6
Federal	531.5	541.9	539.4	528.0	505.7	486.6	470.3	464.2	457.0
National defense	401.6	401.5	397.5	375.8	354.4	336.9	322.6	317.8	308.6
State and local	682.6	708.6	718.7	735.8	746.4	765.7	781.6	793.7	812.7

Source: U.S. Bureau of Economic Analysis, *National Income and Product Accounts of the United States, 1929-94*, Vol 1; and *Survey of Current Business*, August 1997 and May 1998.

No. 716. Gross Domestic Product in Current and Real (1992) Dollars, by Industry: 1990 to 1996

[In billions of dollars. Data are based on the 1987 SIC. Data include nonfactor charges (capital consumption allowances, indirect business taxes, etc.) as well as factor charges against gross product; corporate profits and capital consumption allowances have been shifted from a company to an establishment basis]

INDUSTRY	CURRENT DOLLARS				CHAINED (1992) DOLLARS			
	1990	1994	1995	1996	1990	1994	1995	1996
Gross domestic product	**5,743.8**	**6,947.0**	**7,265.4**	**7,636.0**	**6,136.3**	**6,610.7**	**6,742.1**	**6,928.4**
Private industries	4,951.4	6,013.5	6,301.3	6,639.8	5,246.0	5,763.6	5,921.4	6,094.1
Agriculture, forestry, and fishing	108.7	119.2	111.0	128.9	99.3	119.1	111.4	111.7
Farms	79.5	83.5	73.5	89.4	70.7	84.9	74.2	75.5
Agricultural services	29.1	35.7	37.5	40.5	28.6	34.9	37.0	37.6
Mining [1]	112.3	94.9	99.8	113.6	96.9	102.5	108.4	101.9
Construction	245.2	268.7	286.4	306.1	247.5	249.8	254.1	264.3
Manufacturing	1,031.4	1,216.1	1,286.3	1,332.1	1,090.0	1,193.2	1,273.7	1,323.7
Durable goods	572.8	679.2	716.8	749.0	600.4	671.3	731.2	785.5
Lumber and wood products	31.8	38.4	40.7	41.4	37.0	29.8	31.6	33.6
Furniture and fixtures	15.4	18.5	19.4	20.5	15.8	18.0	18.7	18.8
Stone, clay, and glass products	24.8	28.8	30.7	32.7	25.5	27.0	27.7	29.1
Primary metal industries	42.6	46.3	52.0	50.6	39.0	45.0	44.4	46.8
Fabricated metal products	69.4	84.2	89.5	98.2	72.6	84.5	89.7	94.0
Industrial machinery	114.8	122.3	142.4	150.2	113.2	131.5	164.5	186.1
Electronic & other electric equipment	94.9	132.9	134.0	143.8	92.5	145.8	175.6	217.4
Motor vehicles and equipment	46.1	87.4	87.3	85.1	56.8	78.0	79.3	76.1
Other transportation equipment	60.5	49.5	46.9	49.7	69.1	47.6	43.8	44.5
Instruments and related products	52.2	48.7	49.7	52.3	58.7	45.1	42.6	38.3
Misc. manufacturing industries	20.2	22.2	24.3	24.6	22.2	21.5	22.8	23.3
Nondurable goods	458.6	536.9	569.5	583.1	489.4	522.0	543.2	541.0
Food and kindred products	94.2	109.6	118.7	122.6	103.2	106.5	120.9	112.9
Tobacco manufactures	16.4	16.3	17.6	18.1	24.9	22.3	24.3	23.9
Textile mill products	21.7	25.4	23.6	25.5	22.6	27.3	25.4	26.6
Apparel and other textile products	25.2	28.2	27.3	26.6	26.5	28.3	28.5	26.9
Paper and allied products	45.3	51.3	59.9	57.1	44.1	52.1	45.4	47.3
Printing and publishing	73.9	86.0	85.0	90.4	84.5	78.0	77.5	74.3
Chemicals and allied products	110.3	140.6	155.9	157.8	117.3	131.2	138.9	142.2
Petroleum and coal products	33.0	30.4	30.2	30.1	28.4	27.6	32.2	33.8
Rubber and misc. plastic products	34.0	44.4	46.1	49.7	34.4	45.4	48.2	50.9
Leather and leather products	4.6	4.7	5.1	5.2	4.8	4.5	4.7	4.8
Transportation and public utilities	482.1	598.7	622.4	645.3	491.7	584.1	593.8	608.9
Transportation	176.4	219.9	228.7	235.1	176.7	214.3	216.0	220.8
Railroad transportation	19.6	24.2	24.5	25.3	18.7	25.9	27.7	31.0
Local & interurban passenger transit	9.0	11.4	12.4	13.6	10.3	11.0	12.0	12.2
Trucking and warehousing	75.8	95.0	97.5	92.2	73.7	88.7	87.4	80.3
Water transportation	9.7	10.9	10.8	11.2	10.7	10.8	11.0	10.7
Transportation by air	39.4	51.7	54.9	63.2	39.5	51.4	49.8	59.0
Pipelines, except natural gas	5.0	4.6	5.7	5.5	4.8	4.8	5.4	5.0
Transportation services	17.8	22.1	23.0	24.0	19.2	21.7	23.2	24.0
Communications	146.6	184.6	191.6	200.3	149.2	176.9	178.4	181.6
Telephone and telegraph	119.1	142.1	144.1	149.6	120.6	137.9	136.4	141.2
Radio and television broadcasting	27.6	42.5	47.5	50.6	28.6	38.8	41.7	40.4
Electric, gas, and sanitary services	159.1	194.2	202.0	210.0	168.4	193.1	199.6	207.0
Wholesale trade	367.2	468.0	484.4	516.2	360.5	448.6	457.5	493.3
Retail trade	503.5	615.3	637.6	667.9	546.4	601.2	622.5	648.5
Finance, insurance, and real estate [2]	1,024.1	1,267.6	1,361.3	1,448.5	1,109.0	1,196.9	1,231.1	1,258.5
Depository institutions	169.2	207.4	229.6	247.4	214.9	197.0	193.4	192.0
Nondepository institutions	21.5	36.1	39.0	49.9	25.6	33.9	32.6	35.4
Security and commodity brokers	39.7	78.5	79.5	90.0	41.2	83.0	81.9	92.2
Insurance carriers	69.3	108.8	126.5	136.6	70.2	91.3	105.1	110.1
Insurance agents, brokers & services	37.1	45.0	47.1	50.4	40.8	41.6	42.1	43.6
Real estate	671.9	802.9	842.7	886.2	706.8	758.3	775.6	793.3
Services	1,059.4	1,350.4	1,440.3	1,539.5	1,181.7	1,256.5	1,298.8	1,342.9
Hotels and other lodging places	46.1	57.4	60.6	63.7	49.2	54.4	55.4	55.8
Personal services	38.2	45.8	46.6	49.1	41.7	42.6	42.4	43.3
Business services	199.0	256.0	283.3	318.5	216.5	247.1	271.3	295.7
Auto repair, services, and garages	48.9	59.3	61.1	65.0	54.0	53.3	53.3	55.3
Motion pictures	20.4	23.0	25.9	29.9	22.1	21.8	23.9	26.2
Amusement and recreation services	39.1	51.4	56.2	60.8	42.8	47.5	49.7	51.6
Health services	307.9	410.2	428.9	447.0	356.9	369.7	371.6	376.6
Legal services	80.7	93.8	96.5	100.0	91.5	86.0	85.5	85.1
Educational services	39.8	52.3	55.1	58.2	44.3	48.9	49.6	50.7
Social services & membership organization	29.6	43.2	46.7	49.3	32.5	41.6	43.7	44.9
Other services	147.8	182.6	199.9	215.2	160.4	175.4	184.6	192.9
Government	792.5	933.5	964.1	996.3	867.0	878.3	877.4	874.1
Federal	293.5	324.9	326.2	331.5	327.7	306.9	297.1	290.6
State and local	499.0	608.6	637.9	664.7	539.4	571.3	580.3	583.4

[1] For additional natural resource industries, see Table 1147. [2] For additional finance, insurance, and real estate data, see Table 792.

Source: U.S. Bureau of Economic Analysis, *Survey of Current Business*, August 1997.

No. 717. Gross Domestic Product in Current and Real (1992) Dollars, by Type of Product and Sector: 1990 to 1997

[In billions of dollars. For explanation of chained dollars, see text, Section 14]

ITEM	1990	1991	1992	1993	1994	1995	1996	1997
CURRENT DOLLARS								
Gross domestic	**5,743.8**	**5,916.7**	**6,244.4**	**6,558.1**	**6,947.0**	**7,265.4**	**7,636.0**	**8,079.9**
PRODUCT								
Goods.	2,203.8	2,234.0	2,321.0	2,422.1	2,581.4	2,667.9	2,785.2	2,945.1
Durable goods.	938.2	910.0	955.0	1,028.8	1,106.1	1,163.0	1,228.9	1,317.0
Nondurable goods	1,265.7	1,323.9	1,366.0	1,393.3	1,475.3	1,504.9	1,556.3	1,628.1
Services	3,016.9	3,201.3	3,411.1	3,589.5	3,772.3	3,980.7	4,187.3	4,430.4
Structures	523.1	481.4	512.3	546.5	593.2	616.8	663.6	704.4
SECTOR								
Business	4,796.9	4,908.5	5,184.4	5,453.1	5,801.6	6,074.7	6,401.0	6,794.0
Nonfarm.	4,717.3	4,835.6	5,103.8	5,380.1	5,718.1	6,001.3	6,311.6	6,699.4
Farm	79.6	72.9	80.6	73.0	83.5	73.5	89.4	94.6
Households and institutions.	237.9	257.4	279.1	296.5	312.7	331.8	346.0	366.3
General government	709.0	750.7	781.0	808.5	832.7	858.9	889.0	919.6
Federal	252.7	268.1	274.4	276.9	275.2	275.5	281.4	285.8
State and local	456.3	482.6	506.6	531.6	557.5	583.4	607.6	633.7
CHAINED (1992) DOLLARS								
Gross domestic	**6,136.3**	**6,079.4**	**6,244.4**	**6,389.6**	**6,610.7**	**6,742.1**	**6,928.4**	**7,188.8**
PRODUCT								
Goods.	2,304.8	2,262.7	2,321.0	2,391.5	2,514.2	2,574.2	2,662.6	2,808.3
Durable goods.	966.5	917.2	955.0	1,023.1	1,089.7	1,152.3	1,222.1	1,326.4
Nondurable goods	1,337.9	1,345.6	1,366.0	1,368.5	1,424.9	1,423.4	1,443.7	1488.4
Services	3,295.4	3,332.3	3,411.1	3,469.5	3,542.9	3,614.7	3,686.6	3,789.1
Structures	533.3	484.5	512.3	528.7	554.9	555.0	582.2	598.7
SECTOR								
Business	5,097.0	5,026.4	5,184.4	5,317.2	5,530.6	5,657.4	5,842.9	6,092.1
Nonfarm.	5,026.5	4,954.9	5,103.8	5,246.2	5,446.0	5,582.7	5,766.8	6,011.8
Farm	70.8	71.6	80.6	71.0	85.0	74.2	75.5	79.5
Households and institutions.	264.1	272.1	279.1	290.1	297.9	305.1	311.2	320.5
General government	774.7	781.1	781.0	782.3	782.6	780.3	775.9	779.3
Federal	280.3	281.0	274.4	267.7	258.4	248.1	240.9	235.9
State and local	494.5	500.1	506.6	514.5	524.2	532.2	535.2	543.7

Source: U.S. Bureau of Economic Analysis, *National Income and Product Accounts of the United States, 1929-94*, Vol 1; and *Survey of Current Business*, August 1997 and May 1998.

No. 718. GDP Components—Annual Percent Change: 1988 to 1997

[Change from previous year; for 1988, change from 1987. For explanation of chained dollars, see text, Section 14. Minus sign (-) indicates decrease]

ITEM	1988	1989	1990	1991	1992	1993	1994	1995	1996	1997
CURRENT DOLLARS										
Gross domestic product (GDP). .	**7.6**	**7.7**	**5.6**	**3.0**	**5.5**	**5.0**	**5.9**	**4.6**	**5.1**	**5.8**
Personal consumption expenditures	8.2	7.3	6.8	3.5	6.2	5.7	5.8	5.1	5.0	5.3
Durable goods.	8.2	4.8	0.8	-4.5	7.3	8.5	9.3	5.0	4.3	3.9
Nondurable goods	6.6	7.7	7.0	2.6	3.5	3.7	4.2	3.3	4.0	3.7
Services	9.2	7.7	8.1	5.9	7.5	6.2	5.9	6.1	5.7	6.5
Gross private domestic investment	3.6	7.1	-3.6	-7.9	7.4	10.8	15.0	3.0	7.5	11.3
Fixed investment	5.5	4.5	-0.7	-6.7	6.1	9.2	10.6	6.5	8.2	7.7
Residential	2.2	-0.5	-6.7	-11.4	18.0	11.5	13.7	-0.3	8.5	5.8
Exports	22.3	13.9	9.4	8.0	6.3	3.0	9.5	13.5	6.4	9.9
Imports	8.9	6.6	6.6	-1.0	7.5	7.5	12.9	11.4	6.8	9.6
Govt. consumption expenditures and gross investment	3.9	6.1	7.4	4.2	3.1	1.6	2.3	3.2	3.8	3.3
Federal	0.4	4.4	5.5	3.8	1.0	-1.8	-1.6	-0.1	2.1	0.7
National defense	1.0	1.9	3.5	2.8	-2.0	-4.0	-3.2	-1.3	2.4	-0.7
State and local	7.0	7.5	8.9	4.6	4.6	4.0	4.9	5.4	4.8	4.8
CHAINED (1992) DOLLARS										
Gross domestic product (GDP). .	**3.8**	**3.4**	**1.2**	**-0.9**	**2.7**	**2.3**	**3.5**	**2.0**	**2.8**	**3.8**
Personal consumption expenditures	2.6	1.5	1.1	-0.4	1.9	2.0	2.2	1.7	1.8	2.2
Durable goods.	0.6	0.2	-0.1	-0.5	0.4	0.6	0.6	0.3	0.4	0.4
Nondurable goods	0.6	0.5	0.2	-0.2	0.3	0.5	0.6	0.3	0.3	0.4
Services	1.4	0.8	0.9	0.3	1.1	1.0	1.1	1.0	1.1	1.4
Gross private domestic investment	0.1	0.6	-0.8	-1.3	0.8	1.2	1.7	0.2	1.1	1.6
Fixed investment	0.4	0.3	-0.5	-1.1	0.7	0.9	1.1	0.7	1.1	1.1
Nonresidential	0.5	0.4	-0.1	-0.6	0.1	0.7	0.7	0.8	0.9	1.0
Residential	-0.1	-0.2	-0.4	-0.5	0.5	0.3	0.4	-0.2	0.2	0.1
Exports	1.2	1.0	0.8	0.6	0.6	0.3	0.8	1.1	0.9	1.3
Imports	-0.4	-0.4	-0.4	0.1	-0.7	-0.9	-1.3	-1.0	-1.1	-1.7
Govt. consumption expenditures and gross investment	0.3	0.6	0.6	0.1	0.1	-0.2	0.0	0.0	0.1	0.2
Federal	-0.2	0.1	0.2	0.0	-0.2	-0.4	-0.3	-0.2	-0.1	-0.1
National defense	-0.1	-0.1	0.0	-0.1	-0.4	-0.3	-0.3	-0.2	-0.1	-0.1
State and local	0.4	0.4	0.4	0.2	0.3	0.2	0.3	0.2	0.2	0.3

Source: U.S. Bureau of Economic Analysis, *National Income and Product Accounts of the United States, 1929-94*, Vol. 1; and *Survey of Current Business*, August 1997 and May 1998.

No. 719. Gross State Product in Current and Real (1992) Dollars: 1990 to 1996

[**In billions of dollars.** For definition of gross state product or chained dollars, see text, Section 14]

STATE	CURRENT DOLLARS					CHAINED (1992) DOLLARS				
	1990	1993	1994	1995	1996	1990	1993	1994	1995	1996
United States .	[1]5,659.8	6,440.0	6,868.0	7,228.3	7,631.0	6,046.5	6,274.5	6,535.6	6,707.6	6,923.8
Alabama	71.1	83.0	89.3	95.0	99.2	75.5	80.9	85.5	88.4	90.7
Alaska.	25.4	22.5	21.9	23.7	24.2	25.2	22.1	21.5	22.7	21.4
Arizona	68.5	85.0	95.4	104.0	111.5	72.9	82.8	91.2	97.3	102.6
Arkansas	37.9	46.5	50.4	53.4	56.4	40.0	45.3	48.2	49.9	51.5
California.	792.7	843.1	876.0	913.5	962.7	845.2	819.1	835.5	855.1	880.1
Colorado	74.4	92.9	100.7	107.9	116.2	79.0	90.8	96.8	101.6	106.8
Connecticut	98.5	107.5	112.6	118.6	124.0	105.2	103.9	107.0	110.2	113.0
Delaware.	21.0	23.7	24.1	26.9	28.3	23.2	26.0	26.2	27.1	28.9
District of Columbia . . .	40.7	47.0	48.1	49.7	51.2	45.3	46.8	46.6	46.7	47.8
Florida.	255.2	300.7	321.7	339.0	360.5	273.0	291.6	305.7	314.3	326.1
Georgia	140.5	170.9	186.0	200.8	216.0	150.0	166.4	178.2	187.4	197.1
Hawaii.	32.4	35.2	35.2	36.0	36.3	34.9	36.3	35.6	34.9	34.9
Idaho	17.5	22.4	24.5	26.9	27.9	18.5	21.8	23.5	25.5	25.9
Illinois	273.4	312.3	336.9	352.9	370.8	290.8	306.8	325.6	333.8	345.5
Indiana	109.6	129.7	141.4	148.8	155.8	116.3	126.5	135.1	139.6	144.1
Iowa	55.0	62.0	68.7	71.4	76.3	58.0	60.4	66.0	67.5	70.3
Kansas	51.3	58.2	61.9	64.1	68.0	54.3	56.7	59.4	60.3	62.0
Kentucky	67.7	79.9	86.1	90.6	95.4	72.3	78.2	83.4	86.4	89.3
Louisiana	91.1	94.7	103.9	112.9	121.1	93.7	92.3	100.7	107.5	109.6
Maine	23.2	25.1	26.2	27.7	28.9	24.8	24.4	24.9	25.4	26.0
Maryland	113.7	124.6	132.9	137.4	143.2	122.3	121.4	126.5	127.6	130.2
Massachusetts	158.9	174.0	186.0	195.9	208.6	169.9	168.9	177.3	183.0	191.0
Michigan	188.0	217.3	240.6	251.8	263.3	202.1	211.2	228.9	234.9	241.0
Minnesota	99.5	114.6	124.6	131.4	141.6	105.1	110.9	118.4	122.0	128.7
Mississippi	38.7	46.6	50.8	53.6	56.4	40.8	45.2	48.4	50.2	51.7
Missouri.	104.1	118.3	129.1	137.5	145.1	111.3	115.5	123.4	128.5	132.8
Montana	13.3	16.1	16.9	17.7	18.5	13.9	15.7	16.2	16.6	16.9
Nebraska.	33.2	38.4	42.1	43.7	47.2	34.9	37.4	40.4	41.3	43.2
Nevada	31.3	39.5	44.5	48.7	53.7	33.1	38.6	42.3	44.8	48.3
New Hampshire	23.7	27.2	29.3	31.8	34.1	25.2	26.4	28.0	30.0	31.7
New Jersey	214.1	243.9	255.8	266.1	276.4	227.7	236.4	242.8	246.9	251.1
New Mexico	26.7	36.3	40.9	40.8	42.7	27.9	35.6	39.8	39.6	40.4
New York.	498.3	541.1	565.2	587.7	613.3	535.6	527.6	543.7	549.6	563.3
North Carolina	142.5	168.6	182.3	192.2	204.2	154.5	165.2	177.9	183.9	190.9
North Dakota	11.4	12.7	13.7	14.5	15.7	11.9	12.4	13.2	13.7	14.3
Ohio	227.1	256.6	276.7	292.1	304.4	241.6	250.2	264.7	273.6	280.7
Oklahoma	56.9	64.0	66.0	68.6	72.8	59.5	62.3	63.6	65.0	66.7
Oregon	57.0	68.9	74.7	80.8	87.0	60.8	66.5	70.6	75.0	79.4
Pennsylvania	245.8	283.1	296.8	313.3	328.5	261.9	273.6	281.6	290.6	298.7
Rhode Island	21.5	23.3	23.9	25.0	25.6	23.1	22.6	22.8	23.3	23.3
South Carolina	65.4	75.2	80.7	85.3	89.5	69.5	73.6	77.7	80.1	82.7
South Dakota	12.9	16.3	17.5	18.7	20.3	13.7	15.9	16.8	17.5	18.4
Tennessee	94.2	116.7	127.9	134.9	140.8	100.5	113.4	121.9	125.8	128.7
Texas	388.9	453.0	484.1	514.2	551.8	404.1	438.9	465.5	486.1	502.9
Utah	31.1	38.1	42.0	45.6	50.4	32.9	37.1	40.2	42.4	45.9
Vermont	11.6	13.0	13.6	13.9	14.6	12.3	12.6	13.0	13.0	13.5
Virginia	148.1	170.0	178.8	187.0	197.8	160.6	167.1	173.4	177.0	183.2
Washington	114.1	136.4	144.7	150.0	159.6	122.2	132.1	137.2	138.7	143.8
West Virginia	28.0	31.9	34.5	36.0	37.2	29.3	31.5	33.5	34.3	35.0
Wisconsin	99.2	117.7	125.8	132.7	139.2	105.0	115.1	120.8	124.6	128.7
Wyoming	13.5	14.6	14.9	15.8	16.8	13.4	14.6	15.1	15.7	15.8

[1] For chained (1992) dollar estimates, states will not add to U.S. total.

Source: U.S. Bureau of Economic Analysis, *Survey of Current Business,* June 1998.

No. 720. Gross State Product in Chained (1992) Dollars, by Industry: 1996

[In billions of dollars. For definition of gross state product or chained dollars, see text, Section 14. Industries based on 1987 Standard Industrial Classification]

STATE	Total [1]	Farms, forestry, fisheries [2]	Construction	Manufacturing	Transportation, public utilities	Wholesale trade	Retail trade	Finance, insurance, real estate	Services	Government [3]
United States [4]	6,923.8	111.7	264.3	1,323.7	611.7	493.3	648.5	1,255.9	1,342.9	839.6
Alabama	90.7	1.8	3.6	21.0	8.8	6.0	9.5	10.6	13.9	14.0
Alaska	21.4	0.3	0.8	1.1	3.5	0.7	1.5	2.3	2.5	4.3
Arizona	102.6	1.7	5.6	16.8	8.2	6.7	11.4	18.3	19.6	13.0
Arkansas	51.5	2.5	1.9	13.2	5.9	3.3	5.6	5.5	7.2	6.0
California	880.1	18.1	27.3	138.7	62.8	62.9	83.0	189.7	194.8	99.6
Colorado	106.8	1.8	5.4	14.4	12.1	7.0	10.9	17.7	22.1	13.8
Connecticut	113.0	0.8	3.5	20.8	7.2	7.9	8.9	30.3	23.6	9.9
Delaware	28.9	0.3	0.8	5.6	1.4	1.1	1.6	13.0	3.5	2.4
District of Columbia	47.8	0.0	0.4	1.1	2.6	0.6	1.3	8.7	14.6	18.6
Florida	326.1	5.8	14.7	28.8	30.4	25.2	39.2	67.8	73.4	40.1
Georgia	197.1	3.3	7.2	37.9	22.7	18.1	18.8	29.9	34.0	24.4
Hawaii	34.9	0.4	1.5	1.0	3.5	1.4	4.1	9.3	7.0	7.0
Idaho	25.9	1.5	1.4	5.8	2.4	1.6	2.7	3.0	4.0	3.3
Illinois	345.5	4.4	13.4	71.9	32.3	27.2	29.0	65.3	67.2	33.4
Indiana	144.1	2.4	6.2	48.3	11.9	9.0	13.8	17.4	20.7	13.7
Iowa	70.3	4.9	2.7	18.4	5.8	5.0	6.1	9.3	10.1	7.8
Kansas	62.0	2.6	2.5	11.8	7.1	5.1	6.4	7.4	9.9	8.6
Kentucky	89.3	2.1	3.2	26.6	7.6	5.3	8.2	9.1	12.4	11.7
Louisiana	109.6	1.3	4.4	21.9	10.2	6.2	9.2	13.4	16.5	11.8
Maine	26.0	0.5	1.1	4.9	2.0	1.6	3.1	4.6	4.7	3.5
Maryland	130.2	1.2	6.2	12.0	10.6	8.6	12.2	26.5	29.1	23.6
Massachusetts	191.0	1.1	5.7	33.5	12.4	14.2	15.9	43.9	47.2	17.3
Michigan	241.0	2.2	8.7	68.6	16.5	18.0	22.7	36.0	42.5	24.6
Minnesota	128.7	3.6	5.3	26.7	10.3	11.2	11.9	21.2	24.0	13.8
Mississippi	51.7	1.5	1.9	12.8	5.7	3.0	5.5	5.4	7.8	7.6
Missouri	132.8	2.3	5.8	29.6	14.1	10.2	12.8	18.8	24.1	14.7
Montana	16.9	0.8	0.8	1.3	2.3	1.1	1.8	2.2	3.1	2.7
Nebraska	43.2	3.7	1.8	6.6	4.9	3.3	3.8	5.9	7.0	6.0
Nevada	48.3	0.4	3.9	2.5	3.9	2.4	4.9	8.6	15.1	4.8
New Hampshire	31.7	0.2	1.0	8.1	2.5	2.0	3.0	6.5	5.8	2.8
New Jersey	251.1	1.4	8.4	36.8	25.6	24.0	19.6	55.8	52.8	26.6
New Mexico	40.4	0.7	1.7	8.2	3.2	1.7	3.7	5.1	6.6	6.8
New York	563.3	2.5	15.2	71.7	46.3	36.0	40.8	167.2	122.6	60.9
North Carolina	190.9	4.1	7.4	56.8	15.2	12.5	17.7	25.2	27.4	24.1
North Dakota	14.3	1.4	0.7	1.2	1.7	1.3	1.4	1.7	2.4	2.1
Ohio	280.7	2.9	10.1	80.7	22.3	20.6	27.2	40.3	46.9	28.6
Oklahoma	66.7	1.3	2.0	12.7	6.9	4.2	7.1	7.7	11.0	10.6
Oregon	79.4	2.3	4.1	17.4	6.3	6.6	7.4	12.1	13.9	9.3
Pennsylvania	298.7	2.9	10.8	66.7	27.5	18.4	27.5	51.8	60.5	31.0
Rhode Island	23.3	0.2	0.8	4.3	1.7	1.4	2.2	5.0	5.1	2.8
South Carolina	82.7	1.1	3.6	23.4	6.7	4.9	8.9	10.3	11.7	11.9
South Dakota	18.4	1.7	0.6	3.1	1.5	1.2	1.7	3.4	2.7	2.2
Tennessee	128.7	1.4	4.8	31.1	10.3	9.9	14.9	16.4	24.0	15.4
Texas	502.9	6.4	20.8	90.8	55.4	38.4	46.6	66.6	86.7	57.9
Utah	45.9	0.5	2.5	6.8	4.2	3.0	5.0	7.1	8.6	6.7
Vermont	13.5	0.3	0.5	2.7	1.2	0.9	1.4	2.3	2.6	1.6
Virginia	183.2	1.7	7.5	30.3	16.1	10.6	15.7	31.2	34.7	34.3
Washington	143.8	4.0	6.6	19.4	12.0	11.3	15.0	25.0	28.8	21.5
West Virginia	35.0	0.2	1.5	6.2	4.8	1.9	3.2	3.6	5.3	4.6
Wisconsin	128.7	2.6	5.2	38.3	9.2	8.4	11.7	19.7	20.0	13.5
Wyoming	15.8	0.3	0.5	0.9	2.5	0.5	1.1	1.6	1.4	2.0

[1] Includes mining not shown separately. [2] Includes agricultural services. [3] Includes federal civilian and military and state and local government. [4] States will not add to U.S. total as chained-dollar estimates are usually not additive.

Source: U.S. Bureau of Economic Analysis, *Survey of Current Business,* June 1998.

No. 721. Relation of GDP, GNP, Net National Product, National Income, Personal Income, Disposable Personal Income, and Personal Saving: 1990 to 1997

[In billions of dollars. For definitions, see text, Section 14]

ITEM	1990	1991	1992	1993	1994	1995	1996	1997
Gross domestic product.	5,743.8	5,916.7	6,244.4	6,558.1	6,947.0	7,265.4	7,636.0	8,079.9
Plus: Receipts of factor income from the rest of the world [1]	177.5	156.2	137.9	150.8	176.5	222.8	234.3	262.2
Less: Payments of factor income to the rest of the world [2]	156.4	140.5	126.8	132.1	168.3	217.5	232.6	282.0
Equals: Gross national product.	5,764.9	5,932.4	6,255.5	6,576.8	6,955.2	7,270.6	7,637.7	8,060.1
Less: Consumption of fixed capital	651.5	679.9	713.5	727.9	777.5	796.8	830.1	867.9
Equals: Net national product [3]	5,113.4	5,252.5	5,542.0	5,848.9	6,177.7	6,473.9	6,807.6	7,192.2
Less: Indirect business tax and nontax liability.	442.6	478.1	505.6	532.5	568.5	582.8	604.8	619.4
Plus: Subsidies [4]	25.3	23.6	27.1	31.1	26.6	25.2	25.4	26.1
Equals: National income [3]	4,652.1	4,761.6	4,990.4	5,266.8	5,590.7	5,912.3	6,254.5	6,649.7
Less: Corporate profits [5].	397.1	411.3	428.0	492.8	570.5	650.0	735.9	805.0
Net interest.	467.3	448.0	414.3	402.5	412.3	425.1	425.1	448.7
Contributions for social insurance	518.5	543.5	571.4	596.0	630.5	659.1	692.0	732.1
Wage accruals less disbursements . . .	0.1	-0.1	-15.8	4.4	13.3	13.1	1.1	1.2
Plus: Personal interest income.	704.4	699.2	667.2	651.0	668.1	718.9	735.7	768.6
Personal dividend income	142.9	153.6	159.4	185.3	204.8	251.9	291.2	321.5
Government transfer payments to persons	666.5	749.1	835.7	889.8	930.9	990.0	1,042.0	1,094.1
Business transfer payments to persons	21.3	20.8	22.5	22.1	23.7	25.0	26.0	27.1
Equals: Personal income	4,804.2	4,981.6	5,277.2	5,519.2	5,791.8	6,150.8	6,495.2	6,873.9
Less: Personal tax and nontax payments.	624.8	624.8	650.5	690.0	739.1	795.1	886.9	988.7
Equals: Disposable personal income. .	4,179.4	4,356.8	4,626.7	4,829.2	5,052.7	5,355.7	5,608.3	5,885.2
Less: Personal outlays	3,958.1	4,097.4	4,341.0	4,580.7	4,842.1	5,101.1	5,368.8	5,658.5
Equals: Personal saving.	221.3	259.5	285.6	248.5	210.6	254.6	239.6	226.7

[1] Consists largely of receipts by U.S. residents of interest and dividends and reinvested earnings of foreign affiliates of U.S. corporations. [2] Consists largely of payments to foreign residents of interest and dividends and reinvested earnings of U.S. affiliates of foreign corporations. [3] Includes items not shown separately. [4] Less current surplus of government enterprises. [5] With inventory valuation and capital consumption adjustments.

Source: U.S. Bureau of Economic Analysis, *National Income and Product Accounts of the United States, 1929-94,* Vol 1; and *Survey of Current Business,* August 1997 and May 1998.

No. 722. Selected Per Capita Income and Product Items in Current and Real (1992) Dollars: 1960 to 1997

[In dollars. Based on Bureau of the Census estimated population including Armed Forces abroad; based on quarterly averages. For explanation of chained dollars, see text, Section 14]

YEAR	CURRENT DOLLARS					CHAINED (1992) DOLLARS				
	Gross domestic product	Gross national product	Personal income	Disposable personal income	Personal consumption expenditures	Gross domestic product	Gross national product	Disposable personal income	Personal consumption expenditures
1960	2,913	2,931	2,277	2,008	1,838	12,512	12,585	8,660	7,926
1965	3,700	3,728	2,860	2,541	2,286	14,792	14,897	10,292	9,257
1970	5,050	5,081	4,077	3,545	3,160	16,520	16,616	12,022	10,717
1971	5,419	5,456	4,328	3,805	3,383	16,853	16,959	12,345	10,975
1972	5,894	5,935	4,703	4,074	3,671	17,579	17,694	12,770	11,508
1973	6,524	6,584	5,217	4,553	4,018	18,412	18,572	13,539	11,950
1974	6,998	7,071	5,672	4,928	4,353	18,178	18,360	13,310	11,756
1975	7,550	7,611	6,091	5,367	4,765	17,896	18,032	13,404	11,899
1976	8,341	8,419	6,673	5,837	5,268	18,713	18,878	13,793	12,446
1977	9,201	9,295	7,315	6,362	5,797	19,426	19,611	14,095	12,846
1978	10,292	10,392	8,176	7,097	6,418	20,185	20,367	14,662	13,258
1979	11,361	11,507	9,105	7,861	7,079	20,541	20,794	14,899	13,417
1980	12,226	12,381	10,037	8,665	7,730	20,252	20,497	14,813	13,216
1981	13,547	13,698	11,132	9,566	8,440	20,542	20,756	15,009	13,245
1982	13,961	14,095	11,744	10,145	8,943	19,896	20,076	15,053	13,270
1983	14,998	15,135	12,379	10,803	9,744	20,499	20,675	15,332	13,829
1984	16,508	16,640	13,602	11,929	10,543	21,744	21,904	16,309	14,415
1985	17,529	17,614	14,464	12,629	11,341	22,320	22,418	16,654	14,954
1986	18,374	18,427	15,200	13,289	12,019	22,801	22,857	17,039	15,409
1987	19,323	19,359	16,013	13,896	12,743	23,264	23,300	17,164	15,740
1988	20,605	20,659	17,076	14,905	13,669	23,934	23,988	17,678	16,221
1989	21,984	22,042	18,194	15,790	14,531	24,504	24,559	17,854	16,430
1990	22,979	23,064	19,220	16,721	15,360	24,549	24,632	17,996	16,532
1991	23,416	23,478	19,715	17,242	15,732	24,060	24,121	17,809	16,249
1992	24,447	24,490	20,660	18,113	16,520	24,447	24,490	18,113	16,520
1993	25,403	25,476	21,379	18,706	17,273	24,750	24,822	18,221	16,825
1994	26,647	26,678	22,216	19,381	18,093	25,357	25,389	18,431	17,207
1995	27,605	27,625	23,370	20,349	18,837	25,616	25,642	18,861	17,460
1996	28,752	28,759	24,457	21,117	19,608	26,088	26,101	19,116	17,750
1997	30,161	30,088	25,660	21,969	20,478	26,835	26,781	19,493	18,170

Source: U.S. Bureau of Economic Analysis, *National Income and Product Accounts of the United States, 1929-94,* Vol 2; and *Survey of Current Business,* August 1997 and May 1998.

No. 723. Personal Consumption Expenditures in Current and Real (1992) Dollars, by Type: 1990 to 1996

[**In billions of dollars**. For definition of "chained" dollars, see text, Section 14]

EXPENDITURE	CURRENT DOLLARS				CHAINED (1992) DOLLARS			
	1990	1994	1995	1996	1990	1994	1995	1996
Total expenditures [1]	**3,839.3**	**4,717.0**	**4,957.7**	**5,207.6**	**4,132.2**	**4,486.0**	**4,595.3**	**4,714.1**
Food and tobacco [1]	672.5	761.7	783.8	805.7	713.5	735.0	737.9	736.5
Food purchased for off-premise consumption	404.8	451.6	462.2	478.4	423.3	434.5	433.4	434.7
Purchased meals and beverages [2]	218.0	254.3	264.1	268.7	231.6	245.1	248.7	246.6
Tobacco products	42.0	47.3	48.7	49.6	50.9	47.2	47.4	46.8
Clothing, accessories, and jewelry [1]	262.7	312.7	323.4	336.3	279.4	308.5	321.8	335.3
Shoes	31.9	36.0	36.8	38.1	34.0	35.7	36.6	37.6
Clothing	173.8	211.6	217.7	226.0	183.7	211.2	220.6	229.9
Jewelry and watches	31.2	37.7	39.3	41.6	34.0	35.6	36.8	39.7
Personal care	57.3	68.4	71.9	75.7	60.6	65.5	67.9	70.1
Housing [1]	586.3	712.7	750.3	787.2	627.2	674.3	688.2	700.2
Owner-occupied nonfarm dwellings-space rent	410.7	507.0	532.2	558.3	437.6	479.6	487.2	495.3
Tenant-occupied nonfarm dwellings-space rent	150.1	174.0	184.6	193.6	160.0	165.2	171.1	174.9
Household operation [1]	436.2	535.0	562.8	591.9	457.0	514.5	533.6	548.4
Furniture [3]	39.0	45.9	48.0	49.6	40.6	43.2	44.2	44.6
Semidurable house furnishings [4]	21.2	27.2	28.9	30.1	22.0	25.7	26.9	28.2
Cleaning and polishing preparations	41.9	50.8	52.3	54.5	43.7	50.2	50.0	50.6
Household utilities	138.3	163.8	168.5	177.9	146.7	156.3	159.4	163.1
Electricity	71.9	84.2	88.0	90.3	76.1	82.6	84.3	85.2
Gas	26.8	32.4	31.5	34.9	27.7	30.0	30.7	32.7
Water and other sanitary services	27.5	36.6	38.8	41.1	31.9	33.0	33.8	34.6
Fuel oil and coal	12.0	10.5	10.2	11.6	11.2	10.7	10.5	10.6
Telephone and telegraph	60.4	82.6	90.2	96.9	61.3	79.6	86.6	91.1
Medical care [1]	615.6	826.1	871.6	912.8	691.1	751.0	766.2	782.4
Drug preparations and sundries [5]	65.1	81.6	85.7	90.9	74.5	76.7	79.1	81.7
Physicians	140.8	180.0	191.4	196.5	158.5	162.4	166.1	169.3
Dentists	32.9	43.9	47.6	50.9	37.7	39.8	41.1	42.0
Hospitals and nursing homes [6]	265.7	357.0	375.9	394.2	299.0	331.5	336.6	343.1
Health insurance [7]	37.4	55.0	53.6	56.3	41.3	40.0	37.5	36.9
Medical care [7]	31.3	42.9	40.7	41.8	35.3	36.6	35.2	34.7
Personal business [1]	290.1	370.4	389.1	421.1	331.3	352.1	350.7	363.6
Expense of handling life insurance [8]	56.4	72.6	75.4	79.9	61.2	68.1	67.9	68.5
Legal services	41.8	48.8	49.1	52.2	46.4	45.3	44.0	45.2
Funeral and burial expenses	9.0	11.1	12.2	12.8	10.1	10.1	10.5	10.4
Transportation	463.3	542.2	572.3	602.2	491.3	515.3	528.0	540.3
User-operated transportation [1]	426.9	502.6	530.1	557.7	454.2	476.6	487.8	497.7
New autos	92.4	91.2	87.1	86.1	98.1	86.2	80.6	78.2
Net purchases of used autos	31.6	44.1	52.4	55.3	35.0	37.5	40.8	42.1
Tires, tubes, accessories, etc.	29.4	34.5	35.8	37.9	30.0	35.1	36.2	38.3
Repair, greasing, washing, parking, storage, rental, and leasing	84.1	116.4	128.7	140.1	94.7	108.5	116.5	123.3
Gasoline and oil	96.6	109.4	114.4	122.6	108.1	109.8	113.1	114.1
Purchased local transportation	7.8	8.9	9.2	10.1	8.6	8.6	8.5	8.5
Mass transit systems	5.2	5.9	6.0	6.6	5.7	5.7	5.5	5.6
Taxicab	2.6	3.0	3.2	3.5	2.9	2.9	3.0	3.0
Purchased intercity transportation [1]	28.5	30.7	33.0	34.4	28.6	30.1	31.7	34.2
Railway (commutation)	0.8	0.7	0.8	0.8	0.8	0.7	0.7	0.7
Bus	1.0	1.1	1.3	1.3	1.1	1.1	1.4	1.4
Airline	23.9	25.8	27.7	28.2	23.7	25.5	26.8	28.8
Recreation [1][9]	281.6	370.2	402.5	431.1	291.8	365.2	395.7	424.4
Magazines, newspapers, and sheet music	21.5	24.5	25.5	26.5	23.8	22.9	22.9	22.7
Nondurable toys and sport supplies	31.6	39.7	42.2	45.4	32.6	38.9	41.4	43.9
Video and audio products, computing equipment, musical instruments	53.8	78.5	85.2	89.7	47.9	87.4	101.8	119.5
Education and research	80.7	104.7	112.2	119.6	89.3	96.8	99.4	102.7
Higher education	44.0	59.0	62.2	66.2	50.2	53.1	53.7	54.0
Religious and welfare activities	100.4	131.2	139.8	150.5	106.6	125.6	128.6	136.6
Foreign travel and other, net	-7.4	-18.3	-22.1	-26.5	-8.2	-16.2	-19.5	-21.5
Foreign travel by U.S. residents	41.2	50.1	51.9	54.9	46.1	48.8	48.9	50.8
Less: Expenditures in the United States by nonresidents	51.6	69.7	75.2	82.7	57.7	66.4	69.5	73.5

[1] Includes other expenditures not shown separately.   [2] Consists of purchases (including tips) of meals and beverages from retail, service, and amusement establishments; hotels; dining and buffet cars; schools; school fraternities; institutions; clubs; and industrial lunch rooms. Includes meals and beverages consumed both on and off-premise.   [3] Includes mattresses and bedsprings.   [4] Consists largely of textile house furnishings including piece goods allocated to house furnishing use. Also includes lamp shades, brooms, and brushes.   [5] Excludes drug preparations and related products dispensed by physicians, hospitals, and other medical services.   [6] Consists of (1) current expenditures (including consumption of fixed capital) of nonprofit hospitals and nursing homes and (2) payments by patients to proprietary and government hospitals and nursing homes.   [7] Consists of (1) premiums, less benefits and dividends, for health hospitalization and accidental death and dismemberment insurance provided by commercial insurance carriers and (2) administrative expenses (including consumption of fixed capital) of Blue Cross and Blue Shield plans and of other independent prepaid and self-insured health plans.   [8] Consists of (1) operating expenses of life insurance carriers and private noninsured pension plans and (2) premiums less benefits and dividends of fraternal benefit societies. Excludes expenses allocated by commercial carriers to accident and health insurance.   [9] For additional details, see Table 425.

Source: U.S. Bureau of Economic Analysis, *National Income and Product Accounts of the United States, 1929-94*, Vol 1; and *Survey of Current Business*, August 1997.

No. 724. Personal Income and Its Disposition: 1990 to 1997

[In billions of dollars, except as indicated. For definition of personal income and chained dollars, see text, Section 14]

ITEM	1990	1991	1992	1993	1994	1995	1996	1997
Personal income	**4,804.2**	**4,981.6**	**5,277.2**	**5,519.2**	**5,791.8**	**6,150.8**	**6,495.2**	**6,873.9**
Wage and salary disbursements	2,757.5	2,827.6	2,986.4	3,089.6	3,240.7	3,429.5	3,632.5	3,877.4
Commodity-producing industries [1]	754.2	746.3	765.7	781.2	824.4	864.4	909.1	960.3
Manufacturing	561.2	562.5	583.5	592.9	620.8	648.4	674.7	706.0
Distributive industries [2]	634.1	646.6	680.3	699.4	741.4	783.1	823.3	876.3
Service industries [3]	852.1	888.7	972.6	1,024.7	1,072.7	1,159.0	1,257.5	1,375.5
Government	517.2	546.1	567.8	584.3	602.2	623.0	642.6	665.3
Other labor income	300.6	322.7	351.3	385.1	405.0	406.8	407.6	416.6
Proprietors' income [4]	374.0	376.5	423.8	450.8	471.6	489.0	520.3	544.5
Rental income of persons [5]	61.0	67.9	79.4	105.7	124.4	132.8	146.3	147.9
Personal dividend income	142.9	153.6	159.4	185.3	204.8	251.9	291.2	321.5
Personal interest income	704.4	699.3	667.2	651.0	668.1	718.9	735.7	768.6
Transfer payments to persons	687.8	769.9	858.2	912.0	954.7	1,015.0	1,068.0	1,121.1
Less: Personal contributions for								
social insurance	*223.9*	*235.8*	*248.4*	*260.3*	*277.5*	*293.1*	*306.3*	*323.7*
Less: Personal tax and nontax payments.	*624.8*	*624.8*	*650.6*	*690.0*	*739.1*	*795.1*	*886.9*	*988.7*
Equals: Disposable personal income	**4,179.4**	**4,356.8**	**4,626.7**	**4,829.2**	**5,052.7**	**5,355.7**	**5,608.3**	**5,885.2**
Less: Personal outlays	*3,958.1*	*4,097.4*	*4,341.0*	*4,580.7*	*4,842.1*	*5,101.1*	*5,368.8*	*5,658.5*
Personal consumption expenditures	3,839.3	3,975.1	4,219.8	4,459.2	4,717.0	4,957.7	5,207.6	5,485.8
Interest paid by persons	108.9	111.9	111.7	108.2	110.9	128.5	145.2	154.8
Personal transfer payments to								
the rest of the world (net)	9.9	10.4	9.6	13.3	14.2	14.8	15.9	17.9
Equals: Personal saving	**221.3**	**259.5**	**285.7**	**248.5**	**210.6**	**254.6**	**239.6**	**226.7**
Addenda:								
Disposable personal income:								
Total, billions of chained								
(1992) dollars	4,498.2	4,500.0	4,626.7	4,703.9	4,805.1	4,964.2	5,076.9	5,221.9
Per capita (dollars):								
Current dollars	16,720.0	17,241.8	18,112.2	18,706.0	19,381.0	20,349.0	21,117.0	21,969.0
Chained (1992) dollars	17,996.1	17,808.9	18,112.8	18,221.0	18,431.0	18,861.0	19,116.0	19,493.0
Personal saving as percentage of								
disposable personal income	5.3	6.0	6.2	5.1	4.2	4.8	4.3	3.9

1 Comprises agriculture, forestry, fishing, mining, construction, and manufacturing.   2 Comprises transportation, communication, public utilities, and trade.   3 Comprises finance, insurance, real estate, services, and rest of world.   4 With capital consumption and inventory valuation adjustments.   5 With capital consumption adjustment.

Source: U.S. Bureau of Economic Analysis, *National Income and Product Accounts of the United States, 1929-94,* Vol 1; and *Survey of Current Business,* August 1997 and May 1998.

No. 725. Gross Saving and Investment: 1990 to 1997

[In billions of dollars]

ITEM	1990	1991	1992	1993	1994	1995	1996	1997
Gross saving	**903.1**	**934.0**	**904.3**	**949.5**	**1,079.2**	**1,165.5**	**1,267.8**	**1,394.3**
Gross private saving	860.3	930.6	970.7	979.3	1,030.2	1,093.1	1,125.5	1,164.2
Personal saving	221.3	259.5	285.6	248.5	210.6	254.6	239.6	226.7
Undistributed corporate profits [1]	104.7	114.8	115.5	131.9	167.6	172.4	202.1	219.5
Undistributed profits	79.4	77.7	93.9	104.5	132.3	145.0	142.8	144.2
Inventory valuation adjustment	-13.5	4.0	-7.5	-8.5	-16.1	-24.3	-2.5	5.5
Capital consumption adjustment	38.9	33.1	29.1	36.0	51.4	51.6	61.8	69.7
Corporate consumption of fixed								
capital	350.3	364.5	376.4	388.4	412.3	428.9	452.3	475.6
Noncorporate consumption of fixed								
capital	184.0	191.9	209.0	206.1	226.3	224.1	230.5	241.2
Wage accruals less disbursements	-	-	-15.8	4.4	13.3	13.1	1.1	1.2
Gross government saving	42.7	3.3	-66.5	-29.8	49.0	72.4	142.3	230.0
Federal	-94.0	-132.2	-215.0	-182.7	-117.2	-103.6	-39.2	42.8
State and local	136.7	135.5	148.6	152.9	166.2	176.0	181.5	187.3
Capital grants received by the U.S. (net)	-	-	-	-	-	-	-	-
Gross investment	**920.5**	**944.0**	**949.1**	**1,002.1**	**1,093.8**	**1,137.2**	**1,207.9**	**1,308.3**
Gross private domestic investment	799.7	736.2	790.4	876.2	1,007.9	1,038.2	1,116.5	1,242.5
Gross government investment	199.4	200.5	209.1	204.5	205.9	213.4	224.3	226.0
Net foreign investment	-78.6	7.3	-50.5	-78.6	-120.0	-114.4	-132.9	-160.2
Statistical discrepancy	**17.4**	**10.1**	**44.8**	**52.6**	**14.6**	**-28.2**	**-59.9**	**-86.0**

- Represents or rounds to zero.   1 With inventory valuation and capital consumption adjustments.

Source: U.S. Bureau of Economic Analysis, *National Income and Product Accounts of the United States, 1929-94,* Vol 1; and *Survey of Current Business,* August 1997 and May 1998.

No. 726. Personal Income, by State: 1990 to 1997

[In billions of dollars, except percent. 1997 preliminary. Represents a measure of income received from all sources during the calendar year by residents of each state. Data exclude federal employees overseas and U.S. residents employed by private U.S. firms on temporary foreign assignment. Totals may differ from those in Tables 721, 722, and 724. For definition of average annual percent change, see Guide to Tabular Presentation]

STATE	CURRENT DOLLARS				CONSTANT (1992) DOLLARS [1]				Average annual percent change		Percent distribution	
	1990	1995	1996	1997	1990	1995	1996	1997	1990-96	1996-97	1990	1997
United States . .	4,786.3	6,137.9	6,480.0	6,851.1	5,151.5	5,689.0	5,865.9	6,079.0	2.2	3.6	100.0	100.0
Alabama	61.7	82.1	86.0	90.0	66.4	76.1	77.8	79.9	2.7	2.7	1.3	1.3
Alaska	11.7	14.6	14.9	15.4	12.6	13.5	13.5	13.7	1.2	1.5	0.2	0.2
Arizona	61.2	87.5	94.6	101.9	65.9	81.1	85.6	90.4	4.5	5.6	1.3	1.5
Arkansas	33.1	45.0	47.5	49.4	35.6	41.7	43.0	43.8	3.2	1.9	0.7	0.7
California	640.3	764.6	808.2	857.4	689.1	708.7	731.6	760.7	1.0	4.0	13.4	12.5
Colorado	63.8	91.7	98.2	105.3	68.7	85.0	88.9	93.4	4.4	5.1	1.3	1.5
Connecticut	87.2	106.5	111.7	118.6	93.8	98.7	101.1	105.2	1.3	4.1	1.8	1.7
Delaware	14.5	18.8	20.1	21.2	15.6	17.4	18.2	18.8	2.6	3.3	0.3	0.3
District of Columbia . .	15.5	18.0	18.4	19.0	16.7	16.7	16.7	16.8	0.0	0.6	0.3	0.3
Florida	249.7	328.1	348.9	370.1	268.8	304.1	315.8	328.4	2.7	4.0	5.2	5.4
Georgia	113.3	157.8	168.9	180.1	121.9	146.3	152.9	159.8	3.8	4.5	2.4	2.6
Hawaii	24.0	29.6	30.1	30.9	25.8	27.4	27.2	27.4	0.9	0.7	0.5	0.5
Idaho	15.6	22.4	23.6	24.8	16.7	20.7	21.4	22.0	4.2	2.8	0.3	0.4
Illinois	235.0	301.7	318.1	335.5	253.0	279.6	288.0	297.7	2.2	3.4	4.9	4.9
Indiana	95.5	125.7	131.9	138.4	102.8	116.5	119.4	122.8	2.5	2.8	2.0	2.0
Iowa	47.0	59.2	63.6	65.9	50.6	54.8	57.6	58.5	2.2	1.6	1.0	1.0
Kansas	44.6	56.2	59.7	63.3	48.0	52.1	54.0	56.1	2.0	3.9	0.9	0.9
Kentucky	55.8	72.7	76.8	80.7	60.0	67.4	69.5	71.6	2.5	3.0	1.2	1.2
Louisiana	62.4	82.2	85.6	90.0	67.2	76.2	77.4	79.9	2.4	3.2	1.3	1.3
Maine	21.2	25.0	26.1	27.4	22.8	23.1	23.6	24.3	0.6	3.0	0.4	0.4
Maryland	108.0	133.6	140.0	147.6	116.3	123.8	126.8	130.9	1.5	3.2	2.3	2.2
Massachusetts	139.9	172.1	181.4	192.8	150.6	159.5	164.2	171.1	1.5	4.2	2.9	2.8
Michigan	174.4	229.5	239.3	249.8	187.7	212.7	216.6	221.7	2.4	2.4	3.6	3.6
Minnesota	85.0	111.0	119.5	125.6	91.5	102.9	108.1	111.4	2.8	3.1	1.8	1.8
Mississippi	32.8	45.0	47.6	49.9	35.3	41.8	43.1	44.3	3.4	2.8	0.7	0.7
Missouri	90.6	116.8	123.3	129.7	97.5	108.2	111.6	115.0	2.3	3.0	1.9	1.9
Montana	12.1	16.2	16.9	17.6	13.0	15.0	15.3	15.6	2.8	2.0	0.3	0.3
Nebraska	27.8	35.1	37.9	39.4	29.9	32.5	34.3	35.0	2.3	2.0	0.6	0.6
Nevada	24.7	37.9	41.7	44.9	26.5	35.2	37.8	39.9	6.1	5.6	0.5	0.7
New Hampshire	23.1	29.5	31.1	32.9	24.9	27.3	28.1	29.2	2.0	3.9	0.5	0.5
New Jersey	193.4	238.5	250.2	263.0	208.1	221.1	226.5	233.3	1.4	3.0	4.0	3.8
New Mexico	22.0	30.8	32.2	33.9	23.7	28.5	29.1	30.1	3.5	3.4	0.5	0.5
New York	416.7	505.4	529.9	557.8	448.5	468.4	479.7	494.9	1.1	3.2	8.7	8.1
North Carolina	111.0	152.6	162.6	173.3	119.5	141.4	147.2	153.8	3.5	4.5	2.3	2.5
North Dakota	9.7	11.9	13.2	13.0	10.5	11.0	11.9	11.5	2.1	-3.4	0.2	0.2
Ohio	197.1	251.1	262.2	275.9	212.1	232.8	237.4	244.8	1.9	3.1	4.1	4.0
Oklahoma	49.2	61.3	64.5	68.2	53.0	56.8	58.4	60.5	1.6	3.6	1.0	1.0
Oregon	49.9	68.9	73.9	79.1	53.7	63.8	66.9	70.2	3.7	4.9	1.0	1.2
Pennsylvania	230.9	285.2	299.2	313.2	248.5	264.3	270.9	277.9	1.4	2.6	4.8	4.6
Rhode Island	19.8	23.5	24.3	25.4	21.3	21.8	22.0	22.6	0.5	2.7	0.4	0.4
South Carolina	54.1	70.3	74.0	78.0	58.2	65.1	66.9	69.2	2.3	3.4	1.1	1.1
South Dakota	10.8	14.0	15.3	15.8	11.6	13.0	13.9	14.0	3.1	0.7	0.2	0.2
Tennessee	79.9	111.8	116.9	123.6	85.9	103.6	105.9	109.6	3.6	3.5	1.7	1.8
Texas	295.1	400.6	426.2	459.9	317.6	371.3	385.8	408.0	3.3	5.8	6.2	6.7
Utah	24.6	36.2	39.1	42.1	26.5	33.5	35.4	37.3	4.9	5.4	0.5	0.6
Vermont	10.0	12.6	13.2	13.8	10.8	11.7	12.0	12.2	1.8	1.7	0.2	0.2
Virginia	124.6	160.3	168.4	178.0	134.1	148.6	152.4	158.0	2.2	3.7	2.6	2.6
Washington	96.2	130.3	139.5	149.9	103.6	120.8	126.3	133.0	3.4	5.3	2.0	2.2
West Virginia	25.4	32.0	33.2	34.4	27.4	29.7	30.0	30.5	1.5	1.7	0.5	0.5
Wisconsin	86.9	114.6	120.4	126.5	93.5	106.2	109.0	112.3	2.6	3.0	1.8	1.8
Wyoming	7.8	10.0	10.4	10.9	8.4	9.3	9.4	9.6	1.9	2.1	0.2	0.2

[1] Implicit price deflator for personal consumption expenditures is used as a deflator.

Source: U.S. Bureau of Economic Analysis, *Survey of Current Business*, May 1998, and unpublished data.

No. 727. Personal Income Per Capita in Current and Constant (1992) Dollars, by State: 1990 to 1997

[1997 data preliminary. See headnote, Table 726]

STATE	CURRENT DOLLARS				CONSTANT (1992) DOLLARS [1]				Income rank	
	1990	1995	1996	1997	1990	1995	1996	1997	1990	1997
United States ...	19,188	23,359	24,436	25,598	20,652	21,651	22,120	22,713	(X)	(X)
Alabama............	15,231	19,254	20,056	20,842	16,393	17,846	18,155	18,493	42	38
Alaska.............	21,097	24,214	24,597	25,305	22,707	22,443	22,266	22,453	9	19
Arizona............	16,640	20,316	21,335	22,364	17,910	18,830	19,313	19,844	35	35
Arkansas	14,042	18,144	18,967	19,585	15,114	16,817	17,169	17,378	49	48
California	21,393	24,229	25,368	26,570	23,026	22,457	22,964	23,576	8	13
Colorado...........	19,322	24,517	25,740	27,051	20,796	22,724	23,300	24,003	18	9
Connecticut........	26,507	32,603	34,174	36,263	28,530	30,219	30,935	32,177	1	1
Delaware	21,648	26,235	27,782	29,022	23,300	24,316	25,149	25,752	6	5
District of Columbia	25,701	32,609	34,172	35,852	27,662	30,224	30,933	31,812	(X)	(X)
Florida	19,185	23,139	24,198	25,255	20,649	21,447	21,905	22,409	19	20
Georgia	17,407	21,940	23,028	24,061	18,735	20,336	20,845	21,350	28	25
Hawaii	21,564	25,103	25,421	26,034	23,210	23,267	23,012	23,100	7	16
Idaho	15,368	19,199	19,865	20,478	16,541	17,795	17,982	18,170	41	43
Illinois	20,534	25,580	26,855	28,202	22,101	23,709	24,310	25,024	11	7
Indiana............	17,191	21,716	22,633	23,604	18,503	20,128	20,488	20,944	30	29
Iowa	16,911	20,826	22,330	23,102	18,201	19,303	20,214	20,499	33	32
Kansas............	17,968	21,886	23,133	24,379	19,339	20,285	20,941	21,632	22	24
Kentucky	15,106	18,847	19,773	20,657	16,259	17,469	17,899	18,329	43	41
Louisiana	14,790	18,999	19,709	20,680	15,919	17,610	17,841	18,350	45	40
Maine.............	17,190	20,227	21,087	22,078	18,502	18,748	19,088	19,590	31	36
Maryland	22,517	26,567	27,676	28,969	24,235	24,624	25,053	25,705	5	6
Massachusetts.......	23,249	28,397	29,808	31,524	25,023	26,320	26,983	27,972	3	3
Michigan..........	18,730	23,767	24,588	25,560	20,159	22,029	22,258	22,680	20	18
Minnesota.........	19,378	24,097	25,699	26,797	20,857	22,335	23,263	23,777	16	10
Mississippi	12,719	16,743	17,561	18,272	13,690	15,519	15,897	16,213	50	50
Missouri	17,672	21,927	22,984	24,001	19,021	20,323	20,806	21,296	25	26
Montana..........	15,067	18,602	19,278	20,046	16,217	17,242	17,451	17,787	44	46
Nebraska	17,562	21,424	22,975	23,803	18,902	19,857	20,798	21,121	26	27
Nevada	20,241	24,809	26,059	26,791	21,786	22,995	23,589	23,772	12	11
New Hampshire	20,767	25,726	26,772	28,047	22,352	23,845	24,235	24,886	10	8
New Jersey	24,930	29,982	31,265	32,654	26,832	27,789	28,302	28,974	2	2
New Mexico	14,502	18,246	18,814	19,587	15,609	16,912	17,031	17,380	46	47
New York	23,147	27,850	29,221	30,752	24,913	25,813	26,452	27,287	4	4
North Carolina	16,674	21,233	22,244	23,345	17,946	19,680	20,136	20,714	34	31
North Dakota	15,281	18,504	20,479	20,271	16,447	17,151	18,538	17,987	40	45
Ohio	18,147	22,560	23,493	24,661	19,532	20,910	21,266	21,882	21	21
Oklahoma	15,633	18,748	19,574	20,556	16,826	17,377	17,719	18,240	37	42
Oregon............	17,452	21,915	23,111	24,393	18,784	20,312	20,921	21,644	27	23
Pennsylvania.......	19,410	23,673	24,851	26,058	20,891	21,942	22,496	23,122	17	15
Rhode Island.......	19,729	23,783	24,613	25,760	21,235	22,044	22,280	22,857	14	17
South Carolina	15,448	19,073	19,898	20,755	16,627	17,678	18,012	18,416	39	39
South Dakota	15,510	19,032	20,749	21,447	16,694	17,640	18,782	19,030	38	37
Tennessee	16,328	21,350	22,032	23,018	17,574	19,789	19,944	20,424	36	33
Texas.............	17,310	21,381	22,324	23,656	18,631	19,817	20,208	20,990	29	28
Utah	14,231	18,317	19,384	20,432	15,317	16,977	17,547	18,130	47	44
Vermont	17,721	21,609	22,545	23,401	19,073	20,029	20,408	20,764	24	30
Virginia...........	20,054	24,284	25,255	26,438	21,584	22,508	22,861	23,459	13	14
Washington........	19,637	23,974	25,277	26,718	21,136	22,221	22,881	23,707	15	12
West Virginia.......	14,197	17,576	18,225	18,957	15,280	16,291	16,498	16,821	48	49
Wisconsin..........	17,722	22,416	23,390	24,475	19,074	20,777	21,173	21,717	23	22
Wyoming	17,213	20,954	21,587	22,648	18,527	19,422	19,541	20,096	32	34

X Not applicable.   [1] Implicit price deflator for personal consumption expenditures is used as a deflator.

Source: U.S. Bureau of Economic Analysis, *Survey of Current Business,* May 1998, and unpublished data.

No. 728. Disposable Personal Income Per Capita in Current and Constant (1992) Dollars, by State: 1990 and 1997

[In dollars. 1997 data preliminary]

STATE	CURRENT DOLLARS 1990	CURRENT DOLLARS 1997	CONSTANT (1992) DOLLARS 1990	CONSTANT (1992) DOLLARS 1997
United States	16,689	21,908	17,963	19,439
Alabama	13,572	18,334	14,608	16,268
Alaska	18,148	21,707	19,533	19,261
Arizona	14,663	19,345	15,782	17,165
Arkansas	12,559	17,304	13,517	15,354
California	18,421	22,674	19,827	20,119
Colorado	16,790	22,751	18,071	20,187
Connecticut	22,847	29,598	24,590	26,263
Delaware	18,544	24,430	19,959	21,677
District of Columbia	21,807	30,372	23,471	26,949
Florida	16,959	21,894	18,253	19,427
Georgia	15,236	20,620	16,399	18,296
Hawaii	18,375	22,531	19,777	19,992
Idaho	13,492	17,687	14,522	15,694
Illinois	17,727	23,855	19,080	21,167
Indiana	14,987	20,166	16,131	17,894
Iowa	14,708	20,014	15,830	17,759
Kansas	15,680	20,879	16,877	18,526
Kentucky	13,247	17,918	14,258	15,899
Louisiana	13,289	18,384	14,303	16,312
Maine	15,090	19,256	16,242	17,086
Maryland	19,184	24,386	20,648	21,638
Massachusetts	19,853	25,990	21,368	23,061
Michigan	16,297	21,794	17,541	19,338
Minnesota	16,571	22,205	17,836	19,703
Mississippi	11,587	16,532	12,471	14,669
Missouri	15,476	20,706	16,657	18,373
Montana	13,165	17,465	14,170	15,497
Nebraska	15,428	20,503	16,605	18,193
Nevada	17,560	22,742	18,900	20,179
New Hampshire	18,494	24,438	19,905	21,684
New Jersey	21,547	27,422	23,191	24,332
New Mexico	12,960	17,327	13,949	15,374
New York	19,608	25,713	21,104	22,815
North Carolina	14,578	20,099	15,690	17,834
North Dakota	13,598	17,837	14,636	15,827
Ohio	15,817	21,093	17,024	18,716
Oklahoma	13,620	18,006	14,659	15,977
Oregon	15,128	20,517	16,282	18,205
Pennsylvania	16,925	22,434	18,217	19,906
Rhode Island	17,315	22,297	18,636	19,784
South Carolina	13,671	18,147	14,714	16,102
South Dakota	13,952	19,195	15,017	17,032
Tennessee	14,712	20,390	15,835	18,092
Texas	15,399	20,868	16,574	18,516
Utah	12,422	17,370	13,370	15,413
Vermont	15,477	20,401	16,658	18,102
Virginia	17,362	22,388	18,687	19,865
Washington	17,233	23,154	18,548	20,545
West Virginia	12,673	16,803	13,640	14,909
Wisconsin	15,306	20,634	16,474	18,309
Wyoming	15,207	19,801	16,367	17,570

Source: U.S. Bureau of Economic Analysis, *Survey of Current Business*, May 1998, unpublished data.

No. 729. Personal Income, by Selected Large Metropolitan Area: 1994 to 1996

[As defined June 30, 1994. CMSA=Consolidated Metropolitan Statistical Area; MSA=Metropolitan Statistical Area. See Appendix II]

METROPOLITAN AREA RANKED BY 1997 POPULATION	PERSONAL INCOME 1994 (mil. dol.)	PERSONAL INCOME 1995 (mil. dol.)	PERSONAL INCOME 1996 (mil. dol.)	Annual percent change, 1995-96	PER CAPITA PERSONAL INCOME 1994 (dol.)	PER CAPITA PERSONAL INCOME 1995 (dol.)	PER CAPITA PERSONAL INCOME 1996 (dol.)	Percent of national average, 1996
United States	5,774,875	6,137,878	6,480,031	5.6	22,186	23,359	24,436	100.0
New York-No. New Jersey-Long Island, NY-NJ-CT-PA CMSA	590,202	626,539	659,399	5.2	29,970	31,732	33,303	136.3
Los Angeles-Riverside-Orange County, CA CMSA	341,769	360,329	378,298	5	22,417	23,533	24,522	100.4
Chicago-Gary-Kenosha, IL-IN-WI CMSA	222,978	238,058	250,787	5.3	26,242	27,866	29,195	119.5
Washington-Baltimore, DC-MD-VA-WV CMSA	195,280	205,681	215,836	4.9	27,766	29,018	30,204	123.6
San Francisco-Oakland-San Jose, CA CMSA	188,817	203,046	217,884	7.3	28,990	30,989	32,933	134.8
Philadelphia-Wilmington-Atlantic City, PA-NJ-DE-MD CMSA	152,556	161,128	169,717	5.3	25,587	26,989	28,413	116.3
Boston-Worcester-Lawrence-Lowell-Brockton, MA-NH (NECMA)	154,929	166,492	175,769	5.6	27,095	28,925	30,366	124.3
Detroit-Ann Arbor-Flint, MI CMSA	132,287	141,283	147,044	4.1	24,802	26,264	27,113	111.0
Dallas-Fort Worth, TX CMSA	106,085	114,316	122,834	7.5	24,294	25,663	26,906	110.1
Houston-Galveston-Brazoria, TX CMSA	98,543	105,839	112,597	6.4	24,046	25,424	26,556	108.7
Atlanta, GA	81,442	89,020	96,193	8.1	24,451	25,938	27,241	111.5
Miami-Fort Lauderdale, FL CMSA	75,283	80,181	84,660	5.6	22,150	23,294	24,341	99.6
Seattle-Tacoma-Bremerton, WA CMSA	81,292	87,159	93,546	7.3	25,287	26,716	28,269	115.7
Cleveland-Akron, OH CMSA	68,194	72,543	75,712	4.4	23,485	24,957	26,025	106.5
Phoenix-Mesa, AZ CMSA	53,320	58,994	64,359	9.1		22,166	23,377	95.7
Minneapolis-St. Paul, MN-WI CMSA	70,644	75,469	80,878	7.2	26,246	27,682	29,299	119.9
San Diego, CA	58,171	61,380	65,000	5.9	22,111	23,201	24,282	99.4
St. Louis, MO-IL	60,119	64,142	67,118	4.6	23,733	25,238	26,337	107.8
Pittsburgh, PA	54,830	57,665	60,194	4.4	22,880	24,167	25,359	103.8
Denver-Boulder-Greeley, CO CMSA	56,092	60,771	65,084	7.1	25,657	27,262	28,650	117.2
Tampa-St. Petersburg-Clearwater, FL	46,279	49,670	52,738	6.2	21,503	22,817	23,984	98.2
Portland-Salem, OR-WA CMSA	44,697	48,636	52,531	8	22,508	24,000	25,343	103.7
Cincinnati-Hamilton, OH-KY-IN CMSA	42,644	45,357	47,786	5.4	22,511	23,787	24,901	101.9
Kansas City, MO-KS	38,562	41,353	43,810	5.9	23,281	24,738	25,949	106.2
Sacramento-Yolo, CA	35,322	37,783	39,619	4.9	22,283	23,518	24,288	99.4
Milwaukee-Racine, WI CMSA	39,656	42,156	44,087	4.6	24,268	25,768	26,923	110.2

U.S. Bureau of Economic Analysis, *Survey of Current Business*, April 1998.

No. 730. Projections of Personal Income, Earnings, and Gross State Product in Constant (1987) Dollars, by State: 1993 to 2010

[In billions of dollars. For information on methodology, see source. Gross state product estimates are not available for 1993; therefore, 1992 shown for comparison]

STATE	PERSONAL INCOME			EARNINGS			GROSS STATE PRODUCT		
	1993	2000	2010	1993	2000	2010	1992	2000	2010
United States	4,183.9	4,894.5	5,917.2	3,017.5	3,532.7	4,207.5	5,001.4	6,025.6	7,219.4
Alabama	55.9	64.6	77.5	40.0	46.3	54.7	66.0	79.6	95.2
Alaska	10.8	12.6	15.3	9.0	10.4	12.4	23.0	26.8	30.9
Arizona	55.7	70.4	91.0	38.5	48.7	61.6	62.3	83.3	105.8
Arkansas	30.3	35.2	42.0	21.6	25.3	29.6	37.3	45.6	54.5
California	533.3	638.3	795.5	390.6	468.0	577.1	652.3	783.0	969.0
Colorado	59.8	73.3	92.5	45.0	55.2	68.7	69.0	88.8	110.5
Connecticut	71.5	81.8	97.5	50.8	58.3	68.7	82.5	97.0	115.1
Delaware	11.9	14.0	17.0	9.4	11.0	13.1	18.4	22.7	27.3
District of Columbia	13.5	14.3	15.5	25.1	27.6	30.9	32.0	34.2	37.7
Florida	221.2	276.7	357.2	136.2	170.1	215.3	222.6	288.4	364.2
Georgia	103.7	126.2	157.9	79.0	96.1	118.3	128.6	164.2	203.7
Hawaii	21.4	25.4	31.0	16.4	19.4	23.3	27.2	32.0	38.4
Idaho	15.0	18.2	22.4	11.2	13.5	16.4	17.7	22.9	28.4
Illinois	205.8	234.7	277.7	151.4	173.1	202.1	246.8	292.7	345.1
Indiana	85.5	98.4	116.8	62.4	71.9	83.8	103.3	126.8	150.5
Iowa	40.3	46.3	54.1	27.8	32.3	37.0	50.5	58.9	68.6
Kansas	39.3	45.9	54.8	27.5	32.2	37.8	47.1	56.6	67.2
Kentucky	50.1	57.8	68.6	35.6	41.0	47.9	63.7	76.9	90.9
Louisiana	55.6	63.8	75.8	39.0	44.9	52.4	79.9	92.5	106.8
Maine	18.2	20.9	25.2	12.3	14.2	16.8	20.1	23.8	28.3
Maryland	92.7	108.3	130.4	59.7	69.3	82.0	95.4	111.4	131.7
Massachusetts	114.9	130.8	154.8	84.8	97.6	114.3	135.1	160.0	187.6
Michigan	152.0	170.6	197.5	109.8	123.2	140.1	171.7	201.1	231.4
Minnesota	74.1	86.8	103.6	56.2	65.8	77.5	92.9	112.2	133.8
Mississippi	30.3	35.0	41.6	20.7	24.1	28.1	37.2	45.7	54.3
Missouri	79.9	92.5	110.4	57.6	66.5	77.9	93.6	111.3	131.8
Montana	11.4	13.6	16.6	7.6	9.0	10.8	13.0	16.2	19.6
Nebraska	24.8	28.9	34.4	18.3	21.2	24.8	31.6	37.9	45.2
Nevada	24.7	32.1	42.6	18.5	24.0	31.2	31.4	43.2	56.2
New Hampshire	19.5	23.1	28.0	12.7	15.2	18.2	21.6	26.8	32.4
New Jersey	164.4	189.0	223.1	111.3	128.4	150.1	184.1	215.9	253.4
New Mexico	20.6	25.0	31.4	14.6	17.7	21.9	27.3	35.4	43.7
New York	351.9	387.6	439.6	256.5	285.1	321.6	413.1	464.6	526.9
North Carolina	101.3	122.6	151.4	76.7	92.3	111.2	130.5	164.3	200.1
North Dakota	8.5	9.8	11.4	6.0	7.0	8.0	11.1	12.7	14.9
Ohio	169.9	192.6	225.0	123.1	140.0	161.3	203.2	240.4	279.7
Oklahoma	43.0	49.6	58.9	29.7	34.1	39.7	50.7	60.2	70.4
Oregon	46.0	55.3	68.1	33.2	39.9	48.3	52.5	65.2	79.3
Pennsylvania	199.8	223.9	260.5	137.3	154.6	177.3	222.1	255.7	294.5
Rhode Island	16.6	18.8	22.2	10.8	12.4	14.5	17.8	20.9	24.5
South Carolina	47.8	57.1	70.7	34.7	41.6	50.7	58.9	74.1	91.6
South Dakota	10.0	11.9	14.4	7.2	8.5	10.1	12.7	15.8	19.2
Tennessee	73.3	87.8	107.4	55.5	66.5	79.9	91.3	114.9	139.3
Texas	269.3	323.9	398.5	205.3	245.7	297.4	350.0	433.6	525.2
Utah	23.4	29.9	39.3	18.2	23.2	30.2	30.0	40.6	52.6
Vermont	8.6	10.2	12.4	6.1	7.3	8.7	10.0	12.2	14.6
Virginia	109.2	127.0	154.3	77.0	89.5	107.3	125.1	148.9	179.2
Washington	89.3	107.3	134.7	64.5	77.1	95.3	105.8	128.8	159.7
West Virginia	22.9	25.6	29.6	14.5	16.1	18.3	26.8	30.9	35.6
Wisconsin	78.0	90.8	108.8	55.5	64.5	75.8	92.8	113.2	135.1
Wyoming	7.2	8.5	10.2	5.1	5.9	6.9	12.0	14.7	17.6

Source: U.S. Bureau of Economic Analysis, *BEA Regional Projections to 2045: Volume 1, States.*

No. 731. Flow of Funds Accounts—Composition of Individuals' Savings: 1980 to 1996

[In billions of dollars. Combined statement for households, farm business, and nonfarm noncorporate business. Minus sign (-) indicates decrease]

COMPOSITION OF SAVINGS	1980	1985	1990	1991	1992	1993	1994	1995	1996
Increase in financial assets	323.2	622.5	590.8	418.1	529.8	512.4	542.8	492.7	541.5
Checkable deposits and currency	9.2	41.8	-19.0	43.2	98.9	54.5	-8.9	-38.2	-47.7
Time and savings deposits	125.5	119.7	48.7	-54.2	-76.5	-106.9	-5.8	152.6	144.4
Money market fund shares	23.9	2.3	26.9	9.1	-41.3	5.9	13.7	95.5	90.8
Securities	3.1	81.6	198.1	127.4	252.3	194.3	205.7	-56.5	-35.7
Open market paper..............	-5.0	-7.0	6.2	-29.9	-3.3	15.6	-10.5	0.3	11.4
U.S. savings bonds.............	-7.3	5.3	8.5	11.9	19.1	14.7	8.0	5.1	2.0
Other Treasury securities	19.6	3.7	61.3	-22.0	59.6	11.8	153.2	5.0	-62.1
Agency securities.............	4.8	12.2	41.5	12.3	36.8	-31.4	149.4	-31.9	54.8
Municipal securities...........	8.3	94.9	27.7	40.2	-27.2	-27.2	-51.9	-50.7	-21.4
Corporate and foreign bonds	-14.6	2.6	45.1	29.6	-8.5	37.3	2.1	51.4	27.7
Corporate equities	-4.3	-111.2	-28.8	-23.6	33.1	-57.7	-138.1	-176.1	-245.5
Mutual fund shares............	1.8	81.2	36.6	109.0	142.8	231.3	93.7	140.4	197.4
Private life insurance reserves	9.7	10.4	25.3	25.6	27.7	35.7	34.3	44.8	35.2
Private insured pension reserves	22.3	55.6	95.9	46.4	76.7	86.3	71.2	66.7	69.2
Private noninsured pension reserves	60.2	126.6	64.1	72.5	81.8	82.7	87.1	98.3	85.2
Govt insurance and pension reserves	35.8	69.0	85.7	83.0	83.7	81.8	93.7	75.4	97.4
Investment in tangible assets	4.1	11.2	32.9	17.5	-7.1	0.9	17.8	-49.7	-25.0
Miscellaneous assets	29.2	103.5	30.8	46.4	32.4	76.9	30.8	101.9	123.5
Gross investment in tangible assets	407.5	661.1	815.8	758.3	823.0	897.9	1,021.5	1,050.9	1,107.4
Consumption of fixed capital	296.0	409.8	577.9	612.4	633.9	674.2	716.3	724.5	756.2
Net investment in tangible assets	111.4	251.3	237.9	145.8	189.1	223.7	305.2	326.4	351.2
Residential structures	58.8	105.2	113.3	92.0	114.5	142.3	164.7	164.0	178.9
Other fixed assets [1]	31.5	35.4	23.3	4.1	-10.1	4.8	22.2	53.8	60.5
Consumer durables	27.3	103.9	98.4	50.9	79.6	81.5	104.3	109.1	112.8
Inventories [1]	-6.2	6.8	2.9	-1.1	5.1	-4.8	13.9	-0.5	-1.0
Net increase in liabilities............	196.6	435.5	267.3	217.4	204.0	297.1	401.6	441.9	478.0
Mortgage debt on nonfarm homes	94.1	174.7	226.2	177.7	188.9	186.6	203.4	195.7	277.4
Other mortgage debt [1]	50.9	98.1	16.9	5.3	-28.8	-17.8	3.7	21.5	45.7
Consumer credit	2.3	73.9	16.1	-13.7	5.0	61.5	126.3	141.6	94.4
Policy loans	6.7	-0.1	4.1	4.8	5.7	5.6	7.8	10.5	7.1
Security credit	7.3	18.9	-3.7	16.3	-1.6	22.6	-1.1	3.5	14.5
Other liabilities [1]	35.3	70.1	7.7	27.1	34.8	38.5	61.5	69.1	38.8
Personal saving (Flow of Funds measure) [2] ..	238.0	438.3	561.4	346.5	514.9	439.0	446.4	377.2	414.7
Personal saving as a percentage of of disposable personal income	12.1	14.6	13.5	8.0	11.2	9.2	8.9	7.1	7.4

[1] Includes corporate farms. [2] Net acquisition of financial assets plus net investment in tangible assets minus net increase in liabilities.

Source: Board of Governors of the Federal Reserve System, *Flow of Funds Accounts,* quarterly.

No. 732. Annual Expenditure Per Child by Husband-Wife Families, by Family Income and Expenditure Type: 1996

[In dollars. Expenditures based on data from the 1990-92 Consumer Expenditure Survey updated to 1996 dollars using the Consumer Price Index. For more on the methodology, see report cited below]

AGE OF CHILD	Total	EXPENDITURE TYPE						
		Housing	Food	Trans-por-tation	Clothing	Health care	Child care and educa-tion	Miscel-lan-eous [1]
INCOME: LESS THAN $34,700								
Less than 2 yrs. old...............	5,670	2,160	810	720	370	390	660	560
3 to 5 yrs. old...................	5,780	2,140	900	700	360	370	740	570
6 to 8 yrs. old...................	5,900	2,060	1,160	810	400	420	440	610
9 to 11 yrs. old..................	5,940	1,860	1,380	880	450	460	270	640
12 to 14 yrs. old.................	6,740	2,080	1,450	1,000	750	470	190	800
15 to 17 yrs. old.................	6,650	1,680	1,570	1,340	670	500	310	580
INCOME: $34,700-$58,300								
Less than 2 yrs. old...............	7,860	2,930	960	1,080	440	510	1,080	860
3 to 5 yrs. old...................	8,060	2,900	1,110	1,050	430	490	1,200	880
6 to 8 yrs. old...................	8,130	2,830	1,420	1,170	470	560	770	910
9 to 11 yrs. old..................	8,100	2,630	1,670	1,240	520	600	500	940
12 to 14 yrs. old.................	8,830	2,840	1,680	1,350	880	610	370	1,100
15 to 17 yrs. old.................	8,960	2,440	1,870	1,710	780	640	630	890
INCOME: MORE THAN $58,300								
Less than 2 yrs. old...............	11,680	4,650	1,280	1,510	580	580	1,630	1,450
3 to 5 yrs. old...................	11,910	4,620	1,450	1,480	560	560	1,780	1,460
6 to 8 yrs. old...................	11,870	4,550	1,740	1,600	620	640	1,220	1,500
9 to 11 yrs. old..................	11,790	4,350	2,030	1,670	670	690	850	1,530
12 to 14 yrs. old.................	12,620	4,570	2,130	1,780	1,110	690	650	1,690
15 to 17 yrs. old.................	12,930	4,160	2,240	2,160	1,010	730	1,150	1,480

[1] Expenses include personal care items, entertainment, and reading materials.

Source: Dept. of Agriculture, Center for Nutrition Policy and Promotion, *Expenditures on Children by Families, 1996 Annual Report.*

No. 733. Average Annual Expenditures of All Consumer Units, by Race, Hispanic Origin, and Age of Householder: 1995

[In dollars. Based on Consumer Expenditure Survey. Data are averages for the noninstitutional population. Expenditures reported here are out-of-pocket]

ITEM	All con-sumer units	Black	His-panic	AGE Under 25 yrs.	25 to 34 yrs.	35 to 44 yrs.	45 to 54 yrs.	55 to 64 yrs.	65 yrs. and over
Expenditures, total	**32,277**	**23,750**	**26,794**	**18,429**	**31,488**	**38,425**	**42,181**	**32,604**	**22,265**
Food	4,505	3,446	4,678	2,690	4,470	5,367	5,469	4,539	3,388
Food at home	2,803	2,442	3,370	1,407	2,759	3,345	3,223	2,832	2,367
Cereals and bakery products	441	371	454	227	422	539	501	425	385
Cereals and cereal products	165	163	203	95	172	208	183	151	130
Bakery products	276	208	251	133	251	331	318	274	255
Meats, poultry, fish, and eggs	752	866	1,097	331	724	900	899	807	610
Beef	228	221	331	108	217	273	274	253	175
Pork	156	207	229	61	159	181	184	169	127
Other meats	104	107	121	52	99	129	114	111	86
Poultry	138	172	205	66	132	170	169	127	113
Fish and seafood	97	120	148	27	90	111	125	114	81
Eggs	30	39	62	16	28	36	32	33	28
Dairy products	297	209	347	155	301	352	338	293	248
Fresh milk and cream	123	92	179	66	135	147	134	121	98
Other dairy products	174	117	168	89	167	206	204	171	150
Fruits and vegetables	457	388	593	213	433	509	513	496	437
Fresh fruits	144	117	202	61	137	157	157	153	151
Fresh vegetables	137	108	185	57	122	148	166	157	132
Processed fruits	96	94	117	55	96	110	100	102	87
Processed vegetables	80	69	89	40	78	94	90	84	67
Other food at home	856	609	879	482	878	1,044	973	811	687
Nonalcoholic beverages	240	184	258	155	246	289	283	230	182
Food away from home	1,702	1,004	1,309	1,283	1,711	2,022	2,246	1,707	1,021
Alcoholic beverages	277	157	197	277	299	314	348	253	171
Housing	10,465	8,144	9,223	5,908	10,541	12,631	12,894	10,291	7,590
Shelter	5,932	4,502	5,572	3,625	6,162	7,552	7,560	5,358	3,668
Owned dwellings	3,754	1,922	2,354	485	3,104	5,066	5,576	3,799	2,401
Mortgage interest and charges	2,107	1,097	1,521	306	2,211	3,385	3,201	1,719	511
Property taxes	932	425	466	86	546	986	1,414	1,117	973
Maintenance, repair, insurance, other	716	400	367	93	347	695	961	963	917
Rented dwellings	1,786	2,433	3,102	2,985	2,873	2,102	1,334	986	931
Other lodging	392	147	115	155	185	384	650	572	335
Utilities, fuels, and public services	2,193	2,206	1,958	1,159	1,989	2,388	2,628	2,442	1,982
Natural gas	268	315	223	95	222	279	314	322	284
Electricity	870	840	693	436	762	962	1,034	984	801
Fuel oil and other fuels	87	48	19	17	49	86	92	105	129
Telephone	708	781	796	541	745	778	859	723	517
Water and other public services	260	222	226	69	211	284	329	308	251
Household operations	508	318	316	199	701	604	445	374	466
Personal services	258	226	211	155	559	378	115	65	127
Other household expenses	250	92	104	44	141	226	330	309	339
Housekeeping supplies	430	255	387	135	360	490	501	514	423
Household furnishings and equipment	1,403	862	991	790	1,329	1,597	1,760	1,603	1,051
Household textiles	100	46	59	24	83	112	158	126	67
Furniture	327	319	278	271	391	434	397	279	143
Floor coverings	177	34	122	38	85	142	165	167	366
Major appliances	155	170	118	93	137	171	189	176	132
Small appliances, misc. housewares	85	41	50	63	71	85	101	143	58
Miscellaneous household equipment	557	252	364	301	561	653	750	712	284
Apparel and services	1,704	1,765	1,719	1,206	1,904	2,079	2,090	1,833	876
Men and boys	425	366	422	279	511	536	519	431	191
Women and girls	660	655	507	383	611	774	868	830	407
Children under 2 years old	81	92	158	95	154	106	59	45	18
Footwear	278	405	334	230	334	380	311	207	145
Other apparel products and services	259	247	298	219	294	284	333	320	115
Transportation	6,016	4,515	5,145	4,033	6,188	7,488	8,017	5,726	3,377
Vehicle purchases (net outlay)	2,639	2,077	2,497	1,913	2,846	3,643	3,516	2,108	1,166
Cars and trucks, new	1,194	927	861	555	1,273	1,730	1,332	1,118	680
Cars and trucks, used	1,411	1,111	1,636	1,322	1,531	1,873	2,129	953	485
Gasoline and motor oil	1,006	713	891	701	1,014	1,182	1,324	1,063	604
Other vehicle expenses	2,016	1,453	1,438	1,236	2,029	2,289	2,725	2,142	1,285
Vehicle finance charges	261	245	172	179	347	322	361	223	78
Maintenance and repair	653	507	477	379	579	720	923	709	474
Vehicle insurance	713	503	528	455	668	781	930	792	531
Rent, lease, licenses, other	390	198	261	222	435	465	510	419	201
Public transportation	355	273	319	184	299	374	452	413	323
Health care [1]	1,732	1,059	1,055	465	1,096	1,609	1,850	1,909	2,647
Entertainment [2]	1,612	925	1,060	1,081	1,682	1,951	2,138	1,577	929
Personal care products and services	403	370	369	243	387	450	517	407	326
Reading	163	75	74	71	134	173	199	188	161
Education	471	256	293	667	335	436	1,028	366	155
Tobacco products and smoking supplies	269	176	142	245	270	310	347	314	139
Miscellaneous	766	456	526	347	687	815	1,018	948	603
Cash contributions	925	564	378	114	455	908	1,463	1,043	1,101
Personal insurance and pensions	2,967	1,842	1,936	1,081	3,040	3,894	4,803	3,211	802
Life and other personal insurance	374	345	190	69	251	440	563	555	245
Pensions and Social Security	2,593	1,498	1,746	1,012	2,788	3,453	4,240	2,656	558
Personal taxes	**3,055**	**1,484**	**1,640**	**1,075**	**3,299**	**3,794**	**4,916**	**3,128**	**1,083**

[1] For additional health care expenditures, see Table 180.   [2] For additional recreation expenditures, see Table 426.

Source: U.S. Bureau of Labor Statistics, *Consumer Expenditures in 1995;* and unpublished data.

No. 734. Average Annual Expenditures of All Consumer Units, by Region and Size of Unit: 1995

[See headnote, page 464]

ITEM	REGION				SIZE OF CONSUMER UNIT				
	North-east	Mid-west	South	West	One person	Two per-sons	Three per-sons	Four per-sons	Five or more
Expenditures, total	**33,014**	**31,937**	**30,289**	**35,222**	**19,390**	**33,095**	**37,856**	**42,800**	**41,603**
Food	4,870	4,348	4,272	4,726	2,500	4,366	5,228	6,280	6,805
Food at home	3,122	2,626	2,626	2,998	1,401	2,587	3,276	4,085	4,761
Cereals and bakery products	528	411	404	454	221	402	504	667	747
Cereals and cereal products	195	152	153	171	76	146	190	251	310
Bakery products	333	259	251	282	145	256	314	416	437
Meats, poultry, fish, and eggs	866	669	746	754	343	678	900	1,118	1,359
Beef	232	221	233	223	97	200	280	360	401
Pork	156	137	172	153	67	143	179	240	286
Other meats	131	101	93	97	49	89	129	157	182
Poultry	182	116	131	132	64	121	171	191	263
Fish and seafood	129	70	88	116	50	97	110	131	162
Eggs	36	24	29	34	15	27	32	39	65
Dairy products	328	279	270	331	148	271	339	436	520
Fresh milk and cream	132	118	116	132	60	104	140	184	242
Other dairy products	196	161	154	199	88	166	199	253	278
Fruits and vegetables	552	412	419	480	250	451	518	607	735
Fresh fruits	175	136	126	154	84	146	157	182	232
Fresh vegetables	176	114	127	145	76	141	156	172	215
Processed fruits	120	87	83	104	50	88	113	142	154
Processed vegetables	81	75	84	77	40	77	92	111	135
Other food at home	847	855	787	979	439	786	1,015	1,258	1,400
Nonalcoholic beverages	250	244	226	250	127	219	290	348	386
Food away from home	1,748	1,722	1,646	1,728	1,098	1,778	1,951	2,195	2,043
Alcoholic beverages	327	261	242	307	248	309	265	296	253
Housing	11,485	9,754	9,287	12,265	7,036	10,581	11,768	13,577	13,085
Shelter	6,993	5,198	4,859	7,550	4,359	5,760	6,563	7,717	7,256
Owned dwellings	4,311	3,521	3,026	4,691	1,850	3,901	4,376	5,613	4,935
Mortgage interest and charges	2,212	1,903	1,634	3,026	823	1,857	2,726	3,639	3,253
Property taxes	1,439	955	693	807	496	1,172	954	1,209	971
Maintenance, repair, insurance, other	659	663	700	859	531	872	696	764	711
Rented dwellings	2,164	1,316	1,524	2,416	2,283	1,360	1,770	1,613	1,982
Other lodging	518	361	309	443	226	499	416	492	339
Utilities, fuels, and public services	2,297	2,184	2,266	1,982	1,423	2,265	2,505	2,734	2,839
Natural gas	332	395	159	234	170	286	291	337	352
Electricity	810	783	1,065	713	532	895	1,017	1,119	1,141
Fuel oil and other fuels	223	77	47	33	65	99	88	96	95
Telephone	718	706	715	692	507	714	816	839	894
Water and other public services	214	224	281	311	149	272	293	344	357
Household operations	482	451	544	545	250	429	646	1,006	525
Personal services	238	270	261	258	61	129	414	673	351
Other household expenses	244	180	283	286	189	301	232	334	173
Housekeeping supplies	467	418	393	467	235	476	490	530	586
Household furnishings and equipment	1,245	1,504	1,225	1,721	768	1,651	1,565	1,589	1,879
Household textiles	122	109	100	70	58	130	108	103	111
Furniture	304	313	327	368	167	320	460	438	428
Floor coverings	54	221	50	450	96	332	79	119	165
Major appliances	132	167	166	145	79	168	174	179	263
Small appliances, misc. housewares	84	91	82	85	58	98	85	100	99
Miscellaneous household equipment	548	603	501	604	311	602	658	650	814
Apparel and services	1,751	1,721	1,667	1,697	991	1,524	2,097	2,479	2,499
Men and boys	421	418	414	457	235	353	512	648	720
Women and girls	695	713	622	628	391	642	820	910	853
Children under 2 years old	87	75	81	80	16	43	142	151	178
Footwear	278	277	289	262	176	201	322	483	437
Other apparel products and services	270	237	261	271	173	285	301	288	311
Transportation	5,468	6,378	6,039	6,069	2,916	6,158	7,852	8,156	8,222
Vehicle purchases (net outlay)	2,145	2,954	2,856	2,380	1,036	2,563	3,718	3,789	3,975
Cars and trucks, new	1,111	1,212	1,327	1,036	551	1,293	1,613	1,533	1,530
Cars and trucks, used	975	1,696	1,505	1,332	461	1,226	2,071	2,206	2,434
Gasoline and motor oil	877	1,043	1,031	1,045	531	1,016	1,248	1,376	1,382
Other vehicle expenses	1,960	2,078	1,881	2,214	1,111	2,146	2,552	2,567	2,493
Vehicle finance charges	182	278	305	244	92	277	342	377	382
Maintenance and repair	584	643	632	764	393	702	833	791	742
Vehicle insurance	767	689	682	739	411	752	886	908	878
Rent, lease, licenses, other	427	468	262	467	214	415	492	491	491
Public transportation	486	302	271	429	239	433	334	423	372
Health care [1]	1,757	1,759	1,790	1,584	1,109	2,126	1,775	1,969	1,856
Entertainment [2]	1,544	1,602	1,459	1,939	992	1,667	1,834	2,187	1,986
Personal care products and services	438	373	386	435	236	433	470	533	488
Reading	186	170	135	177	120	187	176	189	146
Education	576	492	436	403	293	360	616	759	665
Tobacco products and smoking supplies	260	299	283	217	172	272	325	323	362
Miscellaneous	708	794	722	860	654	822	768	843	797
Cash contributions	724	962	902	1,113	621	1,213	933	926	883
Personal insurance and pensions	2,920	3,022	2,670	3,432	1,502	3,079	3,751	4,281	3,556
Life and other personal insurance	353	403	392	330	140	422	434	565	508
Pensions and Social Security	2,567	2,619	2,277	3,102	1,363	2,657	3,317	3,716	3,048
Personal taxes	**3,215**	**2,837**	**2,438**	**4,101**	**2,016**	**3,214**	**3,610**	**4,033**	**3,278**

[1] For additional health care expenditures, see Table 180.   [2] For additional recreation expenditures, see Table 426.

Source: U.S. Bureau of Labor Statistics, *Consumer Expenditures in 1995;* and unpublished data.

No. 735. Average Annual Expenditures of All Consumer Units, by Type of Household Unit: 1995

[See headnote, page 464]

ITEM	Husband and wife only	HUSBAND AND WIFE WITH CHILDREN — Total	Oldest child under 6	Oldest child 6 to 17	Oldest child 18 and over	One parent, at least one child under 18	Single person and other consumer units
Expenditures, total	**36,052**	**44,989**	**40,559**	**45,020**	**48,294**	**22,626**	**22,351**
Food	4,722	6,368	5,129	6,592	6,944	3,586	3,017
Food at home	2,772	4,041	3,455	4,181	4,264	2,529	1,830
Cereals and bakery products	430	649	533	688	670	406	284
Cereals and cereal products	151	249	199	273	243	172	105
Bakery products	279	400	334	415	427	234	180
Meats, poultry, fish, and eggs	717	1,078	849	1,115	1,207	752	490
Beef	214	322	248	337	357	241	145
Pork	148	218	179	221	248	164	106
Other meats	93	159	115	165	187	105	66
Poultry	126	201	155	212	222	134	91
Fish and seafood	109	135	119	135	150	79	61
Eggs	28	42	33	45	44	29	21
Dairy products	285	437	378	454	455	273	193
Fresh milk and cream	107	185	164	194	185	128	80
Other dairy products	179	252	214	260	270	146	112
Fruits and vegetables	490	621	549	635	655	372	307
Fresh fruits	161	189	164	194	200	115	98
Fresh vegetables	153	179	153	179	201	90	96
Processed fruits	93	142	140	143	141	90	62
Processed vegetables	82	112	92	119	113	77	51
Other food at home	849	1,256	1,145	1,290	1,276	726	555
Nonalcoholic beverages	230	343	264	362	375	202	166
Food away from home	1,950	2,327	1,675	2,411	2,680	1,057	1,187
Alcoholic beverages	338	303	250	304	350	95	251
Housing	11,512	13,997	14,527	14,318	13,002	8,171	7,643
Shelter	6,176	7,863	8,030	8,201	7,101	4,710	4,577
Owned dwellings	4,637	5,963	5,806	6,199	5,629	1,788	2,022
Mortgage interest and charges	2,190	3,857	4,133	4,179	3,047	1,176	941
Property taxes	1,419	1,263	1,016	1,234	1,495	404	537
Maintenance, repair, insurance, other	1,029	843	657	786	1,087	208	545
Rented dwellings	909	1,376	1,963	1,484	747	2,808	2,341
Other lodging	630	524	262	518	725	114	215
Utilities, fuels, and public services	2,396	2,751	2,346	2,709	3,121	1,880	1,685
Natural gas	304	328	259	320	395	238	208
Electricity	956	1,128	941	1,139	1,241	761	637
Fuel oil and other fuels	112	99	88	89	127	42	70
Telephone	723	845	777	808	965	658	592
Water and other public services	301	351	281	354	395	180	178
Household operations	451	888	1,919	767	376	589	276
Personal services	93	586	1,632	464	66	468	94
Other household expenses	358	302	287	303	311	121	182
Housekeeping supplies	548	584	541	587	615	270	266
Household furnishings and equipment	1,941	1,911	1,691	2,054	1,788	722	839
Household textiles	144	115	112	110	129	54	70
Furniture	367	520	599	531	442	236	183
Floor coverings	437	145	51	199	107	24	91
Major appliances	194	207	179	198	244	92	99
Small appliances, misc. housewares	109	106	63	100	157	51	63
Miscellaneous household equipment	689	818	687	916	709	265	333
Apparel and services	1,588	2,477	2,471	2,453	2,534	1,655	1,188
Men and boys	380	647	536	678	671	441	282
Women and girls	666	914	699	953	1,029	624	471
Children under 2 years old	41	159	470	86	50	120	33
Footwear	199	431	465	428	404	286	202
Other apparel products and services	301	326	301	308	380	184	199
Transportation	6,535	8,936	7,707	8,435	10,798	3,919	3,887
Vehicle purchases (net outlay)	2,584	4,169	3,584	4,060	4,798	1,913	1,635
Cars and trucks, new	1,417	1,776	1,281	1,947	1,808	617	742
Cars and trucks, used	1,128	2,343	2,266	2,078	2,901	1,274	867
Gasoline and motor oil	1,096	1,463	1,221	1,397	1,764	642	669
Other vehicle expenses	2,337	2,899	2,587	2,572	3,771	1,151	1,337
Vehicle finance charges	286	408	414	400	418	167	148
Maintenance and repair	759	888	693	769	1,282	406	461
Vehicle insurance	797	1,002	756	896	1,379	450	496
Rent, lease, licenses, other	494	601	724	507	692	128	232
Public transportation	518	404	315	406	465	213	246
Health care [1]	2,438	2,102	1,746	2,026	2,509	803	1,225
Entertainment [2]	1,830	2,319	1,980	2,501	2,222	1,082	1,099
Personal care products and services	451	530	401	561	573	305	294
Reading	211	206	182	199	235	77	122
Education	391	847	192	773	1,457	264	299
Tobacco products and smoking supplies	242	312	248	316	352	234	239
Miscellaneous	798	822	800	804	874	514	741
Cash contributions	1,457	1,033	500	1,091	1,306	550	646
Personal insurance and pensions	3,541	4,738	4,425	4,646	5,137	1,372	1,699
Life and other personal insurance	505	598	444	628	652	194	176
Pensions and Social Security	3,035	4,140	3,980	4,018	4,486	1,177	1,523
Personal taxes	**3,717**	**4,635**	**4,287**	**4,577**	**5,006**	**830**	**2,039**

[1] For additional health care expenditures, see Table 180.   [2] For additional recreation expenditures, see Table 426.

Source: U.S. Bureau of Labor Statistics, *Consumer Expenditures in 1995;* and unpublished data.

No. 736. Average Annual Expenditures of All Consumer Units, by Type of Expenditure: 1989 to 1995

[In dollars. See headnote, Table 733]

TYPE	1989	1990	1991	1992	1993	1994	1995
Number of consumer units (1,000)	95,818	96,968	97,918	100,019	100,049	102,210	103,024
Total expenditures	**27,810**	**28,381**	**29,614**	**29,846**	**30,692**	**31,731**	**32,277**
Food	4,152	4,296	4,271	4,273	4,399	4,411	4,505
Food at home	2,390	2,485	2,651	2,643	2,735	2,712	2,803
Cereal and bakery products	359	368	404	411	434	429	441
Meats, poultry, fish, and eggs	611	668	709	687	734	732	752
Dairy products	304	295	294	302	295	289	297
Fruits and vegetables	408	408	429	428	444	437	457
Other food at home	708	746	815	814	827	825	856
Food away from home	1,762	1,811	1,620	1,631	1,664	1,698	1,702
Alcoholic beverages	284	293	297	301	268	278	277
Housing	8,434	8,703	9,252	9,477	9,636	10,106	10,465
Shelter	4,660	4,836	5,191	5,411	5,415	5,686	5,932
Fuels, utilities, public services	1,835	1,890	1,990	1,984	2,112	2,189	2,193
Household operations, furnishings	1,546	1,571	1,648	1,649	1,699	1,838	1,911
Housekeeping supplies	394	406	424	433	410	393	430
Apparel and services	1,582	1,618	1,735	1,710	1,676	1,644	1,704
Transportation	5,187	5,120	5,151	5,228	5,453	6,044	6,016
Vehicle purchase	2,291	2,129	2,111	2,189	2,319	2,725	2,639
Gasoline and motor oil	985	1,047	995	973	977	986	1,006
Other transportation	1,911	1,944	2,045	2,066	2,157	2,334	2,371
Health care	1,407	1,480	1,554	1,634	1,776	1,755	1,732
Tobacco products, smoking supplies	261	274	276	275	268	259	269
Life and other personal insurance	346	345	356	353	399	398	374
Pensions and Social Security	2,125	2,248	2,431	2,397	2,509	2,540	2,593
Other expenditures	4,030	4,003	4,291	4,198	4,308	4,297	4,340

Source: U.S. Bureau of Labor Statistics, *Consumer Expenditures in 1995;* and earlier reports.

No. 737. Average Annual Expenditures of All Consumer Units, by Metropolitan Area: 1994-95

[In dollars. Metropolitan areas defined June 30, 1983, CMSA=Consolidated Metropolitan Statistical Area; MSA=Metropolitan Statistical Area; PMSA=Primary Metropolitan Statistical Area. See text, Section 1, and Appendix II. See headnote, Table 733]

METROPOLITAN AREA	Total expenditures [1]	Food	HOUSING Total [1]	HOUSING Shelter	Apparel and services	TRANSPORTATION Total [1]	TRANSPORTATION Vehicle purchases	TRANSPORTATION Gasoline and motor oil	Health care
Anchorage, AK MSA	42,662	5,928	13,474	8,537	2,139	6,710	2,257	1,055	1,944
Atlanta, GA MSA	40,214	4,721	12,315	7,181	2,441	8,284	4,180	991	2,226
Baltimore, MD MSA	35,025	4,483	12,271	7,716	1,459	5,660	2,396	917	1,822
Boston-Lawrence-Salem, MA-NH CMSA	35,529	4,577	12,807	7,846	1,995	5,765	2,284	864	1,878
Buffalo-Niagara Falls, NY CMSA	24,828	4,298	9,174	5,007	1,503	3,619	1,233	781	1,299
Chicago-Gary-Lake County, IL-IN-WI CMSA	37,946	5,099	13,067	7,984	2,525	6,899	3,240	992	1,820
Cincinnati-Hamilton, OH-KY-IN CMSA	32,817	4,344	10,462	5,810	1,492	6,758	3,174	1,088	1,810
Cleveland-Akron-Lorain, OH CMSA	28,199	4,182	9,477	5,175	1,341	5,198	2,081	853	1,466
Dallas-Fort Worth, TX CMSA	38,895	5,300	11,606	6,267	2,152	7,875	3,530	1,272	1,840
Detroit-Ann Arbor, MI CMSA	34,114	4,538	11,025	6,419	1,754	7,520	3,205	1,072	1,400
Honolulu, HI MSA	40,996	5,920	14,161	9,718	1,481	6,349	2,231	911	1,851
Houston-Galveston-Brazoria, TX CMSA	38,347	5,709	10,670	5,588	2,416	8,170	4,152	1,165	2,036
Kansas City, MO-Kansas City, KS CMSA	34,254	4,526	10,016	5,292	1,815	6,579	2,847	1,080	2,090
Los Angeles-Long Beach, CA PMSA	36,324	4,652	13,671	8,978	2,015	6,141	2,296	1,079	1,307
Miami-Fort Lauderdale, FL CMSA	31,764	4,701	10,868	6,250	1,564	6,128	2,423	962	1,389
Milwaukee, WI PMSA	34,907	4,032	11,191	6,868	1,637	7,308	3,828	1,055	1,506
Minneapolis-St. Paul, MN-WI MSA	39,516	4,894	12,283	7,287	1,782	6,884	2,588	1,186	1,727
New York-Northern New Jersey-Long Island, NY-NJ-CT CMSA	36,491	5,442	14,027	8,948	2,323	4,994	1,251	764	1,824
Philadelphia-Wilmington-Trenton, PA-NJ-DE-MD CMSA	31,756	4,647	10,275	6,220	1,667	5,413	2,147	793	1,450
Pittsburgh-Beaver Valley, PA CMSA	27,664	3,888	8,819	4,471	1,543	4,790	2,092	765	1,651
Portland-Vancouver, OR-WA CMSA	34,853	4,414	11,707	7,318	1,777	6,088	2,736	972	1,559
San Diego, CA MSA	34,027	4,077	12,208	8,346	1,490	6,396	2,314	1,114	1,455
San Francisco-Oakland-San Jose, CA CMSA	41,960	5,221	15,989	9,902	2,049	6,465	2,125	1,082	1,582
Seattle-Tacoma, WA CMSA	36,389	4,496	11,938	7,689	1,466	6,789	2,860	998	1,522
St. Louis-East St. Louis-Alton, MO-IL CMSA	31,337	4,208	9,432	4,795	1,566	6,956	3,678	987	1,637
Washington, DC-MD-VA MSA	41,838	4,950	14,447	9,261	2,088	6,775	2,801	1,006	1,783

[1] Includes expenditures not shown separately.

Source: U.S. Bureau of Labor Statistics, *Consumer Expenditures in 1994-95.*

No. 738. Money Income of Households—Percent Distribution, by Income Level, Race, and Hispanic Origin, in Constant (1996) Dollars: 1970 to 1996

[Constant dollars based on CPI-U-X1 deflator. Households as of **March** of **following year.** Based on Current Population Survey; see text, Sections 1 and 14, and Appendix III. For definition of median, see Guide to Tabular Presentation]

YEAR	Number of house-holds (1,000)	PERCENT DISTRIBUTION Under $10,000	$10,000-$14,999	$15,000-$24,999	$25,000-$34,999	$35,000-$49,999	$50,000-$74,999	$75,000 and over	Median income (dollars)
ALL HOUSEHOLDS [1]									
1970	64,778	13.7	7.7	15.6	16.4	21.3	16.8	8.5	33,181
1975	72,867	13.0	8.8	16.2	15.6	19.4	17.8	9.2	32,943
1980	82,368	12.9	8.2	16.4	14.3	19.1	17.9	11.2	33,763
1985	88,458	12.7	8.3	15.6	14.2	17.8	17.8	13.5	34,439
1990	94,312	12.0	7.9	15.0	14.1	17.8	17.9	15.2	35,945
1994	98,990	12.6	8.7	15.8	14.1	16.3	16.9	15.5	34,158
1995	99,627	11.8	8.5	15.6	13.9	16.9	17.4	15.7	35,082
1996	101,018	11.8	8.6	15.4	13.7	16.3	18.0	16.4	35,492
WHITE									
1970	57,575	12.5	7.2	14.9	16.5	22.0	17.7	9.0	34,560
1975	64,392	11.6	8.4	15.9	15.5	20.0	18.8	9.9	34,451
1980	71,872	11.3	7.7	16.0	14.5	19.7	18.9	12.1	35,620
1985	76,576	11.1	7.8	15.2	14.3	18.4	18.6	14.5	36,320
1990	80,968	10.2	7.6	14.8	14.3	18.3	18.8	16.2	37,492
1994	83,737	10.8	8.4	15.5	14.2	16.8	17.7	16.5	36,026
1995	84,511	10.2	8.2	15.4	14.0	17.3	18.1	16.8	36,822
1996	85,059	10.0	8.2	15.1	13.7	16.7	18.8	17.4	37,161
BLACK									
1970	6,180	25.0	12.1	21.5	15.2	14.5	8.7	2.8	21,035
1975	7,489	25.4	13.3	19.0	16.0	14.1	9.4	2.8	20,682
1980	8,847	25.9	12.9	19.8	13.2	14.4	10.0	3.8	20,521
1985	9,797	25.8	11.9	19.1	13.1	13.9	11.0	5.2	21,609
1990	10,671	26.3	11.1	17.0	13.3	14.5	11.2	6.5	22,420
1994	11,655	25.2	11.1	18.3	13.4	13.1	11.7	7.2	22,261
1995	11,577	23.5	11.3	18.5	13.7	14.7	11.5	6.7	23,054
1996	12,109	23.1	11.6	17.7	13.9	14.0	12.4	7.4	23,482
HISPANIC [2]									
1975	2,948	16.8	11.7	22.1	17.5	18.1	10.3	3.5	24,749
1980	3,906	16.7	10.7	21.2	16.2	16.9	12.8	5.5	26,025
1985	5,213	17.9	12.0	19.5	15.2	16.4	12.3	6.6	25,467
1990	6,220	16.7	11.6	18.6	15.8	17.0	12.8	7.5	26,806
1994	7,735	19.2	12.1	19.1	15.2	15.0	11.8	7.6	24,796
1995	7,939	19.2	12.3	21.0	15.2	14.0	11.8	6.5	23,535
1996	8,225	17.2	11.9	21.0	15.0	15.0	12.3	7.7	24,906

[1] Includes other races not shown separately.   [2] Persons of Hispanic origin may be of any race. Income data for Hispanic origin households are not available prior to 1972.

No. 739. Money Income of Households—Median Income, by Race and Hispanic Origin, in Current and Constant (1996) Dollars: 1970 to 1996

[In dollars. See headnote, Table 738]

YEAR	MEDIAN INCOME IN CURRENT DOLLARS All house-holds [1]	White	Black	Asian, Pacific Islander	His-panic [2]	MEDIAN INCOME IN CONSTANT (1996) DOLLARS All house-holds [1]	White	Black	Asian, Pacific Islander	His-panic [2]
1970	8,734	9,097	5,537	(NA)	(NA)	33,181	34,560	21,035	(NA)	(NA)
1980	17,710	18,684	10,764	(NA)	13,651	33,763	35,620	20,521	(NA)	26,025
1981	19,074	20,153	11,309	(NA)	15,300	33,215	35,094	19,693	(NA)	26,643
1982	20,171	21,117	11,968	(NA)	15,178	33,105	34,657	19,642	(NA)	24,910
1983 [3]	20,885	21,902	12,429	(NA)	15,906	32,900	34,502	19,579	(NA)	25,057
1984	22,415	23,647	13,471	(NA)	16,992	33,849	35,709	20,343	(NA)	25,660
1985	23,618	24,908	14,819	(NA)	17,465	34,439	36,320	21,609	(NA)	25,467
1986	24,897	26,175	15,080	(NA)	18,352	35,642	37,471	21,588	(NA)	26,272
1987 [4]	26,061	27,458	15,672	(NA)	19,336	35,994	37,924	21,646	(NA)	26,706
1988	27,225	28,781	16,407	32,267	20,359	36,108	38,172	21,760	42,795	27,002
1989	28,906	30,406	18,083	36,102	21,921	36,575	38,473	22,881	45,681	27,737
1990	29,943	31,231	18,676	38,450	22,330	35,945	37,492	22,420	46,158	26,806
1991	30,126	31,569	18,807	36,449	22,691	34,705	36,367	21,665	41,989	26,140
1992 [5]	30,636	32,209	18,755	37,801	22,597	34,261	36,020	20,974	42,274	25,271
1993	31,241	32,960	19,533	38,347	22,886	33,922	35,788	21,209	41,638	24,850
1994	32,264	34,028	21,027	40,482	23,421	34,158	36,026	22,261	42,858	24,796
1995	34,076	35,766	22,393	40,614	22,860	35,082	36,822	23,054	41,813	23,535
1996	35,492	37,161	23,482	43,276	24,906	35,492	37,161	23,482	43,276	24,906

NA Not available.   [1] Includes other races not shown separately.   [2] Persons of Hispanic origin may be of any race. [3] Beginning 1983, data based on revised Hispanic population controls and not directly comparable with prior years.   [4] Beginning 1987, data based on revised processing procedures and not directly comparable with prior years.   [5] Based on 1990 census population controls.

Source of Tables 738 and 739: U.S. Bureau of the Census, *Current Population Reports,* P60-197; and Internet site <http://www.census.gov/hhes/income/histinc/inchhdet.html> (accessed 25 March 1998).

No. 740. Money Income of Households—Distribution, by Income Level and Selected Characteristics: 1996

[See headnote, Table 738. For composition of regions, see inside front cover]

CHARACTERISTIC	Number of house-holds (1,000)	NUMBER (1,000)							Median income (dollars)
		Under $10,000	$10,000-$14,999	$15,000-$24,999	$25,000-$34,999	$35,000-$49,999	$50,000-$74,999	$75,000 and over	
Total [1]	101,018	11,879	8,659	15,509	13,808	16,466	18,170	16,527	35,492
Age of householder:									
15 to 24 years.	5,160	1,124	636	1,220	864	702	439	176	21,438
25 to 34 years.	19,314	1,790	1,345	2,940	3,322	3,756	3,966	2,195	35,888
35 to 44 years.	23,823	1,711	1,239	2,789	3,173	4,474	5,545	4,893	44,420
45 to 54 years.	18,843	1,354	850	1,895	2,014	3,209	4,211	5,310	50,472
55 to 64 years.	12,469	1,422	975	1,649	1,484	1,991	2,395	2,553	39,815
65 years and over	21,408	4,479	3,614	5,016	2,952	2,334	1,614	1,400	19,448
White	85,059	8,575	6,980	12,853	11,658	14,184	15,998	14,809	37,161
Black	12,109	2,794	1,399	2,144	1,679	1,691	1,502	900	23,482
Hispanic [2]	8,225	1,415	980	1,731	1,230	1,231	1,009	628	24,906
Northeast.	19,724	2,473	1,611	2,689	2,492	3,096	3,670	3,692	37,406
Midwest.	23,972	2,471	1,973	3,700	3,335	4,037	4,696	3,761	36,579
South	35,693	4,604	3,288	5,873	5,166	5,763	5,877	5,123	32,422
West	21,629	2,332	1,787	3,246	2,815	3,569	3,927	3,951	37,125
Size of household:									
One person	25,402	6,728	4,172	5,321	3,516	2,891	1,717	1,057	17,897
Two persons.	32,736	2,406	2,420	5,541	4,945	5,823	6,261	5,339	37,283
Three persons.	17,065	1,336	905	1,969	2,195	3,133	3,804	3,723	44,813
Four persons	15,396	836	606	1,423	1,841	2,660	3,938	4,092	51,405
Five persons.	6,774	361	322	780	790	1,278	1,646	1,598	47,841
Six persons	2,311	138	122	288	346	425	509	483	42,438
Seven or more persons	1,334	74	111	187	174	265	295	236	40,337
Type of household:									
Family households	70,241	4,870	4,154	9,407	9,448	12,593	15,225	14,542	43,082
Married-couple.	53,604	1,635	2,250	6,079	6,821	10,096	13,222	13,499	49,858
Male householder, wife absent	3,847	296	288	666	640	786	735	436	35,658
Female householder, husband	12,790	2,939	1,616	2,663	1,987	1,710	1,268	606	21,564
Nonfamily households. . . .	30,777	7,009	4,504	6,102	4,360	3,872	2,945	1,986	20,973
Male householder.	13,707	2,066	1,534	2,592	2,315	2,218	1,750	1,231	27,266
Female householder . .	17,070	4,942	2,971	3,509	2,045	1,654	1,195	754	16,398
Educational attainment of householder: [3]									
Total.	95,857	10,756	8,023	14,288	12,944	15,764	17,731	16,351	36,516
Less than 9th grade	7,628	2,300	1,427	1,675	945	648	435	197	15,376
9th to 12th grade (no diploma).	9,933	2,377	1,538	2,164	1,369	1,234	875	377	19,652
High school graduate . . .	30,293	3,408	2,811	5,384	4,551	5,609	5,499	3,031	32,295
Some college, no degree	17,078	1,410	1,195	2,439	2,664	3,189	3,582	2,599	38,398
Associate degree.	6,855	430	371	885	952	1,252	1,662	1,303	44,509
Bachelor's degree or more	24,070	831	682	1,741	2,462	3,832	5,678	8,845	59,978
Bachelor's degree. . . .	15,501	556	513	1,272	1,789	2,688	3,791	4,892	55,137
Master's degree	5,705	189	139	332	505	827	1,395	2,318	63,887
Professional degree . . .	1,631	51	14	68	122	184	255	937	90,344
Doctorate degree	1,233	34	16	69	46	133	236	697	81,159
Tenure:									
Owner occupied	66,356	4,795	4,344	8,530	8,568	11,355	14,365	14,400	43,793
Renter occupied	32,968	6,722	4,089	6,606	4,994	4,871	3,651	2,035	23,436
Occupier paid no cash rent	1,693	363	225	373	246	240	155	92	21,479
Work experience of householder:									
Total	101,018	11,879	8,659	15,509	13,808	16,466	18,170	16,527	35,492
Worked	72,377	3,509	3,987	9,529	10,416	13,686	16,216	15,034	43,975
Worked at full-time jobs	62,729	1,881	2,732	7,846	9,089	12,401	14,904	13,876	46,316
50 weeks or more . .	52,699	660	1,695	6,000	7,495	10,763	13,343	12,744	49,530
27 to 49 weeks. . . .	6,649	444	628	1,202	1,097	1,189	1,210	880	34,365
26 weeks or less. . .	3,381	779	410	644	497	449	351	252	22,355
Worked at part-time jobs	9,648	1,627	1,255	1,684	1,327	1,284	1,312	1,159	26,742
50 weeks or more . .	4,744	545	596	880	677	693	671	682	29,719
27 to 49 weeks. . . .	2,240	387	278	362	291	311	336	275	27,589
26 weeks or less. . .	2,664	695	381	442	359	281	305	201	20,662
Did not work	28,641	8,370	4,671	5,979	3,392	2,780	1,954	1,493	16,730

[1] Includes other races not shown separately. [2] Persons of Hispanic origin may be of any race. [3] 25 years old and over.

Source: U.S. Bureau of the Census, *Current Population Reports*, P60-197.

No. 741. Household Income Before and After Taxes in Current and Constant (1996) Dollars: 1980 to 1996

[In dollars, except as indicated. Households as of March of the following year. Income in current and 1996 CPI-U-X1 adjusted dollars]

YEAR	Number of house-holds (1,000)	CURRENT DOLLARS				CONSTANT (1996) DOLLARS			
		Mean		Median		Mean		Median	
		Before taxes	After taxes	Before taxes	After taxes	Before taxes	After taxes	Before taxes	After taxes
1980	82,368	21,063	16,272	17,710	14,551	40,155	31,022	33,763	27,741
1985 [1]	88,458	29,066	22,646	23,618	19,401	42,383	33,022	34,439	28,290
1990	94,312	37,403	29,188	29,943	24,546	44,901	35,039	35,945	29,466
1991 [2]	95,669	37,922	29,640	30,126	24,955	43,685	34,145	34,705	28,748
1992 [2]	96,426	38,840	30,425	30,636	25,474	43,435	34,025	34,261	28,488
1993 [3]	97,107	41,428	32,092	31,241	26,112	44,983	34,846	33,922	28,353
1994 [4]	98,990	43,133	33,315	32,264	26,973	45,665	35,271	34,158	28,556
1995 [5]	99,627	44,938	34,592	34,076	28,249	46,265	35,613	35,082	29,083
1996	101,018	47,123	36,008	35,492	29,312	47,123	36,008	35,492	29,312

[1] Recording of amounts for earnings from longest job increased to $299,999. Full implementation of 1980 census-based sample design. [2] Implementation of 1990 census population controls. [3] Data collection method changed from paper and pencil to computer assisted interviewing. In addition, the March 1994 income supplement was revised to allow for the coding of different income amounts on selected questionnaire items. Limits either increased or decreased in the following categories: earnings increased to $999,999; social security increased to $49,999; supplemental security income and public assistance increased to $24,999; veterans' benefits increased to $99,999; child support and alimony decreased to $49,999. [4] Introduction of 1990 census sample design. [5] Full implementation of the 1990 census-based sample design and metropolitan definitions, 7,000 household sample reduction, and revised race edits.

Source: U.S. Bureau of the Census, Internet site <http://www.census.gov/hhes/income/histinc/rdi01.html> (accessed 27 January 1998).

No. 742. Mean-Taxes Paid and Taxes Paid as a Percentage of Total Mean Before-Tax Income by Type of Tax in Current and Constant (1996) Dollars: 1980 to 1996

[Households as of March of the following year. Mean taxes paid in current and 1996 CPI-U-X1 adjusted dollars]

TYPE OF TAX AND YEAR	Number (1,000)	MEAN TAXES PAID			TYPE OF TAX AND YEAR	Number (1,000)	MEAN TAXES PAID		
		Current dollars	Con-stant 1996 dollars	As a per-cent of mean before-tax income			Current dollars	Con-stant 1996 dollars	As a per-cent of mean before-tax income
One or more taxes paid:					1992 [2]	62,247	1,837	2,054	3.9
1980	76,171	5,180	9,875	23.1	1993 [3]	62,459	2,045	2,220	4.4
1985	81,943	6,947	10,130	22.5	1994 [4]	63,626	2,194	2,323	4.1
1990	87,597	8,896	10,679	22.4	1995 [5]	64,827	2,296	2,364	4.2
1991	88,636	9,007	10,376	22.3	1996	65,856	2,467	2,467	4.3
1992	89,232	9,178	10,264	22.2	FICA payroll taxes:				
1993	89,561	10,217	11,094	23.1	1980	62,061	1,114	2,124	4.6
1994	91,540	10,768	11,400	23.4	1985 [1]	66,090	1,894	2,762	5.6
1995	92,754	11,292	11,625	23.7	1990	70,942	2,692	3,232	6.2
1996	94,236	12,118	12,118	24.3	1991	71,466	2,807	3,234	6.3
Federal income taxes:					1992 [2]	72,516	2,889	3,231	6.3
1980	61,316	4,011	7,647	15.3	1993 [3]	72,264	2,961	3,215	6.1
1985 [1]	68,019	4,675	6,817	13.2	1994 [4]	74,050	3,107	3,289	6.1
1990	70,255	5,806	6,970	12.4	1995 [5]	75,096	3,193	3,287	6.1
1991	69,842	5,901	6,798	12.3	1996	76,724	3,330	3,330	6.0
1992 [2]	68,957	6,029	6,742	12.1	Property taxes on own home:				
1993 [3]	68,786	7,098	7,707	13.3	1980	52,328	575	1,096	2.3
1994 [4]	69,501	7,591	8,037	13.5	1985 [1]	53,298	811	1,183	2.3
1995 [5]	70,926	7,935	8,169	13.7	1990	58,472	1,125	1,351	2.5
1996	72,009	8,637	8,637	14.3	1991	59,403	1,119	1,289	2.5
State income taxes:					1992 [2]	59,838	1,213	1,357	2.6
1980	52,591	859	1,638	3.3	1993 [3]	60,554	1,230	1,336	2.5
1985 [1]	57,033	1,330	1,939	3.8	1994 [4]	62,121	1,257	1,331	2.4
1990	61,875	1,710	2,053	3.8	1995 [5]	63,377	1,361	1,401	2.5
1991	62,314	1,761	2,029	3.8	1996	64,559	1,433	1,433	2.6

[1] Recording of amounts for earnings from longest job increased to $299,999. Full implementation of 1980 census-based sample design. [2] Implementation of 1990 census population controls. [3] Data collection method changed from paper and pencil to computer assisted interviewing. In addition, the March 1994 income supplement was revised to allow for the coding of different income amounts on selected questionnaire items. Limits either increased or decreased in the following categories: earnings increased to $999,999; social security increased to $49,999; supplemental security income and public assistance increased to $24,999; veterans' benefits increased to $99,999; child support and alimony decreased to $49,999. [4] Introduction of 1990 census sample design. [5] Full implementation of the 1990 census-based sample design and metropolitan definitions, 7,000 household sample reduction, and revised race edits.

Source: U.S. Bureau of the Census, Internet site <http://www.census.gov/hhes/income/histinc/rdi02.html> (accessed 27 January 1998).

No. 743. Money Income of Households—Median Income and Income Level, by Household Type: 1996

[See headnote, Table 738]

ITEM	All house-holds	FAMILY HOUSEHOLDS				NONFAMILY HOUSEHOLDS		
		Total	Married couple	Male house-holder, wife absent	Female house-holder, husband absent	Total [1]	Single-person household	
							Male house-holder	Female house-holder
MEDIAN INCOME (dollars)								
All households	**35,492**	**43,082**	**49,858**	**35,658**	**21,564**	**20,973**	**27,266**	**16,398**
White	37,161	45,382	50,302	36,938	24,375	21,536	28,520	16,765
Black	23,482	27,496	42,069	30,995	16,256	15,454	20,525	12,434
Hispanic [2]	24,906	27,152	32,379	28,322	14,535	15,705	19,323	11,770
NUMBER (1,000)								
All households	**101,018**	**70,241**	**53,604**	**3,847**	**12,790**	**30,777**	**13,707**	**17,070**
Under $5,000	3,428	1,730	601	72	1,057	1,698	554	1,144
$5,000 to $9,999	8,452	3,140	1,035	223	1,882	5,312	1,513	3,798
$10,000 to $14,999	8,658	4,154	2,251	288	1,615	4,504	1,533	2,971
$15,000 to $19,999	7,868	4,613	2,845	334	1,434	3,254	1,275	1,980
$20,000 to $24,999	7,641	4,794	3,234	332	1,229	2,847	1,318	1,530
$25,000 to $34,999	13,808	9,448	6,821	639	1,987	4,360	2,315	2,046
$35,000 to $49,999	16,465	12,593	10,096	785	1,710	3,872	2,217	1,654
$50,000 to $74,999	18,172	15,225	13,224	735	1,268	2,946	1,750	1,195
$75,000 to $99,999	8,235	7,189	6,560	254	378	1,043	641	404
$100,000 and over	8,293	7,352	6,939	183	230	941	591	349

[1] Includes other nonfamily households not shown separately. [2] Persons of Hispanic origin may be of any race.

Source: U.S. Bureau of the Census, *Current Population Reports*, P60-197.

No. 744. Money Income of Households—Median Income, by State, in Constant (1996) Dollars: 1986 to 1996

[Constant dollars based on the CPI-U-X1 deflator. Data based on the Current Population Survey; see text, Sections 1 and 14, and Appendix III. The CPS is designed to collect reliable data on income primarily at the national level and secondarily at the regional level. When the income data are tabulated by state, the estimates are considered less reliable and, therefore, particular caution should be used when trying to interpret the results]

STATE	1986	1990	1995 [1]	1996	STATE	1986	1990	1995 [1]	1996
United States	**35,642**	**35,945**	**35,082**	**35,492**	Missouri	31,387	32,811	35,853	34,265
					Montana	29,101	28,061	28,577	28,684
Alabama	27,389	28,039	26,758	30,302	Nebraska	31,168	32,991	33,901	34,014
Alaska	44,888	47,176	49,370	52,779	Nevada	37,531	38,442	37,149	38,540
Arizona	36,505	35,082	31,774	31,637	New Hampshire	43,732	48,985	40,328	39,407
Arkansas	26,813	27,354	26,576	27,123					
California	41,530	39,963	38,102	38,812	New Jersey	45,402	46,499	45,221	47,468
					New Mexico	28,409	30,058	26,758	25,086
Colorado	38,927	36,894	41,908	40,950	New York	35,825	37,924	34,003	35,410
Connecticut	46,842	46,662	41,431	42,119	North Carolina	31,296	31,607	32,923	35,601
Delaware	36,685	36,979	35,959	39,309	North Dakota	30,790	30,328	29,948	31,470
District of Columbia	34,819	32,883	31,656	31,966					
Florida	32,710	32,034	30,623	30,641	Ohio	35,954	36,029	35,973	34,070
					Oklahoma	29,989	29,272	27,088	27,437
Georgia	34,887	33,086	35,106	32,496	Oregon	35,464	35,151	37,448	35,492
Hawaii	41,520	46,723	44,116	41,772	Pennsylvania	34,081	34,819	35,543	34,899
Idaho	29,704	30,378	33,641	34,709	Rhode Island	37,994	38,376	36,403	36,986
Illinois	37,952	39,065	39,195	39,554					
Indiana	32,537	32,326	34,371	35,147	South Carolina	31,449	34,495	29,929	34,665
					South Dakota	28,485	29,496	30,451	29,526
Iowa	32,152	32,758	36,568	33,209	Tennessee	26,135	27,121	29,872	30,790
Kansas	34,252	35,914	31,237	32,585	Texas	34,590	33,887	32,985	33,072
Kentucky	28,451	29,747	30,690	32,413	Utah	37,623	36,184	37,557	37,038
Louisiana	29,905	26,896	28,774	30,262					
Maine	33,533	32,969	34,858	34,696	Vermont	35,215	37,332	34,823	32,358
					Virginia	42,539	42,104	37,292	39,211
Maryland	43,812	46,646	42,253	43,993	Washington	38,482	38,549	36,618	36,676
Massachusetts	43,432	43,513	39,713	39,494	West Virginia	23,569	26,575	25,615	25,247
Michigan	38,087	35,938	37,502	39,225	Wisconsin	37,836	36,867	42,164	40,001
Minnesota	37,855	37,772	39,053	40,991	Wyoming	33,726	35,366	32,460	30,953
Mississippi	23,639	24,223	27,322	26,677					

[1] Full implementation of the 1990 census-based sample design and metropolitan definitions, 7,000 household sample reduction, and revised race edits.

Source: U.S. Bureau of the Census, *Current Population Reports*, P60-197; and Internet site http://www.census.gov/hhes/income/ histinc/inchhdet.html (accessed 25 March 1998).

No. 745. Money Income of Families—Percent Distribution, by Income Level, Race, and Hispanic Origin, in Constant (1996) Dollars: 1970 to 1996

[Constant dollars based on CPI-U-X1 deflator. Families as of **March** of following year. Beginning with 1980, based on householder concept and restricted to primary families. Based on Current Population Survey; see text, Sections 1 and 14, and Appendix III. For definition of median, see Guide to Tabular Presentation]

YEAR	Number of families (1,000)	PERCENT DISTRIBUTION							Median income (dollars)
		Under $10,000	$10,000-$14,999	$15,000-$24,999	$25,000-$34,999	$35,000-$49,999	$50,000-$74,999	$75,000 and over	
ALL FAMILIES [1]									
1970	52,227	7.3	6.4	15.1	17.4	24.4	19.6	9.9	37,485
1975	56,245	6.6	7.0	15.4	16.2	22.3	21.5	11.2	38,301
1980	60,309	6.9	6.3	14.8	14.6	21.5	21.8	14.0	40,079
1985	63,558	7.8	6.3	14.3	14.2	19.4	21.3	16.7	40,443
1990	66,322	7.4	5.9	13.2	13.8	19.3	21.3	19.2	42,440
1994	69,313	8.1	6.4	14.1	14.0	17.8	20.2	19.4	41,059
1995	69,597	7.2	6.3	13.9	13.8	18.3	20.7	19.7	41,810
1996	70,241	7.6	6.1	13.5	13.5	17.7	21.3	20.3	42,300
WHITE									
1970	46,535	6.1	5.8	14.3	17.4	25.2	20.6	10.6	38,887
1975	49,873	5.4	6.3	14.8	16.1	22.9	22.6	11.9	39,834
1980	52,710	5.5	5.5	14.1	14.6	22.2	23.0	15.0	41,759
1985	54,991	6.2	5.6	13.7	14.3	20.0	22.2	18.1	42,509
1990	56,803	5.5	5.2	12.7	13.9	19.8	22.4	20.5	44,315
1994	58,444	6.3	5.7	13.6	14.1	18.4	21.2	20.9	43,284
1995	58,872	5.5	5.7	13.4	13.8	18.7	21.7	21.2	43,905
1996	58,934	5.9	5.4	13.0	13.5	18.3	22.3	21.7	44,756
BLACK									
1970	4,928	17.9	12.3	22.8	16.8	16.8	10.3	3.2	23,854
1975	5,586	17.1	13.6	20.3	17.5	16.4	11.7	3.5	24,509
1980	6,317	18.3	13.1	20.5	14.3	16.4	12.6	4.9	24,162
1985	6,921	20.4	11.6	19.5	13.9	15.4	13.1	6.3	24,477
1990	7,471	20.8	11.2	17.0	13.5	15.8	13.3	8.3	25,717
1994	8,093	20.0	10.9	17.7	14.0	14.4	14.1	9.0	26,148
1995	8,055	18.8	10.6	18.0	14.3	16.1	13.4	8.6	26,737
1996	8,455	18.9	10.7	17.6	14.3	15.1	14.4	9.0	26,522
HISPANIC ORIGIN [2]									
1975	2,499	13.1	11.6	22.3	18.3	19.7	11.2	3.7	26,665
1980	3,235	12.8	10.7	21.2	17.2	18.4	14.0	5.7	28,055
1985	4,206	14.3	12.1	19.6	15.8	17.0	13.8	7.5	27,745
1990	4,981	14.1	11.6	19.1	15.6	17.6	13.8	8.2	28,128
1994	6,202	16.4	12.8	19.4	15.3	15.6	12.4	8.3	25,746
1995	6,287	15.5	11.9	22.3	15.8	14.4	12.8	7.2	25,295
1996	6,631	14.6	11.6	21.5	15.6	15.2	13.0	8.5	26,179

[1] Includes other races not shown separately.   [2] Persons of Hispanic origin may be of any race.

No. 746. Money Income of Families—Median Income, by Race and Hispanic Origin, in Current and Constant (1996) Dollars: 1970 to 1996

[See headnote, Table 738]

YEAR	MEDIAN INCOME IN CURRENT DOLLARS					MEDIAN INCOME IN CONSTANT (1996) DOLLARS				
	All families [1]	White	Black	Asian, Pacific Islander	Hispanic [2]	All families [1]	White	Black	Asian, Pacific Islander	Hispanic [2]
1970	9,867	10,236	6,279	(NA)	(NA)	37,485	38,887	23,854	(NA)	(NA)
1980	21,023	21,904	12,674	(NA)	14,716	40,079	41,759	24,162	(NA)	28,055
1981	22,388	23,517	13,266	(NA)	16,401	38,986	40,952	23,101	(NA)	28,561
1982	23,433	24,603	13,598	(NA)	16,227	38,459	40,379	22,317	(NA)	26,632
1983	24,580	25,757	14,506	(NA)	16,956	38,721	40,575	22,851	(NA)	26,711
1984 [3]	26,433	27,686	15,431	(NA)	18,832	39,917	41,809	23,302	(NA)	28,438
1985 [4]	27,735	29,152	16,786	(NA)	19,027	40,443	42,509	24,477	(NA)	27,745
1986	29,458	30,809	17,604	(NA)	19,995	42,171	44,105	25,201	(NA)	28,624
1987 [5]	30,970	32,385	18,406	(NA)	20,300	42,775	44,729	25,422	(NA)	28,038
1988	32,191	33,915	19,329	36,560	21,769	42,695	44,981	25,636	48,489	28,872
1989	34,213	35,975	20,209	40,351	23,446	43,290	45,520	25,571	51,057	29,667
1990	35,353	36,915	21,423	42,246	23,431	42,440	44,315	25,717	50,715	28,128
1991	35,939	37,783	21,548	40,974	23,895	41,401	43,525	24,823	47,201	27,527
1992 [6]	36,573	38,670	21,103	42,255	23,555	40,900	43,245	23,600	47,255	26,342
1993 [7]	36,959	39,300	21,542	44,456	23,654	40,131	42,672	23,391	48,271	25,684
1994 [8]	38,782	40,884	24,698	46,122	24,318	41,059	43,284	26,148	48,830	25,746
1995 [9]	40,611	42,646	25,970	46,356	24,570	41,810	43,905	26,737	47,725	25,296
1996	42,300	44,756	26,522	49,195	26,179	42,300	44,756	26,522	49,195	26,179

NA Not available.   [1] Includes other races not shown separately.   [2] Persons of Hispanic origin may be of any race. [3] Implementation of Hispanic population weighting controls.   [4] Recording of amounts for earnings from longest job increased to $299,999.   [5] Implementation of a new March CPS processing system.   [6] Implementation of 1990 census population controls. [7] See text, Section 14, for information on data collection change.   [8] Introduction of 1990 census sample design.   [9] Full implementation of the 1990 census-based sample design and metropolitan definitions, 7,000 household sample reduction, and revised race edits.

Source of Tables 745 and 746: U.S. Bureau of the Census, *Current Population Reports*, P60-197.

No. 747. Share of Aggregate Income Received by Each Fifth and Top 5 Percent of Families: 1970 to 1996

[Families as of March of the following year. Income in constant 1996 CPI-U-X1 adjusted dollars]

YEAR	Num-ber (1,000)	INCOME AT SELECTED POSITIONS (dollars)					PERCENT DISTRIBUTION OF AGGREGATE INCOME					
		Upper limit of each fifth				Top 5 percent	Lowest 5th	Second 5th	Third 5th	Fourth 5th	Highest 5th	Top 5 percent
		Lowest	Second	Third	Fourth							
1970	52,227	19,375	31,608	42,925	59,003	92,127	5.4	12.2	17.6	23.8	40.9	15.6
1975	56,245	19,506	32,120	44,669	61,847	96,876	5.6	11.9	17.7	24.2	40.7	14.9
1980	60,309	19,827	33,382	47,280	66,344	104,854	5.3	11.6	17.6	24.4	41.1	14.6
1981	61,019	19,181	32,651	46,596	65,825	104,470	5.3	11.4	17.5	24.6	41.2	14.4
1982	61,393	18,708	32,040	45,872	65,816	107,193	5.0	11.3	17.2	24.4	42.2	15.3
1983 [1]	62,015	18,644	31,933	46,432	66,394	109,268	4.9	11.2	17.2	24.5	42.4	15.3
1984	62,706	18,990	33,032	47,846	68,805	112,654	4.8	11.1	17.1	24.5	42.5	15.4
1985	63,558	19,372	33,372	48,342	70,326	115,145	4.8	11.0	16.9	24.3	43.1	16.1
1986	64,491	20,042	34,501	50,277	72,394	119,393	4.7	10.9	16.9	24.1	43.4	16.5
1987 [2]	65,204	20,162	34,780	50,828	73,657	120,091	4.6	10.7	16.8	24.0	43.8	17.2
1988	65,837	20,030	34,725	51,062	74,148	122,020	4.6	10.7	16.7	24.0	44.0	17.2
1989	66,090	20,249	35,429	51,625	75,350	125,220	4.6	10.6	16.5	23.7	44.6	17.9
1990	66,322	20,223	34,866	50,467	73,816	122,877	4.6	10.8	16.6	23.8	44.3	17.4
1991 [3]	67,173	19,584	33,535	49,535	72,564	118,451	4.5	10.7	16.6	24.1	44.2	17.1
1992 [3]	68,216	18,690	33,185	49,206	71,628	118,555	4.3	10.5	16.5	24.0	44.7	17.6
1993 [4]	68,506	18,426	32,574	48,894	72,526	122,894	4.1	9.9	15.7	23.3	47.0	20.3
1994 [5]	69,313	18,993	33,137	49,759	74,107	127,090	4.2	10.0	15.7	23.3	46.9	20.1
1995	69,597	19,633	33,959	50,431	74,394	127,307	4.4	10.1	15.8	23.2	46.5	20.0
1996	70,241	19,680	34,315	51,086	75,316	128,000	4.2	10.0	15.8	23.1	46.8	20.3

[1] Beginning 1983, data based on revised Hispanic population controls and not directly comparable with prior years. [2] Beginning 1987, data based on revised processing procedures and not directly comparable with prior years. [3] Based on 1990 census population controls. [4] See text, Section 14, for explanation of changes in data collection method. [5] Introduction of new 1990 census sample design.

Source: U.S. Bureau of the Census, *Current Population Reports*, P60-197; and Internet site, <http://www.census.gov/hhes/income/histinc/index.html> (accessed 3 March 1998).

No. 748. Money Income of Families—Distribution, by Family Characteristics, by Income Level: 1996

[See headnote, Table 745. For composition of regions, see inside front cover]

CHARACTERISTIC	Number of families (1,000)	INCOME LEVEL (1,000)							Median income (dollars)
		Under $10,000	$10,000 to $14,999	$15,000 to $24,999	$25,000 to $34,999	$35,000 to $49,999	$50,000 to $74,999	$75,000 and over	
All families	**70,241**	**5,312**	**4,294**	**9,499**	**9,469**	**12,463**	**14,942**	**14,262**	**42,300**
Age of householder:									
15 to 24 years old.	2,964	800	333	619	519	393	215	83	19,937
25 to 34 years old.	13,737	1,498	969	1,906	2,107	2,654	2,949	1,654	37,177
35 to 44 years old.	19,026	1,231	895	2,013	2,311	3,499	4,773	4,304	47,725
45 to 54 years old.	14,384	636	474	1,162	1,338	2,450	3,607	4,716	57,161
55 to 64 years old	8,997	502	500	969	1,064	1,609	2,032	2,320	48,198
65 years old and over	11,133	643	1,123	2,829	2,130	1,858	1,366	1,184	28,983
White.	58,934	3,440	3,191	7,651	7,927	10,761	13,169	12,796	44,756
Black.	8,455	1,601	907	1,487	1,210	1,279	1,214	758	26,522
Hispanic origin [1]	6,631	972	767	1,425	1,036	1,006	862	563	26,179
Northeast	13,404	1,044	677	1,600	1,627	2,270	3,009	3,177	46,553
Midwest	16,457	962	860	2,123	2,228	3,019	3,958	3,308	44,957
South.	25,438	2,223	1,809	3,771	3,699	4,551	4,931	4,454	38,710
West	14,943	1,084	949	2,005	1,915	2,624	3,044	3,323	42,569
Type of family:									
Married-couple families	53,604	1,647	2,268	6,102	6,853	10,097	13,195	13,442	49,707
Male householder, wife absent	3,847	393	341	713	667	744	663	326	31,600
Female householder, husband absent.	12,790	3,272	1,685	2,684	1,949	1,623	1,084	495	19,911
Unrelated subfamilies	615	225	122	129	71	47	15	7	13,131
Education attainment of householder: [2]									
Total	67,277	4,511	3,961	8,879	8,950	12,070	14,727	14,178	43,603
Less than 9th grade	4,767	736	821	1,272	824	572	379	164	20,781
9th to 12th grade (no diploma)	6,771	1,080	825	1,548	1,117	1,082	776	342	24,575
High school graduate (includes equivalency)	21,870	1,526	1,358	3,359	3,441	4,632	4,853	2,700	38,563
Some college, no degree.	12,092	631	569	1,361	1,784	2,472	3,034	2,241	44,814
Associate degree	4,955	229	140	500	598	930	1,399	1,158	51,176
Bachelor's degree or more	16,823	309	249	839	1,187	2,381	4,286	7,572	69,688
Bachelor's degree	10,753	213	200	637	872	1,755	2,900	4,176	64,293
Master's degree	4,009	65	39	131	229	474	1,025	2,046	76,065
Professional degree	1,189	24	8	45	67	96	185	764	102,557
Doctorate degree	872	7	1	27	19	57	176	585	92,316

[1] Persons of Hispanic origin may be of any race. [2] Persons 25 years old and over.

Source: U.S. Bureau of the Census, *Current Population Reports*, P60-197.

No. 749. Money Income of Families—Work Experience, by Income Level: 1996

[See headnote, Table 745]

CHARACTERISTIC	Number of families (1,000)	Under $10,000	$10,000 to $14,999	$15,000 to $24,999	$25,000 to $34,999	$35,000 to $49,999	$50,000 to $74,999	$75,000 and over	Median income (dollars)
All families.............	**70,241**	**5,312**	**4,294**	**9,499**	**9,469**	**12,463**	**14,942**	**14,262**	**42,300**
Number of earners:									
No earners.................	9,947	2,574	1,504	2,469	1,484	1,018	517	381	18,088
One earner.................	20,052	2,335	2,061	4,250	3,488	3,325	2,554	2,037	28,383
Two earners or more	40,242	401	729	2,780	4,496	8,120	11,871	11,844	56,442
Two earners	31,309	366	665	2,466	3,907	6,679	9,051	8,174	53,361
Three earners	6,697	32	59	281	507	1,209	2,163	2,446	63,281
Four earners or more	2,236	3	5	33	82	232	658	1,224	79,371
Work experience of householder:									
Total	70,241	5,312	4,294	9,499	9,469	12,463	14,942	14,262	42,300
Worked....................	53,460	2,221	2,285	5,723	6,898	10,120	13,257	12,955	49,054
Worked at full-time jobs	46,843	1,237	1,702	4,774	5,915	9,085	12,178	11,951	51,083
50 weeks or more	39,796	393	1,059	3,623	4,877	7,931	10,921	10,991	53,752
27 to 49 weeks	4,586	318	380	690	674	815	970	740	38,934
26 weeks or less	2,461	527	263	461	363	339	288	220	24,430
Worked at part-time jobs.	6,616	983	583	949	984	1,035	1,079	1,002	33,042
50 weeks or more	3,229	285	276	471	504	564	552	578	36,838
27 to 49 weeks	1,557	252	114	213	213	252	272	239	34,394
26 weeks or less	1,830	446	193	265	267	219	256	184	25,401

No. 750. Median Income of Families, by Type of Family in Current and Constant (1996) Dollars: 1970 to 1996

[See headnote, Table 745]

	CURRENT DOLLARS						CONSTANT (1996) DOLLARS					
		Married-couple families			Male house-holder, no wife present	Female house-holder, no hus-band present		Married-couple families			Male house-holder, no wife present	Female house-holder, no hus-band present
YEAR	Total	Total	Wife in paid labor force	Wife not in paid labor force			Total	Total	Wife in paid labor force	Wife not in paid labor force		
1970	9,867	10,516	12,276	9,304	9,012	5,093	37,485	39,951	46,637	35,346	34,237	19,348
1980	21,023	23,141	26,879	18,972	17,519	10,408	40,079	44,117	51,243	36,169	33,399	19,842
1985	27,735	31,100	36,431	24,556	22,622	13,660	40,443	45,349	53,123	35,807	32,987	19,919
1986	29,458	32,805	38,346	25,803	24,962	13,647	42,171	46,963	54,895	36,939	35,735	19,537
1987 [1]	30,970	34,879	40,751	26,640	25,208	14,683	42,775	48,174	56,284	36,794	34,816	20,280
1988	32,191	36,389	42,709	27,220	26,827	15,346	42,695	48,262	56,644	36,102	35,580	20,353
1989	34,213	38,547	45,266	28,747	27,847	16,442	43,290	48,774	57,276	36,374	35,235	20,804
1990	35,353	39,895	46,777	30,265	29,046	16,932	42,440	47,892	56,154	36,332	34,869	20,326
1991 [2]	35,939	40,995	48,169	30,075	28,351	16,692	41,401	47,226	55,490	34,646	32,660	19,229
1992 [2]	36,573	41,890	49,775	30,174	27,576	17,025	40,900	46,846	55,664	33,744	30,839	19,039
1993 [3]	36,959	43,005	51,204	30,218	26,467	17,443	40,131	46,695	55,598	32,811	28,738	18,940
1994 [3]	38,782	44,959	53,309	31,176	27,751	18,236	41,059	47,598	56,438	33,006	29,380	19,307
1995 [4]	40,611	47,062	55,823	32,375	30,358	19,691	41,810	48,452	57,471	33,331	31,254	20,272
1996	42,300	49,707	58,381	33,748	31,600	19,911	42,300	49,707	58,381	33,748	31,600	19,911

[1] Beginning 1987, data based on revised processing procedures and not directly comparable with prior years. [2] Based on 1990 census population controls. [3] See text, Section 14, for information on data collection change. [4] Introduction of 1990 census sample design.

No. 751. Married-Couple Families—Number and Median Income, by Work Experience of Husbands and Wives and Presence of Children: 1996

[As of **March 1997**. Based on Current Population Survey; see text, Sections 1 and 14, and Appendix III]

WORK EXPERIENCE OF HUSBAND OR WIFE	NUMBER (1,000)					MEDIAN INCOME (dollars)				
	All married-couple families	No related children	One or more related children under 18 years old			All married-couple families	No related children	One or more related children under 18 years old		
			Total	One child	Two children or more			Total	One child	Two children or more
All married-couple families	53,604	27,420	26,184	10,011	16,173	49,707	46,936	51,768	53,944	50,752
Husband worked	42,953	18,138	24,815	9,343	15,472	55,627	59,124	53,142	55,989	51,730
Wife worked.	32,453	13,848	18,605	7,477	11,128	59,833	62,992	57,637	59,493	56,264
Wife year-round, full-time worker	18,509	8,690	9,819	4,331	5,488	64,278	66,856	61,878	62,845	61,158
Wife did not work	10,500	4,290	6,210	1,866	4,344	40,999	44,512	38,835	38,774	38,858
Husband year-round, full-time worker	35,041	13,809	21,232	7,956	13,276	59,109	63,367	56,186	58,705	54,549
Wife worked.	27,078	11,051	16,028	6,387	9,641	62,234	66,219	59,995	61,776	58,553

Source of Tables 749-751: U.S. Bureau of the Census, *Current Population Reports*, P60-197; and Internet site, <http://www.census.gov/hhes/income/histinc/index.html> (accessed 25 March 1998).

No. 752. Money Income of Persons—Selected Characteristics, by Income Level: 1995

[Constant dollars based on CPI-U-X1 deflator. As of **March of following year.** Covers persons 15 years old and over. For definition of median, see Guide to Tabular Presentation. For composition of regions, see map, inside front cover]

| ITEM | All persons (1,000) | Total (1,000) | PERSONS WITH INCOME Number (1,000) | | | | | | | | Median income (dollars) |
			Under $5,000 [1]	$5,000 to $9,999	$10,000 to $14,999	$15,000 to $24,999	$25,000 to $34,999	$35,000 to $49,999	$50,000 to $74,999	$75,000 and over	
MALE											
Total	100,159	93,439	9,014	10,402	10,931	18,145	14,516	13,996	9,912	6,253	23,834
15 to 24 years old	18,539	14,016	5,572	2,963	2,068	2,216	795	301	75	26	6,960
25 to 34 years old	20,040	19,354	961	1,565	2,157	4,892	4,252	3,256	1,657	613	25,179
35 to 44 years old	21,793	21,181	862	1,363	1,616	3,769	3,717	4,518	3,275	2,062	32,167
45 to 54 years old	16,119	15,748	595	1,069	1,082	2,225	2,516	3,227	2,923	2,111	36,232
55 to 64 years old	10,265	9,966	558	982	1,032	1,649	1,599	1,690	1,287	1,169	29,526
65 yr. old and over	13,404	13,173	465	2,460	2,977	3,395	1,637	1,004	695	542	16,684
Northeast	19,393	18,060	1,740	1,813	1,981	3,392	2,846	2,679	2,096	1,512	25,282
Midwest	22,990	21,908	2,038	2,173	2,321	4,226	3,673	3,677	2,407	1,393	25,406
South	35,026	32,464	3,241	3,909	4,110	6,526	4,998	4,701	3,005	1,974	22,234
West	22,750	21,006	1,994	2,507	2,519	4,002	2,998	2,939	2,403	1,643	23,395
White	84,540	80,041	7,141	8,262	9,125	15,559	12,608	12,326	9,009	6,012	24,949
Black	11,113	9,410	1,395	1,686	1,257	1,887	1,370	1,119	488	209	16,491
Hispanic [2]	10,627	9,305	1,124	1,607	1,781	2,225	1,204	791	408	165	15,437
Education attainment of householder: [3]											
Total	81,620	79,423	3,441	7,439	8,863	15,929	13,721	13,695	9,837	6,497	27,248
Less than 9th grade	6,477	6,139	545	1,766	1,524	1,383	547	215	103	55	12,174
9th to 12th grade [4]	8,212	7,671	638	1,322	1,592	2,132	1,123	545	233	86	16,058
High school graduate [5]	26,226	25,510	1,144	2,421	3,046	6,245	5,120	4,600	2,220	715	24,814
Some college, no degree	14,033	13,756	484	968	1,238	2,880	2,839	2,768	1,814	765	29,160
Associate degree	5,299	5,210	160	238	370	915	1,086	1,287	856	297	33,065
Bachelor's degree or more	21,374	21,136	470	724	1,093	2,375	3,006	4,279	4,611	4,578	44,161
Bachelor's degree	13,672	13,510	332	529	841	1,773	2,199	2,908	2,883	2,045	39,624
Master's degree	4,776	4,709	98	129	168	427	584	947	1,116	1,239	50,003
Professional degree	1,708	1,702	22	44	42	102	136	245	292	818	71,869
Doctorate degree	1,218	1,215	17	21	43	72	85	179	320	477	62,255
FEMALE											
Total	107,076	96,558	19,495	19,854	13,970	19,237	11,278	7,505	3,659	1,560	12,815
15 to 24 years old	18,115	13,502	6,064	3,168	1,913	1,666	495	137	40	18	5,881
25 to 34 years old	20,217	18,481	3,290	2,763	2,532	4,519	3,105	1,475	602	196	16,384
35 to 44 years old	22,167	20,637	3,336	2,789	2,485	4,554	3,309	2,459	1,140	565	18,447
45 to 54 years old	16,894	15,693	2,370	2,048	1,883	3,487	2,338	2,054	1,110	403	19,046
55 to 64 years old	11,210	10,220	2,057	1,982	1,468	2,077	1,099	833	506	197	13,316
65 yr. old and over	18,474	18,026	2,377	7,103	3,690	2,933	933	547	262	180	9,626
Northeast	21,322	19,400	3,803	3,927	2,675	3,728	2,339	1,692	834	403	13,451
Midwest	24,993	23,219	4,597	4,679	3,414	4,876	2,783	1,726	825	320	13,051
South	37,954	33,772	6,916	7,224	4,979	6,805	3,921	2,393	1,094	440	12,357
West	22,807	20,167	4,179	4,024	2,902	3,828	2,235	1,695	906	397	12,831
White	88,756	80,741	16,252	16,242	11,867	15,970	9,481	6,365	3,175	1,389	12,961
Black	13,514	11,817	2,347	2,906	1,585	2,504	1,329	774	297	75	11,772
Hispanic [2]	10,073	7,744	2,036	2,003	1,242	1,366	602	309	148	39	9,484
Education attainment of householder: [3]											
Total	88,961	83,056	13,431	16,686	12,058	17,571	10,783	7,368	3,619	1,541	14,682
Less than 9th grade	6,836	5,775	1,416	2,643	954	546	119	49	34	13	7,276
9th to 12th grade [4]	9,000	7,929	1,787	2,866	1,533	1,241	310	126	41	25	8,544
High school graduate [5]	31,360	29,212	5,002	6,369	5,256	7,287	3,149	1,452	513	185	12,702
Some college, no degree	15,335	14,528	2,225	2,392	2,137	3,603	2,152	1,342	526	151	16,255
Associate degree	7,107	6,839	854	825	883	1,631	1,335	893	335	83	20,460
Bachelor's degree or more	19,323	18,775	2,147	1,591	1,295	3,263	3,718	3,505	2,171	1,084	27,556
Bachelor's degree	13,685	13,247	1,715	1,265	1,025	2,557	2,710	2,182	1,263	531	25,192
Master's degree	4,356	4,285	341	263	227	568	855	1,097	669	265	33,302
Professional degree	739	715	64	33	26	67	93	119	135	178	42,059
Doctorate degree	543	527	29	30	17	71	59	107	104	110	42,431

[1] Includes persons with income deficit.   [2] Persons of Hispanic origin may be of any race.   [3] Persons 25 years and over.
[4] No diploma attained.   [5] Includes high school equivalency.

Source: U.S. Bureau of the Census, *Current Population Reports*, P60-197.

No. 753. Median Income of Persons with Income in Constant (1996) Dollars, by Sex, Race, and Hispanic Origin: 1980 to 1996

[Age as of March of following year. Persons 15 years old and over. Constant dollars based on CPI-U-X1 deflator]

ITEM	MALE				FEMALE			
	1980	1990	1995	1996	1980	1990	1995	1996
NUMBER WITH INCOME (1,000)								
All races	78,661	88,220	92,066	93,439	80,826	92,245	96,007	96,558
White	69,420	76,480	79,022	80,041	70,573	78,566	80,608	80,741
Black	7,387	8,820	9,339	9,410	8,596	10,687	11,607	11,817
Asian and Pacific Islander.	(NA)	2,235	3,095	3,277	(NA)	2,333	3,025	3,226
Hispanic [1]	3,996	6,767	8,577	9,305	3,617	5,903	7,478	7,744
White, not Hispanic origin	65,564	69,987	70,754	71,084	67,084	72,939	73,506	73,445
MEDIAN INCOME IN CONSTANT (1996) DOLLARS (dol.)								
All races	23,888	24,361	23,228	$23,834	9,380	12,089	12,488	$12,815
White	25,409	25,414	24,601	24,949	9,431	12,385	12,680	12,961
Black	15,269	15,448	16,479	16,491	8,731	9,997	11,285	11,772
Asian and Pacific Islander.	(NA)	23,282	22,816	23,374	(NA)	13,308	13,242	14,634
Hispanic [1]	18,414	16,170	15,278	15,437	8,398	9,042	9,192	9,484
White, not Hispanic origin	26,082	26,360	26,233	26,290	9,494	12,702	13,185	13,514

NA Not available.   [1] Persons of Hispanic origin may be of any race.

No. 754. Average Earnings of Year-Round, Full-Time Workers, by Educational Attainment: 1996

[In dollars. For persons 18 years old and over as of March 1997]

AGE AND SEX	All workers	Less than 9th grade	HIGH SCHOOL		COLLEGE		
			9th to 12th grade (no diploma)	High school graduate (includes equivalency)	Some college, no degree	Associate degree	Bachelor's degree or more
Male, total	42,077	20,153	25,283	32,521	38,491	39,873	63,127
18 to 24 years old	18,856	13,336	15,478	18,779	18,336	23,447	27,257
25 to 34 years old	33,055	19,176	19,910	27,349	32,624	34,854	44,355
35 to 44 years old	45,840	19,798	26,116	35,138	39,630	41,558	70,035
45 to 54 years old	51,705	21,600	34,527	39,178	46,499	43,745	72,461
55 to 64 years old	49,916	20,747	32,926	38,032	59,390	55,129	71,070
65 years old and over. . .	42,025	26,566	24,620	33,142	29,810	(B)	65,165
Female, total	28,363	15,150	17,313	21,893	25,889	28,403	41,339
18 to 24 years old	17,002	(B)	12,512	15,219	16,481	16,985	24,980
25 to 34 years old	26,119	14,244	16,826	19,526	23,738	27,020	34,132
35 to 44 years old	30,879	14,650	18,261	23,134	27,853	29,493	46,923
45 to 54 years old	31,222	15,678	18,007	23,833	30,666	31,248	45,012
55 to 64 years old	27,629	17,652	19,039	23,179	27,340	28,982	41,342
65 years old and over. . .	35,170	(B)	(B)	25,878	20,477	(B)	89,165

B Base figure too small to meet statistical standards for reliability of derived figure.

No. 755. Per Capita Money Income in Current and Constant (1996) Dollars, by Race and Hispanic Origin: 1970 to 1996

[In dollars. Constant dollars based on CPI-U-X1 deflator. As of March of following year]

YEAR	CURRENT DOLLARS					CONSTANT (1996) DOLLARS				
	All races [1]	White	Black	Asian, Pacific Islander	His- panic [2]	All races [1]	White	Black	Asian, Pacific Islander	His- panic [2]
1970	3,177	3,354	1,869	(NA)	(NA)	12,070	12,742	7,100	(NA)	(NA)
1980	7,787	8,233	4,804	(NA)	4,865	14,845	15,696	9,159	(NA)	9,275
1985 [3]	11,013	11,671	6,840	(NA)	6,613	16,059	17,018	9,974	(NA)	9,643
1986	11,670	12,352	7,207	(NA)	7,000	16,706	17,683	10,317	(NA)	10,021
1987 [4]	12,391	13,143	7,645	(NA)	7,653	17,114	18,153	10,559	(NA)	10,570
1988	13,123	13,896	8,271	(NA)	7,956	17,405	18,430	10,970	(NA)	10,552
1989	14,056	14,896	8,747	(NA)	8,390	17,785	18,848	11,068	(NA)	10,616
1990	14,387	15,265	9,017	(NA)	8,424	17,271	18,325	10,825	(NA)	10,113
1991	14,617	15,510	9,170	(NA)	8,662	16,839	17,867	10,564	(NA)	9,978
1992 [5]	14,847	15,785	9,239	(NA)	8,591	16,604	17,653	10,332	(NA)	9,607
1993	15,777	16,800	9,863	15,691	8,830	17,131	18,242	10,709	17,037	9,588
1994	16,555	17,611	10,650	16,902	9,435	17,527	18,645	11,275	17,894	9,989
1995	17,227	18,304	10,982	16,567	9,300	17,736	18,844	11,306	17,056	9,575
1996	18,136	19,181	11,899	17,921	10,048	18,136	19,181	11,899	17,921	10,048

NA Not available.   [1] Includes other races not shown separately.   [2] Persons of Hispanic origin may be of any race.
[3] Beginning 1985, data based on revised Hispanic population controls   [4] Beginning 1987, data based on revised processing procedures and not directly comparable with prior years.   [5] Based on 1990 population controls.
Source of Tables 753-755: U.S. Bureau of the Census, Current Population Reports, P60-197; and Internet site, <http://www.census.gov/hhes/income/histinc/index.html\> (accessed 25 March 1998).

No. 756. Persons Below Poverty Level and Below 125 Percent of Poverty Level: 1960 to 1996

[Persons as of **March of the following year**. Based on Current Population Survey; see text, Sections 1 and 14, and Appendix III]

YEAR	NUMBER BELOW POVERTY LEVEL (1,000)				PERCENT BELOW POVERTY LEVEL				BELOW 125 PERCENT OF POVERTY LEVEL		AVERAGE INCOME CUTOFFS FOR NONFARM FAMILY OF FOUR [3]	
	All races [1]	White	Black	His- panic [2]	All races [1]	White	Black	His- panic [2]	Num- ber (1,000)	Per- cent of total popula- tion	At poverty level	At 125 percent of poverty level
1960	39,851	28,309	(NA)	(NA)	22.2	17.8	(NA)	(NA)	54,560	30.4	3,022	3,778
1970	25,420	17,484	7,548	(NA)	12.6	9.9	33.5	(NA)	35,624	17.6	3,968	4,960
1975	25,877	17,770	7,545	2,991	12.3	9.7	31.3	23.0	37,182	17.6	5,500	6,875
1976	24,975	16,713	7,595	2,783	11.8	9.1	31.1	26.9	35,509	16.7	5,815	7,269
1977	24,720	16,416	7,726	2,700	11.6	8.9	31.3	24.7	35,659	16.7	6,191	7,739
1978	24,497	16,259	7,625	2,607	11.4	8.7	30.6	22.4	34,155	15.8	6,662	8,328
1979 [4]	26,072	17,214	8,050	2,921	11.7	9.0	31.0	21.6	36,616	16.4	7,412	9,265
1980	29,272	19,699	8,579	3,491	13.0	10.2	32.5	21.8	40,658	18.1	8,414	10,518
1981	31,822	21,553	9,173	3,713	14.0	11.1	34.2	25.7	43,748	19.3	9,287	11,609
1982	34,398	23,517	9,697	4,301	15.0	12.0	35.6	26.5	46,520	20.3	9,862	12,328
1983 [5]	35,303	23,984	9,882	4,633	15.2	12.1	35.7	29.9	47,150	20.3	10,178	12,723
1984	33,700	22,955	9,490	4,806	14.4	11.5	33.8	28.0	45,288	19.4	10,609	13,261
1985	33,064	22,860	8,926	5,236	14.0	11.4	31.3	28.4	44,166	18.7	10,989	13,736
1986 [6]	32,370	22,183	8,983	5,117	13.6	11.0	31.1	29.0	43,486	18.2	11,203	14,004
1987 [6]	32,221	21,195	9,520	5,422	13.4	10.4	32.4	27.3	43,032	17.9	11,611	14,514
1988	31,745	20,715	9,356	5,357	13.0	10.1	31.3	28.0	42,551	17.5	12,092	15,115
1989	31,528	20,785	9,302	5,430	12.8	10.0	30.7	26.7	42,653	17.3	12,674	15,843
1990	33,585	22,326	9,837	6,006	13.5	10.7	31.9	26.2	44,837	18.0	13,359	16,699
1991	35,708	23,747	10,242	6,339	14.2	11.3	32.7	28.1	47,527	18.9	13,924	17,405
1992 [7]	38,014	25,259	10,827	7,592	14.8	11.9	33.4	29.6	50,592	19.7	14,335	17,919
1993	39,265	26,226	10,877	8,126	15.1	12.2	33.1	30.6	51,801	20.0	14,763	18,454
1994	38,059	25,379	10,196	8,416	14.5	11.7	30.6	30.7	50,401	19.3	15,141	18,926
1995	36,425	24,423	9,872	8,574	13.8	11.2	29.3	30.3	48,761	18.5	15,569	19,461
1996	36,529	24,650	9,694	8,697	13.7	11.2	28.4	29.4	49,310	18.5	16,036	20,045

NA Not available. [1] Includes other races not shown separately. [2] Persons of Hispanic origin may be of any race. [3] Beginning 1981, income cutoffs for nonfarm families are applied to all families, both farm and nonfarm. [4] Population controls based on 1980 census; see text, sections 1 and 14. [5] Beginning 1983, data based on revised Hispanic population controls and not directly comparable with prior years. [6] Beginning 1987, data based on revised processing procedures and not directly comparable with prior years. [7] Beginning 1992, based on 1990 population controls.

Source: U.S. Bureau of the Census, *Current Population Reports,* P60-198.

No. 757. Children Below Poverty Level, by Race and Hispanic Origin: 1970 to 1996

[Persons as of **March of the following year**. Covers only related children in families under 18 years old. Based on Current Population Survey; see text, Sections 1 and 14, and Appendix III]

YEAR	NUMBER BELOW POVERTY LEVEL (1,000)				PERCENT BELOW POVERTY LEVEL			
	All races [1]	White	Black	Hispanic [2]	All races [1]	White	Black	Hispanic [2]
1970	10,235	6,138	3,922	(NA)	14.9	10.5	41.5	(NA)
1980	11,114	6,817	3,906	1,718	17.9	13.4	42.1	33.0
1981	12,068	7,429	4,170	1,874	19.5	14.7	44.9	35.4
1982	13,139	8,282	4,388	2,117	21.3	16.5	47.3	38.9
1983 [3]	13,427	8,534	4,273	2,251	21.8	17.0	46.2	37.7
1984	12,929	8,086	4,320	2,317	21.0	16.1	46.2	38.7
1985	12,483	7,838	4,057	2,512	20.1	15.6	43.1	39.6
1986	12,257	7,714	4,037	2,413	19.8	15.3	42.7	37.1
1987 [4]	12,275	7,398	4,234	2,606	19.7	14.7	44.4	38.9
1988	11,935	7,095	4,148	2,576	19.0	14.0	42.8	37.3
1989	12,001	7,164	4,257	2,496	19.0	14.1	43.2	35.5
1990	12,715	7,696	4,412	2,750	19.9	15.1	44.2	37.7
1991	13,658	8,316	4,637	2,977	21.1	16.1	45.6	39.8
1992 [5]	14,521	8,752	5,015	3,440	21.6	16.5	46.3	39.0
1993	14,961	9,123	5,030	3,666	22.0	17.0	45.9	39.9
1994	14,610	8,826	4,787	3,956	21.2	16.3	43.3	41.1
1995	13,999	8,474	4,644	3,938	20.0	15.5	41.5	39.3
1996	13,764	8,488	4,411	4,090	19.8	15.5	39.5	39.9

NA Not available. [1] Includes other races not shown separately. [2] Persons of Hispanic origin may be of any race. [3] Beginning 1983, data based on revised Hispanic population controls and not directly comparable with prior years. [4] Beginning 1987, data based on revised processing procedures and not directly comparable with prior years. [5] Beginning 1992, based on 1990 population controls.

Source: U.S. Bureau of the Census, *Current Population Reports,* P60-198.

No. 758. Weighted Average Poverty Thresholds: 1980 to 1996

[Official poverty thresholds; see text, Section 14]

SIZE OF UNIT	1980[1]	1989	1990	1991	1992	1993	1994	1995	1996
One person (unrelated individual) . . .	$4,190	$6,310	$6,652	$6,932	$7,143	$7,363	$7,547	$7,763	7,995
Under 65 years	4,290	6,451	6,800	7,086	7,299	$7,518	7,710	7,929	8,163
65 years and over	3,949	5,947	6,268	6,532	6,729	6,930	7,108	7,309	7,525
Two persons	5,363	8,076	8,509	8,865	9,137	9,414	9,661	9,933	10,233
Householder under 65 years	5,537	8,343	8,794	9,165	9,443	9,728	9,976	10,259	10,564
Householder 65 years and over . . .	4,983	7,501	7,905	8,241	8,487	8,740	8,967	9,219	9,491
Three persons	6,565	9,885	10,419	10,860	11,186	11,522	11,821	12,158	12,516
Four persons	8,414	12,674	13,359	13,924	14,335	14,763	15,141	15,569	16,036
Five persons	9,966	14,990	15,792	16,456	16,952	17,449	17,900	18,408	18,952
Six persons	11,269	16,921	17,839	18,587	19,137	19,718	20,235	20,804	21,389
Seven persons	12,761	19,162	20,241	21,058	21,594	22,383	22,923	23,552	24,268
Eight persons	14,199	21,328	22,582	23,605	24,053	24,838	25,427	26,237	27,091
Nine or more persons	16,896	25,480	26,848	27,942	28,745	29,529	30,300	31,280	31,971

[1] Poverty levels for nonfarm families.

Source: U.S. Bureau of the Census, Current Population Reports, P60-198; and earlier reports.

No. 759. Persons Below Poverty Level, by Selected Characteristics: 1996

[Persons as of March 1996. Based on Current Population Survey; see text, Sections 1 and 14, and Appendix III. For composition of regions, see inside front cover]

AGE AND REGION	NUMBER BELOW POVERTY LEVEL (1,000)				PERCENT BELOW POVERTY LEVEL			
	All races [1]	White	Black	Hispanic [2]	All races [1]	White	Black	Hispanic [2]
Total	36,529	24,650	9,694	8,697	13.7	11.2	28.4	29.4
Under 18 years old	14,463	9,044	4,519	4,237	20.5	16.3	39.9	40.3
18 to 24 years old	4,466	3,123	1,095	1,051	17.9	15.6	39.6	29.0
25 to 34 years old	5,093	3,487	1,276	1,259	12.7	10.7	23.8	22.9
35 to 44 years old	4,343	2,976	1,053	1,032	9.9	8.2	23.6	23.5
45 to 54 years old	2,516	1,764	584	416	7.6	6.3	19.4	16.9
55 to 59 years old	1,086	770	257	180	9.4	6.3	16.6	19.2
60 to 64 years old	1,134	820	250	151	9.4	7.7	21.7	22.2
65 years old and over . . .	3,428	2,667	661	370	11.5	9.6	25.4	24.4
65 to 74 years old	1,580	1,170	357	231	10.8	9.4	25.3	23.3
75 years old and over .	1,848	1,497	303	140	8.8	7.3	22.8	26.6
					13.3	12.0	29.0	
Northeast	6,558	4,279	1,987	1,563	12.7	9.9	30.6	33.4
Midwest	6,654	4,794	1,668	596	10.7	8.8	27.8	27.6
South	14,098	8,200	5,378	2,568	15.1	11.4	28.8	26.9
West	9,219	7,377	662	3,969	15.4	14.7	22.6	30.1

[1] Includes other races not shown separately.   [2] Persons of Hispanic origin may be of any race.

Source: U.S. Bureau of the Census, Current Population Reports, P60-198;

No. 760. Persons 65 Years Old and Over Below Poverty Level: 1980 to 1996

[Persons as of March of following year. Based on the Current Population Survey, see text, Sections 1 and 14, and Appendix III]

CHARACTERISTIC	NUMBER BELOW POVERTY LEVEL (1,000)					PERCENT BELOW POVERTY LEVEL				
	1980	1990	1994	1995	1996	1980	1990	1994	1995	1996
Total	3,871	3,658	3,663	3,318	3,428	15.7	12.2	11.7	10.5	10.8
White	3,042	2,707	2,846	2,572	2,667	13.6	10.1	10.2	9.0	9.4
Black	783	860	700	629	661	38.1	33.8	27.4	25.4	25.3
Asian and Pacific Islander	(NA)	62	67	89	63	(NA)	12.1	13.0	14.3	9.7
Hispanic [1]	179	245	323	342	370	30.8	22.5	22.6	23.5	24.4
In families	(NA)	1,172	1,254	1,058	1,190	(NA)	5.8	6.0	5.0	5.6
Unrelated individuals	(NA)	2,479	2,409	2,260	2,237	(NA)	24.7	23.1	21.4	20.9

NA Not available. [1] Persons of Hispanic origin may be of any race.

Source: U.S. Bureau of the Census, Current Population Reports, P60-198; and earlier reports.

No. 761. Persons Below Poverty Level, by State: 1980 to 1996

[Based on the Current Population Survey; see text, Sections 1 and 14, and Appendix III. The CPS is designed to collect reliable data on income primarily at the national level and secondarily at the regional level. When the income data are tabulated by state, the estimates are considered less reliable and, therefore, particular caution should be used when trying to interpret the results; for additional detail, see source]

STATE	NUMBER BELOW POVERTY LEVEL (1,000)					PERCENT BELOW POVERTY LEVEL				
	1980	1990 [1]	1994	1995	1996	1980	1990 [1]	1994	1995	1996
United States	29,272	33,585	38,059	36,425	36,529	13.0	13.5	14.5	13.8	13.7
Alabama.	810	779	704	882	595	21.2	19.2	16.4	20.1	14.0
Alaska	36	57	61	45	54	9.6	11.4	10.2	7.1	8.2
Arizona.	354	484	673	700	980	12.8	13.7	15.9	16.1	20.5
Arkansas	484	472	369	376	449	21.5	19.6	15.3	14.9	17.2
California	2,619	4,128	5,658	5,342	5,472	11.0	13.9	17.9	16.7	16.9
Colorado.	247	461	335	335	412	8.6	13.7	9.0	8.8	10.6
Connecticut.	255	196	344	318	392	8.3	6.0	10.8	9.7	11.7
Delaware	68	48	57	74	63	11.8	6.9	8.3	10.3	8.6
District of Columbia	131	120	129	122	130	20.9	21.1	21.2	22.2	24.1
Florida	1,692	1,896	2,128	2,321	2,037	16.7	14.4	14.9	16.2	14.2
Georgia	727	1,001	1,012	878	1,097	13.9	15.8	14.0	12.1	14.8
Hawaii	81	121	97	122	142	8.5	11.0	8.7	10.3	12.1
Idaho	138	157	137	167	140	14.7	14.9	12.0	14.5	11.9
Illinois	1,386	1,606	1,464	1,459	1,429	12.3	13.7	12.4	12.4	12.1
Indiana.	645	714	816	545	428	11.8	13.0	13.7	9.6	7.5
Iowa	311	289	302	352	279	10.8	10.4	10.7	12.2	9.6
Kansas.	215	259	375	273	287	9.4	10.3	14.9	10.8	11.2
Kentucky	701	628	710	572	658	19.3	17.3	18.5	14.7	17.0
Louisiana	868	952	1,117	849	873	20.3	23.6	25.7	19.7	20.5
Maine.	158	162	113	138	135	14.6	13.1	9.4	11.2	11.2
Maryland	389	468	541	520	522	9.5	9.9	10.7	10.1	10.3
Massachusetts.	542	626	585	665	622	9.5	10.7	9.7	11.0	10.1
Michigan.	1,194	1,315	1,347	1,174	1,068	12.9	14.3	14.1	12.2	11.2
Minnesota.	342	524	523	427	458	8.7	12.0	11.7	9.2	9.8
Mississippi	591	684	515	630	575	24.3	25.7	19.9	23.5	20.6
Missouri	625	700	797	484	500	13.0	13.4	15.6	9.4	9.5
Montana.	102	134	97	133	155	13.2	16.3	11.5	15.3	17.0
Nebraska	199	167	146	159	169	13.0	10.3	8.8	9.6	10.2
Nevada	70	119	168	173	133	8.3	9.8	11.1	11.1	8.1
New Hampshire.	63	68	87	60	73	7.0	6.3	7.7	5.3	6.4
New Jersey.	659	711	730	617	726	9.0	9.2	9.2	7.8	9.2
New Mexico	268	319	356	457	472	20.6	20.9	21.1	25.3	25.5
New York	2,391	2,571	3,097	3,020	3,058	13.8	14.3	17.0	16.5	16.7
North Carolina.	877	829	980	877	885	15.0	13.0	14.2	12.6	12.2
North Dakota.	99	87	65	76	69	15.5	13.7	10.4	12.0	11.0
Ohio	1,046	1,256	1,571	1,285	1,424	9.8	11.5	14.1	11.5	12.7
Oklahoma.	406	481	540	548	556	13.9	15.6	16.7	17.1	16.6
Oregon.	309	267	373	360	382	11.5	9.2	11.8	11.2	11.8
Pennsylvania.	1,142	1,328	1,496	1,464	1,374	9.8	11.0	12.5	12.2	11.6
Rhode Island.	97	71	99	102	104	10.7	7.5	10.3	10.6	11.0
South Carolina.	534	548	501	744	482	16.8	16.2	13.8	19.9	13.0
South Dakota	127	93	107	103	82	18.8	13.3	14.5	14.5	11.8
Tennessee	884	833	779	846	878	19.6	16.9	14.6	15.5	15.9
Texas.	2,247	2,684	3,603	3,270	3,180	15.7	15.9	19.1	17.4	16.6
Utah	148	143	154	168	153	10.0	8.2	8.0	8.4	7.7
Vermont	62	61	45	61	74	12.0	10.9	7.6	10.3	12.6
Virginia.	647	705	710	648	795	12.4	11.1	10.7	10.2	12.3
Washington.	538	434	614	677	666	12.7	8.9	11.7	12.5	11.9
West Virginia.	297	328	336	300	323	15.2	18.1	18.6	16.7	18.5
Wisconsin.	403	448	453	449	460	8.5	9.3	9.0	8.5	8.8
Wyoming	49	51	45	59	58	10.4	11.0	9.3	12.2	11.9

[1] Beginning 1990, data based on revised processing procedures and not directly comparable with prior years.

Source: U.S. Bureau of the Census, *Current Population Reports*, P60-198, and earlier reports.

No. 762. Persons Below Poverty Level, by Race and Family Status: 1979 to 1996

[Persons as of March of following year. Based on Current Population Survey; see text, Sections 1 and 14, and Appendix III]

RACE AND FAMILY STATUS	NUMBER BELOW POVERTY LEVEL (mil.)					PERCENT BELOW POVERTY LEVEL				
	1979 [1]	1990	1994	1995	1996	1979 [1]	1990	1994	1995	1996
All persons [2]	26.1	33.6	38.1	36.4	36.5	11.7	13.5	14.5	13.8	13.7
In families	20.0	25.2	29.0	27.5	27.4	10.2	12.0	13.1	12.3	12.2
Householder.	5.5	7.1	8.1	7.5	7.7	9.2	10.7	11.6	10.8	11.0
Related children under 18 years.	10.0	12.7	14.6	14.0	13.8	16.0	19.9	21.2	20.2	19.8
Unrelated individuals	5.7	7.4	8.3	8.2	8.5	21.9	20.7	21.5	20.9	20.8
Male	2.0	2.9	3.3	3.4	3.3	16.9	16.9	17.8	18.0	17.0
Female	3.8	4.6	5.0	4.9	5.1	26.0	24.0	24.9	23.5	24.2
White [2]	17.2	22.3	25.4	24.4	24.7	9.0	10.7	11.7	11.2	11.2
In families	12.5	15.9	18.5	17.6	17.6	7.4	9.0	10.1	9.6	9.6
Householder.	3.6	4.6	5.3	5.0	5.1	6.9	8.1	9.1	8.5	8.6
Related children under 18 years.	5.9	7.7	8.8	8.5	8.5	11.4	15.1	16.3	15.5	15.5
Unrelated individuals	4.5	5.7	6.3	6.3	6.5	19.7	18.6	19.3	19.0	18.9
Black [2]	8.1	9.8	10.2	9.9	9.7	31.0	31.9	30.6	29.3	28.4
In families	6.8	8.2	8.4	8.2	8.0	30.0	31.0	29.6	28.5	27.6
Householder.	1.7	2.2	2.2	2.1	2.2	27.8	29.3	27.3	26.4	26.1
Related children under 18 years.	3.7	4.4	4.8	4.6	4.4	40.8	44.2	43.3	41.5	39.5
Unrelated individuals	1.2	1.5	1.6	1.6	1.6	37.3	35.1	34.8	32.6	32.2
In families with female										
householder, no spouse present. .	9.4	12.6	14.4	14.2	13.8	34.9	37.2	38.6	36.5	35.8
Householder.	2.6	3.8	4.2	4.1	4.2	30.4	33.4	34.6	32.4	32.6
Related children under 18 years.	5.6	7.4	8.4	8.4	8.0	48.6	53.4	52.9	50.3	49.3

[1] Population controls based on 1980 census; see text, Section 14. [2] Includes other races and members of unrelated subfamilies not shown separately.
Source: U.S. Bureau of the Census, *Current Population Reports*, P60-198; and earlier reports.

No. 763. Monthly Measures of Poverty Status, by Selected Characteristics: 1993-94 Period

[Covers 2-year calendar period. Based on Survey of Income and Program Participation, see text, Section 14]

CHARACTERISTIC	PERSONS POOR IN AN AVERAGE MONTH OF 1994		PERSONS POOR 2 OR MORE MONTHS OF 1994		PERSONS POOR ALL 24 MONTHS OF 1993-94		Median duration of poverty spells (months)
	Number (1,000)	Percent	Number (1,000)	Percent	Number (1,000)	Percent	
Total [1]	37,597	14.6	52,725	20.8	11,887	4.8	4.9
Under 18 years old.	15,464	22.3	20,782	30.3	5,659	8.3	5.2
18 to 64 years old	18,999	12.0	28,066	18.1	4,907	3.2	4.7
65 years old and over	3,134	10.2	3,877	13.3	1,321	4.9	7.2
White.	25,474	11.8	37,195	17.6	6,480	3.1	4.6
Black.	10,346	31.7	13,199	41.1	4,682	15.1	6.2
Hispanic origin [2].	7,553	29.0	10,022	40.0	2,383	10.3	5.8
Region: [3]							
Northeast	6,845	13.3	9,320	18.4	2,560	5.2	5.3
Midwest	8,718	13.3	12,656	19.4	2,668	4.2	5.2
South	14,346	16.4	19,909	23.0	4,939	5.8	5.2
West.	7,688	14.5	10,840	21.4	1,720	3.5	4.0
Educational attainment: [4]							
Less than 4 years of high school . . .	9,224	23.9	12,122	32.4	3,424	9.5	6.5
High school graduate, no college. . .	7,977	11.3	11,853	17.2	2,056	3.0	4.7
One or more years of college	4,931	6.2	7,968	10.2	749	1.0	3.8
Disability status: [5]							
With a work disability.	5,919	21.6	7,984	31.4	2,072	8.2	6.2
With no work disability	15,787	10.5	23,874	15.9	3,595	2.5	4.3
Total [1]	40,009	15.4	54,800	21.4	13,105	5.3	4.5
Under 18 years old.	17,169	24.5	22,529	32.4	6,489	9.4	5.3
18 to 64 years old	19,652	12.3	28,317	18.1	5,156	3.4	4.0
65 years old and over	3,188	10.2	3,954	13.5	1,459	5.4	6.7
White.	27,543	12.7	38,861	18.3	7,793	3.8	4.2
Black.	10,304	31.2	13,059	40.2	4,461	14.1	6.8
Hispanic origin [2].	8,555	31.4	10,940	41.8	3,262	13.5	5.0
Region: [3]							
Northeast	7,303	14.1	9,892	19.3	2,822	5.5	4.4
Midwest	8,740	13.2	12,069	18.4	2,571	4.0	3.9
South	14,701	16.8	20,044	23.3	5,085	6.1	5.6
West.	9,265	16.8	12,795	24.3	2,628	5.2	4.4
Educational attainment: [4]							
Less than 4 years of high school . . .	9,507	24.8	12,221	33.0	3,736	10.5	6.4
High school graduate, no college. . .	8,263	11.6	11,973	17.3	2,120	3.1	4.0
One or more years of college	5,071	6.3	8,077	10.1	759	1.0	3.7
Disability status: [5]							
With a work disability.	7,059	21.6	8,991	29.8	2,519	8.6	5.8
With no work disability	15,539	10.5	23,445	15.9	3,444	2.4	4.0

[1] Includes other characteristics not shown separately. [2] Persons of Hispanic origin may be of any race. [3] For compostion of regions, see inside front cover. [4] Persons 18 years old and over. [5] Persons 15 to 69 years old.
Source: U.S. Bureau of the Census, unpublished data from the Survey of Income and Program Participation.

No. 764. Families Below Poverty Level and Below 125 Percent of Poverty Level: 1960 to 1996

[Families as of **March of the following year.** Based on Current Population Survey, see text, Sections 1 and 14, and Appendix III]

YEAR	NUMBER BELOW POVERTY LEVEL (1,000)				PERCENT BELOW POVERTY LEVEL				BELOW 125 PERCENT OF POVERTY LEVEL	
	All races [1]	White	Black	His-panic [2]	All races [1]	White	Black	His-panic [2]	Number (1,000)	Percent
1960	8,243	6,115	(NA)	(NA)	18.1	14.9	(NA)	(NA)	11,525	25.4
1970	5,260	3,708	1,481	(NA)	10.1	8.0	29.5	(NA)	7,516	14.4
1975	5,450	3,838	1,513	627	9.7	7.7	27.1	25.1	7,974	14.2
1976	5,311	3,560	1,617	598	9.4	7.1	27.9	23.1	7,647	13.5
1977	5,311	3,540	1,637	591	9.3	7.0	28.2	21.4	7,713	13.5
1978	5,280	3,523	1,622	559	9.1	6.9	27.5	20.4	7,417	12.8
1979 [3]	5,461	3,581	1,722	614	9.2	6.9	27.8	20.3	7,784	13.1
1980	6,217	4,195	1,826	751	10.3	8.0	28.9	23.2	8,764	14.5
1981	6,851	4,670	1,972	792	11.2	8.8	30.8	24.0	9,568	15.7
1982	7,512	5,118	2,158	916	12.2	9.6	33.0	27.2	10,279	16.7
1983 [4]	7,647	5,220	2,161	981	12.3	9.7	32.3	25.9	10,358	16.7
1984	7,277	4,925	2,094	991	11.6	9.1	30.9	25.2	9,901	15.8
1985	7,223	4,983	1,983	1,074	11.4	9.1	28.7	25.5	9,753	15.3
1986 [5]	7,023	4,811	1,987	1,085	10.9	8.6	28.0	24.7	9,476	14.7
1987 [5]	7,005	4,567	2,117	1,168	10.7	8.1	29.4	25.5	9,338	14.3
1988	6,874	4,471	2,089	1,141	10.4	7.9	28.2	23.7	9,284	14.1
1989	6,784	4,409	2,077	1,133	10.3	7.8	27.8	23.4	9,267	14.0
1990	7,098	4,622	2,193	1,244	10.7	8.1	29.3	25.0	9,564	14.4
1991 [6]	7,712	5,022	2,343	1,372	11.5	8.8	30.4	26.5	10,244	15.3
1992 [6]	8,144	5,255	2,484	1,529	11.9	9.1	31.1	26.7	10,959	16.1
1993	8,393	5,452	2,499	1,625	12.3	9.4	31.3	27.3	11,203	16.4
1994	8,053	5,312	2,212	1,724	11.6	9.1	27.3	27.8	10,771	15.5
1995	7,532	4,994	2,127	1,695	10.8	8.5	26.4	27.0	10,223	14.7
1996	7,708	5,059	2,206	1,748	11.0	8.6	26.1	26.4	10,476	14.9

NA Not available. [1] Includes other races not shown separately. [2] Persons of Hispanic origin may be of any race. [3] Population controls based on 1980 census; see text, Section 14. [4] Beginning 1983, data based on revised Hispanic population controls and not directly comparable with prior years. [5] Beginning 1987, data based on revised processing procedures and not directly comparable with prior years. [6] Beginning 1992, based on 1990 population controls.

Source: U.S. Bureau of the Census, *Current Population Reports,* P60-198.

No. 765. Families Below Poverty Level, by Selected Characteristics: 1996

[Families as of **March 1997.** Based on Current Population Survey; see text, Sections 1 and 14, and Appendix III. For composition of regions, see map, inside front cover]

CHARACTERISTIC	NUMBER BELOW POVERTY LEVEL (1,000)				PERCENT BELOW POVERTY LEVEL			
	All races [1]	White	Black	His-panic [2]	All races [1]	White	Black	His-panic [2]
Total	**7,708**	**5,059**	**2,206**	**1,748**	**11.0**	**8.6**	**26.1**	**26.4**
Age of householder:								
15 to 24 years old.	970	600	338	227	33.7	27.8	55.7	43.6
25 to 34 years old.	2,293	1,467	701	543	16.7	13.2	35.4	28.5
35 to 44 years old.	2,080	1,381	572	549	10.9	8.8	23.5	28.5
45 to 54 years old.	974	653	245	203	6.8	5.3	15.5	18.9
55 to 64 years old.	690	463	179	126	7.7	6.0	20.0	19.0
65 years old and over	664	474	158	87	6.0	4.8	17.2	16.7
Northeast	1,393	879	441	348	10.4	7.7	28.3	32.0
Midwest	1,382	976	378	124	8.4	6.7	25.1	25.1
South	3,136	1,765	1,264	533	12.3	8.7	26.9	23.6
West	1,797	1,440	123	744	12.0	11.3	17.9	26.6
Education of householder: [3]								
No high school diploma	2,819	1,902	762	1,024	24.4	20.7	39.9	37.5
High school diploma, no college	2,231	1,422	700	291	10.2	7.7	25.1	18.4
Some college, less than bachelor's degree	1,246	821	348	154	7.3	5.7	16.2	13.4
Bachelor's degree or more	404	294	45	39	2.4	2.0	4.6	6.2
Work experience of householder:								
Total [4]	7,037	4,580	2,046	1,657	11.9	9.4	27.2	27.1
Worked during year.	3,886	2,671	1,026	943	7.6	6.2	17.2	19.2
Year-round, full time.	1,202	875	275	398	3.1	2.6	6.6	11.4
Not year-round, full time	2,684	1,796	751	545	22.1	18.4	41.2	38.3
Did not work	3,151	1,909	1,020	714	39.6	32.0	65.5	59.8

[1] Includes other races not shown separately. [2] Hispanic persons may be of any race. [3] Householder 25 years old and over. [4] Persons 16 years old and over.

Source: U.S. Bureau of the Census, *Current Population Reports,* P60-198; and unpublished data.

No. 766. Persons Below Poverty Level, by Definition of Income: 1996

[Persons as of **March 1996.** For explanation of income definitions, see text, Section 14]

Defi-nition num-ber	DEFINITION	NUMBER BELOW POVERTY LEVEL (1,000)				PERCENT BELOW POVERTY LEVEL			
		All races [1]	White	Black	His-panic [2]	All races [1]	White	Black	His-panic [2]
	All persons	266,218	219,656	34,110	29,614	(X)	(X)	(X)	(X)
	INCOME BEFORE TAXES								
1	Money income excluding capital gains [3]	36,529	24,650	9,694	8,697	13.7	11.2	28.4	29.4
2	Definition 1 less government money transfers .	57,476	42,384	12,361	10,467	21.6	19.3	36.2	35.3
3	Definition 2 plus capital gains.	57,292	42,186	12,375	10,413	21.5	19.2	36.3	35.2
4	Definition 3 plus health insurance supplements to wage or salary income [4] . . .	55,447	40,868	11,949	9,993	20.8	18.6	35.0	33.7
	INCOME AFTER TAXES								
5	Definition 4 less social security payroll taxes. .	58,078	42,745	12,583	10,581	21.8	19.5	36.9	35.7
6	Definition 5 less federal income taxes (excluding EITC) [5]	58,598	43,096	12,710	10,671	22.0	19.6	37.3	36.0
7	Definition 6 plus EITC [5]	54,644	40,326	11,744	9,482	20.5	18.4	34.4	32.0
8	Definition 7 less state income taxes	55,119	40,670	11,854	9,524	20.7	18.5	34.8	32.2
9	Definition 8 plus nonmeans-tested government cash transfers [6]	37,075	24,808	10,112	8,260	13.9	11.3	29.6	27.9
10	Definition 9 plus value of medicare	36,044	23,999	9,921	8,065	13.5	10.9	29.1	27.2
11	Definition 10 plus value of regular-price school lunches.	36,017	23,985	9,921	8,059	13.5	10.9	29.1	27.2
12	Definition 11 plus means-tested government cash transfers [7]	33,118	22,109	9,065	7,489	12.4	10.1	26.6	25.3
13	Definition 12 plus value of medicaid	30,647	20,546	8,325	6,857	11.5	9.4	24.4	23.2
14	Definition 13 plus means-tested government noncash transfers [8]	27,133	18,484	7,147	5,991	10.2	8.4	21.0	20.2
15	Definition 14 plus net imputed return on equity in own home [9]	24,650	16,586	6,641	5,737	9.3	7.6	19.5	19.4

X Not applicable.   [1] Includes other races not shown separately.   [2] Persons of Hispanic origin may be of any race.   [3] Official definition based on income before taxes and includes government cash transfers.   [4] Employer contributions to the health insurance plans of employees.   [5] Earned Income Tax Credit.   [6] Includes social security and railroad retirement, veterans payments, unemployment and workers' compensation, Black Lung payments, Pell Grants, and other government educational assistance.   [7] Includes AFDC and other public assistance or welfare payments, Supplemental Security Income, and veterans payments. Households must meet certain eligibility requirements in order to qualify for these benefits.   [8] Includes medicaid, food stamps, subsidies from free or reduced-price school lunches, and rent subsidies.   [9] Estimated amount of income a household would receive if it chose to shift amount held as home equity into an interest bearing account.

Source: U.S. Bureau of the Census, *Current Population Reports,* P60-197.

No. 767. Family Net Worth—Mean and Median Net Worth in Constant (1995) Dollars, by Selected Family Characteristics: 1989 to 1995

[Net worth in thousands of constant (1995) dollars. Constant dollar figures are based on consumer price index for all urban consumers published by U.S. Bureau of Labor Statistics. Families include one-person units and as used in this table are comparable to the Bureau of Census household concept. Based on Survey of Consumer Finance; see Appendix III. For definition of median, see Guide to Tabular Presentation]

FAMILY CHARACTERISTIC	1989			1992			1995		
	Percent of families	Net worth		Percent of families	Net worth		Percent of families	Net worth	
		Mean	Median		Mean	Median		Mean	Median
All families	100.0	225.9	57.0	100.0	201.1	52.9	100.0	208.1	55.6
Age of family head:									
Under 35 years old.	28.1	58.0	9.5	25.8	50.4	10.1	24.8	42.0	10.7
35 to 44 years old	21.5	180.2	67.6	22.8	144.8	46.3	23.0	141.5	51.0
45 to 54 years old	15.1	330.8	114.7	16.2	287.9	84.2	17.9	290.0	90.6
55 to 64 years old	13.9	373.1	118.7	13.2	362.0	122.9	12.5	372.4	111.3
65 to 74 years old	12.5	341.0	93.6	12.6	308.9	105.8	12.0	344.9	106.9
75 years old and over.	8.9	296.2	89.2	9.4	231.3	93.2	9.8	257.2	92.3
Family income in constant (1995) dollars:[1]									
Less than $10,000	15.5	29.0	1.6	15.5	30.8	3.3	16.1	43.6	4.7
$10,000 to $24,999	24.5	70.0	24.0	27.7	69.8	27.6	26.9	77.2	30.0
$25,000 to $49,999	29.8	127.3	56.0	29.6	125.0	55.1	30.6	117.7	53.4
$50,000 to $99,999	22.0	247.2	129.5	20.1	241.3	122.9	19.8	256.0	121.1
$100,000 and more	8.3	1,350.4	547.1	7.1	1,284.2	498.7	6.5	1,435.3	482.0
Education of householder:									
No high school diploma. . . .	24.3	99.1	28.5	20.4	76.2	21.3	18.5	83.2	22.7
High school diploma.	32.2	135.8	45.0	29.9	120.9	41.4	31.7	128.9	50.7
Some college	15.6	226.9	56.5	17.8	186.0	63.2	19.1	184.9	45.2
College degree	27.8	440.6	136.0	31.9	364.3	103.1	30.7	379.4	102.6
Tenure:									
Owner occupied	63.9	326.8	122.0	63.9	290.3	106.5	64.7	297.9	101.4
Renter occupied or other. . . .	36.1	47.5	2.3	63.1	43.0	3.6	35.3	43.5	4.5

[1] Income for year preceding the survey.

Source: Board of Governors of the Federal Reserve System, *Federal Reserve Bulletin, January 1997* and unpublished revisions.

No. 768. Nonfinancial Assets Held by Families, by Type of Asset: 1995

[**Median value in thousands of dollars**. Constant dollar figures are based on consumer price index for all urban consumers published by U.S. Bureau of Labor Statistics. Families include one-person units and, as used in this table, are comparable to the Bureau of Census household concept. for definition of family, see text, Section 1. Based on Survey of Consumer Finance; see Appendix III. For data on financial assets, see Table 798. For definition of median, see Guide to Tabular Presentation]

AGE OF FAMILY HEAD AND FAMILY INCOME	Total	Vehicles	Primary residence	Investment real estate	Business	Other nonfinancial
PERCENT OF FAMILIES OWNING ASSET						
All families, total	**91.1**	**84.2**	**64.7**	**18.0**	**11.1**	**9.0**
Age of family head:						
Under 35 years old	87.4	84.1	37.9	7.0	8.4	7.3
35 to 44 years old	91.0	85.0	64.7	14.7	14.4	10.1
45 to 54 years old	93.8	88.3	75.4	25.0	15.4	11.3
55 to 64 years old	94.1	88.4	82.3	27.3	12.6	10.2
65 to 74 years old	92.7	82.4	79.4	27.9	8.7	9.0
75 years old and over	89.9	72.2	72.5	16.3	3.8	5.6
Family income:						
Less than $10,000	68.6	56.6	37.5	7.2	4.8	3.7
$10,000 to $24,999	90.2	83.3	56.2	11.3	7.0	6.3
$25,000 to $49,999	96.8	92.3	68.0	16.6	9.8	9.7
$50,000 to $99,999	99.0	93.4	84.7	26.9	16.8	11.3
$100,000 and more	99.4	90.8	90.9	51.6	32.6	23.9
Current work status of householder:						
Professional, managerial	96.6	91.1	70.5	24.8	9.7	14.5
Technical, sales, clerical	93.0	88.0	63.4	11.4	6.4	10.9
Precision production	97.1	93.2	67.0	16.1	7.4	8.8
Machine operators and laborers	93.8	92.1	61.0	14.1	5.6	6.8
Service occupations	86.9	83.7	50.4	9.0	3.7	2.1
Self-employed	96.1	86.1	74.2	33.1	58.2	15.5
Retired	88.2	76.3	70.5	18.9	3.3	5.8
Other not working	67.3	59.7	35.3	8.5	4.1	6.0
Tenure:						
Owner occupied	100.0	90.8	100.0	22.8	13.7	10.5
Renter occupied or other	74.8	72.2	-	9.0	6.5	6.5
MEDIAN VALUE [1]						
All families, total	**82.8**	**9.9**	**89.0**	**50.0**	**45.0**	**8.8**
Age of family head:						
Under 35 years old	21.7	8.9	76.0	30.0	22.0	5.0
35 to 44 years old	95.9	10.7	95.0	47.0	35.0	10.0
45 to 54 years old	113.0	12.6	100.0	59.0	70.0	10.0
55 to 64 years old	108.0	11.3	85.0	75.0	65.0	10.0
65 to 74 years old	94.6	8.2	82.5	57.0	100.5	14.0
75 years old and over	79.0	5.3	80.0	22.4	37.5	8.0
Family income:						
Less than $10,000	14.0	3.6	38.5	16.2	50.0	5.2
$10,000 to $24,999	44.7	6.1	65.0	26.4	30.0	7.5
$25,000 to $49,999	81.9	11.0	80.0	45.0	25.0	5.8
$50,000 to $99,999	145.7	16.2	120.0	60.0	33.0	15.0
$100,000 and more	304.5	23.8	200.0	130.0	320.0	18.0
Current work status of householder:						
Professional, managerial	129.1	12.5	130.0	55.5	18.0	10.6
Technical, sales, clerical	82.5	10.3	90.0	44.5	24.0	9.0
Precision production	72.7	12.1	80.0	37.5	20.0	5.0
Machine operators and laborers	56.3	10.8	65.0	30.0	20.0	8.0
Service occupations	36.3	7.0	70.0	30.0	80.2	10.0
Self-employed	180.1	12.7	120.0	100.0	75.0	8.0
Retired	78.0	7.4	75.0	45.0	100.0	10.0
Other not working	22.0	6.4	60.0	50.0	21.0	7.0
Tenure:						
Owner occupied	115.8	11.9	89.0	50.0	55.0	10.0
Renter occupied or other	7.5	6.4	(B)	35.0	22.0	5.0

- Represents zero.   B Base figure too small to meet statistical standards for reliability of derived figure.   [1] Median value of financial asset for families holding such assets.

Source: Board of Governors of the Federal Reserve System, *Federal Reserve Bulletin*, January 1997, and unpublished revisions.

No. 769. Household and Nonprofit Organization Sector Balance Sheet: 1980 to 1997

[In billions of dollars. As of December 31. For details of financial assets and liabilities, see Table 797]

ITEM	1980	1985	1990	1991	1992	1993	1994	1995	1996	1997
Assets	10,923	16,631	24,177	25,904	27,043	28,393	29,378	32,333	35,213	39,254
Tangible assets [1]	4,366	6,535	9,325	9,470	9,733	9,982	10,319	10,805	11,418	12,146
Real estate	3,422	5,235	7,406	7,478	7,666	7,807	8,020	8,404	8,918	9,564
Consumer durable goods	918	1,265	1,866	1,935	2,005	2,108	2,226	2,323	2,415	2,492
Financial assets [1]	6,557	10,096	14,852	16,434	17,310	18,412	19,059	21,528	23,795	27,109
Deposits	1,494	2,461	3,241	3,244	3,227	3,160	3,134	3,346	3,562	3,835
Checkable deposits and currency	228	319	386	427	524	571	540	497	455	426
Time and savings deposits	1,203	1,941	2,478	2,424	2,349	2,236	2,224	2,374	2,540	2,723
Money market fund shares	62	193	365	380	339	338	351	452	531	637
Credit market instruments [1]	425	846	1,493	1,586	1,640	1,631	1,942	1,905	1,965	1,827
U.S. government securities	165	270	519	509	616	595	930	881	956	804
Treasury	160	242	394	381	458	475	662	591	542	305
Savings bonds	73	80	126	138	157	172	180	185	187	187
Corporate equities	903	1,128	1,795	2,578	2,920	3,221	3,049	4,066	4,604	5,738
Mutual fund shares	46	198	468	587		991	1,052	1,255	1,592	1,938
Pension fund reserves	962	2,047	3,388	3,877	4,218	4,662	4,880	5,600	6,314	7,454
Equity in noncorporate business	2,156	2,608	3,247	3,195	3,155	3,219	3,419	3,625	3,836	4,088
Liabilities	1,427	2,330	3,703	3,907	4,085	4,339	4,668	5,049	5,421	5,827
Credit market instruments	1,376	2,239	3,579	3,758	3,933	4,157	4,482	4,851	5,205	5,571
Home mortgages	906	1,411	2,489	2,655	2,798	2,924	3,098	3,275	3,504	3,758
Consumer credit	355	604	805	794	798	859	984	1,123	1,212	1,265
Net worth	9,496	14,302	20,473	21,997	22,958	24,054	24,710	27,284	29,792	33,427

[1] Includes types of assets and/or liabilities not shown separately.

Source: Board of Governors of the Federal Reserve System, *Balance Sheets for the U.S. Economy*.

No. 770. Net Stock of Fixed Reproducible Tangible Wealth: 1980 to 1996

[In billions of dollars. As of December 31]

ITEM	1980	1985	1989	1990	1991	1992	1993	1994	1995	1996
CURRENT DOLLARS										
Net stock	10,323	13,737	17,447	18,284	18,717	19,480	20,508	21,717	22,718	23,774
Private	7,154	9,583	12,149	12,707	12,955	13,484	14,199	15,064	15,739	16,503
Nonresidential equipment	1,375	1,850	2,322	2,452	2,519	2,590	2,687	2,823	2,989	3,169
Information processing and related equipment	225	413	558	586	603	629	650	674	704	785
Industrial equipment	525	646	823	877	898	917	946	991	1,050	1,084
Transportation equipment	306	395	456	473	491	510	539	581	627	660
Other equipment	319	396	485	516	527	534	552	577	608	639
Nonresidential structures	2,266	3,155	3,916	4,107	4,177	4,303	4,529	4,776	4,971	5,163
Nonresidential buildings, excluding farm	1,169	1,787	2,372	2,518	2,594	2,686	2,835	3,011	3,144	3,299
Utilities	695	853	997	1,017	1,032	1,062	1,120	1,160	1,200	1,236
Residential	3,513	4,578	5,911	6,147	6,259	6,591	6,983	7,466	7,779	8,171
Housing units	2,898	3,730	4,808	4,984	5,057	5,327	5,667	6,078	6,322	6,639
Government	2,251	2,889	3,535	3,711	3,827	3,991	4,201	4,426	4,656	4,855
Equipment	300	425	511	552	577	600	618	635	647	656
Structures	1,952	2,464	3,024	3,159	3,250	3,390	3,583	3,791	4,009	4,199
Federal	698	889	1,042	1,090	1,127	1,169	1,227	1,263	1,297	1,333
Defense	483	613	712	744	768	798	839	857	868	884
State and local	1,554	2,000	2,493	2,621	2,701	2,822	2,974	3,163	3,360	3,522
Consumer durable goods	918	1,265	1,763	1,866	1,935	2,005	2,108	2,226	2,323	2,415
Motor vehicles	257	392	564	590	593	607	629	659	679	702
Furniture and household equipment	459	605	804	846	885	926	985	1,046	1,102	1,154
Other	203	268	396	429	457	471	493	521	543	559
CHAINED (1992) DOLLARS										
Net stock	14,269	16,178	18,160	18,586	18,883	19,212	19,603	20,037	20,517	21,071
Private	9,950	11,346	12,617	12,890	13,078	13,278	13,536	13,830	14,163	14,551
Nonresidential equipment	1,855	2,178	2,451	2,507	2,537	2,579	2,649	2,749	2,881	3,035
Nonresidential structures	3,177	3,697	4,051†	4,142	4,205	4,251	4,300	4,345	4,404	4,482
Residential	4,921	5,471	6,115	6,240	6,335	6,448	6,587	6,738	6,886	7,048
Government	3,127	3,382	3,697	3,782	3,860	3,940	4,008	4,069	4,133	4,206
Federal	969	1,022	1,109	1,126	1,139	1,148	1,150	1,147	1,144	1,147
State and local	2,156	2,357	2,584	2,652	2,717	2,787	2,854	2,918	2,986	3,056
Consumer durable goods	1,198	1,455	1,850	1,919	1,950	1,998	2,064	2,144	2,229	2,323

Source: U.S. Bureau of Economic Analysis, *Survey of Current Business,* May 1998, and previous issues.

This section presents indexes of producer and consumer prices, actual prices for selected commodities, and energy prices. The primary sources of these data are monthly publications of the Department of Labor, Bureau of Labor Statistics (BLS), which include *Monthly Labor Review, Consumer Price Index, Detailed Report; Producer Price Indexes;* and *U.S. Import and Export Price Indexes.* The Department of Commerce, Bureau of Economic Analysis, is the source for gross domestic product measures.

Producer price index (PPI)—This index, dating from 1890, is the oldest continuous statistical series published by BLS. It is designed to measure average changes in prices received by producers of all commodities, at all stages of processing, produced in the United States.

The index has undergone several revisions (see *Monthly Labor Review,* February 1962, April 1978, and August 1988). It is now based on approximately 3,200 commodity price series and 80,000 quotations per month. Indexes for the net output of manufacturing and mining industries have been added in recent years. Prices used in constructing the index are collected from sellers and generally apply to the first significant large volume commercial transaction for each commodity—i.e., the manufacturer's or other producer's selling price or the selling price on an organized exchange or at a central market.

The weights used in the index represent the total net selling value of commodities produced or processed in this country. Values are f.o.b. (free-on-board) production point and are exclusive of excise taxes. Effective with the release of data for January 1988, many important producer price indexes were changed to a new reference base year, 1982=100, from 1967=100. The reference year of the PPI shipment weights has been taken primarily from the 1987 Census of Manufactures. For further detail regarding the PPI, see the *BLS Handbook of Methods, Bulletin 2414,* Chapter 16.

In Brief

Consumer price changes: 1996-97:

All items index up 2.3 percent
Medical care index up 2.8 percent
Fuel oil index down –0.1 percent

Consumer price indexes (CPI)—The CPI is a measure of the average change in prices over time in a fixed "market basket" of goods and services purchased either by urban wage earners and clerical workers or by all urban consumers.

In 1919, BLS began to publish complete indexes at semiannual intervals, using a weighting structure based on data collected in the expenditure survey of wage-earner and clerical-worker families in 1917-19 (BLS Bulletin 357, 1924). The first major revision of the CPI occurred in 1940, with subsequent revisions in 1953, 1964, 1978, and 1987.

Beginning with the release of data for January 1988 in February 1988, most Consumer Price Indexes shifted to a new reference base year. All indexes previously expressed on a base of 1967=100, or any other base through December 1981, have been rebased to 1982-84=100. Selection of the 1982-84 period was made to coincide with the updated expenditure weights, which are based upon data tabulated from the Consumer Expenditure Surveys for 1982, 1983, and 1984.

BLS publishes CPI's for two population groups: (1) a CPI for All Urban Consumers (CPI-U) which covers approximately 80 percent of the total population; and (2) a CPI for Urban Wage Earners and Clerical Workers; (CPI-W) which covers 32 percent of the total population. The CPI-U includes, in addition to wage earners and clerical workers, groups which historically have been excluded from CPI coverage, such as professional, managerial, and technical workers; the self-employed, short-term workers, the unemployed, and retirees; and others not in the labor force.

The current CPI is based on prices of food, clothing, shelter, fuels, transportation fares, charges for doctors' and dentists' services, drugs, etc., purchased for day-to-day living. Prices are collected in 85 areas across the country from over 57,000 housing units and 19,000 establishments. Area selection was based on the 1980 census. All taxes directly associated with the purchase and use of items are included in the index. Prices of food, fuels, and a few other items are obtained every month in all 85 locations. Prices of most other commodities and services are collected monthly in the five largest geographic areas and every other month in other areas.

In calculating the index, each item is assigned a weight to account for its relative importance in consumers' budgets. Price changes for the various items in each location are then averaged. Local data are then combined to obtain a U.S. city average. Separate indexes are also published for regions, area size-classes, cross-classifications of regions and size-classes, and for 29 local areas, usually consisting of the Metropolitan Statistical Area (MSA); see Appendix II. Area definitions are those established by the Office of Management and Budget in 1983. Definitions do not include revisions made since 1983. Area indexes do not measure differences in the level of prices among cities; they only measure the average change in prices for each area since the base period. For further detail regarding the CPI, see the BLS *Handbook of Methods,* Bulletin 2414, Chapter 19; the Consumer Price Index, and Report 736, the CPI: 1987 Revision. In January 1983, the method of measuring homeownership costs in the CPI-U was changed to a rental equivalence approach. This treatment calculates homeowner costs of shelter based on the implicit rent owners would pay to rent the homes they own. The rental equivalence approach was introduced into the CPI-W in 1985. The CPI-U was used to prepare the consumer prices tables in this section.

International price indexes—The BLS International Price Program produces export and import price indexes for non-military goods traded between the United States and the rest of the world. The export price index provides a measure of price change for all products sold by U.S. residents to foreign buyers. The import price index provides a measure of price change for goods purchased from other countries by U.S. residents. The reference period for the indexes is 1990=100, unless otherwise indicated.

The product universe for both the import and export indexes includes raw materials, agricultural products, semifinished manufactures, and finished manufactures, including both capital and consumer goods. Price data for these items are collected primarily by mail questionnaire. In nearly all cases, the data are collected directly from the exporter or importer, although in a few cases, prices are obtained from other sources.

To the extent possible, the data gathered refer to prices at the U.S. border for exports and at either the foreign border or the U.S. border for imports. For nearly all products, the prices refer to transactions completed during the first week of the month. Survey respondents are asked to indicate all discounts, allowances, and rebates applicable to the reported prices, so that the price used in the calculation of the indexes is the actual price for which the product was bought or sold.

In addition to general indexes for U.S. exports and imports, indexes are also published for detailed product categories of exports and imports. These categories are defined according to the five-digit level of detail for the Bureau of Economic Analysis End-Use Classification, the three-digit level of detail for the Standard International Trade Classification (SITC), and the four-digit level of detail for the Harmonized System. Aggregate import indexes by country or region of origin are also available.

Other price indexes—Chain-weighted price indexes are weighted averages of the detailed price indexes used in the deflation of goods and services that make up the gross domestic product (GDP). The weights used for the most recent year reflect the composition of goods and services in the preceding year; for all other years, the weights reflect the composition of goods and services in the preceding year and the current year. Chain-weighted price indexes provide the most reliable comparisons of rates of price of goods and services produced in the United States; another index, the gross domestic purchases chained price index, measures the average price of goods and services purchased in the United States. The difference between these two measures is due to net exports. Both price indexes are expressed in terms of the base year value 1992=100.

Measures of inflation—Inflation is defined as a time of generally rising prices for goods and factors of production. The Bureau of Labor Statistics samples prices of items in a representative market basket and publishes the results as the CPI. The media invariably announce the inflation rate as the percent change in the CPI from month to month. A much more meaningful indicator of inflation is the percent change from the same month of the prior year.

The Producer Price Index (PPI) measures prices at the producer/manufacturing level only. The PPI shows the same general pattern of inflation as does the CPI, but is more volatile. The PPI can be roughly viewed as a leading indicator. It often tends to foreshadow trends that later occur in the CPI.

Other measures of inflation include the gross domestic purchases chain-weighted price index, index of industrial materials prices; the Dow Jones Commodity Spot Price Index; Futures Price Index, the Employment Cost Index, the Hourly Compensation Index, or the Unit Labor Cost Index as a measure of the change in cost of the labor factor of production, and changes in long-term interest rates that are often used to measure changes in the cost of the capital factor of production.

Statistical reliability—For a discussion of statistical collection and estimation, sampling procedures, and measures of statistical reliability pertaining to the producer price index and the CPI, see Appendix III.

No. 771. Purchasing Power of the Dollar: 1950 to 1997

[Indexes: PPI, 1982=$1.00; CPI, 1982–84=$1.00. Producer prices prior to 1961, and consumer prices prior to 1964, exclude Alaska and Hawaii. Producer prices based on finished goods index. Obtained by dividing the average price index for the 1982=100, PPI; 1982–84=100, CPI base periods (100.0) by the price index for a given period and expressing the result in dollars and cents. Annual figures are based on average of monthly data]

YEAR	ANNUAL AVERAGE AS MEASURED BY— Producer prices	Consumer prices	YEAR	ANNUAL AVERAGE AS MEASURED BY— Producer prices	Consumer prices	YEAR	ANNUAL AVERAGE AS MEASURED BY— Producer prices	Consumer prices
1950	$3.546	$4.151	1966	2.841	3.080	1982	1.000	1.035
1951	3.247	3.846	1967	2.809	2.993	1983	0.984	1.003
1952	3.268	3.765	1968	2.732	2.873	1984	0.964	0.961
1953	3.300	3.735	1969	2.632	2.726	1985	0.955	0.928
1954	3.289	3.717	1970	2.545	2.574	1986	0.969	0.913
1955	3.279	3.732	1971	2.469	2.466	1987	0.949	0.880
1956	3.195	3.678	1972	2.392	2.391	1988	0.926	0.846
1957	3.077	3.549	1973	2.193	2.251	1989	0.880	0.807
1958	3.012	3.457	1974	1.901	2.029	1990	0.839	0.766
1959	3.021	3.427	1975	1.718	1.859	1991	0.822	0.734
1960	2.994	3.373	1976	1.645	1.757	1992	0.812	0.713
1961	2.994	3.340	1977	1.546	1.649	1993	0.802	0.692
1962	2.985	3.304	1978	1.433	1.532	1994	0.797	0.675
1963	2.994	3.265	1979	1.289	1.380	1995	0.782	0.656
1964	2.985	3.220	1980	1.136	1.215	1996	0.762	0.638
1965	2.933	3.166	1981	1.041	1.098	1997	0.759	0.623

Source: U.S. Bureau of Labor Statistics. Monthly data in U.S. Bureau of Economic Analysis, *Survey of Current Business.*

Figure 15.1
Annual Percent Change in Producer Price Indexes by Stage of Processing: 1970 to 1997

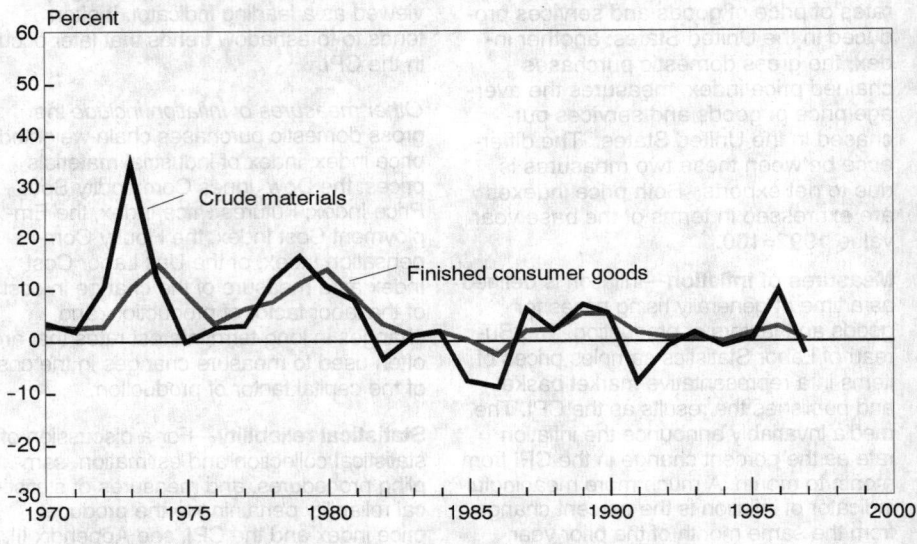

Percent

Crude materials

Finished consumer goods

Source: Chart prepared by U.S. Bureau of the Census. For data, see Table 777.

Figure 15.2
Annual Percent Change in Consumer Price Indexes: 1970 to 1997

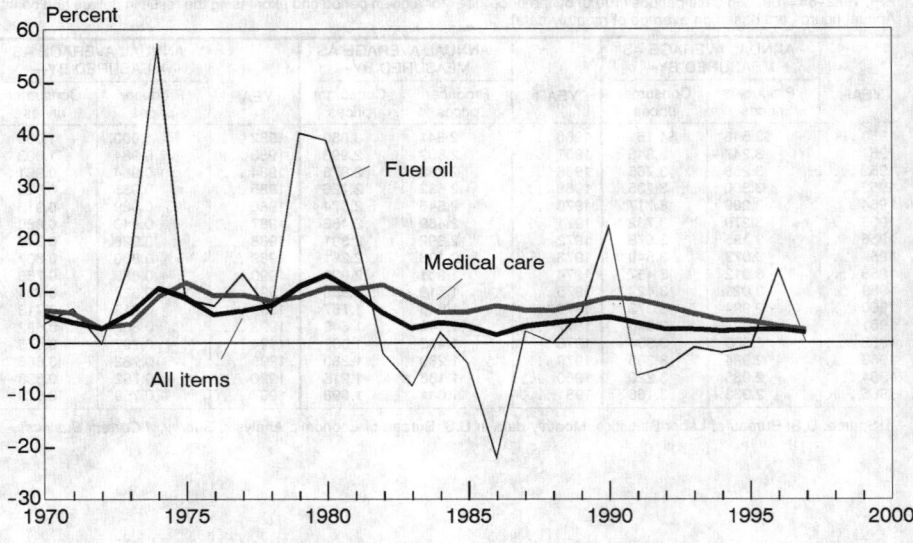

Percent

Fuel oil

Medical care

All items

Source: Chart prepared by U.S. Bureau of the Census. For data, see Table 772.

No. 772. Consumer Price Indexes (CPI-U), by Major Groups: 1939 to 1997

[1982-84=100. Represents annual averages of monthly figures. Reflects buying patterns of all urban consumers. Minus sign (-) indicates decrease. See text, Section 15]

YEAR	All items	Com-modities	Energy	Food	Shelter	Apparel and upkeep	Trans-porta-tion	Med-ical care	Fuel oil	Elec-tricity	Utility (piped) gas	Tele-phone serv-ices
1939	13.9	14.8	(NA)	11.8	(NA)	21.6	14.3	10.3	5.8	28.9	12.9	36.1
1940	14.0	14.9	(NA)	12.0	(NA)	21.8	14.2	10.4	6.1	28.6	12.8	36.1
1945	18.0	20.7	(NA)	17.3	(NA)	31.4	15.9	11.9	7.5	28.0	12.3	41.3
1950	24.1	29.0	(NA)	25.4	(NA)	40.3	22.7	15.1	11.0	27.2	13.2	49.5
1955	26.8	31.3	(NA)	27.8	22.7	42.9	25.8	18.2	13.0	28.5	14.6	52.9
1960	29.6	33.6	(NA)	30.0	25.2	45.7	29.8	22.3	13.5	29.9	17.6	58.3
1965	31.5	35.2	22.9	32.2	27.0	47.8	31.9	25.2	14.3	29.7	18.0	57.7
1966	32.4	36.1	23.3	33.8	27.8	49.0	32.3	26.3	14.7	29.7	18.1	56.5
1967	33.4	36.8	23.8	34.1	28.8	51.0	33.3	28.2	15.1	29.9	18.1	57.3
1968	34.8	38.1	24.2	35.3	30.1	53.7	34.3	29.9	15.6	30.2	18.2	57.3
1969	36.7	39.9	24.8	37.1	32.6	56.8	35.7	31.9	15.9	30.8	18.6	58.0
1970	38.8	41.7	25.5	39.2	35.5	59.2	37.5	34.0	16.5	31.8	19.6	58.7
1971	40.5	43.2	26.5	40.4	37.0	61.1	39.5	36.1	17.6	33.9	21.0	61.6
1972	41.8	44.5	27.2	42.1	38.7	62.3	39.9	37.3	17.6	35.6	22.1	65.0
1973	44.4	47.8	29.4	48.2	40.5	64.6	41.2	38.8	20.4	37.4	23.1	66.7
1974	49.3	53.5	38.1	55.1	44.4	69.4	45.8	42.4	32.2	44.1	26.0	69.5
1975	53.8	58.2	42.1	59.8	48.8	72.5	50.1	47.5	34.9	50.0	31.1	71.7
1976	56.9	60.7	45.1	61.6	51.5	75.2	55.1	52.0	37.4	53.1	36.3	74.3
1977	60.6	64.2	49.4	65.5	54.9	78.6	59.0	57.0	42.4	56.6	43.2	75.2
1978	65.2	68.8	52.5	72.0	60.5	81.4	61.7	61.8	44.9	60.9	47.5	76.0
1979	72.6	76.6	65.7	79.9	68.9	84.9	70.5	67.5	63.1	65.6	55.1	75.8
1980	82.4	86.0	86.0	86.8	81.0	90.9	83.1	74.9	87.7	75.8	65.7	77.7
1981	90.9	93.2	97.7	93.6	90.5	95.3	93.2	82.9	107.3	87.2	74.9	84.6
1982	96.5	97.0	99.2	97.4	96.9	97.8	97.0	92.5	105.0	95.8	89.8	93.2
1983	99.6	99.8	99.9	99.4	99.1	100.2	99.3	100.6	96.5	98.9	104.7	99.2
1984	103.9	103.2	100.9	103.2	104.0	102.1	103.7	106.8	98.5	105.3	105.5	107.5
1985	107.6	105.4	101.6	105.6	109.8	105.0	106.4	113.5	94.6	108.9	104.8	111.7
1986	109.6	104.4	88.2	109.0	115.8	105.9	102.3	122.0	74.1	110.4	99.7	117.2
1987	113.6	107.7	88.6	113.5	121.3	110.6	105.4	130.1	75.8	110.0	95.1	116.5
1988	118.3	111.5	89.3	118.2	127.1	115.4	108.7	138.6	75.8	111.5	94.5	116.0
1989	124.0	116.7	94.3	125.1	132.8	118.6	114.1	149.3	80.3	114.7	97.1	117.2
1990	130.7	122.8	102.1	132.4	140.0	124.1	120.5	162.8	98.6	117.4	97.3	117.7
1991	136.2	126.6	102.5	136.3	146.3	128.7	123.8	177.0	92.4	121.8	98.5	119.7
1992	140.3	129.1	103.0	137.9	151.2	131.9	126.5	190.1	88.0	124.2	100.3	120.4
1993	144.5	131.5	104.2	140.9	155.7	133.7	130.4	201.4	87.2	126.7	106.5	121.2
1994	148.2	133.8	104.6	144.3	160.5	133.4	134.3	211.0	85.6	126.7	108.5	123.1
1995	152.4	136.4	105.2	148.4	165.7	132.0	139.1	220.5	84.8	129.6	102.9	124.0
1996	156.9	139.9	110.1	153.3	171.0	131.7	143.0	228.2	97.0	131.8	107.2	125.9
1997	160.5	141.8	111.5	157.3	176.3	132.9	144.3	234.6	96.9	132.5	114.6	127.7
PERCENT CHANGE												
1940	0.7	0.7	(NA)	1.7	(NA)	0.9	-0.7	1.0	5.2	-1.0	-0.8	-
1945	2.3	3.0	(NA)	2.4	(NA)	5.4	-	2.6	-5.1	-0.7	-0.8	1.5
1950	1.3	0.7	(NA)	1.6	(NA)	-1.2	2.7	2.0	0.9	0.4	0.8	7.6
1955	-0.4	-0.9	(NA)	-1.4	0.9	-0.5	-1.1	2.2	3.2	1.4	3.5	-0.9
1960	1.7	0.9	2.3	1.0	2.0	1.6	-	3.7	-1.5	1.4	6.7	1.6
1965	1.6	1.1	1.8	2.2	1.9	1.1	1.6	2.4	2.1	-0.3	0.6	-1.5
1970	5.7	4.5	2.8	5.7	8.9	4.2	5.0	6.6	3.8	3.2	5.4	1.2
1971	4.4	3.6	3.9	3.1	4.2	3.2	5.3	6.2	6.7	6.6	7.1	4.9
1972	3.2	3.0	2.6	4.2	4.6	2.0	1.0	3.3	0.0	5.0	5.2	5.5
1973	6.2	7.4	8.1	14.5	4.7	3.7	3.3	4.0	15.9	5.1	4.5	2.6
1974	11.0	11.9	29.6	14.3	9.6	7.4	11.2	9.3	57.8	17.9	12.6	4.2
1975	9.1	8.8	10.5	8.5	9.9	4.5	9.4	12.0	8.4	13.4	19.6	3.2
1976	5.8	4.3	7.1	3.0	5.5	3.7	10.0	9.5	7.2	6.2	16.7	3.6
1977	6.5	5.8	9.5	6.3	6.6	4.5	7.1	9.6	13.4	6.6	19.0	1.2
1978	7.6	7.2	6.3	9.9	10.2	3.6	4.6	8.4	5.9	7.6	10.0	1.1
1979	11.3	11.3	25.1	11.0	13.9	4.3	14.3	9.2	40.5	7.7	16.0	-0.3
1980	13.5	12.3	30.9	8.6	17.6	7.1	17.9	11.0	39.0	15.5	19.2	2.5
1981	10.3	8.4	13.6	7.8	11.7	4.8	12.2	10.7	22.3	15.0	14.0	8.9
1982	6.2	4.1	1.5	4.1	7.1	2.6	4.1	11.6	-2.1	9.9	19.9	10.2
1983	3.2	2.9	0.7	2.1	2.3	2.5	2.4	8.8	-8.1	3.2	16.6	6.4
1984	4.3	3.4	1.0	3.8	4.9	1.9	4.4	6.2	2.1	6.5	0.8	8.4
1985	3.6	2.1	0.7	2.3	5.6	2.8	2.6	6.3	-4.0	3.4	-0.7	3.9
1986	1.9	-0.9	-13.2	3.2	5.5	0.9	-3.9	7.5	-21.7	1.4	-4.9	4.9
1987	3.6	3.2	0.5	4.1	4.7	4.4	3.0	6.6	2.3	-0.4	-4.6	-0.6
1988	4.1	3.5	0.8	4.1	4.8	4.3	3.1	6.5	-	1.4	-0.6	-0.4
1989	4.8	4.7	5.6	5.8	4.5	2.8	5.0	7.7	5.9	2.9	2.8	1.0
1990	5.4	5.2	8.3	5.8	5.4	4.6	5.6	9.0	22.8	2.4	0.2	0.4
1991	4.2	3.1	0.4	2.9	4.5	3.7	2.7	8.7	-6.3	3.7	1.2	1.7
1992	3.0	2.0	0.5	1.2	3.3	2.5	2.2	7.4	-4.8	2.0	1.8	0.6
1993	3.0	1.9	1.2	2.2	3.0	1.4	3.1	5.9	-0.9	2.0	6.2	0.7
1994	2.6	1.7	0.4	2.4	3.1	-0.2	3.0	4.8	-1.9	-	1.9	1.6
1995	2.8	1.9	0.6	2.8	3.2	-1.0	3.6	4.5	-0.9	2.3	-5.2	0.7
1996	3.0	2.6	4.7	3.3	3.2	-0.2	2.8	3.5	14.4	1.7	4.2	1.5
1997	2.3	1.4	1.3	2.6	3.1	0.9	0.9	2.8	-0.1	0.5	6.9	1.4

- Represents zero.   NA Not available.

Source: Bureau of Labor Statistics, *Monthly Labor Review and Handbook of Labor Statistics*, periodic.

No. 773. Consumer Price Indexes for All Urban Consumers (CPI-U) for Selected Items and Groups: 1980 to 1997

[1982-84=100. Annual averages of monthly figures. See headnote, Table 772]

ITEM	1980	1990	1991	1992	1993	1994	1995	1996	1997
All items	**82.4**	**130.7**	**136.2**	**140.3**	**144.5**	**148.2**	**152.4**	**156.9**	**160.5**
Food and beverages	86.7	132.1	136.8	138.7	141.6	144.9	148.9	153.7	157.7
Food	86.8	132.4	136.3	137.9	140.9	144.3	148.4	153.3	157.3
Food at home	88.4	132.3	135.8	136.8	140.1	144.1	148.8	154.3	158.1
Cereals and bakery products	83.9	140.0	145.8	151.5	156.6	163.0	167.5	174.0	177.6
Cereals and cereal products	84.2	141.1	147.5	153.3	157.9	164.8	167.1	168.9	169.5
Cereals	76.3	158.6	168.1	175.4	183.3	190.6	192.5	190.0	187.5
Rice, pasta, and cornmeal	90.9	122.0	126.5	128.3	129.7	139.7	140.2	144.2	148.8
Bakery products	83.8	139.2	144.7	150.4	155.7	161.9	167.4	176.1	181.1
White bread	85.9	136.4	139.3	146.2	152.2	159.0	165.5	177.5	183.8
Cookies, cakes, and cupcakes	81.5	142.7	151.1	155.6	159.3	165.1	169.1	174.1	179.2
Meats, poultry, fish and eggs	92.0	130.0	132.6	130.9	135.5	137.2	138.8	144.8	148.5
Meats	92.7	128.5	132.5	130.7	134.6	135.4	135.5	140.2	144.4
Beef and veal	98.4	128.8	132.4	132.3	137.1	136.0	134.9	134.5	136.8
Ground beef excl. canned	104.6	118.1	119.9	118.9	121.7	119.7	116.1	114.3	116.4
Chuck roast	99.8	130.3	135.8	137.1	141.9	140.3	138.7	140.0	142.3
Round steak	98.9	125.1	129.5	129.9	134.4	133.0	130.4	129.3	130.1
Sirloin steak	96.2	130.6	133.5	132.4	138.5	137.5	138.7	137.6	139.0
Pork	81.9	129.8	134.1	127.8	131.7	133.9	134.8	148.2	155.9
Bacon	73.5	113.4	119.8	104.6	110.8	118.1	120.0	148.9	164.0
Chops	82.9	140.2	141.7	138.9	144.6	144.2	144.2	153.0	155.2
Ham	85.5	132.4	139.9	135.6	137.9	139.3	139.6	149.2	156.3
Poultry	93.7	132.5	131.5	131.4	136.9	141.5	143.5	152.4	156.6
Fresh whole chicken	94.4	134.9	131.7	131.9	138.0	140.1	142.2	152.6	158.5
Fresh, frozen chicken parts	91.7	135.9	134.7	134.4	140.1	145.6	146.0	155.0	157.4
Fish and seafood	87.5	146.7	148.3	151.7	156.6	163.7	171.6	173.1	177.1
Canned fish and seafood	93.7	119.5	119.0	118.7	121.5	123.8	125.5	125.9	128.4
Fresh, frozen fish, seafood	84.1	161.4	163.8	168.7	174.5	183.6	194.1	196.0	200.7
Eggs	88.6	124.1	121.2	108.3	117.1	114.3	120.5	142.1	140.0
Dairy products	90.9	126.5	125.1	128.5	129.4	131.7	132.8	142.1	145.5
Fruits and vegetables	82.1	149.0	155.8	155.4	159.0	165.0	177.7	183.9	187.5
Fresh fruits and vegetables	81.8	(NA)	(NA)	(NA)	(NA)	186.7	206.0	211.8	215.4
Fresh fruits	84.8	170.9	193.9	184.2	188.8	201.2	219.0	234.4	236.3
Apples	92.1	147.5	172.8	179.5	169.0	174.0	183.5	202.3	199.6
Bananas	91.5	138.2	145.0	139.9	135.5	143.6	153.8	159.0	159.6
Oranges, tangerines	72.6	160.6	249.4	176.2	190.1	189.9	224.5	239.3	226.1
Fresh vegetables	79.0	151.1	154.4	157.9	168.7	172.3	193.1	189.2	194.6
Potatoes	81.0	162.6	144.6	141.5	154.6	174.3	174.7	180.6	174.2
Lettuce	77.8	150.3	159.8	155.7	178.2	170.3	221.2	185.7	200.1
Tomatoes	81.9	160.8	153.1	171.8	168.0	173.5	188.3	198.2	213.6
Processed fruits and vegetables	82.6	(NA)	(NA)	(NA)	(NA)	134.5	137.5	144.4	147.9
Processed fruits	82.1	136.9	131.8	137.7	132.3	133.1	137.2	145.2	148.8
Processed vegetables	83.1	127.5	128.5	128.8	130.8	136.6	138.3	143.9	147.2
Coffee	111.6	117.5	115.3	110.7	109.8	140.4	163.1	149.2	168.0
Food away from home	83.4	(NA)	(NA)	(NA)	(NA)	145.7	149.0	152.7	157.0
Lunch	83.8	133.9	138.4	141.3	144.0	146.4	149.6	153.3	157.7
Dinner	84.2	132.3	136.3	138.9	141.3	143.8	147.1	150.7	154.7
Alcoholic beverages	86.4	129.3	142.8	147.3	149.6	151.5	153.9	158.5	162.8
Alcoholic beverages at home	87.3	123.0	137.8	141.6	142.2	142.5	143.1	146.8	149.5
Beer and ale	84.8	123.6	138.4	143.5	143.2	143.4	143.9	147.4	148.2
Distilled spirits	89.8	125.7	139.2	141.5	143.2	144.3	145.7	147.5	150.8
Wine	89.5	114.4	129.9	132.6	134.0	133.3	133.6	139.3	145.5
Alcoholic beverages away from home	82.9	144.4	156.9	162.5	167.4	171.6	176.5	182.7	189.4
Housing	81.1	128.5	133.6	137.5	141.2	144.8	148.5	152.8	156.8
Shelter	81.0	140.0	146.3	151.2	155.7	160.5	165.7	171.0	176.3
Renters' cost	(NA)	146.7	155.6	160.9	165.0	169.4	174.3	180.2	186.4
Rent, residential	80.9	138.4	143.3	146.9	150.3	154.0	157.8	162.0	166.7
Tenants' insurance	78.9	130.6	133.2	136.5	140.8	145.8	150.9	154.7	159.2
Homeowners' costs	(NA)	144.6	150.2	155.3	160.2	165.5	171.0	176.5	181.5
Owners' equivalent rent	(NA)	144.8	150.4	155.5	160.5	165.8	171.3	176.8	181.9
Household insurance	(NA)	135.3	138.4	142.2	146.9	152.3	157.4	161.0	165.3
Maintenance and repair	82.4	122.2	126.3	128.6	130.6	130.8	135.0	139.0	143.7
Fuels and other utilities	75.4	111.6	115.3	117.8	121.3	122.8	123.7	127.5	130.8
Fuels	74.8	104.5	106.7	108.1	111.2	111.7	111.5	115.2	117.9
Fuel oil and other	86.1	99.3	94.6	90.7	90.3	88.8	88.1	99.2	99.8
Fuel oil	87.7	98.6	92.4	88.0	87.2	85.6	84.8	97.0	96.9
Gas (piped) and electricity	71.4	109.3	112.6	114.8	118.5	119.2	119.2	122.1	125.1
Electricity	75.8	117.4	121.8	124.2	126.7	126.7	129.6	131.8	132.5
Utility (piped) gas	65.7	97.3	98.5	100.3	106.5	108.5	102.9	107.2	114.6
Telephone services	77.7	117.7	119.7	120.4	121.2	123.1	124.0	125.9	127.7
Local charges	72.8	149.3	153.9	155.7	156.4	156.9	160.4	160.8	163.1
Interstate toll charges	83.3	68.2	67.6	68.0	69.6	75.2	74.9	77.9	77.3
Intrastate toll charges	85.2	95.1	93.1	91.4	90.7	90.2	86.0	89.4	93.9
Water and sewerage maintenance	74.0	150.2	161.1	172.1	181.4	190.6	196.5	204.5	210.0
Cable television	(NA)	158.4	175.7	186.2	198.9	197.4	200.7	212.6	228.7
Refuse collection	(NA)	171.2	189.2	207.3	220.5	231.4	241.2	246.0	250.5

See footnotes at end of table.

No. 773. Consumer Price Indexes for All Urban Consumers (CPI-U) for Selected Items and Groups: 1980 to 1997—Continued

[1982-84=100. Annual averages of monthly figures. See headnote, table 772]

ITEM	1980	1990	1991	1992	1993	1994	1995	1996	1997
Household furnishings and operations	86.3	113.3	116.0	118.0	119.3	121.0	123.0	124.7	125.4
Housefurnishings	88.5	106.7	107.5	109.0	109.5	111.0	111.2	111.3	110.6
Furniture and bedding	88.0	115.7	116.6	120.6	123.5	128.2	130.9	134.1	134.5
Bedroom furniture	83.5	118.5	120.1	126.8	132.5	135.1	136.4	139.3	141.5
Sofas	(NA)	118.4	118.3	119.4	120.1	125.2	132.8	141.5	142.0
Living room chairs and tables	(NA)	116.7	118.4	121.9	125.0	132.7	136.6	136.9	136.7
Appliances and electronic equip.	93.5	87.8	86.0	84.6	83.4	82.3	80.0	77.8	75.3
Video and audio equipment	100.7	80.8	79.4	78.4	77.1	76.0	73.9	71.3	69.1
Television	104.6	74.6	72.9	72.4	70.7	69.9	68.1	64.5	61.7
Video products other than TV	(NA)	91.5	84.6	81.0	78.5	73.8	70.3	66.3	63.4
Audio products	97.7	93.2	94.6	94.4	93.9	93.8	92.1	90.7	88.9
Housekeeping supplies	83.2	125.2	128.9	129.6	130.7	132.3	137.1	141.1	143.1
Housekeeping services	84.3	120.1	127.5	132.1	135.8	138.5	143.7	148.0	151.9
Postage	76.2	125.1	143.6	145.3	145.3	145.3	160.3	160.3	160.3
Apparel and upkeep	90.9	124.1	128.7	131.9	133.7	133.4	132.0	131.7	132.9
Apparel commodities	92.9	122.0	126.4	129.4	131.0	130.4	128.7	128.2	129.1
Apparel commodities less footwear	93.0	122.8	127.4	130.2	131.9	131.2	129.3	128.5	129.4
Men's and boy's apparel	89.4	120.4	124.2	126.5	127.5	126.4	126.2	127.7	130.1
Women's and girl's apparel	96.0	122.6	127.6	130.4	132.6	130.9	126.9	124.7	126.1
Infants' and toddlers'	85.5	125.8	128.9	129.3	127.1	128.1	127.2	129.7	129.0
Footwear	91.8	117.4	120.9	125.0	125.9	126.0	125.4	126.6	127.6
Transportation	83.1	120.5	123.8	126.5	130.4	134.3	139.1	143.0	144.3
Private transportation	84.2	118.8	121.9	124.6	127.5	131.4	136.3	140.0	141.0
New vehicles	88.5	121.4	126.0	129.2	132.7	137.6	141.0	143.7	144.3
New cars	88.4	121.0	125.3	128.4	131.5	136.0	139.0	141.4	141.7
New trucks	(NA)	121.6	127.0	130.9	135.7	141.7	145.9	149.5	151.4
Used cars	62.3	117.6	118.1	123.2	133.9	141.7	156.5	157.0	151.1
Motor fuel	97.4	101.2	99.4	99.0	98.0	98.5	100.0	106.3	106.2
Automobile maintenance and repair	81.5	130.1	136.0	141.3	145.9	150.2	154.0	158.4	162.7
Automobile insurance	82.0	177.9	191.5	205.5	216.7	224.8	234.3	243.9	251.6
Automobile finance charges	86.4	99.6	98.0	86.1	78.6	83.8	99.0	94.4	93.6
Vehicle rental, registration, other	78.3	148.1	154.8	162.3	169.8	174.2	177.9	181.1	185.4
Public transportation	69.0	142.6	148.9	151.4	167.0	172.0	175.9	181.9	186.7
Airline fares	68.0	148.4	155.2	155.2	178.7	185.5	189.7	192.5	199.2
Other intercity transportation	73.1	143.3	149.0	152.5	150.9	152.8	153.3	156.0	155.1
Intracity transportation	69.7	133.5	138.9	146.9	150.7	152.7	157.5	173.2	175.8
Medical care	74.9	162.8	177.0	190.1	201.4	211.0	220.5	228.2	234.6
Medical care commodities	75.4	163.4	176.8	188.1	195.0	200.7	204.5	210.4	215.3
Prescription drugs	72.5	181.7	199.7	214.7	223.0	230.6	235.0	242.9	249.3
Nonprescription drugs, medical sup.	(NA)	120.6	126.3	131.2	135.5	138.1	140.5	143.1	145.4
Medical care services	74.8	162.7	177.1	190.5	202.9	213.4	224.2	232.4	239.1
Professional medical services	77.9	156.1	165.7	175.8	184.7	192.5	201.0	208.3	215.4
Physicians' services	76.5	160.8	170.5	181.2	191.3	199.8	208.8	216.4	222.9
Dental services	78.9	155.8	167.4	178.7	188.1	197.1	206.8	216.5	226.6
Eye care	(NA)	117.3	121.9	127.0	130.4	133.0	137.0	139.3	141.5
Hospital and related services	69.2	178.0	196.1	214.0	231.9	245.6	257.8	269.5	278.4
Hospital rooms	68.0	175.4	191.9	208.7	226.4	239.2	251.2	261.0	(NA)
Entertainment	83.6	132.4	138.4	142.3	145.8	150.1	153.9	159.1	162.5
Entertainment commodities	84.5	124.0	128.6	131.3	133.4	136.1	138.7	143.0	144.2
Reading materials	77.7	136.2	144.7	150.9	156.2	161.3	168.1	176.4	179.0
Newspapers	79.4	134.6	146.5	154.8	161.1	168.2	178.7	188.9	191.3
Magazines, periodicals, and books	75.9	137.9	143.3	147.4	151.8	155.1	158.4	165.0	167.8
Sporting goods, equipment	88.5	114.9	118.5	120.2	120.1	122.2	123.5	123.4	122.6
Sport vehicles, including bicycles	87.9	115.3	117.5	119.7	120.6	122.3	125.3	125.7	124.5
Toys, hobbies; other entertainment	86.5	121.5	123.9	124.7	126.0	127.4	127.8	131.9	133.3
Pet supplies and expenses	83.3	124.6	129.1	128.1	128.8	130.9	132.3	139.0	142.7
Entertainment services	82.3	143.2	150.6	155.9	160.8	166.8	172.0	178.1	183.8
Club membership	(NA)	117.0	122.5	125.2	128.4	130.7	132.8	133.3	132.1
Admissions	83.8	151.2	159.3	164.5	167.3	175.2	182.3	192.1	198.9
Tobacco and smoking products	72.0	181.5	202.7	219.8	228.4	220.0	225.7	232.8	243.7
Personal care	81.9	130.4	134.9	138.3	141.5	144.6	147.1	150.1	152.7
Personal care services	83.7	132.8	137.0	140.0	144.0	144.0	147.9	151.5	156.6	162.4
Beauty parlor services for women	83.4	133.0	137.2	139.8	143.6	147.7	150.9	155.9	161.4
Haircuts, etc. for men	84.4	131.5	135.9	140.3	144.6	147.9	153.4	158.5	165.5
Personal and educational expenses	70.9	170.2	183.7	197.4	210.7	223.2	235.5	247.5	259.7
School books and supplies	71.4	171.3	180.3	190.3	197.6	205.5	214.4	226.9	238.4
Personal and educational services	70.8	170.4	184.2	198.1	211.9	224.8	237.3	249.3	261.6
Tuition and other school fees	71.2	175.7	191.4	208.5	225.3	239.8	253.8	267.1	280.4
College tuition	70.8	175.0	192.8	213.5	233.5	249.8	264.8	279.8	294.1
Elementary and high school tuition	72.3	182.8	198.0	213.7	228.9	242.6	259.2	272.8	288.1
Day care and nursery school	(NA)	(NA)	103.2	108.3	113.6	119.6	124.5	129.4	134.3
All commodities	86.0	122.8	126.6	129.1	131.5	133.8	136.4	139.9	141.8
All commodities less food	85.7	117.4	121.3	124.2	126.3	127.9	129.8	132.6	133.4
Energy	86.0	102.1	102.5	103.0	104.2	104.6	105.2	110.1	111.5

NA Not available.

Source: U.S. Bureau of Labor Statistics, *Monthly Labor Review* and *CPI Detailed Report*, January issues.

No. 774. Consumer Price Indexes (CPI-U)—Selected Areas: 1980 to 1997

[1982-84=100, except as indicated. Represents annual averages of monthly figures. Local area CPI indexes are byproducts of the national CPI program. Each local index has a smaller sample size than the national index and is therefore, subject to substantially more sampling and other measurement error. As a result, local area indexes show greater volatility than the national index, although their long- term trends are similar. Area definitions are those established by the Office of Management and Budget in 1983. For further detail see the U.S. Bureau of Labor Statistics Handbook of Methods, Bulletin 2285, Chapter 19, the Consumer Price Index, and Report 736, the CPI: 1987 Revision. See also text, Section 15]

AREA	1980	1990	1993	1994	1995	1996	1997 All items	1997 Food and beverages	1997 Food	1997 Housing	1997 Apparel and upkeep	1997 Transportation	1997 Medical care	1997 Entertainment	1997 Fuel and other utilities
U.S., all items	**82.4**	**130.7**	**144.5**	**148.2**	**152.4**	**156.9**	**160.5**	**157.7**	**157.3**	**156.8**	**132.9**	**144.3**	**234.6**	**162.5**	**130.8**
Anchorage, AK MSA	85.5	118.6	132.2	135.0	138.5	142.7	144.8	145.8	146.3	129.4	127.0	147.0	248.9	180.3	146.4
Atlanta, GA MSA	80.3	131.7	143.4	146.7	148.7	156.0	158.9	159.5	163.3	156.5	137.0	132.5	243.5	186.6	139.1
Boston-Lawrence-Salem, MA-NH CMSA	80.3	138.9	152.9	154.7	157.4	163.3	167.9	160.4	160.6	162.5	143.8	141.6	293.1	175.4	126.0
Chicago-Gary-Lake County, IL-IN-WI CMSA	82.2	131.7	145.4	148.6	148.4	157.4	161.7	160.5	159.5	160.2	122.3	140.2	235.5	175.3	125.7
Cincinnati-Hamilton, OH-KY-IN CMSA	82.1	126.5	137.8	142.4	143.4	149.6	156.1	145.0	143.5	145.1	132.7	137.6	221.1	163.6	121.9
Cleveland-Akron-Lorain, OH CMSA	78.9	129.0	140.3	144.4	140.2	152.0	152.0	158.1	159.2	153.2	127.8	141.8	211.5	158.4	129.0
Dallas-Fort Worth, TX CMSA	81.5	125.1	137.3	141.2	144.0	148.8	151.4	157.0	154.9	138.8	137.2	142.9	225.3	168.9	128.6
Denver-Boulder, CO CMSA	78.4	120.9	135.8	141.8	144.0	153.1	158.1	148.0	150.0	147.7	104.0	165.6	265.8	155.2	126.6
Detroit-Ann Arbor, MI CMSA	85.3	128.6	139.6	144.0	143.9	152.5	156.3	151.4	150.8	147.1	135.2	149.0	214.1	160.3	126.3
Honolulu, HI MSA	83.0	138.1	160.1	164.5	168.4	170.7	171.9	159.2	159.5	177.1	117.3	166.2	217.3	147.9	137.1
Houston-Galveston-Brazoria, TX CMSA	82.7	120.6	133.4	137.9	139.4	142.7	145.4	147.7	147.5	126.1	142.1	141.4	228.4	161.6	106.9
Kansas City, MO-KS CMSA	83.6	126.0	138.1	141.3	141.7	151.6	155.8	160.0	161.0	146.1	133.4	140.7	210.0	171.0	133.8
Los Angeles-Anaheim-Riverside, CA CMSA	83.7	135.9	150.3	152.3	149.4	157.5	160.0	163.2	161.4	156.6	121.0	145.2	232.0	147.6	154.0
Miami-Fort Lauderdale, FL CMSA	81.1	128.0	139.1	143.6	146.9	153.7	158.4	165.7	166.0	150.2	153.5	147.2	219.2	153.8	119.8
Milwaukee, WI PMSA	81.4	126.2	142.1	147.0	153.5	154.7	157.7	154.5	155.5	156.1	122.9	143.7	230.5	140.1	108.0
Minneapolis-St. Paul, MN-WI MSA	78.9	127.0	139.2	143.6	144.8	151.9	154.8	163.3	161.3	140.8	145.6	144.0	218.8	170.8	120.2
New York-Northern New Jersey-Long Island, NY-NJ-CT CMSA	82.1	138.5	154.5	158.2	158.3	166.9	170.8	163.0	162.3	171.7	130.3	154.1	244.5	167.6	119.2
Philadelphia-Wilmington-Trenton, PA-NJ-DE-MD CMSA	83.6	135.8	150.2	154.6	158.3	162.8	166.5	154.3	153.4	167.3	104.0	152.8	247.8	181.8	131.9
Pittsburgh-Beaver Valley, PA CMSA	81.0	126.2	139.9	144.6	142.9	153.2	157.0	151.8	150.5	156.2	140.9	132.7	228.8	165.7	145.2
Portland-Vancouver, OR-WA CMSA	87.2	127.4	144.7	148.9	149.9	158.6	164.0	148.4	148.4	162.5	131.4	150.9	217.6	172.3	129.9
San Diego, CA MSA	79.4	138.4	150.6	154.5	147.0	160.9	163.7	161.4	159.9	163.5	126.1	152.2	236.8	161.4	123.2
San Francisco-Oakland-San Jose, CA CMSA	80.4	132.1	146.3	148.7	149.3	155.1	160.4	160.1	160.6	165.6	116.1	133.6	224.7	165.7	149.4
Seattle-Tacoma, WA CMSA	82.7	126.8	142.9	147.8	149.3	157.5	163.0	160.2	160.6	164.4	125.9	145.6	226.4	152.3	120.9
St. Louis-East St. Louis, MO-IL CMSA 1	82.5	128.1	137.5	141.3	144.7	149.6	152.9	155.0	153.3	145.5	123.8	143.8	190.5	164.2	123.9
Tampa-St. Petersburg-Clearwater, FL MSA 1	(NA)	111.7	124.0	126.5	128.0	131.6	134.0	131.7	130.3	129.0	120.0	127.0		122.4	119.5
Washington-Baltimore, DC-MD-VA-WV CMSA	82.9	135.6	149.3	152.2	152.7	159.6	162.4	155.3	155.8	157.1	143.4	146.2	231.6	174.6	130.6

NA Not available.   1 1987=100.

Source: U.S. Bureau of Labor Statistics, *Monthly Labor Review* and *CPI Detailed Report*, January issues.

No. 775. Cost of Living Index—Selected Metropolitan Areas: Fourth Quarter 1997

[Measures relative price levels for consumer goods and services in participating areas for a midmanagement standard of living. The nationwide average equals 100, and each index is read as a percent of the national average. The index does not measure inflation, but compares prices at a single point in time. Excludes taxes. Metropolitan areas as defined by the Office of Management and Budget. For definitions and components of MSAs, see source for details]

METROPOLITAN AREAS	Composite index (100%)	Grocery items (16%)	Housing (28%)	Utilities (8%)	Transportation (10%)	Health care (5%)	Misc. goods and services (33%)
Abilene, TX MSA	93.4	86.1	88.0	100.5	105.2	100.3	95.2
Albany, GA MSA	91.8	103.4	74.9	104.7	92.6	87.2	97.9
Albuquerque, NM MSA	103.1	101.7	105.3	102.8	96.5	115.1	101.7
Alexandria, LA MSA	95.1	97.0	87.7	112.0	100.2	80.8	97.6
Altoona, PA MSA	99.5	102.4	97.4	121.7	91.3	90.6	98.5
Amarillo, TX MSA	92.1	92.1	85.7	100.1	103.2	89.0	93.2
Anchorage, AK MSA	123.3	125.8	131.4	87.0	111.5	169.6	118.8
Anniston, AL MSA	91.1	99.9	81.4	103.5	92.2	85.2	92.8
Appleton-Oshkosh-Neenah, WI MSA	99.7	99.7	103.2	86.7	101.7	99.0	99.5
Asheville, NC MSA	104.0	96.5	110.9	119.8	107.5	90.9	99.3
Atlanta, GA MSA	99.4	102.0	97.2	93.8	102.2	103.9	99.7
Augusta-Aiken, GA-SC MSA	90.3	92.4	81.5	109.5	99.9	98.5	88.1
Austin-San Marcos, TX MSA	99.6	88.5	105.5	85.4	96.7	109.9	102.3
Bakersfield, CA MSA	102.5	108.4	89.5	116.5	111.8	107.5	103.8
Baltimore, MD PMSA	98.2	98.0	95.4	110.5	100.9	98.7	96.8
Baton Rouge, LA MSA	100.3	103.4	96.0	105.9	104.3	100.1	100.1
Beaumont-Port Arthur, TX MSA	96.1	88.1	91.5	101.3	103.0	94.9	101.0
Bellingham, WA MSA	104.6	104.5	118.8	88.2	99.6	124.7	94.4
Benton Harbor, MI MSA	107.5	106.3	117.1	102.6	101.1	99.6	104.3
Billings, MT MSA	102.5	102.6	103.5	82.3	112.4	103.7	103.7
Biloxi-Gulfport-Pascagoula, MS MSA	98.6	102.9	86.7	119.9	98.8	89.4	103.1
Binghamton, NY MSA	96.4	102.7	80.9	127.3	103.8	92.7	97.8
Birmingham, AL MSA	98.6	99.6	95.0	101.5	95.7	96.5	101.5
Bismarck, ND MSA	98.1	102.3	98.5	87.1	90.0	98.1	100.6
Bloomington, IN MSA	102.1	112.0	99.9	92.4	101.8	103.4	101.3
Boston, MA-NH PMSA	138.1	112.7	192.6	129.4	123.7	136.5	110.5
Bryan-College Station, TX MSA	90.2	86.9	81.5	110.6	87.6	91.5	94.6
Buffalo-Niagara Falls, NY MSA	97.6	107.1	89.3	125.1	103.7	91.4	92.7
Burlington, VT MSA	113.0	104.9	124.2	129.6	103.4	117.3	105.3
Canton-Massillon, OH MSA	97.1	100.5	93.2	96.1	102.4	87.1	99.3
Cedar Rapids, IA MSA	96.2	92.8	93.6	101.9	101.8	94.6	97.5
Champaign-Urbana, IL MSA	105.2	100.5	109.7	116.4	100.5	100.4	103.0
Charleston-North Charleston, SC MSA	96.8	95.1	92.8	118.4	90.9	104.2	95.9
Charleston, WV MSA	101.0	106.0	98.3	108.2	103.9	90.2	100.4
Charlotte-Gastonia-Rock Hill, NC-SC MSA	100.5	99.1	101.6	103.3	97.0	98.9	100.7
Chattanooga, TN-GA MSA	95.5	97.3	91.7	91.0	93.4	91.4	100.4
Cheyenne, WY MSA	95.8	102.4	89.9	72.4	98.2	100.9	101.6
Cincinnati, OH-KY-IN PMSA	91.1	89.1	84.7	95.0	95.5	102.8	93.1
Cincinnati, OH-KY-IN PMSA	99.5	97.4	98.1	98.2	99.4	98.7	102.2
Clarksville-Hopkinsville, TN-KY MSA	94.7	95.0	90.1	96.1	93.7	90.4	99.3
Colorado Springs, CO MSA	100.8	101.0	115.0	70.9	99.4	126.2	91.8
Columbia, MO MSA	95.7	102.9	85.4	82.2	100.6	103.3	101.4
Columbia, SC MSA	94.9	97.4	87.3	125.3	86.2	87.3	96.5
Columbus, OH MSA	102.4	98.9	105.5	120.6	101.2	91.1	99.4
Cumberland, MD-WV MSA	100.8	97.2	109.0	100.2	92.4	86.9	100.5
Dallas, TX PMSA	98.2	95.7	94.9	96.2	106.6	104.2	99.2
Davenport-Moline-Rock Island, IA-IL MSA	98.9	101.9	90.3	97.4	100.9	96.1	105.2
Dayton-Springfield, OH MSA	103.7	96.5	111.1	103.9	100.2	107.9	101.0
Daytona Beach, FL MSA	94.5	100.3	85.8	94.4	94.2	101.7	98.0
Decatur, AL MSA	95.0	97.3	85.0	88.9	102.5	97.0	101.5
Decatur, IL MSA	93.7	100.4	77.9	117.1	101.5	89.4	96.8
Denver, CO PMSA	105.9	103.2	120.2	82.7	105.4	124.1	97.6
Des Moines, IA MSA	96.5	91.7	95.5	95.9	97.5	100.7	98.9
Dover, DE MSA	101.5	109.2	93.4	113.4	99.6	99.5	102.7

See footnotes at end of table.

No. 775. Cost of Living Index—Selected Metropolitan Areas: Third Quarter 1997—Continued

[See headnote, page 493]

METROPOLITAN AREAS	Com- posite index (100%)	Grocery items (16%)	Housing (28%)	Utilities (8%)	Transpor- tation (10%)	Health care (5%)	Misc. goods and services (33%)
Dubuque, IA MSA	106.7	94.7	123.3	102.7	102.6	97.8	102.0
Eau Claire, WI MSA	100.3	99.8	103.4	99.9	99.1	107.6	97.1
El Paso, TX MSA	94.6	100.5	83.5	85.6	112.7	101.6	97.1
Elkhart-Goshen, IN MSA	93.1	96.1	87.5	93.9	91.8	98.2	95.7
Elmira, NY MSA	112.5	107.7	118.6	150.6	113.0	87.8	104.8
Eugene-Springfield, OR MSA	108.7	100.4	128.3	73.4	108.8	119.1	102.8
Evansville-Henderson, IN-KY MSA	92.6	102.8	84.0	74.1	88.8	88.0	101.3
Evansville-Henderson, IN-KY MSA	96.3	99.5	96.3	90.5	93.5	91.5	97.9
Fargo-Moorhead, ND-MN MSA	98.2	96.9	90.3	98.2	95.2	107.6	104.6
Fitchburg-Leominster, MA PMSA	101.3	108.4	96.1	110.6	104.9	105.7	98.2
Flagstaff, AZ-UT MSA	112.1	109.7	131.7	92.0	120.3	109.6	99.8
Fort Collins-Loveland, CO MSA	104.9	111.2	115.6	74.1	102.2	113.4	99.5
Fort Myers-Cape Coral, FL MSA	99.4	99.7	93.3	109.5	107.2	99.8	99.9
Fort Smith, AR-OK MSA	86.2	92.8	74.7	88.3	82.3	74.7	95.4
Fort Walton Beach, FL MSA	98.6	105.6	96.0	90.0	90.8	98.0	101.8
Fort Wayne, IN MSA	91.1	98.4	85.7	95.5	91.5	90.8	90.9
Fort Worth-Arlington, TX PMSA	88.1	87.2	81.1	84.2	95.2	94.5	92.3
Fresno, CA MSA	103.7	105.7	96.8	113.4	119.5	113.5	100.2
Gadsden, AL MSA	92.8	96.7	78.7	100.7	88.5	90.7	102.4
Gainesville, FL MSA	100.8	104.6	96.8	95.1	101.0	103.5	103.2
Glens Falls, NY MSA	101.6	103.9	92.9	118.2	106.4	107.8	101.3
Grand Forks, ND-MN MSA	98.8	102.1	93.5	93.5	97.9	94.2	104.2
Grand Junction, CO MSA	99.4	103.9	101.9	79.4	110.1	103.3	96.3
Grand Rapids-Muskegon-Holland, MI MSA	104.6	104.0	112.7	105.4	110.6	103.9	96.4
Great Falls, MT MSA	103.9	103.1	105.8	80.2	103.8	102.8	108.5
Greeley, CO MSA	102.1	110.1	106.2	78.9	101.8	109.5	99.2
Green Bay, WI MSA	97.9	93.8	103.4	84.2	98.5	107.7	96.7
Greensboro-Winston-Salem- High Point, NC MSA	100.1	98.1	105.0	104.8	102.9	88.2	97.2
Greenville-Spartanburg-Anderson, SC MSA	98.3	97.5	101.9	96.4	92.4	99.2	97.4
Greenville, NC MSA	96.1	98.2	86.7	120.1	88.5	96.3	99.4
Hagerstown, MD PMSA	97.8	93.9	95.7	97.1	99.1	97.9	101.3
Hattiesburg, MS MSA	96.8	100.3	82.0	113.6	100.7	92.8	103.4
Hickory-Morganton-Lenoir, NC MSA	97.1	98.2	91.7	102.1	88.8	85.4	104.2
Houston, TX PMSA	94.1	90.7	83.2	101.0	105.9	109.9	97.3
Huntsville, AL MSA	97.5	95.7	83.6	100.1	100.2	98.5	108.1
Indianapolis, IN MSA	98.5	102.3	93.2	93.5	99.7	99.5	101.8
Jacksonville, FL MSA	96.8	103.7	84.7	96.7	105.4	92.5	102.3
Jackson, MS MSA	91.1	87.4	92.3	103.4	94.8	84.3	89.2
Jackson, TN MSA	100.5	103.0	99.8	90.6	100.0	89.5	104.5
Janesville-Beloit, WI MSA	102.1	95.1	117.7	95.8	98.4	95.5	96.0
Johnson City-Kingsport-Bristol, TN-VA MSA	95.8	93.2	99.7	84.4	93.6	93.6	97.5
Jonesboro, AR MSA	87.0	92.4	79.0	91.3	80.6	85.2	92.2
Joplin, MO MSA	89.3	92.0	81.3	90.1	83.9	95.7	94.8
Kansas City, MO-KS MSA	96.9	98.6	90.8	91.2	99.3	105.3	100.4
Killeen-Temple, TX MSA	96.8	91.3	93.1	111.1	95.9	107.4	97.6
Knoxville, TN MSA	95.6	93.9	91.3	94.2	93.9	96.9	100.7
Lafayette, IN MSA	93.4	95.9	91.3	90.7	95.9	95.0	93.8
Lafayette, LA MSA	98.1	98.4	99.0	85.6	102.1	90.2	100.6
Lake Charles, LA MSA	96.8	93.8	91.0	111.9	98.6	76.9	102.5

See footnotes at end of table.

No. 775. Cost of Living Index—Selected Metropolitan Areas: Fourth Quarter 1997—Continued

[See headnote, page 493]

METROPOLITAN AREAS	Composite index (100%)	Grocery items (16%)	Housing (28%)	Utilities (8%)	Transportation (10%)	Health care (5%)	Misc. goods and services (33%)
Lancaster, PA MSA	107.4	98.0	113.2	106.3	116.4	96.8	106.8
Lansing-East Lansing, MI MSA	108.5	109.0	130.4	80.2	95.7	105.9	100.6
Las Cruces, NM MSA	100.0	101.3	99.7	100.3	93.3	96.5	101.9
Las Vegas, NV-AZ MSA	94.1	103.2	78.8	114.1	99.9	103.3	94.5
Lawrence, KS MSA	102.3	91.8	111.4	90.7	99.7	93.0	105.0
Lawton, OK MSA	93.1	95.6	80.7	92.9	95.6	92.6	102.0
Lexington, KY MSA	97.9	100.1	94.8	85.0	95.6	102.9	102.3
Lima, OH MSA	99.5	101.4	98.2	95.7	95.7	85.1	104.2
Lincoln, NE MSA	101.9	96.8	116.7	87.4	101.0	88.6	98.0
Little Rock-North Little Rock, AR MSA	89.9	104.4	81.1	109.2	94.6	69.0	88.2
Los Angeles-Long Beach, CA PMSA	117.6	116.3	133.9	114.2	112.7	112.7	107.4
Louisville, KY-IN MSA	96.4	99.8	90.8	94.5	104.0	92.3	98.6
Lubbock, TX MSA	91.1	90.3	86.6	74.4	100.3	92.0	96.6
Macon, GA MSA	96.0	103.4	88.6	105.4	94.7	89.1	97.9
Madison, WI MSA	110.3	98.3	125.9	91.1	102.9	107.2	110.1
Mansfield, OH MSA	97.6	100.7	94.5	120.5	95.3	88.1	95.6
McAllen-Edinburg-Mission, TX MSA	95.6	88.2	95.8	93.9	89.7	91.3	101.9
Memphis, TN-AR-MS MSA	93.2	97.5	90.4	80.5	99.6	96.4	94.3
Miami, FL PMSA	106.7	105.7	107.6	100.1	113.0	105.7	106.6
Minneapolis-St. Paul, MN-WI MSA	103.1	100.0	97.5	100.6	112.9	125.6	103.1
Mobile, Al MSA	93.6	100.0	82.1	104.1	95.4	85.9	98.6
Monroe, LA MSA	99.3	93.5	85.3	144.5	98.9	92.0	104.6
Montgomery AL MSA	100.5	95.7	96.2	100.0	99.5	92.9	108.2
Muncie, IN MSA	96.1	96.3	96.2	94.2	96.6	94.9	94.7
Myrtle Beach, SC MSA	97.2	101.0	96.7	106.1	95.4	92.6	95.1
Nashville, TN MSA	96.8	103.2	94.6	97.1	98.2	93.8	95.8
Nassau-Suffolk, NY PMSA	143.4	124.4	171.4	156.7	121.4	165.8	127.5
New Haven-Meriden, CT PMSA	126.0	115.6	147.8	158.0	117.5	123.6	107.6
New Orleans, LA MSA	94.3	97.7	84.4	134.8	96.9	75.9	94.0
New York, NY PMSA	237.7	144.4	478.8	175.1	124.0	187.1	133.7
Odessa-Midland, TX MSA	90.7	89.7	79.3	82.6	100.3	93.8	99.6
Oklahoma City, OK MSA	91.8	91.1	80.3	96.3	94.8	92.1	99.9
Omaha, NE-IA MSA	92.5	95.9	91.0	94.0	99.2	89.2	90.5
Orlando, FL MSA	100.0	99.9	95.9	99.3	99.5	109.0	102.1
Panama City, FL MSA	95.8	94.2	99.3	89.0	92.0	99.5	95.6
Pensacola, FL MSA	93.9	104.1	78.6	87.0	94.5	109.2	100.7
Peoria-Pekin, IL MSA	103.8	99.1	104.4	95.0	106.0	101.9	107.3
Philadelphia, PA-NJ PMSA	123.6	107.9	142.7	167.9	120.1	105.5	108.5
Phoenix-Mesa, AZ MSA	103.6	104.6	101.0	105.3	114.3	114.4	100.1
Pocatello, ID MSA	93.6	100.5	89.7	74.7	96.6	99.6	96.2
Portland-Vancouver, OR-WA PMSA	107.3	101.6	119.9	76.2	115.0	122.0	102.1
Pueblo, CO MSA	92.2	108.9	81.5	77.7	94.8	108.3	93.1
Raleigh-Durham-Chapel Hill, NC MSA	104.1	101.0	113.0	109.2	97.0	105.1	98.6
Rapid City, SD MSA	100.8	102.4	97.8	100.8	98.4	96.6	103.9
Reading, PA MSA	105.5	101.9	105.3	120.3	96.9	89.9	109.1
Richland-Kennewick-Pasco, WA MSA	99.3	100.1	95.2	79.5	100.8	129.8	101.2
Richmond-Petersburg, VA MSA	103.9	99.5	104.2	125.8	106.7	107.6	99.0
Riverside-San Bernardino, CA PMSA	106.4	105.0	105.8	100.0	115.2	124.7	103.4
Roanoke, VA MSA	95.2	99.7	93.0	87.1	94.3	94.0	97.2
Rochester, MN MSA	101.2	95.6	99.9	97.6	110.3	99.3	103.8
Rockford, IL MSA	101.8	98.0	104.6	103.9	98.7	101.9	101.6
Salem, OR PMSA	102.0	94.3	108.3	74.2	107.5	118.5	102.7
Salinas, CA MSA	131.0	122.2	171.6	96.7	123.2	145.0	108.8
Salt Lake City-Ogden, UT MSA	99.5	107.0	95.0	79.3	109.1	103.1	101.2
San Angelo, TX MSA	91.9	88.2	78.5	85.4	102.8	93.5	103.4
San Antonio, TX MSA	92.6	92.9	88.5	89.6	93.6	95.1	96.0
Santa Barbara-Santa Maria-Lompoc, CA MSA	108.9	111.4	118.9	107.4	114.9	128.0	94.5
Santa Fe, NM MSA	113.7	107.4	134.5	91.7	113.4	105.8	106.1
Sarasota-Bradenton, FL MSA	105.9	98.5	120.2	92.7	99.4	105.4	102.5

See footnotes at end of table.

No. 775. Cost of Living Index—Selected Metropolitan Areas: Fourth Quarter 1997—Continued

[See headnote, page 493]

METROPOLITAN AREAS	Composite index (100%)	Grocery items (16%)	Housing (28%)	Utilities (8%)	Transportation (10%)	Health care (5%)	Misc. goods and services (33%)
Scranton-Wilkes Barre-Hazleton, PA MSA. .	99.7	100.3	100.5	113.9	98.9	88.7	97.6
Sheboygan, WI MSA	98.8	104.0	105.4	76.6	99.2	98.1	96.2
Sioux Falls, SD MSA	95.4	99.9	90.9	96.9	97.4	99.7	95.3
South Bend, IN MSA.	92.3	92.7	90.3	89.2	89.3	103.4	93.5
Spokane, WA MSA.	102.5	101.4	115.1	59.8	96.6	125.7	100.1
Springfield, MO MSA	93.3	96.1	87.3	83.2	96.7	96.7	97.8
St. Cloud, MN MSA	98.7	100.2	88.8	99.9	106.4	102.7	103.2
St. Joseph, MO MSA	94.1	92.9	93.4	81.4	90.3	101.8	98.1
St. Louis, MO-IL MSA	98.1	99.7	97.4	94.8	98.6	110.6	96.4
Sumter, SC MSA	91.4	94.6	74.0	112.3	96.0	92.1	98.2
Syracuse, NY MSA.	102.4	109.1	90.0	135.4	107.5	105.2	99.9
Tacoma, WA PMSA	99.4	101.9	101.9	70.1	107.4	142.6	93.0
Tallahassee, FL MSA	100.0	103.3	97.3	92.4	100.8	107.6	100.9
Tampa-St. Petersburg-Clearwater, FL MSA .	98.6	103.3	89.6	116.6	102.2	109.9	96.6
Toledo, OH MSA	101.8	101.6	91.1	128.4	106.9	100.7	103.3
Tucson, AZ MSA	98.7	107.2	93.6	116.5	94.3	107.1	94.4
Tulsa, OK MSA	92.8	95.9	83.2	92.0	83.2	103.2	100.5
Tyler, TX MSA	96.6	92.2	87.2	101.6	103.4	98.4	103.4
Utica-Rome, NY MSA	102.2	101.7	94.9	134.8	107.1	100.3	99.7
Victoria, TX MSA	93.4	82.9	88.0	103.3	110.0	93.0	96.3
Visalia-Tulare-Porterville, CA MSA	107.5	104.7	104.9	112.6	111.3	114.4	107.6
Waco, TX MSA	90.8	86.1	78.9	113.5	102.2	82.9	96.0
Washington, DC-MD-VA-WV PMSA	121.7	109.7	150.4	91.7	126.1	116.3	110.2
Wausau, WI MSA.	102.4	93.4	116.5	92.1	92.7	108.6	98.9
West Palm Beach-Boca Raton, FL MSA. . .	106.9	100.5	111.2	103.2	108.5	110.4	106.1
Wichita, KS MSA	96.6	91.6	88.3	111.6	99.7	108.3	99.4
Williamsport, PA MSA	101.8	95.5	106.0	135.8	95.7	91.9	96.4
Wilmington-Newark, DE-MD PMSA	111.3	110.9	119.1	128.7	99.6	106.0	104.8
Wilmington, NC MSA	101.6	98.7	108.5	116.7	93.0	97.5	96.6
Yakima, WA MSA.	103.8	102.6	117.2	87.9	104.8	132.5	91.3
York, PA MSA	96.6	96.6	86.6	112.0	108.9	92.1	98.7
Youngstown-Warren, OH MSA	96.5	99.7	97.9	118.3	89.5	88.6	91.7
Yuma, AZ MSA	107.8	106.2	105.0	144.1	115.5	112.2	99.3

Source: ACCRA, 4232 King St., Alexandria, VA 22302-1507, *ACCRA Cost of Living Index*, Fourth Quarter 1997 (copyright).

No. 776. Annual Percent Changes in Consumer Prices—United States and OECD Countries: 1990 to 1996

[Covers member countries of Organization for Economic Cooperation (OECD). For consumer price indexes for OECD countries, see Section 30]

COUNTRY	1990 [1]	1991	1992	1993	1994	1995	1996
United States	5.4	4.2	3.0	3.0	2.6	2.8	2.9
OECD	5.8	5.2	4.0	3.6	4.3	5.5	4.9
Australia	7.3	3.2	1.0	1.8	1.9	4.6	2.6
Canada	4.8	5.6	1.5	1.8	0.2	2.2	1.6
Japan	3.1	3.3	1.7	1.3	0.7	-0.1	0.1
New Zealand	6.1	2.6	1.0	1.3	1.8	3.8	2.3
Austria	3.3	3.3	4.0	3.6	3.0	2.2	1.9
Belgium	3.4	3.2	2.4	2.8	2.4	1.5	2.1
Denmark	2.7	2.4	2.1	1.3	2.0	2.1	2.1
Finland	6.1	4.3	2.9	2.2	1.1	1.0	0.6
France	3.4	3.2	2.4	2.1	1.7	1.7	2.0
Germany	2.7	3.5	4.0	3.6	2.7	1.8	1.5
Greece	20.4	19.5	15.9	14.4	10.9	8.9	8.2
Ireland	3.3	3.2	3.1	1.4	2.3	2.5	1.7
Italy [2]	6.1	6.5	5.3	4.2	3.9	5.4	3.8
Luxembourg	3.7	3.1	3.2	3.6	2.2	1.9	1.4
Netherlands	2.5	3.9	3.2	2.6	2.8	1.9	2.1
Norway	4.1	3.4	2.3	2.3	1.4	2.5	1.3
Portugal [3]	13.4	11.4	8.9	6.5	5.2	4.1	3.1
Spain	6.7	5.9	5.9	4.6	4.7	4.7	3.6
Sweden	10.5	9.3	2.3	4.6	2.4	2.9	0.8
Switzerland	5.4	5.8	4.0	3.3	0.9	1.8	0.8
Turkey [3]	60.3	66.0	70.1	66.1	105.1	89.1	80.4
United Kingdom	9.5	5.9	3.7	1.6	2.5	3.4	2.4

[1] Change from 1989. [2] Households of wage and salary earners. [3] Excludes rent.

Source: Organization for Economic Cooperation and Development, Paris, France, *Main Economic Indicators*, monthly (copyright).

No. 777. Producer Price Indexes, by Stage of Processing: 1960 to 1997

[1982=100. Minus sign (-) indicates decline. See text, Section 15]

YEAR	CRUDE MATERIALS				Inter-mediate materials, supplies, and compon-ents	FINISHED GOODS		CONSUMER FOODS		Finished consumer goods excl. food
	Total	Food-stuffs and feedstuffs	Fuel	Crude nonfood materials except fuel		Con-sumer goods	Capital equip-ment	Crude	Proc-essed	
1960	30.4	38.4	10.5	26.9	30.8	33.6	32.8	39.8	35.2	33.5
1961	30.2	37.9	10.5	27.2	30.6	33.6	32.9	38.0	35.3	33.4
1962	30.5	38.6	10.4	27.1	30.6	33.7	33.0	38.4	35.6	33.4
1963	29.9	37.5	10.5	26.7	30.7	33.5	33.1	37.8	35.2	33.4
1964	29.6	36.6	10.5	27.2	30.8	33.6	33.4	38.9	35.2	33.3
1965	31.1	39.2	10.6	27.7	31.2	34.2	33.8	39.0	36.8	33.6
1966	33.1	42.7	10.9	28.3	32.0	35.4	34.6	41.5	39.2	34.1
1967	31.3	40.3	11.3	26.5	32.2	35.6	35.8	39.6	38.8	34.7
1968	31.8	40.9	11.5	27.1	33.0	36.5	37.0	42.5	40.0	35.5
1969	33.9	44.1	12.0	28.4	34.1	37.9	38.3	45.9	42.3	36.3
1970	35.2	45.2	13.8	29.1	35.4	39.1	40.1	46.0	43.9	37.4
1971	36.0	46.1	15.7	29.4	36.8	40.2	41.7	45.8	44.7	38.7
1972	39.9	51.5	16.8	32.3	38.2	41.5	42.8	48.0	47.2	39.4
1973	54.5	72.6	18.6	42.9	42.4	46.0	44.2	63.6	55.8	41.2
1974	61.4	76.4	24.8	54.5	52.5	53.1	50.5	71.6	63.9	48.2
1975	61.6	77.4	30.6	50.0	58.0	58.2	58.2	71.7	70.3	53.2
1976	63.4	76.8	34.5	54.9	60.9	60.4	62.1	76.7	69.0	56.5
1977	65.5	77.5	42.0	56.3	64.9	64.3	66.1	79.5	72.7	60.6
1978	73.4	87.3	48.2	61.9	69.5	69.4	71.3	85.8	79.4	64.9
1979	85.9	100.0	57.3	75.5	78.4	77.5	77.5	92.3	86.8	73.5
1980	95.3	104.6	69.4	91.8	90.3	88.6	85.8	93.9	92.3	87.1
1981	103.0	103.9	84.8	109.8	98.6	96.6	94.6	104.4	97.2	96.1
1982	100.0	100.0	100.0	100.0	100.0	100.0	100.0	100.0	100.0	100.0
1983	101.3	101.8	105.1	98.8	100.6	101.3	102.8	102.4	100.9	101.2
1984	103.5	104.7	105.1	101.0	103.1	103.3	105.2	111.4	104.9	102.2
1985	95.8	94.8	102.7	94.3	102.7	103.8	107.5	102.9	104.8	103.3
1986	87.7	93.2	92.2	76.0	99.1	101.4	109.7	105.6	107.4	98.5
1987	93.7	96.2	84.1	88.5	101.5	103.6	111.7	107.1	109.6	100.7
1988	96.0	106.1	82.1	85.9	107.1	106.2	114.3	109.8	112.7	103.1
1989	103.1	111.2	85.3	95.8	112.0	112.1	118.8	119.6	118.6	108.9
1990	108.9	113.1	84.8	107.3	114.5	118.2	122.9	123.0	124.4	115.3
1991	101.2	105.5	82.9	97.5	114.4	120.5	126.7	119.3	124.4	118.7
1992	100.4	105.1	84.0	94.2	114.7	121.7	129.1	107.6	124.4	120.8
1993	102.4	108.4	87.1	94.1	116.2	123.0	131.4	114.4	126.5	121.7
1994	101.8	106.5	82.4	97.0	118.5	123.3	134.1	111.3	127.9	121.6
1995	102.7	105.8	72.1	105.8	124.9	125.6	136.7	118.8	129.8	124.0
1996	113.8	121.5	92.6	105.7	125.7	129.5	138.3	129.2	133.8	127.6
1997 prel .	111.1	112.2	101.3	103.5	125.6	130.2	138.2	126.6	135.1	128.2
PERCENT CHANGE										
1960	-2.3	-1.0	1.0	3.7	-	0.9	0.3	6.7	1.4	0.6
1961	-0.7	-1.3	-	-4.3	-0.6	-	0.3	-4.5	0.3	-0.3
1962	1.0	1.8	-1.0	1.1	-	0.3	0.3	1.1	0.8	-
1963	-2.0	-2.8	1.0	-0.4	0.3	-0.6	0.3	-1.6	-1.1	-
1964	-1.0	-2.4	-	-1.5	0.3	0.3	0.9	2.9	-	-0.3
1965	5.1	7.1	1.0	1.9	1.3	1.8	1.2	0.3	4.5	0.9
1966	6.4	8.9	2.8	1.8	2.6	3.5	2.4	6.4	6.5	1.5
1967	-5.4	-5.6	3.7	2.2	0.6	0.6	3.5	-4.6	-1.0	1.8
1968	1.6	1.5	1.8	-6.4	2.5	2.5	3.4	7.3	3.1	2.3
1969	6.6	7.8	4.3	2.3	3.3	3.8	3.5	8.0	5.7	2.3
1970	3.8	2.5	15.0	4.8	3.8	3.2	4.7	0.2	3.8	3.0
1971	2.3	2.0	13.8	2.5	4.0	2.8	4.0	-0.4	1.8	3.5
1972	10.8	11.7	7.0	1.0	3.8	3.2	2.6	4.8	5.6	1.8
1973	36.6	41.0	10.7	9.9	11.0	10.8	3.3	32.5	18.2	4.6
1974	12.7	5.2	33.3	32.8	23.8	15.4	14.3	12.6	14.5	17.0
1975	0.3	1.3	23.4	27.0	10.5	9.6	15.2	0.1	10.0	10.4
1976	2.9	-0.8	12.7	-8.3	5.0	3.8	6.7	7.0	-1.8	6.2
1977	3.3	0.9	21.7	9.8	6.5	6.5	6.4	3.7	5.4	7.3
1978	12.1	12.6	14.8	2.6	7.1	7.9	7.9	7.9	9.2	7.1
1979	17.0	14.5	18.9	9.9	12.8	11.7	8.7	7.6	9.3	13.3
1980	10.9	4.6	21.1	22.0	15.2	14.3	10.7	1.7	6.3	18.5
1981	8.1	-0.7	22.2	21.6	9.2	9.0	10.3	11.2	5.3	10.3
1982	-2.9	-3.8	17.9	19.6	1.4	3.5	5.7	-4.2	2.9	4.1
1983	1.3	1.8	5.1	-8.9	0.6	1.3	2.8	2.4	0.9	1.2
1984	2.2	2.8	-	-1.2	2.5	2.0	2.3	8.8	4.0	1.0
1985	-7.4	-9.5	-2.3	2.2	-0.4	0.5	2.2	-7.6	-0.1	1.1
1986	-8.5	-1.7	-10.2	-6.6	-3.5	-2.3	2.0	2.6	2.5	-4.6
1987	6.8	3.2	-8.8	-19.4	2.4	2.2	1.8	1.4	2.0	2.2
1988	2.5	10.3	-2.4	16.4	5.5	2.5	2.3	2.5	2.8	2.4
1989	7.4	4.8	3.9	-2.9	4.6	5.6	3.9	8.9	5.2	5.6
1990	5.6	1.7	-0.6	11.5	2.2	5.4	3.5	2.8	4.9	5.9
1991	-7.1	-6.7	-2.2	12.0	-0.1	1.9	3.1	-3.0	-	2.9
1992	-0.8	-0.4	1.3	-9.1	0.3	1.0	1.9	-9.8	-	1.8
1993	2.0	3.1	3.7	-3.4	1.3	1.1	1.8	6.3	1.7	0.7
1994	-0.6	-1.8	-5.4	-0.1	2.0	0.2	2.1	-2.7	1.1	-0.1
1995	0.9	-0.7	-12.5	3.1	5.4	1.9	1.9	6.7	1.5	2.0
1996	10.8	14.8	28.4	-0.1	0.6	3.1	1.2	8.8	3.1	2.9
1997 prel..	-2.4	-7.7	9.4	-2.1	-0.1	0.5	-0.1	-2.0	1.0	0.5

- Represents or rounds to zero.
Source: U.S. Bureau of Labor Statistics, Producer Price Indexes, monthly and annual.

No. 778. Producer Price Indexes for Selected Commodity Groupings: 1990 to 1997

[1982=100, except as indicated]

COMMODITY	1990	1991	1992	1993	1994	1995	1996	1997
All commodities	**116.3**	**116.5**	**117.2**	**118.9**	**120.4**	**124.7**	**127.7**	**127.6**
Fresh fruits and melons	118.1	129.9	84.0	84.5	82.7	85.8	100.8	99.4
Fresh and dry vegetables	118.1	103.8	115.0	135.2	129.0	144.4	135.0	123.1
Wheat	87.6	79.4	98.5	98.4	104.8	118.6	136.6	108.2
Slaughter cattle	122.5	115.8	115.4	116.7	105.8	99.5	95.8	97.9
Slaughter hogs	94.1	82.7	70.7	76.1	65.9	70.2	88.6	87.0
Slaughter turkeys	116.9	109.5	106.6	113.1	119.6	120.3	121.5	112.9
Wool	89.6	69.4	81.6	56.5	80.5	99.6	78.1	91.9
Milk eligible for fluid use	101.6	90.0	96.7	94.6	96.3	94.1	108.5	98.1
Milk, manufacturing grade	97.5	87.9	94.3	93.3	94.3	92.9	105.7	95.3
Alfalfa hay	169.2	135.7	124.5	167.8	194.6	164.3	172.5	203.9
Oilseeds	112.1	106.4	107.5	115.9	117.4	112.6	139.4	140.8
Bakery products	141.0	146.6	152.5	156.6	160.0	164.3	169.8	173.9
Flour and flour base mixes and doughs	107.9	103.8	115.0	112.0	113.8	120.8	130.6	122.3
Milled rice	102.5	109.9	108.8	101.3	118.3	113.1	129.4	127.3
Meats	117.0	113.5	106.7	110.6	104.7	102.9	109.0	111.6
Processed poultry	113.6	109.9	109.0	111.7	114.7	114.2	119.7	117.4
Unprocessed and packaged fish	147.2	149.5	156.1	156.5	161.4	170.8	165.9	178.1
Fluid milk products	123.9	121.2	123.9	122.7	125.3	124.9	138.1	135.7
Butter	71.3	69.5	59.3	54.4	50.4	55.4	71.0	76.6
Natural, processed, and imitation cheese	111.7	107.6	111.0	111.6	111.9	112.6	122.1	116.6
Ice cream and frozen desserts	123.1	123.1	124.9	127.2	127.4	128.2	132.6	137.9
Dry, condensed, and evaporated milk products	118.5	117.0	128.0	132.3	134.3	133.6	142.1	139.2
Canned fruits and juices	127.0	128.6	134.5	126.2	125.9	129.4	137.5	137.6
Frozen fruits, juices and ades	139.0	116.3	125.9	110.7	111.9	115.9	123.9	117.2
Dried and dehydrated fruits	106.7	111.8	114.6	117.9	121.0	121.0	124.1	124.9
Frozen vegetables	118.4	117.6	116.4	120.9	125.9	124.2	125.4	125.8
Sugar and confectionery	123.1	128.4	127.7	127.9	132.5	134.0	137.5	137.5
Alcoholic beverages	117.2	123.7	126.1	126.0	124.8	128.5	132.8	135.1
Soft drinks	122.3	125.5	125.6	126.2	127.0	133.1	134.0	133.2
Packaged beverage materials	115.7	111.5	105.1	105.2	127.2	142.4	127.6	147.9
Animal fats and oils	93.4	93.7	92.9	100.0	110.8	132.4	140.1	148.2
Crude vegetable oils	115.8	103.0	97.1	110.5	135.0	130.0	118.1	116.6
Shortening and cooking oil	123.2	116.5	115.1	122.9	138.6	142.5	138.5	137.8
Jams, jellies, and preserves	122.2	126.5	126.4	125.9	127.1	128.9	129.8	129.1
Pickles and pickle products	139.5	148.6	153.5	158.0	162.8	164.7	172.0	172.5
Processed eggs	121.0	117.1	94.7	108.2	104.7	101.3	126.4	122.6
Frozen specialties	131.9	134.4	135.7	136.3	137.6	138.7	141.1	142.6
Vegetable cake and meal feeds	85.4	83.1	86.0	92.0	85.6	79.6	116.4	127.9
Formula feeds	110.2	109.4	111.3	113.5	116.5	115.5	143.2	133.3
Apparel	117.5	119.6	122.2	123.2	123.5	124.2	125.1	125.7
Cattle hides	217.8	173.4	171.4	180.2	200.9	209.9	186.5	196.1
Men's footwear, excluding athletic	132.8	136.9	140.5	142.8	144.7	150.1	152.4	156.4
Women's footwear, excluding athletic	118.8	120.7	124.2	126.9	127.2	129.0	132.1	132.2
Children's footwear, except athletic	130.2	135.5	132.9	137.7	138.8	140.6	142.0	144.0
Luggage and small leather goods	126.7	130.5	133.2	134.4	133.4	133.4	133.8	135.8
Bituminous coal	97.4	97.1	94.9	96.0	96.6	94.9	94.4	96.2
Natural gas (to pipelines)	80.4	79.1	80.6	84.7	78.8	66.6	91.2	101.7
Commercial electric power	115.3	122.3	124.4	127.2	128.8	131.7	131.6	131.7
Industrial electric power	119.6	128.1	129.6	130.6	129.2	130.8	131.6	130.8
Gasoline	78.7	69.9	68.1	63.9	61.7	63.7	72.8	71.9
Light fuel oils	73.5	65.2	61.6	59.8	55.9	56.6	69.3	64.3
Residual fuels	57.7	49.1	45.9	49.6	48.2	52.6	59.8	59.5
Prepared paint	124.8	129.9	131.6	133.2	135.3	142.1	147.2	152.1
Paint materials	136.3	135.8	131.1	131.5	132.1	139.4	141.3	141.5
Medicinal and botanical chemicals	102.2	109.0	111.3	120.7	125.4	128.3	128.6	133.4
Preparations, ethical (prescription)	200.8	217.5	231.7	242.2	250.0	257.0	265.4	273.5
Mixed fertilizers	103.3	105.2	102.6	99.0	105.7	111.1	114.7	113.6
Fertilizer materials	95.2	99.0	94.5	90.7	103.7	119.0	123.5	120.7
Soap and synthetic detergents	117.7	117.5	120.6	122.2	121.4	122.9	125.2	126.4
Cosmetics and other toilet preparations	121.6	124.6	126.7	129.1	128.7	129.0	130.2	130.6
Rubber, except natural rubber	111.2	105.5	103.3	105.3	108.4	125.5	121.5	118.7
Tires, tubes, tread, & repair materials	96.8	98.2	98.9	98.9	98.6	100.2	97.0	95.2
Plastic construction products	117.2	115.1	112.7	116.6	122.9	133.8	130.9	128.2
Softwood lumber	123.8	125.7	148.6	193.0	198.1	178.5	189.5	206.5
Hardwood lumber	131.0	128.5	140.7	163.3	168.3	167.0	163.9	174.1
Prefabricated structural members	122.3	122.4	132.7	159.7	169.3	163.5	167.5	177.8
Softwood plywood	119.6	120.8	147.2	169.7	176.8	188.1	173.7	175.5
Hardwood plywood and related products	102.7	102.8	106.9	115.4	122.3	122.2	124.9	127.1
Boxes	119.1	123.6	127.5	138.2	141.3	145.0	147.1	149.2
Woodpulp	151.3	119.2	118.9	104.2	115.9	183.2	133.1	128.6
Wastepaper	138.9	121.4	117.5	117.4	209.5	371.1	141.6	163.3
Paper	128.8	126.9	123.2	123.8	126.0	159.0	149.4	143.9
Paperboard	135.7	130.2	134.3	130.0	140.5	183.1	155.1	144.4
Converted paper and paperboard products	135.2	134.8	134.8	133.7	136.7	157.0	153.4	148.4
Hardboard, particleboard & fiberboard prods	107.5	106.5	114.9	128.1	139.0	139.6	131.6	123.9
Iron ore	83.3	83.6	83.7	82.7	82.7	91.8	96.7	96.3
Iron and steel scrap	166.0	147.6	139.2	172.5	192.9	202.7	191.1	188.9
Foundry and forge shop products	117.2	119.0	120.1	121.3	123.9	129.3	132.6	134.1
Steel mill products	114.5	112.1	109.5	106.4	108.2	113.4	115.6	116.4
Primary nonferrous metals	149.2	133.4	114.0	108.1	118.1	138.7	126.2	126.2
Metal cans and can components	111.4	114.0	115.6	113.9	109.1	106.6	107.4	105.2
Hand and edge tools	127.7	134.8	141.6	146.1	149.1	152.6	160.9	163.2
Vitreous china fixtures	123.3	125.6	127.0	127.6	127.0	128.9	131.8	131.5

See footnotes at end of table.

No. 778. Producer Price Indexes for Selected Commodity Groupings: 1990 to 1997—Continued

[1982=100, except as indicated]

COMMODITY	1990	1991	1992	1993	1994	1995	1996	1997
Brass fittings	155.8	162.5	167.7	172.3	177.3	185.1	192.0	198.0
Steam and hot water equipment	132.6	135.2	138.0	138.9	138.6	141.6	144.7	147.2
Warm air furnaces	129.6	131.5	134.8	137.3	138.0	141.2	142.9	143.9
Conversion burners and parts	134.4	138.5	142.3	147.1	150.1	154.8	157.9	157.4
Water heaters, domestic	124.3	124.5	127.9	133.4	137.9	146.2	152.9	154.1
Metal doors, sash, and trim	131.4	134.6	135.0	136.6	142.0	156.5	159.3	161.0
Metal tanks	113.8	114.9	115.0	113.9	114.2	118.6	120.9	122.9
Sheet metal products	129.2	129.0	128.0	128.9	131.7	138.9	139.6	140.8
Struct., arch., pre-eng metal products	117.0	115.7	114.7	115.8	120.7	127.7	131.7	135.2
Bolts, nuts, screws, rivets, and washers	116.3	118.3	118.7	119.8	120.9	123.0	125.3	127.1
Lighting fixtures	127.5	129.8	131.0	131.2	132.2	135.9	137.3	137.4
Farm and garden tractors	123.2	128.1	133.4	135.3	138.3	141.5	144.8	146.0
Agricultural machinery excl. tractors	121.5	125.4	128.2	131.8	136.1	142.5	146.9	150.3
Agricultural equipment	119.2	121.3	124.0	129.9	132.1	140.5	143.3	142.3
Power cranes, excavators, and equipment	129.7	133.8	141.3	147.4	148.9	151.9	156.0	159.2
Construction equipment for mounting	119.9	121.3	121.8	125.0	126.1	130.1	133.5	140.5
Specialized construction machinery	124.3	129.1	128.4	129.6	135.5	138.2	140.6	(NA)
Portable air compressors	117.3	117.7	120.4	121.2	120.7	123.1	123.7	124.1
Tractors, other than farm	124.0	128.2	132.7	137.0	140.3	143.1	146.5	148.5
Power driven hand tools	121.1	124.5	127.2	129.5	132.9	135.1	137.0	138.1
Welding machines and equipment	127.5	132.8	137.7	142.5	147.8	153.0	157.4	160.7
Industrial process furnaces and ovens	127.3	131.0	134.2	137.1	139.1	141.9	146.7	(NA)
Cutting tools and accessories	118.5	121.5	123.9	125.8	128.1	131.9	135.1	136.9
Abrasive products	122.3	126.6	130.5	132.4	135.1	138.2	141.3	142.7
Metal cutting machine tools	129.8	134.6	138.9	141.1	143.1	148.0	152.6	156.0
Metal forming machine tools	128.7	133.5	135.9	138.4	141.9	145.7	149.6	153.9
Pumps, compressors, and equipment	119.2	124.6	129.1	132.8	135.2	139.4	143.5	146.5
Elevators, escalators, and other lifts	110.1	108.7	109.4	110.7	112.4	113.0	113.7	114.8
Industrial material handling equipment	115.0	117.4	118.4	120.2	122.4	125.3	127.4	129.7
Mechanical power transmission equipment	125.3	129.1	132.1	136.2	140.5	146.9	151.5	(NA)
Scales and balances	109.1	109.4	105.1	105.6	106.7	108.9	111.5	(NA)
Fans and blowers, except portable	123.7	127.2	129.1	131.8	134.2	138.9	142.4	(NA)
Electronic computers (Dec. 1990=100)	(NA)	88.9	73.2	62.9	58.0	51.8	42.4	33.2
Computer storage devices (Dec. 1992=100)	(NA)	(NA)	(NA)	86.8	74.9	65.7	55.2	47.5
Computer terminals and parts (Dec. 1993=100)	(NA)	(NA)	(NA)	(NA)	99.8	96.6	95.9	95.6
Computer peripheral equipment and parts (Dec. 1993=100)	(NA)	(NA)	(NA)	(NA)	97.5	95.2	91.6	88.5
Food products machinery	133.4	139.3	143.8	147.3	152.6	157.5	161.1	165.4
Textile machinery and equipment	128.8	135.0	138.9	143.7	144.9	146.7	148.4	152.1
Woodworking machinery and equipment	122.1	124.5	128.4	132.8	133.4	137.1	141.9	143.9
Printing trades machinery and equipment	124.9	126.5	126.8	129.5	130.9	133.6	136.8	138.8
Wiring devices	132.2	133.9	134.8	138.6	141.5	147.2	151.2	154.0
Integrating and measuring instruments	126.7	131.0	134.3	136.6	138.9	143.3	143.4	144.7
Motors, generators, motor generator sets	132.9	134.9	136.6	138.6	140.2	143.9	145.6	144.7
Transformers and power regulators	120.9	123.9	123.5	123.0	125.3	128.9	129.7	129.5
Switchgear, switchboard, etc., equipment	124.4	128.5	131.5	134.6	136.8	140.3	142.6	145.6
Communication and related equipment	106.1	107.4	107.9	109.1	110.8	112.1	113.0	114.0
Electric lamps/bulbs and parts	130.7	131.9	132.0	134.8	135.0	137.3	136.7	140.0
Electronic components and accessories	118.4	118.6	117.5	117.7	116.6	113.6	108.9	104.0
Mining machinery and equipment	121.0	125.2	127.4	129.5	131.1	135.6	139.0	140.3
Office and store machines and equipment	109.5	109.8	111.0	111.0	111.3	111.5	112.0	112.4
Internal combustion engines	120.2	126.0	128.4	130.2	132.9	135.6	138.8	140.1
Major appliances	108.7	108.3	108.2	109.6	109.5	108.9	109.3	106.7
Electric housewares and fans	109.7	111.8	112.6	113.4	112.0	110.8	110.6	107.9
Electric lamps	133.0	133.5	134.1	138.6	140.4	142.7	143.9	146.0
Television receivers	78.9	78.9	77.1	74.5	74.3	72.2	71.9	69.4
Household glassware	132.5	136.0	141.6	142.9	147.4	153.2	157.3	161.3
Lawn/garden equipment excl., garden tractors	123.0	124.7	125.3	126.2	128.4	130.4	132.3	132.2
Cutlery, razors and razor blades	129.8	140.9	142.3	146.1	150.0	154.1	158.4	162.5
Flat glass	107.5	105.9	106.5	107.3	110.5	113.2	110.0	108.4
Construction sand/gravel/crushed stone	125.4	128.6	130.6	134.0	137.9	142.3	145.6	148.2
Ceramic floor and wall tile	132.5	131.1	132.6	133.5	135.5	138.0	138.3	138.4
Insulation materials	108.4	110.8	102.3	105.8	111.9	118.8	118.9	117.7
Motor vehicles	120.4	125.9	129.9	134.2	139.1	140.3	141.6	139.7
Truck and bus bodies	127.8	130.9	133.0	134.1	138.1	146.0	150.9	154.8
Truck trailers	110.8	112.1	115.1	118.2	122.2	131.7	130.7	130.3
Aircraft	136.2	145.2	152.0	155.8	160.9	167.7	172.8	175.0
Toys, games, and children's vehicles	118.1	120.2	121.4	121.5	122.4	124.3	125.3	125.2
Sporting and athletic goods	112.6	115.3	118.2	118.6	120.1	122.0	123.3	124.7
Small arms and ammunition	145.3	151.2	152.7	157.0	159.8	162.8	165.5	167.3
Caskets	127.4	132.6	135.9	141.9	147.2	153.5	158.6	163.3
Musical instruments	121.7	126.6	130.3	135.9	141.8	149.1	154.8	159.4
Jewelry and jewelry product	119.3	121.5	122.0	123.5	124.6	125.8	127.6	128.1
Watches, clocks and timing mechanisms	113.7	116.8	117.5	118.1	119.2	121.5	121.3	118.2
Phono records, compact discs, & audio tapes	105.1	107.4	108.1	106.9	106.9	108.6	105.1	102.6
Fire extinguishers	107.6	111.4	115.8	122.6	130.7	134.7	137.3	138.0

NA Not available.

Source: U.S. Bureau of Labor Statistics, *Producer Price Indexes*, monthly and annual.

No. 779. Producer Price Indexes for the Net Output of Selected Industries: 1990 to 1997

[Indexes are based on selling prices reported by establishments of all sizes by probability sampling. Industries selected by value added. N.e.c.= not elsewhere classified. See text, Section 27]

INDUSTRY	SIC code [1]	Index base	1990	1994	1995	1996	1997
Bituminous coal and lignite	1211	12/81	100.5	97.0	95.3	95.0	95.9
Coal Mining Services	1241	06/85	107.0	104.9	105.7	109.2	108.1
Crude petroleum and natural gas	1311	06/84	76.4	62.4	59.0	76.8	79.1
Natural gas liquids	1321	06/84	77.4	59.4	66.6	87.8	88.3
Drilling oil and gas wells	1381	12/85	91.3	103.2	104.2	115.1	143.7
Construction sand and gravel	1442	06/82	126.9	142.8	146.6	151.1	155.3
Industrial sand	1446	06/82	119.3	130.4	134.2	136.6	138.9
Potash, soda, and borate minerals	1474	12/84	116.4	113.0	113.7	121.2	117.4
Sausage and other prepared meats	2013	12/82	112.7	108.9	108.5	115.5	118.8
Poultry slaughtering and processing	2015	12/81	118.9	121.1	120.5	127.1	124.7
Creamery butter	2021	06/84	77.7	62.6	64.7	81.7	84.5
Natural and processed cheese	2022	06/81	110.3	110.3	110.8	119.6	115.7
Ice cream and frozen desserts	2024	06/83	122.2	125.1	125.8	130.5	135.1
Fluid milk	2026	12/82	121.4	123.7	123.3	134.3	133.6
Cereal breakfast foods	2043	12/83	145.2	164.8	169.4	174.5	168.2
Rice milling	2044	06/84	94.0	109.3	104.6	117.5	118.9
Blended and prepared flour	2045	06/85	112.5	115.1	115.6	120.1	121.9
Wet corn milling	2046	06/85	114.7	128.8	124.5	133.6	123.6
Cookies and crackers	2052	06/83	141.9	154.5	156.5	161.4	167.0
Raw cane sugar mills	2061	06/82	115.7	111.7	115.9	115.0	112.9
Cane sugar refining	2062	06/82	124.4	123.3	124.5	127.9	127.1
Beet sugar processing	2063	06/82	120.7	110.0	111.4	117.8	118.4
Candy and other confectionery products, and chewing gum	2064	06/83	122.9	135.7	137.8	143.8	146.2
Chocolate and cocoa products	2066	06/83	109.2	119.6	123.8	127.7	131.5
Processed nuts and seeds (salted/roasted/cooked/blanched/etc.)	2068	06/91	(NA)	106.3	111.8	114.3	114.8
Cottonseed oil mill products	2074	06/85	112.3	119.7	117.5	130.6	122.1
Soybean oil mill products	2075	12/79	84.4	91.9	87.7	98.6	103.2
Vegetable oil mills, n.e.c.	2076	12/85	139.2	121.2	117.5	123.3	125.6
Animal and marine fats and oils	2077	12/82	112.7	112.7	118.1	138.1	145.9
Shortening, cooking oils, and margarine	2079	12/81	124.2	140.8	144.2	140.0	137.7
Malt beverages	2082	06/82	115.2	119.9	124.0	127.7	128.0
Malt	2083	06/85	113.4	103.8	116.0	135.0	122.6
Wines, brandy and brandy spirits	2084	12/83	113.1	119.8	120.6	126.3	135.8
Distilled spirits, except brandy	2085	06/83	121.4	140.4	145.0	149.1	152.0
Canned and cured seafoods	2091	12/84	122.8	116.7	120.4	113.7	113.6
Fresh or frozen packaged fish	2092	12/82	129.4	140.8	149.4	140.0	145.2
Coffee	2095	06/81	120.0	134.7	152.6	138.7	161.8
Potato and corn chips, and similar snacks	2096	06/91	(NA)	103.4	104.3	106.5	109.4
Macaroni, spaghetti, and noodles	2098	06/85	113.1	127.3	125.0	127.4	125.5
Cigarettes	2111	12/82	197.6	198.9	204.3	210.5	223.3
Cigars	2121	12/82	141.4	172.9	186.5	201.8	228.5
Chewing and smoking tobacco and snuff	2131	12/82	166.2	229.5	243.6	253.8	265.3
Cotton broadwoven fabric	2211	12/80	109.3	113.5	118.6	119.1	118.5
Manmade fiber and silk broadwoven fabric	2221	06/81	115.6	109.9	112.4	113.0	115.0
Carpet and rugs	2273	06/90	(NA)	100.7	102.2	104.4	105.9
Hardwood dimension and flooring	2426	06/84	117.2	145.4	146.5	144.1	153.6
Millwork	2431	06/83	120.4	152.8	152.1	153.6	156.4
Wood kitchen cabinets	2434	06/84	120.4	139.1	144.3	147.3	150.4
Hardwood veneer and plywood	2435	06/85	113.1	133.5	137.3	137.8	139.8
Softwood plywood	2436	12/80	102.5	152.9	158.0	139.5	142.4
Mobile homes	2451	06/81	122.5	142.1	151.0	155.3	157.8
Prefabricated wood buildings and components	2452	12/84	114.3	148.0	155.0	158.1	163.8
Wood preserving	2491	06/85	110.9	142.1	146.2	153.3	162.9
Reconstituted wood products	2493	06/91	(NA)	125.2	125.9	119.2	112.8
Upholstered wood household furniture	2512	06/82	121.5	129.7	132.9	136.3	138.1
Metal household furniture	2514	06/84	114.4	121.8	125.3	128.4	130.3
Mattresses and bedsprings	2515	06/83	121.2	131.9	133.6	134.7	135.9
Wood television, radio, phonograph and sewing machine cabinets	2517	12/85	104.6	108.6	108.8	110.1	114.1
Sanitary Paper Products	2676	06/83	130.0	142.5	149.5	150.3	147.8
Envelopes	2677	12/84	114.4	108.5	125.9	124.6	124.0
Stationery products	2678	06/85	122.0	119.5	156.5	143.1	136.5
Newspaper publishing	2711	12/79	220.4	269.5	286.7	306.9	317.7
Periodical publishing	2721	12/79	205.7	239.1	246.3	253.2	263.2
Book Publishing	2731	12/80	175.2	202.8	214.3	224.7	232.1
Book printing	2732	12/83	125.0	140.7	147.6	147.7	145.8
Typesetting	2791	06/85	109.9	116.6	117.8	118.8	119.5
Platemaking services	2796	12/85	107.4	110.7	111.6	112.7	112.8
Toilet preparations	2844	03/80	153.2	166.5	167.1	168.5	168.9
Paints and Allied Products	2851	06/83	125.0	136.0	143.1	147.4	152.1
Petroleum Refining	2911	06/85	90.1	72.2	74.5	85.3	83.1
Men's footwear	3143	12/80	142.0	154.6	160.4	162.7	166.2
Women's footwear	3144	12/80	117.1	127.0	128.6	131.6	131.9
Flat glass	3211	12/80	109.2	113.0	116.6	108.9	104.0
Glass containers	3221	06/82	118.6	125.4	128.3	126.9	123.6
Hydraulic cement	3241	06/82	102.7	118.7	127.2	132.9	138.1
Ceramic wall and floor tile	3253	06/85	112.3	114.7	116.5	116.3	116.0

See footnotes at end of table.

No. 779. Producer Price Indexes for the Net Output of Selected Industries: 1990 to 1997—Continued

[Indexes are based on selling prices reported by establishments of all sizes by probability sampling. Industries selected by value added. N.e.c.= not elsewhere classified. See text, Section 27]

INDUSTRY	SIC code [1]	Index base	1990	1994	1995	1996	1997
Clay refractories	3255	12/85	111.6	118.9	121.2	125.2	127.7
Lime	3274	12/85	107.8	110.4	112.3	115.8	117.7
Gypsum products	3275	06/81	102.3	128.0	145.1	144.5	159.1
Cut stone and stone products	3281	12/84	122.7	131.7	134.0	135.8	138.4
Abrasive products	3291	12/80	141.3	159.5	162.2	165.1	166.5
Primary copper	3331	06/80	152.4	145.9	194.4	144.8	137.3
Primary aluminum	3334	06/80	122.3	108.9	144.6	121.8	128.1
Metal cans	3411	06/81	116.6	110.8	118.7	112.0	110.4
Cutlery	3421	12/83	122.1	141.1	145.0	146.8	149.9
Metal sanitary ware	3431	12/80	138.1	150.2	157.0	162.8	163.7
Iron and steel forgings	3462	12/83	107.3	108.8	112.8	114.6	116.1
Construction machinery	3531	12/80	137.6	153.8	157.2	161.6	164.4
Mining machinery and equipment	3532	06/81	128.1	138.8	143.5	147.6	149.3
Electronic computers	3571	12/90	(NA)	53.8	45.2	36.5	
Computer storage devices	3572	12/92	(NA)	60.1	53.8	45.2	36.5
Computer Terminals	3575	12/93	(NA)	76.8	67.2	57.6	51.1
Calculating and accounting machines	3578	06/85	92.6	90.9	90.3	86.8	88.3
Office machines, not elsewhere classified	3579	06/85	109.4	112.5	115.6	116.1	117.2
Automatic merchandising machines	3581	06/82	116.1	118.2	118.6	123.0	123.9
Commercial laundry equipment	3582	12/82	134.0	149.2	156.6	162.6	165.4
Household cooking equipment and parts	3631	06/81	110.7	114.1	114.2	114.3	113.2
Household refrigerators and freezers	3632	12/81	112.8	115.6	115.5	116.4	112.6
Household laundry equipment	3633	12/79	137.6	135.7	135.5	136.8	132.6
Electric housewares and fans	3634	12/82	109.7	114.2	112.8	112.4	109.8
Household vacuum cleaners	3635	12/82	114.7	123.6	124.0	124.6	112.6
Phonograph records and prerecorded audio tapes and disks	3652	12/84	101.4	100.5	102.0	99.2	97.7
Telephone & telegraph apparatus	3661	12/85	112.0	116.9	118.2	119.7	119.4
Electron tubes, all types	3671	12/85	109.4	114.6	117.2	117.3	116.8
Printed circuit boards	3672	06/91	(NA)	95.0	95.1	95.9	95.0
Semiconductors and related devices	3674	06/81	105.0	97.1	91.3	84.8	76.7
Electronic capacitors	3675	06/81	101.0	100.5	101.9	104.6	103.6
Electronic resistors	3676	12/80	134.1	163.8	166.2	175.6	176.9
Electronic coils, transformers, and other inductors	3677	06/82	124.5	132.0	133.6	135.9	137.5
Connectors for electronic applications	3678	12/80	134.5	150.1	151.1	154.3	155.4
Storage batteries	3691	12/84	114.6	107.6	111.8	115.4	115.2
Motor vehicles and passenger car bodies	3711	06/82	119.9	138.0	139.1	140.4	138.7
Truck and bus bodies	3713	12/82	125.4	136.8	145.5	149.9	153.5
Motor vehicle parts and accessories	3714	12/82	108.9	112.0	113.5	114.0	113.1
Truck trailers	3715	12/79	125.6	138.6	148.6	147.8	147.7
Motor homes built on purchased chassis	3716	06/84	125.8	134.5	137.8	141.6	143.1
Aircraft	3721	12/85	116.0	132.9	137.3	140.5	142.3
Aircraft engines and engine parts	3724	12/85	112.6	129.0	130.9	133.4	134.8
Ship building and repairing	3731	12/85	114.0	126.8	127.6	130.1	133.3
Boat building and repairing	3732	12/81	136.0	150.2	154.6	159.6	165.0
Railroad equipment	3743	06/84	114.2	122.6	127.6	129.6	127.4

NA Not available. [1] Standard Industrial Classification code.
Source: U.S. Bureau of Labor Statistics, Producer Price Indexes, monthly.

No. 780. Chain-Type Price Indexes For Personal Consumption Expenditures (PCE): 1980 to 1997

[1992=100. For explanation of "chain-type," see text, Section 14]

ITEM	1980	1985	1990	1991	1993	1994	1995	1996	1997
Personal consumption expenditures	58.5	75.8	92.9	96.8	102.7	105.2	107.9	110.5	112.7
Durable goods	75.6	87.8	96.6	98.5	101.2	103.3	103.7	102.8	100.7
Motor vehicles and parts	68.3	83.2	93.8	97.1	103.3	107.2	111.0	113.0	113.0
Furniture and household equipment	92.0	100.9	101.5	100.9	98.6	98.6	96.7	93.7	90.3
Nondurable goods	65.3	78.7	94.6	98.1	101.5	102.8	104.5	107.2	109.2
Food	63.6	77.5	95.1	98.5	101.7	103.9	106.5	109.6	112.6
Clothing and shoes	72.5	81.6	94.5	97.9	101.0	100.3	98.9	98.8	99.8
Gasoline and oil	97.8	99.4	101.8	100.5	99.1	99.6	101.2	107.4	107.5
Fuel oil and coal	93.7	104.6	107.8	104.0	99.6	98.0	97.2	108.9	108.8
Services	51.0	71.6	91.2	95.8	103.6	106.9	110.5	113.8	117.0
Housing	52.4	73.9	93.5	97.1	102.8	105.7	109.0	112.4	115.8
Household operation	60.3	87.7	94.2	97.6	102.8	104.9	106.3	109.1	111.3
Electricity and gas	62.1	92.4	95.2	98.1	103.1	103.7	103.9	106.4	108.7
Other household operation	59.1	83.8	93.5	97.3	102.6	105.7	108.0	111.0	113.1
Transportation	56.0	71.1	89.9	95.4	104.3	106.3	109.7	112.2	116.6
Medical care	43.6	65.6	89.2	94.4	102.6	110.5	114.5	117.4	120.1
Other	51.8	69.3	90.2	95.3	102.2	105.4	110.1	113.7	117.5
Addenda:									
Price indexes for PCE:									
Food	63.6	77.5	95.1	98.5	101.7	103.9	106.5	109.6	112.6
Energy	80.8	96.5	98.9	99.5	101.0	101.5	102.3	107.0	108.1
PCE less food and energy	55.7	74.0	92.1	96.3	103.0	105.7	108.5	110.9	113.1

Source: U.S. Bureau of Economic Analysis, The National Income and Product Accounts of the United States, 1929-94, Vol. 2 and Survey of Current Business, August 1997 and May 1998.

No. 781. Chain-Type Price Indexes for Gross Domestic Product: 1990 to 1997

[1992=100. For explanation of "chain-type", see text, Section 14]

ITEM	1990	1991	1993	1994	1995	1996	1997
Gross domestic product	93.6	97.3	102.6	105.1	107.8	110.2	112.5
Personal consumption expenditures	92.9	96.8	102.7	105.2	107.9	110.5	112.7
Durable goods	96.6	98.5	101.2	103.3	104.3	103.8	102.2
Nondurable goods	94.6	98.1	101.5	102.8	104.5	107.2	109.2
Services	91.2	95.8	103.6	106.9	110.5	113.8	117.0
Gross private domestic investment	98.4	99.7	101.5	103.3	104.7	104.5	104.1
Fixed investment	98.2	99.6	101.5	103.4	104.8	104.7	104.5
Nonresidential	98.4	99.9	100.7	101.9	102.3	101.3	99.9
Structures	98.8	100.1	103.3	107.0	111.5	114.1	117.9
Producers' durable equipment	98.2	99.8	99.6	99.9	98.9	96.6	93.6
Residential	97.8	98.9	103.7	107.1	110.9	113.6	117.1
Exports of goods and services	98.7	100.3	100.1	101.2	103.4	101.6	99.4
Exports of goods	101.8	101.7	99.1	100.0	101.7	98.3	94.6
Exports of services	91.7	97.0	102.3	104.3	107.6	110.2	112.0
Imports of goods and services	100.4	100.0	98.8	99.4	101.6	99.4	95.5
Imports of goods	102.2	100.7	98.5	98.9	101.1	98.3	93.9
Imports of services	93.2	97.0	100.0	101.6	104.0	105.1	104.1
Government consumption expend [1]	94.1	97.5	102.5	104.9	108.3	111.8	114.5
Federal	92.9	96.9	102.5	104.8	108.3	112.0	114.7
National defense	92.9	96.5	101.8	103.6	106.8	111.0	113.6
Nondefense	92.8	98.0	104.3	107.7	111.9	114.5	117.4
State and local	94.9	97.9	102.5	104.9	108.2	111.7	114.3

[1] And gross investment.

Source: U.S. Bureau of Economic Analysis, *The National Income and Product Accounts of the United States, 1929-94,* Vol. 2; and *Survey of Current Business,* August 1997 and May 1998.

No. 782. Chain-Type Price Indexes—Annual Percent Change: 1990 to 1997

[1992=100. For explanation of "chain-type", see text, Section 14]

ITEM	1990	1991	1992	1993	1994	1995	1996	1997
Gross domestic product	4.4	3.9	2.8	2.6	2.4	2.5	2.3	2.0
Personal consumption expenditures	5.1	4.2	3.3	2.7	2.4	2.6	2.4	2.0
Durable goods	1.4	2.0	1.5	1.2	2.0	1.0	-0.4	-1.6
Nondurable goods	6.0	3.6	2.0	1.5	1.3	1.7	2.6	1.9
Services	5.4	5.0	4.4	3.6	3.1	3.5	2.9	2.9
Gross private domestic investment	2.4	1.4	0.3	1.5	1.8	1.4	-0.2	-0.4
Fixed investment	2.5	1.4	0.4	1.5	1.8	1.3	-0.1	-0.2
Nonresidential	2.4	1.5	0.1	0.7	1.2	0.4	-1.0	-1.4
Structures	3.3	1.3	-0.1	3.3	3.6	4.2	2.3	3.3
Producers' durable equipment	1.8	1.6	0.2	-0.4	0.3	-1.0	-2.3	-3.1
Residential	2.9	1.1	1.2	3.7	3.3	3.6	2.4	3.0
Exports of goods and services	0.8	1.6	-0.3	0.1	1.2	2.2	-1.8	-2.2
Exports of goods	-1.0	-0.1	-1.7	-0.9	0.8	1.8	-3.4	-3.7
Exports of services	5.8	5.8	3.1	2.3	2.0	3.2	2.4	1.7
Imports of goods and services	2.6	-0.3	0.0	-1.2	0.6	2.2	-2.2	-3.9
Imports of goods	1.8	-1.4	-0.7	-1.5	0.5	2.2	-2.8	-4.5
Imports of services	6.5	4.1	3.1	0.0	1.6	2.4	1.1	-1.0
Gov't consumption expends and gross	4.3	3.6	2.6	2.5	2.3	3.3	3.3	2.4
Federal	3.5	4.3	3.2	2.5	2.3	3.3	3.4	2.4
National defense	3.5	3.8	3.7	1.8	1.8	3.1	3.9	2.4
Nondefense	3.5	5.5	2.1	4.3	3.3	3.9	2.3	2.5
State and local	4.9	3.1	2.2	2.5	2.3	3.2	3.2	2.3

Source: U.S. Bureau of Economic Analysis, *National Income and Product Accounts of the Unites States, 1929-94, vol. 2;* and *Survey of Current Business,* August 1997 and May 1998.

No. 783. Commodity Research Bureau Futures Price Index: 1980 to 1997

[1967=100. Index computed daily. Represents unweighted geometric average of commodity futures prices (through 6 months forward) of 17 major commodity futures markets. Represents end of year index]

ITEM	1980	1985	1987	1988	1989	1990	1991	1992	1993	1994	1995	1996	1997
All commodities	308.5	229.2	232.5	251.8	229.9	222.6	208.0	205.9	212.4	229.7	237.1	247.9	229.1
Imported	426.0	398.2	356.1	365.2	271.7	276.0	264.4	232.4	246.9	352.3	354.4	322.2	408.7
Industrial	324.6	211.7	252.5	248.2	249.6	245.5	217.2	224.7	235.0	263.6	272.5	266.3	210.9
Grains	312.1	198.5	186.1	261.9	205.7	171.2	196.1	196.9	193.8	191.2	218.6	284.7	210.7
Oilseeds	314.6	245.4	223.6	309.6	254.2	223.6	195.4	218.8	239.8	259.9	277.5	307.9	(NA)
Livestock and meats	217.4	206.9	189.9	199.1	206.5	226.2	174.0	179.8	201.4	192.3	192.4	241.7	238.1
Metals (precious)	531.4	256.6	346.4	318.7	296.9	257.8	226.0	228.5	242.2	273.9	276.0	271.3	249.3

NA Not available.

Source: Bridge Commodity Research Bureau (CRB), Chicago, IL, *CRB Commodity Index Report,* weekly. (Copyright.)

No. 784. Indexes of Spot Primary Market Prices: 1980 to 1997

[1967=100. Computed weekly for 1980; daily thereafter. Represents unweighted geometric average of price quotations of 23 commodities; much more sensitive to changes in market conditions than is a monthly producer price index]

ITEMS AND NUMBER OF COMMODITIES	1980 (6-24)	1985 (5-21)	1988 (5-27)	1989 (5-26)	1990 (5-25)	1991 (5-28)	1992 (5-26)	1993 (5-23)	1994 (5-24)	1995 (5-23)	1996 (5-21)	1997 (5-26)
All commodities (23)	**265.1**	**251.4**	**270.3**	**281.3**	**279.2**	**235.3**	**242.3**	**237.7**	**261.5**	**290.6**	**297.7**	**271.8**
Foodstuffs (10).	260.9	248.1	230.1	222.5	231.5	197.7	201.3	208.3	215.5	229.1	251.3	227.3
Raw industrials (13)	268.0	253.6	302.0	329.0	317.0	265.2	275.5	260.4	299.2	348.2	334.9	307.5
Livestock and products (5)	250.5	284.5	316.1	285.2	306.9	286.6	276.4	291.3	296.9	314.6	338.4	306.1
Metals (5)	257.9	220.2	276.7	347.1	313.9	348.8	262.7	236.2	262.1	306.7	296.7	269.8
Textiles and fibers (4)	234.7	220.8	247.3	253.5	259.4	201.8	218.6	205.3	252.6	286.0	274.6	261.5
Fats and oils (4)	229.5	273.1	230.4	208.1	193.3	185.0	180.7	190.1	209.6	228.3	245.7	257.1

Source: Bridge Commodity Research Bureau, Chicago, IL, *CRB Commodity Index Report,* weekly (copyright).

No. 785. Average Prices of Selected Fuels and Electricity: 1980 to 1997

[In dollars per unit, except electricity, in cents per kWh. Represents price to end-users, except as noted]

ITEM	Unit [1]	1980	1985	1990	1991	1992	1993	1994	1995	1996	1997
Crude oil, composite [2]. . .	Barrel	28.07	26.75	22.22	19.06	18.43	16.41	15.59	17.23	20.71	19.08
Motor gasoline: [3]											
Unleaded regular	Gallon.	1.25	1.20	1.16	1.14	1.13	1.11	1.11	1.15	1.23	1.23
Unleaded premium . . .	Gallon.	(NA)	1.34	1.35	1.32	1.32	1.30	1.31	1.34	1.41	1.42
No. 2 heating oil.	Gallon.	0.79	0.85	0.73	0.67	0.63	0.60	0.57	0.56	0.67	0.64
No. 2 diesel fuel.	Gallon.	0.82	0.79	0.73	0.65	0.62	0.60	0.55	0.56	0.68	0.64
Residual fuel oil.	Gallon.	0.61	0.61	0.44	0.34	0.34	0.34	0.35	0.39	0.46	0.42
Natural gas, residential . .	1,000 cu/ft . .	3.68	6.12	5.80	5.82	5.89	6.16	6.41	6.06	6.34	6.93
Electricity, residential. . . .	kWh	5.4	7.4	7.8	8.0	8.2	8.3	8.4	8.4	8.4	8.5

NA Not available. [1] See headnote. [2] Refiner acquisition cost. [3] Average, all service.

Source: U.S. Energy Information Administration, *Monthly Energy Review.*

No. 786. Weekly Food Cost: 1990 and 1997

[In dollars. Assumes that food for all meals and snacks is purchased at the store and prepared at home. See source for details on estimation procedures]

FAMILY TYPE	DECEMBER 1990				NOVEMBER 1997			
	Thrifty plan	Low-cost plan	Moderate-cost plan	Liberal plan	Thrifty plan	Low-cost plan	Moderate-cost plan	Liberal plan
FAMILIES								
Family of two:								
20-50 years.	48.10	60.60	74.70	92.70	57.20	72.30	89.30	111.10
51 years and over	45.60	58.30	71.80	85.80	53.70	69.50	86.00	103.10
Family of four:								
Couple, 20-50 years and children—								
1-2 and 3-5 years	70.10	87.30	106.60	131.00	83.00	104.00	127.30	156.70
6-8 and 9-11 years	80.10	102.60	128.30	154.40	95.50	122.50	152.90	184.30
INDIVIDUALS [1]								
Child:								
1-2 years	12.70	15.40	18.00	21.80	14.90	18.30	21.40	26.00
3-5 years	13.70	16.80	20.70	24.90	16.10	20.00	24.70	29.70
6-8 years	16.60	22.20	27.90	32.50	19.90	26.60	33.10	38.60
9-11 years	19.80	25.30	32.50	37.60	23.60	30.20	38.60	44.70
Male:								
12-14 years.	20.60	28.60	35.70	42.00	24.50	34.10	42.30	49.80
15-19 years.	21.40	29.60	36.80	42.60	25.30	35.20	43.80	50.60
20-50 years.	22.90	29.30	36.60	44.30	27.30	35.00	43.80	53.00
51 years and over	20.90	27.90	34.30	41.10	24.60	33.40	41.20	49.40
Female:								
12-19 years.	20.80	24.80	30.10	36.30	24.40	29.40	35.70	43.10
20-50 years.	20.80	25.80	31.30	40.00	24.70	30.70	37.40	48.00
51 years and over	20.60	25.10	31.00	36.90	24.20	29.80	37.00	44.30

[1] The costs given are for individuals in four-person families. For individuals in other size families, the following adjustments are suggested: one-person, add 20 percent; two-person, add 10 percent; three-person, add 5 percent; five- or six-person, subtract 5 percent; seven- (or more) person, subtract 10 percent.

Source: U.S. Dept. of Agriculture, Agricultural Research Service, unpublished data.

No. 787. Food—Retail Prices of Selected Items: 1990 to 1997

[In dollars per pound, except as indicated. As of December]

FOOD	1990	1992	1993	1994	1995	1996	1997
Cereals and bakery products:							
Flour, white, all purpose	0.24	0.23	0.22	0.23	0.24	0.30	0.28
Rice, white, lg. grain, raw	0.49	0.53	0.50	0.53	0.55	0.55	0.58
Spaghetti and macaroni	0.85	0.86	0.84	0.87	0.88	0.84	0.88
Bread, white, pan	0.70	0.74	0.76	0.75	0.84	0.87	0.88
Meats, poultry, fish and eggs:							
Ground chuck, 100% beef	2.02	1.91	1.91	1.84	1.85	1.85	1.81
Rib roast, USDA Choice	4.54	4.69	4.73	4.88	4.81	5.09	5.21
Round steak, USDA Choice	3.42	3.34	3.32	3.24	3.20	3.22	3.09
Sirloin steak, bone-in	3.65	3.75	3.69	(NA)	(NA)	(NA)	(NA)
T-bone steak	5.45	5.39	5.77	5.86	5.92	5.87	6.07
Pork:							
Bacon, sliced	2.28	1.86	2.02	1.89	2.17	2.64	2.61
Chops, center cut, bone-in	3.32	3.15	3.24	3.03	3.29	3.44	3.39
Shoulder picnic, bone-in, smoked	1.41	1.18	1.19	1.13	1.17	1.31	1.29
Sausage	2.42	2.14	1.99	1.85	1.92	2.15	2.08
Poultry:							
Chicken, fresh, whole	0.86	0.88	0.91	0.90	0.94	1.00	1.00
Chicken breast, bone-in	2.00	2.08	2.17	1.91	1.95	2.09	1.99
Chicken legs, bone-in	1.17	1.14	1.13	1.12	1.20	1.26	1.22
Turkey, frozen, whole	0.96	0.93	0.95	0.98	0.99	1.02	0.98
Eggs, grade A, large, (dozen)	1.00	0.93	0.87	0.87	1.16	1.31	1.17
Dairy products:							
Milk, fresh, whole, fortified (1/2 gal.)	1.39	1.39	1.43	1.44	1.48	1.65	1.61
Butter, salted, grade AA, stick	1.92	1.64	1.61	1.54	1.73	2.17	2.46
Ice cream, prepack., bulk,reg.(1/2 gal.)	2.54	2.49	2.59	2.62	2.68	2.94	3.02
Fresh fruits and vegetables:							
Apples, red delicious	0.77	0.76	0.78	0.72	0.83	0.89	0.90
Bananas	0.43	0.40	0.41	0.46	0.45	0.48	0.46
Oranges, navel.	0.56	0.52	0.56	0.55	0.64	0.59	0.58
Grapefruit	0.56	0.52	0.50	0.47	0.49	0.55	0.53
Lemons.	0.97	0.90	1.05	1.04	1.12	1.14	1.06
Pears, anjou	0.79	0.80	0.89	(NA)	(NA)	1.06	0.85
Potatoes, white	0.32	0.31	0.36	0.34	0.38	0.33	0.37
Lettuce, iceberg	0.58	0.66	0.53	0.91	0.61	0.62	0.70
Tomatoes, field grown	0.86	1.23	1.31	1.43	1.51	1.21	1.62
Cabbage.	0.39	0.38	0.37	0.45	0.41	0.40	0.46
Carrots, short trimmed and topped	0.44	0.44	0.41	0.48	0.53	0.54	0.50
Celery.	0.49	0.48	0.49	0.52	0.54	0.44	0.57
Cucumbers	0.56	0.51	0.93	0.69	0.53	0.60	0.58
Processed fruits and vegetables:							
Orange juice, frozen concentrate, 12 oz. can, per 16 oz. . . .	2.02	1.70	1.67	1.55	1.57	1.73	1.67
Potatoes, frozen, french fried	0.85	0.86	0.87	0.84	0.86	0.90	0.95

NA Not available.

Source: U.S. Bureau of Labor Statistics, *CPI Detailed Report, CPI Detailed Report,* January issues.

No. 788. Average Price of Energy in Selected Metropolitan Areas: 1997

[In dollars per unit shown. As of January. One therm contains approximately 100 cubic feet of natural gas. See Appendix II]

CITY/MSA	Utility (piped) gas (100 therms)	Electricity (500 kWh)	Fuel oil No. 2 (gallon)	GASOLINE All types [1]	Unleaded regular	Unleaded premium
U.S. city average	**70.47**	**48.13**	**0.98**	**1.24**	**1.18**	**1.36**
Baltimore, MD MSA	71.65	47.76	1.11	1.24	1.18	1.33
Boston-Lawrence-Salem, MA-NH CMSA	96.81	63.09	0.99	1.27	1.23	1.39
Chicago-Gary-Lake County, IL-IN-WI CMSA	62.74	58.57	(NA)	1.27	1.21	1.40
Cleveland-Akron-Lorain, OH CMSA	62.66	59.97	(NA)	1.10	1.05	1.22
Dallas-Fort Worth, TX CMSA	59.71	45.47	(NA)	1.16	1.10	1.29
Detroit-Ann Arbor, MI CMSA	53.13	47.32	(NA)	1.13	1.09	1.29
Houston-Galveston-Brazoria, TX CMSA	56.50	40.75	(NA)	1.15	1.09	1.26
Los Angeles-Anaheim-Riverside, CA CMSA	84.89	63.95	(NA)	1.40	1.34	1.52
Miami-Fort Lauderdale, FL CMSA	111.85	43.59	(NA)	1.27	1.20	1.38
New York-N. NJ-Long Island, NY-NJ-CT CMSA	85.96	71.91	1.08	1.30	1.23	1.42
Philadelphia-Wilmington-Trenton, PA-NJ-DE-MD CMSA. .	83.53	62.83	0.90	1.27	1.14	1.33
Pittsburgh-Beaver Valley, PA CMSA.	79.61	52.87	0.81	1.23	1.17	1.37
St. Louis-East St. Louis, MO-IL CMSA	65.86	37.07	(NA)	1.09	1.05	1.25
San Francisco-Oakland-San Jose, CA CMSA	74.82	61.08	(NA)	1.44	1.37	1.60
Washington-Baltimore, DC-MD-VA-WVA	86.29	40.62	1.16	1.26	1.20	1.36

NA Not available.   [1] Includes types of gasoline not shown separately.

Source: U.S. Bureau of Labor Statistics, *CPI Detailed Report,* January issues.

No. 789. Import Price Indexes—Selected Commodities: 1990 to 1997

[1995=100. Indexes are weighted by the 1990 Tariff Schedule of the United States Annotated, a scheme for describing and reporting product composition and value of U.S. imports. Import prices are based on U.S. dollar prices paid by importer. F.o.b. = Free on board; c.i.f. = Cost, insurance, and freight; n.e.s.=Not elsewhere specified]

COMMODITY	1990 [1]	1991	1992	1993	1994	1995	1996	1997
All commodities....................	90.3	92.8	94.3	94.4	95.8	100.8	100.1	98.2
Food and live animals................	84.9	88.1	84.3	87.0	93.9	100.1	94.7	103.7
Meat........................	116.3	122.8	110.4	115.6	105.9	99.1	90.4	101.9
Fish........................	77.9	86.7	86.9	86.9	97.6	101.6	97.5	103.6
Crustaceans; fresh, chilled, frozen, salted or dried..	73.3	80.7	79.3	80.1	97.7	103.4	95.0	103.5
Beverages and tobacco................	86.1	96.1	98.4	97.7	98.2	99.7	103.6	107.5
Beverages.....................	86.4	96.0	97.9	98.2	98.1	99.9	101.4	104.0
Crude materials.....................	82.4	77.5	77.5	77.1	86.3	99.8	94.3	97.4
Crude rubber....................	65.3	63.6	65.1	66.5	68.6	101.3	90.7	83.9
Cork and wood..................	72.5	76.2	82.7	92.2	113.2	92.7	113.6	122.5
Pulp and waste paper	91.5	70.4	66.2	56.7	62.4	103.2	62.1	65.8
Metalliferous ores and metal scrap.........	94.7	88.0	85.7	83.0	84.2	100.0	101.7	105.8
Mineral fuels and related products...........	92.9	105.8	110.1	101.6	96.9	105.1	110.6	104.6
Crude petroleum and petroleum products	91.7	105.5	110.4	100.8	96.4	105.4	111.0	104.0
Crude petroleum	88.4	107.7	116.2	101.4	97.4	104.5	111.2	103.7
Natural gas....................	112.7	111.1	105.5	113.8	105.4	101.2	108.2	113.3
Chemicals and related products	88.3	90.3	91.2	92.1	92.0	100.7	98.8	96.4
Organic chemicals..................	96.7	97.1	95.4	93.2	93.8	99.2	98.4	95.8
Intermediate manufactured products	88.8	88.6	88.8	88.6	90.2	99.8	99.2	96.8
Rubber manufactures	95.1	95.9	97.2	99.0	97.6	100.1	100.2	97.6
Cork and wood manufactures...........	83.9	82.4	90.3	100.8	105.7	99.7	101.3	99.0
Paper and paperboard products	79.9	80.4	75.0	77.0	76.1	99.6	100.9	87.5
Textiles......................	86.8	90.6	93.2	95.0	95.7	101.0	100.1	100.5
Nonmetallic mineral manufactures	89.5	92.7	94.7	96.8	97.4	99.9	101.5	102.6
Iron and steel...................	91.5	91.2	89.6	90.2	91.0	99.6	97.7	96.3
Nonferrous metals.................	93.7	84.5	84.2	72.8	81.0	98.6	93.8	95.1
Silver, platinum and other platinum group metals...	125.4	120.8	101.2	92.6	100.2	104.5	96.2	103.8
Aluminum....................	84.1	73.1	73.6	67.4	76.4	99.5	90.2	93.1
Manufactures of metals, n.e.s...........	89.7	91.8	93.5	94.8	94.9	100.5	100.4	99.0
Machinery and transport equipment.........	90.2	92.8	94.5	95.9	97.6	100.6	98.6	95.7
Machinery specialized for particular industries	84.1	87.9	91.0	92.9	94.7	101.1	101.1	99.3
Metalworking machinery..............	82.3	83.9	86.7	89.9	91.9	102.1	101.3	98.3
General industrial machinery, parts, n.e.s.......	84.4	87.7	90.6	92.4	94.1	100.7	100.5	98.3
Computer equipment and office machines	119.2	116.1	114.2	109.7	104.0	100.4	91.7	81.2
Computer equipment	143.0	138.2	131.7	121.9	109.1	99.7	93.0	80.8
Telecommunications [2]	102.0	99.6	99.0	99.9	99.2	100.5	97.3	93.4
Electrical machinery and equipment	92.0	93.7	95.2	96.9	98.9	101.6	95.5	90.2
Electronic valves, diodes, transistors & integr. cir. ...	93.3	94.6	94.5	99.1	102.7	102.9	89.3	78.3
Road vehicles	84.3	88.7	90.4	92.8	96.6	100.0	100.4	100.8
Miscellaneous manufactured articles	92.1	93.7	96.6	97.9	98.2	100.4	100.7	100.2
Plumbing, heating & lighting fixtures.........	95.3	94.9	98.2	98.8	96.4	100.4	99.5	96.2
Furniture and parts................	93.7	95.7	97.7	98.4	98.2	100.7	100.8	102.9
Articles of apparel and clothing	97.6	95.9	98.8	99.2	99.2	100.1	101.5	102.6
Footwear.....................	97.2	99.1	100.7	99.4	98.4	100.0	101.3	101.1
Prof., scientific & contrlng instr & appratus, n.e.s.....	83.5	87.5	89.4	94.7	96.8	100.5	99.3	97.1
Photographic apparatus [3]	86.1	88.0	90.4	93.9	95.9	101.4	97.4	94.4
Miscellaneous manufactured articles, n.e.s........	88.8	92.3	96.1	98.1	98.3	100.3	100.9	99.4

[1] June 1990 may not equal 100 because indexes were reweighted to an "average" trade value in 1990.   [2] Includes sound recording and reproducing equipment.   [3] Includes photographic supplies, optical goods, watches, and clocks.

Source: U.S. Bureau of Labor Statistics, News, U.S. Import and Export Price Indexes, monthly.

No. 790. Export Price Indexes—Selected Commodities: 1990 to 1997

[1995=100. Indexes are weighted by 1980 export values according to the Schedule B classification system of the U.S. Bureau of the Census. Prices used in these indexes were collected from a sample of U.S. manufacturers of exports and are factory transaction prices, except as noted. F.a.s. = free alongside ship. N.e.s. = not elsewhere specified. F.o.b. = free on board]

COMMODITY	1990 [1]	1991	1992	1993	1994	1995	1996	1997
All commodities....................	91.5	92.5	92.8	93.2	94.8	100.5	101.4	99.3
Food and live animals...................	89.0	86.0	87.8	83.5	88.7	97.4	122.0	98.5
Meat..........................	84.9	87.9	91.5	96.2	92.5	99.9	101.6	95.3
Fish.........................	83.6	80.4	83.3	82.0	83.3	103.2	89.4	85.3
Cereals and cereal preparations	90.6	80.7	87.4	75.7	84.9	95.4	145.6	92.3
Wheat........................	80.4	65.4	77.7	67.4	65.4	91.1	129.3	87.1
Maize........................	97.6	87.8	91.8	78.8	94.9	98	165.3	90.4
Fruits and vegetables	83.6	99.5	82.0	84.4	89.8	96.2	105.7	101.6
Feeding stuff for animals	93.2	95.5	97.6	96.2	101.4	98.3	122.5	127.2
Miscellaneous food products...............	100.4	100.9	100.6	100.8	98.3	101.3	103.2	103.5
Beverages and tobacco................	86.4	92.0	95.5	98.4	98.7	99.9	100.6	100.8
Tobacco and tobacco manufactures	86.6	92.1	95.5	98.3	98.6	100.0	100.6	100.9
Crude materials	80.4	76.3	74.7	79.6	86.4	104.1	90.3	93.4
Raw hides and skins	105.1	81.5	80.8	79.1	94.3	103.4	95.7	100.8
Oil seeds and oleaginous fruits	97.0	99.2	98.3	97.8	112.7	96.6	127.0	134.6
Cork and wood....................	66.4	63.7	71.7	105.1	97.3	102.1	94.7	93.2
Pulp and waste paper	64.7	56.0	53.4	45.4	61.1	111.6	56.8	65.9
Textile fibers......................	81.8	85.3	68.6	66.6	83.7	106.9	91.1	83.4
Cotton textile fibers	83.4	86.7	64.1	62.2	81.4	107.9	90.2	80.6
Crude fertilizers and minerals	101.9	102.9	101.5	96.7	97.3	99.4	96.8	97.8
Metalliferous ores and metal scrap.........	83.4	74.4	71.1	70.1	76.2	104.2	89.3	91.7
Ferrous waste and scrap	85.2	79.7	70.2	84.5	81.6	99.6	93.3	93.5
Nonferrous base metal waste and scrap	85.3	72.3	73.8	62.0	79.6	100.2	86.8	89.2
Mineral fuels and related materials	100.1	98.7	95.0	96.6	96.0	102.0	109.1	110.9
Coal, coke and briquettes.............	103.2	101.7	99.8	96.8	96.8	100.3	103.1	102.0
Crude petroleum and petroleum products	99.9	95.3	92.0	96.0	95.7	103.6	113.7	119.4
Animal and vegetable oils, fats and waxes	86.6	78.9	79.7	82.7	92.5	96.5	95.4	94.7
Chemicals and related products	85.6	87.5	85.5	84.4	86.9	102.6	97.1	96.5
Organic chemicals...................	81.7	81.4	78.8	77.9	79.8	106.8	87.8	84.9
Hydrocarbons, n.e.s. and derivatives, f.a.s.	82.9	67.7	69.1	71.2	82.0	115.7	90.8	95.0
Alcohols, phenols, phenol-alcohols, & deriv., f.a.s..	77.4	81.9	74.9	75.0	71.8	105.9	88.0	81.5
Chemical materials and products, n.e.s.	85.9	90.0	89.5	91.9	94.6	100.0	102.0	103.9
Intermediate manufactured products	86.9	87.1	87.6	87.7	90.9	100.8	97.9	98.2
Rubber manufactures	84.9	90.1	90.6	93.1	93.7	99.8	102.8	103.2
Paper and paperboard products	81.1	81.1	80.2	76.5	78.4	103.3	87.3	83.5
Textiles	89.7	93.7	95.1	96.2	96.1	101.1	103.8	103.3
Nonmetallic mineral manufactures	91.1	92.5	94.6	96.4	98.1	100.1	101.2	104.3
Nonferrous metals..................	88.4	77.7	77.5	71.7	81.6	99.7	93.4	93.4
Manufactures of metals, n.e.s...........	88.0	90.6	91.4	92.7	94.7	100.1	101.5	104.4
Machinery and transport equipment [2]	95.3	98.3	99.7	99.8	99.4	100.0	100.9	100.6
Power generating machinery [3]..........	86.5	90.7	94.9	95.9	97.7	99.4	104.3	106.0
Rotating electric plant and parts thereof, n.e.s.	89.2	91.2	93.7	95.0	96.2	100.4	102.4	103.1
Machinery specialized for particular industries	88.0	91.6	93.5	95.8	97.3	99.9	102.7	104.2
Agricultural machinery and parts [4]	90.3	92.2	94.6	96.8	98.7	100.3	102.0	102.8
Civil engineering and contractors, plant and equip.	87.6	92.1	90.4	93.5	97.1	100.2	101.5	103.1
Metalworking machinery.................	89.0	95.1	97.4	99.1	98.8	100.0	102.3	104.3
General industrial machines, parts, n.e.s.	89.2	92.7	94.9	96.8	98.4	99.4	102.5	105.2
Computer equipment and office machines	132.0	129.4	124.5	115.3	106.5	100.8	93.7	84.7
Computer equipment	148.1	144.4	138.7	123.2	111.0	101.5	90.1	79.1
Telecommunications [5]	94.1	100.0	101.8	102.9	100.9	100.3	101.1	99.6
Electrical machinery and equipment	96.8	97.4	100.3	100.2	99.9	100.7	99.1	96.5
Electronic valves, diodes, transistors & integr. cir. .	101.6	99.5	104.7	103.3	101.0	101.7	97.9	91.8
Road vehicles	92.1	94.7	96.2	97.3	98.4	99.8	101.0	101.8
Miscellaneous manufactured articles	91.7	96.5	98.3	99.0	99.1	99.9	100.8	101.7

[1] June 1990 may not equal 100 because indexes were reweighted to an "average" trade value in 1990.　[2] Excludes military and commercial aircraft.　[3] Includes equipment.　[4] Excludes tractors.　[5] Includes sound recording and reproducing equipment.

Source: U.S. Bureau of Labor Statistics, *News, U.S. Import and Export Price Indexes*, monthly.

No. 791. Refiner/Reseller Sales Price of Gasoline, by State: 1995 to 1997

[In cents per gallon. As of **March**. Represents all refinery and gas plant operators' sales through company-operated retail outlets. Gasoline prices exclude excise taxes]

STATE	Gasoline excise taxes 1997	AVERAGE, ALL GRADES			MIDGRADE			PREMIUM		
		1995	1996	1997	1995	1996	1997	1995	1996	1997
United States	(NA)	63.0	71.5	70.3	67.3	76.0	75.1	72.4	80.4	79.4
Alabama	18	61.3	69.5	67.5	64.2	72.7	70.3	69.1	77.3	75.7
Alaska	8	81.8	90.0	90.9	93.9	103.7	101.8	92.3	102.5	101.9
Arizona	18	70.2	80.3	78.4	73.2	85.6	85.2	81.0	91.1	90.0
Arkansas	19	58.7	67.7	66.2	61.9	70.7	68.8	66.0	75.4	73.5
California	19	68.1	78.0	79.0	71.4	81.1	84.2	79.2	87.7	90.3
Colorado	22	63.6	73.3	72.6	68.4	78.1	76.5	70.9	80.5	79.9
Connecticut	39	72.3	74.7	73.2	72.3	78.2	77.9	78.2	83.6	81.9
Delaware	23	67.4	73.5	71.6	69.6	76.1	74.7	76.0	81.7	80.5
District of Columbia . .	20	77.8	85.4	82.0	75.9	83.8	80.6	83.3	91.2	86.6
Florida	13	63.2	71.2	70.0	65.3	73.6	72.9	72.7	80.4	79.3
Georgia	8	60.5	68.2	66.2	62.9	70.8	69.0	68.3	76.0	74.0
Hawaii	16	96.7	103.7	101.9	98.8	106.7	106.1	104.9	112.7	111.6
Idaho	26	67.3	77.8	79.6	69.8	80.0	82.8	75.0	84.7	88.1
Illinois	20	63.0	73.8	70.9	71.6	82.8	78.4	74.2	84.0	81.6
Indiana	16	61.0	70.2	67.8	65.7	75.2	71.6	69.4	78.6	76.5
Iowa	20	59.5	70.2	68.8	66.8	75.9	72.5	66.3	76.8	75.2
Kansas	18	57.5	67.6	66.4	62.9	73.5	71.9	64.2	74.6	73.1
Kentucky	16	61.9	70.8	69.2	65.5	74.6	73.2	69.3	77.9	77.2
Louisiana	20	58.5	66.2	65.7	63.2	70.2	70.3	66.0	74.2	72.1
Maine	19	64.8	71.4	71.1	70.0	77.0	75.8	72.6	78.7	79.1
Maryland	24	69.2	77.0	73.7	71.2	79.1	76.2	77.2	85.0	81.0
Massachusetts	21	69.5	75.2	74.6	73.5	80.3	80.5	78.3	82.9	83.1
Michigan	16	61.2	71.8	68.4	65.2	76.0	72.5	69.3	79.9	76.8
Minnesota	20	62.6	72.6	71.6	68.0	78.7	74.3	69.5	79.7	78.2
Mississippi	18	58.1	66.4	65.5	61.8	70.1	69.8	66.1	74.2	73.6
Missouri	17	59.4	69.8	68.9	64.5	75.9	74.8	66.6	77.1	77.0
Montana	28	69.0	79.9	77.3	72.0	81.9	79.9	76.4	88.4	86.6
Nebraska	26	59.8	69.9	68.7	63.7	74.0	73.0	66.9	77.1	75.9
Nevada	24	66.9	78.6	78.1	70.3	82.6	81.8	77.1	88.0	87.3
New Hampshire	20	71.5	77.8	76.6	74.9	80.8	81.2	80.2	86.8	86.7
New Jersey	11	66.3	71.6	70.7	73.8	79.9	79.1	75.3	80.9	80.6
New Mexico	19	64.1	74.7	73.3	69.3	78.7	76.0	72.0	82.4	81.6
New York	22	67.8	74.3	74.4	72.3	79.5	79.4	78.4	84.5	83.7
North Carolina	23	60.2	68.5	67.3	62.6	70.9	70.1	68.0	76.2	75.2
North Dakota	20	62.2	72.5	70.4	68.3	77.7	75.8	71.6	81.6	79.1
Ohio	22	61.3	70.6	68.4	65.8	74.5	72.2	70.5	79.3	77.6
Oklahoma	17	56.0	65.5	64.4	63.2	72.8	70.7	63.7	72.9	71.4
Oregon	24	67.7	77.2	76.2	72.6	82.9	82.8	80.4	88.0	86.8
Pennsylvania	22	64.2	70.7	69.1	67.4	73.7	72.3	72.9	78.7	77.4
Rhode Island	29	66.0	73.3	72.6	70.0	76.7	77.4	75.4	81.7	81.6
South Carolina	17	60.5	68.5	66.7	62.6	71.3	69.4	68.7	76.8	74.8
South Dakota	20	62.2	72.6	70.9	67.5	77.0	73.3	70.3	80.4	79.0
Tennessee	21	60.3	68.9	67.4	62.7	71.3	70.5	67.8	76.5	75.2
Texas	20	57.8	65.3	63.8	63.9	71.4	69.9	66.2	73.7	72.3
Utah	19	67.6	77.3	79.3	70.2	79.9	82.0	73.9	83.3	85.8
Vermont	16	72.0	78.8	77.6	74.3	81.6	81.9	80.9	87.7	86.0
Virginia	18	63.8	71.6	69.4	66.1	73.9	72.0	72.2	80.0	77.3
Washington	23	69.9	79.8	77.2	75.0	84.6	82.4	82.0	90.7	88.4
West Virginia	21	65.3	73.6	71.3	68.1	76.4	74.3	73.8	81.9	79.8
Wisconsin	27	61.6	71.8	68.6	65.4	75.9	73.1	69.5	79.2	76.5
Wyoming	9	65.1	76.0	75.4	70.1	80.7	81.8	72.8	83.5	83.8

NA Not available.

Source: U.S. Energy Information Administration, *Petroleum Marketing Monthly*.

Figure 16.1
**Insured Commercial Banks—Income and
Financial Condition: 1980 to 1997**

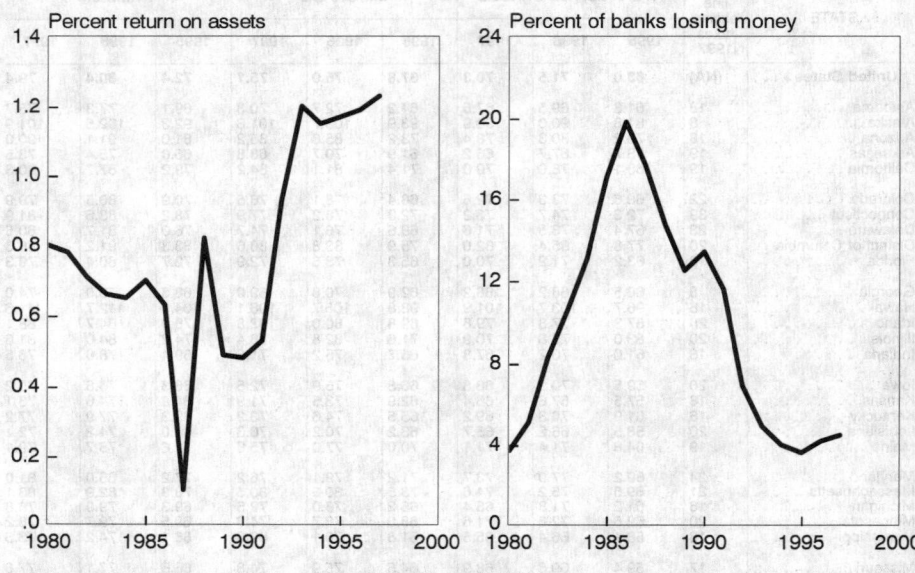

Source: Chart prepared by U.S. Bureau of the Census. For data, see Table 807.

Figure 16.2.
Mutual Fund Shares Holdings: 1997

Total $3.0 trillion

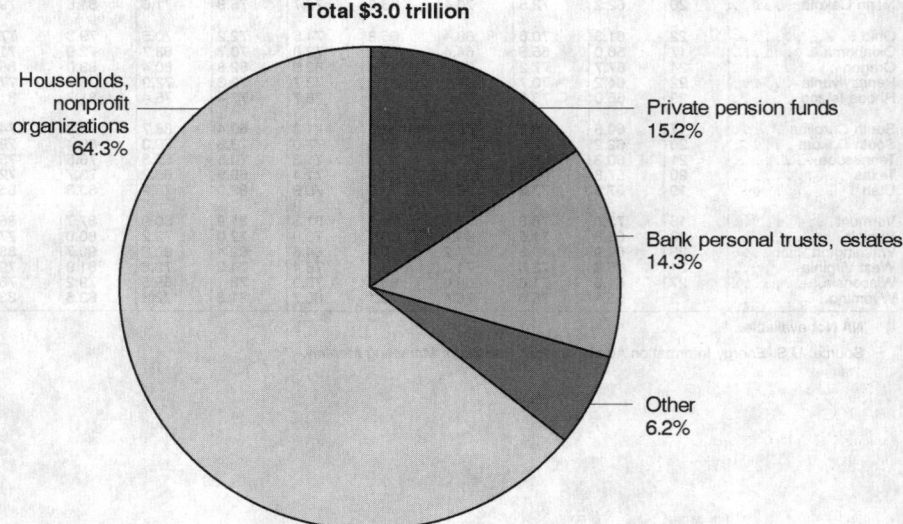

Households,
nonprofit
organizations
64.3%

Private pension funds
15.2%

Bank personal trusts, estates
14.3%

Other
6.2%

Source: Chart prepared by U.S. Bureau of the Census. For data, see Table 843.

Banking, Finance, and Insurance

This section presents data on the Nation's finances, various types of financial institutions, money and credit, securities, and insurance. The primary sources of these data are publications of several departments of the federal government, especially the Treasury Department, and independent agencies such as the Federal Deposit Insurance Corporation, the Federal Reserve System, and the Securities and Exchange Commission. National data on insurance are available primarily from private organizations, such as the American Council of Life Insurance.

In Brief

Conventional new-home mortgage rates:

1990	10.08%
1995	8.05%
1997	7.76%

Dow-Jones industrial average:

1990	2,634
1995	5,117
1997	7,908

Flow of funds—The flow of funds accounts of the Federal Reserve System (see Tables 794 to 797) bring together statistics on all of the major forms of financial instruments to present an economy-wide view of asset and liability relationships. In flow form, the accounts relate borrowing and lending to one another and to the non-financial activities that generate income and production. Each claim outstanding is included simultaneously as an asset of the lender and as a liability of the debtor. The accounts also indicate the balance between asset totals and liability totals over the economy as a whole. Several publications of the Board of Governors of the Federal Reserve System contain information on the flow of funds accounts: Summary data on flows and outstandings, in the *Federal Reserve Bulletin, Flow of Funds Accounts of the United States* (quarterly), and *Annual Statistical Digest;* and concepts and organization of the accounts, in *Guide to the Flow of Funds Accounts* (1993).

Banking system—Banks in this country are organized under the laws of both the states and the federal government and are regulated by several bank supervisory agencies. National banks are supervised by the Comptroller of the Currency. *Reports of Condition* have been collected from national banks since 1863. Summaries of these reports are published in the Comptroller's *Annual Report,* which also presents data on the structure of the national banking system.

The Federal Reserve System was established in 1913 to exercise central banking functions, some of which are shared with the U.S. Treasury. It includes national banks and such state banks that voluntarily join the system. Statements of state bank members are consolidated by the Board of Governors of the Federal Reserve System with data for national banks collected by the Comptroller of the Currency into totals for all member banks of the System. Balance sheet data for member banks and other commercial banks are published quarterly in the *Federal Reserve Bulletin.* The Federal Deposit Insurance Corporation (FDIC), established in 1933, insures each depositor up to $100,000. Major item balance sheet and income data for all commercial banks are published in the *FDIC Quarterly Banking Profile.* This publication is also available on the Internet at the following address: www.fdic.gov. Balance sheet and income data for individual institutions are also available at this site in the Institution Directory (ID) system.

The FDIC is the primary federal regulator of state-chartered banks that are not members of the Federal Reserve System and of most savings banks insured by the Bank Insurance Fund (BIF). The agency also has certain back-up supervisory authority, for safety and soundness purposes, over state-chartered banks that are members of the Federal Reserve System, national banks, and savings associations.

Savings institutions—Savings institutions are primarily involved in credit extension in the form of mortgage loans. Statistics on savings institutions are collected by the U.S. Office of Thrift Supervision and the FDIC. The Financial Institutions Reform, Recovery, and Enforcement Act of 1989 (FIRREA) authorized the establishment of the Resolution Trust Corporation (RTC) which was responsible for the disposal of assets from failed savings institutions. FIRREA gave the FDIC the job of managing the federal deposit insurance fund for savings institutions (SAIF=Savings Association Insurance Fund). Major balance sheet and income data for all insured savings institutions are published in the *FDIC Quarterly Banking Profile.*

Credit Unions—Federally chartered credit unions are under the supervision of the National Credit Union Administration. State-chartered credit unions are supervised by the respective state supervisory authorities. The Administration publishes comprehensive program and statistical information on all federal and federally insured state credit unions in the *Annual Report of the National Credit Union Administration.* Deposit insurance (up to $100,000 per account) is provided to members of all federal and those state credit unions that are federally-insured by the National Credit Union Share Insurance Fund. Deposit insurance for state chartered credit unions is also available in some states under private or state-administered insurance programs.

Other credit agencies—Insurance companies, finance companies dealing primarily in installment sales financing, and personal loan companies represent important sources of funds for the credit market. Statistics on loans, investments, cash, etc., of life insurance companies are published principally by the American Council of Life Insurance in its *Life Insurance Fact Book* and in the *Federal Reserve Bulletin.* Consumer credit data are published currently in the *Federal Reserve Bulletin.*

Government corporations and credit agencies make available credit of specified types or to specified groups of private borrowers, either by lending directly or by insuring or guaranteeing loans made by private lending institutions. Data on operations of government credit agencies, along with other government corporations, are available in reports of individual agencies; data on their debt outstanding are published in the *Federal Reserve Bulletin.*

Currency—Currency, including coin and paper money, represents about 40 percent of all media of exchange in the United States, with most payments made by check. All currency is now issued by the Federal Reserve Banks.

Securities—The Securities and Exchange Commission (SEC) was established in 1934 to protect the interests of the public and investors against malpractices in the securities and financial markets and to provide the fullest possible disclosure of information regarding securities to the investing public. Statistical data are published in the *SEC Annual Report.*

Insurance—Insuring companies, which are regulated by the various states or the District of Columbia, are classified as either life or property. Companies that underwrite accident and health insurance only and those that underwrite accident and health insurance in addition to one or more property lines are included with property insurance. Insuring companies, other than those classified as life, are permitted to underwrite one or more property lines provided they are so licensed and have the necessary capital or surplus.

There are a number of published sources for statistics on the various classes of insurance—life, health, fire, marine, and casualty. Organizations representing certain classes of insurers publish reports for these classes. Among them are the annual commercial publishers, such as The National Underwriter Company whose *Argus Health Chart* (annual) contains financial and operating data for individual health and accident insurance companies, including Blue Cross and Blue Shield Plans. The American Council of Life Insurance publishes statistics on life insurance purchases, ownership, benefit payments, and assets in its *Life Insurance Fact Book.*

No. 792. Gross Domestic Product in Finance, Insurance, and Real Estate, in Current and Real (1992) Dollars: 1990 to 1996

[In billions of dollars, except percent. For definition of gross domestic product, see text, Section 14. Based on 1987 Standard Industrial Classification]

INDUSTRY	CURRENT DOLLARS				CHAINED (1992) DOLLARS [1]			
	1990	1994	1995	1996	1990	1994	1995	1996
Finance, insurance, real estate, total	**1,024.1**	**1,267.6**	**1,361.3**	**1,448.5**	**1,109.0**	**1,196.9**	**1,231.1**	**1,258.5**
Percent of gross domestic product	17.8	18.2	18.7	19.0	18.1	18.1	18.3	18.2
Depository institutions	169.2	207.4	229.6	247.4	214.9	197.0	193.4	192.0
Nondepository institutions	21.5	36.1	39.0	49.9	25.6	33.9	32.6	35.4
Security and commodity brokers	39.7	78.5	79.5	90.0	41.2	83.0	81.9	92.2
Insurance carriers	69.3	108.8	126.5	136.6	70.2	91.3	105.1	110.1
Insurance agents, brokers, and services	37.1	45.0	47.1	50.4	40.8	41.6	42.1	43.6
Real estate	671.9	802.9	842.7	886.2	706.8	758.3	775.6	793.3
Nonfarm housing services	492.2	607.3	642.8	673.3	525.6	573.3	587.9	596.8
Other real estate	179.6	195.6	199.9	212.9	179.8	185.0	187.7	196.6
Holding and other investment offices	15.5	-11.1	-3.2	-12.0	12.3	12.9	12.6	12.6

[1] See text, Section 14.

Source: U.S. Bureau of Economic Analysis, *Survey of Current Business*, August 1997.

No. 793. Finance, Insurance, and Real Estate—Establishments, Employees, and Payroll: 1990 and 1995

[Covers establishments with payroll. Employees are for the week including March 12. Most government employees are excluded. For statement on methodology, see Appendix III]

KIND OF BUSINESS	1987 SIC code [1]	ESTABLISHMENTS (1,000)		EMPLOYEES (1,000)		PAYROLL (bil. dol.)	
		1990	1995	1990	1995	1990	1995
Finance, insurance, real estate	**(H)**	**544.7**	**628.5**	**6,957**	**6,998**	**197.4**	**256.2**
Depository institutions [2][3]	60	81.2	104.7	2,033	2,079	48.4	62.5
Central reserve depositories	601	0.1	0.1	31	25	0.9	1.0
Commercial banks	602	52.3	66.9	1,472	1,532	35.6	45.7
Savings institutions	603	21.7	16.6	417	268	8.8	7.4
Credit unions	606	3.6	15.1	51	158	1.0	3.5
Functions closely related to banking	609	2.8	5.3	44	61	1.4	2.1
Nondepository institutions [2][3]	61	42.0	45.4	506	490	14.0	18.4
Federal and fed.-sponsored credit	611	0.6	1.3	14	24	0.4	1.1
Personal credit institutions	614	25.0	17.9	236	161	5.5	5.4
Business credit institutions	615	3.7	4.8	88	101	3.1	4.4
Mortgage bankers and brokers	616	10.9	20.5	153	202	4.6	7.5
Security and commodity brokers [2]	62	25.2	41.0	411	523	26.6	45.5
Security brokers and dealers	621	15.9	24.3	308	382	20.8	34.4
Commodity contracts brokers, dealers	622	1.2	1.5	15	13	0.7	0.7
Security and commodity exchanges	623	0.2	0.1	9	8	0.5	0.4
Security and commodity services	628	7.1	14.8	76	120	4.5	9.9
Insurance carriers [2]	63	43.3	41.3	1,407	1,503	41.5	56.6
Life insurance	631	14.1	11.8	572	557	16.3	19.7
Medical service and health insurance [2]	632	2.1	3.0	188	271	5.1	9.6
Accident and health insurance	6321	1.1	1.1	48	52	1.3	1.7
Hospital and medical service plans	6324	1.0	1.9	139	219	3.8	8.0
Fire, marine, and casualty insurance	633	18.3	20.8	533	588	17.0	24.2
Surety insurance	635	0.6	0.6	15	11	0.5	0.5
Title insurance	636	3.2	2.5	57	39	1.6	1.4
Pension, health and welfare funds	637	3.8	2.3	25	35	0.6	1.0
Insurance agents, brokers, and service	64	110.8	125.4	712	677	20.3	22.8
Real estate	65	217.0	246.1	1,374	1,403	28.5	32.9
Real estate operators and lessors	651	95.7	100.2	509	492	8.7	9.6
Real estate agents and managers	653	72.2	115.4	585	743	13.3	18.8
Title abstract offices	654	3.1	4.8	24	34	0.5	0.9
Subdividers and developers [2]	655	19.6	17.6	140	119	3.4	3.2
Subdividers and developers, n.e.c. [4]	6552	10.8	10.3	88	69	2.3	2.2
Cemetery subdividers and developers	6553	4.4	6.1	35	46	0.6	0.9
Holding and other investment offices [2]	67	22.6	23.2	263	255	10.0	13.8
Holding offices	671	6.2	8.5	124	137	5.4	8.2
Investment offices	672	1.0	0.9	16	23	1.0	1.7
Trusts	673	7.8	5.2	65	35	1.4	1.0
Educational, religious, etc. trusts	6732	3.6	2.5	42	21	0.9	0.6
Miscellaneous investing	679	5.0	7.5	44	50	1.5	2.7
Patent owners and lessors	6794	0.9	1.4	15	16	0.4	0.7
Administrative and auxiliary	(X)	2.6	1.5	251	69	8.2	3.6

X Not applicable. [1] Standard Industrial Classification; see text, Section 13. [2] Includes industries not shown separately. [3] Includes government employees. [4] N.e.c.=Not elsewhere classified.

Source: U.S. Bureau of the Census, *County Business Patterns*, annual.

No. 794. Flow of Funds Accounts—Financial Assets of Financial and Nonfinancial Institutions, by Holder Sector: 1980 to 1997

[In billions of dollars. As of Dec. 31]

SECTOR	1980	1985	1990	1991	1992	1993	1994	1995	1996	1997
All sectors	14,067	24,023	36,601	39,759	42,131	45,648	47,821	53,620	59,446	67,226
Households [1]	6,557	10,096	14,852	16,434	17,310	18,412	19,059	21,528	23,795	27,109
Nonfinancial business	1,624	2,964	4,168	4,293	4,478	4,860	5,185	5,630	6,083	6,472
Farm business	24	33	47	50	53	57	60	63	65	70
Nonfarm noncorporate	145	435	486	479	492	514	558	592	620	652
Nonfinancial corporations	1,455	2,496	3,634	3,764	3,932	4,289	4,567	4,975	5,398	5,751
State and local government	301	645	963	1,020	1,034	1,083	1,026	976	983	1,028
U.S. government	229	372	440	498	474	489	437	438	438	438
U.S. govt.-sponsored enterprises	195	324	478	497	552	631	782	897	989	1,099
Federally-related mortgage pools	114	369	1,020	1,156	1,272	1,357	1,472	1,570	1,711	1,826
Monetary authorities	174	243	342	365	382	424	452	472	495	534
Commercial banking [2]	1,482	2,369	3,316	3,414	3,630	3,876	4,130	4,488	4,705	5,179
U.S.-chartered commercial banks	1,266	1,983	2,622	2,649	2,750	2,916	3,113	3,316	3,439	3,742
Foreign banking offices in U.S.	98	144	367	438	509	542	590	666	715	817
Nonbank finance	2,876	5,667	9,014	9,918	10,664	11,813	12,352	14,155	16,095	18,887
Funding corporations	16	135	250	278	338	329	368	373	483	572
Savings institutions	792	1,275	1,323	1,145	1,060	1,020	1,009	1,013	1,032	1,025
Credit unions	68	135	217	240	265	282	294	311	330	355
Life insurance	464	796	1,367	1,500	1,610	1,780	1,884	2,087	2,272	2,581
Other insurance	182	299	533	576	598	642	679	741	780	844
Private pension funds	504	1,207	1,572	1,860	1,959	2,193	2,292	2,657	3,037	3,578
State and local govt. retirement funds	197	399	920	1,032	1,168	1,256	1,294	1,518	1,715	2,100
Finance companies	197	338	547	560	556	557	600	672	715	759
Mortgage companies	16	25	49	60	60	60	36	33	41	48
Real estate investment trusts	3	8	13	14	14	17	22	26	27	31
Mutual funds	62	246	608	769	993	1,375	1,477	1,853	2,342	3,014
Closed-end investment funds	8	8	53	71	93	116	118	134	142	154
Money market funds	76	242	493	535	539	560	603	745	891	1,049
Security brokers, dealers	45	156	262	333	382	479	455	568	636	777
Asset-backed securities issuers	-	39	283	337	401	483	552	684	810	988
Bank personal trusts, estates	245	358	522	608	630	661	670	740	842	1,012
Rest of the world	516	974	2,009	2,163	2,336	2,705	2,905	3,466	4,152	4,654

- Represents zero.　[1] Includes nonprofit organizations.　[2] Includes other sectors not shown separately.

No. 795. Flow of Funds Accounts—Credit Market Debt Outstanding: 1980 to 1997

[In billions of dollars. As of Dec. 31. N.e.c.=Not elsewhere classified]

ITEM	1980	1985	1990	1991	1992	1993	1994	1995	1996	1997
Credit market debt	4,734	8,624	13,736	14,373	15,169	16,143	17,182	18,408	19,735	21,119
U.S. government	735	1,590	2,498	2,776	3,080	3,336	3,492	3,637	3,782	3,805
Nonfederal domestic nonfinancial	3,223	5,539	8,338	8,525	8,747	9,095	9,521	10,080	10,655	11,389
Households [1]	1,376	2,239	3,579	3,758	3,933	4,157	4,482	4,851	5,205	5,571
Corporations	910	1,606	2,481	2,423	2,464	2,520	2,658	2,869	3,042	3,283
Nonfarm noncorporate business	431	843	1,148	1,130	1,115	1,119	1,122	1,148	1,189	1,250
Farm business	161	173	135	135	135	138	142	145	150	156
State and local government	344	678	995	1,078	1,100	1,162	1,117	1,068	1,069	1,129
Rest of the world	197	237	286	301	316	386	372	443	513	559
Financial sectors	579	1,258	2,614	2,771	3,026	3,325	3,797	4,248	4,785	5,366
Commercial banking	91	188	198	185	195	208	228	251	264	310
Thrift institutions [2]	55	111	140	95	88	100	113	115	141	161
Life insurance companies	-	-	-	-	-	-	1	1	2	2
Government-sponsored enterprises [3]	163	264	399	408	448	528	701	807	897	996
Federally-related mortgage pools	114	369	1,020	1,156	1,272	1,357	1,472	1,570	1,711	1,826
Asset-backed securities issuers	-	39	285	339	403	485	554	687	819	998
Finance companies	127	224	374	390	386	385	434	484	530	554
Mortgage companies	12	17	25	22	30	30	19	19	32	36
Real estate investment trusts	5	5	12	14	14	17	31	37	50	74
Security brokers, dealers	-	1	15	19	22	34	34	29	27	35
Funding corporations	13	39	147	143	169	180	211	249	313	374
CORPORATE CREDIT MARKET DEBT OUTSTANDING, BY TYPE OF INSTRUMENT										
Total	910	1,606	2,481	2,423	2,464	2,520	2,658	2,869	3,042	3,283
Commercial paper	28	72	117	98	107	118	139	157	156	169
Municipal securities [4]	46	127	115	114	114	114	109	96	79	59
Corporate bonds	366	578	1,008	1,087	1,155	1,230	1,253	1,326	1,399	1,490
Bank loans, n.e.c.	230	424	545	508	488	478	521	584	632	705
Other loans and advances	110	248	473	410	413	388	421	454	472	515
Savings institutions	1	15	17	10	6	5	5	6	8	9
Finance companies	78	135	241	237	238	224	247	271	279	287
U.S. government	8	14	9	8	8	8	8	10	9	8
Acceptance liabilities to banks	17	28	29	23	20	17	15	14	13	11
Rest of the world	5	56	172	125	130	114	122	122	126	139
Asset-backed securities issuers	-	-	4	7	10	19	24	30	38	61
Mortgages	131	156	222	206	187	192	214	252	304	346

- Represents or rounds to zero.　[1] Includes nonprofit organizations.　[2] Covers savings institutions and credit unions.　[3] U.S. government.　[4] Industrial revenue bonds. Issued by state and local governments to finance private investment and secured in interest and principal by the industrial user of the funds.

Source of Tables 794 and 795: Board of Governors of the Federal Reserve System, *Flow of Funds Accounts*, March 1998 quarterly diskettes. Data are also published in the quarterly Z.1 release.

No. 796. Flow of Funds Accounts—Financial Assets and Liabilities of Financial and Nonfinancial Institutions, by Sector and Type of Instrument: 1997

[In billions of dollars. As of Dec. 31. Preliminary. A=Assets; L=Liabilities, SDR=Special drawing rights, IMF=International Monetary Fund. RP's=Repurchase agreements. "N.e.c."=Not elsewhere classified]

TYPE OF INSTRUMENT	All sectors, total A	All sectors, total L	Private domestic nonfinancial — Total A	Private — Total L	Households[1] A	Households[1] L	Business A	Business L	State and local govts. A	State and local govts. L	U.S. Government A	U.S. Government L	Financial Total[2] A	Financial Total[2] L	Commercial banking A	Commercial banking L	Life insurance A	Life insurance L	Federally sponsored credit agencies and mortgage pools A	Federally sponsored credit agencies and mortgage pools L	Foreign sector A	Foreign sector L
Total	67,226	48,860	34,609	15,382	27,109	5,827	6,472	8,392	1,028	1,163	438	4,398	27,524	26,813	5,179	5,052	2,581	2,396	2,925	2,904	4,654	2,267
Gold stock and SDR's	21	18										10	11									
IMF position	18	18									18											18
Official foreign exchange	31	31									14		17									31
Treasury currency, SDR certificates	35	27										27	35									
Checkable deposits, currency	1,268	1,286	874		426		415		33		42		85	1,286	1	656	4		2		267	
Time and savings deposits	3,187	3,187	2,946		2,723		145		79		3		169	3,187		2,363					68	
Fed. funds and security RP's	626	814	116				6		110				433	814		552	3		93		78	
Money market fund shares	1,049	1,049	740		637		103						309	1,049			57					
Foreign deposits	105	527	82		49		32						23								527	527
Life insurance reserves	651	651	651		651							14		637				637				
Pension fund reserves	7,454	7,454	7,454		7,454							450		7,004				1,268				
Interbank claims[3]	227	199											79	199	74	123					149	
Mutual fund shares[3]	3,014	3,014	2,059		1,938		82		40				955	3,014	8		58					
Other corporate equities[4]	12,959	12,959	5,818		5,738				80				6,259		3		582				882	
Credit market instruments[5]	21,119	21,119	2,754	11,389	1,827	5,571	335	4,689	592	1,129	201	3,805	15,894	5,366	4,032	310	1,775		2,734	2,822	2,270	559
U.S. Treasury securities[6]	3,778	3,778	654		305		70		279			3,778	1,859		270		97		16		1,266	
Federal agency securities[7]	2,848	2,848	605		500		10		95			27	1,984	2,822	571		253		315	2,822	259	
Municipal securities	1,366	1,366	492	1,366	449	188	42	59	2	1,120			874		97		15		5			
Corporate and foreign bonds	3,338	3,338	394	1,490	349		100	1,490	45				2,413	1,466	143	193	1,026	2	33		532	383
Mortgages	5,277	5,277	324	5,227	102	3,864	79	1,363	122		46		4,908	50	1,244		211		2,073			
Consumer credit	1,265	1,265	79	1,265		1,265							1,187	83	513							
Bank loans, n.e.c	1,171	1,171		1,036		61		975					1,171	746	1,171	59						
Open-market paper	979	979	206	169	123		34	169	49				699	333	3		68		33			52
Security credit	462	462	211	129	211	129							251								75	65
Trade credit[8]	1,744	1,391	1,466	1,222		107	1,466	1,081			26	98	191	38							61	51
Taxes payable	47	140	27	102				102	27		20			1		5		12				
Proprietors' equity	4,088		4,088		4,088																	
Investment in bank personal trusts	1,051	1,051	1,051		1,051									1,051								
Miscellaneous claims	8,072	6,441	4,275	2,540	318	20	3,889	2,520	68	34	104	4	2,814	2,816	939	1,043	106	477	95	83	880	1,081

- Represents or rounds to zero. [1] Includes nonprofit organizations. [2] Includes other financial institutions, not shown separately. [3] Nonbank finance liability is redemption value of shares of open-end investment companies. [4] Assets shown at market value. No specific liability attributed to issuers of stocks other than open-end investment companies for amounts outstanding. [5] Includes "Other loans," not shown separately. [6] Includes savings bonds and other nonmarketable debt held by public. [7] Issues by agencies in the budget and by government-sponsored enterprises in financial sectors, issues backed by federally-related mortgage pools, and loan participation certificates. [8] Asset is corporate only; noncorporate credit deducted in liability total to conform to quarterly flow tables.

Source: Board of Governors of the Federal Reserve System, Flow of Funds Accounts, quarterly.

No. 797. Flow of Funds Accounts—Financial Assets of Households: 1980 to 1997

[As of **December 31**. Includes nonprofit organizations]

TYPE OF INSTRUMENT	TOTAL (bil. dol.)							PERCENT DISTRIBUTION		
	1980	1985	1990	1994	1995	1996	1997	1980	1990	1997
Total financial assets	**6,557**	**10,096**	**14,852**	**19,059**	**21,528**	**23,795**	**27,109**	**100.0**	**100.0**	**100.0**
Deposits	1,494	2,461	3,241	3,134	3,346	3,562	3,835	22.8	21.8	14.1
Foreign deposits		8	13	19	23	35	49	-	0.1	0.2
Checkable deposits and currency . .	228	319	386	540	497	455	426	3.5	2.6	1.6
Time and savings deposits	1,203	1,941	2,478	2,224	2,374	2,540	2,723	18.4	16.7	10.0
Money market fund shares	62	193	365	351	452	531	637	0.9	2.5	2.3
Credit market instruments	425	846	1,493	1,942	1,905	1,965	1,827	6.5	10.1	6.7
Open-market paper	38	35	63	47	60	83	123	0.6	0.4	0.5
U.S. Government securities	165	270	519	930	881	956	804	2.5	3.5	3.0
Treasury issues	160	242	394	662	591	542	305	2.4	2.6	1.1
Savings bonds	73	80	126	180	185	187	187	1.1	0.8	0.7
Other Treasury	88	162	267	482	406	355	118	1.3	1.8	0.4
Agency issues	5	29	126	267	290	414	500	0.1	0.8	1.8
Municipal securities	104	346	575	502	446	423	449	1.6	3.9	1.7
Corporate and foreign bonds	31	77	199	349	408	396	349	0.5	1.3	1.3
Mortgages	86	116	137	115	110	106	102	1.3	0.9	0.4
Corporate equities [1]	903	1,128	1,795	3,049	4,066	4,604	5,738	13.8	12.1	21.2
Mutual fund shares	46	198	468	1,052	1,255	1,592	1,938	0.7	3.1	7.1
Security credit	16	35	62	109	128	163	211	0.2	0.4	0.8
Life insurance reserves	216	257	381	505	550	594	651	3.3	2.6	2.4
Pension fund reserves [2]	962	2,047	3,388	4,880	5,600	6,314	7,454	14.7	22.8	27.5
Investment in bank personal trusts . .	265	384	552	699	767	872	1,051	4.0	3.7	3.9
Equity in noncorporate business	2,156	2,608	3,247	3,419	3,625	3,836	4,088	32.9	21.9	15.1
Miscellaneous assets	74	133	224	270	285	294	318	1.1	1.5	1.2

- Represents zero. [1] Only those directly held and those in closed-end funds. Other equities are included in mutual funds, life insurance and pension reserves, and bank personal trusts. [2] See also Table 847.

Source: Board of Governors of the Federal Reserve System, *Flow of Funds Accounts*, March 1998 diskettes. Data are also published in the quarterly Z.1 release.

No. 798. Financial Assets Held by Families, by Type of Asset: 1992 and 1995

[**Median value in thousands of constant 1995 dollars**. Constant dollar figures are based on consumer price index data published by U.S. Bureau of Labor Statistics. Families include one-person units; for definition of family, see text, Section 1. Based on Survey of Consumer Finance; see Appendix III. For definition of median, see Guide to Tabular Presentation]

AGE OF FAMILY HEAD AND FAMILY INCOME	Any financial asset [1]	Transaction accounts [2]	Certificates of deposit	Savings bonds	Stocks [3]	Mutual funds [4]	Retirement accounts [5]	Life insurance (cash value)	Other managed [6]
PERCENT OF FAMILIES OWNING ASSET									
1992, total	90.3	87.0	16.7	22.3	17.0	10.4	38.0	34.8	4.0
1995, total	**90.7**	**87.1**	**14.3**	**22.8**	**15.2**	**12.3**	**43.0**	**31.9**	**3.9**
Under 35 years old	86.6	80.8	7.2	20.4	10.8	8.0	38.0	22.7	1.6
35 to 44 years old	91.8	87.3	8.1	31.0	14.6	11.2	52.1	29.2	3.5
45 to 54 years old	92.3	89.0	12.3	25.3	17.6	16.3	55.0	38.4	3.0
55 to 64 years old	90.5	88.2	17.1	20.2	15.0	16.1	47.7	37.4	7.6
65 to 74 years old	92.2	91.3	23.9	16.8	18.6	14.9	35.5	37.4	5.9
75 years old and over	93.9	92.9	34.7	15.3	19.8	10.2	15.5	35.6	5.2
Less than $10,000	67.6	60.6	8.0	5.5	2.6	1.8	6.5	15.9	0.5
$10,000 to $24,999	87.9	82.6	15.8	12.8	8.8	4.8	24.1	25.3	3.6
$25,000 to $49,999	97.7	94.9	13.9	26.9	14.0	12.7	52.2	33.5	4.2
$50,000 to $99,999	99.5	98.6	16.1	39.3	26.7	21.9	70.5	44.4	5.5
$100,000 and more	100.0	99.9	19.6	36.3	43.9	38.1	83.6	52.6	7.7
MEDIAN VALUE [7]									
1992, total	12.2	2.5	11.2	0.7	8.7	17.4	15.5	3.3	21.7
1995, total	**14.0**	**2.1**	**10.0**	**1.0**	**8.8**	**20.0**	**16.0**	**5.0**	**30.0**
Under 35 years old	5.0	1.2	5.3	0.5	3.0	5.5	5.0	3.5	4.5
35 to 44 years old	12.3	2.0	6.0	1.0	4.5	10.0	12.5	5.3	10.8
45 to 54 years old	26.0	3.0	12.0	1.0	10.0	21.0	27.5	7.8	56.7
55 to 64 years old	30.0	3.1	14.0	1.5	19.4	56.0	30.0	5.5	50.0
65 to 74 years old	21.1	3.2	20.0	1.5	20.0	55.0	29.2	5.0	35.0
75 years old and over	22.6	5.0	11.0	4.8	18.0	50.0	23.5	5.0	65.0
Less than $10,000	1.3	0.7	8.0	0.2	2.0	25.0	5.0	1.6	51.0
$10,000 to $24,999	5.5	1.4	10.0	0.8	6.0	8.5	6.0	3.0	24.0
$25,000 to $49,999	12.3	1.9	10.0	0.7	6.0	13.0	10.0	5.0	20.0
$50,000 to $99,999	42.0	4.5	15.0	1.3	7.5	20.0	24.0	8.0	38.0
$100,000 and more	213.3	16.9	17.0	1.2	29.0	58.5	84.0	15.0	70.0

[1] Includes other types of financial assets, not shown separately. [2] Checking, savings, and money market accounts. [3] Covers only those stocks that are directly held by families outside mutual funds, IRA's, Keogh or pension accounts. [4] Excludes money market mutual funds, individual retirement accounts (IRA's), Keogh accounts, and any type of pension plan invested in mutual funds. [5] Covers IRA's, Keogh accounts, and employer-provided pension plans from which withdrawals can be made, such as 401(k) plans. [6] Includes trusts, annuities, managed investment accounts, and other such assets. [7] Median value of financial asset for families holding such assets.

Source: Board of Governors of the Federal Reserve System, *Federal Reserve Bulletin*, January 1997, and unpublished revisions.

No. 799. Flow of Funds Accounts—Liabilities of Households: 1980 to 1997

[As of **December 31**. Includes nonprofit organizations]

TYPE OF INSTRUMENT	TOTAL (bil. dol.)							PERCENT DISTRIBUTION		
	1980	1985	1990	1994	1995	1996	1997	1980	1990	1997
Total liabilities	**1,427**	**2,330**	**3,703**	**4,668**	**5,049**	**5,421**	**5,827**	**100.0**	**100.0**	**100.0**
Credit market instruments	1,376	2,239	3,579	4,482	4,851	5,205	5,571	96.4	96.6	95.6
Home mortgages	906	1,411	2,489	3,098	3,275	3,504	3,758	63.5	67.2	64.5
Consumer credit	355	604	805	984	1,123	1,212	1,265	24.9	21.7	21.7
Municipal securities	17	81	84	126	139	159	188	1.2	2.3	3.2
Bank loans, n.e.c. [1]	28	31	18	40	56	52	61	2.0	0.5	1.0
Other loans	55	79	101	134	160	173	193	3.8	2.7	3.3
Commercial mortgages	15	33	83	102	97	106	106	1.0	2.2	1.8
Security credit	25	51	39	75	79	94	129	1.7	1.0	2.2
Trade payables	14	24	69	94	102	104	107	1.0	1.9	1.8
Unpaid life insurance premiums [2]	13	15	16	17	18	18	20	0.9	0.4	0.3

[1] Not elsewhere classified.   [2] Includes deferred premiums.

Source: Board of Governors of the Federal Reserve System, *Flow of Funds Accounts*, March 1998 diskettes.

No. 800. Financial Debt Held by Families, by Type of Debt: 1992 and 1995

[**Median debt in thousands of constant 1995 dollars**. See headnote, Table 798]

AGE OF FAMILY HEAD AND FAMILY INCOME	Any debt	Mortgage, home equity	Installment	Other lines of credit	Credit card	Investment real estate	Other debt [1]
PERCENT OF FAMILIES HOLDING DEBTS							
1992, total	73.6	39.1	46.2	2.4	43.8	7.8	8.8
1995, total	**74.9**	**41.0**	**46.2**	**1.9**	**47.4**	**6.4**	**8.5**
Under 35 years old	83.7	32.9	62.6	2.7	54.8	2.8	7.6
35 to 44 years old	87.2	54.2	60.2	2.1	56.1	6.8	10.5
45 to 54 years old	86.6	61.9	53.7	2.2	56.6	10.8	12.9
55 to 64 years old	74.1	45.3	34.8	1.6	43.4	11.6	7.7
65 to 74 years old	54.3	25.1	16.7	1.3	30.8	5.3	5.3
75 years old and over	28.7	6.8	9.0	-	17.7	1.7	2.9
Less than $10,000	48.1	9.2	25.8	(B)	24.7	2.0	6.1
$10,000 to $24,999	67.7	25.2	40.7	1.3	42.0	2.3	8.5
$25,000 to $49,999	83.6	47.3	54.2	2.0	55.8	5.9	8.3
$50,000 to $99,999	89.2	68.0	60.2	3.2	63.1	10.1	8.9
$100,000 and more	85.8	73.1	38.7	4.3	38.9	25.9	14.1
MEDIAN DEBT [2]							
1992, total	19.5	47.5	5.0	2.2	1.1	26.0	2.7
1995, total	**22.4**	**51.7**	**6.1**	**3.6**	**1.5**	**30.0**	**2.0**
Under 35 years old	15.0	62.0	7.1	1.4	1.3	22.8	1.5
35 to 44 years old	37.6	61.0	5.6	2.0	1.9	30.0	2.0
45 to 54 years old	40.7	50.0	7.2	5.5	2.0	30.0	3.0
55 to 64 years old	21.5	37.0	5.0	3.4	1.3	40.0	4.0
65 to 74 years old	7.6	19.0	4.9	3.8	0.8	40.0	2.0
75 years old and over	1.9	18.1	3.4	(B)	0.4	8.0	4.0
Less than $10,000	2.5	18.0	2.6	(B)	0.6	11.4	2.7
$10,000 to $24,999	8.8	27.6	3.8	1.5	1.2	10.7	1.2
$25,000 to $49,999	23.9	45.0	6.7	3.9	1.5	26.0	1.7
$50,000 to $99,999	64.3	67.0	9.0	2.2	2.0	35.0	3.5
$100,000 and more	118.0	100.0	8.5	7.0	2.5	48.0	7.0

- Represents or rounds to zero.   B Base figure too small.   [1] Includes loans on insurance policies, loans against pension accounts, and other unclassified loans.   [2] Median amount of financial debt for families holding such debts.

No. 801. Percent Distribution of Amount of Debt Held by Families: 1992 and 1995

[See headnote, Table 802]

TYPE OF DEBT	1992	1995	PURPOSE OF DEBT	1992	1995	TYPE OF LENDING INSTITUTION	1992	1995
Total	**100.0**	**100.0**	**Total . . . .**	**100.0**	**100.0**	**Total . . . .**	**100.0**	**100.0**
Home mortgage and home equity lines of credit	64.1	67.3	Home purchase	59.8	67.0	Commercial bank	33.1	34.7
			Home improvement . .	2.3	1.9	Savings and loan	16.5	10.7
			Investment, excluding real estate	1.6	0.4	Credit union	4.0	4.4
Installment loans	10.3	11.0				Finance or loan company .	13.6	20.8
Credit card balances . .	2.8	3.6	Vehicles	6.2	7.0	Brokerage	3.3	2.1
Other lines of credit . . .	0.7	0.5	Goods and services . .	5.0	4.8	Real estate lender	14.3	13.0
Investment real estate mortgages	19.9	15.0	Investment real estate .	20.7	16.1	Individual lender	4.4	5.3
Other debt	2.1	2.6	Education	2.5	2.6	Other nonfinancial	1.5	0.8
			Other loans	2.1	0.3	Government	2.0	1.3
						Credit and store cards . .	3.0	3.6
						Other loans	4.4	3.3

Source of Tables 800 and 801: Board of Governors of the Federal Reserve System, *Federal Reserve Bulletin*, January 1997 and unpublished revisions.

No. 802. Ratios of Debt Payments to Family Income: 1989 to 1995

[In percent. Constant dollar figures are based on consumer price index data published by U.S. Bureau of Labor Statistics. Families include one-person units; for definition of family, see text, Section 1. Based on Survey of Consumer Finance; see Appendix III. For definition of median, see Guide to Tabular Presentation]

AGE OF FAMILY HEAD AND FAMILY INCOME (constant (1995) dollars)	RATIO OF DEBT PAYMENTS TO FAMILY INCOME						PERCENT OF DEBTORS WITH—					
	Aggregate			Median			Ratios above 40 percent			Any payment 60 days or more past due		
	1989	1992	1995	1989	1992	1995	1989	1992	1995	1989	1992	1995
All families	15.6	15.7	14.8	16.1	16.3	16.3	11.0	11.5	11.0	7.2	6.0	7.0
Under 35 years old	18.1	16.9	17.5	17.2	16.5	16.7	13.0	10.5	11.1	11.1	8.2	8.7
35 to 44 years old	19.3	18.4	17.2	18.4	19.2	18.1	8.9	12.2	10.0	6.4	7.0	7.7
45 to 54 years old	15.3	17.4	15.8	16.6	16.8	16.7	12.5	11.4	10.8	4.5	5.3	7.3
55 to 64 years old	16.9	14.4	14.1	13.6	15.4	14.1	10.4	15.5	15.5	7.3	4.6	3.1
65 to 74 years old	6.5	10.3	9.6	11.3	10.9	13.3	8.3	8.5	8.4	3.3	1.1	5.3
75 years old and over	2.7	4.6	3.5	10.0	5.5	3.8	12.4	9.4	8.7	1.1	2.0	5.3
Less than $10,000	17.9	16.8	22.7	22.0	19.4	16.0	27.9	28.8	27.2	21.2	11.1	8.5
$10,000 to $24,999	12.7	16.3	16.3	17.2	15.5	17.4	14.4	15.7	15.9	11.8	9.2	11.1
$25,000 to $49,999	16.5	17.0	16.9	16.4	16.7	16.9	9.9	9.7	8.3	4.5	6.2	7.8
$50,000 to $99,999	16.8	16.0	16.6	16.1	16.9	16.7	5.5	4.7	4.9	4.6	2.1	2.8
$100,000 and more	14.6	14.1	10.6	13.2	14.6	11.0	7.1	4.3	3.6	1.2	0.5	1.4

Source: Board of Governors of the Federal Reserve System, *Federal Reserve Bulletin*, January 1997, and unpublished revisions.

No. 803. Selected Financial Institutions—Number and Assets, by Asset Size: 1997

[As of December. FDIC=Federal Deposit Insurance Corporation]

ASSET SIZE	NUMBER OF INSTITUTIONS			ASSETS (bil. dol.)		
	F.D.I.C.-insured		Credit unions [1]	F.D.I.C.-insured		Credit unions [1]
	Commercial banks	Savings institutions		Commercial banks [2]	Savings institutions	
Total	9,143	1,779	11,238	5,014.9	1,026.2	351.2
Less than $5.0 million	46	4	5,298	0.2	(Z)	9.8
$5.0 million to $9.9 million	168	32	1,737	1.3	0.3	12.5
$10.0 million to $24.9 million	1,242	106	1,843	22.5	2.0	29.8
$25.0 million to $49.9 million	2,058	233	1,010	76.0	8.9	35.6
$50.0 million to $99.9 million	2,337	389	641	167.7	28.8	45.0
$100.0 million to $499.9 million. . .	2,620	734	622	516.6	165.5	127.3
$500.0 million to $999.9 million. . .	305	124	61	211.4	84.9	39.8
$1.0 billion to $2.9 billion	194	97	24	314.6	150.5	36.9
$3.0 billion or more.	173	60	2	3,704.6	585.4	14.6
	PERCENT DISTRIBUTION					
Total	100.0	100.0	100.0	100.0	100.0	100.0
Less than $5.0 million	0.5	0.2	47.1	(Z)	(Z)	2.8
$5.0 million to $9.9 million	1.8	1.8	15.5	(Z)	(Z)	3.6
$10.0 million to $24.9 million	13.6	6.0	16.4	0.4	0.2	8.5
$25.0 million to $49.9 million	22.5	13.1	9.0	1.5	0.9	10.1
$50.0 million to $99.9 million	25.6	21.9	5.7	3.3	2.8	12.8
$100.0 million to $499.9 million. . .	28.7	41.3	5.5	10.3	16.1	36.2
$500.0 million to $999.9 million. . .	3.3	7.0	0.5	4.2	8.3	11.3
$1.0 billion to $2.9 billion	2.1	5.5	0.2	6.3	14.7	10.5
$3.0 billion or more.	1.9	3.4	(Z)	73.9	57.0	4.2

Z Less than $50 million or 0.05 percent. [1] Source: National Credit Union Administration, *National Credit Union Administration Yearend Statistics 1997.* Excludes nonfederally insured state chartered credit unions and federally insured corporate credit unions. [2] Includes foreign branches of U.S. banks.

Source: Except as noted, U.S. Federal Deposit Insurance Corporation, *Statistics on Banking, 1997.*

No. 804. Banking Offices, by Type of Bank: 1980 to 1997

[As of December 31. Includes Puerto Rico and outlying areas. Covers all FDIC-insured commercial banks and savings institutions. Data for 1980 include automatic teller machines which were reported by many banks as branches]

ITEM	1980	1985	1990	1992	1993	1994	1995	1996	1997
All banking offices	(NA)	82,316	84,363	81,171	80,707	81,709	81,933	82,476	83,914
Number of banks	(NA)	18,043	15,162	13,856	13,222	12,604	11,972	11,452	10,922
Number of branches	(NA)	64,273	69,201	67,315	67,485	69,105	69,961	71,024	72,992
Commercial banks	53,172	57,710	62,753	63,401	63,828	65,597	66,454	67,316	69,463
Number of banks.	14,434	14,417	12,347	11,466	10,960	10,452	9,942	9,528	9,143
Number of branches	38,738	43,293	50,406	51,935	52,868	55,145	56,512	57,788	60,320
Savings institutions	(NA)	24,606	21,610	17,770	16,879	16,112	15,479	15,160	14,451
Number of banks.	(NA)	3,626	2,815	2,390	2,262	2,152	2,030	1,924	1,779
Number of branches	(NA)	20,980	18,795	15,380	14,617	13,960	13,449	13,236	12,672

NA Not available.

Source: U.S. Federal Deposit Insurance Corporation, *Statistics on Banking*, annual and "HSOB 1934-1995"; <http://www.fdic.gov/databank/sob/hist96/index.html>; (accessed 26 September 1997).

No. 805. Retail Fees and Services of Banks: 1996 and 1997

[In dollars, except as noted. Data for 1996 as of November or December; 1997 data as of June. For most services, fees are reported in terms of (1) the proportion of those banks offering a service that charge for the service and (2) the average fee charged by the institutions that charge for the service. Based on a random sample of depository institutions belonging to the Bank Insurance Fund, whose members are predominantly commercial banks]

TYPE OF ACCOUNT OR SERVICE	1996	1997	TYPE OF ACCOUNT OR SERVICE	1996	1997
NONINTEREST CHECKING ACCOUNT			AUTOMATED TELLER MACHINES (ATMs)		
Percent offering.	97.8	98.7	Percent offering.	72.9	79.4
			Annual fee:		
Single-balance, single-fee account: [1]			Percent charging	13.4	16.7
Percent offering	32.9	39.3	Average	7.94	11.51
Monthly fee (low balance)	6.34	6.09	Fees for customer transactions on us: [4]		
Minimum balance to avoid fee	480	479	Withdrawals:		
Minimum balance to open	123	124	Percent charging.	6.8	7.4
			Average	0.59	0.65
Fee-only account: [2]			Balance inquiries:		
Percent offering.	34.2	33.3	Percent charging.	4.4	6.7
Monthly fee	5.02	4.49	Average	0.70	0.65
Check charge:			Fees for customer transactions on		
Percent charging.	45.8	32.4	others: [4]		
Average	0.34	0.38	Withdrawals:		
Minimum balance to open	82	61	Percent charging.	79.8	67.0
			Average	1.10	1.06
NOW ACCOUNTS [3]			Balance inquiries:		
			Percent charging.	64.7	55.2
Percent offering.	97.3	97.6	Average	1.03	0.99
			Surcharge: [5]		
Single-fee account: [1]			Percent charging	44.8	60.1
Percent offering	44.0	56.7	Average	1.19	1.14
Monthly fee (low balance)	8.11	7.81			
Minimum balance to avoid fee	1,079	1,052			
Minimum balance to open	654	663			

[1] A monthly fee for balances below the minimum, no monthly fee for balances above the minimum, and no other charges. [2] A monthly fee, no minimum balance to eliminate the fee, and a charge per check in some cases. [3] NOW (negotiable order of withdrawal) accounts are checking accounts that pay interest and often have fee structures that differ from those of noninterest checking accounts. [4] An institution's "customer" is one who has an account at the institution. A customer's ATM transactions in which the machine used is that of the customer's institution are called "on us"; a customer's transactions in which the machine used is that of another institution are called "on others". [5] An ATM surcharge is a fee imposed by the ATM's institution, typically on every transaction by the machine's noncustomer users.

Source: Board of Governors of the Federal Reserve Systems, *Annual Report to the Congress on Retail Fees and Services of Depository Institutions*, June 1998.

No. 806. Insured Commercial Banks—Assets and Liabilities: 1980 to 1997

[In billions of dollars, except as indicated. As of Dec. 31. Includes outlying areas. Except as noted, includes foreign branches of U.S. banks]

ITEM	1980	1985	1990	1992	1993	1994	1995	1996	1997 [1]
Number of banks reporting	14,435	14,417	12,343	11,462	10,958	10,450	9,940	9,528	9,143
Assets, total.	**1,856**	**2,731**	**3,389**	**3,506**	**3,706**	**4,011**	**4,313**	**4,578**	**5,015**
Net loans and leases.	1,006	1,608	2,055	1,977	2,097	2,306	2,550	2,758	2,916
Real estate loans	269	438	830	868	923	998	1,080	1,139	1,244
Home equity lines of credit [2] . . .	(NA)	(NA)	61	73	73	76	79	85	98
Commercial and industrial loans. . .	391	578	615	536	539	589	661	710	796
Loans to individuals	187	309	404	385	419	487	535	562	561
Credit cards and related plans . .	(NA)	(NA)	134	136	153	187	216	232	231
Farm loans.	32	36	33	35	37	39	40	41	45
Other loans and leases.	158	288	242	216	239	251	292	364	329
Less: Reserve for losses.	10	23	56	54	53	52	53	54	55
Less: Unearned income	21	18	14	9	7	6	6	5	5
Investment securities.	325	439	605	773	837	823	811	801	872
Other	524	684	730	755	772	881	952	1,020	1,227
Domestic office assets.	1,533	2,326	2,999	3,109	3,258	3,483	3,728	3,906	4,267
Foreign office assets	323	406	390	396	448	527	585	672	748
Liabilities and capital, total	1,856	2,731	3,389	3,506	3,706	4,011	4,313	4,578	5,015
Noninterest-bearing deposits [3]	432	471	489	541	572	572	612	664	676
Interest-bearing deposits [4]	1,049	1,646	2,162	2,158	2,182	2,302	2,416	2,533	2,745
Subordinated debt.	7	15	24	34	37	41	44	51	62
Other liabilities	260	429	496	510	618	783	892	954	1,113
Equity capital	108	169	219	263	296	312	350	375	418
Domestic office deposits.	1,187	1,796	2,357	2,412	2,424	2,443	2,573	2,724	2,896
Foreign office deposits.	294	322	293	287	330	432	454	474	526

NA Not available. [1] Preliminary. [2] For one- to four-family residential properties. [3] Prior to 1985, demand deposits. [4] Prior to 1985, time and savings deposits.

Source: U.S. Federal Deposit Insurance Corporation, *The FDIC Quarterly Banking Profile, Annual Report*, and *Statistics on Banking*, annual.

No. 807. Insured Commercial Banks—Income and Selected Measures of Financial Condition: 1980 to 1997

[In billions of dollars, except as indicated. Includes outlying areas. Includes foreign branches of U.S. banks]

ITEM	1980	1985	1990	1992	1993	1994	1995	1996	1997 [1]
Interest income.	177.4	248.2	320.4	255.2	245.1	257.8	302.4	312.8	339.6
Interest expense.	120.1	157.3	204.9	121.8	105.7	111.3	148.2	150.0	165.0
Net interest income	57.3	90.9	115.5	133.4	139.3	146.6	154.2	162.8	174.5
Provisions for loan losses.	4.5	17.8	32.1	26.0	16.8	11.0	12.6	16.3	19.8
Noninterest income.	13.3	31.1	54.9	65.6	75.0	76.3	82.4	93.6	104.5
Noninterest expense	46.7	82.4	115.7	130.9	139.7	144.2	149.7	160.7	170.0
Income taxes	5.0	5.6	7.7	14.5	19.9	22.4	26.1	28.2	31.9
Securities gain/loss, net	-0.5	1.6	0.5	4.0	3.1	-0.6	0.5	1.1	1.8
Extraordinary gains, net	-	0.2	0.6	0.4	2.1	-	-	0.1	-
Net income.	14.0	18.0	16.0	32.0	43.0	44.6	48.7	52.4	59.2
RATIOS OF CONDITION									
Return on assets [2] (percent).	0.80	0.70	0.48	0.93	1.20	1.15	1.17	1.19	1.23
Return on equity [3] (percent)	13.66	11.31	7.45	12.98	15.34	14.61	14.66	14.46	14.70
Equity capital to assets (percent)	5.80	6.20	6.45	7.51	8.00	7.78	8.11	8.20	8.33
Noncurrent assets plus other real estate owned to assets [4] (percent). .	(NA)	1.87	2.94	2.54	1.61	1.01	0.85	0.75	0.66
Net charge-offs [5]	3.6	13.6	29.7	25.6	17.5	11.2	12.2	15.5	18.3
Net charge-offs to loans and leases (percent)	0.36	0.84	1.43	1.27	0.85	0.50	0.49	0.58	0.63
Net interest margin [6] (percent)	3.66	4.09	3.94	4.41	4.40	4.36	4.29	4.27	4.21
Percentage of banks losing money. . .	3.7	17.1	13.4	6.9	4.9	4.0	3.6	4.2	4.5

- Represents or rounds to zero. NA Not available. [1] Preliminary. [2] Net income (including securities transactions and nonrecurring items) as a percentage of average total assets. [3] Net income as a percentage of average total equity capital. [4] The sum of loans, leases, debt securities and other assets that are 90 days or more past due, or in nonaccrual status plus foreclosed property. [5] Total loans and leases charged off (removed from balance sheet because of uncollectibility), less amounts recovered on loans and leases previously charged off. [6] Interest income less interest expense as a percentage of average earning assets (i.e. the profit margin a bank earns on its loans and investments).

Source: U.S. Federal Deposit Insurance Corporation, *Annual Report; Statistics on Banking*, annual; and *FDIC Quarterly Banking Profile*.

No. 808. Insured Commercial Banks—Selected Measures of Financial Condition, by Asset Size and Region: 1997

[In percent, except as indicated. Preliminary. See headnote, Table 807]

ASSET SIZE AND REGION	Number of banks	Return on assets	Return on equity	Equity capital to assets	Noncurrent assets plus other real estate owned to total assets	Net charge-offs to loans and leases	Percentage of banks losing money
Total	9,143	1.23	14.70	8.33	0.66	0.63	4.5
Less than $100 million . .	5,853	1.19	10.91	10.82	0.71	0.27	6.4
$100 million to $1 billion .	2,923	1.34	13.98	9.62	0.65	0.36	1.1
$1 billion to $10 billion. . .	301	1.36	14.92	9.16	0.77	1.08	1.7
$10 billion or more	66	1.18	15.30	7.58	0.62	0.58	(NA)
Northeast [1]	714	1.14	15.40	7.33	0.73	0.73	3.6
Southeast [2]	1,524	1.23	13.69	8.88	0.59	0.46	6.1
Central [3]	1,999	1.29	15.32	8.35	0.58	0.50	3.9
Midwest [4]	2,329	1.44	15.90	9.07	0.69	0.82	2.6
Southwest [5]	1,601	1.22	13.78	8.65	0.52	0.37	3.8
West [6]	976	1.35	13.79	9.82	0.72	0.83	9.7

NA Not available. [1] CT, DE, DC, ME, MD, MA, NH, NJ, NY, PA, PR, RI, and VT. [2] AL, FL, GA, MS, NC, SC, TN, VA, and WV. [3] IL, IN, KY, MI, OH, and WI. [4] IA, KS, MN, MO, NE, ND, and SD. [5] AR, LA, NM, OK, and TX. [6] AK, AZ, CA, CO, HI, ID, MT, NV, OR, Pacific Islands, UT, WA, and WY.

Source: U.S. Federal Deposit Insurance Corporation, *The FDIC Quarterly Banking Profile*, Fourth Quarter 1997.

No. 809. U.S. Banking Offices of Foreign Banks—Summary: 1980 to 1996

[In billions of dollars, except as indicated. As of **December**. Covers agencies, branches, subsidiary commercial banks, and New York State investment companies]

ITEM	1980	1985	1990	1992	1993	1994	1995	1996	SHARE [1] 1980	SHARE [1] 1990	SHARE [1] 1995	SHARE [1] 1996
Assets	200.6	440.8	791.1	869.0	855.7	943.7	983.9	991.6	11.9	21.4	21.7	20.7
Loans, total	121.4	247.4	397.9	407.5	379.6	418.9	461.4	460.7	13.4	18.0	17.3	16.2
Business	59.6	108.8	193.3	208.7	195.6	216.2	249.4	264.4	18.2	30.8	35.1	34.6
Deposits	80.4	236.7	383.9	464.3	465.8	522.7	523.0	529.1	6.6	14.5	17.6	16.8

[1] Percent of "domestically owned" commercial banks plus U.S. offices of foreign banks.

Source: Board of Governors of the Federal Reserve System, unpublished data.

No. 810. Foreign Lending by U.S. Banks, by Type of Borrower and Country: 1997

[In millions of dollars. As of **December**. Covers 109 U.S. banking organizations which do nearly all of the foreign lending in the country. Data represent claims on foreign residents and institutions held at all domestic and foreign offices of covered banks. Data cover only cross-border and nonlocal currency lending. These result from a U.S. bank's office in one country lending to residents of another country or lending in a currency other than that of the borrower's country. Excludes local currency loans and other claims and local currency liabilities held by banks' foreign offices on residents of the country in which the office was located (e.g. Deutsche mark loans to German residents booked at the German branch of the reporting U.S. bank). Criteria for country selection is $4 billion or more]

COUNTRY	Total	Bank	Public	Private non-bank	COUNTRY	Total	Bank	Public	Private non-bank
Total [1]	333,876	118,148	88,973	126,758	Hong Kong	9,033	3,860	83	5,090
					Indonesia	5,035	1,679	388	2,968
Argentina	10,629	1,790	2,520	6,319	Italy	7,136	2,252	3,700	1,184
Australia	4,926	1,583	1,082	2,261	Japan	19,210	6,494	8,320	4,396
Bahamas, The	9,958	8,986	44	928	Korea, South	9,978	5,851	593	3,534
Belgium	7,007	3,324	2,708	975	Mexico	17,200	1,599	7,033	8,569
Brazil	16,351	5,155	5,111	6,086	Netherlands	9,090	2,719	1,955	4,416
Canada	14,376	2,725	6,114	5,538	Russia	7,086	392	5,651	1,043
Cayman Islands	14,891	4,762	159	9,970	Spain	8,310	3,918	2,941	1,452
Chile	4,728	722	965	3,041	Sweden	4,765	1,317	2,569	879
France	14,975	7,068	5,394	2,512	Switzerland	5,800	1,478	318	4,004
Germany	16,953	5,921	9,063	1,969	United Kingdom	33,423	19,227	531	13,666

[1] Includes other countries, not shown separately.

Source: Board of Governors of the Federal Reserve System, Federal Financial Institutions Examination Council, statistical release.

No. 811. Insured Commercial Banks, by State and Other Area: 1997

[In billions of dollars, except number of banks. As of **December 31**. Includes foreign branches of U.S. banks]

STATE	Number	Assets	Deposits	STATE	Number	Assets	Deposits
Total	9,143	5,014.9	3,421.7	Nebraska	326	25.9	21.6
United States	9,124	4,980.2	3,399.2	Nevada	25	25.9	8.1
				New Hampshire	21	11.7	8.5
Alabama	175	101.2	72.7				
Alaska	6	4.8	3.5	New Jersey	71	79.9	62.4
Arizona	41	39.3	22.8	New Mexico	58	11.3	9.0
Arkansas	226	28.7	24.7	New York	153	1,119.2	630.7
California	336	474.7	361.4	North Carolina	60	433.1	270.9
				North Dakota	117	8.9	7.6
Colorado	216	33.9	29.3				
Connecticut	26	4.8	4.0	Ohio	235	230.6	154.4
Delaware	34	127.9	50.8	Oklahoma	320	34.1	28.0
District of Columbia	6	1.2	0.9	Oregon	41	5.8	4.7
Florida	266	116.9	92.1	Pennsylvania	212	267.6	194.8
				Rhode Island	9	77.3	54.8
Georgia	353	69.2	46.9				
Hawaii	14	22.9	15.7	South Carolina	80	17.5	14.5
Idaho	16	1.4	1.2	South Dakota	106	30.3	11.8
Illinois	784	265.4	194.8	Tennessee	232	75.1	56.3
Indiana	185	66.5	50.9	Texas	839	235.1	191.8
				Utah	49	39.6	20.2
Iowa	453	43.3	36.0				
Kansas	403	31.3	26.7	Vermont	21	7.1	5.9
Kentucky	271	51.0	38.2	Virginia	151	77.8	55.9
Louisiana	158	46.7	37.6	Washington	80	11.7	9.9
Maine	17	4.9	3.7	West Virginia	100	21.6	17.5
				Wisconsin	361	72.5	55.4
Maryland	83	35.2	26.9	Wyoming	52	8.3	7.2
Massachusetts	46	123.4	84.2				
Michigan	163	118.8	85.3	American Samoa	1	0.1	(Z)
Minnesota	520	131.9	97.9	Puerto Rico	13	33.7	21.6
Mississippi	107	34.4	27.8	Guam	2	0.8	0.7
				Pacific Islands	1	(Z)	(Z)
Missouri	404	63.4	53.5	Virgin Islands	2	0.1	0.1
Montana	96	9.0	7.5				

Z Less than $50 million.

Source: U.S. Federal Deposit Insurance Corporation, *Statistics on Banking*, annual.

No. 812. Federal and State-Chartered Credit Unions—Summary: 1980 to 1997

[Except as noted, as of **December 31**. Federal data include District of Columbia, Puerto Rico, Canal Zone, Guam, and Virgin Islands. Excludes state-insured, privately-insured, and noninsured state-chartered credit unions and corporate central credit unions which have mainly other credit unions as members]

YEAR	OPERATING CREDIT UNIONS		Number of failed institutions [1]	MEMBERS (1,000)		ASSETS (mil. dol.)		LOANS OUTSTANDING (mil. dol.)		SAVINGS (mil. dol.)	
	Federal	State		Federal	State	Federal	State	Federal	State	Federal	State
1980 ...	12,440	4,910	239	24,519	12,338	40,092	20,870	26,350	14,582	36,263	18,469
1985 ...	10,125	4,920	94	29,579	15,689	78,188	41,525	48,241	26,168	71,616	37,917
1990 ...	8,511	4,349	164	36,241	19,454	130,073	68,133	83,029	44,102	117,892	62,082
1992 ...	7,908	4,686	114	38,124	23,238	162,066	96,312	87,350	52,192	145,637	87,371
1993 ...	7,696	4,621	37	39,756	23,997	172,854	104,316	94,640	57,695	153,506	93,482
1994 ...	7,498	4,493	33	40,837	24,295	182,529	106,937	110,090	65,769	160,226	94,797
1995 ...	7,329	4,358	26	42,163	24,927	193,781	112,860	120,514	71,606	170,300	99,838
1996 ...	7,152	4,240	19	43,546	25,652	206,695	120,193	134,127	79,661	180,969	105,743
1997 ...	6,981	4,257	16	43,491	27,921	215,104	136,074	140,104	92,117	187,822	119,359

[1] Through 1994 for year ending September 30; 1995 reflects 15-month period from October 1994 through December 1995; beginnning 1996 reflects calendar year. A failed institution is defined as a credit union which has ceased operation because it was involuntarily liquidated or merged with assistance from the National Credit Union Share Insurance Fund. Assisted mergers were not identified until 1981.

Source: National Credit Union Administration, *Annual Report of the National Credit Union Administration*, and unpublished data.

No. 813. Insured Savings Institutions—Financial Summary: 1985 to 1997

[**In billions of dollars, except number of institutions**. As of **December 31**. Includes Puerto Rico, Guam, and Virgin Islands. Covers SAIF (Savings Association Insurance Fund)- and BIF (Bank Insurance Fund)-insured savings institutions. Excludes institutions in Resolution Trust Corporation conservatorship and, beginning 1992, excludes one self-liquidating institution. Minus sign (-) indicates loss]

ITEM	1985	1989	1990	1991	1992	1993	1994	1995	1996	1997
Number of institutions	3,626	3,087	2,815	2,561	2,390	2,262	2,152	2,030	1,924	1,779
Assets, total	1,263	1,428	1,259	1,113	1,030	1,001	1,009	1,026	1,028	1,026
Loans and leases, net	821	916	812	724	648	626	635	648	681	692
Liabilities, total	1,218	1,358	1,192	1,044	956	922	929	940	942	937
Deposits	1,023	1,081	987	907	828	774	737	742	728	704
Equity capital.	45	69	68	69	74	78	80	86	86	89
Interest and fee income.	119	134	117	98	78	66	63	71	72	69
Interest expense	101	110	91	70	46	35	33	43	42	41
Net interest income.	17	25	26	28	32	32	30	28	30	29
Net income	6	-6	-5	1	7	7	6	8	7	9

Source: U.S. Federal Deposit Insurance Corporation, *Statistics on Banking*, annual and *FDIC Quarterly Banking Profile*.

No. 814. Volume of Long-Term Mortgage Loans Originated, by Type of Property, 1980 to 1996, and by Lender, 1996

[**In billions of dollars**. Covers credit extended in primary mortgage markets for financing real estate acquisitions]

TYPE OF PROPERTY	1980	1985	1990	1992	1993	1994	1995	1996, BY LENDER				
								Total [1]	Commercial banks	Mortgage companies	Savings and loan	Life insurance companies
Loans, total	197.2	430.0	710.5	1,124.0	1,241.7	1,019.2	930.0	1,125.3	437.7	458.1	132.0	35.1
1-4 unit family home . .	133.8	289.8	458.4	893.7	1,019.9	768.7	639.4	785.2	178.5	445.7	121.7	0.4
New units	49.1	59.0	110.7	132.4	117.3	114.6	110.7	178.2	64.0	98.2	13.1	0.1
Existing units	84.6	230.8	347.7	761.3	902.5	654.2	528.7	607.1	114.5	347.5	108.6	0.3
Multifamily residential .	12.5	31.9	32.6	25.7	31.7	32.7	39.2	47.1	22.6	12.3	4.9	1.6
New units	8.6	10.6	6.5	4.9	4.4	4.5	5.4	8.4	3.7	1.4	0.2	0.6
Existing units	3.9	21.3	26.0	20.9	27.3	28.2	33.8	38.8	18.9	10.9	4.7	1.0
Nonresidential	35.9	99.4	209.5	184.4	172.5	190.0	220.8	267.3	219.4	-	5.3	32.3
Farm properties	15.0	9.0	10.0	20.2	17.6	27.8	30.6	25.6	17.1	-	-	0.7

- Represents zero. [1] Includes other lenders not shown separately.

Source: U.S. Dept. of Housing and Urban Development, monthly and quarterly press releases based on the Survey of Mortgage Lending Activity.

No. 815. Characteristics of Conventional First Mortgage Loans for Purchase of Single-Family Homes: 1990 to 1997

[In percent, except as indicated. Annual averages. Covers fully amortized conventional mortgage loans used to purchase single-family nonfarm homes. Excludes refinancing loans, nonamortized and balloon loans, loans insured by the Federal Housing Administration, and loans guaranteed by the Veterans Administration. Based on a sample of mortgage lenders, including savings and loans associations, savings banks, commercial banks, and mortgage companies]

LOAN CHARACTERISTICS	NEW HOMES						PREVIOUSLY OCCUPIED HOMES					
	1990	1993	1994	1995	1996	1997	1990	1993	1994	1995	1996	1997
Contract interest rate, [1]												
all loans	9.7	7.0	7.3	7.7	7.6	7.6	9.8	6.9	7.3	7.7	7.6	7.5
Fixed-rate loans	10.1	7.3	7.9	8.0	7.8	7.7	10.1	7.3	8.0	8.0	7.8	7.7
Adjustable-rate loans [2]	8.9	5.8	6.5	7.2	7.0	6.9	8.9	5.5	6.2	7.0	6.9	6.7
Initial fees, charges [3]	1.98	1.29	1.29	1.20	1.21	1.01	1.74	1.19	1.07	0.93	0.93	0.97
Effective interest rate, [4]												
all loans	10.1	7.2	7.5	7.9	7.8	7.7	10.1	7.1	7.5	7.8	7.7	7.7
Fixed-rate loans	10.4	7.5	8.1	8.2	8.0	7.9	10.4	7.5	8.2	8.2	8.0	7.9
Adjustable-rate loans [2]	9.2	5.9	6.6	7.4	7.2	7.0	9.2	5.7	6.4	7.1	7.1	6.9
Term to maturity (years)	27.3	26.1	27.5	27.7	27.1	28.2	27.0	25.4	27.1	27.4	26.8	27.3
Purchase price ($1,000)	154.1	163.7	170.7	175.4	182.6	181.4	140.3	139.6	136.4	137.3	150.2	161.0
Loan to price ratio	74.9	78.0	78.7	78.6	78.1	80.4	74.9	77.1	80.1	80.1	79.1	79.2
Percent of number of loans with adjustable rates	31	18	41	37	26	21	27	20	39	31	27	22

[1] Initial interest rate paid by the borrower as specified in the loan contract. [2] Loans with a contractual provision for periodic adjustments in the contract interest rate. [3] Includes all fees, commissions, discounts and "points" paid by the borrower, or seller, in order to obtain the loan. Excludes those charges for mortgage, credit, life or property insurance; for property transfer; and for title search and insurance. [4] Contract interest rate plus fees and charges amortized over a 10-year period.

Source: U.S. Federal Housing Finance Board, *Rates & Terms on Conventional Home Mortgages, Annual Summary.*

No. 816. Mortgage Debt Outstanding, by Type of Property and Holder: 1980 to 1997

[In billions of dollars. As of Dec. 31. Includes Puerto Rico and Guam]

TYPE OF PROPERTY AND HOLDER	1980	1985	1989	1990	1991	1992	1993	1994	1995	1996	1997
Mortgage debt, total.	1,465	2,374	3,580	3,794	3,948	4,063	4,206	4,392	4,606	4,929	5,277
Residential nonfarm	1,111	1,742	2,749	2,961	3,134	3,293	3,448	3,632	3,821	4,074	4,357
One- to four-family homes.	970	1,537	2,461	2,674	2,851	3,019	3,178	3,357	3,533	3,762	4,019
Savings institutions.	487	554	669	600	538	490	470	478	482	514	519
Mortgage pools or trusts [1]	125	407	887	1,046	1,230	1,400	1,519	1,658	1,771	1,941	2,106
Government National Mortgage Assoc.	92	207	358	392	416	411	405	441	461	494	523
Federal Home Loan Mortgage Corp . .	13	100	266	308	352	402	443	488	512	552	577
Federal National Mortgage Association.	(X)	54	220	291	363	436	487	521	570	633	688
Private mortgage conduits [2]	(NA)	(NA)	(NA)	(NA)	(NA)	(NA)	(NA)	209	228	262	318
Commercial banks	162	215	391	458	486	511	561	616	669	699	762
Individuals and others [3]	117	239	370	403	422	414	390	370	376	376	404
Federal and related agencies	61	110	131	153	163	194	230	228	227	225	221
Federal National Mortgage Assoc . . .	52	92	91	94	101	124	151	159	162	161	156
Life insurance companies	18	12	12	13	11	11	9	7	7	7	7
Five or more units	141	205	288	287	283	273	269	275	287	313	338
Commercial	256	526	750	754	735	690	677	677	701	768	829
Farm	97	106	80	79	79	80	81	83	85	87	90
TYPE OF HOLDER											
Savings institutions	603	760	910	802	705	628	598	596	597	628	630
Commercial banks	264	431	771	849	881	901	948	1,013	1,090	1,145	1,244
Life insurance companies.	131	172	254	268	260	242	224	211	207	205	211
Individuals and others [3]	206	404	529	555	569	561	533	524	538	579	617
Mortgage pools or trusts [1]	146	439	918	1,081	1,267	1,445	1,576	1,732	1,867	2,070	2,283
Government National Mortgage Assoc. . . .	94	212	368	404	420	420	414	451	472	506	537
Federal Home Loan Mortgage Corp.	17	100	273	316	359	408	447	491	515	554	579
Federal National Mortgage Association . . .	(X)	55	228	300	372	445	496	530	583	651	710
Farmers Home Administration [4]	32	48	(Z)	(Z)	(Z)	(Z)	(Z)	(Z)	(Z)	(Z)	(Z)
Private mortgage conduits.	(NA)	(NA)	(NA)	(NA)	(NA)	(NA)	(NA)	260	294	359	457
Federal and related agencies	115	167	198	239	266	286	326	316	307	301	293
Federal National Mortgage Association . . .	57	98	99	105	112	137	166	174	177	175	168
Farmers Home Administration [4]	3	1	41	41	42	42	41	42	42	42	41
Federal Land Banks.	38	47	30	29	29	29	28	29	28	30	31
Federal Home Loan Mortgage Corp . . .	5	14	22	22	27	34	47	42	44	47	48
Federal Housing and Veterans Admin	4	4	5	7	9	11	11	10	9	6	3
Government National Mortgage Assoc. . . .	5	1	(Z)	(Z)	(Z)	(Z)	(Z)	(Z)	(Z)	(Z)	(Z)
Federal Deposit Insurance Corp	(X)	(X)	(X)	(X)	(X)	(X)	(X)	14	8	4	1
Resolution Trust Corporation	(X)	(X)	(X)	(X)	33	46	32	17	10	2	(X)

NA Not available.   X Not applicable.   Z Less than $500 million.   [1] Outstanding principal balances of mortgage pools backing securities insured or guaranteed by the agency indicated. Includes other pools not shown separately. [2] Includes securitized home equity loans. [3] Includes mortgage companies, real estate investment trusts, state and local retirement funds, noninsured pension funds, state and local credit agencies, credit unions, and finance companies. [4] FmHA-guaranteed securities sold to the Federal Financing Bank were reallocated from FmHA mortgage pools to FmHA mortgage holdings in 1986 because of accounting changes by the Farmers Home Administration.

Source: Board of Governors of the Federal Reserve System, *Federal Reserve Bulletin,* monthly.

No. 817. Estimated Home Equity Debt Outstanding, by Type and Source of Credit: 1990 to 1997

[In billions of dollars. A "traditional home equity loan" is a closed-end loan extended for a specific period that generally requires repayment of interest and principal in equal monthly installments. Such a loan typically has a fixed interest rate. A "home equity line of credit" is a revolving account that permits borrowing from time to time, at the homeowner's discretion, up to the amount of the credit line. It usually has a more flexible repayment schedule and a variable interest rate. Based on reports from lending institutions and data from the Survey of Consumers, a sample survey of households]

| YEAR | Total | HOME EQUITY LINES OF CREDIT | | | TRADITIONAL HOME EQUITY LOANS | | |
		All lenders	Commercial banks	Other sources	All lenders	Commercial banks	Other sources
1990	258	105	61	44	153	54	99
1991	262	114	70	44	148	53	95
1992	258	114	73	41	144	50	94
1993	261	110	73	37	151	49	102
1994	274	116	76	40	158	54	104
1995	299	123	79	44	176	61	115
1996	347	132	85	47	215	69	146
1997	420	153	98	55	267	76	191

Source: Board of Governors of the Federal Reserve System, *Federal Reserve Bulletin*, July 1994 and April 1998.

No. 818. Home Equity Lending—Percentage of Homeowners with Credit, Sources of Credit, and Uses for Funds Borrowed: 1993-94 and 1997

[In percent. See headnote, Table 817]

| ITEM | HOME EQUITY LINES OF CREDIT | | TRADITIONAL HOME EQUITY LOANS | | USES FOR FUNDS BORROWED | 1997[1] | |
	1993-94	1997	1993-94	1997		Home equity lines of credit	Traditional home equity loans
Percentage of homeowners with home equity credit	8	8	5	5	Home improvement	69	45
					Repayment of other debts	49	61
SOURCE OF HOME EQUITY CREDIT					Education	19	2
Total	100	100	100	100	Real estate	9	10
					Auto or truck	37	6
Commercial banks	60	61	29	44	Medical expenses	10	2
Savings institutions [2]	21	16	30	20	Business expenses	18	4
Credit unions	13	16	11	13	Vacation	13	1
Other creditors [3]	7	7	29	24	Other [4]	1	1

[1] Percentages sum to more than 100 because respondents were allowed to cite multiple uses for a single loan or drawdown and more than one draw for one line of credit.   [2] Includes savings banks and savings and loan associations.   [3] Includes finance and loan companies, brokerage firms, mortgage companies, and individuals.   [4] Includes purchase of furniture or appliance, purchase of boat or other recreational vehicle, payment of taxes, and personal financial investments.

Source: Board of Governors of the Federal Reserve System, *Federal Reserve Bulletin*, April 1998.

No. 819. Mortgage Delinquency and Foreclosure Rates: 1980 to 1997

[In percent, except as indicated. Covers one- to four-family residential nonfarm mortgage loans]

ITEM	1980	1985	1990	1992	1993	1994	1995	1996	1997
Number of mortgage loans outstanding (1,000)	30,033	34,004	40,638	42,562	45,301	47,563	49,214	50,118	51,169
Delinquency rates: [1]									
Total	5.0	5.8	4.7	4.6	4.2	4.1	4.3	4.3	4.3
Conventional loans	3.1	4.0	3.0	2.9	2.7	2.6	2.8	2.8	2.8
VA loans	5.3	6.6	6.4	6.5	6.3	6.3	6.4	6.7	6.9
FHA loans	6.6	7.5	6.7	7.1	7.1	7.3	7.6	8.1	8.1
Foreclosure rates: [2]									
Total	0.5	1.0	0.9	1.0	1.0	0.9	0.9	1.0	1.1
Conventional loans	0.2	0.7	0.7	0.8	0.8	0.7	0.7	0.7	0.7
VA loans	0.6	1.1	1.2	1.3	1.3	1.3	1.3	1.6	1.8
FHA loans	0.7	1.3	1.3	1.4	1.5	1.5	1.4	1.6	2.0

[1] Number of loans delinquent 30 days or more as percentage of mortgage loans serviced in survey. Annual average of quarterly figures.   [2] Percentage of loans in the foreclosure process at yearend, not seasonally adjusted.

Source: Mortgage Bankers Association of America, Washington, DC, *National Delinquency Survey*, quarterly.

No. 820. Consumer Credit Outstanding and Finance Rates: 1980 to 1997

[In billions of dollars, except percent. Estimated amounts of seasonally adjusted credit outstanding as of end of year; finance rates, annual averages]

TYPE OF CREDIT	1980	1985	1990	1991	1992	1993	1994	1995	1996	1997
Total.	350.1	584.7	796.4	777.2	779.9	838.6	959.7	1,094.2	1,179.9	1,235.8
Automobile	112.0	210.9	282.4	263.4	262.7	288.0	327.9	364.2	392.4	414.6
Revolving [1]	55.1	122.1	223.3	263.7	278.2	309.9	365.5	443.0	499.2	528.9
Other [2]	183.0	251.7	290.7	250.1	239.1	240.7	266.4	287.0	288.3	292.4
FINANCE RATES (percent)										
Commercial banks:										
New automobiles (48 months) [3]	14.32	12.91	11.78	11.13	9.28	8.08	8.13	9.57	9.05	9.02
Other consumer goods (24 months) .	15.48	15.94	15.46	15.17	14.04	13.46	13.20	13.94	13.53	13.91
Credit-card plans	17.31	18.69	18.17	18.23	17.77	16.81	15.69	16.02	15.63	15.76
Finance companies:										
New automobiles	14.82	11.98	12.54	12.41	9.93	9.47	9.80	11.19	9.83	7.12
Used automobiles	19.10	17.58	15.99	15.59	13.80	12.78	13.51	14.47	13.54	13.27

[1] Consists mainly of outstanding balances on credit card accounts, but also includes borrowing under check credit and overdraft plans, and unsecured personal lines of credit. [2] Includes noninstallment credit. [3] For 1980, maturities were 36 months for new car loans.

Source: Board of Governors of the Federal Reserve System, *Federal Reserve Bulletin*, monthly; and *Annual Statistical Digest*.

No. 821. Delinquency Rates on Bank Installment Loans, by Type of Loan: 1980 to 1997

[In percent, except as indicated. As of end of year; seasonally adjusted, except as noted. Number of loans having an installment past due for 30 days or more as a percentage of total installment loans outstanding]

TYPE OF CREDIT	1980	1985	1989	1990	1991	1992	1993	1994	1995	1996	1997
DELINQUENCY RATES											
Closed-end installment loans, total	2.82	2.32	2.64	2.57	2.58	2.43	1.77	1.72	2.12	2.34	2.43
Personal loans [1]	3.53	3.63	3.52	3.37	2.95	3.18	2.30	2.38	2.81	3.18	3.21
Automobile, direct loans [2] . . .	1.81	1.64	2.03	2.22	2.14	2.08	1.58	1.46	1.87	2.03	2.29
Automobile, indirect loans [3] . .	2.29	2.02	2.61	2.59	2.66	2.33	1.65	1.65	2.17	2.36	2.46
Property improvement [4]	1.93	1.91	2.25	2.30	2.38	2.18	1.61	1.66	1.77	2.02	2.09
Home equity and second mortgage loans [5] . .	(NA)	2.06	1.85	1.45	2.06	1.89	1.66	1.38	1.41	1.42	1.49
Mobile home loans	3.14	2.39	2.51	3.03	2.86	4.02	3.70	3.68	4.02	4.75	4.91
Recreational vehicle loans	1.94	1.84	2.24	2.63	2.25	2.27	1.26	1.23	1.62	2.16	2.28
Marine financing [5]	(NA)	(NA)	(NA)	(NA)	(NA)	2.52	1.72	1.51	2.22	2.67	2.74
Bank card loans.	2.72	2.95	2.24	2.86	3.29	2.93	2.49	2.93	3.34	3.72	3.04
Revolving credit loans	2.70	1.96	2.92	3.00	2.75	2.63	2.90	2.38	3.14	3.99	3.45
Home equity lines of credit loans (open-end) [5] .	(NA)	(NA)	0.78	0.85	0.88	0.85	0.70	0.63	0.90	1.04	0.96
REPOSSESSIONS PER 1,000 LOANS OUTSTANDING											
Mobile home	1.57	1.21	1.63	1.19	1.62	1.30	1.21	1.18	0.86	1.64	1.89
Automobile, direct loans [2]	1.10	1.11	1.03	1.75	1.17	0.92	0.83	0.53	0.96	0.76	0.90
Automobile, indirect loans [3] . . .	2.75	2.08	1.70	1.61	2.07	1.47	0.97	1.17	1.36	1.61	1.56
Marine financing [5]	(NA)	(NA)	(NA)	(NA)	(NA)	1.21	1.03	0.82	0.81	1.30	1.05

NA Not available. [1] Beginning 1985, includes home appliance loans. [2] Made directly by bank's lending function. [3] Made by automobile dealerships; loans in bank's portfolio. [4] Beginning 1985, own plan and FHA Title I loans. [5] Not seasonally adjusted.

Source: American Bankers Association, Washington, DC, *Consumer Credit Delinquency Bulletin*, quarterly (copyright).

No. 822. Credit Cards—Holders, Numbers, Spending, and Debt, 1990 and 1997, and Projections, 2000

TYPE OF CREDIT CARD	CARDHOLDERS (mil.)			NUMBER OF CARDS (mil.)			CREDIT CARD SPENDING (bil. dol.)			CREDIT CARD DEBT (bil. dol.)		
	1990	1997	2000, proj.	1990	1997	2000, proj.	1990	1997	2000, proj.	1990	1997	2000, proj.
Total [1]	122	149	157	1,013	1,387	1,499	467	1,080	1,419	243	560	677
Bank [2]	79	100	105	213	403	458	243	678	891	154	397	486
Oil company.	85	79	79	123	109	105	28	38	46	3	4	5
Phone.	97	116	126	141	173	183	14	19	22	2	2	3
Retail store	96	108	114	459	614	652	75	121	147	51	88	99
Travel and entertainment [3] . . .	16	23	24	28	31	38	85	160	232	20	33	40
Other [4]	10	7	7	49	57	63	22	64	81	13	36	44

[1] Cardholders may hold more than one type of card. [2] Visa and MasterCard credit cards. Excludes debit cards. [3] Includes American Express and Diners Club. [4] Includes Air Travel Card, automobile rental, Discover (except for cardholders), and miscellaneous cards.

Source: HSN Consultants Inc., Oxnard, CA, *The Nilson Report*, twice-monthly. (Copyright used by permission.)

No. 823. Usage of General Purpose Credit Cards by Families: 1989 to 1995

[General purpose credit cards include Mastercard, Visa, Optima, and Discover cards. All dollar figures are given in constant 1995 dollars based on consumer price index data as published by U.S. Bureau of Labor Statistics. Families include one-person units; for definition of family, see text, Section 1. Based on Survey of Consumer Finance; see Appendix III. For definition of median, see Guide to Tabular Presentation]

AGE OF FAMILY HEAD AND FAMILY INCOME	Percent having a general purpose credit card	Median number of cards	Median new charges on last month's bills	Percent having a balance after last month's bills	Median balance [1]	PERCENT OF CARDHOLDING FAMILIES WHO—		
						Almost always pay off the balance	Some-times pay off the balance	Hardly ever pay off the balance
1989, total	55.8	2	$100	52.0	$1,200	53.1	21.5	25.4
1992, total	62.2	2	100	52.8	1,100	52.8	19.6	27.6
1995, total	66.4	2	200	56.3	1,500	51.9	20.4	27.7
Under 35 years old	59.0	2	100	69.2	1,500	40.2	23.5	36.3
35 to 44 years old	68.5	2	200	68.1	1,900	40.7	26.9	32.4
45 to 54 years old	75.4	2	200	64.8	1,800	47.1	22.5	30.4
55 to 64 years old	71.9	2	200	48.0	1,800	59.3	18.4	22.3
65 to 74 years old	68.3	2	200	30.8	800	72.0	12.9	15.1
75 years old and over	54.6	1	100	18.2	700	85.8	2.5	11.7
Less than $10,000	26.3	1	100	55.8	1,000	56.4	12.4	31.2
$10,000 to $24,999	53.3	2	100	57.0	1,500	50.9	17.2	31.9
$25,000 to $49,999	75.0	2	100	59.2	1,500	47.6	20.9	31.5
$50,000 to $99,999	93.1	2	200	59.4	2,000	49.7	25.3	25.1
$100,000 and more	97.1	3	800	35.4	2,100	73.7	17.2	9.1

[1] Among families having a balance.

Source: Board of Governors of the Federal Reserve System, unpublished data.

No. 824. Debit Cards—Numbers, Transactions, and Volume, 1990 to 1997, and Projections, 2000

TYPE OF DEBIT CARD	NUMBER OF CARDS (mil.)				NUMBER OF TRANSACTIONS (mil.)				VOLUME (bil. dol.)			
	1990	1995	1997	2000, proj.	1990	1995	1997	2000, proj.	1990	1995	1997	2000, proj.
Total [1]	173	240	291	353	273	1,558	3,912	9,408	12	62	163	368
Bank [2]	9	40	80	122	127	829	2,465	6,008	8	36	110	244
EFT systems [3]	160	190	200	219	129	672	1,388	3,335	3	23	49	120
Other [4]	4	10	11	12	17	57	59	65	1	3	4	4

[1] Increasingly, bank cards and EFT cards are the same pieces of plastic that carry multiple brands. The total card figure shown does not include any duplication. [2] Visa Check Card and MasterCard MasterMoney. [3] Cards issued by financial institution members of regional and national switches. EFT=Electronic fund transfer. [4] Commercial fuel cards issued by private-label firms plus retail cards such as those issued by supermarkets and oil companies.

Source: HSN Consultants Inc., Oxnard, CA, The Nilson Report, twice-monthly. (Copyright used by permission.)

No. 825. Electronic Funds Transfer Volume: 1980 to 1997

[Electronic funds transfer cover automated teller machine (ATM) transactions and transactions at point-of-sale (POS) terminals. Point-of-sale terminals are electronic terminals in retail stores that allow a customer to pay for goods through a direct debit to a customer's account at the bank]

ITEM	Unit	1980	1985	1990	1992	1993	1994	1995	1996	1997
Total number of transactions	Million	(NA)	3,579	5,942	7,537	8,135	8,958	10,464	11,830	12,422
ATM transactions	Million	(NA)	3,565	5,751	7,206	7,705	8,334	9,689	10,684	10,980
POS transactions	Million	(NA)	14	191	289	430	624	775	1,146	1,442
ATM terminals, total [1]	1,000	18.5	60.0	80.2	87.3	94.8	109.1	122.7	139.1	165.0
Monthly transactions per terminal	Number	5,405	4,951	5,980	6,876	6,772	6,459	6,580	6,399	5,545
Shared terminals	1,000	(NA)	35.5	75.3	84.7	92.6	108.1	122.6	139.0	165.0
Proprietary terminals	1,000	(NA)	24.5	4.9	2.6	2.3	1.0	0.1	0.1	(NA)
POS terminals, total [2]	1,000	(NA)	(NA)	53	95	155	341	529	875	1,300

NA Not available. [1] As of September. [2] As of June.

Source: Faulkner & Gray, Chicago, IL, Faulkner & Gray/EFT Network Data Book-1998, September 26, 1997 (copyright).

No. 826. Money Stock and Liquid Assets: 1980 to 1997

[In billions of dollars. As of December. Seasonally adjusted averages of daily figures]

ITEM	1980	1981	1982	1983	1984	1985	1986	1987	1988	1989	1990	1991	1992	1993	1994	1995	1996	1997
M1, total [1]	**409**	**437**	**475**	**521**	**552**	**620**	**724**	**750**	**787**	**794**	**826**	**897**	**1,025**	**1,130**	**1,151**	**1,129**	**1,083**	**1,076**
Currency [2]	115	123	133	146	156	168	181	197	212	223	247	267	293	322	354	372	395	426
Travelers checks [2]	4	4	4	5	5	5	6	7	7	7	7	8	8	8	8	8	9	8
Demand deposits [3]	261	231	234	238	244	267	302	287	287	279	277	290	340	385	384	391	404	397
Other checkable deposits [4]	28	79	104	132	147	180	236	260	281	285	294	333	384	415	404	356	276	245
M2, total	**1,601**	**1,756**	**1,911**	**2,128**	**2,312**	**2,498**	**2,734**	**2,833**	**2,996**	**3,161**	**3,280**	**3,380**	**3,435**	**3,488**	**3,503**	**3,651**	**3,826**	**4,046**
M1	409	437	475	521	552	620	724	750	787	794	826	897	1,025	1,130	1,151	1,129	1,083	1,076
Non-M1 components in M2	1,192	1,319	1,436	1,607	1,760	1,878	2,010	2,083	2,209	2,367	2,454	2,483	2,410	2,358	2,352	2,523	2,743	2,970
Money market funds, retail [5]	63	152	185	138	167	177	210	225	246	322	357	372	354	356	385	455	523	603
Savings deposits (including MMDA's [5])	400	344	400	685	705	815	941	937	926	894	924	1,045	1,187	1,219	1,150	1,135	1,272	1,397
Commercial banks	186	159	190	363	389	457	534	535	542	541	582	665	754	785	753	775	905	1,021
Thrift institutions	215	185	210	322	315	359	407	403	384	353	342	380	433	434	397	360	367	377
Small time deposits [6]	729	823	851	784	889	886	858	921	1,037	1,151	1,173	1,065	868	783	817	933	949	970
Commercial banks	286	348	380	351	388	386	369	392	451	534	610	602	508	468	503	576	595	626
Thrift institutions	442	475	471	433	501	499	489	529	586	618	562	463	360	314	314	357	354	344
M3, total	**1,992**	**2,241**	**2,442**	**2,685**	**2,980**	**3,198**	**3,486**	**3,673**	**3,913**	**4,066**	**4,127**	**4,182**	**4,194**	**4,259**	**4,334**	**4,596**	**4,931**	**5,374**
M2	1,601	1,756	1,911	2,128	2,312	2,498	2,734	2,833	2,996	3,161	3,280	3,380	3,435	3,488	3,503	3,651	3,826	4,046
Non-M2 components in M3	391	485	531	557	668	701	752	840	917	905	847	802	759	771	831	944	1,105	1,329
Large time deposits [8]	260	304	325	316	403	422	420	467	518	541	481	417	354	334	363	420	491	594
Commercial banks [8]	215	250	261	220	256	271	270	304	344	380	360	333	286	272	299	345	413	505
Thrift institutions	45	54	64	97	147	152	150	163	175	161	121	83	67	61	65	74	78	88
Repurchase agreements [9]	57	65	67	95	95	120	143	173	189	158	139	120	129	159	183	182	194	235
Eurodollars [9]	58	77	90	105	97	94	104	108	117	95	89	79	67	66	81	89	109	145
Money market funds, institution only	16	39	49	41	62	64	85	92	92	111	139	187	210	213	203	254	310	376
L, total	**2,330**	**2,602**	**2,846**	**3,151**	**3,519**	**3,827**	**4,122**	**4,340**	**4,664**	**4,893**	**4,977**	**5,008**	**5,081**	**5,173**	**5,316**	**5,702**	**6,084**	**6,609**
M3	1,992	2,241	2,442	2,685	2,980	3,198	3,486	3,673	3,913	4,066	4,127	4,182	4,194	4,259	4,334	4,596	4,931	5,374
Savings bonds	72	68	68	71	74	79	92	101	109	118	126	138	157	172	180	185	187	186
Short-term Treasury securities [10]	134	149	183	213	262	298	276	249	267	324	334	329	345	341	383	469	455	430
Bankers acceptances	32	40	44	45	42	42	37	45	40	41	36	24	21	15	14	11	12	12
Commercial paper [11]	100	104	108	136	157	209	231	273	334	345	354	335	366	387	405	441	498	606

[1] Currency outside U.S. Treasury, Federal Reserve Banks and the vaults of depository institutions.   [2] Outstanding amount of nonbank issuers.   [3] At commercial banks and foreign-related institutions.
[4] Consists of negotiable order of withdrawal (NOW) and automatic transfer service (ATS) accounts at all depository institutions, credit union share draft balances, and demand deposits at thrift institutions.
market deposit accounts (MMDA).   [6] Issued in amounts of less than $100,000. Includes retail repurchase agreements. Excludes individual retirement accounts (IRA's) and Keogh accounts.   [7] Issued in amounts
of $100,000 or more. Excludes those booked at international banking facilities.   [8] Excludes those held by money market mutual funds, depository institutions, U.S. Government, foreign banks and official
institutions.   [9] Excludes those held by depository institutions and money market mutual funds.   [10] U.S. Treasury bills and coupons with remaining maturities of less than 12 months held by other than depository
institutions, Federal Reserve banks, money market mutual funds, and foreign entities.   [11] Excludes commercial paper held by money market mutual funds.

Source: Board of Governors of the Federal Reserve System, Federal Reserve Bulletin, monthly, and Money Stock, Liquid Assets, and Debt Measures, Federal Reserve Statistical Release H.6, weekly.

No. 827. Money Market Interest Rates and Mortgage Rates: 1980 to 1997

[Percent per year. Annual averages of monthly data, except as indicated]

TYPE	1980	1985	1986	1987	1988	1989	1990	1991	1992	1993	1994	1995	1996	1997
Federal funds, effective rate [1][2]	13.35	8.10	6.80	6.66	7.57	9.21	8.10	5.69	3.52	3.02	4.21	5.83	5.30	5.46
Commercial paper, 3-month [1][2]	12.61	7.95	6.49	6.82	7.66	8.99	8.06	5.87	3.75	3.22	4.66	5.93	5.41	5.58
Commercial paper, 6-month [1][2]	12.24	8.00	6.39	6.85	7.68	8.80	7.95	5.85	3.80	3.30	4.93	5.93	5.42	5.62
Prime rate charged by banks	15.26	9.93	8.33	8.21	9.32	10.87	10.01	8.46	6.25	6.00	7.15	8.83	8.27	8.44
Eurodollar deposits, 3-month	14.00	8.27	6.70	7.07	7.85	9.16	8.16	5.86	3.70	3.18	4.63	5.93	5.38	5.61
Finance paper, 3-month [2][3]	11.45	7.77	6.38	6.54	7.38	8.72	7.87	5.60	3.65	3.16	4.53	5.78	5.29	5.48
Finance paper, 6-month [2][3]	11.25	7.74	6.31	6.37	7.14	8.16	7.53	5.70	3.63	3.15	4.56	5.68	5.21	5.54
Bankers acceptances, 3-month [2][4]	12.67	7.91	6.38	6.75	7.56	8.87	7.93	5.70	3.62	3.13	4.56	5.81	5.31	5.54
Bankers acceptances, 6-month [2][4]	12.20	7.95	6.28	6.78	7.60	8.67	7.80	5.67	3.67	3.21	4.83	5.80	5.31	5.57
Large negotiable CD's:														
3-month, secondary market	13.07	8.05	6.52	6.86	7.73	9.09	8.15	5.83	3.68	3.17	4.63	5.92	5.39	5.62
6-month, secondary market	12.94	8.24	6.50	7.01	7.91	9.08	8.17	5.91	3.76	3.28	4.96	5.98	5.47	5.73
Taxable money market funds [5]	12.68	7.71	6.26	6.12	7.11	8.87	7.82	5.71	3.36	2.70	3.75	5.48	4.95	5.10
Tax-exempt money market funds [5]	(NA)	4.90	4.31	4.14	4.79	5.90	5.45	4.13	2.58	1.97	2.38	3.39	2.99	3.14
Certificates of deposit (CD's): [6]														
6-month	(NA)	7.83	6.51	6.47	7.18	8.34	7.35	5.67	3.46	2.84	3.37	4.92	4.68	4.86
1-year	(NA)	8.29	6.75	6.77	7.47	8.41	7.42	5.88	3.72	3.12	3.94	5.39	4.95	5.16
2½-year	(NA)	9.00	7.13	7.16	7.77	8.33	7.52	6.29	4.47	3.73	4.49	5.69	5.14	5.40
5-year	(NA)	9.66	7.60	7.66	8.11	8.30	7.71	6.83	5.62	4.88	5.30	6.00	5.46	5.67
U.S. Government securities:														
Secondary market: [7]														
3-month Treasury bill	11.39	7.47	5.97	5.78	6.67	8.11	7.50	5.38	3.43	3.00	4.25	5.49	5.01	5.06
6-month Treasury bill	11.32	7.65	6.02	6.03	6.91	8.03	7.46	5.44	3.54	3.12	4.64	5.56	5.08	5.18
1-year Treasury bill	10.85	7.81	6.07	6.33	7.13	7.92	7.35	5.52	3.71	3.29	5.02	5.60	5.22	5.36
Auction average: [8]														
3-month Treasury bill	11.51	7.47	5.98	5.82	6.68	8.12	7.51	5.42	3.45	3.02	4.29	5.51	5.02	5.07
6-month Treasury bill	11.37	7.64	6.03	6.05	6.92	8.04	7.47	5.49	3.57	3.14	4.66	5.59	5.09	5.18
1-year Treasury bill	10.75	7.76	6.07	6.33	7.17	7.91	7.36	5.54	3.75	3.33	4.98	5.69	5.23	5.36
Home mortgages: [9]														
HUD series: [9]														
FHA insured, secondary market [10]	13.44	12.24	9.91	10.16	10.49	10.24	10.17	9.25	8.46	7.46	8.68	8.18	8.19	7.89
Conventional, new-home [11][12]	13.95	12.28	10.07	10.17	10.30	10.21	10.08	9.20	8.43	7.37	8.58	8.05	8.03	7.76
Conventional, existing-home [11]	13.95	12.29	10.09	10.17	10.31	10.22	10.08	9.20	8.43	7.37	8.59	8.05	8.03	7.76
Conventional, 15 yr. fixed [6]	(NA)	11.53	10.05	10.04	10.14	10.05	9.67	8.76	7.80	6.65	7.77	7.39	7.28	7.16
Conventional, 30 yr. fixed [6]	(NA)	11.90	10.39	10.40	10.38	10.26	10.01	9.09	8.27	7.17	8.28	7.86	7.76	7.57

NA Not available. [1] Based on daily offering rates of dealers. [2] Yields are quoted on a bank-discount basis, rather than an investment yield basis (which would give a higher figure). [3] Placed directly; averages of daily offering rates quoted by finance companies. [4] Based on representative closing yields. From Jan. 1, 1981, rates of top-rated banks only. [5] 12 month return for period ending December 31. Source: IBC Financial Data, Inc., Ashland, MA, *IBC's Money Market Insight*, monthly (copyright). [6] Annual averages. Source: Financial Rates, Inc., North Palm Beach, FL, *Bank Rate Monitor*, weekly (copyright). [7] Averages based on daily offering rates quoted by finance companies. [8] Averages computed on an issue-date basis; bank discount basis. [9] HUD=Housing and Urban Development. [10] Averages based on daily closing bid yields in secondary market, bank discount basis. [11] Primary market. [12] Average contract rates on new commitments.

Source: Except as noted, Board of Governors of the Federal Reserve System, *Federal Reserve Bulletin*, monthly, and *Annual Statistical Digest*.

No. 828. Bond Yields: 1980 to 1997

[**Percent per year**. Annual averages of daily figures, except as indicated]

TYPE	1980	1985	1989	1990	1991	1992	1993	1994	1995	1996	1997
U.S. Treasury, constant maturities: [1] [2]											
1-year..................	12.00	8.42	8.53	7.89	5.86	3.89	3.43	5.32	5.94	5.52	5.63
2-year..................	11.73	9.27	8.57	8.16	6.49	4.77	4.05	5.94	6.15	5.84	5.99
3-year..................	11.51	9.64	8.55	8.26	6.82	5.30	4.44	6.27	6.25	5.99	6.10
5-year..................	11.45	10.12	8.50	8.37	7.37	6.19	5.14	6.69	6.38	6.18	6.22
7-year..................	11.40	10.50	8.52	8.52	7.68	6.63	5.54	6.91	6.50	6.34	6.33
10-year.................	11.43	10.62	8.49	8.55	7.86	7.01	5.87	7.69	6.57	6.44	6.35
20-year.................	(NA)	(NA)	(NA)	(NA)	(NA)	(NA)	6.29	7.47	6.95	6.83	6.69
30-year.................	11.27	10.79	8.45	8.61	8.14	7.67	6.59	7.37	6.88	6.71	6.61
U.S. Govt., long-term bonds [2] [3]	10.81	10.75	8.58	8.74	8.16	7.52	6.45	7.41	6.93	6.80	6.67
State and local govt. bonds, Aaa....	7.86	8.60	7.00	6.97	6.56	6.09	5.38	5.77	5.80	5.52	5.32
State and local govt. bonds, Baa....	9.02	9.58	7.40	7.30	6.99	6.48	5.83	6.17	6.10	5.79	5.50
Municipal (Bond Buyer, 20 bonds)...	8.59	9.10	7.23	7.27	6.92	6.44	5.60	6.18	5.95	5.76	5.52
Corporate Aaa seasoned [4].........	11.94	11.37	9.26	9.32	8.77	8.14	7.22	7.97	7.59	7.37	7.27
Corporate Baa seasoned [4].........	13.67	12.72	10.18	10.36	9.80	8.98	7.93	8.63	8.20	8.05	7.87
Corporate (Moody's) [4] [5].........	12.75	12.05	9.66	9.77	9.23	8.55	7.54	8.26	7.83	7.66	7.54
Industrials (49 bonds) [6]........	12.35	11.80	9.66	9.77	9.25	8.52	7.51	8.21	7.76	7.58	7.47
Public utilities (51 bonds) [7]......	13.15	12.29	9.66	9.76	9.21	8.57	7.56	8.30	7.90	7.74	7.63

NA Not available. [1] Yields on the more actively traded issues adjusted to constant maturities by the U.S. Treasury. [2] Yields are based on closing bid prices quoted by at least five dealers. [3] Averages (to maturity or call) for all outstanding bonds neither due nor callable in less than 10 years, including several very low yielding "flower" bonds. [4] Source: Moody's Investors Service, New York, NY. [5] For 1980 and 1985 includes railroad bonds which were discontinued as part of composite in 1989. [6] Covers 40 bonds for 1980 and 38 bonds for 1985. [7] Covers 40 bonds for 1980 and 1985.
Source: Except as noted, Board of Governors of the Federal Reserve System, *Federal Reserve Bulletin*, monthly.

No. 829. Volume of Debt Markets by Type of Security: 1990 to 1997

[**In billions of dollars**. Covers debt markets as represented by the source]

TYPE OF SECURITY	1990	1992	1993	1994	1995	1996	1997
NEW ISSUE VOLUME							
Total................	**2,780**	**3,995**	**4,829**	**5,268**	**6,745**	**8,159**	**9,406**
U.S. Treasury securities [1]	1,531	1,991	2,066	2,112	2,331	2,485	2,169
Federal agency debt...........	637	913	1,380	2,228	3,506	4,500	5,730
Municipal..................	163	278	340	205	198	226	267
Mortgage-backed securities [2]	235	455	568	359	269	371	368
Asset-backed securities [3].......	42	51	59	75	107	151	185
Corporate debt [4]	173	310	416	289	333	428	687
DAILY TRADING VOLUME							
Total................	**111.2**	**175.2**	**204.6**	**237.7**	**246.3**	**274.0**	**300.5**
U.S. Treasury securities [1] [5] ...	111.2	152.1	173.6	191.3	193.2	203.7	212.1
Federal agency debt [5].........	(NA)	6.1	8.9	16.0	23.7	31.1	40.2
Municipal..................	(NA)	(NA)	(NA)	(NA)	(NA)	1.1	1.1
Mortgage-backed securities [2]	(NA)	17.0	22.1	30.4	29.4	38.1	47.1
VOLUME OF SECURITIES OUTSTANDING							
Total................	**7,431**	**8,504**	**9,093**	**9,633**	**10,404**	**11,231**	**12,099**
U.S. Treasury securities [1]	2,196	2,754	2,990	3,126	3,307	3,460	3,457
Federal agency debt...........	435	484	571	739	845	926	996
Municipal..................	1,184	1,303	1,378	1,342	1,294	1,296	1,366
Mortgage-backed securities [2]	1,024	1,274	1,350	1,442	1,570	1,715	1,827
Asset-backed securities [3].......	102	157	179	205	298	391	517
Money market instruments [6].....	1,157	994	972	1,035	1,177	1,394	1,691
Corporate debt...............	1,334	1,543	1,662	1,747	1,913	2,055	2,214

NA Not available. [1] Marketable public debt. [2] Includes only Government National Mortgage Association (GNMA), Federal National Mortgage Association (FNMA), and Federal Home Loan Mortgage Corporation (FHLMC) mortgage-backed securities. [3] Excludes mortgage-related assets. [4] Nonconvertible corporate debt. [5] Primary dealer transactions. [6] Commercial paper, bankers acceptances, and large time deposits.
Source: PSA, The Bond Market Trade Association, New York, NY. (copyright). Based on data supplied by Board of Governors of the Federal Reserve System, U.S. Dept. of Treasury, Securities Data Company, FHLMC, FNMA, GNMA, Federal Home Loan Banks, Student Loan Marketing Association, Federal Farm Credit Banks, and the Tennessee Valley Authority.

No. 830. Commercial Paper Outstanding, by Type of Company: 1980 to 1997

[**In billions of dollars**. As of **December 31**. Seasonally adjusted. Commercial paper is an unsecured promissory note having a fixed maturity of no more than 270 days]

TYPE OF COMPANY	1980	1985	1989	1990	1991	1992	1993	1994	1995	1996	1997
All issuers	**124.4**	**298.8**	**525.8**	**562.7**	**528.8**	**545.6**	**555.1**	**595.4**	**674.9**	**775.4**	**973.8**
Financial companies [1]..........	87.7	213.8	394.6	414.7	395.5	398.1	399.3	430.7	486.6	590.8	764.9
Dealer-placed paper [2].......	19.9	78.4	183.6	214.7	213.0	226.5	218.9	223.0	275.8	361.1	510.0
Directly-placed paper [3]......	67.8	135.3	210.9	200.0	182.5	171.6	180.4	207.7	210.8	229.7	254.9
Nonfinancial companies [4]	36.7	85.0	131.3	147.9	133.4	147.6	155.7	164.6	188.3	184.6	208.9

[1] Institutions engaged primarily in activities such as, but not limited to, commercial, savings, and mortgage banking; sales, personal, and mortgage financing; factoring, finance leasing, and other business lending; insurance underwriting; and other investment activities. [2] Includes all financial company paper sold by dealers in the open market. [3] As reported by financial companies that place their paper directly with investors. [4] Includes public utilities and firms engaged primarily in such activities as communications, construction, manufacturing, mining, wholesale and retail trade, transportation, and services.
Source: Board of Governors of the Federal Reserve System, *Federal Reserve Bulletin*, monthly.

No. 831. Total Returns of Stocks, Bonds, and Bills: 1950 to 1997

[Stock return data are based on the Standard & Poor's 500 index]

PERIOD	STOCKS				Treasury bills, total return	Bonds (10-year), total return
	Total return	Capital gains	Dividends and reinvestment	Total return after inflation		
1950 to 1997	13.14	8.82	3.97	8.70	5.33	6.05
1950 to 1959	19.28	13.58	5.02	16.69	2.02	0.73
1960 to 1969	7.78	4.39	3.62	5.13	4.06	2.42
1970 to 1979	5.82	1.60	4.15	-0.14	6.42	5.84
1980 to 1989	17.54	12.59	4.42	11.87	9.21	13.06
1990 to 1997	16.63	13.46	2.79	13.09	5.03	9.33

Source: Global Financial Data, Alhambra, CA, "Global Financial Data, US Sector Total Returns;" <http://www.globalfindata.com/april.htm>; (accessed: 27 April 1998); and unpublished data. (Copyright).

No. 832. Equities, Corporate Bonds, and Municipal Securities—Holdings and Net Purchases, by Type of Investor: 1990 to 1997

[In billions of dollars. Holdings as of Dec. 31. Minus sign (-) indicates net sales]

TYPE OF INVESTOR	HOLDINGS					NET PURCHASES				
	1990	1994	1995	1996	1997	1990	1994	1995	1996	1997
EQUITIES [1]										
Total [2]	3,537	6,238	8,331	10,061	12,959	-37.7	24.6	-3.5	-7.0	-41.2
Household sector [3]	1,795	3,049	4,066	4,604	5,738	-26.0	-157.5	-173.2	-290.2	-339.6
State and local governments	5	11	26	50	80	1.5	1.3	12.1	16.9	13.7
Rest of the world [4]	244	369	509	623	882	-16.0	0.9	16.6	12.2	65.1
Bank personal trusts and estates	190	167	203	219	259	0.5	-8.8	-17.9	-23.2	-19.6
Life insurance companies	98	272	344	437	582	-5.7	61.8	18.6	42.1	53.5
Other insurance companies	80	112	134	149	177	-7.0	1.1	-0.6	-6.8	2.5
Private pension funds	562	941	1,179	1,447	1,765	-4.4	-4.0	6.2	-2.3	-23.6
State and local retirement funds	293	543	753	956	1,295	13.2	29.3	41.3	52.2	44.3
Mutual funds	233	710	1,025	1,470	2,049	14.4	100.8	87.4	193.0	167.2
Closed-end funds	16	32	38	44	54	0.1	6.1	-4.6	-1.5	-2.0
CORPORATE & FOREIGN BONDS										
Total [2]	1,704	2,479	2,790	3,069	3,338	123.1	153.2	311.1	278.4	302.8
Household sector [3]	199	349	408	396	349	45.1	35.8	60.0	-12.2	-10.8
Rest of the world [4]	217	311	369	448	532	5.3	38.0	58.1	78.3	84.0
Commercial banking	89	102	111	112	143	4.6	4.3	8.4	1.4	27.9
Savings institutions	76	87	79	69	58	-19.3	-2.4	-8.2	-9.9	-10.2
Life insurance companies	567	779	870	949	1,026	56.5	59.9	90.7	79.2	76.4
Other insurance companies	89	110	123	142	149	10.4	7.2	12.7	18.3	6.9
Private pension funds	146	200	227	250	282	15.2	-7.7	27.0	22.5	32.1
State and local retirement funds	172	168	163	180	202	5.2	1.2	-4.2	16.7	21.8
Mutual funds	59	172	196	229	274	4.7	3.2	23.3	33.8	44.3
Brokers and dealers	29	64	76	91	101	-4.0	-8.7	12.0	14.5	9.8
MUNICIPAL SECURITIES [5]										
Total [2]	1,184	1,342	1,293	1,296	1,366	49.3	-35.9	-48.2	2.6	70.2
Household sector [3]	575	502	446	423	449	27.7	-50.2	-56.3	-22.6	25.8
Commercial banking	117	98	93	94	97	-16.4	-1.6	-4.2	0.9	2.4
Bank personal trusts and estates	81	114	103	104	105	7.7	5.3	-11.1	0.6	1.1
Other insurance companies	137	154	161	175	184	1.8	7.4	7.0	14.4	9.0
Money market mutual funds	84	113	128	144	167	13.9	7.8	14.3	16.8	22.5
Mutual funds	113	207	210	213	222	13.9	-4.3	3.2	3.1	9.0
Closed-end funds	14	53	60	60	61	2.0	1.6	6.2	0.8	0.8

[1] Excludes mutual fund shares.　[2] Includes other types not shown separately.　[3] Includes nonprofit organizations.　[4] Holdings of U.S. issues by foreign residents.　[5] Includes loans.

Source: Board of Governors of the Federal Reserve System, Flow of Funds Accounts, March 1998 quarterly diskettes. Data are also published in the quarterly Z.1 release.

No. 833. Purchases and Sales by U.S. Investors of Foreign Bonds and Stocks, 1980 to 1997, and by Selected Country, 1997

[In billions of dollars. See headnote, Table 834. Minus sign (-) indicates net sales by U.S. investors or a net inflow of capital into the United States]

YEAR AND COUNTRY	NET PURCHASES			TOTAL TRANSACTIONS [1]			BONDS		STOCKS	
	Total	Bonds	Stocks	Total	Bonds	Stocks	Pur-chases	Sales	Pur-chases	Sales
1980	3.1	1.0	2.1	53	35	18	18	17	10	8
1985	7.9	4.0	3.9	212	166	46	85	81	25	21
1990	31.2	21.9	9.2	907	652	255	337	315	132	123
1991	46.8	14.8	32.0	949	675	273	345	330	153	121
1992	47.9	15.6	32.3	1,375	1,043	332	529	514	182	150
1993	143.1	80.4	62.7	2,126	1,572	554	826	746	308	245
1994	57.3	9.2	48.1	2,526	1,706	820	858	848	434	386
1995	98.7	48.4	50.3	2,569	1,827	741	938	890	396	346
1996	110.6	51.4	59.3	3,239	2,279	960	1,165	1,114	510	450
1997, total [2]	87.5	47.2	40.2	4,459	2,981	1,479	1,514	1,467	759	719
United Kingdom	28.2	11.3	16.9	2,077	1,515	561	763	752	289	272
Canada	3.8	2.5	1.3	428	345	84	174	171	42	41
Brazil	5.9	3.8	2.2	192	152	40	78	74	21	19
Japan	10.0	0.5	9.5	189	36	153	18	18	81	72
Bermuda	1.9	1.0	0.9	183	156	27	78	77	14	13
British West Indies	5.2	5.6	-0.5	182	128	54	67	61	27	27
Argentina	6.3	5.8	0.5	155	143	12	74	69	6	6
Netherlands Antilles	1.6	0.2	1.4	115	46	69	23	23	35	34
Bahamas, The	-1.3	-1.0	-0.3	108	96	12	47	48	6	6
Hong Kong	-1.6	-1.5	-0.1	98	19	79	9	10	39	40

[1] Total purchases plus total sales.　[2] Includes other countries, not shown separately.

Source: U.S. Dept. of Treasury, *Treasury Bulletin*, quarterly.

No. 834. Foreign Purchases and Sales of U.S. Securities, by Type of Security, 1980 to 1997, and by Selected Country, 1997

[In billions of dollars. Covers transactions in all types of long-term domestic securities by foreigners as reported by banks, brokers, and other entities in the United States (except nonmarketable U.S. Treasury notes, foreign series; and nonmarketable U.S. Treasury bonds and notes, foreign currency series). Data cover new issues of securities, transactions in outstanding issues, and redemptions of securities. Includes transactions executed in the United States for the account of foreigners, and transactions executed abroad for the account of reporting institutions and their domestic customers. Data by country show the country of domicile of the foreign buyers and sellers of the securities; in the case of outstanding issues, this may differ from the country of the original issuer. The term "foreigner" covers all institutions and individuals domiciled outside the United States, including U.S. citizens domiciled abroad, and the foreign branches, subsidiaries and other affiliates abroad of U.S. banks and businesses; the central governments, central banks, and other official institutions of foreign countries; and international and regional organizations. "Foreigner" also includes persons in the United States to the extent that they are known by reporting institutions to be acting on behalf of foreigners. Minus sign (-) indicates net sales by foreigners or a net outflow of capital from the United States]

YEAR AND COUNTRY	NET PURCHASES					TOTAL TRANSACTIONS [4]				
	Total	Trea-sury bonds and notes [1]	U.S. Govt. corpora-tions [2] bonds	Corpo-rate bonds [3]	Corpo-rate stocks	Total	Trea-sury bonds and notes [1]	U.S. Govt. corpora-tions [2] bonds	Corpo-rate bonds [3]	Corpo-rate stocks
1980	15.8	4.9	2.6	2.9	5.4	198	97	17	9	75
1985	78.3	29.2	4.3	39.8	4.9	1,256	968	46	84	159
1990	18.7	17.9	6.3	9.7	-15.1	4,204	3,620	104	117	362
1991	58.1	19.9	10.2	16.9	11.1	4,706	4,016	124	155	411
1992	73.2	39.3	18.3	20.8	-5.1	5,282	4,444	204	187	448
1993	111.1	23.6	35.4	30.6	21.6	6,314	5,195	263	239	618
1994	140.4	78.8	21.7	38.0	1.9	6,562	5,343	297	222	699
1995	231.9	134.1	28.7	57.9	11.2	7,243	5,828	222	278	915
1996	370.2	232.2	41.7	83.7	12.5	8,965	7,134	241	422	1,169
1997, total [5]	386.1	183.6	49.6	86.9	66.0	12,508	9,554	470	622	1,862
United Kingdom	177.3	98.3	9.6	47.2	22.2	5,731	4,832	80	349	470
Japan	34.5	20.4	7.7	1.6	4.8	1,263	1,083	61	13	106
Canada	4.3	-0.8	0.4	5.8	-1.2	783	618	314	14	81
British West Indies	17.8	4.3	3.8	5.1	4.5	707	380	73	53	201
Bermuda	4.4	-6.4	7.6	5.2	-1.9	632	199	162	35	236
Netherlands Antilles	-0.9	-2.7	0.1	2.0	-0.3	343	187	2	22	133
France	4.4	-2.1	0.1	3.2	3.1	301	235	1	11	54
Germany	34.3	22.5	0.5	2.2	9.1	285	218	4	11	53
Hong Kong	17.6	12.3	3.8	1.8	-0.2	269	240	8	4	17
Singapore	-3.3	-3.7	1.5	1.2	-2.3	252	211	3	4	34

[1] Marketable bonds and notes.　[2] Includes federally-sponsored agencies.　[3] Includes transactions in directly placed issues abroad by U.S. corporations and issues of states and municipalities.　[4] Total purchases plus total sales.　[5] Includes other countries, not shown separately.

Source: U.S. Dept. of Treasury, *Treasury Bulletin*, quarterly.

No. 835. New Security Issues of Corporations, by Type of Offering and Industry Group: 1990 to 1996

[In billions of dollars. Represents gross proceeds of issues maturing in more than one year. Figures are the principal amount or the number of units multiplied by the offering price. Excludes secondary offerings, employee stock plans, investment companies other than closed-end, intracorporate transactions, equities sold abroad, and Yankee bonds. Stock data include ownership securities issued by limited partnerships]

TYPE OF OFFERING AND INDUSTRY GROUP	1990	1993	1994	1995	1996 [1]	TYPE OF OFFERING AND INDUSTRY GROUP	1990	1993	1994	1995	1996 [1]
Total	339.1	769.1	583.2	673.6	665.2	Stocks, total	40.2	122.5	85.2	100.9	116.6
Bonds, total	298.9	646.6	498.0	573.0	548.9	Preferred	4.0	18.9	12.5	11.0	33.2
Public, domestic . . .	188.8	487.0	365.2	408.7	465.5	Common	19.4	82.7	47.8	57.8	83.4
Private placement, domestic	87.0	121.2	76.1	87.5	(NA)	Private place- ment	16.7	20.9	24.8	32.1	(NA)
Sold abroad	23.1	38.4	56.8	76.8	83.4						
Manufacturing	51.8	88.2	43.4	60.8	49.5	Manufacturing	5.6	22.3	17.8	21.8	21.3
Commercial and miscellaneous. . . .	40.7	58.6	40.7	50.7	40.5	Commercial and miscellaneous. . . .	10.2	25.8	15.7	27.8	44.5
Transportation	12.8	10.8	6.9	8.5	5.7	Transportation	0.4	2.2	2.2	0.8	1.7
Public utility	17.6	56.3	13.3	13.8	9.5	Public utility	0.4	7.1	2.2	1.9	3.7
Communication . . .	6.7	31.9	13.3	23.0	14.5	Communication . . .	3.8	3.4	0.5	1.1	4.8
Real estate and financial.	169.3	400.8	380.4	416.2	429.2	Real estate and financial.	19.7	61.0	46.7	47.4	40.5

NA Not available.　[1] Excludes private placements.

Source: Board of Governors of the Federal Reserve System, *Federal Reserve Bulletin*, monthly, and *Annual Statistical Digest*.

No. 836. Stock Prices and Yields: 1990 to 1997

[Closing values as of end of December, except as noted]

INDEX	1990	1992	1993	1994	1995	1996	1997
STOCK PRICES							
Standard & Poor's indices: [1]							
S&P 500 composite (1941-43=10)	330.2	435.7	466.5	459.3	615.9	740.7	970.4
Industrials	387.1	511.4	543.9	548.9	719.7	870.0	1,121.4
Utilities	144.8	159.1	176.4	151.9	201.7	198.8	235.8
S&P 400 Midcap Index (1982=100)	100.0	160.6	179.4	169.4	217.8	255.6	333.4
Russell indices: [2]							
Russell 1000 (Dec. 31, 1986=130)	171.22	233.59	250.71	244.65	328.89	393.75	513.79
Russell 2000 (Dec. 31, 1986=135)	132.16	221.01	258.59	250.36	315.97	362.61	437.02
Russell 3000 (Dec. 31, 1986=140)	180.85	249.80	270.13	263.44	351.91	419.44	543.05
N.Y. Stock Exchange common stock index							
Composite (Dec. 31, 1965=50)	180.49	240.21	259.08	250.94	329.51	392.30	511.19
Yearly high	201.55	242.76	261.16	267.78	331.73	401.08	515.24
Yearly low	161.76	216.86	235.15	241.79	249.86	320.90	386.36
Industrial (Dec. 31, 1965=50).	223.60	294.39	315.26	318.10	413.29	494.38	630.38
Transportation (Dec. 31, 1965=50)	141.49	214.72	270.48	222.46	301.96	352.30	466.25
Utility (Dec. 31, 1965=100)	182.60	209.66	229.92	198.41	252.90	259.91	335.19
Finance (Dec. 31, 1965=50)	122.07	200.83	216.82	195.80	274.25	351.17	495.96
American Stock Exchange Composite Index (Dec. 29, 1996=550)	(NA)	(NA)	(NA)	(NA)	550.00	572.34	684.61
NASDAQ composite index (Feb. 5, 1971=100)	373.8	677.0	776.8	752.0	1,052.1	1,291.0	1,570.4
Industrial	406.1	724.9	805.8	753.8	964.7	1,109.6	1,221.0
Insurance	451.8	803.9	920.6	925.9	1,292.6	1,465.4	1,798.0
Bank	254.9	532.9	689.4	697.1	1,009.4	1,273.5	2,083.2
Dow-Jones and Co., Inc.:							
Composite (65 stocks)	920.6	1,204.6	1,381.0	1,274.4	1,693.2	2,025.8	2,607.4
Industrial (30 stocks)	2,633.7	3,301.1	3,754.1	3,834.4	5,117.1	6,448.3	7,908.3
Transportation (20 stocks).	910.2	1,449.2	1,762.3	1,455.0	1,981.0	2,255.7	3,256.5
Utility (15 stocks).	209.7	221.0	229.3	181.5	225.4	232.5	273.1
Wilshire 5000 equity index (Dec. 31, 1980=1404.596)	3,101.4	4,289.7	4,657.8	4,540.6	6,057.2	7,274.2	9,298.2
COMMON STOCK YIELDS (percent)							
Standard & Poor's composite index (500 stocks): [3]							
Dividend-price ratio [5]	3.61	2.99	2.78	2.82	2.56	2.19	1.77
Earnings-price ratio [5]	6.47	4.22	4.46	5.83	6.09	5.24	4.57

NA Not available.　[1] The S&P 500 composite index includes 400 industrial stocks, 20 transportation, 40 public utility, and 40 financial stocks. The S&P Midcap Index shows the 400 largest capitalization stocks in the United States after the S&P 500.　[2] The Russell 1000 and 3000 indices show respectively the 1000 and 3000 largest capitalization stocks in the United States. The Russell 2000 index shows the 2000 largest capitalization stocks in the United States after the first 1000.　[3] Source: U.S. Council of Economic Advisors, *Economic Report of the President*, annual.　[4] Aggregate cash dividends (based on latest known annual rate) divided by aggregate market value based on Wednesday closing prices. Averages of monthly figures.　[5] Averages of quarterly ratios which are ratio of earnings (after taxes) for 4 quarters ending with particular quarter to price index for last day of that quarter.

Source: Except as noted, Global Financial Data, Alhambra, CA, "GFD Standard and Poor's Sectors;" ; (accessed: 24 April 1998) and "US Stock Market Capitalization Indices;" ; (accessed: 5 February 1998), (Copyright).

No. 837. Dow-Jones U.S. Equity Market Index, by Industry: 1990 to 1997

[As of end of year]

INDUSTRY	1990	1992	1993	1994	1995	1996	1997
U.S. Equity Market Index, total	305.59	413.29	442.19	433.07	581.43	700.56	922.34
Basic materials	299.67	401.09	443.38	456.55	540.47	614.63	680.77
Consumer, cyclical	325.98	527.62	596.43	532.55	635.01	711.02	961.83
Consumer, noncyclical.	543.87	734.03	684.89	740.25	1,052.90	1,287.32	1,738.25
Conglomerates.	354.20	530.30	655.57	638.07	891.54	1,228.43	1,794.92
Energy	262.85	264.73	290.55	286.70	358.74	442.09	533.72
Financial services	233.04	410.85	436.98	408.25	611.76	809.78	1,203.36
Industrial	288.12	390.48	432.52	399.79	499.93	581.94	700.74
Technology	242.10	320.10	361.45	406.48	570.55	730.45	891.62
Utilities	248.91	286.74	316.02	272.82	362.66	359.67	473.01

Source: Dow Jones & Company, Inc., New York, NY, Wall Street Journal, selected issues, (copyright).

No. 838. Sales of Stocks and Options on Registered Exchanges: 1980 to 1996

[Excludes over-the-counter trading]

EXCHANGE	Unit	1980	1985	1989	1990	1991	1992	1993	1994	1995	1996
Market value of all sales, all exchanges [1][2]	Bil. dol	522	1,260	2,010	1,752	1,903	2,149	2,734	2,966	3,690	4,735
New York	Bil. dol	398	1,024	1,581	1,394	1,534	1,759	2,278	2,483	3,078	4,013
American	Bil. dol	47	38	80	65	67	69	83	83	105	131
Chicago	Bil. dol	21	79	101	74	77	87	107	98	114	136
CBOE [3]	Bil. dol	28	38	88	81	74	63	65	87	107	130
Pacific	Bil. dol	13	40	64	53	63	65	70	70	94	108
Philadelphia	Bil. dol	11	23	50	41	39	49	55	51	59	68
STOCKS [4]											
Shares sold, all exchanges [2] . . .	Million.	15,488	37,046	54,239	53,338	58,025	65,463	82,808	90,482	106,393	125,747
New York	Million.	12,390	30,222	44,140	43,829	47,674	53,344	68,732	76,665	90,062	108,151
American	Million.	1,659	2,115	3,248	3,125	3,103	3,631	4,470	4,300	4,843	5,306
Chicago	Million.	598	2,274	2,960	2,511	2,715	3,035	3,792	3,526	3,925	4,247
Pacific	Million.	435	1,352	1,791	1,682	2,068	2,087	2,330	2,147	2,738	3,013
Market value, all exchanges [2] . . .	Bil. dol	476	1,200	1,845	1,612	1,776	2,032	2,610	2,817	3,507	4,511
New York	Bil. dol	398	1,023	1,577	1,390	1,532	1,758	2,276	2,482	3,076	4,011
American	Bil. dol	35	26	43	36	40	42	54	56	73	86
Chicago	Bil. dol	21	79	101	74	77	87	107	98	114	136
Pacific	Bil. dol	11	37	52	45	63	58	62	59	79	92

[1] Includes market value of stocks, rights, warrants, and options trading beginning 1989. [2] Includes other registered exchanges, not shown separately. [3] Chicago Board Options Exchange, Inc. [4] Includes voting trust certificates, American Depository Receipts, and certificate of deposit for stocks.

Source: U.S. Securities and Exchange Commission, SEC Monthly Statistical Review (discontinued Feb. 1989); and unpublished data.

No. 839. NASDAQ—Securities Listed and Volume of Trading: 1980 to 1997

ITEM	Unit	1980	1985	1990	1991	1992	1993	1994	1995	1996	1997
Member firms	Number. . .	2,932	6,307	5,827	5,386	5,254	5,296	5,426	5,451	5,553	5,597
Branch offices	Number. . .	7,555	15,375	24,457	29,158	33,484	44,181	57,105	58,119	60,151	62,966
Companies listed	Number. . .	2,894	4,136	4,132	4,094	4,113	4,611	4,902	5,112	5,556	5,487
Issues	Number. . .	3,050	4,784	4,706	4,684	4,768	5,393	5,761	5,955	6,384	6,208
Shares traded	Million	6,692	20,699	33,380	41,311	48,455	66,541	74,353	101,158	138,112	163,882
Average daily volume . .	Million	26.5	82.1	131.9	163.3	190.8	263.0	295.1	401.4	543.7	647.8
Value of shares traded . . .	Bil. dol. . . .	69	234	452	694	891	1,350	1,449	2,398	2,302	4,482

Source: National Association of Securities Dealers, Washington, DC, Fact Book, annual.

No. 840. Volume of Trading on New York Stock Exchange: 1980 to 1997

[**Round lot:** A unit of trading or a multiple thereof. On the NYSE the unit of trading is generally 100 shares in stocks. For some inactive stocks, the unit of trading is 10 shares. **Odd lot:** An amount of stock less than the established 100-share unit or 10-share unit of trading]

ITEM	Unit	1980	1985	1990	1991	1992	1993	1994	1995	1996	1997
Shares traded	**Million .**	**11,562**	**27,774**	**39,946**	**45,599**	**51,826**	**67,461**	**74,003**	**87,873**	**105,477**	**134,404**
Round lots	Million . .	11,352	27,511	39,665	45,266	51,376	66,923	73,420	87,218	104,636	133,312
Average daily shares	Million . .	45	109	157	179	202	265	291	346	412	527
High day	Million . .	84	181	292	317	389	379	483	653	681	1,201
Low day	Million . .	16	62	57	70	95	90	114	118	130	155
Odd lots	Million . .	209	263	282	333	450	538	583	656	841	1,091
Value of shares traded .	**Bil. dol .**	**382**	**981**	**1,336**	**1,534**	**1,765**	**2,305**	**2,477**	**3,110**	**4,102**	**5,833**
Round lots	Bil. dol. .	375	970	1,325	1,520	1,745	2,283	2,454	3,083	4,064	5,778
Odd lots	Bil. dol. .	8	10	11	[1]13	19	22	22	27	38	56
Bond volume [2]	**Mil. dol .**	**5,190**	**9,047**	**10,893**	**12,698**	**11,629**	**9,743**	**7,197**	**6,979**	**5,529**	**5,046**
Daily average	Mil. dol	20.5	35.9	43.1	50.2	45.8	38.5	28.6	27.7	21.8	19.9

[1] Excludes odd lot statistics for February which were not available. [2] Par value.

Source: New York Stock Exchange, Inc., New York, NY, Fact Book, annual (copyright).

No. 841. Securities Listed on New York Stock Exchange: 1980 to 1997

[As of **December 31**, except **cash dividends** are for **calendar year**]

ITEM	Unit	1980	1985	1989	1990	1991	1992	1993	1994	1995	1996	1997
BONDS												
Number of issuers	Number .	1,045	1,010	794	743	705	636	574	583	564	563	533
Number of issues	Number .	3,057	3,856	2,961	2,912	2,727	2,354	2,103	2,141	2,097	2,064	1,965
Face value	Bil. dol . .	602	1,327	1,435	1,689	2,219	2,009	2,342	2,526	2,773	2,845	2,625
Market value	Bil. dol . .	508	1,339	1,412	1,610	2,227	2,044	2,528	2,367	2,748	2,862	(NA)
Average price	Percent .	84.41	100.90	98.42	95.31	100.34	101.77	107.96	93.73	99.09	100.61	(NA)
STOCKS												
Companies	Number .	1,570	1,541	1,720	1,774	1,885	2,088	2,361	2,570	2,675	2,907	3,047
Number of issues	Number .	2,228	2,298	2,246	2,284	2,426	2,658	2,904	3,060	3,126	3,285	3,358
Shares listed	Billion . .	33.7	52.4	83.0	90.7	99.6	115.8	131.1	142.3	154.7	176.9	207.1
Market value	Bil. dol .	1,243	1,950	3,030	2,820	3,713	4,035	4,541	4,448	6,013	7,300	9,413
Average price	Dollars . .	36.87	37.20	36.51	31.08	37.27	34.83	34.65	31.26	38.86	41.26	45.45
Cash dividends on common stock [1]	Bil. dol . .	53.1	74.2	101.8	103.2	123.4	109.7	120.2	130.0	147.0	150.6	159.4

NA Not available. [1] Beginning 1990 estimate based on average annual yield of the NYSE composite index.

Source: New York Stock Exchange, Inc., New York, NY, *Fact Book*, annual (copyright).

No. 842. Stock Ownership, by Age of Head of Family and Family Income: 1989 to 1995

[**Median value in thousands of constant 1995 dollars**. Constant dollar figures are based on consumer price index data published by U.S. Bureau of Labor Statistics. Families include one-person units; for definition of family, see text, Section 1. Based on Survey of Consumer Finance; see Appendix III. For definition of median, see Guide to Tabular Presentation]

AGE OF FAMILY HEAD AND FAMILY INCOME (constant (1995) dollars)	FAMILIES HAVING DIRECT OR INDIRECT STOCK HOLDINGS (percent)			MEDIAN VALUE AMONG FAMILIES WITH HOLDINGS			STOCK HOLDINGS' SHARE OF GROUP'S FINANCIAL ASSETS (percent)		
	1989	1992	1995	1989	1992	1995	1989	1992	1995
All families	**31.6**	**36.6**	**40.3**	**10.4**	**11.4**	**14.5**	**28.6**	**34.1**	**41.5**
Under 35 years old	22.3	28.4	36.7	3.7	3.8	5.1	20.4	25.2	31.6
35 to 44 years old	38.9	42.5	46.4	6.3	8.1	10.0	30.1	31.4	41.5
45 to 54 years old	41.8	46.2	48.9	16.1	16.3	25.6	36.2	41.1	44.5
55 to 64 years old	36.1	45.3	40.0	22.6	27.1	30.0	28.5	38.3	47.0
65 to 74 years old	26.7	30.0	34.2	24.9	17.9	34.0	26.4	31.6	36.2
75 years old and over	25.9	25.6	27.8	30.7	27.1	20.0	25.0	25.5	39.8
Less than $10,000	3.3	6.8	6.2	35.0	5.9	2.9	12.1	15.3	13.6
$10,000 to $24,999	13.0	18.7	23.2	7.4	4.3	6.0	12.0	15.3	28.1
$25,000 to $49,999	32.3	40.8	47.3	5.5	7.6	9.0	18.3	24.4	32.1
$50,000 to $99,999	52.4	63.4	67.3	10.4	15.2	23.4	23.5	34.5	43.2
$100,000 and more	81.8	78.5	81.1	55.2	75.4	97.7	36.6	40.7	47.3

Source: Board of Governors of the Federal Reserve System, *Federal Reserve Bulletin*, January 1997, and unpublished revisions.

No. 843. Mutual Fund Shares—Holdings and Net Purchases, by Type of Investor: 1990 to 1997

[**In billions of dollars**. Holdings as of **Dec. 31**. Minus sign (-) indicates net sales]

TYPE OF INVESTOR	HOLDINGS					NET PURCHASES				
	1990	1994	1995	1996	1997	1990	1994	1995	1996	1997
Total	**608.4**	**1,477.4**	**1,852.8**	**2,342.4**	**3,013.6**	**53.7**	**100.6**	**147.4**	**237.6**	**259.0**
Households, nonprofit organizations	467.8	1,052.1	1,255.0	1,591.6	1,937.5	27.5	67.4	109.9	180.5	190.9
Nonfinancial corporate business. . .	9.7	31.1	45.7	58.6	81.8	-1.0	2.1	4.6	3.3	3.0
State and local governments	4.8	29.1	35.0	37.0	39.6	3.3	7.8	5.9	2.0	2.6
Commercial banking	1.9	2.0	2.3	2.6	8.1	-0.3	-1.9	0.3	0.3	5.5
Credit unions	1.4	2.6	2.8	2.6	2.5	0.2	-1.6	0.2	-0.3	-0.1
Bank personal trusts and estates . .	62.7	200.4	253.5	322.8	429.5	9.7	21.7	-11.1	16.4	14.3
Life insurance companies	30.7	9.6	27.7	40.0	57.5	12.6	-14.9	13.5	7.0	5.4
Private pension funds	29.2	150.4	230.7	287.2	457.0	1.6	20.1	24.1	28.3	37.4

Source: Board of Governors of the Federal Reserve System, *Flow of Funds Accounts*, March 1998 quarterly diskettes. Data are also published in the quarterly Z.1 release.

No. 844. Mutual Funds—Summary: 1980 to 1997

[Number of funds, accounts, and assets as of **December 31**. A mutual fund is an open-end investment company that continuously issues and redeems shares that represent an interest in a pool of financial assets]

TYPE OF FUND	Unit	1980	1985	1990	1992	1993	1994	1995	1996	1997
Number of funds, total	Number. .	564	1,528	3,105	3,850	4,558	5,357	5,761	6,293	6,778
Equity funds.	Number . .	267	579	1,127	1,356	1,615	1,944	2,211	2,626	3,014
Income and bond funds [1]	Number . .	191	492	1,235	1,629	2,023	2,450	2,553	2,679	2,751
Money market funds, tax-exempt [2] . .	Number . .	10	111	235	279	292	319	325	323	331
Money market funds, taxable [3]	Number . .	96	346	508	586	628	644	672	665	682
Shareholder accounts, total. . . .	Millions. .	12.1	34.7	62.6	80.3	93.6	114.8	131.8	150.8	171.3
Equity funds.	Millions . .	5.8	11.5	23.0	33.2	42.5	59.0	70.7	87.1	103.6
Income and bond funds [1]	Millions . .	1.5	8.3	16.6	23.4	27.5	30.5	30.9	31.5	32.0
Money market funds, tax-exempt [2] . .	Millions . .	(NA)	0.5	1.4	1.9	2.0	2.0	2.3	2.3	2.7
Money market funds, taxable [3]	Millions . .	4.8	14.4	21.6	21.8	21.6	23.3	27.9	29.9	33.0
Assets, total	Bil. dol. .	135	496	1,067	1,646	2,075	2,161	2,820	3,539	4,490
Equity funds.	Bil. dol. . .	44	117	246	523	749	866	1,269	1,751	2,399
Income and bond funds [1]	Bil. dol. . .	14	135	323	577	761	684	798	887	1,032
Money market funds, tax-exempt [2] . .	Bil. dol. . .	2	36	84	95	103	111	123	140	161
Money market funds, taxable [3]	Bil. dol. . .	74	208	415	451	462	500	630	762	898
Sales, total	Bil. dol . .	248	954	1,565	2,751	3,189	3,077	3,602	4,675	5,805
Equity funds.	Bil. dol. . .	6	30	71	145	229	271	307	471	609
Income and bond funds [1]	Bil. dol. . .	4	84	79	220	282	203	170	213	265
Money market funds, tax-exempt [2] . .	Bil. dol. . .	5	109	197	286	342	369	397	468	537
Money market funds, taxable [3]	Bil. dol. . .	232	730	1,219	2,100	2,336	2,234	2,728	3,522	4,393
Redemptions, total	Bil. dol . .	217	865	1,471	2,548	2,905	2,929	3,315	4,267	5,326
Equity funds.	Bil. dol. . .	6	18	45	62	93	142	172	243	364
Income and bond funds [1]	Bil. dol. . .	3	15	53	103	139	188	141	156	178
Money market funds, tax-exempt [2] . .	Bil. dol. . .	4	99	190	282	337	370	386	455	519
Money market funds, taxable [3]	Bil. dol. . .	204	732	1,183	2,101	2,337	2,229	2,616	3,414	4,264

NA Not available. [1] Includes municipal bond funds and, beginning 1996, hybrid funds which invest in both equity and bond. [2] Funds invest in municipal securities with relatively short maturities. [3] Funds invest in short-term, high-grade securities sold in the money market.

No. 845. Individual Retirement Accounts (IRA) Plans—Value, by Type of Holder: 1985 to 1996

[As of **December 31**. Estimated]

TYPE OF HOLDER	AMOUNT (bil. dol.)									PERCENT DISTRIBUTION		
	1985	1989	1990	1991	1992	1993	1994	1995	1996	1985	1990	1996
Total	200	455	529	657	746	868	941	1,170	1,347	100	100	100
Savings institutions	56	98	95	91	85	76	72	73	72	28	18	5
Commercial banks	52	99	119	134	137	134	136	143	144	26	22	11
Mutual funds	32	112	127	169	211	284	305	411	511	16	24	38
Self directed.	29	82	117	181	225	271	318	415	483	15	22	36
Life insurance companies	17	38	42	50	56	70	79	94	106	9	8	8
Credit unions	14	26	29	32	32	32	32	34	33	7	6	2

Source of Tables 844 and 845: Investment Company Institute, Washington, DC, *Mutual Fund Fact Book*, annual (copyright).

No. 846. 401(k) Plan Assets—Summary, 1985 to 1997, and Projections, 2000

YEAR	Total assets (bil. dol.)	TYPE OF ASSET	Percent of companies offering investment option, 1997	ASSETS, 1997		FINANCIAL INSTITUTION MANAGING ASSETS	ASSETS, 1997	
				Amount (bil. dol.)	Percent distribution		Amount (bil. dol.)	Percent distribution
1985	105	Total	(X)	985	100	All defined contribution plans [2]	1,730	100
1989	270	Guaranteed investment						
1990	300	account [1]	52	177	18	Insurance companies . . .	450	26
1991	350	Equity	96	325	33	Banks	433	25
1992	410	Money market.	55	30	3	Mutual fund groups	588	34
1993	475	Balanced account . . .	64	108	11	Other	260	15
1994	525							
1995	675	Bond fund	69	69	7	401(k) plans	985	100
1996	810	Company stock	22	207	21	Insurance companies . . .	217	22
1997	985	Other.	(NA)	(NA)	(NA)	Banks	207	21
						Mutual fund groups	414	42
2000, proj. .	1,475					Other	148	15

NA Not available. X Not applicable. [1] Covers bank certificate of deposits, guaranteed investment contracts (GIC's), GIC alternatives, and insurance company participating contracts. [2] Includes 401(k) plans.

Source: Access Research, Inc., Windsor, CT, *1997 Marketplace Update*, 1997 (copyright).

No. 847. Assets of Private and Public Pension Funds, by Type of Fund: 1980 to 1997

[In billions of dollars. As of end of year. Except for corporate equities, represents book value. Excludes social security trust funds and U.S. government pension funds; see Tables 609 and 613]

TYPE OF PENSION FUND	1980	1985	1990	1992	1993	1994	1995	1996	1997
Total, all types	**873**	**1,866**	**3,088**	**3,869**	**4,286**	**4,471**	**5,173**	**5,835**	**6,946**
Private funds	676	1,467	2,168	2,702	3,030	3,176	3,655	4,120	4,846
Insured	172	260	596	743	836	885	998	1,084	1,268
Noninsured [1] [2]	504	1,207	1,572	1,959	2,193	2,292	2,657	3,037	3,578
Credit market instruments [2]	151	330	487	562	611	657	718	765	832
U.S. government securities [2]	51	196	288	327	351	400	434	453	484
Treasury	32	138	198	224	240	271	292	305	324
Corporate and foreign bonds	78	97	146	186	208	200	227	250	282
Corporate equities	223	495	562	808	938	941	1,179	1,447	1,765
Mutual fund shares	7	11	29	75	116	150	231	287	457
Unallocated insurance contracts [3]	(NA)	132	189	198	207	210	215	231	241
State and local pension funds [2]	197	399	920	1,168	1,256	1,294	1,518	1,715	2,100
Credit market instruments [2]	147	252	424	411	433	456	483	529	577
U.S. government securities [2]	40	124	224	220	231	246	271	299	322
Treasury	21	83	140	148	163	171	176	191	214
Corporate and foreign bonds	92	107	172	153	167	168	163	180	202
Corporate equities	44	120	293	451	531	543	753	956	1,295

NA Not available. [1] Covers all pension funds of corporations, nonprofit organizations, unions, and multi-employer groups. Also includes deferred profit-sharing plans and Federal Employees Retirement System (FERS) Thrift Savings Fund. Excludes health, welfare, and bonus plans. [2] Includes other types of assets not shown separately. [3] Assets held at life insurance companies (e.g., guaranteed investment contracts (GICs), variable annuities).

Source: Board of Governors of the Federal Reserve System, Flow of Funds Accounts, March 1998 quarterly diskettes. Data are also published in the quarterly Z.1 release.

No. 848. Securities Industry—Revenues and Expenses: 1980 to 1996

[In millions of dollars]

TYPE	1980	1985	1989	1990	1991	1992	1993	1994	1995	1996
Revenues, total	**19,829**	**49,844**	**76,864**	**71,356**	**84,890**	**90,584**	**108,844**	**112,758**	**143,414**	**173,164**
Commissions	6,777	10,955	13,452	12,032	14,210	16,249	19,905	19,847	23,215	27,909
Trading/investment gains	5,091	14,549	16,247	15,746	22,641	21,838	25,427	20,219	28,963	30,833
Underwriting profits	1,571	4,987	4,537	3,728	6,593	8,300	11,249	6,844	8,865	12,626
Margin interest	2,151	2,746	3,860	3,179	2,771	2,690	3,235	4,668	6,470	7,390
Mutual fund sales	278	2,754	3,038	3,242	4,176	5,950	8,115	6,887	7,434	10,081
Other	3,960	13,854	35,731	33,428	34,498	35,557	40,913	54,293	68,468	84,324
Expenses, total	**16,668**	**43,342**	**74,041**	**70,566**	**76,234**	**81,467**	**95,805**	**109,266**	**132,089**	**156,160**
Interest expense	3,876	11,470	29,822	28,093	27,512	24,576	26,616	40,250	56,877	65,237
Compensation	7,619	18,112	23,740	22,931	26,916	32,071	39,125	37,595	41,541	51,152
Commissions/clearance paid	1,055	2,314	3,057	2,959	3,200	3,722	5,338	5,360	5,700	7,376
Other	4,119	11,446	17,422	16,583	18,605	21,098	24,726	26,060	27,970	32,395
Net income, pretax	**3,160**	**6,502**	**2,823**	**790**	**8,656**	**9,117**	**13,039**	**3,492**	**11,325**	**17,004**

Source: U.S. Securities and Exchange Commission, Annual Report.

No. 849. Health Insurance—Premium Income and Benefit Payments of Insurance Companies: 1980 to 1995

[In billions of dollars. Includes Puerto Rico and other U.S. outlying areas. Represents premium income of and benefits paid by insurance companies only. Excludes Blue Cross-Blue Shield plans, medical-society sponsored plans, and all other independent plans]

ITEM	1980	1985	1987	1988	1989	1990	1991	1992	1993	1994	1995
Premiums [1]	**43.7**	**75.2**	**84.1**	**98.2**	**108.0**	**112.9**	**116.4**	**125.0**	**124.7**	**129.3**	**133.9**
Group policies [2]	36.8	64.4	74.0	87.6	96.1	100.2	103.0	110.4	110.2	114.1	116.4
Individual and family policies	6.9	10.8	10.1	10.6	11.8	12.7	13.3	14.6	14.5	15.2	17.5
Benefit payments	**37.0**	**60.0**	**72.5**	**83.0**	**89.4**	**92.5**	**97.6**	**104.8**	**103.6**	**106.3**	**110.1**
Group policies [2]	33.0	53.7	66.5	76.4	82.2	84.4	88.8	95.2	94.1	95.9	98.1
Individual and family policies	4.0	6.3	5.9	6.6	7.2	8.2	8.8	9.6	9.3	10.4	12.0
Type of coverage:											
Loss of income	5.3	5.6	6.4	6.4	7.2	7.4	7.5	8.3	8.1	7.8	8.2
Medical expense	27.9	47.2	57.4	66.4	72.0	73.8	77.9	82.9	81.4	84.0	85.8
Dental	2.8	5.3	5.9	6.3	6.5	6.4	6.4	7.1	7.0	7.0	7.7
Medicare supplement	1.0	1.9	2.8	3.8	3.7	5.0	5.8	6.4	6.9	7.5	8.4

[1] Earned premiums. [2] Insurance company group premiums and benefit payments include administrative service agreements and minimum premium plans.

Source: Health Insurance Association of America, Washington, DC, Source Book of Health Insurance Data, annual.

No. 850. Property and Casualty Insurance—Summary: 1989 to 1996

[In billions of dollars. Minus sign (-) indicates loss]

ITEM	1989	1990	1991	1992	1993	1994	1995	1996
Premiums, net written [1]	208.4	217.8	223.0	227.8	241.7	250.7	259.8	268.6
Automobile, private [1]	73.6	78.4	82.8	88.4	93.4	96.8	102.0	107.7
Automobile, commercial [1]	17.3	17.0	16.6	16.1	16.3	16.7	17.2	17.6
Liability other than auto	22.7	22.1	20.9	21.1	22.1	23.6	23.4	24.5
Fire and allied lines	7.0	7.1	7.2	7.1	7.9	8.7	9.4	9.9
Homeowners' multiple peril	17.7	18.6	19.3	20.5	21.5	22.6	24.0	25.4
Commercial multiple peril	17.5	17.7	17.0	16.4	17.3	17.8	18.8	18.9
Workers' compensation	28.5	31.0	31.3	29.7	30.3	28.9	26.2	25.1
Marine, inland and ocean	5.6	5.7	5.5	5.5	6.1	6.7	7.1	7.5
Accident and health	4.6	5.0	5.1	5.4	6.8	7.2	7.8	7.8
Other lines	14.2	15.2	17.4	17.6	20.0	21.7	23.9	24.2
Losses and expenses	223.6	234.7	239.3	259.6	250.7	263.3	268.4	277.1
Underwriting gain/loss	-19.2	-20.9	-19.4	-33.3	-15.1	-19.0	-14.2	-13.8
Net investment income	31.2	32.9	34.2	33.7	32.6	33.7	36.8	38.0
Operating earnings after taxes	9.0	9.0	10.4	5.8	19.3	10.9	20.6	24.4
Assets	527.0	556.3	601.4	637.3	671.5	703.2	756.5	802.3
Policyholders' surplus	134.0	138.4	158.7	163.1	182.3	192.5	224.9	255.5

[1] Includes premiums for automobile liability and physical damage.

Source: Insurance Information Institute, New York, NY, *The Fact Book, Property/Casualty Insurance Facts*, annual (copyright).

No. 851. Automobile Insurance—Average Expenditures Per Insured Vehicle, by State: 1994 to 1996

[In dollars. The average expenditures for automobile insurance in a state are affected by a number of factors, including the underlying rate structure, the coverages purchased, the deductibles and limits selected, the types of vehicles insured, and the distribution of driver characteristics]

STATE	1994	1995	1996	STATE	1994	1995	1996	STATE	1994	1995	1996
U.S.	651	667	685	KS	459	474	495	ND	368	381	402
				KY	526	555	581	OH	517	531	553
AL	524	549	578	LA	767	788	802	OK	503	526	545
AK	720	730	751	ME	471	472	470	OR	566	565	585
AZ	731	727	785	MD	712	732	759	PA	657	667	687
AR	507	500	558	MA	938	898	833	RI	861	870	870
CA	791	794	791	MI	665	645	697	SC	582	582	602
CO	721	722	751	MN	620	628	654	SD	396	428	448
CT	863	881	899	MS	557	579	604	TN	500	519	557
DE	776	784	806	MO	549	573	599	TX	714	711	726
DC	924	959	993	MT	460	468	479	UT	540	547	581
FL	656	739	783	NE	436	452	475	VT	503	512	514
GA	564	597	627	NV	748	759	803	VA	515	553	550
HI	962	963	959	NH	617	609	612	WA	654	650	666
ID	445	447	465	NJ	964	1,013	1,099	WV	619	646	671
IL	587	612	638	NM	628	639	660	WI	496	506	533
IN	529	542	548	NY	870	906	960	WY	422	433	452
IA	422	429	445	NC	462	501	518				

Source: National Association of Insurance Commissioners, Kansas City, MO, *State Average Expenditures and Premiums for Personal Automobile Insurance*, annual (copyright).

No. 852. Life Insurance in Force in the United States—Summary: 1980 to 1996

[As of **December 31** or **calendar year**, as applicable. Covers life insurance with life insurance companies only. Represents all life insurance in force on lives of U.S. residents whether issued by U.S. or foreign companies. For definition of household, see text, Section 1]

YEAR	Number of policies, total (mil.)	LIFE INSURANCE IN FORCE					AVERAGE SIZE POLICY IN FORCE (dollars)				AVERAGE AMOUNT ($1,000)		Disposable personal income per household ($1,000)
		Value (bil. dol.)					Ordinary	Group	Industrial	Credit [1]	Per household	Per insured household	
		Total	Ordinary	Group	Industrial	Credit [1]							
1980	402	3,541	1,761	1,579	36	165	11,920	13,410	620	2,110	41.9	51.1	24.4
1985	386	6,053	3,247	2,562	28	216	22,780	19,720	640	3,100	66.6	82.2	34.6
1990	389	9,393	5,367	3,754	24	248	37,910	26,630	670	3,500	98.4	124.5	44.6
1991	375	9,986	5,678	4,058	22	228	41,450	28,760	680	3,580	102.7	130.0	46.1
1992	366	10,406	5,942	4,241	21	202	42,960	29,930	700	3,610	106.6	136.6	48.2
1993	363	11,105	6,428	4,456	21	200	45,770	31,430	700	3,850	111.6	143.1	49.7
1994	371	11,674	6,835	4,609	20	210	48,950	32,690	700	3,530	118.7	152.2	51.7
1995	392	12,577	7,548	4,778	20	231	49,980	32,950	660	3,530	124.1	159.1	54.3
1996	418	13,760	8,337	5,159	19	246	49,920	34,160	670	3,460	133.3	170.9	56.5

[1] Insures borrower to cover consumer loan in case of death.

Source: American Council of Life Insurance, Washington, DC, *Life Insurance Fact Book*, annual (copyright).

No. 853. Life Insurance Purchases in the United States—Number and Amount: 1980 to 1996

[Excludes revivals, increases, dividend additions, and reinsurance acquired. Includes long-term credit insurance (life insurance on loans of more than 10 years' duration). See also headnote, Table 852]

YEAR	NUMBER OF POLICIES PURCHASED (1,000)				AMOUNT PURCHASED (bil. dol.)			
	Total	Ordinary	Group	Industrial	Total	Ordinary	Group	Industrial
1980	29,007	14,750	11,379	2,878	573	386	183	4
1985	33,880	17,104	16,243	533	[1]1,231	911	[1]320	1
1990	28,791	14,066	14,592	133	1,529	1,070	459	(Z)
1991	29,813	13,471	16,230	112	[2]1,616	1,042	[2]574	(Z)
1992	28,382	13,350	14,930	102	1,489	1,048	441	(Z)
1993	31,238	13,574	17,574	90	1,678	1,101	577	(Z)
1994	31,955	13,780	18,061	114	1,657	1,107	550	(Z)
1995	31,485	13,268	18,105	112	1,600	1,101	499	(Z)
1996	29,908	12,246	17,575	87	1,700	1,118	581	(Z)

Z Less than $500 million.　[1] Includes Federal Employees' Group Life Insurance: $11 billion in 1985.　[2] Includes Servicemen's Group Life Insurance: $167 billion in 1991.

Source: American Council of Life Insurance, Washington, DC, *Life Insurance Fact Book*, annual (copyright).

No. 854. U.S. Life Insurance Companies—Summary: 1980 to 1996

[As of **December 31** or **calendar year**, as applicable. Covers domestic and foreign business of U.S. companies]

ITEM	Unit	1980	1985	1989	1990	1991	1992	1993	1994	1995	1996
U.S. companies	Number	1,958	2,261	2,270	2,195	2,064	1,944	1,844	1,745	1,715	1,695
Sales	**Bil. dol.**	**655**	[1]**1,530**	**1,788**	**2,024**	[2]**2,014**	**1,881**	**2,130**	**2,086**	**2,269**	**(NA)**
Ordinary	Bil. dol	461	1,187	1,343	1,368	1,403	1,395	1,520	1,463	1,650	(NA)
Group	Bil. dol	190	[1]342	444	655	[1]611	485	610	623	618	(NA)
Industrial	Bil. dol	4	1	(Z)	(Z)	(Z)	1	(Z)	(Z)	1	(NA)
Income	**Bil. dol.**	**130.9**	**234.0**	**367.3**	**402.2**	**411.0**	**426.9**	**466.4**	**480.8**	**512.2**	**546.3**
Life insurance premiums	Bil. dol	40.8	60.1	73.3	76.7	79.3	83.9	94.5	96.3	98.9	104.6
Percent of total	Percent	31.2	25.7	20.0	19.1	19.3	19.6	20.3	20.0	19.3	19.2
Annuity considerations	Bil. dol	22.4	53.9	115.0	129.1	123.6	132.6	156.4	153.8	159.9	176.3
Health insurance premiums	Bil. dol	29.4	41.8	56.1	58.2	60.9	65.5	68.7	76.2	80.4	73.2
Investment and other	Bil. dol	38.3	78.2	122.9	138.2	147.2	144.9	146.8	154.5	173.0	192.2
Disbursements	**Bil. dol.**	**88.2**	**151.8**	**246.8**	**277.1**	**299.2**	**305.0**	**318.9**	**346.3**	**381.9**	**(NA)**
Payments to policyholders [2][3]	Bil. dol	59.0	95.7	178.3	200.9	218.6	222.1	231.9	252.9	282.9	(NA)
Percent of total	Percent	66.9	63.0	72.2	72.5	73.1	72.8	72.7	73.1	74.1	(NA)
Death payments	Bil. dol	12.9	18.5	23.5	25.5	26.4	28.0	29.8	31.6	33.0	35.2
Matured endowments	Bil. dol	0.8	0.8	0.8	0.8	0.7	0.7	0.6	0.7	1.0	0.8
Annuity payments	Bil. dol	7.4	19.7	26.0	28.6	31.8	32.4	36.4	40.2	48.1	50.7
Policy dividends	Bil. dol	8.1	12.4	14.9	15.7	15.8	15.3	15.8	16.2	18.1	18.3
Surrender values [3]	Bil. dol	6.4	15.9	73.4	90.2	101.2	100.5	103.1	110.4	124.8	(NA)
Disability benefits	Bil. dol	0.5	0.5	0.5	0.5	0.5	0.6	0.5	0.6	0.8	(NA)
Commissions, expenses, etc. [3]	Bil. dol	27.8	53.1	63.5	70.2	75.1	77.8	80.1	87.4	90.4	(NA)
Dividends to stockholders	Bil. dol	1.4	3.0	5.0	6.0	5.5	5.1	6.9	5.9	8.6	9.2
BALANCE SHEET											
Assets	**Bil. dol.**	**479**	**826**	**1,300**	**1,408**	**1,551**	**1,665**	**1,839**	**1,942**	**2,144**	**2,324**
Government securities	Bil. dol	33	125	178	211	269	320	384	396	409	397
Corporate securities	Bil. dol	227	374	664	711	789	863	982	1,072	1,241	1,429
Percent of total assets	Percent	47.4	45.3	51.1	50.5	50.8	51.8	53.4	55.2	57.9	61.5
Bonds	Bil. dol	180	297	538	583	624	670	730	791	869	952
Stocks	Bil. dol	47	77	126	128	165	193	252	282	372	478
Mortgages	Bil. dol	131	172	254	270	265	247	229	215	212	208
Real estate	Bil. dol	15	29	40	43	47	51	54	54	52	49
Policy loans	Bil. dol	41	54	57	63	66	72	78	85	96	100
Other	Bil. dol	32	72	106	110	115	112	112	120	133	140
Interest earned on assets [4]	Percent	8.02	9.63	9.10	8.89	8.63	8.08	7.52	7.14	7.34	7.17
Liabilities [2][5]	Bil. dol	445	769	1,216	1,317	1,445	1,549	1,711	1,806	1,993	2,158
Policy reserves [2]	**Bil. dol.**	**390**	**665**	**1,084**	**1,197**	**1,305**	**1,407**	**1,550**	**1,644**	**1,812**	**1,965**
Annuities	Bil. dol	181	410	730	815	895	960	1,062	1,118	1,238	1,343
Group	Bil. dol	140	303	474	516	548	560	602	613	619	657
Individual [6]	Bil. dol	41	107	256	299	347	400	460	505	619	686
Life insurance	Bil. dol	198	236	324	349	372	402	436	468	511	553
Health insurance	Bil. dol	11	19	30	33	38	45	52	58	63	69
Asset valuation reserve [7]	Bil. dol	6	11	19	15	19	21	25	25	30	33
Capital and surplus [2]	Bil. dol	34	57	84	91	106	115	128	137	151	166

NA Not available.　Z Less than $500 million.　[1] Data for 1985 include Federal Employees' Group Life Insurance: $11 billion; data for 1991 include Servicemen's Group Life Insurance: $167 billion.　[2] Includes operations of accident and health departments of life insurance companies.　[3] Beginning in 1989, data not comparable to prior years due to change in accounting method.　[4] Net rate.　[5] Includes other obligations not shown separately.　[6] Includes reserves for supplementary contracts with and without life contingencies.　[7] The asset valuation reserve is carried as a liability in financial statements but functions as surplus.

Source: American Council of Life Insurance, Washington, DC, *Life Insurance Fact Book*, annual (copyright).

Business Enterprise

This section relates to the place and behavior of the business firm and to business initiative in the American economy. It includes data on the number, type, and size of businesses; financial data of domestic and multinational U.S. corporations; business investment, expenditures, and profits; sales and inventories; and business failures. Additional business data may be found in other sections, particularly 27 and 28.

The principal sources of these data are the *Survey of Current Business,* published by the Bureau of Economic Analysis (BEA), the *Federal Reserve Bulletin,* issued by the Board of Governors of the Federal Reserve System, the annual *Statistics of Income* reports of the Internal Revenue Service (IRS), *The Business Failure Record* and the *Business Starts Record* issued by The Dun & Bradstreet Corporation, Murray Hill, NJ, and *Fortune* and *The Fortune Directory,* issued by Time, Inc., New York.

Business firms—A **firm** is generally defined as a business organization under a single management and may include one or more establishments. The terms **firm, business, company,** and **enterprise** are used interchangeably throughout this section. A firm doing business in more than one industry is classified by industry according to the major activity of the firm as a whole. The industrial classification is based on the *Standard Industrial Classification (SIC) Manual* (see text, Section 13). The IRS concept of a business firm relates primarily to the legal entity used for tax reporting purposes. The IRS *Statistics of Income* reports present data, based on a sample of tax returns before audit, separately for sole proprietorships, partnerships, and corporations. Data presented are for active enterprises only. A *sole proprietorship* is an unincorporated business owned by one person including large enterprises with many employees and hired managers and part-time operations in which the owner is the only person involved. A *partnership* is an unincorporated business owned by two or more persons, each of whom has a financial interest in the business. The "persons" could be individuals, estates, trusts, other partnerships, or corporations. A *corporation* is a business that is

In Brief

Patents issued in 1996: 121,700
Percent issued to foreign country residents: 43%

Bankruptcies filed in 1997: 1,316,999
Business: 4.1%
Nonbusiness: 95.9%
Change from 1996 26.4%

legally incorporated under state laws. The IRS recognizes many types of businesses as corporations, including joint-stock companies, insurance companies, and unincorporated associations such as business trusts, etc. While many corporations file consolidated tax returns, most corporate tax returns represent individual corporations, some of which are affiliated through common ownership or control with other corporations filing separate returns.

Assets and liabilities—In its annual report, *Statistics of Income, Corporation Income Tax Returns,* the IRS presents balance sheet and income estimates for all active U.S. corporations. The Bureau of the Census issues the *Quarterly Financial Report for Manufacturing, Mining, and Trade Corporations* (QFR), which presents quarterly income account and balance sheet data for manufacturing, mining, and trade industries.

One of the most comprehensive measures of the investment position of the business sector (and the only measure adjusted to current replacement cost) is the BEA capital stock series. See *Survey of Current Business,* May 1997.

Income, profits, dividends, and taxes—Several agencies, among them IRS and BEA, compile corporate income account data. These data, however, are not comparable because of differing definitions and methods of compilation. A reconciliation of the two can be found in Table 8.23 of *Survey of Current Business,* published by BEA. The IRS publishes financial data for all business enterprises. These data appear in *Statistics of Income, Corporation Income Tax Returns,* and the *Statistics of Income Bulletin* (partnerships and sole proprietorships). Data on international income and taxes reported by U.S. corporations are also included in the *Statistics of*

Income Bulletin and in the periodic *Compendium of Studies of International Income and Taxes*. BEA's estimates of international investment income include receipts of income of U.S. direct investment abroad, payments of income on foreign direct investment in the United States, other private investment income receipts and payments (interest and dividends not included in direct investment), and U.S. Government interest receipts and payments. (See Section 28, Foreign Commerce and Aid.)

Corporate data issued by BEA are a part of its national income and product accounts (see text, Section 14). The primary sources for BEA estimates of profits, taxes, dividends, and undistributed profits are from the SOI tabulations. Various adjustments of IRS data are required by the national income treatment—particularly with respect to profits which would be disclosed if all tax returns were audited: depletion, capital gain or loss, treatment of bad debts, measurement of income received from abroad, and intercorporate dividends—to make the figures comparable with other entries in the national income accounts. For a discussion of two types of adjustments (inventory valuation and capital consumption), see text, Section 14. The BEA's corporate profits data also include net earnings of Federal Reserve banks, credit unions, private noninsured pension funds, and several quasi-government credit agencies not included in IRS data.

Changes in industry presentation—The country detail in this presentation is identical to that in the 1989 benchmark survey and in the intervening annual surveys. However, three changes have affected the industry detail. First, beginning with the publication of the preliminary 1994 benchmark survey results, the data for nonbank U.S. parents and foreign affiliates exclude savings institutions and credit unions. The change in coverage reflects the reclassification of savings institutions and credit unions from the "finance, except banking" industry (which is covered by the non-bank data) to the industry "depository institutions" (which will replace the industry "banking" in the publication of the final 1994 benchmark results). This change will not materially affect the comparisons of the data for 1993 with the data for 1994, because in 1993, only one U.S. parent and no foreign affiliates were classified as a savings institution or a credit union.

Second, beginning with the preliminary 1994 benchmark survey results, the "communication and public utilities" group was disaggregated, and the "metal mining" and "nonmetallic minerals mining" groups were aggregated, in the industry table stub. Third, beginning with the revised 1993 annual estimates, the names of two industry groups were changed; the group "machinery, except electrical" is now called "industrial machinery and equipment," and the group "electric and electronic equipment" is now called "electronic and other electric equipment."

Sources and uses of corporate funds—These data show capital requirements of corporations and the manner in which they are financed. Sources of funds should be equal to their uses.

Fortune 500—Sales include service and rental revenues but exclude dividends, interest, and other nonoperating revenues. **Assets** are those shown at the company's yearend. **Net income** is shown after taxes and after extraordinary credits or charges when any are shown on the income statement. **Stockholder's equity** is the sum of capital stock, surplus, and retained earnings at the company's yearend. **Total returns to investors** include both price appreciation and dividend yield. For further discussion, see Time, Inc., New York, NY, *The Fortune Directories*.

Economic censuses—The economic censuses constitute comprehensive and periodic canvasses of the Nation's industrial and business activities. The first economic census of the United States was conducted as part of the 1810 decennial census, when inquiries on manufacturing were included with the census of population. Minerals data were collected in 1840. The first censuses of construction and business were taken for 1929. An integrated economic census program was begun for 1954. In that year, the censuses covered the retail and wholesale trades, selected service industries, manufactures, and mineral industries. In 1992, coverage was expanded to 95 percent of the private U.S. economy. The economic censuses are taken at 5-year intervals covering years ending in "2" and "7." Special surveys are conducted every 5 years as part of the economic censuses to determine the extent of business ownership by specific minority groups and women.

Figure 17.1
Patents Issued: 1980 to 1996

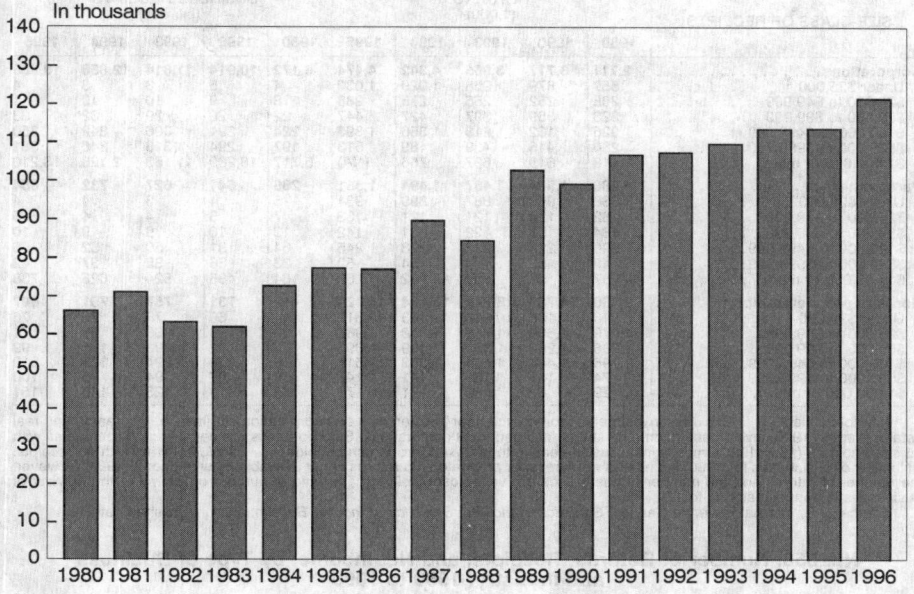

Source: Chart prepared by U.S. Bureau of the Census. For data, see Table 886.

Figure 17.2
Bankruptcy Cases Filed: 1990 to 1997

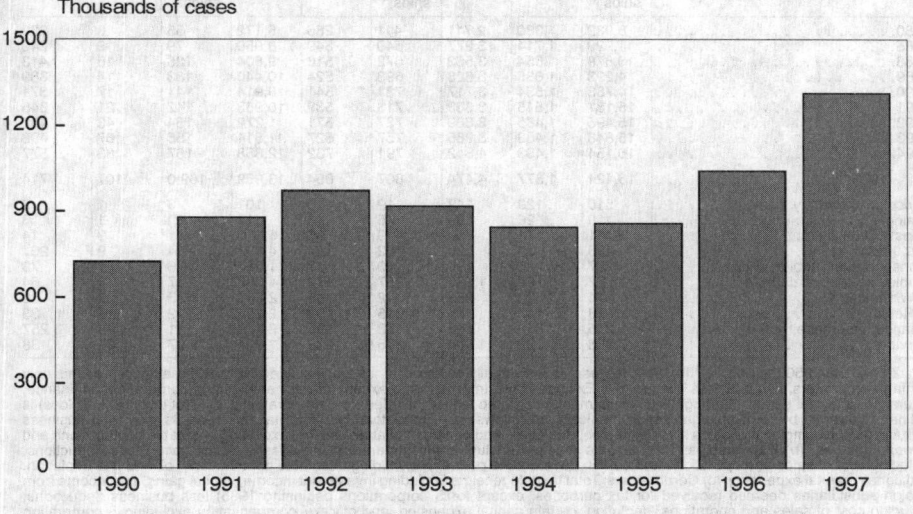

Source: Chart prepared by U.S. Bureau of the Census. For data, see Table 881.

No. 855. Number of Returns and Business Receipts, by Size of Receipts and Type of Business: 1980 to 1995

[Covers active enterprises only. Figures are estimates based on sample of unaudited tax returns; see Appendix III. The industrial distribution is based on data collected from companies; see text, Section 17]

SIZE-CLASS OF RECEIPTS	RETURNS (1,000)					BUSINESS RECEIPTS [1] (bil. dol.)				
	1980	1990	1993	1994	1995	1980	1990	1993	1994	1995
Corporations	2,711	3,717	3,965	4,342	4,474	6,172	10,914	11,814	12,858	13,969
Under $25,000 [2]	557	879	968	1,029	1,030	4	5	3	3	4
$25,000 to $49,999	208	252	256	275	288	8	9	10	10	11
$50,000 to $99,999	323	359	397	427	447	22	26	29	32	33
$100,000 to $499,999	926	1,162	1,218	1,356	1,393	224	291	306	342	350
$500,000 to $999,999	280	416	439	489	513	197	294	313	346	361
$1,000,000 or more	418	649	687	766	(NA)	5,717	10,289	11,153	12,126	13,210
Partnerships	1,380	1,554	1,467	1,494	1,581	286	541	627	732	854
Under $25,000 [2]	638	963	887	899	931	5	4	3	4	4
$25,000 to $49,999	182	126	121	121	133	7	5	4	4	5
$50,000 to $99,999	184	133	129	131	142	13	10	9	9	10
$100,000 to $499,999	290	222	222	228	245	64	51	50	52	56
$500,000 to $999,999	48	52	49	54	59	33	36	35	37	42
$1,000,000 or more	37	57	59	62	69	164	435	524	625	738
Nonfarm proprietorships [3]	9,730	14,783	15,848	16,154	16,424	411	731	757	791	807
Under $25,000 [2]	6,916	10,196	10,615	11,163	11,317	44	69	73	75	76
$25,000 to $49,999	1,079	1,660	1,838	1,868	1,983	39	58	65	67	71
$50,000 to $99,999	836	1,282	1,330	1,409	1,393	59	91	93	101	99
$100,000 to $499,999	796	1,444	1,454	1,503	1,514	159	296	294	308	310
$500,000 to $999,999	74	143	139	141	147	50	97	94	95	100
$1,000,000 or more	29	66	71	70	70	60	119	125	145	151

NA Not available. [1] Excludes investment income except for partnerships and corporations in finance, insurance, and real estate. Starting 1990, investment income no longer included for S corporations. S corporations are certain small companies with 35 shareholders (15 in 1980), mostly individuals, electing to be taxed through shareholders. [2] Includes firms with no receipts. [3] Number of businesses for 1980. Number of nonfarm sole proprietorship returns is not available by size prior to 1981. However, the number of returns and the number of businesses are very closely related. The ratio of number of returns to the number of businesses is approximately 1 to 1.3.

Source: U.S. Internal Revenue Service, *Statistics of Income; Statistics of Income Bulletin;* and unpublished data.

No. 856. Number of Returns, Receipts, and Net Income, by Type of Business and Industry: 1980 to 1995

[See headnote, Table 855. Minus sign (-) indicates net loss]

ITEM	NUMBER OF RETURNS (1,000)			BUSINESS RECEIPTS [2] (bil. dol.)			NET INCOME (less loss) [3] (bil. dol.)		
	Nonfarm proprietorships [1]	Partnerships	Corporations	Nonfarm proprietorships [1]	Partnerships	Corporations	Nonfarm proprietorships [1]	Partnerships	Corporations
1980	8,932	1,380	2,711	411	286	6,172	55	8	239
1985	11,929	1,714	3,277	540	349	8,050	79	-9	240
1988	13,679	1,654	3,563	672	516	9,804	126	15	413
1989	14,298	1,635	3,628	693	524	10,440	133	14	389
1990	14,783	1,554	3,717	731	541	10,914	141	17	371
1991 [4]	15,181	1,515	3,803	713	539	10,963	142	21	345
1992	15,495	1,485	3,869	737	571	11,272	154	43	402
1993	15,848	1,468	3,965	757	627	11,814	156	67	498
1994	16,154	1,493	4,342	791	732	12,858	167	83	577
1995 [4]	16,424	1,577	4,474	807	854	13,969	169.0	107	714
Agriculture, forestry, fishing [5]	510	129	148	19	13	101	3	1	2
Mining	119	26	35	5	18	114	(Z)	1	6
Construction	2,111	71	450	119	36	627.0	21	3	14
Manufacturing	498	30	320	32	124	4,291	4	9	261
Transportation, public utilities	737	26	194	40	77	1,087	6	7	73
Wholesale and retail trade [6]	3,027	164	1,132	257	172	4,206	17	4	64
Wholesale	374	22	352	42	68	2,005	5	2	30
Retail	2,653	143	775	215	103	2,194	12	5	33
Finance, insurance, real estate	1,275	849	683	58	196	2,278	21	45	257
Services	7,958	282	1,504	275	218	1,264	97	37	38

Z Less than $500 million. [1] In 1980, represents individually owned businesses, including farms; thereafter, represents only nonfarm proprietors, i.e., business owners. [2] Excludes investment income except for partnerships and corporations in finance, insurance, and real estate. Starting 1985, investment income no longer included for S corporations. [3] Net income (less loss) is defined differently by form of organization, basically as follows: (a) Proprietorships: Total taxable receipts less total business deductions, including cost of sales and operations, depletion, and certain capital expensing, excluding charitable contributions and owners' salaries; (b) Partnerships: Total taxable receipts (including investment income except capital gains) less deductions, including cost of sales and operations and certain payments to partners, excluding charitable contributions, oil and gas depletion, and certain capital expensing; (c) Corporations: Total taxable receipts (including investment income, capital gains, and income from foreign subsidiaries deemed received for tax purposes, except for S corporations beginning 1985) less business deductions, including cost of sales and operations, depletion, certain capital expensing, and officers' compensation excluding S corporation charitable contributions and investment expenses starting 1985; net income is before income tax. [4] Includes businesses not allocable to individual industries. [5] Represents agricultral services only. [6] Includes trade business not identified as wholesale or retail

Source: U.S. Internal Revenue Service, *Statistics of Income,* various publications.

No. 857. Number of Returns and Business Receipts, by Industry, Type of Business, and Size of Business Receipts: 1994

[Number of returns in thousands; receipts and net income in billions of dollars. Covers active enterprises only. Figures are estimates based on a sample of unaudited tax returns; see Appendix III. The industrial distribution is based on data collected from establishments; see text, Section 17. Minus sign (-) indicates net loss]

INDUSTRY	Nonfarm proprietor-ships	Partner-ships	CORPORATIONS				
			Under $1 mil. [1]	$1 mil.- $4.9 mil.	$5 mil.- $9.9 mil.	$10 mil.- $49.9 mil.	$50 mil. or more
Total: [2]							
Number.	16,154	1,494	3,576	574	92	81	19
Business receipts [3]	791	732	734	1,213	647	1,649	8,617
Net income (less loss)	167	82	-2	26	20	57	477
Agriculture, forestry, fishing:							
Number.	515	123	134	11	1	1	(Z)
Business receipts [3]	19	11	22	24	9	16	23
Mining:							
Number.	126	27	31	3	1	(Z)	(Z)
Business receipts [3]	6	16	4	7	4	10	79
Construction:							
Number.	1,986	66	338	77	10	7	1
Business receipts [3]	116	31	91	164	71	131	125
Manufacturing:							
Number.	513	30	201	73	17	17	6
Business receipts [3]	33	108	51	163	116	340	3,298
Transportation, public utilities:							
Number.	744	23	147	31	4	3	1
Business receipts [3]	40	66	27	65	30	64	856
Wholesale and retail trade:							
Number.	2,954	153	805	219	38	38	7
Business receipts [3]	248	142	217	466	266	796	2,209
Finance, insurance, real estate:							
Number.	1,344	810	628	37	7	7	3
Business receipts [3]	54	161	66	81	50	142	1,638
Services:							
Number.	7,803	261	1,277	123	14	8	1
Business receipts [3]	272	196	253	242	100	149	390

Z Less than 500 returns. [1] Includes businesses without receipts. [2] Includes businesses not allocable to individual industries. [3] Excludes investment income except for partnerships and corporations (other than S corporations) in finance, insurance, and real estate.

Source: U.S. Internal Revenue Service, *Statistics of Income,* various publications; and unpublished data.

No. 858. Sole Proprietorships—Selected Income and Deduction Items: 1980 to 1995

[In millions of dollars, except as indicated. Covers nonfarm sole proprietorships. All figures are estimates based on sample. Tax law changes have affected the comparability of the data over time; see *Statistics of Income* reports for a description]

ITEM	1980	1985	1989	1990	1991	1992	1993	1994	1995
Number of returns (1,000)	8,932	11,929	14,298	14,783	15,181	15,495	15,848	16,154	16,424
Businesses with net income (1,000)	(NA)	8,641	11,018	11,222	11,551	11,720	11,872	12,187	12,213
Inventory, end of year	21,996	24,970	30,060	30,422	29,783	29,898	31,795	33,602	33,356
Business receipts	411,206	540,045	692,811	730,606	712,568	737,082	757,215	790,630	807,364
Income from sales and operations .	407,169	528,675	678,616	719,008	700,681	725,666	746,306	778,494	796,597
Business deductions [1]	356,258	461,273	560,175	589,250	571,154	583,147	600,765	623,833	638,127
Cost of goods sold/operations [1]	209,890	232,294	283,709	291,010	272,627	274,220	289,578	301,004	306,959
Purchases	168,302	(NA)	204,681	204,225	200,861	204,317	210,260	216,365	219,305
Labor costs	10,922	14,504	22,540	22,680	21,918	18,838	20,685	23,497	24,383
Materials and supplies	12,909	(NA)	29,870	30,195	28,072	28,825	32,701	34,304	34,427
Commissions	3,333	(NA)	6,843	8,816	7,628	10,457	8,707	9,029	9,592
Salaries and wages (net)	26,561	38,266	45,469	46,998	48,890	52,316	52,046	53,649	54,471
Car and truck expenses	13,378	17,044	20,789	21,766	22,594	23,920	26,714	30,845	32,785
Rent paid	9,636	15,259	20,952	23,392	23,643	25,148	25,008	26,769	27,503
Repairs	5,032	(NA)	8,149	8,941	9,159	9,706	9,847	10,385	10,172
Taxes paid	7,672	(NA)	9,948	10,342	10,629	12,618	13,062	13,600	13,471
Utilities	4,790	(NA)	13,601	13,539	13,260	14,547	16,069	16,918	17,206
Insurance	6,003	(NA)	12,879	13,358	13,065	13,260	13,173	13,289	12,978
Interest paid	7,190	11,914	13,280	13,312	12,077	10,406	9,431	9,170	10,057
Depreciation	13,953	26,291	24,479	23,735	23,076	23,274	24,964	26,158	26,782
Pension and profit sharing plans . .	141	311	539	586	519	528	636	605	649
Net income (less loss)	54,947	78,773	132,738	141,430	141,516	153,960	156,459	166,799	169,262
Businesses with net income	68,010	98,776	152,416	161,657	162,427	173,473	176,983	187,845	191,729

NA Not available. [1] Includes other amounts not shown separately.

Source: U.S. Internal Revenue Service, *Statistics of Income Bulletin,* quarterly.

No. 859. Partnerships—Selected Items, by Industry: 1980 to 1995

[In millions of dollars, except number of partners and partnerships in thousands. Covers active partnerships only. Includes partnerships not allocable by industry. Figures are estimates based on samples. See Appendix III]

YEAR	NUMBER OF PARTNERSHIPS			Number of part- ners	Total assets [1]	Business re- ceipts [2][3]	Total deduc- tions [3]	Net income less loss [3]	Net in- come [3]	Net loss [3]
	Total	With net income	With net loss							
All industries:										
1980	1,380	774	605	8,420	597,504	285,967	283,749	8,249	45,062	36,813
1985	1,714	876	838	13,245	1,269,434	349,169	376,001	-8,884	77,045	85,928
1990	1,554	854	700	17,095	1,735,285	540,647	549,603	16,610	116,318	99,708
1992	1,485	856	629	15,735	1,907,345	571,427	553,770	42,916	121,834	78,918
1993	1,468	870	598	15,627	2,118,268	626,515	589,358	66,652	137,441	70,788
1994	1,494	890	604	14,990	2,295,212	731,834	680,052	82,183	150,928	68,745
1995	1,581	955	626	15,606	2,718,648	853,831	783,603	106,829	178,651	71,822
Agriculture, forestry, fishing:										
1980	126	72	54	381	24,595	21,611	22,859	472	2,539	2,067
1985	136	76	60	585	27,027	6,529	10,495	-1,049	2,797	3,846
1990	125	77	48	503	27,580	9,497	11,805	1,667	3,905	2,238
1992	125	81	44	504	32,884	8,932	10,547	2,227	3,951	1,724
1993	120	76	44	588	38,947	10,343	12,517	2,019	3,989	1,970
1994	123	72	51	575	41,517	11,324	13,682	1,608	3,985	2,377
1995	129	75	54	603	43,481	13,270	16,207	1,300	4,183	2,853
Mining:										
1980	35	15	20	722	24,742	13,201	18,248	-4,208	3,920	8,128
1985	62	33	30	2,207	66,930	19,922	21,920	1,482	7,884	6,402
1990	41	29	14	2,149	58,246	19,967	20,869	2,183	7,009	4,825
1992	36	23	13	1,389	53,697	16,706	18,230	1,009	5,271	4,263
1993	32	21	11	1,431	51,367	17,364	18,073	2,148	6,070	3,922
1994	27	17	10	1,010	45,532	15,902	17,323	984	5,076	4,092
1995	26	15	11	828	55,503	17,813	19,004	1,111	5,272	4,161
Construction:										
1980	67	51	16	160	9,811	18,407	17,202	1,560	2,119	559
1985	57	41	16	134	15,008	21,476	20,080	2,207	2,743	536
1990	59	45	15	162	17,989	30,716	29,672	1,908	3,020	1,112
1992	59	42	17	158	15,663	25,946	24,501	1,906	2,648	743
1993	62	45	17	154	13,917	26,863	25,279	2,176	2,884	708
1994	66	48	18	159	15,171	31,140	29,065	2,654	3,127	474
1995	71	48	22	167	16,653	35,881	33,936	2,527	3,338	810
Transportation, public utilities:										
1980	20	11	10	73	9,291	5,868	5,821	248	1,092	844
1985	25	15	10	186	26,468	11,253	14,814	-3,006	1,360	4,426
1990	25	14	11	503	63,334	32,800	35,989	-117	5,887	6,004
1992	24	12	12	527	81,070	42,081	43,127	1,054	6,585	5,531
1993	21	11	10	652	115,596	58,852	58,198	4,119	9,319	5,200
1994	23	12	11	635	126,351	66,407	64,863	5,627	11,118	5,491
Manufacturing:										
1980	30	20	10	92	11,252	15,327	16,142	-472	1,199	1,671
1985	30	12	18	105	24,838	22,588	24,225	-1,085	1,228	2,314
1990	28	15	13	246	59,789	65,354	65,833	1,166	4,791	3,626
1992	24	14	11	225	74,240	78,028	78,996	1,870	5,779	3,909
1993	25	16	9	231	84,184	89,861	88,889	3,940	7,482	3,542
1994	30	18	12	224	93,494	107,569	104,551	6,584	9,853	3,268
Wholesale and retail trade:										
1980	200	123	77	487	17,727	65,793	63,988	2,475	3,374	900
1985	201	113	88	493	20,568	69,079	68,119	1,977	3,467	1,490
1990	176	100	77	481	28,423	98,120	97,131	2,610	4,717	2,107
1992	162	86	76	425	32,777	107,870	106,639	2,553	4,758	2,205
1993	157	88	69	471	35,278	110,890	109,854	3,076	5,304	2,229
1994	153	87	66	443	44,367	142,116	140,295	4,301	6,344	2,043
Finance, insurance, and real estate:										
1980	637	313	325	5,566	454,531	87,133	91,382	-4,249	15,169	19,418
1985	844	369	475	7,755	979,787	92,309	118,237	-25,929	30,383	56,311
1990	822	401	422	10,846	1,329,452	64,313	87,011	-19,213	47,577	66,790
1992	797	427	370	10,328	1,438,303	87,773	72,853	-752	50,044	50,796
1993	793	443	350	9,944	1,612,142	127,908	113,480	15,260	59,062	43,802
1994	810	465	345	9,881	1,750,671	161,365	137,240	24,125	65,369	41,245
Services:										
1980	263	169	94	938	45,510	58,627	48,106	12,424	15,649	3,224
1985	341	207	134	1,713	106,597	104,197	96,202	16,541	26,942	10,400
1990	267	173	96	2,153	150,063	161,702	145,789	26,453	39,383	12,930
1992	253	169	84	2,167	178,577	181,603	158,260	33,004	42,748	9,744
1993	256	169	87	2,146	166,806	184,434	162,846	33,887	43,300	9,413
1994	261	170	91	2,060	177,992	195,933	172,926	36,318	46,048	9,730

[1] Total assets are understated because not all partnerships file complete balance sheets.   [2] Includes investment income for partnerships in finance, insurance, and real estate.   [3] Beginning 1985, only net (not gross) income from farming, rents, and royalties are included.

Source: U.S. Internal Revenue Service, *Statistics of Income Bulletin, and Partnerhip Returns—1978-1994.*

No. 860. Partnerships—Selected Income and Balance Sheet Items: 1980 to 1995

[In billions of dollars, except as indicated. Covers active partnerships only. All figures are estimates based on samples. See Appendix III]

ITEM	1980	1985	1989	1990	1991	1992	1993	1994	1995
Number of returns (1,000)	1,380	1,714	1,635	1,554	1,515	1,485	1,468	1,494	1,581
Number with net income (1,000). . . .	774	876	898	854	856	856	870	890	955
Number with balance sheets (1,000).	1,194	1,227	1,149	1,081	1,048	975	977	988	1,053
Number of partners (1,000).	8,420	13,245	18,432	17,095	15,801	15,735	15,627	14,990	15,606
Assets [1] [2]	598	1,269	1,791	1,735	1,817	1,907	2,118	2,295	2,719
Depreciable assets (net).	239	696	670	681	696	701	698	712	767
Inventories, end of year	33	27	59	57	57	62	71	76	88
Land	70	152	214	215	213	213	207	208	221
Liabilities [1] [2]	489	1,069	1,791	1,415	1,460	1,508	1,620	1,662	1,886
Accounts payable	34	41	52	67	63	79	80	81	91
Short-term debt [3].	48	103	87	88	117	115	131	126	124
Long-term debt [4]	178	382	512	498	491	486	489	508	544
Nonrecourse loans.	119	328	461	470	474	476	478	463	466
Partners' capital accounts [2]	109	200	356	320	357	399	499	633	832
Receipts [1]	292	367	551	566	563	597	656	762	890
Business receipts [5]	271	303	524	483	483	515	561	732	854
Interest received [6]	11	21	21	21	20	16	16	19	31
Deductions [1]	284	376	475	550	541	554	589	680	784
Cost of goods sold/operations	114	146	233	243	237	249	273	335	395
Salaries and wages	22	34	54	56	58	62	65	70	80
Taxes paid	10	8	9	9	10	10	11	12	13
Interest paid	28	29	33	30	28	25	27	36	43
Depreciation	22	54	20	60	58	60	60	22	23
Net income (less loss)	8	-9	14	17	21	43	67	82	107
Net income.	45	77	114	116	113	122	137	151	179

[1] Includes items not shown separately.   [2] Assets, liabilities, and partners' capital accounts are understated because not all partnerships file complete balance sheets.   [3] Mortgages, notes, and bonds payable in less than 1 year.   [4] Mortgages, notes, and bonds payable in 1 year or more.

Source: U.S. Internal Revenue Service, Statistics of Income, various issues.

No. 861. Corporate Funds—Sources and Uses: 1980 to 1997

[In billions of dollars, except percent. Covers nonfarm nonfinancial corporate business. See text, Section 17]

ITEM	1980	1985	1990	1991	1992	1993	1994	1995	1996	1997
Sources	**421.8**	**737.9**	**592.6**	**489.3**	**600.0**	**698.1**	**758.9**	**882.0**	**953.8**	**987.2**
Internal	199.9	358.2	409.1	422.2	438.6	480.2	524.3	524.4	588.4	624.8
U.S. undistributed profits.	69.4	26.0	23.6	8.3	33.7	48.2	81.4	86.9	92.7	(NA)
IVA and CCA [1]	-74.5	46.8	-8.9	3.4	-9.1	-7.5	-8.7	-19.0	7.4	(NA)
Capital consumption allowances. .	186.3	264.0	349.5	363.5	372.6	386.1	418.3	430.7	461.3	489.5
Foreign earnings [2]	18.7	21.4	44.8	47.1	41.5	53.4	41.6	59.3	62.0	60.6
External [3]	221.9	379.7	183.5	67.1	161.3	217.9	241.6	403.3	385.5	362.4
Credit market funds	78.7	83.9	47.0	-35.6	60.9	68.9	73.2	123.3	64.7	(NA)
Securities and mortgages	35.9	11.5	-26.6	75.1	66.8	85.3	-37.7	-2.1	-16.4	(NA)
Equity issues	10.4	-84.5	-63.0	18.3	27.0	21.3	-44.9	-74.2	-82.6	(NA)
Bonds and mortgages [4] . . .	25.5	96.0	36.4	56.8	39.8	64.0	7.2	72.2	66.2	(NA)
Loans and short-term paper. . .	42.8	72.4	73.6	-110.7	-5.9	-16.4	110.8	125.3	81.1	(NA)
Other	143.1	295.8	136.5	102.7	100.5	149.1	160.8	214.9	296.3	(NA)
Profit taxes payable	2.9	-3.2	-5.0	-8.2	7.2	2.0	2.4	-0.8	1.1	(NA)
Trade debt	29.1	43.0	28.4	23.1	33.4	36.4	91.8	67.6	59.0	(NA)
Foreign direct investment in U.S	13.2	256.0	55.9	12.0	59.8	42.9	42.9	50.7	59.7	81.8
Miscellaneous liabilities	111.1	256.0	113.1	87.8	59.8	110.6	75.4	171.1	243.3	135.3
Uses	**419.7**	**643.7**	**509.7**	**500.7**	**554.4**	**787.9**	**761.7**	**889.0**	**973.4**	**(NA)**
Capital expenditures	250.7	369.6	394.5	370.9	386.9	430.6	511.1	567.7	592.5	675.7
Increase in financial assets.	168.9	274.1	115.3	129.8	167.5	357.3	278.1	342.4	417.7	(NA)
Discrepancy (sources less uses) . . .	2.1	94.2	82.9	-11.4	45.6	-899.8	-2.9	-7.0	-19.6	(NA)

NA Not available   [1] Inventory valuation and capital consumption adjustment.   [2] Foreign earnings of subsidiaries retained abroad.   [3] Net increases in liability.   [4] Includes industrial pollution control revenue bonds issued by state and local governments.

Source: Board of Governors of the Federal Reserve System. Data derived from Flow of Funds Accounts, annual.

No. 862. Nonfinancial Corporate Business-Sector Balance Sheet: 1987 to 1996

[In billions of dollars. Represents yearend outstandings]

ITEM	1987	1988	1989	1990	1991	1992	1993	1994	1995	1996
Assets	**8,343**	**9,074**	**9,621**	**9,817**	**9,800**	**9,788**	**10,120**	**10,753**	**11,488**	**12,281**
Tangible assets (current cost)	5,440	5,788	6,102	6,183	6,036	5,856	5,831	6,185	6,513	6,876
Real estate [1]	3,083	3,289	3,472	3,429	3,247	3,007	2,874	3,051	3,187	3,383
Equipment [2]	1,568	1,653	1,736	1,828	1,876	1,925	1,994	2,092	2,223	2,361
Inventories [2]	789	847	894	925	913	924	963	1,042	1,103	1,132
Financial assets [3]	2,903	3,286	3,520	3,634	3,764	3,932	4,289	4,567	4,976	5,405
Checkable deposits and currency	105	135	151	167	183	189	203	222	239	286
Time and savings deposits	117	99	90	73	67	52	74	68	66	69
Trade receivables	805	896	938	967	961	989	1,035	1,107	1,206	1,269
Liabilities [3]	3,774	4,192	4,533	4,729	4,830	5,110	5,389	5,627	6,022	6,379
Credit market instruments [3]	1,984	2,188	2,381	2,492	2,432	2,470	2,528	2,667	2,876	3,053
Municipal securities [4]	116	116	116	115	114	114	114	109	96	79
Corporate bonds [5]	784	887	961	1,008	1,087	1,155	1,230	1,253	1,326	1,399
Mortgages	202	208	235	233	215	193	201	223	259	313
Net worth (market value)	4,569	4,882	5,088	5,088	4,970	4,678	4,732	5,125	5,466	5,902

[1] At market value. [2] At replacement (current) cost. [3] Includes items not shown separately. [4] Industrial revenue bonds. Issued by state and local governments to finance private investment and secured in interest and principal by the industrial user of the funds. [5] Through 1992, corporate bonds include net issues by Netherlands Antillean financial subsidiaries, and U.S. direct investment abroad excludes net inflows from those bond issues.

Source: Board of Governors of the Federal Reserve System, *Balance Sheets for the U.S. Economy.*

No. 863. Corporations—Selected Financial Items: 1980 to 1995

[In billions of dollars, except as noted. Covers active corporations only. All corporations are required to file returns except those specifically exempt. See source for changes in law affecting comparability of historical data. Based on samples; see Appendix III]

ITEM	1980	1985	1989	1990	1991	1992	1993	1994	1995
Number of returns (1,000)	2,711	3,277	3,628	3,717	3,803	3,869	3,965	4,342	4,474
Number with net income (1,000)	1,597	1,820	1,922	1,911	1,942	2,064	2,145	2,392	2,455
S Corporation returns [1] (1,000)	545	725	1,423	1,575	1,698	1,785	1,902	2,024	2,153
Assets [2]	7,617	12,773	17,647	18,190	19,030	20,002	21,816	23,446	26,014
Cash	529	683	824	771	787	806	812	853	962
Notes and accounts receivable	1,985	3,318	4,196	4,198	4,191	4,169	4,532	4,768	5,307
Inventories	535	715	879	894	884	915	947	1,126	1,045
Investments in Govt. obligations	266	917	1,262	921	1,069	1,248	1,290	1,309	1,363
Mortgage and real estate	894	1,259	1,610	1,538	1,529	1,567	1,627	1,661	1,713
Other investments	1,214	2,414	3,971	4,137	4,750	4,971	5,701	6,265	7,429
Depreciable assets	2,107	3,174	4,070	4,318	4,549	4,755	4,969	5,284	5,571
Depletable assets	72	112	134	129	142	131	137	148	154
Land	93	141	191	210	215	221	230	239	242
Liabilities [2]	7,617	12,773	17,647	18,190	19,030	20,002	21,816	23,446	26,014
Accounts payable	542	892	1,090	1,094	1,681	1,605	1,466	1,606	1,750
Short-term debt [3]	505	1,001	1,602	1,803	1,500	1,560	1,569	1,831	2,034
Long-term debt [4]	987	1,699	2,490	2,665	2,698	2,742	2,871	3,100	3,335
Capital stock	417	920	1,477	1,585	1,741	1,881	2,042	2,132	2,194
Paid-in or capital surplus	532	1,421	2,595	2,814	3,257	3,656	4,223	4,790	5,446
Retained earnings [5]	1,070	1,366	1,522	1,410	1,441	1,431	1,662	1,698	2,191
Net worth [3] [6]	1,944	3,304	4,603	4,739	5,277	5,700	(NA)	7,031	8,132
Receipts [3] [6]	6,361	8,398	10,935	11,410	11,436	11,742	12,270	13,360	14,539
Business receipts [6] [7]	5,732	7,370	9,427	9,860	9,966	10,360	10,866	11,884	12,786
Interest [8]	367	635	967	977	920	829	808	882	1,039
Rents and royalties	54	105	129	133	137	140	130	132	145
Deductions [3] [6]	6,125	8,158	10,545	11,033	11,087	11,330	11,765	12,775	13,821
Cost of sales and operations [7]	4,205	4,894	6,317	6,611	6,654	6,772	7,052	7,625	8,206
Compensation of officers	109	171	198	205	201	221	226	282	304
Rent paid on business property	72	135	173	185	193	196	201	223	232
Taxes paid	163	201	236	251	258	274	290	322	326
Interest paid	345	569	832	825	733	597	546	611	744
Depreciation	157	304	337	333	334	346	364	403	437
Advertising	52	92	124	126	129	134	140	157	163
Net income (less loss) [6] [9]	239	240	389	371	345	402	498	577	714
Net income	297	364	556	553	536	570	659	740	881
Deficit	58	124	167	182	191	168	161	162	166
Income subject to tax	247	266	371	366	350	378	437	494	565
Income tax before credits [10]	104	109	123	119	116	126	149	168	194
Tax credits [3]	42	48	32	32	29	30	35	37	42
Foreign tax credit	25	24	24	25	21	22	23	25	30
Income tax after credits [11]	62	61	96	96	93	102	(NA)	136	156

NA Not available. [1] Represents certain small corporations with up to 35 shareholders (15 in 1980), mostly individuals, electing to be taxed at the shareholder level. [2] Includes items not shown separately. [3] Payable in less than 1 year. [4] Payable in 1 year or more. [5] Appropriated and unappropriated. [6] Except for 1980, receipts, deductions and net income of S corporations are limited to those from trade or business. Those from investments are excluded. [7] Beginning 1988, includes gross sales and cost of sales of securities, commodities, and real estate by exchanges, brokers, or dealers selling on their own accounts. Previously, net gain included in total receipts only. Excludes investment income. [8] Includes tax-exempt interest in state and local government obligations. [9] Excludes regulated investment companies. [10] Consists of regular (and alternative tax) only. [11] Includes minimum tax, alternative minimum tax, adjustments for prior year credits, and other income-related taxes.

Source: U.S. Internal Revenue Service, *Statistics of Income, Corporation Income Tax Returns,* annual.

No. 864. Corporations—Selected Financial Items, by Industry: 1980 to 1994

[In billions of dollars, except as indicated. Covers active corporations only. Industrial distribution based on data collected from companies; see text, Section 17. Excludes corporations not allocable by industry]

INDUSTRY	1980	1985	1989	1990	1991	1992	1993	1994
Agriculture, forestry, and fishing:								
Returns (1,000)	81	103	123	126	130	138	141	147
Assets [1]	40.7	52.7	63.4	68.3	67.8	71.8	74.6	79.9
Liabilities [1]	29.3	37.2	42.3	45.0	45.0	46.7	46.9	50.6
Receipts [2]	52.1	70.5	86.6	88.1	85.9	95.6	98.3	100.9
Deductions [2]	51.4	70.6	85.1	86.9	85.3	94.0	96.7	99.6
Net income (less loss) [2]	0.7	-0.1	1.6	1.2	0.6	1.6	1.6	1.3
Mining:								
Returns (1,000)	26	41	42	40	39	37	35	35
Assets [1]	126.9	240.8	236.3	219.2	213.0	218.2	224.0	239.7
Liabilities [1]	72.9	136.0	109.9	108.9	106.4	112.1	112.6	121.1
Receipts [2]	176.7	142.0	102.4	111.4	103.3	112.8	112.1	115.7
Deductions [2]	169.1	145.4	99.5	106.5	99.5	110.3	109.6	112.3
Net income (less loss) [2]	7.8	-2.5	3.1	5.3	4.0	2.7	2.6	3.6
Construction:								
Returns (1,000)	272	318	393	407	417	408	417	433
Assets [1]	132.9	215.3	249.7	243.8	243.0	231.1	240.4	249.1
Liabilities [1]	100.1	160.6	183.0	180.0	172.4	159.5	164.6	170.9
Receipts [2]	267.2	387.2	517.5	534.7	515.1	499.4	538.3	592.8
Deductions [2]	262.1	382.8	508.8	527.8	509.2	493.9	530.7	581.2
Net income (less loss) [2]	5.3	4.4	8.7	6.8	6.1	5.5	7.5	11.6
Manufacturing:								
Returns (1,000)	243	277	301	302	300	300	307	312
Assets [1]	1,709.5	2,644.4	3,721.2	3,921.3	4,028.4	4,113.1	4,225.1	4,525.5
Liabilities [1]	960.3	1,544.7	2,347.7	2,529.1	2,547.2	2,701.2	2,784.4	2,936.6
Receipts [2]	2,404.3	2,831.1	3,531.2	3,688.7	3,658.5	3,760.3	3,890.7	4,218.8
Deductions [2]	2,290.6	2,733.1	3,377.1	3,545.1	3,548.7	3,633.8	3,741.6	4,024.3
Net income (less loss) [2]	125.7	113.8	180.5	171.4	132.3	143.6	173.2	219.1
Transportation and public utilities:								
Returns (1,000)	111	138	156	160	165	178	176	187
Assets [1]	758.4	1,246.4	1,474.4	1,522.0	1,573.8	1,642.0	1,770.7	1,826.3
Liabilities [1]	467.7	755.9	963.1	1,013.4	1,044.9	1,106.3	1,190.9	1,207.2
Receipts [2]	523.8	772.4	906.5	936.3	954.9	997.6	1,037.2	1,103.2
Deductions [2]	504.0	747.8	867.6	901.0	917.8	956.5	984.9	1,036.1
Net income (less loss) [2]	20.0	25.1	39.1	35.4	37.7	41.8	52.9	68.3
Wholesale and retail trade:								
Returns (1,000)	800	917	1,013	1,023	1,044	1,053	1,073	1,106
Assets [1]	646.9	1,010.0	1,390.6	1,447.3	1,483.4	1,581.9	1,702.8	1,795.2
Liabilities [1]	424.6	723.7	1,047.8	1,092.5	1,108.6	1,177.7	1,254.2	1,303.1
Receipts [2]	1,955.5	2,473.9	3,184.9	3,309.0	3,380.6	3,503.9	3,709.5	4,052.2
Deductions [2]	1,919.5	2,440.4	3,148.8	3,279.1	3,350.9	3,463.4	3,659.8	3,984.0
Net income (less loss) [2]	38.3	33.1	36.2	30.1	30.0	41.3	49.7	68.5
Finance, insurance, and real estate:								
Returns (1,000)	493	518	593	609	618	635	641	682
Assets [1]	4,022.2	7,029.5	9,957.5	10,193.3	10,780.7	11,480.5	12,831.7	13895.3
Liabilities [1]	3,491.7	5,867.5	7,929.3	8,051.3	8,267.1	8,531.3	9,288.5	10053.1
Receipts [2][3]	697.5	1,182.0	1,868.0	1,954.7	1,924.3	1,900.4	1,940.3	1976.5
Deductions [2]	652.6	1,104.6	1,730.5	1,809.9	1,771.2	1,724.3	1,723.3	1773.1
Net income (less loss) [2]	33.1	60.7	108.9	109.9	124.5	147.0	185.2	169.3
Services:								
Returns (1,000)	671	939	990	1,029	1,062	1,100	1,158	1,424
Assets [1]	178.2	331.0	552.1	572.8	636.8	661.6	744.8	833.9
Liabilities [1]	125.3	241.1	419.8	429.7	459.1	465.0	508.6	570.3
Receipts [2]	279.9	534.6	735.5	779.3	809.7	869.5	941.6	1198.0
Deductions [2]	271.8	528.7	724.9	769.0	800.2	851.1	916.5	1162.5
Net income (less loss) [2]	8.2	5.9	11.0	10.6	9.8	18.5	25.4	35.6
ANNUAL PERCENT CHANGE RECEIPTS [4]								
Agriculture, forestry, and fishing	-2.4	5.9	0.3	1.7	-2.5	11.3	2.8	2.6
Mining	33.3	15.0	2.0	8.8	-7.3	9.2	-0.6	3.1
Construction	5.7	14.4	3.6	3.3	-3.7	-3.0	7.8	10.1
Manufacturing	11.7	2.3	5.4	4.5	-0.8	2.8	3.5	8.4
Transportation and public utilities	17.5	6.4	8.1	3.3	2.0	4.5	4.0	6.3
Wholesale and retail trade	11.6	7.2	6.9	3.9	2.2	3.6	5.9	9.2
Finance, insurance, and real estate	24.3	14.4	9.0	4.6	-1.6	-1.2	2.1	1.8
Services	14.2	9.0	5.8	6.0	3.9	7.4	8.3	27.2

[1] Liabilities does not include net worth. [2] Beginning 1989, receipts, deductions, and net income of S corporations are limited to those from trade or business; those from investments are generally excluded. S corporations are certain small corporations with up to 35 shareholders (15 in 1980), mostly individuals, electing to be taxed at the shareholder level. [3] Beginning 1989, includes gross sales (previously net sales) of securities, commodities, and real estate by exchanges, brokers, or dealers selling on their own account. [4] Change from preceding year.

Source: U.S. Internal Revenue Service, *Statistics of Income, Corporation Income Tax Returns,* annual.

No. 865. Corporations, by Asset-Size Class and Industry: 1995

[In millions of dollars, except number of returns and percent distribution. Covers active corporations only. Excludes corporations not allocable by industry. The industrial distribution is based on data collected from companies; see text, Section 17. Detail may not add to total because of rounding]

INDUSTRY	Total	ASSET-SIZE CLASS					
		Under $10 mil.[1]	$10-$24.9 mil.	$25-$49.9 mil.	$50-$99.9 mil.	$100-$249.9 mil.	$250 mil. and over
Agriculture, forestry, and fishing:							
Returns	147,527	146,887	387	136	55	41	21
Assets	86,299	55,560	5,642	4,725	3,824	5,660	10,888
Receipts	107,582	75,205	5,747	5,945	5,031	7,223	8,432
Deductions	105,967	74,533	5,596	5,781	4,915	7,079	8,063
Net income (less loss)	1,604	650	145	158	117	143	392
Mining:							
Returns	35,123	34,138	467	183	120	100	115
Assets	268,690	18,211	7,230	6,507	8,485	16,194	212,063
Receipts	126,760	23,521	5,339	4,317	4,763	11,239	77,581
Deductions	121,397	23,152	5,276	4,294	4,752	10,903	73,020
Net income (less loss)	5,531	360	58	22	10	336	4,746
Construction:							
Returns	449,882	447,264	1,906	427	169	73	43
Assets	265,813	156,343	27,700	14,806	12,293	10,992	43,677
Receipts	637,090	454,344	59,058	30,389	23,000	19,692	50,605
Deductions	622,622	444,031	57,573	29,734	22,562	19,434	49,289
Net income (less loss)	14,458	10,274	1,460	637	431	251	1,406
Manufacturing:							
Returns	319,699	306,004	6,727	2,855	1,595	1,194	1,324
Assets	4,941,073	218,050	103,637	100,292	113,422	190,677	4,214,995
Receipts	4,585,550	547,130	196,088	163,540	169,611	250,203	3,258,977
Deductions	4,354,564	534,475	189,322	157,593	162,665	237,581	3,072,927
Net income (less loss)	260,910	12,710	6,724	5,944	6,956	12,790	215,786
Transportation and public utilities:							
Returns	194,456	191,553	1,389	525	316	254	419
Assets	1,903,214	67,715	21,130	18,096	22,379	40,655	1,733,237
Receipts	1,156,710	185,736	28,891	20,008	21,793	32,642	867,640
Deductions	1,084,677	184,226	28,073	19,515	21,359	31,627	799,877
Net income (less loss)	72,911	1,495	794	493	437	1,021	68,670
Wholesale and retail trade:							
Returns	1,132,409	1,120,014	8,006	2,212	994	648	536
Assets	1,919,718	469,419	120,773	76,514	70,203	101,492	1,081,317
Receipts	4,310,347	1,731,685	394,155	222,410	174,214	237,623	1,550,260
Deductions	4,247,561	1,714,987	388,541	218,984	171,397	233,806	1,519,846
Net income (less loss)	63,567	16,621	5,600	3,427	2,807	3,798	31,314
Finance, insurance, and real estate:							
Returns	683,211	657,531	6,961	4,958	4,537	4,483	4,740
Assets	15,677,287	279,073	111,614	179,546	324,948	708,041	14,074,066
Receipts[2]	2,278,104	237,842	27,614	29,957	41,127	86,944	1,854,620
Deductions	1,985,796	228,923	27,546	28,185	35,635	69,995	1,595,512
Net income (less loss)	256,811	8,389	(213)	1,233	3,961	13,017	230,424
Services:							
Returns	1,504,230	1,498,591	3,240	1,065	574	422	339
Assets	950,737	250,133	49,105	37,215	41,887	69,641	502,757
Receipts	1,335,695	796,771	70,318	46,706	42,696	63,114	316,089
Deductions	1,297,475	778,225	69,553	45,535	41,953	61,450	300,760
Net income (less loss)	38,408	18,452	751	1,150	727	1,685	15,642
PERCENT DISTRIBUTION RECEIPTS							
Agriculture, forestry, and fishing	100	70	5	6	5	7	8
Mining	100	19	4	3	4	9	61
Construction	100	71	9	5	4	3	8
Manufacturing	100	12	4	4	4	5	71
Transportation and public utilities	100	16	2	2	2	3	75
Wholesale and retail trade	100	40	9	5	4	6	36
Finance, insurance, and real estate[2]	100	10	1	1	2	4	81
Services	100	60	5	3	3	5	24

[1] Includes returns with zero assets.   [2] Includes investment income.

Source: U.S. Internal Revenue Service, *Statistics of Income, Corporation Income Tax Returns*, annual.

No. 866. Employees and Payroll, by Employment-Size Class: 1980 to 1995

[Excludes government employees, railroad employees, self-employed persons, etc. See "General Explanation" in source for definitions and statement on reliability of data. An **establishment** is a single physical location where business is conducted or where services or industrial operations are performed]

EMPLOYMENT-SIZE CLASS	Unit	1980	1985	1989	1990	1991	1992	1993	1994	1995
Employees, total [1]	1,000 .	**74,844**	**81,111**	**91,631**	**93,476**	**92,302**	**92,801**	**94,789**	**96,733**	**100,335**
Under 20 employees	1,000 .	19,423	21,810	23,992	24,373	24,482	25,000	25,233	25,373	25,785
20 to 99 employees	1,000 .	21,168	23,539	26,829	27,414	26,906	27,030	27,443	28,138	29,202
100 to 499 employees	1,000 .	17,840	19,410	22,387	22,926	22,369	22,227	23,195	24,048	25,364
500 to 999 employees	1,000 .	5,689	5,716	6,442	6,551	6,325	6,270	6,449	6,663	7,021
1,000 or more employees	1,000 .	10,716	10,645	11,981	12,212	12,220	12,275	12,470	12,513	12,962
Annual payroll, total [1]	Bil. dol	**1,035**	**1,514**	**1,990**	**2,104**	**2,145**	**2,272**	**2,363**	**2,488**	**2,666**
Under 20 employees	Bil. dol.	231	352	461	485	502	536	554	579	608
20 to 99 employees	Bil. dol.	261	388	514	547	555	586	611	650	696
100 to 499 employees	Bil. dol.	249	362	488	518	523	550	582	621	675
500 to 999 employees	Bil. dol.	91	126	163	174	175	186	191	202	219
1,000 or more employees	Bil. dol.	208	286	364	381	390	413	424	436	467

[1] Prior to 1987, totals for employees and annual payroll have been revised. Detail may not add to totals because revisions for size class are not available.

Source: U.S. Bureau of the Census, *County Business Patterns,* annual.

No. 867. Establishments, Employees, and Payroll, by Industry: 1980 to 1995

[Beginning 1990, data are based on the 1987 Standard Industrial Classification (SIC). Prior to 1990, data are based on the 1972 SIC]

INDUSTRY	ESTABLISHMENTS (1,000)				EMPLOYEES (1,000)				PAYROLL (bil. dol.)			
	1980	1985	1990	1995	1980	1985	1990	1995	1980	1985	1990	1995
All industries [1] . . .	**4,543**	**5,701**	**6,176**	**6,613**	**74,844**	**81,111**	**93,476**	**100,335**	**1,035**	**1,513**	**2,104**	**2,666**
Agricultural services [2] . . .	46	64	85	108	290	380	531	630	3	5	9	12
Mining	30	37	30	27	994	943	723	627	22	28	27	26
Construction	418	476	578	634	4,473	4,480	5,239	5,039	75	98	132	147
Manufacturing	319	358	378	390	21,165	19,429	19,173	18,613	355	458	544	631
Transportation [3]	168	203	235	285	4,623	4,809	5,592	5,924	88	123	166	201
Wholesale trade	385	438	476	518	5,211	5,624	6,328	6,606	89	130	181	227
Retail trade	1,223	1,407	1,530	1,568	15,047	16,851	19,815	21,085	124	178	242	800
Finance and insurance [4] .	421	488	545	628	5,295	6,005	6,956	6,998	77	132	197	256
Services	1,278	1,712	2,059	2,386	17,186	21,549	28,800	34,707	197	346	599	864

[1] Includes nonclassifiable establishments not shown separately. [2] Includes forestry and fisheries. [3] Includes public utilities. [4] Includes real estate.

Source: U.S. Bureau of the Census, *County Business Patterns,* annual.

No. 868. Establishments, Employees, and Payroll, by Employment-Size Class and Industry: 1995

[See headnote, Table 866. Data are based on the 1987 Standard Industrial Classification]

EMPLOYMENT SIZE-CLASS	Unit	All industries [1]	Agricultural services [2]	Mining	Construction	Manufacturing	Transportation [3]	Wholesale trade	Retail trade	Finance and insurance [4]	Services
Establishments, total . . .	1,000 . .	**6,613**	**108**	**27**	**634**	**390**	**285**	**518**	**1,568**	**628**	**2,386**
Under 20 employees	1,000 . .	5,733	103	22	583	261	235	443	1,318	572	2,126
20 to 99 employees	1,000 . .	730	5	4	46	90	40	66	221	48	208
100 to 499 employees	1,000 . .	135	(Z)	1	5	33	8	8	28	7	45
500 to 999 employees	1,000 . .	10	(Z)	(Z)	(Z)	4	1	(Z)	1	1	4
1,000 or more employees	1,000 . .	6	(Z)	(Z)	(Z)	2	(Z)	(Z)	(Z)	(Z)	3
Employees, total	1,000 . .	**100,335**	**630**	**627**	**5,039**	**18,612**	**5,924**	**6,606**	**21,085**	**6,998**	**34,707**
Under 20 employees	1,000 . .	25,785	(D)	(D)	2,242	1,514	1,053	2,261	6,985	2,290	8,885
20 to 99 employees	1,000 . .	29,202	170	171	1,716	3,995	1,663	2,524	8,746	1,853	8,348
100 to 499 employees	1,000 . .	25,364	(D)	(D)	798	6,725	1,569	1,367	4,640	1,454	8,546
500 to 999 employees	1,000 . .	7,021	(D)	(D)	120	2,488	478	233	443	522	2,650
1,000 or more employees	1,000 . .	12,962	(D)	87	163	3,891	1,161	221	271	879	6,278
Annual payroll, total . . .	Bil. dol .	**2,666**	**12**	**26**	**147**	**631**	**201**	**227**	**300**	**256**	**864**
Under 20 employees	Bil. dol	608	(D)	(D)	56	40	29	72	95	70	234
20 to 99 employees	Bil. dol	696	3	7	54	116	51	85	115	67	198
100 to 499 employees	Bil. dol	675	(D)	(D)	28	210	56	51	73	57	191
500 to 999 employees	Bil. dol	219	(D)	(D)	4	87	19	10	9	22	64
1,000 or more employees	Bil. dol	467	(D)	3	5	178	46	10	8	40	177

D Withheld to avoid disclosing data for individual companies; data are included in higher-level totals. Z Less than 500 establishments. [1] Includes nonclassifiable establishments not shown separately. [2] Includes forestry and fisheries. [3] Includes public utilities. [4] Includes real estate.

Source: U.S. Bureau of the Census, *County Business Patterns,* annual.

No. 869. Major Industries—Private Firms, Establishments, Annual Payroll, and Estimated Receipts by Firm Size, 1995

[Firms are an aggregation of all establishments owned by a parent company within an industry. Employment is measured in March and payroll is annual leading to some firms with zero employment]

INDUSTRY AND DATA TYPE	Unit	Total	ALL INDUSTRIES—EMPLOYMENT SIZE OF FIRM							
			0	1 to 4	5 to 9	10 to 19	20 to 99	100 to 499	Less than 500	More than 500
Total:										
Firms	1,000 . .	5,369.1	688.6	2,561.0	981.1	576.9	469.9	76.2	5,353.6	15.4
Establishments	1,000 . .	6,612.7	690.8	2,569.0	998.3	618.3	638.6	284.0	5,798.9	813.8
Employment	1,000 . .	100,314.9	-	5,395.4	6,440.3	7,734.1	18,422.2	14,660.4	52,652.5	47,662.4
Annual payroll.	Bil. dol .	2,665.9	25.8	115.8	137.1	175.4	437.1	361.1	1,252.1	1,413.8
Receipts estimated	Bil. dol .	15,751.4	129.7	790.0	778.9	965.3	2,678.3	2,062.2	7,404.4	8,347.0
Agric. services, forestry, and fishing:										
Firms	1,000 . .	107.3	23.3	49.8	19.3	10.0	4.3	0.4	107.1	0.1
Establishments	1,000 . .	108.7	23.3	49.9	19.3	10.0	4.5	0.6	107.5	1.2
Employment	1,000 . .	630.3	-	103.9	126.8	130.5	147.1	52.1	560.3	70.0
Annual payroll.	Bil. dol .	12.1	0.5	1.8	2.1	2.4	2.8	0.9	10.5	1.6
Receipts estimated	Bil. dol .	37.0	1.5	5.7	5.8	6.2	7.8	3.3	30.3	6.6
Mining:										
Firms	1,000 . .	21.6	2.3	10.0	3.4	2.5	2.5	0.5	21.2	0.4
Establishments	1,000 . .	27.4	2.3	10.0	3.4	2.6	3.0	1.4	22.8	4.6
Employment	1,000 . .	627.5	-	20.2	22.4	33.8	91.5	75.2	243.1	384.4
Annual payroll.	Bil. dol .	25.7	0.1	0.5	0.6	0.9	2.9	2.9	8.1	17.6
Receipts estimated	Bil. dol .	168.1	1.1	5.3	5.2	5.8	18.1	15.6	51.0	117.1
Construction:										
Firms	1,000 . .	630.2	100.6	306.9	111.5	62.8	43.4	4.3	629.5	0.7
Establishments	1,000 . .	636.6	100.6	306.9	111.5	63.0	44.2	5.6	631.8	4.7
Employment	1,000 . .	5,040.6	-	643.6	729.1	838.5	1,594.1	696.3	4,501.6	539.0
Annual payroll.	Bil. dol .	147.3	2.8	13.6	16.3	21.8	48.3	23.9	126.7	20.6
Receipts estimated	Bil. dol .	667.8	13.3	79.1	75.2	92.9	207.5	106.4	574.5	93.3
Manufacturing:										
Firms	1,000 . .	330.3	28.9	100.7	60.4	52.3	66.2	16.8	325.4	4.9
Establishments	1,000 . .	390.4	28.9	100.7	60.5	52.6	70.5	28.5	341.8	48.6
Employment	1,000 . .	18,611.1	-	227.9	405.2	714.8	2,743.2	3,073.0	7,164.0	11,447.1
Annual payroll.	Bil. dol .	631.0	1.8	4.9	9.1	17.6	74.1	86.8	194.2	436.7
Receipts estimated	Bil. dol .	3,417.7	9.5	24.7	40.6	74.8	339.3	460.3	949.1	2,468.6
Transportation, communications & public utilities:										
Firms	1,000 . .	209.0	29.7	96.3	34.2	22.5	20.7	3.9	207.3	1.7
Establishments	1,000 . .	285.7	29.9	96.5	34.7	23.8	27.0	13.0	224.8	60.9
Employment	1,000 . .	5,924.7	-	199.5	223.9	302.3	798.0	628.7	2,152.4	3,772.3
Annual payroll.	Bil. dol .	200.9	1.2	3.9	4.6	6.7	19.5	17.6	53.5	147.4
Receipts estimated	Bil. dol .	1,026.8	5.0	23.3	21.0	28.2	82.7	75.8	236.1	790.6
Wholesale trade:										
Firms	1,000 . .	405.4	41.8	171.7	77.7	54.8	47.8	8.3	402.1	3.3
Establishments	1,000 . .	518.4	41.9	172.3	79.3	59.7	70.0	29.3	452.5	65.9
Employment	1,000 . .	6,606.5	-	370.1	513.7	733.1	1,738.2	1,074.2	4,429.3	2,177.2
Annual payroll.	Bil. dol .	227.0	1.7	10.7	14.6	21.8	53.2	34.9	137.1	89.9
Receipts estimated	Bil. dol .	3,849.0	30.3	246.3	260.6	345.8	969.4	584.3	2,436.6	1,412.4
Retail trade:										
Firms	1,000 . .	1,099.6	135.7	466.5	224.4	141.0	115.7	13.3	1,096.7	2.9
Establishments	1,000 . .	1,571.1	136.8	469.5	230.0	154.1	167.3	78.8	1,236.4	334.7
Employment	1,000 . .	21,086.6	-	1,043.3	1,481.6	1,881.0	4,349.8	2,209.0	10,964.6	10,122.0
Annual payroll.	Bil. dol .	300.1	3.4	12.9	18.1	23.3	62.5	34.3	154.5	145.5
Receipts estimated	Bil. dol .	2,292.7	23.1	129.4	147.5	176.3	519.5	285.0	1,280.7	1,012.0
Finance, insurance & real estate:										
Firms	1,000 . .	433.8	53.6	260.4	58.1	28.6	24.4	5.7	430.8	3.0
Establishments	1,000 . .	629.5	53.7	261.3	60.1	33.5	46.5	30.1	485.1	144.4
Employment	1,000 . .	6,984.8	-	501.7	373.5	377.7	934.4	815.3	3,002.7	3,982.2
Annual payroll.	Bil. dol .	255.9	2.3	11.3	10.2	11.7	29.3	27.9	92.6	163.2
Receipts estimated	Bil. dol .	2,094.2	11.8	75.6	50.1	55.8	169.1	205.1	567.5	1,526.7
Services:										
Firms	1,000 . .	2,114.1	246.9	1,077.1	390.2	204.0	154.9	32.6	2,105.7	8.5
Establishments	1,000 . .	2,392.0	247.4	1,079.7	396.2	217.9	205.2	96.8	2,243.2	148.8
Employment	1,000 . .	34,709.6	-	2,248.0	2,543.3	2,707.7	6,012.7	6,034.0	19,545.8	15,163.9
Annual payroll.	Bil. dol .	864.4	11.4	55.7	61.2	69.0	144.1	131.9	473.4	391.0
Receipts estimated	Bil. dol .	2,188.8	30.9	197.8	171.6	178.8	364.3	326.2	1,269.6	919.3
Unclassified:										
Firms	1,000 . .	53.0	26.0	22.2	3.3	1.1	0.4	(Z)	53.0	(Z)
Establishments	1,000 . .	53.0	26.0	22.2	3.3	1.1	0.4	(Z)	53.0	(Z)
Employment	1,000 . .	93.1	-	37.1	20.8	14.7	13.3	2.7	88.7	4.4
Annual payroll.	Bil. dol .	1.6	0.6	0.4	0.2	0.1	0.1	(Z)	1.5	0.1
Receipts estimated	Bil. dol .	9.4	3.4	2.7	1.2	0.8	0.7	0.2	9.0	0.4

- Represents or rounds to zero.   Z Rounds to less than 50.

Source: Office of Advocacy, U.S. Small Business Administration, based on data provided by the U.S. Department of Commerce, Bureau of the Census, *Statistics of U.S. Businesses*.

No. 870. Private Employer Firms, Establishments, Employment, Annual Payroll and Estimated Receipts by Firm Size: 1990 to 1995

[Firms are an aggregation of all establishments owned by a parent company. Employment is measured in March and payroll is annual leading to some firms with zero employment. This table illustrates the changing importance of firm sizes over time, not job growth as firms can grow or decline and change firm size cells over time]

ITEM	Total	ALL INDUSTRIES—EMPLOYMENT SIZE OF FIRM						
		0-4	5-9	10-19	20-99	100-499	Less than 500	More than 500
EMPLOYER FIRMS								
1990	5,073,795	3,020,935	952,030	562,610	453,732	70,465	5,059,772	14,023
1993	5,193,642	3,139,518	962,481	559,602	445,900	71,512	5,179,013	14,629
1994	5,276,964	3,208,235	964,985	563,097	452,383	73,267	5,261,967	14,997
1995	5,369,068	3,249,573	981,094	576,866	469,869	76,222	5,353,624	15,444
ESTABLISHMENTS								
1990	6,175,559	3,032,253	970,580	599,529	590,496	254,747	5,447,605	727,954
1993	6,401,233	3,147,991	980,865	608,922	631,873	285,184	5,654,835	746,398
1994	6,509,065	3,218,076	982,695	608,804	631,324	283,782	5,724,681	784,384
1995	6,612,721	3,259,795	998,264	618,268	638,616	283,993	5,798,936	813,785
EMPLOYMENT								
1990	93,469,275	5,116,914	6,251,632	7,543,360	17,710,042	13,544,849	50,166,797	43,302,478
1993	94,773,913	5,258,195	6,313,651	7,498,345	17,420,634	13,825,238	50,316,063	44,457,850
1994	96,721,594	5,318,961	6,332,580	7,543,777	17,693,995	14,118,375	51,007,688	45,713,906
1995	100,314,946	5,395,432	6,440,349	7,734,080	18,422,228	14,660,421	52,652,510	47,662,436
ANNUAL PAYROLL ($mil.)								
1990	2,103,971	116,857	114,006	144,451	352,391	279,452	1,007,156	1,096,815
1993	2,363,208	128,968	127,133	159,153	385,005	316,184	1,116,443	1,246,765
1994	2,487,960	134,649	131,667	166,476	408,053	335,574	1,176,419	1,311,541
1995	2,665,922	141,538	137,083	175,388	437,065	361,061	1,252,135	1,413,787
RECEIPTS (est.) ($mil.)								
1990	9,450,656	626,679	569,640	681,192	1,715,443	1,316,747	4,909,700	4,540,956
1993	14,098,572	846,812	730,360	891,635	2,394,813	1,816,355	6,679,975	7,418,597
1994	14,840,452	880,764	752,675	928,380	2,531,403	1,930,758	7,023,980	7,816,472
1995	15,751,365	919,735	778,864	965,259	2,678,293	2,062,235	7,404,386	8,346,979

Source: Office of Advocacy, U.S. Small Business Administration based on data provided by the Department of Commerce, Bureau of Census, unpublished data.

No. 871. New Firms, Births and Deaths, and Employment Changes by Employment Size of Firms: 1992-93

[Longitudinal data for establishments active (payroll) in first quarter of the year (establishments with 0 employment in the first quarter were excluded). New firm births are classified by their employment size at the first quarter. Represents private establishments excluding railroad, domestic and farms. The number of continuing firms was calculated from static and longitudinal data. Existing firms with ownership changes are considered continuing firms]

ITEM	NEW FIRMS (original locations)		ESTABLISHED BIRTHS FOR EXISTING FIRMS		ESTABLISHED DEATHS FOR EXISTING FIRMS	
	Less than 500	More than 500	Less than 500	More than 500	Less than 500	More than 500
FIRMS						
Total, all industries	564,093	411	24,317	55,401	34,694	65,204
Manufacturing	29,001	54	1,249	1,846	1,519	2,243
Transportation, Communications & Public Util.	25,000	11	1,144	5,099	1,611	5,049
Wholesale Trade	37,255	5	2,074	4,590	3,811	5,246
Retail Trade	120,411	19	8,751	20,721	13,863	24,380
Finance, Insurance, and Real Estate	45,867	33	2,685	10,953	4,064	16,022
Services	202,043	281	8,069	11,277	9,195	11,118
Agri. serv., mining, const., & unclassified	104,516	8	345	915	631	1,146
EMPLOYMENT CHANGES						
Total, all industries	3,053,765	384,341	359,765	1,709,668	367,229	1,555,121
Manufacturing	260,029	29,063	45,512	208,257	45,537	240,623
Transportation, Communications & Public Util.	126,877	6,963	23,129	126,030	19,887	101,883
Wholesale Trade	156,809	2,765	21,008	99,991	35,332	96,407
Retail Trade	756,550	8,378	112,141	546,763	122,688	365,770
Finance, Insurance, and Real Estate	182,839	14,812	26,853	250,919	37,534	340,086
Services	1,180,223	318,298	124,719	443,457	95,628	366,287
Agri. serv., mining, const., & unclassified	390,438	4,062	6,403	34,251	10,623	44,065

Source of Tables 870 and 871: Office of Advocacy, U.S. Small Business Administration from data provided by Department of Commerce, Bureau of the Census, unpublished data.

No. 872. Private Employer Firms, Employment, and Estimated Receipts by Firm Size and State: 1995

[Firms are an aggregation of all establishments owned by a parent company within a state. Establishments are locations with active payroll in any quarter. Employment is measured in March and payroll is annual leading to some firms with zero employment]

STATE	EMPLOYER FIRMS (1,000)			EMPLOYMENT (1,000)			ESTIMATED RECEIPTS (bil. dol.)		
	Total	Employment size of firm		Total	Employment size of firm		Total	Employment size of firm	
		Less than 20	More than 500		Less than 20	More than 500		Less than 20	More than 500
United States	5,369	4,808	15	100,315	19,570	47,662	15,751	2,664	8,347
Alabama	79	68	2	1,553	289	783	211	34	114
Alaska	15	13	(Z)	182	50	66	36	8	16
Arizona	83	71	2	1,507	292	714	206	35	112
Arkansas	51	45	1	891	181	437	114	21	60
California	616	544	5	10,958	2,184	5,012	1,835	324	934
Colorado	102	89	2	1,557	346	694	234	45	122
Connecticut	79	68	2	1,411	279	667	290	46	164
Delaware	18	15	1	324	59	172	56	7	37
District of Columbia	16	13	1	414	55	220	61	9	35
Florida	333	300	4	5,208	1,133	2,483	671	143	329
Georgia	145	126	3	2,919	508	1,565	449	71	261
Hawaii	24	21	1	424	91	182	61	13	30
Idaho	29	25	1	379	101	143	55	11	24
Illinois	246	212	4	4,950	878	2,424	856	136	462
Indiana	115	98	3	2,403	426	1,161	363	50	202
Iowa	65	56	1	1,138	234	504	184	29	93
Kansas	59	51	2	982	210	421	157	26	82
Kentucky	70	60	2	1,347	256	636	201	29	113
Louisiana	79	68	2	1,452	292	639	230	34	133
Maine	32	28	1	432	106	171	60	12	28
Maryland	102	88	2	1,821	368	827	269	47	137
Massachusetts	135	117	3	2,735	478	1,340	446	73	234
Michigan	188	163	3	3,704	704	1,763	624	95	351
Minnesota	106	91	2	2,072	380	949	325	53	163
Mississippi	47	41	1	871	169	435	112	19	59
Missouri	117	101	3	2,169	410	1,045	306	52	176
Montana	26	23	1	261	87	72	35	9	14
Nebraska	40	34	1	675	144	307	105	17	53
Nevada	32	27	1	672	109	365	83	14	42
New Hampshire	30	26	1	464	103	197	67	14	30
New Jersey	193	171	3	3,184	649	1,490	624	114	322
New Mexico	35	30	1	507	122	196	66	13	32
New York	407	365	4	6,781	1,352	3,207	1,262	238	638
North Carolina	148	129	3	2,992	533	1,567	425	66	241
North Dakota	18	15	(Z)	230	61	71	35	9	13
Ohio	211	182	3	4,550	791	2,242	683	98	379
Oklahoma	68	60	2	1,055	240	435	147	29	72
Oregon	80	70	2	1,185	282	470	177	34	80
Pennsylvania	233	202	4	4,702	863	2,283	707	109	384
Rhode Island	25	22	1	380	82	159	52	11	23
South Carolina	72	63	2	1,395	259	742	182	30	104
South Dakota	20	17	1	268	69	96	37	8	15
Tennessee	101	87	3	2,153	362	1,141	305	46	169
Texas	351	309	4	6,786	1,269	3,443	1,096	177	624
Utah	39	33	1	744	141	361	103	16	55
Vermont	18	16	1	224	63	74	32	7	13
Virginia	131	114	3	2,481	474	1,237	355	55	200
Washington	130	114	2	1,948	452	805	309	59	147
West Virginia	34	29	1	531	122	235	75	13	41
Wisconsin	112	96	2	2,186	415	968	331	49	173
Wyoming	15	13	1	157	51	49	26	5	13

Z Less than 500.

Source: U.S. Small Business Administration, Office of Advocacy, based on data provided by the U.S. Department of Commerce, Bureau of the Census, unpublished data.

No. 873. Private Establishment, Percent Offering Health Insurance, and Percent With Other Selected Characteristics by State: 1993

[Based on a December 31, 1993 reference period. An establishment is defined as a business at a single physical location]

STATE	Estab-lishments (number)	Percent offering health insur-ance	Percent with 50 percent or more employ-ees that are low-wage [1]	Percent unin-corpor-ated [2]	Percent in busi-ness less than 5 years [2]	Percent in retail	Percent with 75 percent or more employ-ees that are full time	Percent in manu-facturing	Percent in multi-state firm [2]	Percent with union employ-ees [2]	Percent in metro-politan areas
United States . . .	6,276,800	51.6	16.0	33.2	12.4	23.2	60.3	8.1	13.8	3.2	78.7
Alabama.	94,900	52.0	18.7	31.7	11.4	26.3	69.5	9.2	16.5	3.2	73.9
Alaska	15,200	46.2	8.3	31.3	9.1	22.1	59.0	(S)	15.1	(S)	47.6
Arizona.	93,900	49.7	20.2	28.4	13.9	22.8	63.0	8.0	16.3	(S)	85.5
Arkansas	63,600	40.3	21.4	34.6	13.2	25.7	64.6	7.0	10.8	(S)	52.1
California	804,300	47.0	15.9	45.2	13.5	21.7	58.9	10.1	11.0	3.8	95.7
Colorado.	104,100	53.1	15.2	29.5	13.2	21.8	58.0	6.9	17.5	(S)	78.4
Connecticut. . . .	84,200	60.4	10.7	35.4	11.3	19.0	52.6	11.1	12.6	2.2	100.0
Delaware	16,000	64.2	10.5	20.0	11.7	25.9	56.9	6.2	20.7	(S)	80.7
District of Columbia	19,300	66.0	6.7	24.4	12.3	18.0	67.1	(S)	27.1	2.9	100.0
Florida	352,500	47.5	15.8	19.0	17.3	23.0	68.4	5.9	13.8	(S)	94.4
Georgia	166,000	54.8	15.8	27.1	11.7	26.0	68.2	7.3	20.6	(S)	69.8
Hawaii	29,300	85.8	10.6	21.6	11.1	23.5	68.2	4.2	9.8	5.9	69.9
Idaho	33,800	49.9	17.8	44.7	13.6	24.4	56.9	5.6	13.6	(S)	28.0
Illinois	261,600	53.2	16.1	32.9	13.2	23.2	55.0	9.7	13.8	7.1	80.0
Indiana.	137,900	50.3	19.0	31.1	12.1	23.8	57.3	8.3	13.6	3.9	72.2
Iowa	93,300	44.0	23.5	42.6	7.7	25.4	50.2	5.6	10.1	3.0	36.4
Kansas.	72,200	48.3	19.5	36.5	10.7	22.7	53.4	5.2	16.1	2.7	50.1
Kentucky	86,400	49.5	26.8	32.0	12.4	25.6	63.8	8.2	13.7	2.0	53.2
Louisiana	91,400	43.9	22.3	27.4	9.9	24.3	67.4	6.9	15.5	(S)	77.3
Maine.	34,900	56.7	13.9	33.1	11.4	27.3	57.9	7.4	10.6	(S)	59.5
Maryland	114,900	56.8	8.9	25.0	17.0	21.4	57.7	5.5	16.6	2.6	89.3
Massachusetts. .	149,800	60.4	9.9	26.9	10.4	21.2	53.3	9.8	12.4	2.9	99.1
Michigan.	189,100	60.1	17.7	28.0	10.2	23.5	58.2	11.0	11.4	5.7	80.6
Minnesota.	128,500	51.1	15.2	35.0	9.0	22.8	53.6	8.8	14.1	4.0	62.2
Mississippi	56,900	43.3	22.1	39.0	8.6	28.6	65.7	8.1	15.7	0.6	29.2
Missouri	138,000	52.2	20.3	31.1	10.2	24.9	61.8	8.8	15.9	4.6	67.9
Montana.	29,400	40.0	23.4	40.1	11.8	27.7	54.6	6.1	9.9	4.2	23.2
Nebraska	48,000	46.2	18.8	35.1	12.0	26.6	54.8	5.4	15.2	(S)	46.5
Nevada	33,900	52.1	8.1	34.8	13.4	23.6	67.5	5.4	18.9	3.4	83.5
New Hampshire .	33,300	57.5	12.0	37.7	13.6	30.4	56.1	8.3	13.3	0.9	69.1
New Jersey. . . .	178,700	52.0	6.9	27.1	14.5	23.7	55.9	7.7	14.3	5.1	100.0
New Mexico . . .	42,600	49.4	17.0	39.0	12.2	23.5	67.8	4.3	17.2	(S)	57.0
New York	411,900	54.6	13.9	24.8	13.5	24.3	61.0	6.6	12.6	5.2	90.8
North Carolina. .	168,000	51.9	14.5	29.1	10.0	23.9	63.7	10.6	15.6	(S)	68.7
North Dakota. . .	20,700	49.1	16.4	34.9	7.4	22.9	53.5	5.1	16.5	3.0	39.4
Ohio	247,800	54.7	18.3	31.2	12.5	23.7	60.1	8.8	13.5	4.6	83.6
Oklahoma.	84,800	43.9	21.9	37.5	12.7	22.1	62.0	9.1	11.6	(S)	59.5
Oregon.	91,700	51.6	13.3	41.4	13.4	23.5	56.2	8.8	13.4	2.3	69.5
Pennsylvania . . .	259,500	61.0	16.9	39.6	10.1	22.5	60.5	8.1	12.5	4.9	83.6
Rhode Island. . .	25,300	64.5	10.6	20.9	14.8	23.0	55.4	11.8	11.8	4.2	100.0
South Carolina. .	82,200	48.8	18.0	34.1	10.2	28.7	65.6	8.9	16.2	(S)	70.1
South Dakota. . .	23,700	44.7	20.5	45.8	12.0	25.3	56.1	5.0	13.0	(S)	27.3
Tennessee	111,500	48.2	16.6	39.4	10.0	26.8	65.0	8.2	16.1	(S)	71.4
Texas.	409,600	44.7	16.9	36.6	13.1	19.2	67.0	7.7	15.5	(S)	81.4
Utah	44,900	47.3	17.4	30.7	13.9	21.2	54.0	7.9	16.3	(S)	72.7
Vermont	20,400	55.0	14.0	32.2	11.7	25.1	52.9	6.9	10.6	(S)	29.9
Virginia.	152,600	55.7	14.2	26.9	13.6	23.3	59.0	7.8	15.7	(S)	74.9
Washington. . . .	144,700	56.4	9.3	36.5	12.5	22.4	57.5	7.2	12.4	5.4	78.4
West Virginia. . .	37,300	51.9	24.1	34.8	8.9	28.1	64.0	7.1	17.4	3.3	48.2
Wisconsin	125,400	52.6	16.1	37.1	9.1	24.7	48.6	8.3	10.9	4.4	65.7
Wyoming	16,900	47.3	24.1	35.9	12.6	20.9	59.6	5.2	15.1	(S)	30.7

S Does not meet standard of reliability or precision. [1] Low-wage employees earned less than $5 per hour or less than $10,000 per year. Denominators exclude cases with any missing data in wage and salary categories. [2] Denominators exclude cases with missing data.

Source: National Center for Health Statistics, Centers for Disease Control and Prevention, National Employer Health Insurance Survey (NEHIS).

No. 874. Small Establishments, Employees, and Payroll, by Employment-Size Class and Industry: 1995

[See headnote, Table 866. Data are based on the 1987 Standard Industrial Classification]

EMPLOYMENT SIZE-CLASS	Unit	All industries [1]	Agricultural services [2]	Manufacturing	Transportation [3]	Wholesale trade	Retail trade	Finance and insurance [4]	Services
Establishments, total . .	Number.	6,613,218	108,353	389,925	284,986	517,737	1,567,884	628,499	2,385,532
1 to 4 employees. . .	Number.	3,615,126	73,279	135,382	151,898	255,883	709,670	393,204	1,411,854
5 to 9 employees. . .	Number.	1,299,747	19,618	65,750	47,953	108,576	367,964	113,021	456,142
10 to 19 employees .	Number.	817,905	10,257	60,336	35,490	79,004	240,456	65,666	257,549
20 + employees. . . .	Number.	880,440	5,199	128,457	49,645	74,274	249,794	56,608	259,987
Employees, total	1,000 . .	100,335	630	18,612	5,924	6,606	21,085	6,998	34,707
1 to 4 employees. . .	1,000 . .	6,202	(D)	241	253	468	1,301	673	2,450
5 to 9 employees. . .	1,000 . .	8,583	129	442	317	723	2,450	743	2,988
10 to 19 employees .	1,000 . .	11,000	135	830	483	1,070	3,234	874	3,447
20 + employees. . . .	1,000 . .	74,550	(D)	17,099	4,871	4,345	14,100	4,708	25,823
Annual payroll.	Mil. dol .	2,666,412	12,099	631,000	200,880	226,993	300,040	256,153	864,352
1 to 4 employees. . .	Mil. dol .	173,034	(D)	7,752	7,647	16,787	23,366	21,510	74,938
5 to 9 employees. . .	Mil. dol .	185,709	2,171	10,563	7,848	21,769	31,495	21,367	72,585
10 to 19 employees .	Mil. dol .	249,640	2,551	21,828	13,055	33,680	40,269	27,057	86,729
20 + employees. . . .	Mil. dol .	2,058,029	(D)	590,857	172,331	154,757	204,910	186,219	630,100

D Withheld to avoid disclosing data for individual companies; data are included in higher-level totals. [1] Includes establishments not shown separately. [2] Includes forestry and fisheries. [3] Includes public utilities. [4] Includes real estate.
Source: U.S. Bureau of the Census, *County Business Patterns,* annual.

No. 875. Women-Owned Firms by Major Industry Group: 1992

[Based on the 1987 SIC system. Includes individual proprietorships, partnerships and subchapter S corporations. Detail may not add to total due to rounding. N.e.c.=not elsewhere classified]

MAJOR INDUSTRY GROUP	ALL FIRMS		FIRMS WITH PAID EMPLOYEES			
	Firms (number)	Sales and receipts ($1,000)	Firms (number)	Sales and receipts ($1,000)	Employees (number)	Annual payroll ($1,000)
All industries.	5,888,883	642,484,352	817,773	550,425,116	6,252,029	104,786,488
Agricultural services, forestry, & fishing. . . .	82,526	4,987,572	15,254	3,787,251	69,542	1,002,688
Mining	37,205	6,905,374	2,731	5,940,020	30,563	841,127
Construction	183,695	45,978,168	64,746	41,579,094	371,788	8,827,641
Manufacturing	152,346	90,634,753	41,038	88,751,252	803,428	18,574,330
Transportation & public utilities	141,623	25,822,193	31,049	23,026,912	290,081	5,841,177
Wholesale trade.	154,542	12,487,093	45,591	120,625,000	385,814	9,846,339
Retail trade.	1,093,342	155,852,751	244,488	139,694,945	1,850,074	19,926,963
Finance, insurance, and real estate	602,802	51,748,279	56,040	33,084,796	295,871	6,347,967
Services	3,158,444	130,745,314	307,443	92,823,096	2,145,482	33,415,073
Industries not classified	282,358	4,962,855	9,394	1,112,750	9,386	163,185

No. 876. Minority-Owned Firms—Comparison of Business Ownership by Minority Group and Gender: 1987 and 1992

[Based on the 1987 Standard Industrial Classification (SIC). Data includes individual proprietorships, partnerships and subchapter S corporations. Detail may not add to total due to rounding]

SEX AND RACE	FIRMS		Percent change, 1987-1992	PERCENT OF TOTAL		SALES/RECEIPTS		Percent change, 1987-1992	PERCENT OF TOTAL	
	1987	1992		1987	1992	1987 (mil. dol.)	1992 (mil. dol.)		1987	1992
Total.	1,213,750	1,965,565	61.9	(X)	(X)	77,840	202,011	160.0	(X)	(X)
Men	825,441	1,248,130	51.2	68.0	63.5	59,847	152,245	154.9	76.9	75.4
Women.	388,309	717,435	84.8	32.0	36.5	17,993	49,767	176.6	23.1	24.6
Black	424,165	620,912	46.4	34.9	31.6	19,763	32,197	62.9	25.4	15.9
Men	265,887	343,666	29.3	21.9	17.5	13,232	23,688	77.1	17.0	11.7
Women	158,278	277,246	75.2	13.0	14.1	6,531	8,510	30.3	8.4	4.2
Hispanic	422,373	771,708	82.7	34.8	39.3	24,732	72,824	194.5	31.8	36.0
Men	307,348	525,330	70.9	25.3	26.7	20,403	55,645	172.2	26.2	27.5
Women	115,025	246,378	114.2	9.5	12.5	4,328	17,180	297.0	5.6	8.5
API/AIAN: [1]										
Men	258,514	397,779	53.9	21.3	20.2	26,700	74,856	180.4	34.3	37.1
Women	118,197	208,647	76.5	9.7	10.6	7,336	24,853	238.8	9.4	12.3

X Not Applicable. [1] API/AIAN = Asian, Pacific Islander, American Indian, and Alaska Native.

Source of Tables 875-876: U.S. Bureau of the Census, *Survey of Minority-Owned Businesses, Summary 1992, Series MB92-4.*

No. 877. Business Starts and Employment: 1985 to 1997

ITEM	1985	1989	1990	1991	1992	1993	1994	1995	1996	1997
New incorporations (1,000)	664	677	647	629	667	707	741	768	(NA)	(NA)
Failures [1], total	57,078	50,361	60,747	88,140	97,069	86,133	71,558	71,128	71,931	83,384
Rate per 10,000 concerns	115	65	74	107	110	109	86	82	80	88
Current liabilities [2] (mil. dol.)	36,937	42,329	56,130	96,825	94,318	47,756	28,978	37,284	29,569	37,437
Business starts, total	**249,770**	**181,645**	**158,930**	**155,672**	**164,086**	**166,154**	**188,387**	**168,158**	**170,475**	**166,740**
Agriculture, forestry & fishing	3,712	2,828	2,295	2,306	2,160	2,195	2,644	2,199	2,295	2,275
Mining	2,351	1,041	1,054	944	805	772	680	564	589	655
Construction	34,962	25,102	20,801	19,165	18,259	17,533	18,213	16,980	18,624	18,513
Manufacturing	21,976	17,142	15,315	14,927	14,043	13,789	12,927	12,172	12,908	13,144
Transportation & public utilities	8,907	6,653	6,281	6,409	6,578	6,846	7,683	7,161	7,993	8,741
Wholesale trade	29,200	19,091	18,170	18,284	18,419	17,958	16,409	14,956	16,019	15,780
Retail trade	72,744	50,793	43,109	40,653	40,318	38,707	38,949	36,381	38,407	36,377
Finance, insurance & real estate	16,271	11,151	9,550	9,139	9,581	10,314	11,746	10,362	11,222	12,198
Services	57,365	43,556	38,471	39,011	40,555	41,349	49,328	44,586	50,077	50,253
Unclassifiable establishments	2,282	4,288	3,884	4,834	13,368	16,691	29,808	22,797	12,341	8,804
Employment, total	**1,657,383**	**1,212,464**	**827,012**	**731,621**	**800,827**	**780,804**	**758,134**	**738,606**	**846,973**	**939,310**
Agriculture, forestry & fishing	17,267	14,571	8,518	7,344	7,422	5,198	7,099	6,146	7,794	10,001
Mining	20,796	11,651	8,431	6,444	6,519	6,164	4,312	3,184	4,697	4,248
Construction	185,029	125,327	80,096	63,495	59,361	53,432	54,210	53,118	64,478	82,336
Manufacturing	250,020	199,820	139,506	121,238	122,483	119,487	105,255	104,660	108,644	125,007
Transportation & public utilities	72,759	58,575	45,373	38,093	45,227	44,885	41,617	43,583	50,072	59,144
Wholesale trade	153,521	102,822	75,914	69,235	79,247	78,924	66,186	59,933	69,001	73,281
Retail trade	463,416	322,013	207,752	184,698	203,698	191,484	174,270	176,159	200,354	211,007
Finance, insurance & real estate	121,793	81,727	54,872	46,831	56,665	57,199	55,857	54,610	61,185	70,982
Services	369,285	294,207	205,481	192,938	219,120	222,054	243,296	233,482	278,292	299,137
Unclassifiable establishments	3,497	1,751	1,069	1,305	1,085	1,977	6,032	3,731	2,456	4,167

NA Not available.   [1] Includes concerns discontinued following assignment, voluntary or involuntary petition in bankruptcy, attachment, execution, foreclosure, etc.   [2] Liabilities exclude long-term publicly held obligations; offsetting assets are not taken into account.

Source: Dun & Bradstreet Corporation, Murray Hill, NJ,07974-0027 *A Decade of Business Starts*; and *Monthly Failure Report* (copyright).

No. 878. Business Starts and Business Failures, by State: 1996 and 1997

STATE	BUSINESS STARTS		NUMBER OF FAILURES		STATE	BUSINESS STARTS		NUMBER OF FAILURES	
	1996	1997	1996	1997		1996	1997	1996	1997
United States	**170,475**	**166,740**	**71,931**	**83,384**	Missouri	2,502	2,435	1,060	1,490
					Montana	397	419	179	189
Alabama	2,138	2,480	542	635	Nebraska	725	648	392	479
Alaska	235	267	184	177	Nevada	1,534	1,672	476	634
Arizona	3,362	3,110	1,010	1,207	New Hampshire	852	718	375	417
Arkansas	1,258	1,183	1,005	1,117					
California	23,987	22,497	16,879	20,089	New Jersey	7,911	7,481	2,460	2,641
					New Mexico	952	961	423	645
Colorado	3,424	3,276	2,254	3,082	New York	15,174	14,450	4,946	5,054
Connecticut	2,207	2,123	536	635	North Carolina	4,007	4,578	1,038	1,031
Delaware	534	602	49	33	North Dakota	233	255	81	138
District of Columbia	595	696	121	93					
Florida	12,299	13,032	2,676	2,583	Ohio	5,468	5,122	2,280	2,823
					Oklahoma	1,543	1,499	1,560	1,546
Georgia	5,334	5,383	1,306	1,181	Oregon	2,065	1,837	839	1,186
Hawaii	618	696	395	630	Pennsylvania	7,052	6,450	2,922	3,124
Idaho	789	784	539	677	Rhode Island	560	511	134	183
Illinois	6,860	6,525	2,568	3,407					
Indiana	2,955	2,928	850	852	South Carolina	1,903	2,014	372	413
					South Dakota	307	286	159	281
Iowa	1,087	1,199	458	506	Tennessee	3,055	3,239	1,331	1,717
Kansas	1,250	1,109	1,095	1,249	Texas	12,329	11,859	6,058	7,322
Kentucky	1,725	1,859	642	568	Utah	1,523	1,527	378	581
Louisiana	2,110	2,028	272	300					
Maine	712	570	299	395	Vermont	278	291	108	148
Maryland	3,310	3,668	1,621	1,480	Virginia	3,591	3,779	1,058	877
Massachusetts	4,351	3,766	1,612	1,667	Washington	3,165	3,223	2,695	2,977
Michigan	5,489	4,881	1,559	1,934	West Virginia	569	555	300	319
Minnesota	2,286	2,336	596	1,183	Wisconsin	2,508	2,515	934	1,205
Mississippi	1,076	1,171	183	147	Wyoming	281	247	122	137

Source: The Dun & Bradstreet Corporation, Murray Hill, NJ, 07974-0027 A Decade of Business Starts, monthly; (copyright), and *Business Failure Record,* annual (copyright).

No. 879. Business Failures, by Industry: 1990 to 1997

INDUSTRY	NUMBER					RATE PER 10,000 FIRMS				
	1990	1994	1995	1996	1997	1990	1994	1995	1996	1997
Total...................	60,747	71,558	71,128	71,931	83,384	74	86	82	80	88
Agriculture, forestry, fishing	1,733	1,880	2,231	2,723	2,945	50	62	85	102	102
Mining	388	241	200	189	163	88	62	57	60	52
Construction..................	8,162	8,341	9,158	9,801	10,867	91	92	106	112	116
Manufacturing..................	4,740	4,652	4,383	4,093	4,207	92	90	88	83	80
Food and kindred products........	232	207	216	230	222	91	83	91	93	87
Textile mill products	102	100	117	126	127	97	99	122	139	132
Apparel, other textile products	318	409	394	359	364	114	146	151	141	136
Lumber and wood products	420	327	318	375	394	97	86	89	107	106
Furniture and fixtures	258	235	229	184	163	151	140	144	120	101
Paper and allied products	68	71	51	57	47	105	104	76	84	65
Printing and publishing	734	821	815	696	762	74	77	81	69	73
Chemicals and allied products	139	142	126	123	116	86	89	81	78	68
Petroleum refining and coal products .	21	15	14	14	13	83	73	67	64	56
Rubber and misc. products	158	152	128	156	114	101	93	80	98	69
Leather and leather products	40	44	28	32	32	113	133	92	110	105
Stone, clay, and glass products.....	161	133	125	106	118	80	74	74	64	67
Primary metal products	115	83	59	59	68	123	93	69	71	80
Fabricated metal products	397	399	354	311	309	90	90	83	73	70
Machinery, exc. electric	656	615	565	486	506	84	79	75	65	65
Electric and electronic equipment ...	287	272	255	217	228	114	108	104	88	87
Transportation equipment.........	242	168	160	154	137	147	113	114	109	91
Instruments and related equipment ..	120	150	121	92	117	68	82	68	52	61
Miscellaneous	272	309	308	316	368	74	73	76	74	78
Transportation, public utilities........	2,630	2,454	2,733	3,362	4,345	94	77	90	107	130
Wholesale trade...............	4,423	4,648	4,149	3,957	3,874	77	75	71	69	66
Retail trade..................	12,972	12,602	12,952	13,476	15,035	65	66	73	72	78
Finance, insurance, real estate.......	3,819	3,939	4,293	4,138	4,586	60	53	60	57	61
Services....................	16,119	20,619	21,850	22,928	29,359	49	50	54	59	72
Public administration	10	19	24	23	26	(NA)	(NA)	(NA)	(NA)	(NA)
Nonclassifiable establishments........	5,751	12,163	9,221	7,241	7,977	(NA)	(NA)	(NA)	(NA)	(NA)

NA Not available.

Source: The Dun and Bradstreet Corporation, Murray Hill, NJ 07974-0027; *Business Failure Record*, annual (copyright).

No. 880. Bankruptcy Cases, by State: 1993 to 1997

[In thousands. For years ending June 30. Includes outlying areas, not shown separately. Covers only bankruptcy cases filed under the Bankruptcy Reform Act of 1978. **Bankruptcy:** legal recognition that a company or individual is insolvent and must restructure or liquidate. Petitions "filed" means the commencement of a proceeding through the presentation of a petition to the clerk of the court]

STATE	1993	1994	1995	1996	1997	STATE	1993	1994	1995	1996	1997
United States. . .	918.7	845.3	858.1	1,042.1	1,317.0	Missouri	16.6	14.4	15.1	19.8	24.2
						Montana	1.9	1.9	2.1	2.5	3.2
Alabama.........	25.5	23.7	24.3	29.3	33.3	Nebraska	3.9	3.6	3.4	4.6	5.7
Alaska	1.0	0.9	0.9	1.0	1.3	Nevada..........	7.9	7.7	7.3	8.9	12.3
Arizona..........	18.5	17.0	14.8	18.0	23.2	New Hampshire ...	3.7	3.3	3.1	3.4	4.3
Arkansas.........	7.5	6.7	7.9	11.2	14.7						
California.........	159.7	150.9	140.4	164.3	200.1	New Jersey........	24.9	23.8	25.5	30.6	38.8
						New Mexico.......	4.3	3.5	3.7	5.2	6.8
Colorado.........	14.9	13.2	13.1	14.9	17.9	New York	51.3	47.8	48.8	56.1	69.8
Connecticut.......	9.4	8.7	8.5	10.2	12.7	North Carolina	13.8	13.0	14.0	18.9	24.9
Delaware.........	1.6	1.3	1.4	1.9	2.4	North Dakota	1.1	1.1	1.2	1.5	1.9
District of Columbia.	1.4	1.3	1.4	1.6	2.2						
Florida	46.6	41.9	43.4	51.9	67.4	Ohio.............	37.9	32.5	32.4	38.8	50.1
						Oklahoma........	13.9	13.0	13.2	16.1	20.8
Georgia	42.9	40.5	42.1	50.9	59.9	Oregon	13.3	12.7	13.2	15.1	17.9
Hawaii	1.5	1.5	1.8	2.4	3.8	Pennsylvania	23.0	20.2	22.0	28.2	38.3
Idaho	3.9	3.4	3.7	4.8	6.2	Rhode Island	3.5	3.1	3.0	3.8	5.1
Illinois...........	41.4	38.4	39.2	48.5	60.3						
Indiana..........	24.8	22.0	22.3	26.0	33.7	South Carolina	6.8	6.4	6.9	8.5	10.7
						South Dakota.....	1.4	1.3	1.3	1.7	2.1
Iowa............	5.9	5.3	5.9	7.6	9.6	Tennessee........	38.2	35.6	35.5	43.7	52.1
Kansas..........	8.3	7.9	8.5	10.1	12.5	Texas	47.3	41.8	43.8	54.2	69.5
Kentucky.........	12.8	11.6	13.0	16.6	20.6	Utah............	7.5	6.6	6.9	8.0	10.6
Louisiana	13.2	12.3	13.4	17.1	22.6						
Maine...........	2.0	1.8	1.9	2.6	3.6	Vermont	0.9	0.8	0.9	1.2	1.7
						Virginia	26.8	24.4	25.5	31.7	40.7
Maryland.........	16.2	15.4	16.3	20.4	28.8	Washington	17.9	17.5	18.6	25.0	31.7
Massachusetts....	16.4	14.8	14.3	15.9	22.5	West Virginia	4.0	3.6	3.8	4.9	7.6
Michigan.........	25.1	22.9	22.7	28.0	36.1	Wisconsin	11.3	10.2	11.8	14.4	17.9
Minnesota	15.5	13.9	14.1	16.3	19.9	Wyoming.........	1.3	1.2	1.2	1.5	2.0
Mississippi.......	11.1	9.8	10.6	13.3	18.2						

Source: Administrative Office of the U.S. Courts, unpublished data.

No. 881. Bankruptcy Petitions Filed and Pending, by Type and Chapter: 1985 to 1997

[For years ending June 30. Covers only bankruptcy cases filed under the Bankruptcy Reform Act of 1978. **Bankruptcy:** legal recognition that a company or individual is insolvent and must restructure or liquidate. Petitions "filed" means the commencement of a proceeding through the presentation of a petition to the clerk of the court; "pending" is a proceeding in which the administration has not been completed]

ITEM	1985	1990	1991	1992	1993	1994	1995	1996	1997
Total filed	364,536	725,484	880,399	972,490	918,734	845,257	858,104	1,042,110	1,316,999
Business [1]	66,651	64,688	67,714	72,650	66,428	56,748	51,288	52,938	53,993
Nonbusiness [2]	297,885	660,796	812,685	899,840	852,306	788,509	806,816	989,172	1,263,006
Voluntary	362,939	723,886	878,626	971,047	917,350	844,087	856,991	1,040,915	1,315,782
Involuntary	1,597	1,598	1,773	1,443	1,384	1,170	1,113	1,195	1,217
Chapter 7 [3]	244,650	505,337	612,330	679,662	638,916	578,903	581,390	712,129	917,274
Chapter 9 [4]	3	7	20	15	9	17	12	10	9
Chapter 11 [5]	21,425	19,591	22,495	24,029	20,579	17,098	13,221	12,859	11,159
Chapter 12 [6]	(X)	1,351	1,358	1,634	1,434	976	904	1,063	1,006
Chapter 13 [7]	98,452	199,186	244,192	267,121	257,777	248,246	262,551	316,024	387,521
Section 304 [8]	6	12	4	29	19	17	26	24	29
Total pending	608,945	961,919	1,123,433	1,237,357	1,183,009	1,134,036	1,090,446	1,169,112	1,331,290

X Not applicable.   [1] Business bankruptcies include those filed under chapters 7, 9, 11, or 12.   [2] Bankruptcies include those filed under chapters 7, 11, or 13.   [3] Chapter 7, liquidation of nonexempt assets of businesses or individuals.   [4] Chapter 9, adjustment of debts of a municipality.   [5] Chapter 11, individual or business reorganization.   [6] Chapter 12, adjustment of debts of a family farmer with regular income, effective November 26, 1986.   [7] Chapter 13, adjustment of debts of an individual with regular income.   [8] Chapter 11 U.S.C., Section 304, cases ancillary to foreign proceedings.

Source: Administrative Office of the U.S. Courts, *Statistical Tables for the Federal Judiciary.*

No. 882. Small Business Administration Loans to Small Businesses: 1980 to 1996

[For fiscal year ending in year shown; see text, Section 9. A small business must be independently owned and operated, must not be dominant in its particular industry, and must meet standards set by the Small Business Administration as to its annual receipts or number of employees. Loans include both direct and guaranteed loans to small business establishments. Does not include Disaster Assistance Loans]

LOANS APPROVED	Unit	1980	1985	1989	1990	1991	1992	1993	1994	1995	1996
Loans, all businesses	1,000. . .	31.7	19.3	17.0	18.8	20.6	26.4	29.4	40.4	60.1	52.7
Loans, minority-owned businesses . .	1,000. . .	6.0	2.8	2.4	2.4	3.1	3.9	4.5	6.8	10.4	9.1
Percent of all business loans	Percent . .	19	15	14	13	15	15	15	18	19	19
Value of total loans [1]	Mil. dol. .	3,858	3,217	3,490	4,354	4,861	6,596	7,591	9,527	9,854	10,177
Minority business loans [2]	Mil. dol. .	470	324	385	473	764	1,033	1,178	1,754	1,885	2,124

[1] Includes both SBA and bank portions of loans.   [2] SBA direct loans and guaranteed portion of bank loans only.

Source: U.S. Small Business Administration, *Management Information Summary,* unpublished data.

No. 883. Venture Capital Commitments, by Source: 1980 to 1997

[Investment in venture capital partnerships]

SOURCE	1980	1985	1990	1991	1992	1993	1994	1995	1996	1997
Capital commitments (mil. dol.) . .	661	2,327	1,847	1,271	2,548	2,545	3,764	4,227	7,501	9,060
PERCENT DISTRIBUTION										
Individuals/families	16	13	11	12	11	7	12	17	7	13
Endowments/foundations	14	8	13	24	18	11	21	23	11	9
Insurance companies/banks	13	11	9	5	15	11	9	19	3	1
Foreign investors	8	23	7	12	11	4	2	1	2	-
Corporations	19	12	7	5	3	8	9	2	19	29
Pension funds	30	33	53	42	42	59	46	38	55	41

- Represents zero.

Source: Venture Economics Investor Services, Boston, MA, *Venture Capital Journal,* monthly.

No. 884. Mergers and Acquisitions—Summary: 1985 to 1996

[Covers transactions valued at $5 million or more. Values based on transactions for which price data revealed. **All activity** includes mergers, acquisitions, acquisitions of partial interest that involve a 40% stake in the target or an investment of at least $100 million, divestitures, and leveraged transactions that result in a change in ownership. **Divestiture:** sale of a business, division, or subsidiary by corporate owner to another party. **Leveraged buyout:** acquisition of a business in which buyers use mostly borrowed money to finance purchase price and incorporate debt into capital structure of business after change in ownership]

ITEM	Unit	1985	1989	1990	1991	1992	1993	1994	1995	1996
All activity: Number	Number . .	1,719	3,752	4,239	3,446	3,502	3,722	4,383	4,981	5,639
Value	Bil. dol. .	149.6	316.8	205.6	141.5	125.3	420.4	524.9	895.8	1,059.3
Divestitures: Number.	Number . .	780	1,615	1,907	1,759	1,598	1,993	2,005	2,227	2,423
Value	Bil. dol. .	51	94.9	90.8	61.4	57.2	213.4	236.9	365.3	319.0
Leveraged buyouts: Number.	Number . .	154	293	177	171	199	621	173	206	169
Value	Bil. dol. .	16.3	75.5	17.6	7.3	7.2	1.64	10.6	23.6	17.4
Foreign acquisitions of U.S. companies:										
Number	Number . .	259	693	773	504	361	(NA)	(NA)	80	73
Value	Bil. dol. .	27.9	69.2	56.4	29.1	17.6	(NA)	(NA)	3.5	2.9
U.S. acquisitions overseas:										
Number	Number . .	91	347	392	402	455	197	207	317	364
Value	Bil. dol. .	3.7	27.1	20.5	14.8	13.7	19.5	21.1	62.6	59.3

NA Not available.

Source: Securities Data Company, Newark, NJ, Merger & Corporate Transactions Database (copyright).

No. 885. Mergers and Acquisitions, by Industry: 1996

[See headnote, Table 884]

INDUSTRY	U.S. COMPANY ACQUIRING U.S. COMPANY		FOREIGN COMPANY ACQUIRING U.S. COMPANY		U.S. COMPANY ACQUIRING FOREIGN COMPANY	
	Number	Value (mil. dol.)	Number	Value (mil. dol.)	Number	Value (mil. dol.)
Total activity [1]	2,670	556,308.3	73	2,888.0	364	59,302.4
Construction firms	18	1,283.9	3	313.9	6	1,842.5
Food and kindred products	28	5,496.9	3	92.6	16	4,921.6
Tobacco products	2	199.7	(NA)	(NA)	3	601.9
Textile and apparel products	19	1,341.5	1	120.0	4	74.6
Wood products, furniture, and fixtures	20	3,242.8	(NA)	(NA)	3	528.7
Paper and allied products	15	2,329.3	1	138.0	5	469.7
Chemicals and allied products	33	9,208.3	(NA)	(NA)	6	482.8
Drugs	27	9,437.0	5	65.2	16	1,905.4
Stone, clay, glass and concrete products	7	936.2	(NA)	(NA)	4	123.8
Metal and metal products	66	4,306.5	(NA)	(NA)	21	1,214.3
Machinery	49	3,762.9	(NA)	(NA)	22	1,786.6
Computer and office equipment	39	3,642.9	7	411.1	5	202.8
Prepackaged software	84	9,951.0	1	—	11	474.0
Electronic and electrical equipment.	59	14,295.9	7	134.9	12	1,157.4
Communications equipment	33	6,579.8	1	6.6	6	172.3
Transportation equipment	28	6,495.0	(NA)	(NA)	8	1,623.1
Aerospace and aircraft	10	19,628.1	(NA)	(NA)	(NA)	(NA)
Measuring, medical, photo equip; clocks	92	21,064.8	5	83.4	10	1,111.4
Transportation and shipping (except air)	51	28,266.4	(NA)	(NA)	4	606.4
Air transportation and shipping.	2	263.5	(NA)	(NA)	2	458.5
Telecommunications.	58	77,814.6	6	124.0	14	1,363.6
Radio & television broadcasting stations	178	32,064.5	3	58.4	4	457.5
Printing, publishing, and allied services	34	5,393.4	(NA)	(NA)	6	1,098.0
Electric, gas, water distribution.	41	40,355.2	1	195.5	17	9,376.7
Sanitary services.	27	4,889.5	(NA)	(NA)	2	118.0
Hotels and casinos	135	13,991.1	(NA)	(NA)	9	1,365.5
Amusement and recreation services	41	1,755.5	1	300.0	2	33.3
Motion picture production and distribution . . .	17	2,507.2	3	142.5	1	7.0
Personal services	5	714.7	(NA)	(NA)	1	4,031.5
Business services	263	28,632.8	8	134.7	33	5,409.5
Advertising services.	14	843.9	(NA)	(NA)	2	1,487.5
Repair services.	13	6,763.3	1	14.7	6	500.9
Wholesale trade—durable goods	86	4,783.2	(NA)	(NA)	9	939.7
Retail trade—general merchandise and apparel	19	4,178.1	(NA)	(NA)	1	5.0
Commercial banks, bank holding companies .	185	21,259.2	(NA)	(NA)	3	68.9
Real estate, mortgage bankers and brokers . .	122	11,076.5	(NA)	(NA)	3	745.6
Investment & commodity firms, dealers, exchanges	73	12,974.4	6	346.1	10	1,420.3
Insurance	86	15,266.1	1	24.5	11	1,055.4
Other financial	2	18.8	(NA)	(NA)	1	160.0
Agriculture, forestry, and fishing	16	3,140.2	1	5.0	5	90.7
Mining.	17	6,796.7	2	20.5	15	3,074.5
Oil and gas; petroleum refining	138	26,018.1	3	63.2	29	4,189.5
Holding companies, except banks	1	2,251.2	(NA)	(NA)	(NA)	(NA)
Public administration	3	408.1	(NA)	(NA)	1	475.7

- Represents or rounds to zero.   NA Not available.   [1] Includes other items not shown separately.

Source: Securities Data Company, Newark, NJ, Merger & Corporate Transactions Database (copyright).

No. 886. Patents and Trademarks: 1980 to 1996

[In thousands. Calendar year data. Covers patents issued to citizens of the United States and residents of foreign countries. For data on foreign countries, see Table 1376]

ITEM	1980	1985	1990	1991	1992	1993	1994	1995	1996
Patent applications filed	113.0	127.1	176.7	178.4	187.2	189.4	206.9	226.6	211.6
Inventions	104.3	117.0	164.6	164.3	173.1	174.7	189.9	212.4	196.2
Designs	7.8	9.6	11.3	13.1	13.1	13.6	15.8	15.4	15.2
Botanical plants	0.2	0.2	0.4	0.4	0.4	0.4	0.5	0.5	0.7
Reissues	0.6	0.3	0.5	0.6	0.6	0.6	0.7	0.6	0.6
Patents issued	66.2	77.3	99.2	106.8	107.4	109.7	113.6	113.8	121.7
Inventions	61.8	71.7	90.4	96.5	97.4	98.3	101.7	101.4	109.6
Individuals	13.8	12.9	17.3	18.1	17.3	16.5	17.3	17.4	18.2
Corporations: United States	27.7	31.2	36.1	39.2	40.3	41.8	44.0	44.0	45.7
Foreign [1]	19.1	26.4	36.0	38.1	38.7	38.8	38.8	39.1	41.7
U.S. Government	1.2	1.1	1.0	1.2	1.2	1.2	1.3	1.0	0.9
Designs	3.9	5.1	8.0	9.6	9.3	10.6	11.1	11.7	11.4
Botanical plants	0.1	0.2	0.3	0.4	0.3	0.4	0.5	0.4	0.4
Reissues	0.3	0.3	0.4	0.3	0.4	0.3	0.3	0.3	0.3
U.S. residents [2]	40.8	43.3	52.8	57.7	58.7	61.1	64.2	64.4	69.3
Foreign country residents [2]	25.4	33.9	46.2	49.0	48.7	48.7	49.3	49.4	52.4
Percent of total	38.4	43.9	46.7	46.0	45.3	44.3	43.4	43.4	43.0
Other published documents [3]	(Z)	(Z)	0.1	0.1	0.1	0.1	0.1	0.1	0.1
Trademarks:									
Applications filed	46.8	65.1	127.3	123.3	127.8	150.4	161.1	188.9	212.5
Issued	24.7	71.7	60.8	52.4	85.8	86.9	70.1	92.5	101.4
Trademarks	18.9	65.8	53.6	46.6	80.2	80.6	63.9	85.6	93.7
Trademark renewals	5.9	5.9	7.2	5.8	5.6	6.3	6.2	6.9	7.7

Z Less than 50. [1] Includes patents to foreign governments. [2] Includes patents for inventions, designs, botanical plants, and reissues. [3] Includes Defensive Publications, a practice which began in November 1968 and ended in July 1986; and Statutory Invention Registrations, the current practice, which began May 1985. These documents are patent applications, which are published to provide the defensive properties of a patent, but do not have the enforceable rights of a patent.

Source: U.S. Patent and Trademark Office. Fiscal-year figures are published in the *Commissioner of Patents and Trademarks Annual Report.*

No. 887. Patents, by State: 1996

[Includes only U.S. patents granted to residents of the United States and territories]

STATE	Total	Inventions	Designs	Botanical plants	Reissues	STATE	Total	Inventions	Designs	Botanical plants	Reissues
U.S. [1]	69,325	61,104	7,863	183	175	Missouri	762	656	104	-	2
						Montana	141	110	31	-	-
Alabama	336	278	57	1	-	Nebraska	187	167	20	-	-
Alaska	50	36	14	-	-	Nevada	233	195	37	-	1
Arizona	1,153	1,062	83	2	6	New Hampshire	468	419	46	-	3
Arkansas	164	114	49	-	1						
California	11,945	10,473	1,329	107	36	New Jersey	3,374	3,091	275	-	8
						New Mexico	242	225	16	-	1
Colorado	1,320	1,178	139	-	3	New York	5,811	5,176	613	6	16
Connecticut	1,685	1,452	228	2	3	North Carolina	1,450	1,188	255	4	3
Delaware	471	454	13	-	4	North Dakota	72	62	10	-	-
District of Columbia	42	40	2	-	-						
Florida	2,505	2,082	404	15	4	Ohio	3,156	2,616	527	5	8
						Oklahoma	542	481	60	-	1
Georgia	1,135	967	166	1	1	Oregon	965	772	185	5	3
Hawaii	104	80	23	1	-	Pennsylvania	3,225	2,922	293	3	7
Idaho	393	365	27	-	1	Rhode Island	291	235	56	-	-
Illinois	3,672	3,144	508	12	8						
Indiana	1,416	1,277	138	-	1	South Carolina	518	469	48	-	1
						South Dakota	49	43	6	-	-
Iowa	485	432	51	-	2	Tennessee	719	633	82	-	4
Kansas	348	291	54	-	3	Texas	4,490	4,171	309	1	9
Kentucky	397	319	77	-	1	Utah	603	540	59	-	4
Louisiana	444	400	42	-	2						
Maine	113	98	15	-	-	Vermont	282	254	27	-	1
						Virginia	965	859	104	-	2
Maryland	1,203	1,101	97	4	1	Washington	1,330	1,142	183	3	2
Massachusetts	2,710	2,452	245	6	7	West Virginia	139	114	24	-	1
Michigan	3,454	3,179	270	-	5	Wisconsin	1,522	1,321	197	-	4
Minnesota	1,998	1,771	222	-	5	Wyoming	45	33	12	-	-
Mississippi	167	137	25	5	-						

- Represents zero. [1] Includes U.S. territories not shown separately.

Source: U.S. Patent and Trademark Office, Technology Assessment and Forecast Data Base.

No. 888. Patents, by Industry: 1980 to 1996

[Based on the 1972 Standard Industrial Classification (SIC). Includes all patents for inventions granted to residents of the United States, its territories, and foreign citizens. Individual industries may not add to total since a patent may be recorded in more than one industry category. Except for total, data for all years have been revised to reflect the U.S. Patent Classification System as of 1993]

INDUSTRY	SIC code	1980	1985	1990	1994	1995	1996
Total	(X)	61,819	71,661	90,364	101,675	101,419	109,641
Durable goods:							
Stone, clay, and glass products	32	1,243	1,320	1,618	1,732	1,534	1,698
Primary metals	33, 3462-3 .	705	779	913	944	903	842
Fabricated metal products [1]	34	5,013	5,568	6,792	6,360	5,924	6,198
Machinery, except electrical	35	14,378	16,832	19,140	21,436	21,201	23,332
Electronic and other electric equipment	36, 3825 . . .	10,774	13,946	19,203	23,907	25,523	28,035
Transportation equipment . . . . [2]	37, 348	3,091	3,737	4,723	4,479	4,459	4,813
Instruments and related products [2]	38	7,414	8,917	12,252	14,902	14,378	15,493
Nondurable goods:							
Food and kindred products	20	483	546	728	581	600	650
Textile mill products	22	428	513	514	582	629	650
Chemicals and allied products	28	9,879	10,278	12,522	13,349	13,604	14,702
Oil and gas extraction, petroleum products . .	13, 29	595	802	662	797	641	532
Rubber and miscellaneous plastics products .	30	2,581	3,020	3,763	4,162	3,890	3,967
Other industries	(X)	5,235	5,404	7,534	8,443	8,133	8,727

X Not applicable.   [1] Excludes SIC groups 3462, 3463, and 348.   [2] Excludes SIC group 3825.

Source: U.S. Patent and Trademark Office, *Patenting Trends in the United States, State Country Report, 1963-1996.*

No. 889. New Product Introductions of Consumer Packaged Goods: 1980 to 1997

[**Consumer packaged goods:** consumable products packaged by the manufacturer for retail sale primarily through grocery and drug stores. **New product:** a product not previously offered for sale by a particular manufacturer including new varieties, formats, sizes, and packaging for existing products]

ITEM	Food	Beverages	Health and beauty	Household products	Pet products	Miscellaneous products
Domestic and imports:						
1980	1,192	256	834	331	86	197
1985	2,327	585	1,222	463	139	294
1990	3,453	630	1,531	432	164	154
1991	3,130	589	1,614	422	175	113
1992	2,987	587	1,869	417	213	127
1993	3,107	767	2,068	376	173	161
1994	3,883	807	2,655	378	161	97
1995	3,891	809	2,419	314	123	134
1996	3,889	977	3,051	369	160	148
1997, total	3,793	1,205	3,492	366	216	122
Percent:						
New brands [1]	19.8	30.8	20.1	22.7	31.9	34.4
Brand extensions [2]	1.6	1.3	1.1	2.5	-	-
Line extensions [3]	78.6	67.9	78.8	74.8	68.1	65.6
Types of new product innovation (percent): [4]						
Formulation [5]	56.5	61.6	48.4	50.0	47.1	46.9
New market [6]	1.0	-	0.7	3.1	-	3.1
Packaging [8]	14.0	20.2	9.7	17.2	11.8	9.4
Positioning [9]	24.6	18.2	39.8	29.7	41.2	25.0
Technology [9]	-	-	1.4	-	-	12.5
Merchandising	3.9	-	-	-	-	3.1
CUMULATIVE						
Domestic, except imports, 1980-97	47,796	10,093	29,520	6,447	2,575	2,965
Imports, 1980-97 [10]	4,075	1,314	1,389	261	75	178
International, 1985-97 [11]	18,206	5,712	15,534	3,043	2,914	985

- Represents or rounds to zero.   [1] Product introduced under completely or partly new brand name.   [2] Product introduced in a category with an existing brand name which has not been used in the category before.   [3] Introduction of a new variety, format, size, or package of an existing product/brand name.   [4] Product which offers consumers something significantly different from existing products.   [5] Added or new ingredient which offers a benefit not previously provided by existing products in its category.   [6] Special category for new products which do not compete with any existing category of products.   [7] New product packaged in a way that makes it easier to store, handle, prepare, or dispense than others in its category.   [8] New product presented for new users or uses compared to existing products in its category.   [9] New product with added consumer benefits resulting from use of a new technology.   [10] New products introduced in the United States by foreign companies.   [11] New products introduced by U.S. and foreign companies outside the United States.

Source: Marketing Intelligence Service Ltd., Naples, NY, *Product Alert Weekly.* Publication contains extract from data base, Product scan.

No. 890. Net Stock of Fixed Private Capital, by Industry: 1990 to 1996

[Estimates as of **Dec. 31.** Based on the 1987 Standard Industrial Classification]

INDUSTRY	CURRENT DOLLARS (bil. dol.)				QUANTITY INDEXES (1992=100)			
	1990	1994	1995	1996	1990	1994	1995	1996
Fixed private capital	12,707	15,064	15,739	16,503	97.1	104.2	106.7	109.6
Nonresidential	6,559	7,599	7,960	8,332	97.4	103.8	106.6	109.9
Agriculture, forestry, and fishing	317	348	359	367	102.1	100.8	101.4	101.8
Farms	283	302	310	315	103.6	99.3	99.5	99.4
Agricultural services, forestry, and fishing	34	46	49	51	91.0	111.3	115.1	119.4
Mining	441	428	441	436	103.8	98.2	97.7	96.2
Metal mining	29	33	35	35	100.2	102.1	104.8	104.8
Coal mining	32	34	35	36	105.0	101.7	103.9	104.0
Oil and gas extraction	361	342	351	344	104.0	97.5	96.3	94.5
Nonmetallic minerals, except fuels	19	20	20	21	104.5	99.3	100.5	100.1
Construction	77	81	85	88	107.8	100.9	103.2	105.9
Manufacturing	1,203	1,362	1,430	1,480	97.8	102.2	104.9	107.3
Durable goods	630	698	733	759	99.4	101.9	104.6	107.3
Lumber and wood products	25	27	28	29	104.0	101.2	104.0	106.0
Furniture and fixtures	11	12	13	13	100.9	102.8	105.1	107.5
Stone, clay, and glass products	40	41	43	43	102.8	97.6	98.1	98.9
Primary metal industries	118	123	127	128	101.9	97.9	97.7	97.4
Fabricated metal products	68	75	79	82	101.0	101.7	104.6	106.9
Industrial machinery and equipment	110	120	125	129	98.8	101.4	103.3	105.5
Electronic and other electric equipment	91	107	119	129	97.7	107.5	116.8	125.9
Motor vehicles and equipment	63	76	81	86	97.3	106.4	111.3	116.1
Other transportation equipment	49	53	53	53	98.3	98.6	97.6	96.9
Instruments and related products	43	50	52	53	94.4	103.2	104.6	106.3
Miscellaneous manufacturing industries	11	13	13	14	98.3	101.5	104.3	106.9
Nondurable goods	573	664	698	721	96.2	102.5	105.2	107.3
Food and kindred products	117	135	141	146	96.8	102.0	104.4	106.5
Tobacco products	9	9	9	9	102.1	97.8	96.9	96.3
Textile mill products	33	36	37	38	102.1	100.9	101.3	101.1
Apparel and other textile products	11	13	13	13	99.4	103.3	105.1	106.3
Paper and allied products	83	93	97	98	97.1	99.7	101.3	102.1
Printing and publishing	51	57	59	60	97.2	101.7	103.2	104.4
Chemicals and allied products	154	185	197	206	93.8	104.0	108.1	111.9
Petroleum and coal products	74	88	91	93	95.0	102.8	103.9	104.1
Rubber and miscellaneous plastics products	38	46	51	55	95.4	106.6	114.1	121.2
Leather and leather products	3	3	3	3	104.2	97.5	96.3	95.1
Transportation and public utilities	1,849	2,113	2,205	2,302	98.3	102.7	104.8	106.9
Transportation	588	660	692	726	101.6	101.3	103.2	105.4
Railroad transportation	315	342	350	361	102.7	98.4	97.7	97.1
Local and interurban passenger transit	18	18	18	20	108.7	96.5	96.2	102.7
Trucking and warehousing	73	89	99	108	105.0	112.7	122.9	133.3
Water transportation	35	36	36	36	105.3	99.2	97.0	95.0
Transportation by air	82	97	104	110	95.5	100.2	104.2	108.0
Pipelines, except natural gas	38	45	46	48	99.4	102.7	103.8	105.2
Transportation services	27	34	39	43	95.2	112.0	123.2	133.2
Communications	430	493	518	562	95.5	105.3	109.7	114.7
Telephone and telegraph	374	422	437	468	96.4	104.4	107.3	111.0
Radio and television	56	72	82	94	89.9	110.7	124.7	138.1
Electric, gas, and sanitary services	831	959	994	1,014	97.5	102.4	103.5	104.0
Electric services	605	680	706	715	98.9	101.5	102.3	102.8
Gas services	163	195	198	205	95.5	102.2	102.8	102.9
Sanitary services	64	85	91	94	89.6	111.3	115.0	117.5
Wholesale trade	281	346	368	403	95.6	110.1	116.6	127.0
Retail trade	380	469	499	541	94.1	106.4	110.8	118.3
Finance, insurance, and real estate	1,489	1,791	1,871	1,960	95.1	104.5	107.2	110.6
Depository institutions	269	341	354	370	91.5	108.1	110.4	114.1
Nondepository institutions	73	95	107	118	97.4	120.3	134.3	148.7
Security and commodity brokers	10	11	11	12	102.8	103.3	105.5	108.1
Insurance carriers	104	151	164	180	84.2	114.7	123.6	134.8
Insurance agents, brokers, and service	6	6	6	6	101.3	101.7	101.5	101.8
Real estate	998	1,156	1,196	1,240	97.0	101.3	102.6	104.4
Holding and other investment offices	29	31	32	34	102.6	100.3	103.5	106.6
Services	523	661	702	755	94.1	110.3	115.9	123.7
Hotels and other lodging places	101	112	117	127	100.9	101.4	103.5	110.6
Personal services	21	24	25	26	96.9	103.6	106.9	109.7
Business services	87	107	115	126	95.7	115.5	127.0	142.3
Auto repair, services, and parking	68	99	106	115	86.5	114.7	121.2	129.6
Miscellaneous repair services	9	11	12	12	97.0	108.8	111.9	114.7
Motion pictures	16	23	26	29	89.1	118.4	130.9	146.3
Amusement and recreation services	33	42	45	49	97.1	111.5	117.4	124.6
Other services	187	244	256	271	92.6	110.6	114.7	120.0
Health services	100	139	146	154	89.3	113.8	117.7	122.6
Legal services	18	19	19	19	99.5	99.4	99.6	100.1
Educational services	11	15	17	18	93.7	119.4	126.6	136.4
Other [1]	59	71	75	80	96.5	106.4	111.2	117.6
Residential	6,147	7,466	7,779	8,171	96.8	104.5	106.8	109.3
Farms	158	179	183	188	100.1	100.3	100.7	100.8
Real estate	5,989	7,287	7,596	7,983	96.7	104.6	106.9	109.5

[1] Consists of social services, membership organizations, and miscellaneous professional services.

Source: U.S. Bureau of Economic Analysis, *Survey of Current Business,* September 1997.

No. 891. Fixed Nonresidential Private Capital: 1980 to 1996

[In billions of dollars. End-of-year stocks; depreciation over entire calendar year. Data refer to privately owned assets and are based on the fixed capital formation components of the gross domestic product. Excludes residential capital and government enterprises; includes nonprofit institutions. Net stock and depreciation estimates are usually based on geometric depreciation rates]

ITEM	1980	1990	1991	1992	1993	1994	1995	1996
CURRENT DOLLARS								
Net stocks	3,641	6,559	6,697	6,893	7,216	7,599	7,960	8,332
Equipment	1,375	2,452	2,519	2,590	2,687	2,823	2,989	3,169
Structures	2,266	4,107	4,177	4,303	4,529	4,776	4,971	5,163
Depreciation	225	440	457	472	486	513	532	559
Equipment	164	325	339	352	362	379	399	420
Structures	61	114	118	120	124	133	134	138
QUANTITY INDEXES								
Net stocks	73.7	97.4	98.7	100.0	101.7	103.8	106.6	109.9
Equipment	71.9	97.2	98.4	100.0	102.7	106.6	111.7	117.7
Structures	74.7	97.4	98.9	100.0	101.2	102.2	103.6	105.4
Depreciation	65.0	95.5	97.6	100.0	101.5	105.5	108.3	112.9
Equipment	63.0	95.5	97.7	100.0	102.1	106.0	110.8	116.8
Structures	71.2	95.7	97.4	100.0	99.6	103.9	101.3	102.3

Source: U.S. Bureau of Economic Analysis, *Survey of Current Business,* August 1992, September 1993, and August 1994 issues, unpublished data.

No. 892. Gross Private Domestic Investment: 1988 to 1996

[In billions of dollars]

ITEM	1988	1989	1990	1991	1992	1993	1994	1995	1996
CURRENT DOLLARS									
Gross private domestic investment	773.9	829.2	799.7	736.2	790.4	876.2	1,007.9	1,038.2	1,116.5
Net private domestic investment	296.0	314.1	265.4	179.8	205.1	281.7	369.2	385.2	433.8
Fixed investment	763.1	797.5	791.6	738.5	783.4	855.7	946.6	1,008.1	1,090.7
Consumption of fixed capital	478.0	515.1	534.3	556.4	585.4	594.5	638.6	653.0	682.7
Net fixed investment	285.1	282.4	257.4	182.1	198.1	261.2	308.0	355.0	407.9
Nonresidential	530.6	566.2	575.9	547.3	557.9	604.1	660.6	723.0	781.4
Structures	181.3	192.3	200.8	181.7	169.2	176.4	184.5	200.6	215.2
Producers' durable equipment	349.3	373.9	375.1	365.6	388.7	427.7	476.1	522.4	566.2
Residential	232.5	231.3	215.7	191.2	225.6	251.6	286.0	285.1	309.2
Change in business inventories	10.9	31.7	8.0	-2.3	7.0	20.5	61.2	30.1	25.9
Gross government investment	172.9	182.7	199.4	200.5	209.1	204.5	205.9	213.4	224.3
Net government investment	68.7	72.4	82.2	77.0	81.0	71.1	67.1	69.7	76.9
Structures	99.0	102.0	112.6	114.3	123.6	125.0	129.6	138.3	146.6
Equipment	73.9	80.7	86.8	86.2	85.5	79.5	76.4	75.1	77.7
CHAINED (1992) DOLLARS [1]									
Gross private domestic investment	828.2	863.5	815.0	738.1	790.4	863.6	975.7	991.5	1,069.1
Net private domestic investment	311.6	322.6	267.3	177.3	205.1	280.4	360.5	371.9	426.7
Fixed investment	818.3	832.0	805.8	741.3	783.4	842.8	915.5	962.1	1,041.7
Consumption of fixed capital	516.6	540.9	547.7	560.8	585.4	583.1	615.2	619.6	642.4
Net fixed investment	301.7	291.1	258.2	180.4	198.1	259.6	300.4	342.5	399.3
Nonresidential	566.0	588.8	585.2	547.7	557.9	600.2	648.4	706.5	771.7
Structures	196.8	201.2	203.3	181.6	169.2	170.8	172.5	179.9	188.7
Residential	252.5	243.2	220.6	193.4	225.6	242.6	267.0	257.0	272.1
Gross government investment	186.2	192.5	204.6	202.2	209.1	200.4	196.0	197.0	203.3
Net government investment	72.6	74.7	83.0	77.0	81.0	69.9	63.9	64.1	69.1
Federal	14.8	14.2	15.6	12.2	11.1	3.5	-2.1	-3.9	-1.6
	10.1	9.1	9.5	4.9	1.9	-5.7	-8.7	-10.4	-9.2
State and local	57.8	60.5	67.4	64.8	69.9	66.4	66.0	67.9	70.7
Structures	107.6	107.7	115.3	115.3	123.6	121.7	122.0	124.9	128.4
Equipment	78.7	84.7	89.3	86.9	85.5	78.6	73.9	71.9	74.7

[1] See text, Section 14.

Source: U.S. Bureau of Economic Analysis, *National Income and Product Accounts, Volume 1, 1929-94,* and *Survey of Current Business,* August 1997.

No. 893. Business Investment and Plans—Capital Expenditures: 1993 to 1996

[**In millions of dollars.** Based on 1987 Standard Industrial Classification (SIC)]

INDUSTRY	SIC code	1993	1994	1995	1996
Expenditures, total	(X)	489,682	549,274	601,123	642,949
By industry	(X)	488,249	547,859	601,028	642,949
Mining and construction.	10-17	31,227	33,665	38,066	41,211
Manufacturing	(X)	134,066	154,415	180,983	191,179
Durable goods	24-25,32-39	66,361	79,729	97,024	109,695
Nondurable goods.	20-23,26-31	67,705	74,685	83,959	81,484
Transportation	40-42,44-47	30,610	33,335	33,899	35,862
Communications	48	37,050	41,869	46,302	57,106
Utilities	49	41,257	41,463	38,419	36,972
Electric	491	21,029	30,858	26,749	25,459
Gas, water, and other utilities	492-497	20,228	10,605	11,670	11,513
Wholesale and retail trade	(X)	60,316	69,958	76,336	77,371
Wholesale trade	50-51	18,963	23,452	24,457	25,183
Retail trade	52-59	41,353	46,506	51,879	52,188
Finance, insurance, and real estate	(X)	40,242	47,149	50,256	58,790
Finance.	60-62,67	26,024	29,768	30,421	36,320
Insurance and real estate	63-65	14,218	17,381	19,835	22,470
Services	(X)	111,760	123,823	134,243	141,954
Rental and business services	07-09,70,72	(NA)	67,033	72,853	77,641
Health services.	80	30,857	31,754	32,256	33,216
Membership organizations, educational, and miscellaneous services.	81-84,86,87,89	(NA)	25,036	29,133	31,097
Structure and equipment expenditures serving multiple industry categories.	(X)	(NA)	2,183	2,521	2,503
Not distributed by Industry	(X)	(NA)	1,415	96	-

- Represents zero.   NA Not available.   X Not applicable.

Source: U.S. Bureau of the Census. *Annual Capital Exepnditures Survey.*

No. 894. Composite Indexes of Economic Cyclical Indicators: 1980 to 1997

ITEM	Unit	1980	1990	1994	1995	1996	1997
Leading index, composite	1992=100. . .	89.3	99.2	101.3	100.8	102.0	103.8
Average weekly hours, manufacturing. . .	Hours	39.7	40.7	41.9	41.6	41.5	42.0
Average weekly initial claims for unemployment insurance	1,000.	488.9	385.8	341.9	358.2	351.7	319.3
Manufacturers' new orders, consumer goods and materials (1992 dol.)	Mil. dol.	96,153	118,017	136,332	139,218	144,133	153,475
Vendor performance, slower deliveries diffusion index	Percent	40.6	47.9	60.1	52.8	50.5	53.9
Manufacturers' new orders, nondefense capital goods (1992 dol.)	Mil. dol.	27,141.8	34,597.6	34,630.2	38,786.5	41,991.9	45,562.4
Building permits, new private housing units	1,000.	1,246.4	1,155.1	1,366.9	1,335.8	1,418.2	1,437.2
Stock prices, 500 common stocks	1941-43=100	118.8	334.6	460.3	541.6	670.8	872.7
Money supply, M2 (1992 dol.)	Bil. dol.	2,635.5	3,475.6	3,328.1	3,310.8	3,391.5	3,486.4
Interest rate spread, 10-year treasury bonds less federal funds.	Percent	-1.9	0.5	2.9	0.7	1.1	0.9
Index of consumer expectations	Percent	56.8	70.2	83.8	83.2	85.7	97.7
Coincident index, composite.	1992=100. . .	80.1	100.2	106.1	109.6	112.6	116.4
Employees on nonagricultural payrolls	Millions	90,418	109,404	114,145	117,195	119,517	122,264
Personal income less transfer payments (1992 dol.).	Bil. dol.	3,358.2	4,390.4	4,612.8	4,772.5	4,913.8	5,105.4
Industrial production	1992=100. . .	79.7	98.9	109.2	114.5	118.5	124.4
Manufacturing and trade sales (1992 dol.).	Bil. dol.	434,290	562,978	627,972	651,924	678,378	716,102
Lagging index, composite	1992=100. . .	103.7	106.8	100.2	103.5	104.4	104.7
Average duration of unemployment	Weeks	11.9	12.0	18.8	16.6	16.7	15.8
Inventories to sales ratio, manufacturing and trade.	Ratio	1.5	1.4	1.4	1.4	1.4	1.4
Labor cost per unit of output, manufacturing.	Percent	11.1	0.8	-1.8	-1.7	-0.9	-1.1
Average prime rate	Percent	15.3	10.0	7.1	8.8	8.3	8.4
Commercial and industrial loans (1992 dol.)	Bil. dol.	345,348	454,656	460,068	512,382	528,122	548,011
Consumer installment credit to personal income ratio.	Ratio	14.4	14.7	15.6	16.9	17.8	17.7
Consumer price index for services	Percent	14.6	5.8	3.2	3.5	3.3	2.9

Source: The Conference Board, New York, NY 10022-6601, *Business Cycle Indicators,* monthly (copyright).

No. 895. Business Cycle Expansions and Contractions—Months of Duration: 1919 to 1996

[A trough is the low point of a business cycle; a peak is the high point. Contraction, or recession, is the period from peak to subsequent trough; expansion is the period from trough to subsequent peak. Business cycle reference dates are determined by the the National Bureau of Economic Research, Inc.]

BUSINESS CYCLE REFERENCE DATE		Contraction (trough from previous peak)	Expansion (trough to peak)	LENGTH OF CYCLE	
Trough	Peak			Trough from previous trough	Peak from previous peak
March 1919	January 1920	[1]7	10	[2]51	[1]17
July 1921	May 1923	18	22	28	40
July 1924	October 1926	14	27	36	41
November 1927	August 1929	13	21	40	34
March 1933	May 1937	43	50	64	93
June 1938	February 1945	13	80	63	93
October 1945	November 1948	8	37	88	45
October 1949	July 1953	11	45	48	56
May 1954	August 1957	10	39	55	49
April 1958	April 1960	8	24	47	32
February 1961	December 1969	10	106	34	116
November 1970	November 1973	11	36	117	47
March 1975	January 1980	16	58	52	74
July 1980	July 1981	6	12	64	18
November 1982	July 1990	16	92	28	108
March 1991	(X)	8	(X)	100	(X)
Average, all cycles:					
1854 to 1991 (31 cycles) . . .		18	35	53	[3]53
1854 to 1919 (16 cycles) . . .		22	27	48	[4]49
1919 to 1945 (six cycles) . . .		18	35	53	53
1945 to 1991 (nine cycles) . .		11	50	61	61
Average, peacetime cycles:					
1854 to 1991 (26 cycles) . . .		19	29	48	[5]48
1854 to 1919 (14 cycles) . . .		22	24	46	[6]47
1919 to 1945 (five cycles) . . .		20	26	46	45
1945 to 1991 (seven cycles) .		11	43	53	53

X Not applicable.   [1] Previous peak: August 1918.   [2] Previous trough: December 1914.   [3] 30 cycles.   [4] 15 cycles.   [5] 25 cycles.   [6] 13 cycles.

Source: National Bureau of Economic Research, Inc., Cambridge, MA, unpublished data.

No. 896. Manufacturing and Trade—Sales and Inventories: 1980 to 1996

[In billions of dollars, except ratios]

ITEM	1980	1985	1990	1991	1992	1993	1994	1995	1996
Sales, average monthly	393	507	651	646	674	712	768	694	714
Manufacturing	185	233	287	283	293	310	337	304	310
Retail trade	96	138	184	186	195	207	224	198	203
Merchant wholesalers	112	136	179	178	185	194	207	192	201
Inventories [1] **. . . . .**	(NA)	664	834	830	839	861	917	976	1,008
Manufacturing	(NA)	335	399	386	379	377	392	419	438
Retail trade	(NA)	182	240	243	252	268	290	303	314
Merchant wholesalers	(NA)	147	196	200	208	216	235	255	256
Inventory-sales ratios [2] **. . . . .**	(NA)	1.31	1.28	1.28	1.24	1.21	1.19	1.41	1.41
Manufacturing	(NA)	1.44	1.39	1.36	1.29	1.22	1.16	1.38	1.41
Retail trade	(NA)	1.32	1.30	1.31	1.29	1.29	1.29	1.53	1.55
Merchant wholesalers	(NA)	1.08	1.09	1.12	1.12	1.11	1.14	1.33	1.27

NA Not available.   [1] Seasonally adjusted end-of-year data. See text, Section 17.   [2] End-of-year seasonally adjusted inventories to seasonally adjusted sales.

Source: U.S. Bureau of the Census, Current Business Reports, *"Manufacturing and Trade Inventories and Sales"* February 1994, and unpublished data.

No. 897. Manufacturing Corporations—Number, Assets, and Profits, by Asset Size: 1980 to 1997

[Corporations and assets as of **end of 4th quarter**; profits for **entire year.** Based on complete canvass. The asset value for complete canvass was $25 million in 1980 and raised in 1988 to $50 million. Asset sizes less than these values are sampled, except as noted. For details regarding methodology, see source for first quarter, 1988]

YEAR	Unit	Total	ASSET-SIZE CLASS						
			Under [1] $10 mil.	$10-$25 mil.	$25-$50 mil.	$50-$100 mil.	$100-$250 mil.	$250 mil.-$1 bil.	$1 bil. and over
Corporations:									
1980	Number	(NA)	(NA)	1,777	941	590	491	369	244
1985	Number	(NA)	(NA)	(NA)	896	744	608	428	281
1989	Number	(NA)	(NA)	(NA)	(NA)	781	750	579	347
1990	Number	(NA)	(NA)	(NA)	(NA)	834	774	597	367
1991	Number	(NA)	(NA)	(NA)	(NA)	868	799	608	373
1992	Number	(NA)	(NA)	(NA)	(NA)	881	829	621	387
1993	Number	(NA)	(NA)	(NA)	(NA)	956	843	648	407
1994	Number	(NA)	(NA)	(NA)	(NA)	983	903	712	417
1995	Number	(NA)	(NA)	(NA)	(NA)	574	639	727	447
1996	Number	(NA)	(NA)	(NA)	(NA)	532	620	745	484
1997	Number	(NA)	(NA)	(NA)	(NA)	470	615	748	529
Assets:									
1980	Mil. dol.	1,384,474	126,639	43,569	34,930	41,963	75,284	179,959	882,129
1985	Mil. dol.	1,932,766	153,883	64,324	52,669	58,019	96,748	208,403	1,298,720
1989	Mil. dol.	2,501,097	144,814	73,487	56,548	68,149	117,014	282,056	1,759,029
1990	Mil. dol.	2,629,458	142,498	74,477	55,914	72,554	123,967	287,512	1,872,536
1991	Mil. dol.	2,688,422	140,056	70,567	58,549	72,694	127,748	295,743	1,923,066
1992	Mil. dol.	2,798,625	143,766	70,446	65,718	75,967	132,742	302,287	2,007,698
1993	Mil. dol.	2,904,869	149,763	72,854	61,243	81,389	134,388	317,774	2,087,457
1994	Mil. dol.	3,080,231	148,751	81,505	66,405	82,116	138,950	358,100	2,204,404
1995	Mil. dol.	3,309,991	155,818	87,084	68,545	86,856	159,341	367,947	2,384,400
1996	Mil. dol.	3,542,428	164,342	87,256	70,016	93,603	156,754	394,611	2,575,846
1997	Mil. dol.	3,763,096	169,119	87,818	77,074	85,198	158,212	398,608	2,787,067
Net profit: [2]									
1980	Mil. dol.	92,443	7,770	2,235	1,904	2,479	4,532	11,485	62,041
1985	Mil. dol.	87,647	8,601	2,551	2,305	2,819	3,628	7,312	60,431
1989	Mil. dol.	136,490	10,381	5,173	2,921	3,105	4,434	11,824	98,651
1990	Mil. dol.	111,561	8,527	5,160	2,769	2,676	3,531	7,245	81,652
1991	Mil. dol.	67,516	6,820	4,271	2,564	1,714	1,730	5,119	45,299
1992	Mil. dol.	23,212	9,567	4,748	3,245	3,050	4,585	5,976	-7956
1993	Mil. dol.	83,922	11,195	5,415	3,439	3,225	3,624	4,662	52,362
1994	Mil. dol.	176,639	14,131	7,057	4,072	4,999	6,787	14,875	124,719
1995	Mil. dol.	200,443	13,224	5,668	3,775	5,766	7,045	16,994	147,972
1996	Mil. dol.	231,488	15,852	6,881	4,291	5,667	8,004	16,393	174,403
1997	Mil. dol.	246,940	17,872	8,457	4,290	4,771	7,060	18,464	186,029

NA Not available. [1] Beginning 1986, excludes estimates for corporations with less than $250,000 in assets at time of sample selection. Prior periods include estimates for corporations in this size category. [2] After taxes.
Source: U.S. Bureau of the Census, *Quarterly Financial Report for Manufacturing, Mining and Trade Corporations.*

No. 898. U.S. Largest Public Companies—Profitability and Growth: 1997

[In percents. For fiscal years ending in the 12 month period ending September 30. See source for details. Minus sign (-) indicates decrease]

INDUSTRY	PROFITABILITY—RETURN ON CAPITAL [1]		GROWTH				Debt/ capital, latest 12 months (percent)
			Sales [2]		Earnings per share		
	5-year average	Latest 12 months	5-year average	Latest 12 months	5-year average	Latest 12 months	
All industries, median	**10.5**	**10.3**	**8.9**	**7.9**	**6.7**	**14.9**	**32.8**
Aerospace and defense	13.4	12.6	4.0	8.9	7.2	10.7	32.1
Business services and supplies	12.4	10.9	14.9	13.3	9.2	19.8	28.7
Capital goods	13.1	14.7	10.4	7.6	14.0	15.7	30.7
Chemicals	13.2	11.6	6.5	2.0	11.2	12.2	32.0
Computers and software	15.1	14.4	26.0	10.6	16.5	19.6	15.4
Construction	10.1	12.4	11.7	9.9	22.7	25.6	39.9
Consumer durables	10.0	11.1	10.4	6.4	8.0	13.1	33.6
Energy distributors	6.6	6.5	4.6	6.6	3.3	-0.3	36.8
Energy extractors	8.7	11.4	4.7	9.8	-20.7	33.3	30.3
Entertainment and information	10.5	8.7	7.8	9.5	9.0	40.0	40.9
Financial services	12.2	11.7	10.2	11.4	14.4	20.8	41.8
Food distributors	10.1	9.1	7.3	4.7	-17.3	10.4	46.5
Food, drink and tobacco	10.1	10.4	6.2	4.0	-7.3	18.6	40.9
Forest products and packaging	7.6	4.8	7.2	-0.9	(NS)	-44.8	39.6
Health care products	14.6	12.7	11.1	8.8	8.6	15.5	19.4
Health care services	10.4	7.4	24.9	22.3	6.0	23.5	35.4
Household and personal products	9.4	11.7	-7.8	7.0	-11.3	28.8	36.0
Insurance	11.7	12.3	6.2	8.4	7.6	14.9	15.8
Metals	9.7	7.8	7.6	3.8	(NS)	-13.7	30.1
Retailing	9.5	9.0	11.2	9.5	-13.0	16.8	27.9
Telecommunications	10.2	11.3	15.1	11.5	9.3	12.8	28.9
Travel and transport	8.9	10.4	10.4	8.9	-3.0	16.4	38.9

NS Not significant. [1] After-tax profits, the amount remaining if the interest paid on longterm debt was taxed, and minority interest divided by a firm's total capitalization. Total capitalization is long-term debt, common and preferred equity, deferred taxes, investment tax credits, and minority interest in consolidated subsidiaries. [2] Net sales plus other operating revenue.
Source: Forbes, Inc., New York, NY, *Forbes Annual Report on American Industry* (copyright).

No. 899. 500 Largest Industrial Corporations—Sales, Assets, and Profits by Sales Rank: 1990 to 1993

[In billions of dollars. Excludes large privately owned companies that do not publish sales. Includes service and rental revenues, but companies must derive more than 50 percent of revenues from manufacturing or mining for years ending not later than Dec. 31 of year stated; sales exclude excise taxes collected by manufacturer and include discontinued operations Minus sign (-) indicates decrease]

SALES RANK	SALES				ASSETS [1]				PROFITS [2]			
	1990	1991	1992	1993	1990	1991	1992	1993	1990	1991	1992	1993
Total	2,303	2,264	2,365	2,370	2,443	2,466	2,565	2,676	93	[3]55	[3](-Z)	62.6
Top 100.	(NA)	1,619	1,681	1,676	(NA)	1,844	1,902	2,015	(NA)	38	-8	49.0
101-200	(NA)	323	341	343	(NA)	328	351	337	(NA)	9	3	12.0
201-300	(NA)	160	171	175	(NA)	151	160	163	(NA)	4	3	2.0
301-400	(NA)	96	104	107	(NA)	77	91	102	(NA)	3	2	-1.0
401-500	(NA)	65	69	70	(NA)	57	60	59	(NA)	1	(Z)	1.0

NA Not available.　Z Less than $500 million.　[1] Total assets employed in business at end of fiscal year, less depreciation and depletion.　[2] After taxes, special charges, and credits.　[3] Total profits of $55 billion in 1991 and $200 million in 1992 include charge-offs for accounting rule change on retiree health benefits. Profits before charge-offs were $60 billion and $71 billion in 1991 and 1992 respectively.

Source: Time Warner, New York, NY, *The Fortune Directories* (copyright).

No. 900. 500 Largest Industrial Corporations—Selected Financial Items: 1980 to 1996

ITEM	Unit	1980	1990	1991	1992	1993	1994	1995	1996
Sales per employee	$1,000	78.1	153.9	159.2	169.3	174.5	(NA)	(NA)	(NA)
Changes in profits.	Percent . . .	3.6	-11.6	[1]-41.0	[1]-100.4	[1]1.8	13.8	15.0	12.2
Sales per dollar of stockholder's equity . . .	Dollar	3.00	2.97	2.81	2.91	3.02	(NA)	(NA)	(NA)
Return on stockholder's equity	Percent . . .	14.4	12.7	[2]10.2	[2]9.0	[2]10.3	13.7	14.0	13.9
Return on sales	Percent . . .	4.8	4.1	3.1	2.4	2.9	(NA)	(NA)	(NA)
Total return to investors [3]	Percent . . .	21.1	-10.2	29.5	9.1	11.1	-1.0	32.8	30.5

NA Not available.　[1] Changes in profits of -41% in 1991 and -100.4% in 1992 include charge-offs for accounting rule change on retiree health benefits. Changes before charge-offs were -35.8%, 18.3% and 15.1% in 1991, 1992 and 1993 respectively.　[2] For 1991-92 data, the return is on common stockholders' equity. For prior years and again with 1993 data, the return is on total equity.　[3] Includes both price appreciation and dividend yield, i.e., to an investor in the company's stock.

No. 901. 1000 Largest Industrial Corporations—Selected Financial Items, by Industry: 1987 and 1997

[Data are medians. For explanation of terms, see source. Minus sign (-) indicates decrease. For definition of median, see Guide to Tabular Presentation]

INDUSTRY	Rev-enue, percent change from 1996	PROFITS				Earnings per share, 1987-97 ann. rate	TOTAL RETURN TO INVESTORS (percent)	
		Percent change from 1996	As per-cent of revenue	As per-cent of assets	As per-cent of stock-holders' equity		1987-97 ann. rate	1997
Aerospace	13	18	5	6	21	7	21	20
Apparel	7	24	7	9	19	6	12	-1
Beverages	4	17	6	8	17	9	21	32
Building materials, glass	9	66	7	8	23	-2	14	3
Chemicals	2	3	6	6	17	7	14	19
Computer and data services	11	15	5	7	14	14	17	35
Computer peripherals.	13	70	7	12	22	13	22	33
Computers, office equipment	12	21	5	5	16	10	12	24
Diversified outsourcing services	15	21	2	6	21	14	19	64
Electronics, electrical equip	10	11	5	7	15	9	17	20
Electronics, network communications . . .	33	25	14	17	22	27	21	-15
Electronics, semiconductors	4	6	12	10	16	23	15	7
Food.	4	18	3	7	17	10	18	43
Food services.	7	12	2	4	12	15	18	19
Forest and paper products	1	-59	2	2	4	-4	10	6
Industrial and farm equipment	10	17	5	6	16	9	15	31
Insurance: Life, health (stock)	9	36	8	1	11	12	23	42
Insurance: Property and casualty (stock) .	7	28	9	3	12	9	20	41
Metal products	8	20	8	7	17	12	17	36
Metals.	3	19	4	5	13	8	14	-5
Motor vehicles and parts.	6	36	4	4	17	6	14	37
Petroleum refining	-	6	5	6	14	7	14	22
Pharmaceuticals	8	12	14	13	27	14	23	34
Pipelines	37	-19	3	2	8	6	20	16
Publishing, printing	8	-	7	7	15	8	14	38
Savings institutions	10	20	10	1	11	5	22	61
Scientific, photo, and control equip	8	-	7	7	14	10	14	13
Securities.	22	25	10	1	19	15	29	81
Soaps, cosmetics	6	17	7	10	27	13	23	32
Utilities, gas and electric.	6	-	8	3	11	1	14	27
Wholesalers	11	14	1	3	11	9	15	18

- Represents or rounds to zero.
Source of tables 900-901: Time Warner, New York, NY, *The Fortune Directories* (copyright).

No. 902. Corporate Profits, Taxes, and Dividends: 1990 to 1996

[In billions of dollars. Covers corporations organized for profit and other entities treated as corporations. Represents profits to U.S. residents, without deduction of depletion charges and exclusive of capital gains and losses; intercorporate dividends from profits of domestic corporations are eliminated; net receipts of dividends, reinvested earnings of incorporated foreign affiliates, and earnings of unincorporated foreign affiliates are added]

ITEM	1990	1991	1992	1993	1994	1995	1996
Profits before tax	372	374	406	464	531	599	640
Profits tax liability.	141	133	143	164	195	219	233
Profits after tax	231	241	263	301	336	380	407
Dividends	152	163	170	197	211	227	244
Undistributed profits	79	78	94	103	125	153	163
Inventory valuation adjustment (IVA).	-14	4	-8	-7	-13	-28	-9
Capital consumption adjustment	39	33	29	34	36	34	39
Net interest	467	448	414	399	395	404	403
Addenda:							
Corporate profits after tax with IVA/CCA [1] . . .	257	278	285	328	359	386	437
Net cash flow with inventory IVA/CCA [1]	455	479	492	520	564	595	651
Undistributed profits with IVA/CCA [1]	105	115	116	131	148	159	193
Consumption of fixed capital	350	365	376	389	416	436	458
Less: Inventory valuation adjustment (IVA)	-14	4	-8	-7	-13	-28	-9
Equals: Net cash flow	469	475	499	527	577	623	660

[1] Inventory valuation adjustment/capital consumptiom adjustment.

Source: U.S. Bureau of Economic Analysis, *National Income and Product Accounts of the United States,* and *Survey of Current Business,* August 1997.

No. 903. Corporate Profits, by Industry: 1990 to 1996

[In millions of dollars. Profits are without inventory valuation and capital consumption adjustments. Minus sign (-) indicates loss. See headnote, Table 902]

INDUSTRY	BEFORE TAXES				AFTER TAXES			
	1990	1994	1995	1996	1990	1994	1995	1996
Corporate profits	371,685	535,133	622,625	676,576	231,221	348,489	409,401	447,559
Domestic industries	305,945	461,754	535,918	580,659	165,481	275,110	322,694	351,642
Agriculture, forestry, and fishing	1,619	1,384	1,852	2,038	993	681	1,102	1,219
Mining.	2,459	3,416	4,492	6,508	876	2,509	3,073	4,366
Construction.	10,999	13,756	17,789	(NA)	8,781	11,447	14,885	15,791
Manufacturing.	115,543	158,788	193,432	204,520	67,503	97,992	127,143	131,815
Transportation	934	10,408	11,632	12,332	-1,993	6,222	7,238	(NA)
Communications	20,014	36,821	33,448	35,859	11,831	24,758	20,760	21,992
Wholesale trade	19,839	33,311	32,797	(NA)	13,695	24,485	23,181	26,534
Retail trade	24,382	48,803	45,114	(NA)	15,426	35,439	32,603	36,712
Finance, insurance, and real estate	65,354	72,341	101,771	108,550	17,873	11,507	24,312	30,667
Services	20,241	46,817	52,194	59,031	14,901	36,231	41,710	46,627
Rest of the world.	65,740	73,379	86,707	95,917	65,740	73,379	86,707	95,917

NA Not available. [1] Consists of receipts by all U.S. residents, including both corporations and persons, of earnings of unincorporated foreign affiliates, dividends from their incorporated foreign affiliates, and their share of their incorporated foreign affiliates, net of corresponding outflows.

No. 904. Corporate Profits With Inventory Valuation and Capital Consumption Adjustments—Financial and Nonfinancial Industries: 1980 to 1996

[In billions of dollars. Minus sign (-) indicates loss. See headnote, Table 902]

ITEM	1980	1985	1989	1990	1991	1992	1993	1994	1995	1996
Corporate profits with IVA/CCA [1] . .	167.1	304.0	380.0	397.1	411.3	428.0	492.1	554.1	604.8	670.2
Domestic industries	131.6	270.6	322.0	331.3	342.6	363.1	422.5	489.9	528.1	588.2
Rest of the world.	35.5	33.4	58.0	65.7	68.7	64.9	69.6	64.3	76.7	82.0
Corporate profits with IVA [1]	198.3	230.5	330.6	358.2	378.2	398.9	457.7	517.9	570.8	631.0
Domestic industries	162.9	197.1	272.6	292.5	309.5	334.0	388.1	453.7	494.1	548.9
Financial	24.3	29.0	53.1	68.6	87.4	83.7	91.0	94.4	119.1	131.9
Nonfinancial	138.5	168.1	219.6	223.8	222.1	250.3	297.2	359.3	375.0	417.0
Manufacturing	75.8	81.6	109.3	112.3	92.7	96.3	109.7	142.7	145.7	166.5
Transportation and public utilities. .	18.3	34.3	42.6	43.2	53.9	57.8	70.6	81.3	94.8	99.0
Wholesale trade	16.7	20.6	20.4	17.2	20.6	23.0	25.5	34.5	29.6	36.6
Retail trade	6.1	22.5	20.7	20.6	26.1	32.2	39.2	42.2	38.7	41.8
Other	21.6	9.1	26.6	30.6	28.9	41.0	52.1	58.6	66.2	73.1

[1] Inventory valuation adjustment and capital consumption adjustment.

Source of Tables 903-904: U.S. Bureau of Economic Analysis, *National Income and Product Accounts of the Unites States, 1929-94,* forthcoming, and *Survey of Current Business,* May 1997.

No. 905. Manufacturing, Mining, and Trade Corporations—Profits and Stockholders' Equity Ratios: 1990 to 1997

[Averages of quarterly figures at annual rates. Manufacturing data exclude estimates for corporations with less than $250,000 in assets at time of sample selection. Data are not necessarily comparable from year to year due to changes in accounting procedures, industry classifications, sampling procedures, etc.; for detail, see source. Based on sample; see source for discussion of methodology. Minus sign (-) indicates loss]

INDUSTRY	RATIO OF PROFITS TO STOCKHOLDERS' EQUITY (percent)				PROFITS PER DOLLAR OF SALES (cents)				RATIO OF STOCKHOLDERS' EQUITY TO DEBT			
	1990	1995	1996	1997	1990	1995	1996	1997	1990	1995	1996	1997
Manufacturing corporations.	10.7	16.2	17.2	16.9	4.0	5.7	6.2	6.3	1.3	1.4	1.5	1.5
Durable goods	8.0	15.6	15.9	16.2	3.0	5.3	5.5	5.8	1.6	1.9	1.9	1.9
Lumber and wood products	(NA)	12.6	15.0	20.1	(NA)	3.5	3.7	5.6	(NA)	1.8	1.7	1.6
Furniture and fixtures	(NA)	8.1	15.9	16.8	(NA)	2.3	4.2	4.5	(NA)	1.7	1.5	1.8
Stone, clay, and glass products	5.4	12.7	16.7	13.2	1.8	4.6	5.3	4.3	0.8	1.1	1.0	1.1
Primary metal industries	9.5	18.9	11.2	12.7	2.6	5.4	3.6	4.2	1.1	1.3	1.5	1.5
Iron and steel	6.6	14.6	7.7	11.9	1.0	3.8	2.2	3.5	0.6	1.3	1.4	1.4
Nonferrous metals	10.4	22.2	13.8	13.3	4.0	6.8	4.8	5.0	1.6	1.3	1.5	1.6
Fabricated metal products	11.7	13.1	19.5	19.1	3.4	3.5	5.5	5.7	1.3	1.2	1.3	1.3
Machinery, exc. electrical	8.1	12.4	15.5	15.1	4.4	4.4	5.6	5.4	2.2	1.8	1.9	2.0
Electrical and electronic equipment	7.5	18.9	16.2	16.1	3.0	8.5	7.2	7.6	1.6	2.4	2.4	2.6
Transportation equipment	3.8	17.4	18.5	20.9	1.3	4.5	4.9	5.4	1.9	2.1	1.9	2.0
Motor vehicles and equipment	-1.0	21.0	19.8	23.4	-0.5	4.7	4.6	5.5	2.2	2.6	2.7	2.7
Aircraft, guided missiles and parts	11.5	10.8	16.9	17.3	3.4	3.6	5.7	5.2	1.6	1.7	1.4	1.3
Instruments and related products	12.9	14.8	11.4	11.4	6.6	8.3	6.2	6.8	1.6	2.4	2.3	1.9
Miscellaneous manufacturing	(NA)	12.8	14.8	11.3	(NA)	4.1	4.9	4.0	(NA)	1.5	1.6	1.6
Nondurable goods	13.3	16.8	18.5	17.6	4.9	6.1	6.9	6.9	1.2	1.2	1.2	1.3
Food and kindred products [1]	16.1	18.5	19.4	20.1	4.1	5.5	5.6	5.6	0.8	1.0	1.0	0.9
Tobacco products	(¹)	(¹)	(¹)	(¹)	(¹)	(¹)	(¹)	(¹)	(¹)	(¹)	(¹)	(¹)
Textile mill products	3.4	4.9	9.5	10.0	0.8	1.3	2.7	2.8	0.7	0.9	1.0	1.1
Apparel (includes leather)	(NA)	12.4	16.1	24.0	(NA)	2.7	2.7	4.6	(NA)	1.2	0.9	1.0
Paper and allied products	10.6	21.2	10.6	6.4	4.2	7.0	4.0	2.5	1.1	0.9	0.9	0.9
Printing and publishing	8.3	15.0	14.1	11.8	3.6	6.2	6.3	5.8	1.2	1.3	1.3	1.3
Chemicals and allied products	17.3	21.4	23.8	21.6	8.2	9.1	10.9	10.6	1.4	1.2	1.3	1.3
Industrial	13.8	17.0	19.1	16.7	7.0	6.9	7.8	7.1	1.4	1.0	1.0	1.1
Drugs	27.1	26.9	26.2	24.1	15.7	14.5	15.1	14.5	2.2	1.4	1.5	1.7
Residual of chemicals	(NA)	20.3	26.7	24.1	(NA)	7.2	11.0	10.9	(NA)	1.2	1.5	1.5
Petroleum and coal products	12.8	10.8	18.9	19.0	5.7	5.0	8.3	9.2	1.7	1.7	2.1	2.4
Rubber and misc. plastics products	6.9	15.5	13.7	15.9	1.8	4.1	4.0	4.5	1.0	1.3	1.3	1.2
Mining corporations [2]	8.1	2.0	11.1	10.6	5.7	1.8	10.2	10.2	1.3	1.4	1.5	1.6
Retail trade corporations [2]	8.4	10.0	11.4	11.7	1.1	1.6	1.9	2.0	0.6	1.0	1.0	1.1
Wholesale trade corporations [2]	5.0	9.0	10.6	11.0	0.6	1.2	1.5	1.6	1.0	0.8	0.9	1.0

NA Not available. [1] Tobacco included in food and kindred products. [2] Asset cut-off raised to $50 million from $25 million in 1985.

No. 906. Manufacturing Corporations—Selected Finances: 1980 to 1997

[In billions of dollars. Data are not necessarily comparable from year to year due to changes in accounting procedures, industry classifications, sampling procedures, etc.; for detail, see source]

YEAR	ALL MANUFACTURING CORPS.					DURABLE GOODS INDUSTRIES					NONDURABLE GOODS INDUSTRIES				
	Sales	Profits		Stockholders' equity [1]	Debt [1]	Sales	Profits		Stockholders' equity [1]	Debt [1]	Sales	Profits		Stockholders' equity [1]	Debt [1]
		Before taxes	After taxes				Before taxes	After taxes				Before taxes	After taxes		
1980	1,897	145	92	665	292	883	57	36	316	143	1,014	88	57	349	149
1982	2,039	108	71	770	371	913	35	22	356	177	1,126	74	49	415	193
1983	2,114	133	86	813	368	973	49	30	372	168	1,141	84	56	440	200
1984	2,335	166	108	864	405	1,108	76	49	396	166	1,228	90	59	469	239
1985 [2]	2,331	137	88	866	454	1,143	61	39	421	187	1,189	76	49	445	267
1986 [2]	2,221	129	83	875	501	1,126	52	33	436	203	1,096	77	51	438	298
1987	2,378	173	116	901	553	1,178	78	53	444	229	1,200	95	63	457	324
1988	2,596	216	155	958	622	1,285	92	67	469	265	1,312	124	88	489	357
1989	2,745	189	136	999	733	1,357	75	56	501	308	1,388	114	81	498	425
1990	2,812	160	112	1,044	782	1,357	58	41	515	328	1,454	102	71	529	453
1991	2,761	100	68	1,064	814	1,304	14	7	507	338	1,457	86	60	557	476
1992	2,890	33	23	1,035	819	1,390	-34	-24	474	335	1,500	66	47	561	485
1993	3,014	119	84	1,040	819	1,490	39	28	483	327	1,524	79	56	557	492
1994	3,261	244	175	1,114	815	1,660	121	87	533	316	1,601	123	89	581	500
1995	3,586	277	200	1,240	862	1,804	133	96	618	333	1,715	144	104	622	529
1996	3,758	311	227	1,348	920	1,941	147	107	674	366	1,816	162	120	674	554
1997	3,926	335	247	1,461	951	2,079	165	120	740	386	1,847	169	127	722	565

[1] Annual data are average equity or debt for the year using four end-of-quarter figures. [2] Beginning 1986, data exclude estimates for corporations with less than $250,000 in assets at time of sample selection.

Source of Tables 905-906: Through 1981, U.S. Federal Trade Commission; thereafter, U.S. Bureau of Census, *Quarterly Financial Report for Manufacturing, Mining, and Trade Corporations.* In U.S. Council of Economic Advisers, *Economic Report of the President,* annual.

No. 907. U.S. Multinational Companies—Gross Product: 1994 and 1995

[In millions of dollars. Gross product measures valued added by a firm. Consists of nonbank U.S. parent companies and their nonbank foreign affiliates. A U.S. parent comprises the domestic operations of a multinational and is a U.S. person that owns or controls 10 percent or more of the voting securities, or the equivalent, of a foreign business enterprise. A U.S. person can be an incorporated business enterprise. A majority-owned foreign affiliate is a foreign business enterprise in which a U.S. parent company owns or controls 50 percent or more of the voting securities]

INDUSTRY	U.S. MULTINATIONALS		U.S. PARENTS		MAJORITY-OWNED FOREIGN AFFILIATES	
	1994	1995	1994	1995	1994	1995
All industries	1,717,488	1,820,641	1,313,792	1,357,682	403,696	462,959
Petroleum	200,882	213,794	106,877	113,431	94,005	100,363
Manufacturing	902,871	945,908	697,663	713,144	205,208	232,764
Food and kindred products	107,043	108,219	82,293	83,060	24,750	25,159
Chemical and allied products.	156,356	168,657	115,386	120,553	40,970	48,104
Primary and fabricated metals	43,661	51,148	35,610	41,961	8,051	9,187
Industrial machinery and equipment [1]	103,526	108,956	76,036	74,512	27,490	34,444
Electronic and other electric equipment [1]	90,457	102,028	70,591	77,059	19,866	24,969
Transportation equipment	190,124	190,518	154,238	153,613	35,886	36,905
Other	211,704	216,383	163,509	162,386	48,195	53,997
Wholesale trade	77,796	87,233	30,490	31,448	47,306	55,785
Finance (exc, dep. inst.), insurance and real estate [1]	66,138	71,630	57,652	56,804	8,486	14,826
Finance, except depository institutions	24,792	16,135	21,138	5,123	3,654	11,012
Insurance.	41,399	57,988	35,251	49,928	6,148	8,060
Real estate	(D)	(D)	1,366	1,665	541	233
Holding companies	-1,959	-4,392	-103	87	-1,856	-4,479
Services	118,022	129,870	89,822	96,175	28,200	33,695
Hotels and other lodging places	7,061	8,974	5,956	7,773	1,105	1,201
Business services	55,112	58,628	37,630	37,446	17,482	21,182
Advertising	5,147	5,945	2,467	2,823	2,680	3,122
Equipment rental (exc. auto, computers) . . .	1,908	2,524	1,037	1,200	871	1,324
Computer and data processing	25,308	28,919	15,963	18,068	9,345	10,851
Business services, nec	22,750	21,241	18,163	15,355	4,587	5,886
Automotive rental and leasing	4,346	4,670	3,188	3,346	1,158	1,324
Motion pictures, television tape and film	11,191	12,028	10,066	10,421	1,125	1,607
Health services	13,374	15,907	13,064	15,627	310	280
Engineering and architectural services [1]	6,350	8,219	4,646	6,167	1,704	2,052
Management and public relations	6,480	6,127	4,492	3,620	1,988	2,507
Other	14,105	15,316	10,777	11,775	3,328	3,541
Other industries	351,780	372,207	331,289	346,680	20,491	25,527

D Figure withheld to avoid disclosure pertaining to a specific organization or individual.   [1] For changes in industry definition, see text.

Source: U.S. Bureau of Economic Analysis, *Survey of Current Business,* October 1997.

No. 908. U.S. Multinational Companies—Selected Characteristics: 1995

[Preliminary. In billions of dollars, except as indicated. Consists of nonbank U.S. parent companies and their nonbank foreign affiliates. U.S. parent is a U.S. person that owns or controls directly or indirectly, 10 percent or more of the voting securities of an incorporated foreign business enterprise, or an equivalent interest in an unincorporated foreign business enterprise. A U.S. person can be an incorporated business enterprise. A foreign affiliate is a foreign business enterprise owned or controlled by a U.S. parent company]

INDUSTRY [1]	U.S. PARENTS				FOREIGN AFFILIATES				U.S. exports shipped to foreign affiliates	U.S. imports shipped from foreign affiliates
	Total assets	Sales	Employment (1,000)	Employee compensation	Total assets	Sales	Employment (1,000)	Employee compensation		
All industries	7,230.0	4,236.9	18,569.1	815.8	2,815.1	2,140.4	7,377.0	239.7	174.8	153.1
Petroleum	527.0	392.6	472.6	30.4	272.1	428.0	230.9	11.7	3.0	11.1
Manufacturing	2,439.0	2,009.3	9,045.2	446.9	779.3	984.9	4,376.6	136.5	111.0	126.1
Food and kindred products .	259.4	262.6	1,153.9	38.9	99.6	113.2	554.4	13.5	3.4	2.7
Chemical and allied products	441.4	317.9	1,072.6	64.5	181.0	189.1	591.9	24.6	12.7	7.4
Primary and fabricated metals.	115.7	121.7	565.3	26.1	35.3	36.9	195.7	6.2	2.6	2.9
Industrial machinery and equipment	243.1	241.6	1,040.9	52.1	112.9	159.2	529.4	20.8	19.6	30.1
Electronic and electric equipment	338.3	224.7	1,037.4	48.4	71.5	95.4	846.0	14.9	19.5	20.0
Transportation equipment . .	594.3	444.2	1,735.0	111.3	124.7	218.3	697.6	26.5	39.0	49.2
Other manufacturing	447.0	396.6	2,440.1	105.4	154.4	172.8	961.3	30.0	14.2	13.8
Wholesale trade.	138.2	284.2	510.2	20.4	206.0	367.5	538.3	26.7	55.5	13.2
Finance (deposit institutions), insurance, real estate	2,837.1	509.9	1,035.0	65.3	1,229.6	108.4	191.0	10.3	-	-
Services	247.2	192.6	2,192.0	70.4	115.0	100.0	779.8	29.4	2.0	0.4
Other	1,041.5	848.4	5,314.1	182.3	213.1	151.6	1,260.4	25.0	3.3	2.2

- Represents zero.   [1] Represents industry of U.S. parent or industry of foreign affiliate.

Source: U.S. Bureau of Economic Analysis, *Survey of Current Business,* October 1997.

No. 909. Gross Product, Employment, and Capital Expenditures of Nonbank U.S. MNCs, U.S. Parents, and Foreign Affiliates: 1982 to 1995

[Gross product and capital expenditures in millions of dollars; employees in thousands]

ITEM	1990	1991	1992	1993	1994	1995 [1]	PERCENT CHANGE AT ANNUAL RATES 1982-94	1989-94	1994-95
GROSS PRODUCT									
MNCs worldwide:									
Parents and all affiliates . . .	(NA)	(NA)	(NA)	(NA)	(NA)	(NA)	(NA)	(NA)	(NA)
Parents and MOFAs [2]	(NA)	(NA)	(NA)	(NA)	1,717,488	1,820,641	4.4	4.7	6.0
Parents	(NA)	(NA)	(NA)	(NA)	1,313,792	1,357,682	4.2	4.7	3.3
Affiliates, total	(NA)	(NA)	(NA)	(NA)	(NA)	(NA)	(NA)	(NA)	(NA)
MOFAs	356,033	355,963	361,524	359,179	403,696	462,959	5.0	4.8	14.7
Other	(NA)	(NA)	(NA)	(NA)	(NA)	(NA)	(NA)	(NA)	(NA)
EMPLOYEES									
MNCs worldwide:									
Parents and all affiliates . . .	25,264	24,837	24,190	24,222	25,670	25,946	0.1	0.2	1.1
Parents and MOFAs	23,786	23,345	22,812	22,760	24,272	24,541	0.2	0.3	1.1
Parents	18,430	17,959	17,530	17,537	18,565	18,569	-0.1	-0.2	(Z)
Affiliates, total	6,834	6,878	6,660	6,685	7,105	7,377	0.6	1.4	3.8
MOFAs	5,356	5,387	5,282	5,223	5,707	5,972	1.1	2.2	4.6
Other	1,478	1,492	1,378	1,461	1,398	1,405	-1.2	-1.5	0.5
CAPITAL EXPENDITURES									
MNCs worldwide:									
Parents and all affiliates . . .	(NA)	(NA)	(NA)	(NA)	328,240	(NA)	(NA)	3.7	(NA)
Parents and MOFAs	274,614	269,221	272,049	271,661	303,364	327,948	2.2	3.5	8.1
Parents	213,079	206,290	208,834	207,437	231,917	250,677	1.7	3.1	8.1
Affiliates, total	(NA)	(NA)	(NA)	(NA)	96,323	(NA)	(NA)	5.1	(NA)
MOFAs	61,535	62,931	63,215	64,224	71,447	77,271	3.9	4.6	8.2
Other	(NA)	(NA)	(NA)	(NA)	24,876	(NA)	(NA)	6.7	(NA)

NA Not available.   Z Less than .05 percent.   [1] Break-in-series. See source, appendix for details.   [2] Majority-Owned Foreign Affiliate.

Source: U.S. Bureau of Economic Analysis, *Survey of Current Business,* October 1997

No. 910. Nonbank U.S. MNCs, U.S. Parents, and MOFAs by Industry of U.S. Parent: 1989 and 1995

[In billions of dollars, except employees, in thousands]

ITEM	MNC's Gross product	Profit-type return	Capital expenditures	PARENTS Gross product	Profit-type return	Capital expenditures	MOFA's Gross product	Profit-type return	Capital expenditures
1989: All industries	1,364.9	251.4	258.8	1,044.9	164.9	201.8	320.0	86.5	57.0
Petroleum	165.7	31.3	41.5	93.1	15.8	26.8	72.6	15.5	14.7
Manufacturing	793.8	147.0	132.0	586.6	86.2	98.7	207.2	60.8	33.3
Food and kindred products	79.5	19.5	12.0	60.3	14.6	9.4	19.2	5.0	2.7
Chemicals and allied products	141.0	38.4	27.8	97.1	23.4	20.3	43.9	15.0	7.5
Primary and fabricated metals	45.8	9.6	7.3	37.6	6.3	5.4	8.2	3.3	1.9
Industrial machinery and equip. . . .	116.1	16.2	18.5	70.9	1.8	11.5	45.3	14.4	6.9
Electronic/other electric equip	68.5	12.4	13.6	56.1	9.2	11.0	12.4	3.2	2.6
Transportation equipment	160.3	22.0	24.4	121.1	11.6	18.6	39.2	10.4	5.7
Other manufacturing	182.6	28.8	28.4	143.4	19.3	22.4	39.2	9.5	6.0
Wholesale trade	28.8	5.6	6.1	22.6	3.2	5.0	6.2	2.5	1.1
Finance (except banking), insurance and real estate	62.7	20.2	9.4	50.5	16.4	7.6	12.2	3.8	1.9
Services	67.0	7.8	16.7	57.1	5.9	13.6	9.9	1.8	3.1
Other industries	246.9	39.5	53.1	235.0	37.4	50.2	12.0	2.1	3.0
1995: All industries	1,820.6	368.5	328.0	1,357.7	250.5	250.7	463.0	118.0	77.3
Petroleum	209.2	32.7	40.5	113.4	13.5	25.1	95.8	19.2	15.4
Manufacturing	1,002.8	216.0	155.0	713.1	136.4	110.2	289.6	79.6	44.7
Food and kindred products	123.4	31.9	15.8	83.1	21.1	10.8	40.4	10.9	5.0
Chemicals and allied products	188.5	56.6	30.5	120.6	32.4	20.5	68.0	24.3	10.0
Primary and fabricated metals	55.8	10.7	8.3	42.0	6.6	5.9	13.8	4.0	2.4
Industrial machinery and equip. . . .	125.3	24.3	15.5	74.5	10.7	9.9	50.8	13.6	5.6
Electronic/other electric equip	102.6	26.3	24.2	77.1	18.1	19.0	25.5	8.2	5.2
Transportation equipment	205.0	28.7	33.1	153.6	19.6	21.7	51.3	9.1	11.4
Other manufacturing	202.3	37.5	27.6	162.4	27.9	22.3	39.9	9.6	5.3
Wholesale trade	40.5	7.2	7.8	31.5	4.2	6.6	9.0	3.0	1.1
Finance (except banking), insurance and real estate	75.7	33.2	14.1	56.8	25.8	11.5	18.9	7.4	2.6
Services	117.3	15.2	20.0	96.2	12.0	16.9	21.1	3.3	3.1
Other industries	375.2	64.2	90.8	346.7	58.6	80.4	28.5	5.6	10.3

Source: U.S. Bureau of Economic Analysis, *Survey of Current Business,* October 1997.

Communications and Information Technology

This section presents statistics on the various communications media: telephone, telegraph, radio, television, newspapers and periodicals, and the usage, finances, and operations of the Postal Service. Expenditure data for advertising in the media are also included.

Communication media—The Bureau of the Census *Annual Survey of Communication Services* (ASCS) covers all employer firms with one or more establishments that are primarily engaged in providing point-to-point communication services, whether by wire or radio, and whether intended to be received aurally or visually. This includes telephone communications, including cellular and other radiotelephone services; telegraph and other message communications, such as electronic mail services, facsimile transmission services, telex services, and so on; radio and television broadcasting stations and networks; cable and other pay television services; and other communication services, such as radar station operations, satellite earth stations, satellite or missile tracking stations, and so on. The report presents statistics that are summarized by kind-of-business classification based on the 1987 edition of the *Standard Industrial Classification Manual*.

The Federal Communications Commission (FCC), established in 1934, regulates wire and radio communications. Only the largest carriers and holding companies file annual or monthly financial reports. The FCC has jurisdiction over interstate and foreign communication services, but not over intrastate or local services. The gross operating revenues of the telephone carriers reporting annually to the FCC, however, are estimated to cover about 90 percent of the revenues of all U.S. telephone companies. Data are not comparable with Bureau of the Census *Annual Survey of Communication Services* because of coverage (*ASCS* includes all domestic long-distance telephone companies, all local exchange carriers, and all cellular

In Brief	
Consumer spending per person in 1996:	
Basic cable	$140
Books	$83
Home video	$77
Recorded music	$57
Daily newspapers	$51
Magazines	$37
On-line/Internet access services	$20

telephone companies) and different accounting practices for those telephone companies which report to the FCC.

Reports filed by the broadcasting industry cover substantially all radio and television stations operating in the United States. The private radio services represent the largest and most diverse group of licensees regulated by the FCC. These services provide voice, data communications, point-to-point and point-to-multipoint radio communications for fixed and mobile communicators. Major users of these services are small businesses, the aviation industry, the maritime trades, the land transportation industry, manufacturing industries, state and local public safety and governmental authorities, emergency medical service providers, amateur radio operators, and personal radio operations (CB and the General Mobile Radio Service). The FCC also licenses entities as private and common carriers. Private and common carriers provide fixed and land mobile communications service on a for-profit basis. Principal sources of wire, radio, and television data are the FCC's *Annual Report* and its annual *Statistics of Communications Common Carriers.*

Statistics on the printed media are available from the U.S. Bureau of the Census, as well as from various private agencies. The censuses of manufactures (conducted by the Census Bureau every 5 years, for the years ending in "2" and "7") provide statistics on the number and circulation of newspapers and periodicals and on sales of books and pamphlets. Editor & Publisher Co., New York, NY, presents annual data on the number and circulation of daily and Sunday newspapers in its *International Year Book.* Monthly data on new books and new editions appear in *Publishers Weekly,* issued by R. R. Bowker Company, New York. (See Table 937 for annual data.)

Advertising—Data on advertising expenditures are compiled primarily by McCann-Erickson, Inc., (see Table 943). Monthly index figures of advertising in certain media are also published periodically by McCann-Erickson in *Advertising Age.*

The Broadcast Advertisers Reports distinguishes between spot and local advertising primarily on the basis of the type of advertiser to whom the time is sold, rather than how and by whom it is sold. In general, time purchased on behalf of retail or service establishments in the market is considered local, even though the establishments may be part of a national or regional chain. That is, spot advertising promotes a product, while local advertising promotes a given establishment. Network advertising, mutually exclusive of spot and local, is broadcast through the network system.

Postal Service—The Postal Service provides mail processing and delivery services within the United States. The Postal Reorganization Act of 1970 created the Postal Service, effective July 1971, as an independent establishment of the Federal Executive Branch.

Revenue and cost analysis describes the Postal Service's system of attributing revenues and costs to classes of mail and service. This system draws primarily upon probability sampling techniques to develop estimates of revenues, volumes, and weights, as well as costs by class of mail and special service. The costs attributed to classes of mail and special services are primarily incremental costs which vary in response to changes in volume; they account for roughly 60 percent of the total costs of the Postal Service. The balance represents "institutional costs." Statistics on revenues, volume of mail, and distribution of expenditures are presented in the Postal Service's annual report, *Cost and Revenue Analysis,* and its *Annual Report of the Postmaster General* and its *Annual Comprehensive Statement on Postal Operations.*

Statistical reliability—For a discussion of statistical collection and estimation, sampling procedures, and measures of statistical reliability applicable to Census Bureau data, see Appendix III.

No. 911. Gross Domestic Income in Information Technologies (IT) Industries: 1990 to 1998

[In millions of dollars, except as noted]

INDUSTRY	1987 SIC [1] code	1990	1994	1995	1996 est.	1997 est.	1998 est.
Total all IT industries	(X)	346,971	466,604	517,693	571,734	626,744	682,587
Percent share of the economy	(X)	6.1	6.7	7.1	7.5	7.8	8.1
Hardware	(X)	116,145	155,916	183,580	209,581	232,130	254,115
Computers and equipment	3571,2,5,7	28,677	31,352	32,931	37,154	41,273	45,082
Computers and equipment wholesale sales	5045 (pt)	33,599	43,249	50,756	61,129	67,907	74,173
Computers and equipment retail sales	5734 (pt)	1,857	2,505	2,514	2,836	3,151	3,441
Calculating and office machines, n.e.c. [2]	3578, 9	2,607	2,811	3,036	3,173	3,322	3,478
Electron tubes	3671	1,318	1,357	1,473	1,543	1,623	1,717
Printed circuit boards	3672	4,997	5,042	5,719	6,519	7,105	7,603
Semiconductors	3674	17,855	36,266	51,272	57,933	64,305	70,092
Passive electronic components	3675-9	13,099	18,435	19,098	22,111	25,516	29,802
Industrial instruments for measurement	3823	3,765	4,586	4,999	5,140	5,345	5,547
Instruments for measuring electricity	3825	5,352	6,678	7,512	7,766	8,030	8,399
Laboratory analytical instruments	3826	3,019	3,635	4,271	4,279	4,553	4,781
Software/services [3]	(X)	59,661	89,747	102,595	116,959	133,333	151,999
Computer programming services	7371	14,903	22,674	26,178	(NA)	(NA)	(NA)
Prepackaged software	7372	10,615	17,730	19,972	(NA)	(NA)	(NA)
Computer integrated systems design	7373	9,424	13,829	15,025	(NA)	(NA)	(NA)
Computer processing and data preparation	7374	10,256	15,333	17,925	(NA)	(NA)	(NA)
Information retrieval services	7375	2,435	3,188	3,769	(NA)	(NA)	(NA)
Computer services management	7376	1,369	1,932	2,135	(NA)	(NA)	(NA)
Computer rental leasing	7377	1,588	1,324	1,329	(NA)	(NA)	(NA)
Computer maintenance and repair	7378	4,274	4,740	5,024	(NA)	(NA)	(NA)
Computer related services, n.e.c. [2]	7379	3,006	6,686	8,549	(NA)	(NA)	(NA)
Communications hardware [3]	(X)	24,465	36,341	39,918	44,994	48,107	51,289
Telephone and telegraph equipment	3661	9,619	14,236	14,925	15,614	16,464	17,374
Radio and TV and communications equipment	3663	11,278	16,825	19,862	23,020	25,445	27,854
Communications services	48	146,700	184,600	191,600	200,200	213,174	225,184
Telephone and telegraph communications	481, 2, 9	119,100	142,100	144,100	149,600	157,379	163,674
Radio broadcasting	4832	3,743	5,574	6,150	7,292	8,014	8,696
Television broadcasting	4833	11,757	16,027	17,103	18,373	19,354	20,976
Cable and other pay TV services	4841	12,100	21,320	24,248	24,936	28,427	31,838

NA Not available.　X Not applicable.　[1] 1987 Standard Industrial Classification code. See text, Section 13, Labor Force. [2] N.e.c. means not elsewhere classified.　[3] Includes other industries, not shown separately.
Source: U.S. Department of Commerce, Economics and Statistics Administration, *The Emerging Digital Economy*, April 1998.

No. 912. Information Technologies (IT)—Employment and Wages: 1985 to 1996

INDUSTRY	1987 SIC [1] code	EMPLOYMENT (1,000)			ANNUAL WAGES AND EARNINGS (dol.)		
		1985	1990	1996	1985	1990	1996
Total private	(X)	80,992	91,098	100,076	18,843	23,209	28,352
Total IT-producing industries	(X)	4,056	4,134	4,638	27,768	36,248	48,488
Hardware	(X)	1,666	1,574	1,550	28,098	37,598	48,494
Electronic computers	3571	326	279	190	32,689	46,406	62,379
Computers and equipment wholesalers	5045 (pt)	273	295	301	34,908	46,314	57,536
Computers and equipment retailers	5734 (pt)	54	71	104	20,478	29,051	34,605
Computer storage devices & peripheral equipment	3572, 7	98	94	115	28,114	35,938	50,501
Computer terminals, office & accounting, machines, & office machines, n.e.c. [2]	3575, 8, 9,	76	65	58	28,738	39,259	49,537
Electron tubes	3671	47	32	23	26,808	32,257	40,774
Semiconductors	3674	279	240	256	28,206	38,109	55,149
Printed circuit boards, electronic capacitors, resistors, coils, transformers, & connectors	3672, 5-8	171	169	194	18,453	24,209	29,616
Electronic components, n.e.c. [2]	3679	150	141	137	21,772	27,051	34,371
Industrial instruments for measurement	3823	58	67	66	24,528	31,697	40,464
Instruments for measuring electricity	3825	109	91	75	26,661	36,802	54,029
Analytical instruments	3826	25	30	31	27,973	34,400	47,727
Software/services [3]	(X)	558	790	1,228	27,683	38.764	55.760
Computer programming services	7371	79	151	272	29,311	41,857	57,818
Prepackaged software	7372	55	113	199	32,933	45,505	70,821
Computer integrated systems design	7373	60	98	142	31,569	43,795	59,810
Computer processing & data preparation	7374	192	197	231	23,228	30,452	43,098
Information retrieval services	7375	39	48	68	25,121	32,704	46,501
Computer services management, rental & leasing, & maintenance & repair	7376, 7, 9	91	127	242	30,345	41,185	57,150
Computer maintenance & repair	7378	25	40	53	26,929	34,296	40,072
Communications equipment [3]	(X)	514	461	522	23.919	30.195	37.398
Telephone and telegraph equipment	3661	169	126	113	28,281	37,197	55,562
Radio and TV communications equipment & communications equipment, n.e.c. [2]	3663, 9	148	137	157	26,624	34,468	44,173
Communication services	48	1,319	1,309	1,338	28,885	35.239	46.136
Telephone communications	481	921	913	898	30,951	37,230	49,400
Telephone & telegraph communications	482, 489	52	37	26	17,144	39,699	58,258
Radio broadcasting	4832	113	119	115	18,244	22,088	28,964
Television broadcasting	4833	115	115	128	30,880	41,726	50,732
Cable & other pay TV services	4841	118	126	171	21,633	25,994	35,238

X Not applicable.　[1] 1987 Standard Industrial Classification code. See text, Section 13, Labor Force.　[2] N.e.c. means not elsewhere classified.　[3] Includes other industries, not shown separately.
Source: U.S. Department of Commerce, Economics and Statistics Administration, *The Emerging Digital Economy*, April 1998.

No. 913. Communications Industry—Finances: 1993 to 1996

[In millions of dollars. Covers publicly reporting media and communications companies with revenues of over $1 million in 14 media and communication industry segments]

INDUSTRY	REVENUE				OPERATING INCOME			
	1993	1994	1995	1996	1993	1994	1995	1996
Total	141,070	155,318	174,164	195,588	20,700	22,881	24,205	26,341
Television broadcasting	20,448	22,110	23,133	26,963	3,578	4,350	4,320	5,042
Television network companies	15,582	16,613	16,893	19,772	2,540	3,001	2,669	3,105
Television station broadcasters	4,867	5,497	6,239	7,191	1,038	1,349	1,651	1,937
Radio broadcasting	1,700	2,031	2,308	3,114	219	357	421	561
Radio station broadcasters	1,603	1,875	2,139	2,913	226	353	402	539
Radio network companies	97	157	169	201	-7	4	18	23
Subscription video services........	18,869	19,880	24,439	29,490	3,808	3,531	3,730	3,765
Subscription video services operators .	15,213	15,599	19,356	23,885	3,164	2,856	2,817	2,570
Cable and pay-per-view networks	3,656	4,281	5,083	5,605	644	675	913	1,195
Filmed entertainment	14,445	18,102	22,669	25,684	1,240	1,732	2,471	2,622
Recorded music	7,666	8,715	9,248	8,378	827	1,032	1,133	1,033
Newspaper publishing	18,028	19,489	20,872	22,345	2,679	3,130	2,970	3,512
Consumer book publishing	4,207	4,267	4,302	4,413	544	513	543	444
Consumer magazine publishing	8,591	8,658	9,090	9,717	911	943	995	1,038
Business-to-business communications..	1,778	1,973	2,215	2,317	178	219	254	279
Professional and educational publishing .	7,576	8,692	9,764	10,904	828	942	1,001	1,590
Business information services	15,245	17,647	20,297	23,209	2,376	2,984	3,446	3,807
Advertising agencies	7,886	8,420	9,390	10,578	713	858	1,016	1,168
Interactive digital media	7,843	7,812	7,446	8,447	1,785	1,199	750	150
Specialty media and marketing services .	6,788	7,522	8,991	10,030	1,016	1,092	1,156	1,331

Source: Veronis, Suhler & Associates Inc., New York, NY, *Communications Industry Report,* annual (copyright).

No. 914. Media Usage and Consumer Spending: 1990 to 2001

[Estimates of time spent were derived using rating data for television and radio, survey research and consumer purchase data for recorded music, newspapers, magazines, books, home video, admissions for movies, and consumer online/Internet access services. Adults 18 and older except for recorded music, movies in theaters, and video games where estimates include persons 12 years and older]

ITEM	1990	1992	1993	1994	1995	1996	1997, proj.	1998, proj.	1999, proj.	2000, proj.	2001, proj.
HOURS PER PERSON PER YEAR											
Total................	3,263	3,325	3,296	3,395	3,393	3,395	3,402	3,402	3,405	3,429	3,440
Television.................	1,470	1,510	1,535	1,560	1,575	1,567	1,564	1,552	1,548	1,555	1,551
Broadcast TV.............	1,120	1,073	1,082	1,091	1,019	980	942	907	873	854	830
Network stations [1]......	780	914	920	919	836	803	759	730	690	666	642
Independent stations	340	159	162	172	183	177	183	177	183	188	188
Subscription video services ..	350	437	453	469	556	587	622	645	675	701	721
Basic networks [2]	260	359	375	388	468	498	528	547	571	592	612
Premium channels........	90	78	78	81	88	89	94	98	104	109	109
Radio	1,135	1,150	1,082	1,102	1,091	1,091	1,089	1,085	1,076	1,074	1,072
Recorded music	235	233	248	294	289	289	296	303	313	325	336
Daily newspapers	175	172	170	169	165	161	158	157	155	154	153
Consumer books	95	100	99	102	99	99	97	96	97	98	99
Consumer magazines........	90	85	85	84	84	83	81	80	80	79	79
Home video [3]	38	42	43	45	45	49	52	54	56	58	60
Movies in theaters	12	11	12	12	12	12	12	12	12	12	12
Home video games	12	19	19	22	24	26	29	31	33	35	37
Consumer on-line Internet access..	1	2	2	3	7	16	22	30	33	37	39
Educational software	(Z)	1	1	2	2	2	2	2	2	2	2
CONSUMER SPENDING PER PERSON PER YEAR (dol.)											
Total	365.42	398.17	423.82	452.08	479.12	512.05	545.63	582.63	616.66	651.37	685.18
Television	87.90	101.39	109.02	110.89	125.54	140.37	155.70	168.75	178.23	187.60	196.62
Broadcast TV.............	-	-	-	-	-	-	-	-	-	-	-
Subscription video services ..	87.90	101.39	109.02	110.89	125.54	140.37	155.70	168.75	178.23	187.60	196.62
Radio	-	-	-	-	-	-	-	-	-	-	-
Recorded music	36.64	43.05	47.42	56.35	56.93	57.33	59.21	61.54	64.40	67.99	71.56
Daily newspapers	47.55	48.54	48.25	49.12	50.08	50.95	51.59	52.62	54.05	55.27	56.31
Consumer books	63.90	71.39	75.28	80.28	81.39	82.98	84.67	88.09	92.38	97.68	102.86
Consumer magazines........	33.14	34.26	35.27	36.36	36.10	36.63	37.22	37.92	38.91	39.96	40.92
Home video [3]	56.35	59.25	64.17	68.96	70.99	77.43	82.51	88.79	96.33	104.76	113.72
Movies in theaters	24.40	23.24	24.33	25.20	25.39	27.04	26.39	26.62	27.13	27.35	27.56
Home video games	12.39	11.51	12.56	13.15	13.34	14.92	16.86	18.59	19.88	20.87	21.65
Consumer on-line Internet access..	2.93	4.39	5.35	7.44	15.03	20.01	27.23	35.30	40.88	45.35	49.32
Educational software	0.22	1.14	2.17	4.34	4.34	4.38	4.26	4.43	4.46	4.53	4.66

- Represents zero.   Z Less than 1 hour.   [1] Affiliates of the Fox network are counted as network affiliates for part of 1991 and all latter years, but as independent stations in earlier years. Beginning 1995, includes UPN and WB affiliates.   [2] Includes TBS beginning in 1992.   [3] Playback of prerecorded tapes only.

Source: Veronis, Suhler & Associates Inc., New York, NY, *Communications Industry Report,* annual (copyright).

No. 915. Utilization of Selected Media: 1970 to 1996

ITEM	Unit	1970	1980	1985	1990	1991	1992	1993	1994	1995	1996
Households with—											
Telephone service [1]	Percent .	87.0	93.0	91.8	93.3	93.6	93.9	94.2	93.9	93.9	93.8
Radio [2]	Millions .	62.0	78.6	87.1	94.4	95.5	96.6	97.3	98.0	98.0	98.0
Percent of total households . .	Percent .	98.6	99.0	99.0	99.0	99.0	99.0	99.0	99.0	99.0	99.0
Average number of sets	Number .	5.1	5.5	5.5	5.6	5.6	5.6	5.6	5.6	5.6	5.6
Television [3]	Millions .	59	76	85	92	93	92	93	94	95	96
Percent of total households . .	Percent .	95.3	97.9	98.1	98.2	98.2	98.3	98.3	98.3	98.3	98.3
Television sets in homes . . .	Millions .	81	128	155	193	193	192	201	211	217	223
Average number of sets per home	Number .	1.4	1.7	1.8	2.1	2.1	2.1	2.2	2.2	2.3	2.3
Color sets	Millions .	21	63	78	90	91	91	92	93	94	95
Cable television [4]	Millions .	4	15	36	52	55	55	57	59	60	63
Percent of TV households . . .	Percent .	6.7	19.9	42.8	56.4	58.9	60.2	61.4	62.4	63.4	65.3
VCR's [4]	Millions .	(NA)	1	18	63	67	69	72	74	77	79
Percent of TV households . . .	Percent .	(NA)	1.1	20.8	68.6	71.9	75.0	77.1	79.0	81.0	82.2
Commercial radio stations: [2]											
AM	Number .	4,323	4,589	[5]4,718	4,987	4,985	4,961	4,994	4,913	4,150	4,747
FM	Number .	2,196	3,282	[5]3,875	4,392	4,570	4,785	4,971	5,109	5,730	7,566
Television stations: [6] Total	Number .	862	1,011	1,182	1,442	1,459	1,481	1,506	1,512	1,532	1,533
Commercial [3]	Number .	677	734	883	1,092	1,099	1,118	1,137	1,145	1161	1,174
VHF	Number .	501	516	520	547	547	551	552	561	562	554
UHF	Number .	176	218	363	545	552	567	585	584	599	620
Cable television:											
Systems [6]	Number .	2,490	4,225	6,844	9,575	10,704	11,075	11,217	11,214	11,218	11,119
Households served [7]	Millions .	4.5	17.7	39.9	54.9	55.8	56.4	57.2	60.5	64.7	67.0
Daily newspaper circulation [8]	Millions .	62	62	63	62	61	60	60	59	57	57

NA Not available. [1] For occupied housing units. 1970 and 1980 as of April 1; all other years as of March. Source: U.S. Bureau of the Census, *1970* and *1980 Census of Housing*, vol. 1; thereafter Federal Communications Commission, *Trends in Telephone Service*, July 1998. [2] As of December 31, except as noted. Source: Radio Advertising Bureau, New York, NY, through 1992, *Radio Facts*, annual, (copyright); beginning 1993, *Radio Marketing Guide and Fact Book for Advertisers*, annual, (copyright). Number of stations on the air compiled from Federal Communications Commission reports. [3] 1970, as of September of prior year; all other years as of January of year shown. Excludes Alaska and Hawaii. Source: Television Bureau of Advertising, Inc., *Trends in Television*, annual, (copyright). [4] As of February. Excludes Alaska and Hawaii. Source: See footnote 3. [5] As of February 1986. [6] As of January 1. Source: Warren Publishing, Washington DC, *Television and Cable Factbook* (copyright). [7] Source: Nielsen Media Research, *Nielsen Station Index*, November diary estimates (copyright). [8] As of September 30. Source: Editor & Publisher, Co., New York, NY, *Editor & Publisher International Year Book*, annual, (copyright).

Source: Compiled from sources mentioned in footnotes.

No. 916. Multimedia Audiences—Summary: 1998

[In percent, except total. As of **spring**. For persons 18 years old and over. Represents the percent of persons participating during a specified time period. Based on sample and subject to sampling error; see source for details]

ITEM	Total population (1,000)	Television viewing	Television prime time viewing	Cable viewing	Radio listening	Newspaper reading	Accessed Internet [1]
Total	**195,192**	**91.9**	**77.2**	**66.8**	**83.3**	**81.3**	**22.4**
18 to 24 years old.	24,842	89.6	72.4	62.8	90.1	75.6	27.6
25 to 34 years old.	40,972	90.2	76.0	63.4	90.4	79.4	28.9
35 to 44 years old.	43,561	90.3	76.1	69.8	89.4	83.3	28.2
45 to 54 years old	32,521	91.4	78.9	71.4	85.9	84.2	27.7
55 to 64 years old	21,227	95.4	79.3	69.5	77.4	82.7	12.8
65 years old and over	32,069	96.0	81.1	63.9	61.7	81.7	3.0
Male.	93,553	91.9	76.3	67.7	85.2	81.7	25.3
Female	101,639	91.8	78.1	66.0	81.5	81.0	19.6
White	164,831	91.6	77.0	68.3	83.6	82.1	23.2
Black	22,686	94.8	79.7	60.1	83.5	76.5	12.8
Other	7,674	88.6	74.3	54.4	76.2	78.4	32.6
Spanish speaking	19,624	92.6	80.1	48.7	84.6	65.7	13.8
Not high school graduate	36,372	93.1	76.4	50.8	72.2	64.8	3.6
High school graduate	64,868	92.7	78.8	68.9	82.2	80.7	10.8
Attended college.	51,498	91.8	77.5	71.5	87.9	85.8	28.5
College graduate	42,453	89.6	75.4	71.8	88.8	90.9	48.7
Employed:							
Full time	107,605	90.5	75.8	70.4	90.3	83.3	30.0
Part time	19,881	92.1	75.2	66.1	87.4	83.0	26.4
Not employed.	67,705	94.0	80.2	61.4	70.9	77.7	9.0
Household income:							
Less than $10,000.	15,846	93.0	78.3	42.4	71.6	65.3	5.8
$10,000 to $19,999	26,824	93.0	79.7	52.5	70.7	71.9	5.5
$20,000 to $29,999	27,129	92.9	78.3	61.5	79.0	78.5	11.4
$30,000 to $34,999	12,815	91.1	75.7	67.4	80.6	81.2	13.9
$35,000 to $39,999	12,389	92.9	79.1	70.0	86.4	81.6	18.1
$40,000 to $49,999	22,135	92.1	77.8	71.1	86.9	82.9	19.2
$50,000 or more	78,052	90.8	75.6	76.8	90.4	88.3	38.3

[1] In the last 30 days.

Source: Mediamark Research Inc., New York, NY, *Multimedia Audiences*, spring 1998 (copyright).

No. 917. Internet Access and Usage, and Online Service Usage: 1998

[**As of spring.** For persons 18 years old and over. For composition regions, see inside front cover. Based on sample and subject to sampling error; see source for details]

ITEM	Total adults	Any Online/ Internet usage	HAVE INTERNET ACCESS			USED THE INTERNET IN THE LAST 30 DAYS			Used any online service in the past 30 days
			Home or work	Home only	Work only	Home or work	Home only	Work only	
Total adults (1,000)	**195,192**	**44,873**	**62,273**	**37,047**	**29,791**	**43,643**	**27,595**	**20,395**	**34,227**
PERCENT DISTRIBUTION									
Age:									
18 to 34 years old	33.7	42.6	40.9	35.9	33.7	42.8	37.0	35.5	42.2
35 to 54 years old	39.0	48.8	48.2	53.2	57.2	48.8	53.6	57.2	49.2
55 years old and over	27.3	8.6	10.8	10.8	9.1	8.4	9.4	7.3	8.6
Sex:									
Male	47.9	53.9	51.7	52.5	55.7	54.3	55.9	58.4	53.8
Female	52.1	46.1	48.3	47.5	44.3	45.7	44.1	41.6	46.2
Census region:									
Northeast.	20.1	22.4	22.8	23.8	22.4	22.5	23.3	22.4	23.5
Midwest.	23.3	22.5	23.1	21.6	23.6	22.8	21.3	22.5	21.1
South	35.0	29.9	30.0	29.2	29.9	29.7	29.7	30.0	31.5
West	21.6	25.2	24.0	25.3	24.1	25.0	25.6	25.1	23.9
Household size:									
1 to 2 persons	45.3	36.9	35.8	31.6	39.8	37.0	34.4	39.6	36.5
3 to 4 persons	39.3	47.9	48.1	50.8	46.1	47.7	49.6	46.6	48.4
5 or more persons	15.4	15.3	16.1	17.7	14.0	15.3	16.0	13.8	15.1
Any child in household	41.7	46.9	47.4	50.4	48.3	46.8	49.3	47.8	47.3
Marital status:									
Single	23.1	29.3	27.9	23.4	20.7	29.4	24.0	22.7	28.8
Married	57.6	61.4	61.6	68.0	67.5	61.4	68.0	66.7	61.9
Other	19.3	9.3	10.5	8.6	11.7	9.2	8.1	10.6	9.3
Educational attainment:									
Graduated college plus	21.7	46.9	41.8	45.8	54.7	47.4	49.4	60.0	45.9
Attended college	26.4	33.9	34.5	32.3	28.6	33.6	31.8	27.0	34.7
Did not attend college	51.9	19.2	23.7	21.9	16.7	19.1	18.8	13.0	19.4
Household income:									
Less than $50,000.	60.0	31.8	34.3	27.6	24.5	31.6	26.9	21.9	30.7
$50,000 to $74,000	20.3	28.2	28.3	29.0	29.4	28.2	28.4	28.9	28.3
$75,000 to $149,000	16.5	32.5	30.2	34.3	37.9	32.7	35.5	40.3	33.0
$150,000 or more	3.1	7.5	7.1	9.2	8.2	7.5	9.2	8.9	8.0

Source: Mediamark Research Inc., New York, NY, *CyberStats, spring 98* (copyright). Internet site <http://www.mediamart.com/pages/freedata.htm> (accessed 17 June 1998).

No. 918. Telephone Companies—Summary: 1988 to 1995

[**As of Dec. 31** or **calendar year,** as applicable. January 1, 1988, marked the beginning of significant rules changes in the way local exchange carriers account for assets, liabilities, revenue, expenses, and income. Any comparisons with earlier data would not be meaningful]

ITEM	Unit	INDEPENDENT COMPANIES [1]				ALL TELEPHONE COMPANIES			
		1988	1990	1994	1995	1988	1990	1994	1995
All companies	Number .	1,349	1,310	1,314	1,312	1,371	1,332	1,333	1,331
Access lines	Millions .	29	32	37.4	39.8	130	138	157.9	165.8
Total telephone plant	Bil. dol. .	59	65	82.3	85.8	238	256	296.2	308.1
Operating revenues	Bil. dol. .	21	22	29.6	30.2	90	90	103	105
Avg. daily conversations [2] . .	Millions .	(NA)	(NA)	(NA)	(NA)	1,700	9,515	11,158	11,641
Reporting companies [3]	Number .	585	594	563	568	607	616	582	587
Access lines	Millions .	29	30	35.2	36.7	130	136	155.8	162.7
Telephone plant in service . .	Bil. dol. .	57	63	73.8	77.4	233	251	284.1	295.9
Depreciation reserves [4] . . .	Bil. dol. .	20	24	31.1	34.2	80	95	122.7	134.3
Operating revenues	Bil. dol. .	21	22	25.1	26.2	86	89	98.4	101.1
Operating expenses [5]	Bil. dol. .	14	16	18.0	19.6	61	65	73.8	76.5
Net income	Bil. dol. .	3	3	4.0	3.2	12	12	99	11.3
Stockholders' equity	Bil. dol. .	20	22	25.4	25.7	76	80	78.8	78.8
Net income to stockholders equity	Percent .	16	15	15.7	12.5	16	14	12.6	14.3
Employees	1,000. . .	170	161	135	132	639	606	501	477

NA Not available. [1] Companies independent of the Bell System, prior to divestiture of January 1984. [2] Average business day conversations in 1988. Average business day minutes of use beginning in 1990. [3] Comprises only companies submitting operating information to source cited below. [4] Total accumulated depreciation and amortization. [5] Excludes federal income tax.

Source: United States Telephone Association, Washington, DC, *Statistics of the Local Exchange Carriers,* annual (copyright).

No. 919. Telephone Systems: 1985 to 1996

[Covers principal carriers filing annual reports with Federal Communications Commission]

ITEM	Unit	1985	1989	1990	1991	1992	1993	1994	1995	1996
LOCAL EXCHANGE CARRIERS [1]										
Carriers [2]	Number .	55	51	51	52	54	53	52	53	51
Access lines	Millions. .	112	126	130	137	140	149	157	166	178
Business access lines	Millions. .	31	34	36	38	39	41	42	46	49
Residential access lines	Millions. .	79	87	89	91	93	96	98	101	104
Other access lines (public, mobile, special)	Millions. .	2	5	6	7	8	13	17	19	25
Number of local calls (originating)	Billions . .	365	389	402	416	434	447	465	484	504
Number of toll calls (originating)	Billions . .	(NA)	(NA)	63	67	72	78	83	94	95
Gross book cost of plant	Bil. dol.	191	233	240	246	254	264	272	284	296
Depreciation and amortization reserves	Bil. dol.	49	84	89	93	99	107	116	127	138
Net plant.	Bil. dol.	142	150	151	153	155	156	157	157	158
Total assets.	Bil. dol.	162	177	180	184	187	192	196	197	198
Total stockholders equity	Bil. dol.	63	72	74	76	77	73	72	72	74
Operating revenues	Bil. dol.	73	83	84	86	87	90	93	96	101
Local revenues.	Bil. dol.	32	35	37	38	40	42	43	46	50
Operating expenses [3]	Bil. dol.	48	60	62	63	64	66	70	72	74
Net operating income [4]	Bil. dol.	13	14	14	14	14	14	13	14	16
Net income	Bil. dol.	9	10	11	10	9	5	9	11	13
Employees	(1,000) .	(NA)	592	569	538	527	507	474	447	437
Compensation of employees	Bil. dol.	(NA)	21	23	22	22	23	22	21	23
Average monthly residential local telephone rate [5]	Dollars . .	14.54	17.53	17.79	18.66	18.70	18.94	19.07	19.49	19.58
Average monthly single-line business telephone rate [5]	Dollars . .	38.39	41.25	41.21	42.12	42.29	42.57	41.64	41.77	41.83
LONG DISTANCE CARRIERS										
Number of carriers with presubscribed lines.	Number .	(NA)	302	325	388	414	436	511	583	621
Number of presubscribed lines	Millions. .	(NA)	128	132	135	139	143	148	153	159
Total toll service revenues	Bil. dol. .	43	51	52	54	58	62	67	74	82
Interstate switched access minutes	Bil. min. .	167	277	307	328	350	371	401	432	469
INTERNATIONAL TELEPHONE SERVICE [6]										
Number of U.S. billed calls.	Millions. .	411	835	984	1,371	1,643	1,926	2,313	2,821	3,485
Number of U.S. billed minutes	Millions. .	3,446	6,751	8,030	8,986	10,156	11,393	13,393	15,837	19,119
U.S. billed revenues	Mil. dol.	3,487	6,901	8,042	9,096	10,179	11,353	12,255	13,990	14,079
U.S. carrier revenue net of settlements with foreign carriers.	Mil. dol.	2,358	4,503	5,280	5,798	6,835	7,649	7,966	9,053	8,433
Revenue from private-line service	Mil. dol.	172	208	201	303	313	356	440	506	649
Revenue from resale service	Mil. dol.	(NA)	113	167	440	511	593	1,120	1,687	3,457

NA Not available. [1] Gross operating revenues, gross plant, and total assets of reporting carriers estimated at more than 90 percent of total industry. New accounting rules became effective in 1989; prior years may not be directly comparable on a one-to-one basis. Includes Virgin Islands, and prior to 1991, Puerto Rico. [2] The reporting threshold for carriers is $100 million. [3] Excludes taxes. [4] After tax deductions. [5] Based on surveys conducted by FCC. [6] Beginning 1991, includes calls to and from Alaska, Hawaii, Puerto Rico, Canada, and Mexico.

Source: U.S. Federal Communications Commission, *Statistics of Communications Common Carriers,* annual.

No. 920. Telephone Communications—Operating Revenue and Expenses: 1990 to 1996

[Based on a sample of employer firms with one or more establishments that are primarily engaged in providing telephone, voice, and data communication services. For SIC 481. Based on the 1987 Standard Industrial Classification code; see text, Section 13, Labor Force]

ITEM	TOTAL (mil. dol.)					PERCENT DISTRIBUTION		
	1990	1993	1994	1995	1996	1990	1995	1996
OPERATING REVENUE								
Total	160,482	183,538	199,259	216,296	238,063	100.0	100.0	100.0
Local service	40,180	45,178	46,662	49,349	53,403	25.0	22.8	22.4
Long-distance service	67,698	73,923	81,037	86,834	94,039	42.2	40.1	39.5
Network access	30,044	31,658	32,988	34,131	36,101	18.7	15.8	15.2
Cellular and other radiotelephone	6,002	12,401	16,848	22,837	28,520	3.7	10.6	12.0
Directory advertising	8,373	9,117	9,439	9,850	10,214	5.2	4.6	4.3
Other	8,185	11,261	12,285	13,295	15,786	5.1	6.1	6.6
OPERATING EXPENSES								
Total	131,493	160,273	164,936	180,538	192,349	100.0	100.0	100.0
Annual payroll.	34,903	37,106	38,106	40,721	42,087	26.5	22.6	21.9
Employer contributions to Social Security and other supplemental benefits.	8,121	9,379	9,347	9,184	9,611	6.2	5.1	5.0
Access charges	23,214	27,035	30,047	33,748	36,018	17.7	18.7	18.7
Depreciation.	22,927	25,546	28,578	31,651	32,937	17.4	17.5	17.1
Lease and rental.	3,543	3,608	4,037	3,919	4,492	2.7	2.2	2.3
Purchased repairs	2,977	3,474	4,413	4,907	5,243	2.3	2.7	2.7
Insurance	193	228	261	304	336	0.1	0.2	0.2
Telephone and other purchased communication services	504	946	1,321	1,858	2,030	0.4	1.0	1.1
Purchased utilities	1,106	1,315	1,562	1,770	1,961	0.8	1.0	1.0
Purchased advertising	2,328	3,085	3,835	3,607	4,534	1.8	2.0	2.4
Taxes	5,086	5,861	6,603	7,539	7,978	3.9	4.2	4.1
Other	26,591	42,690	36,826	41,330	45,122	20.2	22.9	23.5

Source: U.S. Bureau of the Census, *Annual Survey of Communication Services.*

No. 921. Cellular Telephone Industry: 1990 to 1997

[Calendar year data, except as noted. Based on a survey mailed to all cellular, personal communications services, and enhanced special mobile radio systems. For 1997 data, the universe was 2,228 systems and the response rate was 90 percent]

ITEM	UNIT	1990	1991	1992	1993	1994	1995	1996	1997
Systems.............	Number .	751	1,252	1,506	1,529	1,581	1,627	1,740	2,228
Subscribers.............	1,000 .	5,283	7,557	11,033	16,009	24,134	33,786	44,043	55,312
Cell sites [1].............	Number .	5,616	7,847	10,307	12,805	17,920	22,663	30,045	51,600
Employees.............	Number .	21,382	26,327	34,348	39,775	53,902	68,165	84,161	109,387
Service revenue........[2]	Mil. dol.	4,548	5,708	7,822	10,891	14,229	19,081	23,635	27,486
Roamer revenue [2].....	Mil. dol.	456	704	974	1,360	1,830	2,542	2,781	2,974
Capital investment.......	Mil. dol.	6,282	8,672	11,262	13,946	18,939	24,080	32,574	46,058
Average monthly bill [3].....	Dollars. .	80.90	72.74	68.68	61.48	56.21	51.00	47.70	42.78
Average length of call [3].....	Minutes .	2.20	2.38	2.58	2.41	2.24	2.15	2.32	2.31

[1] The basic geographic unit of a cellular system. A city or county is divided into smaller "cells," each of which is equipped with a low-powered radio transmitter/receiver. The cells can vary in size depending upon terrain, capacity demands, etc. By controlling the transmission power, the radio frequencies assigned to one cell can be limited to the boundaries of that cell. When a cellular phone moves from one cell toward another, a computer at the Switching Office monitors the movement and at the proper time, transfers or hands off the phone call to the new cell and another radio frequency. [2] Service revenue generated by subscribers' calls outside of their system areas. [3] As of December 31.

Source: Cellular Telecommunications Industry Association, Washington, DC, *State of the Cellular Industry*, annual (copyright).

No. 922. Wireless Bureau Stations Authorized, by Class: 1996

[In thousands. For calendar year. Includes Puerto Rico and the Virgin Islands]

CLASS	Number of stations	CLASS	Number of stations
Total................	2,228	Radiolocation	4
Aviation:		Video production	-
Aircraft................	128	Relay press	-
Ground	12	Telephone maintenance	5
Marine:		Land transportation:	
Ship	631	Railroad................	7
Coast	11	Taxicab	2
Public safety:		Automobile emergency	3
Police	27	Interurban passenger	-
Fire................	23	Interurban property	3
Local Government	41	Urban passenger	-
Highway maintenance	9	Urban property	1
Forestry conservation	7	Miscellaneous:	
Special emergency................	19	220 MHz	4
Emergency medical	1	800/900 MHz base................	32
Industrial:		800/900 MHz mobile	113
Special industrial	46	Broadcast auxiliary................	19
Business	282	General mobile	14
Power	24	Interactive video data (IVDS)	1
Petroleum................	12	Amateur	664
Manufacturers................	15	Microwave Part 94	40
Forest products	4	Microwave auxiliary broadcast................	21

- Represents zero.
Source: U.S. Federal Communications Commission, *Annual Report*; and unpublished data.

No. 923. Radio and Television Broadcasting Services—Finances: 1990 to 1996

[In millions of dollars. Based on a sample of taxable employer firms with one or more establishments primarily engaged in broadcasting to the public, except cable and other pay television services. Based on the 1987 Standard Industrial Classification Code; see text, Section 13, Labor Force]

ITEM	TOTAL (SIC 483)			RADIO (SIC 4832)			TELEVISION (SIC 4833)		
	1990	1995	1996	1990	1995	1996	1990	1995	1996
**Operating revenue.......... **	**28,017**	**34,319**	**37,542**	**6,954**	**8,518**	**9,305**	**21,063**	**25,801**	**28,237**
Station time sales	19,019	22,450	24,130	6,397	7,779	8,476	12,622	14,671	15,654
Network compensation	549	564	631	105	71	81	444	493	550
National/regional advertising	7,226	8,166	8,476	1,522	1,765	1,750	5,704	6,401	6,726
Local advertising	11,244	13,720	15,023	4,770	5,943	6,645	6,474	7,777	8,378
Network time sales	7,905	10,319	11,792	305	464	498	7,600	9,855	11,294
Other	1,093	1,550	1,620	252	275	331	841	1,275	1,289
**Operating expenses .... **	**24,145**	**28,038**	**30,721**	**6,317**	**6,997**	**7,499**	**17,828**	**21,041**	**23,222**
Annual payroll................	6,333	7,933	8,497	2,428	2,864	3,065	3,905	5,069	5,432
Employer contributions to social security and other supplemental benefits......	998	1,303	1,400	326	361	389	672	942	1,011
Broadcast rights	7,642	8,260	9,404	264	304	287	7,378	7,956	9,117
Music license fees................	373	405	454	159	204	224	214	201	230
Depreciation................	1,345	1,324	1,455	477	403	440	868	921	1,015
Lease and rental................	469	538	590	197	226	239	272	312	351
Purchased repairs	232	300	331	79	76	78	153	224	253
Insurance	143	168	188	64	69	79	79	99	109
Telephone and other purchased communication services	240	278	319	115	123	134	125	155	185
Purchased utilities................	246	281	310	99	104	110	147	177	200
Purchased advertising	947	1,115	1,195	368	409	407	579	706	788
Taxes................	176	217	229	60	71	71	116	146	158
Other	5,001	5,916	6,349	1,681	1,783	1,976	3,320	4,133	4,373

Source: U.S. Bureau of the Census, *Annual Survey of Communication Services*.

No. 924. Copyright Registration, by Subject Matter: 1990 to 1997

[In thousands. For years ending September 30. Comprises claims to copyrights registered for both U.S. and foreign works]

SUBJECT MATTER	1990	1995	1996	1997	SUBJECT MATTER	1990	1995	1996	1997
Total [1]	643.5	609.2	550.4	569.2	Sound recordings	37.5	34.0	29.9	35.7
Monographs [1]	179.7	196.0	187.2	176.4	Renewals	51.8	30.6	23.7	28.6
Semiconductor chip products	1.0	0.8	0.8	1.0	Musical works [2]	185.3	163.6	133.5	154.4
Serials	111.5	88.7	83.4	83.3	Works of the visual arts [3]	76.7	95.5	91.6	89.6

[1] Includes computer software and machine readable works. [2] Includes dramatic works, accompanying music, choreography, pantomimes motion pictures, and filmstrips. [3] Two-dimensional works of fine and graphic art, including prints and art reproductions; sculptural works; technical drawings and models; photographs; commercial prints and labels; works of applied arts, cartographic works, and multimedia works.

Source: The Library of Congress, Copyright Office, *Annual Report.*

No. 925. Public Television Programming: 1984 to 1996

[For October through September seasons. General programming is directed at the general community. Instructional programming is directed at students in the classroom or otherwise in the general context of formal education]

ITEM	1984	1986	1988	1990	1992	1994	1996
Stations broadcasting	303	305	322	341	349	349	352
Number of broadcasters [1]	169	178	186	193	198	198	201
Average annual hours per broadcaster	5,542	5,650	6,135	6,392	6,303	6,500	6,758
BROADCAST HOURS, PERCENT DISTRIBUTION							
Program content	100	100	100	100	100	100	100
General [2]	88	86	85	86	90	92	92
News and public affairs	14	16	16	18	17	19	19
Information and skills	26	30	32	32	29	27	29
Cultural	20	21	18	19	18	16	17
General children's and youth's	8	7	6	6	15	20	20
Sesame Street	15	11	12	11	11	9	8
Other	6	2	1	1	1	1	1
Instructional [3]	13	15	16	14	12	9	8
Children and youth	12	(NA)	(NA)	(NA)	9	6	5
Adult	1	(NA)	(NA)	(NA)	3	3	3
Producer	100	100	100	100	100	100	100
Local	6	5	5	5	4	5	5
Any public TV source	44	38	27	32	31	33	36
U.S. Coproduction [4]	3	3	10	10	6	6	6
Children's TV Workshop	16	[5]29	16	15	14	12	9
Independent producer	9	([5])	19	19	25	26	27
Foreign producer, international coproduction	13	15	14	12	11	10	10
Commercial producer	3	6	4	4	5	5	4
Other	5	4	4	3	4	4	4
Distributor	100	100	100	100	100	100	100
Local distribution only	6	5	6	6	5	4	5
Public broadcasting service	65	64	62	59	63	63	63
Regional public television network	13	14	18	24	23	23	25
Other	16	17	14	11	9	9	8

NA Not available. [1] Beginning 1988, only broadcasters in the 50 U.S. States were surveyed. In prior years, the stations in the outlying areas were also included. [2] Beginning 1986, this category includes "Business or Consumer." [3] Some general audience programs with instructional applications were double counted if aired during school hours when school was in session. "The Electric Company" was one such program. [4] Prior to 1986, "Consortium." [5] Independent producer included with Children's TV Workshop for 1986.

Source: Corporation for Public Broadcasting, Washington, DC, *Programming Survey*, biennial.

No. 926. Public Broadcasting Systems—Income, by Source: 1980 to 1996

[In millions of dollars, except number of stations and percents. Stations as of Dec. 31; fiscal year data for income. Includes nonbroadcast income]

NUMBER OF STATIONS AND INCOME SOURCE	1980	1985	1990	1993	1994	1995	1996	PERCENT DISTRIBUTION		
								1980	1990	1996
CPB-qualified public radio stations [1]	217	288	318	400	403	407	408	(X)	(X)	(X)
Public television stations	290	317	341	352	351	351	352	(X)	(X)	(X)
Total income	705	1,096	1,581	1,790	1,795	1,917	1,956	100	100	100
Federal government	193	179	267	370	330	338	339	27	17	17
State and local government [2]	272	358	474	475	510	560	518	39	30	27
Subscribers and auction/marathon	102	248	364	412	420	447	477	15	23	24
Business and industry	72	171	262	285	301	294	291	10	17	15
Foundation	24	43	71	100	97	109	159	3	5	8
Other	43	97	143	149	137	169	172	6	9	9

X Not applicable. [1] Includes CPB-supported developmental grantees/stations, and excludes repeater stations. [2] Includes income received from state and other public colleges and universities.

Source: Corporation for Public Broadcasting (CPB), Washington, DC, *Public Broadcasting Income, Fiscal Year, 1996;* and unpublished data.

No. 927. Cable Television—Systems and Subscribers: 1970 to 1997

[Subscribers in thousands, except percent. Estimated]

YEAR (As of Jan. 1)	Sys-tems	Sub-scribers	YEAR (As of Jan. 1)	Sys-tems	Sub-scribers	SUBSCRIBER SIZE-GROUP	NUMBER OF [1]—		PERCENT OF [1]—	
							Sys-tems	Sub-scribers	Sys-tems	Sub-scribers
1970	2,490	4,500	1988	8,500	44,000	**1997, total** [2]	10,838	62,448	100	100
1975	3,506	9,800	1989	9,050	47,500	50,000 and over	265	29,919	2	48
1980	4,225	16,000	1990	9,575	50,000	20,000 to 49,999.	446	13,436	4	22
1981	4,375	18,300	1991	10,704	51,000	10,000 to 19,999.	508	7,181	5	12
1982	4,825	21,000	1992	11,075	53,000	5,000 to 9,999	665	4,570	6	7
1983	5,600	25,000	1993	11,100	55,000	3,500 to 4,999	399	1,662	4	3
1984	6,200	30,000	1994	11,200	57,000	1,000 to 3,499	1,967	3,722	18	6
1985	6,600	32,000	1995	11,126	58,000	500 to 999	1,434	1,034	13	2
1986	7,600	37,500	1996	11,119	60,280	250 to 499	1,468	528	14	1
1987	7,900	41,100	1997	10,850	64,050	Less than 250	3,323	396	31	1

[1] As of October 1. [2] Total number of systems includes 363 not available by subscriber size-group.

Source: Warren Publishing, Inc., Washington, DC, *Television & Cable Factbook,* annual (copyright).

No. 928. Cable and Pay TV—Summary: 1980 to 1997

[Cable TV for calendar year. Pay TV as of **Dec. 31** of year shown]

YEAR	CABLE TV				PAY TV					
	Avg. basic subscrib-ers (1,000)	Avg. monthly basic rate (dol.)	Revenue [1] (mil. dol.)		Units [2] (1,000)		Monthly rate (dol.)		Percent of homes passed by cable with pay TV	Percent of homes with cable TV with pay TV
			Total	Basic	Total [3]	Pay cable	Total pay [3]	Pay cable		
1980	17,500	7.69	2,609	1,615	8,581	7,336	8.91	8.62	26	47
1985	35,440	9.73	8,831	4,138	29,885	29,418	10.29	10.25	46	82
1990	50,520	16.78	17,582	10,174	39,902	39,751	10.35	10.30	46	77
1995	60,900	23.07	25,556	16,860	53,323	44,473	[4]8.54	8.54	50	74
1996	62,800	24.41	27,951	18,395	59,422	46,057	[4]8.35	8.35	51	75
1997	64,210	26.48	30,784	20,405	65,395	46,445	[4]8.29	8.00	51	74

[1] Includes installation revenue, subscriber revenue, and nonsubscriber revenue. [2] Individual program services sold to subscribers. [3] Includes multipoint distribution service (MDS), satellite TV (STV), multipoint multichannel distribution service (MMDS), satellite master antenna TV (SMATV), C-band satellite, and DBS satellite. [4] Direct broadcast satellite average rate not included.

Source: Paul Kagan Associates Inc., Carmel, CA, *The Cable TV Financial Databook,* annual, 1997 (copyright); *The Cable TV Investor,* April 14, 1998; and *The Pay TV Newsletter,* March 31, 1996, and February 28, 1998.

No. 929. Cable and Pay TV—Revenue and Expenses: 1990 to 1996

[Based on a sample of taxable employer firms with one or more establishments that are primarily engaged in the dissemination of visual and textual television programs on a subscription or fee basis. For SIC 4841. Based on the 1987 Standard Industrial Classification code; see text, Section 13, Labor Force]

ITEM	TOTAL (mil. dol.)					PERCENT DISTRIBUTION		
	1990	1993	1994	1995	1996	1990	1995	1996
Revenue	22,165	28,769	29,304	32,541	37,027	100.0	100.0	100.0
Advertising	1,882	2,981	3,597	4,466	5,007	8.5	13.7	13.5
Program revenue	3,816	4,440	4,714	4,843	5,438	17.2	14.9	14.7
Basic service	10,933	14,904	14,547	16,310	18,621	49.3	50.1	50.3
Pay-per-view and other premium service	4,351	4,880	4,662	5,068	5,696	19.6	15.6	15.4
Installation fees	302	417	427	445	508	1.4	1.4	1.4
Other cable and pay TV revenue.	881	1,147	1,357	1,409	1,757	4.0	4.3	4.7
Operating expenses	19,354	22,648	23,492	26,428	30,471	100.0	100.0	100.0
Annual payroll	2,816	3,824	3,931	4,519	5,061	14.5	17.1	16.6
Employer contributions to Social Security and other supplemental benefits	588	866	915	1,000	1,150	3.0	3.8	3.8
Program and production costs [1]	5,926	7,644	8,333	9,442	11,239	30.6	35.7	36.9
Depreciation	3,611	3,848	3,934	4,433	4,990	18.7	16.8	16.4
Lease and rental payments	513	631	648	682	764	2.7	2.6	2.5
Purchased repairs	343	432	459	555	615	1.8	2.1	2.0
Insurance	110	165	162	175	190	0.6	0.7	0.6
Telephone, other purchased communications . .	133	191	225	283	321	0.7	1.1	1.1
Purchased utilities	188	220	210	215	241	1.0	0.8	0.8
Purchased advertising.	467	601	708	891	1,062	2.4	3.4	3.5
Taxes.	310	423	424	429	436	1.6	1.6	1.4
Other operating expenses	4,349	3,803	3,543	3,804	4,402	22.5	14.4	14.4

[1] Includes costs from basic cable, pay-per-view, premium services, in-house programs, and other program and production costs.

Source: U.S. Bureau of the Census, *Annual Survey of Communication Services.*

No. 930. Microcomputer Software Sales: 1995 and 1996

[**In millions of dollars.** Estimated North American retail sales. Figures may not add to totals because individual applications and totals are derived independently]

APPLICATION	1995				1996				
	Total	PC/ MS-DOS	Windows [1]	Macin-tosh	Total	PC/ MS-DOS	Windows 32-bit	Windows 16-bit	Macin-tosh
Total [2]	**9,772.0**	**1,041.2**	**7,333.4**	**1,520.8**	**10,580.4**	**558.2**	**3,199.6**	**5,327.5**	**1,170.8**
Entertainment	826.2	403.5	317.4	105.3	861.9	303.4	343.3	169.6	45.5
Home creativity	300.8	2.9	253.8	44.0	337.7	3.4	118.6	190.5	25.3
Home education	939.7	32.5	728.2	185.1	958.3	22.9	102.0	658.2	174.4
Finance	397.4	80.7	270.6	46.2	467.8	34.2	8.8	388.7	36.2
Word processors	1,085.0	25.0	987.2	63.5	976.3	2.1	373.4	556.7	43.4
Spreadsheets	865.2	12.3	803.4	46.8	881.6	2.4	295.9	547.4	35.2
Databases	336.6	8.7	302.9	24.2	429.8	4.7	174.1	210.1	40.0
Integrated	133.5	2.1	86.9	43.9	107.1	(B)	29.2	48.6	28.5
Utilities	621.0	110.9	371.2	101.9	773.9	30.7	288.5	147.0	114.5
Presentation graphic	462.9	(B)	427.5	30.4	548.8	(B)	175.2	349.4	24.4
Drawing and painting. . . .	461.9	(B)	146.7	309.9	343.4	(B)	14.4	153.3	168.7
Desktop publishing	357.2	(B)	244.6	112.6	357.9	(B)	95.4	183.5	79.1
Other graphics	313.8	22.4	216.1	76.1	275.3	13.5	54.5	138.6	54.3
Project management	164.2	6.7	142.9	14.6	171.9	5.4	47.5	112.1	6.9
Personal info. manager . .	395.2	1.9	343.3	49.7	348.8	2.0	86.7	210.4	39.1
Languages and tools	361.3	11.8	337.2	8.8	418.0	6.7	135.2	271.2	3.6
Other productivity	1,624.7	184.3	1,069.5	279.7	2,321.8	126.3	857.1	992.1	251.8

B Base figure too small to meet statistical standards for reliability of a derived figure. [1] 16- and 32-bit. [2] Includes other software platforms, not shown separately.

Source: Software Publishers Association, Washington, DC, *SPA Software Sales Report*, News Release, March 31, 1997 (copyright).

No. 931. Recording Media—Manufacturers' Shipments and Value: 1982 to 1997

[Domestic shipments based on reports of manufacturers representing more than 85 percent of the market. Domestic value data based on list prices of records and other media]

MEDIUM	1982	1985	1990	1991	1992	1993	1994	1995	1996	1997
UNIT SHIPMENTS [1] (mil.)										
Total [2]	577.4	653.0	865.7	801.0	895.5	955.6	1,122.7	1,112.7	1,137.2	1,063.4
Vinyl singles	137.2	120.7	27.6	22.0	19.8	15.1	11.7	10.2	10.1	7.5
Albums—LPs and EPs.	243.9	167.0	11.7	4.8	2.3	1.2	1.9	2.2	2.9	2.7
CDs	(X)	22.6	286.5	333.3	407.5	495.4	662.1	722.9	778.9	753.1
CD singles.	(X)	(X)	1.1	5.7	7.3	7.8	9.3	21.5	43.2	66.7
Music video	(X)	(X)	9.2	6.1	7.6	11.0	11.2	12.6	16.9	18.6
Cassettes	182.3	339.1	442.2	360.1	366.4	339.5	345.4	272.6	225.3	172.6
Cassette singles	(X)	(X)	87.4	69.0	84.6	85.6	81.1	70.7	59.9	42.2
MANUFACTURES VALUE (mil. dol.)										
Total [2]	3,641.6	4,378.8	7,541.1	7,834.2	9,024.0	10,046.6	12,068.0	12,320.3	12,533.8	12,236.8
Vinyl singles	283.0	281.0	94.4	63.9	66.4	51.2	47.2	46.7	47.5	35.6
Albums—LPs and EPs.	1,925.1	1,280.5	86.5	29.4	13.5	10.6	17.8	25.1	36.8	33.3
CDs	(X)	389.5	3,451.6	4,337.7	5,326.5	6,511.4	8,464.5	9,377.4	9,934.7	9,915.1
CD singles.	(X)	(X)	6.0	35.1	45.1	45.8	56.1	110.9	184.1	272.7
Music video	(X)	(X)	172.3	118.1	157.4	213.3	231.1	220.3	236.1	323.9
Cassettes	1,384.5	2,411.5	3,472.4	3,019.6	3,116.3	2,915.8	2,976.4	2,303.6	1,905.3	1,522.7
Cassette singles	(X)	(X)	257.9	230.4	298.8	298.5	274.9	236.3	189.3	133.5

X Not applicable. [1] Net units, after returns. [2] Includes discontinued media.

Source: Recording Industry Association of America, Washington, DC, Internet site <http://www.riaa.com> (accessed March 25 1998).

No. 932. Publishing Industry—Summary: 1987 to 1996

[**In millions of dollars,** except as noted. Number in parentheses represents Standard Industrial Classification code; see text, Section 13, Labor Force]

ITEM	NEWSPAPERS (SIC 2711)			PERIODICALS (SIC 2721)			BOOKS (SIC 2731)		
	1987	1992	1996	1987	1992	1996	1987	1992	1996
Establishments	9,091	8,679	(NA)	4,020	4,699	(NA)	2,298	2,644	(NA)
With 20 or more employees . . .	2,617	2,629	(NA)	876	991	(NA)	424	500	(NA)
Employees [1] (1,000).	435	417	403	110	116	121	70	80	85
Payroll	9,025	10,506	11,199	2,983	4,075	4,665	1,860	2,676	3,128
Value of receipts	31,849	34,124	39,171	17,329	22,034	24,930	12,620	16,731	21,363
Cost of materials	7,533	6,874	8,483	5,873	6,201	6,940	3,663	5,338	6,601
Value added [2]	24,311	27,247	30,692	11,452	15,833	17,982	9,111	11,494	14,792
New capital expends.	1,523	1,667	1,277	246	234	311	240	327	365
Fixed assets, gross assets.	14,028	20,042	(NA)	2,528	2,769	(NA)	1,680	2,402	(NA)
Inventories, Dec. 31	857	767	894	902	1,067	1,216	2,091	2,944	3,320

NA Not available. [1] Represents the average number of production workers plus the number of other employees in mid-March. [2] By manufacture, derived by subtracting the cost of materials, supplies, containers, fuel, purchased electricity, and contract work from the value of shipments. This result is then adjusted by the addition of value added by merchandising operations, plus the net change in finished goods and work-in-process inventories between the beginning and the end of the year.

Source: U.S. Bureau of the Census, *1992 Census of Manufactures*, Industry Reports, series MC92-I-27A, and *Annual Survey of Manufactures*.

No. 933. Newspapers and Periodicals—Number, by Type: 1980 to 1997

[Data refer to year of compilation of the Directory cited as the source, i.e., generally to year preceding year shown. Data for 1995 and prior years include Canada and Mexico]

TYPE	1980	1985	1989	1990	1991	1992	1993	1994	1995	1996	1997
Newspapers [1]	9,620	9,134	10,457	11,471	11,689	11,339	12,597	12,513	12,246	10,466	10,616
Semiweekly	537	517	567	579	574	562	639	661	705	612	581
Weekly	7,159	6,811	7,622	8,420	8,546	8,293	9,177	9,067	9,011	7,655	7,415
Daily	1,744	1,701	1,773	1,788	1,781	1,755	1,850	1,831	1,710	1,537	1,516
Periodicals [1]	10,236	11,090	11,556	11,092	11,239	11,143	11,863	12,136	11,179	9,843	11,408
Weekly	1,716	1,367	828	553	511	466	485	487	513	442	429
Semimonthly [2]	645	801	622	435	412	371	199	209	216	307	289
Monthly	3,985	4,088	4,445	4,239	4,340	4,326	4,545	4,494	4,067	3,554	3,407
Bimonthly	1,114	1,361	1,880	2,087	2,116	2,143	2,359	2,475	2,568	2,216	2,102
Quarterly	1,444	1,759	2,513	2,758	2,861	3,024	3,199	3,370	3,621	3,280	3,239

[1] Includes other items not shown separately.   [2] Includes fortnightly (every 2 weeks).

Source: Gale Research Inc., Detroit, MI, *1997 Gale Directory of Publications and Broadcast Media*, 129th edition; and earlier editions (copyright).

No. 934. Daily and Sunday Newspapers—Number and Circulation: 1970 to 1997

[Number of newspapers as of **February 1** the following year. Circulation figures as of **September 30** of year shown. For English language newspapers only]

TYPE	1970	1975	1980	1985	1989	1990	1991	1992	1993	1994	1995	1996	1997
NUMBER													
Daily: Total [1]	1,748	1,756	1,745	1,676	1,626	1,611	1,586	1,570	1,556	1,548	1,533	1,520	1,509
Morning	334	339	387	482	530	559	571	596	623	635	656	686	705
Evening	1,429	1,436	1,388	1,220	1,125	1,084	1,042	996	954	935	891	846	816
Sunday	586	639	736	798	847	863	875	891	884	886	888	890	903
CIRCULATION (mil.)													
Daily: Total [1]	62.1	60.7	62.2	62.8	62.6	62.3	60.7	60.1	59.8	59.3	58.2	57.0	56.7
Morning	25.9	25.5	29.4	36.4	40.7	41.3	41.5	42.4	43.1	43.4	44.3	44.8	45.4
Evening	36.2	35.2	32.8	26.4	21.9	21.0	19.2	17.8	16.7	15.9	13.9	12.2	11.3
Sunday	49.2	51.1	54.7	58.8	62.0	62.6	62.1	62.2	62.6	62.3	61.5	60.8	60.5
PER CAPITA CIRCULATION [2]													
Daily: Total [1]	0.30	0.28	0.27	0.26	0.25	0.25	0.24	0.24	0.23	0.23	0.22	0.21	0.21
Morning	0.13	0.12	0.13	0.15	0.16	0.17	0.16	0.17	0.17	0.17	0.17	0.17	0.17
Evening	0.18	0.16	0.14	0.11	0.09	0.08	0.08	0.07	0.06	0.06	0.05	0.05	0.04
Sunday	0.24	0.24	0.24	0.25	0.25	0.25	0.25	0.24	0.24	0.24	0.23	0.23	0.23

[1] All-day newspapers are counted in both morning and evening columns but only once in total. Circulation is divided equally between morning and evening.   [2] Based on U.S. Bureau of the Census estimated resident population as of July 1.

Source: Editor & Publisher Co., New York, NY, *Editor & Publisher International Year Book*, annual (copyright).

No. 935. Daily Newspapers—Number and Circulation, by Size of City: 1980 to 1997

[Number of newspapers as of **February 1** the following year. Circulation as of **September 30** of year shown. For English language newspapers only. See Table 47 for number of cities by population size. All-day newspapers are counted in both morning and evening columns; circulation is divided equally between morning and evening]

TYPE OF DAILY AND POPULATION-SIZE CLASS	NUMBER					NET PAID CIRCULATION (1,000)				
	1980	1985	1990	1995	1997	1980	1985	1990	1995	1997
Morning dailies, total	387	482	559	656	705	29,413	36,361	41,311	44,310	45,434
In cities of—										
1,000,001 or more	20	22	18	25	25	8,795	9,367	6,508	10,173	10,328
500,001 to 1,000,000	27	24	22	22	27	5,705	6,897	4,804	5,587	6,383
100,001 to 500,000	99	121	138	153	153	8,996	12,197	20,051	17,214	16,707
50,001 to 100,000	75	87	100	138	156	2,973	3,653	4,373	5,602	5,869
25,001 to 50,000	64	83	102	115	123	1,701	2,145	3,209	3,150	3,337
Less than 25,000	102	145	179	203	221	1,243	2,099	2,365	2,584	2,810
Evening dailies, total	1,388	1,220	1,084	891	816	32,788	26,407	21,017	13,883	11,294
In cities of—										
1,000,001 or more	11	8	7	3	1	2,984	2,169	1,423	390	2
500,001 to 1,000,000	23	14	12	7	6	4,101	1,626	1,350	1,017	849
100,001 to 500,000	123	102	71	45	39	8,178	6,987	4,687	2,529	1,959
50,001 to 100,000	156	127	94	72	64	4,896	3,942	2,941	2,029	1,719
25,001 to 50,000	246	229	204	158	143	5,106	4,606	4,278	2,819	2,337
Less than 25,000	829	740	696	606	563	7,523	7,075	6,338	5,099	4,428

Source: Editor & Publisher Co., New York, NY, *Editor & Publisher International Year Book*, annual (copyright).

No. 936. Daily and Sunday Newspapers—Number and Circulation, by State: 1997

[Number of newspapers as of February 1 the following year. Circulation as of September 30 of the year shown. For English language newspapers only. New York, Massachusetts, and Virginia Sunday newspapers include national circulation]

STATE	DAILY			SUNDAY		STATE	DAILY			SUNDAY	
	Number	Circulation [1]		Number	Net paid circula-tion [1] (1,000)		Number	Circulation [1]		Number	Net paid circula-tion [1] (1,000)
		Net paid (1,000)	Per capita [2]					Net paid (1,000)	Per capita [2]		
U.S. . . .	1,509	56,728	0.21	903	60,484	MO	45	986	0.18	23	1,289
AL	24	678	0.15	20	749	MT	11	188	0.20	7	196
AK	7	112	0.18	5	132	NE	16	452	0.27	6	434
AZ	16	767	0.16	11	910	NV	9	302	0.17	4	325
AR	31	473	0.18	18	532	NH	12	235	0.20	8	251
CA	95	6,118	0.19	61	6,247	NJ	19	1,422	0.17	16	1,718
CO	30	1,074	0.26	16	1,294	NM	18	295	0.16	13	297
CT	18	769	0.23	12	851	NY	68	6,491	0.35	45	5,475
DE	2	147	0.19	2	171	NC	47	1,362	0.17	36	1,500
DC	2	877	1.64	2	1,161	ND	10	177	0.27	7	181
FL	42	3,013	0.20	36	3,875	OH	84	2,528	0.22	38	2,776
GA	34	1,045	0.13	25	1,338	OK	44	671	0.20	37	813
HI	6	226	0.18	5	258	OR	19	690	0.21	10	711
ID	12	219	0.17	8	237	PA	86	2,869	0.23	41	3,258
IL	68	2,390	0.20	31	2,546	RI	6	237	0.24	3	273
IN	70	1,366	0.23	21	1,299	SC	15	634	0.16	14	750
IA	38	649	0.22	11	667	SD	11	161	0.21	4	134
KS	47	464	0.18	15	425	TN	27	888	0.16	16	1,077
KY	23	624	0.16	14	683	TX	88	2,965	0.15	85	4,000
LA	26	734	0.16	21	827	UT	6	322	0.15	6	365
ME	7	248	0.20	4	203	VT	8	126	0.21	3	102
MD	14	614	0.12	8	890	VA	28	2,692	0.39	15	1,142
MA	33	1,726	0.28	14	1,658	WA	24	1,181	0.20	16	1,275
MI	49	1,792	0.18	26	2,086	WV	22	381	0.20	11	381
MN	25	901	0.19	14	1,153	WI	35	965	0.18	17	1,101
MS	23	393	0.14	18	403	WY	9	89	0.18	4	65

[1] Circulation figures based on the principal community served by a newspaper which is not necessarily the same location as the publisher's office.   [2] Per capita based on estimated resident population as of July 1.

Source: Editor & Publisher Co., New York, NY, *Editor & Publisher International Year Book,* annual (copyright).

No. 937. New Books and Editions Published and Imports, by Subject: 1990 to 1996

[Covers listings in Bowker's Weekly Record in year shown, plus titles issued in that year which were listed in following 6 months. Comprises new books (published for first time) and new editions (with changes in text or format). Excludes government publications; books sold only by subscription; dissertations; periodicals and quarterlies; and pamphlets under 49 pages]

SUBJECT	NEW BOOKS AND NEW EDITIONS						IMPORTS					
	1990	1992	1993	1994	1995	1996	1990	1992	1993	1994	1995	1996
Total	46,738	49,276	49,756	51,663	62,039	68,175	6,414	6,506	7,055	8,172	8,539	9,271
Agriculture	514	565	559	532	673	675	86	93	125	87	97	72
Art	1,262	1,392	1,540	1,621	2,168	2,033	94	156	225	205	273	203
Biography	1,957	2,007	2,071	2,197	2,658	3,007	115	124	136	144	142	221
Business	1,191	1,367	1,442	1,616	1,843	1,788	134	126	253	276	268	238
Education	1,039	1,184	1,247	1,310	1,526	1,595	234	232	246	287	285	280
Fiction	5,764	5,690	5,419	5,415	7,605	8,573	166	246	141	247	251	280
General works	1,760	2,153	1,870	2,208	2,751	3,027	266	313	308	331	367	424
History	2,243	2,322	2,317	2,507	2,999	3,576	329	348	373	447	462	536
Home economics	758	826	881	1,004	1,395	1,447	19	25	24	31	41	22
Juvenile.	5,172	5,144	5,469	5,321	5,678	5,353	103	50	45	45	63	47
Language	649	617	699	700	732	898	202	164	172	199	263	313
Law	896	1,063	1,143	1,168	1,230	1,357	138	197	229	261	215	264
Literature	2,049	2,227	2,169	2,356	2,525	3,082	242	274	286	326	308	428
Medicine	3,014	3,234	3,094	3,147	3,510	4,223	588	514	532	605	611	720
Music	289	346	377	364	479	461	52	69	63	49	73	67
Philosophy, psychology .	1,683	1,806	1,764	1,741	2,068	2,333	284	291	351	379	346	393
Poetry and drama	874	899	1,004	1,065	1,407	1,566	119	136	167	226	206	231
Religion	2,285	2,540	2,633	2,730	3,324	3,803	176	165	186	225	235	310
Science	2,742	2,729	2,678	3,021	3,323	3,725	1,030	840	868	997	1,068	1,058
Sociology, economics. . .	7,042	7,432	7,502	8,038	9,362	10,528	1,368	1,521	1,652	2,121	2,198	2,392
Sports, recreation	973	1,113	1,146	1,161	1,591	1,751	75	112	144	106	118	136
Technology	2,092	2,152	2,247	2,085	2,470	2,629	546	458	476	465	487	520
Travel	495	468	487	556	722	745	48	52	53	113	162	116

Source: R. R. Bowker Co., New York, NY, *Publishers Weekly.* (Copyright by Reed Publishing USA.)

No. 938. Books—Average Retail Prices: 1980 to 1996

[In dollars. Covers listings in Bowker's Weekly Record in year shown, plus titles issued in that year which were listed in following 6 months. Comprises new books (published for first time) and new editions (with changes in text or format)]

SUBJECT	1980	1985	1990	1991	1992	1993	1994	1995	1996
Hardcover [1]	24.64	31.46	42.12	44.17	45.05	34.98	44.65	47.15	50.00
Agriculture	27.55	36.77	54.24	57.73	53.76	41.84	58.10	49.00	45.00
Art	27.70	35.15	42.18	44.99	44.59	39.99	39.97	41.23	53.40
Biography	19.77	22.20	29.58	27.52	30.41	28.37	30.43	30.01	31.67
Business	22.45	28.84	45.48	43.38	43.91	37.95	42.72	46.90	52.62
Education	17.01	27.28	38.72	41.26	48.77	38.60	47.98	43.00	47.09
Fiction	12.46	15.29	19.83	21.30	20.39	19.50	20.95	21.47	22.89
General works	29.84	37.91	54.77	51.74	56.29	45.41	60.41	54.11	68.36
History	22.78	27.02	36.43	39.87	39.19	40.78	40.20	42.19	45.62
Home economics	13.31	17.50	23.80	24.23	24.88	20.55	20.49	22.53	23.39
Juvenile	8.16	9.95	13.01	16.64	14.46	13.87	14.59	14.55	15.97
Language	22.16	28.68	42.98	51.71	49.68	34.02	52.09	54.89	58.81
Law	33.25	41.70	60.78	64.89	76.21	53.94	72.32	73.09	88.51
Literature	18.70	24.53	35.80	36.76	39.23	35.30	37.77	38.49	43.28
Medicine	34.28	44.36	72.24	71.44	75.22	49.78	76.30	75.80	81.48
Music	21.79	28.79	41.86	41.04	47.37	41.44	39.27	43.27	39.21
Philosophy, psychology	21.70	28.11	40.58	42.74	46.85	39.44	44.71	45.26	48.40
Poetry and drama	17.85	22.14	32.19	33.29	36.76	31.06	31.56	34.96	34.15
Religion	17.61	19.13	31.31	32.33	35.31	29.16	30.73	34.27	36.62
Science	37.45	51.19	74.39	80.14	81.95	52.71	90.12	93.52	90.63
Sociology, economics	31.76	33.33	42.10	48.43	45.53	41.32	50.24	55.51	53.82
Sports, recreation	15.92	23.43	30.52	30.68	34.62	32.28	33.39	32.14	34.71
Technology	33.64	50.37	76.80	76.40	82.18	56.31	81.03	88.28	91.59
Travel	16.80	24.66	30.41	32.43	33.28	26.22	32.13	38.30	33.91
Paperbacks:									
Mass market [2]	(NA)	3.63	4.57	5.08	5.22	5.82	5.70	6.53	6.57
Trade	8.60	13.98	17.45	18.40	18.81	20.56	20.56	21.71	21.41

NA Not available. [1] Excludes publications of the United States and other governmental units, books sold only by subscription, and dissertations. [2] "Pocket-sized" books sold primarily through magazine and news outlets, supermarkets, variety stores, etc.

Source: R. R. Bowker Co., New Providence, NJ, *The Bowker Annual: Library and Book Trade Almanac.* (Copyright by Elsevier Inc.); and Publishers Weekly, New York, NY.

No. 939. Periodicals—Average Retail Prices: 1994 to 1998

[In dollars]

SUBJECT	1994	1995	1996	1997	1998
Agriculture	293.56	326.02	383.21	417.56	419.04
Anthropology	143.20	157.10	176.07	189.79	207.45
Art and architecture	87.17	92.24	97.99	101.06	102.30
Astronomy	746.36	840.93	993.03	1,071.36	1,087.53
Biology	556.93	620.18	731.84	824.81	891.40
Botany	422.25	475.10	556.14	607.42	644.47
Business and economics	194.94	227.43	271.13	307.21	339.55
Chemistry	1,006.70	1,106.09	1,319.23	1,467.35	1,577.13
Education	125.39	136.45	150.99	165.03	178.53
Engineering and technology	523.24	575.28	695.69	785.93	866.99
Food science	272.22	308.20	352.20	385.11	440.44
General science	369.40	416.28	487.86	548.10	607.80
General works	63.09	66.73	76.04	80.66	80.53
Geography	305.27	340.79	391.43	452.85	493.93
Geology	469.41	516.08	628.26	703.95	740.14
Health sciences	367.24	403.28	461.07	517.24	573.79
History	76.83	83.27	91.45	95.62	99.26
Language and literature	71.24	77.83	87.34	90.60	92.55
Law	97.22	105.21	119.16	123.80	138.78
Library and information science	136.23	153.58	172.45	181.35	202.30
Math and computer science	566.94	619.31	728.84	805.26	859.91
Military and naval science	133.50	153.75	168.00	184.13	209.50
Music	52.75	57.50	60.89	65.27	67.93
Philosophy and religion	81.48	91.30	101.25	105.99	107.14
Physics	1,035.81	1,144.93	1,358.19	1,510.45	1,601.03
Political science	105.37	119.91	138.24	151.75	166.05
Psychology	163.91	182.67	207.48	234.12	257.69
Recreation	59.82	61.30	68.73	71.54	75.94
Sociology	149.41	156.42	181.84	201.66	222.23
Technology	457.94	519.93	621.97	702.67	775.05
Zoology	421.74	471.55	539.72	594.28	641.06

Source: Library Journal, New York, NY, *Library Journal,* April 15, 1998. (Copyright by Reed Publishing USA.)

No. 940. U.S. Postal Service—Summary: 1980 to 1997

[**Employees in thousands; revenue and expenditures in millions of dollars,** except as indicated. **For fiscal years;** see text, Section 9. Includes Puerto Rico and all outlying areas. See text, Section 18]

ITEM	1980	1990	1993	1994	1995	1996	1997
Offices, stations, and branches	**39,486**	**40,067**	**39,392**	**39,372**	**39,149**	**38,212**	**38,019**
Number of post offices	30,326	28,959	28,728	28,657	28,392	28,189	28,060
Number of stations and branches	9,160	11,108	10,664	10,715	10,757	10,023	9,959
Pieces of mail handled (bil.)	106.3	166.3	171.2	178.0	180.7	183.4	190.9
First class, number (bil.) [1]	60.3	89.3	92.2	95.3	96.3	98.2	99.7
Percent	56.7	53.7	53.8	53.5	53.3	53.3	52.2
Periodicals (bil.)	10.2	10.7	10.3	10.2	10.2	10.1	10.4
Employees, total	**667**	**843**	**818**	**852**	**875**	**886**	**893**
Career	643	761	691	729	753	761	765
Headquarters	3	2	2	2	2	2	2
Headquarters support	(NA)	6	4	4	4	4	4
Inspection Service	5	4	4	4	4	4	4
Field Career	635	747	681	720	745	748	755
Postmasters	29	27	25	27	27	26	26
Supervisors/managers	36	43	32	35	35	35	36
Professional, administrative, and technical.	5	10	10	11	11	11	11
Clerks	263	290	257	265	274	277	281
Mail handlers	37	51	51	55	57	58	59
City carriers	187	236	212	229	240	238	234
Motor vehicle operators.	6	7	7	8	8	8	9
Rural carriers	33	42	44	45	46	48	50
Special delivery messengers	3	2	2	2	2	1	1
Building and equipment maintenance . .	27	33	35	37	38	39	40
Vehicle maintenance	5	5	5	5	5	5	6
Other [2]	4	1	1	1	2	2	2
Noncareer.	25	83	126	123	122	125	128
Casuals.	5	27	27	26	26	25	33
Transitional	(X)	(X)	42	38	32	33	27
Rural substitutes	20	43	44	47	50	54	55
Relief/Leave Replacements.	(X)	12	12	13	13	13	13
Nonbargaining temporary	(X)	(Z)	1	1	1	1	1
Compensation and employee benefits (mil. dol.).	16,541	34,214	38,447	39,609	41,931	42,676	43,835
Avg. salary per employee (dol.) [3]	24,799	37,570	42,711	44,342	45,001	44,718	48,793
Pieces of mail per employee, (1,000)	159	197	209	209	207	207	214
Total revenue [4]	**19,253**	**40,074**	**47,986**	**49,576**	**54,509**	**56,544**	**58,331**
Operating postal revenue.	17,143	39,201	47,418	49,252	54,176	56,309	58,133
Mail revenue [5]	16,377	37,892	45,909	47,739	52,490	54,538	56,267
First class mail	10,146	24,023	28,828	29,377	31,955	33,117	33,398
Priority mail [6]	612	1,555	2,300	2,653	3,075	3,322	3,857
Express mail [7].	184	630	627	671	711	737	825
Mailgram	15	8	7	2	2	2	2
Periodicals (formerly 2d class)	863	1,509	1,740	1,756	1,972	2,014	2,068
Standard mail A (formerly 3d class) . .	2,412	8,082	9,817	10,534	11,792	12,175	12,876
Standard mail B (formerly 4th class) . . .	805	919	1,183	1,353	1,525	1,524	1,628
International surface.	154	222	211	205	205	199	192
International air.	442	941	1,196	1,208	1,254	1,450	1,423
Service revenue	765	1,310	1,510	1,513	1,687	1,771	1,866
Registry	157	174	130	120	116	113	99
Certified	120	310	426	428	560	556	627
Insurance	55	47	52	53	52	49	63
Collection-on-delivery	21	26	20	17	21	21	22
Special delivery	73	6	2	5	3	4	1
Money orders	95	155	166	154	169	221	212
Other.	244	592	713	735	764	803	842
Operating expenses [8]	19,413	40,490	46,322	48,455	50,730	53,113	54,873

NA Not available.   X Not applicable.   Z Fewer than 500.   [1] Items mailed at 1st class rates and weighing 11 ounces or less.   [2] Includes discontinued operations, area offices, and nurses.   [3] For career bargaining unit employees. Includes fringe benefits.   [4] Net revenues after refunds of postage. Includes operating reimbursements, stamped envelope purchases, indemnity claims, and miscellaneous revenue and expenditure offsets. Shown in year which gave rise to the earnings.   [5] For 1980, includes penalty and franked mail, not shown separately. Later years have that mail distributed into the appropriate class.   [6] Provides 2- to 3-day delivery service.   [7] Overnight delivery of packages weighing up to 70 pounds.   [8] Shown in year in which obligation was incurred.

Source: U.S. Postal Service, *Annual Report of the Postmaster General* and *Comprehensive Statement on Postal Operations*, annual; and unpublished data.

No. 941. U.S. Postal Service—Volume of Mail, by Class: 1980 to 1997

[In millions, except percent and per capita. For fiscal years; see text Section 9. Includes Puerto Rico and all outlying areas. For definition of classes of mail, see footnotes, Table 940]

CLASS OF MAIL	PIECES OF MAIL				WEIGHT OF MAIL (lbs.)			
	1980	1990	1995	1997	1980	1990	1995	1997
Total	106,311	166,301	180,734	190,888	12,958	18,826	21,926	23,352
Domestic [1]	105,348	165,503	179,933	189,881	12,742	18,578	21,677	23,093
First class	60,276	89,270	96,296	99,660	2,136	3,340	3,865	4,115
Express.....................	17	59	57	64	78	112	63	76
Priority mail	248	518	869	1,068	591	1,007	1,484	1,861
Periodicals (formerly 2d class)........	10,220	10,680	10,194	10,411	3,478	4,233	4,211	4,338
Standard A (formerly 3d class)........	30,381	63,725	71,112	77,254	3,240	7,648	9,234	9,694
Standard B (formerly 4th class)	633	663	936	988	2,661	2,109	2,709	2,890
Mailgram	39	14	5	5	(X)	(X)	(X)	(X)
U.S. Postal Service	(NA)	538	412	377	(NA)	97	80	88
Free for the blind..............	28	35	52	53	40	30	32	33
International surface.............	450	166	106	97	164	146	114	102
International air	513	632	696	910	52	102	135	157
Percent distribution............	100.0	100.0	100.0	100.0	100.0	100.0	100.0	100.0
Domestic [1]	99.1	99.5	99.6	99.5	98.3	98.7	98.9	98.9
First class mail	56.7	53.7	53.3	52.2	16.5	17.7	17.6	17.6
Express mail	(Z)	(Z)	(Z)	(Z)	0.6	0.6	0.3	0.3
Priority mail	0.6	0.3	0.5	0.6	4.6	5.3	6.8	8.0
Periodicals (formerly 2d class)........	9.6	6.4	5.6	5.4	26.8	22.5	19.2	18.6
Standard A (formerly 3d class)........	28.6	38.3	39.3	40.5	25.0	40.6	42.1	41.5
Standard B (formerly 4th class)........	0.6	0.4	0.5	0.5	20.5	11.2	12.4	12.4
Mailgram	(Z)	(Z)	(Z)	(Z)	(X)	(X)	(X)	(X)
U.S. Postal Service	-	0.3	0.2	0.2	-	0.5	0.4	0.4
Free for the blind..............	(Z)	(Z)	(Z)	(Z)	0.3	0.2	0.1	0.1
International surface.............	0.4	0.1	0.1	0.1	1.3	0.8	0.5	0.4
International air	0.5	0.4	0.4	0.5	0.4	0.5	0.6	0.7
Per capita; [2]								
Domestic mail [3]	475	662	684	708	57	74	82	87
First class..................	272	357	366	372	10	13	15	15
Periodicals	46	43	39	39	16	17	16	16
Standard A	137	255	270	288	15	31	35	36
Standard B	3	3	4	4	12	8	10	11

- Represents zero.   NA Not available.   X Not applicable.   Z Less than .05 percent.   [1] 1980 includes penalty and franked mail, not shown separately. In later years this mail was allocated to the appropriate class.   [2] Based on estimated total population as of July 1, including Armed Forces abroad.   [3] Includes types of mail not shown separately.

Source: U.S. Postal Service, *Annual Report of the Postmaster General;* and unpublished data.

No. 942. U.S. Postal Service Rates for Letters and Post Cards: 1958 to 1995

[Domestic airmail letters discontinued in 1973 at 13 cents per ounce; superseded by express mail. Prior to February 3, 1991, international airmail rates were based on international zones which have been discontinued. Rates exclude Canada and Mexico]

DOMESTIC MAIL DATE OF RATE CHANGE	SURFACE MAIL					INTER-NATIONAL AIR MAIL DATE OF RATE CHANGE	LETTERS				
	Letters			Postal and post cards	Express mail [1]		First 1/2 ounce	Sec-ond 1/2 ounce	Each added 1/2 ounce	Postal and post cards	Aero-grammes
	Each ounce	First ounce	Each added ounce								
1958 (Aug. 1) ..	$0.04	(X)	(X)	$0.03	(X)	1961 (July 1) ..	(X)	(X)	(X)	$0.11	$0.11
1963 (Jan. 7).. .	$0.05	(X)	(X)	$0.04	(X)	1967 (May 1).. .	(X)	(X)	(X)	$0.13	$0.13
1968 (Jan. 7).. .	$0.06	(X)	(X)	$0.05	(X)	1971 (July 1).. .	(X)	(X)	(X)	$0.13	$0.13
1971 (May 16)..	$0.08	(X)	(X)	$0.06	(X)	1974 (Mar. 2) ..	(X)	(X)	(X)	$0.18	$0.18
1974 (Mar. 2).. .	$0.10	(X)	(X)	$0.08	(X)	1976 (Jan. 3) ..	(X)	(X)	(X)	$0.21	$0.22
1975 (Sept. 14) ..	(X)	$0.10	$0.09	$0.07	(X)	1981 (Jan. 1).. .	(X)	(X)	(X)	$0.28	$0.30
1975 (Dec. 31)..	[2](X)	[2]$0.13	[2]$0.11	[2]$0.09	(X)	1985 (Feb. 17) ..	(X)	(X)	(X)	$0.33	$0.36
1978 (May 29)..	(X)	$0.15	$0.13	$0.10	(X)	1988 (Apr. 17) ..	(X)	(X)	(X)	$0.36	$0.39
1981 (Mar. 22)..	(X)	$0.18	$0.17	$0.12	(X)	1991 (Feb. 3) ..	$0.50	$0.45	[3]$0.39	$0.40	$0.45
1981 (Nov. 1) ..	(X)	$0.20	$0.17	$0.13	$9.35	1995 (July 9) ..	$0.60	[3]$0.40	(X)	$0.40	$0.45
1985 (Feb.17)..	(X)	$0.22	$0.17	$0.14	$10.75						
1988 (Apr. 3).. .	(X)	$0.25	$0.20	$0.15	[4]$12.00						
1991 (Feb. 3) ..	(X)	$0.29	$0.23	$0.19	[4]$13.95						
1995 (Jan. 1).. .	(X)	$0.32	$0.23	$0.20	[4]$15.00						

X Not applicable.   [1] Post Office to addressee rates. Rates shown are for weights up to 2 pounds, all zones. Beginning Feb. 17, 1985, for weights between 2 and 5 lbs, $12.85 is charged. Prior to Nov. 1, 1981, rate varied by weight and distances. Over 5 pounds still varies by distance.   [2] As of October 11, 1975, surface mail service upgraded to level of airmail.   [3] Up to the limit of 64 ounces.   [4] Over 8 ounces and up to 2 pounds.

Source: U.S. Postal Service, "United States Domestic Postage Rate: Recent History," and unpublished data.

No. 943. Advertising—Estimated Expenditures, by Medium: 1990 to 1997

[In millions of dollars. See text, Section 18, for definitions of types of advertising]

MEDIUM	1990	1991	1992	1993	1994	1995	1996	1997, prel.
Total	129,590	127,470	132,650	139,540	151,680	162,930	175,230	186,765
National	73,380	73,270	76,710	80,795	88,250	95,360	103,040	109,950
Local	56,210	54,200	55,940	58,745	63,430	67,570	72,190	76,815
Newspapers	32,281	30,409	30,737	32,025	34,356	36,317	38,402	41,220
National	3,867	3,685	3,602	3,620	3,906	3,996	4,400	4,840
Local	28,414	26,724	27,135	28,405	30,450	32,321	34,002	36,380
Magazines	6,803	6,524	7,000	7,357	7,916	8,580	9,010	9,975
Weeklies	2,864	2,670	2,739	2,850	3,140	3,347	3,581	3,890
Women's	1,713	1,671	1,853	2,009	2,106	2,236	2,303	2,595
Monthlies	2,226	2,183	2,408	2,498	2,670	2,997	3,126	3,490
Farm publications	215	215	231	243	262	283	297	315
Television	29,073	28,189	30,450	31,698	35,435	37,828	42,484	44,580
TV networks	9,863	9,533	10,249	10,209	10,942	11,600	13,081	13,275
Three TV networks	9,383	8,933	9,549	9,369	9,959	10,263	11,423	11,525
Syndication (nat'l)	1,860	2,024	2,227	2,586	3,052	3,535	4,472	5,275
Syndication TV	1,109	1,253	1,370	1,576	1,734	2,016	2,218	2,385
Spot (national)	7,788	7,110	7,551	7,800	8,993	9,119	9,803	9,995
Spot (local)	7,856	7,565	8,079	8,435	9,464	9,985	10,944	11,490
Cable (non-network)	597	704	974	1,092	1,250	1,573	1,966	2,160
Radio	8,726	8,476	8,654	9,457	10,529	11,338	12,269	13,180
Network	482	490	424	458	463	480	523	555
Spot	1,635	1,575	1,505	1,657	1,902	1,959	2,135	2,340
Local	6,609	6,411	6,725	7,342	8,164	8,899	9,611	10,285
Yellow Pages	8,926	9,182	9,320	9,517	9,825	10,236	10,849	11,470
National	1,132	1,162	1,188	1,230	1,314	1,410	1,555	1,685
Local	7,794	8,020	8,132	8,287	8,511	8,826	9,294	9,785
Direct mail	23,370	24,460	25,391	27,266	29,638	32,866	34,509	36,925
Business papers	2,875	2,882	3,090	3,260	3,358	3,559	3,808	4,140
Outdoor	1,084	1,077	1,031	1,090	1,167	1,263	1,339	1,410
Miscellaneous	16,237	16,056	16,746	17,627	19,194	20,660	22,263	23,550

Source: McCann-Erickson, Inc., New York, NY. Compiled for Crain Communications, Inc. in *Advertising Age* (copyright).

No. 944. Magazine Advertising—Expenditures, by Product: 1985 to 1997

[In millions of dollars. Space cost based on one-time rate; special rates used where applicable. Year-to-year data not strictly comparable, as a few minor publications are added or deleted]

PRODUCT	1985	1990	1991	1992	1993	1994	1995	1996	1997
Total	4,961	6,753	6,608	7,186	7,667	9,029	10,212	11,282	12,755
Apparel, footwear, accessories	251	428	419	496	513	544	585	671	757
Automotive, accessories, equipment	549	900	941	1,035	1,064	1,223	1,328	1,447	1,777
Beer, wine, and liquor	240	277	279	247	204	199	220	226	270
Computers, office equipment and stationery	250	283	291	354	364	699	951	1,031	1,088
Business and consumer services	463	516	453	513	625	680	782	902	1,020
Drugs and remedies	135	163	167	299	368	438	479	641	816
Food and food products	342	444	437	459	470	512	677	665	684
Household equipment and supplies	100	118	115	161	141	141	170	169	185
Household furnishings	87	116	123	117	146	166	172	161	187
Jewelry, cameras, optical goods	101	157	157	158	168	183	231	270	297
Mail orders/direct response	328	531	574	617	725	904	962	988	1,099
Publishing and media	188	212	197	202	214	259	292	357	407
Retail	121	255	201	190	219	248	256	321	410
Smoking materials	383	305	265	224	210	288	314	333	307
Toiletries and toilet goods	385	679	640	734	811	880	900	989	1,121
Travel, hotels, and resorts	245	380	346	350	378	449	469	518	571
Other	793	989	1,005	1,030	1,047	1,216	1,425	1,593	1,757

Source: Publishers Information Bureau, Inc., New York, NY, as compiled by Competitive Media Reporting.

No. 945. Television—Expenditures for Network Advertising: 1995 to 1997

[In millions of dollars. See text, Section 18, Communications, for a definition of network advertising. Beginning 1996, includes WB and UPN]

PRODUCT	1995	1996	1997	PRODUCT	1995	1996	1997
Total	12,402	14,740	15,225	Home electronics equipment. . . .	203	258	233
Apparel, footwear, accessories . .	340	412	370	Horticulture	37	31	35
Automotive	1,736	1,959	2,323	Household equipment,			
Beer and wine	367	391	402	supplies, and furnishings	382	424	400
Building material, equipment,				Insurance	143	255	189
fixtures	62	53	60	Jewelry, cameras, optical goods .	123	169	176
Computers, office equipment,				Laundry soaps, cleansers,			
and stationery	164	303	380	polishes	267	250	265
Confectionery, soft drinks	673	722	831	Movies	496	668	718
Consumer services	909	1,022	1,028	Pet products	95	110	126
Department, discount stores	393	463	517	Proprietary medicines	1,088	1,405	1,387
Financial planning services.	85	153	177	Publishing and media	31	31	26
Food and food products.	1,422	1,385	1,362	Restaurants and drive-ins.	1,011	1,254	1,216
Freight, industrial development . .	69	137	103	Toiletries and toilet goods.	1,163	1,265	1,376
Gas, lubricants, etc.	60	78	87	Toys and sporting goods	285	351	336
Home centers and hardware				Travel, hotels, and resorts	138	145	141
stores	73	82	75	Other	587	964	886

Source: Television Bureau of Advertising, Inc., New York, NY (copyright). Data compiled by Competitive Media Reporting, New York, NY.

No. 946. Television—Estimated Time Charges for Spot Advertising: 1995 to 1997

[In millions of dollars. Data represent activity in the top 75 markets monitored by Competitive Media Reporting, currently covering approximately 382 stations. Data exclude National Syndicated activity. See text, Section 18, Communications, for definitions of types of advertising]

PRODUCT	1995	1996	1997	PRODUCT	1995	1996	1997
Total.	6,586	7,038	7,219	Horticulture.	42	46	43
Agriculture and farming.	9	11	11	Household equipment, supplies,			
Apparel, footwear, accessories. . . .	59	79	66	and furnishings	156	153	142
Automotive.	2,457	2,678	2,945	Insurance	208	234	270
Beer and wine.	177	152	123	Jewelry, cameras, optical goods . . .	41	44	35
Building material, equipment, fix . . .	51	48	66	Laundry soaps, cleaners, polishes .	88	83	94
Computers, office equipment				Pet products.	35	44	45
and stationery	45	60	62	Political, unions, religious	53	172	31
Confectionery, soft drinks	285	292	290	Proprietary medicines	168	192	220
Consumer services	699	759	863	Publishing and media	83	85	73
Food and food products	883	830	894	Toiletries and toilet goods	241	246	243
Freight, industrial development. . . .	33	48	20	Toys and sporting goods	250	229	191
Gasoline, lubricants, etc.	123	124	118	Travel, hotels, and resorts	193	190	159
Home electronics equipment	151	163	125	Other.	56	76	90

Source: Television Bureau of Advertising, Inc., New York, NY (copright). Data compiled by Competitive Media Reporting, New York, NY, in the top 75 markets.

No. 947. Television—Expenditures for Retail/Local Advertising: 1995 to 1997

[In millions of dollars. See headnote, Table 946]

PRODUCT	1995	1996	1997	PRODUCT	1995	1996	1997
Total	6,608	7,167	7,500	Hotels, resorts, U.S.	107	111	132
Amusements, entertainment	188	194	210	Insurance agencies.	38	37	41
Appliance stores.	309	332	295	Jewelry stores	33	38	40
Auto repair, service stations	103	107	99	Legal services	157	154	168
Auto supply, accessory stores	67	71	94	Leisure time stores and services	225	234	238
Auto, truck dealers	444	482	455	Loan, mortgage companies	75	98	168
Banks, S&L associations	141	172	169	Medical, dental services.	181	214	243
Builders, home improvement.	44	60	53	Movies	383	387	381
Carpet, floor covering stores	72	70	70	Newspapers.	28	30	44
Clothing stores.	168	173	178	Office equipment/supply stores	36	26	31
Department stores	226	202	257	Optical services, supplies.	70	59	51
Discount department stores	152	171	211	Political.	36	260	77
Drug stores	96	116	116	Radio, cable TV	240	220	239
Education services	121	136	158	Realtors, real estate developers	33	36	40
Financial planning services.	28	43	58	Rental services (nonauto).	27	29	22
Food stores, supermarkets	291	309	336	Restaurants, drive-ins	1,116	1,138	1,252
Furniture stores	431	439	453	Shoe stores.	29	39	50
Gas, electric, water companies	41	45	63	Shopping centers	38	41	40
Health clubs, reducing salons	115	120	118	Sport, hobby, toy stores	61	59	55
Home centers and hardware	180	189	195	Other	478	526	600

Source: Television Bureau of Advertising, Inc., New York, NY (copyright). Data compiled by Competitive Media Reporting, New York, NY, in the top 75 markets.

Energy

This section presents statistics on fuel resources, energy production and consumption, electric energy, hydroelectric power, nuclear power, solar energy, wood energy, and the electric and gas utility industries. The principal sources are the U.S. Department of Energy's Energy Information Administration (EIA), the Edison Electric Institute, Washington, DC, and the American Gas Association, Arlington, VA. For additional data on transportation, see Section 21; on fuels, see Section 24; and on energy-related housing characteristics, see Section 25.

The EIA, in its *Annual Energy Review,* provides statistics and trend data on energy supply, demand, and prices. Information is included on petroleum and natural gas, coal, electricity, hydroelectric power, nuclear power, solar, wood, and geothermal energy. Among its annual reports are *Annual Energy Review, Electric Power Annual, Natural Gas Annual, Petroleum Supply Annual, State Energy Data Report, State Energy Price and Expenditure Report, Financial Statistics of Selected Electric Utilities, Performance Profiles of Major Energy Producers, Annual Energy Outlook,* and *International Energy Annual.* These various publications contain state, national, and international data on production of electricity, net summer capability of generating plants, fuels used in energy production, energy sales and consumption, and hydroelectric power. The EIA also issues the *Monthly Energy Review,* which presents current supply, disposition, and price data, and monthly publications on petroleum, coal, natural gas, and electric power. Data on residential energy consumption, expenditures, and conservation activities are available from EIA's Residential Energy Consumption Survey and are published triennially in *Residential Energy Consumption Survey: Consumption and Expenditures,* and *Residential Energy Consumption Survey: Housing Characteristics,* and several other reports.

The Edison Electric Institute's monthly bulletin and annual *Statistical Year Book of the Electric Utility Industry for the Year* contain data on the distribution of electric energy by public utilities; information on the

In Brief

Renewable energy sources provided 6.8 quadrillion Btu's in 1995, which represented 7.5 percent of U.S. consumption.

Crude oil imports surpassed domestic production for the third year in a row in 1997 with 8.0 million barrels per day compared to 6.4 for production.

Net generation of electric energy by utilities reached a record 3.1 trillion kWh in 1996.

electric power supply, expansion of electric generating facilities, and the manufacture of heavy electric power equipment is presented in the annual *Year End Summary of the Electric Power Situation in the United States.* The American Gas Association, in its monthly and quarterly bulletins and its yearbook, *Gas Facts,* presents data on gas utilities, including sales, revenues, customers, prices, and other financial and operating statistics.

Btu conversion factors.—Various energy sources are converted from original units (e.g., short tons, cubic feet, barrels, kilowatt-hours) to the thermal equivalent using British thermal units (Btu). A Btu is the amount of energy required to raise the temperature of 1 pound of water 1 degree Fahrenheit (F) at or near 39.2 degrees F. Factors are calculated annually from the latest final annual data available; some are revised as a result. The following list provides conversion factors used in 1995 for production and consumption, in that order, for various fuels: Petroleum, 5.800 and 5.358 mil. Btu per barrel; total coal, 21.278 and 20.852 mil. Btu per short ton; and natural gas (dry), 1,028 Btu per cubic foot for both. The factors for the production of nuclear power and geothermal power were 10,676 and 20,914 Btu per kilowatt-hour, respectively. The fossil fuel steam-electric power plant generation factor of 10,272 Btu per kilowatt-hour was used for hydroelectric power generation and for wood and waste, wind, photovoltaic, and solar thermal energy consumed at electric utilities.

No. 948. Energy Supply and Disposition, by Type of Fuel: 1970 to 1996

[In quadrillion British thermal units (Btu). For Btu conversion factors, see text, Section 19]

TYPE OF FUEL	1970	1973	1975	1980	1985	1990	1991	1992	1993	1994	1995	1996
Production	62.07	62.06	59.86	64.76	64.87	[1]70.76	70.42	69.96	68.32	70.68	71.12	72.61
Crude oil [2]	20.40	19.49	17.73	18.25	18.99	15.57	15.70	15.22	14.49	14.10	13.89	13.74
Natural gas liquids	2.51	2.57	2.37	2.25	2.24	2.17	2.31	2.36	2.41	2.39	2.44	2.53
Natural gas	21.67	22.19	19.64	19.91	16.98	18.36	18.23	18.38	18.58	19.35	19.10	19.53
Coal	14.61	13.99	14.99	18.60	19.33	22.46	21.59	21.59	20.22	22.07	21.98	22.61
Nuclear electric power	0.24	0.91	1.90	2.74	4.15	6.16	6.58	6.61	6.52	6.84	7.18	7.17
Renewable energy	2.65	2.91	3.23	3.01	3.18	[1]6.07	6.06	5.84	6.13	5.97	6.56	7.06
Hydroelectric power	2.63	2.86	3.15	2.90	2.97	[3]3.01	2.98	2.61	2.88	2.67	3.21	3.59
Geothermal	0.01	(Z)	0.07	0.11	0.20	[1]0.33	0.34	0.35	0.36	0.36	0.31	0.34
Biofuels [4]	(Z)	(Z)	(Z)	(Z)	0.01	[1]2.63	2.64	2.79	2.78	2.84	2.95	3.02
Net trade [5]	**-5.73**	**-12.68**	**-11.75**	**-12.25**	**-7.87**	**-14.08**	**-13.36**	**-14.64**	**-17.18**	**-18.58**	**-17.86**	**-18.99**
Exports	2.66	2.05	2.36	3.72	4.23	4.91	5.22	5.02	4.35	4.12	4.58	4.69
Coal	1.94	1.43	1.76	2.42	2.44	2.77	2.85	2.68	1.96	1.88	2.32	2.37
Natural gas	0.07	0.08	0.07	0.05	0.06	0.09	0.13	0.22	0.14	0.16	0.16	0.16
Petroleum	0.55	0.49	0.44	1.16	1.66	1.82	2.13	2.01	2.12	1.99	1.99	2.06
Imports	8.39	14.73	14.11	15.97	12.10	18.99	18.58	19.66	21.54	22.71	22.48	23.68
Coal	(Z)	(Z)	(Z)	(Z)	0.05	0.07	0.08	0.10	0.18	0.19	0.18	0.18
Natural gas	0.85	1.06	0.98	1.01	0.95	1.55	1.80	2.16	2.40	2.68	2.90	2.90
Petroleum [6]	2.81	13.47	8.72	11.19	6.81	12.77	12.55	13.25	14.75	15.34	15.63	16.24
Consumption	**66.43**	**74.28**	**70.55**	**75.96**	**73.98**	**84.09**	**83.99**	**85.52**	**87.34**	**89.21**	**90.94**	**93.81**
Petroleum [7]	29.52	34.84	32.73	34.20	30.92	33.55	32.85	33.53	33.84	34.73	34.66	35.72
Natural gas [8]	21.79	22.51	19.95	20.39	17.83	19.30	19.61	20.13	20.83	21.29	22.16	22.59
Coal	12.26	12.97	12.66	15.42	17.48	19.10	18.77	19.21	19.83	20.02	20.08	20.99
Nuclear electric power	0.24	0.91	1.90	2.74	4.15	6.16	6.58	6.61	6.52	6.84	7.18	7.17
Renewable energy [9]	2.67	3.06	3.29	3.23	3.61	[1]6.17	6.27	6.11	6.40	6.28	6.85	7.39
Hydroelectric power [9]	2.65	3.01	3.22	3.12	3.40	[3]3.10	3.18	2.85	3.14	2.96	3.47	3.91
Geothermal	0.01	(Z)	0.07	0.11	0.20	[1]0.35	0.35	0.37	0.38	0.38	0.33	0.35
Biofuels [4]	(Z)	(Z)	(Z)	(Z)	0.01	[1]2.63	2.64	2.79	2.78	2.84	2.95	3.02

Z Less than 50 trillion. [1] There is a discontinuity in this time series between 1989 and 1990 due to the expanded coverage of nonelectric utility use of renewable energy beginning in 1990. [2] Includes lease condensate. [3] There is a discontinuity in this time series between 1989 and 1990; beginning in 1990, pumped storage is removed and expanded coverage of industrial use of hydroelectric power is included. [4] Includes wood, wood waste, peat, wood liquors, railroad ties, pitch, wood sludge, municipal solid waste, agricultural waste, straw, tires, landfill gases, fish oils, and/or other waste. [5] Exports minus imports. [6] Includes imports of crude oil for the Strategic Petroleum Reserve, which began in 1977. Includes imports of unfinished oils and natural gas plant liquids. [7] Petroleum products supplied, including natural gas plant liquids and crude oil burned as fuel. [8] Includes supplemental gaseous fuels. [9] Includes net imports of electricity.

Source: U.S. Energy Information Administration, *Annual Energy Review.*

No. 949. Energy Supply and Disposition, by Type of Fuel—Estimates, 1994 to 1996, and Projections, 2005 to 2020

[Quadrillion Btu per year, except percent change. Projections are "reference" or mid-level forecasts. See report for methodology and assumptions used in generating projections]

TYPE OF FUEL	1994	1995	1996	2005	2010	2015	2020
Production, total	**71.55**	**72.31**	**73.80**	**77.98**	**81.00**	**81.97**	**82.77**
Crude oil and lease condensate	14.10	13.89	13.71	12.32	11.79	11.09	10.43
Natural gas plant liquids	2.47	2.37	2.46	2.63	2.95	3.12	3.29
Natural gas	19.27	19.12	19.55	22.88	25.39	26.85	28.21
Coal	22.07	21.98	22.64	25.62	26.62	27.73	28.59
Nuclear power	6.84	7.19	7.20	6.87	6.36	5.12	4.09
Renewable energy and other [1] [2]	5.82	6.40	6.91	7.12	7.41	7.59	7.71
Imports, total	**22.63**	**22.38**	**23.78**	**32.45**	**36.02**	**38.96**	**41.28**
Crude oil [3]	15.35	15.70	16.30	22.01	23.17	24.36	25.30
Petroleum products [4]	3.93	3.19	3.98	5.47	7.61	9.01	10.09
Natural gas	2.68	2.90	2.93	4.39	4.66	5.04	5.34
Other imports [5]	0.67	0.59	0.57	0.58	0.57	0.54	0.56
Exports, total	**4.04**	**4.50**	**4.57**	**4.65**	**4.93**	**5.21**	**5.23**
Petroleum [6]	2.00	2.02	2.04	1.73	1.80	1.89	1.67
Natural gas	0.17	0.16	0.16	0.28	0.29	0.30	0.32
Coal	1.88	2.32	2.37	2.64	2.84	3.03	3.23
Consumption, total	**88.74**	**90.86**	**94.01**	**105.82**	**112.17**	**115.72**	**118.58**
Petroleum products [7]	34.77	34.74	36.01	41.32	44.33	46.20	47.64
Natural gas	21.35	22.18	22.60	26.93	29.63	31.44	33.06
Coal	19.50	19.96	20.90	23.21	24.03	24.95	25.61
Nuclear power	6.84	7.19	7.20	6.87	6.36	5.12	4.09
Renewable energy/other [1] [8]	6.28	6.40	6.91	7.12	7.42	7.62	7.74

[1] Includes utility and nonutility electricity from hydroelectric, wood and wood waste, municipal solid and wood waste, municipal solid waste, other biomass, wind, photovoltaic and solar thermal sources; nonelectric energy from renewable sources, such as active and passive solar systems, and wood; and both the ethanol and gasoline components of E85, but not the ethanol components of blends less than 85 percent. Excludes nonmarketed blends less than 85 percent. Excludes nonmarketed renewable energy. [2] Includes liquid hydrogen, methanol, supplemental natural gas, and some domestic inputs to refineries. [3] Includes imports of crude oil for the Strategic Petroleum Reserve. [4] Includes imports of finished petroleum products, imports of unfinished oils, alcohols, ethers, and blending components. [5] Includes coal, coal coke (net), and electricity (net). [6] Includes crude oil and petroleum products. [7] Includes natural gas plant liquids, crude oil consumed as a fuel, and nonpetroleum based liquids for blending, such as ethanol. [8] Includes net electricity imports, methanol, and liquid hydrogen.

Source: U.S. Energy Information Administration, *Annual Energy Outlook 1998.*

No. 950. Selected Energy Indicators—Summary: 1970 to 1996

[Btu=British thermal unit. For Btu conversion factors, see text, Section 19. Minus sign (-) indicates decrease]

ITEM	1970	1973	1975	1980	1985	1989	1990	1991	1992	1993	1994	1995	1996
AVERAGE ANNUAL PERCENT CHANGE [1]													
Gross domestic product [2] . . .	3.3	1.9	-0.3	-0.1	0.7	3.3	1.3	-1.0	2.7	2.2	3.4	2.0	2.4
Energy production, total [3][4] . .	4.6	-0.2	-1.8	0.3	-0.3	-	6.8	-0.5	-0.6	-2.4	3.3	0.8	2.0
Crude oil [5]	4.2	-0.9	-4.7	0.2	0.2	-6.9	-3.4	0.8	-3.1	-4.9	-2.7	-2.0	-0.6
Natural gas	6.4	-	-6.1	-0.2	-1.2	1.4	2.8	-0.7	0.8	1.1	3.6	-0.2	1.6
Coal	2.2	-0.2	3.4	1.2	-0.4	2.9	5.1	-3.9	(Z)	-6.5	8.8	-0.7	3.2
Energy consumption, total [3][4] .	4.6	1.4	-2.6	-0.8	-	1.4	3.4	-0.1	1.4	2.1	2.1	1.9	3.5
Petroleum products	4.8	1.9	-3.1	-1.6	-0.1	-	-1.9	-2.1	2.1	0.9	2.6	-0.3	3.1
Natural gas (dry)	6.5	-0.3	-6.0	-0.3	-0.7	4.4	-0.5	1.6	2.6	3.4	2.4	4.0	1.7
Coal	1.1	2.4	-1.2	0.5	0.5	0.4	0.9	-1.7	0.5	2.9	0.6	0.4	6.8
PER CAPITA [6] (mil. Btu)													
Energy production	304	294	278	285	273	268	284	279	274	265	271	271	274
Energy consumption	327	351	327	334	311	329	337	333	334	338	341	345	265
Energy consumption per dollar of GDP [2] (1,000 Btu) .	19.6	19.0	18.3	16.5	13.9	13.4	13.7	13.8	13.7	13.6	13.5	13.4	13.6

- Represents zero. Z Less than .05 percent. [1] Represents percent change from immediate prior year; for example, 1970, change from 1965. Percent change derived from Btu values. [2] Gross domestic product in chained (1992) dollars. For definition of chained, see text, Section 14. [3] Includes types of fuel or power, not shown separately. [4] Due to a lack of consistent historical data, some renewable energy sources are not included. [5] Includes lease condensate. [6] Based on resident population estimated as of July 1.

Source: U.S. Energy Information Administration, *Annual Energy Review,* and *Monthly Energy Review.*

No. 951. Energy Consumption, by End-Use Sector: 1970 to 1996

[There exits a discontinuity in the series between 1989 and 1990 due to the expanded coverage of nonelectric utility use of renewable energy beginning 1990. Btu=British thermal units. For Btu conversion factors, see text, Section 19]

YEAR	Total consumption (quad. Btu)	Residential and commercial (quad. Btu)	Industrial and miscellaneous (quad. Btu)	Transportation (quad. Btu)	PERCENT OF TOTAL		
					Residential and commercial	Industrial and miscellaneous	Transportation
1970	66.43	21.71	28.63	16.09	32.7	43.1	24.2
1973	74.28	24.14	31.53	18.60	32.5	42.4	25.0
1975	70.55	23.90	28.40	18.25	33.9	40.3	25.9
1976	74.36	25.02	30.24	19.10	33.6	40.7	25.7
1977	76.29	25.39	31.08	19.82	33.3	40.7	26.0
1978	78.09	26.09	31.39	20.61	33.4	40.2	26.4
1979	78.90	25.81	32.61	20.47	32.7	41.3	25.9
1980	75.96	25.65	30.61	19.69	33.8	40.3	25.9
1981	73.99	25.24	29.24	19.51	34.1	39.5	26.4
1982	70.85	25.63	26.14	19.07	36.2	36.9	26.9
1983	70.52	25.63	25.75	19.13	36.3	36.5	27.1
1984	74.14	26.48	27.86	19.80	35.7	37.6	26.7
1985	73.98	26.70	27.22	20.07	36.1	36.8	27.1
1986	74.30	26.85	26.63	20.81	36.1	35.8	28.0
1987	76.89	27.62	27.83	21.45	35.9	36.2	27.9
1988	80.22	28.92	28.99	22.30	36.1	36.1	27.8
1989	81.32	29.40	29.35	22.56	36.2	36.1	27.7
1990	84.09	29.48	32.14	22.54	35.1	38.2	26.8
1991	83.99	30.09	31.76	22.12	35.8	37.8	26.3
1992	85.52	30.00	33.01	22.46	35.1	38.6	26.3
1993	87.34	31.13	33.30	22.88	35.6	38.1	26.2
1994	89.21	31.29	34.19	23.57	35.1	38.3	26.4
1995	90.94	32.26	34.60	23.96	35.5	38.0	26.3
1996	93.81	33.88	35.43	24.43	36.1	37.8	26.0

Source: U.S. Energy Information Administration, *Annual Energy Review.*

Energy

No. 952. Energy Consumption—End-Use Sector and Selected Source, by State: 1995

[In trillions of Btu, except as indicated. For Btu conversion factors, see text, Section 19]

STATE	Total[1]	Per capita[2] (mil. Btu)	END-USE SECTOR				SOURCE				
			Resi-dential	Com-mercial	Industrial	Trans-porta-tion	Petro-leum	Natural gas (dry)	Coal	Hydro-electric power	Nuclear electric power
United States .	**90,547.4**	**344.4**	**18,056.5**	**13,943.8**	**[3]34,477.8**	**24,071.6**	**34,663.9**	**22,189.1**	**19,673.2**	**3,442.5**	**7,177.1**
Alabama	1,933.3	455.3	331.5	167.4	974.8	459.5	559.6	330.9	826.9	97.9	221.2
Alaska	686.3	1,139.1	49.5	62.7	404.9	169.3	222.2	432.8	12.9	14.1	-
Arizona	1,058.9	246.0	234.2	226.9	223.2	378.0	409.1	124.3	342.4	87.3	287.6
Arkansas	997.9	401.6	187.1	114.0	433.1	263.7	308.8	276.6	237.4	33.1	124.2
California	7,577.0	240.0	1,310.3	1,206.6	2,237.7	2,833.4	3,293.9	1,955.9	61.0	529.6	322.4
Colorado	1,075.2	286.9	242.0	225.0	282.8	325.4	390.5	288.7	337.3	22.9	-
Connecticut	786.3	240.4	242.1	180.1	165.3	204.5	370.4	136.0	23.7	14.0	199.8
Delaware	264.0	368.1	54.3	39.5	109.3	60.9	122.9	62.7	52.4	-	-
Dist. of Columbia .	177.8	320.7	36.3	111.4	3.3	26.8	37.1	33.2	0.1	-	-
Florida	3,518.6	248.1	973.0	750.3	570.0	1,225.3	1,620.2	532.6	653.0	2.4	306.3
Georgia	2,512.1	348.5	530.1	373.4	807.2	801.4	963.6	380.0	728.5	48.8	326.8
Hawaii	254.8	216.1	20.8	24.4	73.7	135.8	234.8	2.9	2.6	1.0	-
Idaho	456.2	391.2	85.6	73.1	184.8	112.8	146.0	65.7	8.9	113.6	-
Illinois	3,804.3	322.7	955.5	703.3	1,333.6	811.9	1,236.6	1,100.1	816.9	1.3	836.4
Indiana	2,592.1	447.2	478.8	295.0	1,185.0	633.4	864.2	541.7	1,341.9	4.8	-
Iowa	1,067.3	375.4	232.2	150.9	422.3	262.0	378.1	263.6	368.8	10.3	39.8
Kansas	1,040.6	405.9	197.7	171.7	391.0	280.2	367.8	369.1	290.9	0.1	107.2
Kentucky	1,770.4	459.0	317.2	196.0	826.4	430.8	620.4	245.6	927.6	35.3	-
Louisiana	3,813.6	879.1	319.3	216.1	2,520.0	758.2	1,476.5	1,778.0	217.5	9.9	167.2
Maine	513.3	414.4	97.9	50.7	278.3	103.4	243.0	5.5	7.1	66.4	2.1
Maryland	1,311.9	260.4	365.3	323.3	270.3	353.0	496.1	199.1	289.6	14.9	137.9
Massachusetts . .	1,493.8	246.1	418.9	356.4	318.7	405.5	682.7	371.7	104.4	11.0	47.8
Michigan	3,157.0	331.0	770.9	561.0	1,073.9	771.9	991.0	987.4	775.8	47.8	260.6
Minnesota	1,622.1	351.5	358.4	214.2	623.6	440.1	615.8	357.7	337.2	46.0	141.1
Mississippi	1,058.8	392.7	192.0	109.7	418.2	338.9	399.6	295.6	103.8	-	85.4
Missouri	1,662.8	312.6	432.6	317.3	363.5	549.3	700.1	281.0	591.4	19.1	87.8
Montana	378.9	435.4	63.8	51.0	162.5	101.7	159.6	59.6	171.2	111.0	-
Nebraska	580.3	354.0	133.0	120.1	159.6	167.6	218.5	133.7	179.5	14.7	79.8
Nevada	537.2	350.3	97.4	81.3	196.1	162.5	202.6	114.7	162.7	20.3	-
New Hampshire . .	284.5	247.8	79.7	52.5	76.3	81.7	151.0	20.1	35.5	24.7	89.3
New Jersey	2,542.9	319.9	529.5	493.5	655.4	864.5	1,238.4	610.9	55.1	[4]-0.9	179.1
New Mexico	575.0	340.3	80.0	96.2	202.4	196.3	208.2	219.4	275.3	2.7	-
New York	3,913.4	215.1	1,053.1	1,088.1	883.8	916.4	1,491.1	1,172.4	287.1	319.3	280.7
North Carolina . . .	2,328.1	323.2	544.8	388.7	784.5	610.1	845.8	209.4	601.1	59.8	382.7
North Dakota . . .	350.1	545.8	57.0	43.6	175.9	74.6	118.0	47.6	399.8	28.5	-
Ohio	4,038.0	362.7	904.5	626.9	1,639.3	867.3	1,190.0	930.1	1,379.8	2.4	178.7
Oklahoma	1,359.6	415.2	253.3	183.6	556.3	366.3	446.2	579.5	343.5	28.0	-
Oregon	1,048.2	332.9	220.1	171.8	365.0	297.3	361.2	151.7	20.2	431.1	-
Pennsylvania . . .	3,885.7	322.2	901.6	585.7	1,484.5	913.9	1,330.5	746.7	1,386.5	8.2	708.3
Rhode Island . . .	235.1	237.0	68.4	49.5	64.3	58.6	98.7	72.0	0.1	10.5	-
South Carolina . .	1,400.7	382.0	275.5	183.5	617.9	323.7	435.5	156.0	314.5	28.8	524.1
South Dakota . . .	235.8	323.2	57.2	39.3	58.1	81.2	114.5	34.8	36.7	61.9	-
Tennessee	1,975.2	376.5	417.3	127.6	896.5	533.8	678.5	264.8	668.2	92.9	167.4
Texas	10,511.5	559.1	1,220.0	1,079.8	6,032.9	2,169.3	4,746.3	3,943.2	1,361.7	17.5	385.3
Utah	638.4	326.0	110.4	100.6	245.8	184.5	234.2	166.7	357.2	10.0	-
Vermont	149.9	256.3	44.1	25.3	34.7	50.6	80.5	7.2	0.1	27.6	41.1
Virginia	2,056.0	310.8	489.8	431.6	530.3	604.3	771.9	254.9	342.2	2.3	267.9
Washington	2,158.6	396.2	406.0	304.3	786.7	635.5	846.9	229.2	69.8	833.2	74.0
West Virginia . . .	818.9	448.7	145.9	93.6	399.5	179.9	272.6	157.4	860.3	12.4	-
Wisconsin	1,749.1	341.5	387.4	263.2	720.8	394.6	535.7	384.7	443.0	55.6	116.9
Wyoming	405.2	845.6	37.8	40.1	227.2	100.0	136.8	103.9	461.9	8.2	-

- Represents zero. [1] Sources of energy includes geothermal, wood and waste, and net interstate sales of electricity, including losses, not shown separately. [2] Based on estimated resident population as of July 1. [3] Includes net imports of coal coke not allocated by state. [4] A negative number occurs when more electricity is expended than is created to provide electricity during peak demand periods.

Source: U.S. Energy Information Administration, *State Energy Data Report,* annual.

No. 953. Energy Expenditures—End-Use Sector and Selected Source, by State: 1994

[In millions of dollars, except as indicated. End-use sector and electric utilities exclude expenditures on energy sources such as hydropower, solar, wind, and geothermal. Also excludes expenditures for reported amounts of energy consumed by the energy industry for production, transportation, and processing operations]

STATE	Total[1]	Per capita[2] (dol.)	END-USE SECTOR				SOURCE			
			Residen-tial	Commer-cial	Industrial	Trans-porta-tion	Petro-leum products	Natural gas	Coal	Electricity sales
U.S.	504,688	1,938	126,859	89,423	[3]108,465	179,941	229,040	77,753	27,251	200,894
AL.	8,912	2,112	2,047	1,046	2,443	3,376	3,978	1,052	1,292	3,560
AK.	1,765	2,928	311	338	159	957	1,140	193	33	462
AZ.	7,545	1,850	1,972	1,586	957	3,030	3,280	523	563	3,748
AR.	5,147	2,098	1,245	656	1,201	2,044	2,351	791	357	2,003
CA.	50,216	1,599	11,587	10,723	7,625	20,281	22,118	8,708	110	20,662
CO	6,100	1,666	1,366	1,184	873	2,678	3,051	943	374	2,076
CT.	6,620	2,022	2,235	1,573	790	2,022	2,983	864	41	2,852
DE.	1,510	2,132	428	244	312	526	761	196	92	627
DC	1,241	2,188	258	717	17	248	293	222	2	731
FL.	21,654	1,551	6,657	4,294	1,950	8,754	10,404	1,198	1,144	11,103
GA	13,777	1,952	3,461	2,402	2,708	5,206	5,994	1,758	1,176	5,872
HI	2,065	1,752	339	346	404	976	1,275	37	4	936
ID	2,176	1,918	417	331	507	921	1,114	230	18	796
IL	22,632	1,925	6,332	4,363	5,275	6,663	8,570	4,966	1,301	8,953
IN	12,825	2,229	2,902	1,561	3,913	4,448	5,497	2,597	1,749	4,356
IA	5,944	2,100	1,444	797	1,635	2,068	2,831	1,081	368	1,957
KS.	5,391	2,113	1,215	952	1,444	1,779	2,353	1,133	309	1,947
KY.	8,046	2,102	1,617	899	2,392	3,137	4,010	814	1,091	3,059
LA.	13,320	3,086	2,097	1,416	5,491	4,316	6,850	2,899	357	4,103
ME	2,807	2,265	749	418	674	965	1,581	32	26	1,119
MD	8,692	1,738	2,691	1,353	1,561	3,087	3,951	999	413	3,846
MA	11,580	1,917	3,706	2,795	1,575	3,504	5,040	2,223	171	4,611
MI	17,777	1,873	4,534	3,459	3,964	5,820	7,234	3,918	1,217	6,423
MN	8,502	1,861	2,017	1,034	1,970	3,481	4,305	1,270	406	2,852
MS	5,282	1,978	1,205	683	1,216	2,177	2,617	650	153	2,139
MO	9,856	1,867	2,620	1,731	1,506	3,999	4,775	1,294	606	3,749
MT	1,918	2,240	338	257	431	891	1,085	226	140	585
NE.	3,279	2,019	721	593	617	1,349	1,670	509	129	1,090
NV.	3,099	2,120	675	484	687	1,254	1,445	459	259	1,253
NH	2,180	1,920	708	468	300	704	1,057	121	51	1,013
NJ.	17,190	2,175	4,689	3,958	2,735	5,808	7,575	3,095	95	6,636
NM	3,113	1,881	577	631	514	1,391	1,689	380	392	1,100
NY.	31,041	1,710	10,303	8,949	3,972	7,818	10,817	6,366	455	14,320
NC	13,677	1,935	3,791	2,250	2,790	4,846	5,987	915	980	6,611
ND	1,645	2,573	307	204	532	602	824	120	474	443
OH	22,892	2,060	5,995	3,909	5,841	7,146	8,871	4,248	1,999	9,476
OK	6,450	1,980	1,562	979	1,292	2,617	3,074	1,367	321	2,391
OR	5,528	1,791	1,155	816	1,033	2,524	2,843	603	51	2,070
PA.	23,542	1,952	7,050	4,050	5,226	7,216	9,506	3,833	2,038	9,617
RI	1,894	1,905	589	407	367	532	784	432	(Z)	674
SC.	7,245	1,989	1,797	1,043	1,909	2,496	2,981	618	528	3,510
SD.	1,429	1,975	334	202	251	642	841	129	47	444
TN.	10,203	1,971	2,409	742	3,037	4,015	4,694	1,070	799	4,265
TX.	47,246	2,566	8,686	6,332	16,749	15,480	25,473	7,800	1,859	16,149
UT.	2,959	1,551	606	480	540	1,333	1,496	458	450	945
VT.	1,158	1,995	364	204	151	439	649	39	(Z)	462
VA.	11,858	1,810	3,390	2,225	1,582	4,662	5,559	1,107	497	5,075
WA	9,185	1,721	1,932	1,315	1,593	4,354	4,836	822	156	3,446
WV	3,858	2,116	849	492	1,123	1,389	1,896	513	1,213	1,289
WI	8,956	1,762	2,398	1,346	1,901	3,311	4,191	1,634	540	3,001
WY	1,672	3,513	191	184	640	657	841	296	405	487

Z Less than $500,000. [1] Includes sources not shown separately. Total expenditures are the sum of purchases for each source (including electricity sales) less electric utility purchases of fuel. [2] Based on estimated resident population as of July 1. [3] Includes net imports of coal coke not shown separately by state.

Source: U.S. Energy Information Administration, *State Energy Price and Expenditure Report*, annual.

No. 954. Energy Expenditures and Average Fuel Prices, by Source and Sector: 1970 to 1994

[For definition of Btu, see text, Section 19. End-use sector and electric utilities exclude expenditures and prices on energy sources such as hydropower, solar, wind, and geothermal. Also excludes expenditures for reported amounts of energy consumed by the energy industry for production, transportation, and processing operations]

SOURCE AND SECTOR	1970	1973	1975	1980	1985	1989	1990	1991	1992	1993	1994
EXPENDITURES (mil. dol.)											
Total [1][2]	82,579	111,638	171,782	373,900	435,597	434,664	471,586	469,283	474,713	491,801	504,688
Natural gas	10,891	13,933	20,061	51,061	72,938	65,383	64,102	64,697	68,401	75,941	77,753
Petroleum products [2] . . .	48,088	65,304	103,858	238,408	223,350	206,588	234,993	222,375	221,897	222,618	229,040
Motor gasoline	31,596	39,667	59,446	124,408	118,044	112,585	126,472	123,051	125,158	126,397	129,900
Coal.	4,594	6,251	13,047	22,648	29,719	28,106	28,381	27,866	27,417	27,857	27,251
Electricity sales	23,351	33,780	50,680	98,098	149,242	169,340	176,742	184,822	186,957	196,586	200,894
Residential sector.	20,083	27,078	36,844	68,825	98,307	108,423	110,144	115,663	116,121	125,257	126,859
Commercial sector	10,668	15,107	22,835	46,881	70,243	75,338	78,845	81,396	82,335	86,543	89,423
Industrial sector . . . . . [2]	16,458	23,549	41,169	94,520	105,897	94,064	102,057	100,802	103,370	105,249	108,465
Transportation sector [2] . .	35,370	45,904	70,934	163,674	161,150	156,839	180,540	171,422	172,886	174,751	179,941
Motor gasoline	30,525	38,598	57,992	121,809	115,201	110,168	123,775	120,557	122,700	124,546	127,945
Electric utilities.	4,316	7,817	16,396	37,435	42,558	38,895	38,441	36,500	35,763	36,651	35,951
AVERAGE FUEL PRICES (dol. per mil. Btu)											
All	**1.65**	**2.02**	**3.33**	**6.91**	**8.43**	**7.69**	**8.29**	**8.24**	**8.17**	**8.27**	**8.31**
Residential sector.	2.12	2.73	3.83	7.55	11.14	11.26	11.44	11.62	11.52	11.89	12.19
Commercial sector	1.97	2.56	4.09	7.88	11.70	11.38	12.02	12.20	12.32	12.72	12.90
Industrial sector	0.83	1.09	2.20	4.71	6.10	5.12	5.29	5.23	5.19	5.19	5.18
Transportation sector . . .	2.31	2.57	4.02	8.61	8.26	7.17	8.27	7.98	7.92	7.87	7.88
Electric utilities.	0.32	0.46	0.96	1.75	1.85	1.48	1.46	1.37	1.34	1.35	1.30

[1] Includes electricity sales; excludes electricity generation. [2] Includes sources or fuel types not shown separately.

Source: U.S. Energy Information Administration, *State Energy Price and Expenditure Report*, annual.

No. 955. Residential Energy Consumption, Expenditures, and Average Price, 1980 to 1993, and by Region, 1993

[For period April to March for 1980-85; January to December for 1987-93. Excludes Alaska and Hawaii in 1980. Covers occupied units only. Excludes household usage of gasoline for transportation and the use of wood or coal. Based on Residential Energy Consumption Survey; see source. For composition of regions, see inside front cover. Btu=British thermal unit; see text, Section 19]

TYPE OF FUEL	Unit	1980	1983	1985	1987	1990	1993				
							Total	North-east	Mid-west	South	West
CONSUMPTION											
Total	Quad. Btu . .	9.74	8.62	9.04	9.13	9.22	10.01	2.38	3.13	2.95	1.55
Avg. per household	Mil. Btu	126	103	105	101	98	103.6	122.4	134.3	87.9	76.0
Natural gas	Quad. Btu . .	5.31	4.77	4.98	4.83	4.86	5.27	1.11	2.07	1.18	0.91
Electricity	Quad. Btu . .	2.42	2.42	2.48	2.76	3.03	3.28	0.47	0.74	1.51	0.56
Fuel oil, kerosene	Quad. Btu . .	1.71	1.14	1.26	1.22	1.04	1.07	0.78	0.13	0.13	0.03
Liquid petroleum gas	Quad. Btu . .	0.31	0.29	0.31	0.32	0.28	0.38	0.03	0.19	0.13	0.04
EXPENDITURES											
Total	Bil. dol.	63.2	87.8	97.0	97.7	110.2	123.91	29.72	31.12	43.67	19.41
Avg. per household	Dollars.	815	1,048	1,123	1,080	1,172	1,282	1,526	1,336	1,304	953
Natural gas	Bil. dol.	17.8	27.1	29.8	26.1	27.3	32.04	8.60	11.13	7.24	5.07
Electricity	Bil. dol.	32.6	48.4	54.5	61.6	71.5	81.08	15.76	17.55	34.08	13.69
Fuel oil, kerosene	Bil. dol.	10.7	9.6	9.6	7.2	8.3	6.98	5.00	0.84	0.9	0.24
Liquid petroleum gas	Bil. dol.	2.1	2.7	3.1	2.8	3.1	3.81	0.35	1.59	1.46	0.41
AVERAGE PRICE											
Total	Dol./mil. Btu.	6.49	10.18	10.73	10.71	12.00	12.38	12.47	9.94	14.82	12.54
Natural gas	Dol./mil. Btu .	3.36	5.67	5.97	5.41	5.60	6.07	7.73	5.38	6.13	5.55
Electricity	Dol./mil. Btu .	13.46	19.98	21.94	22.34	23.60	24.69	33.55	23.67	22.61	24.23
Fuel oil, kerosene	Dol./mil. Btu .	6.29	8.42	7.64	5.89	7.90	6.52	6.41	6.46	6.92	8.00
Liquid petroleum gas	Dol./mil. Btu .	6.71	9.42	9.91	8.91	11.20	10.04	13.90	8.55	11.13	10.99

Source: U.S. Energy Information Administration, *Household Energy Consumption and Expenditures, 1993*, and prior reports. Survey not conducted in 1984, 1986, 1988, and 1989.

No. 956. Residential Energy Consumption and Expenditures, by Type of Fuel and Selected Household Characteristic: 1993

[For period January through December. Quad.=quadrillion. See headnote, Table 955]

CHARACTERISTIC	CONSUMPTION (Btu's)					EXPENDITURES				
	Total [1] (quad.)	Avg. per house-hold[1] (mil.)	Natural gas (quad.)	Elec-tricity (quad.)	Fuel oil[2] (quad.)	Total[1] (bil. dol.)	Avg. per house-hold[1] (dol.)	Natural gas (bil. dol.)	Elec-tricity (bil. dol.)	Fuel oil[2]
Total households	**10.01**	**104**	**5.27**	**3.28**	**1.02**	**123.9**	**1,282**	**32.04**	**81.08**	**6.61**
Single family detached	7.21	121	3.77	2.34	0.78	87.0	1,462	22.23	56.44	5.20
Single family attached	0.70	96	0.41	0.24	0.05	9.3	1,266	2.65	6.22	0.34
Two-to-four unit building	0.80	100	0.54	0.17	0.09	8.9	1,112	3.56	4.72	0.58
Five-or-more unit building	0.83	52	0.43	0.32	0.08	12.0	740	2.84	8.76	0.37
Mobile home	0.46	82	0.14	0.21	0.02	6.7	1,203	0.76	4.93	0.12
Year house built:										
1939 or earlier	2.63	129	1.55	0.51	0.43	27.0	1,325	9.60	13.34	2.75
1940 to 1949	0.77	112	0.44	0.20	0.10	8.6	1,240	2.70	4.91	0.64
1950 to 1959	1.49	114	0.85	0.42	0.19	18.1	1,387	5.28	11.22	1.28
1960 to 1969	1.55	103	0.90	0.49	0.11	18.9	1,257	5.35	12.26	0.69
1970 to 1979	1.59	88	0.69	0.71	0.12	22.2	1,222	3.92	16.74	0.78
1980 to 1984	0.68	80	0.29	0.35	0.02	10.6	1,247	1.73	8.48	0.13
1985 to 1987	0.47	85	0.20	0.23	0.02	7.1	1,284	1.22	5.47	0.11
1988 to 1990	0.43	90	0.18	0.21	0.02	6.2	1,322	1.05	4.81	0.13
1991 to 1993	0.40	89	0.20	0.16	0.01	5.4	1,200	1.19	3.85	0.09
1993 family income:										
Less than $5,000	0.32	80	0.18	0.10	0.03	4.0	991	1.14	2.52	0.18
$5,000 to $9,999	0.86	81	0.48	0.26	0.08	10.3	977	2.94	6.42	0.47
$10,000 to $14,999	1.00	90	0.58	0.29	0.09	11.7	1,051	3.51	7.17	0.58
$15,000 to $19,999	0.95	99	0.52	0.30	0.09	11.2	1,163	3.08	7.08	0.55
$20,000 to $24,999	0.84	97	0.43	0.28	0.08	10.3	1,182	2.62	6.75	0.51
$25,000 to $34,999	1.45	104	0.70	0.51	0.16	18.3	1,302	4.20	12.24	1.05
$35,000 to $49,999	1.90	109	0.96	0.65	0.21	24.1	1,379	5.87	16.18	1.36
$50,000 to $74,999	1.51	119	0.78	0.52	0.17	18.9	1,493	4.66	12.66	1.11
$75,000 or more	1.17	140	0.64	0.38	0.12	15.1	1,809	4.02	10.06	0.81

[1] Includes liquid petroleum gas not shown separately. [2] Includes kerosene.

Source: U.S. Energy Information Administration, *Household Energy Consumption and Expenditures, 1993*.

No. 957. Manufacturing Primary Energy Consumption for all Purposes, by Type of Fuel and Major Industry Group: 1994

[In trillions of Btu. Estimates represented in this table are for the primary consumption of energy for heat and power and as feedstocks or raw material inputs. Primary consumption is defined as the consumption of the energy that was originally produced offsite or was produced onsite from input materials not classified as energy. Examples of the latter are hydrogen produced from the electrolysis of brine; the output of captive (onsite) mines or wells; woodchips, bark, and woodwaste from wood purchased as a raw material input; and waste materials such as wastepaper and packing materials. Primary consumption excludes quantities of energy that are produced from other energy inputs and, therefore, avoids double counting. Based on the 1994 Manufacturing Energy Consumption Survey and subject to sampling variability]

INDUSTRY	SIC[1] code	Total	Net elec-tricity[2]	Residual fuel oil	Distil-late fuel oil[3]	Natural gas[4]	LPG	Coal	Coke and breeze	Other[5]
All industries	**(X)**	**21,663**	**2,656**	**490**	**158**	**6,835**	**1,631**	**2,105**	**449**	**7,926**
Food and kindred products	20	1,193	198	30	19	631	(D)	165	(D)	141
Tobacco products	21	(D)	3	1	(D)	(D)	(D)	(D)	-	(D)
Textile mill products.	22	310	111	17	7	117	4	40	-	14
Apparel and other textile products .	23	(D)	26	(D)	1	25	(D)	(D)	-	(D)
Lumber and wood products	24	491	68	2	25	48	(D)	(D)	-	341
Furniture and fixtures	25	69	22	(Z)	1	24	1	3	-	18
Paper and allied products.	26	2,665	223	173	9	575	5	307	-	1,373
Printing and publishing	27	112	59	(D)	2	48	(D)	-	-	2
Petroleum and coal products	2813	104	80	-	(D)	23	(D)	(Z)	1	1
Rubber and misc. plastic products .	30	287	149	10	4	110	3	5	-	6
Leather and leather products.	31	(D)	3	2	(D)	(D)	(D)	-	-	(Z)
Stone, clay, and glass products . . .	32	944	123	7	23	432	4	274	8	73
Primary metal industries.	33	2,462	493	43	13	811	5	922	424	85
Industrial machinery & equipment .	35	246	109	(D)	4	111	3	11	(D)	5
Electric and electronic equipment .	36	243	113	3	2	88	2	(D)	(D)	(S)
Transportation equipment.	37	363	132	11	7	157	3	28	2	23
Instruments and related products. .	38	107	46	4	1	29	(D)	(D)	-	3
Misc. manufacturing industries . . .	39	(D)	19	1	1	19	1	1	-	(D)

- Represents or rounds to zero. D Withheld to avoid disclosing data for individual establishments. S Withheld because Relative Standard Error is greater than 50 percent. X Not applicable. Z Less than 0.5 trillion Btu. [1] Standard Industrial Classification Code; see text, Section 13. [2] Net electricity is obtained by aggregating purchases, transfers in, and generation from noncombustible renewable resources minus quantities sold and transferred out. Excludes electricity inputs from onsite cogeneration or generation from combustible fuels because that energy has already been included as generating fuel (for example, coal). [3] Includes Nos.1, 2, and 4 fuel oils and Nos. 1, 2, and 4 diesel fuels. [4] Includes natural gas obtained from utilities, transmission pipelines, and any other supplier such as brokers and producers. [5] Includes net steam, and other energy that respondents indicated was used to produce heat and power or as feedstock/raw material inputs.

Source: U.S. Energy Information Administration, *Manufacturing Energy Consumption 1994*.

No. 958. Commercial Buildings—Energy Consumption and Expenditures: 1995

[Covers buildings using one or more major fuel. Excludes industrial buildings, predominantly residential buildings, and buildings of less than 1,000 sq. ft. Based on a sample survey of building representatives and energy suppliers; therefore, subject to sampling variability. For characteristics of commercial buildings, see tables in Section 25. For composition of regions, see inside front cover]

BUILDING CHARACTERISTIC	ALL BUILDINGS USING ANY MAJOR FUEL		CONSUMPTION (tril. Btu)			EXPENDITURES (mil. dol.)		
	Number (1,000)	Square feet (mil.)	Major fuel, total [1]	Electricity	Natural gas	Major fuel, total [1]	Electricity	Natural gas
All buildings	**4,579**	**58,772**	**5,321**	**2,608**	**1,946**	**69,918**	**56,621**	**9,018**
Region:								
Northeast	725	11,883	1,035	436	297	16,479	13,059	1,739
Midwest	1,139	14,322	1,497	558	750	15,076	10,946	2,947
South	1,750	20,830	1,684	1,027	528	22,211	19,009	2,560
West.	964	11,736	1,106	587	371	16,152	13,607	1,772
Year constructed:								
1919 or before	353	3,673	292	99	135	3,310	2,290	655
1920 to 1945	562	6,710	508	173	210	5,665	4,012	966
1946 to 1959	867	9,298	826	325	391	9,813	7,395	1,796
1960 to 1969	718	10,858	1,024	472	375	13,135	10,405	1,750
1970 to 1979	813	11,333	1,125	615	393	15,366	13,005	1,695
1980 to 1989	846	12,252	1,059	648	288	15,895	13,844	1,397
1990 to 1992	218	2,590	297	163	100	4,011	3,318	510
1993 to 1995	202	2,059	190	113	54	2,722	2,353	249
Principal activity within building:								
Assembly [2]	682	8,011	677	252	232	7,876	5,688	1,145
Education	309	7,740	614	221	245	7,129	5,168	1,117
Food sales	137	642	137	119	18	2,634	2,532	97
Food service	285	1,353	332	166	158	4,817	3,931	851
Health care	105	2,333	561	211	258	5,261	3,901	838
Lodging.	158	3,618	461	187	213	5,114	3,838	966
Mercantile/services	1,289	12,728	973	508	395	14,025	11,655	1,979
Office	705	10,478	1,019	676	239	15,849	14,020	1,150
Warehouse and storage	580	8,481	325	176	106	4,709	3,934	559
Other	67	1,004	173	75	55	1,865	1,473	197
Vacant	261	2,384	51	18	26	638	481	119
Square footage:								
1,001 to 5,000	2,399	6,338	708	380	264	11,577	9,696	1,483
5,001 to 10,000	1,035	7,530	624	238	272	8,063	6,055	1,439
10,001 to 25,000	745	11,617	824	384	356	11,099	8,911	1,775
25,001 to 50,000	213	7,676	630	316	231	8,676	7,005	1,159
50,001 to 100,000.	115	7,968	698	363	243	8,824	7,194	1,091
100,001 to 200,000	48	6,776	687	337	244	7,859	6,283	958
200,001 to 500,000	19	5,553	636	307	211	7,291	5,908	729
500,001 and over	6	5,313	514	282	125	6,530	5,568	385

[1] Includes fuel oil, propane, and purchased steam not shown separately.   [2] Includes public assembly, public order and safety, and religious worship.

Source: U.S. Energy Information Administration, *Commercial Buildings Energy Consumption and Expenditures, 1995.*

No. 959. Energy Prices: 1980 to 1996

PRODUCT	Unit	1980	1985	1990	1991	1992	1993	1994	1995	1996
Crude oil domestic first purchase price:										
Nominal	Dol./bbl.	21.6	24.1	20.0	16.5	16.0	14.3	13.2	14.6	18.5
Real [1]	Dol./bbl.	35.8	30.7	21.4	17.0	16.0	13.9	12.6	13.6	16.8
Motor gasoline	Cents/gal.	122.1	119.6	121.7	119.6	119.0	117.3	117.4	120.5	128.8
Leaded regular	Cents/gal.	119.1	111.5	114.9	(NA)	(NA)	(NA)	(NA)	(NA)	(NA)
Unleaded regular	Cents/gal.	124.5	120.2	116.4	114.0	112.7	110.8	111.2	114.7	123.1
Premium	Cents/gal.	(NA)	134.0	134.9	132.1	131.6	130.2	130.5	133.6	141.3
Natural gas, residential	Dol/1000 cu. ft. . . .	3.7	6.1	5.8	5.8	5.9	6.2	6.4	6.1	6.3
Heating oil, residential	Cents/gal.	161.3	134.3	113.6	104.7	93.4	88.8	84.3	80.6	90.1
Coal, all.	Dol/short tons . . .	28.8	34.5	30.5	30.0	29.4	28.6	28.0	27.0	26.5
Electricity, total	Cents/kilowatthour	4.7	6.4	6.6	6.7	6.8	6.9	6.9	6.9	6.9
Uranium, domestic purchases . .	Dol/lb.	(NA)	31.4	15.7	13.7	13.5	13.1	10.3	11.1	13.8

NA Not available.   [1] In chained (1992) dollars, calculated by using gross domestic product implicit price deflators.

Source: U.S. Energy Information Administration, *Annual Energy Review.*

No. 960. Fossil Fuel Prices in Current and Constant (1992) Dollars: 1970 to 1996

[In cents per million British thermal units (Btu), except as indicated. All fuel prices taken as close to the point of production as possible. See text, Section 19, for explanation of Btu conversions from mineral fuels]

FUEL	1970	1973	1975	1980	1985	1989	1990	1991	1992	1993	1994	1995	1996
CURRENT DOLLARS													
Composite [1]	0.32	0.40	0.82	2.04	2.51	1.67	1.84	1.67	1.66	1.67	1.53	1.47	1.85
Crude oil.	0.55	0.67	1.32	3.72	4.15	2.73	3.45	2.85	2.76	2.46	2.27	2.52	3.18
Natural gas	0.15	0.20	0.40	1.45	2.26	1.53	1.55	1.48	1.57	1.84	1.67	1.40	2.03
Bituminous coal [2]	0.26	0.37	0.84	1.09	1.15	1.00	1.00	0.99	0.97	0.93	0.91	0.88	0.86
Anthracite coal	0.49	0.62	1.50	1.86	2.04	1.84	1.75	1.61	1.52	1.46	1.60	1.76	1.80
CONSTANT (1992) DOLLARS													
Composite [1]	1.04	1.12	1.95	3.38	3.20	1.86	1.97	1.72	1.66	1.63	1.46	1.37	1.69
Crude oil.	1.79	1.90	3.13	6.16	5.30	3.05	3.69	2.93	2.76	2.40	2.17	2.34	2.90
Natural gas	0.50	0.57	0.95	2.40	2.88	1.70	1.65	1.52	1.57	1.80	1.60	1.30	1.85
Bituminous coal [2]	0.86	1.03	1.99	1.81	1.46	1.12	1.06	1.02	0.97	0.90	0.86	0.82	0.78
Anthracite coal	1.60	1.74	3.54	3.08	2.61	2.05	1.86	1.66	1.52	1.42	1.52	1.64	1.64

[1] Weighted by relative importance of individual fuels in total fuels production.   [2] Includes subbituminous and lignite.

Source: U.S. Energy Information Administration, *Annual Energy Review.*

No. 961. World Energy Consumption, by Region and Energy Source: 1970 to 1995

[In tons of coal equivalent. Metric ton=1.1023 short tons. Kilogram=2.205 pounds. See text, Section 30, for general comments about the data]

REGION AND ENERGY SOURCE	CONSUMPTION (mil. metric tons)				PER CAPITA (kilograms)				PERCENT DISTRIBUTION			
	1970	1980	1990	1995	1970	1980	1990	1995	1970	1980	1990	1995
World, total . .	6,412	8,783	10,826	11,720	1,208	1,626	2,004	2,055	100.0	100.0	100.0	100.0
North America [1] . .	2,486	2,825	3,196	3,597	5,949	6,667	7,543	7,891	38.8	32.2	29.5	30.7
United States. .	2,205	2,391	2,687	3,021	8,910	9,566	10,749	11,312	34.4	27.2	24.8	25.8
South America . .	142	247	313	407	490	841	1,064	1,281	2.2	2.8	2.9	3.5
Europe	1,709	2,230	2,346	3,600	2,963	3,854	4,056	4,943	26.7	25.4	21.7	30.7
Soviet Union	999	1,592	1,919	([2])	3,476	5,502	6,592	([2])	15.6	18.1	17.7	([2])
Asia	904	1,592	2,624	3,643	292	506	834	1,054	14.1	18.1	24.2	31.1
Oceania	72	107	149	167	2,753	3,993	5,597	5,892	1.1	1.2	1.4	1.4
Africa.	101	191	279	306	(NA)	(NA)	434	428	1.6	2.2	2.6	2.6
Energy source:												
Solid fuels	2,143	2,650	3,238	3,504	586	595	612	615	33.5	30.8	29.9	29.9
Liquid fuels	2,802	3,806	4,000	4,108	770	855	756	721	44.0	44.2	36.9	35.0
Natural gas . . .	1,289	1,838	2,539	2,905	351	413	480	510	20.1	21.5	23.5	24.8
Electricity	178	489	1,049	1,203	48	110	198	211	2.4	3.5	9.7	10.3

NA Not available.   [1] Includes Central America.   [2] Beginning 1992, Soviet Union included with Europe.

Source: Statistical Office of the United Nations, New York, NY, *Energy Statistics Yearbook,* annual (copyright).

No. 962. World Primary Energy Production, by Region and Type: 1980 to 1996

[In quadrillion Btu. Btu=British thermal units. For Btu conversion factors, see source]

REGION AND TYPE	1980	1985	1989	1990	1991	1992	1993	1994	1995	1996
World total	286.38	304.16	339.58	347.71	344.74	346.97	348.69	353.85	364.71	375.37
North America	80.85	84.55	87.53	91.71	92.41	92.53	91.80	95.07	95.89	98.46
United States	64.76	64.87	66.68	70.72	70.39	69.94	68.29	70.65	71.08	72.58
Central and South America	12.11	13.59	15.79	16.67	17.64	18.05	18.98	20.04	21.51	23.21
Western Europe	30.66	37.30	38.46	38.53	38.41	38.77	39.28	40.19	41.30	43.81
Eastern Europe and former USSR	66.72	74.96	80.43	78.93	72.53	68.73	64.68	60.04	58.68	58.29
Middle East	42.17	25.77	39.73	41.03	40.32	43.58	45.78	46.95	47.98	48.99
Africa.	18.05	19.29	20.39	21.40	22.38	22.73	22.58	22.77	24.03	25.13
Far East and Oceania. . .	35.82	48.69	57.24	59.43	61.04	62.59	65.58	68.79	75.32	77.48
Crude oil.	128.12	115.40	127.98	129.50	128.77	129.13	128.86	130.46	133.32	137.39
Natural gas	52.65	61.38	71.12	72.53	73.29	73.70	75.17	76.01	77.77	81.90
Natural gas liquids	5.10	5.82	6.67	6.85	7.13	7.38	7.67	7.84	8.14	8.30
Coal.	74.48	85.77	91.08	92.38	87.76	88.70	86.85	88.87	92.41	93.33
Hydroelectric power	18.05	20.56	21.73	22.61	23.00	23.01	24.39	24.39	25.83	26.28
Nuclear electric power. . .	7.58	15.37	19.82	20.37	21.29	21.36	22.02	22.46	23.31	24.10
Geothermal, solar and wind.	0.40	0.60	1.17	2.79	2.82	2.97	3.05	3.14	3.18	3.35

Source: U.S. Energy Information Administration, *International Energy Annual.*

No. 963. Energy Imports and Exports, by Type of Fuel: 1970 to 1996

[In quadrillion of Btu. For definition of Btu, see text, Section 19]

TYPE OF FUEL	1970	1973	1975	1980	1985	1990	1991	1992	1993	1994	1995	1996
Net imports:[1]												
Coal..............	-1.93	-1.42	-1.74	-2.39	-2.39	-2.70	-2.77	-2.59	-1.78	-1.69	-2.14	-2.19
Natural Gas (dry)	0.77	0.98	0.90	0.96	0.90	1.46	1.67	1.94	2.25	2.52	2.74	2.75
Petroleum	6.92	12.98	12.51	13.50	8.95	15.29	14.22	14.96	16.40	17.26	16.87	18.04
Other [2]	-0.04	0.14	0.08	0.18	0.41	0.03	0.25	0.33	0.32	0.49	0.42	0.40
Imports:												
Coal..............	(Z)	(Z)	0.02	0.03	0.05	0.07	0.08	0.10	0.18	0.19	0.18	0.18
Natural Gas (dry)	0.85	1.06	0.98	1.01	0.95	1.55	1.80	2.16	2.40	2.68	2.90	2.90
Petroleum	7.47	13.47	12.95	14.66	10.61	17.12	16.35	16.97	18.51	19.25	18.86	20.10
Other [2]	0.07	0.20	0.16	0.28	0.49	0.26	0.35	0.44	0.45	0.59	0.54	0.50
Exports:												
Coal..............	1.94	1.43	1.76	2.42	2.44	2.77	2.85	2.68	1.96	1.88	2.32	2.37
Natural Gas (dry)	0.07	0.08	0.07	0.05	0.06	0.09	0.13	0.22	0.14	0.16	0.16	0.15
Petroleum	0.55	0.49	0.44	1.16	1.66	1.82	2.13	2.01	2.12	1.99	1.99	2.06
Other [2]	0.11	0.06	0.08	0.09	0.08	0.23	0.11	0.11	0.13	0.09	0.11	0.10

Z Less than .005 quadrillion Btu.   [1] Net imports equals imports minus exports.   Minus sign (-) denotes an excess of exports over imports.   [2] Coal coke and small amounts of electricity transmitted across U.S. borders with Canada and Mexico.

Source: U.S. Energy Information Administration, *Annual Energy Review*.

No. 964. U.S. Foreign Trade in Selected Mineral Fuels: 1970 to 1997

[Minus sign (-) indicates an excess of imports over exports]

MINERAL FUEL	Unit	1970	1973	1975	1980	1985	1990	1994	1995	1996	1997
NATURAL GAS											
Imports	Bil. cu. ft.....	821	1,033	953	985	950	1,532	2,624	2,841	2,937	2,990
Exports	Bil. cu. ft.....	70	77	73	49	55	86	162	162	154	153
Net trade	Bil. cu. ft.....	-751	-956	-880	-936	-894	-1446	-2462	-2687	-2,784	-2,833
CRUDE OIL											
Imports [1]	Mil. bbl......	483	1,184	1,498	1,926	1,168	2,151	2,578	2,639	2,740	3,002
Exports	Mil. bbl......	5	1	2	105	75	40	36	35	40	39
Net trade	Mil. bbl......	-478	-1,183	-1,496	-1,821	-1,093	-2,112	-2,542	-2,604	-2,700	-2,963
PETROLEUM PRODUCTS											
Imports	Mil. bbl......	765	1,099	712	603	681	775	706	586	719	707
Exports	Mil. bbl......	89	84	74	94	211	273	308	312	318	327
Net trade	Mil. bbl......	-676	-1015	-638	-509	-470	-502	-398	-274	-402	-380
COAL											
Imports	1,000 sh. tons.	36	127	940	1,194	1,952	2,699	7,584	7,201	7,126	7,487
Exports	1,000 sh. tons.	71,733	53,587	66,309	91,742	92,680	105,804	71,359	88,547	90,473	83,545
Net trade	1,000 sh. tons.	71,697	53,460	65,369	90,548	90,728	103,105	63,775	81,346	83,347	76,058

[1] Beginning 1980, includes strategic petroleum reserve imports.

Source: U.S. Energy Information Administration, *Annual Energy Review*.

No. 965. Daily International Flow of Crude Oil, by Area: 1991

[In thousands of barrels per day]

EXPORTING AREA	Total [1]	IMPORTING AREA							
		North America		Central and South America	Western Europe	Eastern Europe	Middle East and Africa	Japan	Other Far East and Oceania
		U.S.	Canada						
World total..........	**28,406**	**5,782**	**551**	**1,641**	**10,245**	**834**	**1,143**	**4,180**	**4,030**
United States	116	(X)	5	[2]111	-	-	-	-	-
North America, except U.S.	2,121	1,502	15	58	346	-	32	157	11
Central and South America	1,842	927	35	615	208	-	-	9	48
Western Europe..............	2,939	183	348	11	2,374	-	23	-	-
Eastern Europe and U.S.S.R.....	1,205	1	-	5	637	493	16	2	51
Middle East................	12,947	1,770	89	682	3,567	246	731	3,034	2,828
Africa.....................	4,969	1,160	59	147	3,101	95	323	11	73
Far East and Oceania........	2,267	239	-	12	12	-	18	967	1,019

- Represents zero.   X Not applicable.   [1] Includes stocks at sea, exchanges, transshipments, and other statistical discrepancies not shown separately.   [2] Includes shipments to Puerto Rico and Virgin Islands.

Source: U.S. Energy Information Administration, *International Energy Annual*.

No. 966. Crude Oil Imports Into United States, by Country of Origin: 1970 to 1997

[In millions of barrels. Barrels contain 42 gallons]

COUNTRY OF ORIGIN	1970	1973	1975	1980	1985	1990	1992	1993	1994	1995	1996	1997
Total imports . . .	483	1,184	1,498	1,921	1,168	2,151	2,220	2,477	2,578	2,643	2,748	2,918
Total OPEC [1]	222	765	1,172	1,410	479	1,283	1,243	1,317	1,307	1,303	1,280	1,349
Persian Gulf [2], total	62	293	409	550	89	657	597	598	589	539	544	591
Iran	12	79	101	3	10	-	-	-	-	-	(NA)	(NA)
Iraq	-	1	1	10	17	188	-	-	-	-	-	32
Kuwait [3]	12	15	1	10	1	29	14	126	112	78	86	92
Qatar	-	3	7	8	-	1	-	-	-	-	-	-
Saudi Arabia [3]	15	169	256	456	48	436	585	468	473	460	457	467
United Arab Emirates. .	23	26	43	63	13	3	-	4	4	1	1	-
Other OPEC [2], total	160	472	763	860	390	625	646	720	717	764	735	755
Algeria	2	44	96	166	31	23	9	9	8	10	3	2
Ecuador [4]	-	17	21	6	20	14	23	(⁴)	(⁴)	(⁴)	35	41
Gabon	-	-	10	9	19	23	45	55	71	84	67	80
Indonesia	26	73	138	115	107	36	26	24	34	23	16	18
Libya	17	49	81	200	-	-	-	-	-	-	(NA)	(NA)
Nigeria	17	164	272	307	102	286	243	264	228	226	218	244
Venezuela	98	126	144	57	112	243	302	369	377	421	477	493
Non-OPEC [5], total . .	245	419	326	511	689	869	977	1,160	1,271	1,340	1,410	1,569
Canada	245	365	219	73	171	235	292	329	359	380	394	412
Malaysia.	(NA)	(NA)	(NA)	(NA)	(NA)	(NA)	(NA)	4	2	2	2	3
Mexico.	-	(Z)	26	185	261	251	288	315	343	375	440	489
Norway.	-	-	4	53	11	35	43	50	69	95	107	104
Trinidad and Tobago	(Z)	22	42	42	36	28	26	20	23	23	21	20
United Kingdom	-	-	(Z)	63	101	57	73	114	145	125	79	61

- Represents zero.   NA Not available.   Z Less than 500,000 barrels.   [1] OPEC (Organization of Petroleum Exporting Countries) includes the Persian Gulf nations shown below, except Bahrain, which is not a member of OPEC, and also includes nations shown under "Other OPEC."   [2] Excludes petroleum imported into the United States indirectly from members of the OPEC countries.   [3] Imports from the Neutral Zone between Kuwait and Saudi Arabia are included in Saudi Arabia.   [4] Ecuador withdrew from OPEC on Dec. 31, 1992; therefore, it is included under OPEC for the period 1973 to 1992.   [5] Includes petroleum imported into the United States indirectly from member of OPEC, primarily from Caribbean and West European areas, as petroleum products that were refined from crude oil produced by OPEC.

Source: 1970, U.S. Bureau of Mines, *Minerals Yearbooks, vol. I;* thereafter, U.S. Energy Information Administration, *Petroleum Supply Annual,* vol. I.

No. 967. Crude Oil and Refined Products—Summary: 1973 to 1997

[Barrels of 42 gallons. Data are averages]

YEAR	CRUDE OIL (1,000 bbl. per day)					REFINED OIL PRODUCTS (1,000 bbl. per day)			Total oil imports[2] (1,000 bbl. per day)	CRUDE OIL STOCKS [3] (mil. bbl.)	
	Input to refiner-ies	Domes-tic pro-duction	Imports		Exports	Domes-tic demand	Imports	Exports		Total	Strategic reserve
			Total [1]	Strate-gic reserve							
1973	12,431	9,208	3,244	(X)	2	17,308	3,012	229	6,256	242	(X)
1974	12,133	8,774	3,477	(X)	3	16,653	2,635	218	6,112	265	(X)
1975	12,442	8,375	4,105	(X)	6	16,322	1,951	204	6,056	271	(X)
1976	13,416	8,132	5,287	(X)	8	17,461	2,026	215	7,313	285	(X)
1977	14,602	8,245	6,615	21	50	18,431	2,193	193	8,807	348	7
1978	14,739	8,707	6,356	161	158	18,847	2,008	204	8,363	376	67
1979	14,648	8,552	6,519	67	235	18,513	1,937	236	8,456	430	91
1980	13,481	8,597	5,263	44	287	17,056	1,646	258	6,909	466	108
1981	12,470	8,572	4,396	256	228	16,058	1,599	367	5,996	594	230
1982	11,774	8,649	3,488	165	236	15,296	1,625	579	5,113	644	294
1983	11,685	8,688	3,329	234	164	15,231	1,722	575	5,051	723	379
1984	12,044	8,879	3,426	197	181	15,726	2,011	541	5,437	796	451
1985	12,002	8,971	3,201	118	204	15,726	1,866	577	5,067	814	493
1986	12,716	8,680	4,178	48	154	16,281	2,045	631	6,224	843	512
1987	12,854	8,349	4,674	73	151	16,665	2,004	613	6,678	890	541
1988	13,246	8,140	5,107	51	155	17,283	2,295	661	7,402	890	560
1989	13,401	7,613	5,843	56	142	17,325	2,217	717	8,061	921	580
1990	13,409	7,355	5,894	27	109	16,988	2,123	748	8,018	908	586
1991	13,301	7,417	5,782	-	116	16,714	1,844	885	7,627	893	569
1992	13,411	7,171	6,083	10	89	17,033	1,805	861	7,888	893	575
1993	13,613	6,847	6,787	15	98	17,237	1,833	904	8,620	922	587
1994	13,866	6,662	7,063	12	99	17,718	1,933	843	8,996	929	592
1995	13,973	6,560	7,230	-	95	17,725	1,605	855	8,835	895	592
1996	14,195	6,465	7,508	-	110	18,309	1,971	871	9,478	850	566
1997	14,626	6,411	7,996	-	108	18,582	1,912	896	9,907	868	563

- Represents zero.   X Not applicable.   [1] Includes Strategic Petroleum Reserve.   [2] Crude oil (including Strategic Petroleum Reserve imports) plus refined products.   [3] End of year.

Source: U.S. Energy Information Administration, *Monthly Energy Review,* February 1996.

No. 968. Petroleum and Coal Products Corporations—Sales, Net Profit, and Profit Per Dollar of Sales: 1980 to 1997

[Represents SIC group 29. Profit rates are averages of quarterly figures at annual rates. Beginning 1988, excludes estimates for corporations with less than $250,000 in assets]

ITEM	Unit	1980	1985	1988	1989	1990	1991	1992	1993	1994	1995	1996	1997
Sales	Bil. dol .	333.2	320.9	252.2	265.3	318.5	282.2	278.0	266.1	268.2	283.1	323.5	313.5
Net profit:													
Before income taxes.	Bil. dol .	39.1	17.7	27.3	23.7	23.3	12.2	2.0	15.0	17.3	16.7	32.9	36.2
After income taxes	Bil. dol .	25.5	12.7	21.2	19.5	18.0	10.9	3.2	13.1	15.0	14.1	26.9	28.9
Depreciation[1]	Bil. dol .	11.6	22.1	20.0	18.5	18.7	18.0	18.3	17.4	17.1	16.7	15.9	15.5
Profits per dollar of sales:													
Before income taxes.	Cents . .	11.7	5.5	10.8	9.0	7.4	4.3	0.4	5.6	6.4	5.9	10.2	11.5
After income taxes	Cents . .	7.7	4.0	8.5	7.4	5.7	3.9	0.9	4.9	5.5	5.0	8.3	9.2
Profits on stockholders' equity:													
Before income taxes.	Percent.	30.7	11.7	19.2	17.8	16.6	8.6	1.5	11.9	13.3	12.7	23.4	23.8
After income taxes	Percent.	20.0	8.5	14.9	14.6	12.8	7.7	2.4	10.3	11.5	10.8	19.1	19.0

[1] Includes depletion and accelerated amortization of emergency facilities.
Source: 1980, U.S. Federal Trade Commission; thereafter, U.S. Bureau of the Census, *Quarterly Financial Report for Manufacturing, Mining and Trade Corporations.*

No. 969. Major Petroleum Companies—Financial Data Summary: 1973 to 1996

[Data represent a composite of approximately 42 major worldwide petroleum companies aggregated on a consolidated, total company basis]

ITEM	1973	1975	1980	1985	1990	1991	1992	1993	1994	1995	1996
FINANCIAL DATA (bil. dol.)											
Net income	11.8	11.6	32.9	19.4	26.8	18.7	12.1	18.8	20.3	24.3	38.1
Depreciation, depletion, etc	10.5	11.3	32.5	53.0	38.7	36.5	43.3	39.0	38.9	43.1	42.7
Cash flow[1]	22.3	22.8	65.4	72.4	65.5	55.2	55.4	57.0	59.2	67.4	80.8
Dividends paid	4.0	4.7	9.3	12.0	15.9	16.3	16.5	15.5	16.4	17.6	18.8
Net internal funds available for investment or debt repayment [2]	18.3	18.1	56.1	60.4	49.6	38.9	38.9	41.5	42.8	49.8	62.0
Capital and exploratory expenditures	16.3	26.9	62.1	58.3	59.6	61.5	53.6	51.8	51.5	57.3	63.7
Long-term capitalization	102.9	121.1	211.4	272.1	300.0	307.4	290.7	291.7	299.0	304.2	317.7
Long-term debt	22.5	28.9	49.8	93.5	90.4	95.9	94.0	91.6	89.1	85.4	77.0
Preferred stock	0.4	0.4	2.0	3.3	5.2	4.1	5.3	5.8	5.4	5.7	7.2
Common stock and retained earnings [3] .	80.0	91.9	159.6	175.3	204.4	207.4	191.4	194.3	204.5	213.1	233.5
Excess of expenditures over cash income [4]	-2.0	8.9	6.0	-2.1	10.0	22.6	14.7	10.3	8.7	7.5	1.7
RATIOS [5] (percent)											
Long-term debt to long-term capitalization	22.0	23.8	23.6	34.4	30.1	31.2	32.3	31.4	29.8	28.1	24.2
Net income to total average capital	12.0	10.0	17.0	7.0	9.1	6.2	4.1	6.5	6.8	7.8	12.3
Net income to average common equity . . .	15.6	13.1	22.5	10.8	13.5	9.1	6.1	9.8	10.1	11.3	17.1

[1] Generally represents internally-generated funds from operations. Sum of net income and noncash charges such as depreciation, depletion, and amortization. [2] Cash flow minus dividends paid. [3] Includes common stock, capital surplus, and earned surplus accounts after adjustments. [4] Capital and exploratory expenditures plus dividends paid minus cash flow. [5] Represents approximate year-to-year comparisons because of changes in the makeup of the group due to mergers and other corporate changes.
Source: Carl H. Pforzheimer & Co., New York, NY, *Comparative Oil Company Statements, 1995-1996,* and earlier reports.

No. 970. Electric Utility Sales and Average Prices, by End-Use Sector: 1970 to 1996

[Prior to 1980, covers Class A and B privately-owned electric utilities; thereafter, Class A utilities whose electric operating revenues were $100 million or more during the previous year]

YEAR	SALES (bil. kWh)				AVERAGE PRICE OF ELECTRICITY SOLD (cents per kWh)							
					Current dollars				Constant (1987) dollars [2]			
	Total [1]	Resi-dential	Com-mercial	Indus-trial	Total [1]	Resi-dential	Com-mercial	Indus-trial	Total [1]	Resi-dential	Com-mercial	Indus-trial
1970	1,392	466	307	571	1.7	2.2	2.1	1.0	5.6	7.2	6.9	3.3
1973	1,713	579	388	686	2.0	2.5	2.4	1.3	5.6	7.1	6.8	3.7
1975	1,747	588	403	688	2.9	3.5	3.5	2.1	6.9	8.3	8.3	5.0
1980	2,094	717	488	815	4.7	5.4	5.5	3.7	7.8	8.9	9.1	6.1
1981	2,147	722	514	826	5.5	6.2	6.3	4.3	8.3	9.4	9.6	6.5
1982	2,086	730	526	745	6.1	6.9	6.9	5.0	8.7	9.8	9.8	7.1
1983	2,151	751	544	776	6.3	7.2	7.0	5.0	8.6	9.8	9.6	6.8
1984	2,286	780	583	838	6.3	7.2	7.1	4.8	8.3	9.5	9.4	6.3
1985	2,324	794	606	837	6.4	7.4	7.3	5.0	8.2	9.4	9.3	6.4
1986	2,369	819	631	831	6.4	7.4	7.2	4.9	7.9	9.2	8.9	6.1
1987	2,457	850	660	858	6.4	7.4	7.1	4.8	7.7	8.9	8.5	5.8
1988	2,578	893	699	896	6.4	7.5	7.0	4.7	7.4	8.7	8.1	5.5
1989	2,647	906	726	926	6.5	7.6	7.2	4.7	7.2	8.5	8.0	5.2
1990	2,713	924	751	946	6.6	7.8	7.3	4.7	7.1	8.3	7.8	5.0
1991	2,762	955	766	947	6.7	8.0	7.5	4.8	6.9	8.2	7.7	4.9
1992	2,763	936	761	973	6.8	8.2	7.7	4.8	6.8	8.2	7.7	4.8
1993	2,861	995	795	977	6.9	8.3	7.7	4.8	6.7	8.1	7.5	4.7
1994	2,935	1,008	820	1,008	6.9	8.4	7.7	4.8	6.6	8.0	7.3	4.6
1995	3,013	1,043	863	1,013	6.9	8.4	7.7	4.7	6.4	7.8	7.2	4.4
1996	3,084	1,078	888	1,017	6.9	8.4	7.6	4.6	6.3	7.7	6.9	4.2

[1] Includes other sectors not shown separately. [2] Based on the GDP implicit price deflator.
Source: U.S. Energy Information Administration, *Annual Energy Review.*

No. 971. Electric Utility Industry—Net Generation, Net Summer Capability, Generating Units, and Consumption of Fuels: 1980 to 1996

[Net Generation for **calendar years**; other data as of **December 31**]

ITEM	Unit	1980	1985	1989	1990	1991	1992	1993	1994	1995	1996
RETAIL SALES											
Retail sales, total	Bil. kWh . .	**2,094**	**2,324**	**2,647**	**2,713**	**2,762**	**2,763**	**2,861**	**2,935**	**3,013**	**3,098**
Net generation by electric utilities	Bil. kWh. .	2,286	2,470	2,784	2,808	2,825	2,797	2,883	2,911	2,995	3,077
Purchases by utilities from nonutility purchasers	Bil. kWh. . .	1	26	90	116	139	166	189	209	222	229
Imports	Bil. kWh. . .	25	46	26	23	31	37	39	52	47	47
Exports	Bil. kWh. . .	4	5	15	21	9	9	11	8	9	9
Losses and unaccounted for . . .	Bil. kWh. . .	214	212	238	214	225	229	238	223	232	277
NET GENERATION											
Total	Bil. kWh . .	**2,286**	**2,470**	**2,784**	**2,808**	**2,825**	**2,797**	**2,883**	**2,911**	**2,995**	**3,077**
Average annual change [1]	Percent . . .	3.5	1.5	2.9	0.9	0.6	-1.0	3.0	1.0	2.8	2.7
Net generation, kWh per kW of net summer capability [2]	Rate	3,951	3,770	4,064	4,067	4,076	4,024	4,119	4,147	4,248	4,333
Source of energy:											
Coal [3]	Percent . . .	50.8	56.8	56.2	55.6	54.9	56.3	56.9	56.2	55.2	57.0
Nuclear	Percent . . .	11.0	15.5	19.0	20.5	21.7	22.1	21.2	22.0	22.5	22.0
Oil.	Percent . . .	10.8	4.0	5.7	4.2	3.9	3.2	3.5	3.1	2.0	2.0
Gas.	Percent . . .	15.1	11.8	9.6	9.4	9.3	9.4	9.0	10.0	10.3	9.0
Hydro	Percent . . .	12.1	11.4	9.5	10.1	9.9	8.7	9.3	8.5	9.9	11.0
Type of prime mover: [4]											
Hydro	Bil. kWh. . .	276	281	265	280	276	240	265	244	294	328
Steam conventional [5]	Bil. kWh. . .	1,726	1,778	1,950	1,919	1,905	1,908	1,964	1,982	1,977	2,018
Gas turbine and internal combustion	Bil. kWh. . .	28	16	29	14	22	21	25	36	44	49
Steam nuclear.	Bil. kWh. . .	251	384	529	577	613	619	610	640	673	675
Other.	Bil. kWh. . .	6	11	11	11	10	10	10	9	6	7
NET SUMMER CAPABILITY											
Total [6]	Mil. kW . . .	**579**	**655**	**685**	**691**	**693**	**695**	**700**	**702**	**705**	**710**
Average annual change [1]	Percent . . .	3.3	2.5	1.1	0.8	0.4	0.3	0.7	0.3	0.4	0.7
Hydro	Mil. kW . . .	82	89	91	91	92	93	96	96	97	94
Steam conventional [7]	Mil. kW . . .	397	437	444	448	447	447	447	446	446	442
Gas turbine	Mil. kW . . .	43	44	45	46	48	50	52	55	57	53
Steam nuclear	Mil. kW . . .	52	79	98	100	100	99	99	99	99	101
Internal combustion	Mil. kW . . .	5	5	5	5	5	5	5	5	5	5
Geothermal and other	Mil. kW . . .	1	2	2	2	2	2	2	2	2	2
Combined cycle	Mil. kW . . .	(NA)	(NA)	(NA)	(NA)	(NA)	(NA)	(NA)	(NA)	(NA)	14
NUMBER OF GENERATING UNITS											
Total [8]	Number . .	**11,084**	**(NA)**	**10,325**	**10,296**	**10,260**	**10,221**	**10,471**	**10,427**	**10,396**	**10,422**
Hydro	Number. . .	3,275	(NA)	3,479	3,479	3,479	3,476	3,388	3,362	3,337	3,480
Steam conventional	Number. . .	2,862	(NA)	2,363	2,354	2,284	2,307	2,221	2,170	2,157	2,153
Gas turbine	Number. . .	1,447	(NA)	1,438	1,460	1,485	1,501	1,411	1,446	1,486	1,542
Steam nuclear	Number. . .	74	(NA)	110	111	111	109	109	109	109	110
Internal combustion	Number. . .	3,410	(NA)	2,889	2,847	2,803	2,807	2,976	2,953	2,920	2,884
CONSUMPTION OF FOSSIL FUELS											
Net generation by fuel [9] . .	Quad. Btu .	**18.56**	**18.79**	**20.54**	**20.32**	**20.07**	**19.99**	**20.58**	**20.92**	**20.92**	**21.44**
Coal	Quad. Btu .	12.12	14.54	15.99	16.19	16.03	16.21	16.79	16.90	16.99	17.91
Percent of total	Percent . . .	65.30	77.38	77.85	79.68	79.87	81.09	81.58	80.78	81.21	83.5
Petroleum	Quad. Btu .	2.63	1.09	1.69	1.25	1.18	0.95	1.05	0.97	0.66	0.73
Gas	Quad. Btu .	3.81	3.16	2.87	2.88	2.86	2.83	2.74	3.05	3.28	2.81
Fuel consumed:											
Coal	Mil. sh. tons	569	694	767	774	772	780	814	817	829	874
Petroleum.	Mil. bbl. . . .	421	175	270	200	189	152	169	155	102	118
Gas.	Bil cu. ft. . .	3,682	3,044	2,787	2,787	2,789	2,766	2,682	2,987	3,197	2,737

NA Not available.   [1] Change from immediate prior year except for 1980, change from 1975. For explanation of average annual percent change, see Guide to Tabular Presentation.   [2] Net summer capability is the steady hourly output that generating equipment is expected to supply to system load, exclusive of auxiliary power as demonstrated by test at the time of summer peak demand.   [3] Includes small percentage (.5 percent) from wood and waste, geothermal, and petroleum coke.   [4] A prime mover is the engine, turbine, water wheel, or similar machine which drives an electric generator.   [5] Fossil fuels only.   [6] Includes wind, solar thermal, and photovoltaic, not shown separately.   [7] Includes fossil steam, wood, and waste.   [8] Each prime mover type in combination plants counted separately. Includes geothermal, wind, and solar, not shown separately.   [9] Includes small amounts of wood, waste, wind, geothermal, solar thermal, and photovoltaic.

Source: U.S. Energy Information Administration, 1980, *Power Production, Fuel Consumption, and Installed Capacity Data-Annual,* and unpublished data; thereafter, *Electric Power Annual, Annual Energy Review,* and unpublished data.

No. 972. Electric Utility Industry—Capability, Peak Load, and Capacity Margin: 1980 to 1996

[Excludes Alaska and Hawaii. Capability represents the maximum kilowatt output with all power sources available and with hydraulic equipment under actual water conditions, allowing for maintenance, emergency outages, and system operating requirements. Capacity margin is the difference between capability and peak load]

| YEAR | CAPABILITY AT THE TIME OF— | | | | NON-COINCIDENT PEAK LOAD | | CAPACITY MARGIN | | | |
| | Summer peak load (1,000 kW) | | Winter peak load (1,000 kW) | | | | Summer | | Winter | |
	Amount	Change from prior year	Amount	Change from prior year	Summer	Winter	Amount (1,000 kW)	Percent of capability	Amount (1,000 kW)	Percent of capability
1980	558,237	13,731	572,195	17,670	427,058	384,567	131,179	23.5	187,628	32.8
1981	572,219	13,982	586,569	14,374	429,349	397,800	142,870	25.0	188,769	32.2
1982	586,142	13,923	598,066	11,497	415,618	373,985	170,524	29.1	224,081	37.5
1983	596,449	10,307	612,453	14,387	447,526	410,779	148,923	25.0	201,674	32.9
1984	604,240	7,791	622,125	9,672	451,150	436,374	153,090	25.3	185,751	29.9
1985	621,597	17,357	636,475	14,350	460,503	423,660	161,094	25.9	212,815	33.4
1986	633,291	11,694	646,721	10,246	476,320	422,857	156,971	24.8	223,864	34.6
1987	648,118	14,827	662,977	16,256	496,185	448,277	151,933	23.4	214,700	32.4
1988	661,580	13,462	676,940	13,963	529,460	466,533	132,120	20.0	210,407	31.1
1989	673,316	11,736	685,249	8,309	523,432	496,378	149,884	22.3	188,871	27.6
1990	685,091	11,775	696,757	11,508	545,537	484,014	139,554	20.4	212,743	30.5
1991	690,915	5,824	703,212	6,455	551,320	485,435	139,595	20.2	217,777	31.0
1992	695,436	4,521	707,752	4,540	548,707	492,983	146,729	21.1	214,769	30.3
1993	694,250	1,186	711,957	4,205	575,356	521,733	118,894	17.1	190,224	26.7
1994	702,985	8,735	715,090	3,133	585,320	518,253	117,665	16.7	196,837	27.5
1995	714,222	11,237	727,679	12,589	620,249	544,684	93,973	13.2	182,995	25.1
1996	723,571	9,349	740,526	12,847	615,529	545,061	108,042	14.9	195,465	26.4

Source: Edison Electric Institute, Washington, DC, *Statistical Yearbook of the Electric Utility Industry,* annual.

No. 973. Electric Energy Sales, by Class of Service, and by State, 1997

[In billions of kilowatt-hours]

STATE	Total[1]	Residential	Commercial	Industrial	STATE	Total[1]	Residential	Commercial	Industrial
Total [2]	**3,119.7**	**1,071.7**	**913.5**	**1,035.9**	Missouri	65.2	26.3	22.8	15.1
Alabama	73.4	24.6	14.1	34.2	Montana	12.5	3.8	3.3	5.1
Alaska	5.0	1.7	2.3	0.8	Nebraska	22.8	8.0	6.5	6.7
Arizona	54.0	20.7	17.9	12.9	Nevada	24.9	7.8	5.4	9.8
Arkansas	36.3	12.9	7.5	15.3	New Hampshire	9.1	3.4	3.2	2.3
California	223.9	72.8	86.9	59.7					
					New Jersey	66.5	22.4	29.8	13.8
Colorado	37.7	12.2	14.9	9.6	New Mexico	17.3	4.5	5.5	5.9
Connecticut	28.4	10.9	11.2	5.9	New York	131.6	39.9	54.3	25.1
Delaware	10.0	3.2	3.0	3.7	North Carolina	108.4	40.3	31.1	35.1
Dist. of Columbia	10.1	1.6	7.9	0.3	North Dakota	8.2	3.5	2.0	2.3
Florida	175.1	88.0	64.3	17.2					
					Ohio	159.9	43.3	36.3	75.8
Georgia	100.4	36.2	29.7	33.3	Oklahoma	44.1	17.3	11.8	12.6
Hawaii	9.4	2.7	2.8	3.9	Oregon	47.1	17.1	13.6	15.7
Idaho	21.3	6.6	6.0	8.4	Pennsylvania	126.5	42.4	35.6	47.3
Illinois	125.9	37.0	38.1	42.1	Rhode Island	6.6	2.5	2.6	1.3
Indiana	88.4	26.3	18.1	43.4					
					South Carolina	67.8	21.3	15.0	30.7
Iowa	35.7	11.6	7.4	15.4	South Dakota	7.7	3.4	2.1	1.9
Kansas	32.2	11.1	11.1	9.6	Tennessee	86.1	33.4	11.6	40.0
Kentucky	75.7	20.7	10.8	41.1	Texas	284.9	101.6	73.6	96.9
Louisiana	75.5	24.3	16.2	32.4	Utah	20.4	5.7	6.5	7.4
Maine	11.9	3.7	3.3	4.9					
					Vermont	5.3	2.0	1.7	1.6
Maryland	56.5	22.1	23.5	10.2	Virginia	87.2	33.9	24.8	19.3
Massachusetts	47.6	16.2	21.0	9.8	Washington	85.1	31.6	21.6	28.0
Michigan	97.4	28.7	32.5	35.3	West Virginia	26.2	9.0	5.9	11.2
Minnesota	55.0	16.9	9.6	27.8	Wisconsin	59.9	18.4	15.7	25.1
Mississippi	39.5	14.5	8.4	15.9	Wyoming	12.2	2.1	2.5	7.1

[1] Includes other service not shown separately.   [2] Preliminary.

Source: U.S. Energy Information Administration, *Electric Power Annual.*

No. 974. Electric Energy—Net Generation and Net Summer Capability, by State: 1990 to 1996

[Capacity as of **Dec. 31.** Covers utilities for public use]

STATE	NET GENERATION (bil. kWh) 1990	1995	1990 Total	1990 Percent from coal	NET SUMMER CAPABILITY (mil. kW) 1995	1996
U.S.	2,808.2	2,994.5	3,077.4	56.5	690.5	709.9
AL	76.2	99.6	115.1	63.9	20.0	20.7
AK	4.5	4.8	5.0	4.6	1.5	1.7
AZ	62.3	69.0	70.9	43.4	14.9	15.1
AR	37.1	39.5	43.7	55.7	9.6	9.6
CA	114.5	121.9	114.7	-	43.7	43.9
CO	31.3	32.7	34.0	94.1	6.6	6.8
CT	32.2	26.9	15.8	15.0	7.1	6.3
DE	7.1	8.3	8.1	52.0	2.0	2.2
DC	0.4	0.2	0.1	-	0.8	0.8
FL	123.6	147.2	145.1	45.3	32.7	36.9
GA	97.6	102.0	98.7	64.1	20.7	22.8
HI	8.0	6.2	6.4	-	1.5	1.6
ID	8.6	10.1	12.2	-	2.3	2.6
IL	127.0	145.2	144.1	49.6	32.6	33.2
IN	97.7	105.2	150.6	69.4	20.6	20.7
IA	29.0	33.5	33.4	84.7	8.0	8.2
KS	33.9	38.2	39.9	74.6	9.6	9.7
KY	73.8	86.2	88.4	95.7	15.5	15.7
LA	58.2	65.6	58.6	31.8	16.8	17.2
ME	9.1	2.7	7.8	-	2.4	2.4
MD	31.5	44.7	44.4	62.6	9.8	11.0
MA	36.5	27.0	27.8	41.4	9.9	9.4
MI	89.1	92.5	95.2	69.5	22.3	22.0
MN	41.6	42.5	41.8	65.4	8.8	9.2
MS	22.9	26.4	28.8	41.6	7.0	7.2
MO	59.0	65.4	67.8	84.3	15.2	16.0
MT	25.7	25.4	26.0	47.0	4.9	4.9
NE	21.6	25.3	27.3	58.7	5.5	5.6
NV	19.3	20.0	21.4	68.6	4.9	5.6
NH	10.8	13.9	15.4	21.5	2.6	2.5
NJ	36.5	27.1	19.8	29.4	13.7	13.6
NM	28.5	29.4	29.4	89.8	5.0	5.1
NY	128.7	101.2	104.4	19.6	31.2	30.1
NC	79.8	96.1	102.8	62.4	20.2	20.9
ND	26.8	28.8	30.8	89.5	4.5	4.2
OH	126.5	137.9	142.9	89.7	27.0	27.3
OK	45.1	48.0	47.5	67.0	12.8	13.1
OR	49.2	44.0	47.9	3.6	11.2	10.5
PA	165.7	168.9	175.0	57.6	33.4	33.7
RI	0.6	0.7	3.3	-	0.3	0.4
SC	69.3	78.4	76.3	39.7	14.9	17.2
SD	6.4	8.8	10.1	20.2	2.7	3.0
TN	73.9	82.3	88.6	62.6	17.0	17.3
TX	234.0	261.7	272.3	48.9	62.0	64.8
UT	32.3	32.1	32.2	95.2	4.8	4.9
VT	5.0	4.8	5.0	-	1.1	1.1
VA	47.2	52.7	56.5	49.4	13.7	14.8
WA	100.5	95.7	112.6	7.1	24.2	24.3
WV	77.4	77.3	84.0	99.1	14.4	14.4
WI	45.6	51.0	51.7	73.9	10.6	11.9
WY	39.4	39.7	40.9	96.8	5.8	6.0

- Represents zero.

Source: U.S. Energy Information Administration, 1980, *Power Production, Fuel Consumption, and Installed Capacity Data,* annual; thereafter, *Electric Power Annual, Electric Power Monthly,* December issues, and *Inventory of Power Plants in the United States,* annual.

No. 975. Nuclear Power Plants—Number of Units, Net Generation, and Net Summer Capability, by State: 1996

STATE	Number of units	NET GENERATION Total (mil. kWh)	Percent of total[1]	NET SUMMER CAPABILITY Total (mil. kW)	Percent of total[1]
U.S.	110	674,729	21.9	100.69	14.3
AL	5	29,708	25.8	4.84	23.6
AZ	3	28,840	40.7	3.81	25.0
AR	2	13,357	30.6	1.69	17.6
CA	4	34,097	29.7	4.31	10.0
CT	4	6,225	39.5	3.19	47.5
FL	5	25,470	17.5	3.82	10.7
GA	4	29,925	30.3	3.90	17.5
IL	13	69,774	48.4	12.61	38.0
IA	1	3,924	11.8	0.53	6.4
KS	1	8,205	20.6	1.17	12.1
LA	2	15,765	26.9	2.01	11.8
ME	1	5,062	64.9	0.87	35.8
MD	2	12,093	27.2	1.68	15.3
MA	1	5,324	19.2	0.67	7.2
MI	5	26,829	28.2	3.99	18.1
MN	3	12,095	28.9	1.57	17.6
MS	1	9,225	32.0	2.26	31.5
MO	1	8,890	13.1	1.13	7.2
NE	2	9,457	34.6	1.25	22.7
NH	1	9,845	63.8	1.16	46.1
NJ	4	11,028	55.7	1.63	11.8
NY	6	35,226	33.8	4.82	15.0
NC	5	33,718	32.8	4.64	22.5
OH	2	13,919	9.7	2.04	7.5
PA	9	68,672	39.2	8.96	26.6
SC	7	43,571	57.1	6.36	38.1
TN	3	22,924	25.9	3.39	21.0
TX	4	35,767	13.1	4.80	7.5
VT	1	3,799	75.9	0.50	45.5
VA	4	26,286	46.5	3.39	23.7
WA	1	5,588	5.0	1.11	4.6
WI	3	10,121	19.6	1.45	12.6

[1] For total capability and generation, see Table 974.

Source: U.S. Energy Information Administration, *Electric Power Annual* and *Electric Power Monthly,* December issues.

No. 976. Nuclear Power Plants—Number, Capacity, and Generation: 1980 to 1996

ITEM	1980	1985	1987	1988	1989	1990	1991	1992	1993	1994	1995	1996
Operable generating units [1]	70	95	107	108	110	111	111	109	109	109	109	110
Net summer capability [1] [2] (mil. kW)	51.8	79.4	93.6	94.7	98.2	99.6	99.6	99.0	99.0	99.1	99.5	100.7
Net generation (bil. kWh)	251.1	383.7	455.3	527.0	529.4	576.9	612.6	618.8	610.3	640.4	673.4	674.8
Percent of total electric utility generation	11.0	15.5	17.7	19.5	19.0	20.5	21.7	22.1	21.2	22.0	22.5	21.9
Capacity factor [3]	56.3	58.0	57.4	63.5	62.2	66.0	70.2	70.9	70.5	73.8	77.4	76.4

[1] As of year-end. [2] Net summer capability is the peak steady hourly output that generating equipment is expected to supply to system load, exclusive of auxiliary and other power plant, as demonstrated by test at the time of summer peak demand. [3] Weighted average of monthly capacity factors. Monthly factors are derived by dividing actual monthly generation by the maximum possible generation for the month (hours in month times net maximum dependable capacity).

Source: U.S. Energy Information Administration, *Annual Energy Review* and *Monthly Energy Review* March 1996.

No. 977. Commercial Nuclear Power Generation, by Country: 1990 to 1997

[Generation for **calendar years**; other data as of **December**]

COUNTRY	REACTORS				GROSS ELECTRICITY GENERATED (bil. kWh)				GROSS CAPACITY (1,000 kW)			
	1990	1995	1996	1997	1990	1995	1996	1997	1990	1995	1996	1997
Total	368	423	424	427	1,743.9	2,271.7	2,372.3	2,352.4	301,745	358,414	364,179	368,471
United States	112	109	110	109	606.4	705.7	704.1	655.1	105,998	105,810	106,957	106,541
Argentina	2	2	2	2	7.0	7.0	7.4	7.9	1,005	1,005	1,005	1,005
Belgium	7	7	7	7	42.7	41.3	43.3	47.4	5,740	5,911	5,911	5,995
Brazil	1	1	1	1	2.0	2.5	2.4	3.1	657	657	657	657
Bulgaria	(NA)	6	6	6	(NA)	17.1	17.6	17.0	(NA)	3,760	3,760	3,760
Canada	19	22	21	21	74.0	100.2	95.2	84.4	13,855	16,699	15,795	15,795
China: Taiwan	6	6	6	6	32.9	35.3	37.7	36.2	5,146	5,144	5,144	5,144
Czech Republic	(NA)	(NA)	(NA)	(NA)	(NA)	(NA)	(NA)	(NA)	(NA)	(NA)	(NA)	(NA)
Finland	4	4	4	4	18.9	18.9	19.4	20.8	2,400	2,400	2,400	2,605
France	58	56	56	56	314.1	377.2	397.1	386.1	58,862	60,674	60,674	60,674
Germany	22	21	20	20	147.2	154.1	161.7	170.3	23,973	24,035	23,431	23,496
Great Britain	42	34	35	35	68.8	82.7	94.7	97.6	15,274	14,022	15,272	15,272
Hungary	4	4	4	4	13.6	14.0	14.1	13.9	1,760	1,840	1,840	1,840
India	6	10	10	10	6.0	7.6	8.5	9.3	1,330	2,270	2,270	2,270
Italy	2	(NA)	(NA)	(NA)	-	(NA)	(NA)	(NA)	1,132	(NA)	(NA)	(NA)
Japan	40	50	51	53	191.9	286.0	293.1	317.8	31,645	41,356	42,712	45,248
Mexico	1	2	2	2	2.1	7.9	7.8	9.5	675	1,350	1,350	1,350
Netherlands	2	2	2	2	3.4	4.0	4.1	2.4	540	540	540	540
Pakistan	1	1	1	1	0.4	0.5	0.3	0.4	137	137	137	137
Russia	(NA)	29	29	29	(NA)	98.7	108.7	108.0	(NA)	21,266	21,266	21,266
Slovenia [1]	1	1	1	1	4.6	4.7	4.5	5.0	664	664	664	664
South Africa	2	2	2	2	8.9	11.9	12.3	13.2	1,930	1,930	1,930	1,930
South Korea	9	10	11	12	52.8	63.9	73.9	76.5	7,616	8,615	9,615	10,315
Spain	10	9	9	9	54.3	55.4	56.2	55.3	7,984	7,400	7,422	7,572
Sweden	12	12	12	12	68.2	69.9	74.4	67.5	10,344	10,442	10,445	10,445
Switzerland	5	5	5	5	23.6	24.8	25.0	25.2	3,079	3,200	3,229	3,229
Ukraine	(NA)	15	15	14	(NA)	70.5	79.5	79.1	(NA)	13,880	13,880	12,880

- Represents zero. NA Not available. [1] Formerly Yugoslavia.

Source: McGraw-Hill, Inc., New York, NY, *Nucleonics Week*, March issues (copyright).

No. 978. Uranium Supply and Discharged Commercial Reactor Fuel: 1980 to 1997

[Years ending **Dec. 31**, except as noted. For additional data on uranium, see Section 24 on mining]

ITEM	Unit	1980	1985	1990	1992	1993	1994	1995	1996	1997
URANIUM CONCENTRATE										
Production	Mil. lb.	43.70	11.31	8.89	5.65	3.06	3.35	6.04	6.32	5.60
Exports	Mil. lb.	5.80	5.30	2.00	2.80	3.00	17.74	9.84	11.50	17.00
Imports	Mil. lb.	3.60	11.70	23.70	23.30	21.00	36.62	41.30	45.42	43.00
Utility purchases from domestic suppliers	Mil. lb.	(NA)	21.7	20.5	23.4	15.5	22.7	22.3	23.7	19.4
Loaded into U.S. Nuclear reactors [1]	Mil. lb.	(NA)	(NA)	(NA)	43.0	45.1	40.4	51.1	46.2	48.7
Inventories, total	Mil. lb.	(NA)	176.9	129.1	117.3	105.7	86.9	72.5	80.0	75.8
At domestic suppliers	Mil. lb.	(NA)	23.7	26.4	25.2	24.5	21.5	13.7	13.9	11.9
At electric utilities	Mil. lb.	(NA)	153.2	102.7	92.1	81.2	65.4	58.7	66.1	63.9
Average prices:										
Purchased imports	Dol. per lb	(NA)	20.08	12.55	11.34	10.53	8.95	10.2	13.2	12.8
Domestic purchases	Dol. per lb	(NA)	31.43	15.70	13.45	13.14	10.30	11.1	13.8	13.4
DISCHARGED COMMERCIAL REACTOR FUEL [2]										
Annual discharge	Metric tons	1,193	1,330	2,084	2,192	2,102	1,809	2,292	2,174	(NA)
Inventory, year-end [3]	Metric tons	6,434	12,481	21,029	24,937	27,039	28,848	31,140	(NA)	(NA)

NA Not available. [1] Does not include any fuel rods removed from reactors and later reloaded into the reactor. [2] Uranium content. Source: Nuclear Assurance Corporation, Atlanta, GA. [3] Reprocessed fuel not included as inventory.

Source: Except as noted, U.S. Energy Information Administration, *Annual Energy Review, Uranium Industry Annual* and unpublished data.

No. 979. Electric Utilities—Generation, Sales, Revenue, and Customers: 1980 to 1996

[Sales and revenue are to and from ultimate customers]

CLASS	Unit	1980	1985	1990	1991	1992	1993	1994	1995	1996
Generation [1]	Bil. kWh..	2,286	2,470	2,808	2,825	2,797	2,883	2,911	2,995	3,077
Sales [2]	**Bil. kWh.**	**2,126**	**2,306**	**2,684**	**2,737**	**2,735**	**2,850**	**2,935**	**3,013**	**3,098**
Residential or domestic.....	Bil. kWh..	734	793	916	949	929	994	1,008	1,043	1,082
Percent of total	Percent...	34.5	34.4	34.1	34.7	34.0	34.9	34.4	(NA)	(NA)
Commercial [3]	Bil. kWh..	524	606	739	753	756	803	820	863	888
Industrial [4]	Bil. kWh..	794	820	932	935	949	957	1,008	1,013	1,030
Revenue [2]	**Bil. dol..**	**95.5**	**149.2**	**176.5**	**185.1**	**187.3**	**197.9**	**202.7**	**207.7**	**212.5**
Residential or domestic....	Bil. dol....	37.6	58.6	71.7	76.4	76.4	82.4	84.6	87.6	90.5
Percent of total	Percent...	39.4	39.3	40.7	41.2	40.8	41.7	41.7	(NA)	(NA)
Commercial [3]	Bil. dol....	27.4	44.1	54.2	56.8	58.0	62.0	63.4	66.4	67.8
Industrial [4]	Bil. dol....	27.3	41.4	44.9	45.9	46.8	46.6	48.1	47.2	47.4
Ultimate customers, Dec. 31 [2]	**Million.....**	**92.7**	**101.6**	**110.1**	**111.4**	**113.1**	**115.2**	**116.5**	**118.3**	**120.0**
Residential or domestic....	Million.....	82.2	89.8	97.0	98.2	99.6	101.3	102.3	103.9	105.3
Commercial [3]	Million.....	9.7	10.9	12.1	12.3	12.5	12.5	12.7	13.0	13.2
Industrial [4]	Million.....	0.5	0.5	0.5	0.5	0.5	0.5	0.6	0.6	0.6
Avg. kWh used per customer .	**1,000 ......**	**23.2**	**22.9**	**24.6**	**24.7**	**24.4**	**24.9**	**25.2**	**(NA)**	**(NA)**
Residential	1,000 ...	9.0	8.9	9.5	9.7	9.4	9.9	9.9	(NA)	(NA)
Commercial [3]	1,000 ...	54.5	56.1	61.3	61.6	61.0	64.4	65.7	(NA)	(NA)
Avg. annual bill per customer .	**Dollar.....**	**1,040**	**1,482**	**1,614**	**1,670**	**1,667**	**1,727**	**1,741**	**(NA)**	**(NA)**
Residential	Dollar.....	462	658	744	782	772	818	827	(NA)	(NA)
Commercial [3]	Dollar.....	2,848	4,080	4,494	4,646	4,681	4,977	5,076	(NA)	(NA)
Avg. revenue per kWh sold. . .	**Cents.....**	**4.49**	**6.47**	**6.57**	**6.76**	**6.85**	**6.94**	**6.91**	**6.89**	**6.86**
Residential	Cents......	5.12	7.39	7.83	8.05	8.22	8.29	8.38	8.40	8.36
Commercial [3]	Cents......	5.22	7.27	7.33	7.55	7.67	7.73	7.73	7.69	7.64
Industrial [4]	Cents......	3.44	5.04	4.81	4.91	4.93	4.87	4.77	4.66	4.60

NA Not available. [1] Source: U.S. Energy Information Administration, *Monthly Energy Review*, monthly. [2] Includes other types not shown separately. [3] Small light and power. [4] Large light and power.

Source: Except as noted, Edison Electric Institute, Washington, DC, *Statistical Yearbook of the Electric Utility Industry*, annual.

No. 980. Major Investor-Owned Electric Utilities—Balance Sheet and Income Account of Privately Owned Companies: 1985 to 1996

[In billions of dollars. As of Dec. 31. As of 1990, covers approximately 180 investor-owned electric utilities that during each of the last 3 years met any one or more of the following conditions — 1 mil. megawatthours of total sales; 100 megawatthours of sales for resale, 500 megawatthours of gross interchange out, and 500 megawatthours of wheeling for other]

ITEM	1985	1989	1990	1991	1992	1993	1994	1995	1996
COMPOSITE BALANCE SHEET									
Total assets and other debits	**404.7**	**465.7**	**477.9**	**487.5**	**506.4**	**566.6**	**574.5**	**578.9**	**582.0**
Total electric utility plant	396.9	462.4	480.6	497.9	518.8	537.3	553.1	567.4	581.4
Electric depreciation and amortization	85.1	125.0	135.7	148.3	160.5	173.4	186.1	201.3	217.5
Net electric utility plant	311.8	337.5	344.9	349.6	358.3	363.8	366.9	366.1	363.9
Total other utility plant	19.9	26.3	28.5	31.0	33.4	36.4	38.6	39.9	41.9
Other utility depreciation and amortization . . .	6.5	9.2	10.0	10.8	11.7	12.4	13.4	13.9	14.7
Net other utility plant	13.4	17.1	18.6	20.2	21.7	24.0	25.2	26.0	27.1
Total all utility plant	431.1	507.9	528.7	548.4	571.9	593.6	610.7	626.7	643.5
All utility plant depreciation and amortization .	97.4	144.6	157.4	171.7	185.1	199.8	212.9	229.3	247.1
Net all utility plant	333.8	363.2	371.3	376.8	386.9	393.8	397.8	397.4	396.4
Other property and investments	12.1	16.1	17.7	17.4	18.0	20.1	23.5	28.0	33.1
Current and accrued assets	39.4	41.5	41.5	43.4	43.4	42.4	41.3	44.1	43.5
Deferred debits	19.4	44.8	47.3	50.0	58.0	110.3	112.0	109.4	108.9
Liabilities and other credits	**404.7**	**465.7**	**477.9**	**487.5**	**506.4**	**566.6**	**574.5**	**578.9**	**582.0**
Capital stock [1]	82.8	82.9	83.2	83.6	86.1	87.1	87.2	84.0	80.7
Other paid-in capital [2]	36.3	39.1	40.5	42.9	44.7	47.2	48.9	50.1	51.8
Retained earnings	41.1	47.7	48.1	49.0	49.7	49.9	51.8	55.7	57.5
Subsidiary earnings	2.2	2.8	2.9	3.0	2.7	2.9	3.2	3.5	4.2
Long-term debt	152.7	162.9	167.9	171.9	174.1	174.9	175.4	173.7	172.6
Current and accrued liabilities	32.0	42.0	44.3	43.4	45.6	48.9	48.0	49.9	49.3
Deferred credits and operating reserves [3] . . .	20.9	28.5	28.8	29.2	31.1	40.9	41.2	40.3	41.0
Deferred income taxes as deferred credits. . .	32.7	53.3	56.5	59.2	65.0	105.0	107.1	108.6	110.5
COMPOSITE INCOME ACCOUNTS									
Electric operating revenues	135.3	150.9	157.3	166.8	169.5	176.4	179.3	183.7	188.9
Electric operating expenses	111.1	121.6	127.9	135.9	139.0	146.1	148.7	150.6	156.9
Net electric utility operating income.	24.1	29.4	29.4	30.9	30.5	30.2	30.6	33.1	32.0
Other than electric utility operating income. . . .	1.2	1.2	1.1	1.2	1.2	1.5	1.3	1.5	1.6
Net utility operating income	25.3	30.6	30.5	32.1	31.8	31.7	32.1	34.6	32.0
Total other income	7.4	5.2	4.1	3.9	2.9	2.8	2.8	3.0	2.8
Total income [4]	32.7	35.8	34.6	36.0	34.7	34.6	34.9	37.6	36.3
Income deductions [5]	14.0	18.5	17.7	19.1	16.3	16.7	15.0	15.5	(NA)
Net income	18.7	17.3	16.9	16.9	18.4	17.9	19.9	22.1	(NA)

NA Not available. [1] Composed of Common Stock Issued and Preferred Stock Issued. [2] Composed of Capital Stock Subscribed, Liability and Premium and Other Paid-in Capital. [3] Composed of Total Deferred Credits less Accumulated Deferred Income Taxes as Deferred Credits. [4] Composed of Net Utility Operating Income plus Total Other Income. [5] Composed of the difference between Total Income less Net Income.

Source: U.S. Energy Information Administration, 1985, *Financial Statistics of Selected Electric Utilities*, annual; thereafter, *Financial Statistics of Major U.S. Investor-Owned Electric Utilities*, annual.

No. 981. Nonutility Electric Power Producers—Summary, by Type of Fuel: 1989 to 1997

TYPE OF FUEL	1989	1990	1991	1992	1993	1994	1995	1996	1997
Installed capacity (megawatts)......	38,851	45,271	49,998	56,814	60,778	68,461	70,255	73,183	78,940
Coal [1]............	6,422	6,937	7,351	8,503	9,772	10,372	10,877	12,122	12,582
Petroleum [2]............	1,129	1,038	1,514	1,730	2,043	2,262	2,116	3,185	3,315
Natural gas [3]...........	14,820	17,430	20,694	21,542	23,463	26,925	27,906	30,840	32,639
Other gas [3]............	([4])	([4])	([4])	([4])	([4])	1,130	1,217	184	184
Petroleum/natural gas (combined) .	4,732	6,468	5,292	8,478	8,505	9,820	10,479	10,875	11,755
Hydroelectric	1,672	1,968	2,072	2,684	2,741	3,364	3,399	3,419	5,041
Geothermal	1,001	1,086	1,103	1,254	1,318	1,335	1,295	1,346	1,446
Solar.....................	200	360	360	360	360	354	354	354	354
Wind....................	1,339	1,405	1,652	1,822	1,813	1,737	1,723	1,670	1,892
Wood [5]................	5,515	6,049	6,708	6,805	7,046	7,416	6,885	5,938	6,079
Waste [6]................	1,825	2,323	2,741	3,006	3,131	3,150	3,430	2,556	2,874
Gross generation (mil. kilowatt hours).	189,896	220,058	251,747	296,001	325,226	354,925	375,901	382,530	421,199
Coal [1]............	31,511	32,131	40,587	47,363	53,367	59,035	60,234	61,424	67,767
Petroleum [2]...........	5,742	7,330	7,814	10,963	13,364	15,069	15,049	14,951	17,267
Natural gas [3]...........	99,632	116,969	131,820	158,798	174,282	179,735	196,633	198,606	219,558
Other gases [3]...........	([4])	([4])	([4])	([4])	([4])	12,480	13,984	14,753	15,123
Hydroelectric	7,124	8,153	8,180	9,446	11,511	13,227	14,774	16,555	18,702
Geothermal	5,416	7,235	8,014	8,578	9,749	10,122	9,912	10,198	11,212
Solar.....................	489	663	779	746	897	824	824	903	994
Wind....................	1,833	2,251	2,606	2,916	3,052	3,482	3,185	3,400	3,727
Wood [5]................	27,835	30,812	33,785	36,255	37,421	38,595	37,283	37,549	39,229
Waste [6]................	8,515	11,688	14,475	17,352	18,325	18,797	20,231	20,449	23,379

[1] Includes coal, anthracite, culm, and coal waste.   [2] Includes petroleum, petroleum coke, diesel, kerosene, and petroleum sludge and tar.   [3] Includes butane, ethane, propane, and other gases.   [4] Included in "Natural gas."   [5] Includes wood, wood waste, peat, wood liquors, railroad ties, pitch, and wood sludge.   [6] Includes municipal solid waste, agricultural waste, straw, tires, landfill gases, and other waste.

Source: Energy Information Administration, *Annual Nonutility Power Producer Report*.

No. 982. Water Power—Developed and Undeveloped Capacity, by Division: 1980 to 1997

[In millions of kilowatts. As of Dec. 31. Excludes all capacity of reversible equipment at pumped storage projects. Also excludes capacity precluded from development due to wild and scenic river legislation. For composition of divisions, see inside front cover]

DIVISION	DEVELOPED INSTALLED CAPACITY							ESTIMATED UNDEVELOPED CAPACITY						
	1980	1990	1993	1994	1995	1996	1997	1980	1990	1993	1994	1995	1996	1997
United State.......	64.4	73.0	74.0	74.1	74.2	74.8	73.5	129.9	73.9	73.6	73.5	71.0	70.0	64.1
New England..........	1.5	1.9	1.9	1.9	1.9	2.0	2.0	4.7	4.4	4.4	4.4	4.4	4.4	3.9
Middle Atlantic.........	4.3	4.9	4.9	4.9	4.9	5.0	5.6	5.1	5.1	4.9	4.9	4.9	4.8	3.6
East North Central	0.9	1.1	1.2	1.2	1.2	1.2	1.2	2.0	1.7	1.7	1.7	1.7	1.6	1.5
West North Central	2.8	3.1	3.1	3.1	3.1	3.0	3.0	3.4	3.1	3.1	3.1	3.1	3.0	2.8
South Atlantic..........	5.9	6.7	6.7	6.7	6.7	6.8	6.8	9.6	7.0	7.2	7.2	7.2	7.3	6.8
East South Central	5.6	5.9	5.9	5.9	5.9	5.9	5.9	3.3	2.4	2.4	2.4	2.3	2.0	2.0
West South Central.....	2.3	2.7	2.7	2.7	2.7	2.8	2.8	4.7	4.6	4.6	4.6	4.6	4.6	4.0
Mountain..............	7.4	9.2	9.5	9.5	9.5	10.0	10.0	34.2	19.4	19.1	19.1	18.8	19.1	18.0
Pacific	33.7	37.5	38.1	38.2	38.3	38.3	36.2	62.9	26.2	26.2	26.1	24.0	22.9	21.5

Source: U.S. Federal Energy Regulatory Commission (formerly U.S. Federal Power Commission), *Hydroelectric Power Resources of the United States, Developed and Undeveloped*, January 1, 1988; and unpublished data.

No. 983. Solar Collector Shipments, by Type, End Use, and Market Sector: 1984 to 1995

[In thousands of square feet, except number of manufacturers. Solar collector is a device for intercepting sunlight, converting the light to heat, and carrying the heat to where it will be either used or stored. 1985 data are not available]

YEAR	Number of manufac- turers	Total ship- ments [1]	COLLECTOR TYPE		END USE			MARKET SECTOR		
			Low tempera- ture	Medium tempera- ture, spe- cial, other	Pool heating	Hot water	Space heating	Resi- dential	Com- mercial	Indus- trial
1984 [2]	225	17,191	4,479	11,939	4,427	8,930	2,370	13,980	2,091	289
1986 [2]	98	9,360	3,751	1,111	3,494	1,181	127	4,131	703	13
1987 [2]	59	7,269	3,157	957	3,111	964	23	3,775	305	11
1988 [2]	51	8,174	3,326	732	3,304	726	7	3,796	255	7
1989 [2]	44	11,482	4,283	1,989	4,688	1,374	205	5,804	424	42
1990	51	11,409	3,645	2,527	5,016	1,091	2	5,835	294	22
1991	48	6,574	5,585	989	5,535	989	24	6,322	225	13
1992	45	7,086	6,187	897	6,210	801	35	6,832	204	27
1993	41	6,968	6,025	931	6,040	880	15	6,694	215	31
1994	41	7,627	6,823	803	6,813	790	19	7,026	583	16
1995	36	7,666	6,813	840	6,763	755	132	6,966	604	82

[1] Includes high temperature collectors, end uses such process heating, and utility and other market sectors not shown separately.   [2] Declines between 1984 and 1989 are primarily due to the expiration of the federal energy tax credit and industry consolidation.

Source: U.S. Energy Information Administration, *Solar Collector Manufacturing Activity*, annual.

No. 984. Renewable Energy Consumption Estimates, by Type: 1990 to 1995

[In quadrillion Btu. Renewable energy is obtained from sources that are essentially inexhaustible unlike fossil fuels of which there is a finite supply]

SOURCE AND SECTOR	1990	1991	1992	1993	1994	1995
SOURCES						
Total	**6.16**	**6.27**	**6.11**	**6.40**	**6.30**	**6.83**
Consumption for electricity	3.94	4.09	3.83	4.15	4.00	4.43
Electric utilities	3.23	3.09	2.70	2.95	2.71	3.16
Hydroelectric power	2.93	2.90	2.51	2.77	2.54	3.04
Geothermal energy	0.18	0.17	0.17	0.16	0.15	0.10
Biofuels [1]	0.02	0.02	0.02	0.02	0.02	0.02
Wind energy [2]	(Z)	(Z)	(Z)	(Z)	(Z)	(Z)
Nonutility power generators	0.70	0.79	0.87	0.94	0.98	0.99
Hydroelectric power	0.08	0.08	0.10	0.12	0.14	0.15
Geothermal, solar, and wind energy	0.18	0.20	0.22	0.24	0.26	0.25
Biofuels [1]	0.44	0.51	0.55	0.57	0.59	0.59
Net imported electricity	0.10	0.21	0.26	0.27	0.31	0.28
Consumption for other uses [3]	2.22	2.17	2.28	2.25	2.30	(NA)
Biofuels [1]	2.63	2.64	2.79	2.78	2.85	(NA)
Solar and photovoltaic energy	0.07	0.07	0.07	0.07	0.07	(NA)
SECTORS						
Total	**6.16**	**6.27**	**6.11**	**6.40**	**6.30**	**6.83**
Residential and commercial	0.64	0.67	0.71	0.65	0.64	0.71
Industrial	2.21	2.22	2.36	2.45	2.54	2.58
Transportation	0.08	0.07	0.08	0.09	0.10	0.11
Electric utilities	3.23	3.30	2.97	3.22	3.01	3.44

NA Not available. Z Less than 0.005 quadrillion Btu. [1] Biofuels are fuelwood, wood byproducts, waste wood, municipal solid waste, manufacturing process waste, and alcohol fuels. [2] Also includes photovoltaic and solar thermal energy. [3] Included are nonutility thermal energy uses, such as space heating and industrial process heat production. Excluded are estimates for mechanical energy, such as shaft power from dams, wind machines, and solar-powered motors and activators.

Source: U.S. Energy Information Administration, *Annual Energy Review.*

No. 985. Privately Owned Gas Utility Industry—Balance Sheet and Income Account: 1980 to 1995

[In millions of dollars. The gas utility industry consists of pipeline and distribution companies. Excludes operations of companies distributing gas in bottles or tanks]

ITEM	1980	1985	1989	1990	1991	1992	1993	1994	1995
COMPOSITE BALANCE SHEET									
Assets, total	**75,851**	**104,478**	**123,820**	**121,686**	**124,120**	**129,400**	**135,813**	**137,911**	**141,965**
Total utility plant	67,071	88,121	106,017	112,863	119,772	129,272	135,859	139,372	143,636
Depreciation and amortization	26,162	36,377	47,054	49,483	52,400	53,005	60,152	61,140	62,723
Utility plant (net)	40,909	51,744	58,963	63,380	67,372	76,267	75,707	78,232	80,912
Investment and fund accounts	15,530	23,871	28,111	23,872	22,883	21,883	23,342	22,658	26,489
Current and accrued assets	17,243	24,771	24,836	23,268	23,023	23,783	21,451	20,728	18,564
Deferred debits [1]	2,169	4,092	10,364	9,576	9,277	9,776	13,369	14,234	13,923
Liabilities, total	**75,851**	**104,478**	**123,820**	**121,686**	**124,120**	**129,400**	**135,813**	**137,911**	**141,965**
Capitalization, total	51,382	65,799	74,753	74,958	75,463	81,183	82,755	85,728	90,581
Capital stock	29,315	39,517	43,889	43,810	43,435	46,318	49,051	50,394	54,402
Long-term debts	22,067	26,282	30,864	31,148	32,028	34,865	33,693	35,296	35,548
Current and accrued liabilities	18,119	26,125	31,005	29,550	28,128	26,438	27,321	25,438	28,272
Deferred income taxes [2]	4,149	7,769	11,292	11,360	10,527	10,952	13,070	13,787	14,393
Other liabilities and credits	2,201	4,785	6,770	5,818	10,002	10,827	12,667	12,955	8,715
COMPOSITE INCOME ACCOUNT									
Operating revenues, total	**85,918**	**103,945**	**70,363**	**66,027**	**63,922**	**66,405**	**69,966**	**63,446**	**58,390**
Operating expenses [3]	81,789	98,320	64,262	60,137	59,165	60,042	62,977	56,789	50,760
Operation and maintenance	74,508	88,572	55,990	51,627	50,867	48,054	50,468	43,879	37,966
Federal, state, and local taxes	4,847	6,590	4,843	4,957	4,446	6,031	6,185	6,613	6,182
Operating income	4,129	5,625	6,101	5,890	4,756	6,363	6,988	6,657	7,630
Utility operating income	4,471	6,030	6,274	6,077	4,962	6,572	7,177	6,851	7,848
Income before interest charges	6,929	7,636	8,764	8,081	5,530	7,223	8,754	8,200	9,484
Net income	4,194	3,785	4,641	4,410	1,894	3,750	5,589	5,011	5,139
Dividends	2,564	4,060	3,113	3,191	4,341	3,889	3,149	3,928	4,037

[1] Includes capital stock discount and expense and reacquired securities. [2] Includes reserves for deferred income taxes. [3] Includes expenses not shown separately.

Source: American Gas Association, Arlington, VA, *Gas Facts,* annual (copyright).

No. 986. Gas Utility Industry—Summary: 1980 to 1996

[Covers natural, manufactured, mixed, and liquid petroleum gas. Based on questionnaire mailed to all privately and municipally owned gas utilities in United States, except those with annual revenues less than $25,000]

ITEM	Unit	1980	1985	1990	1991	1992	1993	1994	1995	1996
End users [1]	1,000	47,223	49,971	54,261	55,174	56,132	57,028	57,960	58,728	59,820
Residential	1,000	43,489	45,929	49,802	50,634	51,525	52,358	53,243	53,955	54,968
Commercial	1,000	3,498	3,816	4,246	4,322	4,397	4,428	4,474	4,530	4,616
Industrial and other	1,000	187	179	166	168	165	181	181	181	183
Sales [2]	Tril. Btu	15,413	12,616	9,842	9,605	9,906	10,021	9,480	9,094	9,532
Residential	Tril. Btu	4,826	4,513	4,468	4,550	4,694	5,054	4,972	4,736	5,198
Percent of total	Percent	31.3	35.8	45.4	47.4	47.4	50.4	52.4	52.0	54.5
Commercial	Tril. Btu	2,453	2,338	2,192	2,198	2,209	2,397	2,351	2,204	2,395
Industrial	Tril. Btu	7,957	5,635	3,010	2,631	2,772	2,404	2,009	1,930	1,791
Other	Tril. Btu	177	130	171	226	231	167	148	224	148
Revenues [2]	Mil. dol	48,303	63,293	45,153	44,647	46,178	49,847	49,864	46,381	51,115
Residential	Mil. dol	17,432	26,864	25,000	25,729	26,702	29,787	30,563	28,741	32,022
Percent of total	Percent	36.1	42.4	55.4	57.6	57.8	59.8	61.3	61.9	62.6
Commercial	Mil. dol	8,183	12,722	10,604	10,669	10,865	12,076	12,254	11,410	12,726
Industrial	Mil. dol	22,215	23,086	8,996	7,576	7,913	7,351	6,475	5,652	5,821
Other	Mil. dol	473	621	553	674	698	632	572	579	546
Prices per mil. Btu [3]	Dollars	3.13	5.02	4.59	4.65	4.66	4.94	5.23	5.10	5.37
Residential	Dollars	3.61	5.95	5.60	5.66	5.69	5.89	6.14	6.06	6.17
Commercial	Dollars	3.34	5.44	4.84	4.85	4.92	5.04	5.21	5.18	5.31
Industrial	Dollars	2.79	4.10	2.99	2.88	2.85	3.02	3.17	3.00	3.32
Gas mains mileage	1,000	1,052	1,119	1,207	1,225	1,254	1,251	1,267	1,262	1,269
Field and gathering	1,000	84	94	90	86	86	73	72	62	58
Transmission	1,000	266	271	280	282	285	270	276	265	260
Distribution	1,000	702	754	837	857	883	908	919	935	952
Construction expenditures [4]	Mil. dol	5,350	5,671	7,899	9,036	11,068	9,140	9,282	10,829	7,722
Transmission	Mil. dol	1,583	1,562	2,886	3,656	5,739	3,288	3,065	3,384	1,316
Distribution	Mil. dol	1,869	2,577	3,714	3,842	3,867	4,286	4,550	5,448	4,234
Production and storage	Mil. dol	1,150	790	309	430	349	253	230	366	651

[1] Annual average.　[2] Excludes sales for resale.　[3] For definition of Btu, see text, Section 19.　[4] Includes general.

Source: American Gas Association, Arlington, VA, *Gas Facts,* annual (copyright).

No. 987. Gas Utility Industry—Customers, Sales, and Revenues, by State: 1996

[See headnote, Table 986. For definition of Btu, see text, Section 19]

STATE	CUSTOM-ERS [1] (1,000) Total [2]	Resi-dential	SALES [3] (tril. Btu) Total [2]	Resi-dential	REVENUES [3] (mil. dol.) Total [2]	Resi-dential	STATE	CUSTOM-ERS [1] (1,000) Total [2]	Resi-dential	SALES [3] (tril. Btu) Total [2]	Resi-dential	REVENUES [3] (mil. dol.) Total [2]	Resi-dential
U.S.	59,820	54,968	9,532	5,198	51,115	32,021	MO	1,383	1,252	209	135	1,172	808
AL	828	764	118	59	680	411	MT	232	205	34	21	178	109
AK	94	81	27	16	89	57	NE	498	438	95	54	404	250
AZ	657	616	54	24	322	187	NV	421	394	39	23	218	140
AR	607	538	96	46	474	275	NH	88	75	17	7	108	50
CA	9,399	8,963	715	477	4,163	3,018							
							NJ	2,358	2,135	471	222	2,786	1,595
CO	1,270	1,148	183	114	736	491	NM	478	436	55	33	224	156
CT	486	435	109	44	821	433	NY	4,380	4,047	646	406	5,049	3,521
DE	114	104	26	9	125	58	NC	794	691	170	60	933	430
DC	146	132	30	14	228	114	ND	111	97	25	13	97	55
FL	629	576	88	19	539	183							
							OH	3,225	2,972	557	383	2,876	2,074
GA	1,649	1,525	243	128	1,407	841	OK	962	870	142	79	681	433
HI	37	34	3	1	49	16	OR	492	434	77	34	383	210
ID	259	179	25	15	120	75	PA	2,623	2,419	456	284	2,883	1,990
IL	3,762	3,465	662	493	3,177	2,422	RI	231	209	36	19	274	165
IN	1,653	1,507	323	186	1,588	1,009							
							SC	468	416	97	29	511	201
IA	849	759	141	83	666	432	SD	143	126	26	14	116	69
KS	890	802	134	86	690	478	TN	906	801	183	69	949	423
KY	770	694	135	72	663	387	TX	3,804	3,474	639	222	2,763	1,302
LA	1,048	982	393	59	1,148	382	UT	586	544	87	57	334	243
ME	22	15	4	-	36	8							
							VT	32	28	8	3	41	18
MD	919	848	138	80	887	574	VA	844	763	149	72	893	526
MA	1,319	1,200	225	119	1,662	1,016	WA	745	668	134	63	614	343
MI	3,040	2,815	543	388	2,725	1,969	WV	400	365	101	40	463	268
MN	1,224	1,114	277	139	1,268	731	WI	1,419	1,291	277	142	1,430	858
MS	447	401	86	31	372	166	WY	138	122	24	13	96	55

- Represents zero.　[1] Averages for the year.　[2] Includes other service, not shown separately.　[3] Excludes sales for resale.

Source: American Gas Association, Arlington, VA, *Gas Facts,* annual (copyright).

Science and Technology

This section presents statistics on scientific, engineering, and technological resources, with emphasis on patterns of research and development (R&D) funding and on scientific, engineering, and technical personnel, education, and employment. Also included are statistics on space program outlays and accomplishments. Principal sources of these data are the National Science Foundation (NSF) and the National Aeronautics and Space Administration (NASA).

NSF gathers data chiefly through recurring surveys. Current NSF publications containing data on funds for research and development and on scientific and engineering personnel include the *Science Resources Studies Highlights* summaries series; Detailed Statistical Tables; and annual, biennial, triennial, and special reports. Titles or the areas of coverage of these reports include the following: *Science and Engineering Indicators; National Patterns of R&D Resources; Science and Engineering Personnel—A National Overview; Women and Minorities in Science and Engineering;* science and technology data presented in chart and tabular form in a pocket-size publication; *International Science and Technology Data Update;* profiles on human resources and funding in individual fields of science and engineering; *Federal Funds for Research and Development; Federal R&D Funding by Budget Function; Federal Support to Universities, Colleges, and Selected Nonprofit Institutions; Scientific and Engineering Facilities at Universities and Colleges; Geographic Distribution of Industrial R&D Expenditures; Research and Development in Industry;* R&D funds and graduate enrollment and support in academic science and engineering; characteristics of doctoral scientists and engineers and of recent graduates in the United States; *U.S. Scientists and Engineers;* and scientists, engineers, and technicians in manufacturing, nonmanufacturing, and trade and regulated industries. Statistical surveys in these areas pose problems of concept

---

In Brief

R&D expenditures:

1990	$151.7 bil.
1995	$183.0 bil.
1997	$205.7 bil.

Federal outlays for space and technologies in constant 1992 dollars:

1970	12.6 bil.
1980	7.6 bil.
1990	12.6 bil.
1998	10.0 bil.

---

and definition and the data should, therefore, be regarded as broad estimates rather than precise quantitative statements. See sources for details.

The National Science Board's biennial *Science and Engineering Indicators* contains data and analyses of international and domestic science and technology, including measures of inputs and outputs. *The Budget of the United States Government,* published by the U.S. Office of Management and Budget, contains summary financial data on federal R&D programs.

Research and development outlays—NSF defines research as a "systematic and intensive study directed toward a fuller knowledge of the subject studied" and development as "the systematic use of scientific knowledge directed toward the production of useful materials, devices, systems, methods, or processes." National coverage of R&D expenditures is developed primarily from periodic surveys in four principal economic sectors: (1) *Government,* made up primarily of federal executive agencies; (2) *industry,* consisting of manufacturing and nonmanufacturing firms and the federally funded research and development centers (FFRDCs) they administer; (3) *universities and colleges,* composed of universities, colleges, and their affiliated institutions, agricultural experiment stations, and associated schools of agriculture, and FFRDCs administered by educational institutions; and (4) *other nonprofit institutions,* consisting of such organizations as private philanthropic foundations, nonprofit research institutes, voluntary health agencies, and FFRDCs administered by nonprofit organizations. The R&D funds reported consist of current operating costs, including planning and administration costs, except as otherwise noted. They exclude funds for routine testing, mapping and surveying, collection of general-purpose data, dissemination of scientific information, and training of scientific personnel.

Scientists, engineers, and technicians—Scientists and engineers are defined as persons engaged in scientific and engineering work at a level requiring a knowledge of sciences equivalent at least to that acquired through completion of a 4-year college course. Technicians are defined as persons engaged in technical work at a level requiring knowledge acquired through a technical institute, junior college, or other type of training less extensive than 4-year college training. Craftsmen and skilled workers are excluded.

Figure 20.1
Top 15 Universities—Federal Research and Development Obligations: 1995

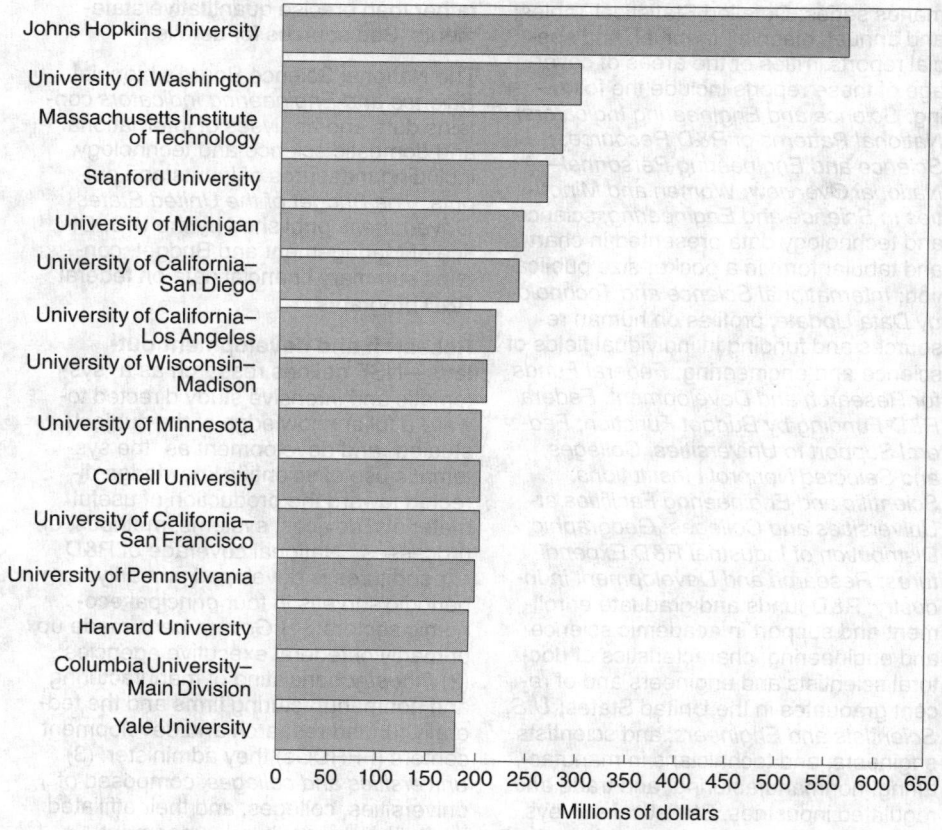

Source: Chart prepared by U.S. Bureau of the Census. For data, see Table 996.

No. 988. R&D Expenditures: 1960 to 1997

[In millions of dollars, except as indicated. For calendar years]

YEAR	Total	SOURCES OF FUNDS					OBJECTIVE (percent of total)			CHARACTER OF WORK		
		Federal government	Industry	Universities/ colleges	Non-profit	Non-federal govern-ment [1]	Defense re-lated [2]	Space re-lated [3]	Other	Basic research	Applied research	Devel-opment
1960......	13,669	8,879	4,516	66	122	88	53	3	44	1,256	3,059	9,355
1961......	14,514	9,441	4,757	72	146	98	50	6	44	1,476	3,115	9,924
1962......	15,577	10,086	5,123	82	177	109	49	7	44	1,780	3,688	10,110
1963......	17,446	11,582	5,456	93	195	122	42	14	45	2,060	3,855	11,531
1964......	19,053	12,726	5,887	108	198	135	37	19	44	2,358	4,189	12,507
1965......	20,192	13,147	6,548	130	221	146	33	21	46	2,618	4,361	13,214
1966......	22,010	14,117	7,330	156	249	158	32	20	48	2,886	4,638	14,486
1967......	23,279	14,511	8,144	190	267	166	35	14	50	3,113	4,838	15,328
1968......	24,646	14,956	9,006	219	286	178	35	14	52	3,361	5,141	16,144
1969......	25,965	15,213	10,010	228	311	203	35	11	54	3,471	5,448	17,046
1970......	26,235	14,970	10,446	251	340	228	33	10	56	3,567	5,742	16,926
1971......	26,910	15,183	10,823	282	364	259	33	10	58	3,698	5,817	17,395
1972......	28,661	15,976	11,713	308	389	276	33	8	59	3,829	6,098	18,734
1973......	30,905	16,563	13,296	331	417	298	32	7	61	4,051	6,662	20,193
1974......	33,238	17,193	14,882	380	470	314	29	7	64	4,439	7,312	21,488
1975......	35,565	18,437	15,823	424	542	340	28	7	65	4,827	8,048	22,691
1976......	39,314	20,179	17,698	463	608	367	27	8	65	5,291	8,964	25,059
1977......	43,233	21,988	19,637	541	683	384	27	7	66	5,925	9,653	27,655
1978......	48,582	24,279	22,456	651	768	429	26	6	68	6,841	10,695	31,047
1979......	55,269	27,100	26,092	760	841	477	25	6	70	7,736	12,073	35,460
1980......	63,076	29,857	30,926	877	911	505	24	5	70	8,651	13,724	40,701
1981......	72,190	33,666	35,956	1,031	974	564	24	5	70	9,741	16,389	46,060
1982......	80,633	37,113	40,705	1,159	1,037	619	26	5	69	10,658	18,261	51,714
1983......	89,742	41,362	45,274	1,329	1,135	642	28	4	68	11,859	20,323	57,560
1984......	101,940	46,319	52,225	1,463	1,228	706	29	3	68	13,176	22,481	66,284
1985......	114,344	52,493	58,013	1,680	1,365	793	30	3	67	14,510	25,389	74,444
1986......	119,907	54,475	61,079	1,944	1,466	942	32	3	65	16,885	27,225	75,796
1987......	125,841	58,254	62,669	2,215	1,658	1,044	32	3	65	18,213	27,819	79,809
1988......	133,463	59,930	68,076	2,441	1,880	1,135	30	3	66	19,381	29,466	84,614
1989......	141,550	60,301	75,091	2,774	2,136	1,248	28	4	68	21,477	32,304	87,767
1990......	151,655	61,456	83,374	3,096	2,367	1,361	25	4	70	22,556	34,981	94,118
1991......	160,521	60,563	92,484	3,412	2,585	1,478	23	4	73	26,629	38,699	95,193
1992......	164,932	60,693	96,404	3,558	2,770	1,508	22	4	74	27,044	37,995	99,894
1993......	165,188	60,350	96,704	3,646	2,928	1,561	22	4	74	28,125	37,318	99,746
1994......	168,554	60,692	99,332	3,867	3,074	1,588	20	4	76	28,934	36,615	103,005
1995......	183,013	63,147	110,998	4,069	3,129	1,670	19	5	77	28,642	40,927	113,445
1996, prel.	193,206	62,810	121,156	4,255	3,250	1,736	18	4	78	29,574	43,353	120,281
1997, prel...	205,742	62,745	133,308	4,457	3,411	1,821	17	4	79	31,212	46,208	128,323

[1] Nonfederal R&D expenditures to university and college performers. [2] R&D spending by the Department of Defense, including space activities, and a portion of the Department of Energy funds. [3] For the National Aeronautics and Space Administration only.

Source: U.S. National Science Foundation, *National Patterns of R&D Resouces*, annual.

No. 989. Federal Obligations for R&D, by Agency: 1980 to 1997

[In millions of dollars. For fiscal years ending in year shown; see text, Section 9, State and Local Government. Includes those agencies with obligations of $1 billion or more in 1997]

AGENCY	1980	1985	1990	1992	1993	1994	1995	1996	1997, prel.
CURRENT DOLLARS									
Obligations, total [1]..........	29,830	48,360	63,559	65,593	67,314	67,256	68,755	69,077	68,064
Dept. of Defense............	13,981	29,792	37,268	36,130	35,849	34,566	34,362	34,284	32,064
Dept. of Health and Human Services .	3,780	5,451	8,406	8,988	10,349	11,022	11,455	11,914	12,185
National Aeronautics and Space Administration.................	3,234	3,327	6,533	7,658	8,020	8,296	9,015	9,614	9,204
Dept. of Energy	4,754	4,966	5,631	6,172	6,262	6,048	6,145	5,676	5,895
National Science Foundation.......	882	1,346	1,690	1,868	1,882	2,040	2,149	2,142	2,279
Dept. of Agriculture	688	943	1,108	1,327	1,328	1,400	1,380	1,352	1,369
CONSTANT (1992) DOLLARS [2]									
Obligations, total [1]..........	50,304	61,683	68,196	65,593	65,608	64,053	63,899	62,740	60,287
Dept. of Defense............	23,577	37,999	39,987	36,130	34,941	32,920	31,935	31,139	28,400
Dept. of Health and Human Services .	6,375	6,953	9,019	8,988	10,087	10,497	10,646	10,821	10,793
National Aeronautics and Space Administration.................	5,454	4,244	7,010	7,658	7,817	7,901	8,378	8,732	8,152
Dept. of Energy	8,016	6,334	6,042	6,172	6,103	5,760	5,711	5,155	5,221
National Science Foundation.......	1,487	1,716	1,813	1,868	1,834	1,943	1,997	1,946	2,019
Dept. of Agriculture...........	1,160	1,203	1,189	1,327	1,294	1,333	1,283	1,228	1,213

[1] Includes other agencies, not shown separately. [2] Based on gross domestic product implicit price deflator.

Source: U.S. National Science Foundation, *Federal Funds for Research and Development*, annual.

No. 990. Performance Sector of R&D Expenditures: 1992 to 1997

[In millions of dollars. For calendar years]

YEAR	RESEARCH AND DEVELOPMENT TOTAL		INDUSTRY				UNIVERSITIES AND COLLEGES						Universities & colleges FFRDCs[3]	OTHER NONPROFIT INSTITUTIONS				Nonprofit FFRDCs[1]
				Funded by—				Funded by—							Funded by—			
	Total	Federal government[1]	Total	Federal government	Industry[2]	Industry FFRDCs[1]	Total	Federal government	Nonfederal government	Industry	Universities & colleges	Nonprofits		Total	Federal government	Industry	Nonprofits	
RESEARCH AND DEVELOPMENT TOTAL																		
1992	164,932	15,853	116,757	22,369	94,388	2,353	19,099	11,306	1,508	1,300	3,558	1,428	5,259	4,864	2,806	716	1,342	748
1993	165,188	16,532	115,435	20,844	94,591	1,965	20,221	12,129	1,561	1,376	3,646	1,510	5,289	4,997	2,841	737	1,419	749
1994	168,554	16,440	117,392	20,261	97,131	2,202	21,305	12,826	1,588	1,437	3,867	1,585	5,305	5,152	2,899	764	1,489	759
1995, prel	183,013	17,231	129,830	21,178	108,652	2,273	22,303	13,434	1,670	1,516	4,069	1,613	5,405	5,167	2,822	830	1,516	804
1996, prel	193,206	16,774	139,579	20,931	118,648	2,273	23,134	13,855	1,736	1,613	4,255	1,676	5,405	5,340	2,871	895	1,575	702
1997, prel	205,742	16,450	151,418	20,787	130,631	2,273	24,031	14,285	1,821	1,710	4,457	1,759	5,405	5,520	2,900	967	1,653	644
BASIC RESEARCH																		
1992	27,044	2,419	6,528	712	5,816	474	12,710	7,886	933	805	2,202	884	2,867	1,980	1,114	329	537	67
1993	28,125	2,623	6,427	466	5,961	492	13,497	8,537	957	843	2,235	925	2,953	2,062	1,155	339	567	72
1994	28,934	2,557	6,514	436	6,078	503	14,267	9,091	970	878	2,361	968	2,944	2,075	1,128	351	596	74
1995, prel	28,642	2,638	5,569	190	5,379	530	14,945	9,547	1,017	923	2,477	982	2,781	2,104	1,116	382	606	74
1996, prel	29,574	2,477	6,056	182	5,874	530	15,500	9,837	1,059	984	2,597	1,023	2,781	2,155	1,114	412	630	74
1997, prel	31,212	2,687	6,645	178	6,467	530	16,101	10,142	1,113	1,046	2,725	1,075	2,781	2,385	1,279	445	661	83
APPLIED RESEARCH																		
1992	37,995	4,337	25,660	4,476	21,184	507	4,810	2,375	471	406	1,111	446	940	1,660	933	243	483	81
1993	37,318	4,838	24,251	4,295	19,956	435	5,068	2,500	495	437	1,157	479	962	1,661	900	251	511	103
1994	36,615	5,006	22,988	3,616	19,372	503	5,272	2,565	507	459	1,235	506	981	1,753	957	260	536	112
1995, prel	40,927	5,054	26,919	3,164	23,755	535	5,532	2,687	536	486	1,305	517	979	1,779	951	282	546	129
1996, prel	43,353	5,000	29,065	3,125	25,940	535	5,779	2,814	555	515	1,360	535	979	1,883	1,012	304	567	111
1997, prel	46,208	5,083	31,663	3,102	28,560	535	5,975	2,869	580	545	1,420	560	979	1,863	940	329	595	110
DEVELOPMENT																		
1992	99,894	9,098	84,569	17,181	67,388	1,373	1,580	1,045	103	89	244	98	1,452	1,223	758	143	322	599
1993	99,746	9,071	84,757	16,083	68,674	1,039	1,656	1,092	109	96	254	105	1,374	1,275	787	147	340	574
1994	103,005	8,877	87,890	16,209	71,681	1,196	1,765	1,171	111	101	271	111	1,380	1,324	814	153	357	574
1995, prel	113,445	9,539	97,342	17,824	79,518	1,209	1,826	1,201	118	107	287	114	1,645	1,284	754	166	364	600
1996, prel	120,281	9,297	104,457	17,624	86,834	1,209	1,855	1,204	122	113	298	118	1,645	1,302	745	179	378	516
1997, prel	128,323	8,681	113,111	17,507	95,604	1,209	1,956	1,274	127	120	312	123	1,645	1,272	682	193	397	451

[1] For R&D funded by the federal government. FFRDCs are federally funded research and development centers. [2] Includes all nonfederal sources. [3] Includes all R&D expenditures of FFRDCs administered by academic institutions and funded by the federal government. In 1994, 99 percent of total funds used were from federal sources.

Source: National Science Foundation, National Patterns of R&D Resources, annual series.

No. 991. Performance Sector of R&D Expenditures, by State: 1995

[In millions of dollars. For the fiscal year]

STATE	Total [1]	Federal government [2]	INDUSTRY			UNIVERSITIES AND COLLEGES					Non-profits [6]
			Total	Funded by—		Total	Funded by—				
				Federal government [3]	Industry [4]		Federal government	Industry	Non-profits	Other [5]	
United States . . .	**183,013**	**17,343**	**132,103**	**23,451**	**108,652**	**22,101**	**13,331**	**1,492**	**1,599**	**5,679**	**5,983**
Alabama	1,681	642	686	273	413	335	190	29	22	94	18
Alaska	163	61	30	(D)	(D)	72	37	5	-	30	1
Arizona	1,995	178	1,356	620	736	380	210	23	12	134	6
Arkansas	330	58	181	(D)	(D)	88	33	8	3	44	3
California	36,133	1,844	28,710	6,925	21,785	2,594	1,797	120	198	480	607
Colorado	2,603	168	1,865	274	1,591	394	260	24	35	74	51
Connecticut	4,311	18	3,906	389	3,517	377	228	20	32	97	10
Delaware	1,149	15	1,077	12	1,065	53	27	4	5	17	3
District of Columbia	3,128	2,106	672	17	656	181	133	13	15	21	169
Florida	5,223	554	4,101	1,634	2,467	559	317	36	29	176	8
Georgia	2,113	272	1,175	142	1,031	658	302	55	25	276	8
Hawaii	509	402	14	(D)	(D)	78	44	-	3	31	15
Idaho	914	28	827	(D)	(D)	59	20	7	2	30	1
Illinois	7,487	81	5,776	146	5,630	818	468	43	65	242	41
Indiana	3,163	62	2,721	382	2,339	376	197	35	20	123	4
Iowa	1,391	37	998	(D)	(D)	323	164	19	15	125	1
Kansas	764	12	569	(D)	(D)	181	70	11	8	92	1
Kentucky	594	6	452	4	448	135	60	17	5	54	1
Louisiana	423	45	61	(D)	(D)	315	136	21	19	138	2
Maine	345	4	286	(D)	(D)	32	16	4	1	11	23
Maryland	6,519	4,159	1,075	287	788	1,160	895	55	50	160	125
Massachusetts	9,969	316	7,416	1,458	5,958	1,147	825	89	128	105	746
Michigan	13,275	82	12,388	148	12,240	755	418	51	57	230	50
Minnesota	3,087		2,636	315	2,321	337	195	23	23	96	85
Mississippi	315		66	(D)	(D)	113	63	9	6	35	3
Missouri	2,499	55	2,028	584	1,443	397	213	37	33	114	18
Montana	119	34	17	(D)	(D)	67	27	6	1	33	2
Nebraska	336	23	150	(D)	(D)	157	55	11	3	88	6
Nevada	445	35	322	(D)	(D)	87	48	7	1	31	1
New Hampshire	598	31	472	36	436	93	60	4	12	17	2
New Jersey	9,128	344	8,200	197	8,002	443	209	26	33	176	15
New Mexico	3,295	481	1,461	1,380	81	230	157	11	7	56	13
New York	10,954	117	8,651	1,821	6,831	1,702	1,107	98	195	302	203
North Carolina	3,191	220	2,226	15	2,212	687	432	74	21	160	59
North Dakota	98	25	12	(D)	(D)	60	28	3	2	27	1
Ohio	5,314	599	4,001	574	3,428	643	375	54	59	155	72
Oklahoma	529	45	288	38	249	186	60	11	17	99	9
Oregon	1,089	56	741	35	706	259	158	12	21	67	33
Pennsylvania	6,919	228	5,331	376	4,955	1,140	754	120	66	199	189
Rhode Island	896	254	520	(D)	(D)	106	72	2	2	29	17
South Carolina	996	34	739	(D)	(D)	220	109	19	19	72	3
South Dakota	55	13	19	-	19	21	11	-	1	9	1
Tennessee	1,402	62	1,003	(D)	(D)	308	192	16	20	80	20
Texas	8,385	538	6,211	912	5,298	1,472	748	102	167	456	164
Utah	1,144	131	803	178	625	202	141	9	9	43	8
Vermont	308	5	248	(D)	(D)	54	33	5	4	12	1
Virginia	3,897	1,581	1,577	743	834	447	262	46	28	111	219
Washington	5,241	160	4,294	(D)	(D)	486	340	39	15	91	301
West Virginia	475	140	243	(D)	(D)	53	30	3	4	15	6
Wisconsin	2,226	40	1,706	33	1,673	473	271	17	15	135	7
Wyoming	87	9	25	(D)	(D)	40	15	2	3	20	13
Other/unknown	5,805	771	1,772	3,502	8,875	548	320	30	30	167	2,620

- Represents or rounds to zero. D Data withheld to avoiding disclosing information about individual companies. [1] Includes university and college Federally Funded Research and Development Centers (FFRDCs), not shown separately. [2] For R&D funded by the federal government. [3] Includes performance at industry FFRDCs. [4] Includes all nonfederal sources. [5] Represents funding by state and local governments and universities and colleges. [6] Data by state are for R&D funded by the federal government. United States total includes other support, not allocated by location.

Source: U.S. National Science Foundation, *National Patterns of R&D Resources, 1997.*

No. 992. Federal Funding for R&D, by Selected Budget Functions: 1970 to 1998

[In millions of dollars. For fiscal years ending in year shown; see text, Section 9, State and Local Government. Excludes R&D plant. Represents budget authority. Functions shown are those for which $1 billion or more was authorized for 1998]

FUNCTION	1970	1980	1985	1990	1994	1995	1996	1997, prel.	1998, prel.
CURRENT DOLLARS									
Total [1]	15,339	29,739	49,887	63,781	68,331	68,791	69,049	70,988	71,602
Eight functions, percent of total	96.6	96.5	98.3	98.0	97.9	97.7	98.0	98.2	98.0
National defense	7,981	14,946	33,698	39,925	37,764	37,204	37,801	39,030	38,726
Health	1,084	3,694	5,418	8,308	10,993	11,407	11,867	12,693	12,998
Space research and technology	3,606	2,738	2,725	5,765	7,414	7,916	7,844	7,795	8,004
Energy	574	3,603	2,389	2,715	2,873	2,844	2,521	2,259	2,229
General science	452	1,233	1,862	2,410	2,712	2,794	2,846	2,962	3,086
Natural resources and environment	340	999	1,059	1,386	2,062	1,988	1,802	1,842	1,902
Transportation	535	887	1,030	1,045	1,888	1,833	1,795	1,827	1,939
Agriculture	238	585	836	950	1,193	1,194	1,176	1,185	1,196
CONSTANT (1992) DOLLARS [2]									
Total [1]	51,113	50,108	63,623	68,448	65,054	63,931	62,728	62,879	61,733
National defense	26,594	25,183	42,977	42,847	35,953	34,575	34,341	34,571	33,388
Health	3,612	6,224	6,910	8,916	10,466	10,601	10,781	11,243	11,206
Space research and technology	12,016	4,613	3,475	6,187	7,059	7,357	7,126	6,904	6,901
Energy	1,913	6,071	3,047	2,925	2,735	2,643	2,290	2,001	1,922
General science	1,506	2,078	2,375	2,586	2,581	2,596	2,586	2,624	2,661
Natural resources and environment	1,133	1,683	1,351	1,487	1,963	1,848	1,637	1,632	1,640
Transportation	1,783	1,495	1,314	1,121	1,798	1,704	1,630	1,618	1,672
Agriculture	793	986	1,066	1,020	1,136	1,109	1,068	1,050	1,031

[1] Includes other functions, not shown separately. [2] Based on gross domestic product implicit price deflator.

Source: U.S. National Science Foundation, *Federal R&D Funding by Budget Function*, annual.

No. 993. National R&D Expenditures as a Percent of Gross Domestic Product, by Country: 1981 to 1996

YEAR	TOTAL R&D						NONDEFENSE R&D [1]					
	United States	Japan	Unified Germany	France	United Kingdom	Italy	United States	Japan	Unified Germany	France	United Kingdom	Italy
1981	2.32	2.13	2.43	1.97	2.37	0.88	1.73	2.12	2.34	1.57	1.84	0.85
1985	2.74	2.58	2.72	2.25	2.23	1.13	1.89	2.56	2.60	1.87	1.76	1.07
1990	2.64	2.85	2.75	2.41	2.18	1.30	1.97	2.83	2.62	1.95	1.84	1.26
1993	2.52	2.68	2.43	2.45	2.15	1.26	1.98	2.65	2.35	2.10	1.85	1.21
1994	2.43	2.64	2.33	2.38	2.11	1.16	1.95	2.60	2.25	2.05	1.84	1.11
1995	2.52	2.78	2.28	2.34	2.05	1.14	2.05	2.74	2.20	(NA)	1.78	1.11
1996	2.55	(NA)	2.26	(NA)	(NA)	1.13	2.10	(NA)	(NA)	(NA)	(NA)	(NA)

NA Not available. [1] Estimated.

Source: National Science Foundation, *National Patterns of R&D Resources*, annual; and Organization for Economic Co-operation and Development.

No. 994. R&D Expenditures in Science and Engineering at Universities and Colleges: 1981 to 1996

[In millions of dollars]

CHARACTERISTIC	1981	1990	1996	CHARACTERISTIC	1981	1990	1996
CURRENT DOLLARS				CONSTANT (1992) DOLLARS [1]			
Total	6,846	16,285	22,995	Total	10,513	17,483	20,846
Basic research	4,593	10,641	15,467	Basic research	7,053	11,424	14,021
Applied R&D	2,253	5,644	7,529	Applied R&D	3,460	6,059	6,825
Source of funds:				Source of funds:			
All governments	5,115	10,960	15,535	All governments	7,855	11,766	14,083
Institutions' own funds	1,004	3,006	4,232	Institutions' own funds	1,542	3,227	3,836
Industry	292	1,128	1,576	Industry	448	1,211	1,429
Other	435	1,191	1,652	Other	668	1,279	1,498
Fields:				Fields:			
Physical sciences	765	1,807	2,260	Physical sciences	1,175	1,940	2,049
Environmental sciences	550	1,068	1,478	Environmental sciences	845	1,147	1,340
Mathematical sciences	87	222	289	Mathematical sciences	134	238	262
Computer sciences	144	515	702	Computer sciences	221	553	636
Life sciences	3,695	8,726	12,697	Life sciences	5,674	9,368	11,510
Psychology	127	253	372	Psychology	195	272	337
Social sciences	366	703	1,104	Social sciences	562	755	1,001
Other sciences	145	336	419	Other sciences	223	361	380
Engineering	967	2,656	3,675	Engineering	1,485	2,851	3,332

[1] Based on gross domestic product implicit price deflator.

Source: U.S. National Science Foundation, *Survey of Rsearch and Development Expenditures at Universities and Colleges*, annual.

No. 995. Federal Obligations to Universities and Colleges: 1970 to 1995

[In millions of dollars, except percent. For fiscal years ending in year shown; see text, Section 9, State and Local Government. Minus sign (-) indicates decrease]

ITEM	1970	1980	1985	1990	1992	1993	1994	1995
CURRENT DOLLARS								
Federal obligations, total	3,237	8,299	10,972	15,200	19,066	(NA)	(NA)	(NA)
Annual percent change [1]	-6.5	9.1	9.3	-2.0	8.6	(NA)	(NA)	(NA)
Academic science/engineering obligations	2,188	4,791	7,258	10,445	12,750	12,751	13,775	14,346
Percent of total	67.6	57.7	66.2	68.7	66.9	(NA)	(NA)	(NA)
Research and development	1,447	4,161	6,246	9,008	10,846	10,943	11,806	12,068
Research and development plant.	45	38	114	125	205	259	214	335
Other science/engineering activities	696	593	898	1,312	1,699	1,548	1,754	1,942
Nonscience/engineering activities	1,049	3,508	3,714	4,755	6,317	(NA)	(NA)	(NA)
CONSTANT (1992) DOLLARS [2]								
Federal obligations, total	10,814	13,999	14,000	16,318	19,066	(NA)	(NA)	(NA)
Annual percent change [1]	-11.2	0.2	5.6	-5.9	5.5	(NA)	(NA)	(NA)
Academic science/engineering obligations	7,309	8,082	9,261	11,214	12,749	12,423	13,104	13,306
Percent of total	67.6	57.7	66.2	68.7	66.9	(NA)	(NA)	(NA)
Research and development	4,833	7,018	7,970	9,671	10,845	10,662	11,231	11,193
Research and development plant.	150	64	145	134	205	253	204	311
Other science/engineering activities	2,326	1,000	1,146	1,409	1,699	1,508	1,669	1,802
Nonscience/engineering activities	3,505	5,917	4,739	5,104	6,317	(NA)	(NA)	(NA)

NA Not available.   [1] Percent change from immediate prior year.   [2] Based on gross domestic product implicit price deflator.
Source: U.S. National Science Foundation, *Survey of Federal S&E Support to Universities, Colleges, and Nonprofit Institutions*, annual.

No. 996. Federal R&D Obligations to Selected Universities and Colleges: 1981 to 1995

[For fiscal years ending in year shown; see text, Section 9, State and Local Government. For the top 45 institutions receiving Federal R&D funds in 1995. Awards to the administrative offices of university systems are excluded from totals for individual institutions because that allocation of funds is unknown, but those awards are included in "total all institutions"]

MAJOR INSTITUTION RANKED BY TOTAL 1995 FEDERAL R&D OBLIGATIONS	OBLIGATIONS ($1,000)			RANK		
	1981	1985	1995	1981	1985	1995
Total, all institutions [1]	4,410,931	6,246,181	12,068,492	(X)	(X)	(X)
45 institutions, percent of total	62.1	60.8	59.3	(X)	(X)	(X)
Johns Hopkins University.	363,429	297,374	569,329	1	1	1
University of Washington.	99,965	146,179	299,631	4	4	2
Massachusetts Institute of Technology	146,035	189,558	282,120	2	2	3
Stanford University.	106,073	174,961	266,744	3	3	4
University of Michigan.	73,999	108,035	243,126	11	11	5
University of California—San Diego	91,403	103,633	239,078	6	13	6
University of California—Los Angeles.	94,945	128,211	216,423	5	5	7
University of Wisconsin—Madison	86,918	124,604	207,504	8	7	8
University of Minnesota	72,001	103,272	202,354	14	14	9
Cornell University.	72,671	119,966	202,077	13	8	10
University of California—San Francisco	64,814	98,536	201,770	15	16	11
University of Pennsylvania	76,136	103,119	197,229	10	15	12
Harvard University.	87,830	109,414	191,499	7	9	13
Columbia University—Main Division.	83,659	127,331	186,179	9	6	14
Yale University.	73,526	109,227	179,542	12	10	15
University of Pittsburgh	38,512	58,620	171,303	29	28	16
Washington University.	54,170	71,978	165,373	17	22	18
University of Colorado.	46,146	71,424	165,373	22	23	17
University of North Carolina at Chapel Hill	38,447	63,105	156,609	30	27	19
Duke University.	44,287	69,169	154,998	23	26	20
Pennsylvania State University.	47,099	76,726	152,382	21	19	21
University Southern California.	49,221	89,706	152,179	20	17	22
University of California—Berkeley	64,065	106,710	142,338	16	12	23
University of Arizona.	36,308	49,740	137,014	33	37	24
Case Western Reserve University	33,744	47,994	127,750	38	40	25
University of Alabama—Birmingham	29,970	44,093	120,191	44	46	26
University of Texas at Austin.	43,756	72,379	115,882	24	21	27
University of Illinois—Urbana Champaign	53,583	83,122	115,717	19	18	28
California Institute of Techology.	32,959	55,083	113,684	40	32	29
University of Rochester.	42,983	70,379	107,604	25	25	30
University of Chicago	53,992	71,194	106,723	18	24	31
Northwestern University.	32,446	48,260	102,561	47	39	32
University of California—Davis	31,757	43,156	98,932	42	47	33
Ohio State University	42,899	56,065	96,429	26	30	34
Vanderbilt University	27,426	39,909	94,421	49	48	35
University of Iowa.	35,300	55,117	93,867	34	31	36
University of Utah.	38,163	50,938	93,783	31	36	37
University of Maryland—College Park	27,313	51,073	92,701	50	35	38
Indiana University.	29,276	39,118	89,030	45	49	39
Georgetown University	10,327	18,194	88,469	103	91	40
Boston University.	27,019	46,152	86,090	51	43	41
New York University.	40,636	74,577	85,543	28	20	42
Baylor College of Medicine.	35,062	45,837	84,076	35	45	43
University of Florida	30,845	47,716	83,702	43	41	44
University of Miami.	28,956	33,709	80,703	46	59	45

X Not applicable.   [1] Includes other institutions, not shown separately.

Source: U.S. National Science Foundation, *Federal S&E Support to Universities and Colleges and Nonprofit Institutions*, annual.

No. 997. Funds for Performance of Industrial R&D, by Source of Funds and Selected Industries: 1980 to 1995

[In millions of dollars. For calendar years. Covers basic research, applied research, and development]

INDUSTRY	1987 SIC [1] code	1980	1985	1990	1993	1994	1995
CURRENT DOLLARS							
Total funds	(X)	**44,505**	**84,239**	**109,727**	**117,400**	**119,595**	**132,103**
Chemicals and allied products	28	4,636	8,540	13,291	(D)	(D)	17,547
Petroleum refining and extraction	13,29	1,552	(D)	2,306	2,152	1,950	1,760
Machinery	35	5,901	12,216	14,446	8,381	8,110	(D)
Electrical equipment	36	9,175	14,432	13,400	13,349	15,338	18,751
Motor vehicles and motor vehicles equipment	371	4,955	6,984	(D)	11,718	(D)	(D)
Aircraft and missiles	372,376	9,198	22,231	20,635	15,056	14,260	16,951
Professional and scientific instruments	38	3,029	5,013	7,055	10,119	11,441	11,976
All other [2]	(X)	6,059	(D)	(D)	(D)	(D)	(D)
Company funds	(X)	**30,476**	**57,043**	**81,602**	**94,591**	**97,131**	**108,652**
Chemicals and allied products	28	4,264	8,310	13,168	16,658	16,559	17,337
Petroleum refining and extraction	13,29	1,401	2,194	2,289	2,138	1,939	1,754
Machinery	35	5,254	10,721	13,575	8,295	8,011	9,676
Electrical equipment	36	5,431	9,271	9,267	11,682	13,537	17,060
Motor vehicles and motor vehicles equipment	371	4,300	6,164	8,594	10,659	11,950	13,590
Aircraft and missiles	372,376	2,570	5,649	5,387	5,684	5,466	5,489
Professional and scientific instruments	38	2,456	4,622	6,318	7,542	8,058	8,516
All other [2]	(X)	4,800	10,112	23,004	31,933	31,611	35,230
CONSTANT (1992) DOLLARS [3]							
Total funds	(X)	**73,769**	**107,270**	**117,230**	**114,380**	**113,802**	**122,590**
Chemicals and allied products	28	7,684	10,875	14,200	(D)	(D)	16,283
Petroleum refining and extraction	13,29	2,573	(D)	2,464	2,097	1,856	1,633
Machinery	35	9,781	15,556	15,434	8,165	7,717	(D)
Electrical equipment	36	15,208	18,378	14,316	13,006	14,595	17,401
Motor vehicles and motor vehicles equipment	371	8,213	8,893	(D)	11,417	(D)	(D)
Aircraft and missiles	372,376	15,246	28,309	22,046	14,669	13,569	15,730
Professional and scientific instruments	38	5,021	6,384	7,537	9,859	10,887	11,114
All other [2]	(X)	10,043	(D)	(D)	(D)	(D)	(D)
Company funds	(X)	**50,515**	**72,638**	**87,182**	**92,158**	**92,426**	**100,828**
Chemicals and allied products	28	7,068	10,582	14,068	16,230	15,757	16,089
Petroleum refining and extraction	13,29	2,322	2,794	2,446	2,083	1,845	1,628
Machinery	35	8,709	13,652	14,503	8,082	7,623	8,979
Electrical equipment	36	9,002	11,806	9,901	11,382	12,881	15,831
Motor vehicles and motor vehicles equipment	371	7,127	7,849	9,182	10,385	11,371	12,611
Aircraft and missiles	372,376	4,260	7,193	5,755	5,538	5,201	5,094
Professional and scientific instruments	38	4,071	5,886	6,750	7,348	7,668	7,903
All other [2]	(X)	7,956	12,877	24,577	31,112	30,080	32,693

D Figure withheld to avoid disclosure of information pertaining to a specific organization or individual.   X Not applicable.   [1] Prior to 1993, 1972 Standard Industrial Classification; beginning 1993, 1987 Standard Industrial Classification; see text, Section 13, Labor Force.   [2] All other manufacturing and nonmanufacturing.   [3] Based on gross domestic product implicit price deflator.

Source: U.S. National Science Foundation, *Research and Development in Industry,* annual.

No. 998. R&D Funds in R&D-Performing Manufacturing Companies, by Industry: 1980 to 1995

INDUSTRY	1987 SIC [1] code	TOTAL R&D FUNDS AS A PERCENT OF NET SALES					COMPANY R&D FUNDS AS A PERCENT OF NET SALES				
		1980	1985	1990	1994	1995	1980	1985	1990	1994	1995
Total [2]	(X)	**3.0**	**4.4**	**4.2**	**3.6**	**3.6**	**2.1**	**3.0**	**3.1**	**2.9**	**2.9**
Food and kindred products [3]	20	0.4	(D)	(D)	0.5	0.5	(D)	0.6	0.5	0.5	0.5
Paper and allied products	26	1.0	(D)	1.0	(D)	(D)	1.0	0.8	1.0	1.0	1.0
Chemicals and allied products	28	3.6	5.0	5.3	(D)	4.7	3.3	4.9	5.3	5.1	4.7
Petroleum refining and extraction	13,29	0.6	(D)	0.9	0.8	0.7	0.5	0.9	0.9	0.8	0.7
Rubber products	30	2.2	(D)	(D)	(D)	(D)	(D)	1.8	2.1	2.3	1.6
Stone, clay, and glass products	32	1.4	(D)	(D)	1.7	1.5	1.3	2.3	1.7	1.5	1.5
Primary metals	33	0.7	(D)	0.8	0.6	0.5	0.5	0.9	0.8	0.6	0.5
Fabricated metal products	34	1.4	1.5	1.4	1.2	1.1	1.4	1.4	1.1	1.0	1.1
Machinery	35	5.0	7.6	7.7	3.8	(D)	4.5	6.7	7.2	3.8	3.6
Electrical equipment	36	6.6	7.6	6.5	5.9	6.0	3.9	4.8	4.5	5.2	5.4
Motor vehicles and motor vehicle equipment	371	4.9	3.8	(D)	(D)	(D)	4.2	3.1	3.7	3.4	3.6
Aircraft and missiles	372,376	13.7	14.9	11.8	13.8	12.9	3.8	3.9	3.1	5.3	4.2
Professional and scientific instruments	38	7.5	8.9	8.0	9.2	10.3	6.1	8.3	7.1	6.5	7.3

D Figure withheld to avoid disclosure of information pertaining to a specific organization or individual.   X Not applicable.   [1] Prior to 1994, 1972 Standard Industrial Classification; beginning 1994, 1987 Standard Industrial Classification; see text, Section 13, Labor Force.   [2] Includes all manufacturing industries.   [3] Includes tobacco products (SIC 21) beginning 1985.

Source: U.S. National Science Foundation, *Research and Development in Industry,* annual.

No. 999. Federal Obligations for Research, by Field of Science: 1980 to 1997

[In millions of dollars. For fiscal years ending in year shown; see text, Section 9, State and Local Government. Excludes R&D plant]

FIELD	1980	1985	1990	1992	1993	1994	1995	1996	1997
CURRENT DOLLARS									
Research, total	11,597	16,133	21,731	24,491	26,890	27,440	28,573	28,578	29,174
Basic	4,674	7,819	11,286	12,490	13,399	13,553	13,895	14,482	14,732
Applied	6,923	8,315	10,446	12,001	13,491	13,887	14,678	14,096	14,441
Life sciences	4,192	6,363	8,830	9,910	10,772	11,079	11,869	12,150	12,300
Psychology	199	327	449	298	551	550	621	641	650
Physical sciences	2,001	3,046	3,809	4,439	4,427	6,793	4,282	4,322	4,398
Environmental sciences	1,261	1,404	2,174	2,208	2,608	2,032	2,947	2,924	2,955
Mathematics and computer sciences . . .	241	575	841	1,160	1,225	1,242	1,531	1,508	1,546
Engineering	2,830	3,618	4,335	4,977	5,499	4,023	5,740	5,509	5,708
Social sciences	524	460	630	690	675	655	682	669	728
Other sciences, n.e.c. [1]	350	342	664	808	1,133	1,066	902	854	889
CONSTANT (1992) DOLLARS [2]									
Research, total	19,557	20,578	23,317	24,491	26,209	26,133	26,555	25,956	25,840
Basic	7,882	9,973	12,109	12,490	13,059	12,908	12,914	13,154	13,049
Applied	11,675	10,605	11,208	12,001	13,149	13,226	13,641	12,803	12,791
Life sciences	7,070	8,115	9,474	9,910	10,499	10,551	11,031	11,036	10,894
Psychology	336	417	482	298	537	524	577	583	576
Physical sciences	3,374	3,885	4,087	4,439	4,315	6,470	3,979	3,926	3,896
Environmental sciences	2,126	1,790	2,333	2,208	2,542	1,935	2,739	2,656	2,617
Mathematics and computer sciences . . .	406	733	902	1,160	1,194	1,183	1,423	1,370	1,369
Engineering	4,773	4,614	4,651	4,977	5,360	3,831	5,335	5,003	5,056
Social sciences	883	587	676	690	658	624	633	608	644
Other sciences, n.e.c. [1]	590	436	712	808	1,104	1,015	838	775	788

[1] N.e.c. = Not elsewhere classified. [2] Based on gross domestic product implicit price deflator.

Source: U.S. National Science Foundation, *Federal Funds for Research and Development,* annual.

No. 1000. R&D Scientists and Engineers—Employment and Cost, by Industry: 1980 to 1995

[Data are estimates; on average full-time-equivalent (FTE) basis]

INDUSTRY	1987 SIC [1] code	1980	1985	1989	1990	1991	1992	1993	1994	1995
EMPLOYED SCIENTISTS										
Average FTE of scientists and engineers (1,000) [2][3]	(X)	469.2	646.8	733.1	758.5	776.4	772.0	766.6	758.9	789.5
Chemicals [4]	28	53.1	71.1	78.3	80.4	81.6	85.6	93.1	92.3	97.0
Machinery	35	65.7	81.7	100.4	113.3	109.7	99.3	97.4	68.4	78.0
Electrical equipment [5]	36	100.7	113.2	122.5	105.2	95.9	91.9	89.2	101.0	114.6
Motor vehicles	371	36.7	28.7	45.8	49.4	45.3	44.5	45.1	51.2	54.1
Aircraft and missiles	372,376	90.6	130.2	134.8	115.3	100.2	92.9	97.9	65.7	79.5
CONSTANT (1992) DOLLARS [6]										
Cost per scientist or engineer ($1,000) [3][7]	(X)	164.8	164.7	153.7	154.9	157.5	155.6	151.5	154.6	155.8
Chemicals [4]	28	152.5	148.6	171.6	174.5	180.4	91.8	0.0	86.1	84.0
Machinery	35	152.3	90.7	149.6	152.9	154.4	126.7	106.9	56.5	70.9
Electrical equipment [5]	36	154.5	156.4	153.4	154.9	152.7	147.4	144.5	150.1	155.7
Motor vehicles	371	234.2	142.0	(D)	(D)	(D)	(D)	(D)	(D)	79.2
Aircraft and missiles	372,376	190.6	198.3	234.6	208.7	183.7	178.5	191.8	204.8	99.0

D Withheld to avoid disclosure. X Not applicable. [1] Prior to 1992, 1972 Standard Industrial Classification; beginning 1992, 1987 Standard Industrial Classification; see text, Section 13, Labor Force. [2] The mean number of FTE R&D scientists and engineers employed in January of the year shown and the following January. [3] Includes industries not shown separately. [4] Includes allied products. [5] Includes communication. [6] Based on gross domestic product implicit price deflator. [7] Represents the arithmetic mean of the numbers of R&D scientists and engineers reported in each industry for January in two consecutive years divided into total R&D expenditures in each industry.

Source: U.S. National Science Foundation, *Research and Development in Industry,* annual.

No. 1001. Civilian Employment of Scientists, Engineers, and Technicians, by Occupation and Industry: 1996

[In thousands. Based on sample and subject to sampling error. For details, see source]

OCCUPATION	Total [1]	WAGE AND SALARY WORKERS								Self em- ployed
		Min- ing [2]	Con- struc- tion	Manu- facturing	Trans- por- tation [3]	Trade	FIRE [4]	Serv- ices	Govern- ment	
Scientists, engineers, and technicians.	4,885.5	54.6	67.2	1,394.5	208.9	236.5	192.1	1,792.2	694.2	235.9
Scientists	665.7	11.4	0.4	79.9	5.4	3.8	11.8	258.9	197.9	92.5
Physical scientists	206.7	9.9	0.4	51.3	3.0	2.4	0.8	81.6	47.2	10.2
Life scientists.	180.0	0.2	0.1	27.1	1.2	1.4	0.4	62.9	74.7	8.3
Mathematical scientists	15.6	(NA)	(NA)	1.5	0.4	0.4	(NA)	3.1	4.5	1.3
Social scientists	263.5	1.3	(NA)	(NA)	0.8	(NA)	7.6	109.9	71.2	72.7
Computer systems analysts, engineers and scientists	932.8	3.7	2.1	196.6	42.2	60.8	86.5	375.0	107.4	58.4
Engineers [5]	1,382.4	18.9	31.0	620.4	68.7	39.1	10.5	370.0	177.9	45.8
Civil engineers.	196.1	0.6	10.9	7.5	5.3	0.5	0.4	86.6	71.3	13.0
Electrical/electronics	367.2	0.6	9.4	163.6	34.6	13.5	1.3	96.1	34.9	13.1
Mechanical engineers	227.9	1.6	5.1	131.2	4.2	7.2	(NA)	61.6	11.8	4.0
Engineering and science technicians	1,235.8	15.7	29.4	432.8	66.9	91.7	4.3	423.0	154.9	11.8
Electrical/electronics technicians	297.4	1.0	7.9	104.3	21.4	69.5	1.4	70.0	20.3	1.7
Engineering technicians.	400.2	4.9	4.2	150.9	25.5	11.4	0.3	105.9	92.9	3.2
Drafters	309.9	1.9	16.9	96.5	16.7	7.1	1.3	152.2	10.2	4.6
Science technicians	228.3	8.0	0.4	81.1	3.3	3.7	1.2	94.9	31.5	2.3
Surveyors.	100.7	2.4	2.6	0.1	2.8	(NA)	0.7	62.5	22.0	7.5
Computer programmers	568.0	2.4	1.5	64.8	22.8	41.0	78.3	302.9	34.0	20.0

NA Not available.   [1] Includes agriculture, forestry, and fishing not shown separately.   [2] Includes oil and gas extraction. [3] Includes communications and public utilities.   [4] Finance, insurance, and real estate.   [5] Includes kinds of engineers and technicians not shown separately.

Source: U.S. Bureau of Labor Statistics, *Monthly Labor Review,* November 1997; and unpublished data. (Data collected biennially.)

No. 1002. Graduate Science/Engineering Students in Doctorate-Granting Colleges: 1985 to 1996

[As of fall. Includes outlying areas]

FIELD OF SCIENCE OR ENGINEERING	TOTAL (1,000)			PERCENT—							
				Female			Foreign		Part time		
	1985	1990	1996	1985	1990	1996	1990	1996	1985	1990	1996
Total, all surveyed fields	355.8	398.8	430.6	34.5	37.6	43.1	25.4	22.8	32.4	31.1	29.5
Science/engineering	317.2	351.7	366.2	29.5	32.4	37.4	27.7	25.5	30.7	28.9	27.4
Engineering, total	90.2	99.8	96.2	11.5	13.6	17.6	36.6	35.1	39.7	35.9	33.5
Sciences, total	226.9	251.9	270.0	36.6	39.8	44.4	24.1	22.1	27.2	26.1	25.3
Physical sciences	29.4	32.5	30.8	20.5	23.4	27.5	37.0	35.2	11.9	11.3	11.4
Environmental.	14.1	12.9	13.7	25.3	29.1	35.2	20.1	19.8	23.8	23.6	25.0
Mathematical sciences . .	15.4	17.5	16.0	29.0	30.6	33.3	35.5	34.4	27.6	24.5	22.9
Computer sciences	24.2	28.1	29.0	25.2	23.2	24.8	32.7	36.1	48.6	47.2	46.3
Agricultural sciences . . .	10.9	10.6	11.2	25.8	29.3	36.5	28.8	25.7	18.4	17.9	20.6
Biological sciences.	42.2	46.4	53.6	42.5	45.5	48.9	24.2	21.0	16.1	14.8	14.5
Psychology.	30.8	35.9	38.7	59.7	65.6	69.4	4.6	4.5	30.6	29.0	26.6
Social sciences	59.9	68.0	77.1	39.8	42.8	47.9	21.7	18.7	34.4	32.9	31.0
Health fields, total.	38.7	47.2	64.4	75.7	76.9	75.4	8.6	7.2	46.2	47.4	41.2

Source: U.S. National Science Foundation, *Survey of Graduate Science Engineering Students and Postdoctorates,* annual.

No. 1003. Science and Engineering Degree Recipients in 1993 and 1994: 1995

[Based on survey and subject to sampling error; see source for details]

DEGREE AND FIELD	Graduates 1993 and 1994 (1,000)	1995 [1]—PERCENT DISTRIBUTION				Median salary [4] ($1,000)
		In school [2]	Employed		Not employed or not FT students	
			In S&E [3]	In other		
Bachelor's recipients	**698.6**	**23**	**19**	**52**	**6**	**25.0**
All science fields	580.2	25	10	59	6	22.8
Computer and mathematical sciences	69.2	13	32	51	4	29.0
Life and related sciences	121.1	37	10	47	5	21.8
Physical and related sciences	33.2	39	27	30	4	25.5
Social and related sciences	356.7	21	5	67	7	21.2
All engineering fields	118.4	15	62	20	4	33.5
Aerospace and related engineering	4.4	25	43	30	2	30.0
Chemical engineering	9.6	23	58	14	5	37.7
Civil and architectural engineering	18.1	13	67	17	3	31.0
Electrical, electronics, computer and communications engineering	38.6	11	64	21	4	35.0
Industrial engineering	6.4	9	59	28	3	34.0
Mechanical engineering	28.9	12	66	17	4	34.0
Other engineering	12.5	26	50	21	3	31.5
Master's recipients	**146.6**	**24**	**43**	**28**	**5**	**39.0**
All science fields	100.0	27	32	36	5	34.8
Computer and mathematical sciences	24.3	14	54	28	4	43.5
Life and related sciences	15.0	35	30	29	6	31.5
Physical and related sciences	9.7	39	41	15	4	35.5
Social and related sciences	51.0	27	21	46	6	30.5
All engineering fields	46.6	20	65	11	4	43.8
Aerospace and related engineering	1.7	24	59	(B)	(B)	43.3
Chemical engineering	1.7	(B)	65	(B)	(B)	42.3
Civil and architectural engineering	6.1	(B)	77	(B)	(B)	39.5
Electrical, electronics, computer and communications engineering	16.5	21	65	(B)	(B)	46.0
Industrial engineering	3.1	(B)	65	(B)	(B)	42.8
Mechanical engineering	7.5	20	65	(B)	(B)	43.0
Other engineering	10.1	21	59	16	4	44.5

B Base figure too small to meet statistical standards of reliability of a derived figure. [1] As of April. [2] Full-time students. [3] In science and engineering. [4] For the principal job. Excludes full-time students, the self-employed, and persons whose principal job is less than 35 hours per week.

Source: National Science Foundation/SRS, *National Survey of Recent College Graduates: 1995.*

No. 1004. Doctorates Conferred, by Recipients' Characteristics: 1990 and 1996

[In percent, except as indicated]

CHARACTERISTIC	1990, total	1996									
		All fields [1]	Engin-eering	Physi-cal sci-ences [2]	Earth sci-ences	Math-ematics	Com-puter sci-ences	Biologi-cal sci-ences [3]	Agri-cul-tural	Social sci-ences [4]	Psy-chol-ogy
Total conferred (number)	36,068	42,415	6,305	3,838	794	1,122	921	6,760	1,037	3,999	3,491
Male	63.7	60	87.7	78.1	78.3	81.9	84.9	60.1	72.8	63.5	33.3
Female	36.3	40	12.3	21.9	21.7	18.1	15.1	39.9	27.2	36.5	66.7
Median age [5]	33.9	33.8	31.7	30.2	33.8	30.9	32.7	31.5	34.3	34.5	33.2
CITIZENSHIP [6]											
Total conferred (number)	34,697	41,116	6099	3707	763	1087	889	5605	1018	3855	3407
U.S. citizen	71.8	67.5	57.6	44.1	39.5	55.2	52.7	36.8	53.6	36.7	8.4
Foreign citizen	28.2	32.5	42.4	55.9	60.5	44.8	47.3	63.2	46.4	63.3	91.6
RACE/ETHNICITY [7]											
Total conferred (number)	26,604	31,506	3383	2568	558	646	513	4365	576	2793	3226
White [8]	86.5	78.3	66.8	73.5	80.4	73.9	69.3	72.6	77	79.1	84.9
Black [8]	3.8	4.6	2.1	2.3	0.7	1.8	2.3	2.2	4.3	5	4.7
Asian/Pacific [8]	4.9	11.7	26.4	19.6	13.7	21.6	21.6	20.3	14	9.7	3.8
Indian/Alaskan [8]	0.4	0.5	0.4	0.2	0.3	0.1	0.7	0.4	0.8	0.8	0.5
Hispanic	3.1	3.5	2.8	2.5	3.4	1.5	3.1	3	2.2	3.4	5.3
Other/unknown	1.4	1.4	1.5	1.9	1.5	1.1	0.3	1.5	1.7	0.2	0.8

[1] Includes other fields, not shown separately. [2] Astronomy, physics, and chemistry. [3] Biochemistry, botany, microbiology, physiology, zoology, and related fields. [4] Anthropology, sociology, political science, economics, international relations and related fields. [5] For definition of median, see Guide to Tabular Presentation. [6] For those with known citizenship. Includes those with temporary visas. [7] Excludes those with temporary visas. [8] Non-Hispanic.

Source: U.S. National Science Foundation, Division of Science Resources Studies, Survey of Earned Doctorates, *Selected Data on Science and Engineering Doctorate Awards,* annual.

No. 1005. Space Vehicle Systems—Net Sales and Backlog Orders: 1965 to 1996

[In millions of dollars. Backlog orders as of Dec. 31. Based on data from major companies engaged in manufacture of aerospace products. Includes parts but excludes engines and propulsion units]

YEAR	NET SALES			BACKLOG ORDERS			YEAR	NET SALES			BACKLOG ORDERS		
	Total	Military	Non-military	Total	Military	Non-military		Total	Military	Non-military	Total	Military	Non-military
1965 .	2,449	602	1,847	2,203	503	1,700	1987 .	8,051	5,248	[1]2,803	12,393	9,460	[1]2,933
1970 .	1,956	1,025	931	1,184	786	398	1988 .	8,622	6,190	[1]2,432	10,838	7,880	[1]2,958
1975 .	2,119	1,096	1,023	1,304	1,019	285	1989 .	9,758	6,457	[1]3,301	13,356	9,192	[1]4,164
1980 .	3,483	1,461	2,022	1,814	951	863	1990 .	9,691	6,556	[1]3,135	12,462	8,130	[1]4,332
1981 .	3,856	1,736	2,120	3,174	2,164	1,010	1991 .	10,515	6,770	[1]3,745	11,664	6,221	[1]5,443
1982 .	4,749	2,606	2,143	4,337	2,403	1,934	1992 .	9,266	5,887	[1]3,379	12,809	7,622	[1]5,187
1983 .	4,940	2,420	2,520	4,865	2,733	2,132	1993 .	8,309	4,175	[1]4,133	15,203	8,332	[1]6,871
1984 .	5,225	3,019	2,206	4,624	3,099	1,525	1994 .	10,594	5,707	[1]4,887	12,888	6,732	[1]6,156
1985 .	6,300	4,241	2,059	6,707	4,941	1,766	1995 .	11,314	4,782	[1]6,532	15,650	5,872	[1]9,778
1986 .	6,304	4,579	[1]1,725	8,063	6,028	[1]2,035	1996 .	11,209	4,777	[1]6,432	18,262	5,864	[1]12,398

[1] Includes data for nonmilitary missile systems and parts.

Source: U.S. Bureau of the Census, *Current Industrial Reports*, MA-37D, *Aerospace Industry (Orders, Sales, and Backlog)* and, beginning 1994, Internet site <http://www.census.gov/cir/www>

No. 1006. Federal Outlays for General Science, Space, and Other Technology: 1970 to 2003

[In billions of dollars. For fiscal years ending in year shown; see text, Section 9, State and Local Governments]

YEAR	CURRENT DOLLARS			CONSTANT (1992) DOLLARS		
	Total	General science/basic research	Space and other technologies	Total	General science/basic research	Space and other technologies
1970	4.5	0.9	3.6	16.0	3.4	12.6
1975	4.0	1.0	3.0	10.0	2.6	7.4
1980	5.8	1.4	4.4	10.0	2.4	7.6
1983	7.9	1.6	6.3	10.9	2.3	8.7
1984	8.3	1.8	6.5	11.1	2.4	8.6
1985	8.6	2.0	6.6	11.1	2.6	8.5
1986	9.0	2.2	6.8	11.3	2.8	8.5
1987	9.2	2.2	7.0	11.2	2.7	8.5
1988	10.8	2.4	8.4	12.7	2.8	9.8
1989	12.8	2.6	10.2	14.4	2.9	11.4
1990	14.4	2.8	11.6	15.6	3.1	12.6
1991	16.1	3.1	13.0	16.5	3.2	13.3
1992	16.4	3.5	12.8	16.4	3.5	12.8
1993	17.0	3.9	13.1	16.4	3.8	12.6
1994	16.2	3.8	12.4	15.1	3.6	11.5
1995	16.7	4.1	12.6	15.2	3.7	11.5
1996	16.7	4.0	12.7	14.8	3.5	11.3
1997	17.1	4.1	13.1	14.9	3.6	11.3
1998, est.	17.1	4.9	12.2	14.3	4.1	10.2
1999, est.	17.6	5.5	12.1	14.5	4.6	10.0
2000, est.	18.1	5.9	12.2	14.7	4.8	9.9
2001, est.	18.4	6.4	12.0	14.6	5.1	9.6
2002, est.	18.7	6.6	12.2	14.5	5.1	9.4
2003, est.	18.9	6.7	12.2	14.3	5.1	9.2

Source: U.S. Office of Management and Budget, *Budget of the United States, Historical Tables, Fiscal Year 1999*, annual.

No. 1007. U.S. Commercial Space Revenues: 1990 to 1995

[In millions of dollars. For calendar years]

INDUSTRY	1990	1991	1992	1993	1994	1995 [1]
Total	3,385	4,370	4,860	5,295	6,640	7,850
Commercial satellites delivered	1,000	1,300	1,300	1,100	1,400	1,550
Satellite services	800	1,200	1,500	1,850	2,330	2,740
Fixed	735	1,115	1,275	1,600	1,980	2,340
Mobile.	65	85	225	250	350	400
Satellite ground equipment.	860	1,300	1,400	1,600	1,970	2,570
Mobile-equipment	145	280	350	420	480	510
Commercial launches	570	380	450	465	580	600
Remote sensing data and services	155	190	210	250	300	330
Commercial R&D infrastructure	-	-	-	30	60	60

- Represents zero. [1] Forecast.

Source: U.S. Department of Commerce, International Trade Administration, *U.S. Industrial Outlook, 1994*; and unpublished data.

No. 1008. National Aeronautics and Space Administration—Budget Summary: 1997 to 2003

[In millions of dollars]

ITEM	1997	1998	1999	2000	2001	2002	2003
Total	**13,709**	**13,638**	**13,465**	**13,278**	**13,315**	**13,394**	**13,435**
Human space flight	5,675	5,680	5,511	5,312	5,156	4,930	4,715
Space station	2,149	2,501	2,270	2,134	1,933	1,766	1,546
U.S. and Russian cooperative program	300	50	-	-	-	-	-
Space shuttle	2,961	2,923	3,059	2,998	3,049	2,989	2,989
Payload and utilization operations	265	205	182	180	174	175	180
Science, aeronautics and technology	5,453	5,552	5,457	5,530	5,726	5,917	6,120
Space science	1,969	1,984	2,058	2,207	2,308	2,387	2,568
Life and microgravity sciences and applications	244	214	242	257	266	264	264
Mission to planet earth	1,362	1,367	1,372	1,492	1,494	1,449	1,407
Aeronautical research and technology	1,340	1,471	1,305	1,092	1,026	1,057	1,071
Mission communication services	419	396	380	382	382	380	380
Academic programs	120	120	100	100	100	100	100
Future planning	(NA)	(NA)	(NA)	(NA)	150	280	330
Mission support	2,564	2,388	2,477	2,416	2,413	2,527	2,580
Safety, reliability and quality assurance	39	38	36	36	36	40	40
Space communication services	291	194	177	136	125	151	121
Research and program management	2,079	2,034	2,099	2,079	2,087	2,171	2,254
Construction of facilities	155	122	165	165	165	165	165
Inspector General	17	18	20	20	20	20	20

- Represents zero. NA Not available.

Source: U.S. National Aeronautics and Space Administration, *NASA Pocket Statistics*, annual.

No. 1009. NASA Space Shuttle Operations Expenditures: 1997 to 1999

[**In millions of dollars.** Data are funding requirements fiscal years shown]

OPERATION	1997	1998	1999
Total	**2,464.9**	**2,369.4**	**2,487.4**
Orbiter and integration	492.6	502.9	573.4
Orbiter	124.7	126.2	113.9
System integration	367.9	376.7	459.5
Propulsion	1,124.7	1,061.8	1,093.4
External tank	352.4	341.3	404.8
Space shuttle main engine	208.3	204.6	175.6
Reusable solid rocket motor	412.8	380.4	362.7
Solid rocket booster	151.2	135.5	150.3
Mission and launch operations	847.6	804.7	820.6
Launch and landing operations	801.4	710.1	728.4
Mission and crew operations	46.2	94.6	92.2

Source: U.S. National Aeronautics and Space Administration, *NASA Pocket Statistics*, annual.

No. 1010. World-Wide Successful Space Launches: 1957 to 1997

[Criterion of success is attainment of Earth orbit or Earth escape]

COUNTRY	Total	1957-1964	1965-1969	1970-1974	1975-1979	1980-1984	1985-1989	1990-1994	1995	1996	1997
Total	**3,892**	**289**	**586**	**555**	**607**	**605**	**550**	**466**	**75**	**73**	**86**
Soviet Union/CIS [1]	2,548	82	302	405	461	483	447	283	32	25	28
United States	1,124	207	279	139	126	93	61	122	27	33	37
Japan	52	-	-	5	10	12	11	9	2	1	2
ESA [2]	96	-	-	-	1	8	21	33	11	10	12
China	49	-	-	2	6	6	9	15	2	3	6
France	10	-	4	3	3	-	-	-	-	-	-
India	8	-	-	-	-	3	-	3	-	1	1
Israel	3	-	-	-	-	-	1	1	1	-	-
Australia	1	-	1	-	-	-	-	-	-	-	-
United Kingdom	1	-	-	1	-	-	-	-	-	-	-

- Represents zero. [1] Commonwealth of Independent States. [2] European Space Agency. Includes launches by Arianespace.

Source: Library of Congress, Congressional Research Service, Science Policy Research Division, *Space Activities of the United States, CIS, and Other Launching Countries/Organizations 1957-1994*, July 31, 1995; and forthcoming report.

No. 1011. Space Shuttle Flights—Summary: 1981 to January 1998

FLIGHT NUMBER	Mission date	Orbiter name	Crew size (up/down)	Days duration	FLIGHT NUMBER	Mission date	Orbiter name	Crew size (up/down)	Days duration
1	4/12/81	Columbia	2	2	45	3/24/92	Atlantis	7	9
2	11/12/81	Columbia	2	2	49	5/7/92	Endeavour	7	9
3	3/22/82	Columbia	2	8	50	6/25/92	Columbia	7	14
4	6/27/82	Columbia	2	7	46	7/31/92	Atlantis	7	8
5	11/11/82	Columbia	4	5	47	9/12/92	Endeavour	7	8
6	4/4/83	Challenger	4	5	52	10/22/92	Columbia	6	10
7	6/18/83	Challenger	5	6	53	12/2/92	Discovery	5	7
8	8/30/83	Challenger	5	6	54	1/13/93	Endeavour	5	6
9	11/28/83	Columbia	6	10	56	4/8/93	Discovery	5	9
10	2/3/84	Challenger	5	8	55	4/26/93	Columbia	7	10
11	4/6/84	Challenger	5	7	57	6/21/93	Endeavour	6	10
12	8/30/84	Discovery	6	7	51	9/12/93	Discovery	5	10
13	10/5/84	Challenger	7	8	58	10/18/93	Columbia	7	14
14	11/8/84	Discovery	5	8	61	12/2/93	Endeavour	7	11
15	1/24/85	Discovery	5	4	60	2/3/94	Discovery	6	8
16	4/12/85	Discovery	7	7	62	3/4/94	Columbia	5	14
17	4/29/85	Challenger	7	7	59	4/9/94	Endeavour	6	11
18	6/17/85	Discovery	7	7	65	7/8/94	Columbia	7	15
19	7/29/85	Challenger	7	8	64	9/9/94	Discovery	6	11
20	8/27/85	Discovery	5	7	68	9/30/94	Endeavour	6	11
21	10/3/85	Atlantis	5	4	66	11/3/94	Atlantis	6	11
22	10/30/85	Challenger	8	7	63	2/3/95	Discovery	6	8
23	11/26/85	Atlantis	7	7	67	3/2/95	Endeavour	7	17
24	1/12/86	Columbia	7	6	71	6/27/95	Atlantis	7/8	10
25	1/28/86	Challenger	7	-	70	7/13/95	Discovery	5	9
26	9/29/88	Discovery	5	4	69	9/7/95	Endeavour	5	11
27	12/2/88	Atlantis	5	4	73	10/20/95	Columbia	7	16
29	3/13/89	Discovery	5	5	74	11/8/95	Atlantis	5	8
30	5/4/89	Atlantis	5	4	72	1/11/96	Endeavour	6	9
28	8/8/89	Columbia	5	5	75	2/22/96	Columbia	7	16
34	10/18/89	Atlantis	5	5	76	3/22/96	Atlantis	6/5	9
33	11/22/89	Discovery	5	5	77	5/19/96	Endeavour	6	10
32	1/9/90	Columbia	5	11	78	6/20/96	Columbia	7	17
36	2/28/90	Atlantis	5	4	79	9/16/96	Atlantis	6	10
31	4/24/90	Discovery	5	5	80	11/20/96	Columbia	5	18
41	10/6/90	Discovery	5	4	81	1/12/97	Atlantis	6	10
38	11/15/90	Atlantis	5	5	82	2/11/97	Discovery	7	10
35	12/2/90	Columbia	7	9	83	4/4/97	Columbia	7	4
37	4/5/91	Atlantis	5	6	84	5/15/97	Atlantis	7/7	9
39	4/28/91	Discovery	7	8	94	7/1/97	Columbia	7	15.7
40	6/5/91	Columbia	7	9	85	8/7/97	Discovery	5	11.85
43	8/2/91	Atlantis	5	9	86	9/25/97	Atlantis	7/7	10.8
48	9/12/91	Discovery	5	5	87	11/19/97	Columbia	6	15.69
44	11/24/91	Atlantis	6	7	89	1/22/98	Endeavor	7/7	8.82
42	1/22/92	Discovery	7	8					

- Represents zero.

Source: U.S. National Aeronautics and Space Administraction, Internet site <http://www.hq.nasa.gov/osf/shuttle> (Accessed 4 May 1998)

No. 1012. Nobel Prize Laureates in Selected Sciences: 1901 to 1996

[Presented by location of award-winning research and by date of award]

COUNTRY	1901-1996				1901-1930	1931-1945	1946-1960	1961-1975	1976-1990	1991-1995	1996
	Total	Physics	Chemistry	Physiology/ Medicine							
Total	441	152	126	163	93	49	74	92	98	27	8
United States	185	66	43	75	6	14	38	41	63	18	5
United Kingdom	70	21	26	24	15	11	14	20	9	-	1
Germany [1]	60	17	28	14	27	11	4	8	7	3	-
France	24	10	7	7	13	2	-	5	2	2	-
Soviet Union	10	7	1	2	2	-	4	3	1	-	-
Japan	4	3	1	-	-	-	-	2	1	-	-
Other countries	88	28	20	41	30	11	13	13	15	4	2

- Represents zero.   [1] Between 1946 and 1991, data are for the former West Germany only.

Source: U.S. National Science Foundation, unpublished data.

Transportation—Land

This section presents statistics on revenues, passenger and freight traffic volume, and employment in various revenue-producing modes of the transportation industry, including motor vehicles, trains, and pipelines. Data are also presented on commuting travel, highway mileage and finances, motor vehicle travel, accidents, sales, and registrations, automobile operating costs, and characteristics of public transit, railroads, and pipelines.

The principal compiler of data on public roads and on operation of motor vehicles is the U.S. Department of Transportation's (DOT) Federal Highway Administration (FHWA). These data appear in FHWA's annual *Highway Statistics* and other publications. The U.S. Interstate Commerce Commission (ICC) presents data on interstate land transport in its publications, the *Annual Report to Congress* and the *Transport Statistics in the United States,* which contain data on railroads and motor carriers subject to ICC regulations.

The U.S. National Highway Traffic Safety Administration issues data on traffic accident deaths and death rates in two annual reports: the *Fact Book* and the *Fatal Accident Reporting System Annual Report.* DOT's Federal Railroad Administration presents data on accidents involving railroads in its annual *Accident/Incident Bulletin,* and the *Rail-Highway Crossing Accident/Incident and Inventory Bulletin.*

Various censuses and surveys conducted by the U.S. Bureau of the Census also provide data. Results of the censuses of transportation are presented in the *Truck Inventory and Use Survey.* The *Annual Survey of Manufactures* and reports of the censuses of manufactures, wholesale and retail trade, and service industries contain statistics on the motor vehicle and equipment industry and on retail, wholesale, and services aspects of this industry. Data on persons commuting to work were collected as part

In Brief

Transportation outlays reached $796.8 billion in 1996

State gasoline tax rates for 1995—
 Lowest rate, 7.5 cents/gallon
  in Georgia
 Highest rate, 34 cents/gallon
  in Connecticut

of the 1980 census and are in various census reports.

Data are also presented in many nongovernment publications. Among them are the weekly and annual *Cars of Revenue Freight Loaded* and the annual *Yearbook of Railroad Facts,* both published by the Association of American Railroads, Washington, DC; and the *Transit Fact Book,* containing electric railway and motorbus statistics, published annually by the American Public Transit Association, Washington, DC. Useful annual handbooks in the field of transportation are *Motor Vehicle Facts and Figures* and *World Motor Vehicle Data,* issued by the American Automobile Manufacturers Association (AAMA), Detroit, MI; *Accident Facts,* issued by the National Safety Council, Chicago, IL; and *Transportation in America,* issued by the ENO Foundation for Transportation, Westport, Connecticut.

Urban and rural highway mileage— Beginning in 1980, mileage is classified in urban and rural categories, rather than municipal and rural. Urban denotes the federal-aid legislation definition of an area. Such areas include, as a minimum, a census place with a population of 5,000 to 49,999 or a designated urbanized area with a population of 50,000 or more. These federal-aid urban areas may extend beyond corporate and census boundaries, and thus are not necessarily coextensive with municipal boundaries. Rural in 1980 refers to nonfederal-aid urban area mileage. Prior to 1980, municipal referred to roads within incorporated places, densely populated New England towns, and certain of the more populous unincorporated areas and rural to nonmunicipal roads.

Federal-Aid Highway Systems—The Intermodal Surface Transportation Efficiency Act (ISTEA of 1991 eliminated the historical Federal-Aid Systems and created the National Highway System (NHS) and other federal-aid highway categories. The final NHS was approved by Congress in December of 1995 under the National Highway System Designation Act.

Functional systems—Roads and streets are assigned to groups according to the character of service they are intended to provide. The functional systems are (1) arterial highways that generally handle the long trips, (2) collector facilities that collect and disperse traffiC between the arterials and the lower systems, and (3) local roads and streets that primarily serve direct access to residential areas.

Regulatory bodies—The ICC, created by the U.S. Congress to regulate transportation in interstate commerce, has jurisdiction over railroads, trucking companies, bus lines, freight forwarders, water carriers, coal slurry pipelines, and transportation brokers. The Federal Energy Regulatory Commission is responsible for setting rates and charges for transportation and sale of natural gas and for establishing rates or charges for transportation.

Motor carriers—For 1960-73, class I for-hire motor carriers of freight were classified by the ICC as those with $1 million or more of gross annual operating revenue; 1974-79, the class I minimum was $3 million. Effective January 1, 1980, class I carriers are those with $5 million or more in revenue. For 1960-68, class I motor carriers of passengers were classified by the ICC as those with $200,000 or more of gross annual operating revenue; for 1969-76, as those with revenues of $1 million or more; and since 1977, as those with $3 million or more. Effective January 1, 1988, class I motor carriers of passengers are those with $5 million or more in

operating revenues; class II less than $5 million in operating revenues.

Railroads—Railroad companies reporting to the ICC are divided into specific groups as follows: (1) Regular line-haul (interstate) railroads (and their nonoperating subsidiaries); (2) switching and terminal railroads; (3) private railroads prior to 1964 (identified by ICC as "circular" because they reported on brief circulars); and (4) unofficial railroads, so designated when their reports are received too late for tabulation. For the most part, the last three groups are not included in the statistics shown here.

For years prior to 1978, class I railroads were those with annual revenues of $1 million or more for 1950-55; $3 million or more for 1956-64; $5 million or more for 1965-75; and $10 million or more for 1976-77. In 1978, the classification became class I, those having more than $50 million gross annual operating revenue; class II, from $10 million to $50 million; and class III, less than $10 million. Effective January 1, 1982, the ICC adopted a procedure to adjust the threshold for inflation by restating current revenues in constant 1978 dollars. In 1990, the criteria for class I and class II railroads were $94.4 million and $18.9 million, respectively. Also effective January 1, 1982, the ICC adopted a *Carrier Classification Index Survey Form* for carriers not filing annual report form R-1 with the commission. Effective January 1, 1992, the ICC adopted new revenue classification levels as follows: Class I–$250 million or more; Class II–less than $250 million but in excess of $20 million; Class III–$20 million or less. The inflation adjustment index still applies. Class II and class III railroads are currently exempted from filing any financial report with the Commission. The form is used for reclassifying carriers.

Statistical reliability—For a discussion of statistical collection and estimation, sampling procedures, and measures of statistical reliability, see Appendix III.

No. 1013. Passenger and Freight Transportation Outlays, by Type of Transport: 1980 to 1996

[In millions of dollars. Freight data include outlays for mail and express. ICC=Interstate Commerce Commission]

TYPE OF TRANSPORT	1980	1985	1990	1991	1992	1993	1994	1995	1996
Total outlays [1]	338,148	492,156	630,419	601,774	644,580	683,697	715,177	759,947	796,826
Passenger:									
Private transportation	284,752	418,213	528,298	498,157	538,223	575,942	604,792	641,250	672,682
Automobiles [2]	276,699	410,313	518,026	488,260	529,309	566,467	594,373	630,559	661,626
New and used cars	73,266	139,300	165,500	153,300	152,900	165,000	184,400	181,800	186,600
Tires, tubes, accessories	22,234	29,647	25,444	25,630	32,780	34,760	31,680	40,667	43,222
Gasoline and oil	93,724	106,588	120,404	113,190	116,050	118,910	117,920	127,333	135,333
Insurance less claims	11,465	11,647	20,111	24,970	28,050	29,480	31,460	31,111	32,556
Interest on debt	17,548	26,743	35,535	25,960	25,740	28,060	34,457	40,693	41,824
Auto registration fees	2,892	4,774	6,054	6,328	7,138	7,369	7,423	7,043	6,951
Operator's permit and fees	370	547	638	702	781	738	823	823	839
Repair, greasing, washing, parking, tolls [3]	37,999	58,118	91,518	89,980	103,840	112,200	116,400	128,700	140,100
Air	8,053	7,900	10,272	9,897	8,914	9,475	10,419	10,691	11,056
For-hire transportation	53,396	73,943	102,121	103,617	106,357	107,755	110,385	118,697	124,143
Local [4]	19,784	27,317	34,169	35,391	36,041	37,401	38,868	42,589	42,005
Bus and transit [5]	9,297	13,548	16,651	17,278	17,932	18,722	20,006	20,963	19,739
School bus	3,833	5,900	7,605	7,879	8,060	7,618	7,847	9,082	10,404
Taxi	5,195	5,636	7,111	7,556	7,333	7,556	7,778	8,046	8,208
Railroad commutation	1,459	2,233	2,802	2,678	2,716	3,505	3,107	4,498	3,654
Intercity	28,345	39,518	53,033	52,613	53,063	52,798	53,798	57,728	63,141
Air	25,098	35,860	49,506	48,938	49,242	49,297	50,514	53,976	59,289
Rail [6]	1,517	1,642	1,750	1,736	1,855	1,773	1,810	2,194	2,231
Bus	1,709	1,989	1,777	1,875	1,899	1,667	1,410	1,481	1,540
International	5,267	7,108	14,919	15,613	17,253	17,556	17,719	18,380	18,996
Freight, total [4]	213,736	273,612	350,949	355,215	375,093	396,306	419,904	444,452	467,208
Highway	155,331	205,645	270,776	274,381	292,930	311,878	330,716	348,109	368,545
Truck, intercity	94,551	123,200	162,300	164,600	176,800	189,700	204,876	219,627	235,440
Truck, local	60,545	82,200	108,350	109,650	116,000	122,050	125,712	128,352	132,973
Rail	27,858	29,150	30,067	30,003	30,473	30,775	33,121	34,343	35,059
Water	15,498	18,448	20,121	20,306	19,895	20,768	21,150	24,873	24,961
Oil pipeline	7,548	8,910	8,505	8,101	8,521	8,421	8,273	9,051	8,625
Air carrier	4,013	6,817	13,706	14,353	14,950	15,805	17,239	18,735	20,118

[1] Total outlays less than sum of passenger and freight totals, as estimated freight costs included in costs of new cars, gasoline, oil, tires, and tubes have been excluded to prevent duplication. [2] Includes business-owned vehicles. [3] Includes storage and rental. [4] Includes items not shown separately. [5] Includes federal, state, and local government operating subsidies and capital grants. [6] Includes federal operating subsidies and capital grants for Amtrak.

Source: Eno Transportation Foundation, Inc., Lansdowne, VA, *Transportation in America*, annual (copyright).

No. 1014. Transportation Industry Summary: 1992

[Includes only establishments with payroll. N.e.c.=Not elsewhere classified]

KIND OF BUSINESS	SIC code [1]	Establishments (number)	Revenue ($1,000)	Annual payroll ($1,000)	First-quarter payroll	Paid employees for pay period including March 12 (number)
Total transportation, except U.S. Post Office.	(X)	(NA)	**327,623**	**92,211**	(NA)	**3,356,872**
Railroad transportation [2]	40	(NA)	28,349	8,753	(NA)	197,421
Passenger transportation	41	17,805	12,649	5,191	1,246	354,913
Local and suburban passenger transportation	411	8,275	5,968	2,624	613	153,278
Local and suburban transit	4111	1,135	1,364	838	199	37,653
Other local passenger transportation	4119	7,140	4,604	1,786	414	115,625
Sightseeing bus	4119 pt	277	342	104	22	5,565
Limousine service	4119 pt	2,430	964	278	64	20,739
Ambulance/rescue service, except by air	4119 pt	3,070	2,507	1,104	256	66,885
Other local passenger transport., n.e.c.	4119 pt	1,363	791	300	72	22,436
Taxicabs	412	3,337	992	306	75	26,338
Other bus transport. and terminal service	413, 4, 5, 7	6,193	5,689	2,261	558	175,297
Intercity and rural bus service	413	607	1,092	483	116	20,404
Charter bus service	414	1,307	1,269	394	86	24,604
Local charter bus	4141	429	375	125	29	7,699
Charter bus, except local	4142	878	894	269	58	16,905
School buses	415	4,260	3,315	1,380	355	130,093
Bus terminal and service facilities	417	19	12	4	1	196
Motor freight transportation and warehousing	42	110,908	143,794	39,896	9,196	1,580,095
Trucking and courier services, except air	421	101,169	135,437	37,760	8,691	1,484,655
Local trucking without storage	4212	49,870	33,554	8,043	1,799	354,742
Household goods moving	4212 pt	2,566	661	196	43	13,237
General freight	4212 pt	12,186	8,404	2,250	522	97,594
Garbage and trash collection	4212 pt	7,405	10,985	2,473	577	94,054
Dump trucking	4212 pt	13,383	6,807	1,418	277	66,956
Other local trucking without storage	4212 pt	14,330	6,698	1,707	380	82,901
Hazardous materials	4212 pt	1,279	885	238	57	9,270
Agricultural products	4212 pt	6,203	2,188	478	106	26,897
Other local trucking without storage, n.e.c.	4212 pt	6,848	3,625	990	218	46,734
Trucking, except local	4213	40,821	78,358	20,974	4,808	758,435
Household goods moving	4213 pt	3,248	7,433	1,354	302	61,592
General freight trucking	4213 pt	25,014	55,257	15,880	3,650	553,202
Other trucking, except local	4213 pt	12,559	15,668	3,741	856	143,641
Hazardous products	4213 pt	1,666	2,759	720	170	25,617
Agricultural products	4213 pt	4,483	3,304	665	146	30,518
Other trucking, except storage, n.e.c	4213 pt	6,410	9,605	2,356	540	87,506
Local trucking with storage	4214	4,512	4,191	1,346	303	64,417
Household goods moving	4214 pt	2,641	2,175	703	155	36,483
Other local trucking with storage	4214 pt	1,871	2,016	643	149	27,934
Courier services, except by air	4215	5,966	19,334	7,396	1,780	307,061
Public warehousing and storage	422	9,718	8,330	2,127	504	95,145
Farm products warehousing and storage	4221	584	656	130	31	6,497
Refrigerated warehousing and storage	4222	929	1,745	464	111	18,963
General warehousing and storage	4225	6,753	3,919	983	233	49,091
General goods warehousing	4225 pt	2,251	2,641	832	196	37,814
Self-service or miniwarehousing	4225 pt	4,502	1,279	151	37	11,277
Special warehousing and storage, n.e.c.	4226	1,452	2,009	551	129	20,594
Trucking terminal facilities	423	21	27	8	2	295
Pipelines, except natural gas	46	844	7,063	821	203	16,779
Refined petroleum pipelines	4613	358	2,010	252	61	5,578
Other pipelines	4612, 9	486	5,053	569	142	11,201
Crude petroleum pipelines	4612	405	4,409	531	132	10,355
Pipelines, n.e.c	4619	81	644	38	10	846
Transportation services	47	46,593	23,890	7,850	1,854	329,202
Arrangement of passenger transportation	472	31,793	10,573	3,921	931	192,981
Travel agencies	4724	27,688	6,964	2,836	673	149,140
Other arrangement of passenger transportation	4725,9	4,105	3,608	1,086	258	43,841
Tour operators	4725	3,008	1,865	690	155	30,519
Arrangement of passenger transportation, n.e.c	4729	1,097	1,744	396	102	13,322
Freight shipping services	473	12,553	9,159	3,233	761	106,979
Freight forwarding	4731 pt	5,308	4,156	1,437	335	48,903
Arrangement of freight and cargo, n.e.c.	4731 pt	7,245	5,002	1,796	426	58,076
Other transportation services	474, 8	2,247	4,158	696	162	29,242
Rental of railroad cars	474	125	1,881	85	23	1,926
Misc. services incidental to transportation.	478	2,122	2,277	612	140	27,316
Packing and crating	4783	835	522	155	33	8,123
Fixed facilities, inspect./weighing services.	4785	263	221	65	15	2,810
Transportation services, n.e.c.	4789	1,024	1,534	392	91	16,383

NA Not available.   X Not applicable.   [1] 1987 Standard Industrial Classification, see text, Section 13.   [2] Includes Class I Freight railroads only. Source: Association of American Railroads, Washington DC, *Railroad Facts,* annual.

Source: Except as noted, U.S. Bureau of the Census, *Census of Transportation, Communications and Utilities: 1992.*

No. 1015. Employment and Earnings in Transportation, by Industry: 1980 to 1997

[Annual averages of monthly figures. Based on Current Employment Statistics program; see Appendix III]

INDUSTRY	SIC [1] code	1980	1985	1990	1992	1993	1994	1995	1996	1997
NUMBER (1,000)										
Total transportation.......	(X)	**2,960**	**2,997**	**3,511**	**3,495**	**3,598**	**3,761**	**3,904**	**4,019**	**4,106**
Railroads..................	40	532	359	279	254	248	241	238	231	227
Class I railroads	4011	482	323	241	222	218	214	212	206	202
Local and interurban passengers ..	41	265	277	338	361	379	404	419	437	451
Trucking and warehousing	42	(NA)	(NA)	1,395	1,385	1,444	1,526	1,587	1,637	1,667
Water transportation	44	211	185	177	173	168	172	175	174	180
Air transportation............	45	(NA)	(NA)	968	964	988	1,023	1,068	1,107	1,128
Pipelines, exc. natural gas	46	21	19	19	19	18	17	15	15	14
Transportation services	47	(NA)	(NA)	336	338	352	378	401	418	439
AVERAGE WEEKLY EARNINGS (dol.)										
Class I railroads	4011	427	595	727	736	782	786	811	850	892
Local and interurban passengers ..	41	217	261	310	334	342	354	358	367	374
Trucking and warehousing	42	358	405	450	467	484	499	501	515	532
Pipelines, exc. natural gas	46	441	629	711	772	817	872	888	909	902

NA Not available.   X Not applicable.   [1] 1987 Standard Industrial Classification, see text, Section 13.

Source: U.S. Bureau of Labor Statistics, Bulletin 2445 and 2481, Employment and Earnings, March and June issues.

No. 1016. Volume of Domestic Intercity Freight and Passenger Traffic, by Type of Transport: 1980 to 1996

[**Freight traffic in bil. ton-miles; passenger traffic in bil. passenger-miles.** A ton-mile is the movement of 1 ton (2,000 pounds) of freight for the distance of 1 mile. A passenger-mile is the movement of 1 passenger for the distance of 1 mile. Comprises public and private traffic, both revenue and nonrevenue]

TYPE OF TRANSPORT	TRAFFIC VOLUME						PERCENT DISTRIBUTION					
	1980	1985	1990	1994	1995	1996	1980	1985	1990	1994	1995	1996
Freight traffic, total	**2,487**	**2,458**	**2,895**	**3,261**	**3,407**	**3,563**	**100.0**	**100.0**	**100.0**	**100.0**	**100.0**	**100.0**
Railroads.........	932	895	1,091	1,275	1,375	1,426	37.5	38.0	35.6	37.7	37.9	37.6
Truck:												
ICC truck........	242	250	311	391	401	437	9.7	9.9	10.4	10.7	11.0	11.3
Non-ICC truck.....	313	360	424	517	520	549	12.6	11.8	14.9	14.6	15.1	15.6
Water:												
Rivers/canals	311	306	390	388	406	417	12.5	12.8	13.0	13.5	13.3	13.0
Great Lakes	96	76	85	87	91	90	3.9	4.0	2.7	2.9	2.5	2.5
Oil pipelines........	588	564	584	591	601	631	23.6	23.2	23.1	20.2	19.9	19.5
Domestic airways [1] ...	5	7	10	12	13	13	0.2	0.2	0.3	0.4	0.3	0.4
Passenger traffic, total ...	**1,468**	**1,636**	**2,034**	**2,280**	**2,354**	**(NA)**	**100.0**	**100.0**	**100.0**	**100.0**	**100.0**	**100.0**
Private automobiles...	1,210	1,310	1,639	1,842	1,898	(NA)	82.5	82.7	79.4	80.6	81.3	81.3
Domestic airways [2] ...	15	12	13	11	11	(NA)	1.0	14.7	0.0	0.6	0.6	0.5
Air, public carrer.....	204	278	346	388	403	(NA)	13.9	0.0	0.0	17.0	16.3	16.5
Bus [3]	27	24	23	25	28	(NA)	1.9	1.8	1.4	1.1	1.1	1.1
Railroads [4]	11	11	13	14	14	(NA)	0.7	0.7	0.7	0.6	0.7	0.7

NA Not available.   [1] Revenue service only for scheduled and nonscheduled carriers, with small section 418 all-cargo carriers included from 1980. Includes express mail, and excess baggage.   [2] Includes general aviation (mostly private business) flying.   [3] Excludes school and urban transit buses.   [4] Includes intercity (Amtrak) and rail commuter service.

Source: Eno Transportation Foundation, Inc., Lansdowne VA, *Transportation in America,* annual (copyright).

No. 1017. Commodity Shipments — Value, Tons and Ton-Miles: 1993

MODE OF TRANSPORTATION	VALUE		TONS		TON-MILES		
	Number (mil. dol.)	Percent	Number (1,000)	Percent	Number (mil.)	Percent	Avg. miles per shipment [1]
All commodities...............	5,846,334	100.0	9,688,493	100.0	2,420,915	100.0	424
Farm products......................	142,442	2.4	636,630	6.6	276,260	11.4	220
Forest products	1,700	-	30,520	0.3	3,635	0.2	222
Fresh fish or other marine products	11,062	0.2	2,995	-	1,746	0.1	159
Metalic ores.......................	20,278	0.3	149,562	1.5	36,895	1.5	358
Coal..............................	23,449	0.4	1,129,945	11.7	487,791	20.1	86
Crude petroleum, natural gas, or gasoline. . .	(S)		(S)		(S)	-	(S)
Nonmetallic minerals.................	20,695	0.4	1,786,381	18.4	155,417	6.4	112
Ordnance or accessories	17,174	0.3	663	-	629	-	919
Food or kindred products.............	856,884	14.7	859,764	8.9	270,984	11.2	102
Tobacco products, excluding insecticides . . .	60,640	1.0	3,225	-	931	-	146
Textile mill products	102,189	1.7	24,757	0.3	11,341	0.5	711
Apparel or other finished textile products . . .	291,203	5.0	15,128	0.2	9,967	0.4	925
Lumber or wood products, excluding furniture	126,662	2.2	663,351	6.8	120,669	5.0	227
Furniture or fixtures.................	69,471	1.2	16,568	0.2	9,789	0.4	547
Pulp, paper, or allied products..........	195,002	3.3	217,233	2.2	100,721	4.2	186
Printed matter	(S)	-	(S)	-	(S)	-	(S)
Chemicals or allied products...........	532,907	9.1	545,405	5.6	236,856	9.8	349
Petroleum or coal products.	359,471	6.1	1,885,833	19.5	287,081	11.9	101
Rubber or miscellaneous plastics products . .	175,267	3.0	52,349	0.5	25,528	1.1	466
Leather or leather products	50,645	0.9	2,401	-	2,182	0.1	941
Clay, concrete, glass, or stone products . . .	91,365	1.6	799,481	8.3	84,032	3.5	349
Primary metal products	228,610	3.9	266,409	2.7	97,266	4.0	275
Fabricated metal products	237,316	4.1	84,895	0.9	30,489	1.3	395
Machinery, excluding electrical	442,770	7.6	34,180	0.4	19,112	0.8	519
Electrical machinery, equipment, or supplies .	411,030	7.0	30,156	0.3	19,591	0.8	660
Transportation equipment..............	652,474	11.2	87,617	0.9	49,098	2.0	339
Instruments, photographic goods, optical goods, watches, or clocks	198,492	3.4	8,600	0.1	5,390	0.2	656
Waste or scrap materials	18,258	0.3	130,894	1.4	27,591	1.1	160
Containers, carriers or devices, shipping, returned empty...................	1,144	-	702	-	230	-	229
Waste hazardous materials/substances	558	-	813	-	314	-	190
Commodity unknown..................	21,941	0.4	7,804	0.1	2,522	0.1	477

- Represents zero.   S Data do not meet publication standards due to high sampling variability or other reasons.   [1] Excludes shipments of STCC 27, printed matter.

Source: U.S. Bureau of Transportation Statistics, *National Transportation Statistics, 1996*. Data from U.S. Bureau of the Census, *1993 Commodity Flow Survey, U.S. Preliminary Report*, TC92-CF-52(P), July 1995.

No. 1018. Transportation Accidents, Deaths, and Injuries: 1990 to 1996

[For related data, see also Table 1047]

YEAR AND CASUALTY	TYPE OF TRANSPORT												
	Motor vehi-cle [1] (1,000)	Rail-road [2]	Air carriers					General aviation	Recre-ational boat-ing [6]	Gas pipe-lines [7]	Liquid pipe-lines [8]	Water-borne [9]	Rail Rapid Trans-it [10]	Haz-ardous materi-als [11]
			Total	Air-lines [3]	Com-muter air car-riers [4]	On demand air car-riers [5]								
Accidents:														
1990....	6,471	2,879	146	24	16	106	2,215	6,411	198	180	3,613	12,178	8,882
1995....	6,699	2,459	123	36	11	75	2,055	8,019	161	188	4,196	14,327	14,741
1996....	6,842	2,443	139	38	12	89	1,905	8,026	185	195	3,799	13,748	13,801
Deaths:														
1990....	44.6	599	95	39	7	50	765	865	6	3	85	117	8
1995....	41.8	567	229	168	9	52	734	829	18	3	46	79	7
1996....	41.9	551	457	380	14	63	631	709	15	5	50	74	120
Injuries:														
1990....	3,231	22,736	86	39	11	36	391	3,822	69	7	175	10,036	443
1995....	3,465	12,546	64	25	25	14	395	4,141	53	11	145	11,238	399
1996....	3,511	10,948	99	77	2	20	359	4,442	72	13	129	11,093	1,168

[1] Data on deaths are from U.S. National Highway Traffic Safety Administration and are based on 30 day definition. Includes only police reported crashes.   [2] Accidents which result in damages to railroad property. Grade crossing accidents are also included when classified as a train accident. Deaths exclude fatalities in railroad-highway grade crossing accidents.   [3] Includes scheduled and nonscheduled (charter) air carriers. Represents serious injuries.   [4] All scheduled service. Represents serious injuries.   [5] All nonscheduled service. Represents serious injuries.   [6] Accidents resulting in death; injury or requiring medical treatment beyond first aid; damages exceeding $500; or a person's disappearance.   [7] Pipeline accidents/incidents are credited to year of occurrence; prior data are credited to the year filed.   [8] Pipelines carrying hazardous materials, petroleum, and liquid petroleum products.   [9] Covers accidents involving commercial vessels which must be reported to U.S. Coast Guard if there is property damage exceeding $25,000; material damage affecting the seaworthiness or efficiency of a vessel; stranding or grounding; loss of life; or injury causing a person's incapacity for more than 3 days.   [10] Reporting criteria and source of data changed between 1989 and 1990; these data from 1990 to present are not comparable to earlier years.   [11] Accidents, deaths, and injuries involving hazardous materials cover all types of transport.

Source: U.S. Bureau of Transportation Statistics, *National Transportation Statistics*, annual.

No. 1019. Highway Mileage—Functional Systems and Urban/Rural: 1996

[As of Dec. 31. For definition of urban, rural, see text, Section 21]

STATE	FUNCTIONAL SYSTEMS					Urban	Rural
	Total	Inter-state [1]	Other arterial	Collector	Local		
U.S [1]	3,933,985	46,286	378,827	795,275	2,704,727	833,623	3,100,362
AL.	93,340	904	8,748	22,473	63,378	20,116	73,224
AK.	13,255	1,086	1,512	2,982	7,904	1,795	11,460
AZ.	54,895	1,169	4,838	10,303	40,334	16,233	38,662
AR.	77,746	541	6,885	21,057	50,192	7,698	70,048
CA.	170,506	2,424	28,067	42,136	107,904	83,109	87,397
CO	84,797	954	8,337	17,885	58,930	13,658	71,139
CT.	20,600	344	3,045	4,162	14,239	11,680	8,920
DE.	5,715	41	626	1,166	4,105	1,982	3,733
DC	1,413	13	271	304	977	1,413	-
FL.	114,422	1,471	12,384	21,135	85,338	48,339	66,083
GA.	111,746	1,241	13,226	25,222	74,166	26,655	85,091
HI	4,142	43	786	1,128	2,524	1,851	2,291
ID	59,674	611	3,678	10,059	45,836	3,773	55,901
IL	137,577	2,163	13,956	25,239	99,981	35,689	101,888
IN	92,970	1,172	8,037	24,803	61,161	19,644	73,326
IA	112,708	781	9,429	32,419	71,010	9,349	103,359
KS.	133,386	872	9,320	34,255	89,948	9,757	123,629
KY.	73,158	762	5,526	18,753	49,263	10,283	62,875
LA.	60,667	893	5,332	13,844	41,905	13,965	46,702
ME	22,577	368	2,327	6,397	13,969	2,615	19,962
MD	29,680	482	3,780	6,292	20,431	13,899	15,781
MA	34,725	565	5,843	8,023	22,828	22,675	12,050
MI	117,620	1,239	12,409	28,343	78,151	28,142	89,478
MN	130,613	913	12,737	31,029	87,462	15,381	115,232
MS	73,202	685	7,093	16,517	49,887	7,921	65,281
MO	122,748	1,178	9,582	26,673	86,921	16,415	106,333
MT	69,809	1,190	6,002	16,703	46,207	2,420	67,389
NE.	92,805	480	7,901	21,183	63,651	5,121	87,684
NV.	45,039	563	2,990	6,105	36,283	5,298	39,741
NH	15,106	224	1,582	2,998	10,586	2,916	12,190
NJ.	35,924	422	5,724	6,752	25,191	24,241	11,683
NM	59,455	1,000	4,516	7,157	47,236	6,133	53,322
NY.	112,347	1,499	14,453	24,543	75,878	40,646	71,701
NC	97,509	981	9,162	19,456	69,578	22,432	75,077
ND	86,808	571	5,872	11,621	68,965	1,823	84,985
OH	114,642	1,573	11,015	25,739	79,872	33,191	81,451
OK	112,664	930	7,973	26,372	78,371	13,034	99,630
OR	83,190	728	6,539	18,970	58,139	10,151	73,039
PA.	118,952	1,750	13,621	23,526	83,809	33,202	85,750
RI	6,001	69	821	1,362	4,254	4,641	1,360
SC.	64,359	829	6,871	14,858	43,267	10,574	53,785
SD.	83,375	678	6,286	19,478	57,132	1,940	81,435
TN.	85,795	1,062	8,713	19,714	57,940	17,277	68,518
TX.	296,259	3,234	29,355	72,163	200,426	82,197	214,062
UT.	41,718	940	3,332	8,368	29,629	6,412	35,306
VT.	14,192	320	1,316	3,326	9,441	1,334	12,858
VA	69,384	1,107	8,304	16,157	45,750	18,530	50,854
WA	79,555	763	7,614	18,829	54,388	17,647	61,908
WV	35,130	550	3,248	9,240	22,537	3,177	31,953
WI	111,435	745	11,857	22,931	77,393	15,982	95,453
WY	34,115	913	3,666	10,997	19,011	2,321	31,794

- Represents zero.   [1] Also includes freeways and expressways.   [2] Includes Puerto Rico not shown separately.

Source: U.S. Federal Highway Administration, *Highway Statistics,* annual.

No. 1020. Highway Mileage—Urban and Rural, by Type and Control, and Federal-Aid Highway System: 1980 to 1996

[In thousands, except percent. As of Dec. 31. Data for urban and rural mileage are not comparable to years prior to 1980 because of classification changes; see text, Section 21]

TYPE AND CONTROL	1980	1985	1990	1991	1992	1993	1994	1995	1996
Total mileage [1]	[2]3,955	3,862	3,880	3,889	3,902	3,905	3,906	3,912	3,934
Urban mileage	624	691	757	750	785	803	814	814	834
Under state control	79	111	96	96	104	106	110	112	113
Under local control	543	578	661	653	680	696	702	706	719
Rural mileage	[2]3,331	3,171	3,123	3,139	3,117	3,102	3,093	3,093	3,100
Under state control	702	773	703	703	697	675	690	691	693
Under local control	2,270	2,173	2,242	2,255	2,239	2,247	2,229	2,231	2,238
Under federal control	262	225	178	182	181	180	174	170	169

[1] Beginning 1985, includes only public road mileage as defined 23 USC 402.   [2] Includes 98,000 miles of nonpublic road mileage previously contained in other rural categories.

Source: U.S. Federal Highway Administration, *Highway Statistics*, annual.

No. 1021. Highway Pavement Condition, by Type of Road System: 1996

CONDITION	URBAN AREAS						RURAL AREAS				
	Total	Inter-state	Other				Total	Inter-state	Other prin-cipal arter-ial	Minor arter-ial	Major collec-tor
			Free-ways and express-ways	Prin-cipal arter-ial	Minor arter-ial	Collec-tor					
Percent of road mileage rated—											
Above Average	35	38	33	25	42	34	42	55	43	39	40
Average	42	53	55	49	37	39	42	41	49	51	38
Below Average	23	9	12	26	21	27	17	4	7	11	22

Source: U.S. Federal Highway Administration, *Highway Statistics*, annual.

No. 1022. Funding for Highways: 1980 to 1996

[In millions of dollars. Data compiled from reports of state and local authorities]

TYPE	1980	1985	1990	1992	1993	1994	1995	1996
Total receipts	39,715	61,506	75,294	86,703	88,380	88,296	95,313	101,497
Current income	37,604	54,957	69,730	77,404	80,610	80,514	87,694	92,179
Other taxes and fees	11,808	15,127	19,827	19,933	19,375	19,872	21,390	21,274
Investment income, other receipts	3,237	4,231	5,639	6,582	6,834	6,166	6,742	7,083
Bond issue proceeds [1]	2,111	6,549	5,564	9,299	7,770	7,782	7,619	9,318
Funds from (+) or to (-) reserves [2]	2,080	-4,058	114	-3,155	-1,955	962	-2,809	-3,339
Total funds available	41,795	57,448	75,408	83,548	86,425	89,258	92,504	98,158
Total disbursements	41,795	57,448	75,408	83,548	86,425	89,258	92,504	98,158
Current disbursements	40,084	54,725	72,457	78,959	81,233	85,109	87,843	93,663
Capital outlay	20,337	27,138	35,151	38,309	39,528	41,780	43,097	46,519
Maintenance and traffic services	11,445	16,032	20,365	22,223	22,894	23,607	24,455	25,803
Administration and research	3,022	4,033	6,501	7,718	7,921	8,398	8,332	8,645
Law enforcement and safety	3,824	5,334	7,235	7,088	7,157	7,518	7,977	8,774
Interest on debt	1,456	2,188	3,205	3,621	3,733	3,806	3,982	3,922
Bond retirement [1]	1,711	2,723	2,951	4,589	5,192	4,149	4,661	4,495

[1] Excludes issue and redemption of short-term notes or refunding bonds.   [2] Plus sign (+) indicates net receipt of funds from other levels of government; minus sign (-) indicates net disbursement of funds to other levels.

Source: U.S. Federal Highway Administration, *Highway Statistics*, annual; and releases.

No. 1023. Disbursement of State Highway Funds, by State: 1990 to 1996

[In millions of dollars. Comprises disbursements from current revenues. Includes transactions by state toll authorities. Excludes amounts allocated for collection expenses and nonhighway purposes, and bonds redeemed by refunding]

STATE	1990	1995	1996	STATE	1990	1995	1996	STATE	1990	1995	1996
U.S.	53,580	67,261	71,736	KS	697	1,019	1,162	ND	189	270	266
				KY	1,008	1,342	1,372	OH	2,271	2,637	2,709
AL	866	1,002	1,064	LA	923	1,195	1,417				
AK	336	438	453	ME	332	379	509	OK	827	828	918
AZ	1,525	1,199	1,532	MD	1,464	1,289	1,449	OR	765	888	995
AR	456	666	755	MA	1,055	2,501	2,545	PA	2,885	3,153	3,118
CA	4,294	5,966	531	MI	1,526	1,974	1,966	RI	214	290	297
CO	714	922	922	MN	1,228	1,210	1,374	SC	585	668	678
CT	1,204	1,153	1,202					SD	232	286	289
DE	315	441	452	MS	529	662	826	TN	1,174	1,230	1,283
DC	273	140	163	MO	937	1,313	1,402	TX	3,001	3,593	4,312
FL	1,677	3,402	3,472	MT	302	388	377	UT	355	431	457
GA	1,278	1,437	1,675	NE	449	578	595	VT	165	194	192
HI	297	307	405	NV	309	484	468	VA	1,874	2,107	2,321
				NH	299	328	346	WA	1,251	1,842	1,766
ID	300	350	359	NJ	1,831	2,102	2,928	WV	650	781	935
IL	2,645	2,985	3,097	NM	409	535	532	WI	979	1,252	1,324
IN	1,218	1,368	1,444	NY	2,874	4,515	4,424	WY	297	272	283
IA	869	1,078	1,128	NC	1,428	1,871	1,939				

Source: U.S. Federal Highway Administration, *Highway Statistics,* annual.

No. 1024. Federal Grants to State and Local Governments for Highway Trust Fund and Federal Transit Administration (FTA), by State: 1997

[Year ending Sept. 30]

STATE	HIGHWAY TRUST FUND		FTA		STATE	HIGHWAY TRUST FUND		FTA		STATE	HIGHWAY TRUST FUND		FTA	
	Total (mil. dol.)	Per cap- ita [1]	Total (mil. dol.)	Per cap- ita [1]		Total (mil. dol.)	Per cap- ita [1]	Total (mil. dol.)	Per cap- ita [1]		Total (mil. dol.)	Per cap- ita [1]	Total (mil. dol.)	Per cap- ita [1]
U.S.	20,467	75.4	4,555	16.8	KS . . .	186	71.7	5	2.1	ND . . .	141	220.5	4	6.8
					KY . . .	293	74.9	16	4.1	OH . . .	763	68.2	94	8.4
AL . . .	299	69.3	10	2.4	LA . . .	256	58.8	48	11.1	OK . . .	270	81.4	13	4.0
AK . . .	240	394.0	2	2.9	ME . . .	118	94.9	3	2.8	OR . . .	340	104.7	164	50.6
AZ . . .	334	73.2	35	7.7	MD . . .	419	82.3	90	17.6	PA . . .	934	77.7	256	21.3
AR . . .	285	113.1	9	3.6	MA . . .	1,025	167.5	225	36.8	RI . . .	106	107.4	7	7.1
CA . . .	2,097	65.0	675	20.9	MI . . .	605	61.9	68	6.9	SC . . .	252	67.0	10	2.8
CO . . .	207	53.3	20	5.2	MN . . .	302	64.5	13	2.7	SD . . .	146	197.3	5	6.6
CT . . .	368	112.7	72	21.9	MS . . .	195	71.4	7	2.6	TN . . .	378	70.5	40	7.4
DE . . .	86	116.9	6	7.6	MO . . .	444	82.2	62	11.5	TX . . .	1,179	60.7	173	8.9
DC . . .	94	178.0	117	220.6	MT . . .	171	195.1	3	2.9	UT . . .	153	74.4	43	20.9
FL . . .	736	50.3	154	10.5	NE . . .	167	101.0	6	3.3	VT . . .	89	151.6	7	12.5
GA . . .	473	63.2	119	15.8	NV . . .	148	88.5	22	13.3	VA . . .	442	65.6	37	5.5
HI . . .	207	174.2	10	8.1	NH . . .	105	89.3	3	2.9	WA . . .	467	83.2	92	16.3
ID . . .	161	133.0	4	3.2	NJ . . .	644	80.0	352	43.7	WV . . .	219	120.3	13	7.1
IL	704	59.1	281	23.6	NM . . .	201	116.3	11	6.6	WI . . .	329	63.7	40	7.7
IN . . .	429	73.1	40	6.8	NY . . .	1,201	66.2	752	41.4	WY . .	134	279.2	1	2.9
IA . . .	229	80.3	20	6.9	NC . . .	448	60.3	35	4.8					

[1] Based on Bureau of the Census resident population as of July 1; excluding population of the territories.
Source: U.S. Bureau of the Census, *Federal Expenditures by State for Fiscal Year,* annual.

No. 1025. State Gasoline Tax Rates, 1994 and 1995, and Motor Fuel Tax Receipts, 1996

STATE	RATE [1] (cents/gal.)		Re- ceipts, 1996 (mil. dol.)	STATE	RATE [1] (cents/gal.)		Re- ceipts, 1996 (mil. dol.)	STATE	RATE [1] (cents/gal.)		Re- ceipts, 1996 (mil. dol.)
	1994	1995			1994	1995			1994	1995	
AL	18.0	18.0	531	KY	16.4	16.4	401	ND	18.0	18.0	93
AK	8.0	8.0	20	LA	20.0	20.0	528	OH	22.0	22.0	1,348
AZ	18.0	18.0	483	ME	19.0	19.0	149	OK	17.0	17.0	367
AR	18.7	18.7	340	MD	23.5	23.5	606	OR	24.0	24.0	372
CA	18.0	18.0	2,721	MA	21.0	21.0	599	PA	22.4	22.4	1,311
CO	22.0	22.0	440	MI	15.0	15.0	762	RI	28.0	29.0	124
CT	31.0	34.0	498	MN	20.0	20.0	516	SC	16.0	16.0	383
DE	22.0	23.0	93	MS	18.4	18.4	336	SD	18.0	18.0	93
DC	20.0	20.0	32	MO	15.1	15.0	589	TN	20.0	20.0	663
FL	12.1	12.3	1,291	MT	27.0	27.0	170	TX	20.0	20.0	2,337
GA	7.5	7.5	411	NE	25.4	25.4	251	UT	19.0	19.0	217
HI	16.0	16.0	68	NV	24.0	24.0	236	VT	16.0	16.0	67
ID	21.0	21.0	185	NH	18.7	18.7	115	VA	17.5	17.5	693
IL	19.0	19.0	1,140	NJ	10.5	10.5	464	WA	23.0	23.0	679
IN	15.0	15.0	663	NM	21.0	18.0	223	WV	25.4	25.4	262
IA	20.0	20.0	376	NY	22.6	21.9	1,326	WI	23.1	23.4	687
KS	18.0	18.0	297	NC	21.3	21.6	1,172	WY	9.0	9.0	54

[1] In effect Dec. 31.
Source: U.S. Federal Highway Administration, *Highway Statistics,* annual.

No. 1026. Price Trends for Federal-Aid Highway Construction: 1980 to 1996

YEAR	Common exca- vation (cu.yd.)	SURFACING			STRUCTURES				Com- posite index
		Portland cement concrete (sq. yd.)	Bitumi- nous concrete (ton)	Index	Rein forcing steel (lb.)	Struc- tural steel (lb.)	Struc- tural concrete (cu. yd.)	Index	
Average contract price:									
1980	1.83	14.92	25.29	(X)	0.48	0.94	226.68	(X)	(X)
1985	2.24	14.31	28.52	(X)	0.44	0.80	243.60	(X)	(X)
1986	2.28	15.63	26.48	(X)	0.44	0.85	236.37	(X)	(X)
1987	2.42	14.80	24.65	(X)	0.44	0.89	240.81	(X)	(X)
1988	2.72	14.33	24.91	(X)	0.49	0.92	274.12	(X)	(X)
1989	2.40	15.17	24.08	(X)	0.56	1.02	283.40	(X)	(X)
1990	2.38	15.91	24.52	(X)	0.53	1.01	286.18	(X)	(X)
1991	2.32	16.58	25.52	(X)	0.51	1.03	264.98	(X)	(X)
1992	2.20	17.80	24.66	(X)	0.52	0.92	259.61	(X)	(X)
1993	2.50	18.81	26.26	(X)	0.47	0.86	261.89	(X)	(X)
1994 (3d qtr.)	3.12	21.09	30.29	(X)	0.49	0.86	285.08	(X)	(X)
Index (1987=100):									
1980	75.5	101.3	102.6	102.2	109.6	106.3	94.1	100.0	97.2
1985	92.4	97.1	115.7	109.6	100.7	89.9	101.2	98.1	102.0
1986	94.0	106.1	107.4	107.0	100.3	96.0	98.2	98.0	101.1
1987	100.0	100.0	100.0	100.0	100.0	100.0	100.0	100.0	100.0
1988	112.2	97.3	101.1	99.8	112.1	104.4	113.8	111.0	106.6
1989	99.0	103.0	97.7	99.4	126.2	115.0	117.7	118.4	107.7
1990	98.1	108.0	99.5	102.3	120.0	114.1	118.8	117.8	108.5
1991	95.5	112.5	103.6	106.5	114.6	116.4	110.0	112.5	107.5
1992	90.8	120.8	100.1	106.9	117.9	103.5	107.8	108.4	105.1
1993	103.2	127.7	106.6	113.5	106.0	97.3	108.7	105.3	108.3
1994	128.6	143.2	122.9	122.3	111.1	96.9	118.4	109.0	115.1
1995	(NA)	(NA)	(NA)	127.9	(NA)	(NA)	(NA)	119.5	121.9
1996	(NA)	(NA)	(NA)	118.7	(NA)	(NA)	(NA)	121.6	120.2

NA Not available.   X Not applicable.

Source: U.S. Federal Highway Administration, *Price Trends for Federal-Aid Highway Construction, Third Quarter 1994.*

No. 1027. Public Highway Debt—State and Local Governments: 1980 to 1995

[**In millions of dollars.** Long-term obligations. Data are for varying calendar and fiscal years. Excludes duplicated and interunit obligations]

ITEM	1980	1985	1988	1989	1990	1991	1992	1993	1994	1995
Total debt issued	2,357	8,194	4,594	5,900	5,838	9,516	12,988	14,178	10,833	11,306
State	1,135	5,397	2,702	3,775	3,277	6,252	9,460	10,035	5,739	4,718
Local	1,222	2,797	1,892	2,125	2,561	3,264	3,528	4,143	5,094	6,587
Total debt redeemed	1,982	4,606	2,774	3,729	5,158	6,138	7,665	10,823	6,103	5,635
State	1,109	3,835	1,547	2,813	2,041	4,352	5,388	8,082	3,622	2,940
Local	873	771	1,227	916	3,117	1,786	2,277	2,741	2,481	2,695
Total debt outstanding	27,519	33,379	41,663	43,834	44,514	47,892	53,539	58,373	63,062	68,733
Local	7,427	12,100	15,927	17,136	16,580	18,058	19,353	22,965	25,613	29,505

Source: U.S. Federal Highway Administration, *Highway Statistics,* annual.

No. 1028. Alternative Fueled Vehicles in Use, by Fuel Type: 1996 to 1998

FUEL	ALTERNATIVE FUELED VEHICLES			FUEL CONSUMPTION (1,000 gasoline-equivalent gallons)		
	1996	1997	1998	1996	1997	1998
Fuels	**352,421**	**380,352**	**402,790**	**297,231**	**321,389**	**342,557**
Liquified petroleum gases (LPG)	263,000	271,000	279,000	239,158	244,612	252,981
Compressed natural gas (CNG)	60,144	73,773	85,122	46,923	63,258	74,998
Liquified natural gas (LNG)	663	965	1,136	3,247	4,567	5,090
M85 (Mixture: 85% methanol + 15% gasoline)	20,265	20,656	21,370	3,390	3,625	3,832
Neat methanol (M100)	172	172	172	347	347	347
E85 (Mixture: 85% ethanol+15% gasoline)	4,536	9,389	10,872	694	1,416	1,614
E95 (Mixture: 95% ethanol + 5% gasoline)	361	357	357	2,699	2,628	2,628
Electricity	3,280	4,040	4,761	773	936	1,067

Source: Energy Information Administration, *Alternatives to Traditional Transportation Fuels 1996.*

No. 1029. Motor Vehicle Registrations, 1980 to 1996, and Drivers Licenses, and Motorcycle Registrations 1996, by State

[In thousands, except as indicated. Motor vehicle registrations cover publicly, privately, and commercially owned vehicles. For uniformity, data have been adjusted to a calendar-year basis as registration years in states differ; figures represent net numbers where possible, excluding re-registrations and nonresident registrations]

| STATE | AUTOMOBILES, TRUCKS, AND BUSES [1] | | | | | | | | 1996 | |
| | 1980 | 1985 | 1990 | 1993 | 1994 | 1995 | 1996 | | Motor-cycle [1] | |
							Total	Auto-mobiles (incl. taxis)	regis-tration (incl. official)	Drivers licenses
U.S	155,796	171,654	188,798	194,063	198,045	201,530	206,365	128,439	3,832	179,539
AL......	2,938	3,338	3,744	3,390	3,177	3,553	3,324	1,746	36	3,138
AK......	262	353	477	489	533	542	531	226	13	440
AZ......	1,917	2,235	2,825	2,892	2,813	2,873	2,983	1,750	71	2,727
AR......	1,574	1,384	1,448	1,528	1,567	1,613	1,633	853	16	1,752
CA......	16,873	18,899	21,926	22,824	22,339	22,432	25,214	15,223	513	20,249
CO	2,342	2,759	3,155	3,032	2,750	2,812	3,433	1,891	94	2,757
CT......	2,147	2,465	2,623	2,594	2,599	2,622	2,609	1,930	48	2,344
DE......	397	465	526	555	578	592	593	391	10	529
DC	268	326	262	264	249	243	237	195	1	333
FL	7,614	9,865	10,950	10,170	10,252	10,369	10,889	7,192	198	11,400
GA	3,818	4,580	5,489	5,632	5,990	6,120	6,283	3,818	73	4,966
HI	570	651	771	763	779	802	786	500	25	733
ID	834	854	1,054	1,023	1,035	1,043	1,061	479	34	820
IL	7,477	7,727	7,873	8,070	8,698	8,973	8,817	6,232	171	7,610
IN	3,826	4,024	4,366	4,670	4,889	5,072	5,216	3,146	96	3,704
IA	2,329	2,696	2,632	2,738	2,766	2,814	2,869	1,642	132	1,956
KS.......	2,007	2,148	2,012	1,922	2,083	2,085	2,110	1,151	49	1,788
KY......	2,593	2,615	2,909	2,629	2,666	2,631	2,696	1,585	37	2,567
LA......	2,779	3,012	2,995	3,166	3,426	3,286	3,318	1,871	37	2,624
ME	724	840	977	1,028	946	967	959	573	27	874
MD	2,803	3,276	3,607	3,560	3,640	3,654	3,635	2,557	38	3,377
MA	3,749	3,738	3,726	3,837	4,027	4,502	4,702	3,528	91	4,355
MI	6,488	6,727	7,209	7,399	7,574	7,674	8,010	5,045	149	6,717
MN	3,091	3,385	3,508	3,716	4,057	3,882	3,861	2,263	116	2,830
MS	1,577	1,746	1,875	2,000	2,063	2,144	2,182	1,257	30	1,700
MO	3,271	3,558	3,905	4,066	4,208	4,255	4,350	2,568	54	3,749
MT	680	652	783	939	950	968	973	431	21	574
NE	1,254	1,257	1,384	1,439	1,458	1,467	1,479	797	18	1,160
NV......	655	709	853	937	985	1,047	1,096	610	22	1,117
NH	704	974	946	959	992	1,122	1,112	733	52	915
NJ	4,761	4,909	5,652	5,641	5,839	5,906	5,822	4,348	91	5,486
NM	1,068	1,176	1,301	1,421	1,422	1,484	1,545	759	31	1,179
NY......	8,002	9,042	10,196	10,163	10,196	10,274	10,636	7,915	135	10,484
NC	4,532	4,450	5,162	5,365	5,443	5,682	5,759	3,474	67	5,187
ND	627	655	630	662	685	695	679	334	16	449
OH	7,771	8,102	8,410	9,279	9,664	9,810	9,770	6,570	219	7,853
OK	2,583	2,864	2,649	2,771	2,806	2,856	3,082	1,675	59	2,396
OR	2,081	2,204	2,445	2,624	2,753	2,785	2,851	1,503	60	2,613
PA......	6,926	7,209	7,971	8,282	8,482	8,481	8,640	5,893	178	8,221
RI	623	610	672	695	699	699	696	508	17	669
SC......	1,996	2,222	2,521	2,684	2,743	2,833	2,791	1,754	39	2,575
SD......	601	650	704	808	769	709	751	366	25	519
TN......	3,271	3,754	4,444	4,964	5,059	5,400	4,830	2,975	79	3,806
TX......	10,475	12,444	12,800	13,118	13,626	13,682	13,487	7,391	144	12,568
UT......	992	1,099	1,206	1,335	1,415	1,447	1,445	802	23	1,319
VT......	347	398	462	483	489	492	503	298	18	469
VA......	3,626	4,253	4,938	5,408	5,507	5,613	5,576	3,603	57	4,692
WA	3,225	3,526	4,257	4,413	4,465	4,503	4,603	2,619	104	3,908
WV	1,320	1,143	1,225	1,345	1,462	1,425	1,406	785	15	1,274
WI	2,941	3,187	3,815	3,815	3,926	3,993	3,972	2,460	169	3,724
WY	467	500	528	558	508	601	562	227	15	343

[1] Excludes vehicles owned by military services.

Source: U.S. Federal Highway Administration, *Highway Statistics,* annual; and *Selected Highway Statistics and Charts,* annual.

No. 1030. Selected Motor Vehicle Indicators, by Model Year: 1992 to 1997

[In thousands of units, except as indicated. A model year begins on Oct. 1, and ends on Sept. 30. It covers the fourth quarter of one calendar year and the first three quarters of the next calendar year]

SALES AND EXPENDITURES	1992	1993	1994	1995	1996	1997
New motor vehicle sales	12,868	13,913	15,179	15,233	15,460	15,380
New-car sales.	8,160	8,428	8,936	8,736	8,654	8,259
Domestic.	6,195	6,595	7,173	7,167	7,361	6,924
U.S. nameplates.	5,048	5,348	5,707	5,518	5,428	4,964
Transplants	1,146	1,247	1,466	1,649	1,933	1,960
Import	1,966	1,833	1,763	1,570	1,293	1,335
New-truck sales	4,707	5,486	6,244	6,498	6,806	7,121
Light	4,446	5,167	5,869	6,070	6,389	6,707
Domestic.	4,026	4,789	5,499	5,666	5,976	6,155
Import.	421	378	370	404	413	552
Other.	261	320	375	427	417	414
Domestic-car production	5,643	5,827	6,548	6,466	6,194	5,879
Avg. expenditure per new car [1] (dollar).	16,893	17,526	18,431	18,849	19,397	20,305
Domestic (dollar).	16,281	16,595	17,406	17,695	18,064	18,580
Import (dollar).	18,861	20,998	22,598	24,111	26,972	29,296

[1] BEA estimate based on the manufacturer's suggested retail price.

Source: U.S. Bureau of Economic Analysis, *Survey of Current Business,* November 1997. Data from American Automobile Manufacturers Assoc., Inc. and Ward's Automotive Reports; seasonally adjusted by BEA.

No. 1031. U.S. Truck Market — Import Penetration: 1975 to 1996

[Represents retail sales]

YEAR	U.S. sales total	DOMESTIC (lbs GVWR) [1][2]				IMPORTS		PERCENT OF U.S. MARKET	
		Total	14,000 lbs. & under	14,001-33,000	Over 33,000	Total imports	From Japan	From Japan	Total imports
1975.	2,478,219	2,248,904	1,973,853	191,903	83,148	229,315	228,097	9.2	9.3
1976.	3,181,254	2,943,872	2,662,587	183,999	97,286	237,382	236,211	7.4	7.5
1977.	3,675,439	3,352,255	3,011,667	199,945	140,643	323,184	321,364	8.7	8.8
1978.	4,109,079	3,773,166	3,406,419	205,139	161,608	335,913	333,662	8.1	8.2
1979.	3,479,794	3,009,867	2,635,604	200,969	173,294	469,701	465,701	13.4	13.5
1980.	2,487,239	2,000,669	1,734,664	149,213	116,792	486,570	480,547	19.3	19.6
1981.	2,260,318	1,809,188	1,587,093	122,395	99,700	451,130	443,504	19.6	20.0
1982.	2,559,881	2,145,947	1,968,473	101,697	75,777	413,934	407,486	15.9	16.2
1983.	3,129,476	2,658,269	2,477,238	99,384	81,647	471,207	463,515	14.8	15.1
1984.	4,093,199	3,475,416	3,208,366	129,357	137,693	617,783	607,758	14.8	15.1
1985.	4,681,698	3,902,417	3,629,080	139,756	133,581	779,281	768,625	16.4	16.6
1986.	4,862,717	3,921,408	3,676,129	133,465	111,814	941,309	926,729	19.1	19.4
1987.	4,912,374	4,054,738	3,790,606	133,872	130,260	857,636	840,297	17.1	17.5
1988.	5,148,964	4,508,059	4,199,643	160,544	147,872	640,905	623,540	12.1	12.4
1989.	4,941,220	4,403,299	4,113,467	145,104	144,728	537,921	514,532	10.4	10.9
1990.	4,846,162	4,215,003	3,956,835	137,031	121,137	631,159	610,688	12.6	13.0
1991.	4,364,672	3,813,173	3,605,779	108,751	98,643	551,499	539,556	12.4	12.6
1992.	4,903,362	4,481,325	4,247,097	115,198	119,030	422,037	412,961	8.4	8.6
1993.	5,680,994	5,287,379	5,000,430	129,063	157,886	393,615	381,433	6.7	6.9
1994.	6,420,857	5,995,227	5,657,634	151,897	185,696	425,630	406,682	6.3	6.6
1995.	6,481,357	6,064,154	5,690,903	171,948	201,303	417,203	393,573	6.1	6.4
1996.	6,929,591	6,477,802	6,131,646	176,147	170,009	451,789	416,211	6.0	6.5

[1] GVWR = Gross vehicle gross weight rating in U.S. pounds.   [2] North American built.

Source: American Automobile Manufacturers Association, Washington, DC, *Motor Vehicle Facts and Figures,* annual (copyright).

No. 1032. Motor Vehicle Production and Trade: 1980 to 1996

ITEM	Unit	1980	1990	1991	1992	1993	1994	1995	1996
United States	1,000. . .	8,010	9,784	8,811	9,702	10,898	12,263	11,985	11,799
Passenger car production	1,000. . .	6,376	6,078	5,439	5,664	5,981	6,614	6,351	6,083
Truck and bus production	1,000. . .	1,634	3,706	3,372	4,038	4,917	5,649	5,635	5,716
Imports:									
Passenger cars (new) [1][2]	1,000. . .	3,116	3,945	3,736	3,575	3,808	4,097	4,114	4,064
Canada	1,000. . .	595	1,220	1,196	1,200	1,468	1,591	1,678	1,688
Germany, Federal Republic of.	1,000. . .	339	245	172	206	184	188	207	234
Japan.	1,000. . .	1,992	1,868	1,789	1,637	1,597	1,593	1,387	1,191
Trucks and buses (new) [2]	1,000. . .	747	766	716	777	722	708	662	688
Japan.	1,000. . .	483	302	283	197	154	170	90	52
All-terrain vehicles	1,000. . .	(NA)	100	(NA)	(NA)	(NA)	(NA)	(NA)	(NA)
Motorcycles, total [3]	1,000. . .	1,120	169	(NA)	(NA)	(NA)	(NA)	(NA)	(NA)
Import value:									
Passenger cars (new) [1]	Mil. dol. .	16,675	45,716	45,564	46,729	52,208	61,367	64,526	66,916
Trucks and buses, (new) [1]	Mil. dol. .	1,985	8,155	8,221	10,000	10,104	10,909	11,792	12,381
Motorcycles [3][4]	Mil. dol. .	1,142	361	(NA)	(NA)	(NA)	(NA)	(NA)	(NA)
Exports, number:									
Passenger cars (new) [1]	1,000. . .	617	794	755	851	864	1,019	989	974
Trucks and buses (new) exports	1,000. . .	186	159	208	161	181	274	254	316
Export value [1][5]	Mil. dol. .	16,015	38,086	(NA)	(NA)	(NA)	(NA)	(NA)	(NA)
Passenger cars (new) [5]	Mil. dol. .	3,932	9,708	9,886	11,893	12,476	14,591	14,251	14,392
Trucks and buses (new) [5]	Mil. dol. .	2,977	3,388	3,388	3,073	3,399	5,238	5,209	6,246
Parts and accessories [6]	Mil. dol. .	9,106	24,996	(NA)	(NA)	(NA)	(NA)	(NA)	(NA)
Factory sales:									
Passenger cars	1,000. . .	6,400	6,050	5,407	5,685	5,962	6,549	6,310	6,140
Trucks and buses	1,000. . .	1,667	3,725	3,387	4,062	4,895	5,640	5,713	5,776
Retail sales:									
Passenger cars (new) [1]	1,000. . .	8,979	9,300	8,175	8,213	8,518	8,991	8,635	8,527
Domestics [7]	1,000. . .	6,581	6,897	6,137	6,277	6,742	7,255	7,129	7,254
Imports [8]	1,000. . .	2,398	2,403	2,038	1,937	1,776	1,735	1,506	1,273
Trucks and buses [9]	1,000. . .	2,232	4,261	3,606	4,247	5,000	5,658	5,691	6,132
Light duty (up to 14,000 GVW) [10] . .	1,000. . .	1,964	3,984	3,621	4,264	5,015	5,673	5,703	(NA)
Med. duty (14,001-26,000 GVW) [10]	1,000. . .	92	71	50	57	64	69	80	(NA)
Heavy duty (over 26,000 GVW) [10] . .	1,000. . .	176	207	171	192	239	284	308	(NA)
Under 6,000 pounds	1,000. . .	985	2,866	2,719	3,212	3,754	4,132	4,031	4,398
Utility	1,000. . .	51	490	549	666	721	1,130	1,258	1,392
Van.	1,000. . .	79	31	17	21	18	12	12	18
Minivan (cargo).	1,000. . .	(X)	83	66	63	70	82	73	64
Station wagon (truck chassis) . . .	1,000. . .	(X)	112	110	201	321	-	-	-
Mini-passenger carrier	1,000. . .	(X)	750	706	840	1,002	1,132	1,113	1,098
6,000 to 10,000 pounds [11]	1,000. . .	975	1,097	876	1,021	1,232	1,506	1,631	1,690
Utility	1,000. . .	108	68	37	51	60	72	144	243
Van.	1,000. . .	172	254	203	241	279	275	274	254
Pickup, conventional	1,000. . .	546	568	476	524	647	883	967	936
Station wagon (truck chassis) . . .	1,000. . .	39	85	55	80	115	125	109	137
10,001 pounds and over	1,000. . .	271	298	242	275	330	388	428	(NA)

- Represents zero.   NA Not available.   X Not applicable.   [1] Based on data from U.S. Dept. of Commerce.   [2] Includes other countries, not shown separately.   [3] Source: Motorcycle Industry Council, Inc., Irvine, CA. Data from U.S. Dept. of Commerce. Excludes mopeds/motorized bicycles and all-terrain vehicles. Excludes moped imports (motorcycle imports less than 51 cc's) from all countries (except Japan).   [4] Represents c.i.f. value.   [5] Covers assembled and unassembled vehicles.   [6] Includes rubber tires and tubes and used vehicles.   [7] Includes domestic models produced in Canada and Mexico.   [8] Excludes domestic models produced in Canada.   [9] Excludes motorcoaches and light-duty imports from foreign manufactures. Includes imports sold by franchised dealers of U.S. manufacturers. Starting in 1987, includes sales of trucks over 10,000 lbs. GVW by foreign manufacturers.   [10] Gross vehicle weight (fully loaded vehicle).   [11] Includes vehicles, not shown separately.

No. 1033. Motor Vehicles in Use: 1980 to 1995

ITEM	Unit	1980	1985	1990	1991	1992	1993	1994	1995
Cars in use, total	Million. .	**104.6**	**114.7**	**123.3**	**123.3**	**120.3**	**121.1**	**122.0**	**123.2**
Under 5 years	Million . .	52.3	48.7	56.5	54.6	50.4	47.0	45.4	46.2
6-8 years.	Million . .	25.2	27.8	22.6	25.5	27.5	28.7	27.7	26.9
9-11 years	Million . .	14.6	17.2	19.1	16.7	16.0	22.5	25.1	23.3
12 years and over	Million . .	12.5	21.0	25.1	26.6	26.4	31.1	31.4	26.8
Average age	Years. . .	6.6	7.6	7.8	7.9	8.1	8.3	8.4	8.5
Cars retired from use [1]	1,000. . .	8,405	7,729	8,897	8,565	11,194	7,366	7,824	7,414
Trucks in use, total	Million. .	**35.2**	**42.4**	**56.0**	**58.2**	**61.2**	**82.5**	**71.4**	**70.2**
Under 3 years	Million . .	8.8	9.0	12.8	12.0	11.3	12.1	13.7	15.4
3-5 years.	Million . .	8.1	6.3	13.2	14.0	14.0	12.9	12.7	12.4
6-8 years.	Million . .	7.4	10.2	8.0	9.9	11.9	14.0	13.6	13.1
9-11 years	Million . .	4.4	6.2	6.6	5.3	5.6	11.7	11.3	10.7
12 years and over	Million . .	6.5	10.7	15.5	17.0	18.3	23.2	20.1	18.6
Average age	Years. . .	7.1	8.1	8.0	8.1	8.4	8.6	8.4	8.4
Trucks retired from use [1]	1,000. . .	1,732	2,100	2,177	2,284	1,587	1,048	4,545	2,918

[1] For years ending June 30. Represents vehicles failing to re-register.

Source of tables 1032 and 1033: Except as noted, American Automobile Manufacturers Association Inc., Washington, DC, *Motor Vehicle Facts and Figures*, annual (copyright); and *World Motor Vehicle Data*, annual (copyright).

No. 1034. Motor Vehicle Registrations: 1980 to 1995

[Compiled principally from information obtained from state authorities, but it was necessary to draw on other sources and to make numerous estimates in order to complete series. Includes Alaska and Hawaii]

ITEM	1980	1990	1992	1993	1994	1995
All motor vehicles	155,796,219	188,797,914	190,362,228	194,063,482	198,045,365	201,530,021
Private and commercial	153,265,069	185,540,912	186,960,290	190,642,869	194,531,748	197,941,202
Publicly owned	2,531,150	3,257,002	3,401,938	3,420,613	3,513,617	3,588,819
Automobiles [1]	121,600,843	133,700,497	126,581,148	127,327,189	127,883,469	128,386,775
Private and commercial	120,743,495	132,164,330	125,087,687	125,843,591	126,396,989	126,899,713
Publicly owned	857,348	1,536,167	1,493,461	1,483,598	1,486,480	1,487,062
Buses	528,789	626,987	644,732	654,432	670,423	685,503
Private and commercial	253,854	275,493	275,245	276,093	282,507	287,873
Publicly owned	274,935	351,494	369,487	378,339	387,916	397,630
Trucks [1]	33,666,587	54,470,430	63,136,348	66,081,861	69,491,473	72,457,743
Private and commercial	32,267,720	53,101,089	61,597,358	64,523,185	67,852,252	70,753,616
Publicly owned	1,398,867	1,369,341	1,538,990	1,558,676	1,639,221	1,704,127

[1] Trucks include pickups, panels and delivery vans. Beginning 1985, personal passenger vans, passenger minivans and utility-type vehicles are no longer included in automobiles but are included in trucks.

Source: U.S. Federal Highway Administration, *Highway Statistics*, annual.

No. 1035. Motor Vehicle Tires and Batteries: 1980 to 1995

[In millions]

ITEM	1980	1985	1990	1991	1992	1993	1994	1995
Tires, passenger car, total [1]	145.9	200.9	218.8	214.8	213.6	214.5	228.6	235.0
Radials	83.5	164.7	200.2	200.4	202.1	205.7	221.4	227.4
Replacement	106.9	141.5	155.3	151.2	152.3	155.4	165.8	165.1
Tires, truck and bus, total [1]	31.1	41.1	46.0	46.9	46.9	42.4	45.0	48.4
Radials	3.8	19.7	29.4	30.6	32.5	32.4	36.1	40.3
Replacement	24.4	32.1	33.9	35.2	36.6	32.9	33.7	35.7
Batteries, total [2]	61.7	74.4	80.1	80.3	79.7	79.8	(NA)	(NA)
Replacement automobile batteries	50.1	58.7	63.5	64.4	65.2	66.6	(NA)	(NA)

[1] Includes original equipment. Also includes exports, not shown separately.　[2] Source: Battery Council International, Chicago, IL, and U.S. Bureau of the Census.

Source: Except as noted, The Rubber Manufacturers Association, Inc., Washington, DC, *RMA Monthly Tire Report*.

No. 1036. Automobile Output and Trade in National Income Accounts in Chained (1992) Dollars: 1990 to 1997

[In billions of dollars. Vehicle output equals final dollar sales value of new vehicles, plus net dollar value of used vehicle sales adjusted for changes in inventories and net balance of vehicle exports and imports]

ITEM	1990	1991	1992	1993	1994	1995	1996	1997
Auto output, total	125.8	111.9	121.6	125.3	132.3	127.6	119.9	120.0
Final sales	129.8	112.9	122.1	125.2	131.8	125.2	124.4	119.6
Personal consumption expenditures	133.3	111.1	117.6	121.6	123.7	122.0	121.2	121.4
Producers' durable equipment	33.0	35.4	35.3	38.8	47.8	43.4	45.1	46.8
Net exports	-38.7	-35.4	-32.8	-36.6	-41.3	-42.2	-43.6	-50.1
Government purchases	2.4	1.8	2.0	1.9	2.0	2.2	2.1	2.0
Change in business inventories	-3.9	-1.0	-0.4	0.1	0.4	2.2	-4.7	0.3
New	-3.6	-1.2	0.1	1.0	0.9	2.5	-5.2	1.1
Used	-0.3	0.2	-0.5	-0.8	-0.4	-0.1	0.3	-0.7

Source: U.S. Bureau of Economic Analysis, *The National Income and Product Accounts of the United States, 1929-94*, forthcoming; and *Survey of Current Business*, May 1997.

No. 1037. Recreational Vehicles—Number and Retail Value of Shipments: 1980 to 1996

ITEM	1980	1985	1987	1988	1989	1990	1991	1992	1993	1994	1995	1996
NUMBER (1,000)												
Total	181.4	351.7	393.6	420.0	388.3	347.3	293.7	382.7	420.2	518.8	475.2	466.8
Motorized homes	99.9	233.5	255.7	277.1	261.6	226.5	172.6	226.3	243.8	306.7	281.0	274.6
Travel trailers	52.0	75.4	86.2	89.6	82.9	80.4	77.6	102.5	113.6	128.0	121.2	123.9
Folding camping trailers	24.5	35.9	41.6	42.3	33.9	30.7	33.9	43.3	51.9	61.7	61.1	57.3
Truck campers	5.0	6.9	10.1	11.0	9.9	9.7	9.6	10.6	10.9	11.4	11.9	11.0
RETAIL VALUE (mil. dol.)												
Total	1,952	6,904	8,288	9,061	9,019	8,101	6,623	8,774	9,518	12,196	12,104	12,365
Motorized homes	1,381	5,724	6,826	7,543	7,420	6,660	5,284	6,963	(NA)	9,897	9,768	9,788
Travel trailers	485	997	1,219	1,254	1,252	1,220	1,107	1,523	1,644	1,912	1,927	2,171
Folding camping trailers	69	137	167	175	147	134	146	189	(NA)	276	290	284
Truck campers	17	46	76	88	81	86	87	99	(NA)	112	119	122

NA Not available.

Source: Recreation Vehicle Industry Association, Reston, VA, *RV's ... A Year-End Report/1989*. Data also in American Automobile Manufacturers Association of the United States, Inc., Washington, DC, *Motor Vehicle Facts and Figures*, annual (copyright).

No. 1038. Transportation to Work: 1990

[In thousands, except as indicated. Based on workers 16 years old or older]

STATE	MEANS OF TRANSPORTATION TO WORK			Worked at home	Average travel time to work [1] (minutes)	HOUSEHOLDS WITH VEHICLES AVAILABLE		
	Car, truck, van		Percent using public transport- ation			None	One vehicle	Two or more vehicles
	Drove alone	Car- pooled						
United States........	84,215	15,378	5.3	3,406	22.4	10,602	31,039	50,306
Alabama..............	1,374	267	0.8	31	21.2	156	466	885
Alaska...............	165	40	2.4	11	16.7	23	64	102
Arizona..............	1,178	239	2.1	48	21.6	107	532	730
Arkansas.............	765	153	0.5	28	19.0	88	303	501
California............	9,982	2,036	4.9	453	24.6	923	3,452	6,006
Colorado.............	1,217	210	2.9	67	20.7	89	412	781
Connecticut...........	1,301	187	3.9	45	21.1	124	386	721
Delaware	258	43	2.4	8	20.0	20	80	147
District of Columbia	107	37	36.6	9	27.1	93	103	53
Florida	4,468	819	2.0	132	21.8	474	2,106	2,555
Georgia	2,379	468	2.8	65	22.7	244	730	1,393
Hawaii	344	116	7.4	19	23.8	35	129	193
Idaho...............	330	53	1.9	21	17.3	17	101	243
Illinois	3,742	653	10.1	144	25.1	588	1,476	2,138
Indiana..............	2,040	332	1.3	73	20.4	175	670	1,221
Iowa	971	157	1.2	89	16.2	75	332	657
Kansas..............	929	136	0.6	49	17.2	60	302	583
Kentucky	1,195	229	1.6	47	20.7	159	447	773
Louisiana	1,239	247	3.0	31	22.3	209	542	749
Maine...............	424	80	0.9	24	19.0	40	159	266
Maryland	1,733	376	8.1	65	27.0	216	554	979
Massachusetts.........	2,148	318	8.3	75	22.7	321	819	1,107
Michigan.............	3,328	429	1.6	100	21.2	344	1,133	1,943
Minnesota............	1,593	247	3.6	116	19.1	142	517	988
Mississippi	777	184	0.8	19	20.6	111	307	494
Missouri	1,816	312	2.0	84	21.6	191	652	1,118
Montana.............	250	41	0.6	22	14.8	20	91	194
Nebraska............	590	87	1.2	44	15.8	43	182	377
Nevada	444	94	2.7	12	19.8	36	174	256
New Hampshire.........	443	70	0.7	20	21.9	26	132	254
New Jersey...........	2,731	472	8.8	80	25.3	360	966	1,468
New Mexico	472	96	1.0	24	19.1	38	185	320
New York	4,461	861	24.8	213	28.6	1,994	2,153	2,492
North Carolina.........	2,528	530	1.0	71	19.8	242	786	1,489
North Dakota..........	210	31	0.6	24	13.0	16	73	152
Ohio	3,889	521	2.5	119	20.7	416	1,351	2,320
Oklahoma............	1,079	191	0.6	41	19.3	91	414	701
Oregon..............	949	165	3.4	56	19.6	88	355	660
Pennsylvania..........	3,818	690	6.4	145	21.6	681	1,589	2,226
Rhode Island..........	376	58	2.5	10	19.2	40	132	206
South Carolina.........	1,235	277	1.1	31	20.5	137	402	720
South Dakota	233	33	0.3	31	13.8	17	76	166
Tennessee	1,763	324	1.3	52	21.5	181	593	1,079
Texas...............	5,821	1,134	2.2	185	22.2	489	2,190	3,392
Utah	541	111	2.3	26	18.9	29	153	355
Vermont	200	36	0.7	17	18.0	17	72	122
Virginia..............	2,281	500	4.0	103	24.0	205	717	1,370
Washington...........	1,701	282	4.5	86	22.0	141	582	1,149
West Virginia	493	107	1.1	16	21.0	94	247	347
Wisconsin............	1,751	270	2.5	114	18.3	170	600	1,052
Wyoming	154	28	1.4	9	15.4	8	48	113

[1] Excludes persons who worked at home.

Source: U.S. Bureau of the Census, Census of Population and Housing, 1990.

No. 1039. National Personal Transportation Survey (NPTS)— Summary of Travel Trends: 1969 to 1990

[Data obtained by collecting information on all trips taken by the respondent on a specific day (known as travel day), combined with longer trips taken over a 2-week period (known as travel period). Contains data from previous NPTS surveys. For compatibility with previous survey data, all data are based only on trips taken during travel day. Be aware that terminology changes from survey to survey. See source for details]

CHARACTERISTIC	Unit	1969	1977	1983	1990	Percent change, 1969-90	Annual percent change, 1969-90
Households, total	1,000	62,504	75,412	85,371	93,347	49.0	1.9
1 person	1,000	10,980	16,214	19,354	22,999	109.0	3.6
2 persons	1,000	18,448	22,925	27,169	30,114	63.0	2.4
3 persons	1,000	10,746	13,046	14,756	16,128	50.0	2.0
4 persons or more	1,000	22,330	23,227	24,092	24,106	8.0	0.4
Persons, total	1,000	197,213	213,141	229,453	[1]239,416	21.0	0.9
Under 16 yrs. old	1,000	60,100	54,958	53,682	54,303	-10.0	-0.5
16-19 yrs. old	1,000	14,598	16,552	15,268	13,851	-5.0	-0.2
20-34 yrs. old	1,000	40,060	52,252	60,788	59,517	49.0	1.9
35-64 yrs. old	1,000	62,982	66,988	75,353	82,480	31.0	1.3
65 yrs. old and over	1,000	19,473	22,391	24,362	26,955	38.0	1.6
5 yrs. old and over	1,000	(NA)	198,434	212,932	222,101	12.0	0.9
Males, total	1,000	94,465	102,521	111,514	114,441	21.0	0.8
16 yrs. old and over	1,000	66,652	74,542	83,645	86,432	30.0	1.1
Females	1,000	102,748	110,620	117,939	124,975	22.0	0.8
16 yrs. old and over	1,000	73,526	83,721	92,080	96,371	31.0	1.1
Licensed drivers	1,000	102,986	127,552	147,015	163,025	58.0	2.2
Male	1,000	57,981	66,199	75,639	80,289	38.0	1.6
Female	1,000	45,005	61,353	71,376	82,707	84.0	2.9
Workers	1,000	75,758	93,019	103,244	118,343	56.0	2.1
Male	1,000	48,487	55,625	58,849	63,996	32.0	1.3
Female	1,000	27,271	37,394	44,395	54,334	99.0	3.3
Households with—							
No vehicle	1,000	12,876	11,538	11,548	8,573	-33.0	-1.9
One vehicle	1,000	30,252	26,092	28,780	30,654	1.0	0.1
Two vehicles	1,000	16,501	25,942	28,632	35,872	117.0	3.8
Three or more Vehicles	1,000	2,875	11,840	16,411	18,248	535.0	9.2
All vehicles available	1,000	72,500	120,098	143,714	165,221	128.0	4.0
Vehicle trips	Millions	87,284	108,826	126,874	158,927	82.0	2.9
Vehicle miles of travel (VMT)	Millions	775,940	907,603	1,002,139	1,409,600	82.0	2.9
Person trips	Millions	145,146	211,778	224,385	249,562	72.0	2.6
Person miles of travel	Millions	1,404,137	1,879,215	1,946,662	2,315,300	65.0	2.4
Ratios:							
Persons per household	Number	[2]3.16	2.83	2.69	2.56	(NA)	(NA)
Vehicles per household	Number	[2]1.16	1.59	1.68	1.77	(NA)	(NA)
Licensed drivers per household	Number	[2]1.65	1.69	1.72	1.75	(NA)	(NA)
Vehicles per licensed driver	Number	[2]0.70	0.94	0.98	1.01	(NA)	(NA)
Workers per household	Number	[2]1.21	1.23	1.21	1.27	(NA)	(NA)
Vehicles per worker	Number	[2]0.96	1.29	1.39	1.40	(NA)	(NA)
Daily vehicle trips per household	Number	[2]3.83	3.95	4.07	4.66	(NA)	(NA)
Daily VMT per household	Number	[2]34.01	32.97	32.16	41.37	(NA)	(NA)
Average vehicle trip length (miles)	Number	[2]8.89	8.34	7.90	8.87	(NA)	(NA)
Average annual VMT	Miles	12,423	12,036	11,739	15,100	22.0	(NA)
Home to work	Miles	4,183	3,815	3,538	4,853	16.0	(NA)
Shopping	Miles	929	1,336	1,567	1,743	88.0	(NA)
Other family or personal business	Miles	1,270	1,444	1,816	3,014	137.0	(NA)
Social and recreational	Miles	4,094	3,286	3,534	4,060	-1.0	(NA)
Average annual vehicle trips	Number	1,396	1,442	1,486	1,702	22.0	(NA)
Home to work	Number	445	423	414	448	0.7	(NA)
Shopping	Number	213	268	297	345	62.0	(NA)
Other family or personal business	Number	195	215	272	411	111.0	(NA)
Social and recreational	Number	312	320	335	349	12.0	(NA)
Average vehicle trip length	Miles	8.9	8.4	7.9	9.0	1.0	(NA)
Home to work	Miles	9.4	9.1	8.5	11.0	17.0	(NA)
Shopping	Miles	4.4	5.0	5.3	5.1	16.0	(NA)
Other family or personal business	Miles	6.5	6.8	6.7	7.4	14.0	(NA)
Social and recreational	Miles	13.1	10.3	10.5	11.8	-10.0	(NA)
Average vehicle occupancy [3]	Persons	(NA)	1.9	1.7	1.6	[4]-1.3	(NA)
Home to work	Persons	(NA)	1.3	1.3	1.1	[4]-1.3	(NA)
Shopping	Persons	(NA)	2.1	1.8	1.7	[4]-1.6	(NA)
Other family or personal business	Persons	(NA)	2.0	1.8	1.8	[4]-0.8	(NA)
Social and recreational	Persons	(NA)	2.4	2.1	2.1	[4]-1.0	(NA)
Journey-to-work trip mode	Percent	100.0	100.0	100.0	100.0	(NS)	(NS)
Auto	Percent	82.7	80.5	77.6	91.4	(NS)	(NS)
Truck [5]	Percent	8.1	12.5	14.8	(NA)	(NS)	(NS)
Public transit	Percent	8.4	4.7	5.8	5.5	(NS)	(NS)
Other	Percent	0.8	2.3	1.8	3.1	(NS)	(NS)

NA Not available. NS Percent change irrelevant. [1] Includes "don't know" and "refusals". [2] Excludes pickups and other light-trucks as household vehicles. [3] Includes other purposes not shown separately. [4] Change from 1977. [5] Household based trucks, primarily pickups.

Source: Federal Highway Administration, *National Personal Transportation Survey, Summary of Travel Trends, 1969, 1977, 1983,* and *1990.*

No. 1040. Roadway Congestion: 1993

[Various federal, state, and local information sources were used to develop the data base with the primary source being the Federal Highway Administration's Highway Performance Monitoring System]

URBANIZED AREA	DAILY VEHICLE MILES OF TRAVEL		VEHICLE HOURS OF DELAY		ANNUAL CONGESTION COST		
	Total miles (1,000)	Per lane-mile of freeway	Total hours	Per 1,000 persons	Per driver (dol.)	Per capita (dol.)	Delay and fuel cost (mil. dol.)
Total, average	17,760	13,180	232,570	90	500	390	1,060
Northeastern cities	28,090	13,100	485,060	100	550	450	2,200
Baltimore MD	18,800	13,570	169,250	80	460	360	770
Boston MA	21,750	14,310	363,330	120	660	550	1,650
Hartford CT	7,070	11,490	45,990	70	450	340	210
New York NY	88,080	13,970	1,729,640	100	580	460	7,900
Philadelphia PA	20,920	12,090	300,170	60	320	250	1,330
Pittsburgh PA	9,420	8,050	134,960	70	380	310	600
Washington DC	30,630	18,230	652,050	190	1,030	860	2,960
Midwestern cities	16,700	12,750	158,690	60	350	270	720
Chicago IL	42,130	16,300	660,800	90	500	390	2,990
Cincinnati OH	13,680	13,680	64,710	50	310	240	300
Cleveland OH	15,410	12,840	78,370	40	260	200	360
Columbus OH	10,180	12,110	55,730	60	320	250	250
Detroit MI	29,600	16,130	541,240	140	820	600	2,420
Indianapolis IN	9,500	11,590	41,460	40	250	200	190
Kansas City MO	15,630	9,990	51,210	40	230	180	230
Louisville KY	7,600	11,780	41,100	50	280	220	180
Milwaukee WI	7,800	12,890	54,100	40	260	200	250
Minn-St. Paul MN	20,700	13,350	135,750	60	360	290	620
Oklahoma City OK	7,750	10,470	29,150	30	200	150	130
St. Louis MO	20,600	11,870	150,670	80	440	340	680
Southern cities	9,020	12,570	103,490	80	460	360	470
Atlanta GA	33,000	15,350	339,210	140	800	640	1,530
Charlotte NC	3,830	11,610	36,660	70	380	310	170
Ft. Lauderdale FL	9,300	12,830	91,720	70	380	320	420
Jacksonville FL	6,520	12,540	71,950	90	540	420	330
Memphis TN	5,400	11,490	32,550	40	210	160	150
Miami FL	10,580	15,900	259,170	130	760	600	1,160
Nashville TN	7,750	11,570	40,060	70	370	300	180
New Orleans LA	5,510	13,280	75,380	70	410	310	340
Norfolk VA	6,080	10,470	76,530	80	440	350	350
Orlando FL	6,730	10,350	60,130	60	350	290	270
Tampa FL	4,500	12,860	55,090	70	400	320	240
Southwestern cities	11,800	12,300	134,270	80	490	380	610
Albuquerque NM	2,920	11,680	32,140	60	350	270	150
Austin TX	6,580	12,180	68,310	120	670	530	310
Corpus Christi TX	2,160	9,370	6,010	20	130	90	30
Dallas TX	25,700	14,120	304,990	140	810	640	1,400
Denver CO	13,480	13,480	172,580	100	580	470	790
El Paso TX	3,820	10,190	15,210	30	170	120	70
Fort Worth TX	13,840	12,300	128,930	100	630	480	590
Houston TX	32,960	14,650	436,450	150	890	680	2,000
Phoenix AZ	10,400	13,870	196,050	90	550	420	890
Salt Lake City UT	6,430	11,800	31,460	40	210	160	140
San Antonio TX	11,530	11,640	84,820	70	420	320	390
Western cities	29,130	15,650	412,630	120	720	570	1,890
Honolulu HI	5,600	14,000	68,750	100	550	470	320
Los Angeles CA	113,000	20,430	1,891,260	160	920	720	8,620
Portland OR.	8,640	13,820	98,450	90	510	410	450
Sacramento CA	10,630	13,040	87,680	70	430	330	400
San Bernardino-Riverside, CA. .	15,500	16,060	232,260	170	1,100	790	1,070
San Diego CA	27,830	15,900	169,010	70	390	310	790
San Fran-Oak CA	42,840	17,480	662,760	170	960	790	3,060
San Jose CA	16,880	13,720	193,680	130	750	580	890
Seattle-Everett WA	21,300	16,380	309,820	160	870	740	1,420

Source: Texas Transportation Institute, College Station, Texas; *Roadway Congestion in Major Urban Areas,* annual (copyright).

No. 1041. Motor Vehicle Accidents—Number and Deaths: 1972 to 1996

ITEM	Unit	1972 [1]	1980	1985	1990	1992	1993	1994	1995	1996
Motor vehicle accidents [2]	Million .	17.0	17.9	19.3	11.5	(NA)	11.9	11.2	10.7	11.2
Cars	Million .	24.5	22.8	25.6	14.3	(NA)	14.1	13.5	12.3	13.3
Trucks	Million .	3.5	5.5	6.1	4.4	(NA)	5.9	5.2	4.5	4.8
Motorcycles	1,000 .	343	560	480	180	(NA)	187	178	152	135
Motor vehicle deaths within 1 yr. [3] . .	1,000 .	56.3	53.2	45.9	46.8	41.0	41.9	42.7	43.9	43.3
Noncollision accidents	1,000 .	15.8	14.7	12.6	4.9	4.1	4.2	4.3	4.4	4.6
Collision accidents:										
With other motor vehicles	1,000 .	23.9	23.0	19.9	19.9	17.6	18.3	19.3	19.4	19.3
With pedestrians	1,000 .	10.3	9.7	8.5	7.3	6.3	6.4	5.9	6.3	6.1
With fixed objects	1,000 .	3.9	3.7	3.2	13.1	11.7	11.5	11.8	12.3	12.0
Deaths within 30 days [4]	1,000 .	54.6	51.1	43.8	44.6	39.3	40.2	40.7	41.8	41.9
Vehicle occupants	1,000 .	41.4	36.8	31.5	33.9	30.5	31.1	32.0	33.1	33.4
Pedestrians	1,000 .	10.2	8.1	6.8	6.5	5.5	5.6	5.5	5.6	5.4
Motorcyclists [5]	1,000 .	3.0	5.1	4.6	3.2	2.4	2.4	2.3	2.2	2.2
Bicyclists . . . . [4][6]	1,000 .	1.0	1.0	0.9	0.9	0.7	0.8	0.8	0.8	0.8
Traffic death rates:										
Per 100,000 resident population. .	Rate . .	26.2	22.5	18.4	17.9	15.4	15.6	15.6	15.9	15.8
Per 100,000 registered vehicles . .	Rate . .	44.5	34.8	26.5	24.3	21.2	21.3	21.2	21.2	20.8
Per 100 million vehicle miles . . .	Rate . .	4.3	3.3	2.5	2.1	1.7	1.7	1.7	1.7	1.7
Per 100,000 licensed drivers	Rate . .	46.1	35.2	27.9	26.7	22.7	23.2	23.2	23.6	23.3
Motor vehicle accidents [7]	Million .	24.9	24.1	32.5	33.4	37.8	32.8	33.9	34.5	35.0
Injuries [7] . . . . [7][8]	1,000 .	5,190	5,230	5,044	5,560	5,445	5,675	5,885	6,025	6,115
Economic loss [7][8]	Bil. dol.	28.7	57.1	76.0	95.9	98.1	104.1	110.5	115.6	120.8

NA Not available.   [1] Represents peak year for deaths from motor vehicle accidents.   [2] Covers only accidents occurring on the road.   [3] Deaths that occur within 1 year of accident. Includes collision categories not shown separately.   [4] Within 30 days of accident. Source: U.S. National Highway Traffic Safety Administration, unpublished data from Fatal Accident Reporting System.   [5] Includes motor scooters and motorized bicycles (mopeds).   [6] Based on 30-day definition of traffic deaths. [7] Source: Insurance Information Institute, New York, NY, *Insurance Facts (copyright)*. Estimates based on official reports from a representative cross-section of states. Includes all motor vehicle accidents on and off the road and all injuries regardless of length of disability.   [8] Wage loss; legal, medical, hospital, and funeral expenses; insurance administrative costs; and property damage.

Source: Except as noted, National Safety Council, Itasca, IL, *Accident Facts,* annual (copyright).

No. 1042. Motor Vehicle Deaths, by State: 1990 to 1996

[Includes both traffic and nontraffic motor vehicle deaths. See source for definitions]

STATE	1990	1994	1995	1996	MILEAGE RATE [1] 1990	MILEAGE RATE [1] 1996	STATE	1990	1994	1995	1996	MILEAGE RATE [1] 1990	MILEAGE RATE [1] 1996
U.S.. .	47,151	42,700	43,363	43,300	2.2	1.8	MO	1,174	1,089	1,110	1,148	2.3	1.9
AL	1,234	1,083	1,111	1,142	2.9	2.2	MT.	225	202	215	198	2.7	2.1
AK	102	85	86	80	2.6	1.9	NE	289	271	254	293	2.1	1.8
AZ	947	915	1,040	993	2.7	2.5	NV	405	294	312	348	4.0	2.4
AR	625	611	631	615	3.0	2.3	NH	154	119	118	134	1.6	1.2
CA	5,411	4,226	4,165	3,972	2.1	1.4	NJ	908	761	776	818	1.5	1.3
CO	583	585	645	434	2.1	1.2	NM	534	447	485	481	3.3	2.2
CT	395	310	318	310	1.5	1.1	NY	2,318	1,658	1,668	1,562	2.2	1.3
DE	151	112	123	120	2.3	1.6	NC	1,489	1,431	1,438	1,492	2.4	1.9
DC	91	-		(NA)	2.7	(NA)	ND	128	88	74	85	2.2	1.3
FL	3,049	2,735	2,812	2,813	2.8	2.2	OH	1,708	1,371	1,357	1,393	2.0	1.4
GA	1,659	1,438	1,494	1,578	2.3	1.8	OK	684	695	674	775	2.1	2.0
HI	186	122	127	145	2.3	1.8	OR	608	491	572	524	2.3	1.7
ID	259	249	263	258	2.6	2.1	PA	1,767	1,441	1,480	1,470	2.1	1.5
IL	1,650	1,554	1,589	1,475	2.0	1.5	RI	104	63	69	69	1.5	1.0
IN	1,097	979	960	981	2.0	1.5	SC	987	847	882	930	2.9	2.4
IA	481	478	527	465	2.1	1.8	SD	166	154	158	175	2.4	2.2
KS	453	442	438	491	2.0	1.9	TN	1,312	1,214	1,240	1,211	2.8	2.1
KY	850	791	856	844	2.5	2.0	TX	3,381	3,142	3,172	3,738	2.1	2.0
LA	1,023	838	880	809	2.7	2.1	UT	296	343	321	321	2.0	1.7
ME	215	188	189	168	1.8	1.3	VT	94	77	106	88	1.6	1.4
MD.	741	656	682	614	1.8	1.3	VA	1,091	930	900	869	1.8	1.2
MA	655	440	448	417	1.4	0.9	WA	875	641	654	690	2.0	1.4
MI	1,633	1,419	1,537	1,505	2.0	1.7	WV	502	356	376	344	3.3	1.9
MN.	644	644	597	576	1.7	1.3	WI	825	712	739	759	1.9	1.5
MS.	863	792	868	811	3.5	2.7	WY	130	144	170	143	2.2	2.0

- Represents zero.   NA Not available.   [1] Deaths per 100 million vehicle miles.

Source: National Safety Council, Itasca, IL, *Accident Facts,* annual (copyright).

No. 1043. Fatal Motor Vehicle Accidents—National Summary: 1980 to 1996

[Based on data from the Fatal Accident Reporting System (FARS). FARS gathers data on accidents that result in loss of human life. FARS is operated and maintained by National Highway Traffic Safety Administration's (NHTSA) National Center for Statistics and Analysis (NCSA). FARS data are gathered on motor vehicle accidents that occurred on a roadway customarily open to the public, resulting in the death of a person within 30 days of the accident. Collection of these data depend on the use of police, hospital, medical examiner/coroner, and Emergency Medical Services reports; state vehicle registration, driver licensing, and highway department files; and vital statistics documents and death certificates. See source for further detail]

ITEM	1980	1985	1990	1992	1993	1994	1995	1996
Fatal accidents, total	45,284	39,196	39,836	34,942	35,780	36,254	37,241	37,351
One vehicle involved	28,306	22,875	23,445	20,388	20,569	20,526	21,256	21,046
Two or more vehicles involved	16,978	16,321	16,391	14,554	15,211	15,728	15,985	16,305
Persons killed in fatal accidents	51,091	43,825	44,599	39,250	40,150	40,716	41,817	41,907
Occupants [1]	41,927	36,043	37,134	32,880	33,574	34,318	35,291	35,579
Drivers	28,816	25,337	25,750	22,584	23,142	23,691	24,390	24,456
Passengers	12,972	10,619	11,276	10,211	10,361	10,518	10,784	11,021
Nonmotorists [1]	9,164	7,782	7,465	6,370	6,576	6,398	6,526	6,328
Pedestrians	8,070	6,808	6,482	5,549	5,649	5,489	5,584	5,412
Pedalcyclists	965	890	859	723	816	802	833	761
Occupant fatalities by type of vehicle, total	41,927	36,043	37,134	32,880	33,574	34,318	35,291	35,579
Passenger cars [1]	27,449	23,212	24,092	21,387	21,566	21,997	22,423	22,416
Mini-compact	3,141	3,571	3,556	2,714	2,635	2,339	2,207	2,011
Subcompact	4,158	4,422	4,753	4,314	4,333	4,721	4,584	4,506
Compact	927	2,635	5,310	5,354	5,707	6,322	6,899	7,161
Intermediate	3,878	4,391	4,849	4,418	4,483	4,407	4,666	4,626
Full size	4,831	2,974	2,386	2,120	2,067	2,074	2,116	2,111
Largest size	6,746	3,612	2,249	1,676	1,608	1,486	1,297	1,246
Motorcycles	4,961	4,417	3,129	2,291	2,336	2,190	2,114	2,045
Other motorized cycles	183	147	115	104	113	130	212	115
Multipurpose vehicles	895	855	1,214	1,335	1,521	1,757	1,935	2,138
Light trucks	6,591	5,834	7,387	6,763	6,990	7,147	7,633	7,763
Pickup	5,483	4,640	5,979	5,385	5,538	5,574	5,938	5,884
Van	1,000	791	1,154	1,292	1,365	1,508	1,639	1,829
Medium trucks	285	157	134	99	90	109	96	89
Heavy trucks	977	820	571	486	515	561	552	532
Buses	46	57	32	28	18	18	33	21
Persons involved in fatal accident	113,289	104,045	107,777	95,691	97,589	98,945	102,102	102,955
Occupants [1]	103,049	95,482	99,297	88,367	90,150	91,644	94,621	95,810
Drivers	62,957	57,883	58,893	51,901	53,401	54,549	56,164	56,793
Passengers	39,892	37,477	40,229	36,330	36,599	36,898	38,252	38,772
Nonoccupants	10,240	8,563	8,480	7,324	7,439	7,301	7,478	7,138
Vehicle miles traveled (VMT) (100 million)	15,273	17,742	21,444	22,471	22,967	23,576	24,227	24,822
Licensed drivers (1,000)	145,295	156,868	167,015	173,125	173,149	175,403	176,628	179,539
Registered vehicles (1,000)	161,490	177,098	192,915	194,427	198,041	201,802	197,065	201,626
Fatalities by road type [1]	(NA)	(NA)	44,599	39,250	40,150	40,716	41,817	41,907
Interstate	4,427	4,148	4,993	4,350	4,566	4,713	4,835	5,231
Federal-aid primary	(NA)	14,526	14,203	12,052	(NA)	(NA)	(NA)	(NA)
Federal-aid secondary	(NA)	6,429	6,892	5,849	(NA)	(NA)	(NA)	(NA)
Federal-aid urban	(NA)	8,116	8,432	6,582	(NA)	(NA)	(NA)	(NA)
Nonfederal-aid	(NA)	10,408	10,039	8,826	(NA)	(NA)	(NA)	(NA)
Fatal accidents by the highest blood alcohol concentration (BAC) in accident:								
0.00 percent	(NA)	48.5	50.6	54.5	56.5	59.3	58.7	59.2
0.01 to 0.09 percent	(NA)	10.3	9.7	9.1	8.5	8.5	8.6	8.7
0.10 percent and over	(NA)	41.2	39.7	36.4	35.0	32.2	32.6	32.2
RATES								
Fatality rate by age group:								
Under 5 years old	6.9	5.2	4.9	4.5	4.5	4.8	4.3	4.6
5 years to 15 years old	8.7	7.4	6.4	5.9	5.8	6.0	5.9	5.7
16 years to 24 years old	46.0	37.1	35.2	29.5	30.2	30.8	31.1	30.5
25 years to 44 years old	24.6	19.6	19.7	16.6	16.9	16.3	17.2	16.9
45 years to 64 years old	17.2	14.5	14.9	13.1	13.0	13.3	13.4	13.7
65 years to 79 years old	19.6	18.0	18.8	17.9	17.9	18.7	18.5	18.6
80 years old and over	25.3	25.1	26.8	26.0	28.0	28.2	27.8	27.9
Fatalities per 100 million VMT	3.3	2.5	2.1	1.8	1.7	1.7	1.7	1.7
Fatalities per 100,000 licensed drivers	35.2	27.9	26.7	22.7	23.2	23.2	23.7	23.3
Licensed driver per person	0.6	0.7	0.7	0.7	0.7	0.7	0.7	0.7
VMT per registered vehicle	9,458	10,018	11,107	11,558	12,189	11,683	11,793	11,807
Fatalities per 100,000 registered vehicles	31.6	24.8	23.1	20.2	21.3	20.2	21.2	20.8
Fatal crashes per 100 million VMT	2.9	2.2	1.9	1.6	1.6	1.5	1.5	1.5
Involved vehicles per fatal crash	1.4	1.5	1.5	1.5	1.5	1.5	1.5	1.5
Fatalities per fatal crash	1.2	1.1	1.1	1.1	1.1	1.1	1.1	1.1
Average occupants per fatal crash	2.3	2.4	2.5	2.5	2.5	2.5	2.5	2.6
Fatalities per 100,000 population	22.5	18.4	17.9	15.4	15.6	15.6	15.8	15.8

NA Not available. [1] Includes items not shown separately.

Source: National Highway Traffic Safety Administration, *Fatal Accident Reporting System,* annual.

No. 1044. Motor Vehicle Occupants and Non-Occupants Killed and Injured: 1985 to 1996

[Vehicle occupants accounted for almost 84 percent of traffic fatalities in 1995. The remaining 16 percent were pedestrians, pedalcyclists, and other non-occupants]

YEAR	Total	OCCUPANTS						NON-OCCUPANTS			
		Total	Passen-ger cars	Light trucks	Large trucks	Motor-cycles	Buses	Total	Ped-estrian	Pedal-cyclist	Other
KILLED											
1985	43,825	36,043	23,212	6,689	977	4,564	57	7,782	6,808	890	84
1986	46,087	38,234	24,944	7,317	926	4,566	39	7,853	6,779	941	133
1987	46,390	38,565	25,132	8,058	852	4,036	51	7,825	6,745	948	132
1988	47,087	39,170	25,808	8,306	911	3,662	54	7,917	6,870	911	136
1989	45,582	38,087	25,063	8,551	858	3,141	50	7,495	6,556	832	107
1990	44,599	37,134	24,092	8,601	705	3,244	32	7,465	6,482	859	124
1991	41,508	34,740	22,385	8,391	661	2,806	31	6,768	5,801	843	124
1992	39,250	32,880	21,387	8,098	585	2,395	28	6,370	5,549	723	98
1993	40,150	33,574	21,566	8,511	605	2,449	18	6,576	5,649	816	111
1994	40,716	34,318	21,997	8,904	670	2,320	18	6,398	5,489	802	107
1995	41,817	35,291	22,423	9,568	648	2,227	33	6,526	5,584	833	109
1996	41,907	35,581	22,416	9,901	621	2,160	21	6,326	5,412	761	153
INJURED											
1988	3,416,000	3,224,000	2,585,000	478,000	37,000	105,000	15,000	192,000	110,000	75,000	8,000
1989	3,284,000	3,088,000	2,431,000	511,000	43,000	83,000	15,000	196,000	112,000	73,000	11,000
1990	3,231,000	3,044,000	2,376,000	505,000	42,000	84,000	33,000	187,000	105,000	75,000	7,000
1991	3,097,000	2,931,000	2,235,000	563,000	28,000	80,000	21,000	166,000	88,000	67,000	11,000
1992	3,070,000	2,908,000	2,232,000	545,000	34,000	65,000	20,000	162,000	89,000	63,000	10,000
1993	3,125,000	2,958,000	2,257,000	590,000	32,000	58,000	17,000	166,000	93,000	65,000	9,000
1994	3,215,000	3,056,000	2,332,000	619,000	30,000	56,000	15,000	159,000	90,000	60,000	9,000
1995	3,386,000	3,232,000	2,416,000	709,000	30,000	55,000	18,000	154,000	84,000	61,000	9,000
1996	3,511,000	3,360,000	2,478,000	768,000	33,000	56,000	20,000	151,000	82,000	59,000	11,000

Source: U.S. National Highway Traffic Safety Administration, *Traffic Safety Facts 1995, Overview,* annual.

No. 1045. Traffic Fatalities in Crashes Involving a Medium/Heavy Truck, by State: 1996

[Medium/heavy trucks represents trucks over 10,000 pounds GVW, including single unit trucks]

STATE	Total	Occu-pant fatali-ties med/heavy trucks	Occu-pant fatali-ties other vehicles	Non-occu-pant fatali-ties	STATE	Total	Occu-pant fatali-ties med/heavy trucks	Occu-pant fatali-ties other vehicles	Non-occu-pant fatali-ties
United States	5,126	621	4,072	433	Missouri	168	19	139	10
					Montana	21	1	18	2
Alabama	151	19	123	9	Nebraska	63	7	55	1
Alaska	6	-	5	1	Nevada	44	5	35	4
Arizona	98	11	78	9	New Hampshire	12	-	11	1
Arkansas	104	24	78	2					
California	390	58	273	59	New Jersey	84	8	64	12
Colorado	63	7	53	3	New Mexico	56	7	39	10
Connecticut	34	5	24	5	New York	161	16	107	38
Delaware	14	1	11	2	North Carolina	183	19	155	9
District of Columbia	4	-	2	2	North Dakota	12	-	12	-
Florida	305	25	250	30	Ohio	225	16	201	8
Georgia	221	37	169	15	Oklahoma	99	23	75	1
Hawaii	13	2	9	2	Oregon	64	9	54	1
Idaho	38	8	29	1	Pennsylvania	185	22	145	18
Illinois	152	16	124	12	Rhode Island	6	1	1	4
Indiana	166	18	141	7					
Iowa	83	5	74	4	South Carolina	111	14	90	7
Kansas	64	15	48	1	South Dakota	24	1	21	2
Kentucky	100	16	75	9	Tennessee	175	23	140	12
Louisiana	94	8	69	17	Texas	450	53	370	27
Maine	15	2	13	-	Utah	35	4	27	4
					Vermont	10	-	9	1
Maryland	70	7	57	6	Virginia	121	20	91	10
Massachusetts	39	2	25	12	Washington	73	10	54	9
Michigan	162	15	135	12	West Virginia	60	19	41	-
Minnesota	77	2	68	7	Wisconsin	105	3	96	6
Mississippi	100	16	77	7	Wyoming	16	2	12	2

- Represents zero.

Source: U.S. National Highway Traffic Safety Administration, *Traffic Safety Facts annual.*

No. 1046. Speeding-Related Traffic Fatalities and Costs by Road Type and Speed Limit: 1996

[Includes fatalities that occurred on roads for which the speed limit was unknown. Includes costs for crashes that occurred on unknown road types. Totals may not equal sum of components due to independent rounding]

STATE	Traffic fatalities, total	SPEEDING-RELATED FATALITIES BY ROAD TYPE AND SPEED							
		Interstate		Noninterstate					
		Over 55 mph	55 mph	55 mph	50 mph	45 mph	40 mph	35 mph	Under 35 mph
United States	41,907	1,210	476	4,439	543	1,429	815	1,316	1,411
Alabama	1,143	37	11	157	16	109	29	39	26
Alaska	80	1	5	6	-	4	1	2	4
Arizona	993	29	19	46	15	49	35	37	38
Arkansas	615	11	9	126	-	21	11	15	17
California	3,989	230	15	385	55	126	113	179	142
Colorado	617	39	8	98	15	27	23	25	30
Connecticut	310	-	8	8	-	10	7	17	37
Delaware	116	-	1	4	11	-	3	2	3
District of Columbia	62	-	1	-	2	4	-	2	21
Florida	2,753	51	36	128	29	119	66	84	92
Georgia	1,574	28	18	168	7	46	13	47	36
Hawaii	148	-	3	5	1	6	-	18	19
Idaho	258	15	1	29	14	7	-	14	10
Illinois	1,477	33	48	215	5	18	30	7	128
Indiana	984	12	11	58	8	17	19	21	32
Iowa	465	9	-	24	5	7	-	10	8
Kansas	491	7	3	52	4	4	8	9	17
Kentucky	841	13	6	165	-	19	-	38	8
Louisiana	781	9	8	73	7	21	7	18	15
Maine	169	2	1	11	16	27	3	9	6
Maryland	608	3	8	10	11	6	17	10	23
Massachusetts	417	19	6	5	2	8	16	23	30
Michigan	1,505	28	19	178	8	35	12	34	45
Minnesota	576	2	8	102	7	8	1	4	21
Mississippi	811	20	7	49	19	16	11	8	9
Missouri	1,149	52	15	216	4	21	27	49	43
Montana	200	5	1	22	-	3	-	4	3
Nebraska	293	16	-	11	29	2	2	3	6
Nevada	348	19	-	9	4	29	-	17	14
New Hampshire	134	-	2	3	3	2	6	7	7
New Jersey	818	-	14	12	20	5	6	2	23
New Mexico	481	30	2	44	15	15	4	24	15
New York	1,564	10	15	163	16	17	26	18	53
North Carolina	1,493	22	15	334	2	79	1	70	6
North Dakota	85	1	-	35	1	1	-	1	3
Ohio	1,395	23	6	203	3	23	12	44	38
Oklahoma	772	47	8	66	15	46	21	14	12
Oregon	524	11	2	90	-	8	12	14	6
Pennsylvania	1,469	28	20	160	12	114	66	87	41
Rhode Island	69	-	4	1	5	1	-	2	12
South Carolina	930	40	14	177	12	89	19	45	38
South Dakota	175	5	2	20	1	8	1	1	1
Tennessee	1,239	23	14	124	10	56	38	26	41
Texas	3,741	163	61	274	48	114	101	115	122
Utah	321	28	2	17	7	3	14	4	10
Vermont	88	5	1	1	22	1	7	8	3
Virginia	875	22	10	129	1	35	4	17	15
Washington	712	22	3	51	49	15	14	45	38
West Virginia	345	12	1	51	2	7	3	15	7
Wisconsin	761	13	4	119	2	16	4	10	26
Wyoming	143	15	-	5	3	5	2	2	11

- Represents or rounds to zero.

Source: U.S. National Highway Traffic Safety Administration, *Traffic Safety Facts 1995, Speeding. Traffic Safety Facts 1995, Speeding.*

No. 1047. Highway Mileage—Travel Summary: 1980 to 1994

YEAR AND TYPE OF SYSTEM	Highway mileage (1,000)	Vehicle miles of travel (bil.)	Daily vehicle miles per mile	FATAL ACCIDENTS		NONFATAL INJURY ACCIDENTS		FATALITIES [2]	
				Number	Rate [1]	Number (1,000)	Rate [1]	Number	Rate [1]
1980	3,857	1,527	1,082	45,284	2.96	2,008	131	51,091	3.35
1985	3,862	1,774	1,259	39,168	2.21	2,219	125	43,825	2.47
1990	3,880	2,148	1,516	39,779	1.85	2,501	116	44,529	2.07
1991	3,889	2,172	1,530	36,895	1.70	2,210	102	41,462	(NA)
1992	3,902	2,240	1,568	34,928	1.56	2,216	99	39,235	1.75
1993	3,905	2,297	1,611	35,750	1.56	(NA)	(NA)	40,115	1.75
1994	3,907	2,360	1,655	36,223	1.53	(NA)	(NA)	40,676	1.72

NA Not available.　[1] Rate per 100 million vehicle miles of travel.　[2] Represents fatalities occurring within 30 days of accident. Excludes nontraffic accidents which, for example, occur outside the rights-of-way or other boundaries of roads that are open for public use.

Source: U.S. Federal Highway Administration, *Fatal and Injury Accident Rates on Public Roads in the United States*, annual.

No. 1048. Alcohol Involvement for Drivers in Fatal Crashes: 1985 and 1995

[BAC = blood alcohol concentration]

DRIVERS INVOLVED IN FATAL CRASHES	1985		1995		Change in percentage, 1985-95
	Number of drivers	Percentage with BAC of .10% or greater	Number of drivers	Percentage with BAC of .10% or greater	
Total drivers [1]	57,883	25.7	56,155	19.3	-25.0
Drivers by age group:					
16 to 20 years old...............	9,386	23.9	7,738	12.7	-47.0
21 to 24 years old...............	9,046	35.3	6,268	27.8	-21.0
25 to 34 years old...............	15,257	32.4	13,029	26.8	-17.0
35 to 44 years old...............	8,892	24.3	10,664	22.8	-6.0
45 to 64 years old...............	9,262	16.7	10,884	14.3	-14.0
65 years old and over	4,479	7.6	6,238	5.0	-34.0
Drivers by sex:					
Male..........................	44,846	28.2	41,216	21.8	-23.0
Female........................	12,142	15.5	14,179	11.2	-28.0
Drivers by vehicle type:					
Passenger cars	34,071	26.1	30,692	19.2	-27.0
Light trucks...................	12,372	28.7	17,420	22.4	-22.0
Large trucks..................	5,091	3.6	4,391	1.3	-62.0
Motorcycles...................	4,598	39.3	2,257	29.1	-26.0

[1] Does not add, due to unknown or other data not included.

Source: National Safety Council, Itasca, IL, *Accident Facts*, 1997 edition (copyright).

No. 1049. Age of Driver and Number in Accidents, 1996

AGE GROUP	Number	Percent	DRIVERS IN ACCIDENTS				Per number of drivers	
			Fatal		All		Fatal [1]	All [2]
			Number	Percent	Number	Percent		
Total.	177,820,000	100.0	57,400	100.0	18,900,000	100.0	32	11
Under 16 years old.	61,000	(Z)	500	0.9	90,000	0.5	(3)	(3)
16 years old	1,578,000	0.9	1,200	2.1	580,000	3.1	76	37
17 years old	2,195,000	1.2	1,600	2.8	670,000	3.5	73	31
18 years old	2,432,000	1.4	1,900	3.3	710,000	3.8	78	29
19 years old	2,653,000	1.5	1,800	3.1	670,000	3.5	68	25
19 years old and under . .	8,919,000	5.0	7,000	12.2	2,720,000	14.4	78	30
20 years old	2,828,000	1.6	1,800	3.1	600,000	3.2	64	21
21 years old	2,864,000	1.6	1,900	3.3	590,000	3.1	66	21
22 years old	2,880,000	1.6	1,800	3.1	560,000	3.0	63	19
23 years old	3,065,000	1.7	1,600	2.8	540,000	2.9	52	18
24 years old	3,625,000	2.0	1,600	2.8	540,000	2.9	44	15
20 to 24 years old	15,262,000	8.6	8,700	15.2	2,830,000	15.0	57	19
25 to 34 years old	37,781,000	21.2	13,000	22.6	4,600,000	24.3	34	12
35 to 44 years old	40,415,000	22.7	11,700	20.4	3,840,000	20.3	29	10
45 to 54 years old	30,928,000	17.4	7,100	12.4	2,360,000	12.5	23	8
55 to 64 years old	19,345,000	10.9	4,100	7.1	1,210,000	6.4	21	6
65 to 74 years old	15,648,000	8.8	3,000	5.2	810,000	4.3	19	5
75 years old and over . . .	9,522,000	5.4	2,800	4.9	530,000	2.8	29	6

Z Less than .05.　[1] Per 100,000 licensed drivers.　[2] Per 100 licensed drivers.　[3] Rates for drivers under age 16 are substantially overstated due to the high proportion of unlicensed drivers involved.

Source: National Safety Council, Itasca, IL, *Accident Facts*, 1997 edition (copyright).

No. 1050. State Legislation—Alcohol and Road Safety Laws: Various Years

STATE	ALCOHOL LEGISLATION				MANDATORY BELT USE LAW		Motor-cycle helmet law [5]	Work zone speed law	1995/96 SPEED LIMIT CHANGES	
	Administrative license revocation since [1]	BAC limit [2]	Zero tolerance limit for minors [3]	Alcohol ignition interlock device [4]	Enforcement	Seating positions			Road types affected [6]	Applicable vehicles
Alabama	No	.10	No	No	Secondary	Front	Yes	Yes	1, 2	Raised to 70
Alaska	5/83	.10	(NA)	Yes	Secondary	All	18	No	No change	Remained at 65
Arizona	1992	.10	.00	No	Secondary	Front	18	No	3	Raised to 75
Arkansas	3/95	.10	.02	Yes	Secondary	Front	Yes	(NA)	No change	Remained at 65
California	1989	.08	.01	Yes	Primary	All	Yes	Yes	4	Raised to 70
Colorado	Yes	.10	No	Yes	Secondary	Front	No	Yes	(NA)	Raised to 65
Connecticut	1/90	.10	.02	No	Primary	[7]Front	18	[8]No	No change	Remained at 55
Delaware	Yes	.10	.02	Yes	Secondary	Front	[9][10]19	Yes	1	Raised to 65
District of Columbia	Yes	.10	.00	No	Secondary	[11]Front	Yes	Yes	No change	Remained at 55
Florida	Yes	.08	No	Yes	Secondary	Front	Yes	Yes	5	Raised to 70
Georgia	(NA)	.10	.04	Yes	Secondary	Front	Yes	Yes	1	Raised to 70
Hawaii	6/90	.08	No	No	Primary	Front	18	No	No change	Remained at 55
Idaho	7/94	.10	.02	Yes	Secondary	Front	18	No	1	Raised to 75
Illinois	1/86	.10	.00	Yes	Secondary	Front	No	Yes	1,2,3,6	Raised to 65
Indiana	Yes	.10	.02	Yes	Secondary	Front	[9]18	Yes	1	Remained at 65
Iowa	(NA)	.10	.02	Yes	Primary	Front	No	Yes	No change	Remained at 65
Kansas	1988	.08	.02	Yes	Secondary	Front	18	Yes	7	Raised to 70
Kentucky	No	.10	.02	No	Secondary	All	Yes	No	1, 5	Raised to 65
Louisiana	1/84	.10	[12].04	Yes	Primary	Front	Yes	No	No change	Remained at 65
Maine [13]	(NA)	.08	(NA)	No	Secondary	(NA)	[9][14]15	(NA)	No change	Remained at 65
Maryland	5/89	[15].10	.01	Yes	Secondary	[7][11]Front	Yes	No	No change	Remained at 65
Massachusetts [13]	(NA)	.10	(NA)	No	Secondary	All	Yes	(NA)	No change	Remained at 65
Michigan	No	.10	.02	Yes	Secondary	[7]Front	Yes	Yes	No change	Remained at 65
Minnesota	1976	.10	.01	No	Secondary	[7]Front	[9]18	Yes	No change	Remained at 65
Mississippi	No	.10	.08	No	Secondary	Front	Yes	Yes	1, 2	Raised to 70
Missouri	1987	.10	No	No	Secondary	Front	Yes	Yes	2, 9	Raised to 70
Montana	No	.10	.02	No	Secondary	All	18	Yes	All	(T)
Nebraska	1/93	.10	.02	Yes	Secondary	Front	Yes	No	1	Raised to 75
Nevada	1983	.10	No	Yes	Secondary	All	Yes	No	All	Raised to 75
New Hampshire	1/94	.08	.01	No		(NA)	18	Yes	1	Remained at 65
New Jersey	(NA)	.10	.01	No	Secondary	Front	Yes	[8]No	No change	Remained at 55
New Mexico [13]	(NA)	.08	.02	No	Primary	[7]Front	18	(NA)	(NA)	Raised to 75
New York	11/94	[15].10	(NA)	[17]Yes	Primary	[7]Front	Yes	(NA)	1	Raised to 65
North Carolina	1983	.08	No	No	Primary	Front	Yes	Yes	8	Raised to 65
North Dakota	1983	.10	No	No	Secondary	Front	18	Yes	No change	Remained at 65
Ohio	9/93	.10	.02	Yes	Secondary	Front	[14]18	[8]No	No change	Remained at 65
Oklahoma	(NA)	.10	.00	Yes	Secondary	Front	18	Yes	Varies	Raised to 75
Oregon	1983	.08	.00	Yes	Primary	All	Yes	No	9	Raised to 65
Pennsylvania	No	.10	No	No	Secondary	Front	Yes	Yes	1	Raised to 65
Rhode Island	No	.10	.04	[17]Yes	Secondary	All	([18])	No	1	Raised to 65
South Carolina	No	.10	No	No	Secondary	[19]Front	21	Yes	No change	Remained at 65
South Dakota	No	.10	No	No	Secondary	Front	18	Yes	All	Raised to 75
Tennessee	No	.10	.02	Yes	Secondary	[7]Front	Yes	Yes	2, 8	Raised to 65
Texas	1995	.10	.07	[17]Yes	Primary	Front	Yes	Yes	1, 2	Raised to 70
Utah	1983	.08	.00	Yes	Secondary	Front	18	(NA)	1	Raised to 75
Vermont	[16]Yes	.08	[12].02	No	Secondary	All	Yes	No	No change	Remained at 65
Virginia	1/95	.08	.02	Yes	Secondary	Front	Yes	No	No change	Remained at 65
Washington	[20]6/94	.10	.02	Yes	Secondary	All	Yes	Yes	1	Raised to 75
West Virginia	(NA)	.10	.02	Yes	Secondary	[7]Front	Yes	Yes	1, 4	Remained at 65
Wisconsin	1/88	[21].10	[22].00	[17]Yes	Secondary	[19]Front	[9]18	Yes	1, 3, 4	Raised to 75
Wyoming	1973	.10	No	No	Secondary	Front	18	No	1, 3, 4	Raised to 75

NA Not available. [1]Year original law became effective, not when grandfather clauses expired. [2]Blood alcohol concentration that constitutes the threshold of legal intoxication. [3]Blood alcohol concentration that constitutes "zero tolerance" threshold for minors less than 21 years old unless noted. [4]Legislation for instruments designed to prevent drivers from starting their cars when breath alcohol content is at or above a set point. [5]Presence of law or age below which riders are required to wear helmet. [6]"1" means rural interstates; "2" means four-lane highways; "3" means rural highways; "4" means inter/intra state freeways; "5" means rural interstates/turnpikes; "6" means county and township roads with no posted speed limit; "7" means separate multilane highways designated/posted by secretary of transportation; "8" means interstates within municipal city limits; "9" means turnpikes; "10" means interstates outside urban areas of population 50,000 or more plus others where posted. [7]Required for certain ages at all seating positions. [8]No work zone speed law per se, but double fine for violation. [9]Plus instruction permit holders. [10]Helmet possession required by all. [11]Excluding front center seat. [12]Blood alcohol concentration that constitutes "zero tolerance" threshold for minors less than 18 years of age. [13]Data from 1994/1995. [14]Plus novice license holders. [15]BAC of .07 is prima facie evidence of DUI (MD); BAC of .05-.10 constitutes driving while ability impaired (NY). [16]Revocation by judicial action (NY) or Dept. of Motor Vehicles (VT). [17]For repeat offenders. [18]Operators under 21 for first year; passengers. [19]Belt use required in rear seat if lap/shoulder belt is available. [20]Applies only to second DUI offense. [21]Different legal limit for repeat offenders. [22]Blood alcohol concentration that constitutes "zero tolerance" threshold for minors less than 19 years of age.
Source: National Safety Council, Itasca, IL, *Accident Facts* (copyright).

No. 1051. Motor Vehicle Safety Defect Recalls, by Domestic and Foreign Manufacturers: 1980 to 1996

[Covers manufacturers reporting to U.S. National Highway Traffic Administration under Section 151 of National Traffic and Motor Vehicle Safety Act of 1966, as amended]

MANUFACTURER	Unit	1980	1985	1989	1990	1991	1992	1993	1994	1995	1996
Motor vehicles:											
Total recall campaigns [1] . .	Number .	167	173	237	208	220	187	221	244	266	265
Domestic	Number .	129	137	182	159	168	142	178	178	190	197
Foreign.	Number .	38	36	55	49	52	45	43	66	76	68
Total vehicles recalled . . .	1,000 . . .	4,868	5,629	7,137	5,985	8,279	10,122	10,922	6,063	18,295	17,084
Domestic	1,000 . . .	3,943	4,995	6,173	4,070	6,646	6,545	7,655	4,280	9,041	15,104
Foreign.	1,000 . . .	925	634	964	1,915	1,633	3,577	3,267	1,784	9,259	1,980
Motor vehicle tires:											
Recall campaigns [1]	Number .	24	19	11	13	12	7	5	5	3	1
Tires recalled	1,000 . . .	7,070	28	115	172	153	8	6	93	10	6

[1] A recall campaign is the notification to the Secretary of the U.S. Dept. of Transportation and to owners, purchasers, and dealers of motor vehicles and motor vehicle equipment.

Source: U.S. National Highway Traffic Safety Administration, *Motor Vehicles Recall Campaigns*, annual.

No. 1052. Cost of Owning and Operating an Automobile: 1980 to 1997

ITEM	Unit	1980	1990	1992	1993	1994	1995	1996	1997
Cost per mile [1]	Cents	27.95	40.96	45.77	45.14	46.65	48.91	51.43	53.08
Cost per 10,000 miles [1] . . .	Dollars. . . .	2,795	4,096	4,577	4,514	4,665	4,891	5,143	5,308
Variable cost	Cents/mile .	7.62	8.40	9.10	9.30	9.20	10.00	10.10	10.80
Gas and oil	Cents/mile .	5.86	5.40	6.00	6.00	5.60	6.00	5.90	6.60
Maintenance.	Cents/mile .	1.12	2.10	2.20	2.40	2.50	2.60	2.80	2.80
Tires	Cents/mile .	0.64	0.90	0.90	0.90	1.10	1.40	1.40	1.40
Fixed cost	Dollars. . . .	(NA)	(NA)	3,667	3,584	3,745	3,891	4,133	4,228
Insurance.	Dollars. . . .	490	675	747	724	697	716	782	809
License and registration	Dollars. . . .	82	165	179	183	204	211	229	220
Depreciation	Dollars. . . .	1,038	2,357	2,780	2,883	2,988	3,099	3,208	3,268
Finance charge	Dollars. . . .	423	680	832	696	695	729	778	793

NA Not available. [1] Beginning 1990, not comparable to previous data.

Source: American Automobile Manufacturers Association Inc., Detroit, MI, *Motor Vehicle Facts and Figures*, annual (copyright).

No. 1053. Domestic Motor Fuel Consumption, by Type of Vehicle: 1970 to 1996

[Comprises all fuel types used for propulsion of vehicles under state motor fuels laws. Excludes federal purchases for military use. Minus sign (-) indicates decrease]

YEAR	FUEL CONSUMPTION					AVG. FUEL CONSUMPTION PER VEHICLE (gal.)			AVG. MILES PER GALLON		
	All vehicles (bil. gal.)	Avg. annual percent change [1]	Cars [2] (bil. gal.)	Buses [3] (bil. gal.)	Trucks [4] (bil. gal.)	Cars [2]	Buses [3]	Trucks [4]	Cars [2]	Buses [3]	Trucks [4]
1970 . .	92.3	5.4	67.7	0.8	11.3	688	2,172	2,467	13.5	5.5	5.5
1975 . .	109.0	2.5	74.1	1.1	14.6	619	2,279	2,722	14.0	5.8	5.6
1980 . .	115.0	-5.9	70.0	1.0	20.0	507	1,926	3,447	16.0	6.0	5.4
1981 . .	114.5	-0.4	69.1	1.1	20.3	496	1,938	3,565	16.4	5.9	5.3
1982 . .	113.4	-0.9	69.1	1.0	20.4	496	1,756	3,647	16.8	5.9	5.5
1983 . .	116.1	2.4	70.3	0.9	20.8	497	1,507	3,769	17.0	5.9	5.6
1984 . .	118.7	2.3	70.6	0.8	21.4	495	1,398	3,967	17.3	5.7	5.7
1985 . .	121.3	2.2	71.5	0.8	21.4	505	1,405	3,570	17.5	5.4	5.8
1986 . .	125.2	3.2	73.2	0.9	21.8	507	1,496	3,821	17.4	5.3	5.8
1987 . .	127.5	1.8	73.3	0.9	22.5	500	1,527	3,937	18.0	5.8	5.9
1988 . .	130.1	2.0	73.3	0.9	22.9	487	1,524	3,736	18.7	5.8	6.0
1989 . .	131.9	1.4	73.9	0.9	23.5	486	1,519	3,776	18.9	6.0	6.1
1990 . .	130.8	-0.8	69.6	0.9	24.5	461	1,428	3,953	20.2	6.4	6.0
1991 . .	128.6	-1.7	64.3	0.9	25.0	443	1,369	4,047	21.1	6.7	6.0
1992 . .	132.9	3.3	65.4	0.9	25.5	455	1,362	4,210	20.9	6.6	6.0
1993 . .	137.3	3.3	67.0	0.9	26.2	462	1,420	4,309	20.5	6.6	6.1
1994 . .	140.8	2.5	67.9	1.0	27.7	462	1,438	4,102	20.7	6.6	6.1
1995 . .	143.8	2.1	68.1	1.0	29.0	530	1,412	4,315	21.1	6.6	6.1
1996 . .	146.7	2.0	68.9	1.0	29.5	531	1,414	4,205	21.3	6.6	6.2

[1] From prior year, except 1970, change from 1965. [2] Includes taxicabs. The format used to report some vehicle types was changed. In previous years, some other two-axle four-tire vehicles were included in the passenger car category. Other two-axle four-tire vehicles are now separate from the truck category. [3] Includes school buses. [4] Includes combinations.

Source: U.S. Federal Highway Administration, *Highway Statistics Summary to 1985*, and *Highway Statistics*, annual.

No. 1054. Motor Vehicle Travel, by Type of Vehicle and by Speed: 1970 to 1996

[Travel in billions of vehicle-miles, except as indicated. Travel estimates based on automatic traffic recorder data. Speed trend data for 1970 were collected by several state highway agencies, normally during summer months; beginning Oct. 1975 all states have monitored speeds at locations on several highway systems Monitoring Program]

| YEAR | VEHICLE-MILES OF TRAVEL (bil.) | | | | AVG. MILES PER VEHICLE (1,000) | | | MOTOR VEHICLE SPEED ON RURAL INTERSTATE | | | | |
| | Total | Cars [1] | Buses | Trucks | Passenger vehicles | | Trucks | Citations recorded (1,000) [2] | Avg. speed (miles per hour) | Percent of vehicles exceeding— | | |
					Cars [1]	Buses				55 mph	60 mph	65 mph
1970	1,110	917	4.5	186	10.3	12.0	9.9	200	63.8	87	69	44
1980	1,527	1,122	6.1	291	8.8	11.5	10.4	667	57.5	66	25	7
1985	1,775	1,256	4.5	391	9.4	7.5	10.5	8,449	59.5	75	44	17
1986	1,835	1,280	4.7	424	9.5	7.9	10.8	8,549	59.7	76	46	18
1987	1,921	1,325	5.3	457	9.7	8.9	11.1	7,992	59.7	74	46	19
1988	2,026	1,380	5.5	502	10.0	8.9	11.5	7,566	59.5	74	46	19
1989	2,096	1,412	5.7	536	10.2	9.1	11.7	7,488	60.1	77	49	22
1990	2,144	1,418	5.7	575	10.3	9.1	11.9	7,511	60.4	78	50	23
1991	2,172	1,367	5.8	649	10.3	9.1	12.2	7,594	59.9	76	48	21
1992	2,247	1,381	5.8	707	10.6	9.0	12.4	7,004	61.2	81	56	28
1993	2,296	1,385	6.1	746	10.5	9.4	12.4	6,433	60.8	78	51	24
1994	2,358	1,416	6.4	765	10.8	9.6	12.2	(NA)	(NA)	(NA)	(NA)	(NA)
1995	2,423	1,448	6.4	790	11.1	9.4	12.0	(NA)	(NA)	(NA)	(NA)	(NA)
1996	2,482	1,468	6.5	815	11.3	9.4	11.8	(NA)	(NA)	(NA)	(NA)	(NA)

NA Not available. [1] Includes motorcycles. [2] Citations issued for 55 mph violations.

Source: U.S. Federal Highway Administration, *Highway Statistics Summary, annual.*

No. 1055. Passenger Transit Industry—Summary: 1985 to 1996

[Includes Puerto Rico. Includes aggregate information for all transit systems in the United States. Excludes nontransit services such as taxicab, school bus, unregulated jitney, sightseeing bus, intercity bus, and special application mass transportation systems (e.g., amusement parks, airports, island, and urban park ferries) Includes active vehicles only]

ITEM	Unit	1985	1990	1992	1993	1994	1995	1996
Operating systems	Number. . .	4,972	5,078	5,086	5,088	5,973	5,973	5,973
Motor bus systems	Number. . .	2,631	2,688	2,693	1,934	2,250	2,250	2,250
Passenger vehicles, active [1] . .	Number. . .	94,368	92,961	102,251	107,316	115,943	115,874	119,556
Motor bus	Number. . .	64,258	58,714	63,080	64,850	68,123	67,107	67,874
Trolley bus.	Number. . .	676	832	907	851	877	885	871
Heavy rail	Number. . .	9,326	10,419	10,245	10,261	10,138	10,157	10,201
Light rail	Number. . .	717	913	1,058	1,025	1,054	999	1,140
Commuter rail	Number. . .	4,035	4,415	4,413	4,494	4,517	4,565	4,665
Demand response.	Number. . .	14,490	16,471	20,695	23,527	28,729	29,352	31,853
Operating funding, total	Mil. dol . . .	12,195	16,053	16,915	17,276	17,968	18,241	19,756
Passenger funding	Mil. dol . . .	4,575	5,891	6,152	6,351	6,756	6,801	7,417
Other operating funding [2] . .	Mil. dol . . .	702	895	646	764	2,271	2,812	3,068
Operating assistance	Mil. dol . . .	6,918	9,267	10,117	10,161	8,941	8,628	9,271
Federal	Mil. dol . . .	940	970	969	966	916	817	567
Local [3]	Mil. dol . . .	[4]5,979	5,327	5,268	5,491	4,171	3,981	4,312
State [3]	Mil. dol . . .	([4])	2,970	3,898	3,704	3,854	3,830	4,392
Total expense	Mil. dol . . .	14,077	17,979	20,034	20,679	21,653	21,540	22,457
Operating expense	Mil. dol . . .	12,381	15,742	16,781	17,350	17,920	17,849	18,503
Vehicle operations	Mil. dol . . .	5,655	6,654	7,660	7,941	8,212	8,282	8,623
Maintenance.	Mil. dol . . .	3,672	4,631	4,831	4,894	5,004	5,047	4,891
General administration . . .	Mil. dol . . .	2,505	3,450	2,674	2,714	2,752	2,590	3,155
Purchased transporta- tion	Mil. dol . . .	549	1,008	1,616	1,800	1,952	1,930	1,834
Reconciling expense	Mil. dol . . .	1,696	2,237	3,253	3,329	3,733	3,691	3,954
Capital expenditure, federal . .	Mil. dol . . .	2,510	2,380	2,613	3,465	3,577	5,481	4,125
Vehicle-miles operated [1] . . .	Mil. dol . . .	2,791	3,242	3,355	3,435	3,467	3,550	3,663
Motor bus	Million . . .	1,863	2,130	2,178	2,210	2,162	2,184	2,165
Trolley bus.	Million . . .	16	14	14	13	14	14	14
Heavy rail	Million . . .	451	537	525	522	532	537	543
Light rail	Million . . .	17	24	29	28	34	35	38
Commuter rail	Million . . .	183	213	219	224	231	238	242
Demand response.	Million . . .	247	306	364	406	464	507	617
Passengers carried [1]	Million . . .	8,636	8,799	8,501	8,217	7,949	7,763	7,975
Motor bus	Million . . .	5,675	5,677	5,517	5,381	4,871	4,848	4,912
Trolley bus.	Million . . .	142	126	126	121	118	119	117
Heavy rail	Million . . .	2,290	2,346	2,207	2,046	2,169	2,033	2,157
Light rail	Million . . .	132	175	188	188	284	251	261
Commuter rail	Million . . .	275	328	314	322	339	344	353
Demand response.	Million . . .	59	68	72	81	88	88	95
Avg. funding per passenger . .	Cents	53.0	66.9	72.4	77.3	85.0	87.1	87.6
Employees, number (avg.) [5] . .	1,000	270	273	279	299	304	311	306
Payroll, employee	Mil. dol . . .	5,843	7,226	7,671	7,932	8,224	8,213	8,687
Fringe benefits, employee . . .	Mil. dol . . .	2,868	3,986	4,319	4,400	4,452	4,484	4,563

[1] Includes other not shown separately. [2] Beginning 1994, includes taxes levied directly by transit agency and other dedicated funds, formerly included in local. [3] Includes other operating revenue, nonoperating revenue, and auxiliary income. [4] For 1985, state and local combined. [5] Through 1992, represents employee equivalents of 2,080 hours = one employee; beginning 1993, equals actual employees.

Source: American Public Transit Association, Washington, DC, *Transit Fact Book,* annual. <http://www.apta.com/pubs/stats/index.htm>.

No. 1056. Class I Intercity Motor Carriers of Passengers: 1980 to 1996

[Carriers subject to ICC regulations. See text, Section 21. Minus sign (-) indicates deficit]

ITEM	Unit	1980	1985	1988	1989	1990	1991	1992	1993	1994	1995	1996
Carriers reporting [1]	Number.	48	43	21	20	21	21	21	21	20	20	17
Number of employees, average. . . .	1,000 . .	31	24	(NA)	(NA)	(NA)	(NA)	(NA)	(NA)	(NA)	(NA)	(NA)
Compensation of employees.	Mil. dol .	599	518	(NA)	(NA)	(NA)	(NA)	(NA)	(NA)	(NA)	(NA)	(NA)
Operating revenue	Mil. dol .	1,397	1,233	1,122	1,205	943	980	938	928	870	917	912
Passenger revenue [2]	Mil. dol .	947	836	825	890	738	793	755	751	721	770	772
Special bus revenue and other . .	Mil. dol .	215	184	155	165	90	187	183	177	149	147	140
Operating expenses	Mil. dol .	1,318	1,168	1,059	1,133	1,015	967	874	880	919	899	878
Net operating revenue	Mil. dol .	79	65	63	72	-72	13	64	48	-49	18	33
Ordinary income:												
Before income taxes	Mil. dol .	107	65	(NA)	(NA)	(NA)	(NA)	(NA)	(NA)	(NA)	(NA)	(NA)
After income taxes.	Mil. dol .	90	53	(NA)	12	-180	162	21	14	-67	-9	13
Passenger vehicles in service [2]	1,000 . .	8.6	8.4	(NA)	(NA)	(NA)	(NA)	(NA)	(NA)	(NA)	(NA)	(NA)
Vehicle-miles, passenger	Million. .	781	567	(NA)	(NA)	(NA)	(NA)	(NA)	(NA)	(NA)	(NA)	(NA)
Revenue passengers carried	Million. .	134	88	55	54	43	42	41	40	41	43	37
Expense per vehicle-mile	Dollar . .	1.69	2.06	(NA)	(NA)	(NA)	(NA)	(NA)	(NA)	(NA)	(NA)	(NA)

NA Not available.　[1] Excludes carriers preponderantly in local or suburban service and carriers engaged in transportation of both property and passengers.　[2] Regular route intercity and local.

Source: Through 1993, U.S. Interstate Commerce Commission, *Transport Statistics in the United States*, part 2, annual, thereafter, U.S. Bureau of Transportation Statistics, *Selected Earnings Data, Class I Motor Carriers of Passengers*.

No. 1057. Passenger Transportation Arrangement: 1993 to 1995

[In millions of dollars, except percent. Represents SIC 4722]

SOURCE OF RECEIPTS	1993	1994	1995	OPERATING EXPENSES	1993	1994	1995
Receipts, total [1] . . .	**11,073**	**11,795**	**12,891**	**Expenses, total [1] . . . . .**	**10,136**	**10,889**	**11,555**
Air carriers	6,138	6,375	6,846	Payroll, annual	4,031	4,526	4,818
Water carriers	528	584	663	Employer contributions [2]. .	558	628	663
Hotels and motels	758	808	867	Lease and rental payments	908	908	1,021
Motor coaches.	388	397	413	Advertising and promotion	713	746	753
Railroads	125	126	145	Taxes and licenses	144	163	181
Rental cars	189	204	242	Utilities	386	388	412
Package tours	2,158	2,425	2,634	Depreciation.	339	361	381
Other	789	876	1,081	Office Supplies	294	325	352
				Repair Services	134	152	168
				Other	2,629	2,692	2,806

[1] Receipts for firms primarily engaged in arranging passenger transportation. These estimates exclude receipts of transportation companies (airlines, railroads, etc.).　[2] Includes contributions to social security and other supplemental benefits.

Source: U.S. Bureau of the Census, *Service Annual Survey*.

No. 1058. Motor Freight Transportation and Warehousing Services—Revenues, Expenses, and Payroll Expenses, and Payroll: 1995 and 1996

[In millions of dollars]

KIND OF BUSINESS	SIC [1] code	OPERATING REVENUE		OPERATING EXPENSES		ANNUAL PAYROLL	
		1995	1996	1995	1996	1995	1996
Motor freight transport. and warehousing services [2]	**42**	**172,727**	**184,259**	**160,321**	**172,058**	**49,373**	**52,522**
Trucking and courier services, except by air [3]	421	161,806	172,743	151,628	162,825	46,478	49,432
Local trucking without storage	4212	43,830	46,589	38,695	41,325	9,885	10,701
Trucking, except local.	4213	91,675	97,586	88,061	94,390	26,635	28,161
Local trucking with storage	4214	5,154	5,502	4,817	5,121	1,633	1,681
Courier services, except by air	4215	21,147	23,066	20,055	21,989	8,325	8,889
Public warehousing and storage	422	10,874	11,463	8,652	9,189	2,883	3,076
Farm product warehousing and storage	4221	749	688	595	560	182	176
Refrigerated warehousing and storage.	4222	2,107	2,203	1,747	1,857	588	617
General warehousing and storage.	4225	6,143	6,522	4,777	5,030	1,613	1,710
Special warehousing and storage [4]	4226	1,875	2,050	1,533	1,742	500	573

[1] Standard Industrial Classification.　[2] Includes terminal and joint terminal maintenance facilities for motor carrier transportation (SIC 4231) not shown separately.　[3] Excludes private motor carriers that operate as auxiliary establishments to nontransportation companies and independent owner-operators with no paid employees.　[4] Includes household goods warehousing.

Source: U.S. Bureau of the Census, *Current Business Reports, 1996 Motor Freight Transportation and Warehousing Survey*.

No. 1059. Bus Profile: 1980 to 1996

ITEM	Unit	1980	1990	1994	1995	1996
FINANCIAL						
Expenditures, school bus	Mil. dol.	3,833	7,605	7,847	9,082	10,404
Operating revenues, intercity buc, Class I	Mil. dol.	1,397	943	870	917	912
Operating expenses, intercity bus, Class I	Mil. dol.	1,318	1,026	919	899	878
INVENTORY						
Operating companies, intercity bus, Class I	Number	61	31	27	28	27
Vehicles:						
Commercial and federal bus	Number	110,576	118,726	122,705	125,057	127,214
School and other bus	Number	418,225	508,261	547,718	560,447	596,395
PERFORMANCE						
Vehicle-miles, all buses:						
Rural and urban highway	Millions	6,059	5,726	6,409	6,383	6,535
Revenue:						
Passenger miles, intercity bus	Millions	(NA)	121,400	135,900	136,104	138,542
Passengers, intercity bus	1,000	370,000	334,000	343,200	366,500	360,000
Avg. miles traveled per vehicle, all buses	Miles	11,458	9,133	9,560	9,312	9,381
Avg. annual fuel consumption, all buses	Gallon	1,926	1,428	1,430	1,412	1,414
Avg. miles per gallon, all buses	Mpg	6.0	6.4	6.6	6.6	6.6
Average revenue per passenger mile	Cents	7.3	11.6	11.6	12.2	12.4
SAFETY						
Fatalities:						
School bus related	Number	150	115	105	122	136
School bus occupants	Number	9	11	3	13	10
Other vehicle occupants	Number	88	64	64	72	101
Nonoccupants	Number	53	40	38	37	25
Fatalities in vehicular accidents, all buses	Number	390	340	286	306	297
Occupant fatality rate:						
Per 100 million vehicle-miles, all buses	Rate	0.8	0.6	0.3	0.5	0.9
Per 10,000 registered vehicles, all buses	Rate	0.9	0.5	0.3	0.5	0.8

NA Not available.

Source: U.S. Bureau of Transportation Statistics, *National Transportation Statistics, 1997*.

No. 1060. Truck Profile: 1980 to 1996

ITEM	Unit	1980	1990	1994	1995	1996
FINANCIAL						
Intercity revenue	Mil. dol	(NA)	127,314	157,910	165,271	(NA)
Class I intercity motor carriers of property:						
Operating revenue, total	Mil. dol	1,290	46,710	(NA)	(NA)	(NA)
Operating expenses, total	Mil. dol	29,012	118,968	147,911	155,920	(NA)
INVENTORY						
Truck registrations, total	1,000	5,791	6,196	6,588	6,719	7,006
PERFORMANCE						
Vehicle miles, total	Millions	108,491	146,242	170,216	178,156	182,756
Average miles traveled per vehicle:						
All trucks, total	Avg. miles	18,736	23,603	25,838	26,514	26,084
Ton-miles, intercity	Millions	555,000	735,000	908,000	921,000	986,000
Average fuel consumption per vehicle	Gallons	3,447	3,953	4,202	4,315	4,205
Highway-user taxes, total	Mil. dol	9,888	19,356	23,836	25,116	(NA)
SAFETY						
Occupant fatalities	Number	8,748	9,306	9,574	10,216	10,522
Vehicle involvement, total (per 100 million vehicle-miles)	Rate	4.5	2.9	2.4	2.4	2.4

NA Not available.

Source: U.S. Bureau of Transportation Statistics, *National Transportation Statistics, 1997*.

No. 1061. Trucking and Courier Services—Operating Revenue, Operating Expenses, and Equipment, by Type of Carrier: 1994 to 1996

[In millions of dollars, except as indicated. Data cover SIC group 421. Excludes private motor carriers that operate as auxiliary establishments to nontransportation companies and independent owner-operators with no paid employees]

ITEM	ALL CARRIERS			SPECIALTY CARRIERS			GENERAL CARRIERS		
	1994	1995	1996	1994	1995	1996	1994	1995	1996
Operating revenues:									
Total [1]	155,713	161,806	172,743	45,034	49,139	52,464	110,679	112,667	120,279
Motor carrier	148,002	153,881	163,786	41,078	44,969	47,883	106,924	108,912	115,903
Local trucking	43,592	48,731	52,301	23,420	27,181	29,045	20,172	21,550	23,256
Long-distance trucking	104,410	105,150	111,485	17,658	17,788	18,838	86,752	87,362	92,647
Operating expenses:									
Total [1]	145,216	151,628	162,825	41,052	44,556	47,685	104,164	107,072	115,140
Annual payroll	43,544	46,478	49,432	10,151	11,254	12,008	33,393	35,224	37,424
Employer contrib. to soc. sec. and other benefits	12,025	12,666	13,020	2,429	2,536	2,699	9,596	10,130	10,321
Purchased fuels	12,114	12,051	13,667	2,880	3,151	3,497	9,234	8,900	10,170
Purchased transportation	28,222	28,757	30,979	7,573	7,449	8,036	20,649	21,308	22,943
Lease and rental	2,664	2,794	2,970	736	738	767	1,928	2,056	2,203
Insurance	5,517	5,638	5,864	1,783	1,888	1,892	3,734	3,750	3,972
Maintenance and repair	8,936	8,876	9,281	2,679	2,894	3,107	6,257	5,982	6,174
Depreciation	8,085	8,702	9,186	2,436	2,882	3,028	5,649	5,820	6,158
Taxes and licenses	3,356	3,410	3,517	807	893	922	2,549	2,517	2,595
Drug and alcohol testing and rehabilitation programs	80	96	102	24	28	28	56	68	74
Other operating expenses	20,673	22,160	24,807	9,554	10,843	11,701	11,119	11,317	13,106
Equipment (1,000 units): [2]									
Trucks	287	295	(NA)	147	154	(NA)	140	141	(NA)
Truck-tractors	681	758	(NA)	133	150	(NA)	548	608	(NA)
Trailers (full and semi)	1,456	1,583	(NA)	212	222	(NA)	1,244	1,361	(NA)

NA Not available. [1] Includes other revenue not shown separately. [2] Represents revenue generating equipment as of December 31, 1994. Includes owned and leased equipment.

Source: U.S. Bureau of the Census, *Current Business Reports, 1995 Motor Freight Transportation and Warehousing Survey.*

No. 1062. Class I Intercity Motor Carriers of Property, by Carrier: 1980 to 1993

[See headnote, Table 1056. Common carriers are carriers offering regular scheduled service. Contract carriers provide service at request of user. Minus sign (-) indicates loss]

ITEM	Unit	1980	1985	1989	1990	1991	1992	1993
Common carriers, gen. freight reporting	Number	298	237	192	191	201	208	220
Number of employees, average	1,000	413	376	461	465	474	490	511
Compensation of employees	Mil. dol	9,803	10,217	12,854	13,556	14,032	14,967	15,987
Operating revenues	Mil. dol	19,725	22,314	27,405	29,682	31,619	34,594	37,600
Operating expenses	Mil. dol	18,870	21,037	26,242	28,340	30,269	32,977	35,729
Ordinary income before taxes	Mil. dol	701	1,198	988	1,146	1,180	1,453	1,641
Net income	Mil. dol	-72	658	659	746	749	878	985
Intercity vehicle-miles	Million	6,547	5,760	6,557	6,804	7,615	8,674	9,770
Intercity revenue freight carried	Mil. ton	178	136	145	157	169	196	225
Common carriers, other reporting [1]	Number	441	397	337	322	295	330	304
Number of employees, average	1,000	101	76	84	87	74	88	83
Compensation of employees	Mil. dol	1,931	1,783	2,105	2,236	1,920	2,358	2,333
Operating revenues	Mil. dol	8,792	7,962	8,321	9,042	7,761	9,367	9,315
Operating expenses	Mil. dol	8,426	7,752	8,081	8,702	7,509	8,942	8,875
Ordinary income before taxes	Mil. dol	230	123	117	198	122	309	354
Net income	Mil. dol	14	94	88	153	85	221	250
Intercity vehicle-miles	Million	6,889	5,714	6,320	6,566	5,372	6,696	6,295
Intercity revenue freight carried	Mil. ton	324	303	278	302	253	298	296
Contract carrier, other [1]	Number	69	64	77	87	83	113	115
Number of employees, average	1,000	14	22	29	34	34	42	40
Compensation of employees	Mil. dol	336	630	893	1,082	989	1,325	1,321
Operating revenues	Mil. dol	1,272	1,942	2,946	3,486	3,644	4,501	4,581
Operating expenses	Mil. dol	1,207	1,807	2,888	3,422	3,547	4,333	4,367
Ordinary income before taxes	Mil. dol	48	103	15	3	53	127	181
Net income	Mil. dol	28	69	3	-13	20	80	123
Intercity vehicle-miles	Million	934	1,227	1,826	2,044	2,339	2,933	2,913
Intercity revenue freight carried	Mil. ton	37	41	80	80	76	110	99
Carriers of household goods reporting	Number	28	40	36	36	36	32	31
Number of employees, average	1,000	10	11	12	13	12	12	10
Compensation of employees	Mil. dol	157	240	276	296	298	291	252
Operating revenues	Mil. dol	1,824	2,684	3,114	3,152	3,026	3,180	3,274
Intercity freight	Mil. dol	1,676	2,388	2,703	2,702	2,318	2,787	2,834
Operating expenses	Mil. dol	1,781	2,635	3,059	3,129	2,973	3,159	3,198
Ordinary income before taxes	Mil. dol	74	79	41	12	27	-1	48
Net income	Mil. dol	42	54	28	8	17	8	62
Power units, intercity service	1,000	25	35	(NA)	(NA)	(NA)	(NA)	(NA)
Intercity vehicle-miles	Million	969	1,171	1,229	1,366	1,086	1,136	949
Intercity revenue freight carried	Mil. ton	5	7	7	8	7	9	5

NA Not available. [1] Other than general freight.

Source: Through 1992, U.S. Interstate Commerce Commission, *Transport Statistics in the United States,* Part 2, annual; thereafter, U.S. Bureau of Transportation Statistics, *National Transportation Statistics,* annual.

No. 1063. Railroads, Class I—Summary: 1980 to 1996

[As of **Dec. 31**, or **calendar year** data, except as noted. Compiled from annual reports of class I railroads only except where noted. Beginning 1985, financial data are not comparable with earlier years due to change in method of accounting for track and related structures. Minus sign (-) indicates deficit]

ITEM	Unit	1980	1985	1990	1991	1992	1993	1994	1995	1996
Class I line-hauling companies [1]	Number.	40	23	14	14	13	13	13	11	10
Employees [2]	1,000 .	458	302	216	206	197	193	190	188	182
Compensation	Mil. dol .	11,318	10,563	8,654	8,695	8,753	8,732	8,874	9,070	9,202
Average per hour	Dollars .	10.2	14.3	15.8	16.8	17.8	17.9	18.5	19.0	20.1
Average per year	Dollars .	24,695	34,991	39,987	42,131	44,336	45,354	46,714	48,188	50,611
Mileage:										
Railroad line owned [3]	1,000 . .	178	162	146	144	141	140	138	137	136
Railroad track owned [4]	1,000 . .	292	269	244	242	238	236	232	228	228
Equipment:										
Locomotives in service	Number.	28,094	22,548	18,835	18,344	18,004	18,161	18,505	18,812	19,269
Average horsepower	1,000 lb	2,302	2,469	2,665	2,714	2,750	2,777	2,832	2,927	2,985
Cars in service:										
Passenger train	Number.	4,347	2,502	(NA)	(NA)	(NA)	(NA)	(NA)	(NA)	(NA)
Freight train [5]	1,000 . .	1,711	1,422	1,212	1,190	1,173	1,173	1,192	1,219	1,241
Freight cars [6]	1,000 . .	1,168	867	659	633	605	587	591	583	571
Income and expenses:										
Operating revenues	Mil. dol.	28,258	27,586	28,370	27,845	28,349	28,825	30,809	32,279	32,693
Operating expenses	Mil. dol.	26,355	25,225	24,652	28,061	25,325	24,517	25,511	27,897	26,331
Net revenue from operations	*Mil. dol* .	*1,902*	*2,361*	*3,718*	*-216*	*3,024*	*4,308*	*5,298*	*4,383*	*6,361*
Income before fixed charges	Mil. dol .	2,897	3,393	4,627	928	4,127	4,990	6,184	5,016	7,055
Provision for taxes [7]	Mil. dol .	592	660	1,088	-156	1,092	1,810	1,935	1,556	2,056
Ordinary income	Mil. dol .	1,129	1,788	1,961	-91	2,055	2,258	3,315	2,439	3,885
Net income	Mil. dol .	1,129	1,882	1,977	-281	1,800	2,240	3,298	2,324	3,885
Net railway operating income	Mil. dol .	1,339	1,746	2,648	-37	1,955	2,517	3,392	2,858	4,338
Total taxes [8]	Mil. dol .	2,585	3,169	3,780	2,649	3,732	4,343	4,512	4,075	4,669
Indus. return on net investment .	Percent.	4.2	4.6	8.1	1.3	6.3	7.1	9.4	7.0	9.4
Gross capital expenditures	Mil. dol .	3,238	4,485	3,591	3,439	3,680	4,504	5,035	5,720	6,550
Balance sheet:										
Total property investment	Mil. dol .	43,923	64,241	70,348	71,622	72,677	75,217	78,384	86,186	90,046
Accrued depreciation and amortization	Mil. dol .	10,706	19,756	22,222	23,057	23,378	23,892	24,200	23,439	23,932
Net investment	Mil. dol .	33,419	46,237	48,126	48,565	49,299	51,325	54,184	62,746	66,113
Shareholder's equity	Mil. dol .	19,860	27,605	23,662	22,603	23,115	24,658	27,389	31,419	32,255
Net working capital	Mil. dol .	922	1,084	-3505	-3988	-4372	-3295	-3059	-2634	-2,942
Cash dividends	Mil. dol .	610	1,444	2,074	915	830	1,054	1,398	1,518	3,937
AMTRAK passenger traffic:										
Passenger revenue	Mil. dol .	(NA)	604.9	941.9	962.3	933.2	777.6	717.9	734.1	756.2
Revenue passengers carried	1,000 . .	21,303	20,945	22,382	21,693	21,678	21,511	21,239	20,349	19,700
Revenue passenger miles	Million. .	4,645	4,977	6,125	6,249	6,181	6,068	5,869	5,401	5,066
Averages:										
Revenue per passenger	Dollars .	(NA)	28.9	42.1	44.4	43.0	36.1	33.8	36.1	38.4
Revenue per passenger mile	Cents . .	(NA)	12.2	15.4	15.4	15.1	12.8	12.2	13.6	14.9
Trip per passenger	Miles . .	218.1	237.6	273.7	288.0	285.1	277.7	(NA)	(NA)	(NA)
Freight service:										
Freight revenue	Mil. dol .	26,200	26,688	24,471	26,949	27,508	27,991	29,931	31,356	31,889
Per ton-mile	Cents . .	2.8	3.0	2.7	2.6	2.6	2.5	2.5	2.4	2.4
Per ton originated	Dollar . .	17.7	20.2	19.3	19.5	19.7	20.0	20.4	20.2	19.8
Revenue-tons originated	Million. .	1,492	1,320	1,425	1,383	1,399	1,397	1,470	1,550	1,611
Revenue-tons carried	Million. .	2,434	1,985	2,024	1,987	2,022	2,047	2,185	2,322	2,229
Tons carried one mile	Billion . .	919	877	1,034	1,039	1,067	1,109	1,201	1,306	1,356
Average miles of road operated	1,000 . .	179	161	133	130	126	124	123	125	127
Revenue ton-miles per mile of road	1,000 . .	5,133	5,446	7,763	8,001	8,451	8,965	9,735	10,439	10,704
Revenue per ton-mile	Cents . .	3	3	3	3	3	3	2	2	2
Train miles	Million. .	428	347	380	375	390	405	441	458	469
Net ton-miles per train-mile [9]	Number.	2,175	2,574	2,755	2,796	2,759	2,759	2,746	2,870	2,912
Net ton-miles per loaded car-mile [9]	Number.	63.5	62.7	69.1	71.6	70.9	71.6	72.2	73.6	75.0
Train-miles per train-hour	Miles . .	18.2	21.9	23.7	23.7	23.7	23.1	22.4	21.8	22.0
Haul per ton, U.S. as a system . .	Miles . .	616	664	726	751	763	794	817	843	842
Accident: [10]										
All railroads	Number.	63,663	35,340	26,440	24,662	22,553	20,400	18,038	15,586	13,108
Persons killed	Number.	1,417	1,036	1,297	1,194	1,170	1,279	1,226	1,146	1,023
Persons injured	Number.	62,246	34,304	25,143	23,468	21,383	19,121	16,812	14,440	12,085
Class I railroads	Number.	57,755	29,388	20,450	18,728	17,055	15,058	12,428	10,565	8,000
Persons killed	Number.	1,344	955	1,166	1,069	1,047	1,124	1,080	994	818
Persons injured	Number.	56,411	28,433	19,284	17,659	16,008	13,934	11,348	9,571	7,182

NA Not available. [1] See text, Section 21, for definition of Class I. [2] Average midmonth count. [3] Represents the aggregate length of roadway of all line-haul railroads. Excludes yard tracks, sidings, and parallel lines. (Includes estimate for class II and III railroads). [4] Includes multiple main tracks, yard tracks, and sidings owned by both line-haul and switching and terminal. (Includes estimate for class II and III railroads). [5] Includes cars owned by all railroads, private car companies, and shippers. [6] Class I railroads only. [7] Includes state income taxes. [8] Includes payroll, income, and other taxes. [9] Revenue and nonrevenue freight. [10] Source: Federal Railroad Admin., *Accident Bulletin*, annual. Includes highway grade crossing casualties.

Source: Except as noted, Association of American Railroads, Washington, DC, *Railroad Facts, Statistics of Railroads of Class I*, annual, and *Analysis of Class I Railroads*, annual.

No. 1064. Railroads, Class I-Cars of Revenue Freight Loaded, 1970 to 1997, and by Commodity Group, 1996 and 1997

[**In thousands.** Figures are 52-week totals. N.e.c.= Not elsewhere classified]

YEAR	CARLOADS Total	Piggy-back	COMMODITY GROUP	CARLOADS 1996	1997	COMMODITY GROUP	CARLOADS 1996	1997
1970 ...	27,160	1,450	Coal..................	6,694	6,709	Metals and products	579	600
1975 ...	23,217	1,308	Metallic ores	443	360	Stone, clay, and glass products ..	477	483
1980 ...	22,598	1,661	Chemicals, allied products ...	1,524	1,578	Crushed stone, gravel, sand ...	679	687
1985 ...	19,574	2,863	Grain	1,235	1,200	Nonmetalic minerals, n.e.c	480	466
1990 ...	16,177	(NA)	Motor vehicles and equipment.	1,003	1,050	Waste and scrap materials	487	489
1993 ...	15,911	(NA)	Pulp, paper, allied products ..	527	525	Lumber, wood products, n.e.c. [1]..	268	275
1994 ...	16,763	(NA)	Primary forest products	352	344	Coke.................	262	242
1995 ...	16,706	(NA)	Food and kindred prod., n.e.c.	415	412	Petroleum product...........	276	291
1996 ...	16,521	(NA)	Grain mill products	490	505	All other carloads	328	346
1997,prel	16,564	(NA)						

NA Not available.　[1] Excludes furniture.

Source: Association of American Railroads, Washington, DC, *Weekly Railroad Traffic,* annual.

No. 1065. Railroads, Class I Line-Haul-Revenue Freight Originated, by Commodity Group: 1980 to 1996

COMMODITY GROUP	1980	1985	1990	1991	1992	1993	1994	1995	1996
Carloads (1,000) [1]	**22,223**	**19,501**	**21,401**	**20,868**	**21,205**	**21,683**	**23,179**	**23,726**	**24,159**
Coal...................	5,789	5,684	5,912	5,683	5,572	5,310	5,681	6,095	6,746
Farm products.............	1,866	1,494	1,689	1,605	1,646	1,636	1,459	1,692	1,530
Chemicals, allied products	1,322	1,296	1,531	1,556	1,568	1,606	1,695	1,642	1,639
Food and kindred products	1,767	1,224	1,307	1,316	1,352	1,380	1,381	1,377	1,302
Nonmetallic minerals [2]	1,474	1,196	1,202	1,075	1,029	1,044	1,138	1,159	1,176
Transportation equipment	1,004	1,202	1,091	1,068	1,181	1,355	1,448	1,473	1,442
Lumber and wood products [3]	1,384	948	780	716	726	710	771	719	682
Pulp, paper, allied products	954	703	611	616	618	620	651	628	589
Petroleum and coal products	596	491	573	533	583	584	602	596	567
Stone, clay, and glass products...	776	551	539	479	483	487	512	516	491
Metallic ores	1,258	511	508	499	489	443	440	463	443
Primary metal products	756	449	477	469	481	528	579	575	597
Waste and scrap materials.....	632	429	439	433	487	558	604	623	605
Machinery, exc. electrical.....	77	35	39	39	39	37	40	41	40
Fabricated metal products [4]	72	31	31	34	32	37	37	32	29
Tons (mil.) [1]	**1,492**	**1,320**	**1,425**	**1,383**	**1,399**	**1,397**	**1,470**	**1,550**	**1,611**
Coal...................	522	538	579	560	554	534	574	627	705
Farm products.............	156	127	147	144	149	147	131	154	142
Chemicals, allied products	108	106	126	127	130	134	142	138	139
Nonmetallic minerals [2]	125	108	109	99	94	96	106	110	113
Food and kindred products	92	74	81	83	86	88	88	91	87
Lumber and wood products [3]	86	63	53	48	50	49	54	51	49
Metallic ores	105	47	47	45	45	41	40	44	42
Stone, clay, and glass products...	54	44	44	39	40	40	42	43	42
Petroleum and coal products ...	38	33	40	37	41	41	43	43	42
Primary metal products	53	34	38	37	39	43	47	47	49
Pulp, paper, allied products	42	36	33	33	34	34	37	36	33
Waste and scrap materials.....	34	26	28	27	30	35	37	38	38
Transportation equipment	24	27	23	22	25	29	30	30	29
Machinery, exc. electrical.....	2	1	1	1	1	1	1	1	1
Fabricated metal products [4]	2	1	1	1	1	1	1	1	1
Gross revenue (mil. dol.) [1] .	**26,938**	**28,225**	**29,775**	**29,319**	**29,777**	**30,376**	**32,424**	**33,782**	**34,310**
Coal...................	4,956	6,556	6,954	6,903	6,717	6,481	7,021	7,356	7,706
Chemicals, allied products	2,946	3,342	3,933	4,043	4,123	4,277	4,520	4,553	4,660
Transportation equipment	1,917	3,110	3,100	2,633	2,753	3,021	3,257	3,269	3,390
Farm products.............	2,801	1,977	2,422	2,332	2,454	2,528	2,407	3,020	2,807
Food and kindred products	2,837	2,256	2,188	2,254	2,308	2,336	2,427	2,464	2,378
Pulp, paper, allied products	1,652	1,641	1,486	1,502	1,508	1,511	1,510	1,543	1,485
Lumber and wood products [3]	1,543	1,525	1,390	1,282	1,342	1,324	1,421	1,385	1,409
Primary metal products	1,332	872	979	977	970	1,021	1,114	1,199	1,254
Stone, clay, and glass products....	1,025	960	931	878	911	944	1,009	1,044	1,033
Petroleum and coal products	865	861	918	888	943	929	967	997	1,013
Nonmetallic minerals [2]	948	949	885	824	812	818	862	875	895
Waste and scrap materials......	513	446	504	515	558	613	655	685	702
Metallic ores	597	403	408	400	409	385	378	394	382
Machinery, exc. electrical.......	176	72	67	62	61	59	65	69	70
Fabricated metal products [4]	110	48	42	48	45	50	50	44	41

[1] Includes commodity groups and small packaged freight shipments, not shown separately.　[2] Except fuels.　[3] Except furniture.　[4] Except ordnance, machinery, and transport.

Source: Association of American Railroads, Washington, DC, *Freight Commodity Statistics,* annual.

No. 1066. Railroad Freight—Producer Price Indexes: 1980 to 1997

[Dec. 1984=100. Reflects prices for shipping a fixed set of commodities under specified and unchanging conditions]

COMMODITY	1980	1985	1990	1991	1992	1993	1994	1995	1996	1997
Total railroad freight	**75.9**	**99.9**	**107.5**	**109.3**	**109.9**	**110.9**	**111.8**	**111.7**	**111.5**	**112.1**
Coal	75.8	100.0	104.2	105.2	105.9	106.6	107.5	107.3	106.7	107.0
Farm products	75.6	99.0	110.4	111.4	111.1	113.7	114.5	115.6	115.7	120.4
Food products	75.2	100.0	105.4	108.1	108.7	109.0	111.0	111.2	108.5	107.6
Metallic ores	74.5	100.2	106.5	106.7	106.6	106.7	104.6	101.9	103.5	103.4
Chemicals or allied products	75.6	100.1	111.7	113.5	115.6	116.2	117.6	120.0	119.2	119.6
Nonmetallic minerals	72.2	100.1	111.7	115.9	117.6	119.3	119.7	119.5	119.2	120.6
Wood or lumber products	72.7	100.0	107.5	108.6	108.8	109.7	110.0	110.0	112.8	111.0
Transportation equipment	81.7	100.0	107.5	109.7	110.8	113.1	115.3	112.8	114.0	113.2
Pulp, paper, or allied products	76.7	100.0	108.0	111.5	111.8	112.6	111.1	108.7	(NA)	111.2
Primary metal products	77.8	99.7	113.1	116.1	117.5	116.3	115.6	115.6	115.4	114.0
Clay, concrete, glass, or stone products .	74.2	100.0	114.1	117.1	116.5	117.9	120.1	121.4	121.1	119.8
Petroleum and coal products	76.1	99.7	109.2	111.6	109.5	110.6	114.8	114.3	114.1	120.5

NA Not available.

Source: U.S. Bureau of Labor Statistics, *Producer Price Indexes,* monthly and annual.

No. 1067. Petroleum Pipeline Companies—Characteristics: 1980 to 1996

[Covers pipeline companies operating in interstate commerce and subject to jurisdiction of Federal Energy Regulatory Commission]

ITEM	Unit	1980	1985	1990	1991	1992	1993	1994	1995	1996
Total miles of pipeline	1,000.	173	171	168	172	164	164	159	177	169
Gathering lines	1,000.	36	35	32	31	29	29	30	35	32
Trunk lines	1,000.	136	136	136	141	136	135	128	142	137
Total deliveries	Mil. bbl.	10,600	10,745	11,378	11,496	11,447	12,219	12,159	12,862	12,635
Crude oil	Mil. bbl.	6,405	6,239	6,563	6,685	6,541	6,708	6,785	6,952	6,975
Products	Mil. bbl.	4,195	4,506	4,816	4,811	4,906	5,511	5,373	5,910	5,660
Total trunk line traffic	Bil. bbl-miles .	3,405	3,342	3,500	3,470	3,428	3,051	3,566	3,619	3,734
Crude oil	Bil. bbl-miles .	1,948	1,842	1,891	1,899	1,853	1,382	1,823	1,899	1,912
Products	Bil. bbl-miles .	1,458	1,500	1,609	1,571	1,575	1,669	1,743	1,720	1,822
Carrier property value	Mil. dol.	19,752	21,605	25,828	26,943	27,106	31,625	26,363	27,460	28,043
Operating revenues.	Mil. dol.	6,356	7,461	7,149	6,798	7,154	6,931	7,281	7,711	7,321
Net income	Mil. dol.	1,912	2,431	2,340	1,788	2,061	1,763	2,148	2,670	2,372

Source: PennWell Publishing Co., Houston, Texas, *Oil & Gas Journal,* annual (copyright).

No. 1068. Major Interstate Natural Gas Pipeline Companies—Summary: 1985 to 1991

[The classification of A and B interstate natural gas pipeline companies changed to major companies and nonmajor companies. Major natural gas pipleline companies are those whose combined sales for resale and natural gas transported or stored for a fee exceed 50 billion cubic feet. They account for more than 85 percent of all interstate natural gas]

ITEM	Unit	1985	1986	1987	1988	1989	1990	1991
Sales	Tril. cu. ft . .	11.3	7.8	6.5	6.4	5.6	4.5	3.9
Residential.	Tril. cu. ft . .	0.3	0.2	0.2	0.3	0.1	0.2	0.2
Commercial, industrial	Tril. cu. ft . .	1.1	0.5	0.4	0.5	0.5	0.4	0.3
For resale	Tril. cu. ft . .	9.9	7.1	5.8	5.6	4.9	3.9	3.3
Operating revenues	Mil. dol . . .	49,106	33,859	27,565	27,501	25,695	22,574	21,420
From sales [1]	Mil. dol . . .	44,996	29,508	22,942	22,512	19,786	15,981	14,135
From transportation of gas of others. . . .	Mil. dol . . .	2,272	3,027	3,622	4,059	4,959	5,505	6,117
Other	Mil. dol . . .	1,838	1,325	1,002	929	950	1,088	1,167
Operation, maintenance expenses.	Mil. dol . . .	42,528	27,460	21,794	22,742	20,829	17,446	17,335
Production.	Mil. dol . . .	36,739	22,208	16,955	17,625	15,257	12,124	11,663
Storage.	Mil. dol . . .	418	420	409	436	458	417	460
Transmission	Mil. dol . . .	3,409	2,984	2,598	2,589	2,589	2,720	2,880
Distribution	Mil. dol . . .	132	80	80	127	94	112	133
Administrative, general, and other	Mil. dol . . .	1,830	1,768	1,752	1,966	2,430	2,074	2,048
Pipeline mileage.	1,000	230.2	217.3	249.5	246.9	253.2	230.2	249.5
Transmission lines	1,000	189.7	184.6	181.2	191.6	194.1	195.5	146.8
Field lines	1,000	69.6	64.5	62.9	55.5	55.1	54.0	50.7
Storage.	1,000	4.8	4.6	4.3	4.8	4.8	5.0	4.7

[1] Includes other ultimate customers not shown separately.

Source: U.S. Energy Information Administration, *Statistics of Interstate Natural Gas Pipeline Companies,* annual.

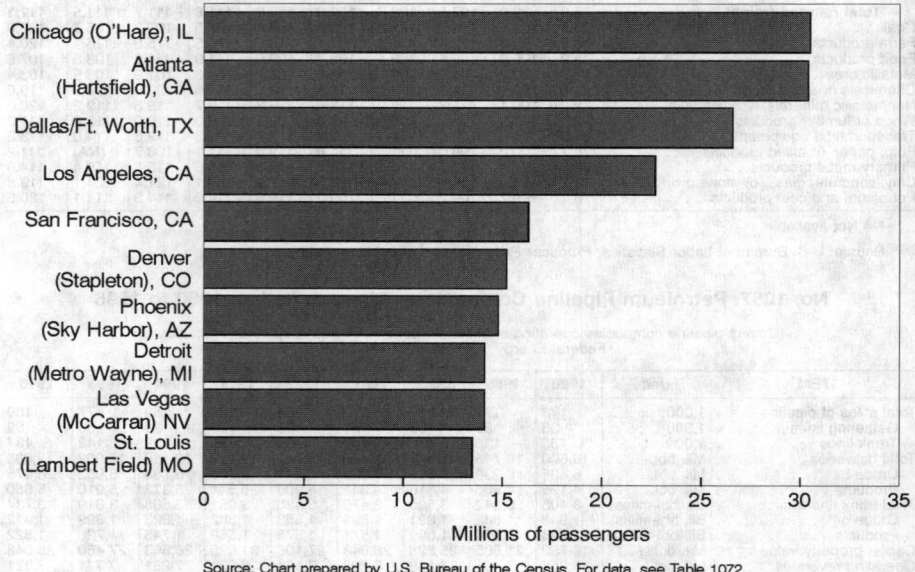

Figure 22.1
**Passengers Enplaned—
Top 10 Airports: 1996**

Millions of passengers

Source: Chart prepared by U.S. Bureau of the Census. For data, see Table 1072.

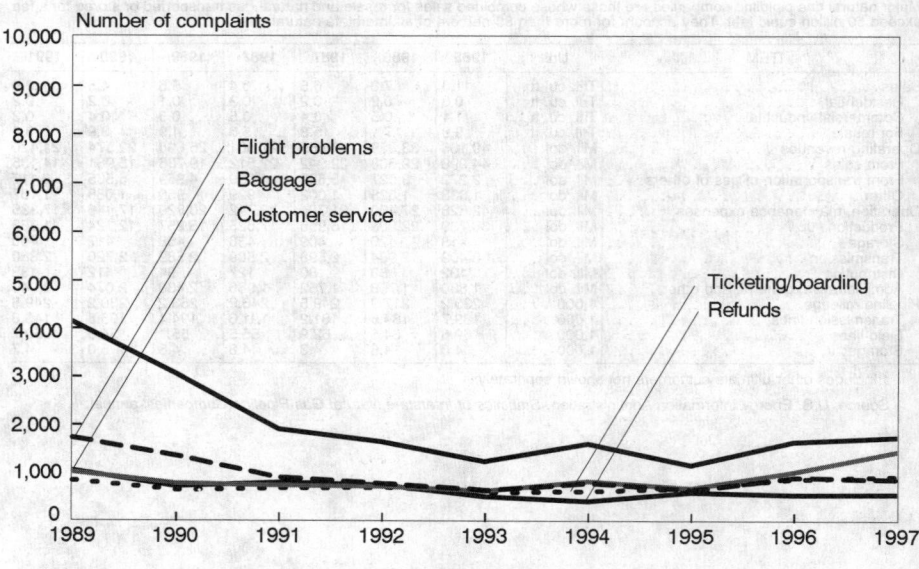

Figure 22.2
**Consumer Complaints Against
U.S. Airlines: 1989 to 1997**

Number of complaints

Flight problems
Baggage
Customer service

Ticketing/boarding
Refunds

Source: Chart prepared by U.S. Bureau of the Census. For data, see Table 1078.

Transportation— Air and Water

This section presents data on civil air transportation and on water transportation, including inland waterways, oceanborne commerce, the merchant marine, cargo and vessel tonnages, and shipbuilding. Comparative data on various types of transportation carriers are presented in Section 21.

Principal sources of these data are the annual *National Transportation Statistics,* issued by the U.S. Bureau of Transportation Statistics; the annual *Air Transport* and *Air Transport Facts and Figures,* issued by the Air Transport Industry Association, Washington, DC, and the annual *Waterborne Commerce of the United States,* issued by the Corps of Engineers of the Department of the Army. In addition, the Bureau of the Census in its commodity transportation survey (part of the census of transportation, taken every 5 years, for years ending in "2" and "7") provides data on the type, weight, and value of commodities shipped by manufacturing establishments in the United States, by means of transportation, origin, and destination.

Additional sources of data on water transportation include *Merchant Fleets of the World,* issued periodically by the U.S. Maritime Administration; *The Bulletin,* issued monthly by the American Bureau of Shipping, New York, NY; and *World Fleet Statistics* and the *Register Book,* published by Lloyd's Register of Shipping, London, England.

Civil aviation—Federal promotion and regulation of civil aviation have been carried out by the FAA and the Civil Aeronautics Board (CAB). The CAB promoted and regulated the civil air transportation industry within the United States and between the United States and foreign countries. The Board granted licenses to provide air transportation service, approved or disapproved proposed rates and fares, and approved or disapproved proposed agreements and corporate

In Brief
SCHEDULED AIR CARRIERS
Revenue passengers enplaned:

1985	382 million
1996	581 million

Net profit:

1985	+$863 million
1996	+$2,824 million

relationships involving air carriers. In December 1984, the CAB ceased to exist as an agency. Some of its functions were transferred to the Department of Transportation (DOT), as outlined below. The responsibility for investigation of aviation accidents resides with the National Transportation Safety Board.

The Office of the Secretary, DOT aviation activities include the following: negotiation of international air transportation rights, selection of U.S. air carriers to serve capacity controlled international markets, oversight of international rates and fares, maintenance of essential air service to small communities, and consumer affairs. DOT's Bureau of Transportation Statistics (BTS) handles aviation information functions formerly assigned to CAB. Prior to BTS, the Research and Special Programs Administration handled these functions.

The principal activities of the FAA include the promotion of air safety, controlling the use of navigable airspace, prescribing regulations dealing with the competency of airmen, airworthiness of aircraft, and air traffic control, operation of air route traffic control centers, airport traffic control towers, and flight service stations, the design, construction, maintenance, and inspection of navigation, traffic control, and communications equipment, and the development of general aviation.

The CAB published monthly and quarterly financial and traffic statistical data for the certificated route air carriers. BTS continues these publications, including both certificated and noncertificated (commuter) air carriers. The FAA publishes data annually on the use of airway facilities; data related to the location of airmen, aircraft, and airports; the volume of activity in the field of nonair carrier (general aviation) flying; and aircraft production and registration.

General aviation comprises all civil flying (including such commercial operations as small demand air taxis, agriculture application, powerline patrol, etc.) but excludes certificated route air carriers, supplemental operators, large-aircraft commercial operators, and commuter airlines.

Air carriers and service—The CAB previously issued "certificates of public convenience and necessity" under Section 401 of the Federal Aviation Act of 1958 for scheduled and nonscheduled (charter) passenger services and cargo services. It also issued certificates under Section 418 of the Act to cargo air carriers for domestic all-cargo service only. The DOT Office of the Secretary now issues the certificates under a "fit, willing, and able" test of air carrier operations. Carriers operating only 60 seat or less aircraft are given exemption authority to carry passengers, cargo, and mail in scheduled and nonscheduled service under Part 298 of the DOT (formerly CAB) regulations. Exemption authority carriers who offer scheduled passenger service to an essential air service point must meet the "fit, willing, and able" test.

Vessel shipments, entrances, and clearances—Shipments by dry cargo vessels comprise shipments on all types of watercraft, except tanker vessels; shipments by tanker vessels comprise all types of cargo, liquid and dry, carried by tanker vessels.

A vessel is reported as entered only at the first port which it enters in the United States, whether or not cargo is unloaded at that port. A vessel is reported as cleared only at the last port at which clearance is made to a foreign port, whether or not it takes on cargo. Army and Navy vessels entering or clearing without commercial cargo are not included in the figures.

Units of measurement—Cargo (or freight) tonnage and shipping weight both represent the gross weight of the cargo including the weight of containers, wrappings, crates, etc. However, shipping weight excludes lift and cargo vans and similar substantial outer containers. Other tonnage figures generally refer to stowing capacity of vessels, 100 cubic feet being called 1 ton. Gross tonnage comprises the space within the frames and the ceiling of the hull, together with those closed-in spaces above deck available for cargo, stores, passengers, or crew, with certain minor exceptions. Net or registered tonnage is the gross tonnage less the spaces occupied by the propelling machinery, fuel, crew quarters, master's cabin, and navigation spaces. Substantially, it represents space available for cargo and passengers. The net tonnage capacity of a ship may bear little relation to weight of cargo. Deadweight tonnage is the weight in long tons required to depress a vessel from light water line (that is, with only the machinery and equipment on board) to load line. It is, therefore, the weight of the cargo, fuel, etc., which a vessel is designed to carry with safety.

No. 1069. Air and Water Transportation Industries—Summary: 1992

[For establishments with payroll]

INDUSTRY	1987 SIC [1] Code	Establish- ments	Revenue (mil. dol.)	Annual payroll (mil. dol.)	Paid employees [2] (1,000)
Air transportation [3]	**45**	**(NA)**	**82,670**	**24,530**	**707**
Air transportation, including air courier services [3]	451,2	(NA)	76,503	22,734	627
Scheduled and air courier services [3]	451	(NA)	73,070	22,026	604
Scheduled [3]	4512	(NA)	62,057	19,090	505
Air courier services.	4513	2,639	11,013	2,935	99
Nonscheduled.	452	1,791	3,433	708	23
Airport terminal services.	458	3,252	6,168	1,796	80
Water transportation	**44**	**8,147**	**29,207**	**5,170**	**171**
Water transportation of freight	441,2,3,4	836	14,704	1,523	37
Deep sea foreign and domestic freight	441, 2	615	11,948	1,148	27
Deep sea foreign freight	4412	334	8,490	629	13
Deep sea domestic freight	4424	281	3,458	519	13
Other water transportation of freight	443,4	221	2,756	375	10
Great Lakes-St. Lawrence Seaway freight	4432	26	559	81	1
Water transportation of freight, n.e.c. [4]	4449	195	2,197	293	9
Water transportation of passengers	448	1,033	4,133	508	23
Ferries.	4482	118	155	51	2
Water transportation of passengers, except by ferry	4481,9	915	3,978	457	22
Deep sea transportation, except by ferry	4481	72	3,268	275	13
Water transportation of passengers, n.e.c. [4] . . .	4489	843	710	182	9
Services incidental to water transportation	449	6,278	10,370	3,140	111
Marinas.	4493	3,348	1,651	346	18
Other services incidental to water transportation . . .	4491,2,9	2,930	8,719	2,794	93
Marine cargo handling.	4491	871	5,066	1,841	59
Towing and tugboat services	4492	941	2,682	689	25
Water transportation services, n.e.c. [4]	4499	1,118	971	263	9

NA Not available. [1] 1987 Standard Industrial Classification code; see text, Section 13, Labor Force. [2] For the pay period including March 12. [3] Revenue for scheduled air transportation includes revenues for large certificated passenger carriers that was reported to the Office of Airline Statistics, U.S. Dept. of Transportation, as published in *Air Carrier Financial Statistics Quarterly*. [4] N.e.c. means not elsewhere classified.

Source: U.S. Bureau of the Census, *Census of Transportation, Communications, and Utilities: 1992*, UC92-A-1.

No. 1070. U. S. Scheduled Airline Industry—Summary: 1985 to 1996

[**For calendar years or Dec. 31.** For domestic and international operations. Covers carriers certificated under Section 401 of the Federal Aviation Act. Minus sign (-) indicates loss]

ITEM	Unit	1985	1990	1991	1992	1993	1994	1995	1996
SCHEDULED SERVICE									
Revenue passengers enplaned .	Mil.	382.0	465.6	452.3	475.1	488.5	528.8	547.8	581.2
Revenue passenger miles.	Bil..	336.4	457.9	448.0	478.6	489.7	519.4	540.7	578.4
Available seat miles.	Bil..	547.8	733.4	715.2	752.8	771.6	784.3	807.1	834.7
Revenue passenger load factor .	Percent .	61.4	62.4	62.6	63.6	63.5	66.2	67.0	69.3
Mean passenger trip length [1] . . .	Miles . . .	881	984	990	1,002	1,002	982	987	995
Freight and express ton miles . . .	Mil. . . .	6,030.5	10,546.3	10,225.2	11,129.7	11,943.6	13,792.2	14,577.5	15,245.0
Aircraft departures.	1,000 . . .	5,835.5	6,923.6	6,782.8	7,050.6	7,245.4	7,531.0	8,061.5	8,227.9
FINANCES									
Total operating revenue [2] . . .	Mil. dol. .	46,664	76,142	75,158	78,140	84,559	88,313	94,578	101,919
Passenger revenue	Mil. dol. .	39,236	58,453	57,092	59,828	63,945	65,422	69,594	75,316
Freight and express revenue. . .	Mil. dol. .	2,681	5,432	5,509	5,916	6,662	7,284	8,616	9,795
Mail revenue	Mil. dol. .	890	970	957	1,184	1,212	1,183	1,266	1,280
Charter revenue	Mil. dol. .	1,280	2,877	3,717	3,082	2,801	3,548	3,485	3,444
Total operating expense	Mil. dol. .	45,238	78,054	76,943	80,585	83,121	85,600	88,718	95,694
Operating profit.	Mil. dol. .	1,426	-1,912	-1,785	-2,444	1,438	2,713	5,860	6,225
Interest expense	Mil. dol. .	1,588	1,978	1,777	2,027	2,347	2,424	1,973
Net profit	Mil. dol. .	863	-3,921	-1,940	-4,791	-2,136	-344	2,314	2,824
Revenue per passenger mile. . .	Cents. . .	11.7	12.8	12.7	12.5	13.1	12.6	12.9	13.0
Rate of return on investment . . .	Percent .	9.6	-6.0	-0.5	-9.3	-0.4	5.2	11.9	11.5
Operating profit margin.	Percent .	3.1	-2.5	-2.4	-3.1	1.7	3.1	6.2	6.1
Net profit margin	Percent .	1.8	-5.1	-2.6	-6.1	-2.5	-0.4	2.4	2.8
EMPLOYEES									
Total	1,000 . . .	355	546	534	540	537	540	547	564
Pilots, copilots, and other flight personnel	1,000 . . .	40	56	57	59	60	61	64	67
Flight attendants	1,000 . . .	63	83	82	86	85	87	87	89
Mechanics	1,000 . . .	43	61	59	59	57	56	50	51
Aircraft and traffic servicing personnel	1,000 . . .	101	251	237	243	243	247	251	266
All other.	1,000 . . .	108	94	98	93	92	90	95	91

[1] For definition of mean, see Guide to Tabular Presentation. [2] Includes other types of revenues, not shown separately.

Source: Air Transport Association of America, Washington, DC, *Air Transport*, annual, and *Air Transport, Facts and Figures*, annual.

No. 1071. Airline Cost Indexes: 1980 to 1996

[Covers U.S. major and national service carriers. Major carriers have operating revenues of $1 billion or more; nationals have operating revenues from $75 million to $1 billion. Minus sign (-) indicates decrease]

INDEX	INDEX (1982=100)								PERCENT DISTRIBUTION OF CASH OPERATING EXPENSES [1]			
	1980	1985	1990	1992	1993	1994	1995	1996	1980	1990	1995	1996
Composite index	86.8	102.8	120.4	126.3	128.2	130.1	131.2	135.2	100.0	100.0	100.0	100.0
Labor cost	85.6	110.6	123.0	136.5	143.4	148.5	155.5	159.5	35.0	29.8	32.3	31.5
Passenger carriers	85.8	110.5	121.7	135.6	143.1	148.7	155.7	159.4	35.2	34.8	33.8
Cargo carriers	78.3	116.0	148.8	150.1	147.0	145.4	151.7	159.6	27.3	14.9	18.1	18.7
Fuel	89.7	79.6	77.2	65.0	59.7	54.4	55.3	64.6	30.0	16.3	10.8	12.2
Aircraft fleet [2] [3]	88.1	123.7	177.0	202.6	208.0	217.5	222.8	229.9	5.2	7.9	9.5	9.6
Interest [2] [4]	88.1	98.0	96.0	79.3	81.2	87.6	93.5	86.9	3.2	2.5	2.8	2.1
Insurance	80.4	155.3	68.2	109.3	139.4	110.8	111.6	111.1	0.3	0.2	0.7	0.7
Maintenance material	104.9	119.9	190.5	177.1	166.2	157.2	153.4	168.9	2.5	3.2	2.5	2.7
Landing fee	87.2	99.9	139.0	168.4	170.1	171.6	176.6	178.0	1.7	1.7	2.0	1.9
Traffic commissions [2]	75.4	112.9	169.2	184.9	193.0	163.3	139.4	130.8	4.9	9.4	8.5	7.9
Communication [2]	65.8	96.6	111.2	124.5	120.0	118.2	116.0	114.7	1.1	1.4	1.5	1.5
Advertising and promotion [2] . .	67.1	96.2	97.8	81.1	72.4	69.7	63.6	58.2	1.6	1.9	1.4	1.2
Passenger food [2]	90.6	98.9	128.4	140.5	128.5	120.6	110.9	104.0	2.9	3.5	3.3	3.1
All other	86.1	111.9	133.4	142.6	146.4	149.9	153.7	157.2	11.8	23.5	26.6	27.6

[1] Total operating expenses plus interest on long term debt, less depreciation and amortization.　[2] Passenger airlines only.
[3] Includes lease, aircraft and engine rentals, depreciation and amortization.　[4] Interest on debt.
Source: Air Transport Association of America, Washington, DC, *Air Transport*, annual; and unpublished data.

No. 1072. Top 40 Airports in 1996—Passengers Enplaned: 1986 and 1996

[In thousands, except rank. For calendar year. Airports ranked by total passengers enplaned]

AIRPORT	1986		1996		AIRPORT	1986		1996	
	Total	Rank	Total	Rank		Total	Rank	Total	Rank
All airports	400,000	(X)	558,184	(X)	New York (JFK), NY	9,125	11	9,703	19
Top 40 airports	304,235	(X)	430,899	(X)	New York (La Guardia), NY.	10,429	8	9,594	20
Chicago (O'Hare), IL . . .	24,794	1	30,526	1	Salt Lake City, UT	4,651	25	9,463	21
Atlanta (Hartsfield Intl), GA.	21,377	2	30,372	2	Pittsburgh, PA	7,470	16	9,348	22
Dallas/Ft. Worth, TX	19,094	3	26,623	3	Honolulu, HI	7,352	17	9,125	23
Los Angeles, CA	17,696	4	22,722	4	Philadelphia, PA	5,424	23	8,572	24
San Francisco, CA.	12,354	7	16,287	5	Cincinnati, OH.	2,136	44	7,300	25
Denver, CO	16,087	5	15,246	6	Washington (National), DC.	4,269	28	6,772	26
Phoenix (Sky Harbor Intl), AZ.	7,720	15	14,807	7	San Diego, CA	4,558	26	6,549	27
Detroit (Wayne County), MI	8,206	13	14,117	8	Portland, OR.	2,415	38	6,126	28
Las Vegas (McCarran Intl), NV	5,329	24	14,054	9	Baltimore, MD.	3,848	31	5,907	29
St. Louis (Lambert-St Louis), MO	9,825	9	13,547	10	Tampa, FL	4,494	27	5,712	30
					Cleveland, OH.	3,093	34	5,287	31
Newark, NJ.	14,405	6	12,916	11	Ft. Lauderdale, FL	3,577	33	4,848	32
Minneapolis/St. Paul, MN . .	7,982	14	12,616	12	San Jose, CA	2,764	36	4,832	33
Miami, FL.	8,589	12	11,906	13	Kansas City, MO	3,911	30	4,820	34
Houston (Intercontinental), TX.	6,560	20	11,622	14	Washington (Dulles Intl), DC	4,269	28	4,750	35
Seattle-Tacoma, WA.	6,652	18	11,489	15	Oakland, CA	1,833	51	4,684	36
Orlando, FL	5,947	21	10,828	16	San Juan (Lewis Munoz Marin Intl), PR	2,156	42	4,550	37
Boston (Logan Intl), MA . .	9,696	10	10,653	17	Chicago (Midway), IL . . .	1,699	54	4,412	38
Charlotte (Douglas Municipal), NC	5,687	22	10,008	18	New Orleans, LA	3,040	35	4,180	39
					Houston (William P. Hobby), TX.	3,722	32	4,026	40

X Not applicable.
Source: U.S. Bureau of Transportation Statistics, *National Transportation Statistics*, 1998, Internet site <http://www.bts.gov/btsprod/nts> (accessed 5 August 1998)

No. 1073. Domestic Airline Markets: 1996

[For calendar year. Data are for the 30 top markets and include all commercial airports in each metro area. Data not include connecting passengers]

MARKET	Passengers	MARKET	Passengers
New York to—from Los Angeles	3,149,020	New York to—from San Juan	1,673,790
New York to—from Chicago	2,996,460	Chicago to—from Los Angeles	1,511,120
New York to—from Miami.	2,777,610	Chicago to—from Detroit	1,506,680
Honolulu to—from Kahului, Maui	2,750,020	Los Angeles to—from Phoenix	1,474,500
New York to—from Boston	2,400,920	New York to—from West Palm Beach. . . .	1,453,700
New York to—from San Francisco	2,282,480	Honolulu to—from Kona, Hawaii	1,391,420
New York to—from Orlando	2,234,940	Los Angeles to—from Honolulu.	1,371,240
Dallas/Ft. Worth to—from Houston	2,205,080	Honolulu to—from Hilo, Hawaii	1,281,090
Los Angeles to—from Las Vegas.	2,102,850	Chicago to—from Minneapolis.	1,275,160
New York to—from Washington	2,087,370	Los Angeles to—from Seattle/Tacoma. . . .	1,259,130
Los Angeles to—from San Francisco	2,034,980	Boston to—from Washington.	1,218,870
New York to—from Atlanta	1,978,680	Chicago to—from Atlanta	1,216,750
Honolulu to—from Lihue, Kauai	1,832,820	New York to—from Dallas/Ft. Worth	1,168,750
New York to—from Ft. Lauderdale	1,768,430	New York to—from Tampa	1,153,880
Los Angeles to—from Oakland	1,710,310	San Francisco to—from San Diego	1,139,240

Source: Air Transport Association of America, Washington, DC, *Air Transport 1997*.

No. 1074. Worldwide Airline Fatalities: 1970 to 1997

[For scheduled air transport operations]

YEAR	Fatal accidents	Passenger deaths	Death rate [1]	Death rate [2]	YEAR	Fatal accidents	Passenger deaths	Death rate [1]	Death rate [2]
1970	29	700	0.29	0.18	1991 [3] . . .	30	653	0.06	0.04
1975	20	467	0.13	0.08	1992 [3] . . .	29	1,097	0.09	0.06
1980	22	814	0.14	0.09	1993 [3] . . .	34	936	0.08	0.05
1985 [3] . . .	22	1,066	0.15	0.09	1994 [3] . . .	28	941	0.07	0.05
1988 [3] . . .	28	729	0.07	0.04	1995 [3] . . .	26	710	0.04	0.03
1989 [3] . . .	27	817	0.07	0.05	1996 [3] . . .	23	1,135	0.08	0.05
1990 [3] . . .	25	495	0.04	0.03	1997 [3][4] . .	26	916	0.06	0.04

[1] Rate per 100 million passenger miles flown. [2] Rate per 100 million passenger kilometers flown. [3] Includes the Commonwealth of Independent States. [4] Preliminary.

Source: International Civil Aviation Organization, Montreal, Canada, *Civil Aviation Statistics of the World,* annual.

No. 1075. Airline Passenger Screening Results: 1980 to 1996

[Calendar year data]

ITEM	1980	1985	1990	1993	1994	1995	1996
Persons screened (mil.)	585	993	1,145	1,150	1,261	1,263	1,382
WEAPONS DETECTED							
Firearms, total	2,022	2,987	2,853	2,798	2,994	2,390	2,147
Handguns	1,878	2,823	2,490	2,707	2,860	2,230	1,999
Long guns	36	90	59	91	134	160	148
Other guns.	108	74	304	(X)	(X)	(X)	(X)
Other dangerous articles [1]	(X)	(X)	(X)	3,867	6,051	4,414	(NA)
Explosive/incendiary devices	8	12	15	251	505	631	(NA)
Persons arrested:							
Carrying firearms/explosives	1,031	1,310	1,337	1,354	1,433	1,194	999
Giving false information	32	42	18	31	35	68	131
Bomb threats received:							
Against airports.	1,179	477	448	304	250	346	284
Against aircraft	268	153	338	248	218	327	419

NA Not available. X Not applicable. [1] For 1980-90 data included firearms; beginning 1993, category includes stunning devices, chemical agents, knives, and other designated items.

Source: U.S. Bureau of Transportation Statistics, *National Transportation Statistics,* 1998, Internet site <http://www.bts.gov/btsprod/nts> (accessed 5 August 1998)

No. 1076. Aircraft Accidents: 1975 to 1997

[For years ending December 31]

ITEM	Unit	1975	1980	1985	1990	1995	1996	1997, prel.
Air carrier accidents, all services [1]	Number. . .	37	19	21	24	36	38	49
Fatal accidents	Number. . .	3	1	7	6	3	5	4
Fatalities	Number. . .	124	1	526	39	168	380	8
Rates per 100,000,000 aircraft miles flown:								
Accidents	Rate	1.5	0.65	0.58	0.49	0.64	0.65	0.76
Fatal accidents	Rate	0.081	0.034	0.19	0.12	0.053	0.086	0.062
Fatalities	Rate	5.0	0.034	14	0.79	3.0	6.5	0.1
Commuter air carrier accidents [2]	Number. . .	48	38	21	16	11	12	16
Fatal accidents	Number. . .	12	8	7	4	2	1	5
Fatalities	Number. . .	28	37	37	7	9	14	46
Rates per 100,000,000 aircraft miles flown:								
Accidents	Rate	(NA)	20	7.0	3.6	1.9	2.4	6.8
Fatal accidents	Rate	(NA)	4.2	2.3	0.9	0.4	0.2	2.1
Fatalities	Rate	(NA)	19	12	1.6	1.6	2.8	20
On-demand air taxi accidents [3]	Number. . .	152	171	154	106	75	89	82
Fatal accidents	Number. . .	24	46	35	28	24	29	16
Fatalities	Number. . .	69	105	76	50	52	63	40
Rates per 100,000 flight hours:								
Accidents	Rate	6.0	4.7	6.0	4.7	3.9	4.6	4.6
Fatal accidents	Rate	0.95	1.3	1.4	1.2	1.3	1.4	1.4
Fatalities	Rate	2.7	2.9	3.0	2.2	2.7	3.2	2.0
General aviation accidents [4]	Number. . .	3,995	3,590	2,739	2,215	2,055	1,905	1,854
Fatal accidents	Number. . .	633	618	498	443	412	359	350
Fatalities	Number. . .	1,252	1,239	956	765	734	631	646
Rates per 100,000 flight hours:								
Accidents	Rate	13.9	9.9	9.7	7.8	8.6	7.9	7.5
Fatal accidents	Rate	2.20	1.70	1.75	1.55	1.74	1.51	1.51
Fatalities	Rate	4.35	3.40	3.38	2.69	3.11	2.67	2.67

NA Not available. [1] U.S. air carriers operating under 14 CFR 121. [2] All scheduled service of U.S. air carriers operating under 14 CFR 135. [3] All nonscheduled service of U.S. air carriers operating under 14 CFR 135. [4] U.S. civil registered aircraft not operated under 14 CFR 121 or 135.

Source: U.S. Bureau of Transportation Statistics, *National Transportation Statistics,* 1998, Internet site <http://www.bts.gov/btsprod/nts> (accessed 3 August 1998)

No. 1077. On-Time Flight Arrivals and Departures at Major U.S. Airports: 1997

[In percent. Quarterly, based on gate arrival and departure times for domestic scheduled operations of U.S. major airlines. All U.S. airlines with 1 percent or more of total U.S. domestic scheduled airline passenger revenues are required to report on-time data. A flight is considered on time if it operated less than 15 minutes after the scheduled time shown in the carrier's computerized reservation system. Cancelled and diverted flights are considered late. See source for data on individual airlines]

AIRPORT	ON-TIME ARRIVALS				ON-TIME DEPARTURES			
	1st. qtr.	2d. qtr.	3d. qtr.	4th. qtr.	1st. qtr.	2d. qtr.	3d. qtr.	4th. qtr.
Total, all airports	73.9	79.0	80.3	77.8	78.9	83.6	84.5	82.6
Total major airports	73.5	78.6	79.9	77.8	77.3	82.4	83.2	81.9
Atlanta, Hartsfield International	70.3	67.8	72.0	70.3	75.4	74.4	80.3	79.4
Baltimore/Washington International	80.0	81.9	83.0	81.5	84.0	86.1	87.3	85.9
Boston, Logan International	74.8	74.2	73.9	73.8	82.4	83.1	83.0	83.2
Charlotte Douglas.	81.3	80.8	84.0	84.2	82.4	81.5	84.7	85.2
Chicago, O'Hare	72.2	80.1	80.3	81.6	73.2	81.7	81.9	82.6
Cincinnati International	72.9	75.8	80.1	80.6	81.3	83.3	86.2	86.9
Dallas/Ft. Worth Regional	74.2	80.0	85.8	79.7	74.4	80.7	85.1	81.1
Denver International	76.6	82.6	80.3	78.8	78.1	85.1	83.7	80.2
Detroit, Metro Wayne	69.2	80.7	80.5	80.5	65.4	78.3	77.6	76.7
Houston George Bush.	78.0	79.1	85.8	80.2	83.0	82.9	87.7	86.1
Las Vegas, McCarran International	76.8	81.8	81.3	78.7	79.3	85.1	83.5	81.0
Los Angeles International.	70.9	75.6	77.1	75.0	74.1	80.2	81.3	79.4
Miami International	70.7	75.3	79.3	75.8	78.9	81.6	84.4	85.1
Minneapolis/St. Paul International	70.5	81.3	78.9	79.5	72.8	81.5	79.4	80.5
Newark International	70.0	71.8	73.8	73.6	76.1	78.6	79.2	80.9
New York, Kennedy International.	73.0	76.9	78.2	74.6	76.7	82.3	84.3	84.1
New York, LaGuardia	74.4	79.0	80.7	79.1	83.2	86.2	86.6	85.8
Orlando International	72.3	77.1	80.8	77.7	82.2	85.0	87.6	86.5
Philadelphia International.	74.2	76.9	77.5	77.9	79.1	82.0	82.3	83.0
Phoenix, Sky Harbor International	75.8	82.1	82.8	78.3	78.3	83.1	83.3	79.6
Pittsburgh, Greater International	80.6	84.3	83.0	83.4	84.6	86.1	84.6	86.6
Portland International	73.9	80.0	79.3	74.1	82.0	85.7	84.9	81.2
St. Louis, Lambert	73.2	82.9	85.7	76.2	74.7	85.4	87.0	78.3
Salt Lake City International	71.1	78.7	80.7	79.9	74.4	84.7	85.3	85.7
San Diego International, Lindbergh	75.5	82.8	81.5	77.2	81.3	88.2	86.1	83.4
San Francisco International	68.1	78.2	74.9	72.7	73.1	83.2	80.2	76.7
Seattle-Tacoma International	69.3	78.3	75.3	71.3	80.5	86.2	80.5	81.0
Washington National.	77.9	79.8	80.0	79.9	85.2	86.0	86.4	86.8

Source: U.S. Department of Transportation, Office of Consumer Affairs, *Air Travel Consumer Report*, monthly.

No. 1078. Consumer Complaints Against U.S. Airlines: 1989 to 1997

[Calendar year data. See source for data on individual airlines]

COMPLAINT CATEGORY	1989	1990	1991	1992	1993	1994	1995	1996	1997
Total	10,553	7,703	6,106	5,639	4,438	5,179	4,629	5,782	6,435
Flight problems [1]	4,111	3,034	1,877	1,624	1,211	1,586	1,133	1,628	1,720
Customer service [2]	1,002	758	714	695	599	805	667	999	1,420
Ticketing/boarding [3]	821	624	659	680	577	598	666	857	909
Baggage.	1,702	1,329	883	752	627	761	628	882	829
Refunds	1,023	701	783	721	482	393	576	521	538
Oversales [4]	607	399	301	265	257	301	263	353	414
Fares [5]	341	312	388	573	398	267	185	180	197
Advertising	89	96	96	54	51	94	66	61	57
Tours	22	29	23	12	16	127	18	16	13
Smoking.	232	74	30	25	30	20	15	13	5
Credit.	19	5	10	10	4	2	4	3	1
Other.	584	342	342	228	186	225	408	269	332

[1] Cancellations, delays, etc. from schedule.   [2] Unhelpful employees, inadequate meals or cabin service, treatment of delayed passengers.   [3] Errors in reservations and ticketing; problems in making reservations and obtaining tickets.   [4] All bumping problems, whether or not airline complied with DOT regulations.   [5] Incorrect or incomplete information about fares, discount fare conditions, and availability, etc.

Source: U.S. Dept. of Transportation, Office of Consumer Affairs, *Air Travel Consumer Report*, monthly.

No. 1079. Commuter/Regional Airline Operations—Summary: 1980 to 1997

[Calendar year data. Commuter/regional airlines operate primarily aircraft of predominately 75 passengers or less and 18,000 pounds of payload capacity serving short haul and small community markets. Represents operations within all North America by U.S. Regional Carriers. Averages are means. For definition of mean, see Guide to Tabular Presentation]

ITEM	Unit	1980	1985	1990	1993	1994	1995	1996	1997
Passenger carriers operating	Number .	214	179	150	130	125	124	109	104
Passengers enplaned	Millions .	14.8	[1]26.0	42.1	52.7	57.1	57.2	61.9	66.3
Average passengers enplaned per carrier. .	1,000 . .	69.2	152.4	277.5	405.2	457.0	461.4	568.3	637.5
Revenue passenger miles (RPM)	Billions .	1.92	[1]4.41	7.61	10.61	12.02	12.75	14.22	15.30
Average RPM's per carrier.	Millions .	8.97	[1]24.64	50.75	81.59	96.15	102.80	130.49	147.09
Airports served	Number .	732	854	811	829	806	780	782	766
Average trip length	Miles. . .	129	173	183	201	210	223	230	231
Passenger aircraft operated	Number .	1,339	1,745	1,917	2,208	2,172	2,138	2,127	2,104
Average seating capacity (seats).	Number .	13.9	19.2	22.1	23.0	23.7	24.6	25.1	25.9
Fleet flying hours [2]	1,000 . .	1,740	2,854	3,447	4,490	4,565	4,659	4,568	4,695
Average annual utilization per aircraft. . . .	Hours . .	1,299	1,635	1,798	2,033	2,102	2,179	2,148	2,231

[1] Adjusted to exclude a merger in 1986.   [2] Prior to 1993, utilization results reflected airborne rather than block hours. Data inclusive of carriers which may have operated during only part of calendar year 1996.

Source: Regional Airline Association, Washington, DC, Annual Report of the Regional Airline Industry (copyright).

No. 1080. Civil Flying—Summary: 1970 to 1996

[As of Dec. 31 or for years ending Dec. 31, except as noted]

ITEM	Unit	1970	1980	1985	1990	1994	1995	1996
Airports in operation [1]	Number . . .	11,261	15,161	16,318	17,490	18,343	18,224	18,292
Heliports	Number . . .	790	2,336	3,120	4,085	4,617	4,559	4,596
Public	Number . . .	4,260	4,814	5,861	5,078	5,137	5,132	5,129
Private	Number . . .	7,001	10,347	10,457	12,412	13,206	13,092	13,163
Airports with runway lights	Number . . .	3,554	4,738	4,941	4,822	4,830	4,838	4,847
Airports with paved runways.	Number . . .	3,805	5,833	6,721	7,694	8,230	8,195	8,218
Airport Improvement Program [2]	Mil. dol. . . .	50.5	639.0	842.1	1,244.7	1,628.0	1,418.1	1,379.9
Total civil aircraft	1,000 . .	154.5	259.4	274.9	275.9	281.0	(NA)	(NA)
Active aircraft [3]	1,000 . .	134.5	214.8	215.4	218.9	180.3	190.0	194.8
Air carriers, total [4]	1,000 . .	2.8	3.8	4.7	6.7	7.4	7.4	7.5
General aviation aircraft [5]	1,000 . .	131.7	211.0	210.7	212.2	172.9	182.6	187.3
Fixed-wing aircraft: Multi-engine . . .	1,000 . .	18.4	31.7	33.6	32.7	22.3	23.7	24.7
Single-engine	1,000 . .	109.5	168.4	164.4	165.1	127.8	134.0	135.9
Rotorcraft [6]	1,000 . .	2.2	6.0	6.4	7.4	4.7	5.6	6.4
Balloons, blimps, gliders, etc	1,000 . .	1.6	5.0	6.3	7.0	5.9	4.5	4.1
Airman certificates held	1,000 . .	1,002	1,195	1,105	1,195	1,225	1,290	1,157
Pilot [7]	1,000 . .	733	827	710	703	654	639	622
Held by women	Percent . . .	4.0	6.4	6.1	5.8	5.9	6.0	5.9
Airline transport	1,000 . .	34	70	83	108	117	124	127
Commercial	1,000 . .	187	183	152	149	139	134	129
Private	1,000 . .	304	357	311	299	284	261	254
Student	1,000 . .	196	200	147	128	96	101	95
Nonpilot [8]	1,000 . .	269	368	395	492	571	651	534
Ground technicians [9]	1,000 . .	241	321	341	421	498	574	459
FAA employees: Total	Number . . .	53,125	55,340	47,245	51,269	48,932	48,324	48,618
Air traffic control specialists [10]	Number . . .	(NA)	27,190	23,580	24,339	23,628	23,208	22,823
Full performance [11]	Number . . .	(NA)	16,317	11,672	12,985	14,997	14,845	15,799
Developmental [11]	Number . . .	(NA)	4,387	4,304	5,042	2,548	2,272	1,999
Assistants [11]	Number . . .	(X)	(X)	1,465	1,153	507	355	335
Traffic management coordinators [12] . .	Number . . .	(X)	(X)	(X)	370	544	561	542
Electronic technicians/ATSS [13]	Number . . .	(NA)	8,871	6,856	6,458	6,531	6,749	6,927
Aviation safety inspectors	Number . . .	(NA)	2,038	1,897	2,984	2,813	2,991	3,265
Engineers	Number . . .	(NA)	2,436	2,457	2,745	2,891	2,810	2,860
Other	Number . . .	(NA)	14,805	12,455	14,743	13,069	12,566	12,743
General aviation: [5]								
Hours flown . . . . [14]	Million	26.0	41.0	34.1	34.8	24.1	25.7	26.1
Fuel consumed: [14]								
Gasoline	Mil. gal. . . .	362	520	420	353	264	276	287
Jet fuel [15].	Mil. gal. . . .	415	766	640	591	663	471	544	568

NA Not available.   X Not applicable.   [1] Existing airports, heliports, seaplane bases, etc. recorded with FAA. Includes military airports with joint civil and military use. Includes U.S. outlying areas. Airport-type definitions: Public—publicly owned and under control of a public agency; private—owned by a private individual or corporation. May or may not be open for public use.   [2] Fiscal year data. Does not include System Planning Grants. Includes U.S. outlying areas. 1970-80 data are obligated federal funds for the Airport Development Aid Program. Thereafter, data are appropriated federal funds under the Airport and Airway Improvement Act of 1982.   [3] Registered aircraft that flew 1 or more hours during the year.   [4] Includes helicopters.   [5] See text, Section 22, Air and Water Transportation. Beginning 1994, excludes commuters and includes experimental aircraft, not shown separately. Prior to 1994, experimental aircraft were included in the appropriate type. Data beginning 1994 have been revised to reflect new information on survey nonresponse.   [6] Includes autogyros; excludes air carrier helicopters.   [7] Includes all active pilots. An active pilot is one with a pilot certificate and a valid medical certificate. Also includes pilots who hold a recreational certificate or only a helicopter, glider, or lighter than air certificate, not shown separately.   [8] Includes dispatchers, flight navigators and engineers, and ground technicians—mechanics, parachute riggers, and ground instructors. Data for 1996 on mechanics, repairmen, parachute riggers, ground instructors, and dispatchers are limited to those ages 70 years and less.   [9] No medical examinations are required, therefore, data represent all certificates on record and include retired or otherwise inactive technicians. See footnote 8.   [10] Includes all air traffic control specialists (staff positions, managers, supervisors, and for 1970-85 traffic management coordinators, not shown separately) and air traffic assistants.   [11] Serving in-flight service stations, towers, and centers.   [12] Prior to 1990, included in total air traffic control specialists.   [13] Airway Transportation Systems Specialists.   [14] Source: 1970, U.S. Bureau of Mines; thereafter, FAA General Aviation Activity and Avionics Survey. Data for 1996 are estimated using new information on survey nonresponse and so are not strictly comparable to earlier years.   [15] Includes kerosene-type and naphtha-type jet fuels.

Source: Except as noted, U.S. Federal Aviation Administration, FAA Statistical Handbook of Aviation, annual, last published in 1993. Internet site <http://api.hq.faa.gov/apohome.htm> and unpublished data.

No. 1081. Net Orders for U.S. Civil Jet Transport Aircraft: 1985 to 1997

[Value in millions of dollars. 1985-1992 are net new firm orders; beginning 1993, net announced orders. Minus sign (-) indicates net cancellations]

TYPE OF AIRCRAFT AND CUSTOMER	1985	1990	1992	1993	1994	1995	1996	1997
Total number [1]	468	670	231	31	79	421	595	512
U.S. customers	242	259	82	44	12	138	408	258
Foreign customers	226	411	149	-13	67	283	187	254
Boeing 737, total	253	189	91	-34	49	189	349	280
U.S. customers	146	38	43	-29	9	85	284	120
Foreign customers	107	151	48	-5	40	104	65	160
Boeing 747, total	37	153	41	-25	-5	35	66	37
U.S. customers	13	24	-	-25	-1	2	22	15
Foreign customers	24	129	41	-	-4	33	44	22
Boeing 757, total	51	66	7	20	5	-7	44	45
U.S. customers	39	33	29	46	-1	-6	35	25
Foreign customers	12	33	-22	-26	6	-1	9	20
Boeing 767, total	10	60	20	43	27	26	10	96
U.S. customers	4	23	10	41	11	4	11	85
Foreign customers	6	37	10	2	16	22	-1	11
Boeing 777, total	-	34	36	29	-	83	88	46
U.S. customers	-	34	-	5	-	-	37	24
Foreign customers	-	-	36	24	-	83	51	22
McDonnell Douglas MD-11, total	-	52	1	-1	2	-6	9	22
U.S. customers	-	16	4	-	2	3	1	-
Foreign customers	-	36	-3	-1	-	-9	8	22
McDonnell Douglas MD-80/90, total	114	116	35	-1	1	51	29	-14
U.S. customers	37	91	-4	6	-8	-	18	-11
Foreign customers	77	25	39	-7	9	51	11	-3
McDonnell Douglas MD-95, total	-	-	-	-	-	50	-	-
U.S. customers	-	-	-	-	-	50	-	-
Foreign customers	-	-	-	-	-	-	-	-

- Represents zero. [1] Includes types of aircraft not shown separately.
Source: Aerospace Industries Association of America, Washington, DC, Research Center, Statistical Series 23.

No. 1082. U.S. Aircraft Shipments: 1971 to 1996

[Value in millions of dollars]

YEAR	TOTAL		CIVIL						MILITARY	
	Units	Value	Large transports		General Aviation [1]		Helicopters		Units	Value
			Units	Value	Units	Value	Units	Value		
1971	11,044	6,555	211	2,542	7,466	322	453	69	2,914	3,622
1975	16,945	8,907	272	3,591	14,056	1,033	838	266	1,779	4,017
1980	14,675	18,950	385	9,916	11,877	2,486	1,366	656	1,047	5,892
1985	3,605	27,225	273	8,404	2,029	1,431	384	506	919	16,884
1990	3,321	38,585	521	22,215	1,144	2,007	603	254	1,053	14,109
1991	3,092	44,657	589	26,856	1,021	1,968	571	211	911	15,622
1992	2,585	47,216	567	28,750	941	1,840	324	142	753	16,484
1993	2,585	41,166	408	24,133	964	2,144	258	113	955	14,776
1994	2,309	38,194	309	19,779	928	2,357	308	185	764	15,873
1995	2,435	36,219	256	17,824	1,077	2,842	292	194	810	15,359
1996, est.	2,374	37,566	269	20,221	1,132	3,142	273	203	700	14,000

[1] Excludes off-the-shelf military aircraft.
Source: U.S. Department of Commerce, International Trade Administration, Internet site <http://www.ita.doc.gov/industry/tai/green/acsh7196.txt> (accessed 4 August 1998).

No. 1083. Employment and Earnings in Aircraft Industries: 1985 to 1997

[Annual averages of monthly figures. See headnote, Table 685]

ITEM	1987 SIC [1] code	Unit	1985	1990	1995	1996	1997
Employment: Total	(X)	1,000	794	898	549	548	591
Aircraft	3721	1,000	326	381	244	243	263
Aircraft engines and engine parts	3724	1,000	148	152	93	95	100
Aircraft equipment, n.e.c. [2]	3728	1,000	143	180	114	120	137
Guided missiles, space vehicles, and parts	376	1,000	177	185	98	90	91
Average weekly earnings: [3]	(X)						
Aircraft	3721	Dollars	(NA)	(NA)	(NA)	(NA)	(NA)
Aircraft engines and parts	3724	Dollars	542	637	770	813	838
Guided missiles, space vehicles, and parts	376	Dollars	515	612	765	790	842
Average hourly earnings: [3]	(X)						
Aircraft [4]	3721	Dollars	13.18	15.66	19.97	20.49	20.76
Aircraft engines and parts	3724	Dollars	12.85	14.84	17.34	18.22	18.58
Guided missiles, space vehicles, and parts	376	Dollars	12.14	14.39	17.74	18.51	19.54

NA Not available. X Not applicable. [1] 1987 Standard Industrial Classification; see text, Section 13, Labor Force. [2] N.e.c. means not elsewhere classified. [3] For production workers. [4] Excludes lump-sum payments. Earnings which include proration of lump-sum payments were: $13.40 in 1985; $16.32 in 1990; $20.02 in 1995; $20.79 in 1996; and $21.09 on 1997.
Source: U.S. Bureau of Labor Statistics, Employment and Earnings, monthly, June issues and Internet site <http://stats.bls.gov/ceshome.htm>

No. 1084. Aerospace—Sales, New Orders, and Backlog: 1990 to 1996

[In billions of dollars, except as indicated. Reported by establishments in which the principal business is the development and/or production of aerospace products]

ITEM	1990	1991	1992	1993	1994	1995	1996
Net sales.	136.6	123.9	118.7	109.9	104.3	102.8	105.7
Percent U.S. Government	54.0	48.9	50.0	49.9	55.6	43.3	40.5
Complete aircraft and parts [1]	49.9	52.9	54.0	48.9	43.3	42.5	45.1
Aircraft engines and parts	16.4	15.6	13.7	12.2	11.3	12.5	15.7
Missiles and space vehicles, parts . . .	22.0	23.3	21.3	18.1	18.4	18.4	17.1
Other products, services	48.3	32.0	29.7	30.7	31.3	29.4	27.9
Net, new orders	146.0	122.5	100.3	79.7	88.7	109.1	126.3
Backlog, Dec. 31	250.1	245.2	236.1	211.8	192.6	202.6	219.6

[1] Except engines sold separately.

Source: U.S. Bureau of the Census, Current Industrial Reports, series MA-37D, Internet site <http://www.census.gov/econ/www/manumenu.htm

No. 1085. Aerospace Industry Sales, by Product Group and Customer: 1985 to 1998

[In billions of dollars. Due to reporting practices and tabulating methods, figures may differ from those in Table 1084]

ITEM	CURRENT DOLLARS					CONSTANT (1987) DOLLARS [3]				
	1985	1990	1995	1997 [1]	1998 [2]	1985	1990	1995	1997 [1]	1998 [2]
Total sales.	96.6	134.4	107.8	129.6	144.5	97.8	121.6	85.5	99.5	108.1
PRODUCT GROUP										
Aircraft, total	50.5	71.4	55.0	69.1	79.5	51.1	64.6	43.7	53.0	59.5
Civil [4]	13.7	31.3	24.0	38.6	49.1	13.9	28.3	19.0	29.7	36.8
Military	36.8	40.1	31.1	30.5	30.4	37.2	36.3	24.6	23.4	22.8
Missiles	11.4	14.2	7.4	8.3	8.0	11.6	12.8	5.9	6.4	6.0
Space	18.6	26.4	27.4	30.6	32.8	18.8	23.9	21.7	23.5	24.6
Related products and services [5] . .	16.1	22.4	18.0	21.6	24.1	16.3	20.3	14.2	16.6	18.0
CUSTOMER GROUP										
Aerospace, total	80.5	112.0	89.8	108.0	120.4	81.5	101.3	71.2	82.9	90.1
DOD [6]	53.2	60.5	42.4	42.3	42.6	53.9	54.8	33.6	32.5	31.9
NASA [7] and other agencies . . .	6.3	11.1	11.4	11.8	11.6	6.3	10.0	9.1	9.0	8.7
Other customers [8]	21.0	40.4	36.0	53.9	66.2	21.3	36.5	28.6	41.4	49.5
Related products and services [5] . .	16.1	22.4	18.0	21.6	24.1	16.3	20.3	14.2	16.6	18.0

[1] Preliminary.   [2] Estimate.   [3] Based on AIA's aerospace composite price deflator.   [4] All civil sales of aircraft (domestic and export sales of jet transports, commuters, business, and personal aircraft and helicopters).   [5] Electronics, software, and ground support equipment, plus sales of non-aerospace products which are produced by aerospace-manufacturing use technology, processes, and materials derived from aerospace products.   [6] Department of Defense.   [7] National Aeronautics and Space Administration.   [8] Includes civil aircraft sales (see footnote 4), commercial space sales, all exports of military aircraft and missiles and related propulsion and parts.

Source: Aerospace Industries Association of America, Inc., Washington, DC, 1995 Year-end Review and Forecast.

No. 1086. Aerospace Industry—Net Profits After Taxes: 1980 to 1997

[For calendar year. Minus sign (-) indicates loss]

YEAR	AEROSPACE INDUSTRY PROFITS				ALL MANUFACTURING CORPORATIONS PROFITS AS A PERCENT OF—		
	Total (mil. dol.)	As percent of—			Sales	Assets	Equity
		Sales	Assets	Equity			
1980	2,588	4.3	5.2	16.0	4.8	6.9	13.9
1982	2,193	3.3	3.7	12.0	3.5	4.5	9.2
1983	2,829	3.5	4.1	12.1	4.1	5.1	10.5
1984	3,639	4.1	4.7	14.1	4.6	6.0	12.5
1985	3,274	3.1	3.6	11.1	3.8	4.6	10.1
1986	3,093	2.8	3.1	9.4	3.7	4.2	9.5
1987	4,582	4.1	4.4	14.6	4.9	5.6	12.8
1988	4,883	4.3	4.4	14.9	6.0	6.9	16.2
1989	3,866	3.3	3.3	10.7	5.0	5.6	13.7
1990	4,487	3.4	3.4	11.5	4.0	4.3	10.7
1991	[1]2,484	1.8	1.9	6.1	2.5	2.6	6.4
1992	[1]-1,836	-1.4	-1.2	-5.2	1.0	1.0	2.6
1993	4,621	3.6	3.5	13.2	2.8	2.9	8.1
1994	5,655	4.7	4.3	14.8	5.4	5.8	15.6
1995	4,633	3.8	3.5	11.1	5.7	6.2	16.2
1996	7,150	5.6	5.1	17.1	6.0	6.5	16.8
1997	7,218	5.2	4.8	17.3	6.3	6.7	16.9

[1] Reflects unusually large nonoperating expenses totalling $3.4 billion in 1991 and $8.7 billion in 1992 due to the initial implementation of a change in accounting for future retirement benefit costs and defense-downsizing restructuring charges. Many large aerospace corporations chose to write off against first quarter earnings amounts required to comply with FASB 106.

Source: Aerospace Industries Association of America, Washington, DC, 1997 Year-end Review and Forecast.

Air and Water Transportation

No. 1087. U.S. Exports of Aerospace Vehicles and Equipment: 1990 to 1997

ITEM	NUMBER OF UNITS				VALUE (mil. dol.)			
	1990	1995	1996	1997	1990	1995	1996	1997
Aerospace vehicles and equipment, total	(NA)	(NA)	(NA)	(NA)	39,119	33,320	40,311	50,614
Total aircraft	(NA)	(NA)	(NA)	(NA)	19,631	13,852	18,984	25,560
Civilian aircraft	(NA)	(NA)	(NA)	(NA)	18,150	12,251	15,160	23,164
Under 4,536 kg. unladen weight, new	1,134	504	507	492	325	296	343	475
4,536-15,000 kg. unladen weight, new.	79	56	52	83	245	306	257	486
Over 15,000 kg. unladen weight, new	306	137	172	252	16,691	10,606	13,624	21,028
Rotorcraft, new	349	208	214	259	161	170	212	208
Used or rebuilt	1,911	614	547	519	712	858	715	959
Nonpowered aircraft	(NA)	(NA)	(NA)	(NA)	15	15	8	8
Military aircraft	445	520	428	416	1,481	1,601	3,824	2,397
New	387	462	316	360	1,406	1,539	3,549	2,297
Used or rebuilt	58	58	112	56	75	62	275	99
Aircraft engines and parts	(NA)	(NA)	(NA)	(NA)	6,918	6,192	6,869	8,618
Piston engines and parts	(NA)	(NA)	(NA)	(NA)	438	369	344	434
Complete engines, new and used	6,411	7,885	7,528	17,749	110	147	144	229
Engine parts	(NA)	(NA)	(NA)	(NA)	328	222	200	205
Reaction/turbine engines and parts	(NA)	(NA)	(NA)	(NA)	6,480	5,823	6,525	8,184
Complete engines, new and used	24,687	7,025	8,638	11,028	1,856	1,802	2,136	2,275
Engine parts	(NA)	(NA)	(NA)	(NA)	4,624	4,020	4,390	5,909
Propellers, rotors, and parts	(NA)	(NA)	(NA)	(NA)	343	334	426	500
Landing gear and parts	(NA)	(NA)	(NA)	(NA)	276	386	527	559
Aircraft parts and accessories, n.e.c. [1]	(NA)	(NA)	(NA)	(NA)	8,982	9,443	10,662	12,090
Avionics	(NA)	(NA)	(NA)	(NA)	747	673	778	871
Flight simulators and parts	(NA)	(NA)	(NA)	(NA)	255	122	166	184
Guided missiles and parts	(NA)	(NA)	(NA)	(NA)	1,306	1,508	1,210	1,149
Space vehicles and parts	(NA)	(NA)	(NA)	(NA)	660	811	689	1,083

NA Not available. [1] N.e.c. means not elsewhere classified.

Source: U.S. Dept. of Commerce, International Trade Administration, Internet site <http://www.ita.doc.gov/aerospace>

No. 1088. International Transportation Transactions of the United States: 1986 to 1997

[In millions of dollars. Data are international transportation transactions recorded for balance of payment purposes (see Table 1302). Receipts include freight on exports carried by U.S.-operated carriers and foreign carrier expenditures in U.S. ports. Payments include freight on imports carried by foreign carriers and U.S. carrier port expenditures abroad. Freight on exports carried by foreign carriers is excluded since such payments are directly or indirectly for foreign account. Similarly, freight on U.S. imports carried by U.S. carriers is a domestic rather than an international transaction. Minus sign (-) indicates excess of payments over receipts]

ITEM	1986	1990	1991	1992	1993	1994	1995	1996	1997
Total receipts	21,020	37,339	38,485	38,147	38,486	40,751	44,990	46,487	47,805
Ocean passenger fares	90	154	156	176	237	287	285	329	329
Other ocean transportation	9,169	12,141	12,252	11,328	11,533	12,404	13,581	12,502	12,201
Freight	3,326	4,326	4,211	4,136	4,056	4,506	5,282	4,703	4,576
Port expenditures	5,843	7,815	8,041	7,192	7,477	7,898	8,299	7,799	7,625
Air passenger fares [1]	5,492	15,144	15,698	16,442	16,291	16,710	18,624	20,084	20,566
Other air transportation	5,420	8,174	8,556	8,374	8,567	9,311	10,016	10,928	11,968
Freight	783	2,432	2,722	2,589	2,814	3,175	3,654	3,958	4,610
Port expenditures	4,637	5,742	5,834	5,785	5,753	6,136	6,362	6,970	7,358
Miscellaneous receipts	849	1,726	1,823	1,827	1,858	2,039	2,484	2,644	2,741
Total payments	24,272	35,497	34,987	34,372	35,933	39,081	41,698	43,222	47,187
Ocean passenger fares	208	248	279	301	341	353	353	453	453
Other ocean transportation	11,299	13,078	12,276	11,781	12,473	13,694	14,068	13,492	14,085
Import freight	9,174	10,904	10,183	9,752	10,462	11,369	11,514	11,259	11,898
Port expenditures	2,125	2,174	2,093	2,029	2,011	2,325	2,554	2,233	2,187
Air passenger fares [1]	6,297	10,283	9,733	10,302	11,069	12,709	14,310	15,365	17,782
Other air transportation	5,127	9,881	10,513	10,468	10,497	10,525	11,061	11,751	12,575
Import freight	2,051	2,207	2,257	2,376	2,580	2,914	3,113	3,201	3,541
Port expenditures	3,076	7,674	8,256	8,092	7,917	7,611	7,948	8,550	9,034
Miscellaneous payments	1,341	2,007	2,186	1,520	1,553	1,800	1,906	2,161	2,292
Balance	-3,252	1,842	3,498	3,775	2,553	1,670	3,292	3,265	618

[1] Beginning 1990, includes interairline settlements.

Source: U.S. Bureau of Economic Analysis, Survey of Current Business, July 1998; and unpublished data.

No. 1089. Federal Expenditures for Civil Functions of the Corps of Engineers, United States Army: 1970 to 1996

[In millions of dollars. For fiscal years ending in year shown, see text, Section 9, State and Local Government. These expenditures represent the work of the Corps of Engineers to plan, design, construct, operate, and maintain civil works projects and activities, particularly in the management and improvement of rivers, harbors, and waterways for navigation, flood control, and multiple purposes. The amounts listed below do not include the expenditure of funds contributed, advanced, or reimbursed by other government agencies or local interests. Includes Puerto Rico and outlying areas]

FISCAL YEAR	Total program [1]	Navigation	Flood control	Multiple purpose	FISCAL YEAR	Total program [1]	Navigation	Flood control	Multiple purpose
1970	1,128	398	379	331	1989	3,252	1,395	1,253	462
1980	3,061	1,225	1,228	551	1990	3,297	1,391	1,397	375
1983	2,959	1,290	1,088	482	1991	3,511	1,473	1,447	443
1984	3,085	1,383	1,154	445	1992	3,675	1,562	1,469	469
1985	2,956	1,234	1,187	419	1993	3,335	1,461	1,243	464
1986	3,163	1,345	1,300	402	1994	3,727	1,607	1,436	521
1987	2,937	1,135	1,272	411	1995	3,796	1,620	1,399	598
1988	3,086	1,271	1,271	423	1996	3,627	1,566	1,349	557

[1] Includes expenditures which are not associated with a specific purpose (e.g., headquarters staff supervision, management, and administration activities, and some research and development activities).

Source: U.S. Army Corps of Engineers, *Report of Civil Works Expenditures by State and Fiscal Year*, annual.

No. 1090. Freight Carried on Major U.S. Waterways: 1975 to 1996

[In millions of tons]

ITEM	1975	1980	1985	1990	1992	1993	1994	1995	1996
Atlantic intracoastal waterway	3.2	4.0	3.1	4.2	3.7	3.8	3.7	3.5	4.3
Great Lakes.	193.8	183.5	148.1	167.1	160.0	159.6	175.3	177.7	181.8
Gulf intracoastal waterway	97.0	94.5	102.5	115.5	112.2	114.9	117.6	117.9	118.0
Mississippi River system [1]	453.4	584.2	527.8	659.6	674.4	660.4	693.3	710.1	701.8
Mississippi River mainstem	311.2	441.5	384.0	475.6	490.7	475.1	496.8	520.2	505.6
Ohio River system [2]	171.4	179.3	203.9	260.0	261.2	257.2	270.5	267.6	270.9
Columbia River.	38.1	49.2	42.4	51.4	49.6	51.2	50.9	57.1	51.2
Snake River.	2.0	5.1	3.5	4.8	4.7	5.3	5.9	6.8	5.7

[1] Main channels and all tributaries of the Mississippi, Illinois, Missouri and Ohio Rivers.   [2] Main channels and all navigable tributaries and embayments of the Ohio, Tennessee, and Cumberland Rivers.

Source: U.S. Army Corps of Engineers, *Waterborne Commerce of the United States*, annual.

No. 1091. Waterborne Commerce, by Type of Commodity: 1990 to 1996

[In millions of short tons. Domestic trade includes all commercial movements between United States ports and on inland rivers, Great Lakes, canals, and connecting channels of the United States, Puerto Rico, and Virgin Islands]

COMMODITY	1990	1994	1995	1996 Total	1996 Domestic	1996 Foreign imports	1996 Foreign exports
Total [1]	2,163.9	2,214.8	2,240.4	2,284.1	1,100.7	732.6	450.8
Coal.	339.9	314.1	324.5	328.7	229.9	8.8	90.1
Petroleum and petroleum products	923.2	961.3	907.1	954.4	398.5	500.0	56.0
Crude petroleum	485.7	531.5	504.6	531.8	128.1	401.7	2.0
Petroleum products [1]	437.5	429.9	402.5	422.7	270.4	98.3	54.0
Gasoline	116.9	119.1	114.4	119.1	95.3	19.6	4.3
Distillate fuel oil	77.4	81.4	76.7	84.5	62.2	16.2	6.2
Residual fuel oil.	145.2	123.4	111.9	112.3	75.1	28.1	9.1
Chemicals and related products	123.8	146.9	153.7	152.3	80.2	24.6	47.5
Crude material, inedible [1]	374.7	369.3	381.7	388.7	233.2	89.5	66.0
Forest products, wood and chips	55.7	47.0	47.2	45.4	18.9	3.6	22.9
Pulp and waste paper	11.8	12.3	14.9	12.6	0.3	0.9	11.3
Soil, sand, gravel, rock, and stone	144.2	147.8	152.5	159.2	127.2	23.8	8.2
Primary manufactured goods [1]	76.0	105.0	106.3	108.9	37.7	55.3	15.9
Papers products	10.7	12.4	13.1	13.7	1.7	3.2	8.8
Lime, cement and glass	28.3	30.9	33.9	33.7	15.6	16.2	1.9
Primary iron and steel products	25.1	46.4	44.1	45.7	14.0	29.3	2.3
Food and farm products [1]	267.5	255.8	303.2	284.9	98.0	25.1	161.7
Fish	3.2	2.7	3.6	2.0	0.1	0.9	1.0
Grain [1]	157.3	133.1	167.9	152.4	55.6	1.2	95.6
Corn	96.1	69.4	105.0	94.0	39.5	(Z)	54.6
Wheat	44.5	47.4	48.5	46.6	12.8	0.2	33.6
Oilseeds	36.0	38.7	46.1	50.1	23.2	0.2	26.7
Soybeans	32.2	35.7	42.0	46.2	19.8	(Z)	26.3
Vegetables products	6.7	8.4	9.0	7.5	1.5	2.2	3.8
Processed grain and animal feed	28.2	29.7	33.0	28.2	8.5	0.8	18.9

Z Rounds to zero.   [1] Includes categories not shown separately.

Source: U.S. Army Corps of Engineers, *Waterborne Commerce of the United States*, annual.

No. 1092. Flag Merchant Vessels—Private Shipyards: 1997

[As of January. Covers ocean-going vessels of 1,000 gross tons and over engaged in foreign and domestic trade, and inactive vessels. Excludes vessels operating exclusively on Great Lakes, inland waterways, and those owned by the United States Army and Navy, and special types such as cable ships, tugs, etc.]

VESSEL TYPE	NUMBER						DEADWEIGHT TONS (1,000)					
	Total	Tank-er [1]	Dry bulk [2]	Con-tainer-ship	Cruise/Pass-en-ger [3]	Other [4]	Total	Tank-er [1]	Dry bulk [2]	Con-tainer-ship	Cruise/Pass-en-ger [3]	Other [4]
Total.........	**495**	**173**	**15**	**83**	**15**	**209**	**17,511**	**10,378**	**575**	**2,639**	**139**	**3,780**
Active vessels........	291	137	11	79	4	60	13,076	8,701	499	2,568	37	1,271
Privately owned.......	282	136	11	79	1	55	12,976	8,684	499	2,568	7	1,218
U.S. foreign trade....	89	13	8	49	-	19	3,392	802	416	1,780	-	394
Foreign-to-foreign....	25	18	1	5	-	1	1,534	1,314	24	187	-	9
Domestic trade.......	130	96	2	22	1	9	7,058	6,301	59	535	7	156
Coastal..........	70	62	2	4	-	2	2,554	2,343	59	114	-	38
Noncontiguous	60	34	-	18	1	7	4,504	3,958	-	421	7	118
Military Sea Lift Command........	38	9	-	3	-	26	992	267	-	66	-	659
Government owned	9	1	-	-	3	5	100	17	-	-	30	53
Ready reserve force ..	2	-	-	-	1	1	24	-	-	-	9	15
Other custody	3	1	-	-	-	2	39	17	-	-	-	22
Other reserve	4	-	-	-	2	2	37	-	-	-	21	16
Inactive vessels	204	36	4	4	11	149	4,435	1,677	76	71	102	2,509
Privately owned.......	20	9	4	-	2	5	968	808	76	-	20	64
Temporarily inactive ..	-	-	-	-	-	-	-	-	-	-	-	-
Laid-up (Not trading) [5].	19	8	4	-	2	5	934	774	76	-	20	64
Laid-up (Marad Custody)	1	1	-	-	-	-	34	34	-	-	-	-
Government owned: National Defense reserve fleet.......	184	27	-	4	9	144	3,467	869	-	71	82	2,445
Ready reserve fleet...	91	10	-	3	-	78	1,897	304	-	51	-	1,542
Other reserve	46	9	-	1	-	36	917	342	-	20	-	555
Nonretention [6]	47	8	-	-	9	30	653	223	-	-	82	348

- Represents zero. [1] Includes liquified natural gas and intergrated tug barge vessels. [2] Includes bulk/oil, ore/oil, ore/bulk/oil carriers and intergrated tug barges. [3] Includes combination passenger and cargo vessels. [4] Breakbulk ships, partial containerships, refrigerated cargo ships, barge, specialized cargo, and roll-on roll-off ships. [5] Vessels idle 30 days or more. [6] Vessels not actively maintained.

Source: Maritime Administration, Office of Statistical and Econimic Analysis.

No. 1093. Private Shipyards—Summary: 1980 to 1997

[For calendar year, unless noted]

ITEM	Unit	1980	1985	1990	1992	1993	1994	1995	1996	1997
Employment [1]........	1,000...	178.0	138.3	130.8	123.8	112.3	107.2	105.0	100.4	94.3
Production workers.....	1,000...	138.8	101.2	93.6	92.7	85.4	79.7	77.8	73.5	67.8
Building activity: Merchant vessels: [2]										
Under construction [3]..	Number .	69	10	-	3	1	1	3	10	14
Ordered	Number .	7	-	3	1	-	3	8	5	6
Delivered	Number .	23	3	-	3	-	1	1	1	4
Cancelled	Number .	4	-	-	-	-	-	-	-	4
Under contract [4].....	Number .	49	7	3	1	1	3	10	14	12
Naval vessels: [2]										
Under construction [3]..	Number .	99	100	95	82	71	60	57	46	46
Ordered	Number .	11	11	7	7	9	12	6	11	4
Delivered	Number .	19	26	15	18	18	15	17	11	8
Under contract [4][5]....	Number .	91	85	87	71	60	57	46	46	42
Repairs/conversions:										
Commercial ships	Mil. dol. .	1,335	852	373	226	292	(NA)	(NA)	(NA)	(NA)
Naval ships........ [3]	Mil. dol. .	1,134	2,311	1,119	526	573	(NA)	(NA)	(NA)	(NA)
Unfinished work: [3]										
Commercial ships	Mil. dol. .	2,070	450	-	156.6	58.3	58.3	93.4	365.4	724.9
Naval ships.........	Mil. dol. .	7,107	12,091	24,495	23,854	21,152	19,679	20,768	17,734	20,116

- Represents zero. NA Not available. [1] Annual average of monthly data. [2] Vessels of 1,000 tons or larger. [3] As of Jan. 1. [4] As of Dec. 31. [5] Two ships were cancelled in 1993.

Source: 1980 and 1985, Shipbuilders Council of America, Arlington, VA., unpublished data; beginning 1990, U.S. Maritime Administration, unpublished data.

No. 1094. Employees in Government and Private Shipyards: 1960 to 1997

[**In thousands.** Annual average employment in establishments primarily engaged in building and repairing of ships, barges, and lighters, whether self-propelled or towed by other craft. Includes all full- and part-time employees]

YEAR	Total	Pri-vate yards	Fed-eral yards	YEAR	Total	Pri-vate yards	Fed-eral yards	YEAR	Total	Pri-vate yards	Fed-eral yards
1960	208	112	96	1988	197	124	73	1993	163	113	50
1970	216	134	83	1989	196	126	71	1994	148	107	41
1975	217	154	65	1990	198	130	68	1995	139	106	33
1980	250	178	72	1991	193	131	62	1996	127	103	24
1985	219	138	80	1992	183	125	58	1997	122	100	22

Source: U.S. Bureau of Labor Statistics, *Employment and Earnings,* monthly, June issues; and Internet cite <http://stats.bls.gov/ceshome/htm>

No. 1095. Employment on U.S. Flag Merchant Vessels and Basic Monthly Wage Scale for Able-Bodied Seamen: 1975 to 1996

[**Employment in thousands**]

YEAR	Employ-ment [1]	YEAR	Employ-ment [1]	YEAR	East coast wage rate [2]	West coast wage rate [2]	YEAR	East coast wage rate [2]	West coast wage rate [2]
1975.	20.5	1991	11.7	1975	612	900	1991	1,518	2,329
1980.	19.6	1992	9.2	1980	967	1,414	1992	1,655	2,438
1985.	13.1	1993	9.3	1985	1,419	2,029	1993	1,721	2,438
1988.	10.7	1994	9.1	1988	1,419	2,175	1994	1,790	2,536
1989.	9.9	1995	7.9	1989	1,448	2,218	1995	1,918	2,637
1990.	11.1	1996	7.5	1990	1,505	2,218	1996	2,014	2,769

[1] As of June 30, except beginning 1980, as of Sept. 30. Estimates of personnel employed on merchant ships, 1,000 gross tons and over. Excludes vessels on inland waterways, Great Lakes, and those owned by, or operated for, U.S. Army and Navy, and special types such as cable ships, tugs, etc.   [2] As of January. Basic monthly wage, over and above subsistence (board and room); excludes overtime and fringe pay benefits. West coast incorporates extra pay for Saturdays and Sundays at sea into base wages but east coast does not.

Source: U.S. Maritime Administration, *U.S. Merchant Marine Data Sheet,* monthly; and unpublished data.

No. 1096. Worldwide Tanker Casualties: 1975 to 1997

[Data for **1975** and **1980** covers tankers, ore/oil carriers and bulk/oil vessels of 6,000 deadweight tons and over; beginning **1985,** 10,000 deadweight tons and over; excludes liquid gas carriers. Incident is counted in the year it is reported. Based on data from "Lloyd's List" published by Lloyd's of London. "Casualties" include weather damage, strandings, collisions and other contact, fires and explosions, machinery damage, and other mishaps]

ITEM	Unit	1975	1980	1985	1990	1992	1993	1994	1995	1996	1997
Casualties.	Number	906	(NA)	340	541	396	314	270	280	241	264
Total losses [1]	Number	22	15	12	10	11	9	11	6	2	7
Deaths	Number	90	132	53	119	86	26	88	8	15	(NA)
Oil spills	Number	45	32	9	31	17	24	29	18	24	22
Amount	1,000 tons	188	136	80	61	152	120	110	4	72	50
Amount	Mil. gallons	58	42	25	19	47	37	33	1	22	15

NA Not available.   [1] Excludes losses due to hostilities.

Source: Tanker Advisory Center, Inc., New York, NY, "Worldwide Tanker Casualty Returns," quarterly.

No. 1097. Merchant Vessels—World and United States: 1970 to 1996

[**Through 1992, as of mid-year; thereafter for year-end.** For propelled sea-going merchant ships of not less than 100 gross tonnage]

YEAR	WORLD: COMPLETED Number	WORLD: COMPLETED Gross tonnage (1,000)	WORLD: OWNED Number	WORLD: OWNED Gross tonnage (1,000)	U.S.: COMPLETED Number	U.S.: COMPLETED Gross tonnage (1,000)	U.S.: REGISTERED Number	U.S.: REGISTERED Gross tonnage (1,000)
1970	2,814	20,980	52,444	227,490	156	375	2,983	18,463
1980	2,412	13,101	73,832	419,911	205	555	5,579	18,464
1985	1,964	18,157	76,395	416,269	66	180	6,447	19,518
1990	1,672	15,885	78,336	423,627	16	15	6,348	21,328
1992	1,506	18,633	79,845	444,305	27	54	5,737	18,228
1993	1,505	20,025	80,655	457,915	30	14	5,646	14,087
1994	1,789	19,612	80,676	475,859	28	29	5,270	13,655
1995	1,856	22,565	82,890	490,662	30	14	5,292	12,760
1996	1,745	25,881	84,264	507,873	29	24	5,289	12,024

Source: Through 1992, Lloyd's Register of Shipping, London, England, *Statistical Tables,* annual; and *Annual Summary of Merchant Ships Completed in the World;* thereafter, *World Fleet Statistics,* annual.

No. 1098. Merchant Vessels—Ships and Tonnage Lost Worldwide: 1980 to 1996

[For merchant vessels of 100 gross tonnage and above. Excludes ships which have been declared constructive losses but have undergone repair during the year. Loss counted in the year the casualty occurred, providing that information was available at time of relevant publication]

TYPE OF SHIP	SHIPS LOST					GROSS TONNAGE LOST (1,000)				
	1980	1990	1994	1995	1996	1980	1990	1994	1995	1996
Total.	363	160	171	190	151	1,791	1,047	1,532	1,055	836
Tankers	24	8	16	12	12	707	138	638	172	179
Ore/bulk carriers [1]	21	15	19	19	18	458	687	590	447	303
General cargo	211	87	76	88	77	478	202	237	218	240
Container ships	2	-	-	-	6	6	-	-	-	94
Passenger [2]	9	-	2	1	-	112	-	26	185	-
Fishing.	96	50	58	70	38	30	20	41	33	20

- Represents zero.   [1] Includes ore/bulk/oil carriers.   [2] Includes passenger cargo/ships.

Source: Lloyd's Register of Shipping, London, England, *Casualty Return*, annual.

No. 1099. Merchant Fleets of the World: 1997

[Vessels of 1,000 gross tons and over. As of Jan. 1. Specified countries have 100 or more ships]

COUNTRY OF REGISTRY	Total	Tanker	Dry Bulk [1]	Container-ship	Roll-on/Roll-off	Cruise/passenger	Other [2]
World total	26,858	6,384	5,694	1,936	946	427	11,471
United States	495	173	15	83	62	15	147
Privately-owned	302	145	15	78	30	3	30
Government-owned . . .	193	28	-	5	32	12	117
Foreign total	26,363	6,211	5,679	1,853	884	412	11,324
Panama	3,998	893	1,086	329	108	54	1,528
Russia	1,655	271	129	27	15	10	1,203
Liberia	1,587	642	461	153	24	38	269
China	1,513	233	345	97	14	33	791
Cyprus	1,476	166	555	108	19	18	610
Malta	1,113	265	337	28	33	9	441
Bahamas.	954	241	142	43	38	47	443
Greece	874	266	406	35	16	19	132
Singapore	753	331	126	114	15	1	166
Japan	744	299	182	37	63	15	148
Saint Vincent	683	99	121	17	25	1	420
Norway (NIS) [3]	626	285	102	5	43	14	177
Philippines.	534	65	232	14	18	6	199
Turkey	516	74	177	4	16	7	238
Korea (South)	449	105	124	65	4	-	151
Netherlands.	445	71	8	40	15	9	302
Indonesia.	444	118	18	5	7	9	287
Ukraine.	415	29	21	11	20	8	326
Germany	404	31	1	180	9	11	172
Antigua & Barbuda . . .	379	11	9	76	19	-	264
Italy	352	194	36	14	41	17	50
Denmark (DIS) [3]	315	71	11	61	9	-	163
India.	305	93	140	6	-	2	64
Malaysia	303	96	50	28	8	-	121
Thailand	286	82	35	8	-	1	160
Honduras	256	28	10	4	5	3	206
Hong Kong	223	15	124	39	-	-	45
Romania	223	12	39	2	9	-	161
Taiwan	202	19	55	87	1	-	40
Sweden	198	69	9	-	48	4	68
Brazil	188	83	53	11	9	1	31
Belize	177	13	13	2	2	-	147
United Kingdom	140	60	6	21	6	20	27
Poland	125	4	69	-	4	1	47
Iran	123	28	47	1	2	-	45
Syria.	119	-	4	-	1	-	114
Norway.	111	24	11	-	7	1	68
Isle of man	110	37	19	17	13	3	21
U.A.R. (Egypt)	110	14	18	-	8	1	69
Vietnam	108	9	5	-	-	-	94
Marshall Islands	106	31	34	19	-	-	22
Bulgaria	105	14	34	5	7	1	44
All others.	2,616	720	275	140	183	48	1,250

- Represents zero.   [1] Includes bulk/oil, ore/oil, and ore/bulk/oil carriers.   [2] Breakbulk ships, partial containerships, refrigerated cargo ships, barge and specialized cargo ships.   [3] International Shipping Registry which is an open registry under which the ship flies the flag of the specified nation but is exempt from certain taxation and other regulations.

Source: U.S. Maritime Administration, *Merchant Fleets of the World*, summary report, annual; and unpublished data.

This section presents statistics on farms and farm operators; land use; farm income, expenditures, and debt; farm output, productivity, and marketings; foreign trade in agricultural products; specific crops; and livestock, poultry, and their products.

The principal sources are the reports issued by the U.S. Bureau of the Census and by the National Agricultural Statistics Service (NASS) and the Economic Research Service (ERS) of the U.S. Department of Agriculture. The 1992 Census of Agriculture is the 24th taken by the Bureau of the Census. The information is available in printed form in the Volume 1, Geographic Area Series, and in electronic format on CD-ROM. The Department of Agriculture publishes annually *Agricultural Statistics*, a general reference book on agricultural production, supplies, consumption, facilities, costs, and returns. The Economic Research Service publishes data on farm assets, debt, and income in the annual *Farm Business Economic Report*. Sources of current data on agricultural exports and imports include *Foreign Agricultural Trade of the United States*, published by the ERS, and the reports of the Bureau of the Census, particularly *U.S. Imports of Merchandise on CD-ROM, U.S. Exports of Merchandise on CD-ROM*, and *U.S. Merchandise Trade: Exports, General Imports, and Imports for Consumption* SITC Revision 3, Commodity by Country (FT925).

The 45 field offices of the NASS collect data on crops, livestock and products, agricultural prices, farm employment, and other related subjects mainly through sample surveys. Information is obtained on some 75 crops and 50 livestock items as well as scores of items pertaining to agricultural production and marketing. State estimates and supporting information are sent to the Agricultural Statistics Board of NASS which reviews the estimates and issues reports containing state and national data. Among these reports are annual

In Brief

Number of farms, 1997: 2.1 million
Leading states:

Texas	205,000
Missouri	102,000
Iowa	98,000

Farm marketings cash receipts, 1996: $202 billion
Leading commodities—

Cattle, calves	$31 billion
Dairy products	$23 billion
Corn	$22 billion

summaries such as *Crop Production, Crop Values, Agricultural Prices*, and *Livestock Production, Disposition and Income*. For more information about concepts and methods underlying USDA's statistical series, see *Major Statistical Series of the U.S. Department of Agriculture* (Agricultural Handbook No. 671), a 12-volume set of publications.

Farms and farmland—The Bureau of the Census has used varying definitions of a farm. Since 1850, when minimum criteria defining a farm for census purposes first were established, the farm definition has been changed nine times. The current definition, first used for the 1974 census, is any place from which $1,000 or more of agricultural products were produced and sold, or normally would have been sold, during the census year.

Acreage designated as "land in farms" consists primarily of agricultural land used for crops, pasture, or grazing. It also includes woodland and wasteland not actually under cultivation or used for pasture or grazing, provided it was part of the farm operator's total operation. Land in farms includes acres set aside under annual commodity acreage programs as well as acres in the Conservation Reserve and Wetlands Reserve Programs for places meeting the farm definition. Land in farms is an operating unit concept and includes land owned and operated as well as land rented from others. All grazing land, except land used under government permits on a per-head basis, was included as "land in farms" provided it was part of a farm or ranch.

Coverage estimates for 1987 and 1992 indicate about 7.2 and 11.1 percent of all farms, respectively, were not included in census totals. Farms undercounted in these censuses were usually small and accounted for approximately 1 percent of the total value of agricultural products sold and approximately 2 percent of the land in farms. For more explanation about mail list compilation and census coverage, see Appendixes A and C, *1992 Census of Agriculture*, Volume 1 reports and *Coverage Evaluation*, Volume 2, Part 2.

Farm income—The final agricultural sector output comprises cash receipts from farm marketings of crops and livestock, federal government payments made directly to farmers for farm-related activities, rental value of farm homes, value of farm products consumed in farm homes, and other farm-related income such as machine hire and custom work. Farm marketings represent quantities of agricultural products sold by farmers multiplied by prices received per unit of production at the local market. Information on prices received for farm products is generally obtained by the NASS Agricultural Statistics Board from surveys of firms (such as grain elevators, packers, and processors) purchasing agricultural commodities directly from producers. In some cases, the price information is obtained directly from the producers.

Crops—Estimates of crop acreage and production by the NASS are based on current sample survey data obtained from individual producers and objective

yield counts, reports of carlot shipments, market records, personal field observations by field statisticians, and reports from other sources. Prices received by farmers are marketing year averages. These averages are based on U.S. monthly prices weighted by monthly marketings during specific periods. U.S. monthly prices are state average prices weighted by marketings during the month. Marketing year average prices do not include allowances for outstanding loans, government purchases, deficiency payments or disaster payments.

All state prices are based on individual state marketing years, while U.S. marketing year averages are based on standard marketing years for each crop. For a listing of the crop marketing years and the participating states in the monthly program, see *Crop Values*, January 1992. Value of production is computed by multiplying state prices by each state's production. The U.S. value of production is the sum of state values for all states. Value of production figures shown in Tables 1128–1131, 1135 and 1136 should not be confused with cash receipts from farm marketings which relate to sales during a calendar year, irrespective of the year of production.

Livestock—Annual inventory numbers of livestock and estimates of livestock, dairy, and poultry production prepared by the Department of Agriculture are based on information from farmers and ranchers obtained by probability survey sampling methods.

Statistical reliability—For a discussion of statistical collection and estimation, sampling procedures, and measures of statistical reliability pertaining to Census Bureau and Department of Agriculture data, see Appendix III.

No. 1100. Farms—Number and Acreage, by Size of Farm: 1982 to 1992

SIZE OF FARM	NUMBER OF FARMS (1,000)			LAND IN FARMS (mil. acres)			CROPLAND HARVESTED (mil. acres)			PERCENT DISTRIBUTION, 1992		
	1982	1987	1992	1982	1987	1992	1982	1987	1992	Number of farms	All land in farms	Cropland harvested
Total	2,241	2,088	1,925	986.8	964.5	945.5	326.3	282.2	295.9	100.0	100.0	100.0
Under 10 acres.	188	183	166	0.7	0.7	0.7	0.3	0.2	0.2	8.6	0.1	0.1
10 to 49 acres	449	412	388	12.1	11.1	10.3	4.5	3.9	3.5	20.1	1.1	1.2
50 to 99 acres	344	311	283	24.8	22.5	20.4	9.5	7.9	7.2	14.7	2.2	2.4
100 to 179 acres.	368	334	301	49.9	45.3	40.7	21.2	17.1	15.4	15.6	4.3	5.2
180 to 259 acres.	211	192	172	45.7	41.5	37.2	21.7	17.2	15.5	8.9	3.9	5.2
260 to 499 acres.	315	286	255	113.0	103.0	91.7	60.5	47.3	43.6	13.3	9.7	14.7
500 to 999 acres.	204	200	186	140.5	138.5	129.3	77.6	67.4	68.6	9.7	13.7	23.2
1,000 to 1,999 acres . .	97	102	102	132.4	138.8	139.0	64.5	61.1	69.3	5.3	14.7	23.4
2,000 acres and over. .	65	67	71	467.5	463.2	476.3	66.6	60.2	72.5	3.7	50.4	24.5

No. 1101. Farms—Number and Acreage, by Tenure of Operator: 1982 to 1992

[*Full owners* own all the land they operate. *Part owners* own a part and rent from others the rest of the land they operate]

ITEM AND YEAR	Unit	Total	Full owner	Part owner	Tenant	PERCENT DISTRIBUTION			
						Total	Full owner	Part owner	Tenant
NUMBER OF FARMS									
1982.	1,000. . . .	2,241	1,326	656	259	100.0	59.2	29.3	11.5
1987.	1,000. . . .	2,088	1,239	609	240	100.0	59.3	29.2	11.5
1992.	1,000. . . .	1,925	1,112	597	217	100.0	57.7	31.0	11.3
Under 50 acres	1,000. . . .	554	444	58	52	100.0	80.1	10.5	9.4
50 to 179 acres.	1,000. . . .	584	395	130	59	100.0	67.6	22.3	10.1
180 to 499 acres.	1,000. . . .	428	190	183	55	100.0	44.4	42.8	12.8
500 to 999 acres.	1,000. . . .	186	48	111	27	100.0	25.8	59.7	14.5
1,000 acres or more.	1,000. . . .	173	35	114	24	100.0	20.2	65.9	13.9
LAND IN FARMS									
1982.	Mil. acres .	987	342	531	114	100.0	34.7	53.8	11.6
1987.	Mil. acres .	964	318	520	127	100.0	32.9	53.9	13.2
1992.	Mil. acres .	946	296	527	123	100.0	31.3	55.7	13.0

No. 1102. Farm Operators—Tenure and Characteristics: 1987 and 1992

[In thousands, except as indicated]

CHARACTERISTIC	ALL FARMS		FARMS WITH SALES OF $10,000 AND OVER		CHARACTERISTIC	ALL FARMS		FARMS WITH SALES OF $10,000 AND OVER	
	1987	1992	1987	1992		1987	1992	1987	1992
Total operators	2,088	1,925	1,060	1,019	Tenant.	240	217	161	148
White	2,043	1,882	1,046	1,003	Principal occupation:				
Black.	23	19	4	5	Farming	1,138	1,053	811	754
American Indian, Eskimo,					Other	950	872	248	265
and Aleut	7	8	2	3	Place of residence: [2]				
Asian or Pacific Islander	8	8	5	5	On farm operated.	1,488	1,379	776	736
Other	7	8	2	3	Not on farm operated	443	409	215	215
Operators of Hispanic origin [1].	17	21	6	8	Years on present farm: [2]				
Female	132	145	42	50	2 years or less.	114	95	49	41
					3 to 4 years	135	133	56	58
Under 25 years old	36	28	21	17	5 to 9 years	304	259	138	121
25 to 34 years old	243	179	147	112	10 years or more	1,163	1,113	653	648
35 to 44 years old	411	382	212	217	Days worked off farm: [2]				
45 to 54 years old	455	429	228	223	None	844	802	561	536
55 to 64 years old	496	430	263	229	Less than 100 days	200	165	124	104
65 years old and over	447	478	188	220	100 to 199 days.	178	162	80	76
Average age (years)	52.0	53.3	50.6	51.9	200 days or more.	737	666	219	226
Full owner	1,239	1,112	445	422					
Part owner	609	597	454	448					

[1] Operators of Hispanic origin may be of any race. [2] Excludes not reported.

Source of Tables 1100-1102: U.S. Bureau of the Census, *Census of Agriculture: 1987*, Vol. 1; and *1992*, Vol. 1.

No. 1103. Farms—Number, Acreage, and Value, by Type of Organization: 1987 and 1992

ITEM	Unit	Total [1]	Individual or family	Partnership	Corporation	PERCENT DISTRIBUTION			
						Total [1]	Individual or family	Partnership	Corporation
ALL FARMS									
Number of farms: 1987	1,000 ...	2,088	1,809	200	67	100.0	86.7	9.6	3.2
1992	1,000 ...	1,925	1,653	187	73	100.0	85.9	9.7	3.8
Land in farms: 1987	Mil. acres.	964	628	153	119	100.0	65.1	15.9	12.4
1992	Mil. acres.	946	604	153	123	100.0	63.9	16.2	13.0
Value of land and buildings: [2] 1987	Bil. dol...	604	424	95	69	100.0	70.1	15.7	11.4
1992	Bil. dol...	687	474	109	85	100.0	69.0	15.8	12.4
Value of farm products sold: 1987	Bil. dol...	136	77	23	35	100.0	56.3	17.1	25.6
1992	Bil. dol...	163	88	29	44	100.0	54.1	18.0	27.2
FARMS WITH SALES OF $10,000 AND OVER									
Number of farms: 1987	1,000 ...	1,060	861	136	56	100.0	81.3	12.8	5.3
1992	1,000 ...	1,019	820	131	61	100.0	80.5	12.8	6.0
Land in farms: 1987	Mil. acres.	829	525	143	116	100.0	63.3	17.3	14.0
1992	Mil. acres.	822	512	143	119	100.0	62.2	17.4	14.4

[1] Includes other types, not shown separately.   [2] Based on a sample of farms.

Source: U.S. Bureau of the Census, *1992 Census of Agriculture*, Vol. 1.

No. 1104. Farms—Number and Acreage: 1980 to 1997

[As of **June 1**. Based on 1974 census definition; for definition of farms and farmland, see text, Section 23. Data for census years (indicated by italics) have been adjusted for underenumeration and are used as reference points along with data from acreage and livestock surveys in estimating data for other years. Minus sign (-) indicates decrease]

YEAR	FARMS		LAND IN FARMS		YEAR	FARMS		LAND IN FARMS	
	Number (1,000)	Annual change [1] (1,000)	Total (mil. acres)	Average per farm (acres)		Number (1,000)	Annual change [1] (1,000)	Total (mil. acres)	Average per farm (acres)
1980	2,440	3	1,039	426	1993	2,083	-25	976	469
1985	2,293	-41	1,012	441	1994	2,065	-18	973	471
1990	2,146	-29	987	460	1995	2,072	7	972	469
1991	2,117	-29	982	464	1996	2,064	-8	970	470
1992	*2,108*	*-9*	*979*	*464*	1997	2,058	-6	968	471

[1] Annual change from immediate preceding year.

No. 1105. Farms—Number and Acreage, by State: 1990 and 1997

[See headnote, Table 1104]

STATE	FARMS (1,000)		ACREAGE (mil.)		ACREAGE PER FARM		STATE	FARMS (1,000)		ACREAGE (mil.)		ACREAGE PER FARM	
	1990	1997	1990	1997	1990	1997		1990	1997	1990	1997	1990	1997
U.S.	2,146	2,058	987	968	460	471	Missouri	108	102	30	30	281	293
							Montana	25	24	61	60	2,449	2,483
Alabama	47	45	10	10	215	216	Nebraska	57	55	47	47	826	855
Alaska	1	1	1	1	1,707	1,804	Nevada	3	3	9	9	3,560	3,520
Arizona	8	8	36	35	4,641	4,720	New Hampshire	3	2	(Z)	(Z)	163	179
Arkansas	47	43	16	15	330	348	New Jersey	8	9	1	1	107	88
California	85	84	31	30	362	357	New Mexico	14	14	45	44	3,296	3,222
Colorado	27	25	33	33	1,249	1,327	New York	39	36	8	8	218	214
Connecticut	4	4	(Z)	(Z)	108	97	North Carolina	62	57	10	9	156	158
Delaware	3	2	1	1	207	235	North Dakota	34	31	41	40	1,209	1,318
Florida	41	40	11	10	266	258	Ohio	83	73	16	15	188	207
Georgia	48	43	13	12	260	274	Oklahoma	70	73	33	34	471	466
Hawaii	5	5	2	2	357	346	Oregon	37	38	18	18	488	467
Idaho	22	22	14	14	628	614	Pennsylvania	53	50	8	8	153	154
Illinois	83	76	28	28	342	368	Rhode Island	1	1	(Z)	(Z)	95	90
Indiana	68	62	16	16	240	256	South Carolina	25	22	5	5	208	233
Iowa	104	98	34	33	322	339	South Dakota	35	33	44	44	1,266	1,354
Kansas	69	64	48	48	694	747	Tennessee	87	80	12	12	139	148
Kentucky	93	88	14	14	152	158	Texas	196	205	132	129	673	629
Louisiana	32	27	9	9	278	321	Utah	13	13	11	11	856	821
Maine	7	7	1	1	201	184	Vermont	7	6	1	1	222	225
Maryland	15	13	2	2	148	162	Virginia	46	47	9	9	193	181
Massachusetts	6	6	1	1	100	92	Washington	37	36	16	16	432	436
Michigan	54	51	11	10	200	206	West Virginia	21	20	4	4	180	185
Minnesota	89	87	30	30	337	343	Wisconsin	80	79	18	17	220	213
Mississippi	40	43	13	13	325	291	Wyoming	9	9	35	35	3,899	3,802

Z Less than 500,000 acres.

Source of Tables 1104 and 1105: U.S. Dept. of Agriculture, National Agricultural Statistics Service, *Farm Numbers, 1975-80; Farms and Land in Farms, Final Estimates by States, 1979-1987; Farms and Land in Farms, Final Estimates, 1988-1992;* and *Farms and Land in Farms*, July releases.

No. 1106. Farm Real Estate—Summary: 1980 to 1997

[1980 and 1989, value data as of **Feb. 1; 1985,** as of **April 1; 1990-98,** as of **January 1.** Excludes Alaska and Hawaii. Total value of land and buildings is estimated by multiplying the number of acres of farmland by the average value per acre of land and buildings. Per acre values are based on data from the census of agriculture. For intercensal years, estimates are based on surveys conducted by the U.S. Dept. of Agriculture]

ITEM	Unit	1980	1985	1989	1990	1991	1992	1993	1994	1995	1996	1997
Total value...............	Bil. dol	763.3	719.4	660.0	671.4	688.0	695.5	717.1	759.2	807.0	860.9	912.3
Average value per acre.......	Dollars.....	737	713	668	683	703	713	736	782	832	890	945
Average value, operating unit...	$1,000.....	313.5	314.5	304.3	313.7	325.9	330.8	345.1	368.7	390.6	417.8	(NA)

NA Not available.

No. 1107. Farm Real Estate—Value of Land and Buildings, by State: 1995 to 1998

[See headnote, Table 1106]

STATE	VALUE OF LAND AND BUILDINGS (mil. dol.)		AVERAGE VALUE OF LAND AND BUILDINGS, PER ACRE			STATE	VALUE OF LAND AND BUILDINGS (mil. dol.)		AVERAGE VALUE OF LAND AND BUILDINGS, PER ACRE		
	1995	1997	1995	1997	1998		1995	1997	1995	1997	1998
U.S.......	807,017	912,344	$832	$945	$1,000	Montana	16,529	18,178	277	305	320
						Nebraska	28,074	31,960	596	680	735
Alabama	12,875	14,356	1,262	1,480	1,570	Nevada......	2,543	3,080	289	350	365
Arizona......	12,282	14,868	347	420	440	New Hampshire	1,094	1,118	2,486	2,600	2,700
Arkansas.....	14,747	14,948	983	1,010	1,050	New Jersey ...	6,844	6,881	8,052	8,290	8,370
California.....	66,456	75,300	2,215	2,510	2,620	New Mexico...	9,883	12,180	225	280	290
Colorado.....	17,020	19,175	520	590	620	New York	10,628	10,703	1,380	1,390	1,390
Connecticut ...	2,495	2,850	6,567	7,500	7,800	North Carolina .	16,092	18,450	1,749	2,050	2,130
Delaware.....	1,533	1,791	2,689	3,170	3,350	North Dakota ..	15,041	16,482	373	410	415
Florida	22,860	23,690	2,219	2,300	2,320	Ohio........	27,359	31,861	1,800	2,110	2,300
Georgia	15,076	16,874	1,256	1,430	1,500	Oklahoma	18,609	19,380	547	570	600
Idaho	11,286	12,960	836	960	1,020	Oregon......	14,776	17,500	844	1,000	1,030
Illinois.......	52,346	61,880	1,863	2,210	2,380	Pennsylvania ..	18,013	20,251	2,339	2,630	2,760
Indiana......	26,302	31,323	1,654	1,970	2,170	Rhode Island ..	438	498	6,947	7,900	8,200
Iowa........	44,786	54,780	1,349	1,650	1,800	South Carolina .	6,749	7,000	1,337	1,400	1,440
Kansas......	25,573	27,485	535	575	590	South Dakota ..	13,306	14,300	302	325	350
Kentucky.....	17,498	20,155	1,250	1,450	1,550	Tennessee....	16,035	19,470	1,336	1,650	1,740
Louisiana	9,199	10,455	1,082	1,230	1,280	Texas.......	70,968	77,400	550	600	650
Maine.......	1,681	1,742	1,245	1,300	1,320	Utah........	6,731	8,250	606	750	780
Maryland.....	8,155	8,400	3,707	4,000	4,120	Vermont	2,026	2,093	1,479	1,550	1,550
Massachusetts .	3,077	3,534	5,398	6,200	6,450	Virginia	15,232	17,255	1,771	2,030	2,100
Michigan	14,219	16,800	1,329	1,600	1,720	Washington ...	16,825	19,311	1,065	1,230	1,280
Minnesota	27,907	30,992	936	1,040	1,090	West Virginia ..	3,368	3,700	910	1,000	1,050
Mississippi....	11,432	11,875	886	950	1,000	Wisconsin	18,004	21,000	1,065	1,250	1,350
Missouri.....	26,411	30,199	880	1,010	1,090	Wyoming.....	6,633	7,612	192	220	230

Source of Tables 1106 and 1107: U.S. Dept. of Agriculture, Economic Research Service (through 1996), and beginning 1997, National Agricultural Statistics Service, 1980, *Farm Real Estate Market Developments,* annual; 1985-88, *Agricultural Resources, Agricultural Land Values and Markets, Situation and Outlook Report,* annual; 1989-98, *Agricultural Land Values,* annual.

No. 1108. Balance Sheet of the Farming Sector: 1980 to 1996

[In billions of dollars, except as indicated. As of **December 31**]

ITEM	1980	1985	1988	1989	1990	1991	1992	1993	1994	1995	1996
Assets	983.2	772.7	792.5	817.7	844.6	848.3	873.8	910.7	943.0	985.4	1,034.9
Real estate...........	782.8	586.2	586.8	604.3	623.3	628.9	646.3	678.3	712.4	761.3	805.4
Livestock and poultry [1]	60.6	46.3	62.2	66.2	70.9	68.1	71.0	72.8	67.9	57.8	60.1
Machinery, motor vehicles [2]	80.3	82.9	81.0	84.1	86.3	85.9	85.3	85.9	86.7	86.7	85.5
Crops [3]	32.7	22.9	23.6	23.7	23.0	22.2	24.2	23.3	23.1	27.2	30.6
Purchased inputs..........	(NA)	1.2	3.5	2.6	2.8	2.6	3.9	3.8	5.0	3.4	4.4
Financial assets..........	26.7	33.3	35.4	36.8	38.3	40.5	43.0	46.5	47.9	49.0	48.9
Claims	983.2	772.7	792.5	817.7	844.6	848.3	873.8	910.7	943.0	985.4	1,034.9
Debt	166.8	177.6	139.8	138.1	138.1	139.4	139.3	142.2	147.1	151.0	156.2
Real estate debt........	89.7	100.1	78.1	76.2	74.9	75.1	75.6	76.3	78.0	79.6	81.9
Nonreal estate debt [4]	77.1	77.5	61.7	61.9	63.2	64.3	63.6	65.9	69.1	71.5	74.2
Equity	816.4	595.1	652.6	679.6	706.4	708.8	734.5	768.5	795.9	834.3	878.7
Farm debt/equity ratio (percent)	20.9	31.0	22.2	21.0	20.3	20.4	19.0	18.5	18.5	18.1	17.8
Farm debt/asset ratio (percent)	17.3	23.7	18.2	17.4	16.9	17.0	15.9	15.6	15.6	15.3	15.1

NA Not available. [1] Excludes horses, mules, and broilers. [2] Include only farm share value for trucks and autos. [3] All non-CCC crops held on farms plus the value above loan rate for crops held under Commodity Credit Corporation. [4] Excludes debt for nonfarm purposes.

Source: U.S. Dept. of Agriculture, Economic Research Service, *Farm Business Economic Report, 1996* (ECI-1997).

No. 1109. Gross Farm Product—Summary: 1980 to 1996

[**In billions of dollars**. For definition of gross product, see text, Section 14. Minus sign (-) indicates decrease]

ITEM	1980	1985	1988	1989	1990	1991	1992	1993	1994	1995	1996
CURRENT DOLLARS											
Farm output, total	142.9	152.7	158.5	177.2	185.6	180.3	187.7	186.5	202.9	197.9	219.9
Cash receipts from farm marketings	140.3	136.3	159.6	166.7	172.3	170.4	172.2	181.7	180.9	193.9	204.2
Farm housing	5.1	5.0	4.8	5.0	5.1	5.2	5.3	5.5	5.8	5.9	6.1
Farm products consumed on farms	1.2	0.9	0.7	0.7	0.7	0.6	0.6	0.5	0.5	0.5	0.4
Other farm income	2.4	4.6	5.2	4.9	4.8	5.1	4.6	4.9	4.9	5.6	6.3
Change in farm inventories	-6.1	5.8	-11.9	-	2.6	-1.1	5.0	-6.2	10.8	-7.9	2.9
Less: Intermediate goods and services purchased [1]	86.8	85.6	94.7	101.0	106.0	107.3	107.1	113.5	119.4	124.4	130.6
Equals: **Gross farm product**	56.1	67.1	63.8	76.2	79.6	72.9	80.6	73.0	83.5	73.5	89.4
Less: Consumption of fixed capital	18.7	20.7	20.5	21.1	21.8	22.4	23.2	23.4	23.7	24.7	25.6
Indirect business tax [2]	3.0	3.3	3.7	3.9	4.4	4.4	4.5	4.4	4.8	5.1	5.1
Plus: Subsidies to operators	1.0	6.3	11.7	9.3	7.5	6.8	7.7	11.3	6.6	6.1	6.1
Equals: **Farm national income**	35.5	49.4	51.4	60.5	61.0	52.9	60.5	56.5	61.5	49.7	64.9
CHAINED (1992) DOLLARS [3]											
Farm output, total	144.5	163.6	160.1	169.7	177.0	178.7	187.7	182.4	199.4	192.0	193.1
Cash receipts from farm marketings	146.3	149.3	161.4	159.7	164.0	168.9	172.2	177.9	178.2	188.5	179.0
Farm housing	7.4	6.2	5.8	5.6	5.6	5.5	5.3	5.2	5.2	5.2	5.1
Farm products consumed on farms	1.4	1.1	0.8	0.7	0.6	0.6	0.6	0.5	0.5	0.5	0.4
Other farm income	2.4	4.7	5.0	4.5	4.7	5.0	4.6	4.8	4.8	5.2	5.3
Change in farm inventories	-7.0	6.9	-12.6	-	2.5	-1.7	5.0	-7.3	11.7	-9.2	2.6
Less: Intermediate goods and services purchased [1]	102.0	96.6	103.0	104.1	106.2	107.1	107.1	111.4	114.7	117.6	117.3
Equals: **Gross farm product**	46.7	66.9	58.2	65.9	70.8	71.6	80.6	71.0	85.0	74.2	75.5

- Represents zero.   [1] Includes rent paid to nonoperator landlords.   [2] Includes nontax liability.   [3] See text, Section 14.

Source: U.S. Bureau of Economic Analysis, *National Income and Product Accounts of the United States 1929-94*, Vol. 2 and *Survey of Current Business*, August 1997.

No. 1110. Value Added to Economy by Agricultural Sector: 1980 to 1996

[**In billions of dollars**. Data include income and expenses related to the farm operator dwellings. The concept presented is consistent with that employed by the Organization for Economic Co-operation and Development]

ITEM	1980	1985	1988	1989	1990	1991	1992	1993	1994	1995	1996
Final agricultural sector output .	148.0	153.5	163.4	181.0	188.8	183.7	191.3	190.2	207.8	203.6	226.2
Final crop output (sales) [1]	64.4	74.1	69.2	81.5	83.3	81.0	89.0	82.0	100.3	96.7	113.5
Final animal output (sales) [1]	70.3	68.7	78.6	83.8	90.2	87.3	87.1	91.7	89.7	87.6	92.0
Services and forestry	13.3	10.7	15.6	15.8	15.3	15.4	15.2	16.6	17.9	19.4	20.7
Machine hire and customwork	0.7	1.5	1.5	1.7	1.8	1.8	1.8	1.9	2.1	1.9	2.2
Forest products sold	1.0	1.4	1.8	2.0	1.9	1.8	2.2	2.6	2.7	2.9	2.9
Other farm income	0.6	3.2	4.5	4.9	4.5	4.7	4.2	4.6	4.4	5.2	5.9
Gross imputed rental value of farm dwellings	11.0	4.7	7.7	7.2	7.2	7.2	7.0	7.6	8.7	9.3	9.8
Less: Intermediate consumption outlays [1]	77.0	73.5	84.3	88.7	92.9	94.6	93.5	100.6	104.9	109.0	112.4
Farm origin [2]	34.9	29.3	37.3	38.1	39.5	38.6	38.6	41.2	41.3	41.6	42.5
Feed purchased	21.0	16.9	20.2	20.7	20.4	19.3	20.1	21.4	22.6	23.8	25.2
Livestock and poultry purchased .	10.7	9.2	13.0	12.9	14.6	14.1	13.6	14.6	13.3	12.3	11.1
Manufactured inputs [2]	22.4	20.2	19.0	20.6	22.0	23.2	22.7	23.1	24.4	26.2	28.4
Fertilizers and lime	9.5	7.5	7.7	8.2	8.2	8.7	8.3	8.4	9.2	10.0	10.9
Pesticides	3.5	4.3	4.1	5.0	5.4	6.3	6.5	6.7	7.2	7.7	8.5
Other intermediate expenses [2]	19.7	24.1	28.0	30.0	31.4	32.8	32.2	36.2	39.2	41.2	41.5
Repair and maintenance of capital items	7.1	6.4	7.7	8.4	8.6	8.6	8.5	9.2	9.1	9.5	10.3
Plus: Net government transactions [3] . .	-2.8	2.9	9.0	5.1	3.1	2.1	2.7	6.9	1.0	0.1	(Z)
Direct government payments	1.3	7.7	14.5	10.9	9.3	8.2	9.2	13.4	7.9	7.3	7.3
Property taxes	3.9	4.5	5.2	5.5	5.9	5.8	6.1	6.2	6.5	6.7	6.8
Equals: **Gross value added**	68.2	82.9	88.1	97.4	98.9	91.2	100.5	96.5	103.9	94.7	113.9
Less: Capital consumption	21.5	19.4	17.6	18.1	18.1	18.2	18.3	18.4	18.7	18.9	18.9
Equals: Net value added	46.7	63.5	70.5	79.3	80.8	73.0	82.1	78.2	85.2	75.8	94.9
Less: Employee compensation	8.3	8.5	9.8	10.7	12.5	12.3	12.3	13.2	13.5	14.3	15.2
Less: Net rent received by nonoperator landlords	6.1	7.7	8.4	9.4	10.1	9.9	11.2	11.0	11.7	12.0	14.3
Less: Real estate and nonreal estate interest	16.3	18.6	14.3	13.9	13.4	12.1	11.1	10.8	11.7	12.7	13.2
Equals: **Net farm income**	16.1	28.6	38.0	45.3	44.8	38.6	47.5	43.1	48.3	36.7	52.2

Z Less than $50 million.   [1] Includes home consumption and value of inventory adjustment.   [2] Includes other outlays not shown separately.   [3] Direct government payments minus motor vehicle registration and licensing fees and property taxes.

Source: U.S. Dept. of Agriculture, Economic Research Service, *Farm Business Economic Report, 1996* (ECI-1997).

No. 1111. Farm Income—Cash Receipts From Farm Marketings: 1990 to 1996

[In millions of dollars. Represents gross receipts from commercial market sales as well as net Commodity Credit Corporation loans. The source estimates and publishes individual cash receipt values only for major commodities and major producing states. The U.S. receipts for individual commodities, computed as the sum of the reported states, may understate the value of sales for some commodities. The degree of underestimation in some of the minor commodities can be substantial]

COMMODITY	1990	1994	1995	1996	COMMODITY	1990	1994	1995	1996
Total	**169,517**	**181,239**	**187,704**	**202,339**	Cabbage	124	240	268	251
					Carrots	281	337	426	378
Livestock and					Cauliflower	188	193	211	218
products [1]	89,220	88,160	87,004	92,914	Celery	215	238	315	198
Cattle and calves	39,302	36,395	34,004	31,138	Corn, sweet	476	635	640	636
Hogs	11,525	9,883	10,264	12,644	Cucumbers	215	284	286	312
Sheep and lambs	414	507	559	601	Lettuce	844	1,278	1,991	1,427
Dairy products	20,153	19,935	19,894	22,834	Onions	486	707	738	701
Broilers	8,365	11,372	11,762	13,906	Peppers, green	150	456	453	462
Chicken eggs	4,010	3,780	3,880	4,757	Tomatoes	1,627	1,746	1,605	1,603
Turkeys	2,393	2,644	2,822	3,056	Cantaloups	195	301	351	401
Horses/mules	490	489	559	628	Watermelons	124	272	357	276
Aquaculture [2]	541	706	757	768					
					Fruits/nuts [1]	9,416	10,335	11,074	11,714
Crops [1]	80,297	93,079	100,700	109,425	Lemons	305	248	268	228
Rice	1,052	1,665	1,282	1,575	Oranges	1,719	1,655	1,712	1,798
Wheat	6,412	7,859	9,115	9,956	Apples	1,078	1,353	1,579	1,846
Barley	823	703	825	992	Avocados	245	260	240	239
Corn	13,348	14,675	18,626	21,573	Cherries	156	249	212	264
Hay	3,271	3,702	3,327	3,574	Grapes	1,677	1,888	2,045	2,334
Sorghum grain	1,002	1,128	1,372	1,813	Peaches	374	315	405	380
Cotton	5,488	6,738	6,851	7,461	Pears	261	227	241	292
Tobacco	2,733	2,656	2,548	2,796	Plums and prunes	295	257	324	295
Peanuts	1,258	1,230	1,001	969	Cranberries	156	231	224	246
Soybeans	10,756	12,826	13,857	16,211	Strawberries	590	837	812	770
Sunflower	217	465	467	432	Almonds	598	965	881	1,009
					Walnuts	236	239	328	318
Vegetables [1]	11,464	13,902	14,891	14,349					
Beans, dry	687	611	609	664	Sugarbeets	1,182	1,234	1,071	1,017
Potatoes	2,502	2,487	2,465	2,699	Cane for sugar	820	899	893	866
Sweetpotatoes	137	181	197	206	Christmas trees	110	436	458	474
Beans, snap	198	293	283	284	Greenhouse/nursery	8,677	10,021	10,441	10,887
Broccoli	268	374	415	403	Mushrooms	667	736	758	753

[1] Includes other commodities not shown separately.   [2] See also Table 1162.

Source: U.S. Dept. of Agriculture, Economic Research Service, *Farm Business Economic Report, 1996* (ECI-1997).

No. 1112. Cash Receipts for Selected Commodities—Leading States: 1996

[See headnote, Table 1111]

STATE	Value of receipts (mil. dol.)	Percent of total receipts	Rank	STATE	Value of receipts (mil. dol.)	Percent of total receipts	Rank
Cattle and calves	31,138	100.0	(X)	Vegetables	14,349	100.0	(X)
Texas	5,331	17.1	1	California	5,474	38.2	1
Nebraska	4,082	13.1	2	Florida	1,303	9.1	2
Kansas	3,995	12.8	3	Idaho	848	5.9	3
Colorado	2,072	6.6	4	Washington	831	5.8	4
Iowa	1,461	4.6	5	Arizona	555	3.9	5
Dairy products	22,834	100.0	(X)	Broilers	13,906	100.0	(X)
California	3,717	16.2	1	Georgia	2,205	15.8	1
Wisconsin	3,262	14.2	2	Arkansas	2,122	15.2	2
New York	1,693	7.4	3	Alabama	1,635	11.7	3
Pennsylvania	1,662	7.2	4	North Carolina	1,310	9.4	4
Minnesota	1,362	5.9	5	Mississippi	1,197	8.6	5
Corn	21,573	100.0	(X)	Hogs	12,644	100.0	(X)
Iowa	4,290	19.8	1	Iowa	3,004	23.7	1
Illinois	3,546	16.4	2	North Carolina	1,749	13.8	2
Nebraska	2,491	11.5	3	Minnesota	1,116	8.8	3
Indiana	1,784	8.2	4	Illinois	1,039	8.2	4
Minnesota	1,704	7.9	5	Nebraska	856	6.7	5
Soybean	16,211	100.0	(X)	Fruits and nuts	11,714	100.0	(X)
Iowa	2,892	17.8	1	California	6,370	57.5	1
Illinois	2,784	17.1	2	Florida	1,774	16.0	2
Minnesota	1,618	9.9	3	Washington	1,466	13.2	3
Indiana	1,453	8.9	4	Oregon	261	2.4	4
Ohio	1,126	6.9	5	Michigan	223	2.0	5

X Not applicable.

Source: U.S. Dept. of Agriculture, Economic Research Service, *Farm Business Economic Report, 1996* (ECI-1997).

No. 1113. Farm Assets, Debt, and Income, by State: 1995 and 1996

[**Assets and debt,** as of **December 31**. Farm income data are after inventory adjustment and include income and expenses related to the farm operator's dwelling. Minus sign (-) indicates loss]

STATE	ASSETS (mil. dol.)		DEBT (mil. dol.)		DEBT/ASSET RATIO (percent)		FINAL AGRICULTURAL SECTOR OUTPUT (mil. dol.)		NET FARM INCOME (mil. dol.)	
	1995	1996	1995	1996	1995	1996	1995	1996	1995	1996
United States	985,364	1,034,871	151,042	156,155	15.3	15.1	203,647	226,212	36,739	52,194
Alabama	14,320	14,615	1,558	1,605	10.9	11.0	3,473	3,831	865	1,074
Alaska.	577	612	12	13	2.1	2.1	35	35	11	10
Arizona	14,559	15,283	1,209	1,057	8.3	6.9	2,286	2,314	661	722
Arkansas	17,579	18,326	3,615	3,687	20.6	20.1	5,475	6,534	1,484	2,101
California	76,064	79,315	14,324	14,917	18.8	18.8	23,372	24,789	4,645	5,663
Colorado	20,560	21,669	3,286	3,505	16.0	16.2	4,630	4,741	636	844
Connecticut	2,432	2,651	200	211	8.2	8.0	509	520	140	154
Delaware	1,743	1,859	314	307	18.0	16.5	755	855	93	138
Florida.	26,051	25,991	3,949	3,895	15.2	15.0	6,200	6,437	1,813	1,769
Georgia	17,969	18,470	3,153	3,316	17.5	18.0	5,821	6,457	1,953	2,234
Hawaii	4,524	4,716	203	207	4.5	4.4	530	520	11	-2
Idaho	14,384	14,940	2,603	2,559	18.1	17.1	3,462	3,739	641	818
Illinois	64,630	68,478	8,085	8,665	12.5	12.7	8,064	10,277	841	2,255
Indiana	31,953	34,447	4,756	4,939	14.9	14.3	5,235	6,133	558	1,241
Iowa	59,366	63,828	10,943	11,642	18.4	18.2	11,433	13,969	2,186	3,969
Kansas	32,117	33,911	6,022	6,039	18.8	17.8	8,017	8,903	1,052	1,729
Kentucky	21,261	21,916	2,871	3,082	13.5	14.1	3,594	3,989	813	1,046
Louisiana	9,313	8,361	1,611	1,461	17.3	17.5	2,225	2,552	521	701
Maine	2,082	2,075	338	350	16.2	16.9	512	549	51	87
Maryland	8,133	8,407	967	982	11.9	11.7	1,589	1,820	193	373
Massachusetts	3,160	3,454	239	258	7.6	7.5	497	527	117	142
Michigan	18,120	19,149	2,722	2,851	15.0	14.9	4,003	3,816	662	376
Minnesota	38,025	39,731	7,707	8,104	20.3	20.4	7,918	9,551	1,058	2,243
Mississippi	13,099	13,654	2,503	2,389	19.1	17.5	3,432	3,994	576	964
Missouri.	32,934	34,598	5,214	5,566	15.8	16.1	4,721	5,922	306	1,195
Montana	19,978	21,056	2,568	2,610	12.9	12.4	2,251	2,192	413	335
Nebraska	37,552	40,719	7,701	8,111	20.5	19.9	9,266	10,860	1,802	3,075
Nevada	3,012	3,181	236	230	7.8	7.2	338	360	48	56
New Hampshire	1,051	1,059	75	80	7.1	7.6	173	182	37	43
New Jersey	6,665	6,681	418	532	6.3	8.0	903	936	227	261
New Mexico	12,390	13,211	1,181	1,272	9.5	9.6	1,582	1,844	307	363
New York.	12,710	13,167	2,178	2,112	17.1	16.0	3,101	3,312	273	462
North Carolina	20,194	20,789	3,280	3,468	16.2	16.7	8,104	9,364	2,680	3,374
North Dakota	21,329	22,308	3,721	3,881	17.4	17.4	3,255	4,099	341	964
Ohio	32,142	34,037	3,443	3,775	10.7	11.1	5,300	5,669	1,100	1,328
Oklahoma	21,613	22,670	3,852	3,993	17.8	17.6	4,029	4,061	488	551
Oregon	17,117	18,182	2,190	2,184	12.8	12.0	3,483	3,801	359	619
Pennsylvania	21,141	22,079	2,496	2,531	11.8	11.5	4,165	4,636	530	946
Rhode Island	425	460	61	35	14.4	7.7	89	92	41	37
South Carolina	7,549	7,685	844	862	11.2	11.2	1,577	1,808	366	493
South Dakota	19,216	20,042	3,714	3,800	19.3	19.0	3,432	4,345	655	1,332
Tennessee	19,567	20,638	2,078	2,152	10.6	10.4	2,638	2,648	470	386
Texas	80,828	85,849	10,159	9,960	12.6	11.6	14,790	14,342	2,524	2,573
Utah	7,982	8,522	690	939	8.6	11.0	965	1,053	179	214
Vermont	2,489	2,507	348	367	14.0	14.7	526	577	92	133
Virginia	17,649	18,533	1,841	1,817	10.4	9.8	2,618	2,757	574	568
Washington	19,412	20,876	3,057	3,126	15.8	15.0	5,828	6,604	933	1,599
West Virginia	3,683	3,792	391	392	10.6	10.4	481	472	41	10
Wisconsin	26,583	27,699	5,200	5,363	19.6	19.4	6,080	6,565	284	560
Wyoming	8,125	8,669	919	955	11.3	11.0	884	860	90	67

Source: U.S. Dept. of Agriculture, Economic Research Service, *Farm Business Economic Report, 1996* (ECI-1997).

No. 1114. Farm Income—Farm Marketings, 1995 and 1996, and Principal Commodities, 1996, by State

[In millions of dollars. Cattle include calves and greenhouse includes nursery]

STATE	1995 Total	1995 Crops	1995 Livestock and products	1996 Total	1996 Crops	1996 Livestock and products	State rank for total farm marketings and four principal commodities in order of marketing receipts
U.S. . . .	187,704	100,700	87,004	202,339	109,425	92,914	Cattle, dairy products, corn, soybeans
AL	2,872	705	2,167	3,174	811	2,363	26-Broilers, cattle, cotton, chicken eggs
AK	30	24	6	29	23	6	50-Greenhouse, dairy products, potatoes, hay
AZ	2,157	1,347	810	2,146	1,308	839	32-Cattle, dairy products, cotton, lettuce
AR	5,090	2,068	3,022	5,887	2,530	3,357	11-Broilers, soybeans, rice, cotton
CA	22,523	16,973	5,549	23,310	17,096	6,213	1-Dairy products, greenhouse, grapes, cotton
CO	4,156	1,414	2,743	4,229	1,470	2,759	17-Cattle, wheat, corn, dairy products
CT	458	230	228	489	252	237	42-Greenhouse, dairy products, aquaculture, chicken eggs
DE	679	162	517	757	184	573	39-Broilers, soybeans, corn, greenhouse
FL	5,956	4,818	1,138	6,131	4,942	1,188	9-Oranges, greenhouse, sugar, dairy products
GA	5,136	2,348	2,789	5,687	2,408	3,279	12-Broilers, cotton, peanuts, chicken eggs
HI	494	423	72	483	417	66	44-Sugar, pineapples, greenhouse, macadamia nuts
ID	3,153	1,932	1,221	3,410	2,081	1,329	25-Potatoes, dairy products, cattle, wheat
IL	8,462	6,537	1,926	9,050	6,989	2,061	5-Corn, soybeans, hogs, cattle
IN	5,187	3,428	1,759	5,558	3,663	1,895	14-Corn, soybeans, hogs, chicken eggs
IA	11,256	6,234	5,022	12,853	7,396	5,457	3-Corn, hogs, soybeans, cattle
KS	7,572	3,035	4,536	7,869	3,299	4,570	7-Cattle, wheat, corn, sorghum grain
KY	3,100	1,485	1,615	3,550	1,831	1,719	22-Tobacco, horses/mules, cattle, corn
LA	2,013	1,383	630	2,342	1,655	687	31-Cotton, sugar, soybeans, rice
ME	450	201	250	485	224	262	43-Potatoes, dairy products, chicken eggs, aquaculture
MD	1,405	572	834	1,534	633	901	36-Broilers, greenhouse, dairy products, corn
MA	436	336	99	478	369	109	45-Greenhouse, cranberries, dairy products, apples
MI	3,626	2,283	1,343	3,643	2,195	1,448	20-Dairy products, corn, greenhouse, soybeans
MN	7,129	3,681	3,448	8,809	4,641	4,168	6-Corn, soybeans, dairy products, hogs
MS	3,134	1,448	1,686	3,463	1,529	1,934	24-Broilers, cotton, soybeans, aquaculture
MO	4,372	2,087	2,285	4,950	2,500	2,450	16-Soybeans, corn, hogs, cattle
MT	1,870	1,074	796	2,027	1,230	797	33-Wheat, cattle, barley, hay
NE	8,953	3,763	5,191	9,454	4,177	5,277	4-Cattle, corn, hogs, soybeans
NV	282	118	164	286	133	153	47-Cattle, hay, dairy products, potatoes
NH	149	86	63	161	89	72	48-Dairy products, greenhouse, apples, cattle
NJ	773	577	196	801	605	196	38-Greenhouse, dairy products, peaches, blueberries
NM	1,458	498	961	1,709	512	1,197	34-Cattle, dairy products, hay, chili peppers
NY	2,859	1,006	1,852	3,043	998	2,045	27-Dairy products, greenhouse, apples, corn
NC	6,891	3,165	3,726	7,831	3,404	4,427	8-Hogs, broilers, tobacco, greenhouse
ND	3,141	2,574	567	3,532	2,996	537	23-Wheat, cattle, barley, sunflower
OH	4,684	3,094	1,589	5,122	3,177	1,945	15-Soybeans, corn, dairy products, greenhouse
OK	3,663	1,091	2,572	3,566	1,126	2,439	21-Cattle, wheat, broilers, hogs
OR	2,709	2,049	660	2,977	2,320	657	28-Greenhouse, wheat, cattle, dairy products
PA	3,769	1,216	2,553	4,143	1,278	2,865	18-Dairy products, cattle, greenhouse, chicken eggs
RI	79	70	9	83	72	11	49-Greenhouse, dairy products, chicken eggs, sweet corn
SC	1,430	816	613	1,602	865	737	35-Broilers, tobacco, greenhouse, cotton
SD	3,396	1,696	1,700	3,684	2,051	1,633	19-Cattle, corn, soybeans, wheat
TN	2,120	1,228	893	2,372	1,374	998	30-Cattle, cotton, soybeans, dairy products
TX	13,108	4,658	8,451	13,053	5,295	7,758	2-Cattle, cotton, dairy products, greenhouse
UT	812	221	591	873	227	646	37-Cattle, dairy products, hay, wheat
VT	470	90	380	535	98	437	41-Dairy products, cattle, greenhouse, maple products
VA	2,230	838	1,393	2,378	900	1,478	29-Broilers, dairy products, cattle, turkeys
WA	5,215	3,631	1,583	5,681	4,017	1,664	13-Apples, dairy products, wheat, cattle
WV	391	79	312	388	80	308	46-Broilers, cattle, dairy products, turkeys
WI	5,674	1,725	3,949	6,062	1,773	4,288	10-Dairy products, corn, cattle, soybeans
WY	728	184	544	662	184	478	40-Cattle, hay, sugar beets, wheat

Source: U.S. Dept. of Agriculture, Economic Research Service, *Farm Business Economic Report, 1996* (ECI-1997).

No. 1115. Indexes of Prices Received and Paid by Farmers: 1990 to 1996

[1990-92=100, except as noted]

ITEM	1990	1994	1995	1996	ITEM	1990	1994	1995	1996
Prices received,					Prices paid, total [3]	99	105	109	114
all products	104	100	102	112	Production	99	106	109	115
					Feed	103	105	104	130
Crops [1]	103	105	112	126	Livestock & poultry	102	94	82	75
Food grains	100	119	134	157	Seed	102	108	110	115
Feed grains and hay	105	106	112	146	Fertilizer	97	105	120	124
Cotton	107	109	127	122	Agricultural chemicals	95	112	115	119
Tobacco	97	101	103	105	Fuels	100	95	94	105
Oil-bearing crops	105	110	104	128	Supplies & repairs	96	109	112	115
Fruits	97	90	99	118	Autos and trucks	97	107	107	108
Commercial vegetables [2]	102	109	120	111	Farm machinery	96	113	120	125
Potatoes & dry beans	133	110	107	114	Building materials	99	109	114	115
					Farm services	96	112	118	118
Livestock and products	105	95	92	99	Interest	107	94	101	105
Meat animals	105	90	85	87	Taxes	95	106	109	112
Dairy products	105	99	98	114	Wage rates	96	110	114	117
Poultry and eggs	105	106	107	120	Parity ratio (1910-14=100) [4]	51	45	45	47

[1] Includes other items not shown separately. [2] Excludes potatoes and dry beans. [3] Includes production items, interest, taxes, wage rates, and a family living component. The family living component is the consumer price index for all urban consumers from the Bureau of Labor Statistics. See text, Section 15, and Table 772. [4] Ratio of prices received by farmers to prices paid.

Source: U.S. Dept. of Agriculture, National Agricultural Statistics Service, *Agricultural Prices: Annual Summary.*

No. 1116. Civilian Consumer Expenditures for Farm Foods—Farm Value and Marketing Bill: 1980 to 1996

[In billions of dollars, except percent. Excludes imported and nonfarm foods, such as coffee and seafood, as well as food consumed by the military, or exported]

ITEM	1980	1985	1988	1989	1990	1991	1992	1993	1994	1995	1996
Consumer expenditures, total	264.4	345.4	398.8	419.4	449.8	465.1	474.5	489.2	512.2	529.5	546.5
Farm value, total	81.7	86.4	96.8	103.8	106.2	101.6	105.1	109.6	109.6	113.8	122.8
Marketing bill, total [1]	182.7	259.0	301.9	315.6	343.6	363.5	369.4	379.6	402.6	415.7	423.7
Percent of total consumer expenditures	69.1	75.0	75.7	75.3	76.4	78.2	77.9	77.6	78.6	78.5	77.5
At-home expenditures [2]	180.1	220.8	242.1	255.5	276.2	286.1	289.6	294.9	308.7	316.9	327.5
Farm value	65.9	66.6	72.5	77.9	80.2	76.7	76.9	76.4	75.3	76.1	81.5
Marketing bill [1]	114.2	154.2	169.6	177.6	196.0	209.4	212.7	218.5	233.4	240.8	246.0
Away-from-home expenditures	84.3	124.6	156.7	163.9	173.6	179.0	184.9	194.3	203.5	212.6	219.0
Farm value	15.8	19.8	24.3	25.9	26.0	24.9	28.2	33.2	34.3	37.7	41.3
Marketing bill [1]	68.5	104.8	132.4	138.0	147.6	154.1	156.7	161.1	169.2	174.9	177.7
Marketing bill cost components:											
Labor cost [3]	81.5	115.6	137.9	145.1	154.0	160.9	168.4	178.0	186.1	196.6	206.3
Packaging materials	21.0	26.9	32.6	35.2	36.5	38.1	40.1	40.9	43.3	47.8	46.9
Rail and truck transport [4]	13.0	16.5	17.8	18.6	19.8	20.4	20.6	21.2	21.8	22.3	22.9
Corporate profits before taxes	9.9	10.4	12.0	12.9	13.2	15.2	15.7	17.2	17.9	18.6	19.3
Fuels and electricity	9.0	13.1	14.1	14.8	15.2	16.3	16.7	18.4	20.5	22.8	24.0
Advertising	7.3	12.5	14.1	15.7	17.1	17.5	18.0	18.6	19.3	20.0	20.8
Depreciation	7.8	15.4	16.2	16.4	16.3	15.8	16.2	17.2	18.1	18.7	19.4
Net interest	3.4	6.1	9.7	12.3	13.5	12.2	10.9	10.1	11.0	11.7	12.1
Net rent	6.8	9.3	11.7	12.7	13.9	15.9	17.2	17.9	18.9	19.6	20.2
Repairs	3.6	4.8	5.2	5.7	6.2	6.4	6.6	7.2	7.8	8.0	8.3
Taxes	8.3	11.7	13.7	14.6	15.7	16.5	17.5	18.2	18.7	19.4	20.1
Other	11.0	16.7	16.8	11.5	22.2	28.3	21.5	14.7	19.2	10.2	3.4

[1] The difference between expenditures for domestic farm-originated food products and the farm value or payment farmers received for the equivalent farm products. [2] Food primarily purchased from retail food stores for use at home. [3] Covers employee wages and salaries, and their health and welfare benefits. Also includes imputed earnings of proprietors, partners, and family workers not receiving stated remuneration. [4] Excludes local hauling.

Source: U.S. Dept. of Agriculture, Economic Research Service, *Food Cost Review,* annual; *Food Review,* periodic; and *Agricultural Statistics,* annual.

No. 1117. Selected Indexes of Farm Inputs: 1980 to 1995

[1992=100. Inputs based on physical quantities of resources used in production]

INPUT	1980	1985	1987	1988	1989	1990	1991	1992	1993	1994	1995
Total	120	106	101	100	99	100	102	100	100	101	101
Farm labor	124	109	102	109	103	103	105	100	97	97	93
Farm real estate	112	107	100	100	102	101	100	100	99	99	98
Durable equipment	166	139	120	113	108	105	103	100	97	94	91
Energy	121	98	102	102	101	100	101	100	100	100	100
Agricultural chemicals [1]	127	96	96	89	92	95	99	100	103	103	108
Other purchased inputs [2]	114	97	93	96	99	101	102	100	108	132	136

[1] Includes fertilizer, lime, and pesticides. [2] Includes purchased services and miscellaneous inputs.

Source: U.S. Dept. of Agriculture, Economic Research Service, *Agricultural Outlook,* monthly.

No. 1118. Farm Output Indexes: 1980 to 1995

[1992=100]

ITEM	1980	1985	1987	1988	1989	1990	1991	1992	1993	1994	1995
Farm output [1]..................	79	89	88	82	89	94	94	100	94	107	101
Per unit of total input...........	66	84	87	82	90	93	93	100	94	106	100
Gross production:											
Livestock and products [2].........	85	89	91	94	94	95	98	100	101	107	110
Meat animals	98	93	95	97	97	97	99	100	100	103	104
Dairy products.............	85	94	94	96	95	98	98	100	99	114	115
Poultry and eggs	64	71	81	83	86	92	96	100	104	109	114
Crops [3]	75	89	85	75	86	92	91	100	89	106	95
Feed crops................	76	100	84	62	85	88	86	100	76	102	83
Food grains	94	95	84	76	83	107	82	100	96	97	90
Oil crops.................	81	96	88	72	88	87	94	100	85	115	99
Cotton and cottonseed	68	82	92	96	75	96	109	100	100	123	110
Tobacco	108	96	69	77	85	95	97	100	94	89	(NA)
Vegetables and melons........	69	81	89	81	84	92	97	100	98	113	108
Fruits and nuts	90	86	95	102	98	97	96	100	107	111	102
Other crops................	57	69	82	86	89	94	96	100	99	105	110

NA Not available. [1] Annual production available for eventual human use. [2] Includes livestock products not shown separately. [3] Includes crops not shown separately.

Source: U.S. Dept. of Agriculture, Economic Research Service, *Agricultural Outlook*, monthly. Also published in the U.S. Council of Economic Advisors, *Economic Report of the President*, annual.

No. 1119. Agricultural Exports and Imports—Volume, by Principal Commodities: 1990 to 1997

[In thousands of metric tons]

EXPORTS	1990	1995	1996	1997	IMPORTS	1990	1995	1996	1997
Animal products [1]	2,737	5,606	5,602	5,723	Fruits, nuts, vegetables ...	4,573	6,214	7,031	7,470
Wheat and products [2] ..	28,282	33,458	31,500	25,851	Bananas..............	3,094	3,664	3,777	3,773
Feed grains and products..	61,397	67,403	58,687	49,032	Green coffee.........	1,174	953	1,077	1,131
Rice	2,509	3,275	2,839	2,508	Cocoa and products	765	620	821	767
Feeds and fodders	10,979	13,338	11,842	12,352	Meat and products [5]	1,165	1,045	1,039	1,154
Protein meal..........	5,138	6,404	6,131	7,311					
Oilseeds and products [3]..	15,778	23,596	26,181	26,764	Vegetable oils	1,183	1,561	1,643	1,880
Vegetable oils.........	1,204	2,510	1,901	2,590	Rubber, crude natural	840	1,044	1,034	1,068
Fruits, nuts, vegetables [4] ..	5,552	6,905	6,831	7,299	Sugar..............	1,856	1,599	2,897	2,975
Cotton and linters	1,733	2,118	1,557	1,652	Spices	129	155	184	184
Tobacco, unmanufactured..	223	209	222	222	Tobacco, unmanufactured .	187	190	302	294

[1] Includes meat and products, poultry meats, dairy products, and fats, oils and greases. Excludes live animals, hides, skins, and eggs. [2] Includes flour and bulgur. [3] Includes soybeans, sunflower seeds, peanuts, cottonseed, safflower seed, flaxseed, and nondefatted soybean flour. [4] Excludes fruit juices. [5] Excludes poultry.

Source: U.S. Dept. of Agriculture, Economic Research Service, *Foreign Agricultural Trade of the United States*, Jan./Feb. 1998, and calendar year supplements.

No. 1120. Agricultural Exports and Imports—Value: 1980 to 1997

[In billions of dollars, except percent. Includes Puerto Rico. Excludes forest products and distilled liquors; includes crude rubber and similar gums (now mainly plantation products). Includes shipments under foreign aid programs]

YEAR	Trade balance	Exports, domestic products	Percent of all exports	Imports for consumption	Percent of all imports	YEAR	Trade balance	Exports, domestic products	Percent of all exports	Imports for consumption	Percent of all imports
1980	23.9	41.2	18	17.4	7	1992	18.3	43.1	10	24.8	5
1985	9.1	29.0	13	20.0	6	1993	17.7	42.9	10	25.2	4
1988	16.1	37.1	12	21.0	5	1994	19.2	46.2	10	27.1	4
1989	18.2	40.1	12	21.9	5	1995	26.0	56.3	10	30.3	4
1990	16.6	39.5	11	22.9	5	1996	26.8	60.4	10	33.6	4
1991	16.5	39.4	10	22.9	5	1997	21.0	57.2	9	36.3	4

Source: U.S. Dept. of Agriculture, Economic Research Service, *Foreign Agricultural Trade of the United States*, Jan.-Feb. issues, and calendar year supplements. Also in *Agricultural Statistics*, annual.

No. 1121. Agricultural Imports—Value, by Selected Commodity, 1980 to 1997, and by Leading Countries of Origin, 1997

[In millions of dollars]

COMMODITY	1980	1985	1990	1994	1995	1996	1997	Leading countries of origin, 1997
Total	17,366	19,968	22,910	27,074	30,336	33,655	36,300	**Canada, Mexico, Indonesia**
Competitive products.	10,374	13,067	17,336	20,316	21,873	25,448	26,948	Canada, Mexico, Italy
Cattle, live	237	307	978	1,152	1,413	1,121	1,124	Canada, Mexico, Japan
Beef and veal	1,780	1,276	1,872	1,798	1,447	1,341	1,609	Canada, Australia, New Zealand
Pork	486	861	938	706	686	728	754	Canada, Denmark, Poland
Dairy products	488	765	891	986	1,118	1,274	1,225	New Zealand, Ireland, Italy
Fruits and preparations. .	564	1,738	2,218	2,137	2,249	2,834	2,847	Mexico, Chile, Argentina
Vegetables and preparations	864	1,385	2,317	2,809	3,189	3,526	3,707	Mexico, Canada, Spain
Wine	692	998	917	1,035	1,153	1,430	1,711	France, Italy, Chile
Malt beverages	367	633	923	1,050	1,166	1,316	1,495	Netherlands, Mexico, Canada
Grains and feeds.	371	623	1,188	2,302	2,312	2,657	2,963	Canada, Thailand, Italy
Sugar and related products.	2,205	1,190	1,213	1,191	1,335	1,889	1,852	Canada, Dominican Republic, Brazil
Oilseeds and products . .	599	756	947	1,548	1,800	2,147	2,242	Canada, Italy, Philippines
Noncompetitive products . .	6,992	6,902	5,574	6,758	8,464	8,207	9,353	Indonesia, Colombia, Mexico
Coffee and products. . . .	4,186	3,322	1,915	2,485	3,263	2,788	3,886	Colombia, Mexico, Brazil
Rubber, crude natural. . .	817	654	707	965	1,629	1,468	1,229	Indonesia, Thailand, Malaysia
Cocoa and products. . . .	920	1,351	1,072	1,013	1,106	1,400	1,471	Canada, Indonesia, Cote d'Ivoire
Bananas and plantains. .	430	763	939	1,072	1,140	1,184	1,220	Costa Rica, Ecuador, Colombia

Source: U.S. Dept. of Agriculture, Economic Research Service, *Foreign Agricultural Trade of the United States*, calendar year supplement.

No. 1122. Imports Share of Food Consumption, by Commodity: 1990 to 1996

[In percent. Import share is the total quantity imported divided by the quantity available for domestic human food consumption. Calculated from supply and utilization balance sheets. A portion of the imports of some commodities is exported; therefore, the ratios presented here may overstate the importance of imports in domestic consumption for some commodity groups. Similarly, a portion of the imports of some commodities is diverted to such nonfood uses as feed, seed, alcohol and fuel production, and industrial uses. This too can overstate the importance of imports]

COMMODITY	1990	1994	1995	1996	COMMODITY	1990	1994	1995	1996
Red meat.	8.1	7.3	6.5	6.4	Bananas.	99.8	99.8	99.8	99.8
Beef	9.8	9.5	8.3	8.0	Grapes.	37.6	40.6	38.8	42.2
Pork	5.6	4.2	3.8	3.7	Fresh vegetables.	8.4	9.3	11.6	12.9
Fish and shellfish	56.3	55.3	55.3	58.5	Cucumbers	33.7	38.4	38.1	42.9
Dairy products [1]	1.9	1.9	1.9	1.9	Tomatoes	20.5	20.3	30.2	36.8
Cheese [2]	4.8	4.7	4.7	4.5					
Salad and cooking oils [3]	5.9	11.1	12.1	12.6	Tree nuts [5]	32.5	37.1	39.9	40.1
Fresh fruits.	30.6	32.3	33.5	34.0	Wheat [6].	4.6	10.8	7.7	10.4
Citrus [4].	3.4	5.7	7.1	6.8	Rice [7].	7.9	10.3	10.2	10.6
Apples	4.7	5.6	7.7	7.2	Cane and beet sugar [8]	24.9	13.6	19.1	33.1

[1] Milk equivalent, milkfat basis. [2] Natural equivalent of cheese and cheese products. [3] Includes edible rapeseed and olive oil. [4] Includes oranges, grapefruits, lemons, limes, tangerines, and tangelos. [5] Includes almonds, filberts, pecans, walnuts, Brazil nuts, pignolias, and miscellaneous tree nuts including chestnuts, cashews, and macadamias. [6] Flour and other wheat products included, grain equivalent. [7] Rough equivalent. Includes milled rice converted to rough basis at annual extraction rate. [8] Import share is the quantity of imports for domestic consumption (net of re-exports) divided by domestic food consumption (disappearance).

Source: U.S. Dept. of Agriculture, Economic Research Service, *Food Consumption, Prices, and Expenditures*, annual.

No. 1123. Selected Farm Products—United States and World Production and Exports: 1995 to 1997

[In metric tons, except as indicated. Metric ton=1.102 short tons or .984 long tons]

ITEM	Unit	AMOUNT						UNITED STATES AS PERCENT OF WORLD		
		United States			World					
		1995	1996	1997	1995	1996	1997	1995	1996	1997
PRODUCTION [1]										
Wheat	Million.	59	62	69	538	582	610	11.0	10.7	11.3
Corn for grain	Million.	187	236	238	515	591	586	36.3	39.9	40.6
Soybeans	Million.	59	65	74	125	132	152	47.4	49.3	48.8
Rice, milled.	Million.	5.6	5.5	5.8	371	380	381	1.5	1.4	1.5
Cotton [2]	Million bales [3].	19.7	17.9	18.9	85.6	93.0	89.2	23.0	19.2	21.2
EXPORTS [4]										
Wheat [5]	Million.	33.8	27.3	28.6	114.2	117.7	114.9	29.6	23.2	24.9
Corn	Million.	56.6	45.6	38.7	78.2	72.4	70.0	72.3	63.0	55.3
Soybeans	Million.	23.2	24.0	24.9	32.0	36.9	39.0	72.5	65.0	63.8
Rice, milled basis.	Million.	2.7	2.5	2.7	20.2	20.2	21.6	13.4	13.0	12.5
Cotton	Million bales [3].	9.4	7.7	6.9	28.4	27.6	26.7	33.0	27.9	25.8

[1] Production years vary by commodity. In most cases, includes harvests from July 1 of the year shown through June 30 of the following year. [2] For production and trade years ending in year shown. [3] Bales of 480 lb. net weight. [4] Trade years may vary by commodity. [5] Includes wheat flour on a grain equivalent.

Source: U.S. Department of Agriculture, Foreign Agricultural Service, *Foreign Agricultural Commodity Circular Series*, periodic.

No. 1124. Agricultural Exports—Value, by Principal Commodities: 1980 to 1997

[See headnote, Table 1120]

COMMODITY	VALUE (mil. dol.)								PERCENT		
	1980	1985	1990	1993	1994	1995	1996	1997	1980	1990	1997
Total agricultural exports [1]	41,234	29,041	39,517	42,911	46,244	56,348	60,445	57,245	100.0	100.0	100.0
Grains and feeds [1]	19,126	11,882	14,409	14,072	13,625	18,644	20,863	15,361	46.4	36.5	26.8
Feed grains and products	9,852	6,112	7,150	5,173	4,912	8,341	9,575	6,211	23.9	18.1	10.8
Corn	8,492	5,206	6,026	4,220	3,936	7,304	8,404	5,172	20.6	15.2	9.0
Wheat and products	6,660	3,898	4,035	4,909	4,316	5,734	6,466	4,302	16.2	10.2	7.5
Rice	1,289	665	801	770	1,008	996	1,029	932	3.2	2.0	1.6
Oilseeds and products [1]	9,394	5,794	5,705	7,264	7,204	8,921	10,792	12,057	22.8	14.4	21.1
Soybeans	5,880	3,732	3,548	4,599	4,330	5,400	7,324	7,379	14.3	9.0	12.9
Soybean oilcake and meal	1,666	870	979	1,071	907	986	1,430	1,865	4.1	2.5	3.3
Vegetable oils and waxes	1,216	870	810	1,056	1,376	1,820	1,375	1,766	3.0	2.1	3.1
Animals and animal products [1]	3,768	4,150	6,696	8,058	9,275	11,018	11,254	11,468	9.2	16.9	20.0
Hides and skins, incl. furskins	1,046	1,295	1,751	1,285	1,523	1,748	1,675	1,651	2.6	4.4	2.9
Cattle hides	637	1,007	1,369	1,079	1,234	1,465	1,327	1,337	1.6	3.5	2.3
Meats and meat products	890	905	2,558	3,325	3,704	4,522	4,590	4,597	2.2	6.5	8.0
Beef and veal	249	467	1,580	1,995	2,304	2,647	2,429	2,497	0.6	4.0	4.4
Fats, oils, and greases	769	619	424	504	594	827	614	562	1.9	1.1	1.0
Poultry and poultry products	603	384	906	1,376	1,880	2,345	2,828	2,779	1.5	2.3	4.9
Cotton, excluding linters	2,864	1,633	2,783	1,528	2,653	3,681	2,715	2,682	7.0	7.0	4.7
Tobacco, unmanufactured	1,334	1,521	1,441	1,306	1,303	1,400	1,390	1,553	3.3	3.6	2.7
Fruits and preparations	1,335	1,186	2,379	2,795	3,127	3,300	3,291	3,451	3.3	6.0	6.0
Fresh fruits	739	743	1,486	1,707	1,954	1,973	1,971	2,100	1.8	3.8	3.7
Vegetables and preparations	1,188	930	2,225	3,027	3,603	3,637	3,822	4,152	2.9	5.6	7.3
Nuts and preparations	757	683	976	1,182	1,285	1,410	1,626	1,446	1.9	2.5	2.5
Other	1,468	1,262	2,903	3,679	4,169	4,337	4,692	5,075	3.6	7.3	8.9

[1] Includes commodities not shown separately.

Source: U.S. Dept. of Agriculture, Economic Research Service, *Foreign Agricultural Trade of the United States*, Jan./Feb. 1998, and calendar year supplements. Also in *Agricultural Statistics*, annual.

No. 1125. Agricultural Exports—Value, by Selected Countries of Destination: 1980 to 1997

[See headnote, Table 1120. Totals include transshipments through Canada, but transshipments are not distributed by country prior to 1982 and beginning 1996]

COUNTRY	VALUE (mil. dol.)								PERCENT		
	1980	1985	1990	1993	1994	1995	1996	1997	1980	1990	1997
Total agricultural exports [1]	41,234	29,041	39,517	42,911	46,244	56,348	60,445	57,245	100.0	100.0	100.0
Asia [1]	15,046	11,191	17,640	18,160	20,621	28,173	28,468	25,624	36.5	44.8	44.8
Japan	6,133	5,409	8,104	8,836	9,457	11,169	11,696	10,532	14.9	20.6	18.4
Korea, South	1,797	1,413	2,644	1,940	2,339	3,759	3,853	2,857	4.4	6.7	5.0
Taiwan [2]	1,095	1,231	1,661	2,046	2,149	2,601	2,965	2,616	2.7	4.2	4.6
China [2]	2,277	157	814	374	1,084	2,635	2,081	1,600	5.6	2.1	2.8
Iraq	256	326	329	3	-	-	3	82	0.7	0.8	0.1
Hong Kong	437	389	701	883	1,244	1,503	1,490	1,712	1.1	1.8	3.0
Pakistan [1][3]	158	266	338	188	245	451	352	442	0.4	0.9	0.8
Western Europe [4]	12,917	7,002	7,353	7,310	7,346	8,811	9,397	9,540	31.4	18.7	16.7
European Union [4]	12,177	6,542	6,851	7,055	7,028	8,465	9,019	8,918	29.6	17.4	15.6
Netherlands	3,476	1,869	1,581	1,682	1,703	2,073	2,051	1,928	8.5	4.0	3.4
Germany	2,373	1,009	1,158	1,077	1,056	1,223	1,464	1,319	5.8	2.9	2.3
Spain [5]	1,488	837	937	779	846	1,169	1,064	1,140	3.6	2.4	2.0
United Kingdom	996	604	829	941	946	1,058	1,216	1,312	2.5	2.1	2.3
Italy	1,203	669	710	601	547	699	788	756	3.0	1.8	1.3
France	765	403	528	596	453	533	524	570	1.9	1.3	1.0
Latin America [1]	6,154	4,224	5,092	6,840	8,170	8,039	10,436	10,363	15.0	13.0	18.1
Mexico	2,469	1,439	2,553	3,619	4,593	3,540	5,447	5,184	6.0	6.5	9.1
Venezuela	703	638	351	484	398	478	474	571	1.7	0.9	1.0
Canada	1,908	1,622	4,197	5,327	5,567	5,812	6,143	6,795	4.7	10.7	11.9
Soviet Union (former)	1,138	1,923	2,271	1,699	1,009	1,333	1,746	1,483	2.8	5.8	2.6
Eastern Europe	1,644	414	537	430	311	290	417	282	4.0	1.4	0.5
Africa [1]	2,237	2,488	1,935	2,394	2,421	2,818	2,723	2,267	5.5	4.9	4.0
Algeria	195	227	513	480	581	388	292	315	0.5	1.3	0.6
Egypt	774	891	693	646	850	1,309	1,256	964	1.9	1.8	1.7

- Represents or rounds to zero.   [1] Includes areas not shown separately.   [2] See text, Section 30.   [3] Includes Canary Islands and Madeira Islands.   [4] Includes Belgium, Luxembourg, Denmark, Greece, Ireland, and Portugal. Beginning 1995, also includes Austria, Finland, and Sweden. As of Jan. 1, 1981, Greece became a member of the European Union. As of Jan. 1, 1986, Spain and Portugal became members of the European Union. For consistency, data for all years are shown on same basis.   [5] As of Jan. 1, 1984, includes Canary Islands and Spanish Africa, not elsewhere classified.

Source: U.S. Dept. of Agriculture, Economic Research Service, *Foreign Agricultural Trade of the United States*, Jan./Feb. 1998, and calendar year supplements. Also in *Agricultural Statistics*, annual.

No. 1126. Cropland Used for Crops and Acreages of Crops Harvested: 1980 to 1997

[In millions of acres, except as indicated]

ITEM	1980	1985	1990	1991	1992	1993	1994	1995	1996	1997
Cropland used for crops	382	372	341	337	337	330	339	332	346	353
Index (1977=100)	101	98	90	89	89	87	90	88	92	93
Cropland harvested [1]	342	334	310	306	305	297	310	302	314	322
Crop failure	10	7	6	7	8	11	7	8	10	8
Cultivated summer fallow	30	31	25	24	24	22	22	22	22	23
Acres of crops harvested [2]	352	342	322	318	317	308	321	314	326	333

[1] Land supporting one or more harvested crops. [2] Area in principal crops harvested as reported by Crop Reporting Board plus acreages in fruits, vegetables for sale, tree nuts, and farm gardens.

Source: U.S. Dept. of Agriculture, Economic Research Service, *Economic Indicators of the Farm Sector: Production and Efficiency Statistics*, annual. Also in *Agricultural Statistics*, annual. Beginning 1991 *Agricultural Resources and Environmental Indicators*, periodical, and *AREI Updates: Cropland Use*, No. 12, annual.

No. 1127. Crops—Acreage and Value, by State: 1995 to 1997

STATE	ACREAGE PLANTED (1,000)			ACREAGE HARVESTED (1,000)			FARM VALUE (mil. dol.)			
	1995	1996	1997	1995	1996	1997	1995	1996	1997 Value	1997 Rank
U.S. [1]	318,237	334,371	334,139	301,032	313,518	319,894	102,032	108,442	108,805	(X)
AL	2,204	2,255	2,373	2,093	2,169	2,188	570	736	576	34
AZ	795	835	808	787	831	800	1,325	1,216	1,232	30
AR	8,435	8,680	8,345	8,198	8,535	8,206	2,239	2,764	2,527	16
CA	5,220	5,202	5,172	4,660	4,770	4,678	13,768	14,155	15,554	1
CO	6,104	6,456	6,479	5,748	5,511	6,100	1,576	1,431	1,580	22
CT	112	120	112	107	115	109	71	82	76	47
DE	507	500	509	499	492	494	151	186	155	44
FL	1,070	1,109	1,089	1,027	1,084	1,060	3,333	3,662	3,793	9
GA	4,237	4,336	4,419	3,864	3,990	4,062	2,099	2,186	2,051	20
HI	53	46	35	53	46	35	320	318	303	40
ID	4,483	4,507	4,493	4,306	4,383	4,336	2,308	2,073	2,193	19
IL	23,221	23,926	23,740	22,526	23,183	23,534	7,048	7,779	7,366	3
IN	11,942	12,648	12,964	11,785	12,395	12,786	3,815	3,868	4,031	8
IA	23,502	24,197	24,711	22,872	24,007	24,513	7,692	8,110	7,830	2
KS	22,428	24,171	23,497	21,363	20,899	22,850	3,474	4,140	4,411	7
KY	5,709	5,844	5,852	5,454	5,640	5,648	1,814	2,125	1,953	21
LA	3,857	4,035	4,040	3,786	3,994	3,963	1,423	1,673	1,490	24
ME	364	327	296	358	316	287	166	152	170	43
MD	1,548	1,575	1,556	1,463	1,521	1,500	434	545	420	36
MA	134	131	133	131	125	128	149	192	220	41
MI	6,790	7,023	7,032	6,647	6,774	6,893	2,458	2,117	2,433	17
MN	19,151	20,001	20,510	18,556	19,722	20,079	5,374	5,553	5,403	4
MS	4,850	4,880	4,770	4,739	4,790	4,696	1,339	1,626	1,498	23
MO	12,056	13,275	13,424	11,689	12,794	13,267	2,480	3,200	3,075	12
MT	9,697	10,774	10,423	9,245	10,342	9,939	1,543	1,399	1,415	27
NE	18,280	18,811	19,121	17,769	18,227	18,696	4,559	5,296	4,873	6
NV	516	525	520	512	522	517	181	180	187	42
NH	85	84	70	83	82	69	31	31	27	48
NJ	452	427	435	413	394	413	298	345	330	38
NM	1,282	1,318	1,290	869	933	1,137	440	436	505	35
NY	3,045	3,018	3,070	2,981	2,941	3,017	1,051	976	1,070	31
NC	4,639	4,757	4,916	4,351	4,525	4,671	2,149	2,508	2,575	15
ND	20,707	22,651	22,271	20,120	22,237	21,091	2,943	3,335	2,593	14
OH	10,025	10,173	10,726	9,883	10,011	10,528	3,097	2,874	3,460	10
OK	10,621	11,341	10,935	8,635	8,935	9,295	1,064	1,155	1,310	28
OR	2,389	2,454	2,390	2,260	2,359	2,293	1,377	1,361	1,423	26
PA	4,146	4,140	4,313	4,050	4,035	4,202	1,403	1,559	1,481	25
RI	11	11	10	11	11	10	6	7	7	49
SC	1,976	1,971	2,030	1,871	1,892	1,962	712	773	737	33
SD	14,334	16,910	17,535	13,947	16,235	16,545	2,219	2,881	2,681	13
TN	4,892	4,999	4,925	4,530	4,703	4,673	1,229	1,306	1,260	29
TX	22,600	24,343	23,389	17,870	18,162	19,979	4,721	4,791	5,038	5
UT	1,099	1,139	1,126	1,042	1,070	1,068	276	278	315	39
VT	387	345	365	379	326	358	67	73	82	46
VA	2,910	2,936	2,926	2,748	2,794	2,774	881	964	829	32
WA	4,144	4,461	4,369	4,011	4,378	4,236	3,666	3,477	3,443	11
WV	650	657	646	642	646	637	111	98	85	45
WI	8,194	8,161	8,012	7,792	7,849	7,677	2,242	2,135	2,373	18
WY	1,883	1,836	1,911	1,820	1,783	1,847	338	313	372	37

X Not applicable. [1] Excludes Alaska. Acreage data include sunflower and sugarbeet acreage unallocated by state.

Source: U.S. Dept. of Agriculture, National Agricultural Statistics Service, *Crop Production*, annual; and *Crop Values*, annual.

No. 1128. Principal Crops—Production, Supply, and Disappearance: 1990 to 1997

[Marketing year beginning May 1 for hay, June 1 for wheat, August 1 for cotton and rice, September 1 for soybeans, corn, and sorghum. Acreage, production, and yield of all crops periodically revised on basis of census data]

CROP AND YEAR	ACREAGE (mil.)— Planted	ACREAGE (mil.)— Harvested	Yield per acre	Production	Farm price[1]	Farm value (mil. dol.)	Total supply[2]	DISAPPEARANCE Total[3]	DISAPPEARANCE Exports	Ending stocks
Corn for grain:			Bu.	Mil. bu.	$/bu.			Mil. bu.		
1990	74.2	67.0	119	7,934	2.28	18,192	9,282	7,761	1,725	1,521
1994	79.2	72.9	139	10,103	2.26	24,118	10,962	9,405	2,177	1,558
1995	71.2	65.0	114	7,374	3.24	24,118	8,948	8,522	2,228	426
1996	79.5	73.1	127	9,293	2.71	25,312	9,733	8,849	1,795	883
1997	80.2	73.7	127	9,366	2.60	24,394	10,259	9,310	1,625	949
Soybeans:			Bu.	Mil. bu.	$/bu.			Mil. bu.		
1990	57.8	56.5	34.1	1,926	5.74	11,042	2,169	1,840	557	329
1994	61.7	60.9	41.4	2,517	5.48	13,756	2,731	2,396	838	335
1995	62.6	61.6	35.3	2,177	6.72	14,617	2,516	2,333	851	183
1996	64.2	63.4	37.6	2,382	7.35	17,455	2,575	2,443	882	131
1997	70.9	69.9	39.0	2,727	6.50	17,705	2,865	2,610	950	255
Hay:			Sh. tons	Mil. sh. tons	$/ton			Mil. sh. tons		
1990	(NA)	61.0	2.40	146	[4][5]80.60	10,462	173	146	(NA)	27
1994	(NA)	58.7	2.55	150	[4][5]86.70	11,114	172	151	(NA)	21
1995	(NA)	59.6	2.59	154	[4][5]82.20	11,042	175	154	(NA)	21
1996	(NA)	60.9	2.45	149	[4][5]95.80	12,723	170	153	(NA)	17
1997	(NA)	60.8	2.50	152	[4][5]102.50	13,417	169	(NA)	(NA)	(NA)
Wheat:			Bu.	Mil. bu.	$/bu.			Mil. bu.		
1990	77.0	69.1	39.5	2,730	2.61	7,184	3,303	2,435	1,069	868
1994	70.3	61.8	37.6	2,321	3.45	7,968	2,981	2,475	1,188	507
1995	69.1	60.9	35.8	2,183	4.55	9,787	2,757	2,381	1,241	376
1996	75.6	62.9	36.3	2,285	4.30	9,815	2,753	2,310	1,001	444
1997	71.0	63.6	39.7	2,527	3.45	8,612	3,060	2,386	1,075	674
Cotton:			Lb.	Mil. bales[6]	cents/lb.			Mil. bales[6]		
1990	12.3	11.7	634	[7]15.5	68.2	5,076	18.5	16.5	7.8	[8]2.3
1994	13.7	13.3	708	[7]19.7	72.0	6,797	23.2	20.6	9.4	[8]2.7
1995	16.9	16.0	537	[7]17.9	76.5	6,575	21.0	18.3	7.7	[8]2.6
1996	14.6	12.9	707	[7]18.9	70.5	6,408	22.0	18.0	7.0	[8]4.1
1997	13.8	13.3	686	[7]19.0	67.4	6,142	23.0	19.0	7.5	[8]4.0
Tobacco:[9]			Lb.	Mil. lb.	$/lb.			Mil. lb.		
1990	(NA)	0.7	2,218	1,626	[5]1.74	2,827	3,969	1,796	631	[10]2,232
1994	(NA)	0.7	2,359	1,583	[5]1.76	2,779	4,057	1,604	523	[10]2,541
1995	(NA)	0.7	1,913	1,269	[5]1.82	2,305	3,666	1,491	533	[10]2,225
1996	(NA)	0.7	2,071	1,517	[5]1.88	2,938	3,727	1,625	628	(NA)
1997	(NA)	0.8	2,106	1,679	[5]1.81	3,039	(NA)	(NA)	(NA)	(NA)
Potatoes:			Cwt.	Mil. cwt.	$/cwt.			Mil. cwt.		
1990	1.4	1.4	293	402	6.08	2,431	582	[11]319	[12]14	(NA)
1994	1.4	1.4	339	467	5.58	2,590	692	[11]367	[12]24	(NA)
1995	1.4	1.4	323	444	6.77	2,992	687	[11]369	[12]30	(NA)
1996	1.5	1.4	350	499	4.93	2,431	(NA)	(NA)	(NA)	(NA)
1997	1.4	1.3	347	460	5.68	2,604	(NA)	(NA)	(NA)	(NA)
Rice, rough:			Lb.	Mil. cwt.	$/cwt.			Mil. cwt.		
1990	2.9	2.8	5,529	156	6.68	1,047	187	163	71	25
1994	3.4	3.3	5,964	198	6.78	1,337	231	200	99	31
1995	3.1	3.1	5,621	174	9.15	1,587	213	188	83	25
1996	2.8	2.8	6,121	171	9.96	1,687	206	179	78	24
1997	3.1	3.0	5,896	179	9.75	1,729	215	189	81	26
Sorghum for grain:			Bu.	Mil. bu.	$/bu.			Mil. bu.		
1990	10.5	9.1	63.1	573	2.12	1,221	793	651	232	143
1994	9.8	8.9	72.8	649	2.13	1,324	697	625	223	72
1995	9.5	8.3	55.6	460	3.19	1,395	532	514	198	18
1996	13.2	11.9	67.5	803	2.34	2,004	821	774	205	47
1997	10.1	9.4	69.5	653	2.25	1,456	701	660	200	41

NA Not available. [1] Except as noted, marketing year average price. U.S. prices are computed by weighting U.S. monthly prices by estimated monthly marketings and do not include an allowance for outstanding loans and government purchases and payments. [2] Comprises production, imports, and beginning stocks. [3] Includes feed, residual, and other domestic uses not shown separately. [4] Prices are for hay sold baled. [5] Season average prices received by farmers. U.S. prices are computed by weighting state prices by estimated sales and include an allowance for outstanding loans and government purchases, if any, for crops under government programs. [6] Bales of 480 pounds, net weight. [7] State production figures, which conform with annual ginning enumeration with allowance for cross-state ginnings, rounded to thousands and added for U.S. totals. [8] Stock estimates based on Census Bureau data which results in an unaccounted difference between supply and use estimates and changes in ending stocks. [9] Flue-cured and cigar wrapper, crop year July-June; all other types October-September. Farm-sales-weight basis. [10] Includes tobacco carried over on farms. [11] Covers potatoes used for table use, feed and canned products, chips, and dehydration. [12] Covers fresh potatoes, chips, frozen and dehydrated products.

Source: Production—U.S. Dept. of Agriculture, National Agricultural Statistics Service. In *Crop Production,* annual; and *Crop Values,* annual. Supply and disappearance—U.S. Dept. of Agriculture, Economic Research Service, *Feed Situation,* quarterly; *Fats and Oils Situation,* quarterly; *Wheat Situation,* quarterly; *Tobacco Situation,* quarterly; *Cotton and Wool Outlook Statistics,* periodic; and *Agricultural Supply and Demand Estimates,* periodic. Data are also in *Agricultural Statistics,* annual; and *Agricultural Outlook,* monthly.

No. 1129. Corn—Acreage, Production, and Value, by Leading States: 1995 to 1997

[One bushel of corn=56 pounds]

STATE	ACREAGE HARVESTED (1,000 acres)			YIELD PER ACRE (bu.)			PRODUCTION (mil. bu.)			PRICE ($/bu.)			FARM VALUE (mil. dol.)		
	1995	1996	1997	1995	1996	1997	1995	1996	1997	1995	1996	1997	1995	1996	1997
U.S. [1]	64,995	73,147	73,720	114	127	127	7,374	9,293	9,366	3.24	2.71	2.60	24,118	25,312	24,394
IA	11,400	12,450	12,000	123	138	138	1,402	1,718	1,656	3.20	2.60	2.50	4,487	4,467	4,140
IL	10,000	10,800	11,050	113	136	129	1,130	1,469	1,425	3.30	2.79	2.70	3,729	4,098	3,849
NE	7,700	8,300	8,725	111	143	132	855	1,187	1,152	3.22	2.64	2.55	2,752	3,133	2,937
MN	6,150	6,950	6,450	119	125	133	732	869	858	3.14	2.47	2.45	2,298	2,146	2,102
IN	5,300	5,450	5,850	113	123	123	599	670	720	3.38	2.78	2.70	2,024	1,864	1,943
OH	3,100	2,750	3,450	121	111	134	375	305	462	3.32	2.95	2.65	1,245	839	1,225
WI	3,050	3,000	3,050	114	111	132	348	333	403	3.11	2.62	2.50	1,081	872	1,007
KS	1,970	2,350	2,700	124	152	153	244	357	386	3.24	2.83	2.65	791	1,011	1,023
SD	2,450	3,700	3,400	79	100	98	194	370	333	3.23	2.31	2.30	625	855	766
MO	1,470	2,650	2,870	102	134	116	150	355	333	3.48	2.77	2.55	522	984	849
MI	2,170	2,300	2,250	115	94	117	250	216	263	3.20	2.66	2.55	799	575	671
TX	1,900	1,800	1,800	114	112	138	217	202	248	3.19	3.19	2.85	691	643	708
CO	830	940	1,030	111	142	146	92	133	150	3.33	2.76	2.65	307	368	399
KY	1,140	1,200	1,170	108	124	103	123	149	121	3.27	3.00	2.70	403	446	325
PA	980	1,070	985	96	119	99	94	127	98	3.86	2.99	3.20	363	381	312
NC	700	900	870	107	95	89	75	86	77	3.54	3.43	2.95	265	293	228
NY	610	630	650	105	107	116	64	67	75	3.85	2.98	2.95	247	201	222
TN	540	680	650	118	116	102	64	79	66	3.50	2.90	2.75	223	229	182
ND	510	720	605	79	91	99	40	66	60	3.16	2.43	2.30	127	159	138
LA	221	523	490	105	125	117	23	65	57	2.95	3.50	2.70	68	229	155
GA	350	525	500	90	95	110	32	50	55	3.55	3.58	2.90	112	179	160

[1] Includes other states, not shown separately.

Source: U.S. Dept. of Agriculture, National Agricultural Statistics Service, *Crop Production*, annual; and *Crop Values*, annual.

No. 1130. Soybeans—Acreage, Production, and Value, by Leading States: 1995 to 1997

[One bushel of soybeans=60 pounds]

STATE	ACREAGE HARVESTED (1,000 acres)			YIELD PER ACRE (bu.)			PRODUCTION (mil. bu.)			PRICE ($/bu.)			FARM VALUE (mil. dol.)		
	1995	1996	1997	1995	1996	1997	1995	1996	1997	1995	1996	1997	1995	1996	1997
U.S. [1]	61,624	63,409	69,884	35	38	39	2,177	2,382	2,727	6.72	7.35	6.50	14,617	17,455	17,705
IA	9,260	9,450	10,400	44	44	47	407	416	484	6.65	7.36	6.40	2,709	3,060	3,095
IL	9,700	9,850	9,950	39	41	43	378	399	428	6.88	7.55	6.55	2,603	3,012	2,802
MN	5,800	5,900	6,700	41	38	39	235	224	261	6.59	7.26	6.30	1,548	1,628	1,646
IN	4,980	5,360	5,400	40	38	44	197	204	238	6.73	7.34	6.55	1,324	1,495	1,556
OH	4,030	4,490	4,490	38	35	44	153	157	198	6.70	7.42	6.45	1,026	1,166	1,274
MO	4,500	4,050	4,850	30	37	37	133	150	177	6.84	7.29	6.35	908	1,092	1,124
NE	3,060	3,010	3,450	33	45	41	101	135	141	6.56	7.19	6.40	662	974	905
SD	2,500	2,670	3,450	30	34	35	75	91	121	6.28	7.08	6.05	471	643	731
AR	3,400	3,500	3,550	26	32	31	88	112	108	6.85	7.36	6.90	606	824	747
KS	2,050	2,000	2,400	25	37	37	51	74	89	6.69	7.17	6.45	343	531	573
MI	1,490	1,640	2,070	40	29	39	60	47	73	6.52	7.15	6.55	389	334	477
MS	1,800	1,750	2,400	21	31	31	38	54	64	6.76	7.34	6.90	256	398	443
KY	1,150	1,180	1,890	36	38	35	41	45	44	7.01	7.43	6.85	290	333	302
TN	1,080	1,150	1,280	32	35	35	35	40	44	6.88	7.25	6.95	238	292	302

[1] Includes other states, not shown separately.

Source: U.S. Dept. of Agriculture, National Agricultural Statistics Service, *Crop Production*, annual; and *Crop Values*, annual.

No. 1131. Wheat—Acreage, Production, and Value, by Leading States: 1995 to 1997

[One bushel of wheat= 60 pounds]

STATE	ACREAGE HARVESTED (1,000 acres)			YIELD PER ACRE (bu.)			PRODUCTION (mil. bu.)			PRICE ($/bu.)			FARM VALUE (mil. dol.)		
	1995	1996	1997	1995	1996	1997	1995	1996	1997	1995	1996	1997	1995	1996	1997
U.S. [1]	60,945	62,927	63,577	35.8	36.3	39.7	2,183	2,285	2,527	4.55	4.30	3.45	9,787	9,815	8,612
KS	11,000	8,800	11,000	26.0	29.0	46.0	286	255	506	4.55	4.63	3.20	1,313	1,182	1,619
ND	11,118	12,515	11,025	27.0	31.6	24.3	300	395	268	5.05	4.19	4.00	1,495	1,638	1,032
MT	5,435	6,360	5,930	36.0	27.8	31.3	196	177	186	4.63	4.24	3.80	904	751	683
OK	5,200	4,900	5,400	21.0	19.0	33.0	109	93	178	4.41	4.73	3.25	482	440	579
WA	2,595	2,745	2,595	59.3	66.5	64.8	154	183	168	4.83	4.14	3.60	743	756	603
TX	2,800	2,900	4,100	27.0	26.0	29.0	76	75	119	4.19	4.98	3.25	317	375	386
ID	1,330	1,560	1,440	77.7	76.4	79.2	103	119	114	4.45	3.96	3.40	460	473	379
SD	2,752	3,854	3,469	33.0	36.1	28.6	91	139	99	4.68	4.07	3.50	420	567	347

[1] Includes other states, not shown separately.

Source: U.S. Dept. of Agriculture, National Agricultural Statistics Service, *Crop Production*, annual; and *Crop Values*, annual.

No. 1132. Greenhouse and Nursery Crops—Summary, by Type of Product: 1990 to 1996

[In millions of dollars, except per capita. Based on a survey of 36 commercial floriculture states and estimates by source]

ITEM	Total	Cut flowers	Potted flowering plants	Foliage plants	Bedding plants	Cut cultivated greens	Other [1]
Domestic production: [2]							
1990..................	8,677	529	701	693	1,032	121	5,601
1994..................	10,006	500	844	714	1,593	135	6,220
1995..................	10,423	479	868	728	1,689	128	6,531
1996..................	10,912	505	874	741	1,759	137	6,896
Imports:							
1990..................	526	326	18	25	(NA)	14	143
1994..................	697	420	28	43	(NA)	20	186
1995..................	855	512	30	53	(NA)	24	236
1996..................	950	573	38	54	(NA)	28	257
RETAIL CONSUMER EXPENDITURES [3]							
Total:							
1990..................	29,273	4,826	2,707	2,510	1,548	679	17,003
1994..................	33,362	5,264	3,288	2,712	2,390	769	18,939
1995..................	35,312	5,758	3,386	2,805	2,533	773	20,057
1996..................	37,247	6,268	3,404	2,899	2,638	840	21,199
Per capita (dol.): [4]							
1990..................	117	19	11	10	6	3	68
1995..................	134	22	13	11	10	3	76
1996..................	140	24	13	11	10	3	80

NA Not available. [1] Includes turfgrass (sod), bulbs, nursery stock, groundcovers, and other greenhouse and nursery products except the following: seeds, cut Christmas trees, and food crops grown under cover. [2] Equivalent wholesale values. [3] Excludes services such as landscaping, installation, and maintenance. [4] Based on U.S. Bureau of the Census estimated resident population as of July 1.

Source: U.S. Dept. of Agriculture, Economic Research Service, unpublished data.

No. 1133. Fresh Fruits and Vegetables—Supply and Use: 1990 to 1997

[In millions of pounds, except per capita in pounds]

YEAR	Utilized production [1]	Imports [2]	Supply, total [1]	CONSUMPTION Total	CONSUMPTION Per capita	Exports [2]
FRUITS						
Citrus:						
1990.................	7,327	184	7,510	5,331	21.4	2,179
1994.................	8,668	372	9,040	6,495	25.0	2,545
1995.................	8,635	449	9,084	6,333	24.1	2,751
1996.................	9,133	445	9,578	7,277	27.5	2,301
Noncitrus: [3]						
1990.................	12,122	7,852	19,974	17,978	70.4	1,995
1994.................	13,078	9,337	22,415	19,594	75.6	2,821
1995.................	12,998	9,388	22,386	19,536	74.3	2,850
1996.................	12,222	9,928	22,150	19,614	74.0	2,536
VEGETABLES & MELONS						
1990.................	34,629	3,265	38,774	34,577	138.4	2,685
1995.................	37,919	4,698	43,697	38,453	146.1	3,525
1996.................	39,849	5,542	46,415	41,252	155.3	3,568
1997.................	41,731	5,858	48,554	43,119	161.0	3,698
POTATOES						
1990.................	11,335	684	12,019	11,691	46.8	327
1995.................	12,849	685	13,534	12,950	49.2	584
1996.................	12,888	987	13,874	13,264	49.9	610
1997.................	12,736	765	13,500	12,830	47.9	670

[1] Crop-year basis for fruits. [2] Fiscal year for fruits; calendar year for vegetables and potatoes. [3] Includes bananas.

No. 1134. Nuts—Supply and Use: 1990 to 1996

[In millions of pounds (shelled)]

YEAR	Beginning stocks	Marketable production [1]	Imports	Supply, total	Consumption	Exports	Ending stocks
1990	326.2	961.5	198.4	1,486.1	609.6	522.6	354.0
1994	279.7	1,061.4	218.9	1,560.1	590.9	635.2	334.1
1995	334.1	771.3	204.0	1,309.5	511.6	540.8	257.1
1996	257.1	827.8	223.4	1,308.3	556.7	572.0	179.6

[1] Utilized production minus inedibles and noncommercial usage.

Source of Tables 1133 and 1134: U.S. Dept. of Agriculture, Economic Research Service, *Fruit and Tree Nuts Situation and Outlook Yearbook* and *Vegetables and Specialties Situation and Outlook Yearbook.*

No. 1135. Commercial Vegetable and Other Specified Crops—Area, Production, and Value, 1995 to 1997, and Leading Producing States, 1997

[Except as noted, relates to commercial production for fresh market and processing combined. Includes market garden areas but excludes minor producing acreage in minor producing states. Excludes production for home use in farm and nonfarm gardens. Value is for season or crop year and should not be confused with calendar-year income]

CROP	AREA [1] (1,000 acres)			PRODUCTION [2] (1,000 short tons)			VALUE [3] (mil. dol.)			Leading states in order of production, 1997
	1995	1996	1997	1995	1996	1997	1995	1996	1997	
Beans, snap	302	283	275	917	960	923	283	293	286	WI, OR, MI [4]
Beans, dry edible. .	1,899	1,753	1,720	1,541	1,398	1,458	636	653	586	ND, MI, NE
Broccoli	129	132	134	791	773	866	443	409	496	CA, AZ
Cabbage	82	83	85	1,324	1,369	1,554	269	251	287	NY, CA, GA [5]
Cantaloups.	103	104	114	964	1,106	1,178	351	401	418	CA, AZ, TX
Carrots	109	117	119	1,760	1,905	2,231	440	394	478	CA, CO, MI [5]
Cauliflower	51	47	47	326	332	324	217	214	198	CA, AZ
Celery	28	27	27	942	943	903	307	199	273	CA, MI, TX
Corn, sweet	703	695	687	4,394	4,432	4,453	640	643	646	(NA)
Fresh market. . .	219	221	223	1,070	1,136	1,129	389	384	398	FL, CA, GA
Processed.	484	474	464	3,324	3,296	3,324	251	259	248	MN, WA, WI
Cucumbers.	177	161	160	1,114	1,053	1,167	302	325	331	MI, FL, NC [4]
Garlic	28	35	37	231	306	278	141	196	262	CA
Lettuce, head	197	203	202	3,117	3,293	3,427	1,463	971	1,188	CA, AZ, CO
Lettuce, leaf	39	41	42	446	458	462	309	246	245	CA, AZ, OH
Mushrooms [6]	140	135	136	391	389	388	731	728	730	(NA)
Onions	164	159	155	3,209	3,068	3,194	634	582	648	CA, OR, WA
Peppers, green . . .	68	69	66	722	848	839	453	475	503	CA, FL, NJ
Potatoes	1,372	1,426	1,326	22,180	24,932	22,996	2,992	2,431	2,604	ID, WA, CO
Strawberries	48	48	45	802	814	816	813	770	908	CA, FL, OR
Sweet potatoes . . .	84	85	84	645	673	651	205	193	213	NC, LA, CA
Tomatoes.	477	464	408	13,013	13,137	11,863	1,605	1,678	1,852	(NA)
Fresh market. . .	133	125	125	1,727	1,728	1,890	891	967	1,247	FL, CA, GA
Processed.	344	339	283	11,286	11,409	9,973	714	711	605	CA, OH, IN
Watermelons. . . .	204	207	185	2,022	2,207	2,037	357	276	309	CA, FL, GA

NA Not available.   [1] Area of crops for harvest for fresh market, including any partially harvested or not harvested because of low prices or other factors, plus area harvested for processing.   [2] Excludes some quantities not marketed.   [3] Fresh market vegetables valued at f.o.b. shipping point. Processing vegetables are equivalent returns at packinghouse door.   [4] Processed only.   [5] Fresh market only.   [6] Area is shown in million square feet. All data are for marketing year ending June 30.

Source: U.S. Dept. of Agriculture, National Agricultural Statistics Service, *Vegetables*, annual summary. Also in *Agricultural Statistics*, annual.

No. 1136. Fruits and Nuts—Utilized Production and Value, 1995 to 1997, and Leading Producing States, 1997

FRUIT OR NUT		UTILIZED PRODUCTION [1]			FARM VALUE (mil. dol.)			Leading states in order of production, 1997
	Unit	1995	1996	1997	1995	1996	1997	
Apples (36 states) [2]	Mil. lb	10,390	10,340	10,227	1,766	1,644	1,688	WA, NY, MI
Apricots	1,000 tons . .	61	79	128	28	35	43	CA, WA, UT
Avocados	1,000 tons . .	190	189	(NA)	245	264	(NA)	CA, FL
Cherries, sweet	1,000 tons . .	153	152	220	193	223	275	WA, OR, CA
Cherries, tart	Mil. lb	311	260	280	18	42	(NA)	MI, UT, NY
Cranberries	1,000 bbl. [3] .	4,193	4,671	5,489	224	308	(NA)	WI, MA, NJ
Dates (CA)	1,000 tons .	23	26	26	18	18	22	CA
Grapefruit (4 states)	Mil. boxes [4] .	71	66	70	308	296	275	FL, CA, TX
Grapes (13 states)	1,000 tons . .	5,913	5,538	6,833	2,047	2,371	2,691	CA, WA, NY
Lemons (2 states)	Mil. boxes [5] .	24	26	23	263	251	294	CA, AZ
Nectarines (CA)	1,000 tons . .	176	247	264	94	117	99	CA
Olives (CA)	1,000 tons . .	78	166	104	50	103	69	CA
Oranges and tangerines (4 states). .	Mil. boxes [6] .	270	272	306	1,724	1,934	2,055	FL, CA, AZ
Papayas	Mil. lb	51	42	41	18	17	19	HI
Peaches (31 states)	Mil. lb	2,191	2,055	2,519	405	394	451	CA, GA, SC
Pears	1,000 tons . .	948	820	1,043	258	308	300	WA, CA, OR
Pineapples	1,000 tons . .	345	347	324	87	96	92	HI
Plums and prunes (fresh)	1,000 tons . .	721	932	855	306	283	(NA)	CA
Tangelos (FL).	Mil. boxes [7] .	3	2	4	15	15	19	FL
Temples (FL)	Mil. boxes [7] .	3	2	2	14	14	13	FL
Almonds (shelled basis) (CA)	Mil. lb	370	510	750	881	1,018	1,080	CA
Hazelnuts (in the shell)	1,000 tons . .	39	19	44	35	16	39	OR, WA
Macadamia nuts	Mil. lb	51	57	58	38	44	43	HI
Pecans (in the shell) (11 states) . . .	Mil. lb	268	222	272	272	141	257	GA, TX, NM
Pistachios	Mil. lb	148	105	178	161	122	201	CA
Walnuts, English (in the shell)	1,000 tons . .	234	208	248	328	327	(NA)	CA

NA Not available.   [1] Excludes quantities not harvested or not marketed.   [2] Production in commercial orchards with 100 or more bearing age trees.   [3] Barrels of 100 pounds.   [4] Approximate average, net weight, is 67 lb. in AZ and CA; 85 in FL; and 80 in TX.   [5] About 76 lb. net.   [6] Net contents of box varies. In CA and AZ approximate average for oranges and tangerines is 75 lb.; FL oranges, 90 lb.; TX oranges, 85 lb.; and FL tangerines, 95 lb.   [7] Approximate net weight is 90 lb.

Source: U.S. Dept. of Agriculture, National Agricultural Statistics Service, *Noncitrus Fruits and Nuts*, annual; and *Citrus Fruits*, annual.

No. 1137. Meat Supply and Use: 1980 to 1997

[**In millions of pounds** (carcass weight equivalent). Carcass weight equivalent is the weight of the animal minus entrails, head, hide, and internal organs; includes fat and bone. Covers federal and state inspected, and farm slaughter]

YEAR AND TYPE OF MEAT	Produc-tion	Imports	Supply, [1] total	Con-sump-tion [2]	Exports	Ending stocks
RED MEAT AND POULTRY						
1980	53,151	2,668	57,036	54,695	1,124	1,217
1985	56,271	3,255	60,631	58,651	926	1,054
1990	62,255	3,295	66,673	62,937	2,472	1,263
1995	74,070	2,837	78,637	69,912	6,956	1,769
1996	75,303	2,769	79,841	70,130	7,976	1,734
1997	76,322	3,065	81,120	70,364	8,831	1,924
ALL RED MEATS						
1980	38,978	2,668	42,481	41,170	429	882
1985	39,409	3,255	43,505	42,311	461	733
1990	38,787	3,295	42,742	40,784	1,250	707
1995	43,677	2,831	47,512	43,968	2,614	930
1996	43,288	2,764	46,982	43,370	2,853	759
1997	43,358	3,059	47,176	43,096	3,185	895
Beef:						
1980	21,643	2,064	24,166	23,560	173	432
1985	23,728	2,071	26,271	25,523	328	420
1990	22,743	2,356	25,434	24,031	1,006	397
1995	25,222	2,103	27,873	25,533	1,821	519
1996	25,525	2,073	28,117	25,863	1,877	377
1997	25,490	2,343	28,210	25,609	2,136	465
Pork:						
1980	16,617	550	17,521	16,838	252	431
1985	14,807	1,128	16,283	15,865	128	289
1990	15,354	898	16,565	16,031	238	296
1995	17,849	664	18,951	17,768	787	396
1996	17,117	618	18,131	16,795	970	366
1997	17,274	633	18,273	16,821	1,044	408
Veal:						
1980	400	21	432	420	2	9
1985	515	20	549	533	4	11
1990	327	(NA)	331	325	(NA)	6
1995	319	(NA)	326	319	(NA)	7
1996	378	(NA)	385	378	(NA)	7
1997	334	(NA)	341	333	(NA)	8
Lamb and mutton:						
1980	318	33	362	351	1	9
1985	359	36	403	389	1	13
1990	363	41	412	397	6	8
1995	287	64	362	348	6	8
1996	268	73	349	334	6	9
1997	260	83	352	333	5	14
POULTRY, TOTAL						
1980	14,173	-	14,555	13,525	695	334
1985	16,862	-	17,126	16,340	465	321
1990	23,468	-	23,931	22,153	1,222	556
1995	30,393	6	31,125	25,944	4,342	839
1996	32,015	5	32,859	26,760	5,123	975
1997	32,964	6	33,944	27,269	5,646	1,029
Broilers:						
1980	11,252	-	11,364	10,682	567	115
1985	13,520	-	13,646	13,072	417	158
1990	18,430	-	18,651	17,266	1,143	242
1995	24,827	1	25,287	20,832	3,894	560
1996	26,124	4	26,688	21,626	4,420	641
1997	27,041	5	27,687	22,416	4,664	607
Mature chicken:						
1980	551	-	581	507	53	21
1985	525	-	537	503	21	13
1990	523	-	530	496	25	9
1995	496	3	513	406	99	7
1996	491	-	498	228	265	6
1997	510	-	516	125	384	7
Turkeys:						
1980	2,370	-	2,610	2,337	75	198
1985	2,817	-	2,943	2,765	27	150
1990	4,514	-	4,750	4,390	54	306
1995	5,069	2	5,326	4,706	348	271
1996	5,401	1	5,673	4,906	438	328
1997	5,412	1	5,741	4,727	598	415

- Represents zero.   NA Not available.   [1] Total supply equals production plus imports plus ending stocks of previous year.
[2] Includes shipments to territories.

Source: U.S. Department of Agriculture, Economic Research Service, *Food Consumption, Prices, and Expenditures, 1997: Annual Data, 1970-1995*; and *Agricultural Outlook*, monthly.

No. 1138. Livestock Inventory and Production: 1980 to 1998

[Production in live weight; includes animals for slaughter market, younger animals shipped to other states for feeding or breeding purposes, farm slaughter and custom slaughter consumed on farms where produced, minus livestock shipped into states for feeding or breeding with an adjustment for changes in inventory]

TYPE OF LIVESTOCK	Unit	1980	1985	1990	1991	1992	1993	1994	1995	1996	1997	1998
ALL CATTLE [1]												
Inventory: [2] Number on farms	Mil	111.2	109.6	95.8	96.4	97.6	99.2	101.0	102.8	103.5	101.5	99.5
Total value	Bil. dol.	55.8	44.0	59.0	63.1	61.5	64.4	66.5	63.2	52.0	53.2	59.9
Value per head	Dol	502	402	616	655	630	649	659	615	503	525	602
Production: Quantity	Bil. lb	40.3	40.1	39.2	39.8	40.3	40.9	42.1	42.7	41.3	41.1	(NA)
Beef, price per 100 lb	Dol	62.40	53.70	74.60	72.70	71.30	72.60	66.70	61.80	58.70	63.10	(NA)
Calves, price per 100 lb	Dol	76.80	62.10	95.60	98.00	89.00	91.20	87.20	73.10	58.40	78.90	(NA)
Value of production	Bil. dol.	25.5	21.2	29.3	29.4	28.6	30.3	26.9	24.8	22.3	24.9	(NA)
HOGS AND PIGS												
Inventory: [3] Number on farms	Mil	67.3	54.1	53.8	54.4	57.6	58.2	57.9	60.0	58.3	56.1	60.9
Total value	Bil. dol.	3.8	4.1	4.3	4.6	4.0	4.1	4.3	3.2	4.1	5.3	5.0
Value per head	Dol	56.00	75.00	79.10	85.40	68.80	71.20	74.90	53.20	70.70	94.00	81.00
Production: Quantity	Bil. lb	23.4	20.2	21.3	22.7	23.9	23.7	24.4	24.4	23.3	24.1	(NA)
Price per 100 lb	Dol	38.00	44.00	53.70	49.10	41.60	45.20	39.90	40.50	51.90	52.90	(NA)
Value of production	Bil. dol.	8.9	8.9	11.3	11.1	9.9	10.6	9.7	9.8	12.0	12.6	(NA)
SHEEP AND LAMBS												
Inventory: [2] Number on farms	Mil	12.7	10.7	11.4	11.2	10.8	10.2	9.7	8.9	8.5	7.9	7.6
Total value	Mil. dol	993	654	901	733	661	714	681	663	732	762	776
Value per head	Dol	78.20	61.10	79.30	65.60	61.20	70.60	69.90	74.70	86.50	96.00	102.00
Production: Quantity	Mil. lb	746	704	781	796	746	689	630	599	566	591	(NA)
Sheep, price per 100 lb	Dol	21.30	23.90	23.20	19.70	25.80	28.60	30.90	28.00	29.90	37.90	(NA)
Lambs, price per 100 lb	Dol	63.60	67.70	55.50	52.20	59.50	64.40	65.60	78.20	82.20	90.30	(NA)
Value of production	Mil. dol	403	434	374	357	394	394	360	410	435	478	(NA)

NA Not available.   [1] Includes milk cows.   [2] As of Jan. 1.   [3] As of Dec. 1 of preceding year.

Source: U.S. Dept. of Agriculture, National Agricultural Statistics Service, *Meat Animals—Production, Disposition, and Income*, annual; and annual livestock summaries. Also in *Agricultural Statistics*, annual.

No. 1139. Cattle and Calves—Number, Production, and Value, by State: 1995 to 1998

[Includes milk cows. See headnote, Table 1138]

STATE	NUMBER ON FARMS [1] (1,000)			QUANTITY PRODUCED (mil. lb.)			VALUE OF PRODUCTION (mil. dol.)			COMMERCIAL SLAUGHTER [2] (mil. lb.)	
	1996	1997	1998	1995	1996	1997	1995	1996	1997	1996	1997
U.S. [3]	103,487	101,460	99,501	42,714	41,329	41,060	24,830	22,277	24,893	42,763	42,605
CA	4,600	4,600	4,600	1,969	1,896	1,997	907	779	953	1,246	1,279
CO	3,100	3,150	3,100	2,011	2,007	2,043	1,184	1,223	1,301	3,106	3,090
ID	1,770	1,750	1,770	873	888	898	487	447	519	903	904
IA	3,950	3,900	3,750	1,910	1,788	1,831	1,160	1,040	1,055	1,529	1,259
KS	6,500	6,600	6,550	3,631	3,590	3,627	2,210	2,074	2,207	8,172	8,547
MN	2,900	2,800	2,600	1,225	1,209	1,183	671	679	701	1,430	1,407
MO	4,550	4,500	4,300	1,168	1,164	1,136	703	592	799	199	121
MT	2,750	2,700	2,600	1,091	1,082	1,084	659	587	716	24	20
NE	6,350	6,550	6,650	3,953	3,886	4,001	2,476	2,565	2,409	8,733	8,925
OK	5,500	5,450	5,450	1,957	1,867	1,974	1,233	995	1,363	48	43
SD	3,850	3,800	3,550	1,420	1,404	1,256	879	796	838	332	318
TX	15,000	14,100	14,300	7,892	7,185	6,964	4,803	4,180	4,341	7,443	7,352
WI	3,800	3,700	3,600	1,100	1,036	1,041	576	491	536	1,908	2,006

[1] As of January 1.   [2] Data cover cattle only. Includes slaughter in federally inspected and other slaughter plants; excludes animals slaughtered on farms.   [3] Includes other states not shown separately.

No. 1140. Hogs and Pigs—Number, Production, and Value, by State: 1995 to 1997

[See headnote, Table 1138]

STATE	NUMBER ON FARMS [1] (1,000)			QUANTITY PRODUCED (mil. lb.)			VALUE OF PRODUCTION (mil. dol.)			COMMERCIAL SLAUGHTER [2] (mil. lb.)	
	1995	1996	1997	1995	1996	1997	1995	1996	1997	1996	1997
U.S. [3]	58,264	56,141	60,915	24,426	23,267	24,094	9,829	12,013	12,634	23,431	23,534
IL	4,800	4,400	4,800	2,202	1,953	1,825	849	981	931	2,252	2,203
IN	4,000	3,750	3,900	1,772	1,589	1,549	685	791	783	1,015	1,231
IA	13,400	12,200	14,500	5,637	5,223	5,348	2,262	2,688	2,770	6,663	6,309
MN	4,950	4,850	5,500	2,003	1,991	2,092	831	1,047	1,118	1,731	1,762
MO	3,550	3,450	3,550	1,461	1,257	1,353	580	641	713	834	897
NE	4,050	3,600	3,550	1,691	1,515	1,468	706	812	809	1,427	1,471
NC	8,200	9,300	9,800	3,157	3,400	3,765	1,322	1,808	2,038	2,187	2,301

[1] As of December 1.   [2] Includes slaughter in federally inspected and other slaughter plants; excludes animals slaughtered on farms.   [3] Includes other states not shown separately.

Source of Tables 1139 and 1140: U.S. Dept. of Agriculture, National Agricultural Statistics Service, *Meat Animals-Production, Disposition and Income*, annual.

No. 1141. Milk Production and Commercial Use: 1980 to 1997

[In billions of pounds milkfat basis]

YEAR	Produc-tion	Farm use	COMMERCIAL Farm market-ings	COMMERCIAL Begin-ning stock	Imports	Commer-cial supply, total	CCC net remov-als [1]	COMMERCIAL Ending stock	COMMERCIAL Disap-pear-ance	Milk price per 100 lb. [2] (dol.)
1980	128.4	2.3	126.1	5.3	2.1	133.5	8.8	5.6	119.0	13.1
1985	143.0	2.5	140.6	4.8	2.8	148.2	13.2	4.5	130.5	12.8
1990	147.7	2.0	145.7	4.1	2.7	152.5	8.5	5.1	138.8	13.7
1995	155.4	1.6	153.9	4.3	2.9	161.1	2.1	4.1	154.8	12.7
1996	154.3	1.5	152.8	4.1	2.9	159.8	0.1	4.7	155.0	14.7
1997	156.6	1.4	155.2	4.7	2.7	162.6	1.3	4.9	156.5	13.4

[1] Removals from commercial supply by Commodity Credit Corporation.   [2] Wholesale price received by farmers for all milk delivered to plants and dealers.

Source: U.S. Dept. of Agriculture, Economic Research Service, *Agricultural Outlook*, monthly.

No. 1142. Milk Cows—Number, Production, and Value, by State: 1995 to 1997

STATE	NUMBER ON FARMS [1] (1,000)			MILK PRODUCED ON FARMS (mil. lb.)			VALUE OF PRODUCTION [2] (mil. dol.)		
	1995	1996	1997	1995	1996	1997	1995	1996	1997
United States [3] . .	9,458	9,361	9,258	155,425	154,259	156,602	20,099	23,044	21,191
California	1,254	1,276	1,325	25,344	25,861	27,628	3,086	3,722	3,633
Idaho.	232	256	272	4,210	4,735	5,193	514	658	639
Michigan.	326	320	306	5,565	5,430	5,410	725	816	738
Minnesota.	599	598	583	9,409	9,440	9,210	1,197	1,378	1,215
New Mexico	191	195	202	3,623	3,753	4,011	433	526	528
New York	703	702	699	11,600	11,510	11,547	1,510	1,717	1,549
Ohio	289	285	280	4,600	4,360	4,415	603	654	587
Pennsylvania.	642	644	639	10,600	10,640	10,742	1,471	1,677	1,538
Texas.	401	398	385	6,113	6,120	5,768	795	924	790
Washington.	266	264	264	5,302	5,279	5,305	688	792	732
Wisconsin.	1,490	1,449	1,393	22,942	22,376	22,368	2,951	3,300	2,982

[1] Average number during year. Represents cows and heifers that have calved, kept for milk; excluding heifers not yet fresh.   [2] Valued at average returns per 100 pounds of milk in combined marketings of milk and cream. Includes value of milk fed to calves.   [3] Includes other states not shown separately.

Source: U.S. Dept. of Agriculture, National Agricultural Statistics Service, *Dairy Products*, annual; and *Milk: Production, Disposition, and Income*, annual.

No. 1143. Milk Production and Manufactured Dairy Products: 1980 to 1997

ITEM	Unit	1980	1985	1990	1992	1993	1994	1995	1996	1997
Number of farms with milk cows	1,000	334	269	193	171	159	149	140	127	117
Cows and heifers that have calved, kept for milk.	Mil. head . .	10.8	11.0	10.0	9.7	9.6	9.5	9.5	9.4	9.3
Milk produced on farms.	Bil. lb	128	143	148	151	151	154	155	154	157
Production per cow	1,000 lb. . .	11.9	13.0	14.8	15.6	15.7	16.2	16.4	16.5	16.9
Whole milk sold from farms [1]	Bil. lb	126	141	146	149	149	152	154	153	155
Sales to plants and dealers	Bil. lb	125	139	145	148	148	151	153	151	154
Value of milk produced	Bil. dol. . . .	16.9	18.4	20.4	20.0	19.5	20.2	20.1	23.0	21.2
Gross farm income, dairy products.	Bil. dol. . . .	16.7	18.1	20.2	19.8	19.3	20.0	19.9	22.9	21.0
Cash receipts from marketing of milk and cream [1]	Bil. dol. . . .	16.6	18.1	20.1	19.7	19.2	19.9	19.9	22.8	21.0
Sales to plants and dealers	Bil. dol. . . .	16.3	17.8	19.9	19.5	19.0	19.6	19.5	22.3	20.6
Number of dairy manufacturing plants	Number. . .	2,257	2,061	1,723	1,603	1,534	1,532	1,495	1,422	1,384
Manufactured dairy products:										
Butter (incl. whey butter)	Mil. lb	1,145	1,248	1,302	1,365	1,315	1,296	1,264	1,174	1,151
Cheese, total [2]	Mil. lb	3,984	5,081	6,059	6,488	6,528	6,735	6,917	7,218	7,329
American (excl. full-skim American). . .	Mil. lb	2,376	2,855	2,894	2,937	2,957	2,974	3,131	3,281	3,285
Cream and Neufchatel	Mil. lb	229	294	431	517	540	573	544	575	615
All Italian varieties	Mil. lb	983	1,491	2,207	2,509	2,495	2,626	2,674	2,812	2,880
Cottage cheese: Creamed [3]	Mil. lb	825	716	832	787	748	731	711	690	706
Curd, pot, and bakers.	Mil. lb	667	599	493	502	471	463	459	448	458
Condensed bulk milk	Mil. lb	952	1,232	1,426	1,624	1,605	1,593	1,372	1,270	1,248
Evaporated and condensed canned milk .	Mil. lb	740	656	615	599	557	565	503	492	579
Nonfat dry milk [4]	Mil. lb	1,168	1,398	902	872	964	1,242	1,243	1,068	1,223
Dry whey [5]	Mil. lb	690	987	1,143	1,237	1,196	1,212	1,147	1,117	1,137
Yogurt, plain and fruit flavored	Mil. lb	(NA)	(NA)	(NA)	(NA)	(NA)	1,393	1,646	1,588	1,574
Ice cream, regular.	Mil. gal . . .	830	901	824	866	866	876	862	879	906
Ice cream, lowfat [6]	Mil. gal . . .	293	301	352	328	325	359	357	366	386
Frozen yogurt.	Mil. gal . . .	(NA)	(NA)	(NA)	(NA)	(NA)	151	152	114	92

NA Not available.   [1] Comprises sales to plants and dealers, and retail sales by farmers direct to consumers.   [2] Includes varieties not shown separately.   [3] Includes partially creamed (low fat).   [4] Includes dry skim milk for animal feed.   [5] Includes animal but excludes modified whey production.   [6] Includes freezer-made milkshake in most states.

Source: U.S. Dept. of Agriculture, National Agricultural Statistics Service, *Dairy Products*, annual; and *Milk: Production, Disposition, and Income*, annual.

No. 1144. Broiler, Turkey, and Egg Production: 1980 to 1997

[For year ending November 30]

ITEM	Unit	1980	1985	1989	1990	1991	1992	1993	1994	1995	1996	1997
Chickens:[1]												
Number [2]	Million . .	392	370	356	352	363	371	380	384	385	387	403
Value per head [2]	Dollars. .	1.88	1.90	2.16	2.29	2.30	2.26	2.37	2.35	2.42	2.65	2.72
Value, total [2]	Mil. dol. .	737	704	771	805	833	838	898	900	930	1,026	1,099
Number sold [3]	Million . .	238	220	199	208	198	207	197	201	179	174	191
Price per lb. [3]	Cents . .	11.0	14.8	14.9	9.3	7.1	8.6	10.0	7.6	6.5	6.7	7.7
Value of sales [3]	Mil. dol. .	129	152	142	94	72	89	96	77	61	61	72
PRODUCTION												
Broilers:[4]												
Number.	Million . .	3,963	4,470	5,517	5,864	6,137	6,402	6,694	7,018	7,326	7,598	7,760
Weight	Bil. lb. .	15.5	18.9	24.0	25.6	27.2	28.8	30.6	32.5	34.2	36.5	37.5
Price per lb	Cents . .	27.7	30.1	36.6	32.6	30.8	31.8	34.0	35.0	34.4	38.1	37.7
Production value.	Mil. dol. .	4,303	5,668	8,778	8,366	8,383	9,174	10,417	11,372	11,762	13,905	14,153
Turkeys:												
Number.	Million . .	165	185	261	282	285	289	288	287	293	303	301
Weight	Bil. lb. .	3.1	3.7	5.5	6.0	6.1	6.3	6.4	6.5	6.8	7.2	7.2
Price per lb	Cents . .	41.3	49.1	40.9	39.4	38.0	37.7	39.0	40.4	41.0	43.3	39.9
Production value.	Mil. dol. .	1,272	1,820	2,235	2,393	2,353	2,396	2,509	2,644	2,776	3,129	2,880
Eggs:												
Number.	Billion . .	69.7	68.4	67.2	67.9	69.0	70.5	71.9	73.9	74.6	76.3	77.4
Price per dozen	Cents . .	56.3	57.2	68.9	70.9	67.8	57.6	63.4	61.4	62.4	74.9	70.2
Production value.	Mil. dol. .	3,268	3,262	3,877	4,021	3,915	3,397	3,800	3,780	3,880	4,762	4,531

[1] Excludes commercial broilers.　　[2] As of December 1.　　[3] Data for 1980 represent number produced and production value.
[4] Young chickens of the heavy breeds and other meat-type birds, to be marketed at 2-5 lbs. live weight and from which no pullets are kept for egg production.

Source: U.S. Dept. of Agriculture, National Agricultural Statistics Service, *Poultry—Production and Value,* annual; *Turkeys,* annual; and *Layers and Egg Production,* annual.

No. 1145. Egg Supply and Use: 1980 to 1997

[In million dozen]

ITEM	1980	1985	1990	1991	1992	1993	1994	1995	1996	1997
Supply, total [1]	5,830	5,734	5,707	5,815	5,922	6,024	6,193	6,235	6,388	6,475
Production	5,806	5,710	5,687	5,801	5,905	6,006	6,179	6,216	6,371	6,460
Imports	5	13	9	2	4	5	4	4	5	9
Use, total	5,811	5,723	5,695	5,802	5,909	6,013	6,178	6,223	6,379	6,468
Consumption [2]	5,169	5,104	4,916	4,939	5,020	5,085	5,185	5,167	5,262	5,348
Hatching use	499	548	679	709	732	770	805	847	865	892
Exports	143	71	101	155	157	159	188	209	253	228

[1] Includes beginning stocks, not shown separately.　　[2] Includes shipments to territories.

Source: U.S. Dept. of Agriculture, Economic Research Service, *Agricultural Outlook,* monthly.

No. 1146. Broiler and Turkey Production, by State: 1995 to 1997

[In millions of pounds, liveweight production]

STATE	BROILERS 1995	BROILERS 1996	BROILERS 1997	TURKEYS 1995	TURKEYS 1996	TURKEYS 1997	STATE	BROILERS 1995	BROILERS 1996	BROILERS 1997	TURKEYS 1995	TURKEYS 1996	TURKEYS 1997
U.S. [1] . .	34,222	36,483	37,523	6,779	7,233	7,216	MO	801	1,059	1,075	551	579	590
AL	4,230	4,192	4,350	(NA)	(NA)	(NA)	NC	3,418	3,542	3,658	1,420	1,458	1,354
AR	4,983	5,660	5,590	536	526	525	OH.	215	240	229	192	227	218
CA	1,179	1,171	1,210	462	493	481	OK.	853	877	869	(NA)	(NA)	(NA)
CO.	(NA)	(NA)	(NA)	159	179	147	OR.	106	107	109	(NA)	(NA)	(NA)
DE	1,394	1,417	1,413	(NA)	(NA)	(NA)	PA	607	654	690	230	246	235
FL	615	591	596	(NA)	(NA)	(NA)	SC.	680	786	830	185	281	368
GA.	5,136	5,655	5,914	44	17	6	SD.	(NA)	(NA)	(NA)	87	99	102
IN	(NA)	(NA)	(NA)	335	351	352	TN	572	603	624	(NA)	(NA)	(NA)
IA	72	77	(NA)	227	222	188	TX	1,747	1,886	2,094	(NA)	(NA)	(NA)
KY	258	331	498	(NA)	(NA)	(NA)	VA	1,197	1,244	1,219	442	485	485
MD.	1,360	1,386	1,417	5	7	9	WA	198	196	194	(NA)	(NA)	(NA)
MN.	250	252	241	855	948	1,026	WV	391	395	381	90	87	87
MS.	2,962	3,109	3,313	(NA)	(NA)	(NA)	WI	104	152	158	(NA)	(NA)	(NA)

NA Not available.　　[1] Includes other states not shown separately.

Source: U.S. Dept. of Agriculture, National Agricultural Statistics Service, *Poultry—Production and Value,* annual; and *Turkeys,* annual.

Natural Resources

This section presents data on the area, ownership, production, trade, reserves, and disposition of natural resources. Natural resources is defined here as including forestry, fisheries, and mining and mineral products.

Forestry—Presents data on the area, ownership, and timber resource of commercial timberland; forestry statistics covering the National Forests and Forest Service cooperative programs; product data for lumber, pulpwood, woodpulp, paper and paperboard, and similar data.

The principal sources of data relating to forests and forest products are *An Analysis of the Timber Situation in the United States, 1989-2040, 1990; Forest Resources of the United States, 1992; U.S. Timber Production, Trade, Consumption, and Price Statistics; Land Areas of the National Forest System,* issued annually by the Forest Service of the Department of Agriculture; *Agricultural Statistics* issued by the Department of Agriculture; and reports of the census of manufactures (taken every 5 years) and the annual Current Industrial Reports, issued by the Bureau of the Census. Additional information is published in the monthly *Survey of Current Business* of the Bureau of Economic Analysis; and the annual *Wood Pulp and Fiber Statistics* and *The Statistics of Paper, Paperboard, and Wood Pulp* of the American Forest and Paper Association, Washington, DC.

The completeness and reliability of statistics on forests and forest products vary considerably. The data for forest land area and stand volumes are much more reliable for areas which have been recently surveyed than for those for which only estimates are available. In general, more data are available for lumber and other manufactured products such as particle board and softwood panels, etc., than for the primary forest products such as poles and piling and fuelwood.

Fisheries—The principal source of data relating to fisheries is *Fisheries of the United States*, issued annually by the National Marine Fisheries Service

In Brief

Real GDP for this sector declined for the second consecutive year to $295 billion in 1996. The sector represents about 4.3 percent of the total U.S. economy.

Lumber consumption in 1996 reached at its highest level since 1987 with just over 9.2 bil. cubic feet being consumed, including 2.6 bil. cubic feet of imports. Producer prices for lumber, after declining in 1995, rose slightly in 1996.

Sixty–six percent of the Nation's 22 billion barrels of proved oil reserves are found in Texas, Alaska, and California. The U.S. continued to import more than it produced in 1996 with 2.7 billion barrels being imported and 2.4 being produced, continuing a trend begun in 1994.

(NMFS), National Oceanic and Atmospheric Administration (NOAA).

The NMFS collects and disseminates data on commercial landings of fish and shellfish. Annual reports include quantity and value of commercial landings of fish and shellfish disposition of landings, and number and kinds of fishing vessels and fishing gear. Reports for the fish-processing industry include annual output for the wholesaling and fish processing establishments, annual and seasonal employment. The Magnuson Fishery Conservation and Management Act of 1976 (Magnuson Act), Public Law 94-265 as amended, provides for the conservation and management of all fishery resources within the U.S. Exclusive Economic Zone (EEZ), and gives the federal government exclusive authority over domestic and foreign fisheries within 200 nautical miles of U.S. shores and over certain living marine resources beyond the EEZ. Within the EEZ, the total allowable level of foreign fishing, if any, is that portion of the "optimum yield" not harvested by

U.S. vessels. Adjustments in the "optimum yield" level may occur periodically. For details, see *Fisheries of the United States, 1996.*

Mining and mineral products—Presents data relating to mineral industries and their products, general summary measures of production and employment, and more detailed data on production, prices, imports and exports, consumption, and distribution for specific industries and products. Data on mining and mineral products may also be found in Sections 26 and 30 of this *Abstract*; data on mining employment may be found in Section 13.

Mining comprises the extraction of minerals occurring naturally (coal, ores, crude petroleum, natural gas) and quarrying, well operation, milling, refining and processing and other preparation customarily done at the mine or well site or as a part of extraction activity. (Mineral preparation plants are usually operated together with mines or quarries.) Exploration for minerals is included as is the development of mineral properties.

The principal governmental sources of these data are the *Minerals Yearbook*, published by the U.S. Geological Survey, Department of the Interior, and various monthly and annual publications of the Energy Information Administration, Department of Energy. See text, Section 19, for list of Department of Energy publications. In addition, the Bureau of the Census conducts a census of mineral industries every 5 years. Nongovernment sources include the *Annual Statistical Report* of the American Iron and Steel Institute, Washington, DC; *Metals Week* and the monthly *Engineering and Mining Journal*, issued by the McGraw-Hill Publishing Co., New York, NY; *The Iron Age*,

issued weekly by the Chilton Co., Philadelphia, PA; and the *Joint Association Survey* of the U.S. Oil and Gas Industry, conducted jointly by the American Petroleum Institute, Independent Petroleum Association of America, and Mid-Continent Oil and Gas Association.

Mineral statistics, with principal emphasis on commodity detail, have been collected by the U.S. Geological Survey since 1880. Current data in U.S. Geological Survey publications include quantity and value of nonfuel minerals produced, sold or used by producers, or shipped; quantity of minerals stocked; crude materials treated and prepared minerals recovered; and consumption of mineral raw materials.

Censuses of mineral industries have been conducted by the Bureau of the Census at various intervals since 1840. Beginning with the 1967 census, legislation provides for a census to be conducted every 5 years for years ending in "2" and "7." The censuses provide, for the various types of mineral establishments, information on operating costs, capital expenditures, labor, equipment, and energy requirements in relation to their value of shipments and other receipts. Commodity statistics on many manufactured mineral products are also collected by the Bureau at monthly, quarterly, or annual intervals and issued in its *Current Industrial Reports* series.

In general, figures shown in the individual commodity tables include data for outlying areas and may therefore not agree with summary tables. Except for crude petroleum and refined products, the export and import figures include foreign trade passing through the customs districts of United States and Puerto Rico, but exclude shipments between U.S. territories and the customs districts.

No. 1147. Gross Domestic Product of Agriculture, Forestry, Fishing, Mining, and Timber-Related Industries in Current and Real (1992) Dollars, by Industry: 1990 to 1996

[In billions of dollars, except as indicated. Industry classifications based on the 1987 Standard Industrial Classification (SIC). Data include nonfactor charges (capital consumption allowances, indirect business taxes, etc.) as well as factor charges against gross product; corporate profits and capital consumption allowances have been shifted from a company to an establishment basis]

INDUSTRY	CURRENT DOLLARS				CHAINED (1992) DOLLARS			
	1990	1994	1995	1996	1990	1994	1995	1996
All industries, total [1]	**5,743.8**	**6,947.0**	**7,265.4**	**7,636.0**	**6,136.3**	**6,610.7**	**6,742.1**	**6,928.4**
Industries covered	**298.1**	**303.9**	**311.4**	**341.9**	**277.3**	**303.6**	**296.7**	**294.6**
Percent of all industries	5.19	4.37	4.29	4.48	4.52	4.59	4.40	4.25
Agriculture, forestry, and fishing	108.7	119.2	111.0	129.8	99.3	119.1	111.4	111.7
Farms	79.5	83.5	73.5	89.4	70.7	84.9	74.2	75.5
Agricultural services	29.1	35.7	37.5	40.5	28.6	34.9	37.0	37.6
Mining [1]	112.3	94.9	99.8	113.6	96.9	102.5	108.4	101.9
Metal mining	4.8	5.9	6.8	6.8	3.7	5.7	5.5	6.3
Coal mining	13.2	13.1	12.3	12.3	12.0	15.5	15.7	16.6
Oil and gas extraction	86.4	66.7	71.0	84.4	73.5	72.2	77.7	69.4
Nonmetallic minerals, except fuels	7.8	9.2	9.6	10.2	7.7	9.2	9.5	10.1
Timber-related manufacturing	77.1	89.8	100.6	98.5	81.1	81.9	77.0	80.9
Lumber and wood products	31.8	38.4	40.7	41.4	37.0	29.8	31.6	33.6
Paper and allied products	45.3	51.3	59.9	57.1	44.1	52.1	45.4	47.3

[1] For additional industries, see Table 716.

Source: U.S. Bureau of Economic Analysis, *Survey of Current Business*, August 1997.

No. 1148. National Forest System—Summary: 1980 to 1996

[For fiscal years ending in year shown; see text, Section 9. Includes Alaska and Puerto Rico, except as noted]

ITEM	Unit	1980	1985	1990	1991	1992	1993	1994	1995	1996
Timber cut, total value	Mil. dol	737	725	1,191	1,012	938	918	786	616	544
Commercial and cost sales: [1]										
Volume	Mil. bd. ft	9,178	10,941	10,500	8,475	7,290	5,917	4,815	3,866	3,725
Value	Mil. dol	730	721	1,188	1,009	935	915	783	616	544
Free use:										
Volume	Mil. bd. ft	2,070	399	151	121	80	80	80	80	80
Value [2]	Mil. dol	5.7	2.2	1	1	1	1	1	1	1
Misc. forest products:										
Value	Mil. dol	1.1	1.7	3	3	3	3	3	3	3
Livestock grazing: [3]										
Cattle and horses [4]	1,000	1,521	1,565	1,236	1,265	1,408	1,318	1,224	1,311	1,167
Sheep and goats	1,000	1,328	1,183	958	1,029	1,183	1,111	925	1,068	859
Roads and trails:										
Road construction [5]	Miles	925	1,903	857	910	853	816	487	424	418
Trail construction [5][6]	Miles	2,419	987	1,635	1,921	1,976	1,976	2,113	2,139	1,696
Receipts, total	Mil. dol	703	636	971	772	614	504	515	387	273
Timber use	Mil. dol	625	515	849	667	520	425	432	303	195
Grazing use	Mil. dol	16	9	10	11	11	11	11	9	7
Special land use, etc	Mil. dol	62	112	112	93	84	68	72	75	71
Payments to local govt. [7]	Mil. dol	240	229	368	335	322	323	309	273	256

[1] Includes land exchanges. [2] Includes some free use timber not reducible to board feet. [3] Covers number actually grazed. Excludes Puerto Rico. [4] Excludes animals under 6 months of age. [5] Includes reconstruction. [6] Includes work accomplished by Human Resource Programs and volunteers. [7] Payments made in following year.

Source: U.S. Forest Service, *Timber Demand and Technology Assessment*, RWU-4861. Also in *Agricultural Statistics*, annual.

No. 1149. National Forest System Land—States and Other Areas: 1996

[In thousands of acres. As of Sept. 30]

STATE AND OTHER AREA	Gross area within unit boundaries[1]	National Forest System Land[2]	Other lands within unit boundaries	STATES AND OTHER AREAS	Gross area within unit boundaries[1]	National Forest System Land[2]	Other lands within unit boundaries
Total	231,744	191,645	40,099	Montana	19,104	16,880	2,224
				Nebraska	442	352	90
United States .	231,687	191,617	40,073	Nevada	6,275	5,819	457
Alabama	1,288	663	625	New Hampshire ...	825	724	102
Alaska	24,355	21,971	2,384	New Jersey	-	-	-
Arizona	11,887	11,251	636	New Mexico	10,367	9,327	1,040
Arkansas	3,504	2,554	950	New York	16	16	-
California	24,403	20,636	3,767	North Carolina	3,165	1,243	1,922
Colorado	16,052	14,505	1,547	North Dakota	1,106	1,106	-
Connecticut	-	-	-	Ohio	834	227	607
Delaware	-	-	-	Oklahoma	465	304	161
Florida	1,408	1,147	261	Oregon	17,507	15,665	1,842
Georgia	1,856	865	991	Pennsylvania	743	513	230
Hawaii	-	-	-	Rhode Island	-	-	-
Idaho	21,658	20,458	1,199	South Carolina	1,376	612	763
Illinois	841	277	565	South Dakota	2,368	2,013	355
Indiana	644	194	450	Tennessee	1,212	633	579
Iowa	-	-	-	Texas	1,994	755	1,240
Kansas	116	108	8	Utah	9,211	8,113	1,098
Kentucky	2,102	692	1,410	Vermont	815	359	456
Louisiana	1,025	604	421	Virginia	3,223	1,656	1,567
Maine	93	53	40	Washington	10,080	9,177	903
Maryland	-	-	-	West Virginia	1,869	1,033	837
Massachusetts	-	-	-	Wisconsin	2,023	1,520	503
Michigan	4,895	2,857	2,038	Wyoming	9,703	9,248	455
Minnesota	5,467	2,837	2,630				
Mississippi	2,310	1,157	1,153	Puerto Rico	56	28	28
Missouri	3,060	1,493	1,567	Virgin Islands	-	-	-

- Represents zero.　[1] Comprises all publicly and privately owned land within authorized boundaries of national forests, purchase units, national grasslands, land utilization projects, research and experimental areas, and other areas.　[2] Federally owned land within the "gross area within unit boundaries."

Source: U.S. Forest Service, *Land Areas of the National Forest System,* annual.

No. 1150. Forest and Timberland Area, Sawtimber and Stock: 1970 to 1992

[As of Jan. 1]

YEAR AND REGION	Total forest land (mil. acres)	TIMBERLAND, OWNERSHIP[1]				SAWTIMBER, NET VOLUME[3]		GROWING STOCK, NET VOLUME[4]	
		All ownerships (mil. acres)	Federally owned or managed[2] (mil. acres)	State, county, and municipal (mil. acres)	Private (mil. acres)	Total (bil. bd. ft.)	Softwood (bil. bd. ft.)	Total (bil. cu. ft.)	Softwood (bil. cu. ft.)
United States, 1970 ..	754	504	116	29	360	2,587	2,035	694	458
North	(NA)	154	11	18	126	295	81	146	39
South	(NA)	203	15	3	185	569	302	191	87
Rocky Mountains........	(NA)	65	42	2	20	398	384	101	95
Pacific Coast	(NA)	82	47	5	29	1,325	1,268	257	238
United States, 1987 ..	731	485	97	34	354	2,853	2,040	766	453
North	165	154	11	19	124	459	126	190	48
South	203	197	16	4	177	781	388	245	106
Rocky Mountains........	142	61	39	3	20	411	394	108	100
Pacific Coast	220	72	31	8	32	1,202	1,132	223	199
United States, 1992 ..	737	490	97	35	358	2,992	2,047	786	450
North	168	158	11	19	127	540	137	207	51
South	212	199	16	4	179	842	389	251	103
Rocky Mountains........	140	63	40	3	20	415	397	110	101
Pacific Coast	217	70	30	8	32	1,196	1,124	218	195

NA Not available.　[1] Timberland is forest land that is producing or is capable of crops of industrial wood and not withdrawn from timber utilization by statute or administrative regulation. Areas qualifying as timberland have the capability of producing in excess of 20 cubic feet per acre per year of industrial wood in natural stands. Currently inaccessible and inoperable areas are included.　[2] Includes Indian lands.　[3] Sawtimber is timber suitable for sawing into lumber. Live trees of commercial species containing at least one 12-foot sawlog or two noncontiguous 8-foot logs, and meeting regional specifications for freedom from defect. Softwood trees must be at least 9.0-inches diameter, and hardwood trees must be at least 11.0-inches diameter at 4 1/2 feet above ground. International 1/4-inch rule.　[4] Live trees of commercial species meeting specified standards of quality or vigor. Cull trees are excluded. Includes only trees 5.0-inches diameter or larger at 4 1/2 feet above ground.

Source: U.S. Forest Service, *Forest Resources of the United States, 1992.*

No. 1151. Timber-Based Industries—Summary of Manufactures: 1992 and 1996

[Data based on *1987 Standard Industrial Classification Manual,* published by the Office of Management and Budget, see text, Manufactures section. N.e.c. = Not elsewhere classified]

INDUSTRY	SIC[1] code	1992			1996		
		All employees		Value of ship-ments (bil. dol.)	All employees		Value of shipments (bil. dol.)
		Number (1,000)	Payroll (mil. dol.)		Number (1,000)	Payroll (mil. dol.)	
Logging and sawmills..................	241/242	221.7	4,739	31.3	254.5	5,984	45.1
Logging..........................	2411	83.6	1,693	13.8	83.0	1,856	15.4
Sawmills/planing mills, general...........	2421	138.1	3,046	21.1	138.0	3,465	26.7
Hardwood dimension and flooring mills	2426	28.5	502	2.0	31.7	631	2.8
Special product sawmills, n.e.c...........	2429	1.8	31	0.1	1.8	32	0.2
Millwork and veneer [2]	243	224.8	5,029	24.8	257.3	6,233	31.8
Millwork.........................	2431	86.3	1,984	9.6	95.3	2,364	11.8
Wood kitchen cabinets	2434	62.8	1,308	4.9	71.7	1,607	6.6
Hardwood veneer and plywood	2435	20.1	395	2.2	21.3	456	2.6
Softwood veneer and plywood	2436	31.3	827	5.4	31.9	931	6.0
Structural wood members, n.e.c...........	2439	24.3	515	2.5	37.1	876	4.7
Wood containers.....................	244	39.9	640	2.9	50.9	893	4.1
Wood buildings, mobile homes	245	56.1	1,227	6.6	81.8	2,077	11.9
Miscellaneous wood products	249	84.6	1,737	10.4	94.2	2,125	13.7
Pulp mills..........................	261	15.9	689	5.5	15.0	701	5.5
Paper mills..........................	262	130.6	5,421	32.8	116.4	5,599	39.6
Paperboard mills.....................	263	51.5	2,136	16.1	54.8	2,599	20.3
Paperboard containers and boxes	265	198.8	5,706	32.6	212.0	6,727	40.4
Setup paperboard boxes...............	2652	6.6	129	0.4	(S)	(S)	(S)
Corrugated and solid fiber boxes	2653	111.7	3,264	19.8	127.4	4,060	25.9
Fiber cans, tubes, drums, and similar products .	2655	12.4	337	1.9	11.9	356	2.1
Sanitary food containers, except folding......	2656	15.4	386	2.5	13.6	389	2.7
Folding paperboard boxes, including sanitary ..	2657	52.7	1,590	7.9	53.2	1,777	9.0
Converted paper and paperboard products [3]	267	229.1	6,525	46.1	232.4	7,321	54.9

S Does not meet publication standards.   [1] Standard Industrial Classification code; see text, Section 13.   [2] Includes plywood and structural members.   [3] Except containers and boxes.

Source: U.S. Bureau of the Census, *Census of Manufactures, 1992 Final Industry Series,* and *Annual Survey of Manufactures.*

No. 1152. Timber Products—Production, Foreign Trade, and Consumption, by Type of Product: 1980 to 1996

[In millions of cubic feet, roundwood equivalent]

ITEM	Unit	1980	1985	1990	1991	1992	1993	1994	1995	1996
Industrial roundwood:										
Domestic production	Mil. cu. ft.	12,123	12,675	14,674	14,051	14,455	14,184	14,515	14,501	14,664
Imports	Mil. cu. ft.	2,570	3,386	3,121	2,841	3,122	3,516	3,701	3,988	4,045
Exports	Mil. cu. ft.	1,857	1,449	2,207	2,287	2,226	2,044	2,042	2,214	2,182
Consumption	Mil. cu. ft.	12,836	14,612	15,597	14,605	15,351	15,656	16,174	16,275	16,527
Lumber:										
Domestic production ...	Mil. cu. ft.	5,305	6,293	7,404	6,858	7,058	6,870	7,082	6,826	7,072
Imports	Mil. cu. ft.	1,545	2,158	1,893	1,698	1,947	2,227	2,384	2,515	2,615
Exports	Mil. cu. ft.	395	297	573	604	548	519	501	481	471
Consumption	Mil. cu. ft.	6,455	8,154	8,725	7,953	8,457	8,577	8,965	8,861	9,215
Plywood and veneer:										
Domestic production ...	Mil. cu. ft.	1,175	1,485	1,422	1,271	1,299	1,300	1,327	1,314	1,297
Imports	Mil. cu. ft.	120	195	97	83	100	100	94	107	97
Exports	Mil. cu. ft.	45	25	109	95	106	100	86	89	87
Consumption	Mil. cu. ft.	1,250	1,655	1,410	1,259	1,293	1,300	1,334	1,333	1,307
Pulp products:										
Domestic production ...	Mil. cu. ft.	4,390	4,432	5,285	5,370	5,488	5,393	5,531	5,847	5,795
Imports	Mil. cu. ft.	880	964	1,083	1,017	1,036	1,128	1,181	1,304	1,262
Exports	Mil. cu. ft.	579	431	673	773	823	753	795	943	925
Consumption	Mil. cu. ft.	4,691	4,965	5,696	5,614	5,702	5,768	5,917	6,208	6,132
Logs:										
Imports	Mil. cu. ft.	25	16	4	2	7	15	18	13	18
Pulpwood chips, exports	Mil. cu. ft.	278	81	178	214	225	211	230	250	278
Fuelwood consumption	Mil. cu. ft.	3,105	3,470	3,177	3,187	3,202	3,244	3,297	3,360	3,420

Source: U.S. Forest Service, *Timber Demand and Technolgy Assessment,* RWU-4861. Also in *Agricultural Statistics,* annual.

No. 1153. Selected Timber Products—Imports and Exports: 1980 to 1996

PRODUCT	Unit	1980	1985	1990	1991	1992	1993	1994	1995	1996
IMPORTS [1]										
Lumber, total [2]	Mil. bd. ft	9,866	14,996	13,063	11,708	13,427	15,369	16,534	17,524	18,363
From Canada	Percent	97.5	97.6	91.2	98.4	98.4	98.2	97.4	97.0	97.1
Logs, total	Mil. bd. ft.[3]	128	99	28	15	45	95	112	80	115
From Canada	Percent	97.4	81.8	70.7	63.4	91.5	93.6	75.9	40.9	57.3
Paper and board [4]	1,000 tons	8,780	11,238	13,148	12,167	12,543	13,971	14,918	15,654	14,418
Woodpulp	1,000 tons	4,051	4,466	4,893	4,997	5,029	5,413	5,650	5,969	5,692
Plywood	Mil. sq. ft.[5]	1,235	1,790	1,687	1,457	1,776	1,786	1,692	1,951	1,772
EXPORTS										
Lumber, total [2]	Mil. bd. ft	2,494	1,793	4,566	3,880	3,498	3,255	3,082	2,929	2,878
To: Canada	Percent	25.3	24.0	14.4	14.6	16.3	17.4	19.8	22.2	23.1
Japan	Percent	26.0	34.5	27.8	31.3	31.8	36.3	34.3	33.4	33.4
Europe	Percent	23.8	15.5	15.0	19.4	21.0	16.8	17.6	17.5	16.9
Logs, total	Mil. bd. ft.[3]	3,261	3,843	4,213	3,761	3,279	2,876	2,684	2,820	2,640
To: Canada	Percent	9.7	11.6	9.4	11.3	12.7	13.6	16.2	25.4	19.7
Japan	Percent	78.0	49.4	62.3	56.5	62.3	65.4	67.9	61.3	68.7
China: Mainland	Percent	2.7	27.8	8.6	9.9	7.2	4.6	2.8	0.7	0.6
Paper and board [4]	1,000 tons	5,214	3,581	6,796	8,331	8,971	9,126	10,097	10,944	12,122
Woodpulp	1,000 tons	3,806	3,796	5,905	6,338	7,222	6,499	6,728	8,261	7,170
Plywood	Mil. sq. ft.[5]	413	365	1,766	1,553	1,760	1,677	1,455	1,517	1,500

[1] Customs value of imports; see text, section 28. [2] Includes railroad ties. [3] Log scale. [4] Includes paper and board products. Excludes hardboard. [5] 3/8 inch basis.

Source: U.S. Forest Service, *Timber Demand and Technolgy Assessment*, RWU-4851. Also in *Agricultural Statistics*, annual.

No. 1154. Lumber Consumption, by Species Group and End Use: 1986 to 1996

[In million board feet, except per capita in board feet. Per capita consumption based on estimated resident population as of July 1]

ITEM	1986	1993	1994	1995	1996	END-USE	1986	1993	1994	1995	1996
Total	**57.8**	**57.4**	**60.0**	**59.1**	**62.4**	New housing	19.3	16.3	16.1	15.9	15.7
Per capita	239	222	230	225	235	Residential upkeep and improvements	10.1	12.0	12.3	12.4	12.6
Species group:						New nonresidential construction [1]	5.3	5.6	5.7	5.8	5.9
Softwoods	47.1	45.7	48.2	47.7	50.5	Manufacturing	4.8	5.5	5.5	5.5	5.5
Hardwoods	10.6	11.7	11.9	11.4	11.9	Shipping	6.8	8.4	8.5	8.5	8.6
						Other [2]	10.9	8.8	8.9	8.8	8.8

[1] In addition to new construction, includes railroad ties laid as replacements in existing track and lumber used by railroads for railcar repair. [2] Includes upkeep and improvement of nonresidential buildings and structures; made-at-home projects, such as furniture, boats, and picnic tables; made-on-the-job items such as advertising and display structures; and miscellaneous products and uses.

Source: U.S. Forest Service, *Timber Demand and Technolgy Assessment*, RWU-4851. Also in *Agricultural Statistics*, annual.

No. 1155. Selected Timber Products—Producer Price Indexes: 1990 to 1997

[1982=100]

PRODUCT	1990	1991	1992	1993	1994	1995	1996	1997
Lumber and wood products	129.7	132.1	146.7	174.0	180.0	178.1	176.1	183.8
Lumber	124.6	124.9	144.7	183.4	188.4	173.4	179.8	194.5
Softwood lumber	123.8	125.7	148.6	193.0	198.1	178.5	189.5	206.5
Hardwood lumber	131.0	128.5	140.7	163.3	168.3	167.0	163.9	174.1
Millwork	130.4	135.5	143.3	156.6	162.4	163.8	166.6	170.9
General millwork	132.0	138.1	144.3	158.5	163.6	165.4	167.9	171.1
Prefabricated structural members	122.3	122.4	132.7	159.7	169.3	163.5	167.5	177.8
Plywood	114.2	114.3	133.3	152.8	158.6	165.3	156.6	159.3
Softwood plywood	119.6	120.8	147.2	169.7	176.8	188.1	173.7	175.5
Hardwood plywood and related products	102.7	102.8	106.9	115.4	122.3	122.2	124.9	127.1
Other wood products	114.7	118.6	124.5	135.3	137.7	143.7	127.5	128.4
Boxes	119.1	123.6	127.5	138.2	141.3	145.0	147.1	149.2
Pulp, paper, and allied products	141.2	142.9	145.2	147.3	152.5	172.2	168.7	167.9
Pulp, paper, and prod, ex bldg paper	132.9	129.8	129.2	127.6	133.1	163.4	149.7	144.7
Woodpulp	151.3	119.2	118.9	104.2	115.9	183.2	133.1	128.6
Wastepaper	138.9	121.4	117.5	117.4	209.5	371.1	141.6	163.3
Paper	128.8	126.9	123.2	123.8	126.0	159.0	149.4	143.9
Writing and printing papers	129.1	124.8	120.2	120.5	121.7	158.4	144.6	140.0
Newsprint	119.6	120.9	109.8	112.1	116.7	161.8	159.5	133.9
Paperboard	135.7	130.2	134.3	130.0	140.5	183.1	155.1	144.4
Converted paper and paperboard products	135.2	134.8	134.8	133.7	136.7	157.0	153.4	148.4
Office supplies and accessories	121.4	119.5	116.4	115.3	116.9	134.9	132.9	131.0
Building paper & building board mill prods	112.2	111.8	119.6	132.7	144.1	144.9	137.2	129.6

Source: U.S. Bureau of Labor Statistics, *Producer Price Indexes*, monthly.

No. 1156. Selected Species—Stumpage Prices In Current and Constant (1982) Dollars: 1990 to 1996

[In dollars per 1,000 board feet. Stumpage prices are based on sales of sawtimber from National Forests]

SPECIES	CURRENT DOLLARS					CONSTANT (1982)DOLLARS [1]				
	1990	1993	1994	1995	1996	1990	1993	1994	1995	1996
Softwoods:										
Douglas fir [2]	466	318	652	453	399	401	270	542	363	312
Southern pine [3]	127	217	266	248	241	109	184	218	199	189
Sugar pine [4]	285	598	625	397	318	245	508	512	318	249
Ponderosa pine [4 5] . . .	218	535	291	158	299	217	455	264	167	234
Western hemlock [6]	203	364	335	292	221	175	309	278	234	173
Hardwoods:										
All eastern hardwoods [7].	146	264	141	150	154	126	224	126	120	121
Oak, white, red, and black [7]	188	195	278	260	209	162	166	231	209	164
Maple, sugar [8]	135	220	313	286	238	116	187	260	209	186

[1] Deflated by the producer price index, all commodities. [2] Western Washington and western Oregon. [3] Southern region. [4] Pacific Southwest region (formerly California region). [5] Includes Jeffrey pine. [6] Pacific Northwest region. [7] Eastern and Southern regions. [8] Eastern region.

Source: U.S. Forest Service, *Timber Demand and Technolgy Assessment*, RWU-4851. Also in *Agricultural Statistics*, annual.

No. 1157. Paper and Paperboard—Production and New Supply: 1980 to 1996

[In thousands of short tons]

ITEM	1980	1985	1990	1991	1992	1993	1994	1995	1996
Production, total	63,600	68,683	80,445	81,234	84,701	86,693	90,897	91,352	92,179
Paper, total.	30,116	34,061	39,361	39,084	40,973	41,745	43,356	42,894	42,460
Paperboard, total.	30,926	32,922	39,318	40,343	41,895	43,113	45,724	46,640	47,901
Unbleached kraft	15,295	16,368	20,357	20,960	21,658	21,447	22,469	22,697	22,179
Semichemical	4,724	5,088	5,640	5,552	5,762	5,672	5,943	5,662	5,619
Bleached kraft	3,836	3,911	4,399	4,572	4,503	4,583	5,029	5,304	5,236
Recycled	7,071	7,555	8,921	9,259	9,973	11,410	12,283	12,977	14,868
Wet machine board E.	138	130	96	96	93	95	96	96	96
Building paper E	1,369	680	723	782	795	797	787	787	787
Insulating board E	1,051	890	946	929	945	943	934	934	934
New supply, all grades, excluding products.	67,783	76,199	87,683	86,014	89,631	93,146	97,447	98,157	96,365
Paper, total.	37,126	43,557	49,485	47,380	49,232	51,246	53,077	52,762	50,759
Newsprint	11,377	12,758	13,412	12,462	12,658	12,750	12,889	12,762	11,768
Printing/writing papers.	16,124	20,658	25,456	24,651	26,013	27,846	29,442	29,543	28,291
Packaging and ind. conv. papers.	5,243	5,163	4,718	4,596	4,783	4,628	4,640	4,241	4,405
Tissue	4,382	4,978	5,899	5,672	5,778	6,022	6,105	6,215	6,294
Paperboard, total.	27,689	30,595	36,301	36,753	38,453	39,950	42,436	43,448	43,611
Construction and other	2,968	2,048	1,897	1,881	1,946	1,949	1,935	1,947	1,994

Source: American Forest and Paper Association, Washington, DC, *Monthly Statistical Summary of Paper, Paperboard and Woodpulp*.

No. 1158. Newsprint—Production, Stocks, Consumption, and Price Index: 1980 to 1996

[In thousands of metric tons, except price index.

COUNTRY AND ITEM	1980	1985	1990	1991	1992	1993	1994	1995	1996
Canada:									
Production	8,625	8,890	9,068	8,855	8,755	9,130	9,299	9,226	9,015
Capacity	(NA)	(NA)	10,100	10,175	9,841	9,604	9,695	9,575	9,769
Stocks at mills, end of year. . . .	165	288	315	565	351	362	225	208	428
United States:									
Capacity	(NA)	(NA)	6,162	6,400	6,625	6,617	6,604	6,580	6,526
Consumption, estimate	10,088	11,507	12,241	12,126	11,268	11,505	11,535	11,826	11,256
Production.	4,239	4,924	5,997	6,206	6,424	6,412	6,336	6,352	6,304
Stocks at mill, end of year	21	57	46	98	59	81	60	76	94
Producer price index (1982=100)	88.5	105.3	119.6	120.9	109.8	112.1	116.7	161.8	159.5

NA Not available. [1] Average for 11 months.

Source: 1980-1993, U.S. Bureau of Economic Analysis, *Survey of Current Business*, monthly; beginning 1994, American Forest and Paper Association, Washington, DC, and Canadian Pulp & Paper Association.

No. 1159. Fishery Products—Domestic Catch, Imports, and Disposition: 1980 to 1996

[**Live weight, in millions of pounds.** For data on commercial catch for selected countries, see Table 1381, Section 30]

ITEM	1980	1985	1988	1989	1990	1991	1992	1993	1994	1995	1996
Total	**11,357**	**15,150**	**14,628**	**15,485**	**16,349**	**16,364**	**16,106**	**20,334**	**19,309**	**16,484**	**16,474**
For human food	8,006	9,337	10,505	12,268	12,662	13,020	13,242	13,821	13,714	13,584	13,625
For industrial use	3,351	5,813	4,123	3,217	3,687	3,344	2,864	6,513	5,595	2,900	2,848
Domestic catch	**6,482**	**6,258**	**7,192**	**8,463**	**9,404**	**9,484**	**9,637**	**10,467**	**10,461**	**9,788**	**9,565**
For human food	3,654	3,294	4,588	6,204	7,041	7,031	7,618	8,214	7,936	7,667	7,476
For industrial use	2,828	2,964	2,604	2,259	2,363	2,453	2,019	2,253	2,525	2,121	2,090
Imports [1]	**4,875**	**8,892**	**7,436**	**7,022**	**6,945**	**6,879**	**6,469**	**9,867**	**8,848**	**6,696**	**6,909**
For human food	4,352	6,043	5,917	6,064	5,621	5,989	5,624	5,607	5,778	5,917	6,150
For industrial use [2]	523	2,849	1,519	958	1,324	890	845	4,260	3,070	779	759
Disposition of											
domestic catch	**6,482**	**6,258**	**7,192**	**8,463**	**9,404**	**9,484**	**9,637**	**10,467**	**10,461**	**9,788**	**9,565**
Fresh and frozen	2,621	2,242	3,813	5,585	6,501	6,541	7,288	7,744	7,475	7,099	7,054
Canned	1,161	1,232	1,017	798	751	674	543	649	622	769	678
Cured	96	70	86	128	126	119	100	115	95	90	93
Reduced to meal, oil, etc.	2,604	2,714	2,276	1,952	2,026	2,150	1,696	1,959	2,269	1,830	1,740

[1] Excludes imports of edible fishery products consumed in Puerto Rico; includes landings of tuna caught by foreign vessels in American Samoa.　[2] Fish meal and sea herring.

No. 1160. Fisheries—Quantity and Value of Domestic Catch: 1980 to 1996

YEAR	QUANTITY (mil. lb. [1])			Value (mil. dol.)	Average price per lb. (cents)	YEAR	QUANTITY (mil. lb. [1])			Value (mil. dol.)	Average price per lb. (cents)
	Total	For human food	For industrial products [2]				Total	For human food	For industrial products [2]		
1980	6,482	3,654	2,828	2,237	34.5	1989	8,463	6,204	2,259	3,238	38.3
1981	5,977	3,547	2,430	2,388	40.0	1990	9,404	7,041	2,363	3,522	37.5
1982	6,367	3,285	3,082	2,390	37.5	1991	9,484	7,031	2,453	3,308	34.9
1983	6,439	3,238	3,201	2,355	36.6	1992	9,637	7,618	2,019	3,678	38.2
1984	6,438	3,320	3,118	2,350	36.5	1993	[3]10,467	8,214	2,253	3,471	33.2
1985	6,258	3,294	2,964	2,326	37.2	1994	10,461	7,936	2,525	3,807	36.8
1986	6,031	3,393	2,638	2,763	45.8	1995	9,788	7,667	2,121	3,770	38.5
1987	6,896	3,946	2,950	3,115	45.2	1996	9,565	7,475	2,090	3,487	36.5
1988	7,192	4,588	2,604	3,520	48.9						

[1] Live weight.　[2] Meal, oil, fish solubles, homogenized condensed fish, shell products, bait, and animal food.　[3] Represents record year.

No. 1161. Domestic Fish and Shellfish Catch and Value, by Species: 1990 to 1996

SPECIES	QUANTITY (1,000 lb.)				VALUE ($1,000)			
	1990	1994	1995	1996	1990	1994	1995	1996
Total	**9,403,571**	**10,461,388**	**9,787,554**	**9,564,888**	**3,521,995**	**3,806,700**	**3,735,615**	**3,486,713**
Fish, total [1]	**8,091,068**	**9,132,276**	**8,520,086**	**8,272,709**	**1,900,097**	**1,984,376**	**1,915,642**	**1,790,966**
Cod:								
Atlantic	95,881	38,653	29,631	31,422	61,329	36,160	28,184	26,634
Pacific	526,396	460,287	591,399	605,314	91,384	95,836	109,680	111,978
Flounder	254,519	426,855	423,443	459,527	112,921	126,580	150,239	154,049
Halibut	70,454	57,900	44,796	49,092	96,700	84,898	66,781	83,468
Menhaden	1,962,160	2,323,537	1,846,959	1,755,471	93,896	128,364	99,131	94,150
Pollock, Alaska	3,108,031	3,124,531	2,852,618	2,623,131	268,344	375,926	259,614	238,129
Sablefish	89,802	71,339	65,904	59,949	58,865	84,827	123,694	109,009
Salmon	733,146	901,086	1,020,765	877,056	612,367	456,407	486,107	368,729
Tuna	62,393	71,795	63,864	85,439	105,040	108,661	102,638	110,256
Shellfish, total [1] . . .	**1,312,503**	**1,329,112**	**1,267,468**	**1,292,179**	**1,621,898**	**1,822,324**	**1,819,973**	**1,695,747**
Clams	139,198	131,427	134,224	123,239	130,194	122,362	140,414	127,779
Crabs	499,416	446,942	363,639	391,797	483,837	532,987	511,987	426,705
Lobsters: American	61,017	66,416	66,406	71,641	154,677	196,175	214,838	241,796
Oysters	29,193	38,086	40,380	38,007	93,718	93,737	101,574	114,839
Scallops:								
Calico	(NA)	7,162	957	(NA)	(NA)	6,944	1,219	(NA)
Sea	39,917	18,228	18,316	18,162	153,696	91,793	92,826	101,823
Shrimp	346,494	2,822,626	306,869	316,879	491,433	564,168	570,034	509,203

NA Not available.　[1] Includes other types of fish and shellfish, not shown separately.

Source of tables 1159-1161: U.S. National Oceanic and Atmospheric Administration, National Marine Fisheries Service, *Fisheries of the United States,* annual.

No. 1162. U.S. Private Aquaculture—Trout and Catfish Production and Value: 1990 to 1997

[Periods are from Sept. 1 of the previous year to Aug. 31 of stated year. Data are for foodsize fish, those over 12 inches long]

ITEM	Unit	1990	1991	1992	1993	1994	1995	1996	1997
TROUT FOODSIZE									
Number sold	Millions .	67.8	67.7	64.5	60.9	58.3	60.2	56.5	59.0
Total weight.	Mil. lb .	56.8	58.9	55.2	54.6	52.1	55.6	53.6	56.7
Total value of sales.	Mil. dol.	64.6	58.3	51.0	54.3	52.7	60.8	57.0	60.2
Average price received	Dol./lb .	1.14	0.99	0.92	0.99	1.01	1.09	1.06	1.06
Percent sold to processors.	Percent .	58	72	71	63	68	68	67	63
CATFISH FOODSIZE									
Number sold	Millions .	272.9	332.7	373.2	379.1	347.6	321.8	375.4	387.1
Total weight.	Mil. lb .	392.4	409.5	497.3	495.8	479.4	481.5	526.3	562.6
Total value of sales.	Mil. dol.	305.1	264.0	302.4	352.9	373.6	378.1	403.3	401.7
Average price received	Dol./lb .	0.78	0.64	0.61	0.71	0.78	0.79	0.77	0.71
Fish sold to processors	Mil. lb .	360.4	390.9	457.4	459.0	439.3	446.9	472.1	524.9
Avg. price paid by processors.	Cents/lb .	75.8	63.1	59.8	70.9	78.4	78.6	77.3	71.2
Processor sales	Mil. lb .	183.1	199.8	231.3	233.5	216.5	227.0	237.2	261.8
Avg. price received by processors . . .	Cents/lb .	224.1	209.0	200.5	218.6	238.5	240.3	236.9	226.0
Inventory (Jan. 1)	Mil. lb .	9.4	9.6	11.6	9.5	11.6	10.9	11.9	11.9

Source: U.S. Dept. of Agriculture, National Agricultural Statistics Service, *Trout Production* released September; *Catfish Production* released February; and *Catfish Processing* released February. Also in annual.

No. 1163. Supply of Selected Fishery Items: 1980 to 1996

[In millions of pounds. Totals available for U.S. consumption are supply minus exports plus imports. Round weight is the complete or full weight as caught]

ITEM	Unit	1980	1985	1989	1990	1991	1992	1993	1994	1995	1996
Tuna, canned	Canned weight. . .	666	759	1,028	856	933	922	835	850	875	859
Shrimp	Heads-off weight. .	425	633	743	734	744	820	808	847	832	845
Salmon, canned	Canned weight. . .	126	113	159	148	131	73	114	117	147	104
Clams	Meat weight.	102	164	150	152	144	155	156	144	144	134
American lobster.	Round weight. . . .	69	108	85	95	107	95	92	101	94	97
Spiny lobster	Round weight. . . .	127	154	89	89	85	81	76	76	89	81
Scallops	Meat weight.	51	72	79	74	62	69	66	76	62	71
Oysters	Meat weight.	71	90	66	56	47	50	48	50	63	58
Sardines, canned	Canned weight. . .	69	76	61	61	52	41	41	48	44	46
Snow crab	Round weight. . . .	54	45	58	37	60	88	66	40	42	46
King crab	Round weight. . . .	133	11	18	19	20	15	8	12	21	30
Crab meat, canned	Canned weight. . .	9	8	8	9	11	9	9	9	12	13

Source: U.S. National Oceanic and Atmospheric Administration, National Marine Fisheries Service, *Fisheries of the United States,* annual.

No. 1164. Canned, Fresh, and Frozen Fishery Products: 1980 to 1996

[Fresh fishery products exclude Alaska and Hawaii. Canned fishery products data are for natural pack only]

PRODUCT	PRODUCTION (mil. lb.)						VALUE (mil. dol.)					
	1980	1990	1993	1994	1995	1996	1980	1990	1993	1994	1995	1996
Canned, [1]	1,516	1,178	1,709	1,768	1,927	2,282	1,928	1,562	1,688	1,796	1,887	1,934
Tuna	602	581	619	610	667	676	1,144	902	904	963	939	957
Salmon.	200	196	198	207	244	197	376	366	307	329	419	284
Clam products	77	110	117	122	129	129	66	76	92	106	110	117
Mackerel [2]	38	23	(NA)	(NA)	(NA)	(NA)	12	11	(NA)	(NA)	(NA)	(NA)
Sardines, Maine.	20	13	14	16	14	18	32	17	25	28	24	30
Shrimp	16	1	1	(Z)	1	1	80	3	4	4	7	6
Crabs.	5	1	(Z)	(Z)	(Z)	(Z)	19	4	1	(Z)	(Z)	(Z)
Oysters [3]	(Z)	1	(Z)	(Z)	(Z)	(Z)	(Z)	1	(Z)	(Z)	(Z)	(Z)
Fish fillets and steaks [4] . .	202	441	420	425	385	398	261	843	847	836	841	886
Cod.	31	65	50	58	65	67	43	132	121	135	152	163
Flounder.	49	54	35	35	35	29	87	154	100	89	86	79
Haddock.	17	7	4	3	3	4	29	24	16	12	11	14
Ocean perch, Atlantic	7	1	1	(Z)	(Z)	(Z)	9	1	2	1	1	1
Rockfish	14	33	18	23	25	20	13	53	30	33	38	42
Pollock, Atlantic	9	12	8	7	4	2	9	21	17	16	10	5
Pollock, Alaska	(NA)	164	161	141	135	136	(NA)	174	185	144	184	159
Other	74	105	143	158	118	140	71	284	376	406	359	423

NA Not available.   Z Less than 500,000 pounds or $500,000.   [1] Includes other products, not shown separately.
[2] Includes Jack and a small amount of Pacific mackerel.   [3] Includes oyster specialties.   [4] Fresh and frozen.

Source: U.S. National Oceanic and Atmospheric Administration, National Marine Fisheries Service, *Fisheries of the United States,* annual.

No. 1165. Summary of Mineral Operations: 1963 to 1992

[Represents mineral operations only. Beginning 1967, excludes single unit establishments without paid employees]

ITEM	Unit	1963	1967	1972	1977	1982	1987	1992
Establishments	Number .	38,651	28,579	25,269	31,359	42,241	33,617	30,787
With 20 or more employees	Number .	5,499	5,682	5,312	6,632	(NA)	6,299	5,600
Including all operations in manufactures . . .	Number .	40,532	29,688	26,178	31,967	42,585	34,041	31,261
Excluding oil and gas extraction.	Number .	17,409	12,221	10,771	12,912	12,267	10,707	9,896
Employees, total . . . . [1]	1,000. . .	616	567	595	799	1,114	698	638
Production workers [1]	1,000. . .	482	433	443	593	762	451	415
All other	1,000. . .	134	134	152	206	352	247	223
Worker-hours, production workers [1]	Million . .	973	892	909	1,183	1,578	942	876
Worker-hours per production workers	1,000. . .	2.0	2.1	2.1	2.1	2.1	2.1	2.1
Payroll, total	Mil. dol. .	3,743	4,187	6,226	13,167	28,637	21,739	24,199
Wages, production workers [1].	Mil. dol. .	2,680	2,888	4,250	9,082	18,030	12,443	13,833
Salaries, all other employees	Mil. dol. .	1,063	1,299	1,976	4,085	10,607	9,296	10,366
Cost of supplies, etc. [2]	Mil. dol. .	8,974	10,576	14,884	46,079	109,697	62,423	65,653
Value added in mining.	Mil. dol. .	15,910	19,330	26,471	68,013	188,055	110,959	113,621
Metal mining	Mil. dol. .	1,418	1,557	2,382	3,504	3,215	4,610	6,724
Coal mining	Mil. dol. .	1,727	2,091	3,754	11,266	18,631	17,068	17,252
Oil and gas extraction	Mil. dol. .	11,020	13,394	17,612	48,587	159,937	80,049	80,016
Nonmetallic minerals mining	Mil. dol. .	1,745	2,288	2,723	4,656	6,273	9,233	9,629
Value of shipments and receipts	Mil. dol. .	18,804	22,784	36,319	96,375	250,000	157,964	162,095
Capital expenditures	Mil. dol. .	3,264	4,058	5,036	17,718	47,753	15,418	17,179

NA Not available. [1] Represents employees up through the working foreman level in manual work. Includes development and exploration workers. [2] Includes purchased machinery installed.

Source: U.S. Bureau of the Census, *Census of Mineral Industries, 1972, 1977, 1982, 1987,* and *1992. Data from the 1997 Census are expected to be released in 1999.*

No. 1166. Mining and Primary Metal Production Indexes: 1980 to 1997

[Index 1992=100]

INDUSTRY GROUP	1980	1985	1990	1991	1992	1993	1994	1995	1996	1997
Mining	**111.5**	**111.0**	**104.8**	**102.6**	**100.0**	**100.1**	**102.6**	**102.3**	**103.9**	**105.8**
Coal	83.4	89.1	103.7	100.1	100.0	95.1	104.1	104.3	106.7	109.9
Oil and gas extraction.	124.4	123.0	106.4	104.7	100.0	101.1	101.7	100.5	101.8	103.1
Crude oil and natural gas. . . .	115.1	111.4	101.6	101.9	100.0	98.0	98.1	96.5	95.9	95.6
Oil and gas drilling	236.8	259.9	151.1	128.6	100.0	122.6	127.0	126.4	138.0	149.7
Metal mining.	65.2	56.6	93.1	93.3	100.0	99.8	100.5	101.5	102.9	107.0
Iron ore	128.5	90.2	101.4	101.7	100.0	100.0	104.3	112.3	111.3	112.7
Nonferrous ores	52.8	50.8	91.9	92.1	100.0	98.6	99.9	100.1	101.8	106.2
Copper ore	65.6	61.2	89.4	92.4	100.0	102.0	104.7	104.8	108.7	109.7
Primary metals, manufacturing . .	**108.0**	**98.4**	**104.0**	**96.7**	**100.0**	**105.7**	**113.4**	**117.2**	**118.9**	**124.5**
Nonferrous metals	92.4	98.2	100.9	97.7	100.0	104.0	113.0	116.5	120.4	126.6
Copper.	75.9	79.7	81.6	88.3	100.0	116.7	111.7	122.0	124.4	132.4
Aluminum	115.1	86.9	100.4	102.2	100.0	91.7	81.8	83.7	88.5	89.4
Iron and steel	119.0	98.8	106.4	96.0	100.0	107.1	113.7	117.7	117.6	122.7

Source: Board of Governors of the Federal Reserve System, *Federal Reserve Bulletin,* monthly; and *Industrial Production and Capacity Utilization,* Statistical Release G.17, monthly.

No. 1167. Mineral Industries—Employment, Hours, and Earnings: 1990 to 1996

ITEM	Unit	1990	1995	1996	ITEM	Unit	1990	1995	1996
All mining:					Avg. weekly hours	Number .	43.9	44.2	44.7
All employees	1,000 . . .	709	580	570	Avg. weekly earnings . .	Dol	568	641	661
Production workers	1,000 . . .	509	424	424	Metal mining:				
Avg. weekly hours	Number .	44.1	44.7	45.3	All employees	1,000 . . .	58	51	52
Avg. weekly earnings . .	Dol	603	684	707	Production workers	1,000 . . .	46	41	41
Coal mining:					Avg. weekly hours	Number .	42.8	43.8	44.0
All employees	1,000 . . .	147	106	100	Avg. weekly earnings . .	Dol	601	735	764
Production workers	1,000 . . .	119	85	82	Nonmetallic minerals,				
Avg. weekly hours	Number .	44.0	44.9	45.8	except fuels:				
Avg. weekly earnings . .	Dol	735	828	857	All employees	1,000 . . .	110	106	108
Oil and gas extraction:					Production workers	1,000 . . .	83	80	82
All employees	1,000 . . .	395	318	311	Avg. weekly hours	Number .	45.3	46.5	47.0
Production workers	1,000 . . .	261	217	220	Avg. weekly earnings . .	Dol	525	624	650

Source: U.S. Bureau of Labor Statistics, *Bulletin 2370* and *Employment and Earnings,* March and June issues.

No. 1168. Mineral Production: 1990 to 1997

[Data represent production as measured by mine shipments, mine sales or marketable production]

MINERAL	Unit	1990	1995	1996	1997, est.
FUEL MINERALS					
Coal, total.	Mil. sh. tons	1,029.1	1,033.0	1,056.7	(NA)
Bituminous	Mil. sh. tons	693.2	613.8	644.9	(NA)
Subbituminous	Mil. sh. tons	244.3	328.0	322.2	(NA)
Lignite	Mil. sh. tons	88.1	86.5	91.6	(NA)
Anthracite	Mil. sh. tons	3.5	4.7	4.2	(NA)
Natural gas (marketed production).	Tril. cu. ft.	18.59	19.51	19.75	19.89
Petroleum (crude).	Mil. bbl. [1]	2,686	2,394	2,360	2,340
Uranium (recoverable content)	Mil. lb.	8.9	6.0	6.3	(NA)
NONFUEL MINERALS					
Abrasive stone [2]	Metric tons	3,710	979	1,290	700
Asbestos (sales)	1,000 metric tons . .	(D)	9.3	9.6	9
Asphalt and related bitumens (native) [3]	Mil. metric tons	25	(³)	(³)	(³)
Barite, primary, sold/used by producers	1,000 metric tons . .	430	543	662	700
Boron minerals, sold or used by producers	1,000 metric tons . .	1,090	1,190	1150	1200
Bromine, sold or used by producers.	1,000 metric tons . .	177	218	227	250
Cement:					
Portland	Mil. metric tons	67.0	73.3	75.8	77.3
Masonry	Mil. metric tons	2.9	3.6	3.5	3.6
Clays.	1,000 metric tons . .	42,900	43,100	43,100	43,900
Diatomite	1,000 metric tons . .	631	687	698	705
Feldspar [4]	1,000 metric tons . .	630	880	890	930
Fluorspar, finished all grades	1,000 metric tons . .	64	51	8	-
Garnet (abrasive)	1,000 metric tons . .	47.0	53.0	68.2	71.0
Gypsum, crude	Mil. metric tons	14.9	16.6	17.5	17.0
Helium [5]	Mil. cu. meters	84.8	99	97	98
Lime, sold or used by producers	Mil. metric tons	15.8	18.5	19.1	19.3
Mica, scrap & flake, sold/used by prod	1,000 metric tons . .	109	108	97	91
Peat, sales by producers	1,000 metric tons . .	721	660	640	620
Perlite, processed, sold or used	1,000 metric tons . .	576	700	684	703
Phosphate rock (marketable)	Mil. metric tons	46.3	43.5	45.4	46.3
Potash (K_2O equivalent) sales	1,000 metric tons . .	1,710	1,400	1,430	1,430
Pumice & pumicite, producer sales	1,000 metric tons . .	443	529	612	538
Pyrites	1,000 metric tons . .	(D)	(NA)	(NA)	(NA)
Salt, common, sold/used by producers	Mil. metric tons	36.9	40.8	42.9	41.4
Sand & gravel, sold/used by producer	Mil. metric tons	855	935	942	989
Construction	Mil. metric tons	829	907	914	961
Industrial	Mil. metric tons	26	28	28	28
Sodium carbonate (natural) (soda ash).	1,000 metric tons . .	9,100	10,100	10,200	10,400
Sodium sulfate (natural).	1,000 metric tons . .	349	327	306	320
Stone [6]	Mil. metric tons	1,110	1,260	1,330	1,390
Crushed and broken	Mil. metric tons	1,110	1,260	1,330	1,390
Dimension [7]	1,000 metric tons . .	1,120	1,160	1,150	1,160
Sulfur: Frasch mines (shipments)	1,000 metric tons . .	3,680	3,150	2,900	2,900
Talc, and pyrophyllite, crude	1,000 metric tons . .	1,270	1,060	994	1,060
Tripoli.	1,000 metric tons . .	81	80	80	(NA)
Vermiculite concentrate	1,000 metric tons . .	209	171	(D)	(D)
METALS					
Antimony ore and concentrate	Metric tons.	(D)	262	242	(NA)
Bauxite (dried).	1,000 metric tons . .	(D)	(D)	(NA)	(NA)
Copper (recoverable content)	1,000 metric tons . .	1,590	1,850	1,920	1,920
Gold (recoverable content)	Metric tons.	294	317	318	325
Iron ore (gross weight) [8]	Mil. metric tons	57.0	61.1	62.2	60
Lead (recoverable content)	1,000 metric tons . .	484	386	426	441
Magnesium metal.	1,000 metric tons . .	139	142	133	120
Manganiferous ore (gross weight) [9]	1,000 metric ton . .	(D)	(D)	(D)	(D)
Mercury [10]	Metric tons.	562	(D)	(D)	(D)
Molybdenum (concentrate).	1,000 metric tons . .	61.6	60.9	54.9	55.5
Nickel.	1,000 metric tons . .	0.3	1.6	1.3	(D)
Palladium metal.	Kilograms	5,930	5,260	6,100	8,300
Platinum metal.	Kilograms	1,810	1,590	1,840	2,500
Silver (recoverable content)	Metric tons.	2,120	1,560	1,570	1,600
Titanium concentrate: Ilmenite (gross weight) . .	1,000 metric tons . .	(D)	(D)	(D)	(D)
Tungsten ore and concentrate [11]	Metric tons.	(D)	(D)	(D)	(D)
Vanadium (recoverable content)	Metric tons.	(D)	(D)	(D)	(D)
Zinc (recoverable content)	1,000 metric tons . .	515	614	600	607

- Represents zero. D Withheld to avoid disclosing individual company data. NA Not available. [1] 42 gal. bbl.
[2] Includes grindstones, oilstones, whetstones, and deburring media. Excludes grinding pebbles, and tubemill liners. [3] Contains bituminous limestone and sandstone, and gilsonite. Includes road oil, 1990-93. Discontinued. [4] Includes aplite, 1992-93.
[5] Refined only. [6] Excludes abrasive stone, bituminous limestone and sandstone, and ground soapstone, all included elsewhere in table. Includes calcareous marl and slate. [7] Includes Puerto Rico, 1990-97. [8] Represents shipments; includes byproduct ores. [9] 5 to 35 percent manganiferous ore. [10] Mercury produced as a byproduct of gold ores only. [11] Content of ore and concentrate.

Source: Nonfuels, through 1994, U.S. Bureau of Mines, thereafter, U.S. Geological Survey, Minerals Yearbook and Mineral Commodities Summaries, annual; fuels, U.S. Energy Information Administration, Annual Energy Review and Monthly Energy Review.

No. 1169. Mineral Production Value: 1990 to 1995

[**In millions of dollars**. Value derived by multiplying production times price at source of production]

MINERAL	1990	1992	1993	1994	1995
Mineral production, total	**141,597**	**127,486**	**125,265**	**122,015**	**118,614**
Mineral fuels, total	**108,133**	**95,453**	**93,265**	**86,815**	**80,114**
Coal, total [1]	22,404	20,976	18,766	20,076	19,709
Natural gas (wellhead)	31,789	32,555	38,834	34,819	28,828
Petroleum (crude)	53,801	41,846	35,625	31,920	31,577
Uranium U_3O_8	140	76	40	(NA)	(NA)
Industrial minerals, total	**21,022**	**20,496**	**21,200**	**23,100**	**24,400**
Abrasive stone [2]	(Z)	(Z)	(Z)	(NA)	(NA)
Asbestos (sales)	([4])	6	6	5	(D)
Asphalt, related bitumens (native) [3]	3,480	2,794	(NA)	(NA)	(NA)
Barite, primary, sold/used by producers	16	20	19	22	17
Boron minerals, sold/used by producers	436	339	373	443	372
Bromine, sold/used by producers	173	170	123	155	186
Calcium chloride (natural)	([4])	([4])	(X)	(X)	(X)
Cement:					
Portland	3,683	3,500	3,920	4,460	4,920
Masonry	225	195	229	286	307
Clays	1,620	1,482	1,480	1,600	1,730
Diatomite	138	141	150	152	171
Feldspar [5]	28	29	31	31	37
Fluorspar, finished shipments	([4])	([4])	([4])	([4])	([4])
Garnet (abrasive)	7	5	(D)	15	10
Gemstones (estimate)	53	66	58	51	74
Gypsum, crude	100	101	107	115	121
Helium [6]	113	187	189	199	196
Lime, sold/used by producers	902	950	965	1,020	1,100
Mica, scrap and flake, sold/used by producers	6	5	4	6	6
Peat (sales by producers)	19	17	17	15	17
Perlite, processed, sold/used by producers	17	16	17	19	22
Phosphate rock (marketable)	1,075	1,058	759	839	945
Potash (K_2O equivalent)	303	334	286	285	284
Pumice and pumicite (sales by producers)	11	15	12	12	13
Salt (common), sold/used by producers	827	803	893	990	1,000
Sand and gravel, sold/used by producers	3,686	3,766	3,980	4,230	4,410
Sodium carbonate (natural) (soda ash)	836	836	734	724	829
Sodium sulfate (natural)	34	26	(D)	24	29
Stone [7]	5,822	5,775	6,030	6,620	6,750
Crushed and broken	5,591	5,594	6,030	6,620	6,750
Dimension	231	181	216	(D)	(D)
Sulfur: Frasch mines (shipments)	335	159	101	162	207
Talc and pyrophyllite, crude [8]	31	31	(D)	32	(4/)
Tripoli	3	3	4	11	11
Vermiculite concentrate	19	15	15	14	(D)
Industrial minerals, undistributed	504	478	417	531	622
Metals, total	**12,442**	**11,537**	**10,800**	**12,100**	**14,100**
Antimony ore and concentrate [9]	([10])	([10])	([10])	([10])	([10])
Bauxite (dried equivalent)	([10])	([10])	([10])	([10])	([10])
Copper (recoverable content)	4,311	4,179	3,640	4,430	5,640
Gold (recoverable content)	3,650	3,662	3,840	4,050	3,990
Iron ore (gross weight) [11]	1,741	1,732	1,640	1,580	1,710
Lead (recoverable content)	491	308	249	298	359
Magnesium metal [12]	433	360	377	389	476
Manganiferous ore (gross weight) [13]	([10])	([10])	([10])	([10])	([10])
Mercury [14]	([10])	0.4	(D)	(D)	([10])
Molybdenum (concentrate)	348	209	165	284	(D)
Palladium metal	22	18	25	29	22
Platinum metal	27	21	21	25	21
Silver (recoverable content)	329	229	227	253	271
Titanium concentrate: Ilmenite (gross weight)	([10])	([10])	([10])	([10])	([10])
Tungsten ore and concentrate	([10])	([10])	([10])	([10])	([10])
Vanadium (recoverable content)	([10])	([10])	([10])	([10])	([10])
Zinc mine production (recoverable content)	847	674	497	619	756
Metals, undistributed	242	156	132	147	812

D Withheld to avoid disclosing individual company data.   NA Not available.   X Not applicable.   Z Less than $500,000.
[1] Includes subbituminous and lignite.   [2] Includes grindstones, oilstones, whetstones, and deburring media.   [3] 1990-92, excluded from industrial minerals.   [4] Included in "Industrial minerals, undistributed."   [5] 1992-93, includes aplite.   [6] Refined only.   [7] Excludes abrasive stone, bituminous limestone and sandstone, and ground soapstone; 1993 excludes dimension stone. State ranks based on publishable data. Includes calcareous marl and slate.   [8] 1990-92, talc only.   [9] Antimony content. [10] Included with "Metals, undistributed".   [11] Represents shipments; includes byproduct ores.   [12] Canvass for magnesium chloride for magnesium metal discontinued in 1986.   [13] 5 to 35 percent manganiferous ore.   [14] Mercury produced as a byproduct of gold ores only.

Source: Nonfuels, through 1994, U.S. Bureau of Mines,thereafter, U.S. Geological Survey, *Minerals Yearbook* and *Mineral Commodities Summaries*, annual; fuels, U.S. Energy Information Administration, *Annual Energy Review.*

No. 1170. Nonfuel Mineral Commodities—Summary: 1997

[Preliminary estimates. Average price in dollars per metric tons except as noted]

MINERAL	Unit	Production	Exports	Net import reliance [1] (percent)	Consumption, apparent	Average price per unit (dollars)	Employment (number)
Aluminum	1,000 metric tons	5,300	1,600	23	6,900	[2]0.75	18,000
Antimony (contained)	Metric tons	[3]31,000	4,500	(NA)	(NA)	[2]1.10	100
Asbestos	1,000 metric tons	9	13	38	21	(D)	30
Barite	1,000 metric tons	700	35	71	2,435	[4]25.00	380
Bauxite and alumina	1,000 metric tons	(NA)	1,300	100	4,300	[4]27.00	(NA)
Beryllium (contained)	Metric tons	210	45	[5]	205	[2 6]327	425
Bismuth (contained)	Metric tons	(D)	200	(D)	(D)	[2]3.50	30
Boron (B_2O_3 content)	1,000 metric tons	622	(NA)	[5]	(NA)	[4 7]340	900
Bromine (contained)	1,000 metric tons	250	14	-	341	[8 9]0.988	1,700
Cadmium (contained)	Metric tons	[3]1,750	100	33	2,600	[2 10]1.00	150
Cement	1,000 metric tons	80,900	850	14	93,602	[4]74.50	17,900
Chromium	1,000 metric tons	[11]124	33	76	513	[4 12]150	(NA)
Clays	1,000 metric tons	43,900	4,970	[5]	39,000	(NA)	13,900
Cobalt (contained)	Metric tons	[11]2,000	1,700	78	9,200	[2]23.00	(NA)
Copper (Mine, contained)	1,000 metric tons	1,920	670	12	2,830	[2]1.08	13,300
Diamond (industrial)	Million carats	135	139	(NA)	244	[14]0.44	(NA)
Diatomite	1,000 metric tons	705	144	[5]	561	[4]252	1,000
Feldspar	1,000 metric tons	930	8	-	931	[4]45.09	400
Fluorspar	1,000 metric tons	121	60	100	609	(NA)	-
Garnet (industrial)	Metric tons	71,000	13,000	[5]	59,000	[4]50-2,000	250
Gemstones	Million dollars	67	2,700	99	5,370	(NA)	800
Germanium (contained)	Kilograms	20,000	(NA)	(NA)	30,000	[8 16]1,475	115
Gold (contained)	Metric tons	325	550	[5]	(NA)	[17]325	14,000
Graphite (crude)	1,000 metric tons	-	27	100	28	[4 18]716	(NA)
Gypsum (crude)	1,000 short tons	17,000	200	30	26,300	[4]7.10	[19]6,000
Iodine	Metric tons	1,330	2,400	65	3,700	[8 20]14.60	40
Iron ore (usable)	Million metric tons	62	5	15	73.7	[4 21]30.41	7,500
Iron and steel scrap (metal)	Million metric tons	78	9	[5]	[15]70	[4 22]124.00	38,000
Iron and steel slag (metal)	1,000 metric tons	21,000	3	1	21,400	[4]7.00	2,500
Lead (contained)	1,000 metric tons	450	30	14	1,660	[2]0.470	1,200
Lime	1,000 metric tons	19,300	58	1	19,500	[4]55.40	5,700
Magnesium compounds	1,000 metric tons	400	55	33	595	(NA)	600
Magnesium metal	1,000 metric tons	190	40	10	166	[2 23]1.65	1,400
Manganese (gross weight)	1,000 metric tons	-	63	100	715	[4 24]2.44	(NA)
Mercury	Metric tons	[11]400	60	(D)	(D)	[26]200.00	(NA)
Mica, scrap and flake	1,000 metric tons	91	7	3	100	[4]91.00	(NA)
Molybdenum (contained)	Metric tons	55,500	50,000	[5]	11,700	[2]8.50	700
Nickel (contained)	Metric tons	16,100	17,300	54	150,000	[4 27]6,931	4
Nitrogen (fixed)-ammonia	1,000 metric tons	13,000	500	14	15,100	[4 28]192	2,500
Peat	1,000 metric tons	500	20	58	1,200	[4]26.00	800
Perlite	1,000 metric tons	703	38	11	790	[4]31.82	140
Phosphate rock	1,000 metric tons	46,300	600	[5]	42,500	[4]23.70	5,000
Platinum-group metals	Kilograms	10,800	60,100	(NA)	(NA)	[17 29]394.83	550
Potash (K_2O equivalent)	1,000 metric tons	1,430	450	76	5,890	[4 30]140	1,650
Pumice and pumicite	1,000 metric tons	538	13	21	680	[4]26.29	70
Salt	1,000 metric tons	41,700	675	14	48,700	[4 31]120.00	4,150
Silicon (contained)	1,000 metric tons	424	41	34	637	[2 32]0.55	(NA)
Silver (contained)	Metric tons	1,600	3,000	(NA)	(NA)	[17]4.62	1,400
Sodium carbonate (soda ash)	1,000 metric tons	10,400	4,000	[5]	6,480	[33]105	2,800
Sodium sulfate	1,000 metric tons	320	80	12	659	[34]114	240
Stone (crushed)	Million metric tons	1,390	4	-	1,397	[4]5.55	78,000
Sulfur (all forms)	1,000 metric tons	11,900	730	11	13,500	[4 35]38.00	3,100
Talc	1,000 metric tons	1,060	197	[5]	955	[4]22	750
Tin (contained)	Metric tons	[11]11,000	4,500	85	49,000	[2]2.65	(NA)
Titanium dioxide	1,000 metric tons	1,330	368	[5]	1,150	[2 36]0.93	4,600
Tungsten (contained)	Metric tons	(D)	20	85	11,400	[37]66	60
Vermiculite	1,000 metric tons	(D)	8	(D)	(D)	(D)	230
Zinc (contained)	1,000 metric tons	607	427	35	[38]1,500	[20]0.810	2,700
Zirconium (ZrO2) content	Metric tons	(D)	26,590	(D)	(D)	[4 39]400	(NA)

- Represents or rounds to zero. D Withheld to avoid disclosure. NA Not available. [1] Calculated as a percent of apparent consumption. [2] Price per pound. [3] Refinery production. [4] Price per metric ton. [5] Net exporter. [6] Metal, vacuum-cast ingot. [7] Granulated pentahydrate borax in bulk, f.o.b mine. [8] Dollars per kilogram. [9] Cents per kilogram, bulk, purified bromine. [10] 1- to 5-short ton lots. [11] Secondary production. [12] Turkish, chromite price. [13] Columbite price. [14] Value of imports per carat. [15] Zone refined, first reduction quality. [16] Price per kilogram. [17] Price per troy ounce. [18] Includes employment at calcining plants. [19] 99.97% indium, per kilogram. [20] O.i.f. value, crude, per kilogram. [21] Lake Superior pellets. Cents per long ton unit of iron. [22] Delivered, No. 1 Heavy Melting composite price. [23] Year-end price. [24] 46%-48% Mn metallurgical ore, per unit contained Mn, c.i.f. U.S. ports. [25] Delivered. [26] Dollars per 76-pound flask. [27] London Metal Exchange cash price. [28] F.o.b. gulf coast. [29] Dealer price of platinum. [30] Price of K20, muriate. [31] Vacuum and open pan, bulk, pellets and packaged, f.o.b. mine and plant. [32] Ferrosilicon, 50% Si. [33] Quoted year-end price, dense, bulk, f.o.b. Green River, WY, dollars per short ton. [34] Quoted price, bulk, f.o.b. works, East, dollars per short ton. [35] Elemental sulfur, f.o.b. mine and/or plant. [36] Rutile, list, year-end. [37] Dollars per unit W03 (7.93 kilograms of contained tungsten per unit). [38] All forms. [39] Price for imported zircon, f.o.b. U.S. east coast. [40] Estimated.

Source: U.S. Geological Survey, Mineral Commodity Summaries, annual.

No. 1171. Selected Mineral Products—Average Prices: 1980 to 1997

[Excludes Alaska and Hawaii, except as noted]

YEAR	Copper, electrolytic [1] (cents per lb.)	Platinum [2] (dol./ troy oz.)	Gold (dol./ fine oz.)	Silver (dol./ fine oz.)	Lead [3] (cents per lb.)	Tin (New York) [4] (cents per lb.)	Zinc [5] (cents per lb.)	Sulfur, crude [6] (dol./ metric ton)	Bituminous coal [7] (dol./ short ton)	Crude petroleum [7] (dol./ bbl.)	Natural gas [7] (dol./ 1,000 cu. ft.)
1980	101	677	613	20.63	43	846	37	89.06	24.52	21.59	1.59
1981	84	446	460	10.52	37	733	45	111.48	26.29	31.77	1.98
1982	73	327	376	7.95	26	654	39	108.27	27.14	28.52	2.46
1983	77	424	424	11.44	22	655	41	87.24	25.85	26.19	2.59
1984	67	357	361	8.14	26	624	49	94.31	25.51	25.88	2.66
1985	67	291	318	6.14	19	596	40	106.46	25.10	24.09	2.51
1986	66	461	368	5.47	22	383	38	105.22	23.70	12.51	1.94
1987	83	553	478	7.01	36	419	42	89.78	23.00	15.40	1.67
1988	121	523	438	6.53	37	441	60	85.95	22.00	12.58	1.69
1989	131	507	383	5.50	39	520	82	86.62	21.76	15.86	1.69
1990	123	467	385	4.82	46	386	75	80.14	21.71	20.03	1.71
1991	109	371	363	4.04	34	363	53	71.45	21.45	16.54	1.64
1992	107	360	345	3.94	35	402	58	48.14	20.98	15.99	1.74
1993	92	374	361	4.30	32	350	46	31.86	19.79	14.25	2.04
1994	111	411	385	5.29	37	369	49	28.60	19.35	13.19	1.85
1995	138	425	386	5.15	42	416	56	43.74	18.74	14.62	1.55
1996	109	398	389	5.19	49	412	51	34.48	18.24	18.46	2.17
1997	107	397	333	4.9	45	381	65	38.00	(NA)	17.24	2.42

NA Not available.   [1] Domestic market prices for wirebar, 1970, 1975-77; prices for cathode thereafter.   [2] Average annual dealer prices.   [3] 1970, New York prices; beginning 1975, nationwide delivered basis.   [4] Straits tin through 1975; thereafter, composite price.   [5] Prime western. Beginning 1975, delivered price.   [6] F.o.b. works.   [7] Average value at the point of production or domestic first purchase price.

Source: Nonfuels, through 1994, U.S. Bureau of Mines, thereafter, U.S. Geological Survey, *Minerals Yearbook* and *Mineral Commodities Summaries*, annual; fuels, U.S. Energy Information Administration, *Annual Energy Review* and *Monthly Energy Review*.

No. 1172. Value of Domestic Nonfuel Mineral Production: 1990 to 1997

[**In millions of dollars**. Data may not add due to rounding]

STATE	1990	1995	1996	1997	STATE	1990	1995	1996	1997
United States .	33,445	37,992	39,967	38,989	Montana	573	574	491	4,983
Alabama	559	706	778	805	Nebraska	90	146	148	161
Alaska	577	538	[1]613	827	Nevada	2,621	3,060	3,230	3,030
Arizona	3,085	4,190	3,580	3,520	New Hampshire	36	50	[1]52	[1]60
Arkansas	381	492	435	535	New Jersey	229	243	[1]246	[1]296
California	2,771	2,760	2,830	2,810					
					New Mexico	1,103	1,130	992	994
Colorado	377	570	513	521	New York	773	886	891	904
Connecticut	122	93	82	[1]65	North Carolina	586	735	690	758
Delaware [2]	10	9	[1]7	[1]6	North Dakota	25	31	31	32
Florida	1,574	1,540	1,760	1,740	Ohio	733	891	969	984
Georgia	1,504	1,690	1,740	1,770					
					Oklahoma	259	357	369	411
Hawaii	106	[1]114	[1]110	[1]100	Oregon	205	239	265	272
Idaho	375	510	449	442	Pennsylvania	1,031	1,080	[1]1,170	1,240
Illinois	667	828	846	880	Rhode Island	18	31	[1]23	[1]23
Indiana	428	589	628	669	South Carolina	450	447	493	507
Iowa	310	456	470	493					
					South Dakota	319	332	357	340
Kansas	349	498	530	547	Tennessee	663	665	662	786
Kentucky	359	432	442	476	Texas	1,459	1,680	1,730	1,700
Louisiana	368	434	393	379	Utah	1,335	1,850	1,730	1,760
Maine	55	68	69	88	Vermont	87	60	[1]66	[1]68
Maryland	368	324	[1]332	401					
					Virginia	507	515	549	600
Massachusetts	128	190	200	213	Washington	483	582	535	522
Michigan	1,440	1,520	1,540	1,560	West Virginia	133	181	185	190
Minnesota	1,482	1,530	1,540	1,160	Wisconsin	215	416	396	389
Mississippi	111	131	144	137	Wyoming	911	973	1,080	996
Missouri	1,105	1,140	1,250	1,320					

[1] Partial data only.   [2] Includes District of Columbia.

Source: 1990, U.S. Bureau of Mines, *Minerals Yearbook*, annual, and *Mineral Commodities Summaries*, annual; thereafter, U.S. Geological Survey.

No. 1173. Principal Fuels, Nonmetals, and Metals—World Production and the U.S. Share: 1980 to 1997

MINERAL	Unit	WORLD PRODUCTION				PERCENT U.S. OF WORLD			
		1980	1990	1995	1997	1980	1990	1995	1997
Fuels: [1]									
Coal	Bil. sh. ton	4.2	5.4	5.1	(NA)	20	19	20	(NA)
Petroleum (crude)	Bil. bbl	21.7	22.1	22.8	24.2	14	12	11	10
Natural gas (dry, marketable)	Tril. cu. ft	53.1	73.6	77.9	(NA)	37	24	24	(NA)
Natural gas plant liquids	Bil. bbl	1.4	1.7	2.0	(NA)	43	34	32	(NA)
Nonmetals:									
Asbestos	1,000 metric tons	4,699	4,003	2,420	2,260	2	(D)	(2)	(2)
Barite	1,000 metric tons	7,495	5,633	4,300	4,600	27	8	13	15
Feldspar	1,000 metric tons	3,202	5,456	6,780	6,800	20	12	13	14
Fluorspar	1,000 metric tons	5,006	5,131	4,050	4,110	2	1	1	-
Gypsum	Mil. metric tons	78	100	97	100	14	15	17	17
Mica (incl. scrap)	1,000 metric tons	228	215	253	220	46	51	43	41
Nitrogen, (fixed) - ammonia	Mil. metric tons	74	97	96	96	20	13	14	14
Phosphate rock, gross wt.	Mil. metric tons	144	162	130	136	38	29	33	34
Potash (k2O equivalent)	Mil. metric tons	28	28	25	24	8	6	6	6
Sulfur, elemental	Mil. metric tons	55	58	53	54	22	20	22	22
Metals, mine basis:									
Bauxite	Mil. metric tons	89	109	107	115	2	(D)	(D)	(D)
Columbian concentrates (Nb content)	1,000 metric tons	15	15	18	17	(NA)	(NA)	-	-
Copper	1,000 metric tons	7,405	9,017	10,100	11,300	16	18	18	17
Gold	Metric tons	1,219	2,133	2,220	2,300	2	14	14	14
Iron ore [2]	Mil. metric tons	891	982	1,027	1,030	8	6	6	6
Lead [2]	1,000 metric tons	3,470	3,353	2,780	2,900	17	15	14	16
Mercury	Metric tons	6,806	4,523	3,160	3,000	16	12	(D)	(D)
Molybdenum	1,000 metric tons	111	128	141	131	62	48	43	42
Nickel [2]	1,000 metric tons	779	965	1,030	1,080	2	(Z)	-	-
Silver	1,000 metric tons	11	16	15	15	9	13	10	10
Tantalum concentrates	Metric tons	544	400	362	395	(NA)	(NA)	-	-
Titanium concentrates:									
Ilmenite	1,000 metric tons	3,726	4,072	3,970	3,500	14	(D)	(D)	(D)
Rutile	1,000 metric tons	436	481	416	414	(D)	(D)	(D)	(D)
Tungsten [2]	1,000 metric tons	52	43	39	32	5	14	(D)	(D)
Vanadium [2]	1,000 metric tons	37	31	35	35	12	(D)	(D)	(D)
Zinc [2]	1,000 metric tons	5,954	7,184	7,240	7,800	6	8	9	8
Metals, smelter basis:									
Aluminum	1,000 metric tons	15,383	19,292	19,900	21,200	30	21	17	17
Cadmium	1,000 metric tons	18	20	19	20	9	8	7	9
Copper	1,000 metric tons	7,649	9,472	10,200	11,000	14	15	16	16
Iron, pig	Mil. metric tons	514	532	533	536	12	9	10	9
Lead [3]	1,000 metric tons	5,430	5,763	5,590	5,980	23	23	25	24
Magnesium [4]	1,000 metric tons	316	354	389	336	49	39	37	36
Raw Steel	Mil. metric tons	717	771	755	773	14	12	13	12
Tin [5]	1,000 metric tons	251	223	201	201	1	-	-	-
Zinc	1,000 metric tons	6,049	7,060	7,550	7,430	6	5	5	5

- Represents or rounds to zero.   D Withheld to avoid disclosing company data.   NA Not available.   Z Less than half the unit of measure.   [1] Source: Energy Information Administration, *International Energy Annual.*   [2] Content of ore and concentrate.   [3] Refinery production.   [4] Primary production; no smelter processing necessary.   [5] Production from primary sources only.

Source: Nonfuels, through 1994, U.S. Bureau of Mines, thereafter, U.S. Geological Survey, *Minerals Yearbook,* annual, and *Mineral Commodities Summaries,* annual; fuels, U.S. Energy Information Administration, *Annual Energy Review.*

No. 1174. Federal Strategic and Critical Materials Inventory: 1980 to 1994

[As of **Dec. 31.** Covers strategic and critical materials essential to military and industrial requirements in time of national emergency]

MINERAL	Unit	QUANTITY [1]				VALUE (mil. dol.) [2]			
		1980	1985	1990	1994	1980	1985	1990	1994
Tin	1,000 metric ton	200	185	169	145	3,158	2,324	962	684
Silver	1,000 troy oz	139,500	136,006	92,151	59,507	2,288	801	374	158
Cobalt	Mil. lb	41	53	53	52	1,020	590	443	561
Bauxite [3]	1,000 lg. ton	14,333	17,957	18,033	16,549	583	871	888	191
Manganese [4]	1,000 sh. ton	5,130	4,470	4,017	2,792	599	520	962	468
Tungsten [5]	Mil. lb	97	87	82	82	817	369	253	178
Zinc	1,000 sh. ton	380	378	379	360	317	268	483	307
Titanium	1,000 sh. ton	43	48	37	37	432	405	402	221
Platinum	1,000 troy oz	466	466	453	453	215	154	186	131
Chromium [6]	1,000 sh. ton	804	854	1,074	1,149	773	836	917	837
Diamonds: Stones	Carat 1,000	19,224	12,549	7,777	6,457	349	336	267	533
Industrial, bort	Carat 1,000	23,693	22,001	17,353	4,012	73	39	16	3

[1] Consists of stockpile and nonstockpile grades and reflects uncommitted balances.   [2] Market values are estimated trade values of similar materials and not necessarily amounts that would be realized at time of sale.   [3] Consists of abrasive grade, metallic grade Jamaica, metallic grade Suriname, and refractory.   [4] Consists of chemical grade, dioxide battery natural, dioxide battery synthetic, electrolytic, ferro-high carbon, ferro-med. carbon, ferro-silicon, and metal.   [5] Consists of carbide powder, ferro, metal powder, and ores and concentrates.   [6] Consists of ferro-high carbon, ferro-low carbon, ferro-silicon, and metal.

Source: U.S. Defense Logistics Agency, *Statistical Supplement, Stockpile Report to the Congress* (AP-3).

No. 1175. Net U.S. Imports of Selected Minerals and Metals as Percent of Apparent Consumption: 1980 to 1997

[In percent. Based on net imports which equal the difference between imports and exports plus or minus government stockpile and industry stock changes]

MINERAL	1980	1990	1991	1992	1993	1994	1995	1996	1997
Columbium	100	100	100	100	100	100	100	100	100
Manganese. . . .	98	100	100	100	100	100	100	100	100
Mica (sheet) . . .	100	100	100	100	100	100	100	100	100
Strontium	100	100	100	100	100	100	100	100	100
Bauxite [1]	94	98	100	100	100	99	99	100	100
Tin.	79	71	74	80	84	83	84	83	85
Tungsten	53	81	91	86	81	95	90	90	85
Cobalt	93	86	86	85	85	80	80	80	80
Chromium.	91	84	80	76	79	81	82	81	78
Tantalum	90	71	73	73	81	75	80	79	76
Potash	65	68	69	68	72	76	75	77	76
Barite.	44	71	66	52	72	64	65	70	71
Nickel.	76	64	61	59	63	64	60	59	54
Selenium	59	46	50	48	39	31	38	40	41
Zinc [2]	60	41	24	33	36	35	35	33	35
Gypsum	35	46	46	50	64	3	21	32	33
Aluminum	(³)	36	31	31	31	31	32	29	30
Cadmium	55	(³)	(³)	1	19	30	23	22	23
Iron and steel . .	13	13	12	13	15	22	21	20	21
Sulfur.	14	21	11	12	14	18	14	14	15
Iron ore	25	3	(³)	2	7	13	7	14	12
Copper.	16	15	19	20	12	12	21	10	11
Titanium	32	(³)	(D)	(D)	(D)	(D)	(³)	(D)	(D)
Platinum group .	87	88	(NA)	(NA)	(NA)	(NA)	(NA)	(NA)	(NA)
Silver.	7	(NA)	(NA)	(NA)	(NA)	(NA)	(NA)	(NA)	(NA)
Mercury	27	(D)	(D)	(D)	(D)	(D)	(D)	(D)	(D)
Vanadium	35	(D)	(D)	(D)	(D)	(D)	(D)	(D)	(D)

D Withheld to avoid disclosure.　　NA Not available.　　[1] Includes alumina.　　[2] Beginning 1990, effect of sharp rise in exports of concentrates. If calculated on a refined zinc-only basis, reliance would be about the same as pre-1990 level; 1990, 64%; 1991, 61%; 1992, 61%; 1993, 67%; 1994, 70%; 1995, 71%; and 1996 and 1997, 70%.　　[3] Net exports.

Source: Through 1994, U.S. Bureau of Mines; thereafter, U.S. Geological Survey, *Mineral Commodity Summaries;* import and export data from U.S. Bureau of the Census.

No. 1176. Federal Offshore Leasing, Exploration, Production, and Revenue: 1990 to 1997

[See source for explanation of terms and for reliability statement]

ITEM	Unit	1990	1991	1992	1993	1994	1995	1996	1997
Tracts offered	Number. .	10,459	16,600	9,618	10,164	10,861	10,995	(NA)	(NA)
Tracts leased.	Number. .	825	676	204	336	560	835	1,537	1,780
Acres offered.	1,000 . . .	56,789	90,288	52,380	55,070	58,895	59,700	(NA)	(NA)
Acres leased	1,000 . . .	4,263	3,414	1,021	1,714	2,775	4,342	8,149	9,637
Bonus paid for leased tracts	Bil. dol. . .	0.6	0.3	0.1	0.1	0.3	0.4	0.9	1.4
New wells being drilled:									
Active	Number. .	120	64	104	129	120	124	(NA)	(NA)
Suspended	Number. .	266	249	180	193	222	247	(NA)	(NA)
Wells completed.	Number. .	13,167	13,184	13,209	13,181	13,342	13,475	(NA)	(NA)
Wells plugged and abandoned	Number. .	14,677	15,430	16,348	16,709	17,427	18,008	(NA)	(NA)
Revenue, total [1]	Bil. dol. . .	3.4	2.8	2.6	2.9	2.6	2.6	3.9	4.8
Bonuses	Bil. dol. . .	0.6	0.3	0.1	0.1	0.3	0.4	0.6	1.2
Oil and gas royalties [1]	Bil. dol. . .	2.6	2.3	2.3	2.5	2.3	2.1	3.0	3.5
Rentals	Bil. dol. . .	0.1	0.1	0.1	(Z)	(Z)	0.9	0.1	0.1
Sales value [2]	Bil. dol. . .	17.0	14.9	15.1	16.4	15.0	13.8	28.0	31.1
Crude oil	Bil. dol. . .	5.9	5.2	5.3	4.9	4.4	5.4	6.8	7.5
Condensate	Bil. dol. . .	1.1	1.1	1.0	0.9	0.7	0.9	1.3	1.4
Natural gas	Bil. dol. . .	9.5	7.9	8.2	9.9	9.8	7.5	11.8	13.3
Sales volume:									
Crude oil	Mil. bbls. .	274	263	302	307	319	357	373	404
Condensate	Mil. bbls. .	51	52	52	55	51	51	65	75
Natural gas	Bil. cu. ft .	5,093	4,516	4,686	4,533	4,700	4,692	5,024	5,077

Z Less than $50 million.　　NA Not available.　　[1] Includes condensate royalties.　　[2] Production value is value at time of production, not current value.

Source: U.S. Dept. of the Interior, Minerals Management Service, *Federal Offshore Statistics,* annual.

No. 1177. Petroleum Industry—Summary: 1980 to 1996

[Includes all costs incurred for drilling and equipping wells to point of completion as productive wells or abandonment after drilling becomes unproductive. Based on sample of operators of different size drilling establishments]

ITEM	Unit	1980	1985	1990	1991	1992	1993	1994	1995	1996
Crude oil producing wells (Dec. 31).	1,000...	548	647	602	614	594	584	582	574	574
Daily output per well.........	Bbl.....	15.9	13.9	12.2	12.1	12.1	11.7	11.4	11.4	11.3
Completed wells drilled, total.....	1,000...	56.9	57.9	26.3	24.8	20.2	21.8	17.4	15.1	18.0
Crude oil.................	1,000...	30.5	33.1	11.5	11.3	8.5	8.3	6.2	6.1	6.8
Gas.....................	1,000...	15.1	13.0	10.1	8.9	7.7	9.4	8.2	6.5	8.1
Dry....................	1,000...	11.3	11.8	4.8	4.5	4.0	4.2	3.1	2.5	3.0
Average depth per well [1]	Feet ...	4,188	4,262	4,759	4,836	5,193	5,494	5,994	5,740	5,932
Average cost per well [1]	$1,000..	368	349	384	422	383	427	483	(NA)	(NA)
Average cost per foot [1]	Dollars..	77.02	75.35	76.07	82.64	70.27	75.30	79.49	(NA)	(NA)
Crude oil production, total.......	Mil. bbl.	3,138	3,274	2,685	2,707	2,617	2,499	2,432	2,394	2,362
Value at wells.............	Bil. dol.	67.7	78.9	53.8	44.8	41.8	35.6	32.1	35.0	43.6
Average price per barrel......	Dollars..	21.59	24.09	20.03	16.54	15.99	14.25	13.19	14.62	18.46
Lower 48 states............	Mil. bbl.	2,548	2,608	2,037	2,051	1,992	1,921	1,863	1,853	1,853
Alaska.................	Mil. bbl.	590	666	647	656	626	577	569	542	510
Onshore.................	Mil. bbl.	2,760	2,819	2,290	2,279	2,173	2,046	1,931	1,838	1,800
Offshore................	Mil. bbl.	377	456	395	428	445	453	500	557	562
Imports: Crude oil..........	Mil. bbl.	1,920	1,168	2,150	2,110	2,219	2,478	2,577	2,639	2,730
Refined petroleum products....	Mil. bbl.	602	683	774	672	657	668	704	588	701
Exports: Crude oil...........	Mil. bbl.	104.8	74.5	39.8	42.3	32.5	35.8	36.1	34.7	40.2
Proved reserves............	Bil. bbl.	29.8	28.4	26.3	24.7	23.7	23.0	22.5	22.40	(NA)
Operable refineries..........	Number.	319	223	205	202	199	187	179	175	171
Capacity (Jan. 1)..........	Mil. bbl.	6,566	5,716	5,683	5,723	5,731	5,519	5,486	5,632	5,595
Refinery input, total..........	Mil. bbl.	5,117	4,814	5,325	5,307	5,340	5,482	5,482	5,555	5,639
Crude oil..............	Mil. bbl.	4,920	4,380	4,895	4,855	4,895	4,968	5,063	5,099	5,176
Natural gas plant liquids.....	Mil. bbl.	168	186	172	172	172	179	172	172	164
Other liquids............	Mil. bbl.	29	248	259	281	274	336	252	285	299
Refinery output, total.........	Mil. bbl.	5,336	5,019	5,574	5,570	5,621	5,763	5,763	5,836	5,946
Motor gasoline..........	Mil. bbl.	2,369	2,343	2,540	2,548	2,577	2,665	2,621	2,723	2,752
Jet fuel..............	Mil. bbl.	365	434	544	526	511	518	529	518	555
Distillate fuel oil........	Mil. bbl.	971	982	1,066	1,080	1,084	1,142	1,168	1,153	1,215
Residual fuel oil........	Mil. bbl.	577	321	347	339	325	307	303	288	263
Liquefied petroleum gases ...	Mil. bbl.	120	142	183	197	223	215	223	237	241
Other products..........	Mil. bbl.	934	796	894	880	902	913	920	920	920
Utilization rate............	Percent .	75.4	77.6	87.1	86.0	87.9	91.5	92.6	92.0	93.5

NA Not available.   [1] Source: American Petroleum Institute, *Joint Association Survey on Drilling Costs*, annual.

Source: Except as noted, U.S. Energy Information Administration, *Annual Energy Review, Petroleum Supply Annual; U.S. Crude Oil, Natural Gas*, and *Natural Gas Liquids Reserves*; and *Monthly Energy Review*.

No. 1178. U.S. Petroleum Balance: 1980 to 1996

[In millions of barrels]

ITEM	1980	1990	1991	1992	1993	1994	1995	1996
Petroleum products supplied for domestic use..................	**6,242**	**6,201**	**6,101**	**6,234**	**6,291**	**6,467**	**7,087**	**6,701**
Production of products..............	5,765	5,934	5,933	6,050	6,182	6,244	6,940	6,511
Crude input to refineries.........	4,934	4,894	4,855	4,909	4,969	5,061	5,718	5,195
Oil, field production...............	3,138	2,685	2,707	2,617	2,499	2,431	2,406	2,366
Alaska.....................	592	647	656	627	577	569	542	510
Lower 48 States...............	2,555	2,037	2,050	1,997	1,922	1,863	1,853	1,856
Net imports...................	1,821	2,112	2,068	2,194	2,441	2,542	2,604	2,708
Imports (gross excluding SPR) [1]....	1,910	2,142	2,111	2,223	2,472	2,574	2,639	2,748
SPR [1] imports................	16	10	-	4	5	4	-	-
Exports....................	-105	40	42	32	36	36	35	40
Other sources.................	33	98	80	90	28	88	102	-
Natural gas liquids (NGL), supply.......	577	574	613	628	664	694	708	716
Other liquids.................	253	465	466	513	550	489	514	599
Net imports of refined products.........	484	326	177	156	134	217	101	181
Imports...................	578	598	500	471	461	518	407	491
Exports...................	94	272	323	315	327	302	307	310
Stock withdrawal, refined products.......	-7	-59	-10	28	-24	6	46	9
TYPE OF PRODUCT SUPPLIED								
Total products supplied for domestic use	**6,242**	**6,201**	**6,101**	**6,234**	**6,291**	**6,467**	**6,469**	**6,701**
Finished motor gasoline.............	2,407	2,641	2,623	2,660	2,729	2,774	2,843	2,888
Distillate fuel oil.................	1,049	1,103	1,066	1,090	1,110	1,154	1,170	1,232
Residual fuel oil.................	918	449	423	401	394	373	311	311
Liquified petroleum gases [2]..........	414	568	616	642	633	686	693	736
Other......................	1,454	1,440	1,373	1,441	1,425	1,480	1,452	1,535
ENDING STOCKS								
Ending stocks, all oils...........	**1,392**	**1,621**	**1,617**	**1,592**	**1,647**	**1,653**	**1,563**	**1,052**
Crude oil and lease condensate.......	358	323	325	318	335	337	303	284
Strategic Petroleum Reserve (SPR) [1].....	108	586	569	575	587	592	592	566
Other.....................	926	712	723	699	725	724	668	202

- Represents zero.   [1] SPR=Strategic petroleum reserve. (See Table 967.)   [2] Includes ethane.

Source: U.S. Energy Information Administration, *Petroleum Supply Annual*.

No. 1179. Crude Petroleum and Natural Gas—Production and Value, by Major Producing States: 1990 to 1996

STATE	CRUDE PETROLEUM						NATURAL GAS MARKETED PRODUCTION [1]					
	Quantity (mil. bbl.)			Value (mil. dol.)			Quantity (bil. cu. ft.)			Value (mil. dol.)		
	1990	1995	1996	1990	1995	1996	1990	1995	1996	1990	1995	1996
Total [2] . . .	2,685	2,406	2,366	53,772	35,004	43,677	18,594	19,506	19,751	31,658	30,286	42,818
AL.	18	19	17	387	306	341	135	520	531	373	948	1,390
AK.	658	542	510	10,086	6,088	7,859	403	470	481	554	771	772
AR.	10	9	9	222	132	165	175	187	222	360	565	847
CA.	322	279	282	5,732	3,906	4,722	363	280	286	857	483	521
CO	31	29	25	722	466	511	243	523	572	377	497	783
FL	6	6	6	(NA)	(NA)	(NA)	6	6	6	15	8	(NA)
IL	20	16	16	467	274	325	1	(Z)	(Z)	1	(NA)	(NA)
IN	3	3	3	73	47	52	(Z)	(Z)	(Z)	1	(Z)	1
KS.	59	44	42	1,359	709	855	574	721	713	893	985	1,366
KY.	5	3	4	124	57	73	75	75	81	169	123	207
LA.	148	131	132	3,409	2,096	2,759	5,242	5,108	5,241	9,587	8,048	12,194
MI	20	11	11	458	189	220	140	238	246	420	399	544
MS	30	20	20	630	294	370	95	96	103	167	118	172
MT	20	17	16	429	247	301	50	50	51	90	68	72
NE.	5	4	4	119	58	69	1	2	2	2	3	3
NM	66	65	64	1,472	1,080	1,340	965	1,626	1,554	1,629	2,056	2,589
NY	(Z)	(Z)	(Z)	9	(Z)	(Z)	25	18	18	55	42	(NA)
ND	39	29	32	849	457	629	52	49	50	93	(NA)	(NA)
OH	8	8	8	196	138	166	155	126	119	393	294	314
OK	117	88	85	2,690	1,459	1,759	2,258	1,812	1,735	3,548	2,616	3,840
PA.	2	2	2	54	33	36	178	111	135	417	315	(NA)
TX.	674	560	543	15,060	9,167	11,035	6,343	6,330	6,449	9,939	10,208	14,768
UT.	23	20	19	524	354	409	146	241	251	249	277	347
WV	2	2	2	43	32	33	178	186	179	568	414	(NA)
WY	103	79	73	2,169	1,223	1,435	736	674	666	856	1,198	1,715

NA Not available.   Z Less than 500 million cubic feet or less than $500,000.   [1] Excludes nonhydrocarbon gases.
[2] Includes other states not shown separately. State production does not include state offshore production.

Source: U.S. Energy Information Administration, *Energy Data Reports, Petroleum Supply Annual, Natural Gas Annual*, and *Natural Gas Monthly*.

No. 1180. Crude Oil, Natural Gas, and Natural Gas Liquids—Reserves by State: 1990 and 1996

[As of **December 31**. Proved reserves are estimated quantities of the mineral, which geological and engineering data demonstrate with reasonable certainty, to be recoverable in future years from known reservoirs under existing economic and operating conditions. Indicated reserves of crude oil are quantities other than proved reserves, which may become economically recoverable from existing productive reservoirs through the application of improved recovery techniques using current technology. Based on a sample of operators of oil and gas wells]

AREA	1990				1996			
	Crude oil		Natural gas (bil. cu. ft.)	Natural gas liquids (mil. bbl.)	Crude oil		Natural gas (bil. cu. ft.)	Natural gas liquids (mil. bbl.)
	Proved (mil. bbl.)	Indicated			Proved (mil. bbl.)	Indicated		
United States	26,254	3,483	169,346	7,586	22,017	2,876	166,474	7,823
Lower 48 States	19,730	2,514	160,046	7,246	16,743	1,924	157,180	7,486
Alabama.	44	(Z)	[1]4,125	170	45	-	5,033	119
Alaska	6,524	969	9,300	340	5,274	952	9,294	337
Arkansas	60	1	1,731	9	58	-	1,470	4
California	[2]4,658	[2]1,425	[2]3,185	[2]105	[2]3,437	[2]905	[2]2,082	[2]92
Colorado.	305	8	4,555	169	231	22	7,710	287
Florida	(NA)	(NA)	(NA)	(NA)	97	-	96	22
Illinois	(NA)	(NA)	(NA)	(NA)	94	-	(NA)	(NA)
Indiana.	131	-	(NA)	(NA)	11	-	(NA)	(NA)
Kansas.	(NA)	(NA)	(NA)	(NA)	266	-	7,694	338
Kentucky	321	(Z)	9,614	313	21	-	983	46
Louisiana	33	-	1,016	25	658	331	9,543	543
Michigan.	(NA)	(NA)	(NA)	(NA)	74	-	2,061	53
Mississippi	(NA)	(NA)	(NA)	(NA)	164	6	631	7
Montana	(NA)	(NA)	(NA)	(NA)	168	-	796	7
Nebraska	221	-	899	15	28	-	(NA)	(NA)
New Mexico	(NA)	(NA)	(NA)	(NA)	744	148	16,485	1,059
New York	687	256	17,260	990	(NA)	(NA)	232	(NA)
North Dakota.	285	-	586	60	248	6	462	48
Ohio	65	-	1,214	(NA)	53	-	1,113	(NA)
Oklahoma.	734	37	16,151	657	632	43	13,074	684
Pennsylvania.	22	-	1,720	(NA)	10	-	1,696	(NA)
Texas.	[2]7,106	618	[2]38,192	[2]2,575	[2]5,736	[2]358	[2]38,270	2,606
Utah	249	44	1,510	([3])	237	46	1,633	([3])
Virginia.	(NA)	(NA)	138	(NA)	(NA)	(NA)	1,930	(NA)
West Virginia	31	-	2,207	86	25	-	2,703	61
Wyoming	794	42	9,944	[4]812	603	14	12,320	[4]727
Federal offshore.	2,805	49	31,433	619	3,085	45	29,096	776

- Represents or rounds to zero.   NA Not available.   [1] Includes state offshore.   [2] Excludes federal offshore.   [3] Included with Wyoming.   [4] Includes Utah.

Source: Energy Information Administration, *U.S. Crude Oil, Natural Gas, and Natural Gas Liquids Reserves, Annual Report 1996*.

No. 1181. World Crude Oil Production, by Major Producing Country: 1980 to 1996

[In thousands of barrels per day]

COUNTRY	1980	1985	1990	1991	1992	1993	1994	1995	1996
World, total [1]	59,599	53,981	60,566	60,207	60,212	60,238	60,992	62,331	64,054
Saudi Arabia	9,900	3,388	6,410	8,115	8,332	8,198	8,120	8,231	8,218
United States	8,597	8,971	7,355	7,417	7,171	6,847	6,662	6,560	6,465
Russia	(X)	(X)	(X)	(X)	7,632	6,730	6,135	5,995	5,850
Iran	1,662	2,250	3,088	3,312	3,429	3,540	3,618	3,643	3,686
China	2,114	2,505	2,774	2,835	2,845	2,890	2,939	2,990	3,131
Norway	528	788	1,704	1,890	2,229	2,350	2,521	2,768	3,104
Venezuela	2,168	1,677	2,137	2,375	2,371	2,450	2,588	2,750	3,053
Mexico	1,936	2,745	2,553	2,680	2,669	2,673	2,685	2,618	2,855
United Kingdom	1,622	2,530	1,820	1,797	1,825	1,915	2,375	2,489	2,568
United Arab Emirates	1,709	1,193	2,117	2,386	2,266	2,159	2,193	2,233	2,278
Nigeria	2,055	1,495	1,810	1,892	1,943	1,960	1,931	1,993	2,188
Kuwait	1,656	1,023	1,175	190	1,058	1,852	2,025	2,057	2,062
Canada	1,435	1,471	1,553	1,548	1,605	1,679	1,746	1,805	1,837
Indonesia	1,577	1,325	1,462	1,592	1,504	1,511	1,510	1,503	1,547
Libya	1,787	1,059	1,375	1,483	1,433	1,361	1,378	1,390	1,401
Algeria	1,106	1,037	1,175	1,230	1,214	1,162	1,180	1,202	1,242
Egypt	595	887	873	874	881	890	896	920	922
Oman	282	498	685	700	740	776	810	851	883
Brazil	182	564	631	630	626	643	671	695	795
Argentina	491	460	483	485	553	594	650	715	756
Angola	150	231	475	500	526	509	536	646	709
Malaysia	283	440	619	646	653	640	645	682	695
India	182	620	660	615	561	534	590	703	651
Colombia	126	176	440	419	433	456	450	585	623
Syria	164	178	388	492	481	554	560	575	604
Iraq	2,514	1,433	2,040	305	425	512	553	560	579
Australia	380	575	575	545	535	503	536	562	570
Qatar	472	301	406	395	423	413	415	442	510

X Not applicable.   [1] Includes countries not shown separately.

Source: U. S. Energy Information Administration, *International Energy Annual, 1996.*

No. 1182. Liquefied Petroleum Gases—Summary: 1980 to 1996

[In millions of 42-gallon barrels. Includes ethane]

ITEM	1980	1985	1990	1991	1992	1993	1994	1995	1996
Production	**561**	**622**	**638**	**683**	**720**	**850**	**734**	**760**	**789**
At natural gas plants	441	479	456	488	500	634	511	521	547
At refineries	121	143	182	196	222	216	223	234	242
Imports	79	68	68	54	57	70	67	53	61
Refinery input	85	111	107	111	172	179	108	105	102
Exports	9	23	14	15	18	16	14	21	19
Stocks, Dec. 31	116	74	98	92	98	117	99	93	86

Source: U.S. Energy Information Administration, *Petroleum Supply Annual.*

No. 1183. Natural Gas Plant Liquids—Production and Value: 1980 to 1996

[Barrels of 42 gallons]

ITEM	Unit	1980	1985	1990	1991	1992	1993	1994	1995	1996
Field production [1]	Mil. bbl	576	587	566	606	621	634	630	643	670
Pentanes plus	Mil. bbl	126	103	112	118	121	122	119	122	123
Liquefied petroleum gases	Mil. bbl	441	479	454	488	500	512	511	521	547
Natural gas processed	Tril. cu. ft.	15	13	15	16	16	16	16	17	17

[1] Includes other finished petroleum products, not shown separately.

Source: U.S. Energy Information Administration, *Energy Data Reports, Petroleum Statement Annual, Petroleum Supply Annual,* and *Natural Gas Annual.*

No. 1184. Natural Gas—Supply, Consumption, Reserves, and Marketed Production: 1980 to 1997

ITEM	Unit	1980	1985	1990	1991	1992	1993	1994	1995	1996	1997, prel.
Producing wells (year-end) .	1,000	182	243	269	276	276	282	292	299	302	(NA)
Production value at wells . .	Bil. dol	32.1	43.4	31.8	30.3	32.6	38.7	36.5	30.2	42.9	48.1
Avg. per 1,000 cu. ft. . .	Dollars	1.59	2.51	1.71	1.64	1.74	2.04	1.85	1.55	2.17	2.42
Proved reserves [1]	Tril. cu. ft . .	199	193	169	167	165	162	164	165	166	(NA)
Marketed production [2] . .	**Tril. cu. ft. .**	**20.2**	**17.3**	**18.6**	**18.5**	**18.7**	**19.0**	**19.7**	**19.5**	**19.8**	**19.9**
Minus: Extraction losses [3] .	Tril. cu. ft . .	0.8	0.8	0.8	0.8	0.9	0.9	0.9	0.9	1.0	0.9
Equals: Dry production	Tril. cu. ft . .	19.4	16.5	17.8	17.7	17.8	18.1	18.8	18.6	18.8	19.0
Plus: Withdrawals from											
storage	Tril. cu. ft . .	2.0	2.4	2.0	2.8	2.8	2.8	2.6	3.0	2.9	2.8
Plus: Imports [4]	Tril. cu. ft . .	1.0	0.9	1.5	1.8	2.1	2.4	2.6	2.8	2.9	3.0
Plus: Balancing item	Tril. cu. ft . .	-0.6	-0.4	-0.2	-0.5	-0.5	-0.1	-0.4	-0.2	0.3	(NA)
Equals: Total supply.	Tril. cu. ft . .	21.9	19.5	21.3	21.8	22.8	23.6	24.2	24.8	25.6	(NA)
Minus: Exports	Tril. cu. ft . .	0.5	0.6	0.9	0.1	0.2	0.1	0.2	0.2	0.2	0.2
Minus: Additions to											
storage [5]	Tril. cu. ft . .	1.9	2.2	2.5	2.7	2.6	2.8	2.9	2.6	3.0	(NA)
Equals: Consumption,											
total	**Tril. cu. ft. .**	**19.9**	**17.3**	**18.7**	**19.0**	**19.5**	**20.3**	**20.7**	**21.6**	**22.0**	**22.0**
Lease and plant fuel. . . .	Tril. cu. ft . .	1.0	1.0	1.2	1.1	1.2	1.2	1.1	1.2	1.3	1.3
Pipeline fuel	Tril. cu. ft . .	0.6	0.5	0.7	0.6	0.6	0.6	0.7	0.7	0.7	0.7
Residential	Tril. cu. ft . .	4.8	4.4	4.4	4.6	4.7	5.0	4.8	4.9	5.2	5.0
Commercial [6]	Tril. cu. ft . .	2.6	2.4	2.6	2.7	2.8	2.9	2.9	3.0	3.2	3.2
Industrial	Tril. cu. ft . .	7.2	5.9	7.0	7.2	7.5	8.0	8.2	8.6	8.9	8.8
Vehicle fuel.	Tril. cu. ft . .	(NA)	(NA)	(Z)	(Z)	(Z)	(Z)	(Z)	(Z)	(Z)	(NA)
Electric utilities	Tril. cu. ft . .	3.7	3.0	2.8	2.8	2.8	2.7	3.0	3.2	2.7	3.0
World production (dry)	Quad. Btu. .	53.1	62.0	73.6	74.8	74.9	76.3	76.8	77.9	82.0	(NA)
U.S. production (dry) . . .	Quad. Btu. .	19.4	16.5	17.8	17.7	17.8	18.1	18.8	18.6	18.8	19.0
Percent U.S. of world . .	Percent . . .	36.5	26.4	24.2	23.7	23.8	23.7	24.5	23.9	22.9	(NA)

NA Not available.   Z Less than .05 trillion cubic feet.   [1] Estimated, end of year. Source: U.S. Energy Information Administration, *U.S. Crude Oil, Natural Gas,* and *Natural Gas Liquids Reserves,* annual.   [2] Marketed production includes gross withdrawals from reservoirs less quantities used for reservoir repressuring and quantities vented or flared. For 1980 and thereafter, it excludes the nonhydrocarbon gases subsequently removed.   [3] Volumetric reduction in natural gas resulting from the extraction of natural gas constituents at natural gas processing plants.   [4] Includes imports of liquefied natural gas.   [5] Includes liquefied natural gas (LNG) storage in above ground tanks.   [6] Includes deliveries to municipalities and public authorities for institutional heating and other purposes.

Source: Except as noted, U.S. Energy Information Administration, *Annual Energy Review, International Energy Annual, Natural Gas Annual,* Volume I and II and *Monthly Energy Review.*

No. 1185. World Natural Gas Production, by Major Producing Country: 1980 to 1996

[In quadrillion Btu's]

COUNTRY	1980	1985	1990	1991	1992	1993	1994	1995	1996
World, total [1]	**53.45**	**62.32**	**73.61**	**74.81**	**74.87**	**76.30**	**76.80**	**77.92**	**81.96**
Russia	(X)	(X)	(X)	(X)	22.62	21.81	21.45	21.01	21.23
United States	**19.40**	**16.45**	**17.81**	**17.70**	**17.84**	**18.10**	**18.82**	**18.60**	**19.02**
Canada.	2.76	3.04	3.85	4.06	4.52	4.91	5.26	5.64	5.85
Netherlands.	3.40	3.01	2.69	3.04	3.06	3.11	2.95	2.97	3.37
United Kingdom	1.32	1.52	1.75	2.01	1.93	2.31	2.47	2.67	3.17
Indonesia	0.63	1.23	1.53	1.72	1.79	1.97	2.21	2.24	2.38
Algeria	0.41	1.36	1.79	1.93	1.97	1.90	1.81	2.05	2.19
Uzbekistan	(X)	(X)	(X)	(X)	1.51	1.59	1.67	1.70	1.70
Saudi Arabia	0.33	0.72	1.08	1.13	1.20	1.27	1.33	1.34	1.46
Norway.	0.92	0.94	0.98	0.97	1.04	0.97	1.04	1.08	1.45
Iran	0.25	0.60	0.84	0.92	0.88	0.96	1.12	1.25	1.38
Turkmenistan	0.00	0.00	0.00	0.00	2.02	2.29	1.26	1.14	1.31
Malaysia	0.06	0.44	0.65	0.75	0.80	0.88	0.92	1.02	1.30
United Arab Emirates.	0.20	0.48	0.78	0.92	1.02	0.94	0.91	1.11	1.28
Australia	0.33	0.46	0.72	0.75	0.82	0.86	0.92	1.03	1.06
Argentina	0.28	0.50	0.63	0.70	0.71	0.76	0.79	0.88	1.02
Mexico	1.01	0.95	0.94	0.94	0.92	0.90	0.91	0.94	0.99
Venezuela.	0.52	0.62	0.76	0.79	0.76	0.82	0.88	0.89	0.96
Germany.	0.00	0.00	0.00	0.67	0.68	0.68	0.67	0.71	0.78
Italy	0.44	0.50	0.61	0.61	0.64	0.69	0.73	0.72	0.71
India.	0.05	0.14	0.40	0.45	0.48	0.53	0.59	0.63	0.70
Pakistan	0.29	0.37	0.48	0.53	0.55	0.58	0.63	0.65	0.70
China	0.51	0.46	0.51	0.53	0.53	0.56	0.59	0.60	0.67
Ukraine	(X)	(X)	(X)	(X)	0.74	0.68	0.64	0.62	0.64
Romania	1.20	1.27	1.00	0.88	0.78	0.75	0.69	0.68	0.63
Qatar	0.18	0.19	0.28	0.33	0.40	0.48	0.48	0.48	0.48
Egypt	0.03	0.18	0.29	0.32	0.35	0.40	0.42	0.44	0.47
Thailand	0.00	0.13	0.21	0.24	0.25	0.31	0.34	0.37	0.43

X Not applicable.   [1] Includes countries not shown separately.

Source: U. S. Energy Information Administration, *International Energy Annual, 1996.*

No. 1186. Coal and Coke—Summary: 1980 to 1997

[Includes coal consumed at mines. Demonstrated coal reserve base for United States on Jan. 1, 1995, was an estimated 496 billion tons. Recoverability varies between 40 and 90 percent for individual deposits; 50 percent or more of overall U.S. coal reserve base is believed to be recoverable]

ITEM	Unit	1980	1985	1990	1993	1994	1995	1996	1997, prel.
COAL									
Coal production, total [1]	Mil. sh. tons	830	884	1,029	945	1,034	1,033	1,064	1,089
Value	Mil. dol.	20,453	22,277	22,404	18,624	20,076	19,460	19,480	(NA)
Anthracite production	Mil. sh. tons	6.1	4.7	3.5	4.3	4.6	4.7	4.8	4.9
Bituminous coal and lignite:									
Production	Mil. sh. tons	824	879	1,026	945	1,034	1,033	1,064	1,084
Underground	Mil. sh. tons	337	350	425	351	399	396	410	(NA)
Surface	Mil. sh. tons	487	529	605	594	634	637	654	(NA)
Exports	Mil. sh. tons	92	93	106	75	71	89	90	84
Imports	Mil. sh. tons	1.2	2.0	2.7	7.3	7.6	7.2	7.1	7.5
Consumption [2]	Mil. sh. tons	703	818	896	926	930	941	983	1,008
Electric power utilities	Mil. sh. tons	569	694	774	814	817	829	875	902
Industrial	Mil. sh. tons	126	116	115	106	107	106	103	100
Number of mines	Number	5,598	4,547	3,243	2,475	2,354	2,104	1,903	(NA)
Daily employment	1,000	225	169	131	101	98	90	83	(NA)
Production, by state:									
Alabama	Mil. sh. tons	26	28	29	25	23	25	25	24
Illinois	Mil. sh. tons	63	59	60	41	53	48	47	42
Indiana	Mil. sh. tons	31	33	36	29	31	26	30	35
Kentucky	Mil. sh. tons	150	152	173	156	162	154	153	156
Montana	Mil. sh. tons	30	33	38	36	42	39	38	41
Ohio	Mil. sh. tons	39	36	35	29	30	26	29	31
Pennsylvania	Mil. sh. tons	93	71	71	60	62	62	68	73
Virginia	Mil. sh. tons	41	41	47	39	37	34	36	36
West Virginia	Mil. sh. tons	122	128	169	131	162	163	170	173
Wyoming	Mil. sh. tons	95	141	184	210	237	264	278	282
Other states	Mil. sh. tons	140	162	187	189	195	192	192	196
World production	Mil. sh. tons	4,103	4,779	5,356	4,930	5,033	5,144	5,185	(NA)
COKE									
Coke production [3]	Mil. sh. tons	46.13	28.44	27.62	23.18	22.69	23.75	23.08	(NA)
Imports	Mil. sh. tons	0.66	0.58	0.77	1.53	1.61	1.82	1.11	(NA)
Exports	Mil. sh. tons	2.07	1.12	0.57	0.84	0.66	0.75	1.12	(NA)
Consumption	Mil. sh. tons	41.28	29.06	27.82	24.29	24.00	24.45	23.09	(NA)

NA Not available. [1] Includes bituminous coal, lignite, and anthracite. [2] Includes some categories not shown separately. [3] Includes beehive coke.

Source: U.S. Energy Information Administration, Coal Industry, annual; Annual Energy Review, and Quarterly Coal Report, and unpublished data.

No. 1187. World Coal Production, by Major Producing Country: 1980 to 1996

[In millions of short tons]

COUNTRY	1980	1985	1990	1991	1992	1993	1994	1995	1996
World	4,193	4,900	5,356	5,033	5,052	4,930	5,033	5,144	5,185
China	684	962	1,190	1,199	1,229	1,304	1,404	1,537	1,550
United States	830	884	1,029	996	998	945	1,034	1,033	1,064
India	126	191	233	253	270	281	291	301	311
Russia	(X)	(X)	(X)	(X)	406	364	320	310	302
Australia	116	172	226	236	249	248	248	267	274
Germany	532	578	514	388	346	315	292	274	264
South Africa	132	191	193	196	203	207	216	227	227
Poland	254	275	237	231	219	219	221	221	219
Kazakhstan	(X)	(X)	(X)	(X)	140	124	115	92	84
Canada	40	67	75	78	72	76	80	83	84
Korea, North	51	59	71	73	74	78	78	78	81
Ukraine	(X)	(X)	(X)	(X)	147	128	104	92	77
Czech Republic	(X)	(X)	(X)	(X)	(X)	77	82	79	77
Greece	26	40	57	58	61	60	63	64	66
Turkey	20	44	52	51	57	54	60	61	62
United Kingdom	144	104	106	107	95	76	54	52	56
Indonesia	1	2	12	15	25	32	33	45	53
Romania	39	51	42	36	42	43	45	44	45
Serbia and Montenegro	(X)	(X)	(X)	(X)	47	41	40	44	43
Colombia	5	10	23	26	26	24	25	29	33
Spain	41	53	40	37	37	35	33	31	33
Bulgaria	33	34	35	31	33	32	32	31	32
Thailand	2	6	14	16	17	17	19	20	21
Hungary	28	27	19	19	17	16	16	15	17
Estonia	(X)	(X)	(X)	(X)	21	16	16	15	12
Mexico	4	7	7	6	7	8	10	10	10
France	25	21	15	14	13	12	10	9	10
Mongolia	5	8	10	9	8	8	8	8	9

X Not applicable.

Source: U.S. Energy Information Administration, International Energy Annual.

No. 1188. Demonstrated Coal Reserves, by Type of Coal and Major Producing State: 1995

[In millions of short tons. As of January 1. The demonstrated reserve base represents the sum of coal in both measured and indicated resource categories of reliability. Measured resources of coal are estimates that have a high degree of geologic assurance from sample analyses and measurements from closely spaced and geological well known sample sites. Indicated resources are estimates based partly from sample and analyses and measurements and partly from reasonable geologic projections. For more information on the classification of coal resources and related terminology, see report cited below]

AREA	Total reserves	TYPE OF COAL				METHOD OF MINING	
		Anthracite	Bituminous	Sub-bituminous	Lignite	Under ground	Surface
United States.	**495,666**	**7,483**	**257,780**	**185,950**	**44,453**	**328,552**	**167,113**
Alabama.	4,635	-	3,552	-	1,083	1,362	3,273
Alaska	6,130	-	698	5,418	14	5,423	707
Colorado.	16,844	26	8,777	3,852	4,190	12,049	4,795
Illinois	89,956	-	89,956	-	-	73,781	16,175
Indiana.	9,991	-	9,991	-	-	8,873	1,118
Iowa	2,190	-	2,190	-	-	1,733	457
Kentucky	32,565	-	32,565	-	-	18,885	13,680
Kentucky, Eastern.	12,485	-	12,485	-	-	2,525	9,960
Kentucky, Western	20,080	-	20,080	-	-	16,360	3,720
Missouri	5,996	-	5,996	-	-	1,479	4,517
Montana	119,773	-	1,385	102,627	15,761	70,959	48,815
New Mexico	12,547	2	3,741	8,804	-	6,205	6,341
North Dakota.	9,470	-	-	-	9,470	-	9,470
Ohio	23,754	-	23,754	-	-	17,847	5,907
Oklahoma.	1,580	-	1,580	-	-	1,237	342
Pennsylvania.	28,868	7,225	21,643			24,408	4,460
Anthracite	7,225	7,225				3,850	3,375
Bituminous	21,643		21,643			20,558	1,085
Texas.	13,065	-	-	-	13,065	-	13,065
Utah	5,956	-	5,955	1	-	5,688	268
Virginia.	2,327	126	2,202	-	-	1,630	697
Washington.	1,401	-	304	1,089	8	1,332	69
West Virginia.	35,983	-	35,983	-	-	31,420	4,564
Wyoming.	68,496	-	4,354	64,141	-	42,525	25,971
East of the MS River.	229,779	7,351	221,346	-	1,083	179,529	50,250
West of the MS River	265,886	132	36,434	185,950	43,370	149,023	116,863

- Represents or rounds to zero.

Source: U.S. Energy Information Administration, *U.S. Coal Reserves: A Review and Update*, August 1996.

No. 1189. Uranium Concentrate (U$_3$O$_8$) Industry—Summary: 1980 to 1996

[Middle demand case. See Table 978]

ITEM	Unit	1980	1985	1990	1991	1992	1993	1994	1995	1996
Production	1,000 sh. tons. . . .	21.9	5.7	4.4	4.0	2.8	1.5	1.7	3.0	3.2
Net imports (U$_3$O$_8$)	1,000 sh. tons. . . .	-1.1	3.2	10.9	6.4	10.3	9.0	9.5	15.8	17.0
Utility and suppliers inventories										
(U$_3$O$_8$ equivalent)	1,000 sh. tons. . . .	(NA)	[1]88.5	[1]64.6	[1]59.4	[1]58.7	[1]52.9	[1]43.4	[1]36.2	[1]40.0
Price (1992 dol./lb. U$_3$O$_8$):										
Long-term contract price	Dollars.	48.62	28.88	(NA)	(NA)	(NA)	(NA)	11.55	11.68	13.44
Spot market price.	Dollars.	52.63	19.90	10.43	8.94	7.95	9.73	[2]8.87	[2]10.65	[2]14.20
Delivered price	Dollars.	46.61	[3]40.09	16.77	14.04	13.45	12.81	9.81	10.46	12.87
Capital expenditures										
(1992 dollars)	Mil. dol.	1308	50	86	68	52	(NA)	(NA)	(NA)	(NA)
Employment.	1,000 person years.	19.9	2.4	1.3	1.0	0.7	0.9	[4]1.0	[4]1.1	1.1

NA Not available.   [1] Includes natural U$_3$O$_8$ (uranium oxide), natural UF$_6$ (uranium hexafluoride), natural UF$_6$ under usage agreement, UF$_6$ at enrichment suppliers, enriched UF$_6$ and fabricated fuel.   [2] Tradetech's restricted exchange value.   [3] Average U.S. contract prices and market price settlements.   [4] Includes reclamation activities (491 person years in 1993, 528 person years in 1994, 573 person years in 1995, and 429 person years in 1996).

Source: U.S. Department of Energy, *Domestic Uranium Mining and Milling Industry*, annual, and *Uranium Industry*, annual.

Construction and Housing

This section presents data on the construction industry and on various indicators of its activity and costs; on housing units and their characteristics and occupants; and on the characteristics and vacancy rates for commercial buildings. There are new data from the 1995 American Housing Survey and the Property Owners and Managers Survey.

The principal source of these data is the U.S. Bureau of the Census, which issues a variety of current publications. Construction statistics compiled by the Bureau appear in its monthly *Current Construction Reports* series with various quarterly or annual supplements; *Housing Starts* and *Housing Completions* present data by type of structure and by four major census regions; *New One-Family Houses Sold and For Sale* also provides statistics annually on physical and financial characteristics for all new housing by the four major census regions; *Price Index of New One-Family Houses Sold* presents quarterly figures and annual regional data; and *Housing Units Authorized by Building Permits* covers approximately 19,000 permit-issuing jurisdictions in the United States (prior to 1995, 17,000 places). Statistics on expenditures by owners of residential properties are issued quarterly and annually in *Expenditures for Residential Upkeep and Improvements. Value of Construction Put in Place* presents data on all types of construction and includes monthly composite cost indexes. Reports of the censuses of construction industries (see below) are also issued on various topics.

Other Census Bureau publications include the *Current Housing Reports* series, which comprises the quarterly *Housing Vacancies,* the quarterly *Market Absorption of Apartments,* the American Housing Survey (formerly Annual Housing Survey) and reports of the censuses of housing and of construction industries. *Construction Review,* published quarterly by the International Trade Administration, U.S. Department of Commerce, contains many of the census series and other construction

In Brief

Value of new construction in constant (1992) dollars reached $520 billion in 1997, an increase of 3% over 1996.

Sales of existing one-family homes increased 3.1% between 1996 and 1997 to just over 4.2 million units.

In 1995, there were 63.5 million owner-occupied housing units. Of these, 61.4% were mortgaged.

statistics series from the federal government and private agencies.

Other sources include the monthly *Dodge Construction Potentials* of F. W. Dodge Division, McGraw-Hill Information Systems Company, New York, NY, which presents national and state data on construction contracts; the National Association of Home Builders with state-level data on housing starts; the NATIONAL ASSOCIATION OF REALTORS, which presents data on existing home sales; the Society of Industrial and Office Realtors and Oncor International on commercial office space; and the U.S. Energy Information Administration, which provides data on commercial buildings through its periodic sample surveys.

Censuses and surveys—Censuses of the construction industry were first conducted by the Bureau of the Census for 1929, 1935, and 1939; beginning in 1967, a census has been taken every 5 years (for years ending in "2" and "7"). The latest reports are for 1992.

The 1992 Census of Construction Industries, in accordance with the 1987 *Standard Industrial Classification Manual* (see text, Section 13), covers all employer establishments primarily engaged in (1) building construction by general contractors or operative builders; (2) heavy (nonbuilding) construction by general contractors; and (3) construction by special trade contractors.

From 1850 through 1930, the Bureau of the Census collected some housing data as part of its censuses of population and agriculture. Beginning in 1940, separate censuses of housing have been taken at 10-year intervals. For the 1970 and 1980 censuses, data on year-round housing units were collected and issued on occupancy and structural characteristics, plumbing facilities, value, and rent; for 1990 such characteristics were presented for all housing units.

The American Housing Survey (*Current Housing Reports* Series H-150 and H-170), which began in 1973, provided an annual and ongoing series of data on selected housing and demographic characteristics until 1983. In 1984, the name of the survey was changed from the Annual Housing Survey. It is currently based on a biennial national sample and on 11 annual MSA samples. All samples represent a cross section of the housing stock in their respective areas. Estimates are subject to both sampling and nonsampling errors; caution should therefore, be used in making comparisons with 1970 and 1980 census data.

Data on residential mortgages were collected continuously from 1890 to 1970, except 1930, as part of the decennial census by the Bureau of the Census. Since 1973, mortgage status data, limited to single family homes on less than ten acres with no business on the property, have been presented in the American Housing Survey. Data on mortgage activity are covered in Section 16.

Housing units—In general, a housing unit is a group of rooms or a single room occupied or intended for occupancy as separate living quarters; that is, the occupants do not live and eat with any other persons in the structure and there is direct access from the outside or through a common hall. Transient accommodations, barracks for workers, and institutional-type quarters are not counted as housing units.

Statistical reliability—For a discussion of statistical collection and estimation, sampling procedures, and measures of statistical reliability applicable to Census Bureau data, see Appendix III.

No. 1190. Construction Industries—Summary, by Industry: 1992

[Based on a probability sample of about 167,000 construction establishments with payroll in 1992; see Appendix III. N.e.c.= Not elsewhere classified]

INDUSTRY	1987 SIC [1] code	Estab-lish-ments with payroll (1,000)	EMPLOYEES (1,000)		PAYROLL (mil. dol.)		VALUE OF CONSTRUC-TION WORK (mil. dol.)		Value added [3] (mil. dol.)
			Total	Con-struction workers	Total	Con-struction workers	Total	Net [2]	
All industries, total	(X)	572.9	4,668	3,596	117,730	83,048	528,106	391,190	234,618
General building contractors	15	168.4	1,097	759	27,078	16,125	215,629	114,722	63,117
Single-family houses	1521	107.5	404	296	7,278	4,869	48,633	33,660	17,183
Other residential buildings	1522	6.5	49	35	1,161	718	7,835	4,338	2,454
Operative builders	1531	17.0	114	50	3,359	1,045	44,588	26,843	15,289
Industrial buildings and warehouses	1541	7.7	123	92	3,476	2,310	20,586	10,967	6,438
Nonresidential buildings, n.e.c	1542	29.7	407	286	11,804	7,183	93,987	38,913	21,754
Heavy construction contractors	16	37.2	799	647	23,728	17,622	95,571	57,526	49,165
Highway and street construction	1611	10.1	257	211	7,358	5,457	35,332	27,863	15,711
Bridge, tunnel, and elevated highway	1622	1.0	44	36	1,485	1,125	7,198	5,316	3,078
Water, sewer, and utility lines	1623	10.2	194	160	5,624	4,252	20,205	17,587	11,734
Heavy construction, n.e.c	1629	15.8	304	240	9,261	6,788	32,837	26,760	18,642
Special trade contractors	17	367.3	2,772	2,190	66,924	49,302	216,905	198,942	122,336
Plumbing, heating, air-conditioning	1711	75.4	613	455	16,613	11,781	56,902	50,756	29,432
Painting and paperhanging	1721	32.0	163	136	3,164	2,470	8,690	8,095	5,855
Electrical work	1731	54.0	487	379	13,624	10,039	40,259	38,541	23,548
Masonry and other stonework	1741	22.6	148	130	2,883	2,366	8,458	7,956	5,146
Plastering, drywall, insulation	1742	18.6	207	173	4,910	3,826	14,056	12,824	8,143
Terrazzo, tile, marble, and mosaic work	1743	6.5	34	27	775	568	2,439	2,323	1,358
Carpentry	1751	38.2	178	145	3,489	2,683	12,852	11,334	6,760
Floorlaying and other floor work	1752	10.2	49	36	1,065	724	4,428	4,032	2,166
Roofing, siding, and sheet metal work	1761	27.6	216	169	4,623	3,230	16,788	15,590	8,906
Concrete work	1771	26.1	193	161	4,038	3,093	14,423	13,179	7,703
Water well drilling	1781	3.6	19	15	444	323	1,727	1,676	995
Structural steel erection	1791	3.8	58	47	1,629	1,227	4,952	4,487	3,021
Glass and glazing work	1793	4.6	32	21	796	495	2,724	2,634	1,424
Excavation work	1794	13.9	77	62	1,817	1,401	6,870	6,129	4,340
Wrecking and demolition work	1795	1.0	13	10	296	215	1,059	928	775
Installing building equipment, n.e.c	1796	3.9	83	64	2,324	1,742	6,611	6,132	4,494
Special trade contractors, n.e.c	1799	25.3	204	157	4,435	3,120	13,667	12,325	8,270

X Not applicable. [1] Based on the 1987 Standard Industrial Classification code; see text, Section 13, Labor Force. [2] Value of construction work less payments for construction work subcontracted to others, not shown separately. [3] Dollar value of business done less (a) payments for materials, components, and supplies, and (b) payments for construction work subcontracted to others.

Source: U.S. Bureau of the Census, *Census of Construction Industries, 1992,* Series CC92-I-1(P) through CC92-I-27(P).

No. 1191. Construction Materials—Producer Price Indexes: 1980 to 1997

[1982=100, except as noted. For discussion of producer price index, see text, Section 15, Prices. This index, more formally known as the special commodity grouping index for construction materials, covers materials incorporated as integral part of a building or normally installed during construction and not readily removable. Excludes consumer durables such as kitchen ranges, refrigerators, etc. This index is not the same as the stage-of-processing index of intermediate materials and components for construction]

COMMODITY	1980	1985	1990	1991	1992	1993	1994	1995	1996	1997 [1]
Construction materials	92.5	107.6	119.6	120.4	122.5	128.6	133.8	138.8	139.6	142.1
Interior solvent based paint	91.3	107.3	133.0	140.2	141.7	142.9	148.1	164.5	175.6	180.5
Plastic construction products	103.9	108.6	117.2	115.1	112.7	116.6	122.9	133.8	130.9	128.2
Douglas fir, dressed	132.6	126.5	138.4	139.6	169.5	237.6	236.2	198.8	227.1	221.3
Southern pine, dressed	104.0	105.2	111.2	111.0	130.6	168.8	182.6	166.9	177.9	201.2
Millwork	93.2	111.7	130.4	135.5	143.3	156.6	162.4	163.8	166.6	170.9
Softwood plywood	109.5	107.4	119.6	120.8	147.2	169.7	176.8	188.1	173.7	175.5
Hardwood plywood and related products	97.5	89.9	102.7	102.8	106.9	115.4	122.3	122.2	124.9	127.1
Softwood plywood veneer, ex. reinforced/backed	126.0	100.1	142.3	138.5	168.3	216.0	207.8	203.5	189.3	201.7
Building paper and building board mill products	86.1	107.4	112.2	111.8	119.6	132.7	144.1	144.9	137.2	129.6
Steel pipe and tubes [2]	(NA)	93.3	102.6	100.8	94.1	92.8	96.9	104.4	103.2	106.9
Builders hardware	84.9	113.5	133.0	138.1	141.4	144.9	148.0	153.2	156.5	158.4
Plumbing fixtures and brass fittings	88.5	111.9	144.3	149.7	153.1	155.9	159.6	166.0	171.1	174.5
Heating equipment	87.0	109.5	131.6	134.1	137.3	140.4	142.5	147.5	151.2	152.4
Metal doors, sash, and trim	87.8	107.3	131.4	134.6	135.0	136.6	142.0	156.5	159.3	161.0
Siding, aluminum [3]	(NA)	101.1	(NA)	(NA)	116.7	117.2	119.4	132.4	125.5	132.1
Incandescent outdoor lighting fixtures	82.7	109.2	137.3	136.5	139.1	138.5	141.5	151.8	152.9	149.8
Commercial fluorescent fixtures [4]	85.7	121.8	113.0	116.5	117.6	117.4	116.2	121.0	123.4	122.8
Architectural and ornamental metalwork [5]	(NA)	104.5	118.7	119.2	117.7	119.5	123.4	128.0	131.3	133.5
Fabricated ferrous wire products [2]	(NA)	99.3	114.6	115.9	117.5	119.3	122.6	125.7	126.8	128.0
Elevators, escalators, and other lifts	87.3	97.7	110.1	108.7	109.4	110.7	112.4	113.0	113.7	114.8
Stamped metal outlet box	82.7	119.7	158.0	160.8	166.5	172.9	179.1	183.5	186.3	189.0
Concrete ingredients and related products	88.4	108.5	115.3	118.4	119.4	123.4	128.7	134.7	138.8	142.5
Concrete products	92.0	107.5	113.5	116.6	117.2	120.2	124.6	129.4	133.2	136.0
Clay construction products exc. refractories	88.8	113.5	129.9	130.2	132.0	135.1	138.3	141.3	142.3	143.5
Prep. asphalt and tar roofing and siding products	105.5	100.5	95.8	96.2	94.3	94.9	92.9	97.8	97.4	96.5
Gypsum products	100.1	132.3	105.2	99.3	99.9	108.3	136.1	154.5	154.0	170.8
Insulation materials	80.7	105.2	108.4	110.8	102.3	105.8	111.9	118.8	118.9	117.7
Paving mixtures and blocks	83.7	111.6	101.2	103.2	100.2	102.0	103.2	105.8	107.6	113.2

NA Not available. [1] Preliminary. [2] June 1982=100. [3] December 1982=100. [4] Recessed nonair. [5] December 1983=100.
Source: U.S. Bureau of Labor Statistics, *Producer Price Indexes,* monthly and annual.

No. 1192. Price and Cost Indexes for Construction: 1980 to 1997

[1992=100. Excludes Alaska and Hawaii. Indexes of certain of these sources are published on bases different from those shown here]

NAME OF INDEX	1980	1985	1990	1992	1993	1994	1995	1996	1997
Bureau of the Census:									
Composite fixed-weighted [1]	68.6	82.9	98.5	100.0	103.7	108.0	112.5	115.0	118.7
Implicit price deflator [2]	67.8	81.8	97.8	100.0	103.8	108.1	112.6	115.2	118.9
Bureau of the Census houses under construction: [3]									
Fixed-weighted	67.6	81.4	98.6	100.0	104.9	109.7	114.4	116.4	119.9
Price deflator	66.4	79.6	97.2	100.0	104.8	109.5	114.3	116.5	119.9
Federal Highway Administration, composite [4]	92.5	97.1	103.2	100.0	103.0	109.5	115.9	116.1	124.7
Bureau of Reclamation composite [5]	70	84	96	100	103	106	110	112	116
Turner Construction Co.: Building construction [6]	61	83	98	100	102	105	109	112	117
E. H. Boeckh, building cost index: [7]									
Residences	(NA)	82.4	94.2	100.0	103.9	107.4	111.0	112.9	115.8
Apartments, hotels, and office buildings	(NA)	83.8	94.9	100.0	102.8	105.6	109.0	111.1	113.9
Commercial and factory buildings	(NA)	82.3	94.4	100.0	102.6	105.7	108.3	110.7	114.7
Engineering News-Record: [8]									
Buildings	68.5	85.7	95.4	100.0	105.7	109.8	109.8	113.0	118.7
Construction	64.9	84.2	94.9	100.0	104.5	108.5	109.8	112.8	116.9
Handy-Whitman public utility: [9]									
Buildings	78	90	101	100	105	112	115	118	122
Electric [10]	68	83	97	100	103	107	111	112	115
Gas	67	85	96	100	103	109	111	112	115
Water [11]	73	88	98	100	104	109	112	115	118
C. A. Turner Telephone Plant [12]	90	89	99	100	102	103	110	115	117

NA Not available.   [1] Weighted average of the various indexes used to deflate the Construction Put in Place series. In calculating the index, the weights (i.e., the composition of current dollar estimates in 1992 by category) are held constant. [2] Derived ratio of total current to constant dollar Construction Put in Place (multiplied by 100).   [3] Excludes value of site.   [4] Based on average contract unit bid prices for composite mile (involving specific average amounts of excavation, paving, reinforcing steel, structural steel, and structural concrete).   [5] Derived from the four quarterly indexes which are weighted averages of costs of labor, materials, and equipment for the construction of dams and reclamation projects.   [6] Based on firm's cost experience with respect to labor rates, materials prices, competitive conditions, efficiency of plant and management, and productivity.   [7] Average of 20 cities for types shown. Weights based on surveys of building costs. Wage rates used for both common and skilled labor. [8] Building construction index computed on the basis of a hypothetical unit of construction requiring 6 bbl. of portland cement, 1,088 M bd. ft. of 2" x 4" lumber, 2,500 lb. of structural steel, and 68.38 hours of skilled labor. General construction index based on same materials components combined with 200 hours of common labor.   [9] Based on data covering public utility construction costs in six geographic regions. Covers skilled and common labor.   [10] As derived by U.S. Bureau of the Census. Covers steam generation plants only.   [11] As derived by U.S. Bureau of the Census. Reflects costs for structures and improvements at water pumping and treatment plants.   [12] Computed by the Census Bureau by averaging the weighted component indexes published for six geographic regions.

Source: U.S. Bureau of the Census. In U.S. Department of Commerce, International Trade Administration, *Construction Review*, quarterly.

No. 1193. Value of New Construction Put in Place: 1964 to 1997

[In millions of dollars. Represents value of construction put in place during year; differs from building permit and construction contract data in timing and coverage. Includes installed cost of normal building service equipment and selected types of industrial production equipment (largely site fabricated). Excludes cost of shipbuilding, land, and most types of machinery and equipment. For methodology, see Appendix III]

YEAR	CURRENT DOLLARS					CONSTANT (1992) DOLLARS				
	Total	Private			Public	Total	Private			Public
		Total [1]	Residential buildings	Nonresidential buildings			Total [1]	Residential buildings	Nonresidential buildings	
1964	75,097	54,893	30,526	17,385	20,203	351,300	259,680	145,486	84,232	91,620
1970	105,890	77,982	35,863	28,171	27,908	372,274	279,212	133,133	100,780	93,062
1975	152,635	109,342	51,581	35,409	43,293	351,973	259,048	128,254	84,282	92,925
1977	200,501	157,418	92,004	38,245	43,083	408,528	324,777	193,479	81,170	83,751
1978	239,867	189,721	109,838	46,224	50,146	439,075	350,182	203,568	93,436	88,893
1979	272,873	216,228	116,444	64,765	56,646	446,503	357,949	192,873	111,235	88,554
1980	273,936	210,290	100,381	72,480	63,646	403,900	315,821	150,943	112,874	88,079
1981	289,070	224,378	99,241	85,569	64,691	396,267	313,358	139,656	122,748	82,910
1982	279,332	216,268	84,676	92,690	63,064	369,135	290,057	115,525	126,705	79,077
1983	311,576	248,126	125,521	87,069	63,450	403,929	324,785	166,981	114,716	79,144
1984	369,025	298,787	153,849	107,680	70,238	463,057	377,445	197,126	135,650	85,612
1985	401,370	323,555	158,474	127,466	77,815	490,943	399,530	199,105	156,349	91,413
1986	429,924	345,342	187,148	120,917	84,582	507,275	411,174	224,557	143,070	96,101
1987	441,647	350,999	194,656	123,247	90,648	502,468	401,642	223,516	140,110	100,826
1988	455,618	360,883	198,101	130,854	94,735	499,621	397,693	218,972	143,467	101,928
1989	469,797	371,623	196,551	139,953	98,174	495,387	393,262	208,748	147,825	102,124
1990	468,532	361,054	182,856	143,506	107,478	479,016	370,102	188,045	146,661	108,914
1991	424,176	314,067	157,835	116,570	110,109	429,592	319,248	160,989	118,266	110,345
1992	452,086	336,239	187,819	105,646	115,847	451,998	336,126	187,687	105,615	115,872
1993	478,648	362,688	210,455	110,635	115,960	461,078	347,851	200,502	106,729	113,227
1994	519,539	399,346	238,874	120,285	120,193	480,620	367,247	218,005	111,416	113,373
1995	538,134	407,477	230,688	135,022	130,657	478,069	360,040	201,677	120,627	118,029
1996	583,638	446,306	256,460	150,350	137,333	506,655	385,967	220,017	131,188	120,688
1997	618,217	471,159	265,610	165,146	147,058	520,117	395,321	221,546	139,067	124,796

[1] Includes other types of private construction, not shown separately.

Source: U.S. Bureau of the Census, *Current Construction Reports*, Series C30, *Value of Construction*, monthly.

No. 1194. Value of New Construction Put in Place: 1990 to 1997

[In millions of dollars. Represents value of construction put in place during year; differs from building permit and construction contract data in timing and coverage. Includes installed cost of normal building service equipment and selected types of industrial production equipment (largely site fabricated). Excludes cost of shipbuilding, land, and most types of machinery and equipment. For methodology, see Appendix III]

TYPE OF CONSTRUCTION	CURRENT DOLLARS					CONSTANT (1992) DOLLARS				
	1990	1994	1995	1996	1997 prel. [1]	1990	1994	1995	1996	1997 prel. [1]
Total new construction .	468,532	519,539	538,134	583,638	618,217	479,016	480,620	478,069	506,655	520,117
Private construction	361,054	399,346	407,477	446,306	471,159	370,102	367,247	360,040	385,967	395,321
Residential buildings	182,856	238,874	230,688	256,460	265,610	188,045	218,005	201,677	220,017	221,546
New housing units	127,987	167,919	162,898	179,448	187,075	131,632	153,250	142,413	153,966	156,038
One unit	108,737	153,838	145,009	159,124	164,444	111,832	140,416	126,773	136,516	137,156
Two or more units . . .	19,250	14,081	17,889	20,324	22,631	19,800	12,833	15,640	17,450	18,882
Improvements	54,869	70,955	67,790	77,012	78,535	56,414	64,755	59,264	66,052	65,508
Nonresidential buildings . . .	143,506	120,285	135,022	150,350	165,146	146,661	111,416	120,627	131,188	139,067
Industrial	33,636	28,947	32,505	32,657	31,394	34,373	26,803	29,043	28,503	26,440
Office	35,055	22,178	25,613	27,886	32,816	35,838	20,553	22,891	24,329	27,631
Hotels, motels	10,679	4,648	7,112	10,912	12,752	10,917	4,308	6,351	9,521	10,741
Other commercial	40,047	37,551	42,654	48,188	50,763	40,922	34,756	38,098	42,042	42,748
Religious	3,566	3,869	4,326	4,534	5,885	3,642	3,584	3,864	3,955	4,951
Educational	4,616	4,822	5,493	6,742	8,437	4,715	4,471	4,908	5,880	7,101
Hospital and institutional .	10,868	12,268	11,248	11,780	13,741	11,103	11,377	10,051	10,280	11,576
Miscellaneous [2]	5,040	6,002	6,071	7,650	9,358	5,151	5,565	5,421	6,677	7,880
Farm nonresidential	2,801	3,226	3,014	3,804	3,956	2,862	2,990	2,692	3,319	3,329
Public utilities	28,933	34,071	35,859	33,261	34,188	29,537	32,074	32,401	29,286	29,448
Telecommunications	9,803	10,121	11,093	11,772	11,626	9,891	9,785	10,073	10,245	9,918
Other public utilities	19,130	23,950	24,766	21,489	22,562	19,646	22,289	22,328	19,041	19,529
Railroads	2,600	3,340	3,509	4,398	5,059	2,633	3,186	3,201	3,894	4,321
Electric light and power .	11,299	14,918	14,049	11,211	12,144	11,572	13,877	12,656	9,914	10,545
Gas	4,820	4,694	6,279	4,865	4,390	5,013	4,308	5,637	4,330	3,820
Petroleum pipelines . . .	411	998	929	1,015	969	428	918	834	903	843
All other private [3]	2,957	2,890	2,893	2,431	2,258	2,997	2,763	2,643	2,156	1,931
Public construction	107,478	120,193	130,657	137,333	147,058	108,914	113,373	118,029	120,688	124,796
Buildings	43,615	49,446	55,700	58,659	63,603	44,583	45,728	49,683	51,119	53,515
Housing and redevelopment	3,808	3,835	4,491	4,614	4,861	3,914	3,495	3,928	3,958	4,055
Industrial	1,434	1,465	1,508	1,389	998	1,465	1,358	1,348	1,214	842
Educational	16,055	20,361	23,278	24,112	27,065	16,398	18,838	20,800	21,035	22,786
Hospital	2,860	3,951	4,332	4,638	5,042	2,924	3,663	3,871	4,050	4,247
Other [4]	19,458	19,834	22,089	23,907	25,637	19,882	18,373	19,737	20,863	21,585
Highways and streets	32,105	37,419	38,498	41,243	45,197	31,777	36,219	35,303	36,483	38,605
Military facilities	2,665	2,318	3,011	2,634	2,620	2,683	2,196	2,728	2,317	2,223
Conservation and development	4,686	6,363	6,368	6,011	5,658	4,870	5,996	5,779	5,335	4,841
Sewer systems	10,276	8,700	9,435	10,433	10,463	10,670	8,199	8,557	9,260	8,951
Water supply facilities	4,909	4,647	5,283	5,964	6,339	4,987	4,237	4,695	5,187	5,393
Miscellaneous public [5]	9,223	11,301	12,362	12,388	13,177	9,344	10,799	11,284	10,987	11,267

[1] Includes estimates for types of construction indicated as (NA).   [2] Includes amusement and recreational buildings, bus and airline terminals, animal hospitals and shelters, etc.   [3] Includes privately owned streets and bridges, parking areas, sewer and water facilities, parks and playgrounds, golf courses, airfields, etc.   [4] Includes federal administrative buildings, prisons, police and fire stations, courthouses, civic centers, passenger terminals, space facilities, postal facilities, etc.   [5] Includes open amusement and recreational facilities, power generating facilities, transit systems, airfields, open parking facilities, etc.

Source: U.S. Bureau of the Census, *Current Construction Reports*, Series C30, *Value of Construction*, monthly.

No. 1195. Construction Contracts—Value of Construction and Floor Space of Buildings, by Class of Construction: 1980 to 1997

[Building construction includes new structures and additions; nonbuilding construction includes major alterations to existing structures which affect only valuation, since no additional floor area is created by "alteration"]

YEAR	Total	Resi-dential build-ings	NONRESIDENTIAL BUILDINGS									Non-build-ing con-struc-tion
			Total	Com-mer-cial [1]	Manu-fac-turing	Educa-tional [2]	Hos-pital	Public build-ings	Reli-gious	Social and recrea-tional	Mis-cella-neous	
VALUE (bil. dol.)												
1980	151.8	60.4	56.9	27.7	9.2	7.4	5.4	1.6	1.2	2.7	1.7	34.5
1985	235.6	102.1	92.1	54.6	8.1	10.0	7.8	3.1	2.0	4.0	2.5	41.4
1987	259.0	114.1	98.8	53.7	8.6	13.2	9.0	4.7	2.1	4.3	3.2	46.1
1988	262.2	116.2	97.9	51.6	9.5	14.1	8.2	4.4	2.2	4.7	3.2	48.1
1989	271.3	116.2	106.1	53.6	12.7	15.9	8.8	5.2	2.0	5.0	2.9	49.0
1990	246.0	100.9	95.4	44.8	8.4	16.6	9.2	5.7	2.2	5.3	3.1	49.7
1991	230.8	94.4	86.2	32.7	8.3	19.0	9.6	6.2	2.4	5.1	3.0	50.2
1992	252.2	110.6	87.0	32.8	8.9	17.6	10.9	5.8	2.5	5.5	3.1	54.6
1993	271.5	123.9	88.8	34.2	9.0	19.3	10.5	3.9	2.4	6.8	2.6	58.9
1994	296.7	133.6	101.5	40.8	11.2	21.0	10.5	6.1	2.5	6.5	3.0	61.6
1995	306.4	127.8	114.1	46.6	13.8	22.9	10.8	6.2	2.8	7.1	3.8	64.4
1996	331.2	146.3	120.0	51.7	13.1	22.9	11.0	6.3	2.9	8.1	4.0	64.9
1997	352.4	151.5	132.8	57.0	13.3	27.3	11.4	6.7	3.7	9.6	3.9	68.1
FLOOR SPACE (mil. sq. ft.)												
1980	3,102	1,839	1,263	738	220	103	55	18	28	49	52	(X)
1985	3,853	2,324	1,529	1,039	165	111	73	28	32	44	38	(X)
1987	3,756	2,288	1,469	933	160	139	78	42	32	46	38	(X)
1988	3,594	2,181	1,413	883	162	142	71	38	32	49	37	(X)
1989	3,516	2,115	1,400	867	158	151	72	41	27	48	35	(X)
1990	3,020	1,817	1,203	694	128	152	69	47	29	51	32	(X)
1991	2,634	1,653	981	476	100	177	72	50	29	45	33	(X)
1992	2,799	1,864	936	462	95	156	77	41	30	42	32	(X)
1993	3,062	2,091	971	481	110	165	75	30	30	51	29	(X)
1994	3,410	2,267	1,144	600	143	172	72	45	30	51	31	(X)
1995	3,452	2,172	1,280	700	163	186	70	39	33	56	33	(X)
1996	3,769	2,476	1,293	721	155	176	76	41	32	60	32	(X)
1997	4,058	2,574	1,484	827	182	195	85	46	41	75	34	(X)

X Not applicable.   [1] Includes nonindustrial warehouses.   [2] Includes science.

Source: F.W. Dodge, a Division of the McGraw-Hill Companies, New York, NY (copyright).

No. 1196. Construction Contracts—Value, by State: 1990 to 1997

[In millions of dollars. Represents value of construction in states in which work was actually done. See headnote, Table 1195]

STATE	1990	1996	1997			STATE	1990	1996	1997		
			Total [1]	Resi-dential	Non-residen-tial				Total [1]	Resi-dential	Non-residen-tial
U.S . .	**246,022**	**306,351**	**352,422**	**151,522**	**132,813**	MO	3,833	6,438	5,846	2,536	2,179
AL	2,939	4,308	4,793	1,962	1,841	MT	332	865	822	333	272
AK	1,919	1,660	1,047	371	359	NE	1,318	1,694	2,043	803	769
AZ	4,553	8,784	10,030	6,106	2,693	NV	3,334	5,555	6,695	2,638	3,245
AR	1,438	2,903	2,941	1,232	822	NH	1,021	1,039	1,339	580	522
CA	37,318	28,932	36,456	15,669	13,711	NJ	6,141	6,456	8,151	2,586	3,420
CO	3,235	6,476	9,167	4,757	3,257	NM	1,124	2,108	1,915	786	634
CT	3,058	3,124	3,708	1,244	1,733	NY	14,137	13,380	15,713	4,241	7,513
DE	787	871	934	416	285	NC	6,614	10,574	14,021	7,113	5,178
DC	795	656	672	28	512	ND	506	791	781	213	244
FL	16,975	21,450	25,068	12,994	8,294	OH	9,885	12,430	14,617	5,461	6,135
GA	7,120	12,156	13,541	7,299	4,549	OK	2,164	2,967	3,119	1,335	1,029
HI	2,831	2,273	1,616	616	693	OR	3,101	5,451	5,928	2,788	2,190
ID	986	1,864	1,760	1,022	499	PA	10,117	9,346	10,046	3,800	3,959
IL	10,796	11,739	12,367	5,474	4,716	RI	594	465	773	288	337
IN	6,350	7,896	9,169	3,995	3,686	SC	3,664	4,580	5,977	2,802	2,437
IA	2,034	2,883	3,263	1,065	1,233	SD	468	706	742	265	254
KS	2,193	3,264	3,752	1,540	1,342	TN	4,388	7,167	8,167	3,808	2,758
KY	3,174	4,462	4,755	2,125	1,857	TX	13,197	22,999	27,073	11,943	10,446
LA	3,191	4,354	4,643	1,420	1,922	UT	1,884	4,218	5,245	1,851	1,407
ME	897	1,076	1,137	479	398	VT	515	484	620	230	297
MD	6,056	6,299	5,847	2,625	2,347	VA	7,180	8,794	10,040	4,592	3,779
MA	5,135	7,411	10,219	2,649	3,701	WA	6,185	7,334	8,470	3,905	3,072
MI	7,646	9,946	10,636	5,036	4,022	WV	1,253	1,215	1,188	229	494
MN	4,953	5,607	6,229	2,579	2,246	WI	4,654	5,651	6,124	2,597	2,324
MS	1,569	2,718	2,591	914	1,038	WY	462	532	624	181	163

[1] Includes nonbuilding construction, not shown separately.

Source: F.W. Dodge, a Division of the McGraw-Hill Companies, New York, NY (copyright).

No. 1197. New Privately-Owned Housing Units Authorized, by State: 1996 and 1997

[Based on about 19,000 places in United States having building permit systems]

STATE	HOUSING UNITS (1,000)			VALUATION (mil. dol.)			STATE	HOUSING UNITS (1,000)			VALUATION (mil. dol.)		
	1996	1997		1996	1997			1996	1997		1996	1997	
		Total	1 unit		Total	1 unit			Total	1 unit		Total	1 unit
U.S .	1,425.6	1,441.1	1,062.4	134,176	141,004	121,194	MO ...	26.3	25.2	18.8	2,276	2,265	1,967
							MT ...	2.7	2.5	1.5	209	204	152
AL ...	19.9	17.7	13.6	1,509	1,537	1,353	NE ...	10.1	9.9	5.6	681	711	548
AK ...	2.6	2.6	1.9	316	334	272	NV ...	37.2	34.8	23.5	2,854	2,788	2,278
AZ ...	53.7	57.8	44.4	5,449	5,776	5,075	NH ...	4.9	5.4	4.6	517	572	530
AR ...	11.1	11.0	6.8	777	761	621	NJ ...	24.2	28.0	23.5	2,134	2,533	2,332
CA ...	92.1	109.6	84.1	12,472	15,396	13,539	NM ...	10.2	10.3	8.2	1,084	887	795
CO ...	41.1	43.1	31.9	4,275	4,659	3,974	NY ...	34.9	32.9	19.6	3,110	3,064	2,390
CT ...	8.5	9.3	7.8	987	1,101	1,023	NC ...	67.0	73.0	55.5	6,043	6,723	5,987
DE ...	4.4	4.7	4.1	352	381	354	ND ...	2.3	3.2	1.5	181	222	146
DC ...	-	(Z)	(Z)	-	1	1	OH ...	49.3	46.5	32.7	5,001	4,795	4,187
FL....	125.0	134.0	90.3	11,472	12,205	9,551	OK ...	10.6	11.2	8.5	981	1,014	899
GA ...	74.9	75.1	59.6	6,075	6,460	5,747	OR ...	27.8	27.0	16.3	2,760	2,838	2,183
HI....	3.9	3.7	2.6	486	507	364	PA ...	37.9	39.9	32.3	3,550	3,802	3,420
ID....	10.8	10.3	8.8	1,059	1,042	964	RI ...	2.5	2.7	2.3	220	250	236
IL....	49.6	46.3	32.8	5,199	5,087	4,267	SC ...	29.4	30.1	22.2	2,464	2,651	2,247
IN....	37.2	35.2	28.1	3,719	3,706	3,381	SD ...	3.6	3.2	2.5	279	256	221
IA....	12.0	10.7	7.4	1,051	1,012	845	TN ...	40.5	34.1	26.7	3,334	3,104	2,738
KS ...	14.7	13.6	9.7	1,322	1,350	1,155	TX ...	118.8	126.0	82.2	9,935	10,725	8,953
KY ...	18.8	18.1	13.7	1,484	1,484	1,321	UT ...	23.5	19.3	14.8	2,111	1,880	1,629
LA ...	18.0	15.1	13.2	1,436	1,332	1,257	VT ...	2.1	1.8	1.6	201	192	182
ME ...	4.7	4.7	4.3	436	451	429	VA ...	45.9	45.5	35.9	3,947	4,119	3,749
MD ...	25.1	26.0	21.1	2,284	2,357	2,073	WA ...	39.6	41.1	27.8	3,773	4,225	3,337
MA ...	17.3	17.2	15.2	2,055	2,172	2,024	WV ...	3.6	4.1	2.9	276	309	264
MI....	52	49.2	40.2	5,179	5,102	4,628	WI....	33.3	31.9	20.6	3,047	2,998	2,394
MN ...	27.0	24.9	20.1	2,903	2,758	2,410	WY ...	2.2	1.7	1.3	201	190	172
MS ...	10.4	10.1	7.8	710	716	630							

- Represents zero.   Z Less than 50 units.

Source: U.S. Bureau of the Census, *Construction Reports*, Series C40, *Building Permits*, monthly.

No. 1198. New Privately-Owned Housing Units Started—Selected Characteristics: 1970 to 1997

[**In thousands.** For composition of regions, see map, inside front cover]

YEAR	Total units	STRUCTURES WITH—			REGION				CONDOMINIUM UNITS [1]		
		One unit	Two to four units	Five or more units	North-east	Mid-west	South	West	Total	Single-family	Multi-family
1970	1,434	813	85	536	218	294	612	311	(NA)	(NA)	(NA)
1972	2,357	1,309	141	906	330	443	1,057	527	(NA)	(NA)	(NA)
1973	2,045	1,132	118	795	277	440	899	429	241	69	172
1974	1,338	888	68	382	183	317	553	285	175	46	130
1975	1,160	892	64	204	149	294	442	275	65	20	45
1976	1,538	1,162	86	289	169	400	569	400	95	30	64
1977	1,987	1,451	122	414	202	465	783	538	118	41	77
1978	2,020	1,433	125	462	200	451	824	545	156	42	114
1979	1,745	1,194	122	429	178	349	748	470	198	43	156
1980	1,292	852	110	331	125	218	643	306	186	35	150
1981	1,084	705	91	288	117	165	562	240	181	36	145
1982	1,062	663	80	320	117	149	591	205	170	40	130
1983	1,703	1,068	113	522	168	218	935	382	276	77	199
1984	1,750	1,084	121	544	204	243	866	436	291	96	194
1985	1,742	1,072	93	576	252	240	782	468	225	79	146
1986	1,805	1,179	84	542	294	296	733	483	214	80	134
1987	1,621	1,146	65	409	269	298	634	420	196	73	123
1988	1,488	1,081	59	348	235	274	575	404	148	53	95
1989	1,376	1,003	55	318	179	266	536	396	118	37	82
1990	1,193	895	37	260	131	253	479	329	75	22	53
1991	1,014	840	36	138	113	233	414	254	60	21	39
1992	1,200	1,030	31	139	127	288	497	288	74	35	40
1993	1,288	1,126	29	133	126	298	562	302	86	45	41
1994	1,457	1,198	35	224	138	329	639	351	96	48	48
1995	1,354	1,076	34	244	118	290	615	331	93	47	47
1996	1,477	1,161	45	271	132	322	662	361	107	53	54
1997	1,474	1,134	44	296	137	304	670	363	110	56	54

NA Not available.   [1] Type of ownership under which the owners of the individual housing units are also joint owners of the common areas of the building or community. Includes a small number of cooperatively-owned units.

Source: U.S. Bureau of the Census, *Current Construction Reports*, Series C20, *Housing Starts*, monthly.

No. 1199. New Privately-Owned Housing Units Started, by State: 1995 to 1998

[In thousands of units]

STATE	1995	1996	1997	1998, est. Total units	1998, est. Single-family units	STATE	1995	1996	1997	1998, est. Total units	1998, est. Single-family units
U.S.	**1,354.0**	**1,476.0**	**1,462.0**	**1,390.0**	**1,080.0**	MO	25.6	27.4	25.5	24.1	19.7
AL.	21.2	20.3	18.7	17.3	13.8	MT.	3.1	2.8	2.4	2.4	1.5
AK.	2.5	2.2	2.2	2.0	1.5	NE.	8.0	10.2	9.7	9.5	5.5
AZ.	53.5	58.3	58.2	53.9	42.2	NV.	33.8	39.5	35.9	32.4	23.0
AR.	12.2	11.5	10.5	9.8	7.0	NH.	4.3	4.9	5.3	5.4	4.7
CA.	86.9	97.7	113.3	121.6	95.5	NJ	25.3	26.0	29.4	27.4	24.3
CO.	39.7	42.5	43.1	36.6	27.2	NM.	9.7	9.7	9.5	8.8	6.6
CT.	9.1	9.8	10.9	10.8	9.5	NY.	23.4	28.7	27.6	28.1	18.8
DE.	5.3	5.5	5.6	5.3	5.0	NC.	64.4	70.6	75.9	70.7	57.0
DC.	0.1	-	-	-	-	ND.	3.2	2.4	2.4	2.3	1.2
FL.	123.4	140.1	145.1	138.1	100.9	OH.	43.6	50.5	46.3	43.3	32.3
GA.	77.2	78.4	72.2	66.7	53.4	OK.	11.8	11.7	12.0	11.6	9.3
HI	6.9	4.0	3.9	3.7	2.3	OR.	25.0	28.0	26.8	25.4	16.5
ID	9.5	9.5	8.9	7.9	6.6	PA	31.1	34.8	36.0	35.9	31.3
IL.	48.8	51.8	48.5	46.2	35.7	RI	2.5	2.7	2.9	2.8	2.5
IN	36.8	39.7	37.0	34.1	28.4	SC	26.1	32.2	34.2	31.4	25.2
IA	9.4	9.9	9.7	9.4	6.0	SD	3.9	3.8	3.1	3.0	2.2
KS	11.0	14.0	11.6	11.6	8.9	TN	36.4	40.9	35.8	33.3	27.2
KY	18.9	19.1	19.3	18.2	14.7	TX	112.5	124.5	130.2	116.4	85.7
LA	14.4	16.5	16.1	14.9	12.3	UT	20.7	22.4	17.9	17.3	13.4
ME.	4.2	4.6	4.3	4.4	4.1	VT	2.0	2.3	2.1	2.0	1.7
MD.	28.9	28.3	27.0	25.7	22.7	VA	45.2	47.2	45.9	44.9	36.9
MA.	16.3	18.2	19.3	19.6	17.4	WA	37.9	42.4	42.1	42.2	29.2
MI	47.6	54.5	51.6	48.3	40.0	WV	4.8	4.0	4.3	4.0	3.3
MN.	25.0	26.7	24.2	23.6	20.0	WI	27.1	30.0	25.5	24.8	17.4
MS.	12.2	11.2	10.5	9.5	7.5	WY	1.9	2.0	1.6	1.4	1.2

- Represents or rounds to zero.

Source: National Association of Home Builders, Economics Division, Washington, DC. Data provided by the Econometric Forecasting Service.

No. 1200. Characteristics of New Privately Owned One-Family Houses Completed: 1970 to 1997

[Percent distribution, except as indicated. Data beginning 1980 show percent distribution of characteristics for all houses completed (includes new houses completed, houses built for sale completed, contractor-built and owner-built houses completed, and houses completed for rent). Data for 1970 cover contractor-built, owner-built, and houses for rent for year construction started and houses sold for year of sale. Percents exclude houses for which characteristics specified were not reported]

CHARACTERISTIC	1970	1980	1990	1995	1997	CHARACTERISTIC	1970	1980	1990	1995	1997
Total houses (1,000). . . .	793	957	966	1,066	1,116	**Bedrooms . . . .**	100	100	100	100	100
						2 or less.	13	17	15	13	13
Financing	100	100	100	100	100	3.	63	63	57	57	56
Mortgage	84	82	82	88	88	4 or more	24	20	29	30	31
FHA-insured	30	16	14	8	8	**Bathrooms . . . .**	100	100	100	100	100
VA-guaranteed	7	8	4	5	4	1 1/2 or less	52	27	13	11	9
Conventional	47	55	62	74	77	2.	32	48	42	41	41
Rural Housing						2 1/2 or more	16	25	45	48	50
Service [1]	(²)	3	2	1	1	**Heating fuel . . . .**	100	100	100	100	100
Cash or equivalent. . . .	16	18	18	12	10	Electricity	28	50	33	28	26
						Gas.	62	41	59	67	69
Floor area.	100	100	100	100	100	Oil.	8	3	5	3	3
Under 1,200 sq. ft	36	21	11	10	8	Other.	1	5	3	1	1
1,200 to 1,599 sq. ft . . .	28	29	22	22	21	**Heating system . . . .**	100	100	100	100	100
1,600 to 1,999 sq. ft . . .	16	22	22	23	22	Warm air furnace	71	57	65	67	70
2,000 to 2,399 sq. ft . . .	21	13	17	17	18	Electric heat pump	(NA)	24	23	25	23
2,400 sq. ft. and over . .	(³)	15	29	28	31	Other.	29	19	12	9	7
Average (sq. ft.).	1,500	1,740	2,080	2,095	2,150	**Central air-conditioning .**	100	100	100	100	100
Median (sq. ft.)	1,385	1,595	1,905	1,920	1,975	With	34	63	76	80	82
						Without	66	37	24	20	18
Number of stories	100	100	100	100	100	**Fireplaces. . . . .**	100	100	100	100	100
1.	74	60	46	49	49	No fireplace	65	43	34	37	39
2 or more	17	31	49	48	49	1 or more	35	56	66	63	61
Split level	10	8	4	3	3	**Parking facilities . . . . . .**	100	100	100	100	100
Foundation	100	100	100	100	100	Garage	58	69	82	84	86
Full or partial basement.	37	36	38	39	37	Carport	17	7	2	2	1
Slab	36	45	40	42	45	No garage or carport . .	25	24	16	14	13
Crawl space	27	19	21	19	19						

NA Not available. [1] Prior to 1997, Farmers Home Administration. [2] Included with "Conventional" financing. [3] Included with floor area of 2,000 to 2,399 square feet.

Source: U.S. Bureau of the Census and U.S. Dept. of Housing and Urban Development, Current Construction Reports, Series C25, New One-Family Houses Sold, monthly, and Characteristics of New Housing, annual.

No. 1201. New Privately Owned One-Family Houses Sold, by Region and Type of Financing, 1980 to 1997, and by Sales-Price Group, 1997

[In thousands. Based on a national probability sample of monthly interviews with builders or owners of one-family houses for which building permits have been issued or, for nonpermit areas, on which construction has started. For details, see source. For composition of regions, see map, inside front cover]

YEAR AND SALES-PRICE GROUP	Total sales	REGION				FINANCING TYPE			
		North-east	Midwest	South	West	Conventional	FHA and VA	Rural Housing Service [1]	Cash
1980	545	50	81	267	145	302	196	14	32
1985	688	112	82	323	170	403	208	11	64
1987	671	117	97	271	186	408	190	8	64
1988	676	101	97	276	202	437	171	6	62
1989	650	86	102	260	202	416	162	14	58
1990	534	71	89	225	149	337	138	10	50
1991	509	57	93	215	144	329	128	9	43
1992	610	65	116	259	170	428	134	7	41
1993	666	60	123	295	188	476	147	6	37
1994	670	61	123	295	191	490	130	9	41
1995	667	55	125	300	187	490	129	9	39
1996	757	74	137	337	209	570	140	9	38
1997	804	78	140	363	223	616	137	6	46
Under $70,000	22	(B)	(B)	19	(B)	11	9	(B)	(B)
$70,000 to $79,999	28	(B)	3	21	3	13	13	(B)	(B)
$80,000 to $99,999	93	4	17	60	12	53	36	(B)	3
$100,000 to $119,999	103	4	18	54	26	65	31	(B)	6
$120,000 to $149,999	173	11	30	76	56	125	34	(B)	14
$150,000 to $199,999	177	20	32	69	55	153	14	(B)	10
$200,000 to $249,999	83	12	16	29	26	77	(B)	(B)	4
$250,000 to $299,999	46	8	8	15	15	44	(B)	(B)	3
$300,000 and over	78	16	13	20	30	74	(B)	(B)	4

B Withheld because estimate did not meet publication standards on the basis of sample size.   [1] Prior to 1996, the Farmers Home Administration.

Source: U.S. Bureau of the Census and U.S. Dept. of Housing and Urban Development, *Current Construction Reports*, series C25, *Characteristics of New Housing*, annual; and *New One-Family Houses Sold*, monthly.

No. 1202. Median Sales Price of New Privately Owned One-Family Houses Sold, by Region: 1980 to 1997

[In dollars. For definition of median, see Guide to Tabular Presentation. For composition of regions, see map, inside front cover]

YEAR	U.S.	North-east	Midwest	South	West	YEAR	U.S.	North-east	Midwest	South	West
1980	64,600	69,500	63,400	59,600	72,300	1990	122,900	159,000	107,900	99,000	147,500
1983	75,300	82,200	79,500	70,900	80,100	1991	120,000	155,900	110,000	100,000	141,100
1984	79,900	88,600	85,400	72,000	87,300	1992	121,500	169,000	115,600	105,500	130,400
1985	84,300	103,300	80,300	75,000	92,600	1993	126,500	162,600	125,000	115,000	135,000
1986	92,000	125,000	88,300	80,200	95,700	1994	130,000	169,000	132,900	116,900	140,400
1987	104,500	140,000	95,000	88,000	111,000	1995	133,900	180,000	134,000	124,500	141,400
1988	112,500	149,000	101,600	92,000	126,500	1996	140,000	186,000	138,000	126,200	153,900
1989	120,000	159,600	108,800	96,400	139,000	1997	146,000	190,000	149,900	129,600	160,000

Source: U.S. Bureau of the Census and U.S. Dept. of Housing and Urban Development, *Current Construction Reports*, Series C25, *Characteristics of New Housing*, annual; and *New One-Family Houses Sold*, monthly.

No. 1203. New Mobile Homes Placed for Residential Use and Average Sales Price, by Region: 1980 to 1997

[A mobile home is a moveable dwelling, 10 feet or more wide and 35 feet or more long, designed to be towed on its own chassis and without need of permanent foundation. Excluded are travel trailers, motor homes, and modular housing. Data are based on a probability sample and subject to sampling variability; see source. For composition of region, see map, inside front cover]

YEAR	UNITS PLACED (1,000)					AVERAGE SALES PRICE (dol.)				
	Total	North-east	Mid-west	South	West	U.S.	North-east	Mid-west	South	West
1980	233.7	12.3	32.3	140.3	48.7	19,800	18,500	18,600	18,200	25,400
1985	283.4	20.2	38.6	187.6	36.9	21,800	22,700	21,500	20,400	28,700
1987	239.2	23.6	40.0	145.5	30.1	23,700	25,600	23,700	21,900	31,000
1988	224.3	22.7	39.1	130.7	31.8	25,100	27,000	24,600	22,700	33,900
1989	202.8	20.2	39.1	112.8	30.6	27,200	30,200	26,700	24,100	37,800
1990	195.4	18.8	37.7	108.4	30.6	27,800	30,000	27,000	24,500	39,300
1991	174.3	14.3	35.4	97.6	27.0	27,700	30,400	27,000	24,500	38,600
1992	212.0	15.0	42.2	124.4	30.4	28,400	30,900	28,800	25,400	39,000
1993	242.5	15.4	44.5	146.7	35.9	30,500	32,000	31,400	27,700	40,500
1994	286.1	16.2	53.0	174.4	42.5	33,500	33,900	34,600	30,500	44,600
1995	310.7	14.6	56.0	198.3	41.8	36,300	36,600	36,600	34,000	46,800
1996	319.7	15.4	56.6	205.1	42.6	38,400	40,200	39,600	36,100	47,700
1997	296.5	13.7	50.9	188.8	43.1	41,100	43,900	41,600	38,700	50,900

Source: U.S. Bureau of the Census, *Current Construction Reports*, Series C20, *Housing Starts*, monthly.

No. 1204. Existing One-Family Houses Sold and Price, by Region: 1970 to 1997

[Based on data (adjusted and aggregated to regional and national totals) reported by participating real estate multiple listing services. For definition of median, see Guide to Tabular Presentation. For composition of regions, see inside front cover]

YEAR	HOUSES SOLD (1,000)					MEDIAN SALES PRICE (dol.)				
	Total	North-east	Mid-west	South	West	Total	North-east	Mid-west	South	West
1970	1,612	251	501	568	292	23,000	25,700	20,100	22,200	24,300
1971	2,018	311	583	735	389	24,800	27,100	22,100	24,300	26,500
1972	2,252	361	630	788	473	26,700	29,800	23,900	26,400	28,400
1973	2,334	367	674	847	446	28,900	32,800	25,300	29,000	31,000
1974	2,272	354	645	839	434	32,000	35,800	27,700	32,200	34,800
1975	2,476	370	701	862	543	35,300	39,300	30,100	34,800	39,600
1976	3,064	439	881	1,033	712	38,100	41,800	32,900	36,500	46,100
1977	3,650	515	1,101	1,231	803	42,900	44,400	36,700	39,800	57,300
1978	3,986	516	1,144	1,416	911	48,700	47,900	42,200	45,100	66,700
1979	3,827	526	1,061	1,353	887	55,700	53,600	47,800	51,300	77,400
1980	2,973	403	806	1,092	672	62,200	60,800	51,900	58,300	89,300
1981	2,419	353	632	917	516	66,400	63,700	54,300	64,400	96,200
1982	1,990	354	490	780	366	67,800	63,500	55,100	67,100	98,900
1983	2,697	477	692	1,004	524	70,300	72,200	56,600	69,200	94,900
1984	2,829	478	720	1,006	624	72,400	78,700	57,100	71,300	95,800
1985	3,134	561	806	1,063	704	75,500	88,900	58,900	75,200	95,400
1986	3,474	635	922	1,145	773	80,300	104,800	63,500	78,200	100,900
1987	3,436	618	892	1,163	763	85,600	133,300	66,000	80,400	113,200
1988	3,513	606	865	1,224	817	89,300	143,000	68,400	82,200	124,900
1989	3,346	531	855	1,185	775	93,100	145,200	71,300	84,500	139,900
1990	3,211	469	831	1,202	709	95,500	141,200	74,000	85,900	139,600
1991	3,220	479	840	1,199	702	100,300	141,900	77,800	88,900	147,200
1992	3,520	534	939	1,292	755	103,700	140,000	81,700	92,100	143,800
1993	3,802	571	1,007	1,416	808	106,800	139,500	85,200	95,000	142,600
1994	3,967	595	1,038	1,469	865	109,900	139,100	87,900	96,000	147,000
1995	3,812	577	992	1,431	813	113,100	136,900	93,600	97,800	148,300
1996	4,087	611	1,048	1,516	912	118,200	140,900	99,800	102,800	152,900
1997	4,215	632	1,067	1,575	942	124,100	145,100	106,100	109,000	160,400

Source: NATIONAL ASSOCIATION OF REALTORS, Washington, DC, prior to 1990, *Home Sales,* monthly, and *Home Sales Yearbook: 1990;* (copyright); thereafter, *Real Estate Outlook; Market Trends & Insights,* monthly, (copyright).

No. 1205. Median Sales Price of Existing One-Family Homes, by Selected Metropolitan Area: 1994 to 1997

[In thousands of dollars. For the top 60 areas in sales price in 1996. Areas are metropolitan statistical areas (MSAs) except as indicated; areas defined as of 1992]

METROPOLITAN AREA	1994	1995	1996	1997	METROPOLITAN AREA	1994	1995	1996	1997
U.S., all areas	109.9	113.1	118.2	124.1	Milwaukee, WI PMSA.....	109.0	114.7	119.4	125.3
Albuquerque, NM........	110.0	117.0	122.3	126.7	Minneapolis-St. Paul, MN-WI..	101.5	106.8	113.9	118.4
Anaheim-Santa Ana, CA					Nashville, TN	96.5	107.3	112.7	115.2
PMSA (Orange Co.) [1]......	211.0	208.4	213.4	229.8	New Haven-Meriden, CT.....	139.6	135.1	133.3	134.1
Atlanta, GA............	93.6	97.5	100.7	108.4	NY: Bergen-Passaic, NJ				
Atlantic City, NJ.........	107.6	107.0	108.0	109.7	PMSA	192.7	190.1	199.4	205.4
Aurora-Elgin, IL.........	124.4	131.6	137.0	141.8	NY: Middlesex-Somerset-				
Austin-San Marcos, TX.....	96.2	101.4	108.1	118.0	Hunterdon, NJ PMSA	170.7	171.4	175.9	176.7
Baltimore, MD...........	115.4	111.3	113.0	118.2	NY: Monmouth-Ocean, NJ....	137.0	137.2	144.7	147.7
Birmingham, AL..........	100.2	103.6	114.1	118.9	NY: Nassau-Suffolk, NY PMSA.	159.3	155.3	159.8	164.0
Boston, MA PMSA.........	179.3	179.0	189.3	196.2	NY: Newark, NJ...........	187.3	185.1	(NA)	193.0
Charlotte-Gastonia-					NY:New York-North NJ				
Rock Hill, NC-SC.........	106.5	107.8	116.8	124.2	Long Island, NY CMSA.....	173.2	169.7	174.5	177.9
Chicago, IL PMSA........	144.1	147.9	153.2	158.9	Phoenix, AZ	91.4	96.8	105.3	113.7
Cincinnati, OH-KY-IN PMSA ..	96.5	100.4	104.8	110.5	Portland, OR PMSA........	116.9	128.4	141.5	152.4
Cleveland, OH PMSA.......	98.5	104.7	111.9	116.8	Providence, RI PMSA.......	116.4	115.6	118.1	119.6
Colorado Springs, CO......	104.2	114.7	126.6	130.5	Raleigh-Durham, NC	115.2	127.0	145.4	152.8
Columbus, OH	94.8	99.1	108.2	117.6	Reno, NV	133.6	137.1	140.0	143.4
Dallas, TX PMSA.........	95.0	96.4	103.5	112.0	Richmond-Petersburg, VA	95.4	103.1	108.7	114.2
Denver, CO PMSA........	116.8	127.3	133.4	140.6	Riverside-San Bernadino, CA				
Detroit, MI PMSA.........	87.0	98.2	111.4	119.6	PMSA [1]	129.1	120.9	115.2	114.3
Eugene-Springfield, OR	96.2	104.9	116.2	119.4	Sacramento, CA [1]	124.5	119.5	115.3	116.1
Ft. Lauderdale-Hollywood-					Salt Lake City-Ogden, UT	98.0	113.7	122.7	128.6
Pompano Beach, FL......	103.1	105.9	112.3	123.7	San Diego, CA [1]	176.0	171.6	174.5	185.2
Greensboro-Winston Salem-					San Francisco, CA Area [1] ...	255.6	254.4	266.7	292.6
High Point, NC	96.6	102.5	112.7	117.3	Sarasota, FL...........	97.0	104.5	107.7	114.1
Greenville-Spartanburg, SC ...	87.4	92.4	105.5	112.8	Seattle, WA	155.9	159.0	164.6	171.3
Hartford, CT PMSA	133.4	133.4	139.2	138.1	Springfield, MA	107.7	106.1	106.0	106.5
Honolulu, HI	360.0	349.0	335.0	307.0	Tallahassee, FL..........	97.8	99.8	109.8	111.7
Kansas City, MO-KS........	87.1	91.7	98.8	106.8	Trenton, NJ	131.3	129.0	136.4	137.7
Lake County, IL	130.8	136.2	144.7	153.5	Tucson, AZ.............	95.4	100.5	105.5	106.8
Las Vegas, NV	110.5	113.5	118.5	123.2	Washington, DC-MD-VA	157.9	156.5	160.7	166.3
Los Angeles-Long Beach,					West Palm Beach-Boca Raton				
CA PMSA [1]...........	189.1	179.9	172.9	176.5	Delray Beach, FL........	117.6	121.3	126.6	133.4
Madison, WI	116.0	124.5	122.2	126.8	Worcester, MA	130.6	130.1	131.2	135.8
Miami-Hialeah, FL PMSA	103.2	107.1	113.2	117.7					

NA Not available.   [1] Data from the California Association of REALTORS.
Source: NATIONAL ASSOCIATION OF of REALTORS, Washington, DC, *Real Estate Outlook: Market Trends & Insights,* monthly, (copyright).

No. 1206. Existing Home Sales, by State: 1990 to 1997

[In thousands]

STATE	1990	1994	1995	1996	1997	STATE	1990	1994	1995	1996	1997
United States [1]	3,560	4,404	4,240	4,559	4,730	Missouri	84.1	110.2	108.3	113.7	115.9
Alabama	61.1	77.4	74.2	76.8	82.2	Montana	12.7	15.6	13.8	14.2	14.9
Alaska	(NA)	(NA)	(NA)	(NA)	(NA)	Nebraska	19.3	23.3	21.1	20.3	23.4
Arizona	86.3	123.8	122.0	128.2	135.1	Nevada	26.2	32.9	29.6	31.8	29.7
Arkansas [2]	44.8	52.3	57.5	59.7	58.7	New Hampshire	7.9	16.2	(NA)	(NA)	(NA)
California [2]	453.0	482.5	425.6	505.4	555.4	New Jersey	114.8	145.4	138.3	147.8	157.3
Colorado	54.2	80.6	76.9	81.6	86.6	New Mexico	23.6	30.4	28.9	26.7	25.5
Connecticut	34.3	49.8	51.4	49.2	55.0	New York	125.5	156.3	150.4	165.8	171.0
Delaware	9.7	10.4	10.2	(NA)	(NA)	North Carolina	135.9	204.1	201.0	212.5	228.0
District of Columbia	13.1	12.3	11.6	10.8	14.2	North Dakota	10.4	10.9	10.6	12.0	11.9
Florida	183.3	229.7	220.3	225.5	234.4	Ohio	151.6	186.4	182.8	192.7	187.3
Georgia	73.2	(NA)	(NA)	(NA)	(NA)	Oklahoma	53.4	59.7	57.7	60.6	64.2
Hawaii	19.2	13.1	10.0	9.8	11.1	Oregon	56.6	58.1	59.0	58.9	60.1
Idaho	18.1	23.1	20.5	20.2	20.7	Pennsylvania	182.7	216.4	217.2	224.3	233.3
Illinois	160.9	188.4	183.5	191.6	199.7	Rhode Island	7.8	11.6	11.5	12.9	14.3
Indiana	80.1	103.3	100.6	103.5	111.5	South Carolina	57.8	67.3	68.9	74.2	81.5
Iowa	51.9	54.3	51.6	56.4	57.7	South Dakota	11.6	13.2	13.3	13.9	15.2
Kansas	38.8	55.7	54.4	59.9	61.6	Tennessee	92.7	129.8	133.6	142.9	149.9
Kentucky	66.4	81.1	78.2	78.8	81.1	Texas	240.0	266.9	256.8	275.0	293.1
Louisiana	41.6	51.4	50.4	50.9	52.9	Utah	22.1	32.4	31.6	33.8	30.0
Maine	(NA)	13.1	13.1	14.2	14.7	Vermont	6.1	10.9	8.8	8.4	8.1
Maryland	67.1	69.5	58.7	60.3	66.4	Virginia	96.9	99.5	92.2	92.2	98.5
Massachusetts	44.0	68.7	68.1	81.9	94.3	Washington	87.7	101.2	95.5	101.5	116.5
Michigan	145.0	184.2	176.3	179.8	180.3	West Virginia	42.0	45.8	44.2	43.8	45.2
Minnesota	64.8	82.1	76.7	85.8	88.0	Wisconsin	74.2	94.3	93.2	101.0	104.6
Mississippi	34.7	43.5	46.1	46.7	47.7	Wyoming	7.4	11.0	9.4	8.6	9.5

NA Not available.   [1] U.S. totals are derived independently and therefore are not equal to the sum of the states.   [2] Data from the California Association of Realtors.

Source: NATIONAL ASSOCIATION OF REALTORS, Washington, DC, *Real Estate Outlook: Market Trends & Insights,* monthly, (copyright).

No. 1207. New Apartments Completed and Rented in 3 Months, by Region: 1980 to 1996

[Structures with five or more units, privately financed, nonsubsidized, unfurnished rental apartments. Based on sample and subject to sampling variability; see source for details. For composition of regions, see inside front cover]

YEAR AND RENT	NUMBER (1,000)					PERCENT RENTED IN 3 MONTHS				
	U.S.	North-east	Mid-west	South	West	U.S.	North-east	Mid-west	South	West
1980	196.1	14.2	43.8	91.5	46.6	75	77	77	74	75
1981	135.3	4.9	36.9	68.4	25.1	80	85	86	78	75
1982	117.0	4.6	21.9	66.8	23.7	72	74	79	70	72
1983	191.5	3.5	41.1	115.1	31.8	69	73	86	63	69
1984	313.2	3.8	41.2	194.4	73.9	67	64	79	63	70
1985	365.2	8.1	54.0	166.1	137.0	65	69	72	59	68
1986	407.6	16.9	64.5	171.7	154.5	66	70	70	62	67
1987	345.6	11.3	66.0	124.5	143.9	63	73	65	59	64
1988	284.5	8.7	60.4	91.7	123.8	66	52	73	58	69
1989	247.8	13.4	45.8	86.3	102.3	70	74	74	68	69
1990 [1]	214.3	12.7	44.3	77.2	80.0	67	66	75	64	65
1991	165.3	6.8	37.9	63.6	57.0	70	83	78	65	68
1992	110.2	10.9	34.0	37.4	28.0	74	75	80	72	70
1993	77.2	3.7	25.3	27.7	20.5	75	37	81	76	73
1994	104.0	3.7	32.2	44.5	23.6	80	96	78	78	85
1995	155.0	7.1	31.7	78.5	37.7	73	74	75	72	73
1996	191.3	6.1	37.2	96.9	51.1	72	61	77	69	75
Less than $350	4.3	1.0	0.4	1.3	1.5	70	19	83	77	96
$350 to $549	47.4	1.2	19.7	20.5	5.9	79	73	80	77	88
$350 to $449	14.7	0.1	6.0	6.2	2.4	82	69	81	80	93
$450 to $549	32.7	1.1	13.7	14.3	3.5	78	73	79	76	85
$550 to $749	70.9	2.3	11.2	35.5	22.0	71	53	79	67	74
$550 to $649	36.2	0.9	8.5	18.5	8.4	72	49	77	69	78
$650 to $749	34.7	1.4	2.7	17.0	13.6	69	55	85	65	72
$750 or more	68.8	1.7	5.9	39.6	21.6	69	91	65	67	70
Median monthly asking rent	$672	$650	$538	$697	$721	(X)	(X)	(X)	(X)	(X)

X Not applicable.   [1] Due to revised estimation procedures, data beginning 1990 not strictly comparable with prior years.

Source: U.S. Bureau of the Census, *Current Housing Reports,* Series H130, *Market Absorption of Apartments,* and unpublished data.

No. 1208. Recent Home Buyers—General Characteristics: 1976 to 1997

[As of **October**. Based on a sample survey; subject to sampling variability]

ITEM	Unit	1976	1980	1985	1990	1993	1994	1995	1996	1997
Median purchase price ...	Dollars ..	43,340	68,714	90,400	131,200	141,900	145,400	147,700	153,200	159,700
First-time buyers.....	Dollars ..	37,670	61,450	75,100	106,000	121,100	125,000	128,300	130,100	135,400
Repeat buyers [1]	Dollars ..	50,090	75,750	106,200	149,400	159,600	163,500	164,300	170,700	178,700
Average monthly										
mortgage payment	Dollars ..	329	599	896	1,127	1,015	1,028	1,062	1,087	1,114
Percent of income....	Percent..	24.0	32.4	30.0	33.8	31.5	31.4	32.6	32.6	32.8
Percent buying—										
New houses.........	Percent..	15.1	22.4	23.8	21.2	22.3	22.0	21.5	22.7	20.9
Existing houses	Percent..	84.9	77.6	76.2	78.8	77.7	78.0	78.5	77.3	79.1
Single-family houses ..	Percent..	88.8	82.4	87.0	83.8	84.2	83.9	83.1	82.6	81.6
Other houses [2]	Percent..	11.2	17.6	13.0	16.2	15.8	16.1	16.9	17.4	18.4
For the first time.....	Percent..	44.8	32.9	36.6	41.9	46.0	47.1	46.2	44.7	46.8
Average age:										
First-time buyers.....	Years ...	28.1	28.3	28.4	30.5	31.6	31.6	32.1	32.4	32.1
Repeat buyers [1].....	Years ...	35.9	36.4	38.4	39.1	41.0	41.7	40.7	41.1	41.1
Downpayment/sales										
price........	Percent..	25.2	28.0	24.8	23.3	20.2	20.2	20.4	19.5	20.3
First-time buyers.....	Percent..	18.0	20.5	11.4	15.7	14.0	13.7	13.3	12.4	13.7
Repeat buyers [1]	Percent..	30.8	32.7	32.7	28.9	25.4	26.1	26.8	25.3	26.1

[1] Buyers who previously owned a home.　　[2] Includes multifamily, condominums and co-ops.
Source: Chicago Title Insurance Company, Chicago, IL, *The Guarantor,* quarterly (copyright).

No. 1209. Total Housing Inventory for the United States: 1970 to 1997

[**In thousands.** Based on the Current Population Survey and the Housing Vacancy Survey and subject to sampling error; see source for details]

ITEM	1970	1975	1980	1985	1990	1992	1993	1994	1995	1996	1997
All housing units ...	**69,778**	**78,821**	**87,739**	**97,333**	**106,283**	**108,316**	**109,611**	**110,952**	**112,655**	**114,139**	**115,621**
Vacant...............	6,137	6,896	8,101	9,446	12,059	11,926	11,894	12,257	12,669	13,155	13,419
Year-round vacant	4,391	5,202	5,996	7,400	9,128	8,932	8,937	9,229	9,570	9,945	10,114
For rent........	1,299	1,647	1,575	2,221	2,662	2,769	2,809	2,858	2,946	3,008	2,978
For sale only	427	591	734	1,006	1,064	970	894	953	1,022	1,082	1,133
Rented or sold	427	536	623	664	660	628	625	772	810	834	867
Held off market	2,238	2,429	3,064	3,510	4,742	4,564	4,609	4,646	4,793	5,022	5,136
Occasional use....	615	649	814	977	1,485	1,443	1,508	1,612	1,667	1,709	1,818
Usual residence elsewhere	429	470	568	659	1,068	1,011	994	815	801	852	885
Other	1,195	1,309	1,683	1,875	2,189	2,111	2,108	2,219	2,325	2,461	2,433
Seasonal [1]	1,746	1,694	2,106	2,046	2,931	2,994	2,957	3,028	3,099	3,209	3,305
Total occupied	63,640	71,925	79,638	87,887	94,224	96,391	97,717	98,695	99,985	100,984	102,202
Owner............	40,834	46,463	52,223	56,152	60,248	61,823	62,533	63,136	64,739	66,041	67,143
Renter............	22,806	25,462	27,415	31,736	33,976	34,568	35,184	35,558	35,246	34,943	35,059
Percent distribution:											
All housing units.....	100.0	100.0	100.0	100.0	100.0	100.0	100.0	100.0	100.0	100.0	100.0
Vacant.........	8.8	8.7	9.2	9.7	11.3	11.0	10.9	11.0	11.2	11.5	11.6
Total occupied	91.2	91.3	90.8	90.3	88.7	89.0	89.1	89.0	88.8	88.5	88.4
Owner............	58.5	58.9	59.5	57.7	56.7	57.1	57.0	56.9	57.5	57.9	58.1
Renter............	32.7	32.3	31.2	32.6	32.0	31.9	32.1	32.0	31.3	30.6	30.3

[1] Beginning 1990 includes vacant seasonal mobile homes. For years shown, seasonal vacant housing units were underreported prior to 1990.
Source: U.S. Bureau of the Census, Internet site <http://www.census.gov/hhes/www/housing/hvs/historic/index.html>

No. 1210. Vacancy Rates for Housing Units—Characteristics: 1990 to 1997

[**In percent.** Rate is relationship between vacant housing for rent or for sale and the total rental and homeowner supply, which comprises occupied units, units rented or sold and awaiting occupancy, and vacant units available for rent or sale. For composition of regions, see map, inside front cover. Based on the Current Population Survey/Housing Vacancy Survey; see source for details]

CHARACTERISTIC	RENTAL UNITS					HOMEOWNER UNITS				
	1990	1994 [1]	1995	1996	1997	1990	1994 [1]	1995	1996	1997
Total units	**7.2**	**7.4**	**7.6**	**7.8**	**7.7**	**1.7**	**1.5**	**1.5**	**1.6**	**1.6**
Inside MSAs.........	7.1	7.3	7.6	7.7	7.5	1.7	1.5	1.5	1.6	1.6
Outside MSAs	7.6	7.7	7.9	8.7	8.8	1.8	1.5	1.6	1.7	1.9
Northeast..........	6.1	7.1	7.2	7.4	6.7	1.6	1.5	1.5	1.6	1.6
Midwest..........	6.4	6.8	7.2	7.9	8.0	1.3	1.1	1.3	1.3	1.2
South	8.8	8.0	8.3	8.6	9.1	2.1	1.7	1.7	1.8	1.9
West.............	6.6	7.1	7.5	7.2	6.6	1.8	1.6	1.7	1.7	1.8
Units in structure:										
One unit.........	4.0	4.5	5.4	5.5	5.8	1.4	1.3	1.4	1.4	1.5
Two units or more ..	9.0	9.1	9.0	9.3	9.0	7.1	4.9	4.8	5.2	4.4
Five units or more ..	9.6	9.8	9.5	9.6	9.1	8.4	5.6	5.1	5.9	4.6
Units with—										
Three rooms or less .	10.3	11.1	11.4	11.3	11.1	10.2	9.7	9.2	10.0	9.6
Four rooms........	8.0	7.9	8.2	8.9	8.6	3.2	3.0	2.8	3.2	3.3
Five rooms	5.7	5.7	5.8	5.8	6.0	2.0	1.8	1.8	1.9	1.9
Six rooms or more ..	3.0	3.4	3.8	3.7	3.9	1.1	0.9	1.1	1.1	1.1

[1] Beginning 1994, based on 1990 population census controls.
Source: Bureau of the Census, Internet site <http://www.census.gov/ftp/pub/hhes/www/hvs.html>

No. 1211. Housing Units—Characteristics, by Tenure and Region: 1995

[In thousands of units, except as indicated. **As of Oct. 1.** Based on the American Housing Survey; see Appendix III. For composition of regions, see map, inside front cover]

CHARACTERISTIC	Total housing units	Sea-sonal	YEAR-ROUND UNITS Occupied Total	Owner	Renter	North-east	Mid-west	South	West	Vacant
Total units	**109,457**	**3,054**	**97,693**	**63,544**	**34,150**	**19,200**	**23,662**	**34,236**	**20,596**	**8,710**
Percent distribution	100.0	2.8	89.3	58.1	31.2	17.5	21.6	31.3	18.8	8.0
Units in structure:										
Single family detached	66,169	1,804	60,826	52,257	8,569	9,818	16,175	22,406	12,427	3,539
Single family attached	6,213	41	5,545	2,936	2,609	1,571	1,053	1,867	1,055	627
2 to 4 units	10,700	124	9,299	1,734	7,565	3,126	2,168	2,083	1,922	1,277
5 to 9 units	5,594	102	4,803	520	4,283	970	1,023	1,592	1,218	690
10 to 19 units	5,092	93	4,342	368	3,974	791	880	1,575	1,096	657
20 to 49 units	3,901	74	3,244	342	2,903	896	559	856	933	583
50 or more units	4,140	55	3,470	550	2,920	1,470	668	641	691	615
Mobile home or trailer	7,647	761	6,164	4,837	1,328	557	1,136	3,216	1,254	722
Stories in structure: [1]										
One story	3,065	35	2,678	279	2,399	158	374	1,204	942	352
2 stories	10,828	149	9,318	1,055	8,263	1,065	1,321	3,594	3,338	1,361
3 stories	8,268	152	7,056	1,179	5,877	2,363	2,451	1,249	992	1,060
4 to 6 stories	4,652	79	3,904	591	3,312	2,287	793	395	429	670
7 or more stories	2,627	32	2,213	415	1,799	1,382	359	312	160	381
Foundation: [2]										
Full or partial basement	32,423	367	30,635	27,080	3,554	9,859	13,077	4,894	2,803	1,420
Crawlspace	18,891	762	16,727	13,155	3,572	573	2,413	9,007	4,735	1,402
Concrete slab	19,255	358	17,722	13,988	3,734	855	1,556	9,610	5,702	1,175
Other	1,813	358	1,287	970	317	101	181	762	243	168
Year structure built:										
1939 and earlier	22,116	544	19,308	11,068	8,239	7,162	6,228	3,574	2,345	2,263
1940 to 1949	8,400	228	7,487	4,671	2,817	1,680	1,750	2,500	1,558	685
1950 to 1959	13,569	371	12,398	8,798	3,600	2,546	3,245	3,936	2,670	800
1960 to 1969	15,806	472	14,267	9,349	4,918	2,415	3,266	5,286	3,300	1,068
1970 to 1979	23,717	784	21,033	13,347	7,685	2,716	4,872	8,358	5,086	1,899
1980 or later	25,849	654	23,201	16,311	6,890	2,679	4,301	10,582	5,639	1,994
Median year	1967	1968	1967	1968	1965	1953	1962	1972	1971	1966
Main heating equipment:										
Warm-air furnace	57,840	838	53,165	38,301	14,863	6,881	17,711	17,212	11,361	3,837
Electric heat pump	10,614	311	9,406	7,027	2,379	433	692	7,003	1,278	897
Steam or hot water system	14,895	87	13,669	7,323	6,345	9,503	2,587	834	745	1,139
Floor, wall, or pipeless furnace	5,674	128	4,963	2,148	2,815	234	389	1,534	2,806	583
Built-in electric units	8,344	422	7,035	2,870	4,166	1,303	1,342	2,286	2,104	887
Room heaters with flue	2,083	178	1,620	869	752	187	245	864	324	285
Room heaters without flue	1,886	49	1,642	964	678	43	31	1,500	69	194
Stoves	2,877	339	2,320	1,735	585	360	379	962	619	218
Fireplaces	1,066	141	850	661	187	37	81	385	347	75
None	1,795	359	1,044	463	581	38	31	457	518	393
Portable electric heaters	950	78	809	413	395	19	18	576	195	63
Other	1,432	124	1,171	768	403	162	156	623	231	137
Kitchen equipment:										
Lacking complete facilities	3,629	391	1,075	461	614	241	281	302	252	2,163
With complete facilities	105,827	2,662	96,618	63,083	33,536	18,959	23,382	33,934	20,344	6,546
Kitchen sink	108,395	2,903	97,034	63,231	33,803	19,033	23,484	34,065	20,452	8,458
Refrigerator	106,872	2,739	97,433	63,469	33,964	19,133	23,597	34,180	20,523	6,701
Burners and oven	107,394	2,795	97,207	63,443	33,764	19,093	23,528	34,113	20,473	7,392
Burners only	151	21	105	31	74	28	17	40	20	25
Oven only	119	4	99	32	68	14	44	19	22	16
Dishwasher	56,635	818	52,508	40,236	12,272	9,084	11,160	19,210	13,054	3,309
Washing machine	79,403	1,129	75,745	60,034	15,711	13,526	18,804	28,015	15,399	2,530
Clothes dryer	74,165	1,062	70,756	57,184	13,571	12,150	18,341	25,694	14,571	2,347
Disposal in kitchen sink	46,353	717	42,451	28,793	13,659	4,159	10,301	14,086	13,906	3,185
Air conditioning:										
Central	50,824	780	46,577	34,161	12,415	3,856	11,694	23,772	7,255	3,467
Percent of total units	46.4	25.5	47.7	53.8	36.4	20.1	49.4	69.4	35.2	39.8
One or more room units	29,141	530	27,181	16,126	11,054	8,732	7,107	8,361	2,982	1,431
Source of water:										
Public system or private company	94,108	1,767	84,818	52,643	32,175	16,307	19,749	29,445	19,318	7,523
Percent of total units	86.0	57.9	86.8	82.8	94.2	84.9	83.5	86.0	93.8	86.4
Well serving 1 to 5 units	14,265	955	12,270	10,463	1,807	2,783	3,778	4,498	1,211	1,041
Other	1,083	332	606	438	167	110	136	293	67	146
Means of sewage disposal:										
Public sewer	83,308	1,222	75,282	44,527	30,755	14,859	18,618	24,111	17,694	6,804
Percent of total units	76.1	40.0	77.1	70.1	90.1	77.4	78.7	70.4	85.9	78.1
Septic tank, cesspool, chemical toilet	25,635	1,521	22,296	18,937	3,359	4,335	5,029	10,041	2,891	1,819
Other	513	311	116	80	36	6	15	83	11	87

[1] Limited to multiunit structures. [2] Limited to single-family units.

Source: U.S. Bureau of the Census, *Current Housing Reports,* Series H-150-95, *American Housing Survey in the United States.*

No. 1212. Housing Inventory for Selected Metropolitan Areas— Summary Characteristics: 1994 to 1996

[Based on the American Housing Survey and subject source for details. For definition of median, see Guide to Tabular Presentation]

YEAR AND METROPOLITAN AREA	Total units (1,000)	PERCENT							OWNER OCCUPIED					RENTER OCCUPIED		
		Owner occupied	Renter occupied	Vacant and seasonal	Single-family	Multi-family	Central heat	Central air	Median monthly housing costs Total (dol.)	Percent of income	Median value (dol.)	Median monthly real estate taxes (dol.)	Median monthly electricity costs (dol.)	Median monthly housing costs Total (dol.)	Percent of income	Median monthly electricity costs (dol.)
1994																
Anaheim-Santa Ana, CA PMSA	918.0	56.0	36.8	7.2	59.8	40.2	70.0	41.4	1,127	23	216,962	121	56	805	32	39
Buffalo, NY CMSA	503.2	60.9	30.2	8.8	61.7	38.3	89.5	14.6	589	21	85,378	188	65	446	29	43
Dallas, TX PMSA	1,152.8	51.3	39.1	9.7	64.4	35.6	82.2	87.1	783	19	87,615	119	114	532	26	73
Fort Worth-Arlington, TX PMSA	555.4	57.9	32.4	9.7	72.7	27.3	74.1	81.2	668	19	70,759	109	117	509	27	83
Milwaukee, WI PMSA	593.0	58.5	35.9	5.6	60.2	39.8	92.7	38.8	684	20	101,407	(²)	47	498	29	32
Phoenix, AZ MSA	1,032.8	56.2	30.7	13.2	73.7	26.3	86.3	86.1	664	19	88,269	55	111	509	29	78
Riverside-San Bernardino-Ontario, CA PMSA	1,121.4	56.5	26.7	16.8	78.5	21.5	72.0	64.4	807	25	123,491	78	63	592	35	43
San Diego, CA MSA	993.3	50.4	39.8	9.7	60.9	39.1	54.3	26.5	873	23	176,277	104	46	640	33	33
1995																
Charlotte, NC-SC MSA	539.4	62.7	30.6	6.7	79.2	20.8	80.6	72.2	532	17	86,763	61	87	489	25	66
Chicago, IL Area PMSAs	2,987.1	59.6	33.8	6.6	55.5	44.5	90.2	47.7	850	21	136,362	185	68	584	29	40
Columbus, OH MSA	604.9	57.9	34.0	8.1	78.6	21.4	91.4	63.7	654	18	92,664	97	61	484	26	43
Denver, CO PMSA	773.9	61.2	32.6	6.2	71.2	28.8	95.5	25.7	763	20	119,694	91	47	539	27	27
Detroit, MI PMSA	1,802.7	66.3	26.9	6.7	77.1	22.9	93.8	44.6	551	17	89,648	126	50	508	27	37
Kansas City, MO-KS MSA	715.5	61.9	30.2	7.9	79.0	21.0	93.1	73.6	565	17	78,542	73	68	481	26	49
Los Angeles-Long Beach, CA PMSA	3,276.0	42.0	48.0	10.0	56.0	44.0	45.3	32.1	943	23	192,803	109	55	654	36	49
Miami-Fort Lauderdale, FL CMSA	1,483.8	52.1	31.8	16.1	53.5	46.5	69.1	76.9	729	24	97,058	110	93	609	35	63
New Orleans, LA MSA	547.7	54.6	33.9	11.5	69.8	30.2	67.9	66.8	404	15	75,768	(¹)	100	441	28	72
New York-Nassau-Suffolk-Orange County, NY PMSAs	4,577.3	41.0	50.9	8.1	32.6	67.4	94.7	11.1	931	22	172,651	(²)	81	650	32	41
Northern New Jersey PMSAs	2,442.2	56.0	34.2	9.8	60.0	40.0	89.5	35.1	976	21	176,713	(²)	72	669	31	42
Philadelphia, PA-NJ PMSA	1,986.6	63.7	28.0	8.4	74.2	25.8	90.4	38.8	673	22	112,769	166	82	578	31	49
Pittsburgh, PA MSA	1,051.7	66.5	25.7	7.8	78.5	21.5	93.9	37.4	416	18	73,383	118	57	417	27	43
Portland, OR-WA PMSA	702.6	60.3	32.9	6.8	76.1	23.9	59.4	18.0	704	19	127,731	147	49	566	28	43
San Antonio, TX MSA	538.7	55.4	34.6	10.0	72.7	27.3	65.2	67.8	507	18	62,577	85	80	475	27	55
1996																
Atlanta, GA MSA	1,421.1	58.6	33.4	8.1	71.4	28.6	88.7	82.6	803	18	105,037	85	81	651	29	64
Cleveland, OH PMSA	829.6	62.4	30.7	6.9	68.5	31.5	94.8	39.3	552	17	99,263	116	64	492	28	39
Hartford, CT MSA	480.2	60.5	31.1	8.4	63.5	36.5	87.9	19.0	888	21	139,641	(²)	69	616	29	46
Indianapolis, IN MSA	640.8	62.2	30.2	7.6	77.5	22.5	89.9	71.6	603	17	91,213	74	63	507	26	47
Memphis, TN-AR-MS MSA	442.0	59.3	31.5	9.2	73.9	26.1	77.1	71.7	592	18	76,175	62	69	477	26	60
Oklahoma City, OK MSA	446.4	57.8	28.7	13.5	77.9	22.1	79.7	76.4	461	15	65,638	41	76	434	26	65
Sacramento, CA MSA	625.4	55.1	34.1	10.8	76.0	24.0	67.5	71.7	874	21	140,758	84	60	590	30	41
St. Louis, MO-IL MSA	1,170.0	64.3	26.5	9.2	76.4	23.6	92.6	76.5	557	21	82,111	77	75	462	27	58
Seattle-Everett, WA PMSA	965.3	58.3	35.1	6.5	66.1	33.9	55.9	6.0	897	21	164,554	151	54	630	28	42

¹ Less than $25. ² More than $200.

Source: U.S. Bureau of the Census, American Housing Survey for Selected Metropolitan Areas, annual.

No. 1213. Housing Units—Size of Units and Lot: 1995

[In thousands, except as indicated. As of Oct. 1. Based on the American Housing Survey; see Appendix III. For composition of regions, see map, inside front cover]

ITEM	Total housing units	Seasonal	YEAR-ROUND UNITS								
			Occupied								Vacant
			Total	Owner	Renter	Northeast	Midwest	South	West	
Total units	109,457	3,054	97,693	63,544	34,150	19,200	23,662	34,236	20,596	8,710
Rooms:										
1 room.	862	104	550	22	528	246	109	72	123	208
2 rooms	1,422	215	958	60	898	279	139	235	305	249
3 rooms	10,166	484	8,311	859	7,452	2,299	1,691	2,240	2,081	1,371
4 rooms	20,789	1,070	17,062	6,069	10,993	3,124	3,858	6,135	3,945	2,656
5 rooms	24,328	660	21,600	13,895	7,705	3,749	5,292	8,380	4,178	2,068
6 rooms	22,151	327	20,700	16,686	4,014	3,797	5,122	7,725	4,055	1,125
7 rooms	14,183	88	13,560	12,007	1,554	2,606	3,467	4,781	2,706	536
8 rooms or more	15,555	106	14,952	13,946	1,006	3,100	3,985	4,667	3,202	496
Median number of rooms.	5.4	4.2	5.5	6.2	4.2	5.5	5.6	5.5	5.4	4.5
Complete bathrooms:										
No bathrooms	1,201	468	465	195	270	133	116	159	57	268
1 bathroom	50,700	1,703	43,777	19,069	24,709	10,472	11,456	13,627	8,221	5,219
1 and one-half bathrooms	15,887	237	14,780	11,319	3,461	3,610	4,889	4,008	2,273	870
2 or more bathrooms	41,669	645	38,671	32,961	5,710	4,984	7,201	16,442	10,044	2,353
Square footage of unit:										
Single detached and mobile homes [1]	73,816	2,564	66,990	57,094	9,897	10,375	17,312	25,622	13,682	4,261
Less than 500	1,242	360	667	379	288	59	107	295	206	216
500 to 749	3,293	483	2,356	1,386	969	244	521	1,166	424	455
750 to 999	6,676	393	5,697	4,126	1,571	521	1,400	2,675	1,101	586
1,000 to 1,499	16,741	406	15,450	12,697	2,753	1,408	3,327	7,147	3,568	885
1,500 to 1,999	14,576	202	13,785	12,218	1,567	1,839	3,288	5,343	3,314	589
2,000 to 2,499	10,344	69	9,943	9,211	732	1,913	2,960	3,124	1,947	333
2,500 to 2,999	5,739	39	5,486	5,147	339	1,265	1,689	1,590	942	214
3,000 to 3,999	5,178	55	4,956	4,737	219	1,214	1,532	1,449	761	167
4,000 or more	2,938	31	2,785	2,597	189	739	814	879	353	121
Other [2]	7,089	527	5,867	4,596	1,271	1,174	1,673	1,953	1,066	695
Median square footage	1,686	862	1,732	1,814	1,270	2,139	1,875	1,552	1,652	1,297
Lot size:										
Single detached and attached units and mobile homes	(NA)	(NA)	72,522	60,020	12,500	11,943	18,364	27,480	14,735	(NA)
Less than one-eighth acre	(NA)	(NA)	6,292	5,367	924	1,324	1,528	1,710	1,730	(NA)
One-eighth to one-quarter acre .	(NA)	(NA)	12,184	11,077	1,107	1,777	3,212	3,725	3,470	(NA)
One-quarter to one-half acre. . .	(NA)	(NA)	10,077	9,303	774	1,707	2,643	3,741	1,986	(NA)
One-half up to one acre.	(NA)	(NA)	7,394	6,656	738	1,537	1,635	3,275	947	(NA)
1 to 4 acres.	(NA)	(NA)	10,450	9,398	1,051	2,138	2,188	4,990	1,134	(NA)
5 to 9 acres.	(NA)	(NA)	1,713	1,574	139	225	477	768	244	(NA)
10 acres or more	(NA)	(NA)	3,670	3,185	485	452	1,258	1,529	431	(NA)
Other [2]	(NA)	(NA)	20,742	13,460	7,282	2,783	5,423	7,742	4,793	(NA)
Median acreage	(NA)	(NA)	0.43	0.43	0.44	0.44	0.47	0.41	0.61	(NA)

NA Not available. [1] Does not include selected vacant units. [2] Represents units not reported or size unknown.
Source: U.S. Bureau of the Census, *Current Housing Reports,* Series H150/95, *American Housing Survey in the United States.*

No. 1214. Occupied Housing Units—Tenure, by Race of Householder: 1991 to 1995

[In thousands, except percent. As of fall. Based on the American Housing Survey; see Appendix III]

RACE OF HOUSEHOLDER AND TENURE	1991	1993	1995
ALL RACES [1]			
Occupied units, total	93,147	94,724	97,693
Owner occupied.	59,796	61,252	63,544
Percent of occupied	64.2	64.7	65.0
Renter occupied	33,351	33,472	34,150
WHITE			
Occupied units, total	79,140	80,029	81,611
Owner occupied.	53,749	54,878	56,507
Percent of occupied	67.9	68.6	69.2
Renter occupied	25,391	25,151	25,104
BLACK			
Occupied units, total	10,832	11,128	11,773
Owner occupied.	4,635	4,788	5,137
Percent of occupied	42.8	43.0	43.6
Renter occupied	6,197	6,340	6,637
HISPANIC ORIGIN [2]			
Occupied units, total	6,239	6,614	7,757
Owner occupied.	2,423	2,788	3,245
Percent of occupied	38.8	42.2	41.8
Renter occupied	3,816	3,826	4,512

[1] Includes oher races, not shown separately. [2] Persons of Hispanic origin may be of any race.
Source: U.S. Bureau of the Census, *Current Housing Reports,* Series H150/91, H150/93, and H150/95, *American Housing Survey in the United States.*

No. 1215. Homeownership Rates, by Age of Householder and Family Status: 1985 to 1997

[**In percent**. Represents the proportion of owner households to the total number of occupied households. Based on the Current Population Survey/Housing Vacancy Survey; see source for details]

AGE OF HOUSEHOLDER AND FAMILY STATUS	1985	1989	1990	1991	1992	1993 [1]	1994	1995	1996	1997
United States	**63.9**	**63.9**	**63.9**	**64.1**	**64.1**	**64.0**	**64.0**	**64.7**	**65.4**	**65.7**
AGE OF HOUSEHOLDER										
Less than 25 years old.	17.2	16.6	15.7	15.3	14.9	14.8	14.9	15.9	18.0	17.7
25 to 29 years old.	37.7	35.3	35.2	33.8	33.6	33.6	34.1	34.4	34.7	35.0
30 to 34 years old.	54.0	53.2	51.8	51.2	50.5	50.8	50.6	53.1	53.0	52.6
35 to 39 years old.	65.4	63.4	63.0	62.2	61.4	61.8	61.2	62.1	62.1	62.6
40 to 44 years old.	71.4	70.2	69.8	69.5	69.1	68.6	68.2	68.6	69.0	69.7
45 to 49 years old.	74.3	74.1	73.9	73.7	74.2	73.7	73.8	73.7	74.4	74.2
50 to 54 years old.	77.5	77.2	76.8	76.1	76.2	77.2	76.8	77.0	77.2	77.7
55 to 59 years old.	79.2	79.1	78.8	79.5	79.3	78.9	78.4	78.8	79.4	79.7
60 to 64 years old.	79.9	80.1	79.8	80.5	81.2	80.9	80.1	80.3	80.7	80.5
65 to 69 years old.	79.5	80.0	80.0	81.4	80.8	80.7	80.6	81.0	82.4	81.9
70 to 74 years old.	76.8	77.8	78.4	78.8	79.0	79.9	80.1	80.9	81.4	82.0
75 years old and over	69.8	71.2	72.3	73.1	73.3	73.4	73.5	74.6	75.3	75.8
Less than 35 years old.	39.9	39.1	38.5	37.8	37.6	37.3	37.3	38.6	39.1	38.7
35 to 44 years old.	68.1	66.6	66.3	65.8	65.1	65.1	64.5	65.2	65.5	66.1
45 to 54 years old.	75.9	75.5	75.2	74.8	75.1	75.3	75.2	75.2	75.6	75.8
55 to 64 years old.	79.5	79.6	79.3	80.0	80.2	79.9	79.3	79.5	80.0	80.1
65 years and over.	74.8	75.8	76.3	77.2	77.1	77.3	77.4	78.1	78.9	79.1
FAMILY STATUS										
Family households:										
Married-couple families.	78.2	78.3	78.1	78.5	78.7	78.7	78.8	79.6	80.2	80.8
Male householder, no spouse present.	57.8	55.7	55.2	54.3	53.6	53.7	52.8	55.3	55.5	54.0
Female householder, no spouse present.	45.8	44.1	44.0	43.9	43.6	43.9	44.2	45.1	46.1	46.1
Nonfamily households:										
One-person	45.8	48.2	49.0	49.4	49.8	49.8	49.8	50.5	51.4	51.8
Male householder.	38.8	41.8	42.4	43.1	43.5	42.8	43.1	43.8	44.9	45.2
Female householder.	51.3	52.6	53.6	53.8	54.1	54.6	54.5	55.4	56.0	56.7
Other:										
Male householder.	30.1	31.5	31.7	31.8	32.4	32.6	33.6	34.2	35.5	35.9
Female householder	30.6	30.8	32.5	33.8	34.0	35.0	34.3	33.0	35.9	39.5

[1] Based on 1990 census controls.

Source: Bureau of the Census, <http://www.census.gov/ftp/pub/hhes/www/hvs.html> (accessed 21 August 1998)

No. 1216. Homeownership Rates, by State: 1985 to 1997

[**In percent**. See headnote, Table 1215]

STATE	1985	1990	1994	1995	1996	1997	STATE	1985	1990	1994	1995	1996	1997
United States	**63.9**	**63.9**	**64.0**	**64.7**	**65.4**	**65.7**	Missouri	69.2	64.0	68.4	69.4	70.2	70.5
Alabama	70.4	68.4	68.5	70.1	71.0	71.3	Montana	66.5	69.1	68.8	68.7	68.6	67.5
Alaska	61.2	58.4	58.8	60.9	62.9	67.2	Nebraska	68.5	67.3	68.0	67.1	66.8	66.7
Arizona	64.7	64.5	67.7	62.9	62.0	63.0	Nevada	57.0	55.8	55.8	58.6	61.1	61.2
Arkansas.	66.6	67.8	68.1	67.2	66.6	66.7	New Hampshire . . .	65.5	65.0	65.1	66.0	65.0	66.8
California.	54.2	53.8	55.5	55.4	55.0	55.7	New Jersey	62.3	65.0	64.1	64.9	64.6	63.1
Colorado	63.6	59.0	62.9	64.6	64.5	64.1	New Mexico	68.2	68.6	66.8	67.0	67.1	69.6
Connecticut	69.0	67.9	63.8	68.2	69.0	68.1	New York	50.3	53.3	52.5	52.7	52.7	52.6
Delaware.	70.3	67.7	70.5	71.7	71.5	69.2	North Carolina	68.0	69.0	68.7	70.1	70.4	70.2
Dist of Columbia. . .	37.4	36.4	37.8	39.2	40.4	42.5	North Dakota	69.9	67.2	63.3	67.3	68.2	68.1
Florida	67.2	65.1	65.7	66.6	67.1	66.9	Ohio	67.9	68.7	67.4	67.9	69.2	69.0
Georgia	62.7	64.3	63.4	66.6	69.3	70.9	Oklahoma	70.5	70.3	68.5	69.8	68.4	68.5
Hawaii	51.0	55.5	52.3	50.2	50.6	50.2	Oregon	61.5	64.4	63.9	63.2	63.1	61.0
Idaho	71.0	69.4	70.7	72.0	71.4	72.3	Pennsylvania	71.6	73.8	71.8	71.5	71.7	73.3
Illinois.	60.6	63.0	64.2	66.4	68.2	68.1	Rhode Island	61.4	58.5	56.5	57.9	56.6	58.7
Indiana	67.6	67.0	68.4	71.0	74.2	74.1	South Carolina	72.0	71.4	72.0	71.3	72.9	74.1
Iowa	69.9	70.7	70.1	71.4	72.8	72.7	South Dakota	67.6	66.2	66.4	67.5	67.8	67.6
Kansas	68.3	69.0	69.0	67.5	67.5	66.5	Tennessee.	67.6	68.3	65.2	67.0	68.8	70.2
Kentucky	68.5	65.8	70.6	71.2	73.2	75.0	Texas	60.5	59.7	59.7	61.4	61.8	61.5
Louisiana	70.2	67.8	65.8	65.3	64.9	66.4	Utah	71.5	70.1	69.3	71.5	72.7	72.5
Maine.	73.7	74.2	72.6	76.7	76.5	74.9	Vermont	69.5	72.6	69.4	70.4	70.3	69.1
Maryland.	65.6	64.9	64.1	65.8	66.9	70.5	Virginia	68.5	69.8	69.3	68.1	68.5	68.4
Massachusetts	60.5	58.6	60.6	60.2	61.7	62.3	Washington	66.8	61.8	62.4	61.6	63.1	62.9
Michigan	70.7	72.3	72.0	72.2	73.3	73.3	West Virginia	75.9	72.0	73.7	73.1	74.3	74.6
Minnesota	70.0	68.0	68.9	73.3	75.4	75.4	Wisconsin	63.8	68.3	64.2	67.5	68.2	68.3
Mississippi.	69.6	69.4	69.2	71.1	73.0	73.7	Wyoming	73.2	68.9	65.8	69.0	68.0	67.6

Source: U.S. Bureau of the Census, Internet site <http://www.census.gov/ftp/pub/hhes/www/hvs.html>

No. 1217. Occupied Housing Units—Costs, by Region: 1995

[As of fall. Specified owner-occupied units are limited to one-unit structures on less than 10 acres and no business on property. Specified renter-occupied units exclude one-unit structures on 10 acres or more. See headnote Table 1218 for an explanation of housing costs. For composition of regions, see map, inside front cover. Based on the American Housing Survey; see Appendix III]

CATEGORY	NUMBER (1,000)					PERCENT DISTRIBUTION				
	Total units	North-east	Mid-west	South	West	Total units	North-east	Mid-west	South	West
OWNER OCCUPIED UNITS										
Total	63,544	11,861	16,567	22,959	12,157	100.0	100.0	100.0	100.0	100.0
Monthly housing costs:										
Less than $300	17,027	1,694	4,633	8,008	2,692	26.8	14.3	27.9	34.9	22.1
$300 to $399	6,360	1,341	1,838	2,144	1,036	10.0	11.3	11.1	9.4	8.5
$400 to $499	5,268	1,143	1,594	1,801	730	8.3	9.6	9.6	7.8	6.0
$500 to $599	4,921	914	1,452	1,811	744	7.7	7.7	8.8	7.9	6.1
$600 to $699	4,356	838	1,267	1,572	679	6.9	7.1	7.6	6.8	5.6
$700 to $799	4,142	751	1,180	1,459	753	6.5	6.3	7.1	6.4	6.2
$800 to $999	6,684	1,373	1,717	2,337	1,257	10.5	11.6	10.4	10.2	10.3
$1,000 to $1,249	5,477	1,253	1,293	1,650	1,280	8.6	10.6	7.8	7.2	10.5
$1,250 to $1,499	3,518	939	685	848	1,047	5.5	7.9	4.1	3.7	8.6
$1,500 or more	5,791	1,616	908	1,328	1,939	9.1	13.6	5.5	5.8	15.9
Median (dol.) [1]	563	700	515	474	726	(X)	(X)	(X)	(X)	(X)
RENTER OCCUPIED UNITS										
Total	34,150	7,338	7,096	11,277	8,439	100.0	100.0	100.0	100.0	100.0
Monthly housing costs:										
Less than $300	4,815	1,003	1,318	1,766	729	14.1	13.7	18.6	15.7	8.6
$300 to $399	4,285	669	1,265	1,722	629	12.5	9.1	17.8	15.3	7.5
$400 to $499	5,645	956	1,455	2,029	1,206	16.5	13.0	20.5	18.0	14.3
$500 to $599	5,076	1,106	1,070	1,609	1,292	14.9	15.1	15.1	14.3	15.3
$600 to $699	4,188	1,024	730	1,199	1,235	12.3	14.0	10.3	10.6	14.6
$700 to $799	2,910	726	372	846	966	8.5	9.9	5.2	7.5	11.4
$800 to $999	2,856	788	292	694	1,081	8.4	10.7	4.1	6.2	12.8
$1,000 to $1,249	1,244	380	97	239	528	3.6	5.2	1.4	2.1	6.3
$1,250 to $1,499	420	122	25	88	185	1.2	1.7	0.4	0.8	2.2
$1,500 or more	365	114	30	68	152	1.1	1.6	0.4	0.6	1.8
No cash rent	2,344	451	442	1,017	435	6.9	6.1	6.2	9.0	5.2
Median (dol.) [1]	523	574	451	479	612	(X)	(X)	(X)	(X)	(X)

X Not applicable.   [1] For explanation of median, see Guide to Tabular Presentation.

No. 1218. Occupied Housing Units—Financial Summary, by Selected Characteristics of the Householder: 1995

[In thousands of units, except as indicated. As of fall. Housing costs include real estate taxes, property insurance, utilities, fuel, water, garbage collection, and mortgage. Based on the American Housing Survey; see Appendix III]

CHARACTERISTIC	Total occupied units	TENURE		BLACK		HISPANIC ORIGIN [1]		ELDERLY [2]		HOUSEHOLDS BELOW POVERTY LEVEL	
		Owner	Renter	Owner	Renter	Owner	Renter	Owner	Renter	Owner	Renter
Total units [3]	97,693	63,544	34,150	5,137	6,637	3,245	4,512	16,299	4,542	6,034	8,661
Monthly housing costs:											
Less than $300	21,844	17,027	4,815	1,721	1,423	883	549	8,833	1,364	3,015	2,682
$300-$399	10,644	6,360	4,285	555	1,004	287	529	2,560	558	710	1,305
$400-$499	10,913	5,268	5,645	444	1,182	249	762	1,479	583	510	1,345
$500-$599	9,997	4,921	5,076	430	928	227	797	947	485	389	904
$600-$699	8,544	4,356	4,188	381	698	219	652	585	389	258	621
$700-$799	7,052	4,142	2,910	323	409	209	388	455	240	227	420
$800-$999	9,540	6,684	2,856	496	417	296	369	582	245	282	309
$1,000 or more	16,815	14,786	2,029	786	167	877	201	855	196	644	166
Median amount (dol.) [4]	543	563	523	465	459	590	535	282	418	300	391
Monthly housing costs as percent of income: [5]											
Less than 5 percent	3,036	2,845	191	174	16	104	19	669	14	17	15
5 to 9 percent	10,508	9,570	938	677	121	455	88	2,749	67	88	55
10 to 14 percent	14,002	11,260	2,741	827	446	444	216	3,222	129	223	116
15 to 19 percent	14,673	10,637	4,035	755	727	470	424	2,382	192	296	194
20 to 24 percent	12,318	8,174	4,144	668	796	397	482	1,724	381	348	297
25 to 29 percent	9,519	5,523	3,996	405	758	293	517	1,196	556	319	578
30 to 34 percent	6,514	3,586	2,928	298	540	205	410	866	485	338	472
35 to 39 percent	4,703	2,402	2,301	227	421	164	370	662	325	262	418
40 percent or more	18,234	8,377	9,857	964	2,219	649	1,639	2,515	1,826	3,007	4,999
Median amount (percent) . . .	22	19	29	20	31	21	34	18	38	52	62
Median monthly costs (dol.): [4]											
Electricity	63	69	48	71	52	64	44	59	40	62	46
Piped gas	38	42	29	46	35	29	25	41	26	38	30
Fuel oil	59	61	52	57	54	60	43	61	54	53	52

[1] Persons of Hispanic origin may be of any race.   [2] Householders 65 years old and over.   [3] Includes units with mortgage payment not reported and no cash rent not shown separately.   [4] For explanation of median, see Guide to Tabular Presentation.   [5] Money income before taxes.

Source of Tables 1217 and 1218: U.S. Bureau of the Census, *Current Housing Reports*, Series H-150/95RV, *American Housing Survey in the United States (Revised)*. Internet site <http://www.census.gov/prod/2/constr/h150/h15095rv.pdf> (accessed 25 August 1997).

No. 1219. Owner Occupied Housing Units—Mortgage Characteristics, by Region: 1995

[As of fall. Based on the American Housing Survey; see Appendix III. For composition of regions, see map, inside front cover]

CHARACTERISTIC	NUMBER (1,000)					PERCENT DISTRIBUTION				
	Total units	North-east	Mid-west	South	West	Total units	North-east	Mid-west	South	West
ALL OWNERS										
Total units	63,544	11,861	16,567	22,959	12,157	100.0	100.0	100.0	100.0	100.0
Mortgages currently on property:										
None, owned free and clear. . . .	24,518	4,607	6,479	9,666	3,765	38.6	38.8	39.1	42.1	31.0
Mortgaged	39,026	7,254	10,088	13,292	8,392	61.4	61.2	60.9	57.9	69.0
One mortgage or land contract.	34,730	6,326	8,913	12,183	7,307	54.7	53.3	53.8	53.1	60.1
Two mortgages	4,244	914	1,167	1,102	1,062	6.7	7.7	7.0	4.8	8.7
Three mortgages or more . . .	52	14	7	7	23	0.1	0.1	0.0	0.0	0.2
OWNERS WITH MORTGAGES										
Total units	39,026	7,254	10,088	13,292	8,392	100.0	100.0	100.0	100.0	100.0
Type of primary mortgage:										
FHA	5,172	514	1,182	2,252	1,225	13.3	7.1	11.7	16.9	14.6
VA	2,356	170	467	1,086	632	6.0	2.3	4.6	8.2	7.5
Farmers Home Administration [1] .	381	47	114	158	62	1.0	0.6	1.1	1.2	0.7
Other types.	27,906	5,732	7,793	8,583	5,798	71.5	79.0	77.3	64.6	69.1
Don't know	1,336	265	202	585	284	3.4	3.7	2.0	4.4	3.4
Not reported	1,875	527	330	628	390	4.8	7.3	3.3	4.7	4.6
Payment plan of primary mortgage:										
Fixed payment, self amortizing . .	30,002	5,392	7,925	10,519	6,166	76.9	74.3	78.6	79.1	73.5
Adjustable rate mortgage	4,473	900	1,116	1,233	1,224	11.5	12.4	11.1	9.3	14.6
Graduated payment mortgage . .	370	67	79	114	109	0.9	0.9	0.8	0.9	1.3
Balloon	586	53	244	178	112	1.5	0.7	2.4	1.3	1.3
Other.	567	102	144	200	121	1.5	1.4	1.4	1.5	1.4
Combination	336	71	93	103	69	0.9	1.0	0.9	0.8	0.8
Not reported	2,691	669	486	946	590	6.9	9.2	4.8	7.1	7.0
Home equity loan:										
With a home equity loan	8,474	1,771	2,271	2,384	2,048	21.7	24.4	22.5	17.9	24.4
No home equity loan	27,696	4,906	7,243	9,776	5,770	71.0	67.6	71.8	73.5	68.8
Not reported	2,857	576	574	1,132	574	7.3	7.9	5.7	8.5	6.8

[1] Due to a reorganization, now the Rural Housing Service handles these mortgage functions.

Source: U.S. Bureau of the Census, *Current Housing Reports*, series H-150/95, *American Housing Survey in the United States*.

No. 1220. Debt Status of Homeowners, by Selected Characteristic: 1997

[In percent. See headnote, Table 817]

HOMEOWNER CHARACTERISTIC	All home-owners	No mortgage debt	First mortgage only [1]	Home equity line of credit	Traditional home equity loan	Either type of home equity loan
All homeowners	100	100	100	100	100	100
Age of head:						
18 to 34 years old	16	7	24	6	23	12
35 to 44 years old	23	9	31	28	32	30
45 to 54 years old	20	12	24	34	27	31
55 to 64 years old	16	18	13	20	11	17
65 years old and over	26	55	8	12	6	10
Family income:						
Less than $15,000.	10	20	4	2	2	2
$15,000 to $24,999	16	26	11	3	6	4
$25,000 to $49,999	34	32	38	25	32	27
$50,000 to $74,999	23	12	26	38	42	39
$75,000 to $99,999	10	5	13	16	8	14
$100,000 or more	8	5	8	16	11	14
Home equity [2]:						
Less than $50,000.	41	24	55	21	69	38
$50.00 to $99,999	33	38	29	40	21	34
$100,000 or more	26	37	16	39	10	28
Census region: [3]						
West.	17	14	18	18	27	21
North Central	30	29	30	33	30	32
Northeast.	17	16	17	24	24	24
South	36	42	35	25	19	23

[1] Excludes those who have only a home equity line of credit.   [2] Home equity consists of the market value of the home less all debts secured by the home, including balances outstanding on equity lines of credit and traditional home equity loans.   [3] For composition of regions, see map, inside front cover.

Source: Board of Governors of the Federal Reserve System, *Federal Reserve Bulletin*, April 1998.

No. 1221. Heating Equipment and Fuels for Occupied Units: 1991 to 1995

[**As of fall.** Based on American Housing Survey. See Appendix III]

TYPE OF EQUIPMENT OR FUEL	NUMBER (1,000)			PERCENT DISTRIBUTION		
	1991	1993	1995	1991	1993	1995
Occupied units, total	93,147	94,724	97,692	100.0	100.0	100.0
Heating equipment:						
Warm air furnace.	49,423	51,248	53,165	53.1	54.1	54.4
Heat pumps.	7,638	8,422	9,406	8.2	8.9	9.6
Steam or hot water	13,929	13,657	13,669	15.0	14.4	14.0
Floor, wall, or pipeless furnace.	4,291	4,746	4,963	4.6	5.0	5.1
Built-in electric units.	6,755	6,722	7,035	7.3	7.1	7.2
Room heaters with flue.	2,549	1,766	1,620	2.7	1.9	1.7
Room heaters without flue	2,111	1,597	1,642	2.3	1.7	1.7
Fireplaces, stoves, portable heaters or other . .	5,590	5,654	5,150	6.0	6.0	5.3
None.	861	911	1,044	0.9	1.0	1.1
House main heating fuel:						
Utility gas.	47,018	47,669	49,203	50.5	50.3	50.4
Fuel oil, kerosene, etc	12,462	12,189	12,029	13.4	12.9	12.3
Electricity	23,714	25,107	26,771	25.5	26.5	27.4
Bottled, tank, or LP gas	3,882	3,922	4,251	4.2	4.1	4.4
Coal or coke.	319	297	210	0.3	0.3	0.2
Wood and other fuel	4,890	4,630	4,186	5.2	4.9	4.3
None.	862	910	1,043	0.9	1.0	1.1
Cooking fuel:						
Electricity	54,232	55,887	57,621	58.2	59.0	59.0
Gas [1]	38,119	37,996	39,218	40.9	40.1	40.1
Other fuel	424	479	566	0.5	0.5	0.6
None.	372	362	287	0.4	0.4	0.3

[1] Includes utility, bottled, tank, and LP gas.

Source: U.S. Bureau of the Census, *Current Housing Reports,* series H150/91, H150/93, and H150/95, *American Housing Survey in the United States.*

No. 1222. Occupied Housing Units—Housing Indicators, by Selected Characteristics of the Householder: 1995

[**In thousands of units. As of fall.** Based on the American Housing Survey. See Appendix III]

CHARACTERISTIC	Total occupied units	TENURE		BLACK		HISPANIC ORIGIN [1]		ELDERLY [2]		HOUSEHOLDS BELOW POVERTY LEVEL	
		Owner	Renter	Owner	Renter	Owner	Renter	Owner	Renter	Owner	Renter
Total units	97,693	63,544	34,150	5,137	6,637	3,245	4,512	16,299	4,542	6,034	8,661
Amenities:											
Porch, deck, balcony or patio .	75,657	54,319	21,338	4,052	3,873	2,597	2,408	13,572	2,492	4,804	4,841
Usable fireplace	31,734	27,280	4,454	1,438	554	992	430	5,611	354	1,661	596
Separate dining room	46,657	36,374	10,283	2,934	2,074	1,652	1,155	8,293	1,028	2,800	2,140
With 2 or more living rooms or recreation rooms	28,941	26,179	2,762	1,659	355	925	197	5,680	277	1,578	428
Garage or carport with home .	57,352	46,906	10,446	2,804	1,171	2,326	1,363	12,268	1,190	3,598	1,880
Cars and trucks available:											
No cars, trucks, or vans.	9,583	2,491	7,092	538	2,375	125	1,202	1,745	2,100	881	3,565
Other households without cars	7,006	4,669	2,337	201	165	347	355	758	108	549	444
1 car with or without trucks or vans.	48,263	30,648	17,615	2,399	3,176	1,464	2,100	9,870	2,074	3,180	3,869
2 cars.	26,149	19,986	6,163	1,544	819	996	721	3,397	228	1,147	678
3 or more cars	6,692	5,750	942	455	102	314	133	529	33	276	106
With cars, no trucks or vans . .	52,068	32,256	19,812	3,093	3,702	1,557	2,282	9,950	2,153	3,035	4,092
1 truck or van with or without cars	28,423	22,304	6,119	1,276	523	1,168	875	3,848	269	1,650	880
2 or more trucks or vans	7,619	6,493	1,126	230	37	396	153	756	20	467	125
Internal deficiencies:											
Signs of rats in last 3 months .	2,708	1,219	1,489	230	555	193	463	263	132	235	637
Holes in floors	1,074	503	571	106	177	71	125	84	36	126	222
Open cracks or holes	4,527	1,943	2,584	356	750	168	426	347	176	346	921
Broken plaster or peeling paint (interior of unit)	3,673	1,672	2,002	273	584	145	333	375	167	304	729
No electrical wiring	26	22	4	-	-	-	-	3	2	15	-
Exposed wiring	1,760	873	887	88	240	80	175	260	105	104	306
Rooms without electric outlet .	1,816	891	925	130	269	44	147	276	98	187	353
Water leakage [3]	11,411	6,325	5,086	641	1,197	354	662	1,067	443	616	1,434

- Represents zero.   [1] Persons of Hispanic origin may be of any race.   [2] Householders 65 years old and over.   [3] During the 12 months prior to the survey.

Source: U.S. Bureau of the Census, *Current Housing Reports,* series H150/95, *American Housing Survey in the United States.*

No. 1223. Appliances and Office Equipment Used by Households, by Region and Family Income: 1997

[Preliminary. Represents appliances possessed and generally used by the household. Based on Residential Energy Consumption Survey; see source. For composition of regions, see inside front cover]

TYPE OF APPLIANCE	House-holds using appli-ance	REGION				FAMILY INCOME IN 1997			
		North-east	Midwest	South	West	Under $10,000	$10,000 -$24,999	$25,000 -$49,999	$50,000 and over
Total households (mil.)	101.5	19.7	24.1	35.9	21.8	13.3	29.1	31.1	27.9
PERCENT WITH—									
Air conditioner:									
Central system	47.1	22.3	51.4	69.7	27.6	27.7	37.7	50.7	62.2
Room	26.1	41.4	27.4	24.3	13.9	33.9	29.8	25.4	19.2
Clothes washer	77.4	76.0	78.9	81.9	69.6	52.7	69.0	81.5	93.4
Clothes dryer [1]	71.1	66.7	75.7	74.2	65.1	36.2	61.0	77.1	91.8
Electric	55.0	48.2	50.1	66.3	48.2	31.0	49.0	59.9	67.5
Natural gas	15.3	17.9	23.9	7.4	16.6	4.8	11.1	16.4	23.6
Dishwasher	50.2	48.5	46.9	51.5	53.1	15.7	35.5	53.6	78.2
Ceiling fan	60.1	51.3	63.6	71.2	46.0	39.3	55.2	64.4	70.3
Freezer	33.2	25.7	41.8	36.9	24.2	25.7	30.0	35.1	37.9
1	30.2	24.2	38.4	33.1	22.0	23.6	27.5	32.2	34.1
2 or more	2.9	1.5	3.4	3.8	2.2	2.0	2.5	2.9	3.8
Microwave oven	83.0	78.7	86.9	82.4	83.3	60.3	81.1	86.7	91.5
Oven	98.8	99.3	99.1	98.6	98.2	96.4	98.7	99.4	99.3
Electric	61.5	49.7	56.6	72.0	60.1	49.2	58.7	63.9	67.5
Natural gas	33.2	44.8	38.1	22.1	35.7	41.8	34.8	31.5	29.5
Self cleaning oven	44.0	48.5	45.0	41.8	42.7	18.1	31.1	47.0	66.6
Range	99.2	99.6	99.4	99.0	98.8	96.8	99.1	99.6	99.6
Electric	60.3	48.8	55.6	70.9	58.4	49.2	58.4	62.9	64.6
Natural gas	34.6	45.5	39.4	23.5	37.7	42.0	35.5	32.8	32.1
Refrigerator	99.9	99.9	99.9	99.9	99.7	99.3	99.9	99.9	100.0
Frost free	86.8	85.2	85.1	90.0	84.7	73.0	83.1	88.5	95.2
Water heater [1]	100.0	100.0	100.0	100.0	100.0	100.0	100.0	100.0	100.0
Electric	39.5	26.5	27.6	58.3	33.3	41.9	43.9	39.9	33.1
Natural gas	51.7	46.8	66.4	37.4	63.2	46.3	48.0	51.7	58.0
Stereo equipment	68.8	66.7	67.0	67.8	74.4	45.2	60.1	73.7	83.7
Color TV	98.7	98.8	99.0	98.7	98.2	96.1	98.4	99.2	99.6
1	31.9	31.8	32.1	29.1	36.1	55.6	40.5	27.3	16.6
2	37.4	36.1	36.2	38.9	37.2	30.9	37.7	41.6	35.4
3	19.1	20.8	20.4	18.4	17.3	7.5	15.5	20.4	26.8
4	7.6	7.5	7.8	8.9	5.5	1.7	3.6	8.2	14.0
5 or more	2.8	2.6	2.5	3.4	2.2	(S)	1.1	1.7	6.8
VCR	87.6	86.1	89.7	86.0	89.0	66.8	84.0	91.6	96.6
Personal computers	35.0	31.9	38.0	31.0	41.3	9.7	16.5	36.9	64.5
1	29.2	27.2	32.4	25.9	32.8	7.9	14.5	32.8	50.6
2 or more	5.9	4.7	5.6	5.1	8.5	(S)	2.0	4.1	13.8
With modem	20.4	17.8	21.7	18.2	24.9	5.2	8.6	19.7	40.7
With laser printer	12.4	11.3	12.9	11.7	14.2	2.5	4.4	12.8	25.1
Used 15 hrs. per week or less	25.2	21.5	27.7	23.0	29.2	6.3	12.2	28.2	44.4
Used 16 hrs. per week or more . . .	9.9	10.4	10.2	8.0	12.1	3.4	4.2	8.7	20.0
Personal use only	4.7	4.5	5.2	4.2	5.3	2.3	2.3	4.1	9.1
Business use only	2.1	2.3	2.5	1.1	3.1	(S)	(S)	1.4	5.0
Both	3.1	3.6	2.6	2.7	3.7	(S)	1.2	3.3	6.0
Cordless phone	61.4	59.6	63.8	61.4	60.2	35.3	51.5	66.9	77.9
Facsimile machine	6.2	6.5	5.3	5.6	8.1	(S)	2.5	5.3	13.3
Photocopier	3.7	3.8	3.9	3.5	3.9	(S)	1.5	3.9	7.3
Answering machine	58.4	62.2	61.0	54.2	59.1	30.2	49.1	62.3	77.2

S Figure does not meet publication standards.   [1] Includes other types, not shown separately.
Source: U.S. Energy Information Administration, Internet site <http://www.eia.doe/emeu/consumption> (accessed 20 May 1998).

No. 1224. Net Stock of Residential Capital: 1985 to 1996

[In billions of dollars. End of year estimates]

ITEM	1985	1987	1988	1989	1990	1991	1992	1993	1994	1995	1996
Total residential capital [1] .	4,683.3	5,386.5	5,737.1	6,054.7	6,295.7	6,407.8	6,749.5	7,152.5	7,643.5	7,965.6	8,362.5
By type of owner and legal form of organization:											
Private	4,578.2	5,267.7	5,602.7	5,911.1	6,147.3	6,258.5	6,591.4	6,983.1	7,465.8	7,778.5	8,171.2
Corporate	55.6	62.6	65.3	67.1	68.6	69.4	72.3	74.0	76.1	78.4	81.9
Noncorporate	4,522.6	5,205.0	5,537.4	5,844.0	6,078.7	6,189.1	6,519.1	6,909.2	7,389.6	7,700.2	8,089.3
Government	105.1	118.9	134.4	143.6	148.4	149.3	158.2	169.4	177.7	187.1	191.3
Federal	32.0	35.4	46.2	50.3	51.4	50.1	52.9	56.1	58.7	61.5	61.4
State and local	73.1	83.4	88.3	93.3	97.0	99.2	105.3	113.3	119.1	125.6	129.9
By tenure group:											
Owner-occupied	3,254.0	3,774.7	4,043.9	4,298.3	4,494.3	4,597.9	4,870.7	5,211.9	5,629.7	5,899.0	6,224.1
Farm	128.6	138.4	142.5	146.9	151.2	152.0	156.8	162.2	170.7	175.0	179.6
Nonfarm	3,125.3	3,636.3	3,901.4	4,151.4	4,343.1	4,445.9	4,713.9	5,049.6	5,459.0	5,724.0	6,044.6
Tenant-occupied	1,302.3	1,469.1	1,534.0	1,587.1	1,626.7	1,634.7	1,694.1	1,743.4	1,807.1	1,850.2	1,917.2
Farm	5.6	6.1	6.3	6.4	6.7	6.7	6.9	7.3	7.8	8.0	8.2
Nonfarm	1,296.7	1,463.0	1,527.7	1,580.7	1,620.1	1,628.0	1,687.2	1,736.2	1,799.3	1,842.2	1,909.0

[1] Includes stocks of other nonfarm residential capital, which consists of dormitories, fraternity and sorority houses, and nurses' homes.
Source: U.S. Bureau of Economic Analysis, Survey of Current Business, monthly, September 1997 issue.

No. 1225. Expenditures by Residential Property Owners for Improvements and Maintenance and Repairs, by Type of Property and Activity: 1980 to 1996

[In millions of dollars]

YEAR AND TYPE OF EXPENDITURE	Total	1-unit properties with owner occupant	Other properties	ADDITIONS AND ALTERATIONS					Major replacements	Mainternance and repairs
				Total	To structures			To property outside of structures		
					Additions	Alterations				
1980	46,338	31,481	14,857	21,336	4,183	11,193		5,960	9,816	15,187
1982	45,291	29,779	15,512	18,774	2,641	10,711		5,423	9,707	16,810
1983	49,295	32,524	16,771	20,271	4,739	11,673		3,859	10,895	18,128
1984	69,784	43,781	26,003	27,822	6,007	14,486		7,329	13,067	28,894
1985	80,267	47,742	32,525	28,775	3,966	17,599		7,211	16,134	35,358
1986	91,274	54,298	36,976	38,608	7,377	21,192		10,040	16,695	35,971
1987	94,082	54,791	39,291	39,978	9,557	21,641		8,779	15,875	38,229
1988	101,117	60,822	40,295	43,339	11,333	22,703		9,303	16,893	40,885
1989	100,891	59,858	41,033	39,786	6,828	23,129		9,828	18,415	42,689
1990	106,773	59,683	47,090	37,253	8,561	21,920		6,771	18,215	51,305
1991	97,528	58,083	39,445	30,944	7,914	16,076		6,954	16,744	49,840
1992	103,734	67,316	36,418	40,186	6,783	22,700		10,704	18,393	45,154
1993	108,305	70,746	37,559	45,797	12,757	24,781		8,259	20,809	41,699
1994	115,030	77,270	37,760	48,828	9,647	28,672		10,509	23,248	42,953
1995, total [1]	**111,683**	**75,362**	**36,321**	**44,726**	**7,936**	**26,893**		**9,897**	**24,910**	**42,047**
Heating and air conditioning [2]	10,151	7,480	2,671	1,872	(NA)	1,872		(NA)	5,639	2,640
Plumbing	9,489	5,145	4,344	2,354	(NA)	2,354		(NA)	3,053	4,082
Roofing	10,415	6,972	3,443	(NA)	(NA)	(NA)		(NA)	6,280	4,135
Painting	10,910	6,169	4,741	(NA)	(NA)	(NA)		(NA)	(NA)	10,910
1996, total [1]	**114,919**	**76,094**	**38,825**	**53,456**	**12,035**	**30,064**		**11,357**	**24,465**	**36,997**
Heating and air conditioning [2]	10,315	7,028	3,287	2,637	(NA)	2,637		(NA)	4,741	2,937
Plumbing	7,884	4,398	3,486	1,892	(NA)	1,892		(NA)	2,239	3,753
Roofing	9,964	6,435	3,529	(NA)	(NA)	(NA)		(NA)	6,809	3,155
Painting	12,126	6,658	5,474	(NA)	(NA)	(NA)		(NA)	(NA)	12,126

NA Not available.   [1] Includes types of expenditures not separately specified.   [2] Central air-conditioning.

Source: U.S. Bureau of the Census, *Current Construction Reports*, series C50, *Expenditures for Resiential Improvement*, quarterly.

No. 1226. Properties, by Type of Owner: 1995

[In thousands. For privately owned rental properties. Based on the Property Owners and Managers Survey and subject to sampling error; see source for details]

CHARACTERISTIC	SINGLE FAMILY PROPERTIES		MULTI FAMILY PROPERTIES						
	Total	Detached	Total	2 units	3 to 4 units	5 to 9 units	10 to 19 units	20 to 49 units	50 units or more
All properties [1]	**8,773**	**6,438**	**20,585**	**3,085**	**2,471**	**1,894**	**1,468**	**2,224**	**9,443**
With individual or partnership owners [2]	7,746	5,752	16,915	2,953	2,347	1,713	1,236	1,858	6,808
Under 25 years old	-	-	14	5	3	-	3	-	3
25 to 34 years old	218	118	490	155	130	68	24	44	69
35 to 44 years old	1,146	823	1,514	475	281	232	114	122	289
45 to 54 years old	1,663	1,237	2,808	670	496	372	184	341	744
55 to 64 years old	1,747	1,336	2,698	561	494	337	218	373	716
65 to 74 years old	1,425	1,093	1,995	428	349	232	167	201	618
75 years or older	891	713	958	270	200	94	109	65	221
Male	5,130	3,814	9,584	1,866	1,540	1,103	768	1,181	3,125
Female	2,316	1,744	2,261	838	545	347	150	174	206
White	6,307	4,654	10,400	2,264	1,731	1,270	825	1,234	3,077
Black	595	499	599	241	197	79	17	14	51
American Indian or Alaskan Native	41	30	22	4	8	3	-	-	7
Asian or Pacific Islander	254	192	442	90	79	53	50	63	107
Other	174	127	217	56	49	32	7	30	43
Hispanic	436	322	479	135	126	80	27	59	52
Non-Hispanic	6,719	5,017	11,104	2,492	1,925	1,334	864	1,276	3,213
Percent of rental income spent on maintenance:									
None	1,261	1,020	283	185	27	27	7	-	36
1 to 4 percent	1,426	1,022	1,530	407	280	141	105	122	475
5 to 9 percent	1,429	1,057	2,844	513	385	275	230	338	1,103
10 to 19 percent	1,741	1,303	4,446	784	658	400	380	431	1,793
20 to 29 percent	764	516	2,287	317	283	256	145	263	1,023
30 to 39 percent	316	211	1,270	158	118	103	58	162	671
40 to 49 percent	182	114	751	78	35	95	83	89	370
50 to 74 percent	231	174	935	73	128	73	65	130	466
75 percent or more	300	219	639	132	123	78	26	91	190

- Represents zero.   [1] Includes properties with other owners not shown separately.   [2] Includes properties with owners not reporting.

Source: U.S. Bureau of the Census, Internet site <http://www.census.gov/hhes/www/poms.html> (accessed 23 April 1997).

No. 1227. Commercial Office Space—Overview for Selected Market Areas: 1997

[As of **mid-October.** For the 75 market areas with the highest vacancy rates in 1997. Data based on responses from individuals knowledgeable in the local markets]

MARKET AREA	Inventory (1,000 sq. ft.)	Vacant space (1,000 sq. ft.)	Vacancy rate (percent)	Construction (1,000 sq. ft.)	Net absorption [1] (1,000 sq. ft.)
United States, all market areas [2]	3,477,314	334,139	9.6	57,647	93,123
Albany, NY	13,987	1,268	9.1	268	310
Albuquerque, NM.	10,065	1,093	10.9	-	395
Allentown, PA	6,933	1,014	14.6	208	-208
Annapolis, MD	2,651	253	9.5	-	-81
Baltimore, MD	39,205	4,885	12.5	680	1,308
Bridgeport, CT	7,320	970	13.2	124	16
Buffalo, NY	7,853	1,166	14.8	454	191
Charleston, SC	3,635	349	9.6	-	238
Chicago, IL	108,520	11,230	10.3	-	3,104
Cleveland, OH	36,131	4,716	13.1	194	831
Colorado Springs, CO	16,168	1,399	8.7	660	638
Columbia, SC	9,955	1,200	12.0	225	43
Dallas, TX	117,009	17,521	15.0	5,257	2,983
Danbury, CT	3,662	689	18.8	300	93
Dayton, OH	11,632	1,586	13.6	-	154
Denver, CO	61,463	7,071	11.5	2,604	722
Des Moines, IA	8,494	902	10.6	150	-256
El Paso, TX	6,586	774	11.8	(NA)	134
Fort Lauderdale, FL	14,669	1,307	8.9	226	912
Fort Worth, TX	18,312	2,114	11.5	75	315
Fresno, CA	12,771	1,189	9.3	41	310
Greensboro, NC	13,408	1,455	10.9	501	610
Greenville, SC	4,497	542	12.1	251	359
Hartford, CT	22,325	4,900	21.9	-	(NA)
Honolulu, HI	14,939	2,166	14.5	-	243
Houston, TX	108,069	10,372	9.6	290	6,500
Indianapolis, IN	18,836	2,212	11.7	832	-361
Knoxville, TN	9,715	950	9.8	-	135
Las Vegas, NV	11,733	1,199	10.2	940	1,259
Little Rock, AR	10,267	1,043	10.2	75	126
Los Angeles-Central, CA	29,431	5,841	19.8	-	980
Los Angeles-East, CA	2,700	324	12.0	-	81
Los Angeles-Inland Empire, CA.	6,285	1,241	19.7	51	259
Los Angeles-Orange County, CA.	54,212	5,819	10.7	-	1,593
Los Angeles-San Fernando Valley, CA. . . .	31,040	3,725	12.0	520	314
Los Angeles-South Bay, CA	29,707	6,491	21.9	-	1,278
Los Angeles-Ventura County, CA.	8,526	1,285	15.1	105	75
Los Angeles-West, CA	57,000	6,000	10.5	1,500	(NA)
Louisville, KY	14,026	1,995	14.2	270	140
Medford, OR	5,574	482	8.7	129	153
Melbourne, FL	4,132	602	14.6	31	320
Miami, FL	27,726	2,855	10.3	630	1,058
Milwaukee, WI	25,353	2,782	11.0	(NA)	627
Mobile, AL	3,150	417	13.2	(NA)	161
Nashua, NH	1,891	171	9.0	-	121
New Haven, CT	12,100	2,605	21.5	-	360
New Jersey-Central	52,421	5,370	10.2	650	1,679
New Jersey-Northern	86,469	11,244	13.0	584	6,287
New Jersey-Southern	14,580	2,408	16.5	876	603
New Orleans, LA	17,982	3,114	17.3	(NA)	189
New York-Brooklyn/Queens, NY	67,563	6,738	10.0	(NA)	(NA)
New York-Long Island, NY	37,593	4,749	12.6	(NA)	1,368
New York-Manhattan, NY.	335,402	35,410	10.6	(NA)	9,297
New York-Westchester, NY	24,638	4,087	16.6	1,600	1,271
Norfolk, VA	15,397	1,416	9.2	-	624
Oakland, CA	26,221	3,727	14.2	-	-476
Oklahoma City, OK.	13,841	2,096	15.1	(NA)	-199
Philadelphia, PA.	84,445	9,270	11.0	1,107	3,413
Pittsburgh, PA	31,830	3,526	11.1	(NA)	455
Providence, RI.	8,869	1,330	15.0	40	507
Rochester, NY	11,505	1,269	11.0	(NA)	850
Sacramento, CA.	26,282	2,344	8.9	989	343
Saint Louis, MO.	34,047	3,182	9.3	649	1,568
San Antonio, TX	16,312	1,481	9.1	-	782
San Diego, CA.	59,468	5,513	9.3	240	1,378
Shreveport, LA	3,658	942	25.8	(NA)	-90
Sious Falls, SD	1,772	239	13.5	33	39
South Bend, IN	2,715	288	10.6	172	197
Stamford, CT	25,816	2,703	10.5	790	1,020
Syracuse, NY	9,211	1,667	18.1	-	138
Tampa, FL	21,137	1,834	8.7	(NA)	729
Toledo, OH	6,500	1,283	19.7	(NA)	-146
Tulsa, OK	14,249	1,556	10.9	-	887
Washington, DC-Suburban MD	60,850	5,294	8.7	165	1,659
Youngstown, OH	2,500	370	14.8	25	-5

- Represents zero.   NA Not available.   [1] Net change in occupied stock.   [2] Includes other market areas, not shown separately.

Source: Society of Industrial and Office REALTORS®, Washington DC, *1998 Comparative Statistics of Industrial and Office Real Estate Markets* (copyright).

No. 1228. Commercial Buildings—Selected Characteristics, by Square Footage of Floorspace: 1995

[Excludes buildings 1,000 square feet or smaller. Building type based on predominant activity in which the occupants were engaged. Based on a sample survey of buillding representatives conducted between August and December 1995; therefore, subject to sampling variability. For composition of regions, see map, inside front cover]

CHARACTERISTIC	Number of build-ings (1,000)	FLOORSPACE (mil. sq. ft.)							Mean sq. ft. per build-ing (1,000)	Median sq. ft. per building (1,000)
		Total	Within buildings having square footage of—							
			5,000 or less	5,001 to 10,000	10,001 to 25,000	25,001 to 50,000	50,001 to 100,000	100,001 and over		
All buildings.	4,579	58,772	6,338	7,530	11,617	7,676	7,968	17,643	12.8	5.0
Region:										
Northeast	725	11,883	995	1,223	2,118	1,380	1,371	4,795	16.4	5.0
Midwest	1,139	14,322	1,772	1,678	2,701	1,726	1,920	4,526	12.6	4.5
South	1,750	20,830	2,428	2,786	4,481	2,664	2,980	5,491	11.9	4.8
West	964	11,736	1,144	1,842	2,317	1,905	1,697	2,831	12.2	5.5
Year constructed:										
1919 or before	353	3,673	442	756	957	407	386	[3]340	10.4	5.5
1920 to 1945	562	6,710	855	981	1,241	595	750	2,288	11.9	4.8
1946 to 1959	867	9,298	1,180	1,710	1,942	1,260	1,293	1,913	10.7	4.3
1960 to 1969	718	10,858	889	1,132	2,163	1,650	1,453	3,572	15.1	5.5
1970 to 1979	813	11,333	1,245	1,186	2,071	1,337	1,453	4,040	13.9	5.0
1980 to 1989	846	12,252	1,087	1,102	2,809	1,701	1,816	3,737	14.5	5.0
1990 to 1992	218	2,590	316	368	251	378	410	867	11.9	3.5
1993 to 1995	202	2,059	324	296	184	349	407	[4]264	10.2	3.5
Principal activity within building:										
Education.	309	7,740	250	404	1,045	1,825	1,752	[1]2,216	25.1	8.5
Food sales	137	642	234	(S)	(S)	(S)	(S)	(NA)	4.7	2.5
Food service	285	1,353	550	390	(S)	(S)	(S)	(NA)	4.8	3.0
Health care	105	2,333	152	(S)	243	175	(S)	1,483	22.2	4.5
Lodging	158	3,618	150	269	748	512	613	[1]1,105	22.8	9.0
Mercantile/services.	1,289	12,728	1,841	2,202	2,939	1,180	1,274	3,292	9.9	4.0
Office	705	10,478	1,084	915	1,580	1,293	1,542	4,064	14.9	4.0
Public assembly	326	3,948	312	786	940	485	499	[1]655	12.1	6.0
Public order and safety	87	1,271	(S)	(S)	368	(S)	(S)	(NA)	14.6	5.0
Religious worship.	269	2,792	301	662	1,120	392	(S)	(NA)	10.4	8.0
Warehouse	580	8,481	807	991	1,530	1,165	1,147	2,841	14.6	5.5
Other.	67	1,004	(S)	(S)	(S)	(S)	(S)	(NA)	14.9	5.0
Vacant	261	2,384	399	497	503	148	225	(NA)	9.1	4.0
Government owned	553	12,076	630	924	1,546	2,023	2,211	4,741	21.8	7.0
Nongovernment owned	4,025	46,696	5,709	6,606	10,071	5,653	5,757	9,209	11.6	4.8
Fuels used alone or in combination:										
Electricity	4,358	57,275	6,008	7,064	11,310	7,641	7,925	17,326	13.1	5.0
Natural gas	2,522	38,838	3,020	4,542	7,654	5,309	5,658	12,655	15.4	5.5
Fuel oil	634	14,670	987	713	1,445	1,164	1,992	8,368	23.1	4.8
Propane	589	5,344	997	881	1,342	562	637	[1]772	9.1	4.0
District heat	115	5,941	(S)	(S)	407	673	792	3,848	51.6	12.5
District chilled water	53	2,521	(S)	(S)	239	275	348	1,576	47.7	12.5
Any other	213	2,336	278	414	413	223	419	[2]252	16.2	4.0
Workers:										
Fewer than 5	2,505	13,885	4,184	3,636	3,806	770	518	[3]415	5.5	3.0
5 to 9	798	6,291	1,202	1,608	2,090	529	567	(NA)	7.9	4.8
10 to 19	625	7,102	695	1,637	2,399	1,099	557	[3]480	11.4	7.5
20 to 49	400	9,132	225	615	2,513	2,620	2,087	[1]940	22.8	16.3
50 to 99	138	6,931	(S)	(S)	567	1,644	2,108	[1]2,325	50.3	37.5
100 to 249	71	5,988	(S)	(S)	155	913	1,472	3,431	84.4	55.0
250 or more	43	9,443	(S)	(S)	(S)	(S)	658	8,598	220.1	120.0
Weekly operating hours:										
39 or less	899	6,143	1,544	1,619	1,354	576	426	(NA)	6.8	4.0
40 to 48	1,257	13,233	1,701	2,033	3,382	1,981	1,776	[1]2,144	10.5	4.8
49 to 60	969	12,242	1,264	1,707	2,562	2,103	1,897	2,709	12.6	5.5
61 to 84	567	10,052	653	1,020	1,873	1,182	1,354	3,970	17.7	6.0
85 to 167	420	6,202	618	503	1,024	749	988	2,319	14.8	4.3
168 (open continuously)	466	10,908	559	647	1,422	1,085	1,527	5,670	23.4	6.0

NA Not available. S Figure does not meet publication standards. [1] 100,001 to 500,000 square feet. [2] 200,001 to 500,000 square feet. [3] 100,001 to 200,000 square feet. [4] 200,001 square feet and over.

Source: U.S. Energy Information Administration, *Commercial Buildings Energy Consumption Survey, 1995*, Internet site <http://www.eia.doe.gov/emeu/cbecs/contents.html> (accessed 26 August 1998).

No. 1229. Commercial Buildings—Number and Size, by Principal Activity: 1995

[See headnote, Table 1228. For composition of regions, see inside front cover]

BUILDING CHARACTERISTICS	All build-ings [1]	Educa-tion	Food sales	Food service	Health care	Lodg-ing	Mer-cantile/ serv-ices	Offices	Public assem-bly	Reli-gious wor-ship	Ware-house
NUMBER (1,000)											
All buildings	**4,579**	**309**	**137**	**285**	**105**	**158**	**1,289**	**705**	**326**	**269**	**580**
Region: Northeast	725	39	(S)	41	14	10	241	112	46	41	88
Midwest	1,139	42	(S)	69	19	38	390	157	89	57	163
South	1,750	111	73	109	51	51	457	298	134	97	223
West.	964	117	32	66	21	59	201	138	57	74	105
Year constructed:											
1919 or before	353	18	(S)	(S)	(S)	(S)	112	57	37	20	31
1920 to 1945	562	42	(S)	(S)	(S)	7	154	74	72	(S)	59
1946 to 1959	867	72	(S)	(S)	19	33	278	128	38	65	79
1960 to 1969	718	66	(S)	25	7	53	229	75	63	50	68
1970 to 1979	813	45	42	66	34	24	207	158	60	53	73
1980 to 1986	846	36	(S)	74	(S)	25	212	151	33	58	161
1990 to 1992	218	17	(S)	(S)	(S)	(S)	47	38	20	(S)	38
1993 to 1995	202	13	(S)	(S)	(S)	(S)	49	23	(S)	(S)	71
FLOORSPACE (mil. sq. ft.)											
All buildings	**58,772**	**7,740**	**642**	**1,353**	**2,333**	**3,618**	**12,728**	**10,478**	**3,948**	**2,792**	**8,481**
Region: Northeast	11,883	1,930	(S)	166	408	350	2,838	2,154	694	442	1,480
Midwest	14,322	1,997	(S)	474	466	909	3,203	2,338	957	633	2,044
South	20,830	2,315	287	443	916	1,313	4,864	3,483	1,367	1,006	3,436
West.	11,736	1,498	209	271	543	1,047	1,822	2,503	930	711	1,522
Year constructed:											
1919 or before	3,673	521	(S)	(S)	(S)	(S)	816	599	381	266	192
1920 to 1945	6,710	1,080	(S)	(S)	(S)	170	1,118	1,155	706	(S)	1,076
1946 to 1959	9,298	1,921	(S)	(S)	356	607	1,895	1,262	498	637	1,236
1960 to 1969	10,858	1,841	(S)	192	428	972	2,342	1,206	821	535	1,530
1970 to 1979	11,333	1,232	165	285	748	576	2,749	2,095	736	510	1,616
1980 to 1986	12,252	614	(S)	305	425	829	2,727	3,377	399	598	2,104
1990 to 1992	2,590	238	(S)	(S)	(S)	(S)	632	568	221	(S)	318
1993 to 1995	2,059	293	(S)	(S)	(S)	(S)	449	217	(S)	(S)	409

S Figure does not meet publication standards. [1] Includes other commercial buildings, not shown separately.
Source: U.S. Energy Information Administration, *Commercial Buildings Energy Consumption Survey, 1995*, Internet site <http://www.eia.doe.gov/emeu/cbecs/contents.html> (accessed 28 August 1998).

No. 1230. Office Buildings—Vacancy Rates for Major Markets: 1980 to 1997

[As of end of year. Excludes government owned and and occupied, owner-occupied, and medical office buildings]

MARKET	1980	1985	1989	1990	1991	1992	1993	1994	1995	1996	1997
Total [1]	**4.6**	**16.9**	**19.5**	**20.0**	**20.2**	**20.5**	**19.4**	**16.2**	**14.3**	**12.4**	**10.1**
Atlanta, GA.	10.0	21.0	19.9	19.1	19.5	19.4	16.8	13.0	10.4	9.2	10.5
Baltimore, MD	7.2	11.5	16.4	20.0	21.0	20.6	17.3	15.5	17.0	14.3	11.6
Boston, MA.	3.8	13.1	15.3	19.6	19.1	17.5	17.7	13.3	10.4	6.2	4.4
Charlotte, NC	(NA)	16.7	14.3	16.5	19.4	(NA)	(NA)	10.0	8.9	8.2	7.1
Cincinnati, OH.	(NA)	(NA)	16.6	(NA)	(NA)	19.4	(NA)	15.3	(NA)	13.1	11.5
Dallas, TX	8.6	23.0	26.9	25.8	26.0	31.3	29.5	21.7	18.7	16.2	14.7
Denver, CO	6.6	24.7	26.1	24.8	23.0	21.5	15.9	12.8	12.1	10.8	9.3
Detroit, MI	(NA)	(NA)	(NA)	(NA)	(NA)	(NA)	21.4	19.7	16.9	11.1	8.5
Fort Lauderdale, FL	(NA)	(NA)	26.3	23.0	24.9	22.9	(NA)	10.8	(NA)	10.5	10.4
Houston, TX	4.0	27.6	27.5	24.9	27.3	27.0	25.1	24.7	21.9	17.5	12.1
Indianapolis, IN	(NA)	(NA)	20.0	21.2	21.4	22.4	18.8	18.4	14.3	(NA)	14.2
Las Vegas, NV	(NA)	(NA)	(NA)	(NA)	(NA)	(NA)	(NA)	8.7	(NA)	10.5	11.8
Los Angeles, CA	0.9	15.3	19.7	16.8	20.2	21.2	21.0	19.6	23.2	22.1	13.8
Memphis, TN	(NA)	(NA)	(NA)	(NA)	(NA)	(NA)	(NA)	(NA)	(NA)	13.6	12.0
Miami, FL.	2.4	20.9	22.0	23.4	22.6	18.5	19.0	15.4	13.8	12.4	11.2
Minneapolis, MN	(NA)	(NA)	20.2	(NA)	18.9	19.9	(NA)	8.2	(NA)	6.5	6.2
Nashville, TN	(NA)	(NA)	(NA)	25.1	18.4	(NA)	(NA)	7.5	(NA)	6.9	6.0
New Jersey (Central)	(NA)	(NA)	(NA)	(NA)	(NA)	(NA)	(NA)	20.7	(NA)	16.0	11.2
New Jersey (North)	(NA)	(NA)	(NA)	(NA)	(NA)	(NA)	(NA)	16.5	(NA)	14.5	11.9
Orlando, FL	(NA)	(NA)	(NA)	(NA)	(NA)	(NA)	(NA)	12.1	(NA)	6.5	6.4
Philadelphia, PA	6.3	14.5	16.3	18.2	17.3	19.0	17.8	16.3	16.2	13.7	10.9
Phoenix, AZ	(NA)	(NA)	(NA)	27.6	24.8	24.4	(NA)	11.8	(NA)	11.5	9.3
Pittsburgh, PA	1.2	(NA)	16.3	16.3	14.2	(NA)	17.0	15.8	14.5	(NA)	15.4
Portland, OR.	(NA)	(NA)	(NA)	(NA)	(NA)	14.5	(NA)	9.4	(NA)	5.8	5.6
Richmond, VA.	(NA)	(NA)	(NA)	(NA)	(NA)	(NA)	(NA)	11.9	(NA)	9.7	9.7
Sacramento, CA	(NA)	(NA)	(NA)	(NA)	(NA)	(NA)	(NA)	14.1	(NA)	12.4	12.3
San Diego, CA	(NA)	24.7	17.6	19.5	23.7	23.8	22.1	18.8	17.4	14.1	10.1
San Francisco, CA.	0.4	13.7	15.7	14.7	13.3	12.5	13.7	11.7	10.2	5.4	4.0
Seattle, WA	(NA)	(NA)	12.4	12.3	12.8	15.9	17.6	14.7	7.1	5.3	4.5
Silicon Valley, CA.	(NA)	(NA)	(NA)	(NA)	(NA)	(NA)	(NA)	12.7	(NA)	8.7	5.8
St Louis, MO.	(NA)	(NA)	22.6	21.0	20.5	21.8	(NA)	19.1	18.1	12.7	12.3
St Paul, MN	(NA)	(NA)	(NA)	(NA)	19.7	18.5	(NA)	15.2	(NA)	12.5	9.9
Tampa/St. Petersburg	(NA)	(NA)	(NA)	(NA)	(NA)	(NA)	(NA)	(NA)	(NA)	13.0	9.1
Washington, DC	2.5	9.0	14.4	19.0	17.6	15.4	14.1	13.4	10.8	9.3	8.0
West Palm Beach, CA	(NA)	(NA)	(NA)	(NA)	(NA)	(NA)	(NA)	16.8	(NA)	12.0	12.3
Wilmington, DE	(NA)	(NA)	12.4	20.3	21.0	19.8	(NA)	16.7	(NA)	9.5	9.7
Winston-Salem/Greensboro	(NA)	(NA)	(NA)	(NA)	(NA)	(NA)	(NA)	13.2	(NA)	14.1	12.3

NA Not available. [1] Includes other North American markets not shown separately. In 1997, 41 markets were covered.
Source: ONCOR International, Houston, TX, 1980 and 1985, *National Office Market Report*, semi-annual; 1989-1990, *International Office Market Report*, semi-annual; thereafter, *Year-End (year) Market Data Book*, annual (copyright).

Manufactures

This section presents summary data for manufacturing as a whole and more detailed information for major industry groups and selected products. The types of measures shown at the different levels include data for establishments, employment and wages, plant and equipment expenditures, value and quantity of production and shipments, value added by manufacture, inventories, and various indicators of financial status.

The principal sources of these data are Bureau of the Census reports of the censuses of manufactures conducted every 5 years; the *Annual Survey of Manufactures;* and *Manufacturing Profiles,* an annual compilation of the formerly printed series of *Current Industrial Reports.* Indexes of industrial production are presented monthly in the Federal Reserve Board's *Federal Reserve Bulletin.* These numbers were changed to a new index base year (1992 = 100) as of early 1997. Reports on current activities of industries, or current movements of individual commodities, are compiled by such government agencies as the Bureau of Labor Statistics; the Economic Research Service of the Department of Agriculture; the International Trade Administration; and by private research or trade associations such as The Conference Board, Inc., the American Iron and Steel Institute, the Electronic Industries Association, and Dataquest, Inc.

Data on financial aspects of manufacturing industries are collected by the Bureau of Economic Analysis (BEA) and the Bureau of the Census. Industry aggregates in the form of balance sheets, profit and loss statements, analyses of sales and expenses, lists of subsidiaries, and types and amounts of security issues are published for leading manufacturing corporations registered with the Securities and Exchange Commission. The BEA issues data on capital in manufacturing industries and capacity utilization rates in manufacturing. See also Section 17, Business Enterprise.

In Brief

Real GDP for the manufacturing sector increased for the fifth straight year to almost $7 trillion in 1996, up 2.8 percent from the previous year.

Production workers saw their average hourly earnings increase to $13.20 in 1997, a 3-percent rise over the previous year. Production workers in Michigan had the highest average hourly earnings with at just over $17, followed by Ohio ($15.30) and Washington ($15.16).

Net profits for manufacturing corporations reached a record level of $335 billion before taxes in 1997. After taxes, profits were $247 billion. The industrial production index for manufacturing also reached an all-time high at 127 (based on 1992=100) in 1997.

Censuses and annual surveys—The first census of manufactures covered the year 1809. Between 1809 and 1963, a census was conducted at periodic intervals. Since 1967, it has been taken every 5 years (for years ending in "2" and "7"). Results from the 1997 census are expected in 1999. Census data, either direct reports or estimates from administrative records, are obtained for every manufacturing plant with one paid employee or more.

The *Annual Survey of Manufactures (ASM),* conducted for the first time in 1949, collects data for the years between censuses for the more general measures of manufacturing activity covered in detail by the censuses. The annual survey data are estimates derived from a scientifically selected sample of establishments. The 1996 annual survey is based on a sample of about 58,000 establishments of an approximate total of 230,000. These establishments represent all manufacturing establishments of multiunit companies and all single-establishment manufacturing companies mailed schedules in the 1992 Census of Manufactures. For the current panel of the ASM sample, all establishments of companies with 1992 shipments in manufacturing in excess of $500 million were included in the survey with certainty. For the remaining portion of the mail survey, the establishment was defined as the sampling unit. For this portion, all establishments with 250 employees or more and establishments with a very large value of shipments also were included. Therefore, of the 58,000 establishments included in the ASM panel, approximately 33,000 are selected with certainty. These establishments account for approximately 80 percent of total value of shipments in the 1992 census. Smaller establishments in the remaining portion of the mail survey were selected by sample.

Establishments and classification— The censuses of manufactures for 1947 through 1992 cover manufacturing establishments as defined in the *Standard Industrial Classification Manual (SIC)*, issued by the U.S. Office of Management and Budget (see text, Section 13). The *Manual* is also used for classifying establishments in the annual surveys. The comparability of manufactures data over time is affected by changes in the official definitions of industries as presented in the *Manual.* It is important to note, therefore, that the 1987 edition of the *Manual* was used for the 1987 and 1992 censuses; and the 1972 edition of the *Manual* and the *1977 Supplement* were used for the 1972 through 1982 censuses. For the censuses from 1947 to 1963, reports were required from all establishments employing one or more persons at any time during the census year. Beginning with the 1967 census, an effort was made to relieve the very small establishments from the necessity of filing a census report. Approximately 150,000 small single-unit manufacturing firms identified as having less than 20 employees (cutoff varied by industry) benefited from this procedure. Data for these single-unit companies were estimated on the basis of government administrative

records and industry averages. Each of the establishments tabulated was classified in 1 of the approximately 459 manufacturing industries as defined by the *SIC Manual* in 1987. The *Manual* defines an industry as a number of establishments producing a single product or a closely related group of products. In the main, an establishment is classified in a particular industry if its production of a product or product group exceeds in value added its production of any other product group. While some establishments produce only the products of the industry in which they are classified, few within an industry specialize to that extent. The statistics on employment, payrolls, value added, inventories, and expenditures, therefore, reflect both the primary and secondary activities of the establishments in that industry. For this reason, care should be exercised in relating such statistics to the total shipments figures of products primary to the industry.

The censuses for 1947 through 1992 were conducted on an establishment basis. The term "establishment" signifies a single physical plant site or factory. It is not necessarily identical to the business unit or company, which may consist of one or more establishments. A company operating establishments at more than one location is required to submit a separate report for each location. An establishment engaged in distinctly different lines of activity and maintaining separate payroll and inventory records is also required to submit separate reports.

Durable goods—Items with a normal life expectancy of 3 years or more. Automobiles, furniture, household appliances, and mobile homes are common examples.

Nondurable goods—Items which generally last for only a short time (3 years or less). Food, beverages, clothing, shoes, and gasoline are common examples.

Statistical reliability—For a discussion of statistical collection and estimation, sampling procedures and measures of statistical reliability applicable to Census Bureau data, see Appendix III.

No. 1231. Gross Domestic Product in Manufacturing in Current and Real (1992) Dollars, by Industry: 1990 to 1996

[In millions of dollars. Data are based on the 1987 Standard Industrial Classification (SIC). Data include nonfactor charges (capital consumption allowances, indirect business taxes, etc.) as well as factor charges against gross product; corporate profits and capital consumption allowances have been shifted from a company to an establishment basis]

INDUSTRY	1990	1991	1992	1993	1994	1995	1996
CURRENT DOLLARS							
Gross domestic product	5,743,837	5,916,668	6,244,445	6,558,092	6,946,974	7,265,390	7,636,036
Manufacturing	1,031,425	1,028,081	1,063,628	1,116,501	1,216,094	1,286,286	1,332,093
Durable goods	572,838	558,312	573,373	615,659	679,184	716,820	749,041
Lumber and wood products	31,799	29,972	32,016	34,645	38,443	40,708	41,398
Furniture and fixtures	15,404	15,056	16,208	17,684	18,536	19,374	20,541
Stone, clay, and glass products	24,836	22,932	25,076	25,139	28,774	30,717	32,662
Primary metal industries	42,638	39,571	38,999	42,023	46,254	52,001	50,600
Fabricated metal products	69,383	67,590	70,055	73,680	84,232	89,486	98,181
Industrial machinery	114,831	105,739	108,640	110,934	122,306	142,368	150,198
Electronic & other electric equipment	94,926	98,191	98,601	114,560	132,923	134,048	143,753
Motor vehicles and equipment	46,102	42,328	52,848	71,529	87,354	87,293	85,054
Other transportation equipment	60,470	62,029	56,535	53,485	49,460	46,913	49,744
Instruments and related products	52,212	54,625	54,246	50,883	48,721	49,657	52,280
Misc. manufacturing industries	20,237	20,279	20,149	21,097	22,181	24,255	24,630
Nondurable goods	458,587	469,769	490,255	500,842	536,910	569,466	583,052
Food and kindred products	94,226	99,164	102,147	103,239	109,573	118,719	122,556
Tobacco manufactures	16,380	17,790	18,365	15,169	16,268	17,586	18,100
Textile mill products	21,742	22,279	25,434	25,494	25,411	23,631	25,519
Apparel and other textile products	25,151	25,890	27,190	27,432	28,241	27,323	26,610
Paper and allied products	45,323	44,849	45,828	47,668	51,337	59,899	57,068
Printing and publishing	73,875	75,870	79,743	80,018	86,000	84,989	90,433
Chemicals and allied products	110,348	114,148	120,457	124,646	140,605	155,852	157,821
Petroleum and coal products	32,985	29,702	28,225	31,343	30,382	30,242	30,122
Rubber and misc. plastic products	33,963	35,650	38,095	41,289	44,378	46,091	49,658
Leather and leather products	4,594	4,427	4,771	4,544	4,715	5,134	5,165
CHAINED (1992) DOLLARS							
Gross domestic product, total [1]	6,136,291	6,079,404	6,244,445	6,389,566	6,610,744	6,742,065	6,928,399
Manufacturing	1,089,974	1,050,216	1,063,628	1,100,823	1,193,167	1,273,695	1,323,717
Percent of all industries	17.8	17.3	17.0	17.2	18.0	18.9	19.1
Durable goods	600,425	567,955	573,373	608,326	671,305	731,200	785,481
Lumber and wood products	36,971	34,127	32,016	28,544	29,817	31,599	33,550
Furniture and fixtures	15,843	14,947	16,208	17,866	18,031	18,663	18,804
Stone, clay, and glass products	25,513	22,916	25,076	24,474	26,979	27,704	29,100
Primary metal industries	38,983	38,637	38,999	43,173	45,014	44,359	46,808
Fabricated metal products	72,567	68,210	70,055	73,381	84,547	89,697	94,019
Industrial machinery	113,182	103,560	108,640	115,056	131,537	164,522	186,068
Electronic & other electric equipment	92,474	95,925	98,601	118,316	145,778	175,583	217,424
Motor vehicles and equipment	56,840	46,784	52,848	66,679	78,000	79,271	76,066
Other transportation equipment	69,059	63,957	56,535	52,302	47,597	43,759	44,483
Instruments and related products	58,656	58,044	54,246	48,681	45,127	42,618	38,322
Misc. manufacturing industries	22,154	21,068	20,149	20,517	21,527	22,811	23,314
Nondurable goods	489,402	482,249	490,255	492,495	521,970	543,163	541,036
Food and kindred products	103,196	102,262	102,147	103,800	106,477	120,852	112,853
Tobacco manufactures	24,851	21,527	18,365	16,140	22,306	24,280	23,930
Textile mill products	22,573	23,068	25,434	25,975	27,346	25,437	26,610
Apparel and other textile products	26,487	26,378	27,190	27,229	28,341	28,501	26,931
Paper and allied products	44,146	44,622	45,828	50,152	52,127	45,373	47,341
Printing and publishing	84,498	80,822	79,743	75,270	77,989	77,508	74,305
Chemicals and allied products	117,260	115,813	120,457	120,606	131,216	138,915	142,183
Petroleum and coal products	28,434	28,281	28,225	27,820	27,624	32,156	33,764
Rubber and misc. plastic products	34,436	35,337	38,095	41,268	45,400	48,218	50,901
Leather and leather products	4,767	4,527	4,771	4,466	4,460	4,690	4,814

[1] For additional industry detail, see Table 716.

Source: U.S. Bureau of Economic Analysis, *Survey of Current Business*, August 1997.

No. 1232. Manufactures—Summary: 1982 to 1996

[For establishment coverage, see text, Manufactures section]

ITEM	Unit	1982	1987	1992	1994 [1]	1995 [1]	1996 [1]
ALL ESTABLISHMENTS							
Number of establishments [2]	1,000 ...	358	369	382	(NA)	(NA)	(NA)
With 20 or more employees	1,000 ...	123	126	125	(NA)	(NA)	(NA)
Employee size-class:							
Establishments [3]	1,000 ...	348	359	371	(NA)	(NA)	(NA)
Under 20	1,000 ...	230	238	252	(NA)	(NA)	(NA)
20 to 99	1,000 ...	84	86	85	(NA)	(NA)	(NA)
100 to 249	1,000 ...	21	22	22	(NA)	(NA)	(NA)
250 to 999	1,000 ...	11	11	11	(NA)	(NA)	(NA)
1,000 and over	1,000 ...	2	2	2	(NA)	(NA)	(NA)
Form of organization:							
Corporate	1,000 ...	283.2	287.4	304.0	(NA)	(NA)	(NA)
Noncorporate [4]	1,000 ...	74.0	81.5	77.7	(NA)	(NA)	(NA)
Individual proprietorship	1,000 ...	45.6	35.4	40.9	(NA)	(NA)	(NA)
Partnership	1,000 ...	15.0	13.2	10.3	(NA)	(NA)	(NA)
All employees: [5]							
Annual average [6]	Million...	19.1	19.0	18.2	18.3	18.7	18.7
Payroll	Bil. dol...	379.6	475.7	559.9	594.0	624.0	645.0
Payroll per employee	$1,000 ..	19.9	25.2	30.7	32.4	33.3	34.5
Production workers:							
Annual average	Million...	12.4	12.2	11.6	11.9	12.3	12.2
Percent of all employees	Percent..	64.9	64.6	63.8	65.1	65.4	65.2
Hours	Billion..	23.5	24.3	23.6	24.5	25.1	25.0
Hours per worker	1,000 ..	1.9	2.0	2.0	2.1	2.0	2.1
Wages	Bil. dol...	204.8	251.4	281.5	304.0	318.0	324.0
Percent of payroll for all employees	Percent..	53.9	52.8	50.4	51.4	50.9	50.3
Wages per worker	$1,000 ..	16.5	20.6	24.2	25.5	25.9	26.7
Wages per worker hour	Dollar ...	8.72	10.35	11.95	12.40	12.68	12.98
Value added by manufacture [7]	Bil. dol...	824.1	1,165.7	1,425.2	1,598.0	1,711.4	1,749.7
Per production worker	$1,000 ..	66.5	95.5	122.6	134.4	139.7	143.8
Per production worker hour	Dollar ..	35.06	47.97	60.56	65.39	68.26	69.96
Per dollar of workers' wages	Dollar ...	4.02	4.64	5.07	5.27	5.39	5.39
Cost of materials	Bil. dol...	1,130	1,320	1,573	1,752	1,897	1,975
Value of shipments [8]	Bil. dol...	1,960	2,476	3,005	3,340	3,594	3,715
Per production worker	$1,000 ..	158.1	203.0	258.0	280.2	293.3	305.4
End-of-year inventories	Bil. dol...	307	333	374	397	421	427
New capital expenditures [9]	Bil. dol...	74.6	78.6	103.2	112.0	128.4	139.3
Gross book value of depreciable assets	Bil. dol...	692	868	1,128	(NA)	(NA)	(NA)
Machinery and equipment	Bil. dol...	527	671	896	(NA)	(NA)	(NA)
Assets per employee	$1,000 ..	36.2	48.6	66.6	(NA)	(NA)	(NA)
Operation ratios:							
Value added to shipments	Ratio ...	42.0	47.1	47.9	48.0	47.7	47.1
Inventories to shipments	Ratio ...	15.7	13.4	12.5	11.9	11.7	11.5
Payroll to value added	Ratio ...	46.1	40.8	34.7	37.2	36.5	36.9
MULTIUNIT COMPANIES							
Establishments	1,000 ...	81.7	80.9	81.0	(NA)	(NA)	(NA)
Employees	Million...	14.3	13.8	13.1	(NA)	(NA)	(NA)
Production workers	Million...	8.8	8.5	8.0	(NA)	(NA)	(NA)
Payroll	Bil. dol...	307.5	377.3	436.0	(NA)	(NA)	(NA)
Wages, production workers	Bil. dol...	159.1	191.8	211.2	(NA)	(NA)	(NA)
Value added by manufacture	Bil. dol...	678.4	953.6	1,160	(NA)	(NA)	(NA)
New capital expenditures	Bil. dol...	65.2	66.5	87.8	(NA)	(NA)	(NA)
SINGLE UNIT COMPANIES							
Establishments	1,000 ...	276.3	288.0	300.7	(NA)	(NA)	(NA)
Employees	Million...	4.8	5.1	5.1	(NA)	(NA)	(NA)
Payroll	Bil. dol...	72.1	98.3	123.1	(NA)	(NA)	(NA)
Value added by manufacture	Bil. dol...	145.7	212.1	265.0	(NA)	(NA)	(NA)

NA Not available. [1] Estimated data based on *Annual Survey of Manufactures;* see text, Manufactures section. [2] Includes administrative and auxiliary units. [3] Excludes administrative offices and auxiliary units. [4] Includes forms of organization not shown separately. [5] Includes data for employees of manufacturing establishments engaged in distribution and construction work. [6] Data are based on pay periods ending nearest 15th of March, May, August, and November. [7] Adjusted value added; takes into account (a) value added by merchandising operations (that is, difference between the sales value and cost of merchandise sold without further manufacture, processing, or assembly), plus (b) net change in finished goods and work-in-process inventories between beginning and end of year. [8] Includes extensive and unmeasurable duplication from shipments between establishments in the same industry classification. [9] Includes plants under construction and not yet in operation.

Source: Except as noted, U.S. Bureau of the Census, *Census of Manufactures, 1982, 1987* and *1992;* and *Annual Survey of Manufactures.*

No. 1233. Manufactures—Summary, by Industry: 1992 and 1996

[Data based on various editions of the *Standard Industrial Classification (SIC) Manual*, published by the Office of Management and Budget; see text, Section 26. N.e.c.=Not elsewhere classified]

INDUSTRY	SIC code	1992					1996						
		All employees		Production workers (1,000)	Value added by manufacture (mil. dol.)	Value of shipments (mil. dol.)	All employees			Production workers (1,000)	Value added by manufacture		Value of shipments (mil. dol.)
		Number [1] (1,000)	Payroll (mil. dol.)				Number [1] (1,000)	Payroll Total (mil. dol.)	Payroll Per employee (dol.)		Total (mil. dol.)	Per production worker (dol.)	
All manufacturing establishments	(X)	16,949	494,109	11,641	1,424,700	3,004,723	18,665.6	645,032	34,557	12,168.0	1,749,662	143,792	3,715,428
Food and kindred products	**20**	1,503	36,772	1,100	157,260	406,963	1,516.6	40,380	26,625	1,112.6	178,783	160,689	461,324
Meat products	201	400	7,564	343	19,141	94,072	433.4	8,921	20,584	370.2	23,518	63,528	102,103
Dairy products	202	135	3,720	85	15,258	52,720	130.9	4,018	30,695	82.8	15,724	189,903	58,123
Preserved fruits and vegetables	203	216	4,825	179	23,644	47,806	204.4	5,131	25,103	169.4	24,506	144,664	51,708
Grain mill products	204	107	3,375	74	21,000	49,957	100.3	3,425	34,148	70.1	21,667	309,087	58,473
Bakery products	205	215	5,599	133	17,905	28,494	219.9	6,158	28,004	136.6	20,712	151,625	32,741
Sugar and confectionery products	206	91	2,402	71	10,990	22,710	88.6	2,603	29,379	68.7	12,640	183,998	26,265
Fats and oils	207	28	778	19	3,770	18,724	25.8	813	31,512	17.8	4,258	239,213	23,388
Beverages	208	144	4,786	74	29,260	57,957	142.8	5,103	35,735	71.5	35,210	492,448	68,387
Miscellaneous foods and kindred products	209	166	3,723	121	16,333	34,523	170.9	4,209	24,628	125.5	20,548	163,729	40,136
Tobacco products	21	38	1,524	27	27,207	35,198	31.4	1,522	48,471	22.7	25,860	1,139,207	34,482
Cigarettes	211	25	1,205	19	24,802	29,746	20.5	1,236	60,293	14.7	23,442	1,594,694	28,987
Cigars	212	3	53	2	190	287	2.9	66	22,759	2.2	287	130,455	450
Chewing and smoking tobacco	213	3	92	2	1,213	1,608	2.4	76	31,667	1.8	1,508	837,778	1,818
Tobacco stemming and redrying	214	7	174	5	1,002	3,557	5.5	144	26,182	4.0	624	156,000	3,228
Textile mill products	22	616	12,398	529	30,060	70,753	576.4	13,215	22,927	489.0	32,555	66,575	80,242
Broadwoven fabric mills, cotton	221	56	1,147	50	2,504	5,811	51.9	1,216	23,430	46.7	2,471	52,912	6,699
Broadwoven fabric mills, manmade	222	87	1,850	77	4,008	8,767	73.9	1,816	24,574	63.0	4,307	68,365	9,750
Broadwoven fabric mills, wool	223	14	279	12	691	1,612	13.4	298	22,239	11.7	673	57,521	1,756
Narrow fabric mills	224	17	323	14	706	1,274	16.7	370	22,156	13.4	817	60,970	1,524
Knitting mills	225	195	3,400	170	8,052	16,985	169.3	3,405	20,112	147.1	8,986	61,088	19,517
Textile finishing, except wool	226	51	1,143	41	2,786	7,089	51.0	1,307	25,627	41.1	3,145	76,521	7,271
Carpets and rugs	227	49	1,088	39	3,480	9,828	55.0	1,368	24,873	43.8	4,076	93,059	11,184
Yarn and thread mills	228	92	1,744	84	4,059	11,274	83.9	1,805	21,514	75.7	3,806	50,277	12,823
Miscellaneous textile goods	229	55	1,423	42	3,775	8,113	61.3	1,630	26,591	46.6	4,276	91,760	9,720
Apparel and other textile products	23	985	15,325	824	36,423	71,658	864.9	14,920	17,251	726.5	38,366	52,809	77,628
Men's and boys' suits and coats	231	44	723	37	1,375	2,430	27.1	516	19,041	22.2	1,239	55,811	1,968
Men's and boys' furnishings	232	261	3,649	228	9,864	17,867	199.7	3,094	15,493	177.6	9,423	53,057	18,507
Women's and misses' outerwear	233	306	4,597	256	10,836	21,631	294.1	4,606	15,661	249.5	11,045	44,269	22,282
Women's and children's undergarments	234	54	798	46	2,193	3,943	38.1	645	16,929	32.0	1,916	59,875	4,244

See footnotes at end of table.

No. 1233. Manufactures—Summary, by Industry: 1992 and 1996—Continued

[See headnote, page 739]

INDUSTRY	SIC code	1992 All employees Number (1,000)	1992 All employees Payroll (mil. dol.)	1992 Production workers (1,000)	1992 Value added by manufacture (mil. dol.)	1992 Value of shipments (mil. dol.)	1996 All employees Number [1] (1,000)	1996 All employees Payroll Total (mil. dol.)	1996 All employees Payroll Per employee (dol.)	1996 Production workers (1,000)	1996 Value added by manufacture Total (mil. dol.)	1996 Value added by manufacture Per production worker (dol.)	1996 Value of shipments (mil. dol.)
Apparel, other textile products—Con.													
Hats, caps, and millinery	235	19	280	16	572	976	17	307	17,953	14	599	41,888	977
Girls' and children's outerwear	236	53	775	44	1,667	3,145	34	542	16,179	28	2,063	75,018	3,874
Fur goods	237	1	21	1	68	172	1	14	17,500	1	34	68,000	104
Miscellaneous apparel and accessories	238	37	566	30	1,260	2,378	31	554	18,105	25	1,445	58,980	2,738
Miscellaneous fabricated textile products	239	211	3,918	169	8,586	19,118	224	4,641	20,737	179	10,603	59,401	22,934
Lumber and wood products	24	656	13,882	540	33,154	81,565	739	17,314	23,438	613	41,486	67,699	106,518
Logging	241	83	1,689	69	5,017	13,592	83	1,856	22,361	68	5,775	84,553	15,411
Sawmills and planing mills	242	168	3,585	144	8,848	23,294	172	4,129	24,076	147	10,404	70,583	29,697
Millwork, plywood, and structural members	243	224	5,005	181	10,844	24,744	257	6,233	24,225	209	13,274	63,451	31,798
Wood containers	244	40	645	33	1,321	2,942	51	893	17,544	43	1,909	44,707	4,059
Wood buildings and mobile homes	245	56	1,234	44	2,531	6,645	82	2,077	25,391	68	4,606	68,237	11,889
Miscellaneous Wood Products	249	84	1,725	69	4,593	10,348	94	2,125	22,558	78	5,518	70,925	13,664
Furniture and fixtures [2]	25	471	10,227	372	22,840	43,826	515	12,414	24,128	414	27,200	65,669	55,697
Household furniture	251	253	4,804	213	10,942	20,508	273	5,674	20,769	233	12,464	53,609	25,426
Office Furniture	252	68	1,868	51	4,626	7,979	70	2,172	31,252	53	5,447	102,195	9,444
Public building and related furniture	253	30	732	23	1,736	4,483	37	1,031	27,567	29	2,290	78,694	7,366
Partitions and fixtures	254	75	1,818	55	3,633	6,580	81	2,246	27,728	61	4,182	68,896	7,951
Miscellaneous furniture and fixtures	259	45	1,005	31	2,353	4,276	54	1,290	24,112	39	2,818	72,817	5,510
Paper and allied products	26	626	20,492	479	60,174	133,201	631	22,947	36,389	488	72,290	148,287	160,661
Pulp mills	261	16	689	12	2,554	5,466	15	701	46,733	11	2,201	198,288	5,508
Paper mills	262	131	5,421	100	14,848	32,786	116	5,599	48,101	90	18,848	208,726	39,566
Paperboard mills	263	52	2,136	39	8,195	16,140	55	2,599	47,427	42	9,655	231,535	20,271
Paperboard containers and boxes	265	199	5,722	151	12,406	32,655	212	6,727	31,731	163	15,668	96,300	40,389
Miscellaneous converted paper products	267	229	6,524	176	22,171	46,154	232	7,321	31,502	182	25,918	142,720	54,927
Printing and publishing	27	1,492	41,136	785	112,446	166,153	1,515	46,175	30,479	801	130,946	163,539	195,435
Newspapers	271	414	10,437	134	26,920	33,782	403	11,199	27,768	136	30,692	226,342	39,171
Periodicals	272	115	4,077	20	15,880	22,104	121	4,665	38,714	16	17,982	1,096,463	24,930
Books	273	130	4,037	57	14,325	21,378	136	4,675	34,451	57	17,857	313,281	26,696
Miscellaneous publishing	274	65	1,720	24	8,473	10,908	69	2,049	29,782	25	9,699	381,850	12,511
Commercial printing	275	567	15,337	408	31,898	56,229	604	18,015	29,806	437	38,407	87,828	67,842
Manifold business forms	276	48	1,341	34	3,922	7,429	41	1,263	30,507	28	3,878	138,996	7,724
Greeting cards	277	23	584	12	3,389	4,190	21	636	29,720	12	3,989	335,210	5,011
Blankbooks and bookbinding	278	66	1,461	51	3,640	5,049	65	1,598	24,775	50	4,388	87,936	6,428
Printing trade services	279	65	2,142	46	3,999	5,086	55	2,074	37,778	39	4,055	103,444	5,123

See footnotes at end of table.

No. 1233. Manufactures—Summary, by Industry: 1992 and 1996—Continued

[See headnote, page 739]

SIC code	INDUSTRY	1992 All employees, Number [1] (1,000)	1992 All employees, Payroll (mil. dol.)	1992 Production workers (1,000)	1992 Value added by manufacture (mil. dol.)	1992 Value of shipments (mil. dol.)	1996 All employees, Number [1] (1,000)	1996 All employees, Payroll Total (mil. dol.)	1996 All employees, Payroll Per employee (dol.)	1996 Production workers (1,000)	1996 Value added by manufacture, Total (mil. dol.)	1996 Value added by manufacture, Per production worker (dol.)	1996 Value of shipments (mil. dol.)
28	**Chemicals and allied products**	849	32,502	479	164,346	305,420	824	36,331	44,086	477	194,412	407,743	367,442
281	Industrial inorganic chemicals	103	4,214	55	16,724	27,331	80	3,749	46,804	45	16,567	366,527	27,741
282	Plastics materials and synthetics	129	5,137	86	20,979	48,698	115	5,086	44,188	79	25,025	315,574	59,567
283	Drugs	194	7,840	93	48,602	67,792	213	9,891	46,393	106	59,813	562,152	86,533
284	Soap, cleaners, and toilet goods	123	3,927	75	26,182	42,875	126	4,389	34,778	75	31,801	425,716	51,809
285	Paints and allied products	51	1,710	26	7,154	14,973	51	1,940	37,965	28	8,497	304,552	18,257
286	Industrial organic chemicals	125	5,495	72	26,132	64,397	126	6,765	53,733	75	28,886	386,693	75,672
287	Agricultural chemicals	40	1,451	25	8,659	18,841	37	1,593	43,406	24	12,277	520,212	23,356
289	Miscellaneous chemical products	84	2,727	48	9,915	20,512	76	2,919	38,408	45	11,547	256,031	24,508
29	**Petroleum and coal products**	114	4,967	74	23,408	150,227	106	5,238	49,415	69	31,656	458,119	174,285
291	Petroleum refining	75	3,640	48	18,607	136,551	67	3,738	55,625	43	26,006	599,217	158,068
295	Asphalt paving and roofing materials	26	846	18	3,006	7,749	25	988	39,206	18	3,464	191,381	9,611
299	Miscellaneous petroleum and coal products	14	481	7	1,796	5,927	14	512	37,647	8	2,187	287,763	6,605
30	**Rubber and misc. plastics products**	907	23,156	698	58,652	113,593	1,018	28,436	27,936	800	74,945	93,716	150,468
301	Tires and inner tubes	65	2,499	53	6,504	11,814	65	2,701	41,682	54	7,079	131,093	14,209
302	Rubber and plastics footwear	14	216	11	464	868	8	165	20,122	7	442	65,970	936
305	Hose and belting and plastics and packing	52	1,411	38	3,290	7,290	61	1,859	30,626	46	4,528	98,649	8,232
306	Fabricated rubber products, n.e.c	105	2,617	79	6,024	11,474	122	3,137	25,819	95	7,275	76,418	14,468
308	Miscellaneous plastics products, n.e.c.	671	16,413	516	42,370	83,487	763	20,574	26,975	598	55,621	93,027	112,623
31	**Leather and leather products**	101	1,806	83	4,527	9,694	77	1,600	20,725	65	4,742	73,406	9,309
311	Leather tanning and finishing	17	420	13	891	2,905	15	393	26,554	12	1,313	105,887	3,134
313	Footwear cut stock	4	63	3	149	317	3	58	21,481	2	162	77,143	326
314	Footwear, except rubber	49	762	41	2,060	3,898	37	704	19,183	31	1,907	61,516	3,605
315	Leather gloves and mittens	3	35	2	69	140	2	45	19,565	2	53	26,500	145
316	Luggage	10	191	8	509	968	6	151	26,034	4	747	173,721	1,115
317	Handbags and personal leather goods	11	202	9	470	861	8	139	16,951	7	328	49,697	580
319	Leather goods, n.e.c	8	133	6	304	575	7	110	16,176	6	233	37,581	404

See footnotes at end of table.

No. 1233. Manufactures—Summary, by Industry: 1992 and 1996—Continued

[See headnote, page 739]

INDUSTRY	SIC code	1992					1996						
		All employees		Production workers (1,000)	Value added by manufacture (mil. dol.)	Value of shipments (mil. dol.)	All employees			Production workers (1,000)	Value added by manufacture		Value of shipments (mil. dol.)
		Number [1] (1,000)	Payroll (mil. dol.)				Number [1] (1,000)	Payroll			Total (mil. dol.)	Per production worker (dol.)	
								Total (mil. dol.)	Per employee (dol.)				
Stone, clay, and glass products	32	469	13,113	357	34,641	62,521	520	15,857	30,471	402	46,055	114,479	82,441
Flat glass	321	12	451	10	1,311	2,073	12	524	45,565	9	1,717	184,624	2,671
Glass and glassware, pressed or blown	322	66	2,075	56	5,900	9,033	60	2,029	34,101	51	6,532	127,082	10,057
Products of purchased glass	323	55	1,369	42	3,757	6,904	64	1,771	27,890	50	4,850	97,782	9,060
Cement, hydraulic	324	17	595	13	2,149	4,051	17	693	41,006	13	3,509	280,720	5,818
Structural clay products	325	31	734	24	1,695	2,857	31	845	27,083	25	2,176	86,693	3,566
Pottery and related products	326	37	863	29	1,995	2,817	45	1,149	25,647	36	2,696	74,066	3,830
Concrete, gypsum, and plaster products	327	174	4,741	126	11,008	23,024	205	6,083	29,746	152	15,739	103,410	32,691
Cut stone and stone products	328	12	282	9	604	1,007	17	412	24,094	13	999	76,846	1,512
Miscellaneous nonmetallic mineral products	329	66	2,004	49	6,222	10,756	72	2,350	32,867	53	7,838	148,166	13,237
Primary metal industries [2]	33	662	22,202	508	52,027	138,287	687	25,644	37,306	543	69,539	128,088	178,298
Blast furnace and basic steel products	331	239	9,179	182	22,173	58,449	221	9,950	45,023	174	29,180	167,701	74,552
Iron and steel foundries	332	122	3,739	99	6,873	11,860	128	4,373	34,111	106	9,061	85,240	15,937
Primary nonferrous metals	333	35	1,334	27	3,391	13,905	35	1,408	40,344	26	4,200	159,091	15,424
Secondary nonferrous metals	334	13	407	9	1,233	6,131	15	500	33,333	11	1,410	125,893	7,127
Nonferrous rolling and drawing	335	147	4,635	109	12,335	37,101	162	5,627	34,670	123	16,670	135,971	48,820
Nonferrous foundries (castings)	336	75	1,942	59	3,927	7,002	94	2,662	28,349	79	5,856	73,939	10,519
Miscellaneous primary metal products	339	31	966	22	2,097	3,837	32	1,125	35,047	23	3,164	137,565	5,919
Fabricated metal products	34	1,362	38,962	994	83,761	166,532	1,483	46,130	31,106	1,114	107,990	96,904	214,006
Metal cans and shipping containers	341	40	1,465	33	3,736	13,263	33	1,369	41,485	27	3,999	148,111	13,454
Cutlery, handtools, and hardware	342	134	3,648	99	9,044	15,448	140	4,220	30,164	107	11,750	109,506	20,197
Plumbing and heating, except electric	343	42	1,152	29	3,105	5,825	45	1,246	27,566	32	4,412	139,620	7,836
Fabricated structural metal products	344	389	10,362	275	21,256	44,876	432	12,555	29,042	315	27,974	88,863	59,388
Screw machine products, bolts, etc.	345	91	2,624	68	5,269	9,026	104	3,265	31,515	81	6,936	85,524	11,797
Metal forgings and stampings	346	234	7,749	185	14,913	30,621	259	9,696	37,407	211	19,880	94,352	41,282
Metal services, n.e.c.	347	108	2,652	83	5,679	9,553	129	3,454	26,754	99	7,793	78,638	14,003
Ordnance and accessories, n.e.c	348	62	2,124	35	4,536	6,855	40	1,466	36,377	24	3,528	146,390	5,222
Miscellaneous fabricated metal products	349	263	7,185	186	16,224	30,667	300	8,858	29,497	219	21,718	99,350	40,828
Industrial machinery and equipment.	35	1,739	57,231	1,086	132,923	258,661	1,981	70,730	35,713	1,287	187,218	145,469	381,794
Engines and turbines	351	83	3,135	52	7,738	17,549	79	3,186	40,534	55	10,513	192,899	23,554
Farm and garden machinery	352	86	2,354	63	7,318	14,784	94	2,918	31,209	70	9,545	136,357	21,292
Construction and related machinery	353	176	5,664	108	12,489	27,193	205	7,157	34,929	133	18,178	136,677	41,509
Metalworking machinery	354	255	8,571	178	16,542	26,474	295	10,985	37,263	211	22,673	107,252	36,841
Special industry machinery	355	162	5,515	91	11,667	21,522	192	7,311	38,019	110	19,221	174,895	35,751
General industrial machinery	356	244	7,742	154	17,817	31,443	265	9,130	34,466	172	23,110	134,439	41,458
Computer and office equipment	357	251	10,143	89	29,229	66,709	259	11,211	43,286	96	41,135	428,044	103,270
Refrigeration and service machinery	358	179	5,264	125	13,597	27,544	201	6,493	32,384	147	17,521	119,029	39,197
Industrial machinery, n.e.c	359	304	8,843	227	16,527	25,443	392	12,340	31,496	293	25,322	86,423	38,922

See footnotes at end of table.

No. 1233. Manufactures—Summary, by Industry: 1992 and 1996—Continued

[See headnote, page 739]

INDUSTRY	SIC code	1992 All employees Number [1] (1,000)	1992 All employees Payroll (mil. dol.)	1992 Production workers (1,000)	1992 Value added by manufacture (mil. dol.)	1992 Value of shipments (mil. dol.)	1996 All employees Number [1] (1,000)	1996 All employees Payroll Total (mil. dol.)	1996 All employees Payroll Per employee (dol.)	1996 Production workers (1,000)	1996 Value added by manufacture Total (mil. dol.)	1996 Value added by manufacture Per production worker (dol.)	1996 Value of shipments (mil. dol.)
Electronics; other electric equipment	**36**	**1,439**	**44,197**	**911**	**121,158**	**216,764**	**1,557**	**54,311**	**34,893**	**1,006**	**184,013**	**182,861**	**320,615**
Electric distribution equipment	361	68	1,946	48	5,437	9,797	74	2,499	33,954	51	6,700	130,350	12,331
Electrical industrial apparatus	362	157	4,387	106	10,850	19,266	171	5,373	31,366	120	14,278	119,182	26,926
Household appliances	363	103	2,571	83	7,964	18,633	108	3,072	28,418	87	9,466	108,680	22,157
Electric lighting and wiring equipment	364	148	3,974	107	11,307	19,844	157	4,617	29,370	117	13,428	114,769	24,562
Household audio and video equipment	365	47	1,123	35	3,486	10,614	49	1,333	27,428	37	3,459	93,235	11,266
Communications equipment	366	239	9,111	114	26,522	42,955	258	11,522	44,590	120	38,705	323,891	68,232
Electronic components and accessories	367	530	16,752	317	44,305	73,642	588	20,830	35,431	368	84,059	228,359	127,996
Misc. electrical equipment and supplies	369	147	4,332	100	11,287	22,013	151	5,067	33,490	106	13,920	130,827	27,146
Transportation equipment	**37**	**1,647**	**62,735**	**1,080**	**158,326**	**399,269**	**1,467**	**63,532**	**43,310**	**1,032**	**176,598**	**171,089**	**465,172**
Motor vehicles and equipment	371	703	26,213	565	80,935	238,384	772	32,867	42,574	634	105,899	167,139	329,155
Aircraft and parts	372	548	22,647	281	47,661	104,858	377	18,733	49,729	190	45,220	237,500	83,394
Ship and boat building and repairing	373	163	4,634	122	8,560	15,249	141	4,353	30,807	108	7,903	72,906	15,634
Railroad equipment	374	28	900	21	2,015	4,714	31	1,141	37,288	23	2,590	114,097	7,067
Motorcycles, bicycles, and parts	375	13	343	10	891	2,134	18	565	30,707	14	1,435	103,986	3,094
Guided missiles, space vehicles, parts	376	146	6,780	50	15,246	26,508	81	4,632	57,185	29	9,986	346,736	17,928
Miscellaneous transportation equipment	379	46	1,218	33	3,018	7,423	47	1,241	26,461	35	3,564	103,304	8,900
Instruments and related products	**38**	**907**	**33,067**	**460**	**89,394**	**134,940**	**821**	**33,783**	**41,164**	**423**	**97,987**	**231,593**	**151,016**
Search and navigation equipment	381	253	10,962	103	24,299	35,039	186	9,540	51,208	68	21,071	310,782	30,371
Measuring and controlling devices	382	276	9,632	138	21,775	34,730	272	10,562	38,817	141	29,028	205,435	46,741
Medical instruments and supplies	384	264	8,522	154	26,082	39,535	268	9,957	37,098	157	31,051	197,777	47,406
Ophthalmic goods	385	29	714	20	1,938	2,675	27	757	28,037	17	2,390	140,588	3,417
Photographic equipment and supplies	386	77	3,061	39	14,862	22,119	61	2,798	46,096	36	14,032	393,053	22,297
Watches, clocks, watchcases and parts	387	8	177	6	438	843	6	169	26,825	4	415	96,512	785
Misc. manufacturing industries	**39**	**366**	**8,417**	**255**	**21,975**	**39,498**	**397**	**10,042**	**25,276**	**283**	**27,021**	**95,346**	**48,597**
Jewelry, silverware, and plated ware	391	46	1,068	32	2,501	5,731	43	1,070	24,711	30	2,761	92,651	6,360
Musical instruments	393	12	273	9	589	982	13	328	25,426	10	685	66,505	1,173
Toys and sporting goods	394	98	2,133	71	6,816	12,123	103	2,489	24,189	76	8,327	109,422	14,748
Pens, pencils, office, and art supplies	395	30	684	21	2,030	3,515	35	838	24,220	26	2,643	102,442	4,351
Costume jewelry and notions	396	27	557	19	1,366	2,316	24	560	23,045	19	1,406	75,187	2,389
Miscellaneous manufactures	399	153	3,702	103	8,674	14,832	179	4,757	26,531	123	11,199	91,271	19,575

X Not applicable. [1] Represents the average of production workers plus all other employees for the payroll period ended nearest the 15th of March. [2] Includes other industries not shown separately.

Source: U.S. Bureau of the Census, 1992 Census of Manufactures and Annual Survey of Manufactures.

No. 1234. Manufactures—Summary, by Selected Industry Based on Value Added: 1992 and 1996

[Data based on various editions of the *Standard Industrial Classification (SIC) Manual*, published by the Office of Management and Budget; see text, Section 26. N.e.c.=Not elsewhere classified]

INDUSTRY	SIC code	1992 All employees: Number [1] (1,000)	1992 Payroll (mil. dol.)	1992 Production workers (1,000)	1992 Value added by manufacture (mil. dol.)	1992 Value of shipments (mil. dol.)	1996 All employees: Number [1] (1,000)	1996 Payroll Total (mil. dol.)	1996 Payroll Per employee (dol.)	1996 Production workers (1,000)	1996 Value added Total (mil. dol.)	1996 Value added Per production worker (dol.)	1996 Value of shipments (mil. dol.)
Meat packing plants	2011	121.2	2,441	105.0	6,958	50,167	130.0	2,991	23,008	110.7	8,278	74,778	51,089
Sausages and other prepared meats	2013	85.4	2,023	65.6	5,480	19,940	88.1	2,175	24,688	69.5	5,954	85,669	20,854
Poultry slaughtering and processing	2015	193.8	3,100	172.8	6,703	23,965	215.3	3,755	17,441	190.0	9,285	48,868	30,160
Fluid milk	2026	63.4	1,840	32.5	5,965	21,926	59.3	1,910	32,209	30.0	6,300	210,000	23,455
Canned fruits and vegetables	2033	63.6	1,465	53.2	6,976	15,071	56.4	1,481	26,259	46.4	6,215	133,944	14,894
Frozen specialties, n.e.c.	2038	46.7	972	38.3	4,076	7,886	42.9	975	22,727	35.9	5,027	140,027	9,404
Cereal breakfast foods	2043	16.1	745	13.1	7,259	9,737	13.8	717	51,957	11.2	6,470	577,679	9,105
Bread, cake, and related products	2051	154.9	4,059	88.1	11,453	18,130	156.3	4,330	27,703	86.0	12,760	148,372	19,859
Cookies and crackers	2052	47.0	1,247	35.0	5,513	8,668	47.4	1,386	29,241	37.2	6,598	177,366	10,347
Candy and other confectionery products	2064	51.5	1,261	41.0	6,347	10,202	53.1	1,433	26,987	41.9	7,740	184,726	12,453
Malt beverages	2082	34.5	1,567	25.1	10,189	17,340	53.1	1,538	45,235	24.6	11,139	452,805	18,220
Bottled and canned soft drinks	2086	77.1	2,163	30.5	9,592	25,423	73.5	2,286	31,102	28.1	12,867	457,900	32,024
Flavoring extracts and syrups, n.e.c.	2087	10.3	342	5.8	5,275	6,923	10.5	409	38,952	5.6	6,172	1,102,143	8,068
Food preparations, n.e.c.	2099	61.4	1,413	43.7	5,881	12,165	69.5	1,682	24,191	49.8	7,617	152,952	14,971
Cigarettes	2111	25.4	1,205	18.1	24,802	29,746	20.5	1,236	60,293	14.7	23,442	1,594,694	28,987
Logging	2411	83.2	1,689	69.2	5,017	13,592	83.0	1,856	22,361	68.3	5,775	84,553	15,411
Sawmills and planing mills, general	2421	137.6	3,040	117.7	7,755	21,061	138.0	3,465	25,109	117.9	9,035	76,633	26,740
Wood household furniture	2511	121.1	2,174	105.2	4,726	8,730	125.4	2,467	19,673	108.8	5,356	49,228	10,517
Paper mills	2621	130.6	5,421	100.4	14,848	32,786	116.4	5,598	48,093	90.3	18,848	208,726	39,566
Paperboard mills	2631	51.5	2,136	39.4	8,195	16,140	54.8	2,599	47,427	41.7	9,655	231,535	25,914
Corrugated and solid fiber boxes	2653	112.3	3,276	81.4	6,760	19,834	127.4	4,060	31,868	94.7	9,360	98,838	17,304
Sanitary paper products	2676	40.6	1,454	32.8	8,226	15,647	36.0	1,464	40,667	29.9	9,097	304,247	
Newspapers	2711	413.9	10,437	133.8	26,920	33,782	403.3	11,199	27,768	135.6	30,692	226,342	39,171
Periodicals	2721	79.0	2,676	20.2	15,880	22,104	120.5	4,665	38,714	16.4	17,982	1,096,463	24,930
Book publishing	2731	115.1	4,077	20.2	11,494	16,698	85.4	3,128	36,628	18.5	14,792	799,568	21,363
Miscellaneous publishing	2741	65.1	1,720	18.2	8,473	10,908	68.8	2,049	29,782	25.4	9,699	381,850	12,511
Commercial printing, lithographic	2752	438.2	12,016	316.2	24,704	43,352	448.9	13,592	30,278	326.3	28,797	88,253	50,614
Commercial printing, n.e.c.	2759	107.4	2,588	74.2	5,484	9,265	133.4	3,691	27,669	92.1	7,765	84,311	13,415
Manifold business forms	2761	47.9	1,341	33.7	3,922	7,429	41.4	1,263	30,507	27.9	3,878	138,996	7,724
Industrial inorganic chemicals, n.e.c.	2819	78.9	3,266	39.7	11,212	18,129	57.0	2,745	48,158	31.0	10,515	339,194	17,862
Plastics materials and resins	2821	61.2	2,698	36.5	12,599	31,601	58.6	2,864	48,873	36.3	15,310	421,763	40,097
Organic fibers, noncellulosic	2824	44.4	1,545	33.9	5,661	11,113	38.5	1,452	37,714	30.3	6,748	222,706	12,912
Pharmaceutical preparations	2834	122.9	4,958	62.4	37,224	50,415	136.9	6,197	45,267	72.3	43,410	600,415	61,554
Soap and other detergents	2841	32.8	1,171	19.9	7,709	14,729	30.3	1,173	38,713	16.8	9,022	537,024	15,779
Polishes and sanitation goods	2842	22.0	662	13.4	4,219	6,659	24.2	737	30,455	14.2	5,425	382,042	8,602
Toilet preparations	2844	59.8	1,774	37.0	13,084	18,629	62.9	2,079	33,052	39.1	15,155	387,596	22,688
Paints and allied products	2851	51.1	1,710	25.7	7,154	14,973	51.1	1,940	37,965	27.9	8,497	304,552	18,257
Industrial organic chemicals, n.e.c.	2869	99.8	4,494	57.2	22,423	54,103	100.3	5,590	55,733	59.3	23,721	400,017	62,739
Agricultural chemicals, n.e.c.	2879	16.8	669	9.6	5,514	9,142	13.8	670	48,551	7.8	7,000	897,436	10,903
Chemical preparations, n.e.c.	2899	37.1	1,233	21.4	5,048	9,927	35.1	1,389	39,573	19.3	5,937	307,617	11,872

See footnotes at end of table.

INDUSTRY	SIC code	1992 All employees		Production workers (1,000)	Value added by manufacture (mil. dol.)	Value of shipments (mil. dol.)	1996 All employees			Production workers (1,000)	Value added by manufacture		Value of shipments (mil. dol.)
		Number[1] (1,000)	Payroll (mil. dol.)				Number[1] (1,000)	Payroll Total (mil. dol.)	Payroll Per employee (dol.)		Total (mil. dol.)	Per production worker (dol.)	
Petroleum refining	2911	74.9	3,640	47.9	18,607	136,551	67.2	3,738	55,625	43.4	26,006	599,217	158,068
Tires and inner tubes	3011	64.6	2,499	52.8	6,504	11,814	64.8	2,701	41,682	54.0	7,079	131,093	14,209
Unsupported plastics film and sheet	3081	54.7	1,680	39.0	5,268	10,619	59.5	1,979	33,261	43.4	6,893	158,825	14,399
Plastics products, n.e.c.	3089	427.8	9,998	332.4	24,398	45,376	500.5	12,901	25,776	395.2	32,282	81,685	61,096
Ready-mixed concrete	3273	82.4	2,293	61.0	5,346	12,015	94.5	2,926	30,963	73.9	7,296	98,728	16,225
Blast furnaces and steel mills	3312	170.1	7,022	131.0	16,541	42,154	149.2	7,452	49,946	117.7	22,112	187,867	54,511
Nonferrous wiredrawing and insulating	3357	60.6	1,724	44.8	4,841	13,044	69.2	2,175	31,431	51.2	6,629	129,473	17,533
Hardware, n.e.c.	3429	75.4	2,063	56.3	4,824	8,806	76.0	2,278	29,974	58.7	5,935	101,107	11,049
Fabricated structural metal	3441	72.0	1,964	50.8	3,947	8,919	75.5	2,300	30,464	55.7	5,159	92,621	11,744
Fabricated plate work (boiler shops)	3443	78.4	2,312	55.4	4,789	8,975	88.0	2,703	30,716	64.5	5,737	88,946	11,269
Sheet metal work	3444	103.9	2,834	75.3	5,715	11,299	119.1	3,536	29,689	88.2	7,513	85,181	14,784
Automotive stampings	3465	105.1	4,094	87.0	7,231	15,803	119.5	5,124	42,879	100.5	10,057	100,070	21,692
Metal stampings, n.e.c.	3469	91.8	2,470	70.0	5,100	9,559	101.1	3,162	31,276	79.8	6,771	84,850	13,096
Internal combustion engines, n.e.c.	3519	55.5	2,029	37.0	4,786	11,707	56.9	2,237	39,315	41.2	7,345	178,277	17,286
Farm machinery and equipment	3523	61.5	1,786	42.6	5,167	9,620	66.6	2,216	33,273	48.5	7,176	147,959	14,469
Construction machinery	3531	74.6	2,458	47.8	5,683	13,139	88.7	3,112	35,085	61.1	8,941	146,334	21,627
Special dies, tools, jigs, and fixtures	3544	110.8	3,883	84.9	6,617	9,265	133.3	5,099	38,252	104.0	9,094	87,442	12,949
Special industry machinery, n.e.c.	3559	83.3	2,947	44.7	6,331	11,479	103.5	4,126	39,865	59.0	12,460	211,186	22,661
Electronic computers	3571	110.6	4,849	31.1	16,129	38,202	103.8	4,500	44,204	31.0	23,153	746,871	59,414
Refrigeration and heating equipment	3585	120.7	3,594	89.0	9,450	19,739	134.9	4,480	33,210	104.0	12,287	118,144	28,094
Industrial machinery, n.e.c.	3599	248.9	7,040	189.1	12,882	19,117	335.3	10,277	30,650	253.0	20,854	82,427	30,751
Motors and generators	3621	67.9	1,762	51.9	4,328	8,168	75.2	2,129	28,311	59.9	5,513	92,037	11,477
Relays and industrial controls	3625	62.5	1,864	36.0	4,686	7,741	66.2	2,325	35,121	38.6	6,247	161,839	10,862
Telephone and telegraph apparatus	3661	91.1	3,739	44.8	12,475	20,510	93.6	4,469	47,746	38.1	18,820	493,963	31,727
Radio and TV communications equip.	3663	124.9	4,721	58.6	12,279	19,521	140.0	6,202	44,300	68.9	17,219	249,913	32,080
Semiconductors and related devices	3674	172.0	6,884	84.8	22,343	32,191	189.6	9,042	47,690	96.2	56,311	585,353	71,413
Electronic components, n.e.c.	3679	180.2	5,119	107.8	11,818	23,670	205.8	6,265	30,442	129.2	14,125	109,327	32,969
Motor vehicles and car bodies	3711	227.8	10,434	192.8	45,983	151,682	225.2	12,310	54,663	196.3	55,369	282,063	200,704
Motor vehicle parts and accessories	3714	400.0	13,955	313.4	31,074	75,058	459.9	18,171	39,511	368.3	44,210	120,038	110,992
Aircraft	3721	264.6	11,493	122.0	23,107	62,940	188.3	9,839	52,252	84.5	25,137	297,479	47,313
Aircraft engines and engine parts	3724	120.4	4,966	66.5	11,726	22,408	75.1	3,640	48,469	41.4	9,037	218,285	18,769
Aircraft parts and equipment, n.e.c.	3728	163.1	6,187	92.0	12,827	19,511	113.4	5,253	46,323	64.5	11,047	171,271	17,312
Ship building and repairing	3731	118.2	3,631	87.0	6,558	10,601	92.1	3,175	34,473	68.4	5,447	79,635	9,811
Search and navigation equipment	3812	253.0	10,962	30.1	24,299	35,039	186.3	9,540	51,208	18.6	21,071	401,613	13,777
Guided missiles and space vehicles	3761	68.5	2,544	32.2	5,685	8,826	63.2	2,720	43,038	33.0	8,613	310,782	30,371
Instruments to measure electricity	3825	98.2	3,099	58.5	9,400	13,396	103.5	3,769	36,415	61.8	12,075	195,388	13,371
Surgical and medical instruments	3841	96.4	2,846	61.6	8,901	13,801	93.1	2,980	32,000	59.7	10,247	171,642	17,042
Surgical appliances and supplies	3842	77.3	3,061	39.2	14,862	22,119	60.7	2,798	46,096	35.7	14,032	393,053	22,297
Photographic equipment and supplies	3861	15,874											

[1] Represents the average of production workers plus all other employees for the payroll period ended nearest the 15th of the month.

Source: U.S. Bureau of the Census, 1992 Census of Manufactures and Annual Survey of Manufactures.

No. 1235. Manufactures Summary: 1996

[Sum of state totals may not add to U.S. total because U.S. and state figures were independently derived]

STATE	ALL EMPLOYEES [1]			PRODUCTION WORKERS [1]		VALUE ADDED BY MANUFACTURES [2]		Value of ship-ments [3] (mil. dol.)
	Number (1,000)	Payroll		Total (1,000)	Wages (mil. dol.)	Total (mil. dol.)	Per production worker (dol.)	
		Total (mil. dol.)	Per employee (dol.)					
United States	18,667	645,140	34,561	12,169	324,612	1,750,493	143,847	3,719,743
Alabama.	383	10,587	27,679	285	6,675	27,451	96,422	66,257
Alaska	16	488	30,873	12	339	1,470	124,568	3,939
Arizona.	208	7,191	34,554	120	2,857	22,850	189,782	36,961
Arkansas	239	5,829	24,410	188	4,036	18,512	98,414	44,310
California	1,938	71,164	36,724	1,162	29,028	188,805	162,427	368,329
Colorado.	196	6,792	34,686	118	3,122	19,215	162,704	39,191
Connecticut.	299	12,785	42,802	153	4,699	24,772	161,484	44,369
Delaware	60	2,840	47,178	27	784	5,791	212,890	13,601
District of Columbia	13	630	49,180	3	97	1,512	504,133	1,975
Florida	486	14,853	30,554	297	6,553	38,621	130,170	76,387
Georgia	585	17,593	30,100	411	9,634	51,753	125,797	115,898
Hawaii	17	509	29,789	10	251	1,609	159,257	3,146
Idaho	74	2,383	32,152	53	1,312	7,977	149,944	18,315
Illinois	996	36,986	37,124	625	17,625	92,011	147,171	196,845
Indiana.	660	22,976	34,812	477	14,290	61,896	129,678	133,787
Iowa	250	7,839	31,307	177	4,725	27,021	153,092	61,981
Kansas.	209	6,902	32,994	145	4,006	18,820	129,970	46,152
Kentucky	296	9,162	30,933	216	5,752	35,040	162,524	82,531
Louisiana	175	6,037	34,439	123	3,706	25,125	203,606	75,961
Maine.	89	2,674	30,175	66	1,760	6,675	100,988	14,445
Maryland	192	6,968	36,309	112	3,226	17,455	155,707	35,700
Massachusetts.	475	19,026	40,071	264	7,723	44,047	166,655	79,254
Michigan.	967	41,782	43,230	629	22,643	85,688	136,186	205,744
Minnesota.	432	15,590	36,071	256	6,886	34,716	135,399	73,273
Mississippi	239	5,654	23,666	190	3,838	17,295	91,024	39,564
Missouri	415	13,572	32,712	263	6,743	40,208	152,650	85,222
Montana.	22	588	26,584	15	376	1,707	111,582	4,930
Nebraska	110	3,086	28,033	80	1,916	9,218	115,229	25,023
Nevada	41	1,195	29,299	27	627	3,275	120,408	6,194
New Hampshire	107	3,576	33,293	71	1,848	10,815	152,969	19,348
New Jersey.	540	22,919	42,419	279	7,905	49,995	179,257	96,001
New Mexico	43	1,304	30,053	28	651	11,745	427,087	16,364
New York	950	35,641	37,533	555	14,541	90,665	163,484	163,697
North Carolina	856	23,796	27,815	628	13,879	76,475	121,814	155,911
North Dakota.	22	570	25,796	15	340	1,808	117,390	4,794
Ohio	1,074	39,790	37,065	720	22,618	105,497	146,462	232,721
Oklahoma.	167	4,859	29,098	119	2,963	15,875	133,856	35,220
Oregon.	232	7,869	33,859	157	4,317	21,838	138,917	45,022
Pennsylvania	918	31,978	34,849	590	16,026	82,922	140,594	165,889
Rhode Island.	83	2,565	30,870	55	1,261	5,407	97,779	9,959
South Carolina.	366	10,658	29,112	272	6,557	30,769	113,162	66,794
South Dakota	46	1,220	26,746	32	651	3,974	125,753	10,488
Tennessee	533	15,394	28,877	397	9,449	42,288	106,411	95,851
Texas.	1,055	36,008	34,131	665	17,032	116,631	175,464	284,151
Utah	119	3,511	29,576	79	1,924	11,239	141,731	22,010
Vermont	48	1,483	30,969	33	788	3,986	122,652	8,554
Virginia.	399	12,555	31,474	284	7,100	42,519	149,926	80,795
Washington	342	13,197	38,610	207	6,429	31,929	154,169	71,874
West Virginia	76	2,521	33,083	55	1,607	8,965	163,885	17,679
Wisconsin	601	19,779	32,910	416	11,324	53,619	128,984	114,464
Wyoming	10	268	27,608	7	175	999	140,746	2,874

[1] Includes employment and payroll at administrative offices and auxiliary units. All employees represents the average of production workers plus all other employees for the payroll period ended nearest the 12th of March. Production workers represents the average of the employment for the payroll periods ended nearest the 12th of March, May, August, and November. [2] Adjusted value added; takes into account (a) value added by merchandising operations (that is, difference between the sales value and cost of merchandise sold without further manufacture, processing, or assembly), plus (b) net change in finished goods and work-inprocess inventories between beginning and end of year. [3] Includes extensive and unmeasurable duplication from shipments between establishments in the same industry classification.

Source: U.S. Bureau of the Census, *Annual Survey of Manufactures, Geographic Area Statistics*, Series M96(AS)-3.

No. 1236. Average Hourly Earnings of Production Workers in Manufacturing Industries, by State: 1980 to 1997

[In dollars]

STATE	1980	1990	1995	1996	1997	STATE	1980	1990	1995	1996	1997
United States ..	7.27	10.83	12.37	12.78	13.17	Missouri........	7.26	10.74	12.17	12.57	12.99
Alabama	6.49	9.39	11.14	11.55	11.85	Montana	8.78	11.51	12.94	13.00	13.28
Alaska.........	10.22	12.46	11.00	11.14	11.78	Nebraska	7.38	9.66	11.19	11.51	12.09
Arizona	7.29	10.21	11.16	11.49	11.68	Nevada	7.72	11.05	12.62	13.59	14.15
Arkansas........	5.71	8.51	10.05	10.41	10.78	New Hampshire....	5.87	10.83	11.94	12.23	12.54
California	7.70	11.48	12.55	12.84	13.22	New Jersey	7.31	11.76	13.56	13.85	14.21
Colorado	7.63	10.94	12.51	12.83	13.33	New Mexico	5.79	9.04	10.68	10.99	11.74
Connecticut	7.08	11.53	13.71	14.01	14.45	New York	7.18	11.11	12.50	12.78	13.19
Delaware	7.58	12.39	14.20	14.02	14.81	North Carolina.....	5.37	8.79	10.56	10.97	11.41
District of Columbia [1]	8.46	12.51	13.66	13.68	14.05	North Dakota	6.56	9.27	10.75	10.95	11.31
Florida.........	5.98	8.98	10.18	10.55	10.95	Ohio...........	8.57	12.64	14.42	14.70	15.30
Georgia	5.77	9.17	10.71	11.19	11.64	Oklahoma	7.36	10.73	11.52	11.78	12.36
Hawaii..........	6.83	10.99	12.82	12.79	13.08	Oregon	8.65	11.15	12.75	13.01	13.38
Idaho..........	7.55	10.60	11.46	12.15	12.46	Pennsylvania	7.59	11.04	12.81	13.40	13.78
Illinois..........	8.02	11.44	12.64	13.03	13.35	Rhode Island	5.59	9.45	10.62	10.95	11.31
Indiana.........	8.49	12.03	13.91	14.33	14.80	South Carolina	5.59	8.84	10.16	10.25	10.34
Iowa...........	8.67	11.27	12.73	13.13	13.57	South Dakota	6.50	8.48	9.36	9.59	9.96
Kansas	7.37	10.94	12.39	12.88	13.46	Tennessee	6.08	9.55	10.78	11.30	11.71
Kentucky	7.34	10.70	12.22	12.70	13.17	Texas	7.15	10.47	11.47	11.81	12.03
Louisiana	7.74	11.61	13.43	13.65	14.16	Utah	7.02	10.32	11.62	12.21	12.85
Maine	6.00	10.59	12.39	12.71	13.10	Vermont........	6.14	10.52	12.21	12.42	12.70
Maryland	7.61	11.57	13.49	13.73	14.14	Virginia	6.22	10.07	11.72	12.19	12.51
Massachusetts	6.51	11.39	12.79	13.05	13.42	Washington	(NA)				
Michigan	9.52	13.86	16.31	16.67	17.17	West Virginia	8.08	11.53	12.64	12.96	13.18
Minnesota	7.61	11.23	12.79	13.16	13.62	Wisconsin........	8.03	11.11	12.76	13.14	13.66
Mississippi	5.44	8.37	9.76	10.18	10.41	Wyoming	7.01	10.83	11.96	13.17	14.56

NA Not available. [1] Washington PMSA (Primary Metropolitan Statistical Area).

Source: U.S. Bureau of Labor Statistics, *Employment and Earnings,* May 1998 issue and earlier issues.

No. 1237. Manufacturers' Shipments, Inventories, and Orders: 1970 to 1997

[In billions of dollars, except ratio]

YEAR	Ship- ments	Inven- tories (Dec. 31)[1]	Ratio of inven- tories to ship- ments[2]	New orders	Unfilled orders (Dec. 31)	YEAR	Ship- ments	Inven- tories (Dec. 31)[1]	Ratio of inven- tories to ship- ments[2]	New orders	Unfilled orders (Dec. 31)
1970	634	101	1.91	625	106	1984	2,288	334	1.75	2,315	370
1971	671	102	1.76	672	107	1985	2,334	330	1.72	2,348	384
1972	756	108	1.58	770	120	1986	2,336	318	1.63	2,342	390
1973	875	124	1.63	913	158	1987	2,476	333	1.58	2,513	427
1974	1,018	158	1.86	1,047	187	1988	2,695	363	1.56	2,739	471
						1989	2,840	385	1.65	2,875	505
1975	1,039	160	1.77	1,023	171						
1976	1,186	175	1.66	1,194	180	1990	2,912	398	1.70	2,934	527
1977	1,358	188	1.58	1,381	202	1991	2,878	384	1.65	2,866	515
1978	1,523	209	1.55	1,580	259	1992	3,005	375	1.47	2,979	489
1979	1,727	239	1.61	1,771	303	1993	3,128	376	1.44	3,092	453
						1994	3,348	396	1.38	3,357	462
1980	1,853	262	1.61	1,876	326						
1981	2,018	280	1.74	2,015	323	1995	3,595	421	1.42	3,608	475
1982	1,960	307	1.97	1,946	309	1996	3,715	427	1.39	3,749	509
1983	2,071	308	1.67	2,105	343	1997	3,929	446	1.36	3,952	532

[1] Beginning in 1982, inventories are stated at current cost and are not comparable to the book value estimates for prior years. [2] Ratio based on December seasonally adjusted data.

Source: U.S. Bureau of the Census, Current Industrial Reports, *Manufacturers' Shipments, Inventories, and Orders: 1987-1997,* Series M3-1(97); and earlier reports.

No. 1238. Value of Manufactures Shipments, Inventories, and New Orders, by Industry: 1993 to 1997

INDUSTRY	SIC code	SHIPMENTS					INVENTORIES (Dec. 31)					NEW ORDERS				
		1993	1994	1995	1996	1997	1993	1994	1995	1996	1997	1993	1994	1995	1996	1997
All manufacturing industries	(X)	3,127,625	3,348,019	3,594,663	3,715,460	3,929,419	375,982	395,974	421,285	427,130	446,131	3,092,381	3,356,797	3,607,586	3,749,299	3,952,025
Durable goods	(X)	1,630,635	1,789,576	1,927,029	2,004,159	2,158,699	233,306	247,001	261,138	266,547	278,766	1,596,974	1,794,508	1,941,378	2,036,536	2,180,708
Stone, clay, and glass	32	65,610	71,230	75,932	82,442	90,221	7,443	7,688	8,359	8,679	8,832	65,945	71,562	76,085	82,142	89,893
Primary metals	33	142,685	161,188	180,314	178,297	188,916	20,093	22,555	24,052	24,385	24,785	144,018	167,685	178,702	180,362	193,987
Fabricated metal products	34	175,118	190,544	204,384	214,007	226,120	23,402	25,127	26,507	27,384	29,046	172,121	191,099	205,388	215,791	228,567
Industrial machinery and equipment	35	278,063	313,047	353,338	381,795	408,860	47,092	51,189	57,108	55,912	58,164	277,416	325,788	358,910	383,749	409,215
Computer and office equipment	357	69,249	78,230	91,343	103,270	111,334	10,473	10,640	12,630	10,277	9,869	68,497	81,595	91,045	103,689	108,986
Electronic and other	36	233,622	266,405	301,447	320,616	351,554	30,765	34,571	37,991	37,953	39,102	233,991	266,386	307,634	319,157	356,557
Electronic components [1]	367	81,236	97,131	120,129	127,996	143,750	10,311	11,391	12,720	13,145	13,778	79,822	97,910	125,680	126,130	145,674
Transportation equipment [1]	37	414,694	450,809	461,806	465,173	502,301	59,140	59,364	57,663	62,347	66,877	386,643	440,817	465,839	495,239	507,667
Motor vehicles and parts	371	267,365	314,637	327,908	329,155	346,606	13,865	15,341	15,838	15,852	15,568	268,545	316,146	328,390	328,914	346,901
Aircraft, missiles, and parts	372, 6	116,345	103,316	100,063	101,322	121,393	9,536	9,403	9,573	9,995	11,255	88,070	90,217	106,062	129,688	124,151
Instruments and related products	38	137,387	138,400	144,719	151,017	162,981	22,492	22,273	24,233	24,517	25,143	133,249	133,232	144,175	149,344	165,453
All other durable goods	(X)	183,456	197,953	205,089	210,812	227,746	22,879	24,234	25,225	25,370	26,817	183,591	197,939	204,645	210,752	229,369
Nondurable goods [1]	(X)	1,496,990	1,558,443	1,667,634	1,711,301	1,770,720	142,676	148,973	160,147	160,583	167,365	1,495,407	1,562,289	1,666,208	1,712,763	1,771,317
Food and kindred products [1]	20	422,220	430,963	446,961	461,297	470,447	31,529	32,652	34,827	35,973	37,301	(NA)	(NA)	(NA)	(NA)	(NA)
Beverages	208	58,562	61,347	64,398	68,387	70,768	5,721	5,902	6,489	7,199	7,871	(NA)	(NA)	(NA)	(NA)	(NA)
Tobacco products	21	28,383	30,021	32,984	34,482	38,693	6,575	6,063	6,100	6,256	6,149	(NA)	(NA)	(NA)	(NA)	(NA)
Textile mill products	22	73,955	78,027	79,874	80,243	83,871	8,821	9,346	9,841	9,479	9,743	(NA)	(NA)	(NA)	(NA)	(NA)
Paper and allied products	26	133,263	143,649	173,716	160,661	161,992	13,795	14,290	17,173	15,887	16,108	(NA)	(NA)	(NA)	(NA)	(NA)
Chemicals and allied products [1]	28	314,907	333,905	361,391	367,674	389,189	35,505	36,737	39,604	40,794	43,880	(NA)	(NA)	(NA)	(NA)	(NA)
Industrial chemicals	2812,6,8,9	158,771	169,909	186,970	184,018	193,265	17,142	17,710	19,157	19,603	20,335	(NA)	(NA)	(NA)	(NA)	(NA)
Drugs, soaps, toiletries	283-4	117,888	122,352	130,932	138,573	150,016	13,964	14,425	15,596	16,099	18,195	(NA)	(NA)	(NA)	(NA)	(NA)
Petroleum and coal products	29	144,834	143,328	151,439	174,284	177,314	9,865	10,661	10,829	12,046	11,806	(NA)	(NA)	(NA)	(NA)	(NA)
Rubber and plastics products	30	122,777	135,145	145,739	150,467	156,599	12,770	14,145	15,093	15,584	16,300	(NA)	(NA)	(NA)	(NA)	(NA)

NA Not available.   X Not applicable.   [1] Includes industries not shown separately.

Source: U.S. Bureau of the Census, Current Industrial Reports, Series M3-1(97), *Manufactures' Shipments, Inventories, and Orders: 1987-1997*.

No. 1239. Value of Manufactures Shipments, Inventories, and New Orders, by Market Grouping: 1993 to 1997

[In millions of dollars. Based on 1987 Standard Industrial Classification (SIC). For definition of individual market groupings, see publication cited below. Based on a sample survey of most manufacturing companies with $500 million or more in annual shipments]

MARKET GROUPING	SHIPMENTS 1993	1994	1995	1996	1997	INVENTORIES (Dec. 31) 1993	1994	1995	1996	1997	NEW ORDERS 1993	1994	1995	1996	1997
All manufacturing industries	3,127,625	3,348,019	3,594,663	3,715,460	3,929,419	375,982	395,974	421,285	427,130	446,131	3,092,381	3,356,797	3,607,586	3,749,299	3,952,025
Market categories:															
Automotive equipment	134,229	155,406	160,793	162,253	169,145	6,776	7,284	7,537	7,697	7,755	134,526	155,702	160,887	162,310	169,310
Home goods and apparel	195,574	205,985	210,653	210,324	220,994	27,423	29,409	30,359	28,056	29,226	194,976	205,505	211,040	209,912	222,405
Consumer staples	691,292	706,036	742,164	780,340	809,598	59,946	61,776	65,704	67,944	71,473	691,346	706,182	742,360	780,545	809,563
Machinery and equipment	524,479	569,333	613,526	652,978	711,993	86,613	92,596	99,957	104,241	111,413	505,542	567,922	624,687	672,605	729,607
Business supplies	248,468	258,551	276,451	289,085	302,490	21,886	23,155	25,052	25,326	26,644	248,203	258,913	276,675	289,251	302,437
Construction materials and supplies	199,227	217,556	228,247	238,116	252,549	23,488	24,939	26,381	26,721	27,689	198,463	219,305	228,242	239,060	253,766
Defense products	86,034	80,793	78,031	75,896	79,523	21,858	19,230	17,146	16,067	16,442	73,530	76,283	76,598	81,145	72,066
Other material, supplies and intermediate products	1,048,322	1,154,359	1,284,798	1,306,468	1,383,127	127,992	137,585	149,149	151,078	155,489	1,045,795	1,166,985	1,287,097	1,314,471	1,392,871
Durable goods industries:															
Nondefense capital goods	400,882	429,272	475,387	512,068	563,933	80,561	86,884	94,498	98,027	104,787	380,329	428,364	486,134	535,575	577,978
Excluding aircraft and parts	330,245	368,193	413,760	448,495	483,149	55,908	60,949	68,579	66,453	69,237	331,278	380,160	418,414	450,084	490,101
Defense capital goods	84,085	77,096	73,415	71,947	75,194	22,557	19,665	17,305	16,178	16,693	71,904	71,683	70,903	77,283	67,706
Durables excluding capital goods	1,145,668	1,283,208	1,378,227	1,420,144	1,519,572	130,188	140,452	149,335	152,342	157,286	1,144,741	1,294,461	1,384,341	1,423,678	1,535,024
Miscellaneous series:															
Producers' durable equipment	1,032,475	1,143,391	1,225,170	1,285,908	1,383,145	144,239	155,298	165,868	171,014	179,571	1,016,530	1,151,557	1,240,694	1,304,326	1,405,864
Household durable goods	88,522	95,167	98,645	98,437	106,074	12,499	13,834	14,676	14,160	14,549	88,914	95,500	98,500	97,963	107,403
Information technology industries	179,581	199,492	223,048	247,295	270,844	28,506	29,923	34,170	31,765	32,528	178,434	202,336	223,687	246,156	272,605
Health care equipment and products	106,335	108,896	114,691	122,805	132,540	14,233	14,422	15,621	16,505	17,853	105,737	107,266	114,183	122,984	133,451

Source: U.S. Bureau of the Census, Current Industrial Reports, Series M3-1(97), Manufacturers' Shipments, Inventories, and Orders: 1987-1997.

No. 1240. Ratios of Manufacturers' Inventories to Shipments and Unfilled Orders to Shipments, by Industry Group: 1993 to 1997

[Based on seasonally adjusted data]

INDUSTRY	INVENTORY/SHIPMENTS RATIO					UNFILLED ORDERS/SHIPMENTS RATIO				
	1993	1994	1995	1996	1997	1993	1994	1995	1996	1997
All manufacturing industries.	1.44	1.38	1.42	1.39	1.36	3.14	2.92	2.81	2.93	2.80
Durable goods industries	1.67	1.61	1.64	1.62	1.54	3.80	3.50	3.38	3.40	3.33
Stone, clay, and glass products .	1.32	1.25	1.31	1.31	1.18	1.23	1.17	1.14	1.05	0.87
Primary metals	1.62	1.46	1.62	1.59	1.57	1.85	1.92	1.89	1.97	2.24
Fabricated metal products	1.55	1.56	1.56	1.56	1.53	1.45	1.40	1.38	1.44	1.47
Industrial machinery and equipment.	1.95	1.92	1.91	1.77	1.69	2.26	2.53	2.43	2.36	2.18
Electronic and other electrical equipment.	1.57	1.55	1.50	1.44	1.33	2.21	1.94	1.96	1.82	1.81
Transportation equipment	1.68	1.55	1.54	1.67	1.59	11.47	10.61	10.43	11.66	10.87
Instruments and related products.	2.00	1.94	2.00	1.97	1.84	4.10	4.18	3.91	3.69	3.54
Nondurable goods industries	1.17	1.10	1.16	1.13	1.13	0.71	0.75	0.68	0.72	0.69
Food and kindred products	0.88	0.85	0.90	0.93	0.92	(NA)	(NA)	(NA)	(NA)	(NA)
Tobacco products.	2.57	2.25	2.09	1.95	1.78	(NA)	(NA)	(NA)	(NA)	(NA)
Textile mill products	1.50	1.44	1.58	1.44	1.45	(NA)	(NA)	(NA)	(NA)	(NA)
Paper and allied products	1.25	1.10	1.23	1.22	1.13	(NA)	(NA)	(NA)	(NA)	(NA)
Chemicals and allied products . .	1.36	1.25	1.33	1.32	1.34	(NA)	(NA)	(NA)	(NA)	(NA)
Petroleum and coal products . . .	0.95	0.89	0.89	0.81	0.88	(NA)	(NA)	(NA)	(NA)	(NA)
Rubber and plastics products. . .	1.21	1.17	1.25	1.26	1.22	(NA)	(NA)	(NA)	(NA)	(NA)

NA Not available.

Source: U.S. Bureau of the Census, Current Industrial Reports, *Manufacturers' Shipments, Inventories, and Orders: 1987-1997*, Series M3-1(97).

No. 1241. Industrial Production Indexes, by Industry: 1980 to 1997

[**1992=100.** Beginning 1990, data based on 1987 Standard Industrial Classification (SIC), earlier years based on 1977 SIC; see text, Section 26]

INDUSTRY	SIC code	1980	1985	1990	1991	1992	1993	1994	1995	1996	1997
Total index	(X)	79.7	88.0	98.9	97.0	100.0	103.6	109.2	114.5	118.5	124.5
Manufacturing.	(X)	75.5	85.7	98.5	96.2	100.0	103.8	110.0	116.0	120.2	127.0
Durable goods	(X)	73.4	85.6	99.0	95.5	100.0	105.7	114.4	123.9	131.7	142.3
Lumber and products	24	80.4	92.0	101.6	94.5	100.0	100.8	105.9	107.8	111.8	115.0
Furniture and fixtures	25	79.1	88.9	100.9	94.8	100.0	104.9	108.1	111.7	116.0	122.7
Stone, clay, and glass products . . .	32	96.5	98.0	105.0	97.2	100.0	102.1	107.9	111.1	114.6	120.5
Primary metals	33	108.0	98.4	104.0	96.7	100.0	105.7	113.4	117.2	118.9	124.5
Fabricated metal products . . . . . . [1]	34	94.4	96.5	101.2	96.2	100.0	104.4	112.2	116.6	119.6	122.9
Industrial, commercial machinery [1] .	35	70.5	81.2	100.1	95.4	100.0	109.9	124.8	142.7	155.3	171.3
Computer and office equipment. .	357	13.9	50.3	81.4	82.3	100.0	120.5	149.1	208.1	281.6	381.9
Electrical machinery	36	48.6	68.4	87.7	89.6	100.0	110.7	133.2	170.9	199.3	231.5
Transportation equipment	37	70.3	88.8	102.3	96.5	100.0	103.8	107.1	105.7	106.5	115.5
Motor vehicles and parts	371	65.8	95.0	95.3	88.5	100.0	113.6	129.8	131.0	130.2	137.0
Instruments	38	73.6	89.3	98.4	99.8	100.0	100.8	99.7	100.6	105.1	108.0
Nondurable goods	(X)	78.3	86.0	97.9	97.0	100.0	101.7	105.2	107.4	108.0	111.2
Foods	20	79.7	88.9	97.0	98.4	100.0	102.0	103.7	106.8	107.3	109.6
Tobacco products	21	108.5	101.8	105.4	98.9	100.0	84.2	104.5	111.8	113.4	113.2
Textile mill products	22	89.0	86.5	93.2	92.7	100.0	105.2	110.6	109.9	106.7	109.6
Paper and products	26	75.2	83.8	96.0	96.8	100.0	104.0	108.4	109.7	107.9	112.9
Printing and publishing	27	72.4	90.2	103.1	99.1	100.0	100.6	100.7	101.5	101.5	104.9
Chemicals and products	28	75.9	79.4	97.3	96.4	100.0	101.4	104.7	107.5	110.5	115.2
Petroleum products	29	95.9	89.5	100.3	99.1	100.0	102.9	102.7	104.5	106.5	109.5
Rubber and plastics products.	30	53.3	73.8	92.2	90.7	100.0	106.9	116.5	119.5	122.5	126.5
Leather and products	31	181.6	126.1	107.8	98.4	100.0	100.9	93.6	83.9	78.3	73.7
Mining	(X)	111.5	111.0	104.8	102.6	100.0	100.1	102.6	102.3	103.9	105.8
Utilities.	(X)	87.3	88.8	98.3	100.4	100.0	103.9	105.3	109.0	112.5	112.6

X Not applicable. [1] Includes computer equipment.

Source: Board of Governors of the Federal Reserve System, *Federal Reserve Bulletin*, monthly; and *Industrial Production and Capacity Utilization*, Statistical Release G.17, monthly.

No. 1242. Index of Manufacturing Capacity: 1980 to 1997

[1992 output=100. Annual figures are averages of quarterly data. Capacity represents estimated quantity of output relative to output in 1992 which the *current* stock of plant and equipment in manufacturing industries was capable of producing. Primary processing industries comprise textiles, lumber, paper and pulp, petroleum, rubber, stone, clay, glass, primary metals, fabricated metals, and a portion of chemicals. Advanced processing industries comprise chemical products, food, beverages, tobacco, apparel, furniture, printing and publishing, leather, machinery, transportation equipment, instruments, ordnance, and miscellaneous industry groups]

YEAR	Index of capacity	RELATION OF OUTPUT TO CAPACITY (percent)			YEAR	Index of capacity	RELATION OF OUTPUT TO CAPACITY (percent)		
		All manu-facturing	Primary process-ing	Advanced process-ing			All manu-facturing	Primary process-ing	Advanced process-ing
1980	95	79	77	81	1989	118	84	86	82
1981	98	78	77	79	1990	121	81	84	80
1982	100	72	69	73	1991	123	78	80	77
1983	102	74	74	74	1992	126	79	82	78
1984	105	80	80	80	1993	129	80	84	79
1985	109	79	79	79	1994	133	82	87	80
1986	112	79	80	78	1995	140	83	87	81
1987	114	81	84	80	1996	148	81	86	80
1988	116	84	87	82	1997	155	82	86	80

Source: Board of Governors of the Federal Reserve System, *Capacity Utilization In Manufacturing, Mining, Utilities, and Industrial Materials,* G.3., monthly.

No. 1243. Finances and Profits of Manufacturing Corporations: 1980 to 1997

[In billions of dollars. Beginning 1989, data exclude estimates for corporations with less than $250,000 in assets at time of sample selection. Prior years include estimates for corporations in this size category. See Table 905 for individual industry data]

ITEM	1980	1985	1990	1991	1992	1993	1994	1995	1996	1997
Net sales...............	1,897	2,331	2,811	2,761	2,890	3,015	3,261	3,519	3,758	3,926
Net operating profit	129	138	173	133	151	180	241	268	277	299
Net profit:										
Before taxes..............	145	137	160	100	33	119	244	277	311	335
After taxes	92	88	112	68	23	84	175	200	227	247
Cash dividends.............	36	46	62	60	63	67	70	81	96	108
Net income retained in business ..	58	42	49	7	-40	17	105	120	132	139

Source: 1980, U.S. Federal Trade Commission; thereafter, U.S. Bureau of the Census, *Quarterly Financial Report for Manufacturing, Mining, and Trade Corporations.*

No. 1244. U.S. Exports of Manufactures, Origin of World Exports of Manufacture: 1981 to 1995

[In billions of dollars, except percents]

ITEM	1981-85, average	1986-90, average	1991	1992	1993	1994	1995
U.S. manufactures export value	**143**	**212**	**305**	**327**	**339**	**381**	**429**
Machinery & transport equipment.......	93	135	190	203	211	233	257
Chemicals.....................	21	31	40	44	45	52	61
Other	29	46	75	80	83	97	111
Origin of world exports of manufactures (percent):							
United States [1] **.................**	**12.7**	**10.7**	**12.0**	**11.8**	**12.1**	**11.8**	**11.5**
Machinery & transport equipment	17.1	14.2	15.1	14.9	15.2	14.4	13.5
Chemicals	15.0	12.9	13.3	13.1	13.6	13.2	13
Other.	8.5	5.9	7.6	7.4	7.8	7.9	8.2
Germany [2]...................	13.4	14.6	14.2	13.9	12.0	11.7	12.2
Japan	13.4	12.4	11.9	11.8	12.5	11.8	11.4
Other G-7 countries [3]............	21.7	21.5	21.6	21.0	19.9	19.7	20.4
East Asian NICs [4]...............	6.4	7.8	8.2	8.1	8.9	8.8	9.4

[1] U.S. exports are domestic exports only.   [2] Prior to 1991, data for are for former West Germany only.   [3] Other Group of Seven (G-7) Countries: Canada, France, Italy, United Kingdom.   [4] East Asian newly industrialized countries (NICs): Hong Kong, S. Korea, Singapore, Taiwan.

Source: U.S. Dept. of Commerce, International Trade Administration, Office of Trade and Economic Analysis. Based on United Nations Commodity Trade Statistics, *Statistical Yearbook of the Republic of China (Taiwan),* and unpublished data.

No. 1245. Alcoholic Beverages—Summary: 1980 to 1996

[For **1980-1985**, stocks on hand for years ending June 30; later data for years ending September 30. All other items for fiscal years ending in year shown; see text, State and Local Government Finances and Employment section. Includes Puerto Rico. Excludes imports]

ITEM	Unit	1980	1985	1990	1992	1993	1994	1995	1996, prel.
Beer: Breweries operated	Number	86	103	286	392	480	619	879	1,504
Production [1]	Mil. bbl. [2]	193	194	202	202	202	203	200	199
Value of shipments [3]	Mil. dol.	9,362	12,216	15,186	17,302	16,629	16,714	17,108	18,196
Tax-paid withdrawals	Mil. bbl. [2]	172	175	182	182	180	180	177	177
Stocks on hand	Mil. bbl. [2]	15	14	14	13.4	13.7	13.4	13.5	13.3
Distilled spirits:									
Production facilities operated	Number	143	117	143	143	132	150	153	(NA)
Production [1][4]	Mil. tax gal. [5] . .	236	117	122	110	111	99	104	(NA)
Tax-paid withdrawals [6]	Mil. tax gal. [5] . .	330	306	251	246	240	229	235	(NA)
Stocks on hand [4]	Mil. tax gal. [5] . .	696	588	451	365	420	410	452	(NA)
Whiskey: Production [1]	Mil. tax gal. [5] . .	87	65	77	62	59	59	69	(NA)
Stocks on hand	Mil. tax gal. [5] . .	566	467	365	309	361	354	358	(NA)
Still wines: Production	Mil. wine gal. [7] .	982	622	577	484	417	438	412	577
Tax-paid withdrawals [8]	Mil. wine gal. [7] .	340	414	468	387	354	356	366	382
Stocks on hand [9]	Mil. wine gal. [7] .	486	602	562	525	520	477	398	473
Effervescent wines [10]**:** Production. . . .	Mil. wine gal. [7] .	26.8	32.0	26.9	24.7	27.7	23.7	24.3	22.3
Tax-paid withdrawals	Mil. wine gal. [7] .	24.1	30.9	26.2	24.1	24.4	23.7	22.8	22.0
Stocks on hand	Mil. wine gal. [7] .	11.9	21.3	22.1	18.8	19.5	16.5	16.8	23.6

NA Not available. [1] Production represents total amount removed from fermenters, including distilling material, and includes increase after fermentation (by amelioration, sweetening, and addition of wine spirits). [2] Barrels of 31 wine gallons. [3] Source: U.S. Bureau of the Census, *Census of Manufactures*, and *Annual Survey of Manufactures*. [4] Excludes alcohol produced for industrial use. Also excludes vodka and gin production. [5] For spirits of 100 proof or over, a tax gallon is equivalent to the proof gallon; for spirits of less than 100 proof, the tax gallon is equivalent to the wine gallon. A proof gallon is the alcoholic equivalent of a U.S. gallon at 60 degrees F, containing 50 percent of ethyl alcohol by volume. [6] Includes ethyl alcohol. [7] A wine gallon is the U.S. gallon equivalent to the volume of 231 cubic inches. [8] Includes special natural wines. [9] Excludes distilling materials. [10] Includes champagne, other effervescent wines, and artificially carbonated wines.

Source: Except as noted, U.S. Bureau of Alcohol, Tobacco, and Firearms, *Alcohol and Tobacco Summary Statistics*, annual; beginning 1985, *Monthly Statistical Release, Distilled Spirits*, Report Symbol 76; and *Wines*, Report Symbol, ATF A:I 5120-3.

No. 1246. Tobacco Products—Production, Consumption, and Expenditures: 1980 to 1996

[Production data are for calendar years. Excludes cigars produced in customs bonded manufacturing warehouses]

ITEM	Unit	1980	1985	1990	1991	1992	1993	1994	1995	1996
PRODUCTION										
Cigarettes	Billions .	714	665	710	695	719	661	726	747	758
Cigars	Billions .	3	3	2	2	2	2	2	2	2
Tobacco [1]	Mil. lb. .	163	158	142	142	141	133	132	131	131
Consumption per person . .	Lb. [3] . . .	7.9	6.8	5.5	5.4	5.4	5.0	5.0	5.0	5
Cigarettes	1,000 .	4	3	3	3	3	3	3	3	3
Cigars [4]	Number.	24	18	13	12	12	11	12	15	18
Consumer expenditures . . .	Bil. dol. .	21.0	32.2	43.8	47.4	48.4	49.0	47.7	48.6	52
Cigarettes	Bil. dol. .	19.4	30.3	41.6	45.2	45.8	46.2	44.5	45.1	49
Cigars	Bil. dol. .	0.7	0.7	0.7	0.7	0.6	0.7	0.9	1.0	916
Other	Bil. dol. .	0.9	1.2	1.5	1.8	2.0	2.1	2.3	2.5	2,217

[1] Smoking and chewing tobaccos and snuff output. [2] Based on estimated population 18 years old and over, as of July 1, including Armed Forces abroad. [3] Unstemmed processing weight equivalent. [4] Weighing over 3 pounds per 1,000.

Source: U.S. Dept. of Agriculture, Economic Research Service, *Tobacco Situation and Outlook,* quarterly.

No. 1247. Textiles and Apparel Products—U.S. Exports and Imports: 1993 to 1995

[**In millions of dollars.** Excludes glass fibers, rubber and leather apparel, and clothing donated for charity. Minus sign (-) indicates deficit]

PRODUCT	EXPORTS			GENERAL IMPORTS			MERCHANDISE TRADE BALANCE		
	1993	1994	1995	1993	1994	1995	1993	1994	1995
Total	10,977	12,208	14,023	42,225	45,952	49,348	-31,248	-33,744	-35,325
Textile yarn fabrics	6,025	6,592	7,372	8,438	9,208	9,910	-2,413	-2,616	-2,538
Textile yarn	1,045	1,213	1,530	1,146	1,335	1,407	-101	-122	123
Cotton fabric, woven	641	725	834	1,552	1,498	1,613	-911	-773	-779
Woven fabric of manmade textiles . .	883	925	952	1,261	1,291	1,224	-378	-366	-272
Woven fabric of textile material	210	236	258	662	695	690	-452	-459	-432
Special yarns	1,418	1,588	1,748	878	977	1,040	540	611	708
Other	1,828	1,905	2,050	2,939	3,412	3,936	-1,111	-1,507	-1,886
Apparel	4,952	5,616	6,651	33,787	36,744	39,438	-28,835	-31,128	-32,787

Source: U.S. Bureau of the Census, *U.S. Merchandise Trade: Exports, General Imports, and Imports for Consumption,* Report FT925, monthly.

No. 1248. Cotton, Wool, and Manmade Fibers — Consumption, by End-Use: 1996

[Represents products manufactured by U.S. mills. Excludes glass fiber]

YEAR	Total (mil. lb.)	COTTON		WOOL		MANUFACTURED FIBERS					
								Artificial [1]		Synthetic [2]	
		Total (mil. lb.)	Percent of end-use	Total (mil. lb.)	Percent of end-use	Total (mil. lb.)	Percent of end-use	Total (mil. lb.)	Percent of end-use	Total (mil. lb.)	Percent of end-use
Total	16,754	5,348	31.9	169	1.0	11,237	67.1	468	2.8	10,769	64.3
Apparel	6,644	3,557	53.5	117	1.8	2,970	44.7	278	4.2	2,692	40.5
Home textiles . .	2,528	1,427	56.4	12	0.5	1,089	43.1	78	3.1	1,011	40.0
Floor coverings .	4,002	25	0.6	24	0.6	3,953	98.8	-	0.0	3,953	98.8
Industrial [3]	3,579	339	9.5	15	0.4	3,225	90.1	112	3.1	3,113	87.0

- Represents or rounds to zero. [1] Rayon and acetate. [2] Nylon, polyester, acrylic, and olefin. [3] Includes consumer-type products.

Source: Fiber Economics Bureau, Inc., Washington, DC, *Textile Organon*, monthly (copyright).

No. 1249. Broadwoven and Knit Fabrics—Shipments, Foreign Trade, and Apparent Consumption: 1996

[Fabric blends as shown in the CIR report, MQ22T are reported based on the chief weight of the fiber; whereas, fabrics blends as shown for imports are based on the chief value of the fiber. Apparent consumption represents new domestic supply and is derived by subtracting exports for the total manufacturers' shipments plus imports]

PRODUCT DESCRIPTION	Manufacturers' shipments (quantity)	IMPORTS FOR CONSUMPTION		Percent imports to manufacturers' shipments	EXPORTS OF DOMESTIC MERCHANDISE		Percent exports to manufacturers' shipments	Apparent consumption (quantity)
		Quantity	Value [1] ($1,000)		Quantity	Value ($1,000)		
BROADWOVEN FABRICS (quantity 1,000 sq. meters)								
Cotton fabrics [2]	3,614,846	1,326,114	1,638,830	36.7	279,080	659,646	7.7	4,661,880
Manmade fiber fabrics	9,522,420	888,246	1,228,633	9.3	387,704	882,069	4.1	10,022,962
Silk fabrics	519	30,933	311,318	5,957.5	3,404	27,145	655.6	28,048
Wool fabrics	127,069	27,112	278,211	21.3	10,681	58,341	8.4	143,500
KNIT FABRICS (quantity in 1,000 kilograms)								
Total	889,481	45,877	454,617	5.2	58,764	495,184	6.6	876,594
Pile fabrics	64,132	19,961	214,933	31.1	12,644	139,321	19.7	71,449
Elastic fabric	(D)	198	4,007	(D)	9,314	88,108	(D)	(D)
Other warp knit fabrics	95,398	5,479	55,102	5.7	3,893	44,250	4.1	96,984
Other narrow knit fabrics	(D)	464	7,101	(D)	2,930	30,440	(D)	-2,466
Other knit fabrics	676,793	19,775	173,474	2.9	29,983	193,065	4.4	666,585

D Data withheld to avoid disclosing figures for individual companies. [1] Dollar value represents the c.i.f. (cost, insurance, and freight) at the first port of entry in the United States plus calculated import duty. [2] Includes all cotton and chiefly cotton mixed with manmade fiber.

Source: U.S. Bureau of the Census, *Manufacturing Profiles*, Series MP/96.

No. 1250. Selected Apparel—Shipments, Foreign Trade, and Apparent Consumption: 1996

[Quantity in thousands of units, value in millions of dollars]

PRODUCT DESCRIPTION	MANUFACTURERS' SHIPMENTS		EXPORTS OF DOMESTIC MERCHANDISE		IMPORTS FOR CONSUMPTION		APPARENT CONSUMPTION	
	Quantity	Value	Quantity	Value	Quantity	Value	Quantity	Value
Men's and boys' apparel:								
Sweaters	14,869	214.4	22,488	100.6	35,568	466.7	27,949	580.5
Tops, except sweaters	(D)	(D)	371,352	1,020.3	1,352,496	6,722.8	(D)	(D)
Bottoms	625,097	7,963.3	256,728	1,032.4	610,488	3,926.8	978,857	10,857.7
Coats:								
Suit type, dress and sport . . .	11,268	711.7	6,816	57.0	11,472	414.4	15,924	1,069.1
Other coats	53,205	1,491.0	20,376	99.1	117,528	1,840.4	150,357	3,232.3
Suits	(D)	(D)	5,184	54.0	79,584	532.1	(D)	(D)
Swimwear	2,269	21.7	1,320	6.3	42,456	149.2	43,405	164.6
Women's and girls' apparel:								
Sweaters	46,996	611.5	3,972	22.7	152,088	1,601.2	195,112	2,190.0
Dresses	182,780	4,373.5	21,432	114.1	189,564	1,928.0	350,912	6,187.4
Tops, except sweaters	596,810	4,156.1	176,748	434.6	1,013,892	5,433.2	1,433,954	9,154.7
Skirts	83,820	1,208.7	10,248	43.8	137,760	1,063.2	211,332	2,228.1
Coats and jackets	48,320	1,816.9	16,632	124.7	127,560	2,847.6	159,248	4,539.8
Bottoms, except skirts	481,963	4,971.8	139,896	480.3	597,072	3,800.5	939,139	8,292.0
Suits	(D)	(D)	7,032	62.4	105,288	361.1	(D)	(D)
Swimwear	51,153	741.7	7,332	37.6	30,780	189.3	74,601	893.4
Infants' apparel	151,677	785.8	104,952	135.7	424,260	1,039.9	470,985	1,690.0

D Data withheld to avoid disclosing figures for individual companies.
Source: U.S. Bureau of the Census, *Manufacturing Profiles*, Series MP/96.

No. 1251. Footwear—Production, Foreign Trade, and Apparent Consumption: 1996

[Quantity in thousands of pairs, value in thousands of dollars]

PRODUCT DESCRIPTION	Manufac-turers' ship-ments (quantity)	EXPORTS OF DOMESTIC MERCHANDISE		Percent exports to domestic produc-tion	IMPORTS FOR CONSUMPTION		Apparent consump-tion (quantity)	Percent imports to apparent consump-tion
		Quantity	Value		Quantity	Value		
Total	192,680	27,904	414,615	14.5	1,351,683	13,839,766	1,516,459	89.1
Rubber or plastic uppers and rubber or plastic soles	25,074	4,954	48,146	19.8	468,874	2,977,616	488,994	95.9
Waterproof.	12,934	502	5,571	3.9	2,927	20,901	15,359	19.1
Not waterproof	12,140	4,452	42,575	36.7	465,947	2,956,715	473,635	98.4
Leather uppers	77,562	12,078	285,534	15.6	587,077	9,040,167	652,561	90.0
Athletic	5,055	7,454	158,522	147.5	415,187	5,613,759	412,788	100.6
Leather soles	25,962	3,040	85,349	11.7	54,080	1,384,093	77,002	70.2
Made with steel safety toes . .	1,545	199	10,585	12.9	6,925	147,212	8,271	83.7
Boots, ex. with steel safety toes	6,355	484	15,248	7.6	4,024	101,116	9,895	40.7
Shoes, ex. with steel safety toes	17,572	2,357	59,516	13.4	43,131	1,135,765	58,346	73.9
Other soles	46,545	1,584	41,663	3.4	117,810	2,042,315	162,771	72.4
Made with steel safety toes . .	1,998	-	-	(NA)	-	-	1,998	(NA)
Boots, ex. with steel safety toes	7,103	1,584	41,663	22.3	117,810	2,042,315	123,329	95.5
Shoes, ex. with steel safety toes	37,444	-	-	(NA)	-	-	37,444	(NA)
Fabric uppers	86,381	10,872	80,935	12.6	295,732	1,821,983	371,241	79.7
Rubber or plastic soles	59,095	6,210	66,269	10.5	246,525	1,538,385	299,410	82.3
Athletic	(D)	4,662	47,219	(D)	82,655	929,803	(D)	(D)
All other.	(D)	1,548	19,050	(D)	163,870	608,582	(D)	(D)
With all other soles	27,286	4,662	14,666	17.1	49,207	283,598	71,831	68.5

- Represents zero.   D Data withheld to avoid disclosure.   NA Not available.

Source: U.S. Bureau of the Census, *Manufacturing Profiles,* Series MP/96, annual.

No. 1252. Inorganic Chemicals and Pharmaceutical Preparations—Value of Shipments: 1990 to 1996

PRODUCT	Product code	Unit	1990	1993	1994	1995	1996
INORGANIC CHEMICAL SHIPMENTS							
Alkalies and chlorine.	2812	Mil. dol . . .	3,187	2,278	2,281	3,169	3,212
Inorganic color pigments	2816	Mil. dol . . .	2,261	2,391	2,471	2,284	2,487
Inorganic chemicals n.e.c.	2819	Mil. dol . . .	13,612	11,860	12,442	14,179	14,454
Household bleaching compounds	28422 00	Mil. dol . . .	724	915	950	923	870
PHARMACEUTICAL PREP. SHIPMENTS							
Affecting neoplasms, endocrine systems, and metabolic disease	28341	Mil. dol . . .	2,743	3,820	4,132	4,076	4,775
Acting on the central nervous system and sense organs.	28342	Mil. dol . . .	7,219	8,927	9,065	9,228	10,207
Acting on the cardiovascular system	28343	Mil. dol . . .	4,815	5,234	5,547	5,988	6,965
Acting on the respiratory system	28344	Mil. dol . . .	3,724	5,510	5,675	5,196	5,179
Acting on the digestive system	28345	Mil. dol . . .	4,840	7,996	8,827	8,593	8,603
Acting on the skin.	28346	Mil. dol . . .	1,558	1,980	2,219	2,171	2,074
Vitamin, nutrient, and hematinic preps.	28347	Mil. dol . . .	2,588	3,560	4,408	4,812	5,413
Affecting parasitic and infective disease . . .	28348	Mil. dol . . .	5,411	7,234	8,189	7,196	7,218
Pharmaceutical preps. for veterinary use . .	28349	Mil. dol . . .	1,057	1,353	1,315	1,605	1,750

Source: U.S. Bureau of the Census, through 1992, *Current Industrial Reports,* MA28A, and MA28G, annual; thereafter, *Manufacturing Profiles,* Series MP, annual.

No. 1253. Fiber, Rugs, Carpeting, and Sheets—Shipments: 1990 to 1996

PRODUCT	Unit	1990	1991	1992	1993	1994	1995	1996
All fibers [1]	Mil. lbs. .	812	837	926	1,008	1,036	953	890
Raw wool [2][3]	Mil. lbs. .	133	152	151	157	153	142	123
Noils, and fiber [4]	Mil. lbs. .	20	21	21	23	19	20	19
Other fibers	Mil. lbs. .	659	664	754	829	864	792	748
Knit fabric production	Mil. lbs. .	1,901	1,963	2,179	2,188	2,230	2,131	1,897
Rugs, carpet and carpeting	Mil. dol. .	8,527	7,980	8,749	9,283	9,895	9,770	10,117
Sheets	1,000 doz.	15,408	14,001	15,198	16,331	16,190	15,282	16,277
Pillow cases	1,000 doz.	12,665	11,301	12,523	14,464	14,622	14,232	14,330
Terry towels	1,000 doz.	42,376	43,158	48,789	47,161	48,348	47,939	46,955

[1] Includes man-made fiber top converted from tow without combing. A number of companies were added for 1990 based on information in the 1987 Census of Manufactures. Data were received from these companies for 1990; therefore, the information shown for years prior to 1990 may not be directly comparable. These changes represent approximately 20 percent of the total fibers consumed on the woolen system and worsted combing.   [2] Data are shown on a scoured basis for greasy wool.
[3] Shorn and pulled wool of sheep excludes raw wool consumed in cotton system spinning to avoid disclosing figures for individual companies.   [4] Includes reprocessed and reused wool, mohair, alpaca, vicuna, and other specialty fibers as well as tops and noils consumed in woolen spinning and mohair consumed in worsted combing. Does not include wool tops consumed in cotton system spinning.

Source: U.S. Bureau of the Census, 1990-1992, *Current Industrial Reports,* MA22K, MA22Q, and MQ23X, annual; thereafter, *Manufacturing Profiles,* Series MP, annual.

No. 1254. Glass Containers, Clay Construction Products, and Refractories—Shipments: 1990 to 1996

[In millions of dollars]

PRODUCT	1990	1991	1992	1993	1994	1995	1996
Glass container shipments	285	279	283	290	285	269	257
Brick shipments [1]	1,014	883	920	990	1,103	1,092	1,235
Clay tile shipments [2]	687	639	646	687	756	728	776
Clay pipe and fittings shipments	60	51	38	32	33	35	36
Refractory shipments	2,003	1,947	1,956	1,930	2,047	2,222	2,296
Clay	771	784	786	773	906	941	945
Nonclay	1,232	1,163	1,170	1,157	1,141	1,281	1,351

NA Not available.   [1] Building or common and face bricks.   [2] Floor and wall tile including quarry tile.

Source: U.S. Bureau of the Census, 1990-1992, *Current Industrial Reports,* M32G, MQ32D, and MA32C, annual; thereafter, *Manufacturing Profiles,* Series MP, annual.

No. 1255. Aluminum Mill Products—Shipments, by Product: 1995 and 1996

[Quantity in thousands of pounds, receipts in thousands of dollars]

PRODUCT DESCRIPTION	1995			1996		
	Gross shipments	Total receipts	Net shipments [1]	Gross shipments	Total receipts	Net shipments [1]
Aluminum mill products . . .	**15,723,667**	**1,316,423**	**14,407,244**	**15,602,233**	**1,321,279**	**14,280,954**
Sheet, plate, and foil	10,807,903	801,942	10,005,961	10,565,874	788,995	9,776,879
Sheet and plate	9,745,709	801,942	8,943,767	9,432,563	788,995	8,643,568
Sheet	9,407,190	801,942	8,605,248	9,130,558	788,995	8,341,563
Plate	338,519	-	338,519	302,005	-	302,005
Foil	1,062,194	-	1,062,194	1,133,311	-	1,133,311
Rod, wire, and cable	1,159,235	382,325	776,910	1,210,469	438,015	772,454
Rod and bare wire	552,322	382,325	169,997	586,058	438,015	148,043
Cable and insulated wire	606,913	(D)	606,913	624,411	-	624,411
Rod, bar, pipe, tube and shapes	3,396,583	132,156	3,264,427	3,492,033	94,269	3,397,764
Rod and bar (rolled and extruded)	431,121	132,156	3,264,427	432,676	94,269	338,407
Pipe and tube (extruded and drawn)	317,648	(D)	317,648	328,540	(D)	328,540
Extruded shapes	2,647,814	-	2,647,814	2,730,817	-	2,730,817
All other	359,946	-	359,946	333,857	-	333,857

- Represents zero.   D Withheld to avoid disclosure of individual companies.   [1] Net shipments are derived by subtracting domestic receipts from gross shipments.   [2] Included "Rod and bare wire."   [3] Included in "Rod and bar."

Source: U.S. Bureau of the Census, *Manufacturing Profiles, 1996,* Series MP/96.

No. 1256. Iron and Steel Industry—Summary: 1990 to 1997

[For financial data, the universe in 1992 consists of the companies that produced 68 percent of the total reported raw steel production. The financial data represent the operations of the steel segment of the companies. Minus sign (-) indicates net loss]

ITEM	Unit	1990	1991	1992	1993	1994	1995	1996	1997
Steel mill products, apparent supply . . .	Mil. tons [1] . .	97.8	88.3	95.0	104.6	121.3	114.8	125.0	131.0
Net shipments	Mil. tons [1] . .	85.0	78.8	82.2	89.0	95.1	97.5	100.9	105.9
Exports	Mil. tons [1] . .	4.3	6.3	4.3	4.0	3.8	7.1	5.0	6.0
Imports	Mil. tons [1] . .	17.2	15.8	17.1	19.5	30.1	24.4	29.2	31.2
Scrap consumed	Mil. tons [1] . .	50.1	50.5	51.9	58.5	60.0	62.0	62.0	64.0
Scrap inventory	Mil. tons [1] . .	3.6	3.7	3.3	3.6	4.0	4.1	5.3	5.0
Iron and steel products: Exports	Mil. tons [1] . .	5.3	7.4	5.3	4.7	4.9	8.2	6.2	7.4
Imports	Mil. tons [1] . .	21.9	20.2	21.9	21.8	32.7	27.3	32.1	34.4
Capacity by steelmaking process	Mil. net tons	116.7	117.6	113.1	109.9	108.2	112.4	116.1	121.4
Revenue	Bil. dol.	30.9	27.1	26.9	29.5	33.5	35.1	35.0	(NA)
Net income	Bil. dol.	0.1	-2.0	-4.1	1.9	1.3	1.5	0.4	(NA)
Stockholders' equity	Bil. dol.	4.3	2.8	-0.6	3.7	7.1	8.6	9.2	(NA)
Total assets	Bil. dol.	28.3	27.4	28.8	30.6	32.0	35.3	35.1	(NA)
Capital expenditures [2]	Bil. dol.	2.6	2.3	1.8	1.5	2.2	2.5	2.1	(NA)
Working capital ratio [2]	Ratio	1.6	1.4	1.4	1.3	1.6	1.5	1.7	(NA)
Inventories	Bil. dol.	4.7	4.4	4.5	4.6	4.9	0.3	0.3	(NA)
Average employment	1,000	164	146	140	127	126	123	119	112
Hours worked	Million	350	304	293	274	273	269	259	247
Index of output, all employees [3]	1987=100 . .	110.5	108.2	117.7	134.2	144.6	145.4	(NA)	(NA)
Producer price indexes: [4]									
Iron and steel, total	1982=100 . .	117.2	114.1	111.5	116.0	122.0	128.8	125.8	126.5
Steel mill products	1982=100 . .	112.1	109.5	106.4	108.2	113.4	120.1	115.6	116.4
Electrometallurgical products	1982=100 . .	120.1	116.9	115.5	115.7	117.0	126.0	157.7	163.0
Iron ore	1982=100 . .	83.3	83.6	83.7	82.7	82.7	91.8	96.7	96.3
Scrap, iron and steel	1982=100 . .	166.0	147.6	139.2	172.5	192.9	202.7	191.1	188.9
Foundry and forge shop products . .	1982=100 . .	117.2	119.0	120.1	121.3	123.9	129.3	132.6	134.1

NA Not available.   [1] In millions of short tons.   [2] Current assets to current liabilities.   [3] Source: U.S. Bureau of Labor Statistics.   [4] Source: U.S. Bureau of Labor Statistics, *Producer Price Indexes*, monthly and annual.

Source: American Iron and Steel Institute, Washington, DC, *Annual Statistical Report* (copyright).

No. 1257. Raw Steel, Pig Iron, and Ferroalloys Production: 1990 to 1997

[In millions, except percent]

ITEM	1990	1991	1992	1993	1994	1995	1996	1997
Raw steel (net tons):								
World production	848.8	811.1	810.2	814.6	800.1	833.8	826.9	874.9
U.S. production	**98.9**	**87.9**	**92.9**	**97.9**	**100.6**	**104.9**	**105.3**	**108.6**
Percent of world	11.6	10.8	11.8	12.0	12.6	12.6	12.7	12.4
Furnace:								
Basic oxygen process . .	58.5	52.7	57.6	59.3	61.0	62.5	60.4	61.1
Electric	36.9	33.8	35.3	38.5	39.6	42.4	44.9	47.5
Open hearth	3.5	1.4	-	-	-	-	-	-
Grade:								
Carbon	86.6	77.9	82.5	86.9	89.5	92.7	93.6	95.9
Alloy and stainless	12.3	10.0	10.4	11.0	11.1	12.3	11.7	12.6
Pig iron and ferroalloys, production (sh. tons)	54.8	48.6	52.2	53.1	54.4	56.1	54.5	54.7

- Represents or rounds to zero.

Source: American Iron and Steel Institute, Washington, DC, *Annual Statistical Report* (copyright).

No. 1258. Steel Products—Net Shipments, by Market Classes: 1990 to 1997

[In thousands of short tons. Comprises carbon, alloy, and stainless steel]

MARKET CLASS	1990	1991	1992	1993	1994	1995	1996	1997
Total [1]	**84,981**	**78,846**	**82,241**	**89,022**	**95,084**	**97,494**	**100,878**	**105,858**
Automotive	11,100	10,015	11,092	12,719	14,753	14,622	14,665	15,251
Steel service centers, distributors	21,111	19,464	21,328	23,714	24,153	23,751	27,124	27,800
Construction, incl. maintenance [2]	9,245	9,161	9,536	13,429	10,935	14,892	15,561	15,885
Containers, packaging, shipping	4,474	4,278	3,974	4,355	4,495	4,139	4,101	4,163
Machinery, industrial equipment, tools . .	2,388	1,982	1,951	2,191	2,427	2,310	2,410	2,355
Steel for converting and processing . . .	9,441	8,265	9,226	9,451	10,502	10,440	10,245	11,263
Rail transportation	1,080	999	1,052	1,223	1,248	1,373	1,400	1,410
Contractors' products	2,870	2,306	2,694	2,913	3,348	(2)	(2)	(2)
Oil and gas industries	1,892	1,425	1,454	1,526	1,703	2,643	3,254	3,811
Electrical equipment	2,453	2,102	2,136	2,213	2,299	2,397	2,401	2,434
Appliances, utensils, and cutlery	1,540	1,388	1,503	1,592	1,736	1,589	1,713	1,635

[1] Includes nonclassified shipments and other classes not shown separately.   [2] Beginning 1994, contractors' products included with construction.

Source: American Iron and Steel Institute, Washington, DC, *Annual Statistical Report* (copyright).

No. 1259. Machine Tools—New Orders and Shipments: 1970 to 1996

[**In millions of dollars.** Data represents total industry volume based on reports from over 200 manufacturers]

YEAR	METAL CUTTING TOOLS					METAL FORMING TOOLS				
	New orders (net)		Shipments		Order backlog, end of period	New orders (net)		Shipments		Order backlog, end of period
	Total	Domestic	Total	Domestic		Total	Domestic	Total	Domestic	
1970	651	507	993	827	471	261	227	450	412	235
1971	609	524	672	554	408	252	223	326	286	162
1972	1,009	877	714	627	702	403	368	304	267	260
1973	1,825	1,550	1,074	935	1,454	787	717	427	388	621
1974	2,017	1,716	1,445	1,241	2,025	566	470	585	522	600
1975	916	781	1,879	1,548	1,062	361	284	573	485	388
1976	1,662	1,477	1,482	1,270	1,243	541	485	578	474	351
1977	2,202	1,981	1,651	1,470	1,794	793	729	630	560	515
1978	3,373	3,043	2,189	1,960	2,981	973	901	825	729	663
1979	4,495	3,866	2,930	2,606	4,546	1,126	991	947	860	843
1980	3,885	3,496	3,681	3,206	4,750	870	744	1,011	879	701
1981	2,228	1,946	4,105	3,552	2,873	717	617	991	824	427
1982	1,064	890	2,895	2,599	1,043	433	372	710	600	151
1983	1,152	1,069	1,372	1,200	823	545	489	474	430	222
1984	1,916	1,700	1,607	1,484	1,132	1,000	932	679	609	542
1985	1,853	1,652	1,742	1,549	1,243	675	610	803	743	414
1986	1,544	1,377	1,890	1,685	897	581	507	688	621	307
1987	1,451	1,294	1,677	1,499	672	667	536	647	538	327
1988	2,708	2,316	1,575	1,400	1,806	883	749	825	702	386
1989	1,977	1,723	2,359	2,059	1,423	832	719	837	704	380
1990	2,070	1,772	2,330	2,004	1,164	894	761	970	851	304
1991	1,894	1,549	1,872	1,595	1,186	748	546	802	625	251
1992	1,756	1,532	1,918	1,605	1,025	726	609	678	547	299
1993	2,322	2,177	2,160	1,955	1,187	971	825	1,044	881	225
1994	2,989	2,833	2,640	2,424	1,535	1,698	1,519	1,370	1,196	554
1995	3,105	2,770	3,195	2,923	1,445	1,748	1,398	1,671	1,347	630
1996, est.	3,489	3,180	3,050	2,708	1,665	1,752	1,173	1,973	1,583	520

Source: The Association For Manufacturing Technology, McLean, VA, *The Economic Handbook of The Machine Tool Industry,* annual (copyright).

No. 1260. Metalworking Machinery—Shipments: 1990 to 1997

[**In thousands of dollars**]

PRODUCT	Product code	1990	1993	1994	1995	1996	1997
Metalworking machinery	(X)	3,426,081	3,222,456	3,780,074	4,547,133	4,607,757	5,010,262
Metal cutting type [1]	(X)	2,371,266	2,084,864	2,463,001	3,036,592	3,141,128	3,583,298
Boring machines	3541D	(2)	84,667	129,835	172,417	88,929	80,161
Drilling machines [2]	3541D	184,118	37,076	51,987	78,936	99,453	89,219
Gear cutting machines	35413	102,678	87,662	100,612	137,121	164,258	213,507
Grinding and polishing machines	35414	433,574	360,894	443,262	549,580	541,277	595,014
Lathes [3]	35415	355,632	305,488	390,843	478,003	451,115	480,672
Milling machines [4]	35416	214,254	180,174	138,852	194,757	199,667	280,158
Machining centers [5]	3541A	436,999	485,375	552,358	698,780	779,433	931,566
Station type machines	3541B	502,066	374,772	455,138	477,021	498,592	551,870
Other metal cutting machine tools [6]	3541C	141,945	166,248	200,114	246,237	315,977	358,299
Metal forming type	(X)	1,080,181	1,139,581	1,277,187	1,510,541	1,466,629	1,426,964
Punching and shearing machines	35421 pt.	200,050	213,402	294,441	326,318	331,382	319,208
Bending and forming machines	35421 pt.	222,861	255,299	253,219	256,882	283,020	258,479
Presses, except forging	35422	308,338	345,653	376,398	379,203	401,990	422,396
Forging machines [7]	35423 pt.	73,947	(D)	(D)	(D)	(D)	(D)
Other metal forming [7]	35423 pt.	274,985	325,227	393,015	548,138	450,237	426,881

D Data withheld to avoid disclosure. X Not applicable. [1] Data for "All lathes (turning machines)" and "All milling machines," valued at under $3,025 each are included in total "Metal cutting type". [2] For 1990, data for "Boring machines" were combined with "Drilling machines" to avoid disclosing individual company data. [3] For 1993 through 1997 product code 35415, "Lathes," excludes the value for product code 35415 09, All Lathes valued under $3,025 each. [4] For 1993 through 1997 product code 35416, "Milling machines," excludes the value for product code 35416 09, "All milling machines valued under $3,025 each." [5] Multi-function numerically controlled machines. [6] Excludes those designed primarily for home workshops, labs, etc. [7] For 1991 through 1997, and 1988 data for "Forging machines" have been combined with "Other metal forming machines" to avoid disclosing individual company

Source: U.S. Bureau of the Census, *Manufacturing Profiles,* Series MP, annual; and release date: July 14, 1998, <http://www.census.gov/ftp/pub/industry/mq35w97a>.

No. 1261. Selected Types of Construction Machinery—Value of Shipments: 1990 to 1996

[In millions of dollars]

PRODUCT DESCRIPTION	Product code	1990	1992	1993	1994	1995	1996
Off-highway wheel and crawler tractors, dozers and self-propelled log skidders; except shovel loader	35315	1,453.1	1,099.5	(D)	(D)	1,597.4	1,690.8
Tractor shovel loaders	3531C	2,235.9	1,833.1	2,354.4	2,632.6	3,041.8	3,340.1
Power cranes, draglines, and shovels	3531E	1,511.8	1,582.3	1,719.4	2,252.5	2,561.4	2,719.5
Mixers, pavers, and related equipment	3531F	609.6	635.8	877.1	1,079.8	1,168.8	1,146.5
Scrapers; graders; compactors; rollers; off-highway trucks, trailers, and wagons; and rough terrain forklifts	3531G	2,023.7	1,560.7	(D)	2,164.2	2,654.3	3,193.2
Equipment for mounting on tractors	3531N	258.6	256.1	249.8	286.6	310.1	(D)
Self-propelled continuous ditchers and trenchers	3531P 20	129.7	124.1	143.6	174.0	193.5	209.1
Aerial work platforms	3531P 90	814.9	590.3	637.4	844.9	1,131.1	(D)

D Data withheld to avoid disclosing figures for individual companies.

Source: U.S. Bureau of the Census, through 1992, *Current Industrial Reports*, series MA35D; thereafter, *Manufacturing Profiles*, Series MP, annual.

No. 1262. Mining and Mineral Processing Equipment—Shipments: 1995 and 1996

PRODUCT	Product code	Number of companies 1996	QUANTITY (units)		VALUE (mil. dol.)	
			1995	1996	1995	1996
Mining and mineral processing equipment	(X)	(X)	(X)	(X)	1,629	1,751
Portable crushing, screening, washing, and combination plants	3531K	17	649	676	96	97
Underground mining machinery [1]	35325	34	4,396	6,838	463	434
Crushing/pulverizing/screening machinery [2]	35327	46	3,871	4,026	295	332
Drills and other mining machinery, n.e.c. [1][3]	35328	30	13,473,018	16,735,391	382	446
Portable drilling rigs and parts	3533A	30	2,155,275	2,267,380	393	443

X Not applicable. [1] Excludes parts. [2] Excludes portables and parts. [3] n.e.c. = Not elsewhere classified.

Source: U.S. Bureau of the Census, *Manufacturing Profiles, 1996*, Series MP/96.

No. 1263. Engines, Refrigeration and Heating Equipment, and Pumps and Compressors—Shipments: 1993 to 1996

PRODUCT	Product code	Unit	1993	1994	1995	1996
Internal combustion engines produced	(X)	1,000	21,342	24,178	23,274	23,559
Gasoline (except outboard, aircraft, and auto)	35191	1,000	20,561	23,287	22,287	22,621
Nonautomotive diesel (except aircraft)	35193	1,000	197	220	246	242
Automotive diesel	35194	1,000	608	661	732	687
Natural gas and LPG	35196	1,000	6	9	9	9
Air-conditioning, heating equipment shipments:						
Heat transfer equipment	35851	Mil. dol	4,951	5,509	6,170	6,409
Unitary air-conditioners	35852	Mil. dol	3,937	4,339	4,807	5,539
Commercial refrigeration equipment	35853 pt	Mil. dol	183	220	203	220
Compressors and compressor units	35854	Mil. dol	3,101	3,717	4,307	4,618
Condensing units, refrigeration (complete)	35855	Mil. dol	240	277	286	296
Room air-conditioners and dehumidifiers	35856	Mil. dol	824	1,106	1,359	1,497
Nonelectric warm air furnaces and humidifiers	3585C pt	Mil. dol	1,334	1,426	1,522	1,639
Pumps and compressors [1]	(X)	Mil. dol	6,216	6,563	6,435	6,974
Domestic water systems	35613	Mil. dol	330	339	329	351
Oil well, oilfield, and other pumps (including laboratory pumps)	35615	Mil. dol	916	907	664	704
Compressors and vacuum pumps	35631	Mil. dol	2,400	2,680	2,742	2,908

X Not applicable. [1] Excludes hand pumps, automotive circulating pumps, compressors for icemaking and refrigeration equipment, air conditioning units, and replacements and repair parts for pumps and compressors.

Source: U.S. Bureau of the Census, *Manufacturing Profiles*, Series MP, annual.

No. 1264. Computer Shipments and Revenues: 1990 to 1995

[Revenue is in if-sold, end-user dollars]

SELECTED AREA AND PRODUCT	FACTORY REVENUE (mil. dol.)			SHIPMENTS (units)		
	1990	1994	1995	1990	1994	1995
United States:						
Supercomputer	789	856	631	531	821	735
Mainframe	12,538	5,120	3,753	3,952	2,662	2,095
Midrange	9,816	7,752	8,623	208,102	141,147	206,008
Workstation	3,147	4,976	5,715	161,488	316,083	357,765
Personal computer	18,661	37,313	47,708	9,848,593	18,605,000	22,582,900
Canada:						
Supercomputer	30	40	34	19	45	46
Mainframe	892	187	220	257	125	157
Midrange	744	459	711	17,832	9,598	20,145
Workstation	226	256	292	12,077	18,627	19,949
Personal computer	1,448	3,586	4,292	857,706	1,732,564	2,043,438
Western Europe:						
Supercomputer	506	493	480	291	341	647
Mainframe	10,862	5,339	4,894	4,307	2,031	2,111
Midrange	10,062	5,831	5,890	243,340	152,665	162,726
Workstation	2,396	2,862	3,752	121,577	202,048	235,171
Personal computer	14,810	22,861	29,483	7,954,834	11,760,736	14,672,340
Japan:						
Supercomputer	470	755	729	116	297	380
Mainframe	5,698	4,933	4,551	6,222	3,982	3,401
Midrange	5,392	4,781	5,494	231,571	175,716	187,124
Workstation	1,512	2,276	2,435	96,267	146,232	156,198
Personal computer	4,746	8,753	13,943	2,243,500	3,344,710	5,695,389

Source: Gartner Group (formerly Dataquest Inc.), San Jose, CA, Consolidated Data Base.

No. 1265. Computers and Office and Accounting Machines—Value of Shipments: 1990 to 1996

[In millions of dollars]

SELECTED PRODUCTS	Product class	1990	1991	1992	1993	1994	1995	1996
Electronic computers	3571	25,630.1	26,274.1	28,571.2	29,659.1	38,260.7	49,038.1	50,681.5
Large-scale processing equipment [1]	35713	(NA)	(NA)	5,267.1	4,104.4	4,458.5	5,288.8	5,962.3
Medium-scale & small-scale processing equipment	35714	(NA)	(NA)	3,347.3	2,442.3	2,815.5	2,278.6	2,401.6
Personal computers and workstations [1]	35715	(NA)	(NA)	17,059.6	18,888.8	24,298.0	34,349.3	35,767.9
Portable computers [1]	35716	(NA)	(NA)	1,644.2	2,575.6	5,028.3	5,774.3	5,290.8
Other general purpose digital processing units [1]	35717	(NA)	(NA)	493.5	946.2	958.8	457.9	432.0
Other computers [1]	35718	(NA)	(NA)	759.4	701.8	701.6	889.3	826.8
Loaded computer processor boards and board subassemblies [2]	36798	2,247.2	12,590.4	13,745.8	15,087.1	17,514.8	24,447.7	24,133.8
Computer storage devices & equipment	35721	7,488.2	5,609.7	6,282.4	5,730.7	5,555.6	7,903.0	8,160.7
Parts for computer storage devices & sub-assemblies	35722	955.2	780.4	1,357.1	1,496.4	1,951.9	2,235.6	1,775.8
Computer terminals	35751	2,066.7	1,729.5	1,707.9	1,531.3	1,243.5	1,086.0	1,062.3
Computer peripheral equipment, n.e.c.	35771	7,696.6	7,763.6	8,505.6	9,810.1	11,943.6	12,331.0	12,783.9
Parts for input/output equipment	35772	3,705.5	4,186.9	3,053.2	2,554.3	2,498.7	2,391.0	5,441.6
Calculating and accounting machines [3]	35784	(D)	973.5	967.5	1,454.2	1,261.5	1,278.9	1,456.2
Magnetic and optical recording media	36950	3,695.4	3,894.4	4,336.8	4,483.3	4,777.1	5,106.2	5,155.8

D Withheld to avoid disclosing data for individual companies.   NA Not available.   [1] Prior to 1992, product class separation for computers is not available.   [2] These data are collected on two Current Industrial Report forms, MA35R, "Computers and Office and Accounting Machines (Shipments) and MA36Q, Semiconductors, Printed Circuit Boards, And Other Electronic Components. [3] Product classes 35781 and 35782 were combined to product class 35784 beginning 1991.

Source: U.S. Bureau of the Census, Manufacturing Profiles, Series MP, annual.

No. 1266. Computers and Industrial Electronics—Factory Shipments: 1990 to 1996

[In millions of dollars]

ITEM	1990	1991	1992	1993	1994	1995	1996
Computer and peripheral equipment, total	50,793	50,121	51,932	54,821	59,254	73,555	78,673
Computers	25,973	26,691	29,036	30,002	38,261	49,038	50,682
Peripheral equipment	24,820	23,430	22,896	24,819	20,993	24,517	27,992
Industrial electronics, total	26,183	26,126	26,778	27,250	29,927	33,732	35,300
Controlling, processing equipment	12,728	12,633	12,881	13,961	15,014	16,450	16,986
Testing, measuring equipment	6,859	7,492	7,484	7,332	8,416	10,109	10,874
Nuclear electronic equipment	567	571	533	519	477	501	503
Robots, accessories, and components	275	294	(NA)	(NA)	(NA)	(NA)	(NA)
Other electronic equipment	5,754	5,137	5,880	5,438	6,020	6,672	6,937

NA Not available.

Source: Electronic Industries Association, Washington, DC, Electronic Market Data Book, annual (copyright).

No. 1267. Computers and Office and Accounting Machines—Shipments: 1995 and 1996

PRODUCT	Product code	Number of companies, 1996	QUANTITY (1,000)		VALUE (mil. dol.)	
			1995	1996	1995	1996
Electronic computers (automatic data processors)	3571	201	20,386	19,939	49,038	50,682
Large-scale processing equipment [1]	35713	29	60	101	5,289	5,962
Medium- and small-scale processing equipment [2]	35714	39	225	268	2,279	2,402
Personal computers and workstations	35715	86	15,308	14,423	34,349	35,768
Portable computers	35716	39	3,964	4,374	5,774	5,291
Computer storage devices and equipment	35721	91	(X)	(X)	7,903	8,161
Parts for computer storage devices and subassemblies	35722	21	(X)	(X)	2,236	1,776
Computer terminals	35751	54	(X)	(X)	1,086	1,062
Parts for computer terminals	35752	13	(X)	(X)	(D)	165
Computer peripheral equipment, n.e.c. [4]	35771	260	(X)	(X)	12,331	12,784
Calculating and accounting machines	35784	43	(X)	(X)	1,279	1,465
Automatic typing and word processing machines	35792	3	(D)	(D)	(D)	(D)
Mailing, letter handling, addressing machines	35795	32	(X)	(X)	1,280	1,235
Other office machines, n.e.c. [4]	35799	45	(X)	(X)	558	576
Printed circuit assemblies	36798	674	(X)	(X)	24,448	24,134
Magnetic and optical recording media	36950	57	(X)	(X)	5,106	5,156

D Data withheld to avoid disclosing figures for individual companies. X Not applicable. [1] 64 megabytes in MINIMUM main memory configuration. [2] Up to 64 megabytes in MINIMUM main memory configuration. [3] Data not shown because it is not comparable to prior years. [4] N.e.c. = Not elsewhere classsified.
Source: U.S. Bureau of the Census, *Manufacturing Profiles,* Series MP, annual.

No. 1268. Consumer Electronics and Electronic Components— Factory Sales, by Product Category: 1990 to 1996

[In millions of dollars. Factory sales include imports]

PRODUCT CATEGORY	1990	1991	1992	1993	1994	1995	1996
Total	43,033	42,668	47,408	52,469	58,230	62,541	65,440
Video products:							
Direct-view color TV	6,197	5,979	6,591	7,316	7,225	6,798	6,492
LCD color TV	50	56	51	45	42	44	39
Projection TV	626	683	714	841	1,117	1,417	1,426
TV/VCR combinations	178	265	375	599	710	723	697
Monochrome TV	99	61	47	40	38	34	29
LCD Monochrome TV	33	31	32	33	32	31	32
Other video:							
VCR decks	2,439	2,454	2,947	2,851	2,869	2,767	2,621
Camcorders	2,260	2,013	1,841	1,958	1,985	2,135	2,084
Laserdisc players	72	81	93	123	122	108	66
Home satellite earth stations	421	370	379	408	900	1,265	1,493
Videocassette players	65	71	49	61	64	59	43
Home and portable products:							
Compact audio systems	1,270	1,264	1,370	1,464	1,703	1,677	1,537
Separate audio components	1,935	1,805	1,586	1,635	1,686	1,911	1,808
Home radios	360	310	324	307	306	284	291
Portable audio equipment	1,645	1,780	2,096	2,187	2,495	2,506	2,150
Mobile electronics:							
Aftermarket autosound equipment	1,192	1,232	1,467	1,604	1,898	1,931	1,814
Factory installed autosound	3,100	2,875	2,990	3,199	3,225	3,100	2,512
Cellular telephones	1,133	962	1,146	1,257	1,275	1,431	1,656
Pagers	118	139	168	198	230	300	370
Vehicle security	190	210	240	294	401	464	478
Home office products:							
Cordless telephones	842	1,125	1,091	1,046	1,106	1,141	1,176
Corded telephones	638	605	575	617	610	557	553
Telephone answering devices	827	1,000	934	1,026	1,153	1,077	1,004
Home computers	4,187	4,287	6,825	8,190	10,088	12,600	15,040
Computer peripherals	1,980	2,060	2,220	2,450	3,100	3,850	4,500
Computer software (inc. CD-ROM)	971	1,045	1,250	1,600	2,050	2,500	3,000
Personal Wordprocessors	656	600	555	558	504	451	404
Home fax machines	920	869	826	888	964	919	839
Home security systems	1,440	1,030	830	940	1,110	1,130	1,350
Electronic gaming:							
Electronic Gaming Hardware	975	1,275	1,575	1,650	1,575	1,500	1,600
Electronic Gaming Software	2,400	2,325	2,400	2,625	2,925	3,000	3,500
Blank media:							
Blank audio cassettes	376	373	376	362	353	334	314
Blank videocassettes	948	980	872	779	730	708	725
Blank floppy diskettes	314	308	320	345	353	373	300
Accessories and batteries:							
Electronic accessories	793	721	715	759	874	816	821
Total primary batteries	1,383	1,424	1,538	2,215	2,412	2,600	2,676
U.S. electronic	61,303	61,698	65,295	71,480	95,704	121,721	129,844
Electron tubes	2,646	2,586	2,655	3,038	3,647	3,675	3,868
Solid State products	23,543	26,238	27,292	31,534	46,379	60,181	67,532
Passive and other components	35,114	32,874	35,349	36,909	45,677	57,865	58,444

Source: Electronic Industries Association, Washington, DC, *Electronic Market Data Book,* annual (copyright).

No. 1269. Semiconductors, Printed Circuit Boards, and Other Electronic Components—Value of Shipments, by Class of Product: 1990 to 1996

[In millions of dollars. N.e.c.=not elsewhere classified]

CLASS OF PRODUCT	Product code	1990	1992	1993	1994	1995	1996
Transmittal, industrial, and special-purpose electron tubes (except x-ray)	36713	1,096.5	868.4	677.6	1,120.5	854.9	645.3
Electron tubes, receiving type	36714	24.2	24.6	27.1	(¹)	(¹)	(¹)
Cathode ray picture tubes, including rebuilt	36714	1,344.1	2,022.8	2,231.5	¹2,627.1	¹2,907.0	¹3,272.0
Electron tube parts	36715	142.6	129.5	160.1	114.9	120.2	153.1
Printed circuit boards	36720	7,174.5	5,721.7	6,273.0	6,812.3	8,367.3	8,302.9
Integrated microcircuits (semiconductor networks)	36741	16,623.3	20,065.4	23,636.1	36,020.4	48,437.9	54,072.5
Transistors	36742	682.3	674.8	704.5	834.6	942.3	1,405.0
Diodes and rectifiers	36743	668.2	652.2	640.7	829.5	1,066.7	918.8
Other semiconductor devices	36749	5,741.0	5,899.2	6,908.2	9,915.4	12,639.4	11,135.3
Capacitors for electronic applications	36750	1,391.5	1,288.0	1,294.3	1,512.3	1,785.3	1,630.5
Resistors	36760	799.8	708.3	716.5	869.5	953.2	906.5
Coils, transformers, reactors, and chokes for electronic applications	36770	975.6	1,095.3	1,121.4	1,250.7	1,411.8	1,368.5
Coaxial connectors	36781	420.0	424.5	419.0	642.4	731.6	636.0
Cylindrical connectors	36782	513.6	503.9	482.8	511.3	552.9	608.8
Rack and panel connectors	36783	500.0	461.9	427.6	545.6	540.5	508.0
Printed circuit connectors	36784	804.9	855.2	859.4	923.4	1,026.4	1,066.9
Other connectors including parts	36785	1,085.0	1,123.3	1,152.8	1,377.2	1,401.9	1,370.1
Filters (except microwave) and piezoelectric devices	36791	457.4	448.8	534.3	674.1	729.2	720.5
Microwave components and devices	36793	1,368.7	1,258.4	1,136.3	1,227.2	1,233.4	1,346.6
Transducers, electrical/electronic input or output	36795	741.1	810.3	832.5	970.5	1,111.3	1,174.9
Switches, mechanical types for electronic circuitry	36796	579.4	541.7	572.6	621.5	666.3	731.8
Printed circuit assemblies	36798	8,269.3	13,745.8	15,087.1	17,514.8	24,447.7	24,133.8
All other electronic components n.e.c	36799	4,898.3	5,260.3	5,257.6	6,149.7	6,978.1	7,273.5

¹ Product codes combined to avoid disclosing figures for individual companies.

Source: U.S Bureau of the Census, *Manufacturing Profiles,* Series MP, annual.

No. 1270. Selected Instruments and Related Products—Shipments: 1990 to 1996

[In millions of dollars]

PRODUCT	Product code	1990	1992	1993	1994	1995	1996
Automatic regulating and control valves	34918	1,418	1,579	1,648	1,807	1,860	1,905
Solenoid-operated valves (except nuclear and fluid power transfer)	34919	346	405	406	452	464	505
Aeronautical, nautical, and navigational instruments	38121	2,518	2,517	2,121	1,859	2,125	2,350
Search & detection, navigation & guidance systems and equipment	38122	32,420	31,311	28,604	25,567	24,697	23,856
Laboratory apparatus and laboratory furniture ¹	38210	1,675	1,715	1,598	1,811	1,837	1,945
Controls for monitoring residential and commercial environments and appliance	38220	1,982	2,197	2,310	2,521	2,533	2,619
Process control instruments	38230	5,224	5,731	5,935	6,240	6,439	6,759
Integrating and totalizing meters for gas and liquids	38242	725	727	777	859	915	963
Counting devices	38243	210	273	285	354	364	363
Motor vehicle instruments ²	38244	1,457	1,576	1,768	2,092	2,193	2,205
Integrating instruments, electrical	38251	396	439	461	440	445	432
Test equipment for testing electrical, radio and communication circuits, and motors	38252	6,156	6,493	6,572	7,582	9,255	10,311
Instruments to measure electricity	38253	586	558	526	554	555	555
Analytical, scientific instruments (except optical)	38260	4,412	4,886	4,766	5,534	5,737	6,093
Sighting, tracking, and fire-control equipment, optical type	38271	581	771	769	652	655	616
Optical instruments and lenses ³	38274	1,252	1,322	1,456	1,597	1,579	1,762
Aircraft engine instruments (except flight)	38291	579	590	552	430	430	447
Physical properties and kinematic testing equip.	38292	1,012	1,149	1,175	1,199	1,374	1,378
Nuclear radiation detection and monitoring instruments	38294	567	533	519	489	501	503
Commercial, geophysical, meteorological, and general purpose instruments	38295	1,140	1,361	1,271	1,344	1,373	1,386
Surveying and drafting instruments	38296	274	255	301	324	356	398

¹ Includes laboratory furniture. Prior to 1990, laboratory furniture was included in product class 38296. ² Includes some data previously classified in product class 37149, "Other motor vehicle parts and accessories, new, n.e.c." ³ Beginning 1992, product classes 38272, "Binoculars and astronomical instruments," and 38273, "Other optical instruments and lenses" were combined into product class 38274; prior years have been restated to reflect revision.

Source: U.S. Bureau of the Census, through 1992, *Current Industrial Reports,* MA38B; thereafter *Manufacturing Profiles,* Series MP, annual.

No. 1271. Fluid Power Products—Shipments: 1991 to 1996

[In millions of dollars. Includes aerospace]

PRODUCT	Product code	1991	1992	1993	1994	1995	1996
Fluid power products, total [1]	(X)	**6,477**	**6,330**	**6,742**	**7,914**	**9,011**	**9,416**
Nonaerospace-type hydraulic directional control valves	3492C	314	316	292	429	467	477
Nonaerospace-type hydraulic valves, except directional control	3492D	292	267	473	561	727	725
Nonaerospace-type pneumatic directional control valves	3492E	294	318	283	382	440	476
Nonaerospace-type flareless fittings and couplings (including nonmetal fittings) used in fluid power transfer systems	3492K	323	326	320	368	447	455
Nonaerospace-type hydraulic and pneumatic fittings, fittings and couplings for hose, and manifolds	3492M	413	423	489	629	676	725
Aerospace-type hydraulic and pnuematic hose or tube end fittings and assemblies and manifolds	3492H	386	354	304	324	358	403
Nonaerospace-type hydraulic fluid power cylinders and actuators, linear and rotary	35934	517	523	786	917	1,071	1,154
Nonaerospace-type pneumatic fluid power cylinders and actuators, linear and rotary	35935	284	341	289	368	400	424
Nonaerospace-type reciprocating pumps	35943	280	251	288	344	491	522
Nonaerospace-type rotary and other fluid power pumps	35944	318	375	339	413	444	423
Nonaerospace-type fluid power motors	35945	194	202	325	433	510	506
Parts for fluid power pumps, motors, and hydrostatic transmissions	35949	354	312	321	334	390	405

X Not applicable. [1] Includes products, not shown separately.

Source: U.S. Bureau of the Census, *Manufacturing Profiles*, Series MP, annual.

No. 1272. Switchgear, Switchboard Apparatus, Relays, and Industrial Controls—Shipments: 1990 to 1996

[In millions of dollars]

PRODUCT	Product code	Companies, 1996 (number)	1990	1992	1993	1994	1995	1996
Power circuit breakers	36132	34	388	481	516	531	443	421
Low volt panelboards & dist. boards	36133	134	1,722	1,531	1,681	1,744	2,025	2,153
Fuses and fuse equipment	36134	24	419	413	320	332	500	522
Molded case circuit breakers, 1,000 volts and under	36135	36	959	955	1,010	1,107	1,173	1,218
Duct, 1,000 volts and under	36136	23	194	189	200	228	239	255
Switchgear, except ducts	36139	129	1,324	1,615	1,581	1,636	1,758	1,864
General purpose and other relays	36251	119	805	782	751	676	808	807
Specific purpose industrial controls	36252	246	2,020	1,916	2,322	2,732	3,312	3,467
General purpose industrial controls	36253	268	2,912	2,778	3,326	3,699	4,189	4,427
Motor controller accessories & parts for industrial controls	36254	131	452	448	476	502	503	497

Source: U.S. Bureau of the Census, through 1992, *Current Industrial Reports*, MA36A, annual; thereafter, *Manufacturing Profiles*, Series MP, annual.

No. 1273. Selected Industrial Air Pollution Control Equipment—Shipments: 1996

[Quantity in number of units, value in millions of dollars]

PRODUCT	Product code	Number of companies	NEW ORDERS		SHIPMENTS		BACKLOG (Dec. 31)	
			Quantity	Value	Quantity	Value	Quantity	Value
Selected industrial air pollution control equipment	**35646**	**110**	**83,936**	**826,871**	**83,545**	**706,959**	**9,799**	**411,697**
Particulate emissions collectors	(X)	86	74,536	495,969	74,150	518,368	9,181	180,301
Electrostatic precipitators	35646 51	15	(D)	108,430	(D)	118,512	(D)	78,467
Fabric filters	35646 54	53	56,240	280,852	55,510	286,828	7,291	54,218
Mechanical collectors	35646 55	37	(D)	57,309	(D)	63,479	(D)	20,265
Wet scrubbers	35646 58	28	1,205	49,378	1,238	49,549	226	27,351
Gaseous emissions control devices	(X)	38	1,068	311,492	1,020	164,034	281	223,510
Catalytic oxidation systems	35646 70	11	196	44,458	189	19,943	50	37,289
Thermal and direct oxidation systems	35646 72	16	251	66,108	242	64,475	47	10,906
Scrubbers (gas absorber)	35646 73	10	516	29,173	525	26,661	106	6,327
Gas absorbers	35646 76	8	(D)	(D)	43	24,487	(D)	(D)
Other	35646 79	18	8,332	19,410	8,375	24,557	337	7,886

D Data withheld to avoid disclosure of company data. X Not applicable.

Source: U.S. Bureau of the Census, *Manufacturing Profiles*, Series MP, annual.

Domestic Trade and Services

This section presents statistics relating to the distributive trades and service industries. Data shown for the trades, classified by kind of business, and for the various categories of services (e.g., personal, business, repair, hotel) cover sales or receipts, establishments, employees, payrolls, and other items. The principal sources of these data are census reports and survey reports of the Bureau of the Census. Data on gross product in trade and service industries usually appear in the *Survey of Current Business*, issued by the U.S. Bureau of Economic Analysis. Financial data for firms engaged in retail, wholesale, or service activities appear in the annual *Statistics of Income*, published by the Internal Revenue Service.

Censuses—Censuses of retail trade and wholesale trade have been taken at various intervals since 1929. Limited coverage of the service industries started in 1933. Beginning with the 1967 census, legislation provides for a census of each area to be conducted every 5 years (for years ending in "2" and "7"). The industries covered in the censuses and surveys of business are those classified in three divisions defined in the *Standard Industrial Classification Manual* (see text, Section 13). *Retail trade* refers to places of business primarily engaged in selling merchandise for personal or household consumption; *wholesale trade*, to establishments primarily engaged in selling goods to dealers and distributors for resale or to purchasers who buy for business and farm uses; and *services*, to establishments primarily engaged in providing a wide range of services for individuals and for businesses.

Beginning with the 1954 Censuses of Retail Trade and Service Industries, data for nonemployer establishments are included and published separately. The census of wholesale trade excludes establishments with no paid employees. Beginning in 1977, sales taxes and finance charges are excluded from sales (or receipt) figures of the three censuses.

In Brief

Retail sales, 1997:
Total	*$2.6 trillion*
Automotive dealers	*$.6 trillion*
Food stores	*$.4 trillion*

Annual receipts of taxable service firms ($ billions):

	1990	1996
Business services	*281*	*485*
Health services	*271*	*399*

In 1982 and prior censuses, the count of establishments represented the number in business at the end of the year. Beginning 1987, the count of establishments represents those in business at any time during the year.

For the 1987 and 1992 Censuses of Service Industries, hospitals operated by governmental organizations are included. Government-operated facilities in other service kind-of-business classifications are excluded from the census. In 1987 and 1992, data were not collected for elementary and secondary schools, colleges and universities, labor unions and similar organizations, and political organizations.

The census of retail trade beginning in 1977, excludes nonemployer direct sellers. Beginning 1982, the census treated each leased department in a store as a separate establishment and classified it according to the kind of business it conducted. In prior years, data for leased departments were consolidated with the data for stores in which they were located.

Current surveys—Current sample surveys conducted by the Bureau of the Census cover various aspects of the retail and wholesale trade and selected service industries. Its *Monthly Retail Trade Report* contains monthly estimates of sales, inventories, and inventory/sales ratios for the United States, by kind of business. Annual figures on sales, year-end inventories, and sales/inventory ratios, by kind of business, appear in the *Annual Benchmark Report for Retail Trade.*

Statistics from the Bureau's monthly wholesale trade survey include national estimates of merchant wholesalers' sales, inventories, and stock-sales ratios by major summary groups—durable and nondurable—and selected kinds of business. Merchant wholesalers are those wholesalers who take title to the goods they sell (e.g., jobbers, exporters, importers, major distributors). These data, based on reports submitted by a sample of firms, appear in the *Monthly Wholesale Trade Report.* Annual figures on sales, sales-inventory ratios, and year-end inventories appear in the *Annual Benchmark Report for Wholesale Trade.* The *Service Annual Survey* provides annual estimates of receipts for selected service industries on a national basis. The *Transportation Annual Survey* and

the *Annual Survey of Communication Services,* (see text, Section 18) furnish the same type of information for services in those respective industries.

For the current sample survey programs, retail trade coverage is the same as for the census; wholesale trade coverage is limited to merchant wholesalers; and selected services coverage is less inclusive than the census.

Estimates obtained from annual and monthly surveys are based on sample data and are not expected to agree exactly with results that would be obtained from a complete census of all establishments. Data include estimates for sampling units not reporting.

Statistical reliability—For a discussion of statistical collection and estimation, sampling procedures, and measures of statistical reliability applicable to Census Bureau data, see Appendix III.

Figure 27.1
U.S. Mail Order Sales, by Kind of Business: 1995

1995 Mail Order Sales: $219.9 Billion

Consumer products 39.3%

Consumer services 25.2%

Generalized mail order marketers[1] 15.8%

Business services 6.1%

Business supplies 10.0%

Industrial 3.7%

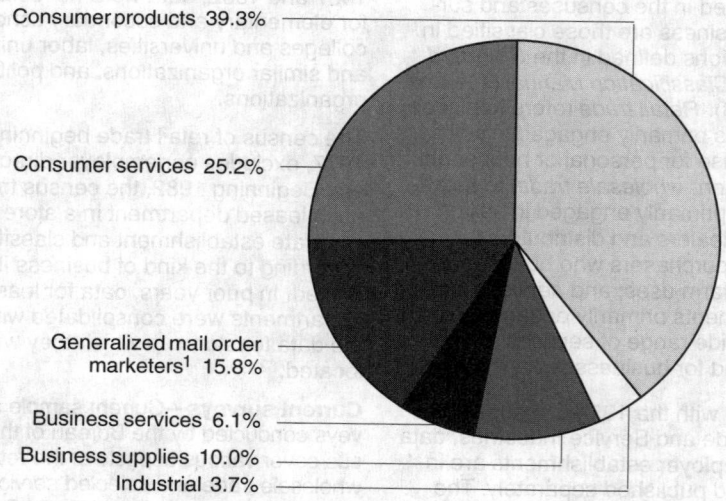

[1]Mail order as part of the overall selling channel mix of multichannel industrial marketers not specializing in mail order selling.

Source: Chart prepared by U.S. Bureau of the Census. For data, see Table 1287.

No. 1274. Gross Domestic Product in Domestic Trade and Service Industries in Current and Real (1992) Dollars: 1990 to 1996

[In billions of dollars, except percent. For definition of gross domestic product, see text, Section 14. Based on 1987 Standard Industrial Classification]

INDUSTRY	CURRENT DOLLARS				CHAINED (1992) DOLLARS [1]			
	1990	1994	1995	1996	1990	1994	1995	1996
Wholesale and retail trade	870.7	1,083.3	1,122.0	1,184.7	906.9	1,049.7	1,080.0	1,141.9
Percent of gross domestic product	15.2	15.6	15.4	15.5	14.8	15.9	16.0	16.5
Wholesale trade	367.2	468.0	484.4	516.8	360.5	448.6	457.5	493.3
Retail trade	503.5	615.3	637.6	667.9	546.4	601.2	622.5	648.5
Services	1,059.4	1,350.4	1,440.3	1,539.5	1,181.7	1,256.5	1,298.8	1,342.9
Percent of gross domestic product	18.4	19.4	19.8	20.2	19.3	19.0	19.3	19.4
Hotels and other lodging places	46.1	57.4	60.6	63.7	49.2	54.4	55.4	55.8
Personal services	38.2	45.8	46.6	49.1	41.7	42.6	42.4	43.3
Business services	199.0	256.0	283.3	318.5	216.5	247.1	271.3	295.7
Auto repair, services, and garages	48.9	59.3	61.1	65.0	54.0	53.3	53.3	55.3
Miscellaneous repair services	17.7	19.2	20.7	22.5	21.5	16.7	17.0	15.9
Motion pictures	20.4	23.0	25.9	29.9	22.1	21.8	23.9	26.2
Amusement and recreation services	39.1	51.4	56.2	60.8	42.8	47.5	49.7	51.6
Health services	307.9	410.2	428.9	447.0	356.9	369.7	371.6	376.6
Legal services	80.7	93.8	96.5	100.0	91.5	86.0	85.5	85.1
Educational services	39.8	52.3	55.1	58.2	44.3	48.9	49.6	50.7
Social services	29.6	43.2	46.7	49.3	32.5	41.6	43.7	44.9
Membership organizations	35.0	45.1	47.0	48.9	38.3	42.1	42.5	43.1
Other services	147.8	182.6	199.9	215.2	160.4	175.4	184.6	192.9
Private households	9.4	11.0	11.8	11.5	10.2	10.4	10.8	10.1

[1] See text, Section 14.

Source: U.S. Bureau of Economic Analysis, *Survey of Current Business*, August 1997.

No. 1275. Retail Trade—Summary: 1972 to 1992

[1972 through 1982 based on 1972 Standard Industrial Classification (SIC) code; beginning 1987 based on 1987 SIC code. Comparability of data over time is affected by changes in the SIC code]

ITEM	Unit	1972	1977	1982	1987	1992
Firms, total [1]	1,000	1,665	1,567	1,573	1,992	2,212
Multiunit establishments [1] [2]	1,000	301	343	415	498	528
Establishments, total [1]	1,000	1,780	1,855	1,923	2,420	2,672
With payroll	1,000	1,265	1,304	1,324	1,504	1,526
With sales of $1,000,000 or more [3]	1,000	74	119	193	259	326
Consumer Price Index: [4]						
All items	1982-84=100 . .	41.8	60.6	96.5	113.6	140.3
All commodities	1982-84=100 . .	44.5	64.2	97.0	107.7	129.1
Sales	Bil. dol.	457	723	1,066	1,540	1,949
By establishments with payroll	Bil. dol.	440	700	1,039	1,493	1,895
By multiunit establishments [2]	Bil. dol.	202	341	567	844	1,137
Percent of total sales	Percent	44.0	47.1	53.2	54.8	58.3
Percent of multiunit sales by 100-or-more establishment multiunits [2] [5]	Percent	55.8	55.8	54.5	54.6	57.0
In 1987 dollars [6]	Bil. dol.	1,042	1,170	1,175	1,540	1,669
Percent of sales by corporations [3]	Percent	76.4	79.8	84.6	88.9	89.9
Per capita sales: [7]						
Current dollars	Dollars	2,186	3,291	4,601	6,357	7,643
Constant (1987) dollars [6]	Dollars	4,978	5,325	5,073	6,357	6,544
Sales as percent of personal income	Percent	46.6	45.2	39.6	40.5	37.9
Payroll, entire year	Bil. dol.	55.4	85.9	123.6	177.5	222.9
Percent of sales [8]	Percent	12.6	12.3	11.9	11.9	11.8
Paid employees, March 12 pay period	1,000	11,211	13,040	14,468	17,780	18,407

[1] Through 1982, represents the number of establishments and firms in business at the end of year. Beginning 1987, represents the number of establishments and firms in business at any time during year. [2] Establishments of firms that operate at two or more locations. [3] Through 1982, represents establishments with and without payroll. Beginning 1987, represents only establishments with payroll. [4] Source: U.S. Bureau of Labor Statistics, *Monthly Labor Review*. Beginning 1982, CPI-U annual averages, see text, Section 15. [5] Prior to 1982, data provided for percent of multiunit sales by 101-or-more establishment units. [6] Based on implicit price deflators for retail sales supplied by U.S. Bureau of Economic Analysis. [7] Based on estimated resident population as of July 1. [8] Covers only establishments with payroll.

Source: Except as noted, U.S. Bureau of the Census, *Census of Retail Trade, 1972*, RC72-S-1; *1977*, RC77-52; *1982*, RC82-A-52 and RC82-I-1; *1987*, RC87-A-52, RC87-N-1, and RC87-S-1; and *1992*, RC92-A-52, RC92-N-1, and RC92-S-1.

No. 1276. Retail Trade—Establishments, Employees, and Payroll: 1990 and 1995

[Covers establishments with payroll. Employees are for the week including March 12. Most government employees are excluded. For statement on methodology, see Appendix III]

KIND OF BUSINESS	1987 SIC code [1]	ESTABLISHMENTS (1,000)		EMPLOYEES (1,000)		PAYROLL (bil. dol.)	
		1990	1995	1990	1995	1990	1995
Retail trade, total	(G)	1,529.7	1,567.9	19,815	21,085	241.7	300.0
Building materials and garden supplies [2]	52	71.9	64.4	703	740	11.9	14.5
Lumber and other building materials	521	27.5	24.0	403	455	7.5	9.5
Paint, glass, and wallpaper stores	523	10.2	9.9	54	50	0.9	1.0
Hardware stores	525	19.0	13.9	143	120	1.9	1.7
Retail nurseries and garden stores	526	10.1	11.7	76	80	1.0	1.3
Mobile home dealers	527	4.2	4.5	23	33	0.4	0.9
General merchandise stores [2]	53	36.6	36.2	2,135	2,291	22.9	29.1
Department stores	531	10.1	10.8	1,710	1,874	18.3	23.6
Variety stores	533	10.0	10.5	109	93	1.0	0.9
Misc. general merchandise stores.	539	15.0	14.3	310	323	3.6	4.5
Food stores [2]	54	186.1	181.9	3,124	3,188	35.8	41.5
Grocery stores	541	132.5	130.8	2,757	2,871	32.4	38.0
Meat and fish markets	542	9.3	8.2	54	45	0.6	0.6
Fruit and vegetable markets	543	2.9	3.1	19	18	0.2	0.2
Candy, nut, confectionery stores.	544	5.4	4.8	29	27	0.2	0.2
Retail bakeries	546	19.9	20.2	176	153	1.5	1.6
Automotive dealers and service stations [2] . . .	55	207.3	199.8	2,104	2,190	40.0	51.2
New and used car dealers	551	26.1	24.2	917	991	23.9	32.4
Used car dealers	552	14.3	19.7	56	78	1.0	1.7
Auto and home supply stores	553	43.4	42.6	305	318	5.1	6.1
Gasoline service stations	554	104.8	97.4	701	702	7.5	8.7
Boat dealers	555	4.6	4.8	34	31	0.6	0.7
Recreational vehicle dealers	556	2.7	2.9	24	28	0.5	0.7
Motorcycle dealers.	557	3.4	3.6	22	27	0.4	0.6
Apparel and accessory stores [2]	56	150.2	135.3	1,193	1,148	12.2	12.9
Men's and boys' clothing stores	561	14.7	13.9	108	107	1.5	1.5
Women's clothing stores.	562	50.2	42.2	439	370	4.0	3.5
Women's accessory and specialty stores . .	563	7.7	8.0	46	46	0.5	0.5
Children's and infants' wear stores	564	5.6	5.1	36	42	0.3	0.4
Family clothing stores.	565	17.8	19.0	283	336	3.0	4.0
Shoe stores	566	37.4	33.0	206	185	2.2	2.2
Misc. apparel and accessory stores	569	9.1	9.6	47	52	0.5	0.6
Furniture and homefurnishings stores [2]	57	108.1	116.7	749	859	12.3	15.7
Furniture and homefurnishings stores [2] . . .	571	61.1	67.3	430	476	7.2	8.9
Furniture stores	5712	30.8	32.9	245	264	4.3	5.3
Floor covering stores	5713	13.2	14.6	77	80	1.5	1.8
Drapery and upholstery stores	5714	3.4	2.6	16	11	0.2	0.2
Misc. homefurnishings stores	5719	13.3	16.7	92	120	1.1	1.6
Household appliance stores	572	10.0	9.7	63	64	1.1	1.2
Radio, television, and computer stores [2] . .	573	34.2	38.9	245	318	3.9	5.5
Radio, TV, and electronic stores	5731	16.5	17.0	120	155	2.1	2.9
Computer and software stores	5734	5.1	8.5	33	58	0.8	1.3
Record and prerecorded tape stores . . .	5735	7.1	8.8	60	78	0.6	0.8
Eating and drinking places [2]	58	402.6	456.7	6,461	7,208	49.6	64.7
Eating places	5812	286.8	344.9	5,700	6,568	43.8	58.7
Drinking places	5813	43.8	47.8	267	305	2.0	2.5
Miscellaneous retail [2]	59	349.0	360.8	2,487	2,611	33.2	40.7
Drug stores and proprietary stores	591	50.0	44.6	593	599	8.3	10.1
Liquor stores [3]	592	30.8	29.0	141	128	1.6	1.6
Used merchandise stores	593	15.0	21.6	79	112	0.9	1.5
Sporting goods and bicycle shops	5941	21.4	24.8	139	173	1.6	2.3
Book stores	5942	11.7	13.4	86	111	0.8	1.3
Stationery stores	5943	4.8	4.4	34	34	0.4	0.5
Jewelry stores.	5944	26.6	27.5	161	143	2.3	2.6
Hobby, toy, and game shops	5945	9.4	10.3	83	104	0.8	1.2
Camera, photo supply stores	5946	3.6	2.9	22	18	0.4	0.3
Gift, novelty, and souvenir shops	5947	29.5	33.8	164	181	1.4	1.8
Sewing, needlework, and piece goods. . . .	5949	8.2	7.0	68	54	0.5	0.5
Catalog and mail-order houses	5961	7.2	7.2	141	181	2.6	3.9
Merchandising machine operators	5962	5.1	6.1	76	72	1.3	1.4
Direct selling establishments	5963	8.8	13.4	107	123	1.7	2.3
Fuel dealers	598	12.0	11.5	100	95	2.2	2.3
Florists	5992	25.8	26.4	131	124	1.2	1.3
Optical goods stores	5995	13.2	14.5	66	73	1.1	1.3
Administrative and auxiliary	(X)	18.0	16.1	860	850	23.7	29.8

X Not applicable.   [1] Based on 1987 Standard Industrial Classification; see text, Section 13.   [2] Includes kinds of business not shown separately.   [3] Includes government employees.

Source: U.S. Bureau of the Census, *County Business Patterns*, annual.

No. 1277. Retail Trade Establishments—Number, Sales, Payroll, and Employees, by Kind of Business: 1987 and 1992

[Each kind-of-business classification includes leased departments classified in that kind of business as if they were separate establishments]

KIND OF BUSINESS	1987 SIC code[1]	ALL ESTABLISHMENTS				ESTABLISHMENTS WITH PAYROLL		
		Number[2] (1,000)		Sales (mil. dol.)		Annual payroll, 1992 (mil. dol.)	Paid employees[3] (1,000)	
		1987	1992	1987	1992		1987	1992
Retail trade, total[4]		**2,420**	**2,672**	**1,540,263**	**1,949,193**	**222,868**	**17,780**	**18,407**
Building materials & garden supplies ..	52	107	105	83,454	100,837	11,790	668	666
Building materials, supply stores ...	521, 3	51	51	61,302	75,358	8,423	432	435
Lumber and other building materials	521	36	36	55,868	68,930	7,519	380	386
Paint, glass, and wallpaper stores	523	15	15	5,434	6,428	903	52	49
Hardware stores	525	27	25	11,036	12,729	1,871	138	136
Retail nurseries and garden stores..	526	21	22	5,809	6,773	1,018	71	71
Mobile home dealers	527	8	7	5,307	5,978	478	27	23
General merchandise stores..	53	57	63	181,971	246,420	24,503	2,003	2,079
Department stores (incl. leased depts.)[5]	531	10	11	153,679	190,785	(NA)	(NA)	(NA)
Department stores (excl. leased depts.)[5]	531	10	11	144,017	186,423	20,136	1,651	1,719
Variety stores	533	21	23	7,134	9,516	1,088	121	116
Misc. general merchandise stores	539	26	29	30,819	50,481	3,279	231	243
Food stores[6]	54	290	278	309,460	377,098	37,228	2,855	2,969
Grocery stores	541	197	186	290,979	358,148	34,425	2,502	2,682
Meat and fish markets	542	[7]11	[7]9	[7]5,616	[7]5,041	556	59	45
Retail bakeries	546	31	31	5,194	5,732	1,407	185	157
Automotive dealers[6]	55 ex. 554	194	207	342,896	406,936	31,807	1,373	1,268
New and used car dealers	551	28	24	280,529	333,801	24,421	940	860
Used car dealers	552	75	92	18,295	25,511	1,132	55	63
Auto and home supply stores	553	67	63	26,622	29,817	4,683	286	269
Boat dealers	555	[7]5	[7]5	[7]6,824	[7]5,537	558	35	27
Recreational vehicle dealers	556	[7]3	[7]3	[7]5,538	[7]6,314	514	25	22
Motorcycle dealers	557	[7]4	[7]4	[7]3,475	[7]4,163	427	27	22
Gasoline service stations	554	137	120	104,769	136,950	7,569	702	675
Apparel and accessory stores	56	197	221	79,322	104,211	12,039	1,121	1,145
Men's and boys' clothing stores	561	19	19	9,017	10,197	1,440	115	105
Women's clothing, specialty stores..	562, 3	77	87	29,208	35,749	4,170	455	467
Women's clothing stores	562	64	65	26,366	31,828	3,690	419	423
Family clothing stores	565	27	33	21,472	33,222	3,469	268	310
Shoe stores	566	43	42	14,594	18,122	2,185	205	184
Furniture and homefurnishings stores.	57	180	189	78,072	96,947	11,869	703	702
Furniture stores	5712	46	48	26,740	31,216	4,355	247	233
Homefurnishings stores	5713, 4, 9	63	64	17,737	21,132	2,835	176	181
Floor covering stores	5713	[7]14	[7]14	[7]9,226	[7]9,616	1,382	75	69
Household appliance stores	572	17	16	8,642	8,407	965	65	54
Radio, television, computer stores[6]	573	54	61	24,953	36,192	3,714	215	235
Radio, TV, and electronic stores.	5731	31	28	15,679	20,275	2,112	123	121
Computer and software stores	5734	8	15	2,799	7,120	607	22	30
Record and prerecorded tape stores	5735	[7]6	[7]8	[7]3,930	[7]5,860	593	44	60
Eating and drinking places	58	490	558	153,462	200,163	52,570	6,100	6,548
Eating places[6]	5812	402	474	142,627	187,758	50,307	5,787	6,244
Restaurants	5812 pt.	[7]155	[7]170	[7]66,364	[7]85,178	25,369	2,822	2,989
Refreshment places	5812 pt.	[7]138	[7]164	[7]56,870	[7]77,686	18,808	2,352	2,652
Cafeterias	5812 pt.	[7]7	[7]6	[7]3,778	[7]3,619	1,037	138	109
Drinking places	5813	88	84	10,834	12,406	2,263	313	304
Drug stores and proprietary stores.	591	56	51	54,142	77,788	9,060	574	588
Miscellaneous retail stores[4][6]	59 ex. 591	710	881	152,716	201,842	24,434	1,682	1,769
Liquor stores	592	45	40	19,826	21,698	1,523	157	133
Used merchandise stores	593	89	124	5,217	8,219	1,124	69	93
Misc. shopping goods stores[6]	594	263	311	53,777	71,650	8,563	706	750
Sporting goods and bicycle shops	5941	50	55	11,256	15,617	1,733	121	137
Book stores	5942	19	23	5,338	8,329	928	72	92
Jewelry stores	5944	50	55	12,925	15,259	2,224	163	148
Hobby, toy, and game shops	5945	28	38	7,451	11,298	992	76	95
Gift, novelty, souvenir shops	5947	79	104	8,446	12,036	1,467	151	164
Nonstore retailers[4]	596	66	116	34,878	52,790	6,280	318	339
Catalog and mail-order houses	5961	31	66	20,765	35,538	3,079	123	150
Merchandising machine operators	5962	24	36	6,258	7,082	1,232	74	70
Direct selling establishments[4]	5963	11	14	7,855	10,170	1,969	121	119
Fuel dealers	598	17	15	14,503	14,202	1,928	99	82
Florists	5992	50	55	5,441	6,433	1,207	125	122
Optical goods stores	5995	15	16	3,480	4,917	1,114	54	65

NA Not available. [1] Based on 1987 Standard Industrial Classification; see text, Section 13. [2] Represents the number of establishments in business at any time during year. [3] For pay period including March 12. [4] Excludes nonemployer direct sellers, SIC 5963. [5] Includes sales from catalog order desks. Data for leased departments not included in broader kind-of-business totals. [6] Includes other kinds of businesses, not shown separately. [7] Covers only establishments with payroll.

Source: U.S. Bureau of the Census, *1987* and *1992 Census of Retail Trade*, RC87-A:52, RC87-N-1, RC92-A-52, and RC92-N-1.

No. 1278. Retail Trade Sales—Summary: 1980 to 1997

[Sales and inventories for leased departments and concessions are tabulated in the kind-of-business category of the leased department or concession. Based on Current Business Survey, see Appendix III]

YEAR	SALES							Inventories at cost [4] (bil. dol.)	Inventory/ sales ratios [4][5]
	Total (bil. dol.)	Annual percent change [1]	Per capita [2] (dol.)	Index of sales (1982= 100)	Durable goods (bil. dol.)	Nondurable goods (bil. dol.)			
						Total	Dept. stores [3]		
1980	957	6.7	4,213	89.5	299	658	85	121	(NA)
1985	1,375	6.9	5,779	128.6	498	877	126	182	1.55
1988	1,656	7.5	6,774	154.9	629	1,027	152	219	1.53
1989	1,759	6.2	7,127	164.5	657	1,102	161	237	1.59
1990	1,845	4.9	7,395	172.5	669	1,176	166	240	1.56
1991	1,856	0.6	7,361	173.6	650	1,206	173	243	1.57
1992	1,952	5.2	7,653	182.5	704	1,248	186	252	1.50
1993	2,074	6.3	8,046	193.9	780	1,294	200	268	1.50
1994	2,230	7.5	8,567	208.5	882	1,348	217	292	1.53
1995	2,329	4.5	8,865	217.8	940	1,390	231	307	1.54
1996	2,461	5.7	9,281	230.2	1,009	1,453	244	316	1.52
1997	2,566	4.3	9,588	240.0	1,058	1,508	261	324	1.49

NA Not available.　[1] Change from immediate prior year.　[2] Based on Bureau of the Census estimates of resident population as of July 1.　[3] Excludes leased departments.　[4] As of Dec. 31. Includes warehouses. Adjusted for seasonal variations. [5] Sales data also adjusted for holiday and trading-day differences.

No. 1279. Retail Trade—Sales, by Kind of Business: 1980 to 1997

[In billions of dollars. See headnote, Table 1278. Based on Current Business Survey, see Appendix III]

KIND OF BUSINESS	1987 SIC code [1]	1980	1985	1990	1993	1994	1995	1996	1997
Retail trade, total.		957.4	1,375.0	1,844.6	2,073.8	2,229.9	2,329.3	2,461.2	2,566.2
Durable goods stores, total [2]		299.2	498.1	668.8	780.0	882.1	939.7	1,008.5	1,058.2
Building materials and garden supplies [2]	52	50.8	71.2	94.6	110.6	124.9	130.1	140.3	150.5
Building materials, supply stores	521,3	35.0	50.8	70.3	83.2	94.6	98.2	106.2	116.1
Hardware stores	525	8.3	10.5	12.5	13.2	14.0	14.1	14.4	14.6
Automotive dealers	55 exc. 554	164.1	303.2	387.6	457.8	521.8	556.7	599.7	625.7
Motor vehicle, misc. automotive dealers. . .	551,2,5,6,7,9	146.2	278.0	356.8	426.4	487.6	520.8	561.3	587.7
Motor vehicle dealers	551,2	137.7	263.1	338.7	405.7	463.7	493.7	531.9	553.2
New and used car dealers	551	130.5	251.6	316.0	377.3	430.6	456.2	490.0	507.5
Auto and home supply stores	553	18.0	25.2	30.8	31.4	34.1	40.0	38.4	38.0
Furniture and homefurnishings stores [2]	57	44.2	68.3	91.5	106.1	120.3	130.3	137.9	146.7
Furniture, homefurnishings stores [2]	571	26.3	38.3	50.5	55.2	59.9	62.3	66.0	71.6
Furniture stores	5712	(NA)	23.9	30.8	33.1	35.4	36.7	39.0	42.8
Floor covering stores	5713	(NA)	7.9	10.7	10.8	11.7	12.0	12.1	13.1
Household appliance, radio, TV, and computer stores	5722,31,34	14.0	25.1	33.0	41.5	50.1	57.2	60.7	64.0
Household appliance stores	5722	(NA)	8.4	8.8	9.0	8.8	9.6	9.7	10.3
Radio, TV, and computer stores	5731,34	(NA)	16.7	24.3	32.5	41.3	47.6	51.1	53.8
Sporting goods and bicycle shops	5941	(NA)	8.7	15.0	16.9	19.0	20.2	21.2	22.1
Book stores	5942	(NA)	4.5	7.4	9.2	10.3	11.5	12.4	12.7
Jewelry stores	5944	(NA)	11.2	15.2	16.6	18.0	19.1	20.2	19.5
Nondurable goods stores, total [2]		658.1	876.9	1,175.8	1,293.9	1,347.8	1,389.6	1,452.7	1,508.0
General merchandise stores	53	109.0	158.6	215.5	264.2	282.3	298.0	313.2	331.5
Department stores [3]	531	85.5	126.4	165.8	199.8	217.4	231.1	244.5	261.2
Variety stores	533	7.8	8.5	8.3	9.8	9.5	9.9	10.6	11.5
Misc. general merchandise stores.	539	15.7	23.8	41.4	54.6	55.4	57.0	58.1	58.8
Food stores	54	220.2	285.1	368.3	384.2	397.4	407.4	421.0	429.8
Grocery stores	541	205.6	269.5	348.2	364.5	376.5	385.0	397.0	403.0
Gasoline service stations	554	94.1	113.3	138.5	139.3	143.9	149.6	157.6	158.7
Apparel and accessory stores [2]	56	49.3	70.2	95.8	107.2	110.0	110.9	114.6	117.8
Men's and boys' clothing stores	561	7.7	8.5	10.5	10.0	10.1	9.4	9.6	10.6
Women's clothing specialty stores	562,3	17.6	26.1	32.8	35.9	34.0	32.2	31.8	31.5
Women's clothing stores	562	15.9	23.6	29.8	32.0	29.9	27.8	27.0	26.2
Family clothing stores.	565	10.8	17.8	28.4	35.5	38.5	40.6	43.0	45.1
Shoe stores	566	10.5	13.1	18.0	18.4	19.1	19.3	20.0	20.4
Eating and drinking places	58	90.1	127.9	190.1	210.4	217.1	222.1	228.2	236.2
Eating places [2]	5812	80.4	117.6	178.7	198.0	204.9	209.0	214.4	222.0
Restaurants, lunchrooms, cafeterias . . .	5812 pt	(NA)	68.2	99.9	107.3	111.6	111.7	114.9	119.5
Refreshment places	5812 pt	(NA)	48.1	75.7	87.9	90.4	93.9	95.7	98.5
Drinking places	5813	(NA)	10.3	11.5	12.4	12.2	13.0	13.7	14.1
Drug stores and proprietary stores	591	31.0	47.0	70.6	79.3	81.3	84.7	90.5	98.2
Liquor stores	592	16.9	19.5	21.7	21.4	21.9	21.7	22.7	24.0
Nonstore retailers	596	22.8	28.3	45.6	57.9	62.5	62.8	68.8	74.9
Catalog and mail-order houses	5961	(NA)	15.8	26.6	37.7	39.9	40.0	43.8	48.7
Fuel dealers	598	(NA)	16.8	15.6	15.1	16.0	16.9	19.0	17.7

NA Not available.　[1] Based on 1987 Standard Industrial Classification code; see text, Section 13.　[2] Includes kinds of business, not shown separately.　[3] Excludes leased departments.

Source of Tables 1278 and 1279: U.S. Bureau of the Census, *Current Business Reports, Annual Benchmark Report for Retail Trade, January 1988 Through December 1997*, (BR/97-RV) and prior issues.

No. 1280. Retail Trade—Merchandise Inventories and Inventory/Sales Ratios, by Kind of Business: 1990 to 1997

[As of **Dec. 31**. Includes warehouses. Adjusted for seasonal variations. Sales data also adjusted for holiday and trading-day differences. See headnote, Table 1278]

KIND OF BUSINESS	1987 SIC code [1]	INVENTORIES AT COST [2] (bil. dol.)				INVENTORY/SALES RATIOS			
		1990	1995	1996	1997	1990	1995	1996	1997
Total		239.8	307.1	316.5	323.6	1.57	1.54	1.52	1.49
Excluding automotive group		*176.7*	*220.6*	*226.7*	*232.1*	*1.45*	*1.46*	*1.43*	*1.42*
Durable goods stores [3]		121.1	163.4	168.9	174.4	2.27	2.01	1.99	1.92
Building materials and garden supplies. . . .	52	17.0	22.5	23.5	25.2	2.28	1.99	1.96	1.97
Automotive dealers.	55 exc. 554	63.1	86.5	89.8	91.5	2.05	1.80	1.78	1.70
Furniture and homefurnishings stores.	57	17.4	24.7	25.1	24.6	2.36	2.18	2.17	1.93
Nondurable goods stores [3]		118.7	143.7	147.6	149.2	1.19	1.22	1.19	1.18
General merchandise stores.	53	42.4	58.3	59.2	58.9	2.34	2.31	2.20	2.10
Department stores	531	33.4	46.5	47.8	48.6	2.40	2.38	2.26	2.19
Food stores.	54	25.0	28.0	29.0	28.9	0.81	0.81	0.81	0.80
Apparel and accessory stores.	56	19.7	22.6	22.7	24.2	2.50	2.41	2.38	2.45

[1] Based on 1987 Standard Industrial Classification code; see text, Section 13. [2] Excludes supplies and equipment used in store and warehouse operations that are not for resale. [3] Includes kinds of business not shown separately.

Source: U.S. Bureau of the Census, *Current Business Reports, Annual Benchmark Report for Retail Trade, January 1988 Through December 1997* (BR/97-RV).

No. 1281. Franchised New Car Dealerships—Summary: 1980 to 1997

ITEM	Unit	1980	1985	1990	1991	1992	1993	1994	1995	1996	1997
Dealerships [1].	Number .	27,900	24,725	24,825	24,200	23,500	22,950	22,850	22,800	22,750	22,700
Sales.	Bil. dol .	130.5	251.6	316.0	301.3	333.8	377.3	430.6	456.2	490.0	507.5
New cars sold [2]	1,000. .	8,979	10,983	9,296	8,176	8,211	8,519	8,991	8,635	8,526	8,272
Used vehicles sold	1,000. .	9,717	13,300	14,180	14,270	15,140	16,300	17,760	18,480	19,170	19,190
Employment	1,000. .	745	857	925	879	875	908	963	996	1,032	1,056
Annual payroll	Bil. dol .	11.0	20.1	24.1	23.5	25.1	26.7	29.8	31.8	34.0	(NA)
Advertising expenses	Bil. dol .	1.2	2.8	3.7	3.5	3.8	4.1	4.3	4.6	5.0	5.1
Dealer pretax profits as a percentage of sales	Percent .	0.6	2.2	1.0	1.0	1.4	1.6	1.8	1.4	1.5	1.4
Inventory: [3] Domestic: [4]											
Total	1,000. .	2,112	2,339	2,537	2,259	2,334	2,487	2,521	2,974	2,856	2,813
Days' supply.	Days . . .	57	60	73	71	68	64	61	71	66	66
Imported: [4]											
Total	1,000. .	269	345	707	694	614	533	453	445	317	338
Days' supply.	Days . . .	31	30	72	83	81	76	67	72	58	54

NA Not available. [1] At beginning of year. [2] Data provided by Ward's Automotive Reports. [3] Annual average. Includes light trucks. [4] Classification based on where automobiles are produced (i.e., automobiles manufactured by foreign companies but produced in the United States are classified as domestic).

Source: National Automobile Dealers Association, McLean, VA, *NADA Data*, annual.

No. 1282. Motor Vehicle Factory Sales and Retail Sales: 1980 to 1997

[In thousands]

YEAR	1980	1985	1989	1990	1991	1992	1993	1994	1995	1996	1997
Factory sales, total	8,067	11,359	10,869	9,769	8,783	9,747	10,857	12,189	12,023	11,916	(NA)
Passenger cars	6,400	8,002	6,807	6,050	5,407	5,685	5,962	6,549	6,310	6,140	(NA)
Trucks and buses	1,667	3,357	4,062	3,719	3,375	4,062	4,895	5,640	5,713	5,776	(NA)
Retail sales, total.	11,466	15,724	14,713	14,146	12,539	13,116	14,199	15,411	15,116	15,456	15,500
Passenger cars (new), total	8,979	11,042	9,772	9,300	8,175	8,213	8,517	8,990	8,634	8,527	8,272
Domestic [1]	6,581	8,205	7,073	6,897	6,137	6,277	6,741	7,255	7,128	7,254	6,917
Imports	2,398	2,838	2,699	2,403	2,038	1,936	1,776	1,735	1,506	1,273	1,355
Trucks (new), total	2,487	4,682	4,941	4,846	4,365	4,903	5,681	6,421	6,481	6,930	7,228
Domestic [1]	2,001	3,902	4,403	4,215	3,813	4,481	5,287	5,995	6,064	6,478	6,633
Imports	486	780	538	631	551	422	394	426	417	452	595

NA Not available. [1] North American built.

Source: American Automobile Manufacturers Association, Detroit, MI, *Motor Vehicle Facts and Figures*, annual (copyright).

No. 1283. Retail Foodstores—Number and Sales, by Type: 1990 to 1996

TYPE OF FOODSTORE	NUMBER [1] (1,000)					SALES [2] (bil. dol.)					PERCENT DISTRIBUTION			
											Number		Sales	
	1990	1993	1994	1995	1996	1990	1993	1994	1995	1996	1990	1996	1990	1996
Total.	254.4	249.3	248.3	247.3	246.3	368.3	385.4	399.3	410.5	423.3	100.0	100.0	100.0	100.0
Grocery stores	172.9	166.9	165.6	164.3	163.0	348.2	365.7	378.6	389.1	400.5	67.7	66.2	94.5	94.6
Supermarkets [3]	25.0	25.6	24.6	24.1	23.8	260.1	281.0	289.0	293.3	302.5	9.9	9.7	70.6	71.5
Conventional	13.7	13.3	12.0	11.1	7.9	90.7	78.6	81.5	69.0	69.2	5.7	3.2	24.6	16.3
Superstore [4]	5.8	6.3	6.5	7.1	8.8	87.6	100.6	107.6	116.7	127.0	2.2	3.6	23.8	30.0
Warehouse [5]	3.4	3.1	2.9	2.8	2.4	33.1	31.9	27.7	26.0	24.3	1.3	1.0	9.0	5.7
Combination food and drug [6]	1.6	2.2	2.4	2.4	4.0	34.8	45.8	51.7	59.3	61.3	0.5	1.6	9.4	14.5
Superwarehouse [7] . . .	0.3	0.5	0.5	0.5	0.5	12.6	15.3	16.2	17.8	15.3	0.2	0.2	3.4	3.6
Hypermarket [8]	0.1	0.2	0.2	0.2	0.2	1.3	8.8	4.3	4.5	5.4	(Z)	0.1	0.4	1.3
Convenience stores [9] . .	59.2	60.9	61.5	62.1	62.7	37.0	39.8	40.3	40.9	38.8	19.1	25.5	10.0	9.2
Superette [10]	88.7	80.4	79.6	78.4	76.5	51.1	44.9	49.2	54.9	59.2	38.6	31.1	13.9	14.0
Specialized food stores [11]	81.5	82.4	82.7	83.0	83.3	20.1	19.7	20.7	21.4	22.9	32.3	33.8	5.5	5.4

Z Less than 0.05 percent. [1] Estimated. [2] Includes nonfood items. [3] A grocery store, primarily self-service in operation, providing a full range of departments, and having at least $2.5 million in annual sales in 1985 dollars. [4] Contains greater variety of products than conventional supermarkets, including specialty and service departments, and considerable nonfood (general merchandise) products. [5] Contains limited product variety and fewer services provided, incorporating case lot stocking and shelving practices. [6] Contains a pharmacy, a nonprescription drug department, and a greater variety of health and beauty aids than that carried by conventional supermarkets. [7] A larger warehouse store that offers expanded product variety and often service meat, deli, or seafood departments. [8] A very large store offering a greater variety of general merchandise—like clothes, hardware, and seasonal goods—and personal care products than other grocery stores. [9] A small grocery store selling a limited variety of food and nonfood products, typically open extended hours. [10] A grocery store, primarily self-service in operation, selling a wide variety of food and nonfood products with annual sales below $2.5 million (1985 dollars). [11] Primarily engaged in the retail sale of a single food category such as meat and seafood stores and retail bakeries.

Source: U.S. Dept. of Agriculture, Economic Research Service, *Food Marketing Review,* annual.

No. 1284. Percent of Supermarkets Offering Selected Services and Product Lines: 1990 to 1997

[In percent. Based on a sample survey of chain and independent supermarkets and subject to sampling variability; for details, see source]

SERVICE OR PRODUCT LINE OFFERED	1990	1996	1997	SERVICE OR PRODUCT LINE OFFERED	1990	1996	1997
Service delicatessen.	73	80	81	Salad bar	18	27	24
Service bakery	60	69	69	Automated teller machines (ATM's).	20	60	62
Service meat.	42	74	60	Banking in store	(NA)	14	22
Service fish.	33	46	43	Pharmacy.	15	26	26
Separate cheese department	33	31	30	Warehouse aisle	(NA)	10	16

NA Not available.

Source: Progressive Grocer Assocs., Darien, CT, *Progressive Grocer Annual Report* (copyright).

No. 1285. Food and Alcoholic Beverage Sales, by Sales Outlet: 1985 to 1996

[In billions of dollars]

SALES OUTLET	1985	1988	1989	1990	1991	1992	1993	1994	1995	1996
Food sales, total [1]	397.5	477.2	510.4	552.1	572.9	584.2	605.8	636.3	662.0	685.3
Off-premise use	228.7	259.9	278.9	303.9	317.3	319.3	325.1	341.3	354.1	369.3
Food stores	204.9	227.4	241.9	262.1	271.2	270.1	273.1	286.7	294.6	304.4
Other stores	16.4	22.9	26.3	30.2	33.7	36.0	38.3	39.8	44.1	49.7
Home-delivered, mail order	2.8	4.0	4.6	5.3	5.8	6.4	6.8	7.8	7.8	7.5
Farmers, manufacturers, wholesalers.	4.6	5.6	6.1	6.3	6.6	6.7	7.0	7.0	7.5	7.8
Food service [2]	168.8	217.3	231.5	248.2	255.6	264.9	280.7	295.0	307.9	316.0
Alcoholic beverage sales, total.	64.0	72.7	75.6	81.1	82.5	82.5	83.2	85.7	88.4	91.7
Packaged alcoholic beverages. . . .	38.2	41.0	43.1	46.4	47.3	46.3	46.1	47.7	48.4	50.3
Liquor stores.	17.1	17.1	17.3	18.6	19.1	18.4	18.3	18.6	18.6	19.4
Food stores	17.0	18.7	19.8	21.2	21.2	20.9	20.8	21.9	22.4	23.3
All other.	4.2	5.3	6.0	6.7	7.0	7.0	7.1	7.1	7.3	7.6
Alcoholic drinks.	25.8	31.7	32.5	34.6	35.2	36.2	37.1	38.1	40.0	41.5
Eating and drinking places [3] . . .	20.7	24.4	25.0	26.8	27.3	27.8	28.5	29.0	30.3	31.3
Hotels and motels [3]	3.4	3.9	3.8	3.8	3.7	3.8	3.8	4.0	4.3	4.6
All other.	1.8	3.4	3.7	4.0	4.2	4.6	4.8	5.0	5.4	5.6

[1] Includes taxes and tips. Excludes home food production. [2] Includes food furnished and donations. [3] Includes tips.

Source: U.S. Dept. of Agriculture, Economic Research Service, *Food Marketing Review, 1994-95* (Agricultural Economic Report No. 743) and unpublished data.

No. 1286. Commercial and Institutional Groups—Food and Drink Sales: 1980 to 1998

[Excludes military. Data refer to sales to consumers of food and alcoholic beverages. Sales are estimated. For details, see source]

TYPE OF GROUP	Num-ber, 1995	SALES (mil. dol.)							
		1980	1985	1990	1994	1995	1996	1997	1998 [1]
Total	797,727	119,004	172,787	238,149	280,442	294,631	306,543	320,146	335,259
Commercial restaurant services [2][3]	621,690	101,529	151,762	211,606	251,935	265,910	276,831	290,131	304,747
Eating places [2]	385,442	72,276	111,657	155,552	187,514	198,293	207,873	215,246	225,984
Full-service restaurants	180,048	39,307	57,939	77,811	91,457	96,396	100,256	105,064	110,317
Limited-service restaurants [4]	180,205	28,699	47,477	69,798	87,395	92,901	98,397	100,575	105,704
Bars and taverns [5]	36,435	7,785	8,338	9,533	9,928	9,948	9,370	10,543	10,881
Food contractors [2]	19,117	6,818	9,460	14,149	16,948	18,186	18,913	20,516	21,673
Manufacturing and industrial plants .	(NA)	2,121	2,721	3,856	4,453	4,814	4,956	5,384	5,671
Colleges and universities	(NA)	1,140	1,738	2,788	3,693	3,989	4,264	4,631	4,988
Lodging places [2]	27,304	6,768	10,557	13,568	14,863	15,561	15,938	16,879	17,638
Hotel restaurants	17,768	4,964	8,986	12,355	13,813	14,516	14,923	15,852	16,619
Motel restaurants	7,993	1,151	975	483	428	618	600	605	600
Retail hosts [2][6]	132,217	3,264	5,254	9,513	11,884	12,589	13,239	14,280	15,229
Department store restaurants	4,721	857	865	876	993	1,038	(NA)	(NA)	(NA)
Grocery store restaurants [6]	57,860	830	2,074	5,432	6,307	6,624	(NA)	(NA)	(NA)
Gasoline service stations	41,690	492	1,052	1,718	2,359	2,520	(NA)	(NA)	(NA)
Recreation and sports.	14,870	1,452	1,972	2,871	3,642	3,866	3,795	4,382	4,626
Institutional restaurant services [2]	176,037	17,475	21,025	26,543	28,508	28,722	29,712	30,015	30,512
Employee restaurant services	6,784	1,635	1,971	1,864	1,483	1,364	1,490	1,238	1,159
Industrial, commercial organizations.	2,453	1,377	1,682	1,603	1,253	1,129	(NA)	(NA)	(NA)
Educational restaurant services	96,287	4,610	5,978	7,671	8,868	9,059	9,298	9,479	9,653
Elementary and secondary schools .	93,368	2,312	2,919	3,700	4,358	4,533	4,725	4,901	5,054
Hospitals	6,265	6,668	7,104	8,968	9,173	9,219	9,391	9,415	9,422
Miscellaneous [2]	32,167	1,521	2,077	2,892	3,493	3,673	3,896	4,064	4,276
Clubs	10,410	1,056	1,537	1,993	2,166	2,278	(NA)	(NA)	(NA)

NA Not available. [1] Projection. [2] Includes other types of groups, not shown separately. [3] Data for establishments with payroll. [4] Fast-food restaurants. [5] For establishments serving food. [6] Beginning 1990, a portion of delicatessen sales in grocery stores are considered food service.

Source: National Restaurant Association, Washington, DC, *Restaurant Numbers: A Statistical Digest for the Restaurant Industry*, 1998; *Restaurant Industry in Review*, annual; and National Restaurant Association *Restaurant Industry Forecast*, December 1997, (copyright).

No. 1287. U.S. Mail Order Sales, by Kind of Business: 1990 to 1995

[In millions of dollars. Mail order sales represent orders placed by mail, phone, or electronically without the person ordering coming to the point of sale to place the order, or the seller coming to the office or home of the orderer to take the order or using an agent to collect the order. Excludes orders placed at catalog desks or elsewhere in stores even in response to a catalog but does include products or services delivered in the store as long as the order was placed by mail, phone, or electronically. Statistics are generated independently each year and are not adjusted for any discontinuities of available data]

KIND OF BUSINESS	1990	1991	1992	1993	1994	1995
Total mail order sales	151,640	162,050	168,050	186,700	200,760	219,900
Consumer, total	98,190	107,970	110,740	118,970	129,740	141,810
Products	57,500	64,940	65,210	71,960	78,460	86,350
Specialty [1]	44,520	50,010	50,560	57,720	64,810	70,920
Apparel.	4,250	4,410	4,820	5,230	6,160	6,800
Books.	2,760	2,770	3,120	3,100	3,200	3,950
Collectibles	1,690	1,810	2,000	2,360	2,200	2,140
Computer software & hardware	1,000	1,330	2,160	3,350	4,430	3,250
Health products	2,480	2,770	2,940	4,010	5,080	5,840
Magazines.	6,020	6,580	6,340	6,280	6,600	6,900
Multi-products	7,410	8,440	6,860	10,190	10,760	11,340
Newspapers	3,020	3,020	3,020	3,020	3,080	3,080
Sporting goods.	3,460	3,910	3,650	4,030	4,610	4,580
General merchandise.	12,980	14,930	14,650	14,240	13,650	15,430
Services	40,690	43,030	45,530	47,010	51,280	55,460
Nonfinancial	21,660	25,740	26,620	26,980	28,400	29,530
Financial	19,030	17,290	18,910	20,030	22,880	25,930
Business products and services	53,450	54,080	57,310	67,730	71,020	78,090
Business supplies [1]	7,160	9,180	10,060	14,080	16,420	21,940
Data processing-oriented supplies. ...	1,520	2,060	2,320	1,840	770	710
Computer hardware	700	1,800	2,400	6,000	8,000	11,300
Business services [1]	8,900	8,940	10,410	13,300	12,640	13,310
Communications	4,240	4,140	5,580	8,050	7,900	7,900
Information	2,500	2,500	2,500	2,850	2,310	2,710
Industrial	5,390	5,560	6,440	8,150	8,160	8,040
Generalized mail order marketers [2]	32,000	30,400	30,400	32,200	33,800	34,800

[1] Includes other kinds of business not shown separately. [2] Mail order as part of the overall selling channel mix of multichannel industrial marketers not specializing in mail order selling.

Source: Fishman, Arnold L., data are extracted from *Annual Guides to Mail Order Sales, 1990-1996*, Marketing Logistics, Inc., Highland Park, IL, 60035 (copyright). For 1990-92, *Portable Mail Order Industry Statistics, 1993 Edition*, Richard D. Irwin, Inc., Burr Ridge, IL, 1994 (copyright).

No. 1288. Retail Trade—Summary of Establishments, by State: 1995

[Covers establishments with payroll. Employees are for the week including March 12. Most government employees are excluded. Kind-of-business classification based on 1987 Standard Industrial Classification (SIC) code; see text, Section 13. For statement on methodology, see Appendix III]

STATE	ESTABLISHMENTS (1,000)				PAID EMPLOYEES (1,000)				ANNUAL PAYROLL (mil. dol.)			
	Total¹	Food stores (SIC 54)	Automotive dealers and service stations (SIC 55)	Eating and drinking places (SIC 58)	Total¹	Food stores (SIC 54)	Automotive dealers and service stations (SIC 55)	Eating and drinking places (SIC 58)	Total¹	Food stores (SIC 54)	Automotive dealers and service stations (SIC 55)	Eating and drinking places (SIC 58)
U.S.	1,567.9	181.9	199.8	456.7	21,085	3,188	2,190	7,208	300,040	41,522	51,229	64,675
AL.	25.3	3.2	4.4	5.8	335	65	38	107	3,964	557	796	794
AK.	3.9	0.4	0.4	1.3	45	8	4	15	854	153	140	210
AZ.	22.9	2.2	2.6	7.3	350	49	40	132	4,984	781	993	1,112
AR.	15.9	1.9	2.7	3.7	190	26	23	59	2,499	287	435	437
CA.	160.1	18.3	16.9	51.8	2,195	286	211	796	35,392	5,532	5,496	7,726
CO	25.4	1.9	2.9	7.9	349	45	33	137	5,045	795	852	1,234
CT.	21.0	2.3	2.5	6.1	265	47	26	76	4,449	716	710	788
DE.	4.9	0.5	0.6	1.3	67	9	7	23	930	139	173	215
DC	3.7	0.4	0.2	1.5	52	5	2	27	951	96	31	371
FL.	90.9	9.8	11.4	24.0	1,260	208	128	438	17,589	2,442	3,254	3,948
GA	43.4	5.0	6.3	11.3	640	115	66	218	8,578	1,074	1,585	1,897
HI	8.0	0.9	0.6	2.6	111	14	8	47	1,790	234	212	572
ID	7.8	0.7	1.2	2.3	93	12	13	32	1,233	171	267	237
IL	66.4	6.8	7.7	21.4	948	129	92	324	13,833	1,655	2,229	2,955
IN	34.8	3.0	5.2	10.4	516	67	57	187	6,475	786	1,195	1,502
IA	19.8	1.9	3.1	6.0	250	42	31	83	2,958	463	584	601
KS.	16.8	1.5	2.6	4.9	217	30	24	78	2,817	364	518	591
KY.	22.5	2.9	3.7	5.6	310	48	36	109	3,796	504	683	877
LA.	23.4	3.7	3.2	6.0	325	59	36	109	4,017	600	800	911
ME	9.6	1.4	1.3	2.5	103	19	12	30	1,464	226	235	293
MD	28.3	3.1	3.0	7.9	410	59	45	132	6,309	999	1,090	1,259
MA	39.4	4.5	4.2	12.4	533	92	43	173	8,377	1,158	1,037	1,832
MI	55.1	6.9	7.2	16.2	797	104	83	278	11,071	1,248	2,116	2,280
MN	28.5	2.6	4.0	7.9	433	54	48	141	5,945	656	944	1,195
MS	15.7	2.4	2.6	3.2	179	32	22	55	2,169	337	454	400
MO	33.1	3.3	5.2	9.4	447	58	53	160	6,092	721	1,154	1,360
MT	7.5	0.7	1.0	2.5	75	10	10	29	898	131	182	221
NE.	11.5	1.2	1.8	3.5	147	23	16	51	1,712	240	321	387
NV.	8.4	0.9	0.9	2.8	123	17	14	44	1,974	311	366	454
NH	8.7	1.1	1.1	2.2	111	19	11	32	1,618	239	287	306
NJ	50.1	6.6	5.5	14.3	593	99	57	163	10,201	1,607	1,535	1,801
NM	10.0	0.9	1.4	3.0	131	16	16	51	1,731	246	332	423
NY.	110.9	16.9	9.7	33.4	1,182	202	91	371	18,789	2,730	2,209	4,126
NC	45.9	5.2	7.1	11.5	607	95	65	207	8,187	1,012	1,530	1,761
ND	4.9	0.5	0.8	1.5	58	8	8	20	647	79	153	141
OH	64.6	7.1	8.6	20.3	989	141	98	349	13,230	1,645	2,139	2,800
OK	20.0	2.6	3.0	5.7	242	34	29	89	3,005	400	598	708
OR	20.7	2.3	2.4	6.7	268	35	31	98	3,976	508	743	882
PA.	71.7	8.1	8.7	21.4	954	158	102	295	13,082	1,887	2,211	2,511
RI	6.6	0.8	0.8	2.3	77	13	7	28	1,077	165	143	262
SC.	23.9	2.8	3.6	6.1	306	52	33	109	3,835	529	725	898
SD.	5.8	0.5	0.9	1.7	66	10	9	22	750	101	168	165
TN.	32.1	4.1	4.8	7.7	455	73	49	154	6,151	715	1,182	1,322
TX.	103.3	13.1	14.4	29.1	1,467	229	156	510	20,778	2,722	3,885	4,605
UT.	10.3	0.9	1.5	3.0	161	22	19	54	2,162	298	389	424
VT.	5.3	0.8	0.6	1.3	52	10	6	17	688	115	122	150
VA.	38.7	4.9	5.1	10.1	550	84	63	177	7,662	1,086	1,460	1,604
WA	33.2	3.6	3.8	10.9	432	62	45	158	6,692	1,024	1,133	1,496
WV	10.8	1.5	1.8	2.8	127	22	16	40	1,511	249	292	312
WI	32.3	2.7	4.5	11.2	451	63	52	160	5,583	712	1,023	1,187
WY	4.0	0.3	0.7	1.2	42	5	6	16	520	74	120	133

¹ Includes other kinds of business not shown separately.

Source: U.S. Bureau of the Census, County Business Patterns, annual.

No. 1289. Shopping Centers—Number, Gross Leasable Area, and Retail Sales, by Gross Leasable Area: 1990 to 1997

[As of **December 31.** A shopping center is a group of architecturally unified commercial establishments built on a site that is planned, developed, owned, and managed as an operating unit related in its location, size, and type of shops to the trade area that the unit serves. The unit provides on-site parking in definite relationship to the types and total size of the stores. The data base attempts to include all centers with three or more stores. Estimates are based on a sample of data available on shopping center properties; for details, contact source]

YEAR	Total	GROSS LEASABLE AREA (sq. ft.)					
		Less than 100,001	100,001-200,000	200,001-400,000	400,001-800,000	800,001-1,000,000	More than 1 million
NUMBER							
1990	36,515	23,231	8,756	2,781	1,102	288	357
1995	41,235	26,001	9,974	3,345	1,234	301	380
1996	42,130	26,497	10,186	3,477	1,276	309	385
1997	42,953	26,928	10,400	3,595	1,324	316	390
Percent distribution	100.0	62.7	24.2	8.4	3.1	0.7	0.9
Percent change, 1996-97	2.0	1.6	2.1	3.4	3.8	2.3	1.3
GROSS LEASABLE AREA							
1990 (mil. sq. ft.)	4,390	1,125	1,197	734	618	259	457
1995 (mil. sq. ft.)	4,967	1,267	1,368	886	689	271	486
1996 (mil. sq. ft.)	5,101	1,293	1,399	926	711	278	493
1997 (mil. sq. ft.)	5,229	1,318	1,431	960	736	285	500
Percent distribution	100.0	25.2	27.4	18.3	14.1	5.4	9.6
Percent change, 1996-97	2.5	1.9	2.3	3.7	3.5	2.3	1.4
RETAIL SALES							
1990 (bil. dol.)	706.4	205.1	179.5	108.0	91.7	45.1	77.0
1995 (bil. dol.)	893.8	259.6	227.1	136.4	115.8	57.0	97.8
1996 (bil. dol.)	933.9	271.2	237.3	142.6	121.0	60.0	102.2
1997 (bil. dol.)	980.0	284.6	249.0	149.7	126.9	62.5	107.4
Percent distribution	100.0	29.0	25.4	15.3	13.0	6.4	10.9
Percent change, 1996-97	4.9	4.9	4.9	5.0	4.9	4.1	5.1

No. 1290. Shopping Centers—Number, Gross Leasable Area, and Retail Sales, by State: 1997

[See headnote, Table 1289. Minus sign (-) indicates decrease]

STATE	Num-ber	Gross leas-able area (mil. sq. ft.)	Retail sales (bil. dol.)	PERCENT CHANGE, 1996-97			STATE	Num-ber	Gross leas-able area (mil. sq. ft.)	Retail sales (bil. dol.)	PERCENT CHANGE, 1996-97		
				Num-ber	Gross leas-able area	Retail sales per sq. ft.					Num-ber	Gross leas-able area	Retail sales per sq. ft.
U.S.	**42,953**	**5,229**	**980.0**	**2.0**	**2.5**	**2.4**	MO	879	110	21.6	2.1	2.5	2.2
							MT	94	10	1.9	3.3	4.8	0.1
AL	625	73	14.8	1.1	1.9	2.2	NE	257	33	5.5	1.6	0.4	4.2
AK	68	8	1.9	3.0	0.3	5.9	NV	331	41	6.3	4.7	5.0	0.3
AZ	1,014	120	23.2	2.3	3.2	1.9	NH	218	23	4.0	1.9	5.2	1.9
AR	366	36	7.2	3.4	3.9	(Z)							
CA	5,774	664	118.0	1.9	2.7	2.2	NJ	1,198	163	26.6	4.8	5.2	0.4
							NM	300	29	6.1	0.3	0.9	3.5
CO	728	95	21.6	4.0	4.0	1.5	NY	1,702	235	42.4	2.5	3.0	1.7
CT	773	94	17.4	2.1	3.8	2.2	NC	1,554	165	27.6	2.0	2.7	1.9
DE	138	21	4.1	3.8	5.7	0.2	ND	87	9	2.0	-	-	4.9
DC	85	9	1.6	7.6	4.7	0.2							
FL	3,216	407	88.0	1.1	1.0	4.5	OH	1,684	243	39.6	2.2	2.9	1.7
							OK	567	60	12.7	0.7	0.7	3.0
GA	1,546	167	30.0	3.3	3.5	1.1	OR	482	55	8.8	1.9	1.7	3.6
HI	182	19	3.9	4.0	6.8	0.5	PA	1,615	231	38.2	2.4	2.3	2.7
ID	157	19	3.2	4.7	4.3	-0.2	RI	200	18	3.6	1.5	2.4	2.6
IL	2,059	250	39.6	2.0	1.6	3.6							
IN	893	118	20.4	1.6	1.3	3.2	SC	789	76	14.9	1.3	1.9	2.6
							SD	56	7	1.2	3.7	0.7	3.9
IA	301	40	7.1	2.0	2.8	1.8	TN	1,190	132	21.8	1.4	3.2	1.5
KS	476	55	11.1	0.4	2.7	1.8	TX	2,936	354	83.1	1.0	2.4	2.3
KY	613	66	13.2	0.8	1.7	2.7	UT	232	32	6.2	3.1	3.1	1.0
LA	693	83	17.8	0.4	2.1	2.5							
ME	200	17	3.9	-	-	6.2	VT	113	8	1.7	1.8	0.4	5.6
							VA	1,242	163	29.9	2.3	2.7	2.5
MD	879	122	23.6	2.2	3.3	1.6	WA	746	98	16.8	3.3	4.6	0.5
MA	979	111	22.0	1.6	2.0	3.3	WV	159	22	3.6	-	-	3.8
MI	993	131	24.0	1.1	1.0	3.8	WI	614	75	13.8	0.7	1.2	3.8
MN	468	67	13.2	2.4	3.5	1.4	WY	53	6	1.3	-	-	4.2
MS	429	41	7.9	0.7	2.0	1.6							

- Represents zero.   Z Less than 0.05 percent.

Source of tables 1289 and 1290: National Research Bureau, Chicago, IL. Data for 1990 published by Monitor Publishing, Clearwater, FL, in *Monitor Magazine*, November/December 1991, (copyright). Data for 1995-97 published by International Council of Shopping Centers in *Shopping Centers Today*, April issues, (copyright—Interactive Market Systems, Inc.).

No. 1291. Retail Sales, by Type of Store and State: 1995 and 1996

[In millions of dollars, except as indicated. Kind-of-business classification based on 1987 Standard Industrial Classification (SIC) code; see text, Section 13. Data are estimates]

STATE	ALL STORES [1]				FOOD STORES				GENERAL MERCHANDISE STORES			
	1995, total	1996			Total (SIC 54)		Grocery stores (SIC 541)		Total (SIC 53)		Department stores (SIC 531)	
		Total	Sales per household [2]		1995	1996	1995	1996	1995	1996	1995	1996
			Amount (dol.)	Percent change, 1995-96								
U.S. . . .	2,355,242	2,465,147	24,992	3.6	409,318	424,091	387,499	401,246	297,878	309,404	230,899	240,828
AL	35,946	36,729	22,643	0.9	6,138	6,485	5,877	6,203	5,180	5,487	4,122	4,387
AK	6,405	6,816	32,397	7.3	1,357	1,424	1,320	1,385	900	946	638	657
AZ	39,322	42,748	25,391	3.5	7,862	8,276	7,625	8,017	5,023	5,409	3,779	4,079
AR	20,999	22,053	22,936	3.8	3,432	3,613	3,336	3,508	3,370	3,585	2,716	2,892
CA	257,662	268,442	24,216	3.4	47,256	48,393	44,162	45,194	31,892	32,989	21,645	22,541
CO	36,808	39,777	26,403	6.4	6,783	7,083	6,579	6,863	4,521	4,816	3,481	3,723
CT	31,844	34,037	27,605	6.8	6,293	6,278	5,893	5,872	3,414	3,416	2,681	2,691
DE	7,545	7,902	28,892	3.0	1,235	1,289	1,154	1,203	1,140	1,179	892	927
DC	3,760	3,760	16,639	1.4	631	620	556	546	224	218	195	190
FL	145,665	158,978	27,505	7.1	23,421	25,542	22,259	24,253	17,155	18,540	12,697	13,793
GA	65,389	70,003	25,809	4.7	11,162	11,932	10,676	11,405	8,641	9,153	6,926	7,376
HI	12,806	13,322	34,308	4.2	2,209	2,266	2,052	2,103	2,115	2,197	888	957
ID	10,766	11,661	26,875	6.2	2,160	2,252	2,110	2,198	1,214	1,296	900	966
IL	104,528	105,802	24,272	0.7	15,348	15,454	14,377	14,460	12,536	12,628	10,357	10,466
IN	53,056	54,930	24,890	2.6	7,698	7,913	7,334	7,531	7,182	7,397	5,836	6,031
IA	26,968	28,189	25,545	4.1	5,219	5,363	4,977	5,110	3,490	3,669	2,884	3,034
KS	22,943	23,538	23,872	2.1	4,137	4,175	4,024	4,057	3,203	3,304	2,460	2,550
KY	33,020	33,815	23,021	1.6	5,760	6,095	5,581	5,900	4,847	5,153	4,053	4,324
LA	37,668	37,956	24,339	0.3	7,268	7,347	6,963	7,030	5,584	5,703	4,383	4,510
ME	11,568	12,355	25,929	6.5	2,612	2,610	2,496	2,492	1,199	1,201	740	744
MD	45,644	46,228	24,804	1.0	8,558	8,645	8,089	8,169	5,375	5,388	4,081	4,109
MA	53,873	57,583	25,075	6.0	10,714	10,722	9,816	9,809	5,566	5,578	3,995	4,006
MI	91,524	94,787	26,567	2.7	12,127	12,478	11,266	11,586	14,541	14,960	12,744	13,146
MN	44,277	45,256	25,661	1.1	7,179	7,208	6,759	6,780	5,390	5,541	4,397	4,535
MS	19,109	19,021	19,581	-0.9	3,716	3,813	3,503	3,592	3,166	3,259	2,421	2,501
MO	52,511	52,460	25,427	-0.6	9,080	8,920	8,776	8,616	7,392	7,434	6,361	6,424
MT	7,831	8,296	24,387	5.2	1,507	1,542	1,461	1,493	887	929	636	676
NE	15,731	15,599	24,585	-1.9	2,773	2,698	2,641	2,564	1,945	1,942	1,542	1,547
NV	16,678	18,443	28,506	6.0	3,243	3,474	3,141	3,360	2,085	2,282	1,675	1,844
NH	12,997	14,175	32,526	7.6	2,807	2,861	2,688	2,735	1,754	1,796	1,182	1,219
NJ	74,425	76,932	26,695	2.8	13,283	13,630	12,315	12,628	7,567	7,550	5,986	5,974
NM	14,634	15,786	25,577	6.5	2,706	2,829	2,619	2,736	1,864	1,989	1,497	1,606
NY	137,771	140,700	21,135	1.8	24,651	25,031	22,168	22,514	13,792	13,646	10,839	10,766
NC	65,781	72,058	25,500	7.6	11,888	12,982	11,389	12,429	7,804	8,452	6,264	6,789
ND	6,381	6,619	26,689	3.1	1,009	1,028	974	992	946	985	769	804
OH	104,900	110,692	26,118	5.2	16,896	17,734	16,003	16,783	13,938	14,621	11,447	12,044
OK	25,998	26,793	21,207	2.3	4,318	4,457	4,130	4,259	3,740	3,904	3,007	3,156
OR	31,193	33,367	26,619	4.7	5,049	5,300	4,854	5,090	4,952	5,241	3,445	3,664
PA	104,471	113,492	24,724	8.7	17,841	19,216	16,698	17,981	11,736	12,320	9,777	10,290
RI	7,359	7,801	21,037	6.4	1,551	1,542	1,409	1,400	782	782	573	577
SC	31,320	33,343	24,427	5.3	5,981	6,355	5,818	6,177	3,762	3,963	3,068	3,244
SD	7,244	7,651	27,984	5.2	1,211	1,257	1,177	1,221	892	948	698	746
TN	49,132	51,706	25,325	4.2	7,695	8,363	7,472	8,115	6,977	7,623	5,529	6,079
TX	165,526	170,864	25,050	1.6	28,491	29,494	27,354	28,293	22,564	23,601	17,630	18,572
UT	15,331	16,871	26,653	7.0	3,196	3,395	3,115	3,306	1,969	2,136	1,494	1,629
VT	5,144	5,652	25,153	8.8	1,214	1,244	1,170	1,197	358	368	262	271
VA	66,648	67,433	26,958	0.1	12,560	12,675	12,061	12,158	8,098	8,095	5,842	5,855
WA	49,551	51,953	24,316	3.2	9,004	9,271	8,664	8,914	6,457	6,708	4,633	4,830
WV	13,616	14,177	19,919	3.8	2,826	2,937	2,760	2,866	1,975	2,036	1,561	1,608
WI	49,473	51,825	26,741	3.9	7,451	7,749	7,060	7,339	6,204	6,443	4,859	5,049
WY	4,501	4,769	26,162	5.6	813	830	799	815	569	594	412	432

See footnotes at end of table.

No. 1291. Retail Sales, by Type of Store and State: 1995 and 1996—Continued

[See headnote, page 774]

STATE	AUTOMOTIVE DEALERS (SIC 55 exc. 554)		EATING AND DRINKING PLACES (SIC 58)		GASOLINE SERVICE STATIONS (SIC 554)		BUILDING MATERIALS AND GARDEN SUPPLIES (SIC 52)		APPAREL AND ACCESSORY STORES (SIC 56)		FURNITURE AND HOME FURNISHINGS STORES (SIC 57)	
	1995	1996	1995	1996	1995	1996	1995	1996	1995	1996	1995	1996
U.S. . . .	569,571	605,128	241,780	243,843	153,262	160,271	119,570	128,045	110,165	113,103	128,362	134,370
AL	9,377	9,613	3,168	3,140	2,791	2,763	2,081	2,061	1,572	1,594	1,568	1,554
AK	1,162	1,249	728	732	384	408	413	462	281	307	249	259
AZ	8,572	10,013	5,342	5,486	2,408	2,658	1,870	2,108	1,455	1,503	2,190	2,354
AR	5,990	6,334	1,672	1,733	1,754	1,820	1,247	1,291	674	712	731	757
CA	56,523	59,854	26,812	25,916	17,058	17,754	13,575	14,929	12,919	13,923	17,200	17,652
CO	7,805	8,998	5,145	5,255	2,085	2,290	1,978	2,207	1,310	1,348	2,417	2,573
CT	6,015	7,072	2,663	2,575	2,210	2,418	1,720	1,896	1,769	1,846	1,477	1,629
DE	1,650	1,673	714	777	425	439	441	480	318	326	489	505
DC	162	155	1,065	1,093	189	185	51	53	349	337	283	276
FL	41,680	44,202	14,261	16,230	7,652	8,272	6,506	7,403	7,083	7,583	8,747	9,428
GA	16,396	17,038	6,760	7,539	4,350	4,600	3,502	3,906	3,067	3,217	3,735	3,948
HI	1,951	2,073	1,951	1,892	652	680	429	472	979	1,058	601	619
ID	2,692	3,108	1,227	1,252	756	824	799	891	346	355	608	649
IL	26,068	26,900	11,703	11,413	6,052	6,254	4,381	4,464	5,280	5,017	6,862	7,076
IN	13,224	13,943	5,706	5,683	3,874	4,091	2,671	2,778	1,761	1,714	2,765	2,918
IA	7,030	7,421	2,539	2,538	2,251	2,407	1,484	1,563	834	856	1,166	1,252
KS	6,119	6,347	2,293	2,250	1,648	1,730	1,000	1,034	754	757	1,127	1,186
KY	7,584	7,804	3,314	3,290	2,958	2,942	2,059	2,046	1,095	1,115	1,362	1,354
LA	9,523	9,659	3,661	3,645	2,743	2,725	1,818	1,809	1,517	1,542	1,514	1,508
ME	2,092	2,460	899	871	750	823	768	848	578	603	364	401
MD	10,644	10,455	4,640	4,889	2,702	2,705	2,098	2,214	2,464	2,438	2,843	2,839
MA	9,988	11,769	5,779	5,635	3,422	3,753	2,531	2,794	3,410	3,576	2,464	2,728
MI	24,771	26,146	9,284	9,260	5,784	6,122	4,498	4,678	3,947	3,830	5,314	5,598
MN	10,847	11,205	4,270	4,172	3,382	3,531	2,537	2,610	1,613	1,619	2,183	2,287
MS	4,737	4,720	1,549	1,493	1,386	1,335	1,061	1,022	663	653	717	690
MO	13,840	13,982	5,606	5,355	4,255	4,342	2,401	2,419	1,788	1,749	2,324	2,381
MT	1,731	1,962	1,123	1,122	546	588	564	618	241	242	424	442
NE	3,844	3,857	1,627	1,542	1,205	1,223	668	667	556	540	889	902
NV	3,288	3,904	2,262	2,362	912	1,026	911	1,044	673	708	962	1,050
NH	2,526	3,035	960	950	704	786	821	925	623	666	592	669
NJ	18,433	19,859	6,378	5,966	4,175	4,238	3,269	3,432	5,143	5,119	4,415	4,641
NM	3,012	3,481	2,053	2,094	1,102	1,209	786	877	526	540	784	835
NY	26,921	28,702	14,415	13,367	6,941	6,974	6,631	6,890	10,205	10,096	7,764	8,093
NC	16,423	17,447	6,462	7,372	4,131	4,473	4,463	5,085	2,887	3,099	3,807	4,118
ND	1,780	1,865	593	587	548	581	351	367	193	196	237	251
OH	26,058	28,007	11,827	12,015	6,987	7,522	4,778	5,071	3,804	3,762	5,733	6,163
OK	7,699	7,984	2,564	2,613	1,894	1,923	1,084	1,102	983	1,025	1,038	1,058
OR	7,655	8,302	2,899	2,873	1,994	2,128	2,041	2,300	1,238	1,365	1,668	1,753
PA	25,873	29,267	9,379	9,216	6,078	6,486	5,128	5,657	4,979	5,217	4,552	5,030
RI	1,249	1,466	794	765	567	618	327	359	353	367	297	327
SC	7,550	7,797	3,233	3,583	2,223	2,338	2,032	2,255	1,549	1,615	1,660	1,744
SD	1,969	2,099	697	704	654	705	368	392	235	244	306	331
TN	13,377	14,143	4,861	4,967	3,768	3,839	2,768	2,823	1,948	2,037	2,222	2,273
TX	46,063	47,877	16,621	16,945	11,053	11,262	6,749	6,879	7,620	7,927	7,660	7,808
UT	3,428	4,033	1,838	1,909	1,016	1,130	866	983	614	643	1,038	1,124
VT	1,013	1,223	443	440	374	420	401	455	219	234	170	193
VA	15,386	15,093	6,294	6,636	4,196	4,199	3,302	3,474	3,414	3,388	4,393	4,397
WA	11,117	11,826	4,873	4,733	3,279	3,433	3,360	3,718	2,125	2,300	2,880	2,965
WV	3,307	3,344	1,136	1,234	1,002	1,032	882	957	451	460	573	590
WI	12,481	13,294	5,082	5,119	3,467	3,703	2,898	3,050	1,619	1,591	2,826	3,014
WY	944	1,068	615	613	523	562	205	225	141	142	171	178

[1] Includes other types of stores, not shown separately. [2] Based on number of households as of July 1 as estimated by source. Minus sign (-) indicates decrease.

Source: Market Statistics, New York, NY, *The Survey of Buying Power Data Service*, annual (copyright).

No. 1292. Merchant Wholesalers—Summary: 1990 to 1997

[**Inventories and stock/sales ratios**, as of **December, seasonally adjusted**. Data reflect latest revision. Based on Current Business Survey; see Appendix III]

KIND OF BUSINESS	1987 SIC code [1]	1990	1993	1994	1995	1996	1997
SALES (bil. dol.)							
Merchant wholesalers		1,793.8	1,940.2	2,075.7	2,265.7	2,420.7	2,527.4
Durable goods	50	881.2	986.9	1,082.3	1,179.2	1,245.8	1,305.2
Motor vehicles, parts, and supplies	501	173.9	179.3	197.2	202.6	211.1	218.4
Furniture and homefurnishings	502	33.9	34.9	36.7	40.9	43.6	42.7
Lumber and construction materials	503	63.6	71.5	78.1	77.1	85.8	88.2
Professional and commercial equipment	504	114.3	159.2	165.7	194.6	231.4	256.2
Metals and minerals, except petroleum	505	77.8	80.2	92.4	100.5	98.4	106.0
Electrical goods	506	116.5	131.9	150.2	169.8	173.8	178.1
Hardware, plumbing and heating equipment	507	52.7	55.5	63.7	67.6	70.5	75.5
Machinery, equipment and supplies	508	157.0	160.6	169.8	182.7	187.3	193.4
Miscellaneous durable goods	509	91.4	113.8	128.3	143.3	143.9	146.6
Nondurable goods	51	912.6	953.3	993.4	1,086.5	1,174.9	1,222.2
Paper and paper products	511	51.6	59.2	67.6	82.0	82.7	89.2
Drugs, proprietaries, and sundries	512	51.5	72.2	83.2	95.0	102.9	119.6
Apparel, piece goods, and notions	513	64.9	70.4	72.5	70.6	75.5	87.2
Groceries and related products	514	272.5	285.3	288.6	304.7	315.4	329.0
Farm-product raw materials	515	107.6	96.0	95.4	113.7	130.2	118.1
Chemicals and allied products	516	35.7	39.1	41.8	47.8	53.5	56.0
Petroleum and petroleum products	517	148.5	139.3	143.0	150.6	177.8	181.2
Beer, wine, and distilled beverages	518	49.3	51.3	53.0	54.1	56.4	57.9
Miscellaneous nondurable goods	519	131.0	140.4	148.2	168.2	180.7	183.6
INVENTORIES (bil. dol.)							
Merchant wholesalers		195.6	215.9	234.9	253.1	256.2	272.5
Durable goods	50	126.2	135.6	149.0	160.3	161.7	171.3
Motor vehicles, parts, and supplies	501	23.5	24.4	25.5	27.0	26.6	28.2
Furniture and homefurnishings	502	4.6	4.8	4.9	5.1	5.3	5.3
Lumber and construction materials	503	6.0	6.7	7.4	7.4	7.7	7.6
Professional and commercial equipment	504	15.8	17.9	20.5	22.8	22.3	23.9
Metals and minerals, except petroleum	505	10.7	11.1	12.8	12.8	12.7	13.8
Electrical goods	506	15.9	17.5	20.2	23.5	23.0	24.1
Hardware, plumbing and heating equipment	507	8.5	9.3	10.8	11.0	12.1	12.4
Machinery, equipment and supplies	508	31.5	29.2	31.6	34.7	35.9	39.6
Miscellaneous durable goods	509	9.8	14.6	15.2	15.8	16.0	16.4
Nondurable goods	51	69.4	80.2	85.9	92.8	94.5	101.2
Paper and paper products	511	4.9	6.3	7.0	8.3	8.6	9.7
Drugs, proprietaries, and sundries	512	6.5	10.4	11.6	12.0	13.7	15.8
Apparel, piece goods, and notions	513	9.8	11.4	12.2	11.9	11.8	13.1
Groceries and related products	514	14.7	15.7	16.1	16.7	17.8	17.7
Farm-product raw materials	515	8.8	10.0	10.4	12.3	9.6	10.5
Chemicals and allied products	516	3.1	3.7	4.1	4.6	4.7	4.9
Petroleum and petroleum products	517	4.4	4.0	4.9	4.9	5.7	5.1
Beer, wine, and distilled beverages	518	4.4	4.5	4.6	4.8	5.0	5.1
Miscellaneous nondurable goods	519	12.7	14.2	14.9	17.3	17.7	19.3
STOCK/SALES RATIO							
Merchant wholesalers		1.31	1.33	1.28	1.28	1.25	1.28
Durable goods	50	1.75	1.61	1.55	1.56	1.54	1.56
Motor vehicles, parts, and supplies	501	1.66	1.63	1.50	1.54	1.47	1.61
Furniture and homefurnishings	502	1.71	1.69	1.45	1.48	1.44	1.46
Lumber and construction materials	503	1.33	1.01	1.03	1.13	1.07	1.02
Professional and commercial equipment	504	1.58	1.35	1.37	1.29	1.13	1.04
Metals and minerals, except petroleum	505	1.60	1.62	1.54	1.54	1.52	1.53
Electrical goods	506	1.71	1.50	1.51	1.58	1.68	1.62
Hardware, plumbing and heating equipment	507	1.90	1.94	1.90	1.89	2.04	1.96
Machinery, equipment and supplies	508	2.49	2.16	2.11	2.10	2.29	2.40
Miscellaneous durable goods	509	1.27	1.52	1.35	1.31	1.31	1.37
Nondurable goods	51	0.90	1.03	0.99	0.99	0.94	0.99
Paper and paper products	511	1.16	1.21	1.11	1.20	1.21	1.27
Drugs, proprietaries, and sundries	512	1.49	1.65	1.59	1.44	1.52	1.48
Apparel, piece goods, and notions	513	1.77	2.12	2.07	2.00	1.73	1.77
Groceries and related products	514	0.66	0.67	0.64	0.63	0.69	0.64
Farm-product raw materials	515	1.04	1.20	1.19	1.25	0.89	1.05
Chemicals and allied products	516	0.97	1.14	1.09	1.08	1.05	1.04
Petroleum and petroleum products	517	0.33	0.39	0.40	0.37	0.35	0.36
Beer, wine, and distilled beverages	518	0.95	1.06	1.02	1.03	1.08	0.99
Miscellaneous nondurable goods	519	1.17	1.22	1.13	1.18	1.17	1.24

[1] Based on 1987 Standard Industrial Classification code; see text, Section 13.

Source: U.S. Bureau of the Census, *Current Business Reports, Annual Benchmark Report for Wholesale Trade, January 1988 Through February 1998*, (BW/97-RV).

No. 1293. Wholesale Trade, by Kind of Business: 1987 and 1992

[Based on 1987 Standard Industrial Classification (SIC) code; see text, Section 13]

KIND OF BUSINESS	ESTABLISH-MENTS [1] (1,000)		SALES (mil. dol.)		ANNUAL PAYROLL (mil. dol.)		PAID EMPLOYEES [2] (1,000)	
	1987	1992	1987	1992	1987	1992	1987	1992
Wholesale trade	**469.5**	**495.5**	**2,508,258**	**3,238,520**	**133,357**	**173,272**	**5,596**	**5,791**
Durable goods	297.3	313.5	1,262,302	1,593,874	82,767	105,155	3,332	3,349
Motor vehicles, parts, and supplies	45.8	47.3	326,625	394,104	9,872	12,065	483	489
Furniture and home furnishings	14.5	16.5	48,123	58,927	3,652	4,612	153	161
Lumber and construction materials	19.1	19.5	79,946	89,764	5,476	6,060	231	211
Professional & commercial equipment	44.2	46.8	175,149	262,974	19,728	26,380	698	685
Metals and minerals, except petroleum	11.1	11.2	114,528	118,322	4,038	4,684	143	138
Electrical goods	35.3	39.3	179,727	227,784	12,104	15,070	441	436
Hardware, plumbing, heating equipment	23.1	24.7	57,126	76,088	5,610	7,106	235	241
Machinery, equipment, supplies	71.7	73.9	178,892	230,004	16,731	21,267	682	690
Miscellaneous durable goods	32.3	34.3	102,185	135,906	5,556	7,912	266	299
Nondurable goods	172.2	182.0	1,245,956	1,644,647	50,589	68,117	2,264	2,442
Paper and paper products	16.8	19.7	83,173	106,580	5,202	6,939	228	269
Drugs, proprietaries, and sundries	4.9	6.1	64,280	129,306	2,968	5,368	120	158
Apparel, piece goods, and notions	16.9	19.6	81,476	109,203	4,661	6,522	181	196
Groceries and related products	42.1	42.9	380,945	504,567	16,729	21,723	763	812
Farm-product raw materials	12.6	11.6	117,606	136,869	1,847	2,100	117	109
Chemicals and allied products	12.7	14.2	94,620	132,471	3,847	5,596	131	147
Petroleum and petroleum products	16.7	16.1	234,874	281,585	3,658	4,447	175	169
Beer, wine, and distilled beverages	5.8	5.3	49,433	59,487	3,849	4,670	146	142
Misc. nondurable goods	43.7	46.8	139,550	184,577	7,828	10,754	404	441

[1] Number of establishments in business at any time during the year.   [2] For pay period including March 12.

Source: U.S. Bureau of the Census, *Census of Wholesale Trade: 1987*, WC87-A-52 and *1992*, WC92-A-52.

No. 1294. Selected Service Industries—Summary: 1987 and 1992

[For establishments with payroll]

KIND OF BUSINESS	1987 SIC code [1]	ESTABLISH-MENTS [2] (1,000)		RECEIPTS OR EXPENSES [3] (mil. dol.)		PAID EMPLOYEES [4] (1,000)	
		1987	1992	1987	1992	1987	1992
Firms subject to Federal income tax [5]	(X)	**1,626**	**1,825**	**772,194**	**1,202,613**	**16,055**	**19,290**
Hotels and other lodging places [6]	70 ex. 704	47	49	51,865	69,204	1,411	1,489
Personal services	72	185	197	31,491	43,280	1,105	1,218
Business services	73	252	307	166,322	274,892	4,414	5,542
Automotive repair, services, and parking	75	151	172	51,423	70,033	785	864
Miscellaneous repair services	76	66	72	20,838	30,732	346	428
Amusement and recreation services and museums [7]	78, 79, 84	99	115	57,638	92,915	1,094	1,382
Health services	80	407	442	182,289	299,067	3,592	4,453
Legal services	81	138	152	66,998	101,114	808	924
Social services	83	43	59	7,330	13,349	357	505
Engineering and management services [8]	87 ex. 8733	205	233	127,344	192,819	1,969	2,271
Firms exempt from Federal income tax [5]	(X)	**176**	**209**	**253,284**	**423,900**	**6,737**	**8,109**
Selected health services	8011 pt.; 8021 pt.; 805, 6, 8, 9	19	24	184,920	312,050	4,648	5,565
Social services	83	63	82	26,884	47,170	1,110	1,407
Selected membership organizations	861, 2, 4, 9	68	72	22,028	33,795	539	603

X Not applicable.   [1] Based on 1987 Standard Industrial Classification; see text, Section 13.   [2] Number of establishments in business at any time during the year.   [3] Receipts refer to establishments subject to Federal income tax. Expenses refer to establishments exempt from Federal income tax.   [4] For pay period including March 12.   [5] Includes other kinds of business, not shown separately.   [6] Excludes membership lodging.   [7] Includes motion pictures.   [8] Except noncommercial research organizations.

Source: U.S. Bureau of the Census, *1992 Census of Service Industries*, Geographic Area Series, SC92-A-52.

No. 1295. National Nonprofit Associations—Number, by Type: 1980 to 1997

[Data compiled during last few months of year previous to year shown and the beginning months of year shown]

TYPE	1980	1990	1995	1997	TYPE	1980	1990	1995	1997
Total	**14,726**	**22,289**	**22,663**	**22,901**	Fraternal, foreign interest,				
Trade, business, commercial	3,118	3,918	3,757	3,755	nationality, ethnic	435	573	552	541
Agriculture	677	940	1,122	1,124	Religious	797	1,172	1,230	1,230
Legal, governmental,					Veteran, hereditary, patriotic	208	462	686	745
public admin., military	529	792	776	780	Hobby, avocational	910	1,475	1,549	1,548
Scientific, engineering, tech	1,039	1,417	1,355	1,381	Athletic sports	504	840	838	836
Educational	[1]2,376	1,291	1,290	1,310	Labor unions	235	253	245	245
Cultural	([1])	1,886	1,918	1,918	Chambers of Commerce [2]	105	168	168	162
Social welfare	994	1,705	1,885	1,934	Greek and non-Greek				
Health, medical	1,413	2,227	2,348	2,453	letter societies	318	340	336	335
Public affairs	1,068	2,249	2,148	2,113	Fan clubs	(NA)	581	460	491

NA Not available.   [1] Data for cultural associations included with educational associations.   [2] National and binational.

Source: Gale Research Inc., Detroit, MI. Compiled from *Encyclopedia of Associations*, annual (copyright).

No. 1296. Service Industries—Summary of Taxable Firms: 1992

KIND OF BUSINESS	1987 SIC code [1]	ALL ESTABLISHMENTS		ESTABLISHMENTS WITH PAYROLL			
		Establishments [2] (1,000)	Receipts (mil. dol.)	Establishments [2] (1,000)	Receipts (mil. dol.)	Annual payroll (mil. dol.)	Paid employees [3] (1,000)
Firms subject to Federal income tax [4]	(X)	8,593.5	1,345,146	1,825.4	1,202,613	452,697	19,290
Hotels and other lodging places [4] [5]	70 ex. 704	92.9	71,038	48.6	69,204	19,633	1,489
Hotels and motels	701	69.1	68,508	41.7	67,193	19,187	1,456
Personal services [4]	72	1,320.9	59,598	197.1	43,280	14,379	1,218
Laundry, cleaning, and garment services	721	124.4	18,805	55.8	17,140	5,588	426
Photographic studios, portrait	722	64.3	4,280	11.4	3,191	853	67
Beauty and barber shops	723, 4	471.6	15,951	87.7	10,347	4,428	402
Funeral service and crematories	726	25.2	7,588	15.6	7,145	1,856	88
Business services [4]	73	2,056.2	309,439	306.6	274,892	109,299	5,542
Advertising [4]	731	91.6	22,673	19.0	19,456	7,223	196
Advertising agencies	7311	(NA)	(NA)	13.9	13,608	5,649	132
Credit reporting and collection	732	14.6	6,377	7.5	6,151	2,163	98
Mailing, reproduction, stenographic [4]	733	154.5	20,990	32.1	18,339	5,522	235
Direct mail advertising services	7331	(NA)	(NA)	3.9	6,434	1,777	79
Services to dwellings and other buildings	734	460.5	23,586	57.6	19,003	9,164	818
Miscellaneous equipment rental and leasing	735	52.4	22,782	24.8	21,778	4,905	200
Personnel supply services [4]	736	54.1	38,709	31.2	38,163	26,436	1,975
Help supply services	7363	(NA)	(NA)	19.0	33,587	24,075	1,842
Computer and data processing services [4]	737	223.6	104,650	59.1	101,073	35,598	886
Computer programming services	7371	(NA)	(NA)	23.3	23,548	10,890	243
Prepackaged software	7372	(NA)	(NA)	7.1	20,802	6,614	131
Computer integrated systems design	7373	(NA)	(NA)	5.0	14,805	4,151	98
Data processing and preparation	7374	(NA)	(NA)	7.3	20,200	6,796	230
Information retrieval services	7375	(NA)	(NA)	1.1	3,900	1,098	32
Computer maintenance and repair	7378	(NA)	(NA)	5.0	7,353	2,300	63
Detective and armored car services	7381	(NA)	(NA)	11.6	9,193	5,794	482
Photofinishing laboratories	7384	(NA)	(NA)	7.8	4,415	1,200	69
Auto repair, services, and parking [4]	75	454.3	78,512	172.0	70,033	15,550	864
Automotive rentals, no drivers [4]	751	22.2	20,906	10.6	20,574	2,757	132
Truck rental and leasing, no drivers	7513	(NA)	(NA)	4.3	7,445	1,029	42
Passenger car rental	7514	(NA)	(NA)	4.9	10,280	1,475	81
Automotive repair shops [4]	753	334.5	46,200	128.7	39,746	10,337	520
Top and body repair and paint shops	7532	(NA)	(NA)	35.0	12,262	3,445	166
General automotive repair shops	7538	(NA)	(NA)	64.8	17,773	4,406	230
Automotive services, except repair	754	85.8	7,661	22.5	6,047	1,776	160
Miscellaneous repair services [4]	76	269.8	35,237	71.6	30,732	9,695	428
Electrical repair shops	762	71.6	11,875	21.2	10,667	3,707	162
Amusement and recreation services [4] [6]	78, 79, 84	691.7	103,556	114.8	92,915	25,357	1,382
Motion picture prod., distribution, services	781, 2	54.1	34,289	13.0	33,062	8,084	249
Motion picture theaters	783	8.1	5,879	6.9	5,817	788	105
Video tape rental	784	33.7	5,495	22.0	5,075	944	124
Producers, orchestras, entertainers [7]	792	288.6	13,054	10.1	8,625	2,895	69
Commercial sports	794	71.6	9,010	3.8	7,594	4,022	90
Physical fitness facilities	7991	29.6	4,135	9.2	3,824	1,043	130
Health services [4]	80	1,005.5	321,650	441.7	299,067	129,093	4,453
Offices and clinics of doctors of medicine	801	328.9	151,824	197.7	141,429	68,732	1,357
Offices and clinics of dentists	802	138.5	36,939	108.8	35,523	13,039	555
Offices, clinics of doctors of osteopathy	803	14.2	4,008	8.7	3,638	1,650	47
Offices of other health practitioners [4]	804	243.0	23,892	74.7	18,926	6,150	283
Offices and clinics of chiropractors	8041	41.4	6,555	27.3	5,918	1,652	85
Offices and clinics of optometrists	8042	26.0	5,333	17.1	4,940	1,301	69
Nursing and personal care facilities	805	51.8	34,742	15.0	33,990	15,954	1,135
Hospitals [4]	806	(NA)	(NA)	1.4	31,083	10,556	428
General medical and surgical hospitals	8062	(NA)	(NA)	0.7	24,162	8,013	323
Medical and dental laboratories [4]	807	29.4	15,172	16.0	14,460	4,804	178
Medical laboratories	8071	(NA)	(NA)	8.4	12,511	3,980	139
Home health care services	808	(NA)	(NA)	8.0	10,414	4,853	342
Legal services	81	326.9	108,443	151.7	101,114	39,328	924
Selected educational services	823, 4, 9	240.7	9,158	14.7	7,242	2,457	133
Social services [4]	83	617.4	18,201	59.1	13,349	5,466	505
Child day care services	835	524.4	8,708	35.3	5,270	2,388	283
Engineering and architectural services [4]	871	225.4	83,033	68.1	78,770	32,745	825
Engineering services	8711	131.3	67,716	41.8	65,245	27,247	658
Architectural services	8712	71.6	12,682	17.9	11,244	4,408	122
Accounting, auditing, and bookkeeping	872	325.5	37,191	79.1	34,038	14,001	521
Research and testing services [8]	873 ex. 8733	30.4	22,910	13.5	22,690	9,227	282
Management and public relations [4]	874	735.8	72,490	72.1	57,321	23,371	644
Management services	8741	111.0	23,774	19.7	21,728	8,516	278
Management consulting services	8742	(NA)	(NA)	33.8	22,629	9,620	212

[2] NA Not available.   X Not applicable.   [1] Based on 1987 Standard Industrial Classification; see text, Section 13. [2] Represents the number of establishments in business at any time during year.   [3] For pay period including March 12. [4] Includes other kinds of business, not shown separately.   [5] Excludes membership lodging.   [6] Includes motion pictures and museums.   [7] Excludes motion picture producers.   [8] Excludes noncommercial research organizations.

Source: U.S. Bureau of the Census, *1992 Census of Service Industries*, SC92-A-52 and SC92-N-1.

No. 1297. Services—Establishments, Employees, and Payroll: 1990 and 1995

[Covers establishments with payroll. Employees are for the week including March 12. Most government employees are excluded. For statement on methodology, see Appendix III]

KIND OF BUSINESS	1987 SIC code [1]	ESTABLISHMENTS (1,000)		EMPLOYEES (1,000)		PAYROLL (bil. dol.)	
		1990	1995	1990	1995	1990	1995
Services, total [2]	(I)	2,059.3	2,385.5	28,800	34,707	599.4	864.4
Hotels and other lodging places	70	50.6	54.1	1,529	1,575	19.1	23.9
Hotels and motels	701	39.2	43.3	1,463	1,519	18.3	23.0
Personal services [2]	72	186.1	202.3	1,196	1,282	13.5	16.6
Laundry, cleaning, and garment services	721	50.4	56.3	418	443	5.2	6.3
Beauty shops	723	76.1	81.7	371	395	3.9	4.8
Barber shops	724	5.1	4.5	16	14	0.2	0.2
Funeral service and crematories	726	14.9	15.8	85	100	1.7	2.2
Business services [2]	73	292.3	352.7	5,119	6,825	98.1	157.7
Advertising	731	19.1	20.6	204	226	7.3	9.1
Advertising agencies	7311	11.1	13.7	137	142	5.4	6.9
Credit reporting and collection	732	6.6	7.2	94	106	2.0	2.6
Mailing, reproduction, stenographic [2]	733	26.2	33.9	233	279	5.1	7.3
Direct mail advertising services	7331	3.5	4.1	84	88	1.7	2.2
Commercial art and graphic design	7336	9.0	12.9	52	59	1.5	2.0
Services to buildings	734	48.5	62.9	802	902	8.3	11.2
Misc. equipment rental and leasing	735	22.6	25.5	209	227	4.9	6.3
Personnel supply services [2]	736	27.0	35.6	1,518	2,648	20.6	44.2
Employment agencies	7361	12.8	13.2	247	249	4.3	5.2
Help supply services	7363	13.3	22.2	1,210	2,397	15.6	38.9
Computer and data processing services [2]	737	40.5	75.2	773	1,118	28.5	53.2
Computer programming services	7371	12.4	25.5	217	311	8.9	16.3
Prepackaged software	7372	3.8	7.0	76	162	3.5	10.1
Computer integrated systems design	7373	3.3	5.8	82	111	3.5	5.3
Data processing and preparation	7374	6.8	7.9	229	270	6.4	9.5
Information retrieval services	7375	0.5	1.7	17	39	0.5	1.7
Computer maintenance and repair	7378	3.3	4.9	53	63	1.9	2.6
Miscellaneous business services	738	62.7	77.1	1,093	1,298	17.2	23.2
Detective and armored car services	7381	9.4	12.4	467	534	5.2	7.2
Photofinishing laboratories	7384	6.2	7.2	76	72	1.2	1.4
Automotive repair, services, and parking [2]	75	156.6	181.3	877	991	15.2	19.4
Automotive rentals, no drivers [2]	751	10.5	10.6	147	141	2.9	3.2
Truck rental and leasing, no drivers	7513	4.0	4.8	51	38	1.2	1.1
Passenger car rental	7514	4.5	4.3	78	92	1.3	1.9
Automotive repair shops [2]	753	112.7	134.3	507	581	9.6	12.8
Top and body repair and paint shops	7532	30.5	34.7	164	186	3.2	4.3
General automotive repair shops	7538	54.8	69.5	214	262	3.8	5.5
Automotive services, except repair	754	18.1	25.4	145	200	1.5	2.5
Miscellaneous repair services	76	67.4	73.6	403	456	8.7	11.8
Electrical repair shops	762	17.2	20.2	115	154	2.6	4.2
Motion pictures [2]	78	35.4	42.9	430	512	8.6	11.2
Motion picture production and services	781	9.2	12.9	189	217	5.9	7.9
Motion picture distribution and services	782	1.0	1.4	24	22	0.9	1.2
Motion picture theaters	783	7.0	6.6	107	112	0.8	0.9
Video tape rental	784	16.4	21.2	103	160	0.8	1.2
Amusement and recreation services [2]	79	75.2	93.5	1,032	1,324	16.1	25.3
Producers, orchestras, entertainers	792	9.7	14.7	126	154	3.3	5.0
Commercial sports	794	3.3	4.4	79	95	3.0	5.5
Sports clubs, managers, & promoters	7941	0.9	1.5	27	41	2.2	4.5
Amusement parks	7996	0.7	1.0	69	96	1.1	1.5
Membership sports and recreation clubs	7997	13.1	14.5	242	278	3.4	4.6
Health services [2]	80	436.7	478.3	8,811	10,851	213.8	314.7
Offices and clinics of medical doctors	801	193.6	194.3	1,387	1,664	63.0	85.6
Offices and clinics of dentists	802	104.7	111.2	533	615	11.6	16.1
Offices of other health practitioners	804	62.5	80.1	250	335	5.0	7.9
Offices and clinics of chiropractors	8041	22.9	29.0	73	89	1.3	1.8
Nursing and personal care facilities	805	19.1	22.0	1,461	1,756	18.6	28.1
Hospitals [3]	806	6.3	7.4	4,325	5,091	99.2	146.1
Medical and dental laboratories	807	14.4	16.1	158	196	3.8	5.5
Medical laboratories	8071	7.1	8.6	118	156	3.0	4.6
Home health care services	808	7.7	14.0	351	749	4.8	13.2
Legal services	81	142.4	163.6	932	961	36.0	43.2
Elementary and secondary schools	821	14.3	17.1	451	589	6.6	10.2
Colleges and universities	822	3.0	3.5	1,082	1,251	19.2	27.0
Social services [2]	83	115.6	155.8	1,750	2,263	20.9	32.1
Child day care services	835	39.0	49.1	405	535	3.4	5.5
Residential care	836	21.0	29.9	417	550	5.4	8.2
Museums, botanical, zoological gardens	84	3.2	3.8	64	76	1.1	1.5
Business associations	861	12.7	14.6	99	111	2.7	3.8
Civic and social associations	864	40.0	41.8	366	386	3.7	4.4
Engineering and management services [2]	87	201.1	269.2	2,473	2,795	79.8	108.3
Engineering services	8711	33.1	43.8	652	688	24.9	31.2
Architectural services	8712	15.7	18.6	140	134	4.8	5.5
Accounting, auditing, and bookkeeping	872	67.9	84.9	524	588	13.8	18.4
Research and testing services	873	14.9	19.6	393	462	12.3	17.3
Management services	8741	15.3	21.7	286	313	7.7	9.9
Management consulting services	8742	24.5	41.3	226	352	8.6	17.0

[1] Based on 1987 Standard Industrial Classification; see text, Section 13. [2] Includes kinds of business not shown separately. [3] Includes government employees.

Source: U.S. Bureau of the Census, *County Business Patterns,* annual.

No. 1298. Service Industries—Annual Receipts of Taxable Firms: 1985 to 1996

[In billions of dollars. Covers employer and nonemployer firms except as noted. Estimated]

KIND OF BUSINESS	1987 SIC code [1]	1985	1990	1992	1993	1994	1995	1996
Hotels and other lodging places [2]	70 ex. 704	45.4	64.2	71.0	74.1	79.6	84.1	88.9
Hotels and motels	701	43.5	62.0	68.5	71.5	76.7	81.1	85.7
Personal services [3]	72	36.7	54.7	59.6	62.6	66.1	70.6	73.2
Laundry, cleaning, and garment services	721	12.8	17.3	18.8	19.1	19.7	20.7	21.5
Beauty shops	7231	9.0	12.8	14.4	14.6	15.2	16.4	16.9
Barber shops	7241	1.2	1.4	1.5	1.5	1.6	1.6	1.6
Funeral service and crematories	726	5.2	6.8	7.6	8.2	8.6	9.4	10.0
Business services [3]	73	155.9	280.7	309.4	337.4	375.1	425.1	485.2
Advertising	731	14.9	22.0	22.7	23.4	24.2	27.1	30.7
Advertising agencies	7311	11.1	16.1	16.0	16.7	17.3	19.3	21.4
Credit reporting and collection	732	3.7	5.8	6.4	7.0	7.1	7.7	8.6
Mailing, reproduction, stenographic [3]	733	14.5	20.8	21.0	21.9	22.3	24.4	25.8
Direct mail advertising services	7331	3.8	7.0	6.8	7.3	7.3	7.5	8.2
Commercial art and graphic design	7336	(NA)	6.1	6.2	6.0	6.3	6.8	7.3
Services to dwellings and other buildings	734	13.3	22.3	23.6	23.5	25.7	27.5	30.5
Miscellaneous equipment rental and leasing	735	(NA)	23.1	22.8	24.6	26.4	29.5	30.7
Personnel supply services	736	14.7	32.5	38.7	42.1	48.0	59.4	68.5
Employment agencies	7361	3.7	6.2	5.0	5.6	6.5	7.7	8.9
Help supply services	7363	(NA)	26.4	33.7	36.5	41.4	51.6	59.6
Computer and data processing services [3]	737	45.1	88.3	104.7	117.9	135.6	156.4	184.4
Computer programming services	7371	(NA)	21.3	25.0	27.4	31.1	35.1	42.2
Prepackaged software	7372	(NA)	16.5	21.2	25.2	28.9	33.2	39.3
Computer integrated systems design	7373	(NA)	12.9	15.2	16.2	17.0	17.5	20.2
Data processing and preparation	7374	(NA)	17.8	20.4	23.7	29.2	35.6	41.0
Information retrieval services	7375	(NA)	3.5	3.9	4.3	4.6	5.3	6.9
Computer maintenance and repair	7378	(NA)	7.0	7.7	8.3	9.3	10.7	12.0
Miscellaneous business services [3]	738	(NA)	65.8	69.7	77.0	85.7	93.1	106.0
Detective and armored car services	7381	(NA)	9.0	9.7	10.3	10.8	11.9	13.5
Photofinishing laboratories	7384	4.3	5.6	5.7	6.4	6.6	6.8	7.2
Automotive repair, services, and parking [3]	75	51.7	73.7	78.5	84.3	91.9	99.2	106.7
Automotive rentals, no drivers [3]	751	14.6	20.8	20.9	22.7	24.4	26.6	29.4
Truck rental and leasing, without drivers	7513	5.5	8.5	7.6	8.1	9.0	10.1	11.2
Passenger car rental	7514	(NA)	9.0	10.4	11.4	12.2	12.9	14.5
Automotive repair shops [3]	753	30.5	43.5	46.2	49.7	54.6	58.6	62.2
Top & body repair & paint shops	7532	(NA)	13.5	13.9	15.0	16.4	17.8	18.8
General automotive repair shops	7538	(NA)	19.6	21.3	22.7	25.2	27.3	28.9
Automotive services, except repair	754	(NA)	6.5	7.7	8.3	9.3	10.4	11.5
Miscellaneous repair services	76	20.7	32.8	35.2	36.8	40.7	44.9	46.2
Electrical repair shops	762	(NA)	11.3	11.9	12.4	13.1	14.5	14.6
Motion pictures	78	21.5	40.0	45.7	49.8	53.5	57.2	60.2
Motion picture produc., distribution, allied services	781,2	15.0	28.9	34.3	37.7	40.3	43.3	46.2
Motion picture theaters	783	3.8	6.1	5.9	6.0	6.2	6.5	7.0
Video tape rental	784	(NA)	5.0	5.5	6.2	7.0	7.4	6.9
Amusement and recreation services [3]	79	31.2	50.1	57.7	63.7	68.5	77.5	85.8
Producers, orchestras, entertainers	792	6.4	10.7	13.1	15.4	16.1	17.5	19.7
Commercial sports	794	5.0	8.6	9.0	9.9	11.1	13.1	14.6
Sports clubs, managers, & promoters	7941	(NA)	3.7	4.0	5.1	6.1	7.7	8.9
Amusement parks	7996	2.6	4.9	5.4	5.6	5.9	6.3	6.8
Membership sports and recreation clubs	7997	3.5	4.8	5.4	6.0	6.4	6.8	7.4
Health services [3]	80	147.4	271.2	321.7	335.1	351.4	376.3	399.2
Offices and clinics of doctors of medicine	801	72.1	128.9	151.8	154.2	159.6	168.0	173.5
Offices and clinics of dentists	802	20.6	31.5	36.9	38.9	41.7	44.9	47.4
Offices of other health practitioners	804	7.9	20.1	23.9	25.4	25.9	27.4	28.6
Offices and clinics of chiropractors	8041	2.7	5.5	6.6	6.9	6.8	6.7	7.0
Nursing and personal care facilities	805	17.5	30.2	34.7	36.2	37.3	41.1	44.3
Hospitals [4]	806	15.7	26.5	31.1	33.3	35.1	38.4	44.7
Medical and dental laboratories	807	5.4	12.0	15.2	15.1	15.4	15.5	16.0
Medical laboratories	8071	3.9	10.0	12.9	12.7	13.0	12.9	13.3
Home health care services	808	(NA)	7.6	11.2	13.2	15.4	18.0	19.5
Legal services	81	52.8	97.6	108.4	112.1	114.6	116.0	124.6
Social services	83	(NA)	15.5	18.2	20.1	22.5	24.9	28.0
Child day care services	8351	2.6	7.1	8.7	9.4	10.1	10.9	11.4
Residential care	8361	(NA)	4.6	4.9	5.4	5.9	6.4	7.2
Museums, botanical, zoological gardens	84	(NA)	0.1	0.2	0.2	0.2	0.2	0.3
Engineering and management services [3]	87	(NA)	198.4	215.6	222.9	235.4	263.8	292.5
Engineering services	8711	(NA)	64.8	67.7	67.1	68.1	73.9	80.3
Architectural services	8712	(NA)	13.0	12.7	13.5	14.8	16.5	18.5
Accounting, auditing, & bookkeeping	8721	21.2	32.6	37.2	39.8	42.6	48.8	54.5
Research and testing services [5]	873, ex. 87	(NA)	20.4	22.9	24.6	25.6	26.8	30.8
Management services	8741	(NA)	20.6	23.8	23.4	24.3	27.6	27.6
Management consulting services	8742	(NA)	28.9	31.9	34.5	38.5	46.4	53.7
Arrangement of passenger transportation	472	6.3	12.3	11.9	12.4	13.1	14.2	15.3
Real estate agents and managers	653	31.3	63.0	73.1	79.2	80.9	82.7	89.0

NA Not available. [1] Standard Industrial Classification; see text, Section 13. [2] Excludes those on membership basis. [3] Includes other kinds of businesses, not shown separately. [4] Covers employer firms only. [5] Excludes noncommercial research organizations.

Source: U.S. Bureau of the Census, *Current Business Reports, Service Annual Survey: 1996* (BS/96); and unpublished data.

No. 1299. Lodging Industry Summary: 1990 to 1996

YEAR	Average occu-pancy rate (percent)	Average room rate (dol.)	ROOM SIZE OF PROPERTY	1996 Estab-lishments	1996 Rooms (mil.)	ITEM	1996 Business traveler	1996 Leisure traveler
1990	63.3	57.96	Total	47,000	3.6	Typical night:		
1991	60.9	58.08				Made reservations .	91%	81%
1992	61.7	58.91	Percent:			Amount paid	$73.00	$67.60
1993	63.6	60.53	Under 75 rooms . . .	66.6	25.6			
1994	65.2	62.86	75-149 rooms	21.9	31.0	Length of stay:		
1995	65.5	65.81	150-299 rooms . . .	8.5	22.3	One night	37%	46%
1996	65.2	69.66	300 or more	3.0	21.1	Two nights	23%	26%
						Three or more	39%	29%

Source: American Hotel & Motel Association, Washington, DC, *Lodging Industry Profile* (copyright).

No. 1300. Service Industries—Summary of Tax-Exempt Firms: 1992

[Covers establishments with payroll]

KIND OF BUSINESS	1987 SIC code [1]	Establish-ments [2] (1,000)	Reve-nues (mil. dol.)	Annual payroll (mil. dol.)	Paid employ-ees [3] (1,000)
Firms exempt from Federal income tax [4] .	(X)	**208.9**	**446,256**	**186,672**	**8,109**
Nursing and personal care facilities.	805	5.9	15,220	7,591	498
Hospitals	806	5.7	279,735	126,202	4,566
Hospitals, excluding government	806	3.6	203,360	87,062	3,252
Social services [4]	83	81.7	53,672	19,331	1,407
Individual and family social services.	832	28.9	16,046	6,381	434
Residential care	836	15.0	10,615	4,830	319
Business associations	861	14.3	11,068	3,157	102
Civic, social, and fraternal associations	864	41.8	13,176	3,657	355
Research and testing services	873	3.8	12,535	4,511	126

X Not applicable. [1] Based on 1987 Standard Industrial Classification; see text, Section 13. [2] Represents the number of establishments in business at any time during year. [3] For pay period including March 12. [4] Includes other kinds of business, not shown separately.

Source: U.S. Bureau of the Census, *1992 Census of Service Industries*, SC92-A-52 and SC92-N-1.

No. 1301. Selected Service Industries—Revenue and Expenses for Tax-Exempt Firms: 1990 to 1996

[**In billions of dollars**. Estimated from a sample of employer firms only]

KIND OF BUSINESS	1987 SIC code [1]	REVENUE 1990	REVENUE 1995	REVENUE 1996	EXPENSES 1990	EXPENSES 1995	EXPENSES 1996
Selected amusement and recreation services [2]	792, 7991, 7997, 7999	7.9	12.8	13.3	(NA)	12.1	12.5
Offices and clinics of doctors of medicine	801	12.9	24.9	26.2	12.5	24.1	25.5
Nursing and personal care facilities	805	12.1	17.6	18.5	(NA)	16.8	18.2
Hospitals	806	233.6	325.0	337.8	225.6	314.9	327.8
Home health care services.	808	3.9	7.9	8.0	3.6	7.7	7.9
Health and allied services, n.e.c.	809	5.3	9.7	10.4	5.2	9.3	9.9
Social services.	83	45.3	70.3	75.2	39.4	63.4	67.9
Individual and family social services	8322	13.0	20.8	22.3	12.6	19.4	20.9
Job training and related services	8331	4.9	6.5	6.8	4.5	6.5	6.7
Child day care services	8351	2.9	5.4	5.6	3.0	5.2	5.3
Residential care	8361	8.8	13.5	15.4	8.6	12.8	14.8
Selected membership organizations [3]	86 (pt)	31.5	45.9	48.9	28.6	42.7	45.4
Research and testing services	873	11.0	14.5	14.9	10.0	13.9	14.7

NA Not available. [1] Standard Industrial Classification; see text, Section 13. [2] Covers theatrical producers, bands, orchestras, and entertainers (SIC 792); physical fitness facilities (SIC 7991); membership sports and recreation clubs (SIC 7997); and amusement and recreation services, not elsewhere classified (SIC 7999). [3] Includes business associations (SIC 861); professional membership organizations (SIC 862); civic, social, and fraternal organizations (SIC 864); and other membership organizations, except labor unions and political and religious organizations (SIC 869).

Source: U.S. Bureau of the Census, *Current Business Reports, Service Annual Survey: 1996* (BS/96).

Figure 28.1
U.S. International Transaction Balances: 1960 to 1997

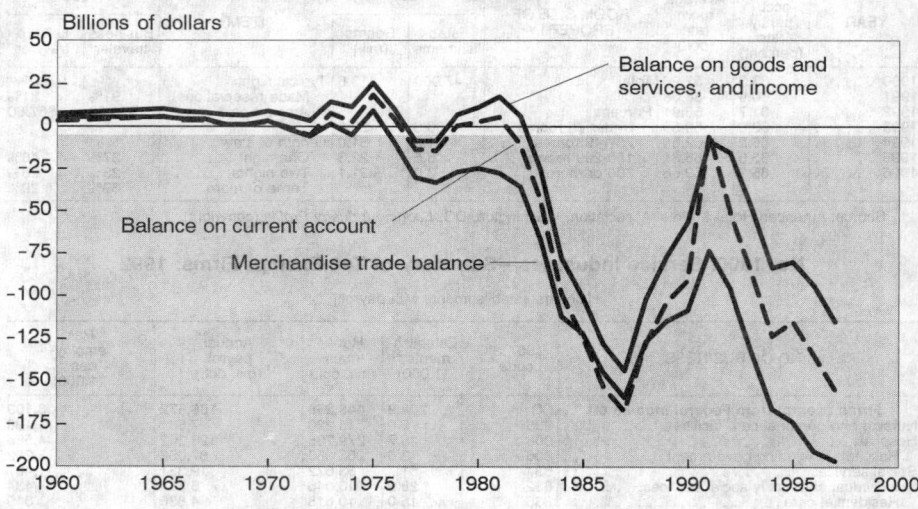

Source: Chart prepared by U.S. Bureau of the Census. For data, see Table 1302.

Figure 28.2
**Top Purchasers of U.S. Exports and Suppliers
of U.S. General Imports: 1997**

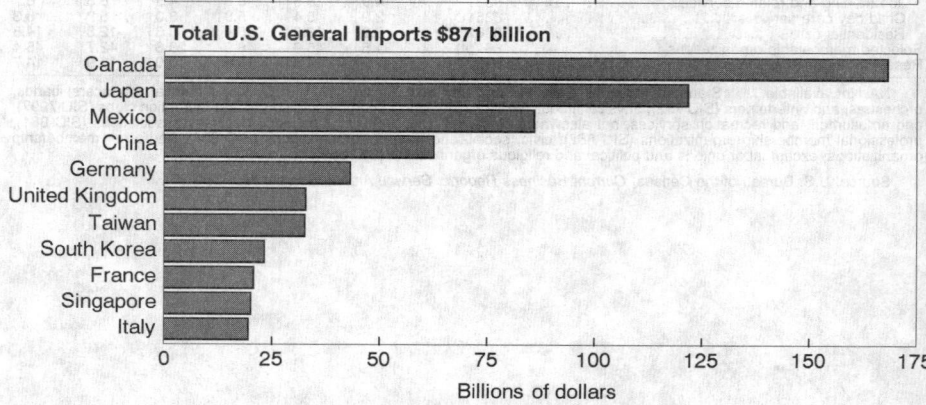

Source: Chart prepared by U.S. Bureau of the Census. For data, see Table 1323.

Foreign Commerce and Aid

This section presents data on the flow of goods, services, and capital between the United States and other countries; changes in official reserve assets of the United States; international investments; foreign assistance programs; and import duties.

The Bureau of Economic Analysis publishes current figures on U.S. international transactions and the U.S. international investment position in its monthly *Survey of Current Business.* Statistics for the foreign aid programs are presented by the Agency for International Development (AID) in its annual *U.S. Overseas Loans and Grants and Assistance from International Organizations;* and by the Department of Agriculture in its *Foreign Agricultural Trade of the United States.*

The principal source of merchandise import and export data is the Bureau of the Census. Current data are presented monthly in *U.S. Merchandise Trade,* (beginning 1994, retitled *U.S. International Trade in Goods and Services*) report Series FT900, and *U.S. Merchandise Trade: Exports, General Imports, and Imports for Consumption*, report Series FT925 (discontinued after 1996). The *Bureau of the Census Catalog* and the *Guide to Foreign Trade Statistics* lists the Bureau's monthly and annual reports in this field. In addition, the International Trade Administration and the Bureau of Economic Analysis present summary as well as selected commodity and country data for U.S. foreign trade in the *U.S. Industry and Trade Outlook* (formerly *U.S. Industrial Outlook*), the *Survey of Current Business,* and *U.S. Foreign Trade Highlights,* respectively. The merchandise trade data in the latter source include balance of payments adjustments to the census data. The Treasury Department's *Monthly Treasury Statement of Receipts and Outlays of the United States Government* contains information on import duties.

International accounts—The international transactions tables (Nos. 1302 to 1304) show, for given time periods, the transfer of goods, services, grants, and financial assets and liabilities between the United States and the rest of the

In Brief

The U.S. current account and merchandise trade deficits both increased to record levels in 1997 at $155 and $191 billion, respectively. The balance on service transactions in 1997 showed a record surplus of $88 billion.

The U.S. direct investment position abroad increased almost 11 percent to $860 billion in 1997 over the previous year. The foreign direct investment position in the United States was up 15 percent to $682 billion.

The U.S. merchandise trade deficit with Japan increased to $56 billion in 1997 after declining the previous 2 years. The next largest deficits to Japan were with China and Germany at $50 billion and $19 billion, respectively.

world. The major revisions to this series were incorporated this year due to the first benchmark survey of the stock of U.S. portfolio investment abroad in over 50 years. The international investment position table (No. 1305) presents, for specific dates, the value of U.S. investments abroad and of foreign investments in the United States. The movement of foreign and U.S. capital as presented in the balance of payments is not the only factor affecting the total value of foreign investments. Among the other factors are changes in the valuation of assets or liabilities, including changes in prices of securities, defaults, expropriations, and write-offs.

Direct investment abroad means the ownership or control, directly or indirectly, by one person of 10 percent or more of the voting securities of an incorporated business enterprise or an equivalent interest in an unincorporated business enterprise. Direct investment position is the value of U.S. parents' claims on the equity of, and receivables due from, foreign affiliates, less foreign affiliates' receivables due from their U.S. parents.

Income consists of parents' shares in the earnings of their affiliates plus net interest received by parents on intercompany accounts, less withholding taxes on dividends and interest.

Foreign aid—Foreign assistance is divided into three major categories—grants (military supplies and services and other grants), credits, and other assistance (through net accumulation of foreign currency claims from the sale of agricultural commodities). *Grants* are transfers for which no payment is expected (other than a limited percentage of the foreign currency "counterpart" funds generated by the grant), or which at most involve an obligation on the part of the receiver to extend aid to the United States or other countries to achieve a common objective. *Credits* are loan disbursements or transfers under other agreements which give rise to specific obligations to repay, over a period of years, usually with interest. All known returns to the U.S. Government stemming from grants and credits (reverse grants, returns of grants, and payments of principal) are taken into account in net grants and net credits, but no allowance is made for interest or commissions. *Other assistance* represents the transfer of U.S. farm products in exchange for foreign currencies (plus, since enactment of Public Law 87-128, currency claims from principal and interest collected on credits extended under the farm products program), *less* the government's disbursements of the currencies as grants, credits, or for purchases. The net acquisition of currencies represents net transfers of resources to foreign countries under the agricultural programs, in addition to those classified as grants or credits.

The basic instrument for extending military aid to friendly nations has been the Mutual Defense Assistance Program authorized by the Congress in 1949. Prior to 1952, economic and technical aid was authorized in the Foreign Assistance Act of 1948, the 1950 Act for International Development, and other legislation which set up programs for specific countries. In 1952, these economic, technical, and military aid programs were combined under the Mutual Security Act, which in turn was followed by the Foreign Assistance Act passed in 1961.

Appropriations to provide military assistance were also made in the Department of Defense Appropriation Act (rather than the Foreign Assistance Appropriation Act) beginning in 1966 for certain countries in Southeast Asia and in other legislation concerning program for specific countries (such as Israel). Figures on activity under the Foreign Assistance Act as reported in the *Foreign Grants and Credits* series differ from data published by AID or its immediate predecessors, due largely to differences in reporting, timing, and treatment of particular items.

Exports—The Bureau of the Census compiles export data primarily from Shipper's Export Declarations required to be filed with customs officials for shipments leaving the United States. They include U.S. exports under mutual security programs and exclude shipments to U.S. Armed Forces for their own use.

The value reported in the export statistics is generally equivalent to a free alongside ship (f.a.s.) value at the U.S. port of export, based on the transaction price, including inland freight, insurance, and other charges incurred in placing the merchandise alongside the carrier at the U.S. port of exportation. This value, as defined, excludes the cost of loading merchandise aboard the exporting carrier and also excludes freight, insurance, and any other charges or transportation and other costs beyond the U.S. port of exportation. The country of destination is defined as the country of ultimate destination or country where the merchandise is to be consumed, further processed, or manufactured, as known to the shipper at the time of exportation. When ultimate destination is not known, the shipment is statistically credited to the last country to which the shipper knows the merchandise will be shipped in the same form as exported.

For certain "low-valued" shipments, the export statistics include estimates based upon selected samples of such shipments. The dollar value of the "low-valued" shipments has varied. For instance, effective January 1987 through September 1989, data are estimated for shipments valued under $1,501; from October 1989 through December 1989, data are estimated for shipments valued under $2,501 to all countries.

Effective January 1990, the United States began substituting Canadian import statistics for U.S. exports to Canada. As a result of the data exchange between the United States and Canada, the United States has adopted the Canadian import exemption level for its export statistics based on shipments to Canada.

Data are estimated for shipments valued under $2,501 to all countries, except Canada, using factors based on the ratios of low-valued shipments to individual country totals. These shipments represent slightly less than 2.5 percent of the monthly value of U.S. exports to those countries. Data are estimated for shipments reported on Canadian import documents which total less than $900 (Canadian). Such shipments represent 2 percent of the monthly value of U.S. exports to Canada.

Prior to 1989, exports were based on Schedule B, Statistical Classification of Domestic and Foreign Commodities Exported from the United States. These statistics were retabulated and published using Schedule E, Standard International Trade Classification, Revision 2. Beginning in 1989, Schedule B classifications were based on the Harmonized System and made to coincide with the Standard International Trade Classification, Revision 3. This revision will affect the comparability of most export series beginning with the 1989 data for commodities.

Imports—The Bureau of the Census compiles import data from various customs forms required to be filed with customs officials. Data on import values are presented on two bases in this section: the c.i.f. (cost, insurance, and freight) and the customs import value (as appraised by the U.S. Customs Service in accordance with legal requirements of the Tariff Act of 1930, as amended). This latter valuation, primarily used for collection of import duties, frequently does not reflect the actual transaction value. Country of origin is defined as country where the merchandise was grown, mined, or manufactured. If country of origin is unknown, country of shipment is reported.

Imports are classified either as "General imports" or "Imports for consumption."

General imports are a combination of entries for immediate consumption, entries into customs bonded warehouses, and entries into U.S. Foreign Trade Zones, thus generally reflecting total arrivals of merchandise. *Imports for consumption* are a combination of entries for immediate consumption, withdrawals from warehouses for consumption, and entries of merchandise into U.S. customs territory from U.S. Foreign Trade Zones, thus generally reflecting the total of the commodities entered into U.S. consumption channels.

Since July 1953, the import statistics include estimates, not classified by commodity, for certain low-valued shipments. For instance, from January 1985 through September 1989, import statistics include estimates for shipments valued under $1,001. Effective October 1989, import statistics are fully compiled on shipments valued over $1,250 or, under certain textile programs, for any article which must be reported on a formal entry. Value data for shipments valued under $1,251 and not required to be reported on formal entries are estimated for individual countries using factors based on the ratios of low-valued shipments to individual country totals for past periods. The estimated low-valued shipments generally amount to slightly less than 4 percent of the import total.

Prior to 1989, imports were based on the Tariff Schedule of the United States Annotated. The statistics were retabulated and published using Schedule A, Standard International Trade Classification, Revision 2. Beginning in 1989, the statistics are based on the Harmonized Tariff Schedule of the United States, which coincides with the Standard International Trade Classification, Revision 3. This revision will affect the comparability of most import commodity series beginning with the 1989 data.

Area coverage—Except as noted, the geographic area covered by the export and import trade statistics is the United States Customs area (includes the 50 states, the District of Columbia and Puerto Rico), the U.S. Virgin Islands (effective January 1981), and U.S. Foreign Trade Zones (effective July 1982). Data for selected tables and total values for 1980, have been revised to reflect the U.S. Virgin Islands' trade with foreign countries, where possible.

No. 1302. U.S. International Transactions, by Type of Transaction: 1980 to 1997

[In millions of dollars. Minus sign (-) indicates debits]

TYPE OF TRANSACTION	1980	1985	1989	1990	1991	1992	1993	1994	1995	1996	1997
Exports of goods and services [1]	344,440	382,749	643,012	700,552	722,653	742,337	769,919	861,574	999,491	1,063,971	1,179,380
Merchandise, excl. military [2][3]	224,250	215,915	362,120	389,307	416,913	440,352	456,832	502,398	575,845	611,983	679,325
Foods, feeds, and beverages	36,278	24,566	37,475	35,172	35,829	40,336	40,692	41,957	50,475	55,533	51,507
Industrial supplies and materials	72,088	61,159	99,826	105,503	109,826	109,592	111,870	121,547	146,372	147,980	158,274
Capital goods, except automotive	76,283	79,322	138,908	152,543	166,453	176,070	182,096	205,248	233,778	253,143	295,288
Automotive vehicles and parts [4]	17,443	24,945	34,888	36,465	40,008	47,027	52,534	57,776	61,829	65,021	74,029
Consumer goods (nonfood) [5]	17,751	14,593	37,317	43,719	46,858	51,424	54,655	59,981	64,425	70,136	77,445
Services	47,584	73,155	127,233	147,922	164,333	176,982	186,385	201,434	219,802	238,792	258,268
Transfers under U.S. military agency sales contracts	9,029	8,718	8,564	9,932	11,135	12,387	13,471	12,787	14,755	15,765	18,269
Travel	10,588	17,762	36,205	43,007	48,385	54,742	57,875	58,417	63,395	69,751	73,268
Passenger fares	2,591	4,411	10,657	15,298	15,854	16,618	16,528	16,997	18,909	20,413	20,895
Other transportation	11,618	14,674	20,526	22,042	22,631	21,531	21,958	23,754	26,081	26,074	26,911
Royalties and license fees	7,085	6,678	13,818	16,634	17,819	20,841	21,695	26,712	30,289	32,823	33,676
Other private services	6,276	20,035	36,875	40,341	47,821	50,022	53,975	61,880	65,555	73,073	84,465
U.S. government misc. services	398	878	587	668	690	841	883	887	818	893	784
Income on U.S. assets abroad	72,606	93,679	153,659	163,324	141,408	125,003	126,702	157,742	203,844	213,196	241,787
Direct investment	37,146	30,547	55,368	58,740	52,198	51,912	61,241	72,391	93,164	99,802	109,407
Other private receipts	32,898	57,633	92,638	94,072	81,186	65,977	60,353	81,230	105,967	108,733	128,845
U.S. government receipts	2,562	5,499	5,653	10,512	8,023	7,114	5,108	4,121	4,713	4,661	3,535
Imports of goods, services, and income	-333,774	-484,037	-720,189	-757,507	-732,068	-758,481	-817,910	-946,008	-1,080,107	-1,158,309	-1,294,904
Merchandise, excl. military [2][3]	-249,750	-338,088	-477,365	-498,337	-490,981	-536,458	-589,441	-668,590	-749,574	-803,320	-877,279
Foods, feeds, and beverages	-18,564	-21,850	-24,898	-26,407	-26,205	-27,610	-27,866	-30,958	-33,176	-35,711	-39,694
Industrial supplies and materials	-132,472	-114,008	-135,363	-145,188	-132,963	-140,591	-152,437	-164,946	-185,005	-209,469	-217,304
Capital goods, except automotive	-31,576	-61,287	-112,156	-116,061	-120,802	-134,252	-152,305	-184,369	-221,429	-229,050	-254,175
Automotive vehicles and parts [4]	-28,257	-64,905	-87,356	-88,480	-85,696	-91,787	-102,420	-118,271	-123,797	-128,938	-140,778
Consumer goods (nonfood) [5]	-34,268	-66,336	-103,621	-105,053	-107,777	-122,656	-134,076	-146,274	-160,030	-171,115	-193,042
Services	-41,491	-72,862	-104,185	-120,019	-121,196	-119,561	-125,715	-136,155	-145,964	-156,029	-170,520
Direct defense expenditures	-10,851	-13,108	-15,313	-17,531	-16,409	-13,835	-12,202	-10,292	-9,986	-11,081	-11,488
Travel	-10,397	-24,558	-33,416	-37,349	-35,322	-38,552	-40,713	-43,782	-44,916	-48,048	-51,220
Passenger fares	-3,607	-6,444	-8,249	-10,531	-10,012	-10,603	-11,410	-13,062	-14,663	-15,818	-18,235
Other transportation	-11,790	-15,643	-22,172	-24,966	-24,975	-23,767	-24,524	-26,019	-27,034	-27,403	-28,949
Royalties and license fees	-724	-1,170	-2,528	-3,135	-4,035	-5,161	-5,032	-5,852	-6,919	-7,854	-9,411
Other private services	-2,909	-10,203	-20,636	-24,590	-28,328	-25,381	-29,580	-34,588	-39,823	-43,138	-48,421
U.S. government miscellaneous services	-1,214	-1,735	-1,871	-1,919	-2,116	-2,263	-2,255	-2,560	-2,623	-2,687	-2,796
Income on foreign assets in the United States	-42,532	-73,087	-138,639	-139,149	-119,891	-102,462	-102,754	-141,263	-184,569	-198,960	-247,105
Direct investment	-8,635	-7,213	-6,507	-2,871	3,433	-302	-5,574	-20,621	-30,195	-33,641	-45,674
Other private payments	-21,214	-42,745	-93,768	-95,508	-82,452	-63,079	-57,804	-76,450	-97,004	-97,901	-113,959
U.S. government payments	-12,684	-23,129	-38,364	-40,770	-40,872	-39,081	-39,376	-44,192	-57,370	-67,418	-87,472
Unilateral transfers (excl. military grants, net)	-8,349	-22,700	-26,963	-34,669	5,032	-35,230	-38,142	-39,391	-34,638	-40,577	-39,691
U.S. government grants	-5,486	-11,268	-10,911	-17,433	24,160	-15,826	-16,821	-16,508	-11,170	-15,023	-12,090
U.S. government pensions and other transfers	-1,818	-2,138	-2,744	-3,184	-3,730	-4,018	-4,081	-4,545	-3,433	-4,442	-4,193
Private remittances and other transfers	-1,044	-9,295	-13,308	-14,053	-15,399	-15,386	-17,240	-19,338	-20,035	-21,112	-23,408

TYPE OF TRANSACTION	1980	1985	1989	1990	1991	1992	1993	1994	1995	1996	1997
U.S. assets abroad, net (increase/capital outflow (-))	-86,967	-39,889	-168,744	-74,011	-57,881	-68,774	-194,537	-171,102	-327,453	-368,801	-478,502
U.S. official reserve assets, net	-8,155	-3,858	-25,293	-2,158	5,763	3,901	-1,379	5,346	-9,742	6,668	-1,010
Special drawing rights	-16	-897	-535	-192	-177	2,316	-537	-441	-808	370	-350
Reserve position in the International Monetary Fund	-1,667	908	471	731	-367	-2,692	-44	494	-2,466	-1,280	-3,575
Foreign currencies	-6,472	-3,869	-25,229	-2,697	6,307	4,277	-797	5,293	-6,468	7,578	2,915
U.S. govt. assets, other than official reserve assets, net	-5,162	-2,821	1,259	2,307	2,911	-1,657	-342	-389	-589	-708	174
U.S. credits and other long-term assets	-9,860	-7,657	-5,590	-8,430	-12,874	-7,398	-6,299	-5,272	-4,843	-5,011	-5,302
Repayments on U.S. credits and other long-term assets	4,456	4,719	6,723	10,867	16,776	5,807	6,270	5,068	4,115	4,197	5,504
U.S. foreign currency holdings and U.S. short-term assets, net	242	117	125	-130	-992	-66	-313	-185	139	106	-28
U.S. private assets, net	-73,651	-33,211	-144,710	-74,160	-66,555	-71,018	-192,817	-176,059	-317,122	-374,761	-477,666
Direct investments abroad	-19,222	-14,065	-36,834	-29,950	-31,369	-42,640	-77,945	-75,214	-96,654	-81,072	-121,843
Foreign securities	-3,568	-7,481	-22,070	-28,765	-45,673	-49,166	-146,253	-60,309	-100,074	-115,801	-87,981
U.S. claims on unaffiliated foreigners reported by U.S. nonbanking concerns	-4,023	-10,342	-27,646	-27,824	11,097	-387	766	-36,336	-45,286	-86,333	-120,403
U.S. claims reported by U.S. banks, n.i.e. [8]	-46,838	-1,323	-58,160	12,379	-610	21,175	30,615	-4,200	-75,108	-91,555	-147,439
Foreign assets in the U.S., net (increase/capital inflow (+))	58,112	141,183	224,390	140,992	109,641	168,776	279,671	304,460	465,449	563,357	733,441
Foreign official assets in the U.S., net	15,497	-1,119	8,503	33,910	17,389	40,477	71,753	39,583	109,768	127,344	15,817
U.S. government securities	11,895	-1,139	1,532	30,243	16,147	22,403	53,014	36,827	72,712	120,679	-2,936
U.S. Treasury securities	9,708	-838	149	29,576	14,846	18,454	48,952	30,750	68,977	115,671	-7,270
Other	2,187	-301	1,383	657	1,301	3,949	4,062	6,077	3,735	5,008	4,334
Other U.S. government liabilities	615	844	160	1,868	1,367	2,191	1,313	1,564	-217	-362	-2,521
U.S. liabilities reported by U.S. banks, n.i.e. [8]	-159	645	4,976	3,385	-1,484	16,571	14,841	3,665	34,008	5,704	21,928
Other foreign official assets	3,145	-1,469	1,835	-1,586	1,359	-688	2,585	-2,473	3,265	1,323	-654
Other foreign assets in the United States, net	42,615	142,301	215,887	107,082	92,253	128,299	207,918	264,877	355,681	436,013	717,624
Direct investments in the United States, net	16,918	20,010	67,736	47,915	22,004	17,936	48,993	44,592	57,653	77,622	93,449
U.S. Treasury securities	2,645	20,433	29,618	-2,534	18,826	37,131	24,381	34,274	99,548	154,996	146,710
U.S. securities other than U.S. Treasury securities	5,457	50,962	38,767	1,592	35,144	30,043	80,092	56,971	96,367	130,151	196,845
U.S. currency flows	4,500	5,200	5,900	18,800	15,400	13,400	18,900	23,400	12,300	17,362	24,782
U.S. liabilities to unaffiliated foreigners reported by U.S. nonbanking concerns	6,852	9,851	22,086	45,133	-3,115	13,573	10,489	1,302	59,637	39,404	107,779
U.S. liabilities reported by U.S. banks, n.i.e. [8]	10,743	41,045	51,780	-3,824	3,994	16,216	25,063	104,338	30,176	16,478	148,059
Allocations of special drawing rights	1,152	(X)	(X)	(X)	(X)	(X)	(X)	(X)	(X)	(X)	(X)
Statistical discrepancy	25,386	22,950	48,494	24,643	-47,378	-48,628	999	-9,533	-22,742	-59,641	-99,724
Balance on merchandise trade	-25,500	-122,173	-115,245	-109,030	-74,068	-96,106	-132,609	-166,192	-173,729	-191,337	-197,954
Balance on services	6,093	294	23,048	27,901	43,137	57,421	60,670	65,279	73,838	82,763	87,748
Balance on investment income	30,073	20,590	15,020	24,174	21,517	22,541	23,948	16,479	19,275	14,236	-5,318
Balance on goods, services, and income	10,666	-101,290	-77,177	-56,955	-9,414	-16,144	-47,991	-84,434	-80,616	-94,338	-115,524
Unilateral transfers, net	-8,349	-22,954	-26,963	-34,669	5,032	-35,230	-38,142	-39,391	-34,638	-40,577	-39,691
Balance on current account	2,317	-124,243	-104,139	-91,624	-4,383	-51,374	-86,133	-123,825	-115,254	-134,915	-155,215

X Not applicable. [1] Excludes transfers of goods and services under U.S. military grant programs. [2] Excludes exports of goods under U.S. military agency sales contracts identified in Bureau of the Census export documents, excludes imports of goods under direct defense expenditures identified in Census import documents, and reflects various other adjustments (for valuation, coverage, and timing) of Census statistics to a balance of payments basis. [3] Includes other end-use items, not shown separately. [4] Includes engines. [5] Excludes automotive. [6] Break in series due to inclusion of new data. See Technical Note in Survey of Current Business, June 1979. [7] Includes sales of foreign obligations to foreigners. [8] Not included elsewhere. [9] Includes foreign currency notes sold to private residents abroad.

Source: U.S. Bureau of Economic Analysis, Survey of Current Business, July 1998 and previous issues.

No. 1303. U.S. Balances on International Transactions, by Area and Selected Country: 1995 to 1997

[In millions of dollars. Minus sign (-) indicates debits]

AREA OR COUNTRY	1995, BALANCE ON—			1996, BALANCE ON—			1997, BALANCE ON—		
	Mer-chandise trade [1]	Goods, services, and income	Current account	Mer-chandise trade [1]	Goods, services, and income	Current account	Mer-chandise trade [1]	Goods, services, and income	Current account
All areas	**-173,729**	**-80,616**	**-115,254**	**-191,337**	**-94,338**	**-134,915**	**-197,954**	**-115,524**	**-155,215**
Western Europe	-15,241	-3,856	-3,376	-23,326	-9,927	-9,671	-22,808	-22,499	-22,730
European Economic	-12,819	-1,533	-318	-21,568	-9,227	-8,069	-21,294	-21,927	-21,127
Belgium-Luxembourg . . .	4,078	5,321	5,260	3,184	4,185	4,122	3,045	4,573	4,497
France	-2,939	-126	-283	-4,191	-588	-709	-4,803	-3,633	-3,784
Germany	-14,893	-12,119	-10,693	-15,874	-14,304	-12,993	-18,816	-18,128	-17,259
Italy	-7,661	-4,853	-5,159	-9,678	-6,984	-7,276	-10,455	-7,909	-8,211
Netherlands	9,818	15,619	15,572	9,017	16,002	15,952	12,070	20,235	20,178
United Kingdom	1,244	-14,077	-12,933	1,399	-13,219	-11,998	3,416	-21,510	-20,187
Eastern Europe	-1,293	-1,075	-4,150	285	917	-2,415	-731	615	-2,165
Canada	-19,589	-3,033	-3,430	-24,153	-6,616	-6,964	-18,977	-405	-771
Latin America, other Western									
Hemisphere	-9,438	4,418	-5,714	-16,038	-805	-11,289	-6,106	15,259	4,023
Mexico	-16,598	-16,469	-20,292	-18,340	-17,180	-21,346	-15,509	-14,771	-19,318
Venezuela	-5,162	-3,009	-3,077	-8,755	-6,792	-6,854	-6,893	-4,742	-4,815
Japan [2]	-60,330	-55,296	-55,436	-49,202	-46,314	-46,444	-57,058	-63,956	-64,093
Other Asia and Africa	-74,937	-49,431	-61,893	-86,749	-59,413	-76,698	-99,306	-73,229	-88,651
Australia	7,099	13,241	13,125	7,844	14,084	13,979	7,032	14,696	14,579
South Africa	567	1,381	1,205	803	1,407	1,227	476	1,273	1,053
International and unallocated .	-	14,416	5,620	2	13,736	4,587	-	13,995	4,593

- Represents zero.   [1] Adjusted to balance of payments basis; excludes exports under U.S. military sales contracts and imports under direct defense expenditures.   [2] Includes Ryukyu Islands.
Source: U.S. Bureau of Economic Analysis, *Survey of Current Business*, July 1998 issue.

No. 1304. Private Services Transaction, by Type of Service and Country: 1990 to 1996

[In millions of dollars]

TYPE OF SERVICE AND COUNTRY	EXPORTS				IMPORTS			
	1990	1994	1995	1996	1990	1994	1995	1996
Total private services	137,224	184,195	204,165	221,224	100,570	122,620	134,523	143,086
Travel	43,007	58,417	63,395	69,908	37,349	43,782	46,053	48,739
Overseas	30,806	47,299	54,331	60,144	28,929	34,534	36,418	38,162
Canada	7,093	6,252	6,207	6,763	3,541	3,914	4,319	4,606
Mexico	5,108	4,866	2,857	3,001	4,879	5,334	5,316	5,971
Passenger fares	15,298	17,083	19,125	20,557	10,531	12,885	14,433	15,776
Other transportation	22,745	24,941	27,412	27,216	25,168	27,255	28,249	28,453
Freight	8,063	9,697	11,420	11,161	14,353	16,324	16,759	16,879
Port services	13,662	14,180	14,810	14,691	9,920	10,013	10,579	10,792
Other	1,020	1,065	1,184	1,364	895	919	911	783
Royalties and license fees	16,634	22,661	27,383	29,974	3,135	5,560	6,503	7,322
Other private services	39,540	61,093	66,850	73,569	24,387	33,138	39,285	42,796
Affiliated services	13,622	18,651	20,272	22,810	9,118	11,860	13,597	16,026
Unaffiliated services	25,918	42,442	46,578	50,759	15,269	21,278	25,689	26,770
Education	5,126	7,175	7,512	7,807	658	816	949	1,041
Financial services	4,417	5,763	7,029	8,034	2,475	1,654	2,472	3,184
Insurance, net	230	1,676	1,390	2,121	1,910	4,034	5,383	4,387
Telecommunications	2,735	2,865	3,183	3,405	5,583	6,928	7,773	8,385
Business, prof., & tech. services . . .	6,951	15,893	17,765	19,247	1,891	3,628	4,691	5,253
Advertising	130	487	558	597	243	728	718	971
Computer & data processing services	1,031	2,796	3,197	3,142	44	244	422	334
Management, consulting, and public relations services	354	1,134	1,456	1,473	135	321	475	543
Legal services	451	1,617	1,664	1,910	111	383	468	516
Construction, engineering, architectural, & mining services .	867	2,474	2,848	2,990	170	280	339	489
Canada	15,743	17,251	18,247	19,951	9,307	11,180	12,542	13,818
Europe	48,716	65,567	73,090	80,230	40,030	49,026	53,604	55,815
Belgium-Luxembourg	1,796	2,517	2,719	2,800	1,027	1,248	1,522	1,611
France	5,573	6,508	7,991	8,749	4,187	5,671	6,175	6,309
Germany	7,489	11,405	12,919	13,790	6,852	7,294	7,895	8,586
Italy	3,324	4,154	4,569	4,750	3,485	3,446	3,732	3,724
Netherlands	3,281	5,106	5,927	6,421	1,945	2,585	3,171	3,238
United Kingdom	13,050	17,327	18,546	20,482	11,624	14,627	16,359	17,128
Other	(NA)	9,635	10,694	12,397	(NA)	8,429	9,366	9,401
Other Western Europe	(NA)	(NA)	(NA)	(NA)	(NA)	(NA)	(NA)	(NA)
Eastern Europe	1,009	2,198	2,614	3,028	815	1,998	2,235	2,241
Latin America and other Western Hemisphere	21,718	31,722	32,113	34,073	20,298	25,309	27,212	30,070
Mexico	7,875	9,870	7,290	7,923	8,279	10,467	10,687	11,562
Venezuela	1,284	2,129	2,489	2,312	670	754	701	728
Other	(NA)	7,701	8,771	8,839	(NA)	4,324	4,666	4,863
Other countries	45,726	65,141	75,744	81,280	28,225	35,352	38,873	40,356
Int'l organizations and unallocated	5,325	4,508	4,970	5,691	2,706	1,754	2,290	3,026

NA Not available.
Source: U.S. Bureau of Economic Analysis, *Survey of Current Business*, October 1997.

No. 1305. International Investment Position: 1990 to 1997

[In millions of dollars. Estimates for end of year; subject to considerable error due to nature of basic data]

TYPE OF INVESTMENT	1990	1991	1992	1993	1994	1995	1996	1997
U.S. net international investment position:								
Current cost	-206,287	-269,131	-398,173	-275,626	-351,897	-603,100	-767,076	-1,223,568
Market value	-166,845	-263,096	-454,604	-180,371	-232,943	-537,064	-743,656	-1,322,455
U.S. assets abroad:								
Current cost	2,180,003	2,285,121	2,324,992	2,742,525	2,901,776	3,296,785	3,767,018	4,237,311
Market value	2,291,734	2,468,351	2,464,196	3,055,316	3,217,431	3,754,289	4,347,148	5,007,119
U.S. official reserve assets	174,664	159,223	147,435	164,945	163,394	176,061	160,739	134,836
Gold	102,406	92,561	87,168	102,556	100,110	101,279	96,698	75,929
Special drawing rights	10,989	11,240	8,503	9,039	10,039	11,037	10,312	10,027
Reserve position in IMF	9,076	9,488	11,759	11,818	12,030	14,649	15,435	18,071
Foreign currencies	52,193	45,934	40,005	41,532	41,215	49,096	38,294	30,809
U.S. government assets, other	81,993	79,144	80,722	81,029	80,430	81,005	81,677	81,483
U.S. loans and other long-term assets	81,365	77,498	79,087	79,106	78,249	78,975	79,786	79,573
Repayable in dollars	80,040	76,272	77,987	78,100	77,474	78,252	79,114	78,942
Other	1,325	1,226	1,100	1,006	775	723	672	631
U.S. foreign currency holdings and short-term assets	628	1,646	1,635	1,923	2,181	2,030	1,891	1,910
U.S. private assets:								
Current cost	1,923,346	2,046,754	2,096,835	2,496,551	2,657,952	3,039,719	3,524,602	4,020,992
Market value	2,035,077	2,229,984	2,236,039	2,809,342	2,973,607	3,497,223	4,104,732	4,790,800
Direct investments abroad:								
Current cost	620,031	644,307	659,426	714,756	752,148	849,651	936,954	1,023,872
Market value	731,762	827,537	798,630	1,027,547	1,067,803	1,307,155	1,517,084	1,793,680
Foreign securities	342,313	455,750	515,083	853,528	889,706	1,054,352	1,280,159	1,446,301
Bonds	144,717	176,774	200,817	309,666	303,079	355,284	403,373	445,049
Corporate stocks	197,596	278,976	314,266	543,862	586,627	699,068	876,786	1,001,252
U.S. claims on unaffiliated foreigners [1]	265,315	256,295	254,303	242,022	322,980	367,567	449,978	562,396
U.S. claims reported by U.S. banks [2]	695,687	690,402	668,023	686,245	693,118	768,149	857,511	988,423
Foreign assets in the U.S.								
Current cost	2,386,290	2,554,252	2,723,165	3,018,151	3,253,673	3,899,885	4,534,094	5,460,879
Market value	2,458,579	2,731,447	2,918,800	3,235,687	3,450,374	4,291,353	5,090,804	6,329,574
Foreign official assets in the U.S.	373,293	398,538	437,263	509,422	535,217	671,631	801,062	833,901
U.S. government securities	291,228	311,199	329,317	381,687	407,152	497,810	612,656	614,390
U.S. Treasury securities	285,911	305,994	322,600	373,050	396,887	482,807	592,891	589,850
Other	5,317	5,205	6,717	8,637	10,265	15,003	19,765	24,540
Other U.S. government liabilities	17,243	18,610	20,801	22,113	23,678	23,460	23,099	20,577
U.S. liabilities reported by U.S. banks [2]	39,880	38,396	54,967	69,721	73,386	107,394	113,098	135,026
Other foreign official assets	24,942	30,333	32,178	35,901	31,001	42,967	52,209	63,908
Other foreign assets in the U.S.:								
Current cost	2,012,997	2,155,714	2,285,902	2,508,729	2,718,456	3,228,254	3,733,032	4,626,978
Market value	2,085,286	2,332,909	2,481,537	2,726,265	2,915,157	3,619,722	4,289,742	5,495,673
Direct investments:								
Current cost	467,312	491,942	500,542	550,862	561,152	614,258	666,962	751,845
Market value	539,601	669,137	696,177	768,398	757,853	1,005,726	1,223,672	1,620,540
U.S. Treasury securities	152,452	170,295	197,739	221,501	235,684	357,691	504,792	661,961
U.S. currency	85,932	101,316	114,803	133,732	157,183	169,482	186,843	211,625
U.S. securities other than U.S. Treasury securities	460,644	546,008	599,447	696,449	739,695	971,356	1,199,460	1,577,984
Corporate and other bonds	238,903	274,136	299,287	355,822	368,077	481,214	588,043	718,076
Corporate stocks	221,741	271,872	300,160	340,627	371,618	490,142	611,417	859,908
U.S. liabilities to unaffiliated foreigners [1]	213,406	208,908	220,666	229,038	239,817	300,424	346,727	453,555
U.S. liabilities reported by U.S. banks [2]	633,251	637,245	652,705	677,147	784,925	815,043	828,248	970,008

[1] Reported by U.S. nonbanking concerns. [2] Not included elsewhere.

Source: U.S. Bureau of Economic Analysis, *Survey of Current Business*, July 1998.

No. 1306. U.S. Reserve Assets: 1980 to 1997

[In billions of dollars. As of end of year, except as indicated]

TYPE	1980	1985	1990	1991	1992	1993	1994	1995	1996	1997
Total	26.8	43.2	83.3	77.7	71.3	73.4	74.3	85.8	75.1	70.0
Gold stock [1]	11.2	11.1	11.1	11.1	11.1	11.1	11.1	11.1	11.0	11.0
Special drawing rights	2.6	7.3	11.0	11.2	8.5	9.0	10.0	11.0	10.3	10.0
Foreign currencies	10.1	12.9	52.2	45.9	40.0	41.5	41.2	49.1	38.3	30.9
Reserve position in IMF [2]	2.9	11.9	9.1	9.5	11.8	11.8	12.0	14.6	15.4	18.1

[1] Includes gold in Exchange Stabilization Fund; excludes gold held under earmark at Federal Reserve banks for foreign and international accounts. Beginning 1975, gold assets were valued at $42.22 pursuant to the amending of Section 2 of the Par Value Modification Act, PL-93-110, approved September 21, 1973. [2] International Monetary Fund.

Source: Board of Governors of the Federal Reserve System, *Federal Reserve Bulletin*, monthly; and Department of the Treasury, *Treasury Bulletin*, monthly.

No. 1307. Foreign Direct Investment Position in the United States on a Historical-Cost Basis, by Industry and Selected Countries: 1996 and 1997

[In millions of dollars]

COUNTRY	1996				1997			
	Total [1]	Petro- leum	Manufac- turing, total	Whole- sale	Total [1]	Petro- leum	Manufac- turing, total	Whole- sale
All countries............	594,088	43,770	242,320	75,115	681,651	47,679	267,070	87,564
Canada........................	54,799	3,515	22,298	4,020	64,022	3,446	27,759	3,273
Europe.......................	368,322	29,285	174,326	32,743	425,220	32,627	195,135	41,289
Austria.....................	1,769	(D)	261	361	1,831	(D)	306	9
Belgium....................	4,838	(D)	2,219	482	6,771	1,265	3,690	812
Denmark...................	2,765	5	745	1,455	3,025	5	636	1,892
Finland....................	2,495	(D)	1,798	369	3,089	(D)	2,387	(D)
France.....................	41,132	429	26,978	1,694	47,088	(D)	29,157	2,507
Germany...................	59,863	(D)	28,752	10,176	69,701	(D)	33,063	12,468
Ireland....................	6,621	401	2,125	1,067	10,514	390	2,919	1,157
Italy.......................	3,327	(D)	738	558	3,318	579	591	444
Luxembourg...............	4,276	-	2,127	1,344	6,218	-	2,820	2,494
Netherlands...............	74,320	12,516	25,914	5,651	84,862	13,561	29,411	5,074
Norway....................	2,484	356	1,490	82	3,971	(D)	1,601	(D)
Spain......................	2,405	-1	449	111	2,643	4	632	113
Sweden....................	9,479	(D)	6,463	1,962	13,147	(D)	7,683	2,077
Switzerland...............	30,390	478	15,602	1,850	38,574	195	18,923	3,326
United Kingdom...........	121,288	10,856	58,554	5,176	129,551	11,568	61,204	7,465
Latin America and other Western Hemisphere...........	29,180	3,160	4,333	1,275	35,701	3,766	3,861	1,779
South and Central America........	8,802	-98	355	99	10,049	3	148	176
Mexico.................	1,436	-18	504	149	1,723	-12	470	222
Panama.................	5,817	(D)	166	-41	6,645	-71	9	-49
Other Western Hemisphere......	20,378	3,258	3,978	1,176	25,652	3,763	3,712	1,603
Bahamas................	1,806	(D)	151	263	1,986	(D)	130	355
Netherlands Antilles.......	9,311	2,701	2,510	(D)	7,701	2,561	1,168	207
United Kingdom Islands, Caribbean.	7,614	(D)	1,453	500	11,954	(D)	1,942	748
Africa.......................	645	(D)	219	-4	1,608	(D)	204	-53
Middle East..................	5,977	(D)	942	119	6,882	(D)	480	420
Israel......................	1,857	-	914	109	2,292	-	459	410
Kuwait.....................	2,572	4	(D)	2	2,881	4	7	1
Saudi Arabia...............	1,390	(D)	-1	8	1,573	(D)	1	9
Asia and Pacific.............	135,166	6,454	40,201	36,961	148,218	6,350	39,631	40,856
Australia...................	13,877	(D)	2,890	274	16,229	6,528	3,130	12
Hong Kong.................	1,644	4	235	647	1,757	-16	313	637
Japan.....................	114,534	118	35,178	34,972	123,514	214	33,379	39,567
Singapore..................	1,232	-13	273	142	2,776	23	1,085	212
Taiwan.....................	2,225	-1	1,201	375	2,778	-1	1,552	373

- Represents or rounds to zero.   D Suppressed to avoid disclosure of data of individual companies.   [1] Includes other industries not shown separately.

Source: U.S. Bureau of Economic Analysis, *Survey of Current Business*, July 1998.

No. 1308. U.S. Affiliates of Foreign Companies—Assets, Sales, Employment, Land, Exports, and Imports: 1996

[A U.S. affiliate is a U.S. business enterprise in which one foreign owner (individual, branch, partnership, association, trust, corporation, or government) has a direct or indirect voting interest of 10 percent or more. Universe estimates based on a sample survey of nonbank affiliates with assets, sales, or net income of $10 million or more]

INDUSTRY	Total assets (mil. dol.)	Sales (mil. dol.) [1]	Employ- ment (1,000) [2]	Employee compen- sation (mil. dol.)	GROSS BOOK VALUE (mil. dol.)		Merchan- dise exports[4] (mil. dol.)	Merchan- dise imports[4] (mil. dol.)
					Plant and equip- ment [3]	Land		
Total..............	2,613,985	1,596,022	4,977.5	210,378	738,447	59,200	136,588	252,990
Petroleum....................	114,735	152,832	111.8	6,525	116,331	2,257	9,984	21,080
Manufacturing.................	578,886	552,023	2,213.6	104,004	273,201	12,828	58,821	78,531
Chemicals and allied products..	180,996	134,451	409.8	24,633	85,931	5,074	15,656	14,254
Wholesale trade [5].............	233,829	466,700	488.6	24,338	83,954	2,802	62,792	147,958
Motor vehicles and auto parts and supplies..............	79,527	101,416	68.9	4,033	45,655	663	4,341	40,678
Farm-product raw materials ...	8,668	34,508	18.1	650	2,068	75	15,740	3,120
Retail trade.................	50,063	94,028	821.0	15,094	28,484	3,016	1,507	3,408
Finance, except banking.......	705,181	58,230	49.3	8,018	7,621	717	15	21
Insurance....................	575,947	89,625	152.0	9,167	27,864	1,091	-	-
Real estate..................	100,549	13,903	27.1	1,006	67,763	22,418	7	1
Services.....................	105,297	56,247	633.8	18,801	43,680	8,109	738	1,173
Other.......................	149,497	112,434	480.3	23,424	89,550	5,962	2,725	818

- Represents zero.   [1] Excludes returns, discounts, allowances, and sales and excise taxes.   [2] Average number of full-time and part-time employees.   [3] Includes mineral rights and minor amounts of property other than land.   [4] F.a.s. value at port of exportation.   [5] Includes industries not shown separately.

Source: U.S. Bureau of Economic Analysis, *Survey of Current Business*, June 1998; and *Foreign Direct Investment in the United States, Operations of U.S. Affiliates of Foreign Companies*, Revised 1995 Estimates and Preliminary 1996 Estimates.

No. 1309. Foreign Direct Investment in the United States—Gross Book Value and Employment of U.S. Affiliates of Foreign Companies, by State: 1981 to 1996

[A U.S. affiliate is a U.S. business enterprise in which one foreign owner (individual, branch, partnership, association, trust corporation, or government) has a direct or indirect voting interest of 10 percent or more. Universe estimates based on a sample survey of nonbank affiliates with assets, sales, or net income of $10 million or more]

STATE AND OTHER AREA	GROSS BOOK VALUE OF PROPERTY, PLANT, AND EQUIPMENT (mil. dol.)				TOTAL EMPLOYMENT				
								1996	
	1981	1990	1995	1996	1981 (1,000)	1990 (1,000)	1995 (1,000)	Total (1,000)	Percent of all businesses
Total	187,956	578,355	769,491	797,647	2,416.6	4,734.5	4,941.8	4,977.5	(X)
United States	178,003	552,902	733,089	758,356	2,402.3	4,704.4	4,898.9	4,941.4	4.8
Alabama	2,776	7,300	10,598	11,635	27.0	55.7	60.6	61.4	4.0
Alaska	(D)	19,435	25,558	25,904	8.8	13.2	9.8	10.1	5.1
Arizona	2,949	7,234	6,699	9,101	30.6	57.1	51.9	56.7	3.4
Arkansas	636	2,344	3,666	3,657	17.5	29.2	32.1	35.1	3.8
California	20,404	75,768	96,576	100,718	248.4	555.9	548.6	545.3	4.8
Colorado	2,369	6,544	8,602	8,440	24.7	56.3	72.2	69.8	4.2
Connecticut	1,254	5,357	8,466	8,641	40.8	75.9	73.3	83.3	5.9
Delaware	1,869	5,818	2,919	3,103	36.0	43.1	15.8	15.4	4.6
District of Columbia	547	3,869	4,983	4,951	3.2	11.4	13.4	11.8	2.9
Florida	6,295	18,659	24,865	28,952	73.9	205.7	210.0	214.4	3.9
Georgia	4,558	16,729	22,432	22,491	78.5	161.0	180.1	185.9	6.1
Hawaii	(D)	11,830	15,972	15,547	17.0	53.0	48.9	48.6	11.0
Idaho	312	776	1,026	1,171	3.8	11.7	11.3	11.7	2.8
Illinois	5,646	23,420	34,305	33,687	113.6	245.8	237.0	229.7	4.6
Indiana	1,883	13,426	18,782	16,022	47.0	126.9	136.9	124.9	5.0
Iowa	1,032	2,712	4,527	5,096	21.6	32.8	35.8	36.3	3.1
Kansas	877	5,134	3,233	4,680	14.6	29.6	34.0	41.3	4.0
Kentucky	1,848	9,229	15,136	14,785	26.0	65.7	83.4	84.1	5.9
Louisiana	7,872	17,432	20,543	21,774	47.0	61.4	51.0	54.4	3.6
Maine	1,637	2,080	3,885	3,846	17.7	26.6	29.1	30.6	6.6
Maryland	2,103	5,713	9,197	9,670	45.1	79.6	95.0	94.4	5.1
Massachusetts	1,712	8,890	12,707	13,749	55.6	131.2	141.5	163.2	6.0
Michigan	4,188	12,012	21,370	17,913	65.9	139.6	170.3	157.3	4.1
Minnesota	2,902	11,972	8,688	9,514	33.0	89.8	79.8	88.9	4.2
Mississippi	1,431	2,989	3,055	2,465	11.3	23.6	22.6	21.6	2.4
Missouri	1,894	5,757	8,327	10,016	32.6	73.7	79.3	83.6	3.7
Montana	1,235	2,181	1,938	1,865	3.0	5.1	4.4	4.2	1.4
Nebraska	241	776	1,320	1,645	5.6	14.9	15.7	18.1	2.6
Nevada	556	5,450	8,242	8,287	6.9	22.7	25.0	25.0	3.2
New Hampshire	409	1,446	2,212	2,141	13.9	25.9	30.0	30.2	6.2
New Jersey	6,552	18,608	26,175	26,688	134.9	227.0	205.2	206.5	6.6
New Mexico	997	4,312	4,363	4,451	7.9	17.4	16.2	15.4	2.8
New York	7,892	36,424	52,992	52,752	210.3	347.5	343.8	345.4	5.1
North Carolina	5,543	15,234	21,475	22,913	89.0	181.0	225.3	225.8	7.3
North Dakota	1,155	1,251	915	911	3.5	3.1	3.2	4.8	1.9
Ohio	5,178	20,549	29,932	32,617	99.9	219.1	222.1	223.6	4.8
Oklahoma	2,760	6,049	5,448	5,410	25.0	43.6	34.2	35.0	3.1
Oregon	845	3,427	5,807	5,349	13.1	39.1	49.7	49.1	3.9
Pennsylvania	5,772	16,587	24,432	24,448	135.0	221.6	231.6	234.3	5.0
Rhode Island	359	1,120	2,240	2,573	9.9	13.3	16.2	19.3	4.9
South Carolina	5,318	10,067	13,438	15,124	65.1	104.7	111.6	116.0	8.1
South Dakota	299	553	665	665	1.3	4.5	4.6	5.2	1.8
Tennessee	3,747	10,280	14,227	14,999	57.4	116.9	136.3	133.6	6.0
Texas	23,383	57,079	68,142	72,315	179.0	299.5	326.4	316.9	4.5
Utah	1,791	3,918	5,612	6,287	16.8	21.0	28.6	32.9	4.0
Vermont	315	631	1,037	1,017	6.0	7.7	10.4	9.8	4.1
Virginia	3,046	10,702	15,129	16,999	49.8	113.3	141.4	141.2	5.4
Washington	2,430	7,985	11,462	11,621	26.0	77.5	83.0	86.0	4.2
West Virginia	3,992	7,975	7,809	7,389	35.4	34.9	31.9	26.3	4.7
Wisconsin	2,320	5,088	7,415	7,792	62.2	81.4	71.5	70.7	3.1
Wyoming	2,144	2,782	4,544	4,569	4.2	5.8	6.9	6.1	3.6
Puerto Rico	413	1,499	2,174	1,763	9.5	16.1	27.4	19.4	(NA)
Other territories and offshore	7,496	18,484	17,798	18,901	3.1	9.0	13.1	10.3	(NA)
Foreign	2,044	5,470	16,430	18,627	1.6	5.0	2.4	6.4	(NA)

D Withheld to avoid disclosure of data of individual companies. NA Not available. X Not applicable.

Source: U.S. Bureau of Economic Analysis, *Survey of Current Business*, June 1998, and *Foreign Direct Investment in the United States, Operations of U.S. Affiliates of Foreign Companies*, annual.

No. 1310. U.S. Businesses Acquired or Established by Foreign Direct Investors—Investment Outlays, by Industry of U.S. Business Enterprise and Country of Ultimate Beneficial Owner: 1990 to 1997

[**In millions of dollars.** Foreign direct investment is the ownership or control, directly or indirectly, by one foreign individual branch, partnership, association, trust, corporation, or government of 10 percent or more of the voting securities of a U.S. business enterprise or an equivalent interest in an unincorporated one. Data represent number and full cost of acquisitions of existing U.S. business enterprises, including business segments or operating units of existing U.S. business enterprises and establishments of new enterprises. Investments may be made by the foreign direct investor itself, or indirectly by an existing U.S. affiliate of the foreign direct investor. Covers investments in U.S. business enterprises with assets of over $1 million, or ownership of 200 acres of U.S. land]

INDUSTRY AND COUNTRY	1990	1991	1992	1993	1994	1995	1996	1997, prel.
Total	65,932	25,538	15,333	26,229	45,626	57,195	79,929	70,819
INDUSTRY								
Petroleum	1,141	702	463	882	469	1,520	1,059	688
Manufacturing	23,898	11,461	6,014	11,090	21,218	26,643	27,835	19,963
Wholesale trade	1,676	623	698	837	2,156	1,168	4,746	2,578
Retail trade	1,250	1,605	256	1,495	1,542	2,838	2,988	438
Depository institutions [1]	897	482	529	958	2,026	2,301	1,944	3,935
Finance, except depository institutions [1] . .	2,121	2,199	797	1,599	2,195	7,837	8,676	6,536
Insurance	2,093	2,102	291	1,105	450	654	4,688	8,639
Real estate	7,771	3,823	2,161	1,883	2,647	2,996	4,175	3,831
Services	19,369	2,256	2,023	4,162	7,163	5,881	15,292	12,407
Other [2]	5,716	284	2,101	2,218	5,760	5,359	8,528	11,802
COUNTRY								
Canada	3,430	3,454	1,351	3,797	4,128	8,029	9,700	10,764
Europe	36,011	13,994	8,344	16,845	31,920	38,195	49,427	46,190
France	10,217	4,976	406	1,249	1,404	1,129	6,021	2,772
Germany [3]	2,363	1,922	1,964	2,841	3,328	13,117	12,858	6,412
Netherlands	2,247	1,661	1,331	2,074	1,537	1,061	6,476	11,255
Switzerland	3,905	1,327	1,259	804	5,044	7,533	4,910	6,351
United Kingdom	13,096	2,169	2,255	8,238	17,261	9,094	14,757	13,355
Other Europe	4,183	1,939	1,129	1,639	3,346	6,261	4,405	6,045
Latin America and other Western Hemisphere	796	375	1,438	874	1,352	1,550	1,790	923
South and Central America	399	108	1,152	527	(D)	1,283	(D)	(D)
Other Western Hemisphere	397	267	286	347	(D)	267	(D)	(D)
Africa	(D)	(D)	(D)	(D)	(D)	(D)	(D)	(D)
Middle East	472	1,006	238	1,308	(D)	447	(D)	918
Asia and Pacific	23,170	6,560	3,716	3,004	5,263	8,688	12,751	11,993
Australia	1,412	251	164	129	1,522	2,270	2,222	8,421
Japan	19,933	5,357	2,921	2,065	2,715	3,602	8,813	1,845
Other Asia and Pacific	1,825	952	631	810	1,026	2,816	1,716	1,727

D Suppressed to avoid disclosure of data of individual companies. [1] Prior to 1992, "depository institutions" excludes, and "finance, depository institutions" includes, savings institutions and credit unions. Beginning with 1992, savings institutions and credit unions have been reclassified from "finance, except depository institutions" to "depository institutions". [2] For investments in which more than one investor participated, each investor and each investor's shares are classified by country of each ultimate beneficial owner. [3] Prior to 1990, this line includes data only for the Federal Republic of Germany. Beginning in 1990, this line also includes the former German Democratic Republic (GDR). This change has no effect on the data because, prior to 1991, there were no U.S. affiliates of the former GDR.
Source: U.S. Bureau of Economic Analysis, *Survey of Current Business,* June 1997 and June 1998.

No. 1311. U.S. Businesses Acquired by Foreign Direct Investors—Assets, Sales, and Employment, by Industry of U.S. Business Enterprise: 1996 and 1997

[See headnote, Table 1310. Minus sign (-) indicates loss]

INDUSTRY	1996					1997, prel.				
	Total assets (mil. dol.)	Sales (mil. dol.)	Net income (mil. dol.)	Employ-ment (1,000)	Acres of land owned (1,000)	Total assets (mil. dol.)	Sales (mil. dol.)	Net income (mil. dol.)	Employ-ment (1,000)	Acres of land owned
Total	241,008	83,544	2,608	436.9	797,284	179,476	63,579	2,375	297.6	558,943
Petroleum	2,133	4,816	20	(2)	(D)	3,989	5,251	(D)	2.4	12,928
Manufacturing	33,796	25,156	120	132.7	(D)	21,144	21,297	696	95.5	(D)
Wholesale trade	4,625	4,677	44	12.7	(D)	3,907	6,836	(D)	(3)	(D)
Retail trade	4,295	6,384	79	(4)	1,376	521	(D)	-1	(3)	5
Depository institutions . . .	(D)	(D)	(D)	35.3	(D)	29,288	(D)	147	(5)	546
Finance, except depository institutions	25,334	3,531	(D)	7.3	(D)	15,051	2,591	293	(3)	(D)
Insurance	(D)	(D)	-37	(6)	(D)	72,704	8,411	360	(3)	719
Real estate	4,571	559	123	(7)	(D)	4,196	508	94	(7)	(D)
Services	17,109	9,571	308	99.9	(D)	12,873	6,296	170	100.4	(D)
Other [1]	26,042	17,309	506	74.1	159,251	15,802	9,024	70	40.1	(D)

D Withheld to avoid disclosure of data of individual companies. [1] Includes agriculture, forestry, and fishing; mining; construction; transportation; and communication and public utilities. [2] Employment size class of 1,000 to 2,499 employees. [3] Employment size class of 10,000 to 24,999 employees. [4] Employment size class of 50,000 to 99,999 employees. [5] Employment size class of 5,000 to 9,999 employees. [6] Employment size class of 2,500 to 4,999 employees. [7] Employment size class of 1 to 499 employees.
Source: U.S. Bureau of Economic Analysis, *Survey of Current Business,* June 1997 and 1998 issues.

No. 1312. U.S. Direct Investment Position Abroad on a Historical-Cost Basis, by Country: 1990 to 1997

[In millions of dollars. U.S. investment abroad is the ownership or control by one U.S. person of 10% or more of the voting securities of an incorporated foreign business enterprise or an equivalent interest in a unincorporated foreign business enterprise. Negative position can occur when a U.S. parent company's liabilities to the foreign affiliate are greater that its equity in, and loans to the foreign affiliate]

COUNTRY	1990	1991	1992	1993	1994	1995	1996	1997
All countries	430,521	467,844	502,063	564,283	612,893	699,015	777,203	860,723
Canada	69,508	70,711	68,690	69,922	74,221	83,498	91,301	99,859
Europe	214,739	235,163	248,744	285,735	297,133	344,596	382,366	420,934
Austria	1,113	1,268	1,371	1,312	2,197	2,829	2,929	2,621
Belgium	9,464	10,611	11,381	11,697	14,714	18,706	17,985	17,403
Denmark	1,726	1,940	1,676	1,735	2,030	2,161	2,664	2,576
Finland	544	386	343	414	761	965	1,115	1,338
France	19,164	21,569	25,157	24,312	27,322	33,358	33,746	34,615
Germany	27,609	32,411	33,003	36,811	38,878	44,242	44,651	43,931
Greece	282	306	372	410	482	533	567	638
Ireland	5,894	6,471	7,607	9,019	7,239	7,996	10,198	14,476
Italy	14,063	15,085	13,015	12,748	14,808	17,096	17,994	17,749
Luxembourg	1,697	1,734	2,031	5,611	6,310	5,929	7,666	9,796
Netherlands	19,120	20,293	20,700	20,91	29,889	42,113	54,437	64,648
Norway	4,209	4,318	3,825	3,757	5,026	4,741	5,787	6,262
Portugal	897	1,034	1,290	1,264	1,181	1,413	1,490	1,498
Spain	7,868	8,088	8,757	6,689	9,572	10,856	12,227	11,642
Sweden	1,787	2,323	1,881	2,374	1,905	6,816	6,823	7,299
Switzerland	25,099	25,682	28,698	33,056	27,908	31,125	30,208	35,203
Turkey	522	545	732	995	874	973	1,059	1,076
United Kingdom	72,707	79,819	85,176	109,208	100,817	106,332	122,692	138,765
Other	974	1,282	1,729	3,411	5,219	6,412	8,127	9,396
Latin America	43,348	48,546	54,339	59,302	116,478	131,377	147,535	172,481
South America	22,933	24,607	28,760	31,210	37,673	49,170	55,687	67,112
Argentina	2,531	2,831	3,327	4,442	5,692	7,660	7,930	9,766
Brazil	14,384	14,997	16,313	16,772	17,885	25,002	28,699	35,727
Chile	1,896	2,069	2,544	2,749	5,062	6,216	7,075	7,767
Colombia	1,677	1,876	3,053	2,930	3,463	3,506	3,610	3,727
Ecuador	280	321	295	555	784	889	920	1,175
Peru	599	492	620	622	971	1,335	2,094	2,595
Venezuela	1,087	1,427	1,972	2,362	3,087	3,634	4,346	5,176
Other	479	594	636	778	728	928	1,013	1,177
Central America	20,415	23,939	25,579	28,092	30,083	33,493	38,007	48,881
Costa Rica	251	417	274	298	607	921	1,284	1,580
Guatemala	130	107	115	139	200	233	331	357
Honduras	262	255	239	159	140	68	129	183
Mexico	10,313	12,501	13,730	15,221	16,968	16,873	19,900	25,395
Panama	9,289	10,484	11,038	12,043	11,905	15,123	16,065	20,958
Other	169	175	182	233	262	273	298	408
Other Western Hemisphere	28,065	29,131	36,969	41,180	48,722	48,714	53,841	56,489
Bahamas	4,004	3,864	4,167	3,138	2,808	1,768	1,836	1,515
Barbados	252	291	340	471	391	698	922	801
Bermuda	20,169	22,262	26,736	28,666	28,355	28,374	30,919	33,092
Dominican Republic	529	661	779	1,039	266	330	400	476
Jamaica	625	763	892	1,049	1,167	1,287	1,494	1,687
Netherlands Antilles	-4,501	-5,072	-1,989	-62	6,739	6,835	7,401	5,393
Trinidad and Tobago	485	510	565	691	529	673	786	602
U.K. Islands, Caribbean	5,929	5,397	5,401	5,544	7,858	8,358	9,492	12,143
Other	574	455	75	645	608	392	589	777
Africa	3,650	4,427	4,469	5,469	5,760	6,017	6,832	10,253
Egypt	1,231	1,246	1,334	1,510	1,090	1,093	1,297	1,570
Nigeria	-401	529	301	478	605	627	627	1,465
South Africa	775	868	879	900	1,132	1,422	1,488	2,347
Other	2,045	1,784	1,955	2,581	2,933	2,873	3,420	4,872
Middle East	3,959	4,963	5,759	6,571	6,367	7,198	7,793	8,959
Israel	746	826	1,335	1,604	1,483	1,831	2,062	2,286
Saudi Arabia	1,899	2,303	2,351	2,587	2,100	2,741	2,592	3,079
United Arab Emirates	409	416	429	524	357	500	594	682
Other	905	1,419	1,644	1,856	2,427	2,126	2,545	2,912
Asia and Pacific	254,887	284,299	304,681	92,671	108,528	122,711	136,481	142,704
Australia	15,110	16,072	16,928	19,047	20,196	24,328	28,409	26,125
China	354	426	563	916	2,557	2,765	3,843	5,013
Hong Kong	6,055	6,656	8,693	10,063	11,092	11,768	14,690	19,065
India	372	415	484	599	1,030	1,105	1,353	1,684
Indonesia	3,207	3,826	4,384	4,864	6,355	6,777	7,520	7,395
Japan	22,599	25,403	26,591	31,095	34,117	37,309	35,684	35,569
Korea, South	2,695	2,900	2,912	3,427	4,334	5,557	6,516	6,528
Malaysia	1,466	1,774	1,596	1,975	3,148	4,237	5,300	5,623
New Zealand	3,156	2,949	3,314	3,064	3,893	4,601	5,225	5,191
Philippines	1,355	1,395	1,666	1,953	2,484	2,719	3,519	3,403
Singapore	3,975	5,363	6,715	8,875	10,940	12,140	14,019	17,514
Taiwan	2,226	2,666	2,827	3,113	3,775	4,293	4,640	4,944
Thailand	1,790	2,025	2,594	2,943	3,585	4,283	4,777	3,537
Other	356	348	696	737	1,022	830	986	1,113
International	2,535	2,684	3,131	3,433	4,406	3,618	4,896	5,533
Addenda:								
Eastern Europe	(D)	307	731	2,356	4,029	5,136	6,651	7,743
European Communities(12)	180,491	199,361	210,164	240,414	253,242	301,345	337,184	368,997
OPEC	7,145	9,729	10,692	11,737	13,794	15,546	17,641	20,554

D Withheld to avoid disclosure of data of individual companies.   ¹ OPEC=Organization of Petroleum Exporting Countries. Includes Algeria, Ecuador, Gabon, Indonesia, Iran, Iraq, Kuwait, Libya, Nigeria, Qatar, Saudi Arabia, United Arab Emirates, and Venezuela. Prior to 1993, Ecuador was also a member and was included in this line.
Source: U.S. Bureau of Economic Analysis, *Survey of Current Business*, July 1998, and earlier issues.

No. 1313. U.S. Government Foreign Grants and Credits, by Type and Country: 1966 to 1996

[In millions of dollars. See text, Section 28. Negative figures (-) occur when the total of grant returns, principal repayments, and/or foreign currencies disbursed by the U.S. government exceeds new grants and new credits utilized and/or acquisitions of foreign currencies through new sales of farm products]

TYPE AND COUNTRY	1966-1975, total	1976-1985, total	1990	1991	1992	1993	1994	1995	1996
Total, net	**70,356**	**104,190**	**14,253**	**-32,040**	**17,718**	**17,110**	**15,835**	**12,090**	**15,937**
Western Europe	**1,004**	**1,618**	**-103**	**-6,040**	**325**	**300**	**128**	**155**	**271**
Austria	-19	34	-10	-19	-1	-1	-1	-1	-1
Belgium and Luxembourg	17	-46	-9	-3	-	-	-	-	-
Bosnia and Hercegovina	-	-	-	-	40	30	50	59	186
Croatia	-	-	-	-	62	37	50	9	-14
Denmark	64	-58	-	-	-	-	-	-	-
Finland	-19	21	-8	-5	-5	-26	-1	-1	-1
France	-93	-222	-15	-8	-2	-2	-1	-	-
Germany	-117	-117	-338	-6,117	-	-1	-	(Z)	(Z)
Iceland	-8	-12	(Z)	-	-	-	-	-	-
Ireland	-51	7	2	-6	-6	-8	25	21	24
Italy	85	133	-30	-14	-	(Z)	-	(Z)	-
Macedonia	-	-	-	-	67	1	3	1	2
Netherlands	116	-180	-	-	-	-	-	-	-
Norway	379	-257	-	-1	-15	4	-	-	-
Portugal	34	1,003	56	44	159	113	115	-18	-9
Slovenia	-	-	-	-	118	-6	-18	-24	-27
Spain	607	965	-122	-76	-54	31	-55	-59	-48
Sweden	17	-1	-	-	-	-	-	-	-
United Kingdom	-546	-964	-111	-113	-115	-118	-120	-123	-125
Yugoslavia	84	174	-39	-58	-308	1	-1	(Z)	-1
Other [1] and unspecified	455	1,139	520	335	386	246	82	290	285
Eastern Europe	**226**	**1,029**	**948**	**779**	**731**	**2,862**	**2,713**	**1,757**	**1,853**
Albania	-	-	-	9	59	29	10	9	53
Armenia	-	-	-	-	19	62	78	60	73
Azerbaijan	-	-	-	-	(Z)	-	14	11	8
Belarus	-	-	-	-	27	74	37	47	30
Bulgaria	-	-	-	17	1	20	5	6	11
Czechoslovakia	-	-5	(Z)	1	1	15	1	-2	3
Czech Republic	-	-	-	-	-	2	2	3	9
Estonia	-	-	-	-	21	1	(Z)	1	3
Georgia	-	-	-	-	5	65	53	53	49
Hungary	-5	6	1	3	2	3	4	5	13
Kazakhstan	-	-	-	-	17	9	12	16	57
Kyrgyzstan	-	-	-	-	1	63	22	18	25
Latvia	-	-	-	-	21	1	3	2	6
Lithuania	-	-	-	-	21	24	15	27	14
Moldova	-	-	-	-	9	25	22	15	13
Poland	-75	1,017	902	646	77	21	5	5	40
Romania	92	55	64	39	10	14	9	8	28
Russia	-	-	-	-	149	1,895	1,134	427	400
Slovakia	-	-	-	-	-	1	1	2	11
Soviet Union	214	-44	-30	3	-	5	-	-	-
Tajikistan	-	-	-	-	10	17	19	18	20
Turkmenistan	-	-	-	-	7	24	13	16	19
Ukraine	-	-	-	-	8	50	103	165	257
Uzbekistan	-	-	-	-	(Z)	1	4	1	5
Other [2] and unspecified	-	-	11	60	265	442	1,148	842	706
Near East and South Asia	**17,195**	**50,777**	**6,605**	**-24,670**	**8,121**	**7,933**	**7,023**	**2,946**	**7,322**
Afghanistan	185	56	57	59	70	49	8	8	10
Bangladesh	701	1,670	175	168	154	109	178	73	22
Cyprus	20	138	16	18	10	14	16	6	10
Egypt	271	13,600	4,976	2,508	2,537	2,760	2,240	1,637	1,548
Greece	905	362	282	-179	665	315	266	243	-12
India	3,810	1,021	-8	100	78	54	32	39	39
Iran	914	-847	-	-23	(Z)	-	-	-	-21
Iraq [3]	-5	5	-7	365	119	135	135	128	112
Israel	3,760	25,417	4,379	2,002	4,691	3,276	3,134	420	5,301
Jordan	618	1,320	139	67	112	127	95	128	163
Kuwait	-	-	-2,506	-13,550	-2	-	-	-	-
Lebanon	90	233	8	5	11	7	5	4	11
Nepal	105	177	20	16	19	20	20	19	17
Oman	(Z)	79	4	3	13	24	1	4	11
Pakistan	2,048	1,971	526	346	123	-39	-162	-190	-167
Saudi Arabia	23	-20	-1,614	-13,913	-1,328	-	-	-	-
Sri Lanka	153	512	72	109	53	72	35	25	3
Syria	15	262	(Z)	-	-	2	-	-	-
Turkey	2,703	3,760	367	798	673	823	241	150	-61
United Arab Emirates	-	-361	-3,709	-	-	-	-	-	-
Yemen (Sanaa)	24	216	14	-	-	-	-	-	-
Yemen	-	-	28	19	14	21	1	3	4
UNRWA [4]	296	596	7	76	69	140	7	103	72
West Bank-Gaza	11	13	1	5	11	19	64	57	27
Other and unspecified	548	236	29	40	31	26	705	91	233

See footnotes at end of table.

No. 1313. U.S. Government Foreign Grants and Credits, by Type and Country: 1966 to 1996—Continued

[In millions of dollars. See headnote, p. 794]

COUNTRY	1966-1975, total	1976-1985, total	1990	1991	1992	1993	1994	1995	1996
Africa	3,610	11,066	1,853	1,484	1,624	1,779	1,802	1,968	1,431
Algeria	263	345	59	-42	-14	-11	28	759	365
Angola	6	115	-15	-4	-20	8	39	25	28
Benin	12	44	5	10	17	12	16	12	7
Botswana	35	169	17	11	8	15	14	15	6
Burkina	40	287	15	32	17	20	13	16	9
Burundi	5	62	18	6	16	19	36	23	2
Cameroon	50	150	42	57	42	23	13	4	3
Cape Verde	1	68	6	7	9	5	6	8	8
Chad	20	145	24	26	26	22	9	13	5
Eritrea	-	-	-	-	-	4	19	5	11
Ethiopia	297	310	54	123	88	137	126	91	76
Ghana	203	152	14	32	36	48	54	57	30
Guinea	68	74	15	22	21	34	33	28	24
Cote d'Ivoire	57	57	25	58	46	21	38	17	22
Kenya	76	549	110	87	90	79	41	34	-6
Lesotho	27	197	15	11	16	7	6	12	3
Liberia	86	459	31	64	40	29	42	40	35
Madagascar	13	86	33	31	20	26	22	26	33
Malawi	30	56	34	48	47	41	33	58	32
Mali	58	199	31	44	31	37	30	31	5
Mauritania	20	161	11	6	3	7	2	2	2
Morocco	413	948	95	100	26	21	26	-53	-24
Mozambique	1	175	80	89	72	75	68	100	46
Niger	64	223	33	44	34	29	16	31	12
Nigeria	284	267	156	34	31	18	52	1	-5
Rwanda	13	91	13	27	10	32	200	70	47
Senegal	48	361	60	39	47	54	32	24	36
Sierra Leone	36	85	2	10	16	8	7	8	17
Somalia	47	582	77	11	338	506	24	17	7
South Africa	-11	2	20	28	44	66	71	112	76
Sudan	52	1,358	145	113	32	35	44	8	10
Swaziland	8	58	14	13	13	14	10	12	10
Tanzania	123	259	51	42	27	28	24	17	13
Togo	18	60	10	19	12	8	7	3	1
Tunisia	376	563	38	5	16	-4	1	-5	-25
Uganda	33	40	43	39	26	58	51	51	30
Zaire	342	938	241	48	33	9	1	1	(Z)
Zambia	35	331	63	50	76	52	21	25	18
Zimbabwe	(Z)	271	10	27	67	28	34	29	17
Other and unspecified	361	769	156	113	165	160	491	240	444
Far East and Pacific	34,767	9,651	38	-8,966	801	13	747	751	747
Australia	276	-12	-34	-26	-18	-2	-1	-	-
Burma	43	31	1	-3	(Z)	-2	-2	-2	-2
Cambodia	1,760	87	5	6	14	29	16	37	29
China	-	49	71	55	31	14	6	136	113
Hong Kong	41	11	-8	-	-	1	1	73	133
Indonesia	1,390	1,661	46	23	82	-64	23	25	39
Japan and Ryukyu Islands	-345	-210	-635	-9,377	-30	-2	-1	(Z)	(Z)
Laos	1,868	8	(Z)	(Z)	1	(Z)	(Z)	3	3
Malaysia	86	39	-1	-2	-	-	1	-	1
Mongolia	-	-	-	17	2	36	17	11	6
New Zealand	95	-68	-2	-2	-1	-	-	-	-
Pacific Islands, Trust Territory of the [5]	488	1,260	220	179	204	152	317	209	215
Philippines	729	1,466	556	391	543	129	-53	54	48
Singapore	78	110	(Z)	(Z)	(Z)	(Z)	(Z)	1	(Z)
South Korea	5,426	3,518	-192	-331	-133	-431	-55	-50	-62
Taiwan	1,523	648	-7	-8	-7	-9	-8	-5	-3
Thailand	996	733	-19	49	44	84	245	207	195
Vietnam	19,720	18	-	-	-	-	-	-	-
Other and unspecified	595	302	39	64	71	75	242	51	32
Western Hemisphere	6,816	9,848	2,002	2,020	2,462	678	796	441	328
Argentina	34	21	64	87	90	80	26	-30	-53
Bolivia	270	413	112	197	185	129	115	92	86
Brazil	1,518	399	260	-22	410	-188	-60	-204	-192
Canada	272	317	-41	-50	-38	-41	-120	-	-
Chile	724	-565	-32	-40	-55	-39	-36	-27	-6
Colombia	846	298	-30	7	-78	-235	-4	-6	9
Costa Rica	103	687	108	63	24	15	-1	-30	-50
Dominican Republic	360	550	27	25	3	163	9	-21	-14
Ecuador	144	153	61	26	30	17	19	5	3
El Salvador	93	1,681	303	308	278	212	87	114	65
Guatemala	160	270	96	82	109	74	52	37	-1
Guyana	71	36	42	11	9	6	9	9	11
Haiti	42	370	53	69	54	59	122	199	70
Honduras	113	801	223	193	126	92	49	72	27
Jamaica	120	643	108	109	84	34	99	27	-18

See footnotes at end of table.

No. 1313. U.S. Government Foreign Grants and Credits, by Type and Country: 1966 to 1996—Continued

[In millions of dollars. See headnote, p. 794]

COUNTRY	1966-1975, total	1976-1985, total	1990	1991	1992	1993	1994	1995	1996
Western Hemisphere—Continued:									
Mexico	305	1,162	140	38	-109	-160	-231	-201	-131
Nicaragua	150	197	100	396	207	37	41	27	28
Panama	210	205	102	153	193	49	6	8	-8
Paraguay	86	22	(Z)	1	(Z)	1	2	1	2
Peru	274	757	87	139	672	113	44	138	55
Trinidad and Tobago	21	151	5	5	-10	-11	-9	-14	-15
Uruguay	116	-9	-4	-5	2	-1	2	(Z)	1
Venezuela	115	-35	-18	-14	-2	1	(Z)	(Z)	1
Other [6] and unspecified	671	1,325	236	242	280	271	575	250	460
Other international organizations and unspecified areas	**4,018**	**9,768**	**1,610**	**1,854**	**2,236**	**2,413**	**1,209**	**2,574**	**2,170**

Z Less than $500,000.   [1] Includes European Atomic Energy Community, European Coal and Steel Community, European Payments Union, European Productivity Agency, North Atlantic Treaty Organization, and Organization for European Economic Cooperation.   [2] Foreign assistance in 1989-94 to the countries of Eastern Europe and to the Newly Independent States of the former Soviet Union was reported primarily on a regional basis.   [3] Foreign assistance to Iraq in 1991-94 was direct humanitarian assistance to ethnic minorities of Northern Iraq after the conflict in the Persian Gulf.   [4] United Nations Relief and Works Agency for Palestine refugees.   [5] Excludes transactions with Commonwealth of the Northern Mariana Islands after October 1986; includes transactions with Federated States of Micronesia, Republic of the Marshall Islands, and Republic of Palau.   [6] Includes Andean Development Corporation, Caribbean Development Bank, Central American Bank for Economic Integration, Eastern Caribbean Central Bank, Inter-American Institute of Agricultural Science, Organizations of American States, and Pan American Health Organization.

Source: U.S. Bureau of Economic Analysis, press releases, and unpublished data.

No. 1314. U.S. Foreign Economic and Military Aid Programs: 1970 to 1996

[In millions of dollars. For years ending June 30 except, beginning 1977, ending Sept. 30. Economic aid shown here represents U.S. economic aid—not just aid under the Foreign Assistance Act. Major components in recent years include AID, Food for Peace, Peace Corps, and paid-in subscriptions to international financial institutions, such as IBRD, and IDB. Annual figures are gross unadjusted program figures]

PERIOD OR YEAR	Total economic and military aid	ECONOMIC AID			MILITARY AID		
		Total	Loans	Grants	Total	Loans	Grants
1970	6,568	3,676	1,389	2,288	2,892	70	2,822
1975	6,916	4,908	1,679	3,229	2,009	750	1,259
1976	6,412	3,878	1,759	2,119	2,535	1,442	1,093
1976, TQ [1]	2,603	1,931	840	1,091	672	494	178
1977	7,784	5,594	2,083	3,511	2,190	1,411	779
1978	9,014	6,661	2,530	4,131	2,353	1,601	752
1979	13,845	7,120	1,900	5,220	6,725	5,173	1,552
1980	9,695	7,573	1,993	5,580	2,122	1,450	672
1981	10,550	7,305	1,460	5,845	3,245	2,546	699
1982	12,324	8,129	1,454	6,675	4,195	3,084	1,111
1983	14,202	8,603	1,619	6,984	5,599	3,932	1,667
1984	15,524	9,038	1,621	7,417	6,486	4,401	2,085
1985	18,128	12,327	1,579	10,748	5,801	2,365	3,436
1986	16,739	10,900	1,330	9,570	5,839	1,980	3,859
1987	14,488	9,386	1,138	8,248	5,102	953	4,149
1988	13,792	8,961	852	8,109	4,831	763	4,068
1989	14,688	9,860	694	9,166	4,828	410	4,418
1990	15,727	10,834	756	10,078	4,893	404	4,489
1991	16,663	11,904	354	11,550	4,760	428	4,332
1992	15,589	11,242	494	10,748	4,347	345	4,002
1993	28,196	24,054	462	23,593	4,143	855	3,288
1994	15,870	11,940	887	11,053	3,931	770	3,161
1995	15,108	11,295	190	11,105	3,813	558	3,255
1996	13,559	9,589	329	9,260	3,970	544	3,426

[1] Transition quarter, July-Sept.

Source: U.S. Agency for International Development, *U.S. Overseas Loans and Grants and Assistance from International Organizations*, annual.

No. 1315. U.S. Foreign Military Aid, by Region and Selected Countries: 1994 to 1996

[In thousands of dollars. For years ending **Sept. 30**. Military aid data include Military Assistance Program (MAP) grants, foreign military credit sales, International Military Education and Training, and excess defense articles. N.I.S.=New Independent States]

REGION AND COUNTRY	1994	1995	1996	REGION AND COUNTRY	1994	1995	1996
Total	3,930,672	3,812,746	3,970,233	Panama.	-	425	-
				Asia [1]	2,847	3,804	6,508
Near East [1]	3,112,098	3,111,501	3,204,683	Malaysia	318	504	613
Egypt	1,300,800	1,301,000	1,301,009	Philippines	876	-	1,210
Israel	1,800,000	1,800,000	1,800,000	Thailand	895	96	1,445
Jordan.	9,800	8,303	101,202	Viet Nam	-	999	-
Morocco	528	724	830	Europe [1]	774,776	566,928	606,598
Tunisia	500	800	816	Bulgaria.	300	400	708
Sub-Saharan Africa [1] . .	4,506	4,955	11,046	Czech Republic.	500	500	795
Ghana.	514	222	257	Greece	283,600	229,683	224,054
Kenya	288	283	297	Hungary	700	796	1,034
Senegal.	450	598	637	Latvia	195	903	388
Latin America [1]	17,301	21,881	10,717	Poland	700	1,747	1,021
Bolivia.	3,406	3,597	547	Portugal.	81,500	500	769
Colombia.	8,600	10,588	95	Turkey.	406,006	329,152	321,095
Dominican Rep.	608	213	507	N.I.S.	1,481	1,722	4,508
Ecuador.	509	293	547	Russia.	471	413	760
El Salvador	400	404	535	Ukraine	600	707	1,019
Honduras.	524	325	500	Oceania and other	88	376	420
Jamaica.	501	174	469				
Mexico	201	400	992	**Nonregional . . . .**	**17,575**	**101,579**	**125,753**

- Represents zero.   [1] Includes countries not shown separately.

Source: U.S. Agency for International Development, *U.S. Overseas Loans and Grants and Assistance from International Organizations*, annual.

No. 1316. U.S. Foreign Aid—Economic Assistance, by Region and Selected Countries: 1994 to 1996

[In thousands of dollars. For years ending **Sept. 30**. N.I.S.=New Independent States]

REGION AND COUNTRY	1994	1995	1996	REGION AND COUNTRY	1994	1995	1996
Total	11,939,559	11,294,639	9,589,560	Honduras.	47,229	29,685	25,800
				Jamaica.	32,095	23,967	32,097
Near East [1]	1,972,814	2,310,372	2,146,415	Latin America			
Egypt	606,486	975,825	824,262	Regional	53,655	51,542	50,549
Israel	1,200,000	1,200,000	1,200,000	Mexico	11,426	9,931	25,276
Jordan.	46,979	13,506	32,466	Nicaragua	93,053	31,373	27,254
Lebanon	1,661	13,380	1,026	Peru	156,044	131,576	103,366
Morocco	42,947	15,035	15,821	Asia [1]	596,349	571,818	462,682
West Bank/Gaza	58,480	80,909	63,448	Bangladesh	125,223	146,774	55,142
Sub-Saharan Africa [1] . . .	1,457,752	1,306,081	1,106,508	India	155,419	164,429	157,175
Angola	66,656	44,760	83,470	Indonesia.	24,371	61,564	33,459
Benin	25,251	20,337	16,389	Kampuchea	29,694	42,115	27,500
Botswana.	15,325	31,905	1,776	Nepal	19,333	100	15,667
Eritrea.	40,546	10,452	13,550	Pakistan	49,608	16,993	16,493
Ethiopa	145,179	119,494	110,810	Philippines	77,565	17,121	57,042
Ghana.	55,004	39,172	43,501	Thailand	12,113	13,255	5,287
Guinea	31,394	19,671	15,671	Europe [1]	693,480	686,098	562,140
Kenya	48,533	26,450	16,122	Bosnia Hercegovina. . .	86,271	71,900	245,325
Liberia.	60,107	51,643	57,912	Bulgaria.	7,817	38,525	32,633
Madagascar	33,318	30,015	19,684	Croatia	18,367	12,345	15,630
Malawi.	54,554	67,820	31,354	Cyprus	29,999		9,376
Mali	41,458	34,758	30,912	Hungary	2,308	26,012	19,564
Mozambique.	74,745	66,709	59,273	Lithuania	15,015	22,252	17,989
Namibia.	18,367	16,815	6,766	Macedonia	12,000	13,512	9,655
Niger.	26,696	18,895	4,846	Portugal.			-
Rwanda	54,171	166,021	120,527	Ireland, Republic of . .	39,408	39,200	-
Senegal.	35,524	24,386	19,776	N.I.S [1]	2,118,374	842,503	628,663
Somalia.	24,815	14,778	9,399	Armenia	89,174	52,526	70,724
South Africa	133,674	100,120	116,709	Azerbaijan	21,274	9,848	5,625
Sudan	66,331	30,067	23,521	Belarus	50,718	11,067	25,041
Tanzania	25,955	31,469	11,788	Georgia	36,816	39,273	20,023
Uganda	47,370	57,826	39,519	Kazakhstan	104,623	40,191	29,725
Zambia	35,190	29,555	10,978	Kyrgyz Republic	42,650	25,104	17,034
Zimbabwe	40,246	21,584	19,497	Moldova	62,368	21,723	31,769
Latin America [1]	941,698	717,121	680,509	Russia.	1,410,594	353,196	178,060
Bolivia.	106,059	65,570	90,062	Tajikistan	46,233	8,401	3,368
Colombia.	21,593	17,306	16,766	Turkemenistan	27,871	5,343	28,952
Costa Rica	12,110	6,244	2,139	Ukraine	160,771	178,779	120,771
Dominican Rep	90,731	15,692	13,831	Uzberistan	24,723	11,515	10,874
Ecuador.	19,392	14,286	13,559	Oceania and other	26,538	6,765	21,769
El Salvador	56,807	63,214	78,436				
Guatemala	67,878	39,199	37,333	**Nonregional . . . .**	**4,132,554**	**4,853,881**	**3,980,874**
Haiti	106,024	157,592	99,325				

- Represents zero.   [1] Includes countries and regional organizations not shown separately.

Source: U.S. Agency for International Development, *U.S. Overseas Loans and Grants and Assistance from International Organizations*, annual.

No. 1317. U.S. International Trade in Goods and Services: 1995 to 1997

[In millions of dollars. Data presented on a balance of payments basis and will not agree with the following merchandise trade Tables 1318 to 1326]

CATEGORY	EXPORTS			IMPORTS			TRADE BALANCE		
	1995	1996	1997	1995	1996	1997	1995	1996	1997
Total	795,647	850,775	937,593	895,538	959,349	1,047,799	-99,891	-108,574	-110,207
Goods.	575,845	611,983	679,325	749,574	803,320	877,279	-173,729	-191,337	-197,955
Services	219,802	238,792	258,268	145,964	156,029	170,520	73,838	82,763	87,748
Travel	63,395	69,751	73,268	44,916	48,048	51,220	18,479	21,703	22,048
Passenger fares	18,909	20,413	20,895	14,663	15,818	18,235	4,246	4,595	2,660
Other transportation	26,081	26,074	26,911	27,034	27,403	28,949	-953	-1,329	-2,038
Royalties and license fees.	30,289	32,823	33,676	6,919	7,854	9,411	23,370	24,969	24,265
Other private services. . .	65,555	73,073	84,465	39,823	43,138	48,421	25,732	29,935	36,044
Other [1]	14,755	15,765	18,269	9,986	11,081	11,488	4,769	4,684	6,781
U.S. government miscel. services	818	893	784	2,623	2,687	2,796	-1,805	-1,794	-2,012

[1] Represents transfers under U.S. military sales contracts for exports and direct defense expenditures for imports.

Source: U.S. Bureau of the Census, *U.S. International Trade in Goods and Services*, series FT-900(97).

No. 1318. U.S. Exports and General Imports in Goods: 1970 to 1997

[In billions of dollars. Domestic and foreign exports, are f.a.s. value basis; general imports are on customs value basis]

YEAR	TOTAL GOODS [1]			MANUFACTURED GOODS [2][3]			AGRICULTURAL PRODCTS [4]			MINERAL FUELS [3][5]		
	Exports	Imports	Bal-ance	Exports	Imports	Bal-ance	Exports	Imports	Bal-ance	Exports	Imports	Balance
1970	43.8	40.4	3.4	31.7	27.3	4.4	7.3	5.8	1.6	1.6	3.1	-1.5
1971	44.7	46.2	-1.5	32.9	32.1	0.8	7.8	5.8	2.0	1.5	3.7	-2.2
1972	50.5	56.4	-5.9	36.5	39.7	-3.2	9.5	6.5	3.0	1.6	4.8	-3.2
1973	72.5	70.5	2.0	48.5	47.1	1.3	17.9	8.5	9.4	1.7	8.2	-6.5
1974	100.0	102.6	-2.5	68.5	57.8	10.7	22.3	10.4	11.9	3.4	25.5	-22.0
1975	109.3	98.5	10.8	76.9	54.0	22.9	22.1	9.5	12.6	4.5	26.5	-22.0
1976	117.0	123.5	-6.5	83.1	67.6	15.5	23.3	11.2	12.1	4.2	34.0	-29.8
1977	123.2	151.0	-27.8	88.9	80.5	8.4	24.2	13.6	10.6	4.2	47.2	-43.0
1978	145.9	174.8	-28.8	103.6	104.3	-0.7	29.8	15.0	14.8	3.9	42.0	-38.1
1979	186.5	209.5	-22.9	132.7	117.1	15.6	35.2	16.9	18.3	5.7	59.9	-54.2
1980	225.7	245.3	-19.5	160.7	133.0	27.7	41.8	17.4	24.3	8.2	78.9	-70.7
1981	238.7	261.0	-22.3	171.7	149.8	22.0	43.8	17.2	26.6	10.3	81.2	-70.9
1982	216.4	244.0	-27.5	155.3	151.7	3.6	37.0	15.7	21.3	12.8	65.3	-52.5
1983	205.6	258.0	-52.4	148.5	171.2	-22.7	36.5	16.5	19.9	9.8	57.8	-48.0
1983	205.6	258.0	-52.4	148.7	170.9	-22.2	36.1	16.0	20.2	9.8	57.8	-48.0
1984	224.0	330.7	-106.7	164.1	230.9	-66.8	37.9	19.3	18.6	9.7	60.8	-51.1
1985	218.8	336.5	-117.7	168.0	257.5	-89.5	29.3	19.5	9.8	10.3	53.7	-43.4
1986	227.2	365.4	-138.3	179.8	296.7	-116.8	26.3	20.9	5.4	8.4	37.2	-28.8
1987	254.1	406.2	-152.1	199.9	324.4	-124.6	28.7	20.3	8.4	8.0	44.1	-36.1
1988	322.4	441.0	-118.5	255.6	361.4	-105.7	37.1	20.7	16.4	8.5	41.0	-32.5
1989	363.8	473.2	-109.4	287.0	379.4	-92.4	41.6	21.1	20.5	9.9	52.6	-42.7
1990	393.6	495.3	-101.7	315.4	388.8	-73.5	39.6	22.3	17.2	12.4	64.7	-52.3
1991	421.7	488.5	-66.7	345.1	392.4	-47.3	39.4	22.1	17.2	12.3	54.1	-41.8
1992	448.2	532.7	-84.5	368.5	434.3	-65.9	43.1	23.4	19.8	11.3	55.3	-43.9
1993	465.1	580.7	-115.6	388.7	479.9	-91.2	42.8	23.6	19.2	9.9	55.9	-46.0
1994	512.6	663.3	-150.6	431.1	557.3	-126.3	45.9	26.0	20.0	9.0	56.4	-47.4
1995	584.7	743.4	-158.7	486.7	629.7	-143.0	56.0	29.3	26.8	10.5	59.1	-48.6
1996	625.1	795.3	-170.2	524.7	658.8	-134.1	60.6	32.6	28.1	12.4	78.1	-65.7
1997	689.2	870.7	-181.5	592.5	728.9	-136.4	57.1	35.2	21.9	13.0	78.3	-65.3

[1]Includes nonmonetary gold, military grant aid, special category shipments, trade between the U.S. Virgin Islands and foreign countries and undocumented exports to Canada. Adjustments were also made for carryover. Import values are based on transaction prices whenever possible ("f.a.s." for 1974-79 and Customs value thereafter). Import data before 1974 do not exist on a transaction price valuation basis. [2]Manufactured goods include commodity sections 5-9 under Schedules A and E for 1970-82 and SITC Rev. 3 for 1983-forward. Manufactures include undocumented exports to Canada, nonmonetary gold (excluding gold ore, scrap, and base bullion), and special category shipments. [3]Data for 1970-80 exclude trade between the U.S. Virgin Islands and foreign countries. Census data concordances link the 1980-92 trade figures into time series that are as consistent as possible. Data for 1970-79 are not linked and are from published sources. Import values are "f.a.s." for 1974-79 and Customs value thereafter; these values are based on transaction prices while maintaining a data series as consistent as possible over time. Import data before 1974 do not exist on a transaction price valuation basis. 1991 imports include revisions for passenger cars, trucks, petroleum and petroleum products not included elsewhere; see footnote 7 on page 18 for more details. [4]Agricultural products for 1983-forward utilize the latest census definition that excludes manufactured goods that were previously classified as manufactured agricultural products. [5]Mineral fuels include commodity section 3 under SITC Rev. 1 for 1970-76, SITC Rev. 2 for 1977-82 and SITC Rev. 3 for 1983-forward.

Source: U.S. International Trade Administration, through 1996, *U.S. Foreign Trade Highlights,* annual; and thereafter, release date: June 30, 1998; http://www.ita.doc.gov/industry/otea/usfth/t03.prn>.

No. 1319. U.S. Exports and Imports for Consumption of Merchandise, by Major Customs District: 1980 to 1997

[In billions of dollars. Exports are f.a.s. (free alongside ship) value all years; imports are on customs value basis]

CUSTOMS DISTRICT	EXPORTS					IMPORTS FOR CONSUMPTION				
	1980	1990	1995	1996	1997	1980	1990	1995	1996	1997
Total [1]	220.8	393.0	584.7	625.1	689.2	244.0	490.6	738.6	789.9	862.7
Anchorage, AK.	1.0	3.7	5.9	6.1	7.6	0.2	0.7	5.7	6.9	7.2
Baltimore, MD	9.0	6.7	9.0	8.3	7.6	6.0	11.2	14.4	14.0	14.7
Boston.	0.8	5.6	4.6	5.0	5.7	5.0	12.2	13.4	13.7	14.7
Buffalo, NY . . . [2] . . .	6.3	15.8	30.5	32.3	39.2	7.4	19.2	29.1	29.3	30.6
Charleston, SC [2]	3.1	6.7	10.1	10.8	12.3	1.8	6.8	10.4	11.6	12.3
Chicago, IL	4.2	10.2	18.4	18.7	19.6	4.1	18.3	31.3	33.5	37.1
Cleveland, OH	1.8	4.0	7.8	10.2	14.0	1.5	11.3	21.7	23.6	26.2
Dallas/Fort Worth, TX	0.5	3.4	4.4	3.8	5.3	1.2	4.8	8.8	9.8	11.4
Detroit, MI.	14.6	35.6	56.8	60.8	66.7	12.7	37.8	64.7	69.4	76.4
Duluth, MN	1.5	0.8	1.4	1.5	1.4	3.0	3.9	6.0	6.5	6.5
El Paso, TX.	1.8	3.9	7.9	9.6	10.2	1.4	5.0	12.9	13.6	14.9
Great Falls, MT	1.8	2.4	3.0	3.2	4.3	3.2	4.7	6.9	8.0	8.9
Honolulu, HI.	0.2	0.5	1.1	1.3	1.6	1.8	2.1	2.7	2.7	2.7
Houston/Galveston, TX . . .	15.7	17.6	27.4	27.1	28.5	20.1	21.6	23.4	28.2	28.9
Laredo, TX	8.3	15.2	24.3	29.7	39.1	2.7	10.0	24.7	31.9	38.1
Los Angeles, CA.	14.8	42.1	67.0	69.0	74.2	20.0	64.1	96.3	99.9	110.3
Miami, FL	6.9	11.2	22.7	24.5	29.5	2.6	7.1	11.9	13.5	16.2
Milwaukee, WI	0.4	0.1	0.1	0.1	0.2	0.4	1.1	1.5	1.4	1.5
Minneapolis, MN.	0.1	0.9	1.3	1.4	1.6	0.3	2.0	2.8	3.3	3.7
Mobile, AL [2].	2.6	1.9	3.4	3.4	3.8	3.0	3.4	3.9	4.9	4.8
New Orleans, LA	19.5	18.0	28.4	31.0	30.4	22.5	24.1	34.4	35.4	35.4
New York, NY	38.9	50.9	61.4	61.9	67.1	43.4	68.0	87.6	93.4	103.1
Nogales, AZ.	0.8	2.1	4.0	4.2	4.9	1.2	4.2	7.7	7.2	8.6
Norfolk, VA [2]	8.0	11.7	14.4	15.2	16.1	4.7	7.4	8.6	9.4	9.9
Ogdensburg, NY.	3.8	7.9	9.2	9.9	10.6	4.6	9.8	14.4	15.9	17.4
Pembina, ND.	2.3	3.4	5.5	5.9	7.1	3.0	4.1	7.2	7.4	7.7
Philadelphia, PA	3.2	4.0	6.7	9.2	7.7	15.6	18.3	18.3	19.0	19.0
Port Arthur, TX	2.0	0.9	1.3	1.0	1.3	9.4	3.2	4.8	6.0	6.4
Portland, ME	4.3	1.7	2.1	2.1	2.1	1.6	4.3	4.4	5.2	5.3
Portland, OR	3.8	5.8	10.2	10.0	8.5	2.6	5.6	7.9	7.5	9.6
Providence, RI	2.7	(Z)	0.1	(Z)	0.1	1.5	1.3	0.9	1.3	1.3
San Diego, CA	1.4	3.4	6.1	7.5	9.0	1.0	4.3	8.9	11.0	14.0
San Francisco, CA	10.6	23.1	43.7	47.8	48.1	8.3	28.0	58.8	57.7	58.7
San Juan, PR	0.9	2.5	2.6	2.5	2.8	3.7	5.4	6.8	7.2	8.0
Savannah, GA	2.4	7.4	10.9	10.9	13.4	2.2	9.8	14.7	16.1	18.0
Seattle, WA	12.0	32.6	31.4	37.1	44.8	9.2	20.9	24.1	25.1	30.1
St. Albans, VT	0.7	4.0	4.4	4.1	3.0	1.6	5.2	7.4	7.9	8.1
St. Louis, MO.	0.2	0.3	0.3	1.6	1.3	0.9	3.0	4.4	4.8	5.7
Tampa, FL.	2.8	4.3	6.7	6.9	7.4	3.7	7.0	9.2	9.2	9.4
Virgin Islands of the U.S. . .	0.1	0.2	0.2	0.2	0.2	4.1	2.1	2.1	2.8	3.3
Washington, DC	0.3	1.1	2.3	2.1	2.2	0.4	0.8	1.2	1.3	1.6
Wilmington, NC	1.3	3.0	4.4	4.2	4.0	1.1	3.3	7.4	7.8	8.9

Z Less than $50 million.　[1] Totals shown for exports reflect the value of estimated parcel post and Special Category shipments, and beginning 1990, adjustments for undocumented exports to Canada which are not distributed by customs district. Beginning 1990, the value of bituminous coal exported through Norfolk, VA; Charleston, SC; and Mobile, AL is reflected in the total but not distributed by district.　[2] Beginning 1990, excludes exports of bituminous coal.

Source: U.S. Bureau of the Census, 1980, *Highlights of U.S. Export and Import Trade*, FT 990; 1990, *U.S. Merchandise Trade: Selected Highlights,* series FT 920, monthly; and beginning 1995, *U.S. Export History* and *U.S. Import History* on compact disc.

No. 1320. Export and Import Unit Value Indexes—Selected Countries: 1992 to 1996

[Indexes in U.S. dollars, 1990=100. A unit value is an implicit price derived from value and quantity data]

COUNTRY	EXPORT UNIT VALUE					IMPORT UNIT VALUE				
	1992	1993	1994	1995	1996	1992	1993	1994	1995	1996
United States	101.0	101.4	103.6	108.8	109.4	100.8	100.1	101.8	106.4	107.4
Australia.	87.7	82.3	86.0	93.6	94.7	99.3	99.4	104.3	109.6	109.5
Austria	98.0	88.6	(NA)	(NA)	(NA)	102.2	93.4	(NA)	(NA)	(NA)
Belgium-Luxembourg	100.5	(NA)	(NA)	(NA)	(NA)	99.2	(NA)	(NA)	(NA)	(NA)
Canada	95.3	94.4	94.6	101.2	104.3	99.2	98.6	99.1	102.6	104.4
Denmark	101.6	91.4	94.1	106.8	106.2	99.7	89.2	92.0	106.8	104.1
France	99.6	90.1	98.3	111.1	108.2	97.9	87.0	92.4	104.5	102.6
Germany	102.1	92.0	92.9	107.6	(NA)	102.0	91.1	94.6	110.0	(NA)
Italy	100.8	87.9	88.9	96.2	(NA)	95.9	83.9	85.2	(NA)	(NA)
Japan	114.0	124.5	134.1	144.8	(NA)	96.3	97.0	97.2	105.3	(NA)
Netherlands	98.4	90.1	92.4	106.7	101.9	101.0	89.7	91.6	104.4	100.3
Norway	88.7	77.7	75.4	86.6	92.1	97.2	85.8	86.4	97.2	95.4
Sweden	98.9	81.2	78.1	(NA)	(NA)	98.4	80.9	75.8	(NA)	(NA)
United Kingdom	101.8	97.6	101.5	111.6	111.9	100.9	94.3	99.4	112.5	111.8

NA Not available.

Source: International Monetary Fund, Washington, DC, *International Financial Statistics*, monthly (copyright).

No. 1321. U.S. Exports, by State of Origin: 1990 to 1997

[In millions of dollars. Exports are on a f.a.s. value basis]

STATE AND OTHER AREA	1990	1996	1997 Total	1997 Rank	STATE AND OTHER AREA	1990	1996	1997 Total	1997 Rank
Total	**394,045**	**624,767**	**688,896**	**(X)**	Montana	229	440	530	48
					Nebraska	693	1,907	1,971	39
United States	**315,065**	**555,960**	**615,788**	**(X)**	Nevada	394	1,268	1,075	45
Alabama	2,834	5,170	5,932	26	New Hampshire	973	1,481	1,597	43
Alaska	2,850	2,879	2,721	34					
Arizona	3,729	10,503	13,820	14	New Jersey	7,633	13,119	15,167	13
Arkansas	920	2,003	2,305	35	New Mexico	249	931	1,776	40
California	44,520	93,418	99,161	1	New York	22,072	34,230	37,979	3
Colorado	2,274	4,883	5,120	28	North Carolina	8,010	15,734	16,402	11
Connecticut	4,356	6,100	7,058	24	North Dakota	360	707	778	46
Delaware	1,344	1,594	2,067	38	Ohio	13,378	22,677	24,903	7
District of Columbia. ...	320	305	485	(X)	Oklahoma	1,646	2,365	2,728	33
Florida	11,634	20,744	23,234	8	Oregon	4,065	8,948	9,151	21
					Pennsylvania	8,491	14,364	16,069	12
Georgia	5,763	10,982	12,949	15	Rhode Island	595	919	1,088	44
Hawaii	179	284	334	50					
Idaho	898	1,571	1,664	42	South Carolina	3,116	6,698	7,517	23
Illinois	12,965	24,176	26,455	6	South Dakota	205	443	517	49
Indiana	5,273	10,984	12,029	17	Tennessee	3,746	8,094	9,233	20
Iowa	2,189	4,400	5,118	29	Texas	32,931	66,862	76,184	2
Kansas	2,113	3,784	4,292	30	Utah	1,596	3,296	3,239	32
Kentucky	3,175	6,385	7,953	22	Vermont	1,154	3,302	3,811	31
Louisiana	14,199	21,667	18,732	9	Virginia	9,333	12,215	12,755	16
Maine	870	1,380	1,723	41	Washington	24,432	26,482	32,752	4
					West Virginia	1,550	2,169	2,276	37
Maryland	2,592	5,019	5,214	27	Wisconsin	5,158	9,504	10,125	18
Massachusetts	9,501	14,524	16,526	10	Wyoming	264	481	560	47
Michigan	18,474	27,553	32,254	5					
Minnesota	5,091	8,992	9,447	19	Puerto Rico	3,600	5,134	5,601	(X)
Mississippi	1,605	2,623	2,290	36	Virgin Islands	51	184	233	(X)
Missouri	3,130	5,404	6,724	25	Other [1]	75,328	63,490	67,275	(X)

X Not applicable.   [1] Includes unreported, not specified, special category, estimated shipments, foreign trade zone, re-exports, and any timing adjustments.

Source: U.S. Bureau of the Census, *U.S. Merchandise Trade,* series FT 900, December issues.

No. 1322. U.S. Exporting Companies Profile, by Company Type and Employment-Size-Class: 1987 and 1992

COMPANY TYPE AND EMPLOYMENT-SIZE-CLASS	NUMBER OF EXPORTERS		KNOWN EXPORT VALUE [1] (mil. dol.)		PERCENT OF—			
					Number of exporters		Known export value	
	1987	1992	1987	1992	1987	1992	1987	1992
All companies, total	**69,354**	**112,854**	**159,913**	**348,960**	**100.0**	**100.0**	**100.0**	**100.0**
No employees	8,351	15,534	8,293	9,178	12.0	13.8	5.2	2.6
1 to 19 employees	30,818	51,186	11,911	29,397	44.4	45.4	7.4	8.4
20 to 49 employees	11,619	18,501	5,058	17,005	16.8	16.4	3.2	4.9
50 to 99 employees	6,911	10,505	5,235	13,840	10.0	9.3	3.3	4.0
100 to 249 employees	5,703	8,679	6,100	18,371	8.2	7.7	3.8	5.3
250 to 499 employees	2,469	3,621	5,616	15,055	3.6	3.2	3.5	4.3
500 or more employees	3,483	4,828	117,700	246,114	5.0	4.3	73.6	70.5
Manufacturers	**29,127**	**42,763**	**115,740**	**241,522**	**42.0**	**37.9**	**72.4**	**69.2**
No employees	1,561	1,949	1,565	1,971	2.3	1.7	1.0	0.6
1 to 19 employees	7,998	12,342	810	2,534	11.5	10.9	0.5	0.7
20 to 49 employees	6,301	9,949	1,115	4,217	9.1	8.8	0.7	1.2
50 to 99 employees	4,523	6,781	1,639	4,897	6.5	6.0	1.0	1.4
100 to 249 employees	4,182	5,999	3,376	9,809	6.0	5.3	2.1	2.8
250 to 499 employees	1,881	2,594	3,130	8,990	2.7	2.3	2.0	2.6
500 or more employees	2,681	3,149	104,105	209,104	3.9	2.8	65.1	59.9
Wholesalers	**23,114**	**39,713**	**25,471**	**50,989**	**33.3**	**35.2**	**15.9**	**14.6**
No employees	1,859	4,503	1,166	1,882	2.7	4.0	0.7	0.5
1 to 19 employees	14,697	25,296	7,358	16,730	21.2	22.4	4.6	4.8
20 to 49 employees	3,583	5,673	3,100	7,128	5.2	5.0	1.9	2.0
50 to 99 employees	1,546	2,182	3,064	5,419	2.2	1.9	1.9	1.6
100 to 249 employees	869	1,338	2,042	4,820	1.3	1.2	1.3	1.4
250 to 499 employees	305	406	1,543	1,942	0.4	0.4	1.0	0.6
500 or more employees	255	315	7,197	13,068	0.4	0.3	4.5	3.7
Other companies	**15,907**	**26,910**	**15,267**	**53,158**	**22.9**	**23.8**	**9.5**	**15.2**
No employees	3,972	6,030	2,221	2,754	5.7	5.3	1.4	0.8
1 to 19 employees	7,975	13,364	3,714	9,934	11.5	11.8	2.3	2.8
20 to 49 employees	1,706	2,826	835	5,625	2.5	2.5	0.5	1.6
50 to 99 employees	825	1,488	524	3,380	1.2	1.3	0.3	1.0
100 to 249 employees	622	1,271	666	3,547	0.9	1.1	0.4	1.0
250 to 499 employees	270	586	924	3,998	0.4	0.5	0.6	1.1
500 or more employees	537	1,345	6,384	23,921	0.8	1.2	4.0	6.9
Unclassified companies	1,206	3,468	3,436	3,291	1.7	3.1	2.1	0.9

[1] Known value is defined as the value of exports by known exporters, i.e., those export transactions that could be matched to specific companies. Export values are on f.a.s. or "free alongside ship basis." Total export value was $251 billion in 1987 and $448 billion in 1992.

Source: U.S. Bureau of the Census, *A Profile of U.S. Exporting Companies, 1992,* CB-97-135 press release.

No. 1323. U.S. Exports, Imports, and Merchandise Trade Balance, by Country: 1993 to 1997

[In millions of dollars. Includes silver ore and bullion. Country totals include exports of special category commodities, if any. Data include nonmonetary gold and includes trade of Virgin Islands with foreign countries, see footnote 2 for exception. Minus sign (-) denotes an excess of imports over exports]

COUNTRY	EXPORTS, DOMESTIC AND FOREIGN					GENERAL IMPORTS [1]					MERCHANDISE TRADE BALANCE				
	1993	1994	1995	1996	1997	1993	1994	1995	1996	1997	1993	1994	1995	1996	1997
Total	465,091.0	512,626.5	584,742.5	625,075.0	689,182.4	580,659.4	663,255.7	743,542.8	795,289.3	870,670.7	-115,568.4	-150,629.2	-158,800.8	-170,214.3	-181,488.2
Afghanistan	9.5	5.4	4.1	16.9	11.5	6.1	6.1	5.4	16.4	10.0	3.4	-0.6	-1.3	0.5	1.5
Albania	34.3	16.0	13.5	12.1	12.1	7.5	6.1	9.5	10.3	11.7	26.8	9.9	4.0	1.7	-8.6
Algeria	938.0	1,191.5	774.0	635.2	691.6	1,583.0	1,526.9	1,749.5	2,125.7	2,439.5	-644.9	-335.4	-975.5	-1,490.5	-1,747.9
Andorra	14.6	4.8	16.4	24.5	21.7	0.1	0.1	0.2	2.5	0.3	14.5	4.7	16.2	22.0	21.4
Angola	173.8	197.3	259.6	268.3	280.6	2,092.2	2,061.3	2,232.3	2,901.5	2,779.1	-1,918.4	-1,864.0	-1,972.6	-2,633.2	-2,498.6
Anguilla	14.3	12.8	14.6	12.8	18.1	0.3	0.3	0.1	0.8	0.7	13.9	12.5	14.5	12.0	17.4
Antigua	73.0	64.8	97.1	82.4	84.5	14.6	5.3	3.1	8.9	4.8	58.4	59.5	94.1	73.5	79.6
Argentina	3,775.7	4,461.6	4,189.2	4,516.8	5,810.0	1,205.7	1,725.4	1,760.9	2,279.2	2,228.2	2,570.0	2,736.2	2,428.3	2,237.6	3,581.8
Armenia	77.8	73.9	70.4	57.4	62.1	0.7	1.0	1.0	1.5	6.0	77.1	73.0	54.2	56.0	56.1
Aruba	265.8	273.6	247.4	234.6	238.4	457.0	461.2	420.6	558.1	610.2	-191.2	-187.5	-173.2	-323.5	-371.8
Australia	8,276.5	9,780.5	10,789.1	12,008.4	12,062.9	3,297.3	3,202.0	3,322.9	3,868.9	4,602.3	4,979.2	6,578.5	7,466.2	8,139.6	7,460.6
Austria	1,325.8	1,371.7	2,017.2	2,009.8	2,074.7	1,410.7	1,749.7	1,963.3	2,200.3	2,368.4	-85.0	-378.0	53.9	-190.5	-293.7
Azerbaijan	36.6	27.4	35.6	54.0	62.3	0.2	0.3	0.8	4.5	5.7	36.4	27.1	34.8	49.5	56.6
Bahamas, The	704.4	684.9	661.3	726.0	809.5	328.4	202.8	156.5	164.9	154.9	376.0	482.0	504.8	561.1	654.6
Bahrain	636.0	443.9	254.9	244.2	406.1	97.1	147.5	134.2	116.3	116.4	538.8	296.4	120.8	127.9	289.8
Bangladesh	254.5	232.1	325.1	210.1	259.0	886.5	1,080.1	1,257.2	1,343.0	1,679.4	-632.0	-848.0	-932.2	-1,132.9	-1,420.4
Barbados	145.5	161.1	185.7	222.5	280.9	34.1	34.5	37.7	41.2	42.1	111.4	126.6	148.0	181.3	238.7
Byelarus	92.2	46.4	48.0	53.1	40.6	33.9	53.5	44.9	52.2	66.0	58.4	-7.1	3.1	0.9	-25.4
Belgium	8,878.4	10,939.3	12,465.5	12,532.2	13,420.3	5,149.1	6,354.3	6,053.9	6,775.7	7,911.9	3,729.4	4,585.0	6,411.6	5,756.5	5,508.4
Belize	135.6	115.2	99.8	106.6	114.8	53.7	50.8	52.2	68.2	77.3	82.0	64.4	47.6	38.5	37.5
Benin	22.3	25.9	34.1	27.4	51.6	15.8	10.1	9.8	13.6	7.7	6.5	15.8	24.3	13.8	43.9
Bermuda	264.8	299.9	298.5	281.9	295.1	9.1	9.1	10.3	11.5	29.8	250.2	290.8	288.2	270.4	265.3
Bolivia	218.2	184.9	213.5	269.5	102.5	190.8	260.3	262.5	275.2	223.3	27.4	-75.4	-49.0	-5.7	-120.8
Bosnia and Hercegovina	24.8	39.0	28.4	58.8	43.1	7.2	4.5	3.3	10.1	8.3	17.6	34.5	25.1	48.6	34.8
Botswana	24.9	22.7	35.8	28.9	121.4	8.0	13.6	21.2	3.9	24.6	16.9	9.1	14.5	25.1	96.8
Brazil	6,058.0	8,101.6	11,439.4	12,717.5	15,914.7	7,478.8	8,682.6	8,832.9	8,773.4	9,625.5	-1,420.8	-581.0	2,606.6	3,944.2	6,289.2
British Virgin Islands	46.1	47.1	49.3	53.9	64.6	14.1	14.6	9.1	6.6	13.1	31.9	32.5	40.2	47.3	51.5
Brunei	472.5	375.8	189.9	374.7	178.1	30.2	45.6	38.3	48.3	55.8	442.4	330.3	151.6	326.4	122.3
Bulgaria	115.3	110.0	131.8	137.5	109.6	158.9	215.5	188.5	126.5	171.4	-43.6	-105.5	-56.7	11.0	-61.8
Burkina Faso	17.7	7.3	14.6	10.4	18.3	0.4	0.5	0.4	3.9	1.0	17.3	6.8	14.2	6.5	17.3
Cameroon	48.5	53.7	45.5	71.3	101.1	101.1	55.0	57.3	64.5	57.2	-52.6	-1.3	-11.7	6.8	64.3
Canada	100,443.7	114,438.5	127,226.1	134,210.3	151,766.7	111,216.4	128,405.9	144,369.8	155,892.6	168,200.9	-10,772.7	-13,967.4	-17,143.7	-21,682.3	-16,434.2
Cayman Islands	164.3	202.2	180.3	208.0	270.3	34.7	52.5	18.3	16.9	2.9	129.6	149.6	162.0	191.2	250.7
Chad	7.8	7.5	10.8	3.4	3.1	0.3	0.3	3.2	7.1	7.6	7.5	7.6	7.6	-3.7	-4.0
Chile	2,598.5	2,773.8	3,614.9	4,139.5	4,368.4	1,462.0	1,820.5	1,930.8	2,262.2	2,293.1	1,136.5	953.3	1,684.1	1,877.3	2,075.3
China	8,762.8	9,281.8	11,753.6	11,992.6	12,862.3	31,539.9	38,786.7	45,543.2	51,512.6	62,557.6	-22,777.1	-29,504.9	-33,789.6	-39,520.0	-49,695.3
Colombia	3,234.5	4,064.3	4,624.4	4,714.3	5,197.0	3,031.6	3,171.0	3,791.1	4,423.8	4,737.3	202.9	893.3	833.3	290.5	459.7
Congo (Brazzaville)	27.4	38.0	54.7	62.9	74.7	500.1	179.6	206.9	315.3	471.5	-472.6	-140.1	-152.2	-252.4	-396.8
Congo (Kinshawa)	35.4	38.0	77.1	73.3	37.8	238.1	206.9	266.9	258.7	281.8	-202.7	-185.3	-189.9	-185.3	-244.0
Costa Rica	1,542.2	1,870.0	1,736.5	1,816.4	2,024.4	1,541.4	1,647.1	1,843.1	1,974.2	2,323.2	0.8	222.9	-106.6	-157.9	-298.8
Croatia	103.4	146.8	139.9	106.0	138.7	106.0	114.7	93.0	71.2	82.8	-2.7	32.0	46.2	34.8	55.9
Cyprus	137.8	208.8	257.8	256.9	244.5	15.6	17.9	13.3	17.4	16.4	122.2	190.9	244.4	239.6	228.1
Czech Republic	266.8	296.8	362.7	412.2	589.8	277.0	315.8	363.4	482.3	609.8	-10.2	-19.0	-0.7	-70.1	-20.0
Denmark	1,091.8	1,214.8	1,517.7	1,731.0	1,756.9	1,664.0	2,121.6	1,945.0	2,141.5	2,137.7	-572.2	-906.8	-427.3	-410.5	-380.8

See footnotes at end of table.

No. 1323. U.S. Exports, Imports, and Merchandise Trade Balance, by Country: 1993 to 1997—Continued

[See headnote, page 801]

COUNTRY	EXPORTS, DOMESTIC AND FOREIGN					GENERAL IMPORTS					MERCHANDISE TRADE BALANCE				
	1993	1994	1995	1996	1997	1993	1994	1995	1996	1997	1993	1994	1995	1996	1997
Djibouti	13.2	6.7	8.5	8.3	7.3	-	0.1	-	-	-	13.2	6.7	8.4	8.3	7.3
Dominica	27.4	25.6	26.5	34.2	37.4	5.8	6.9	6.6	7.7	9.1	21.6	18.6	19.9	26.5	28.3
Dominican Republic	2,349.8	2,798.8	3,014.9	3,190.5	3,924.0	2,671.7	3,090.6	3,399.9	3,574.8	4,326.8	-322.0	-291.8	-384.0	-384.3	-402.8
Ecuador	1,100.0	1,194.6	1,538.3	1,258.5	1,525.9	1,399.4	1,726.2	1,939.9	1,958.1	2,054.8	-299.4	-531.6	-401.6	-699.6	-528.9
Egypt	2,767.8	2,854.8	2,985.1	3,153.3	3,835.4	613.1	548.7	606.4	680.5	657.5	2,154.8	2,306.0	2,378.7	2,472.9	3,177.9
El Salvador	873.3	931.2	1,110.6	1,074.5	1,400.1	487.8	609.2	812.2	975.4	1,346.2	385.5	322.0	298.4	99.1	53.8
Estonia	54.3	33.3	138.9	83.6	47.4	20.2	29.3	62.3	55.1	76.8	34.1	4.0	76.6	28.5	-29.3
Ethiopia	75.4	143.8	147.5	148.1	121.2	12.2	-	-	-	-	63.2	143.8	147.6	148.1	121.2
Federated States of Micronesia	25.1	24.6	23.3	24.7	29.0	14.0	13.2	13.0	11.2	11.9	11.1	11.3	10.2	13.5	17.2
Fiji	26.9	118.2	31.6	27.5	32.8	68.6	97.1	78.0	74.7	84.6	-41.8	21.1	-46.4	-47.2	-51.8
Finland	847.6	1,068.3	1,249.7	2,438.6	1,741.1	1,608.3	1,800.7	2,270.0	2,388.8	2,391.5	-760.7	-732.4	-1,020.3	49.8	-650.4
France	13,266.8	13,618.7	14,249.7	14,455.5	15,964.9	15,279.3	16,699.9	17,209.4	18,645.8	20,636.4	-2,012.5	-3,080.2	-2,964.3	-4,190.3	-4,671.5
French Guiana	323.2	195.6	441.7	300.7	493.7	2.7	3.2	5.3	4.7	2.4	320.4	192.5	436.4	296.0	491.4
French Polynesia	102.2	72.0	88.7	88.7	105.3	8.5	14.3	20.5	17.2	35.4	93.7	57.7	68.2	71.5	69.9
Gabon	48.2	40.2	54.4	56.1	84.6	961.0	1,134.3	1,464.0	1,983.7	2,202.3	-912.8	-1,094.1	-1,409.6	-1,927.6	-2,117.7
Gambia	9.9	3.9	6.2	8.4	9.7	2.3	2.4	2.3	1.9	2.9	7.6	1.5	3.9	6.5	6.8
Georgia	47.9	78.2	95.2	81.4	140.6	21.1	1.3	10.6	6.5	7.0	26.8	76.9	84.6	74.9	133.6
Germany	18,932.2	19,229.0	22,394.3	23,495.0	24,458.3	28,562.1	31,744.3	36,844.0	38,945.1	43,121.5	-9,629.9	-12,515.3	-14,449.8	-15,450.1	-18,663.2
Ghana	215.0	124.5	167.2	295.7	315.0	215.5	198.5	196.1	171.4	155.3	-0.5	-74.0	-28.9	124.3	159.8
Gibraltar	8.3	23.1	18.4	11.7	8.8	3.8	4.0	4.9	6.5	2.8	4.5	19.1	13.5	5.2	6.0
Greece	880.4	829.0	1,518.8	824.5	949.3	347.5	455.3	397.3	506.0	453.2	532.8	373.7	1,121.5	318.5	496.2
Greenland	2.7	3.3	2.4	4.1	4.9	13.1	9.5	7.4	6.4	7.9	-10.4	-6.2	-5.0	-2.2	-3.0
Grenada	23.9	23.5	26.8	35.7	40.6	8.1	7.2	5.3	3.6	6.5	15.8	16.2	21.5	32.1	34.1
Guadeloupe	48.5	51.2	69.3	66.0	57.6	4.8	1.9	1.2	1.4	3.5	43.7	49.3	68.0	64.6	54.1
Guatemala	1,312.3	1,352.2	1,646.6	1,566.1	1,729.6	1,194.4	1,282.7	1,526.7	1,678.5	1,990.2	117.9	69.5	119.9	-112.4	-260.6
Guinea	59.4	49.8	66.7	87.1	82.8	117.3	92.1	99.0	116.5	127.7	-57.9	-42.3	-32.3	-29.4	-44.9
Guyana	122.4	109.8	141.2	136.9	142.5	154.2	98.0	107.4	109.5	112.8	-31.8	11.7	33.8	27.4	29.7
Haiti	228.5	204.5	550.2	474.8	499.1	90.7	58.7	129.8	143.6	188.2	137.8	145.8	420.4	331.3	310.9
Honduras	898.9	1,011.8	1,278.9	1,642.6	2,018.9	913.9	1,097.6	1,441.3	1,795.4	2,322.2	-15.0	-85.8	-162.4	-152.8	-303.4
Hong Kong	9,873.8	11,441.0	14,231.1	13,966.3	15,117.1	9,554.4	9,695.6	10,291.2	9,864.5	10,287.8	319.4	1,745.4	3,939.9	4,101.8	4,829.3
Hungary	434.8	309.0	295.3	330.7	485.5	400.5	470.3	547.0	676.2	1,078.9	34.3	-161.3	-251.7	-345.5	-593.5
Iceland	146.9	111.8	170.6	257.1	179.2	232.6	248.7	232.7	236.0	230.8	-85.6	-136.9	-62.2	21.2	-51.6
India	2,778.1	2,294.0	3,295.8	3,328.3	3,607.6	4,553.7	5,309.5	5,726.2	6,169.5	7,322.4	-1,775.6	-3,015.5	-2,430.5	-2,841.2	-3,714.8
Indonesia	2,770.3	2,808.8	3,359.6	3,976.8	4,522.3	5,435.4	6,546.9	7,435.3	8,249.9	9,188.4	-2,665.1	-3,738.2	-4,075.7	-4,273.1	-4,666.1
Iran	616.2	328.9	277.3	0.3	1.1	0.2	0.9	0.2	-	0.1	616.0	328.0	277.1	0.3	1.0
Iraq	4.0	0.8	0.2	2.8	82.0	-	-	-	-	311.9	4.0	0.8	0.2	2.8	-229.9
Ireland	2,728.4	3,418.6	4,108.8	3,668.7	4,642.2	2,519.4	2,893.5	4,078.7	4,803.9	5,866.6	209.0	525.2	30.1	-1,135.2	-1,224.4
Israel	4,429.1	4,995.8	5,621.1	6,011.9	5,994.9	4,420.2	5,229.4	5,708.7	6,433.6	7,326.0	8.8	-233.6	-87.6	-421.7	-1,331.0
Italy	6,463.8	7,182.7	8,861.6	8,797.1	8,994.7	13,215.6	14,802.2	16,348.3	18,324.8	19,407.5	-6,751.9	-7,619.4	-7,486.7	-9,527.8	-10,412.8
Ivory Coast	88.6	111.2	173.2	141.1	150.9	178.3	185.4	214.1	397.4	289.0	-89.6	-74.2	-40.9	-256.3	-138.1
Jamaica	1,116.2	1,065.5	1,420.4	1,491.0	1,416.5	719.7	746.6	847.0	838.2	738.0	396.5	318.9	573.4	652.9	678.4
Japan	47,891.5	53,487.7	64,342.6	67,606.8	65,548.9	107,246.4	119,155.7	123,479.1	115,187.0	121,663.2	-59,354.9	-65,668.0	-59,136.5	-47,580.2	-56,114.8
Jordan	360.5	287.3	335.3	345.2	402.5	18.7	29.0	28.8	25.2	25.3	341.8	258.3	306.5	320.1	377.1
Kazakhstan	68.1	130.2	80.9	138.3	346.3	41.3	62.3	122.9	121.2	128.9	26.8	67.9	-42.1	17.2	217.4
Kenya	131.1	169.6	114.0	104.6	225.3	92.4	108.8	101.5	106.5	114.0	38.8	60.8	12.5	-2.0	111.4
Kiribati	30.7	23.4	2.3	4.2	2.7	1.5	0.9	1.2	1.2	1.7	29.2	22.4	1.1	3.0	1.0

See footnotes at end of table.

COUNTRY	EXPORTS, DOMESTIC AND FOREIGN					GENERAL IMPORTS					MERCHANDISE TRADE BALANCE				
	1993	1994	1995	1996	1997	1993	1994	1995	1996	1997	1993	1994	1995	1996	1997
Kuwait	999.4	1,175.9	1,437.3	1,983.6	1,390.0	1,818.5	1,457.5	1,335.5	1,651.2	1,816.4	-819.0	-281.5	101.8	332.4	-426.4
Kyrgyzstan	18.4	6.0	24.7	46.9	28.4	2.0	7.7	8.3	5.0	2.4	16.4	-1.8	16.3	41.9	25.9
Latvia	89.5	101.1	89.5	166.6	217.8	22.4	41.4	81.9	102.9	145.1	67.1	59.7	7.6	63.7	72.7
Lebanon	377.3	442.0	592.3	627.0	551.9	26.8	25.4	35.1	41.5	77.8	350.5	416.6	557.2	585.6	474.2
Lesotho	7.4	3.4	2.0	2.6	2.4	55.7	63.0	62.1	65.4	86.5	-48.3	-59.6	-60.2	-62.7	-84.2
Liberia	38.9	46.4	41.7	49.8	42.9	3.1	3.5	9.8	26.9	4.8	35.8	42.9	31.9	22.9	38.1
Liechtenstein	10.9	13.9	14.9	8.9	12.5	100.2	98.3	126.2	91.1	116.5	-89.3	-84.4	-111.3	-82.3	-104.0
Lithuania	56.9	41.2	52.0	62.9	87.4	16.2	15.3	26.4	34.4	79.8	40.8	25.9	25.6	28.6	7.6
Luxembourg	560.4	228.4	374.4	242.2	712.1	253.0	287.5	234.0	203.8	238.8	307.4	-59.1	140.4	38.3	473.2
Macau	27.5	21.2	29.9	29.8	65.0	668.5	791.3	895.3	857.6	1,021.0	-641.0	-770.1	-865.5	-827.9	-956.0
Macedonia	11.4	14.0	21.3	14.4	33.8	111.4	82.1	88.8	124.8	147.1	-100.0	-68.1	-67.6	-110.5	-113.3
Madagascar	10.9	47.9	10.0	17.8	11.5	42.8	57.1	57.3	51.8	62.6	-31.9	-9.2	-47.3	-34.0	-51.0
Malawi	25.8	18.7	17.8	13.3	17.5	57.8	56.5	40.9	72.5	82.8	-32.0	-37.8	-23.1	-59.2	-65.3
Malaysia	6,064.4	6,969.0	8,816.1	8,546.2	10,780.0	10,563.0	13,981.7	17,454.7	17,828.8	18,026.7	-4,498.6	-7,012.6	-8,638.6	-9,282.6	-7,246.7
Mali	32.7	19.0	23.2	18.4	26.2	1.2	6.7	3.6	4.9	3.8	31.4	13.0	19.6	13.5	22.3
Malta	171.6	87.6	106.7	125.2	120.9	103.6	95.7	132.4	208.6	223.6	68.0	-8.0	-25.8	-83.5	-102.7
Marshall Islands	35.6	33.1	31.7	29.4	23.6	11.5	8.0	11.0	3.9	7.3	24.1	25.2	20.6	25.5	16.3
Martinique	32.5	31.1	38.4	35.3	33.9	1.1	3.5	2.1	1.0	2.4	31.4	27.5	36.3	34.3	31.4
Mauritania	19.8	14.0	43.1	15.1	20.9	6.5	3.5	5.5	5.3	0.2	13.3	10.5	37.6	9.8	20.6
Mauritius	18.0	23.7	24.7	25.2	31.4	197.9	216.6	229.7	217.0	238.4	-179.9	-192.9	-204.9	-191.8	-207.0
Mexico	41,581.1	50,843.5	46,292.1	56,791.5	71,388.4	39,917.4	49,493.8	62,100.6	74,297.3	85,937.5	1,663.7	1,349.7	-15,808.6	-17,505.8	-14,549.1
Moldova	31.2	23.4	10.2	21.6	19.7	0.4	3.0	12.2	15.9	53.7	30.8	20.4	-2.0	5.7	-34.0
Monaco	5.9	5.6	9.5	3.1	6.9	16.1	17.5	24.1	15.9	19.6	-10.2	-11.9	-14.6	-12.8	-12.7
Morocco	600.1	408.7	517.4	476.3	434.7	184.9	192.0	239.3	247.1	295.9	415.2	216.7	278.1	229.2	138.9
Mozambique	59.0	39.4	49.3	23.0	45.6	8.7	15.3	27.6	26.6	30.5	50.3	24.1	21.7	-3.5	15.1
Namibia	21.5	16.4	26.5	22.7	25.0	22.1	27.8	11.5	27.1	63.0	-0.6	-11.4	15.0	-4.5	-38.1
Netherlands	12,838.5	13,581.6	16,557.7	16,662.6	19,826.7	5,443.3	6,006.8	6,405.0	6,583.1	7,292.8	7,395.2	7,574.8	10,152.7	10,079.4	12,533.8
Netherlands Antilles	519.2	521.0	504.0	529.6	475.2	396.6	425.3	289.9	684.8	579.8	122.6	95.7	214.1	-155.2	-104.6
New Caledonia	22.5	27.3	22.4	28.7	34.4	24.3	22.7	40.2	54.8	51.9	-1.8	4.7	-17.8	-26.1	-17.5
New Zealand	1,248.6	1,507.8	1,691.4	1,728.5	1,962.1	1,207.6	1,421.1	1,451.8	1,463.2	1,579.2	41.0	86.6	239.6	265.4	382.9
Nicaragua	150.2	185.7	249.7	262.3	289.8	128.4	167.2	238.7	350.4	439.3	21.8	18.5	11.0	-88.1	-149.5
Niger	16.3	12.0	39.5	24.8	24.8	3.0	2.4	1.5	1.6	29.8	13.3	9.6	38.0	23.2	-5.0
Nigeria	894.7	509.1	602.8	818.4	813.1	5,301.4	4,429.9	4,930.4	5,978.3	6,349.4	-4,406.7	-3,920.9	-4,327.7	-5,159.9	-5,536.4
Norway	1,212.4	1,267.3	1,293.0	1,559.0	1,721.3	1,957.5	2,353.4	3,086.7	3,992.5	3,752.0	-745.1	-1,086.1	-1,793.7	-2,433.5	-2,030.7
Oman	251.4	219.1	222.0	216.8	340.8	277.2	458.3	294.9	414.4	242.4	-25.8	-239.2	-72.9	-197.7	98.4
Pakistan	811.3	718.3	941.2	1,271.4	1,240.1	897.2	1,011.6	1,197.1	1,265.7	1,442.2	-85.9	-293.3	-255.8	5.7	-202.2
Panama	1,187.4	1,277.0	1,389.6	1,380.5	1,536.1	279.7	322.4	307.1	346.1	367.2	907.7	954.6	1,082.5	1,034.4	1,168.9
Papua New Guinea	50.4	65.7	50.8	69.2	116.6	97.9	114.8	55.0	85.6	64.5	-47.4	-49.1	-4.2	-16.4	52.1
Paraguay	521.1	787.6	992.4	897.5	913.4	49.6	80.1	55.0	42.3	40.7	471.5	707.5	937.4	855.2	872.8
Peru	1,071.9	1,407.5	1,775.3	1,773.8	1,953.3	753.9	841.1	1,034.5	1,260.9	1,772.3	318.0	566.4	740.8	512.9	181.0
Philippines	3,529.2	3,886.0	5,294.8	6,142.4	7,417.3	4,893.6	5,719.1	7,006.5	8,161.4	10,445.0	-1,364.4	-1,833.0	-1,711.7	-2,019.0	-3,027.6
Poland	911.6	625.2	776.1	968.3	1,169.9	453.8	651.2	663.9	627.9	695.6	457.8	-26.0	112.2	340.4	474.4
Portugal	726.5	1,054.3	898.1	960.7	954.2	785.2	898.5	1,056.6	1,016.5	1,138.0	-58.7	155.8	-158.5	-55.8	-183.8
Qatar	166.4	161.9	225.9	207.7	379.0	65.3	80.9	90.9	157.1	157.4	101.1	81.0	135.0	50.6	221.7
Romania	323.6	339.7	253.1	265.6	258.0	69.2	194.7	222.4	248.5	399.8	254.4	145.0	30.7	17.1	-141.8

See footnotes at end of table.

No. 1323. U.S. Exports, Imports, and Merchandise Trade Balance, by Country: 1993 to 1997—Continued

[See headnote, page 801]

COUNTRY	EXPORTS, DOMESTIC AND FOREIGN					GENERAL IMPORTS					MERCHANDISE TRADE BALANCE				
	1993	1994	1995	1996	1997	1993	1994	1995	1996	1997	1993	1994	1995	1996	1997
Russia	2,970.3	2,578.1	2,823.3	3,345.8	3,364.9	1,743.3	3,245.0	4,030.0	3,576.8	4,319.0	1,227.0	-666.9	-1,206.6	-231.0	-954.0
Saudi Arabia	6,661.2	6,013.4	6,154.9	7,311.3	8,437.8	7,707.8	7,688.0	8,376.7	10,467.2	9,364.8	-1,046.6	-1,674.6	-2,221.8	-3,155.9	-927.0
Senegal	70.3	42.4	67.9	55.8	51.8	7.6	11.3	5.0	5.5	6.8	62.7	31.2	62.9	50.3	44.9
Singapore	11,678.0	13,019.9	15,333.2	16,720.0	17,696.2	12,798.2	15,357.7	18,560.5	20,343.1	20,074.6	-1,120.2	-2,337.8	-3,227.3	-3,623.1	-2,378.4
Slovakia	33.9	42.8	61.0	62.6	82.0	64.6	130.7	129.5	124.6	165.6	-30.7	-87.9	-68.5	-62.0	-83.6
Somalia	46.4	29.9	8.1	4.2	2.8	0.1	0.2	0.1	0.3	0.3	46.1	29.7	7.9	4.1	2.4
South Africa	2,188.4	2,172.3	2,750.6	3,111.9	2,997.2	1,844.8	2,030.5	2,208.0	2,323.3	2,510.1	343.7	141.8	542.6	788.5	487.2
South Korea	14,782.0	18,025.4	25,379.9	26,621.1	25,046.1	17,118.0	19,629.3	24,183.9	22,655.1	23,173.1	-2,336.0	-1,603.9	1,195.9	3,966.0	1,873.0
Spain	4,168.1	4,622.3	5,526.0	5,499.6	5,538.7	2,991.9	3,554.9	3,879.5	4,279.8	4,605.5	1,176.2	1,067.4	1,646.5	1,219.8	933.3
Sri Lanka	203.2	197.7	279.1	211.1	154.7	1,001.7	1,093.0	1,259.7	1,393.0	1,620.0	-798.5	-895.2	-980.5	-1,181.9	-1,465.3
St. Lucia	98.7	80.5	80.9	84.5	89.3	31.3	26.5	35.2	34.2	34.2	67.4	54.0	45.7	62.2	55.1
St. Vincent	37.7	38.2	42.2	45.0	54.4	4.9	5.4	7.8	6.8	4.3	32.8	32.7	34.4	38.2	50.0
Sudan	58.6	54.5	43.4	51.3	36.4	11.7	35.1	22.7	18.7	12.1	46.9	19.4	20.7	32.6	24.3
Suriname	114.4	121.8	189.7	222.7	183.0	58.3	43.3	100.2	96.6	91.5	56.1	78.5	89.5	126.0	91.5
Sweden	2,353.7	2,518.4	3,079.8	3,430.5	3,314.1	4,533.7	5,040.9	6,256.4	7,152.7	7,298.9	-2,180.0	-2,522.5	-3,176.6	-3,722.2	-3,984.8
Switzerland	6,806.5	5,624.0	6,227.5	8,373.4	8,306.9	5,972.9	6,373.1	7,593.8	7,792.6	8,405.1	833.6	-749.1	-1,366.4	580.8	-98.2
Syria	186.5	197.9	223.4	226.3	180.4	130.4	64.3	61.2	15.2	27.9	56.1	133.6	162.1	211.1	152.6
Taiwan	16,167.8	17,108.8	19,289.6	18,460.2	20,365.7	25,101.5	26,705.8	28,971.8	29,907.3	32,628.5	-8,933.7	-9,597.0	-9,682.2	-11,447.1	-12,262.8
Tajikistan	11.7	15.2	17.7	17.2	18.6	17.7	59.6	40.9	32.8	8.5	-6.1	-44.5	-23.2	-15.6	10.0
Tanzania	32.6	48.9	66.3	50.2	64.9	11.4	17.4	22.4	18.9	26.6	21.1	34.0	43.9	31.3	38.3
Thailand	3,766.2	4,865.1	6,665.0	7,197.5	7,349.4	8,541.5	10,305.8	11,348.1	11,336.1	12,601.5	-4,775.4	-5,440.7	-4,683.1	-4,138.6	-5,252.1
Togo	12.8	12.4	18.5	20.0	25.6	3.4	4.1	3.5	4.2	9.4	9.4	8.4	15.1	15.8	16.2
Trinidad and Tobago	528.6	540.5	689.2	665.5	1,105.9	802.7	1,113.2	1,086.2	1,313.2	1,134.3	-274.1	-572.7	-397.1	-647.7	-28.3
Tunisia	232.3	327.2	215.0	189.2	252.3	40.7	53.9	70.4	75.8	63.1	191.6	273.3	144.6	113.4	189.2
Turkey	3,428.9	2,752.4	2,768.1	2,846.6	3,539.5	1,197.5	1,574.9	1,797.9	1,778.2	2,121.1	2,231.4	1,177.5	970.3	1,068.4	1,418.5
Turkmenistan	45.6	137.4	34.2	200.8	117.7	2.0	1.7	1.2	0.5	2.1	43.7	135.7	33.0	200.3	115.6
Turks and Caicos Islands	21.9	29.2	33.5	43.5	58.6	4.1	4.4	5.0	5.1	5.3	17.9	24.7	28.6	38.4	53.3
Uganda	20.9	27.7	22.1	17.2	35.2	9.9	34.9	13.2	15.9	37.8	11.0	-7.1	8.9	1.3	-2.5
Ukraine	310.3	180.3	223.4	395.1	402.9	165.5	323.4	405.6	506.9	410.0	144.8	-143.1	-182.2	-111.9	-7.1
United Arab Emirates	1,810.6	1,598.7	2,006.5	2,533.2	2,607.1	726.7	448.6	459.2	498.8	920.1	1,083.8	1,150.1	1,547.2	2,034.4	1,687.0
United Kingdom	26,438.3	26,899.5	28,856.5	30,962.5	36,425.3	21,730.1	25,057.5	26,929.5	28,978.8	32,659.3	4,708.1	1,842.1	1,927.0	1,983.7	3,766.0
Uruguay	253.5	310.7	395.4	482.9	547.6	265.5	167.7	167.2	260.5	228.9	-12.0	143.0	228.7	222.4	318.7
Uzbekistan	73.0	89.6	63.4	351.8	234.1	7.3	2.9	18.7	159.0	39.1	65.7	86.7	44.7	192.8	195.1
Venezuela	4,590.2	4,039.3	4,640.4	4,749.4	6,601.6	8,139.8	8,371.3	9,764.0	13,173.1	13,477.2	-3,549.7	-4,332.0	-5,123.6	-8,423.7	-6,875.6
Vietnam	7.0	172.7	252.5	616.4	286.6	-	50.6	198.9	331.8	388.5	7.0	122.2	53.6	284.7	-101.9
Western Samoa	10.4	7.3	7.6	11.9	11.1	1.2	0.3	1.0	2.5	1.0	9.2	7.0	7.0	9.4	10.9
Yemen, Republic of	322.3	178.0	185.2	255.9	153.4	98.1	182.7	41.6	31.2	16.0	224.2	-4.7	143.6	224.7	137.4
Yugoslavia, Fed. Rep. of	1.7	0.5	2.2	46.0	49.1	-	-	-	8.2	10.4	1.7	0.5	2.2	37.8	38.7
Zambia	42.4	32.6	48.9	46.0	29.3	40.8	63.5	32.9	64.2	55.9	1.6	-30.9	16.0	-18.3	-26.6
Zimbabwe	84.4	92.8	122.0	90.7	81.9	109.9	102.4	97.7	133.0	139.5	-25.4	-9.6	24.3	-42.3	-57.5

- Represents zero or rounds to zero.

Source: U.S. Bureau of the Census, *U.S. International Trade in Goods and Services*, series FT 900, December issues.

No. 1324. U.S. Exports and General Imports, by Selected SITC Commodity Groups: 1994 to 1997

[**In millions of dollars.** SITC = Standard International Trade Classification. N.e.s. = Not elsewhere specified]

COMMODITY GROUP	EXPORTS [1]				GENERAL IMPORTS [2]			
	1994	1995	1996	1997	1994	1995	1996	1997
Total	512,626	584,742	624,767	689,182	663,256	743,445	791,364	870,671
Agricultural commodities	44,936	54,850	59,311	55,639	25,955	29,258	32,565	35,164
Animal feeds	3,353	3,667	4,183	4,621	433	472	633	648
Cereal flour	1,159	1,163	1,170	1,241	970	1,082	1,213	1,328
Coffee	53	15	4	7	2,270	2,985	2,491	3,575
Corn	4,197	7,521	8,623	5,426	85	66	116	103
Cotton, raw and linters	2,641	3,711	2,740	2,716	21	29	300	20
Hides and skins	1,391	1,621	1,515	1,503	126	140	133	130
Live animals	587	521	533	685	1,392	1,729	1,595	1,655
Meat and preparations	5,195	6,450	6,958	6,885	2,627	2,317	2,317	2,656
Oils/fats, vegetable	963	1,293	1,024	1,398	1,051	1,157	1,416	1,381
Rice	1,009	994	1,029	933	130	121	157	217
Soybeans	4,355	5,422	7,447	7,479	46	32	31	86
Sugar	5	5	5	3	552	682	1,001	956
Tobacco, unmanufactured	1,304	1,397	1,390	1,548	697	555	1,053	1,129
Vegetables and fruits	6,757	7,098	7,313	7,472	6,075	6,581	7,514	7,752
Wheat	4,055	5,464	6,302	4,196	291	238	247	359
Other agricultural	7,912	8,508	9,075	9,526	9,189	11,072	12,348	13,169
Manufactured goods	402,674	451,828	483,874	550,529	557,310	629,685	659,867	728,928
ADP equipment, office machinery . .	30,867	36,410	39,666	43,698	52,058	62,703	66,499	74,993
Airplane parts	9,824	10,349	11,723	13,266	2,727	2,616	3,464	4,917
Airplanes	18,803	13,836	18,962	25,552	3,719	3,651	3,943	4,557
Alcoholic bev, distilled	355	390	385	385	1,826	1,844	2,048	2,186
Aluminum	2,787	3,775	3,485	3,768	4,943	5,819	4,828	5,558
Artwork/antiques	1,184	1,071	887	1,120	2,432	2,666	2,791	3,587
Basketware, etc	1,816	1,996	2,239	2,494	2,588	2,942	3,014	3,364
Chemicals, cosmetics	3,537	3,835	4,323	4,873	1,998	2,307	2,443	2,677
Chemicals, dyeing	2,330	2,585	2,716	3,294	1,869	2,079	2,165	2,485
Chemicals, fertilizers	2,703	3,219	3,070	3,123	1,298	1,391	1,400	1,374
Chemicals, inorganic	4,067	4,541	4,657	5,264	4,087	4,658	4,954	5,132
Chemicals, medicinal	6,096	6,434	7,160	8,087	4,674	5,543	7,076	8,748
Chemicals, n.e.s.	7,657	9,131	9,651	11,160	3,235	3,925	4,568	4,821
Chemicals, organic	12,789	16,106	14,744	16,408	10,805	13,334	14,820	16,874
Chemicals, plastics	12,485	14,958	15,467	17,274	5,941	7,155	7,443	8,237
Cigarettes	4,965	4,770	4,736	4,417	70	64	69	75
Clothing	5,461	6,482	7,285	8,396	36,748	39,523	41,559	48,408
Copper	1,266	1,728	1,553	1,441	2,295	2,983	2,953	3,254
Cork, wood, lumber	5,572	5,637	5,501	5,146	6,680	6,149	7,532	8,179
Crude fertilizers	1,446	1,525	1,526	1,621	1,026	1,164	1,176	1,334
Electrical machinery	44,454	53,139	56,637	65,816	57,750	75,051	75,525	80,370
Fish and preparations	3,036	3,177	2,930	2,624	6,590	6,739	6,657	7,687
Footwear	646	671	761	800	11,712	12,098	12,749	14,026
Furniture and parts	3,131	3,125	3,323	3,942	7,565	8,338	9,431	11,144
Gem diamonds	184	171	151	108	5,756	5,951	6,588	7,595
General industrial machinery	21,813	24,394	26,599	30,603	21,330	24,125	25,286	26,321
Glassware	560	630	680	813	1,158	1,333	1,413	1,553
Glass	1,503	1,644	1,814	2,125	1,350	1,468	1,679	1,750
Gold, nonmonetary	5,689	5,055	6,641	5,673	1,933	2,155	2,737	3,035
Iron and steel mill products	3,554	5,349	4,795	5,637	12,896	12,279	13,368	14,285
Lighting, plumbing	1,249	1,293	1,358	1,535	2,024	2,284	2,579	2,944
Metal manufactures, n.e.s.	7,034	8,060	9,234	10,309	8,847	10,010	10,843	12,242
Metal ores; scrap	3,713	5,564	4,278	4,662	3,262	4,004	4,048	4,156
Metalworking machinery	3,897	4,626	5,241	5,702	4,596	5,926	6,789	7,325
Nickel	210	284	307	347	735	1,197	1,137	1,144
Optical goods	965	1,113	1,378	1,697	1,817	2,148	2,327	2,493
Paper and paperboard	7,448	9,572	9,837	10,283	9,066	12,470	11,637	11,697
Photographic equipment	3,016	3,351	3,743	3,865	4,676	5,145	5,271	5,759
Plastic articles, n.e.s.	3,574	3,847	4,439	5,092	4,517	5,101	5,306	5,676
Platinum	306	318	248	437	1,325	1,694	1,716	1,973
Pottery	104	99	95	101	1,555	1,667	1,569	1,683
Power generating machinery	20,346	21,856	22,292	27,221	19,543	20,493	22,499	24,601
Printed materials	3,971	4,325	4,346	4,605	2,234	2,584	2,700	2,871
Pulp and waste paper	3,794	6,206	4,034	3,868	2,315	3,827	2,648	2,639
Records/magnetic media	5,864	6,263	6,555	6,815	3,612	3,896	4,078	4,137
Rubber articles, n.e.s.	795	888	972	1,256	1,253	1,415	1,465	1,553
Rubber tires and tubes	1,614	1,858	1,959	2,394	3,034	3,144	3,074	3,417

See footnotes at end of table.

No. 1324. U.S. Exports and General Imports, by Selected SITC Commodity Groups: 1994 to 1997—Continued

[In millions of dollars]

COMMODITY GROUP	EXPORTS [1]				GENERAL IMPORTS [2]			
	1994	1995	1996	1997	1994	1995	1996	1997
Manufactured goods—Continued								
Scientific instruments	16,475	18,616	20,599	24,039	9,963	11,581	12,385	13,969
Ships, boats	1,165	1,178	1,064	1,366	808	816	1,029	875
Silver and bullion	256	663	638	641	488	580	569	472
Spacecraft	444	655	636	994	219	169	232	239
Specialized industrial machinery	19,677	23,311	25,659	29,162	16,733	18,972	18,509	21,182
Television, VCR, etc	(NA)	(NA)	(NA)	24,093	(NA)	(NA)	(NA)	36,771
Textile yarn, fabric	6,445	7,192	7,814	8,975	9,207	9,980	10,248	11,951
Toys/games/sporting goods	3,079	3,560	3,693	3,827	11,824	13,074	14,734	17,374
Travel goods	233	253	306	330	3,085	3,408	3,581	3,841
Watches/clocks/parts	276	248	277	310	2,641	2,785	2,805	2,838
Wood manufactures	1,543	1,633	1,685	1,958	3,390	3,687	4,037	4,668
Mineral fuel	8,911	10,358	12,057	12,682	56,391	59,109	73,028	78,277
Coal	2,966	3,714	3,849	3,849	646	703	606	655
Crude oil	49	6	460	1,040	38,479	42,814	50,582	54,226
Petroleum preparations	3,167	3,244	3,948	3,899	10,270	9,096	13,858	13,904
Liquified propane/butane	195	316	302	298	873	852	1,263	1,158
Natural gas	254	266	261	275	3,937	3,182	4,002	5,477
Other mineral	2,280	2,812	3,237	3,584	2,186	2,462	2,717	2,857
Reexports	29,981	36,581	40,690	44,153	(X)	(X)	(X)	(X)
Agricultural commodities	987	1,174	1,252	1,439	(X)	(X)	(X)	(X)
Manufactured goods	28,383	34,848	38,798	41,958	(X)	(X)	(X)	(X)
Mineral fuels	78	120	168	284	(X)	(X)	(X)	(X)
Other, reexports	532	439	472	472	(X)	(X)	(X)	(X)

NA Not available.　X Not applicable.　[1] F.A.S. basis.　[2] Customs value basis.

Source: U.S. Bureau of the Census, *U.S. International Trade in Goods and Services*, Series FT-900(97).

No. 1325. Imports for Consumption—Values and Duties: 1980 to 1996

[Imports are on customs value basis. Beginning 1970, includes silver ores and bullion, and beginning 1980, includes trade of Virgin Islands with foreign countries. For basis of dollar values and for area coverage, see text, Section 28]

YEAR	VALUES				Duties cal-culated [1] (mil. dol.)	RATIO OF DUTIES TO VALUES		Duties per capita [2] (dollar)
	Total (mil. dol.)	Free (mil. dol.)	Dutiable (mil. dol.)	Percent free		Total imports (percent)	Dutiable imports (percent)	
1980	[3]244,007	106,992	132,951	45	7,535	3.1	5.7	33.09
1981	259,012	76,338	182,674	29	8,893	3.4	4.9	38.67
1982	242,340	75,856	166,484	31	8,688	3.6	5.2	37.40
1983	256,679	83,397	173,283	32	9,430	3.7	5.4	40.21
1984	322,989	102,977	220,012	32	12,042	3.7	5.5	50.90
1985	343,553	106,035	237,518	31	13,067	3.8	5.5	54.73
1986	368,657	121,742	246,915	33	13,312	3.6	5.4	55.10
1987	402,066	132,152	269,914	33	13,923	3.5	5.2	57.08
1988	437,140	151,693	285,447	35	15,054	3.4	5.3	61.12
1989	468,012	156,365	311,647	33	16,096	3.4	5.2	64.70
1990	490,554	161,108	329,446	33	16,339	3.3	5.0	65.38
1991	483,028	167,641	315,386	35	16,197	3.4	5.1	64.10
1992	525,091	194,583	330,508	37	17,164	3.3	5.2	67.12
1993	574,863	236,007	338,856	41	18,334	3.2	5.4	70.99
1994	657,885	292,257	365,628	44	19,846	3.0	5.6	73.64
1995	739,660	373,948	365,713	51	18,597	2.5	5.1	64.70
1996	790,470	406,640	383,829	51	18,005	2.3	4.7	67.87

[1] Customs duties (including import excise taxes) calculated on the basis of reports of quantity and value of imports of merchandise entered directly for consumption or withdrawn from bonded customs warehouses.　[2] Based on estimated population including Armed Forces abroad as of July 1.　[3] Total includes revisions not carried to free and dutiable values.

Source: U.S. Bureau of the Census, 1970-1988, *Highlights of U.S. Export and Import Trade*, series FT 990, monthly; beginning 1989, *U.S. Merchandise Trade: Selected Highlights*, series FT 920, monthly; and unpublished data.

No. 1326. Domestic Exports and Imports for Consumption of Merchandise, by Selected SIC-Based Product Category: 1990 to 1996

[In millions of dollars. Includes nonmonetary gold]

SIC-BASED PRODUCT CATEGORY	SIC [1] code	1990	1991	1992	1993	1994	1995	1996
Domestic exports, total [2]	(X)	374,537	400,842	425,377	439,282	482,141	547,300	583,221
Agricultural, forestry and fishery products	(X)	26,225	25,052	26,785	25,324	26,102	33,418	36,234
Agricultural products	01	22,597	21,075	22,633	21,615	22,189	29,391	32,380
Livestock and livestock products	02	829	970	871	836	973	920	989
Forestry products	08	281	306	324	276	263	272	271
Fish, fresh or chilled; and other marine products [3]	09	2,518	2,701	2,959	2,596	2,677	2,836	2,594
Mineral commodities	(X)	7,335	7,442	7,210	5,584	5,650	7,159	7,284
Metallic ores and concentrates	10	1,137	1,014	1,084	799	1,018	1,562	1,091
Bituminous, lignite and anthracite coal	11,12	4,513	4,623	4,241	3,090	2,858	3,572	3,694
Crude petroleum and natural gas	13	638	675	737	588	576	729	1,197
Nonmetallic minerals, exc. fuels	14	1,047	1,130	1,148	1,107	1,199	1,296	1,302
Manufactured commodities	(X)	330,403	359,635	383,082	400,721	441,501	496,421	530,484
Food and kindred products	20	16,160	17,492	19,761	20,509	23,094	26,021	27,041
Tobacco manufactures	21	5,040	4,574	4,509	4,253	5,367	5,222	5,238
Textile mill products	22	3,635	4,108	4,473	4,687	5,151	5,696	6,177
Apparel and related products	23	2,848	3,679	4,599	5,433	6,145	7,190	8,104
Lumber and related products	24	6,523	6,477	6,802	7,361	7,252	7,424	7,401
Furniture and fixtures	25	1,589	2,086	2,518	2,818	3,030	2,953	3,101
Paper and allied products	26	8,631	9,214	9,969	9,457	11,000	14,943	14,002
Printing and publishing	27	3,150	3,590	3,808	4,057	4,070	4,471	4,534
Chemicals and allied products	28	37,806	41,483	41,953	42,742	48,950	57,897	58,503
Petroleum and coal products	29	6,794	7,026	6,403	6,163	5,510	6,014	7,158
Rubber and misc. plastics products	30	6,398	7,049	7,872	8,554	9,942	11,025	12,093
Leather and leather products	31	1,388	1,413	1,541	1,536	1,539	1,565	1,725
Stone, clay, and glass products	32	3,295	3,533	3,855	3,844	4,215	4,796	5,097
Primary metal products	33	13,116	15,243	15,105	18,669	16,327	20,191	21,279
Fabricated metal products	34	11,138	11,962	13,265	13,497	13,395	15,161	16,612
Machinery, except electrical	35	61,229	65,300	68,554	72,279	82,120	95,909	104,055
Electric and electronic machinery	36	39,807	42,330	45,992	52,947	63,839	76,235	79,533
Transportation equipment	37	68,113	76,172	82,862	80,196	85,068	82,699	92,887
Instruments and related products	38	19,524	21,699	22,815	24,699	26,560	29,581	32,842
Misc. manufactured commodities	39	4,296	4,621	5,446	5,288	5,813	7,383	6,763
Imports for consumption, total [2]	(X)	490,554	483,028	525,091	574,863	657,884	739,661	790,470
Agricultural, forestry and fishery products	(X)	12,750	13,148	14,216	15,866	17,427	19,799	20,661
Agricultural products	01	5,925	6,107	6,716	7,839	8,657	9,803	10,950
Livestock and livestock products	02	1,453	1,501	1,873	2,161	2,047	2,450	2,377
Forestry products	08	1,015	978	1,088	1,068	1,208	1,932	1,810
Fish, fresh or chilled; and other marine products [3]	09	4,357	4,562	4,540	4,798	5,515	5,614	5,525
Mineral commodities	(X)	51,391	44,581	44,823	45,965	47,300	51,050	57,144
Metallic ores and concentrates	10	1,500	1,244	1,167	1,108	1,283	1,413	1,407
Bituminous, lignite and anthracite coal	11,12	93	112	127	218	229	248	238
Crude petroleum and natural gas	13	48,917	42,415	42,796	43,871	44,949	48,495	54,463
Nonmetallic minerals, exc. fuels	14	881	810	734	767	839	894	1,035
Manufactured commodities	(X)	407,043	406,550	445,127	490,289	567,052	639,729	680,609
Food and kindred products	20	16,564	16,298	17,445	16,090	17,342	18,326	20,948
Tobacco manufactures	21	94	199	285	467	163	169	245
Textile mill products	22	6,807	7,132	7,808	6,161	6,534	6,965	7,169
Apparel and related products	23	24,644	25,497	30,533	35,475	38,561	41,208	43,075
Lumber and related products	24	5,446	5,229	6,700	8,901	10,528	10,406	12,194
Furniture and fixtures	25	5,235	5,130	5,601	6,242	7,522	8,303	9,320
Paper and allied products	26	11,669	10,431	10,382	10,891	11,772	16,757	14,784
Printing and publishing	27	1,849	1,878	2,046	2,211	2,422	2,902	2,996
Chemicals and allied products	28	21,611	22,999	25,849	27,259	31,697	38,079	42,826
Petroleum and coal products	29	14,472	11,097	10,410	9,906	9,504	8,971	18,768
Rubber and misc. plastics products	30	9,731	9,855	11,287	13,053	14,393	15,973	16,891
Leather and leather products	31	10,944	10,714	11,342	11,692	12,977	13,628	14,187
Stone, clay, and glass products	32	5,845	5,558	5,951	6,431	7,594	8,498	9,088
Primary metal products	33	23,232	22,262	22,891	22,772	30,106	33,519	34,583
Fabricated metal products	34	11,608	11,396	12,436	12,941	14,664	16,213	17,492
Machinery, except electrical	35	55,021	55,578	62,274	73,370	89,705	106,391	112,907
Electric and electronic machinery	36	55,736	58,610	65,596	76,869	94,332	114,912	114,066
Transportation equipment	37	89,599	88,004	92,930	102,259	115,998	122,344	129,235
Instruments and related products	38	16,846	18,668	20,338	22,080	24,410	27,473	28,747
Misc. manufactured commodities	39	20,090	20,015	23,025	25,219	26,830	28,694	31,088

X Not applicable. [1] Standard Industrial Classification. [2] Includes scrap and waste, used or secondhand merchandise, manufactured commodities not identified by kind, and timing adjustments. [3] Includes frozen and packaged fish.

Source: U.S. Bureau of the Census, 1985 and 1988, *Highlights of U.S. Export and Import Trade*, series FT 990; beginning 1990, *U.S. Merchandise Trade*, series FT 900, December issues.

Figure 29.1
Selected Outlying Areas of the United States

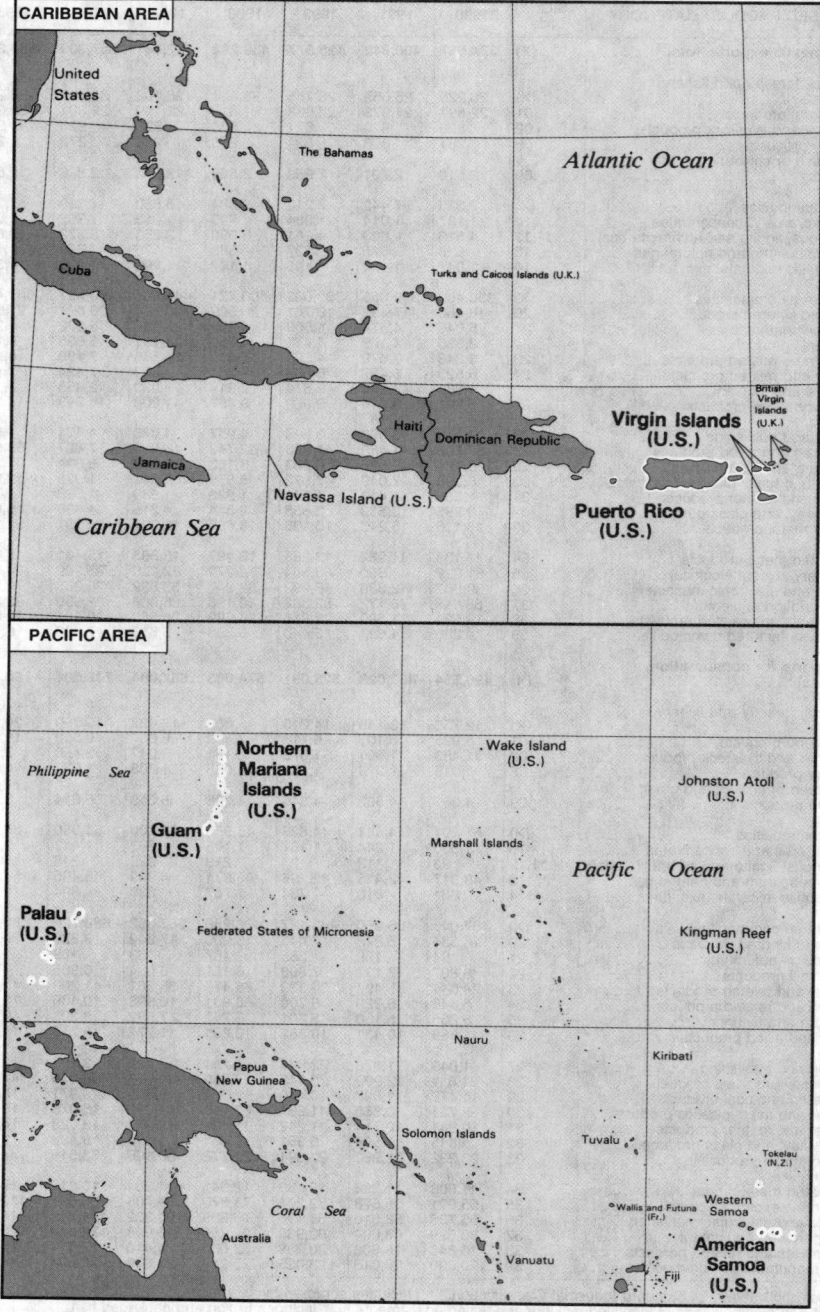

Outlying Areas

This section presents summary economic and social statistics for Puerto Rico, Virgin Islands, Guam, American Samoa, and the Northern Mariana Islands.

Primary sources are the decennial censuses of population and housing, and the censuses of agriculture, business, manufactures, and construction (taken every 5 years) conducted by the Bureau of the Census; the annual *Vital Statistics of the United States,* issued by the National Center for Health Statistics; and the annual *Income and Product* of the Puerto Rico Planning Board, San Juan.

Jurisdiction—The United States gained jurisdiction over these areas as follows:

The islands of *Puerto Rico* and *Guam,* surrendered by Spain to the United States in October 1898, were ceded to the United States by the Treaty of Paris, ratified in 1899. Puerto Rico became a commonwealth on July 25, 1952, thereby achieving a high degree of local autonomy under its own constitution. The *Virgin Islands,* comprising 50 islands and cays, was purchased by the United States from Denmark in 1917. *American Samoa,* a group of seven islands, was acquired by the United States in accordance with a convention among the United States, Great Britain, and Germany, ratified in 1900 (Swains Island was annexed in 1925).

By an agreement approved by the Security Council and the United States, the Northern Mariana Islands, previously under Japanese mandate, was administered by the United States between 1947 and 1986 under the United Nations trusteeship system. The Northern Mariana Islands became a commonwealth in 1986.

Censuses—Because characteristics of the outlying areas differ, the presentation of census data for them is not uniform.

In Brief

Persons per household, 1990:

Puerto Rico	*3.3*
Virgin Islands	*3.1*
Guam	*4.0*
American Samoa	*7.0*
Northern Mariana Islands	*4.6*

The 1960 Census of Population covered all of the places listed above except the Northern Mariana Islands (their census was conducted in April 1958 by the Office of the High Commissioner), while the 1960 Census of Housing also excluded American Samoa. The 1970, 1980, and 1990 Censuses of Population and Housing covered all five areas. Beginning in 1967, Congress authorized the economic censuses, to be taken at 5-year intervals, for years ending in "2" and "7." Prior economic censuses were conducted in Puerto Rico for 1949, 1954, 1958, and 1963 and in Guam and the Virgin Islands for 1958 and 1963. In 1967, the census of construction industries was added for the first time in Puerto Rico; in 1972, Virgin Islands and Guam were covered. For 1982, 1987, and 1992 the economic censuses covered the Northern Mariana Islands.

Information in other sections—In addition to the statistics presented in this section, other data are included as integral parts of many tables showing distribution by states in various sections of the *Abstract.* See "Outlying areas of the United States" in the index. For definition and explanation of terms used, see Section 1, Population; Section 4, Education; Section 23, Agriculture; Section 25, Construction and Housing; Section 26, Manufactures; and Section 27, Domestic Trade and Services.

Outlying Areas

No. 1327. Estimated Resident Population With Projections: 1960 to 2020

[**In thousands.** Population data generally are de facto figures for the present territory. Population estimates were derived from information available as of early 1998. See text, Section 30, for general comments regarding the data. For details of methodology, coverage, and reliability, see source]

AREA	1960	1970	1980	1990	1995	1997	1998	2000, proj.	2010, proj.	2020, proj.
Puerto Rico..............	2,358	2,722	3,210	3,537	3,731	3,827	3,857	3,908	4,087	4,180
American Samoa...........	20	27	32	47	57	60	62	65	81	96
Guam	67	86	107	134	144	146	148	152	178	204
Virgin Islands.............	33	63	98	104	114	117	118	121	132	141
Northern Mariana Island	9	12	17	44	58	64	67	72	99	124

Source: U.S. Bureau of the Census, International Data Base.

No. 1328. Vital Statistics—Specified Areas: 1960 to 1996

[Births, deaths, and infant deaths by place of residence. Rates for 1960, 1970, 1980, and 1990 based on population enumerated as of **April 1;** for other years, on population estimated as of **July 1**]

AREA AND YEAR	BIRTHS		DEATHS		INFANT DEATHS	
	Number	Rate [1]	Number	Rate [1]	Number	Rate [2]
Puerto Rico: 1960	76,314	32.5	15,791	6.7	3,307	43.3
1970.............	67,628	24.8	18,080	6.7	1,930	28.5
1980.............	72,986	22.8	20,413	6.4	1,351	18.5
1990.............	66,417	18.8	25,957	7.3	888	13.4
1995.............	63,425	17.0	30,138	8.1	653	10.3
1996.............	63,108	16.7	28,721	7.6	561	8.9
Guam: 1965	2,523	32.8	336	4.4	82	32.5
1970.............	2,842	28.8	355	5.8	62	21.6
1980.............	2,945	27.8	393	3.7	43	14.6
1990.............	3,839	28.6	520	3.9	31	8.1
1995.............	4,180	29.0	(NA)	(NA)	(NA)	(NA)
1996.............	(NA)	(NA)	(NA)	(NA)	(NA)	(NA)
Virgin Islands: 1960	1,180	36.8	332	10.3	42	35.6
1970.............	2,898	46.8	469	7.9	72	24.8
1980.............	2,504	25.9	504	5.2	61	24.4
1990.............	2,267	21.8	480	4.6	33	14.6
1995.............	2,063	18.1	(NA)	(NA)	(NA)	(NA)
1996.............	(NA)	(NA)	(NA)	(NA)	(NA)	(NA)

NA Not available.   [1] Per 1,000 population.   [2] Per 1,000 live births.

Source: U.S. National Center for Health Statistics, *Vital Statistics of the United States,* annual.

No. 1329. Land Area and Population Characteristics, by Area: 1990

[As of **April 1.** For definition of median, see Guide to Tabular Presentation]

ITEM	United States	Puerto Rico	Virgin Islands	Guam	American Samoa	Northern Mariana Islands
Land area (sq. miles)	3,536,338	3,427	134	210	77	179
Total resident population......	**248,709,873**	**3,522,037**	**101,809**	**133,152**	**46,773**	**43,345**
Per square mile..........	70.3	1,027.9	760.9	634.1	607.4	242.2
Percent increase, 1980-90 ..	9.8	10.2	5.4	25.6	44.8	158.3
Urban	187,053,487	2,508,346	37,885	50,801	15,599	12,151
Rural	61,656,386	1,013,691	63,924	82,351	31,174	31,194
Male	121,239,418	1,705,642	49,210	70,945	24,023	22,802
Female	127,470,455	1,816,395	52,599	62,207	22,750	20,543
Males per 100 females	95.1	93.9	93.6	114.0	105.6	111.0
Median age (years).........	32.9	28.4	28.2	25.0	20.9	27.4
Male (years)	31.7	27.2	27.1	25.2	20.6	29.9
Female (years)	34.1	29.6	29.2	24.9	21.2	24.9
Marital status, persons						
15 years and over	195,142,002	2,563,818	72,365	93,200	28,952	33,030
Never married	52,559,853	711,470	27,539	30,759	11,412	13,810
Married [1]	111,498,578	1,499,449	35,199	54,717	15,958	17,869
Widowed or divorced........	31,083,571	352,899	9,627	7,724	1,582	1,351
Households and families:						
Households	91,947,410	1,054,924	32,020	31,373	6,607	6,873
Persons in households	242,012,129	3,487,567	100,488	124,596	46,267	31,856
Persons per household.....	2.63	3.31	3.14	3.97	7.00	4.63
Families	64,517,947	886,339	23,012	27,313	6,301	5,312
Husband-wife families......	50,708,322	634,872	13,197	21,342	5,153	3,947
Children ever born per						
1,000 females 15 to 44 years ..	1,223	1,512	1,662	1,523	1,757	1,226

[1] For Puerto Rico, includes consensually married couples and for all areas, includes separated couples.

Source: U.S. Bureau of the Census, *1990 Census of Population,* CP-1 and CP-2 parts 1, (United States), 53 (Puerto Rico), 55 (Virgin Islands); *1990 Census of Population and Housing,* CPH-1, parts 53A and 55; CPH-6, parts G (Guam), AS (American Samoa), and CNMI (Commonwealth of the Northern Mariana Islands); and Summary Tape File, parts 3C, (United States), 3A (Puerto Rico), and 3 (Virgin Islands).

No. 1330. Selected Social and Economic Characteristics, by Area: 1990

[As of April 1]

CHARACTERISTIC	United States	Puerto Rico	Virgin Islands	Guam	American Samoa	Northern Mariana Islands
EDUCATIONAL ATTAINMENT						
Persons 25 years and over.........	158,868,436	1,952,297	55,639	66,700	19,570	24,633
Less than 9th grade	16,502,211	691,835	12,908	9,238	3,664	4,285
9th to 12th grade, no diploma.........	22,841,507	290,173	11,278	8,602	5,239	4,016
High school graduate	47,642,763	410,559	14,021	22,220	6,253	8,659
Some college or associate degree.......	39,571,702	281,248	9,011	14,984	3,062	3,818
Bachelor's degree or higher	32,310,253	278,482	8,421	11,656	1,352	3,855
EMPLOYMENT STATUS						
Total persons, 16 years old and over ...	191,829,271	2,497,078	70,323	90,990	27,991	32,522
In labor force....................	125,182,378	1,180,162	47,553	66,138	14,198	26,589
Percent of total	65.3	47.3	67.6	72.7	50.7	81.8
Armed forces....................	1,708,928	5,486	110	11,952	11	8
Civilian labor force	123,473,450	1,174,676	47,443	54,186	14,187	26,581
Employed...................	115,681,202	934,736	44,267	52,144	13,461	25,965
Unemployed...............	7,792,248	239,940	3,176	2,042	726	616
Percent of civilian labor force	6.3	20.4	6.7	3.8	5.1	2.3
Not in labor force	66,646,893	1,316,916	22,770	24,852	13,793	5,933
FAMILY INCOME IN 1989						
Families, census year	65,049,428	889,998	23,012	27,313	6,301	5,312
Percent distribution by income class	100.0	100.0	100.0	100.0	100.0	100.0
Less than $5,000	4.0	25.1	8.8	4.0	11.0	8.2
$5,000 to $9,999	5.6	24.9	9.5	4.7	19.2	13.9
$10,000 to $14,999.............	7.2	16.5	12.8	8.3	17.0	13.1
$15,000 to $24,999.............	16.4	17.5	20.6	21.1	23.6	21.6
$25,000 or more................	66.9	16.0	48.3	61.9	29.1	43.2
Median income (dollars)	35,225	9,988	24,036	31,178	15,979	21,275
RESIDENCE IN 1985						
Persons 5 years and over	230,445,777	3,219,765	92,579	118,055	39,821	39,206
Same house	122,796,970	2,190,479	56,098	54,665	30,759	11,479
Different house in this area	102,540,097	879,691	25,003	24,763	2,763	6,870
Outside area	5,108,710	149,595	11,478	38,627	6,299	20,857
LANGUAGE SPOKEN AT HOME						
Persons 5 years and over	230,445,777	3,219,765	92,579	118,055	39,821	39,206
Speak only English at home...........	198,600,798	(NA)	70,442	44,048	1,203	1,878

NA Not available.

Source: U.S. Bureau of the Census, *1990 Census of Population and Housing*, Summary Tape File, parts 3C, (United States), 3A, and unpublished data, (Puerto Rico), and 3 (Virgin Islands); *1990 Census of Population*, CP-2 parts 1,(United States), 53 (Puerto Rico), 55 (Virgin Islands); CPH-L-98, *The Foreign Born Population in the United States: 1990; 1990 Census of Population and Housing*, CPH-6, parts G (Guam), AS (American Samoa), and CNMI (Commonwealth of the Northern Mariana Islands).

No. 1331. Federal Direct Payments for Individuals: 1990 and 1997

[In thousands of dollars. For fiscal years ending September 30]

SELECTED PROGRAM PAYMENTS	1990				1997			
	Puerto Rico	Guam	Virgin Islands	American Samoa	Puerto Rico	Guam	Virgin Islands	American Samoa
Total	**3,487,697**	**83,199**	**95,396**	**14,615**	**5,800,327**	**191,662**	**149,099**	**24,619**
Pell Grants	240,545	1,260	432	113	295,055	1,458	1,548	250
Medicare: Hospital Insurance [1] .	186,950	2,273	4,977	-	505,971	721	12,684	-
Supplemental medical insurance [1].............	209,525	2,227	3,722	-	580,859	355	6,381	-
Social Security:								
Disability insurance	560,910	1,907	5,692	2,410	952,257	6,417	10,450	5,891
Retirement insurance.......	1,077,133	11,372	31,601	4,330	1,633,467	36,189	52,892	6,687
Survivors insurance	461,999	6,430	11,056	3,873	736,452	18,045	17,002	6,941
Federal workers compensation .	7,342	734	50	85	6,434	894	231	89
Veterans:								
Pension and disability......	280,799	3,578	1,794	1,354	357,976	6,206	1,655	2,588
Education assistance	3,086	178	28	37	5,084	518	116	313
Federal retirement and disability [2]	161,315	34,150	8,326	1,605	193,467	65,947	7,305	1,837
Federal payments for unemployment compensation	129,298	-	4,659	-	303,474	-	4,888	-
Food Stamps	(3)	14,362	18,403	-	(3)	48,606	27,946	-
Housing assistance [4]........	123,848	4,043	3,233	777	196,789	6,104	-	-
Other	44,947	685	1,423	31	33,042	202	6,001	23

- Represents or rounds to zero. [1] Figures have been adjusted proportionately to exclude obligations unpaid as of Sept. 30,1997. [2] Includes retirement and disability payments to former U.S. Postal Service employees. [3] Food stamp program in Puerto Rico was replaced by the Nutritional Assistance Grant Program in 1982. [4] Amounts shown for housing assistance for nonpublic agencies reflects reductions to allow for offsetting amounts included for payments to public agencies. Also includes FEMA .

Source: U.S. Bureau of the Census, *Federal Expenditures by State*, annual.

No. 1332. Public Elementary and Secondary Schools, by Areas: 1996

[For school year ending in year shown, unless otherwise indicated]

ITEM	Puerto Rico	Guam	Virgin Islands	American Samoa	ITEM	Puerto Rico	Guam	Virgin Islands	American Samoa
PUBLIC EL/SEC					School staff	47,199	2,490	2,244	909
Enrollment, fall	627,620	32,960	22,737	14,576	Teachers	39,328	1,802	1,622	728
Elementary (kindergarten-					Other support services staff	21,489	917	1,068	414
grade 8)	460,585	24,877	16,342	11,207	Current expenditures ($1,000) [1]	1,646,313	173,721	135,291	30,372
Secondary (grades 9-12 and post									
graduates)	167,035	8,083	6,395	3,369	HIGHER EDUCATION				
Staff, fall	69,731	3,728	3,421	1,417	Enrollment, fall	170,337	6,010	3,054	1,232
School district staff . .	1,043	321	379	94					

[1] Public elementary and secondary day schools.

Source: U.S. National Center for Education Statistics, *Digest of Education Statistics,* annual, and unpublished data.

No. 1333. Puerto Rico—Summary: 1970 to 1997

ITEM	Unit	1970	1980	1985	1990	1994	1995	1996	1997
POPULATION									
Total [1]	1,000	2,722	3,184	3,378	3,527	3,686	3,719	3,733	3,806
Persons per family	Number. . .	4.6	4.3	3.9	3.7	3.6	3.5	3.5	3.5
EDUCATION [2]									
Enrollment, total.	1,000	922.6	1,090.9	1,107.9	(NA)	(NA)	(NA)	(NA)	(NA)
Public day school	1,000	672.3	716.1	692.9	651.2	631.4	621.4	627.6	618.9
Other public	1,000	103.9	149.5	152.0	(NA)	(NA)	(NA)	(NA)	(NA)
Private schools	1,000	89.1	95.2	102.7	145.8	140.0	145.9	148.0	(NA)
College and university	1,000	57.3	130.1	155.5	156.0	161.7	165.4	168.7	159.3
Expenses	Mil. dol. . .	288.8	825.0	1,171.8	1,686.4	2,251.4	2,555.8	2,787.7	2,846.8
As percent of GNP	Percent . . .	6.2	7.5	7.8	7.8	8.5	9.0	9.1	8.9
P.R. Dept. of Education	Mil. dol. . .	254.6	612.2	810.2	1,054.2	1,467.9	1,689.4	1,903.0	1,910.9
Personal consumption	Mil. dol. . . .	34.2	212.8	361.6	644.2	783.5	866.4	884.7	935.9
LABOR FORCE [3]									
Total [4]	1,000	765	907	985	1,124	1,203	1,219	1,268	1,298
Employed [5]	1,000	686	753	774	963	1,011	1,051	1,092	1,128
Agriculture [6]	1,000	68	38	39	36	34	34	32	31
Manufacturing	1,000	132	143	141	168	166	172	167	162
Trade	1,000	128	138	150	185	201	211	218	228
Government	1,000	106	184	183	222	224	232	246	261
Unemployed	1,000	79	154	211	161	192	168	175	170
Unemployment rate [7]	Rate	10	17	21	14	16	14	14	13
Compensation of employees	Mil. dol. . .	2,800	7,200	9,442	13,639	16,764	17,773	18,990	19,920
Avg. compensation	Dollar	4,082	9,563	12,456	14,854	16,582	16,911	17,390	17,660
Salary and wages	Mil. dol. . .	2,555	6,290	8,137	11,681	14,420	15,300	16,350	17,156
INCOME [8]									
Personal income:									
Current dollars	Mil. dol. . . .	3,753	11,002	14,588	21,105	25,864	27,378	30,122	32,076
Constant (1954) dollars	Mil. dol. . . .	2,654	3,985	4,274	5,551	6,243	6,547	7,119	7,454
Disposable personal income:									
Current dollars	Mil. dol. . . .	3,565	10,403	13,760	19,914	24,248	25,591	28,184	30,020
Constant (1954) dollars	Mil. dol. . . .	2,521	3,768	4,032	5,238	5,853	6,119	6,661	6,977
Average family income:									
Current dollars	Dollar . . .	6,366	14,858	16,914	22,234	25,484	25,881	28,293	29,783
Constant (1954) dollars	Dollar . . .	4,503	5,381	4,957	5,848	6,151	6,177	6,646	6,915
BANKING [9]									
Assets	Mil. dol. . . .	3,322	10,223	21,209	27,902	32,778	39,859	39,671	42,380
TOURISM [8]									
Number of visitors	1,000	1,225.0	2,140.0	2,061.6	3,425.8	4,022.6	4,086.6	4,110.2	4,349.7
Visitor expenditures	Mil. dol. . . .	235.4	618.7	757.7	1,366.4	1,728.3	1,827.6	1,898.3	2,046.3
Average per visitor	Dollar	192	289	368	399	430	447	462	470
Net income from tourism	Mil. dol. . . .	89.8	202.2	223.1	383.3	469.2	498.7	526.8	553.5

NA Not available. [1] 1970, 1980, and 1990 enumerated as of April 1; all other years estimated as of July 1. [2] Enrollment for the first school month. Expenses for school year ending in year shown. Since 1990, does not include all public schools or enrollment. [3] Annual average of monthly figures, for fiscal years. [4] Beginning 1980, for population 16 years old and over; 1970, for population 14 years and over. [5] Includes other employment not shown separately. [6] Includes forestry and fisheries. [7] Percent unemployed of the labor force. [8] For fiscal years. [9] As of June 30. Does not include federal savings banks and international banking entities.

Source: Puerto Rico Planning Board, San Juan, PR, *Income and Product,* annual; and *Socioeconomics Statistics,* annual.

No. 1334. Puerto Rico—Gross Product and Net Income: 1980 to 1997

[In millions of dollars. For fiscal years ending June 30. Data for 1997 are preliminary]

ITEM	1980	1985	1990	1993	1994	1995	1996	1997
Gross domestic product	**11,065**	**15,002**	**21,619**	**25,133**	**26,641**	**28,452**	**30,331**	**32,102**
Agriculture	380	357	434	411	369	318	375	368
Manufacturing	5,306	7,909	12,126	15,428	16,748	17,867	19,040	19,797
Contract construction and mining [1]	369	334	720	874	928	1,006	1,095	1,217
Transportation & other public services [2]	1,279	1,709	2,468	3,009	3,134	3,276	3,557	3,726
Trade	2,273	3,160	4,728	5,303	5,635	5,989	6,290	6,495
Finance, insurance, real estate	1,486	2,547	3,896	4,897	5,246	5,730	5,084	6,522
Services	1,279	1,837	3,015	3,909	4,332	4,724	5,075	5,348
Government	1,897	2,346	3,337	3,881	3,987	4,440	4,841	5,220
Commonwealth	1,574	1,996	2,884	3,327	3,395	3,793	4,122	4,457
Municipalities	323	350	453	555	592	647	719	763
Rest of the world	-3,372	-5,287	-8,985	-11,790	-13,050	-14,195	-15,925	-16,754
Statistical discrepancy	166	91	-121	-789	-689	-703	-846	-591
Domestic net income	**9,007**	**12,182**	**17,941**	**21,185**	**22,041**	**23,653**	**25,266**	**26,534**
Agriculture	435	410	486	469	420	442	474	514
Manufacturing	4,756	7,117	11,277	14,462	15,688	16,685	17,796	18,473
Mining	9	10	26	25	28	30	33	37
Contract construction	337	309	679	805	830	903	985	1,097
Transportation and other public services [2]	1,022	1,248	1,778	2,132	2,193	2,360	2,521	2,620
Trade	1,609	2,285	3,420	3,712	3,875	4,108	4,352	4,546
Finance, insurance, and real estate	1,200	2,141	3,280	4,073	4,294	4,735	5,015	5,346
Services	1,114	1,606	2,643	3,415	3,775	4,146	4,431	4,682
Commonwealth government [3]	1,897	2,346	3,337	3,881	3,987	4,440	4,841	5,220
Rest of the world	-3,372	-5,287	-8,985	-11,790	-13,050	-14,195	-15,181	-16,001

[1] Mining includes only quarries. [2] Includes other public utilities, and radio and television broadcasting. [3] Includes public enterprises not elsewhere classified.

Source: Puerto Rico Planning Board, San Juan, PR, *Economic Report of the Governor, 1996-97.*

No. 1335. Puerto Rico—Transfer Payments: 1985 to 1997

[In millions of dollars. Data represent transfer payments between federal and state governments and other nonresidents. See headnote, Table 1334]

ITEM	1985	1990	1993	1994	1995	1996	1997
Total receipts	**3,531**	**4,871**	**5,478**	**5,957**	**6,236**	**7,033**	**7,660**
Federal government	3,348	4,649	5,279	5,630	5,912	6,748	7,337
Transfers to individuals [1]	3,283	4,577	5,186	5,532	5,838	6,675	7,255
Veterans benefits	317	349	405	414	440	472	484
Medicare	220	368	517	570	661	1,061	1,299
Old age, disability, survivors (social security)	1,581	2,055	2,463	2,722	2,912	3,101	3,282
Nutritional assistance	780	880	975	995	1,063	1,071	1,087
Industry subsidies	65	72	93	98	74	73	82
U.S. state governments	17	18	33	23	18	17	17
Other nonresidents	166	205	166	304	307	268	306
Total payments	**1,180**	**1,801**	**2,089**	**2,211**	**2,301**	**2,348**	**2,387**
Federal government	1,145	1,756	2,021	2,055	2,132	2,268	2,349
Transfers from individuals	508	817	980	1,003	1,052	1,127	1,156
Contribution to Medicare	44	97	122	142	162	167	165
Employee contribution for social security	463	720	856	859	888	958	988
Transfers from industries	13	16	26	32	49	37	47
Unemployment insurance	189	247	208	211	184	191	203
Employer contribution for social security	435	675	807	810	847	914	944
Other nonresidents [2]	35	45	69	155	169	78	39
Net balance	**2,351**	**3,070**	**3,389**	**3,746**	**3,935**	**4,685**	**5,272**
Federal government	2,203	2,893	3,258	3,575	3,780	4,479	4,988
U.S. state governments	14	16	27	16	13	12	13
Other nonresidents	134	162	104	155	143	193	271

[1] Includes other receipts and payments not shown separately. [2] Includes U.S. state governments

Source: Puerto Rico Planning Board, San Juan, PR, *Economic Report of the Governor, 1996-97.*

No. 1336. Puerto Rico—Merchandise Imports and Exports: 1980 to 1997

[In millions of dollars. Imports are imports for consumption; see text, Section 28]

ITEM	1980	1985	1988	1989	1990	1991	1992	1993	1994	1995	1996	1997
Imports	9,018	10,162	13,096	15,010	16,200	15,079	16,476	16,124	17,152	18,969	19,422	21,928
From U.S	5,345	6,130	8,788	10,193	10,792	10,306	11,463	11,179	11,455	12,213	12,220	13,904
From other	3,673	4,032	4,308	4,817	5,408	4,773	5,013	4,945	5,697	6,756	7,202	8,024
Exports	6,576	11,087	14,436	17,455	20,402	21,128	20,455	20,351	22,711	23,573	22,379	26,653
To U.S	5,643	9,873	12,756	15,334	17,915	18,729	17,990	17,613	20,098	20,986	19,907	25,045
To other	933	1,214	1,680	2,121	2,487	2,399	2,465	2,738	2,613	2,587	2,472	1,608

Source: U.S. Bureau of the Census, *Foreign Commerce and Navigation of the United States*, annual; *U.S. Trade with Puerto Rico and U.S. Possessions, FT 895;* and, through 1988, *Highlights of U.S. Export and Import Trade, FT990;* thereafter, *FT920* supplement.

No. 1337. Puerto Rico—Economic Summary, by Industry: 1995

[Covers establishments with payroll. Employees are for the week including March 12. Most government employees are excluded. For statement on methodology, see Appendix III]

INDUSTRY	1987 SIC code [1]	Total establishments	1 to 4	5 to 9	10 to 19	20 to 49	50 or more	Employees [2]	Annual payroll (mil. dol.)
Total [2]	(X)	38,832	23,314	6,304	4,075	3,105	2,034	617,986	9,736.0
Agricultural services, forestry, and fishing	A	95	73	13	5	4	-	389	3.6
Mining	B	32	10	3	9	6	4	866	10.6
Nonmetallic minerals, except fuels	14	23	6	2	7	5	3	666	8.8
Construction [2]	C	1,406	613	232	177	210	174	40,323	494.4
General contractors and operative builders	15	516	196	88	58	91	83	17,209	204.3
Special trade contractors	17	751	377	128	98	88	60	13,820	176.1
Manufacturing [2]	D	1,978	564	225	308	362	519	156,237	3,040.4
Food and kindred products	20	294	91	37	52	59	55	20,825	364.4
Textile mill products	22	23	5	4	1	4	9	2,881	35.0
Apparel and other textile products	23	216	45	15	27	35	94	24,409	246.6
Furniture and fixtures	25	125	49	18	29	22	7	2,027	23.6
Paper and allied products	26	40	3	3	8	10	16	1,967	37.6
Printing and publishing	27	201	105	25	37	21	13	4,615	86.9
Chemicals and allied products	28	187	19	15	20	33	100	32,423	1,007.4
Petroleum and coal products	29	27	5	5	5	5	7	1,293	40.3
Rubber and misc. plastic products	30	80	20	7	12	20	21	4,141	80.2
Leather and leather products	31	22	4	1	1	2	14	6,893	80.7
Stone, clay, and glass products	32	152	42	22	29	44	15	4,450	91.8
Fabricated metal products	34	176	56	24	36	38	22	4,517	67.7
Industrial machinery and equip	35	70	30	7	8	10	15	6,493	128.9
Electronic and other electronic equip	36	91	4	6	9	10	62	19,717	357.4
Instruments and related products	38	59	5	5	3	7	39	11,469	241.6
Transportation and public utilities [2]	E	1,045	635	154	102	84	70	27,752	640.3
Trucking and warehousing	42	301	186	49	30	26	10	3,385	65.0
Water transportation	44	53	16	8	5	12	12	5,600	86.3
Air transportation	45	62	20	10	10	9	13	2,475	49.4
Transportation services	47	412	320	50	24	9	9	2,697	47.3
Communication	48	114	34	20	21	22	17	12,034	363.9
Electric, gas, and sanitary services	49	25	10	1	4	3	7	1,033	19.8
Wholesale trade [2]	F	2,325	997	499	387	290	152	34,764	751.4
Durable goods	50	1,216	523	263	223	158	49	14,751	311.3
Nondurable goods	51	1,090	472	229	161	128	100	19,487	424.1
Retail trade [2]	G	12,366	6,848	2,466	1,533	1,072	447	134,430	1,424.8
Building materials, garden supplies	52	853	538	164	81	56	14	6,157	73.3
General merchandise stores	53	456	159	64	93	66	74	18,307	193.0
Food stores	54	1,736	1,058	256	148	118	156	27,140	233.4
Automotive dealers and service stations	55	2,015	1,317	418	151	94	35	12,744	167.2
Apparel and accessory stores	56	1,814	689	578	376	150	21	15,939	140.0
Furniture and home furnishings	57	864	478	200	131	49	6	5,791	72.5
Eating and drinking places	58	2,391	1,268	322	317	390	94	30,059	296.3
Finance, insurance, and real estate [2]	H	1,860	863	395	294	209	99	38,242	822.5
Depository institutions	60	334	60	72	127	52	23	14,051	333.5
Nondepository institutions	61	402	103	118	77	78	26	9,050	151.9
Insurance carriers	63	74	21	13	6	18	16	4,093	104.1
Insurance agents, brokers, and service	64	228	122	46	22	24	14	3,516	94.1
Real estate	65	745	506	135	58	31	15	6,612	92.6
Services [2]	I	10,422	6,921	1,502	879	634	486	152,447	2,131.8
Personal services	72	766	554	114	64	32	2	3,721	39.2
Business services	73	1,284	642	215	155	119	153	43,078	522.3
Auto repair, services, and parking	75	896	647	142	64	29	14	4,913	65.4
Motion pictures	78	122	55	12	32	21	2	1,492	15.6
Amusement and recreation services	79	246	142	44	20	31	9	3,565	31.2
Health services	80	3,170	2,487	386	143	76	78	33,367	474.2
Legal services	81	1,092	921	79	66	20	6	3,987	79.2
Education services	82	439	105	56	65	110	103	21,449	302.4
Social services	83	313	138	70	46	31	28	5,611	61.5
Membership organizations	86	528	337	75	52	39	25	6,165	68.8
Engineering and management services	87	916	559	179	86	64	28	8,974	201.5

- Represents or rounds to zero.   X Not applicable.   [1] 1987 Standard Industrial Classification (SIC) code; see text, Section 13.   [2] Includes other establishments not shown separately.

Source: U.S. Bureau of the Census, *County Business Patterns*, annual.

No. 1338. Highway Statistics (Most Current Year) for Puerto Rico and the Territories

ITEM	Puerto Rico, 1994	Virgin Islands, 1996	Guam, 1996	American Samoa, 1993	Northern Mariana Islands, 1995
Motor-vehicle registrations:					
Total.	1,661,000	57,135	112,893	5,117	15,133
Automobiles	1,432,000	43,754	79,080	4,628	14,559
Buses	4,000	1,121	858	203	200
Trucks	225,000	12,260	32,955	286	374
Trailers	17,000	158	3,621	52	36
Motorcycles	22,000	226	617	29	57
Driver licenses in force [1]	1,529,000	(NA)	47,928	4,111	11,481
Learner permits issued.	81,000	4,550	6,008	36	3,530
Operator licenses issued	314,000	22,728	36,008	3,644	7,951
Chauffeur licenses issued.	87,000	(NA)	5,692	398	-
Motorcycle licenses issued	-	(NA)	220	-	-
Motor vehicle tax receipts ($1,000)	71,216	1,613	6,277	250	1,028
Registration fees.	61,305	1,314	5,789	219	849
Driver licenses	4,823	299	488	27	179
Motor carriers.	332	(NA)	(NA)	2	-
Other	4,755	(NA)	(NA)	2	-
Motor-fuel consumption: [2]					
Territorial tax rate (cents/gal.)on Dec. 31:					
Gasoline	16	14	11	11.5	10
Diesel and LPG.	8	14	10	11.5	10
Net gallons taxed (1,000)	1,200,751	38,746	90,866	3,150	65,932
At prevailing rates	1,198,377	(NA)	(NA)	3,150	65,932
At other rates	2,374	(NA)	(NA)	-	-
Motor-fuel tax receipts: [2] ($1,000)					
Gross gallonage receipts	170,988	5,425	3,132	61	6,593
Less:					
Refunds paid	799	(NA)	(NA)	116	-
Dedicated gallonage tax	119	(NA)	(NA)	-	-
Other receipts	852	(NA)	(NA)	-	-
Net total receipts.	170,922	5,425	5,363	(-55)	6,593
Highway receipts ($1,000)	650,455	31,422	486	19,497	5,448
Highway-user revenue	290,753	772	(NA)	195	-
General funds	299,974	5,038	(NA)	277	899
FHWA funds	54,204	14,504	54	18,908	3,749
Other federal funds	-	11,108	432	117	800
Highway disbursements ($1,000).	650,455	20,558	17,081	622	5,448
Capital outlay	484,860	14,100	9,631	19	3,749
Maintenance	42,468	952	4,337	422	587
Administration	103,282	6,353	2,627	181	172
Highway law enforcement.	19,845	105	486	-	940

- Represents or rounds to zero.   NA Not available.   [1] For American Samoa, data are licenses in force instead of license issued.   [2] 1996 data for Puerto Rico.

Source: U.S. Federal Highway Administration, *Highway Statistics,* annual.

No. 1339. Guam, Virgin Islands, and Northern Mariana Islands— Economic Summary: 1992

[Sales and payroll in millions of dollars]

ITEM	Guam	Virgin Islands	No. Mariana Islands	ITEM	Guam	Virgin Islands	No. Mariana Islands
Total:				Wholesale trade:			
Establishments	1,955	2,932	1,266	Establishments	154	114	60
Sales.	3,018	2,281	1,132	Sales.	428	414	132
Annual payroll	567	338	161	Annual payroll	32	21	6
Paid employees [1]	33,057	20,968	20,105	Paid employees [1].	1,715	1,030	534
Unpaid family workers [2] . . .	337	330	268	Unpaid family workers [2] . . .	4	1	3
Construction:				Retail trade:			
Establishments	240	147	103	Establishments	886	1,339	616
Sales.	709	169	88	Sales.	1,114	881	384
Annual payroll	178	44	18	Annual payroll	141	120	38
Paid employees [1]	9,131	2,224	3,036	Paid employees [1]	9,565	8,859	4,715
Unpaid family workers [2] . . .	17	3	20	Unpaid family workers [2] . . .	237	239	157
Manufacturing:				Services:			
Establishments	48	78	73	Establishments	627	1,254	414
Sales.	110	134	264	Sales.	656	682	264
Annual payroll	23	23	49	Annual payroll	193	130	51
Paid employees [1]	1,130	1,196	6,267	Paid employees [1]	11,516	7,659	5,553
Unpaid family workers [2] . . .	8	3	4	Unpaid family workers [2] . . .	71	84	84

[1] For pay period including March 12.   [2] Includes those who worked 15 hours or more during the week including March 12.

Source: U.S. Bureau of the Census, *1992 Economic Census of Outlying Areas,* OA92-E-5 to OA92-E-7.

Comparative International Statistics

This section presents statistics for the world as a whole and for many countries on a comparative basis with the United States. Data are shown for population, births and deaths, social and industrial indicators, finances, agriculture, communication, and military affairs.

Statistics of the individual nations may be found primarily in official national publications, generally in the form of yearbooks, issued by most of the nations at various intervals in their own national languages and expressed in their own or customary units of measure. (For a listing of selected publications, see Guide to Sources.) For handier reference, especially for international comparisons, the Statistical Office of the United Nations compiles data as submitted by member countries and issues a number of international summary publications, generally in English and French. Among these are the *Statistical Yearbook;* the *Demographic Yearbook*; the *Yearbook of International Trade Statistics*; the *Yearbook of National Accounts Statistics: Vol. II, International Tables; Population and Vital Statistics Reports* (quarterly); the *Monthly Bulletin of Statistics*; and the *Energy Statistics Yearbook*. Specialized agencies of the United Nations also issue international summary publications on agricultural, labor, health, and education statistics. Among these are the *Production Yearbook* and *Trade Yearbook* issued by the Food and Agriculture Organization, the *Yearbook of Labour Statistics* issued by the International Labour Office, *World Health Statistics* issued by World Health Organization, and the *Statistical Yearbook* issued by the Educational, Scientific, and Cultural Organization.

The Bureau of the Census presents estimates and projections of basic demographic measures for countries and regions of the world in the *World Population Profile* series. The *International Population Reports* (Series IPC, formerly P95) and *International Briefs* (Series IB) also present population figures for many foreign

In Brief

Ten most populous countries in 1998:

	(million persons)
China	1,237
India	984
United States	270
Indonesia	213
Brazil	170
Russia	147
Pakistan	135
Bangladesh	128
Japan	126
Nigeria	111

countries. Detailed population statistics are also available from the Bureau of the Census' International Data Base.

The U.S. Arms Control and Disarmament Agency and the International Monetary Fund (IMF) also compile data on international statistics. In its annual *World Military Expenditures and Arms Transfers*, the Arms Control and Disarmament Agency presents data on various economic indicators, as well as basic military data. Among the topics presented have been military expenditures, gross national product, imports and exports, and armed forces. The IMF publishes a series of reports relating to financial data. These include *International Financial Statistics, Direction of Trade,* and *Balance of Payments Yearbook*, published in English, French, and Spanish.

Statistical coverage, country names, and classifications— Problems of space and availability of data limit the number of countries and the extent of statistical coverage shown. The list of countries included and the spelling of country names are based almost entirely on the list of sovereign nations, dependencies, and areas of special sovereignty provided by the U.S. Department of State.

In recent years, several important changes took place in the status of the world's nations. In 1990, a unified Germany was formed from the Federal Republic of

Germany (West) and the German Democratic Republic (East). The Republic of Yemen was formed by union of the Yemen Arab Republic and the People's Democratic Republic of Yemen. Also in 1990, Namibia, once a United Nations mandate, realized its independence from South Africa.

In 1991, the Soviet Union broke up into 15 independent countries: Armenia, Azerbaijan, Belarus, Estonia, Georgia, Kazakhstan, Kyrgyzstan, Latvia, Lithuania, Moldova, Russia, Tajikistan, Turkmenistan, Ukraine, and Uzbekistan.

In 1992, the Socialist Federal Republic of Yugoslavia dissolved; none of the successor states has been recognized as its continuation. The United States recognizes Bosnia and Herzegovina, Croatia, Slovenia, and The Former Yugoslav Republic of Macedonia as independent countries. Serbia and Montenegro have asserted the formation of a joint independent state, but this entity has not been formally recognized as a state by the United States.

On January 1, 1993, Czechoslovakia was succeeded by two independent countries: the Czech Republic and Slovakia. Eritrea announced its independence from Ethiopia in April 1993, and was subsequently recognized as an independent nation by the United States.

The population estimates and projections used in Tables 1343-1345 were prepared by the Census Bureau. For each country, the data on population, by age and sex, fertility, mortality, and international migration were evaluated and, where necessary, adjusted for inconsistencies and errors in the data. In most instances, comprehensive projections were made by the component method, resulting in distributions of the population by age and sex, and requiring an assessment of probable future trends of fertility, mortality, and international migration.

Economic associations—The Organization for European Economic Cooperation (OEEC), a regional grouping of Western European countries established in 1948 for the purpose of harmonizing national economic policies and conditions, was succeeded on September 30, 1961, by the Organization for Economic Cooperation and Development (OECD). The member nations of the OECD are Australia, Austria, Belgium, Canada, Czech Republic, Denmark, Finland, France, Germany, Greece, Hungary, Iceland, Ireland, Italy, Japan, Luxembourg, Mexico, the Netherlands, New Zealand, Norway, Poland, Portugal, South Korea, Spain, Sweden, Switzerland, Turkey, the United Kingdom, and the United States.

Quality and comparability of the data— The quality and comparability of the data presented here are affected by a number of factors:

(1) The year for which data are presented may not be the same for all subjects for a particular country, or for a given subject for different countries, though the data shown are the most recent available. All such variations have been noted. The data shown are for calendar years except as otherwise specified.

(2) The bases, methods of estimating, methods of data collection, extent of coverage, precision of definition, scope of territory, and margins of error may vary for different items within a particular country, and for like items for different countries.

Footnotes and headnotes to the tables give a few of the major time-period and coverage qualifications attached to the figures; considerably more detail is presented in the source publications. Many of the measures shown are, at best, merely rough indicators of magnitude.

(3) Figures shown in this section for the United States may not always agree with figures shown in the preceding sections. Disagreements may be attributable to the use of differing original sources, a difference in the definition of geographic limits (the 50 states, conterminous United States only, or the United States including certain outlying areas and possessions), or to possible adjustments made in the United States figures by the United Nations or other sources in order to make them more comparable with figures from other countries.

International comparisons of national accounts data—In order to compare national accounts data for different countries, it is necessary to convert each country's data into a common unit of currency, usually the U.S. dollar. The market exchange rates which are often used in converting national currencies do not necessarily reflect the relative purchasing power in the various countries. It is necessary that the goods and services produced in different countries be valued consistently if the differences observed are meant to reflect real differences in the volumes of goods and services produced. The use of purchasing power parities (see Table 1355) instead of exchange rates is intended to achieve this objective.

The method used to present the data shown in Table 1355 is to construct volume measures directly by revaluing the goods and services sold in different countries at a common set of international prices. By dividing the ratio of the gross domestic products of two countries expressed in their own national currencies by the corresponding ratio calculated at constant international prices, it is possible to derive the implied purchasing power parity (PPP) between the two currencies concerned. PPP s show how many units of currency are needed in one country to buy the same amount of goods and services which one unit of currency will buy in the other country. For further information, see *National Accounts, Main Aggregates*, Volume I, issued annually by the Organization for Economic Cooperation and Development, Paris, France.

International Standard Industrial Classification—The original version of the International Standard Industrial Classification of All Economic Activities (ISIC) was adopted in 1948. Wide use has been made both nationally and internationally in classifying data according to kind of economic activity in the fields of production, employment, national income, and other economic statistics. A number of countries have utilized the ISIC as the basis for devising their industrial classification scheme.

Substantial comparability has been attained between the industrial classifications of many other countries, including the United States, and the ISIC by ensuring, as far as practicable, that the categories at detailed levels of classification in national schemes fitted into only one category of the ISIC. For more detail, see Bureau of the Census, The *International Standard Industrial Classification and the U.S. Standard Industrial Classification*, Technical Paper No. 14 and text, Section 27. The United Nations, the International Labour Organisation, the Food and Agriculture Organization, and other international bodies have utilized the ISIC in publishing and analyzing statistical data. Revisions of the ISIC were issued in 1958, 1968, and 1989.

International maps—A series of regional world maps is provided on pages 816 and 820-825. References are included in Table 1343 for easy location of individual countries on the maps. The Robinson map projection is used for this series of maps. A map projection is used to portray all or part of the round earth on a flat surface, but this cannot be done without some distortion. For the Robinson projection, distortion is very low along the equator and within 45 degrees of the center but is greatest near the poles. For additional information on map projections and maps, please contact the Earth Science Information Center, U.S. Geological Survey, 507 National Center, Reston, VA 22092.

Spain
Morocco
Tunisia
Malta
Greece
Cyprus
Lebanon
West Bank
Gaza Strip
Syria
Iraq
Iran
Afghanistan
Western Sahara
Algeria
Libya
Israel
Jordan
Kuwait
Bahrain
Qatar
Saudi Arabia
Egypt
Pakistan
United Arab Emirates
Mauritania
Mali
Niger
Chad
Oman
Yemen
Nigeria
Sudan
Eritrea
Djibouti
Ethiopia
See Inset
Cameroon
Central African Republic
Uganda
Somalia
Sao Tome & Principe
Congo
Rwanda
Kenya
Indian Ocean
Gabon
Democratic Republic of the Congo
Burundi
Equatorial Guinea
Tanzania
Seychelles
Comoros
Mayotte
St. Helena
Angola
Zambia
Malawi
Madagascar
Mauritius
Zimbabwe
Mozambique
Namibia
Botswana
Reunion
Atlantic Ocean
Swaziland
South Africa
Lesotho

Inset
Mauritania
Mali
Niger
Senegal
Burkina Faso
The Gambia
Guinea-Bissau
Guinea
Benin
Nigeria
Sierra Leone
Cote d' Ivoire
Ghana
Liberia
Togo

Nepal   Bhutan   China

Macau   Hong
Kong
Burma   Taiwan

Bangladesh
India

see inset

Pacific Ocean

Marshall Islands

Federated States of Micronesia

Kiribati

Papua New Guinea   Nauru

Solomon Islands   Tuvalu

Vanuatu   Wallis & Futuna

New Caledonia   Fiji

Indian Ocean

Australia

New Zealand

Pacific Ocean

inset

Thailand   Vietnam

Philippines   Mariana Islands

Guam

Cambodia

Trust Ter. of the
Pac. Isl. (Palau)

Brunei

Malaysia
Singapore

Indonesia

Indian Ocean

No. 1340. Total World Population: 1980 to 2050

[As of midyear]

YEAR	Popula-tion (mil.)	AVERAGE ANNUAL [1]		YEAR	Popula-tion (mil.)	AVERAGE ANNUAL [1]		YEAR	Popula-tion (mil.)	AVERAGE ANNUAL [1]	
		Growth rate (per-cent)	Popula-tion change (mil.)			Growth rate (per-cent)	Popula-tion change (mil.)			Growth rate (per-cent)	Popula-tion change (mil.)
1980	4,454	1.69	76.1	1997	5,847	1.34	79.1	2020	7,585	0.91	69.1
1985	4,851	1.69	82.5	1998	5,926	1.32	78.5	2030	8,247	0.76	63.2
1990	5,279	1.56	82.9	2000	6,083	1.27	77.5	2040	8,850	0.62	55.3
1995	5,688	1.39	79.4	2010	6,849	1.11	76.4	2050	9,346	(NA)	(NA)

NA Not available. [1] Represents change from year shown to immediate succeeding year.
Source: U.S. Bureau of the Census, "Total Midyear Population for the World: 1950-2050", published 15 June 1998; <http://www.census.gov/ipc/www/worldpop.html>.

No. 1341. World Summary: 1980 to 1996

[See text, Section 30, for general comments concerning quality of the data]

ITEM	Unit	1980	1985	1990	1991	1992	1993	1994	1995	1996
Agriculture, forestry, fishing:										
Coffee...............	Mil. metric tons.	4.8	5.8	6.1	6.1	6.1	5.6	5.8	5.8	6.2
Cotton (lint)...........	Mil. metric tons.	13.8	17.3	18.5	20.6	18.1	16.7	18.7	20.2	19.7
Tobacco..............	Mil. metric tons.	5.3	7.0	7.0	7.5	8.3	8.4	6.5	6.4	7.3
Roundwood...........	Mil. cubic meters	2,932	3,189	3,498	3,389	3,329	3,335	3,376	3,411	(NA)
Fish catches..........	Mil. metric tons.	72.0	86.3	96.4	96.4	98.8	101.6	109.1	111.5	(NA)
Industrial production:										
Wine................	Mil. metric tons.	35.3	29.5	28.0	27.5	25.8	22.4	22.7	22.4	(NA)
Sugar...............	Mil. metric tons.	84.4	98.5	111.0	112.2	117.7	112.2	109.8	117.0	126.6
Wheat flour [1]	Mil. metric tons.	237.2	267.6	293.1	308.6	315.1	306.9	300.5	(NA)	(NA)
Electricity...........	Bil. kWh.	8,247	9,747	11,788	12,017	12,142	12,420	12,708	13,098	(NA)
Pig iron and ferroalloys..	Mil. metric tons.	542	507	529	501	500	502	523	(NA)	(NA)
Sawnwood...........	Mil. cubic meters	451	468	505	457	437	431	435	427	(NA)
Woodpulp...........	Mil. metric tons.	125.8	141.8	155.1	155.2	152.0	151.2	161.9	161.9	(NA)
Newsprint...........	Mil. metric tons.	25.4	28.3	32.6	32.4	32.3	32.5	33.8	34.7	(NA)
Merchant vessels, launched .	Mil. gross tons.	13.9	17.3	14.7	16.7	20.5	18.7	16.3	(NA)	15.5
External trade:										
Imports, c.i.f...........	Bil. U.S. dollars.	2,047	2,028	3,555	3,539	3,797	3,727	4,245	5,063	5,300
Exports, f.o.b...........	Bil. U.S. dollars.	1,998	1,927	3,425	3,410	3,661	3,652	4,165	4,968	5,161
Civil aviation, kilometers flown [2]	Millions	9,362	10,565	14,350	14,240	15,310	17,072	18,223	19,345	(NA)

NA Not available. [1] Source: U.S. Department of Agriculture, Economic Research Service, World Agriculture-Trends and Indicators. See also Table 1380. [2] Scheduled services of members of International Civil Aviation Organization.
Source: Except as noted, Statistical Division of the United Nations, New York, NY, Monthly Bulletin of Statistics, (copyright).

No. 1342. Religious Population of the World: 1996

[In thousands, except percent. Refers to adherents of all religions as defined and enumerated for each of the world's countries in World Encyclopedia (1982), projected to mid-1996, adjusted for recent data]

RELIGION	Total	Percent distri-bution	Africa	Asia	Latin America	Northern America	Europe [1]	Oceania
Total population...	5,804,120	100.0	748,130	3,513,218	490,444	295,677	727,678	28,973
Christians...........	1,955,229	33.7	360,874	303,127	455,819	255,542	555,614	24,253
Roman Catholics	981,465	16.9	125,376	94,250	408,968	75,398	269,021	8,452
Protestants	404,020	7.0	114,726	45,326	34,816	121,361	79,534	8,257
Orthodox...........	218,350	3.8	25,215	13,970	460	6,390	171,665	650
Anglicans	69,136	1.2	27,200	650	1,089	6,300	28,357	5,540
Other Christians	282,258	4.9	68,357	148,931	10,486	46,093	7,037	1,354
Muslims...........	1,126,325	19.4	308,660	778,362	1,356	5,530	32,032	385
Nonreligious [2]	886,929	15.3	3,567	752,759	16,053	21,315	90,390	2,845
Hindus.............	793,076	13.7	1,986	786,991	760	1,365	1,650	323
Buddhists...........	325,275	5.6	38	321,985	569	920	1,563	200
Atheists	222,195	3.8	440	175,450	3,010	1,850	40,845	600
Chinese folk-religionists [3].	220,971	3.8	13	220,653	68	100	120	17
New-religionists [4]	106,016	1.8	21	103,361	919	900	803	11
Ethnic religionists	102,945	1.8	70,250	30,350	1,042	45	1,150	108
Sikhs.............	19,508	0.3	37	18,465	9	496	494	7
Jews..............	13,866	0.2	165	4,257	1,084	5,836	2,432	92
Spiritists...........	10,293	0.2	5	1,120	8,834	315	18	1
Baha'is.............	6,404	0.1	1,923	3,230	722	357	95	77
Confucians	5,086	0.1	1	5,050	3	27	5	1
Jains	4,920	0.1	59	4,835	5	5	16	1
Shintoists...........	2,898	-	-	2,893	1	2	1	1
Other religionists	1,952	-	90	100	190	1,072	450	50
Parsees............	191	-	2	185	1	1	1	1
Mandeans...........	45	-	-	45	-	-	-	-

- Represents or rounds to zero. [1] Includes Russia. [2] Persons professing no religion, nonbelievers, agnostics, freethinkers, and dereligionized secularists indifferent to all religion. [3] Followers of traditional Chinese religion. [4] Followers of Asiatic 20th-century New Religions, New Religious movements, radical new crisis religions, and non-Christian syncretistic mass religions.
Source: Encyclopaedia Britannica, Inc., Chicago, IL, Britannica Book of the Year. Reprinted with permission from Britannica Book of the Year, 1997 © 1997 Encyclopaedia Britannica, Inc.

No. 1343. Population, by Country: 1980 to 2000

[Population data generally are de facto figures for the present territory. Population estimates were derived from information available as of early 1998. See text, Section 30, for general comments concerning the data. For details of methodology, coverage, and reliability, see source. Minus sign (-) indicates decrease]

COUNTRY OR AREA	Map reference	MID-YEAR POPULATION (1,000)				Population rank, 1998	Annual rate of growth,[1] 1990-2000 (percent)	Population per sq. mile, 1998	Area (sq. mile)
		1980	1990	1998	2000, proj.				
World	S0	4,453,832	5,278,640	5,926,467	6,082,966	(X)	1.4	117	50,627,993
Afghanistan	S5	14,985	14,767	24,792	26,668	39	5.9	99	250,000
Albania	S3	2,699	3,273	3,331	3,401	129	0.4	315	10,579
Algeria	S4	18,862	25,352	30,481	31,788	35	2.3	33	919,591
Andorra	S3	34	53	65	68	203	2.5	372	174
Angola	S4	6,794	8,430	10,865	11,487	68	3.1	23	481,351
Antigua and Barbuda	S1	69	63	64	64	205	0.3	377	170
Argentina	S2	28,237	32,634	36,265	37,215	31	1.3	34	1,056,637
Armenia	S5	3,115	3,366	3,422	3,396	126	0.1	297	11,506
Australia	S6	14,616	17,033	18,613	18,950	52	1.1	6	2,941,285
Austria	S3	7,549	7,718	8,134	8,148	84	0.5	255	31,942
Azerbaijan	S5	6,173	7,200	7,856	7,956	87	1.0	235	33,436
Bahamas, The	S1	210	251	280	288	176	1.3	72	3,888
Bahrain	S4	348	502	616	642	162	2.5	2,579	239
Bangladesh	S5	88,077	110,118	127,567	131,999	8	1.8	2,467	51,703
Barbados	S1	252	255	259	259	178	0.2	1,560	166
Belarus	S3	9,644	10,215	10,409	10,391	71	0.2	130	80,154
Belgium	S3	9,847	9,962	10,175	10,186	74	0.2	872	11,672
Belize	S1	144	190	230	242	181	2.4	26	8,803
Benin	S4	3,444	4,676	6,101	6,517	95	3.3	143	42,710
Bhutan	S5	1,281	1,585	1,908	1,996	144	2.3	105	18,147
Bolivia	S2	5,439	6,620	7,826	8,139	88	2.1	19	418,683
Bosnia and Herzegovina . . .	S3	4,092	4,360	3,366	3,592	128	-1.9	170	19,741
Botswana	S4	903	1,304	1,448	1,479	147	1.3	6	226,012
Brazil	S2	122,936	151,040	169,807	173,791	5	1.4	52	3,265,061
Brunei	S6	185	254	315	331	174	2.6	155	2,035
Bulgaria	S3	8,844	8,966	8,240	8,156	83	-0.9	193	42,683
Burkina Faso	S4	6,939	9,024	11,266	11,892	65	2.8	107	105,714
Burma	S5	33,766	41,068	47,305	48,852	25	1.7	186	253,954
Burundi	S4	4,138	5,285	5,537	5,931	101	1.2	559	9,903
Cambodia	S5	6,499	8,717	11,340	11,919	64	3.1	166	68,154
Cameroon	S4	8,761	11,894	15,029	15,892	59	2.9	83	181,251
Canada	S1	24,593	27,791	30,675	31,330	33	1.2	9	3,560,219
Cape Verde	S1	296	349	400	411	172	1.6	257	1,556
Central African Republic . . .	S4	2,244	2,798	3,376	3,516	127	2.3	14	240,533
Chad	S4	4,507	5,889	7,360	7,760	90	2.8	15	486,178
Chile .[2]	S2	11,094	13,128	14,788	15,155	60	1.4	51	289,112
China[2]	S5	984,736	1,138,895	1,236,915	1,256,168	1	1.0	343	3,600,930
Colombia	S2	26,583	32,985	38,581	40,037	30	1.9	96	401,042
Comoros	S4	334	429	546	581	163	3.0	651	838
Congo (Brazzaville)[3] . . .	S4	1,620	2,206	2,658	2,776	133	2.3	20	131,853
Congo (Kinshasa)[3]	S4	28,129	37,978	49,001	51,988	24	3.1	56	875,521
Costa Rica	S2	2,307	3,022	3,605	3,744	122	2.1	184	19,560
Cote d'Ivoire	S4	8,261	11,904	15,446	16,190	58	3.1	126	122,780
Croatia	S3	4,593	4,754	4,672	4,681	110	-0.2	214	21,829
Cuba	S1	9,653	10,545	11,051	11,139	66	0.5	258	42,803
Cyprus	S5	611	681	749	759	157	1.1	210	3,568
Czech Republic	S3	10,289	10,310	10,286	10,284	72	-	212	48,440
Denmark	S3	5,123	5,141	5,334	5,375	103	0.4	326	16,359
Djibouti	S4	279	370	441	454	166	2.0	52	8,486
Dominica	S1	75	72	66	64	202	-1.2	227	290
Dominican Republic	S1	5,697	6,997	7,999	8,262	85	1.7	428	18,680
Ecuador	S2	8,123	10,308	12,337	12,782	62	2.2	115	106,888
Egypt	S4	42,441	56,106	66,050	68,495	16	2.0	172	384,344
El Salvador	S1	4,527	5,041	5,752	5,925	98	1.6	719	8,000
Equatorial Guinea	S4	256	369	454	478	164	2.6	42	10,830
Eritrea	S4	2,555	2,945	3,842	4,142	119	3.4	82	46,842
Estonia	S3	1,482	1,573	1,421	1,398	148	-1.2	82	17,413
Ethiopia	S4	36,413	48,015	58,390	60,967	21	2.4	135	432,310
Fiji	S6	635	738	803	823	156	1.1	114	7,054
Finland	S3	4,780	4,986	5,149	5,165	106	0.4	44	117,942
France	S3	53,870	56,735	58,805	59,128	20	0.4	279	210,668
Gabon	S4	808	1,078	1,208	1,244	150	1.4	12	99,486
Gambia, The	S4	676	964	1,292	1,381	149	3.6	335	3,861
Georgia	S5	5,048	5,457	5,109	5,034	107	-0.8	190	26,911
Germany	S3	78,298	79,357	82,079	82,081	12	0.3	607	135,236
Ghana	S4	10,880	15,190	18,497	19,272	53	2.4	208	88,811
Greece	S3	9,643	10,123	10,662	10,751	69	0.6	211	50,502
Grenada	S2	90	94	96	98	195	0.4	735	131
Guatemala	S1	7,232	9,631	12,008	12,670	63	2.7	287	41,865
Guinea	S4	4,320	5,936	7,477	7,611	89	2.5	79	94,927
Guinea-Bissau	S4	789	998	1,206	1,263	151	2.4	112	10,811
Guyana	S2	759	748	708	703	158	-0.6	9	76,004
Haiti	S1	5,056	6,048	6,781	6,992	93	1.4	637	10,641
Honduras	S1	3,625	4,740	5,862	6,130	97	2.6	136	43,201
Hungary	S3	10,711	10,352	10,208	10,167	73	-0.2	286	35,653
Iceland	S1	228	255	271	274	177	0.7	7	38,707
India	S5	690,462	850,558	984,004	1,017,645	2	1.8	857	1,147,950
Indonesia	S6	154,936	187,728	212,942	219,267	4	1.6	302	705,189
Iran	S5	39,274	56,946	68,960	71,879	15	2.3	109	631,660

See footnotes at end of table.

No. 1343. Population, by Country: 1980 to 2000—Continued

[See headnote, page 827]

COUNTRY OR AREA	Map refer-ence	MID-YEAR POPULATION (1,000)				Popu-lation rank, 1998	Annual rate of growth, [1] 1990-2000 (percent)	Popula-tion per sq. mile, 1998	Area (sq. mile)
		1980	1990	1998	2000, proj.				
Iraq	S5	13,233	18,135	21,722	23,151	46	2.4	130	167,556
Ireland	S3	3,401	3,508	3,619	3,647	121	0.4	136	26,598
Israel	S4	3,737	4,512	5,644	5,852	100	2.6	719	7,849
Italy	S3	56,451	56,761	56,783	56,687	22	0.0	500	113,521
Jamaica	S1	2,229	2,466	2,635	2,669	134	0.8	630	4,181
Japan	S5	116,807	123,537	125,932	126,434	9	0.2	826	152,411
Jordan	S4	2,168	3,277	4,435	4,701	115	3.6	125	35,344
Kazakhstan	S5	14,994	16,708	16,847	16,816	54	0.1	16	1,049,150
Kenya	S4	16,685	23,674	28,337	29,251	37	2.1	129	219,788
Kiribati	S6	58	72	84	87	197	1.9	303	277
Korea, North	S5	17,114	20,019	21,234	21,688	47	0.8	457	46,490
Korea, South	S5	38,124	42,869	46,417	47,351	26	1.0	1,224	37,911
Kuwait	S5	1,370	2,131	1,913	2,068	143	-0.3	278	6,880
Kyrgyzstan	S5	3,623	4,390	4,522	4,584	113	0.4	59	76,641
Laos	S5	3,293	4,191	5,261	5,557	105	2.8	59	89,112
Latvia	S3	2,525	2,672	2,385	2,327	137	-1.4	96	24,903
Lebanon	S4	3,075	3,130	3,506	3,620	124	1.5	888	3,950
Lesotho	S4	1,346	1,744	2,090	2,167	140	2.2	178	11,718
Liberia	S4	1,900	2,265	2,772	3,090	131	3.1	75	37,189
Libya	S4	3,119	4,338	5,691	6,122	99	3.4	8	679,359
Liechtenstein	S3	25	29	32	32	214	1.2	510	62
Lithuania	S5	3,436	3,702	3,600	3,572	123	-0.4	143	25,174
Luxembourg	S3	364	382	425	433	169	1.2	426	998
Macedonia, The Former Yugoslav Republic of	S3	1,893	2,031	2,009	2,035	141	0.0	202	9,928
Madagascar	S4	8,678	11,525	14,463	15,295	61	2.8	64	224,533
Malawi	S4	6,129	9,139	9,840	10,154	77	1.1	271	36,324
Malaysia	S6	13,764	17,507	20,933	21,820	48	2.2	165	126,853
Maldives	S5	154	218	290	310	175	3.5	2,505	116
Mali	S4	6,731	8,231	10,109	10,751	75	2.7	21	471,042
Malta	S4	364	354	380	383	173	0.8	3,063	124
Marshall Islands	S6	31	46	63	68	206	3.9	902	70
Mauritania	S4	1,550	1,979	2,511	2,660	136	3.0	6	397,838
Mauritius	S4	964	1,074	1,168	1,196	152	1.1	1,636	714
Mexico	S1	68,686	84,748	98,553	102,027	11	1.9	133	742,486
Micronesia, Federated States of	S6	77	109	130	133	191	2.0	478	271
Moldova	S5	3,996	4,398	4,458	4,467	114	0.2	343	13,012
Monaco	S3	27	30	32	32	213	0.7	41,485	1
Mongolia [4]	S5	1,662	2,216	2,579	2,655	135	1.8	4	604,247
Montenegro [4]	S3	579	616	680	681	161	1.0	127	5,333
Morocco	S4	19,487	24,685	29,114	30,205	36	2.0	169	172,317
Mozambique	S4	12,103	14,056	18,641	19,614	51	3.3	62	302,737
Namibia	S4	975	1,409	1,622	1,674	145	1.7	5	317,873
Nauru	S6	8	9	11	11	224	1.3	1,295	8
Nepal	S5	15,016	19,333	23,698	24,920	41	2.5	449	52,819
Netherlands	S3	14,144	14,952	15,731	15,878	57	0.6	1,200	13,104
New Zealand	S6	3,113	3,299	3,625	3,698	120	1.1	35	103,734
Nicaragua	S2	2,776	3,591	4,583	4,851	112	3.0	99	46,430
Niger	S4	5,629	7,644	9,672	10,260	79	2.9	20	489,073
Nigeria	S4	65,699	86,530	110,532	117,171	10	3.0	314	351,649
Norway	S3	4,086	4,242	4,420	4,456	116	0.5	37	118,865
Oman	S5	1,175	1,773	2,364	2,533	138	3.6	29	82,031
Pakistan	S5	85,219	113,914	135,135	141,145	7	2.1	449	300,664
Palau	S6	13	15	18	19	219	2.1	102	177
Panama	S2	1,956	2,388	2,736	2,821	132	1.7	93	29,340
Papua New Guinea	S6	2,991	3,823	4,600	4,812	111	2.3	26	174,405
Paraguay	S2	3,193	4,236	5,291	5,580	104	2.8	34	153,398
Peru	S2	17,295	21,989	26,111	27,136	38	2.1	53	494,208
Philippines	S6	51,092	65,037	77,726	80,961	13	2.2	675	115,124
Poland	S3	35,578	38,109	38,607	38,644	29	0.1	328	117,571
Portugal	S3	9,778	9,871	9,928	9,902	76	-	281	35,382
Qatar	S5	231	482	697	750	160	4.4	164	4,247
Romania	S5	22,109	22,775	22,396	22,291	43	-0.2	252	88,934
Russia	S5	139,045	148,088	146,861	145,905	6	-0.1	22	6,592,817
Rwanda	S4	5,170	7,161	7,956	8,337	86	1.5	826	9,633
Saint Kitts and Nevis	S1	44	40	42	43	210	0.8	304	139
Saint Lucia	S1	122	140	152	156	187	1.1	646	236
Saint Vincent and the Grenadines	S1	98	113	120	121	192	0.7	915	131
San Marino	S3	21	23	25	25	216	0.9	1,075	23
Sao Tome and Principe	S4	94	119	150	160	188	2.9	405	371
Saudi Arabia	S4	9,949	15,871	20,786	22,246	49	3.4	25	829,996
Senegal	S4	5,640	7,408	9,723	10,390	78	3.4	131	74,131
Serbia [4]	S3	9,262	9,705	10,526	10,530	70	0.8	309	34,116
Seychelles	S4	66	73	79	80	198	0.8	447	176
Sierra Leone	S4	3,333	4,283	5,080	5,509	108	2.5	184	27,653
Singapore	S6	2,414	3,039	3,490	3,572	125	1.6	14,487	241
Slovakia	S3	4,966	5,263	5,393	5,401	102	0.3	111	48,440
Slovenia	S3	1,885	1,969	1,972	1,970	142	-	252	7,819
Solomon Islands	S6	233	336	441	470	165	3.4	41	10,633
Somalia	S4	5,791	6,675	6,842	7,434	92	1.1	28	242,216

See footnotes at end of table.

No. 1343. Population, by Country: 1980 to 2000—Continued

[See headnote, page 827]

COUNTRY OR AREA	Map reference	MID-YEAR POPULATION (1,000)				Population rank, 1998	Annual rate of growth,[1] 1990-2000 (percent)	Population per sq. mile, 1998	Area (sq. mile)
		1980	1990	1998	2000, proj.				
South Africa	S4	29,252	37,191	42,835	43,982	27	1.7	91	471,444
Spain	S3	37,488	38,793	39,134	39,208	28	0.1	203	192,819
Sri Lanka	S5	14,900	17,193	18,934	19,355	50	1.2	757	24,996
Sudan	S4	19,064	26,628	33,551	35,530	32	2.9	37	917,375
Suriname	S2	355	396	428	434	168	0.9	7	62,344
Swaziland	S4	607	840	966	1,004	155	1.8	146	6,641
Sweden	S3	8,310	8,559	8,887	8,939	82	0.4	56	158,927
Switzerland	S3	6,385	6,844	7,260	7,289	91	0.6	473	15,355
Syria[2]	S4	8,774	12,620	16,673	17,759	55	3.4	235	71,062
Taiwan[2]	S5	17,848	20,279	21,908	22,319	45	1.0	1,759	12,456
Tajikistan	S5	3,969	5,332	6,020	6,194	96	1.5	109	55,251
Tanzania	S4	18,690	24,886	30,609	31,963	34	2.5	89	342,100
Thailand	S5	47,026	55,052	60,037	61,164	18	1.1	304	197,595
Togo	S4	2,596	3,680	4,906	5,263	109	3.6	234	21,000
Tonga	S0	93	101	108	110	194	0.8	391	277
Trinidad and Tobago	S2	1,091	1,198	1,117	1,087	153	-1.0	564	1,981
Tunisia	S4	6,443	8,207	9,380	9,645	81	1.6	156	59,985
Turkey	S5	45,121	56,123	64,567	66,618	17	1.7	217	297,591
Turkmenistan	S5	2,875	3,668	4,298	4,436	117	1.9	23	188,456
Tuvalu	S6	7	9	10	11	225	1.6	1,040	10
Uganda	S4	12,298	17,227	22,167	23,452	44	3.1	287	77,108
Ukraine	S5	50,047	51,600	50,125	49,507	23	-0.4	215	233,089
United Arab Emirates	S5	1,000	1,952	2,303	2,386	139	2.0	71	32,278
United Kingdom	S3	56,314	57,507	58,970	59,247	19	0.3	632	93,278
United States	S1	227,726	249,949	270,312	274,943	3	1.0	76	3,539,227
Uruguay	S2	2,920	3,106	3,285	3,333	130	0.7	49	67,035
Uzbekistan	S5	16,000	20,624	23,784	24,423	40	1.7	138	172,741
Vanuatu	S6	117	154	185	193	185	2.2	32	5,699
Venezuela	S2	14,768	19,325	22,803	23,596	42	2.0	67	340,560
Vietnam	S5	53,661	66,314	76,236	78,350	14	1.7	607	125,622
Western Samoa	S0	155	186	225	235	182	2.3	204	1,100
Yemen	S5	8,527	12,023	16,388	17,521	56	3.8	80	203,849
Zambia	S4	5,638	7,957	9,461	9,872	80	2.2	33	285,992
Zimbabwe	S4	7,298	9,958	11,044	11,272	67	1.2	74	149,293
AREAS OF SPECIAL SOVEREIGNTY AND DEPENDENCIES									
American Samoa	S0	32	47	62	65	207	3.3	808	77
Anguilla	S1	7	8	11	12	223	3.5	317	35
Aruba	S1	60	67	68	69	200	0.4	917	75
Bermuda	S1	55	58	62	63	208	0.9	3,278	19
Cayman Islands	S1	17	27	38	41	212	4.3	376	100
Cook Islands	S0	18	18	20	20	217	1.1	215	93
Faroe Islands	S3	43	47	42	40	211	-1.7	77	541
French Guiana	S2	68	116	163	173	186	4.0	5	34,421
French Polynesia	S0	151	201	238	246	179	2.0	168	1,413
Gaza Strip[5]	S4	453	635	1,054	1,163	154	6.0	7,166	147
Gibraltar	S3	29	31	29	29	215	-0.6	12,538	2
Greenland	S1	50	56	59	60	209	0.8	(Z)	131,931
Guadeloupe	S1	337	378	416	425	170	1.2	612	680
Guam	S6	107	134	148	152	189	1.3	709	209
Guernsey	S3	53	61	65	66	204	0.8	862	75
Hong Kong	S5	5,063	5,688	6,707	6,967	94	2.0	17,564	382
Jersey	S3	76	84	89	90	196	0.8	1,973	45
Macau	S6	256	352	429	445	167	2.4	69,469	6
Man, Isle of	S3	64	69	75	76	199	1.0	331	227
Martinique	S1	339	374	407	416	171	1.1	996	409
Mayotte	S4	52	90	142	157	190	5.6	978	145
Montserrat	S1	12	13	13	13	222	0.3	332	39
Netherlands Antilles	S2	173	189	206	210	183	1.1	554	371
New Caledonia	S6	139	168	194	200	184	1.7	27	7,243
Northern Mariana Islands	S6	17	44	67	72	201	4.9	361	184
Puerto Rico	S1	3,210	3,537	3,857	3,908	118	1.0	1,115	3,459
Reunion	S4	507	600	705	730	159	2.0	731	965
Saint Helena	S4	6	7	7	7	226	0.8	45	158
Saint Pierre and Miquelon	S1	6	6	7	7	227	0.8	74	93
Turks and Caicos Islands	S1	7	12	16	17	220	4.2	98	166
Virgin Islands	S1	100	104	118	121	193	1.5	875	135
Virgin Islands, British	S1	11	16	19	20	218	2.2	323	58
Wallis and Futuna	S6	11	14	15	-15	221	1.1	142	106
West Bank[5]	S4	833	1,080	1,557	1,662	146	4.3	715	2,178
Western Sahara	S4	126	191	234	245	180	2.5	2	102,703

- Represents or rounds to zero. X Not applicable. Z Less than one person per square mile. [1] Computed by the exponential method. For explanation of average annual percent change, see Guide to Tabular Presentation. [2] With the establishment of diplomatic relations with China on January 1, 1979, the U.S. government recognized the People's Republic of China as the sole legal government of China and acknowledged the Chinese position that there is only one China and that Taiwan is part of China. [3] "Congo" is the official short-form name for both the Republic of Congo and the Democratic Republic of the Congo. To distinguish one from the other the U.S. Dept. of State adds the capital in parentheses. This practice is unofficial and provisional. [4] The U.S. view is that the Socialist Federal Republic of Yugoslavia has dissolved and no successor state represents its continuation. Serbia and Montenegro have asserted the formation of a joint independent state, but this entity has not been recognized by the United States. [5] The Gaza Strip and West Bank are Israeli occupied with interim status subject to Israeli/Palestinian negotiations. The final status is to be determined.

Source: U.S. Bureau of the Census, unpublished data from the International Data Base.

No. 1344. Age Distribution, by Country: 1998 and 2000

[In percent. Covers countries with 10 million or more population in 1998]

COUNTRY OR AREA	1998 Under 15 years old	1998 65 years old and over	2000, proj. Under 15 years old	2000, proj. 65 years old and over	COUNTRY OR AREA	1998 Under 15 years old	1998 65 years old and over	2000, proj. Under 15 years old	2000, proj. 65 years old and over
World	30.7	6.8	30.1	6.9	Kenya	43.6	2.7	42.1	2.8
Afghanistan	42.9	2.7	42.7	2.8	Korea, North	25.8	6.0	25.6	6.5
Algeria	38.2	3.8	36.4	3.9	Korea, South	22.4	6.4	21.9	6.9
Angola	44.9	2.7	44.9	2.8	Madagascar	44.7	3.3	44.5	3.3
Argentina	27.5	10.2	27.3	10.3	Malaysia	35.7	3.9	35.0	4.1
Australia	21.2	12.4	20.8	12.6	Mali	47.4	3.2	47.4	3.1
Bangladesh	37.4	3.2	36.0	3.3	Mexico	35.6	4.1	34.8	4.3
Belarus	20.0	13.4	18.8	13.6	Morocco	36.4	4.5	35.2	4.6
Belgium	17.3	16.8	17.0	17.1	Mozambique	44.9	2.3	44.7	2.3
Brazil	30.2	5.1	29.4	5.3	Nepal	41.6	3.3	41.1	3.4
Burkina Faso	48.0	3.0	47.9	2.9	Netherlands	18.3	13.5	18.2	13.7
Burma	36.5	4.2	36.0	4.2	Nigeria	44.8	2.9	44.8	3.0
Cambodia	45.4	3.0	45.0	3.0	Pakistan	41.8	4.0	40.9	4.1
Cameroon	45.9	3.3	45.8	3.3	Peru	35.7	4.5	35.1	4.7
Canada	19.8	12.5	19.3	12.6	Philippines	37.6	3.6	37.0	3.6
Chile [1]	28.3	7.0	27.6	7.2	Poland	20.6	11.8	19.2	12.2
China [1]	25.8	6.6	25.1	7.0	Romania	19.0	13.0	18.1	13.5
Colombia	33.2	4.5	32.7	4.6	Russia	19.7	12.5	18.4	12.6
Congo (Kinshasa) [2]	48.2	2.6	48.2	2.6	Saudi Arabia	43.0	2.4	42.9	2.6
Cote d'Ivoire	46.7	2.2	46.4	2.2	Serbia [3]	20.6	12.7	19.9	13.5
Cuba	22.0	9.5	21.4	9.7	South Africa	34.7	4.5	34.1	4.6
Czech Republic	17.2	13.7	16.6	13.8	Spain	15.2	16.3	14.8	16.8
Ecuador	35.9	4.4	34.5	4.5	Sri Lanka	27.6	6.3	26.6	6.5
Egypt	36.1	3.7	35.2	3.7	Sudan	45.4	2.2	44.8	2.3
Ethiopia	46.0	2.8	46.3	2.8	Syria	46.1	2.9	45.3	2.9
France	18.9	15.8	18.5	16.1	Taiwan [1]	22.4	8.2	21.6	8.6
Germany	15.6	15.9	15.2	16.5	Tanzania	44.6	2.9	44.3	2.9
Ghana	42.9	3.1	41.7	3.2	Thailand	24.3	6.0	23.5	6.5
Greece	16.1	16.5	15.6	17.2	Turkey	30.9	5.7	29.9	6.0
Guatemala	42.9	3.5	42.5	3.6	Uganda	51.1	2.2	51.2	2.2
Hungary	17.5	14.4	17.3	14.6	Ukraine	19.0	14.0	17.9	13.9
India	34.5	4.6	33.7	4.7	United Kingdom	19.3	15.7	19.1	15.7
Indonesia	30.8	4.0	30.1	4.3	United States	21.6	12.7	21.4	12.6
Iran	43.3	4.1	41.7	4.2	Uzbekistan	38.0	4.7	36.3	4.7
Iraq	44.1	3.2	43.4	3.1	Venezuela	33.8	4.5	32.8	4.6
Italy	14.4	17.6	14.2	18.2	Vietnam	34.6	5.3	32.7	5.4
Japan	15.2	16.0	14.9	17.0	Yemen	48.1	3.3	47.5	3.1
Kazakhstan	29.1	7.0	27.8	7.0	Zimbabwe	43.8	2.6	42.6	2.7

[1] See footnote 2, Table 1343.   [2] See footnote 3, Table 1343.   [3] See footnote 4, Table 1343.

Source: U.S. Bureau of the Census, unpublished data from the International Data Base.

No. 1345. Vital Statistics, by Country: 1998 and 2000

[Covers countries with 6 million or more population in 1998]

COUNTRY OR AREA	CRUDE BIRTH RATE [1] 1998	CRUDE BIRTH RATE [1] 2000, proj.	CRUDE DEATH RATE [2] 1998	CRUDE DEATH RATE [2] 2000, proj.	EXPECTATION OF LIFE AT BIRTH (years) 1998	EXPECTATION OF LIFE AT BIRTH (years) 2000, proj.	INFANT MORTALITY RATE [3] 1998	INFANT MORTALITY RATE [3] 2000, proj.	TOTAL FERTILITY RATE [4] 1998	TOTAL FERTILITY RATE [4] 2000, proj.
United States	14.4	14.2	8.8	8.8	76.1	76.3	6.4	6.7	2.07	2.07
Afghanistan	42.4	41.6	17.4	16.6	46.8	47.8	143.6	137.5	6.01	5.87
Algeria	27.5	26.5	5.6	5.4	68.9	69.6	45.4	42.2	3.38	3.16
Angola	43.6	42.6	16.8	15.9	47.9	48.9	132.4	125.9	6.20	6.05
Argentina	20.0	19.9	7.7	7.6	74.5	75.0	19.0	17.8	2.68	2.64
Australia	13.5	13.0	6.9	6.9	79.9	80.4	5.3	5.0	1.82	1.80
Austria	9.9	9.4	10.1	10.0	77.3	77.6	5.2	5.0	1.37	1.37
Azerbaijan	22.2	21.1	9.4	9.6	63.3	62.9	81.6	83.4	2.72	2.62
Bangladesh	28.9	27.2	10.6	10.1	56.7	57.5	97.7	93.0	3.32	3.08
Belarus	9.7	9.7	13.5	13.9	68.3	68.0	14.2	14.6	1.34	1.31
Belgium	10.2	9.7	10.4	10.5	77.4	77.7	6.3	6.1	1.49	1.48
Benin	45.8	44.9	12.8	12.0	53.6	54.6	100.2	95.3	6.48	6.32
Bolivia	31.4	30.0	9.9	9.3	60.9	62.0	63.9	60.2	4.05	3.81
Brazil	20.9	19.9	8.5	9.1	64.4	63.8	37.0	33.8	2.33	2.23
Bulgaria	8.1	9.3	13.2	13.2	72.0	72.6	12.8	12.0	1.14	1.32
Burkina Faso	46.2	45.5	17.7	17.5	46.1	45.7	109.2	105.2	6.64	6.48
Burma	29.0	28.0	12.5	12.3	54.5	55.0	78.4	74.2	3.70	3.57
Cambodia	41.6	40.8	16.5	15.9	48.0	48.5	106.8	103.4	5.81	5.81
Cameroon	42.1	41.6	14.0	13.9	51.4	51.2	76.9	74.5	5.86	5.73
Canada	12.1	11.6	7.3	7.3	79.2	79.6	5.6	5.4	1.65	1.64
Chad	43.5	42.8	16.9	16.3	48.2	48.9	117.0	113.6	5.74	5.64
Chile	18.3	17.4	5.6	5.5	75.2	75.8	10.4	9.6	2.30	2.21
China [5]	15.7	14.6	7.0	7.0	69.6	70.3	45.5	41.1	1.80	1.79
Colombia	24.9	24.0	5.7	5.5	70.1	70.9	25.4	23.2	2.90	2.85

See footnotes at end of table.

No. 1345. Vital Statistics, by Country: 1998 and 2000—Continued

[See headnote, page 830]

COUNTRY OR AREA	CRUDE BIRTH RATE [1]		CRUDE DEATH RATE [2]		EXPECTATION OF LIFE AT BIRTH (years)		INFANT MORTALITY RATE [3]		TOTAL FERTILITY RATE [4]	
	1998	2000, proj.	1998	2000, proj.	1998	2000, proj.	1998	2000, proj.	1998	2000, proj.
Congo (Kinshasa) [6]	46.8	46.0	15.2	14.8	49.3	49.6	101.6	97.3	6.51	6.39
Cote d'Ivoire	42.2	41.4	16.1	16.2	46.2	45.9	96.0	92.4	5.97	5.80
Cuba	13.1	12.7	7.4	7.4	75.6	75.9	7.9	7.7	1.57	1.60
Czech Republic	9.0	10.7	10.9	10.8	74.1	74.6	6.8	6.6	1.17	1.39
Dominican Republic	26.4	25.5	5.7	5.6	69.7	70.4	44.3	40.8	3.06	3.00
Ecuador	23.2	21.4	5.2	5.0	71.8	72.5	32.1	29.3	2.75	2.51
Egypt	27.3	26.3	8.4	8.1	62.1	62.7	69.2	65.7	3.41	3.24
Ethiopia	44.7	44.0	21.3	21.6	40.9	40.1	125.7	123.5	6.88	6.75
France	11.7	11.1	9.1	9.2	78.5	78.8	5.7	5.6	1.63	1.58
Germany	8.8	8.5	10.8	10.8	77.0	77.3	5.2	5.1	1.25	1.27
Ghana	32.8	30.8	10.6	10.2	56.8	57.5	77.5	74.8	4.27	3.95
Greece	9.7	9.4	9.4	9.5	78.3	78.6	7.3	7.0	1.31	1.29
Guatemala	36.0	35.1	7.0	6.6	66.0	66.9	47.7	44.6	4.81	4.66
Guinea	41.3	40.0	17.8	16.9	46.0	47.0	128.9	123.7	5.59	5.46
Haiti	32.8	32.3	14.2	13.8	51.4	51.9	99.0	96.3	4.67	4.50
Hong Kong	12.9	12.9	5.9	6.1	78.8	79.0	5.2	5.2	1.36	1.42
Hungary	10.7	10.9	13.5	13.1	70.8	71.5	9.7	9.2	1.45	1.45
India	25.9	24.9	8.7	8.3	62.9	63.9	63.1	58.5	3.24	3.11
Indonesia	23.1	22.4	8.2	8.1	62.5	63.4	59.2	55.4	2.61	2.53
Iran	31.4	29.2	6.2	5.8	68.3	69.1	49.0	45.1	4.31	3.90
Iraq	38.6	38.2	6.6	6.6	66.5	66.5	62.4	62.4	5.23	5.01
Italy	9.1	9.4	10.2	10.4	78.4	78.6	6.4	6.2	1.19	1.25
Japan	10.3	10.6	7.9	8.3	80.0	80.2	4.1	4.1	1.46	1.50
Kazakhstan	17.2	17.1	10.2	10.5	63.6	63.2	58.3	59.4	2.12	2.07
Kenya	31.7	29.9	14.2	15.0	47.6	46.5	59.4	58.8	4.07	3.69
Korea, North	15.3	20.4	15.6	6.9	51.3	70.7	87.8	24.3	1.60	2.30
Korea, South	16.1	15.8	5.7	5.7	74.0	74.7	7.8	7.4	1.79	1.80
Madagascar	41.9	41.2	13.8	13.3	52.9	53.6	90.6	87.6	5.76	5.64
Malawi	40.2	38.9	23.7	24.0	36.6	36.0	133.8	130.5	5.62	5.33
Malaysia	26.5	25.6	5.4	5.2	70.4	71.0	22.5	20.9	3.37	3.32
Mali	49.9	49.1	19.0	18.1	47.0	48.0	121.7	117.2	7.02	6.89
Mexico	25.5	24.5	4.9	4.8	71.6	72.4	25.8	23.4	2.91	2.79
Morocco	26.4	25.2	6.2	6.0	68.5	69.2	53.0	48.9	3.35	3.13
Mozambique	43.5	42.0	17.8	16.8	45.4	46.4	120.3	114.9	6.00	5.76
Nepal	35.7	35.0	10.4	9.9	57.9	59.0	76.0	71.2	4.87	4.68
Netherlands	11.6	11.1	8.7	8.7	78.0	78.3	5.2	5.1	1.49	1.48
Niger	53.0	51.6	23.4	22.2	41.5	42.4	114.4	111.2	7.30	7.17
Nigeria	42.2	41.4	13.0	13.0	53.6	53.1	70.7	68.2	6.09	5.95
Pakistan	34.4	32.6	10.7	10.2	59.1	59.7	93.5	90.3	4.91	4.56
Peru	26.7	25.5	5.8	5.6	70.0	70.8	43.4	39.4	3.31	3.14
Philippines	28.4	27.3	6.5	6.4	66.4	66.8	34.6	33.2	3.54	3.38
Poland	9.8	11.5	9.8	9.7	72.8	73.3	13.2	12.4	1.36	1.54
Portugal	10.6	10.3	10.3	10.3	75.7	76.1	6.9	6.6	1.35	1.32
Romania	9.3	10.9	11.6	11.5	70.5	71.2	18.8	17.5	1.17	1.36
Russia	9.6	9.7	14.9	15.0	65.0	65.3	23.3	22.7	1.34	1.33
Rwanda	39.0	38.9	19.0	20.0	41.9	40.7	113.3	112.4	5.86	5.73
Saudi Arabia	37.6	37.2	5.0	4.7	70.0	71.1	41.3	36.3	6.38	6.30
Senegal	44.4	43.4	11.1	10.4	57.4	58.3	61.2	58.4	6.18	6.04
Serbia [7]	12.6	12.5	9.7	9.7	73.2	73.7	17.1	15.9	1.75	1.73
Somalia	46.8	47.5	18.5	18.7	46.2	46.2	125.8	125.8	7.01	7.18
South Africa	26.4	25.5	12.3	13.3	55.7	53.9	52.0	52.0	3.16	3.02
Spain	9.7	10.2	9.6	9.8	77.6	77.9	6.5	6.3	1.21	1.27
Sri Lanka	18.4	17.9	6.0	6.1	72.6	72.8	16.3	15.9	2.12	2.08
Sudan	39.9	38.8	10.9	10.3	56.0	56.8	72.6	69.2	5.68	5.47
Sweden	11.7	12.3	10.8	10.8	79.2	79.4	3.9	3.9	1.76	1.89
Switzerland	10.8	10.3	9.0	9.1	78.9	79.1	4.9	4.8	1.46	1.46
Syria [5]	37.8	36.1	5.6	5.3	67.8	68.4	37.6	35.2	5.55	5.19
Taiwan [5]	14.8	14.5	5.4	5.2	76.8	78.2	6.3	5.7	1.77	1.77
Tajikistan	27.7	27.3	7.8	8.0	64.5	64.1	112.1	117.4	3.53	3.43
Tanzania	40.8	40.0	16.7	16.8	46.4	46.0	96.9	93.6	5.49	5.31
Thailand	16.8	16.2	7.1	7.2	69.0	69.4	30.8	28.3	1.84	1.80
Tunisia	20.1	19.4	5.1	5.0	73.1	73.6	32.6	30.1	2.44	2.32
Turkey	21.4	20.4	5.4	5.2	72.8	73.8	38.3	33.3	2.47	2.35
Uganda	49.2	48.0	19.0	17.9	42.6	43.5	92.9	88.5	7.09	6.96
Ukraine	9.5	9.6	16.3	16.4	65.8	66.0	21.8	21.7	1.35	1.32
United Kingdom	12.0	11.8	10.7	10.6	77.2	77.5	5.9	5.7	1.70	1.72
Uzbekistan	23.7	23.2	7.7	7.9	64.1	63.7	71.0	72.1	2.87	2.77
Venezuela	23.0	21.5	5.0	4.9	72.7	73.3	27.5	25.5	2.70	2.53
Vietnam	21.6	20.0	6.7	6.5	67.7	68.5	36.0	33.7	2.50	2.31
Yemen	43.4	43.3	10.3	9.5	59.5	60.5	72.2	67.4	7.14	6.99
Zambia	44.6	44.4	22.6	22.6	37.1	36.9	92.6	91.1	6.41	6.28
Zimbabwe	31.3	30.0	20.1	20.8	39.2	38.6	61.8	60.7	3.86	3.56

[1] Number of births during 1 year per 1,000 persons (based on midyear population). [2] Number of deaths during 1 year per 1,000 persons (based on midyear population). [3] Number of deaths of children under 1 year of age per 1,000 live births in a calendar year. [4] Average number of children that would be born if all women lived to the end of their childbearing years and, at each year of age, they experienced the birth rates occurring in the specified year. [5] See footnote 2, table 1343. [6] See footnote 3, Table 1343. [7] Serbia and Montenegro have asserted the formation of a joint independent state, but this entity has not been recognized by the United States. Data in this table are for Serbia alone.

Source: U.S. Bureau of the Census, unpublished data from the International Data Base.

No. 1346. Marriage and Divorce Rates, by Country: 1980 to 1995

COUNTRY	MARRIAGE RATE PER 1,000 POPULATION, 15 TO 64 YEARS OLD						DIVORCE RATE PER 1,000 MARRIED WOMEN					
	1980	1990	1992	1993	1994	1995	1980	1990	1992	1993	1994	1995
United States [1]	16	15	14	14	14	14	23	21	21	21	20	20
Canada	12	10	9	8	8	8	10	11	11	11	11	11
Denmark	8	9	9	9	10	10	11	13	13	13	13	12
France [3]	10	8	7	7	7	[2]7	6	8	8	8	9	[2]9
Germany [3]	9	9	8	9	8	8	6	8	7	9	9	9
Italy	9	8	8	8	7	[2]7	1	2	2	2	2	2
Japan	10	8	9	9	9	9	5	5	6	6	6	6
Netherlands	10	9	9	8	8	8	8	8	9	9	10	10
Sweden	7	7	7	6	6	[2]6	11	12	13	13	14	14
United Kingdom	12	10	9	9	9	[2]8	[4]12	13	12	12	13	[2]13

[1] Includes unlicensed marriages registered in California. [2] Preliminary. [3] Prior to 1991, data are for former West Germany. [4] England and Wales only.

No. 1347. Births to Unmarried Women, by Country: 1980 to 1995

[For U.S. figures, marital status is inferred from a comparison of the child's and parents' surnames on the birth certificate for those states that do not report on marital status. No estimates are included for misstatements on birth records or failures to register births]

COUNTRY	1980		1990		1994		1995	
	Total live births (1,000)	Percent born to unmarried women	Total live births (1,000)	Percent born to unmarried women	Total live births (1,000)	Percent born to unmarried women	Total live births (1,000)	Percent born to unmarried women
United States	3,612	18	4,158	28	3,953	33	3,900	32
Canada [1]	360	13	398	24	385	25	378	26
Denmark	57	33	63	46	70	47	70	46
France [3]	800	11	762	30	711	36	[2]728	[2]37
Germany [3]	621	8	906	11	770	15	765	16
Italy	640	4	554	6	527	8	[2]521	[2]8
Japan	1,616	1	1,222	1	1,238	1	1,187	1
Netherlands	181	4	198	11	196	14	191	16
Sweden	97	40	124	47	112	52	103	53
United Kingdom	754	12	799	28	751	32	732	34

[1] 1980 through 1990 excludes Newfoundland. After 1990, a significant number of births are not allocated according to marital status, resulting in an understatement of the proportion of births to unmarried women. [2] Preliminary. [3] Prior to 1990, data are for former West Germany.

Source of Tables 1346 and 1347: U.S. Bureau of Labor Statistics, *Monthly Labor Review*, March 1990 and unpublished data.

No. 1348. Death Rates, by Cause and Country

[Age-standardized death rate per 100,000 population. For explanation of age-adjustment, see text, Section 2. The standard population for this table is the old European standard; see source for details. Deaths classified to ninth revision of *International Classification of Diseases*; see text, Section 2]

COUNTRY	Year	Ischemic heart disease	Cerebrovascular disease	CANCER OF —			Bronchitis, [1] emphysema, asthma	Chronic liver disease and cirrhosis	Motor vehicle traffic accidents	Suicide and self-inflicted injury
				Lung, trachea, bronchus	Stomach	Female breast				
United States	1992	164.4	47.3	57.3	5.0	30.5	8.9	10.5	15.2	11.8
Australia	1993	162.1	63.9	37.1	7.0	29.2	11.0	6.3	10.6	11.4
Austria	1994	148.9	83.6	33.9	15.9	31.0	12.1	24.8	14.5	20.4
Bulgaria	1994	231.4	230.3	33.5	19.6	22.0	9.9	20.1	13.3	15.9
Canada	1993	146.2	48.7	53.8	6.7	31.1	6.9	8.2	11.6	12.8
Czech Republic	1993	276.6	168.0	53.1	17.4	31.2	19.6	16.5	13.6	18.1
Denmark	1992	190.3	72.0	51.1	7.8	40.6	36.5	13.5	10.2	20.4
Finland	1994	206.8	86.4	31.0	11.2	23.2	14.1	9.6	8.6	26.4
France	1993	58.0	49.7	35.3	8.0	28.4	9.5	15.6	14.4	19.8
Germany	1994	152.3	82.5	35.8	14.3	31.3	16.8	21.3	11.1	13.8
Hungary	1994	250.2	161.0	65.9	22.4	35.4	39.6	81.3	16.0	33.5
Italy	1992	90.4	86.6	42.8	17.2	28.4	21.4	20.8	15.2	7.1
Japan	1994	36.4	75.8	28.0	31.2	9.6	10.1	11.2	9.9	15.1
Netherlands	1994	112.4	64.0	51.1	11.1	38.4	13.5	4.6	7.5	9.7
New Zealand	1993	195.1	76.1	40.7	8.2	34.0	11.3	4.1	16.6	12.6
Norway	1993	161.9	80.0	30.0	9.8	27.7	12.6	4.5	5.9	13.0
Poland	1994	110.1	79.0	52.1	18.3	22.3	17.7	12.8	18.8	14.8
Portugal	1994	75.6	187.1	22.0	22.8	25.0	9.7	21.3	20.9	7.1
Russia	1994	409.0	297.0	44.7	34.2	22.1	40.7	(NA)	23.2	41.7
Spain	1992	73.0	81.9	34.1	14.1	24.4	7.3	17.7	16.0	6.6
Sweden	1993	172.0	65.8	23.3	8.2	24.7	10.6	5.6	6.3	14.7
Switzerland	1994	100.4	48.8	33.7	8.6	33.1	17.7	8.4	8.4	19.6
United Kingdom:										
England and Wales	1994	181.5	71.5	48.2	10.7	37.0	9.0	5.9	5.9	6.7
Scotland	1994	223.9	114.9	67.2	11.3	38.3	8.4	9.4	7.3	11.7

NA Not available. [1] Chronic and unspecified.

Source: World Health Organization, Geneva, Switzerland, *World Health Statistics Annual*.

No. 1349. Health Expenditures as Percent of GDP, by Country: 1980 to 1997

[In percent. G.D.P.=gross domestic product; for explanation, see text, Section 14]

COUNTRY	TOTAL HEALTH EXPENDITURES					PUBLIC HEALTH EXPENDITURES				
	1980	1985	1990	1995	1997	1980	1985	1990	1995	1997
United States	9.1	10.6	12.6	14.1	14.0	3.9	4.3	5.1	6.5	6.5
Australia.	7.3	7.7	8.3	8.4	8.3	4.6	5.5	5.6	5.6	5.7
Austria	7.7	6.7	7.2	8.0	7.9	5.3	5.1	5.3	5.8	5.7
Belgium	6.5	7.3	7.5	7.9	7.6	5.4	6.0	6.7	6.9	6.7
Canada	7.3	8.4	9.2	9.7	9.3	5.5	6.4	6.9	6.9	6.4
Czech Republic	3.8	4.5	5.4	7.5	7.0	3.7	4.1	5.2	6.9	6.4
Denmark.	8.7	8.2	8.2	8.0	7.7	7.7	7.3	7.1	6.8	5.0
Finland.	6.5	7.3	8.0	7.6	7.3	5.1	5.7	6.5	5.7	5.6
France	7.6	8.5	8.9	9.9	9.9	6.0	6.5	6.6	8.0	7.7
Germany [1]	8.8	9.3	8.7	10.4	10.4	7.0	7.2	6.7	8.1	8.1
Greece.	3.6	4.0	4.2	5.8	7.1	2.9	3.3	3.5	4.4	5.3
Hungary	(NA)	(NA)	6.1	7.1	6.5	(NA)	(NA)	(NA)	4.9	4.5
Iceland.	6.2	7.3	7.9	8.2	8.0	5.5	6.3	6.9	6.9	6.7
Ireland	8.7	7.9	6.7	7.0	7.0	7.1	6.0	4.9	5.2	5.3
Italy	7.0	7.1	8.1	7.7	7.6	5.6	5.5	6.3	5.4	5.3
Japan	6.4	6.7	6.0	7.2	7.3	4.5	4.7	4.6	5.6	5.7
Korea, South.	2.9	3.9	3.9	3.9	4.0	0.8	1.2	1.7	1.9	2.3
Luxembourg	6.2	6.1	6.6	6.7	7.1	5.7	5.5	6.1	6.2	6.5
Mexico	(NA)	(NA)	3.6	4.9	4.7	(NA)	(NA)	2.1	2.8	2.8
Netherlands	7.9	7.9	8.3	8.8	8.5	5.9	5.9	6.1	6.7	6.1
New Zealand.	6.0	5.3	7.0	7.3	7.6	5.3	(NA)	5.8	5.6	5.8
Norway.	7.0	6.7	7.8	8.0	7.4	5.9	5.7	6.5	6.6	6.1
Poland	(NA)	(NA)	4.4	4.5	5.3	(NA)	(NA)	(NA)	4.2	4.9
Portugal	5.8	6.3	6.5	8.2	8.2	3.7	3.4	4.3	5.0	4.9
Spain.	5.6	5.6	6.9	7.3	7.4	4.5	4.6	5.4	5.7	5.8
Sweden	9.4	9.0	8.8	8.5	8.6	8.7	8.1	7.9	7.1	7.1
Switzerland	6.9	7.7	8.3	9.6	10.2	4.6	5.1	5.7	6.9	7.1
Turkey	3.3	2.2	3.6	3.3	(NA)	0.9	1.1	2.2	2.4	(NA)
United Kingdom	5.6	5.9	6.0	6.9	6.7	5.0	5.0	5.1	5.8	5.7

NA Not available.   [1] Data prior to 1991 are for former West Germany.

Source: Organization for Economic Cooperation and Development, Paris, France, *OECD Health Data 98*; and *OECD in Figures, 1998 Edition.*

No. 1350. Selected Environmental Data—OECD Countries

[Figures are for the latest available year. Varying definitions and survey methods can limit the comparability across countries]

COUNTRY	AIR POLLUTANT EMISSIONS PER CAPITA			WASTE GENERATED			
	Sulfur oxides (kilograms)	Nitrogen oxides (kilograms)	Carbon dioxide [1] (tons)	Municipal [2], mid-1990s (kilograms per capita)	Nuclear [3], 1995		
					Amount (tons)	Per unit of energy (tons per Mtoe [4])	Per 1,000 persons (kilograms)
Australia.	119	120	16	690	-	-	-
Austria	8	22	7	480	-	-	-
Belgium	24	33	12	470	121	2.3	11.9
Canada	91	68	16	630	1,690	7.2	57.1
Czech Republic	106	40	12	230	46	1.2	4.5
Denmark.	28	48	12	530	-	-	-
Finland.	19	51	11	410	68	2.4	13.3
France	17	26	6	560	1,200	5.0	20.6
Germany	37	27	11	400	470	1.4	5.8
Greece.	51	34	7	310	-	-	-
Hungary	69	18	6	420	52	2.1	5.1
Iceland.	30	106	9	560	-	-	-
Ireland	46	32	10	430	-	-	-
Italy	25	37	7	470	-	-	-
Japan	7	12	9	400	914	1.8	7.3
Korea, South.	34	26	8	390	216	1.5	4.8
Luxembourg	19	48	22	530	-	-	-
Mexico	23	16	3	330	20	0.1	0.2
Netherlands	10	35	12	580	14	0.2	0.9
New Zealand.	11	58	8	(NA)	-	-	-
Norway.	8	51	8	620	-	-	-
Poland	61	29	9	290	(NA)	(NA)	(NA)
Portugal	26	26	5	350	-	-	-
Spain.	53	31	6	370	168	1.6	4.3
Sweden	11	41	6	440	213	4.2	24.1
Switzerland	5	19	6	610	77	3.1	10.9
Turkey	29	9	3	590	-	-	-
United Kingdom	40	39	10	490	1,713	7.7	29.2
United States	63	75	20	720	2,100	1.0	8.0

- Represents zero.   NA Not available.   [1] Carbon dioxide from energy use only. Excludes international marine bunkers.
[2] Municipal waste is that which is collected and treated by or for municipalities: household waste and bulky waste as well as comparable waste from small communities or industrial enterprises; and market and garden residue.   [3] Wastes from spent fuel measured in terms of heavy metal.   [4] Mtoe=million tons of oil equivalent (primary energy supply).

Source: Organization for Economic Cooperation and Development, Paris, France, *Toward Sustainable Development: Environmental Indicators*, July 1998 and *OECD in Figures*, annual.

No. 1351. Educational Attainment, by Country: 1995

[Percent distribution. Persons 25 to 64 years old]

COUNTRY	Total	Early childhood, primary, and lower secondary education only	Upper secondary education only	Non-university tertiary education only	University education only
Australia	100	47	29	10	14
Austria	100	31	62	2	6
Belgium	100	47	29	14	11
Canada	100	25	28	30	17
Denmark	100	38	42	6	14
Finland	100	35	45	9	12
France	100	32	50	8	11
Germany	100	16	61	10	13
Greece	100	57	25	6	11
Ireland	100	53	27	10	10
Italy	100	65	27	(1)	[1]8
Netherlands	100	39	39	(1)	[1]22
New Zealand	100	41	34	15	10
Norway	100	19	53	11	18
Portugal	100	80	9	4	7
Spain	100	72	12	4	12
Sweden	100	25	46	14	14
Switzerland	100	18	61	12	9
Turkey	100	77	15	(1)	[1]8
United Kingdom	100	24	54	9	12
United States	100	14	53	8	25

[1] Non-university tertiary education included in university education only.

Source: Organization for Economic Cooperation and Development, Paris, France, *Education at a Glance*, annual, (copyright).

No. 1352. Participation in Job-Related Continuing Education and Training, by Country

[**Percentage of the employed population 25 to 64 years old**. Data refer to all job-related education and training organized, financed, or sponsored by authorities, provided by employers, or self-financed. Job-related continuing education and training refers to all organized, systematic education and training activities in which people take part in order to obtain knowledge and/or learn new skills for a current or a future job, to increase earnings, improve job and/or career opportunities in current or other fields, and generally to improve their opportunities for advancement and promotion]

COUNTRY	Year	Total	Male	Female	COUNTRY	Year	Total	Male	Female
United States [1][2]	1995	34	31	36	Germany [1][7]	1994	33	35	31
Australia [1][3]	1995	38	38	38	Greece [4]	1994	1	1	1
Austria [4]	1995	8	8	7	Ireland [4]	1994	4	3	6
Belgium [4][5]	1994	3	3	2	Italy [4][8]	1995	1	1	1
Canada [1]	1993	28	27	30	Spain [4]	1995	3	2	5
Denmark [4]	1995	15	13	17	Sweden [9]	1996	42	39	44
Finland [1][6]	1995	45	45	45	Switzerland [1]	1996	35	38	31
France [1]	1994	40	38	43	United Kingdom [4]	1995	12	11	13

[1] During the 12-month period preceding the survey.   [2] Excludes full-time students.   [3] Excludes persons enrolled only in full-time programs at any time during the survey period and people pursuing only on-the-job training.   [4] During the 4-week period preceding the survey.   [5] Covers all forms of continuing education and training.   [6] Includes only the training of employees which is sponsored by employers.   [7] Excludes initial training of students over 25 years old in vocational schools and in the dual system and forms of continuing vocational training other than formal courses.   [8] Excludes persons enrolled in ordinary school courses.   [9] During the 6-month period preceding the survey. Includes only training supplied or sponsored by employers.

Source: Organization for Economic Cooperation and Development, Paris, France, *Education at a Glance*, annual (copyright).

No. 1353. Number of Foreign Students in Selected OECD Countries: 1995

[Covers students enrolled in a program at the university level or its equivalent]

COUNTRY OF ORIGIN	Total [1]	COUNTY OF DESTINATION					
		United States	Canada	France	Germany	Japan	United Kingdom
Total [1]	1,313,064	452,599	54,712	165,350	154,536	53,511	156,977
United States	23,276	(X)	3,742	2,945	4,512	1,164	6,243
Canada	27,250	22,747	(X)	1,035	463	131	1,713
Mexico	12,075	9,003	783	605	277	98	598
Japan	56,668	45,276	4,530	1,219	1,599	(X)	2,673
Korea, South	61,382	33,599	1,360	1,601	4,799	17,788	784
France	32,433	5,843	(NA)	(X)	5,872	131	8,936
Germany	41,220	8,592	722	5,332	(X)	270	9,518
Greece	36,638	3,699	198	2,806	8,231	14	10,374
Ireland	12,407	909	99	547	541	15	9,799
Italy	29,742	2,704	148	3,372	5,890	57	3,107
Netherlands	11,945	1,847	153	841	2,564	39	2,009
Spain	21,142	5,126	142	3,263	4,241	44	4,983
United Kingdom	24,161	786	1,938	4,217	3,535	218	(X)
Turkey	35,305	6,716	151	1,734	22,747	37	1,183
Russia	10,116	4,832	-	891	2,727	122	302

- Represents zero.   NA Not available.   X Not applicable.   [1] Includes other countries, not shown separately.

Source: Organization for Economic Cooperation and Development, Paris, France, *Education at a Glance*, annual (copyright).

No. 1354. Gross National Product, by Country: 1985 to 1995

[In billions of dollars, except per capita. For most countries, data for GNP are based on local currencies which are deflated to constant 1995 local currency values before conversion to U.S. dollar equivalents. In general, rates used for conversion are the 1995 average par/market exchange rates as supplied by the International Bank for Reconstruction and Development]

COUNTRY	CURRENT DOLLARS				CONSTANT (1995) DOLLARS				Per capita (dollars)		
	1985	1990	1994	1995	1985	1990	1994	1995	1985	1990	1995
United States	4,201	5,765	6,932	7,247	5,758	6,625	7,106	7,247	24,140	26,510	27,550
Algeria	28	34	37	39	39	39	38	39	1,744	1,544	1,365
Argentina	147	181	278	271	201	209	285	271	6,627	6,437	7,909
Australia	185	250	324	342	254	288	332	342	16,070	16,900	18,920
Austria	132	183	221	231	182	210	226	231	24,010	27,630	28,860
Bangladesh	14	21	27	29	19	24	28	29	194	215	240
Belgium	158	219	262	269	217	252	268	269	21,970	25,300	26,550
Brazil	371	502	610	657	509	576	626	657	3,718	3,841	4,084
Bulgaria	41	45	37	38	56	52	38	38	6,316	5,805	4,394
Canada	319	436	517	542	437	501	530	542	17,370	18,810	19,000
Chile [1]	20	36	53	59	28	41	55	59	2,322	3,109	4,173
China [1]	799	1,382	2,461	2,759	1,095	1,588	2,523	2,759	1,040	1,401	2,303
Colombia . . . . . . [2] . .	35	52	71	76	48	60	73	76	1,627	1,818	2,107
Congo (Kinshasa) [2] . . .	6	8	5	5	8	9	5	5	235	230	114
Croatia [1]	(X)	(X)	19	20	(X)	(X)	20	20	(X)	(X)	4,045
Cuba [1]	30	34	22	23	40	39	23	23	4,014	3,672	2,068
Czech Republic [1]	(X)	(X)	94	101	(X)	(X)	96	101	(X)	(X)	9,779
Denmark	110	141	173	170	151	162	178	170	29,570	31,540	32,540
Egypt	24	37	44	46	34	42	45	46	677	750	746
El Salvador	5	6	9	10	6	7	9	10	1,311	1,325	1,671
Ethiopia	3	4	5	5	4	5	5	5	92	102	96
Finland	86	121	121	119	118	139	124	119	24,150	27,820	23,410
France	895	1,251	1,452	1,521	1,226	1,438	1,488	1,521	22,330	25,460	26,290
Germany [3]	1,232	1,738	2,079	2,172	1,689	1,998	2,131	2,172	27,670	25,170	26,190
Ghana	3	4	6	6	4	5	6	6	306	330	357
Greece	56	72	87	91	76	82	89	91	7,656	8,144	8,696
Hungary [1]	53	63	64	66	72	72	65	66	6,767	6,949	6,519
India [1]	142	229	299	326	195	263	307	326	252	307	348
Indonesia	67	113	172	189	92	130	177	189	532	694	931
Iran [1]	111	134	158	158	152	154	162	158	3,200	2,702	2,449
Iraq [1]	31	23	(NA)	(NA)	42	26	(NA)	(NA)	2,683	1,435	(NA)
Israel	38	57	83	91	52	65	85	91	12,870	14,470	17,070
Italy	644	886	1,025	1,082	882	1,019	1,050	1,082	15,430	17,670	18,850
Japan	2,809	4,187	4,981	5,153	3,849	4,811	5,106	5,153	31,880	38,950	41,160
Kenya [1]	4	6	7	8	5	7	7	8	262	286	274
Korea, North [1]	26	(NA)	21	21	36	(NA)	22	21	1,839	(NA)	894
Korea, South	130	259	380	425	179	297	390	425	4,380	6,935	9,437
Kuwait [1]	26	25	28	30	36	25	28	30	20,930	13,400	16,500
Malaysia	27	46	71	81	37	53	73	81	2,386	3,033	4,134
Mexico	157	204	254	237	215	235	261	237	2,806	2,756	2,521
Morocco	18	26	33	32	25	30	34	32	1,064	1,162	1,107
Netherlands	224	310	373	391	307	356	382	391	21,180	23,830	25,240
Nigeria	51	72	94	95	70	83	96	95	935	958	946
Norway	74	95	121	128	101	109	124	128	24,320	25,700	29,350
Pakistan	29	44	57	61	40	51	59	61	402	445	482
Peru	33	37	51	57	46	43	53	57	2,331	1,961	2,363
Philippines	37	57	71	77	51	66	73	77	877	1,011	1,052
Poland [1]	144	163	188	209	198	188	193	209	5,318	4,925	5,404
Portugal	53	84	98	103	73	97	100	103	7,292	9,826	10,430
Romania	99	105	91	99	136	121	93	99	6,134	5,294	4,513
Russia [1]	(X)	(X)	93	76	(X)	(X)	95	76	(X)	(X)	478
Saudi Arabia [1]	94	113	121	128	129	130	124	128	9,769	8,157	6,815
Serbia and Montenegro [1]	(X)	(X)	(NA)	21	(X)	(X)	(NA)	21	(X)	(X)	1,948
Slovakia [1]	(X)	(X)	18	19	(X)	(X)	19	19	(X)	(X)	3,619
Slovenia [1]	(X)	(X)	21	23	(X)	(X)	22	23	(X)	(X)	11,550
South Africa	83	107	124	131	113	123	127	131	3,394	3,317	3,185
Spain	303	451	525	554	415	519	538	554	10,810	13,370	14,160
Sri Lanka	6	9	12	13	8	10	12	13	521	572	699
Sweden	145	192	207	219	199	221	212	219	23,800	25,830	24,730
Switzerland	198	267	302	316	271	307	309	316	41,440	45,270	44,070
Syria	25	30	45	50	34	34	46	50	3,258	2,730	3,283
Taiwan	91	169	243	264	125	194	249	264	6,440	9,575	12,390
Tanzania	2	3	4	4	2	3	4	4	115	131	134
Thailand	49	96	147	163	67	111	151	163	1,310	2,012	2,806
Turkey	78	124	153	167	106	142	157	167	2,100	2,536	2,714
United Kingdom	653	903	1,058	1,110	895	1,037	1,084	1,110	15,800	18,070	19,020
Venezuela	41	56	71	75	56	65	73	75	3,298	3,339	3,457

NA Not available.   X Not applicable.   [1] Estimated.   [2] See footnote 3, Table 1343.   [3] Prior to 1991, data are for former West Germany.

Source: U.S. Arms Control and Disarmament Agency, *World Military Expenditures and Arms Transfers*, annual. Data from International Bank for Reconstruction and Development and U.S. Central Intelligence Agency.

No. 1355. Gross Domestic Product, by Country: 1980 to 1997

Column groups: **PURCHASING POWER PARITY BASIS [1]** — Amount (bil. dol.) and Per capita (dollars). **CONSTANT (1990) PRICE LEVELS AND EXCHANGE RATES [2]** — Amount (bil. dol.) and Annual growth rate [3] (percent).

COUNTRY	PPP Amount 1980	1985	1990	1994	1995	1996	PPP Per cap. 1980	1985	1990	1994	1995	1996	Const. Amount 1980	1985	1990	1994	1995	1996	1997	Growth 1996	1997
OECD, total [4][5]	7,405	10,818	15,163	18,344	19,084	20,038	8,539	11,990	16,133	18,864	19,469	20,289	12,828	14,390	16,932	17,990	18,383	18,854	19,369	2.6	2.7
OECD Europe [4]	3,089	4,369	6,115	7,265	7,569	7,893	7,525	10,400	14,155	16,392	16,993	17,630	5,718	6,201	7,240	7,566	7,760	7,901	8,108	1.8	2.6
European Union [6]	2,873	4,036	5,628	6,675	6,937	7,216	8,083	11,246	15,440	17,992	18,644	19,333	5,349	5,777	6,739	7,036	7,211	7,333	7,521	1.7	2.6
Australia	127	194	272	332	352	373	8,671	12,293	15,942	18,583	19,519	20,376	214	251	295	326	339	351	361	3.4	2.9
Austria	67	93	129	161	166	172	8,850	12,278	16,712	20,040	20,613	21,395	128	137	159	172	176	179	183	1.6	2.1
Belgium	87	118	166	208	214	222	8,851	11,976	16,668	20,105	21,105	21,856	160	166	196	204	208	211	216	1.5	2.4
Canada	246	370	509	594	622	645	10,020	14,262	18,304	20,314	20,992	21,529	427	493	568	598	612	621	644	1.5	3.6
Czech Republic	(NA)	(NA)	(NA)	(NA)	(NA)	(NA)	(NA)	(NA)	(NA)	(NA)	(NA)	(NA)	(NA)	(NA)	34	30	31	33	33	4.1	0.9
Denmark	45	67	85	106	112	118	8,749	12,997	16,552	20,422	21,491	22,418	106	120	129	139	142	146	151	2.7	3.4
Finland	38	57	81	83	92	97	8,004	11,682	16,193	16,340	17,921	18,871	99	114	135	125	131	135	142	3.3	4.6
France	511	711	984	1,116	1,157	1,199	9,475	12,851	17,347	19,272	19,908	20,533	963	1,030	1,195	1,234	1,260	1,276	1,305	1.3	2.3
Germany	658	921	1,269	1,608	1,675	1,736	8,407	11,862	15,991	19,754	20,510	21,200	1,321	1,421	1,640	1,750	1,781	1,805	1,848	1.4	2.4
Greece	51	71	93	121	127	134	5,315	7,175	9,187	11,613	12,174	12,743	71	76	83	88	90	92	95	2.6	3.4
Hungary	(NA)	(NA)	(NA)	(NA)	(NA)	(NA)	(NA)	(NA)	(NA)	(NA)	(NA)	(NA)	(NA)	(NA)	36	31	32	32	33	1.1	3.0
Iceland	2	3	4	5	6	6	9,492	13,100	17,294	19,459	21,755	23,242	5	5	6	6	6	7	7	5.2	4.9
Ireland	18	27	40	57	62	69	5,291	7,501	11,375	15,766	17,201	18,988	32	36	46	54	61	66	71	8.6	7.5
Italy	476	668	922	1,069	1,115	1,148	8,440	11,782	16,257	18,682	19,460	19,974	877	945	1,094	1,124	1,157	1,165	1,180	0.7	1.3
Japan	958	1,472	2,202	2,652	2,752	2,925	8,204	12,188	17,824	21,223	21,916	23,235	2,007	2,369	2,970	3,144	3,191	3,316	3,332	3.9	0.5
Korea, South	(NA)	(NA)	340	507	565	619	(NA)	(NA)	7,928	11,353	12,518	13,580	110	165	254	334	364	390	414	7.1	6.2
Luxembourg	4	5	9	12	13	14	9,970	14,566	22,809	30,176	31,210	32,416	7	8	10	13	13	14	14	3.0	3.6
Mexico	251	360	466	728	698	751	3,606	4,617	5,411	7,824	7,367	7,776	220	242	263	302	283	298	318	5.2	6.7
Netherlands	124	172	239	289	307	325	8,750	11,839	15,962	18,802	19,874	20,905	229	243	284	308	315	325	335	3.3	3.2
New Zealand	24	37	45	58	61	64	7,731	11,218	13,352	16,331	16,963	17,473	36	42	43	48	50	51	52	2.4	1.9
Norway	37	57	74	95	99	107	9,124	13,775	17,512	21,937	22,743	24,364	90	106	115	133	138	145	151	5.3	4.0
Poland	(NA)	(NA)	(NA)	(NA)	(NA)	(NA)	(NA)	(NA)	(NA)	(NA)	(NA)	(NA)	(NA)	(NA)	59	66	68	70	74	6.1	5.6
Portugal	45	61	93	119	124	130	4,588	6,087	9,372	12,042	12,457	13,100	51	53	67	71	72	75	77	3.0	3.4
Spain	219	308	461	538	561	587	5,849	8,018	11,856	13,743	14,318	14,954	366	395	495	515	529	541	559	2.3	3.2
Sweden	77	109	146	155	166	171	9,250	13,057	17,004	17,616	18,750	19,258	188	205	230	226	235	238	243	1.3	1.8
Switzerland	75	104	144	170	177	181	11,720	15,969	21,242	24,198	24,984	25,402	184	197	228	226	228	228	229	-0.2	0.5
Turkey	102	169	264	320	350	383	2,299	3,351	4,691	5,276	5,682	6,114	91	115	151	165	176	189	201	7.0	6.3
United Kingdom	453	649	912	1,032	1,047	1,096	8,039	11,449	15,847	17,680	17,862	18,636	752	828	976	1,013	1,040	1,065	1,101	2.3	3.4
United States	**2,708**	**4,017**	**5,554**	**6,716**	**7,030**	**7,388**	**11,892**	**16,844**	**22,224**	**25,764**	**26,711**	**27,821**	**4,205**	**4,793**	**5,554**	**6,005**	**6,147**	**6,316**	**6,555**	**2.8**	**3.8**

NA Not available. [1] The goods and services produced in different countries should be valued consistently if the differences observed are meant to reflect real differences in the volumes of goods and services produced. The use of purchasing power parities (PPP) instead of exchange rates is intended to achieve this objective. PPP's show how many units of currency are needed in one country to buy the same amount of goods and services which one unit of currency will buy in the other country. See text, Section 30. [2] Based on constant (1990) price data converted to U.S. dollars using 1990 exchange rates. [3] Percent change from immediate prior year. Minus sign (-) indicates decrease. [4] Excludes Czech Republic, Hungary, and Poland. [5] Excludes South Korea. [6] For countries, see text, Section 30.

Source: Organization for Economic Cooperation and Development, Paris, France, National Accounts, Main Aggregates, vol. I, annual; and "OECD Statistics GDP;" published February 1998; <http://www.oecd.org/std/gdp.htm> (copyright).

No. 1356. International Economic Composite Indexes, by Country: 1980 to 1997

[Average annual percent change from previous year; derived from indexes with base 1990=100. The coincident index changes are for calendar years and the leading index changes are for years ending June 30 because they lead the coincident indexes by about 6 months, on average. The G-7 countries are United States, Canada, France, Germany, Italy, United Kingdom, and Japan. Minus sign (-) indicates decrease]

COUNTRY	1980	1985	1988	1989	1990	1991	1992	1993	1994	1995	1996	1997
LEADING INDEX												
Total, 13 countries	2.4	2.4	6.9	4.5	2.0	-1.6	-0.7	-0.4	3.7	5.1	2.5	3.1
12 countries, excluding U.S.	6.7	4.5	8.2	6.6	3.5	-2.0	2.3	-2.6	3.7	5.3	3.5	3.2
G-7 countries	2.2	2.1	6.8	4.5	1.8	-2.1	-1.0	-0.9	3.5	4.7	2.4	3.2
North America	-2.7	-0.4	5.2	1.8	-0.5	-1.9	2.0	3.2	4.7	4.5	0.9	3.2
United States	-3.1	-0.8	5.2	2.0	-0.4	-1.6	2.3	3.0	4.3	4.3	1.0	3.2
Canada	2.6	4.2	5.7	0.3	-2.5	-5.8	-0.8	5.9	9.4	6.8	-0.1	3.8
Four European countries	2.9	2.4	2.3	3.7	1.7	-0.5	0.8	-0.3	3.6	3.9	0.8	2.7
France	3.1	0.9	3.3	4.2	-0.2	0.6	2.3	-	4.2	3.4	-0.6	3.4
Germany	2.0	2.1	2.3	3.9	3.5	2.7	0.2	-1.8	2.4	3.6	0.5	3.3
Italy	5.7	5.2	-0.2	2.9	2.5	-2.3	0.9	-0.3	5.5	4.9	2.2	1.3
United Kingdom.	2.2	3.0	2.7	3.3	0.2	-1.3	0.5	2.5	3.6	4.0	2.5	1.5
Seven Pacific region countries.	12.5	7.0	15.1	9.0	5.7	-3.0	-5.8	-5.3	2.1	7.4	6.7	3.5
Australia	5.3	7.5	5.6	3.3	-0.4	-3.6	4.7	5.5	7.3	3.4	1.7	2.5
Taiwan.	4.0	5.8	13.0	11.1	6.0	0.8	7.4	4.8	7.1	7.3	3.9	7.9
Thailand.	2.0	5.1	16.8	11.5	12.7	4.5	5.5	7.3	10.2	9.8	5.6	0.3
Japan.	15.0	7.4	16.5	9.2	6.1	-4.0	-8.8	-8.5	-0.4	7.4	7.9	3.6
Korea, South	-2.1	5.4	15.2	11.5	5.6	4.5	5.4	4.7	12.5	11.1	4.9	2.2
Malaysia	4.0	-1.5	5.6	2.6	1.4	2.3	-1.6	0.2	6.6	3.4	0.2	2.3
New Zealand	2.2	5.9	-1.4	1.6	1.7	-2.3	3.4	3.9	3.1	1.7	1.4	1.9
COINCIDENT INDEX												
Total, 13 countries	0.3	3.4	5.8	4.4	3.4	0.3	0.9	0.1	2.8	3.0	2.4	2.8
12 countries, excluding U.S.	1.9	3.1	6.3	5.4	5.2	2.5	0.5	-1.3	1.8	2.5	1.9	1.7
G-7 countries	0.1	3.3	5.6	4.2	3.2	0.1	0.6	-0.2	2.5	2.6	2.2	2.7
North America	-2.3	3.9	4.9	2.8	0.2	-3.7	1.2	2.8	4.7	3.7	3.0	4.4
United States	-2.7	3.7	4.8	2.8	0.2	-3.7	1.3	2.8	4.8	3.8	3.2	4.4
Canada	2.2	5.8	6.0	2.8	0.1	-4.3	0.2	2.4	4.4	2.9	1.4	3.5
Four European countries	0.8	2.2	5.1	4.3	4.4	1.1	-0.5	-3.3	1.7	2.7	1.7	2.4
France.	-0.5	-0.4	5.5	6.4	4.5	-0.1	-1.1	-4.0	2.0	3.5	1.2	2.8
Germany	1.1	2.1	3.1	3.3	5.5	4.2	0.8	-2.4	0.9	1.6	0.5	0.4
Italy.	6.1	3.9	6.4	3.4	5.9	3.2	-	-7.3	-	2.5	2.1	2.3
United Kingdom.	-2.0	4.2	6.9	4.1	0.8	-4.9	-2.5	0.1	4.4	4.3	4.2	5.8
Seven Pacific region countries.	3.0	3.8	7.6	6.6	6.3	4.1	1.4	-0.1	1.6	2.0	2.0	1.6
Australia	4.3	7.0	7.4	8.9	0.3	-8.2	-1.8	1.8	9.4	8.8	3.0	2.9
Taiwan.	8.5	5.1	9.5	8.7	4.1	7.2	7.5	6.5	7.1	4.7	2.9	7.3
Thailand.	3.0	1.9	15.4	13.3	13.0	3.9	6.3	8.3	7.8	7.7	5.9	-3.8
Japan	3.4	3.8	7.3	6.5	6.8	4.9	0.8	-1.0	-	0.6	1.4	0.4
Korea, South	-3.5	6.1	11.1	7.0	9.3	8.4	5.1	4.6	9.5	9.6	6.6	2.5
Malaysia	-0.1	-5.8	3.4	3.9	2.4	5.4	1.2	2.4	3.0	2.5	0.4	-1.2
New Zealand	1.5	1.4	-1.4	-0.9	0.7	-1.1	0.9	3.2	5.2	4.3	4.2	3.2

- Represents or rounds to zero.

Source: Center for International Business Cycle Research, Columbia Business School, New York, NY, *International Economic Indicators,* monthly.

No. 1357. Selected International Economic Indicators, by Country: 1980 to 1996

[Data cover gross domestic product (GDP) at market prices. Gross fixed capital formation covers private and government sectors except military. Savings data are calculated by deducting outlays—such as personal consumption expenditures, interest paid, and transfer payments to foreigners—from disposable personal income]

YEAR	United States	France	Ger-many	Italy	Nether-lands	United Kingdom	Japan	Canada
Ratio of gross fixed capital formation to GDP (current prices):								
1980	19.6	23.0	22.6	24.3	21.6	17.9	31.6	23.3
1985	18.8	19.3	19.5	20.7	19.7	17.0	27.5	19.7
1990	16.2	21.4	20.9	20.3	20.9	19.5	31.7	21.1
1994	16.2	18.5	22.0	16.6	18.7	14.9	28.6	18.5
1995	16.6	17.9	21.7	17.3	19.4	15.1	28.3	17.3
1996	17.0	17.5	21.0	17.0	19.9	15.0	29.6	17.5
Ratio of savings to disposable personal income:								
1980	8.5	17.6	14.2	21.6	11.0	13.4	17.9	13.3
1985	7.2	14.0	12.8	19.2	13.1	10.7	15.6	13.1
1990	5.3	12.5	14.7	18.5	15.5	8.1	12.1	9.5
1994	3.9	13.6	12.3	14.7	11.4	10.1	12.8	7.5
1995	4.9	14.3	12.3	14.4	12.8	11.0	13.0	6.9
1996	4.9	12.5	12.4	13.4	(NA)	11.6	13.2	4.6

NA Not available.

Source: U.S. Dept. of Commerce, International Trade Administration, Office of Trade and Economic Analysis, based on official statistics of listed countries.

No. 1358. Annual Percent Change in Consumer Prices, by Country: 1993 to 1997

[Change from previous year. See text, Section 30, for general comments concerning the data. For additional qualifications of the data for individual countries, see source]

COUNTRY	1993	1994	1995	1996	1997	COUNTRY	1993	1994	1995	1996	1997
United States	3.0	2.6	2.8	2.9	2.3	Korea, South	4.8	6.2	4.5	4.9	4.4
Argentina	10.6	4.2	3.4	0.2	0.5	Malaysia	3.5	3.7	5.3	3.5	2.7
Australia	1.8	1.9	4.6	2.6	0.3	Mexico	9.8	7.0	35.0	34.4	20.6
Belgium	2.8	2.4	1.5	2.1	1.6	Netherlands	2.1	1.8	2.8	3.6	3.3
Brazil	2,148	2,076	66.0	15.8	6.9	Nigeria	57.2	57.0	72.8	29.3	8.2
Canada.	1.8	0.2	2.2	1.6	1.6	Norway.	2.3	1.4	2.5	1.3	2.6
Chile	12.7	11.4	8.2	7.4	6.1	Pakistan	10.0	12.4	12.3	10.4	11.4
Colombia.	22.6	23.8	21.0	20.2	18.5	Philippines.	7.6	9.1	8.1	8.4	5.1
France	2.1	1.7	1.8	2.0	1.2	Russia	(NA)	307.4	197.4	47.6	14.6
Germany.	5.0	2.7	1.8	1.5	1.8	South Africa.	9.7	9.0	8.6	7.4	8.5
India.	6.4	10.2	10.2	9.0	7.2	Spain	4.6	4.7	4.7	3.6	2.0
Indonesia	9.7	9.6	9.0	6.6	11.6	Sweden	4.6	2.2	2.5	0.5	0.5
Iran	21.2	31.5	49.6	28.9	17.2	Switzerland	3.3	0.8	1.8	0.8	0.5
Israel	10.9	12.3	10.0	11.3	9.0	Turkey	66.1	106.3	88.1	80.3	85.7
Italy	4.5	4.0	5.2	4.0	2.0	United Kingdom	1.6	2.5	3.4	2.4	3.1
Japan.	1.3	0.7	-0.1	0.1	1.7	Venezuela	38.1	60.8	59.9	99.9	50.0

NA Not available.

Source: International Monetary Fund, Washington, DC, *International Financial Statistics*, monthly (copyright).

No. 1359. Comparative Price Levels—Selected OECD Countries: 1998

[As of May. Example of data: An item that costs $1.00 in the United States would cost $1.38 (U.S. dollars) in Japan]

COUNTRY	United States (U.S. dollar)	Canada (Canadian dollar)	Japan (yen)	France (franc)	Germany (Deutsche mark)	Italy (lire)	Nether-lands (guilder)	United Kingdom (pound)
United States	100	116	73	87	88	107	93	85
Australia.	85	99	61	74	74	90	78	72
Austria	114	133	83	100	100	122	106	97
Belgium	109	127	79	95	96	116	101	92
Canada	86	100	62	75	75	92	80	73
Denmark.	138	161	100	121	121	148	128	117
Finland.	121	141	88	106	106	129	112	103
France	115	134	83	100	101	122	106	97
Germany	114	133	83	99	100	121	105	96
Greece.	84	98	61	73	74	90	78	71
Iceland.	126	147	92	110	111	135	117	107
Ireland	95	111	69	83	83	101	88	80
Italy	94	109	68	82	82	100	87	79
Japan	138	160	100	120	121	147	127	117
Luxembourg	104	121	76	91	91	111	96	88
Netherlands	108	126	78	94	95	115	100	91
New Zealand.	84	98	61	74	74	90	78	72
Norway.	138	161	100	120	121	147	128	117
Portugal	77	89	56	67	67	82	71	65
Spain.	87	101	63	75	76	92	80	73
Sweden	129	150	94	112	113	137	119	109
Switzerland	135	157	98	118	119	144	125	114
Turkey	55	64	40	48	48	59	51	46
United Kingdom	118	137	86	103	104	126	109	100

Source: Organization for Economic Cooperation and Development, Paris, France, *Main Economic Indicators*, August 1998 (copyright).

No. 1360. At-Home Food and Beverage Expenditures, by Country: 1993

[Percent of total personal consumption expenditures. Expenditures spent on food and alcoholic beverages that were consumed at home]

COUNTRY	Food [1]	Alcoholic beverages	COUNTRY	Food [1]	Alcoholic beverages
United States	7.7	1.1	Mexico	[4]33.2	(NA)
			Netherlands	11.6	1.5
Australia	14.6	4.3	Pakistan [2]	39.3	(NA)
Bangladesh [2]	62.6	(NA)	Philippines	[3]54.6	(NA)
Canada.	10.1	2.3	Singapore	14.8	1.6
France	15.2	2.0	South Africa	27.0	5.9
Germany	[3]17.7	(NA)	Spain	[4]21.0	(NA)
Greece	30.8	3.1	Sweden	14.5	2.7
India.	51.4	0.6	Switzerland	17.9	(NA)
Israel	21.0	0.7	Turkey [2]	25.3	(NA)
Italy	17.6	1.0	United Kingdom	11.5	6.0
Japan.	[4]17.8	(NA)	Venezuela	[3]37.3	(NA)

NA Not available.   [1] Food expenditures include nonalcoholic beverages.   [2] Calculated by using World Bank data on food as a share of gross domestic product.   [3] Food expenditures include nonalcoholic and alcoholic beverages.   [4] Food expenditures include all beverages and tobacco.

Source: U.S. Dept. of Agriculture, Economic Research Service, *Food Consumption, Prices, and Expenditures, 1997: Annual Data, 1970-95.*

No. 1361. Per Capita Consumption of Meat and Poultry: 1997

[Preliminary. In kilograms per capita. Beef, veal, and pork quantities are as of September and in carcass-weight equivalents; poultry quantities are as of July and are on ready-to-cook basis]

COUNTRY	PORK		COUNTRY	POULTRY		COUNTRY	BEEF AND VEAL	
	Quantity	Rank		Quantity	Rank		Quantity	Rank
Czech Republic	67.4	1	Hong Kong	53.8	1	Argentina.	60.8	1
Denmark.	64.5	2	United States	47.0	2	United States	43.8	2
Belgium-Luxembourg	61.2	3	Israel	45.4	3	Brazil	36.4	3
Austria	58.1	4	Singapore	34.1	4	Australia	33.7	4
Spain	54.4	5	Canada	33.8	5	New Zealand	33.7	5
Germany	51.2	6	Saudi Arabia	33.2	6	Canada	31.7	6
Hong Kong	50.5	7	Taiwan	32.5	7	Czech Republic. . . .	29.4	7
Netherlands	44.1	8	Australia	27.4	8	France	26.7	8
Hungary	41.3	9	United Kingdom . . .	26.7	9	Kazakhstan	25.9	9
Taiwan	39.6	10	Ireland	26.6	10	Italy	25.0	10
United States	28.0	21						

Source: U.S. Department of Agriculture, Foreign Agricultural Service, *Livestock and Poultry: World Markets and Trade,* annual.

No. 1362. Motor Vehicle Registrations, by Country: 1995

COUNTRY	ALL VEHICLES		PASSENGER CARS		COUNTRY	ALL VEHICLES		PASSENGER CARS	
	Number (mil.)	Persons per vehicle	Number (mil.)	Persons per car		Number (mil.)	Persons per vehicle	Number (mil.)	Persons per car
Argentina	5.9	6	4.7	7	Israel	1.4	4	1.1	5
Australia	11.2	2	9.0	2	Italy	32.8	2	30.0	2
Austria	4.4	2	3.6	2	Japan.	66.9	2	44.7	3
Belgium	4.8	2	4.2	2	Kuwait	0.7	3	0.5	4
Bulgaria	1.8	5	1.6	5	Netherlands . . .	6.3	2	5.6	3
Canada.	16.7	2	13.2	2	New Zealand . .	2.0	2	1.7	2
Chile	1.4	11	0.9	16	Norway	2.1	2	1.7	3
Costa Rica . . .	0.1	26	0.1	60	Panama	0.2	12	0.1	19
Denmark	2.0	3	1.7	3	Paraguay	0.1	44	0.1	73
Dominican					Poland	3.9	10	3.5	11
Republic	0.2	40	0.1	67	Portugal	3.4	3	2.6	4
Ecuador	0.5	24	0.2	57	Puerto Rico . . .	1.7	2	1.4	3
Finland	2.2	2	1.9	3	Singapore	0.5	7	0.3	10
France	30.3	2	25.1	2	Sweden	4.0	2	3.6	2
Germany	43.6	2	40.5	2	Switzerland . . .	3.5	2	3.2	2
Greece	3.1	3	2.2	5	Syria	0.3	56	0.1	130
Hong Kong . . .	0.5	13	0.3	21	Thailand	5.0	12	1.4	44
Hungary	2.5	4	2.2	5	United States .	200.4	1	135.0	2
Ireland	1.2	3	1.0	4	Uruguay	0.5	7	0.4	7

Source: American Automobile Manufactures Association, Inc., Detroit, MI, *AAMA Motor Vehicle Facts & Figures,* annual, (copyright).

No. 1363. Telephones, Newspapers, Television, and Radio, by Country

[See text, Section 30, for general comments about the data. For data qualifications for countries, see source]

COUNTRY	Telephone main lines per 100 people, [1] 1995	Cellular telephone subscribers per 100,000 people, [1] 1995	Daily newspaper circulation per 1,000 people, [2] 1994	Television receivers per 1,000 people, [3] 1995	Radio receivers per 1,000 people, [4] 1994
Algeria	4	17	46	[5]71	236
Argentina	16	985	138	347	673
Australia	51	12,767	258	482	1,291
Austria	47	4,762	472	497	619
Belgium	46	2,321	321	464	774
Brazil	7	795	45	278	393
Bulgaria	30	193	209	358	454
Canada	[5]59	8,647	189	[5]647	1,051
Chile	13	1,382	100	280	345
China	3	302	23	250	184
Colombia	10	707	64	188	178
Costa Rica	16	549	99	220	260
Cuba	3	18	120	200	347
Cyprus	47	6,065	110	143	300
Czech Republic	24	473	219	406	631
Denmark	61	15,728	365	536	1,036
Dominican Republic	[5]8	422	34	87	173
Ecuador	6	462	72	148	327
Egypt	5	13	64	126	307
Finland	55	19,922	473	519	1,003
France	56	2,375	237	579	891
Germany	49	4,275	317	550	935
Ghana	-	36	18	(NA)	229
Greece	49	2,608	156	442	418
Guatemala	3	282	23	54	68
Honduras	3	-	44	80	408
Hungary	19	2,594	228	441	625
Iceland	55	11,524	515	447	793
India	1	15	(NA)	61	81
Indonesia	2	112	20	[5]147	148
Iran	8	[5]14	(NA)	140	237
Iraq	3	-	27	(NA)	218
Ireland	37	4,406	170	382	636
Israel	42	5,349	281	[5]295	478
Italy	43	6,738	105	436	802
Jamaica	12	1,789	66	285	436
Japan	49	8,149	576	619	912
Korea, South	41	3,659	404	[5]323	1,017
Kuwait	23	7,068	401	379	445
Lebanon	8	2,996	172	268	889
Luxembourg	56	6,578	384	[5]591	636
Malaysia	17	4,337	142	[5]231	432
Mexico	10	699	113	192	256
Morocco	4	110	13	[5]145	219
Netherlands	53	3,318	334	495	909
New Zealand	48	10,801	297	[5]508	991
Norway	56	22,445	607	561	799
Pakistan	2	33	21	[5]22	88
Panama	11	-	62	169	227
Paraguay	[5]3	320	42	73	172
Peru	5	313	86	100	255
Philippines	2	730	65	[5]121	144
Poland	15	194	141	408	441
Portugal	36	3,434	41	332	441
Puerto Rico	33	4,756	184	322	233
Romania	13	40	297	[5]201	713
Russia	17	60	267	[5]379	204
Saudi Arabia	10	90	54	257	339
Singapore	48	9,773	364	362	294
South Africa	9	1,290	33	101	645
Spain	39	2,408	104	490	314
Sweden	68	22,936	483	476	312
Switzerland	61	6,352	409	461	879
Syria	6	-	18	89	841
Taiwan	[6]47	3,616	[6]165	317	257
Thailand	6	1,852	48	[5]221	190
Trinidad and Tobago	16	430	135	318	(NA)
Tunisia	6	36	46	156	491
Turkey	21	699	44	240	199
United Kingdom	50	9,799	351	612	162
United States	**63**	**12,840**	**228**	**776**	1,429
Uruguay	20	1,258	237	305	2,122
Venezuela	11	1,801	215	180	606
					443

- Represents or rounds to zero.   NA Not available.   [1] As of December 31.   [2] Publications containing general news and appearing at least 4 times a week; may range in size from a single sheet to 50 or more pages. Circulation data refer to average circulation per issue or number of printed copies per issue and include copies sold outside the country.   [3] Estimated number of sets in use.   [4] Data cover estimated number of receivers in use and apply to all types of receivers for radio broadcasts to the public, including receivers connected to a radio "redistribution system" but excluding television sets.   [5] For 1994.   [6] Source: U.S. Bureau of the Census. Data from Republic of China publications. Telephone data for 1996; newspaper data for 1995.

Source: International Telecommunications Union, Geneva, Switzerland, *World Telecommunication Indicators*, (copyright); and United Nations Educational, Scientific, and Cultural Organization, Paris, France, *Statistical Yearbook*, (copyright).

No. 1364. Gross Public Debt, Expenditures, and Taxes, by Country: 1970 to 1996

[Percent of gross domestic product]

COUNTRY	GROSS DEBT			EXPENDITURES			TAXES		
	1970	1980	1996	1970	1980	1996	1970	1980	1996
United States	41.5	37.0	63.9	30.0	31.4	33.3	28.9	30.0	31.7
Australia	(NA)	(NA)	43.8	(NA)	31.4	36.6	(NA)	27.7	31.6
Austria	19.4	37.7	69.8	38.5	48.1	51.7	38.5	44.5	46.1
Belgium	63.7	78.2	130.1	41.8	57.8	54.3	38.3	47.4	49.9
Canada	52.8	44.0	100.3	33.5	38.8	44.7	31.3	30.3	37.2
Denmark	(NA)	44.7	74.8	(NA)	56.2	61.5	40.4	48.1	54.4
Finland	15.9	14.1	61.4	30.0	38.1	57.4	33.0	38.4	50.0
France	(NA)	30.9	63.0	38.5	46.1	54.5	37.4	43.6	47.6
Germany	18.1	31.1	64.9	38.3	47.9	49.0	37.2	43.9	44.1
Greece	17.6	22.9	111.9	(NA)	30.4	44.7	21.6	25.1	33.9
Iceland	(NA)	25.2	57.6	(NA)	32.5	38.1	(NA)	31.8	33.5
Ireland	(NA)	72.7	76.5	(NA)	48.2	37.6	(NA)	33.1	35.3
Italy	38.1	58.1	125.2	33.0	42.1	52.9	27.9	32.4	44.8
Japan	11.5	51.2	86.4	19.0	32.0	36.2	19.7	25.6	29.0
Korea, South	23.5	16.0	2.7	(NA)	19.3	21.2	(NA)	18.7	24.3
Netherlands	51.5	46.9	78.5	41.3	55.8	49.9	37.7	45.9	44.8
Norway	42.9	47.6	40.1	36.7	43.8	45.5	37.3	45.8	44.7
Portugal	19.0	32.8	67.6	19.8	23.6	47.0	20.9	27.9	41.3
Spain	(NA)	18.3	74.6	21.6	32.2	43.3	20.9	29.1	37.6
Sweden	30.5	44.3	79.8	42.8	60.1	64.7	43.4	50.6	55.6
United Kingdom	77.1	54.0	61.3	36.7	43.0	41.9	35.6	35.1	35.5

NA Not available.

Source: Organization for Economic Cooperation and Development, Paris, France, *The OECD Observer*, February/March 1998 (copyright).

No. 1365. Percent Distribution of Tax Receipts, by Country: 1980 to 1995

COUNTRY	Total [1]	INCOME AND PROFITS TAXES [2]			SOCIAL SECURITY CONTRIBUTIONS			TAXES ON GOODS AND SERVICES [5]		
		Total [3]	Individual	Corporate	Total [4]	Employees	Employers	Total [3]	General consumption taxes [6]	Taxes on specific goods, services [7]
United States: 1980	100.0	49.8	39.1	10.8	21.9	9.2	11.9	17.6	7.0	8.3
1990	100.0	45.4	37.7	7.7	25.8	11.0	13.4	17.3	8.0	7.1
1995	100.0	45.8	36.3	9.4	25.1	10.7	13.1	17.9	8.0	7.7
Canada: 1980	100.0	46.6	34.1	11.6	10.5	3.7	6.6	32.6	11.5	13.0
1990	100.0	48.6	41.0	7.0	14.3	4.4	9.7	25.9	14.4	9.5
1995	100.0	45.9	37.3	8.1	16.8	5.4	11.1	25.5	15.2	8.4
France: 1980	100.0	18.1	12.9	5.1	42.7	11.1	28.4	30.4	21.1	8.4
1990	100.0	17.2	11.8	5.3	44.1	13.2	27.2	28.4	18.8	8.7
1995	100.0	17.6	13.9	3.7	43.3	13.1	26.8	27.3	17.4	9.0
Germany [8]: 1980	100.0	35.1	29.6	5.5	34.3	15.3	18.4	27.1	16.6	9.3
1990	100.0	32.4	27.6	4.8	37.5	16.2	19.1	26.7	16.6	9.2
1995	100.0	30.1	27.3	2.8	39.4	17.1	20.0	27.8	17.3	9.4
Italy: 1980	100.0	31.1	23.1	7.8	38.0	6.9	28.4	26.5	15.6	9.7
1990	100.0	36.5	26.3	10.0	32.9	6.3	23.6	28.0	14.7	10.6
1995	100.0	35.1	26.2	8.7	31.7	6.7	20.9	27.3	13.9	11.2
Japan: 1980	100.0	46.1	24.3	21.8	29.1	10.2	14.8	16.3	-	14.1
1990	100.0	48.5	26.8	21.6	29.0	11.0	15.0	13.2	4.3	7.3
1995	100.0	36.6	21.4	15.2	36.3	14.4	18.3	15.1	5.2	8.0
Netherlands: 1980	100.0	32.8	26.3	6.6	38.1	15.7	17.8	25.2	15.8	7.3
1990	100.0	32.2	24.7	7.5	37.4	23.1	7.5	26.4	16.5	7.5
1995	100.0	26.4	18.9	7.5	41.8	27.1	6.7	27.4	15.6	9.2
Sweden: 1980	100.0	43.5	41.0	2.5	28.8	0.1	27.6	24.0	13.4	9.2
1990	100.0	41.6	38.5	3.1	27.2	0.1	26.0	25.0	14.9	9.2
1995	100.0	41.4	35.3	6.1	29.1	3.5	24.9	24.3	15.1	8.6
United Kingdom: 1980	100.0	38.2	29.8	8.3	16.6	6.7	9.5	29.2	14.4	13.1
1990	100.0	39.3	28.5	10.8	17.1	6.5	9.9	30.8	16.6	12.7
1995	100.0	36.9	27.4	9.5	17.7	7.4	9.6	34.7	19.0	14.1

- Represents zero. [1] Includes property taxes, employer payroll taxes other than social security contributions, and miscellaneous taxes, not shown separately. [2] Includes taxes on capital gains. [3] Includes other taxes not shown separately. [4] Includes contributions of self-employed not shown separately. [5] Taxes on the production, sales, transfer, leasing, and delivery of goods and services and rendering of services. [6] Primary value-added and sales taxes. [7] For example, excise taxes on alcohol, tobacco, and gasoline. [8] Prior to 1990, data are for former West Germany.

Source: Organization for Economic Cooperation and Development, Paris, France, *Revenue Statistics of OECD Member Countries*, annual (copyright).

No. 1366. Civilian Labor Force, Employment, and Unemployment, by Country: 1980 to 1996

[Data based on U.S. labor force definitions (see source) except that minimum age for population base varies as follows: United States, France, Sweden, and United Kingdom, 16 years; Australia, Canada, Japan, Netherlands, Germany, and Italy (beginning 1994), 15 years; and Italy (prior to 1994) 14 years]

YEAR	United States	Australia	Canada	France	Germany[1]	Italy	Japan	Netherlands	Sweden	United Kingdom
Civilian labor force (mil.):										
1980	106.9	6.7	12.0	22.9	27.3	21.1	55.7	5.9	4.3	26.5
1985	115.5	7.3	13.1	23.6	28.0	21.8	58.8	6.2	4.4	27.2
1990	[2]125.8	8.4	14.3	24.3	29.4	22.7	63.0	6.7	[2]4.6	28.5
1994	[2]131.1	8.8	14.8	24.8	[3]29.9	[2][3]22.6	65.8	7.2	4.4	28.3
1995	132.3	9.0	14.9	24.9	[3]29.7	[3]22.7	66.0	7.3	4.5	28.5
1996	133.9	9.1	15.1	25.1	[3]29.6	[3]22.8	66.4	7.3	4.5	[3]28.6
Labor force participation rate:[4]										
1980	63.8	62.1	64.6	57.5	54.7	48.2	62.6	55.4	66.9	62.5
1985	64.8	61.6	65.8	56.8	54.7	47.2	62.3	55.5	66.9	62.1
1990	[2]66.5	64.6	67.3	56.0	55.3	47.2	62.6	56.1	[2]67.4	63.7
1994	[2]66.6	63.9	65.3	55.5	[3]53.7	[2][3]47.5	63.1	59.0	63.8	62.5
1995	66.6	64.6	64.8	55.3	[3]53.2	[3]47.6	62.9	59.3	[3]64.3	[3]62.7
1996	66.8	64.6	64.9	55.5	[3]52.8	[3]47.7	63.0	[3]59.4	[3]64.3	[3]62.7
Civilian employment (mil.):										
1980	99.3	6.3	11.1	21.4	26.5	20.2	54.6	5.5	4.2	24.7
1985	107.2	6.7	11.7	21.2	26.0	20.5	57.3	5.6	4.3	24.3
1990	[2]118.8	7.9	13.2	22.1	28.0	21.1	61.7	6.2	[2]4.5	26.7
1994	[2]123.1	7.9	13.3	21.7	[3]27.9	[2][3]20.1	63.9	6.7	4.0	25.6
1995	124.9	8.2	13.5	21.9	[3]27.8	[3]20.0	63.9	6.8	4.1	26.0
1996	126.7	8.3	13.7	22.0	[3]27.5	[3]20.0	64.2	6.8	4.0	[3]26.3
Employment-population ratio:[5]										
1980	59.2	58.3	59.7	53.8	53.1	46.1	61.3	52.1	65.6	58.1
1985	60.1	56.5	58.9	50.9	50.7	44.4	60.6	50.1	65.0	55.5
1990	[2]62.8	60.1	61.9	50.9	52.6	43.9	61.3	52.6	[2]66.1	59.6
1994	[2]62.5	57.7	58.5	48.7	[3]50.2	[2][3]42.1	61.3	54.7	57.6	56.5
1995	62.9	59.1	58.6	48.8	[3]49.7	[3]41.8	60.9	[3]55.2	[3]58.4	[3]57.2
1996	63.2	59.1	58.6	48.5	[3]49.0	[3]41.9	60.9	[3]55.6	[3]57.9	[3]57.6
Unemployment rate:										
1980	7.1	6.1	7.5	6.5	2.8	4.4	2.0	6.0	2.0	7.0
1985	7.2	8.3	10.5	10.5	7.2	6.0	2.6	9.6	2.8	11.2
1990	[2]5.6	6.9	8.1	9.1	5.0	7.0	2.1	6.2	[2]1.8	7.0
1994	[2]6.1	9.7	10.4	12.3	[3]6.5	[2][3]11.3	2.9	7.2	9.6	9.7
1995	5.6	8.5	9.5	11.8	[3]6.5	[3]12.0	3.2	7.0	9.1	8.7
1996	5.4	8.6	9.7	12.6	[3]7.2	[3]12.1	3.4	6.4	9.9	[3]8.2
Under 25 years old	12.0	15.7	16.1	[6]27.8	(NA)	(NA)	6.7	(NA)	21.4	[6]14.7
Teenagers[7]	16.7	20.8	20.1	(NA)	(NA)	(NA)	9.3	(NA)	22.8	[6]17.8
20 to 24 years old	9.3	12.3	13.6	(NA)	(NA)	(NA)	6.2	(NA)	21.0	[6]13.0
25 years old and over	4.2	6.7	8.5	[6]10.8	(NA)	(NA)	2.9	(NA)	8.5	[6]6.9

NA Not available.　[1] Former West Germany.　[2] Break in series. Data not comparable with prior years.　[3] Preliminary.
[4] Civilian labor force as a percent of the civilian working age population. Germany and Japan include the institutionalized population as part of the working age population.　[5] Civilian employment as a percent of the civilian working age population. Germany and Japan include the institutionalized population as part of the working age population.　[6] French data are for March; United Kingdom data are for the spring quarter.　[7] 16 to 19 years old in the United States, Sweden, and United Kingdom; 15 to 19 years old in Canada, Australia, and Japan.

Source: U.S. Bureau of Labor Statistics, *Comparative Labor Force Statistics for Ten Countries, 1959-1997*, March 1998, and *Monthly Labor Review*.

No. 1367. Unemployment Rates, by Country: 1995 to 1997

[Annual averages. The standardized unemployment rates shown here are calculated as the number of unemployed persons as a percentage of the civilian labor force. The unemployed are persons of working age who, in the reference period, are without work, available for work and have taken specific steps to find work]

COUNTRY	1995	1996	1997	COUNTRY	1995	1996	1997
OECD, total	7.5	7.6	7.3	Ireland	12.3	11.6	10.1
European Union	10.7	10.9	10.7	Italy	11.9	12.0	12.1
				Japan	3.1	3.4	3.4
United States	5.6	5.4	4.9	Luxembourg	2.9	3.0	2.6
Australia	8.6	8.6	8.7	Netherlands	6.9	6.3	5.2
Austria	3.9	4.3	4.4	New Zealand	6.3	6.1	6.7
Belgium	9.9	9.7	9.2	Norway	5.0	4.9	4.1
Canada	9.5	9.7	9.2	Portugal	7.3	7.3	6.8
Denmark	7.2	6.8	5.5	Spain	22.9	22.2	20.8
Finland	16.2	15.3	13.1	Sweden	8.8	9.6	9.9
France	11.7	12.4	12.4	Switzerland	3.5	3.9	(NA)
Germany	8.2	8.9	10.0	United Kingdom	8.7	8.2	7.0

NA Not available.

Source: Organization for Economic Cooperation and Development, Paris, France, *OECD News Release, Standardised Unemployment Rates*, 21 July 1998.

No. 1368. Civilian Employment-Population Ratio and Females as Percent of Total Civilian Employment, by Country: 1980 to 1996

[See headnote, Table 1366]

COUNTRY	CIVILIAN EMPLOYMENT-POPULATION RATIO [1]								CIVILIAN EMPLOYMENT, PERCENT FEMALE			
	Women				Men							
	1980	1990	1995	1996	1980	1990	1995	1996	1980	1990	1995	1996
United States . .	47.7	[2]54.3	[2]55.6	56.0	72.0	[2]72.0	[2]70.8	70.9	42.4	[2]45.2	[2]46.1	46.2
Australia	41.9	49.3	50.3	50.4	75.1	71.2	68.1	67.9	36.4	41.5	43.1	43.1
Canada	46.7	54.0	52.1	52.1	73.1	70.1	65.5	65.2	39.6	44.4	45.2	45.3
France . [3]	40.3	41.6	41.3	41.1	68.9	61.3	57.3	56.8	39.5	43.0	44.4	44.5
Germany [3]	38.9	[2]40.9	(NA)	(NA)	69.9	[2]65.6	(NA)	(NA)	39.2	[2]41.0	(NA)	(NA)
Italy	27.9	29.2	[2][4]28.4	[4]28.8	66.0	60.0	[2][4]56.5	[4]56.2	31.7	34.7	[2][4]35.3	[4]35.7
Japan	45.7	48.0	47.7	47.7	77.9	75.4	75.0	74.9	38.4	40.3	40.3	40.3
Sweden	58.0	[2]61.8	[4]54.9	[4]54.2	73.6	[2]70.6	[4]62.2	[4]61.8	45.2	[2]47.8	48.1	47.9
United Kingdom .	44.8	49.6	[4]49.6	[4]50.1	72.8	70.3	[4]65.5	[4]65.7	40.4	43.4	44.9	[4]45.0

NA Not available.   [1] Civilian employment as a percent of the civilian working age population.   [2] Break in series. Data not comparable with prior years.   [3] Former West Germany.   [4] Preliminary.

Source: U.S. Bureau of Labor Statistics, *Comparative Labor Force Statistics for Ten Countries, 1959-1997*, March 1998 and *Monthly Labor Review*.

No. 1369. Female Labor Force Participation Rates, by Country: 1980 to 1995

[In percent. Female labor force of all ages divided by female population 15-64 years old]

COUNTRY	1980	1985	1990	1995	COUNTRY	1980	1985	1990	1995
Australia	52.1	54.9	62.9	64.8	Korea, South	(NA)	45.3	51.3	53.2
Austria.	48.7	51.0	55.4	(NA)	Luxembourg	39.9	43.2	50.7	46.8
Belgium	47.0	49.3	52.4	56.1	Mexico	(NA)	(NA)	(NA)	40.1
Canada	59.1	65.1	67.8	67.6	Netherlands	35.5	40.9	53.1	57.1
Czech Republic.	(NA)	(NA)	69.1	65.4	New Zealand	44.5	47.6	62.9	65.8
Denmark	71.4	74.5	78.5	73.6	Norway	62.3	68.0	71.2	72.4
Finland	70.1	73.7	72.9	70.3	Poland.	(NA)	(NA)	(NA)	61.1
France.	54.4	54.8	57.6	59.5	Portugal.	54.3	56.1	62.9	62.4
Germany [1]	52.8	52.9	57.4	61.0	Spain	32.2	33.4	41.2	45.1
Greece	33.0	41.8	43.6	45.9	Sweden	74.1	78.1	80.1	74.5
Hungary.	(NA)	(NA)	(NA)	50.5	Switzerland	54.1	56.2	59.6	67.1
Iceland	55.9	66.2	66.0	81.9	Turkey.	46.3	36.7	36.7	34.2
Ireland.	36.3	36.6	38.9	47.6	United Kingdom	58.3	60.6	65.5	66.0
Italy	39.1	40.5	45.9	42.7	United States	59.7	63.9	68.8	70.7
Japan	54.9	57.2	60.4	62.2					

NA Not available.   [1] Prior to 1991 data are for former West Germany.

Source: Organization for Economic Cooperation and Development, Paris, France, *Labour Force Statistics*, annual (copyright).

No. 1370. Civilian Employment, by Industry and Country: 1990 and 1996

[Data based on U.S. labor force definitions except that minimum age for population base varies as follows: United States, France, Sweden, and United Kingdom, 16 years; Australia, Canada, Germany, Italy (1996), Japan, 15 years; and Italy (1990), 14 years. For the United States and Italy the data are not comparable between 1990 and 1996. Industries based on International Standard Industrial Classification; see text, Section 30]

INDUSTRY	United States	Austra-lia	Canada	France	Germany	Italy	Japan	Sweden	United Kingdom
TOTAL EMPLOYMENT (1,000)									
1990, total	118,793	7,859	13,165	22,098	27,952	21,080	61,710	4,501	26,818
Agriculture, forestry, fishing.	3,394	440	551	1,248	965	1,879	4,270	178	573
Industry [1]	29,834	1,865	3,117	6,425	10,875	[2]6,842	20,890	1,268	8,128
Manufacturing.	21,346	1,170	2,105	4,708	8,839	4,755	15,010	943	[3]5,971
Services	85,565	5,554	9,497	14,425	16,112	12,355	36,550	3,056	18,117
1996, total	126,708	8,344	13,676	21,925	(NA)	20,053	64,200	4,007	26,088
Agriculture, forestry, fishing.	3,570	424	565	1,004	(NA)	1,392	3,390	131	511
Industry [1]	29,030	1,807	2,969	5,479	(NA)	[2]6,471	21,130	1,008	7,006
Manufacturing.	20,518	1,120	2,083	(NA)	(NA)	4,873	14,420	773	5,066
Services	94,108	6,113	10,142	15,442	(NA)	12,190	39,680	2,868	18,571
PERCENT DISTRIBUTION									
1990, total	100	100	100	100	100	100	100	100	100
Agriculture, forestry, fishing.	3	6	4	6	3	9	7	4	2
Industry [1]	25	24	24	29	39	[2]32	34	28	30
Manufacturing.	18	15	16	21	32	23	24	21	[3]22
Services	72	71	72	65	58	59	59	68	68
1996, total	100	100	100	100	(NA)	100	100	100	100
Agriculture, forestry, fishing.	3	5	4	5	(NA)	7	5	3	2
Industry [1]	23	22	22	25	(NA)	[2]32	33	25	27
Manufacturing.	16	13	15	(NA)	(NA)	24	23	19	19
Services	74	73	74	70	(NA)	61	62	72	71

NA Not available.   [1] Includes mining and construction.   [2] Public utilities included in industry.   [3] Includes mining.

Source: U.S. Bureau of Labor Statistics, Office of Productivity and Technology, *Comparative Civilian Labor Force Statistics, 10 Countries, 1959-1997*, March 1998 and unpublished data.

844   Comparative International Statistics

No. 1371. Index of Industrial Production, by Country: 1980 to 1997

[Industrial production index measures output in the manufacturing, mining, and electric and gas utilities industries. Minus sign (-) indicates decrease]

COUNTRY	INDEX (1990=100)								ANNUAL PERCENT CHANGE				
	1980	1985	1992	1993	1994	1995	1996	1997	1992-93	1993-94	1994-95	1995-96	1996-97
OECD, total	79.3	86.3	99.3	98.7	103.2	107.0	109.3	114.2	-0.6	4.6	3.7	2.1	4.5
Australia	76.6	84.9	98.3	101.1	107.1	107.6	110.4	112.1	2.8	5.9	0.5	2.6	1.5
Austria	76.0	82.9	100.7	99.2	103.2	108.3	109.6	(NA)	-1.5	4.0	4.9	1.2	(NA)
Belgium	82.1	85.5	98.0	92.9	94.6	100.7	101.6	106.0	-5.2	1.8	6.4	0.9	4.3
Canada [1]	81.4	93.9	97.2	102.1	108.3	112.7	114.4	120.1	5.0	6.1	4.1	1.5	5.0
Czech Republic	(NA)	(NA)	71.8	68.1	69.5	75.6	77.0	80.5	-5.2	2.1	8.8	1.9	4.5
Finland	75.3	87.8	92.2	97.2	108.3	117.1	121.0	131.8	5.4	11.4	8.1	3.3	8.9
France	89.2	89.2	97.6	93.9	97.6	99.6	99.8	103.6	-3.8	3.9	2.0	0.2	3.8
Germany [2]	83.0	85.6	100.9	93.6	96.9	98.9	99.3	103.3	-7.2	3.5	2.1	0.4	4.0
Greece	90.9	97.4	98.0	95.2	96.4	98.2	99.3	100.6	-2.9	1.3	1.9	1.1	1.3
Hungary	102.9	112.6	73.8	76.6	84.0	87.9	90.9	100.9	3.8	9.7	4.6	3.4	11.0
Ireland	54.2	69.5	112.7	119.0	133.2	158.3	170.9	197.1	5.6	11.9	18.8	8.0	15.3
Italy	87.5	84.8	97.8	95.7	101.7	107.9	104.8	107.7	-2.1	6.3	6.1	-2.9	2.8
Japan	67.3	79.8	96.0	92.0	93.1	96.2	98.5	101.9	-4.2	1.2	3.3	2.4	3.5
Korea, South	33.1	54.5	116.0	121.1	134.5	150.5	161.6	172.6	4.4	11.1	11.9	7.4	6.8
Luxembourg	69.7	84.7	99.5	95.2	100.9	102.3	100.4	107.4	-4.3	6.0	1.4	-1.9	7.0
Mexico [3]	84.0	88.8	107.9	108.2	113.4	104.5	115.2	125.9	0.3	4.8	-7.8	10.2	9.3
Netherlands	86.8	91.7	101.5	100.3	104.6	106.7	111.2	113.4	-1.2	4.3	2.0	4.2	2.0
Norway	58.3	79.0	108.3	112.2	120.0	127.2	134.1	138.6	3.6	7.0	6.0	5.4	3.4
Poland	(NA)	122.4	87.4	91.6	103.6	114.3	125.0	139.1	4.8	13.1	10.3	9.4	11.3
Portugal	62.8	73.9	97.7	95.2	95.0	99.4	100.8	103.3	-2.6	-0.2	4.6	1.4	2.5
Spain	83.0	85.7	96.3	91.8	98.6	103.3	102.0	109.1	-4.7	7.4	4.8	-1.3	7.0
Sweden [4]	83.0	91.5	93.8	94.3	105.5	117.8	120.5	129.4	0.5	11.9	11.7	2.3	7.4
Switzerland	82	85	99	97	102	104	103	109	-2.0	5.2	2.0	-1.0	5.8
United States	80.5	89.0	101.1	104.7	110.3	115.8	119.8	125.8	3.6	5.3	5.0	3.5	5.0

NA Not available.   [1] Gross domestic product in industry at factor cost and 1986 prices.   [2] 1980-90 former West Germany; later data use 1990 annual average data for West Germany as base year.   [3] Includes construction.   [4] Mining and manufacturing.

Source: Organization for Economic Cooperation and Development, Paris, France, *Main Economic Indicators, Historical Statistics, 1969-1988*, 1990; and *Main Economic Indicators*, monthly (copyright).

No. 1372. Indexes of Hourly Compensation Costs for Production Workers in Manufacturing, by Country: 1980 to 1996

[United States=100. Compensation costs include all pay made directly to the worker—pay for time worked and not worked (eg. leave, except sick leave), other direct pay, employer expenditures for legally required insurance programs and contractual and private benefit plans, and for some countries, other labor taxes. Data adjusted for exchange rates. Area averages are trade-weighted to account for difference in countries' relative importance to U.S. trade in manufactured goods. The trade weights used are the sum of U.S. imports of manufactured products for consumption (customs value) and U.S. domestic exports of manufactured products (f.a.s. value) in 1992; see source for detail]

AREA OR COUNTRY	1980	1985	1990	1994	1995	1996	AREA OR COUNTRY	1980	1985	1990	1994	1995	1996
United States	100	100	100	100	100	100	Austria [6]	90	58	119	128	148	141
Total [1]	67	52	83	89	95	91	Belgium	133	69	129	138	156	147
OECD [2]	74	57	90	96	103	98	Denmark	110	62	120	121	141	137
Europe	101	61	116	114	128	125	Finland [7]	83	63	141	113	144	138
Asian newly industrial-							France	91	58	102	101	113	109
izing economies [3] . . .	12	13	25	34	37	39	Germany [6,8]	125	74	147	159	185	180
Canada	88	84	106	94	93	94	Greece	38	28	45	45	52	(NA)
Mexico	22	12	11	15	9	8	Ireland	60	46	79	75	80	80
Australia [4]	86	63	88	83	88	93	Italy	83	59	119	95	96	102
Hong Kong [5]	15	13	21	27	28	29	Luxembourg	121	59	110	119	134	(NA)
Israel	38	31	57	54	61	62	Netherlands	122	67	123	124	141	132
Japan	56	49	86	125	138	119	Norway	117	80	144	124	142	141
Korea, South	10	9	25	38	43	46	Portugal	21	12	25	27	31	(NA)
New Zealand	54	34	56	53	59	62	Spain	60	36	76	68	74	75
Singapore	15	19	25	37	43	47	Sweden	127	74	140	112	126	138
Sri Lanka.	2	2	2	3	3	(NA)	Switzerland	112	74	140	148	170	160
Taiwan	10	12	26	33	34	33	United Kingdom	77	48	85	76	80	80

NA Not available.   [1] The 28 foreign economies shown below.   [2] Organization for Economic Cooperation and Development; see text, Section 30.   [3] Hong Kong, South Korea, Singapore, and Taiwan.   [4] Includes non-production workers, except in managerial, executive, professional, and higher supervisory positions.   [5] Average of selected manufacturing industries.   [6] Excludes workers in establishments considered handicraft manufactures (including all printing and publishing and miscellaneous manufacturing in Austria).   [7] Includes workers in mining and electrical power plants.   [8] Former West Germany.

Source: U.S. Bureau of Labor Statistics, *News Release* USDL 97-213, June 27, 1997.

No. 1373. Selected Indexes of Manufacturing Activity, by Country: 1980 to 1996

[1992=100. Data relate to employees (wage and salary earners) in Belgium, Italy, the Netherlands, and the United Kingdom, and to all employed persons (employees and self-employed workers) in the other countries. Minus sign (-) indicates decrease. For explanation of average annual percent change, see Guide to Tabular Presentation]

INDEX	United States	Canada	Japan	Belgium	France	Germany [1]	Italy	Netherlands	Norway	Sweden	United Kingdom
Output per hour:											
1980	71.9	78.5	63.9	64.5	70.5	77.3	64.0	69.8	76.7	74.0	54.4
1985	87.7	94.1	77.3	86.3	83.8	88.9	81.5	89.7	90.2	87.1	71.2
1990	97.7	95.8	95.4	96.9	99.1	99.0	92.8	98.5	96.6	95.0	89.3
1994	108.1	106.2	101.8	110.0	110.4	108.4	107.4	114.2	101.4	116.1	109.3
1995	115.1	107.5	109.2	109.4	114.5	112.0	110.7	119.6	102.5	122.4	107.6
1996	120.2	108.6	114.3	110.6	117.0	117.0	113.3	122.6	103.3	125.4	106.1
Average annual percent change:											
1979-85	3.3	2.4	3.5	6.1	3.0	2.0	4.9	4.4	2.4	3.0	4.4
1985-90	2.2	0.4	4.3	2.3	3.4	2.2	2.6	1.9	1.4	1.8	4.6
1990-96	3.5	2.1	3.0	2.2	2.8	2.8	3.4	3.7	1.1	4.7	2.9
Compensation per hour, national currency basis: [2]											
1980	55.8	50.2	58.6	52.7	41.3	53.8	27.9	64.7	39.0	37.4	33.8
1985	75.3	74.6	72.5	74.5	73.7	70.2	60.1	81.9	63.4	58.4	54.7
1990	91.0	91.3	90.7	89.9	91.8	89.4	84.0	90.8	92.3	87.6	83.5
1994	105.6	102.1	106.7	108.4	106.2	112.1	106.6	108.2	104.4	101.1	108.3
1995	108.7	103.9	110.0	111.6	107.7	117.4	109.2	111.1	109.2	106.2	108.7
1996	112.2	108.5	111.6	114.3	109.6	123.5	117.1	114.5	114.0	113.4	110.8
Average annual percent change:											
1979-85	7.1	8.7	4.7	7.8	12.8	5.9	16.7	4.9	10.0	9.6	11.8
1985-90	3.9	4.1	4.6	3.8	4.5	5.0	6.9	2.1	7.8	8.5	8.8
1990-96	3.6	2.9	3.5	4.1	3.0	5.5	5.7	3.9	3.6	4.4	4.8
Real hourly compensation: [2][3]											
1980	94.9	95.7	75.4	87.0	80.6	74.8	78.8	87.8	86.0	87.5	70.3
1985	98.1	99.4	81.4	87.5	90.9	80.7	88.9	90.6	90.8	87.2	80.1
1990	97.6	97.8	95.3	95.1	97.3	96.4	94.3	96.5	97.7	97.4	91.7
1994	100.0	100.1	104.7	103.1	102.4	105.2	98.4	102.7	100.7	96.2	104.1
1995	100.1	99.7	107.9	104.6	102.0	108.3	95.6	103.6	102.8	96.8	101.0
1996	100.3	102.5	109.4	104.9	101.8	112.4	98.9	104.6	105.9	102.7	100.5
Average annual percent change:											
1979-85	0.3	0.7	1.1	0.8	2.3	1.8	1.5	0.3	0.6	-0.5	2.6
1985-90	-0.1	-0.3	3.2	1.7	1.4	3.6	1.2	1.3	1.5	2.2	2.7
1990-96	0.4	0.8	2.3	1.6	0.8	2.6	0.8	1.3	1.4	0.9	1.5
Unit labor costs, national currency:											
1980	77.6	63.9	91.7	81.8	58.6	69.6	43.7	92.7	50.8	50.6	62.1
1985	85.8	79.3	93.8	86.3	88.0	78.9	73.8	91.3	70.2	67.1	76.9
1990	93.1	95.2	95.0	92.7	92.6	90.3	90.5	92.1	95.6	92.3	93.5
1994	97.7	96.1	104.9	98.6	96.2	103.5	99.2	94.8	102.9	87.0	99.1
1995	94.5	96.7	100.7	102.0	94.0	104.8	98.6	92.9	106.5	86.8	101.0
1996	93.3	99.9	97.7	103.3	93.7	105.5	103.3	93.4	110.3	90.4	104.4
Average annual percent change:											
1979-85	3.7	6.1	1.2	1.6	9.5	3.8	11.2	0.5	7.4	6.4	7.1
1985-90	1.6	3.7	0.3	1.5	1.0	2.7	4.2	0.2	6.4	6.6	4.0
1990-96	-	0.8	0.5	1.8	0.2	2.6	2.2	0.2	2.4	-0.3	1.9
Unit labor costs, U.S. dollar basis: [4]											
1980	77.6	66.1	51.5	90.0	73.5	59.9	62.9	82.1	63.9	69.6	81.7
1985	85.8	70.1	49.9	46.8	51.9	41.9	47.6	48.4	50.8	45.4	56.5
1990	93.1	98.6	83.1	89.2	90.0	87.2	93.0	88.9	95.0	90.8	94.5
1994	97.7	85.0	130.1	94.8	91.8	99.6	75.8	91.6	90.7	65.7	86.0
1995	94.5	85.2	135.9	111.3	99.8	114.3	74.6	101.8	104.5	70.8	90.2
1996	93.3	88.5	113.8	107.2	96.9	109.5	82.5	97.4	106.1	78.5	92.3
Average annual percent change:											
1979-85	3.7	3.4	-0.3	-9.7	-3.3	-4.1	-3.2	-7.6	-1.7	-5.2	-1.3
1985-90	1.6	7.1	10.8	13.8	11.7	15.8	14.3	12.9	13.3	14.8	10.8
1990-96	-	-1.8	5.4	3.1	1.2	3.9	-2.0	1.5	1.9	-2.4	-0.4
Employment:											
1980	111.6	110.5	87.4	120.9	124.7	102.2	126.4	107.5	134.5	130.9	159.0
1985	106.0	105.6	91.9	104.6	110.0	94.9	105.4	94.9	120.7	122.0	123.3
1990	105.5	111.6	95.8	102.5	105.1	100.3	106.8	101.1	105.4	117.2	116.2
1994	101.3	103.5	95.9	91.1	92.7	89.3	94.1	91.3	104.7	94.2	97.0
1995	102.5	105.8	93.5	95.5	92.6	87.3	93.6	89.6	107.6	98.8	99.4
1996	102.0	106.7	92.7	94.2	91.2	84.6	92.8	88.8	109.8	98.1	100.7
Average annual percent change:											
1979-85	-1.4	-0.8	1.2	-2.7	-2.3	-1.1	-2.9	-2.3	-1.8	-1.2	-4.9
1985-90	-0.1	1.1	0.8	-0.4	-0.9	1.1	0.3	1.3	-2.7	-0.8	-1.2
1990-96	-0.6	-0.7	-0.5	-1.4	-2.3	-2.8	-2.3	-2.1	0.7	-2.9	-2.4
Aggregate hours:											
1980	107.6	109.5	93.8	121.4	131.5	110.3	123.0	111.4	135.0	124.0	160.3
1985	104.7	104.8	98.4	103.0	108.9	99.4	101.4	96.1	120.2	119.4	125.1
1990	104.9	110.8	100.9	104.3	104.5	100.1	108.2	101.6	103.7	116.4	118.0
1994	103.8	106.2	93.7	92.2	91.8	86.3	94.8	91.3	100.2	99.6	97.2
1995	104.1	108.9	92.0	95.6	92.0	84.1	97.2	89.8	107.2	106.3	100.3
1996	103.5	109.1	92.0	94.6	90.8	80.3	94.3	89.0	109.3	106.0	102.1
Average annual percent change:											
1979-85	-1.2	-0.9	1.1	-3.3	-3.3	-1.8	-3.1	-2.5	-1.8	-0.8	-5.3
1985-90	-	1.1	0.5	0.2	-0.8	0.2	1.3	1.1	-2.9	-0.5	-1.2
1990-96	-0.2	-0.3	-1.5	-1.6	-2.3	-3.6	-2.3	-2.2	0.9	-1.6	-2.4

- Represents or rounds to zero. [1] Former West Germany. [2] Compensation includes, but real hourly compensation excludes, adjustments for payroll and employment taxes that are not compensation to employees, but are labor costs to employers. [3] Index of hourly compensation divided by the index of consumer prices to adjust for changes in purchasing power. [4] Indexes in national currency adjusted for changes in prevailing exchange rates.
Source: Bureau of Labor Statistics, *Manufacturing Productivity and Unit Labor Cost Trends, 1996*, March 28, 1998.

No. 1374. Relative Labor Productivity Levels in Manufacturing in Selected OECD Countries: 1973 to 1996

[United States=100. The productivity levels for the United States, Canada, Japan, Australia, France, Germany, the Netherlands, Sweden, and the United Kingdom are based on the estimates presented in Table 1375. The estimates for other countries are derived from various industry-of-origin studies, using a standardized methodology. For details, see source]

| | VALUE ADDED | | | | | |
| | 1973 | | 1985 | | 1996 [1] | |
COUNTRY	Per person engaged	Per hour worked	Per person engaged	Per hour worked	Per person engaged	Per hour worked
United States	100	100	100	100	100	100
Canada	81	82	82	84	67	68
Mexico	34	32	34	31	33	(NA)
Japan	55	48	78	69	76	74
Australia	50	50	54	56	50	51
France	66	70	72	86	69	84
Germany [2]	73	76	76	86	63	82
Netherlands	77	88	86	107	75	97
Sweden	66	80	68	87	74	90
United Kingdom	52	54	55	60	58	67

NA Not available.   [1] 1990 for Mexico; 1994 for Australia; and 1995 for Netherlands.   [2] Data are for former West Germany.

Source: Organization for Economic Cooperation and Development, Paris, France, *Science, Technology and Industry Outlook 1998*, 1998 (copyright).

No. 1375. Manufacturing Labor Productivity Levels in Major OECD Economies: 1993

[Value added per hour worked, leader country=100 (the productivity level of the leader country in each industry is indicated in bold). Data are updated from benchmark productivity comparisons for 1987 using output and employment series from OECD's STAN database. The trend in total hours worked at the sectoral level is assumed to be identical to the trend for total manufacturing. A mix of industry-of-origin and expenditure purchasing power parities (PPPs) (see text, Section 30) for the conversion of value added to a common currency were used. Industry-of-origin price comparisons were used where possible and were applied in more than 65 percent of all cases. These price ratios are all based on price comparisons between the United States and one other country. Conversion factors from sector-specific private studies were used for Japan and Germany for those industries where these estimates were available. For the other cases expenditure PPPs, adjusted for net indirect tax rates and industry-specific distribution margins were applied. Estimates of productivity levels were derived from a combination of PPPs, hours worked, employment, and value added]

SECTOR	United States	Japan	Germany [1]	France	United Kingdom	Canada	Australia	Netherlands	Sweden
Total manufacturing	100.0	76.6	79.8	84.2	64.1	71.3	52.0	95.6	91.8
Food, beverages and tobacco	100.0	35.6	88.7	87.0	41.7	64.3	51.1	96.6	72.8
Textiles, clothing & footwear	78.3	41.9	72.1	67.1	51.5	46.3	32.3	100.0	66.5
Wood products & furniture	56.0	17.6	55.7	55.3	28.1	52.6	27.1	100.0	71.9
Paper products & printing	85.0	49.7	59.0	64.3	76.4	67.6	53.7	64.5	100.0
Chemical products	66.9	52.6	55.4	56.9	79.7	52.6	39.8	100.0	89.4
Non-metallic mineral products	81.8	62.9	79.5	99.4	70.6	78.4	77.4	100.0	81.0
Basic metal products	76.8	78.3	72.9	63.3	61.4	87.9	56.8	70.4	100.0
Metal products	68.9	67.6	64.6	46.4	42.5	54.8	35.9	54.0	100.0
Machinery & equipment	100.0	67.4	49.2	67.3	47.9	55.5	46.4	34.6	45.2
Electrical machinery	80.3	89.0	49.9	78.9	48.2	51.9	28.0	82.2	100.0
Transport equipment	88.4	100.0	68.0	85.0	47.8	71.9	45.5	41.8	49.5
Other manufacturing	100.0	41.4	43.1	31.4	43.5	33.5	22.1	27.0	47.4

[1] Data are for former West Germany.

Source: Pilat, Dirk, "Labour Productivity Levels in OECD Countries: Estimates for Manufacturing and Selected Service Sectors", *Economics Department Working Papers, No. 169*, Organisation for Economic Cooperation and Development, Paris, France, 1996 (copyright) and unpublished data.

No. 1376. Patents, by Country: 1996

[Includes only U.S. patents granted to residents of areas outside of the United States and its territories]

COUNTRY	Total [1]	Inventions	Designs	COUNTRY	Total [1]	Inventions	Designs
Total	52,372	48,542	3,547	Switzerland	1,191	1,112	74
				Sweden	971	854	115
Japan	24,047	23,053	936	Netherlands	885	797	44
Germany	7,125	6,818	250	Australia	566	471	87
France	3,016	2,788	201	Israel	525	484	32
United Kingdom	2,674	2,453	202	Belgium	516	488	26
Canada	2,639	2,233	401	Finland	453	444	9
Taiwan	2,419	1,897	522	Austria	387	362	25
Korea, South	1,567	1,493	72	Denmark	334	241	66
Italy	1,385	1,200	179	Other countries	1,672	1,354	306

[1] Includes patents for botanical plants and reissues, not shown separately.

Source: U.S. Patent and Trademark Office, Technology Assessment and Forecast Data Base.

No. 1377. World Production of Major Mineral Commodities: 1990 to 1997

COUNTRY	Unit	1990	1995	1996	1997, est.	Leading producers, 1996
MINERAL FUELS						
Coal.	Mil. short tons. .	5,356	5,144	5,185	(NA)	China, United States, India
Dry natural gas	Tril. cu. ft. . . .	73.6	77.9	82.0	(NA)	Russia, United States, Canada
Natural gas plant liquids [1] . . .	Mil. barrels [2]. .	1,691	2,002	2,037	(NA)	United States, Saudi Arabia, Canada
Petroleum, crude	Mil. barrels [2]. .	22,107	22,751	23,380	(NA)	Saudi Arabia, United States, Russia
NONMETALLIC MINERALS						
Cement, hydraulic	Mil. metric tons .	1,160	1,444	1,485	1,500	China, Japan, United States
Diamond, gem and industrial .	Mil. carats	111	113	117	118	Australia, Russia, Congo (Kinshasa)
Nitrogen in ammonia.	Mil. metric tons .	97.5	96.1	97.5	96.0	China, United States, India
Phosphate rock	Mil. metric tons .	162	130	133	136	United States, China, Morocco
Potash, marketable.	Mil. metric tons .	27.5	24.7	23.9	23.5	Canada, Germany, Belarus
Salt.	Mil. metric tons .	183	192	192	192	United States, China, Canada
Sulfur, elemental basis	Mil. metric tons .	57.8	53.2	52.2	54.0	United States, Canada, China
METALS						
Aluminum [3]	Mil. metric tons .	19.3	19.9	20.7	21.2	United States, Russia, Canada
Bauxite, gross weight	Mil. metric tons .	113.0	107.0	114.0	115.0	Australia, Guinea, Jamaica
Chromite, gross weight [1]	1,000 metric tons	13,200	14,300	12,200	12,000	South Africa, Turkey, India
Copper, metal content [4]	1,000 metric tons	8,950	10,100	11,000	11,300	Chile, United States, Canada
Gold, metal content	Metric tons. . . .	2,180	2,220	2,250	2,300	South Africa, United States, Australia
Iron ore, gross weight [5]	Mil. metric tons .	983	1,030	1,020	1,030	China, Brazil, Australia
Lead, metal content [4]	1,000 metric tons	3,370	2,780	2,920	2,900	Australia, China, United States
Manganese ore, gross weight.	Mil. metric tons .	26.1	23.0	22.3	(NA)	China, South Africa, Ukraine
Nickel, metal content [4]	1,000 metric tons	974	1,030	1,080	1,080	Russia, Canada, New Caledonia
Steel, crude	Mil. metric tons .	771	755	758	773	European Union, Japan, China
Tin, metal content [4]	1,000 metric tons	221	195	196	201	China, Indonesia, Peru
Zinc, metal content [4]	1,000 metric tons	7,150	7,240	7,440	7,800	Canada, Australia, China

NA Not available.   [1] Excludes China.   [2] 42-gallon barrels.   [3] Unalloyed ingot metal.   [4] Mine output.   [5] Includes iron ore concentrates and iron ore agglomerates.

Source: Mineral fuels, Energy Information Administration, *International Energy Annual;* nonmetallic minerals and metals, 1990, U.S. Bureau of Mines, thereafter, U.S. Geological Survey, *Minerals Yearbook; Annual Reports;* and *Mineral Commodity Summaries, 1997.*

No. 1378. Selected Petroleum Product Prices, by Country: 1997

[Data are averages for the available time period (daily, monthly, quarterly, year) that is closest to January 1, 1997. Includes taxes]

COUNTRY	AUTOMOTIVE FUELS (U.S. dollars per gallon)		RESIDENTIAL (U.S. dollars per gallon)				INDUSTRIAL (U.S. dollars per barrel)	
	Premium gasoline	Diesel fuel	Light fuel oil	Kerosene	Liquified petroleum gases	Light fuel oil	Heavy fuel oil
United States	**1.42**	**1.29**	**1.08**	**0.89**	**0.92**	**31.71**	**20.62**
Argentina	3.10	1.00	0.87	1.15	2.39	41.81	23.31
Australia	2.20	2.27	(NA)	(NA)	(NA)	(NA)	(NA)
Belgium	4.20	3.02	1.04	(NA)	(NA)	36.04	20.10
Brazil.	2.30	1.31	1.04	1.38	1.21	54.82	28.97
Canada	1.92	1.56	1.15	(NA)	(NA)	29.60	18.67
Chile	2.16	1.41	0.99	1.17	1.57	59.01	28.68
France	4.22	3.08	1.63	(NA)	(NA)	48.60	23.55
Germany	3.87	2.91	1.18	(NA)	(NA)	43.22	20.95
Greece	3.06	2.43	1.71	(NA)	(NA)	60.70	31.07
India [1]	[2]2.25	0.92	(NA)	(NA)	(NA)	30.77	24.51
Ireland	3.74	(NA)	1.53	(NA)	(NA)	45.91	25.78
Italy	4.21	3.38	3.29	(NA)	(NA)	116.23	25.79
Japan	[2]3.28	2.34	1.55	1.56	(NA)	44.14	25.00
Korea, South	3.82	1.74	(NA)	1.72	2.27	(NA)	35.71
Mexico	1.41	1.05	0.86	1.05	0.67	44.12	19.72
Netherlands	4.57	3.92	1.54	(NA)	(NA)	(NA)	32.06
Norway.	4.97	4.41	2.38	(NA)	(NA)	76.77	55.40
Peru	2.68	1.40	(NA)	1.14	1.70	58.71	27.68
Philippines [1]	1.38	1.08	(NA)	1.08	0.81	(NA)	17.12
Russia	[2]0.46	0.48	0.22	(NA)	(NA)	9.31	(NA)
Saudi Arabia	[2]0.61	0.37	0.15	0.44	(NA)	0.37	(NA)
Spain	3.10	2.53	1.35	(NA)	(NA)	48.74	27.31
Sweden	4.34	3.55	2.30	(NA)	(NA)	39.93	30.94
Switzerland	3.29	3.47	0.98	(NA)	(NA)	33.39	21.55
Turkey	2.55	1.87	2.02	(NA)	(NA)	(NA)	26.12
United Kingdom	4.25	3.78	1.04	(NA)	(NA)	38.45	24.30
Venezuela.	0.47	0.38	0.07	0.55	0.29	15.86	1.18

NA Not available.   [1] Data for 1995.   [2] Regular gasoline.

Source: Energy Information Administration, *International Energy Annual.*

No. 1379. Energy Consumption and Production, by Country: 1990 and 1996

[See text, Section 30, for general comments about the data. For data qualifications for countries, see source]

| COUNTRY | PRIMARY ENERGY CONSUMED | | | | DRY NATURAL GAS PRODUCTION (quad. Btu) | | CRUDE PETROLEUM PRODUCTION (1,000 barrels per day) | | COAL PRODUCTION (mil. short tons) | |
| | Total (quad. Btu) | | Per capita (mil. Btu) | | | | | | | |
	1990	1996	1990	1996	1990	1996	1990	1996	1990	1996
World	344.0	375.1	65	65	72.53	81.90	60,566	64,054	5,356	5,185
United States	84.2	93.4	337	352	18.36	19.54	7,355	6,465	1,029	1,064
Algeria	1.1	1.4	45	47	1.90	2.56	1,175	1,242	(Z)	(Z)
Argentina	1.8	2.6	57	74	0.59	1.11	483	756	(Z)	(Z)
Australia...........	3.7	4.1	217	223	0.76	1.12	575	570	226	274
Austria	1.2	1.3	154	158	0.05	0.06	22	21	3	1
Bahrain	0.3	0.3	532	517	0.21	0.26	42	35	(NA)	(NA)
Bangladesh.........	0.3	0.4	2	3	0.15	0.25	1	1	(NA)	(NA)
Belarus...........	(X)	1.0	(X)	100	(X)	0.01	(X)	36	(X)	(NA)
Belgium	2.2	2.5	216	247	(Z)	(Z)	(NA)	(NA)	3	1
Brazil	5.7	7.2	39	46	0.11	0.24	631	795	5	5
Bulgaria	1.3	1.0	141	115	-	(Z)	4	1	35	32
Burma	(NA)	(NA)	2	2	0.04	0.06	13	15	(Z)	(Z)
Canada	10.9	12.2	392	407	3.90	5.97	1,553	1,837	75	84
Chile	0.6	0.8	43	55	0.07	0.06	20	9	2	1
China.............	27.0	37.0	23	30	0.56	0.78	2,774	3,131	1,190	1,550
Colombia	1.0	1.3	30	36	0.14	0.17	440	623	23	33
Congo (Kinshasa) [1]	(NA)	(NA)	3	2	(NA)	(NA)	29	30	(Z)	(Z)
Cuba	0.5	0.4	46	37	(Z)	(Z)	14	30	(NA)	(NA)
Czech Republic	(X)	2.3	(X)	227	(X)	0.01	(X)	4	(X)	77
Denmark...........	0.8	0.9	156	173	0.12	0.25	121	208	(NA)	(NA)
Ecuador...........	(NA)	(NA)	25	29	0.01	0.01	285	396	(NA)	(NA)
Egypt.............	1.4	1.6	27	27	0.30	0.50	873	922	(NA)	(NA)
Finland............	1.1	1.1	229	208	(NA)	(NA)	(NA)	(NA)	(NA)	(NA)
France	8.8	9.9	156	169	0.11	0.10	61	43	15	10
Germany	(X)	14.4	(X)	176	(X)	0.70	(X)	60	(X)	264
Greece............	1.1	1.2	103	112	0.01	(Z)	15	8	57	66
Hong Kong	0.5	0.6	85	97	(NA)	(NA)	(NA)	(NA)	(NA)	(NA)
Hungary	1.3	1.1	120	112	0.15	0.16	40	32	19	17
India	7.7	11.6	9	12	0.41	0.80	660	651	233	311
Indonesia	2.2	3.5	12	18	1.53	2.65	1,462	1,547	12	53
Iran	3.1	4.0	57	66	0.88	1.45	3,088	3,686	1	1
Iraq	0.9	1.2	51	58	0.15	0.12	2,040	579	(NA)	(NA)
Ireland	0.4	0.5	105	127	0.08	0.10	(NA)	(NA)	(Z)	(Z)
Israel	0.5	0.6	96	112	(Z)	(Z)	(Z)	(Z)	(NA)	(NA)
Italy	7.0	7.6	122	131	0.63	0.72	87	101	1	(Z)
Japan	18.1	21.4	147	170	0.08	0.09	11	12	11	7
Korea, North	2.1	2.2	103	96	(NA)	(NA)	(NA)	(NA)	71	81
Korea, South	3.7	7.2	86	157	(NA)	(NA)	(NA)	(NA)	19	5
Kuwait	0.5	0.5	208	319	0.19	0.22	1,175	2,062	(NA)	(NA)
Libya	0.5	0.6	123	102	0.23	0.24	1,375	1,401	(NA)	(NA)
Malaysia...........	1.0	1.7	55	81	0.68	1.36	619	695	(Z)	(Z)
Mexico	4.9	5.6	57	58	0.96	1.08	2,553	2,855	7	10
Morocco	0.3	0.4	13	14	(Z)	(Z)	(Z)	(Z)	1	1
Netherlands	3.4	3.8	225	242	2.41	3.01	70	56	(NA)	(NA)
New Zealand........	0.7	0.9	218	247	0.17	0.20	40	37	3	4
Nigeria	0.7	0.9	6	7	0.14	0.19	1,810	2,188	(Z)	(Z)
Norway............	1.6	1.7	373	397	1.06	1.61	1,704	3,104	(Z)	(Z)
Pakistan	1.2	1.7	10	13	0.45	0.65	62	55	3	4
Peru	(NA)	(NA)	18	21	0.02	0.03	129	120	(Z)	(Z)
Philippines	0.7	1.0	12	14	-	(Z)	5	2	1	2
Poland	3.9	3.8	103	98	0.12	0.13	2	5	237	219
Portugal	0.7	0.9	75	87	(NA)	(NA)	(NA)	(NA)	(Z)	(Z)
Romania	2.9	2.1	124	93	1.07	0.67	163	135	42	45
Russia	(X)	26.0	(X)	176	(X)	19.35	(X)	5,850	(X)	302
Saudi Arabia	3.2	4.0	212	214	1.13	1.53	6,410	8,218	(NA)	(NA)
Serbia	(X)	0.5	(X)	51	(X)	0.02	(X)	22	(X)	43
South Africa	3.4	4.3	91	100	-	0.07	(NA)	(NA)	193	227
Spain	3.9	4.5	101	115	0.06	0.02	16	15	40	33
Sweden	2.2	2.3	252	255	(NA)	(NA)	(Z)	(Z)	(Z)	(Z)
Switzerland	1.2	1.2	174	172	(Z)	-	(NA)	(NA)	(NA)	(NA)
Syria	0.6	0.7	50	45	0.11	0.10	388	604	(NA)	(NA)
Taiwan	2.0	3.1	100	145	0.08	0.04	3	1	1	(Z)
Tajikistan	(NA)	(NA)	(X)	30	(X)	(Z)	(X)	2	(X)	(Z)
Thailand	1.3	2.3	22	39	0.21	0.43	44	61	14	21
Trinidad and Tobago	(NA)	(NA)	185	284	0.18	0.32	150	130	(NA)	(NA)
Tunisia............	(NA)	(NA)	25	27	0.01	0.03	93	87	(NA)	(NA)
Turkey	2.0	2.7	35	43	0.01	0.01	73	67	52	63
Ukraine	(X)	6.3	(X)	122	(X)	0.59	(X)	66	(X)	77
United Arab Emirates ...	1.2	1.8	640	793	0.82	1.34	2,117	2,278	(NA)	(NA)
United Kingdom	9.5	10.1	165	171	1.92	3.34	1,820	2,568	106	56
Venezuela..........	2.1	2.6	108	117	0.91	1.06	2,137	3,053	2	4
Vietnam...........	0.3	0.5	4	6	(Z)	0.03	50	175	5	9

- Represents zero.   NA Not available.   X Not applicable.   Z Less than 5 tril. Btu, 500 barrels per day, or 500,000 short tons.   [1] See footnote 3, Table 1343.

Source: U.S. Energy Information Administration, *International Energy Annual*.

No. 1380. World Food Production, by Commodity: 1990 to 1997

[In millions of metric tons]

COMMODITY	1990	1991	1992	1993	1994	1995	1996	1997, prel.
Grains, total	1,768.6	1,708.0	1,789.8	1,714.3	1,762.7	1,710.6	1,870.4	1,890.1
Wheat	588.0	543.0	562.3	559.3	524.6	537.5	582.4	609.8
Coarse grains	828.6	810.3	871.8	799.5	873.6	801.9	908.1	898.9
Corn	482.3	491.2	538.5	475.5	561.8	515.5	591.4	585.8
Rice, milled.	352.0	354.7	355.7	355.5	364.5	371.2	379.9	381.4
Oils.	58.3	61.0	61.7	63.7	70.1	73.0	74.9	77.2
Soybeans	104.2	107.4	117.4	117.8	137.7	125.0	131.6	152.2
Rapeseed	25.1	28.3	25.3	26.8	30.4	34.5	31.4	33.7
Pulses [1] [2]	58.4	53.4	51.0	55.7	57.2	55.3	55.3	57.7
Vegetables and melons [1]	461.4	462.4	478.6	509.5	532.9	559.9	589.1	595.6
Fruits [1]	352.2	350.8	379.0	384.7	390.4	404.9	426.7	429.4
Nuts [1]	4.6	4.8	5.0	5.0	5.3	4.9	5.1	5.2
Red meat.	116.0	117.8	118.6	117.7	119.9	124.4	128.6	130.2
Poultry	37.4	38.9	40.6	42.2	44.8	48.4	51.1	53.4
Milk	441.3	428.4	423.7	393.5	383.7	380.8	379.8	381.3

[1] Data from Food and Agriculture Organization of the United Nations.   [2] Edible seeds of peas, beans, lentils and similar crops.

Source: U.S. Department of Agriculture, Economic Research Service, *Agricultural Outlook*, monthly.

No. 1381. Fisheries—Commercial Catch, by Country: 1990 to 1995

[In thousands of metric tons, live weight. Catch of fish, crustaceans, mollusks (including weight of shells). Does not include marine mammals and aquatic plants]

COUNTRY	1990	1993	1994	1995	COUNTRY	1990	1993	1994	1995
World [1]	97,854	103,172	100,538	112,910	Korea, South	1,745	2,649	2,700	2,688
Canada.	1,626	1,212	1,089	901	Mexico	1,401	1,201	1,264	1,358
Chile	5,195	6,035	7,838	7,591	Norway.	1,745	2,562	2,551	2,808
China	12,095	17,568	20,719	24,433	Peru.	6,875	9,010	11,997	8,943
Denmark.	1,518	1,656	1,916	2,041	Philippines.	2,210	2,264	2,276	2,269
Iceland	1,508	1,718	1,560	1,616	Russia	7,808	4,461	3,781	4,374
India.	3,794	4,546	4,738	4,904	Spain	1,380	1,255	1,372	1,320
Indonesia	3,044	3,685	3,917	4,118	Thailand	2,786	3,395	3,537	3,502
Japan.	10,354	8,081	7,396	6,758	United States	5,868	5,934	5,922	5,634
Korea, North (est.) .	1,753	1,782	1,802	1,850	Vietnam	960	1,100	1,150	1,200

[1] Includes other countries, not shown separately.

Source: U.S. National Oceanic and Atmospheric Administration, National Marine Fisheries Service, *Fisheries of the United States,* annual. Data from Food and Agriculture Organization of the United Nations, Rome, Italy.

No. 1382. Meat Production, by Country: 1990 to 1997

[In thousands of metric tons, carcass weight. Covers beef and veal (incl. buffalo meat), pork (incl. bacon and ham), mutton and lamb (incl. goat meat), horsemeat, and poultry. Refers to meat from animals slaughtered within the national boundaries irrespective of origin of animals, and relates to commercial and farm slaughter. Excludes lard, tallow, and edible offals. See text, Section 30, for general comments concerning the data]

COUNTRY	1990	1995	1996	1997	COUNTRY	1990	1995	1996	1997
World [1]	178,830	208,931	217,594	221,025	Italy	3,948	3,983	4,057	4,018
Argentina.	3,290	3,413	3,266	3,514	Japan.	3,503	3,201	3,081	3,028
Brazil	7,709	10,082	10,785	11,222	Mexico	2,801	3,799	3,684	3,902
China	28,584	52,622	59,114	62,001	Russia.	(X)	5,749	5,277	4,800
France	5,744	6,306	6,524	6,321	Spain	3,467	3,975	4,133	3,986
Germany	7,259	5,798	5,855	5,881	United Kingdom .	3,319	3,821	3,564	3,646
India.	3,830	4,391	4,451	4,553	United States . .	28,610	33,882	34,294	34,718

X Not applicable.   [1] Includes other countries, not shown separately.

Source: Food and Agriculture Organization of the United Nations, Rome, Italy, FAOSTAT database.

No. 1383. Wheat, Rice, and Corn Production, by Country: 1990 to 1997

[In thousands of metric tons. Rice data cover paddy. Data for each country pertain to the calendar year in which all or most of the crop was harvested. See text, Section 30, for general comments concerning quality of the data]

COUNTRY	WHEAT			RICE			CORN		
	1990	1995	1997	1990	1995	1997	1990	1995	1997
World	588,037	537,532	609,797	520,382	550,939	564,740	482,323	515,499	585,833
Argentina	10,990	8,600	14,500	460	877	1,185	7,600	11,100	18,500
Australia	15,066	16,504	19,000	787	951	1,217	205	317	330
Bangladesh	1,004	1,370	1,500	26,781	26,533	27,340	-	-	-
Brazil	3,300	1,540	2,830	10,000	10,050	9,559	24,330	32,480	33,000
Burma	135	150	150	13,695	17,000	15,345	186	270	250
Canada	32,098	25,037	24,300	-	-	-	7,067	7,271	7,180
China	98,229	102,215	124,000	189,331	185,214	197,857	96,820	112,000	110,000
Egypt	4,268	5,700	5,850	3,167	4,399	5,000	4,598	5,353	6,010
France	33,600	30,862	34,000	125	124	125	9,500	12,394	16,800
Germany	(NA)	17,763	19,867	-	-	-	(NA)	2,395	3,027
Hungary	6,161	4,600	5,270	38	15	15	4,317	4,600	6,400
India	49,850	65,470	69,000	111,448	119,442	123,012	8,962	9,440	9,800
Indonesia	-	-	-	44,680	51,100	47,538	5,000	6,000	5,700
Iran	8,000	11,300	10,000	1,970	2,327	2,402	50	70	100
Italy	8,108	7,653	6,705	1,451	1,311	1,394	5,864	8,454	9,778
Japan	952	444	573	13,124	13,435	12,532	2	2	1
Kazakhstan	16,197	6,490	8,650	578	185	262	442	158	100
Korea, South	1	10	7	7,732	6,386	7,365	120	70	87
Mexico	3,930	3,468	3,800	300	349	508	14,100	17,780	18,000
Nigeria	50	50	40	4,167	3,767	3,083	5,810	6,500	5,000
Pakistan	14,429	17,002	16,650	4,898	5,905	6,547	1,185	1,283	1,300
Philippines	-	-	-	9,885	11,174	10,769	5,102	4,324	4,200
Romania	7,311	7,700	7,186	68	24	15	6,800	9,923	12,680
Russia	49,596	30,100	44,200	895	462	331	2,451	1,700	2,700
South Africa	1,702	1,950	2,283	-	-	-	8,615	10,200	8,000
Thailand	-	-	-	17,192	21,800	21,667	3,800	3,700	3,500
Turkey	16,000	15,500	16,000	246	346	346	2,100	1,800	2,100
Ukraine	30,374	16,273	18,400	117	80	65	4,737	3,392	5,300
United Kingdom	14,000	14,310	15,050	-	-	-	-	-	-
United States	74,292	59,400	68,761	7,081	7,887	8,115	201,534	187,305	237,897

- Represents or rounds to zero.   NA Not available.

No. 1384. Wheat, Rice, and Corn—Exports and Imports of 10 Leading Countries: 1995 to 1997

[In thousands of metric tons. Wheat data are for trade year beginning in July of year shown; rice data are for calendar year; corn data are for trade year beginning in October of year shown. Countries listed are the ten leading exporters or importers in 1997]

LEADING EXPORTERS	EXPORTS			LEADING IMPORTERS	IMPORTS		
	1995	1996	1997		1995	1996	1997
WHEAT				WHEAT			
European Union	32,003	33,350	32,675	European Union	21,505	18,240	20,600
United States	33,681	27,039	28,000	Egypt	5,919	7,000	7,200
Canada	16,850	18,135	20,000	Japan	6,101	6,264	6,200
Australia	12,086	17,845	15,000	Brazil	5,470	5,200	5,700
Argentina	4,416	9,700	9,000	Algeria	3,401	3,600	4,800
Kazakhstan	4,356	2,250	3,100	Iran	2,744	7,000	4,500
Hungary	1,599	400	1,200	Indonesia	3,612	4,195	4,500
Russia	177	600	1,000	Pakistan	1,903	3,012	4,000
Turkey	963	1,000	1,000	Korea, South	2,554	3,465	3,800
Romania	1,487	4	750	Yemen	2,026	2,400	2,500
RICE				RICE			
Thailand	5,931	5,281	5,272	European Union	1,685	1,732	1,473
Vietnam	2,308	3,040	3,268	Brazil	987	786	1,000
United States	3,073	2,624	2,292	Iran	1,633	1,294	1,000
Pakistan	1,592	1,677	1,982	Philippines	277	687	816
India	4,201	3,556	1,959	Indonesia	3,011	1,233	800
European Union	696	1,284	1,156	Nigeria	450	500	800
China	32	265	938	Iraq	92	236	720
Australia	519	475	700	Saudi Arabia	615	786	659
Uruguay	470	596	680	Malaysia	402	573	645
Argentina	327	367	500	South Africa	634	709	621
CORN				CORN			
United States	52,681	46,579	37,500	Japan	15,976	15,963	15,700
Argentina	6,946	10,203	13,000	European Union	9,693	10,407	9,995
European Union	7,436	8,111	7,900	Korea, South	8,963	8,336	7,500
China	227	3,892	5,000	Taiwan	5,733	5,744	5,000
Hungary	500	100	1,500	Mexico	6,379	3,141	3,700
Romania	750	522	700	Egypt	2,225	3,123	3,100
Mexico	50	43	500	Malaysia	2,444	2,500	2,100
South Africa	1,640	2,200	500	Colombia	1,180	1,518	1,700
Ukraine	50	-	400	Saudi Arabia	923	1,273	1,300
Canada	414	284	300	Venezuela	1,205	1,350	1,300

- Represents or rounds to zero.

Source of Tables 1383 and 1384: U.S. Department of Agriculture, Economic Research Service, unpublished data from the PS&D (Production, supply and distribution) database.

No. 1385. United States and Foreign Stock Markets—Market Capitalization and Value of Shares Traded: 1990 to 1997

[In millions of U.S. dollars. Market capitalization is the total amount of the various securities (bonds, debentures, and stock) issued by corporations]

COUNTRY	MARKET CAPITALIZATION [1]				VALUE OF SHARES TRADED [2]		
	1990	1995	1996	1997	1990	1995	1996
United States	3,059,434	6,857,622	8,484,433	11,308,779	1,815,476	5,108,591	7,121,487
Argentina	3,268	37,783	44,679	59,252	852	4,594	4,382
Australia	107,611	245,218	311,988	696,656	39,333	97,884	145,482
Austria	11,476	32,513	33,953	35,724	18,609	25,759	20,528
Belgium	65,449	104,960	119,831	136,965	6,425	15,249	26,120
Brazil	16,354	147,636	216,990	255,478	5,598	79,186	112,108
Canada	241,920	366,344	486,268	567,635	71,278	183,686	265,360
Chile	13,645	73,860	65,940	72,046	783	11,072	8,460
China	(NA)	42,055	113,755	206,366	(NA)	49,774	256,008
Colombia	1,416	17,893	17,137	19,529	71	1,254	1,360
Czech Republic	(NA)	15,664	18,077	12,786	(NA)	3,630	8,431
Denmark	39,063	56,223	71,688	93,766	11,105	25,942	34,667
Finland	22,721	44,138	63,078	73,322	3,933	19,006	22,422
France	314,384	522,053	591,123	674,368	116,893	364,550	277,100
Germany	355,073	577,365	670,997	825,233	501,805	573,549	768,745
Greece	15,228	17,060	24,178	34,164	3,924	6,091	8,283
Hong Kong	83,397	303,705	449,381	413,323	34,633	106,888	166,419
India	38,567	127,199	122,605	128,466	21,918	13,738	109,448
Indonesia	8,081	66,585	91,016	29,105	3,992	14,403	32,142
Italy	148,766	209,522	258,160	344,665	42,566	86,904	102,351
Japan	2,917,679	3,667,292	3,088,850	2,216,699	1,602,388	1,231,552	1,251,998
Korea, South	110,594	181,955	138,817	41,881	75,949	185,197	177,266
Luxembourg	10,456	30,443	32,692	33,892	87	205	534
Malaysia	48,611	222,729	307,179	93,608	10,871	76,822	173,568
Mexico	32,725	90,694	106,540	156,595	12,212	34,377	43,040
Netherlands	119,825	356,481	378,721	468,736	40,199	248,606	339,500
New Zealand	8,835	31,950	38,288	90,483	1,933	8,407	9,871
Norway	26,130	44,587	57,423	66,503	13,996	24,420	35,882
Pakistan	2,850	9,286	10,639	10,966	231	3,210	6,054
Peru	812	11,795	12,291	17,586	99	3,935	3,805
Philippines	5,927	58,859	80,649	31,361	1,216	14,727	25,519
Portugal	9,201	18,362	24,660	38,954	1,687	4,233	7,147
South Africa	137,540	280,526	241,571	232,069	8,158	17,048	27,202
Spain	111,404	197,788	242,779	290,383	40,967	59,791	249,128
Sweden	92,102	178,049	247,217	272,730	15,718	93,197	136,898
Switzerland	160,044	433,621	402,104	575,338	(NA)	310,928	392,783
Taiwan	100,710	187,206	273,608	287,813	715,005	383,099	470,193
Thailand	23,896	141,507	99,828	23,538	22,894	57,000	44,365
Turkey	19,065	20,772	30,020	61,090	5,841	51,392	36,831
United Kingdom	848,866	1,407,737	1,740,246	1,996,225	278,740	510,131	578,471
Venezuela	8,361	3,655	10,055	14,581	2,232	510	1,275

NA Not available. [1] Year-end total market values of listed domestic companies. [2] Annual total turnover of listed company shares.

Source: International Finance Corporation, Washington, DC, *Emerging Stock Markets Factbook*, annual, (copyright).

No. 1386. Dow-Jones World Stock Index, by Country and Industry: 1994 to 1997

[Index figures shown are as of **December 31. Indexes based on June 30, 1982=100 for United States; December 31, 1991=100 for World**. Based on share prices denominated in U.S. dollars. Stocks in countries that impose significant restrictions on foreign ownership are included in the world index in the same proportion that shares are available to foreign investors]

INDUSTRY	1994	1995	1996	1997	INDUSTRY	1994	1995	1996	1997
World, total	113.91	133.46	147.57	166.63	United Kingdom	107.34	124.49	152.02	198.16
					Asia/Pacific	119.39	119.80	108.93	77.93
Americas	108.53	143.61	173.40	227.09	Australia	114.89	127.90	148.78	156.23
United States	433.07	581.43	700.56	922.35	Hong Kong	184.08	223.67	299.50	223.42
Canada	95.23	108.25	135.41	190.22	Indonesia	176.25	172.48	187.42	145.78
Mexico	107.06	77.96	94.31	375.72	Japan	116.21	114.08	95.63	73.63
Europe	115.70	136.54	162.41	191.64	Malaysia	216.69	223.08	265.49	114.64
Austria	104.36	101.29	110.00	126.68	New Zealand	155.86	176.17	203.35	155.58
Belgium	115.75	142.56	158.64	210.25	Singapore	178.06	196.51	199.84	127.74
Denmark	98.16	112.42	137.26	213.02	Thailand	207.44	196.76	126.66	59.94
Finland	205.90	202.88	280.72	411.28					
France	109.17	120.03	142.38	182.44	Basic materials	124.40	130.91	136.62	119.65
Germany	122.57	138.24	161.41	232.98	Conglomerate	127.47	146.57	171.32	169.13
Ireland	122.90	152.83	196.04	274.91	Consumer, cyclical . . .	124.27	135.13	148.64	160.15
Italy	109.54	103.51	113.62	223.02	Consumer, noncyclical . .	98.64	130.19	152.04	188.21
Netherlands	133.88	167.30	207.58	316.06	Energy	110.23	132.32	163.27	188.61
Norway	122.41	129.21	159.87	209.76	Financial services	112.75	134.62	142.64	168.20
Spain	89.33	114.31	149.44	286.63	Industrial	112.24	118.38	122.31	117.79
Sweden	119.43	163.14	213.88	341.28	Technology	134.91	168.07	197.94	242.59
Switzerland	162.99	232.62	236.03	352.50	Utilities	101.12	118.44	123.90	152.77

Source: Dow Jones & Company, Inc., New York, NY, *Wall Street Journal*, selected issues (copyright).

No. 1387. Foreign Stock Market Activity—Morgan Stanley Capital International Indexes: 1995 to 1997

[Index figures shown are as of **December 31. January 1, 1970=100, except as noted**. Based on share prices denominated in U.S. dollars. EMG=Emerging Markets Global. GDP=Gross Domestic Product]

INDEX AND COUNTRY	INDEX			PERCENT CHANGE [1]		INDEX AND COUNTRY	INDEX			PERCENT CHANGE [1]	
	1995	1996	1997	1996	1997		1995	1996	1997	1996	1997
DEVELOPED MARKETS						United Kingdom	716	883	1,052	23.3	19.1
World index [2]	734	820	937	11.7	14.2	Hong Kong	4,818	6,213	4,609	29.0	-25.8
EAFE index [3]	1,136	1,186	1,188	4.4	0.2	Japan	3,348	2,813	2,133	-16.0	-24.2
Europe index	733	869	1,057	18.5	21.6	Singapore	2,735	2,515	1,733	-8.1	-31.1
Pacific index	2,362	2,139	1,576	-9.4	-26.3						
Far East index	3,384	3,015	2,188	-10.9	-27.4	EMERGING MARKETS					
GDP-weighted indexes:						EMG Far East index	263.7	273.1	135.5	3.6	-50.4
World index [2]	874	974	1,104	11.5	13.4	India [5]	98.8	95.1	104.2	-3.8	9.6
EAFE index [3]	1,205	1,278	1,334	6.1	4.4	Indonesia	508.2	637.2	163.0	25.4	-74.2
						Korea, South	173.8	107.1	35.1	-38.4	-67.3
United States	581.1	705.2	928.9	21.4	31.7	Malaysia	347.0	432.1	135.0	24.5	-68.8
Canada	403.9	510.3	567.5	26.4	11.2	Pakistan [5]	91.5	73.8	91.6	-19.4	24.2
						Philippines	442.5	509.3	199.8	15.1	-60.8
Australia	304.2	345.1	301.7	13.4	-12.6	Sri Lanka [5]	105.6	88.4	98.6	-16.3	11.5
New Zealand [4]	114.2	129.6	107.9	13.5	-16.7	Taiwan	227.9	316.6	294.8	38.9	-6.9
						Thailand	523.3	324.7	72.9	-38.0	-77.5
Austria	890	919	922	3.2	0.3						
Belgium	897	976	1,081	8.8	10.8	EMG Latin America	782	928	1,192	18.7	28.4
Denmark	1,124	1,349	1,794	20.0	33.0	Argentina	1,239	1,447	1,764	16.9	21.9
Finland [4]	128.8	169.7	196.8	31.7	16.0	Brazil	578	798	984	38.0	23.4
France	672	802	887	19.4	10.6	Chile	903	754	770	-16.4	2.0
Germany	818	917	1,131	12.1	23.3	Colombia [5]	110.2	117.6	162.0	6.6	37.8
Ireland [4]	215.7	277.8	314.8	28.8	13.3	Mexico	744	864	1,304	16.1	50.9
Italy	208.6	231.3	309.0	10.9	33.6	Peru [5]	221.3	215.2	253.3	-2.8	17.7
Netherlands	1,192	1,485	1,805	24.5	21.6	Venezuela	75.4	171.7	218.8	127.9	27.4
Norway	1,023	1,296	1,358	26.8	4.8	Greece [4]	238.2	241.6	320.5	1.4	32.7
Portugal [4]	68.4	90.5	130.2	32.3	43.9	Jordan	96.1	85.2	83.7	-11.4	-1.8
Spain	162.3	221.5	272.6	36.5	23.1	Turkey	103.1	136.0	287.5	31.9	111.4
Sweden	1,796	2,431	2,713	35.4	11.6						
Switzerland	1,569	1,589	2,274	1.2	43.2						

[1] Percent change during calendar year (e.g. December 31, 1995, through December 31, 1996). Adjusted for foreign exchange fluctuations relative to U.S. dollar. [2] Includes South African gold mines quoted in London. [3] Europe, Australasia, Far East Index. Comprises all European and Far East countries listed under developed markets plus Australia, Malaysia, and New Zealand. [4] January 1, 1988=100. [5] December 1992=100.

Source: Morgan Stanley Capital International, New York, NY, unpublished data (copyright). This information may not be reproduced or redisseminated in any form without prior written permission from Morgan Stanley Capital International. This information is provided on an "as is" basis. Neither Morgan Stanley or any other party makes any representation or warranty of any kind either express or implied, with respect to this information (or the results to be obtained by the use thereof) and Morgan Stanley expressly disclaims any and all warranties of originality, accuracy, completeness, merchantability, and fitness for any particular purpose. The user of this information assumes the entire risk of any use made of the information. In no event shall Morgan Stanley or any other part be liable to the user for any direct or indirect damages, including without limitation, any lost profits, lost savings, or other incidental or consequential damages arising out of use of this information.

No. 1388. Foreign Stock Market Indices: 1980 to 1997

[**As of year end**. The DAX index is a total return index which includes dividends, whereas the other foreign indices are price indices which exclude dividends]

YEAR	London FTSE 100	Tokyo Nikkei 225	Hong Kong Hang Seng	Germany DAX-30	Paris CAC-40
1980	647	7,116	1,477	481	(X)
1985	1,413	13,113	1,752	1,366	(X)
1990	2,144	23,849	3,025	1,398	1,518
1991	2,493	22,984	4,297	1,578	1,766
1992	2,847	16,925	5,512	1,545	1,858
1993	3,418	17,417	11,888	2,267	2,268
1994	3,066	19,723	8,191	2,107	1,881
1995	3,689	19,868	10,073	2,254	1,872
1996	4,119	19,361	13,452	2,889	2,316
1997	5,136	15,259	10,723	4,250	2,999

X Not applicable.

Source: Global Financial Data, Alhambra, CA (http://www.globalfindata.com), unpublished data. (Copyright.)

No. 1389. Reserve Assets and International Transaction Balances, by Country: 1995 to 1997

[**In millions of U.S. dollars.** Assets include holdings of convertible foreign currencies, special drawing rights, and reserve position in International Monetary Fund and exclude gold holdings. Minus sign (-) indicates debits]

COUNTRY	TOTAL RESERVE ASSETS		1997		CURRENT ACCOUNT BALANCE			MERCHANDISE TRADE BALANCE		
	1995	1996	Total	Currency holdings [1]	1995	1996	1997	1995	1996	1997
United States	74,780	64,040	58,910	30,810	-129,190	-148,730	-166,800	-171,690	-189,250	-197,000
Algeria	2,005	4,235	8,047	8,046	(NA)	(NA)	(NA)	(NA)	(NA)	(NA)
Argentina	14,288	18,104	22,320	22,153	-2,768	-3,787	-10,119	2,238	1,622	-3,195
Australia	11,896	14,485	16,845	16,099	-19,668	-15,762	-12,928	-4,223	-635	-1,807
Austria	18,730	22,865	19,736	18,605	-4,841	-3,990	-3,865	-7,203	-7,786	-4,043
Bangladesh	2,340	1,835	1,582	1,552	-824	-962	(NA)	-2,324	-2,252	(NA)
Belgium	16,177	16,953	16,190	14,519	14,410	13,999	13,954	9,463	8,516	8,343
Brazil	49,708	58,323	50,827	50,826	-18,136	(NA)	(NA)	-3,157	(NA)	(NA)
Burma	561	229	250	250	(NA)	(NA)	(NA)	(NA)	(NA)	(NA)
Cameroon	4	3	1	(Z)	90	(NA)	(NA)	627	(NA)	(NA)
Canada	15,049	20,422	17,823	15,122	-4,586	3,323	-9,261	25,429	30,720	17,556
Chile	14,140	14,833	17,306	16,991	-1,403	-3,742	-4,062	1,368	-1,094	-1,296
China	75,377	107,039	142,762	139,890	1,618	7,243	29,718	18,050	19,535	46,222
Colombia	8,102	9,597	9,507	8,979	-4,101	-4,754	(NA)	-2,699	-2,133	(NA)
Congo (Kinshasa) [2] .	147	83	(NA)	(NA)	(NA)	(NA)	(NA)	(NA)	(NA)	(NA)
Cote d'Ivoire	529	606	618	618	-447	204	(NA)	1,345	1,860	(NA)
Denmark	11,016	14,140	19,124	18,157	1,607	2,865	(NA)	6,820	7,532	(NA)
Ecuador	1,628	1,859	2,093	2,069	-735	111	-743	354	1,220	598
Egypt	16,181	17,398	18,665	18,479	-254	-192	(NA)	-7,597	-8,390	(NA)
Finland	10,038	6,916	8,417	7,532	5,202	4,787	6,022	12,346	11,082	11,590
France	26,853	26,796	30,927	27,097	10,840	20,560	39,470	11,000	14,940	28,070
Germany	85,005	83,178	77,587	69,853	-22,560	-13,780	-1,190	65,110	71,210	74,700
Ghana	698	829	(NA)	(NA)	-145	-324	(NA)	-257	-366	(NA)
Greece	14,780	17,501	12,595	12,441	-2,864	-4,554	(NA)	-14,425	-15,505	(NA)
Hungary	12,052	9,795	8,476	8,400	-2,535	-1,689	(NA)	-2,433	-2,652	(NA)
India	17,922	20,170	24,688	24,324	-5,563	-5,299	(NA)	-6,719	-9,462	(NA)
Indonesia	13,708	18,251	16,587	16,088	-6,431	-7,663	-4,816	6,533	5,948	10,090
Ireland	8,630	8,205	6,526	6,020	1,721	1,908	1,984	13,557	15,754	18,646
Israel	8,119	11,415	20,332	20,332	-6,205	-6,646	-5,014	-7,597	-7,646	-5,848
Italy	34,905	45,948	55,739	53,431	25,141	41,108	33,425	44,759	60,862	46,785
Japan	183,250	216,648	219,648	207,866	111,040	65,880	94,350	131,790	83,560	101,600
Kenya	353	747	580	562	-480	-166	(NA)	-738	-510	(NA)
Korea, South	32,678	34,037	20,368	19,710	-8,507	-23,006	-8,167	-4,444	-14,965	-3,179
Kuwait	3,561	3,515	3,452	3,126	5,019	7,071	7,671	5,582	6,964	6,296
Malaysia	23,774	27,009	20,788	20,013	-7,362	(NA)	(NA)	-100	(NA)	(NA)
Mexico	16,847	19,433	28,797	28,136	-1,576	-1,923	(NA)	7,089	6,531	(NA)
Morocco	3,601	3,794	3,993	3,951	-1,521	-627	(NA)	-2,397	-2,111	(NA)
Nepal	586	571	(NA)	(NA)	-356	-327	-418	-961	-1,106	-1,308
Netherlands	33,714	26,767	24,865	21,881	24,391	22,779	21,242	22,102	21,777	17,752
Nigeria	1,443	4,075	(NA)	(NA)	-3,123	3,092	(NA)	2,125	8,482	(NA)
Norway	22,518	26,517	23,400	22,074	4,854	10,632	8,112	8,571	12,923	11,062
Pakistan	1,733	548	1,195	1,184	-3,333	(NA)	(NA)	-2,878	(NA)	(NA)
Peru	8,222	10,578	10,982	10,982	-4,314	-3,619	-3,407	-2,168	-1,985	-1,739
Philippines	6,372	10,030	7,266	7,147	-1,980	-3,953	-4,303	-8,944	-11,342	-11,127
Poland	14,774	17,844	20,407	20,298	854	-3,264	(NA)	-1,646	-7,287	(NA)
Portugal	15,850	15,918	15,660	15,130	-144	-1,491	-1,877	-8,910	-9,340	-9,551
Romania	1,579	2,103	3,803	3,700	-1,780	-2,579	(NA)	-1,577	-2,470	(NA)
Saudi Arabia	8,622	6,794	7,353	5,944	-5,325	681	254	24,390	35,370	33,530
Singapore	68,695	76,847	71,289	70,883	14,361	14,723	14,803	977	2,224	1,145
South Africa	2,820	942	4,799	4,790	-2,756	-1,715	-1,931	1,715	2,330	1,992
Spain	34,485	57,927	68,398	66,023	513	503	2,486	-18,244	-16,027	-13,347
Sri Lanka	2,088	1,962	2,024	1,996	-770	-683	-388	-985	-800	-629
Sudan	163	107	82	82	-500	-827	(NA)	-510	-719	(NA)
Sweden	24,051	19,107	10,824	9,656	4,940	5,892	7,301	15,978	18,636	17,921
Switzerland	36,413	38,433	39,028	36,899	21,879	20,470	(NA)	3,223	1,836	(NA)
Syria	(NA)	(NA)	(NA)	(NA)	367	165	564	-143	-338	454
Thailand	35,982	37,731	26,179	25,697	-13,554	-14,692	-2,917	-7,969	-9,488	1,564
Trinidad and Tobago .	358	544	706	706	294	(NA)	(NA)	588	(NA)	(NA)
Turkey	12,442	16,436	18,658	18,614	-2,338	-2,437	-2,750	-13,212	-10,582	-15,466
United Kingdom	42,020	39,900	32,320	28,880	-5,860	-3,690	6,810	-18,310	-19,610	-20,540
Venezuela	6,283	11,788	14,378	14,000	2,014	8,824	5,999	7,013	13,756	11,592

NA Not available.   Z Less than $500,000.   [1] Holdings of convertible foreign currencies.   [2] See footnote 3, Table 1343.

Source: International Monetary Fund, Washington, DC, *International Financial Statistics*, monthly, (copyright).

No. 1390. Foreign Trade—Source of Imports and Destination of Exports, by Country: 1996

[In billions of dollars. All exports are f.o.b. (free on board) and all imports are c.i.f. (cost insurance freight) except for United States, Australian, and Canadian imports, which are f.o.b.]

COUNTRY	Total [1]	O.E.C.D. [2] Total	E.U. [3]	C.E.E.C. [4]	China, Vietnam, North Korea	O.P.E.C. [5]	Other developing countries [6]	Africa	America [7]	Middle East [8]	Far East [9]
IMPORTS											
Australia	61.5	44.6	15.3	-	3.5	2.8	10.5	0.5	0.5	1.7	12.7
Belgium-Luxembourg	150.5	132.6	112.8	0.6	1.6	1.5	14.1	5.6	2.3	1.6	6.1
Canada	171.0	150.6	16.7	0.1	3.7	2.5	14.0	1.5	3.3	0.9	11.0
Czech Republic	27.8	19.9	16.2	2.9	0.3	0.1	4.6	0.1	0.3	0.1	1.0
Denmark	44.8	39.7	31.8	0.4	0.8	0.3	3.6	0.4	1.0	0.1	2.5
Finland	30.7	24.8	18.0	0.5	0.5	0.2	4.7	0.2	0.6	0.1	1.6
France	279.1	227.6	175.8	2.0	6.4	9.6	33.5	12.0	4.8	5.9	18.0
Germany	444.5	364.5	245.1	7.8	12.6	8.6	51.1	9.7	8.6	3.8	36.4
Hungary	16.2	12.1	9.7	0.6	0.2	0.1	3.2	0.1	0.2	0.1	0.6
Iceland	2.0	1.9	1.2	-	-	-	0.1	-	-	-	0.1
Ireland	35.0	29.0	19.8	0.1	0.4	0.1	5.4	0.4	0.2	0.1	3.7
Italy	193.0	148.6	117.4	3.6	3.9	12.0	24.8	14.1	4.5	5.0	9.9
Japan	349.6	179.5	49.5	0.2	42.7	47.2	80.0	5.0	9.4	35.2	114.9
Korea, South	209.4	97.0	20.5	-	8.7	24.6	79.1	1.8	3.2	34.7	22.1
Mexico	86.7	75.6	6.6	0.2	0.9	0.5	9.6	1.0	2.6	0.1	4.2
Netherlands	133.9	105.2	76.0	1.1	2.3	7.0	18.3	3.4	3.8	5.1	13.6
New Zealand	14.7	11.9	3.0	-	0.6	0.5	1.8	0.1	0.1	0.3	2.1
Norway	33.8	29.5	23.9	0.2	0.7	0.1	3.2	0.4	0.7	0.1	2.2
Poland	47.9	36.6	24.7	0.8	0.8	0.5	9.2	3.6	0.7	1.0	1.6
Portugal	31.6	27.1	23.9	0.1	0.2	1.5	2.8	1.7	0.8	0.6	0.9
Spain	121.9	98.5	80.7	0.5	2.5	7.8	12.5	7.3	4.0	3.1	6.8
Sweden	64.2	58.1	44.4	1.1	0.5	0.8	3.7	0.4	0.7	0.5	2.8
Switzerland	78.2	71.4	61.8	0.3	1.0	1.2	4.4	1.3	0.8	0.7	3.3
United Kingdom	287.2	236.2	155.3	1.7	3.7	5.2	40.4	6.3	4.9	3.9	30.4
United States	791.3	531.0	142.7	1.0	51.8	44.0	163.5	18.3	48.8	18.1	168.9
EXPORTS											
Australia	60.2	34.5	6.5	0.1	3.2	4.0	18.5	1.4	0.6	1.9	18.5
Belgium-Luxembourg	163.8	141.7	122.2	0.8	1.0	2.4	17.9	3.6	1.8	4.9	8.2
Canada	202.4	189.2	11.5	0.1	2.2	2.7	8.0	1.2	3.3	1.4	6.7
Czech Republic	21.9	15.6	12.7	3.6	0.1	0.2	2.4	0.3	0.2	0.3	0.5
Denmark	50.9	44.0	33.4	0.6	0.4	0.8	5.1	0.6	1.2	0.9	2.2
Finland	40.4	30.4	21.8	1.7	0.6	1.2	6.6	0.6	0.6	1.0	3.2
France	284.5	229.6	181.7	2.2	3.2	9.0	40.5	16.2	5.2	6.7	17.0
Germany	512.8	422.7	289.6	8.6	7.6	11.2	62.6	10.3	10.2	10.4	34.8
Hungary	13.1	9.8	8.3	0.9	-	0.1	2.3	0.1	0.1	0.2	0.2
Iceland	1.9	1.7	1.2	-	-	-	0.1	-	0.1	-	0.2
Ireland	47.4	42.0	32.9	0.1	0.1	0.6	4.6	0.7	0.4	0.6	1.8
Italy	233.8	178.9	129.4	5.1	2.8	8.1	38.8	7.8	8.7	8.7	15.6
Japan	411.3	228.5	63.1	0.2	23.2	17.4	142.1	5.8	13.2	9.7	151.6
Korea, South	199.9	57.4	13.6	0.1	11.5	10.5	120.4	2.1	5.8	9.4	43.6
Mexico	95.5	81.6	3.2	-	0.2	0.7	13.1	0.2	10.7	0.2	1.5
Netherlands	150.3	131.0	112.4	1.0	0.8	2.7	14.9	3.1	2.2	2.5	6.7
New Zealand	14.5	9.8	2.1	-	0.4	0.7	3.6	0.2	0.5	0.4	2.6
Norway	48.8	45.4	37.6	0.3	0.2	0.2	2.6	0.3	0.7	0.3	1.3
Poland	26.3	18.7	15.3	0.8	0.1	0.8	5.9	0.9	1.0	0.8	0.6
Portugal	22.1	19.9	17.7	0.1	-	0.1	2.0	0.9	0.4	0.2	0.3
Spain	102.1	83.8	72.5	0.5	0.6	2.9	14.3	3.6	5.6	2.2	3.4
Sweden	83.0	70.5	46.7	0.9	1.5	1.6	8.5	1.4	1.6	1.3	6.2
Switzerland	79.8	64.7	48.4	0.5	0.8	2.2	11.5	1.4	1.8	3.0	7.5
United Kingdom	262.2	212.3	149.2	1.2	1.3	10.8	36.7	8.1	4.3	11.6	20.4
United States	622.8	439.5	127.5	0.9	12.6	23.5	146.3	10.6	52.5	19.9	93.0

- Represents or rounds to zero.   [1] Includes other areas not shown separately.   [2] Organization for Economic Cooperation and Development. For member countries, see text, Section 30.   [3] European Union comprises Austria, Belgium-Luxembourg, Denmark, Finland, France, Germany, Greece, Ireland, Italy, Netherlands, Portugal, Spain, Sweden, and United Kingdom.   [4] Central and Eastern European countries comprises Albania, Bulgaria, Estonia, Latvia, Lithuania, Romania, Slovakia, and Slovenia.   [5] Organization of Petroleum Exporting Countries comprises Algeria, Ecuador, Gabon, Indonesia, Iran, Iraq, Kuwait, Libya, Nigeria, Qatar, Saudi Arabia, United Arab Emirates, and Venezuela.   [6] Comprises trade with all countries other than China, North Korea, Vietnam, and members of OPEC, CEEC, and OECD.   [7] All countries comprising the continent except Canada, Mexico, and the United States.   [8] Comprises Syria, Lebanon, Israel, Gaza Strip, Jordan, Iraq, Saudi Arabia, Yemen, Kuwait, Bahrain, United Arab Emirates, Qatar, Oman, and Iran.   [9] All countries comprising the continent of Asia except Japan, China, North Korea, Vietnam, and those countries listed under Middle East.

Source: Organization for Economic Cooperation and Development, Paris, France. Data derived from *Monthly Statistics of Foreign Trade,* (copyright).

No. 1391. Foreign Exchange Rates: 1997

[**Foreign currency units per U.S. dollar; annual average, except as noted**. Rates shown include market, official, and principal rates, as published by the International Monetary Fund in *International Financial Statistics*]

COUNTRY	Currency	1997	COUNTRY	Currency	1997
Afghanistan	Afghanis	3,000	Latvia	Lats	0.581
Albania	Leks	148.9	Lebanon	Lebanese Pounds	1,540
Algeria	Algerian Dinar	57.71	Lesotho	Loti	4.608
Antigua and Barbuda [1]	E.Caribbean Dollar	2.700	Liberia [1]	Liberian Dollar	1.000
Argentina	Pesos	1.000	Libya [1]	Libyan Dinars	0.389
Armenia	Dram	490.9	Lithuania	Litai	4.000
Aruba	Aruban Florins	1.790	Luxembourg	Francs	35.77
Australia	Australian Dollar	1.344	Macedonia, The Former		
Austria	Schillings	12.20	Yugoslav Republic of	Denar	50.00
Bahamas, The	Bahamian Dollar	1.225	Madagascar	Malagasy Francs	5,091
Bahrain	Dinars	0.376	Malaysia	Ringgit	2.813
Bangladesh	Taka	43.89	Maldives	Rufiyaa	11.77
Barbados [1]	Barbados Dollar	2.000	Mali	Cfa Francs	583.7
Belarus [1]	Rubel	25,964	Malta	Maltese Liri	0.360
Belgium	Francs	35.77	Mauritania	Ouguiyas	151.9
Belize [1]	Belize Dollar	2.000	Mauritius	Rupees	20.56
Benin	Cfa Francs	583.7	Mexico	New Pesos	7.914
Bhutan	Ngultrum	36.31	Moldova	Lei	4.624
Botswana	Pula	3.651	Mongolia	Tugriks	790.0
Brazil	Reais	1.078	Morocco	Dirhams	9.527
Bulgaria	Leva	1,682	Mozambique	Meticais	11,544
Burkina Faso	Cfa Francs	583.7	Namibia	Namibia Dollar	4.608
Burma	Kyats	6.242	Nepal	Rupees	58.01
Cambodia	Riels	2,946	Netherlands	Guilders	1.951
Cameroon	Cfa Francs	583.7	Netherlands Antilles [1]	Guilders	1.790
Canada	Canadian Dollar	1.385	New Zealand	New Zealand Dollar	1.508
Cape Verde	Escudos	93.18	Nicaragua	Cordobas	9.450
Central African Republic	Cfa Francs	583.7	Niger	Cfa Francs	583.7
Chad	Cfa Francs	583.7	Norway	Kroner	7.073
Chile	Pesos	419.3	Oman [1]	Rials Omani	0.385
China	Yuan	8.290	Pakistan	Rupees	41.11
Comoros	Comorian Francs	437.8	Panama [1]	Balboas	1.000
Congo (Brazzaville)	Cfa Francs	583.7	Papua New Guinea	Kina	1.434
Costa Rica	Colones	232.6	Paraguay	Guaranies	2,191
Cote d'Ivoire	Cfa Francs	583.7	Philippines	Pesos	29.47
Croatia	Kuna	6.101	Poland	Zlotys	3.279
Cyprus	Cyprus Pounds	0.513	Portugal	Escudos	175.3
Czech Republic	Koruny	31.70	Qatar	Riyals	3.640
Denmark	Kroner	6.604	Russia	Rubles	5.784
Djibouti	Djibouti Francs	177.7	Rwanda	Rwanda Francs	301.5
Dominica [1]	E.Caribbean Dollar	2.700	Saint Kitts and Nevis [1]	E.Caribbean Dollar	2.700
Dominican Republic	Pesos	14.27	Saint Lucia [1]	E.Caribbean Dollar	2.700
Ecuador	Sucres	3,998	Saint Vincent and the		
Egypt [1]	Egyptian Pounds	3.388	Grenadines [1]	E.Caribbean Dollar	2.700
El Salvador [1]	Colones	8.755	Saudi Arabia	Riyals	3.745
Equatorial Guinea	Cfa Francs	583.7	Senegal	Cfa Francs	583.7
Estonia	Krooni	13.88	Seychelles	Rupees	5.026
Ethiopia	Birr	6.709	Sierra Leone	Leones	967.7
Fiji	Fiji Dollar	1.444	Singapore	Singapore Dollar	1.485
Finland	Markkaa	5.191	Slovakia	Koruny	33.62
France	Francs	5.837	Slovenia	Tolars	159.7
Gabon	Cfa Francs	583.7	Solomon Islands	Solomon Isl Dollar	3.717
Germany	Deutsche Mark	1.734	South Africa	Rand	4.608
Greece	Drachmas	273.1	Spain	Pesetas	146.4
Grenada [1]	E.Caribbean Dollar	2.700	Sri Lanka	Rupees	59.00
Guatemala	Quetzales	6.065	Suriname	Guilders	401.0
Guyana	Guyana Dollar	142.4	Swaziland	Langeni	4.603
Haiti	Gourdes	16.66	Sweden	Kronor	7.635
Honduras	Lempiras	13.00	Switzerland	Swiss Francs	1.451
Hong Kong	Hong Kong Dollar	7.742	Syria [1]	Syrian Pounds	11.23
Hungary	Forint	186.8	Tanzania	Tanzania Shilling	612.1
Iceland	Kronur	70.90	Thailand	Baht	31.36
India	Rupees	36.31	Togo	Cfa Francs	583.7
Indonesia	Rupiah	2,909	Tonga	Pa'Anga	1.264
Iran	Rials	1,753	Trinidad and Tobago	Tt Dollars	6.250
Iraq	Dinars	0.311	Tunisia	Dinars	1.106
Ireland	Irish Pounds	0.659	Turkey	Liras	151,865
Israel	New Sheqalim	3.449	Uganda	Uganda Shilling	10,830
Italy	Lire	1,703	Ukraine	Hryvnias	1.862
Jamaica	Jamaica Dollars	35.40	United Arab Emirates	Dirhams	3.671
Japan	Yen	121.0	United Kingdom	Pounds Sterling	0.638
Jordan	Dinars	0.709	Uruguay	Pesos	9.445
Kazakhstan	Tenge	75.44	Vanuatu	Vatu	115.9
Kenya	Kenya Shillings	58.73	Venezuela	Venezuela	488.6
Korea, South	Won	951.3	Yemen	Rials	129.2
Kuwait	Dinars	0.303	Zambia	Kwacha	1,334
Kyrgyzstan	Soms	17.36	Zimbabwe	Zimbabwe Dollar	11.89
Laos	Kip	1,257			

[1] End-of-year value.

Source: U.S. Dept. of Commerce, International Trade Administration, "Foreign Exchange Rates, 1992-97;" published 28 August 1998; <http://www.ita.doc.gov/industry/otea/usfth/t37.prn>.

No. 1392. International Tourism Receipts—Leading Countries: 1990 to 1997

[In millions of dollars, except as indicated. Minus sign (-) indicates decrease]

COUNTRY	TOTAL RECEIPTS				Percent change, 1996-97	PERCENT OF WORLD TOTAL	
	1990	1995	1996	1997		1990	1997
World, total [1]	268,310	401,475	433,863	443,770	2.3	100.0	100.0
United States	43,007	63,395	69,908	75,056	7.4	16.0	16.9
Italy	20,016	27,723	30,018	30,000	-0.1	7.5	6.8
France	20,184	27,527	28,357	27,947	-1.5	7.5	6.3
Spain	18,593	25,701	27,654	27,190	-1.7	6.9	6.1
United Kingdom	14,940	18,554	19,296	20,569	6.6	5.6	4.6
Germany	14,288	18,028	17,567	16,418	-6.5	5.3	3.7
Austria	13,417	14,593	13,990	12,393	-11.4	5.0	2.8
China	2,218	8,733	10,200	12,074	18.4	0.8	2.7
Australia	4,088	7,375	8,811	9,324	5.8	1.5	2.1
Hong Kong	5,032	9,604	10,836	9,242	-14.7	1.9	2.1
Canada	6,339	7,994	8,868	8,928	0.7	2.4	2.0
Thailand	4,326	7,664	8,664	8,700	0.4	1.6	2.0
Poland	358	6,600	8,400	8,700	3.6	0.1	2.0
Singapore	4,904	8,378	7,961	7,993	0.4	1.8	1.8
Switzerland	7,411	9,365	8,891	7,960	-10.5	2.8	1.8
Mexico	5,467	6,179	6,934	7,530	8.6	2.0	1.7
Turkey	3,225	4,957	5,962	7,000	17.4	1.2	1.6
Indonesia	2,105	5,228	6,087	6,589	8.3	0.8	1.5
Belgium	3,721	5,719	5,893	5,997	1.8	1.4	1.4

[1] Includes other countries not shown separately.

Source: World Tourism Organization, Madrid, Spain, unpublished data (copyright).

No. 1393. Net Flow of Financial Resources to Developing Countries: 1980 to 1995

[In billions of U.S. dollars. Net flow covers loans, grants, and grant-like flows minus amortization on loans. Military flows are excluded. Developing countries cover countries designated by Development Assistance Committee (DAC) as developing. Official development assistance covers all flows to developing countries and multilateral institutions provided by official agencies, including state and local governments, or by their executive agencies, which are administered with the promotion of economic development and welfare of developing countries as their main objective and whose financial terms are intended to be concessional in character with grant element of at least 25 percent. Other official flows cover export credits and portfolio investment from the official sector]

ORIGIN AND TYPE OF RESOURCE	1980	1985	1989	1990	1991	1992	1993	1994	1995
DAC countries [1]	75.4	45.2	84.3	76.4	94.7	115.8	136.1	165.9	166.7
Official development assistance	27.3	29.4	45.7	53.0	56.7	60.9	56.5	59.2	58.9
Other official flows	5.3	3.4	5.8	8.6	7.1	8.9	7.9	10.1	9.8
Private flows at market terms	40.4	9.4	28.8	9.8	25.5	40.1	66.0	90.7	92.0
Private voluntary agencies	2.4	2.9	4.0	5.1	5.4	6.0	5.7	6.0	6.0
Total net flow to developing countries, by DAC country [1]	75.4	45.2	87.1	76.4	94.7	115.8	136.1	165.9	166.7
United States	13.9	1.8	16.4	11.1	20.8	33.5	58.2	59.7	47.8
Official development assistance	7.1	9.4	7.7	11.4	11.3	11.7	10.1	9.9	7.4
Other official flows	1.1	0.2	-0.5	-0.4	-0.8	1.3	0.1	0.9	1.5
Private flows at market terms	4.3	-9.3	7.3	-2.4	7.6	17.7	45.4	46.3	36.5
Private voluntary agencies	1.3	1.5	1.9	2.5	2.7	2.8	2.6	2.6	2.5
Australia	0.9	1.2	1.5	1.5	-2.1	4.2	2.1	2.1	2.5
Austria	0.3	0.2	0.2	0.6	0.7	0.8	0.7	1.0	0.9
Belgium	2.9	1.3	1.5	0.1	1.5	2.2	0.7	2.2	-0.2
Canada	3.2	1.7	2.7	3.5	4.0	4.2	5.3	5.6	4.7
Denmark	0.8	0.4	0.9	1.1	1.1	1.6	1.4	1.3	1.8
Finland	0.2	0.3	0.9	1.0	1.0	0.8	0.3	0.6	0.6
France [2]	11.6	8.9	5.3	5.7	6.5	10.8	10.9	12.7	12.8
Germany [2]	10.6	5.8	12.1	13.6	13.1	8.9	15.4	23.9	21.2
Ireland	(Z)	0.1	0.1	0.2	0.1	0.2	0.1	0.2	0.2
Italy	4.0	2.2	5.8	3.2	7.5	4.2	2.4	3.4	2.8
Japan	6.8	11.6	22.0	17.2	24.5	16.2	15.9	28.5	42.3
Luxembourg	(NA)	(NA)	(NA)	(NA)	(Z)	5.9	0.1	0.1	0.1
Netherlands	2.4	2.6	2.5	4.0	4.4	3.4	5.6	4.7	6.8
New Zealand	0.1	0.1	0.1	0.1	0.1	0.1	0.1	0.1	0.2
Norway	0.9	0.6	0.9	1.2	1.4	1.4	1.2	1.5	1.5
Portugal	(NA)	(NA)	0.1	0.3	0.2	0.4	0.2	0.2	0.3
Spain	(NA)	(NA)	0.4	1.0	1.3	1.6	1.4	3.5	1.6
Sweden	1.9	1.4	2.3	2.8	1.8	3.0	2.5	2.4	2.2
Switzerland	2.7	2.5	1.8	3.4	3.0	3.1	2.9	0.1	0.9
United Kingdom	12.2	2.5	9.5	6.5	5.6	9.3	8.8	12.0	15.5

NA Not available. Z Less than $50 million. [1] DAC countries listed below. Country totals may not add to DAC total because debt forgiveness of non-official development assistance claims is not included in DAC totals. [2] Former West Germany.

Source: Organization for Economic Cooperation and Development, Paris, France, *Annual Reports of the Development Assistance Committee.*

No. 1394. External Public Debt, by Country: 1990 to 1996

[External public debt is defined as debt repayable to external creditors in foreign currency, goods, or services, with an original or extended maturity of more than 1 year, which is a direct obligation of, or has repayment guaranteed by, a public body in the borrowing country. Excludes undisbursed debt (amounts not yet drawn by recipient) and unguaranteed private debt, which for some countries is substantial. Debt contracted for the purchase of military equipment is not usually reported. **Debt service payments** represent the sum of interest payments and repayments of principal on external public debt]

COUNTRY	TOTAL EXTERNAL PUBLIC DEBT (mil. dol.)			1996					DEBT SERVICE RATIO [3] (percent)			
	1990	1994	1995	Total [1]	Bilateral official	Banks	Multilateral organizations	Bonds [2]	1990	1994	1995	1996
Argentina	46,902	55,829	55,967	62,389	10,027	1,049	9,891	41,159	37	31	34	44
Bangladesh	11,973	15,353	15,469	15,401	5,323	25	9,859	-	29	14	15	12
Bolivia	3,684	4,114	4,448	4,236	1,564	11	2,629	17	39	29	29	31
Brazil	87,669	94,916	97,180	94,584	16,803	8,784	9,426	56,076	22	31	37	41
Bulgaria	9,831	8,414	8,716	8,135	1,403	269	1,238	5,154	19	13	17	21
Cameroon	5,366	7,301	8,059	7,999	5,614	364	1,567	-	22	22	20	24
Chile	10,424	8,992	7,181	4,887	626	2,151	2,091	-	26	20	26	32
China	45,512	82,388	94,671	102,257	21,737	24,437	17,695	11,105	12	9	10	9
Colombia	14,667	14,354	13,946	14,811	1,738	4,054	4,765	3,409	41	43	29	35
Congo (Brazzaville) [4]	4,203	4,772	4,952	4,663	3,124	770	674	-	35	54	14	21
Congo (Kinshasa) [4]	9,004	9,278	9,618	9,258	6,081	517	2,319	4	15	1	2	2
Costa Rica	3,060	3,215	3,123	2,887	964	40	1,285	564	24	15	16	14
Cote d'Ivoire	10,663	11,239	11,899	11,364	5,122	2,525	3,664	-	35	36	23	26
Croatia	(X)	1,541	1,590	3,098	942	1,481	578	21	10	16	12	11
Dominican Republic	3,417	3,609	3,638	3,511	1,861	36	1,019	519	33	22	26	23
Ecuador	9,864	10,550	12,062	12,432	2,198	1,055	2,909	6,013	27	15	13	12
Egypt	27,347	29,925	30,584	28,915	23,370	445	4,192	-	35	20	19	42
Ethiopia	8,479	9,568	9,772	9,480	6,643	26	2,485	-	6	10	15	11
Gabon	3,147	3,516	3,987	3,872	3,146	117	582	-	37	26	25	26
Ghana	2,773	4,146	4,569	4,680	1,117	181	3,117	-	13	12	11	11
Guatemala	2,464	2,727	2,832	2,763	1,131	125	1,035	231	35	30	31	29
Honduras	3,423	3,899	3,979	3,852	1,410	112	2,118	125	34	49	39	41
Hungary [5]	18,002	22,237	23,782	18,420	678	1,545	2,761	13,263	31	28	28	24
India [5]	71,058	87,605	80,369	74,403	23,915	14,182	29,331	1,088	33	31	31	37
Indonesia	48,042	63,922	65,305	60,105	28,911	6,003	17,248	1,141	27	18	18	18
Jamaica	3,930	3,434	3,404	3,180	1,741	203	1,104	77	20	14	13	12
Jordan	7,040	6,881	7,017	7,134	4,071	216	1,385	796	35	33	30	28
Kenya	4,758	5,536	5,891	5,645	2,134	498	2,935	-	(NA)	(NA)	(NA)	(NA)
Lebanon	356	776	1,549	1,931	303	481	325	800	(X)	13	2	4
Macedonia, The Former Yugoslav Republic of	(X)	637	768	860	366	79	348	-	44	10	8	9
Madagascar	3,360	3,561	3,707	3,587	1,900	27	1,608	-	13	9	7	8
Malaysia	11,589	13,648	16,023	15,697	2,815	3,084	1,403	7,788	12	18	14	18
Mali	2,333	2,544	2,737	2,774	1,313	-	1,461	-	21	28	28	35
Mexico	75,970	79,332	94,384	93,435	10,936	7,154	17,756	53,595	22	36	33	28
Morocco	22,307	20,793	22,110	20,771	8,840	3,294	6,527	286	4	42	40	24
Nicaragua	8,277	9,757	8,537	5,119	3,114	409	1,550	-	12	9	8	10
Oman	2,397	2,605	2,636	2,643	472	1,438	220	-	23	35	27	27
Pakistan	16,504	22,683	23,804	23,692	10,261	309	12,194	300	6	5	4	11
Panama	3,986	3,927	3,910	5,133	392	690	677	3,326	37	31	21	13
Papua New Guinea	1,519	1,730	1,666	1,520	493	127	859	-	11	18	16	35
Peru	13,625	17,676	18,922	20,412	11,344	122	3,594	4,773	27	19	16	14
Philippines	24,037	30,272	29,905	27,934	12,084	589	7,938	5,707	5	12	11	6
Poland	39,259	39,500	41,071	39,215	28,335	323	2,175	8,270	20	16	16	6
Senegal	2,931	3,038	3,171	3,101	1,238	-	1,849	-	(NA)	(NA)	(NA)	(NA)
Sierra Leone	600	846	904	889	415	-	468	-	(X)	5	6	9
Slovenia	(X)	1,356	1,489	2,035	203	280	553	973	14	8	7	7
Sri Lanka	4,947	6,648	7,008	6,816	3,426	266	2,941	-	6	1	9	5
Sudan	9,153	9,398	9,778	9,368	5,692	1,589	2,083	-	23	7	5	4
Syria	14,915	16,538	16,755	16,696	14,523	-	1,029	-	34	22	21	19
Tanzania	5,734	6,127	6,205	6,102	2,837	(NA)	2,903	-	17	14	12	12
Thailand	12,452	16,188	16,951	17,037	7,623	3,319	2,984	1,905	25	19	17	17
Tunisia	6,659	8,025	8,721	8,687	3,154	1,090	3,631	474	29	31	28	22
Turkey	38,869	48,440	50,313	48,168	7,494	15,324	7,707	14,174	29	31	28	22
Uganda	2,157	2,866	3,059	3,148	789	14	2,284	3	60	44	20	20
Uruguay	3,043	3,749	3,830	4,093	265	509	1,204	2,110	41	15	22	16
Venezuela	24,506	28,039	28,491	28,450	1,269	1,985	2,787	20,659	23	19	22	17
Yemen	5,152	5,457	5,526	5,619	2,544	80	1,357	-	6	4	3	2
Yugoslavia, former [6]	12,985	8,509	8,724	8,479	3,112	4,126	1,234	-	(NA)	(NA)	(NA)	(NA)
Zambia	4,876	4,863	5,073	5,305	2,961	9	2,214	-	15	31	186	25
Zimbabwe	2,464	3,418	3,523	3,335	1,179	162	1,583	90	23	25	24	21

- Represents or rounds to zero. NA Not available. X Not applicable. [1] Includes other types of creditors not shown separately. [2] Covers publicly issued and privately placed bonds. [3] Debt service payments as percent of exports. [4] See footnote 3, Table 1343. [5] Fiscal year basis. [6] The bulk of the debt of Yugoslavian enterprises is reported as nonguaranteed.

Source: The World Bank, Washington, DC, *World Debt Tables*, periodic.

No. 1395. Military Expenditures, by Country: 1985 to 1995

[**In millions of dollars,** except as indicated. See also Table 576. For most countries, data for expenditures and for gross national product (GNP) were based on local currencies which were deflated to constant 1995 local currency values before conversion to U.S. dollar equivalents. In general, the rates used for conversion are the 1995 average par/market exchange rates as supplied by the International Bank for Reconstruction and Development]

COUNTRY	CURRENT DOLLARS				CONSTANT (1995) DOLLARS		1995		
	1985	1990	1994	1995	1985	1990	Total	Percent of GNP	Per capita (dollars)
United States	258,200	306,200	288,100	277,800	353,800	351,900	277,800	3.8	1,056
Algeria [1]	716	697	1,226	1,238	982	801	1,238	3.2	43
Angola [1]	(NA)	(NA)	453	225	(NA)	(NA)	225	3.0	22
Argentina	5,599	3,436	4,724	4,684	7,673	3,949	4,684	1.7	137
Australia	4,960	5,866	8,358	8,401	6,798	6,741	8,401	2.5	465
Bangladesh	245	317	475	502	336	365	502	1.7	4
Belgium	4,880	5,356	4,498	4,449	6,688	6,155	4,449	1.7	439
Brazil	3,044	8,555	7,185	10,900	4,172	9,832	10,900	1.7	68
Bulgaria [1]	5,808	3,887	982	1,073	7,960	4,467	1,073	2.8	125
Burma	877	1,093	1,698	1,833	1,202	1,256	1,833	3.9	41
Canada	7,169	9,187	9,408	9,077	9,825	10,560	9,077	1.7	318
Chile [2]	821	1,154	1,832	2,243	1,125	1,327	2,243	3.8	158
China [1]	39,010	48,440	57,040	63,510	53,470	55,660	63,510	2.3	53
Colombia	559	1,225	1,302	2,000	766	1,408	2,000	2.6	55
Congo (Kinshasa) [3]	68	(NA)	36	17	93	(NA)	17	0.3	-
Croatia [1]	(X)	(X)	1,827	2,114	(X)	(X)	2,114	10.5	425
Cuba	1,335	1,400	600	350	1,830	1,609	350	1.6	32
Czech Republic [1]	(X)	(X)	2,495	2,368	(X)	(X)	2,368	2.3	229
Egypt [1]	3,129	1,468	1,835	2,653	4,289	1,687	2,653	5.7	43
France [4]	35,740	44,800	48,960	47,770	48,990	51,480	47,770	3.1	826
Germany [4]	39,400	48,540	41,020	41,160	54,000	55,790	41,160	1.9	496
Greece	3,898	4,182	4,811	5,056	5,343	4,806	5,056	5.5	482
Hungary [1]	3,782	1,277	1,203	961	5,183	1,468	961	1.5	95
India	5,022	6,635	8,294	7,831	6,883	7,626	7,831	2.4	8
Indonesia [2]	1,600	1,699	2,364	3,398	2,193	1,952	3,398	1.8	17
Iran [1]	8,523	8,098	5,449	4,191	11,680	9,307	4,191	2.6	65
Iraq [1]	12,650	14,110	(NA)	(NA)	17,340	16,210	(NA)	(NA)	(NA)
Israel	7,773	7,168	8,171	8,734	10,650	8,237	8,734	9.6	1,646
Italy	14,200	19,150	20,700	19,380	19,460	22,010	19,380	1.8	338
Japan	27,400	40,740	49,300	50,240	37,550	46,820	50,240	1.0	401
Jordan	620	397	437	481	849	456	481	7.7	117
Kazakhstan [1]	(X)	(X)	450	426	(X)	(X)	426	0.9	25
Kenya	89	173	147	173	122	198	173	2.3	6
Korea, North [1]	5,260	5,940	5,500	6,000	7,209	6,827	6,000	28.6	255
Korea, South	6,507	10,780	13,930	14,410	8,919	12,390	14,410	3.4	320
Kuwait	1,501	13,170	3,069	3,488	2,057	15,130	3,488	11.6	1,919
Libya [2]	(NA)	(NA)	1,297	1,999	(NA)	(NA)	1,999	6.0	381
Malaysia	1,023	1,271	2,247	2,444	1,402	1,461	2,444	3.0	125
Mexico	1,063	1,058	1,992	2,321	1,457	1,215	2,321	1.0	25
Netherlands	6,792	8,129	8,034	8,012	9,309	9,343	8,012	2.1	518
New Zealand	702	897	702	740	962	1,030	740	1.3	211
Nigeria [2]	757	674	793	(NA)	1,038	775	(NA)	(NA)	(NA)
Pakistan	1,809	3,120	3,933	3,740	2,480	3,586	3,740	6.1	30
Peru	2,244	683	847	989	3,075	784	989	1.7	41
Philippines	506	1,232	1,368	1,151	693	1,416	1,151	1.5	16
Poland [1]	14,670	8,752	4,644	4,887	20,110	10,060	4,887	2.3	127
Romania [1]	6,840	3,869	2,178	2,520	9,374	4,446	2,520	2.5	115
Russia [1]	(X)	(X)	93,000	76,000	(X)	(X)	76,000	11.4	513
Saudi Arabia	21,340	23,160	17,200	17,210	29,240	26,620	17,210	13.5	919
Singapore	1,687	2,106	3,304	3,970	2,312	2,421	3,970	4.7	1,191
Slovakia [1]	(X)	(X)	440	577	(X)	(X)	577	3.0	108
Slovenia [1]	(X)	(X)	438	344	(X)	(X)	344	1.5	176
South Africa	3,124	4,545	3,015	2,895	4,282	5,223	2,895	2.2	71
Spain	7,338	8,382	8,156	8,652	10,060	9,633	8,652	1.6	221
Sri Lanka	174	411	541	585	238	472	585	4.6	32
Sweden	4,308	5,138	5,832	6,042	5,904	5,905	6,042	2.8	683
Syria [1][2]	5,432	4,391	(NA)	3,563	7,445	5,046	3,563	7.2	236
Taiwan	6,395	8,938	11,480	13,140	8,765	10,270	13,140	5.0	618
Tanzania	68	98	82	69	94	112	69	1.8	2
Thailand	2,066	2,372	3,970	4,014	2,832	2,726	4,014	2.5	69
Turkey	3,568	4,323	6,168	6,606	4,890	4,968	6,606	4.0	108
Ukraine	(X)	(X)	4,378	3,588	(X)	(X)	3,588	2.9	70
United Kingdom	33,450	37,090	35,440	33,400	45,850	42,630	33,400	3.0	572
Vietnam [1]	(NA)	723	435	544	(NA)	831	544	2.6	7

- Represents or rounds to zero.   NA Not available.   X Not applicable.   [1] Estimated.   [2] Data probably omit a major share of total military expenditures, probably including most arms acquisitions.   [3] See footnote 3, Table 1343.   [4] Prior to 1990, data for former West Germany.

Source: U.S. Arms Control and Disarmament Agency, *World Military Expenditures and Arms Transfers,* annual.

No. 1396. Armed Forces Personnel, by Country: 1985 to 1995

[**Personnel data as of July.** Armed Forces refer to active-duty military personnel, including paramilitary forces where those forces resemble regular units in their organization, equipment, training, or mission. Reserve forces are not included]

COUNTRY	ARMED FORCES PERSONNEL (1,000)					ARMED FORCES PER 1,000 POPULATION				
	1985	1990	1993	1994	1995	1985	1990	1993	1994	1995
United States	2,244	2,181	1,815	1,715	1,620	9.4	8.7	7.0	6.6	6.2
Algeria	170	126	139	126	120	7.7	5.0	5.1	4.5	4.2
Angola	66	115	128	120	82	8.7	13.6	13.4	12.2	8.1
Argentina.	129	85	65	69	65	4.2	2.6	1.9	2.0	1.9
Australia	70	68	68	59	58	4.4	4.0	3.8	3.3	3.2
Bangladesh	91	103	107	113	115	0.9	0.9	0.9	1.0	1.0
Belgium.	107	106	70	53	47	10.9	10.6	6.9	5.2	4.6
Brazil	496	295	296	296	285	3.6	2.0	1.9	1.9	1.8
Bulgaria.	189	129	52	80	86	21.2	14.4	6.1	9.4	10.0
Burma.	186	230	286	370	322	5.0	5.6	6.6	8.4	7.1
Canada	83	87	76	75	70	3.3	3.3	2.7	2.7	2.5
Chile.	124	95	92	102	102	10.3	7.2	6.7	7.3	7.2
China	4,100	3,500	3,031	2,930	2,930	3.9	3.1	2.6	2.5	2.4
Colombia	66	110	139	146	146	2.2	3.3	4.0	4.1	4.0
Congo (Kinshasa) [1]	62	55	55	53	49	1.9	1.5	1.3	1.2	1.1
Croatia	(X)	(X)	(NA)	80	60	(X)	(X)	(NA)	16.2	12.1
Cuba	297	297	175	140	70	29.5	28.1	16.2	12.9	6.4
Czech Republic	(X)	(X)	107	90	68	(X)	(X)	10.3	8.7	6.6
Egypt	466	434	424	430	430	9.4	7.7	7.1	7.0	6.9
France . [2]	563	550	506	506	504	10.2	9.7	8.8	8.8	8.7
Germany [2].	495	545	398	362	352	8.1	6.9	4.9	4.4	4.2
Greece	201	201	213	206	213	20.2	19.9	20.5	19.7	20.3
Hungary	117	94	(NA)	60	71	11.0	9.1	(NA)	5.9	7.0
India	1,260	1,262	1,265	1,305	1,265	1.6	1.5	1.4	1.4	1.4
Indonesia.	278	283	271	280	280	1.6	1.5	1.4	1.4	1.4
Iran	345	440	528	528	440	7.3	7.7	8.5	8.4	6.8
Iraq	788	1,390	407	425	390	50.2	75.4	21.2	21.4	18.9
Israel	195	190	181	185	185	47.9	42.1	35.8	35.7	34.9
Italy	504	493	450	436	435	8.8	8.5	7.9	7.6	7.6
Japan	241	250	242	233	240	2.0	2.0	1.9	1.9	1.9
Jordan	81	100	100	100	112	30.6	30.5	25.7	25.0	27.3
Kazakhstan	(X)	(X)	44	18	28	(X)	(X)	2.6	1.1	1.7
Kenya.	19	20	24	22	22	0.9	0.8	0.9	0.8	0.8
Korea, North	784	1,200	1,200	1,200	1,040	40.0	56.0	53.0	52.0	44.3
Korea, South	600	650	750	750	655	14.7	15.2	17.0	16.8	14.5
Kuwait	16	7	12	15	20	9.3	3.3	7.8	8.9	11.0
Libya	91	86	85	80	76	24.6	19.7	17.4	15.8	14.5
Malaysia	110	130	115	115	122	7.1	7.4	6.1	6.0	6.2
Mexico	140	175	175	175	175	1.8	2.1	1.9	1.9	1.9
Netherlands	103	104	86	77	67	7.1	7.0	5.6	5.0	4.3
New Zealand	13	11	11	10	10	4.0	3.3	3.2	2.9	2.9
Nigeria	134	94	76	80	89	1.8	1.1	0.8	0.8	0.9
Pakistan	483	550	580	540	587	4.9	4.8	4.8	4.4	4.6
Peru	128	125	112	112	115	6.5	5.7	4.8	4.7	4.8
Philippines	115	109	107	109	110	2.0	1.7	1.5	1.5	1.5
Poland	439	313	180	255	278	11.8	8.2	4.7	6.6	7.2
Romania	237	126	167	200	209	10.5	5.5	7.4	9.0	9.5
Russia	(X)	(X)	1,500	1,400	1,400	(X)	(X)	10.1	9.4	9.4
Saudi Arabia	80	146	172	164	175	6.1	9.2	9.9	9.1	9.3
Singapore	56	56	56	56	60	20.7	18.4	17.4	17.1	18.0
Slovakia	(X)	(X)	33	47	52	(X)	(X)	6.2	8.8	9.7
Slovenia	(X)	(X)	12	17	10	(X)	(X)	6.1	8.7	5.1
South Africa	95	85	72	102	100	2.8	2.3	1.8	2.5	2.4
Spain	314	263	204	213	210	8.2	6.8	5.2	5.5	5.4
Sri Lanka.	22	22	110	110	110	1.4	1.3	6.1	6.1	6.0
Sweden.	69	65	44	70	51	8.3	7.6	5.0	8.0	5.8
Syria.	402	408	408	320	320	38.2	32.3	29.0	22.0	21.2
Taiwan	444	370	442	425	425	23.0	18.2	21.2	20.2	20.0
Tanzania	43	40	46	50	35	2.0	1.6	1.7	1.8	1.2
Thailand	235	283	295	290	288	4.6	5.1	5.2	5.0	4.9
Turkey	814	769	686	811	805	16.1	13.7	11.6	13.4	13.1
Ukraine	(X)	(X)	510	495	476	(X)	(X)	9.9	9.6	9.3
United Kingdom	334	308	271	257	233	5.9	5.4	4.7	4.4	4.0
Vietnam.	1,027	1,052	550	550	550	16.9	15.9	7.8	7.7	7.6

NA Not available.   X Not applicable.   [1] See footnote 3, Table 1343.   [2] Prior to 1990, data for former West Germany.

Source: U.S. Arms Control and Disarmament Agency, *World Military Expenditures and Arms Transfers*, annual.

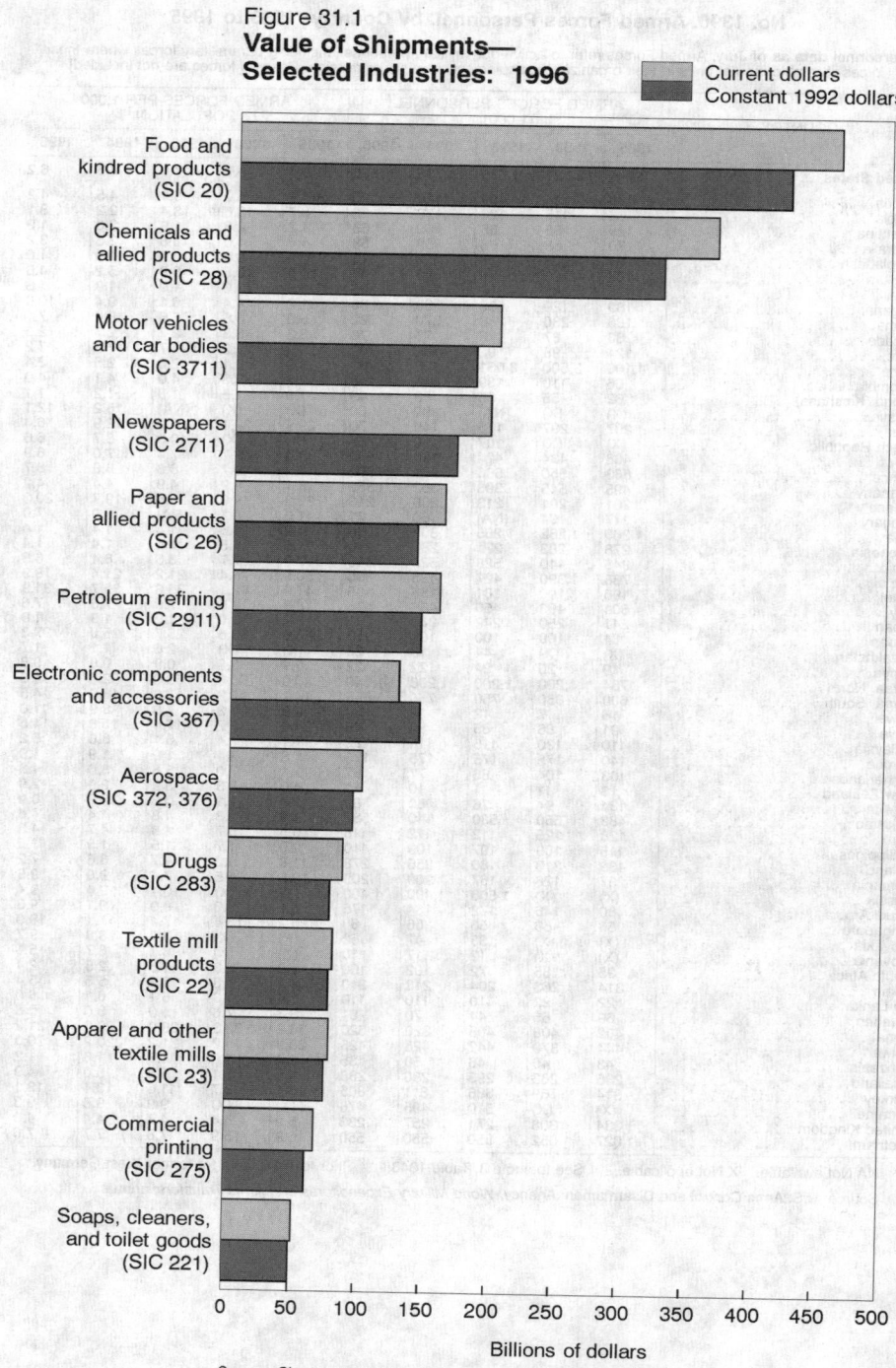

Figure 31.1
**Value of Shipments—
Selected Industries: 1996**

Current dollars
Constant 1992 dollars

Billions of dollars

Source: Chart prepared by U.S. Bureau of the Census. For data, see Section 31.

Industrial Outlook

This section presents industry statistics for selected manufacturing industries. The industry groupings correspond to those used in the *1994 U.S. Industrial Outlook*. The tables contain new and revised data from the *1995 Annual Survey of Manufactures* along with revised industry data for 1987 through 1992 from the *1992 Census of Manufactures: General Summary.*

To provide a more accurate picture of industry trends, the value of shipments shown in these tables are expressed both in "current dollars" and in inflation–adjusted or "constant dollars." Current dollars show the value of the goods in the year they are produced. Constant dollars (or "real" dollars) show the value of shipments as they would be valued if produced in the base year. This permits shipment levels from different years to be compared. The constant dollar shipments (base year 1992) were derived by deflating the product class shipments from the Bureau of the Census using the Bureau of Labor Statistics' producer price indexes.

The tables contain both "industry" and "product" shipments. The Bureau of the Census collects shipments data from individual factories (or establishments) rather than at the company level. Most factories make a variety of products, but for statistical purposes each factory is classified in the industry associated with its major product. For instance, the total output of a plant may consist of 80 percent tires and 20 percent hose and belting. In this case, the total output of the plant would be credited to the tire industry, and the shipments of all plants so classified would make up the "industry shipments" of the tire industry. The value of all tires shipped by all establishments is aggregated to derive "product shipments."

Trade data were tabulated following the Bureau of the Census's 1997 trade concordance (with a few exceptions) to approximate the Standard Industrial Classification (SIC) industry groupings. Exports are limited to domestic exports and are valued "free alongside ship" or f.a.s. Imports are restricted to goods imported for consumption and are on a customs value basis. Trade data should only be compared with product shipments data.

Researchers who once relied on the *U.S. Industrial Outlook* will be greatly assisted by the publication of the *U.S. Industry and Trade Outlook 1998* in the fall of 1997. This new publication is the result of an innovative public–private partnership between the International Trade Administration of the Department of Commerce and the McGraw–Hill companies. Authorship is shared by the Commerce Department, other government agencies, and McGraw–Hill. As in years past, the new *Outlook* is anchored by historical statistical data provided by the Bureau of the Census.

The *Outlook* is a basic resource for industry analysis and business development. The 1998 edition will contain 50 chapters covering important manufacturing and service sectors, along with industry snapshots, and hundreds of industry reviews, analyses, and forecasts. This new publication continues the legacy of the *U.S. Industrial Outlook*, the most widely read and respected single source industry–by–industry overview of the U.S. economy. Like its predecessor, the *Industry and Trade Outlook* is a single source reference for business planners, investors, researchers, and students who need to know where major sectors of the U.S. economy have been and where they are going in an increasingly global marketplace. For sales information contact the National Technical Information Service, 703/487–4650.

No. 1397. Recent Trends in Food and Kindred Products (SIC 20): 1991 to 1997

ITEM	Unit	1991	1992	1993	1994	1995	1996	1997
INDUSTRY DATA								
Value of shipments [1]	Mil. dol.	397,892	406,963	422,220	430,963	446,869	461,324	(NA)
Value of shipments (1992 dollars)	Mil. dol.	398,551	406,963	415,112	419,160	431,001	422,973	(NA)
Total employment	1,000.	1,511	1,503	1,520	1,511	1,520	1,517	(NA)
Production workers	1,000.	1,101	1,100	1,118	1,112	1,120	1,113	(NA)
Average hourly earnings	Dollar	10.15	10.41	10.58	10.74	10.96	11.17	(NA)
Capital expenditures	Mil. dol.	9,993	9,898	9,389	10,093	11,812	11,717	(NA)
PRODUCT DATA								
Value of shipments [2]	Mil. dol.	363,943	382,889	397,633	405,490	421,507	435,009	(NA)
Value of shipments (1992 dollars)	Mil. dol.	364,419	382,889	391,090	394,447	406,291	398,717	(NA)
TRADE DATA								
Value of imports	Mil. dol.	19,780	20,883	20,890	22,842	23,956	26,498	29,052
Value of exports	Mil. dol.	20,083	22,642	23,138	25,801	28,868	29,667	30,893

NA Not available.   [1] Value of all products and services sold by establishments in the food and kindred products industry. [2] Value of products classified in the food and kindred products industry produced by all industries.

Source: U.S. Department of Commerce, Bureau of the Census, International Trade Administration (ITA).

No. 1398. Recent Trends in Higher Value Added Foods and Beverages and Lower Value Foods and Feeds: 1991 to 1997

ITEM	Unit	1991	1992	1993	1994	1995	1996	1997
HIGHER VALUE ADDED FOODS AND BEVERAGES [1]								
Industry data:								
Value of shipments [2]	Mil. dol.	196,594	202,519	209,326	216,694	224,783	230,574	(NA)
Value of shipments (1992 dollars)	Mil. dol.	199,523	202,519	206,564	209,893	212,907	213,512	(NA)
Total employment	1,000.	830	830	836	826	829	826	(NA)
Production workers	1,000.	570	574	578	572	575	570	(NA)
Average hourly earnings	Dollar	11.33	11.57	11.83	12.08	12.08	12.41	(NA)
Capital expenditures	Mil. dol.	6,312	6,405	5,935	6,247	7,235	7,032	(NA)
Product data:								
Value of shipments [3]	Mil. dol.	182,570	191,278	197,567	204,380	213,482	218,210	(NA)
Value of shipments (1992 dollars)	Mil. dol.	185,227	191,278	195,162	198,230	202,518	202,242	(NA)
Trade data:								
Value of imports	Mil. dol.	8,722	9,727	9,459	10,360	11,333	13,004	14,322
Value of exports	Mil. dol.	5,735	6,688	7,532	8,659	9,187	9,956	10,615
LOWER VALUE ADDED FOODS AND FEEDS [4]								
Industry data:								
Value of shipments [2]	Mil. dol.	201,297	204,444	212,894	214,269	222,086	230,750	(NA)
Value of shipments (1992 dollars)	Mil. dol.	199,028	204,444	208,548	209,267	218,095	209,461	(NA)
Total employment	1,000.	679	673	684	685	691	690	(NA)
Production workers	1,000.	528	527	540	540	546	543	(NA)
Average hourly earnings	Dollar	8.94	9.21	9.29	9.39	9.81	9.89	(NA)
Capital expenditures	Mil. dol.	3,680	3,494	3,454	3,846	4,577	4,686	(NA)
Product data:								
Value of shipments [3]	Mil. dol.	181,373	191,611	200,065	201,110	208,024	216,799	(NA)
Value of shipments (1992 dollars)	Mil. dol.	179,192	191,611	195,928	196,217	203,773	196,475	(NA)
Trade data:								
Value of imports	Mil. dol.	11,058	11,155	11,431	12,482	12,623	13,494	14,730
Value of exports	Mil. dol.	14,348	15,954	15,606	17,142	19,681	19,711	20,278

NA Not available.   [1] SIC's 2023, 24, 32-38, 43, 45, 47, 51-53, 64-68, 82, 84-86, 95, 96, 98, and 99. This aggregation includes those industries defined as higher value added.   [2] Value of all products and services sold by establishments in this industry. [3] Value of products classified in this industry produced by all industries.   [4] SIC 20 excluding 2023, 24, 32-38, 43, 45, 47, 51-53, 64-68, 82, 84-86, 95, 96, 98, and 99. This aggregation includes those industries defined as lower value added.

Source: U.S. Department of Commerce, Bureau of the Census, International Trade Administration (ITA).

No. 1399. Recent Trends in Red Meat and Poultry Slaughtering and Processing: 1991 to 1997

ITEM	Unit	1991	1992	1993	1994	1995	1996	1997
RED MEAT (SIC 2011, 2013)								
Industry data:								
Value of shipments [1]	Mil. dol.	69,795	70,107	73,941	70,701	72,025	71,943	(NA)
Value of shipments (1992 dollars)	Mil. dol.	66,307	70,107	71,389	71,609	74,312	71,003	(NA)
Total employment	1,000.	205	207	209	204	214	218	(NA)
Production workers	1,000.	167	171	173	169	178	180	(NA)
Average hourly earnings	Dollar	8.74	8.99	9.06	9.43	9.81	9.64	(NA)
Capital expenditures	Mil. dol.	811	719	703	699	862	1,135	(NA)
Product data:								
Value of shipments [2]	Mil. dol.	62,676	64,351	68,216	64,839	65,878	65,839	(NA)
Value of shipments (1992 dollars)	Mil. dol.	59,535	64,351	65,856	65,679	67,977	64,988	(NA)
Trade data:								
Value of imports	Mil. dol.	3,140	2,926	3,070	2,984	2,662	2,638	2,989
Value of exports	Mil. dol.	4,348	4,807	4,698	5,273	6,303	6,226	6,233
POULTRY SLAUGHTERING AND PROCESSING (SIC 2015)								
Industry data:								
Value of shipments [1]	Mil. dol.	22,379	23,965	25,501	27,415	28,929	30,160	(NA)
Value of shipments (1992 dollars)	Mil. dol.	22,070	23,965	24,783	25,937	27,525	27,122	(NA)
Total employment	1,000.	194	194	205	216	214	215	(NA)
Production workers	1,000.	173	173	184	193	192	190	(NA)
Average hourly earnings	Dollar	7.02	7.39	7.40	7.49	8.09	8.27	(NA)
Capital expenditures	Mil. dol.	635	469	555	594	726	697	(NA)
Product data:								
Value of shipments [2]	Mil. dol.	21,246	23,592	24,983	27,027	28,708	29,981	(NA)
Value of shipments (1992 dollars)	Mil. dol.	20,953	23,592	24,279	25,570	27,315	26,961	(NA)
Trade data:								
Value of imports	Mil. dol.	35.7	25.8	29.9	25.3	30.5	44.7	45.6
Value of exports	Mil. dol.	879	990	1,157	1,633	2,097	2,585	2,509

NA Not available.   [1] Value of all products and services sold by establishments in this industry.   [2] Value of products classified in this industry produced by all industries.
Source: U.S. Department of Commerce, Bureau of the Census, International Trade Administration (ITA).

No. 1400. Recent Trends in Alcoholic Beverages (SIC 2082, 2084, 2085): 1991 to 1997

ITEM	Unit	1991	1992	1993	1994	1995	1996	1997
INDUSTRY DATA								
Value of shipments [1]	Mil. dol.	23,888	25,035	24,739	24,983	25,652	27,441	(NA)
2082 Malt beverages	Mil. dol.	16,421	17,340	16,656	16,795	17,151	18,220	(NA)
2084 Wines & brandy	Mil. dol.	3,697	4,301	4,514	4,301	4,798	5,548	(NA)
2085 Distilled liquor	Mil. dol.	3,770	3,394	3,569	3,888	3,703	3,673	(NA)
Value of shipments (1992 dollars)	Mil. dol.	24,337	25,035	24,802	25,333	25,251	26,160	(NA)
2082 Malt beverages	Mil. dol.	16,722	17,340	16,859	17,332	17,100	17,655	(NA)
2084 Wines & brandy	Mil. dol.	3,781	4,301	4,465	4,267	4,723	5,175	(NA)
2085 Distilled liquor	Mil. dol.	3,835	3,394	3,478	3,734	3,429	3,330	(NA)
Total employment	1,000.	54.8	55.6	56.4	53.8	55.6	57.6	(NA)
2082 Malt beverages	1,000.	33.1	34.5	35.3	33.5	32.6	34.0	(NA)
2084 Wines & brandy	1,000.	14.2	14.0	14.1	13.7	16.3	17.0	(NA)
2085 Distilled liquor	1,000.	7.5	7.1	7.0	6.6	6.7	6.6	(NA)
Production workers	1,000.	36.3	36.7	37.0	34.9	35.9	36.8	(NA)
2082 Malt beverages	1,000.	24.1	25.1	25.3	23.6	23.6	24.6	(NA)
2084 Wines & brandy	1,000.	6.9	6.5	6.6	6.6	7.5	7.5	(NA)
2085 Distilled liquor	1,000.	5.3	5.1	5.1	4.7	4.8	4.7	(NA)
Average hourly earnings	Dollar	19.26	19.83	19.81	20.15	20.37	20.22	(NA)
2082 Malt beverages	Dollar	22.49	22.89	22.71	23.01	23.92	23.39	(NA)
2084 Wines & brandy	Dollar	12.26	12.68	12.80	13.53	13.05	13.56	(NA)
2085 Distilled liquor	Dollar	14.44	15.05	15.49	15.43	15.38	16.07	(NA)
Capital expenditures	Mil. dol.	871	736	668	754	1,138	1,200	(NA)
2082 Malt beverages	Mil. dol.	702	565	479	564	861	877	(NA)
2084 Wines & brandy	Mil. dol.	105	115	146	151	209	269	(NA)
2085 Distilled liquor	Mil. dol.	63.9	56.3	42.1	39.7	67.3	54.0	(NA)
PRODUCT DATA								
Value of shipments [2]	Mil. dol.	22,758	24,607	24,324	24,370	25,155	26,794	(NA)
2082 Malt beverages	Mil. dol.	15,887	17,302	16,629	16,714	17,108	18,196	(NA)
2084 Wines & brandy	Mil. dol.	3,467	4,050	4,355	4,196	4,675	5,411	(NA)
2085 Distilled liquor	Mil. dol.	3,404	3,255	3,340	3,460	3,372	3,188	(NA)
Value of shipments (1992 dollars)	Mil. dol.	23,186	24,607	24,394	24,735	24,780	25,568	(NA)
2082 Malt beverages	Mil. dol.	16,178	17,302	16,831	17,249	17,057	17,631	(NA)
2084 Wines & brandy	Mil. dol.	3,545	4,050	4,308	4,163	4,601	5,047	(NA)
2085 Distilled liquor	Mil. dol.	3,463	3,255	3,255	3,324	3,122	2,890	(NA)
TRADE DATA								
Value of imports	Mil. dol.	3,065	3,527	3,387	3,668	3,980	4,619	5,198
2082 Malt beverages	Mil. dol.	840	881	961	1,072	1,192	1,341	1,514
2084 Wines & brandy	Mil. dol.	1,094	1,347	1,152	1,268	1,402	1,724	2,031
2085 Distilled liquor	Mil. dol.	1,131	1,299	1,274	1,328	1,386	1,554	1,653
Value of exports	Mil. dol.	655	742	766	973	1,242	1,342	1,409
2082 Malt beverages	Mil. dol.	207	221	234	391	526	453	418
2084 Wines & brandy	Mil. dol.	155	182	184	201	246	330	423
2085 Distilled liquor	Mil. dol.	294	339	349	380	470	559	568

NA Not available.   [1] Value of all products and services sold by establishments in the alcoholic beverages industry.   [2] Value of products classified in the alcoholic beverages industry industry produced by all industries.
Source: U.S. Department of Commerce, Bureau of the Census, International Trade Administration (ITA).

No. 1401. Recent Trends in Textile Mill Products (SIC 22): 1991 to 1997

ITEM	Unit	1991	1992	1993	1994	1995	1996	1997
INDUSTRY DATA								
Value of shipments [1]	Mil. dol. . .	65,439	70,753	73,955	78,027	79,874	80,242	(NA)
Value of shipments (1992 dollars)	Mil. dol. . .	65,979	70,753	74,276	78,223	77,725	77,246	(NA)
Total employment	1,000. . . .	594	617	610	624	610	577	(NA)
Production workers	1,000. . . .	510	528	524	534	520	489	(NA)
Average hourly earnings	Dollar . .	8.17	8.62	8.92	9.29	9.38	9.62	(NA)
PRODUCT DATA								
Value of shipments [2]	Mil. dol. . .	65,266	70,008	73,216	77,249	79,200	79,334	(NA)
Value of shipments (1992 dollars)	Mil. dol. . .	65,807	70,008	73,530	77,459	77,045	76,355	(NA)
TRADE DATA								
Value of imports	Mil. dol. . .	5,375	5,843	6,161	6,534	6,965	7,169	8,370
Value of exports	Mil. dol. . .	4,101	4,467	4,687	5,151	5,696	6,177	7,081

NA Not available.　[1] Value of all products and services sold by establishments in the textile mill products industry.　[2] Value of products classified in the textile mill products industry produced by all industries.

Source: U.S. Department of Commerce, Bureau of the Census, International Trade Administration (ITA).

No. 1402. Recent Trends in Cotton, Manmade, and Wool Broadwoven Fabric Mills: 1991 to 1997

ITEM	Unit	1991	1992	1993	1994	1995	1996	1997
COTTON BROADWOVEN FABRIC MILLS (SIC 221)								
Industry data:								
Value of shipments [1]	Mil. dol. . .	5,583	5,811	5,990	6,172	6,751	6,699	(NA)
Value of shipments (1992 dollars)	Mil. dol. . .	5,756	5,811	5,930	6,068	6,375	6,325	(NA)
Total employment	1,000. . .	65.0	55.9	55.0	55.0	55.8	51.9	(NA)
Production workers	1,000. . .	57.8	50.1	49.9	50.0	50.4	46.7	(NA)
Average hourly earnings	Dollar . .	8.43	8.92	9.38	9.82	9.96	10.32	(NA)
Product data:								
Value of shipments [2]	Mil. dol. . .	5,498	5,708	5,863	6,084	6,640	6,582	(NA)
Value of shipments (1992 dollars)	Mil. dol. . .	5,668	5,708	5,805	5,982	6,270	6,215	(NA)
Trade data:								
Value of imports	Mil. dol. . .	1,277	1,475	1,525	1,482	1,614	1,507	1,689
Value of exports	Mil. dol. . .	542	579	621	705	813	881	938
MANMADE BROADWOVEN FABRIC MILLS (SIC 222)								
Industry data:								
Value of shipments [1]	Mil. dol. . .	8,153	8,767	9,145	9,605	9,810	9,750	(NA)
Value of shipments (1992 dollars)	Mil. dol. . .	8,345	8,767	9,294	9,974	9,959	9,701	(NA)
Total employment	1,000. . .	77.2	87.2	85.8	81.5	80.8	73.9	(NA)
Production workers	1,000. . .	67.3	76.7	75.0	71.4	69.7	63.0	(NA)
Average hourly earnings	Dollar . .	8.77	9.21	9.46	9.91	10.20	10.48	(NA)
Product data:								
Value of shipments [2]	Mil. dol. . .	7,898	8,500	8,853	9,442	9,716	9,549	(NA)
Value of shipments (1992 dollars)	Mil. dol. . .	8,084	8,500	8,997	9,805	9,864	9,502	(NA)
Trade data:								
Value of imports	Mil. dol. . .	1,381	1,468	1,541	1,586	1,550	1,598	1,777
Value of exports	Mil. dol. . .	791	891	974	1,049	1,099	1,209	1,303
WOOL BROADWOVEN FABRIC MILLS (SIC 223)								
Industry data:								
Value of shipments [1]	Mil. dol. . .	1,725	1,612	1,681	1,861	1,829	1,756	(NA)
Value of shipments (1992 dollars)	Mil. dol. . .	1,669	1,612	1,693	1,884	1,840	1,761	(NA)
Total employment	1,000. . .	14.6	13.7	13.8	14.6	13.9	13.4	(NA)
Production workers	1,000. . .	12.5	11.8	11.9	12.6	12.1	11.7	(NA)
Average hourly earnings	Dollar . . .	8.36	8.46	8.87	9.70	9.92	9.78	(NA)
Product data:								
Value of shipments [2]	Mil. dol. . .	1,492	1,388	1,502	1,518	1,463	1,427	(NA)
Value of shipments (1992 dollars)	Mil. dol. . .	1,444	1,388	1,513	1,537	1,472	1,431	(NA)
Trade data:								
Value of imports	Mil. dol. . .	247	240	230	242	252	267	292
Value of exports	Mil. dol. . .	62.4	99.3	84.6	87.2	114.0	116.0	134.1

NA Not available.　[1] Value of all products and services sold by establishments in this industry.　[2] Value of products classified in this industry produced by all industries.

Source: U.S. Department of Commerce, Bureau of the Census, International Trade Administration (ITA).

No. 1403. Recent Trends in Broadwoven Fabric Mills (SIC 221, 222, 223): 1991 to 1997

ITEM	Unit	1991	1992	1993	1994	1995	1996	1997
INDUSTRY DATA								
Value of shipments [1]	Mil. dol.	15,460	16,190	16,816	17,638	18,389	18,204	(NA)
Value of shipments (1992 dollars)	Mil. dol.	15,770	16,190	16,917	17,926	18,174	17,788	(NA)
Total employment	1,000.	157	157	155	151	151	139	(NA)
Production workers	1,000.	138	139	137	134	132	121	(NA)
Average hourly earnings	Dollar	8.59	9.04	9.38	9.86	10.08	10.35	(NA)
PRODUCT DATA								
Value of shipments [2]	Mil. dol.	14,888	15,597	16,218	17,045	17,819	17,558	(NA)
Value of shipments (1992 dollars)	Mil. dol.	15,196	15,597	16,315	17,324	17,605	17,148	(NA)
TRADE DATA								
Value of imports	Mil. dol.	2,905	3,183	3,295	3,310	3,417	3,372	3,758
Value of exports	Mil. dol.	1,395	1,569	1,680	1,840	2,027	2,206	2,376

NA Not available.   [1] Value of all products and services sold by establishments in the food and kindred products industry.
[2] Value of products classified in the food and kindred products industry produced by all industries.

Source: U.S. Department of Commerce, Bureau of the Census, International Trade Administration (ITA).

No. 1404. Recent Trends in Carpets and Rugs, Weft, Lace, and Knit, and Yarn Spinning Mills: 1991 to 1997

ITEM	Unit	1991	1992	1993	1994	1995	1996	1997
CARPETS AND RUGS (SIC 227)								
Industry data:								
Value of shipments [1]	Mil. dol.	9,045	9,828	10,234	10,600	10,762	11,184	(NA)
Value of shipments (1992 dollars)	Mil. dol.	9,008	9,828	10,286	10,537	10,551	10,722	(NA)
Total employment	1,000.	48.3	49.4	50.6	55.1	55.5	55.0	(NA)
Production workers	1,000.	37.8	38.9	39.6	42.9	43.5	43.8	(NA)
Average hourly earnings	Dollar	8.33	8.83	9.17	9.54	9.58	9.55	(NA)
Product data:								
Value of shipments [2]	Mil. dol.	8,555	9,518	9,953	10,141	10,405	10,806	(NA)
Value of shipments (1992 dollars)	Mil. dol.	8,521	9,518	10,003	10,081	10,201	10,360	(NA)
Trade data:								
Value of imports	Mil. dol.	584	700	660	736	843	820	925
Value of exports	Mil. dol.	683	705	698	667	632	702	793
WEFT, LACE, AND WARP KNIT FABRIC MILLS (SIC 2257, 2258)								
Industry data:								
Value of shipments [1]	Mil. dol.	6,274	7,270	7,526	8,110	7,858	7,537	(NA)
Value of shipments (1992 dollars)	Mil. dol.	6,289	7,270	7,544	8,182	7,752	7,414	(NA)
Total employment	1,000.	52.5	63.9	60.6	61.2	57.7	54.8	(NA)
Production workers	1,000.	43.9	53.9	50.6	51.5	48.5	46.3	(NA)
Average hourly earnings	Dollar	8.17	8.54	8.90	9.43	9.47	9.58	(NA)
Product data:								
Value of shipments [2]	Mil. dol.	6,542	7,436	7,478	8,102	7,841	7,580	(NA)
Value of shipments (1992 dollars)	Mil. dol.	6,558	7,436	7,492	8,172	7,736	7,459	(NA)
Trade data:								
Value of imports	Mil. dol.	200	233	302	354	356	542	805
Value of exports	Mil. dol.	334	377	375	400	495	547	676
YARN SPINNING MILLS (SIC 2281)								
Industry data:								
Value of shipments [1]	Mil. dol.	7,123	7,669	7,618	7,999	8,465	8,543	(NA)
Value of shipments (1992 dollars)	Mil. dol.	7,109	7,669	7,960	8,289	8,324	8,526	(NA)
Total employment	1,000.	68.9	68.7	65.6	66.1	64.5	60.6	(NA)
Production workers	1,000.	62.5	62.6	59.7	60.2	58.8	55.1	(NA)
Average hourly earnings	Dollar	8.36	8.48	8.62	8.95	9.13	9.47	(NA)
Product data:								
Value of shipments [2]	Mil. dol.	7,519	7,756	7,696	8,196	8,619	8,771	(NA)
Value of shipments (1992 dollars)	Mil. dol.	7,504	7,756	8,041	8,493	8,475	8,753	(NA)
Trade data:								
Value of imports	Mil. dol.	264	321	337	388	400	420	529
Value of exports	Mil. dol.	202	169	146	209	299	327	355

NA Not available.   [1] Value of all products and services sold by establishments in this industry.   [2] Value of products classified in this industry produced by all industries.

Source: U.S. Department of Commerce, Bureau of the Census, International Trade Administration (ITA).

No. 1405. Recent Trends in Apparel and Other Textile Products (SIC 23): 1991 to 1997

ITEM	Unit	1991	1992	1993	1994	1995	1996	1997
INDUSTRY DATA								
Value of shipments [1]	Mil. dol.	68,309	71,658	74,010	76,979	78,103	77,628	(NA)
Value of shipments (1992 dollars)	Mil. dol.	69,578	71,658	73,339	76,063	76,601	74,976	(NA)
Total employment	1,000	982	985	980	954	947	865	(NA)
Production workers	1,000	832	824	825	799	792	726	(NA)
Average hourly earnings	Dollar	6.93	7.12	7.34	7.44	7.56	7.67	(NA)
PRODUCT DATA								
Value of shipments [2]	Mil. dol.	62,649	68,844	70,986	73,258	73,780	73,319	(NA)
Value of shipments (1992 dollars)	Mil. dol.	63,780	68,844	70,345	72,382	72,370	70,843	(NA)
TRADE DATA								
Value of imports	Mil. dol.	27,377	32,644	35,475	38,561	41,208	43,075	50,191
Value of exports	Mil. dol.	3,746	4,659	5,433	6,009	6,979	7,836	8,930

NA Not available.   [1] Value of all products and services sold by establishments in the apparel and other textile products industry.   [2] Value of products classified in the apparel and other textile products industry produced by all industries.

Source: U.S. Department of Commerce, Bureau of the Census, International Trade Administration (ITA).

No. 1406. Recent Trends in Selected Men's and Boys' Apparel (SIC 231, 2321, -3, -5, -6): 1991 to 1997

ITEM	Unit	1991	1992	1993	1994	1995	1996	1997
INDUSTRY DATA								
Value of shipments [1]	Mil. dol.	16,083	16,991	16,819	17,088	17,426	17,208	(NA)
2311 Men/boys' suits/coats	Mil. dol.	2,579	2,430	2,463	2,362	2,078	1,968	(NA)
2321 Men's and boys' shirts	Mil. dol.	4,698	5,921	5,012	5,082	5,186	4,939	(NA)
2323 Men's and boys' neckwear	Mil. dol.	556	618	619	705	792	652	(NA)
2325 Men/boys' trousers	Mil. dol.	6,760	6,519	7,055	7,226	7,506	7,658	(NA)
2326 Men/boys' work clothing	Mil. dol.	1,491	1,503	1,670	1,714	1,863	1,991	(NA)
Value of shipments (1992 dollars)	Mil. dol.	16,640	16,991	16,538	16,669	16,837	16,437	(NA)
2311 Men/boys' suits/coats	Mil. dol.	2,639	2,430	2,471	2,338	2,044	1,915	(NA)
2321 Men's and boys' shirts	Mil. dol.	4,888	5,921	4,938	5,017	5,104	4,880	(NA)
2323 Men's and boys' neckwear	Mil. dol.	565	618	611	695	772	628	(NA)
2325 Men/boys' trousers	Mil. dol.	7,042	6,519	6,889	6,975	7,169	7,190	(NA)
2326 Men/boys' work clothing	Mil. dol.	1,506	1,503	1,629	1,644	1,748	1,823	(NA)
Total employment	1,000	235.0	245.0	229.0	225.0	216.0	185.0	(NA)
2311 Men/boys' suits/coats	1,000	44.6	44.0	41.2	34.0	31.1	27.1	(NA)
2321 Men's and boys' shirts	1,000	70.3	84.4	72.7	73.8	71.0	59.1	(NA)
2323 Men's and boys' neckwear	1,000	6.5	7.5	6.3	6.2	5.6	4.7	(NA)
2325 Men/boys' trousers	1,000	82.3	78.9	78.5	82.2	79.4	70.9	(NA)
2326 Men/boys' work clothing	1,000	31.5	30.4	30.0	28.5	28.6	23.4	(NA)
Production workers	1,000	204	214	199	197	190	163	(NA)
2311 Men/boys' suits/coats	1,000	37.2	37.4	34.7	28.7	26.3	22.2	(NA)
2321 Men's and boys' shirts	1,000	62.1	74.2	64.1	67.0	64.4	53.1	(NA)
2323 Men's and boys' neckwear	1,000	5.2	5.8	4.8	4.6	4.0	3.5	(NA)
2325 Men/boys' trousers	1,000	72.2	69.8	68.4	71.9	70.4	64.3	(NA)
2326 Men/boys' work clothing	1,000	27.7	26.4	26.5	24.4	24.8	19.6	(NA)
Average hourly earnings	Dollar	7.00	6.94	7.21	7.18	7.45	7.67	(NA)
2311 Men/boys' suits/coats	Dollar	8.39	7.96	8.32	8.35	8.13	8.40	(NA)
2321 Men's and boys' shirts	Dollar	7.08	6.85	6.90	6.96	7.20	7.38	(NA)
2323 Men's/boys' neckwear	Dollar	8.32	7.39	8.43	9.21	9.82	10.16	(NA)
2325 Men/boys' trousers	Dollar	6.55	6.81	7.15	7.03	7.40	7.69	(NA)
2326 Men/boys' work clothing	Dollar	5.86	6.06	6.47	6.49	7.19	7.17	(NA)
PRODUCT DATA								
Value of shipments [2]	Mil. dol.	14,143	15,810	15,405	16,129	16,096	15,441	(NA)
2311 Men/boys' suits/coats	Mil. dol.	2,450	2,387	2,257	2,417	2,020	1,913	(NA)
2321 Men's and boys' shirts	Mil. dol.	3,915	5,318	4,632	4,709	4,792	4,303	(NA)
2323 Men's and boys' neckwear	Mil. dol.	525	544	529	594	618	574	(NA)
2325 Men/boys' trousers	Mil. dol.	5,911	6,065	6,338	6,636	6,771	6,757	(NA)
2326 Men/boys' work clothing	Mil. dol.	1,341	1,495	1,650	1,773	1,895	1,894	(NA)
Value of shipments (1992 dollars)	Mil. dol.	14,628	15,810	15,147	15,733	15,550	14,744	(NA)
2311 Men/boys' suits/coats	Mil. dol.	2,508	2,387	2,263	2,393	1,986	1,861	(NA)
2321 Men's and boys' shirts	Mil. dol.	4,074	5,318	4,563	4,649	4,717	4,252	(NA)
2323 Men's and boys' neckwear	Mil. dol.	533	544	521	586	602	553	(NA)
2325 Men/boys' trousers	Mil. dol.	6,158	6,065	6,190	6,405	6,467	6,344	(NA)
2326 Men/boys' work clothing	Mil. dol.	1,355	1,495	1,609	1,700	1,777	1,734	(NA)
TRADE DATA								
Value of imports	Mil. dol.	6,168	7,624	8,281	9,178	10,873	11,426	13,282
2311 Men/boys' suits/coats	Mil. dol.	678	789	824	954	1,042	1,134	1,317
2321 Men's and boys' shirts	Mil. dol.	3,039	4,028	4,519	4,917	5,875	6,006	6,810
2323 Men's and boys' neckwear	Mil. dol.	140	151	158	156	167	174	184
2325 Men/boys' trousers	Mil. dol.	2,310	2,657	2,780	3,151	3,789	4,113	4,972
2326 Men/boys' work clothing	Mil. dol.	(NA)	(NA)	(NA)	(NA)	(NA)	(NA)	(NA)
Value of exports	Mil. dol.	1,140	1,478	1,795	2,036	2,158	2,374	2,661
2311 Men/boys' suits/coats	Mil. dol.	161	197	237	292	269	264	251
2321 Men's and boys' shirts	Mil. dol.	333	457	595	721	842	919	1,091
2323 Men's and boys' neckwear	Mil. dol.	14.5	15.5	21.1	17.9	18.4	21.1	20.6
2325 Men/boys' trousers	Mil. dol.	631	809	942	1,005	1,029	1,170	1,298
2326 Men/boys' work clothing	Mil. dol.	(NA)	(NA)	(NA)	(NA)	(NA)	(NA)	(NA)

NA Not available.   [1] Value of all products and services sold by establishments in the selected men's and boys' apparel industry.   [2] Value of products classified in the selected men's and boys' apparel industry produced by all industries.

Source: U.S. Department of Commerce, Bureau of the Census, International Trade Administration (ITA).

No. 1407. Recent Trends in Men's and Boys' Underwear and Nightwear (SIC 2322): 1991 to 1997

ITEM	Unit	1991	1992	1993	1994	1995	1996	1997
INDUSTRY DATA								
Value of shipments [1]	Mil. dol. . .	742	820	581	664	592	590	(NA)
Value of shipments (1992 dollars)	Mil. dol. . .	755	820	578	660	586	578	(NA)
Total employment	1,000. . . .	12.0	14.2	11.3	10.5	7.8	6.9	(NA)
Production workers	1,000. . . .	11.1	13.1	10.5	10.1	7.5	6.5	(NA)
Average hourly earnings	Dollar . . .	7.66	6.67	6.48	7.03	7.10	6.46	(NA)
PRODUCT DATA								
Value of shipments [2]	Mil. dol. . .	744	808	689	743	674	578	(NA)
Value of shipments (1992 dollars)	Mil. dol. . .	757	808	685	738	667	567	(NA)
TRADE DATA								
Value of imports	Mil. dol. . .	289	396	528	652	963	1,229	1,661
Value of exports	Mil. dol. . .	157	219	314	331	431	531	624

NA Not available. [1] Value of all products and services sold by establishments in the men's and boys' underwear and nightwear industry. [2] Value of products classified in the men's and boys' underwear and nightwear industry produced by all industries.

Source: U.S. Department of Commerce, Bureau of the Census, International Trade Administration (ITA).

No. 1408. Recent Trends in Selected Women's Outerwear (SIC 2331, 2335, 2337): 1991 to 1997

ITEM	Unit	1991	1992	1993	1994	1995	1996	1997
INDUSTRY DATA								
Value of shipments [1]	Mil. dol. . .	14,415	13,733	14,123	14,598	14,413	13,851	(NA)
2331 Women's/misses' blouses	Mil. dol. . .	3,973	3,970	4,012	4,147	3,797	3,649	(NA)
2335 Women's/misses' dresses	Mil. dol. . .	5,922	5,366	5,602	6,396	6,928	6,606	(NA)
2337 Women's suits and coats	Mil. dol. . .	4,520	4,397	4,509	4,055	3,688	3,596	(NA)
Value of shipments (1992 dollars)	Mil. dol. . .	14,610	13,733	14,063	14,644	14,604	14,248	(NA)
2331 Women's/misses' blouses	Mil. dol. . .	4,096	3,970	3,976	4,053	3,686	3,563	(NA)
2335 Women's/misses' dresses	Mil. dol. . .	5,957	5,366	5,597	6,507	7,128	6,896	(NA)
2337 Women's suits and coats	Mil. dol. . .	4,556	4,397	4,491	4,084	3,790	3,789	(NA)
Total employment	1,000. . . .	214.0	188.0	190.0	182.0	186.0	169.0	(NA)
2331 Women's/misses' blouses	1,000. . . .	60.8	56.1	52.9	51.8	47.8	42.9	(NA)
2335 Women's/misses' dresses	1,000. . . .	105.0	83.2	87.1	87.5	99.3	93.3	(NA)
2337 Women's suits and coats	1,000. . . .	49.0	48.3	49.6	43.1	38.8	33.0	(NA)
Production workers	1,000. . . .	182.0	156.0	159.0	151.0	156.0	143.0	(NA)
2331 Women's/misses' blouses	1,000. . . .	50.3	47.1	44.7	42.2	39.3	35.6	(NA)
2335 Women's/misses' dresses	1,000. . . .	91.3	71.0	74.5	74.8	85.1	80.5	(NA)
2337 Women's suits and coats	1,000. . . .	40.0	37.8	40.0	34.1	31.1	26.8	(NA)
Average hourly earnings	Dollar . . .	6.57	6.88	7.02	7.09	6.99	6.92	(NA)
2331 Women's/misses' blouses	Dollar . . .	6.11	6.44	6.96	6.61	6.55	6.35	(NA)
2335 Women's/misses' dresses	Dollar . . .	6.49	6.82	6.71	7.10	6.93	6.87	(NA)
2337 Women's suits and coats	Dollar . . .	7.31	7.56	7.64	7.68	7.75	7.95	(NA)
PRODUCT DATA								
Value of shipments [2]	Mil. dol. . .	12,805	13,581	14,275	14,400	14,083	13,734	(NA)
2331 Women's/misses' blouses	Mil. dol. . .	3,618	4,195	4,580	4,425	4,012	3,752	(NA)
2335 Women's/misses' dresses	Mil. dol. . .	5,443	5,278	5,431	6,042	6,397	6,336	(NA)
2337 Women's suits and coats	Mil. dol. . .	3,745	4,108	4,264	3,933	3,674	3,646	(NA)
Value of shipments (1992 dollars)	Mil. dol. . .	12,980	13,581	14,211	14,433	14,253	14,119	(NA)
2331 Women's/misses' blouses	Mil. dol. . .	3,730	4,195	4,539	4,325	3,896	3,664	(NA)
2335 Women's/misses' dresses	Mil. dol. . .	5,475	5,278	5,426	6,146	6,582	6,614	(NA)
2337 Women's suits and coats	Mil. dol. . .	3,775	4,108	4,247	3,961	3,775	3,842	(NA)
TRADE DATA								
Value of imports	Mil. dol. . .	6,119	7,073	7,718	7,960	8,430	8,943	9,768
2331 Women's/misses' blouses	Mil. dol. . .	2,923	3,501	3,864	3,948	3,906	3,980	4,658
2335 Women's/misses' dresses	Mil. dol. . .	981	1,054	1,130	1,339	1,688	1,870	1,930
2337 Women's suits and coats	Mil. dol. . .	2,215	2,518	2,724	2,673	2,836	3,093	3,180
Value of exports	Mil. dol. . .	362	519	590	591	714	725	820
2331 Women's/misses' blouses	Mil. dol. . .	101	171	213	243	342	339	376
2335 Women's/misses' dresses	Mil. dol. . .	65	98	105	103	113	115	148
2337 Women's suits and coats	Mil. dol. . .	197	250	272	245	259	272	297

NA Not available. [1] Value of all products and services sold by establishments in the selected women's outerwear industry. [2] Value of products classified in the selected women's outerwear industry produced by all industries.

Source: U.S. Department of Commerce, Bureau of the Census, International Trade Administration (ITA).

No. 1409. Recent Trends in Women's and Children's Undergarments (SIC 234): 1991 to 1997

ITEM	Unit	1991	1992	1993	1994	1995	1996	1997
INDUSTRY DATA								
Value of shipments [1]	Mil. dol.	3,850	3,943	3,943	4,245	4,577	4,244	(NA)
2341 Women/child's underwear	Mil. dol.	2,494	2,368	2,155	2,438	2,494	2,330	(NA)
2342 Bras and allied garments	Mil. dol.	1,356	1,575	1,789	1,807	2,083	1,914	(NA)
Value of shipments (1992 dollars)	Mil. dol.	3,947	3,943	3,884	4,129	4,418	4,071	(NA)
2341 Women/child's underwear	Mil. dol.	2,561	2,368	2,135	2,390	2,431	2,264	(NA)
2342 Bras and allied garments	Mil. dol.	1,386	1,575	1,748	1,739	1,988	1,807	(NA)
Total employment	1,000.	58.7	53.7	52.1	47.1	45.9	38.1	(NA)
2341 Women/child's underwear	1,000.	47.9	41.6	38.0	33.5	30.2	25.5	(NA)
2342 Bras and allied garments	1,000.	10.8	12.1	14.1	13.6	15.7	12.6	(NA)
Production workers	1,000.	49.4	45.4	43.7	39.4	38.0	32.0	(NA)
2341 Women/child's underwear	1,000.	41.5	35.8	33.0	29.0	26.3	22.6	(NA)
2342 Bras and allied garments	1,000.	7.9	9.6	10.7	10.4	11.7	9.4	(NA)
Average hourly earnings	Dollar	6.43	6.74	6.89	6.70	7.01	7.31	(NA)
2341 Women/child's underwear	Dollar	6.28	6.46	6.54	6.51	6.96	7.21	(NA)
2342 Bras + allied garments	Dollar	7.22	7.80	7.93	7.22	7.09	7.53	(NA)
PRODUCT DATA								
Value of shipments [2]	Mil. dol.	3,660	3,821	3,587	3,917	4,180	3,922	(NA)
2341 Women/child's underwear	Mil. dol.	2,260	2,237	1,928	2,128	2,135	1,980	(NA)
2342 Bras and allied garments	Mil. dol.	1,400	1,584	1,659	1,789	2,045	1,941	(NA)
Value of shipments (1992 dollars)	Mil. dol.	3,752	3,821	3,532	3,808	4,032	3,758	(NA)
2341 Women/child's underwear	Mil. dol.	2,320	2,237	1,911	2,086	2,081	1,924	(NA)
2342 Bras and allied garments	Mil. dol.	1,431	1,584	1,621	1,722	1,951	1,833	(NA)
TRADE DATA								
Value of imports	Mil. dol.	1,256	1,519	1,787	2,067	2,443	2,492	2,885
2341 Women/child's underwear	Mil. dol.	829	985	1,168	1,342	1,540	1,646	1,939
2342 Bras and allied garments	Mil. dol.	427	534	619	725	903	845	946
Value of exports	Mil. dol.	355	407	466	521	654	650	816
2341 Women/child's underwear	Mil. dol.	136	155	186	222	267	274	347
2342 Bras and allied garments	Mil. dol.	219	252	280	299	387	376	468

NA Not available.   [1] Value of all products and services sold by establishments in the women's and children's undergarments industry.   [2] Value of products classified in the women's and children's undergarments industry produced by all industries.

Source: U.S. Department of Commerce, Bureau of the Census, International Trade Administration (ITA).

No. 1410. Recent Trends in Girls' and Children's Outerwear (SIC 236): 1991 to 1997

ITEM	Unit	1991	1992	1993	1994	1995	1996	1997
INDUSTRY DATA								
Value of shipments [1]	Mil. dol.	3,741	3,145	3,221	3,926	3,605	3,874	(NA)
2361 Child's dresses/blouses	Mil. dol.	1,881	1,619	1,567	1,716	1,631	1,636	(NA)
2369 Children's outerwear n.e.c.	Mil. dol.	1,860	1,525	1,655	2,210	1,973	2,238	(NA)
Value of shipments (1992 dollars)	Mil. dol.	3,785	3,145	3,203	3,932	3,594	3,832	(NA)
2361 Child's dresses/blouses	Mil. dol.	1,912	1,619	1,570	1,728	1,572	1,567	(NA)
2369 Children's outerwear n.e.c.	Mil. dol.	1,873	1,525	1,633	2,203	2,022	2,265	(NA)
Total employment	1,000.	60.0	53.3	49.2	48.0	42.7	33.5	(NA)
2361 Child's dresses/blouses	1,000.	30.8	23.9	23.1	19.5	17.3	11.6	(NA)
2369 Children's outerwear n.e.c.	1,000.	29.2	29.4	26.1	28.5	25.4	21.9	(NA)
Production workers	1,000.	50.6	43.6	39.8	38.4	34.1	27.4	(NA)
2361 Child's dresses/blouses	1,000.	26.1	19.1	18.6	15.2	13.1	8.8	(NA)
2369 Children's outerwear n.e.c.	1,000.	24.5	24.5	21.2	23.2	21.0	18.6	(NA)
Average hourly earnings	Dollar	5.90	6.36	6.63	6.78	6.54	7.01	(NA)
2361 Child's dresses/blouses.	Dollar	6.13	6.49	6.24	6.53	6.33	7.36	(NA)
2369 Children's outerwear n.e.c.	Dollar	5.68	6.26	6.97	6.96	6.65	6.87	(NA)
PRODUCT DATA								
Value of shipments [2]	Mil. dol.	3,592	3,503	3,452	3,636	3,565	3,585	(NA)
2361 Child's dresses/blouses	Mil. dol.	1,812	1,719	1,626	1,680	1,616	1,590	(NA)
2369 Children's outerwear n.e.c.	Mil. dol.	1,780	1,784	1,826	1,957	1,949	1,995	(NA)
Value of shipments (1992 dollars)	Mil. dol.	3,634	3,503	3,432	3,642	3,554	3,542	(NA)
2361 Child's dresses/blouses	Mil. dol.	1,841	1,719	1,629	1,692	1,557	1,523	(NA)
2369 Children's outerwear n.e.c.	Mil. dol.	1,792	1,784	1,803	1,951	1,997	2,019	(NA)
TRADE DATA								
Value of imports	Mil. dol.	6,694	8,016	8,196	8,926	8,890	9,191	11,258
2361 Child's dresses/blouses	Mil. dol.	-	-	-	-	-	-	-
2369 Children's outerwear n.e.c.	Mil. dol.	6,694	8,016	8,196	8,926	8,890	9,191	11,258
Value of exports	Mil. dol.	458	625	703	920	1,273	1,723	1,977
2361 Child's dresses/blouses	Mil. dol.	-	-	-	-	-	-	-
2369 Children's outerwear n.e.c.	Mil. dol.	458	625	703	920	1,273	1,723	1,977

- Represents or rounds to zero.   NA Not available.   [1] Value of all products and services sold by establishments in the girls' and children's outerwear industry.   [2] Value of products classified in the girls' and children's outerwear industry produced by all industries.

Source: U.S. Department of Commerce, Bureau of the Census, International Trade Administration (ITA).

No. 1411. Recent Trends in Misc. Fabricated Textile Products (SIC 239): 1991 to 1997

ITEM	Unit	1991	1992	1993	1994	1995	1996	1997
INDUSTRY DATA								
Value of shipments [1]	Mil. dol. . .	17,660	19,118	20,264	21,738	22,488	22,934	(NA)
239A Homefurnishings	Mil. dol. . .	6,777	6,886	7,154	7,411	7,616	7,517	(NA)
239B Misc. textile products	Mil. dol. . .	10,883	12,232	13,110	14,327	14,872	15,418	(NA)
Value of shipments (1992 dollars)	Mil. dol. . .	17,906	19,118	20,034	21,318	21,740	21,236	(NA)
239A Homefurnishings	Mil. dol. . .	6,870	6,886	7,022	7,217	7,305	7,002	(NA)
239B Misc. textile products	Mil. dol. . .	11,037	12,232	13,012	14,101	14,436	14,234	(NA)
Total employment	1,000. .	190	211	212	222	228	224	(NA)
239A Homefurnishings	1,000. .	68.6	73.7	72.1	71.3	74.4	68.6	(NA)
239B Misc. textile products	1,000. .	122	137	140	151	154	155	(NA)
Production workers	1,000. .	154	168	171	179	182	179	(NA)
239A Homefurnishings	1,000. .	56.3	61.0	59.5	59.0	60.0	55.8	(NA)
239B Misc. textile products	1,000. .	98.0	107.0	112.0	120.0	122.0	123.0	(NA)
Average hourly earnings	Dollar . . .	8.45	8.34	8.61	8.78	8.90	9.02	(NA)
239A Homefurnishings	Dollar . . .	6.85	7.24	7.79	7.90	7.98	8.20	(NA)
239B Misc. textile products	Dollar . . .	9.42	8.98	9.06	9.21	9.33	9.39	(NA)
PRODUCT DATA								
Value of shipments [2]	Mil. dol. . .	16,207	18,220	19,555	20,738	21,240	21,866	(NA)
239A Homefurnishings	Mil. dol. . .	6,100	6,540	6,980	7,230	7,096	7,071	(NA)
239B Misc. textile products	Mil. dol. . .	10,108	11,681	12,575	13,508	14,143	14,795	(NA)
Value of shipments (1992 dollars)	Mil. dol. . .	16,423	18,220	19,331	20,339	20,534	20,243	(NA)
239A Homefurnishings	Mil. dol. . .	6,184	6,540	6,851	7,043	6,808	6,587	(NA)
239B Misc. textile products	Mil. dol. . .	10,240	11,681	12,480	13,296	13,726	13,657	(NA)
TRADE DATA								
Value of imports	Mil. dol. . .	2,316	2,698	3,116	3,428	3,556	3,614	4,186
239A Homefurnishings	Mil. dol. . .	1,000	1,178	1,334	1,553	1,736	1,734	2,078
239B Misc. textile products	Mil. dol. . .	1,315	1,520	1,782	1,875	1,820	1,880	2,108
Value of exports	Mil. dol. . .	780	862	972	944	939	1,018	1,110
239A Homefurnishings	Mil. dol. . .	317	338	349	362	350	371	439
239B Misc. textile products	Mil. dol. . .	463	524	623	582	590	647	671

NA Not available. [1] Value of all products and services sold by establishments in the misc. fabricated textile products industry. The designation 239A represents SIC's 2391 and 2392; 239B represents SIC 239 less SIC's 2391 and 2392. [2] Value of products classified in the misc. fabricated textile products industry produced by all industries

Source: U.S. Department of Commerce, Bureau of the Census, International Trade Administration (ITA).

No. 1412. Recent Trends in Logging and Sawmills and Planing Mills, General: 1991 to 1997

ITEM	Unit	1991	1992	1993	1994	1995	1996	1997
LOGGING (SIC 2411)								
Industry data:								
Value of shipments [1]	Mil. dol. . .	11,422	13,592	15,976	16,488	16,465	15,411	(NA)
Value of shipments (1992 dollars)	Mil. dol. . .	12,635	13,592	13,085	13,148	13,026	12,811	(NA)
Total employment	1,000. . .	77.2	83.2	86.2	87.0	84.8	83.0	(NA)
Production workers	1,000. . .	64.3	69.2	71.6	71.7	69.9	68.3	(NA)
Average hourly earnings	Dollar . . .	9.98	10.01	9.86	9.98	10.52	10.76	(NA)
Capital expenditures	Mil. dol. . .	322	374	366	472	589	539	(NA)
Product data:								
Value of shipments [2]	Mil. dol. . .	10,728	12,962	15,362	15,648	15,794	14,831	(NA)
Value of shipments (1992 dollars)	Mil. dol. . .	11,868	12,962	12,581	12,479	12,495	12,328	(NA)
Trade data:								
Value of imports	Mil. dol. . .	199	219	265	273	293	291	323
Value of exports	Mil. dol. . .	2,715	2,749	3,077	2,915	3,026	2,851	2,366
SAWMILLS AND PLANING MILLS, GENERAL (SIC 2421)								
Industry data:								
Value of shipments [1]	Mil. dol. . .	17,466	21,061	24,460	26,964	25,776	26,740	(NA)
Value of shipments (1992 dollars)	Mil. dol. . .	20,052	21,061	19,662	21,181	21,716	22,700	(NA)
Total employment	1,000. . .	128	138	142	142	143	138	(NA)
Production workers	1,000. . .	114	118	122	122	122	118	(NA)
Average hourly earnings	Dollar . . .	9.49	9.65	9.83	9.97	10.24	10.51	(NA)
Capital expenditures	Mil. dol. . .	511	459	548	694	852	1,000	(NA)
Product data:								
Value of shipments [2]	Mil. dol. . .	17,515	20,347	23,641	26,001	24,945	25,849	(NA)
Value of shipments (1992 dollars)	Mil. dol. . .	20,109	20,347	19,004	20,425	21,015	21,943	(NA)
Trade data:								
Value of imports	Mil. dol. . .	2,638	3,472	5,022	6,039	5,505	6,813	7,305
Value of exports	Mil. dol. . .	2,203	2,323	2,450	2,428	2,412	2,393	2,472

NA Not available. [1] Value of all products and services sold by establishments in this industry. [2] Value of products classified in this industry produced by all industries.

Source: U.S. Department of Commerce, Bureau of the Census, International Trade Administration (ITA).

No. 1413. Recent Trends in Hardwood Veneer and Softwood Veneer: 1991 to 1997

ITEM	Unit	1991	1992	1993	1994	1995	1996	1997
HARDWOOD VENEER AND PLYWOOD (SIC 2435)								
Industry data:								
Value of shipments [1]	Mil. dol. . .	1,894	2,238	2,537	2,609	2,642	2,623	(NA)
Value of shipments (1992 dollars) . . .	Mil. dol. . .	1,975	2,238	2,371	2,292	2,277	2,236	(NA)
Total employment	1,000. . .	17.1	19.9	19.8	21.9	22.0	21.3	(NA)
Production workers	1,000. . .	14.5	16.9	16.8	18.8	18.8	18.3	(NA)
Average hourly earnings	Dollar	8.18	8.12	8.55	8.21	8.75	8.95	(NA)
Capital expenditures	Mil. dol. . .	50.0	45.1	46.6	52.5	32.2	37.7	(NA)
Product data:								
Value of shipments [2]	Mil. dol. . .	1,743	2,023	2,305	2,444	2,520	2,556	(NA)
Value of shipments (1992 dollars) . . .	Mil. dol. . .	1,817	2,023	2,154	2,148	2,173	2,179	(NA)
Trade data:								
Value of imports	Mil. dol. . .	588	729	857	890	924	997	994
Value of exports	Mil. dol. . .	244	273	292	343	372	369	419
SOFTWOOD VENEER AND PLYWOOD (SIC 2436)								
Industry data:								
Value of shipments [1]	Mil. dol. . .	4,587	5,350	6,035	6,544	6,828	6,033	(NA)
Value of shipments (1992 dollars) . . .	Mil. dol. . .	5,013	5,350	5,172	5,417	5,376	5,264	(NA)
Total employment	1,000. . .	31.3	30.9	30.7	30.3	32.4	31.9	(NA)
Production workers	1,000. . .	28.1	27.7	27.7	27.2	29.1	28.6	(NA)
Average hourly earnings	Dollar . . .	10.97	11.08	11.42	11.83	12.14	12.36	(NA)
Capital expenditures	Mil. dol. . .	95	95	118	150	184	208	(NA)
Product data:								
Value of shipments [2]	Mil. dol. . .	3,972	4,778	5,321	5,700	5,953	5,225	(NA)
Value of shipments (1992 dollars) . . .	Mil. dol. . .	4,341	4,778	4,560	4,719	4,688	4,559	(NA)
Trade data:								
Value of imports	Mil. dol. . .	35.5	59.0	76.9	96.4	99.4	88.4	109.4
Value of exports	Mil. dol. . .	279	341	373	327	339	317	392

NA Not available.   [1] Value of all products and services sold by establishments in this industry.   [2] Value of products classified in this industry produced by all industries.

Source: U.S. Department of Commerce, Bureau of the Census, International Trade Administration (ITA).

No. 1414. Recent Trends in Reconstituted Wood Products (SIC 2493): 1991 to 1997

ITEM	Unit	1991	1992	1993	1994	1995	1996	1997
INDUSTRY DATA								
Value of shipments [1]	Mil. dol. . .	3,037	3,986	4,669	5,344	5,202	5,141	(NA)
Value of shipments (1992 dollars)	Mil. dol. . .	3,177	3,986	4,180	4,388	4,264	4,470	(NA)
Total employment	1,000. . .	20.7	22.8	23.5	24.3	25.0	26.1	(NA)
Production workers	1,000. . .	16.8	18.6	19.2	19.7	20.4	21.1	(NA)
Average hourly earnings	Dollar . . .	10.91	11.49	11.72	11.85	11.92	12.73	(NA)
Capital expenditures	Mil. dol. . .	206	143	171	333	438	573	(NA)
PRODUCT DATA								
Value of shipments [2]	Mil. dol. . .	3,046	3,987	4,658	5,338	5,160	5,111	(NA)
Value of shipments (1992 dollars)	Mil. dol. . .	3,186	3,987	4,170	4,382	4,229	4,444	(NA)
TRADE DATA								
Value of imports	Mil. dol. . .	234	402	581	834	963	1,067	1,146
Value of exports	Mil. dol. . .	225	244	256	292	308	308	355

NA Not available.   [1] Value of all products and services sold by establishments in the reconstituted wood products industry.   [2] Value of products classified in the reconstituted wood products industry produced by all industries.

Source: U.S. Department of Commerce, Bureau of the Census, International Trade Administration (ITA).

No. 1415. Recent Trends in Household Furniture (SIC 251): 1991 to 1997

ITEM	Unit	1991	1992	1993	1994	1995	1996	1997
INDUSTRY DATA								
Value of shipments [1]	Mil. dol.	19,396	20,507	21,906	23,603	24,458	25,426	(NA)
2511 Wood furniture, house	Mil. dol.	7,938	8,730	9,267	9,921	10,242	10,517	(NA)
2512 Upholstered furniture, house	Mil. dol.	5,828	6,231	6,690	7,458	7,810	8,075	(NA)
2514 Metal furniture, house	Mil. dol.	2,079	1,955	2,141	2,126	2,012	2,096	(NA)
2515 Mattresses and bedsprings	Mil. dol.	2,907	2,821	3,001	3,255	3,478	3,754	(NA)
2517 Wood TV & radio cabinets	Mil. dol.	234	319	315	391	461	471	(NA)
2519 Other furniture	Mil. dol.	410	451	493	451	456	513	(NA)
Value of shipments (1992 dollars)	Mil. dol.	19,697	20,507	21,373	22,363	22,563	23,010	(NA)
2511 Wood furniture, house	Mil. dol.	8,141	8,730	8,911	9,136	9,112	9,177	(NA)
2512 Upholstered furniture, house	Mil. dol.	5,875	6,231	6,591	7,206	7,375	7,422	(NA)
2514 Metal furniture, house	Mil. dol.	2,117	1,955	2,118	2,072	1,905	1,930	(NA)
2515 Mattresses and bedsprings	Mil. dol.	2,919	2,821	2,950	3,121	3,300	3,538	(NA)
2517 Wood TV & radio cabinets	Mil. dol.	235	319	311	381	444	449	(NA)
2519 Other furniture	Mil. dol.	410	451	492	446	427	493	(NA)
Total employment	1,000.	255	253	255	267	271	273	(NA)
Production workers	1,000.	213	213	217	229	231	232	(NA)
Average hourly earnings	Dollar	8.04	8.36	8.77	8.83	8.89	9.21	(NA)
Capital expenditures	Mil. dol.	294	346	393	436	528	481	(NA)
2511 Wood furniture, house	Mil. dol.	165	197	238	257	271	273	(NA)
2512 Upholstered furniture, house	Mil. dol.	49.4	73.9	70.2	79.6	83.7	80.8	(NA)
2514 Metal furniture, house	Mil. dol.	33.8	29.2	27.1	49.8	116.0	43.2	(NA)
2515 Mattresses and bedsprings	Mil. dol.	35.1	30.9	38.6	29.5	36.4	58.0	(NA)
2517 Wood TV & radio cabinets	Mil. dol.	3.7	3.7	5.8	6.4	6.6	3.8	(NA)
2519 Other furniture	Mil. dol.	7.5	10.8	13.9	13.7	14.7	21.6	(NA)
PRODUCT DATA								
Value of shipments [2]	Mil. dol.	18,842	19,517	20,825	22,690	23,530	24,571	(NA)
2511 Wood furniture, house	Mil. dol.	7,592	7,976	8,398	9,251	9,315	9,625	(NA)
2512 Upholstered furniture, house	Mil. dol.	5,402	5,811	6,235	7,125	7,565	7,804	(NA)
2514 Metal furniture, house	Mil. dol.	1,982	1,792	1,957	1,882	1,924	2,158	(NA)
2515 Mattresses and bedsprings	Mil. dol.	3,182	3,079	3,282	3,528	3,750	3,990	(NA)
2517 Wood TV & radio cabinets	Mil. dol.	292	376	435	468	529	541	(NA)
2519 Other furniture	Mil. dol.	392	483	520	437	447	453	(NA)
Value of shipments (1992 dollars)	Mil. dol.	19,130	19,517	20,328	21,508	21,739	22,270	(NA)
2511 Wood furniture, house	Mil. dol.	7,787	7,976	8,075	8,518	8,287	8,399	(NA)
2512 Upholstered furniture, house	Mil. dol.	5,446	5,811	6,143	6,884	7,143	7,173	(NA)
2514 Metal furniture, house	Mil. dol.	2,019	1,792	1,936	1,834	1,822	1,987	(NA)
2515 Mattresses and bedsprings	Mil. dol.	3,195	3,079	3,227	3,382	3,558	3,761	(NA)
2517 Wood TV & radio cabinets	Mil. dol.	293	376	429	457	510	515	(NA)
2519 Other furniture	Mil. dol.	392	483	519	432	418	436	(NA)
TRADE DATA								
Value of imports	Mil. dol.	2,729	2,995	3,397	3,965	4,448	4,988	5,882
Value of exports	Mil. dol.	955	1,113	1,184	1,307	1,320	1,326	1,530

NA Not available.   [1] Value of all products and services sold by establishments in the household furniture industry.
[2] Value of products classified in the household furniture industry produced by all industries.

Source: U.S. Department of Commerce, Bureau of the Census, International Trade Administration (ITA).

No. 1416. Recent Trends in Office Furniture (SIC 252): 1991 to 1997

ITEM	Unit	1991	1992	1993	1994	1995	1996	1997
INDUSTRY DATA								
Value of shipments [1]	Mil. dol.	7,224	7,979	8,265	8,664	8,899	9,444	(NA)
Value of shipments (1992 dollars)	Mil. dol.	7,207	7,979	8,142	8,163	8,161	8,498	(NA)
Total employment	1,000.	65.0	68.0	69.5	69.6	69.4	69.5	(NA)
Production workers	1,000.	46.9	50.5	52.2	53.3	53.6	53.3	(NA)
Average hourly earnings	Dollar	11.03	10.85	11.19	11.07	11.7	11.86	(NA)
Capital expenditures	Mil. dol.	171	200	235	243	303	358	(NA)
PRODUCT DATA								
Value of shipments [2]	Mil. dol.	7,130	7,676	7,885	8,428	8,884	9,351	(NA)
Value of shipments (1992 dollars)	Mil. dol.	7,116	7,676	7,766	7,942	8,146	8,412	(NA)
TRADE DATA								
Value of imports	Mil. dol.	513	534	646	787	935	1,114	1,425
Value of exports	Mil. dol.	317	379	427	446	413	459	561

NA Not available.   [1] Value of all products and services sold by establishments in the office furniture industry.   [2] Value of products classified in the office furniture industry produced by all industries.

Source: U.S. Department of Commerce, Bureau of the Census, International Trade Administration (ITA).

No. 1417. Recent Trends in Household Consumer Durables (SIC 251, 3524, 363, 3651): 1991 to 1997

ITEM	Unit	1991	1992	1993	1994	1995	1996	1997
INDUSTRY DATA								
Value of shipments [1]	Mil. dol.	49,379	53,098	57,329	63,369	64,805	63,394	(NA)
Value of shipments (1992 dollars)	Mil. dol.	49,694	53,098	56,685	61,865	62,791	60,491	(NA)
Total employment	1,000.	412	412	416	434	443	439	(NA)
Production workers	1,000.	335	339	345	363	366	364	(NA)
Average hourly earnings	Dollar	8.99	9.30	9.69	9.73	9.86	10.25	(NA)
Capital expenditures	Mil. dol.	1,175	1,280	1,178	1,301	1,568	1,598	(NA)
PRODUCT DATA								
Value of shipments [2]	Mil. dol.	46,353	48,314	51,650	56,958	58,980	60,334	(NA)
Value of shipments (1992 dollars)	Mil. dol.	46,640	48,314	51,046	55,542	57,039	57,622	(NA)
TRADE DATA								
Value of imports	Mil. dol.	21,033	23,037	24,506	28,300	30,543	29,878	31,480
Value of exports	Mil. dol.	5,889	6,531	7,072	7,774	8,100	8,441	9,434

NA Not available. [1] Value of all products and services sold by establishments in the household consumer durables industry. [2] Value of products classified in the household consumer durables industry produced by all industries.
Source: U.S. Department of Commerce, Bureau of the Census, International Trade Administration (ITA).

No. 1418. Recent Trends in Paper and Allied Products (SIC 26): 1991 to 1997

ITEM	Unit	1991	1992	1993	1994	1995	1996	1997
INDUSTRY DATA								
Value of shipments [1]	Mil. dol.	130,131	133,201	133,262	143,649	173,716	160,661	(NA)
Value of shipments (1992 dollars)	Mil. dol.	129,289	133,201	135,059	141,192	141,915	140,102	(NA)
Total employment	1,000.	625	627	626	622	629	631	(NA)
Production workers	1,000.	477	479	479	480	487	488	(NA)
Average hourly earnings	Dollar	13.39	13.81	14.09	14.52	14.73	15.02	(NA)
Capital expenditures	Mil. dol.	9,206	7,963	7,370	7,731	8,369	9,302	(NA)
PRODUCT DATA								
Value of shipments [2]	Mil. dol.	124,658	128,941	128,695	138,560	168,137	155,319	(NA)
Value of shipments (1992 dollars)	Mil. dol.	123,908	128,941	130,523	136,231	137,048	135,455	(NA)
TRADE DATA								
Value of imports	Mil. dol.	10,423	10,356	10,787	11,668	16,624	14,610	14,664
Value of exports	Mil. dol.	9,263	10,042	9,457	11,000	14,943	14,002	14,512

NA Not available. [1] Value of all products and services sold by establishments in the paper and allied products industry. [2] Value of products classified in the paper and allied products produced by all industries.
Source: U.S. Department of Commerce, Bureau of the Census, International Trade Administration (ITA).

No. 1419. Recent Trends in Pulp Mills and Paper and Paperboard Mills: 1991 to 1997

ITEM	Unit	1991	1992	1993	1994	1995	1996	1997
PULP MILLS (SIC 2611)								
Industry data:								
Value of shipments [1]	Mil. dol	5,363	5,466	4,282	4,827	7,513	5,508	(NA)
Value of shipments (1992 dollars)	Mil. dol	5,243	5,466	4,758	4,992	4,920	4,931	(NA)
Total employment	1,000	17.1	15.9	14.2	13.3	14.6	15.0	(NA)
Production workers	1,000	13.0	12.1	10.8	10.2	11.3	11.1	(NA)
Average hourly earnings	Dollar	18.31	19.15	19.49	20.08	20.4	20.16	(NA)
Capital expenditures	Mil. dol	985	772	426	315	564	698	(NA)
Product data:								
Value of shipments [2]	Mil. dol	5,741	6,104	4,995	5,952	8,911	6,329	(NA)
Value of shipments (1992 dollars)	Mil. dol	5,612	6,104	5,550	6,156	5,836	5,666	(NA)
Trade data:								
Value of imports	Mil. dol	2,142	2,104	1,868	2,285	3,745	2,601	2,572
Value of exports	Mil. dol	2,920	3,236	2,482	2,954	4,698	3,358	3,253
PAPER AND PAPERBOARD MILLS (SIC 262, 263)								
Industry data:								
Value of shipments [1]	Mil. dol	48,427	48,926	48,267	53,381	69,638	59,837	(NA)
Value of shipments (1992 dollars)	Mil. dol	47,612	48,926	48,625	52,187	53,571	51,107	(NA)
Total employment	1,000	181	182	180	177	175	171	(NA)
Production workers	1,000	138	140	138	136	135	132	(NA)
Average hourly earnings	Dollar	17.57	17.97	18.22	19.17	19.76	20.34	(NA)
Capital expenditures	Mil. dol	5,883	4,952	4,507	4,960	4,859	5,502	(NA)
Product data:								
Value of shipments [2]	Mil. dol	47,148	47,232	46,513	51,110	67,052	57,971	(NA)
Value of shipments (1992 dollars)	Mil. dol	46,414	47,232	46,866	49,945	51,571	49,514	(NA)
Trade data:								
Value of imports	Mil. dol	6,925	6,736	7,224	7,371	10,235	9,154	9,055
Value of exports	Mil. dol	4,056	4,263	4,190	4,813	6,437	6,339	6,545

NA Not available. [1] Value of all products and services sold by establishments in this industry. [2] Value of products classified in this industry produced by all industries.
Source: U.S. Census Bureau, Bureau of the Census, International Trade Administration (ITA).

No. 1420. Recent Trends in Printing and Publishing (SIC 27): 1991 to 1997

ITEM	Unit	1991	1992	1993	1994	1995	1996	1997
INDUSTRY DATA								
Value of shipments [1]	Mil. dol. . .	160,271	166,153	172,633	176,876	188,133	195,435	(NA)
2711 Newspapers	Mil. dol. . .	34,474	33,782	34,651	36,091	37,732	39,171	(NA)
2721 Periodicals	Mil. dol. . .	20,811	22,104	22,653	21,892	23,743	24,930	(NA)
2731 Book publishing	Mil. dol. . .	16,976	16,698	18,616	19,695	20,484	21,363	(NA)
2732 Book printing	Mil. dol. . .	4,235	4,681	4,810	4,745	5,392	5,333	(NA)
2741 Misc publishing	Mil. dol. . .	9,985	10,908	11,807	11,976	12,025	12,511	(NA)
275 Commercial printing	Mil. dol. . .	53,137	56,229	58,173	60,411	65,101	67,842	(NA)
2761 Manifold business forms	Mil. dol. . .	7,399	7,429	7,491	6,958	7,894	7,724	(NA)
2771 Greeting cards	Mil. dol. . .	3,897	4,190	4,275	4,546	4,689	5,011	(NA)
2782 Blankbooks and binders	Mil. dol. . .	3,317	3,758	3,771	4,276	4,544	4,820	(NA)
2789 Bookbinding	Mil. dol. . .	1,359	1,291	1,258	1,367	1,509	1,608	(NA)
279 Printing trade services	Mil. dol. . .	4,681	5,085	5,129	4,920	5,020	5,123	(NA)
Value of shipments (1992 dollars)	Mil. dol. . .	165,225	166,153	167,352	167,099	168,181	168,517	(NA)
2711 Newspapers	Mil. dol. . .	36,441	33,782	33,222	33,294	32,782	31,718	(NA)
2721 Periodicals	Mil. dol. . .	21,999	22,104	22,014	20,849	21,903	22,379	(NA)
2731 Book publishing	Mil. dol. . .	17,519	16,698	18,180	18,493	18,257	18,166	(NA)
2732 Book printing	Mil. dol. . .	4,588	4,681	4,777	4,647	5,043	5,008	(NA)
2741 Misc publishing	Mil. dol. . .	10,412	10,908	11,320	11,048	10,604	10,504	(NA)
275 Commercial printing	Mil. dol. . .	53,478	56,229	56,764	58,252	59,454	60,555	(NA)
2761 Manifold business forms	Mil. dol. . .	7,261	7,429	7,027	6,240	5,762	5,494	(NA)
2771 Greeting cards	Mil. dol. . .	4,030	4,190	4,040	4,016	3,960	4,064	(NA)
2782 Blankbooks and binders	Mil. dol. . .	3,392	3,758	3,668	4,049	4,058	4,152	(NA)
2789 Bookbinding	Mil. dol. . .	1,364	1,291	1,249	1,343	1,431	1,501	(NA)
279 Printing trade services	Mil. dol. . .	4,741	5,085	5,090	4,867	4,928	4,977	(NA)

NA Not available.   [1] Value of all products and services sold by establishments in the printing and publishing industry.

Source: U.S. Department of Commerce, Bureau of the Census, International Trade Administration (ITA).

No. 1421. Recent Trends in Periodicals, Book Publishing, and Commercial Printing: 1991 to 1997

ITEM	Unit	1991	1992	1993	1994	1995	1996	1997
PERIODICALS (SIC 2721)								
Industry data:								
Value of shipments [1]	Mil. dol. . .	20,811	22,104	22,653	21,892	23,743	24,930	(NA)
Value of shipments (1992 dollars)	Mil. dol. . .	21,999	22,104	22,014	20,849	21,903	22,379	(NA)
Total employment	1,000. . .	113	115	117	117	122	121	(NA)
Production workers	1,000. . .	21.1	20.2	19.7	18.2	17.8	16.4	(NA)
Average hourly earnings	Dollar . .	13.28	13.40	12.51	12.78	13.58	14.85	(NA)
Capital expenditures	Mil. dol. . .	241	235	290	308	332	311	(NA)
Product data:								
Value of shipments [2]	Mil. dol. . .	19,424	20,942	21,692	21,642	22,951	24,352	(NA)
Value of shipments (1992 dollars)	Mil. dol. . .	20,533	20,942	21,080	20,611	21,173	21,860	(NA)
Trade data:								
Value of imports	Mil. dol. . .	121	134	194	209	222	217	204
Value of exports	Mil. dol. . .	705	732	737	789	825	819	864
BOOK PUBLISHING (SIC 2731)								
Industry data:								
Value of shipments [1]	Mil. dol. . .	16,976	16,698	18,616	19,695	20,484	21,363	(NA)
Value of shipments (1992 dollars)	Mil. dol. . .	17,519	16,698	18,180	18,493	18,257	18,166	(NA)
Total employment	1,000. . .	78.8	79.0	83.2	83.5	83.5	85.4	(NA)
Production workers	1,000. . .	17.4	18.2	18.2	18.2	18.5	18.5	(NA)
Average hourly earnings	Dollar . .	12.78	12.51	12.90	13.56	13.61	13.27	(NA)
Capital expenditures	Mil. dol. . .	357	327	282	283	345	365	(NA)
Product data:								
Value of shipments [2]	Mil. dol. . .	15,215	14,761	16,596	17,229	18,409	19,114	(NA)
Value of shipments (1992 dollars)	Mil. dol. . .	15,701	14,761	16,207	16,177	16,407	16,254	(NA)
Trade data:								
Value of imports	Mil. dol. . .	868	953	966	1,023	1,185	1,240	1,298
Value of exports	Mil. dol. . .	1,505	1,637	1,664	1,703	1,780	1,776	1,897
COMMERCIAL PRINTING (SIC 275)								
Industry data:								
Value of shipments [1]	Mil. dol. . .	53,137	56,229	58,173	60,411	65,101	67,842	(NA)
Value of shipments (1992 dollars)	Mil. dol. . .	53,478	56,229	56,764	58,252	59,454	60,555	(NA)
Total employment	1,000. . .	567	567	572	577	598	604	(NA)
Production workers	1,000. . .	409	408	415	417	433	437	(NA)
Average hourly earnings	Dollar . .	10.80	11.50	11.69	11.75	11.86	12.31	(NA)
Capital expenditures	Mil. dol. . .	2,215	2,144	2,234	2,708	2,680	2,959	(NA)
Product data:								
Value of shipments [2]	Mil. dol. . .	51,761	54,902	56,960	58,902	63,819	66,624	(NA)
Value of shipments (1992 dollars)	Mil. dol. . .	52,096	54,902	55,577	56,791	58,277	59,466	(NA)
Trade data:								
Value of imports	Mil. dol. . .	420	442	505	585	756	748	825
Value of exports	Mil. dol. . .	1,026	1,056	1,201	1,061	1,197	1,195	1,248

NA Not available.   [1] Value of all products and services sold by establishments in this industry.   [2] Value of products classified in this industry produced by all industries.

Source: U.S. Department of Commerce, Bureau of the Census, International Trade Administration (ITA).

No. 1422. Recent Trends in Chemicals and Allied Products (SIC 28): 1991 to 1997

ITEM	Unit	1991	1992	1993	1994	1995	1996	1997
INDUSTRY DATA								
Value of shipments [1]	Mil. dol. . .	298,544	305,420	314,907	333,905	361,161	367,442	(NA)
Value of shipments (1992 dollars)	Mil. dol. . .	302,217	305,420	307,625	317,588	323,024	325,552	(NA)
Total employment	1,000. .	867	849	838	823	839	825	(NA)
Production workers	1,000. .	484	479	474	472	487	477	(NA)
Average hourly earnings	Dollar . . .	14.94	15.27	15.62	16.25	16.56	17.22	(NA)
Capital expenditures	Mil. dol. . .	16,599	16,381	15,690	15,411	17,557	20,041	(NA)
PRODUCT DATA								
Value of shipments [2]	Mil. dol. . .	268,935	282,242	292,416	309,592	337,103	343,338	(NA)
Value of shipments (1992 dollars)	Mil. dol. . .	271,466	282,242	285,763	294,588	300,900	304,212	(NA)
TRADE DATA								
Value of imports	Mil. dol. . .	23,324	26,221	27,586	32,117	38,679	43,609	49,206
Value of exports	Mil. dol. . .	41,878	42,366	43,041	49,301	58,363	59,055	65,709

NA Not available.   [1] Value of all products and services sold by establishments in the chemicals and allied products industry.   [2] Value of products classified in the chemicals and allied products industry produced by all industries.

Source: U.S. Department of Commerce, Bureau of the Census, International Trade Administration (ITA).

No. 1423. Recent Trends in Industrial Inorganic Chemicals, Except Pigments (SIC 2812, 2813, 2819): 1991 to 1997

ITEM	Unit	1991	1992	1993	1994	1995	1996	1997
INDUSTRY DATA								
Value of shipments [1]	Mil. dol. . .	23,792	24,012	23,063	21,676	23,447	24,271	(NA)
Value of shipments (1992 dollars)	Mil. dol. . .	23,652	24,012	22,766	20,956	21,636	21,748	(NA)
Total employment	1,000. .	95.8	94.6	85	77.9	73.1	71.5	(NA)
Production workers	1,000. .	51.1	49.3	44.1	41.0	39.7	39.4	(NA)
Average hourly earnings	Dollar . . .	16.17	16.65	16.90	17.82	18.87	20.92	(NA)
PRODUCT DATA								
Value of shipments [2]	Mil. dol. . .	19,083	18,607	18,425	17,783	20,618	21,339	(NA)
Value of shipments (1992 dollars)	Mil. dol. . .	18,944	18,607	18,197	17,163	18,807	18,923	(NA)
TRADE DATA								
Value of imports	Mil. dol. . .	4,284	4,166	4,039	4,707	5,607	6,250	6,216
Value of exports	Mil. dol. . .	4,990	5,130	4,822	5,215	6,178	6,373	7,282

NA Not available.   [1] Value of all products and services sold by establishments in the industrial inorganic chemicals., except pigments industry.   [2] Value of products classified in the industrial inorganic chemicals, except pigments industry produced by all industries.

Source: U.S. Department of Commerce, Bureau of the Census, International Trade Administration (ITA).

No. 1424. Recent Trends in Petrochemicals (SIC 2821, 2822, 2824, 2843, 2865, 2869, 2873): 1991 to 1997

ITEM	Unit	1991	1992	1993	1994	1995	1996	1997
INDUSTRY DATA								
Value of shipments [1]	Mil. dol. . .	116,681	117,277	119,225	132,458	147,754	143,152	(NA)
Value of shipments (1992 dollars)	Mil. dol. . .	115,894	117,277	115,987	124,809	125,548	122,517	(NA)
Total employment	1,000. . .	263	257	255	252	253	250	(NA)
Production workers	1,000. . .	162	159	158	156	157	158	(NA)
Average hourly earnings	Dollar . . .	17.08	17.62	17.93	18.63	19.11	19.86	(NA)
Capital expenditures	Mil. dol. . .	9,255	7,837	7,554	7,319	8,526	10,627	(NA)
PRODUCT DATA								
Value of shipments [2]	Mil. dol. . .	112,464	113,476	115,269	126,971	142,673	139,399	(NA)
Value of shipments (1992 dollars)	Mil. dol. . .	111,539	113,476	112,268	119,759	121,105	119,659	(NA)
TRADE DATA								
Value of imports	Mil. dol. . .	9,936	11,084	12,099	14,599	17,671	18,745	20,723
Value of exports	Mil. dol. . .	23,089	22,150	22,047	26,555	32,763	31,582	34,207

NA Not available.   [1] Value of all products and services sold by establishments in the petrochemicals industry.   [2] Value of products classified in the petrochemicals industry produced by all industries.

Source: U.S. Department of Commerce, Bureau of the Census, International Trade Administration (ITA).

No. 1425. Recent Trends in Plastics Materials and Resins and Synthetic Rubber: 1991 to 1997

ITEM	Unit	1991	1992	1993	1994	1995	1996	1997
PLASTIC MATERIALS AND RESINS (SIC 2821)								
Industry data:								
Value of shipments [1]	Mil. dol.	29,842	31,601	31,546	37,305	43,453	40,097	(NA)
Value of shipments (1992 dollars)	Mil. dol.	28,945	31,601	31,172	35,327	35,156	34,567	(NA)
Total employment	1,000.	60.6	61.2	62.2	68.9	70.0	58.6	(NA)
Production workers	1,000.	36.7	36.5	36.6	40.4	41.6	36.3	(NA)
Average hourly earnings	Dollars	17.27	18.61	18.75	19.39	20.04	20.5	(NA)
Capital expenditures	Mil. dol.	2,289	1,712	1,926	2,536	2,324	2,784	(NA)
Product data:								
Value of shipments [2]	Mil. dol.	31,723	33,299	33,589	38,043	44,017	42,751	(NA)
Value of shipments (1992 dollars)	Mil. dol.	30,769	33,299	33,191	36,025	35,612	36,854	(NA)
Trade data:								
Value of imports	Mil. dol.	1,775	2,062	2,518	3,280	4,084	4,176	4,649
Value of exports	Mil. dol.	7,383	7,007	7,181	8,427	10,337	10,587	11,746
SYNTHETIC RUBBER (SIC 2822)								
Industry data:								
Value of shipments [1]	Mil. dol.	4,127	4,235	4,739	4,964	5,475	5,291	(NA)
Value of shipments (1992 dollars)	Mil. dol.	4,098	4,235	4,623	4,755	4,543	4,537	(NA)
Total employment	1,000.	11.5	11.9	12.2	11.9	12.0	12.0	(NA)
Production workers	1,000.	7.4	7.6	7.7	7.7	8.0	7.9	(NA)
Average hourly earnings	Dollar	17.85	18.73	19.27	19.52	20.61	20.68	(NA)
Capital expenditures	Mil. dol.	366	321	256	266	268	279	(NA)
Product data:								
Value of shipments [2]	Mil. dol.	3,939	4,318	4,643	4,983	5,430	5,139	(NA)
Value of shipments (1992 dollars)	Mil. dol.	3,912	4,318	4,530	4,773	4,507	4,407	(NA)
Trade data:								
Value of imports	Mil. dol.	466	530	555	624	691	681	725
Value of exports	Mil. dol.	900	1,010	947	1,081	1,264	1,344	1,304

NA Not available. [1] Value of all products and services sold by establishments in this industry. [2] Value of products classified in this industry produced by all industries.

Source: U.S. Department of Commerce, Bureau of the Census, International Trade Administration (ITA).

No. 1426. Recent Trends in Man-Made Fibers (SIC 2823, 2824): 1991 to 1997

ITEM	Unit	1991	1992	1993	1994	1995	1996	1997
INDUSTRY DATA								
Value of shipments [1]	Mil. dol.	12,698	12,861	13,293	13,366	14,035	14,179	(NA)
Value of shipments (1992 dollars)	Mil. dol.	12,713	12,861	13,289	13,217	13,421	13,425	(NA)
Total employment	1,000.	57.5	55.4	51.6	46.9	44.7	44.5	(NA)
Production workers	1,000.	42.7	41.7	39.8	36.6	35.0	35.1	(NA)
Average hourly earnings	Dollar	14.50	14.22	14.63	14.23	14.87	15.28	(NA)
PRODUCT DATA								
Value of shipments [2]	Mil. dol.	10,930	10,924	11,092	11,779	12,529	12,383	(NA)
Value of shipments (1992 dollars)	Mil. dol.	10,938	10,924	11,092	11,709	12,023	11,768	(NA)
TRADE DATA								
Value of imports	Mil. dol.	784	907	1,127	1,302	1,384	1,401	1,558
Value of exports	Mil. dol.	1,694	1,473	1,407	1,594	2,078	2,113	2,168

NA Not available. [1] Value of all products and services sold by establishments in the man-made fibers industry. [2] Value of products classified in the man-made fibers industry produced by all industries.

Source: U.S. Department of Commerce, Bureau of the Census, International Trade Administration (ITA).

No. 1427. Recent Trends in Drugs (SIC 283): 1991 to 1997

ITEM	Unit	1991	1992	1993	1994	1995	1996	1997
INDUSTRY DATA								
Value of shipments [1]	Mil. dol. . .	64,829	67,792	70,985	75,804	80,907	86,532	(NA)
2833 Medicinals and botanicals	Mil. dol. . .	6,722	6,526	5,926	6,093	7,027	8,884	(NA)
2834 Pharmaceutical preps.	Mil. dol. . .	50,486	50,415	53,281	56,123	58,405	61,554	(NA)
2835 Diagnostic substances	Mil. dol. . .	5,058	6,857	6,864	8,278	9,248	9,692	(NA)
2836 Bio. prod. exc. diagnostic	Mil. dol. . .	2,564	3,993	4,914	5,310	6,227	6,402	(NA)
Value of shipments (1992 dollars)	Mil. dol. . .	68,803	67,792	68,179	71,142	73,820	76,824	(NA)
2833 Medicinals and botanicals	Mil. dol. . .	6,866	6,526	5,523	5,460	6,164	7,739	(NA)
2834 Pharmaceutical preps.	Mil. dol. . .	54,111	50,415	51,084	52,159	52,475	53,386	(NA)
2835 Diagnostic substances	Mil. dol. . .	5,156	6,857	6,750	8,245	9,058	9,465	(NA)
2836 Bio. prod. exc. diagnostic	Mil. dol. . .	2,670	3,993	4,822	5,279	6,122	6,234	(NA)
Total employment	1,000. . . .	203	194	200	205	216	213	(NA)
2833 Medicinals and botanicals	1,000. . . .	13.7	13.1	13.0	12.9	14.1	16.8	(NA)
2834 Pharmaceutical preps.	1,000. . . .	142	123	128	133	143	137	(NA)
2835 Diagnostic substances	1,000. . . .	33.5	39.9	39.3	39.1	38.2	39.9	(NA)
2836 Bio. prod. exc. diagnostic	1,000. . . .	13.3	18.5	19.0	19.8	21.1	19.6	(NA)
Production workers	1,000. . . .	90.1	92.7	94.6	102.0	113.0	106.0	(NA)
2833 Medicinals and botanicals	1,000. . . .	7.8	7.5	7.7	7.5	7.5	8.9	(NA)
2834 Pharmaceutical preps.	1,000. . . .	64.6	62.4	62.8	68.0	78.7	72.3	(NA)
2835 Diagnostic substances	1,000. . . .	10.8	14.7	14.9	16.1	15.3	15.5	(NA)
2836 Bio prod ex diagnostic	1,000. . . .	6.9	8.1	9.2	9.9	11.0	9.7	(NA)
Average hourly earnings	Dollar . . .	15.00	14.78	15.80	16.34	15.99	16.63	(NA)
2833 Medicinals and botanicals	Dollar . . .	19.67	18.93	19.62	19.70	20.27	20.83	(NA)
2834 Pharmaceutical preps.	Dollar . . .	14.41	14.71	15.81	16.11	15.40	15.88	(NA)
2835 Diagnostic substances	Dollar . . .	17.80	14.09	15.64	17.23	18.08	19.15	(NA)
2836 Bio. prod. exc. diagnostic	Dollar . . .	10.79	12.50	12.57	13.81	13.74	14.06	(NA)
Capital expenditures	Mil. dol. . .	3,038	3,887	4,047	4,034	4,503	4,301	(NA)
2833 Medicinals and botanicals	Mil. dol. . .	555	554	482	483	384	835	(NA)
2834 Pharmaceutical preps.	Mil. dol. . .	2,017	2,450	2,493	2,618	3,134	2,588	(NA)
2835 Diagnostic substances	Mil. dol. . .	344	588	667	573	532	518	(NA)
2836 Bio. prod. exc. diagnostic	Mil. dol. . .	123	295	405	361	453	360	(NA)
PRODUCT DATA								
Value of shipments [2]	Mil. dol. . .	51,880	60,793	63,970	67,751	71,528	76,293	(NA)
2833 Medicinals and botanicals	Mil. dol. . .	6,647	7,002	6,749	6,772	7,345	8,999	(NA)
2834 Pharmaceutical preps.	Mil. dol. . .	37,416	43,082	45,522	48,086	49,965	52,932	(NA)
2835 Diagnostic substances	Mil. dol. . .	4,973	6,196	6,453	7,179	7,926	8,036	(NA)
2836 Bio. prod. exc. diagnostic	Mil. dol. . .	2,844	4,512	5,246	5,715	6,293	6,326	(NA)
Value of shipments (1992 dollars)	Mil. dol. . .	54,924	60793	61428	63588	65,285	67,754	(NA)
2833 Medicinals and botanicals	Mil. dol. . .	6,790	7002	6290	6068	6,443	7,839	(NA)
2834 Pharmaceutical preps.	Mil. dol. . .	40,102	43082	43645	44690	44,892	45,908	(NA)
2835 Diagnostic substances	Mil. dol. . .	5,070	6196	6345	7150	7,763	7,848	(NA)
2836 Bio. prod. exc. diagnostic	Mil. dol. . .	2,963	4512	5148	5681	6,188	6,159	(NA)
TRADE DATA								
Value of imports	Mil. dol. . .	4,812	5,958	6,094	6,966	8,583	11,161	14,196
2833 Medicinals and botanicals	Mil. dol. . .	2,854	3,277	3,101	3,366	4,632	6,121	7,298
2834 Pharmaceutical preps.	Mil. dol. . .	1,442	1,859	2,096	2,517	2,877	3,702	5,358
2835 Diagnostic substances	Mil. dol. . .	191	336	379	530	465	546	601
2836 Bio. prod. exc. diagnostic	Mil. dol. . .	325	486	518	553	608	792	939
Value of exports	Mil. dol. . .	5,731	6,774	7,222	7,565	7,996	8,889	10,375
2833 Medicinals and botanicals	Mil. dol. . .	2,064	2,444	2,401	2,281	2,445	2,511	2,942
2834 Pharmaceutical preps.	Mil. dol. . .	1,478	1,819	2,027	2,315	2,247	2,718	3,335
2835 Diagnostic substances	Mil. dol. . .	1,160	1,370	1,485	1,507	1,741	1,891	2,171
2836 Bio. prod. exc. diagnostic	Mil. dol. . .	1,028	1,142	1,309	1,462	1,563	1,769	1,928

NA Not available.   [1] Value of all products and services sold by establishments in the drugs industry.   [2] Value of products classified in the drugs industry produced by all industries.

Source: U.S. Department of Commerce, Bureau of the Census, International Trade Administration (ITA).

No. 1428. Recent Trends in Soap, Cleaners, and Toilet Goods (SIC 284): 1991 to 1997

ITEM	Unit	1991	1992	1993	1994	1995	1996	1997
INDUSTRY DATA								
Value of shipments [1]	Mil. dol.	42,245	42,875	46,903	46,548	49,795	51,809	(NA)
2841 Soap and other detergents	Mil. dol.	15,442	14,729	15,458	14,603	15,735	15,779	(NA)
2842 Polishes/sanitation goods	Mil. dol.	6,229	6,659	8,079	8,405	8,679	8,602	(NA)
2843 Surface active agents	Mil. dol.	3,330	2,859	3,661	3,721	4,860	4,741	(NA)
2844 Toilet preparations	Mil. dol.	17,245	18,629	19,706	19,820	20,522	22,688	(NA)
Value of shipments (1992 dollars)	Mil. dol.	43,103	42,875	46,174	45,873	48,469	49,766	(NA)
2841 Soap and other detergents	Mil. dol.	15,854	14,729	15,259	14,530	15,487	15,230	(NA)
2842 Polishes/sanitation goods	Mil. dol.	6,324	6,659	8,014	8,264	8,353	8,239	(NA)
2843 Surface active agents	Mil. dol.	3,346	2,859	3,599	3,609	4,529	4,248	(NA)
2844 Toilet preparations	Mil. dol.	17,579	18,629	19,301	19,469	20,100	22,048	(NA)
Total employment	1,000	123	123	124	119	123	126	(NA)
2841 Soap and other detergents	1,000	36.7	32.8	31.2	31.3	31.6	30.3	(NA)
2842 Polishes/sanitation goods	1,000	19.6	22.0	22.8	21.4	23.1	24.2	(NA)
2843 Surface active agents	1,000	9.3	8.2	8.6	8.1	7.9	8.8	(NA)
2844 Toilet preparations	1,000	57.5	59.8	61.7	58.1	60.2	62.9	(NA)
Production workers	1,000	75.7	74.5	74.6	71.1	73.8	74.6	(NA)
2841 Soap and other detergents	1,000	23.1	19.9	17.9	18.6	18.0	16.8	(NA)
2842 Polishes/sanitation goods	1,000	12.2	13.4	13.8	13.1	14.0	14.2	(NA)
2843 Surface active agents	1,000	4.8	4.2	4.3	3.9	3.9	4.5	(NA)
2844 Toilet preparations	1,000	35.6	37.0	38.6	35.5	37.9	39.1	(NA)
Average hourly earnings	Dollars	12.28	12.32	12.26	12.36	12.75	13.02	(NA)
2841 Soap and other detergents	Dollars	14.70	14.86	15.06	14.89	15.40	15.68	(NA)
2842 Polishes/sanitation goods	Dollars	11.13	11.84	11.94	11.12	11.49	11.49	(NA)
2843 Surface active agents	Dollars	14.33	15.09	15.95	16.80	16.20	16.55	(NA)
2844 Toilet preparations	Dollars	10.83	10.80	10.59	10.93	11.44	11.89	(NA)
Capital expenditures	Mil. dol.	1,245	1,290	1,320	1,334	1,041	1,304	(NA)
2841 Soap and other detergents	Mil. dol.	641	571	514	494	356	427	(NA)
2842 Polishes/sanitation goods	Mil. dol.	139	121	130	124	154	173	(NA)
2843 Surface active agents	Mil. dol.	160	92	203	225	120	161	(NA)
2844 Toilet preparations	Mil. dol.	304	506	473	491	411	543	(NA)
PRODUCT DATA								
Value of shipments [2]	Mil. dol.	38,695	39,999	43,293	42,622	45,775	47,797	(NA)
2841 Soap and other detergents	Mil. dol.	11,785	11,022	11,594	11,089	12,205	12,467	(NA)
2842 Polishes/sanitation goods	Mil. dol.	5,546	6,477	7,492	7,601	7,755	7,327	(NA)
2843 Surface active agents	Mil. dol.	3,975	3,776	4,032	3,648	4,703	4,836	(NA)
2844 Toilet preparations	Mil. dol.	17,390	18,724	20,175	20,284	21,112	23,168	(NA)
Value of shipments (1992 dollars)	Mil. dol.	39,450	39,999	42,603	41,971	44,538	45,900	(NA)
2841 Soap and other detergents	Mil. dol.	12,099	11,022	11,445	11,033	12,013	12,033	(NA)
2842 Polishes/sanitation goods	Mil. dol.	5,630	6,477	7,433	7,474	7,464	7,018	(NA)
2843 Surface active agents	Mil. dol.	3,995	3,776	3,965	3,538	4,383	4,333	(NA)
2844 Toilet preparations	Mil. dol.	17,726	18,724	19,760	19,926	20,678	22,515	(NA)
TRADE DATA								
Value of imports	Mil. dol.	1,076	1,308	1,463	1,689	1,936	2,100	2,318
2841 Soap and other detergents	Mil. dol.	179	213	254	335	421	486	510
2842 Polishes/sanitation goods	Mil. dol.	33.5	46.0	49.8	56.3	61.6	69.4	92.7
2843 Surface active agents	Mil. dol.	152	158	204	263	296	288	305
2844 Toilet preparations	Mil. dol.	712	892	956	1,035	1,157	1,257	1,410
Value of exports	Mil. dol.	2,235	2,529	2,853	3,358	3,710	4,132	4,759
2841 Soap and other detergents	Mil. dol.	511	583	644	716	828	899	975
2842 Polishes/sanitation goods	Mil. dol.	130	144	170	174	205	212	216
2843 Surface active agents	Mil. dol.	477	548	604	734	790	826	940
2844 Toilet preparations	Mil. dol.	1,118	1,254	1,437	1,733	1,887	2,195	2,628

NA Not available.   [1] Value of all products and services sold by establishments in the soap, cleaners, and toilet goods industry.   [2] Value of products classified in the soap, cleaners, and toilet goods industry produced by all industries.

Source: U.S. Department of Commerce, Bureau of the Census, International Trade Administration (ITA).

No. 1429. Recent Trends in Paints and Allied Products (SIC 2851): 1991 to 1997

ITEM	Unit	1991	1992	1993	1994	1995	1996	1997
INDUSTRY DATA								
Value of shipments [1]	Mil. dol.	14,388	14,973	16,030	17,404	17,744	18,257	(NA)
Value of shipments (1992 dollars)	Mil. dol.	14,607	14,973	15,840	16,897	16,415	16,345	(NA)
Total employment	1,000.	51.2	51.1	50.3	50.0	52.4	51.1	(NA)
Production workers	1,000.	25.2	25.7	25.9	27.0	27.8	27.9	(NA)
Average hourly earnings	Dollar	12.12	12.71	13.00	14.00	14.02	14.61	(NA)
Capital expenditures	Mil. dol.	260	273	256	280	409	404	(NA)
PRODUCT DATA								
Value of shipments [2]	Mil. dol.	13,722	14,283	15,356	16,426	16,726	17,376	(NA)
Value of shipments (1992 dollars)	Mil. dol.	13,931	14,283	15,174	15,947	15,472	15,556	(NA)
TRADE DATA								
Value of imports	Mil. dol.	141	184	197	261	343	393	440
Value of exports	Mil. dol.	686	754	811	936	1,009	1,091	1,318

NA Not available. [1] Value of all products and services sold by establishments in the paints and allied products industry. [2] Value of products classified in the paints and allied products industry produced by all industries.

Source: U.S. Department of Commerce, Bureau of the Census, International Trade Administration (ITA).

No. 1430. Recent Trends in Organic Chemicals, Except Gum and Wood (SIC 2865, 2869): 1991 to 1997

ITEM	Unit	1991	1992	1993	1994	1995	1996	1997
INDUSTRY DATA								
Value of shipments [1]	Mil. dol.	64,317	63,663	63,541	69,205	75,912	74,863	(NA)
Value of shipments (1992 dollars)	Mil. dol.	64,490	63,663	61,113	64,865	65,287	63,179	(NA)
Total employment	1,000.	125	122	121	113	115	123	(NA)
Production workers	1,000.	72.5	70.4	70.9	66.0	67.4	72.5	(NA)
Average hourly earnings	Dollar	18.32	18.72	18.88	20.23	20.56	21.61	(NA)
Capital expenditures	Mil. dol.	5,338	4,749	4,028	3,509	4,891	6,242	(NA)
PRODUCT DATA								
Value of shipments [2]	Mil. dol.	59,326	58,655	59,135	65,003	72,306	70,532	(NA)
Value of shipments (1992 dollars)	Mil. dol.	59,427	58,655	56,974	61,125	62,389	60,085	(NA)
TRADE DATA								
Value of imports	Mil. dol.	6,579	7,243	7,332	8,656	10,567	11,535	12,896
Value of exports	Mil. dol.	10,112	10,081	10,452	12,387	15,619	14,194	15,473

NA Not available. [1] Value of all products and services sold by establishments in the organic chemicals, except gum and wood industry. [2] Value of products classified in the organic chemicals, except gum and wood industry produced by all industries.

Source: U.S. Department of Commerce, Bureau of the Census, International Trade Administration (ITA).

No. 1431. Recent Trends in Nitrogenous Fertilizers and Phosphatic Fertilizers: 1991 to 1997

ITEM	Unit	1991	1992	1993	1994	1995	1996	1997
NITROGENOUS FERTILIZERS (SIC 2873)								
Industry data:								
Value of shipments [1]	Mil. dol.	3,268	3,177	3,467	4,246	4,446	4,376	(NA)
Value of shipments (1992 dollars)	Mil. dol.	3,146	3,177	3,340	3,617	3,267	3,196	(NA)
Total employment	1,000.	7.3	7.0	7.0	8.0	7.3	7.5	(NA)
Production workers	1,000.	4.7	4.7	4.7	5.4	5.1	5.1	(NA)
Average hourly earnings	Dollar	14.82	15.66	16.11	16.69	16.37	16.95	(NA)
Capital expenditures	Mil. dol.	224	209	186	175	176	305	(NA)
Product data:								
Value of shipments [2]	Mil. dol.	3,438	3,589	3,737	4,428	4,761	4,864	(NA)
Value of shipments (1992 dollars)	Mil. dol.	3,309	3,589	3,600	3,772	3,498	3,553	(NA)
PHOSPHATIC FERTILIZERS (SIC 2874)								
Industry data:								
Value of shipments [1]	Mil. dol.	5,030	4,318	3,648	4,597	5,337	5,684	(NA)
Value of shipments (1992 dollars)	Mil. dol.	4,401	4,318	4,155	4,152	4,083	4,031	(NA)
Total employment	1,000.	10.3	9.5	9.4	8.5	8.6	7.8	(NA)
Production workers	1,000.	7.3	6.7	6.6	6.2	6.5	5.8	(NA)
Average hourly earnings	Dollar	14.70	13.84	14.70	16.69	16.75	17.30	(NA)
Capital expenditures	Mil. dol.	200	307	150	159	194	200	(NA)
Product data:								
Value of shipments [2]	Mil. dol.	4,572	3,929	3,397	4,272	4,983	5,364	(NA)
Value of shipments (1992 dollars)	Mil. dol.	4,000	3,929	3,869	3,859	3,813	3,804	(NA)

NA Not available. [1] Value of all products and services sold by establishments in this industry. [2] Value of products classified in this industry produced by all industries.

Source: U.S. Department of Commerce, Bureau of the Census, International Trade Administration (ITA).

No. 1432. Recent Trends in Agricultural Chemicals, n.e.c. (SIC 2879): 1991 to 1997

ITEM	Unit	1991	1992	1993	1994	1995	1996	1997
INDUSTRY DATA								
Value of shipments [1]	Mil. dol.	8,424	9,142	9,554	9,636	10,079	10,903	(NA)
Value of shipments (1992 dollars)	Mil. dol.	8,639	9,142	9,142	8,800	8,991	9,597	(NA)
Total employment	1,000.	16.4	16.8	16.3	15.3	14.8	13.8	(NA)
Production workers	1,000.	9.1	9.6	9.2	8.8	8.7	7.8	(NA)
Average hourly earnings	Dollar	15.21	15.57	16.41	18.40	19.85	19.45	(NA)
Capital expenditures	Mil. dol.	489	428	356	299	318	463	(NA)
PRODUCT DATA								
Value of shipments [2]	Mil. dol.	7,448	8,225	8,737	8,848	9,623	10,038	(NA)
Value of shipments (1992 dollars)	Mil. dol.	7,639	8,225	8,361	8,080	8,585	8,837	(NA)

NA Not available. [1] Value of all products and services sold by establishments in the agricultural chemicals, n.e.c. industry. [2] Value of products classified in the agricultural chemicals, n.e.c. industry produced by all industries.

Source: U.S. Department of Commerce: Bureau of the Census, International Trade Administration (ITA).

No. 1433. Recent Trends in Adhesives and Sealants (SIC 2891): 1991 to 1997

ITEM	Unit	1991	1992	1993	1994	1995	1996	1997
INDUSTRY DATA								
Value of shipments [1]	Mil. dol.	5,615	5,657	5,859	5,859	5,991	6,466	(NA)
Value of shipments (1992 dollars)	Mil. dol.	5,655	5,657	5,711	5,537	5,345	5,667	(NA)
Total employment	1,000.	20.9	21.1	20.9	19.2	19.0	17.3	(NA)
Production workers	1,000.	11.7	11.7	11.5	11.3	11.4	11.1	(NA)
Average hourly earnings	Dollar	11.48	12.36	12.57	13.37	13.39	14.04	(NA)
Capital expenditures	Mil. dol.	142	188	183	204	198	188	(NA)
PRODUCT DATA								
Value of shipments [2]	Mil. dol.	5,382	5,415	5,807	5,427	5,594	6,141	(NA)
Value of shipments (1992 dollars)	Mil. dol.	5,420	5,415	5,660	5,129	4,990	5,382	(NA)
TRADE DATA								
Value of imports	Mil. dol.	94.1	112	119	135	140	145	153
Value of exports	Mil. dol.	169	202	241	283	316	369	433

NA Not available. [1] Value of all products and services sold by establishments in the adhesives and sealants industry. [2] Value of products classified in the adhesives and sealants industry produced by all industries.

Source: U.S. Department of Commerce, Bureau of the Census, International Trade Administration (ITA).

No. 1434. Recent Trends in Petroleum Refining (SIC 2911): 1991 to 1997

ITEM	Unit	1991	1992	1993	1994	1995	1996	1997
INDUSTRY DATA								
Value of shipments [1]	Mil. dol.	146,357	136,551	129,961	128,686	136,173	158,068	(NA)
Value of shipments (1992 dollars)	Mil. dol.	141,408	136,551	135,376	139,120	142,441	144,751	(NA)
Total employment	1,000.	75.5	74.9	73.1	72.0	70.4	67.2	(NA)
Production workers	1,000.	48.4	47.9	47.3	46.6	45.6	43.4	(NA)
Average hourly earnings	Dollar	19.35	19.76	21.04	21.16	21.79	22.41	(NA)
Capital expenditures	Mil. dol.	5,633	6,182	5,986	5,524	5,866	5,197	(NA)
PRODUCT DATA								
Value of shipments [2]	Mil. dol.	138,322	131,640	125,456	123,825	131,086	151,857	(NA)
Value of shipments (1992 dollars)	Mil. dol.	133,645	131,640	130,683	133,865	137,119	139,063	(NA)
TRADE DATA								
Value of imports	Mil. dol.	10,895	10,185	9,742	9,274	8,765	18,510	21,838
Value of exports	Mil. dol.	6,371	5,759	5,641	4,958	5,333	6,300	6,436

NA Not available. [1] Value of all products and services sold by establishments in the petroleum refining industry. [2] Value of products classified in the petroleum refining industry produced by all industries.

Source: U.S. Department of Commerce, Bureau of the Census, International Trade Administration (ITA).

No. 1435. Recent Trends in Tires and Inner Tubes (SIC 3011): 1991 to 1997

ITEM	Unit	1991	1992	1993	1994	1995	1996	1997
INDUSTRY DATA								
Value of shipments [1]	Mil. dol. . .	11,822	11,814	12,601	13,183	14,145	14,209	(NA)
Value of shipments (1992 dollars)	Mil. dol. . .	11,953	11,814	12,614	13,249	14,061	14,604	(NA)
Total employment	1,000. . . .	64.7	64.6	65.1	65.1	65.9	64.8	(NA)
Production workers	1,000. . . .	52.2	52.8	53.3	54.0	54.3	54.0	(NA)
Average hourly earnings	Dollar . . .	17.64	18.54	18.63	19.00	18.89	19.48	(NA)
Capital expenditures	Mil. dol. . .	514	506	490	518	467	579	(NA)
PRODUCT DATA								
Value of shipments [2]	Mil. dol. . .	11,303	11,316	12,241	12,816	13,835	13,753	(NA)
Value of shipments (1992 dollars)	Mil. dol. . .	11,428	11,316	12,253	12,880	13,753	14,134	(NA)
TRADE DATA								
Value of imports	Mil. dol. . .	2,271	2,463	2,681	2,979	3,089	3,020	3,357
Value of exports	Mil. dol. . .	1,262	1,395	1,453	1,598	1,856	1,955	2,394

NA Not available. [1] Value of all products and services sold by establishments in the tires and inner tubes industry. [2] Value of products classified in the tires and inner tubes industry produced by all industries.

Source: U.S. Department of Commerce, Bureau of the Census, International Trade Administration (ITA).

No. 1436. Recent Trends in Fabricated Rubber Products, n.e.c. (SIC 3069): 1991 to 1997

ITEM	Unit	1991	1992	1993	1994	1995	1996	1997
INDUSTRY DATA								
Value of shipments [1]	Mil. dol. . .	6,842	6,933	7,608	7,748	8,327	8,481	(NA)
Value of shipments (1992 dollars)	Mil. dol. . .	6,883	6,933	7,474	7,442	7,632	7,654	(NA)
Total employment	1,000. . . .	57.9	56.5	58.4	57.9	58.1	58.1	(NA)
Production workers	1,000. . . .	43.2	42.0	43.4	43.1	43.9	43.5	(NA)
Average hourly earnings	Dollar . . .	9.87	10.08	10.33	10.31	10.86	10.93	(NA)
Capital expenditures	Mil. dol. . .	175	205	222	215	226	269	(NA)
PRODUCT DATA								
Value of shipments [2]	Mil. dol. . .	6,490	6,600	7,179	7,384	7,720	7,875	(NA)
Value of shipments (1992 dollars)	Mil. dol. . .	6,530	6,600	7,052	7,093	7,076	7,108	(NA)
TRADE DATA								
Value of imports	Mil. dol. . .	796	1,045	1,279	1,504	1,758	1,952	2,010
Value of exports	Mil. dol. . .	708	725	773	916	969	1,044	1,252

NA Not available. [1] Value of all products and services sold by establishments in the fabricated rubber products, n.e.c. industry. [2] Value of products classified in the fabricated rubber products, n.e.c., industry produced by all industries.

Source: U.S. Department of Commerce, Bureau of the Census, International Trade Administration (ITA).

No. 1437. Recent Trends in Miscellaneous Plastic Products Excluding Bottles and Plumbing (SIC 3081-4, -6, -7, -9): 1990 to 1996

ITEM	Unit	1991	1992	1993	1994	1995	1996	1997
INDUSTRY DATA								
Value of shipments [1]	Mil. dol. . .	71,938	77,891	84,160	93,893	100,989	104,807	(NA)
Value of shipments (1992 dollars)	Mil. dol. . .	71,681	77,891	83,236	95,677	97,096	100,986	(NA)
Total employment	1,000. . . .	612	627	650	682	715	714	(NA)
Production workers	1,000. . . .	465	480	504	533	560	558	(NA)
Average hourly earnings	Dollar . . .	9.71	9.96	10.23	10.34	10.44	10.68	(NA)
Capital expenditures	Mil. dol. . .	3,353	3,449	3,465	4,033	4,862	5,213	(NA)
PRODUCT DATA								
Value of shipments [2]	Mil. dol. . .	66,669	75,532	81,512	90,577	97,398	101,470	(NA)
Value of shipments (1992 dollars)	Mil. dol. . .	66,453	75,532	80,622	92,240	93,548	97,645	(NA)
TRADE DATA								
Value of imports	Mil. dol. . .	3,686	4,272	4,631	5,236	6,000	6,373	6,913
Value of exports	Mil. dol. . .	3,796	4,387	4,925	5,814	6,362	7,003	8,097

NA Not available. [1] Value of all products and services sold by establishments in the miscellaneous plastic products excluding bottles and plumbing industry. [2] Value of products classified in the miscellaneous plastic products excluding bottles and plumbing industry produced by all industries.

Source: U.S. Department of Commerce, Bureau of the Census, International Trade Administration (ITA).

No. 1438. Recent Trends in Footwear, Except Rubber (SIC 314): 1991 to 1997

ITEM	Unit	1991	1992	1993	1994	1995	1996	1997
INDUSTRY DATA								
Value of shipments [1]	Mil. dol. . .	3,588	3,898	3,974	3,923	3,688	3,605	(NA)
3142 House slippers	Mil. dol. . .	264	285	302	204	113	128	(NA)
3143 Men's footwear	Mil. dol. . .	1,962	2,210	2,351	2,461	2,420	2,413	(NA)
3144 Women's footwear	Mil. dol. . .	1,097	1,095	1,010	950	758	555	(NA)
3149 Footwear n.e.c.	Mil. dol. . .	266	309	310	309	397	509	(NA)
Value of shipments (1992 dollars)	Mil. dol. . .	3,680	3,898	3,907	3,816	3,477	3,345	(NA)
3142 House slippers	Mil. dol. . .	258	285	310	205	109	122	(NA)
3143 Men's footwear	Mil. dol. . .	2,016	2,210	2,305	2,382	2,257	2,218	(NA)
3144 Women's footwear	Mil. dol. . .	1,135	1,095	987	927	730	522	(NA)
3149 Footwear n.e.c.	Mil. dol. . .	271	309	305	302	381	483	(NA)
Total employment	1,000. . . .	51.1	48.8	48.5	46.8	44.4	36.7	(NA)
Production workers	1,000. . . .	44.0	41.4	41.3	40.3	37.7	31.1	(NA)
Average hourly earnings	Dollar . . .	7.14	7.33	7.43	7.44	7.85	8.32	(NA)
Capital expenditures	Mil. dol. . .	28.1	51.2	40.3	58.8	34.1	34.5	(NA)
3142 House slippers	Mil. dol. . .	2.1	2.1	2.5	4.8	1.5	1.2	(NA)
3143 Men's footwear	Mil. dol. . .	16.2	32.8	26.1	43.3	23.6	25.8	(NA)
3144 Women's footwear	Mil. dol. . .	8.1	10.5	6.8	7.6	4.3	2.4	(NA)
3149 Footwear n.e.c.	Mil. dol. . .	1.7	5.8	4.9	3.1	4.7	5.1	(NA)
PRODUCT DATA								
Value of shipments [2]	Mil. dol. . .	3,495	3,608	3,707	3,739	3,402	3,128	(NA)
3142 House slippers	Mil. dol. . .	256	259	256	208	122	116	(NA)
3143 Men's footwear	Mil. dol. . .	1,763	1,807	1,970	2,040	1,926	1,924	(NA)
3144 Women's footwear	Mil. dol. . .	1,186	1,229	1,188	1,190	959	735	(NA)
3149 Footwear n.e.c.	Mil. dol. . .	289	314	293	301	394	354	(NA)
Value of shipments (1992 dollars)	Mil. dol. . .	3,586	3,608	3,643	3,639	3,217	2,906	(NA)
3142 House slippers	Mil. dol. . .	251	259	263	209	118	110	(NA)
3143 Men's footwear	Mil. dol. . .	1,812	1,807	1,931	1,975	1,797	1,768	(NA)
3144 Women's footwear	Mil. dol. . .	1,228	1,229	1,160	1,161	924	692	(NA)
3149 Footwear n.e.c.	Mil. dol. . .	295	314	289	294	378	336	(NA)
TRADE DATA								
Value of imports	Mil. dol. . .	8,336	8,616	9,290	9,698	9,984	10,478	11,544
Value of exports	Mil. dol. . .	307	343	332	382	370	385	378

NA Not available.   [1] Value of all products and services sold by establishments in the footwear, except rubber industry.
[2] Value of products classified in the footwear, except rubber industry produced by all industries.

Source: U.S. Department of Commerce, Bureau of the Census, International Trade Administration (ITA).

No. 1439. Recent Trends in Leather Tanning and Finishing (SIC 3111): 1991 to 1997

ITEM	Unit	1991	1992	1993	1994	1995	1996	1997
INDUSTRY DATA								
Value of shipments [1]	Mil. dol. . .	2,075	2,905	3,198	3,041	3,119	3,134	(NA)
Value of shipments (1992 dollars)	Mil. dol. . .	2,067	2,905	3,096	2,808	2,717	2,821	(NA)
Total employment	1,000. . . .	11.1	16.6	16.9	15.9	15.3	14.8	(NA)
Production workers	1,000. . . .	9.4	13.3	13.8	13.4	12.5	12.4	(NA)
Average hourly earnings	Dollar . . .	11.10	10.56	10.65	10.62	10.54	10.98	(NA)
Capital expenditures	Mil. dol. . .	37.1	48.5	52.2	45.5	57.6	51.9	(NA)
PRODUCT DATA								
Value of shipments [2]	Mil. dol. . .	2,226	2,952	3,218	3,064	3,138	3,184	(NA)
Value of shipments (1992 dollars)	Mil. dol. . .	2,217	2,952	3,115	2,829	2,733	2,866	(NA)
TRADE DATA								
Value of imports	Mil. dol. . .	571	631	736	960	1,089	1,139	1,376
Value of exports	Mil. dol. . .	680	705	764	812	870	951	1,146

NA Not available.   [1] Value of all products and services sold by establishments in the leather tanning and finishing industry.
[2] Value of products classified in the leather tanning and finishing industry produced by all industries.

Source: U.S. Department of Commerce, Bureau of the Census, International Trade Administration (ITA).

No. 1440. Recent Trends in Luggage and Personal Leather Goods (SIC 2386, 315, 316, 317): 1991 to 1997

ITEM	Unit	1991	1992	1993	1994	1995	1996	1997
INDUSTRY DATA								
Value of shipments [1]	Mil. dol.	2,252	2,207	2,106	2,070	1,891	2,030	(NA)
2386 Leather and sheep-lined clothing	Mil. dol.	166	209	224	237	206	190	(NA)
3151 Leather gloves/mittens	Mil. dol.	134	140	169	145	114	145	(NA)
3161 Luggage	Mil. dol.	1,091	968	930	991	946	1,115	(NA)
3171 Women's handbags/purses	Mil. dol.	518	463	387	304	305	286	(NA)
3172 Personal leather goods	Mil. dol.	344	428	395	393	321	294	(NA)
Value of shipments (1992 dollars)	Mil. dol.	2,289	2,207	2,090	2,064	1,888	2,007	(NA)
2386 Leather and sheep-lined clothing	Mil. dol.	165	209	225	247	218	201	(NA)
3151 Leather gloves/mittens	Mil. dol.	136	140	168	137	103	125	(NA)
3161 Luggage	Mil. dol.	1,115	968	922	979	942	1,102	(NA)
3171 Women's handbags/purses	Mil. dol.	522	463	385	313	307	291	(NA)
3172 Personal leather goods	Mil. dol.	351	428	389	388	317	289	(NA)
Total employment	1,000.	28.2	26.4	24.3	22.1	18.5	18.1	(NA)
Production workers	1,000.	22.0	21.1	19.0	17.7	14.8	14.4	(NA)
Average hourly earnings	Dollar	7.69	7.43	7.41	7.55	7.85	8.13	(NA)
Capital expenditures	Mil. dol.	16.1	27.9	28.2	26.8	30.9	36.7	(NA)
2386 Leather and sheep-lined clothing	Mil. dol.	0.3	1.3	1.6	0.1	0.6	0.2	(NA)
3151 Leather gloves/mittens	Mil. dol.	0.1	0.5	0.3	12.2	18.4	12.3	(NA)
3161 Luggage	Mil. dol.	8.6	15.9	16.4	9.5	6.1	17.8	(NA)
3171 Women's handbags/purses	Mil. dol.	2.7	3.4	4.2	3.1	3.7	3.6	(NA)
3172 Personal leather goods	Mil. dol.	4.4	6.8	5.7	1.9	2.1	2.8	(NA)
PRODUCT DATA								
Value of shipments [2]	Mil. dol.	2,164	2,109	2,013	2,050	1,818	1,822	(NA)
2386 Leather and sheep-lined clothing	Mil. dol.	201	199	216	222	194	183	(NA)
3151 Leather gloves/mittens	Mil. dol.	127	114	115	115	94	125	(NA)
3161 Luggage	Mil. dol.	1,028	864	814	880	778	830	(NA)
3171 Women's handbags/purses	Mil. dol.	432	411	366	328	315	301	(NA)
3172 Personal leather goods	Mil. dol.	375	522	503	505	438	384	(NA)
Value of shipments (1992 dollars)	Mil. dol.	2,199	2,109	1,997	2,045	1,816	1,804	(NA)
2386 Leather and sheep-lined clothing	Mil. dol.	201	199	217	231	205	193	(NA)
3151 Leather gloves/mittens	Mil. dol.	129	114	114	109	85	108	(NA)
3161 Luggage	Mil. dol.	1,052	864	807	869	775	820	(NA)
3171 Women's handbags/purses	Mil. dol.	436	411	364	338	318	305	(NA)
3172 Personal leather goods	Mil. dol.	383	522	495	498	433	378	(NA)
TRADE DATA								
Value of imports	Mil. dol.	3,557	3,884	4,069	4,562	4,675	4,774	5,106
2386 Leather and sheep-lined clothing	Mil. dol.	1,080	1,231	1,222	1,241	994	912	977
3151 Leather gloves/mittens	Mil. dol.	158	171	214	261	291	295	309
3161 Luggage	Mil. dol.	1,129	1,273	1,403	1,700	1,965	2,042	2,312
3171 Women's handbags/purses	Mil. dol.	898	890	910	959	972	1,055	1,051
3172 Personal leather goods	Mil. dol.	292	319	321	401	454	470	457
Value of exports	Mil. dol.	230	270	283	311	355	384	408
2386 Leather and sheep-lined clothing	Mil. dol.	57.3	65.5	69.5	64.9	88.7	67.6	71.0
3151 Leather gloves/mittens	Mil. dol.	13.1	12.2	14.0	13.8	13.4	10.0	6.6
3161 Luggage	Mil. dol.	109.0	135.0	138.0	166.0	176.0	231.0	250.2
3171 Women's handbags/purses	Mil. dol.	29.2	35.1	41.3	42.4	49.6	46.0	46.5
3172 Personal leather goods	Mil. dol.	21.3	22.8	20.0	23.9	27.2	29.3	33.7

Not available.   [1] Value of all products and services sold by establishments in the luggage and personal leather goods industry.   [2] Value of products classified in the luggage and personal leather goods industry produced by all industries.
Source: U.S. Department of Commerce, Bureau of the Census, International Trade Administration (ITA).

No. 1441. Recent Trends in Flat Glass (SIC 3211): 1991 to 1997

ITEM	Unit	1991	1992	1993	1994	1995	1996	1997
INDUSTRY DATA								
Value of shipments [1]	Mil. dol.	2,065	2,073	2,283	2,600	2,598	2,671	(NA)
Value of shipments (1992 dollars)	Mil. dol.	2,056	2,073	2,234	2,346	2,213	2,417	(NA)
Total employment	1,000.	12.9	11.8	11.3	11.2	11.2	11.5	(NA)
Production workers	1,000.	10.5	9.7	9.2	9.1	9.1	9.3	(NA)
Average hourly earnings	Dollar	16.92	17.45	18.03	19.01	19.73	19.39	(NA)
Capital expenditures	Mil. dol.	163	148	159	137	170	248	(NA)
PRODUCT DATA								
Value of shipments [2]	Mil. dol.	2,089	1,994	2,151	2,474	2,474	2,555	(NA)
Value of shipments (1992 dollars)	Mil. dol.	2,081	1,994	2,105	2,233	2,107	2,312	(NA)
TRADE DATA								
Value of imports	Mil. dol.	283	278	342	416	399	463	492
Value of exports	Mil. dol.	497	499	583	620	687	793	810

NA Not available.   [1] Value of all products and services sold by establishments in the flat glass industry.   [2] Value of products classified in the flat glass industry produced by all industries.
Source: U.S. Department of Commerce, Bureau of the Census, International Trade Administration (ITA).

No. 1442. Recent Trends in Hydraulic Cement, Ceramic Tile, and Gypsum Products: 1991 to 1997

ITEM	Unit	1991	1992	1993	1994	1995	1996	1997
HYDRAULIC CEMENT (SIC 3241)								
Industry data:								
Value of shipments [1]	Mil. dol. . .	3,811	4,051	4,187	4,808	5,342	5,818	(NA)
Value of shipments (1992 dollars) . . .	Mil. dol. . .	3,796	4,051	3,987	4,278	4,437	4,618	(NA)
Total employment	1,000. . .	16.3	17.0	16.6	16.6	16.8	16.9	(NA)
Production workers	1,000. . .	12.0	12.8	12.5	12.4	12.6	12.5	(NA)
Average hourly earnings	Dollar	15.17	15.15	15.48	15.80	16.40	16.75	(NA)
Capital expenditures	Mil. dol. . .	232	226	227	280	282	495	(NA)
Product data:								
Value of shipments [2]	Mil. dol. . .	3,701	3,929	4,051	4,699	5,172	5,650	(NA)
Value of shipments (1992 dollars) . . .	Mil. dol. . .	3,686	3,929	3,858	4,180	4,296	4,484	(NA)
Trade data:								
Value of imports	Mil. dol. . .	335	251	285	444	542	596	753
Value of exports	Mil. dol. . .	47.2	50.3	49.3	46.8	56.0	59.1	60.2
CERAMIC WALL AND FLOOR TILE (SIC 3253)								
Industry data:								
Value of shipments [1]	Mil. dol. . .	757	731	811	847	938	989	(NA)
Value of shipments (1992 dollars) . . .	Mil. dol. . .	766	731	806	829	902	949	(NA)
Total employment	1,000. . .	9.4	8.9	8.7	8.6	9.4	9.2	(NA)
Production workers	1,000. . .	7.6	7.3	7.3	7.1	7.8	7.7	(NA)
Average hourly earnings	Dollar	9.16	9.50	10.41	9.92	10.35	10.41	(NA)
Capital expenditures	Mil. dol. . .	22.7	48.9	68.0	73.1	61.5	45.6	(NA)
Product data:								
Value of shipments [2]	Mil. dol. . .	683	678	739	735	790	839	(NA)
Value of shipments (1992 dollars) . . .	Mil. dol. . .	690	678	734	719	760	805	(NA)
Trade data:								
Value of imports	Mil. dol. . .	365	419	472	519	562	628	716
Value of exports	Mil. dol. . .	21.0	19.3	22.6	23.5	26.1	24.6	28.9
GYPSUM PRODUCTS (SIC 3275)								
Industry data:								
Value of shipments [1]	Mil. dol. . .	2,026	2,100	2,290	2,954	3,476	3,826	(NA)
Value of shipments (1992 dollars) . . .	Mil. dol. . .	2,020	2,100	2,069	2,161	2,249	2,481	(NA)
Total employment	1,000. . .	10.2	10.6	10.4	10.8	11.3	13.2	(NA)
Production workers	1,000. . .	8.0	8.5	8.3	8.6	9.0	10.4	(NA)
Average hourly earnings	Dollar	13.11	12.70	13.06	13.42	14.28	14.09	(NA)
Capital expenditures	Mil. dol. . .	35.1	43.8	39.8	74.6	154.0	123.0	(NA)
Product data:								
Value of shipments [2]	Mil. dol. . .	1,899	1,948	2,133	2,729	3,221	3,712	(NA)
Value of shipments (1992 dollars) . . .	Mil. dol. . .	1,893	1,948	1,927	1,996	2,083	2,407	(NA)
Trade data:								
Value of imports	Mil. dol. . .	12.8	13.2	24.5	50.6	75.2	101.0	125.3
Value of exports	Mil. dol. . .	65.6	71.2	55.3	50.5	52.9	60.3	65.8

NA Not available. [1] Value of all products and services sold by establishments in this industry. [2] Value of products classified in this industry produced by all industries.

Source: U.S. Department of Commerce: Bureau of the Census, International Trade Administration (ITA).

No. 1443. Recent Trends in Steel Mill Products (SIC 3312, 3315, 3316, 3317): 1991 to 1997

ITEM	Unit	1991	1992	1993	1994	1995	1996	1997
INDUSTRY DATA								
Value of shipments [1]	Mil. dol. . .	56,103	57,187	61,301	68,753	73,716	73,238	(NA)
Value of shipments (1992 dollars)	Mil. dol. . .	54,965	57,187	60,338	64,732	65,687	67,422	(NA)
Total employment	1,000. . .	244	234	225	222	221	217	(NA)
Production workers	1,000. . .	185	179	173	172	173	171	(NA)
Capital expenditures	Mil. dol. . .	3,399	2,568	2,166	3,130	3,283	3,402	(NA)
PRODUCT DATA								
Value of shipments [2]	Mil. dol. . .	53,968	56,132	60,199	67,681	72,347	71,293	(NA)
Value of shipments (1992 dollars)	Mil. dol. . .	52,866	56,132	59,266	63,733	64,472	65,609	(NA)
TRADE DATA								
Value of imports	Mil. dol. . .	8,344	8,508	9,300	13,445	12,908	13,853	14,815
Value of exports	Mil. dol. . .	3,868	3,191	2,988	3,205	4,893	4,346	5,117

NA Not available. [1] Value of all products and services sold by establishments in the steel mill products industry. [2] Value of products classified in the steel mill products industry produced by all industries.

Source: U.S. Department of Commerce, Bureau of the Census, International Trade Administration (ITA).

No. 1444. Recent Trends in General Components (SIC 345, 3491, 3494, 3562): 1991 to 1997

[The code 349A in the table represents an aggregation of SIC's 3491 and 3494]

ITEM	Unit	1991	1992	1993	1994	1995	1996	1997
INDUSTRY DATA								
Value of shipments [1]	Mil. dol.	21,515	22,038	23,202	25,014	27,310	28,648	(NA)
3451 Screw machine products	Mil. dol.	3,007	3,831	4,170	4,686	5,044	5,278	(NA)
3452 Industrial fasteners	Mil. dol.	5,570	5,195	5,373	5,819	6,385	6,519	(NA)
349A Valves and pipe fittings	Mil. dol.	8,872	8,723	9,102	9,618	10,600	11,405	(NA)
3562 Ball and roller bearings	Mil. dol.	4,066	4,290	4,557	4,891	5,281	5,446	(NA)
Value of shipments (1992 dollars)	Mil. dol.	21,670	22,038	22,866	24,174	25,593	26,221	(NA)
3451 Screw machine products	Mil. dol.	3,023	3,831	4,137	4,599	4,841	4,993	(NA)
3452 Industrial fasteners	Mil. dol.	5,586	5,195	5,320	5,699	6,145	6,209	(NA)
349A Valves and pipe fittings	Mil. dol.	8,925	8,723	8,928	9,174	9,731	10,178	(NA)
3562 Ball and roller bearings	Mil. dol.	4,136	4,290	4,481	4,702	4,876	4,841	(NA)
Total employment	1,000	198	194	194	196	207	212	(NA)
3451 Screw machine products	1,000	40.7	46.4	47.1	51.9	54.2	57.1	(NA)
3452 Industrial fasteners	1,000	50.2	44.1	43.7	43.4	46.0	46.5	(NA)
349A Valves and pipe fittings	1,000	71.2	68.0	69.0	66.8	71.3	71.9	(NA)
3562 Ball and roller bearings	1,000	35.9	35.0	33.8	33.4	35.6	36.0	(NA)
Production workers	1,000	145.0	142.0	144.0	147.0	156.0	159.0	(NA)
3451 Screw machine products	1,000	32.3	36.5	38.5	41.9	44.0	46.0	(NA)
3452 Industrial fasteners	1,000	36.3	31.9	32.0	31.9	34.1	35.1	(NA)
349A Valves and pipe fittings	1,000	47.7	45.6	46.6	45.8	48.9	48.5	(NA)
3562 Ball and roller bearings	1,000	29.1	28.2	27.3	27.2	29.2	29.5	(NA)
Average hourly earnings	Dollar	11.95	12.57	12.70	12.90	13.25	13.52	(NA)
3451 Screw machine products	Dollar	10.28	11.29	11.36	11.25	11.55	12.26	(NA)
3452 Industrial fasteners	Dollar	11.88	12.80	12.74	12.76	13.58	13.36	(NA)
349A Valves and pipe fittings	Dollar	12.14	12.39	12.76	12.76	13.17	13.55	(NA)
3562 Ball and roller bearings	Dollar	13.83	14.35	14.48	15.97	15.65	15.72	(NA)
Capital expenditures	Mil. dol.	845	758	778	825	1,194	1,024	(NA)
3451 Screw machine products	Mil. dol.	108	135	152	226	250	231	(NA)
3452 Industrial fasteners	Mil. dol.	186	151	163	157	386	190	(NA)
349A Valves and pipe fittings	Mil. dol.	263	265	257	269	310	331	(NA)
3562 Ball and roller bearings	Mil. dol.	288	207	206	173	248	273	(NA)
PRODUCT DATA								
Value of shipments [2]	Mil. dol.	20,407	20,754	21,930	23,702	25,871	27,030	(NA)
3451 Screw machine products	Mil. dol.	2,926	3,660	3,986	4,642	5,324	5,608	(NA)
3452 Industrial fasteners	Mil. dol.	5,275	4,854	5,043	5,439	5,916	6,115	(NA)
349A Valves and pipe fittings	Mil. dol.	8,313	8,100	8,461	8,828	9,501	10,049	(NA)
3562 Ball and roller bearings	Mil. dol.	3,893	4,140	4,440	4,794	5,129	5,258	(NA)
Value of shipments (1992 dollars)	Mil. dol.	20,544	20,754	21,616	22,913	24,262	24,772	(NA)
3451 Screw machine products	Mil. dol.	2,941	3,660	3,954	4,555	5,109	5,305	(NA)
3452 Industrial fasteners	Mil. dol.	5,291	4,854	4,993	5,327	5,694	5,824	(NA)
349A Valves and pipe fittings	Mil. dol.	8,353	8,100	8,303	8,422	8,723	8,969	(NA)
3562 Ball and roller bearings	Mil. dol.	3,960	4,140	4,366	4,609	4,736	4,674	(NA)
TRADE DATA								
Value of imports	Mil. dol.	3,863	4,221	4,630	5,490	6,264	6,458	7,019
3451 Screw machine products	Mil. dol.	(NA)	(NA)	(NA)	(NA)	(NA)	(NA)	(NA)
3452 Industrial fasteners	Mil. dol.	1,121	1,231	1,386	1,666	1,894	1,847	1,907
349A Valves and pipe fittings	Mil. dol.	1,931	2,096	2,240	2,653	2,988	3,221	3,650
3562 Ball and roller bearings	Mil. dol.	812	895	1,004	1,171	1,381	1,389	1,462
Value of exports	Mil. dol.	2,974	3,154	3,332	3,849	4,570	5,167	5,568
3451 Screw machine products	Mil. dol.	(NA)	(NA)	(NA)	(NA)	(NA)	(NA)	(NA)
3452 Industrial fasteners	Mil. dol.	634	685	710	905	1,061	1,366	1,333
349A Valves and pipe fittings	Mil. dol.	1,666	1,810	1,965	2,211	2,620	2,890	3,239
3562 Ball and roller bearings	Mil. dol.	674	659	658	733	889	912	996

NA Not available. [1] Value of all products and services sold by establishments in the general components industry. [2] Value of products classified in the general components industry produced by all industries.

Source: U.S. Department of Commerce, Bureau of the Census, International Trade Administration (ITA).

No. 1445. Recent Trends in Automotive Parts and Accessories (SIC 3465, 3592, 3647, 3691, 3694, 3714): 1991 to 1997

ITEM	Unit	1991	1992	1993	1994	1995	1996	1997
INDUSTRY DATA								
Value of shipments [1]	Mil. dol. . .	91,215	105,841	119,678	138,982	147,773	152,134	(NA)
Value of shipments (1992 dollar)	Mil. dol. . .	91,624	105,841	119,264	137,842	145,124	148,775	(NA)
Total employment	1,000. . .	580	609	633	679	706	691	(NA)
Production workers	1,000. . .	457	482	506	548	566	558	(NA)
Average hourly earnings	Dollar . . .	15.61	15.84	16.22	16.57	17.05	17.05	(NA)
Capital expenditures	Mil. dol. . .	4,690	4,585	5,308	6,010	7,824	7,572	(NA)
PRODUCT DATA								
Value of shipments [2]	Mil. dol. . .	88,768	104,109	118,293	134,462	143,859	148,201	(NA)
Value of shipments (1992 dollar)	Mil. dol. . .	89,150	104,109	117,882	133,371	141,294	144,954	(NA)
TRADE DATA								
Value of imports	Mil. dol. . .	18,438	21,055	23,461	27,267	28,800	30,837	33,093
Value of exports	Mil. dol. . .	18,987	22,437	26,064	27,927	29,323	30,285	35,150

NA Not available.   [1] Value of all products and services sold by establishments in the automotive parts and accessories industry.   [2] Value of products classified in the automotive parts and accessories industry produced by all industries.

Source: U.S. Department of Commerce, Bureau of the Census, International Trade Administration (ITA).

No. 1446. Recent Trends in Farm Machinery and Equipment (SIC 3523): 1991 to 1997

ITEM	Unit	1991	1992	1993	1994	1995	1996	1997
INDUSTRY DATA								
Value of shipments [1]	Mil. dol. . .	10,522	9,620	11,190	12,759	13,757	14,469	(NA)
Value of shipments (1992 dollars)	Mil. dol. . .	10,870	9,620	10,938	12,163	12,773	13,070	(NA)
Total employment	1,000. . .	65.1	61.5	63.5	66.5	65.7	66.6	(NA)
Production workers	1,000. . .	45.4	42.6	45.8	47.7	48.3	48.5	(NA)
Average hourly earnings	Dollar . . .	12.80	13.18	13.18	13.60	14.37	14.24	(NA)
Capital expenditures	Mil. dol. . .	220	196	229	260	290	294	(NA)
PRODUCT DATA								
Value of shipments [2]	Mil. dol. . .	9,724	8,940	10,340	11,911	12,599	13,191	(NA)
Value of shipments (1992 dollars)	Mil. dol. . .	10,045	8,940	10,108	11,355	11,698	11,916	(NA)
TRADE DATA								
Value of imports	Mil. dol. . .	1,911	2,022	2,148	2,917	3,089	2,990	3,404
Value of exports	Mil. dol. . .	2,130	2,176	2,473	2,647	3,119	3,804	4,620

NA Not available.   [1] Value of all products and services sold by establishments in the farm machinery and equipment industry.   [2] Value of products classified in the farm machinery and equipment industry produced by all industries.

Source: U.S. Department of Commerce, Bureau of the Census, International Trade Administration (ITA).

No. 1447. Recent Trends in Lawn and Garden Equipment (SIC 3524): 1991 to 1997

ITEM	Unit	1991	1992	1993	1994	1995	1996	1997
INDUSTRY DATA								
Value of shipments [1]	Mil. dol. . .	4,901	5,164	5,828	6,836	6,971	6,823	(NA)
Value of shipments (1992 dollars)	Mil. dol. . .	4,946	5,164	5,788	6,682	6,723	6,480	(NA)
Total employment	1,000. . .	24.4	24.9	25.7	28.0	27.7	27.0	(NA)
Production workers	1,000. . .	18.9	19.9	20.5	22.4	22.3	21.5	(NA)
Average hourly earnings	Dollar . . .	9.99	10.73	10.88	10.56	10.26	11.05	(NA)
Capital expenditures	Mil. dol. . .	98.2	125.0	92.1	129.0	126.0	120.0	(NA)
PRODUCT DATA								
Value of shipments [2]	Mil. dol. . .	4,267	4,344	4,884	5,730	6,061	5,908	(NA)
Value of shipments (1992 dollars)	Mil. dol. . .	4,306	4,344	4,850	5,601	5,845	5,611	(NA)
TRADE DATA								
Value of imports	Mil. dol. . .	118	135	162	175	172	225	264
Value of exports	Mil. dol. . .	562	612	686	740	765	721	788

NA Not available.   [1] Value of all products and services sold by establishments in the lawn and garden equipment industry.
[2] Value of products classified in the lawn and garden equipment industry produced by all industries.

Source: U.S. Department of Commerce, Bureau of the Census, International Trade Administration (ITA).

No. 1448. Recent Trends in Construction Machinery (SIC 3531): 1991 to 1997

ITEM	Unit	1991	1992	1993	1994	1995	1996	1997
INDUSTRY DATA								
Value of shipments [1]	Mil. dol. . .	13,710	13,139	15,444	17,697	19,911	21,627	(NA)
Value of shipments (1992 dollars)	Mil. dol. . .	14,076	13,139	15,097	17,049	18,714	19,860	(NA)
Total employment	1,000	81.0	74.6	74.7	77.9	85.4	88.7	(NA)
Production workers	1,000	53.6	47.8	49.1	52.9	58.4	61.1	(NA)
Average hourly earnings	Dollar . . .	15.32	15.13	15.33	14.84	14.81	14.93	(NA)
Capital expenditures	Mil. dol. . .	485	395	346	359	443	450	(NA)
PRODUCT DATA								
Value of shipments [2]	Mil. dol. . .	12,297	12,001	14,122	16,123	18,299	20,259	(NA)
Value of shipments (1992 dollars)	Mil. dol. . .	12,626	12,001	13,804	15,532	17,198	18,604	(NA)
TRADE DATA								
Value of imports	Mil. dol. . .	2,109	2,574	3,403	4,277	4,458	4,433	5,364
Value of exports	Mil. dol. . .	4,404	4,280	4,361	5,210	5,471	5,792	6,649

NA Not available.   [1] Value of all products and services sold by establishments in the construction machinery industry.
[2] Value of products classified in the construction machinery industry produced by all industries.

Source: U.S. Department of Commerce, Bureau of the Census, International Trade Administration (ITA).

No. 1449. Recent Trends in Mining Machinery (SIC 3532): 1991 to 1997

ITEM	Unit	1991	1992	1993	1994	1995	1996	1997
INDUSTRY DATA								
Value of shipments [1]	Mil. dol. . .	1,655	1,548	1,881	1,715	2,181	2,397	(NA)
Value of shipments (1992 dollars)	Mil. dol. . .	1,682	1,548	1,844	1,659	2,038	2,193	(NA)
Total employment	1,000	14.2	12.6	12.6	12.6	13.8	13.7	(NA)
Production workers	1,000	8.4	7.4	7.7	8.0	8.9	8.4	(NA)
Average hourly earnings	Dollar . . .	10.91	11.92	12.21	13.08	13.30	13.87	(NA)
Capital expenditures	Mil. dol. . .	33.3	33.0	58.9	29.5	29.8	43.8	(NA)
PRODUCT DATA								
Value of shipments [2]	Mil. dol. . .	1,584	1,417	1,745	1,639	2,100	2,202	(NA)
Value of shipments (1992 dollars)	Mil. dol. . .	1,610	1,417	1,711	1,585	1,962	2,014	(NA)
TRADE DATA								
Value of imports	Mil. dol. . .	317	268	307	379	466	515	553
Value of exports	Mil. dol. . .	764	811	846	987	1,111	1,235	1,523

NA Not available.   [1] Value of all products and services sold by establishments in the mining machinery industry.   [2] Value
of products classified in the mining machinery industry produced by all industries.

Source: U.S. Department of Commerce, Bureau of the Census, International Trade Administration (ITA).

No. 1450. Recent Trends in Oil and Gas Field Machinery (SIC 3533): 1991 to 1997

ITEM	Unit	1991	1992	1993	1994	1995	1996	1997
INDUSTRY DATA								
Value of shipments [1]	Mil. dol. . .	4,102	3,921	3,740	3,758	3,803	4,646	(NA)
Value of shipments (1992 dollars)	Mil. dol. . .	4,030	3,921	3,762	3,677	3,619	4,290	(NA)
Total employment	1,000	28.1	26.3	24.5	25.5	24.3	26.4	(NA)
Production workers	1,000	15.9	15.4	13.8	14.7	15.0	17.0	(NA)
Average hourly earnings	Dollar . . .	13.52	13.63	14.22	15.57	15.05	16.07	(NA)
Capital expenditures	Mil. dol. . .	102.0	105.0	79.8	77.7	123.0	157.0	(NA)
PRODUCT DATA								
Value of shipments [2]	Mil. dol. . .	3,400	2,981	2,939	2,976	3,023	3,814	(NA)
Value of shipments (1992 dollars)	Mil. dol. . .	3,339	2,981	2,956	2,912	2,876	3,521	(NA)
TRADE DATA								
Value of imports	Mil. dol. . .	64.0	36.2	47.1	67.5	93.2	145.0	204.3
Value of exports	Mil. dol. . .	3,938	3,986	3,746	3,546	4,168	5,236	5,907

NA Not available.   [1] Value of all products and services sold by establishments in the oil and gas field machinery industry.
[2] Value of products classified in the oil and gas field machinery industry produced by all industries.

Source: U.S. Department of Commerce, Bureau of the Census, International Trade Administration (ITA).

No. 1451. Recent Trends in Machine Tools (SIC 3541, 3542): 1991 to 1997

ITEM	Unit	1991	1992	1993	1994	1995	1996	1997
INDUSTRY DATA								
Value of shipments [1]	Mil. dol. . .	4,702	5,102	5,231	5,366	6089	6357	(NA)
3541 Metal cutting machines	Mil. dol. . .	3,250	3,618	3,518	3,672	4065	4143	(NA)
3542 Metal forming machines	Mil. dol. . .	1,452	1,484	1,713	1,694	2024	2213	(NA)
Value of shipments (1992 dollars)	Mil. dol. . .	4,831	5,102	5,154	5,196	5695	5771	(NA)
3541 Metal cutting machines	Mil. dol. . .	3,351	3,618	3,476	3,579	3817	3770	(NA)
3542 Metal forming machines	Mil. dol. . .	1,480	1,484	1,677	1,617	1877	2001	(NA)
Total employment	1,000. . . .	39.8	39.9	38.0	37.1	40.4	40.4	(NA)
3541 Metal cutting machines	1,000. . . .	26.9	27.4	25.3	24.0	27.0	26.9	(NA)
3542 Metal forming machines	1,000. . . .	12.9	12.5	12.7	13.1	13.4	13.5	(NA)
Production workers	1,000. . . .	23.9	23.3	22.3	22.0	24.5	24.7	(NA)
3541 Metal cutting machines	1,000. . . .	15.8	15.4	14.5	13.7	16.0	16.2	(NA)
3542 Metal forming machines	1,000. . . .	8.1	7.9	7.8	8.3	8.5	8.5	(NA)
Average hourly earnings	Dollar . . .	14.76	15.34	15.72	16.16	16.25	16.74	(NA)
3541 Metal cutting machines	Dollar . . .	14.81	15.54	15.75	16.31	16.26	16.85	(NA)
3542 Metal forming machines	Dollar . . .	14.67	14.93	15.68	15.91	16.24	16.52	(NA)
Capital expenditures	Mil. dol. . .	98.0	124.0	95.7	131.0	190.0	169.0	(NA)
3541 Metal cutting machines	Mil. dol. . .	66.4	82.8	63.0	106.0	134.0	117.0	(NA)
3542 Metal forming machines	Mil. dol. . .	31.6	40.7	32.7	25.4	56.2	52.0	(NA)
PRODUCT DATA								
Value of shipments [2]	Mil. dol. . .	4,291	4,521	4,524	5,098	5,747	6,088	(NA)
3541 Metal cutting machines	Mil. dol. . .	2,838	3,093	2,915	3,435	3,906	4,082	(NA)
3542 Metal forming machines	Mil. dol. . .	1,453	1,428	1,609	1,663	1,841	2,006	(NA)
Value of shipments (1992 dollars)	Mil. dol. . .	4,407	4,521	4,456	4,934	5,375	5,528	(NA)
3541 Metal cutting machines	Mil. dol. . .	2,926	3,093	2,881	3,347	3,668	3,714	(NA)
3542 Metal forming machines	Mil. dol. . .	1,481	1,428	1,576	1,587	1,707	1,814	(NA)
TRADE DATA								
Value of imports	Mil. dol. . .	2,587	2,311	2,596	3,389	4,380	4,770	5,329
3541 Metal cutting machines	Mil. dol. . .	1,926	1,681	1,882	2,385	3,101	3,415	3,828
3542 Metal forming machines	Mil. dol. . .	661	630	714	1,004	1,279	1,356	1,501
Value of exports	Mil. dol. . .	1,555	1,836	1,744	2,179	2,265	2,753	2,886
3541 Metal cutting machines	Mil. dol. . .	878	1,017	975	1,353	1,350	1,662	1,768
3542 Metal forming machines	Mil. dol. . .	678	819	769	826	914	1,090	1,118

NA Not available. [1] Value of all products and services sold by establishments in the machine tools industry. [2] Value of products classified in the machine tools industry produced by all industries.

Source: U.S. Department of Commerce, Bureau of the Census, International Trade Administration (ITA).

No. 1452. Recent Trends in Special Dies, Tools, Jigs and Fixtures (SIC 3544): 1991 to 1997

ITEM	Unit	1991	1992	1993	1994	1995	1996	1997
INDUSTRY DATA								
Value of shipments [1]	Mil. dol. . .	8,575	9,265	9,951	11,145	12,656	12,949	(NA)
Value of shipments (1992 dollars)	Mil. dol. . .	8,706	9,265	9,708	10,604	11,839	11,902	(NA)
Total employment	1,000. . . .	110	111	118	119	131	133	(NA)
Production workers	1,000. . . .	84.0	84.9	90.7	91.8	102.0	104.0	(NA)
Average hourly earnings	Dollar . . .	13.87	14.58	14.70	15.03	15.35	15.64	(NA)
Capital expenditures	Mil. dol. . .	387	369	532	541	722	699	(NA)
PRODUCT DATA								
Value of shipments [2]	Mil. dol. . .	9,692	10,230	10,990	12,235	13,595	13,834	(NA)
Value of shipments (1992 dollars)	Mil. dol. . .	9,839	10,230	10,722	11,641	12,717	12,715	(NA)
TRADE DATA								
Value of imports	Mil. dol. . .	1,662	1,399	1,880	2,608	2,948	2,656	2,924
Value of exports	Mil. dol. . .	863	1,033	1,239	1,306	1,480	1,616	1,958

NA Not available. [1] Value of all products and services sold by establishments in the special dies, tools, jigs and fixtures industry. [2] Value of products classified in the special dies, tools, jigs and fixtures industry produced by all industries.

Source: U.S. Department of Commerce, Bureau of the Census, International Trade Administration (ITA).

No. 1453. Recent Trends in Power-Driven Handtools and Welding Apparatus: 1991 to 1997

ITEM	Unit	1991	1992	1993	1994	1995	1996	1997
POWER-DRIVEN HANDTOOLS (SIC 3546)								
Industry data:								
Value of shipments [1]	Mil. dol.	2,489	2,873	3,480	3,608	3,791	3,744	(NA)
Value of shipments (1992 dollars)	Mil. dol.	2,556	2,873	3,405	3,450	3,566	3,470	(NA)
Total employment	1,000.	16.8	16.1	17.0	16.1	17.0	16.3	(NA)
Production workers	1,000.	10.9	10.6	11.7	11.2	11.9	11.3	(NA)
Average hourly earnings	Dollar	11.08	11.08	10.98	11.27	12.13	12.17	(NA)
Capital expenditures	Mil. dol.	74.8	72.3	112.0	106.0	118.0	118.0	(NA)
Product data:								
Value of shipments [2]	Mil. dol.	2,239	2,415	3,074	3,281	3,368	3,426	(NA)
Value of shipments (1992 dollars)	Mil. dol.	2,298	2,415	3,008	3,137	3,168	3,175	(NA)
Trade data:								
Value of imports	Mil. dol.	690	766	824	953	1,085	1,209	1,388
Value of exports	Mil. dol.	550	568	600	699	738	720	916
WELDING APPARATUS (SIC 3548)								
Industry data:								
Value of shipments [1]	Mil. dol.	2,557	2,738	3,101	3,086	3,303	3,496	(NA)
Value of shipments (1992 dollars)	Mil. dol.	2,650	2,738	2,984	2,871	2,970	3,067	(NA)
Total employment	1,000.	18.7	19.6	20.3	18.6	18.9	19.7	(NA)
Production workers	1,000.	11.3	11.7	13.1	12.0	12.7	13.0	(NA)
Average hourly earnings	Dollar	13.39	13.87	14.76	15.28	15.92	16.05	(NA)
Capital expenditures	Mil. dol.	50.5	65.3	80.6	73.5	89.3	124.0	(NA)
Product data:								
Value of shipments [2]	Mil. dol.	2,434	2,391	2,717	3,043	3,336	3,452	(NA)
Value of shipments (1992 dollars)	Mil. dol.	2,523	2,391	2,615	2,830	3,000	3,028	(NA)
Trade data:								
Value of imports	Mil. dol.	480	382	535	530	659	751	882
Value of exports	Mil. dol.	599	624	655	685	770	851	1,081

NA Not available. [1] Value of all products and services sold by establishments in this industry. [2] Value of products classified in this industry produced by all industries.

Source: U.S. Department of Commerce, Bureau of the Census, International Trade Administration (ITA).

No. 1454. Recent Trends in Textile Machinery and Paper Industries Machinery: 1991 to 1997

ITEM	Unit	1991	1992	1993	1994	1995	1996	1997
TEXTILE MACHINERY (SIC 3552)								
Industry data:								
Value of shipments [1]	Mil. dol.	1,446	1,571	1,853	1,908	1,997	1,877	(NA)
Value of shipments (1992 dollars)	Mil. dol.	1,492	1,571	1,792	1,837	1,904	1,769	(NA)
Total employment	1,000.	15.3	15.0	16.5	16.7	16.9	16.3	(NA)
Production workers	1,000.	10.1	9.6	10.1	10.6	10.6	10.2	(NA)
Average hourly earnings	Dollar	11.27	11.06	10.96	11.92	13.00	13.17	(NA)
Capital expenditures	Mil. dol.	36.1	39.5	46.9	71.4	66.4	41.1	(NA)
Product data:								
Value of shipments [2]	Mil. dol.	1,235	1,334	1,612	1,615	1,620	1,475	(NA)
Value of shipments (1992 dollars)	Mil. dol.	1,274	1,334	1,559	1,554	1,545	1,390	(NA)
Trade data:								
Value of imports	Mil. dol.	1,165	1,464	1,781	1,772	1,687	1,447	1,624
Value of exports	Mil. dol.	534	547	553	567	602	581	680
PAPER INDUSTRIES MACHINERY (SIC 3554)								
Industry data:								
Value of shipments [1]	Mil. dol.	2,286	2,524	2,529	2,828	3,418	3,419	(NA)
Value of shipments (1992 dollars)	Mil. dol.	2,328	2,524	2,496	2,751	3,283	3,216	(NA)
Total employment	1,000.	18.3	18.2	18.1	17.5	19.3	19.5	(NA)
Production workers	1,000.	9.6	10.2	9.8	9.8	10.9	11.2	(NA)
Average hourly earnings	Dollar	14.63	14.76	15.24	16.11	16.55	17.56	(NA)
Capital expenditures	Mil. dol.	68.8	65.4	55.9	49.7	90.6	75.3	(NA)
Product data:								
Value of shipments [2]	Mil. dol.	2,061	2,225	2,253	2,479	2,970	3,039	(NA)
Value of shipments (1992 dollars)	Mil. dol.	2,099	2,225	2,224	2,411	2,853	2,859	(NA)
Trade data:								
Value of imports	Mil. dol.	694	637	709	907	981	1,182	1,109
Value of exports	Mil. dol.	637	583	652	653	862	853	990

NA Not available. [1] Value of all products and services sold by establishments in this industry. [2] Value of products classified in this industry produced by all industries.

Source: U.S. Department of Commerce, Bureau of the Census, International Trade Administration (ITA).

No. 1455. Recent Trends in Printing Trades Machinery, Food Products Machinery, and Packaging Machinery: 1991 to 1997

ITEM	Unit	1991	1992	1993	1994	1995	1996	1997
PRINTING TRADES MACHINERY (SIC 3555)								
Industry data:								
Value of shipments [1]	Mil. dol.	3,665	2,635	2,727	3,079	3,498	3,654	(NA)
Value of shipments (1992 dollars)	Mil. dol.	3,688	2,635	2,668	2,972	3,300	3,371	(NA)
Total employment	1,000.	24.6	19.2	18.9	21.4	21.6	21.8	(NA)
Production workers	1,000.	12.1	10.7	10.3	11.7	12.1	11.0	(NA)
Average hourly earnings	Dollar	13.09	13.65	14.59	14.48	14.80	15.90	(NA)
Capital expenditures	Mil. dol.	82.1	62.7	52.9	74.0	101.0	106.0	(NA)
Product data:								
Value of shipments [2]	Mil. dol.	3,171	2,342	2,345	2,814	3,213	3,019	(NA)
Value of shipments (1992 dollars)	Mil. dol.	3,190	2,342	2,294	2,716	3,031	2,785	(NA)
Trade data:								
Value of imports	Mil. dol.	1,143	1,217	1,347	1,553	1,988	1,776	2,019
Value of exports	Mil. dol.	1,072	1,054	1,064	1,029	1,215	1,338	1,407
FOOD PRODUCTS MACHINERY (SIC 3556)								
Industry data:								
Value of shipments [1]	Mil. dol.	2,272	2,417	2,630	2,674	2,819	2,798	(NA)
Value of shipments (1992 dollars)	Mil. dol.	2,342	2,417	2,564	2,520	2,579	2,502	(NA)
Total employment	1,000.	18.4	18.9	18.8	19.8	19.9	21.1	(NA)
Production workers	1,000.	10.5	11.2	11.3	12.0	12.1	12.1	(NA)
Average hourly earnings	Dollar	12.53	13.08	13.23	13.05	13.46	13.66	(NA)
Capital expenditures	Mil. dol.	46.3	46.8	48.8	48.5	43.0	67.0	(NA)
Product data:								
Value of shipments [2]	Mil. dol.	1,970	2,102	2,311	2,266	2,347	2,490	(NA)
Value of shipments (1992 dollars)	Mil. dol.	2,030	2,102	2,252	2,136	2,147	2,227	(NA)
Trade data:								
Value of imports	Mil. dol.	427	474	439	481	591	545	575
Value of exports	Mil. dol.	621	687	696	734	792	821	817
PACKAGING MACHINERY (SIC 3565)								
Industry data:								
Value of shipments [1]	Mil. dol.	2,890	3,150	3,418	3,690	4,185	4,056	(NA)
Value of shipments (1992 dollars)	Mil. dol.	2,952	3,150	3,322	3,491	3,864	3,667	(NA)
Total employment	1,000.	23.4	26.4	24.9	24.8	28.0	27.2	(NA)
Production workers	1,000.	13.4	15.6	14.2	14.9	16.9	16.3	(NA)
Average hourly earnings	Dollar	13.97	13.86	14.29	14.52	14.69	14.68	(NA)
Capital expenditures	Mil. dol.	64.5	70.6	90.2	98.6	87.0	111.0	(NA)
Product data:								
Value of shipments [2]	Mil. dol.	2,767	2,861	3,098	3,257	3,658	3,435	(NA)
Value of shipments (1992 dollars)	Mil. dol.	2,826	2,861	3,011	3,081	3,377	3,105	(NA)
Trade data:								
Value of imports	Mil. dol.	643	699	719	842	932	1,042	1,104
Value of exports	Mil. dol.	611	606	672	792	839	841	871

NA Not available. [1] Value of all products and services sold by establishments in this industry. [2] Value of products classified in this industry produced by all industries.

Source: U.S. Department of Commerce, Bureau of the Census, International Trade Administration (ITA).

No. 1456. Recent Trends in Computers and Peripherals (SIC 3571,2,5,7): 1991 to 1997

[Census reclassified some parts for electronic computers (3571) to component industries (367) for 1989-1990]

ITEM	Unit	1991	1992	1993	1994	1995	1996	1997
INDUSTRY DATA								
Value of shipments [1]	Mil. dol.	56,236	61,969	64,374	73,345	86,078	97,592	(NA)
Total employment	1,000.	232	221	211	201	210	221	(NA)
Production workers	1,000.	75.8	74.2	73.9	75.8	78.9	83.4	(NA)
Average hourly earnings	Dollar	12.45	12.26	12.77	13.67	13.49	14.84	(NA)
Capital expenditures	Mil. dol.	1,817	2,137	2,045	1,907	1,902	2,684	(NA)
PRODUCT DATA								
Value of shipments [2]	Mil. dol.	49,144	54,722	57,928	65,635	81,356	85,441	(NA)
TRADE DATA								
Value of imports	Mil. dol.	25,215	30,710	36,978	45,124	55,185	60,245	68,433
Value of exports	Mil. dol.	23,893	24,879	25,276	28,956	34,294	37,621	41,380

NA Not available. [1] Value of all products and services sold by establishments in the computers and peripherals industry. [2] Value of products classified in the computers and peripherals industry produced by all industries.

Source: U.S. Department of Commerce, Bureau of the Census, International Trade Administration (ITA).

No. 1457. Recent Trends in Electrical Equipment (SIC 361, 3621, 3625): 1991 to 1997

ITEM	Unit	1991	1992	1993	1994	1995	1996 [1]	1997
INDUSTRY								
Value of shipments (1992 dollars)	Mil. dol. . .	24,290	25,706	27,329	29,082	31,833	32,536	(NA)
3612 Transformers	Mil. dol. . .	3,833	4,118	4,028	4,819	5,192	5,051	(NA)
3613 Switchgear and apparatus.	Mil. dol. . .	5,302	5,679	5,723	5,889	6,363	6,603	(NA)
3621 Motors and generators	Mil. dol. . .	7,675	8,168	9,064	9,267	10,621	10,787	(NA)
3625 Relays and controls	Mil. dol. . .	7,478	7,741	8,514	9,108	9,657	10,095	(NA)

NA Not available. [1] Estimate.

Source: U.S. Department of Commerce, Bureau of the Census, International Trade Administration (ITA). Estimates by ITA.

No. 1458. Recent Trends in Transformers, except Electronic (SIC 3612): 1991 to 1997

ITEM	Unit	1991	1992	1993	1994	1995	1996	1997
INDUSTRY DATA								
Value of shipments [1]	Mil. dol. . .	3,952	4,118	3,940	4,708	5,213	5,147	(NA)
Value of shipments (1992 dollars)	Mil. dol. . .	3,833	4,118	4,028	4,819	5,192	5,051	(NA)
Total employment.	1,000. . . .	30.8	29.0	27.9	30.7	32.3	32.1	(NA)
Production workers.	1,000. . . .	23.5	22.0	21.1	21.7	23.0	22.4	(NA)
Average hourly earnings.	Dollar . . .	11.20	11.62	12.00	11.91	11.93	12.68	(NA)
Capital expenditures	Mil. dol. . .	122.0	85.3	77.8	166.0	132.0	144.0	(NA)
PRODUCT DATA								
Value of shipments [2]	Mil. dol. . .	3,956	4,066	3,906	4,485	4,632	4,746	(NA)
Value of shipments (1992 dollars)	Mil. dol. . .	3,837	4,066	3,994	4,591	4,614	4,657	(NA)
TRADE DATA								
Value of imports.	Mil. dol. . .	435	500	608	592	815	828	975
Value of exports.	Mil. dol. . .	301	338	359	384	469	518	659

NA Not available. [1] Value of all products and services sold by establishments in the transformers, except electronic industry. [2] Value of products classified in the transformers, except electronic industry produced by all industries.

Source: U.S. Department of Commerce, Bureau of the Census, International Trade Administration (ITA).

No. 1459. Recent Trends in Household Appliances (SIC 363): 1991 to 1997

ITEM	Unit	1991	1992	1993	1994	1995	1996	1997
INDUSTRY DATA								
Value of shipments [1]	Mil. dol. . .	17,175	18,633	20,435	22,829	21,776	22,157	(NA)
3631 Household cooking equipment . .	Mil. dol. . .	2,806	2,950	3,010	3,849	3,918	3,565	(NA)
3632 Household refrigerators	Mil. dol. . .	3,613	4,232	4,463	5,149	5,200	5,605	(NA)
3633 Household laundry equipment . .	Mil. dol. . .	3,112	3,329	3,871	4,612	4,133	4,233	(NA)
3634 Electric housewares and fans . .	Mil. dol. . .	3,021	2,897	3,106	3,053	3,298	3,032	(NA)
3635 Household vacuums.	Mil. dol. . .	1,752	1,905	2,096	1,933	2,045	2,425	(NA)
3639 Home appliances, n.e.c.	Mil. dol. . .	2,872	3,320	3,889	4,233	3,183	3,297	(NA)
Value of shipments (1992 dollars)	Mil. dol. . .	17,246	18,633	20,179	22,512	21,498	21,717	(NA)
3631 Household cooking equipment . .	Mil. dol. . .	2,806	2,950	2,911	3,755	3,856	3,481	(NA)
3632 Household refrigerators	Mil. dol. . .	3,616	4,232	4,436	5,068	5,154	5,538	(NA)
3633 Household laundry equipment . .	Mil. dol. . .	3,075	3,329	3,887	4,668	4,191	4,258	(NA)
3634 Electric housewares and fans . .	Mil. dol. . .	3,061	2,897	3,087	3,065	3,328	3,066	(NA)
3635 Household vacuums.	Mil. dol. . .	1,743	1,905	2,037	1,843	1,941	2,303	(NA)
3639 Home appliances, n.e.c.	Mil. dol. . .	2,945	3,320	3,820	4,114	3,028	3,070	(NA)
Total employment.	1,000. . .	101	103	105	111	110	108	(NA)
Production workers.	1,000. . . .	81.1	83.2	85.0	90.6	87.7	87.0	(NA)
Average hourly earnings.	Dollar . . .	11.13	11.34	11.72	11.74	12.23	12.81	(NA)
Capital expenditures	Mil. dol. . .	487	556	481	517	630	721	(NA)
PRODUCT DATA								
Value of shipments [2]	Mil. dol. . .	16,089	16,789	18,027	19,841	20,095	20,581	(NA)
3631 Household cooking equipment . .	Mil. dol. . .	2,942	3,007	3,162	3,821	3,904	3,766	(NA)
3632 Household refrigerators	Mil. dol. . .	3,621	4,048	4,309	4,995	5,121	5,356	(NA)
3633 Household laundry equipment . .	Mil. dol. . .	2,860	2,995	3,299	3,671	3,541	3,699	(NA)
3634 Electric housewares and fans . .	Mil. dol. . .	2,608	2,653	2,710	2,651	2,875	2,501	(NA)
3635 Household vacuums.	Mil. dol. . .	1,834	1,809	2,015	1,788	1,907	2,341	(NA)
3639 Home appliances, n.e.c.	Mil. dol. . .	2,224	2,279	2,531	2,916	2,748	2,919	(NA)
Value of shipments (1992 dollars)	Mil. dol. . .	16,141	16,789	17,792	19,559	19,834	20,160	(NA)
3631 Household cooking equipment . .	Mil. dol. . .	2,942	3,007	3,058	3,727	3,842	3,677	(NA)
3632 Household refrigerators	Mil. dol. . .	3,625	4,048	4,283	4,916	5,075	5,292	(NA)
3633 Household laundry equipment . .	Mil. dol. . .	2,826	2,995	3,312	3,715	3,592	3,721	(NA)
3634 Electric housewares and fans . .	Mil. dol. . .	2,642	2,653	2,694	2,662	2,902	2,529	(NA)
3635 Household vacuums.	Mil. dol. . .	1,825	1,809	1,958	1,705	1,809	2,223	(NA)
3639 Home appliances, n.e.c.	Mil. dol. . .	2,281	2,279	2,486	2,834	2,614	2,717	(NA)
TRADE DATA								
Value of imports.	Mil. dol. . .	3,675	4,322	4,535	4,915	5,131	5,444	5,764
Value of exports.	Mil. dol. . .	2,066	2,307	2,482	2,568	2,621	2,791	2,958

NA Not available. [1] Value of all products and services sold by establishments in the household appliances industry. [2] Value of products classified in the household appliances industry produced by all industries.

Source: U.S. Department of Commerce, Bureau of the Census, International Trade Administration (ITA).

No. 1460. Recent Trends in Lighting Fixtures and Wiring Devices: 1991 to 1997

ITEM	Unit	1991	1992	1993	1994	1995	1996	1997
LIGHTING FIXTURES (SIC 3645, 3646, 3648)								
Industry data:								
Value of shipments [1]	Mil. dol.	6,247	6,727	7,075	8,050	8,404	8,846	(NA)
Value of shipments (1992 dollars)	Mil. dol.	6,303	6,727	7,041	7,945	8,047	8,363	(NA)
Total employment	1,000.	51.8	51.6	52.4	54.1	56.5	56.4	(NA)
Production workers	1,000.	35.5	35.9	36.5	38.5	40.5	40.8	(NA)
Average hourly earnings	Dollar	9.30	9.36	9.50	10.08	10.2	10.22	(NA)
Product data:								
Value of shipments [2]	Mil. dol.	6,194	6,720	7,150	7,806	8,297	8,596	(NA)
3645 Residential lighting fixtures.	Mil. dol.	1,409	1,681	1,896	2,041	1,990	1,988	(NA)
3646 Commercial lighting fixtures	Mil. dol.	2,955	3,047	3,122	3,294	3,620	3,777	(NA)
3648 Lighting equipment, n.e.c.	Mil. dol.	1,830	1,993	2,132	2,472	2,687	2,832	(NA)
Value of shipments (1992 dollars)	Mil. dol.	6,249	6,720	7,111	7,699	7,942	8,125	(NA)
3645 Residential lighting fixtures.	Mil. dol.	1,423	1,681	1,861	1,977	1,886	1,868	(NA)
3646 Commercial lighting fixtures	Mil. dol.	2,984	3,047	3,110	3,242	3,435	3,527	(NA)
3648 Lighting equipment, n.e.c.	Mil. dol.	1,841	1,993	2,141	2,480	2,622	2,730	(NA)
WIRING DEVICES (SIC 3643, 3644)								
Industry data:								
Value of shipments (1992 dollars)	Mil. dol.	7,175	7,804	7,905	8,402	8,354	8,651	(NA)
3643 Wiring devices, current	Mil. dol.	4,316	4,585	4,585	4,695	4,827	5,083	(NA)
3644 Wiring goods, noncurrent.	Mil. dol.	2,859	3,220	3,320	3,707	3,527	3,568	(NA)

NA Not available. [1] Value of all products and services sold by establishments in this industry. [2] Value of products classified in this industry produced by all industries.

Source: U.S. Department of Commerce, Bureau of the Census, International Trade Administration (ITA).

No. 1461. Recent Trends in Household Audio and Video Equipment (SIC 3651): 1991 to 1997

ITEM	Unit	1991	1992	1993	1994	1995	1996	1997
INDUSTRY DATA								
Value of shipments [1]	Mil. dol.	7,907	8,794	9,159	10,102	11,600	8,988	(NA)
Value of shipments (1992 dollars)	Mil. dol.	7,805	8,794	9,346	10,308	12,008	9,285	(NA)
Total employment	1,000.	31.4	31.3	31.2	28.5	33.4	31.0	(NA)
Production workers	1,000.	22.0	22.4	22.6	21.7	24.6	23.3	(NA)
Average hourly earnings	Dollar	9.39	9.55	9.60	9.74	10.05	10.17	(NA)
Capital expenditures	Mil. dol.	295	253	212	219	284	276	(NA)
PRODUCT DATA								
Value of shipments [2]	Mil. dol.	7,154	7,664	7,915	8,697	9,294	9,274	(NA)
Value of shipments (1992 dollars)	Mil. dol.	7,062	7,664	8,076	8,874	9,621	9,581	(NA)
TRADE DATA								
Value of imports	Mil. dol.	14,511	15,585	16,412	19,246	20,792	19,221	19,570
Value of exports	Mil. dol.	2,306	2,499	2,721	3,158	3,394	3,603	4,159

NA Not available. [1] Value of all products and services sold by establishments in the household audio and video equipment industry. [2] Value of products classified in the household audio and video equipment industry produced by all industries.

Source: U.S. Department of Commerce, Bureau of the Census, International Trade Administration (ITA).

No. 1462. Recent Trends in Telecommunications Equipment (SIC 3661, 3663): 1991 to 1997

ITEM	Unit	1991	1992	1993	1994	1995	1996	1997
INDUSTRY DATA								
Value of shipments [1]	Mil. dol.	35,719	40,031	42,190	49,371	54,915	63,807	(NA)
Value of shipments (1992 dollars)	Mil. dol.	36,178	40,031	41,736	48,498	54,166	62,619	(NA)
Total employment	1,000.	217	216	208	220	216	234	(NA)
Production workers	1,000.	99	103	95	100	103	107	(NA)
Average hourly earnings	Dollar	13.52	14.28	14.35	14.25	15.69	16.33	(NA)
Capital expenditures	Mil. dol.	1,080	1,317	1,445	1,518	1,899	2,088	(NA)
PRODUCT DATA								
Value of shipments [2]	Mil. dol.	32,531	36,106	38,151	45,495	52,481	60,706	(NA)
Value of shipments (1992 dollars)	Mil. dol.	32,973	36,106	37,742	44,695	51,762	59,582	(NA)
TRADE DATA								
Value of imports	Mil. dol.	6,370	7,307	8,066	10,218	10,883	11,895	12,981
Value of exports	Mil. dol.	5,095	6,199	7,884	9,904	12,341	12,773	15,674

NA Not available. [1] Value of all products and services sold by establishments in the telecommunications equipment industry. [2] Value of products classified in the telecommunications equipment industry produced by all industries.

Source: U.S. Department of Commerce, Bureau of the Census, International Trade Administration (ITA).

No. 1463. Recent Trends in Telephone and Telegraph Apparatus, and Radio and TV Communications Equipment: 1991 to 1997

ITEM	Unit	1991	1992	1993	1994	1995	1996	1997
TELEPHONE AND TELEGRAPH APPARATUS (SIC 3661)								
Industry data:								
Value of shipments [1]	Mil. dol. . .	17,488	20,510	21,540	23,243	26,183	31,727	(NA)
Value of shipments (1992 dollars) . . .	Mil. dol. . .	17,384	20,510	21,411	23,081	26,052	31,412	(NA)
Total employment	1,000. .	94.0	91.1	84.9	86.5	89.3	93.6	(NA)
Production workers	1,000. .	46.0	44.8	38.5	41.3	40.8	38.1	(NA)
Average hourly earnings	Dollar	14.61	14.90	15.34	15.35	16.65	16.57	(NA)
Capital expenditures	Mil. dol. . .	471	615	595	662	742	731	(NA)
Product data:								
Value of shipments [2]	Mil. dol. . .	15,284	18,328	19,589	21,661	24,816	30,516	(NA)
Value of shipments (1992 dollars) . . .	Mil. dol. . .	15,193	18,328	19,472	21,510	24,692	30,214	(NA)
RADIO AND TV COMMUNICATIONS EQUIPMENT (SIC 3663)								
Industry data:								
Value of shipments [1]	Mil. dol. . .	18,231	19,521	20,650	26,128	28,733	32,080	(NA)
Value of shipments (1992 dollars) . . .	Mil. dol. . .	18,795	19,521	20,325	25,416	28,114	31,206	(NA)
Total employment	1,000. .	123	125	123	133	127	140	(NA)
Production workers	1,000. .	52.7	58.6	56.0	59.0	61.7	68.9	(NA)
Average hourly earnings	Dollar	12.63	13.82	13.66	13.51	15.08	16.18	(NA)
Capital expenditures	Mil. dol. . .	609	702	851	856	1,157	1,357	(NA)
Product data:								
Value of shipments [2]	Mil. dol. . .	17,247	17,778	18,562	23,834	27,665	30,190	(NA)
Value of shipments (1992 dollars) . . .	Mil. dol. . .	17,781	17,778	18,269	23,185	27,069	29,368	(NA)

NA Not available.   [1] Value of all products and services sold by establishments in this industry.   [2] Value of products classified in this industry produced by all industries.

Source: U.S. Department of Commerce, Bureau of the Census, International Trade Administration (ITA).

No. 1464. Recent Trends in Electronic Components and Accessories (SIC 367): 1991 to 1997

ITEM	Unit	1991	1992	1993	1994	1995	1996	1997
INDUSTRY DATA								
Value of shipments [1]	Mil. dol. . .	67,547	73,642	81,236	97,131	120,129	127,996	(NA)
Value of shipments (1992 dollars)	Mil. dol. . .	66,557	73,642	81,129	97,838	126,734	144,213	(NA)
Total employment	1,000. . .	537	530	531	551	584	588	(NA)
Production workers	1,000. . .	320	317	321	340	364	368	(NA)
Average hourly earnings	Dollar	10.33	10.83	10.98	11.14	11.41	11.70	(NA)
PRODUCT DATA								
Value of shipments [2]	Mil. dol. . .	62,766	71,372	77,840	92,719	115,202	126,997	(NA)
Value of shipments (1992 dollars)	Mil. dol. . .	61,920	71,372	77,739	93,343	121,272	142,543	(NA)
TRADE DATA								
Value of imports	Mil. dol. . .	20,648	23,116	27,963	36,086	51,505	49,293	51,458
Value of exports	Mil. dol. . .	16,761	17,381	20,144	26,178	33,440	35,048	42,695

NA Not available.   [1] Value of all products and services sold by establishments in the electronic components and accessories industry.   [2] Value of products classified in the electronic components and accessories industry produced by all industries.

Source: U.S. Department of Commerce, Bureau of the Census, International Trade Administration (ITA).

No. 1465. Recent Trends in Electron Tubes (SIC 3671): 1991 to 1997

ITEM	Unit	1991	1992	1993	1994	1995	1996	1997
INDUSTRY DATA								
Value of shipments [1]	Mil. dol. . .	2,659	3,145	3,052	3,148	3,500	3,779	(NA)
Value of shipments (1992 dollars)	Mil. dol. . .	2,618	3,145	3,085	3,126	3,434	3,701	(NA)
Total employment	1,000. . .	22.8	22.2	20.2	20.4	21.6	23.3	(NA)
Production workers	1,000. . .	16.6	16.8	15.3	15.8	16.6	17.9	(NA)
Average hourly earnings	Dollar	12.9	13.21	13.73	13.25	13.1	12.95	(NA)
Capital expenditures	Mil. dol. . .	81.0	61.7	85.5	132.0	142.0	181.0	(NA)
PRODUCT DATA								
Value of shipments [2]	Mil. dol. . .	2,659	3,357	3,330	3,561	3,894	4,178	(NA)
Value of shipments (1992 dollars)	Mil. dol. . .	2,617	3,357	3,367	3,536	3,822	4,092	(NA)
TRADE DATA								
Value of imports	Mil. dol. . .	817	928	990	1,218	1,390	1,239	1,123
Value of exports	Mil. dol. . .	759	771	929	1,232	1,541	1,720	2,258

NA Not available.   [1] Value of all products and services sold by establishments in the electron tubes industry.   [2] Value of products classified in the electron tubes industry produced by all industries.

Source: U.S. Department of Commerce, Bureau of the Census, International Trade Administration (ITA).

No. 1466. Recent Trends in Printed Circuit Boards and Semiconductors and Related Devices: 1991 to 1997

ITEM	Unit	1991	1992	1993	1994	1995	1996	1997
PRINTED CIRCUIT BOARDS (SIC 3672)								
Industry data:								
Value of shipments [1]	Mil. dol.	6,578	7,320	7,378	8,416	9,498	10,702	(NA)
Value of shipments (1992 dollars)	Mil. dol.	6,532	7,320	7,551	8,803	9,924	11,067	(NA)
Total employment	1,000.	72.2	76.0	73.6	76.9	81.6	88.3	(NA)
Production workers	1,000.	48.1	51.0	50.5	54.0	59.6	63.9	(NA)
Average hourly earnings	Dollar	9.92	10.16	10.58	10.49	10.36	10.75	(NA)
Capital expenditures	Mil. dol.	326	318	283	381	453	585	(NA)
Product data:								
Value of shipments [2]	Mil. dol.	5,899	6,293	6,930	7,555	8,543	8,949	(NA)
Value of shipments (1992 dollars)	Mil. dol.	5,858	6,293	7,093	7,902	8,926	9,254	(NA)
Trade data:								
Value of imports	Mil. dol.	1,904	1,243	1,289	1,468	1,840	1,849	2,071
Value of exports	Mil. dol.	1,374	1,092	973	1,377	1,651	1,694	2,007
SEMICONDUCTORS AND RELATED DEVICES (SIC 3674)								
Industry data:								
Value of shipments [1]	Mil. dol.	30,721	32,191	35,152	47,265	65,922	71,413	(NA)
Value of shipments (1992 dollars)	Mil. dol.	29,230	32,191	35,222	47,790	71,810	85,833	(NA)
Total employment	1,000.	181	172	163	183	192	190	(NA)
Production workers	1,000.	88.1	84.8	82.2	92.9	98.1	96.2	(NA)
Average hourly earnings	Dollar	12.68	13.55	14.08	14.46	14.89	15.29	(NA)
Product data:								
Value of shipments [2]	Mil. dol.	27,438	29,391	33,689	44,064	60,330	67,070	(NA)
Value of shipments (1992 dollars)	Mil. dol.	26,106	29,391	33,757	44,554	65,719	80,613	(NA)
Trade data:								
Value of imports	Mil. dol.	12,928	15,275	19,244	25,670	38,618	36,256	36,267
Value of exports	Mil. dol.	10,831	11,465	13,744	17,991	23,189	24,001	28,861

NA Not available.   [1] Value of all products and services sold by establishments in this industry.   [2] Value of products classified in this industry produced by all industries.

Source: U.S. Department of Commerce, Bureau of the Census, International Trade Administration (ITA).

No. 1467. Recent Trends in Passive Components (SIC 3675-9): 1991 to 1997

ITEM	Unit	1991	1992	1993	1994	1995	1996	1997
INDUSTRY DATA								
Value of shipments [1]	Mil. dol.	27,588	30,986	35,656	38,302	41,209	42,102	(NA)
Value of shipments (1992 dollars)	Mil. dol.	28,177	30,986	35,270	38,119	41,565	43,612	(NA)
Total employment	1,000.	261	260	275	271	290	287	(NA)
Production workers	1,000.	168	165	173	177	190	190	(NA)
Average hourly earnings	Dollar	8.99	9.45	9.48	9.53	9.86	10.16	(NA)
Capital expenditures	Mil. dol.	833	983	1,314	1,248	1,436	1,587	(NA)
PRODUCT DATA								
Value of shipments [2]	Mil. dol.	26,771	32,330	33,892	37,540	42,435	46,800	(NA)
Value of shipments (1992 dollars)	Mil. dol.	27,339	32,330	33,523	37,350	42,805	48,584	(NA)
TRADE DATA								
Value of imports	Mil. dol.	5,000	5,671	6,440	7,730	9,658	9,949	11,997
Value of exports	Mil. dol.	3,797	4,053	4,498	5,578	7,060	7,633	9,568

NA Not available.   [1] Value of all products and services sold by establishments in the passive components industry.   [2] Value of products classified in the passive components industry produced by all industries.

Source: U.S. Department of Commerce, Bureau of the Census, International Trade Administration (ITA).

No. 1468. Recent Trends in Motor Vehicles and Car Bodies (SIC 3711): 1991 to 1997

ITEM	Unit	1991	1992	1993	1994	1995	1996	1997
INDUSTRY DATA								
Value of shipments [1]	Mil. dol.	135,881	151,682	167,826	197,514	201,171	200,704	(NA)
Value of shipments (1992 dollars)	Mil. dol.	140,228	151,682	162,151	184,076	185,753	183,292	(NA)
Total employment	1,000.	224	228	224	234	238	225	(NA)
Production workers	1,000.	182	193	191	203	208	196	(NA)
Average hourly earnings	Dollar	21.07	21.96	22.61	23.39	24.48	24.60	(NA)
Capital expenditures	Mil. dol.	3,447	2,988	4,034	4,247	4,521	4,382	(NA)
PRODUCT DATA								
Value of shipments [2]	Mil. dol.	128,754	147,447	163,324	194,977	198,252	198,112	(NA)
Value of shipments (1992 dollars)	Mil. dol.	132,873	147,447	157,801	181,712	183,058	180,924	(NA)
TRADE DATA								
Value of imports	Mil. dol.	58,355	59,659	67,613	78,614	83,837	86,772	92,536
Value of exports	Mil. dol.	15,058	17,447	18,270	20,973	21,390	22,793	24,363

NA Not available.   [1] Value of all products and services sold by establishments in the motor vehicles and car bodies industry.   [2] Value of products classified in the motor vehicles and car bodies industry produced by all industries.

Source: U.S. Department of Commerce, Bureau of the Census, International Trade Administration (ITA).

No. 1469. Recent Trends in Aerospace (SIC 372, 376): 1991 to 1997

ITEM	Unit	1991	1992	1993	1994	1995	1996	1997
INDUSTRY DATA								
Value of shipments [1]	Mil. dol.	132,182	131,367	116,346	103,316	100,062	101,322	(NA)
Value of shipments (1992 dollars)	Mil. dol.	137,510	131,367	113,815	98,831	94,046	93,799	(NA)
Total employment	1,000.	752	694	612	525	471	458	(NA)
Production workers	1,000.	362	331	279	241	221	219	(NA)
Average hourly earnings	Dollar	16.75	18.74	19.05	20.00	20.37	21.33	(NA)
Capital expenditures	Mil. dol.	3,400	3,837	2,725	2,363	2,114	2,513	(NA)
PRODUCT DATA								
Value of shipments [2]	Mil. dol.	124,109	122,800	110,312	97,156	95,311	96,222	(NA)
Value of shipments (1992 dollars)	Mil. dol.	129,081	122,800	107,905	92,937	89,576	88,974	(NA)
TRADE DATA								
Value of imports	Mil. dol.	12,531	13,026	11,648	11,802	11,045	13,241	17,376
Value of exports	Mil. dol.	42,374	43,594	37,934	35,789	31,331	38,580	48,181

NA Not available. [1] Value of all products and services sold by establishments in the aerospace industry. [2] Value of products classified in the aerospace industry produced by all industries.

Source: U.S. Department of Commerce, Bureau of the Census, International Trade Administration (ITA).

No. 1470. Recent Trends in Aircraft and Aircraft Engines and Engine Parts: 1991 to 1997

ITEM	Unit	1991	1992	1993	1994	1995	1996	1997
AIRCRAFT (SIC 3721)								
Industry data:								
Value of shipments [1]	Mil. dol.	58,486	62,940	55,120	50,970	47,028	47,313	(NA)
Value of shipments (1992 dollars)	Mil. dol.	60,796	62,940	53,775	48,131	42,909	41,870	(NA)
Total employment	1,000.	260	265	241	218	189	188	(NA)
Production workers	1,000.	125	122	104	93	84	85	(NA)
Average hourly earnings	Dollar	17.86	20.00	19.90	20.75	22.15	23.12	(NA)
Capital expenditures	Mil. dol.	1,043	1,660	1,154	877	586	622	(NA)
Product data:								
Value of shipments [2]	Mil. dol.	52,514	56,569	51,006	46,814	44,457	44,584	(NA)
Value of shipments (1992 dollars)	Mil. dol.	54,588	56,569	49,762	44,206	40,563	39,455	(NA)
Trade data:								
Value of imports	Mil. dol.	3,438	3,921	3,738	3,809	3,557	3,948	4,669
Value of exports	Mil. dol.	24,173	26,419	21,306	18,831	13,614	18,970	25,509
AIRCRAFT ENGINES AND ENGINE PARTS (SIC 3724)								
Industry data:								
Value of shipments [1]	Mil. dol.	22,901	22,408	18,946	16,584	17,519	18,769	(NA)
Value of shipments (1992 dollars)	Mil. dol.	24,157	22,408	18,538	15,855	16,450	17,315	(NA)
Total employment	1,000.	123	120	103	84	76	75	(NA)
Production workers	1,000.	67.2	66.5	53.6	45.5	41.9	41.4	(NA)
Average hourly earnings	Dollar	15.60	17.25	17.15	18.79	18.17	19.98	(NA)
Capital expenditures	Mil. dol.	768	598	440	435	475	485	(NA)
Product data:								
Value of shipments [2]	Mil. dol.	21,315	20,933	17,995	15,218	15,811	17,017	(NA)
Value of shipments (1992 dollars)	Mil. dol.	22,484	20,933	17,608	14,549	14,846	15,698	(NA)
Trade data:								
Value of imports	Mil. dol.	5,100	5,864	5,366	5,430	4,875	5,829	7,867
Value of exports	Mil. dol.	7,025	6,674	6,243	6,451	6,130	6,798	8,542

NA Not available. [1] Value of all products and services sold by establishments in this industry. [2] Value of products classified in this industry produced by all industries.

Source: U.S. Department of Commerce, Bureau of the Census, International Trade Administration (ITA).

No. 1471. Recent Trends in Aircraft Parts and Equipment, n.e.c. (SIC 3728): 1991 to 1997

ITEM	Unit	1991	1992	1993	1994	1995	1996	1997
INDUSTRY DATA								
Value of shipments [1]	Mil. dol.	21,691	19,511	18,264	17,049	16,848	17,312	(NA)
Value of shipments (1992 dollars)	Mil. dol.	22,713	19,511	17,750	16,206	15,939	16,029	(NA)
Total employment	1,000.	189	163	139	122	116	113	(NA)
Production workers	1,000.	107.0	92.0	78.4	66.1	64.0	64.5	(NA)
Average hourly earnings	Dollar	15.09	16.71	18.37	19.20	19.73	19.98	(NA)
Capital expenditures	Mil. dol.	1,003	1,112	713	656	673	916	(NA)
PRODUCT DATA								
Value of shipments [2]	Mil. dol.	25,288	21,940	18,684	17,710	17,701	18,832	(NA)
Value of shipments (1992 dollars)	Mil. dol.	26,480	21,940	18,157	16,835	16,747	17,437	(NA)
TRADE DATA								
Value of imports	Mil. dol.	3,888	3,132	2,437	2,476	2,515	3,337	4,687
Value of exports	Mil. dol.	9,953	9,050	9,133	9,472	10,070	11,497	12,973

NA Not available. [1] Value of all products and services sold by establishments in the aircraft parts and equipment, n.e.c. industry. [2] Value of products classified in the aircraft parts and equipment, n.e.c. industry produced by all industries.

Source: U.S. Department of Commerce, Bureau of the Census, International Trade Administration (ITA).

No. 1472. Recent Trends in Ship Building and Repairing (SIC 3731): 1991 to 1997

ITEM	Unit	1991	1992	1993	1994	1995	1996	1997
INDUSTRY DATA								
Value of shipments [1]	Mil. dol. . .	10,935	10,601	9,964	9,865	9,613	9,811	(NA)
Value of shipments (1992 dollars)	Mil. dol. . .	11,068	10,601	9,436	9,017	8,819	8,807	(NA)
Total employment	1,000. . . .	122	118	112	102	95	92	(NA)
Production workers	1,000. . . .	90.9	87.0	81.9	76.0	70.4	68.4	(NA)
Average hourly earnings	Dollar . . .	12.79	13.05	13.45	14.00	14.63	14.39	(NA)
Capital expenditures	Mil. dol. . .	180	128	156	166	232	242	(NA)
PRODUCT DATA								
Value of shipments [2]	Mil. dol. . .	10,700	10,381	9,801	9,877	9,590	9,722	(NA)
Value of shipments (1992 dollars)	Mil. dol. . .	10,830	10,381	9,282	9,028	8,798	8,727	(NA)
TRADE DATA								
Value of imports	Mil. dol. . .	14.4	50.9	517.0	12.4	29.4	54.0	30.1
Value of exports	Mil. dol. . .	321	652	379	595	483	346	610.7

NA Not available.   [1] Value of all products and services sold by establishments in the ship building and repairing industry.   [2] Value of products classified in the ship building and repairing industry produced by all industries.

Source: U.S. Department of Commerce, Bureau of the Census, International Trade Administration (ITA).

No. 1473. Recent Trends in Boat Building and Repairing (SIC 3732): 1991 to 1997

ITEM	Unit	1991	1992	1993	1994	1995	1996	1997
INDUSTRY DATA								
Value of shipments [1]	Mil. dol. . .	3,705	4,648	4,975	5,334	5,597	5,823	(NA)
Value of shipments (1992 dollars)	Mil. dol. . .	3,800	4,648	4,887	5,154	5,255	5,284	(NA)
Total employment	1,000. . . .	41.0	44.5	47.0	47.6	47.9	49.2	(NA)
Production workers	1,000. . . .	31.9	34.6	36.8	38.4	38.9	40.1	(NA)
Average hourly earnings	Dollar . . .	9.04	9.58	9.57	9.70	10.49	10.57	(NA)
Capital expenditures	Mil. dol. . .	40.5	63.6	83.2	98.9	89.0	109.0	(NA)
PRODUCT DATA								
Value of shipments [2]	Mil. dol. . .	3,518	4,331	4,632	4,887	5,072	5,214	(NA)
Value of shipments (1992 dollars)	Mil. dol. . .	3,608	4,331	4,550	4,722	4,763	4,732	(NA)
TRADE DATA								
Value of imports	Mil. dol. . .	207	257	425	564	807	997	814
Value of exports	Mil. dol. . .	774	714	534	507	658	621	673

NA Not available.   [1] Value of all products and services sold by establishments in the boat building and repairing industry.   [2] Value of products classified in the boat building and repairing industry produced by all industries.

Source: U.S. Department of Commerce, Bureau of the Census, International Trade Administration (ITA).

No. 1474. Recent Trends in Motorcycles, Bicycles, and Parts (SIC 3751): 1991 to 1997

ITEM	Unit	1991	1992	1993	1994	1995	1996	1997
INDUSTRY DATA								
Value of shipments [1]	Mil. dol. . .	1,582	2,134	2,566	2,632	2,833	3,094	(NA)
Value of shipments (1992 dollars)	Mil. dol. . .	1,615	2,134	2,513	2,546	2,663	2,865	(NA)
Total employment	1,000. . . .	9.5	12.8	14.1	15.7	16.1	18.4	(NA)
Production workers	1,000. . . .	7.3	9.9	10.5	11.7	12.0	13.8	(NA)
Average hourly earnings	Dollar . . .	11.73	12.18	13.53	14.50	13.91	13.85	(NA)
Capital expenditures	Mil. dol. . .	56.6	62.0	50.6	92.3	118.0	131.0	(NA)
PRODUCT DATA								
Value of shipments [2]	Mil. dol. . .	2,112	2,153	2,640	2,549	2,654	2,839	(NA)
Value of shipments (1992 dollars)	Mil. dol. . .	2,155	2,153	2,585	2,465	2,494	2,629	(NA)
TRADE DATA								
Value of imports	Mil. dol. . .	1,329	1,537	1,717	1,763	2,130	2,015	2,084
Value of exports	Mil. dol. . .	615	671	703	711	850	906	977

NA Not available.   [1] Value of all products and services sold by establishments in the motorcycles, bicycles, and parts industry.   [2] Value of products classified in the motorcycles, bicycles, and parts industry produced by all industries.

Source: U.S. Department of Commerce, Bureau of the Census, International Trade Administration (ITA).

No. 1475. Recent Trends in Guided Missiles and Space Vehicles and Space Propulsion Units and Parts: 1991 to 1997

ITEM	Unit	1991	1992	1993	1994	1995	1996	1997
GUIDED MISSILES AND SPACE VEHICLES (SIC 3761)								
Industry data:								
Value of shipments [1]	Mil. dol.	23,513	19,423	15,800	13,954	14,315	13,777	(NA)
Value of shipments (1992 dollars)	Mil. dol.	24,165	19,423	15,628	13,899	14,373	14,262	(NA)
Total employment	1,000.	138.0	97.7	86.6	68.5	60.8	55.7	(NA)
Production workers	1,000.	45.1	30.1	27.6	23.8	20.0	18.6	(NA)
Average hourly earnings	Dollar	18.94	22.58	20.88	21.30	20.65	21.81	(NA)
Capital expenditures	Mil. dol.	452	313	308	297	294	367	(NA)
Product data:								
Value of shipments [2]	Mil. dol.	16,075	13,972	13,452	10,983	11,756	10,536	(NA)
Value of shipments (1992 dollars)	Mil. dol.	16,521	13,972	13,306	10,939	11,804	10,907	(NA)
Trade data:								
Value of imports	Mil. dol.	1.8	4.1	5.2	1.6	2.7	1.1	0.2
Value of exports	Mil. dol.	318	599	507	364	718	608	462
SPACE PROPULSION UNITS AND PARTS (SIC 3764)								
Industry data:								
Value of shipments [1]	Mil. dol.	3,676	5,121	6,201	3,374	2,954	2,715	(NA)
Value of shipments (1992 dollars)	Mil. dol.	3,778	5,121	6,134	3,360	2,968	2,819	(NA)
Total employment	1,000.	28.0	32.0	29.2	22.8	19.6	17.2	(NA)
Production workers	1,000.	9.5	13.2	8.9	7.8	6.7	5.5	(NA)
Average hourly earnings	Dollar	18.98	23.81	22.03	22.10	19.6	20.61	(NA)
Capital expenditures	Mil. dol.	103.0	121.0	85.4	68.9	48.8	77.5	(NA)
Product data:								
Value of shipments [2]	Mil. dol.	4,530	5,207	5,862	3,705	2,984	2,803	(NA)
Value of shipments (1992 dollars)	Mil. dol.	4,656	5,207	5,799	3,690	2,999	2,911	(NA)
Trade data:								
Value of imports	Mil. dol.	0.5	0.4	0.2	(NA)	0.1	14.6	43.1
Value of exports	Mil. dol.	6.7	12.6	1.1	1.6	40.1	22.3	5.4

NA Not available. [1] Value of all products and services sold by establishments in this industry. [2] Value of products classified in this industry produced by all industries.

Source: U.S. Department of Commerce, Bureau of the Census, International Trade Administration (ITA).

No. 1476. Recent Trends in Space Vehicle Equipment, n.e.c. (SIC 3769): 1991 to 1997

ITEM	Unit	1991	1992	1993	1994	1995	1996	1997
INDUSTRY DATA								
Value of shipments [1]	Mil. dol.	1,917	1,964	2,015	1,386	1,398	1,436	(NA)
Value of shipments (1992 dollars)	Mil. dol.	1,901	1,964	1,991	1,381	1,406	1,504	(NA)
Total employment	1,000.	14.3	16.2	12.3	9.1	8.8	8.1	(NA)
Production workers	1,000.	7.7	6.8	5.6	4.7	4.6	4.8	(NA)
Average hourly earnings	Dollar	18.27	18.04	19.95	20.29	21.49	20.98	(NA)
Capital expenditures	Mil. dol.	31.5	33.8	25.3	29.1	37.0	45.0	(NA)
PRODUCT DATA								
Value of shipments [2]	Mil. dol.	4,387	4,179	3,313	2,727	2,602	2,451	(NA)
Value of shipments (1992 dollars)	Mil. dol.	4,352	4,179	3,273	2,718	2,618	2,567	(NA)
TRADE DATA								
Value of imports	Mil. dol.	103	104	102	86	96	112	110
Value of exports	Mil. dol.	899	839	745	669	759	684	690

NA Not available. [1] Value of all products and services sold by establishments in the space vehicle equipment, n.e.c. industry. [2] Value of products classified in the space vehicle equipment, n.e.c., industry produced by all industries.

Source: U.S. Department of Commerce, Bureau of the Census, International Trade Administration (ITA).

No. 1477. Recent Trends in Search and Navigation Equipment (SIC 3812): 1991 to 1997

ITEM	Unit	1991	1992	1993	1994	1995	1996	1997
INDUSTRY DATA								
Value of shipments [1]	Mil. dol.	38,612	35,039	33,546	30,110	32,000	30,371	(NA)
Value of shipments (1992 dollars)	Mil. dol.	39,360	35,039	32,856	29,204	30,506	28,925	(NA)
Total employment	1,000.	298	253	225	199	200	186	(NA)
Production workers	1,000.	119.0	103.0	88.5	80.3	71.6	67.8	(NA)
Average hourly earnings	Dollar	16.74	17.28	18.79	18.84	19.95	20.31	(NA)
Capital expenditures	Mil. dol.	909	849	706	688	730	1,223	(NA)
PRODUCT DATA								
Value of shipments [2]	Mil. dol.	34,173	34,171	31,203	29,160	27,755	26,653	(NA)
Value of shipments (1992 dollars)	Mil. dol.	34,835	34,171	30,561	28,283	26,458	25,383	(NA)
TRADE DATA								
Value of imports	Mil. dol.	955	965	862	863	994	1,044	1,273
Value of exports	Mil. dol.	2,241	2,133	2,105	2,031	1,978	2,046	2,515

NA Not available. [1] Value of all products and services sold by establishments in the search and navigation equipment industry. [2] Value of products classified in the search and navigation equipment industry produced by all industries.

Source: U.S. Department of Commerce, Bureau of the Census, International Trade Administration (ITA).

No. 1478. Recent Trends in Laboratory Instruments (SIC 3821, 3826, 3827): 1991 to 1997

ITEM	Unit	1991	1992	1993	1994	1995	1996	1997
INDUSTRY DATA								
Value of shipments [1]	Mil. dol.	9,534	9,823	10,384	11,119	12,254	13,039	(NA)
3821 Lab apparatus and furniture.	Mil. dol.	1,840	2,111	2,173	2,453	2,349	2,455	(NA)
3826 Analytical instruments.	Mil. dol.	5,236	5,223	5,657	6,023	7,178	7,714	(NA)
3827 Optical instruments	Mil. dol.	2,458	2,489	2,554	2,643	2,727	2,870	(NA)
Value of shipments (1992 dollars)	Mil. dol.	9,787	9,823	10,229	10,842	11,761	12,310	(NA)
3821 Lab apparatus and furniture.	Mil. dol.	1,929	2,111	2,089	2,303	2,145	2,192	(NA)
3826 Analytical instruments.	Mil. dol.	5,342	5,223	5,596	5,888	6,915	7,340	(NA)
3827 Optical instruments	Mil. dol.	2,516	2,489	2,544	2,651	2,700	2,779	(NA)
Total employment	1,000.	76.5	78.2	78.0	76.6	76.8	77.4	(NA)
3821 Lab apparatus and furniture.	1,000.	15.2	17.8	16.9	18.5	17.4	17.6	(NA)
3826 Analytical instruments.	1,000.	38.2	40.1	40.3	38.7	40.2	40.8	(NA)
3827 Optical instruments	1,000.	23.1	20.3	20.8	19.4	19.2	19.0	(NA)
Production workers	1,000.	33.6	34.3	34.0	35.2	35.1	34.5	(NA)
3821 Lab apparatus and furniture.	1,000.	7.1	9.0	8.2	9.2	8.9	8.7	(NA)
3826 Analytical instruments.	1,000.	15.1	15.3	15.5	15.2	15.0	15.3	(NA)
3827 Optical instruments	1,000.	11.4	10.0	10.3	10.8	11.2	10.5	(NA)
Average hourly earnings.	Dollar	12.42	12.74	13.06	13.47	14.14	14.65	(NA)
3821 Lab apparatus and furniture.	Dollar	11.43	11.58	11.86	12.28	12.35	12.32	(NA)
3826 Analytical instruments	Dollar	12.33	13.35	13.51	14.14	15.13	15.98	(NA)
3827 Optical instruments.	Dollar	13.15	12.90	13.35	13.53	14.24	14.75	(NA)
Capital expenditures	Mil. dol.	323	355	330	325	371	401	(NA)
3821 Lab apparatus and furniture.	Mil. dol.	52.2	55.8	42.9	41.2	45.0	48.0	(NA)
3826 Analytical instruments.	Mil. dol.	194.0	228.0	213.0	178.0	197.0	225.0	(NA)
3827 Optical instruments	Mil. dol.	76.8	71.4	74.5	106.0	129.0	128.0	(NA)
PRODUCT DATA								
Value of shipments [2]	Mil. dol.	8,464	9,481	9,654	10,014	11,062	11,451	(NA)
3821 Lab apparatus and furniture.	Mil. dol.	1,673	1,846	1,833	1,941	1,982	2,119	(NA)
3826 Analytical instruments.	Mil. dol.	4,763	5,126	5,267	5,647	6,527	6,650	(NA)
3827 Optical instruments	Mil. dol.	2,029	2,509	2,554	2,425	2,554	2,682	(NA)
Value of shipments (1992 dollars)	Mil. dol.	8,690	9,481	9,516	9,775	10,626	10,815	(NA)
3821 Lab apparatus and furniture.	Mil. dol.	1,754	1,846	1,762	1,823	1,810	1,892	(NA)
3826 Analytical instruments.	Mil. dol.	4,860	5,126	5,210	5,520	6,288	6,327	(NA)
3827 Optical instruments	Mil. dol.	2,077	2,509	2,544	2,432	2,528	2,596	(NA)
TRADE DATA								
Value of imports	Mil. dol.	1,835	1,998	2,069	2,367	2,761	3,095	3,413
3821 Lab apparatus and furniture.	Mil. dol.	121	116	126	181	202	195	111
3826 Analytical instruments.	Mil. dol.	799	897	897	994	1,129	1,298	1,474
3827 Optical instruments	Mil. dol.	915	985	1,046	1,192	1,430	1,601	1,827
Value of exports	Mil. dol.	2,975	3,104	3,263	3,585	4,114	4,565	5,279
3821 Lab apparatus and furniture.	Mil. dol.	240	216	253	299	336	327	362
3826 Analytical instruments.	Mil. dol.	1,784	1,927	2,094	2,227	2,528	2,683	2,923
3827 Optical instruments	Mil. dol.	951	961	917	1,059	1,250	1,555	1,993

NA Not available. [1] Value of all products and services sold by establishments in the laboratory instruments industry. [2] Value of products classified in the laboratory instruments industry produced by all industries.

Source: U.S. Department of Commerce, Bureau of the Census, International Trade Administration (ITA).

No. 1479. Recent Trends in Measuring and Controlling Instruments (SIC 3822, 3823, 3824, 3829): 1991 to 1997

ITEM	Unit	1991	1992	1993	1994	1995	1996	1997
INDUSTRY DATA								
Value of shipments [1]	Mil. dol.	15,270	16,081	16,279	17,689	19,059	20,331	(NA)
3822 Environmental controls	Mil. dol.	2,317	2,594	2,813	2,896	3,175	3,488	(NA)
3823 Process controls	Mil. dol.	6,096	6,470	6,356	7,038	7,764	8,271	(NA)
3824 Fluid meters and devices	Mil. dol.	2,320	2,601	2,824	3,300	3,260	3,294	(NA)
3829 Instruments, n.e.c.	Mil. dol.	4,538	4,416	4,287	4,456	4,861	5,278	(NA)
Value of shipments (1992 dollars)	Mil. dol.	15,617	16,081	15,871	17,062	18,250	19,102	(NA)
3822 Environmental controls	Mil. dol.	2,357	2,594	2,614	2,630	2,865	3,108	(NA)
3823 Process controls	Mil. dol.	6,239	6,470	6,219	6,800	7,472	7,744	(NA)
3824 Fluid meters and devices	Mil. dol.	2,372	2,601	2,818	3,290	3,243	3,275	(NA)
3829 Instruments, n.e.c.	Mil. dol.	4,650	4,416	4,219	4,343	4,669	4,974	(NA)
Total employment	1,000.	128	129	126	126	132	132	(NA)
3822 Environmental controls	1,000.	23.2	24.7	24.4	24.5	27.4	26.5	(NA)
3823 Process controls	1,000.	52.0	50.5	50.0	50.6	52.2	51.8	(NA)
3824 Fluid meters and devices	1,000.	13.2	16.2	15.8	16.6	16.5	16.2	(NA)
3829 Instruments, n.e.c.	1,000.	39.9	37.6	35.7	34.5	35.9	37.0	(NA)
Production workers	1,000.	68.3	71.3	69.4	71.3	75.4	73.7	(NA)
3822 Environmental controls	1,000.	15.3	16.8	17.2	17.2	18.2	17.8	(NA)
3823 Process controls	1,000.	24.4	24.1	23.6	24.4	25.8	24.6	(NA)
3824 Fluid meters and devices	1,000.	8.5	11.3	10.7	11.8	12.0	11.7	(NA)
3829 Instruments, n.e.c.	1,000.	20.1	19.1	17.9	17.9	19.4	19.6	(NA)
Average hourly earnings	Dollar	11.78	12.61	12.91	12.97	13.37	13.54	(NA)
3822 Environmental controls	Dollar	11.29	11.04	11.29	11.30	11.30	11.30	(NA)
3823 Process controls	Dollar	11.41	12.25	12.32	12.28	12.80	13.01	(NA)
3824 Fluid meters and devices	Dollar	13.20	15.29	15.55	16.70	18.18	18.27	(NA)
3829 Instruments, n.e.c.	Dollar	11.98	12.85	13.56	12.92	13.06	13.44	(NA)
Capital expenditures	Mil. dol.	610	501	420	498	579	596	(NA)
3822 Environmental controls	Mil. dol.	55.4	80.6	87.6	75.9	138.0	113.0	(NA)
3823 Process controls	Mil. dol.	344	165	133	227	223	231	(NA)
3824 Fluid meters and devices	Mil. dol.	81.0	74.1	76.1	92.3	93.7	97.6	(NA)
3829 Instruments, n.e.c.	Mil. dol.	130	181	123	102	125	154	(NA)
PRODUCT DATA								
Value of shipments [2]	Mil. dol.	14,121	15,448	16,071	17,181	17,803	18,812	(NA)
3822 Environmental controls	Mil. dol.	2,164	2,370	2,433	2,755	2,740	2,920	(NA)
3823 Process controls	Mil. dol.	5,304	5,997	6,213	6,599	6,923	7,456	(NA)
3824 Fluid meters and devices	Mil. dol.	2,300	2,731	3,066	3,509	3,513	3,547	(NA)
3829 Instruments, n.e.c.	Mil. dol.	4,353	4,350	4,359	4,318	4,627	4,889	(NA)
Value of shipments (1992 dollars)	Mil. dol.	14,442	15,448	15,690	16,585	17,076	17,718	(NA)
3822 Environmental controls	Mil. dol.	2,202	2,370	2,261	2,502	2,473	2,603	(NA)
3823 Process controls	Mil. dol.	5,429	5,997	6,079	6,376	6,663	6,981	(NA)
3824 Fluid meters and devices	Mil. dol.	2,352	2,731	3,059	3,498	3,496	3,526	(NA)
3829 Instruments, n.e.c.	Mil. dol.	4,460	4,350	4,291	4,208	4,445	4,608	(NA)
TRADE DATA								
Value of imports	Mil. dol.	1,863	2,199	2,611	3,521	4,019	4,010	4,309
3822 Environmental controls	Mil. dol.	183	225	254	277	278	351	409
3823 Process controls	Mil. dol.	970	1,142	1,223	1,586	1,953	1,974	2,125
3824 Fluid meters and devices	Mil. dol.	208	296	554	954	974	861	904
3829 Instruments, n.e.c.	Mil. dol.	501	536	581	703	813	825	872
Value of exports	Mil. dol.	3,833	3,926	4,487	4,953	5,321	5,407	6,383
3822 Environmental controls	Mil. dol.	614	716	778	825	760	668	753
3823 Process controls	Mil. dol.	1,389	1,383	1,688	1,891	2,164	2,242	2,740
3824 Fluid meters and devices	Mil. dol.	159	170	272	427	406	417	469
3829 Instruments, n.e.c.	Mil. dol.	1,670	1,657	1,749	1,810	1,991	2,081	2,421

NA Not available.   [1] Value of all products and services sold by establishments in the measuring and controlling instruments industry.   [2] Value of products classified in the measuring and controlling instruments industry produced by all industries.

Source: U.S. Department of Commerce, Bureau of the Census, International Trade Administration (ITA).

No. 1480. Recent Trends in Instruments to Measure Electricity (SIC 3825): 1991 to 1997

ITEM	Unit	1991	1992	1993	1994	1995	1996	1997
INDUSTRY DATA								
Value of shipments [1]	Mil. dol.	8,508	8,826	8,746	10,124	12,418	13,371	(NA)
Value of shipments (1992 dollars)	Mil. dol.	8,726	8,826	8,608	9,800	11,649	12,543	(NA)
Total employment	1,000.	71.5	68.5	64.9	63.0	62.3	63.2	(NA)
Production workers	1,000.	35.0	32.2	30.5	32.0	31.0	33.0	(NA)
Average hourly earnings	Dollar	12.49	14.20	14.56	14.84	15.07	15.53	(NA)
Capital expenditures	Mil. dol.	255	324	402	334	398	469	(NA)
PRODUCT DATA								
Value of shipments [2]	Mil. dol.	7,804	7,985	8,180	9,020	10,882	11,964	(NA)
Value of shipments (1992 dollars)	Mil. dol.	8,004	7,985	8,051	8,731	10,208	11,224	(NA)
TRADE DATA								
Value of imports	Mil. dol.	1,240	1,200	1,341	1,536	1,966	2,271	2,686
Value of exports	Mil. dol.	2,739	2,957	3,054	3,388	4,166	4,897	5,764

NA Not available. [1] Value of all products and services sold by establishments in the instruments to measure electricity industry. [2] Value of products classified in the instruments to measure electricity industry produced by all industries.
Source: U.S. Department of Commerce, Bureau of the Census, International Trade Administration (ITA).

No. 1481. Recent Trends in Surgical and Medical Instruments and Surgical Appliances and Supplies: 1991 to 1997

ITEM	Unit	1991	1992	1993	1994	1995	1996	1997
SURGICAL AND MEDICAL INSTRUMENTS (SIC 3841)								
Industry data:								
Value of shipments [1]	Mil. dol.	11,420	13,396	15,113	14,809	15,681	17,042	(NA)
Value of shipments (1992 dollars)	Mil. dol.	11,689	13,396	14,860	14,448	15,136	16,262	(NA)
Total employment	1,000.	93.4	98.2	103.0	99.7	101.0	104.0	(NA)
Production workers	1,000.	56.1	58.5	61.4	59.6	60.4	61.8	(NA)
Average hourly earnings	Dollar	10.6	10.9	11.3	11.5	11.8	12.2	(NA)
Capital expenditures	Mil. dol.	586	689	809	619	619	673	(NA)
Product data:								
Value of shipments [2]	Mil. dol.	10,474	13,276	14,759	14,264	14,936	16,192	(NA)
Value of shipments (1992 dollars)	Mil. dol.	10,720	13,276	14,512	13,916	14,417	15,450	(NA)
Trade data:								
Value of imports	Mil. dol.	1,050	1,182	1,378	1,471	1,674	1,863	2,018
Value of exports	Mil. dol.	2,145	2,427	2,519	2,467	2,784	3,423	3,986
SURGICAL APPLIANCES AND SUPPLIES (SIC 3842)								
Industry data:								
Value of shipments [1]	Mil. dol.	13,386	13,801	14,553	14,423	14,759	15,874	(NA)
Value of shipments (1992 dollars)	Mil. dol.	13,786	13,801	14,034	13,479	13,794	14,630	(NA)
Total employment	1,000.	99.3	96.4	98.0	95.4	92.4	93.1	(NA)
Production workers	1,000.	64.1	61.6	61.9	58.9	58.2	59.7	(NA)
Average hourly earnings	Dollar	10.16	10.84	10.93	11.14	11.51	11.58	(NA)
Capital expenditures	Mil. dol.	466	504	433	372	396	519	(NA)
Product data:								
Value of shipments [2]	Mil. dol.	11,514	12,438	13,285	12,285	13,317	14,304	(NA)
Value of shipments (1992 dollars)	Mil. dol.	11,858	12,438	12,811	12,285	12,446	13,184	(NA)
Trade data:								
Value of imports	Mil. dol.	580	807	818	870	1,060	1,148	1,364
Value of exports	Mil. dol.	1,425	1,662	1,805	1,968	2,194	2,372	2,673

NA Not available. [1] Value of all products and services sold by establishments in this industry. [2] Value of products classified in this industry produced by all industries.
Source: U.S. Department of Commerce, Bureau of the Census, International Trade Administration (ITA).

No. 1482. Recent Trends in Dental Equipment and Supplies (SIC 3843): 1991 to 1997

ITEM	Unit	1991	1992	1993	1994	1995	1996	1997
INDUSTRY DATA								
Value of shipments [1]	Mil. dol.	1,681	1,914	2,012	2,191	2,237	2,366	(NA)
Value of shipments (1992 dollars)	Mil. dol.	1,692	1,914	1,946	2,087	2,100	2,196	(NA)
Total employment	1,000.	14.6	15.1	15.4	15.2	16.5	16.4	(NA)
Production workers	1,000.	9.1	8.9	9.2	9.7	10.5	11.2	(NA)
Average hourly earnings	Dollar	11.30	11.50	11.89	11.49	11.66	11.46	(NA)
Capital expenditures	Mil. dol.	35.2	48.6	58.5	51.7	75.6	45.8	(NA)
PRODUCT DATA								
Value of shipments [2]	Mil. dol.	1,397	1,621	1,664	1,917	2,027	2,172	(NA)
Value of shipments (1992 dollars)	Mil. dol.	1,407	1,621	1,609	1,826	1,903	2,017	(NA)
TRADE DATA								
Value of imports	Mil. dol.	183	230	226	221	262	274	312
Value of exports	Mil. dol.	376	448	498	512	574	632	637

NA Not available. [1] Value of all products and services sold by establishments in the dental equipment and supplies industry. [2] Value of products classified in the dental equipment and supplies industry produced by all industries.
Source: U.S. Department of Commerce, Bureau of the Census, International Trade Administration (ITA).

No. 1483. Recent Trends in X-Ray Apparatus and Tubes and Electromedical Equipment: 1991 to 1997

ITEM	Unit	1991	1992	1993	1994	1995	1996	1997
X-RAY APPARATUS AND TUBES (SIC 3844)								
Industry data:								
Value of shipments [1]	Mil. dol.	3,211	3,235	3,372	3,373	3,620	3,634	(NA)
Value of shipments (1992 dollars)	Mil. dol.	3,240	3,235	3,352	3,330	3,549	3,528	(NA)
Total employment	1,000.	13.8	14.3	14.2	14.0	13.9	13.4	(NA)
Production workers	1,000.	6.9	7.1	6.9	6.6	6.6	6.3	(NA)
Average hourly earnings	Dollar	14.42	14.79	15.44	15.28	15.35	16.05	(NA)
Capital expenditures	Mil. dol.	71.4	63.6	85.6	84.8	95.9	60.0	(NA)
Product data:								
Value of shipments [2]	Mil. dol.	2,201	2,360	2,510	2,494	2,695	2,960	(NA)
Value of shipments (1992 dollars)	Mil. dol.	2,221	2,360	2,495	2,462	2,642	2,874	(NA)
Trade data:								
Value of imports	Mil. dol.	1,075	1,102	1,167	1,062	1,139	1,170	1,161
Value of exports	Mil. dol.	742	782	824	966	1,158	1,182	1,287
ELECTROMEDICAL EQUIPMENT (SIC 3845)								
Industry data:								
Value of shipments [1]	Mil. dol.	6,123	7,189	7,186	7,512	7,116	8,491	(NA)
Value of shipments (1992 dollars)	Mil. dol.	6,223	7,189	7,193	7,713	7,382	9,013	(NA)
Total employment	1,000.	35.3	40.1	39.9	39.2	41.1	42.0	(NA)
Production workers	1,000.	15.3	18.1	17.6	17.6	17.8	18.0	(NA)
Average hourly earnings	Dollar	11.82	11.94	12.12	12.60	12.88	13.43	(NA)
Capital expenditures	Mil. dol.	198	255	241	306	290	350	(NA)
Product data:								
Value of shipments [2]	Mil. dol.	5,194	6,306	6,515	6,894	6,988	8,502	(NA)
Value of shipments (1992 dollars)	Mil. dol.	5,278	6,306	6,521	7,078	7,249	9,025	(NA)
Trade data:								
Value of imports	Mil. dol.	1,273	1,263	1,281	1,289	1,399	1,480	1,699
Value of exports	Mil. dol.	2,043	2,256	2,396	2,820	3,092	3,552	3,636

NA Not available.　[1] Value of all products and services sold by establishments in this industry.　[2] Value of products classified in this industry produced by all industries.

Source: U.S. Department of Commerce, Bureau of the Census, International Trade Administration (ITA).

No. 1484. Recent Trends in Photographic Equipment and Supplies (SIC 3861): 1991 to 1997

ITEM	Unit	1991	1992	1993	1994	1995	1996	1997
INDUSTRY DATA								
Value of shipments [1]	Mil. dol.	21,420	22,119	22,368	23,261	21,654	22,297	(NA)
Value of shipments (1992 dollars)	Mil. dol.	21,208	22,119	23,276	24,825	23,135	23,796	(NA)
Total employment	1,000.	79.0	77.3	75.7	63.9	61.1	60.7	(NA)
Production workers	1,000.	40.5	39.2	38.0	34.7	35.2	35.7	(NA)
Average hourly earnings	Dollar	14.70	14.65	14.64	15.82	16.41	16.72	(NA)
Capital expenditures	Mil. dol.	1,102	805	775	753	746	724	(NA)
PRODUCT DATA								
Value of shipments [2]	Mil. dol.	18,518	18,861	19,686	20,227	19,159	19,129	(NA)
Value of shipments (1992 dollars)	Mil. dol.	18,334	18,861	20,485	21,586	20,469	20,415	(NA)
TRADE DATA								
Value of imports	Mil. dol.	5,798	6,401	7,017	7,702	8,399	8,440	9,083
Value of exports	Mil. dol.	3,782	3,758	3,631	3,702	4,074	4,483	4,687

NA Not available.　[1] Value of all products and services sold by establishments in the photographic equipment and supplies industry.　[2] Value of products classified in the photographic equipment and supplies industry produced by all industries.

Source: U.S. Department of Commerce, Bureau of the Census, International Trade Administration (ITA).

No. 1485. Recent Trends in Jewelry, Precious Metal (SIC 3911): 1991 to 1997

ITEM	Unit	1991	1992	1993	1994	1995	1996	1997
INDUSTRY DATA								
Value of shipments [1]	Mil. dol.	3,895	4,190	4,278	4,459	4,444	4,443	(NA)
Value of shipments (1992 dollars)	Mil. dol.	3,887	4,190	4,215	4,350	4,297	4,243	(NA)
Total employment	1,000.	33.1	32.5	34.0	31.1	30.1	29.4	(NA)
Production workers	1,000.	21.9	22.5	23.6	20.1	20.3	20.1	(NA)
Average hourly earnings	Dollar	9.01	9.41	9.53	9.78	9.61	10.06	(NA)
Capital expenditures	Mil. dol.	41.9	36.8	45.3	49.2	58	91.4	(NA)
PRODUCT DATA								
Value of shipments [2]	Mil. dol.	3,502	3,739	4,006	4,063	4,034	4,016	(NA)
Value of shipments (1992 dollars)	Mil. dol.	3,495	3,739	3,947	3,964	3,902	3,836	(NA)
TRADE DATA								
Value of imports	Mil. dol.	2,451	2,711	3,142	3,438	3,573	3,766	3,959
Value of exports	Mil. dol.	414	476	388	366	375	392	471

NA Not available.　[1] Value of all products and services sold by establishments in the jewelry, precious metal industry.　[2] Value of products classified in the jewelry, precious metal industry produced by all industries.

Source: U.S. Department of Commerce, Bureau of the Census, International Trade Administration (ITA).

No. 1486. Recent Trends in Dolls, Toys, and Games (SIC 3942, 3944): 1991 to 1997

ITEM	Unit	1991	1992	1993	1994	1995	1996	1997
INDUSTRY DATA								
Value of shipments [1]	Mil. dol.	4,494	4,542	4,968	4,550	5,092	4,867	(NA)
3942 Dolls and stuffed toys	Mil. dol.	438	251	273	239	227	253	(NA)
3944 Games and toys	Mil. dol.	4,056	4,291	4,696	4,311	4,866	4,614	(NA)
Value of shipments (1992 dollars)	Mil. dol.	4,570	4,542	4,954	4,510	4,967	4,708	(NA)
3942 Dolls and stuffed toys	Mil. dol.	445	251	268	234	220	246	(NA)
3944 Games and toys	Mil. dol.	4,126	4,291	4,686	4,276	4,747	4,462	(NA)
Total employment	1,000.	32.4	35.5	39.0	35.3	38.7	36.8	(NA)
3942 Dolls and stuffed toys	1,000.	5.0	3.6	4.2	3.2	2.9	3.5	(NA)
3944 Games and toys	1,000.	27.4	31.9	34.8	32.1	35.8	33.3	(NA)
Production workers	1,000.	22.9	26.8	28.8	27.5	30.0	28.5	(NA)
3942 Dolls and stuffed toys	1,000.	3.7	2.8	3.1	2.5	2.2	2.6	(NA)
3944 Games and toys	1,000.	19.2	24.0	25.7	25.0	27.8	25.9	(NA)
Average hourly earnings	Dollar	8.56	8.43	9.03	9.31	9.58	9.59	(NA)
3942 Dolls and stuffed toys	Dollar	9.09	6.88	6.73	7.66	7.45	7.74	(NA)
3944 Games and toys	Dollar	8.48	8.60	9.31	9.45	9.73	9.76	(NA)
Capital expenditures	Mil. dol.	107.0	146.0	142.0	140.0	138.0	142.0	(NA)
3942 Dolls and stuffed toys	Mil. dol.	11.8	3.0	2.7	1.7	1.8	1.0	(NA)
3944 Games and toys	Mil. dol.	95.4	143.0	139.0	139.0	136.0	141.0	(NA)
PRODUCT DATA								
Value of shipments [2]	Mil. dol.	3,840	3,983	4,248	4,170	4,495	4,154	(NA)
3942 Dolls and stuffed toys	Mil. dol.	399	291	294	290	241	265	(NA)
3944 Games and toys	Mil. dol.	3,440	3,693	3,955	3,880	4,254	3,890	(NA)
Value of shipments (1992 dollars)	Mil. dol.	3,905	3,983	4,235	4,132	4,384	4,019	(NA)
3942 Dolls and stuffed toys	Mil. dol.	405	291	289	283	234	257	(NA)
3944 Games and toys	Mil. dol.	3,500	3,693	3,947	3,849	4,150	3,762	(NA)
TRADE DATA								
Value of imports	Mil. dol.	5,752	7,111	7,897	7,445	8,041	9,523	12,063
3942 Dolls and stuffed toys	Mil. dol.	1,466	1,661	1,687	1,711	2,034	2,464	3,578
3944 Games and toys	Mil. dol.	4,286	5,450	6,210	5,734	6,008	7,059	8,484
Value of exports	Mil. dol.	568	720	744	867	916	898	973
3942 Dolls and stuffed toys	Mil. dol.	39.3	54.5	45.1	56.1	59.0	54.5	62.6
3944 Games and toys	Mil. dol.	529	665	698	811	857	844	910

NA Not available. [1] Value of all products and services sold by establishments in the dolls, toys, and games industry.
[2] Value of products classified in the dolls, toys, and games industry produced by all industries.

Source: U.S. Department of Commerce, Bureau of the Census, International Trade Administration (ITA).

No. 1487. Recent Trends in Sporting and Athletic Goods, n.e.c. and Costume Jewelry: 1991 to 1997

ITEM	Unit	1991	1992	1993	1994	1995	1996	1997
SPORTING AND ATHLETIC GOODS, n.e.c. (SIC 3949)								
Industry data:								
Value of shipments [1]	Mil. dol.	7,340	7,581	8,459	8,943	9,543	9,882	(NA)
Value of shipments (1992 dollars)	Mil. dol.	7,552	7,581	8,401	8,734	9,149	9,340	(NA)
Total employment	1,000.	62.2	62.0	64.4	68.2	67.7	66.1	(NA)
Production workers	1,000.	44.9	44.2	46.8	49.7	48.8	47.6	(NA)
Average hourly earnings	Dollar	8.43	8.52	8.74	8.67	9.26	9.51	(NA)
Capital expenditures	Mil. dol.	143	178	218	192	222	254	(NA)
Product data:								
Value of shipments [2]	Mil. dol.	6,504	6,994	7,865	8,285	8,802	9,203	(NA)
Value of shipments (1992 dollars)	Mil. dol.	6,691	6,994	7,810	8,091	8,440	8,698	(NA)
Trade data:								
Value of imports	Mil. dol.	2,080	2,518	2,543	3,129	3,392	3,472	3,531
Value of exports	Mil. dol.	1,148	1,289	1,490	1,758	2,171	2,313	2,366
COSTUME JEWELRY (SIC 3961)								
Industry data:								
Value of shipments [1]	Mil. dol.	1,430	1,444	1,429	1,627	1,660	1,525	(NA)
Value of shipments (1992 dollars)	Mil. dol.	1,460	1,444	1,417	1,603	1,624	1,472	(NA)
Total employment	1,000.	17.8	17.4	17.1	18.8	16.1	16.2	(NA)
Production workers	1,000.	12.2	12.5	12.0	14.3	12.4	12.5	(NA)
Average hourly earnings	Dollar	7.15	7.25	7.50	8.06	7.77	8.41	(NA)
Capital expenditures	Mil. dol.	9.7	12.8	9.7	13.6	11.8	10.1	(NA)
Product data:								
Value of shipments [2]	Mil. dol.	1,399	1,532	1,556	1,679	1,770	1,666	(NA)
Value of shipments (1992 dollars)	Mil. dol.	1,428	1,532	1,542	1,654	1,732	1,608	(NA)
Trade data:								
Value of imports	Mil. dol.	514	550	561	586	514	484	486
Value of exports	Mil. dol.	128	121	135	149	150	152	166

NA Not available. [1] Value of all products and services sold by establishments in this industry. [2] Value of products classified in this industry produced by all industries.

Source: U.S. Department of Commerce, Bureau of the Census, International Trade Administration (ITA).

Guide to—Sources of Statistics, State Statistical Abstracts, and Foreign Statistical Abstracts

Alphabetically arranged by subject, this guide contains references to the important primary sources of statistical information for the United States published since 1990. Secondary sources have been included if the information contained in them is presented in a particularly convenient form or if primary sources are not readily available. Nonrecurrent publications presenting compilations or estimates for years later than 1990 or types of data not available in regular series are also included.

Much valuable information may also be found in state reports, foreign statistical abstracts, which are included at the end of this appendix and in reports for particular commodities, industries, or similar segments of our economic and social structures, many of which are not included here.

Publications listed under each subject are divided into two main groups: "U.S. Government" and "Other." The location of the publisher of each report is given except for federal agencies located in Washington, DC. Most federal publications may be purchased from the Superintendent of Documents, U.S. Government Printing Office, Washington, DC 20402, tel. 202-512-1800, or from Government Printing Office bookstores in certain major cities. In some cases, federal publications may be obtained from the issuing agency.

Major reports, such as the Census of Population, which consist of many volumes, are listed by their general, all-inclusive titles.

Bureau of the Census Publications

In most cases, separate reports of the most recent censuses are available for each state, subject, industry, etc. Complete information on publications of all the censuses and current surveys conducted by the Bureau of the Census appears in the *Bureau of the Census Catalog,* published annually and available from the Superintendent of Documents.

Abortions—*see* Vital Statistics.

Accidents —*see also* Health; Insurance; and Vital Statistics

U.S. Government

Bureau of Labor Statistics

Occupational Injuries and Illnesses in the United States by Industry. Annual.

Department of Transportation

Transportation Safety Information Report. Quarterly.

Federal Railroad Administration

Accident/Incident Bulletin. Summary, statistics, and analysis of accidents on railroads in the United States. Annual.

Rail-Highway Crossing Accident/Incident and Inventory Bulletin. Annual.

Mine Safety and Health Administration

Informational Reports by Mining Industry: Coal; Metallic Minerals; Nonmetallic Minerals (except stone and coal); Stone, Sand, and Gravel. Annual.

Accidents —Con.

U.S. Government —Con.

Mine Injuries and Worktime. (Some preliminary data.) Quarterly.

National Center for Health Statistics

Vital Statistics of the United States. Annual.

Volume I, Natality

Volume II, Mortality

National Transportation Safety Board

Accidents; Air Carriers. Annual.

Accidents; General Aviation. Annual.

Other

Metropolitan Life Insurance Company, New York, NY

Health and Safety Education.

Statistical Bulletin. Quarterly.

National Fire Protection Association, Quincy, MA

NFPA Journal. Bimonthly.

Climate —*see also* Agriculture

  U.S. Government

    National Oceanic and Atmospheric Administration

      Climatography of the United States, No. 20, Supplement No. 1, Freeze/Frost Data.

      Climatological Data. Issued in sections for states and outlying areas. Monthly with annual summary.

      General Summary of Tornadoes. Annual.

      Hourly Precipitation Data. Monthly with annual summary; for each state.

      Local Climatological Data. Monthly with annual summary; for major cities.

      Storm Data. Monthly.

      Weekly Weather and Crop Bulletin. National summary.

Commerce —*see* Foreign Commerce; Retail and Wholesale Trade; *and* Transportation.

Commodity Prices —*see also* Economic Indexes

  U.S. Government

    Board of Governors of the Federal Reserve System

      Annual Statistical Digest.

      Federal Reserve Bulletin. Monthly.

    Bureau of Labor Statistics

      Consumer Prices: Energy and Food. Monthly.

      CPI Detailed Report. Monthly.

      Monthly Labor Review.

      Producer Price Indexes. Monthly, with annual supplement.

      Relative Importance of Components in the Consumer Price Indexes. Annual.

      U.S. Import and Export Price Indexes. Monthly.

    Department of Agriculture

      Agricultural Price Reports. Monthly and annual.

  Other

    Bridge Commodity Research Bureau, a Bridge Information Systems Inc. Chicago, IL.

      Commodity Year Book Update Disk. (Three editions annually.)

      CRB Commodity Index Report. Weekly.

      CRB Commodity Year Book. Annual.

      CRB Futures Perspective. Weekly.

      CRB Infotech. CD

      Electronic Futures Trend Analyzer. Daily.

      Final Markets. End of day.

      Futures Market Service. Weekly.

      Futures Market Service Fundamental & Technical Commentary. Daily and weekly.

      Bridge News Summaries. Daily

      Price Service. Daily

      The Blue Line. Daily

Commodity Prices —Con.

  Other —Con.

      Wall Street Journal. (Dow Jones & Co., New York, NY.) Daily except Saturdays, Sundays, and holidays.

Communications —*see also* Newspapers

  U.S. Government

    Bureau of the Census

      Census of Transportation, Communications and Utilities. Quinquennial. (1992, most recent.)

    Federal Communications Commission

      Annual Report.

      Statistics of Communications Common Carriers. Annual.

    Rural Electrification Administration

      Annual Statistical Report—Rural Telephone Borrowers.

    U.S. Postal Service

      Annual Report of the Postmaster General.

      Cost and Revenue Analysis. Annual.

  Other

    John Blair & Company, New York, NY

      Statistical Trends in Broadcasting. Annual.

    Book Industry Study Group, Inc., New York, NY

      Consumer Research Study on Book Purchasing. Annual.

    Reed Publishing USA, Newton, MA

      Broadcasting & Cable Market Place. Annual.

      Broadcasting Magazine. Weekly.

    Corporation for Public Broadcasting, Washington, DC

      Average Revenue Profiles for Public Broadcasting Grantees. Annual.

    Frequently asked Questions About Public Broadcasting Periodic.

      Public Broadcasting Stations' Income from State Governments and State Colleges & Universities Ranked State-By-State. Annual.

      Public Radio and Television Programming Content by Category. Biennial.

    Editor & Publisher Co., New York, NY

      International Year Book. Annual.

      Market Guide. Annual.

    Electronic Industries Alliance, Arlington, VA

      Electronic Market Data Book. Annual.

      Electronic Market Trends. Monthly.

      Electronics Foreign Trade. Monthly.

    Radio Advertising Bureau, New York, NY

      Radio Facts. Annual.

    United States Telephone Association, Washington, DC

      Statistics of the Local Exchange Carriers. Annual.

    Warren Publishing, Inc., Washington, DC

      Cable Action Update. Weekly.

Communications —Con.
> *Other* —Con.
>> Cable and Station Coverage Atlas. Annual.
>>
>> Television Action Update. Weekly.
>>
>> Television and Cable Factbook. Annual.
>>
>> TV Station & Cable Ownership Directory. Semi-annual.

Construction, Housing, and Real Estate —*see also* Money *and* Transportation

> *U.S. Government*

>> Board of Governors of the Federal Reserve System

>>> Annual Statistical Digest.
>>>
>>> Federal Reserve Bulletin. Monthly.

>> Bureau of Census

>>> Census of Construction Industries. Quinquennial. (1992, most recent.)
>>>
>>> Census of Housing. Decennial. (1990, most recent.)

>>> Current Construction Reports: Housing Starts, C20 (monthly); New Residential Construction in Selected Metropolitan Statistical Areas, C21 (quarterly); Housing Completions, C22 (monthly); New One-Family Houses Sold and for Sale, C25 (monthly with annual report, Characteristics of New Housing); Price Index of New One-Family Houses Sold, C27 (quarterly); Value of Construction Put in Place, C30 (monthly with occasional historical supplement); Housing Units Authorized by Building Permits, C40 (monthly and annual); Residential Improvements and Repairs, C50 (quarterly and annual).

>>> Current Housing Reports: Housing Vacancies, H-111 (quarterly and annual); Market Absorption of Apartments, H-130 (quarterly and annual); Characteristics of Apartments Completed, H-131 (annual); Annual Housing Survey, H-150 (series of six biennial reports); Annual Housing Survey—Housing Characteristics for Selected Metropolitan Areas, H-170.

>> Bureau of Economic Analysis

>>> Business Statistics, 1963-91. 1992. (Discontinued).
>>>
>>> The National Income and Product Accounts of the United States, 1929-94: Statistical Tables, 1998.
>>>
>>> Survey of Current Business. Monthly.

>> Bureau of Labor Statistics

>>> Compensation and Working Conditions. Quarterly.
>>>
>>> Employment and Earnings. Monthly.
>>>
>>> Employment, Hours, and Earnings, United States, 1909-94. 1994. (Bulletin 2445.)
>>>
>>> Employment, Hours, and Earnings, United States, 1988-96. 1996. (Bulletin 2481.)

Construction, Housing, and Real Estate —Con.

> *U.S. Government* —Con.

>> Evaluating Your Firm's Injury and Illness Record, Construction Industries Report 812, (1991).
>>
>> Monthly Labor Review.
>>
>> Occupational Employment in Mining, Construction, Finance, and Services. 1995. (Bulletin 2460.)
>>
>> Occupational Injuries and Illnesses in the United States by Industry. Annual.

>> Department of Housing and Urban Development

>>> Survey of Mortgage Lending Activity. Monthly and quarterly press releases.

>> Department of Veterans Affairs

>>> Loan Guaranty Highlights. Quarterly.

>> Energy Information Administration

>>> Residential Energy Consumption Survey: Housing Characteristics. Triennial.

>> International Trade Administration

>>> Construction Review. Quarterly.

>> Office of Thrift Supervision

>>> Annual Report.

> *Other*

>> Dodge, F.W., National Information Services Division, McGraw-Hill Information Systems Co., New York, NY

>>> Dodge Construction Potentials. Monthly.

>> NATIONAL ASSOCIATION OF REALTORS, Washington, DC

>>> Real Estate Outlook: Market Trends & Insights, Monthly.

Consumer Income and Expenditures, and Personal Income —*see also* Agriculture; Economic Indexes; Investments; *and* National Income

> *U.S. Government*

>> Board of Governors of the Federal Reserve System

>>> Annual Statistical Digest.
>>>
>>> Federal Reserve Bulletin. Monthly.

>> Bureau of the Census

>>> Census of Population. Decennial. (1990, most recent.)
>>>
>>> Current Population Reports. (Series on Consumer Income, P60.)
>>>
>>> Current Population Reports. (Series on Household Economic Studies, P70.)
>>>
>>> Special Studies Reports. (Series on Special Studies, P23.)

>> Bureau of Economic Analysis

>>> Business Statistics, 1963-91. 1992. (Discontinued.)
>>>
>>> Survey of Current Business. Monthly.

>> Bureau of Labor Statistics

>>> Consumer Expenditure Survey, Integrated Diary and Interview Survey data.
>>>
>>> Annual press releases and reports, biannual bulletins.
>>>
>>> Consumer Expenditure Survey: 1988-89. 1991. (Bulletin 2383.)

Education —Con.
 U.S. Government —Con.
  Revenues and Expenditures for Public
   Elementary and Secondary Education.
   Annual.

 National Science Foundation

  Academic Research and Development
   Expenditures. Detailed Statistical
   Tables. Annual

  Academic Science and Engineering:
   Graduate Enrollment and Support:
   Detailed Statistical Tables. Annual

  Characteristics of Doctoral Scientists and
   Engineers in the United States. Detailed
   Statistical Tables. Biennial.

  Characteristics of Recent
   Science/Engineering Graduates.
   Detailed Statistical Tables. Biennial.

  Characteristics of Recent Scientists and
   Engineers. Detailed Statistical Tables.
   Biennial.

  Federal Funds for Research and
   Development. Detailed Statistiscal
   Tables. Annual.

  Federal R&D Funding by Budget
   Function. Report. Annual.

  Federal Science and Engineering Support
   to Universities, Colleges, and Nonprofit
   Institutions. Detailed Statistical Tables.
   Annual.

  Federal Scientists and Engineers.
   Detailed Statistical Tables. Quinquennial.

  Graduate Students and Post-doctorates
   in Science and Engineering. Annual.

  Immigrant Scientists, Engineers and
   Technicians. Detailed Statistical Tables.
   Annual.

  International Science and Technology
   Data Update. Report. Annual.

  National Patterns of R&D Resources.
   Report. Annual.

  Research and Development in
   Industry. Detailed Statistical Tables.
   Annual.

  Science and Engineering Degrees.
   Detailed Statistical Tables. Annual.

  Science and Engineering Degrees,
   by Race/Ethnicity of Recipients.
   Detailed Statistical Tables. Annual.

  Science and Engineering Doctorates
   Awards. Detailed Statistical Tables.
   Annual.

  Science and Engineering Indicators.
   Report. Biennial.

  Science and Engineering Profiles.
   Annual.

  Scientific and Engineering Research
   Facilities at Universities and Colleges.
   Report. Biennial.

  Science and Technology Pocket Data
   Book. Report. Annual.

  Scientists, Engineers, and Technicians in
   Manufacturing Industries. Detailed
   Statistical Tables. Triennial.

Education —Con.
 U.S. Government —Con.
  Scientists, Engineers, and Technicians in
   Nonmanufacturing Industries. Detailed
   Statistical Tables. Triennial.

  Scientists, Engineers, and Technicians in
   Trade and Regulated Industries.
   Detailed Statistical Tables. Triennial.

  U.S. Scientists and Engineers. Detailed
   Statistical Tables. Biennial.

  Women, Minorities, and Persons with
   Disabilities. Report. Biennial.

 Other

  American Council on Education,
   Washington, DC

   A Fact Book on Higher Education.
    Quarterly.

   National Norms for Entering College
    Freshmen. Annual.

  Bowker (R.R.) Company, New Providence,
   NJ

   American Library Directory. Annual.

   Bowker Annual Library and Book Trade
    Almanac.

  Chronicle of Higher Education, Inc.,
   Washington, DC

   Almanac. Annual.

  College Entrance Examination Board, New
   York, NY

   National Report on College-Bound
    Seniors. Annual.

  National Catholic Educational Association,
   Washington, DC

   Catholic Schools in America. Annual.

   United States Catholic Elementary and
    Secondary Schools. Staffing and
    Enrollment. Annual.

   U.S. Catholic Elementary Schools and
    their Finances. Biennial.

   U.S. Catholic Secondary Schools and
    their Finances. Biennial.

  National Education Association, Washington,
   DC

   Estimates of School Statistics. Annual.

   Rankings of the States. Annual.

   Status of the American Public School
    Teacher, 1995-96. Quinquennial.

  Research Associates of Washington,
   Arlington, VA

   Inflation Measures for Schools, Colleges,
    and Libraries. Annual.

   State Profiles: Financing Public Higher
    Education Rankings. Annual.

   Wages and Cost of Living: 508 County
    Indexes. (1995, most recent.)

Elections

 U.S. Government

  Bureau of the Census

   Congressional District Data:

Energy —Con.

Other

American Gas Association, Arlington, VA

Gas Facts. Annual.

American Petroleum Institute, Washington, DC

The Basic Petroleum Data Book. Annual.

Edison Electric Institute, Washington, DC

Statistical Yearbook of the Electric Utility Industry. Annual.

McGraw-Hill Publications Co., New York, NY

Electrical World Directory of Electric Utilities. Annual.

National Coal Association, Washington, DC

Steam-Electric Plant Factors. Annual.

U.S. Council for Energy Awareness, Washington, DC

U.S. Public Opinion on Nuclear Energy. (Polling reports updated periodically.)

Environment

U.S. Government

Bureau of the Census

Current Industrial Report, Survey of Pollution Abatement Costs and Expenditures, series MA-200.

Council on Environmental Quality

Environmental Quality. Annual.

Environmental Protection Agency

Air Quality Data. Annual.

Cost of Clean Water. Annual.

Federal Certification Test Results for Motor Vehicles. Annual.

Municipal Water Facilities Inventory. Quinquennial.

National Air Pollutant Emission Trends, 1900-96.

National Air Quality and Emissions Trends Report. 1996.

Needs Survey, Conveyance and Treatment of Municipal Wastewater Summaries of Technical Data. Biennial.

Pesticides Monitoring Journal. Quarterly.

Radiation Data and Reports. Monthly.

Sewage Facility Construction. Annual.

Summary of Water Enforcement Actions Pursued by EPA since December 3, 1970. (Updated continuously.)

Geological Survey

A Statistical Summary of Data from the U.S. Geological Survey's National Water Quality Networks. (Open-File Report 83-533.)

Other

American Petroleum Institute, Washington, DC

Petroleum Industry Environmental Report. Annual.

Executions —*see* Law Enforcement.

Exports —*see* Foreign Commerce.

Family Characteristics —*see* Population.

Farms and Farm Characteristics —*see* Agriculture.

Federal Government Finances and Employment

—*see also* Elections; Science Resources; *and* State and Local Government

U.S. Government

Board of Governors of the Federal Reserve System

Annual Statistical Digest.

Federal Reserve Bulletin. Monthly.

Bureau of the Census

Federal Expenditures by State for Fiscal Year. Annual.

Bureau of Economic Analysis

Business Statistics, 1963-91. 1992. (Discontinued.)

Survey of Current Business. Monthly.

Council of Economic Advisers

Economic Indicators. Monthly.

Economic Report of the President. Annual.

Council on Environmental Quality

Environmental Quality. Annual.

Department of Labor

Annual Report of the Secretary.

Department of the Treasury

Consolidated Financial Statements of the United States Government. (Prototype.)

Daily Treasury Statement.

Monthly Statement of the Public Debt of the United States.

Monthly Treasury Statement of Receipts and Outlays of the United States Government.

Treasury Bulletin. Quarterly.

United States Government Annual Report and Appendix.

Internal Revenue Service

IRS Data Book.

Statistics of Income Division.

Corporation Income Tax Returns. Annual.

Statistics of Income Bulletin. Quarterly.

National Science Foundation

Federal Funds for Research and Development. Detailed Statistical Tables. Annual.

Federal R&D Funding by Budget Function. Report. Annual.

Federal Scientists and Engineers. Detailed Statistical Tables. Annual.

Federal Support to Universities, Colleges, and Nonprofit Institutions. Detailed Statistical Tables. Annual.

International Science and Technology Data Update. Report. Annual.

National Patterns of R&D Resources. Report. Annual.

Science and Engineering Indicators. Report. Biennial.

Science and Engineering Personnel: A National Overview. Report. Biennial.

Federal Government Finances and Employment —Con.

U.S. Government —Con.

Office of Management and Budget

The Budget of the United States Government. Annual.

Office of Personnel Management

Civil Service Retirement and Disability Fund. Report. Annual.

Demographic Profile of the Federal Workforce. Biennial. (Even years.)

Employment by Geographic Area. Biennial. (Even years.)

Employment and Trends. Bimonthly. (Odd months.)

Occupations of Federal White-Collar and Blue-Collar Workers. Biennial. (Odd years.)

Pay Structure of the Federal Civil Service. Annual.

Statistical Abstract for the Federal Employee Benefit Programs. Annual.

Work Years and Personnel Costs. Annual.

Other

Advisory Commission on Intergovernmental Relations, Washington, DC

Characteristics of Federal Grant-in-Aid Programs to State and Local Governments: Grants Funded FY 93. (Every 3 years.)

Changing Public Attitudes on Governments and Taxes. Annual.

Significant Features of Fiscal Federalism. Annual.

Moody's Investors Service, New York, NY

Moody's Municipal and Government Manual. Annual with weekly supplements.

Tax Foundation, Washington, DC

Facts and Figures on Government Finance. Annual.

Finance —*see* Federal Government; Investments; Money; *and* State and Local Government.

Fisheries

U.S. Government

Department of Agriculture

CATFISH. 12 issues of Catfish processing, plus 4 issues of catfish production and annual issue of Trout Production.

National Oceanic and Atmospheric Administration, National Marine Fisheries Service

Fisheries of the United States. Annual.

Food —*see also* Agriculture

U.S. Government

Bureau of Labor Statistics

Consumer Expenditure Survey, integrated Diary and Interview Survey data. Annual press releases and reports, biannual bulletins.

Consumer Expenditure Survey, 1988-89. 1991. (Bulletin 2383.)

Food —Con.

U.S. Government —Con.

Consumer Expenditure Survey, 1987. (Bulletin 2354.) 1990.

Consumer Prices: Energy and Food. Monthly.

CPI Detailed Report. Monthly.

Monthly Labor Review.

Producer Price Indexes. Monthly, with annual supplement.

Department of Agriculture

Agricultural Outlook. 11 issues per year.

Food Consumption, Prices, and Expenditures, 1996 (SB-928). Revised annually.

Food Cost Review. 1995. (Agricultural Economic Report No. 729.) Revised annually.

Food Review. Quarterly.

Department of Agriculture, Food and Consumer Service

Annual Historical Review:

Food and Consumer Service Programs.

Department of Agriculture, Science and Education Administration.

Family Economics Review. Quarterly.

Other

American Frozen Food Institute, Burlingame, CA

Frozen Food Pack Statistics. Annual.

National Food Processors Association, Washington, DC

Canned Fruit and Vegetable Pack and Stock Situation Reports. Quarterly.

Foreign Commerce —*see also* Economic Indexes; *and* International Accounts and Aid

U.S. Government

Army, Corps of Engineers

Waterborne Commerce of the United States (in five parts). Annual.

Bureau of the Census

Summary of U.S. Export and Import Merchandise Trade. Monthly; includes cumulative data. (FT 900.)

Survey of the Origin of Exports of Manufacturing Establishments. Triennial. (Current Industrial Reports M76 (AS)-8.)

U.S. Commodity Exports and Imports as Related to Output. Annual. (Series ES 2.)

U.S. Trade with Puerto Rico and U.S. Possessions. Monthly and Annual. (FT 895.)

Bureau of Economic Analysis

Business Statistics, 1963-91. 1992. (Discontinued.)

Survey of Current Business. Monthly. (June issue contains detailed data on merchandise trade.)

U.S. Merchandise Trade: Exports and Imports by End-Use Category. Annually.

Foreign Commerce —Con.
U.S. Government —Con.
Department of Agriculture
Foreign Agricultural Trade of the United States (FATUS). Bimonthly with annual supplements on calendar year and fiscal year trade statistics.
World Agricultural Trends and Indicators, 1970-88 Statistical Bulletin No. 781. Annual.
Energy Information Administration
Annual Energy Review.
Monthly Energy Review.
International Trade Administration
Business America. Monthly. (Issues in March, June, September, and December contain quarterly data on key International comparisons.)
Overseas Business Reports. Irregular.
U.S. Foreign Trade Highlights. Annual.
U.S. Global Trade Outlook. Annual.
Maritime Administration
Annual Report.
National Science Foundation
International Science and Technology Data Update. Report. Annual.
Science and Engineering Indicators. Report. Biennial.
Science and Technology Pocket Data Book. Report. Annual.
Other
Aerospace Industries Association of America, Washington, DC
Exports of Aerospace Products. Quarterly.
Imports of Aerospace Products. Quarterly.
Bridge Commodity Research Bureau, Chicago, IL
Commodity Yearbook. Annual.
Forests and Lumber —*see also* Economic Indexes
U.S. Government
Bureau of the Census
Census of Manufactures. Quinquennial. (1992, most recent.)
Current Industrial Reports. Monthly, quarterly, and annual series on various industries.
Forest Service
An Analysis of the Timber Situation in the United States: 1989-2040. 1990.
Forest Resources of the United States, 1992.
Land Areas of the National Forest System. Annual.
The 1993 RPA Timber Assessment Update. Forthcoming.
U.S. Timber Production, Trade, Consumption, and Price Statistics, 1960-88. Annual.
International Trade Administration
Construction Review. Quarterly.

Forests and Lumber —Con.
Other
American Forest & Paper Association, Washington, DC
Statistics of Paper, Paperboard, and Wood Pulp. Annual.
Statistical Roundup.
Wood Pulp and Fiber Statistics. Annual.
Gas Utilities —*see* Energy.
Geography —*see also* Environment *and* Public Lands
U.S. Government
Government —*see* Federal Government; *and* State and Local Government.
Guam —*see* Outlying Areas.
Health Insurance —*see* Insurance.
Health and Medical Care —*see also* Accidents; Environment; Food; Insurance; Social Insurance; *and* Vital Statistics
U.S. Government
Bureau of Labor Statistics
Consumer Expenditure Survey; Integrated Diary and Interview Survey Data.
Annual press releases and biannual bulletins.
CPI Detailed Report. Monthly.
Employee Benefits in Medium and Large Firms. Biennial.
Employee Benefits in Small Private Establishments. Biennial.
Employee Benefits in State and Local Governments. Biennial.
Monthly Labor Review.
Centers for Disease Control and Prevention, Atlanta, GA
Morbidity and Mortality Weekly Report. Annual summary also.
Department of Agriculture, Food and Consumer Service
Annual Historical Review, Food and Consumer Service Programs.
Department of Health and Human Services
Annual Report.
Department of Veterans Affairs
Annual Report of The Secretary of Veterans Affairs.
Summary of Medical Programs. Semiannual.
Drug Enforcement Administration
Drug Abuse and Law Enforcement Statistics. Irregular.
Health Care Financing Administration
Health Care Financing Review. Medicare and Medicaid Statistical Supplement. Annual.
Health Care Financing Research Reports. Occasional.
Health Care Financing Review. Quarterly.
National Center for Health Statistics
Health: United States. Annual. (DHHS Pub. No. PHS *year*-1232.)

Health and Medical Care —Con.

U.S. Government —Con.

Vital and Health Statistics. (A series of statistical reports covering health-related topics.)

Series 10: Health Interview Survey Statistics. Irregular.

Current Estimates from the Health Interview Survey. Annual.

Series 11: Health and Nutrition Examination Survey Statistics. Irregular.

Series 13: Health Resources Utilization Statistics. Irregular.

National Hospital Discharge Survey: Annual Summary. Annual.

Ambulatory Care, Visits to Physician Offices, Hospital Outpatient Departments and Emergency Departments. Annual.

Internet address: http://www.cdc.gov/nchswww/

Series 14: Health Resources: Manpower and Facilities Statistics. Irregular.

Substance Abuse and Mental Health Services Administration

National Household Survey on Drug Abuse. Advance Reports, Main Findings, Population Estimates, latest year available 1993.

Social Security Administration

Social Security Bulletin. Quarterly with annual statistical supplement.

Other

American Dental Association, Chicago, IL

Dental Statistics Handbook. Triennial.

Dental Students' Register. Annual.

Distribution of Dentists in the United States by Region and State. Triennial.

Survey of Dental Practice. Annual.

American Hospital Association, Chicago, IL

Hospital Statistics. Annual.

American Medical Association, Chicago, IL

Physician Characteristics and Distribution in the U.S. Annual.

Socioeconomic Characteristics of Medical Practice. 1995.

Physicians' Visits, Hours, Earnings and Expenses.

U.S. Medical Licensure Statistics, and License Requirements. Annual.

American Osteopathic Association, Chicago, IL

Yearbook and Directory of Osteopathic Physicians. Annual.

Metropolitan Life Insurance Company, New York, NY

Health and Safety Education.

Statistical Bulletin. Quarterly.

Hospitals —*see* Health.

Hotels —*see* Service Establishments.

Household Appliances —*see* Construction, Housing, and Real Estate. Housing—*see* Construction.

Immigration and Naturalization

U.S. Government

Department of State, Bureau of Consular Affairs

Report of the Visa Office. Annual. (Dept. of State Pub. 8810.)

Department of Transportation

Report of Passenger Travel Between the United States and Foreign Countries. Annual, semiannual, quarterly, monthly.

Immigration and Naturalization Service

I&N Reporter. Quarterly.

Statistical Yearbook of the Immigration and Naturalization Service. Annual.

National Science Foundation

Immigrant Scientists and Engineers. Detailed Statistical Tables. Annual.

Science and Engineering Doctoral Awards Reached Record Highs in 1990. SRS Data Brief. (NSF 91-308.)

Survey of Direct U.S. Private Capital Investment in Research and Development Facilities in Japan. (NSF 91-312)

Science and Engineering Doctorates. Detailed Statistical Tables. Annual.

Imports —*see* Foreign Commerce.

Income —*see* Consumer Income; *and* National Income.

Industry —*see* Business; Economic Indexes; *and* Manufactures.

Institutions —*see* Education; Health; *and* Law Enforcement.

Insurance—*see also* Social Insurance

U.S. Government

Bureau of the Census

Census of Finance, Insurance, and Real Estate. Quinquennial. (1992, most recent)

Department of Veterans Affairs

Annual Report of The Secretary of Veterans Affairs.

Government Life Insurance Programs for Veterans and Members of the Service. Annual.

Other

American Council of Life Insurance, Washington, DC

Life Insurance Fact Book. Biennial. (Odd years)

Health Insurance Association of America, Washington, DC

Source Book of Health Insurance Data. Annual.

Insurance Information Institute, New York, NY

Internet address: http://www.iii.org

Insurance Facts. Annual.

National Association of Insurance Commissioners, Washington DC

International Statistics —Con.
Other —Con.

Revenue Statistics of OECD Member Countries. Annual.

Review of Fisheries in OECD Member Countries. Annual.

Statistical Trends in Transport (ECMT.)

Statistics of Area Production and Field of Crop Products in OECD Member Countries.

Statistics of Foreign Trade:

Monthly Statistics of Foreign Trade. (Series A.)

Foreign Trade by Commodities. (Series C.) Annual.

Tourism Policy and International Tourism in OECD Member Countries. Annual.

Uranium Resources Production and Demand. Biennial.

World Energy Statistics and Balances.

Pan American Health Organization, Washington DC

Health Conditions in the Americas. 1990 Edition. Quadrennial.

United Nations Educational, Scientific and Cultural Organization, Paris, France

Statistical Yearbook.

United Nations Statistics Division, New York, NY

Compendium of Human Settlements Statistics. (Series N.)

Demographic Yearbook. (Series R.)

Energy Balances and Electricity Profiles. (Series W.)

Energy Statistics Yearbook. (Series J.)

Industrial Statistics Yearbook: (Series P.)

Commodity Production Statistics.

International Trade Statistics Yearbook. (Series G.)

Monthly Bulletin of Statistics. (Series Q.)

National Accounts Statistics: (Series X, Annually.)

Main Aggregates and Detailed Tables.

Analysis of Main Aggregates.

Population and Vital Statistics Report. (Series A, Quarterly.)

Social Statistics and Indicators: (Series K, Occasional.)

The World's Women: Trends and Statistics.

Women's Indicators and Statistics Database (CD and diskette only.)

Statistical Yearbook. (Series; also available in CD-ROM, Series S/CD)

World Statistics Pocketbook. (Series V, Annually.)

World Health Organization, Geneva, Switzerland

World Health Statistics Annual.

International Trade —see Foreign Commerce; and International Statistics.

Investments and Securities —see also Business; Construction; Insurance; International Accounts; and Money
U.S. Government

Board of Governors of the Federal Reserve System

Annual Statistical Digest.

Federal Reserve Bulletin. Monthly.

Commodity Futures Trading Commission. Annual.

Commitment of Traders in Commodity Futures. Internet address: http://www.cftc.gov

Securities and Exchange Commission

Annual Report.

Other

William B. Dana Co., New York, NY

Commercial and Financial Chronicle. Semi-weekly.

Investment Company Institute, Washington, DC

Mutual Fund Fact Book. Annual.

Moody's Investors Service, New York, NY

Moody's Manuals. (Volumes on Industriales, OTC, Banks and Finance, International, Municipals and Governments, Transportation, and Public Utilities.) Annual with weekly supplements.

New York Stock Exchange, Inc., New York, NY

Fact Book. Annual.

Securities Industry Association, New York, NY

Foreign Activity Report. Quarterly.

Securities Industry Trends. Periodic.

SIA Securities Industry Fact Book. Annual.

Standard and Poor's Corporation, New York, NY

Analyst's Handbook. Annual with monthly cumulative supplements.

Corporation Records. Six basic volumes; News Supplements, daily; Dividend Record, daily, and cumulative monthly and annual.

Daily Stock Price Records. Quarterly.

Security Owner's Stock Guide. Monthly.

Statistical Service. (Security Price Index Record; business and financial basic statistics with monthly supplement.)

Wall Street Journal. (Dow Jones & Co., New York, NY.) Daily except Saturdays, Sundays, and holidays.

Irrigation, Drainage, and Soil Conservation —see Agriculture

Juvenile Court —see Law Enforcement.

Labor —see also Accidents; Business; Economic Indexes; International Statistics; Science Resources; and Social Insurance
U.S. Government

Board of Governors of the Federal Reserve System

Labor —Con.
  U.S. Government —Con.
    Annual Statistical Digest.

    Federal Reserve Bulletin. Monthly.

  Bureau of the Census

    Census of Population. Decennial. (1990, most recent.)

    County Business Patterns. Annual.

    Current Governments Reports: Public Employment, GE No. 1 (annual); City Employment, GE No. 2 (annual); Local Government Employment in Selected Metropolitan Areas and Large Counties, GE No. 3 (annual); County Government Employment, GE No. 4 (annual).

    Population Profile of the United States. (Biennial Series P23.)

  Bureau of Justice Statistics and Bureau of the Census

    Justice Expenditure and Employment in the U.S. Annual.

  Bureau of Labor Statistics

    Compensation and Working Conditions. Quarterly.

    Employee Benefits in Medium and Large Firms. Biennial.

    Employee Benefits in Small Private Establishments. Biennial.

    Employee Benefits in State and Local Governments. Biennial.

    Employer Costs for Employee Compensation. Annual.

    Employment and Earnings. Monthly.

    Employment and Wages. Annual.

    Employment Cost Index. Quarterly.

    Employment, Hours, and Earnings, United States, 1909-94. 1994. (Bulletin 2445.)

    Employment, Hours, and Earnings, United States, 1988-96. 1996. (Bulletin 2481.)

    Employment Outlook: 1994-2005. Job Quality and Other Aspects of Projected Employment Growth. 1995. (Bulletin 2472.)

    The Employment Situation. Monthly.

    Geographic Profile of Employment and Unemployment. Annual.

    Monthly Labor Review.

    Occupational Employment in Manufacturing Industries. 1994. (Bulletin 2437.)

    Occupational Employment in Mining, Construction, Finance, and Services. 1995. (Bulletin 2460.)

    Occupational Employment Statistics. 1994.(Bulletin 2468.)

    Occupational Injuries and Illnesses in the United States, by Industry. Annual.

    Occupational Projections and Training Data. Biennial.

    Productivity Measures for Selected Industries and Government Services. Annual.

    Real Earnings. Monthly.

Labor —Con.
  U.S. Government —Con.
    State and Metropolitan Area Employment and Unemployment. Monthly.

    Usual Weekly Earnings of Wage and Salary Workers. Quarterly.

    Work Experience of the Population. Annual.

  Department of Agriculture

    Farm Labor. Quarterly.

  Department of Labor

    Annual Report of the Secretary.

  Employment and Training Administration

    Employment and Training Report of the President. Annual.

    Unemployment Insurance Claims. Weekly.

  Interstate Commerce Commission

    Monthly Report of Class I Railroad Employees, by Group. (Statement No. 350.)

    Wage Statistics of Class I Railroads in the United States. Annual. (Statement No. 300.)

  Maritime Administration

    Employment Report of United States Flag Merchant Fleet Ocean-going Vessels 1,000 Gross Tons and Over. Quarterly.

    Seafaring Wage Rates. Biennial.

  National Science Foundation

    Characteristics of Doctoral Scientists and Engineers in the United States. Detailed Statistical Tables. Biennial.

    Characteristics of Recent Science and Engineering Graduates. Detailed Statistical Tables. Biennial.

    Immigrant Scientists and Engineers. Detailed Statistical Tables. Annual.

    U.S. Scientists and Engineers. Detailed Statistical Tables. Biennial.

    Woman, Minorities in Science and Engineering. Report. Biennial.

  Office of Personnel Management

    Demographic Profile of the Federal Workforce. Biennial. (Even years.)

    Occupations of Federal White-Collar and Blue-Collar Workers. Biennial. (Odd years.)

  Women's Bureau

    Handbook on Women Workers. Periodic.

Other

  Aerospace Industries Association of America, Washington, DC

    Employment in the Aerospace Industry. Monthly.

    Survey of Aerospace Employment. Annual.

  The Bureau of National Affairs, Inc., Washington, DC

    Basic Patterns in Union Contracts. Annual.

    BNA's Employment Outlook. Quarterly.

Labor —Con.

Other —Con.

BNA's Job Absence and Turnover. Quarterly.

Briefing Sessions on Employee Relations Workbook. Annual.

Calendar of Negotiations. Annual.

Directory of U.S. Labor Organizations. Annual.

National Labor Relations Board Election Statistics. Annual.

NLRB Representation and Decertification Elections Statistics. Quarterly.

PPF Survey (Personnel Policies Forum.) Three times a year.

Law Enforcement, Courts, and Prisons

U.S. Government

Administrative Office of the United States Courts

Judicial Business of the United States Courts.

Calendar Year Reports on Authorized Wiretaps. (State and Federal.)

Federal Court Management Statistics. Annual.

Federal Judicial Case Statistics. Annual.

Statistical Tables for the Federal Judiciary. Semiannual.

Bureau of the Census

Census of Population. Decennial. (1990, most recent.)

Bureau of Justice Statistics

Age patterns of victims of serious violent crimes. September 1997.

Alcohol and crime: An analysis of national data on the prevalence of alcohol involvement in crime. April 1998.

Campus law enforcement agencies, 1995. December 1996.

Capital punishment. Annual. 1996. December 1997.

Carjacking. March 1994.

Census of state and local law enforcement agencies, 1992. July 1993.

Changes in criminal victimization, 1994-95. April 1997.

Characteristics of adults on probation, 1995, December 1997.

Child victimizers: Violent offenders and their victims. March 1996.

Civil jury cases and verdicts in large counties: Civil justice survey of state courts, 1992.

Civil Justice Survey of State Courts, 1992, CD-ROM. July 1996.

Comparing case processing statistics. September 1996.

Comparing federal and state prison inmates, 1991. October 1994.

Contract cases in large counties: Civil Justice Survey of State Courts, 1992. February 1996.

Law Enforcement, Courts, and Prisons —Con.

U.S. Government —Con.

Correctional populations in the United States annual.

Costs of crime to victims. March 1994.

Criminal Victimization. Annual.

Criminal Victimization in the United States Annual.

Drugs and crime facts, 1994. June 1995.

Drugs, crime and the justice system: A national report. May 1993.

Elderly crime victims: Selected findings. March 1994.

Expenditure and Employment Data for the Criminal Justice System. Annual.

Federal criminal case processing, 1997. June 1998.

Federal firearms-related offenses: Federal offenses and offenders. July 1995.

Federal law enforcement officers, 1996. January 1998.

Federal tort trials and verdicts, 1994-95. January 1998.

Felony defendants in large urban counties: Biennial.

Felony sentences in state courts: Biennial.

Felony sentences in the United States Biennial.

Female victims of violent crime. December 1996.

Firearms and crimes of violence: Selected findings from national statistical series. February 1994.

Firearm injury from crime: Firearms, crime, and criminal justice. April 1996.

Guns and crime: Handgun victimization, firearm self-defense, and firearm theft. May 1994.

Guns used in crime: Firearms, crime, and criminal justice. July 1995.

Highlights from 20 years of surveying crime victims: The National Crime Victimization Survey, 1973-92. November 1993.

HIV in prisons and jails 1995. August 1997.

Households Touched by Crime. Annual.

Indigent defense. February 1996.

Injuries from crime. May 1989.

Jails and jail inmates: 1993-94: Census of jails and survey of jails. May 1995.

Justice expenditure and employment in the United States, 1990. May 1998.

Juvenile delinquents in the federal criminal justice system. February 1997.

Juveniles prosecuted in state criminal courts, 1994: National Survey of Prosecutors. March 1997.

Law enforcement management and administrative statistics: Data for individual agencies with 100 or more officers, 1993. September 1995.

Law Enforcement, Courts, and Prisons —Con.
U.S. Government —Con.

Lifetime likelihood of going to state or federal prison. March 1997.

Local police departments, 1993: A LEMAS report. April 1996.

Motor Vehicle Theft

Murder in families. July 1994.

Murder in large urban counties, 1988. May 1993.

National Corrections Reporting Program. Annual.

Nation's two crime measures: The Uniform Crime Reports and the National Crime Survey. November 1995.

Noncitizens in the federal criminal justice system: Federal Justice Statistics Program. August 1996.

Parole in the United States Annual.

Population density in state prisons. December 1986.

Presale firearm checks: A national estimate. February 1997.

Pretrial release of federal felony defendants: Federal Justice Statistics Program, 1990, February 1994.

Pretrial release of felony defendants, 1992: National Pretrial Reporting Program, 1992. November. 1994.

Prison and jail inmates 1995. August 1996.

Prison and jail inmates at midyear, 1997. January 1998.

Prisoner petitions in the federal courts, 1980-96

Prisoners in State and Federal Institutions. Annual.

Probation and parole populations, 1996. August 1997.

Profile of inmates in the United States and in England and Wales. October. 1994.

Profile of jail inmates, 1996. April 1998.

Prosecutors in state courts. Biennial.

Sentencing in the federal courts: Does race matter? The transition to sentencing guidelines, 1986-90. December 1993.

Sex differences in violent victimization, 1994. September 1997.

Sex offenses and offenders. January 1997.

Sheriffs' departments 1993. June 1996.

Sourcebook of criminal justice statistics, 1994-95 editions, CDROM. October 1997.

Spouse murder defendants in large urban counties. September 1995.

State court sentencing of convicted felons. Biennial.

Students' reports of school crime: 1989 and 1995. April 1998.

Law Enforcement, Courts, and Prisons —Con.
U.S. Government —Con.

Substance abuse and treatment of adults on probation, 1995. March 1998.

Survey of state criminal history information systems, 1995. May 1997.

Survey of state prison inmates, 1991. May 1993.

Tort cases in large counties: Civil justice survey of state courts, 1992. April 1995.

Violence against women: Estimates from the redesigned survey. August 1995.

Violence and theft in the workplace. July 1994.

Violence by intimates: Analysis of data on crimes by current or former spouses, boyfriends, and girlfriends. March 1998.

Violence-related injuries treated in hospital emergency departments. August 1997.

Violent crime. April 1994.

Violent offenders in state prison: Sentences and time served— state inmates, 1992-94. July 1995.

Weapons offenses and offenders: Firearms, crime and criminal justice. November 1995.

Women in prison. March 1994.

Young black male victims. December 1994.

Drug Enforcement Administration

Drug Abuse and Law Enforcement Statistics. Irregular.

Federal Bureau of Investigation

Bomb Summary. Annual.

Crime in the United States. Annual.

Law Enforcement Officers Killed and Assaulted. Annual.

Other

Institute for Criminal Justice Ethics, New York, NY

Criminal Justice Ethics. Semiannual.

National Center for State Courts, Williamsburg, VA

State Court Caseload Statistics. Annual.

Libraries — *see* Education.

Livestock —*see* Agriculture.

Lumber —*see* Forests and Lumber.

Manufactures —*see also* Agriculture; Business; Economic Indexes; Forests and Lumber; Investments; Labor; *and* Minerals
U.S. Government

Board of Governors of the Federal Reserve System

Annual Statistical Digest.

Federal Reserve Bulletin. Monthly.

Industrial Production and Capacity Utilization G.17. Monthly.

Bureau of Alcohol, Tobacco, and Firearms

Alcohol and Tobacco Summary Statistics. Annual.

Bureau of the Census

Manufactures —Con.
  U.S. Government —Con.
    Annual Survey of Manufactures. (1995, most recent.)
    Census of Manufactures. Quinquennial. (1992, most recent.)
    Concentration Ratios in Manufacturing Industry. (1992, most recent.)
    Cotton Production and Distribution. Annual.
    County Business Patterns. Annual.
    Current Industrial Reports. Monthly, quarterly, and annual series on various industries.
    Manufacturers' Shipments, Inventories, and Orders. Monthly.
    Manufacturers' Shipments, Inventories, and Orders: 1987-96. Annual summary. (Current Industrial Reports M3-1(95).)
    Manufacturing Profiles. (series MP-1.) Annual.
    Plant and Equipment Expenditures and Plans. Quarterly.
    Pollution Abatement Cost and Expenditures. (Current Industrial Reports MA-200.)
    Quarterly Financial Report for Manufacturing, Mining, and Trade Corporations.
    Survey of Plant Capacity Utilization. (Current Industrial Reports MQ-C1.) Discontinued March 1992.
    U.S. Commodity Exports and Imports as Related to Output. Annual. (Series ES2.)
  Bureau of Economic Analysis
    Business Statistics, 1963-91. 1992. (Discontinued.)
    Survey of Current Business. Monthly.
  Bureau of Labor Statistics
    Compensation and Working Conditions. Quarterly.
    Employment and Earnings. Monthly.
    Employment, Hours, and Earnings, United States, 1909-94. 1994. (Bulletin 2445.)
    Employment, Hours, and Earnings, United States, 1988-96. 1996. (Bulletin 2481.)
    Monthly Labor Review.
    Occupational Employment in Manufacturing Industries. 1994. (Bulletin 2437.)
    Occupational Injuries and Illnesses in the United States by Industry. Annual.
    Producer Price Indexes. Monthly, with annual supplement.
    Productivity Measures for Selected Industries and Government Services. Annual.
    White-Collar Pay: Private Goods-Producing Industries, March 1990. 1990. (Bulletin 2374.)
  International Trade Administration
    U.S. Industrial Outlook. Annual. (1994, most recent.)

Manufactures —Con.
  U.S. Government —Con.
    International Trade Commission
      Synthetic Organic Chemicals, U.S. Production and Sales. Annual.
    National Science Foundation
      International Science and Technology Data Update. Report. Annual.
      Planned R&D Expenditures of Major U.S. Firms. Special Report. (NSF 91-306.)
      Research and Development in Industry. Detailed Statistical Tables. Annual.
      Science and Engineering Indicators. Report. Biennial.
      Science and Engineering Personnel: A National Overview, Report. Biennial.
      Scientists, Engineers, and Technicians in Manufacturing Industries. Detailed Statistical Tables. Triennial.
      Scientists, Engineers, and Technicians in Nonmanufacturing Industries. Detailed Statistical Tables. Triennial.
      Scientists, Engineers, and Technicians in Trade and Regulated Industries. Detailed Statistical Tables. Triennial.
  Other
    Aerospace Industries Association of America, Washington, DC
      Aerospace Facts and Figures. Annual.
      Aerospace Industry Year-End Review and Forecast. Annual.
      Commercial Helicopter Shipments. Quarterly.
      Manufacturing Production, Capacity, and Utilization in Aerospace and Aircraft and Parts. Quarterly.
      Orders, Shipments, Backlog and Inventories for Aircraft, Missiles, & Parts. Quarterly.
    American Automobile Manufacturers Association of the United States, Inc., Detroit MI
      Motor Vehicle Facts and Figures. Annual.
    American Frozen Food Institute, Burlingame, CA
      Frozen Food Pack Statistics. Annual.
    American Iron and Steel Institute, Washington, DC
      Annual Statistical Report.
    Bridge Commodity Research Bureau, New York, NY
    Commodity Yearbook. Annual.
    Dataquest Inc., San Jose, CA
      Consolidated Data Base.
    Dealerscope Merchandising, Philadelphia, PA
      Merchandising. Annual.
    Electronic Industries Alliance, Arlington, VA
      Electronic Market Data Book. Annual.
      Electronic Market Trends. Monthly.
      Electronics Foreign Trade. Monthly.
    National Association of Hosiery Manufacturers, Charlotte, NC

Manufactures —Con.
  Other —Con.
    Hosiery Statistics. Annual.
    National Food Processors Association, Washington, DC
      Canned Fruit and Vegetable Pack and Stock Situation Reports. Quarterly.

Marine Corps —*see* National Defense.

Marriage —*see* Vital Statistics.

Medical Care; Mental Health —*see* Health.

Merchant Vessels —*see* Transportation

Military Services —see National Defense.

Minerals and Metals —*see also* Economic Indexes; Energy; Foreign Commerce; *and* Manufactures
  U.S. Government
    Bureau of the Census
      Census of Mineral Industries. Quinquennial.(1992, most recent.)
    U.S. Geological Survey
      Mineral Commodity Summaries. Annual.
      Mineral Industry Surveys. (Monthly, quarterly, or annual report.)
      Minerals Yearbook. (Monthly, quarterly, or annual report.)
    Department of the Treasury
      Treasury Bulletin. Quarterly.
    Energy Information Administration
      Annual Energy Review.
      Coal Industry Annual.
      International Energy Outlook.
      International Energy Annual.
      Monthly Energy Review.
      Natural Gas Annual.
      Petroleum Supply Annual.
      Quarterly Coal Report.
      U.S. Crude Oil, Natural Gas, and Natural Gas Liquids Reserves. Annual.
  Other
    American Bureau of Metal Statistics, Inc., Secaucus, NJ
      Non-Ferrous Metal Data.
    American Gas Association, Arlington, VA
      Gas Facts. Annual.
      Year Book.
    American Metal Market, New York, NY
      Daily Newspapers.
      Metal Statistics. Annual.
    American Petroleum Institute, Washington, DC
      Quarterly Well Completion Report.
    American Petroleum Institute, Independent Petroleum Association of America, and Mid-Continent Oil and Gas Association
      Joint Association Survey on Drilling Costs. Annual.
    Knight-Ridder Commodity Research Bureau, Chicago, IL
      Commodity Yearbook. Annual.

Minerals and Metals —Con.
  Other —Con.
    Independent Petroleum Association of America, Washington, DC
      IPAA Weekly Oil Trends.
      IPAA Wholesale Oil Prices. Monthly.
      The Oil & Natural Gas Producing Industry in Your State. Annual.
      U.S. Petroleum Statistics. Semiannual.
    McGraw-Hill Publications Co., New York, NY
      Engineering and Mining Journal. Monthly.
      Keystone Coal Industry Manual. Annual.
    National Coal Association, Washington, DC
      Coal Data. Annual.
    PennWell Publishing Co., Tulsa, OK
      Offshore. Monthly.
      Oil and Gas Journal. Weekly.
    Carl H. Pforzheimer & Co., New York, NY
      Comparative Oil Company Statistics, 1991-1990. Annual.

Money and Banking —*see also* Construction; Insurance; International Accounts; *and* Investments
  U.S. Government
    Board of Governors of the Federal Reserve System
      Annual Statistical Digest.
      Domestic Offices, Commercial Bank Assets and Liabilities Consolidated Report of Condition. Quarterly.
      Federal Reserve Bulletin. Monthly.
      Flow of Funds Accounts: Seasonally Adjusted and Unadjusted. Z.1(780). Quarterly.
      Money Stock, Liquid Assets, and Debt Measures. H.6. Weekly.
    Bureau of the Census
      Census of Finance, Insurance, and Real Estate. Quinquennial. (1992, most recent.)
    Bureau of the Mint
      Annual Report of the Director.
    Comptroller of the Currency
      Quarterly Journal.
    Department of the Treasury
      Daily Treasury Statement.
      Monthly Treasury Statement of Receipts and Outlays of the United States Government.
      Statement of United States Currency and Coin. Monthly.
      Treasury Bulletin. Quarterly.
    Farm Credit Administration
      Annual Report on the Work of the Cooperative Farm Credit System.
      Production Credit Association: Summary of Operations. Annual.
      Report to the Federal Land Bank Associations. Annual.
    Federal Deposit Insurance Corporation
      Annual Report.

Money and Banking —Con.
  U.S. Government —Con.
      Data Book-Operating Banks and
        Branches. Annual.
      Quarterly Banking Profile.
      Statistics on Banking. Annual, and Histori-
        cal 1934-1996, Volume I.
      Trust Assets of Insured Commercial
        Banks. Annual.
      Quarterly Banking Review.
    National Credit Union Administration
      Annual Report.
      Yearend Statistics.
      Midyear Statistics.
    Office of Thrift Supervision
      Annual Report.

  Other
    Credit Union National Association, Inc.,
      Madison, WI
      Credit Union Services Profile. Annual.
      The Credit Union Report. Annual.
      Operating Ratios and Spreads. Semian-
        nual.
    William B. Dana Co., New York, NY
      The Market Chronicle. Weekly.
    Federal National Mortgage Association,
      Washington, DC
      Annual Report.
    Investment Company Institute, Washington,
      DC
      Mutual Fund Fact Book. Annual.
    National Council of Savings Institutions,
      Washington, DC
      Fact Book of National Council of Savings
        Institutions. Annual.
    United States League of Savings Institu-
      tions, Chicago, IL
      Savings Institutions Sourcebook. Annual.
Mortgages —*see* Construction; *and* Money.
Motor Carriers and Vehicles —*see* Transportation
National Defense —*see also* Federal Government
  U.S. Government
    Bureau of the Census
      Manufacturers' Shipments to Federal
        Government Agencies. (Current Indus-
        trial Reports MA-175.) Conducted for
        economic census years ending in 2 and
        7.)
    Department of Defense
      Annual Fact Sheet of Department of
        Defense.
      Annual Report of Secretary of Defense.
      Atlas/Data Abstract for the United States
        and Selected Areas. Annual.
      The Black in the Armed Forces. Statistical
        Fact Book. Annual.
      Five Year Defense Plan. Annual.
      Foreign Military Sales and Military Assis-
        tance Facts. Annual.
      Military Manpower Statistics. Quarterly.

National Defense —Con.
  U.S. Government —Con.
      Military Posture Report. Annual.
      Prime Contract Awards. Semiannual.
      Prime Contract Awards by State. Semian-
        nual.
      Selected Defense Department Economic
        Indicators. Monthly.
      Selected Manpower Statistics. Annual.
    Department of Veterans Affairs
      Annual Report of the Secretary of Veter-
        ans Affairs.
    National Guard Bureau
      Annual Review of the Chief.
    Office of Civil Defense
      Annual Statistical Report.
    Office of Management and Budget
      The Budget of the United States Govern-
        ment. Annual.
    Selective Service System, National Head-
      quarters
      Semiannual Report of the Director of
        Selective Service
    U.S. Arms Control and Disarmament Agency
      World Military Expenditures and Arms
        Transfers. Annual.
National Income and Wealth —*see also* Con-
  sumer Income; *and* Money and Banking
  U.S. Government
    Bureau of Economic Analysis
      Business Statistics, 1963-91. 1992. (Dis-
        continued.)
      The National Income and Product
        Accounts of the United States, 1929-94:
        Statistical tables, 1998.
      Survey of Current Business. Monthly.
    Council of Economic Advisers
      Economic Indicators. Monthly.
      Economic Report of the President.
        Annual.
    Internal Revenue Service
      Statistics of Income Bulletin. Quarterly.
Naturalization —*see* Immigration.
Navy —*see* National Defense.
Newspapers, Periodicals, and Books —*see also*
  Communications
  U.S. Government
    Bureau of the Census
      Annual Survey of Manufactures. (1996,
        most recent.)
      Census of Manufactures. Quinquennial.
        (1992, most recent.)
    Library of Congress
      Annual Report.
    The National Library of Medicine (for clinical
      medical reports)
      Annual Report.
    The National Agricultural Library (for techni-
      cal agricultural publications)
      Annual Report

Retail and Wholesale Trade —Con.
  U.S. Government —Con.
    Annual Benchmark Report for Retail
      Trade.
    Annual Benchmark Report for Wholesale
      Trade.
    Census of Retail Trade. Quinquennial.
      (1992, most recent.)
    Census of Wholesale Trade. Quinquen-
      nial. (1992, most recent.)
    County Business Patterns. Annual.
    Merchant Wholesalers Measures of Value
      Produced, Capital Expenditures, Depre-
      ciable Assets, and Operating Expenses.
      (1992, most recent.)
    Monthly Retail Trade Report. Sales and
      Inventories.
    Monthly Wholesale Trade Report. Sales
      and Inventories.
    Selected Characteristics of Retail Trade-
      Measures of Value Produced, Capital
      Expenditures, Depreciable Assets, and
      Operating Expenses. (1992, most
      recent.)
  Bureau of Economic Analysis
    Business Statistics, 1963-91. 1992. (Dis-
      continued.)
    Survey of Current Business. Monthly.
  Bureau of Labor Statistics
    Compensation and Working Conditions.
      Quarterly.
    CPI Detailed Report. Monthly.
    Employment and Earnings. Monthly.
    Employment, Hours, and Earnings,
      United States, 1909-94. 1994. (Bulletin
      2445.)
    Employment, Hours, and Earnings,
      United States, 1988-96. 1996. (Bulletin
      2481.)
    Monthly Labor Review.
    Occupational Employment Statistics,
      1994. 1996. (Bulletin 2468.)
    Occupational Injuries and Illnesses in the
      United States by Industry. Annual.
    Producer Price Indexes. Monthly, with
      annual supplement.
    Productivity Measures for Selected Indus-
      tries and Government Services. Annual.
    Technology and Labor in Three Service
      Industries: Utilities, Retail Trade, and
      Lodging. 1990. (Bulletin 2367.)
  Other
    Dealerscope Merchandising, Philadelphia,
      PA
      Merchandising. Annual.
    Lebhar-Friedman, Inc., New York, NY
      Accounting Today. Biweekly.
      Apparel Merchandising. Monthly.
    Market Statistics, New York, NY
      The Survey of Buying Power Data Serv-
        ice. Annual.

Retail and Wholesale Trade —Con.
  Other —Con.
    National Restaurant Association, Washing-
      ton, DC
      Restaurant Economic Trends. Monthly.
      Restaurant Industry Employee Profile.
        1998.
      Restaurant Industry Forecast. Annual.
      Restaurant Industry in Review. Annual.
      Restaurant Industry Operations Report.
        Annual.
      Restaurant Industry Pocket Factbook.
        Annual.
      Restaurant Numbers: A Statistical Digest
        for the Restaurant Industry. 1998.
      Restaurant Spending. Annual.
      Restaurants USA. Monthly.
      Survey of Wage Rates for Hourly Restau-
        rant Employees. Biennial.
      Survey of Benefits for Hourly Restaurant
        Employees. 1998.
      Limited-Service Restaurant Trends.
        Annual.
      Tableservice Restaurant Trends. Annual.
      Internet address:
        http://www.restaurant.org
Roads —*see* Transportation.
Sales —*see* Retail and Wholesale Trade.
Savings Institutions —*see* Money.
Science Resources
  U.S. Government
    Bureau of the Census
      Current Industrial Reports, MA37D.
        Annual.
    Energy Research and Development Admin-
      istration
      The Nuclear Industry. Annual.
    National Aeronautics and Space Administra-
      tion
      Annual Procurement Report.
      The Civil Service Work Force.
      Pocket Statistics. Annual.
    National Science Foundation
      Academic Research and Development
        Expenditures. Detailed Statistical
        Tables. Annual
      Academic Science and Engineering:
        Graduate Enrollment and Support:
        Detailed Statistical Tables. Annual
      Characteristics of Doctoral Scientists and
        Engineers in the United States. Detailed
        Statistical Tables. Biennial.
      Characteristics of Recent
        Science/Engineering Graduates.
        Detailed Statistical Tables. Biennial.
      Characteristics of Recent Scientists and
        Engineers. Detailed Statistical Tables.
        Biennial.
      Federal Funds for Research and Devel-
        opment. Detailed Statistiscal Tables.
        Annual.

Science Resources —Con.

U.S. Government —Con.

Federal R&D Funding by Budget Function. Report. Annual.

Federal Science and Engineering Support to Universities, Colleges, and Nonprofit Institutions. Detailed Statistical Tables. Annual.

Federal Scientists and Engineers. Detailed Statistical Tables. Quinquennial.

Graduate Students and Post-doctorates in Science and Engineering. Annual.

Immigrant Scientists, Engineers and Technicians. Detailed Statistical Tables. Annual.

International Science and Technology Data Update. Report. Annual.

National Patterns of R&D Resources. Report. Annual.

Research and Development in Industry. Detailed Statistical Tables. Annual.

Science and Engineering Degrees. Detailed Statistical Tables. Annual.

Science and Engineering Degrees, by Race/Ethnicity of Recipients. Detailed Statistical Tables. Annual.

Science and Engineering Doctorates Awards. Detailed Statistical Tables. Annual.

Science and Engineering Indicators. Report. Biennial.

Science and Engineering Profiles. Annual.

Scientific and Engineering Research Facilities at Universities and Colleges. Report. Biennial.

Science and Technology Pocket Data Book. Report. Annual.

Scientists, Engineers, and Technicians in Manufacturing Industries. Detailed Statistical Tables. Triennial.

Scientists, Engineers, and Technicians in Nonmanufacturing Industries. Detailed Statistical Tables. Triennial.

Scientists, Engineers, and Technicians in Trade and Regulated Industries. Detailed Statistical Tables. Triennial.

U.S. Scientists and Engineers. Detailed Statistical Tables. Biennial.

Women, Minorities, and Persons with Disabilities. Report. Biennial.

Patent and Trademark Office

Commissioner of Patents and Trademarks Annual Report.

Technology Assessment and Forecast Reports

"All Technologies." Annual.

"State Country." Annual.

"Patenting Trends in the United States." Annual.

Other

National Academy of Sciences, Washington, DC

Science Resources —Con.

Other —Con.

Science, Engineering, and Humanities Doctorates in the United States. Biennial. Summary Report. Doctorate Recipients from United States Universities. Annual.

Securities —see Investments; and Money.

Service Establishments—see also Retail and Wholesale Trade

U.S. Government

Bureau of the Census

Annual Survey of Communication Services.

Census of Service Industries. Quinquennial. (1992, most recent.)

Transportation Annual Survey.

Selected Characteristics of Selected Service Industries—Capital Expenditures, Depreciable Assets, and Operating Expenses. (1992, most recent.)

Service Annual Survey Report.

Internal Revenue Service

Statistics of Income Division. (Annual report on Corporation Income Tax Returns. Periodic compendiums on Studies of International Income and Taxes.)

Statistics of Income Bulletin. Quarterly.

Other

Decker Communications, Inc., New York, NY

Marketing Communications. (Advertising.) Monthly.

Laventhol & Horwath, Philadelphia, PA

The Executive Conference Center: A Statistical and Financial Profile. Annual.

Gaming Industry Study. Annual.

Lifecare Industry. Annual. (Analysis of facilities by size and section of the country for selected financial data, resident census information, and medical costs.)

National Trends of Business in the Lodging Industry. Monthly. (Analysis of nationwide trends in sales, occupancy, and room rates of hotels, motor hotels, and economy lodging facilities.)

Separate reports on the segments of lodging industries. Annuals. (Reports covering economy, all-suite, and resort.)

U.S. Lodging Industry. Annual. (Report on hotel and motor hotel operations.)

Worldwide Lodging Industry. Annual. (Report on international hotel operations.)

Pannell Kerr Forster, Houston, TX

Clubs in Town and Country. Annual.

Trends in the Hotel Industry, International Edition. Annual.

Trends in the Hotel Industry, U.S.A. Edition. Annual.

Social Insurance and Human Services —see also Insurance and Labor

State and Local Government —Con.
U.S. Government —Con.
County Government Employment. Annual. (GE No. 4.)

County Government Finances. Annual. (GF No. 8.)

Federal Expenditures by State. Annual.

Finances of Employee-Retirement Systems of State and Local Governments. Annual. (GF No. 2.)

Finances of Public School Systems. Annual. (GF No. 10.)

Finances of Selected Public Employee Retirement Systems. Quarterly. (GR Nos. 1-4.)

Government Finances. Annual. Covers federal, state, and local governments. (GF No. 5.)

Local Government Employment in Major County Areas. Annual. (GE No. 3.)

Local Government Finances in Major County Areas. Annual. (GF No. 6.)

Public Employment. Annual. (GE No. 1.)

Quarterly Summary of Federal, State, and Local Tax Revenue. (GT Nos. 1-4.)

State Government Finances. Annual. (GF No. 3.)

State Government Tax Collections. Annual. (GF No. 1.)

Bureau of Labor Statistics
Employee Benefits in State and Local Governments. Biennial.

Employment and Earnings. Monthly.

Employment, Hours, and Earnings, United States, 1909-94. 1994. (Bulletin 2445.)

Employment, Hours, and Earnings, United States, 1988-96. 1996. (Bulletin 2481.)

Occupational Employment Statistics, 1994. 1996. (Bulletin 2468.)

Federal Highway Administration
Highway Statistics. Annual.

Office of Management and Budget
The Budget of the United States Government. Annual.

Social Security Administration
Benefits and Beneficiaries Under Public Employee Retirement Systems, Fiscal Year 1991, Social Security Bulletin, Spring 1995.

Other
Advisory Commission on Intergovernmental Relations,Washington, DC

1991: State Revenue Capacity and Effort.

Significant Features of Fiscal Federalism. Annual.

The Council of State Governments, Lexington, KY

The Book of the States. Biennial.

State Administrative Officials Classified by Function. Biennial.

International City Management Association, Washington, DC

State and Local Government —Con.
Other —Con.
Baseline Data Reports. Bimonthly.

Compensation: An Annual Report on Local Government Executive Salaries and Fringe Benefits.

Municipal Year Book. Annual.

Special Data Issues. Periodical.

National Governors' Association, Washington, DC

Directory of Governors of the American States, Commonwealths & Territories. Annual.

Governors' Staff Directory. Biannual.

National Governors' Association and National Association of State Budget Officers, Washington, DC

The Fiscal Survey of States. Biannual.

Tax Foundation, Washington, DC

Facts and Figures on Government Finance. Annual.

Stocks and Bonds —*see* Investments.

Stores —*see* Retail and Wholesale Trade *and* Service Establishments.

Tax Collections —*see* Federal Government; *and* State and Local Government.

Telephone and Telegraph Systems —*see* Communications.

Television —*see* Communications.

Trade —*see* Foreign Commerce; Retail and Wholesale Trade; *and* Service Establishments.

Transportation —*see also* Foreign Commerce.
U.S. Government
Army, Corps of Engineers

Waterborne Commerce of the United States (in five parts). Annual.

Bureau of the Census

Census of Transportation, Communications and Utilities. Quinquennial. (1992, most recent.)

Commodity Flow Survey. 1993.

Transportation Annual Survey.

Truck Inventory and Use Survey. Quinquennial. (1992, most recent.)

Vessel Entrances and Clearances. Annual. (FT 975.)

Bureau of Economic Analysis

Business Statistics, 1963-91. 1992. (Discontinued.)

Survey of Current Business. Monthly.

Bureau of Transportation Statistics

Coast Guard

Annual Report of the Secretary of Transportation.

Marine Casualty Statistics. Annual.

Polluting Incidents In And Around U.S. Waters. Annual.

Department of State, Bureau of Consular Affairs

Summary of Passport Statistics. Annual.

Department of Transportation

Transportation —Con.
U.S. Government —Con.

Airport Activity Statistics of Certified Route Air Carriers. Annual.

Transportation Safety Information Report. Quarterly.

U.S. International Air Travel Statistics. Annual.

Federal Highway Administration

Highway Statistics. Annual.

Highway Statistics, Summary to 1995.

Interstate Commerce Commission

Class I Freight Railroads Selected Earnings Data. Quarterly.

Quarterly Report.

Transport Statistics in the United States. Issued annually in two separate parts:

    Part 1: Railroads

    Part 2: Motor Carriers

Maritime Administration

Annual Report.

Employment Report of United States Flag Merchant Fleet Ocean-going Vessels 1,000 Gross Tons and Over. Quarterly.

Foreign Flag Merchant Ships Owned by U.S. Parent Companies. Annual.

Maritime Manpower Report. Quarterly.

Research and Special Programs Administration

Other

Aerospace Industries Association of America, Washington, DC

Aerospace Facts and Figures. Annual.

Commercial Helicopter Shipments. Quarterly.

Air Transport Association of America, Washington, DC

Air Transport Association Annual Report.

American Automobile Manufacturers Association, Detroit, MI.

Motor Vehicle Facts and Figures. Annual.

World Motor Vehicle Data. Annual.

American Bureau of Shipping, Paramus, NJ

The Record. Annual with one supplement.

American Public Transit Association, Washington, DC

Internet address: http://www.apta.com

   Transit Fact Book. Annual.

Association of American Railroads, Washington, DC

Analysis of Class I Railroads. Annual.

Cars of Revenue Freight Loaded. Weekly with annual summary.

Freight Commodity Statistics, Class I Railroads in the United States. Annual.

Yearbook of Railroad Facts.

ENO Transportation Foundation, Leesburg, VA

Transportation in America. mid-year, annually with periodic supplements.

Transportation —Con.
Other —Con.

General Aviation Manufacturers Association, Washington, DC

Shipment Report. Quarterly and Annual.

Statistical Databook. Annual.

Lake Carriers' Association, Cleveland, OH

Annual Report.

Monthly Bulk Commodities Report.

Lloyd's Register of Shipping, London, England

Casualty Return. (Annual statistical summary of all merchant ships totally lost or reported broken up during year.)

Merchant Shipbuilding Returns. (Quarterly Statistical summary of world shipbuilding.)

World Fleet Statistics. (An end-year analysis of world merchant fleet.)

National Air Carrier Association, Washington, DC

Annual Report.

Regional Airline Association, Washington, DC

Annual Report.

Shipbuilders Council of America, Arlington, VA

Annual Report.

Tanker Advisory Center, Inc., New York, NY

Worldwide Tanker Casualty Returns. Annual.

Travel —*see* Recreation *and* Transportation.

Unemployment Insurance —*see* Labor; *and* Social Insurance.

Utilities, Public—*see* Communications; Energy; Public Utilities *and* Transportation.

Veterans —*see* National Defense; *and* Population.

Virgin Islands of the United States —*see* Outlying Areas.

Vital Statistics —*see also* Accidents; *and* Health
U.S. Government

Centers for Disease Control and Prevention, Atlanta, GA

Morbidity and Mortality Weekly Report. Annual summary also.

National Center for Health Statistics

Monthly Vital Statistics Report. Preliminary data births and deaths: United States, 1995.

Vital and Health Statistics. (A series of statistical reports covering health-related topics.)

    Series 20: Mortality Data. Irregular.

    Series 21: Natality, Marriage, and Divorce Data. Irregular.

    Series 23: National Survey of Family Growth Statistics. Irregular.

Vital Statistics of the United States. Annual.

Other

The Alan Guttmacher Institute, New York, NY

Family Planning Perspectives. Monthly.

United Nations Statistics Division, New York, NY

Guide to State Statistical Abstracts

This bibliography includes the most recent statistical abstracts for states published since 1987 plus those that will be issued in late 1998. For some states, a near equivalent has been listed in substitution for, or in addition to, a statistical abstract. All sources contain statistical tables on a variety of subjects for the state as a whole, its component parts, or both. The page counts given for publications are approximate. Internet sites also contain statistical data.

Alabama

University of Alabama, Center for Business and Economic Research, Box 870221, Tuscaloosa 35487   205-348-6191. Internet site <http://www.cba.ua.edu/~cber/>

*Economic Abstract of Alabama.*1997. 488 pp.

Alaska

Department of Commerce and Economic Development, Division of Trade & Development, P.O. Box 110804, Juneau 99811-0804 907-465-2017. Internet site <http://www. commerce.state.ak.us/trade/>

The Alaska Economy Performance Report. 1996

Arizona

University of Arizona, Economic and Business Research, College of Business and Public Administration, McClelland Hall 204 Tucson, Arizona 85721-0001   520-621-2155 fax 520-621-2150. Internet site <http://www. bpa.arizona.edu/newpage>

Arizona Statistical Abstract: A 1993 Data Handbook. 616 pp.

Arizona Economic Indicators. 52 pp. Biennial.

Arizona's Economy. 20 pp. (Quarterly newsletter and data.)

Arkansas

University of Arkansas at Little Rock, Institute for Economic Advancement, Economic Research, 2801 South University, Little Rock 72204   501-569-8550

Arkansas State and County Economic Data. 1997. 16 pp. (Revised annually.)

University of Arkansas at Little Rock, Institute for Economic Advancement, Census State Data Center, Little Rock 72204 501-569-8530

Arkansas Statistical Abstract, 1998. 700 pp. (Revised biennially.)

California

Department of Finance, 915 L Street, 8th Floor, Sacramento 95814   916-322-2263. Internet site <http://www.dof.ca.gov/>

California Statistical Abstract, 1997.

Pacific Data Resources, P.O. Box 1922, Santa Barbara, CA 93116-1922   800-422-2546

California Almanac, 6th ed. Biennial. 275 pp.

Colorado

University of Colorado, Business Research Division, Campus Box 420, Boulder 80309 303-492-8227. Internet site <http://www. colorado.edu/ libraries/govpubs/online/htm>

Statistical Abstract of Colorado, 1987. 600 pp. (Latest and last edition).

Connecticut

Connecticut Department of Economic & Community Development, 505 Hudson St., Hartford 06106 1-860-270-8165. Internet site <http://www.state.ct.us/ecd/>

Connecticut Market Data. Fall/winter 1998. (Diskette also available.)

Connecticut Town Profiles, 1996-97. 340 pp.

Delaware

Delaware Economic Development Office, 99 Kings Highway, Dover 19901 302-739-4271. Internet site <http://www. state.de.us/govern/ agencies/dedo/index.htm>

Delaware Statistical Overview, 1997.

District of Columbia

Office of Planning, Data Management Division, Presidential Bldg., Suite 500, 415 12th St., N.W. Washington 20004   202-727-6533

1990 Census, Population and Housing for the District of Columbia. 72 pp.

1990 Census: Social, Economic and Housing. (44 pp. for each of nine volumes).

Socio-Economic Indicators by Census Tract. 221 pp.

Socio-Economic Indicators of Change by Census Tract, 1980-1990. 146 pp.

Office of Policy and Evaluation, Executive Office of the Mayor, 1 Judiciary Square, Suite 920, 441 4th St., N.W., Washington 20001   202-727-6979

Indices—A Statistical Index to DC Services, Dec. 1994-96. 331 pp.

Florida

University of Florida, Bureau of Economic and Business Research, Box 117145, Gainesville 32611-7145   352-392-0171. Internet site <http://www.cba.ufl.edu/bebr/>

Florida Statistical Abstract, 1997. 31st ed. 800 pp. Also available on diskette.

Florida County Perspectives, 1997. One profile for each county. Annual.

Florida County Rankings, 1997.

Florida and the Nation, 1998.

Georgia

University of Georgia, Selig Center for Economic Growth, Terry College of Business, Athens 30602-6269 706-542-4085. Internet site <http://www.selig.uga.edu/>

Georgia Statistical Abstract, 1997-98. 500 pp.

University of Georgia, College of Agricultural and Environmental Sciences, Athens 30602-4356   706-542-8938 Fax 706542-8934. Internet site <http://www.uga.edu/~caes/>

The Georgia County Guide. 1998. 17th ed. Annual. 200 pp.

Hawaii

Hawaii State Department of Business, and Economic Development & Tourism, Research and Economic Analysis Division, Statistics Branch P.O. Box 2359, Honolulu 96804. Inquiries 808-586-2481; Copies 808-586-2424. Internet site <http://www.hawaii.gov/dbedt>

The State of Hawaii Data Book 1997: A Statistical Abstract. 30th ed. 700 pp.

Idaho

Department of Commerce, 700 West State St., Boise 83720-0093   208-334-2470. Internet site <http://www.idoc.state.id.us>

County Profiles of Idaho, 1998.
Idaho Community Profiles, 1997.
Idaho Facts, 1998.
Idaho Facts Data Book, 1995.
Profile of Rural Idaho 1998.

University of Idaho, Center for Business Development and Research, Moscow 83844-3227   208-885-6611. Internet site <http://www.daho.edu/cbdr>

Idaho Statistical Abstract, 4th ed. 1996.

Illinois

University of Illinois, Bureau of Economic and Business Research, 428 Commerce West, 1206 South 6th Street, Champaign 61820 217-333-2332

Illinois Statistical Abstract. 1997. 850 pages

Indiana

Indiana University, Indiana Business Research Center, School of Business, 801 W. Michigan BS4015 Indianapolis 46202-5151 317-274-2204. Internet site <http://www.iupui.edu/it/ibrc/>

Indiana Factbook, 1998-99. 393 pages.

Iowa

Public Interest Institute, 600 N. Jackson Street, Mount Pleasant, IA 52641   319-385-3462

1996 Statistical Profile of Iowa.

Kansas

University of Kansas, Institute for Public Policy and Business Research, 607 Blake Hall, Lawrence 66045-2960   785-864-3701. Internet site <http://www.ukans.edu/cwis/units/IPPBR/>

Kansas Statistical Abstract, 1997. 32nd ed. 1998.

Kentucky

Kentucky Cabinet for Economic Development, Division of Research, 500 Mero Street, Capital Plaza Tower, Frankfort 40601 502-564-4886. Internet site <http://www.state.ky.us/edc/cabmain.htm>

Kentucky Deskbook of Economic Statistics. 34th ed. 1998.

Louisiana

University of New Orleans, Division of Business and Economic Research, New Orleans 70148 504-280-6240. Internet site <http://leap.nlu.edu/STAAB.HTM>

Statistical Abstract of Louisiana. 10th ed. 1997.

Maine

Maine Department of Economic and Community Development, State House Station 59, Augusta 04333   207-287-2656

Maine: A Statistical Summary. (Updated periodically.)

Maryland

Regional Economic Studies Institute (RESI), Towson University, Towson 21252-7097 410-830-3778

Maryland Statistical Abstract. 1997. 356 pp.

Massachusetts

Massachusetts Institute for Social and Economic Research, Box 37515, University of Massachusetts at Amherst 01003-7515 413-545-3460 Fax 413-545-3686. Internet site <http://www.umass.edu/miser/>

Population Estimates for Massachusetts Cities and Towns. 1995.

Projection of the Population, Mass., Cities and Towns, Years 1990-2010.

Journey to work in Mass., 1990.

Minnesota

Department of Trade and Economic Development, Business and Community Development Division, 500 Metro Square Building, St. Paul 55101   651-297-1291

Compare Minnesota: An Economic and Statistical Factbook, 1994-95. 165 pp.

Economic Report to the Governor: State of Minnesota, 1992. 148 pp.

Office of State Demographer, Minnesota Planning, 300 Centennial Bldg., St. Paul 55155   651-296-2557. Internet site <http://www.mnplan.state.mn.us/demography/>

Minnesota Population and Household Estimates, 1997. Available diskette in Lotus, dBase or ASCII formats.

Minnesota Population Projections, 2025.

Mississippi

Mississippi State University, College of Business and Industry, Division of Research, P.O. Box 5288 Mississippi State 39762 601-325-3817/3571

Mississippi Statistical Abstract. 1997. 554 pp.

Missouri

University of Missouri, Business and Public Administration Research Center, Columbia 65211   573-882-4805. Internet site <http://tiger.bpa.missouri.edu/bparc/>

Statistical Abstract for Missouri, 1997 Biennial. 256 pp.

Montana

Montana Department of Commerce, Census and Economic Information Center, 1424 9th Ave., Helena 59620   406-444-2896. Internet site <http://commerce.state.mt.us/ceic/>

Statistical Reports from the Montana County Database. (Separate county and State reports; available by subject section as well as complete reports by county and State, updated periodically.)

Nebraska

Department of Economic Development, Division of Research, Box 94666, Lincoln 68509   402-471-3784 . Internet site <http://www.ded.state.ne.us/>

Nebraska Statistical Handbook. 1997-1998. 300 pp. (Available only on internet).

Nevada

Department of Administration, Budget and Planning Division, 209 East Musser Street, Suite 200, Carson City 89710   702-687-4065

Nevada Statistical Abstract. 1996. Biennial. 225 pp.

New Hampshire

Office of State Planning, 2 1/2 Beacon St., Concord 03301-4497   603-271-2155 Internet site <http://www.state.nh.us/osp/nhresnet/>

Current Estimates and Trends in New Hampshire's Housing Supply. Update: 1996. 32 pp.

1996 Population Estimates for New Hampshire Cities and Towns

New Hampshire Population Projections for Counties by Age & Sex, Apr. 1997, 2000-2020.

New Jersey

New Jersey State Data Center, NJ Department of Labor, P.O. Box 388, Trenton 08625-0388 609-984-2595. Internet site <http://www. state.nj.us/labor/lra/njsdc.html>

New Jersey Source Book, 1993. 156 pp.

New Mexico

University of New Mexico, Bureau of Business and Economic Research, 1919 Lomas N.E. Albuquerque 87131-6021   505-277-6626 Fax 505-277-2773. Internet site <http://www. unm.edu/bber/>

County Profiles. *1997.* 72 pp.

Community Profiles for Selected New Mexico cities.

Population Projections for the State of New Mexico, 1997.

New York

Nelson A. Rockefeller Institute of Government, 411 State Street, Albany 12203-1003 518-443-5522. Internet site <http://www. rockinst.org/>

New York State Statistical Yearbook, 1997. 21st ed. 582 pp.

North Carolina

Office of Governor Office of State Planning, 116 West Jones Street, Raleigh 27603-8003 919-733-4131. Internet site <http://www.ospl. state.nc.us/#Demographer>

Statistical Abstract of North Carolina Counties, 1991. 6th edition. (No longer being published.)

North Dakota

University of North Dakota, Box 8369, Bureau of Business and Economic Research, Grand Forks 58202   701-777-2637

The Statistical Abstract of North Dakota. 1988. 700 pp.

North Dakota Department of Economic Development & Finance, 1833 E. Bismark Expressway, Bismark 58504-6708 701-231-7441

State of North Dakota Economic, Demographic, Public Services, and Fiscal Condition. May 1998. 155 pp.

Ohio

Department of Development, Office of Strategic Research, P.O. Box 1001, Columbus 43216-1001   614-466-2115. Internet site <http://www.odod.ohio.gov/>

Research products and services. (Updated continuously.)

The Ohio State University, School of Public Policy and Management, 1775 College Road, Columbus 43210-1399   614-292-8696

Benchmark Ohio, 1993. Biennial. 300 pp.

Oklahoma

University of Oklahoma, Center for Economic and Management Research, 307 West Brooks Street, Room 4, Norman 73019 405-325-2931. Internet site <http://www.nt. cba.ou.edu/>

Statistical Abstract of Oklahoma, 1997. Annual. 441 pp.

Oregon

Secretary of State, Business Services Division, Publication Services Bldg., 2555 Capital Street, NE, Suite 180, Salem 97310 503-986-2234. Internet site <http://www.sos. state.or.us/bluebook/1997-98/toc.htm>

Oregon Blue Book. 1997-1998. Biennial. 476 pp.

Pennsylvania

Pennsylvania State Data Center, Institute of State and Regional Affairs, Penn State Harrisburg, 777 West Harrisburg Pike, Middletown Pennsylvania 17057-4898 717-948-6336. Internet site <http://howard. hbg.psu.edu/psdc/psdchome1.1.html>

Pennsylvania Statistical Abstract, 1998. 301 pp.

Rhode Island

Rhode Island Economic Development Corporation, 1 West Exchange Street, Providence 02903   401-222-2601 Fax 401-222-2102. Internet site <http://www. riedc.com/>

Rhode Island 1990 Census of Population and Housing Summary. May 1994.

The Rhode Island Economy. July 1998.

South Carolina

Budget and Control Board, Office of Research and Statistical Services, R. C. Dennis Building, Room 425, Columbia 29201 803-734-3781. Internet site <http://www.state.sc.us/drss/>

South Carolina Statistical Abstract: 1997. 440 pp.

South Dakota

University of South Dakota, State Data Center, Business Research Bureau, Vermillion 57069-2390   605-677-5287

1997 South Dakota Community Abstracts. 400 pp.

Tennessee

University of Tennessee at Knoxville, Center for Business and Economic Research, 100 Glocker, Knoxville 37996-4170 615-974-6075. Internet site <http://cber.bus.utk.edu/>

Tennessee Statistical Abstract, 1996-97. 16th ed. 807 pp. Biennial.

Texas

Dallas Morning News, Communications Center, P.O. Box 655237, Dallas 75265-5237 214-977-8261

Texas Almanac, 1998-99. 672 pp.

Utah

University of Utah, Bureau of Economic and Business Research, 1645 East Campus Center Drive, Salt Lake City 84112-9302 801-581-6333. Internet site <http://www.business.utah.edu/BEBR/>

Statistical Abstract of Utah. 1996. (Centennial.)

Utah Foundation, 10 West 100 South, Suite 323, Salt Lake City 84101-1544 801-364-1837

Statistical Review of Government in Utah. 1997.

Vermont

Labor Market Information, Department of Employment and Training, 5 Green Mountain Drive, P.O. Box 488, Montpelier 05601-0488 802-828-4202. Internet site <http://www.det.state.vt.us/>

Demographic and Economic Profiles. Annual. Regional county reports also available.

Virginia

University of Virginia, Weldon Cooper Center for Public Service, 918 Emmet Street, North Suite 300, Charlottesville 22903-4832 804-982-5585. Internet site <http://www.virginia.edu/cpserz/>

Virginia Statistical Abstract, 1996-97. Biennial. 950 pp.

Washington

Washington State Office of Financial Management, Forecasting Division P.O. Box 43113 Olympia 98504-3113   360-902-0599. Internet site <http://www.wa.gov/ofm/>

Washington State Data Book, 1997. 300 pp.

Population Trends for Washington State. Annual. 48 pages.

West Virginia

West Virginia University, College of Business and Economics, Bureau of Business and Economic Research, P.O. Box 6025, Morgantown 26506-6026   304-293-7831. Internet site <http://www.wvu.edu/colbe/research/bureau/home.htm>

West Virginia Statistical Abstract, 1995, Biennial. 400 pp.

County Data Profiles. Annual. 50 pp.

Census Data Profiles. Decennial. 30 pp.

West Virginia Economic Outlook. Annual. 50 pp.

West Virginia Research League, Inc., P.O. Box 11176, Charleston 25339 304-346-9451

Economic Indicators. 1995. 215 pp.

The 1997 Statistical Handbook. 94 pp.

Wisconsin

Wisconsin Legislative Reference Bureau, P.O. Box 2037, Madison 53701-2037 608-266-7098

1997-1998 Wisconsin Blue Book. 950 pp. Biennial.

Wyoming

Department of Administration and Information, Division of Economic Analysis, 327 E. Emerson Building, Cheyenne 82002-0060 307-777-7504. Internet site <http://www.state.wy.us/ai/ai.html>

The Equality State Almanac 1997. 120 pp.

Guide to Foreign Statistical Abstracts

This bibliography presents recent statistical abstracts for Mexico, Russia, and member nations of the Organization for Economic Cooperation and Development. All sources contain statistical tables on a variety of subjects for the individual countries. Many of the following publications provide text in English as well as in the national language(s). For further information on these publications, contact the named statistical agency which is responsible for editing the publication.

Austria

Osterreichisches Statistisches Zentralamt, P.O. Box 9000, A-1033 Vienna

Statistisches Jahrbuch for die Republik Osterreich. Annual. 1997   554 pp. (In German.)

Australia

Australian Bureau of Statistics, Canberra

Yearbook Australia. Annual. 1998   809 pp. (In English.)

Belgium

Institut National de Statistique, 4 4 rue de Louvain, 1000 Brussels

Annuaire statistique de la Belgique. Annual. 1994   822 pp. (In French and Dutch.)

Canada

Statistics Canada, Ottawa, Ontario, KIA OT6

Canada Yearbook: A review of economic, social and political developments in Canada. 1997   515 pp. Irregular. (In English and French.)

Croatia

Republika Hrvatska, Republicki Zavod Za Statistiku

Statisticki ljetopis 1995   644 pp. (In English and Serbo-Croatian.)

Czech Republic

Czech Statistical Office, Sokolovska 142, 186 04 Praha 8

Statisticka Rocenka Ceske Rpubliky 1997   711 pp. (In English and Czech.)

Denmark

Danmarks Statistik, Postboks 2550 Sejrogade 11, DK 2100, Copenhagen

Statistical Yearbook. 1997. Annual. 559 pp. (In Danish with English translations of table headings.)

Finland

Central Statistical Office of Finland, Box 504 SF-00101 Helsinki

Statistical Yearbook of Finland. Annual. 1997   663 pp. (In English, Finnish, and Swedish.)

France

Institut National de la Statistique et des Etudes Economiques, Paris 18, Bld. Adolphe Pinard, 75675 Paris (Cedex 14)

Annuaire Statistique de la France. Annual. 1998   981 pp. (In French.)

Greece

National Statistical Office, 14-16 Lycourgou St., 101-66 Athens

Concise Statistical Yearbook 1995   254 pp. (In English.)

Statistical Yearbook of Greece. Annual. 1996 532 pp. (plus seven pages of diagrams). (In English and Greek.)

Iceland

Hagstofa Islands/Statistical Bureau, Hverfisgata 8-10, Reykjavik.

Statistical Abstract of Iceland. 1994. Irregular. 303 pp. (In English and Icelandic.)

Ireland

Central Statistics Office, Earlsfort Terrace, Dublin 2

Statistical Abstract. Annual. 1997   411 pp. (In English.)

Italy

ISTAT (Istituto Centrale di Statistica), Via Cesare Balbo 16, 00100 Rome

Annuario Statistico Italiano. Annual. 1997 791 pp. (In Italian.)

Japan

Statistics Bureau, Management & Coordination Agency, 19-1 Wakamatsucho, Shinjuku Tokyo 162

Japan Statistical Yearbook. Annual. 1998 918 pp. (In English and Japanese.)

Luxembourg

STATEC (Service Central de la Statistique et des Etudes), P.O. Box 304, L-2013, Luxembourg

Annuaire Statistique. Annual. 1997. (In French.)

Mexico

Instituto Nacional de Estadistica Geografia e Informatica, Avda. Insurgentes Sur No. 795-PH Col. Napoles, Del. Benito Juarez 03810 Mexico, D.F.

Anuario estadistico de los Estados Unidos Mexicanos. Annual. 1996 646 pp. Also on disc. (In Spanish.) *Agenda Estadistica 1994* 186 pp.

Netherlands

Centraal Bureau voor de Statistiek. 428 Prinses Beatrixlaan P.O. Box 959, 2270 AZ Voorburg

Statistisch Yearbook 1998. 585 pp. (In English.)

New Zealand

Department of Statistics, Wellington

New Zealand Official Yearbook. Annual. 1998   606 pp. (In English.)

Norway

Central Bureau of Statistics, Skippergate 15,
P.B. 8131 Dep. N-Oslo 1

Statistical Yearbook. Annual. 1997   475 pp.
(In English and Norwegian.)

Portugal

INE (Instituto Nacional de Estatistica), Avenida
Antonio Jose de Almeida, P-1078 Lisbon
Codex

Anuario Estatistico: de Portugal. 1995
339 pp. (In Portugese.)

Russia

State Committee of Statistics of Russia,
Moscow

Russian Federation in the Year 1993. Statistical Yearbook. 1997   746 pp. (In Russian.)

Slovakia

Statistical Office of the Slovak Republic,
Mileticova 3, 824 67 Bratislava

Statisticka Rocenka Slovensak 1997.
727 pp. (In English and Slovak)

Slovenia

Statistical Office of the Republic of Slovenia,
Vozarski Pot 12, 61000 Ljubljana

Statisticni Letopis Republike Slovenije 1997.
657 pp. (In Slovenian.)

Spain

INE (Instituto Nacional de Estadistica), Paseo
de la Castellana, 183, Madrid 16

Anuario Estadistico de Espana. Annual.
1996   848 pp. (In Spanish.)

Anuario Estadistico. 1988. (Edicion Manual.)
976 pp.

Sweden

Statistics Sweden, S-11581 Stockholm

Statistical Yearbook of Sweden. Annual.
1998   559 pp. (In English and Swedish.)

Switzerland

Bundesamt fur Statistik, Hallwylstrasse 15,
CH-3003, Bern

Statistisches Jahrbuch der Schweiz. Annual.
1998   549 pp. (In French and German.)

Turkey

State Institute of Statistics, Prime Ministry,
114 Necatibey Caddesi, Bakanliklar,
Yenisehir, Ankara

Statistical Yearbook of Turkey. 1996
690 pp. (In English and Turkish.)

Turkey in Statistics 1994   150 pp.
(In English and Turkish.)

United Kingdom

Central Statistical Office, Great George Street,
London SW1P 3AQ

Annual Abstract of Statistics. Annual. 1991
349 pp. (In English.)

West Germany

Statistische Bundesamt, Postfach 5528,
6200 Wiesbaden

*Statistisches Jahrbuch fur die
Bundesrepublic Deutschland.* Annual. 1997
755 pp. (In German.)

Statistisches Jahrbuch fur das Ausland.
1997. 398 pp.

Metropolitan Areas: Concepts, Components, and Population

Statistics for metropolitan areas (MAs) shown in the *Statistical Abstract* represent areas defined by the U.S. Office of Management and Budget (OMB) according to published standards that are applied to Census Bureau data. The general concept of an MA is that of a core area containing a large population nucleus, together with adjacent communities having a high degree of economic and social integration with that core. Currently defined MAs are based on application of 1990 standards (which appeared in the Federal Register on March 30, 1990) to 1990 decennial census data and to subsequent Census Bureau population estimates and special census data. Current MA definitions were announced by OMB effective June 30, 1998. MAs include metropolitan statistical areas (MSAs), consolidated metropolitan statistical areas (CMSAs), and primary metropolitan statistical areas (PMSAs).

In this appendix, Table B presents geographic components and 1997 population estimates for each MSA, CMSA, and PMSA outside of New England. Table A presents definitions and data for New England county metropolitan areas (NEC-MAs), the county-based alternative metropolitan areas for the city- and town-based MSAs and CMSAs of the six New England states.

Standard definitions of metropolitan areas were first issued in 1949 by the then Bureau of the Budget (predecessor of OMB), under the designation "standard metropolitan area" (SMA). The term was changed to "standard metropolitan statistical area" (SMSA) in 1959, and to "metropolitan statistical area" (MSA) in 1983. The collective term "metropolitan area" (MA) became effective in 1990.

OMB has been responsible for the official metropolitan areas since they were first defined, except for the period 1977 to 1981, when they were the responsibility of the Office of Federal Statistical Policy and Standards, Department of Commerce. The standards for defining metropolitan areas were modified in 1958, 1971, 1975, 1980, and 1990.

Defining MSAs, CMSAs, and PMSAs— The current standards provide that each newly qualifying MSA must include at least: one city with 50,000 or more inhabitants, or a Census Bureau-defined urbanized area (of at least 50,000 inhabitants) and a total metropolitan population of at least 100,000 (75,000 in New England). Under the standards, the county (or counties) that contains the largest city becomes the "central county" (counties), along with any adjacent counties that have at least 50 percent of their population in the urbanized area surrounding the largest city. Additional "outlying counties" are included in the MSA if they meet specified requirements of commuting to the central counties and other selected requirements of metropolitan character (such as population density and percent urban). In New England, the MSAs are defined in terms of cities and towns rather than counties. An area that meets these requirements for recognition as an MSA and also has a population of 1 million or more may be recognized as a CMSA if: separate component areas can be identified within the entire area by meeting statistical criteria specified in the standards, and local opinion indicates there is support for the component areas. If recognized, the component areas are designated PMSAs, and the entire area becomes a CMSA. PMSAs, like the CMSAs that contain them, are composed of entire counties, except in New England where they are composed of cities and towns. If no PMSAs are recognized, the entire area is designated as an MSA. As of the June 30, 1998, OMB announcement, there were 256 MSAs, and 18 CMSAs comprising 73 PMSAs in the United States. In addition, there were three MSAs, one CMSA, and three PMSAs in Puerto Rico.

Central cities and MA titles—The largest city in each MSA/CMSA is designated a "central city." Additional cities qualify if specified requirements are met concerning population size and commuting patterns. The title of each MSA consists of the names of up to three of its central cities and the name of each state into which the

MSA extends. However, a central city with less than 250,000 population and less than one-third the population of the area's largest city is not included in an MSA title unless local opinion supports its inclusion. Titles of PMSAs also typically are based on central city names but in certain cases consist of county names. Generally, titles of CMSAs are based on the titles of their component PMSAs.

Defining New England County Metropolitan Areas (NECMAs)—The OMB defines NECMAs as a county-based alternative to the city- and town-based New England MSAs and CMSAs. The NECMA defined for an MSA or a CMSA includes: the county containing the first-named city in that MSA/CMSA title (this county may include the first-named cities of other MSAs/CMSAs as well), and each additional county having at least half its population in the MSAs/CMSAs whose first-named cities are in the previously identified county. NECMAs are not identified for individual PMSAs. There are 12 NECMAs, including 1 for the Boston-Worcester-Lawrence, MA-NH-ME-CT CMSA and 1 for the Connecticut portion of the New York-Northern New Jersey-Long Island, NY-NJ-CT-PA CMSA. Central cities of a NECMA are those cities in the

NECMA that qualify as central cities of an MSA or a CMSA. NECMA titles derive from names of central cities.

Changes in MA definitions over time—Changes in the definitions of MAs since the 1950 census have consisted chiefly of the recognition of new areas as they reached the minimum required city or urbanized area population, and the addition of counties (or cities and towns in New England) to existing areas as new decennial census data showed them to qualify. In some instances, formerly separate MAs have been merged, components of an MA have been transferred from one MA to another, or components have been dropped from an MA. The large majority of changes have taken place on the basis of decennial census data. However, Census Bureau population estimates and special censuses serve as the basis for intercensal updates.

Because of these historical changes in geographic definitions, users must be cautious in comparing MA data from different dates. For some purposes, comparisons of data for MAs as defined at given dates may be appropriate; for other purposes, it may be preferable to maintain consistent MA definitions.

Table A. New England County Metropolitan Areas (NECMAs)

[In thousands. As of July 1]

NECMA	Population, 1997	NECMA	Population, 1997	NECMA	Population, 1997
Bangor, ME	143	Burlington, VT	191	New London-Norwich, CT	253
Penobscot County	143	Chittenden County	141	New London County	253
		Franklin County	44		
Barnstable-Yarmouth, MA	205	Grand Isle County	6	Pittsfield, MA	134
Barnstable County	205			Berkshire County	134
		Hartford, CT	1,105		
Boston-Worcester-Lawrence-		Hartford County	825	Portland, ME	251
Lowell-Brockton, MA-NH	5,828	Middlesex County	149	Cumberland County	251
Bristol County, MA	516	Tolland County	131		
Essex County, MA	691			Providence-Warwick-	
Middlesex County, MA	1,418	Lewiston-Auburn, ME	101	Pawtucket, RI	905
Norfolk County, MA	639	Androscoggin County	101	Bristol County	49
Plymouth County, MA	462			Kent County	162
Suffolk County, MA	643	New Haven-Bridgeport-		Providence County	574
Worcester County, MA	726	Stamford-Waterbury-		Washington County	120
Hillsborough County, NH	358	Danbury, CT	1,626		
Rockingham County, NH	267	Fairfield County	833	Springfield, MA	591
Strafford County, NH	108	New Haven County	792	Hampden County	441
				Hampshire County	150

Source: U.S. Bureau of the Census, "Estimates of the Population of Counties and Demographic Components of Population Change: April 1, 1990, to July 1, 1997"; published 17 March 1998; <http://www.census.gov/population/estimates/county/co-97-5/97C500.txt>.

Table B. Metropolitan Areas Outside of New England and Their Components as of June 30, 1998

[Population estimated as of **July 1, 1997**. All metropolitan areas are arranged alphabetically. PMSAs are included under their respective CMSAs, see CMSA entry. This table presents data for MAs outsideNew England only]

	Population, 1997 (1,000)
Abilene, TX MSA	**121**
Taylor County	121
Albany, GA MSA	**118**
Dougherty County	96
Lee County	22
Albany-Schenectady-Troy, NY MSA	**876**
Albany County	294
Montgomery County	51
Rensselaer County	154
Saratoga County	197
Schenectady County	147
Schoharie County	32
Albuquerque, NM MSA	**675**
Bernalillo County	526
Sandoval County	86
Valencia County	63
Alexandria, LA MSA	**126**
Rapides Parish	126
Allentown-Bethlehem-Easton, PA MSA	**614**
Carbon County	59
Lehigh County	298
Northampton County	257
Altoona, PA MSA	**131**
Blair County	131
Amarillo, TX MSA	**208**
Potter County	109
Randall County	99
Anchorage, AK MSA	**251**
Anchorage Borough	251
Anniston, AL MSA	**117**
Calhoun County	117
Appleton-Oshkosh-Neenah, WI MSA	**342**
Calumet County	38
Outagamie County	154
Winnebago County	150
Asheville, NC MSA	**211**
Buncombe County	193
Madison County	19
Athens, GA MSA	**139**
Clarke County	91
Madison County	24
Oconee County	23
Atlanta, GA MSA	**3,627**
Barrow County	39
Bartow County	69
Carroll County	81
Cherokee County	127
Clayton County	204
Cobb County	551
Coweta County	81
DeKalb County	588
Douglas County	87
Fayette County	85
Forsyth County	76
Fulton County	723
Gwinnett County	501
Henry County	98
Newton County	55

	Population, 1997 (1,000)
Paulding County	69
Pickens County	19
Rockdale County	67
Spalding County	57
Walton County	52
Augusta-Aiken, GA-SC MSA	**457**
Columbia County, GA	89
McDuffie County, GA	22
Richmond County, GA	193
Aiken County, SC	134
Edgefield County, SC	20
Austin-San Marcos, TX MSA.	**1,071**
Bastrop County	49
Caldwell County	32
Hays County	86
Travis County	694
Williamson County	210
Bakersfield, CA MSA	**629**
Kern County	629
Baton Rouge, LA MSA	**570**
Ascension Parish	70
East Baton Rouge Parish	394
Livingston Parish	85
West Baton Rouge Parish	20
Beaumont-Port Arthur, TX MSA	**375**
Hardin County	48
Jefferson County	242
Orange County	85
Bellingham, WA MSA	**154**
Whatcom County	154
Benton Harbor, MI MSA	**161**
Berrien County	161
Billings, MT MSA	**126**
Yellowstone County	126
Biloxi-Gulfport-Pascagoula, MS MSA	**343**
Hancock County	39
Harrison County	176
Jackson County	129
Binghamton, NY MSA	**252**
Broome County	199
Tioga County	53
Birmingham, AL MSA	**900**
Blount County	45
Jefferson County	659
St. Clair County	61
Shelby County	135
Bismarck, ND MSA	**91**
Burleigh County	67
Morton County	24
Bloomington, IN MSA	**117**
Monroe County	117
Bloomington-Normal, IL MSA	**141**
McLean County	141
Boise City, ID MSA	**384**
Ada County	267
Canyon County	117

	Population, 1997 (1,000)
Brownsville-Harlingen, TX MSA	**321**
Cameron County	321
Bryan-College Station, TX MSA	**133**
Brazos County	133
Buffalo-Niagara Falls, NY MSA	**1,165**
Erie County	944
Niagara County	220
Canton-Massillon, OH MSA	**403**
Carroll County	29
Stark County	374
Casper, WY MSA	**64**
Natrona County	64
Cedar Rapids, IA MSA	**182**
Linn County	182
Champaign-Urbana, IL MSA	**168**
Champaign County	168
Charleston-North Charleston, SC MSA	**510**
Berkeley County	134
Charleston County	285
Dorchester County	91
Charleston, WV MSA	**254**
Kanawha County	204
Putnam County	50
Charlotte-Gastonia-Rock Hill, NC-SC MSA	**1,350**
Cabarrus County, NC	116
Gaston County, NC	183
Lincoln County, NC	57
Mecklenburg County, NC	613
Rowan County, NC	124
Union County, NC	106
York County, SC	151
Charlottesville, VA MSA	**147**
Albemarle County	78
Fluvanna County	18
Greene County	13
Charlottesville city	38
Chattanooga, TN-GA MSA	**447**
Hamilton County, TN	295
Marion County, TN	27
Catoosa County, GA	50
Dade County, GA	15
Walker County, GA	62
Cheyenne, WY MSA	**78**
Laramie County	78
Chicago-Gary-Kenosha, IL-IN-WI CMSA	**8,642**
Chicago, IL PMSA	**7,774**
Cook County, IL	5,077
DeKalb County, IL	84
DuPage County, IL	870
Grundy County, IL	36
Kane County, IL	381
Kendall County, IL	50
Lake County, IL	595
McHenry County, IL	237
Will County, IL	444

	Population, 1997 (1,000)
Gary, IN PMSA	**623**
Lake County, IN	479
Porter County, IN	144
Kankakee, IL PMSA	**102**
Kankakee County, IL	102
Kenosha, WI PMSA	**143**
Kenosha County, WI	143
Chico-Paradise, CA MSA	**194**
Butte County	194
Cincinnati-Hamilton, OH-KY-IN CMSA	**1,934**
Cincinnati, OH-KY-IN PMSA	**1,607**
Brown County, OH	40
Clermont County, OH	173
Hamilton County, OH	852
Warren County, OH	140
Boone County, KY	76
Campbell County, KY	87
Gallatin County, KY	7
Grant County, KY	20
Kenton County, KY	146
Pendleton County, KY	14
Dearborn County, IN	47
Ohio County, IN	5
Hamilton-Middletown, OH PMSA	**327**
Butler County, OH	327
Clarksville-Hopkinsville, TN-KY MSA	**197**
Montgomery County, TN	124
Christian County, KY	73
Cleveland-Akron, OH CMSA	**2,908**
Akron, OH PMSA	**682**
Portage County	151
Summit County	532
Cleveland-Lorain-Elyria, OH PMSA	**2,226**
Ashtabula County	103
Cuyahoga County	1,387
Geauga County	88
Lake County	224
Lorain County	282
Medina County	142
Colorado Springs, CO MSA	**480**
El Paso County	480
Columbia, MO MSA	**128**
Boone County	128
Columbia, SC MSA	**504**
Lexington County	200
Richland County	304
Columbus, GA-AL MSA	**272**
Chattahoochee County, GA	16
Harris County, GA	22
Muscogee County, GA	183
Russell County, AL	51
Columbus, OH MSA	**1,460**
Delaware County	87
Fairfield County	121
Franklin County	1,017
Licking County	139
Madison County	41
Pickaway County	53
Corpus Christi, TX MSA	**387**
Nueces County	317
San Patricio County	70
Cumberland, MD-WV MSA	**99**
Allegany County, MD	72
Mineral County, WV	27
Dallas-Fort Worth, TX CMSA	**4,683**
Dallas, TX PMSA	**3,127**
Collin County	401
Dallas County	2,023

	Population, 1997 (1,000)
Denton County	365
Ellis County	101
Henderson County	67
Hunt County	69
Kaufman County	64
Rockwall County	36
Fort Worth-Arlington, TX PMSA	**1,556**
Hood County	36
Johnson County	114
Parker County	79
Tarrant County	1,327
Danville, VA MSA	**109**
Pittsylvania County	58
Danville city	51
Davenport-Moline-Rock Island, IA-IL MSA	**357**
Scott County, IA	157
Henry County, IL	51
Rock Island County, IL	148
Dayton-Springfield, OH MSA	**945**
Clark County	146
Greene County	140
Miami County	98
Montgomery County	561
Daytona Beach, FL MSA	**466**
Flagler County	46
Volusia County	420
Decatur, AL MSA	**142**
Lawrence County	33
Morgan County	108
Decatur, IL MSA	**114**
Macon County	114
Denver-Boulder-Greeley, CO CMSA	**2,318**
Boulder-Longmont, CO PMSA	**262**
Boulder County	262
Denver, CO PMSA	**1,901**
Adams County	316
Arapahoe County	463
Denver County	499
Douglas County	126
Jefferson County	497
Greeley, CO PMSA	**156**
Weld County	156
Des Moines, IA MSA	**430**
Dallas County	36
Polk County	354
Warren County	40
Detroit-Ann Arbor-Flint, MI CMSA	**5,439**
Ann Arbor, MI PMSA	**539**
Lenawee County	98
Livingston County	142
Washtenaw County	300
Detroit, MI PMSA	**4,464**
Lapeer County	87
Macomb County	783
Monroe County	142
Oakland County	1,167
St. Clair County	158
Wayne County	2,127
Flint, MI PMSA	**435**
Genesee County	435
Dothan, AL MSA	**134**
Dale County	49
Houston County	85
Dover, DE MSA	**123**
Kent County	123
Dubuque, IA MSA	**88**
Dubuque County	88

	Population, 1997 (1,000)
Duluth, MN-WI MSA	**238**
St. Louis County, MN	195
Douglas County, WI	43
Eau Claire, WI MSA	**143**
Chippewa County	54
Eau Claire County	89
El Paso, TX MSA	**702**
El Paso County	702
Elkhart-Goshen, IN MSA	**171**
Elkhart County	171
Elmira, NY MSA	**93**
Chemung County	93
Enid, OK MSA	**57**
Garfield County	57
Erie, PA MSA	**279**
Erie County	279
Eugene-Springfield, OR MSA	**311**
Lane County	311
Evansville-Henderson, IN-KY MSA	**289**
Posey County, IN	27
Vanderburgh County, IN	167
Warrick County, IN	51
Henderson County, KY	45
Fargo-Moorhead, ND-MN MSA	**166**
Cass County, ND	115
Clay County, MN	52
Fayetteville, NC MSA	**284**
Cumberland County	284
Fayetteville-Springdale-Rogers, AR MSA	**267**
Benton County	130
Washington County	137
Flagstaff, AZ-UT MSA	**120**
Coconino County, AZ	114
Kane County, UT	6
Florence, AL MSA	**137**
Colbert County	53
Lauderdale County	84
Florence, SC MSA	**124**
Florence County	124
Fort Collins-Loveland, CO MSA	**226**
Larimer County	226
Fort Myers-Cape Coral, FL MSA	**387**
Lee County	387
Fort Pierce-Port St. Lucie, FL MSA	**296**
Martin County	116
St. Lucie County	180
Fort Smith, AR-OK MSA	**192**
Crawford County, AR	50
Sebastian County, AR	106
Sequoyah County, OK	37
Fort Walton Beach, FL MSA	**168**
Okaloosa County	168
Fort Wayne, IN MSA	**478**
Adams County	33
Allen County	312
De Kalb County	39
Huntington County	37
Wells County	27
Whitley County	30

	Population, 1997 (1,000)			Population, 1997 (1,000)			Population, 1997 (1,000)
Fresno, CA MSA	**869**	**Galveston-Texas City, TX**		**Kalamazoo-Battle Creek, MI**	
Fresno County	754	**PMSA**	**243**	**MSA**	**447**
Madera County	114	Galveston County	243	Calhoun County	142
Gadsden, AL MSA	**104**	**Houston, TX PMSA**	**3,852**	Kalamazoo County	229
Etowah County	104	Chambers County	24	Van Buren County	76
		Fort Bend County	321		
Gainesville, FL MSA	**198**	Harris County	3,158	**Kansas City, MO-KS MSA**	**1,709**
Alachua County	198	Liberty County	64	Cass County, MO	78
		Montgomery County	258	Clay County, MO	174
Glens Falls, NY MSA	**123**	Waller County	27	Clinton County, MO	19
Warren County	62			Jackson County, MO	648
Washington County	61	**Huntington-Ashland,**		Lafayette County, MO	33
		WV-KY-OH MSA	**315**	Platte County, MO	69
Goldsboro, NC MSA	**112**	Cabell County, WV	95	Ray County, MO	23
Wayne County	112	Wayne County, WV	42	Johnson County, KS	417
		Boyd County, KY	50	Leavenworth County, KS	70
Grand Forks, ND-MN MSA	**102**	Carter County, KY	27	Miami County, KS	26
Grand Forks County, ND	70	Greenup County, KY	37	Wyandotte County, KS	153
Polk County, MN	32	Lawrence County, OH	64		
				Killeen-Temple, TX MSA	**300**
Grand Junction, CO MSA	**111**	**Huntsville, AL MSA**	**333**	Bell County	222
Mesa County	111	Limestone County	61	Coryell County	77
		Madison County	272		
Grand Rapids-Muskegon-				**Knoxville, TN MSA**	**654**
Holland, MI MSA	**1,026**	**Indianapolis, IN MSA**	**1,503**	Anderson County	71
Allegan County	101	Boone County	43	Blount County	100
Kent County	539	Hamilton County	155	Knox County	366
Muskegon County	166	Hancock County	53	Loudon County	38
Ottawa County	220	Hendricks County	92	Sevier County	63
		Johnson County	107	Union County	16
Great Falls, MT MSA	**79**	Madison County	132		
Cascade County	79	Marion County	814	**Kokomo, IN MSA**	**100**
		Morgan County	65	Howard County	84
Green Bay, WI MSA	**214**	Shelby County	43	Tipton County	16
Brown County	214				
		Iowa City, IA MSA	**102**	**La Crosse, WI-MN MSA**	**122**
Greensboro—Winston-		Johnson County	102	La Crosse County, WI	102
Salem—High Point, NC				Houston County, MN	19
MSA	**1,153**	**Jackson, MI MSA**	**155**		
Alamance County	118	Jackson County	155	**Lafayette, LA MSA**	**372**
Davidson County	139			Acadia Parish	58
Davie County	31	**Jackson, MS MSA**	**425**	Lafayette Parish	184
Forsyth County	286	Hinds County	247	St. Landry Parish	83
Guilford County	382	Madison County	71	St. Martin Parish	47
Randolph County	120	Rankin County	107		
Stokes County	43			**Lafayette, IN MSA**	**172**
Yadkin County	35	**Jackson, TN MSA**	**99**	Clinton County	33
		Chester County	15	Tippecanoe County	138
Greenville, NC MSA	**121**	Madison County	85		
Pitt County	121			**Lake Charles, LA MSA**	**179**
		Jacksonville, FL MSA	**1,035**	Calcasieu Parish	179
Greenville-Spartanburg-		Clay County	135		
Anderson, SC MSA	**905**	Duval County	733	**Lakeland-Winter Haven, FL**	
Anderson County	158	Nassau County	54	**MSA**	**449**
Cherokee County	48	St. Johns County	113	Polk County	449
Greenville County	349				
Pickens County	105	**Jacksonville, NC MSA**	**143**	**Lancaster, PA MSA**	**454**
Spartanburg County	245	Onslow County	143	Lancaster County	454
				Lansing-East Lansing, MI	
Harrisburg-Lebanon-		**Jamestown, NY MSA**	**140**	**MSA**	**447**
Carlisle, PA MSA	**615**	Chautauqua County	140	Clinton County	63
Cumberland County	208			Eaton County	100
Dauphin County	246	**Janesville-Beloit, WI MSA**	**150**	Ingham County	284
Lebanon County	117	Rock County	150		
Perry County	44			**Laredo, TX MSA**	**183**
		Johnson City-Kingsport-		Webb County	183
Hattiesburg, MS MSA	**110**	**Bristol, TN-VA MSA**	**460**		
Forrest County	74	Carter County, TN	53	**Las Cruces, NM MSA**	**168**
Lamar County	36	Hawkins County, TN	49	Dona Ana County	168
		Sullivan County, TN	151		
Hickory-Morganton, NC MSA	**318**	Unicoi County, TN	17	**Las Vegas, NV-AZ MSA**	**1,262**
Alexander County	31	Washington County, TN	102	Clark County, NV	1,106
Burke County	82	Scott County, VA	23	Nye County, NV	27
Caldwell County	76	Washington County, VA	49	Mohave County, AZ	129
Catawba County	130	Bristol city, VA	17		
				Lawrence, KS MSA	**91**
Honolulu, HI MSA	**870**	**Johnstown, PA MSA**	**238**	Douglas County	91
Honolulu County	870	Cambria County	157		
		Somerset County	80	**Lawton, OK MSA**	**114**
Houma, LA MSA	**191**			Comanche County	114
Lafourche Parish	88	**Jonesboro, AR MSA**	**77**		
Terrebonne Parish	103	Craighead County	77	**Lexington, KY MSA**	**444**
				Bourbon County	19
Houston-Galveston-		**Joplin, MO MSA**	**147**	Clark County	32
Brazoria, TX CMSA	**4,320**	Jasper County	99	Fayette County	240
Brazoria, TX PMSA	**225**	Newton County	48	Jessamine County	36
Brazoria County	225			Madison County	65

	Popu-lation, 1997 (1,000)
Scott County	29
Woodford County	22
Lima, OH MSA	**155**
Allen County	108
Auglaize County	47
Lincoln, NE MSA	**233**
Lancaster County	233
Little Rock-North Little Rock, AR MSA	**552**
Faulkner County	77
Lonoke County	49
Pulaski County	350
Saline County	76
Longview-Marshall, TX MSA	**208**
Gregg County	113
Harrison County	60
Upshur County	35
Los Angeles-Riverside-Orange County, CA CMSA	**15,609**
Los Angeles-Long Beach, CA PMSA	**9,145**
Los Angeles County	9,145
Orange County, CA PMSA	**2,674**
Orange County	2,674
Riverside-San Bernardino, CA PMSA	**3,064**
Riverside County	1,448
San Bernardino County	1,616
Ventura, CA PMSA	**726**
Ventura County	726
Louisville, KY-IN MSA	**993**
Bullitt County, KY	58
Jefferson County, KY	671
Oldham County, KY	43
Clark County, IN	93
Floyd County, IN	71
Harrison County, IN	34
Scott County, IN	23
Lubbock, TX MSA	**231**
Lubbock County	231
Lynchburg, VA MSA	**207**
Amherst County	30
Bedford County	56
Campbell County	50
Bedford city	6
Lynchburg city	65
Macon, GA MSA	**316**
Bibb County	156
Houston County	104
Jones County	23
Peach County	24
Twiggs County	10
Madison, WI MSA	**398**
Dane County	398
Mansfield, OH MSA	**175**
Crawford County	47
Richland County	128
McAllen-Edinburg-Mission, TX MSA	**511**
Hidalgo County	511
Medford-Ashland, OR MSA	**171**
Jackson County	171
Melbourne-Titusville-Palm Bay, FL MSA	**461**
Brevard County	461
Memphis, TN-AR-MS MSA	**1,083**
Fayette County, TN	30
Shelby County, TN	866
Tipton County, TN	46
Crittenden County, AR	50
DeSoto County, MS	92

	Popu-lation, 1997 (1,000)
Merced, CA MSA	**196**
Merced County	196
Miami-Fort Lauderdale, FL CMSA	**3,515**
Fort Lauderdale, FL PMSA	**1,471**
Broward County	1,471
Miami, FL PMSA	**2,045**
Dade County	2,045
Milwaukee-Racine, WI CMSA	**1,637**
Milwaukee-Waukesha, WI PMSA	**1,451**
Milwaukee County	909
Ozaukee County	81
Washington County	113
Waukesha County	349
Racine, WI PMSA	**185**
Racine County	185
Minneapolis-St. Paul, MN-WI MSA	**2,792**
Anoka County, MN	287
Carver County, MN	63
Chisago County, MN	39
Dakota County, MN	335
Hennepin County, MN	1,053
Isanti County, MN	30
Ramsey County, MN	484
Scott County, MN	76
Sherburne County, MN	58
Washington County, MN	192
Wright County, MN	83
Pierce County, WI	35
St. Croix County, WI	57
Missoula, MT MSA	**89**
Missoula County	89
Mobile, AL MSA	**527**
Baldwin County	129
Mobile County	398
Modesto, CA MSA	**422**
Stanislaus County	422
Monroe, LA MSA	**147**
Ouachita Parish	147
Montgomery, AL MSA	**319**
Autauga County	41
Elmore County	60
Montgomery County	218
Muncie, IN MSA	**118**
Delaware County	118
Myrtle Beach, SC MSA	**169**
Horry County	169
Naples, FL MSA	**196**
Collier County	196
Nashville, TN MSA	**1,135**
Cheatham County	34
Davidson County	534
Dickson County	41
Robertson County	51
Rutherford County	160
Sumner County	122
Williamson County	111
Wilson County	81
New Orleans, LA MSA	**1,308**
Jefferson Parish	451
Orleans Parish	469
Plaquemines Parish	26
St. Bernard Parish	66
St. Charles Parish	48
St. James Parish	21
St. John the Baptist Parish	42
St. Tammany Parish	185
New York-Northern New Jersey-Long Island, NY-NJ-CT-PA CMSA (pt.) [1]	**18,251**
Bergen-Passaic, NJ PMSA	**1,335**
Bergen County, NJ	851
Passaic County, NJ	484

	Popu-lation, 1997 (1,000)
Dutchess County, NY PMSA	**265**
Dutchess County, NY	265
Jersey City, NJ PMSA	**551**
Hudson County, NJ	551
Middlesex-Somerset-Hunterdon, NJ PMSA	**1,106**
Hunterdon County, NJ	121
Middlesex County, NJ	708
Somerset County, NJ	277
Monmouth-Ocean, NJ PMSA	**1,077**
Monmouth County, NJ	596
Ocean County, NJ	481
Nassau-Suffolk, NY PMSA	**2,666**
Nassau County, NY	1,304
Suffolk County, NY	1,363
New York, NY PMSA	**8,611**
Bronx County, NY	1,188
Kings County, NY	2,240
New York County, NY	1,536
Putnam County, NY	92
Queens County, NY	1,976
Richmond County, NY	402
Rockland County, NY	280
Westchester County, NY	896
Newark, NJ PMSA	**1,943**
Essex County, NJ	751
Morris County, NJ	454
Sussex County, NJ	142
Union County, NJ	498
Warren County, NJ	98
Newburgh, NY-PA PMSA	**366**
Orange County, NY	327
Pike County, PA	39
Trenton, NJ PMSA	**330**
Mercer County, NJ	330
Norfolk-Virginia Beach-Newport News, VA-NC MSA	**1,545**
Gloucester County, VA	34
Isle of Wight County, VA	29
James City County, VA	43
Mathews County, VA	9
York County, VA	57
Chesapeake city, VA	196
Hampton city, VA	139
Newport News city, VA	176
Norfolk city, VA	229
Poquoson city, VA	11
Portsmouth city, VA	100
Suffolk city, VA	61
Virginia Beach city, VA	433
Williamsburg city, VA	12
Currituck County, NC	17
Ocala, FL MSA	**237**
Marion County	237
Odessa-Midland, TX MSA	**243**
Ector County	125
Midland County	119
Oklahoma City, OK MSA	**1,031**
Canadian County	85
Cleveland County	197
Logan County	31
McClain County	26
Oklahoma County	630
Pottawatomie County	62
Omaha, NE-IA MSA	**687**
Cass County, NE	24
Douglas County, NE	441
Sarpy County, NE	119
Washington County, NE	18
Pottawattamie County, IA	85
Orlando, FL MSA	**1,467**
Lake County	196
Orange County	784
Osceola County	142
Seminole County	345
Owensboro, KY MSA	**91**
Daviess County	91
Panama City, FL MSA	**146**
Bay County	146

	Population, 1997 (1,000)		Population, 1997 (1,000)		Population, 1997 (1,000)
Parkersburg-Marietta, WV-OH MSA	**151**	Orange County	109	St. Charles County, MO	264
Wood County, WV	87	Wake County	552	St. Louis County, MO	1,004
Washington County, OH	64			Warren County, MO	24
		Rapid City, SD MSA	**87**	St. Louis city, MO	342
Pensacola, FL MSA	**397**	Pennington County	87	Clinton County, IL	35
Escambia County	283			Jersey County, IL	21
Santa Rosa County	114	**Reading, PA MSA**	**354**	Madison County, IL	259
		Berks County	354	Monroe County, IL	26
Peoria-Pekin, IL MSA	**346**			St. Clair County, IL	264
Peoria County	183	**Redding, CA MSA**	**163**		
Tazewell County	129	Shasta County	163	**Salinas, CA MSA**	**362**
Woodford County	35			Monterey County	362
		Reno, NV MSA	**306**		
Philadelphia-Wilmington-Atlantic City, PA-NJ-DE-MD CMSA	**5,972**	Washoe County	306	**Salt Lake City-Ogden, UT MSA**	**1,248**
Atlantic-Cape May, NJ PMSA	**335**	**Richland-Kennewick-Pasco, WA MSA**	**183**	Davis County	226
Atlantic County, NJ	237	Benton County	136	Salt Lake County	840
Cape May County, NJ	98	Franklin County	47	Weber County	182
Philadelphia, PA-NJ PMSA	**4,941**			**San Angelo, TX MSA**	**103**
Bucks County, PA	583	**Richmond-Petersburg, VA MSA**	**943**	Tom Green County	103
Chester County, PA	417	Charles City County	7	**San Antonio, TX MSA**	**1,511**
Delaware County, PA	543	Chesterfield County	243	Bexar County	1,333
Montgomery County, PA	712	Dinwiddie County	24	Comal County	71
Philadelphia County, PA	1,451	Goochland County	18	Guadalupe County	78
Burlington County, NJ	418	Hanover County	79	Wilson County	30
Camden County, NJ	505	Henrico County	244		
Gloucester County, NJ	246	New Kent County	12	**San Diego, CA MSA**	**2,723**
Salem County, NJ	66	Powhatan County	21	San Diego County	2,723
Vineland-Millville-Bridgeton, NJ PMSA	**141**	Prince George County	30		
Cumberland County, NJ	141	Colonial Heights city	17	**San Francisco-Oakland-San Jose, CA CMSA**	**6,701**
Wilmington-Newark, DE-MD PMSA	**556**	Hopewell city	22	**Oakland, CA PMSA**	**2,270**
New Castle County, DE	475	Petersburg city	34	Alameda County	1,371
Cecil County, MD	81	Richmond city	192	Contra Costa County	899
				San Francisco, CA PMSA	**1,662**
Phoenix-Mesa, AZ MSA	**2,840**	**Roanoke, VA MSA**	**229**	Marin County	236
Maricopa County	2,696	Botetourt County	28	San Francisco County	732
Pinal County	143	Roanoke County	81	San Mateo County	694
Pine Bluff, AR MSA	**82**	Roanoke city	94	**San Jose, CA PMSA**	**1,609**
Jefferson County	82	Salem city	25	Santa Clara County	1,609
		Rochester, MN MSA	**115**	**Santa Cruz-Watsonville, CA PMSA**	**240**
Pittsburgh, PA MSA	**2,361**	Olmsted County	115	Santa Cruz County	240
Allegheny County	1,281			**Santa Rosa, CA PMSA**	**429**
Beaver County	186	**Rochester, NY MSA**	**1,086**	Sonoma County	429
Butler County	169	Genesee County	62	**Vallejo-Fairfield-Napa, CA PMSA**	**490**
Fayette County	145	Livingston County	66	Napa County	119
Washington County	206	Monroe County	718	Solano County	371
Westmoreland County	375	Ontario County	100		
		Orleans County	45	**San Luis Obispo-Atascadero-Paso Robles, CA MSA**	**233**
Pocatello, ID MSA	**74**	Wayne County	95	San Luis Obispo County	233
Bannock County	74				
		Rockford, IL MSA	**355**	**Santa Barbara-Santa Maria-Lompoc, CA MSA**	**390**
Portland-Salem, OR-WA CMSA	**2,113**	Boone County	38	Santa Barbara County	390
Portland-Vancouver, OR-WA PMSA	**1,788**	Ogle County	50		
Clackamas County, OR	331	Winnebago County	267	**Santa Fe, NM MSA**	**140**
Columbia County, OR	44			Los Alamos County	18
Multnomah County, OR	625	**Rocky Mount, NC MSA**	**146**	Santa Fe County	122
Washington County, OR	391	Edgecombe County	56		
Yamhill County, OR	80	Nash County	90	**Sarasota-Bradenton, FL MSA**	**539**
Clark County, WA	317			Manatee County	237
Salem, OR PMSA	**325**	**Sacramento-Yolo, CA CMSA**	**1,656**	Sarasota County	302
Marion County, OR	265	**Sacramento, CA PMSA**	**1,503**		
Polk County, OR	60	El Dorado County	156	**Savannah, GA MSA**	**284**
		Placer County	221	Bryan County	23
Provo-Orem, UT MSA	**328**	Sacramento County	1,126	Chatham County	226
Utah County	328	**Yolo, CA PMSA**	**153**	Effingham County	35
		Yolo County	153		
Pueblo, CO MSA	**133**			**Scranton—Wilkes-Barre-Hazleton, PA MSA**	**622**
Pueblo County	133	**Saginaw-Bay City-Midland, MI MSA**	**403**	Columbia County	64
		Bay County	110	Lackawanna County	210
Punta Gorda, FL MSA	**134**	Midland County	81	Luzerne County	318
Charlotte County	134	Saginaw County	211	Wyoming County	29
Raleigh-Durham-Chapel Hill, NC MSA	**1,050**	**St. Cloud, MN MSA**	**161**	**Seattle-Tacoma-Bremerton, WA CMSA**	**3,368**
Chatham County	45	Benton County	34	**Bremerton, WA PMSA**	**235**
Durham County	200	Stearns County	128	Kitsap County	235
Franklin County	44	**St. Joseph, MO MSA**	**97**	**Olympia, WA PMSA**	**200**
Johnston County	102	Andrew County	15	Thurston County	200
		Buchanan County	82		
		St. Louis, MO-IL MSA	**2,558**		
		Franklin County, MO	91		
		Jefferson County, MO	193		
		Lincoln County, MO	35		

	Population, 1997 (1,000)		Population, 1997 (1,000)		Population, 1997 (1,000)
Seattle-Bellevue-Everett, WA PMSA	**2,268**	Hillsborough County	909	Arlington County, VA	173
Island County	71	Pasco County	320	Clarke County, VA	13
King County	1,633	Pinellas County	872	Culpeper County, VA	33
Snohomish County	565	**Terre Haute, IN MSA**	**148**	Fairfax County, VA	914
Tacoma, WA PMSA	**665**	Clay County	27	Fauquier County, VA	53
Pierce County	665	Vermillion County	17	King George County, VA . .	17
Sharon, PA MSA	**122**	Vigo County	105	Loudoun County, VA	133
Mercer County	122	**Texarkana, TX-Texarkana,**		Prince William County, VA .	254
Sheboygan, WI MSA	**110**	**AR MSA**	**123**	Spotsylvania County, VA . .	81
Sheboygan County	110	Bowie County, TX	84	Stafford County, VA	88
Sherman-Denison, TX		Miller County, AR	40	Warren County, VA	30
MSA	**102**	**Toledo, OH MSA**	**612**	Alexandria city, VA	116
Grayson County	102	Fulton County	41	Fairfax city, VA	20
Shreveport-Bossier City, LA		Lucas County	451	Falls Church city, VA	10
MSA	**379**	Wood County	119	Fredericksburg city, VA . . .	21
Bossier Parish	93	**Topeka, KS MSA**	**165**	Manassas city, VA	34
Caddo Parish	243	Shawnee County	165	Manassas Park city, VA . .	8
Webster Parish	43	**Tucson, AZ MSA**	**780**	Berkeley County, WV	69
Sioux City, IA-NE MSA	**121**	Pima County	780	Jefferson County, WV	40
Woodbury County, IA	102	**Tulsa, OK MSA**	**764**		
Dakota County, NE	19	Creek County	66	**Waterloo-Cedar Falls, IA**	
Sioux Falls, SD MSA	**161**	Osage County	43	**MSA**	**122**
Lincoln County	20	Rogers County	66	Black Hawk County	122
Minnehaha County	141	Tulsa County	536	**Wausau, WI MSA**	**122**
South Bend, IN MSA	**258**	Wagoner County	54	Marathon County	122
St. Joseph County	258	**Tuscaloosa, AL MSA**	**161**	**West Palm Beach-Boca**	
Spokane, WA MSA	**405**	Tuscaloosa County	161	**Raton, FL MSA**	**1,019**
Spokane County	405	**Tyler, TX MSA**	**167**	Palm Beach County	1,019
Springfield, IL MSA	**204**	Smith County	167	**Wheeling, WV-OH MSA**	**154**
Menard County	12	**Utica-Rome, NY MSA**	**299**	Marshall County, WV	36
Sangamon County	192	Herkimer County	66	Ohio County, WV	49
Springfield, MO MSA	**301**	Oneida County	233	Belmont County, OH	70
Christian County	47	**Victoria, TX MSA**	**82**	**Wichita, KS MSA**	**531**
Greene County	226	Victoria County	82	Butler County	60
Webster County	28	**Visalia-Tulare-Porterville,**		Harvey County	32
State College, PA MSA	**133**	**CA MSA**	**353**	Sedgwick County	439
Centre County	133	Tulare County	353	**Wichita Falls, TX MSA**	**137**
Steubenville-Weirton, OH-		**Waco, TX MSA**	**203**	Archer County	8
WV MSA	**137**	McLennan County	203	Wichita County	129
Jefferson County, OH	76	**Washington-Baltimore, DC-MD-**		**Williamsport, PA MSA**	**118**
Brooke County, WV	26	**VA-WV CMSA**	**7,207**	Lycoming County	118
Hancock County, WV	34	**Baltimore, MD PMSA**	**2,475**	**Wilmington, NC MSA**	**214**
Stockton-Lodi, CA MSA	**543**	Anne Arundel County, MD .	470	Brunswick County	66
San Joaquin County	543	Baltimore County, MD	721	New Hanover County	148
Sumter, SC MSA	**107**	Carroll County, MD	147	**Yakima, WA MSA**	**218**
Sumter County	107	Harford County, MD	213	Yakima County	218
Syracuse, NY MSA	**741**	Howard County, MD	229	**York, PA MSA**	**371**
Cayuga County	82	Queen Anne's County, MD .	39	York County	371
Madison County	72	Baltimore city, MD	657	**Youngstown-Warren, OH**	
Onondaga County	461	**Hagerstown, MD PMSA** . . .	**128**	**MSA**	**595**
Oswego County	125	Washington County, MD . .	128	Columbiana County	112
Tallahassee, FL MSA	**261**	**Washington, DC-MD-VA-WV**		Mahoning County	257
Gadsden County	45	**PMSA**	**4,603**	Trumbull County	226
Leon County	215	District of Columbia, DC. . .	529	**Yuba City, CA MSA**	**139**
Tampa-St. Petersburg-		Calvert County, MD	69	Sutter County	78
Clearwater, FL MSA	**2,227**	Charles County, MD	115	Yuba County	62
Hernando County	126	Frederick County, MD	183	**Yuma, AZ MSA**	**130**
		Montgomery County, MD . .	827	Yuma County	130
		Prince George's County, MD	771		

[1] Five PMSAs of the New York-Northern New Jersey-Long Island, NY-NJ-CT-PA CMSA are in Connecticut and therefore do not appear in this table; also, the CMSA's population shown here reflects the absence of those PMSAs.

Source: U.S. Bureau of the Census, "Estimates of the Population of Counties and Demographic Components of Population Change: April 1, 1990, to July 1, 1997"; published 17 March 1998; <http://www.census.gov/population/estimates/county/co-97-5/97C500.txt>.

Limitations of the Data

Introduction.—The data presented in this *Statistical Abstract* came from many sources. The sources include not only federal statistical bureaus and other organizations that collect and issue statistics as their principal activity, but also governmental administrative and regulatory agencies, private research bodies, trade associations, insurance companies, health associations, and private organizations such as the National Education Association and philanthropic foundations. Consequently, the data vary considerably as to reference periods, definitions of terms and, for ongoing series, the number and frequency of time periods for which data are available.

The statistics presented were obtained and tabulated by various means. Some statistics are based on complete enumerations or censuses while others are based on samples. Some information is extracted from records kept for administrative or regulatory purposes (school enrollment, hospital records, securities registration, financial accounts, social security records, income tax returns, etc.), while other information is obtained explicitly for statistical purposes through interviews or by mail. The estimation procedures used vary from highly sophisticated scientific techniques, to crude "informed guesses."

Each set of data relates to a group of individuals or units of interest referred to as the *target universe* or *target population,* or simply as the *universe* or *population.* Prior to data collection the target universe should be clearly defined. For example, if data are to be collected for the universe of households in the United States, it is necessary to define a "household." The target universe may not be completely tractable. Cost and other considerations may restrict data collection to a *survey universe* based on some available list, such list may be out of date. This list is called a *survey frame* or *sampling frame.*

The data in many tables are based on data obtained for all population units, *a census,* or on data obtained for only a portion, or *sample,* of the population units.

When the data presented are based on a sample, the sample is usually a scientifically selected *probability sample.* This is a sample selected from a list or sampling frame in such a way that every possible sample has a known chance of selection and usually each unit selected can be assigned a number, greater than zero and less than or equal to one, representing its likelihood or probability of selection.

For large-scale sample surveys, the probability sample of units is often selected as a multistage sample. The first stage of a multistage sample is the selection of a probability sample of large groups of population members, referred to as primary sampling units (PSUs). For example, in a national multistage household sample, PSUs are often counties or groups of counties. The second stage of a multistage sample is the selection, within each PSU selected at the first stage, of smaller groups of population units, referred to as secondary sampling units. In subsequent stages of selection, smaller and smaller nested groups are chosen until the ultimate sample of population units is obtained. To qualify a multistage sample as a probability sample, all stages of sampling must be carried out using probability sampling methods.

Prior to selection at each stage of a multistage (or a single stage) sample, a list of the sampling units or sampling frame for that stage must be obtained. For example, for the first stage of selection of a national household sample, a list of the counties and county groups that form the PSUs must be obtained. For the final stage of selection, lists of households, and sometimes persons within the households, have to be compiled in the field. For surveys of economic entities and for the economic censuses the Bureau generally uses a frame constructed from the Bureau's Standard Statistical Establishment List (SSEL). The SSEL contains all establishments with payroll in the United States including small single establishment firms as well as large multi-establishment firms.

Wherever the quantities in a table refer to an entire universe, but are constructed from data collected in a sample survey, the table quantities are referred to as *sample estimates*. In constructing a sample estimate, an attempt is made to come as close as is feasible to the corresponding universe quantity that would be obtained from a complete census of the universe. Estimates based on a sample will, however, generally differ from the hypothetical census figures. Two classifications of errors are associated with estimates based on sample surveys: (1) *sampling error*—the error arising from the use of a sample, rather than a census, to estimate population quantities and (2) *nonsampling error*—those errors arising from nonsampling sources. As discussed below, the magnitude of the sampling error for an estimate can usually be estimated from the sample data. However, the magnitude of the nonsampling error for an estimate can rarely be estimated. Consequently, actual error in an estimate exceeds the error that can be estimated.

The particular sample used in a survey is only one of a large number of possible samples of the same size which could have been selected using the same sampling procedure. Estimates derived from the different samples would, in general, differ from each other. The *standard error* (SE) is a measure of the variation among the estimates derived from all possible samples. The standard error is the most commonly used measure of the sampling error of an estimate. Valid estimates of the standard errors of survey estimates can usually be calculated from the data collected in a probability sample. For convenience, the standard error is sometimes expressed as a percent of the estimate and is called the relative standard error or *coefficient of variation* (CV). For example, an estimate of 200 units with an estimated standard error of 10 units has an estimated CV of 5 percent.

A sample estimate and an estimate of its standard error or CV can be used to construct interval estimates that have a prescribed confidence that the interval includes the average of the estimates derived from all possible samples with a known probability. To illustrate, if all possible samples were selected under essentially the same general conditions, and

using the same sample design, and if an estimate and its estimated standard error were calculated from each sample, then: 1) Approximately 68% of the intervals from one standard error below the estimate to one standard error above the estimate would include the average estimate derived from all possible samples; 2) approximately 90% of the intervals from 1.6 standard errors below the estimate to 1.6 standard errors above the estimate would include the average estimate derived from all possible samples; and 3) approximately 95% of the intervals from two standard errors below the estimate to two standard errors above the estimate would include the average estimate derived from all possible samples.

Thus, for a particular sample, one can say with the appropriate level of confidence (e.g., 90% or 95%) that the average of all possible samples is included in the constructed interval. Example of a confidence interval: An estimate is 200 units with a standard error of 10 units. An approximately 90% confidence interval (plus or minus 1.6 standard errors) is from 184 to 216.

All surveys and censuses are subject to nonsampling errors. Nonsampling errors are of two kinds—*random* and *nonrandom*. Random nonsampling errors arise because of the varying interpretation of questions (by respondents or interviewers) and varying actions of coders, keyers, and other processors. Some randomness is also introduced when respondents must estimate values. These same errors usually have a nonrandom component. Nonrandom nonsampling errors result from total nonresponse (no usable data obtained for a sampled unit), partial or item nonresponse (only a portion of a response may be usable), inability or unwillingness on the part of respondents to provide correct information, difficulty interpreting questions, mistakes in recording or keying data, errors of collection or processing, and coverage problems (overcoverage and undercoverage of the target universe). Random nonresponse errors usually, but not always, result in an understatement of sampling errors and thus an overstatement of the precision of survey estimates. Estimating the magnitude of nonsampling errors would require special experiments or access to independent data and, consequently, the magnitudes are seldom available.

Nearly all types of nonsampling errors that affect surveys also occur in complete censuses. Since surveys can be conducted on a smaller scale than censuses, nonsampling errors can presumably be controlled more tightly. Relatively more funds and effort can perhaps be expended toward eliciting responses, detecting and correcting response error, and reducing processing errors. As a result, survey results can sometimes be more accurate than census results.

To compensate for suspected nonrandom errors, adjustments of the sample estimates are often made. For example, adjustments are frequently made for nonresponse, both total and partial. Adjustments made for either type of nonresponse are often referred to as *imputations*. Imputation for total nonresponse is usually made by substituting for the questionnaire responses of the nonrespondents the "average" questionnaire responses of the respondents. These imputations usually are made separately within various groups of sample members, formed by attempting to place respondents and nonrespondents together that have "similar" design or ancillary characteristics. Imputation for item nonresponse is usually made by substituting for a missing item the response to that item of a respondent having characteristics that are "similar" to those of the nonrespondent.

For an estimate calculated from a sample survey, the *total error* in the estimate is composed of the sampling error, which can usually be estimated from the sample, and the nonsampling error, which usually cannot be estimated from the sample. The total error present in a population quantity obtained from a complete census is composed of only nonsampling errors. Ideally, estimates of the total error associated with data given in the *Statistical Abstract* tables should be given. However, due to the unavailability of estimates of nonsampling errors, only estimates of the levels of sampling errors, in terms of estimated standard errors or coefficients of variation, are available. To obtain estimates of the estimated standard errors from the sample of interest, obtain a copy of the referenced report which appears at the end of each table.

Principal data bases.—Beginning below are brief descriptions of many of the sample surveys and censuses that provide a substantial portion of the data contained in this *Abstract*.

SECTION 1. POPULATION

Source and Title: Bureau of the Census, *Census of Population*

Tables: See tables citing *Census of Population* in Section 1 and also in Sections 2, 4, 6, 8, 13, 14, 21, and 29.

Universe, Frequency, and Types of Data: Complete count of U.S. population conducted every 10 years since 1790. Data obtained on number and characteristics of inhabitants.

Type of Data Collection Operation: In 1970, 1980, and 1990 complete census for some items—age, sex, race, marital status, and relationship to household head. In 1970, other items collected from a 5% and a 15% probability (systematic) sample of the population. In 1980, approximately 19% of the housing units were included in the sample; in 1990, approximately 17%.

Data Collection and Imputation Procedures: In 1970, extensive use of mail questionnaires in urban areas; personal interviews in most rural areas. In 1980 and 1990, mail questionnaires were used in even more areas than in 1970, with personal interviews in the remainder. Extensive telephone and personal followup for nonrespondents was done in the censuses. Imputations were made for missing characteristics.

Estimates of Sampling Error: Sampling errors for data are estimated for all items collected by sample and vary by characteristic and geographic area. The CVs for national and state estimates are generally very small.

Other (nonsampling) Errors: Since 1950, evaluation programs have been conducted to provide information on the magnitude of some sources of nonsampling errors such as response bias and undercoverage in each census. Results from the evaluation program for the 1990 census indicate that the net under coverage amounted to about 1.5 to 2 % of the total resident population.

Sources of Additional Material: U.S. Bureau of the Census, *The Coverage of Population in the 1980 Census*, PHC80-E4; *Content Reinterview Study: Accuracy of*

Data for Selected Population and Housing Characteristics as Measured by Reinterview, PHC80-E2; *1980 Census of Population*, Vol. 1., (PC80-1), Appendixes B, C, and D.

Source and Title: U.S. Bureau of the Census, *Current Population Survey (CPS)*

Tables: See tables citing *Current Population Reports* primarily in Section 1, but also in Sections 2, 3, 4, 8, 12, 13, 14, 18, 23, and 29. Many Bureau of Labor Statistics' (BLS) tables in Section 13 are CPS based.

Universe, Frequency, and Types of Data: Nationwide monthly sample survey of civilian noninstitutional population, 15 years old or over, to obtain data on employment, unemployment, and a number of other characteristics.

Type of Data Collection Operation: Multistage probability sample of about 60,000 households in 729 PSUs in 1993. Oversampling in some states and the largest MSAs to improve reliability for those areas of employment data on annual average basis. A continual sample rotation system is used. Households are in sample 4 months, out for 8 months, and in for 4 more. Month-to-month overlap is 75%; year-to-year overlap is 50%.

Data Collection and Imputation Procedures: For first and fifth months that a household is in sample, personal interviews; other months, approximately, 85% of the data collected by phone. Imputation is done for both item and total nonresponse. Adjustment for total nonresponse is done by a predefined cluster of units, by MSA size and residence; for item nonresponse imputation varies by subject matter.

Estimates of Sampling Error: Estimated CVs on national annual averages for labor force, total employment, and nonagricultural employment, 0.2%; for total unemployment and agricultural employment, 1.0% to 2.5%. The estimated CVs for family income and poverty rate for all persons in 1986 are 0.5% and 1.5%, respectively. CVs for subnational areas, such as states, would be larger and would vary by area.

Other (nonsampling) Errors: Estimates of response bias on unemployment are not available, but estimates of unemployment are usually 5% to 9% lower than estimates from reinterviews. Four to 5.0% of sample households unavailable for interviews.

Sources of Additional Material: U.S. Bureau of the Census and Bureau of Labor Statistics, *Concepts and Methods Used in Labor Force Statistics from Current Population Survey* (Census Series P-23, No. 62; BLS Report No. 463) and Bureau of the Census, *Current Population Survey* (Tech.

Paper 40) and Bureau of Labor Statistics, *Employment and Earnings*, monthly, Explanatory Notes and Estimates of Error, Tables 1-A through 1-H and *BLS Handbook of Methods*, Chapter 1 (Bulletin 2414.)

SECTION 2. VITAL STATISTICS

Source and Title: U.S. National Center for Health Statistics (NCHS), *Vital Registration System*

Tables: See tables citing *Vital Statistics of the United States;* 341 in Section 5; and 1328 in Section 29.

Universe, Frequency, and Types of Data: Annual data on births and deaths in the United States.

Type of Data Collection Operation: Mortality data based on complete file of death records, except 1972, based on 50% sample. Natality statistics 1951-71, based on 50% sample of birth certificates, except a 20% to 50% in 1967, received by NCHS. Beginning 1972, data from some states received through Vital Statistics Cooperative Program (VSCP) and complete file used; data from other states based on 50% sample. Beginning 1986, all reporting areas participated in the VSCP.

Data Collection and Imputation Procedures: Reports based on records from registration offices of all states, District of Columbia, New York City, Puerto Rico, Virgin Islands, and Guam.

Estimates of Sampling Error: For recent years, CVs for births are small due to large portion of total file in sample (except for very small estimated totals).

Other (nonsampling) Errors: Data on births and deaths believed to be at least 99% complete.

Sources of Additional Material: U.S. National Center for Health Statistics, *Vital Statistics of the United States,* Vol. I and Vol. II, annual, and *Monthly Vital Statistics Report.*

(See Section 1 above for information pertaining to Tables 107-110.)

SECTION 3. HEALTH AND NUTRITION

Source and Title: U.S. National Center for Health Statistics, *National Health Interview Survey (NHIS)*

Tables: 194, 197, 199, 220, 221, 228, 229, 231, 232, and 238.

Universe, Frequency, and Types of Data: Continuous data collection covering the civilian noninstitutional population to obtain information on personal and demographic characteristics, illnesses, injuries, impairments, and other health topics.

Type of Data Collection Operation: Multistage probability sample of 49,000 households (in 198 PSUs) from 1985 to 1994; 45,000 households (358 design PSUs) from 1995 on, selected in groups of about four adjacent households.

Data Collection and Imputation Procedures: Some missing data items (e.g., age) are imputed using an average value. Unit nonresponse is compensated for by an adjustment to the survey weights

Estimates of Sampling Error: Estimated CVs: For physician visits by males, 1.5%; for workdays lost by males, 3.5%; for persons injured at home, 4.7%.

Other (nonsampling) Errors: Response rate was 93.8% in 1995 for the NHIS.

Sources of Additional Material: U.S. National Center for Health Statistics, "Current Estimates from the National Health Interview Survey, U.S., 1995," Vital and Health Statistics, Series 10.

(See Section 13 for information pertaining to Table 189, Section 15 for Table 179, and Section 27 for Table 188.)

SECTION 4. EDUCATION

Source and Title: U.S. Department of Education, National Center for Education Statistics, *Higher Education General Information Survey (HEGIS), Fall Enrollment in Institutions of Higher Education;* beginning 1986, *Integrated Postsecondary Education Data Survey (IPEDS), Fall Enrollment.*

Tables: 302, 303, 306, and 307.

Universe, Frequency, and Types of Data: Annual survey of all institutions and branches listed in the *Directory* to obtain data on total enrollment by sex, level of enrollment, type of program, racial/ethnic characteristics (every other year prior to 1990, then annually) and attendance status of student, and on first-time students.

Type of Data Collection Operation: Complete census.

Data Collection and Imputation Procedures: Survey package is usually mailed in the spring with surveys due at varying dates in the summer and fall; mail and phone followup procedures for nonrespondents. Missing data are imputed by using data of similar institutions.

Estimates of Sampling Error: Not applicable.

Other (nonsampling) Errors: Approximately 97% response rate in fall 1995.

Sources of Additional Material: U.S. Department of Education, National Center for Education Statistics, *Fall Enrollment in Higher Education,* annual.

Source and Title: U.S. Department of Education, National Center for Education Statistics, *Higher Education General Information Survey (HEGIS), Financial Statistics of Institutions of Higher Education;* beginning 1986, *Integrated Postsecondary Education Data Survey (IPEDS), Finance.*

Tables: 251, 254, 306, and 309.

Universe, Frequency, and Types of Data: Annual survey of all institutions and branches listed in the *Education Directory, Colleges and Universities* to obtain data on financial status and operations, including current funds revenues, current funds expenditures, and physical plant assets.

Type of Data Collection Operation: Complete census.

Data Collection and Imputation Procedures: Survey package is usually mailed in the spring with surveys due at varying dates in the summer and fall; mail and phone followup procedures for nonrespondents. Missing data are imputed by using data of similar institutions.

Estimates of Sampling Error: Not applicable.

Other (nonsampling) Errors: For 1995, a 94% response rate..

Sources of Additional Material: U.S. Department of Education, National Center for Education Statistics, *Financial Statistics.*

Source and Title: U.S. Department of Education, National Center for Education Statistics, *Higher Education General Information Survey (HEGIS), Degrees and Other Formal Awards Conferred.* Beginning 1986, *Integrated Postsecondary Education Data Survey (IPEDS), Completions.*

Tables: 323-328.

Universe, Frequency, and Types of Data: Annual survey of all institutions and branches listed in the *Education Directory, Colleges and Universities* to obtain data on earned degrees and other formal awards, conferred by field of study, level of degree, sex, and by racial/ethnic characteristics (every other year prior to 1990, then annually).

Type of Data Collection Operation: Complete census.

Data Collection and Imputation Procedures: Survey package is usually mailed in the spring with surveys due at varying dates in the summer and fall; mail and phone followup procedures for nonrespondents. Missing data are imputed by using data of similar institutions.

Estimates of Sampling Error: Not applicable.

Other (nonsampling) Errors: For 1994-95, approximately 97% response rate.

Sources of Additional Material: U.S. Department of Education, National Center for Education Statistics, *Completions,* annual.

(See Sections 1 and 9 for information pertaining to the Bureau of the Census.)

SECTION 5. LAW ENFORCEMENT, COURTS, AND PRISONS

Source and Title: U.S. Federal Bureau of Investigation, *Uniform Crime Reporting (UCR) Program*

Tables: 335-340, 342-345, 353-355, and 357.

Universe, Frequency, and Types of Data: Monthly reports on the number of criminal offenses that become known to law enforcement agencies. Data are collected on crimes cleared by arrest, by age, sex, and race of offender, and on assaults on law enforcement officers.

Type of Data Collection Operation: Crime statistics are based on reports of crime data submitted either directly to the FBI by contributing law enforcement agencies or through cooperating state UCR programs.

Data Collection and Imputation Procedures: States with UCR programs collect data directly from individual law enforcement agencies and forward reports, prepared in accordance with UCR standards, to FBI. Accuracy and consistency edits are performed by FBI.

Estimates of Sampling Error: Not applicable.

Other (nonsampling) Errors: Coverage of 95% of the population (90.1% in MSAs, 78.6% in "other cities," and 75.9% in rural areas) by UCR program, though varying number of agencies report. Some error may be present through incorrect reporting.

Sources of Additional Material: U.S. Federal Bureau of Investigation, *Crime in the United States.*

Source and Title: U.S. Bureau of Justice Statistics (BJS), *National Crime Victimization Survey*

Tables: 346-350.

Universe, Frequency, and Types of Data: Monthly survey of individuals and households in the United States to obtain data on criminal victimization of those units for compilation of annual estimates.

Type of Data Collection Operation: National probability sample survey of about 50,000 interviewed households in 376 PSUs selected from a list of addresses from the 1980 census, supplemented by new construction permits and an area sample where permits are not required.

Data Collection and Imputation Procedures: Interviews are conducted every 6 months for 3 years for each household in the sample; 8,000 households are interviewed monthly. Personal interviews are used in the first and fifth interviews; the intervening interviews are conducted by telephone whenever possible.

Estimates of Sampling Error: CVs in 1994: 2.7% for crimes of violence; 8.5% for estimate of rape/sexual assault counts; 5.5% for robbery counts; 2.8% for assault counts; 8.0% for personal theft counts; 1.9% for property crimes; 3.0% for burglary counts; 2.0% for theft; and 4.4% for motor vehicle theft counts.

Other (nonsampling) Errors: Respondent recall errors which may include reporting incidents for other than the reference period; interviewer coding and processing errors; and possible mistaken reporting or classifying of events. Adjustment is made for a household noninterview rate of about 4% and for a within-household noninterview rate of 7%.

Sources of Additional Material: U.S. Bureau of Justice Statistics, *Criminal Victimization in the United States,* annual.

(See Section 2 for details on Table 341.)

SECTION 7. PARKS AND RECREATION

(See Section 27 for details on Tables 427 and 452.)

SECTION 8. ELECTIONS

(See Section 1 above for information pertaining to Tables 483 and 484 and Section 9 for information pertaining to Table 477.)

SECTION 9. STATE AND LOCAL GOVERNMENT FINANCES AND EMPLOYMENT

Source and Title: U.S. Bureau of the Census, *Census of Governments*

Tables: See tables in Section 9 citing *Census of Governments* and Table 477 in Section 8.

Universe, Frequency, and Types of Data: Survey of all governmental units in the United States conducted every 5 years to obtain data on government revenue, expenditures, debt, assets, employment and employee retirement systems, property values, public school systems, and number, size, and structure of governments.

Type of Data Collection Operation: Complete census. List of units derived through classification of government units recently authorized in each state and identification, counting, and classification of existing local governments and public school systems.

Data Collection and Imputation Procedures: Data collected through field and office compilation of financial data from official records and reports for states and large local governments; mail canvass of selected data items, like state tax revenue and employee retirement systems; and collection of local government statistics through central collection arrangements with state governments.

Estimates of Sampling Error: Not applicable.

Other (nonsampling) Errors: Some nonsampling errors may arise due to possible inaccuracies in classification, response, and processing.

Sources of Additional Material: U.S. Bureau of the Census, *Census of Governments, 1997,* various reports, and *State Government Finances in 1990,* GF 90, No. 3.

Source and Title: U.S. Bureau of the Census, *Annual Surveys of State and Local Government*

Tables: See tables citing *Public Employment* and *Government Finances* in Section 9, Table 279 in Section 4, and Table 614 in Section 12.

Universe, Frequency, and Types of Data: Sample survey conducted annually to obtain data on revenue, expenditure, debt, and employment of state and local governments. Universe is all governmental units in the United States (about 87,000).

Type of Data Collection Operation: Sample of about 22,000 units includes all state governments, county governments with 50,000+ population, municipalities and townships with 25,000+ population, all school districts with 10,000+ enrollment in October 1986, and other governments meeting certain criteria; probability sample for remaining units.

Data Collection and Imputation Procedures: Field and office compilation of data from official records and reports for states and large local governments; central collection of local governmental financial data through cooperative agreements with a number of state governments; mail canvass of other units with mail and telephone followups of nonrespondents. Data for nonresponses are imputed from previous year data or obtained from secondary sources, if available.

Estimates of Sampling Error: CVs for estimates of major employment and financial items are generally less than 2% for most states and less than 1.2% for the majority of states.

Other (nonsampling) Errors: Nonresponse rate is less than 15% for number of units. Other possible errors may result from undetected inaccuracies in classification, response, and processing.

Sources of Additional Material: U.S. Bureau of the Census, *Public Employment in 1990,* GE 90, No. 1, *Governmental Finances in 1989-90,* GF 90, No. 5, and *Census of Governments, 1987,* various reports.

SECTION 10. FEDERAL GOVERNMENT

Source and Title: U.S. Internal Revenue Service, *Statistics of Income, Individual Income Tax Returns*

Tables: 552-556.

Universe, Frequency, and Types of Data: Annual study of unaudited individual income tax returns, forms 1040, 1040A, and 1040EZ, filed by U.S. citizens and residents. Data provided on various financial characteristics by size of adjusted gross income, marital status, and by taxable and nontaxable returns. Data by state, based on 100% file, also include returns from 1040NR, filed by nonresident aliens plus certain self-employment tax returns.

Type of Data Collection Operation: Annual stratified probability sample of approximately 125,000 returns broken into sample strata based on the larger of total income or total loss amounts as well as the size of business plus farm receipts. Sampling rates for sample strata varied from .025% to 100%.

Data Collection and Imputation Procedures: Computer selection of sample of tax return records. Data adjusted during editing for incorrect, missing, or inconsistent entries to ensure consistency with other entries on return.

Estimates of Sampling Error: Estimated CVs for tax year 1987: Adjusted gross income less deficit 0.13%; salaries and wages 0.20%; and tax-exempt interest received 4.51%. (State data not subject to sampling error.)

Other (nonsampling) Errors: Processing errors and errors arising from the use of tolerance checks for the data.

Sources of Additional Material: U.S. Internal Revenue Service, *Statistics of Income, Individual Income Tax Returns,* annual.

SECTION 12. SOCIAL INSURANCE AND HUMAN SERVICES

Source and Title: U.S. Social Security Administration, *Benefit Data*

Tables: 610 and 611.

Universe, Frequency, and Types of Data: All persons receiving monthly benefits under Title II of Social Security Act. Data on number and amount of benefits paid by type and state.

Type of Data Collection Operation: Data based on administrative records. Data based on 100% files, as well as 10% and 1% sample files.

Data Collection and Imputation Procedures: Records used consist of actions pursuant to applications dated by subsequent post-entitlement actions.

Estimates of Sampling Error: Varies by size of estimate and sample file size.

Other (nonsampling) Errors: Processing errors, which are believed to be small.

Sources of Additional Material: U.S. Social Security Administration, *Annual Statistical Supplement to the Social Security Bulletin.*

Source and Title: U.S. Social Security Administration, *Supplemental Security Income (SSI) Program*

Tables: 625 and 626.

Universe, Frequency, and Types of Data: All eligible aged, blind, or disabled persons receiving SSI benefit payments under SSI program. Data include number of persons receiving federally administered SSI, amounts paid, and state administered supplementation.

Type of Data Collection Operation: Data based on administrative records.

Data Collection and Imputation Procedures: Data adjusted to reflect returned checks and overpayment refunds. For federally administered payments, actual adjusted amounts are used.

Estimates of Sampling Error: Not applicable.

Other (nonsampling) Errors: Processing errors, which are believed to be small.

Sources of Additional Material: U.S. Social Security Administration, *Annual Statistical Supplement to the Social Security Bulletin.*

(See Section 1 above for information pertaining to the Current Population Survey, Section 3 for information pertaining to the National Center for Health Statistics, and Section 9 for information pertaining to Annual Surveys of State and Local Government.)

SECTION 13. LABOR FORCE, EMPLOYMENT, AND EARNINGS

Source and Title: U.S. Bureau of Labor Statistics (BLS), *Current Employment Statistics (CES) Program*

Tables: 685-687, 692; in Section 3, Table 189; in Section 21, Table 1015; and in Section 22, Table 1083.

Universe, Frequency, and Types of Data: Monthly survey covering about 6 million nonagricultural establishments to obtain data on employment, hours, and earnings, by industry.

Type of Data Collection Operation: Sample survey of about 390,000 establishments in June 1997.

Data Collection and Imputation Procedures: Cooperating state agencies mail questionnaires to sample establishments to develop state and local estimates; information is forwarded to BLS where national estimates are prepared.

Estimates of Sampling Error: Estimated CVs for employment, 0.1%, for average weekly hours paid, 0.1% and for average hourly earnings, 0.2%.

Other (nonsampling) Errors: Estimates of employment adjusted annually to reflect complete universe. Average adjustment is 0.2%.

Sources of Additional Material: U.S. Bureau of Labor Statistics, *Employment and Earnings,* monthly, Explanatory Notes and Estimates of Error, Tables 2-A through 2-G.

(See Section 1 above for information pertaining to the Current Population Survey.)

SECTION 14. INCOME, EXPENDITURES, AND WEALTH

Source and Title: Board of Governors of the Federal Reserve System, *Survey of Consumer Finances*

Tables: 767 and 768; and in Section 16, Tables 798, 800-802, and 823.

Universe, Frequency, and Types of Data: Periodic sample survey of families. In this survey a given household is divided into a primary economic unit and other economic units. The primary economic unity, which may be a single individual, is generally chosen as the unit that contains the person who either holds the title to the home or is the first person listed on the lease. The primary unit is used as the reference family. The survey collects detailed data on the composition of family balance sheets, the terms of loans, and relationships with financial institutions. It also gathered information on the employment history and pension rights of the survey respondent and the spouse or partner of the respondent.

Type of Data Collection Operation: The survey employs a two-part strategy for sampling families. Some families were selected by standard multistage area-probability sampling methods from the forty-eight contiguous states. The remaining families in the survey were selected using tax data under the strict rules governing confidentiality and the rights of potential respondents to refuse participation.

Data Collection and Imputation Procedures: The Survey Research Center at the University of Michigan collected the 1989 survey data between August 1989 and

March 1990. Adjustments for nonresponse errors are made through systematic imputation of unanswered questions and through weighting adjustments based on data used in the sample design for families that refused participation.

Estimates of Sampling Error: Because of the complex design of the survey, the estimation of potential sampling errors is not straightforward.

Other (nonsampling) Errors: The achieved sample of 3,143 families represents a response rate of about 69 percent in the area-probability sample and a rate of about 34 percent in the tax-data sample. Proper training of interviewers and careful design of questionnaires were used to control inaccurate survey responses.

Sources of Additional Material: Board of Governors of the Federal Reserve System, "Changes in Family Finances from 1983 to 1989: Evidence from the Survey of Consumer Finances," *Federal Reserve Bulletin,* January 1992.

(See Section 1 above for information pertaining to the Bureau of the Census.)

SECTION 15. PRICES

Source and Title: U.S. Bureau of Labor Statistics (BLS), *Consumer Price Index (CPI)*

Tables: 771-774, 787, 788; and in Section 3, Table 179.

Universe, Frequency, and Types of Data: Monthly survey of price changes of all types of consumer goods and services purchased by urban wage earners and clerical workers prior to 1978, and urban consumers thereafter. Both indexes continue to be published.

Type of Data Collection Operation: Prior to 1978, sample of various consumer items in 56 urban areas; thereafter, in 85 PSUs, except from January 1987 through March 1988, when 91 areas were sampled.

Data Collection and Imputation Procedures: Prices of consumer items are obtained from about 57,000 housing units, and 19,000 other reporters in 85 areas. Prices of food, fuel, and a few other items are obtained monthly; prices of most other commodities and services are collected every month in the five largest geographic areas and every other month in others.

Estimates of Sampling Error: Estimates of standard errors are not available at present.

Other (nonsampling) Errors: Errors result from inaccurate reporting, difficulties in defining concepts and their operational implementation, and introduction of product quality changes and new products.

Sources of Additional Material: U.S. Bureau of Labor Statistics, *The Consumer Price Index:* 1987 Revision, Report 736, and *BLS Handbook of Methods,* Chapter 19, Bulletin 2414.

Source and Title: U.S. Bureau of Labor Statistics, *Producer Price Index (PPI)*

Tables: 771, 777-779; in Section 21, Table 1066; in Section 24, Table 1155; and in Section 25, Table 1191.

Universe, Frequency, and Types of Data: Monthly survey of producing companies to determine price changes of all commodities produced in the United States for sale in commercial transactions. Data on agriculture, forestry, fishing, manufacturing, mining, gas, electricity, public utilities, and a few services.

Type of Data Collection Operation: Probability sample of approximately 3,100 about 75,000 quotations per month.

Data Collection and Imputation Procedures: Data are collected by mail. If transaction prices are not supplied, list prices are used. Some prices are obtained from trade publications, organized exchanges, and government agencies. To calculate index, price changes are multiplied by their relative weights based on total net selling value of all commodities in 1982.

Estimates of Sampling Error: Not applicable.

Other (nonsampling) Errors: Not available at present.

Sources of Additional Material: U.S. Bureau of Labor Statistics, *BLS Handbook of Methods,* Chapter 16, Bulletin 2414.

SECTION 16. BANKING, FINANCE, AND INSURANCE

(See Section 14 for information pertaining to Tables 798, 800-802, and 823 and Section 17 for information pertaining to Table 793.)

SECTION 17. BUSINESS ENTERPRISE

Source and Title: U.S. Bureau of the Census, *County Business Patterns*

Tables: 866-868, 874; in Section 16, Table 793; in Section 27, Tables 1276 and 1297; and in Section 29, Table 1337.

Universe, Frequency, and Types of Data: Annual tabulation of basic data items extracted from the Standard Statistical Establishment List, a file of all known single and multiestablishment companies maintained and updated by the Bureau of the Census. Data include number of establishments, number of employees, first-quarter and annual payrolls, and number of establishments by employment size class. Data are excluded for self-employed persons, domestic service workers, railroad employees, agricultural production workers, and most government employees.

Type of Data Collection Operation: The annual Company Organization Survey provides individual establishment data for multiestablishment companies. Data for single establishment companies are obtained from various Census Bureau programs, such as the Annual Survey of Manufactures and Current Business Surveys, as well as from administrative records of the Internal Revenue Service and the Social Security Administration.

Estimates of Sampling Error: Not Applicable.

Other (nonsampling) Error: Response rates of greater than 90% for the 1993 Company Organization Survey.

Sources of Additional Materials: U.S. Bureau of the Census, *General Explanation of County Business Patterns.*

Source and Title: U.S. Internal Revenue Service, *Statistics of Income, Sole Proprietorship Returns* and *Statistics of Income Bulletin*

Tables: 855-858.

Universe, Frequency, and Types of Data: Annual study of unaudited income tax returns of nonfarm sole proprietorships, form 1040 with business schedules. Data provided on various financial characteristics by industry.

Type of Data Collection Operation: Stratified probability sample of approximately 31,000 sole proprietorships for tax year 1990. The sample is classified based on presence or absence of certain business schedules; the larger of total income or loss; and size of business plus farm receipts. Sampling rates vary from 0.043% to 100%.

Data Collection and Imputation Procedures: Computer selection of sample of tax return records. Data adjusted during editing for incorrect, missing, or inconsistent entries to ensure consistency with other entries on return.

Estimates of Sampling Error: Estimated CVs for tax year 1990 are not available; for 1987 (the latest available): For sole proprietorships, business receipts, 1.66%; net income, (less loss), 1.33%; depreciation 2.17%; interest expense 2.80%; and employee benefit programs 7.55%.

Other (nonsampling) Errors: Processing errors and errors arising from the use of tolerance checks for the data.

Sources of Additional Material: U.S. Internal Revenue Service, *Statistics of Income, Sole Proprietorship Returns* (for years through 1980) and *Statistics of Income Bulletin,* Vol. 10, No. 1 (summer 1990).

Source and Title: U.S. Internal Revenue Service, *Statistics of Income, Partnership Returns* and *Statistics of Income Bulletin*

Tables: 855-857, 859, and 860.

Universe, Frequency, and Types of Data: Annual study of unaudited income tax returns of partnerships, Form 1065. Data provided on various financial characteristics by industry.

Type of Data Collection Operation: Stratified probability sample of approximately 28,000 partnership returns from a population of 1,660,000 filed during calendar year 1990. The sample is classified based on combinations of gross receipts, net income or loss, and total assets, and on industry. Sampling rates vary from 0.04% to 100%.

Data Collection and Imputation Procedures: Computer selection of sample of tax return records. Data are adjusted during editing for incorrect, missing, or inconsistent entries to ensure consistency with other entries on return. Data not available due to regulations are not imputed.

Estimates of Sampling Error: Estimated CVs for tax year 1988 (latest available): For number of partnerships, 0.51%; business receipts, 0.78%; net income, 3.03%; net loss, 2.21% and total assets, 1.22%.

Other (nonsampling) Errors: Processing errors and errors arising from the use of tolerance checks for the data.

Sources of Additional Material: U.S. Internal Revenue Service, *Statistics of Income, Partnership Returns* and *Statistics of Income Bulletin,* Vol. 10, No. 1 (summer 1990).

Source and Title: U.S. Internal Revenue Service, *Corporation Income Tax Returns*

Tables: 855-857 and 863-865.

Universe, Frequency, and Types of Data: Annual study of unaudited corporation income tax returns, forms 1120 and 1120 (A, F, L, PC, REIT, RIC, and S), filed by corporations or businesses legally defined as corporations. Data provided on various financial characteristics by industry and size of total assets, and business receipts.

Type of Data Collection Operation: Stratified probability sample of approximately 85,000 returns for 1987, distributed by sample classes generally based on type of return, size of total assets, size of net income or deficit, and selected business activity. Sampling rates for sample strata varied from 0.25% to 100%.

Data Collection and Imputation Procedures: Computer selection of sample of tax return records. Data adjusted during editing for incorrect, missing, or inconsistent entries to ensure consistency with other entries on return and to achieve statistical definitions.

Estimates of Sampling Error: Estimated CVs for 1988: Number of returns in subgroups ranged from 1.4% with assets under $100,000, to 0% with assets over $100 mil.; for amount of net income and amount of income tax, 0.18%

Other (nonsampling) Errors: Processing errors and errors arising from the use of tolerance checks for the data.

Sources of Additional Material: U.S. Internal Revenue Service, *Statistics of Income, Corporation Income Tax Returns*, annual.

SECTION 18. COMMUNICATIONS

(See Section 26 for information pertaining to Table 932.)

SECTION 19. ENERGY

Source and Title: U.S. Energy Information Administration, *Residential Energy Consumption Survey*

Tables: 955, 956; and Table 1223 in Section 25.

Universe, Frequency, and Types of Data: Triennial survey of households and fuel suppliers. Data are obtained on energy-related household characteristics, housing unit characteristics, use of fuels, and energy consumption and expenditures by fuel type.

Type of Data Collection Operation: Probability sample of 7,183 eligible units in 129 PSUs. For responding units, fuel consumption and expenditure data obtained from fuel suppliers to those households.

Data Collection and Imputation Procedures: Personal interviews. Extensive followup of nonrespondents including mail questionnaires for some households. Adjustments for nonrespondents were made in weighting for respondents. Most item nonresponses were imputed.

Estimates of Sampling Error: Estimated CVs for household averages: For consumption, 1.3%; for expenditures, 1.0%; for various fuels, values ranged from 1.4% for electricity to 5.9% for LPG.

Other (nonsampling) Errors: Household response rate of 86.7%. Nonconsumption data were mostly imputed for mail respondents (5.2% of eligible units). Usable responses from fuel suppliers for various fuels ranged from 82.8% for electricity to 55.7% for fuel oil.

Sources of Additional Material: U.S. Energy Information Administration, *Household Energy Consumption and Expenditures, 1990* and *Housing Characteristics, 1990.*

SECTION 21. TRANSPORTATION—LAND

(See Section 1 for information pertaining to Table 1038, Section 13 for Table 1015, Section 15 for Table 1066, and Section 27 for Table 1057.)

SECTION 22. TRANSPORTATION—AIR AND WATER

(See Section 13 for information pertaining to Table 1083.)

SECTION 23. AGRICULTURE

Source and Title: U.S. Bureau of the Census, *Census of Agriculture.*

Tables: 1100-1103.

Universe, Frequency, and Types of Data: Complete count of U.S. farms and ranches conducted once every 5 years with data at the national, state, and county level. Data published on farm numbers and related items/characteristics.

Type of Data Collection Operation: Complete census for— number of farms; land in farms; estimated market value of land and buildings, machinery and equipment, agriculture products sold; total cropland; irrigated land; total farm production expenses; farm operator characteristics; livestock and poultry inventory and sales; and selected crops harvested.

Data Collection and Imputation Procedures: Data collection is by mailing questionnaires to all farmers and ranchers. Nonrespondents are conducted by telephone and correspondence followups. Imputations were made for all nonresponse item/characteristics.

Estimates of Sampling Error: Variability in the estimates is due to the sample selection and estimation for items collected by sample and census nonresponse estimation procedures. The CVs for national and state estimates are generally very small. Approximately 85% response rate.

Other (nonsampling) Errors: Nonsampling errors are due to incompleteness of the census mailing list, duplications on the list, respondent reporting errors, errors in editing reported data, and in imputation for missing data. Evaluation studies are conducted to measure certain nonsampling errors such as list coverage and classification error.

Results from the evaluation program for the 1987 census indicate the net under coverage amounted to about 7.2% of the Nation's total farms.

Sources of Additional Material: U.S. Bureau of the Census, *1992 Census of Agriculture,* Volume 2, Subject Series—Part 1, *Agriculture Atlas of the U.S.,* Part 2, *Coverage Evaluation,* Part 3, *Rankings of States and Counties,* Part 4, *History,* Part 5, *ZIP Code Tabulation of Selected Items* ; and Volume 4, *Farm and Ranch Irrigation Survey.*

Source and Title: U.S. Department of Agriculture, National Agricultural Statistics Service (NASS), *Basic Area Frame Sample*

Tables: See tables citing NASS in source notes in Section 23, which pertain to this or the following two surveys.

Universe, Frequency, and Types of Data: Two annual area sample surveys of U.S. farm operators: June agricultural survey collects data on planted acreage and livestock inventories; and a February Farm Costs and Returns survey that collects data on total farm production, expenses and specific commodity costs of production.

Type of Data Collection Operation: Stratified probability sample of about 16,000 land area units of about 1 sq. mile (range from 0.1 sq. mile in cities to several sq. miles in open grazing areas). Sample includes 60,000 parcels of agricultural land. About 20% of the sample replaced annually.

Data Collection and Imputation Procedures: Data collection is by personal enumeration. Imputation is based on enumerator observation or data reported by respondents having similar agricultural characteristics.

Estimates of Sampling Error: Estimated CVs range from 1% to 2% for regional estimates to 3% to 6% for state estimates of livestock inventories.

Other (nonsampling) Errors: Minimized through rigid quality controls on the collection process and careful review of all reported data.

Sources of Additional Material: U.S. Department of Agriculture, SRS, *Scope and Methods of the Statistical Reporting Service,* (name changed to National Agricultural Statistics Service), Miscellaneous Publication No. 1308, September 1983 (revised).

Source and Title: U.S. Department of Agriculture National Agricultural Statistics Service (NASS), *Multiple Frame Surveys*

Tables: See tables citing NASS in source notes in Section 23, which pertain to this or the following survey.

Universe, Frequency, and Types of Data: Surveys of U.S. farm operators to obtain data on major livestock inventories, selected crop acreages and production, grain stocks, and farm labor characteristics; and to obtain farm economic data for price indexing.

Type of Data Collection Operation: Primary frame is obtained from general or special purpose lists, supplemented by a probability sample of land areas used to estimate for list incompleteness.

Data Collection and Imputation Procedures: Mail, telephone, or personal interviews used for initial data collection. Mail nonrespondent followup by phone and personal interviews. Imputation based on average of respondents.

Estimates of Sampling Error: Estimated CV for number of hired farm workers is about 3%. Estimated CVs range from 1% to 2% for regional estimates to 3% to 6% for state estimates of livestock inventories.

Other (nonsampling) Errors: In addition to above, replicated sampling procedures used to monitor effects of changes in survey procedures.

Sources of Additional Material: U.S. Department of Agriculture, SRS, *Scope and Methods of the Statistical Reporting Service,* (name changed to National Agricultural Statistics Service), Miscellaneous Publication No. 1308, September 1983 (revised).

Source and Title: U.S. Department of Agriculture, National Agricultural Statistics Service (NASS), *Objective Yield Surveys*

Tables: See tables citing NASS in source notes in Section 23, which pertain to this or the preceding survey.

Universe, Frequency, and Types of Data: Surveys for data on corn, cotton, potatoes, soybeans, wheat, and rice to forecast and estimate yields.

Type of Data Collection Operation: Random location of plots in probability samples selected in June from Basic Area Frame Sample (see above).

Data Collection and Imputation Procedures: Enumerators count and measure plant characteristics in sample fields. Production measured from plots at harvest. Harvest loss measured from post harvest gleanings.

Estimates of Sampling Error: CVs for national estimates of production are about 2-3%.

Other (nonsampling) Errors: In addition to above, replicated sampling procedures used to monitor effects of changes in survey procedures.

Sources of Additional Material: U.S. Department of Agriculture, SRS, *Scope and Methods of the Statistical Reporting Service,* (name changed to National Agricultural Statistics Service), Miscellaneous Publication No. 1308, September 1983 (revised).

(See Section 1 above for information pertaining to the Census of Population and Current Population Survey.)

SECTION 24. NATURAL RESOURCES

(See Section 15 for Table 1155.)

SECTION 25. CONSTRUCTION AND HOUSING

Source and Title: U.S. Bureau of the Census, *Monthly Survey of Construction*
Tables: 1198 and 1200-1203.
Universe, Frequency, and Types of Data: Survey conducted monthly of newly constructed housing units (excluding mobile homes). Data are collected on the start, completion, and sale of housing. (Annual figures are aggregates of monthly estimates.)
Type of Data Collection Operation: Probability sample of housing units obtained from building permits selected from 17,000 places. For nonpermit places, multistage probability sample of new housing units selected in 169 PSUs. In those areas, all roads are canvassed in selected enumeration districts.
Data Collection and Imputation Procedures: Data are obtained by telephone inquiry and field visit.
Estimates of Sampling Error: Estimated CV of 3% to 4% for estimates of national totals, but are as high as 20% for estimated totals of more detailed characteristics, such as housing units in multiunit structures.
Other (nonsampling) Errors: Response rate is over 90% for most items. Nonsampling errors are attributed to definitional problems, differences in interpretation of questions, incorrect reporting, inability to obtain information about all cases in the sample, and processing errors.
Sources of Additional Material: U.S. Bureau of the Census, *Construction Reports,* series C20, *Housing Starts;* C22, *Housing Completions;* and C25, *New One-Family Houses Sold and For Sale.*

Source and Title: U.S. Bureau of the Census, *Value of Construction Put in Place*
Tables: 1193 and 1194.
Universe, Frequency, and Types of Data: Survey conducted monthly on total value of all construction put in place in the current month, both public and private projects. Construction values include costs of materials and labor, contractors' profits, overhead costs, cost of architectural and engineering work, and miscellaneous project costs. (Annual figures are aggregates of monthly estimates.)
Type of Data Collection Operation: Varies by type of activity: Total cost of private one-family houses started each month is distributed into value put in place using fixed patterns of monthly construction progress; using a multistage probability sample, data for private multifamily housing are obtained by mail from owners of multiunit projects. Data for residential additions and alterations are obtained in a quarterly survey measuring expenditures; monthly estimates are interpolated from quarterly data. Estimates of value of private nonresidential construction, and state and local government construction are obtained by mail from owners (or agents) for a probability sample of projects. Estimates of farm nonresidential construction expenditures are based on U.S. Department of Agriculture annual estimates of construction; public utility estimates are obtained from reports submitted to federal regulatory agencies and from private utility companies; estimates of federal construction are based on monthly data supplied by federal agencies.
Data Collection and Imputation Procedures: See "Type of Data Collection Operation." Imputation accounts for approximately 20% of estimated value of construction each month.
Estimates of Sampling Error: CV estimates for private nonresidential construction range from 3% for estimated value of industrial buildings to 9% for religious buildings. CV is approximately 2% for total new private nonresidential buildings.
Other (nonsampling) Errors: For directly measured data series based on samples, some nonsampling errors may arise from processing errors, imputations, and misunderstanding of questions. Indirect data series are dependent on the validity of the underlying assumptions and procedures.
Sources of Additional Material: U.S. Bureau of the Census, *Construction Reports,* Series C30, *Value of Construction Put in Place.*

Source and Title: U.S. Bureau of the Census, *American Housing Survey*
Tables: See Tables citing *American Housing Survey* in source notes.
Universe, Frequency, and Types of Data: Conducted nationally in the fall in odd numbered years to obtain data on the approximately 103 million occupied or vacant housing units in the United States (group quarters are excluded). Data include characteristics of occupied housing units, vacant

units, new housing and mobile home units, financial characteristics, recent mover households, housing and neighborhood quality indicators, and energy characteristics.

Type of Data Collection Operation: The national sample was a multistage probability sample with about 51,300 units eligible for interview in 1987. Sample units, selected within 394 PSUs, were surveyed over a 5-month period.

Data Collection and Imputation Procedures: For 1987, the survey was conducted by personal interviews. The interviewers obtained the information from the occupants or, if the unit was vacant, from informed persons such as landlords, rental agents, or knowledgeable neighbors.

Estimates of Sampling Error: For the national sample, illustrations of the S.E. of the estimates are provided in the Appendix B of the 1987 report. As an example, the estimated CV is about 0.5% for the estimated percentage of owner occupied units with two persons.

Other (nonsampling) Errors: Response rate was about 97%. Nonsampling errors may result from incorrect or incomplete responses, errors in coding and recording, and processing errors. For the 1985 national sample, approximately 6% of the total housing inventory was not adequately represented by the AHS sample.

Sources of Additional Material: U.S. Bureau of the Census, *Current Housing Reports,* Series H-150 and H-170, *American Housing Survey.*

(See Section 1 above for information pertaining to the Census of Population, Section 15 pertaining to Table 1191, and Section 19 for Table 1223.)

SECTION 26. MANUFACTURES

Source and Title: U.S. Bureau of the Census, *Census of Manufactures*

Tables: See tables citing *Census of Manufactures* in source notes in Section 26 and also Table 932 in Section 18 and Table 1339 in Section 29.

Universe, Frequency, and Types of Data: Conducted every 5 years to obtain information on labor, materials, capital input and output characteristics, plant location, and legal form of organization for all plants in the United States with one or more paid employees. Universe was 350,000 manufacturing establishments in 1987.

Type of Data Collection Operation: Complete enumeration of data items obtained from 200,000 firms. Administrative records from Internal Revenue Service and Social Security Administration are used for 150,000 smaller single-location firms, which were determined by various cutoffs based on size and industry.

Data Collection and Imputation Procedures: Five mail and telephone followups for larger nonrespondents. Data for small single-location firms (generally those with fewer than 10 employees) not mailed census questionnaires were estimated from administrative records of IRS and SSA. Data for nonrespondents were imputed from related responses or administrative records from IRS and SSA. Approximately 8% of total value of shipments was represented by fully imputed records in 1987.

Estimates of Sampling Error: Not applicable.

Other (nonsampling) Errors: Based on evaluation studies, estimates of nonsampling errors for 1972 were about 1.3% for estimated total payroll; 2% for total employment; and 1% for value of shipments. Estimates for later years are not available.

Sources of Additional Material: U.S. Bureau of the Census, *1987 Census of Manufactures, Industry Series, Geographic Area Series, and Subject Series.*

Source and Title: U.S. Bureau of the Census, *Annual Survey of Manufactures*

Tables: See Tables citing *Annual Survey of Manufactures* in source notes.

Universe, Frequency, and Types of Data: Conducted annually to provide basic measures of manufacturing activity for intercensal years for all manufacturing establishments having one or more paid employees.

Type of Data Collection Operation: Sampling frame is 350,000 establishments in the 1987 Census of Manufactures (see above), supplemented by Social Security Administration lists of new manufacturers and new manufacturing establishments of multiestablishment companies identified annually by the Census Bureau's Company Organization Survey. A probability sample of about 55,000 establishments is selected. All establishments of companies with more than $500 million of manufacturing shipments in 1987 are included with certainty. All establishments with 250+ employees are also included with certainty along with a probability sample of smaller establishments.

Data Collection and Imputation Procedures: Survey is conducted by mail with phone and mail followups of nonrespondents. Imputation (for all nonresponse items) is based on previous year reports, or for new establishments in survey, on industry averages.

Estimates of Sampling Error: Estimated standard errors for number of employees, new expenditure, and for value added totals are given in annual publications. For U.S. level industry statistics, most estimated standard errors are 2% or less, but vary considerably for detailed characteristics.

Other (nonsampling) Errors: Response rate is about 85%. Nonsampling errors include those due to collection, reporting, and transcription errors, many of which are corrected through computer and clerical checks.

Sources of Additional Material: U.S. Bureau of the Census, *Annual Survey of Manufactures,* and Technical Paper 24.

SECTION 27. DOMESTIC TRADE AND SERVICES

Source and Title: U.S. Bureau of the Census, *Census of Wholesale Trade, Census of Retail Trade, Census of Service Industries*

Tables: See tables citing the above censuses in source notes in Section 27 and Table 1339 in Section 29.

Universe, Frequency, and Types of Data: Conducted every 5 years to obtain data on number of establishments, number of employees, total payroll size, total sales, and other industry-specific statistics. In 1987, the universe was all employer establishments primarily engaged in wholesale trade, and employer and nonemployer establishments in retail trade or service industries.

Type of Data Collection Operation: All wholesale firms with paid employees surveyed; all retail and service large employer firms surveyed (i.e. all employer firms above the payroll size cutoff established to separate large from small employers) plus a 10-percent sample of smaller employer firms. Firms with no employees were not required to file a census return.

Data Collection and Imputation Procedures: Mail questionnaire is utilized with both mail and telephone followups for nonrespondents. Data for nonrespondents and all employer firms in retail trade and service industries are obtained from administrative records of IRS and the Social Security Administration.

Estimates of Sampling Error: Not applicable.

Other (nonsampling) Errors: Response rate in 1987 of 80% for single establishment firms; 83% for multi-establishment firms. Item response ranged from 60% to 90% with higher rates for less detailed questions.

Sources of Additional Material: U.S. Bureau of the Census, Appendix A of *Census of Retail Trade; Census of Service Industries; Census of Wholesale Trade;* and *History of the 1987 Economic Censuses,* April 1992.

Source and Title: U.S. Bureau of the Census, *Current Business Surveys*

Tables: 1278-1280, 1292, 1298, 1301; Table 188 in Section 3; Tables 427 and 452 in Section 7; and Table 1057 in Section 21.

Universe, Frequency, and Types of Data: Provides monthly estimates of retail sales by kind of business and geographic area, and end-of-month inventories of retail stores; wholesale sales and end-of-month inventories; and annual receipts of selected service industries.

Type of Data Collection Operation: Probability sample of all firms from a list frame and, additionally, for retail and service an area frame. The list frame is the Bureau's Standard Statistical Establishment List (SSEL) updated quarterly for recent birth Employer Identification (EI) Numbers issued by the Internal Revenue Service and assigned a kind-of-business code by the Social Security Administration. The largest firms are included monthly; a sample of others is included every three months on a rotating basis. The area frame covers businesses not subjected to sampling on the list frame.

Data Collection and Imputation Procedures: Data are collected by mail questionnaire with telephone followups for nonrespondents. Imputation made for each nonresponse item and each item failing edit checks.

Estimates of Sampling Error: For the 1989 monthly surveys, CVs are about 0.6% for estimated total retail sales, 1.7% for wholesale sales, 1.3% for wholesale inventories. For dollar volume of receipts, CVs from the *Service Annual Survey* vary by kind of business and range between 1.5% to 15.0%. Sampling errors are shown in monthly publications.

Other (nonsampling) Errors: Imputation rates are about 18% to 23% for monthly retail sales, 20% to 25% for wholesale sales, about 25% to 30% for monthly wholesale inventories and 14% for the *Service Annual Survey.*

Sources of Additional Material: U.S. Bureau of the Census, *Current Business Reports, Monthly Retail Trade, Monthly Wholesale Trade,* and *Service Annual Survey.*

(See Section 17 for information pertaining to Tables 1276 and 1297.)

SECTION 28. FOREIGN COMMERCE AND AID

Source and Title: U.S. Bureau of the Census, *Foreign Trade—Export Statistics*

Tables: See Bureau of the Census citations for export statistics in source notes in Section 28 and also Table 1336 in Section 29.

Universe, Frequency, and Types of Data: The export declarations collected by Customs are processed each month to obtain data on the movement of U.S. merchandise exports to foreign countries. Data obtained include value, quantity, and shipping weight of exports by commodity, country of destination, Customs district of exportation, and mode of transportation.

Type of Data Collection Operation: Shipper's Export Declarations are required to be filed for the exportation of merchandise valued over $1,500. Customs officials collect and transmit the documents to the Bureau of the Census on a flow basis for data compilation. Value data for shipments valued under $1,501 are estimated, based on established percentages of individual country totals.

Data Collection and Imputation Procedures: Statistical copies of Shipper's Export Declarations are received on a daily basis from Customs ports throughout the country and subjected to a monthly processing cycle. They are fully processed to the extent they reflect items valued over $1,500. Estimates for shipments valued at $1,500 or less are made, based on established percentages of individual country totals.

Estimates of Sampling Error: Not applicable.

Other (nonsampling) Errors: Clerical and complex computer checks intercept most processing errors and minimize otherwise significant reporting errors; other nonsampling errors are caused by undercounting of exports to Canada due to the nonreceipt of some Shipper's Export Declarations.

Sources of Additional Material: U.S. Bureau of the Census, *U.S. Merchandise Trade: Exports, General Imports, and Imports for Consumption, SITC, Commodity by Country*, FT 925 (discontinued after 1996).

Source and Title: U.S. Bureau of the Census, *Foreign Trade—Import Statistics*

Tables: See Bureau of the Census citations for import statistics in source notes in Section 28 and also Table 1336 in Section 29.

Universe, Frequency, and Types of Data: The import entry documents collected by Customs are processed each month to obtain data on the movement of merchandise imported into the United States. Data obtained include value, quantity, and shipping weight by commodity, country of origin, Customs district of entry, and mode of transportation.

Type of Data Collection Operation: Import entry documents are required to be filed for the importation of goods into the United States valued over $1,000 or for articles which must be reported on formal entries. Customs officials collect and transmit statistical copies of the documents to the Bureau of the Census on a flow basis for data compilation. Estimates for shipments valued under $1,001 and not reported on formal entries are based on established percentages of individual country totals.

Data Collection and Imputation Procedures: Statistical copies of import entry documents, received on a daily basis from Customs ports of entry throughout the country, are subjected to a monthly processing cycle. They are fully processed to the extent they reflect items valued at $1,001 and over or items which must be reported on formal entries.

Estimates of Sampling Error: Not applicable.

Other (nonsampling) Errors: Verification of statistical data reporting by Customs officials prior to transmittal and a subsequent program of clerical and computer checks are utilized to hold nonsampling errors arising from reporting and/or processing errors to a minimum.

Sources of Additional Material: U.S. Bureau of the Census, *U.S. Merchandise Trade: Exports, General Imports and Imports for Consumption, SITC, Commodity by Country*, FT 925 (discontinued after 1996).

(See Section 13 for information pertaining to Table 1083.)

SECTION 29. OUTLYING AREAS

(See Section 1 for information pertaining to Tables 1329 and 1330, Section 2 for Table 1328, Section 17 for Table 1337, Section 22 for Table 1336, Sections 26 and 27 for Table 1339.)

Tables Deleted From the 1997 Edition of the Statistical Abstract

Index

NOTE: Index citations refer to table numbers, not page numbers.

NOTE: Index citations refer to table numbers, not page numbers.

NOTE: Index citations refer to table numbers, not page numbers.

NOTE: Index citations refer to table numbers, not page numbers.

NOTE: Index citations refer to table numbers, not page numbers.

NOTE: Index citations refer to table numbers, not page numbers.

Table

NOTE: Index citations refer to table numbers, not page numbers.

NOTE: Index citations refer to table numbers, not page numbers.

NOTE: Index citations refer to table numbers, not page numbers.

NOTE: Index citations refer to table numbers, not page numbers.

NOTE: Index citations refer to table numbers, not page numbers.

NOTE: Index citations refer to table numbers, not page numbers.

NOTE: Index citations refer to table numbers, not page numbers.

NOTE: Index citations refer to table numbers, not page numbers.

NOTE: Index citations refer to table numbers, not page numbers.

NOTE: Index citations refer to table numbers, not page numbers.

NOTE: Index citations refer to table numbers, not page numbers.

NOTE: Index citations refer to table numbers, not page numbers.

NOTE: Index citations refer to table numbers, not page numbers.

NOTE: Index citations refer to table numbers, not page numbers.

NOTE: Index citations refer to table numbers, not page numbers.

NOTE: Index citations refer to table numbers, not page numbers.

NOTE: Index citations refer to table numbers, not page numbers.

NOTE: Index citations refer to table numbers, not page numbers.

NOTE: Index citations refer to table numbers, not page numbers.

	Table

NOTE: Index citations refer to table numbers, not page numbers.

NOTE: Index citations refer to table numbers, not page numbers.

NOTE: Index citations refer to table numbers, not page numbers.

NOTE: Index citations refer to table numbers, not page numbers.

NOTE: Index citations refer to table numbers, not page numbers.

NOTE: Index citations refer to table numbers, not page numbers.

NOTE: Index citations refer to table numbers, not page numbers.

NOTE: Index citations refer to table numbers, not page numbers.

NOTE: Index citations refer to table numbers, not page numbers.

NOTE: Index citations refer to table numbers, not page numbers.

NOTE: Index citations refer to table numbers, not page numbers.

NOTE: Index citations refer to table numbers, not page numbers.

NOTE: Index citations refer to table numbers, not page numbers.

NOTE: Index citations refer to table numbers, not page numbers.

NOTE: Index citations refer to table numbers, not page numbers.

NOTE: Index citations refer to table numbers, not page numbers.

NOTE: Index citations refer to table numbers, not page numbers.

NOTE: Index citations refer to table numbers, not page numbers.

NOTE: Index citations refer to table numbers, not page numbers.

NOTE: Index citations refer to table numbers, not page numbers.

Table

NOTE: Index citations refer to table numbers, not page numbers.

NOTE: Index citations refer to table numbers, not page numbers.

NOTE: Index citations refer to table numbers, not page numbers.

NOTE: Index citations refer to table numbers, not page numbers.

NOTE: Index citations refer to table numbers, not page numbers.

NOTE: Index citations refer to table numbers, not page numbers.

NOTE: Index citations refer to table numbers, not page numbers.

NOTE: Index citations refer to table numbers, not page numbers.

›duct Announcement

'mmediate Release

For additional information contact:
Renee Edwards, Public Affairs Director (703) 605-6400
redwards@ntis.fedworld.gov

west Data Released From The U.S. Bureau of the Census

S Offers The *State and Metropolitan Area Data Book 1997-98*

›tate and Metropolitan Area Data Book 1997-98, the highly respected companion report to the
us Bureau's *Statistical Abstract of the United States*, is now available from the National Technical
mation Service. While the *Statistical Abstract* provides general social, political, and economic data
ιe U.S. as a whole, the *Data Book* contains similar information, but focuses on the local areas.

Data Book is designed to serve as a statistical reference and guide to other statistical publications
ources. It includes a selection of data from statistical publications and electronic sources, both
·nment and private. Although emphasis is primarily given to state and metropolitan area data, U.S.
and data for component counties and central cities are also provided

Data Book tracts local trends and developments in such diverse areas as:

- Population
- Income
- Labor force
- Construction

- Health care
- Business enterprises
- Education
- Crime

dition to its extensive tables, the report includes maps, source notes, and appendixes. For the
rs' convenience, source notes now appear at the bottom of each table page, as well as in the source
and explanations appendix.

›tate and Metropolitan Area Data Book 1997-98 is available from NTIS, 1-800-553-NTIS
'), for $22.50 plus $5 handling fee, no additional charge for shipping; quote order number
;-124407KMW. Most major credit cards accepted. Order via e-mail:
·s@ntis.fedworld.gov. Fax order to: (703) 605-6900.

; is the central source for worldwide scientific, technical, and related business information.
; also offers thousands of multimedia and educational programs produced by federal
:ies. As a self-sustaining agency of the U.S. Department of Commerce, NTIS covers its
ιess and operating expenses with the sale of its products and services.

U.S. DEPARTMENT OF COMMERCE
Technology Administration
National Technical Information Service
Springfield, VA 22161   (703) 605-6000

PA/852
6/98

*O*ut Goes the SIC, In Comes the NAICS

Official Government Version
Now Available at NTIS

Just released

The North American Industry Classification System (NAICS) - United States 1997 replaces the U.S. Standard Industrial Classification (SIC) system which was last updated in 1987. The new codes are available in printed copy and CD-ROM. Each is the U.S. government's official version as prepared by the Office of Management and Budget's Economic Classification Policy Committee. They are produced and distributed by the National Technical Information Service.

NAICS is the first-ever North American industry classification system. It was developed by the U.S., Canada, and Mexico to provide comparable statistics across the three countries.

NAICS - United States 1997 will reshape the way we view our changing economy. It features:

- More than 350 new industries and definitions for each
- Economy groupings in 20 broad sectors, up from the 10 divisions of the SIC
- Tables showing correspondence between NAICS 1997 and 1987 SICs
- An index of 18,000 business activities with their corresponding NAICS code

The CD-ROM version offers a powerful search capability making it easy to find what you want. It provides links from sector codes to descriptions, a documented history, and downloadable files. Visit our NAICS Web site: www.ntis.gov/naics.

In addition to the CD-ROM, NAICS comes in paper copy with either a soft cover or hard cover. To order, call the NTIS Sales Desk at 1-800-553-NTIS (6847).

U.S. DEPARTMENT OF COMMERCE
Technology Administration
National Technical Information Service
Springfield, VA 22161   (703) 605-6000